			4/81

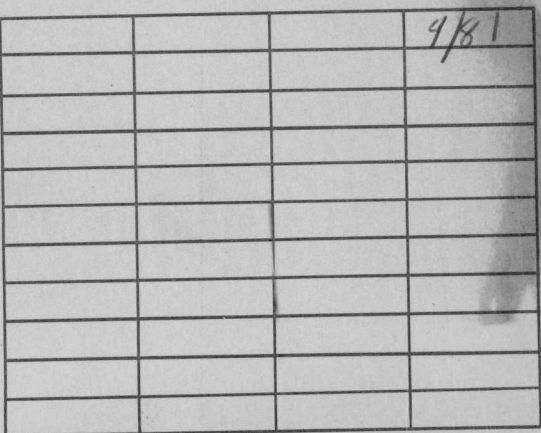

The
Poetical Works
of
Robert Browning

The
Poetical Works
of
Robert Browning

Cambridge Edition

With a New Introduction
by G. Robert Stange

Houghton Mifflin Company Boston

Library of Congress Cataloging in Publication Data

Browning, Robert, 1812–1889.
The poetical works of Robert Browning.

Based on the 1895 Cambridge ed. published by
Houghton, Mifflin, Boston under title: The complete
poetic and dramatic works of Robert Browning.
I. Stange, George Robert, 1919–   ed.
II. Title.
PR4200.F74   821'.8   74-5216
ISBN 0-395-18485-1

Printed in the United States of America

v 10 9 8 7 6 5 4 3

EDITOR'S NOTE

In the Publisher's Note to the Cambridge Edition of Browning's poetical works, first published in 1895, it is explained that the aim was to bring, "by a careful study of condensation . . . the entire body of Browning's work into a single volume, and to equip the edition with the requisite apparatus." It goes on to mention that the order of arrangement is chronological, "with one or two obvious divergences," and that "the exigencies of the volume" have forced the editor, Horace E. Scudder, to be "very frugal" with his explanatory notes.

Scudder's edition was a notable achievement; for over three quarters of a century it has been by far the best (if not the most legible) one-volume edition of the poetry. The present edition might better be described as a reissue. The main improvement is physical: the type has been renewed, darkened, and enlarged. The Biographical Sketch of 1895 has been replaced by a general introduction and a chronology of Browning's life. No attempt has been made to replace or revise the original Notes and Illustrations, first because a reasonably complete annotation of Browning's poetry would require another hundred pages of text, and also because Scudder's notes are still useful to a modern reader. Fragmentary and sometimes dated though they may be, they contain a good deal of usable information and have the additional value of showing us how a devoted nineteenth-century reader responded to a great poet who was, to him, still a contemporary.

G. R. S.

CONTENTS

INTRODUCTION

Overshadowed by whole libraries of criticism and exegesis, an introductory statement to a collection of Browning's poetry can only justify itself by modesty of aim. In a few pages one can do no more than try to establish the general impression that this poetry leaves with us almost a century after Browning's death. But that impression, the total effect, is the result of something more than the work itself; our experience of Browning involves a commingling of the poet's character — partly fictive, partly real — with the poems, assigned to many voices, but distinctly the utterance of that character. To define, then, that special thing that "Browning" means to readers of the 1970s, one must begin by considering his present reputation, then turn to his characterizing qualities: the language of his poetry and its dominant themes.

Browning wrote copiously and published for over thirty years without achieving recognition. Tennyson, who was only three years older than he, had become famous in his early thirties; and, indeed, Elizabeth Barrett was, throughout their married life, much more widely known than her husband. However, when Browning's success finally came in the 1860s it was of a peculiarly vivid sort. Hungry as he may have been for admiration, he must occasionally have quailed at his new following — the bands of earnest seekers after "thoughts," the tremulous enthusiasts and the formidably systematic Browning societies. Nevertheless, he endured and the fame — curiously — has lasted. The course of Browning's posthumous reputation is different from that of other major poets; there has been no marked reaction against him (as there was in the case of Pope or Tennyson); his simple-minded followers remained loyal (as late as the 1930s Browning enthusiasts at Yale belonged to a group called *The T.B.I.Y.T.B.'s* — "the best is yet to be"); and among many of the most brilliant modern writers there has been, as we shall see, sustained appreciation. Even the twentieth-century attacks on Browning are oddly consistent with those of his own time. Many of his contemporaries found Browning "coarse," discerned that, in spite of his interests in the manifestations of religion, he was incapable of profound religious feeling, and — most important of all — saw in his poetry a force subversive of classical order and restraint. The same objections have been expressed by twentieth-century critics whose *parti pris* involves a taste for classicism and an attachment to traditional Christianity.

The consistency of attitude toward Browning over so long a period of time can, perhaps, be traced to that sense of the *modern* that remains — however ambiguously — as a primary quality of his work. In the 1860s, the beginning of his years of fame, it was the characteristic most frequently commented on. His poetry represented a new wave of literary interest; no matter that he was almost the same age as Tennyson and a good deal older than Arnold, his younger readers considered him the representative of a new poetic generation, and they were right in doing so. For, looking back at Browning through the poetic movements of the twentieth century, we can see that his development as a poet involved two main accomplishments: first, a revival of the vernacular language of poetry and the creation of a more vigorous and economical poetic style; second, the development of a totally new dramatic method. It could be said that in doing both these things he performed in his own career the kind of redirection of interest that, repeated by twentieth-century poets, was defined as a literary revolution.

In his earlier years Browning was an ardent disciple of Shelley's. He apostrophized him as the "Sun-treader" and wished to be, like him, an ideal "subjective" poet. Browning's single piece of literary criticism is an *Essay on Shelley* in which he observed that the subjective poet does not "deal with the doings of men (the result of which dealing, in its pure form . . . is what we call dramatic poetry)," but that his study is himself, and he selects as subjects those silent scenes "in which he can best hear the beating of his individual heart." The weakness of Browning's early poetry (*Pauline*, which opens this volume, is the best example) is precisely in the sedulous attention the poet pays to the beating of his own heart. As Browning matured he advanced toward dramatic — what he called "objective" — poetry and was increasingly influenced by the later Shakespeare and by Donne. The fully evolved dramatic monologues which began to appear in the 1840s employ a new and concise technique; they are not contemplations of the poet's own soul, but exposures of character through speech, revelations of an indirect, ironic sort that the reader is led to arrive at on his own. The "truth" that these poems permit us to glimpse must be continually reassessed, revised. The dramatic monologue, as Browning shaped it, became — in a variety of adaptations — the dominant form of twentieth-century poetry. Poets who were looking for a new style found in Browning's work a special freshness and vigor; they learned from him how to incorporate into verse the rhythms of ordinary speech. Since the best of Browning's dramatic poetry is flexible and informal enough to adapt to a great variety of subject matter, his practice obtained for poets the kind of freedom in the handling of their materials that only novelists had until then enjoyed. Modern writers have also been attracted by a quality less easy to define, but touching even more directly on what we think of as the modern spirit, this is Browning's tentativeness of assertion, his delight in refusing the Olympian security of "high" poetry and insisting on the value of the quotidian.

Appropriately enough, it was Ezra Pound, involved as poet or critic in every significant literary innovation in the twentieth century, who was most explicit in drawing attention to what modern writers could find in Browning. In an early poem, "Mesmerism," Pound addressed him as the "old mesmerizer, / Tyin' your meanin' in seventy swadelin's," but

> True to the Truth's sake and crafty dissector,
> You grabbed at the gold sure; had no need to pack cents
> Into your versicles
> Clear sight's elector!

"I stem from Browning," Pound said. "Why deny one's father?" And in his program for the reform of English poetry his first aim, which he claimed to have derived from Browning, was the elimination from poetry of all superfluous language.

Neither Eliot nor Yeats went so far as Pound in admiration and imitation of Browning. But both poets found their mature style in working toward dramatic poetry, and they had in common the aim of discovering, as Eliot put it, "a contemporary idiom." Tempering his praise with some disparaging remarks about Browning's unacceptable "optimism." Eliot spoke of him as the only nineteenth-century poet "to devise a way of speech which might be useful for others," to teach the possibility of using "non-poetic material," and to reassert "the relation of poetry to speech."

But Browning's "modernism" is also the result of factors unrelated to his direct influence on the major poets of our century. It is a quality still operative for us — ordinary readers of a later day — , and to explain that fact one needs to understand that Browning's relation to the main lines of English poetry is appreciably different from that of his great contemporaries. Tennyson, for example, attached himself to the major traditions of Western poetry; in an intensely self-conscious way he seems to have planned his career in the model of Virgil's progress from pastoral to epic, trying to make his life as a poet assume the pattern already defined by Milton and Pope. Perhaps it is a necessary corollary to this great and learned effort that Tennyson's work should now appear to mark the end of a tradition, to come to a close in itself. Certainly it would be hard to imagine any fruitful, innovative continuance along the lines of practice he established.

For Browning, on the contrary, the idea was to "make it new." He learned, as we know, from Shakespeare and Donne and in his eccentric way was a proficient classicist; but his poetry does not demand or profit from allusion to earlier masters. He exists totally in the cultural matrix of Romanticism and is happiest when he gives himself to the elaboration of its major themes. It was Browning's special virtue to touch, as it were, both ends of this diverse and long-lived movement. If, in his beginning, he absorbs and transforms a Shelleyan impulse, in his ripest work he gives the first expression in English poetry to modes of thought that we now call Vitalist and Existentialist.

What such poets as Ezra Pound or, more recently, Robert Lowell have found in Browning might best be described as a distinctive attitude toward poetry, an original sense of what the process of poetic expression is. For most readers the easiest way to perceive these special virtues is to look at Browning's language and recurrent themes as they appear in a few representative poems.

The "Browningesque" style which perturbed so many Victorian readers is largely a matter of a certain briskness of approach, the manipulation of calculated shock. "Old Hippety-hop o' the accents"; Pound's phrase leads one to think of such lines as:

> If at night when doors are shut,
>   And the wood-worm picks
> And the death-watch ticks,
> And the bar has a flag of smut,
> And a cat's in the water-butt —

The passage is likely to jolt any reader, but though it is technically adept, it achieves its effect through what Pope called Imitative Metre, an entirely conventional technique. The heavily stressed string of monosyllables reproduce the nervous starts, the tossing, the picking and ticking that punctuate a sleepless night. Such passages are characteristic of Browning, but they are much less experimental — and demand much less of the reader — than, let us say, the opening lines of "Caliban upon Setebos":

> 'Will sprawl, now that the heat of day is best,
> Flat on his belly in the pit's much mire,
> With elbows wide, fists clenched to prop his chin.
> And, while he kicks both feet in the cool slush,
> And feels about his spine small eft-things course,
> Run in and out each arm, and make him laugh:
> And while . . . etc.

Here the roughness of sound — a matter of knotted consonants, irregular (but highly controlled) rhythms and elliptical syntax — is not simply a *tour de main*. Caliban's character, an ingenious variation on Shakespeare's theme, emerges more from the texture of the language than from what the poem actually *says*. The jagged, congealed sounds, the distortion of syntax, both express an internal emotional reality and — in a typical display of Browning's wit — begin to make a statement about the nature of theological speculation. The subtitle of the poem is "Natural Theology in the Island," and it is both a poetic gloss on *The Tempest* and a satire on "reason" and religious thought in the island of John Bull.

But there is more, even in Browning's most clotted poems, than mere "hippety-hop." His technique involves a process of skipping, but in more than one sense. When Ruskin objected to the poet's habit of making things difficult for the reader by omitting transitions, Browning replied:

> You would have me paint it all plain out, which can't be; but by various artifices I try to make shift with touches and bits of outlines which *succeed* if they bear the conception from me to you. You ought, I think, to keep pace with the thought tripping from ledge to ledge of my "glaciers," as you call them; not stand poking your alpenstock into the holes and demonstrating that no foot could have stood there; suppose it sprang over there?

One might hope that Ruskin came to realize that the devices that make Browning's language peculiar do finally conduce to the achievement of a single end. When the poet suppresses transitions, makes rhythm appeal to the intellectual sense as well as to the motor faculty, places words so that they have more than one referent, and may be said to "swing" syntactically, he is finding ways of packing more meaning into less room. The effect of his diction when Browning is at his best is of a fine denseness of significance along with a startling economy of expression. He did not altogether escape mistakes of taste and, in his later years, fell into a kind of complacency that sometimes allowed him to relish the defects of his stylistic virtues. But the assumption that he was a bumbler when it came to language, or that he had a faulty ear for the sonorities of English verse, is one of the more irritating of vulgar errors. He was, as often as any other major poet of the last two centuries, in complete control of his language, and when he avoided smoothness he did so intentionally. It may be, however, that we have come to speak too much of the "Calibanesque" Browning; the reader who wishes to see what the old master can do in the way of classical restraint and controlled poignancy need only look at "Eurydice to Orpheus" on the page after "Caliban":

> But give them me, the mouth, the eyes, the brow!
> Let them once more absorb me! One look now
>   Will lap me round forever, not to pass
> Out of its light, though darkness lie beyond:
> Hold me but safe again within the bond
>   Of one immortal look! All woe that was,
> Forgotten, and all terror that may be,
> Defied, — no past is mine, no future: look at me!

Inevitably, one discovers that Browning's language is indistinguishable from the themes of his poetry. A diction so consciously intensified and directed makes, by its very nature, a statement about reality. The patterns of Browning's speech are affective: he avoids sequential discourse and arranges his "meanings" in a kind of syntactic perspective by which we see them first in one way then in another. We are not led by easy stages to comprehension; it assails us in flashes. Such techniques do not merely convince us of the poet's versatility, they posit a world without rational sequence, in which there is no completeness, no assured order, no finished truth — a world in which knowledge is only fragmentary.

Though the two main themes of Browning's poetry — love and art — are not uniquely his in the way his language is, both aspects of his work are clearly products of the same impulse and are charged with the same kind of poetic energy. Browning sees love and art (and for him the two are often inseparable) as the means by which men fulfill their humanity. It would not be oversimplifying to say that Browning sees *true* love and *true* art as our ways to the Good; by experiencing them fully men learn to give themselves to life.

It is in his definition of love that Browning may appear to the reader of our time to be most lacking in sophistication. The ancient distinction between Agape and Eros has acquired new force in the twentieth century, and when Browning's poetry is regarded in the context of these traditional views, it is obvious that he was quite innocent of the opposition. Certainly he never had any serious conception of Agape, the theocentric love which exists regardless of human merit, creating goodness rather than being attracted by it. Eros, the love centered in man, rooted in physical passion, leading to the desire to possess, is the only love Browning knew, and under the aegis of Eros he concerned himself only with that relatively recent conception of love which we call Romantic. His poems, in fact, have helped to extend — or even create — several ideas of Romantic love that are recurrent in literature and life. For example, it is one of the principal tenets of Romantic love that physical passion, in achieving its satisfaction, becomes also a means of achieving certain spiritual and transcendental values. Lovers are believed to be able to realize themselves by merging their individual identities in what has been called an "exchange of individual fatalities." No writer, with the possible exception of Wagner, has expressed this paradox more fully than Browning. Here, for example, is how the lover speaks in "Two in the Campagna":

> How say you? Let us, O my dove,
>   Let us be unashamed of soul,
> As earth lies bare to heaven above!
>   How is it under our control
> To love or not to love?
>
> I would that you were all to me,
>   You that are just so much, no more.
> Nor yours, nor mine, nor slave nor free!

We have become so used to both popular and literary expressions of Romantic love that we no longer question the assumption that by full possession of the physical being the lover makes a kind of leap to a spiritual good. Yet the notion that the way to the ideal is through bodily passion is a rather recent one.

Another aspect of Romantic love is the annihilation of time; by achieving union the lovers are transposed to the absolute. Browning's poetry offers many versions of what he called "the instant made eternity," a state which, we are to understand, comes only through the fullness of love. The idea is most concisely (if not most beautifully) expressed in the late sonnet, "Now":

> Out of your whole life give but a moment!
> All of your life that has gone before,
> All to come after it, — so you ignore,
> So you make perfect the present, — condense,
> In a rapture of rage, for perfection's endowment,
> Thought and feeling and soul and sense —
> Merged in a moment which gives me at last
> You around me for once, you beneath me, above me —
> Me — sure that despite of time future, time past, —
> This tick of our life-time's one moment you love me!
> How long such suspension may linger? Ah, Sweet —
> The moment eternal — just that and no more —
> When ecstasy's utmost we clutch at the core
> While cheeks burn, arms open, eyes shut and lips meet!

It is suggested in "Dîs Aliter Visum" and in "The Statue and the Bust" that it is a sin not to give oneself fully in "good faith" to the experience of love — even to a love that is adulterous. One comes to feel that for Browning love — along with art, the supremely valuable human activity — is prized not for the joy it produces or the life it sustains, but as a kind of exercise in commitment. The total giving of the self to the all-encompassing Other becomes the paradigm of an action which finally transcends all morality and all social value.

In treating the theme of art Browning, like so many other nineteenth- and twentieth-century poets, was concerned with problems quite different from those one finds in Horace or in works like Boileau's *Art poétique*. For the post-Romantic poets reflection on the nature and meaning of poetry became an almost obsessive theme, attended often with a certain anxiety. Reading their poetry and letters one is led to infer that the value of all art has been called into question by bourgeois society and that the poet must, at the outset of his career, define and defend his function. Browning's first three long poems were all — directly or indirectly — on the subject of the poet and his role. *Pauline, Paracelsus,* and *Sordello* mark the stages of the poet's own advance toward a dramatic, "objective" art — the only kind Browning would defend morally and aesthetically. In *Sordello* a careful distinction is made among three kinds of poet who might be called, in order of ascending value, the Subjective, the Descriptive, the Dramatic:

> . . . seeing somewhat of man's estate, — has been,
> For the worst of us to say they so have seen;
> For the better what it was they saw; the best
> Impart the gift of seeing to the rest:
> "So that I glance," says such an one, "around,
> And there's no face but I can read profound
> Disclosures in.". . .

The somewhat feeble virtues of *Pauline* depend on mere subjectivity, on an ability to see "somewhat of man's estate" and to report the fact. But the mature poems do indeed "Impart the gift of seeing to the rest." Browning does not, however, see this accomplishment as sufficient in itself: in a long series of poems on the nature of art he sets himself the task of both explaining what makes for good art, what for false, and illustrating his beliefs by the operation of the poem itself. He counters with ingenuity — or sometimes casuistry — not only the arguments of the Philistines who say that art is useless to a progressive society, but the more important objections about the "good" of poetry which he himself raises and which seem to have plagued him all his life.

Of the nearly two dozen poems that make art their theme, "Fra Lippo Lippi" is the most approachable; it illustrates Browning's style of argument most clearly and gives full treatment to his recurrent speculations. The poet has succeeded in making "Fra Lippo" both a delightful dramatic monologue and a disquisition — the most elaborate that Browning was to write — on a theory of naturalistic art. Being uneasily both artist and monk, lover of flesh and ostensible ascetic, Lippo embodies the conflict between the natural and spiritual man. He enacts the contradictions of an art which has as its object the interpretation of the real world, but which must, at the same time, justify its existence by demonstrating its spiritual value through the transformation and transcendence of phenomena. The problem is obviously not one to trouble our contemporary practitioners of the *nouveau roman* or the new *Sachlichkeit*, but to Browning and most of his serious contemporaries it was crucial. In "Fra Lippo" contraries and oppositions are set forth on a series of planes as the poem proceeds to show how in life and art at its most real contradictions are reconciled precisely by being *realized*.

The argument that the poet gives to Lippo to express is too complicated to trace in detail, but in its main points it outlines the theoretical foundations of Browning's own practice. It is with flesh, Lippo asserts, with concrete reality that the artist must begin. By being entirely true to sense he arrives at soul, and in defending this commitment to naturalism Lippo invokes the most illustrious of parallels:

> For me, I think I speak as I was taught;
> I always see the garden and God there
> A-making man's wife: and, my lesson learned,

> The value and significance of flesh,
> I can't unlearn ten minutes afterwards.

The artist as maker (*poètes*) is, then, analogous to God ("God is the perfect poet," as it is expressed in *Paracelsus*). Lippo, rejoicing in

> — The beauty and the wonder and the power,
> The shapes of things, their colors, lights and shades,
> Changes and surprises,

concludes " — and God made it all! / For what?" The question applies more directly to a work of art than to divine creation and leads to Browning's problem of affirming the artistic purpose and value of fidelity to the truth of experience. The artist must not despise any of God's works: "count it crime / To let a truth slip." And to the objection that his kind of art merely reproduces an already accomplished Creation, the naturalistic artist replies that men are made

> . . . so that we love
> First when we see them painted, things we have passed
> Perhaps a hundred times nor cared to see;
> And so they are better, painted — better to us,
> Which is the same thing.

As Browning would have it, it is the artist's function to prefigure — or to preenact — the awareness that his audience can achieve. Because the viewer/reader repeats an act of insight that would otherwise have been impossible for him, the artist has created a new value by his faithful imitation. It is characteristic that Browning should make love the animating force of art; to perceive is to love, and the artist arouses our unexercised capacities for perceiving by the application of his own more intense love of the world around him. The suggested hierarchy of value mounts from perception to love to the godlike activity of creation. It is only, I would suggest, by likening the artist to the creator of the universe that Browning is able to resolve the contradiction he feels between the artist's simple joy in the phenomenological world, the delight he takes in reproducing crude fact, and the achievement of that higher spirituality which Browning — still the earnest Victorian — had to believe was the attendant of aesthetic value. The problem is interestingly like that of Romantic love, in which we must assume that the lovers — by the very intensity of their physical passion — are spiritualized. In his idea of art, however, Browning goes farther and evolves a poetic myth based on the theological doctrine of the Incarnation. As, by the ultimate, divine act of love, flesh is made spirit, so the "objective artist" performs a lesser incarnation by his love of things around him.

The notion of a literary parallel to the Incarnation appears in several of Browning's poems on art and gives him an answer to the nagging demands of Victorian morality. Browning was always interested in paradox and by allusion to the greatest of paradoxes he could satisfy both himself and his critics. Since no man or object is unworthy in the eyes of the creator, it follows that for the poet all experience is potentially valuable and all subjects worthy of treatment. Furthermore, the poet's status is honorably defined: he stands somewhere between the ordinary man and God (in one poem he is happily referred to as "God's spy"). But most important for Browning — and for his readers — is the belief that the poet rejoices more fully than others in the multiple possibilities of life, the diversities of human kind. The poems on art are essential Browning: they celebrate the values of acceptance, commitment, and vigorous action. They are all, in a way, manifestoes of the convictions and qualities which make for the continuing excitement of his poetry.

G. ROBERT STANGE

CHRONOLOGY OF BROWNING'S LIFE

1812   Born in Camberwell, London, on May 7.

1828   Matriculates at the newly established London University, which he leaves during his second term.

1833   *Pauline* published anonymously.

1833–34   Period of travel, including a trip to Russia.

1835   *Paracelsus* published (the first poem to which Browning attached his name).

1837   *Strafford: An Historical Tragedy* produced at Covent Garden Theatre, published later in the year.

1840   *Sordello* published.

1841   *Bells and Pomegranates* No. I published (*Pippa Passes*). Seven more numbers followed, the last appearing in 1846.

1845   Makes the acquaintance of Elizabeth Barrett (born 1806).

1846   Elizabeth and Robert Browning are married on September 12. They go first to France, then to Italy, where they eventually take up residence at Florence in the Casa Guidi.

1850   *Christmas-Eve and Easter-Day* published.

1855   *Men and Women* published in two volumes.

1861   Mrs. Browning dies in Florence. Browning, with his son, leaves Florence for England.

1864   *Dramatis Personae* published.

1868   *The Ring and the Book* published in four successive volumes.

1876   *Pacchiarotto, with Other Poems.*

1879   *Dramatic Idylls* published (Second Series appeared in 1880).

1881   The English Browning Society is founded.

1884   *Ferishtah's Fancies.*

1887   *Parleyings with Certain People of Importance in their Day.*

1889   Browning dies on December 12 at his son's house in Venice. Burial on December 31 in Poet's Corner, Westminster Abbey.

1890   *Asolando: Fancies and Facts* published posthumously.

The
Poetical Works
of
Robert Browning

PAULINE: THE FRAGMENT OF A CONFESSION

THE history of the earliest printed of Browning's writings is so curious that it seems worth while to give it at greater length than its intrinsic merit would require. As a boy Browning wrote an inordinate amount of verse, imitative largely of Byron, and some of it written when he was twelve struck his father as good enough to deserve printing, but no publisher could be found ready to confirm this faith. Then Browning fell into a Shelleyan mood, and when he was twenty projected a great work of which the introduction only was written. This introduction was *Pauline*, which to be precise was completed October 22, 1832. Browning's aunt volunteered to pay the expenses of publication, and it was published anonymously early in 1833 by Saunders & Otley. The most authoritative person on literary matters in the young poet's circle of friends was the Rev. William Johnson Fox, a Unitarian clergyman and editor of the *Monthly Repository*. He had a few years before given emphatic commendation to the boy's verse, and now reviewed the poem with great warmth in his own magazine, so winning the poet's gratitude as to draw from him the extravagant expression: "I shall never write a line without thinking of the source of my first praise, be assured." The poem missed what would have been from its writer a more notable review. Mr. John Stuart Mill, six years Browning's senior, was so delighted with *Pauline* that he wrote to the editor of *Tait's Magazine*, the only periodical in which he could write freely, asking leave to review the poem. The editor replied that he had just printed a curt, contemptuous notice, and could not at once take the other track. When Mill died his copy of *Pauline*, crowded with annotations, fell into Browning's hands and may now be seen in the South Kensington Museum.

In spite of such hopeful promise the poem was still-born from the press. Five years later, Browning wrote in a copy "the only remaining crab of the shapely Tree of Life in my Fool's Paradise." He appears never to have spoken of it until a striking circumstance brought it again into light. Many years after it was printed Dante Gabriel Rossetti was browsing among the volumes of forgotten poetry in the British Museum. He came upon a book in which a number of pamphlet poems were bound in a heterogeneous collection. Among these was *Pauline*. He read it, and from its internal evidence was convinced that it was an unacknowledged poem of Browning's. The book was wholly out of print, and he made a copy of it. He wrote to Browning afterwards taxing the poet with the production, and Browning, greatly surprised at Rossetti's discovery, acknowledged the authorship. In 1865, the editor of this Cambridge edition, meeting Rossetti in London, mentioned the fact that he had been copying at the British Museum Browning's prose introduction to the suppressed spurious collection of Shelley's Letters, whereupon Rossetti told him of this other rare book. Afterwards on learning that he had copied *Pauline* also he said: "I suppose you will print it when you go back to America." "By no means," replied the editor; "that would be a breach of faith. I copied it as a student of Browning. I never would make it public without Browning's consent." A year or two later therefore when a new edition of the collected poems was published, he thought himself not unlikely the unwitting occasion of the inclusion of *Pauline*, for in the introduction Browning wrote as follows:

"The first piece in the series (*Pauline*), I acknowledge and retain with extreme repugnance, indeed purely of necessity ; for not long ago I inspected one, and am certified of the existence of other transcripts, intended sooner or later to be published abroad: by forestalling these, I can at least correct some misprints (no syllable is changed) and introduce a boyish work by an exculpatory word. The thing was my earliest attempt at "poetry always dramatic in principle, and so many utterances of so many imaginary persons, not mine," which I have since written according to a scheme less extravagant and scale less impracticable than were ventured upon in this crude preliminary sketch, — a sketch that, on reviewal, appears not altogether wide of some hint of the characteristic features of that particular *dramatis persona* it would fain have reproduced : good draughtsmanship, however, and right handling were far beyond the artist at that time.

LONDON, *December* 25, 1867. R. B."

Twenty years later, upon sending out his final collective edition, Browning added to the preface just quoted the following sentences : —

"I preserve, in order to supplement it, the foregoing preface. I had thought, when compelled to include in my collected works the poem to which it refers, that the honest course would be to reprint, and leave mere literary errors unaltered. Twenty years' endurance of an eyesore seems more than sufficient : my faults remain duly recorded against me, and I claim permission to somewhat diminish these, so far as style is concerned, in the present and final edition, where *Pauline* must needs, first of my performances, confront the reader. I have simply removed solecisms, mended the metre a little and endeavored to strengthen the phraseology — experience helping, in some degree, the helplessness of juvenile haste and heat in their untried adventure long ago."

LONDON, *February* 27, 1888.

The text here given, as throughout this volume, is that of Mr. Browning's latest revision. The text of the first revision, i. e. 1867, may be found at the close of volume i. of the Riverside edition.

The quotations from Marot and Cornelius Agrippa which follow were prefixed to the original edition of the poem. The note enclosed in brackets was Browning's comment on reprinting the poem the last time.

PAULINE

Plus ne suis ce que j'ai été,
Et ne le sçaurois jamais être.
Marot.

Non dubito, quin titulus libri nostri raritate sua quamplurimos alliciat ad legendum : inter quos nonnulli obliquæ opinionis, mente languidi, multi etiam maligni, et in ingenium nostrum ingrati accedent, qui temeraria sua ignorantia, vix conspecto titulo clamabunt. Nos vetita docere, hæresium semina jacere : piis auribus offendiculo, præclaris ingeniis scandalo esse : . . . adeo conscientiæ suæ consulentes, ut nec Apollo, nec Musæ omnes, neque Angelus de cœlo me ab illorum execratione vindicare queant : quibus et ego nunc consulo, ne scripta nostra legant, nec intelligant, nec meminerint : nam noxia sunt, venenosa sunt : Acherontis ostium est in hoc libro, lapides loquitur, caveant, ne cerebrum illis excutiat. Vos autem, qui æqua mente ad legendum venitis, si tantam prudentiæ discretionem adhibueritis, quantam in melle legendo apes, jam securi legite. Puto namque vos et utilitatis haud parum et voluptatis plurimum accepturos. Quod si qua repereritis, quæ vobis non placeant, mittite illa, nec utimini; NAM ET EGO VOBIS ILLA NON PROBO, SED NARRO. Cætera tamen propterea non respuite . . . Ideo, si quid liberius dictum sit, ignoscite adolescentiæ nostræ, qui minor quam adolescens hoc opus composui. — *Hen. Corn. Agrippa, De Occult. Philosoph. in Præfat.*

LONDON : *January*, 1833.
V. A. XX.

[This introduction would appear less absurdly pretentious did it apply, as was intended, to a completed structure of which the poem was meant for only a beginning and remains a fragment.]

PAULINE, mine own, bend o'er me — thy soft breast
Shall pant to mine — bend o'er me — thy sweet eyes,
And loosened hair and breathing lips, and arms
Drawing me to thee — these build up a screen
To shut me in with thee, and from all fear ;
So that I might unlock the sleepless brood
Of fancies from my soul, their lurking-place,
Nor doubt that each would pass, ne'er to return
To one so watched, so loved and so secured.
But what can guard thee but thy naked love ?
Ah dearest, whoso sucks a poisoned wound
Envenoms his own veins ! Thou art so good,
So calm — if thou shouldst wear a brow less light
For some wild thought which, but for me, were kept
From out thy soul as from a sacred star !
Yet till I have unlocked them it were vain
To hope to sing ; some woe would light on me ;
Nature would point at one whose quivering lip
Was bathed in her enchantments, whose brow burned
Beneath the crown to which her secrets knelt,
Who learned the spell which can call up the dead,
And then departed smiling like a fiend
Who has deceived God, — if such one should seek
Again her altars and stand robed and crowned
Amid the faithful ! Sad confession first,
Remorse and pardon and old claims renewed·
Ere I can be — as I shall be no more.

I had been spared this shame if I had sat
By thee forever from the first, in place
Of my wild dreams of beauty and of good,
Or with them, as an earnest of their truth :
No thought nor hope having been shut from thee,
No vague wish unexplained, no wandering aim
Sent back to bind on fancy's wings and seek
Some strange fair world where it might be a
    law ;
But, doubting nothing, had been led by thee,
Through youth, and saved, as one at length
    awaked
Who has slept through a peril. Ah vain, vain !

Thou lovest me ; the past is in its grave
Though its ghost haunts us ; still this much is
    ours,
To cast away restraint, lest a worse thing
Wait for us in the dark. Thou lovest me ;
And thou art to receive not love but faith,
For which thou wilt be mine, and smile and
    take
All shapes and shames, and veil without a fear
That form which music follows like a slave :
And I look to thee and I trust in thee,
As in a Northern night one looks alway
Unto the East for morn and spring and joy.
Thou seest then my aimless, hopeless state,
And, resting on some few old feelings won
Back by thy beauty, wouldst that I essay
The task which was to me what now thou art :
And why should I conceal one weakness more ?

Thou wilt remember one warm morn when
    winter
Crept aged from the earth, and spring's first
    breath
Blew soft from the moist hills ; the black-thorn
    boughs,
So dark in the bare wood, when glistening
In the sunshine were white with coming buds,
Like the bright side of a sorrow, and the banks
Had violets opening from sleep like eyes.
I walked with thee who knew'st not a deep
    shame
Lurked beneath smiles and careless words
    which sought
To hide it till they wandered and were mute,
As we stood listening on a sunny mound
To the wind murmuring in the damp copse,
Like heavy breathings of some hidden thing
Betrayed by sleep ; until the feeling rushed
That I was low indeed, yet not so low
As to endure the calmness of thine eyes.
And so I told thee all, while the cool breast
I leaned on altered not its quiet beating :
And long ere words like a hurt bird's complaint
Bade me look up and be what I had been,
I felt despair could never live by thee :
Thou wilt remember. Thou art not more dear
Than song was once to me ; and I ne'er sung
But as one entering bright halls where all
Will rise and shout for him : sure I must own
That I am fallen, having chosen gifts
Distinct from theirs — that I am sad and fain
Would give up all to be but where I was,
Not high as I had been if faithful found,
But low and weak yet full of hope, and sure

Of goodness as of life — that I would lose
All this gay mastery of mind, to sit
Once more with them, trusting in truth and love
And with an aim — not being what I am.

O Pauline, I am ruined who believed
That though my soul had floated from its
    sphere
Of wild dominion into the dim orb
Of self — that it was strong and free as ever !
It has conformed itself to that dim orb,
Reflecting all its shades and shapes, and now
Must stay where it alone can be adored.
I have felt this in dreams — in dreams in which
I seemed the fate from which I fled ; I felt
A strange delight in causing my decay.
I was a fiend in darkness chained forever
Within some ocean-cave ; and ages rolled,
Till through the cleft rock, like a moonbeam,
    came
A white swan to remain with me ; and ages
Rolled, yet I tired not of my first free joy
In gazing on the peace of its pure wings :
And then I said, "It is most fair to me,
Yet its soft wings must sure have suffered
    change
From the thick darkness, sure its eyes are dim.
Its silver pinions must be cramped and numbed
With sleeping ages here ; it cannot leave me,
For it would seem, in light beside its kind,
Withered, though here to me most beautiful."
And then I was a young witch whose blue eyes,
As she stood naked by the river springs,
Drew down a god : I watched his radiant form
Growing less radiant, and it gladdened me ;
Till one morn, as he sat in the sunshine
Upon my knees, singing to me of heaven,
He turned to look at me, ere I could lose
The grin with which I viewed his perishing :
And he shrieked and departed and sat long
By his deserted throne, but sunk at last
Murmuring, as I kissed his lips and curled
Around him, "I am still a god — to thee."

Still I can lay my soul bare in its fall,
Since all the wandering and all the weakness
Will be a saddest comment on the song :
And if, that done, I can be young again,
I will give up all gained, as willingly
As one gives up a charm which shuts him out
From hope or part or care in human kind.
As life wanes, all its care and strife and toil
Seem strangely valueless, while the old trees
Which grew by our youth's home, the waving
    mass
Of climbing plants heavy with bloom and dew,
The morning swallows with their songs like
    words,
All these seem clear and only worth our
    thoughts :
So, aught connected with my early life,
My rude songs or my wild imaginings,
How I look on them — most distinct amid
The fever and the stir of after years !

I ne'er had ventured e'en to hope for this,
Had not the glow I felt at His award,
Assured me all was not extinct within :

His whom all honor, whose renown springs up
Like sunlight which will visit all the world,
So that e'en they who sneered at him at first,
Come out to it, as some dark spider crawls
From his foul nets which some lit torch invades,
Yet spinning still new films for his retreat.
Thou didst smile, poet, but can we forgive?

Sun-treader, life and light be thine forever!
Thou art gone from us; years go by and spring
Gladdens and the young earth is beautiful,
Yet thy songs come not, other bards arise,
But none like thee: they stand, thy majesties,
Like mighty works which tell some spirit there
Hath sat regardless of neglect and scorn,
Till, its long task completed, it hath risen
And left us, never to return, and all
Rush in to peer and praise when all in vain.
The air seems bright with thy past presence yet,
But thou art still for me as thou hast been
When I have stood with thee as on a throne
With all thy dim creations gathered round
Like mountains, and I felt of mould like them,
And with them creatures of my own were
        mixed,
Like things half-lived, catching and giving life.
But thou art still for me who have adored
Though single, panting but to hear thy name
Which I believed a spell to me alone,
Scarce deeming thou wast as a star to men!
As one should worship long a sacred spring
Scarce worth a moth's flitting, which long
        grasses cross,
And one small tree embowers droopingly —
Joying to see some wandering insect won
To live in its few rushes, or some locust
To pasture on its boughs, or some wild bird
Stoop for its freshness from the trackless air:
And then should find it but the fountain-head,
Long lost, of some great river washing towns
And towers, and seeing old woods which will live
But by its banks untrod of human foot,
Which, when the great sun sinks, lie quivering
In light as some thing lieth half of life
Before God's foot, waiting a wondrous change;
Then girt with rocks which seek to turn or stay
Its course in vain, for it does ever spread
Like a sea's arm as it goes rolling on,
Being the pulse of some great country — so
Wast thou to me, and art thou to the world!
And I, perchance, half feel a strange regret
That I am not what I have been to thee:
Like a girl one has silently loved long
In her first loneliness in some retreat,
When, late emerged, all gaze and glow to view
Her fresh eyes and soft hair and lips which
        bloom
Like a mountain berry: doubtless it is sweet
To see her thus adored, but there have been
Moments when all the world was in our praise,
Sweeter than any pride of after hours.
Yet, sun-treader, all hail! From my heart's
        heart
I bid thee hail! E'en in my wildest dreams,
I proudly feel I would have thrown to dust
The wreaths of fame which seemed o'erhanging
        me,
To see thee for a moment as thou art.

And if thou livest, if thou lovest, spirit!
Remember me who set this final seal
To wandering thought — that one so pure as thou
Could never die. Remember me who flung
All honor from my soul, yet paused and said,
"There is one spark of love remaining yet,
For I have naught in common with him, shapes
Which followed him avoid me, and foul forms
Seek me, which ne'er could fasten on his mind;
And though I feel how low I am to him,
Yet I aim not even to catch a tone
Of harmonies he called profusely up;
So, one gleam still remains, although the last."
Remember me who praise thee e'en with tears,
For never more shall I walk calm with thee;
Thy sweet imaginings are as an air,
A melody some wondrous singer sings,
Which, though it haunt men oft in the still eve,
They dream not to essay; yet it no less
But more is honored. I was thine in shame,
And now when all thy proud renown is out,
I am a watcher whose eyes have grown dim
With looking for some star which breaks on him
Altered and worn and weak and full of tears.

Autumn has come like spring returned to us,
Won from her girlishness; like one returned
A friend that was a lover, nor forgets
The first warm love, but full of sober thoughts
Of fading years; whose soft mouth quivers yet
With the old smile, but yet so changed and still!
And here am I the scoffer, who have probed
Life's vanity, won by a word again
Into my own life — by one little word
Of this sweet friend who lives in loving me,
Lives strangely on my thoughts and looks and
        words,
As fathoms down some nameless ocean thing
Its silent course of quietness and joy.
O dearest, if indeed I tell the past,
May'st thou forget it as a sad sick dream!
Or if it linger — my lost soul too soon
Sinks to itself and whispers we shall be
But closer linked, two creatures whom the earth
Bears singly, with strange feelings unrevealed
Save to each other; or two lonely things
Created by some power whose reign is done,
Having no part in God or his bright world.
I am to sing whilst ebbing day dies soft,
As a lean scholar dies worn o'er his book,
And in the heaven stars steal out one by one
As hunted men steal to their mountain watch.
I must not think, lest this new impulse die
In which I trust; I have no confidence:
So, I will sing on fast as fancies come;
Rudely, the verse being as the mood it paints

I strip my mind bare, whose first elements
I shall unveil — not as they struggle forth
In infancy, nor as they now exist,
When I am grown above them and can rule —
But in that middle stage when they were full
Yet ere I had disposed them to my will;
And then I shall show how these elements
Produced my present state, and what it is.

I am made up of an intensest life,
Of a most clear idea of consciousness

Of self, distinct from all its qualities,
From all affections, passions, feelings, powers;
And thus far it exists, if tracked, in all:
But linked, in me, to self-supremacy,
Existing as a centre to all things,
Most potent to create and rule and call
Upon all things to minister to it;
And to a principle of restlessness
Which would be all, have, see, know, taste,
    feel, all —
This is myself; and I should thus have been
Though gifted lower than the meanest soul.

And of my powers, one springs up to save
From utter death a soul with such desire
Confined to clay — of powers the only one
Which marks me — an imagination which
Has been a very angel, coming not
In fitful visions, but beside me ever
And never failing me; so, though my mind
Forgets not, not a shred of life forgets,
Yet I can take a secret pride in calling
The dark past up to quell it regally.

A mind like this must dissipate itself,
But I have always had one lode-star; now,
As I look back, I see that I have halted
Or hastened as I looked towards that star —
A need, a trust, a yearning after God:
A feeling I have analyzed but late,
But it existed, and was reconciled
With a neglect of all I deemed his laws,
Which yet, when seen in others, I abhorred.
I felt as one beloved, and so shut in
From fear: and thence I date my trust in signs
And omens, for I saw God everywhere;
And I can only lay it to the fruit
Of a sad after-time that I could doubt
Even his being — e'en the while I felt
His presence, never acted from myself,
Still trusted in a hand to lead me through
All danger; and this feeling ever fought
Against my weakest reason and resolve.

And I can love nothing — and this dull truth
Has come the last: but sense supplies a love
Encircling me and mingling with my life.

These make myself: I have long sought in vain
To trace how they were formed by circumstance,
Yet ever found them mould my wildest youth
Where they alone displayed themselves, con-
    verted
All objects to their use: now see their course!

They came to me in my first dawn of life
Which passed alone with wisest ancient books
All halo-girt with fancies of my own;
And I myself went with the tale — a god
Wandering after beauty, or a giant
Standing vast in the sunset — an old hunter
Talking with gods, or a high-crested chief
Sailing with troops of friends to Tenedos.
I tell you, naught has ever been so clear
As the place, the time, the fashion of those
    lives:
I had not seen a work of lofty art,
Nor woman's beauty nor sweet nature's face,

Yet, I say, never morn broke clear as those
On the dim clustered isles in the blue sea,
The deep groves and white temples and wet
    caves:
And nothing ever will surprise me now —
Who stood beside the naked Swift-footed,
Who bound my forehead with Proserpine's hair.

And strange it is that I who could so dream
Should e'er have stooped to aim at aught be
    neath —
Aught low or painful; but I never doubted:
So, as I grew, I rudely shaped my life
To my immediate wants; yet strong beneath
Was a vague sense of power though folded up —
A sense that, though those shades and time
    were past,
Their spirit dwelt in me, with them should rule.

Then came a pause, and long restraint chained
    down
My soul till it was changed. I lost myself,
And were it not that I so loathe that loss,
I could recall how first I learned to turn
My mind against itself; and the effects
In deeds for which remorse were vain as for
The wanderings of delirious dream; yet thence
Came cunning, envy, falsehood, all world's
    wrong
That spotted me: at length I cleansed my soul.
Yet long world's influence remained; and
    naught
But the still life I led, apart once more,
Which left me free to seek soul's old delights,
Could e'er have brought me thus far back to
    peace.

As peace returned, I sought out some pursuit;
And song rose, no new impulse but the one
With which all others best could be combined.
My life has not been that of those whose heaven
Was lampless save where poesy shone out;
But as a clime where glittering mountain-tops
And glancing sea and forests steeped in light
Give back reflected the far-flashing sun;
For music (which is earnest of a heaven,
Seeing we know emotions strange by it,
Not else to be revealed,) is like a voice,
A low voice calling fancy, as a friend,
To the green woods in the gay summer time:
And she fills all the way with dancing shapes
Which have made painters pale, and they go or
Till stars look at them and winds call to them
As they leave life's path for the twilight world
Where the dead gather. This was not at first.
For I scarce knew what I would do. I had
An impulse but no yearning — only sang.

And first I sang as I in dream have seen
Music wait on a lyrist for some thought,
Yet singing to herself until it came.
I turned to those old times and scenes where all
That's beautiful had birth for me, and made
Rude verses on them all; and then I paused —
I had done nothing, so I sought to know
What other minds achieved, No fear outbroke
As on the works of mighty bards I gazed,
In the first joy at finding my own thoughts

Recorded, my own fancies justified,
And their aspirings but my very own.
With them I first explored passion and mind, —
All to begin afresh! I rather sought
To rival what I wondered at than form
Creations of my own; if much was light
Lent by the others, much was yet my own.

I paused again: a change was coming — came:
I was no more a boy, the past was breaking
Before the future and like fever worked.
I thought on my new self, and all my powers
Burst out. I dreamed not of restraint, but
        gazed
On all things: schemes and systems went and
        came,
And I was proud (being vainest of the weak)
In wandering o'er thought's world to seek some
        one
To be my prize, as if you wandered o'er
The White Way for a star.

                        And my choice fell
Not so much on a system as a man —
On one, whom praise of mine shall not offend,
Who was as calm as beauty, being such
Unto mankind as thou to me, Pauline, —
Believing in them and devoting all
His soul's strength to their winning back to
        peace;
Who sent forth hopes and longings for their sake,
Clothed in all passion's melodies: such first
Caught me and set me, slave of a sweet task,
To disentangle, gather sense from song:
Since, song-inwoven, lurked there words which
        seemed
A key to a new world, the muttering
Of angels, something yet unguessed by man.
How my heart leapt as still I sought and found
Much there, I felt my own soul had conceived,
But there living and burning! Soon the orb
Of his conceptions dawned on me; its praise
Lives in the tongues of men, men's brows are
        high
When his name means a triumph and a pride,
So, my weak voice may well forbear to shame
What seemed decreed my fate: I threw myself
To meet it, I was vowed to liberty,
Men were to be as gods and earth as heaven,
And I — ah, what a life was mine to prove!
My whole soul rose to meet it. Now, Pauline,
I shall go mad, if I recall that time!

Oh let me look back ere I leave forever
The time which was an hour one fondly waits
For a fair girl that comes a withered hag!
And I was lonely, far from woods and fields,
And amid dullest sights, who should be loose
As a stag; yet I was full of bliss, who lived
With Plato and who had the key to life;
And I had dimly shaped my first attempt,
And many a thought did I build up on thought,
As the wild bee hangs cell to cell; in vain,
For I must still advance, no rest for mind.

'T was in my plan to look on real life,
The life all new to me; my theories
Were firm, so them I left, to look and learn

Mankind, its cares, hopes, fears, its woes and joys
And, as I pondered on their ways, I sought
How best life's end might be attained — an end
Comprising every joy. I deeply mused.

And suddenly without heart-wreck I awoke
As from a dream: I said, "'T was beautiful,
Yet but a dream, and so adieu to it!"
As some world-wanderer sees in a far meadow
Strange towers and high-walled gardens thick
        with trees,
Where song takes shelter and delicious mirth
From laughing fairy creatures peeping over,
And on the morrow when he comes to lie
Forever 'neath those garden-trees fruit-flushed
Sung round by fairies, all his search is vain.
First went my hopes of perfecting mankind,
Next — faith in them, and then in freedom's self
And virtue's self, then my own motives, ends
And aims and loves, and human love went last.
I felt this no decay, because new powers
Rose as old feelings left — wit, mockery,
Light-heartedness; for I had oft been sad,
Mistrusting my resolves, but now I cast
Hope joyously away: I laughed and said,
"No more of this!" I must not think: at
        length
I looked again to see if all went well.

My powers were greater: as some temple seemed
My soul, where naught is changed and incense
        rolls
Around the altar, only God is gone
And some dark spirit sitteth in his seat.
So, I passed through the temple and to me
Knelt troops of shadows, and they cried, "Hail,
        king!
We serve thee now and thou shalt serve no
        more!
Call on us, prove us, let us worship thee!"
And I said, "Are ye strong? Let fancy bear me
Far from the past!" And I was borne away,
As Arab birds float sleeping in the wind,
O'er deserts, towers and forests, I being calm.
And I said, "I have nursed up energies,
They will prey on me." And a band knelt low
And cried, "Lord, we are here and we will
make
Safe way for thee in thine appointed life!
But look on us!" And I said, "Ye will worship
Me; should my heart not worship too?" They
        shouted,
"Thyself, thou art our king!" So, I stood
        there
Smiling — oh, vanity of vanities!
For buoyant and rejoicing was the spirit
With which I looked out how to end my course;
I felt once more myself, my powers — all mine;
I knew while youth and health so lifted me
That, spite of all life's nothingness, no grief
Came nigh me, I must ever be light-hearted;
And that this knowledge was the only veil
Betwixt joy and despair: so, if age came,
I should be left — a wreck linked to a soul
Yet fluttering, or mind-broken and aware
Of my decay. So a long summer morn
Found me; and ere noon came, I had resolved
No age should come on me ere youth was spent

For I would wear myself out, like that morn
Which wasted not a sunbeam ; every hour
I would make mine, and die.

           And thus I sought
To chain my spirit down which erst I freed
For flights to fame : I said, "The troubled life
Of genius, seen so gay when working forth
Some trusted end, grows sad when all proves
    vain —
How sad when men have parted with truth's
    peace
For falsest fancy's sake, which waited first
As an obedient spirit when delight
Came without fancy's call : but alters soon,
Comes darkened, seldom, hastens to depart,
Leaving a heavy darkness and warm tears.
But I shall never lose her ; she will live
Dearer for such seclusion. I but catch
A hue, a glance of what I sing : so, pain
Is linked with pleasure, for I ne'er may tell
Half the bright sights which dazzle me ; but
    now
Mine shall be all the radiance : let them fade
Untold — others shall rise as fair, as fast !
And when all 's done, the few dim gleams trans-
    ferred," —
(For a new thought sprang up how well it were,
Discarding shadowy hope, to weave such lays
As straight encircle men with praise and love,
So, I should not die utterly, — should bring
One branch from the gold forest, like the knight
Of old tales, witnessing I had been there) —
"And when all 's done, how vain seems e'en
    success —
The vaunted influence poets have o'er men !
'T is a fine thing that one weak as myself
Should sit in his lone room, knowing the words
He utters in his solitude shall move
Men like a swift wind — that though dead and
    gone,
New eyes shall glisten when his beauteous
    dreams
Of love come true in happier frames than his.
Ay, the still night brings thoughts like these,
    but morn
Comes and the mockery again laughs out
At hollow praises, smiles allied to sneers ;
And my soul's idol ever whispers me
To dwell with him and his unhonored song :
And I foreknow my spirit, that would press
First in the struggle, fail again to make
All bow enslaved, and I again should sink.

"And then know that this curse will come on us,
To see our idols perish ; we may wither,
No marvel, we are clay, but our low fate
Should not extend to those whom trustingly
We sent before into time's yawning gulf
To face what dread may lurk in darkness there.
To find the painter's glory pass, and feel
Music can move us not as once, or, worst,
To weep decaying wits ere the frail body
Decays ! Naught makes me trust some love is
    true,
But the delight of the contented lowness
With which I gaze on him I keep forever
Above me ; I to rise and rival him ?

Feed his fame rather from my heart's best blood,
Wither unseen that he may flourish still."

Pauline, my soul's friend, thou dost pity yet
How this mood swayed me when that soul found
    thine,
When I had set myself to live this life,
Defying all past glory. Ere thou camest
I seemed defiant, sweet, for old delights
Had flocked like birds again ; music, my life,
Nourished me more than ever ; then the lore
Loved for itself and all it shows — that king
Treading the purple calmly to his death,
While round him, like the clouds of eve, all
    dusk,
The giant shades of fate, silently flitting,
Pile the dim outline of the coming doom ;
And him sitting alone in blood while friends
Are hunting far in the sunshine ; and the boy
With his white breast and brow and clustering
    curls
Streaked with his mother's blood, but striving
    hard
To tell his story ere his reason goes.
And when I loved thee as love seemed so oft,
Thou lovedst me indeed : I wondering searched
My heart to find some feeling like such love,
Believing I was still much I had been.
Too soon I found all faith had gone from me,
And the late glow of life, like change on clouds,
Proved not the morn-blush widening into day,
But eve faint-colored by the dying sun
While darkness hastens quickly. I will tell
My state as though 't were none of mine --
    despair
Cannot come near us — this it is, my state.

Souls alter not, and mine must still advance ;
Strange that I knew not, when I flung away
My youth's chief aims, their loss might lead to
    loss
Of what few I retained, and no resource
Be left me : for behold how changed is all !
I cannot chain my soul : it will not rest
In its clay prison, this most narrow sphere :
It has strange impulse, tendency, desire,
Which nowise I account for nor explain,
But cannot stifle, being bound to trust
All feelings equally, to hear all sides :
How can my life indulge them ? yet they live,
Referring to some state of life unknown.

My selfishness is satiated not,
It wears me like a flame ; my hunger for
All pleasure, howsoe'er minute, grows pain ;
I envy — how I envy him whose soul
Turns its whole energies to some one end,
To elevate an aim, pursue success
However mean ! So, my still baffled hope
Seeks out abstractions ; I would have one joy,
But one in life, so it were wholly mine,
One rapture all my soul could fill : and this
Wild feeling places me in dream afar
In some vast country where the eye can see
No end to the far hills and dales bestrewn
With shining towers and towns, till I grow
    mad
Well-nigh, to know not one abode but holds

Some pleasure, while my soul could grasp the
          world,
But must remain this vile form's slave.   I look
With hope to age at last, which quenching much,
May let me concentrate what sparks it spares.

This restlessness of passion meets in me
A craving after knowledge : the sole proof
Of yet commanding will is in that power
Repressed ; for I beheld it in its dawn,
The sleepless harpy with just-budding wings,
And I considered whether to forego
All happy ignorant hopes and fears, to live,
Finding a recompense in its wild eyes.
And when I found that I should perish so,
I bade its wild eyes close from me forever,
And I am left alone with old delights ;
See ! it lies in me a chained thing, still prompt
To serve me if I loose its slightest bond :
I cannot but be proud of my bright slave.

How should this earth's life prove my only
          sphere ?
Can I so narrow sense but that in life
Soul still exceeds it ?   In their elements
My love outsoars my reason ; but since love
Perforce receives its object from this earth
While reason wanders chainless, the few truths
Caught from its wanderings have sufficed to
          quell
Love chained below ; then what were love, set
          free,
Which, with the object it demands, would pass
Reason companioning the seraphim ?
No, what I feel may pass all human love
Yet fall far short of what my love should be.
And yet I seem more warped in this than aught,
Myself stands out more hideously : of old
I could forget myself in friendship, fame,
Liberty, nay, in love of mightier souls ;
But I begin to know what thing hate is —
To sicken and to quiver and grow white —
And I myself have furnished its first prey.
Hate of the weak and ever-wavering will,
The selfishness, the still-decaying frame . . .
But I must never grieve whom wing can waft
Far from such thoughts — as now.   Andromeda !
And she is with me : years roll, I shall change,
But change can touch her not — so beautiful
With her fixed eyes, earnest and still, and hair
Lifted and spread by the salt-sweeping breeze,
And one red beam, all the storm leaves in
          heaven,
Resting upon her eyes and hair, such hair,
As she awaits the snake on the wet beach
By the dark rock and the white wave just
          breaking
At her feet ; quite naked and alone ; a thing
I doubt not, nor fear for, secure some god
To save will come in thunder from the stars.
Let it pass !   Soul requires another change.
I will be gifted with a wondrous mind,
Yet sunk by error to men's sympathy,
And in the wane of life, yet only so
As to call up their fears ; and there shall come
A time requiring youth's best energies ;
And lo, I fling age, sorrow, sickness off,
And rise triumphant, triumph through decay.

And thus it is that I supply the chasm
'Twixt what I am and all I fain would be :
But then to know nothing, to hope for nothing,
To seize on life's dull joys from a strange fear
Lest, losing them, all 's lost and naught remains !

There 's some vile juggle with my reason here ;
I feel I but explain to my own loss
These impulses : they live no less the same.
Liberty ! what though I despair ? my blood
Rose never at a slave's name proud as now.
Oh sympathies, obscured by sophistries ! —
Why else have I sought refuge in myself,
But from the woes I saw and could not stay ?
Love ! is not this to love thee, my Pauline ?
I cherish prejudice, lest I be left
Utterly loveless ? witness my belief
In poets, though sad change has come there too ;
No more I leave myself to follow them —
Unconsciously I measure me by them —
Let me forget it : and I cherish most
My love of England — how her name, a word
Of hers in a strange tongue makes my heart
          beat !

Pauline, could I but break the spell ! Not
          now —
All 's fever — but when calm shall come again,
I am prepared : I have made life my own.
I would not be content with all the change
One frame should feel, but I have gone in
          thought
Through all conjuncture, I have lived all life
When it is most alive, where strangest fate
New-shapes it past surmise — the throes of men
Bit by some curse or in the grasps of doom
Half-visible and still-increasing round,
Or crowning their wide being's general aim.

These are wild fancies, but I feel, sweet friend,
As one breathing his weakness to the ear
Of pitying angel — dear as a winter flower,
A slight flower growing alone, and offering
Its frail cup of three leaves to the cold sun,
Yet joyous and confiding like the triumph
Of a child : and why am I not worthy thee ?
I can live all the life of plants, and gaze
Drowsily on the bees that flit and play,
Or bare my breast for sunbeams which will
          kill,
Or open in the night of sounds, to look
For the dim stars ; I can mount with the bird
Leaping airily his pyramid of leaves
And twisted boughs of some tall mountain tree
Or rise cheerfully springing to the heavens ;
Or like a fish breathe deep the morning air
In the misty sun-warm water ; or with flower
And tree can smile in light at the sinking sun
Just as the storm comes, as a girl would look
On a departing lover — most serene.

Pauline, come with me, see how I could build
A home for us, out of the world, in thought !
I am uplifted : fly with me, Pauline !

Night, and one single ridge of narrow path
Between the sullen river and the woods
Waving and muttering, for the moonless night

Has shaped them into images of life,
Like the uprising of the giant-ghosts,
Looking on earth to know how their sons fare :
Thou art so close by me, the roughest swell
Of wind in the tree-tops hides not the panting
Of thy soft breasts. No, we will pass to morn-
    ing —
Morning, the rocks and valleys and old woods.
How the sun brightens in the mist, and here,
Half in the air, like creatures of the place,
Trusting the element, living on high boughs
That swing in the wind — look at the silver
    spray
Flung from the foam-sheet of the cataract
Amid the broken rocks ! Shall we stay here
With the wild hawks ? No, ere the hot noon
    come,
Dive we down — safe ! See this our new retreat
Walled in with a sloped mound of matted
    shrubs,
Dark, tangled, old and green, still sloping down
To a small pool whose waters lie asleep
Amid the trailing boughs turned water-plants :
And tall trees overarch to keep us in,
Breaking the sunbeams into emerald shafts,
And in the dreamy water one small group
Of two or three strange trees are got together
Wondering at all around, as strange beasts herd
Together far from their own land : all wildness,
No turf nor moss, for boughs and plants pave all,
And tongues of bank go shelving in the lymph,
Where the pale-throated snake reclines his head,
And old gray stones lie making eddies there,
The wild-mice cross them dry-shod. Deeper in !
Shut thy soft eyes — now look — still deeper in !
This is the very heart of the woods all round
Mountain-like heaped above us ; yet even here
One pond of water gleams ; far off the river
Sweeps like a sea, barred out from land ; but
    one —
One thin clear sheet has overleaped and wound
Into this silent depth, which gained, it lies
Still, as but let by sufferance ; the trees bend
O'er it as wild men watch a sleeping girl,
And through their roots long creeping plants
    out-stretch
Their twined hair, steeped and sparkling ; far-
    ther on,
Tall rushes and thick flag-knots have combined
To narrow it ; so, at length, a silver thread,
It winds, all noiselessly through the deep wood
Till through a cleft-way, through the moss and
    stone,
It joins its parent-river with a shout.

Up for the glowing day, leave the old woods !
See, they part like a ruined arch : the sky !
Nothing but sky appears, so close the roots
And grass of the hill-top level with the air —
Blue sunny air, where a great cloud floats laden
With light, like a dead whale that white birds
    pick,
Floating away in the sun in some north sea.
Air, air, fresh life-blood, thin and searching air,
The clear, dear breath of God that loveth us,
Where small birds reel and winds take their de-
    light !
Water is beautiful, but not like air :

See, where the solid azure waters lie
Made as of thickened air, and down below,
The fern-ranks like a forest spread themselves
As though each pore could feel the element ;
Where the quick glancing serpent winds his
    way,
Float with me there, Pauline ! — but not like air.

Down the hill ! Stop — a clump of trees, see, set
On a heap of rock, which look o'er the far plain :
So, envious climbing shrubs would mount to rest
And peer from their spread boughs ; wide they
    wave, looking
At the muleteers who whistle on their way,
To the merry chime of morning bells, past all
The little smoking cots, mid fields and banks
And copses bright in the sun. My spirit wan-
    ders :
Hedgerows for me — those living hedgerows
    where
The bushes close and clasp above and keep
Thought in — I am concentrated — I feel ;
But my soul saddens when it looks beyond :
I cannot be immortal, taste all joy.

O God, where do they tend — these struggling
    aims ?
What would I have ? What is this "sleep"
    which seems
To bound all ? can there be a "waking" point
Of crowning life ? The soul would never rule :
It would be first in all things, it would have
Its utmost pleasure filled, but, that complete,
Commanding, for commanding, sickens it.
The last point I can trace — rest beneath
Some better essence than itself, in weakness ;
This is "myself," not what I think should be :
And what is that I hunger for but God ?

My God, my God, let me for once look on thee
As though naught else existed, we alone !
And as creation crumbles, my soul's spark
Expands till I can say, — Even from myself
I need thee and I feel thee and I love thee.
I do not plead my rapture in thy works
For love of thee, nor that I feel as one
Who cannot die : but there is that in me
Which turns to thee, which loves or which
    should love.

Why have I girt myself with this hell-dress ?
Why have I labored to put out my life ?
Is it not in my nature to adore,
And e'en for all my reason do I not
Feel him, and thank him, and pray to him —
    now ?
Can I forego the trust that he loves me ?
Do I not feel a love which only ONE . . .
O thou pale form, so dimly seen, deep-eyed !
I have denied thee calmly — do I not
Pant when I read of thy consummate power,
And burn to see thy calm pure truths out-flash
The brightest gleams of earth's philosophy ?
Do I not shake to hear aught question thee ?
If I am erring save me, madden me,
Take from me powers and pleasures, let me die
Ages, so I see thee ! I am knit round
As with a charm by sin and lust and pride.

Yet though my wandering dreams have seen
    all shapes
Of strange delight, oft have I stood by thee —
Have I been keeping lonely watch with thee
In the damp night by weeping Olivet,
Or leaning on thy bosom, proudly less,
Or dying with thee on the lonely cross,
Or witnessing thine outburst from the tomb.

A mortal, sin's familiar friend, doth here
Avow that he will give all earth's reward,
But to believe and humbly teach the faith,
In suffering and poverty and shame,
Only believing he is not unloved.

And now, my Pauline, I am thine forever!
I feel the spirit which has buoyed me up
Desert me, and old shades are gathering fast;
Yet while the last light waits, I would say much,
This chiefly, it is gain that I have said
Somewhat of love I ever felt for thee
But seldom told; our hearts so beat together
That speech seemed mockery; but when dark
    hours come,
And joy departs, and thou, sweet, deem'st it
    strange
A sorrow moves me, thou canst not remove,
Look on this lay I dedicate to thee,
Which through thee I began, which thus I end,
Collecting the last gleams to strive to tell
How I am thine, and more than ever now
That I sink fast: yet though I deeplier sink,
No less song proves one word has brought me
    bliss,
Another still may win bliss surely back.
Thou knowest, dear, I could not think all calm,
For fancies followed thought and bore me off,
And left all indistinct; ere one was caught
Another glanced; so, dazzled by my wealth,
I knew not which to leave nor which to choose,
For all so floated, naught was fixed and firm.
And then thou said'st a perfect bard was one
Who chronicled the stages of all life,
And so thou bad'st me shadow this first stage.
'T is done, and even now I recognize
The shift, the change from last to past — discern
Faintly how life is truth and truth is good.
And why thou must be mine is, that e'en now
In the dim hush of night, that I have done,
Despite the sad forebodings, love looks
    through —
Whispers, — E'en at the last I have her still,
With her delicious eyes as clear as heaven
When rain in a quick shower has beat down
    mist,
And clouds float white above like broods of
    swans.
How the blood lies upon her cheek, outspread
As thinned by kisses! only in her lips
It wells and pulses like a living thing,
And her neck looks like marble misted o'er
With love-breath, — a Pauline from heights
    above,
Stooping beneath me, looking up — one look
As I might kill her and be loved the more.

So, love me — me, Pauline, and naught but me,
Never leave loving! Words are wild and weak,

Believe them not, Pauline! I stained myself
But to behold thee purer by my side,
To show thou art my breath, my life, a last
Resource, an extreme want: never believe
Aught better could so look on thee; nor seek
Again the world of good thoughts left for mine!
There were bright troops of undiscovered suns,
Each equal in their radiant course; there were
Clusters of far fair isles which ocean kept
For his own joy, and his waves broke on them
Without a choice; and there was a dim crowd
Of visions, each a part of some grand whole:
And one star left his peers and came with peace
Upon a storm, and all eyes pined for him;
And one isle harbored a sea-beaten ship,
And the crew wandered in its bowers and
    plucked
Its fruits and gave up all their hopes of home;
And one dream came to a pale poet's sleep,
And he said, "I am singled out by God,
No sin must touch me." Words are wild and
    weak,
But what they would express is, — Leave me
    not,
Still sit by me with beating breast and hair
Loosened, be watching earnest by my side,
Turning my books or kissing me when I
Look up — like summer wind! Be still to me
A help to music's mystery which mind fails
To fathom, its solution, no mere clue!
O reason's pedantry, life's rule prescribed!
I hopeless, I the loveless, hope and love.
Wiser and better, know me now, not when
You loved me as I was. Smile not! I have
Much yet to dawn on you, to gladden you.
No more of the past! I 'll look within no more.
I have too trusted my own lawless wants,
Too trusted my vain self, vague intuition —
Draining soul's wine alone in the still night,
And seeing how, as gathering films arose,
As by an inspiration life seemed bare
And grinning in its vanity, while ends
Foul to be dreamed of, smiled at me as fixed
And fair, while others changed from fair to foul
As a young witch turns an old hag at night.
No more of this! We will go hand in hand,
I with thee, even as a child — love's slave,
Looking no farther than his liege commands.

And thou hast chosen where this life shall be:
The land which gave me thee shall be our home,
Where nature lies all wild amid her lakes
And snow-swathed mountains and vast pines
    begirt
With ropes of snow — where nature lies all bare,
Suffering none to view her but a race
Or stinted or deformed, like the mute dwarfs
Which wait upon a naked Indian queen.
And there (the time being when the heavens
    are thick
With storm) I 'll sit with thee while thou dost
    sing
Thy native songs, gay as a desert bird
Which crieth as it flies for perfect joy,
Or telling me old stories of dead knights;
Or I will read great lays to thee — how she,
The fair pale sister, went to her chill grave
With power to love and to be loved and live:

Or we will go together, like twin gods
Of the infernal world, with scented lamp
Over the dead, to call and to awake,
Over the unshaped images which lie
Within my mind's cave : only leaving all,
That tells of the past doubt.   So, when spring
 comes
With sunshine back again like an old smile,
And the fresh waters and awakened birds
And budding woods await us, I shall be
Prepared, and we will question life once more,
Till its old sense shall come renewed by change,
Like some clear thought which harsh words
 veiled before ;
Feeling God loves us, and that all which errs
Is but a dream which death will dissipate.
And then what need of longer exile ? Seek
My England, and, again there, calm approach
All I once fled from, calmly look on those
The works of my past weakness, as one views
Some scene where danger met him long before.
Ah that such pleasant life should be but
 dreamed !

But whate'er come of it, and though it fade,
And though ere the cold morning all be gone,
As it may be ; — though music wait to wile,
And strange eyes and bright wine lure, laugh
 like sin
Which steals back softly on a soul half saved,
And I the first deny, decry, despise,
With this avowal, these intents so fair, —
Still be it all my own, this moment's pride !
No less I make an end in perfect joy.
E'en in my brightest time, a lurking fear
Possessed me : I well knew my weak resolves,
I felt the witchery that makes mind sleep
Over its treasure, as one half afraid
To make his riches definite : but now
These feelings shall not utterly be lost,
I shall not know again that nameless care
Lest, leaving all undone in youth, some new
And undreamed end reveal itself too late :
For this song shall remain to tell forever
That when I lost all hope of such a change,
Suddenly beauty rose on me again.
No less I make an end in perfect joy,
For I, who thus again was visited,
Shall doubt not many another bliss awaits,
And, though this weak soul sink and darkness
 whelm,
Some little word shall light it, raise aloft,

To where I clearlier see and better love,
As I again go o'er the tracts of thought
Like one who has a right, and I shall live
With poets, calmer, purer still each time,
And beauteous shapes will come for me to seize.
And unknown secrets will be trusted me
Which were denied the waverer once ; but now
I shall be priest and prophet as of old.

Sun-treader, I believe in God and truth
And love ; and as one just escaped from death
Would bind himself in bands of friends to feel
He lives indeed, so, I would lean on thee !
Thou must be ever with me, most in gloom
If such must come, but chiefly when I die,
For I seem, dying, as one going in the dark
To fight a giant : but live thou forever,
And be to all what thou hast been to me !
All in whom this wakes pleasant thoughts of me
Know my last state is happy, free from doubt
Or touch of fear.   Love me and wish me well.

SONNET.

Mr. Gosse in his *Personalia* copies from the
Monthly Repository the following sonnet. Three
other pieces first printed in the same periodical
will be found as afterward grouped in *Bells
and Pomegranates*.

EYES, calm beside thee (Lady, couldst thou
 know !)
 May turn away thick with fast gathering
  tears :
I glance not where all gaze : thrilling and low
 Their passionate praises reach thee — my
  cheek wears
 Alone no wonder when thou passest by ;
 Thy tremulous lids, bent and suffused, reply
To the irrepressible homage which doth glow
 On every lip but mine : if in thine ears
Their accents linger — and thou dost recall
 Me as I stood, still, guarded, very pale,
 Beside each votarist whose lighted brow
Wore worship like an aureole, " O'er them all
 My beauty," thou wilt murmur, " did pre-
  vail
 Save that one only : " — Lady, couldst thou
  know !
August 17, 1834.

PARACELSUS

INSCRIBED TO

AMÉDÉE DE RIPERT-MONCLAR

BY HIS AFFECTIONATE FRIEND

LONDON, March 15, 1835.   R. B.

THE dedication of *Paracelsus* was, in a degree, the payment of a debt, for it was the young count, four years older than Browning, and at the time a private agent in England between the Duchesse de Berri and her royalist friends in France, who suggested the subject to the poet. When first published *Paracelsus* had the following Preface : " I am anxious that the reader should not, at the very outset, — mistaking my performance for one of a class with which it has nothing in common, — judge it by principles on which it was never moulded, and subject it to a standard to which it was never meant to conform. I therefore anticipate his discovery, that it is an attempt, probably more novel than happy, to reverse the method usually adopted by writers whose aim it is to set forth any phenomena of the mind or the passions, by the operation of persons and events ; and that, instead of having recourse to an external machinery of incidents to create and evolve the crisis I desire to produce, I have ventured to display somewhat minutely the mood itself in its rise and progress, and have suffered the agency by which it is influenced and determined, to be generally discernible in its effects alone, and subordinate throughout, if not altogether excluded : and this for a reason. I have endeavored to write a poem, not a drama : the canons of the drama are well known, and I cannot but think that, inasmuch as they have immediate regard to stage representation, the peculiar advantages they hold out are really such only so long as the purpose for which they were at first instituted is kept in view. I do not very well understand what is called a Dramatic Poem, wherein all those restrictions only submitted to on account of compensating good in the original scheme are scrupulously retained, as though for some special fitness in themselves — and all new facilities placed at an author's disposal by the vehicle he selects, as pertinaciously rejected. It is certain, however, that a work like mine depends on the intelligence and sympathy of the reader for its success, — indeed were my scenes stars, it must be his coöperating fancy which, supplying all chasms, shall collect the scattered lights into one constellation — a Lyre or a Crown. I trust for his indulgence towards a poem which had not been imagined six months ago : and that even should he think slightingly of the present (an experiment I am in no case likely to repeat) he will not be prejudiced against other productions which may follow in a more popular, and perhaps less difficult form."

Mr. Browning, senior, paid for the publication of *Paracelsus*. In its final form, as here given, it is greatly changed, not in structure but in phrase. Mr. Cooke states that the change affects nearly a third of the lines.

PERSONS

AUREOLUS PARACELSUS, a student.
FESTUS and MICHAL, his friends.
APRILE, an Italian poet.

I. PARACELSUS ASPIRES

SCENE, *Würzburg : a garden in the environs.* 1512.

FESTUS, PARACELSUS, MICHAL.

Paracelsus. Come close to me, dear friends ;
   still closer ; thus !
Close to the heart which, though long time roll by
Ere it again beat quicker, pressed to yours,
As now it beats — perchance a long, long time —
At least henceforth your memories shall make
Quiet and fragrant as befits their home.
Nor shall my memory want a home in yours —
Alas, that it requires too well such free
Forgiving love as shall embalm it there !

For if you would remember me aright,
As I was born to be, you must forget
All fitful, strange and moody waywardness
Which e'er confused my better spirit, to dwell
Only on moments such as these, dear friends !
— My heart no truer, but my words and ways
More true to it : as Michal, some months
   hence,
Will say, " this autumn was a pleasant time,"
For some few sunny days ; and overlook
Its bleak wind, hankering after pining leaves.
Autumn would fain be sunny ; I would look
Liker my nature's truth : and both are frail,
And both beloved, for all our frailty.
   Michal.   Aureole !
   Par. Drop by drop ! she is weeping like a
   child !
Not so ! I am content — more than content ;
Nay, autumn wins you best by this its mute
Appeal to sympathy for its decay :
Look up, sweet Michal, nor esteem the less

Your stained and drooping vines their grapes
    bow down,
Nor blame those creaking trees bent with their
    fruit,
That apple-tree with a rare after-birth
Of peeping blooms sprinkled its wealth among!
Then for the winds — what wind that ever raved
Shall vex that ash which overlooks you both,
So proud it wears its berries? Ah, at length,
The old smile meet for her, the lady of this
Sequestered nest! — this kingdom, limited
Alone by one old populous green wall
Tenanted by the ever-busy flies.
Gray crickets and shy lizards and quick spiders,
Each family of the silver-threaded moss —
Which, look through near, this way, and it
    appears
A stubble-field or a cane-brake, a marsh
Of bulrush whitening in the sun : laugh now!
Fancy the crickets, each one in his house,
Looking out, wondering at the world — or best,
Yon painted snail with his gay shell of dew,
Travelling to see the glossy balls high up
Hung by the caterpillar, like gold lamps.
    Mich. In truth we have lived carelessly and
    well.
    Par. And shall, my perfect pair! — each,
    trust me, born
For the other ; nay, your very hair, when mixed,
Is of one hue. For where save in this nook
Shall you two walk, when I am far away,
And wish me prosperous fortune? Stay : that
    plant
Shall never wave its tangles lightly and softly,
As a queen's languid and imperial arm
Which scatters crowns among her lovers, but you
Shall be reminded to predict to me
Some great success! Ah see, the sun sinks broad
Behind Saint Saviour's : wholly gone, at last!
    Festus. Now, Aureole, stay those wandering
    eyes awhile!
You are ours to-night, at least ; and while you
    spoke
Of Michal and her tears, I thought that none
Could willing leave what he so seemed to love :
But that last look destroys my dream — that
    look
As if, where'er you gazed, there stood a star!
How far was Würzburg with its church and spire
And garden-walls and all things they contain,
From that look's far alighting?
    Par.   I but spoke
And looked alike from simple joy to see
The beings I love best, shut in so well
From all rude chances like to be my lot,
That, when afar, my weary spirit, — disposed
To lose awhile its care in soothing thoughts
Of them, their pleasant features, looks and
    words, —
Needs never hesitate, nor apprehend
Encroaching trouble may have reached them
    too,
Nor have recourse to fancy's busy aid
And fashion even a wish in their behalf
Beyond what they possess already here ;
But, unobstructed, may at once forget
Itself in them, assured how well they fare.
Beside, this Festus knows he holds me one

Whom quiet and its charms arrest in vain,
One scarce aware of all the joys I quit,
Too filled with airy hopes to make account
Of soft delights his own heart garners up :
Whereas behold how much our sense of all
That 's beauteous proves alike! When Festus
    learns
That every common pleasure of the world
Affects me as himself ; that I have just
As varied appetite for joy derived
From common things ; a stake in life, in short,
Like his ; a stake which rash pursuit of aims
That life affords not, would as soon destroy ; —
He may convince himself that, this in view,
I shall act well advised. And last, because,
Though heaven and earth and all things were
    at stake,
Sweet Michal must not weep, our parting eve.
    Fest. True : and the eve is deepening, and
    we sit
As little anxious to begin our talk
As though to-morrow I could hint of it
As we paced arm-in-arm the cheerful town
At sun-dawn ; or could whisper it by fits
(Trithemius busied with his class the while)
In that dim chamber where the noon-streaks peer
Half-frightened by the awful tomes around ;
Or in some grassy lane unbosom all
From even-blush to midnight : but, to-morrow!
Have I full leave to tell my inmost mind?
We have been brothers, and henceforth the
    world
Will rise between us : — all my freest mind?
'T is the last night, dear Aureole!
    Par.   Oh, say on!
Devise some test of love, some arduous feat
To be performed for you : say on! If night
Be spent the while, the better! Recall how oft
My wondrous plans and dreams and hopes and
    fears
Have — never wearied you, oh no! — as I
Recall, and never vividly as now,
Your true affection, born when Einsiedeln
And its green hills were all the world to us ;
And still increasing to this night which ends
My further stay at Würzburg. Oh, one day
You shall be very proud! Say on, dear friends!
    Fest. In truth? 'T is for my proper peace, in-
    deed,
Rather than yours ; for vain all projects seem
To stay your course : I said my latest hope
Is fading even now. A story tells
Of some far embassy despatched to win
The favor of an eastern king, and how
The gifts they offered proved but dazzling dust
Shed from the ore-beds native to his clime.
Just so, the value of repose and love,
I meant should tempt you, better far than I
You seem to comprehend ; and yet desist
No whit from projects where repose nor love
Has part.
    Par.   Once more? Alas! As I foretold.
    Fest. A solitary brier the bank puts forth
To save our swan's nest floating out to sea.
    Par. Dear Festus, hear me. What is it you
    wish?
That I should lay aside my heart's pursuit,
Abandon the sole ends for which I live,

Reject God's great commission, and so die !
You bid me listen for your true love's sake :
Yet how has grown that love ?   Even in a long
And patient cherishing of the self-same spirit
It now would quell ; as though a mother hoped
To stay the lusty manhood of the child
Once weak upon her knees.   I was not born
Informed and fearless from the first, but shrank
From aught which marked me out apart from
      men :
I would have lived their life, and died their
      death,
Lost in their ranks, eluding destiny :
But you first guided me through doubt and fear,
Taught me to know mankind and know myself ;
And now that I am strong and full of hope,
That, from my soul, I can reject all aims
Save those your earnest words made plain to me,
Now that I touch the brink of my design,
When I would have a triumph in their eyes,
A glad cheer in their voices — Michal weeps,
And Festus ponders gravely !
      Fest.   When you deign
To hear my purpose . . .
      Par.   Hear it ?   I can say
Beforehand all this evening's conference !
'T is this way, Michal, that he uses : first,
Or he declares, or I, the leading points
Of our best scheme of life, what is man's end
And what God's will ; no two faiths e'er agreed
As his with mine.   Next, each of us allows
Faith should be acted on as best we may ;
Accordingly, I venture to submit
My plan, in lack of better, for pursuing
The path which God's will seems to authorize.
Well, he discerns much good in it, avows
This motive worthy, that hope plausible,
A danger here to be avoided, there
An oversight to be repaired : in fine,
Our two minds go together — all the good
Approved by him, I gladly recognize,
All he counts bad, I thankfully discard,
And naught forbids my looking up at last
For some stray comfort in his cautious brow.
When lo ! I learn that, spite of all, there lurks
Some innate and inexplicable germ
Of failure in my scheme ; so that at last
It all amounts to this — the sovereign proof
That we devote ourselves to God, is seen
In living just as though no God there were ;
A life which, prompted by the sad and blind
Folly of man, Festus abhors the most ;
But which these tenets sanctify at once,
Though to less subtle wits it seems the same,
Consider it how they may.
      Mich.   Is it so, Festus ?
He speaks so calmly and kindly : is it so ?
      Par. Reject those glorious visions of God's
      love
And man's design ; laugh loud that God should
      send
Vast longings to direct us ; say how soon
Power satiates these, or lust, or gold ; I know
The world's cry well, and how to answer it.
But this ambiguous warfare . . . .
      Fest.   . . . Wearies so
That you will grant no last leave to your friend
To urge it ? — for his sake, not yours ?   I wish

To send my soul in good hopes after you ;
Never to sorrow that uncertain words
Erringly apprehended, a new creed
Ill understood, begot rash trust in you,
Had share in your undoing.
      Par.   Choose your side,
Hold or renounce : but meanwhile blame me not
Because I dare to act on your own views,
Nor shrink when they point onward, nor espy
A peril where they most ensure success.
      Fest.   Prove that to me — but that !   Prove
      you abide
Within their warrant, nor presumptuous boast
God's labor laid on you ; prove, all you covet,
A mortal may expect ; and, most of all,
Prove the strange course you now affect, will
      lead
To its attainment — and I bid you speed,
Nay, count the minutes till you venture forth !
You smile ; but I had gathered from slow
      thought —
Much musing on the fortunes of my friend —
Matter I deemed could not be urged in vain ;
But it all leaves me at my need : in shreds
And fragments I must venture what remains.
      Mich.   Ask at once, Festus, wherefore he
      should scorn. . . .
      Fest.   Stay, Michal : Aureole, I speak guard-
      edly
And gravely, knowing well, whate'er your error,
This is no ill-considered choice of yours,
No sudden fancy of an ardent boy.
Not from your own confiding words alone
Am I aware your passionate heart long since
Gave birth to, nourished and at length matures
This scheme.   I will not speak of Einsiedeln,
Where I was born your elder by some years
Only to watch you fully from the first :
In all beside, our mutual tasks were fixed
Even then — 't was mine to have you in my view
As you had your own soul and those intents
Which filled it when, to crown your dearest
      wish,
With a tumultuous heart, you left with me
Our childhood's home to join the favored few
Whom, here, Trithemius condescends to teach
A portion of his lore : and not one youth
Of those so favored, whom you now despise,
Came earnest as you came, resolved, like you,
To grasp all, and retain all, and deserve
By patient toil a wide renown like his.
Now, this new ardor which supplants the old
I watched, too ; 't was significant and strange,
In one matched to his soul's content at length
With rivals in the search for wisdom's prize,
To see the sudden pause, the total change ;
From contest, the transition to repose —
From pressing onward as his fellows pressed,
To a blank idleness, yet most unlike
The dull stagnation of a soul, content,
Once foiled, to leave betimes a thriveless quest.
That careless bearing, free from all pretence
Even of contempt for what it ceased to seek —
Smiling humility, praising much, yet waiving
What it professed to praise — though not so well
Maintained but that rare outbreaks, fierce and
      brief,
Revealed the hidden scorn, as quickly curbed.

That ostentatious show of past defeat,
That ready acquiescence in contempt,
I deemed no other than the letting go
His shivered sword, of one about to spring
Upon his foe's throat; but it was not thus:
Not that way looked your brooding purpose
    then.
For after-signs disclosed, what you confirmed,
That you prepared to task to the uttermost
Your strength, in furtherance of a certain aim
Which — while it bore the name your rivals gave
Their own most puny efforts — was so vast
In scope that it included their best flights.
Combined them, and desired to gain one prize
In place of many, — the secret of the world,
Of man, and man's true purpose, path and fate.
— That you, not nursing as a mere vague dream
This purpose, with the sages of the past,
Have struck upon a way to this, if all
You trust be true, which following, heart and
    soul,
You, if a man may, dare aspire to KNOW:
And that this aim shall differ from a host
Of aims alike in character and kind,
Mostly in this, — that in itself alone
Shall its reward be, not an alien end
Blending therewith; no hope nor fear nor joy
Nor woe, to elsewhere move you, but this pure
Devotion to sustain you or betray:
Thus you aspire.
    Par.   You shall not state it thus:
I should not differ from the dreamy crew
You speak of. I profess no other share
In the selection of my lot, than this
My ready answer to the will of God
Who summons me to be his organ. All
Whose innate strength supports them shall suc-
    ceed
No better than the sages.
    Fest.   Such the aim, then,
God sets before you; and 't is doubtless need
That he appoint no less the way of praise
Than the desire to praise; for, though I hold,
With you, the setting forth such praise to be
The natural end and service of a man,
And hold such praise is best attained when man
Attains the general welfare of his kind —
Yet this, the end, is not the instrument.
Presume not to serve God apart from such
Appointed channel as he wills shall gather
Imperfect tributes, for that sole obedience
Valued perchance! He seeks not that his altars
Blaze, careless how, so that they do but blaze.
Suppose this, then; that God selected you
To KNOW (heed well your answers, for my faith
Shall meet implicitly what they affirm),
I cannot think you dare annex to such
Selection aught beyond a steadfast will,
An intense hope; nor let your gifts create
Scorn or neglect of ordinary means
Conducive to success, make destiny
Dispense with man's endeavor. Now, dare you
    search
Your inmost heart, and candidly avow
Whether you have not rather wild desire
For this distinction than security
Of its existence? whether you discern
The path to the fulfilment of your purpose

Clear as that purpose — and again, that purpose
Clear as your yearning to be singled out
For its pursuer. Dare you answer this?
    Par. (after a pause). No, I have naught to
        fear! Who will may know
The secret'st workings of my soul. What
        though
It be so? — if indeed the strong desire
Eclipse the aim in me? — if splendor break
Upon the outset of my path alone,
And duskest shade succeed? What fairer sea¹
Shall I require to my authentic mission
Than this fierce energy? — this instinct striving
Because its nature is to strive? — enticed
By the security of no broad course,
Without success forever in its eyes!
How know I else such glorious fate my own,
But in the restless irresistible force
That works within me? Is it for human will
To institute such impulses? — still less,
To disregard their promptings! What should I
Do, kept among you all; your loves, your cares,
Your life — all to be mine? Be sure that God
Ne'er dooms to waste the strength he deigns
    impart!
Ask the geier-eagle why she stoops at once
Into the vast and unexplored abyss,
What full-grown power informs her from the
    first,
Why she not marvels, strenuously beating
The silent boundless regions of the sky!
Be sure they sleep not whom God needs! Nor
    fear
Their holding light his charge, when every hour
That finds that charge delayed, is a new death.
This for the faith in which I trust; and hence
I can abjure so well the idle arts
These pedants strive to learn and teach; Black
    Arts,
Great Works, the Secret and Sublime, forsooth—
Let others prize: too intimate a tie
Connects me with our God! A sullen fiend
To do my bidding, fallen and hateful sprites
To help me — what are these, at best, beside
God helping, God directing everywhere,
So that the earth shall yield her secrets up,
And every object there be charged to strike,
Teach, gratify her master God appoints?
And I am young, my Festus, happy and free!
I can devote myself; I have a life
To give; I, singled out for this, the One!
Think, think! the wide East, where all Wis-
    dom sprung;
The bright South, where she dwelt; the hopeful
    North,
All are passed o'er — it lights on me! 'T is time
New hopes should animate the world, new light
Should dawn from new revealings to a race
Weighed down so long, forgotten so long; thus
    shall
The heaven reserved for us at last receive
Creatures whom no unwonted splendors blind,
But ardent to confront the unclouded blaze,
Whose beams not seldom blessed their pilgrim-
    age,
Not seldom glorified their life below.
    Fest. My words have their old fate and
        make faint stand

Against your glowing periods. Call this, truth —
Why not pursue it in a fast retreat,
Some one of Learning's many palaces,
After approved example ? — seeking there
Calm converse with the great dead, soul to soul,
Who laid up treasure with the like intent
— So lift yourself into their airy place,
And fill out full their unfulfilled careers,
Unravelling the knots their baffled skill
Pronounced inextricable, true ! — but left
Far less confused. A fresh eye, a fresh hand,
Might do much at their vigor's waning-point ;
Succeeding with new-breathed new-hearted
    force,
As at old games the runner snatched the torch
From runner still : this way success might be.
But you have coupled with your enterprise
An arbitrary self-repugnant scheme
Of seeking it in strange and untried paths.
What books are in the desert ? Writes the sea
The secret of her yearning in vast caves
Where yours will fall the first of human feet ?
Has wisdom sat there and recorded aught
You press to read ? Why turn aside from her
To visit, where her vesture never glanced,
Now — solitudes consigned to barrenness
By God's decree, which who shall dare impugn ?
Now — ruins where she paused but would not
    stay,
Old ravaged cities that, renouncing her,
She called an endless curse on, so it came :
Or worst of all, now — men you visit, men,
Ignoblest troops who never heard her voice
Or hate it, men without one gift from Rome
Or Athens, — these shall Aureole's teachers be !
Rejecting past example, practice, precept,
Aidless 'mid these he thinks to stand alone :
Thick like a glory round the Stagirite
Your rivals throng, the sages : here stand you !
Whatever you may protest, knowledge is not
Paramount in your love ; or for her sake
You would collect all help from every source —
Rival, assistant, friend, foe, all would merge
In the broad class of those who showed her
    haunts,
And those who showed them not.
    Par.   What shall I say ?
Festus, from childhood I have been possessed
By a fire — by a true fire, or faint or fierce,
As from without some master, so it seemed,
Repressed or urged its current : this but ill
Expresses what I would convey : but rather
I will believe an angel ruled me thus,
Than that my soul's own workings, own high
    nature,
So became manifest. I knew not then
What whispered in the evening, and spoke out
At midnight. If some mortal, born too soon,
Were laid away in some great trance — the ages
Coming and going all the while — till dawned
His true time's advent ; and could then record
The words they spoke who kept watch by his
    bed, —
Then I might tell more of the breath so light
Upon my eyelids, and the fingers light
Among my hair. Youth is confused ; yet never
So dull was I but, when that spirit passed,
I turned to him, scarce consciously, as turns

A water-snake when fairies cross his sleep.
And having this within me and about me
While Einsiedeln, its mountains, lakes and
    woods
Confined me — what oppressive joy was mine
When life grew plain, and I first viewed the
    thronged,
The everlasting concourse of mankind !
Believe that ere I joined them, ere I knew
The purpose of the pageant, or the place
Consigned me in its ranks — while, just awake,
Wonder was freshest and delight most pure —
'T was then that least supportable appeared
A station with the brightest of the crowd,
A portion with the proudest of them all.
And from the tumult in my breast, this only
Could I collect, that I must thenceforth die
Or elevate myself far, far above
The gorgeous spectacle. I seemed to long
At once to trample on, yet save mankind,
To make some unexampled sacrifice
In their behalf, to wring some wondrous good
From heaven or earth for them, to perish, win-
    ning
Eternal weal in the act : as who should dare
Pluck out the angry thunder from its cloud,
That, all its gathered flame discharged on him,
No storm might threaten summer's azure sleep :
Yet never to be mixed with men so much
As to have part even in my own work, share
In my own largess. Once the feat achieved,
I would withdraw from their officious praise,
Would gently put aside their profuse thanks.
Like some knight traversing a wilderness,
Who, on his way, may chance to free a tribe
Of desert-people from their dragon-foe ;
When all the swarthy race press round to kiss
His feet, and choose him for their king, and yield
Their poor tents, pitched among the sand-hills,
    for
His realm : and he points, smiling, to his scarf
Heavy with riveled gold, his burgonet
Gay set with twinkling stones — and to the East,
Where these must be displayed !
    Fest.   Good : let us hear
No more about your nature, " which first shrank
From all that marked you out apart from men ! "
    Par. I touch on that ; these words but analyze
The first mad impulse : 't was as brief as fond,
For as I gazed again upon the show,
I soon distinguished here and there a shape
Palm-wreathed and radiant, forehead and full
    eye.
Well pleased was I their state should thus at once
Interpret my own thoughts : — " Behold the clue
To all," I rashly said, " and what I pine
To do, these have accomplished : we are peers.
They know and therefore rule : I, too, will
    know ! "
You were beside me, Festus, as you say ;
You saw me plunge in their pursuits whom fame
Is lavish to attest the lords of mind,
Not pausing to make sure the prize in view
Would satiate my cravings when obtained,
But since they strove I strove. Then came a
    slow
And strangling failure. We aspired alike,
Yet not the meanest plodder, Tritheim counts

A marvel, but was all-sufficient, strong
Or staggered only at his own vast wits ;
While I was restless, nothing satisfied,
Distrustful, most perplexed.   I would slur over
That struggle ; suffice it, that I loathed myself
As weak compared with them, yet felt somehow
A mighty power was brooding, taking shape
Within me ; and this lasted till one night
When, as I sat revolving it and more,
A still voice from without said — " Seest thou
    not,
Desponding child, whence spring defeat and
    loss ?
Even from thy strength.   Consider : hast thou
    gazed
Presumptuously on wisdom's countenance,
No veil between ; and can thy faltering hands,
Unguided by the brain the sight absorbs,
Pursue their task as earnest blinkers do
Whom radiance ne'er distracted ? Live their life
If thou wouldst share their fortune, choose their
    eyes
Unfed by splendor.   Let each task present
Its petty good to thee.   Waste not thy gifts
In profitless waiting for the gods' descent,
But have some idol of thine own to dress
With their array.   Know, not for knowing's sake,
But to become a star to men forever ;
Know, for the gain it gets, the praise it brings,
The wonder it inspires, the love it breeds :
Look one step onward, and secure that step ! "
And I smiled as one never smiles but once,
Then first discovering my own aim's extent,
Which sought to comprehend the works of God,
And God himself, and all God's intercourse
With the human mind ; I understood, no less,
My fellows' studies, whose true worth I saw,
But smiled not, well aware who stood by me.
And softer came the voice — " There is a way :
'T is hard for flesh to tread therein, imbued
With frailty — hopeless, if indulgence first
Have ripened inborn germs of sin to strength :
Wilt thou adventure for my sake and man's,
Apart from all reward ?" And last it breathed —
" Be happy, my good soldier ; I am by thee,
Be sure, even to the end ! " — I answered not,
Knowing him.   As he spoke, I was endued
With comprehension and a steadfast will ;
And when he ceased, my brow was sealed his
    own.
If there took place no special change in me,
How comes it all things wore a different hue
Thenceforward ? — pregnant with vast conse-
    quence,
Teeming with grand result, loaded with fate ?
So that when, quailing at the mighty range
Of secret truths which yearn for birth, I haste
To contemplate undazzled some one truth,
Its bearings and effects alone — at once
What was a speck expands into a star,
Asking a life to pass exploring thus,
Till I near craze.   I go to prove my soul !
I see my way as birds their trackless way.
I shall arrive ! what time, what circuit first,
I ask not : but unless God send his hail
Or blinding fireballs, sleet or stifling snow,
In some time, his good time, I shall arrive :
He guides me and the bird.   In his good time !

Mich.   Vex him no further, Festus ; it is so !
Fest.   Just thus you help me ever.   This
    would hold
Were it the trackless air, and not a path
Inviting you, distinct with footprints yet
Of many a mighty marcher gone that way.
You may have purer views than theirs, perhaps
But they were famous in their day — the proofs
Remain.   At least accept the light they lend.
Par.   Their light ! the sum of all is briefly
    this :
They labored and grew famous, and the fruits
Are best seen in a dark and groaning earth
Given over to a blind and endless strife
With evils, what of all their lore abates ?
No ; I reject and spurn them utterly
And all they teach.   Shall I still sit beside
Their dry wells, with a white lip and filmed eye,
While in the distance heaven is blue above
Mountains where sleep the unsunned tarns ?
Fest.   And yet
As strong delusions have prevailed ere now.
Men have set out as gallantly to seek
Their ruin.   I have heard of such : yourself
Avow all hitherto have failed and fallen.
Mich.   Nay, Festus, when but as the pilgrims
    faint
Through the drear way, do you expect to see
Their city dawn amid the clouds afar ?
Par.   Ay, sounds it not like some old well-
    known tale ?
For me, I estimate their works and them
So rightly, that at times I almost dream
I too have spent a life the sages' way,
And tread once more familiar paths.   Perchance
I perished in an arrogant self-reliance
Ages ago ; and in that act, a prayer
For one more chance went up so earnest, so
Instinct with better light let in by death,
That life was blotted out — not so completely
But scattered wrecks enough of it remain,
Dim memories, as now, when once more seems
The goal in sight again.   All which, indeed,
Is foolish, and only means — the flesh I wear,
The earth I tread, are not more clear to me
Than my belief, explained to you or no.
Fest.   And who am I, to challenge and dis-
    pute
That clear belief ?   I will divest all fear.
Mich.   Then Aureole is God's commissary !
    he shall
Be great and grand — and all for us !
Par.   No, sweet !
Not great and grand.   If I can serve mankind
'T is well ; but there our intercourse must end
I never will be served by those I serve.
Fest.   Look well to this ; here is a plague
    spot, here,
Disguise it how you may !   'T is true, you utter
This scorn while by our side and loving us ;
'T is but a spot as yet : but it will break
Into a hideous blotch if overlooked.
How can that course be safe which from the first
Produces carelessness to human love ?
It seems you have abjured the helps which men
Who overpass their kind, as you would do,
Have humbly sought ; I dare not thoroughly
    probe

This matter, lest I learn too much.   Let be
That popular praise would little instigate
Your efforts, nor particular approval
Reward you ; put reward aside ; alone
You shall go forth upon your arduous task,
None shall assist you, none partake your toil,
None share your triumph : still you must retain
Some one to cast your glory on, to share
Your rapture with.   Were I elect like you,
I would encircle me with love, and raise
A rampart of my fellows ; it should seem
Impossible for me to fail, so watched
By gentle friends who made my cause their
      own.
They should ward off fate's envy — the great
      gift,
Extravagant when claimed by me alone,
Being so a gift to them as well as me.
If danger daunted me or ease seduced,
How calmly their sad eyes should gaze re-
      proach !
   Mich.   O Aureole, can I sing when all alone,
Without first calling, in my fancy, both
To listen by my side — even I !   And you ?
Do you not feel this ?   Say that you feel this !
   Par.   I feel 't is pleasant that my aims, at
      length
Allowed their weight, should be supposed to
      need
A further strengthening in these goodly helps !
My course allures for its own sake, its sole
Intrinsic worth ; and ne'er shall boat of mine
Adventure forth for gold and apes at once.
Your sages say, " if human, therefore weak : "
If weak, more need to give myself entire
To my pursuit ; and by its side, all else . . .
No matter !   I deny myself but little
In waiving all assistance save its own.
Would there were some real sacrifice to make !
Your friends the sages threw their joys away,
While I must be content with keeping mine.
   Fest.   But do not cut yourself from human
      weal !
You cannot thrive — a man that dares effect
To spend his life in service to his kind
For no reward of theirs, unbound to them
By any tie ; nor do so, Aureole !   No —
There are strange punishments for such.   Give
      up
(Although no visible good flow thence) some
      part
Of the glory to another ; hiding thus,
Even from yourself, that all is for yourself.
Say, say almost to God — " I have done all
For her, not for myself ! "
   Par.   And who but lately
Was to rejoice in my success like you ?
Whom should I love but both of you ?
   Fest.   I know not :
But know this, you, that 't is no will of mine
You should abjure the lofty claims you make ;
And this the cause — I can no longer seek
To overlook the truth, that there would be
A monstrous spectacle upon the earth,
Beneath the pleasant sun, among the trees :
— A being knowing not what love is.   Hear
      me !
You are endowed with faculties which bear

Annexed to them as 't were a dispensation
To summon meaner spirits to do their will
And gather round them at their need ; inspiring
Such with a love themselves can never feel,
Passionless 'mid their passionate votaries.
I know not if you joy in this or no,
Or ever dream that common men can live
On objects you prize lightly, but which make
Their heart's sole treasure : the affections seem
Beauteous at most to you, which we must taste
Or die : and this strange quality accords,
I know not how, with you ; sits well upon
That luminous brow, though in another it
      scowls
An eating brand, a shame.   I dare not judge
      you.
The rules of right and wrong thus set aside,
There 's no alternative — I own you one
Of higher order, under other laws
Than bind us ; therefore, curb not one bold
      glance !
'T is best aspire.   Once mingled with us all . . .
   Mich.   Stay with us, Aureole !   cast those
      hopes away,
And stay with us !   An angel warns me, too,
Man should be humble ; you are very proud :
And God, dethroned, has doleful plagues for
      such !
— Warns me to have in dread no quick repulse,
No slow defeat, but a complete success :
You will find all you seek, and perish so !
   Par.   *(after a pause).*   Are these the barren
      first-fruits of my quest ?
Is love like this the natural lot of all ?
How many years of pain might one such hour
O'erbalance ?   Dearest Michal, dearest Festus,
What shall I say, if not that I desire
To justify your love ; and will, dear friends,
In swerving nothing from my first resolves.
See, the great moon ! and ere the mottled owls
Were wide awake, I was to go.   It seems
You acquiesce at last in all save this —
If I am like to compass what I seek
By the untried career I choose ; and then,
If that career, making but small account
Of much of life's delight, will yet retain
Sufficient to sustain my soul : for thus
I understand these fond fears just expressed.
And first ; the lore you praise and I neglect,
The labors and the precepts of old time,
I have not lightly disesteemed.   But, friends,
Truth is within ourselves ; it takes no rise
From outward things, whate'er you may be-
      lieve.
There is an inmost centre in us all,
Where truth abides in fulness ; and around,
Wall upon wall, the gross flesh hems it in,
This perfect, clear perception — which is truth.
A baffling and perverting carnal mesh
Binds it, and makes all error : and, to KNOW,
Rather consists in opening out a way
Whence the imprisoned splendor may escape,
Than in effecting entry for a light
Supposed to be without.   Watch narrowly
The demonstration of a truth, its birth,
And you trace back the effluence to its spring
And source within us ; where broods radiance
      vast,

To be elicited ray by ray, as chance
Shall favor : chance — for hitherto, your sage
Even as he knows not how those beams are
    born,
As little knows he what unlocks their fount :
And men have oft grown old among their books
To die case-hardened in their ignorance,
Whose careless youth had promised what long
    years
Of unremitted labor ne'er performed :
While, contrary, it has chanced some idle day,
To autumn loiterers just as fancy-free
As the midges in the sun, gives birth at last
To truth — produced mysteriously as cape
Of cloud grown out of the invisible air.
Hence, may not truth be lodged alike in all,
The lowest as the highest ? some slight film
The interposing bar which binds a soul
And makes the idiot, just as makes the sage
Some film removed, the happy outlet whence
Truth issues proudly ? See this soul of ours !
How it strives weakly in the child, is loosed
In manhood, clogged by sickness, back com-
    pelled
By age and waste, set free at last by death :
Why is it, flesh enthralls it or enthrones ?
What is this flesh we have to penetrate ?
Oh, not alone when life flows still, do truth
And power emerge, but also when strange
    chance
Ruffles its current ; in unused conjuncture,
When sickness breaks the body — hunger,
    watching,
Excess or languor — oftenest death's approach,
Peril, deep joy or woe. One man shall crawl
Through life surrounded with all stirring things,
Unmoved ; and he goes mad : and from the
    wreck
Of what he was, by his wild talk alone,
You first collect how great a spirit he hid.
Therefore, set free the soul alike in all,
Discovering the true laws by which the flesh
Accloys the spirit ! We may not be doomed
To cope with seraphs, but at least the rest
Shall cope with us. Make no more giants, God,
But elevate the race at once ! We ask
To put forth just our strength, our human
    strength,
All starting fairly, all equipped alike,
Gifted alike, all eagle-eyed, true-hearted —
See if we cannot beat thine angels yet !
Such is my task. I go to gather this
The sacred knowledge, here and there dispersed
About the world, long lost or never found.
And why should I be sad or lorn of hope ?
Why ever make man's good distinct from God's,
Or, finding they are one, why dare mistrust ?
Who shall succeed if not one pledged like me ?
Mine is no mad attempt to build a world
Apart from his, like those who set themselves
To find the nature of the spirit they bore,
And, taught betimes that all their gorgeous
    dreams
Were only born to vanish in this life,
Refused to fit them to its narrow sphere,
But chose to figure forth another world
And other frames meet for their vast desires, —
And all a dream ! Thus was life scorned : but life

Shall yet be crowned : twine amaranth ! I am
    priest !
And all for yielding with a lively spirit
A poor existence, parting with a youth
Like those who squander every energy
Convertible to good, on painted toys,
Breath-bubbles, gilded dust ! And though
    spurn
All adventitious aims, from empty praise
To love's award, yet whoso deems such helps
Important, and concerns himself for me,
May know even these will follow with the rest —
As in the steady rolling Mayne, asleep
Yonder, is mixed its mass of schistous ore.
My own affections, laid to rest awhile,
Will waken purified, subdued alone
By all I have achieved. Till then — till then . . .
Ah, the time-wiling loitering of a page
Through bower and over lawn, till eve shall
    bring
The stately lady's presence whom he loves —
The broken sleep of the fisher whose rough coat
Enwraps the queenly pearl — these are faint
    types !
See, see, they look on me : I triumph now !
But one thing, Festus, Michal ! I have told
All I shall e'er disclose to mortal : say —
Do you believe I shall accomplish this ?
    Fest. I do believe !
    Mich.   I ever did believe !
    Par. Those words shall never fade from out
        my brain !
This earnest of the end shall never fade !
Are there not, Festus, are there not, dear
    Michal,
Two points in the adventure of the diver,
One — when, a beggar, he prepares to plunge,
One — when, a prince, he rises with his pearl ?
Festus, I plunge !
    Fest.   We wait you when you rise !

II. PARACELSUS ATTAINS

Scene, *Constantinople : the house of a Greek conjurer.*
        1521.

PARACELSUS.

Over the waters in the vaporous West
The sun goes down as in a sphere of gold
Behind the arm of the city, which between,
With all that length of domes and minarets,
Athwart the splendor, black and crooked runs
Like a Turk verse along a scimitar.
There lie, sullen memorial, and no more
Possess my aching sight ! 'T is done at last.
Strange — and the juggles of a sallow cheat
Have won me to this act ! 'T is as yon cloud
Should voyage unwrecked o'er many a moun-
    tain-top
And break upon a molehill. I have dared
Come to a pause with knowledge ; scan for once
The heights already reached, without regard
To the extent above ; fairly compute
All I have clearly gained ; for once excluding
A brilliant future to supply and perfect
All half-gains and conjectures and crude hopes;
And all because a fortune-teller wills

His credulous seekers should inscribe thus
    much
Their previous life's attainment, in his roll,
Before his promised secret, as he vaunts,
Make up the sum: and here, amid the scrawled
Uncouth recordings of the dupes of this
Old arch-genethliac, lie my life's results!

A few blurred characters suffice to note
A stranger wandered long through many lands
And reaped the fruit he coveted in a few
Discoveries, as appended here and there,
The fragmentary produce of much toil,
In a dim heap, fact and surmise together
Confusedly massed as when acquired; he was
Intent on gain to come too much to stay
And scrutinize the little gained: the whole
Slipt in the blank space 'twixt an idiot's gibber
And a mad lover's ditty — there it lies.

And yet those blottings chronicle a life —
A whole life, and my life! Nothing to do,
No problem for the fancy, but a life
Spent and decided, wasted past retrieve
Or worthy beyond peer. Stay, what does this
Remembrancer set down concerning "life"?
" 'Time fleets, youth fades, life is an empty
    dream,'
It is the echo of time; and he whose heart
Beat first beneath a human heart, whose speech
Was copied from a human tongue, can never
Recall when he was living yet knew not this.
Nevertheless long seasons pass o'er him
Till some one hour's experience shows what no-
    thing,
It seemed, could clearer show; and ever after,
An altered brow and eye and gait and speech
Attest that now he knows the adage true,
'Time fleets, youth fades, life is an empty
    dream.'"

Ay, my brave chronicler, and this same hour
As well as any: now, let my time be!

Now! I can go no farther; well or ill,
'T is done. I must desist and take my chance.
I cannot keep on the stretch: 't is no back-
    shrinking —
For let but some assurance beam, some close
To my toil grow visible, and I proceed
At any price, though closing it, I die.
Else, here I pause. The old Greek's prophecy
Is like to turn out true: "I shall not quit
His chamber till I know what I desire!"
Was it the light wind sang it o'er the sea?

An end, a rest! strange how the notion, once
Encountered, gathers strength by moments!
    Rest!
Where has it kept so long? this throbbing brow
To cease, this beating heart to cease, all cruel
And gnawing thoughts to cease! To dare let
    down
My strung, so high-strung brain, to dare unnerve
My harassed o'ertasked frame, to know my
    place,
My portion, my reward, even my failure,
Assigned, made sure forever! To lose myself

Among the common creatures of the world,
To draw some gain from having been a man,
Neither to hope nor fear, to live at length!
Even in failure, rest! But rest in truth
And power and recompense . . . I hoped that
    once!

What, sunk insensibly so deep? Has all
Been undergone for this? This the request
My labor qualified me to present
With no fear of refusal? Had I gone
Slightingly through my task, and so judged fit
To moderate my hopes; nay, were it now
My sole concern to exculpate myself,
End things or mend them, — why, I could not
    choose
A humbler mood to wait for the event!
No, no, there needs not this; no, after all,
At worst I have performed my share of the
    task:
The rest is God's concern; mine, merely this,
To know that I have obstinately held
By my own work. The mortal whose brave foot
Has trod, unscathed, the temple-court so far
That he descries at length the shrine of shrines,
Must let no sneering of the demons' eyes,
Whom he could pass unquailing, fasten now
Upon him, fairly past their power; no, no —
He must not stagger, faint, fall down at last,
Having a charm to baffle them; behold,
He bares his front: a mortal ventures thus
Serene amid the echoes, beams and glooms!
If he be priest henceforth, if he wake up
The god of the place to ban and blast him there,
Both well! What 's failure or success to me?
I have subdued my life to the one purpose
Whereto I ordained it; there alone I spy,
No doubt, that way I may be satisfied.

Yes, well have I subdued my life! beyond
The obligation of my strictest vow,
The contemplation of my wildest bond,
Which gave my nature freely up, in truth,
But in its actual state, consenting fully
All passionate impulses its soil was formed
To rear, should wither; but foreseeing not
The tract, doomed to perpetual barrenness,
Would seem one day, remembered as it was,
Beside the parched sand-waste which now it is,
Already strewn with faint blooms, viewless then.
I ne'er engaged to root up loves so frail
I felt them not; yet now, 't is very plain
Some soft spots had their birth in me at first,
If not love, say, like love: there was a time
When yet this wolfish hunger after knowledge
Set not remorselessly love's claims aside.
This heart was human once, or why recall
Einsiedeln, now, and Würzburg which the
    Mayne
Forsakes her course to fold as with an arm?

And Festus — my poor Festus, with his praise
And counsel and grave fears — where is he now
With the sweet maiden, long ago his bride?
I surely loved them — that last night, at least,
When we . . . gone! gone! the better. I am
    saved
The sad review of an ambitious youth

Choked by vile lusts, unnoticed in their birth,
But let grow up and wind around a will
Till action was destroyed. No, I have gone
Purging my path successively of aught
Wearing the distinct likeness of such lusts.
I have made life consist of one idea:
Ere that was master, up till that was born,
I bear a memory of a pleasant life
Whose small events I treasure; till one morn
I ran o'er the seven little grassy fields,
Startling the flocks of nameless birds, to tell
Poor Festus, leaping all the while for joy,
To leave all trouble for my future plans,
Since I had just determined to become
The greatest and most glorious man on earth.
And since that morn all life has been forgotten:
All is one day, one only step between
The outset and the end: one tyrant all-
Absorbing aim fills up the interspace,
One vast unbroken chain of thought, kept up
Through a career apparently adverse
To its existence: life, death, light and shadow,
The shows of the world, were bare receptacles
Or indices of truth to be wrung thence,
Not ministers of sorrow or delight:
A wondrous natural robe in which she went.
For some one truth would dimly beacon me
From mountains rough with pines, and flit and
     wink
O'er dazzling wastes of frozen snow, and tremble
Into assured light in some branching mine
Where ripens, swathed in fire, the liquid gold —
And all the beauty, all the wonder fell
On either side the truth, as its mere robe;
I see the robe now — then I saw the form.
So far, then, I have voyaged with success,
So much is good, then, in this working sea
Which parts me from that happy strip of land:
But o'er that happy strip a sun shone, too!
And fainter gleams it as the waves grow rough,
And still more faint as the sea widens; last
I sicken on a dead gulf streaked with light
From its own putrefying depths alone.
Then, God was pledged to take me by the hand;
Now, any miserable juggle can bid
My pride depart. All is alike at length:
God may take pleasure in confounding pride
By hiding secrets with the scorned and base —
I am here, in short: so little have I paused
Throughout! I never glanced behind to know
If I had kept my primal light from wane,
And thus insensibly am — what I am!

Oh, bitter; very bitter!
                    And more bitter,
To fear a deeper curse, an inner ruin,
Plague beneath plague, the last turning the first
To light beside its darkness. Let me weep
My youth and its brave hopes, all dead and gone,
In tears which burn! Would I were sure to win
Some startling secret in their stead, a tincture
Of force to flush old age with youth, or breed
Gold, or imprison moonbeams till they change
To opal shafts! — only that, hurling it
Indignant back, I might convince myself
My aims remained supreme and pure as ever!
Even now, why not desire, for mankind's sake,
That if I fail, some fault may be the cause,

That, though I sink, another may succeed?
O God, the despicable heart of us!
Shut out this hideous mockery from my heart!

'T was politic in you, Aureole, to reject
Single rewards, and ask them in the lump;
At all events, once launched, to hold straight on:
For now 't is all or nothing. Mighty profit
Your gains will bring if they stop short of such
Full consummation! As a man, you had
A certain share of strength; and that is gone
Already in the getting these you boast.
Do not they seem to laugh, as who should say —
"Great master, we are here indeed, dragged
     forth
To light; this hast thou done: be glad! Now,
     seek
The strength to use which thou hast spent in
     getting!"

And yet 't is much, surely 't is very much,
Thus to have emptied youth of all its gifts,
To feed a fire meant to hold out till morn
Arrived with inexhaustible light; and lo,
I have heaped up my last, and day dawns not!
And I am left with gray hair, faded hands,
And furrowed brow. Ha, have I, after all,
Mistaken the wild nursling of my breast?
Knowledge it seemed, and power, and recom-
     pense!
Was she who glided through my room of nights,
Who laid my head on her soft knees and
     smoothed
The damp locks, — whose sly soothings just began
When my sick spirit craved repose awhile —
God! was I fighting sleep off for death's sake?

God! Thou art mind! Unto the master-mind
Mind should be precious. Spare my mind alone!
All else I will endure; if, as I stand
Here, with my gains, thy thunder smite me
     down,
I bow me; 't is thy will, thy righteous will;
I o'erpass life's restrictions, and I die;
And if no trace of my career remain
Save a thin corpse at pleasure of the wind
In these bright chambers level with the air,
See thou to it! But if my spirit fail,
My once proud spirit forsake me at the last,
Hast thou done well by me? So do not thou!
Crush not my mind, dear God, though I be
     crushed!
Hold me before the frequence of thy seraphs
And say, — "I crushed him, lest he should dis-
     turb
My law. Men must not know their strength:
     behold,
Weak and alone, how he had raised himself!"

But if delusions trouble me, and thou,
Not seldom felt with rapture in thy help
Throughout my toils and wanderings, dost in-
     tend
To work man's welfare through my weak en-
     deavor,
To crown my mortal forehead with a beam
From thine own blinding crown, to smile, and
     guide

This puny hand and let the work so wrought
Be styled my work, — hear me! I covet not
An influx of new power, an angel's soul:
It were no marvel then — but I have reached
Thus far, a man; let me conclude, a man!
Give but one hour of my first energy,
Of that invincible faith, but only one!
That I may cover with an eagle-glance
The truths I have, and spy some certain way
To mould them, and completing them, possess!

Yet God is good: I started sure of that,
And why dispute it now? I 'll not believe
But some undoubted warning long ere this
Had reached me: a fire-labarum was not deemed
Too much for the old founder of these walls.
Then, if my life has not been natural,
It has been monstrous: yet, till late, my course
So ardently engrossed me, that delight,
A pausing and reflecting joy, 't is plain,
Could find no place in it. True, I am worn;
But who clothes summer, who is life itself?
God, that created all things, can renew!
And then, though after-life to please me now
Must have no likeness to the past, what hinders
Reward from springing out of toil, as changed
As bursts the flower from earth and root and
    stalk?
What use were punishment, unless some sin
Be first detected? let me know that first!
No man could ever offend as I have done . . .
    (*A voice from within.*)
I hear a voice, perchance I heard
Long ago, but all too low,
So that scarce a care it stirred
If the voice were real or no:
I heard it in my youth when first
The waters of my life outburst:
But, now their stream ebbs faint, I hear
That voice, still low, but fatal-clear —
As if all poets, God ever meant
Should save the world, and therefore lent
Great gifts to, but who, proud, refused
To do his work, or lightly used
Those gifts, or failed through weak endeavor,
So, mourn cast off by him forever, —
As if these leaned in airy ring
To take me; this the song they sing.

"Lost, lost! yet come,
With our wan troop make thy home.
Come, come! for we
Will not breathe, so much as breathe
Reproach to thee,
Knowing what thou sink'st beneath.
So sank we in those old years,
We who bid thee, come! thou last
Who, living yet, hast life o'erpast.
And altogether we, thy peers,
Will pardon crave for thee, the last
Whose trial is done, whose lot is cast
With those who watch but work no more,
Who gaze on life but live no more
Yet we trusted thou shouldst speak
The message which our lips, too weak,
Refused to utter, — shouldst redeem
Our fault: such trust, and all a dream!
Yet we chose thee a birthplace

Where the richness ran to flowers:
Couldst not sing one song for grace?
Not make one blossom man's and ours?
Must one more recreant to his race
Die with unexerted powers,
And join us, leaving as he found
The world, he was to loosen, bound?
Anguish! ever and forever;
Still beginning, ending never!
Yet, lost and last one, come!
How couldst understand, alas,
What our pale ghosts strove to say,
As their shades did glance and pass
Before thee night and day?
Thou wast blind as we were dumb:
Once more, therefore, come, O come!
How should we clothe, how arm the spirit
Shall next thy post of life inherit —
How guard him from thy speedy ruin?
Tell us of thy sad undoing
Here, where we sit, ever pursuing
Our weary task, ever renewing
Sharp sorrow, far from God who gave
Our powers, and man they could not save!"
    (APRILE *enters.*)
Ha, ha! our king that wouldst be, here at last?
Art thou the poet who shall save the world?
Thy hand to mine! Stay, fix thine eyes on
    mine!
Thou wouldst be king? Still fix thine eyes on
    mine!
Par. Ha, ha! why crouchest not? Am I
    not king?
So torture is not wholly unavailing!
Have my fierce spasms compelled thee from
    thy lair?
Art thou the sage I only seemed to be,
Myself of after-time, my very self
With sight a little clearer, strength more firm,
Who robes him in my robe and grasps my
    crown
For just a fault, a weakness, a neglect?
I scarcely trusted God with the surmise
That such might come, and thou didst hear
    the while!
Aprile. Thine eyes are lustreless to mine:
    my hair
Is soft, nay silken soft: to talk with thee
Flushes my cheek, and thou art ashy-pale.
Truly, thou hast labored, hast withstood her
    lips,
The siren's! Yes, 't is like thou hast attained!
Tell me, dear master, wherefore now thou
    comest?
I thought thy solemn songs would have their
    meed
In after-time; that I should hear the earth
Exult in thee and echo with thy praise,
While I was laid forgotten in my grave.
Par. Ah fiend, I know thee, I am not thy
    dupe!
Thou art ordained to follow in my track,
Reaping my sowing, as I scorned to reap
The harvest sown by sages passed away.
Thou art the sober searcher, cautious striver,
As if, except through me, thou hast searched
    or striven!
Ay, tell the world! Degrade me after all,

To an aspirant after fame, not truth —
To all but envy of thy fate, be sure!
  Apr. Nay, sing them to me; I shall envy
    not:
Thou shalt be king! Sing thou, and I will sit
Beside, and call deep silence for thy songs,
And worship thee, as I had ne'er been meant
To fill thy throne: but none shall ever know!
Sing to me; for already thy wild eyes
Unlock my heart-strings, as some crystal-shaft
Reveals by some chance blaze its parent fount
After long time: so thou reveal'st my soul.
All will flash forth at last, with thee to hear!
  Par. (His secret! I shall get his secret —
    fool!)
I am he that aspired to KNOW: and thou?
  Apr. I would LOVE infinitely, and be loved!
  Par. Poor slave! I am thy king indeed.
  Apr.   Thou deem'st
That —born a spirit, dowered even as thou,
Born for thy fate — because I could not curb
My yearnings to possess at once the full
Enjoyment, but neglected all the means
Of realizing even the frailest joy,
Gathering no fragments to appease my want,
Yet nursing up that want till thus I die —
Thou deem'st I cannot trace thy safe sure
    march
O'er perils that o'erwhelm me, triumphing,
Neglecting naught below for aught above,
Despising nothing and ensuring all —
Nor that I could (my time to come again)
Lead thus my spirit securely as thine own.
Listen, and thou shalt see I know thee well.
I would love infinitely . . .
          Ah, lost! lost!
    Oh ye who armed me at such cost,
    How shall I look on all of ye
    With your gifts even yet on me?
  Par. (Ah, 't is some moonstruck creature
    after all!
Such fond fools as are like to haunt this den:
They spread contagion, doubtless: yet he
    seemed
To echo one foreboding of my heart
So truly, that . . . no matter! How he stands
With eve's last sunbeam staying on his hair
Which turns to it as if they were akin:
And those clear smiling eyes of saddest blue
Nearly set free, so far they rise above
The painful fruitless striving of the brow
And enforced knowledge of the lips, firm-set
In slow despondency's eternal sigh!
Has he, too, missed life's end, and learned the
    cause?)
I charge thee, by thy fealty, be calm!
Tell me what thou wouldst be, and what I am.
  Apr. I would love infinitely, and be loved.
First: I would carve in stone, or cast in brass,
The forms of earth. No ancient hunter lifted
Up to the gods by his renown, no nymph
Supposed the sweet soul of a woodland tree
Or sapphirine spirit of a twilight star,
Should be too hard for me; no shepherd-king
Regal for his white locks; no youth who
    stands
Silent and very calm amid the throng,
His right hand ever hid beneath his robe

Until the tyrant pass; no lawgiver,
No swan-soft woman rubbed with lucid oils
Given by a god for love of her — too hard!
Every passion sprung from man, conceived by
    man,
Would I express and clothe it in its right form,
Or blend with others struggling in one form,
Or show repressed by an ungainly form.
Oh, if you marvelled at some mighty spirit
With a fit frame to execute its will —
Even unconsciously to work its will —
You should be moved no less beside some strong
Rare spirit, fettered to a stubborn body,
Endeavoring to subdue it and inform it
With its own splendor! All this I would do:
And I would say, this done, "His sprites
    created,
God grants to each a sphere to be its world,
Appointed with the various objects needed
To satisfy its own peculiar want;
So, I create a world for these my shapes
Fit to sustain their beauty and their strength!"
And, at the word, I would contrive and paint
Woods, valleys, rocks and plains, dells, sands
    and wastes,
Lakes which, when morn breaks on their quiv-
    ering bed,
Blaze like a wyvern flying round the sun,
And ocean isles so small, the dog-fish tracking
A dead whale, who should find them, would
    swim thrice
Around them, and fare onward — all to hold
The offspring of my brain. Nor these alone:
Bronze labyrinth, palace, pyramid and crypt,
Baths, galleries, courts, temples and terraces,
Marts, theatres, and wharfs — all filled with
    men,
Men everywhere! And this performed in turn,
When those who looked on, pined to hear the
    hopes
And fears and hates and loves which moved the
    crowd,
I would throw down the pencil as the chisel,
And I would speak; no thought which ever
    stirred
A human breast should be untold; all passions,
All soft emotions, from the turbulent stir
Within a heart fed with desires like mine,
To the last comfort shutting the tired lids
Of him who sleeps the sultry noon away
Beneath the tent-tree by the wayside well:
And this in language as the need should be,
Now poured at once forth in a burning flow
Now piled up in a grand array of words.
This done, to perfect and consummate all,
Even as a luminous haze links star to star,
I would supply all chasms with music, breathing
Mysterious motions of the soul, no way
To be defined save in strange melodies.
Last, having thus revealed all I could love,
Having received all love bestowed on it,
I would die: preserving so throughout my course
God full on me, as I was full on men:
He would approve my prayer, "I have gone
    through
The loveliness of life; create for me
If not for men, or take me to thyself,
Eternal, infinite love!"

                              If thou hast ne'er
Conceived this mighty aim, this full desire,
Thou hast not passed my trial, and thou art
No king of mine.
       Par.   Ah me!
       Apr.   But thou art here!
Thou didst not gaze like me upon that end
Till thine own powers for compassing the bliss
Were blind with glory ; nor grow mad to grasp
At once the prize long patient toil should claim,
Nor spurn all granted short of that.   And I
Would do as thou, a second time : nay, listen!
Knowing ourselves, our world, our task so great,
Our time so brief, 't is clear if we refuse
The means so limited, the tools so rude
To execute our purpose, life will fleet,
And we shall fade, and leave our task undone.
We will be wise in time : what though our work
Be fashioned in despite of their ill-service,
Be crippled every way ?   'T were little praise
Did full resources wait on our goodwill
At every turn.   Let all be as it is.
Some say the earth is even so contrived
That tree and flower, a vesture gay, conceal
A bare and skeleton framework.   Had we means
Answering to our mind!   But now I seem
Wrecked on a savage isle : how rear thereon
My palace ?   Branching palms the props shall be,
Fruit glossy mingling ; gems are for the East ;
Who heeds them ?   I can pass them.   Serpents'
       scales,
And painted birds' down, furs and fishes' skins
Must help me ;   and a little here and there
Is all I can aspire to : still my art
Shall show its birth was in a gentler clime.
" Had I green jars of malachite, this way
I 'd range them : where those sea-shells glisten
       above,
Cressets should hang, by right : this way we set
The purple carpets, as these mats are laid,
Woven of fern and rush and blossoming flag."
Or if, by fortune, some completer grace
Be spared to me, some fragment, some slight
       sample
Of the prouder workmanship my own home
       boasts,
Some trifle little heeded there, but here
The place's one perfection — with what joy
Would I enshrine the relic, cheerfully
Foregoing all the marvels out of reach!
Could I retain one strain of all the psalm
Of the angels, one word of the fiat of God,
To let my followers know what such things are!
I would adventure nobly for their sakes :
When nights were still, and still the moaning sea,
And far away I could descry the land
Whence I departed, whither I return,
I would dispart the waves, and stand once more
At home, and load my bark, and hasten back,
And fling my gains to them, worthless or true.
" Friends," I would say, " I went far, far for
       them,
Past the high rocks the haunt of doves, the
       mounds
Of red earth from whose sides strange trees
       grow out,
Past tracts of milk-white minute blinding sand,
Till, by a mighty moon, I tremblingly

Gathered these magic herbs, berry and bud,
In haste, not pausing to reject the weeds,
But happy plucking them at any price.
To me, who have seen them bloom in their own
       soil,
They are scarce lovely : plait and wear them,
       you!
And guess, from what they are, the springs that
       fed them,
The stars that sparkled o'er them, night by
       night,
The snakes that travelled far to sip their dew ! "
Thus for my higher loves ; and thus even weak-
       ness
Would win me honor.   But not these alone
Should claim my care; for common life, its wants
And ways, would I set forth in beauteous hues :
The lowest hind should not possess a hope,
A fear, but I 'd be by him, saying better
Than he his own heart's language.   I would live
Forever in the thoughts I thus explored,
As a discoverer's memory is attached
To all he finds ; they should be mine henceforth,
Imbued with me, though free to all before :
For clay, once cast into my soul's rich mine,
Should come up crusted o'er with gems.   Nor
       this
Would need a meaner spirit than the first;
Nay, 't would be but the selfsame spirit, clothed
In humbler guise, but still the selfsame spirit :
As one spring wind unbinds the mountain snow
And comforts violets in their hermitage.

But, master, poet, who hast done all this,
How didst thou 'scape the ruin whelming me ?
Didst thou, when nerving thee to this attempt,
Ne'er range thy mind's extent, as some wide
       hall,
Dazzled by shapes that filled its length with
       light,
Shapes clustered there to rule thee, not obey,
That will not wait thy summons, will not rise
Singly, nor when thy practised eye and hand
Can well transfer their loveliness, but crowd
By thee forever, bright to thy despair ?
Didst thou ne'er gaze on each by turns, and ne'er
Resolve to single out one, though the rest
Should vanish, and to give that one, entire
In beauty, to the world ; forgetting, so,
Its peers, whose number baffles mortal power ?
And, this determined, wast thou ne'er seduced
By memories and regrets and passionate love,
To glance once more farewell ? and did their
       eyes
Fasten thee, brighter and more bright, until
Thou couldst but stagger back unto their feet,
And laugh that man's applause or welfare ever
Could tempt thee to forsake them ?   Or when
       years
Had passed and still their love possessed thee
       wholly,
When from without some murmur startled thee
Of darkling mortals famished for one ray
Of thy so-hoarded luxury of light,
Didst thou ne'er strive even yet to break those
       spells
And prove thou couldst recover and fulfil
Thy early mission, long ago renounced.

And to that end, select some shape once more?
And did not mist-like influences, thick films,
Faint memories of the rest that charmed so long
Thine eyes, float fast, confuse thee, bear thee off,
As whirling snow-drifts blind a man who treads
A mountain ridge, with guiding spear, through storm?
Say, though I fell, I had excuse to fall;
Say, I was tempted sorely: say but this,
Dear lord, Aprile's lord!
    Par.   Clasp me not thus,
Aprile! That the truth should reach me thus!
We are weak dust. Nay, clasp not or I faint!
    Apr. My king! and envious thoughts could
      outrage thee?
Lo, I forget my ruin, and rejoice
In thy success, as thou! Let our God's praise
Go bravely through the world at last! What care
Through me or thee? I feel thy breath. Why, tears?
Tears in the darkness, and from thee to me?
    Par. Love me henceforth, Aprile, while I learn
To love; and, merciful God, forgive us both!
We wake at length from weary dreams; but both
Have slept in fairy-land: though dark and drear
Appears the world before us, we no less
Wake with our wrists and ankles jewelled still.
I too have sought to KNOW as thou to LOVE —
Excluding love as thou refusedst knowledge.
Still thou hast beauty and I, power. We wake:
What penance canst devise for both of us?
    Apr. I hear thee faintly. The thick darkness! Even
Thine eyes are hid. 'T is as I knew: I speak,
And now I die. But I have seen thy face!
O poet, think of me, and sing of me!
But to have seen thee and to die so soon!
    Par. Die not, Aprile! We must never part.
Are we not halves of one dissevered world,
    nom this strange chance unites once more?
Part? never!
Till thou the lover, know; and I, the knower,
Love — until both are saved. Aprile, hear!
We will accept our gains, and use them — now I
God, he will die upon my breast! Aprile!
    Apr. To speak but once, and die! yet by his side.
Hush! hush!
              Ha! go you ever girt about
With phantoms, powers? I have created such,
But these seem real as I.
    Par.   Whom can you see
Through the accursed darkness?
    Apr.   Stay; I know,
I know them: who should know them well as I?
White brows, lit up with glory; poets all!
    Par. Let him but live, and I have my reward!
    Apr. Yes; I see now. God is the perfect poet,
Who in his person acts his own creations.
Had you but told me this at first! Hush! hush!
    Par. Live! for my sake, because of my great sin.

To help my brain, oppressed by these wild words
And their deep import. Live! 't is not too late.
I have a quiet home for us, and friends.
Michal shall smile on you. Hear you? Lean thus,
And breathe my breath. I shall not lose one word
Of all your speech, one little word, Aprile!
    Apr. No, no. Crown me? I am not one of you!
'T is he, the king, you seek. I am not one.
    Par. Thy spirit, at least, Aprile! Let me love.

I have attained, and now I may depart.

III. PARACELSUS

SCENE, *Basel: a chamber in the house of* PARACELSUS.
1526.

PARACELSUS, FESTUS.

    Par. Heap logs and let the blaze laugh out!
    Fest.   True, true!
'T is very fit all, time and chance and change
Have wrought since last we sat thus, face to face
And soul to soul — all cares, far-looking fears,
Vague apprehensions, all vain fancies bred
By your long absence, should be cast away,
Forgotten in this glad unhoped renewal
Of our affections.
    Par.   Oh, omit not aught
Which witnesses your own and Michal's own
Affection: spare not that! Only forget
The honors and the glories and what not,
It pleases you to tell profusely out.
    Fest. Nay, even your honors, in a sense, I waive:
The wondrous Paracelsus, life's dispenser,
Fate's commissary, idol of the schools
And courts, shall be no more than Aureole still,
Still Aureole and my friend as when we parted
Some twenty years ago, and I restrained
As best I could the promptings of my spirit
Which secretly advanced you, from the first,
To the pre-eminent rank which, since, your own
Adventurous ardor nobly triumphing,
Has won for you.
    Par.   Yes, yes. And Michal's face
Still wears that quiet and peculiar light
Like the dim circlet floating round a pearl?
    Fest. Just so.
    Par.   And yet her calm sweet countenance,
Though saintly, was not sad; for she would sing
Alone. Does she still sing alone, bird-like,
Not dreaming you are near? Her carols dropt
In flakes through that old leafy bower built under
The sunny wall at Würzburg, from her lattice
Among the trees above, while I, unseen,
Sat conning some rare scroll from Tritheim's shelves,
Much wondering notes so simple could divert
My mind from study. Those were happy days.
Respect all such as sing when all alone!

Fest. Scarcely alone : her children, you may
  guess,
Are wild beside her.
  Par. Ah, those children quite
Unsettle the pure picture in my mind :
A girl, she was so perfect, so distinct :
No change, no change ! Not but this added
  grace
May blend and harmonize with its compeers,
And Michal may become her motherhood ;
But 't is a change, and I detest all change,
And most a change in aught I loved long since.
So, Michal — you have said she thinks of me ?
  Fest. O very proud will Michal be of you !
Imagine how we sat, long winter-nights,
Scheming and wondering, shaping your pre-
  sumed
Adventure, or devising its reward ;
Shutting out fear with all the strength of hope.
For it was strange how, even when most secure
In our domestic peace, a certain dim
And flitting shade could sadden all ; it seemed
A restlessness of heart, a silent yearning,
A sense of something wanting, incomplete —
Not to be put in words, perhaps avoided
By mute consent — but, said or unsaid, felt
To point to one so loved and so long lost.
And then the hopes rose and shut out the fears —
How you would laugh should I recount them
  now !
I still predicted your return at last
With gifts beyond the greatest of them all,
All Tritheim's wondrous troop ; did one of which
Attain renown by any chance, I smiled,
As well aware of who would prove his peer.
Michal was sure some woman, long ere this,
As beautiful as you were sage, had loved . . .
  Par. Far-seeing, truly, to discern so much
In the fantastic projects and day-dreams
Of a raw restless boy !
  Fest. Oh, no : the sunrise
Well warranted our faith in this full noon !
Can I forget the anxious voice which said,
" Festus, have thoughts like these e'er shaped
  themselves
In other brains than mine ? have their possessors
Existed in like circumstance ? were they weak
As I, or ever constant from the first,
Despising youth's allurements and rejecting
As spider-films the shackles I endure ?
Is there hope for me ?" — and I answered gravely
As an acknowledged elder, calmer, wiser,
More gifted mortal. O you must remember,
For all your glorious . . .
  Par. Glorious ? ay, this hair,
These hands — nay, touch them, they are mine !
  Recall
With all the said recallings, times when thus
To lay them by your own ne'er turned you pale
As now. Most glorious, are they not ?
  Fest. Why — why —
Something must be subtracted from success
So wide, no doubt. He would be scrupulous,
  truly,
Who should object such drawbacks. Still, still,
  Aureole,
You are changed, very changed ! 'T were los-
  ing nothing

To look well to it : you must not be stolen
From the enjoyment of your well-won meed.
  Par. My friend ! you seek my pleasure, past
  a doubt :
You will best gain your point, by talking, not
Of me, but of yourself.
  Fest. Have I not said
All touching Michal and my children ? Sure
You know, by this, full well how Aennchen looks
Gravely, while one disparts her thick brown hair;
And Aureole's glee when some stray gannet
  builds
Amid the birch-trees by the lake. Small hope
Have I that he will honor (the wild imp)
His namesake. Sigh not ! 't is too much to ask
That all we love should reach the same proud
  fate.
But you are very kind to humor me
By showing interest in my quiet life ;
You, who of old could never tame yourself
To tranquil pleasures, must at heart despise . .
  Par. Festus, strange secrets are let out by
  death
Who blabs so oft the follies of this world :
And I am death's familiar, as you know.
I helped a man to die, some few weeks since,
Warped even from his go-cart to one end —
The living on princes' smiles, reflected from
A mighty herd of favorites. No mean trick
He left untried, and truly well-nigh wormed
All traces of God's finger out of him :
Then died, grown old. And just an hour before
Having lain long with blank and soulless eyes,
He sat up suddenly, and with natural voice
Said that in spite of thick air and closed doors
God told him it was June ; and he knew well,
Without such telling, harebells grew in June ;
And all that kings could ever give or take
Would not be precious as those blooms to him.
Just so, allowing I am passing sage,
It seems to me much worthier argument
Why pansies,[1] eyes that laugh, bear beauty's
  prize
From violets, eyes that dream — (your Michal's
  choice) —
Than all fools find to wonder at in me
Or in my fortunes. And be very sure
I say this from no prurient restlessness,
No self-complacency, itching to turn,
Vary and view its pleasure from all points,
And, in this instance, willing other men
May be at pains, demonstrate to itself
The realness of the very joy it tastes.
What should delight me like the news of friends
Whose memories were a solace to me oft,
As mountain-baths to wild fowls in their flight?
Ofter than you had wasted thought on me
Had you been wise, and rightly valued bliss.
But there 's no taming nor repressing hearts:
God knows I need such ! — So, you heard me
  speak ?
  Fest. Speak ? when ?
  Par. When but this morning at my class ?
There was noise and crowd enough. I saw you
  not.
Surely you know I am engaged to fill

1 Citrinula (flammula) herba Paracelso multum famil
iaris. — DORN.

The chair here? — that 't is part of my proud
    fate
To lecture to as many thick-skulled youths
As please, each day, to throng the theatre,
To my great reputation, and no small
Danger of Basel's benches long unused
To crack beneath such honor?
    Fest.   I was there ;
I mingled with the throng : shall I avow
Small care was mine to listen ? — too intent
On gathering from the murmurs of the crowd
A full corroboration of my hopes !
What can I learn about your powers ? but they
Know, care for naught beyond your actual state,
Your actual value ; yet they worship you,
Those various natures whom you sway as one !
But ere I go, be sure I shall attend . . .
    Par. Stop, o' God's name : the thing 's by no
    means yet
Past remedy ! Shall I read this morning's labor
— At least in substance ? Naught so worth the
    gaining
As an apt scholar ! Thus then, with all due
Precision and emphasis — you, beside, are clearly
Guiltless of understanding more, a whit,
The subject than your stool — allowed to be
A notable advantage.
    Fest.   Surely, Aureole,
You laugh at me !
    Par.   I laugh ? Ha, ha ! thank heaven,
I charge you, if 't be so ! for I forget
Much, and what laughter should be like. No
    less,
However, I forego that luxury
Since it alarms the friend who brings it back.
True, laughter like my own must echo strangely
To thinking men ; a smile were better far ;
So, make me smile ! If the exulting look
You wore but now be smiling, 't is so long
Since I have smiled ! Alas, such smiles are
    born
Alone of hearts like yours, or herdsmen's souls
Of ancient time, whose eyes, calm as their flocks,
Saw in the stars mere garnishry of heaven,
And in the earth a stage for altars only.
Never change, Festus : I say, never change !
    Fest. My God, if he be wretched after all !
    Par. When last we parted, Festus, you de-
    clared,
— Or Michal, yes, her soft lips whispered words
I have preserved. She told me she believed
I should succeed (meaning, that in the search
I then engaged in, I should meet success)
And yet be wretched : now, she augured false.
    Fest. Thank heaven ! but you spoke strangely :
    could I venture
To think bare apprehension lest your friend,
Dazzled by your resplendent course, might find
Henceforth less sweetness in his own, could move
Such earnest mood in you ? Fear not, dear
    friend,
That I shall leave you, inwardly repining
Your lot was not my own !
    Par.   And this forever !
Forever ! gull who may, they will be gulled !
They will not look nor think ; 't is nothing new
In them : but surely he is not of them !
My Festus, do you know, I reckoned, you —

Though all beside were sand-blind — you, my
    friend,
Would look at me, once close, with piercing eye
Untroubled by the false glare that confounds
A weaker vision : would remain serene,
Though singular amid a gaping throng.
I feared you, or I had come, sure, long ere this,
To Einsiedeln. Well, error has no end,
And Rhasis is a sage, and Basel boasts
A tribe of wits, and I am wise and blest
Past all dispute ! 'T is vain to fret at it.
I have vowed long ago my worshippers
Shall owe to their own deep sagacity
All further information, good or bad.
Small risk indeed my reputation runs,
Unless perchance the glance now searching me
Be fixed much longer ; for it seems to spell
Dimly the characters a simpler man
Might read distinct enough. Old eastern books
Say, the fallen prince of morning some short
    space
Remained unchanged in semblance ; nay, his
    brow
Was hued with triumph : every spirit then
Praising, *his* heart on flame the while : — a tale !
Well, Festus, what discover you, I pray ?
    Fest. Some foul deed sullies then a life which
    else
Were raised supreme ?
    Par.   Good : I do well, most well !
Why strive to make men hear, feel, fret them-
    selves
With what is past their power to comprehend ?
I should not strive now : only, having nursed
The faint surmise that one yet walked the earth,
One, at least, not the utter fool of show,
Not absolutely formed to be the dupe
Of shallow plausibilities alone :
One who, in youth, found wise enough to choose
The happiness his riper years approve,
Was yet so anxious for another's sake,
That, ere his friend could rush upon a mad
And ruinous course, the converse of his own,
His gentle spirit essayed, prejudged for him
The perilous path, foresaw its destiny,
And warned the weak one in such tender words,
Such accents — his whole heart in every tone —
That oft their memory comforted that friend
When it by right should have increased despair :
— Having believed, I say, that this one man
Could never lose the light thus from the first
His portion — how should I refuse to grieve
At even my gain if it disturb our old
Relation, if it make me out more wise ?
Therefore, once more reminding him how well
He prophesied, I note the single flaw
That spoils his prophet's title. In plain words,
You were deceived, and thus were you de-
    ceived —
I have not been successful, and yet am
Most miserable ; 't is said at last ; nor you
Give credit, lest you force me to concede
That common sense yet lives upon the world !
    Fest. You surely do not mean to banter me ?
    Par. You know, or — if you have been wise
    enough
To cleanse your memory of such matters —
    knew,

As far as words of mine could make it clear,
That 't was my purpose to find joy or grief
Solely in the fulfilment of my plan
Or plot or whatsoe'er it was ; rejoicing
Alone as it proceeded prosperously,
Sorrowing then only when mischance retarded
Its progress. That was in those Würzburg days !
Not to prolong a theme I thoroughly hate,
I have pursued this plan with all my strength ;
And having failed therein most signally,
Cannot object to ruin utter and drear
As all-excelling would have been the prize
Had fortune favored me. I scarce have right
To vex your frank good spirit late so glad
In my supposed prosperity, I know,
And, were I lucky in a glut of friends,
Would well agree to let your error live,
Nay, strengthen it with fables of success.
But mine is no condition to refuse
The transient solace of so rare a godsend,
My solitary luxury, my one friend :
Accordingly I venture to put off
The wearisome vest of falsehood galling me,
Secure when he is by. I lay me bare,
Prone at his mercy — but he is my friend !
Not that he needs retain his aspect grave ;
That answers not my purpose ; for 't is like,
Some sunny morning — Basel being drained
Of its wise population, every corner
Of the amphitheatre crammed with learned
    clerks,
Here Œcolampadius, looking worlds of wit,
Here Castellanus, as profound as he,
Munsterus here, Frobenius there, all squeezed
And staring, — that the zany of the show,
Even Paracelsus, shall put off before them
His trappings with a grace but seldom judged
Expedient in such cases : — the grim smile
That will go round ! Is it not therefore best
To venture a rehearsal like the present
In a small way ? Where are the signs I seek,
The first-fruits and fair sample of the scorn
Due to all quacks ? Why, this will never do !
    Fest. These are foul vapors, Aureole ; naught
        beside !
The effect of watching, study, weariness.
Were there a spark of truth in the confusion
Of these wild words, you would not outrage thus
Your youth's companion. I shall ne'er regard
These wanderings, bred of faintness and much
    study.
'T is not thus you would trust a trouble to me,
To Michal's friend.
    Par.   I have said it, dearest Festus !
For the manner, 't is ungracious probably ;
You may have it told in broken sobs, one day,
And scalding tears, ere long : but I thought best
To keep that off as long as possible.
Do you wonder still ?
    Fest.   No ; it must oft fall out
That one whose labor perfects any work,
Shall rise from it with eye so worn that he
Of all men least can measure the extent
Of what he has accomplished. He alone
Who, nothing tasked, is nothing weary too,
May clearly scan the little he effects :
But we, the bystanders, untouched by toil,
Estimate each aright.

    Par.   This worthy Festus
Is one of them, at last ! 'T is so with all !
First, they set down all progress as a dream ;
And next, when he whose quick discomfiture
Was counted on, accomplishes some few
And doubtful steps in his career, — behold,
They look for every inch of ground to vanish
Beneath his tread, so sure they spy success !
    Fest. Few doubtful steps ? when death re-
        tires before
Your presence — when the noblest of mankind,
Broken in body or subdued in soul,
May through your skill renew their vigor, raise
The shattered frame to pristine stateliness ?
When men in racking pain may purchase dreams
Of what delights them most, swooning at once
Into a sea of bliss or rapt along
As in a flying sphere of turbulent light ?
When we may look to you as one ordained
To free the flesh from fell disease, as frees
Our Luther's burning tongue the fettered soul ?
When . . .
    Par.   When and where, the devil, did you get
This notable news ?
    Fest.   Even from the common voice ;
From those whose envy, daring not dispute
The wonders it decries, attributes them
To magic and such folly.
    Par.   Folly ? Why not
To magic, pray ? You find a comfort doubtless
In holding, God ne'er troubles him about
Us or our doings : once we were judged worth
The devil's tempting . . . I offend : forgive me,
And rest content. Your prophecy on the whole
Was fair enough as prophesyings go ;
At fault a little in detail, but quite
Precise enough in the main ; and hereupon
I pay due homage : you guessed long ago
(The prophet !) I should fail — and I have failed.
    Fest. You mean to tell me, then, the hopes
        which fed
Your youth have not been realized as yet ?
Some obstacle has barred them hitherto ?
Or that their innate . . .
    Par.   As I said but now,
You have a very decent prophet's fame,
So you but shun details here. Little matter
Whether those hopes were mad, — the aims
        they sought,
Safe and secure from all ambitious fools ;
Or whether my weak wits are overcome
By what a better spirit would scorn : I fail.
And now methinks 't were best to change a
        theme
I am a sad fool to have stumbled on.
I say confusedly what comes uppermost ;
But there are times when patience proves at
        fault,
As now : this morning's strange encounter — you
Beside me once again ! you, whom I guessed
Alive, since hitherto (with Luther's leave)
No friend have I among the saints at peace,
To judge by any good their prayers effect.
I knew you would have helped me — why not he,
My strange competitor in enterprise,
Bound for the same end by another path,
Arrived, or ill or well, before the time,
At our disastrous journey's doubtful close ?

How goes it with Aprile? Ah, they miss
Your lone sad sunny idleness of heaven,
Our martyrs for the world's sake; heaven shuts
fast:
The poor mad poet is howling by this time!
Since you are my sole friend then, here or there,
I could not quite repress the varied feelings
This meeting wakens; they have had their vent,
And now forget them. Do the rear-mice still
Hang like a fretwork on the gate (or what
In my time was a gate) fronting the road
From Einsiedeln to Lachen?
   Fest.   Trifle not:
Answer me, for my sake alone! You smiled
Just now, when I supposed some deed, unworthy
Yourself, might blot the else so bright result;
Yet if your motives have continued pure,
Your will unfaltering, and in spite of this,
You have experienced a defeat, why then
I say not you would cheerfully withdraw
From contest — mortal hearts are not so fash-
   ioned —
But surely you would ne'ertheless withdraw.
You sought not fame nor gain nor even love,
No end distinct from knowledge, — I repeat
Your very words: once satisfied that knowledge
Is a mere dream, you would announce as much,
Yourself the first. But how is the event?
You are defeated — and I find you here!
   Par. As though "here" did not signify de-
feat!
I spoke not of my little labors here,
But of the break-down of my general aims:
For you, aware of their extent and scope,
To look on these sage lecturings, approved
By beardless boys, and bearded dotards worse,
As a fit consummation of such aims,
Is worthy notice. A professorship
At Basel! Since you see so much in it,
And think my life was reasonably drained
Of life's delights to render me a match
For duties arduous as such post demands, —
Be it far from me to deny my power
To fill the petty circle lotted out
Of infinite space, or justify the host
Of honors thence accruing. So, take notice,
This jewel dangling from my neck preserves
The features of a prince, my skill restored
To plague his people some few years to come:
And all through a pure whim. He had eased
   the earth
For me, but that the droll despair which seized
The vermin of his household, tickled me.
I came to see. Here drivelled the physician,
Whose most infallible nostrum was at fault;
There quaked the astrologer, whose horoscope
Had promised him interminable years;
Here a monk fumbled at the sick man's mouth
With some undoubted relic — a sudary
Of the Virgin; while another piebald knave
Of the same brotherhood (he loved them ever)
Was actively preparing 'neath his nose
Such a suffumigation as, once fired,
Had stunk the patient dead ere he could groan.
I cursed the doctor and upset the brother,
Brushed past the conjurer, vowed that the first
   gust
Of stench from the ingredients just alight

Would raise a cross-grained devil in my sword,
Not easily laid: and ere an hour the prince
Slept as he never slept since prince he was.
A day — and I was posting for my life,
Placarded through the town as one whose spite
Had near availed to stop the blessed effects
Of the doctor's nostrum which, well seconded
By the sudary, and most by the costly smoke —
Not leaving out the strenuous prayers sent up
Hard by in the abbey — raised the prince to life:
To the great reputation of the seer
Who, confident, expected all along
The glad event — the doctor's recompense —
Much largess from his highness to the monks —
And the vast solace of his loving people,
Whose general satisfaction to increase,
The prince was pleased no longer to defer
The burning of some dozen heretics
Remanded till God's mercy should be shown
Touching his sickness: last of all were joined
Ample directions to all loyal folk
To swell the complement by seizing me
Who — doubtless some rank sorcerer — endeav-
   ored
To thwart these pious offices, obstruct
The prince's cure, and frustrate heaven by help
Of certain devils dwelling in his sword.
By luck, the prince in his first fit of thanks
Had forced this bauble on me as an earnest
Of further favors. This one case may serve
To give sufficient taste of many such,
So, let them pass. Those shelves support a pile
Of patents, licenses, diplomas, titles
From Germany, France, Spain, and Italy;
They authorize some honor; ne'ertheless,
I set more store by this Erasmus sent;
He trusts me; our Frobenius is his friend,
And him "I raised" (nay, read it) "from the
   dead."
I weary you, I see. I merely sought
To show, there's no great wonder after all
That, while I fill the class-room and attract
A crowd to Basel, I get leave to stay,
And therefore need not scruple to accept
The utmost they can offer, if I please:
For 't is but right the world should be prepared
To treat with favor e'en fantastic wants
Of one like me, used up in serving her.
Just as the mortal, whom the gods in part
Devoured, received in place of his lost limb
Some virtue or other — cured disease, I think;
You mind the fables we have read together.
   Fest. You do not think I comprehend a word.
The time was, Aureole, you were apt enough
To clothe the airiest thoughts in specious
   breath;
But surely you must feel how vague and strange
These speeches sound.
   Par.   Well, then: you know my hopes;
I am assured, at length, those hopes were vain;
That truth is just as far from me as ever;
That I have thrown my life away; that sorrow
On that account is idle, and further effort
To mend and patch what's marred beyond re-
   pairing,
As useless: and all this was taught your friend
By the convincing good old-fashioned method
Of force — by sheer compulsion. Is that plain?

Fest. Dear Aureole, can it be my fears were
    just ?
God wills not . . .
    Par.   Now, 't is this I most admire —
The constant talk men of your stamp keep up
Of God's will, as they style it ; one would swear
Man had but merely to uplift his eye,
And see the will in question charactered
On the heaven's vault. 'T is hardly wise to moot
Such topics : doubts are many and faith is weak.
I know as much of any will of God
As knows some dumb and tortured brute what
    Man,
His stern lord, wills from the perplexing blows
That plague him every way ; but there, of
    course,
Where least he suffers, longest he remains —
My case ; and for such reasons I plod on,
Subdued but not convinced. I know as little
Why I deserve to fail, as why I hoped
Better things in my youth. I simply know
I am no master here, but trained and beaten
Into the path I tread ; and here I stay,
Until some further intimation reach me,
Like an obedient drudge. Though I prefer
To view the whole thing as a task imposed
Which, whether dull or pleasant, must be done —
Yet, I deny not, there is made provision
Of joys which tastes less jaded might affect ;
Nay, some which please me too, for all my
    pride —
Pleasures that once were pains : the iron ring
Festering about a slave's neck grows at length
Into the flesh it eats. I hate no longer
A host of petty vile delights, undreamed of
Or spurned before ; such now supply the place
Of my dead aims : as in the autumn woods
Where tall trees used to flourish, from their
    roots
Springs up a fungous brood sickly and pale,
Chill mushrooms colored like a corpse's cheek.
    Fest. If I interpret well your words, I own
It troubles me but little that your aims,
Vast in their dawning and most likely grown
Extravagantly since, have baffled you.
Perchance I am glad ; you merit greater praise ;
Because they are too glorious to be gained,
You do not blindly cling to them and die ;
You fell, but have not sullenly refused
To rise, because an angel worsted you
In wrestling, though the world holds not your
    peer ;
And though too harsh and sudden is the change
To yield content as yet, still you pursue
The ungracious path as though 't were rosy-
    strewn.
'T is well : and your reward, or soon or late,
Will come from him whom no man serves in
    vain.
    Par. Ah, very fine ! For my part, I conceive
The very pausing from all further toil,
Which you find heinous, would become a seal
To the sincerity of all my deeds.
To be consistent I should die at once ;
I calculated on no after-life ;
Yet (how crept in, how fostered, I know not)
Here am I with as passionate regret
For youth and health and love so vainly lavished,

As if their preservation had been first
And foremost in my thoughts ; and this strange
    fact
Humbled me wondrously, and had due force
In rendering me the less averse to follow
A certain counsel, a mysterious warning —
You will not understand — but 't was a man
With aims not mine and yet pursued like mine,
With the same fervor and no more success,
Perishing in my sight ; who summoned me,
As I would shun the ghastly fate I saw,
To serve my race at once ; to wait no longer
That God should interfere in my behalf,
But to distrust myself, put pride away,
And give my gains, imperfect as they were,
To men. I have not leisure to explain
How, since, a singular series of events
Has raised me to the station you behold,
Wherein I seem to turn to most account
The mere wreck of the past, — perhaps receive
Some feeble glimmering token that God views
And may approve my penance : therefore here
You find me, doing most good or least harm.
And if folks wonder much and profit little
'T is not my fault ; only, I shall rejoice
When my part in the farce is shuffled through,
And the curtain falls : I must hold out till then.
    Fest. Till when, dear Aureole ?
    Par.   Till I 'm fairly thrust
From my proud eminence. Fortune is fickle
And even professors fall : should that arrive,
I see no sin in ceding to my bent.
You little fancy what rude shocks apprise us
We sin ; God's intimations rather fail
In clearness than in energy : 't were well
Did they but indicate the course to take
Like that to be forsaken. I would fain
Be spared a further sample. Here I stand,
And here I stay, be sure, till forced to flit.
    Fest. Be you but firm on that head ! long
    ere then
All I expect will come to pass, I trust :
The cloud that wraps you will have disappeared.
Meantime, I see small chance of such event :
They praise you here as one whose lore, already
Divulged, eclipses all the past can show,
But whose achievements, marvellous as they be,
Are faint anticipations of a glory
About to be revealed. When Basel's crowds
Dismiss their teacher, I shall be content
That he depart.
    Par.   This favor at their hands
I look for earlier than your view of things
Would warrant. Of the crowd you saw to-day,
Remove the full half sheer amazement draws,
Mere novelty, naught else ; and next, the tribe
Whose innate blockish dulness just perceives
That unless miracles (as seem my works)
Be wrought in their behalf, their chance is
    slight
To puzzle the devil ; next, the numerous set
Who bitterly hate established schools, and help
The teacher that oppugns them, till he once
Have planted his own doctrine, when the
    teacher
May reckon on their rancor in his turn ;
Take, too, the sprinkling of sagacious knaves
Whose cunning runs not counter to the vogue.

But seeks, by flattery and crafty nursing,
To force my system to a premature
Short-lived development. Why swell the list?
Each has his end to serve, and his best way
Of serving it: remove all these, remains
A scantling, a poor dozen at the best,
Worthy to look for sympathy and service,
And likely to draw profit from my pains.
   Fest. 'T is no encouraging picture: still
    these few
Redeem their fellows. Once the germ im-
   planted,
Its growth, if slow, is sure.
   Par. God grant it so!
I would make some amends: but if I fail,
The luckless rogues have this excuse to urge,
That much is in my method and my manner,
My uncouth habits, my impatient spirit,
Which hinders of reception and result
My doctrine: much to say, small skill to speak!
These old aims suffered not a looking-off
Though for an instant; therefore, only when
I thus renounce them and resolved to reap
Some present fruit — to teach mankind some
   truth
So dearly purchased — only then I found
Such teaching was an art requiring cares
And qualities peculiar to itself:
That to possess was one thing — to display
Another. With renown first in my thoughts,
Or popular praise, I had soon discovered it:
One grows but little apt to learn these things.
   Fest. If it be so, which nowise I believe,
There needs no waiting fuller dispensation
To leave a labor of so little use.
Why not throw up the irksome charge at once?
   Par. A task, a task!
           But wherefore hide the whole
Extent of degradation once engaged
In the confessing vein? Despite of all
My fine talk of obedience and repugnance,
Docility and what not, 't is yet to learn
If when the task shall really be performed,
My inclination free to choose once more,
I shall do aught but slightly modify
The nature of the hated task I quit.
In plain words, I am spoiled; my life still tends
As first it tended; I am broken and trained
To my old habits: they are part of me.
I know, and none so well, my darling ends
Are proved impossible: no less, no less,
Even now what humors me, fond fool, as when
Their faint ghosts sit with me and flatter me
And send me back content to my dull round?
How can I change this soul? — this apparatus
Constructed solely for their purposes,
So well adapted to their every want,
To search out and discover, prove and perfect;
This intricate machine whose most minute
And meanest motions have their charm to me
Though to none else — an aptitude I seize,
An object I perceive, a use, a meaning,
A property, a fitness, I explain
And I alone: — how can I change my soul?
And this wronged body, worthless save when
   tasked
Under that soul's dominion — used to care
For its bright master's cares and quite subdue

Its proper cravings — not to ail nor pine
So he but prosper — whither drag this poor
Tried patient body? God! how I essayed
To live like that mad poet, for a while,
To love alone; and how I felt too warped
And twisted and deformed! What should I do
Even though released from drudgery, but re-
   turn
Faint, as you see, and halting, blind and sore,
To my old life and die as I began?
I cannot feed on beauty for the sake
Of beauty only, nor can drink in balm
From lovely objects for their loveliness;
My nature cannot lose her first imprint;
I still must hoard and heap and class all truths
With one ulterior purpose: I must know!
Would God translate me to his throne, believe
That I should only listen to his word
To further my own aim! For other men,
Beauty is prodigally strewn around,
And I were happy could I quench as they
This mad and thriveless longing, and content
   me
With beauty for itself alone: alas,
I have addressed a frock of heavy mail
Yet may not join the troop of sacred knights;
And now the forest-creatures fly from me,
The grass-banks cool, the sunbeams warm no
   more.
Best follow, dreaming that ere night arrive,
I shall o'ertake the company and ride
Glittering as they!
   Fest. I think I apprehend
What you would say: if you, in truth, design
To enter once more on the life thus left,
Seek not to hide that all this consciousness
Of failure is assumed!
   Par. My friend, my friend,
I toil, you listen; I explain, perhaps
You understand: there our communion ends.
Have you learnt nothing from to-day's dis-
   course?
When we would thoroughly know the sick
   man's state
We feel awhile the fluttering pulse, press soft
The hot brow, look upon the languid eye,
And thence divine the rest. Must I lay bare
My heart, hideous and beating, or tear up
My vitals for your gaze, ere you will deem
Enough made known? You! who are you,
   forsooth?
That is the crowning operation claimed
By the arch-demonstrator — heaven the hall,
And earth the audience. Let Aprile and you
Secure good places: 't will be worth the while.
   Fest. Are you mad, Aureole? What can I
    have said
To call for this? I judged from your own
   words.
   Par. Oh, doubtless! A sick wretch de-
   scribes the ape
That mocks him from the bed-foot, and all
   gravely
You thither turn at once: or he recounts
The perilous journey he has late performed,
And you are puzzled much how that could be!
You find me here, half stupid and half mad;
It makes no part of my delight to search

Into these matters, much less undergo
Another's scrutiny ; but so it chances
That I am led to trust my state to you :
And the event is, you combine, contrast
And ponder on my foolish words as though
They thoroughly conveyed all hidden here —
Here, loathsome with despair and hate and
    rage !
Is there no fear, no shrinking and no shame ?
Will you guess nothing ? will you spare me no-
    thing ?
Must I go deeper ? Ay or no ?
    Fest.   Dear friend . . .
    Par.   True : I am brutal — 't is a part of it ;
The plague's sign — you are not a lazar-haunter,
How should you know ? Well then, you think
    it strange
I should profess to have failed utterly,
And yet propose an ultimate return
To courses void of hope : and this, because
You know not what temptation is, nor how
'T is like to ply men in the sickliest part.
You are to understand that we who make
Sport for the gods, are hunted to the end :
There is not one sharp volley shot at us,
Which 'scaped with life, though hurt, we
    slacken pace
And gather by the wayside herbs and roots
To stanch our wounds, secure from further
    harm :
We are assailed to life's extremest verge.
It will be well indeed if I return,
A harmless busy fool, to my old ways !
I would forget hints of another fate,
Significant enough, which silent hours
Have lately scared me with.
    Fest.   Another ! and what ?
    Par.   After all, Festus, you say well : I am
A man yet : I need never humble me.
I would have been — something, I know not
    what ;
But though I cannot soar, I do not crawl.
There are worse portions than this one of mine.
You say well !
    Fest.   Ah !
    Par.   And deeper degradation !
If the mean stimulants of vulgar praise,
If vanity should become the chosen food
Of a sunk mind, should stifle even the wish
To find its early aspirations true,
Should teach it to breathe falsehood like life-
    breath —
An atmosphere of craft and trick and lies ;
Should make it proud to emulate, surpass
Base natures in the practices which woke
Its most indignant loathing once . . . No, no !
Utter damnation is reserved for hell !
I had immortal feelings ; such shall never
Be wholly quenched : no, no !
                     My friend, you wear
A melancholy face, and certain 't is
There 's little cheer in all this dismal work.
But was it my desire to set abroach
Such memories and forebodings ? I foresaw
Where they would drive. 'T were better we
    discuss
News from Lucerne or Zurich ; ask and tell
Of Egypt's flaring sky or Spain's cork-groves.

    Fest.   I have thought : trust me, this mood
    will pass away !
I know you and the lofty spirit you bear,
And easily ravel out a clue to all.
These are the trials meet for such as you,
Nor must you hope exemption : to be mortal
Is to be plied with trials manifold.
Look round ! The obstacles which kept the rest
From your ambition, have been spurned by you ;
Their fears, their doubts, the chains that bind
    them all,
Were flax before your resolute soul, which
    naught
Avails to awe save these delusions bred
From its own strength, its selfsame strength dis-
    guised,
Mocking itself. Be brave, dear Aureole ! Since
The rabbit has his shade to frighten him,
The fawn a rustling bough, mortals their cares,
And higher natures yet would slight and laugh
At these entangling fantasies, as you
At trammels of a weaker intellect, —
Measure your mind's height by the shade it
    casts !
I know you.
    Par.   And I know you, dearest Festus !
And how you love unworthily ; and how
All admiration renders blind.
    Fest.   You hold
That admiration blinds ?
    Par.   Ay and alas !
    Fest.   Naught blinds you less than admiration,
    friend !
Whether it be that all love renders wise
In its degree ; from love which blends with
    love —
Heart answering heart — to love which spends
    itself
In silent mad idolatry of some
Pre-eminent mortal, some great soul of souls,
Which ne'er will know how well it is adored.
I say, such love is never blind ; but rather
Alive to every the minutest spot
Which mars its object, and which hate (supposed
So vigilant and searching) dreams not of.
Love broods on such : what then ? When first
    perceived
Is there no sweet strife to forget, to change,
To overflush those blemishes with all
The glow of general goodness they disturb ?
— To make those very defects an endless source
Of new affection grown from hopes and fears ?
And, when all fails, is there no gallant stand
Made even for much proved weak ? no shrinking-
    back
Lest, since all love assimilates the soul
To what it loves, it should at length become
Almost a rival of its idol ? Trust me,
If there be fiends who seek to work our hurt,
To ruin and drag down earth's mightiest spirits
Even at God's foot, 't will be from such as love,
Their zeal will gather most to serve their cause ;
And least from those who hate, who most essay
By contumely and scorn to blot the light
Which forces entrance even to their hearts :
For thence will our defender tear the veil
And show within each heart, as in a shrine,
The giant image of perfection, grown

In hate's despite, whose calumnies were spawned
In the untroubled presence of its eyes.
True admiration blinds not ; nor am I
So blind. I call your sin exceptional ;
It springs from one whose life has passed the
    bounds
Prescribed to life. Compound that fault with
    God !
I speak of men ; to common men like me
The weakness you reveal endears you more,
Like the far traces of decay in suns.
I bid you have good cheer !
    Par.   *Præclare ! Optime !*
Think of a quiet mountain-cloistered priest
Instructing Paracelsus ! yet 't is so.
Come, I will show you where my merit lies.
'T is in the advance of individual minds
That the slow crowd should ground their expec-
    tation
Eventually to follow ; as the sea
Waits ages in its bed till some one wave
Out of the multitudinous mass, extends
The empire of the whole, some feet perhaps,
Over the strip of sand which could confine
Its fellows so long time : thenceforth the rest,
Even to the meanest, hurry in at once,
And so much is clear gained. I shall be glad
If all my labors, failing of aught else,
Suffice to make such inroad and procure
A wider range for thought : nay, they do this ;
For, whatsoe'er my notions of true knowledge
And a legitimate success, may be,
I am not blind to my undoubted rank
When classed with others : I precede my age :
And whoso wills is very free to mount
These labors as a platform whence his own
May have a prosperous outset. But, alas !
My followers — they are noisy as you heard ;
But, for intelligence, the best of them
So clumsily wield the weapons I supply
And they extol, that I begin to doubt
Whether their own rude clubs and pebble-stones
Would not do better service than my arms
Thus vilely swayed — if error will not fall
Sooner before the old awkward batterings
Than my more subtle warfare, not half learned.
    Fest. I would supply that art, then, or with-
    hold
New arms until you teach their mystery.
    Par. Content you, 't is my wish ; I have
    recourse
To the simplest training. Day by day I seek
To wake the mood, the spirit which alone
Can make those arms of any use to men.
Of course they are for swaggering forth at once
Graced with Ulysses' bow, Achilles' shield —
Flash on us, all in armor, thou Achilles !
Make our hearts dance to thy resounding step !
A proper sight to scare the crows away !
    Fest. Pity you choose not then some other
    method
Of coming at your point. The marvellous art
At length established in the world bids fair
To remedy all hindrances like these :
Trust to Frobenius' press the precious lore
Obscured by uncouth manner, or unfit
For raw beginners ; let his types secure
A deathless monument to after-time :

Meanwhile wait confidently and enjoy
The ultimate effect : sooner or later
You shall be all-revealed.
    Par.   The old dull question
In a new form ; no more. Thus : I possess
Two sorts of knowledge ; one, — vast, shadowy,
Hints of the unbounded aim I once pursued :
The other consists of many secrets, caught
While bent on nobler prize, — perhaps a few
Prime principles which may conduct to much :
These last I offer to my followers here.
Now, bid me chronicle the first of these,
My ancient study, and in effect you bid
Revert to the wild courses just abjured :
I must go find them scattered through the world.
Then, for the principles, they are so simple
(Being chiefly of the overturning sort),
That one time is as proper to propound them
As any other — to-morrow at my class,
Or half a century hence embalmed in print.
For if mankind intend to learn at all,
They must begin by giving faith to them
And acting on them : and I do not see
But that my lectures serve indifferent well :
No doubt these dogmas fall not to the earth,
For all their novelty and rugged setting.
I think my class will not forget the day
I let them know the gods of Israel,
Aëtius, Oribasius, Galen, Rhasis,
Serapion, Avicenna, Averröes,
Were blocks !
    Fest. And that reminds me, I heard some-
    thing
About your waywardness : you burned their
    books,
It seems, instead of answering those sages.
    Par. And who said that?
    Fest.   Some I met yesternight
With Œcolampadius. As you know, the purpose
Of this short stay at Basel was to learn
His pleasure touching certain missives sent
For our Zuinglius and himself. 'T was he
Apprised me that the famous teacher here
Was my old friend.
    Par.   Ah, I forgot : you went . . .
    Fest. From Zurich with advices for the ear
Of Luther, now at Wittenberg — (you know,
I make no doubt, the differences of late
With Carolostadius) — and returning sought
Basel and . . .
    Par. I remember. Here 's a case, now,
Will teach you why I answer not, but burn
The books you mention. Pray, does Luther
    dream
His arguments convince by their own force
The crowds that own his doctrine ? No, indeed !
His plain denial of established points
Ages had sanctified and men supposed
Could never be oppugned while earth was under
And heaven above them — points which chance
    or time
Affected not — did more than the array
Of argument which followed. Boldly deny !
There is much breath-stopping, hair-stiffening
Awhile ; then, amazed glances, mute awaiting
The thunderbolt which does not come : and next
Reproachful wonder and inquiry ; those
Who else had never stirred, are able now

To find the rest out for themselves, perhaps
To outstrip him who set the whole at work,
— As never will my wise class its instructor.
And you saw Luther?
    Fest.   'T is a wondrous soul!
    Par. True : the so-heavy chain which galled
        mankind
Is shattered, and the noblest of us all
Must bow to the deliverer — nay, the worker
Of our own project — we who long before
Had burst our trammels, but forgot the crowd,
We should have taught, still groaned beneath
        their load :
This he has done and nobly. Speed that may!
Whatever be my chance or my mischance,
What benefits mankind must glad me too ;
And men seem made, though not as I believed,
For something better than the times produce.
Witness these gangs of peasants your new lights
From Suabia have possessed, whom Münzer
        leads,
And whom the duke, the landgrave and the
        elector
Will calm in blood! Well, well; 't is not my
        world!
    Fest. Hark!
    Par.   'T is the melancholy wind astir
Within the trees ; the embers too are gray:
Morn must be near.
    Fest.   Best ope the casement . see,
The night, late strewn with clouds and flying
        stars,
Is blank and motionless : how peaceful sleep
The tree-tops altogether! Like an asp,
The wind slips whispering from bough to bough.
    Par. Ay ; you would gaze on a wind-shaken
        tree
By the hour, nor count time lost.
    Fest.   So you shall gaze :
Those happy times will come again.
    Par.   Gone, gone,
Those pleasant times! Does not the moaning
        wind
Seem to bewail that we have gained such gains
And bartered sleep for them ?
    Fest.   It is our trust
That there is yet another world to mend
All error and mischance.
    Par.   Another world!
And why this world, this common world, to be
A make-shift, a mere foil, how fair soever,
To some fine life to come ? Man must be fed
With angels' food, forsooth ; and some few
        traces
Of a diviner nature which look out
Through his corporeal baseness, warrant him
In a supreme contempt of all provision
For his inferior tastes — some straggling marks
Which constitute his essence, just as truly
As here and there a gem would constitute
The rock, their barren bed, one diamond.
But were it so — were man all mind — he gains
A station little enviable. From God
Down to the lowest spirit ministrant,
Intelligence exists which casts our mind
Into immeasurable shade. No, no :
Love, hope, fear, faith — these make humanity ;
These are its sign and note and character,

And these I have lost! — gone, shut from me
        forever,
Like a dead friend safe from unkindness more!
See, morn at length. The heavy darkness seems
Diluted, gray and clear without the stars ;
The shrubs bestir and rouse themselves as if
Some snake, that weighed them down all night,
        let go
His hold ; and from the East, fuller and fuller
Day, like a mighty river, flowing in ;
But clouded, wintry, desolate and cold.
Yet see how that broad prickly star-shaped
        plant,
Half-down in the crevice, spreads its woolly
        leaves
All thick and glistering with diamond dew.
And you depart for Einsiedeln this day,
And we have spent all night in talk like this!
If you would have me better for your love,
Revert no more to these sad themes.
    Fest.   One favor,
And I have done. I leave you, deeply moved ;
Unwilling to have fared so well, the while
My friend has changed so sorely. If this mood
Shall pass away, if light once more arise
Where all is darkness now, if you see fit
To hope and trust again, and strive again,
You will remember — not our love alone —
But that my faith in God's desire that man
Should trust on his support, (as I must think
You trusted) is obscured and dim through you :
For you are thus, and this is no reward.
Will you not call me to your side, dear Aureole?

IV. PARACELSUS ASPIRES

SCENE, *Colmar in Alsatia : an Inn.* 1528.

PARACELSUS, FESTUS.

Par. (to JOHANNES OPORINUS, *his Secretary*).
        Sic itur ad astra! Dear Von Visenburg
Is scandalized, and poor Torinus paralyzed,
And every honest soul that Basel holds
Aghast ; and yet we live, as one may say,
Just as though Liechtenfels had never set
So true a value on his sorry carcass,
And learned Pütter had not frowned us dumb.
We live ; and shall as surely start to-morrow
For Nuremberg, as we drink speedy scathe
To Basel in this mantling wine, suffused
A delicate blush, no fainter tinge is born
I' the shut heart of a bud. Pledge me, good
        John —
"Basel ; a hot plague ravage it, and Pütter
Oppose the plague!" Even so ? Do you too share
Their panic, the reptiles ? Ha, ha ; faint through
        these,
Desist for these! They manage matters so
At Basel, 't is like : but others may find means
To bring the stoutest braggart of the tribe
Once more to crouch in silence — means to breed
A stupid wonder in each fool again,
Now big with admiration at the skill
Which stript a vain pretender of his plumes:
And, that done, — means to brand each slavish
        brow

So deeply, surely, ineffaceably,
That henceforth flattery shall not pucker it
Out of the furrow ; there that stamp shall stay
To show the next they fawn on, what they are,
This Basel with its magnates, — fill my cup, —
Whom I curse soul and limb. And now dispatch,
Dispatch, my trusty John ; and what remains
To do, whate'er arrangements for our trip
Are yet to be completed, see you hasten
This night ; we 'll weather the storm at least :
     to-morrow
For Nuremberg ! Now leave us ; this grave clerk
Has divers weighty matters for my ear :
                    [OPORINUS *goes out.*
And spare my lungs. At last, my gallant Festus,
I am rid of this arch-knave that dogs my heels
As a gaunt crow a gasping sheep ; at last
May give a loose to my delight. How kind,
How very kind, my first best only friend !
Why, this looks like fidelity. Embrace me !
Not a hair silvered yet ? Right ! you shall live
Till I am worth your love ; you shall be proud,
And I — but let time show ! Did you not won-
     der ?
I sent to you because our compact weighed
Upon my conscience — (you recall the night
At Basel, which the gods confound !) — because
Once more I aspire. I call you to my side :
You come. You thought my message strange ?
  Fest.   So strange
That I must hope, indeed, your messenger
Has mingled his own fancies with the words
Purporting to be yours.
  Par.   He said no more,
'T is probable, than the precious folk I leave
Said fiftyfold more roughly. Welladay,
'T is true ! poor Paracelsus is exposed
At last ; a most egregious quack he proves :
And those he overreached must spit their hate
On one who, utterly beneath contempt,
Could yet deceive their topping wits. You
     heard
Bare truth ; and at my bidding you come here
To speed me on my enterprise, as once
Your lavish wishes sped me, my own friend !
  Fest. What is your purpose, Aureole ?
  Par.   Oh, for purpose,
There is no lack of precedents in a case
Like mine ; at least, if not precisely mine,
The case of men cast off by those they sought
To benefit.
  Fest.   They really cast you off ?
I only heard a vague tale of some priest,
Cured by your skill, who wrangled at your
     claim,
Knowing his life's worth best ; and how the
     judge
The matter was referred to saw no cause
To interfere, nor you to hide your full
Contempt of him ; nor he, again, to smother
His wrath thereat, which raised so fierce a
     flame
That Basel soon was made no place for you.
  Par. The affair of Liechtenfels ? the shal-
     lowest fable,
The last and silliest outrage — mere pretence !
I knew it, I foretold it from the first,
How soon the stupid wonder you mistook

For genuine loyalty — a cheering promise
Of better things to come — would pall and pass ;
And every word comes true. Saul is among
The prophets ! Just so long as I was pleased
To play off the mere antics of my art,
Fantastic gambols leading to no end,
I got huge praise : but one can ne'er keep down
Our foolish nature's weakness. There they
     flocked,
Poor devils, jostling, swearing and perspiring,
Till the walls rang again ; and all for me !
I had a kindness for them, which was right ;
But then I stopped not till I tacked to that
A trust in them and a respect — a sort
Of sympathy for them ; I must needs begin
To teach them, not amaze them, '' to impart
The spirit which should instigate the search
Of truth,'' just what you bade me ! I spoke out.
Forthwith a mighty squadron, in disgust,
Filed off — '' the sifted chaff of the sack,'' I
     said,
Redoubling my endeavors to secure
The rest. When lo ! one man had tarried so
     long
Only to ascertain if I supported
This tenet of his, or that ; another loved
To hear impartially before he judged,
And having heard, now judged ; this bland
     disciple
Passed for my dupe, but all along, it seems,
Spied error where his neighbors marvelled
     most ;
That fiery doctor who had hailed me friend,
Did it because my by-paths, once proved wrong
And beaconed properly, would commend again
The good old ways our sires jogged safely o'er,
Though not their squeamish sons ; the other
     worthy
Discovered divers verses of St. John,
Which, read successively, refreshed the soul,
But, muttered backwards, cured the gout, the
     stone,
The colic and what not. *Quid multa ?* The end
Was a clear class-room, and a quiet leer
From grave folk, and a sour reproachful glance
From those in chief who, cap in hand, installed
The new professor scarce a year before ;
And a vast flourish about patient merit
Obscured awhile by flashy tricks, but sure
Sooner or later to emerge in splendor —
Of which the example was some luckless wight
Whom my arrival had discomfited,
But now, it seems, the general voice recalled
To fill my chair and so efface the stain
Basel had long incurred. I sought no better,
Only a quiet dismissal from my post,
And from my heart I wished them better suited
And better served. Good night to Basel,
     then !
But fast as I proposed to rid the tribe
Of my obnoxious back, I could not spare them
The pleasure of a parting kick.
  Fest.   You smile :
Despise them as they merit !
  Par.   If I smile,
'T is with as very contempt as ever turned
Flesh into stone. This courteous recompense,
This grateful . . . Festus, were your nature fit

To be defiled, your eyes the eyes to ache
At gangrene-blotches, eating poison-blains,
The ulcerous barky scurf of leprosy
Which finds — a man, and leaves — a hideous
　　thing
That cannot but be mended by hell-fire,
— I would lay bare to you the human heart
Which God cursed long ago, and devils make
　　since
Their pet nest and their never-tiring home.
Oh, sages have discovered we are born
For various ends — to love, to know: has ever
One stumbled, in his search, on any signs
Of a nature in us formed to hate? To hate?
If that be our true object which evokes
Our powers in fullest strength, be sure 't is hate!
Yet men have doubted if the best and bravest
Of spirits can nourish him with hate alone.
I had not the monopoly of fools,
It seems, at Basel.
　　Fest.　　　　　　But your plans, your plans!
I have yet to learn your purpose, Aureole!
　　Par.　Whether to sink beneath such ponder-
　　ous shame,
To shrink up like a crushed snail, undergo
In silence and desist from further toil,
And so subside into a monument
Of one their censure blasted? or to bow
Cheerfully as submissively, to lower
My old pretensions even as Basel dictates,
To drop into the rank her wits assign me
And live as they prescribe, and make that use
Of my poor knowledge which their rules allow,
Proud to be patted now and then, and careful
To practise the true posture for receiving
The amplest benefit from their hoofs' appliance
When they shall condescend to tutor me?
Then, one may feel resentment like a flame
Within, and deck false systems in truth's garb,
And tangle and entwine mankind with error,
And give them darkness for a dower and false-
　　hood
For a possession, ages: or one may mope
Into a shade through thinking, or else drowse
Into a dreamless sleep and so die off.
But I, — now Festus shall divine! — but I
Am merely setting out once more, embracing
My earliest aims again! What thinks he now?
　　Fest.　Your aims? the aims? — to Know?
　　and where is found
The early trust . . .
　　Par.　　　　　　Nay, not so fast; I say.
The aims — not the old means. You know
　　they made me
A laughing-stock; I was a fool; you know
The when and the how: hardly those means
　　again!
Not but they had their beauty; who should
　　know
Their passing beauty, if not I? Still, dreams
They were, so let them vanish, yet in beauty
If that may be. Stay: thus they pass in song!
　　　　　　　　　　　　　　　　　[*He sings.*
Heap cassia, sandal-buds and stripes
Of labdanum, and aloe-balls,
Smeared with dull nard an Indian wipes
　　From out her hair: such balsam falls
　　Down sea-side mountain pedestals,

From tree-tops where tired winds are fain,
Spent with the vast and howling main,
To treasure half their island-gain.

And strew faint sweetness from some old
　　Egyptian's fine worm-eaten shroud
Which breaks to dust when once unrolled;
　　Or shredded perfume, like a cloud
From closet long to quiet vowed,
With mothed and dropping arras hung,
Mouldering her lute and books among,
As when a queen, long dead, was young.

Mine, every word! And on such pile shall die
My lovely fancies, with fair perished things,
Themselves fair and forgotten; yes, forgotten,
Or why abjure them? So, I made this rhyme
That fitting dignity might be preserved;
No little proud was I; though the list of drugs
Smacks of my old vocation, and the verse
Halts like the best of Luther's psalms.
　　Fest.　　　　　　　　But, Aureole,
Talk not thus wildly and madly. I am here —
Did you know all! I have travelled far, in-
　　deed,
To learn your wishes. Be yourself again!
For in this mood I recognize you less
Than in the horrible despondency
I witnessed last. You may account this, joy;
But rather let me gaze on that despair
Than hear these incoherent words and see
This flushed cheek and intensely-sparkling eye.
　　Par.　Why, man, I was light-hearted in my
　　prime,
I am light-hearted now; what would you have?
Aprile was a poet, I make songs —
'T is the very augury of success I want!
Why should I not be joyous now as then?
　　Fest.　Joyous! and how? and what remains
　　for joy?
You have declared the ends (which I am sick
Of naming) are impracticable.
　　Par.　　　　　　　　　　Ay,
Pursued as I pursued them — the arch-fool!
Listen: my plan will please you not, 't is like,
But you are little versed in the world's ways.
This is my plan — (first drinking its good luck) —
I will accept all helps; all I despised
So rashly at the outset, equally
With early impulses, late years have quenched:
I have tried each way singly: now for both!
All helps! no one sort shall exclude the rest.
I seek to know and to enjoy at once,
Not one without the other as before.
Suppose my labor should seem God's own cause
Once more, as first I dreamed, — it shall not
　　balk me
Of the meanest earthliest sensualest delight
That may be snatched; for every joy is gain,
And gain is gain, however small. My soul
Can die then, nor be taunted — "what was
　　gained?"
Nor, on the other hand, should pleasure follow
As though I had not spurned her hitherto,
Shall she o'ercloud my spirit's rapt communion
With the tumultuous past, the teeming future
Glorious with visions of a full success.
　　Fest.　Success!

Par. And wherefore not? Why not prefer
Results obtained in my best state of being,
To those derived alone from seasons dark
As the thoughts they bred? When I was best,
    my youth
Unwasted, seemed success not surest too?
It is the nature of darkness to obscure.
I am a wanderer: I remember well
One journey, how I feared the track was missed,
So long the city I desired to reach
Lay hid; when suddenly its spires afar
Flashed through the circling clouds; you may
    conceive
My transport. Soon the vapors closed again,
But I had seen the city, and one such glance
No darkness could obscure: nor shall the pres-
    ent —
A few dull hours, a passing shame or two,
Destroy the vivid memories of the past.
I will fight the battle out; a little spent
Perhaps, but still an able combatant.
You look at my gray hair and furrowed brow?
But I can turn even weakness to account:
Of many tricks I know, 't is not the least
To push the ruins of my frame, whereon
The fire of vigor trembles scarce alive,
Into a heap, and send the flame aloft.
What should I do with age? So, sickness lends
An aid; it being, I fear, the source of all
We boast of: mind is nothing but disease,
And natural health is ignorance.
Fest.   I see
But one good symptom in this notable scheme.
I feared your sudden journey had in view
To wreak immediate vengeance on your foes.
'T is not so: I am glad.
Par.   And if I please
To spit on them, to trample them, what then?
'T is sorry warfare truly, but the fools
Provoke it. I would spare their self-conceit,
But if they must provoke me, cannot suffer
Forbearance on my part, if I may keep
No quality in the shade, must needs put forth
Power to match power, my strength against
    their strength,
And teach them their own game with their
    own arms —
Why, be it so and let them take their chance!
I am above them like a god, there 's no
Hiding the fact: what idle scruples, then,
Were those that ever bade me soften it,
Communicate it gently to the world,
Instead of proving my supremacy,
Taking my natural station o'er their head,
Then owning all the glory was a man's!
— And in my elevation man's would be.
But live and learn, though life 's short, learn-
    ing hard!
And therefore, though the wreck of my past self,
I fear, dear Pütter, that your lecture-room
Must wait awhile for its best ornament,
The penitent empiric, who set up
For somebody, but soon was taught his place;
Now, but too happy to be let confess
His error, snuff the candles, and illustrate
(*Fiat experientia corpore vili*)
Your medicine's soundness in his person. Wait,
Good Pütter!

Fest.   He who sneers thus, is a god!
Par. Ay, ay, laugh at me! I am very glad
You are not gulled by all this swaggering; you
Can see the root of the matter! — how I strive
To put a good face on the overthrow
I have experienced, and to bury and hide
My degradation in its length and breadth;
How the mean motives I would make you think
Just mingle as is due with nobler aims,
The appetites I modestly allow
May influence me as being mortal still —
Do goad me, drive me on, and fast supplant
My youth's desires. You are no stupid dupe
You find me out! Yes, I had sent for you
To palm these childish lies upon you, Festus!
Laugh — you shall laugh at me!
Fest.   The past, then, Aureole,
Proves nothing? Is our interchange of love
Yet to begin? Have I to swear I mean
No flattery in this speech or that? For you,
Whate'er you say, there is no degradation;
These low thoughts are no inmates of your mind,
Or wherefore this disorder? You are vexed
As much by the intrusion of base views,
Familiar to your adversaries, as they
Were troubled should your qualities alight
Amid their murky souls: not otherwise,
A stray wolf which the winter forces down
From our bleak hills, suffices to affright
A village in the vales — while foresters
Sleep calm, though all night long the famished
    troop
Snuff round and scratch against their crazy huts.
These evil thoughts are monsters, and will flee.
Par. May you be happy, Festus, my own
    friend!
Fest. Nay, further; the delights you fain
    would think
The superseders of your nobler aims,
Though ordinary and harmless stimulants,
Will ne'er content you. . . .
Par.   Hush! I once despised them,
But that soon passes. We are high at first
In our demand, nor will abate a jot
Of toil's strict value; but time passes o'er,
And humbler spirits accept what we refuse:
In short, when some such comfort is doled out
As these delights, we cannot long retain
Bitter contempt which urges us at first
To hurl it back, but hug it to our breast
And thankfully retire. This life of mine
Must be lived out and a grave thoroughly
    earned:
I am just fit for that and naught beside.
I told you once, I cannot now enjoy,
Unless I deem my knowledge gains through joy;
Nor can I know, but straight warm tears reveal
My need of linking also joy to knowledge:
So, on I drive, enjoying all I can,
And knowing all I can. I speak, of course,
Confusedly; this will better explain — feel here!
Quick beating, is it not? — a fire of the heart
To work off some way, this as well as any.
So, Festus sees me fairly launched; his calm
Compassionate look might have disturbed me
    once,
But now, far from rejecting, I invite
What bids me press the closer, lay myself

Open before him, and be soothed with pity ;
I hope, if he command hope, and believe
As he directs me — satiating myself
With his enduring love.   And Festus quits me
To give place to some credulous disciple
Who holds that God is wise, but Paracelsus
Has his peculiar merits : I suck in
That homage, chuckle o'er that admiration,
And then dismiss the fool ; for night is come,
And I betake myself to study again,
Till patient searchings after hidden lore
Half wring some bright truth from its prison ;
     my frame
Trembles, my forehead's veins swell out, my
     hair
Tingles for triumph.   Slow and sure the morn
Shall break on my pent room and dwindling
     lamp
And furnace dead, and scattered earths and
     ores ;
When, with a failing heart and throbbing brow,
I must review my captured truth, sum up
Its value, trace what ends to what begins,
Its present power with its eventual bearings,
Latent affinities, the views it opens,
And its full length in perfecting my scheme.
I view it sternly circumscribed, cast down
From the high place my fond hopes yielded it,
Proved worthless — which, in getting, yet had
     cost
Another wrench to this fast-falling frame.
Then, quick, the cup to quaff, that chases sor-
     row !
I lapse back into youth, and take again
My fluttering pulse for evidence that God
Means good to me, will make my cause his own.
See ! I have cast off this remorseless care
Which clogged a spirit born to soar so free,
And my dim chamber has become a tent,
Festus is sitting by me, and his Michal . . .
Why do you start ?   I say, she listening here,
(For yonder — Würzburg through the orchard-
     bough !)
Motions as though such ardent words should
     find
No echo in a maiden's quiet soul,
But her pure bosom heaves, her eyes fill fast
With tears, her sweet lips tremble all the while !
Ha, ha !
     Fest.   It seems, then, you expect to reap
No unreal joy from this your present course,
But rather . . .
     Par.   Death ! To die ! I owe that much
To what, at least, I was.   I should be sad
To live contented after such a fall,
To thrive and fatten after such reverse !
The whole plan is a makeshift, but will last
My time.
     Fest.   And you have never mused and said,
" I had a noble purpose, and the strength
To compass it ; but I have stopped half-way,
And wrongly given the first-fruits of my toil
To objects little worthy of the gift.
Why linger round them still ? why clench my
     fault ?
Why seek for consolation in defeat,
In vain endeavors to derive a beauty
From ugliness ? why seek to make the most

Of what no power can change, nor strive instead
With mighty effort to redeem the past
And, gathering up the treasures thus cast down,
To hold a steadfast course till I arrive
At their fit destination and my own ? "
You have never pondered thus ?
     Par.   Have I, you ask ?
Often at midnight, when most fancies come,
Would some such airy project visit me :
But ever at the end . . . or will you hear
The same thing in a tale, a parable ?
You and I, wandering over the world wide,
Chance to set foot upon a desert coast.
Just as we cry, " No human voice before
Broke the inveterate silence of these rocks ! "
— Their querulous echo startles us ; we turn :
What ravaged structure still looks o'er the sea ?
Some characters remain, too !   While we read,
The sharp salt wind, impatient for the last
Of even this record, wistfully comes and goes,
Or sings what we recover, mocking it.
This is the record ; and my voice, the wind's.
                                        [*He sings*

Over the sea our galleys went,
With cleaving prows in order brave
To a speeding wind and a bounding wave
     A gallant armament :
Each bark built out of a forest-tree
     Left leafy and rough as first it grew,
And nailed all over the gaping sides,
Within and without, with black bull-hides,
Seethed in fat and suppled in flame,
To bear the playful billows' game :
So, each good ship was rude to see,
Rude and bare to the outward view,
     But each upbore a stately tent
Where cedar pales in scented row
Kept out the flakes of the dancing brine,
And an awning drooped the mast below,
In fold on fold of the purple fine,
That neither noontide nor starshine
Nor moonlight cold which maketh mad,
     Might pierce the regal tenement.
When the sun dawned, oh, gay and glad
We set the sail and plied the oar ;
But when the night-wind blew like breath,
For joy of one day's voyage more,
We sang together on the wide sea,
Like men at peace on a peaceful shore ;
Each sail was loosed to the wind so free,
Each helm made sure by the twilight star,
And in a sleep as calm as death,
We, the voyagers from afar,
Lay stretched along, each weary crew
In a circle round its wondrous tent
Whence gleamed soft light and curled rich
     scent,
     And with light and perfume, music too :
So the stars wheeled round, and the darkness
     past,
And at morn we started beside the mast,
And still each ship was sailing fast.

Now, one morn, land appeared — a speck
Dim trembling betwixt sea and sky :
" Avoid it," cried our pilot, " check
     The shout, restrain the eager eye ! "
But the heaving sea was black behind

For many a night and many a day,
And land, though but a rock, drew nigh ;
So, we broke the cedar pales away,
Let the purple awning flap in the wind,
And a statue bright was on every deck !
We shouted, every man of us,
And steered right into the harbor thus,
With pomp and pæan glorious.

A hundred shapes of lucid stone !
All day we built its shrine for each,
A shrine of rock for every one,
Nor paused till in the westering sun
We sat together on the beach
To sing because our task was done.
When lo ! what shouts and merry songs !
What laughter all the distance stirs !
A loaded raft with happy throngs
Of gentle islanders !
"Our isles are just at hand," they cried,
"Like cloudlets faint in even sleeping.
Our temple-gates are opened wide,
Our olive-groves thick shade are keeping
For these majestic forms " — they cried.
Oh, then we awoke with sudden start
From our deep dream, and knew, too late,
How bare the rock, how desolate,
Which had received our precious freight :
Yet we called out — " Depart !
Our gifts, once given, must here abide.
Our work is done ; we have no heart
To mar our work," — we cried.

   Fest. In truth ?
   Par.   Nay, wait : all this in tracings faint
On rugged stones strewn here and there, but
   piled
In order once : then follows — mark what fol-
   lows !
" The sad rhyme of the men who proudly clung
To their first fault, and withered in their pride."
   Fest. Come back then, Aureole ; as you fear
God, come !
This is foul sin ; come back ! Renounce the past,
Forswear the future ; look for joy no more,
But wait death's summons amid holy sights,
And trust me for the event — peace, if not joy.
Return with me to Einsiedeln, dear Aureole !
   Par. No way, no way ! it would not turn to
good.
A spotless child sleeps on the flowering moss —
'T is well for him ; but when a sinful man,
Envying such slumber, may desire to put
His guilt away, shall he return at once
To rest by lying there ? Our sires knew well
(Spite of the grave discoveries of their sons)
The fitting course for such : dark cells, dim
   lamps,
A stone floor one may writhe on like a worm :
No mossy pillow blue with violets !
   Fest. I see no symptom of these absolute
And tyrannous passions. You are calmer now.
This verse-making can purge you well enough
Without the terrible penance you describe.
You love me still : the lusts you fear will never
Outrage your friend. To Einsiedeln, once more !
Say but the word !
   Par.   No, no ; those lusts forbid :

They crouch, I know, cowering with half-shut
   eye
Beside you ; 't is their nature. Thrust yourself
Between them and their prey ; let some fool
   style me
Or king or quack, it matters not — then try
Your wisdom, urge them to forego their treat !
No, no ; learn better and look deeper, Festus !
If you knew how a devil sneers within me
While you are talking now of this, now that,
As though we differed scarcely save in trifles !
   Fest. Do we so differ ? True, change must
proceed,
Whether for good or ill ; keep from me, which !
Do not confide all secrets : I was born
To hope, and you . . .
   Par.   To trust : you know the fruits !
   Fest. Listen : I do believe, what you call trust
Was self-delusion at the best : for, see !
So long as God would kindly pioneer
A path for you, and screen you from the world,
Procure you full exemption from man's lot,
Man's common hopes and fears, on the mere
   pretext
Of your engagement in his service — yield you
A limitless license, make you God, in fact,
And turn your slave — you were content to say
Most courtly praises ! What is it, at last,
But selfishness without example ? None
Could trace God's will so plain as you, while
   yours
Remained implied in it ; but now you fail,
And we, who prate about that will, are fools !
In short, God's service is established here
As he determines fit, and not your way,
And this you cannot brook. Such discontent
Is weak. Renounce all creatureship at once !
Affirm an absolute right to have and use
Your energies ; as though the rivers should
   say —
" We rush to the ocean ; what have we to do
With feeding streamlets, lingering in the vales,
Sleeping in lazy pools ? " Set up that plea,
That will be bold at least !
   Par.   'T is like enough.
The serviceable spirits are those, no doubt,
The East produces : lo, the master bids, —
They wake, raise terraces and garden-grounds
In one night's space ; and, this done, straight
   begin
Another century's sleep, to the great praise
Of him that framed them wise and beautiful,
Till a lamp's rubbing, or some chance akin,
Wake them again. I am of different mould.
I would have soothed my lord, and slaved for
   him
And done him service past my narrow bond,
And thus I get rewarded for my pains !
Beside, 't is vain to talk of forwarding
God's glory otherwise ; this is alone
The sphere of its increase, as far as men
Increase it ; why, then, look beyond this sphere ?
We are his glory ; and if we be glorious,
Is not the thing achieved ?
   Fest.   Shall one like me
Judge hearts like yours ? Though years have
   changed you much,
And you have left your first love, and retain

Its empty shade to veil your crooked ways,
Yet I still hold that you have honored God.
And who shall call your course without reward?
For, wherefore this repining at defeat
Had triumph ne'er inured you to high hopes?
I urge you to forsake the life you curse,
And what success attends me? — simply talk
Of passion, weakness and remorse; in short,
Anything but the naked truth — you choose
This so-despised career, and cheaply hold
My happiness, or rather other men's.
Once more, return!

    Par.   And quickly. John the thief
Has pilfered half my secrets by this time:
And we depart by daybreak. I am weary,
I know not how; not even the wine-cup soothes
My brain to-night . . .
Do you not thoroughly despise me, Festus?
No flattery! One like you needs not be told
We live and breathe deceiving and deceived.
Do you not scorn me from your heart of hearts,
Me and my cant, each petty subterfuge,
My rhymes and all this frothy shower of words,
My glozing self-deceit, my outward crust
Of lies which wrap, as tetter, morphew, furfur
Wrap the sound flesh? — so, see you flatter not!
Even God flatters: but my friend, at least,
Is true. I would depart, secure henceforth
Against all further insult, hate and wrong
From puny foes; my one friend's scorn shall
    brand me:
No fear of sinking deeper!

    Fest.   No, dear Aureole!
No, no; I came to counsel faithfully.
There are old rules, made long ere we were
    born,
By which I judge you. I, so fallible,
So infinitely low beside your mighty
Majestic spirit! — even I can see
You own some higher law than ours which call
Sin, what is no sin — weakness, what is strength.
But I have only these, such as they are,
To guide me; and I blame you where they bid,
Only so long as blaming promises
To win peace for your soul: the more, that
    sorrow
Has fallen on me of late, and they have helped me
So that I faint not under my distress.
But wherefore should I scruple to avow
In spite of all, as brother judging brother,
Your fate is most inexplicable to me?
And should you perish without recompense
And satisfaction yet — too hastily
I have relied on love: you may have sinned,
But you have loved. As a mere human mat-
    ter —
As I would have God deal with fragile men
In the end — I say that you will triumph yet!

    Par. Have you felt sorrow, Festus? — 't is
    because
You love me. Sorrow, and sweet Michal yours!
Well thought on: never let her know this last
Dull winding-up of all: these miscreants dared
Insult me — me she loved: — so, grieve her not!

    Fest. Your ill success can little grieve her
    now.

    Par. Michal is dead! pray Christ we do not
    craze!

    Fest. Aureole, dear Aureole, look not on me
    thus!
Fool, fool! this is the heart grown sorrow-
    proof —
I cannot bear those eyes.

    Par.   Nay, really dead?

    Fest. 'T is scarce a month.

    Par. Stone dead! — then you have laid her
Among the flowers ere this. Now, do you
    know,
I can reveal a secret which shall comfort
Even you. I have no julep, as men think,
To cheat the grave; but a far better secret.
Know, then, you did not ill to trust your love
To the cold earth: I have thought much of it:
For I believe we do not wholly die.

    Fest. Aureole!

    Par. Nay, do not laugh; there is a reason
For what I say: I think the soul can never
Taste death. I am, just now, as you may see,
Very unfit to put so strange a thought
In an intelligible dress of words;
But take it as my trust, she is not dead.

    Fest. But not on this account alone? you
    surely,
—Aureole, you have believed this all along?

    Par. And Michal sleeps among the roots
    and dews,
While I am moved at Basel, and full of schemes
For Nuremberg, and hoping and despairing,
As though it mattered how the farce plays out,
So it be quickly played. Away, away!
Have your will, rabble! while we fight the
    prize,
Troop you in safety to the snug back-seats
And leave a clear arena for the brave
About to perish for your sport! — Behold!

V. PARACELSUS ATTAINS

SCENE, *Salzburg: a cell in the Hospital of St. Sebastian.*
    1541.

FESTUS, PARACELSUS.

    Fest. No change! The weary night is well-
    nigh spent,
The lamp burns low, and through the casement-
    bars
Gray morning glimmers feebly: yet no change!
Another night, and still no sigh has stirred
That fallen discolored mouth, no pang relit
Those fixed eyes, quenched by the decaying
    body,
Like torch-flame choked in dust. While all
    beside
Was breaking, to the last they held out bright,
As a stronghold where life intrenched itself;
But they are dead now — very blind and dead:
He will drowse into death without a groan.

My Aureole — my forgotten, ruined Aureole!
The days are gone, are gone! How grand thou
    wast!
And now not one of those who struck thee
    down —
Poor glorious spirit — concerns him even to stay

And satisfy himself his little hand
Could turn God's image to a livid thing.

Another night, and yet no change! 'T is much
That I should sit by him, and bathe his brow,
And chafe his hands; 't is much: but he will
    sure
Know me, and look on me, and speak to me
Once more — but only once! His hollow cheek
Looked all night long as though a creeping
    laugh
At his own state were just about to break
From the dying man: my brain swam, my
    throat swelled,
And yet I could not turn away. In truth,
They told me how, when first brought here, he
    seemed
Resolved to live, to lose no faculty;
Thus striving to keep up his shattered strength,
Until they bore him to this stifling cell:
When straight his features fell, an hour made
    white
The flushed face, and relaxed the quivering
    limb,
Only the eye remained intense awhile
As though it recognized the tomb-like place,
And then he lay as here he lies.
                      Ay, here!
Here is earth's noblest, nobly garlanded —
Her bravest champion with his well-won
    prize —
Her best achievement, her sublime amends
For countless generations fleeting fast
And followed by no trace; — the creature-god
She instances when angels would dispute
The title of her brood to rank with them.
Angels, this is our angel! Those bright forms
We clothe with purple, crown and call to
    thrones,
Are human, but not his; those are but men
Whom other men press round and kneel before;
Those palaces are dwelt in by mankind;
Higher provision is for him you seek
Amid our pomps and glories: see it here!
Behold earth's paragon! Now, raise thee,
    clay!

God! Thou art love! I build my faith on that.
Even as I watch beside thy tortured child
Unconscious whose hot tears fall fast by him,
So doth thy right hand guide us through the
    world
Wherein we stumble. God! what shall we say?
How has he sinned? How else should he have
    done?
Surely he sought thy praise — thy praise, for all
He might be busied by the task so much
As half forget awhile its proper end.
Dost thou well, Lord? Thou canst not but pre-
    fer
That I should range myself upon his side —
How could he stop at every step to set
Thy glory forth? Hadst thou but granted him
Success, thy honor would have crowned success,
A halo round a star. Or, say he erred, —
Save him, dear God; it will be like thee: bathe
    him
In light and life! Thou art not made like us;

We should be wroth in such a case; but thou
Forgivest—so, forgive these passionate thoughts
Which come unsought and will not pass away!
I know thee, who hast kept my path, and made
Light for me in the darkness, tempering sorrow
So that it reached me like a solemn joy;
It were too strange that I should doubt thy love.
But what am I? Thou madest him and knowest
How he was fashioned. I could never err
That way: the quiet place beside thy feet,
Reserved for me, was ever in my thoughts:
But he — thou shouldst have favored him as
    well!

Ah! he wakens! Aureole, I am here! 't is
    Festus!
I cast away all wishes save one wish —
Let him but know me, only speak to me!
He mutters; louder and louder; any other
Than I, with brain less laden, could collect
What he pours forth. Dear Aureole, do but
    look!
Is it talking or singing, this he utters fast?
Misery that he should fix me with his eye,
Quick talking to some other all the while!
If he would husband this wild vehemence
Which frustrates its intent! — I heard, I know
I heard my name amid those rapid words.
Oh, he will know me yet! Could I divert
This current, lead it somehow gently back
Into the channels of the past! — His eye
Brighter than ever! It must recognize me!

I am Erasmus: I am here to pray
That Paracelsus use his skill for me.
The schools of Paris and of Padua send
These questions for your learning to resolve.
We are your students, noble master: leave
This wretched cell, what business have you
    here?
Our class awaits you; come to us once more!
(O agony! the utmost I can do
Touches him not; how else arrest his ear?)
I am commissioned . . . I shall craze like him.
Better be mute and see what God shall send.
    Par. Stay, stay with me!
    Fest.   I will; I am come here
To stay with you — Festus, you loved of old;
Festus, you know, you must know!
    Par.   Festus! Where 's
Aprile, then? Has he not chanted softly
The melodies I heard all night? I could not
Get to him for a cold hand on my breast,
But I made out his music well enough,
O well enough! If they have filled him full
With magical music, as they freight a star
With light, and have remitted all his sin,
They will forgive me too, I too shall know!
    Fest. Festus, your Festus!
    Par.   Ask him if Aprile
Knows as he Loves — if I shall Love and Know?
I try; but that cold hand, like lead — so cold!
    Fest. My hand, see!
    Par.   Ah, the curse, Aprile, Aprile!
We get so near — so very, very near!
'T is an old tale: Jove strikes the Titans down
Not when they set about their mountain-piling
But when another rock would crown the work

And Phaeton—doubtless his first radiant plunge
Astonished mortals, though the gods were calm,
And Jove prepared his thunder: all old tales!
  Fest. And what are these to you?
  Par.   Ay, fiends must laugh
So cruelly, so well! most like I never
Could tread a single pleasure underfoot,
But they were grinning by my side, were chuck-
  ling
To see me toil and drop away by flakes!
Hell-spawn! I am glad, most glad, that thus I
  fail!
Your cunning has o'ershot its aim. One year,
One month, perhaps, and I had served your
  turn!
You should have curbed your spite awhile. But
  now,
Who will believe 't was you that held me back?
Listen: there's shame and hissing and con-
  tempt,
And none but laughs who names me, none but
  spits
Measureless scorn upon me, me alone,
The quack, the cheat, the liar, — all on me!
And thus your famous plan to sink mankind
In silence and despair, by teaching them
One of their race had probed the inmost truth,
Had done all man could do, yet failed no less —
Your wise plan proves abortive. Men despair?
Ha, ha! why, they are hooting the empiric,
The ignorant and incapable fool who rushed
Madly upon a work beyond his wits;
Nor doubt they but the simplest of themselves
Could bring the matter to triumphant issue.
So, pick and choose among them all, accursed!
Try now, persuade some other to slave for you,
To ruin body and soul to work your ends!
No, no; I am the first and last, I think.
  Fest. Dear friend, who are accursed? who
  has done . . .
  Par. What have I done? Fiends dare ask
  that? or you,
Brave men? Oh, you can chime in boldly,
  backed
By the others! What had you to do, sage peers?
Here stand my rivals; Latin, Arab, Jew,
Greek, join dead hands against me: all I ask
Is, that the world enroll my name with theirs,
And even this poor privilege, it seems,
They range themselves, prepared to disallow.
Only observe! why, fiends may learn from them!
How they talk calmly of my throes, my fierce
Aspirings, terrible watchings, each one claiming
Its price of blood and brain; how they dissect
And sneeringly disparage the few truths
Got at a life's cost; they too hanging the while
About my neck, their lies misleading me
And their dead names browbeating me! Gray
  crew,
Yet steeped in fresh malevolence from hell,
Is there a reason for your hate? My truths
Have shaken a little the palm about each prince?
Just think, Aprile, all these leering dotards
Were bent on nothing less than to be crowned
As we! That yellow blear-eyed wretch in chief
To whom the rest cringe low with feigned re-
  spect,
Galen of Pergamos and hell — nay speak

The tale, old man! We met there face to face:
I said the crown should fall from thee. Once
  more
We meet as in that ghastly vestibule:
Look to my brow! Have I redeemed my pledge?
  Fest. Peace, peace; ah, see!
  Par.   Oh, emptiness of fame!
O Persic Zoroaster, lord of stars!
— Who said these old renowns, dead long ago,
Could make me overlook the living world
To gaze through gloom at where they stood, in-
  deed,
But stand no longer? What a warm light life
After the shade! In truth, my delicate witch,
My serpent-queen, you did but well to hide
The juggles I had else detected. Fire
May well run harmless o'er a breast like yours!
The cave was not so darkened by the smoke
But that your white limbs dazzled me: oh, white,
And panting as they twinkled, wildly dancing!
I cared not for your passionate gestures then,
But now I have forgotten the charm of charms,
The foolish knowledge which I came to seek,
While I remember that quaint dance; and thus
I am come back, not for those mummeries,
But to love you, and to kiss your little feet
Soft as an ermine's winter coat!
  Fest.   A light
Will struggle through these thronging words at
  last,
As in the angry and tumultuous West
A soft star trembles through the drifting clouds.
These are the strivings of a spirit which hates
So sad a vault should coop it, and calls up
The past to stand between it and its fate.
Were he at Einsiedeln — or Michal here!
  Par. Cruel! I seek her now — I kneel — I
  shriek —
I clasp her vesture — but she fades, still fades;
And she is gone; sweet human love is gone!
'T is only when they spring to heaven that angels
Reveal themselves to you; they sit all day
Beside you, and lie down at night by you
Who care not for their presence, muse or sleep,
And all at once they leave you, and you know
  them!
We are so fooled, so cheated! Why, even now
I am not too secure against foul play;
The shadows deepen and the walls contract:
No doubt some treachery is going on.
'T is very dusk. Where are we put, Aprile?
Have they left us in the lurch? This murky
  loathsome
Death-trap, this slaughter-house, is not the hall
In the golden city! Keep by me, Aprile!
There is a hand groping amid the blackness
To catch us. Have the spider-fingers got you,
Poet? Hold on me for your life! If once
They pull you! — Hold!
              'T is but a dream — no more!
I have you still; the sun comes out again;
Let us be happy: all will yet go well!
Let us confer: is it not like, Aprile,
That spite of trouble, this ordeal passed,
The value of my labors ascertained,
Just as some stream foams long among the
  rocks
But after glideth glassy to the sea,

So, full content shall henceforth be my lot?
What think you, poet? Louder! Your clear voice
Vibrates too like a harp-string. Do you ask
How could I still remain on earth, should God
Grant me the great approval which I seek?
I, you, and God can comprehend each other,
But men would murmur, and with cause enough;
For when they saw me, stainless of all sin,
Preserved and sanctified by inward light,
They would complain that comfort, shut from them,
I drank thus unespied; that they live on,
Nor taste the quiet of a constant joy,
For ache and care and doubt and weariness,
While I am calm; help being vouchsafed to me,
And hid from them. — 'T were best consider that!
You reason well, Aprile; but at least
Let me know this, and die! Is this too much?
I will learn this, if God so please, and die!

If thou shalt please, dear God, if thou shalt please!
We are so weak, we know our motives least
In their confused beginning. If at first
I sought . . . but wherefore bare my heart to thee?
I know thy mercy; and already thoughts
Flock fast about my soul to comfort it,
And intimate I cannot wholly fail,
For love and praise would clasp me willingly
Could I resolve to seek them. Thou art good,
And I should be content. Yet — yet first show
I have done wrong in daring! Rather give
The supernatural consciousness of strength
Which fed my youth! Only one hour of that,
With thee to help — O what should bar me then!

Lost, lost! Thus things are ordered here! God's creatures,
And yet he takes no pride in us! — none, none!
Truly there needs another life to come!
If this be all — (I must tell Festus that)
And other life await us not — for one,
I say 't is a poor cheat, a stupid bungle,
A wretched failure. I, for one, protest
Against it, and I hurl it back with scorn.

Well, onward though alone! Small time remains,
And much to do: I must have fruit, must reap
Some profit from my toils. I doubt my body
Will hardly serve me through; while I have labored
It has decayed; and now that I demand
Its best assistance, it will crumble fast:
A sad thought, a sad fate! How very full
Of wormwood 't is, that just at altar-service,
The rapt hymn rising with the rolling smoke,
When glory dawns and all is at the best,
The sacred fire may flicker and grow faint
And die for want of a wood-piler's help!
Thus fades the flagging body, and the soul
Is pulled down in the overthrow. Well, well —
Let men catch every word, let them lose naught
Of what I say; something may yet be done.

They are ruins! Trust me who am one of you!
All ruins, glorious once, but lonely now.
It makes my heart sick to behold you crouch
Beside your desolate fane: the arches dim,
The crumbling columns grand against the moon,
Could I but rear them up once more — but that
May never be, so leave them! Trust me, friends,
Why should you linger here when I have built
A far resplendent temple, all your own?
Trust me, they are but ruins! See, Aprile,
Men will not heed! Yet were I not prepared
With better refuge for them, tongue of mine
Should ne'er reveal how blank their dwelling is:
I would sit down in silence with the rest.

Ha, what? you spit at me, you grin and shriek
Contempt into my ear — my ear which drank
God's accents once? you curse me? Why men, men,
I am not formed for it! Those hideous eyes
Will be before me sleeping, waking, praying,
They will not let me even die. Spare, spare me,
Sinning or no, forget that, only spare me
The horrible scorn! You thought I could support it.
But now you see what silly fragile creature
Cowers thus. I am not good nor bad enough,
Not Christ nor Cain, yet even Cain was saved
From Hate like this. Let me but totter back!
Perhaps I shall elude those jeers which creep
Into my very brain, and shut these scorched
Eyelids and keep those mocking faces out.

Listen, Aprile! I am very calm:
Be not deceived, there is no passion here
Where the blood leaps like an imprisoned thing:
I am calm: I will exterminate the race!
Enough of that: 't is said and it shall be.
And now be merry: safe and sound am I
Who broke through their best ranks to get at you.
And such a havoc, such a rout, Aprile!
 Fest. Have you no thought, no memory for me,
Aureole? I am so wretched — my pure Michal
Is gone, and you alone are left me now,
And even you forget me. Take my hand —
Lean on me thus. Do you not know me, Aureole?
 Par. Festus, my own friend, you are come at last?
As you say, 't is an awful enterprise;
But you believe I shall go through with it:
'T is like you, and I thank you. Thank him for me,
Dear Michal! See how bright St. Saviour's spire
Flames in the sunset; all its figures quaint
Gay in the glancing light: you might conceive them
A troop of yellow-vested white-haired Jews
Bound for their own land where redemption dawns.
 Fest. Not that blest time — not our youth's time, dear God!
 Par. Ha — stay! true, I forget — all is done since,
And he is come to judge me. How he speaks,

How calm, how well! yes, it is true, all true;
All quackery; all deceit; myself can laugh
The first at it, if you desire: but still
You know the obstacles which taught me tricks
So foreign to my nature — envy and hate,
Blind opposition, brutal prejudice,
Bald ignorance — what wonder if I sunk
To humor men the way they most approved?
My cheats were never palmed on such as you,
Dear Festus! I will kneel if you require me,
Impart the meagre knowledge I possess,
Explain its bounded nature, and avow
My insufficiency — whate'er you will:
I give the fight up: let there be an end,
A privacy, an obscure nook for me.
I want to be forgotten even by God.
But if that cannot be, dear Festus, lay me,
When I shall die, within some narrow grave,
Not by itself — for that would be too proud —
But where such graves are thickest; let it look
Nowise distinguished from the hillocks round,
So that the peasant at his brother's bed
May tread upon my own and know it not;
And we shall all be equal at the last,
Or classed according to life's natural ranks,
Fathers, sons, brothers, friends — not rich, nor
          wise,
Nor gifted: lay me thus, then say, "He lived
Too much advanced before his brother men;
They kept him still in front: 't was for their
          good,
But yet a dangerous station. It were strange
That he should tell God he had never ranked
With men: so, here at least he is a man."
    Fest. That God shall take thee to his breast,
          dear spirit,
Unto his breast, be sure! and here on earth
Shall splendor sit upon thy name forever.
Sun! all the heaven is glad for thee: what care
If lower mountains light their snowy phares
At thine effulgence, yet acknowledge not
The source of day? Their theft shall be their
          bale:
For after-ages shall retrack thy beams,
And put aside the crowd of busy ones
And worship thee alone — the master-mind,
The thinker, the explorer, the creator!
Then, who should sneer at the convulsive throes
With which thy deeds were born, would scorn
          as well
The sheet of winding subterraneous fire
Which, pent and writhing, sends no less at last
Huge islands up amid the simmering sea.
Behold thy might in me! thou hast infused
Thy soul in mine; and I am grand as thou,
Seeing I comprehend thee — I so simple,
Thou so august. I recognize thee first;
I saw thee rise, I watched thee early and late,
And though no glance reveal thou dost accept
My homage — thus no less I proffer it,
And bid thee enter gloriously thy rest.
    Par. Festus!
    Fest.   I am for noble Aureole, God!
I am upon his side, come weal or woe.
His portion shall be mine. He has done well.
I would have sinned, had I been strong enough,
As he has sinned. Reward him or I waive
Reward! If thou canst find no place for him,

He shall be king elsewhere, and I will be
His slave forever. There are two of us.
    Par. Dear Festus!
    Fest.   Here, dear Aureole! ever by you!
    Par. Nay, speak on, or I dream again.
          Speak on!
Some story, anything — only your voice.
I shall dream else. Speak on! ay, leaning so!
    Fest. Thus the Mayne glideth
          Where my Love abideth.
          Sleep 's no softer: it proceeds
          On through lawns, on through meads,
          On and on, whate'er befall,
          Meandering and musical,
          Though the niggard pasturage
          Bears not on its shaven ledge
          Aught but weeds and waving grasses
          To view the river as it passes,
          Save here and there a scanty patch
          Of primroses too faint to catch
          A weary bee.
    Par. More, more; say on!
    Fest.   And scarce it pushes
          Its gentle way through strangling rushes
          Where the glossy kingfisher
          Flutters when noon-heats are near,
          Glad the shelving banks to shun,
          Red and steaming in the sun,
          Where the shrew-mouse with pale throat
          Burrows, and the speckled stoat;
          Where the quick sandpipers flit
          In and out the marl and grit
          That seems to breed them, brown as they:
          Naught disturbs its quiet way,
          Save some lazy stork that springs,
          Trailing it with legs and wings,
          Whom the shy fox from the hill
          Rouses, creep he ne'er so still.
    Par. My heart! they loose my heart, those
          simple words;
Its darkness passes, which naught else could
          touch:
Like some dark snake that force may not expel,
Which glideth out to music sweet and low.
What were you doing when your voice broke
          through
A chaos of ugly images? You, indeed!
Are you alone here?
    Fest.   All alone: you know me?
This cell?
    Par.   An unexceptionable vault:
Good brick and stone: the bats kept out, the
          rats
Kept in: a snug nook: how should I mistake it?
    Fest. But wherefore am I here?
    Par.   Ah, well remembered!
Why, for a purpose — for a purpose, Festus!
'T is like me: here I trifle while time fleets,
And this occasion, lost, will ne'er return.
You are here to be instructed. I will tell
God's message; but I have so much to say,
I fear to leave half out. All is confused
No doubt; but doubtless you will learn in time.
He would not else have brought you here: no
          doubt
I shall see clearer soon.
    Fest.   Tell me but this —
You are not in despair?

Par.   I ? and for what ?
Fest. Alas, alas ! he knows not, as I feared !
Par. What is it you would ask me with that earnest
Dear searching face ?
Fest.   How feel you, Aureole ?
Par.   Well :
Well. 'T is a strange thing : I am dying, Festus,
And now that fast the storm of life subsides,
I first perceive how great the whirl has been.
I was calm then, who am so dizzy now —
Calm in the thick of the tempest, but no less
A partner of its motion and mixed up
With its career. The hurricane is spent,
And the good boat speeds through the brighten-
      ing weather ;
But is it earth or sea that heaves below ?
The gulf rolls like a meadow-swell, o'erstrewn
With ravaged boughs and remnants of the shore ;
And now some islet, loosened from the land,
Swims past with all its trees, sailing to ocean ;
And now the air is full of uptorn canes,
Light strippings from the fan-trees, tamarisks
Unrooted, with their birds still clinging to them,
All high in the wind. Even so my varied life
Drifts by me ; I am young, old, happy, sad,
Hoping, desponding, acting, taking rest,
And all at once : that is, those past conditions
Float back at once on me. If I select
Some special epoch from the crowd, 't is but
To will, and straight the rest dissolve away,
And only that particular state is present
With all its long-forgotten circumstance
Distinct and vivid as at first — myself
A careless looker-on and nothing more,
Indifferent and amused, but nothing more.
And this is death : I understand it all.
New being waits me ; new perceptions must
Be born in me before I plunge therein ;
Which last is Death's affair ; and while I speak,
Minute by minute he is filling me
With power ; and while my foot is on the thresh-
      old
Of boundless life — the doors unopened yet,
All preparations not complete within —
I turn new knowledge upon old events,
And the effect is . . . but I must not tell ;
It is not lawful. Your own turn will come
One day. Wait, Festus ! You will die like me.
Fest. 'T is of that past life that I burn to
      hear.
Par. You wonder it engages me just now ?
In truth, I wonder too. What 's life to me ?
Where'er I look is fire, where'er I listen
Music, and where I tend bliss evermore.
Yet how can I refrain ? 'T is a refined
Delight to view those chances, — one last view.
I am so near the perils I escape,
That I must play with them and turn them over,
To feel how fully they are past and gone.
Still, it is like, some further cause exists
For this peculiar mood — some hidden purpose ;
Did I not tell you something of it, Festus ?
I had it fast, but it has somehow slipt
Away from me ; it will return anon.
Fest. (Indeed his cheek seems young again,
      his voice
Complete with its old tones : that little laugh

Concluding every phrase, with upturned eye,
As though one stooped above his head to whom
He looked for confirmation and approval,
Where was it gone so long, so well preserved ?
Then, the forefinger pointing as he speaks,
Like one who traces in an open book
The matter he declares ; 't is many a year
Since I remarked it last : and this in him,
But now a ghastly wreck !)
                    And can it be,
Dear Aureole, you have then found out at last
That worldly things are utter vanity ?
That man is made for weakness, and should wait
In patient ignorance, till God appoint . . .
Par. Ha, the purpose : the true purpose :
      that is it !
How could I fail to apprehend ! You here,
I thus ! But no more trifling : I see all,
I know all : my last mission shall be done
If strength suffice. No trifling ! Stay ; this
      posture
Hardly befits one thus about to speak :
I will arise.
Fest.   Nay, Aureole, are you wild ?
You cannot leave your couch.
Par.   No help ; no help ;
Not even your hand. So ! there, I stand once
      more !
Speak from a couch ? I never lectured thus.
My gown — the scarlet lined with fur ; now put
The chain about my neck ; my signet-ring
Is still upon my hand, I think — even so ;
Last, my good sword ; ah, trusty Azoth, leapest
Beneath thy master's grasp for the last time ?
This couch shall be my throne : I bid these walls
Be consecrate, this wretched cell become
A shrine, for here God speaks to men through
      me.
Now, Festus, I am ready to begin.
Fest. I am dumb with wonder.
Par.   Listen, therefore, Festus !
There will be time enough, but none to spare.
I must content myself with telling only
The most important points. You doubtless feel
That I am happy, Festus ; very happy.
Fest. 'T is no delusion which uplifts him thus !
Then you are pardoned, Aureole, all your sin ?
Par. Ay, pardoned : yet why pardoned ?
Fest.   'T is God's praise
That man is bound to seek, and you . . .
Par.   Have lived !
We have to live alone to set forth well
God's praise. 'T is true, I sinned much, as I
      thought,
And in effect need mercy, for I strove
To do that very thing ; but, do your best
Or worst, praise rises, and will rise forever.
Pardon from him, because of praise denied —
Who calls me to himself to exalt himself ?
He might laugh as I laugh !
Fest.   But all comes
To the same thing. 'T is fruitless for man-
      kind
To fret themselves with what concerns them not ;
They are no use that way : they should lie down
Content as God has made them, nor go mad
In thriveless cares to better what is ill.
Par. No, no ; mistake me not ; let me not work

More harm than I have worked! This is my
  case :
If I go joyous back to God, yet bring
No offering, if I render up my soul
Without the fruits it was ordained to bear,
If I appear the better to love God
For sin, as one who has no claim on him,
Be not deceived! It may be surely thus
With me, while higher prizes still await
The mortal persevering to the end.
Beside I am not all so valueless :
I have been something, though too soon I left
Following the instincts of that happy time.
  Fest. What happy time? For God's sake,
    for man's sake,
What time was happy? All I hope to know
That answer will decide. What happy time?
  Par. When but the time I vowed myself to
    man?
  Fest. Great God, thy judgments are inscruta-
    ble!
  Par. Yes, it was in me; I was born for it —
I, Paracelsus : it was mine by right.
Doubtless a searching and impetuous soul
Might learn from its own motions that some task
Like this awaited it about the world ;
Might seek somewhere in this blank life of ours
For fit delights to stay its longings vast ;
And, grappling Nature, so prevail on her
To fill the creature full she dared thus frame
Hungry for joy ; and, bravely tyrannous,
Grow in demand, still craving more and more,
And make each joy conceded prove a pledge
Of other joy to follow — bating naught
Of its desires, still seizing fresh pretence
To turn the knowledge and the rapture wrung
As an extreme, last boon, from destiny,
Into occasion for new covetings,
New strifes, new triumphs : — doubtless a strong
    soul,
Alone, unaided might attain to this,
So glorious is our nature, so august
Man's inborn uninstructed impulses,
His naked spirit so majestical !
But this was born in me; I was made so ;
Thus much time saved : the feverish appetites,
The tumult of unproved desire, the unaimed
Uncertain yearnings, aspirations blind,
Distrust, mistake, and all that ends in tears
Were saved me ; thus I entered on my course.
You may be sure I was not all exempt
From human trouble ; just so much of doubt
As bade me plant a surer foot upon
The sun-road, kept my eye unruined 'mid
The fierce and flashing splendor, set my heart
Trembling so much as warned me I stood there
On sufferance — not to idly gaze, but cast
Light on a darkling race ; save for that doubt,
I stood at first where all aspire at last
To stand : the secret of the world was mine.
I knew, I felt, (perception unexpressed,
Uncomprehended by our narrow thought,
But somehow felt and known in every shift
And change in the spirit, — nay, in every pore
Of the body, even,) — what God is, what we are,
What life is — how God tastes an infinite joy
In infinite ways — one everlasting bliss,
From whom all being emanates, all power

Proceeds ; in whom is life forevermore,
Yet whom existence in its lowest form
Includes ; where dwells enjoyment there is he,
With still a flying point of bliss remote,
A happiness in store afar, a sphere
Of distant glory in full view ; thus climbs
Pleasure its heights forever and forever.
The centre-fire heaves underneath the earth,
And the earth changes like a human face ;
The molten ore bursts up among the rocks,
Winds into the stone's heart, outbranches bright
In hidden mines, spots barren river-beds,
Crumbles into fine sand where sunbeams bask —
God joys therein. The wroth sea's waves are
    edged
With foam, white as the bitten lip of hate,
When, in the solitary waste, strange groups
Of young volcanos come up, cyclops-like,
Staring together with their eyes on flame —
God tastes a pleasure in their uncouth pride.
Then all is still ; earth is a wintry clod :
But spring-wind, like a dancing psaltress, passes
Over its breast to waken it, rare verdure
Buds tenderly upon rough banks, between
The withered tree-roots and the cracks of frost,
Like a smile striving with a wrinkled face ;
The grass grows bright, the boughs are swoln
    with blooms
Like chrysalids impatient for the air,
The shining dorrs are busy, beetles run
Along the furrows, ants make their ado ;
Above, birds fly in merry flocks, the lark
Soars up and up, shivering for very joy ;
Afar the ocean sleeps ; white fishing-gulls
Flit where the strand is purple with its tribe
Of nested limpets ; savage creatures seek
Their loves in wood and plain — and God renews
His ancient rapture. Thus he dwells in all,
From life's minute beginnings, up at last
To man — the consummation of this scheme
Of being, the completion of this sphere
Of life : whose attributes had here and there
Been scattered o'er the visible world before,
Asking to be combined, dim fragments meant
To be united in some wondrous whole,
Imperfect qualities throughout creation,
Suggesting some one creature yet to make,
Some point where all those scattered rays should
    meet
Convergent in the faculties of man.
Power — neither put forth blindly, nor con-
    trolled
Calmly by perfect knowledge ; to be used
At risk, inspired or checked by hope and fear :
Knowledge — not intuition, but the slow
Uncertain fruit of an enhancing toil,
Strengthened by love : love — not serenely pure,
But strong from weakness, like a chance-sown
    plant
Which, cast on stubborn soil, puts forth changed
    buds
And softer stains, unknown in happier climes ;
Love which endures and doubts and is oppressed
And cherished, suffering much and much sus-
    tained,
And blind, oft-failing, yet believing love,
A half-enlightened, often-checkered trust : —
Hints and previsions of which faculties.

Are strewn confusedly everywhere about
The inferior natures, and all lead up higher,
All shape out dimly the superior race,
The heir of hopes too fair to turn out false,
And man appears at last. So far the seal
Is put on life ; one stage of being complete,
One scheme wound up : and from the grand
  result
A supplementary reflux of light,
Illustrates all the inferior grades, explains
Each back step in the circle. Not alone
For their possessor dawn those qualities,
But the new glory mixes with the heaven
And earth ; man, once descried, imprints forever
His presence on all lifeless things : the winds
Are henceforth voices, wailing or a shout,
A querulous mutter or a quick gay laugh,
Never a senseless gust now man is born.
The herded pines commune and have deep
  thoughts,
A secret they assemble to discuss
When the sun drops behind their trunks which
  glare
Like grates of hell : the peerless cup afloat
Of the lake-lily is an urn, some nymph
Swims bearing high above her head : no bird
Whistles unseen, but through the gaps above
That let light in upon the gloomy woods,
A shape peeps from the breezy forest-top,
Arch with small puckered mouth and mocking
  eye.
The morn has enterprise, deep quiet droops
With evening, triumph takes the sunset hour,
Voluptuous transport ripens with the corn
Beneath a warm moon like a happy face :
— And this to fill us with regard for man,
With apprehension of his passing worth,
Desire to work his proper nature out,
And ascertain his rank and final place,
For these things tend still upward, progress is
The law of life, man is not Man as yet.
Nor shall I deem his object served, his end
Attained, his genuine strength put fairly forth,
While only here and there a star dispels
The darkness, here and there a towering mind
O'erlooks its prostrate fellows : when the host
Is out at once to the despair of night,
When all mankind alike is perfected,
Equal in full-blown powers — then, not till then,
I say, begins man's general infancy.
For wherefore make account of feverish starts
Of restless members of a dormant whole,
Impatient nerves which quiver while the body
Slumbers as in a grave ? Oh, long ago
The brow was twitched, the tremulous lids
  astir,
The peaceful mouth disturbed ; half uttered
  speech
Ruffled the lip, and then the teeth were set,
The breath drawn sharp, the strong right-hand
  clenched stronger,
As it would pluck a lion by the jaw ;
The glorious creature laughed out even in
  sleep !
But when full roused, each giant-limb awake,
Each sinew strung, the great heart pulsing fast,
He shall start up and stand on his own earth,
Then shall his long triumphant march begin,

Thence shall his being date, — thus wholly
  roused,
What he achieves shall be set down to him.
When all the race is perfected alike
As man, that is ; all tended to mankind,
And, man produced, all has its end thus far :
But in completed man begins anew
A tendency to God. Prognostics told
Man's near approach ; so in man's self arise
August anticipations, symbols, types
Of a dim splendor ever on before
In that eternal circle life pursues.
For men begin to pass their nature's bound,
And find new hopes and cares which fast sup
  plant
Their proper joys and griefs ; they grow too
  great
For narrow creeds of right and wrong, which
  fade
Before the unmeasured thirst for good : while
  peace
Rises within them ever more and more.
Such men are even now upon the earth,
Serene amid the half-formed creatures round
Who should be saved by them and joined with
  them.
Such was my task, and I was born to it —
Free, as I said but now, from much that chains
Spirits, high-dowered but limited and vexed
By a divided and delusive aim,
A shadow mocking a reality
Whose truth avails not wholly to disperse
The flitting mimic called up by itself,
And so remains perplexed and nigh put out
By its fantastic fellow's wavering gleam.
I, from the first, was never cheated thus ;
I never fashioned out a fancied good
Distinct from man's ; a service to be done,
A glory to be ministered unto
With powers put forth at man's expense, with-
  drawn
From laboring in his behalf ; a strength
Denied that might avail him. I cared not
Lest his success ran counter to success
Elsewhere : for God is glorified in man,
And to man's glory vowed I soul and limb.
Yet, constituted thus, and thus endowed,
I failed : I gazed on power till I grew blind.
Power ; I could not take my eyes from that :
That only, I thought, should be preserved, in
  creased
At any risk, displayed, struck out at once —
The sign and note and character of man.
I saw no use in the past : only a scene
Of degradation, ugliness and tears,
The record of disgraces best forgotten.
A sullen page in human chronicles
Fit to erase. I saw no cause why man
Should not stand all-sufficient even now,
Or why his annals should be forced to tell
That once the tide of light, about to break
Upon the world, was sealed within its spring :
I would have had one day, one moment's space,
Change man's condition, push each slumbering
  claim
Of mastery o'er the elemental world
At once to full maturity, then roll
Oblivion o'er the work, and hide from man

What night had ushered morn. Not so, dear
    child
Of after-days, wilt thou reject the past
Big with deep warnings of the proper tenure
By which thou hast the earth : for thee the
    present
Shall have distinct and trembling beauty, seen
Beside that past's own shade when, in relief,
Its brightness shall stand out : nor yet on thee
Shall burst the future, as successive zones
Of several wonder open on some spirit
Flying secure and glad from heaven to heaven :
But thou shalt painfully attain to joy,
While hope and fear and love shall keep thee
    man !
All this was hid from me : as one by one
My dreams grew dim, my wide aims circum-
    scribed,
As actual good within my reach decreased,
While obstacles sprung up this way and that
To keep me from effecting half the sum,
Small as it proved ; as objects, mean within
The primal aggregate, seemed, even the least,
Itself a match for my concentred strength —
What wonder if I saw no way to shun
Despair ? The power I sought for man, seemed
    God's.
In this conjuncture, as I prayed to die,
A strange adventure made me know, one sin
Had spotted my career from its uprise ;
I saw Aprile — my Aprile there !
And as the poor melodious wretch disburdened
His heart, and moaned his weakness in my ear,
I learned my own deep error ; love's undoing
Taught me the worth of love in man's estate,
And what proportion love should hold with
    power
In his right constitution ; love preceding
Power, and with much power, always much
    more love ;
Love still too straitened in his present means,
And earnest for new power to set love free.
I learned this, and supposed the whole was
    learned :
And thus, when men received with stupid won-
    der
My first revealings, would have worshipped me,
And I despised and loathed their proffered
    praise —

When, with awakened eyes, they took revenge
For past credulity in casting shame
On my real knowledge, and I hated them —
It was not strange I saw no good in man,
To overbalance all the wear and waste
Of faculties, displayed in vain, but born
To prosper in some better sphere : and why ?
In my own heart love had not been made wise
To trace love's faint beginnings in mankind,
To know even hate is but a mask of love's,
To see a good in evil, and a hope
In ill-success ; to sympathize, be proud
Of their half-reasons, faint aspirings, dim
Struggles for truth, their poorest fallacies,
Their prejudice and fears and cares and doubts
All with a touch of nobleness, despite
Their error, upward tending all though weak,
Like plants in mines which never saw the sun,
But dream of him, and guess where he may
    be,
And do their best to climb and get to him.
All this I knew not, and I failed. Let men
Regard me, and the poet dead long ago
Who loved too rashly ; and shape forth a third
And better-tempered spirit, warned by both :
As from the over-radiant star too mad
To drink the life-springs, beamless thence it-
    self —
And the dark orb which borders the abyss,
Ingulfed in icy night, — might have its course,
A temperate and equidistant world.
Meanwhile, I have done well, though not all
    well.
As yet men cannot do without contempt ;
'T is for their good, and therefore fit awhile
That they reject the weak, and scorn the false,
Rather than praise the strong and true, in me :
But after, they will know me. If I stoop
Into a dark tremendous sea of cloud,
It is but for a time ; I press God's lamp
Close to my breast ; its splendor, soon or late,
Will pierce the gloom : I shall emerge one day.
You understand me ? I have said enough !
    Fest. Now die, dear Aureole !
    Par.   Festus, let my hand —
This hand, lie in your own, my own true friend !
Aprile ! Hand in hand with you, Aprile !

    Fest. And this was Paracelsus !

STRAFFORD

A TRAGEDY

DEDICATED, IN ALL AFFECTIONATE ADMIRATION,

TO

WILLIAM C. MACREADY

LONDON, APRIL 23, 1837

Paracelsus found an enthusiastic reader in the actor Macready, who begged Browning to write him a play, even suggesting the subject to him, which did not awaken the poet's interest. More than a year passed, when the two met at a supper given by Macready after the successful presentation of Talfourd's *Ion*. As the guests were leaving, Macready said to Browning : " Write a play, Browning, and keep me from going to America." "Shall it be historical and English? " replied Browning. " What do you say to a drama on Strafford? " and the poet now had his subject. His choice is readily explained by the fact that he was at this time helping his friend John Forster with his Life of Strafford contained in *Lives of Eminent British Statesmen*. Indeed, Mr. Furnivall says without hesitation that the agreement of the Strafford of the play with the Strafford of Forster's biography is due to the fact that Browning wrote the whole of the Life of Strafford after the first seven paragraphs.

When the play was rehearsing Browning gave Macready a lilt which he had composed for the children's song in Act V. It was not used, because the two children who were to sing wished a more pretentious song. The lilt which Browning composed was purposely no more than a *crooning* measure. He afterward gave it to Miss Hickey for her special edition of *Strafford*, and it is reproduced here in its place. The following is Browning's preface to the first edition : —

" I had for some time been engaged in a Poem of a very different nature, when induced to make the present attempt ; and am not without apprehension that my eagerness to freshen a jaded mind by diverting it to the healthy natures of a grand epoch, may have operated unfavorably on the represented play, which is one of Action in Character, rather than Character in Action. To remedy this, in some degree, considerable curtailment will be necessary, and, in a few instances, the supplying details not required, I suppose, by the mere reader. While a trifling success would much gratify, failure will not wholly discourage me from another effort : experience is to come ; and earnest endeavor may yet remove many disadvantages.

" The portraits are, I think, faithful ; and I am exceedingly fortunate in being able, in proof of this, to refer to the subtle and eloquent exposition of the characters of Eliot and Strafford, in the *Lives of Eminent British Statesmen*, now in the course of publication in Lardner's *Cyclopedia*, by a writer [John Forster] whom I am proud to call my friend ; and whose biographies of Hampden, Pym, and Vane, will, I am sure, fitly illustrate the present year — the Second Centenary of the Trial concerning Ship-Money. My Carlisle, however, is purely imaginary : I at first sketched her singular likeness roughly in, as suggested by Matthews and the memoir-writers — but it was too artificial, and the substituted outline is exclusively from Voiture and Waller.

" The Italian boat-song in the last scene is from Redi's ' Bacco,' long since naturalized in the joyous and delicate version of Leigh Hunt."

PERSONS

CHARLES I.
Earl of HOLLAND.
Lord SAVILE.
Sir HENRY VANE.
WENTWORTH, Viscount WENTWORTH, Earl of STRAFFORD.
JOHN PYM.
JOHN HAMPDEN.
The younger VANE.
DENZIL HOLLIS.
BENJAMIN RUDYARD.
NATHANIEL FIENNES.
Earl of LOUDON.
MAXWELL, *Usher of the Black Rod.*

BALFOUR, *Constable of the Tower.*
A PURITAN.
Queen HENRIETTA.
LUCY PERCY, *Countess of Carlisle.*
Presbyterians, Scots Commissioners, Adherents of Strafford, Secretaries, Officers of the Court, etc.
Two of Strafford's CHILDREN.

ACT I

SCENE I. *A House near Whitehall.* HAMPDEN, HOLLIS, *the* younger VANE, RUDYARD, FIENNES *and many of the Presbyterian Party :* LOUDON *and other Scots Commissioners.*

Vane. I say, if he be here —
Rudyard.   (And he is here !) —
Hollis. For England's sake let every man be still
Nor speak of him, so much as say his name,
Till Pym rejoin us ! Rudyard ! Henry Vane !
One rash conclusion may decide our course
And with it England's fate — think — England's fate !
Hampden, for England's sake they should be still !
Vane. You say so, Hollis ? Well, I must be still.
It is indeed too bitter that one man,
Any one man's mere presence, should suspend
England's combined endeavor : little need
To name him !
Rud.   For you are his brother, Hollis !
Hampden. Shame on you, Rudyard ! time to tell him that
When he forgets the Mother of us all.
Rud. Do I forget her ?
Hamp.   You talk idle hate
Against her foe : is that so strange a thing ?
Is hating Wentworth all the help she needs ?
A Puritan. The Philistine strode, cursing as he went :
But David — five smooth pebbles from the brook
Within his scrip . . .
Rud.   Be you as still as David !
Fiennes. Here 's Rudyard not ashamed to wag a tongue
Stiff with ten years' disuse of Parliaments ;
Why, when the last sat, Wentworth sat with us !
Rud. Let 's hope for news of them now he returns —
He that was safe in Ireland, as we thought !
— But I 'll abide Pym's coming.
Vane.   Now, by Heaven,
Then may be cool who can, silent who will —
Some have a gift that way ! Wentworth is here,
Here, and the King 's safe closeted with him
Ere this. And when I think on all that 's past
Since that man left us, how his single arm
Rolled the advancing good of England back
And set the woeful past up in its place,
Exalting Dagon where the Ark should be, —
How that man has made firm the fickle King
(Hampden, I will speak out !) — in aught he feared
To venture on before ; taught tyranny
Her dismal trade, the use of all her tools,
To ply the scourge yet screw the gag so close
That strangled agony bleeds mute to death —
How he turns Ireland to a private stage
For training infant villanies, new ways
Of wringing treasure out of tears and blood,
Unheard oppressions nourished in the dark
To try how much man's nature can endure
— If he dies under it, what harm ? if not,
Why, one more trick is added to the rest
Worth a king's knowing, and what Ireland bears
England may learn to bear : — how all this while
That man has set himself to one dear task,
The bringing Charles to relish more and more
Power, power without law, power and blood too
— Can I be still ?
Hamp.   For that you should be still.

Vane. Oh Hampden, then and now ! The year he left us,
The People in full Parliament could wrest
The Bill of Rights from the reluctant King ;
And now, he 'll find in an obscure small room
A stealthy gathering of great-hearted men
That take up England's cause : England is here !
Hamp. And who despairs of England ?
Rud.   That do I,
If Wentworth comes to rule her. I am sick
To think her wretched masters, Hamilton,
The muckworm Cottington, the maniac Laud,
May yet be longed-for back again. I say,
I do despair.
Vane. And, Rudyard, I 'll say this —
Which all true men say after me, not loud
But solemnly and as you 'd say a prayer !
This King, who treads our England underfoot,
Has just so much . . . it may be fear or craft,
As bids him pause at each fresh outrage : friends,
He needs some sterner hand to grasp his own,
Some voice to ask, " Why shrink ? Am I not by ? "
Now, one whom England loved for serving her,
Found in his heart to say, " I know where best
The iron heel shall bruise her, for she leans
Upon me when you trample." Witness, you !
So Wentworth heartened Charles, so England fell.
But inasmuch as life is hard to take
From England . . .
Many Voices. Go on, Vane ! 'T is well said, Vane !
Vane. Who has not so forgotten Runnymede ! —
Voices. 'T is well and bravely spoken, Vane ! Go on !
Vane. There are some little signs of late she knows
The ground no place for her. She glances round,
Wentworth has dropped the hand, is gone his way
On other service : what if she arise ?
No ! the King beckons, and beside him stands
The same bad man once more, with the same smile
And the same gesture. Now shall England crouch,
Or catch at us and rise ?
Voices.   The Renegade !
Haman ! Ahithophel !
Hamp.   Gentlemen of the North,
It was not thus the night your claims were urged,
And we pronounced the League and Covenant,
The cause of Scotland, England's cause as well :
Vane there, sat motionless the whole night through.
Vane. Hampden !
Fien.   Stay, Vane !
Loudon.   Be just and patient, Vane !
Vane. Mind how you counsel patience, Loudon ! you
Have still a Parliament, and this your League
To back it ; you are free in Scotland still :
While we are brothers, hope 's for England yet.
But know you wherefore Wentworth comes ? to quench

This last of hopes? that he brings war with him?
Know you the man's self? what he dares?
Lou.   We know,
All know — 't is nothing new.
Vane.   And what 's new, then,
In calling for his life? Why, Pym himself —
You must have heard — ere Wentworth dropped
    our cause
He would see Pym first; there were many more
Strong on the people's side and friends of his,
Eliot that 's dead, Rudyard and Hampden here,
But for these Wentworth cared not; only, Pym
He would see — Pym and he were sworn, 't is
    said,
To live and die together; so, they met
At Greenwich. Wentworth, you are sure, was
    long,
Specious enough, the devil's argument
Lost nothing on his lips; he 'd have Pym own
A patriot could not play a purer part
Than follow in his track; they two combined
Might put down England. Well, Pym heard
    him out;
One glance — you know Pym's eye — one word
    was all:
"You leave us, Wentworth! while your head
    is on,
I 'll not leave you."
Hamp.   Has he left Wentworth, then?
Has England lost him? Will you let him speak,
Or put your crude surmises in his mouth?
Away with this! Will you have Pym or Vane?
Voices. Wait Pym's arrival! Pym shall speak.
Hamp.   Meanwhile
Let Loudon read the Parliament's report
From Edinburgh: our last hope, as Vane says,
Is in the stand it makes. Loudon!
Vane.   No, no!
Silent I can be: not indifferent!
Hamp. Then each keep silence, praying God
    to spare
His anger, cast not England quite away
In this her visitation!
A Puritan.   Seven years long
The Midianite drove Israel into dens
And caves. Till God sent forth a mighty man,
            (PYM *enters.*)
Even Gideon!
Pym. Wentworth 's come: nor sickness, care,
The ravaged body nor the ruined soul,
More than the winds and waves that beat his
    ship,
Could keep him from the King. He has not
    reached
Whitehall: they 've hurried up a Council there
To lose no time and find him work enough.
Where 's Loudon? your Scots' Parliament . . .
Lou.   Holds firm:
We were about to read reports.
Pym.   The King
Has just dissolved your Parliament.
Lou. and other Scots.   Great God!
An oath-breaker! Stand by us, England, then!
Pym. The King 's too sanguine; doubtless
    Wentworth 's here:
But still some little form might be kept up.
Hamp. Now speak, Vane! Rudyard, you
    had much to say!

Hol. The rumor 's false, then . . .
Pym.   Ay, the Court gives out
His own concerns have brought him back: I
    know
'T is the King calls him. Wentworth supersedes
The tribe of Cottingtons and Hamiltons
Whose part is played; there 's talk enough, by
    this, —
Merciful talk, the King thinks: time is now
To turn the record's last and bloody leaf
Which, chronicling a nation's great despair,
Tells they were long rebellious, and their lord
Indulgent, till, all kind expedients tried,
He drew the sword on them and reigned in
    peace.
Laud's laying his religion on the Scots
Was the last gentle entry: the new page
Shall run, the King thinks, "Wentworth thrust
    it down
At the sword's point."
A Puritan.   I 'll do your bidding, Pym,
England's and God's — one blow!
Pym.   A goodly thing —
We all say, friends, it is a goodly thing
To right that England. Heaven grows dark
    above:
Let 's snatch one moment ere the thunder fall,
To say how well the English spirit comes out
Beneath it! All have done their best, indeed,
From lion Eliot, that grand Englishman,
To the least here: and who, the least one here,
When she is saved (for her redemption dawns
Dimly, most dimly, but it dawns — it dawns)
Who 'd give at any price his hope away
Of being named along with the Great Men?
We would not — no, we would not give that up!
Hamp. And one name shall be dearer than all
    names,
When children, yet unborn, are taught that
    name
After their fathers', — taught what matchless
    man . . .
Pym. . . . Saved England? What if Went-
    worth 's should be still
That name?
Rud. and others. We have just said it, Pym!
    His death
Saves her! We said it — there 's no way be-
    side!
I 'll do God's bidding, Pym! They struck
    down Joab
And purged the land.
Vane.   No villanous striking-down!
Rud. No, a calm vengeance: let the whole
    land rise
And shout for it. No Feltons!
Pym.   Rudyard, no!
England rejects all Feltons; most of all
Since Wentworth . . . Hampden, say the trust
    again
Of England in her servants — but I 'll think
You know me, all of you. Then, I believe,
Spite of the past, Wentworth rejoins you,
    friends!
Vane and others. Wentworth? Apostate!
    Judas! Double-dyed
A traitor! Is it Pym, indeed . . .
Pym.   . . . Who says

Vane never knew that Wentworth, loved that
    man,
Was used to stroll with him, arm locked in arm,
Along the streets to see the people pass,
And read in every island-countenance
Fresh argument for God against the King, —
Never sat down, say, in the very house
Where Eliot's brow grew broad with noble
    thoughts,
(You 've joined us, Hampden — Hollis, you as
    well,)
And then left talking over Gracchus's death . .
    Vane. To frame, we know it well, the choi-
    cest clause
In the Petition of Right: he framed such clause
One month before he took at the King's hand
His Northern Presidency, which that Bill
Denounced.
    Pym. Too true! Never more, never more
Walked we together! Most alone I went.
I have had friends — all here are fast my
    friends —
But I shall never quite forget that friend.
And yet it could not but be real in him!
You, Vane, — you, Rudyard, have no right to
    trust
To Wentworth : but can no one hope with me ?
Hampden, will Wentworth dare shed English
    blood
Like water ?
    Hamp.   Ireland is Aceldama.
    Pym. Will he turn Scotland to a hunting-
    ground
To please the King, now that he knows the
    King?
The People or the King? and that King,
    Charles?
    Hamp. Pym, all here know you: you 'll not
    set your heart
On any baseless dream. But say one deed
Of Wentworth's, since he left us . . . [*Shouting
    without.*
    Vane.   There ! he comes,
And they shout for him ! Wentworth's at
    Whitehall,
The King embracing him, now, as we speak,
And he, to be his match in courtesies,
Taking the whole war's risk upon himself,
Now, while you tell us here how changed he is !
Hear you ?
    Pym.   And yet if 't is a dream, no more,
That Wentworth chose their side, and brought
    the King
To love it as though Laud had loved it first,
And the Queen after ; that he led their cause
Calm to success, and kept it spotless through,
So that our very eyes could look upon
The travail of our souls, and close content
That violence, which something mars even right
Which sanctions it, had taken off no grace
From its serene regard. Only a dream !
    Hamp. We meet here to accomplish certain
    good
By obvious means, and keep tradition up
Of free assemblages, else obsolete,
In this poor chamber : nor without effect
Has friend met friend to counsel and confirm,
As, listening to the beats of England's heart,

We spoke its wants to Scotland's prompt reply
By these her delegates. Remains alone
That word grow deed, as with God's help it
    shall —
But with the devil's hindrance, who doubts too ?
Looked we or no that tyranny should turn
Her engines of oppression to their use ?
Whereof, suppose the worst be Wentworth
    here —
Shall we break off the tactics which succeed
In drawing out our formidablest foe,
Let bickering and disunion take their place ?
Or count his presence as our conquest's proof,
And keep the old arms at their steady play ?
Proceed to England's work ! Fiennes, read the
    list !
    Fien. Ship-money is refused or fiercely
    paid
In every county, save the northern parts
Where Wentworth's influence . . . [*Shouting.*
    Vane.   I, in England's name,
Declare her work, this day, at end ! Till now,
Up to this moment, peaceful strife was best.
We English had free leave to think ; till now,
We had a shadow of a Parliament
In Scotland. But all 's changed : they change
    the first,
They try brute-force for law, they, first of
    all . . .
    Voices. Good ! Talk enough ! The old true
    hearts with Vane !
    Vane. Till we crush Wentworth for her,
    there 's no act
Serves England !
    Voices.   Vane for England !
    Pym.   Pym should be
Something to England. I seek Wentworth,
    friends.

Scene II. *Whitehall.*

Lady Carlisle *and* Wentworth.

Wentworth. And the King ?
    Lady Carlisle. Wentworth, lean on me !
    Sit then !
I 'll tell you all ; this horrible fatigue
Will kill you.
    Went. No ; — or, Lucy, just your arm ;
I 'll not sit till I 've cleared this up with him:
After that, rest. The King ?
    Lady Car.   Confides in you.
    Went. Why? or, why now ? — They have
    kind throats, the knaves !
Shout for me — they !
    Lady Car. You come so strangely soon :
Yet we took measures to keep off the crowd —
Did they shout for you ?
    Went.   Wherefore should they not ?
Does the King take such measures for himself ?
Beside, there 's such a dearth of malcontents,
You say !
    Lady Car. I said but few dared carp at you.
    Went. At me ? at us, I hope ! The King
    and I !
He 's surely not disposed to let me bear
The fame away from him of these late deeds
In Ireland ? I am yet his instrument
Be it for well or ill ? He trusts me. too

Lady Car. The King, dear Wentworth, pur-
poses, I said,
To grant you, in the face of all the Court . . .
Went. All the Court! Evermore the Court
about us!
Savile and Holland, Hamilton and Vane
About us, — then the King will grant me —
what?
That he for once put these aside and say —
"Tell me your whole mind, Wentworth!"
Lady Car. You professed
You would be calm.
Went. Lucy, and I am calm!
How else shall I do all I come to do,
Broken, as you may see, body and mind,
How shall I serve the King? Time wastes mean-
while,
You have not told me half. His footstep! No,
Quick, then, before I meet him, — I am calm —
Why does the King distrust me?
Lady Car. He does not
Distrust you.
Went. Lucy, you can help me; you
Have even seemed to care for me: one word!
Is it the Queen?
Lady Car. No, not the Queen: the party
That poisons the Queen's ear, Savile and Hol-
land.
Went. I know, I know: old Vane, too, he's
one too?
Go on — and he's made Secretary. Well?
Or leave them out and go straight to the charge;
The charge!
Lady Car. Oh, there's no charge, no precise
charge;
Only they sneer, make light of — one may say,
Nibble at what you do.
Went. I know! but, Lucy,
I reckoned on you from the first! — Go on!
— Was sure could I once see this gentle friend
When I arrived, she'd throw an hour away
To help her . . . what am I?
Lady Car. You thought of me,
Dear Wentworth?
Went. But go on! The party here!
Lady Car. They do not think your Irish
government
Of that surpassing value . . .
Went. The one thing
Of value! The one service that the crown
May count on! All that keeps these very Vanes
In power, to vex me — not that they do vex,
Only it might vex some to hear that service
Decried, the sole support that's left the King!
Lady Car. So the Archbishop says.
Went. Ah? well, perhaps
The only hand held up in my defence
May be old Laud's! These Hollands then, these
Saviles
Nibble? They nibble? — that's the very word!
Lady Car. Your profit in the Customs, Bris-
tol says,
Exceeds the due proportion: while the tax . . .
Went. Enough! 'tis too unworthy, — I am not
So patient as I thought! What's Pym about?
Lady Car. Pym?
Went. Pym and the People.
Lady Car. Oh, the Faction!

Extinct — of no account: there'll never be
Another Parliament.
Went. Tell Savile that!
You may know — (ay, you do — the creatures
here
Never forget!) that in my earliest life
I was not . . . much that I am now! The King
May take my word on points concerning Pym
Before Lord Savile's, Lucy, or if not,
I bid them ruin their wise selves, not me,
These Vanes and Hollands! I'll not be their
tool
Who might be Pym's friend yet.
But there's the King!
Where is he?
Lady Car. Just apprised that you arrive.
Went. And why not here to meet me? I was
told
He sent for me, nay, longed for me.
Lady Car. Because, —
He is now . . . I think a Council's sitting now
About this Scots affair.
Went. A Council sits?
They have not taken a decided course
Without me in the matter?
Lady Car. I should say . . .
Went. The war? They cannot have agreed
to that?
Not the Scots' war? — without consulting me —
Me, that am here to show how rash it is,
How easy to dispense with? — Ah, you too
Against me! well, — the King may take his
time.
— Forget it, Lucy! Cares make peevish: mine
Weigh me (but 't is a secret) to my grave.
Lady Car. For life or death I am your own,
dear friend! [*Goes out.*
Went. Heartless! but all are heartless here.
Go now,
Forsake the People! I did not forsake
The People: they shall know it, when the King
Will trust me! — who trusts all beside at once,
While I have not spoke Vane and Savile fair,
And am not trusted: have but saved the throne;
Have not picked up the Queen's glove prettily,
And am not trusted. But he'll see me now.
Weston is dead: the Queen's half English now —
More English: one decisive word will brush
These insects from . . . the step I know so well!
The King! But now, to tell him . . . no — to
ask
What's in me he distrusts: — or, best begin
By proving that this frightful Scots affair
Is just what I foretold. So much to say,
And the flesh fails, now, and the time is come,
And one false step no way to be repaired.
You were avenged, Pym, could you look on me.
(PYM *enters.*)
Went. I little thought of you just then.
Pym. No? I
Think always of you, Wentworth.
Went. The old voice!
I wait the King, sir.
Pym. True — you look so pale!
A Council sits within; when that breaks up
He'll see you.
Went. Sir, I thank you.
Pym. Oh, thank Laud!

You know when Laud once gets on Church af-
 fairs
The case is desperate : he 'll not be long
To-day : he only means to prove, to-day,
We English all are mad to have a hand
In butchering the Scots for serving God
After their fathers' fashion : only that !
 Went. Sir, keep your jests for those who
 relish them !
(Does he enjoy their confidence ?) 'T is kind
To tell me what the Council does.
 Pym.   You grudge
That I should know it had resolved on war
Before you came ? no need : you shall have all
The credit, trust me !
 Went.   Have the Council dared —
They have not dared . . . that is — I know you
 not.
Farewell, sir : times are changed.
 Pym.   — Since we two met
At Greenwich ? Yes : poor patriots though we
 be,
You cut a figure, makes some slight return
For your exploits in Ireland ! Changed indeed,
Could our friend Eliot look from out his grave !
Ah, Wentworth, one thing for acquaintance'
 sake,
Just to decide a question ; have you, now,
Felt your old self since you forsook us ?
 Went.   Sir !
 Pym. Spare me the gesture ! you misappre-
 hend.
Think not I mean the advantage is with me.
I was about to say that, for my part,
I never quite held up my head since then —
Was quite myself since then : for first, you see,
I lost all credit after that event
With those who recollect how sure I was
Wentworth would outdo Eliot on our side.
Forgive me : Savile, old Vane, Holland here,
Eschew plain-speaking : 't is a trick I keep.
 Went. How, when, where, Savile, Vane, and
 Holland speak,
Plainly or otherwise, would have my scorn,
All of my scorn, sir . . .
 Pym.   . . . Did not my poor thoughts
Claim somewhat ?
 Went. Keep your thoughts ! believe the King
Mistrusts me for their prattle, all these Vanes
And Saviles ! make your mind up, o' God's love,
That I am discontented with the King !
 Pym. Why, you may be : I should be, that
 I know,
Were I like you.
 Went.   Like me ?
 Pym.   I care not much
For titles : our friend Eliot died no lord,
Hampden 's no lord, and Savile is a lord ;
But you care, since you sold your soul for one.
I can't think, therefore, your soul's purchaser
Did well to laugh you to such utter scorn
When you twice prayed so humbly for its price,
The thirty silver pieces . . . I should say,
The Earldom you expected, still expect,
And may. Your letters were the movingest !
Console yourself : I 've borne him prayers just
 now
From Scotland not to be oppressed by Laud,

Words moving in their way : he 'll pay, be sure,
As much attention as to those you sent.
 Went. False, sir ! Who showed them you ?
 Suppose it so,
The King did very well . . . nay, I was glad
When it was shown me : I refused, the first !
John Pym, you were my friend — forbear me
 once !
 Pym. Oh, Wentworth, ancient brother of
 my soul,
That all should come to this !
 Went.   Leave me !
 Pym.   My friend,
Why should I leave you ?
 Went.   To tell Rudyard this,
And Hampden this !
 Pym.   Whose faces once were bright
At my approach, now sad with doubt and fear,
Because I hope in you — yes, Wentworth, you
Who never mean to ruin England — you
Who shake off, with God's help, an obscene
 dream
In this Ezekiel chamber, where it crept
Upon you first, and wake, yourself, your true
And proper self, our Leader, England's Chief,
And Hampden's friend !
              This is the proudest day !
Come, Wentworth ! Do not even see the King !
The rough old room will seem itself again !
We 'll both go in together : you 've not seen
Hampden so long : come : and there 's Fiennes :
 you 'll have
To know young Vane. This is the proudest day !
 [*The* KING *enters.* WENTWORTH *lets fall* PYM'S *hand.*
 Charles. Arrived, my lord ? — This gentle-
 man, we know
Was your old friend.
              The Scots shall be informed
What we determine for their happiness.
              [PYM *goes out.*
You have made haste, my lord.
 Went.   Sir, I am come . . .
 Cha. To see an old familiar — nay, 't is well ;
Aid us with his experience : this Scots' League
And Covenant spreads too far, and we have
 proofs
That they intrigue with France : the Faction
 too,
Whereof your friend there is the head and front,
Abets them, — as he boasted, very like.
 Went. Sir, trust me ! but for this once, trust
 me, sir !
 Cha. What can you mean ?
 Went.   That you should trust me, sir !
Oh — not for my sake ! but 't is sad, so sad
That for distrusting me, you suffer — you
Whom I would die to serve : sir, do you think
That I would die to serve you ?
 Cha.   But rise, Wentworth !
 Went. What shall convince you ? What does
 Savile do
To prove him . . . Ah, one can't tear out one's
 heart
And show it, how sincere a thing it is !
 Cha. Have I not trusted you ?
 Went.   Say aught but that !
There is my comfort, mark you : all will be
So different when you trust me — as you shall !

It has not been your fault, — I was away,
Mistook, maligned, how was the King to know?
I am here, now — he means to trust me, now —
All will go on so well!
Cha.   Be sure I do —
I've heard that I should trust you: as you came,
Your friend, the Countess, told me . . .
Went.   No, — hear nothing —
Be told nothing about me! — you're not told
Your right-hand serves you, or your children
     love you!
Cha.   You love me, Wentworth: rise!
Went.   I can speak now.
I have no right to hide the truth. 'T is I
Can save you: only I. Sir, what must be?
Cha.   Since Laud's assured (the minutes are
     within)
— Loath as I am to spill my subjects' blood . . .
Went.   That is, he'll have a war: what's
     done is done!
Cha.   They have intrigued with France;
     that's clear to Laud.
Went.   Has Laud suggested any way to meet
The war's expense?
Cha.   He'd not decide so far
Until you joined us.
Went.   Most considerate!
He's certain they intrigue with France, these
     Scots?
The People would be with us.
Cha.   Pym should know.
Went.   The People for us — were the People
     for us!
Sir, a great thought comes to reward your trust:
Summon a Parliament! in Ireland first,
Then, here.
Cha.   In truth?
Went.   That saves us! that puts off
The war, gives time to right their grievances —
To talk with Pym. I know the Faction — Laud
So styles it — tutors Scotland: all their plans
Suppose no Parliament: in calling one
You take them by surprise. Produce the proofs
Of Scotland's treason; then bid England help:
Even Pym will not refuse.
Cha.   You would begin
With Ireland?
Went.   Take no care for that: that's sure
To prosper.
Cha.   You shall rule me. You were best
Return at once: but take this ere you go!
Now, do I trust you? You're an Earl: my
     Friend
Of Friends: yes, while . . . You hear me not!
Went.   Say it all o'er again — but once again:
The first was for the music: once again!
Cha.   Strafford, my friend, there may have
     been reports,
Vain rumors. Henceforth touching Strafford is
To touch the apple of my sight: why gaze
So earnestly?
Went.   I am grown young again,
And foolish. What was it we spoke of?
Cha.   Ireland,
The Parliament, —
Went.   I may go when I will?
— Now?
Cha.   Are you tired so soon of us?

Went.   My King!
But you will not so utterly abhor
A Parliament? I'd serve you any way.
Cha.   You said just now this was the only
     way.
Went.   Sir, I will serve you!
Cha.   Strafford, spare yourself:
You are so sick, they tell me.
Went.   'T is my soul
That's well and prospers now.
             This Parliament —
We'll summon it, the English one — I'll care
For everything. You shall not need them much.
Cha.   If they prove restive . . .
Went.   I shall be with you.
Cha.   Ere they assemble?
Went.   I will come, or else
Deposit this infirm humanity
I' the dust. My whole heart stays with you,
     my King!
     [*As* WENTWORTH *goes out, the* QUEEN *enters.*
Cha.   That man must love me.
Queen.   Is it over then?
Why, he looks yellower than ever! Well,
At least we shall not hear eternally
Of service — services: he's paid at least.
Cha.   Not done with: he engages to surpass
All yet performed in Ireland.
Queen.   I had thought
Nothing beyond was ever to be done.
The war, Charles — will he raise supplies
     enough?
Cha.   We've hit on an expedient; he . . .
     that is,
I have advised . . . we have decided on
The calling — in Ireland — of a Parliament.
Queen.   O truly! You agree to that? Is that
The first-fruit of his counsel? But I guessed
As much.
Cha.   This is too idle, Henriette!
I should know best. He will strain every nerve,
And once a precedent established . . .
Queen.   Notice
How sure he is of a long term of favor!
He'll see the next, and the next after that;
No end to Parliaments!
Cha.   Well, it is done.
He talks it smoothly, doubtless. If, indeed,
The Commons here . . .
Queen.   Here! you will summon them
Here? Would I were in France again to see
A King!
Cha.   But, Henriette . . .
Queen.   Oh, the Scots see clear!
Why should they bear your rule?
Cha.   But listen, sweet!
Queen.   Let Wentworth listen — you confide
     in him!
Cha.   I do not, love, — I do not so confide!
The Parliament shall never trouble us!
. . Nay, hear me! I have schemes, such
     schemes: we'll buy
The leaders off: without that, Wentworth's
     counsel
Had ne'er prevailed on me. Perhaps I call it
To have excuse for breaking it forever,
And whose will then the blame be? See you
     not?

Come, dearest! — look, the little fairy, now,
That cannot reach my shoulder! Dearest,
come!

ACT II

SCENE I. (As in Act I. Scene 1.)

The same Party enters.

Rud. Twelve subsidies!
Vane. O Rudyard, do not laugh
At least!
Rud. True: Strafford called the Parlia-
ment —
'T is he should laugh!
A Puritan. Out of the serpent's root
Comes forth a cockatrice.
Fien. — A stinging one,
If that 's the Parliament: twelve subsidies!
A stinging one! but, brother, where 's your
word
For Strafford's other nest-egg, the Scots' war?
The Puritan. His fruit shall be a fiery flying
serpent.
Fien. Shall be? It chips the shell, man;
peeps abroad.
Twelve subsidies! — Why, how now, Vane?
Rud. Peace, Fiennes!
Fien. Ah? — But he was not more a dupe
than I,
Or you, or any here, the day that Pym
Returned with the good news. Look up, friend
Vane!
We all believe that Strafford meant us well
In summoning the Parliament.
(HAMPDEN *enters.*)
Vane. Now, Hampden,
Clear me! I would have leave to sleep again:
I 'd look the People in the face again:
Clear me from having, from the first, hoped,
dreamed
Better of Strafford!
Hamp. You may grow one day
A steadfast light to England, Henry Vane!
Rud. Meantime, by flashes I make shift to
see
Strafford revived our Parliaments; before,
War was but talked of; there 's an army, now:
Still, we 've a Parliament! Poor Ireland bears
Another wrench (she dies the hardest death!) —
Why, speak of it in Parliament! and lo,
'T is spoken, so console yourselves!
Fien. The jest!
We clamored, I suppose, thus long, to win
The privilege of laying on our backs
A sorer burden than the King dares lay.
Rud. Mark now: we meet at length, com-
plaints pour in
From every county, all the land cries out
On loans and levies, curses ship-money,
Calls vengeance on the Star Chamber; we lend
An ear. " Ay, lend them all the ears you
have! "
Puts in the King; " my subjects, as you find,
Are fretful, and conceive great things of you.
Just listen to them, friends; you 'll sanction me
The measures they most wince at, make them
yours,

Instead of mine, I know: and, to begin,
They say my levies pinch them, — raise me
straight
Twelve subsidies! "
Fien. All England cannot furnish
Twelve subsidies!
Hol. But Strafford, just returned
From Ireland — what has he to do with that?
How could he speak his mind? He left be-
fore
The Parliament assembled. Pym, who knows
Strafford . . .
Rud. Would I were sure we know ourselves!
What is for good, what, bad — who friend, who
foe!
Hol. Do you count Parliaments no gain?
Rud. A gain?
While the King's creatures overbalance us?
— There 's going on, beside, among ourselves
A quiet, slow, but most effectual course
Of buying over, sapping, leavening
The lump till all is leaven. Glanville's gone.
I 'll put a case; had not the Court declared
That no sum short of just twelve subsidies
Will be accepted by the King — our House,
I say, would have consented to that offer
To let us buy off ship-money!
Hol. Most like,
If, say, six subsidies will buy it off,
The House . . .
Rud. Will grant them! Hampden, do you
hear?
Congratulate with me! the King 's the king,
And gains his point at last — our own assent
To that detested tax! All 's over, then
There 's no more taking refuge in this room,
Protesting, " Let the King do what he will,
We, England, are no party to our shame:
Our day will come! " Congratulate with me!
(PYM *enters.*)
Vane. Pym, Strafford called this Parliament
you say,
But we 'll not have our Parliaments like those
In Ireland, Pym!
Rud. Let him stand forth, your friend!
One doubtful act hides far too many sins;
It can be stretched no more, and, to my mind,
Begins to drop from those it covered.
Other Voices. Good!
Let him avow himself! No fitter time!
We wait thus long for you.
Rud. Perhaps, too long!
Since nothing but the madness of the Court,
In thus unmasking its designs at once,
Has saved us from betraying England. Stay
This Parliament is Strafford's: let us vote
Our list of Grievances too black by far
To suffer talk of subsidies: or best,
That ship-money 's disposed of long ago
By England: any vote that 's broad enough:
And then let Strafford, for the love of it,
Support his Parliament!
Vane. And vote as well
No war to be with Scotland! Hear you, Pym?
We 'll vote, no war! No part nor lot in it
For England!
Many Voices. Vote, no war! Stop the new
levies!

No Bishops' war! At once! When next we
meet!
 Pym. Much more when next we meet!
Friends, which of you
Since first the course of Strafford was in doubt,
Has fallen the most away in soul from me?
 Vane. I sat apart, even now under God's eye,
Pondering the words that should denounce you,
Pym,
In presence of us all, as one at league
With England's enemy.
 Pym.   You are a good
And gallant spirit, Henry. Take my hand
And say you pardon me for all the pain
Till now! Strafford is wholly ours.
 Many Voices.   Sure? sure?
 Pym. Most sure: for Charles dissolves the
Parliament
While I speak here.
     — And I must speak, friends, now!
Strafford is ours. The King detects the change,
Casts Strafford off forever, and resumes
His ancient path: no Parliament for us,
No Strafford for the King!
      Come, all of you,
To bid the King farewell, predict success
To his Scots' expedition, and receive
Strafford, our comrade now. The next will be
Indeed a Parliament!
 Vane.   Forgive me, Pym!
 Voices. This looks like truth: Strafford can
have, indeed,
No choice.
 Pym. Friends, follow me! He's with the
King.
Come, Hampden, and come, Rudyard, and
come, Vane!
This is no sullen day for England, sirs!
Strafford shall tell you!
 Voices.   To Whitehall then! Come!

   Scene II. *Whitehall.*

   Charles *and* Strafford.

 Cha. Strafford!
 Strafford. Is it a dream? my papers, here —
Thus, as I left them, all the plans you found
So happy — (look! the track you pressed my
hand
For pointing out) — and in this very room,
Over these very plans, you tell me, sir,
With the same face, too — tell me just one thing
That ruins them! How's this? What may
this mean?
Sir, who has done this?
 Cha.   Strafford, who but I?
You bade me put the rest away: indeed
You are alone.
 Straf. Alone, and like to be!
No fear, when some unworthy scheme grows
ripe,
Of those, who hatched it, leaving me to loose
The mischief on the world! Laud hatches war,
Falls to his prayers, and leaves the rest to me,
And I'm alone.
 Cha.   At least, you knew as much
When first you undertook the war.

 Straf.   My liege,
Was this the way? I said, since Laud would lap
A little blood, 't were best to hurry over
The loathsome business, not to be whole months
At slaughter — one blow, only one, then, peace,
Save for the dreams. I said, to please you both
I'd lead an Irish army to the West,
While in the South an English . . . but you look
As though you had not told me fifty times
'T was a brave plan! My army is all raised,
I am prepared to join it . . .
 Cha.   Hear me, Strafford!
 Straf. . . . When, for some little thing, my
whole design
Is set aside — (where is the wretched paper?)
I am to lead — (ay, here it is) — to lead
The English army: why? Northumberland,
That I appointed, chooses to be sick —
Is frightened: and, meanwhile, who answers for
The Irish Parliament? or army, either?
Is this my plan?
 Cha. . So disrespectful, sir?
 Straf. My liege, do not believe it! I am yours,
Yours ever: 't is too late to think about:
To the death, yours. Elsewhere, this untoward
step
Shall pass for mine; the world shall think it
mine.
But here! But here! I am so seldom here,
Seldom with you, my King! I, soon to rush
Alone upon a giant in the dark!
 Cha. My Strafford!
 Straf. [*Examines papers awhile.*] "Seize
the passes of the Tyne!"
But, sir, you see — see all I say is true?
My plan was sure to prosper, so, no cause
To ask the Parliament for help; whereas
We need them frightfully.
 Cha.   Need the Parliament?
 Straf. Now, for God's sake, sir, not one error
more!
We can afford no error; we draw, now,
Upon our last resource: the Parliament
Must help us!
 Cha. I've undone you, Strafford!
 Straf.   Nay —
Nay — why despond, sir, 't is not come to that!
I have not hurt you? Sir, what have I said
To hurt you? I unsay it! Don't despond!
Sir, do you turn from me?
 Cha.   My friend of friends!
 Straf. We'll make a shift. Leave me the
Parliament!
Help they us ne'er so little and I'll make
Sufficient out of it. We'll speak them fair.
They're sitting, that's one great thing; that
half gives
Their sanction to us; that's much: don't de-
spond!
Why, let them keep their money, at the worst!
The reputation of the People's help
Is all we want: we'll make shift yet!
 Cha.   Good Strafford!
 Straf. But meantime, let the sum be ne'er so
small
They offer, we'll accept it: any sum —
For the look of it: the least grant tells the Scots
The Parliament is ours — their stanch ally

Turned ours : that told, there 's half the blow to
  strike !
What will the grant be ? What does Glanville
  think ?
  Cha. Alas !
  Straf.   My liege ?
  Cha.   Strafford !
  Straf.   But answer me !
Have they . . . Oh surely not refused us half ?
Half the twelve subsidies ? We never looked
For all of them. How many do they give ?
  Cha. You have not heard . . .
  Straf. (What has he done ?) — Heard what ?
But speak at once, sir, this grows terrible !
                    [*The King continuing silent.*
You have dissolved them ! — I 'll not leave this
  man.
  Cha. 'T was old Vane's ill-judged vehemence.
  Straf.   Old Vane ?
  Cha. He told them, just about to vote the
  half,
That nothing short of all twelve subsidies
Would serve our turn, or be accepted.
  Straf.   Vane !
Vane ! Who, sir, promised me, that very
  Vane . . .
O God, to have it gone, quite gone from me,
The one last hope — I that despair, my hope —
That I should reach his heart one day, and cure
All bitterness one day, be proud again
And young again, care for the sunshine too,
And never think of Eliot any more, —
God, and to toil for this, go far for this,
Get nearer, and still nearer, reach this heart
And find Vane there !
[*Suddenly taking up a paper, and continuing with a
  forced calmness.*
                    Northumberland is sick :
Well, then, I take the army : Wilmot leads
The horse, and he, with Conway, must secure
The passes of the Tyne : Ormond supplies
My place in Ireland. Here, we 'll try the City :
If they refuse a loan — debase the coin
And seize the bullion ! we 've no other choice.
Herbert . . .
          And this while I am here ! with you !
And there are hosts such, hosts like Vane ! I go,
And, I once gone, they 'll close around you, sir,
When the least pique, pettiest mistrust, is sure
To ruin me — and you along with me !
Do you see that ? And you along with me !
— Sir, you 'll not ever listen to these men,
And I away, fighting your battle ? Sir,
If they — if She — charge me, no matter how —
Say you, " At any time when he returns
His head is mine ! " Don't stop me there ! You
  know
My head is yours, but never stop me there !
  Cha. Too shameful, Strafford ! You advised
  the war,
And . . .
  Straf. I ! I ! that was never spoken with
Till it was entered on ! That loathe the war !
That say it is the maddest, wickedest . . .
Do you know, sir, I think within my heart,
That you would say I did advise the war ;
And if, through your own weakness, or, what 's
  worse.

These Scots, with God to help them, drive me
  back,
You will not step between the raging People
And me, to say . . .
              I knew it ! from the first
I knew it ! Never was so cold a heart !
Remember that I said it — that I never
Believed you for a moment !
              — And, you loved me !
You thought your perfidy profoundly hid
Because I could not share the whisperings
With Vane, with Savile ? What, the face was
  masked ?
I had the heart to see, sir ! Face of flesh,
But heart of stone — of smooth cold frightful
  stone !
Ay, call them ! Shall I call for you ? The Scots
Goaded to madness ? Or the English — Pym —
Shall I call Pym, your subject ? Oh, you think
I 'll leave them in the dark about it all ?
They shall not know you ? Hampden, Pym
  shall not ?
          (Pym, Hampden, Vane, *etc.,* enter.)
[*Dropping on his knee.*] Thus favored with your
  gracious countenance
What shall a rebel League avail against
Your servant, utterly and ever yours ?
So, gentlemen, the King 's not even left
The privilege of bidding me farewell
Who haste to save the People — that you style
Your People — from the mercies of the Scots
And France their friend ?
[*To* Charles.] Pym's grave gray eyes are fixed
Upon you, sir !
              Your pleasure, gentlemen.
  Hamp. The King dissolved us — 't is the King
  we seek
And not Lord Strafford.
  Straf.   Strafford, guilty too
Of counselling the measure. [*To* Charles.]
  (Hush . . . you know —
You have forgotten — sir, I counselled it)
A heinous matter, truly ! But the King
Will yet see cause to thank me for a course
Which now, perchance . . . (Sir, tell them so !)
  — he blames.
Well, choose some fitter time to make your
  charge :
I shall be with the Scots, you understand ?
Then yelp at me !
              Meanwhile, your Majesty
Binds me, by this fresh token of your trust
[*Under the pretence of an earnest farewell,* Strafford
  conducts Charles *to the door, in such a manner as to
  hide his agitation from the rest : as the King disap-
  pears, they turn as by one impulse to* Pym, *who has
  not changed his original posture of surprise.*
  Hamp. Leave we this arrogant strong wicked
  man !
  Vane and others. Hence, Pym ! Come out of
  this unworthy place
To our old room again ! He 's gone.
[Strafford, *just about to follow the King, looks back.*
  Pym.   Not gone !
[*To* Strafford.] Keep tryst ! the old appoint-
  ment 's made anew :
Forget not we shall meet again !
  Straf.   So be it !

And if an army follows me?
Vane. His friends
Will entertain your army!
Pym. I'll not say
You have misreckoned, Strafford: time shows.
Perish
Body and spirit! Fool to feign a doubt,
Pretend the scrupulous and nice reserve
Of one whose prowess shall achieve the feat!
What share have I in it? Do I affect
To see no dismal sign above your head
When God suspends his ruinous thunder there?
Strafford is doomed. Touch him no one of you!
[PYM, HAMPDEN, *etc., go out.*
Straf. Pym, we shall meet again!
(Lady CARLISLE *enters.*)
You here, child?
Lady Car. Hush—
I know it all: hush, Strafford!
Straf. Ah! you know?
Well. I shall make a sorry soldier, Lucy!
All knights begin their enterprise, we read,
Under the best of auspices; 't is morn,
The Lady girds his sword upon the Youth
(He 's always very young) — the trumpets sound,
Cups pledge him, and, why, the King blesses
him —
You need not turn a page of the romance
To learn the Dreadful Giant's fate. Indeed,
We 've the fair Lady here; but she apart, —
A poor man, rarely having handled lance,
And rather old, weary, and far from sure
His Squires are not the Giant's friends. All 's
one:
Let us go forth!
Lady Car. Go forth?
Straf. What matters it?
We shall die gloriously — as the book says.
Lady Car. To Scotland? not to Scotland?
Straf. Am I sick
Like your good brother, brave Northumber-
land?
Beside, these walls seem falling on me.
Lady Car. Strafford,
The wind that saps these walls can undermine
Your camp in Scotland, too. Whence creeps
the wind?
Have you no eyes except for Pym? Look here!
A breed of silken creatures lurk and thrive
In your contempt. You 'll vanquish Pym? Old
Vane
Can vanquish you. And Vane you think to fly?
Rush on the Scots! Do nobly! Vane's slight
sneer
Shall test success, adjust the praise, suggest
The faint result: Vane's sneer shall reach you
there.
— You do not listen!
Straf. Oh, — I give that up!
There 's fate in it: I give all here quite up!
Care not what old Vane does or Holland does
Against me! 'T is so idle to withstand!
In no case tell me what they do!
Lady Car. But, Strafford . . .
Straf. I want a little strife, beside; real strife;
This petty palace-warfare does me harm:
I shall feel better, fairly out of it.
Lady Car. Why do you smile?

Straf. I got to fear them, child!
I could have torn his throat at first, old Vane's,
As he leered at me on his stealthy way
To the Queen's closet. Lord, one loses heart!
I often found it on my lips to say,
"Do not traduce me to her!"
Lady Car. But the King . . .
Straf. The King stood there, 't is not so long
ago,
— There; and the whisper, Lucy, "Be my friend
Of friends!" — My King! I would have . . .
Lady Car. . . . Died for him?
Straf. Sworn him true, Lucy: I can die for
him.
Lady Car. But go not, Strafford! But you
must renounce
This project on the Scots! Die, wherefore die?
Charles never loved you.
Straf. And he never will.
He 's not of those who care the more for men
That they 're unfortunate.
Lady Car. Then wherefore die
For such a master?
Straf. You that told me first
How good he was — when I must leave true
friends
To find a truer friend! — that drew me here
From Ireland, — "I had but to show myself,
And Charles would spurn Vane, Savile, and the
rest" —
You, child, to ask me this?
Lady Car. (If he have set
His heart abidingly on Charles!)
Then, friend,
I shall not see you any more.
Straf. Yes, Lucy.
There 's one man here I have to meet.
Lady Car. (The King!
What way to save him from the King?
My soul —
That lent from its own store the charmed dis-
guise
Which clothes the King — he shall behold my
soul!)
Strafford, — I shall speak best if you 'll not gaze
Upon me: I had never thought, indeed,
To speak, but you would perish too, so sure!
Could you but know what 't is to bear, my
friend,
One image stamped within you, turning blank
The else imperial brilliance of your mind, —
A weakness, but most precious, — like a flaw
I' the diamond, which should shape forth some
sweet face
Yet to create, and meanwhile treasured there
Lest nature lose her gracious thought forever!
Straf. When could it be? no! Yet . . . was
it the day
We waited in the anteroom, till Holland
Should leave the presence-chamber?
Lady Car. What?
Straf. — That I
Described to you my love for Charles?
Lady Car. (Ah, no —
One must not lure him from a love like that!
Oh, let him love the King and die! 'T is past.
I shall not serve him worse for that one brief
And passionate hope, silent forever now!)

And you are really bound for Scotland then?
I wish you well: you must be very sure
Of the King's faith, for Pym and all his crew
Will not be idle — setting Vane aside!

Straf. If Pym is busy, — you may write of
Pym.

Lady Car. What need, since there's your
King to take your part?
He may endure Vane's counsel; but for Pym —
Think you he'll suffer Pym to . . .

Straf. Child, your hair
Is glossier than the Queen's!

Lady Car. Is that to ask
A curl of me?

Straf. Scotland — the weary way!

Lady Car. Stay, let me fasten it.
— A rival's, Strafford?

Straf. [*showing the George.*] He hung it
there: twine yours around it, child!

Lady Car. No — no — another time — I trifle
so!
And there's a masque on foot. Farewell. The
Court
Is dull; do something to enliven us
In Scotland: we expect it at your hands.

Straf. I shall not fail in Scotland.

Lady Car. Prosper — if
You'll think of me sometimes!

Straf. How think of him
And not of you? of you, the lingering streak
(A golden one) in my good fortune's eve.

Lady Car. Strafford . . . Well, when the
eve has its last streak
The night has its first star. [*She goes out.*

Straf. That voice of hers —
You'd think she had a heart sometimes! His
voice
Is soft too.
Only God can save him now.
Be Thou about his bed, about his path!
His path! Where's England's path? Diverg-
ing wide,
And not to join again the track my foot
Must follow — whither? All that forlorn way
Among the tombs! Far — far — till . . . What,
they do
Then join again, these paths? For, huge in the
dusk,
There's — Pym to face!
Why then, I have a foe
To close with, and a fight to fight at last
Worthy my soul! What, do they beard the
King,
And shall the King want Strafford at his need?
Am I not here?
Not in the market-place,
Pressed on by the rough artisans, so proud
To catch a glance from Wentworth! They lie
down
Hungry yet smile, "Why, it must end some
day:
Is he not watching for our sake?" Not there!
But in Whitehall, the whited sepulchre,
The . . .
Curse nothing to-night! Only one name
They'll curse in all those streets to-night.
Whose fault?
Did I make kings? set up, the first, a man

To represent the multitude, receive
All love in right of them — supplant them so,
Until you love the man and not the king —
The man with the mild voice and mournful eyes
Which send me forth.
— To breast the bloody sea
That sweeps before me: with one star for guide.
Night has its first, supreme, forsaken star.

ACT III

SCENE I. *Opposite Westminster Hall.*

Sir HENRY VANE, LORD SAVILE, LORD HOLLAND *and
others of the Court.*

Sir H. Vane. The Commons thrust you out?

Savile. And what kept you
From sharing their civility?

Vane. Kept me?
Fresh news from Scotland, sir! worse than the
last,
If that may be. All's up with Strafford there:
Nothing to bar the mad Scots marching hither
Next Lord's-day morning. That detained me,
sir!
Well now, before they thrust you out, — go on, —
Their Speaker — did the fellow Lenthal say
All we set down for him?

Holland. Not a word missed.
Ere he began, we entered, Savile, I
And Bristol and some more, with hope to breed
A wholesome awe in the new Parliament.
But such a gang of graceless ruffians, Vane,
As glared at us!

Vane. So many?

Sav. Not a bench
Without its complement of burly knaves;
Your hopeful son among them: Hampden leant
Upon his shoulder — think of that!

Vane. I'd think
On Lenthal's speech, if I could get at it.
Urged he, I ask, how grateful they should prove
For this unlooked-for summons from the King?

Holl. Just as we drilled him.

Vane. That the Scots will march
On London?

Holl. All, and made so much of it,
A dozen subsidies at least seemed sure
To follow, when . . .

Vane. Well?

Holl. 'T is a strange thing now!
I've a vague memory of a sort of sound,
A voice, a kind of vast unnatural voice —
Pym, sir, was speaking! Savile, help me out.
What was it all?

Sav. Something about "a matter" —
No, — "work for England."

Holl. "England's great revenge"
He talked of.

Sav. How should I get used to Pym
More than yourselves?

Holl. However that may be,
'T was something with which we had naught to
do,
For we were "strangers," and 't was "Eng-
land's work" —
(All this while looking us straight in the face)

In other words, our presence might be spared.
So, in the twinkling of an eye, before
I settled to my mind what ugly brute
Was likest Pym just then, they yelled us out,
Locked the doors after us, and here are we.

Vane. Eliot's old method . . .

Sav. Prithee, Vane, a truce
To Eliot and his times, and the great Duke,
And how to manage Parliaments ! 'T was you
Advised the Queen to summon this : why, Strafford
('To do him justice) would not hear of it.

Vane. Say rather, you have done the best of turns
To Strafford : he 's at York, we all know why.
I would you had not set the Scots on Strafford
Till Strafford put down Pym for us, my lord !

Sav. Was it I altered Strafford's plans ? did I . . .

(*A Messenger enters.*)

Mes. The Queen, my lords — she sends me : follow me
At once ; 't is very urgent ! she requires
Your counsel : something perilous and strange
Occasions her command.

Sav. We follow, friend !
Now, Vane ; — your Parliament will plague us all !

Vane. No Strafford here beside !

Sav. If you dare hint
I had a hand in his betrayal, sir . . .

Holl. Nay, find a fitter time for quarrels — Pym
Will overmatch the best of you ; and, think,
The Queen !

Vane. Come on, then : understand, I loathe
Strafford as much as any — but his use !
To keep off Pym, to screen a friend or two,
I would we had reserved him yet awhile.

Scene II. *Whitehall.*

The Queen *and* Lady Carlisle.

Queen. It cannot be.

Lady Car. It is so.

Queen. Why, the House
Have hardly met.

Lady Car. They met for that.

Queen. No, no !
Meet to impeach Lord Strafford ? 'T is a jest.

Lady Car. A bitter one.

Queen. Consider ! 'T is the House
We summoned so reluctantly, which nothing
But the disastrous issue of the war
Persuaded us to summon. They 'll wreak all
Their spite on us, no doubt ; but the old way
Is to begin by talk of grievances :
They have their grievances to busy them.

Lady Car. Pym has begun his speech.

Queen. Where 's Vane ? — That is,
Pym will impeach Lord Strafford if he leaves
His Presidency ; he 's at York, we know,
Since the Scots beat him : why should he leave York ?

Lady Car. Because the King sent for him.

Queen. Ah — but if
The King did send for him, he let him know
We had been forced to call a Parliament —

A step which Strafford, now I come to think,
Was vehement against.

Lady Car. The policy
Escaped him, of first striking Parliaments
To earth, then setting them upon their feet
And giving them a sword : but this is idle.
Did the King send for Strafford ? He will come.

Queen. And what am I to do ?

Lady Car. What do ? Fail, madam !
Be ruined for his sake ! what matters how,
So it but stand on record that you made
An effort, only one ?

Queen. The King away
At Theobald's !

Lady Car. Send for him at once : he must
Dissolve the House.

Queen. Wait till Vane finds the truth
Of the report : then . . .

Lady Car. — It will matter little
What the King does. Strafford that lends his arm
And breaks his heart for you !

(*Sir H. Vane enters.*)

Vane. The Commons, madam,
Are sitting with closed doors. A huge debate,
No lack of noise ; but nothing, I should guess,
Concerning Strafford : Pym has certainly
Not spoken yet.

Queen. [*To* Lady Carlisle.] You hear ?

Lady Car. I do not hear
That the King 's sent for !

Vane. Savile will be able
To tell you more.

(*Holland enters.*)

Queen. The last news, Holland ?

Holl. Pym
Is raging like a fire. The whole House means
To follow him together to Whitehall
And force the King to give up Strafford.

Queen. Strafford ?

Holl. If they content themselves with Strafford ! Laud
Is talked of, Cottington and Windebank too.
Pym has not left out one of them — I would
You heard Pym raging !

Queen. Vane, go find the King !
Tell the King, Vane, the People follow Pym
To brave us at Whitehall !

(*Savile enters.*)

Sav. Not to Whitehall —
'T is to the Lords they go : they seek redress
On Strafford from his peers — the legal way,
They call it.

Queen. (Wait, Vane !)

Sav. But the adage gives
Long life to threatened men. Strafford can save
Himself so readily : at York, remember,
In his own county : what has he to fear ?
The Commons only mean to frighten him
From leaving York. Surely, he will not come.

Queen. Lucy, he will not come !

Lady Car. Once more, the King
Has sent for Strafford. He will come.

Vane. Oh doubtless !
And bring destruction with him : that 's his way.
What but his coming spoilt all Conway's plan ?
The King must take his counsel, choose his friends,

Be wholly ruled by him! What's the result?
The North that was to rise, Ireland to help, —
What came of it? In my poor mind, a fright
Is no prodigious punishment.
    Lady Car.   A fright?
Pym will fail worse than Strafford if he thinks
To frighten him. [*To the* QUEEN.] You will
    not save him then?
    Sav. When something like a charge is made,
        the King
Will best know how to save him : and 't is clear,
While Strafford suffers nothing by the matter,
The King may reap advantage : this in question,
No dinning you with ship-money complaints!
    Queen. [*To* Lady CARLISLE.] If we dissolve
    them, who will pay the army?
Protect us from the insolent Scots?
    Lady Car.   In truth,
I know not, madam. Strafford's fate concerns
Me little : you desired to learn what course
Would save him : I obey you.
    Vane.   Notice, too,
There can't be fairer ground for taking full
Revenge — (Strafford's revengeful) — than he 'll
    have
Against his old friend Pym.
    Queen.   Why, he shall claim
Vengeance on Pym!
    Vane.   And Strafford, who is he
To 'scape unscathed amid the accidents
That harass all beside? I, for my part,
Should look for something of discomfiture
Had the King trusted me so thoroughly
And been so paid for it.
    Holl.   He 'll keep at York :
All will blow over : he 'll return no worse,
Humbled a little, thankful for a place
Under as good a man. Oh, we 'll dispense
With seeing Strafford for a month or two!
            (STRAFFORD *enters.*)
    Queen. You here!
    Straf. The King sends for me, madam.
    Queen.   Sir,
The King . . .
    Straf.   An urgent matter that imports
        the King!
[*To* Lady CARLISLE.] Why, Lucy, what's in
    agitation now,
That all this muttering and shrugging, see,
Begins at me? They do not speak!
    Lady Car.   'T is welcome!
For we are proud of you — happy and proud
To have you with us, Strafford! You were
    stanch
At Durham : you did well there! Had you not
Been stayed, you might have . . . we said, even
    now,
Our hope 's in you!
    Vane. [*To* Lady CARLISLE.] The Queen
    would speak with you.
    Straf. Will one of you, his servants here,
        vouchsafe
To signify my presence to the King?
    Sav. An urgent matter?
    Straf.   None that touches you,
Lord Savile! Say, it were some treacherous
Sly pitiful intriguing with the Scots —
You would go free, at least! (They half divine

My purpose!) Madam, shall I see the King?
The service I would render, much concerns
His welfare.
    Queen.   But his Majesty, my lord,
May not be here, may . . .
    Straf.   Its importance, then.
Must plead excuse for this withdrawal, madam,
And for the grief it gives Lord Savile here.
    Queen. [*Who has been conversing with* VANE
        and HOLLAND.] The King will see you,
        sir!
[*To* Lady CARLISLE.] Mark me : Pym's worst
Is done by now : he has impeached the Earl,
Or found the Earl too strong for him, by now.
Let us not seem instructed! We should work
No good to Strafford, but deform ourselves
With shame in the world's eye. [*To* STRA-
        FORD.] His Majesty
Has much to say with you.
    Straf.   Time fleeting, too!
[*To* Lady CARLISLE.] No means of getting
        them away? And She —
What does she whisper? Does she know my
        purpose?
What does she think of it? Get them away!
    Queen. [*To* Lady CARLISLE.] He comes to
        baffle Pym — he thinks the danger
Far off : tell him no word of it! a time
For help will come ; we 'll not be wanting then.
Keep him in play, Lucy — you, self-possessed
And calm! [*To* STRAFFORD.] To spare your
        lordship some delay
I will myself acquaint the King. [*To* LADY
        CARLISLE.] Beware!
        [*The* QUEEN, VANE, HOLLAND, *and* SAVILE *go out.*
    Straf. She knows it?
    Lady Car.   Tell me, Strafford!
    Straf.   Afterward!
This moment 's the great moment of all time.
She knows my purpose?
    Lady Car.   Thoroughly : just now
She bade me hide it from you.
    Straf.   Quick, dear child,
The whole o' the scheme?
    Lady Car.   (Ah, he would learn if they
Connive at Pym's procedure! Could they but
Have once apprised the King! But there 's no
        time
For falsehood, now.) Strafford, the whole is
        known.
    Straf. Known and approved?
    Lady Car.   Hardly discountenanced.
    Straf. And the King — say, the King con-
        sents as well?
    Lady Car. The King 's not yet informed,
        but will not dare
To interpose.
    Straf.   What need to wait him, then?
He 'll sanction it! I stayed, child, tell him,
        long!
It vexed me to the soul — this waiting here.
You know him, there 's no counting on the
        King.
Tell him I waited long!
    Lady Car.   (What can he mean?
Rejoice at the King's hollowness?)
    Straf.   I knew
They would be glad of it, — all over once.

I knew they would be glad: but he 'd contrive,
The Queen and he, to mar, by helping it,
An angel's making.
    Lady Car.   (Is he mad?) Dear Strafford,
You were not wont to look so happy.
    Straf.   Sweet,
I tried obedience thoroughly. I took
The King's wild plan: of course, ere I could
    reach
My army, Conway ruined it. I drew
The wrecks together, raised all heaven and
    earth,
And would have fought the Scots: the King at
    once
Made truce with them. Then, Lucy, then,
    dear child,
God put it in my mind to love, serve, die
For Charles, but never to obey him more!
While he endured their insolence at Ripon
I fell on them at Durham. But you 'll tell
The King I waited? All the anteroom
Is filled with my adherents.
    Lady Car.   Strafford — Strafford,
What daring act is this you hint?
    Straf.   No, no!
'T is here, not daring if you knew? all here!
              [*Drawing papers from his breast.*
Full proof; see, ample proof — does the Queen
    know
I have such damning proof? Bedford and
    Essex,
Brooke, Warwick, Savile (did you notice Sa-
    vile?
The simper that I spoilt?), Saye, Mandeville —
Sold to the Scots, body and soul, by Pym!
    Lady Car.   Great heaven!
    Straf.   From Savile and his lords, to Pym
And his losels, crushed! — Pym shall not ward
    the blow
Nor Savile creep aside from it! The Crew
And the Cabal— I crush them!
    Lady Car.   And you go —
Strafford, — and now you go? —
    Straf.   — About no work
In the background, I promise you! I go
Straight to the House of Lords to claim these
    knaves.
Mainwaring!
    Lady Car.   Stay — stay, Strafford!
    Straf.   She 'll return,
The Queen — some little project of her own!
No time to lose: the King takes fright perhaps.
    Lady Car.   Pym 's strong, remember!
    Straf.   Very strong, as fits
The Faction's head — with no offence to Hamp-
    den,
Vane, Rudyard, and my loving Hollis: one
And all they lodge within the Tower to-night
In just equality. Bryan! Mainwaring!
            [*Many of his Adherents enter.*
The Peers debate just now (a lucky chance)
On the Scots' war; my visit 's opportune.
When all is over, Bryan, you proceed
To Ireland: these dispatches, mark me, Bryan,
Are for the Deputy, and these for Ormond:
We want the army here — my army, raised
At such a cost, that should have done such good,
And was inactive all the time! no matter,

We 'll find a use for it. Willis . . . or, no —
    you!
You, friend, make haste to York: bear this, at
    once . . .
Or, — better stay for form's sake, see yourself
The news you carry. You remain with me
To execute the Parliament's command,
Mainwaring! Help to seize these lesser knaves
Take care there 's no escaping at backdoors:
I 'll not have one escape, mind me — not one!
I seem revengeful, Lucy? Did you know
What these men dare!
    Lady Car.   It is so much they dare.
    Straf. I proved that long ago; my turn is
    now.
Keep sharp watch, Goring, on the citizens!
Observe who harbors any of the brood
That scramble off: be sure they smart for it!
Our coffers are but lean.
                And you, child, too,
Shall have your task; deliver this to Laud
Laud will not be the slowest in my praise:
"Thorough," he 'll cry! — Foolish, to be so
    glad!
This life is gay and glowing, after all:
'T is worth while, Lucy, having foes like mine
Just for the bliss of crushing them. To-day
Is worth the living for.
    Lady Car.   That reddening brow!
You seem . . .
    Straf. Well — do I not? I would be well —
I could not but be well on such a day!
And, this day ended, 't is of slight import
How long the ravaged frame subjects the soul
In Strafford.
    Lady Car.   Noble Strafford!
    Straf.   No farewell!
I 'll see you anon, to-morrow — the first thing.
— If She should come to stay me!
    Lady Car.   Go — 't is nothing —
Only my heart that swells: it has been thus
Ere now: go, Strafford!
    Straf.   To-night, then, let it be.
I must see Him: you, the next after Him.
I 'll tell you how Pym looked. Follow me,
    friends!
You, gentlemen, shall see a sight this hour
To talk of all your lives. Close after me!
"My friend of friends!"
            [STRAFFORD *and the rest go out.*
    Lady Car. The King — ever the King!
No thought of one beside, whose little word
Unveils the King to him — one word from me,
Which yet I do not breathe!
                 Ah, have I spared
Strafford a pang, and shall I seek reward
Beyond that memory? Surely too, some way
He is the better for my love. No, no —
He would not look so joyous — I 'll believe
His very eye would never sparkle thus,
Had I not prayed for him this long, long while.

SCENE III. *The Antechamber of the House of Lords.*

Many of the Presbyterian Party. The Adherents of
    STRAFFORD, *etc.*

A Group of Presbyterians. — 1. I tell you he
    struck Maxwell: Maxwell sought

To stay the Earl: he struck him and passed on.
2. Fear as you may, keep a good countenance
Before these rufflers.
3.   Strafford here the first,
With the great army at his back!
4.   No doubt.
I would Pym had made haste: that's Bryan,
    hush —
The gallant pointing.
    Strafford's Followers. — 1. Mark these wor-
        thies, now!
2. A goodly gathering! "Where the carcass
    is
There shall the eagles" — What's the rest?
3.   For eagles
Say crows.
    A Presbyterian. Stand back, sirs!
    One of Strafford's Followers. Are we in
        Geneva?
    A Presbyterian. No, nor in Ireland; we have
        leave to breathe.
    One of Strafford's Followers. Truly? Be-
        hold how privileged we be
That serve "King Pym"! There's Some-one
    at Whitehall
Who skulks obscure; but Pym struts . . .
    The Presbyterian.   Nearer.
    A Follower of Strafford.   Higher,
We look to see him. [*To his* Companions.] I'm
    to have St. John,
In charge; was he among the knaves just now
That followed Pym within there?
    Another.   The gaunt man
Talking with Rudyard. Did the Earl expect
Pym at his heels so fast? I like it not.
            (MAXWELL *enters.*)
    Another. Why, man, they rush into the net!
Here's Maxwell —
Ha, Maxwell? How the brethren flock around
The fellow! Do you feel the Earl's hand yet
Upon your shoulder, Maxwell?
    Maxwell.   Gentlemen,
Stand back! a great thing passes here.
    A Follower of Strafford. [*To another.*] The
        Earl
Is at his work! [*To* M.] Say, Maxwell, what
    great thing!
Speak out! [*To a* Presbyterian.] Friend, I've
    a kindness for you! Friend,
I've seen you with St. John: O stockishness!
Wear such a ruff, and never call to mind
St. John's head in a charger? How, the plague,
Not laugh?
    Another. Say, Maxwell, what great thing!
    Another.   Nay, wait:
The jest will be to wait.
    First.   And who's to bear
These demure hypocrites? You'd swear they
    came . . .
Came . . . just as we come!
[*A Puritan enters hastily and without observing* STRAF-
    FORD'S *Followers.*
    The Puritan.   How goes on the work?
Has Pym . . .
    A Follower of Strafford. The secret's out at
        last. Aha,
The carrion's scented! Welcome, crow the
    first!

Gorge merrily, you with the blinking eye!
"King Pym has fallen!"
    The Puritan.   Pym?
    A Strafford.   Pym!
    A Presbyterian.   Only Pym?
    Many of Strafford's Followers. No, brother,
        not Pym only; Vane as well,
Rudyard as well, Hampden, St. John as well!
    A Presbyterian. My mind misgives: can it be
        true?
    Another. Lost! Lost!
    A Strafford. Say we true, Maxwell?
    The Puritan.   Pride before destruction,
A haughty spirit goeth before a fall.
    Many of Strafford's Followers. Ah now! The
        very thing! A word in season!
A golden apple in a silver picture
To greet Pym as he passes!
    [*The doors at the back begin to open, noise and light
        issuing.*
    Max.   Stand back, all!
    Many of the Presbyterians. I hold with Pym!
        And I!
    Strafford's Followers.   Now for the text!
He comes! Quick!
    The Puritan. How hath the oppressor ceased!
The Lord hath broken the staff of the wicked!
The sceptre of the rulers, he who smote
The people in wrath with a continual stroke,
That ruled the nations in his anger — he
Is persecuted and none hindereth!
    [*The doors open, and* STRAFFORD *issues in the greatest
        disorder, and amid cries from within of* "Void the
        House!"
    Straf. Impeach me! Pym! I never struck, I
        think,
The felon on that calm insulting mouth
When it proclaimed — Pym's mouth proclaimed
    me . . . God!
Was it a word, only a word that held
The outrageous blood back on my heart —
    which beats!
Which beats! Some one word — "Traitor,"
    did he say,
Bending that eye, brimful of bitter fire,
Upon me?
    Max. In the Commons' name, their servant
Demands Lord Strafford's sword.
    Straf.   What did you say?
    Max. The Commons bid me ask your lord-
        ship's sword.
    Straf. Let us go forth: follow me, gentlemen!
Draw your swords too: cut any down that bar
    us.
On the King's service! Maxwell, clear the way!
    [*The Presbyterians prepare to dispute his passage.*
    Straf. I stay: the King himself shall see me
        here.
Your tablets, fellow!
    [*To* MAINWARING.] Give that to the King!
Yes, Maxwell, for the next half-hour, let be!
Nay, you shall take my sword!
            [MAXWELL *advances to take it.*
            Or, no — not that!
Their blood, perhaps, may wipe out all thus far
All up to that — not that! Why, friend, you see
When the King lays your head beneath my foot
It will not pay for that. Go, all of you!

Max. I dare, my lord, to disobey : none stir !
Straf. This gentle Maxwell ! — Do not touch
    him, Bryan !
    [*To the* Presbyterians.] Whichever cur of you
        will carry this
Escapes his fellow's fate. None saves his life ?
None?   [*Cries from within of "* STRAFFORD *!"*
Slingsby, I've loved you at least : make haste !
Stab me ! I have not time to tell you why.
You then, my Bryan ! Mainwaring, you then !
Is it because I spoke so hastily
At Allerton?   The King had vexed me.
    [*To the* Presbyterians.]   You !
— Not even you ? If I live over this,
The King is sure to have your heads, you know !
But what if I can't live this minute through ?
Pym, who is there with his pursuing smile !
                [*Louder cries of "* STRAFFORD *! "*
The King ! I troubled him, stood in the way
Of his negotiations, was the one
Great obstacle to peace, the Enemy
Of Scotland : and he sent for me, from York,
My safety guaranteed — having prepared
A Parliament — I see ! And at Whitehall
The Queen was whispering with Vane — I see
The trap !   [*Tearing off the George.*
        I tread a gewgaw underfoot,
And cast a memory from me. One stroke, now !
    [*His own* Adherents *disarm him. Renewed cries
        of "* STRAFFORD *! "*
England ! I see thy arm in this and yield.
Pray you now — Pym awaits me — pray you
    now !

[STRAFFORD *reaches the doors : they open wide.* HAMP-
    DEN *and a crowd discovered, and, at the bar,* PYM
    standing apart. As STRAFFORD *kneels, the scene
    shuts.*

ACT IV

SCENE I. *Whitehall.*

The KING, *the* QUEEN, HOLLIS, *Lady* CARLISLE. (VANE,
    HOLLAND, SAVILE, *in the background.*)

Lady Car. Answer them, Hollis, for his
    sake ! One word !
Cha. [*To* HOLLIS.] You stand, silent and
    cold, as though I were
Deceiving you — my friend, my playfellow
Of other times. What wonder after all ?
Just so, I dreamed my People loved me.
    Hol.   Sir,
It is yourself that you deceive, not me.
You'll quit me comforted, your mind made up
That, since you've talked thus much and
    grieved thus much,
All you can do for Strafford has been done.
    Queen. If you kill Strafford — (come, we
    grant you leave.
Suppose) —
    Hol.   I may withdraw, sir ?
    Lady Car.   Hear them out !
'T is the last chance for Strafford ! Hear them
    out !
    Hol. " If we kill Strafford " — on the eigh-
        teenth day
Of Strafford's trial — " We ! "
    Cha.   Pym, my good Hollis —

Pym, I should say !
    Hol.   Ah, true — sir, pardon me !
You witness our proceedings every day ;
But the screened gallery, I might have guessed,
Admits of such a partial glimpse at us,
Pym takes up all the room, shuts out the view,
Still, on my honor, sir, the rest of the place
Is not unoccupied. The Commons sit
— That's England ; Ireland sends, and Scot-
        land too,
Their representatives ; the Peers that judge
Are easily distinguished ; one remarks
The People here and there : but the close cur-
        tain
Must hide so much !
    Queen.   Acquaint your insolent crew,
This day the curtain shall be dashed aside !
It served a purpose.
    Hol.   Think ! This very day ?
Ere Strafford rises to defend himself ?
    Cha. I will defend him, sir ! — sanction the
        past
This day : it ever was my purpose. Rage
At me, not Strafford !
    Lady Car.   Nobly ! — will he not
Do nobly ?
    Hol. Sir, you will do honestly ;
And, for that deed, I too would be a king.
    Cha. Only, to do this now ! — " deaf " (in
        your style)
" To subjects' prayers," — I must oppose them
        now !
It seems their will the trial should proceed, —
So palpably their will !
    Hol.   You peril much,
But it were no bright moment save for that.
Strafford, your prime support, the sole roof-
        tree
Which props this quaking House of Privilege,
(Flood comes, winds beat, and see — the treach-
        erous sand !)
Doubtless, if the mere putting forth an arm
Could save him, you'd save Strafford.
    Cha.   And they dare
Consummate calmly this great wrong ! No
        hope ?
This ineffaceable wrong ! No pity then ?
    Hol. No plague in store for perfidy ? —
        Farewell !
You call me, sir — [*To* Lady CARLISLE.] You,
        lady, bade me come
To save the Earl : I came, thank God for it,
To learn how far such perfidy can go !
You, sir, concert with me on saving him
Who have just ruined Strafford !
    Cha.   I ? — and how ?
    Hol. Eighteen days long he throws, one after
        one,
Pym's charges back : a blind moth-eaten law !
— He'll break from it at last : and whom to
        thank ?
The mouse that gnawed the lion's net for him
Got a good friend, — but he, the other mouse,
That looked on while the lion freed himself —
Fared he so well, does any fable say ?
    Cha. What can you mean ?
    Hol.   Pym never could have proved
Strafford's design of bringing up the troops

To force this kingdom to obedience : Vane —
Your servant, not our friend, has proved it.
Cha.   Vane ?
Hol. This day. Did Vane deliver up or no
Those notes which, furnished by his son to Pym,
Seal Strafford's fate ?
Cha.   Sir, as I live, I know
Nothing that Vane has done ! What treason
      next ?
I wash my hands of it. Vane, speak the truth !
Ask Vane himself !
Hol.   I will not speak to Vane,
Who speak to Pym and Hampden every day.
Queen. Speak to Vane's master then !
      What gain to him
Were Strafford's death ?
Hol.   Ha ? Strafford cannot turn
As you, sir, sit there — bid you forth, demand
If every hateful act were not set down
In his commission ? — whether you contrived
Or no, that all the violence should seem
His work, the gentle ways — your own, — his
      part,
To counteract the King's kind impulses —
While . . . but you know what he could say !
      And then
He might produce — mark, sir ! — a certain
      charge
To set the King's express command aside,
If need were, and be blameless. He might
      add . . .
Cha. Enough !
Hol. — Who bade him break the Parlia-
      ment,
Find some pretence for setting up sword-law !
Queen. Retire !
Cha. Once more, whatever Vane dared do,
I know not : he is rash, a fool — I know
Nothing of Vane !
Hol.   Well — I believe you. Sir,
Believe me, in return, that . . .
[*Turning to* Lady CARLISLE.] Gentle lady,
The few words I would say, the stones might
      hear
Sooner than these, — I rather speak to you,
You, with the heart ! The question, trust me,
      takes
Another shape, to-day : not, if the King
Or England shall succumb, — but, who shall pay
The forfeit, Strafford or his master. Sir,
You loved me once : think on my warning now !
                                        [*Goes out.*
Cha. On you and on your warning both ! —
      Carlisle !
That paper !
Queen.   But consider !
Cha.   Give it me !
There, signed — will that content you ? Do not
      speak !
You have betrayed me, Vane ! See ! any day,
According to the tenor of that paper,
He bids your brother bring the army up,
Strafford shall head it and take full revenge.
Seek Strafford ! Let him have the same, before
He rises to defend himself !
Queen.   In truth ?
That your shrewd Hollis should have worked a
      change

Like this ! You, late reluctant . . .
Cha.   Say, Carlisle,
Your brother Percy brings the army up,
Falls on the Parliament — (I 'll think of you,
My Hollis !) say, we plotted long — 't is mine,
The scheme is mine, remember ! Say, I cursed
Vane's folly in your hearing ! If the Earl
Does rise to do us shame, the fault shall lie
With you, Carlisle !
Lady Car. Nay, fear not me ! but still
That 's a bright moment, sir, you throw away.
Tear down the veil and save him !
Queen.   Go, Carlisle !
Lady Car. (I shall see Strafford — speak to
      him : my heart
Must never beat so, then ! And if I tell
The truth ? What 's gained by falsehood ?
      There they stand
Whose trade it is, whose life it is ! How vain
To gild such rottenness ! Strafford shall know,
Thoroughly know them !)
Queen. Trust to me ! [*To* CARLISLE.]
      Carlisle,
You seem inclined, alone of all the Court,
To serve poor Strafford : this bold plan of yours
Merits much praise, and yet . . .
Lady Car. Time presses, madam.
Queen. Yet — may it not be something pre-
      mature ?
Strafford defends himself to-day — reserves
Some wondrous effort, one may well suppose !
Lady Car. Ay, Hollis hints as much.
Cha. Why linger then ?
Haste with the scheme — my scheme : I shall
      be there
To watch his look. Tell him I watch his look !
Queen. Stay, we 'll precede you !
Lady Car. At your pleasure.
Cha. Say —
Say, Vane is hardly ever at Whitehall !
I shall be there, remember !
Lady Car. Doubt me not.
Cha. On our return, Carlisle, we wait you
      here !
Lady Car. I 'll bring his answer. Sir, I fol-
      low you.
(Prove the King faithless, and I take away
All Strafford cares to live for : let it be —
'T is the King's scheme !
                              My Strafford, I can save,
Nay, I have saved you, yet am scarce content,
Because my poor name will not cross your mind.
Strafford, how much I am unworthy you !)

SCENE II. *A passage adjoining Westminster Hall.*

Many groups of Spectators *of the Trial.* Officers *of the
      Court, etc.*

1st Spec. More crowd than ever ! Not know
      Hampden, man ?
That 's he, by Pym, Pym that is speaking now.
No, truly, if you look so high you 'll see
Little enough of either !
2d Spec. Stay : Pym's arm
Points like a prophet's rod.
3d Spec. Ay, ay, we 've heard
Some pretty speaking : yet the Earl escapes.
4th Spec. I fear it : just a foolish word or two

About his children — and we see, forsooth,
Not England's foe in Strafford, but the man
Who, sick, half-blind . . .
   2d Spec.   What 's that Pym 's saying now
Which makes the curtains flutter? look! A
   hand
Clutches them. Ah! The King's hand!
   5th Spec.   I had thought
Pym was not near so tall. What said he,
   friend?
   2d Spec.   "Nor is this way a novel way of
   blood,"
And the Earl turns as if to . . . Look! look!
   Many Spectators.   There!
What ails him? No — he rallies, see — goes on,
And Strafford smiles. Strange!
   An Officer.   Haselrig!
   Many Spectators.   Friend? Friend?
   The Officer. Lost, utterly lost: just when
   we looked for Pym
To make a stand against the ill effects
Of the Earl's speech! Is Haselrig without?
Pym's message is to him.
   3d Spec.   Now, said I true?
Will the Earl leave them yet at fault or no?
   1st Spec. Never believe it, man! These
Ruin the Earl.
   5th Spec.   A brave end: not a whit
Less Pym, less Pym all over. Then, the trial
Is closed. No — Strafford means to speak
   again?
   An Officer. Stand back, there!
   5th Spec. Why, the Earl is coming hither!
Before the court breaks up! His brother,
   look, —
You 'd say he 'd deprecated some fierce act
In Strafford's mind just now.
   An Officer.   Stand back, I say!
   2d Spec. Who 's the veiled woman that he
   talks with?
   Many Spectators. Hush —
The Earl! the Earl!
[*Enter* STRAFFORD, SLINGSBY, *and other* Secretaries,
HOLLIS, Lady CARLISLE, MAXWELL, BALFOUR, *etc.*
STRAFFORD *converses with* Lady CARLISLE.
   Hol.   So near the end! Be patient —
Return!
   Straf. [*To his* Secretaries.] Here — any-
   where — or, 't is freshest here!
To spend one's April here, the blossom-month:
Set it down here!
        [*They arrange a table, papers, etc.*
         So, Pym can quail, can cower
Because I glance at him, yet more 's to do.
What 's to be answered, Slingsby? Let us end!
[*To* Lady CARLISLE.] Child, I refuse his offer;
   whatsoe'er
It be! Too late! Tell me no word of him!
'T is something, Hollis, I assure you that —
To stand, sick as you are, some eighteen days
Fighting for life and fame against a pack
Of very curs, that lie through thick and thin,
Eat flesh and bread by wholesale, and can't say
"Strafford" if it would take my life!
   Lady Car.   Be moved!
Glance at the paper!
   Straf.   Already at my heels!

Pym's faulting bloodhounds scent the track
   again.
Peace, child! Now, Slingsby!
[Messengers *from* LANE *and other of* STRAFFORD's Coun-
sel *within the Hall are coming and going during the
Scene.*
   Straf. [*setting himself to write and dictate.*]
         I shall beat you, Hollis!
Do you know that? In spite of St. John's tricks,
In spite of Pym — your Pym who shrank from
   me!
Eliot would have contrived it otherwise.
[*To a* Messenger.] In truth? This slip, tell
   Lane, contains as much
As I can call to mind about the matter.
Eliot would have disdained . . .
   [*Calling after the* Messenger.] And Radcliffe,
   say,
The only person who could answer Pym,
Is safe in prison, just for that.
                Well, well!
It had not been recorded in that case,
I baffled you.
   [*To* Lady CARLISLE.] Nay, child, why look so
   grieved?
All 's gained without the King! You saw Pym
   quail?
What shall I do when they acquit me, think
   you,
But tranquilly resume my task as though
Nothing had intervened since I proposed
To call that traitor to account! Such tricks,
Trust me, shall not be played a second time,
Not even against Laud, with his gray hair —
Your good work, Hollis! Peace! To make
   amends,
You, Lucy, shall be here when I impeach
Pym and his fellows.
   Hol.   Wherefore not protest
Against our whole proceeding, long ago?
Why feel indignant now? Why stand this while
Enduring patiently?
   Straf.   Child, I 'll tell you —
You, and not Pym — you, the slight graceful girl
Tall for a flowering lily, and not Hollis —
Why I stood patient! I was fool enough
To see the will of England in Pym's will;
To fear, myself had wronged her, and to wait
Her judgment: when, behold, in place of it . . .
[*To a* Messenger *who whispers.*] Tell Lane to
   answer no such question! Law, —
I grapple with their law! I 'm here to try
My actions by their standard, not my own!
Their law allowed that levy: what 's the rest
To Pym, or Lane, any but God and me?
   Lady Car. The King 's so weak! Secure
   this chance! 'T was Vane,
Never forget, who furnished Pym the notes . . .
   Straf. Fit, — very fit, those precious notes
Of Vane,
To close the Trial worthily! I feared
Some spice of nobleness might linger yet
And spoil the character of all the past.
Vane eased me . . . and I will go back and say
As much — to Pym, to England! Follow me,
I have a word to say! There, my defence
Is done!
         Stay! why be proud? Why care to own

My gladness, my surprise? — Nay, not surprise!
Wherefore insist upon the little pride
Of doing all myself, and sparing him
The pain? Child, say the triumph is my King's!
When Pym grew pale, and trembled, and sank
    down,
One image was before me: could I fail?
Child, care not for the past, so indistinct,
Obscure — there's nothing to forgive in it,
'T is so forgotten! From this day begins
A new life, founded on a new belief
In Charles.
    Hol.   In Charles? Rather believe in Pym!
And here he comes in proof! Appeal to Pym!
Say how unfair . . .
    Straf.   To Pym? I would say nothing!
I would not look upon Pym's face again.
    Lady Car. Stay, let me have to think I
pressed your hand!
    [STRAFFORD *and his* Friends *go out*.
    (*Enter* HAMPDEN *and* VANE.)
    Vane. O Hampden, save the great misguided
    man!
Plead Strafford's cause with Pym! I have re-
    marked
He moved no muscle when we all declaimed
Against him: you had but to breathe — he turned
Those kind calm eyes upon you.
    [*Enter* PYM, *the* Solicitor-General ST. JOHN, *the* Mana-
    gers *of the Trial,* FIENNES, RUDYARD, *etc.*
    Rud.   Horrible!
Till now all hearts were with you: I withdraw
For one. Too horrible! But we mistake
Your purpose, Pym: you cannot snatch away
The last spar from the drowning man.
    Fien.   He talks
With St. John of it — see, how quietly!
[*To other* Presbyterians.] You'll join us?
    Strafford may deserve the worst:
But this new course is monstrous. Vane, take
    heart!
This Bill of his Attainder shall not have
One true man's hand to it.
    Vane.   Consider, Pym!
Confront your Bill, your own Bill: what is
    it?
You cannot catch the Earl on any charge, —
No man will say the law has hold of him
On any charge; and therefore you resolve
To take the general sense on his desert,
As though no law existed, and we met
To found one. You refer to Parliament
To speak its thought upon the abortive mass
Of half-borne-out assertions, dubious hints
Hereafter to be cleared, distortions — ay,
And wild inventions. Every man is saved
The task of fixing any single charge
On Strafford: he has but to see in him
The enemy of England.
    Pym.   A right scruple!
I have heard some called England's enemy
With less consideration.
    Vane.   Pity me!
Indeed you make me think I was your friend!
I who have murdered Strafford, how remove
That memory from me?
    Pym.   I absolve you, Vane.
Take you no care for aught that you have done!

    Vane. John Hampden, not this Bill! Re-
    ject this Bill!
He staggers through the ordeal: let him go,
Strew no fresh fire before him! Plead for us!
When Strafford spoke, your eyes were thick
    with tears!
    Hamp. England speaks louder: who are we,
    to play
The generous pardoner at her expense,
Magnanimously waive advantages,
And, if he conquer us, applaud his skill?
    Vane. He was your friend.
    Pym.   I have heard that before
    Fien. And England trusts you.
    Hamp.   Shame be his, who turns
The opportunity of serving her
She trusts him with, to his own mean account —
Who would look nobly frank at her expense!
    Fien. I never thought it could have come to
    this.
    Pym. But I have made myself familiar,
    Fiennes,
With this one thought — have walked, and sat,
    and slept,
This thought before me. I have done such
    things,
Being the chosen man that should destroy
The traitor. You have taken up this thought
To play with, for a gentle stimulant,
To give a dignity to idler life
By the dim prospect of emprise to come,
But ever with the softening, sure belief,
That all would end some strange way right at
    last.
    Fien. Had we made out some weightier
    charge!
    Pym.   You say
That these are petty charges: can we come
To the real charge at all? There he is safe
In tyranny's stronghold. Apostasy
Is not a crime, treachery not a crime:
The cheek burns, the blood tingles, when you
    speak
The words, but where's the power to take re-
    venge
Upon them? We must make occasion serve, —
The oversight shall pay for the main sin
That mocks us.
    Rud.   But this unexampled course,
This Bill!
    Pym.   By this, we roll the clouds away
Of precedent and custom, and at once
Bid the great beacon-light God sets in all,
The conscience of each bosom, shine upon
The guilt of Strafford: each man lay his hand
Upon his breast, and judge!
    Vane.   I only see
Strafford, nor pass his corpse for all beyond!
    Rud. and others. Forgive him! He would
    join us, now he finds
What the King counts reward! The pardon,
    too,
Should be your own. Yourself should bear to
    Strafford
The pardon of the Commons.
    Pym.   Meet him? Strafford!
Have we to meet once more, then? Be it so!
And yet — the prophecy seemed half fulfilled

When, at the Trial, as he gazed, my youth,
Our friendship, divers thoughts came back at
once
And left me, for a time . . . 'Tis very sad!
To-morrow we discuss the points of law
With Lane — to-morrow?
    Vane.   Not before to-morrow —
So, time enough! I knew you would relent!
    Pym. The next day, Haselrig, you introduce
The Bill of his Attainder. Pray for me!

Scene III. *Whitehall.*

The King.

    Cha. My loyal servant! To defend himself
Thus irresistibly,— withholding aught
That seemed to implicate us!
                  We have done
Less gallantly by Strafford. Well, the future
Must recompense the past.
                  She tarries long.
I understand you, Strafford, now!
                  The scheme —
Carlisle's mad scheme — he 'll sanction it, I fear,
For love of me. 'T was too precipitate:
Before the army 's fairly on its march,
He 'll be at large: no matter.
                  Well, Carlisle?
    (*Enter* Pym.)
    Pym. Fear me not, sir:— my mission is to
save,
This time.
    Cha. To break thus on me! unannounced!
    Pym. It is of Strafford I would speak.
    Cha.   No more
Of Strafford! I have heard too much from
you.
    Pym. I spoke, sir, for the People; will you
hear
A word upon my own account?
    Cha.   Of Strafford?
(So turns the tide already? Have we tamed
The insolent brawler? — Strafford's eloquence
Is swift in its effect.) Lord Strafford, sir,
Has spoken for himself.
    Pym.   Sufficiently.
I would apprise you of the novel course
The People take: the Trial fails.
    Cha.   Yes, yes:
We are aware, sir: for your part in it
Means shall be found to thank you.
    Pym.   Pray you, read
This schedule! I would learn from your own
mouth
— (It is a matter much concerning me) —
Whether, if two Estates of us concede
The death of Strafford, on the grounds set forth
Within that parchment, you, sir, can resolve
To grant your own consent to it. This Bill
Is framed by me. If you determine, sir,
That England's manifested will should guide
Your judgment, ere another week such will
Shall manifest itself. If not, — I cast
Aside the measure.
    Cha.   You can hinder, then,
The introduction of this Bill?
    Pym.   I can.

    Cha. He is my friend, sir: I have wronged
him: mark you,
Had I not wronged him, this might be. You
think
Because you hate the Earl . . . (turn not away,
We know you hate him) — no one else could love
Strafford: but he has saved me, some affirm.
Think of his pride! And do you know one
strange,
One frightful thing? We all have used the mar
As though a drudge of ours, with not a source
Of happy thoughts except in us; and yet
Strafford has wife and children, household cares,
Just as if we had never been. Ah, sir,
You are moved, even you, a solitary man
Wed to your cause — to England if you will!
    Pym. Yes — think, my soul — to England!
Draw not back!
    Cha. Prevent that Bill, sir! All your course
seems fair
Till now. Why, in the end, 't is I should sign
The warrant for his death! You have said much
I ponder on; I never meant, indeed,
Strafford should serve me any more. I take
The Commons' counsel; but this Bill is yours —
Nor worthy of its leader: care not, sir,
For that, however! I will quite forget
You named it to me. You are satisfied?
    Pym. Listen to me, sir! Eliot laid his hand,
Wasted and white, upon my forehead once;
Wentworth — he 's gone now! — has talked on,
whole nights,
And I beside him; Hampden loves me: sir,
How can I breathe and not wish England well,
And her King well?
    Cha.   I thank you, sir, who leave
That King his servant. Thanks, sir!
    Pym.   Let me speak!
— Who may not speak again; whose spirit yearns
For a cool night after this weary day:
— Who would not have my soul turn sicker yet
In a new task, more fatal, more august,
More full of England's utter weal or woe.
I thought, sir, could I find myself with you,
After this trial, alone, as man to man —
I might say something, warn you, pray you,
save —
Mark me, King Charles, save — you!
But God must do it. Yet I warn you, sir —
(With Strafford's faded eyes yet full on me)
As you would have no deeper question moved
— " How long the Many must endure the One,"
Assure me, sir, if England give assent
To Strafford's death, you will not interfere!
Or —
    Cha. God forsakes me. I am in a net
And cannot move. Let all be as you say!
    (*Enter* Lady Carlisle.)
    Lady Car. He loves you — looking beautiful
with joy
Because you sent me! he would spare you all
The pain! he never dreamed you would forsake
Your servant in the evil day — nay, see
Your scheme returned! That generous heart
of his!
He needs it not — or, needing it, disdains
A course that might endanger you — you, sir,
Whom Strafford from his inmost soul . . .

[*Seeing* PYM.] Well met!
No fear for Strafford! All that 's true and brave
On your own side shall help us: we are now
Stronger than ever.
                    Ha — what, sir, is this?
All is not well! What parchment have you
    there?
    Pym. Sir, much is saved us both.
    Lady Car.   This Bill! Your lip
Whitens — you could not read one line to me
Your voice would falter so!
    Pym.   No recreant yet!
The great word went from England to my soul,
And I arose. The end is very near.
    Lady Car. I am to save him! All have
    shrunk beside;
'T is only I am left. Heaven will make strong
The hand now as the heart. Then let both die!

ACT V

SCENE I. *Whitehall.*

HOLLIS, Lady CARLISLE.

    Hol. Tell the King then! Come in with me!
    Lady Car.   Not so!
He must not hear till it succeeds.
    Hol.   Succeed?
No dream was half so vain — you 'd rescue Straf-
    ford
And outwit Pym! I cannot tell you . . . lady,
The block pursues me, and the hideous show.
To-day . . . is it to-day? And all the while
He 's sure of the King's pardon. Think, I have
To tell this man he is to die. The King
May rend his hair, for me! I 'll not see Straf-
    ford
    Lady Car. Only, if I succeed, remember —
    Charles
Has saved him. He would hardly value life
Unless his gift. My stanch friends wait. Go in —
You must go in to Charles!
    Hol.   And all beside
Left Strafford long ago. The King has signed
The warrant for his death! the Queen was
    sick
Of the eternal subject. For the Court, —
The Trial was amusing in its way,
Only too much of it: the Earl withdrew
In time. But you, fragile, alone, so young,
Amid rude mercenaries — you devise
A plan to save him! Even though it fails,
What shall reward you!
    Lady Car.   I may go, you think,
To France with him? And you reward me,
    friend,
Who lived with Strafford even from his youth
Before he set his heart on state-affairs
And they bent down that noble brow of his.
I have learned somewhat of his latter life,
And all the future I shall know: but, Hollis,
I ought to make his youth my own as well.
Tell me, — when he is saved!
    Hol.   My gentle friend,
He should know all and love you, but 't is vain!
    Lady Car. Love? no — too late now! Let
    him love the King!

'T is the King's scheme! I have your word,
    remember!
We 'll keep the old delusion up. But, quick!
Quick! Each of us has work to do, beside!
Go to the King! I hope — Hollis — I hope!
Say nothing of my scheme! Hush, while we
    speak
Think where he is! Now for my gallant friends!
    Hol. Where he is? Calling wildly upon
    Charles,
Guessing his fate, pacing the prison-floor.
Let the King tell him! I 'll not look on Straf-
    ford.

SCENE II. *The Tower.*

STRAFFORD *sitting with his* Children.   *They sing.*

O bell' andare
Per barca in mare,
Verso la sera,
Di Primavera!

Andante.

O bell' an-da-re, Per bar-ca in

ma-re, Ver-so la se-ra, Di prima-

slentando e diminuendo.

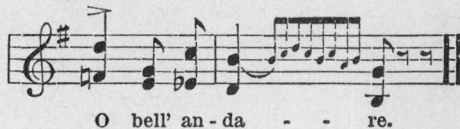

O bell' an-da - - re.

William. The boat 's in the broad moonlight
    all this while —

Verso la sera
Di Primavera!

And the boat shoots from underneath the moon
Into the shadowy distance; only still
You hear the dipping oar —

Verso la sera,

And faint, and fainter, and then all 's quite gone,
Music and light and all, like a lost star.
    Anne. But you should sleep, father: you
    were to sleep.
    Straf. I do sleep, Anne; or if not — you must
    know
There 's such a thing as . . .

Wil.   You 're too tired to sleep ?
Straf. It will come by-and-by and all day long,
In that old quiet house I told you of :
We sleep safe there.
Anne.   Why not in Ireland ?
Straf.   No !
Too many dreams ! — That song 's for Venice,
      William :
You know how Venice looks upon the map —
Isles that the mainland hardly can let go ?
Wil. You 've been to Venice, father ?
Straf.   I was young, then.
Wil. A city with no King ; that 's why I like
Even a song that comes from Venice.
Straf.   William ?
Wil. Oh, I know why ! Anne, do you love
      the King ?
But I 'll see Venice for myself one day.
Straf. See many lands, boy — England last
      of all, —
That way you 'll love her best.
Wil.   Why do men say
You sought to ruin her, then ?
Straf.   Ah, — they say that.
Wil. Why ?
Straf. I suppose they must have words to say,
As you to sing.
Anne.   But they make songs beside :
Last night I heard one, in the street beneath,
That called you . . . Oh, the names !
Wil.   Don't mind her, father !
They soon left off when I cried out to them.
Siraf. We shall so soon be out of it, my boy !
'T is not worth while : who heeds a foolish song ?
Wil. Why, not the King.
Straf.   Well : it has been the fate
Of better ; and yet, — wherefore not feel sure
That Time, who in the twilight comes to mend
All the fantastic day's caprice, consign
To the low ground once more the ignoble Term,
And raise the Genius on his orb again, —
That Time will do me right ?
Anne.   (Shall we sing, William ?
He does not look thus when we sing.)
Straf.   For Ireland,
Something is done : too little, but enough
To show what might have been.
Wil.   (I have no heart
To sing now ! Anne, how very sad he looks !
Oh, I so hate the King for all he says !)
Straf. Forsook them ? What, the common
      songs will run
That I forsook the People ? Nothing more ?
Ay, Fame, the busy scribe, will pause, no doubt,
Turning a deaf ear to her thousand slaves
Noisy to be enrolled, — will register
The curious glosses, subtle notices,
Ingenious clearings-up one fain would see
Beside that plain inscription of The Name —
The Patriot Pym, or the Apostate Strafford !
[*The* Children *resume their song timidly, but break off.*
      (*Enter* HOLLIS *and an* Attendant.)
Straf. No, — Hollis ? in good time ! — Who
      is he ?
Hol.   One
That must be present.
Straf.   Ah — I understand.
They will not let me see poor Laud alone.

How politic ! They 'd use me by degrees
To solitude : and, just as you came in,
I was solicitous what life to lead
When Strafford 's " not so much as Constable
In the King's service." Is there any means
To keep one's self awake ? What would you do
After this bustle, Hollis, in my place ?
Hol. Strafford !
Straf.   Observe, not but that Pym and you
Will find me news enough — news I shall hear
Under a quince-tree by a fish-pond side
At Wentworth. Garrard must be re-engaged
My newsman. Or, a better project now —
What if when all 's consummated, and the Saints
Reign, and the Senate's work goes swim-
      ingly, —
What if I venture up, some day, unseen,
To saunter through the Town, notice how Pym,
Your Tribune, likes Whitehall, drop quietly
Into a tavern, hear a point discussed,
As, whether Strafford's name were John or
      James —
And be myself appealed to — I, who shall
Myself have near forgotten !
Hol.   I would speak . . .
Straf. Then you shall speak, — not now. I
      want just now,
To hear the sound of my own tongue. This
      place
Is full of ghosts.
Hol.   Nay, you must hear me, Strafford !
Straf. Oh, readily ! Only, one rare thing
      more, —
The minister ! Who will advise the King,
Turn his Sejanus, Richelieu and what not,
And yet have health — children, for aught I
      know —
My patient pair of traitors ! Ah, — but, Wil-
      liam —
Does not his cheek grow thin ?
Wil.   'T is you look thin,
Father !
Straf. A scamper o'er the breezy wolds
Sets all to-rights.
Hol.   You cannot sure forget
A prison-roof is o'er you, Strafford ?
Straf.   No,
Why, no. I would not touch on that, the first.
I left you that. Well, Hollis ? Say at once,
The King can find no time to set me free !
A mask at Theobald's ?
Hol.   Hold : no such affair
Detains him.
Straf. True : what needs so great a matter ?
The Queen's lip may be sore. Well : when he
      pleases, —
Only, I want the air : it vexes flesh
To be pent up so long.
Hol.   The King — I bear
His message, Strafford : pray you, let me speak !
Straf. Go, William ! Anne, try o'er your
      song again !
                    [*The* Children *retire.*
They shall be loyal, friend, at all events.
I know your message : you have nothing new
To tell me : from the first I guessed as much.
I know, instead of coming here himself,
Leading me forth in public by the hand,

The King prefers to leave the door ajar
As though I were escaping — bids me trudge
While the mob gapes upon some show prepared
On the other side of the river ! Give at once
His order of release ! I 've heard, as well,
Of certain poor manœuvres to avoid
The granting pardon at his proper risk ;
First, he must prattle somewhat to the Lords,
Must talk a trifle with the Commons first,
Be grieved I should abuse his confidence,
And far from blaming them, and . . . Where 's
      the order ?
  Hol. Spare me !
  Straf. Why, he 'd not have me steal away ?
With an old doublet and a steeple hat
Like Prynne's ? Be smuggled into France,
      perhaps ?
Hollis, 't is for my children ! 'T was for them
I first consented to stand day by day
And give your Puritans the best of words,
Be patient, speak when called upon, observe
Their rules, and not return them prompt their
      lie !
What 's in that boy of mine that he should prove
Son to a prison-breaker ? I shall stay
And he 'll stay with me. Charles should know
      as much,
He too has children !
[*Turning to* HOLLIS's *companion.*] Sir, you
      feel for me !
No need to hide that face ! Though it have
      looked
Upon me from the judgment-seat . . . I know
Strangely, that somewhere it has looked on
      me . . .
Your coming has my pardon, nay, my thanks :
For there is one who comes not.
  Hol.   Whom forgive,
As one to die !
  Straf.   True, all die, and all need
Forgiveness : I forgive him from my soul.
  Hol. 'T is a world's wonder : Strafford, you
      must die !
  Straf. Sir, if your errand is to set me free
This heartless jest mars much. Ha ! Tears in
      truth ?
We 'll end this ! See this paper, warm — feel
      — warm
With lying next my heart ! Whose hand is
      there ?
Whose promise ? Read, and loud for God to
      hear !
"Strafford shall take no hurt " — read it, I say !
" In person, honor, nor estate " —
  Hol.   The King . . .
  Straf. I could unking him by a breath !
      You sit
Where Loudon sat, who came to prophesy
The certain end, and offer me Pym's grace
If I 'd renounce the King : and I stood firm
On the King's faith. The King who lives . . .
  Hol.   To sign
The warrant for your death.
  Straf.   " Put not your trust
In princes, neither in the sons of men,
In whom is no salvation ! "
  Hol.   Trust in God !
The scaffold is prepared : they wait for you :

He has consented. Cast the earth behind !
  Cha. You would not see me, Strafford, at
      your foot !
It was wrung from me ! Only, curse me not !
  Hol. [*To* STRAFFORD.] As you hope grace
      and pardon in your need,
Be merciful to this most wretched man.
                         [*Voices from within.*

      Verso la sera
      Di Primavera.

  Straf. You 'll be good to those children, sir ?
      I know
You 'll not believe her, even should the Queen
Think they take after one they rarely saw.
I had intended that my son should live
A stranger to these matters : but you are
So utterly deprived of friends ! He too
Must serve you — will you not be good to him ?
Or, stay, sir, do not promise — do not swear !
You, Hollis — do the best you can for me !
I 've not a soul to trust to : Wandesford 's dead.
And you 've got Radcliffe safe, Laud's turn
      comes next :
I 've found small time of late for my affairs,
But I trust any of you, Pym himself —
No one could hurt them : there 's an infant,
      too, —
These tedious cares ! Your Majesty could spare
      them.
Nay — pardon me, my King ! I had forgotten
Your education, trials, much temptation,
Some weakness : there escaped a peevish
      word —
'T is gone : I bless you at the last. You know
All 's between you and me : what has the world
To do with it ? Farewell !
  Cha. [*at the door.*]   Balfour ! Balfour !
            (*Enter* BALFOUR.)
The Parliament ! — go to them : I grant all
Demands. Their sittings shall be permanent :
Tell them to keep their money if they will :
I 'll come to them for every coat I wear
And every crust I eat : only I choose
To pardon Strafford. As the Queen shall
      choose !
— You never heard the People howl for blood,
Beside !
  Balfour. Your Majesty may hear them now :
The walls can hardly keep their murmurs out :
Please you retire !
  Cha.   Take all the troops, Balfour !
  Bal. There are some hundred thousand of
      the crowd.
  Cha. Come with me, Strafford ! You 'll not
      fear, at least !
  Straf. Balfour, say nothing to the world of
      this !
I charge you, as a dying man, forget
You gazed upon this agony of one . . .
Of one . . . or if . . . why, you may say, Bal
      four,
The King was sorry : 't is no shame in him :
Yes, you may say he even wept, Balfour.
And that I walked the lighter to the block
Because of it. I shall walk lightly, sir !
Earth fades, heaven breaks on me : I shall
      stand next

Before God's throne : the moment's close at
  hand
When man the first, last time, has leave to lay
His whole heart bare before its Maker, leave
To clear up the long error of a life
And choose one happiness for evermore.
With all mortality about me, Charles,
The sudden wreck, the dregs of violent death —
What if, despite the opening angel-song,
There penetrate one prayer for you ? Be saved
Through me ! Bear witness, no one could pre-
  vent
My death ! Lead on ! ere he awake — best,
  now !
All must be ready : did you say, Balfour,
The crowd began to murmur ? They 'll be
  kept
Too late for sermon at St. Antholin's !
Now ! But tread softly — children are at play
In the next room. Precede ! I follow —
  (*Enter* Lady CARLISLE, *with many* Attendants.)
  Lady Car.   Me !
Follow me, Strafford, and be saved ! The
  King ?
[*To the* KING.] Well — as you ordered, they
  are ranged without,
The convoy . . . [*seeing the* KING's *state.*]
[*To* STRAFFORD.] You know all, then ! Why,
  I thought
It looked best that the King should save you,
  — Charles
Alone ; 't is a shame that you should owe me
  aught.
Or no, not shame ! Strafford, you 'll not feel
  shame
At being saved by me ?
  Hol.   All true ! Oh Strafford,
She saves you ! all her deed ! this lady's deed !
And is the boat in readiness ? You, friend,
Are Billingsley, no doubt. Speak to her,
  Strafford !
See how she trembles, waiting for your voice !
The world 's to learn its bravest story yet.
  Lady Car. Talk afterward ! Long nights
  in France enough,
To sit beneath the vines and talk of home.
  Straf. You love me, child ? Ah, Strafford
  can be loved
As well as Vane ! I could escape, then ?
  Lady Car.   Haste !
Advance the torches, Bryan !
  Straf.   I will die.
They call me proud : but England had no right,
When she encountered me — her strength to
  mine —
To find the chosen foe a craven. Girl,
I fought her to the utterance, I fell,
I am hers now, and I will die. Beside,
The lookers-on ! Eliot is all about
This place, with his most uncomplaining brow.
  Lady Car. Strafford !
  Straf. I think if you could know how much
I love you, you would be repaid, my friend !
  Lady Car. Then, for my sake !
  Straf.   Even for your sweet sake,
I stay.
  Hol. For *their* sake !
  Straf.   To bequeath a stain ?

Leave me ! Girl, humor me and let me die !
  Lady Car. Bid him escape — wake, King !
  Bid him escape !
  Straf. True, I will go ! Die and forsake the
  King ?
I 'll not draw back from the last service.
  Lady Car. Strafford !
  Straf. And, after all, what is disgrace to me ?
Let us come, child ! That it should end this
  way !
Lead then ! but I feel strangely : it was not
To end this way.
  Lady Car. Lean — lean on me !
  Straf.   My King !
Oh, had he trusted me — his friend of friends !
  Lady Car. I can support him, Hollis !
  Straf.   Not this way !
This gate — I dreamed of it, this very gate.
  Lady Car. It opens on the river : our good
  boat
Is moored below, our friends are there.
  Straf.   The same :
Only with something ominous and dark,
Fatal, inevitable.
  Lady Car.   Strafford ! Strafford !
  Straf. Not by this gate ! I feel what will
  be there !
I dreamed of it, I tell you : touch it not !
  Lady Car. To save the King, — Strafford,
  to save the King !
[*As* STRAFFORD *opens the door,* PYM *is discovered with*
  HAMPDEN, VANE, *etc.* STRAFFORD *falls back :* PYM
  follows slowly and confronts him.
  Pym. Have I done well ? Speak, England !
  Whose sole sake
I still have labored for, with disregard
To my own heart, — for whom my youth was
  made
Barren, my manhood waste, to offer up
Her sacrifice — this friend, this Wentworth
  here —
Who walked in youth with me, loved me, it
  may be,
And whom, for his forsaking England's cause,
I hunted by all means (trusting that she
Would sanctify all means) even to the block
Which waits for him. And saying this, I
  feel
No bitterer pang than first I felt, the hour
I swore that Wentworth might leave us, but I
Would never leave him : I do leave him now.
I render up my charge (be witness, God !)
To England who imposed it. I have done
Her bidding — poorly, wrongly, — it may be,
With ill effects — for I am weak, a man :
Still, I have done my best, my human best,
Not faltering for a moment. It is done.
And this said, if I say . . . yes, I will say
I never loved but one man — David not
More Jonathan ! Even thus, I love him now :
And look for my chief portion in that world
Where great hearts led astray are turned again
(Soon it may be, and, certes, will be soon :
My mission over, I shall not live long,) —
Ay, here I know I talk — I dare and must,
Of England, and her great reward, as all
I look for there ; but in my inmost heart,
Believe, I think of stealing quite away

To walk once more with Wentworth — my
    youth's friend
Purged from all error, gloriously renewed.
And Eliot shall not blame us. Then indeed . . .
This is no meeting, Wentworth! Tears in-
    crease
Too hot. A thin mist — is it blood? — enwraps
The face I loved once. Then, the meeting be!
    Straf. I have loved England too; we 'll meet
    then, Pym;
As well die now! Youth is the only time
To think and to decide on a great course :
Manhood with action follows ; but 't is dreary
To have to alter our whole life in age —
The time past, the strength gone! As well die
    now.
When we meet, Pym, I 'd be set right — not
    now!
Best die. Then if there 's any fault, fault too
Dies, smothered up. Poor gray old little Laud
May dream his dream out, of a perfect Church,
In some blind corner. And there 's no one
    left.
I trust the King now wholly to you, Pym !
And yet, I know not : I shall not be there :
Friends fail — if he have any. And he 's weak,
And loves the Queen, and . . . Oh, my fate is
    nothing —
Nothing ! But not that awful head — not that !
    Pym. If England shall declare such will to
    me . . .
    Straf. Pym, you help England! I, that am
    to die,
What I must see! 't is here — all here! My
    God,
Let me but gasp out, in one word of fire,
How thou wilt plague him, satiating hell !

What? England that you help, become through
    you
A green and putrefying charnel, left
Our children . . . some of us have children,
    Pym —
Some who, without that, still must ever wear
A darkened brow, an over-serious look,
And never properly be young! No word?
What if I curse you? Send a strong curse
    forth
Clothed from my heart, lapped round with hor-
    ror till
She 's fit with her white face to walk the world,
Scaring kind natures from your cause and you —
Then to sit down with you at the board-head,
The gathering for prayer . . . O speak, but
    speak !
. . . Creep up, and quietly follow each one home,
You, you, you, be a nestling care for each
To sleep with, — hardly moaning in his dreams,
She gnaws so quietly, — till, lo he starts,
Gets off with half a heart eaten away !
Oh, shall you 'scape with less if she 's my child ?
You will not say a word — to me — to Him ?
    Pym. If England shall declare such will to
    me . . .
    Straf. No, not for England now, not for
    Heaven now, —
See, Pym, for my sake, mine who kneel to you !
There, I will thank you for the death, my
    friend !
This is the meeting: let me love you well !
    Pym. England, — I am thine own! Dost
    thou exact
That service? I obey thee to the end.
    Straf. O God, I shall die first — I shall die
    first !

SORDELLO

BROWNING began *Sordello* in 1837, inter-
rupted his work to write the earlier parts of
Bells and Pomegranates, but resumed it and
completed it in 1840, when it was published by
Moxon. In 1863, when reprinting the poem,
Browning dedicated it as below to M. Milsand,
and in his dedication wrote practically a pre-
face to the poem.

TO J. MILSAND, OF DIJON

DEAR FRIEND, — Let the next poem be in-
troduced by your name, therefore remembered
along with one of the deepest of my affections,
and so repay all trouble it ever cost me. I wrote
it twenty-five years ago for only a few, counting
even in these on somewhat more care about its
subject than they really had. My own faults of
expression were many ; but with care for a man

or book such would be surmounted, and with-
out it what avails the faultlessness of either ?
I blame nobody, least of all myself, who did my
best then and since ; for I lately gave time and
pains to turn my work into what the many
might — instead of what the few must — like ;
but after all, I imagined another thing at first,
and therefore leave as I find it. The historical
decoration was purposely of no more importance
than a background requires ; and my stress lay
on the incidents in the development of a soul :
little else is worth study. I, at least, always
thought so ; you, with many known and un-
known to me, think so ; others may one day
think so ; and whether my attempt remain for
them or not, I trust, though away and past it
to continue ever yours,

                       R. B.

LONDON, *June* 9, 1863.

Concerning this revised edition he wrote to a friend : —

"I do not understand what —— can mean by saying that Sordello has been 'rewritten.' I did certainly at one time intend to rewrite much of it, but changed my mind, — and the edition which I reprinted was the same in all respects as its predecessors — only with an elucidatory heading to each page, and some few alterations,

presumably for the better, in the text, such as occur in most of my works. I cannot remember a single instance of any importance that is re-written, and I only suppose that —— has taken project for performance, and set down as 'done' what was for a while intended to be done."

For the sake of such elucidation as these head-lines give, they are introduced here as side-notes.

SORDELLO

BOOK THE FIRST

WHO will, may hear Sordello's story told :
His story? Who believes me shall behold
The man, pursue his fortunes to the end,
Like me : for as the friendless-people's friend

<small>A Quixotic attempt.</small> Spied from his hill-top once, despite the din
And dust of multitudes, Pentapolin
Named o' the Naked Arm, I single out
Sordello, compassed murkily about
With ravage of six long sad hundred years.
Only believe me. Ye believe ?
                 Appears
Verona . . . Never, I should warn you first,
Of my own choice had this, if not the worst
Yet not the best expedient, served to tell
A story I could body forth so well
By making speak, myself kept out of view,
The very man as he was wont to do,
And leaving you to say the rest for him.
Since, though I might be proud to see the dim
Abysmal past divide its hateful surge,
Letting of all men this one man emerge
Because it pleased me, yet, that moment past,
I should delight in watching first to last
His progress as you watch it, not a whit
More in the secret than yourselves who sit
Fresh-chapleted to listen. But it seems
Your setters-forth of unexampled themes,
Makers of quite new men, producing them,
Would best chalk broadly on each vesture's hem
The wearer's quality ; or take their stand,
Motley on back and pointing-pole in hand,
Beside him. So, for once I face ye, friends,

<small>Why the Poet himself ad-dresses his audience—</small> Summoned together from the world's four ends,
Dropped down from heaven or cast up from hell,
To hear the story I propose to tell.
Confess now, poets know the dragnet's trick,
Catching the dead, if fate denies the quick,
And shaming her ; 't is not for fate to choose
Silence or song because she can refuse
Real eyes to glisten more, real hearts to ache
Less oft, real brows turn smoother for our sake :
I have experienced something of her spite ;
But there 's a realm wherein she has no right
And I have many lovers. Say, but few
Friends fate accords me ? Here they are : now view
The host I muster ! Many a lighted face
Foul with no vestige of the grave's disgrace ;

What else should tempt them back to taste our air
Except to see how their successors fare ?
My audience ! and they sit, each ghostly man
Striving to look as living as he can,
Brother by breathing brother ; thou art set,
Clear-witted critic, by . . . but I 'll not fret
A wondrous soul of them, nor move death's spleen
Who loves not to unlock them. Friends ! I mean

<small>Few liv-ing, many dead.</small> The living in good earnest — ye elect
Chiefly for love — suppose not I reject
Judicious praise, who contrary shall peep,
Some fit occasion, forth, for fear ye sleep,
To glean your bland approvals. Then, appear,
Verona ! stay — thou, spirit, come not near

<small>Shelley de-parting,</small> Now — not this time desert thy cloudy place

<small>Verona ap-pears.</small> To scare me, thus employed, with that pure face !
I need not fear this audience, I make free
With them, but then this is no place for thee !
The thunder-phrase of the Athenian, grown
Up out of memories of Marathon,
Would echo like his own sword's griding screech
Braying a Persian shield, — the silver speech
Of Sidney's self, the starry paladin,
Turn intense as a trumpet sounding in
The knights to tilt, — wert thou to hear ! What heart
Have I to play my puppets, bear my part
Before these worthies ?
               Lo, the past is hurled
In twain : up-thrust, out-staggering on the world
Subsiding into shape, a darkness rears
Its outline, kindles at the core, appears
Verona. 'T is six hundred years and more
Since an event. The Second Friedrich wore
The purple, and the Third Honorius filled
The holy chair. That autumn eve was stilled :
A last remains of sunset dimly burned
O'er the far forests, like a torch-flame turned
By the wind back upon its bearer's hand
In one long flare of crimson ; as a brand,
The woods beneath lay black. A single eye
From all Verona cared for the soft sky.
But, gathering in its ancient market-place,
Talked group with restless group ; and not a face
But wrath made livid, for among them were
Death's stanch purveyors, such as have in care
To feast him. Fear had long since taken root
In every breast, and now these crushed its fruit.
The ripe hate, like a wine : to note the way
It worked while each grew drunk ! Men grave and gray

Stood, with shut eyelids, rocking to and fro,
Letting the silent luxury trickle slow

How her Guelfs are discomfited. About the hollows where a heart
should be ;
But the young gulped with a delirious
glee
Some foretaste of their first debauch in blood
At the fierce news : for, be it understood,
Envoys apprised Verona that her prince
Count Richard of Saint Boniface, joined since
A year with Azzo, Este's Lord, to thrust
Taurello Salinguerra, prime in trust
With Ecelin Romano, from his seat
Ferrara, — over-zealous in the feat
And stumbling on a peril unaware,
Was captive, trammelled in his proper snare,
They phrase it, taken by his own intrigue.

Why they entreat the Lombard League, Immediate succor from the Lombard
League
Of fifteen cities that affect the Pope,
For Azzo, therefore, and his fellow-
hope
Of the Guelf cause, a glory overcast !
Men's faces, late agape, are now aghast.
" Prone is the purple pavis ; Este makes
Mirth for the devil when he undertakes
To play the Ecelin ; as if it cost
Merely your pushing-by to gain a post
Like his ! The patron tells ye, once for all,
There be sound reasons that preferment fall
On our beloved " . . .
" Duke o' the Rood, why not ? "
Shouted an Estian, " grudge ye such a lot ?
The hill-cat boasts some cunning of her own,
Some stealthy trick to better beasts unknown,
That quick with prey enough her hunger blunts,
And feeds her fat while gaunt the lion hunts."
" Taurello," quoth an envoy, " as in wane
Dwelt at Ferrara. Like an osprey fain
To fly but forced the earth his couch to make
Far inland, till his friend the tempest wake,
Waits he the Kaiser's coming ; and as yet
That fast friend sleeps, and he too sleeps : but let
Only the billow freshen, and he snuffs
The aroused hurricane ere it enroughs
The sea it means to cross because of him.
Sinketh the breeze ? His hope-sick eye grows
dim ;
Creep closer on the creature ! Every day
Strengthens the Pontiff ; Ecelin, they say,
Dozes now at Oliero, with dry lips
Telling upon his perished finger-tips
How many ancestors are to depose
Ere he be Satan's Viceroy when the doze
Deposits him in hell. So, Guelfs rebuilt
Their houses ; not a drop of blood was spilt
When Cino Bocchimpane chanced to meet
Buccio Virtù — God's wafer, and the street
Is narrow ! Tutti Santi, think, a-swarm
With Ghibellins, and yet he took no harm !
This could not last. Off Salinguerra went
To Padua, Podestà, ' with pure intent,'
Said he, ' my presence, judged the single bar
To permanent tranquillity, may jar
No longer ' — so ! his back is fairly turned ?
The pair of goodly palaces are burned,
The gardens ravaged, and our Guelfs laugh,
drunk

A week with joy. The next, their laughter sunk
In sobs of blood, for they found, some strange
way,
Old Salinguerra back again — I say,

In their changed fortune at Ferrara : Old Salinguerra in the town once
more
Uprooting, overturning, flame before,
Blood fetlock-high beneath him.
Azzo fled ;
Who 'scaped the carnage followed ; then the
dead
Were pushed aside from Salinguerra's throne,
He ruled once more Ferrara, all alone,
Till Azzo, stunned awhile, revived, would
pounce
Coupled with Boniface, like lynx and ounce,
On the gorged bird. The burghers ground their
teeth
To see troop after troop encamp beneath
I' the standing corn thick o'er the scanty patch
It took so many patient months to snatch
Out of the marsh ; while just within their walls
Men fed on men. At length Taurello calls
A parley : ' let the Count wind up the war !
Richard, light-hearted as a plunging star,
Agrees to enter for the kindest ends
Ferrara, flanked with fifty chosen friends,
No horse-boy more, for fear your timid sort
Should fly Ferrara at the bare report.
Quietly through the town they rode, jog-jog ;
'Ten, twenty, thirty, — curse the catalogue
Of burnt Guelf houses ! Strange, Taurello shows
Not the least sign of life ' — whereat arose
A general growl : ' How ? With his victors by ?
I and my Veronese ? My troops and I ?
Receive us, was your word ? ' So jogged they on,
Nor laughed their host too openly : once gone
Into the trap ! " —
Six hundred years ago !
Such the time's aspect and peculiar woe
(Yourselves may spell it yet in chronicles,
Albeit the worm, our busy brother, drills
His sprawling path through letters anciently
Made fine and large to suit some abbot's eye)
When the new Hohenstauffen dropped the mask,
Flung John of Brienne's favor from his casque,
Forswore crusading, had no mind to leave
Saint Peter's proxy leisure to retrieve
Losses to Otho and to Barbaross,
Or make the Alps less easy to recross ;
And, thus confirming Pope Honorius' fear,
Was excommunicate that very year.
" The triple-bearded Teuton come to life ! "
Groaned the Great League ; and, arming for the
strife,

For the times grow stormy again. Wide Lombardy, on tiptoe to begin,
Took up, as it was Guelf or Ghibellin,
Its cry ; what cry ?
" The Emperor to come ! "
His crowd of feudatories, all and some,
That leapt down with a crash of swords, spears,
shields,
One fighter on his fellow, to our fields,
Scattered anon, took station here and there,
And carried it, till now, with little care —
Cannot but cry for him ; how else rebut
Us longer ? Cliffs, an earthquake suffered jut
In the mid-sea, each domineering crest

Which naught save such another throe can wrest
From out (conceive) a certain chokeweed grown
Since o'er the waters, twine and tangle thrown
Too thick, too fast accumulating round,
Too sure to over-riot and confound
Ere long each brilliant islet with itself,
Unless a second shock save shoal and shelf,
Whirling the sea-drift wide : alas, the bruised
And sullen wreck ! Sunlight to be diffused
For that ! Sunlight, 'neath which, a scum at first,
The million fibres of our chokeweed nurst
Dispread themselves, mantling the troubled main,
And, shattered by those rocks, took hold again,
So kindly blazed it — that same blaze to brood
O'er every cluster of the multitude
Still hazarding new clasps, ties, filaments,
An emulous exchange of pulses, vents
Of nature into nature ; till some growth
Unfancied yet, exuberantly clothe

The Ghi-bellins' wish : the Guelfs' wish.
A surface solid now, continuous, one :
"The Pope, for us the People, who begun
The People, carries on the People thus,
To keep that Kaiser off and dwell with us ! "
See you ?
        Or say, Two Principles that live
Each fitly by its Representative.
" Hill-cat " — who called him so ? — the grace-fullest
Adventurer, the ambiguous stranger-guest
Of Lombardy (sleek but that ruffling fur,
Those talons to their sheath !) whose velvet purr
Soothes jealous neighbors when a Saxon scout
— Arpo or Yoland, is it ? — one without
A country or a name, presumes to couch
Beside their noblest ; until men avouch
That, of all Houses in the Trevisan,
Conrad descries no fitter, rear or van,

How Ece-lo's house grew head of those,
            Than Ecelo ! They laughed as they enrolled
That name at Milan on the page of gold,
Godego's lord, — Ramon, Marostica,
Cartiglion, Bassano, Loria,
And every sheep-cote on the Suabian's fief !
No laughter when his son, " the Lombard Chief "
Forsooth, as Barbarossa's path was bent
To Italy along the Vale of Trent,
Welcomed him at Roncaglia ! Sadness now —
The hamlets nested on the Tyrol's brow,
The Asolan and Euganean hills,
The Rhetian and the Julian, sadness fills
Them all, for Ecelin vouchsafes to stay
Among and care about them ; day by day
Choosing this pinnacle, the other spot,
A castle building to defend a cot,
A cot built for a castle to defend,
Nothing but castles, castles, nor an end
To boasts how mountain ridge may join with ridge
By sunken gallery and soaring bridge.
He takes, in brief, a figure that beseems
The griesliest nightmare of the Church's dreams,
-- A Signory firm-rooted, unestranged

From its old interests, and nowise changed
By its new neighborhood : perchance the vaunt
Of Otho, " my own Este shall supplant
Your Este," come to pass. The sire led in
A son as cruel ; and this Ecelin
Had sons, in turn, and daughters sly and tall
And curling and compliant ; but for all
Romano (so they styled him) throve, that neck
Of his so pinched and white, that hungry cheek
Proved 't was some fiend, not him, the man's-flesh went
To feed : whereas Romano's instrument,
Famous Taurello Salinguerra, sole
I' the world, a tree whose boughs were slipt the bole
Successively, why should not he shed blood
To further a design ? Men understood
Living was pleasant to him as he wore
His careless surcoat, glanced some missive o'er,
Propped on his truncheon in the public way,
While his lord lifted writhen hands to pray,
Lost at Oliero's convent.
                        Hill-cats, face
Our Azzo, our Guelf-Lion ! Why disgrace
As Azzo Lord of Este heads these.
A worthiness conspicuous near and far
(Atii at Rome while free and consu-lar,
Este at Padua who repulsed the Hun)
By trumpeting the Church's princely son ?
— Styled Patron of Rovigo's Polesine,
Ancona's march, Ferrara's . . . ask, in fine,
Our chronicles, commenced when some old monk
Found it intolerable to be sunk
(Vexed to the quick by his revolting cell)
Quite out of summer while alive and well :
Ended when by his mat the Prior stood,
'Mid busy promptings of the brotherhood,
Striving to coax from his decrepit brains
The reason Father Porphyry took pains
To blot those ten lines out which used to stand
First on their charter drawn by Hildebrand.
The same night wears. Verona's rule of yore
Was vested in a certain Twenty-four ;
Count Richard's Palace at Verona.
And while within his palace these debate
Concerning Richard and Ferrara's fate,
Glide we by clapping doors, with sudden glare
Of cressets vented on the dark, nor care
For aught that 's seen or heard until we shut
The smother in, the lights, all noises but
The carroch's booming : safe at last ! Why strange
Such a recess should lurk behind a range.
Of banquet-rooms ? Your finger — thus — you push
A spring, and the wall opens, would you rush
Upon the banqueters, select your prey,
Waiting (the slaughter-weapons in the way
Strewing this very bench) with sharpened ear
A preconcerted signal to appear ;
Or if you simply crouch with beating heart,
Of the couple found therein,
Bearing in some voluptuous pageant part
To startle them. Nor mutes nor masquers now ;
Nor any . . . does that one man sleep whose brow

The dying lamp-flame sinks and rises o'er?
What woman stood beside him? not the more
Is he unfastened from the earnest eyes
Because that arras fell between! Her wise
And lulling words are yet about the room,
Her presence wholly poured upon the gloom
Down even to her vesture's creeping stir.
And so reclines he, saturate with her,
Until an outcry from the square beneath
Pierces the charm: he springs up, glad to
    breathe,
Above the cunning element, and shakes
The stupor off as (look you) morning breaks
On the gay dress, and, near concealed by it,
The lean frame like a half-burnt taper, lit
Erst at some marriage-feast, then laid away
Till the Armenian bridegroom's dying day,
In his wool wedding-robe.
              For he — for he,
Gate-vein of this hearts' blood of Lombardy,
(If I should falter now) — for he is thine!
Sordello, thy forerunner, Florentine!
A herald-star I know thou didst absorb
Relentless into the consummate orb
That scared it from its right to roll along
A sempiternal path with dance and song
Fulfilling its allotted period,
Serenest of the progeny of God —
Who yet resigns it not! His darling stoops
With no quenched lights, desponds with no blank
    troops
Of disenfranchised brilliances, for, blent
Utterly with thee, its shy element
Like thine upburneth prosperous and clear.
Still, what if I approach the august sphere
Named now with only one name, disentwine
That under-current soft and argentine
From its fierce mate in the majestic mass
Leavened as the sea whose fire was mixt with
    glass
In John's transcendent vision, — launch once
    more
That lustre? Dante, pacer of the shore
Where glutted hell disgorgeth filthiest gloom,
Unbitten by its whirring sulphur-spume —
Or whence the grieved and obscure waters slope
Into a darkness quieted by hope;
Plucker of amaranths grown beneath God's eye
In gracious twilights where his chosen lie, —
I would do this! If I should falter now!

          In Mantua territory half is slough,
One be-   Half pine-tree forest; maples, scarlet
longs to   oaks
Dante; his Breed o'er the river-beds; even Min-
Birthplace. cio chokes
With sand the summer through: but 't is mo-
    rass
In winter up to Mantua walls. There was,
Some thirty years before this evening's coil,
One spot reclaimed from the surrounding spoil,
Goito; just a castle built amid
A few low mountains; firs and larches hid
Their main defiles, and rings of vineyard bound
The rest. Some captured creature in a pound,
Whose artless wonder quite precludes distress,
Secure beside in its own loveliness,
So peered with airy head, below, above,
The castle at its toils, the lapwings love

To glean among at grape-time. Pass within.
A maze of corridors contrived for sin,
Dusk winding-stairs, dim galleries got past,
You gain the inmost chambers, gain at last
A maple-panelled room: that haze which seems
Floating about the panel, if there gleams
A sunbeam over it, will turn to gold
And in light-graven characters unfold
The Arab's wisdom everywhere; what shade
Marred them a moment, those slim pillars made
Cut like a company of palms to prop
The roof, each kissing top entwined with top,
Leaning together; in the carver's mind
Some knot of bacchanals, flushed cheek com-
    bined
With straining forehead, shoulders purpled, hair
Diffused between, who in a goat-skin bear
A vintage; graceful sister-palms! But quick
To the main wonder, now. A vault, see; thick
            Black shade about the ceiling, though
A Vault   fine slits
inside the Across the buttress suffer light by fits
Castle at   Upon a marvel in the midst. Nay,
Goito,   stoop —
A dullish gray-streaked cumbrous font, a group
Round it, — each side of it, where'er one sees, —
Upholds it; shrinking Caryatides
Of just-tinged marble like Eve's lilied flesh
Beneath her maker's finger when the fresh
First pulse of life shot brightening the snow.
The font's edge burdens every shoulder, so
They muse upon the ground, eyelids half closed;
Some, with meek arms behind their backs dis-
    posed,
Some, crossed above their bosoms, some, to veil
Their eyes, some, propping chin and cheek so
    pale,
Some, hanging slack an utter helpless length
Dead as a buried vestal whose whole strength
Goes when the grate above shuts heavily.
So dwell these noiseless girls, patient to see,
Like priestesses because of sin impure
Penanced forever, who resigned endure,
Having that once drunk sweetness to the dregs,
And every eve, Sordello's visit begs
Pardon for them: constant as eve he came
To sit beside each in her turn, the same
As one of them, a certain space: and awe
And what   Made a great indistinctness till he saw
Sordello   Sunset slant cheerful through the
would see   buttress-chinks,
there.   Gold seven times globed; surely our
           maiden shrinks
And a smile stirs her as if one faint grain
Her load were lightened, one shade less the stain
Obscured her forehead, yet one more bead slipt
From off the rosary whereby the crypt
Keeps count of the contritions of its charge?
Then with a step more light, a heart more large
He may depart, leave her and every one
To linger out the penance in mute stone.
Ah, but Sordello? 'T is the tale I mean
To tell you.
          In this castle may be seen,
On the hill-tops, or underneath the vines,
Or eastward by the mound of firs and pines
That shuts out Mantua, still in loneliness,
A slender boy in a loose page's dress,

Sordello: do but look on him awhile
Watching ('t is autumn) with an earnest smile
The noisy flock of thievish birds at work
Among the yellowing vineyards ; see him lurk
    ('T is winter with its sullenest of
His boy-   storms)
hood in Beside that arras-length of broidered
the domain forms,
of Ecelin. On tiptoe, lifting in both hands a light
Which makes yon warrior's visage flutter bright
— Ecelo, dismal father of the brood,
And Ecelin, close to the girl he wooed,
Auria, and their Child, with all his wives
From Agnes to the Tuscan that survives,
Lady of the castle, Adelaide. His face
— Look, now he turns away ! Yourselves shall
    trace
(The delicate nostril swerving wide and fine,
A sharp and restless lip, so well combine
With that calm brow) a soul fit to receive
Delight at every sense ; you can believe
Sordello foremost in the regal class
Nature has broadly severed from her mass
Of men, and framed for pleasure, as she frames
Some happy lands, that have luxurious names,
For loose fertility ; a footfall there
Suffices to upturn to the warm air
Half-germinating spices ; mere decay
Produces richer life ; and day by day
New pollen on the lily-petal grows,
And still more labyrinthine buds the rose.
You recognize at once the finer dress
Of flesh that amply lets in loveliness
At eye and ear, while round the rest is furled
(As though she would not trust them with her
    world)
A veil that shows a sky not near so blue,
And lets but half the sun look fervid through.
    How can such life ? — like souls on
How a   each full-fraught
poet's soul Discovery brooding, blind at first to
comes into aught
play. Beyond its beauty, till exceeding love
Becomes an aching weight ; and, to remove
A curse that haunts such natures — to preclude
Their finding out themselves can work no good
To what they love nor make it very blest
By their endeavor, — they are fain invest
The lifeless thing with life from their own soul,
Availing it to purpose, to control,
To dwell distinct and have peculiar joy
And separate interests that may employ
That beauty fitly, for its proper sake.
Nor rest they here ; fresh births of beauty wake
Fresh homage, every grade of love is past,
With every mode of loveliness : then cast
Inferior idols off their borrowed crown
Before a coming glory. Up and down
Runs arrowy fire, while earthly forms com-
    bine
To throb the secret forth ; a touch divine —
And the scaled eyeball owns the mystic rod ;
Visibly through his garden walketh God.
What de-   So fare they. Now revert. One
notes such   character
a soul's Denotes them through the progress
progress. and the stir, —
A need to blend with each external charm,

Bury themselves, the whole heart wide and
    warm, —
In something not themselves ; they would be
    long
To what they worship — stronger and more
    strong
Thus prodigally fed — which gathers shape
And feature, soon imprisons past escape
The votary framed to love and to submit
Nor ask, as passionate he kneels to it,
Whence grew the idol's empery. So runs
A legend ; light had birth ere moons and suns,
Flowing through space a river and alone,
Till chaos burst and blank the spheres were
    strown
Hither and thither, foundering and blind :
When into each of them rushed light — to find
Itself no place, foiled of its radiant chance.
Let such forego their just inheritance !
For there's a class that eagerly looks, too
On beauty, but, unlike the gentler crew,
Proclaims each new revealment born a twin
With a distinctest consciousness within,
Referring still.the quality, now first
Revealed, to their own soul — its instinct nursed
In silence, now remembered better, shown
More thoroughly, but not the less their own ;
A dream come true ; the special exercise
How poets Of any special function that implies
class at The being fair, or good, or wise, or
length — strong,
Dormant within their nature all along —
Whose fault ? So, homage, other souls direct
Without, turns inward. "How should this de-
    ject
Thee, soul ?" they murmur ; "wherefore
    strength be quelled
Because, its trivial accidents withheld,
Organs are missed that clog the world, inert,
Wanting a will, to quicken and exert,
Like thine — existence cannot satiate,
Cannot surprise ? Laugh thou at envious fate,
Who, from earth's simplest combination stampt
With individuality — uncrampt
By living its faint elemental life,
Dost soar to heaven's complexest essence, rife
With grandeurs, unaffronted to the last,
For honor, Equal to being all !"
    In truth ? Thou hast
Life, then — wilt challenge life for us: our race
Is vindicated so, obtains its place
In thy ascent, the first of us ; whom we
May follow, to the meanest, finally,
Or shame — With our more bounded wills ?
    Ah, but to find
A certain mood enervate such a mind,
Counsel it slumber in the solitude
Thus reached, nor, stooping, task for man
    kind's good
Its nature just as life and time accord
" — Too narrow an arena to reward
Emprise — the world's occasion worthless since
Not absolutely fitted to evince
Its mastery !" Or if yet worse befall,
And a desire possess it to put all
That nature forth, forcing our straitened sphere
Contain it, — to display completely here
The mastery another life should learn,

Thrusting in time eternity's concern, —
So that Sordello . . .

     Fool, who spied the mark

Which may the Gods avert Of leprosy upon him, violet-dark
Already as he loiters? Born just now,
With the new century, beside the glow
And efflorescence out of barbarism;
Witness a Greek or two from the abysm
That stray through Florence-town with studi-
 ous air,
Calming the chisel of that Pisan pair:
If Nicolo should carve a Christus yet!
While at Siena is Guidone set,
Forehead on hand; a painful birth must be
Matured ere Saint Eufemia's sacristy
Or transept gather fruits of one great gaze
At the moon: look you! The same orange
 haze, —
The same blue stripe round that — and, in the
 midst,
Thy spectral whiteness, Mother-maid, who didst
Pursue the dizzy painter!
     Woe, then, worth
Any officious babble letting forth
The leprosy confirmed and ruinous
To spirit lodged in a contracted house!
Go back to the beginning, rather; blend
It gently with Sordello's life; the end
Is piteous, you may see, but much between
Pleasant enough. Meantime, some pyx to screen
The full-grown pest, some lid to shut upon
The goblin! So they found at Babylon,
(Colleagues, mad Lucius and sage Antoine)
Sacking the city, by Apollo's shrine,
In rummaging among the rarities,
A certain coffer; he who made the prize
Opened it greedily; and out there curled
Just such another plague, for half the world
Was stung. Crawl in then, hag, and couch
 asquat,
Keeping that blotchy bosom thick in spot
Until your time is ripe! The coffer-lid
Is fastened, and the coffer safely hid
Under the Loxian's choicest gifts of gold.
Who will may hear Sordello's story told,
And how he never could remember when
He dwelt not at Goito. Calmly, then,

From Sordello, now in childhood. About this secret lodge of Ade-
 laide's
Glided his youth away; beyond the
 glades
On the fir-forest border, and the rim
Of the low range of mountain, was for him
No other world: but this appeared his own
To wander through at pleasure and alone.
The castle too seemed empty; far and wide
Might he disport; only the northern side
Lay under a mysterious interdict —
Slight, just enough remembered to restrict
His roaming to the corridors, the vault
Where those font-bearers expiate their fault,
The maple-chamber, and the little nooks
And nests, and breezy parapet that looks
Over the woods to Mantua: there he strolled.
Some foreign women-servants, very old,
Tended and crept about him — all his clue
To the world's business and embroiled ado

Distant a dozen hill-tops at the most.

The delights of his childish fancy, And first a simple sense of life
 engrossed
Sordello in his drowsy Paradise;
The day's adventures for the day
 suffice —
Its constant tribute of perceptions strange.
With sleep and stir in healthy interchange,
Suffice, and leave him for the next at ease
Like the great palmer-worm that strips tne
 trees,
Eats the life out of every luscious plant,
And, when September finds them sere or scant,
Puts forth two wondrous winglets, alters quite,
And hies him after unforeseen delight.
So fed Sordello, not a shard dissheathed;
As ever, round each new discovery, wreathed
Luxuriantly the fancies infantine
His admiration, bent on making fine
Its novel friend at any risk, would fling
In gay profusion forth; a ficklest king,
Confessed those minions! — eager to dispense
So much from his own stock of thought and
 sense
As might enable each to stand alone
And serve him for a fellow; with his own,
Joining the qualities that just before
Had graced some older favorite. Thus they
 wore
A fluctuating halo, yesterday
Set flicker and to-morrow filched away, —
Those upland objects each of separate name,
Each with an aspect never twice the same,
Waxing and waning as the new-born host
Of fancies, like a single night's hoar-frost,

Which could blow out a great bubble. Gave to familiar things a face gro-
 tesque;
Only, preserving through the mad
 burlesque
A grave regard. Conceive! the
 orpine patch
Blossoming earliest on the log-house thatch
The day those archers wound along the vines —
Related to the Chief that left their lines
To climb with clinking step the northern stair
Up to the solitary chambers where
Sordello never came. Thus thrall reached
 thrall;
He o'er-festooning every interval,
As the adventurous spider, making light
Of distance, shoots her threads from depth to
 height,
From barbican to battlement: so flung
Fantasies forth and in their centre swung
Our architect, — the breezy morning fresh
Above, and merry, — all his waving mesh
Laughing with lucid dew-drops rainbow-edged.
 This world of ours by tacit pact is pledged
To laying such a spangled fabric low
Whether by gradual brush or gallant blow.
But its abundant will was balked here: doubt

Being secure awhile from intrusion. Rose tardily in one so fenced about
From most that nurtures judgment,
 care and pain:
Judgment, that dull expedient we
 are fain,
Less favored, to adopt betimes and force
Stead us, diverted from our natural course

Of joys — contrive some yet amid the dearth,
Vary and render them, it may be, worth
Most we forego. Suppose Sordello hence
Selfish enough, without a moral sense
However feeble; what informed the boy
Others desired a portion in his joy?
Or say a ruthful chance broke woof and
    warp —
A heron's nest beat down by March winds sharp,
A fawn breathless beneath the precipice,
A bird with unsoiled breast and unfilmed eyes
Warm in the brake — could these undo the
    trance
Lapping Sordello? Not a circumstance
That makes for you, friend Naddo! Eat fern-
    seed
And peer beside us and report indeed
If (your word) "genius" dawned with throes
    and stings
And the whole fiery catalogue, while springs,
Summers and winters quietly came and went.
    Time put at length that period to content,
By right the world should have imposed: be-
    reft
Of its good offices, Sordello, left
To study his companions, managed rip
Their fringe off, learn the true relationship,
Core with its crust, their nature with his own:
Amid his wild-wood sights he lived alone.
As if the poppy felt with him! Though he
Partook the poppy's red effrontery
Till Autumn spoiled their fleering quite with
    rain,
And, turbanless, a coarse brown rattling crane
Lay bare. That's gone: yet why renounce,
    for that,
His disenchanted tributaries — flat
Perhaps, but scarce so utterly forlorn,
Their simple presence might not well be borne
Whose parley was a transport once: recall
The poppy's gifts, it flaunts you, after all,
A poppy: — why distrust the evidence
Of each soon satisfied and healthy sense?

But it comes; and new-born judgment The new-born judgment answered,
    "little boots
Beholding other creatures' attributes
And having none!" or, say that it
    sufficed,
"Yet, could one but possess, one's self," (enticed
Judgment) "some special office!" Naught
    beside
Serves you? "Weil then, be somehow justi-
    fied
For this ignoble wish to circumscribe
And concentrate, rather than swell, the tribe
Of actual pleasures: what, now, from without
Effects it? — proves, despite a lurking doubt,
Mere sympathy sufficient, trouble spared?
That, tasting joys by proxy thus, you fared

Decides that he needs sympa- thizers.
    The better for them?" Thus much
    craved his soul.
Alas, from the beginning love is
    whole
And true; if sure of naught beside,
    most sure
Of its own truth at least; nor may endure
A crowd to see its face, that cannot know
How hot the pulses throb its heart below.

While its own helplessness and utter want
Of means to worthily be ministrant
To what it worships, do but fan the more
Its flame, exalt the idol far before
Itself as it would have it ever be.
Souls like Sordello, on the contrary,
Coerced and put to shame, retaining will,
Care little, take mysterious comfort still,
But look forth tremblingly to ascertain
If others judge their claims not urged in vain,
And say for them their stifled thoughts aloud.
So, they must ever live before a crowd:
— "Vanity," Naddo tells you.
                        Whence contrive
A crowd, now? From these women just alive,
That archer-troop? Forth glided — not alone
Each painted warrior, every girl of stone,
Nor Adelaide (bent double o'er a scroll,
One maiden at her knees, that eve, his soul
Shook as he stumbled through the arras'd
    glooms
On them, for, 'mid quaint robes and weird per-
    fumes,
Started the meagre Tuscan up, — her eyes,
The maiden's, also, bluer with surprise)
— But the entire out-world: whatever, scraps
And snatches, song and story, dreams per-
    haps,
Conceited the world's offices, and he
Had hitherto transferred to flower or tree,
Not counted a befitting heritage
Each, of its own right, singly to engage
Some man, no other, — such now dared to stand
Alone. Strength, wisdom, grace on every hand
Soon disengaged themselves, and he discerned
A sort of human life: at least, was turned

He there- fore creates such a company;
    A stream of lifelike figures through
    his brain.
Lord, liegeman, valvassor and suze-
    rain,
Ere he could choose, surrounded
    him; a stuff
To work his pleasure on; there, sure enough:
But as for gazing, what shall fix that gaze?
Are they to simply testify the ways
He who convoked them sends his soul along
With the cloud's thunder or a dove's brood-
    song?
— While they live each his life, boast each his

Each of which, leading its own life,
    own
Peculiar dower of bliss, stand each
    alone
In some one point where something
    dearest loved
Is easiest gained — far worthier to be proved
Than aught he envies in the forest-wights!
No simple and self-evident delights,
But mixed desires of unimagined range,
Contrasts or combinations, new and strange,
Irksome perhaps, yet plainly recognized
By this, the sudden company — loves prized
By those who are to prize his own amount
Of loves. Once care because such make ac
    count,
Allow that foreign recognitions stamp
The current value, and his crowd shall vamp
Him counterfeits enough; and so their print
Be on the piece, 't is gold, attests the mint.

And "good," pronounce they whom his new appeal
Is made to: if their casual print conceal —
This arbitrary good of theirs o'ergloss
What he has lived without, nor felt the loss —
Qualities strange, ungainly, wearisome,
— What matter? So must speech expand the dumb
Part-sigh, part-smile with which Sordello, late
Whom no poor woodland-sights could satiate,
Betakes himself to study hungrily
Just what the puppets his crude fantasy
Supposes notablest, — popes, kings, priests, knights, —
May please to promulgate for appetites;
Accepting all their artificial joys
Not as he views them, but as he employs
Each shape to estimate the other's stock
Of attributes, whereon — a marshalled flock
Of authorized enjoyments — he may spend
Himself, be men, now, as he used to blend
With tree and flower — nay more entirely, else
'Twere mockery: for instance, " How excels
My life that chieftain's?" (who apprised the youth
Ecelin, here, becomes this month, in truth,
Imperial Vicar ?) " Turns he in his tent
Remissly? Be it so — my head is bent
Deliciously amid my girls to sleep.
What if he stalks the Trentine-pass? Yon steep
I climbed an hour ago with little toil:
We are alike there. But can I, too, foil
The Guelf's paid stabber, carelessly afford
Saint Mark's a spectacle, the sleight o' the sword
Baffling the treason in a moment?" Here
No rescue! Poppy he is none, but peer
To Ecelin, assuredly: his hand,
Fashioned no otherwise, should wield a brand
With Ecelin's success — try, now ! He soon
Was satisfied, returned as to the moon
From earth; left each abortive boy's-attempt
Has quali- For feats, from failure happily ex-
ties impos- empt,
sible to a In fancy at his beck. " One day I
boy, will
Accomplish it ! Are they not older still
— Not grown up men and women ? 'T is be-side
Only a dream; and though I must abide
With dreams now, I may find a thorough vent
For all myself, acquire an instrument
For acting what these people act; my soul
Hunting a body out may gain its whole
Desire some day !" How else express chagrin
And resignation, show the hope steal in
With which he let sink from an aching wrist
The rough-hewn ash-bow? Straight, a gold shaft hissed
Into the Syrian air, struck Malek down
Superbly ! " Crosses to the breach ! God's Town
Is gained him back !" Why bend rough ash-bows more ?
Thus lives he: if not careless as before,
Comforted : for one may anticipate,
Rehearse the future, be prepared when fate

Shall have prepared in turn real men whose names
Startle, real places of enormous fames,
Este abroad and Ecelin at home
To worship him, — Mantua, Verona, Rome
To witness it. Who grudges time so spent ?
Rather test qualities to heart's content —
Summon them, thrice selected, near and far —
Compress the starriest into one star,
So, only to And grasp the whole at once !
be appro- The pageant thinnec
priated in Accordingly ; from rank to rank
fancy, like wind
His spirit passed to winnow and divide;
Back fell the simpler phantasms ; every side
The strong clave to the wise ; with either classed
The beauteous ; so, till two or three amassed
Mankind's beseemingnesses, and reduced
Themselves eventually, graces loosed,
Strengths lavished, all to heighten up One Shape
Whose potency no creature should escape.
Can it be Friedrich of the bowmen's talk ?
Surely that grape-juice, bubbling at the stalk,
Is some gray scorching Sarasenic wine
The Kaiser quaffs with the Miramoline —
Those swarthy hazel-clusters, seamed and chapped,
Or filberts russet-sheathed and velvet-capped,
Are dates plucked from the bough John Bri-enne sent,
To keep in mind his sluggish armament
Of Canaan: — Friedrich's, all the pomp and fierce
Demeanor ! But harsh sounds and sights trans-pierce
So rarely the serene cloud where he dwells,
And prac- Whose looks enjoin, whose lightest
tised on words are spells
till the real On the obdurate ! That right arm in-
come. deed
Has thunder for its slave; but where 's the need
Of thunder if the stricken multitude
Hearkens, arrested in its angriest mood,
While songs go up exulting, then dispread,
Dispart, disperse, lingering overhead
Like an escape of angels ? 'T is the tune,
Nor much unlike the words his women croon
Smilingly, colorless and faint-designed
Each, as a worn-out queen's face some remind
Of her extreme youth's love-tales. " Eglamor
Made that !" Half minstrel and half emperor,
What but ill objects vexed him ? Such he slew.
The kinder sort were easy to subdue
By those ambrosial glances, dulcet tones;
And these a gracious hand advanced to thrones
Beneath him. Wherefore twist and torture this,
Striving to name afresh the antique bliss,
Instead of saying, neither less nor more,
He means He had discovered, as our world be
to be per- fore,
fect — say, Apollo? That shall be the name
Apollo; nor bid
Me rag by rag expose how patchwork hid

The youth — what thefts of every clime and
    day
Contributed to purfle the array
He climbed with (June at deep) some close
    ravine
'Mid clatter of its million pebbles sheen,
Over which, singing soft, the runnel slipped
Elate with rains: into whose streamlet dipped
He foot, yet trod, you thought, with unwet
    sock —
Though really on the stubs of living rock
Ages ago it crenelled; vines for roof,
Lindens for wall; before him, aye aloof,
Flittered in the cool some azure damsel-fly,
Born of the simmering quiet, there to die.
Emerging whence, Apollo still, he spied
Mighty descents of forest; multiplied
Tuft on tuft, here, the frolic myrtle-trees,
There gendered the grave maple stocks at ease,
And, proud of its observer, straight the wood
Tried old surprises on him; black it stood
A sudden barrier ('t was a cloud passed o'er)
So dead and dense, the tiniest brute no more
Must pass; yet presently (the cloud dispatched)
Each clump, behold, was glistening detached
A shrub, oak-boles shrunk into ilex-stems!
Yet could not he denounce the stratagems
He saw thro', till, hours thence, aloft would
    hang
White summer-lightnings; as it sank and
    sprang
To measure, that whole palpitating breast
Of heaven, 't was Apollo, nature prest
At eve to worship.
        Time stole: by degrees
The Pythons perish off; his votaries
Sink to respectful distance; songs redeem
Their pains, but briefer; their dismissals seem
Emphatic; only girls are very slow
To disappear — his Delians! Some that glow
O' the instant, more with earlier loves to wrench
Away, reserves to quell, disdains to quench;
Alike in one material circumstance —
All soon or late adore Apollo! Glance
The bevy through, divine Apollo's choice,

And Apollo must one day find Daphne. His Daphne! "We secure Count
    Richard's voice
In Este's counsels, good for Este's
    ends
As our Taurello," say his faded friends,
" By granting him our Palma! " — the sole
    child,
They mean, of Agnes Este who beguiled
Ecelin, years before this Adelaide
Wedded and turned him wicked : "but the
    maid
Rejects his suit," those sleepy women boast.
She, scorning all beside, deserves the most
Sordello: so, conspicuous in his world
Of dreams sat Palma. How the tresses curled
Into a sumptuous swell of gold and wound
About her like a glory! even the ground
Was bright as with spilt sunbeams; breathe
    not, breathe
Not! — poised, see, one leg doubled underneath,
Its small foot buried in the dimpling snow,
Rests, but the other, listlessly below,
O'er the couch-side swings feeling for cool air,

The vein-streaks swollen a richer violet where
The languid blood lies heavily; yet calm
On her slight prop, each flat and outspread palm,
As but suspended in the act to rise
By consciousness of beauty, whence her eyes
But when will this dream turn truth? Turn with so frank a triumph, for
    she meets
    Apollo's gaze in the pine glooms.
                Time fleets:
That 's worst! Because the pre-appointed age
Approaches. Fate is tardy with the stage
And crowd she promised. Lean he grows and
    pale,
Though restlessly at rest. Hardly avail
Fancies to soothe him. Time steals, yet alone
He tarries here! The earnest smile is gone.
How long this might continue matters not;
For the time is ripe, and he ready. — Forever, possibly; since to the spot
    None come: our lingering Taurello
    quits
    Mantua at last, and light our lady flits
Back to her place disburdened of a care.
Strange — to be constant here if he is there!
Is it distrust? Oh, never! for they both
Goad Ecelin alike, Romano's growth
Is daily manifest, with Azzo dumb
And Richard wavering : let but Friedrich come,
Find matter for the minstrelsy's report!
— Lured from the Isle and its young Kaiser's
    court
To sing us a Messina morning up,
And, double rillet of a drinking cup,
Sparkle along to ease the land of drouth,
Northward to Provence that, and thus far south
The other. What a method to apprise
Neighbors of births, espousals, obsequies!
Which in their very tongue the Troubadour
Records; and his performance makes a tour,
For Trouveres bear the miracle about,
Explain its cunning to the vulgar rout,
Until the Formidable House is famed
Over the country — as Taurello aimed,
Who introduced, although the rest adopt,
The novelty. Such games, her absence stopped,
Begin afresh now Adelaide, recluse
No longer, in the light of day pursues
Her plans at Mantua : whence an accident
Which, breaking on Sordello's mixed content,
Opened, like any flash that cures the blind,
The veritable business of mankind.

BOOK THE SECOND

The woods were long austere with snow : at last
This bubble of fancy. Pink leaflets budded on the beech,
    and fast
    Larches, scattered through pine-tree
    solitudes,
Brightened, "as in the slumbrous heart o' the
    woods
Our buried year, a witch, grew young again
To placid incantations, and that stain
About were from her caldron, green smoke blent
With those black pines " — so Eglamor gave
    vent
To a chance fancy. Whence a just rebuke
From his companion; brother Naddo shook

The solemnest of brows ; " Beware," he said,
" Of setting up conceits in nature's stead ! "
Forth wandered our Sordello. Naught so sure
As that to-day's adventure will secure
Palma, the visioned lady — only pass
O'er yon damp mound and its exhausted grass,
Under that brake where sundawn feeds the
    stalks
Of withered fern with gold, into those walks
Of pine and take her ! Buoyantly he went.
Again his stooping forehead was besprent
With dew-drops from the skirting ferns. Then
    wide
Opened the great morass, shot every side
With flashing water through and through ;
    a-shine,
Thick steaming, all alive. Whose shape di-
    vine,
Quivered i' the farthest rainbow-vapor, glanced
Athwart the flying herons ? He advanced,
But warily ; though Mincio leaped no more,
Each footfall burst up in the marish-floor
A diamond jet : and if he stopped to pick
Rose-lichen, or molest the leeches quick,
And circling blood-worms, minnow, newt or
    loach,
A sudden pond would silently encroach
This way and that. On Palma passed. The
    verge
Of a new wood was gained. She will emerge
Flushed, now, and panting, — crowds to see, —
    will own
She loves him — Boniface to hear, to groan,
To leave his suit ! One screen of pine-trees still
Opposes : but — the startling spectacle —
Mantua, this time ! Under the walls — a crowd
Indeed, real men and women, gay and loud
Round a pavilion. How he stood !

            In truth

When greatest and brightest, bursts. No prophecy had come to pass : his
    youth
In its prime now — and where was
    homage poured
Upon Sordello ? — born to be adored,
And suddenly discovered weak, scarce made
To cope with any, cast into the shade
By this and this. Yet something seemed to
    prick
And tingle in his blood ; a sleight — a trick —
And much would be explained. It went for
    naught —
The best of their endowments were ill bought
With his identity : nay, the conceit,
That this day's roving led to Palma's feet
Was not so vain — list ! The word, " Palma ! "
    Steal
Aside, and die, Sordello ; this is real,
And this — abjure !

         What next ? The curtains see
Dividing ! She is there ; and presently
He will be there — the proper You, at length —
In your own cherished dress of grace and
    strength :
Most like, the very Boniface !

            Not so.
It was a showy man advanced ; but though
A glad cry welcomed him, then every sound
Sank and the crowd disposed themselves around,

— " This is not he," Sordello felt ; while, " Place
For the best Troubadour of Boniface ! "
Hollaed the Jongleurs, — " Eglamor, whose lay
Concludes his patron's Court of Love to-day ! "
Obsequious Naddo strung the master's lute
With the new lute-string, " Elys," named to suit

At a Court of Love a minstrel sings. The song : he stealthily at watch, the
    while,
Biting his lip to keep down a great
    smile
Of pride : then up he struck. Sordello's brain
Swam ; for he knew a sometime deed again ;
So, could supply each foolish gap and chasm
The minstrel left in his enthusiasm,
Mistaking its true version — was the tale
Not of Apollo ? Only, what avail
Luring her down, that Elys an he pleased,
If the man dared no further ? Has he ceased ?
And, lo, the people's frank applause half done,
Sordello was beside him, had begun
(Spite of indignant twitchings from his friend
The Trouvere) the true lay with the true end,
Taking the other's names and time and place
For his. On flew the song, a giddy race,

Sordello, before Palma, conquers him, After the flying story ; word made
    leap
Out word, rhyme — rhyme ; the lay
    could barely keep
Pace with the action visibly rushing past :
Both ended. Back fell Naddo more aghast
Than some Egyptian from the harassed bull
That wheeled abrupt and, bellowing, fronted
    full
His plague, who spied a scarab 'neath the
    tongue,
And found 't was Apis' flank his hasty prong
Insulted. But the people — but the cries,
The crowding round, and proffering the prize !
— For he had gained some prize. He seemed
    to shrink
Into a sleepy cloud, just at whose brink
One sight withheld him. There sat Adelaide,
Silent ; but at her knees the very maid
Of the North Chamber, her red lips as rich,
The same pure fleecy hair ; one weft of which,
Golden and great, quite touched his cheek as
    o'er
She leant, speaking some six words and no more.
He answered something, anything ; and she
Unbound a scarf and laid it heavily
Upon him, her neck's warmth and all. Again
Moved the arrested magic ; in his brain
Noises grew, and a light that turned to glare,
And greater glare, until the intense flare
Engulfed him, shut the whole scene from his
    sense.
And when he woke 't was many a furlong
    thence,
At home ; the sun shining his ruddy wont ;
The customary birds'-chirp ; but his front

Receives the prize, and ruminates. Was crowned — was crowned ! Her
    scented scarf around
His neck ! Whose gorgeous vesture
    heaps the ground ?
A prize ? He turned, and peeringly on him
Brooded the women-faces, kind and dim,
Ready to talk — " The Jongleurs in a troop
Had brought him back, Naddo and Squarcialup.

And Tagliafer; how strange! a childhood spent
In taking, well for him, so brave a bent!
Since Eglamor," they heard, "was dead with spite,
And Palma chose him for her minstrel."
                                        Light
Sordello rose — to think, now; hitherto
He had perceived. Sure, a discovery grew
Out of it all! Best live from first to last
The transport o'er again. A week he passed,
Sucking the sweet out of each circumstance,
From the bard's outbreak to the luscious trance
Bounding his own achievement. Strange! A man
Recounted an adventure, but began
Imperfectly; his own task was to fill
The frame-work up, sing well what he sung ill,
Supply the necessary points, set loose
As many incidents of little use
— More imbecile the other, not to see
Their relative importance clear as he!
But, for a special pleasure in the act
Of singing — had he ever turned, in fact,
From Elys, to sing Elys? — from each fit
Of rapture to contrive a song of it?
True, this snatch or the other seemed to wind
Into a treasure, helped himself to find
A beauty in himself; for, see, he soared
By means of that mere snatch, to many a hoard
Of fancies; as some falling cone bears soft
The eye along the fir-tree spire, aloft
To a dove's nest. Then, how divine the cause
Why such performance should exact applause
From men, if they had fancies too? Did fate
Decree they found a beauty separate
In the poor snatch itself? — "Take Elys, there,
— 'Her head that's sharp and perfect like a
        pear,
So close and smooth are laid the few fine locks
Colored like honey oozed from topmost rocks
Sun-blanched the livelong summer' — if they
        heard
Just those two rhymes, assented at my word,
And loved them as I love who have run
These fingers through those pale locks, let the
        sun
Into the white cool skin — who first could clutch,
Then praise — I needs must be a god to such.
Or what if some, above themselves, and yet
How had he been superior to Eglamor? Beneath me, like their Eglamor, have set
An impress on our gift? So, men believe
And worship what they know not, nor receive
Delight from. Have they fancies — slow, perchance,
Not at their beck, which indistinctly glance
Until, by song, each floating part be linked
To each, and all grow palpable, distinct?"
He pondered this.
                  Meanwhile, sounds low and drear
Stole on him, and a noise of footsteps, near
And nearer, while the underwood was pushed
Aside, the larches grazed, the dead leaves
        crushed
At the approach of men. The wind seemed laid;
Only, the trees shrunk slightly and a shade
Came o'er the sky although 't was mid-day yet:

You saw each half-shut downcast floweret
Flutter — "a Roman bride, when they'd dispart
Her unbound tresses with the Sabine dart,
Holding that famous rape in memory still,
Felt creep into her curls the iron chill,
And looked thus," Eglamor would say — indeed
This is answered by Eglamor himself: 'T is Eglamor, no other, these precede
Home hither in the woods. "'T were surely sweet
Far from the scene of one's forlorn defeat
To sleep!" judged Naddo, who in person led
Jongleurs and Trouveres, chanting at their head,
A scanty company; for, sooth to say,
Our beaten Troubadour had seen his day.
Old worshippers were something shamed, old
        friends
Nigh weary; still the death proposed amends.
"Let us but get them safely through my song
And home again!" quoth Naddo.
                              All along,
This man (they rest the bier upon the sand)
— This calm corpse with the loose flowers in his
        hand,
Eglamor, lived Sordello's opposite.
For him indeed was Naddo's notion right,
And verse a temple-worship vague and vast,
A ceremony that withdrew the last
Opposing bolt, looped back the lingering veil
Which hid the holy place: should one so frail
Stand there without such effort? or repine
If much was blank, uncertain at the shrine
He knelt before, till, soothed by many a rite,
The power responded, and some sound or sight
                Grew up, his own forever, to be fixed,
One who belonged to what he loved, In rhyme, the beautiful, forever! — mixed
With his own life, unloosed when he
        should please,
Having it safe at hand, ready to ease
All pain, remove all trouble; every time
He loosed that fancy from its bonds of rhyme,
(Like Perseus when he loosed his naked love)
Faltering; so distinct and far above
Himself, these fancies! He, no genius rare,
Transfiguring in fire or wave or air
At will, but a poor gnome that, cloistered up
In some rock-chamber with his agate cup,
His topaz rod, his seed-pearl, in these few
And their arrangement finds enough to do
For his best art. Then, how he loved that art!
The calling marking him a man apart
From men — one not to care, take counsel for
Cold hearts, comfortless faces — (Eglamor
Was neediest of his tribe) — since verse, the gift,
Was his, and men, the whole of them, must shift
Without it, e'en content themselves with wealth
And pomp and power, snatching a life by stealth.
So, Eglamor was not without his pride!
Loving his art and rewarded by it, The sorriest bat which cowers
        throughout noontide
While other birds are jocund, has one
        time
When moon and stars are blinded, and the prime
Of earth is his to claim, nor find a peer;
And Eglamor was noblest poet here —
He well knew, 'mid those April woods, he cast
Conceits upon in plenty as he passed,

That Naddo might suppose him not to think
Entirely on the coming triumph : wink
At the one weakness ! 'T was a fervid child,
That song of his ; no brother of the guild
Had e'er conceived its like. The rest you know,
The exaltation and the overthrow :
Our poet lost his purpose, lost his rank,
His life — to that it came. Yet envy sank
Within him, as he heard Sordello out,
And, for the first time, shouted — tried to shout
Like others, not from any zeal to show
Pleasure that way : the common sort did so.
What else was Eglamor? who, bending down
As they, placed his beneath Sordello's crown,
Printed a kiss on his successor's hand,
Left one great tear on it, then joined his band
— In time ; for some were watching at the door :
Who knows what envy may effect?   "Give o'er,
Nor charm his lips, nor craze him ! " (here one spied
And disengaged the withered crown) — " Beside
His crown? How prompt and clear those verses rang
To answer yours ! nay, sing them ! "   And he sang
Them calmly. Home he went ; friends used to wait
His coming, zealous to congratulate ;
But, to a man, — so quickly runs report, —
Could do no less than leave him, and escort
His rival. That eve, then, bred many a thought :
What must his future life be ? was he brought
So low, who stood so lofty this Spring morn?
At length he said, " Best sleep now with my scorn,
And by to-morrow I devise some plain
Expedient ! " So, he slept, nor woke again.
Ending with what had possessed him. They found as much, those friends, when they returned
O'erflowing with the marvels they had learned
About Sordello's paradise, his roves
Among the hills and vales and plains and groves,
Wherein, no doubt, this lay was roughly cast,
Polished by slow degrees, completed last
To Eglamor's discomfiture and death.
    Such form the chanters now, and, out of breath,
They lay the beaten man in his abode,
Naddo reciting that same luckless ode,
Doleful to hear. Sordello could explore
By means of it, however, one step more
In joy ; and, mastering the round at length,
Learnt how to live in weakness as in strength,
When from his covert forth he stood, addressed
Eglamor, bade the tender ferns invest,
Primæval pines o'ercanopy his couch,
And, most of all, his fame — (shall I avouch
Eglamor heard it, dead though he might look,
And laughed as from his brow Sordello took
The crown, and laid on the bard's breast, and said
It was a crown, now, fit for poet's head ?)
— Continue. Nor the prayer quite fruitless fell,
A plant they have, yielding a three-leaved bell
Which whitens at the heart ere noon, and ails
Till evening ; evening gives it to her gales

To clear away with such forgotten things
As are an eyesore to the morn : this brings
Him to their mind, and bears his very name.
Eglamor done with, So much for Eglamor. My own month came ;
Sordello begins. 'T was a sunrise of blossoming and May.
Beneath a flowering laurel thicket lay
Sordello ; each new sprinkle of white stars
That smell fainter of wine than Massic jars
Dug up at Baiæ, when the south wind shed
The ripest, made him happier ; filleted
And robed the same, only a lute beside
Lay on the turf. Before him far and wide
The country stretched : Goito slept behind
— The castle and its covert, which confined
Him with his hopes and fears ; so fain of old
To leave the story of his birth untold.
At intervals, 'spite the fantastic glow
Of his Apollo-life, a certain low
And wretched whisper, winding through the bliss,
Admonished, no such fortune could be his,
All was quite false and sure to fade one day :
The closelier drew he round him his array
Of brilliance to expel the truth. But when
A reason for his difference from men
Surprised him at the grave, he took no rest
While aught of that old life, superbly dressed
Down to its meanest incident, remained
A mystery : alas, they soon explained
Away Apollo ! and the tale amounts
To this : when at Vicenza both her counts
Who he really was, Banished the Vivaresi kith and kin,
Those Maltraversi hung on Ecelin,
and why at Goito. Reviled him as he followed ; he for spite
Must fire their quarter, though that self-same night
Among the flames young Ecelin was born
Of Adelaide, there too, and barely torn
From the roused populace hard on the rear,
By a poor archer when his chieftain's fear
Grew high ; into the thick Elcorte leapt,
Saved her, and died ; no creature left except
His child to thank. And when the full escape
Was known — how men impaled from chine to nape
Unlucky Prata, all to pieces spurned
Bishop Pistore's concubines, and burned
Taurello's entire household, flesh and fell,
Missing the sweeter prey — such courage well
Might claim reward. The orphan, ever since,
Sordello, had been nurtured by his prince
Within a blind retreat where Adelaide —
(For, once this notable discovery made,
The past at every point was understood)
— Might harbor easily when times were rude,
When Azzo schemed for Palma, to retrieve
That pledge of Agnes Este — loth to leave
Mantua unguarded with a vigilant eye,
While there Taurello bode ambiguously —
He who could have no motive now to moil
For his own fortunes since their utter spoil —
As it were worth while yet (went the report)
To disengage himself from her. In short,
Apollo vanished ; a mean youth, just named
His lady's minstrel, was to be proclaimed

—How shall I phrase it? — Monarch of the World!

He, so little, would fain be so much:

For, on the day when that array was furled
Forever, and in place of one a slave
To longings, wild indeed, but longings save
In dreams as wild, suppressed — one daring not
Assume the mastery such dreams allot,
Until a magical equipment, strength,
Grace, wisdom, decked him too, — he chose at length,
Content with unproved wits and failing frame,
In virtue of his simple will, to claim
That mastery, no less — to do his best
With means so limited, and let the rest
Go by, — the seal was set: never again
Sordello could in his own sight remain

Leaves the dream he may be something,

One of the many, one with hopes and cares
And interests nowise distinct from theirs,
Only peculiar in a thriveless store
Of fancies, which were fancies and no more;
Never again for him and for the crowd
A common law was challenged and allowed
If calmly reasoned of, howe'er denied
By a mad impulse nothing justified
Short of Apollo's presence. The divorce
Is clear: why needs Sordello square his course
By any known example? Men no more
Compete with him than tree and flower before.
Himself, inactive, yet is greater far
Than such as act, each stooping to his star,
Acquiring thence his function; he has gained
The same result with meaner mortals trained
To strength or beauty, moulded to express
Each the idea that rules him; since no less
He comprehends that function, but can still
Embrace the others, take of might his fill
With Richard as of grace with Palma, mix
Their qualities, or for a moment fix
On one; abiding free meantime, uncramped
By any partial organ, never stamped
Strong, and to strength turning all energies —
Wise, and restricted to becoming wise —
That is, he loves not, nor possesses One
Idea that, star-like over, lures him on
To its exclusive purpose. " Fortunate!
This flesh of mine ne'er strove to emulate
A soul so various — took no casual mould
Of the first fancy and, contracted, cold,
Clogged her forever —soul averse to change
As flesh: whereas flesh leaves soul free to range,
Remains itself a blank, cast into shade,
Encumbers little, if it cannot aid.

For the fact that he can do nothing,

So, range, free soul! — who, by self-consciousness,
The last drop of all beauty dost express —
The grace of seeing grace, a quintessence
For thee: while for the world, that can dispense
Wonder on men who, themselves, wonder — make
A shift to love at second-hand, and take
For idols those who do but idolize,
Themselves, — the world that counts men strong or wise,

Who, themselves, court strength, wisdom, — it shall bow
Surely in unexampled worship now,
Discerning me! " —
(Dear monarch, I beseech,
Notice how lamentably wide a breach
Is here: discovering this, discover too
What our poor world has possibly to do
With it! As pigmy natures as you please —
So much the better for you; take your ease,
Look on, and laugh; style yourself God alone;
Strangle some day with a cross olive-stone!
All that is right enough: but why want us
To know that you yourself know thus and thus?)
"The world shall bow to me conceiving all
Man's life, who see its blisses, great and small,
Afar — not tasting any; no machine
To exercise my utmost will is mine:
Be mine mere consciousness! Let men perceive
What I could do, a mastery believe,
Asserted and established to the throng
By their selected evidence of song
Which now shall prove, whate'er they are, or seek
To be, I am — whose words, not actions speak,
Who change no standards of perfection, vex
With no strange forms created to perplex,
But just perform their bidding and no more,
At their own satiating-point give o'er,
While each shall love in me the love that leads
His soul to power's perfection." Song, not deeds,
(For we get tired) was chosen. Fate would brook
Mankind no other organ; he would look
For not another channel to dispense
His own volition by, receive men's sense
Of its supremacy — would live content,
Obstructed else, with merely verse for vent.

Yet is able to imagine everything,

Nor should, for instance, strength an outlet seek
And, striving, be admired; nor grace bespeak
Wonder, displayed in gracious attitudes;
Nor wisdom, poured forth, change unseemly moods:
But he would give and take on song's one point.
Like some huge throbbing stone that, poised a-joint,
Sounds, to affect on its basaltic bed,
Must sue in just one accent; tempests shed
Thunder, and raves the windstorm: only let
That key by any little noise be set —
The far benighted hunter's halloo pitch
On that, the hungry curlew chance to scritch
Or serpent hiss it, rustling through the rift,
However loud, however low — all lift
The groaning monster, stricken to the heart.
Lo ye, the world's concernment, for its part,

If the world esteem this equivalent.

And this, for his, will hardly interfere!
Its businesses in blood and blaze this year
But while the hour away — a pastime slight
Till he shall step upon the platform: right!
And, now thus much is settled, cast in rough,
Proved feasible, be counselled! thought enough, —

Slumber, Sordello! any day will serve:
Were it a less digested plan! how swerve
To-morrow? Meanwhile eat these sun-dried
   grapes,
And watch the soaring hawk there! Life es-
   capes
Merrily thus.
         He thoroughly read o'er
His truchman Naddo's missive six times more,
Praying him visit Mantua and supply
A famished world.
         The evening star was high
When he reached Mantua, but his fame ar-
   rived
Before him: friends applauded, foes connived,
And Naddo looked an angel, and the rest
Angels, and all these angels would be blest
Supremely by a song — the thrice-renowned
Goito-manufacture. Then he found
(Casting about to satisfy the crowd)

He has   That happy vehicle, so late allowed,
loved   A sore annoyance; 't was the song's
song's re-   effect
sults, not   He cared for, scarce the song itself:
song;   reflect!
In the past life, what might be singing's use?
Just to delight his Delians, whose profuse
Praise, not the toilsome process which procured
That praise, enticed Apollo: dreams abjured,
No overleaping means for ends — take both
For granted or take neither! I am loth
To say the rhymes at last were Eglamor's;
But Naddo, chuckling, bade competitors
Go pine; "the master certes meant to waste
No effort, cautiously had probed the taste
He 'd please anon: true bard, in short, disturb
His title if they could; nor spur nor curb,
Fancy nor reason, wanting in him; whence
The staple of his verses, common sense:
He built on man's broad nature — gift of gifts,
That power to build! The world contented
   shifts
With counterfeits enough, a dreary sort
Of warriors, statesmen, ere it can extort
Its poet-soul — that 's, after all, a freak
(The having eyes to see and tongue to speak)
With our herd's stupid sterling happiness
So plainly incompatible that — yes —
Yes — should a son of his improve the breed
And turn out poet, he were cursed indeed!"
"Well, there 's Goito and its woods anon,
If the worst happen; best go stoutly on
Now!" thought Sordello.

So, must   Ay, and goes on yet!
effect this   You pother with your glossaries to
to obtain   get
those.   A notion of the Troubadour's intent
In rondel, tenzon, virlai, or sirvent —
Much as you study arras how to twirl
His angelot, plaything of page and girl
Once; but you surely reach, at last, — or, no!
Never quite reach what struck the people so,
As from the welter of their time he drew
Its elements successively to view,
Followed all actions backward on their course,
And catching up, unmingled at the source,
Such a strength, such a weakness, added then
A touch or two, and turned them into men.

Virtue took form, nor vice refused a shape;
Here heaven opened, there was hell agape,
As Saint this simpered past in sanctity,
Sinner the other flared portentous by
A greedy people. Then why stop, surprised
At his success? The scheme was realized
Too suddenly in one respect: a crowd
Praising, eyes quick to see, and lips as loud
To speak, delicious homage to receive,
The woman's breath to feel upon his sleeve,
Who said, "But Anafest — why asks he less
Than Lucio, in your verses? how confess,
It seemed too much but yestereve!" — the
   youth,
Who bade him earnestly, "Avow the truth!
You love Bianca, surely, from your song;
I knew I was unworthy!" — soft or strong,
In poured such tributes ere he had arranged
Ethereal ways to take them, sorted, changed,
Digested. Courted thus at unawares,
In spite of his pretensions and his cares,
He caught himself shamefully hankering
After the obvious petty joys that spring
From true life, fain relinquish pedestal

He suc-   And condescend with pleasures —
ceeds a   one and all
little, but   To be renounced, no doubt; for, thus
fails   to chain
more;   Himself to single joys and so refrain
From tasting their quintessence, frustrates,
   sure,
His prime design; each joy must he abjure
Even for love of it.
         He laughed: what sage
But perishes if from his magic page
He look because, at the first line, a proof
'T was heard salutes him from the cavern roof?
"On! Give yourself, excluding aught beside,
To the day's task; compel your slave provide
Its utmost at the soonest; turn the leaf
Thoroughly conned. These lays of yours, in
   brief —
Cannot men bear, now, something better? —
   fly
A pitch beyond this unreal pageantry
Of essences? the period sure has ceased
For such: present us with ourselves, at least,
Not portions of ourselves, mere loves and hates
Made flesh: wait not!"

Tries   Awhile the poet waits
again, is   However. The first trial was
no better   enough:
satisfied,   He left imagining, to try the stuff
That held the imaged thing, and, let it writhe
Never so fiercely, scarce allowed a tithe
To reach the light — his Language. How he
   sought
The cause, conceived a cure, and slow re-
   wrought
That Language, — welding words into the crude
Mass from the new speech round him, till a
   rude
Armor was hammered out, in time to be
Approved beyond the Roman panoply
Melted to make it, — boots not. This obtained
With some ado, no obstacle remained
To using it; accordingly he took
An action with its actors, quite forsook

Himself to live in each, returned anon
With the result — a creature, and, by one
And one, proceeded leisurely to equip
Its limbs in harness of his workmanship.
"Accomplished! Listen, Mantuans!" Fond
    essay!
Piece after piece that armor broke away,
Because perceptions whole, like that he sought
To clothe, reject so pure a work of thought
As language : thought may take perception's
    place
But hardly co-exist in any case,
Being its mere presentment — of the whole
By parts, the simultaneous and the sole
By the successive and the many. Lacks
The crowd perception? painfully it tacks
Thought to thought, which Sordello, needing
    such,
Has rent perception into : it 's to clutch
And reconstruct — his office to diffuse,
Destroy : as hard, then, to obtain a Muse
As to become Apollo. "For the rest,
E'en if some wondrous vehicle expressed
The whole dream, what impertinence in me
So to express it, who myself can be
The dream! nor, on the other hand, are those
I sing to, over-likely to suppose

And declines from the ideal of song.

        A higher than the highest I present
        Now, which they praise already : be
            content
        Both parties, rather — they with the
            old verse,
And I with the old praise — far go, fare
    worse!"
A few adhering rivets loosed, upsprings
The angel, sparkles off his mail, which rings
Whirled from each delicatest limb it warps,
So might Apollo from the sudden corpse
Of Hyacinth have cast his luckless quoits.
He set to celebrating the exploits
Of Montfort o'er the Mountaineers.
                        Then came
The world's revenge: their pleasure, now his aim
Merely, — what was it? "Not to play the fool
So much as learn our lesson in your school!"
Replied the world. He found that, every time
He gained applause by any ballad-rhyme,
His auditory recognized no jot
As he intended, and, mistaking not
Him for his meanest hero, ne'er was dunce
Sufficient to believe him — all, at once.
His will . . . conceive it caring for his will!
— Mantuans, the main of them, admiring still
How a mere singer, ugly, stunted, weak,
Had Montfort at completely (so to speak)
His fingers' ends; while past the praise-tide
    swept
To Montfort, either's share distinctly kept :
The true meed for true merit! — his abates

What is the world's recognition worth?

        Into a sort he most repudiates,
        And on them angrily he turns. Who
            were
        The Mantuans, after all, that he
            should care
        About their recognition, ay or no?
In spite of the convention months ago,
(Why blink the truth?) was not he forced to
    help

This same ungrateful audience, every whelp
Of Naddo's litter, make them pass for peers
With the bright band of old Goito years,
As erst he toiled for flower or tree? Why,
    there
Sat Palma! Adelaide's funereal hair
Ennobled the next corner. Ay, he strewed
A fairy dust upon that multitude,
Although he feigned to take them by them-
    selves ;
His giants dignified those puny elves,
Sublime their faint applause. In short, he
    found
Himself still footing a delusive round,
Remote as ever from the self-display
He meant to compass, hampered every way
By what he hoped assistance. Wherefore then
Continue, make believe to find in men
A use he found not ?
            Weeks, months, years went by,
And lo, Sordello vanished utterly,
Sundered in twain; each spectral part at strife
With each ; one jarred against another life ;

How, poet no longer in unity with man,

How, poet   The Poet thwarting hopelessly the
no longer   Man,
in unity   Who, fooled no longer, free in fancy
with man,   ran
Here, there, — let slip no opportunities
As pitiful, forsooth, beside the prize
To drop on him some no-time and acquit
His constant faith (the Poet-half's to wit —
That waiving any compromise between
No joy and all joy kept the hunger keen
B yond most methods) — of incurring scoff
From the Man-portion — not to be put off
With self-reflectings by the Poet's scheme,
Though ne'er so bright. Who sauntered forth
    in dream,
Dressed anyhow, nor waited mystic frames,
Immeasurable gifts, astounding claims,
But just his sorry self ? — who yet might be
Sorrier for aught he in reality
Achieved, so pinioned Man's the Poet-part,
Fondling, in turn of fancy, verse ; the Art
Developing his soul a thousand ways —
Potent, by its assistance, to amaze
The multitude with majesties, convince
Each sort of nature, that the nature's prince
Accosted it. Language, the makeshift, grew
Into a bravest of expedients, too ;
Apollo, seemed it now, perverse had thrown
Quiver and bow away, the lyre alone
Sufficed. While, out of dream, his day's work
    went
To tune a crazy tenzon or sirvent —
So hampered him the Man-part, thrust to judge
Between the bard and the bard's audience,
    grudge
A minute's toil that missed its due reward !
But the complete Sordello, Man and Bard,

The whole visible Sordello goes wrong

            John's cloud-girt angel, this foot on
    the land,
        That on the sea, with, open in his
        hand,
        A bitter-sweetling of a book — was
        gone.
Then, if internal struggles to be one
Which frittered him incessantly piecemeal.

Referred, ne'er so obliquely, to the real
Intruding Mantuans! ever with some call
To action while he pondered, once for all,
Which looked the easier effort — to pursue
This course, still leap o'er paltry joys, yearn
　　　through
The present ill-appreciated stage
Of self-revealment, and compel the age
Know him; or else, forswearing bard-craft, wake
From out his lethargy and nobly shake
Off timid habits of denial, mix
With men, enjoy like men. Ere he could fix
On aught, in rushed the Mantuans; much they
　　　cared
For his perplexity! Thus unprepared,
The obvious if not only shelter lay
With those In deeds, the dull conventions of his
too hard　　day
for half of Prescribed the like of him: why not
him,　　be glad
'T is settled Palma's minstrel, good or bad,
Submits to this and that established rule?
Let Vidal change, or any other fool,
His murrey-colored robe for filamot,
And crop his hair; too skin-deep, is it not,
Such vigor? Then, a sorrow to the heart,
His talk! Whatever topics they might start
Had to be groped for in his consciousness
Straight, and as straight delivered them by
　　　guess.
Only obliged to ask himself, "What was,"
A speedy answer followed; but, alas,
One of God's large ones, tardy to condense
Itself into a period; answers whence
A tangle of conclusions must be stripped
At any risk ere, trim to pattern clipped,
They matched rare specimens the Mantuan flock
Regaled him with, each talker from his stock
Of sorted-o'er opinions, every stage,
Juicy in youth or desiccate with age,
Fruits like the fig-tree's, rathe-ripe, rotten-rich,
Sweet-sour, all tastes to take: a practice which
He too had not impossibly attained,
Once either of those fancy-flights restrained;
(For, at conjecture how might words appear
To others, playing there what happened here,
And occupied abroad by what he spurned
At home, 't was slipped, the occasion he returned
To seize :) he 'd strike that lyre adroitly —
　　　speech,
Would but a twenty-cubit plectre reach;
A clever hand, consummate instrument,
Were both brought close; each excellency went
For nothing, else. The question Naddo asked,
Had just a lifetime moderately tasked
To answer, Naddo's fashion. More disgust
Of whom And more: why move his soul, since
he is also　　move it must
too con- At minute's notice or as good it
temptuous.　　failed
To move at all? The end was, he retailed
Some ready-made opinion, put to use
This quip, that maxim, ventured reproduce
Gestures and tones — at any folly caught
Serving to finish with, nor too much sought
If false or true 't was spoken; praise and blame
Of what he said grew pretty nigh the same
—Meantime awards to meantime acts: his soul,

Unequal to the compassing a whole,
Saw, in a tenth part, less and less to strive
About. And as for men in turn . . . contrive
Who could to take eternal interest
In them, so hate the worst, so love the best!
Though, in pursuance of his passive plan,
He hailed, decried, the proper way.
　　　　　　　　　　　　As Man.
So figured he; and how as Poet? Verse
Came only not to a stand-still. The worse,
That his poor piece of daily work to do
Was, not sink under any rivals; who
He pleases Loudly and long enough, without
neither　　these qualms,
himself Turned, from Bocafoli's stark-naked
nor them :　　psalms,
To Plara's sonnets spoilt by toying with,
"As knops that stud some almug to the pith
Pricked for gum, wry thence, and crinklèd
　　　worse
Than pursèd eyelids of a river-horse
Sunning himself o' the slime when whirrs the
　　　breeze " —
Gad-fly, that is. He might compete with these!
But — but —
　　　　　"Observe a pompion-twine afloat;
Pluck me one cup from off the castle-moat!
Which the Along with cup you raise leaf, stalk
best judges　　and root,
account The entire surface of the pool to
for.　　boot.
So could I pluck a cup, put in one song
A single sight, did not my hand, too strong,
Twitch in the least the root-strings of the whole.
How should externals satisfy my soul?"
"Why that 's precise the error Squarcialupe "
(Hazarded Naddo) "finds; ' the man can't stoop
To sing us out,' quoth he, ' a mere romance;
He 'd fain do better than the best, enhance
The subjects' rarity, work problems out
Therewith.' Now, you 're a bard, a bard past
　　　doubt,
And no philosopher; why introduce
Crotchets like these? fine, surely, but no use
In poetry — which still must be, to strike,
Based upon common sense; there 's nothing like
Appealing to our nature! what beside
Was your first poetry? No tricks were tried.
In that, no hollow thrills, affected throes!
' The man,' said we, ' tells his own joys and
　　　woes :
We 'll trust him.' Would you have your songs
　　　endure?
Build on the human heart! — why, to be sure
Yours is one sort of heart — but I mean theirs,
Ours, every one's, the healthy heart one cares
To build on! Central peace, mother of strength,
That 's father of . . . nay, go yourself that
　　　length,
Ask those calm-hearted doers what they do
When they have got their calm! And is it
　　　true,
Fire rankles at the heart of every globe?
Perhaps. But these are matters one may probe
Too deeply for poetic purposes:
Rather select a theory that . . . yes,
Laugh! what does that prove? — stations you
　　　midway

And saves some little o'er-refining. Nay,
That's rank injustice done me! I restrict
The poet? Don't I hold the poet picked
Out of a host of warriors, statesmen . . . did
I tell you? Very like! As well you hid
That sense of power, you have! True bards
believe
All able to achieve what they achieve —
That is, just nothing — in one point abide
Profounder simpletons than all beside.
Oh, ay! The knowledge that you are a bard
Must constitute your prime, nay sole, reward!"
So prattled Naddo, busiest of the tribe
Of genius-haunters — how shall I describe
What grubs or nips or rubs or rips — your louse
For love, your flea for hate, magnanimous,

Their criticisms give small comfort: Malignant, Pappacoda, Tagliafer,
Picking a sustenance from wear and
tear
By implements it sedulous employs
To undertake, lay down, mete out, o'er-toise
Sordello? Fifty creepers to elude
At once! They settled stanchly: shame ensued:
Behold the monarch of mankind succumb
To the last fool who turned him round his
thumb,
As Naddo styled it! 'T was not worth oppose
The matter of a moment, gainsay those
He aimed at getting rid of; better think
Their thoughts and speak their speech, secure
to slink
Back expeditiously to his safe place,
And chew the cud — what he and what his race
Were really, each of them. Yet even this
Conformity was partial. He would miss
Some point, brought into contact with them ere
Assured in what small segment of the sphere
Of his existence they attended him;
Whence blunders, falsehoods rectified — a grim
List — slur it over! How? If dreams were
tried,
His will swayed sicklily from side to side,
Nor merely neutralized his waking act
But tended e'en in fancy to distract
The intermediate will, the choice of means.
He lost the art of dreaming: Mantuan scenes
Supplied a baron, say, he sang before,
Handsomely reckless, full to running o'er
Of gallantries; "abjure the soul, content
With body, therefore!" Scarcely had he bent
Himself in dream thus low, when matter fast
Cried out, he found, for spirit to contrast
And task it duly; by advances slight,
The simple stuff becoming composite,
Count Lori grew Apollo — best recall
His fancy! Then would some rough peasant-
Paul,
Like those old Ecelin confers with, glance
His gay apparel o'er; that countenance
Gathered his shattered fancies into one,
And, body clean abolished, soul alone

And his own degradation is complete. Sufficed the gray Paulician: by and by,
To balance the ethereality,
Passions were needed; foiled he sank
again.
Meanwhile the world rejoiced ('t is
time explain)
Because a sudden sickness set it free

From Adelaide. Missing the mother-bee,
Her mountain-hive Romano swarmed; at once
A rustle-forth of daughters and of sons
Blackened the valley. "I am sick too, old,
Half-crazed I think; what good's the Kaiser's
gold
To such an one? God help me! for I catch
My children's greedy sparkling eyes at watch —
'He bears that double breastplate on,' they say,
'So many minutes less than yesterday!'
Beside, Monk Hilary is on his knees
Now, sworn to kneel and pray till God shall
please
Exact a punishment for many things
You know, and some you never knew; which
brings
To memory, Azzo's sister Beatrix
And Richard's Giglia are my Alberic's
And Ecelin's betrothed; the Count himself
Must get my Palma: Ghibellin and Guelf
Mean to embrace each other." So began

Adelaide's death: what happens on it: Romano's missive to his fighting
man
Taurello — on the Tuscan's death,
away
With Friedrich sworn to sail from Naples' bay
Next month for Syria. Never thunder-clap
Out of Vesuvius' throat, like this mishap
Startled him. "That accursed Vicenza! I
Absent, and she selects this time to die!
Ho, fellows, for Vicenza!" Half a score
Of horses ridden dead, he stood before
Romano in his reeking spurs: too late —
"Boniface urged me, Este could not wait,"
The chieftain stammered; "let me die in
peace —
Forget me! Was it I who craved increase
Of rule? Do you and Friedrich plot your worst
Against the Father: as you found me first
So leave me now. Forgive me! Palma, sure,
Is at Goito still. Retain that lure —
Only be pacified!"

The country rung
With such a piece of news: on every tongue,
How Ecelin's great servant, congeed off,
Had done a long day's service, so, might doff
The green and yellow, and recover breath
At Mantua, whither, — since Retrude's death,
(The girlish slip of a Sicilian bride
From Otho's house, he carried to reside
At Mantua till the Ferrarese should pile
A structure worthy her imperial style,
The gardens raise, the statues there enshrine,
She never lived to see) — although his line
Was ancient in her archives and she took
A pride in him, that city, nor forsook
Her child when he forsook himself and spent
A prowess on Romano surely meant
For his own growth — whither he ne'er resorts
If wholly satisfied (to trust reports)
With Ecelin. So, forward in a trice
Were shows to greet him. "Take a friend's
advice,"
Quoth Naddo to Sordello, "nor be rash
Because your rivals (nothing can abash
Some folks) demur that we pronounced you best
To sound the great man's welcome; 't is a test,
Remember! Stroiavacca looks asquint.

The rough fat sloven; and there's plenty hint
Your pinions have received of late a shock —
Outsoar them, cobswan of the silver flock!
And a trouble it occasions Sordello. Sing well!" A signal wonder, song's
no whit
Facilitated.
            Fast the minutes flit;
Another day, Sordello finds, will
     bring
The soldier, and he cannot choose but sing;
So, a last shift, quits Mantua — slow, alone:
Out of that aching brain, a very stone,
Song must be struck. What occupies that
     front?
Just how he was more awkward than his wont
The night before, when Naddo, who had seen
Taurello on his progress, praised the mien
For dignity no crosses could affect —
Such was a joy, and might not he detect
A satisfaction if established joys
Were proved imposture? Poetry annoys
Its utmost: wherefore fret? Verses may come
Or keep away! And thus he wandered, dumb
Till evening, when he paused, thoroughly spent,
On a blind hill-top: down the gorge he went,
Yielding himself up as to an embrace.
The moon came out; like features of a face,
A querulous fraternity of pines,
Sad blackthorn clumps, leafless and grovelling
     vines
Also came out, made gradually up
The picture; 't was Goito's mountain-cup
And castle. He had dropped through one de-
     file
He never dared explore, the Chief erewhile
He chances upon his old environment, Had vanished by. Back rushed the
dream, enwrapped
Him wholly. 'T was Apollo now
they lapped,
Those mountains, not a pettish min-
strel meant
To wear his soul away in discontent,
Brooding on fortune's malice. Heart and brain
Swelled; he expanded to himself again,
As some thin seedling spice-tree starved and
     frail,
Pushing between cat's head and ibis' tail
Crusted into the porphyry pavement smooth,
—Suffered remain just as it sprung, to soothe
The Soldan's pining daughter, never yet
Well in her chilly green-glazed minaret,—
When rooted up, the sunny day she died,
And flung into the common court beside
Its parent tree. Come home, Sordello! Soon
Was he low muttering, beneath the moon,
Of sorrow saved, of quiet evermore, —
Since from the purpose, he maintained before,
Only resulted wailing and hot tears.
Sees but failure in all done since, Ah, the slim castle! dwindled of
late years,
But more mysterious; gone to ruin
— trails
Of vine through every loop-hole. Naught avails
The night as, torch in hand, he must explore
The maple chamber: did I say, its floor
Was made of intersecting cedar beams?
Worn now with gaps so large, there blew cold
     streams

Of air quite from the dungeon; lay your ear
Close and 't is like, one after one, you hear
In the blind darkness water drop. The nests
And nooks retain their long ranged vesture-
     chests
Empty and smelling of the iris root
The Tuscan grated o'er them to recruit
Her wasted wits. Palma was gone that day,
Said the remaining women. Last, he lay
Beside the Carian group reserved and still.
The Body, the Machine for Acting Will,
Had been at the commencement proved unfit:
That for Demonstrating, Reflecting it,
Mankind — no fitter: was the Will Itself
In fault?
         His forehead pressed the moonlit shelf
Beside the youngest marble maid awhile;
Then, raising it, he thought, with a long smile,
and resolves to desist from the like. "I shall be king again!" as he
withdrew
The envied scarf; into the font he
threw
His crown.
    Next day, no poet! "Wherefore?" asked
Taurello, when the dance of Jongleurs, masked
As devils, ended; "don't a song come next?"
The master of the pageant looked perplexed
Till Naddo's whisper came to his relief.
"His Highness knew what poets were: in brief,
Had not the tetchy race prescriptive right
To peevishness, caprice? or, call it spite,
One must receive their nature in its length
And breadth, expect the weakness with the
     strength!"
—So phrasing, till, his stock of phrases spent,
The easy-natured soldier smiled assent,
Settled his portly person, smoothed his chin,
And nodded that the bull-bait might begin.

BOOK THE THIRD

And the font took them: let our laurels lie!
Braid moonfern now with mystic trifoly
Because once more Goito gets, once more,
Sordello to itself! A dream is o'er,
And the suspended life begins anew;
Quiet those throbbing temples, then, subdue
Nature may triumph therefore; That cheek's distortion! Nature's
strict embrace,
Putting aside the past, shall soon
efface
Its print as well — factitious humors grown
Over the true — loves, hatreds not his own —
And turn him pure as some forgotten vest
Woven of painted byssus, silkiest
Tufting the Tyrrhene whelk's pearl-sheeted
     lip,
Left welter where a trireme let it slip
I' the sea, and vexed a satrap; so the stain
O' the world forsakes Sordello, with its pain,
Its pleasure: how the tinct loosening escapes,
Cloud after cloud! Mantua's familiar shapes
Die, fair and foul die, fading as they flit,
Men, women, and the pathos and the wit,
Wise speech and foolish, deeds to smile or sigh
For, good, bad, seemly or ignoble, die.
The last face glances through the eglantines.

The last voice murmurs, 'twixt the blossomed vines,
Of Men, of that machine supplied by thought
To compass self-perception with, he sought
By forcing half himself — an insane pulse
Of a god's blood, on clay it could convulse,
Never transmute — on human sights and sounds,
To watch the other half with; irksome bounds
It ebbs from to its source, a fountain sealed
Forever. Better sure be unrevealed
Than part revealed: Sordello well or ill
Is finished: then what further use of Will,
Point in the prime idea not realized,
An oversight? inordinately prized,
No less, and pampered with enough of each
Delight to prove the whole above its reach.
" To need become all natures, yet retain
The law of my own nature — to remain
Myself, yet yearn . . . as if that chestnut, think,
Should yearn for this first larch-bloom crisp and pink,
Or those pale fragrant tears where zephyrs stanch
March wounds along the fretted pine-tree branch!
Will and the means to show will, great and small,
Material, spiritual, — abjure them all
Save any so distinct, they may be left
To amuse, not tempt become! and, thus bereft,
Just as I first was fashioned would I be!
Nor, moon, is it Apollo now, but me
For her   Thou visitest to comfort and be-
son, lately   friend!
alive, dies   Swim thou into my heart, and there
again,   an end,
Since I possess thee! — nay, thus shut mine eyes
And know, quite know, by this heart's fall and rise,
When thou dost bury thee in clouds, and when
Out-standest: wherefore practise upon men
To make that plainer to myself? "
                                        Slide here
Over a sweet and solitary year
Wasted; or simply notice change in him —
How eyes, once with exploring bright, grew dim
And satiate with receiving. Some distress
Was caused, too, by a sort of consciousness
Under the imbecility, — naught kept
That down; he slept, but was aware he slept,
So, frustrated: as who brainsick made pact
Erst with the overhanging cataract
To deafen him, yet still distinguished plain
His own blood's measured clicking at his brain.
To finish. One declining Autumn day —
Few birds about the heaven chill and gray,
No wind that cared trouble the tacit woods —
He sauntered home complacently, their moods
According, his and nature's. Every spark
Was found   Of Mantua life was trodden out; so
and is lost.   dark
The embers, that the Troubadour, who sung
Hundreds of songs, forgot, its trick his tongue,
Its craft his brain, how either brought to pass
Singing at all; that faculty might class
With any of Apollo's now. The year
Began to find its early promise sere
As well. Thus beauty vanishes; thus stone

Outlingers flesh: nature's and his youth gone,
They left the world to you, and wished you joy,
When, stopping his benevolent employ,
A presage shuddered through the welkin; harsh
The earth's remonstrance followed. 'T was the marsh
Gone of a sudden. Mincio, in its place,
Laughed, a broad water, in next morning's face,
And, where the mists broke up immense and white
I' the steady wind, burned like a spilth of light
Out of the crashing of a myriad stars.
And here was nature, bound by the same bars
Of fate with him!
But nature   "No! youth once gone is gone:
is one   Deeds let escape are never to be done.
thing, man   Leaf-fall and grass-spring for the
another —   year; for us —
Oh forfeit I unalterably thus
My chance? nor two lives wait me, this to spend,
Learning save that? Nature has time, may mend
Mistake, she knows occasion will recur;
Landslip or seabreach, how affects it her
With her magnificent resources? — I
Must perish once and perish utterly.
Not any strollings now at even-close
Down the field-path, Sordello! by thorn-rows
Alive with lamp-flies, swimming spots of fire
And dew, outlining the black cypress' spire
She waits you at, Elys, who heard you first
Woo her, the snow-month through, but ere she durst
Answer 't was April. Linden-flower-time-long
Her eyes were on the ground; 't is July, strong
Now; and because white dust-clouds overwhelm
The woodside, here or by the village elm
That holds the moon, she meets you, somewhat pale,
But letting you lift up her coarse flax veil
And whisper (the damp little hand in yours)
Of love, heart's love, your heart's love that endures
Till death. Tush! No mad mixing with the rout
Of haggard ribalds wandering about
The hot torchlit wine-scented island-house
Where Friedrich holds his wickedest carouse,
Parading, — to the gay Palermitans,
Soft Messinese, dusk Saracenic clans
Having   Nuocera holds, — those tall grave
multifari-   dazzling Norse,
ous sym-   High-cheeked, lank-haired, toothed
pathies,   whiter than the morse,
Queens of the caves of jet stalactites,
He sent his barks to fetch through icy seas,
The blind night seas without a saving star,
And here in snowy birdskin robes they are,
Sordello! — here, mollitious alcoves gilt
Superb as Byzant domes that devils built!
— Ah, Byzant, there again! no chance to go
Ever like august cheery Dandolo,
Worshipping hearts about him for a wall,
Conducted, blind eyes, hundred years and all,
Through vanquished Byzant where friends note for him
What pillar, marble massive, sardius slim,
'T were fittest he transport to Venice' Square —

Flattered and promised life to touch them there
Soon, by those fervid sons of senators!
No more lifes, deaths, loves, hatreds, peaces, wars!
Ah, fragments of a whole ordained to be,
Points in the life I waited! what are ye
But roundels of a ladder which appeared
Awhile the very platform it was reared
To lift me on? — that happiness I find
Proofs of my faith in, even in the blind
Instinct which bade forego you all unless
Ye led me past yourselves. Ay, happiness

He may neither renounce nor satisfy;

Awaited me; the way life should be used
Was to acquire, and deeds like you conduced
To teach it by a self-revealment, deemed
Life's very use, so long! Whatever seemed
Progress to that, was pleasure; aught that stayed
My reaching it — no pleasure. I have laid
The ladder down; I climb not; still, aloft
The platform stretches! Blisses strong and soft,
I dared not entertain, elude me; yet
Never of what they promised could I get
A glimpse till now! The common sort, the crowd,
Exist, perceive; with Being are endowed,
However slight, distinct from what they See,
However bounded; Happiness must be,
To feed the first by gleanings from the last,
Attain its qualities, and slow or fast
Become what they behold; such peace-in-strife
By transmutation, is the Use of Life,
The Alien turning Native to the soul
Or body — which instructs me; I am whole
There and demand a Palma; had the world
Been from my soul to a like distance hurled,
'T were Happiness to make it one with me:
Whereas I must, ere I begin to Be,
Include a world, in flesh, I comprehend
In spirit now; and this done, what 's to blend
With? Naught is Alien in the world — my Will

In the process to which is pleasure,

Owns all already; yet can turn it — still
Less — Native, since my Means to correspond
With Will are so unworthy, 't was my bond
To tread the very joys that tantalize
Most now, into a grave, never to rise.
I die then! Will the rest agree to die?
Next Age or no? Shall its Sordello try
Clue after clue, and catch at last the clue
I miss? — that 's underneath my finger too,
Twice, thrice a day, perhaps, — some yearning traced
Deeper, some petty consequence embraced
Closer! Why fled I Mantua, then? — complained
So much my Will was fettered, yet remained
Content within a tether half the range
I could assign it? — able to exchange
My ignorance (I felt) for knowledge, and
Idle because I could thus understand —
Could e'en have penetrated to its core
Our mortal mystery, yet — fool — forbore,
Preferred elaborating in the dark

My casual stuff, by any wretched spark
Born of my predecessors, though one stroke
Of mine had brought the flame forth! Mantua's yoke,
My minstrel's-trade, was to behold mankind, —
My own concern was just to bring my mind
Behold, just extricate, for my acquist,
Each object suffered stifle in the mist
Which hazard, custom, blindness interpose
Betwixt things and myself."
                Whereat he rose
The level wind carried above the firs
Clouds, the irrevocable travellers,
Onward.
      " Pushed thus into a drowsy copse,
Arms twine about my neck, each eyelid drops
Under a humid finger; while there fleets
Outside the screen, a pageant time repeats
Never again! To be deposed, immured

While renunciation ensures despair.

Clandestinely — still petted, still assured
To govern were fatiguing work — the Sight
Fleeting meanwhile! 'T is noontide: wreak ere night
Somehow my will upon it, rather! Slake
This thirst somehow, the poorest impress take
That serves! A blasted bud displays you, torn,
Faint rudiments of the full flower unborn;
But who divines what glory coats o'erclasp
Of the bulb dormant in the mummy's grasp
Taurello sent?" . . .
             " Taurello? Palma sent
Your Trouvere," (Naddo interposing leant
Over the lost bard's shoulder) — " and, believe,
You cannot more reluctantly receive
Than I pronounce her message: we depart
Together. What avail a poet's heart
Verona's pomps and gauds? five blades of grass
Suffice him. News? Why, where your marish was,
On its mud-banks smoke rises after smoke
I' the valley, like a spout of hell new-broke.
Oh, the world's tidings! small your thanks, I guess,
For them. The father of our Patroness
Has played Taurello an astounding trick,
Parts between Ecelin and Alberic
His wealth and goes into a convent: both
Wed Guelfs: the Count and Palma plighted troth
A week since at Verona: and they want
You doubtless to contrive the marriage-chant
Ere Richard storms Ferrara." Then was told
The tale from the beginning — how, made bold
By Salinguerra's absence, Guelfs had burned
And pillaged till he unawares returned
To take revenge: how Azzo and his friend
Were doing their endeavor, how the end
O' the siege was nigh, and how the Count, released
From further care, would with his marriage

There is yet a way of escaping this;

feast
Inaugurate a new and better rule,
Absorbing thus Romano.
           " Shall I school
My master," added Naddo, " and suggest

How you may clothe in a poetic vest
These doings, at Verona? Your response
To Palma! Wherefore jest? 'Depart at once?'
A good resolve! In truth, I hardly hoped
So prompt an acquiescence. Have you groped
Out wisdom in the wilds here? — Thoughts
    may be
Over-poetical for poetry.
Pearl-white, you poets liken Palma's neck;
And yet what spoils an orient like some speck
Of genuine white, turning its own white gray?
You take me? Curse the cicala!"
                                        One more day,
One eve — appears Verona! Many a group,
(You mind) instructed of the osprey's swoop
On lynx and ounce, was gathering — Christendom
Sure to receive, whate'er the end was, from
The evening's purpose cheer or detriment,
Since Friedrich only waited some event
Like this, of Ghibellins establishing
Themselves within Ferrara, ere, as King
Of Lombardy, he'd glad descend there, wage
Old warfare with the Pontiff, disengage
His barons from the burghers, and restore
The rule of Charlemagne, broken of yore
By Hildebrand.
Which he   I' the palace, each by each,
now takes   Sordello sat and Palma: little speech
by obeying   At first in that dim closet, face with
Palma: face
(Despite the tumult in the market-place)
Exchanging quick low laughters: now would
    rush
Word upon word to meet a sudden flush,
A look left off, a shifting lips' surmise —
But for the most part their two histories
Who there- Ran best through the locked fingers
upon be-   and linked arms.
comes his   And so the night flew on with its
associate.   alarms
Till in burst one of Palma's retinue;
"Now, Lady!" gasped he. Then arose the
    two
And leaned into Verona's air, dead-still.
A balcony lay black beneath until
Out, 'mid a gush of torchfire, gray-haired men
Came on it and harangued the people: ther
Sea-like that people surging to and fro
Shouted, "Hale forth the carroch — trumpets,
    ho,
A flourish! Run it in the ancient grooves!
Back from the bell! Hammer — that whom
    behooves
May hear the League is up! Peal — learn who
    list,
Verona means not first of towns break tryst
To-morrow with the League!"
                                        Enough. Now turn —
Over the eastern cypresses: discern!
Is any beacon set a-glimmer?
                                        Rang
The air with shouts that overpowered the clang
Of the incessant carroch, even: "Haste —
The candle's at the gateway! ere it waste,
Each soldier stand beside it, armed to march
With Tiso Sampier through the eastern arch!"
Ferrara's succored, Palma!

                                        Once again
They sat together; some strange thing in train
To say, so difficult was Palma's place
In taking, with a coy fastidious grace
Like the bird's flutter ere it fix and feed.
But when she felt she held her friend indeed
Safe, she threw back her curls, began implant
Her lessons; telling of another want
As her   Goito's quiet nourished than his
own histo-   own;
ry will ac-   Palma — to serve him — to be served
count for,   alone
Importing; Agnes' milk so neutralized
The blood of Ecelin. Nor be surprised
If, while Sordello fain had captive led
Nature, in dream was Palma subjected
To some out-soul, which dawned not though she
    pined
Delaying till its advent, heart and mind,
Their life. "How dared I let expand the force
Within me, till some out-soul, whose resource
It grew for, should direct it? Every law
Of life, its every fitness, every flaw,
Must One determine whose corporeal shape
Would be no other than the prime escape
And revelation to me of a Will
Orb-like o'ershrouded and inscrutable
Above, save at the point which, I should know,
Shone that myself, my powers, might overflow
So far, so much; as now it signified
Which earthly shape it henceforth chose my
    guide,
Whose mortal lip selected to declare
Its oracles, what fleshly garb would wear
— The first of intimations, whom to love;
The next, how love him. Seemed that orb,
    above
The castle-covert and the mountain-close,
Slow in appearing, — if beneath it rose
Cravings, aversions, — did our green precinct
Take pride in me, at unawares distinct
With this or that endowment, — how, repressed
At once, such jetting power shrank to the rest!
Was I to have a chance touch spoil me, leave
My spirit thence unfitted to receive
The consummating spell? — that spell so near
Moreover! 'Waits he not the waking year?
His almond-blossoms must be honey-ripe
By this; to welcome him, fresh runnels stripe
The thawed ravines; because of him, the wind
Walks like a herald. I shall surely find
Him now!'
                "And chief, that earnest April morn
Of Richard's Love-court, was it time, so worn
A reverse   And white my cheek, so idly my
to, and   blood beat,
comple-   Sitting that morn beside the Lady's
tion of, his.   feet
And saying as she prompted; till outburst
One face from all the faces. Not then first
I knew it; where in maple chamber glooms,
Crowned with what sanguine-heart pomegranate blooms
Advanced it ever? Men's acknowledgment
Sanctioned my own: 'twas taken, Palma's
    bent, —
Sordello, — recognized, accepted.
                                        "Dumb

Sat she still scheming. Ecelin would come
Gaunt, scared, ' Cesano baffles me,' he 'd say :
' Better I fought it out, my father's way !
Strangle Ferrara in its drowning flats,
And you and your Taurello yonder ! — what 's
Romano's business there ? ' An hour's concern
To cure the froward Chief ! — induce return
As heartened from those overmeaning eyes,
Wound up to persevere, — his enterprise
Marked out anew, its exigent of wit
Apportioned, — she at liberty to sit
And scheme against the next emergence, I —
To covet her Taurello-sprite, made fly
Or fold the wing — to con your horoscope
For leave command those steely shafts shoot
    ope,
Or straight assuage their blinding eagerness
In blank smooth snow. What semblance of
    success
To any of my plans for making you

How she ever aspired for his sake,
    Mine and Romano's ? Break the
        first wall through,
    Tread o'er the ruins of the Chief,
        supplant
His sons beside, still, vainest were the vaunt :
There, Salinguerra would obstruct me sheer,
And the insuperable Tuscan, here,
Stay me ! But one wild ève that Lady died
In her lone chamber : only I beside :
Taurello far at Naples, and my sire
At Padua, Ecelin away in ire
With Alberic. She held me thus — a clutch

Circumstances helping or hindering.
    To make our spirits as our bodies
        touch —
    And so began flinging the past up,
        heaps
Of uncouth treasure from their sunless sleeps
Within her soul ; deeds rose along with dreams,
Fragments of many miserable schemes,
Secrets, more secrets, then — no, not the last —
'Mongst others, like a casual trick o' the past,
How . . . ay, she told me, gathering up her
    face,
All left of it, into one arch-grimace
To die with . . .
        " Friend, 't is gone ! but not the fear
Of that fell laughing, heard as now I hear.
Nor faltered voice, nor seemed her heart grow
    weak
When i' the midst abrupt she ceased to speak
— Dead, as to serve a purpose, mark ! — for in
Rushed o' the very instant Ecelin
(How summoned, who divines ?) — looking as if
He understood why Adelaide lay stiff
Already in my arms ; for, ' Girl, how must
I manage Este in the matter thrust
Upon me, how unravel your bad coil ? —
Since ' (he declared) ' 't is on your brow — a soil
Like hers there ! ' then in the same breath,
    ' he lacked
No counsel after all, had signed no pact
With devils, nor was treason here or there,
Goito or Vicenza, his affair :
He buried it in Adelaide's deep grave,
Would begin life afresh, now, — would not
    slave
For any Friedrich's nor Taurello's sake !
What booted him to meddle or to make

In Lombardy ? ' And afterward I knew
The meaning of his promise to undo
All she had done — why marriages were made,
New friendships entered on, old followers paid
With curses for their pains, — new friends'
    amaze
At height, when, passing out by Gate Saint
    Blaise,
He stopped short in Vicenza, bent his head
Over a friar's neck, — ' had vowed,' he said,
' Long since, nigh thirty years, because his wife
And child were saved there, to bestow his life
On God, his gettings on the Church.'
                        " Exiled
Within Goito, still one dream beguiled
My days and nights ; 't was found, the orb I
    sought

How success at last seemed possible,
    To serve, those glimpses came of
        Fomalhaut,
    No other : but how serve it ? —
        authorize
You and Romano mingled destinies ?
And straight Romano's angel stood beside
Me who had else been Boniface's bride,
For Salinguerra 't was, with neck low bent,
And voice lightened to music, (as he meant
To learn, not teach me,) who withdrew the pall
From the dead past and straight revived it all,
Making me see how first Romano waxed,
Wherefore he waned now, why, if I relaxed
My grasp (even I !) would drop a thing effete,
Frayed by itself, unequal to complete
Its course, and counting every step astray

By the intervention of Salinguerra :
    A gain so much. Romano, every
        way
    Stable, a Lombard House now — why
        start back
Into the very outset of its track ?
This patching principle which late allied
Our House with other Houses — what beside
Concerned the apparition, the first Knight
Who followed Conrad hither in such plight
His utmost wealth was summed in his one
    steed ?
For Ecelo, that prowler, was decreed
A task, in the beginning hazardous
To him as ever task can be to us ;
But did the weather-beaten thief despair
When first our crystal cincture of warm air.
That binds the Trevisan, — as its spice-belt
(Crusaders say) the tract where Jesus dwelt, —
Furtive he pierced, and Este was to face —
Despaired Saponian strength of Lombard
    grace ?
Tried he at making surer aught made sure,
Maturing what already was mature ?
No ; his heart prompted Ecelo, ' Confront
Este, inspect yourself. What 's nature ? Wont.
Discard three-parts your nature, and adopt

Who remedied ill wrought by Ecelin,
    The rest as an advantage ! ' Old
        strength propped
    The man who first grew Podestà
        among
The Vicentines, no less than, while there
    sprung
His palace up in Padua like a threat,
Their noblest spied a grace, unnoticed yet
In Conrad's crew. Thus far the object gained

Romano was established —·has remained —
'For are you not Italian, truly peers
With Este? "Azzo" better soothes our ears
Than "Alberic"? or is this lion's-crine
From over-mounts' (this yellow hair of mine)
'So weak a graft on Agnes Este's stock?'
(Thus went he on with something of a mock)
'Wherefore recoil, then, from the very fate
Conceded you, refuse to imitate
Your model farther? Este long since left
Being mere Este: as a blade its heft,
Este required the Pope to further him:
And you, the Kaiser—whom your father's whim
Foregoes or, better, never shall forego
If Palma dare pursue what Ecelo
Commenced, but Ecelin desists from: just
As Adelaide of Susa could intrust
Her donative, — her Piedmont given the Pope,
Her Alpine-pass for him to shut or ope
'Twixt France and Italy, — to the superb
Matilda's perfecting, — so, lest aught curb
Our Adelaide's great counter-project for
Giving her Trentine to the Emperor
With passage here from Germany, — shall you
Take it, — my slender plodding talent, too!'
— Urged me Taurello with his half-smile.
            "He

As Patron of the scattered family
Conveyed me to his Mantua, kept in bruit
Azzo's alliances and Richard's suit
Until, the Kaiser excommunicate,
'Nothing remains,' Taurello said, 'but wait
Some rash procedure: Palma was the link,
As Agnes' child, between us, and they shrink
And had a project for her own glory, From losing Palma: judge if we
     advance,
 Your father's method, your inherit-
     ance!'
    The day I was betrothed to Boniface
At Padua by Taurello's self, took place
The outrage of the Ferrarese: again,
The day I sought Verona with the train
Agreed for, — by Taurello's policy
Convicting Richard of the fault, since we
Were present to annul or to confirm, —
Richard, whose patience had outstayed its
   term,
Quitted Verona for the siege.
         "And now
What glory may engird Sordello's brow
Through this? A month since at Oliero slunk
All that was Ecelin into a monk;
But how could Salinguerra so forget
His liege of thirty years as grudge even yet
One effort to recover him? He sent
Forthwith the tidings of this last event
To Ecelin — declared that he, despite
The recent folly, recognized his right
To order Salinguerra: 'Should he wring
Its uttermost advantage out, or fling
This chance away? Or were his sons now
   Head
O' the House?' Through me Taurello's mis-
   sive sped;
My father's answer will by me return.
Behold! 'For him,' he writes, 'no more con-
   cern

With strife than, for his children, with fresh
   plots
Of Friedrich. Old engagements out he blots
For aye: Taurello shall no more subserve,
Nor Ecelin impose.' Lest this unnerve
Taurello at this juncture, slack his grip
Of Richard, suffer the occasion slip, —
I, in his sons' default (who, mating with
Este, forsake Romano as the frith
Its mainsea for that firmland, sea makes head
Against) I stand, Romano, — in their stead
Assume the station they desert, and give
Still, as the Kaiser's representative,
Taurello license he demands. Midnight —
Morning — by noon to-morrow, making light
Which she would change to Sordello's.   Of the League's issue, we, in some
     gay weed
   Like yours, disguised together, may
     precede
    The arbitrators to Ferrara: reach
Him, let Taurello's noble accents teach
The rest! Then say if I have misconceived
Your destiny, too readily believed
The Kaiser's cause your own!' "
         And Palma's fled.
Though no affirmative disturbs the head,
A dying lamp-flame sinks and rises o'er,
Like the alighted planet Pollux wore,
Until, morn breaking, he resolves to be
Gate-vein of this heart's blood of Lombardy,
Soul of this body — to wield this aggregate
Of souls and bodies, and so conquer fate
Though he should live — a centre of disgust
Even — apart, core of the outward crust
He vivifies, assimilates. For thus
I bring Sordello to the rapturous
Thus then, having completed a circle, Exclaim at the crowd's cry, becaus
     one round
   Of life was quite accomplished; and
     he found
Not only that a soul, whate'er its might,
Is insufficient to its own delight,
Both in corporeal organs and in skill
By means of such to body forth its Will —
And, after, insufficient to apprise
Men of that Will, oblige them recognize
The Hid by the Revealed — but that, the last
Nor lightest of the struggles overpast,
Will he bade abdicate, which would not void
The throne, might sit there, suffer he enjoyed
Mankind, a varied and divine array
Incapable of homage, the first way,
Nor fit to render incidentally
Tribute connived at, taken by the by,
In joys. If thus with warrant to rescind
The ignominious exile of mankind —
Whose proper service, ascertained intact
As yet, (to be by him themselves made act,
Not watch Sordello acting each of them)
Was to secure — if the true diadem
Seemed imminent while our Sordello drank
The wisdom of that golden Palma, — thank
Verona's Lady in her citadel
Founded by Gaulish Brennus, legends tell:
And truly when she left him, the sun reared
A head like the first clamberer's who peered
A-top the Capitol, his face on flame
With triumph, triumphing till Manlius came.

Nor slight too much my rhymes — that spring, dispread,
Dispart, disperse, lingering overhead
Like an escape of angels ! Rather say,

The poet may pause and breathe, My transcendental platan ! mounting gay
(An archimage so courts a novice-queen)
With tremulous silvered trunk, whence branches sheen
Laugh out, thick foliaged next, a-shiver soon
With colored buds, then glowing like the moon
One mild flame, — last a pause, a burst, and all
Her ivory limbs are smothered by a fall,
Bloom-flinders and fruit-sparkles and leaf-dust,
Ending the weird work prosecuted just
For her amusement ; he decrepit, stark,
Dozes ; her uncontrolled delight may mark
Apart —
        Yet not so, surely never so !
Only, as good my soul were suffered go
O'er the lagune : forth fare thee, put aside —
Entrance thy synod, as a god may glide
Out of the world he fills, and leave it mute
For myriad ages as we men compute,
Returning into it without a break

Being really in the flesh at Venice, O' the consciousness ! They sleep, and I awake
O'er the lagune, being at Venice. Note,
In just such songs as Eglamor (say) wrote
With heart and soul and strength, for he believed
Himself achieving all to be achieved
By singer — in such songs you find alone
Completeness, judge the song and singer one,
And either purpose answered, his in it
Or its in him : while from true works (to wit
Sordello's dream-performances that will
Never be more than dreamed) escapes there still
Some proof, the singer's proper life was 'neath
The life his song exhibits, this a sheath
To that ; a passion and a knowledge far
Transcending these, majestic as they are,
Smouldered ; his lay was but an episode
In the bard's life : which evidence you owed
To some slight weariness, some looking-off
Or start-away. The childish skit or scoff
In " Charlemagne," (his poem, dreamed divine
In every point except one silly line
About the restiff daughters) — what may lurk
In that ? "My life commenced before this work,"
(So I interpret the significance
Of the bard's start aside and look askance) —
" My life continues after : on I fare
With no more stopping, possibly, no care

And watching his own life sometimes, To note the undercurrent, the why and how,
Where, when, o' the deeper life, as thus just now.
But, silent, shall I cease to live ?
        Alas
For you ! who sigh, ' When shall it come to pass
We read that story ? How will he compress
The future gains, his life's true business,

Into the better lay which — that one flout,
Howe'er inopportune it be, lets out —
Engrosses him already, though professed
To meditate with us eternal rest,
And partnership in all his life has found ? ' "
'T is but a sailor's promise, weather-bound :
" Strike sail, slip cable, here the bark be moored
For once, the awning stretched, the poles assured !
Noontide above ; except the wave's crisp dash,
Or buzz of colibri, or tortoise' splash,
The margin 's silent : out with every spoil
Made in our tracking, coil by mighty coil,
This serpent of a river to his head
I' the midst ! Admire each treasure, as we spread
The bank, to help us tell our history
Aright : give ear, endeavor to descry
The groves of giant rushes, how they grew
Like demons' endlong tresses we sailed through,
What mountains yawned, forests to give us vent
Opened, each doleful side, yet on we went
Till . . . may that beetle (shake your cap) attest
The springing of a land-wind from the West !"
— Wherefore ? Ah yes, you frolic it to-day !
To-morrow, and, the pageant moved away
Down to the poorest tent-pole, we and you
Part company : no other may pursue
Eastward your voyage, be informed what fate
Intends, if triumph or decline await
The tempter of the everlasting steppe.
I muse this on a ruined palace-step
At Venice : why should I break off, nor sit
Longer upon my step, exhaust the fit
England gave birth to ? Who 's adorable
Enough reclaim a —— no Sordello's Will
Alack ! — be queen to me ? That Bassanese
Busied among her smoking fruit-boats ? These
Perhaps from our delicious Asolo
Who twinkle, pigeons o'er the portico
Not prettier, bind June lilies into sheaves
To deck the bridge-side chapel, dropping leaves

Because it is pleasant to be young, Soiled by their own loose gold-meal ?
Ah, beneath
The cool arch stoops she, brownest cheek ! Her wreath
Endures a month — a half month — if I make
A queen of her, continue for her sake
Sordello's story ? Nay, that Paduan girl
Splashes with barer legs where a live whirl
In the dead black Giudecca proves sea-weed
Drifting has sucked down three, four, all indeed
Save one pale-red striped, pale-blue turbaned post
For gondolas.
        You sad dishevelled ghost
That pluck at me and point, are you advised
I breathe ? Let stay those girls (e'en her disguised
— Jewels i' the locks that love no crownet like
Their native field-buds and the green wheat spike,
So fair ! — who left this end of June's turmoil,
Shook off, as might a lily its gold soil,
Pomp, save a foolish gem or two, and free
In dream, came join the peasants o'er the sea)
Look they too happy, too tricked out ? Confess

There is such niggard stock of happiness
To share, that, do one's uttermost, dear wretch,
One labors ineffectually to stretch
Would but suffering humanity allow! It o'er you so that mother and children, both
May equitably flaunt the sumpter-cloth!
Divide the robe yet farther : be content
With seeing just a score pre-eminent
Through shreds of it, acknowledged happy wights,
Engrossing what should furnish all, by rights!
For, these in evidence, you clearlier claim
A like garb for the rest, — grace all, the same
As these my peasants. I ask youth and strength
And health for each of you, not more — at length
Grown wise, who asked at home that the whole race
Might add the spirit's to the body's grace,
And all be dizened out as chiefs and bards.
But in this magic weather one discards
Much old requirement. Venice seems a type
Of Life — 'twixt blue and blue extends, a stripe,
As Life, the somewhat, hangs 'twixt naught and naught :
'T is Venice, and 't is Life — as good you sought
To spare me the Piazza's slippery stone
Or keep me to the unchoked canals alone,
As hinder Life the evil with the good
Which make up Living, rightly understood.
Which instigates to tasks like this, Only, do finish something! Peasants, queens,
Take them, made happy by whatever means,
Parade them for the common credit, vouch
That a luckless residue, we send to crouch
In corners out of sight, was just as framed
For happiness, its portion might have claimed
As well, and so, obtaining joy, had stalked
Fastuous as any! — such my project, balked
Already ; I hardly venture to adjust
The first rags, when you find me. To mistrust
Me ! — nor unreasonably. You, no doubt,
Have the true knack of tiring suitors out
With those thin lips on tremble, lashless eyes
Inveterately tear-shot — there, be wise,
Mistress of mine, there, there, as if I meant
You insult ! — shall your friend (not slave) be shent
For speaking home ? Beside, care-bit erased
Broken-up beauties ever took my taste
Supremely ; and I love you more, far more
Than her I looked should foot Life's temple-floor.
Years ago, leagues at distance, when and where
A whisper came, " Let others seek ! — thy care
And doubtlessly compensates them, Is found, thy life's provision ; if thy race
Should be thy mistress, and into one face
The many faces crowd ? " Ah, had I, judge,
Or no, your secret ? Rough apparel — grudge
All ornaments save tag or tassel worn
To hint we are not thoroughly forlorn —
Slouch bonnet, unloop mantle, careless go
Alone (that 's saddest, but it must be so)
Through Venice, sing now and now glance aside,

Aught desultory or undignified, —
Then, ravishingest lady, will you pass
Or not each formidable group, the mass
Before the Basilic (that feast gone by,
God's great day of the Corpus Domini)
And, wistfully foregoing proper men,
Come timid up to me for alms ? And then
The luxury to hesitate, feign do
Some unexampled grace ! — when, whom but you
Dare I bestow your own upon ? And hear
Further before you say, it is to sneer
I call you ravishing ; for I regret
Little that she, whose early foot was set
Forth as she 'd plant it on a pedestal,
Now, i' the silent city, seems to fall
Toward me — no wreath, only a lip's unrest
To quiet, surcharged eyelids to be pressed
Dry of their tears upon my bosom. Strange
Such sad chance should produce in thee such change,
My love ! Warped souls and bodies ! yet God spoke
Of right-hand, foot and eye — selects our yoke,
Sordello, as your poetship may find !
So, sleep upon my shoulder, child, nor mind
Their foolish talk ; we 'll manage reinstate
Your old worth ; ask moreover, when they prate
Of evil men past hope, " Don't each contrive,
Despite the evil you abuse, to live ? —
Keeping, each losel, through a maze of lies,
His own conceit of truth ? to which he hies
By obscure windings, tortuous, if you will,
But to himself not inaccessible ;
He sees truth, and his lies are for the crowd
Who cannot see ; some fancied right allowed
His vilest wrong, empowered the losel clutch
One pleasure from a multitude of such
As those who desist should remember. Denied him." Then assert, " All men appear
To think all better than themselves, by here
Trusting a crowd they wrong ; but really," say,
" All men think all men stupider than they,
Since, save themselves, no other comprehends
The complicated scheme to make amends
— Evil, the scheme by which, through Ignorance,
Good labors to exist." A slight advance, —
Merely to find the sickness you die through,
And naught beside ! but if one can't eschew
One's portion in the common lot, at least
One can avoid an ignorance increased
Tenfold by dealing out hint after hint
How naught were like dispensing without stint
The water of life — so easy to dispense
Beside, when one has probed the centre whence
Commotion 's born — could tell you of it all !
" — Meantime, just meditate my madrigal
O' the mugwort that conceals a dewdrop safe ! "
What, dullard ? we and you in smothery chafe,
Babes, baldheads, stumbled thus far into Zin
The Horrid, getting neither out nor in,
A hungry sun above us, sands that bung
Our throats, — each dromedary lolls a tongue,
Each camel churns a sick and frothy chap,
And you, 'twixt tales of Potiphar's mishap,
And sonnets on the earliest ass that spoke,

—Remark, you wonder any one needs choke
With founts about! Potsherd him, Gibeon-
     ites!
While awkwardly enough your Moses smites
The rock, though he forego his Promised Land
Thereby, have Satan claim his carcass, and
Figure as Metaphysic Poet . . . ah,
Mark ye the dim first oozings? Meribah!
Then, quaffing at the fount my courage gained,
Recall — not that I prompt ye — who ex-
     plained . . .
" Presumptuous ! " interrupts one. You, not I
'T is, brother, marvel at and magnify

Let the Such office : " office," quotha? can
poet take we get
his own To the beginning of the office yet?
part, then, What do we here? simply experiment
Each on the other's power and its intent
When elsewhere tasked, — if this of mine were
     trucked
For yours to either's good, — we watch con-
     struct,
In short, an engine : with a finished one,
What it can do, is all, — naught, how 't is done.
But this of ours yet in probation, dusk
A kernel of strange wheelwork through its husk
Grows into shape by quarters and by halves;
Remark this tooth's spring, wonder what that
     valve's
Fall bodes, presume each faculty's device,
Make out each other more or less precise —
The scope of the whole engine 's to be proved;
We die : which means to say, the whole 's
     removed,
Dismounted wheel by wheel, this complex
     gin, —
To be set up anew elsewhere, begin
A task indeed, but with a clearer clime
Than the murk lodgment of our building-time.
And then, I grant you, it behoves forget
How 't is done — all that must amuse us yet
So long : and, while you turn upon your heel,
Pray that I be not busy slitting steel
Should any Or shredding brass, camped on some
object that virgin shore
he was Under a cluster of fresh stars, be-
dull fore
I name a tithe o' the wheels I trust to do!
So occupied, then, are we : hitherto,
At present, and a weary while to come,
The office of ourselves, — nor blind nor dumb,
And seeing somewhat of man's state, — has been,
For the worst of us, to say they so have seen;
For the better, what it was they saw; the best
Impart the gift of seeing to the rest :
"So that I glance," says such an one, " around,
And there 's no face but I can read profound
Disclosures in ; this stands for hope, that — fear,
And for a speech, a deed in proof, look here!
' Stoop, else the strings of blossom, where the
     nuts
O'erarch, will blind thee! Said I not? She
     shuts
Both eyes this time, so close the hazels meet!
Thus, prisoned in the Piombi, I repeat
Events one rove occasioned, o'er and o'er,
Putting 'twixt me and madness evermore
Thy sweet shape, Zanze! Therefore stoop!'

                              'That 's truth!'
(Adjudge you) ' the incarcerated youth
Would say that!'
          Youth? Plara the bard? Set down
That Plara spent his youth in a grim town
Whose cramped ill-featured streets huddled
     about
The minster for protection, never out
Of its black belfry's shade and its bells' roar.
The brighter shone the suburb, — all the more
Ugly and absolute that shade's reproof
Of any chance escape of joy, — some roof,
Taller than they, allowed the rest detect, —
Before the sole permitted laugh (suspect
Who could, 't was meant for laughter, that
     ploughed cheek's
Repulsive gleam!) when the sun stopped both
     peaks
Of the cleft belfry like a fiery wedge,
Then sank, a huge flame on its socket edge,
With leavings on the gray glass oriel-pane
Ghastly some minutes more. No fear of rain —
The minster minded that! in heaps the dust
Lay everywhere. This town, the minster's trust,
Beside his Held Plara; who, its denizen, bade
sprightlier hail
predeces- In twice twelve sonnets, Tempe's
sors. dewy vale."
" 'Exact the town, the minster and the
     street!' "
" As all mirth triumphs, sadness means defeat :
Lust triumphs and is gay, Love 's triumphed
     o'er
And sad : but Lucio 's sad. I said before,
Love 's sad, not Lucio ; one who loves may
     be
As gay his love has leave to hope, as he
Downcast that lusts' desire escapes the springe :
' T is of the mood itself I speak, what tinge
Determines it, else colorless, — or mirth,
Or melancholy, as from heaven or earth."
" 'Ay, that 's the variation's gist!'
                              Indeed?
Thus far advanced in safety then, proceed!
And having seen too what I saw, be bold
And next encounter what I do behold
(That 's sure) but bid you take on trust!"
                              Attack
The use and purpose of such sights? Alack,
Not so unwisely does the crowd dispense
On Salinguerras praise in preference
One ought To the Sordellos : men of action,
not blame these!
but praise Who, seeing just as little as you
this; please,
Yet turn that little to account, — engage
With, do not gaze at, — carry on, a stage,
The work o' the world, not merely make report
The work existed ere their day! In short,
When at some future no-time a brave band
Sees, using what it sees, then shake my hand
In heaven, my brother! Meanwhile where 's
     the hurt
Of keeping the Makers-see on the alert,
At whose defection mortals stare aghast
As though heaven's bounteous windows were
     slammed fast
Incontinent? Whereas all you, beneath,

Should scowl at, bruise their lips and break their
　　teeth
Who ply the pullies, for neglecting you:
And therefore have I moulded, made anew
A Man, and give him to be turned and tried,
Be angry with or pleased at. On your side,
Have ye times, places, actors of your own?
　　　　Try them upon Sordello when full-
At all events, his own audience may:　grown,
　　　　And then—ah then! If Hercules
　　　　first parched
　　　　His foot in Egypt only to be marched
A sacrifice for Jove with pomp to suit,
What chance have I? The demigod was mute
Till, at the altar, where time out of mind
Such guests became oblations, chaplets twined
His forehead long enough, and he began
Slaying the slayers, nor escaped a man.
Take not affront, my gentle audience! whom
No Hercules shall make his hecatomb,
Believe, nor from his brows your chaplet rend—
That's your kind suffrage, yours, my patron-
　　friend,
Whose great verse blares unintermittent on
Like your own trumpeter at Marathon,—
You who, Platæa and Salamis being scant,
Put up with Ætna for a stimulant—
And did well, I acknowledged, as he loomed
Over the midland sea last month, presumed
Long, lay demolished in the blazing West
At eve, while towards him tilting cloudlets
　　pressed
Like Persian ships at Salamis. Friend, wear
A crest proud as desert while I declare
Had I a flawless ruby fit to wring
Tears of its color from that painted king
Who lost it, I would, for that smile which
　　went
To my heart, fling it in the sea, content,
What if things brighten, who knows?　Wearing your verse in place, an
　　amulet
　　Sovereign against all passion, wear
　　and fret!
My English Eyebright, if you are not glad
That, as I stopped my task awhile, the sad
Dishevelled form, wherein I put mankind
To come at times and keep my pact in mind,
Renewed me,—hear no crickets in the hedge,
Nor let a glowworm spot the river's edge
At home, and may the summer showers gush
Without a warning from the missel thrush!
So, to our business, now—the fate of such
As find our common nature—overmuch
Despised because restricted and unfit
To bear the burden they impose on it—
Cling when they would discard it; craving
　　strength
To leap from the allotted world, at length
They do leap,—flounder on without a term,
Each a god's germ, doomed to remain a germ
In unexpanded infancy, unless ...
But that's the story—dull enough, confess!
There might be fitter subjects to allure;
Still, neither misconceive my portraiture
Nor undervalue its adornments quaint:
What seems a fiend perchance may prove a saint.
Ponder a story ancient pens transmit,
Then say if you condemn me or acquit.

John the Beloved, banished Antioch
For Patmos, bade collectively his flock
Where-upon, with a story to the point,　Farewell, but set apart the closing
　　eve
　　To comfort those his exile most
　　would grieve,
He knew: a touching spectacle, that house
In motion to receive him! Xanthus' spouse
You missed, made panther's meat a month
　　since; but
Xanthus himself (his nephew 't was, they shut
'Twixt boards and sawed asunder), Polycarp,
Soft Charicle, next year no wheel could warp
To swear by Cæsar's fortune, with the rest
Were ranged; through whom the gray disciple
　　pressed,
Busily blessing right and left, just stopped
To pat one infant's curls, the hangman cropped
Soon after, reached the portal. On its hinge
The door turns and he enters: what quick
　　twinge
Ruins the smiling mouth, those wide eyes fix
Whereon, why like some spectral candlestick's
Branch the disciple's arms? Dead swooned he,
　　woke
Anon, heaved sigh, made shift to gasp, heart-
　　broke,
"Get thee behind me, Satan! Have I toiled
To no more purpose? Is the gospel foiled
Here too, and o'er my son's, my Xanthus'
　　hearth,
Portrayed with sooty garb and features
　　swarth—
Ah, Xanthus, am I to thy roof beguiled
To see the—the—the Devil domiciled?"
Whereto sobbed Xanthus, "Father, 't is your-
　　self
Installed, a limning which our utmost pelf
Went to procure against to-morrow's loss;
He takes up the thread of discourse.　And that's no twy-prong, but a pas-
　　toral cross,
　　You 're painted with!"
　　　　His puckered brows unfold—
And you shall hear Sordello's story told.

BOOK THE FOURTH

Meantime Ferrara lay in rueful case;
The lady-city, for whose sole embrace
Her pair of suitors struggled, felt their arms
A brawny mischief to the fragile charms
They tugged for—one discovering that to
　　twist
Her tresses twice or thrice about his wrist
Secured a point of vantage—one, how best
He 'd parry that by planting in her breast
His elbow spike—each party too intent
Men suffered much,　For noticing, howe'er the battle went,
　　The conqueror would but have a
　　corpse to kiss.
"May Boniface be duly damned for this!"
—Howled some old Ghibellin, as up he turned,
From the wet heap of rubbish where they
　　burned
His house, a little skull with dazzling teeth:
"A boon, sweet Christ—let Salinguerra seethe
In hell forever, Christ, and let myself

Be there to laugh at him!"—moaned some
    young Guelf
Stumbling upon a shrivelled hand nailed fast
To the charred lintel of the doorway, last
His father stood within to bid him speed.
The thoroughfares were overrun with weed
—Docks, quitchgrass, loathy mallows no man
    plants.
The stranger, none of its inhabitants

Whichever of the parties was victor. Crept out of doors to taste fresh air
    again,
And ask the purpose of a splendid
    train
Admitted on a morning; every town
Of the East League was come by envoy down
To treat for Richard's ransom: here you saw
The Vicentine, here snowy oxen draw
The Paduan carroch, its vermilion cross
On its white field. A-tiptoe o'er the fosse
Looked Legate Montelungo wistfully
After the flock of steeples he might spy
In Este's time, gone (doubts he) long ago
To mend the ramparts: sure the laggards know
The Pope's as good as here! They paced the
    streets
More soberly. At last, "Taurello greets
The League," announced a pursuivant,—"will
    match
Its courtesy, and labors to dispatch
At earliest Tito, Friedrich's Pretor, sent
On pressing matters from his post at Trent,
With Mainard Count of Tyrol,—simply waits
Their going to receive the delegates."
"Tito!" Our delegates exchanged a glance,
And, keeping the main way, admired askance
The lazy engines of outlandish birth,
Couched like a king each on its bank of earth—
Arbalist, manganel and catapult;
While stationed by, as waiting a result,
Lean silent gangs of mercenaries ceased
Working to watch the strangers. "This, at
    least,
Were better spared; he scarce presumes gainsay
The League's decision! Get our friend away
And profit for the future: how else teach
Fools 't is not safe to stray within claw's reach
Ere Salinguerra's final gasp be blown?
Those mere convulsive scratches find the bone.
Who bade him bloody the spent osprey's nare?"
    The carrochs halted in the public square.
Pennons of every blazon once a-flaunt,
Men prattled, freelier that the crested gaunt

How Guelfs criticise Ghibellin work White ostrich with a horse-shoe in
    her beak
Was missing, and whoever chose
    might speak
"Ecelin" boldly out: so,—"Ecelin
Needed his wife to swallow half the sin
And sickens by himself: the devil's whelp,
He styles his son, dwindles away, no help
From conserves, your fine triple-curded froth
Of virgin's blood, your Venice viper-broth—
Eh? Jubilate!"—"Peace! no little word
You utter here that's not distinctly heard
Up at Oliero: he was absent sick
When we besieged Bassano—who, i' the thick
O' the work, perceived the progress Azzo made,
Like Ecelin, through his witch Adelaide?

She managed it so well that, night by night,
At their bed-foot stood up a soldier-sprite,
First fresh, pale by-and-by without a wound,
And, when it came with eyes filmed as in swound,
They knew the place was taken."—"Ominous
That Ghibellins should get what cautelous
Old Redbeard sought from Azzo's sire to wrench
Vainly; Saint George contrived his town a
    trench
O' the marshes, an impermeable bar."
"—Young Ecelin is meant the tutelar
Of Padua, rather; veins embrace upon
His hand like Brenta and Bacchiglion."
What now?—"The founts! God's bread,
    touch not a plank!
A crawling hell of carrion—every tank

As unusually energetic in this case. Choke full!—found out just now to
    Cino's cost—
The same who gave Taurello up for
    lost,
And, making no account of fortune's freaks,
Refused to budge from Padua then, but sneaks
Back now with Concorezzi—'faith! they drag
Their carroch to San Vitale, plant the flag
On his own palace, so adroitly razed
He knew it not; a sort of Guelf folk gazed
And laughed apart; Cino disliked their air—
Must pluck up spirit, show he does not care—
Seats himself on the tank's edge—will begin
To hum, za, za, Cavaler Ecelin—
A silence; he gets warmer, clinks to chime,
Now both feet plough the ground, deeper each
    time,
At last, za, za, and up with a fierce kick
Comes his own mother's face caught by the
    thick
Gray hair about his spur!"
                Which means, they lift
The covering, Salinguerra made a shift
To stretch upon the truth; as well avoid
Further disclosures; leave them thus employed.
Our dropping Autumn morning clears apace,
And poor Ferrara puts a softened face
On her misfortunes. Let us scale this tall
Huge foursquare line of red brick garden-wall

How, passing through the rare garden, Bastioned within by trees of every
    sort
On three sides, slender, spreading,
    long and short;
Each grew as it contrived, the poplar
    ramped,
The fig-tree reared itself,—but stark and
    cramped,
Made fools of, like tamed lions: whence, on the
    edge,
Running 'twixt trunk and trunk to smooth one
    ledge
Of shade, were shrubs inserted, warp and woof,
Which smothered up that variance. Scale the
    roof
Of solid tops, and o'er the slope you slide
Down to a grassy space level and wide,
Here and there dotted with a tree, but trees
Of rarer leaf, each foreigner at ease,
Set by itself: and in the centre spreads,
Borne upon three uneasy leopards' heads,
A laver, broad and shallow, one bright spirt
Of water bubbles in. The walls begirt

With trees leave off on either hand; pursue
Your path along a wondrous avenue
Those walls abut on, heaped of gleamy stone,
With aloes leering everywhere, gray-grown
From many a Moorish summer: how they wind
Out of the fissures! likelier to bind
The building than those rusted cramps which
    drop
Already in the eating sunshine. Stop,
You fleeting shapes above there! Ah, the pride
Or else despair of the whole country-side!
A range of statues, swarming o'er with wasps,

Salinguer- God, goddess, woman, man, the
ra con-   Greek rough-rasps
trived for In crumbling Naples marble — meant
a purpose,   to look
Like those Messina marbles Constance took
Delight in, or Taurello's self conveyed
To Mantua for his mistress, Adelaide,
A certain font with caryatides
Since cloistered at Goito; only, these
Are up and doing, not abashed, a troop
Able to right themselves — who see you, stoop
Their arms o' the instant after you! Unplucked
By this or that, you pass; for they conduct
To terrace raised on terrace, and, between,
Creatures of brighter mould and braver mien
Than any yet, the choicest of the Isle
No doubt. Here, left a sullen breathing-while,
Up-gathered on himself the Fighter stood
For his last fight, and, wiping treacherous
    blood
Out of the eyelids just held ope beneath
Those shading fingers in their iron sheath,
Steadied his strengths amid the buzz and stir
Of the dusk hideous amphitheatre
At the announcement of his over-match
To wind the day's diversion up, dispatch
The pertinacious Gaul: while, limbs one heap,
The Slave, no breath in her round mouth,
    watched leap
Dart after dart forth, as her hero's car
Clove dizzily the solid of the war
— Let coil about his knees for pride in him.
We reach the farthest terrace, and the grim
San Pietro Palace stops us.

              Such the state
Of Salinguerra's plan to emulate
Sicilian marvels, that his girlish wife
Retrude still might lead her ancient life
In her new home: whereat enlarged so much
Neighbors upon the novel princely touch
He took, — who here imprisons Boniface.
Here must the Envoys come to sue for grace;
And here, emerging from the labyrinth
Below, Sordello paused beside the plinth
Of the door-pillar.

Sordello   He had really left
ponders all Verona for the cornfields (a poor theft
seen and   From the morass) where Este's camp
heard,   was made.
The Envoys' march, the Legate's cavalcade —
All had been seen by him, but scarce as when, —
Eager for cause to stand aloof from men
At every point save the fantastic tie
Acknowledged in his boyish sophistry, —
He made account of such. A crowd, — he meant
To task the whole of it; each part's intent

Concerned him therefore: and, the more he
    pried,
The less became Sordello satisfied
With his own figure at the moment. Sought
He respite from his task? Descried he aught
Novel in the anticipated sight
Of all these livers upon all delight?
This phalanx, as of myriad points combined,
Whereby he still had imaged the mankind
His youth was passed in dreams of rivalling,
His age — in plans to prove at least such thing
Had been so dreamed, — which now he must
    impress
With his own will, effect a happiness
By theirs, — supply a body to his soul
Thence, and become eventually whole
With them as he had hoped to be without —

Finds in   Made these the mankind he once
men no   raved about?
machine   Because a few of them were notable,
for his   Should all be figured worthy note?
sake,   As well
Expect to find Taurello's triple line
Of trees a single and prodigious pine.
Real pines rose here and there; but, close among,
Thrust into and mixed up with pines, a throng
Of shrubs, he saw, — a nameless common sort
O'erpast in dreams, left out of the report
And hurried into corners, or at best
Admitted to be fancied like the rest.
Reckon that morning's proper chiefs — how few!
And yet the people grew, the people grew,
Grew ever, as if the many there indeed,
More left behind and most who should suc-
    ceed, —
Simply in virtue of their mouths and eyes,
Petty enjoyments and huge miseries, —
Mingled with, and made veritably great
Those chiefs: he overlooked not Mainard's state
Nor Concorezzi's station, but instead
Of stopping there, each dwindled to be head
Of infinite and absent Tyrolese
Or Paduans; startling all the more, that these
Seemed passive and disposed of, uncared for,
Yet doubtless on the whole (like Eglamor)
Smiling; for if a wealthy man decays
And out of store of robes must wear, all days,
One tattered suit, alike in sun and shade,
'T is commonly some tarnished gay brocade
Fit for a feast-night's flourish and no more:
Nor otherwise poor Misery from her store
Of looks is fain upgather, keep unfurled
For common wear as she goes through the world,
The faint remainder of some worn-out smile
Meant for a feast-night's service merely. While
Crowd upon crowd rose on Sordello thus, —
(Crowds no way interfering to discuss,
Much less dispute, life's joys with one employed
In envying them, — or, if they aught enjoyed,
Where lingered something indefinable
In every look and tone, the mirth as well
As woe, that fixed at once his estimate
Of the result, their good or bad estate) —

But a   Old memories returned with new
thing with effect:
life of its And the new body, ere he could sus-
own,   pect,
Cohered, mankind and he were really fused,

The new self seemed impatient to be used
By him, but utterly another way
Than that anticipated: strange to say,
They were too much below him, more in thrall
Than he, the adjunct than the principal.
What booted scattered units? — here a mind
And there, which might repay his own to find,
And stamp, and use? — a few, howe'er august,
If all the rest were grovelling in the dust?
No: first a mighty equilibrium, sure,
Should he establish, privilege procure
For all, the few had long possessed! He felt
An error, an exceeding error melt —
While he was occupied with Mantuan chants,
Behoved him think of men, and take their
    wants,
Such as he now distinguished every side,
As his own want which might be satisfied, —
And, after that, think of rare qualities
Of his own soul demanding exercise.
It followed naturally, through no claim
On their part, which made virtue of the aim
At serving them, on his, — that, past retrieve,
He felt now in their toils, theirs, — nor could
    leave
Wonder how, in the eagerness to rule,
Impress his will on mankind, he (the fool!)
Had never even entertained the thought
That this his last arrangement might be fraught
With incidental good to them as well,
And rights hitherto ignored by him, And that mankind's delight would
    help to swell
His own. So, if he sighed, as for-
    merly.
Because the merry time of life must fleet,
'T was deeplier now, — for could the crowds re-
    peat
Their poor experiences? His hand that shook
Was twice to be deplored. "The Legate, look!
With eyes, like fresh-blown thrush-eggs on a
    thread,
Faint-blue and loosely floating in his head,
Large tongue, moist open mouth; and this long
    while
That owner of the idiotic smile
A fault he is now anxious to repair, Serves them!" He fortunately saw in time
His fault however, and since the of-
    fice prime
Includes the secondary — best accept
Both offices; Taurello, its adept,
Could teach him the preparatory one,
And how to do what he had fancied done
Long previously, ere take the greater task,
How render first these people happy? Ask
The people's friends: for there must be one
    good,
One way to it — the Cause! — he understood
The meaning now of Palma; why the jar
Else, the ado, the trouble wide and far
Of Guelfs and Ghibellins, the Lombard hope
And Rome's despair? — 'twixt Emperor and
    Pope
The confused shifting sort of Eden tale —
Hardihood still recurring, still to fail —
That foreign interloping fiend, this free
And native overbrooding deity —
Yet a dire fascination o'er the palms
The Kaiser ruined, troubling even the calms

Of paradise — or, on the other hand,
Since he apprehends its full extent, The Pontiff, as the Kaisers under-
    stand,
One snake-like cursed of God to love
    the ground,
Whose heavy length breaks in the noon profound
Some saving tree — which needs the Kaiser,
    dressed
As the dislodging angel of that pest,
Yet flames that pest bedropped, flat head, full
    fold,
With coruscating dower of dyes. "Behold
The secret, so to speak, and master-spring
O' the contest! — which of the two Powers shall
    bring
Men good — perchance the most good — ay, it
    may
Be that! — the question, which best knows the
    way."
And hereupon Count Mainard strutted past
Out of San Pietro; never seemed the last
Of archers, slingers: and our friend began
To recollect strange modes of serving man,
Arbalist, catapult, brake, manganel,
And more. "This way of theirs may, — who
    can tell? —
Need perfecting," said he: "let all be solved
At once! Taurello 't is, the task devolved
On late — confront Taurello!"
                And at last
He did confront him. Scarce an hour had past
When forth Sordello came, older by years
Than at his entry. Unexampled fears
Oppressed him, and he staggered off, blind, mute
And deaf, like some fresh-mutilated brute,
Into Ferrara — not the empty town
That morning witnessed: he went up and down
Streets whence the veil had been stripped shred
    by shred,
So that, in place of huddling with their dead
Indoors, to answer Salinguerra's ends,
Townsfolk make shift to crawl forth, sit like
    friends
With any one. A woman gave him choice
Of her two daughters, the infantile voice
Or the dimpled knee, for half a chain, his throat
Was clasped with; but an archer knew the
    coat —
Its blue cross and eight lilies, — bade beware
One dogging him in concert with the pair
Though thrumming on the sleeve that hid his
    knife.
Night set in early, autumn dews were rife,
They kindled great fires while the Leaguers'
    mass
Began at every carroch — he must pass
Between the kneeling people. Presently
The carroch of Verona caught his eye
With purple trappings; silently he bent
Over its fire, when voices violent
Began, "Affirm not whom the youth was like
That struck me from the porch, I did not strike
Again: I too have chestnut hair; my kin
And would fain have helped some way, Hate Azzo and stand up for Ece-
    lin.
Here, minstrel, drive bad thoughts
    away! Sing! Take
My glove for guerdon!" And for that man's
    sake

He turned: "A song of Eglamor's!" — scarce
   named,
When, "Our Sordello's rather!" — all ex-
   claimed;
"Is not Sordello famousest for rhyme?"
He had been happy to deny, this time, —
Profess as heretofore the aching head
And failing heart, — suspect that in his stead
Some true Apollo had the charge of them,
Was champion to reward or to condemn,
So his intolerable risk might shift
Or share itself; but Naddo's precious gift
Of gifts, he owned, be certain! At the close —
"I made that," said he to a youth who rose
As if to hear: 't was Palma through the band
Conducted him in silence by her hand.

   Back now for Salinguerra. Tito of Trent
Gave place to Palma and her friend; who went
In turn at Montelungo's visit — one
After the other were they come and gone, —
These spokesmen for the Kaiser and the Pope,
This incarnation of the People's hope,
Sordello, — all the say of each was said;
And Salinguerra sat, himself instead
Of these to talk with, lingered musing yet.
'T was a drear vast presence-chamber roughly
   set
In order for the morning's use; full face,
The Kaiser's ominous sign-mark had first place,
The crowned grim twy-necked eagle, coarsely-
   blacked
With ochre on the naked wall; nor lacked
Romano's green and yellow either side;
But the new token Tito brought had tried
The Legate's patience — nay, if Palma knew
What Salinguerra almost meant to do
Until the sight of her restored his lip
A certain half-smile, three months' chieftainship
Had banished! Afterward, the Legate found
No change in him, nor asked what badge he
   wound
And unwound carelessly. Now sat the Chief
But Salin- Silent as when our couple left, whose
guerra is brief
also pre- Encounter wrought so opportune ef-
occupied;   fect
In thoughts he summoned not, nor would reject,
Though time 't was now if ever, to pause — fix
On any sort of ending: wiles and tricks
Exhausted, judge! his charge, the crazy town,
Just managed to be hindered crashing down —
His last sound troops ranged — care observed to
   post
His best of the maimed soldiers innermost —
So much was plain enough, but somehow struck
Him not before. And now with this strange luck
Of Tito's news, rewarding his address
So well, what thought he of? — how the success
With Friedrich's rescript there would either
   hush
Old Ecelin's scruples, bring the manly flush
To his young son's white cheek, or, last, exempt
Himself from telling what there was to tempt?
No: that this minstrel was Romano's last
Resem- Servant — himself the first! Could
bling Sor- he contrast
dello inno- The whole! — that minstrel's thirty
thing else. years just spent

In doing naught, their notablest event
This morning's journey hither, as I told —
Who yet was lean, outworn and really old,
A stammering awkward man that scarce dared
   raise
His eye before the magisterial gaze —
And Salinguerra with his fears and hopes
Of sixty years, his Emperors and Popes,
Cares and contrivances, yet, you would say,
'T was a youth nonchalantly looked away
Through the embrasure northward o'er the sick
Expostulating trees — so agile, quick
How he And graceful turned the head on the
was made broad chest
in body Encased in pliant steel, his constant
and spirit, vest,
Whence split the sun off in a spray of fire
Across the room; and, loosened of its tire
Of steel, that head let breathe the comely brown
Large massive locks discolored as if a crown
Encircled them, so frayed the basnet where
A sharp white line divided clean the hair;
Glossy above, glossy below, it swept
Curling and fine about a brow thus kept
Calm, laid coat upon coat, marble and sound:
This was the mystic mark the Tuscan found,
Mused of, turned over books about. Square-
   faced,
No lion more; two vivid eyes, enchased
In hollows filled with many a shade and streak
Settling from the bold nose and bearded cheek.
Nor might the half-smile reach them that de-
   formed
A lip supremely perfect else — unwarmed,
Unwidened, less or more; indifferent
Whether on trees or men his thoughts were bent,
Thoughts rarely, after all, in trim and train
As now a period was fulfilled again:
Of such, a series made his life, compressed
In each, one story serving for the rest —
And what How his life-streams rolling arrived
had been at last
his career At the barrier, whence, were it once
of old. overpast,
They would emerge, a river to the end, —
Gathered themselves up, paused, bade fate be-
   friend,
Took the leap, hung a minute at the height,
Then fell back to oblivion infinite:
Therefore he smiled. Beyond stretched gar-
   den-grounds
Where late the adversary, breaking bounds,
Had gained him an occasion, That above,
That eagle, testified he could improve
Effectually. The Kaiser's symbol lay
Beside his rescript, a new badge by way
Of baldric; while, — another thing that marred
Alike emprise, achievement and reward, —
Ecelin's missive was conspicuous too.
   What past life did those flying thoughts pur
   sue?
As his, few names in Mantua half so old;
But at Ferrara, where his sires enrolled
It latterly, the Adelardi spared
No pains to rival them: both factions shared
Ferrara, so that, counted out, 't would yield
A product very like the city's shield,
Half black and white, or Ghibellin and Guelf

As after Salinguerra styled himself
And Este, who, till Marchesalla died,
(Last of the Adelardi) -- never tried
His fortune there : with Marchesalla's child
Would pass — could Blacks and Whites be rec-
  onciled,
And young Taurello wed Linguetta — wealth
And sway to a sole grasp. Each treats by stealth
Already : when the Guelfs, the Ravennese
Arrive, assault the Pietro quarter, seize
Linguetta, and are gone ! Men's first dismay
Abated somewhat, hurries down, to lay
The after indignation, Boniface,
This Richard's father. " Learn the full disgrace
Averted, ere you blame us Guelfs, who rate
Your Salinguerra, your sole potentate
That might have been, 'mongst Este's valvas-
  sors —
Ay, Azzo's — who, not privy to, abhors
Our step ; but we were zealous." Azzo 's then
To do with ! Straight a meeting of old men:
" Old Salinguerra dead, his heir a boy,
What if we change our ruler and decoy
The Lombard Eagle of the azure sphere
With Italy to build in, fix him here,
Settle the city's troubles in a trice ?
For private ends, let public good suffice ! "

The origi-nal check to his for-tunes, In fine, young Salinguerra's stanch-
  est friends
Talked of the townsmen making him
  amends,
Gave him a goshawk, and affirmed there was
Rare sport, one morning, over the green grass
A mile or so. He sauntered through the plain,
Was restless, fell to thinking, turned again
In time for Azzo's entry with the bride ;
Count Boniface rode smirking at their side ;
" She brings him half Ferrara," whispers flew,
" And all Ancona ! If the stripling knew ! "
Anon the stripling was in Sicily
Where Heinrich ruled in right of Constance ; he
Was gracious nor his guest incapable ;
Each understood the other. So it fell,
One Spring, when Azzo, thoroughly at ease,
Had near forgotten by what precise degrees
He crept at first to such a downy seat,
The Count trudged over in a special heat
To bid him of God's love dislodge from each
Of Salinguerra's palaces, — a breach
Might yawn else, not so readily to shut,
For who was just arrived at Mantua but
The youngster, sword on thigh and tuft on chin,
Which he was in the way to re-trieve, With tokens for Celano, Ecelin,
Pistore, and the like ! Next news, —
  no whit
Do any of Ferrara's domes befit
His wife of Heinrich's very blood : a band
Of foreigners assemble, understand
Garden-constructing, level and surround,
Build up and bury in. A last news crowned
The consternation : since his infant's birth,
He only waits they end his wondrous girth
Of trees that link San Pietro with Tomà,
To visit Mantua. When the Podestà
Ecelin, at Vicenza, called his friend
Taurello thither, what could be their end
But to restore the Ghibellins' late Head,
The Kaiser helping ? He with most to dread

From vengeance and reprisal, Azzo, there
With Boniface beforehand, as aware
Of plots in progress, gave alarm, expelled
Both plotters : but the Guelfs in triumph yelled
Too hastily. The burning and the flight,
And how Taurello, occupied that night
With Ecelin, lost wife and son, I told :
When a fresh ca-lamity de-stroyed all: — Not how he bore the blow, re-
  tained his hold,
Got friends safe through, left ene-
  mies the worst
O' the fray, and hardly seemed to care at first :
But afterward men heard not constantly
Of Salinguerra's House so sure to be !
Though Azzo simply gained by the event
A shifting of his plagues — the first, content
To fall behind the second and estrange
So far his nature, suffer such a change
That in Romano sought he wife and child
And for Romano's sake seemed reconciled
To losing individual life, which shrunk
As the other prospered — mortised in his trunk,
Like a dwarf palm which wanton Arabs foil
Of bearing its own proper wine and oil,
By grafting into it the stranger-vine,
Which sucks its heart out, sly and serpentine,
Till forth one vine-palm feathers to the root,
And red drops moisten the insipid fruit.
Once Adelaide set on, — the subtle mate
Of the weak soldier, urged to emulate
The Church's valiant women deed for deed,
And paragon her namesake, win the meed
O' the great Matilda, — soon they overbore
The rest of Lombardy, — not as before
By an instinctive truculence, but patched
The Kaiser's strategy until it matched
The Pontiff's, sought old ends by novel means.
" Only, why is it Salinguerra screens
Himself behind Romano ? — him we bade
Enjoy our shine i' the front, not seek the shade ! "
— Asked Heinrich, somewhat of the tardiest
To comprehend. Nor Philip acquiesced
At once in the arrangement ; reasoned, plied
His friend with offers of another bride,
A statelier function — fruitlessly : 't was plain
He sank into a sec-ondary personage, Taurello through some weakness
  must remain
Obscure. And Otho, free to judge of
  both,
— Ecelin the unready, harsh and loth,
And this more plausible and facile wight
With every point a-sparkle — chose the right,
Admiring how his predecessors harped
On the wrong man : " thus." quoth he, " wits
  are warped
By outsides ! " Carelessly, meanwhile, his life
Suffered its many turns of peace and strife
In many lands — you hardly could surprise
The man ; who shamed Sordello (recognize !)
In this as much beside, that, unconcerned
What qualities were natural or earned,
With no ideal of graces, as they came
He took them, singularly well the same —
Speaking the Greek's own language, just be-
  cause
Your Greek eludes you, leave the least of flaws
In contracts with him ; while, since Arab lore
Holds the stars' secret — take one trouble more

And master it ! 'T is done, and now deter
Who may the Tuscan, once Jove trined for her,
From Friedrich's path ! — Friedrich, whose pil-
    grimage
The same man puts aside, whom he 'll engage
To leave next year John Brienne in the lurch,
Come to Bassano, see Saint Francis' church
And judge of Guido the Bolognian's piece
Which, lend Taurello credit, rivals Greece —
Angels, with aureoles like golden quoits
Pitched home, applauding Ecelin's exploits.
For elegance, he strung the angelot,

With the   Made rhymes thereto ; for prowess,
appropri-   clove he not
ate graces   Tiso, last siege, from crest to crup-
of such.   per ? Why

Detail you thus a varied mastery
But to show how Taurello, on the watch
For men, to read their hearts and thereby catch
Their capabilities and purposes,
Displayed himself so far as displayed these :
While our Sordello only cared to know
About men as a means whereby he 'd show
Himself, and men had much or little worth
According as they kept in or drew forth
That self ; the other's choicest instruments
Surmised him shallow.
                Meantime, malcontents
Dropped off, town after town grew wiser. "How
Change the world's face ? " asked people ; " as
    't is now
It has been, will be ever : very fine
Subjecting things profane to things divine,
In talk ! This contumacy will fatigue
The vigilance of Este and the League !
The Ghibellins gain on us ! " — as it happed.
Old Azzo and old Boniface, entrapped
By Ponte Alto, both in one month's space
Slept at Verona : either left a brace
Of sons — but, three years after, either's pair
Lost Guglielm and Aldobrand its heir :
Azzo remained and Richard — all the stay
Of Este and Saint Boniface, at bay

But Ece-   As 't were. Then, either Ecelin
in, he set   grew old
in front,   Or his brain altered — not o' the
'alling,   proper mould
For new appliances — his old palm-stock
Endured no influx of strange strengths. He 'd
    rock
As in a drunkenness, or chuckle low
As proud of the completeness of his woe,
Then weep real tears ; — now make some mad
    onslaught
On Este, heedless of the lesson taught
So painfully, — now cringe for peace, sue peace
At price of past gain, bar of fresh increase
To the fortunes of Romano. Up at last
Rose Este, down Romano sank as fast.
And men remarked these freaks of peace and
    war
Happened while Salinguerra was afar :
Whence every friend besought him, all in vain,
To use his old adherent's wits again.
Not he ! — " who had advisers in his sons,
Could plot himself, nor needed any one's
Advice." 'T was Adelaide's remaining stanch

Prevented his destruction root and branch
Forthwith ; but when she died, doom fell, for
    gay
He made alliances, gave lands away
To whom it pleased accept them, and withdrew
Forever from the world. Taurello, who
Was summoned to the convent, then refused
A word at the wicket, patience thus abused.
Promptly threw off alike his imbecile
Ally's yoke, and his own frank, foolish smile.
Soon a few movements of the happier sort
Changed matters, put himself in men's report
As heretofore ; he had to fight, beside,
                And that became him ever. So, in
Salin-   pride
guerra   And flushing of this kind of second
must again   youth,
come for- He dealt a good-will blow. Este in
ward,   truth
Lay prone — and men remembered, somewhat
    late,
A laughing old outrageous stifled hate
He bore to Este — how it would outbreak
At times spite of disguise, like an earthquake
In sunny weather — as that noted day
When with his hundred friends he tried to slay
Azzo before the Kaiser's face : and how,
On Azzo's calm refusal to allow
A liegeman's challenge, straight he too was
    calmed :
As if his hate could bear to lie embalmed,
Bricked up, the moody Pharaoh, and survive
All intermediate crumblings, to arrive
At earth's catastrophe — 't was Este's crash,
Not Azzo's he demanded, so, no rash
Procedure ! Este's true antagonist
Rose out of Ecelin : all voices whist,
All eyes were sharpened, wits predicted. He
'T was, leaned in the embrasure absently,
Why and   Amused with his own efforts, now,
how, is let   to trace
out in   With his steel-sheathed forefinger
soliloquy.   Friedrich's face
I' the dust : but as the trees waved sere, his
    smile
Deepened, and words expressed its thought
    erewhile.
" Ay, fairly housed at last, my old compeer ?
That we should stick together, all the year
I kept Vicenza ! — How old Boniface,
Old Azzo caught us in its market-place,
He by that pillar, I at this, — caught each
In mid swing, more than fury of his speech,
Egging the rabble on to disavow
Allegiance to their Marquis — Bacchus, how
They boasted ! Ecelin must turn their drudge.
Nor, if released, will Salinguerra grudge
Paying arrears of tribute due long since —
Bacchus ! My man could promise then, nor
    wince,
The bones-and-muscles ! Sound of wind and
    limb,
Spoke he the set excuse I framed for him :
And now he sits me, slavering and mute,
Intent on chafing each starved purple foot
Benumbed past aching with the altar slab —
Will no vein throb there when some monk shall
    blab

Spitefully to the circle of bald scalps,
Ecelin, he did all for, 'Friedrich's affirmed to be our side the Alps'
Is a monk now, — Eh, brother Lactance, brother Anaclet?
Sworn to abjure the world, its fume and fret,
God's own now? Drop the dormitory bar,
Enfold the scanty gray serge scapular
Twice o'er the cowl to muffle memories out!
So! But the midnight whisper turns a shout,
Eyes wink, mouths open, pulses circulate
In the stone walls: the past, the world you hate
Is with you, ambush, open field — or see
The surging flame — we fire Vicenza — glee!
Follow, let Pilio and Bernardo chafe!
Bring up the Mantuans — through San Biagio — safe!
Ah, the mad people waken? Ah, they writhe
And reach us? If they block the gate? No tithe
Can pass — keep back, you Bassanese! The edge,
Use the edge — shear, thrust, hew, melt down the wedge,
Let out the black of those black upturned eyes!
Hell — are they sprinkling fire too? The blood fries
And hisses on your brass gloves as they tear
Those upturned faces choking with despair.
Brave! Slidder through the reeking gate!
    'How now?
You six had charge of her?' And then the vow
Comes, and the foam spirts, hair's plucked, till one shriek
(I hear it) and you fling — you cannot speak —
Your gold-flowered basnet to a man who haled
The Adelaide he dared scarce view unveiled
This morn, naked across the fire: how crown
The archer that exhausted lays you down
Your infant, smiling at the flame, and dies?
While one, while mine . . .
        "Bacchus! I think there lies
More than one corpse there " (and he paced the room)
" — Another cinder somewhere: 't was my doom
Beside, my doom! If Adelaide is dead,
I live the same, this Azzo lives instead
Of that to me, and we pull, any how,
Este into a heap: the matter's now
Just when the prize awaits somebody; At the true juncture slipping us so oft.
        Ay, Heinrich died and Otho, please you, doffed
His crown at such a juncture! Still, if holds
Our Friedrich's purpose, if this chain enfolds
The neck of . . . who but this same Ecelin
That must recoil when the best days begin!
Recoil? that's naught; if the recoiler leaves
His name for me to fight with, no one grieves:
But he must interfere, forsooth, unlock
His cloister to become my stumbling-block
Just as of old! Ay, ay, there't is again —
The land's inevitable Head — explain
The reverences that subject us! Count
These Ecelins now! Not to say as fount,
Originating power of thought, — from twelve
That drop i' the trenches they joined hands to delve,

Six shall surpass him, but . . . why, men must twine
Somehow with something! Ecelin's a fine
Himself, if it were only worth while, Clear name! 'T were simpler, doubt-less, twine with me
At once our cloistered friend's capacity
Was of a sort! I had to share myself
In fifty portions, like an o'ertasked elf
That's forced illume in fifty points the vast
Rare vapor he's environed by. At last
My strengths, though sorely frittered, e'en con-verge
And crown . . . no, Bacchus, they have yet to urge
The man be crowned!
        "That aloe, an he durst,
Would climb! Just such a bloated sprawler first
I noted in Messina's castle-court
The day I came, when Heinrich asked in sport
If I would pledge my faith to win him back
His right in Lombardy: 'for, once bid pack
Marauders,' he continued, 'in my stead
You rule, Taurello!' and upon this head
Laid the silk glove of Constance — I see her
Too, mantled head to foot in miniver,
Retrude following!
        "I am absolved
From further toil: the empery devolved
On me, 't was Tito's word: I have to lay
For once my plan, pursue my plan my way,
Prompt nobody, and render an account
Taurello to Taurello! Nay, I mount
To Friedrich: he conceives the post I kept,
— Who did true service, able or inept,
Who's worthy guerdon, Ecelin or I.
Me guerdoned, counsel follows: would he vie
With the Pope really? Azzo, Boniface
Compose a right-arm Hohenstauffen's race
Must break ere govern Lombardy. I point
How easy 't were to twist, once out of joint,
The socket from the bone: my Azzo's stare
Meanwhile! for I, this idle strap to wear,
Shall — fret myself abundantly, what end
To serve? There's left me twenty years to
As it may be — but also, as it may not be — spend
        — How better than my old way?
        Had I one
        Who labored to o'erthrow my work
        — a son
Hatching with Azzo superb treachery,
To root my pines up and then poison me,
Suppose — 't were worth while frustrate that!
        Beside,
Another life's ordained me: the world's tide
Rolls, and what hope of parting from the press
Of waves, a single wave through weariness
Gently lifted aside, laid upon shore?
My life must be lived out in foam and roar,
No question. Fifty years the province held
Taurello; troubles raised, and troubles quelled,
He in the midst — who leaves this quaint stone place,
These trees a year or two, then not a trace
Of him! How obtain hold, fetter men's tongues
Like this poor minstrel with the foolish songs —

To which, despite our bustle, he is linked?
— Flowers one may tease, that never grow extinct.
Ay, that patch, surely, green as ever, where
I set Her Moorish lentisk, by the stair,
To overawe the aloes; and we trod
Those flowers, how call you such? — into the sod;
A stately foreigner — a world of pain
To make it thrive, arrest rough winds — all vain!
It would decline; these would not be destroyed:
And now, where is it? where can you avoid
The flowers? I frighten children twenty years
Longer! — which way, too, Ecelin appears
To thwart me, for his son's besotted youth
Gives promise of the proper tiger-tooth:
They feel it at Vicenza! Fate, fate, fate,
My fine Taurello! Go you, promulgate
Friedrich's decree, and here 's shall aggrandize
Young Ecelin — your Prefect's badge! a prize

The supposition he most inclines to;
Too precious, certainly.
                "How now? Compete
With my old comrade? shuffle from their seat
His children? Paltry dealing! Don't I know
Ecelin? now, I think, and years ago!
What 's changed — the weakness? did not I compound
For that, and undertake to keep him sound
Despite it? Here 's Taurello hankering
After a boy's preferment — this plaything
To carry, Bacchus!" And he laughed.
                        Remark
Why schemes wherein cold-blooded men embark
Prosper, when your enthusiastic sort
Fail: while these last are ever stopping short —
(So much they should — so little they can do!)
The careless tribe see nothing to pursue
If they desist; meantime their scheme succeeds.
    Thoughts were caprices in the course of deeds
Methodic with Taurello; so, he turned,
Enough amused by fancies fairly earned
Of Este's horror-struck submitted neck,
And Richard, the cowed braggart, at his beck,

Being contented with mere vengeance.
To his own petty but immediate doubt
If he could pacify the League without
Conceding Richard; just to this was brought
That interval of vain discursive thought!
As, shall I say, some Ethiop, past pursuit
Of all enslavers, dips a shackled foot
Burnt to the blood, into the drowsy black
Enormous watercourse which guides him back
To his own tribe again, where he is king;
And laughs because he guesses, numbering
The yellower poison-wattles on the pouch
Of the first lizard wrested from its couch
Under the slime (whose skin, the while he strips
To cure his nostril with, and festered lips,
And eyeballs bloodshot through the desert-blast)
That he has reached its boundary, at last

May breathe; — thinks o'er enchantments of the South
Sovereign to plague his enemies, their mouth,
Eyes, nails, and hair; but, these enchantments tried
In fancy, puts them soberly aside
For truth, projects a cool return with friends,
The likelihood of winning mere amends
Ere long; thinks that, takes comfort silently,
Then, from the river's brink, his wrongs and he,
Hugging revenge close to their hearts, are soon
Off-striding for the Mountains of the Moon.
    Midnight: the watcher nodded on his spear,
Since clouds dispersing left a passage clear
For any meagre and discolored moon
To venture forth; and such was peering soon
Above the harassed city — her close lanes
Closer, not half so tapering her fanes,
As though she shrunk into herself to keep
What little life was saved, more safely. Heap
By heap the watch-fires mouldered, and beside
The blackest spoke Sordello and replied
Palma with none to listen. " 'T is your cause:

Sordello, taught what Ghibellins are,
            What makes a Ghibellin? There
        should be laws —
    (Remember how my youth escaped!
        I trust
    To you for manhood, Palma; tell me just
As any child) — there must be laws at work
Explaining this. Assure me, good may lurk
Under the bad, — my multitude has part
In your designs, their welfare is at heart
With Salinguerra, to their interest
Refer the deeds he dwelt on, — so divest
Our conference of much that scared me. Why
Affect that heartless tone to Tito? I
Esteemed myself, yes, in my inmost mind
This morn, a recreant to my race — mankind
O'erlooked till now: why boast my spirit's force,
—Such force denied its object? why divorce
These, then admire my spirit's flight the same
As though it bore up, helped some half-orbed flame
Else quenched in the dead void, to living space?
That orb cast off to chaos and disgrace,
Why vaunt so much my unencumbered dance,
Making a feat's facilities enhance
Its marvel? But I front Taurello, one
Of happier fate, and all I should have done,
He does; the people's good being paramount
With him, their progress may perhaps account
For his abiding still; whereas you heard
The talk with Tito — the excuse preferred
For burning those five hostages, — and broached
By way of blind, as you and I approached,
I do believe."
                She spoke: then he, "My thought
Plainlier expressed! All to your profit — naught
Meantime of these, of conquests to achieve
For them, of wretchedness he might relieve

And what Guelfs approves of neither.
    While profiting your party. Azzo too,
Supports a cause: what cause? Do Guelfs pursue

Their ends by means like yours, or better ? "
                                    When
The Guelfs were proved alike, men weighed
    with men,
And deed with deed, blaze, blood, with blood
    and blaze,
Morn broke : " Once more, Sordello, meet its
    gaze
Proudly — the people's charge against thee fails
In every point, while either party quails !
These are the busy ones : be silent thou !
Two parties take the world up, and allow
No third, yet have one principle, subsist
By the same injustice ; whoso shall enlist
With either, ranks with man's inveterate foes.
So there is one less quarrel to compose :
The Guelf, the Ghibellin may be to curse —
I have done nothing, but both sides do worse
Than nothing. Nay, to me, forgotten, reft
Of insight, lapped by trees and flowers, was
    left
The notion of a service — ha ? What lured
Me here, what mighty aim was I assured
Must move Taurello ? What if there remained
Have men   A cause, intact, distinct from these,
a cause   ordained
distinct   For me, its true discoverer ? "
from   Some one pressed
both ?   Before them here, a watcher, to
                          suggest
The subject for a ballad : " They must know
The tale of the dead worthy, long ago
Consul of Rome — that 's long ago for us,
Minstrels and bowmen, idly squabbling thus
In the world's corner — but too late no doubt,
For the brave time he sought to bring about.
Who was   — Not know Crescentius Nomen-
the famed   tanus ? " Then
Roman   He cast about for terms to tell him,
Crescen-   when
tius ?   Sordello disavowed it, how they
                          used
Whenever their Superior introduced
A novice to the Brotherhood — (" for I
Was just a brown-sleeve brother, merrily
Appointed too," quoth he, " till Innocent
Bade me relinquish, to my small content,
My wife or my brown sleeves ") — some brother
    spoke
Ere nocturns of Crescentius, to revoke
The edict issued, after his demise,
Which blotted fame alike and effigies,
All out except a floating power, a name
Including, tending to produce the same
Great act. Rome, dead, forgotten, lived at least
Within that brain, though to a vulgar priest
And a vile stranger, — two not worth a slave
Of Rome's, Pope John, King Otho, — fortune
    gave
The rule there : so, Crescentius, haply dressed
In white, called Roman Consul for a jest,
Taking the people at their word, forth stepped
As upon Brutus' heel, nor ever kept
Rome waiting, — stood erect, and from his brain
Gave Rome out on its ancient place again,
Ay, bade proceed with Brutus' Rome, Kings
    styled
Themselves mere citizens of, and, beguiled

Into great thoughts thereby, would choose the
    gem
Out of a lapfull, spoil their diadem
— The Senate's cypher was so hard to scratch
He flashes like a phanal, all men catch
The flame, Rome 's just accomplished ! when
    returned
Otho, with John, the Consul's step had spurned
And Hugo Lord of Este, to redress
The wrongs of each. Crescentius in the stress
Of adverse fortune bent. " They crucified
Their Consul in the Forum ; and abide
E'er since such slaves at Rome, that I — (for I
Was once a brown-sleeve brother, merrily
Appointed) — I had option to keep wife
Or keep brown sleeves, and managed in the strife
Lose both. A song of Rome ! "
                            And Rome, indeed,
Robed at Goito in fantastic weed,
The Mother-City of his Mantuan days,
Looked an established point of light whence rays
Traversed the world ; for, all the clustered
    homes
Beside of men, seemed bent on being Romes
In their degree ; the question was, how each
Should most resemble Rome, clean out of reach.
Nor, of the Two, did either principle
How if, in   Struggle to change — but to possess
the reinte-   — Rome, still,
gration of   Guelf Rome or Ghibellin Rome.
Rome,   Let Rome advance !
Rome, as she struck Sordello's ignorance —
How could he doubt one moment ? Rome 's the
    Cause !
Rome of the Pandects, all the world's new
    laws —
Of the Capitol, of Castle Angelo ;
New structures, that inordinately glow,
Subdued, brought back to harmony, made ripe
By many a relic of the archetype
Extant for wonder ; every upstart church
That hoped to leave old temples in the lurch,
Corrected by the Theatre forlorn
That, — as a mundane shell, its world late
    born, —
Lay and o'ershadowed it. These hints combined,
Be typified   Rome typifies the scheme to put man-
the tri-   kind
umph of   Once more in full possession of their
mankind ?   rights.
" Let us have Rome again ! On me it lights
To build up Rome — on me, the first and last :
For such a future was endured the past ! "
And thus, in the gray twilight, forth he sprung
To give his thought consistency among
The very People — let their facts avail
Finish the dream grown from the archer's tale

BOOK THE FIFTH

Is it the same Sordello in the dusk
As at the dawn ? — merely a perished husk
Now, that arose a power fit to build
Mankind   Up Rome again ? The proud con-
triumph of   ception chilled
a sudden ?   So soon ? Ay, watch that latest
                          dream of thine

— A Rome indebted to no Palatine —
Drop arch by arch, Sordello! Art possessed
Of thy wish now, rewarded for thy quest
To-day among Ferrara's squalid sons?
Are this and this and this the shining ones
Meet for the Shining City? Sooth to say,
Your favored tenantry pursue their way
After a fashion! This companion slips
On the smooth causey, t' other blinkard trips
At his mooned sandal. "Leave to lead the
    brawls
Here i' the atria?" No, friend! He that sprawls
On aught but a stibadium . . . what his dues
Who puts the lustral vase to such an use?
Oh, huddle up the day's disasters! March,
Ye runagates, and drop thou, arch by arch,
Rome!
    Yet before they quite disband — a whim —
Study mere shelter, now, for him, and him,
Nay, even the worst, — just house them! Any
    cave
Suffices: throw out earth! A loophole? Brave!
They ask to feel the sun shine, see the grass
Grow, hear the larks sing? Dead art thou, alas,
And I am dead! But here's our son excels
At hurdle-weaving any Scythian, fells
Oak and devises rafters, dreams and shapes
His dream into a door-post, just escapes
The mystery of hinges. Lie we both
Perdue another age. The goodly growth
Of brick and stone! Our building-pelt was
    rough,
But that descendant's garb suits well enough
A portico-contriver. Speed the years —

Why, the work should be one of ages, What's time to us? At last, a city
    rears
Itself! nay, enter — what's the grave
    to us?
Lo, our forlorn acquaintance carry thus
The head! Successively sewer, forum, cirque —
Last age, an aqueduct was counted work,
But now they tire the artificer upon
Blank alabaster, black obsidion,
— Careful, Jove's face be duly fulgurant,
And mother Venus' kiss-creased nipples pant
Back into pristine pulpiness, ere fixed
Above the baths. What difference betwixt
This Rome and ours — resemblance what, be-
    tween
That scurvy dumb - show and this pageant
    sheen —
These Romans and our rabble? Use thy wit!
The work marched: step by step, — a workman
    fit
Took each, nor too fit, — to one task, one time, —
No leaping o'er the petty to the prime,

If per-formed equally and thor-oughly; When just the substituting osier lithe
For brittle bulrush, sound wood for
    soft withe,
To further loam-and-roughcast-work
    a stage, —
Exacts an architect, exacts an age:
No tables of the Mauritanian tree
For men whose maple log's their luxury!
That way was Rome built. "Better" (say
    you) "merge
At once all workmen in the demiurge,
All epochs in a lifetime, every task

In one!" So should the sudden city bask
I' the day — while those we'd feast there, want
    the knack
Of keeping fresh-chalked gowns from speck and
    brack,
Distinguish not rare peacock from vile swan
Nor Mareotic juice from Cæcuban.
"Enough of Rome! 'T was happy to conceive
Rome on a sudden, nor shall fate bereave
Me of that credit: for the rest, her spite
Is an old story — serves my folly right
By adding yet another to the dull
List of abortions — things proved beautiful
Could they be done, Sordello cannot do."
He sat upon the terrace, plucked and threw
The powdery aloe-cusps away, saw shift
Rome's walls, and drop arch after arch, and
    drift
Mist-like afar those pillars of all stripe,
Mounds of all majesty. "Thou archetype,
Last of my dreams and loveliest, depart!"
    And then a low voice wound into his heart
"Sordello!" (low as some old Pythoness
Conceding to a Lydian King's distress
The cause of his long error — one mistake
Of her past oracle) "Sordello, wake!
God has conceded two sights to a man —

And a man can do but a man's portion. One, of men's whole work, time's
    completed plan,
The other, of the minute's work,
    man's first
Step to the plan's completeness: what's dis-
    persed
Save hope of that supreme step which, descried
Earliest, was meant still to remain untried
Only to give you heart to take your own
Step, and there stay — leaving the rest alone?
Where is the vanity? Why count as one
The first step, with the last step? What is gone
Except Rome's aëry magnificence,
That last step you'd take first? — an evidence
You were God: be man now! Let those glances
    fall!
The basis, the beginning step of all,
Which proves you just a man — is that gone too?
Pity to disconcert one versed as you
In fate's ill-nature! but its full extent
Eludes Sordello, even: the veil rent,
Read the black writing — that collective man
Outstrips the individual! Who began

The last of each series of work-men The acknowledged greatnesses? Ay,
    your own art
Shall serve us: put the poet's mimes
    apart —
Close with the poet's self, and lo, a dim
Yet too plain form divides itself from him!
Alcamo's song enmeshes the lulled Isle,
Woven into the echoes left erewhile
By Nina, one soft web of song: no more
Turning his name, then, flower-like o'er and
    o'er!
An elder poet in the younger's place;
Nina's the strength, but Alcamo's the grace:
Each neutralizes each then! Search your fill;
You get no whole and perfect Poet — still
New Ninas, Alcamos, till time's mid-night
Shrouds all — or better say, the shutting light
Of a forgotten yesterday. Dissect

Every ideal workman — (to reject
In favor of your fearful ignorance
The thousand phantasms eager to advance,
Sums up in himself all predecessors. And point you but to those within
your reach) —
predecessors. Were you the first who brought —
(in modern speech)
The Multitude to be materialized?
That loose eternal unrest — who devised
An apparition i' the midst? The rout
Was checked, a breathless ring was formed
about
That sudden flower: get round at any risk
The gold-rough pointel, silver-blazing disk
O' the lily! Swords across it! Reign thy reign
We just see Charlemagne, And serve thy frolic service, Charle-
magne!
lemagne, — The very child of over-joyousness,
Hildebrand, Unfeeling thence, strong therefore:
Strength by stress
Of Strength comes of that forehead confident,
Those widened eyes expecting heart's content,
A calm as out of just-quelled noise; nor swerves
For doubt, the ample cheek in gracious curves
Abutting on the upthrust nether lip:
He wills, how should he doubt then? Ages slip:
Was it Sordello pried into the work
So far accomplished, and discovered lurk
A company amid the other clans,
Only distinct in priests for castellans
And popes for suzerains (their rule confessed
Its rule, their interest its interest,
Living for sake of living — there an end, —
Wrapt in itself, no energy to spend
In making adversaries or allies), —
Dived you into its capabilities
And dared create, out of that sect, a soul
Should turn a multitude, already whole,
Into its body? Speak plainer! Is 't so sure
God's church lives by a King's investiture?
Look to last step! A staggering — a shock —
What 's mere sand is demolished, while the rock
Endures: a column of black fiery dust
Blots heaven — that help was prematurely thrust
Aside, perchance! — but air clears, naught 's
erased
Of the true outline! Thus much being firm
based,
The other was a scaffold. See him stand
Buttressed upon his mattock, Hildebrand
Of the huge brain-mask welded ply o'er ply
As in a forge; it buries either eye
White and extinct, that stupid brow; teeth
clenched,
The neck tight-corded, too, the chin deep-
trenched,
As if a cloud enveloped him while fought
Under its shade, grim prizers, thought with
thought
At dead-lock, agonizing he, until
The victor thought leap radiant up, and Will,
The slave with folded arms and drooping lids
They fought for, lean forth flame-like as it
bids.
Call him no flower — a mandrake of the earth,
Thwarted and dwarfed and blasted in its birth,
Rather, — a fruit of suffering's excess,
Thence feeling, therefore stronger: still by stress

Of Strength, work Knowledge! Full three hun-
dred years
Have men to wear away in smiles and tears
Between the two that nearly seemed to touch
In composite work they end and name. Observe you! quit one workman and
you clutch
Another, letting both their trains go
by —
The actors-out of either's policy,
Heinrich, on this hand, Otho, Barbaross,
Carry the three Imperial crowns across,
Aix' Iron, Milan's Silver, and Rome's Gold —
While Alexander, Innocent uphold
On that, each Papal key — but, link on link,
Why is it neither chain betrays a chink?
How coalesce the small and great? Alack,
For one thrust forward, fifty such fall back!
Do the popes coupled there help Gregory
Alone? Hark — from the hermit Peter's cry
At Claremont, down to the first serf that says
Friedrich 's no liege of his while he delays
Getting the Pope's curse off him! The Cru-
sade —
Or trick of breeding Strength by other aid
Than Strength, is safe. Hark — from the wild
harangue
Of Vimmercato, to the carroch's clang
Yonder! The League — or trick of turning
Strength
Against Pernicious Strength, is safe at length.
Yet hark — from Mantuan Albert making cease
The fierce ones, to Saint Francis preaching peace
Yonder! God's Truce — or trick to supersede
The very Use of Strength, is safe. Indeed
We trench upon the future. Who is found
To take next step, next age — trail o'er the
ground —
Shall I say, gourd-like? — not the flower's dis-
play
Nor the root's prowess, but the plenteous way
O' the plant — produced by joy and sorrow,
whence
Unfeeling and yet feeling, strongest thence?
Knowledge by stress of merely Knowledge?
No —
E'en were Sordello ready to forego
His life for this, 't were overleaping work
Some one has first to do, howe'er it irk,
Nor stray a foot's breadth from the beaten road.
Who means to help must still support the load
Hildebrand lifted — 'why hast Thou,' he
groaned,
'Imposed on me a burden, Paul had moaned,
And Moses dropped beneath?' Much done —
and yet
Doubtless that grandest task God ever set
On man, left much to do: at his arm's wrench,
Charlemagne's scaffold fell; but pillars blench
Merely, start back again — perchance have been
Taken for buttresses: crash every screen,
Hammer the tenons better, and engage
A gang about your work, for the next age
Or two, of Knowledge, part by Strength and part
By Knowledge! Then, indeed, perchance may
start
Sordello on his race — would time divulge
Such secrets! If one step 's awry, one bulge
Calls for correction by a step we thought

Got over long since, why, till that is wrought,
No progress! And the scaffold in its turn
Becomes, its service o'er, a thing to spurn.
Meanwhile, if your half-dozen years of life
In store dispose you to forego the strife,
Who takes exception? Only bear in mind,
Ferrara's reached, Goito's left behind:

If associates trouble you, stand off! As you then were, as half yourself, desist!
— The warrior-part of you may, an it list,
Finding real falchions difficult to poise,
Fling them afar and taste the cream of joys
By wielding such in fancy, — what is bard
Of you may spurn the vehicle that marred
Elys so much, and in free fancy glut
His sense, yet write no verses — you have but
To please yourself for law, and once could please
What once appeared yourself, by dreaming these
Rather than doing these, in days gone by.
But all is changed the moment you descry
Mankind as half yourself, — then, fancy's trade
Ends once and always: how may half evade
The other half? men are found half of you.
Out of a thousand helps, just one or two
Can be accomplished presently: but flinch
From these (as from the falchion, raised an inch,
Elys, described a couplet) and make proof
Of fancy, — then, while one half lolls aloof
I' the vines, completing Rome to the tip-top —
See if, for that, your other half will stop

Should the new sympathies allow you. A tear, begin a smile! The rabble's woes,
Ludicrous in their patience as they chose
To sit about their town and quietly
Be slaughtered, — the poor reckless soldiery,
With their ignoble rhymes on Richard, how
'Polt-foot,' sang they, 'was in a pitfall now,'
Cheering each other from the engine-mounts, —
That crippled sprawling idiot who recounts
How, lopped of limbs, he lay, stupid as stone,
Till the pains crept from out him one by one,
And wriggles round the archers on his head
To earn a morsel of their chestnut bread, —
And Cino, always in the self-same place
Weeping; beside that other wretch's case,
Eyepits to ear, one gangrene since he plied
The engine in his coat of raw sheep's hide
A double watch in the noon sun; and see
Lucchino, beauty, with the favors free,
Trim hacqueton, spruce beard and scented hair,
Campaigning it for the first time — cut there
In two already, boy enough to crawl
For latter orpine round the southern wall,
Tomà, where Richard's kept, because that whore
Marfisa, the fool never saw before,
Sickened for flowers this wearisomest siege:
And Tiso's wife — men liked their pretty liege,
Cared for her least of whims once, — Berta, wed
A twelvemonth gone, and, now poor Tiso's dead,
Delivering herself of his first child
On that chance heap of wet filth, reconciled
To fifty gazers!" — (Here a wind below
Made moody music augural of woe
From the pine barrier) — "What if, now the scene

Draws to a close, yourself have really been
Time having been lost, — You, plucking purples in Goito's moss
choose quick! Like edges of a trabea (not to cross
Your consul-humor) or dry aloe-shafts
For fasces, at Ferrara — he, fate wafts,
This very age, her whole inheritance
Of opportunities? Yet you advance
Upon the last! Since talking is your trade,
There's Salinguerra left you to persuade:
Fail! then" —
    "No — no — which latest chance secure!"
Leaped up and cried Sordello: "this made sure,
The past were yet redeemable; its work
Was — help the Guelfs, whom I, howe'er it irk,
Thus help!" He shook the foolish aloe-haulm
He takes his first step as a Guelf; Out of his doublet, paused, proceeded calm
To the appointed presence. The large head
Turned on its socket; "And your spokesman," said
The large voice, " is Elcorte's happy sprout?
Few such " — (so finishing a speech no doubt
Addressed to Palma, silent at his side)
"— My sober councils have diversified.
Elcorte's son! good: forward as you may,
Our lady's minstrel with so much to say!"
The hesitating sunset floated back,
Rosily traversed in the wonted track
The chamber, from the lattice o'er the girth
Of pines, to the huge eagle blacked in earth
Opposite, — outlined sudden, spur to crest,
That solid Salinguerra, and caressed
Palma's contour; 't was day looped back night's pall;
Sordello had a chance left spite of all.
And much he made of the convincing speech
Meant to compensate for the past and reach
Through his youth's daybreak of unprofit, quite
To his noon's labor, so proceed till night
Leisurely! The great argument to bind
Taurello with the Guelf Cause, body and mind,
— Came the consummate rhetoric to that?
Yet most Sordello's argument dropped flat
Through his accustomed fault of breaking yoke,
Disjoining him who felt from him who spoke.
Was't not a touching incident — so prompt
A rendering the world its just accompt,
Once proved its debtor? Who'd suppose, before
This proof, that he, Goito's god of yore,
At duty's instance could demean himself
So memorably, dwindle to a Guelf?
Be sure, in such delicious flattery steeped,
His inmost self at the out-portion peeped,
Thus occupied; then stole a glance at those
Appealed to, curious if her color rose
Or his lip moved, while he discreetly urged
The need of Lombardy becoming purged
At soonest of her barons; the poor part
Abandoned thus, missing the blood at heart
And spirit in brain, unseasonably off
Elsewhere! But, though his speech was worthy scoff,
Good-humored Salinguerra, famed for tact
And tongue, who, careless of his phrase, ne'er lacked

The right phrase, and harangued Honorius
    dumb
At his accession, — looked as all fell plumb
To purpose and himself found interest
In every point his new instructor pressed
— Left playing with the rescript's white wax
    seal
To scrutinize Sordello head and heel.
He means to yield assent sure? No, alas!
All he replied was, "What, it comes to pass
That poesy, sooner than politics,
Makes fade young hair?" To think such
    speech could fix
Taurello!
      Then a flash of bitter truth:
So fantasies could break and fritter youth
That he had long ago lost earnestness,

But to will and to do are different: Lost will to work, lost power to even express
The need of working! Earth was
    turned a grave:
No more occasions now, though he should crave
Just one, in right of superhuman toil,
To do what was undone, repair such spoil,
Alter the past — nothing would give the chance!
Not that he was to die; he saw askance
Protract the ignominious years beyond
To dream in — time to hope and time despond,
Remember and forget, be sad, rejoice
As saved a trouble; he might, at his choice,
One way or other, idle life out, drop

He may sleep on the bed he has made.   No few smooth verses by the way — for prop,
A thyrsus, these sad people, all the same,
Should pick up, and set store by, — far from
    blame,
Plant o'er his hearse, convinced his better part
Survived him. "Rather tear men out the heart
O' the truth!" — Sordello muttered, and re-
    newed
His propositions for the Multitude.
But Salinguerra, who at this attack
Had thrown great breast and ruffling corselet
    back
To hear the better, smilingly resumed
His task; beneath, the carroch's warning
    boomed;
He must decide with Tito; courteously
He turned then, even seeming to agree
With his admonisher — "Assist the Pope,
Extend Guelf domination, fill the scope
O' the Church, thus based on All, by All, for
    All —
Change Secular to Evangelical" —
Echoing his very sentence: all seemed lost,
When suddenly he looked up, laughingly al-
    most,
To Palma: "This opinion of your friend's —
For instance, would it answer Palma's ends?
Best, were it not, turn Guelf, submit our
    Strength" —
(Here he drew out his baldric to its length)
— "To the Pope's Knowledge — let our captive
    slip,
Wide to the walls throw ope our gates, equip
Azzo with ... what I hold here! Who'll
    subscribe

To a trite censure of the minstrel tribe
Henceforward? or pronounce, as Heinrich used,
'Spear-heads for battle, burr-heads for the
    joust!'
— When Constance, for his couplets, would
    promote
Alcamo, from a parti-colored coat,
To holding her lord's stirrup in the wars.
Not that I see where couplet-making jars
With common sense: at Mantua I had borne
This chanted, better than their most forlorn
Of bull-baits, — that's indisputable!"
                Brave
Whom vanity nigh slew, contempt shall save!
All's at an end: a Troubadour suppose
Mankind will class him with their friends or
    foes?

Scorn flings cold water in his face,   A puny uncouth ailing vassal think
The world and him bound in some
    special link?
Abrupt the visionary tether burst.
What were rewarded here, or what amerced
If a poor drudge, solicitous to dream
Deservingly, got tangled by his theme
So far as to conceit the knack or gift
Or whatsoe'er it be, of verse, might lift
The globe, a lever like the hand and head
Of — "Men of Action," as the Jongleurs said,
— "The Great Men," in the people's dialect?
And not a moment did this scorn affect

Arouses him at last, to some purpose,   Sordello: scorn the poet? They, for once,
Asking "what was," obtained a full response.
Bid Naddo think at Mantua, he had but
To look into his promptuary, put
Finger on a set thought in a set speech:
But was Sordello fitted thus for each
Conjecture? Nowise; since within his soul,
Perception brooded unexpressed and whole.
A healthy spirit like a healthy frame
Craves aliment in plenty — all the same,
Changes, assimilates its aliment.
Perceived Sordello, on a truth intent?
Next day no formularies more you saw
Than figs or olives in a sated maw.
'T is Knowledge, whither such perceptions tend;
They lose themselves in that, means to an end,
The many old producing some one new,
A last unlike the first. If lies are true,
The Caliph's wheel-work man of brass receives
A meal, munched millet grains and lettuce
    leaves
Together in his stomach rattle loose;
You find them perfect next day to produce:
But ne'er expect the man, on strength of that,
Can roll an iron camel-collar flat
Like Haroun's self! I tell you, what was stored

And thus gets the utmost out of him.   Bit by bit through Sordello's life, outpoured
That eve, was, for that age, a novel
    thing:
And round those three the People formed a ring
Of visionary judges whose award
He recognized in full — faces that barred
Henceforth return to the old careless life,
In whose great presence, therefore, his first strife
For their sake must not be ignobly fought:

All these, for once, approved of him, he thought,
Suspended their own vengeance, chose await
The issue of this strife to reinstate
Them in the right of taking it — in fact
He must be proved king ere they could exact
Vengeance for such king's defalcation. Last,
A reason why the phrases flowed so fast
Was in his quite forgetting for a time
Himself in his amazement that the rhyme
Disguised the royalty so much : he there —
And Salinguerra yet all unaware
Who was the lord, who liegeman !
 " Thus I lay
On thine my spirit and compel obey
His lord, — my liegeman, —impotent to build
Another Rome, but hardly so unskilled
In what such builder should have been, as brook
One shame beyond the charge that I forsook
His function ! Free me from that shame, I bend
A brow before, suppose new years to spend, —
Allow each chance, nor fruitlessly, recur —
Measure thee with the Minstrel, then, demur

He asserts the poet's rank and right,   At any crowd he claims ! That I must cede
Shamed now, my right to my especial meed —
Confess thee fitter help the world than I
Ordained its champion from eternity,
Is much : but to behold thee scorn the post
I quit in thy behalf — to hear thee boast
What makes my own despair !" And while he rung
The changes on this theme, the roof up-sprung,
The sad walls of the presence-chamber died
Into the distance, or embowering vied
With far-away Goito's vine-frontier ;
And crowds of faces — (only keeping clear
The rose-light in the midst, his vantage-ground
To fight their battle from) — deep clustered round
Sordello, with good wishes no mere breath,
Kind prayers for him no vapor, since, come death,
Come life, he was fresh-sinewed every joint,
Each bone new-marrowed as whom gods anoint
Though mortal to their rescue. Now let sprawl
The snaky volumes hither ! Is Typhon all
For Hercules to trample — good report
From Salinguerra only to extort ?
" So was I " (closed he his inculcating,
A poet must be earth's essential king)

Basing these on their proper ground,   " So was I, royal so, and if I fail,
'T is not the royalty, ye witness quail,
But one deposed who, caring not exert
Its proper essence, trifled malapert
With accidents instead — good things assigned
As heralds of a better thing behind —
And, worthy through display of these, put forth
Never the inmost all-surpassing worth
That constitutes him king precisely since
As yet no other spirit may evince
Its like : the power he took most pride to test,
Whereby all forms of life had been professed
At pleasure, forms already on the earth,
Was but a means to power beyond, whose birth

Should, in its novelty, be kingship's proof.
Now, whether he came near or kept aloof
The several forms he longed to imitate,
Not there the kingship lay, he sees too late.
Those forms, unalterable first as last,
Proved him her copier, not the protoplast
Of nature : what would come of being free,
By action to exhibit tree for tree,
Bird, beast, for beast and bird, or prove earth bore
One veritable man or woman more ?
Means to an end, such proofs are : what the end ?
Let essence, whatsoe'er it be, extend —
Never contract. Already you include
The multitude ; then let the multitude
Include yourself ; and the result were new :
Themselves before, the multitude turn you.
This were to live and move and have, in them,
Your being, and secure a diadem
You should transmit (because no cycle yearns
Beyond itself, but on itself returns)
When, the full sphere in wane, the world o'er laid
Long since with you, shall have in turn obeyed
Some orb still prouder, some displayer, still
More potent than the last, of human will,

Recognizing true dignity in service,   And some new king depose the old.
 Of such
Am I — whom pride of this elates too much ?
Safe, rather say, 'mid troops of peers again ;
I, with my words, hailed brother of the train
Deeds once sufficed : for, let the world roll back,
Who fails, through deeds howe'er diverse, re-track
My purpose still, my task ? A teeming crust —
Air, flame, earth, wave at conflict ! Then, needs must
Emerge some Calm embodied, these refer
The brawl to — yellow-bearded Jupiter ?
No ! Saturn ; some existence like a pact
And protest against Chaos, some first fact
I' the faint of time. My deep of life, I know,
Is unavailing e'en to poorly show " . . .
For here the Chief immeasurably yawned)
. . . " Deeds in their due gradation till Song dawned —
The fullest effluence of the finest mind,
All in degree, no way diverse in kind
From minds about it, minds which, more or less,
Lofty or low, move seeking to impress

Whether successively that of epoist,   Themselves on somewhat ; but one mind has climbed
Step after step, by just ascent sublimed.
Thought is the soul of act, and, stage by stage,
Soul is from body still to disengage
As tending to a freedom which rejects
Such help and incorporeally affects
The world, producing deeds but not by deeds,
Swaying, in others, frames itself exceeds,
Assigning them the simpler tasks it used
To patiently perform till Song produced
Acts, by thoughts only, for the mind : divest
Mind of e'en Thought, and, lo, God's unexpressed

Will draws above us ! All then is to win
Save that. How much for me, then? where begin
My work? About me, faces ! and they flock,
The earnest faces. What shall I unlock
By song? behold me prompt, whate'er it be,
To minister : how much can mortals see
Of Life ? No more than so? I take the task
And marshal you Life's elemental masque,
Show Men, on evil or on good lay stress,

Dramatist, or, so to call him, analyst, This light, this shade make promi-
nent, suppress
All ordinary hues that softening blend
Such natures with the level. Apprehend
Which sinner is, which saint, if I allot
Hell, Purgatory, Heaven, a blaze or blot,
To those you doubt concerning ! I enwomb
Some wretched Friedrich with his red-hot tomb ,
Some dubious spirit, Lombard Agilulph
With the black chastening river I engulf !
Some unapproached Matilda I enshrine
With languors of the planet of decline —
These, fail to recognize, to arbitrate
Between henceforth, to rightly estimate
Thus marshalled in the masque ! Myself, the while,
As one of you, am witness, shrink or smile
At my own showing ! Next age — what 's to do?
The men and women stationed hitherto
Will I unstation, good and bad, conduct
Each nature to its farthest, or obstruct
At soonest, in the world : light, thwarted, breaks
A limpid purity to rainbow flakes,
Or shadow, massed, freezes to gloom : behold
How such, with fit assistance to unfold,
Or obstacles to crush them, disengage
Their forms, love, hate, hope, fear, peace make, war wage,
In presence of you all ! Myself, implied
Superior now, as, by the platform's side,
I bade them do and suffer, — would last content
The world . . . no — that 's too far ! I cir-
cumvent
A few, my masque contented, and to these
Offer unveil the last of mysteries —
Man's inmost life shall have yet freer play :
Once more I cast external things away,
And natures composite, so decompose
That " . . . Why, he writes Sordello!
"How I rose,
And how have you advanced ! since evermore
Yourselves effect what I was fain before
Effect, what I supplied yourselves suggest,
What I leave bare yourselves can now invest.
How we attain to talk as brothers talk,
In half-words, call things by half-names, no balk
From discontinuing old aids. To-day
Takes in account the work of Yesterday :
Has not the world a Past now, its adept
Consults ere he dispense with or accept
New aids? a single touch more may enhance,
A touch less turned to insignificance
Those structures' symmetry the past has strewed

The world with, once so bare. Leave the mere rude
Who turns in due course synthetist. Explicit details ! 't is but brother's speech
We need, speech where an accent's change gives each
The other's soul — no speech to understand
By former audience : need was then to expand,
Expatiate — hardly were we brothers ! true —
Nor I lament my small remove from you,
Nor reconstruct what stands already. Ends
Accomplished turn to means : my art intends
New structure from the ancient : as they changed
The spoils of every clime at Venice, ranged
The horned and snouted Libyan god, upright
As in his desert, by some simple bright
Clay cinerary pitcher — Thebes as Rome,
Athens as Byzant rifled, till their Dome
From earth's reputed consummations razed
A seal the all-transmuting Triad blazed
Above. Ah, whose that fortune ? Ne'erthe-
less
E'en he must stoop contented to express
No tithe of what 's to say — the vehicle
Never sufficient : but his work is still
For faces like the faces that select
This for one day: now, serve as Guelf ! The single service I am bound
effect, —
That bid me cast aside such fancies,
bow
Taurello to the Guelf cause, disallow
The Kaiser's coming — which with heart, soul, strength,
I labor for, this eve, who feel at length
My past career's outrageous vanity,
And would, as it amends, die, even die
Now I first estimate the boon of life,
If death might win compliance — sure, this strife
Is right for once — the People my support."
My poor Sordello ! what may we extort
By this, I wonder? Palma's lighted eyes
Turned to Taurello who, long past surprise,
Began, "You love him — what you 'd say at large
Let me say briefly. First, your father's charge
To me, his friend, peruse : I guessed indeed
You were no stranger to the course decreed.
Salin- guerra, dislodged from his post, He bids me leave his children to the saints :
As for a certain project, he acquaints
The Pope with that, and offers him the best
Of your possessions to permit the rest
Go peaceably — to Ecelin, a stripe
Of soil the cursed Vicentines will gripe,
— To Alberic, a patch the Trevisan
Clutches already ; extricate, who can,
Treville, Villarazzi, Puissolo,
Loria and Cartiglione ! — all must go,
And with them go my hopes. 'T is lost, there !
Lost
This eve, our crisis, and some pains it cost
Procuring ; thirty years — as good I 'd spent
Like our admonisher ! But each his bent
Pursues : no question, one might live absurd
One's self this while, by deed as he by word
Persisting to obtrude an influence where

'T is made account of, much as . . . nay, you
        fare
With twice the fortune, youngster ! — I submit,
Happy to parallel my waste of wit
With the renowned Sordello's : you decide
A course for me. Romano may abide
Romano, — Bacchus !   After all, what dearth
Of Ecelins and Alberics on earth ?
Say there 's a prize in prospect, must disgrace
Betide competitors, unless they style
Themselves Romano ? Were it worth my while
To try my own luck ! But an obscure place
Suits me — there wants a youth to bustle,
        stalk
And attitudinize — some fight, more talk,
Most flaunting badges — how, I might make
        clear
Since Friedrich's very purposes lie here
— Here, pity they are like to lie ! For me,
With station fixed unceremoniously
Long since, small use contesting ; I am but
The liegeman — you are born the lieges — shut
That gentle mouth now ! or resume your kin
In your sweet self ; were Palma Ecelin
For me to work with ! Could that neck en-
        dure
This bauble for a cumbrous garniture,
She should . . . or might one bear it for her ?
        Stay —
I have not been so flattered many a day
As by your pale friend — Bacchus !   The least
        help
Would lick the hind's fawn to a lion's whelp :
His neck is broad enough — a ready tongue
Beside — too writhled — but, the main thing,
        young —
I could . . . why, look ye ! "
                        And the badge was thrown

In mov-
ing, opens
a door to
Sordello,
Across Sordello's neck : "This
        badge alone
Makes you Romano's Head — be-
        comes superb
On your bare neck, which would, on mine, dis-
        turb
The pauldron," said Taurello. A mad act,
Nor even dreamed about before — in fact,
Not when his sportive arm rose for the nonce —
But he had dallied overmuch, this once,
With power : the thing was done, and he, aware
The thing was done, proceeded to declare —
(So like a nature made to serve, excel·
In serving, only feel by service well !)
— That he would make Sordello that and more.
" As good a scheme as any. What 's to pore
At in my face ? " he asked — " ponder instead
This piece of news ; you are Romano's Head !
One cannot slacken pace so near the goal,
Suffer my Azzo to escape heart-whole
This time ! For you there 's Palma to
        espouse —
For me, one crowning trouble ere I house
Like my compeer."
                        On which ensued a strange
And solemn visitation ; there came change
O'er every one of them ; each looked on each :
Up in the midst a truth grew, without speech.
And when the giddiness sank and the haze
Subsided, they were sitting, no amaze,

Sordello with the baldric on, his sire
Who is de-
clared Sal-
inguerra's
son,
Silent, though his proportions seemed
        aspire
Momently ; and, interpreting the
        thrill
Right at its ebb, Palma was found there still
Relating somewhat Adelaide confessed
A year ago, while dying on her breast, —
Of a contrivance that Vicenza night
When Ecelin had birth. "Their convoy's flight,
Cut off a moment, coiled inside the flame
That wallowed like a dragon at his game
The toppling city through — San Biagio rocks !
And wounded lies in her delicious locks
Retrude, the frail mother, on her face,
None of her wasted, just in one embrace
Covering her child : when, as they lifted her,
Cleaving the tumult, mighty, mightier
And mightiest Taurello's cry outbroke,
Leapt like a tongue of fire that cleaves the
        smoke,
Midmost to cheer his Mantuans onward —
        drown
His colleague Ecelin's clamor, up and down
The disarray : failed Adelaide see then
Who was the natural chief, the man of men ?
Outstripping time, her infant there burst
        swathe,
Stood up with eyes haggard beyond the scathe
From wandering after his heritage
Lost once and lost for aye — and why that rage,
That deprecating glance ? A new shape leant
On a familiar shape — gloatingly bent
O'er his discomfiture ; 'mid wreaths it wore,
Still one outflamed the rest — her child's be-
        fore
'T was Salinguerra's for his child : scorn, hate,
Rage now might startle her when all too late !
Then was the moment ! — rival's foot had
        spurned
Hidden
hitherto
by Ade-
laide's
policy.
Never that House to earth else !
        Sense returned —
The act conceived, adventured and
        complete,
They bore away to an obscure retreat
Mother and child — Retrude's self not slain "
(Nor even here Taurello moved) " though pain
Was fled : and what assured them most 't was
        fled,
All pain, was, if they raised the pale hushed
        head
'T would turn this way and that, waver awhile,
And only settle into its old smile —
(Graceful as the disquieted water-flag
Steadying itself, remarked they, in the quag
On either side their path) — when suffered look
Down on her child. They marched : no sign
        once shook
The company's close litter of crossed spears
Till, as they reached Goito, a few tears
Slipped in the sunset from her long black lash,
And she was gone. So far the action rash ;
No crime. They laid Retrude in the font,
Taurello's very gift, her child was wont
To sit beneath — constant as eve he came
To sit by its attendant girls the same
As one of them. For Palma, she would blend
With this magnific spirit to the end.

That ruled her first; but scarcely had she
    dared
To disobey the Adelaide who scared
Her into vowing never to disclose
A secret to her husband, which so froze
His blood at half-recital, she contrived
To hide from him Taurello's infant lived,
Lest, by revealing that, himself should mar
Romano's fortunes. And, a crime so far,
Palma received that action: she was told
Of Salinguerra's nature, of his cold
Calm acquiescence in his lot! But free
To impart the secret to Romano, she

How the   Engaged to repossess Sordello of
discovery His heritage, and hers, and that way
moves   doff
Salin-   The mask, but after years, long years:
guerra,   while now,
Was not Romano's sign-mark on that brow?"
  Across Taurello's heart his arms were locked:
And when he did speak 't was as if he mocked
The minstrel, "who had not to move," he said,
" Nor stir — should fate defraud him of a shred
Of his son's infancy? much less his youth!"
(Laughingly all this) — " which to aid, in truth,
Himself, reserved on purpose, had not grown
Old, not too old — 't was best they kept alone
Till now, and never idly met till now; "
— Then, in the same breath, told Sordello how
All intimations of this eve's event
Were lies, for Friedrich must advance to Trent,
Thence to Verona, then to Rome, there stop,
Tumble the Church down, institute a-top
The Alps a Prefecture of Lombardy:
— " That 's now! — no prophesying what may
    be
Anon, with a new monarch of the clime,
Native of Gesi, passing his youth's prime
At Naples. Tito bids my choice decide
On whom" . . .
    " Embrace him, madman!" Palma cried,
Who through the laugh saw sweat-drops burst
    apace,
And his lips blanching: he did not embrace
Sordello, but he laid Sordello's hand
On his own eyes, mouth, forehead.
                Understand,
This while Sordello was becoming flushed

And Sor- Out of his whiteness; thoughts
dello the rushed, fancies rushed;
finally-de- He pressed his hand upon his head
termined, and signed
Both should forbear him. " Nay, the best 's be-
    hind!"
Taurello laughed — not quite with the same
    laugh:
" The truth is, thus we scatter, ay, like chaff
These Guelfs, a despicable monk recoils
From: nor expect a fickle Kaiser spoils
Our triumph! — Friedrich? Think you, I in-
    tend
Friedrich shall reap the fruits of blood I spend
And brain I waste? Think you, the people clap
Their hands at my out-hewing this wild gap
For any Friedrich to fill up? 'T is mine —
That 's yours: I tell you, towards some such
    design
Have I worked blindly, yes, and idly, yes,

And for another, yes — but worked no less
With instinct at my heart; I else had swerved,
While now — look round! My cunning has pre-
    served
Samminiato — that 's a central place
Secures us Florence, boy, — in Pisa's case,
By land as she by sea; with Pisa ours,
And Florence, and Pistoia, one devours
The land at leisure! Gloriously dispersed —
Brescia, observe, Milan, Piacenza first
That flanked us (ah, you know not!) in the
    March;
On these we pile, as keystone of our arch,
Romagna and Bologna, whose first span
Covered the Trentine and the Valsugan;
Sofia's Egna by Bolgiano 's sure!" . . .
So he proceeded: half of all this, pure

The devil Delusion, doubtless, nor the rest too
putting   true,
forth his But what was undone he felt sure to
potency: do,
As ring by ring he wrung off, flung away
The pauldron-rings to give his sword-arm play —
Need of the sword now! That would soon ad-
    just
Aught wrong at present; to the sword intrust
Sordello's whiteness, undersize: 't was plain
He hardly rendered right to his own brain —
Like a brave hound, men educate to pride
Himself on speed or scent nor aught beside,
As though he could not, gift by gift, match men!

Since Sor- Palma had listened patiently: but
dello, who when
began by 'T was time expostulate, attempt
rhyming, withdraw
Taurello from his child, she, without awe
Took off his iron arms from, one by one,
Sordello's shrinking shoulders, and, that done,
Made him avert his visage and relieve
Sordello (you might see his corselet heave
The while) who, loose, rose — tried to speak,
    then sank:
They left him in the chamber. All was blank.
  And even reeling down the narrow stair
Taurello kept up, as though unaware
Palma was by to guide him, the old device
— Something of Milan — " how we muster
    thrice
The Torriani's strength there; all along
Our own Visconti cowed them" — thus the song
Continued even while she bade him stoop,
Thrid somehow, by some glimpse of arrow-loop,
The turnings to the gallery below,
Where he stopped short as Palma let him
    go.
When he had sat in silence long enough
Splintering the stone bench, braving a rebuff
She stopped the truncheon; only to commence
One of Sordello's poems, a pretence
For speaking, some poor rhyme of " Elys' hair
And head that 's sharp and perfect like a pear,
So smooth and close are laid the few fine locks

May, even Stained like pale honey oozed from
from the   topmost rocks
depths of Sun-blanched the livelong summer "
failure   — from his worst
Performance, the Goito, as his first:
And that at end, conceiving from the brow

And open mouth no silence would serve now,
Went on to say the whole world loved that man
And, for that matter, thought his face, though
   wan,
Eclipsed the Count's — he sucking in each
   phrase
As if an angel spoke. The foolish praise
Ended, he drew her on his mailed knees, made
Her face a framework with his hands, a shade,
A crown, an aureole : there must she remain
(Her little mouth compressed with smiling pain
As in his gloves she felt her tresses twitch)
To get the best look at, in fittest niche
Dispose his saint. That done, he kissed her
   brow,
— " Lauded her father for his treason now,"
He told her, " only, how could one suspect
The wit in him ? — whose clansman, recollect,
Was ever Salinguerra — she, the same,
Romano and his lady — so, might claim
To know all, as she should " — and thus begun
Schemes with a vengeance, schemes on schemes,
   " not one
Fit to be told that foolish boy," he said,
" But only let Sordello Palma wed,
   — Then ! "
'T was a dim long narrow place at best :
Midway a sole grate showed the fiery
   West,
As shows its corpse the world's end
   some split tomb —
A gloom, a rift of fire, another gloom,
Faced Palma — but at length Taurello set
Her free ; the grating held one ragged jet
Of fierce gold fire : he lifted her within
The hollow underneath — how else begin
Fate's second marvellous cycle, else renew
The ages than with Palma plain in view ?
Then paced the passage, hands clenched, head
   erect,
Pursuing his discourse ; a grand unchecked
Monotony made out from his quick talk
And the recurring noises of his walk ;
— Somewhat too much like the o'ercharged as-
   sent
Of two resolved friends in one danger blent,
Who hearten each the other against heart ;
Boasting there 's naught to care for, when,
   apart
The boaster, all 's to care for. He, beside
Some shape not visible, in power and pride
Approached, out of the dark, ginglingly near,
Nearer, passed close in the broad light, his ear
Crimson, eyeballs suffused, temples full-
   fraught,
Just a snatch of the rapid speech you caught,
And on he strode into the opposite dark,
Till presently the harsh heel's turn, a spark
I' the stone, and whirl of some loose embossed
   thong
That crashed against the angle aye so long
After the last, punctual to an amount
Of mailed great paces you could not but count, —
Prepared you for the pacing back again.
And by the snatches you might ascertain
That, Friedrich's Prefecture surmounted, left
By this alone in Italy, they cleft
Asunder, crushed together, at command

[Marginal note:] Yet spring to the summit of success,

Of none, were free to break up Hildebrand,
Rebuild, he and Sordello, Charle-
   magne —
But garnished, Strength with Know-
   ledge, " if we deign
Accept that compromise and stoop to give
Rome law, the Cæsar's Representative."
Enough, that the illimitable flood
Of triumphs after triumphs, understood
In its faint reflux (you shall hear) sufficed
Young Ecelin for appanage, enticed
Him on till, these long quiet in their graves,
He found 't was looked for that a whole life's
   braves
Should somehow be made good ; so, weak and
   worn,
Must stagger up at Milan, one gray morn
Of the to-come, and fight his latest fight.
But, Salinguerra's prophecy at height —
He voluble with a raised arm and
   stiff,
A blaring voice, a blazing eye, as if
   He had our very Italy to keep
Or cast away, or gather in a heap
To garrison the better — ay, his word
Was, " run the cucumber into a gourd,
Drive Trent upon Apulia " — at their pitch
Who spied the continents and islands which
Grew mulberry-leaves and sickles, in the
   map —
(Strange that three such confessions so should
   hap
To Palma, Dante spoke with in the clear
Amorous silence of the Swooning-sphere, —
Cunizza, as he called her ! Never ask
Of Palma more ! She sat, knowing her task
Was done, the labor of it, — for, success
Concerned not Palma, passion's votaress)
Triumph at height, and thus Sordello crowned —
Above the passage suddenly a sound
Stops speech, stops walk : back shrinks Tau-
   rello, bids
With large involuntary asking lids,
Palma interpret. " 'T is his own foot-stamp —
Your hand ! His summons ! Nay, this idle
   damp
Befits not ! " Out they two reeled dizzily.
" Visconti 's strong at Milan," resumed he,
In the old, somewhat insignificant way —
(Was Palma wont, years afterward, to say)
As though the spirit's flight, sustained thus
   far,
Dropped at that very instant.
              Gone they are —
Palma, Taurello ; Eglamor anon,
Ecelin, — only Naddo 's never gone !
— Labors, this moonrise, what the Master
   meant —
" Is Squarcialupo speckled ? — purulent,
I 'd say, but when was Providence put out ?
He carries somehow handily about
His spite nor fouls himself ! " Goito's vines
Stand like a cheat detected — stark rough
   lines,
The moon breaks through, a gray mean scale
   against
The vault where, this eve's Maiden, thou re-
   main'st

[Marginal notes:] If he consent to oppress the world. / Just this decided, as it now may be,

Like some fresh martyr, eyes fixed — who can tell?
As Heaven, now all's at end, did not so well,
And we have done.   Spite of the faith and victory, to leave
     Its virgin quite to death in the lone eve.
While the persisting hermit-bee . . . ha! wait
No longer: these in compass, forward fate!

BOOK THE SIXTH

The thought of Eglamor's least like a thought,
At the close of a day or a life,   And yet a false one, was, "Man shrinks to naught
     If matched with symbols of immensity;
Must quail, forsooth, before a quiet sky
Or sea, too little for their quietude : "
And, truly, somewhat in Sordello's mood
Confirmed its speciousness, while eve slow sank
Down the near terrace to the farther bank,
And only one spot left from out the night
Glimmered upon the river opposite —
A breadth of watery heaven like a bay,
A sky-like space of water, ray for ray,
And star for star, one richness where they mixed
As this and that wing of an angel, fixed,
Tumultuary splendors folded in
To die. Nor turned he till Ferrara's din
(Say, the monotonous speech from a man's lip
Who lets some first and eager purpose slip
In a new fancy's birth ; the speech keeps on
Though elsewhere its informing soul be gone)
— Aroused him, surely offered succor. Fate
Paused with this eve ; ere she precipitate
Herself, — best put off new strange thoughts awhile,
That voice, those large hands, that portentous smile, —
What help to pierce the future as the past,
Lay in the plaining city?
     And at last
The main discovery and prime concern,
All that just now imported him to learn,
Truth's self, like yonder slow moon to complete
Heaven, rose again, and, naked at his feet,
Lighted his old life's every shift and change,
Past procedure is fitliest reviewed,   Effort with counter-effort ; nor the range
     Of each looked wrong except wherein it checked
Some other — which of these could he suspect,
Prying into them by the sudden blaze?
The real way seemed made up of all the ways —
Mood after mood of the one mind in him ;
Tokens of the existence, bright or dim,
Of a transcendent all-embracing sense
Demanding only outward influence,
A soul, in Palma's phrase, above his soul,
Power to uplift his power, — such moon's control
Over such sea-depths, — and their mass had swept
Onward from the beginning and still kept

Its course : but years and years the sky above
Held none, and so, untasked of any love,
His sensitiveness idled, now amort,
Alive now, and, to sullenness or sport
Given wholly up, disposed itself anew
At every passing instigation, grew
And dwindled at caprice, in foam-showers spilt,
Wedge-like insisting, quivered now a gilt
Shield in the sunshine, now a blinding race
Of whitest ripples o'er the reef — found place
For much display ; not gathered up and, hurled
Right from its heart, encompassing the world.
So had Sordello been, by consequence,
Without a function : others made pretence
To strength not half his own, yet had some core
Within, submitted to some moon, before
Them still, superior still whate'er their force, —
Were able therefore to fulfil a course,
Nor missed life's crown, authentic attribute.
To each who lives must be a certain fruit
Of having lived in his degree, — a stage,
Earlier or later in men's pilgrimage,
To stop at ; and to this the spirits tend
Who, still discovering beauty without end,
Amass the scintillations, make one star
— Something   unlike   them,   self-sustained, afar, —
And meanwhile nurse the dream of being blest
By winning it to notice and invest
Their souls with alien glory, some one day
As more appreciable in its entirety.   Whene'er the nucleus, gathering shape alway,
     Round to the perfect circle — soon or late,
According as themselves are formed to wait ;
Whether mere human beauty will suffice
— The yellow hair and the luxurious eyes,
Or human intellect seem best, or each
Combine in some ideal form past reach
On earth, or else some shade of these, some aim,
Some love, hate even, take their place, the same,
So to be served — all this they do not lose,
Waiting for death to live, nor idly choose
What must be Hell — a progress thus pursued
Through all existence, still above the food
That's offered them, still fain to reach beyond
The widened range, in virtue of their bond
Of sovereignty. Not that a Palma's Love,
A Salinguerra's Hate, would equal prove
To swaying all Sordello : but why doubt
Strong, he needed some moon without external strength :   Some love meet for such strength,
     Would match his sea? — or fear, Good manifest,
Only the Best breaks faith? — Ah, but the Best
Somehow eludes us ever, still might be
And is not! Crave we gems? No penury
Of their material round us! Pliant earth
And plastic flame — what balks the mage his birth
— Jacinth in balls or lodestone by the block?
Flinders enrich the strand, veins swell the rock ;
Naught more! Seek creatures? Life's i' the tempest, thought
Clothes the keen hill-top, mid-day woods are fraught
With fervors : human forms are well enough!
But we had hoped, encouraged by the stuff

Profuse at nature's pleasure, men beyond
These actual men! — and thus are over-fond
In arguing, from Good — the Best, from force
Divided — force combined, an ocean's course
From this our sea whose mere intestine pants
Might seem at times sufficient to our wants.
　External power? If none be adequate,
And he stand forth ordained (a prouder fate)
Himself a law to his own sphere? — remove
All incompleteness, for that law, that love?
Nay, if all other laws be feints, — truth veiled
Helpfully to weak vision that had failed
To grasp aught but its special want, — for lure,
Embodied? Stronger vision could endure
The unbodied want: no part — the whole of
　truth!
The People were himself; nor, by the ruth
At their condition, was he less impelled

Even now, where can he perceive much? To alter the discrepancy beheld,
Than if, from the sound whole, a
　sickly part
Subtracted were transformed, decked
　out with art,

Then palmed on him as alien woe — the Guelf
To succor, proud that he forsook himself.

Internal strength must suffice then, All is himself; all service, therefore,
　rates
Alike, nor serving one part, immo-
　lates

The rest: but all in time! "That lance of
　yours
Makes havoc soon with Malek and his Moors,
That buckler 's lined with many a giant's beard,
Ere long, our champion, be the lance upreared,
The buckler wielded handsomely as now!
But view your escort, bear in mind your vow,
Count the pale tracts of sand to pass ere that,
And, if you hope we struggle through the flat,
Put lance and buckler by! Next half-month
　lacks
Mere sturdy exercise of mace and axe
To cleave this dismal brake of prickly-pear
Which bristling holds Cydippe by the hair,
Lames barefoot Agathon: this felled, we 'll
　try
The picturesque achievements by and by —
Next life!"
　　　　　Ay, rally, mock, O People, urge
Your claims! — for thus he ventured, to the
　verge,
Push a vain mummery which perchance dis-
　trust
Of his fast-slipping resolution thrust
Likewise: accordingly the Crowd — (as yet
He had unconsciously contrived forget,
I' the whole, to dwell o' the points . . . one
　might assuage
The signal horrors easier than engage
With a dim vulgar vast unobvious grief
Not to be fancied off, nor gained relief
In brilliant fits. cured by a happy quirk,
But by dim vulgar vast unobvious work
To corrrespond . . .) — this Crowd then, forth
　they stood.
"And now content thy stronger vision, brood
On thy bare want; uncovered, turf by turf,
Study the corpse-face through the taint-worms'
　scurf!"

Down sank the People's Then; up-rose their
　Now

His sympathy with the people, to wit; These sad ones render service to! And how
Piteously little must that service
　prove
— Had surely proved in any case!
　for, move
Each other obstacle away, let youth

Become aware it had surprised a truth
'T were service to impart — can truth be seized,
Settled forthwith, and, of the captive eased,
Its captor find fresh prey, since this alit
So happily, no gesture luring it,
The earnest of a flock to follow? Vain,
Most vain! a life to spend ere this he chain
To the poor crowd's complacence: ere the crowd
Pronounce it captured, he descries a cloud
Its kin of twice the plume; which he, in turn,
If he shall live as many lives, may learn
How to secure: not else. Then Mantua called
Back to his mind how certain bards were
　thralled
— Buds blasted, but of breath more like per-
　fume
Than Naddo's staring nosegay's carrion bloom;
Some insane rose that burnt heart out in sweets,
A spendthrift in the spring, no summer greets;
Some Dularete, drunk with truths and wine,
Grown bestial, dreaming how become divine.
Yet to surmount this obstacle, commence
With the commencement, merits crowning!
　Hence
Must truth be casual truth, elicited
In sparks so mean, at intervals dispread
So rarely, that 't is like at no one time
Of the world's story has not truth, the prime
Of truth, the very truth which, loosed, had
　hurled
The world's course right, been really in the
　world
— Content the while with some mean spark by
　dint
Of some chance-blow, the solitary hint
Of buried fire, which, rip earth's breast, would
　stream
Sky-ward!
　　　　　Sordello's miserable gleam
Was looked for at the moment: he would dash
This badge, and all it brought, to earth, — abash
Taurello thus, perhaps persuade him wrest
The Kaiser from his purpose, — would attest
His own belief, in any case. Before

Of which, try now the inherent force! He dashes it however, think once
　more!
For, were that little, truly service?
"Ay,
I' the end, no doubt; but meantime? Plain
　you spy
Its ultimate effect, but many flaws
Of vision blur each intervening cause.
Were the day's fraction clear as the life's sum
Of service, Now as filled as teems To-come
With evidence of good — nor too minute
A share to vie with evil! No dispute,
'T were fitliest maintain the Guelfs in rule:
That makes your life's work: but you have to
　school
Your day's work on these natures circumstanced

Thus variously, which yet, as each advanced
Or might impede the Guelf rule, must be moved
Now, for the Then's sake, — hating what you
loved,
Loving old hatreds! Nor if one man bore
Brand upon temples while his fellow wore
The aureole, would it task you to decide:
But, portioned duly out, the future vied
Never with the unparcelled present! Smite
Or spare so much on warrant all so slight?
The present's complete sympathies to break,
Aversions bear with, for a future's sake
So feeble? Tito ruined through one speck,
The Legate saved by his sole lightish neck?
This were work, true, but work performed at
cost
Of other work; aught gained here, elsewhere
lost.
For a new segment spoil an orb half-done?
Rise with the People one step, and sink — one?
Were it but one step, less than the whole face
Of things, your novel duty bids erase!
Harms to abolish! What, the prophet saith,
The minstrel singeth vainly then? Old faith,
Old courage, only born because of harms,
Were not, from highest to the lowest, charms?
Flame may persist; but is not glare as stanch?
Where the salt marshes stagnate, crystals
branch;
Blood dries to crimson; Evil's beautified
In every shape. Thrust Beauty then aside
And banish Evil! Wherefore? After all,
Is Evil a result less natural
Than Good? For overlook the seasons' strife
With tree and flower, — the hideous animal life,
(Of which who seeks shall find a grinning taunt
How much of man's ill may be removed? For his solution, and endure the vaunt
Of nature's angel, as a child that knows
Himself befooled, unable to propose
Aught better than the fooling) — and but care
For men, for the mere People then and there, —
In these, could you but see that Good and Ill
Claimed you alike! Whence rose their claim
but still
From Ill, as fruit of Ill? What else could knit
You theirs but Sorrow? Any free from it
Were also free from you! Whose happiness
Could be distinguished in this morning's press
Of miseries? — the fool's who passed a gibe
'On thee,' jeered he, 'so wedded to thy tribe,
Thou carriest green and yellow tokens in
Thy very face that thou art Ghibellin!'
Much hold on you that fool obtained! Nay
mount
How much of ill ought to be removed? Yet higher — and upon men's own account
Must evil stay: for, what is joy? —
to heave
Up one obstruction more, and com-
mon leave
What was peculiar, by such act destroy
Itself; a partial death is every joy;
The sensible escape, enfranchisement
Of a sphere's essence: once the vexed — content,
The cramped — at large, the growing circle —
round,
All's to begin again — some novel bound
To break, some new enlargement to entreat;

The sphere though larger is not more complete.
Now for Mankind's experience: who alone
Might style the unobstructed world his own?
Whom palled Goito with its perfect things?
Sordello's self: whereas for Mankind springs
Salvation by each hindrance interposed.
They climb; life's view is not at once disclosed
To creatures caught up, on the summit left,
Heaven plain above them, yet of wings bereft:
But lower laid, as at the mountain's foot.
So, range on range, the girdling forests shoot
Twixt your plain prospect and the throngs who
scale
Height after height, and pierce mists, veil by
veil,
Heartened with each discovery; in their soul,
The Whole they seek by Parts — but, found that
Whole,
Could they revert, enjoy past gains? The space
Of time you judge so meagre to embrace
The Parts were more than plenty, once attained
The Whole, to quite exhaust it: naught were
gained
But leave to look — not leave to do: Beneath
Soon sates the looker — look above, and Death
Tempts ere a tithe of Life be tasted. Live
First, and die soon enough, Sordello! Give
If removed, at what cost to Sordello? Body and spirit the first right they
claim,
And pasture soul on a voluptuous
shame
That you, a pageant-city's denizen,
Are neither vilely lodged 'midst Lombard men —
Can force joy out of sorrow, seem to truck
Bright attributes away for sordid muck,
Yet manage from that very muck educe
Gold; then subject nor scruple, to your cruce
The world's discardings! Though real ingots
pay
Your pains, the clods that yielded them are
clay
To all beside, — would clay remain, though
quenched
Your purging-fire; who's robbed then? Had
you wrenched
An ampler treasure forth! — As 't is, they crave
A share that ruins you and will not save
Them. Why should sympathy command you
quit
The course that makes your joy, nor will remit
Their woe? Would all arrive at joy? Reverse
Men win little thereby; he loses all: The order (time instructs you) nor
coerce
Each unit till, some predetermined
mode,
The total be emancipate; men's road
Is one, men's times of travel many; thwart
No enterprising soul's precocious start
Before the general march! If slow or fast
All straggle up to the same point at last,
Why grudge your having gained, a month ago,
The brakes at balm-shed, asphodels in blow,
While they were landlocked? Speed their Then,
but how
This badge would suffer you improve your
Now!"
His time of action for, against, or with
Our world (I labor to extract the pith

Of this his problem) grew, that even-tide,
Gigantic with its power of joy, beside
The world's eternity of impotence
To profit though at his whole joy's expense.

For he can infinitely enjoy him-self, use grief

"Make nothing of my day because so brief?
Rather make more: instead of joy,
Before its novelty have time subside!
Wait not for the late savor, leave untried
Virtue, the creaming honey-wine, quick squeeze
Vice like a biting spirit from the lees
Of life! Together let wrath, hatred, lust,
All tyrannies in every shape, be thrust
Upon this Now, which time may reason out
As mischiefs, far from benefits, no doubt;
But long ere then Sordello will have slipped
Away; you teach him at Goito's crypt,
There 's a blank issue to that fiery thrill.
Stirring, the few cope with the many, still:
So much of sand as, quiet, makes a mass
Unable to produce three tufts of grass,
Shall, troubled by the whirlwind, render void
The whole calm glebe's endeavor: be employed!
And e'en though somewhat smart the Crowd for
    this,
Contribute each his pang to make your bliss,
'T is but one pang — one blood-drop to the bowl
Which brimful tempts the sluggish asp uncowl
At last, stains ruddily the dull red cape,
And, kindling orbs gray as the unripe grape
Before, avails forthwith to disentrance
The portent, soon to lead a mystic dance
Among you! For, who sits alone in Rome?
Have those great hands indeed hewn out a home,
And set me there to live? Oh life, life-breath,
Life-blood, — ere sleep, come travail, life ere
    death!
This life stream on my soul, direct, oblique,
But always streaming! Hindrances? They
    pique:
Helps? such . . . but why repeat, my soul o'er-
    tops
Each height, then every depth profoundlier
    drops?
Enough that I can live, and would live! Wait
For some transcendent life reserved by Fate
To follow this? Oh, never! Fate, I trust
The same, my soul to; for, as who flings dust,
Perchance (so facile was the deed) she checked
The void with these materials to affect
My soul diversely: these consigned anew
To naught by death, what marvel if she threw
A second and superber spectacle
Before me? What may serve for sun, what still
Wander a moon above me? What else wind
About me like the pleasures left behind,
And how shall some new flesh that is not flesh
Cling to me? What 's new laughter? Soothes
    the fresh
Sleep like sleep? Fate 's exhaustless for my sake
In brave resource: but whether bids she slake
My thirst at this first rivulet, or count
No draught worth lip save from some rocky
    fount
Above i' the clouds, while here she 's provident
Of pure loquacious pearl, the soft tree-tent
Guards, with its face of reate and sedge, nor fail

The silver globules and gold-sparkling grail
At bottom? Oh, 't were too absurd to slight
For the hereafter the to-day's delight!
Quench thirst at this, then seek next well-spring:
    wear
Home-lilies ere strange lotus in my hair!
Here is the Crowd, whom I with freest heart

Freed from a problem-atic obli-gation,

Offer to serve, contented for my part
To give life up in service, — only grant
That I do serve; if otherwise, why want
Aught further of me? If men cannot choose
But set aside life, why should I refuse
The gift? I take it — I, for one, engage
Never to falter through my pilgrimage —
Nor end it howling that the stock or stone
Were enviable, truly: I, for one,
Will praise the world, you style mere anteroom
To palace — be it so! shall I assume
— My foot the courtly gait, my tongue the trope,
My mouth the smirk, before the doors fly ope
One moment? What? with guarders row on
    row,
Gay swarms of varletry that come and go,
Pages to dice with, waiting-girls unlace
The plackets of, pert claimants help displace,
Heart-heavy suitors get a rank for, — laugh
At yon sleek parasite, break his own staff
'Cross Beetle-brows the Usher's shoulder, — why,
Admitted to the presence by and by,
Should thought of having lost these make me
    grieve
Among new joys I reach, for joys I leave?
Cool citrine-crystals, fierce pyropus-stone,
Are floor-work there! But do I let alone
That black-eyed peasant in the vestibule
Once and forever? — Floor-work? No such fool!
Rather, were heaven to forestall earth, I 'd say
I, is it, must be blessed? Then, my own way

And ac-cepting life on its own terms,

Bless me! Give firmer arm and
    fleeter foot,
I 'll thank you: but to no mad wings
    transmute
These limbs of mine — our greensward was so
    soft!
Nor camp I on the thunder-cloud aloft:
We feel the bliss distinctlier, having thus
Engines subservient, not mixed up with us.
Better move palpably through heaven: nor,
    freed
Of flesh, forsooth, from space to space proceed
'Mid flying synods of worlds! No: in heaven's
    marge
Show Titan still, recumbent o'er his targe
Solid with stars — the Centaur at his game,
Made tremulously out in hoary flame!

Which, yet, others have re-nounced: how?

"Life! Yet the very cup whose extreme dull
Dregs, even, I would quaff, was dashed, at full,
Aside so oft; the death I fly, revealed
So oft a better life this life concealed,
And which sage, champion, martyr, through
    each path
Have hunted fearlessly — the horrid
    bath,
The crippling-irons and the fiery
    chair.
'T was well for them: let me become aware

As they, and I relinquish life, too! Let
What masters life disclose itself! Forget
Vain ordinances, I have one appeal —
I feel, am what I feel, know what I feel;
So much is truth to me. What Is, then? Since
One object, viewed diversely, may evince
Beauty and ugliness — this way attract,
That way repel, — why gloze upon the fact?
Why must a single of the sides be right?
What bids choose this and leave the opposite?
Where's abstract Right for me? — in youth en-
dued
With Right still present, still to be pursued,
Through all the interchange of circles, rife
Each with its proper law and mode of life,
Each to be dwelt at ease in: where, to sway
Absolute with the Kaiser, or obey
Implicit with his serf of fluttering heart,
Or, like a sudden thought of God's, to start
Up, Brutus in the presence, then go shout
That some should pick the unstrung jewels out—
Each, well!"
                And, as in moments when the past
Gave partially enfranchisement, he cast
Himself quite through mere secondary states
Of his soul's essence, little loves and hates,

Because there is a life beyond life, Into the mid deep yearnings overlaid
By these; as who should pierce hill,
plain, grove, glade,
And on into the very nucleus probe
That first determined there exist a globe.
As that were easiest, half the globe dissolved,
So seemed Sordello's closing-truth evolved
By his flesh-half's break up; the sudden swell
Of his expanding soul showed Ill and Well,
Sorrow and Joy, Beauty and Ugliness,
Virtue and Vice, the Larger and the Less,
All qualities, in fine, recorded here,
Might be but modes of Time and this one sphere,
Urgent on these, but not of force to bind
Eternity, as Time — as Matter — Mind,
If Mind, Eternity, should choose assert
Their attributes within a Life: thus girt
With circumstance, next change beholds them
cinct
Quite otherwise — with Good and Ill distinct,
Joys, sorrows, tending to a like result —
Contrived to render easy, difficult,
This or the other course of . . . what new bond
In place of flesh may stop their flight beyond
Its new sphere, as that course does harm or good
To its arrangements. Once this understood,
As suddenly he felt himself alone,
Quite out of Time and this world: all was
known.
What made the secret of his past despair?
— Most imminent when he seemed most aware
Of his own self-sufficiency; made mad
By craving to expand the power he had,
And not new power to be expanded? — just
This made it; Soul on Matter being thrust,
Joy comes when so much Soul is wreaked in
Time
On Matter, — let the Soul's attempt sublime
Matter beyond the scheme and so prevent
By more or less that deed's accomplishment,
And Sorrow follows: Sorrow how avoid?
Let the employer match the thing employed,

Fit to the finite his infinity,
And thus proceed forever, in degree
And with new conditions of success, Changed but in kind the same, still
limited
To the appointed circumstance and
dead
To all beyond. A sphere is but a sphere;
Small, Great, are merely terms we bandy here;
Since to the spirit's absoluteness all
Are like. Now, of the present sphere we call
Life, are conditions; take but this among
Many; the body was to be so long
Youthful, no longer: but, since no control
Tied to that body's purposes his soul,
She chose to understand the body's trade
More than the body's self — had fain conveyed
Her boundless, to the body's bounded lot.
Hence, the soul permanent, the body not, —
Scarcely its minute for enjoying here, —
The soul must needs instruct her weak compeer,
Run o'er its capabilities and wring
A joy thence, she held worth experiencing:
Which, far from half discovered even, — lo,
The minute gone, the body's power let go
Apportioned to that joy's acquirement! Broke
Nor such as, in this, produce failure. Morning o'er earth, he yearned for
all it woke —
From the volcano's vapor-flag, winds
hoist
Black o'er the spread of sea, — down to the moist
Dale's silken barley-spikes sullied with rain,
Swayed earthwards, heavily to rise again —
The Small, a sphere as perfect as the Great
To the soul's absoluteness. Meditate
Too long on such a morning's cluster-chord
And the whole music it was framed afford, —
The chord's might half discovered, what should
pluck
One string, his finger, was found palsy-struck.
And then no marvel if the spirit, shown
A saddest sight — the body lost alone
Through her officious proffered help, deprived
Of this and that enjoyment Fate contrived, —
Virtue, Good, Beauty, each allowed slip hence, —
Vaingloriously were fain, for recompense,
To stem the ruin even yet, protract
The body's term, supply the power it lacked
From her infinity, compel it learn
These qualities were only Time's concern,
And body may, with spirit helping, barred —
Advance the same, vanquished — obtain reward,
Reap joy where sorrow was intended grow,
Of Wrong make Right, and turn Ill Good below.
And the result is, the poor body soon
Sinks under what was meant a wondrous boon,
Leaving its bright accomplice all aghast.
So much was plain then, proper in the past;
To be complete for, satisfy the whole
Series of spheres — Eternity, his soul
Needs must exceed, prove incomplete for, each
Single sphere — Time. But does our know-
ledge reach
No farther? Is the cloud of hindrance broke
But, even here, is failure inevitable? But by the failing of the fleshly yoke,
Its loves and hates, as now when
death lets soar
Sordello, self-sufficient as before,
Though during the mere space that shall elapse

'Twixt his enthralment in new bonds, perhaps?
Must life be ever just escaped, which should
Have been enjoyed? — nay, might have been
    and would,
Each purpose ordered right — the soul's no whit
Beyond the body's purpose under it —
Like yonder breadth of watery heaven, a bay,
And that sky-space of water, ray for ray
And star for star, one richness where they mixed
As this and that wing of an angel, fixed,
Tumultuary splendors folded in
To die — would soul, proportioned thus, begin
Exciting discontent, or surelier quell
The body if, aspiring, it rebel?
But how so order life? Still brutalize
The soul, the sad world's way, with muffled eyes
To all that was before, all that shall be
After this sphere — all and each quality
Save some sole and immutable Great-Good
And Beauteous whither fate has loosed its hood
Or may   To follow? Never may some soul
failure   see All
here be   — The Great Before and After, and
success   the Small
also   Now, yet be saved by this the sim-
    plest lore,
And take the single course prescribed before,
As the king-bird with ages on his plumes
Travels to die in his ancestral glooms?
But where descry the Love that shall select
That course? Here is a soul whom, to affect,
Nature has plied with all her means, from trees
And flowers e'en to the Multitude! — and these,
Decides he save or no? One word to end!
  Ah, my Sordello, I this once befriend
And speak for you. Of a Power above you still
Which, utterly incomprehensible,
Is out of rivalry, which thus you can
When in- Love, though unloving all conceived
duced by by man —
love?   What need! And of — none the
    minutest duct
To that out-nature, naught that would instruct
And so let rivalry begin to live —
But of a Power its representative
Who, being for authority the same,
Communication different, should claim
A course, the first chose but this last revealed —
This Human clear, as that Divine concealed —
What utter need!
        What has Sordello found?
Or can his spirit go the mighty round,
End where poor Eglamor begun? So, says
Old fable, the two eagles went two ways
About the world: where, in the midst, they met,
Though on a shifting waste of sand, men set
Jove's temple. Quick, what has Sordello found?
Sordello For they approach — approach — that
knows: foot's rebound
    Palma? No, Salinguerra though in
    mail;
They mount, have reached the threshold, dash
    the veil
Aside — and you divine who sat there dead,
Under his foot the badge: still, Palma said,
A triumph lingering in the wide eyes,
Wider than some spent swimmer's if he spies
Help from above in his extreme despair,

And, head far back on shoulder thrust, turns
    there
With short quick passionate cry: as Palma
    pressed
In one great kiss, her lips upon his breast,
It beat.
    By this, the hermit-bee has stopped
His day's toil at Goito: the new-cropped
Dead vine-leaf answers, now 'tis eve, he bit,
Twirled so, and filed all day: the mansion's fit,
God counselled for. As easy guess the word
That passed betwixt them, and become the
    third
To the soft small unfrighted bee, as tax
Him with one fault — so, no remembrance
But too   racks
late: an Of the stone maidens and the font of
insect   stone
knows   He, creeping through the crevice,
sooner. leaves alone.
    Alas, my friend, alas Sordello, whom
Anon they laid within that old font-tomb,
And, yet again, alas!
        And now is 't worth
Our while bring back to mind, much less set
    forth
How Salinguerra extricates himself
Without Sordello? Ghibellin and Guelf
May fight their fiercest out? If Richard
    sulked
In durance or the Marquis paid his mulct,
Who cares, Sordello gone? The upshot, sure,
On his dis- Was peace; our chief made some
appear- frank overture
ance from That prospered; compliment fell
the stage, thick and fast
On its disposer, and Taurello passed
With foe and friend for an outstripping soul,
Nine days at least. Then, — fairly reached the
    goal, —
He, by one effort, blotted the great hope
Out of his mind, nor further tried to cope
With Este, that mad evening's style, but sent
Away the Legate and the League, content
No blame at least the brothers had incurred,
— Dispatched a message to the Monk, he heard
Patiently first to last, scarce shivered at,
Then curled his limbs up on his wolfskin mat
And ne'er spoke more, — informed the Fer-
    rarese
He but retained their rule so long as these
Lingered in pupilage, — and last, no mode
Apparent else of keeping safe the road
From Germany direct to Lombardy
For Friedrich, — none, that is, to guarantee
The faith and promptitude of who should next
Obtain Sofia's dowry, — sore perplexed —
(Sofia being youngest of the tribe
The next Of daughters, Ecelin was wont to
aspirant bribe
can press The envious magnates with — nor,
forward; since he sent
Henry of Egna this fair child, had Trent
Once failed the Kaiser's purposes — " we lost
Egna last year, and who takes Egna's post —
Opens the Lombard gate if Friedrich knock?")
Himself espoused the Lady of the Rock
In pure necessity, and, so destroyed

His slender last of chances, quite made void
Old prophecy, and spite of all the schemes
Overt and covert, youth's deeds, age's dreams,
Was sucked into Romano. And so hushed
He up this evening's work, that, when 't was
    brushed
Somehow against by a blind chronicle
Which, chronicling whatever woe befell
Ferrara, noted this the obscure woe
Of "Salinguerra's sole son Giacomo
Deceased, fatuous and doting, ere his sire,"
The townsfolk rubbed their eyes, could but
    admire
Which of Sofia's five was meant.
                    The chaps
Of earth's dead hope were tardy to collapse,
Obliterated not the beautiful
Distinctive features at a crash: but dull
And duller these, next year, as Guelfs withdrew
Each to his stronghold. Then (securely too
Ecelin at Campese slept; close by,
Who likes may see him in Solagna lie,
With cushioned head and gloved hand to denote
The cavalier he was) — then his heart smote
Young Ecelin at last; long since adult.
And, save Vicenza's business, what result
In blood and blaze? (So hard to intercept
Sordello till his plain withdrawal!) Stepped

Salin-   Then this new lord on Lombardy. I'
guerra's   the nick
part laps- Of time when Ecelin and Alberic
ing to   Closed with Taurello, come pre-
Ecelin,   cisely news

That in Verona half the souls refuse
Allegiance to the Marquis and the Count —
Have cast them from a throne they bid him
    mount,
Their Podestà, through his ancestral worth.
Ecelin flew there, and the town henceforth
Was wholly his — Taurello sinking back
From temporary station to a track
That suited. News received of this acquist,
Friedrich did come to Lombardy: who missed
Taurello then? Another year: they took
Vicenza, left the Marquis scarce a nook
For refuge, and, when hundreds two or three
Of Guelfs conspired to call themselves "The
    Free,"
Opposing Alberic, — vile Bassanese, —
(Without Sordello!) — Ecelin at ease
Slaughtered them so observably, that oft
A little Salinguerra looked with soft
Blue eyes up, asked his sire the proper age
To get appointed his proud uncle's page.
More years passed, and that sire had dwindled
    down
To a mere showy turbulent soldier, grown
Better through age, his parts still in repute,
Subtle — how else? — but hardly so astute
As his contemporaneous friends professed;
Undoubtedly a brawler: for the rest,
Known by each neighbor, and allowed for, let
Keep his incorrigible ways, nor fret
Men who would miss their boyhood's bugbear:
    "trap
The ostrich, suffer our bald osprey flap
A battered pinion!" — was the word. In fine,
One flap too much and Venice's marine

Was meddled with; no overlooking that!
She captured him in his Ferrara, fat
And florid at a banquet, more by fraud
Than force, to speak the truth; there's slander
    laud
Ascribed you for assisting eighty years
To pull his death on such a man; fate shears
The life-cord prompt enough whose last fine
    thread
You fritter: so, presiding his board-head,
The old smile, your assurance all went well
With Friedrich (as if he were like to tell!)
In rushed (a plan contrived before) our friends,
Made some pretence at fighting, some amends
For the shame done his eighty years — (apart
The principle, none found it in his heart
To be much angry with Taurello) — gained
Their galleys with the prize, and what remained
But carry him to Venice for a show?
— Set him, as 't were, down gently — free to go
His gait, inspect our square, pretend observe
The swallows soaring their eternal curve
'Twixt Theodore and Mark, if citizens
Gathered importunately, fives and tens,
To point their children the Magnifico,

Who, with   All but a monarch once in firm-land,
his   go
brother,   His gait among them now — "it
played it   took, indeed,
out,   Fully this Ecelin to supersede

That man," remarked the seniors. Singular!
Sordello's inability to bar
Rivals the stage, that evening, mainly brought
About by his strange disbelief that aught
Was ever to be done, — this thrust the Twain
Under Taurello's tutelage, — whom, brain
And heart and hand, he forthwith in one rod
Indissolubly bound to baffle God
Who loves the world — and thus allowed the
    thin
Gray wizened dwarfish devil Ecelin,
And massy-muscled big-boned Alberic
(Mere man, alas!) to put his problem quick
To demonstration — prove wherever 's will
To do, there 's plenty to be done, or ill
Or good. Anointed, then, to rend and rip —
Kings of the gag and flesh-hook, screw and
    whip,
They plagued the world: a touch of Hilde-
    brand
(So far from obsolete!) made Lombards band
Together, cross their coats as for Christ's cause,
And saving Milan win the world's applause.
Ecelin perished: and I think grass grew
Never so pleasant as in Valley Rù

And went   By San Zenon where Alberic in turn
home duly   Saw his exasperated captors burn
to their   Seven children and their mother;
reward.   then, regaled

So far, tied on to a wild horse, was trailed
To death through raunce and bramble-bush. I
    take
God's part and testify that 'mid the brake
Wild o'er his castle on the pleasant knoll,
You hear its one tower left, a belfry, toll —
The earthquake spared it last year, laying flat
The modern church beneath, — no harm in
    that!

Chirrups the contumacious grasshopper,
Rustles the lizard and the cushats chirre
Above the ravage : there, at deep of day
A week since, heard I the old Canon say
He saw with his own eyes a barrow burst
And Alberic's huge skeleton unhearsed
Only five years ago. He added, "June's
The month for carding off our first cocoons
The silkworms fabricate" — a double news,
Nor he nor I could tell the worthier. Choose !
  And Naddo gone, all 's gone ; not Eglamor !
Believe, I knew the face I waited for,
A guest my spirit of the golden courts !
Oh strange to see how, despite ill-reports,
Disuse, some wear of years, that face retained
Its joyous look of love ! Suns waxed and
    waned,
And still my spirit held an upward flight,
Spiral on spiral, gyres of life and light
More and more gorgeous — ever that face there
The last admitted ! crossed, too, with some care
As perfect triumph were not sure for all,
Good will But, on a few, enduring damp must
— ill luck, fall,
get second — A transient struggle, haply a pain-
prize : ful sense
Of the inferior nature's clinging — whence
Slight starting tears easily wiped away,
Fine jealousies soon stifled in the play
Of irrepressible admiration — not
Aspiring, all considered, to their lot
Who ever, just as they prepare ascend
Spiral on spiral, wish thee well, impend
Thy frank delight at their exclusive track,
That upturned fervid face and hair put back !
  Is there no more to say ? He of the rhymes —
Many a tale, of this retreat betimes,
Was born : Sordello die at once for men ?
The Chroniclers of Mantua tired their pen
Telling how *Sordello Prince Visconti* saved
Mantua, and elsewhere notably behaved —
Who thus, by fortune ordering events,
Passed with posterity, to all intents,
For just the god he never could become.
As Knight, Bard, Gallant, men were never
    dumb
In praise of him : while what he should have
    been,
Could be, and was not — the one step too mean
For him to take, — we suffer at this day
Because of : Ecelin had pushed away
Its chance ere Dante could arrive and take
What least That step Sordello spurned, for the
one may I world's sake :
award He did much — but Sordello's chance
Sordello ? was gone.
Thus, had Sordello dared that step alone,
Apollo had been compassed — 't was a fit

He wished should go to him, not he to it
— As one content to merely be supposed
Singing or fighting elsewhere, while he dozed
Really at home — one who was chiefly glad
To have achieved the few real deeds he had,
Because that way assured they were not worth
Doing, so spared from doing them henceforth —
A tree that covets fruitage and yet tastes
Never itself, itself. Had he embraced
Their cause then, men had plucked Hesperian
    fruit
And, praising that, just thrown him in to boot
All he was anxious to appear, but scarce
Solicitous to be. A sorry farce
Such life is, after all ! Cannot I say
This — that He lived for some one better thing ?
must per- this way. —
force con- Lo, on a heathy brown and nameless
tent him, hill
By sparkling Asolo, in mist and chill,
Morning just up, higher and higher runs
A child barefoot and rosy. See ! the sun 's
On the square castle's inner-court's low wall
Like the chine of some extinct animal
Half turned to earth and flowers ; and through
    the haze
(Save where some slender patches of gray
    maize
Are to be overleaped) that boy has crossed
The whole hill-side of dew and powder-frost
Matting the balm and mountain camomile.
Up and up goes he, singing all the while
Some unintelligible words to beat
The lark, God's poet, swooning at his feet,
So worsted is he at "the few fine locks
Stained like pale honey oozed from topmost
    rocks
Sun-blanched the livelong summer," — all that 's
    left
Of the Goito lay ! And thus bereft,
Sleep and forget, Sordello ! In effect
He sleeps, the feverish poet — I suspect
As no prize Not utterly companionless ; but,
at all, has friends,
contented Wake up ! The ghost 's gone, and
me. the story ends
I 'd fain hope, sweetly; seeing, peri or ghoul,
That spirits are conjectured fair or foul,
Evil or good, judicious authors think,
According as they vanish in a stink
Or in a perfume. Friends, be frank ! ye snuff
Civet, I warrant. Really ? Like enough !
Merely the savor's rareness ; any nose
May ravage with impunity a rose :
Rifle a musk-pod and 't will ache like yours !
I 'd tell you that same pungency ensures
An after-gust, but that were overbold.
Who would has heard Sordello's story told.

PIPPA PASSES

A DRAMA

Sordello did not prove commercially successful, and Browning was reluctant to go on publishing his poetry at his father's expense. "One day," Mr. Gosse says, "as the poet was discussing the matter with Mr. Edward Moxon, the publisher, the latter remarked that at that time he was bringing out some editions of the old Elizabethan dramatists in a comparatively cheap form, and that if Mr. Browning would consent to print his poems as pamphlets, using this cheap type, the expense would be very inconsiderable." Browning accepted the suggestion at once and began the issue of a cheap series of pamphlets, each sixteen octavo pages in double column, printed on poor paper and sold first for a sixpence each, the price afterward being raised to a shilling and then to half a crown. The series consisted of eight numbers under the general fanciful title *Bells and Pomegranates*. Apparently the passage in Exodus xxviii. 33, "And beneath upon the hem of it [the priest's robe] thou shalt make pomegranates of blue, and of purple, and of scarlet, round about the hem thereof; and bells of gold between them round about," suggested the title, but as all sorts of speculations sprang up about its significance, Browning appended the following note to the eighth and final number of the series: —

"Here ends my first series of *Bells and Pomegranates*, and I take the opportunity of explaining, in reply to inquiries, that I only meant by that title to indicate an endeavor towards something like an alteration, or mixture, of music with discoursing, sound with sense, poetry with thought; which looks too ambitious, thus expressed, so the symbol was preferred. It is little to the purpose, that such is actually one of the most familiar of the many Rabbinical (and Patristic) acceptations of the phrase; because I confess that, letting authority alone, I suppose the bare words, in such juxtaposition, would sufficiently convey the desired meaning. 'Faith

and good works' is another fancy, for instance, and perhaps no easier to arrive at; yet Giotto placed a pomegranate fruit in the hand of Dante, and Raffaello crowned his Theology (in the *Camera della Segnatura*) with blossoms of the same; as if the Bellari and Vasari would be sure to come after, and explain that it was merely '*simbolo delle buone opere — il qual Pomo-granato fu però usato nelle veste del Pontefice appresso gli Ebrei.*'

            "R. B."

The first number of *Bells and Pomegranates* contained *Pippa Passes*. It was published in 1841 and was introduced by the following dedicatory preface : —

ADVERTISEMENT

Two or three years ago I wrote a Play, about which the chief matter I much care to recollect at present is, that a Pitfull of good-natured people applauded it: ever since, I have been desirous of doing something in the same way that should better reward their attention. What follows, I mean for the first of a series of Dramatical Pieces, to come out at intervals; and I amuse myself by fancying that the cheap mode in which they appear, will for once help me to a sort of Pit-audience again. Of course such a work must go on no longer than it is liked; and to provide against a too certain and but too possible contingency, let me hasten to say now — what, if I were sure of success, I would try to say circumstantially enough at the close — that I dedicate my best intentions most admiringly to the Author of *Ion* — most affectionately to Sergeant Talfourd.

         ROBERT BROWNING.

The phrases in the closing sentence were afterward used by Browning as a dedication when he discarded the advertisement in the collective editions of his poems.

PERSONS

PIPPA.
OTTIMA.
SEBALD.
Foreign Students.
GOTTLIEB.
SCHRAMM.

JULES.
PHENE.
Austrian Police.
BLUPHOCKS.
LUIGI and his mother.
Poor Girls.
MONSIGNOR and his attendants.

INTRODUCTION

NEW YEAR'S DAY AT ASOLO IN THE TREVISAN

A large mean airy chamber. A girl, PIPPA, *from the silk-mills, springing out of bed.*

DAY!
Faster and more fast,
O'er night's brim, day boils at last :
Boils, pure gold, o'er the cloud-cup's brim
Where spurting and suppressed it lay,
For not a froth-flake touched the rim
Of yonder gap in the solid gray
Of the eastern cloud, an hour away ;
But forth one wavelet, then another, curled,
Till the whole sunrise, not to be suppressed,
Rose, reddened, and its seething breast
Flickered in bounds, grew gold, then overflowed
     the world.

Oh Day, if I squander a wavelet of thee,
A mite of my twelve-hours' treasure,
The least of thy gazes or glances,
(Be they grants thou art bound to or gifts above
     measure)
One of thy choices or one of thy chances,
(Be they tasks God imposed thee or freaks at
     thy pleasure)
— My Day, if I squander such labor or leisure,
Then shame fall on Asolo, mischief on me !

Thy long blue solemn hours serenely flowing,
Whence earth, we feel, gets steady help and
     good —
Thy fitful sunshine-minutes, coming, going,
As if earth turned from work in gamesome
     mood —
All shall be mine ! But thou must treat me not
As prosperous ones are treated, those who live
At hand here, and enjoy the higher lot,
In readiness to take what thou wilt give,
And free to let alone what thou refusest ;
For, Day, my holiday, if thou ill-usest
Me, who am only Pippa, — old-year's sorrow,
Cast off last night, will come again to-morrow :
Whereas, if thou prove gentle, I shall borrow
Sufficient strength of thee for new-year's sorrow.
All other men and women that this earth
Belongs to, who all days alike possess,
Make general plenty cure particular dearth,
Get more joy one way, if another, less :
Thou art my single day, God lends to leaven
What were all earth else, with a feel of
     heaven, —
Sole light that helps me through the year, thy
     sun's !
Try now ! Take Asolo's Four Happiest Ones —
And let thy morning rain on that superb
Great haughty Ottima ; can rain disturb
Her Sebald's homage ? All the while thy rain
Beats fiercest on her shrub-house window-pane
He will but press the closer, breathe more warm
Against her cheek ; how should she mind the
     storm ?
And, morning past, if mid-day shed a gloom
O'er Jules and Phene, — what care bride and
     groom

Save for their dear selves ? 'Tis their mar-
     riage-day ;
And while they leave church and go home their
     way,
Hand clasping hand, within each breast would be
Sunbeams and pleasant weather spite of thee.
Then, for another trial, obscure thy eve
With mist, — will Luigi and his mother grieve —
The lady and her child, unmatched, forsooth,
She in her age, as Luigi in his youth,
For true content ? The cheerful town, warm,
     close
And safe, the sooner that thou art morose,
Receives them. And yet once again, outbreak
In storm at night on Monsignor, they make
Such stir about, — whom they expect from
     Rome
To visit Asolo, his brothers' home,
And say here masses proper to release
A soul from pain, — what storm dares hurt his
     peace ?
Calm would he pray, with his own thoughts to
     ward
Thy thunder off, nor want the angels' guard.
But Pippa — just one such mischance would
     spoil
Her day that lightens the next twelvemonth's
     toil
At wearisome silk-winding, coil on coil !
     And here I let time slip for naught !
Aha, you foolhardy sunbeam, caught
With a single splash from my ewer !
You that would mock the best pursuer,
Was my basin over-deep ?
One splash of water ruins you asleep,
And up, up, fleet your brilliant bits
Wheeling and counterwheeling,
Reeling, broken beyond healing :
Now grow together on the ceiling !
That will task your wits.
Whoever it was quenched fire first, hoped to see
Morsel after morsel flee
As merrily, as giddily . . .
Meantime, what lights my sunbeam on,
Where settles by degrees the radiant cripple ?
Oh, is it surely blown, my martagon ?
New-blown and ruddy as St. Agnes' nipple,
Plump as the flesh-bunch on some Turk bird's
     poll !
Be sure if corals, branching 'neath the ripple
Of ocean, bud there, — fairies watch unroll
Such turban-flowers ; I say, such lamps disperse
Thick red flame through that dusk green uni-
     verse !
I am queen of thee, floweret !
And each fleshy blossom
Preserve I not — (safer
Than leaves that embower it,
Or shells that embosom)
— From weevil and chafer ?
Laugh through my pane then ; solicit the bee ;
Gibe him, be sure ; and, in midst of thy glee,
Love thy queen, worship me !

— Worship whom else ? For am I not, this day,
Whate'er I please ? What shall I please to-day ?
My morn, noon, eve and night — how spend my
     day ?

To-morrow I must be Pippa who winds silk,
The whole year round, to earn just bread and
    milk :
But, this one day, I have leave to go,
And play out my fancy's fullest games ;
I may fancy all day — and it shall be so —
That I taste of the pleasures, am called by the
    names
Of the Happiest Four in our Asolo !

See ! Up the hillside yonder, through the morn-
    ing,
Some one shall love me, as the world calls love :
I am no less than Ottima, take warning !
The gardens, and the great stone house above,
And other house for shrubs, all glass in front,
Are mine ; where Sebald steals, as he is wont,
To court me, while old Luca yet reposes:
And therefore, till the shrub-house door un-
    closes,
I . . . what now ? — give abundant cause for
    prate
About me — Ottima, I mean — of late,
Too bold, too confident she 'll still face down
The spitefullest of talkers in our town.
How we talk in the little town below !
    But love, love, love — there 's better love, I
        know !
This foolish love was only day's first offer ;
I choose my next love to defy the scoffer :
For do not our Bride and Bridegroom sally
Out of Possagno church at noon ?
Their house looks over Orcana valley :
Why should not I be the bride as soon
As Ottima ? For I saw, beside,
Arrive last night that little bride —
Saw, if you call it seeing her, one flash
Of the pale snow-pure cheek and black bright
    tresses,
Blacker than all except the black eyelash ;
I wonder she contrives those lids no dresses !
— So strict was she, the veil
Should cover close her pale
Pure cheeks — a bride to look at and scarce
    touch,
Scarce touch, remember, Jules ! For are not such
Used to be tended, flower-like, every feature,
As if one's breath would fray the lily of a
    creature !
A soft and easy life these ladies lead :
Whiteness in us were wonderful indeed.
Oh, save that brow, its virgin dimness,
Keep that foot its lady primness,
Let those ankles never swerve
From their exquisite reserve,
Yet have to trip along the streets like me,
All but naked to the knee !
How will she ever grant her Jules a bliss
So startling as her real first infant kiss ?
Oh, no — not envy, this !

— Not envy, sure ! — for if you gave me
Leave to take or to refuse,
In earnest, do you think I 'd choose
That sort of new love to enslave me ?
Mine should have lapped me round from the
    beginning ;
As little fear of losing it as winning :

Lovers grow cold, men learn to hate their wives,
And only parents' love can last our lives.
At eve the Son and Mother, gentle pair,
Commune inside our turret : what prevents
My being Luigi ? While that mossy lair
Of lizards through the winter-time is stirred
With each to each imparting sweet intents
For this new-year, as brooding bird to bird —
(For I observe of late, the evening walk
Of Luigi and his mother, always ends
Inside our ruined turret, where they talk,
Calmer than lovers, yet more kind than friends)
— Let me be cared about, kept out of harm,
And schemed for, safe in love as with a charm;
Let me be Luigi ! If I only knew
What was my mother's face — my father, too !
    Nay, if you come to that, best love of all
Is God's ; then why not have God's love be-
    fall
Myself as, in the palace by the Dome,
Monsignor ? — who to-night will bless the home
Of his dead brother ; and God bless in turn
That heart which beats, those eyes which
    mildly burn
With love for all men ! I, to-night at least,
Would be that holy and beloved priest.

Now wait ! — even I already seem to share
In God's love : what does New-year's hymn
    declare ?
What other meaning do these verses bear ?

All service ranks the same with God :
If now, as formerly he trod
Paradise, his presence fills
Our earth, each only as God wills
Can work — God's puppets, best and worst,
Are we ; there is no last nor first.

Say not "a small event ! "   Why "small" ?
Costs it more pain that this, ye call
A " great event," should come to pass,
Than that ?   Untwine me from the mass
Of deeds which make up life, one deed
Power shall fall short in or exceed !

And more of it, and more of it ! — oh yes —
I will pass each, and see their happiness,
And envy none — being just as great, no doubt,
Useful to men, and dear to God, as they !
A pretty thing to care about
So mightily, this single holiday !
But let the sun shine ! Wherefore repine ?
— With thee to lead me, O Day of mine,
Down the grass path gray with dew,
Under the pine-wood, blind with boughs,
Where the swallow never flew
Nor yet cicala dared carouse —
No, dared carouse !   [*She enters the street.*

I. MORNING

Up the Hillside, inside the Shrub-house. LUCA's *Wife,*
    OTTIMA, *and her Paramour, the German* SEBALD.

Sebald. [*sings.*]   *Let the watching lids wink !*
                          Day's ablaze with eyes, think !
                          Deep into the night, drink !

Ottima. Night? Such may be your Rhine-
land nights, perhaps;
But this blood-red beam through the shutter's
chink
—We call such light, the morning: let us see!
Mind how you grope your way, though! How
these tall
Naked geraniums straggle! Push the lattice
Behind that frame!—Nay, do I bid you?—
Sebald,
It shakes the dust down on me! Why, of
course
The slide-bolt catches. Well, are you content,
Or must I find you something else to spoil?
Kiss and be friends, my Sebald! Is't full
morning?
Oh, don't speak then!
Seb.   Ay, thus it used to be!
Ever your house was, I remember, shut
Till mid-day; I observed that, as I strolled
On mornings through the vale here; country
girls
Were noisy, washing garments in the brook,
Hinds drove the slow white oxen up the hills:
But no, your house was mute, would ope no eye!
And wisely: you were plotting one thing there,
Nature, another outside. I looked up—
Rough white wood shutters, rusty iron bars,
Silent as death, blind in a flood of light.
Oh, I remember!—and the peasants laughed
And said, "The old man sleeps with the young
wife."
This house was his, this chair, this window—
his.
Otti. Ah, the clear morning! I can see Saint
Mark's;
That black streak is the belfry. Stop: Vicenza
Should lie . . . there's Padua, plain enough,
that blue!
Look o'er my shoulder, follow my finger!
Seb.   Morning?
It seems to me a night with a sun added.
Where's dew, where's freshness? That bruised
plant, I bruised
In getting through the lattice yestereve,
Droops as it did. See, here's my elbow's mark
I' the dust o' the sill.
Otti.   Oh, shut the lattice, pray!
Seb. Let me lean out. I cannot scent blood
here,
Foul as the morn may be.
                    There, shut the world out!
How do you feel now, Ottima? There, curse
The world and all outside! Let us throw off
This mask: how do you bear yourself? Let's
out
With all of it!
Otti.   Best never speak of it.
Seb. Best speak again and yet again of it,
Till words cease to be more than words. "His
blood,"
For instance—let those two words mean, "His
blood"
And nothing more. Notice, I'll say them now,
"His blood."
Otti.   Assuredly if I repented
The deed—
Seb. Repent? Who should repent, or why?

What puts that in your head? Did I once say
That I repented?
Otti.   No; I said the deed . . .
Seb. "The deed" and "the event"—just
now it was
"Our passion's fruit"—the devil take such
cant!
Say, once and always, Luca was a wittol,
I am his cut-throat, you are . . .
Otti.   Here's the wine;
I brought it when we left the house above,
And glasses too—wine of both sorts. Black?
White then?
Seb. But am not I his cut-throat? What
are you?
Otti. There trudges on his business from the
Duomo
Benet the Capuchin, with his brown hood
And bare feet; always in one place at church,
Close under the stone wall by the south entry.
I used to take him for a brown cold piece
Of the wall's self, as out of it he rose
To let me pass—at first, I say, I used:
Now, so has that dumb figure fastened on me,
I rather should account the plastered wall
A piece of him, so chilly does it strike.
This, Sebald?
Seb. No, the white wine—the white wine!
Well, Ottima, I promised no new year
Should rise on us the ancient shameful way;
Nor does it rise. Pour on! To your black
eyes!
Do you remember last damned New Year's day?
Otti. You brought those foreign prints. We
looked at them
Over the wine and fruit. I had to scheme
To get him from the fire. Nothing but saying
His own set wants the proof-mark, roused him
up
To hunt them out.
Seb.   'Faith, he is not alive
To fondle you before my face.
Otti.   Do you
Fondle me then! Who means to take your life
For that, my Sebald?
Seb.   Hark you, Ottima!
One thing to guard against. We'll not make
much
One of the other—that is, not make more
Parade of warmth, childish officious coil,
Than yesterday: as if, sweet, I supposed
Proof upon proof were needed now, now first,
To show I love you—yes, still love you—love
you
In spite of Luca and what's come to him
—Sure sign we had him ever in our thoughts,
White sneering old reproachful face and all!
We'll even quarrel, love, at times, as if
We still could lose each other, were not tied
By this: conceive you?
Otti.   Love!
Seb.   Not tied so sure!
Because though I was wrought upon, have
struck
His insolence back into him—am I
So surely yours?—therefore forever yours?
Otti. Love, to be wise, (one counsel pays
another,)

Should we have — months ago, when first we
    loved,
For instance that May morning we two stole
Under the green ascent of sycamores —
If we had come upon a thing like that
Suddenly . . .
    Seb. " A thing "— there again—" a thing ! "
    Otti. Then, Venus' body, had we come upon
My husband Luca Gaddi's murdered corpse
Within there, at his couch-foot, covered close —
Would you have pored upon it ? Why persist
In poring now upon it ? For 't is here
As much as there in the deserted house :
You cannot rid your eyes of it. For me,
Now he is dead I hate him worse : I hate . . .
Dare you stay here ? I would go back and hold
His two dead hands, and say, " I hate you worse,
Luca, than " . . .
    Seb. Off, off — take your hands off mine,
'T is the hot evening — off ! oh, morning is it ?
    Otti. There 's one thing must be done ; you
        know what thing.
Come in and help to carry. We may sleep
Anywhere in the whole wide house to-night.
    Seb. What would come, think you, if we let
        him lie
Just as he is ? Let him lie there until
The angels take him ! He is turned by this
Off from his face beside, as you will see.
    Otti. This dusty pane might serve for look-
        ing-glass.
Three, four—four gray hairs ! Is it so you said
A plait of hair should wave across my neck ?
No — this way.
    Seb.   Ottima, I would give your neck,
Each splendid shoulder, both those breasts of
    yours,
That this were undone ! Killing ! Kill the
    world,
So Luca lives again ! — ay, lives to sputter
His fulsome dotage on you — yes, and feign
Surprise that I return at eve to sup,
When all the morning I was loitering here —
Bid me dispatch my business and begone.
I would . . .
    Otti.   See !
    Seb.   No, I 'll finish. Do you think
I fear to speak the bare truth once for all ?
All we have talked of, is, at bottom, fine
To suffer ; there 's a recompense in guilt ;
One must be venturous and fortunate :
What is one young for, else ? In age we 'll sigh
O'er the wild reckless wicked days flown over ;
Still, we have lived : the vice was in its place.
But to have eaten Luca's bread, have worn
His clothes, have felt his money swell my
    purse —
Do lovers in romances sin that way ?
Why, I was starving when I used to call
And teach you music, starving while you
    plucked me
These flowers to smell !
    Otti.   My poor lost friend !
    Seb.   He gave me
Life, nothing less : what if he did reproach
My perfidy, and threaten, and do more —
Had he no right ? What was to wonder at ?
He sat by us at table quietly :

Why must you lean across till our cheeks
    touched ?
Could he do less than make pretence to strike ?
'T is not the crime's sake — I 'd commit ten
    crimes
Greater, to have this crime wiped out, undone !
And you — O how feel you ? Feel you for me ?
    Otti. Well then, I love you better now than
    ever,
And best (look at me while I speak to you) —
Best for the crime ; nor do I grieve, in truth,
This mask, this simulated ignorance,
This affectation of simplicity,
Falls off our crime ; this naked crime of ours
May not now be looked over : look it down !
Great ? let it be great ; but the joys it brought,
Pay they or no its price ? Come : they or it !
Speak not ! The past, would you give up the
    past
Such as it is, pleasure and crime together ?
Give up that noon I owned my love for you ?
The garden's silence : even the single bee
Persisting in his toil, suddenly stopped,
And where he hid you only could surmise
By some campanula chalice set a-swing.
Who stammered — " Yes, I love you ? "
    Seb.   And I drew
Back ; put far back your face with both my hands
Lest you should grow too full of me — your face
So seemed athirst for my whole soul and body !
    Otti. And when I ventured to receive you
    here,
Made you steal hither in the mornings —
    Seb.   When
I used to look up 'neath the shrub-house here,
Till the red fire on its glazed windows spread
To a yellow haze ?
    Otti.   Ah — my sign was, the sun
Inflamed the sere side of yon chestnut-tree
Nipped by the first frost.
    Seb.   You would always laugh
At my wet boots : I had to stride through grass
Over my ankles.
    Otti.   Then our crowning night !
    Seb. The July night ?
    Otti.   The day of it too, Sebald !
When heaven's pillars seemed o'erbowed with
    heat,
Its black-blue canopy suffered descend
Close on us both, to weigh down each to each,
And smother up all life except our life.
So lay we till the storm came.
    Seb.   How it came !
    Otti. Buried in woods we lay, you recollect ;
Swift ran the searching tempest overhead ;
And ever and anon some bright white shaft
Burned through the pine-tree roof, here burned
    and there,
As if God's messenger through the close wood
    screen
Plunged and replunged his weapon at a venture,
Feeling for guilty thee and me : then broke
The thunder like a whole sea overhead —
    Seb. Yes !
    Otti. —While I stretched myself upon you
    hands
To hands, my mouth to your hot mouth, and
    shook

All my locks loose, and covered you with
      them —
You, Sebald, the same you!
Seb.   Slower, Ottima!
Otti.   And as we lay —
Seb.   Less vehemently! Love me!
Forgive me! Take not words, mere words, to
      heart!
Your breath is worse than wine. Breathe slow,
      speak slow!
Do not lean on me!
Otti.   Sebald, as we lay,
Rising and falling only with our pants,
Who said, "Let death come now! 'T is right
      to die!
Right to be punished! Naught completes such
      bliss
But woe!" Who said that?
Seb.   How did we ever rise?
Was 't that we slept? Why did it end?
Otti.   I felt you
Taper into a point the ruffled ends
Of my loose locks 'twixt both your humid lips.
My hair is fallen now: knot it again!
Seb.   I kiss you now, dear Ottima, now and
      now!
This way? Will you forgive me — be once
      more
My great queen?
Otti.   Bind it thrice about my brow;
Crown me your queen, your spirit's arbitress,
Magnificent in sin. Say that!
Seb.   I crown you
My great white queen, my spirit's arbitress,
Magnificent . . .

> [*From without is heard the voice of* PIPPA *singing —*
>
> The year 's at the spring
> And day 's at the morn;
> Morning 's at seven;
> The hillside 's dew-pearled;
> The lark 's on the wing;
> The snail 's on the thorn:
> God 's in his heaven —
> All 's right with the world!
>
> [PIPPA *passes.*

Seb.   God 's in his heaven! Do you hear
      that? Who spoke?
You, you spoke!
Otti.   Oh — that little ragged girl!
She must have rested on the step: we give
      them
But this one holiday the whole year round.
Did you ever see our silk-mills — their inside?
There are ten silk-mills now belong to you.
She stoops to pick my double heartsease . . .
      Sh!
She does not hear: call you out louder!
Seb.   Leave me!
Go, get your clothes on — dress those shoulders!
Otti.   Sebald?
Seb.   Wipe off that paint! I hate you.
Otti.   Miserable!
Seb.   My God, and she is emptied of it now!
Outright now! — how miraculously gone
As of the grace — had she not strange grace
      once?

Why, the blank cheek hangs listless as it likes,
No purpose holds the features up together,
Only the cloven brow and puckered chin
Stay in their places: and the very hair,
That seemed to have a sort of life in it,
Drops, a dead web!
Otti.   Speak to me — not of me!
Seb. — That round great full-orbed face,
      where not an angle
Broke the delicious indolence — all broken!
Otti.   To me — not of me! Ungrateful, per-
      jured cheat!
A coward too: but ingrate 's worse than all!
Beggar — my slave — a fawning, cringing lie!
Leave me! Betray me! I can see your drift!
A lie that walks and eats and drinks!
Seb.   My God!
Those morbid olive faultless shoulder-blades —
I should have known there was no blood be-
      neath!
Otti.   You hate me then? You hate me
      then?
Seb.   To think
She would succeed in her absurd attempt,
And fascinate by sinning, show herself
Superior — guilt from its excess superior
To innocence! That little peasant's voice
Has righted all again. Though I be lost,
I know which is the better, never fear,
Of vice or virtue, purity or lust,
Nature or trick! I see what I have done,
Entirely now! Oh I am proud to feel
Such torments — let the world take credit
      thence —
I, having done my deed, pay too its price!
I hate, hate — curse you! God 's in his heaven!
Otti.   — Me!
Me! no, no, Sebald, not yourself — kill me!
Mine is the whole crime. Do but kill me —
      then
Yourself — then — presently — first hear me
      speak!
I always meant to kill myself — wait, you!
Lean on my breast — not as a breast; don't
      love me
The more because you lean on me, my own
Heart's Sebald! There, there, both deaths
      presently!
Seb.   My brain is drowned now — quite
      drowned: all I feel
Is . . . is, at swift-recurring intervals,
A hurry-down within me, as of waters
Loosened to smother up some ghastly pit:
There they go — whirls from a black fiery sea!
Otti.   Not me — to him, O God, be merciful!

Talk by the way, while PIPPA *is passing from the hill-*
side to Orcana. Foreign Students of painting and
sculpture, from Venice, assembled opposite the house
of JULES, *a young French statuary, at Passagno.*

1st Student. Attention! My own post is be-
neath this window, but the pomegranate clump
yonder will hide three or four of you with a
little squeezing, and Schramm and his pipe
must lie flat in the balcony. Four, five —
who 's a defaulter? We want everybody, for
Jules must not be suffered to hurt his bride
when the jest 's found out.

2d Stud. All here! Only our poet's away — never having much meant to be present, moonstrike him! The airs of that fellow, that Giovacchino! He was in violent love with himself, and had a fair prospect of thriving in his suit, so unmolested was it, — when suddenly a woman falls in love with him, too; and out of pure jealousy he takes himself off to Trieste, immortal poem and all: whereto is this prophetical epitaph appended already, as Bluphocks assures me, — "*Here a mammoth-poem lies, Fouled to death by butterflies.*" His own fault, the simpleton! Instead of cramp couplets, each like a knife in your entrails, he should write, says Bluphocks, both classically and intelligibly. — *Æsculapius, an Epic. Catalogue of the drugs: Hebe's plaister — One strip Cools your lip. Phœbus' emulsion — One bottle Clears your throttle. Mercury's bolus — One box Cures* . . .

3d Stud. Subside, my fine fellow! If the marriage was over by ten o'clock, Jules will certainly be here in a minute with his bride.

2d Stud. Good! — only, so should the poet's muse have been universally acceptable, says Bluphocks, *et canibus nostris* . . . and Delia not better known to our literary dogs than the boy Giovacchino!

1st Stud. To the point, now. Where's Gottlieb, the new-comer? Oh, — listen, Gottlieb, to what has called down this piece of friendly vengeance on Jules, of which we now assemble to witness the winding-up. We are all agreed, all in a tale, observe, when Jules shall burst out on us in a fury by and by: I am spokesman — the verses that are to undeceive Jules bear my name of Lutwyche — but each professes himself alike insulted by this strutting stonesquarer, who came along from Paris to Munich, and thence with a crowd of us to Venice and Possagno here, but proceeds in a day or two alone again — oh, alone indubitably! — to Rome and Florence. He, forsooth, take up his portion with these dissolute, brutalized, heartless bunglers! — so he was heard to call us all. Now, is Schramm brutalized, I should like to know? Am I heartless?

Gottlieb. Why, somewhat heartless; for, suppose Jules a coxcomb as much as you choose, still, for this mere coxcombry, you will have brushed off — what do folks style it? — the bloom of his life. Is it too late to alter? These love-letters now, you call his — I can't laugh at them.

4th Stud. Because you never read the sham letters of our inditing which drew forth these.

Gott. His discovery of the truth will be frightful.

4th Stud. That's the joke. But you should have joined us at the beginning: there's no doubt he loves the girl — loves a model he might hire by the hour!

Gott. See here! "He has been accustomed," he writes, "to have Canova's women about him, in stone, and the world's women beside him, in flesh; these being as much below, as those above, his soul's aspiration: but now he is to have the reality." There you laugh

again! I say, you wipe off the very dew of his youth.

1st Stud. Schramm! (Take the pipe out of his mouth, somebody!) Will Jules lose the bloom of his youth?

Schramm. Nothing worth keeping is ever lost in this world : look at a blossom — it drops presently, having done its service and lasted its time; but fruits succeed, and where would be the blossom's place could it continue? As well affirm that your eye is no longer in your body, because its earliest favorite, whatever it may have first loved to look on, is dead and done with — as that any affection is lost to the soul when its first object, whatever happened first to satisfy it, is superseded in due course. Keep but ever looking, whether with the body's eye or the mind's, and you will soon find something to look on! Has a man done wondering at women? — there follow men, dead and alive, to wonder at. Has he done wondering at men? — there's God to wonder at: and the faculty of wonder may be, at the same time, old and tired enough with respect to its first object, and yet young and fresh sufficiently, so far as concerns its novel one. Thus . . .

1st Stud. Put Schramm's pipe into his mouth again! There, you see! Well, this Jules . . . a wretched fribble — oh, I watched his disportings at Possagno, the other day! Canova's gallery — you know : there he marches first resolvedly past great works by the dozen without vouchsafing an eye: all at once he stops full at the *Psiche-fanciulla* — cannot pass that old acquaintance without a nod of encouragement — "In your new place, beauty? Then behave yourself as well here as at Munich — I see you!" Next he posts himself deliberately before the unfinished *Pietà* for half an hour without moving, till up he starts of a sudden, and thrusts his very nose into — I say, into — the group; by which gesture you are informed that precisely the sole point he had not fully mastered in Canova's practice was a certain method of using the drill in the articulation of the knee-joint — and that, likewise, has he mastered at length! Good-by, therefore, to poor Canova — whose gallery no longer needs detain his successor Jules, the predestinated novel thinker in marble!

5th Stud. Tell him about the women: go on to the women!

1st Stud. Why, on that matter he could never be supercilious enough. How should we be other (he said) than the poor devils you see, with those debasing habits we cherish? He was not to wallow in that mire, at least: he would wait, and love only at the proper time, and meanwhile put up with the *Psiche-fanciulla.* Now, I happened to hear of a young Greek — real Greek girl at Malamocco; a true Islander, do you see, with Alciphron's "hair like sea-moss" — Schramm knows! — white and quiet as an apparition, and fourteen years old at farthest, — a daughter of Natalia, so she swears — that hag Natalia, who helps us to models at three *lire* an hour. We selected this girl for the heroine of our jest. So first, Jules received a scented letter — somebody had seen his Tydeus at the Academy, and my picture was nothing to it: a profound admirer bade him persevere — would make herself known to him ere long. (Paolina, my little friend of the *Fenice*, transcribes divinely.) And in due time, the mysterious correspondent gave certain hints of her peculiar charms — the pale cheeks, the black hair — whatever, in short, had struck us in our Malamocco model: we retained her name, too — Phene, which is, by interpretation, sea-eagle. Now, think of Jules finding himself distinguished from the herd of us by such a creature! In his very first answer he proposed marrying his monitress: and fancy us over these letters, two, three times a day, to receive and dispatch! I concocted the main of it: relations were in the way — secrecy must be observed — in fine, would he wed her on trust, and only speak to her when they were indissolubly united? St — st — Here they come!

6th Stud. Both of them! Heaven's love, speak softly, speak within yourselves!

5th Stud. Look at the bridegroom! Half his hair in storm and half in calm, — patted down over the left temple, — like a frothy cup one blows on to cool it: and the same old blouse that he murders the marble in.

2d Stud. Not a rich vest like yours, Hannibal Scratchy! — rich, that your face may the better set it off.

6th Stud. And the bride! Yes, sure enough, our Phene! Should you have known her in her clothes? How magnificently pale!

Gott. She does not also take it for earnest, I hope!

1st Stud. Oh, Natalia's concern, that is! We settle with Natalia.

6th Stud. She does not speak — has evidently let out no word. The only thing is, will she equally remember the rest of her lesson, and repeat correctly all those verses which are to break the secret to Jules?

Gott. How he gazes on her! Pity — pity!

1st Stud. They go in: now, silence! You three, — not nearer the window, mind, than that pomegranate: just where the little girl, who a few minutes ago passed us singing, is seated!

II. NOON

Over Orcana. The house of JULES, *who crosses its threshold with* PHENE: *she is silent, on which* JULES *begins —*

Do not die, Phene! I am yours now, you
Are mine now; let fate reach me how she likes,
If you'll not die: so, never die! Sit here —
My work-room's single seat. I over-lean
This length of hair and lustrous front; they turn
Like an entire flower upward: eyes, lips, last
Your chin — no, last your throat turns: 't is their scent
Pulls down my face upon you. Nay, look ever
This one way till I change, grow you — I could
Change into you, beloved!
                    You by me,
And I by you; this is your hand in mine,

And side by side we sit: all's true. Thank God!
I have spoken: speak you!
                    O my life to come!
My Tydeus must be carved that 's there in clay;
Yet how be carved, with you about the room?
Where must I place you? When I think that once
This room-full of rough block-work seemed my heaven
Without you! Shall I ever work again,
Get fairly into my old ways again,
Bid each conception stand while, trait by trait,
My hand transfers its lineaments to stone?
Will my mere fancies live near you, their truth —
The live truth, passing and repassing me,
Sitting beside me?
                    Now speak!
                              Only first,
See, all your letters! Was 't not well contrived?
Their hiding-place is Psyche's robe; she keeps
Your letters next her skin: which drops out foremost?
Ah, — this that swam down like a first moonbeam
Into my world!
                    Again those eyes complete
Their melancholy survey, sweet and slow,
Of all my room holds; to return and rest
On me, with pity, yet some wonder too:
As if God bade some spirit plague a world,
And this were the one moment of surprise
And sorrow while she took her station, pausing
O'er what she sees, finds good, and must destroy!
What gaze you at? Those? Books, I told you of;
Let your first word to me rejoice them, too:
This minion, a Coluthus, writ in red,
Bistre and azure by Bessarion's scribe —
Read this line . . . no, shame — Homer's be the Greek
First breathed me from the lips of my Greek girl!
This Odyssey in coarse black vivid type
With faded yellow blossoms 'twixt page and page,
To mark great places with due gratitude;
"He said, and on Antinous directed
A bitter shaft" . . . a flower blots out the rest!
Again upon your search? My statues, then!
— Ah, do not mind that — better that will look
When cast in bronze — an Almaign Kaiser, that,
Swart-green and gold, with truncheon based on hip.
This, rather, turn to! What, unrecognized?
I thought you would have seen that here you sit
As I imagined you, — Hippolyta,
Naked upon her bright Numidian horse.
Recall you this then? "Carve in bold relief" —
So you commanded — "carve, against I come,
A Greek, in Athens, as our fashion was,
Feasting, bay-filleted and thunder-free,
Who rises 'neath the lifted myrtle-branch.
'Praise those who slew Hipparchus!' cry the guests,

'While o'er thy head the singer's myrtle waves
As erst above our champion : stand up, all ! '"
See, I have labored to express your thought.
Quite round, a cluster of mere hands and arms
(Thrust in all senses, all ways, from all sides,
Only consenting at the branch's end
They strain toward) serves for frame to a sole
    face,
The Praiser's, in the centre : who with eyes
Sightless, so bend they back to light inside
His brain where visionary forms throng up,
Sings, minding not that palpitating arch
Of hands and arms, nor the quick drip of wine
From the drenched leaves o'erhead, nor crowns
    cast off,
Violet and parsley crowns to trample on —
Sings, pausing as the patron-ghosts approve,
Devoutly their unconquerable hymn.
But you must say a " well " to that — say
    " well ! "
Because you gaze — am I fantastic, sweet ?
Gaze like my very life's-stuff, marble — mar-
    bly
Even to the silence ! Why, before I found
The real flesh Phene, I inured myself
To see, throughout all nature, varied stuff
For better nature's birth by means of art :
With me, each substance tended to one form
Of beauty — to the human archetype.
On every side occurred suggestive germs
Of that — the tree, the flower — or take the
    fruit, —
Some rosy shape, continuing the peach,
Curved beewise o'er its bough ; as rosy limbs,
Depending, nestled in the leaves ; and just
From a cleft rose-peach the whole Dryad sprang.
But of the stuffs one can be master of,
How I divined their capabilities !
From the soft-rinded smoothening facile chalk
That yields your outline to the air's embrace,
Half-softened by a halo's pearly gloom ;
Down to the crisp imperious steel, so sure
To cut its one confided thought clean out
Of all the world. But marble ! — 'neath my
    tools
More pliable than jelly — as it were
Some clear primordial creature dug from depths
In the earth's heart, where itself breeds itself,
And whence all baser substance may be worked ;
Refine it off to air, you may, — condense it
Down to the diamond ; — is not metal there,
When o'er the sudden speck my chisel trips ?
— Not flesh, as flake off flake I scale, approach,
Lay bare those bluish veins of blood asleep ?
Lurks flame in no strange windings where, sur-
    prised
By the swift implement sent home at once,
Flushes and glowings radiate and hover
About its track ?
                    Phene ? what — why is this ?
That whitening cheek, those still dilating eyes !
Ah, you will die — I knew that you would die !

PHENE *begins, on his having long remained silent.*

Now the end 's coming ; to be sure, it must
Have ended sometime ! Tush, why need I speak
Their foolish speech ? I cannot bring to mind
One half of it, beside ; and do not care

For old Natalia now, nor any of them.
Oh, you — what are you ? — if I do not try
To say the words Natalia made me learn,
To please your friends, — it is to keep myself
Where your voice lifted me, by letting that
Proceed : but can it ? Even you, perhaps,
Cannot take up, now you have once let fall,
The music's life, and me along with that —
No, or you would ! We 'll stay, then, as we are :
Above the world.
                    You creature with the eyes !
If I could look forever up to them,
As now you let me, — I believe, all sin,
All memory of wrong done, suffering borne,
Would drop down, low and lower, to the earth
Whence all that 's low comes, and there touch
    and stay
— Never to overtake the rest of me,
All that, unspotted, reaches up to you,
Drawn by those eyes ! What rises is myself,
Not me the shame and suffering ; but they sink,
Are left, I rise above them. Keep me so,
Above the world !
                    But you sink, for your eyes
Are altering — altered ! Stay — " I love you,
    love " . . .
I could prevent it if I understood :
More of your words to me : was 't in the tone
Or the words, your power ?
                    Or stay — I will repeat
Their speech, if that contents you ! Only change
No more, and I shall find it presently
Far back here, in the brain yourself filled up.
Natalia threatened me that harm should follow
Unless I spoke their lesson to the end,
But harm to me, I thought she meant, not you.
Your friends, — Natalia said they were your
    friends
And meant you well, — because, I doubted it,
Observing (what was very strange to see)
On every face, so different in all else,
The same smile girls like me are used to bear,
But never men, men cannot stoop so low ;
Yet your friends, speaking of you, used that
    smile,
That hateful smirk of boundless self-conceit
Which seems to take possession of the world
And make of God a tame confederate,
Purveyor to their appetites . . . you know !
But still Natalia said they were your friends,
And they assented though they smiled the more.
And all came round me, — that thin Englishman
With light lank hair seemed leader of the rest ;
He held a paper — " What we want," said he,
Ending some explanation to his friends —
" Is something slow, involved and mystical,
To hold Jules long in doubt, yet take his taste
And lure him on until, at innermost
Where he seeks sweetness' soul, he may find
    — this !
— As in the apple's core, the noisome fly :
For insects on the rind are seen at once,
And brushed aside as soon, but this is found
Only when on the lips or loathing tongue."
And so he read what I have got by heart :
I 'll speak it, — " Do not die, love ! I am
    yours " . . .
No — is not that, or like that, part of words

Yourself began by speaking? Strange to lose
What cost such pains to learn! Is this more
  right?

I am a painter who cannot paint;
In my life, a devil rather than saint;
In my brain, as poor a creature too:
No end to all I cannot do!
Yet do one thing at least I can —
Love a man or hate a man
Supremely: thus my lore began.
Through the Valley of Love I went,
In the lovingest spot to abide,
And just on the verge where I pitched my tent,
I found Hate dwelling beside.
(Let the Bridegroom ask what the painter meant,
Of his Bride, of the peerless Bride!)
And further, I traversed Hate's grove,
In the hatefullest nook to dwell;
But lo, where I flung myself prone, couched Love
Where the shadow threefold fell.
(The meaning — those black bride's-eyes above,
Not a painter's lip should tell!)

"And here," said he, "Jules probably will
  ask,
'You have black eyes, Love, — you are, sure
  enough,
My peerless bride, — then do you tell indeed
What needs some explanation! What means
  this?'"
— And I am to go on, without a word —

So, I grew wise in Love and Hate,
From simple that I was of late.
Once, when I loved, I would enlace
Breast, eyelids, hands, feet, form and face
Of her I loved, in one embrace —
As if by mere love I could love immensely!
Once, when I hated, I would plunge
My sword, and wipe with the first lunge
My foe's whole life out like a sponge —
As if by mere hate I could hate intensely!
But now I am wiser, know better the fashion
How passion seeks aid from its opposite pas-
  sion:
And if I see cause to love more, hate more
Than ever man loved, ever hated before —
And seek in the Valley of Love
The nest, or the nook in Hate's Grove
Where my soul may surely reach
The essence, naught less, of each,
The Hate of all Hates, the Love
Of all Loves, in the Valley or Grove, —
I find them the very warders
Each of the other's borders.
When I love most, Love is disguised
In Hate; and when Hate is surprised
In Love, then I hate most: ask
How Love smiles through Hate's iron casque,
Hate grins through Love's rose-braided mask, —
And how, having hated thee,
I sought long and painfully
To reach thy heart, nor prick
The skin but pierce to the quick —
Ask this, my Jules, and be answered straight
By thy bride — how the painter Lutwyche can
  hate!

JULES *interposes.*

Lutwyche! Who else? But all of them, no
  doubt,
Hated me: they at Venice — presently
Their turn, however! You I shall not meet:
If I dreamed, saying this would wake me.
                                   Keep
What's here, the gold — we cannot meet again,
Consider! and the money was but meant
For two years' travel, which is over now,
All chance or hope or care or need of it.
This — and what comes from selling these, my
  casts
And books and medals, except . . . let them go
Together, so the produce keeps you safe
Out of Natalia's clutches! If by chance
(For all's chance here) I should survive the gang
At Venice, root out all fifteen of them,
We might meet somewhere, since the world is
  wide.

[*From without is heard the voice of* PIPPA, *singing —*

Give her but a least excuse to love me!
When — where —
How — can this arm establish her above me,
If fortune fixed her as my lady there,
There already, to eternally reprove me?
(" Hist!" — said Kate the Queen;
But " Oh!" cried the maiden, binding her
  tresses,
"'Tis only a page that carols unseen,
Crumbling your hounds their messes!")

Is she wronged? — To the rescue of her honor,
My heart!
Is she poor? — What costs it to be styled a do-
  nor?
Merely an earth to cleave, a sea to part.
But that fortune should have thrust all this upon
  her!
(" Nay, list!" — bade Kate the Queen;
And still cried the maiden, binding her tresses,
"'Tis only a page that carols unseen,
Fitting your hawks their jesses!")
                              [PIPPA *passes.*

JULES *resumes.*

What name was that the little girl sang forth?
Kate? The Cornaro, doubtless, who renounced
The crown of Cyprus to be lady here
At Asolo, where still her memory stays,
And peasants sing how once a certain page
Pined for the grace of her so far above
His power of doing good to, " Kate the Queen —
She never could be wronged, be poor," he
  sighed,
" Need him to help her!"
                        Yes, a bitter thing
To see our lady above all need of us;
Yet so we look ere we will love; not I,
But the world looks so. If whoever loves
Must be, in some sort, god or worshipper,
The blessing or the blest one, queen or page,
Why should we always choose the page's part?
Here is a woman with utter need of me, —
I find myself queen here, it seems!
                                  How strange!
Look at the woman here with the new soul,
Like my own Psyche, - fresh upon her lips

Alit, the visionary butterfly,
Waiting my word to enter and make bright,
Or flutter off and leave all blank as first.
This body had no soul before, but slept
Or stirred, was beauteous or ungainly, free
From taint or foul with stain, as outward
    things
Fastened their image on its passiveness :
Now, it will wake, feel, live — or die again !
Shall to produce form out of unshaped stuff
Be Art — and further, to evoke a soul
From form be nothing ? This new soul is
    mine !

Now, to kill Lutwyche, what would that do ? —
    save
A wretched dauber, men will hoot to death
Without me, from their hooting. Oh, to hear
God's voice plain as I heard it first, before
They broke in with their laughter ! I heard
    them
Henceforth, not God.
                    To Ancona — Greece — some isle !
I wanted silence only ; there is clay
Everywhere. One may do whate'er one likes
In Art : the only thing is, to make sure
That one does like it — which takes pains to
    know.
Scatter all this, my Phene — this mad dream !
Who, what is Lutwyche, what Natalia's friends,
What the whole world except our love — my
    own,
Own Phene ? But I told you, did I not,
Ere night we travel for your land — some isle
With the sea's silence on it ? Stand aside —
I do but break these paltry models up
To begin Art afresh. Meet Lutwyche, I —
And save him from my statue meeting him ?
Some unsuspected isle in the far seas !
Like a god going through his world, there
    stands
One mountain for a moment in the dusk,
Whole brotherhoods of cedars on its brow :
And you are ever by me while I gaze
— Are in my arms as now — as now — as now !
Some unsuspected isle in the far seas !
Some unsuspected isle in far-off seas !

Talk by the way, while PIPPA *is passing from Orcana to
the Turret. Two or three of the Austrian Police
loitering with* BLUPHOCKS, *an English vagabond, just
in view of the Turret.*

Bluphocks.[1] So, that is your Pippa, the lit-
tle girl who passed us singing ? Well, your
Bishop's Intendant's money shall be honestly
earned : — now, don't make me that sour face
because I bring the Bishop's name into the busi-
ness ; we know he can have nothing to do with
such horrors : we know that he is a saint and
all that a bishop should be, who is a great man
beside. *Oh were but every worm a maggot,
Every fly a grig, Every bough a Christmas fagot,
Every tune a jig !* In fact, I have abjured all
religions ; but the last I inclined to was the
Armenian : for I have travelled, do you see,
and at Koenigsberg, Prussia Improper (so

[1] " He maketh his sun to rise on the evil and on the
good, and sendeth rain on the just and on the unjust."

styled because there 's a sort of bleak hungry
sun there), you might remark, over a venerable
house-porch, a certain Chaldee inscription ; and
brief as it is, a mere glance at it used absolutely
to change the mood of every bearded passenger.
In they turned, one and all ; the young and
lightsome, with no irreverent pause, the aged
and decrepit, with a sensible alacrity : 't was
the Grand Rabbi's abode, in short. Struck
with curiosity, I lost no time in learning Syriac
— (these are vowels, you dogs, — follow my
stick's end in the mud — *Celarent, Darii,
Ferio !*) and one morning presented myself,
spelling-book in hand, a, b, c, — I picked it out
letter by letter, and what was the purport of
this miraculous posy ? Some cherished legend
of the past, you 'll say — " *How Moses hocus-
pocussed Egypt's land with fly and locust,*" —
or, " *How to Jonah sounded harshish, Get thee
up and go to Tarshish,* " — or " *How the angel
meeting Balaam, Straight his ass returned
a salaam.*" In no wise ! "*Shackabrack —
Boach — somebody or other — Isaach, Re-cei-ver,
Pur - cha - ser and Ex - chan - ger of — Stolen
Goods !* " So, talk to me of the religion of
a bishop ! I have renounced all bishops save
Bishop Beveridge ! — mean to live so — and
die — *As some Greek dog-sage, dead and merry,
Hellward bound in Charon's wherry, With food
for both worlds, under and upper, Lupine-seed
and Hecate's supper, And never an obolus
. . . (though thanks to you, or this Intendant
through you, or this Bishop through his Inten-
dant — I possess a burning pocket-full of zwan-
zigers) . . .To pay the Stygian Ferry !*

1st Policeman. There is the girl, then ; go
and deserve them the moment you have pointed
out to us Signor Luigi and his mother. [*To the
rest.*] I have been noticing a house yonder, this
long while : not a shutter unclosed since morn-
ing !

2d Pol. Old Luca Gaddi's, that owns the
silk-mills here : he dozes by the hour, wakes
up, sighs deeply, says he should like to be
Prince Metternich, and then dozes again, after
having bidden young Sebald, the foreigner, set
his wife to playing draughts. Never molest
such a household, they mean well.

Blup. Only, cannot you tell me something of
this little Pippa, I must have to do with ? One
could make something of that name. Pippa —
that is, short for Felippa — rhyming to *Panurge
consults Hertrippa — Believest thou, King Agrip-
pa ?* Something might be done with that name.

2d Pol. Put into rhyme that your head and
a ripe muskmelon would not be dear at half a
zwanziger ! Leave this fooling, and look out ;
the afternoon 's over or nearly so.

3d Pol. Where in this passport of Signor
Luigi does our Principal instruct you to watch
him so narrowly ? There ? What 's there be-
side a simple signature ? (That English fool 's
busy watching.)

2d Pol. Flourish all round — " Put all possi-
ble obstacles in his way ; " oblong dot at the
end — " Detain him till further advices reach
you ; " scratch at bottom — " Send him back
on pretence of some informality in the above ; "

ink-spirt on righthand side (which is the case here) — "Arrest him at once." Why and wherefore, I don't concern myself, but my instructions amount to this : if Signor Luigi leaves home to-night for Vienna — well and good, the passport deposed with us for our *visa* is really for his own use, they have misinformed the Office, and he means well ; but let him stay over to-night — there has been the pretence we suspect, the accounts of his corresponding and holding intelligence with the Carbonari are correct, we arrest him at once, to-morrow comes Venice, and presently Spielberg. Bluphocks makes the signal, sure enough ! That is he, entering the turret with his mother, no doubt.

III. EVENING

Inside the Turret on the Hill above Asolo. LUIGI *and his* MOTHER *entering.*

Mother. If there blew wind, you 'd hear a
  long sigh, easing
The utmost heaviness of music's heart.
  Luigi. Here in the archway ?
  Mother.   Oh no, no — in farther,
Where the echo is made, on the ridge.
  Luigi.   Here surely, then.
How plain the tap of my heel as I leaped up !
Hark — "Lucius Junius ! " The very ghost of
  a voice
Whose body is caught and kept by . . . what
  are those ?
Mere withered wallflowers, waving overhead ?
They seem an elvish group with thin bleached
  hair
That lean out of their topmost fortress — look
And listen, mountain men, to what we say,
Hand under chin of each grave earthy face.
Up and show faces all of you ! — "All of you ! "
That 's the king dwarf with the scarlet comb ;
  old Franz,
Come down and meet your fate ? Hark —
  "Meet your fate ! "
  Mother. Let him not meet it, my Luigi — do
  not
Go to his City ! Putting crime aside,
Half of these ills of Italy are feigned :
Your Pellicos and writers for effect,
Write for effect.
  Luigi.   Hush ! Say A writes, and B.
  Mother. These A's and B's write for effect,
  I say.
Then, evil is in its nature loud, while good
Is silent ; you hear each petty injury,
None of his virtues ; he is old beside,
Quiet and kind, and densely stupid. Why
Do A and B kill not him themselves ?
  Luigi.   They teach
Others to kill him — me — and, if I fail,
Others to succeed ; now, if A tried and failed,
I could not teach that : mine 's the lesser task.
Mother, they visit night by night . . .
  Mother.   — You, Luigi ?
Ah, will you let me tell you what you are ?
  Luigi. Why not ? Oh, the one thing you fear
  to hint,
You may assure yourself I say and say
Ever to myself ! At times — nay, even as now

We sit — I think my mind is touched, suspect
All is not sound : but is not knowing that,
What constitutes one sane or otherwise ?
I know I am thus — so, all is right again.
I laugh at myself as through the town I walk,
And see men merry as if no Italy
Were suffering ; then I ponder — " I am rich,
Young, healthy ; why should this fact trouble me,
More than it troubles these ? " But it does
  trouble.
No, trouble 's a bad word : for as I walk
There 's springing and melody and giddiness,
And old quaint turns and passages of my youth,
Dreams long forgotten, little in themselves,
Return to me — whatever may amuse me :
And earth seems in a truce with me, and heaven
Accords with me, all things suspend their strife,
The very cicala laughs " There goes he, and
  there !
Feast him, the time is short ; he is on his way
For the world's sake : feast him this once, our
  friend ! "
And in return for all this, I can trip
Cheerfully up the scaffold-steps. I go
This evening, mother !
  Mother.   But mistrust yourself —
Mistrust the judgment you pronounce on him !
  Luigi. Oh, there I feel — am sure that I am
  right !
  Mother. Mistrust your judgment then, of the
  mere means
To this wild enterprise : say, you are right, —
How should one in your state e'er bring to pass
What would require a cool head, a cool heart,
And a calm hand ? You never will escape.
  Luigi. Escape ? To even wish that, would
  spoil all.
The dying is best part of it. Too much
Have I enjoyed these fifteen years of mine,
To leave myself excuse for longer life :
Was not life pressed down, running o'er with
  joy,
That I might finish with it ere my fellows
Who, sparelier feasted, make a longer stay ?
I was put at the board-head, helped to all
At first ; I rise up happy and content.
God must be glad one loves his world so much.
I can give news of earth to all the dead
Who ask me : — last year's sunsets, and great
  stars
Which had a right to come first and see ebb
The crimson wave that drifts the sun away —
Those crescent moons with notched and burn-
  ing rims
That strengthened into sharp fire, and there
  stood,
Impatient of the azure — and that day
In March, a double rainbow stopped the storm —
May's warm slow yellow moonlit summer
  nights —
Gone are they, but I have them in my soul !
  Mother. (He will not go !)
  Luigi.   You smile at me ? 'T is true, —
Voluptuousness, grotesqueness, ghastliness,
Environ my devotedness as quaintly
As round about some antique altar wreathe
The rose festoons, goats' horns, and oxen's
  skulls.

Mother. See now: you reach the city, you must cross
His threshold — how?
Luigi. Oh, that 's if we conspired!
Then would come pains in plenty, as you guess —
But guess not how the qualities most fit
For such an office, qualities I have,
Would little stead me, otherwise employed,
Yet prove of rarest merit only here.
Every one knows for what his excellence
Will serve, but no one ever will consider
For what his worst defect might serve: and yet
Have you not seen me range our coppice yonder
In search of a distorted ash? — I find
The wry spoilt branch a natural perfect bow.
Fancy the thrice-sage, thrice-precautioned man
Arriving at the palace on my errand!
No, no! I have a handsome dress packed up —
White satin here, to set off my black hair;
In I shall march — for you may watch your life out
Behind thick walls, make friends there to betray you;
More than one man spoils everything. March straight —
Only, no clumsy knife to fumble for,
Take the great gate, and walk (not saunter) on
Through guards and guards — I have rehearsed it all
Inside the turret here a hundred times.
Don't ask the way of whom you meet, observe!
But where they cluster thickliest is the door
Of doors; they 'll let you pass — they 'll never blab
Each to the other, he knows not the favorite,
Whence he is bound and what 's his business now.
Walk in — straight up to him; you have no knife:
Be prompt, how should he scream? Then, out with you!
Italy, Italy, my Italy!
You 're free, you 're free! Oh mother, I could dream
They got about me — Andrea from his exile,
Pier from his dungeon, Gualtier from his grave!
Mother. Well, you shall go. Yet seems this patriotism
The easiest virtue for a selfish man
To acquire: he loves himself — and next, the world —
If he must love beyond, — but naught between:
As a short-sighted man sees naught midway
His body and the sun above. But you
Are my adored Luigi, ever obedient
To my least wish, and running o'er with love:
I could not call you cruel or unkind.
Once more, your ground for killing him! — then go!
Luigi. Now do you try me, or make sport of me?
How first the Austrians got these provinces . . .
(If that is all, I 'll satisfy you soon)
— Never by conquest but by cunning, for
That treaty whereby . . .
Mother. Well?
Luigi. (Sure, he 's arrived,
The tell-tale cuckoo: spring 's his confidant,

And he lets out her April purposes!)
Or . . . better go at once to modern time.
He has . . . they have . . . in fact, I understand
But can't restate the matter; that 's my boast:
Others could reason it out to you, and prove
Things they have made me feel.
Mother. Why go to-night?
Morn 's for adventure. Jupiter is now
A morning-star. I cannot hear you, Luigi!
Luigi. "I am the bright and morning-star,"
saith God —
And, "to such an one I give the morning-star."
The gift of the morning-star! Have I God's gift
Of the morning-star?
Mother. Chiara will love to see
That Jupiter an evening-star next June.
Luigi. True, mother. Well for those who live through June!
Great noontides, thunder-storms, all glaring pomps
That triumph at the heels of June the god
Leading his revel through our leafy world.
Yes, Chiara will be here.
Mother. In June: remember,
Yourself appointed that month for her coming.
Luigi. Was that low noise the echo?
Mother. The night-wind.
She must be grown — with her blue eyes upturned
As if life were one long and sweet surprise:
In June she comes.
Luigi. We were to see together
The Titian at Treviso. There, again!
[*From without is heard the voice of* PIPPA, *singing —*

A king lived long ago,
In the morning of the world,
When earth was nigher heaven than now;
And the king's locks curled,
Disparting o'er a forehead full
As the milk-white space 'twixt horn and horn
Of some sacrificial bull —
Only calm as a babe new-born:
For he was got to a sleepy mood,
So safe from all decrepitude,
Age with its bane, so sure gone by,
(The gods so loved him while he dreamed)
That, having lived thus long, there seemed
No need the king should ever die.

Luigi. No need that sort of king shoul l
ever die!

Among the rocks his city was:
Before his palace, in the sun,
He sat to see his people pass,
And judge them every one
From its threshold of smooth stone.
They haled him many a valley-thief
Caught in the sheep-pens, robber-chief
Swarthy and shameless, beggar-cheat,
Spy-prowler, or rough pirate found
On the sea-sand left aground;
And sometimes clung about his feet,
With bleeding lip and burning cheek,
A woman, bitterest wrong to speak
Of one with sullen thickset brows:
And sometimes from the prison-house

The angry priests a pale wretch brought,
Who through some chink had pushed and pressed
On knees and elbows, belly and breast,
Worm-like into the temple, — caught
He was by the very god,
Who ever in the darkness strode
Backward and forward, keeping watch
O'er his brazen bowls, such rogues to catch!
These, all and every one,
The king judged, sitting in the sun.

Luigi. That king should still judge sitting in
the sun!

His councillors, on left and right,
Looked anxious up, — but no surprise
Disturbed the king's old smiling eyes
Where the very blue had turned to white.
'T is said, a Python scared one day
The breathless city, till he came,
With forky tongue and eyes on flame,
Where the old king sat to judge alway;
But when he saw the sweepy hair
Girt with a crown of berries rare
Which the god will hardly give to wear
To the maiden who singeth, dancing bare
In the altar-smoke by the pine-torch lights,
At his wondrous forest rites, —
Seeing this, he did not dare
Approach that threshold in the sun,
Assault the old king smiling there.
Such grace had kings when the world begun!
[Pippa *passes.*

Luigi. And such grace have they, now that
the world ends!
The Python at the city, on the throne,
And brave men, God would crown for slaying
him,
Lurk in by-corners lest they fall his prey.
Are crowns yet to be won in this late time,
Which weakness makes me hesitate to reach?
'T is God's voice calls: how could I stay?
Farewell!

Talk by the way, while Pippa *is passing from the Turret
to the Bishop's Brother's House, close to the Duomo
S. Maria. Poor* Girls *sitting on the steps.*

1st Girl. There goes a swallow to Venice —
the stout seafarer!
Seeing those birds fly, makes me wish for wings.
Let us all wish; you, wish first!
2d Girl. I? This sunset
To finish.
3d Girl. That old — somebody I know,
Grayer and older than my grandfather,
To give me the same treat he gave last week —
Feeding me on his knee with fig-peckers,
Lampreys and red Breganze-wine, and mum-
bling
The while some folly about how well I fare,
Let sit and eat my supper quietly:
Since had he not himself been late this morning
Detained at — never mind where, — had he
not . . .
" Eh, baggage, had I not! " —
2d Girl. How she can lie!
3d Girl. Look there — by the nails!
2d Girl. What makes your fingers red?
3d Girl. Dipping them into wine to write bad
words with

On the bright table: how he laughed!
1st Girl. My turn.
Spring 's come and summer 's coming. I would
wear
A long loose gown, down to the feet and hands,
With plaits here, close about the throat, all day;
And all night lie, the cool long nights, in bed;
And have new milk to drink, apples to eat,
Deuzans and junetings, leather-coats . . . ah, I
should say,
This is away in the fields — miles!
3d Girl. Say at once
You 'd be at home: she 'd always be at home!
Now comes the story of the farm among
The cherry orchards, and how April snowed
White blossoms on her as she ran. Why, fool,
They 've rubbed the chalk-mark out, how tall
you were,
Twisted your starling's neck, broken his cage,
Made a dung-hill of your garden!
1st Girl. They destroy
My garden since I left them? well — perhaps
I would have done so: so I hope they have!
A fig-tree curled out of our cottage wall;
They called it mine, I have forgotten why,
It must have been there long ere I was born:
Cric — cric — I think I hear the wasps o'er-
head
Pricking the papers strung to flutter there
And keep off birds in fruit-time — coarse long
papers,
And the wasps eat them, prick them through
and through.
3d Girl. How her mouth twitches! Where
was I? — before
She broke in with her wishes and long gowns
And wasps — would I be such a fool! — Oh,
here!
This is my way: I answer every one
Who asks me why I make so much of him —
(If you say, " you love him " — straight " he 'll
not be gulled! ")
" He that seduced me when I was a girl
Thus high — had eyes like yours, or hair like
yours,
Brown, red, white," — as the case may be:
that pleases!
See how that beetle burnishes in the path!
There sparkles he along the dust: and, there —
Your journey to that maize-tuft spoiled at least!
1st Girl. When I was young, they said if you
killed one
Of those sunshiny beetles, that his friend
Up there, would shine no more that day nor
next.
2d Girl. When you were young? Nor are
you young, that 's true.
How your plump arms, that were, have dropped
away!
Why, I can span them. Cecco beats you still?
No matter, so you keep your curious hair.
I wish they 'd find a way to dye our hair
Your color — any lighter tint, indeed,
Than black: the men say they are sick of black,
Black eyes, black hair!
4th Girl. Sick of yours, like enough.
Do you pretend you ever tasted lampreys
And ortolans? Giovita, of the palace,

Engaged (but there's no trusting him) to slice
   me
Polenta with a knife that had cut up
An ortolan.
   2d Girl. Why, there ! Is not that Pippa
We are to talk to, under the window, —
   quick ! —
Where the lights are ?
   1st Girl. That she ? No, or she would sing,
For the Intendant said . . .
   3d Girl.   Oh, you sing first !
Then, if she listens and comes close . . . I 'll
   tell you, —
Sing that song the young English noble made,
Who took you for the purest of the pure,
And meant to leave the world for you — what
   fun !
   2d Girl. [*Sings.*]

You 'll love me yet ! — and I can tarr j
   Your love's protracted growing :
June reared that bunch of flowers you carry,
   From seeds of April's sowing.

I plant a heartfull now : some seed
   At least is sure to strike,
And yield — what you 'll not pluck indeed,
   Not love, but, may be, like.

You 'll look at least on love's remains,
   A grave's one violet :
Your look ? — that pays a thousand pains.
   What 's death ? You 'll love me yet !

   3d Girl. [*To* PIPPA *who approaches.*] Oh, you
may come closer — we shall not eat you ! Why,
you seem the very person that the great rich
handsome Englishman has fallen so violently in
love with. I 'll tell you all about it.

IV. NIGHT

Inside the Palace by the Duomo. MONSIGNOR, *dismissing his* Attendants.

   Monsignor. Thanks, friends, many thanks !
I chiefly desire life now, that I may recompense
every one of you. Most I know something of
already. What, a repast prepared ? *Benedicto
benedicatur* . . . ugh, ugh ! Where was I ? Oh,
as you were remarking, Ugo, the weather is mild,
very unlike winter-weather : but I am a Sicilian,
you know, and shiver in your Julys here. To
be sure, when 't was full summer at Messina, as
we priests used to cross in procession the great
square on Assumption Day, you might see our
thickest yellow tapers twist suddenly in two,
each like a falling star, or sink down on themselves in a gore of wax. But go, my friends, but
go ! [*To the* Intendant.] Not you, Ugo ! [*The
others leave the apartment.*] I have long wanted
to converse with you, Ugo.
   Intendant. Uguccio —
   Mon. . . . 'guccio Stefani, man ! of Ascoli,
Fermo and Fossombruno ; — what I do need instructing about, are these accounts of your administration of my poor brother's affairs. Ugh !
I shall never get through a third part of your
accounts : take some of these dainties before we

attempt it, however. Are you bashful to that
degree ? For me, a crust and water suffice.
   Inten. Do you choose this especial night to
question me ?
   Mon. This night, Ugo. You have managed
my late brother's affairs since the death of our
elder brother : fourteen years and a month, all
but three days. On the Third of December, I
find him . . .
   Inten. If you have so intimate an acquaintance
with your brother's affairs, you will be tender
of turning so far back : they will hardly bear
looking into, so far back.
   Mon. Ay, ay, ugh, ugh, — nothing but disappointments here below ! I remark a considerable payment made to yourself on this Third of
December. Talk of disappointments ! There
was a young fellow here, Jules, a foreign sculptor
I did my utmost to advance, that the Church
might be a gainer by us both : he was going on
hopefully enough, and of a sudden he notifies to
me some marvellous change that has happened in
his notions of Art. Here 's his letter, — " He
never had a clearly conceived Ideal within his
brain till to-day. Yet since his hand could manage a chisel, he has practised expressing other
men's Ideals ; and, in the very perfection he has
attained to, he foresees an ultimate failure : his
unconscious hand will pursue its prescribed
course of old years, and will reproduce with a
fatal expertness the ancient types, let the novel
one appear never so palpably to his spirit.
There is but one method of escape : confiding
the virgin type to as chaste a hand, he will turn
painter instead of sculptor, and paint, not carve,
its characteristics," — strike out, I dare say, a
school like Correggio : how think you, Ugo ?
   Inten. Is Correggio a painter ?
   Mon. Foolish Jules ! and yet, after all, why
foolish ? He may — probably will — fail egregiously ; but if there should arise a new painter,
will it not be in some such way, by a poet now,
or a musician (spirits who have conceived and
perfected an Ideal through some other channel),
transferring it to this, and escaping our conventional roads by pure ignorance of them ; eh,
Ugo ? If you have no appetite, talk at least,
Ugo !
   Inten. Sir, I can submit no longer to this
course of yours. First, you select the group
of which I formed one, — next you thin it
gradually, — always retaining me with your
smile, — and so do you proceed till you have
fairly got me alone with you between four stone
walls. And now then ? Let this farce, this
chatter end now : what is it you want with me ?
   Mon. Ugo !
   Inten. From the instant you arrived, I felt
your smile on me as you questioned me about
this and the other article in those papers —
why your brother should have given me this
villa, that *podere*, — and your nod at the end
meant, — what ?
   Mon. Possibly that I wished for no loud talk
here. If once you set me coughing, Ugo ! —
   Inten. I have your brother's hand and seal
to all I possess : now ask me what for ! what
service I did him — ask me !

Mon. I would better not: I should rip up old disgraces, let out my poor brother's weaknesses. By the way, Maffeo of Forli, (which, I forgot to observe, is your true name,) was the interdict ever taken off you for robbing that church at Cesena?

Inten. No, nor needs be: for when I murdered your brother's friend, Pasquale, for him . . .

Mon. Ah, he employed you in that business, did he? Well, I must let you keep, as you say, this villa and that *podere*, for fear the world should find out my relations were of so indifferent a stamp? Maffeo, my family is the oldest in Messina, and century after century have my progenitors gone on polluting themselves with every wickedness under heaven: my own father . . . rest his soul! — I have, I know, a chapel to support that it may rest: my dear two dead brothers were, — what you know tolerably well; I, the youngest, might have rivalled them in vice, if not in wealth: but from my boyhood I came out from among them, and so am not partaker of their plagues. My glory springs from another source; or if from this, by contrast only, — for I, the bishop, am the brother of your employers, Ugo. I hope to repair some of their wrong, however; so far as my brother's ill-gotten treasure reverts to me, I can stop the consequences of his crime: and not one *soldo* shall escape me. Maffeo, the sword we quiet men spurn away, you shrewd knaves pick up and commit murders with; what opportunities the virtuous forego, the villanous seize. Because, to pleasure myself apart from other considerations, my food would be millet-cake, my dress sackcloth, and my couch straw, — am I therefore to let you, the off-scouring of the earth, seduce the poor and ignorant by appropriating a pomp these will be sure to think lessens the abominations so unaccountably and exclusively associated with it? Must I let villas and *poderi* go to you, a murderer and thief, that you may beget by means of them other murderers and thieves? No — if my cough would but allow me to speak!

Inten. What am I to expect? You are going to punish me?

Mon. Must punish you, Maffeo. I cannot afford to cast away a chance. I have whole centuries of sin to redeem, and only a month or two of life to do it in. How should I dare to say . . .

Inten. "Forgive us our trespasses"?

Mon. My friend, it is because I avow myself a very worm, sinful beyond measure, that I reject a line of conduct you would applaud perhaps. Shall I proceed, as it were, a-pardoning? — I? — who have no symptom of reason to assume that aught less than my strenuousest efforts will keep myself out of mortal sin, much less keep others out. No: I do trespass, but will not double that by allowing you to trespass.

Inten. And suppose the villas are not your brother's to give, nor yours to take? Oh, you are hasty enough just now!

Mon. 1, 2 — N° 3! — ay, can you read the substance of a letter, N° 3, I have received

from Rome? It is precisely on the ground there mentioned, of the suspicion I have that a certain child of my late elder brother, who would have succeeded to his estates, was murdered in infancy by you, Maffeo, at the instigation of my late younger brother — that the Pontiff enjoins on me not merely the bringing that Maffeo to condign punishment, but the taking all pains, as guardian of the infant's heritage for the Church, to recover it parcel by parcel, howsoever, whensoever, and wheresoever. While you are now gnawing those fingers, the police are engaged in sealing up your papers, Maffeo, and the mere raising my voice brings my people from the next room to dispose of yourself. But I want you to confess quietly, and save me raising my voice. Why, man, do I not know the old story? The heir between the succeeding heir, and this heir's ruffianly instrument, and their complot's effect, and the life of fear and bribes and ominous smiling silence? Did you throttle or stab my brother's infant? Come now!

Inten. So old a story, and tell it no better? When did such an instrument ever produce such an effect? Either the child smiles in his face; or, most likely, he is not fool enough to put himself in the employer's power so thoroughly: the child is always ready to produce — as you say — howsoever, wheresoever, and whensoever.

Mon. Liar!

Inten. Strike me? Ah, so might a father chastise! I shall sleep soundly to-night at least, though the gallows await me to-morrow; for what a life did I lead! Carlo of Cesena reminds me of his connivance, every time I pay his annuity; which happens commonly thrice a year. If I remonstrate, he will confess all to the good bishop — you!

Mon. I see through the trick, caitiff! I would you spoke truth for once. All shall be sifted, however — seven times sifted.

Inten. And how my absurd riches encumbered me! I dared not lay claim to above half my possessions. Let me but once unbosom myself, glorify Heaven, and die!

Sir, you are no brutal dastardly idiot like your brother I frightened to death: let us understand one another. Sir, I will make away with her for you — the girl — here close at hand; not the stupid obvious kind of killing; do not speak — know nothing of her nor of me! I see her every day — saw her this morning: of course there is to be no killing; but at Rome the courtesans perish off every three years, and I can entice her thither — have indeed begun operations already. There's a certain lusty blue-eyed florid-complexioned English knave, I and the Police employ occasionally. You assent, I perceive — no, that's not it — assent I do not say — but you will let me convert my present havings and holdings into cash, and give me time to cross the Alps? 'T is but a little black-eyed pretty singing Felippa, gay silk-winding girl. I have kept her out of harm's way up to this present; for I always intended to make your life a plague to you with her. 'T is as well settled once and forever. Some women I have procured will pass Bluphocks, my handsome scoundrel, off for somebody; and once Pippa entangled!— you conceive? Through her singing? Is it a bargain?

[From without is heard the voice of PIPPA, *singing* —

> *Overhead the tree-tops meet,*
> *Flowers and grass spring 'neath one's feet;*
> *There was naught above me, naught below,*
> *My childhood had not learned to know:*
> *For, what are the voices of birds*
> *— Ay, and of beasts, — but words, our words,*
> *Only so much more sweet?*
> *The knowledge of that with my life begun.*
> *But I had so near made out the sun,*
> *And counted your stars, the seven and one,*
> *Like the fingers of my hand:*
> *Nay, I could all but understand*
> *Wherefore through heaven the white moon ranges;*
> *And just when out of her soft fifty changes*
> *No unfamiliar face might overlook me —*
> *Suddenly God took me.*

*[*PIPPA *passes.*

Mon. [Springing up.] My people — one and all — all — within there! Gag this villain — tie him hand and foot! 'He dares . . . I know not half he dares — but remove him — quick! *Miserere mei, Domine!* Quick, I say!

PIPPA'S *Chamber again. She enters it.*

The bee with his comb,
The mouse at her dray,
The grub in his tomb,
While winter away;
But the fire-fly and hedge-shrew and lob-worm,
I pray,
How fare they?
Ha, ha, thanks for your counsel, my Zanze!
" Feast upon lampreys, quaff Breganze " —
The summer of life so easy to spend,
And care for to-morrow so soon put away!
But winter hastens at summer's end,
And fire-fly, hedge-shrew, lob-worm, pray,
How fare they?
No bidding me then to . . . what did Zanze say?
" Pare your nails pearlwise, get your small feet shoes
More like " . . . (what said she?) — " and less like canoes! "
How pert that girl was! — would I be those pert Impudent staring women! It had done me, However, surely no such mighty hurt To learn his name who passed that jest upon me:
No foreigner, that I can recollect,
Came, as she says, a month since, to inspect Our silk-mills — none with blue eyes and thick rings
Of raw-silk-colored hair, at all events.
Well, if old Luca keep his good intents,
We shall do better, see what next year brings!
I may buy shoes, my Zanze, not appear
More destitute than you perhaps next year!
Bluph . . . something! I had caught the uncouth name

But for Monsignor's people's sudden clatter
Above us — bound to spoil such idle chatter
As ours: it were indeed a serious matter
If silly talk like ours should put to shame
The pious man, the man devoid of blame,
The . . . ah but — ah but, all the same,
No mere mortal has a right
To carry that exalted air;
Best people are not angels quite:
While — not the worst of people's doings scare
The devil; so there 's that proud look to spare!
Which is mere counsel to myself, mind! for
I have just been the holy Monsignor:
And I was you too, Luigi's gentle mother,
And you too, Luigi! — how that Luigi started
Out of the turret — doubtlessly departed
On some good errand or another,
For he passed just now in a traveller's trim,
And the sullen company that prowled
About his path, I noticed, scowled
As if they had lost a prey in him.
And I was Jules the sculptor's bride,
And I was Ottima beside,
And now what am I? — tired of fooling.
Day for folly, night for schooling!
New year 's day is over and spent,
Ill or well, I must be content.
Even my lily 's asleep, I vow:
Wake up — here 's a friend I've plucked you!
Call this flower a heart's-ease now!
Something rare, let me instruct you,
Is this, with petals triply swollen,
Three times spotted, thrice the pollen;
While the leaves and parts that witness
Old proportions and their fitness,
Here remain unchanged, unmoved now;
Call this pampered thing improved now!
Suppose there 's a king of the flowers
And a girl-show held in his bowers —
" Look ye, buds, this growth of ours,"
Says he, " Zanze from the Brenta,
I have made her gorge polenta
Till both cheeks are near as bouncing
As her . . . name there 's no pronouncing!
See this heightened color too,
For she swilled Breganze wine
Till her nose turned deep carmine;
'T was but white when wild she grew.
And only by this Zanze's eyes
Of which we could not change the size,
The magnitude of all achieved
Otherwise, may be perceived."

Oh what a drear dark close to my poor day!
How could that red sun drop in that black cloud?
Ah Pippa, morning's rule is moved away,
Dispensed with, never more to be allowed!
Day 's turn is over, now arrives the night's.
Oh lark, be day's apostle
To mavis, merle and throstle,
Bid them their betters jostle
From day and its delights!
But at night, brother owlet, over the woods,
Toll the world to thy chantry;
Sing to the bats' sleek sisterhoods
Full complines with gallantry:
Then, owls and bats,

Cowls and twats,
Monks and nuns, in a cloister's moods,
Adjourn to the oak-stump pantry!
        [*After she has begun to undress herself.*
Now, one thing I should like to really know:
How near I ever might approach all these
I only fancied being, this long day :
— Approach, I mean, so as to touch them, so
As to . . . in some way . . . move them — if
        you please,
Do good or evil to them some slight way.
For instance, if I wind
Silk to-morrow, my silk may bind
        [*Sitting on the bedside.*

And border Ottima's cloak's hem.
Ah me, and my important part with them,
This morning's hymn half promised when I
        rose !
True in some sense or other, I suppose.
        [*As she lies down.*
God bless me ! I can pray no more to-night.
No doubt, some way or other, hymns say
        right.

        All service ranks the same with God —
        With God, whose puppets, best and worst,
        Are we ; there is no last nor first.
                [*She sleeps.*

KING VICTOR AND KING CHARLES

A TRAGEDY

THIS was No. II. of *Bells and Pomegranates* and was issued in 1842, though it appears to have been written before the publication of *Pippa Passes.* The following is the advertisement prefixed to the tragedy when first published and always afterward retained.

"So far as I know, this tragedy is the first artistic consequence of what Voltaire termed ' a terrible event without consequences ; ' and although it professes to be historical, I have taken more pains to arrive at the history than most readers would thank me for particularizing : since acquainted, as I will hope them to be, with the chief circumstances of Victor's remarkable European career — nor quite ignorant of the sad and suprising facts I am about to reproduce (a tolerable account of which is to be found, for instance, in Abbe Roman's *Récit*, or even the fifth of Lord Orrery's Letters from Italy) — I cannot expect them to be versed, nor desirous

of becoming so, in all the detail of the memoirs, correspondence, and relations of the time. From these only may be obtained a knowledge of the fiery and audacious temper, unscrupulous selfishness, profound dissimulation, and singular fertility in resources, of Victor — the extreme and painful sensibility, prolonged immaturity of powers, earnest good purpose and vacillating will of Charles — the noble and right woman's manliness of his wife — and the illconsidered rascality and subsequent betteradvised rectitude of D'Ormea. When I say, therefore, that I cannot but believe my statement (combining as it does what appears correct in Voltaire and plausible in Condorcet) more true to person and thing than any it has hitherto been my fortune to meet with, no doubt my word will be taken, and my evidence spared as readily.   R. B."

LONDON, 1842.

PERSONS

VICTOR AMADEUS, first King of Sardinia.
CHARLES EMANUEL, his son, Prince of Piedmont.
POLYXENA, wife of Charles.
D'ORMEA, minister.

FIRST YEAR, 1730. — KING VICTOR

PART I

SCENE. — *The Council Chamber of Rivoli Palace, near Turin, communicating with a Hall at the back, an Apartment to the left, and another to the right of the stage.*

TIME, 1730–31.

CHARLES, POLYXENA.

Charles. You think so ? Well, I do not

Polyxena.   My beloved,
All must clear up ; we shall be happy yet :
This cannot last forever — oh, may change
To-day or any day !
        Cha.   — May change ? Ah yes —
May change !
        Pol.   Endure it, then.
        Cha.   No doubt a life
Like this drags on, now better and now worse.
My father may . . . may take to loving me ;
And he may take D'Ormea closer yet
To counsel him ; — may even cast off her
— That bad Sebastian ; but he also may
. . . Or no, Polyxena, my only friend,
He may not force you from me ?
        Pol.   Now, force me

From you!—me, close by you as if there
    gloomed
No Sebastians, no D'Ormeas on our path—
At Rivoli or Turin, still at hand,
Arch-counsellor, prime confidant . . . force
    me!
  Cha. Because I felt as sure, as I feel sure
We clasp hands now, of being happy once.
Young was I, quite neglected, nor concerned
By the world's business that engrossed so much
My father and my brother: if I peered
From out my privacy,—amid the crash
And blaze of nations, domineered those two.
'T was war, peace—France our foe, now—
    England, friend—
In love with Spain—at feud with Austria!
    Well—
I wondered, laughed a moment's laugh for pride
In the chivalrous couple, then let drop
My curtain—" I am out of it," I said—
When . . .
  Pol.   You have told me, Charles.
  Cha.   Polyxena—
When suddenly,—a warm March day, just
    that!
Just so much sunshine as the cottage child
Basks in delighted, while the cottager
Takes off his bonnet, as he ceases work,
To catch the more of it—and it must fall
Heavily on my brother! Had you seen
Philip—the lion-featured! not like me!
  Pol. I know—
  Cha.   And Philip's mouth yet fast to mine,
His dead cheek on my cheek, his arm still
    round
My neck,—they bade me rise, " for I was heir
To the Duke," they said, "the right hand of
    the Duke: "
Till then he was my father, not the Duke.
So . . . let me.finish . . . the whole intricate
World's-business their dead boy was born to, I
Must conquer,—ay, the brilliant thing he was
I of a sudden must be: my faults, my follies,
—All bitter truths were told me, all at once,
To end the sooner. What I simply styled
Their overlooking me, had been contempt:
How should the Duke employ himself, forsooth,
With such an one, while lordly Philip rode
By him their Turin through? But he was
    punished,
And must put up with—me! 'T was sad
    enough
To learn my future portion and submit.
And then the wear and worry, blame on blame!
For, spring-sounds in my ears, spring-smells
    about,
How could I but grow dizzy in their pent
Dim palace-rooms at first? My mother's look
As they discussed my insignificance,
She and my father, and I sitting by,—
I bore; I knew how brave a son they missed;
Philip had gayly run state-papers through,
While Charles was spelling at them painfully!
But Victor was my father spite of that.
" Duke Victor's entire life has been," I said,
" Innumerable efforts to one end;
And on the point now of that end's success,
Our Ducal turning to a Kingly crown,

Where 's time to be reminded 't is his child
He spurns?" And so I suffered—scarcely
    suffered,
Since I had you at length!
  Pol.   To serve in place
Of monarch, minister and mistress, Charles!
  Cha. But, once that crown obtained, then
    was 't not like
Our lot would alter? " When he rests, takes
    breath,
Glances around, sees who there 's left to love—
Now that my mother's dead, sees I am left—
Is it not like he 'll love me at the last? "
Well, Savoy turns Sardinia; the Duke 's King:
Could I—precisely then—could you expect
His harshness to redouble? These few months
Have been . . . have been . . . Polyxena, do you
And God conduct me, or I lose myself!
What would he have? What is 't they want
    with me?
Him with this mistress and this minister,
—You see me and you hear him; judge us
    both!
Pronounce what I should do, Polyxena!
  Pol. Endure, endure, beloved! Say you
    not
He is your father? All 's so incident
To novel sway! Beside, our life must change:
Or you 'll acquire his kingcraft, or he 'll find
Harshness a sorry way of teaching it.
I bear this—not that there 's so much to bear.
  Cha. You bear? Do not I know that you,
    though bound
To silence for my sake, are perishing
Piecemeal beside me? And how otherwise
When every creephole from the hideous Court
Is stopped; the Minister to dog me, here—
The Mistress posted to entrap you, there!
And thus shall we grow old in such a life;
Not careless, never estranged,—but old: to
    alter
Our life, there is so much to alter!
  Pol.   Come—
Is it agreed that we forego complaint
Even at Turin, yet complain we here
At Rivoli? 'T were wiser you announced
Our presence to the King. What 's now afoot
I wonder? Not that any more 's to dread
Than every day's embarrassment: but guess
For me, why train so fast succeeded train
On the high-road, each gayer still than each!
I noticed your Archbishop's pursuivant,
The sable cloak and silver cross; such pomp
Bodes . . . what now, Charles? Can you con-
    ceive?
  Cha. Not I.
  Pol. A matter of some moment—
  Cha.   There 's our life!
Which of the group of loiterers that stare
From the lime-avenue, divines that I—
About to figure presently, he thinks,
In face of all assembled—am the one
Who knows precisely least about it?
  Pol.   Tush!
D'Ormea's contrivance!
  Cha.   Ay, how otherwise
Should the young Prince serve for the old King's
    foil?

— So that the simplest courtier may remark
'T were idle raising parties for a Prince
Content to linger the court's laughing-stock.
Something, 't is like, about that weary business
[*Pointing to papers he has laid down, and which*
POLYXENA examines.

— Not that I comprehend three words, of course,
After all last night's study.

Pol. The faint heart!
Why, as we rode and you rehearsed just now
Its substance . . . (that's the folded speech I
mean,
Concerning the Reduction of the Fiefs)
— What would you have? — I fancied while
you spoke,
Some tones were just your father's.

Cha. Flattery!
Pol. I fancied so: — and here lurks, sure
enough,
My note upon the Spanish Claims! You've
mastered
The fief-speech thoroughly: this other, mind,
Is an opinion you deliver, — stay,
Best read it slowly over once to me;
Read — there's bare time; you read it firmly —
loud
— Rather loud, looking in his face, — don't sink
Your eye once — ay, thus! "If Spain claims"
. . . begin
— Just as you look at me!

Cha. At you! Oh truly,
You have I seen, say, marshalling your troops,
Dismissing councils, or, through doors ajar,
Head sunk on hand, devoured by slow chagrins
— Then radiant, for a crown had all at once
Seemed possible again! I can behold
Him, whose least whisper ties my spirit fast,
In this sweet brow, naught could divert me from
Save objects like Sebastian's shameless lip,
Or worse, the clipped gray hair and dead white
face
And dwindling eye as if it ached with guile,
D'Ormea wears . . .
(*As he kisses her, enter from the* KING'S *apartment*
D'ORMEA.)
I said he would divert
My kisses from your brow!

D'Ormea. [*Aside.*] Here! So, King Victor
Spoke truth for once: and who's ordained.
but I
To make that memorable? Both in call,
As he declared! Were 't better gnash the teeth.
Or laugh outright now?

Cha. [*to* POL.] What's his visit for?
D'O. [*Aside.*] I question if they even speak
to me.
Pol. [*to* CHA.] Face the man! He'll sup-
pose you fear him else.
[*Aloud.*] The Marquis bears the King's com-
mand, no doubt?
D'O. [*Aside.*] Precisely! — If I threatened
him, perhaps?
Well, this at least is punishment enough!
Men used to promise punishment would come.
Cha. Deliver the King's message, Marquis!
D'O. [*Aside.*] Ah —
So anxious for his fate? [*Aloud.*] A word,
my Prince,

Before you see your father — just one word
Of counsel!
Cha. Oh, your counsel certainly!
Polyxena, the Marquis counsels us!
Well, sir? Be brief, however!
D'O. What? You know
As much as I? — preceded me, most like,
In knowledge! So! ('T is in his eye, beside —
His voice: he knows it, and his heart's on flame
Already!) You surmise why you, myself,
Del Borgo, Spava, fifty nobles more,
Are summoned thus?
Cha. Is the Prince used to know,
At any time, the pleasure of the King,
Before his minister? — Polyxena,
Stay here till I conclude my task: I feel
Your presence (smile not) through the walls,
and take
Fresh heart. The King's within that chamber?
D'O. [*Passing the table whereon a paper lies,*
exclaims, as he glances at it] "Spain!"
Pol. [*Aside to* CHA.] Tarry awhile: what
ails the minister?
D'O. Madam, I do not often trouble you.
The Prince loathes, and you scorn me — let that
pass!
But since it touches him and you, not me,
Bid the Prince listen!
Pol [*to* CHA.] Surely you will listen:
— Deceit? — Those fingers crumpling up his
vest?
Cha. Deceitful to the very fingers' ends!
D'O. [*who has approached them, overlooks the*
other paper CHARLES *continues to hold*].
My project for the Fiefs! As I supposed!
Sir, I must give you light upon those measures
— For this is mine, and that I spied of Spain,
Mine too!
Cha. Release me! Do you gloze on me
Who bear in the world's face (that is, the world
You make for me at Turin) your contempt?
— Your measures? — When was not a hateful
task
D'Ormea's imposition? Leave my robe!
What post can I bestow, what grant concede?
Or do you take me for the King?
D'O. Not I!
Not yet for King, — not for, as yet, thank God,
One who in . . . shall I say a year, a month?
Ay! — shall be wretcheder than e'er was slave
In his Sardinia, — Europe's spectacle
And the world's by-word! What? The Prince
aggrieved
That I excluded him our counsels? Here
[*Touching the paper in* CHARLES'S *hand.*
Accept a method of extorting gold
From Savoy's nobles, who must wring its worth
In silver first from tillers of the soil,
Whose hinds again have to contribute brass
To make up the amount: there's counsel, sir,
My counsel, one year old; and the fruit, this —
Savoy's become a mass of misery
And wrath, which one man has to meet — the
King:
You're not the King! Another counsel, sir!
Spain entertains a project (here it lies)
Which, guessed, makes Austria offer that same
King

Thus much to baffle Spain; he promises;
Then comes Spain, breathless lest she be fore-
   stalled,
Her offer follows; and he promises . . .
  Cha. — Promises, sir, when he has just agreed
To Austria's offer?
  D'O.   That's a counsel, Prince!
But past our foresight, Spain and Austria
   (choosing
To make their quarrel up between themselves
Without the intervention of a friend)
Produce both treaties, and both promises . . .
  Cha. How?
  D'O. Prince, a counsel! And the fruit of
   that?
Both parties covenant afresh, to fall
Together on their friend, blot out his name,
Abolish him from Europe. So, take note,
Here's Austria and here's Spain to fight
   against,
And what sustains the King but Savoy here,
A miserable people mad with wrongs?
·You're not the King!
  Cha.   Polyxena, you said
All would clear up: all does clear up to me.
  D'O. Clear up! 'T is no such thing to
   envy, then?
You see the King's state in its length and
   breadth?
You blame me now for keeping you aloof
From counsels and the fruit of counsels? Wait
Till I explain this morning's business!
  Cha. [*Aside.*]   No —
Stoop to my father, yes, — D'Ormea, no;
— The King's son, not to the King's counsel-
   lor!
I will do something, but at least retain
The credit of my deed! [*Aloud.*] Then it is
   this
You now expressly come to tell me?
  D'O.   This
To tell! You apprehend me?
  Cha.   Perfectly.
Further, D'Ormea, you have shown yourself,
For the first time these many weeks and
   months,
Disposed to do my bidding?
  D'O.   From the heart!
  Cha. Acquaint my father, first, I wait his
   pleasure:
Next . . . or, I'll tell you at a fitter time.
Acquaint the King!
  D'O. [*Aside.*]   If I 'scape Victor yet!
First, to prevent this stroke at me: if not, —
Then, to avenge it! [*To* Cha.] Gracious sir,
   I go.   [*Goes.*
  Cha. God, I forbore! Which more offends,
   that man
Or that man's master? Is it come to this?
Have they supposed (the sharpest insult yet)
I needed e'en his intervention? No!
No — dull am I, conceded, — but so dull,
Scarcely! Their step decides me.
  Pol.   How decides?
  Cha. You would be freed D'Ormea's eye
   and hers?
— Could fly the court with me and live content?
So, this it is for which the knights assemble!

The whispers and the closeting of late,
The savageness and insolence of old,
— For this!
  Pol. What mean you?
  Cha.   How? You fail to catch
Their clever plot? I missed it, but could you?
These last two months of care to inculcate
How dull I am, — D'Ormea's present visit
To prove that, being dull, I might be worse
Were I a King — as wretched as now dull —
You recognize in it no winding up
Of a long plot?
  Pol.   Why should there be a plot?
  Cha. The crown's secure now; I should
   shame the crown —
An old complaint; the point is, how to gain
My place for one more fit in Victor's eyes,
His mistress the Sebastian's child.
  Pol.   In truth?
  Cha. They dare not quite dethrone Sardi-
   nia's Prince:
But they may descant on my dulness till
They sting me into even praying them
Grant leave to hide my head, resign my state,
And end the coil. Not see now? In a word,
They'd have me tender them myself my rights
As one incapable; — some cause for that,
Since I delayed thus long to see their drift!
I shall apprise the King he may resume
My rights this moment.
  Pol.   Pause! I dare not think
So ill of Victor.
  Cha.   Think no ill of him!
  Pol. — Nor think him, then, so shallow as to
   suffer
His purpose be divined thus easily.
And yet — you are the last of a great line;
There's a great heritage at stake; new days
Seemed to await this newest of the realms
Of Europe: — Charles, you must withstand
   this!
  Cha.   Ah!
You dare not then renounce the splendid court
For one whom all the world despises? Speak!
  Pol. My gentle husband, speak I will, and
   truth.
Were this as you believe, and I once sure
Your duty lay in so renouncing rule,
I could . . . could? Oh what happiness it
   were
To live, my Charles, and die, alone with you!
  Cha. I grieve I asked you. To the pres-
   ence, then!
By this, D'Ormea acquaints the King, no
   doubt,
He fears I am too simple for mere hints,
And that no less will serve than Victor's mouth
Demonstrating in council what I am.
I have not breathed, I think, these many years!
  Pol. Why, it may be! — if he desire to wed
That woman, call legitimate her child.
  Cha. You see as much? Oh, let his will
   have way!
You'll not repent confiding in me, love?
There's many a brighter spot in Piedmont, far,
Than Rivoli. I'll seek him: or, suppose
You hear first how I mean to speak my mind?
Loudly and firmly both, this time, be sure!

I yet may see your Rhine-land, who can tell?
Once away, ever then away! I breathe.
Pol. And I too breathe.
Cha. Come, my Polyxena!

KING VICTOR

PART II

Enter KING VICTOR, *bearing the regalia on a cushion,
from his apartment. He calls loudly —*

D'Ormea! — for patience fails me, treading thus
Among the obscure trains I have laid, — my
    knights
Safe in the hall here — in that anteroom,
My son, — D'Ormea, where? Of this, one
    touch —   [*Laying down the crown.*
This fireball to these mute black cold trains —
    then
Outbreak enough!
[*Contemplating it.*] To lose all, after all!
This, glancing o'er my house for ages — shaped,
Brave meteor, like the crown of Cyprus now,
Jerusalem, Spain, England, every change
The braver, — and when I have clutched a
    prize
My ancestry died wan with watching for,
To lose it! — by a slip, a fault, a trick
Learnt to advantage once and not unlearned
When past the use, — "just this once more" (I
    thought)
"Use it with Spain and Austria happily,
And then away with trick!" An oversight
I'd have repaired thrice over, any time
These fifty years, must happen now! There's
    peace
At length; and I, to make the most of peace,
Ventured my project on our people here,
As needing not their help: which Europe
    knows,
And means, cold-blooded, to dispose herself
(Apart from plausibilities of war)
To crush the new-made King — who ne'er till
    now
Feared her. As Duke, I lost each foot of earth
And laughed at her: my name was left, my
    sword
Left, all was left! But she can take, she
    knows,
This crown, herself conceded . . .
                That's to try,
Kind Europe! — My career's not closed as
    yet,
This boy was ever subject to my will,
Timid and tame — the fitter! — D'Ormea, too
What if the sovereign also rid himself
Of thee, his prime of parasites? I delay!
D'Ormea!
    (*As* D'ORMEA *enters, the King seats himself.*)
        My son, the Prince — attends he?
D'O.   Sir,
He does attend. The crown prepared! — it
    seems
That you persist in your resolve.
Victor.   Who's come?
The chancellor and the chamberlain? My
    knights?

D'O. The whole Annunziata. If, my liege,
Your fortune had not tottered worse than
    now . . .
Vic. Del Borgo has drawn up the schedules?
    mine —
My son's, too? Excellent! Only, beware
Of the least blunder, or we look but fools.
First, you read the Annulment of the Oaths;
Del Borgo follows . . . no, the Prince shall sign;
Then let Del Borgo read the Instrument:
On which, I enter.
D'O.   Sir, this may be truth;
You, sir, may do as you affect — may break
Your engine, me, to pieces: try at least
If not a spring remain worth saving! Take
My counsel as I've counselled many times!
What if the Spaniard and the Austrian threat?
There's England, Holland, Venice — which ally
Select you?
Vic.   Aha! Come, D'Ormea, — "truth"
Was on your lip a minute since. Allies?
I've broken faith with Venice, Holland, Eng-
    land
— As who knows if not you?
D'O.   But why with me
Break faith — with one ally, your best, break
    faith?
Vic. When first I stumbled on you, Marquis
    — 't was
At Mondovi — a little lawyer's clerk . . .
D'O. Therefore your soul's ally! — who
brought you through
Your quarrel with the Pope, at pains enough —
Who simply echoed you in these affairs —
On whom you cannot therefore visit these
Affairs' ill fortune — whom you trust to guide
You safe (yes, on my soul) through these affairs!
Vic. I was about to notice, had you not
Prevented me, that since that great town kept
With its chicane D'Ormea's satchel stuffed
And D'Ormea's self sufficiently recluse,
He missed a sight, — my naval armament
When I burned Toulon. How the skiff exults
Upon the galliot's wave! — rises its height,
O'ertops it even; but the great wave bursts,
And hell-deep in the horrible profound
Buries itself the galliot: shall the skiff
Think to escape the sea's black trough in turn?
Apply this: you have been my minister
— Next me, above me possibly; — sad post,
Huge care, abundant lack of peace of mind;
Who would desiderate the eminence?
You gave your soul to get it; you'd yet give
Your soul to keep it, as I mean you shall,
D'Ormea! What if the wave ebbed with me?
Whereas it cants you to another crest;
I toss you to my son; ride out your ride!
D'O. Ah, you so much despise me?
Vic.   You, D'Ormea?
Nowise: and I'll inform you why. A king
Must in his time have many ministers,
And I've been rash enough to part with mine
When I thought proper. Of the tribe, not one
(. . . Or wait, did Pianezze? . . . ah, just the
    same!)
Not one of them, ere his remonstrance reached
The length of yours, but has assured me (com-
    monly

Standing much as you stand, — or nearer, say,
The door to make his exit on his speech)
— I should repent of what I did.   D'Ormea,
Be candid, you approached it when I bade you
Prepare the schedules! But you stopped in
    time,
You have not so assured me : how should I
Despise you then ?
                    (*Enter* CHARLES.)
    Vic. [*Changing his tone.*] Are you instructed ?
        Do
My order, point by point! About it, sir !
    D'O. You so despise me! [*Aside.*] One last
        stay remains —
the boy's discretion there.
            [*To* CHA.] For your sake, Prince,
I pleaded, wholly in your interest,
To save you from this fate !
    Cha. [*Aside.*]   Must I be told
The Prince was supplicated for — by him ?
    Vic. [*To D'O.*] Apprise Del Borgo, Spava,
        and the rest,
Our son attends them ; then return.
    D'O.   One word !
    Cha. [*Aside.*] A moment's pause and they
        would drive me hence,
I do believe !
    D'O. [*Aside.*] Let but the boy be firm !
    Vic. You disobey ?
    Cha. [*To D'O.*]   You do not disobey
Me, at least. Did you promise that or no ?
    D'O. Sir, I am yours: what would you ?
        Yours am I !
    Cha. When I have said what I shall say,
        'tis like
Your face will ne'er again disgust me. Go !
Through you, as through a breast of glass, I see.
And for your conduct, from my youth till now,
Take my contempt! You might have spared
    me much,
Secured me somewhat, nor so harmed yourself :
That's over now. Go, ne'er to come again !
    D'O. As son, the father — father, as the son !
My wits! My wits !   [*Goes.*
    Vic. [*Seated.*] And you, what meant you,
        pray,
Speaking thus to D'Ormea ?
    Cha.   Let us not
Waste words upon D'Ormea ! Those I spent
Have half unsettled what I came to say.
His presence vexes to my very soul.
    Vic. One called to manage a kingdom, Charles,
        needs heart
To bear up under worse annoyances
Than seems D'Ormea — to me, at least.
    Cha. [*Aside.*]   Ah, good !
He keeps me to the point ! Then be it so.
[*Aloud.*] Last night, sir, brought me certain
    papers — these —
To be reported on, — your way of late.
Is it last night's result that you demand ?
    Vic. For God's sake, what has night brought
        forth ? Pronounce
The . . . what's your word ? — result !
    Cha.   Sir, that had proved
Quite worthy of your sneer, no doubt : — a few
Lame thoughts, regard for you alone could
    wring,

Lame as they are, from brains like mine, be-
    lieve !
As 'tis, sir, I am spared both toil and sneer.
These are the papers.
    Vic.   Well, sir ? I suppose
You hardly burned them. Now for your result !
    Cha. I never should have done great things,
        of course,
But . . . oh my father, had you loved me more !
    Vic. Loved ? [*Aside.*] Has D'Ormea played
        me false, I wonder ?
[*Aloud.*] Why, Charles, a king's love is diffused
    — yourself
May overlook, perchance, your part in it.
Our monarchy is absolutest now
In Europe, or my trouble's thrown away.
I love, my mode, that subjects each and all
May have the power of loving, all and each,
Their mode : I doubt not, many have their sons
To trifle with, talk soft to, all day long :
I have that crown, this chair, D'Ormea, Charles !
    Cha. 'Tis well I am a subject then, not you.
    Vic. [*Aside.*] D'Ormea has told him every-
        thing. [*Aloud.*] Aha,
I apprehend you : when all's said, you take
Your private station to be prized beyond
My own, for instance ?
    Cha.   — Do and ever did
So take it : 'tis the method you pursue
That grieves . . .
    Vic. These words ! Let me express, my
        friend,
Your thoughts. You penetrate what I supposed
Secret. D'Ormea plies his trade betimes !
I purpose to resign my crown to you.
    Cha. To me ?
    Vic.   Now, — in that chamber.
    Cha.   You resign
The crown to me ?
    Vic.   And time enough, Charles, sure ?
Confess with me, at four-and-sixty years
A crown's a load. I covet quiet once
Before I die, and summoned you for that.
    Cha. 'Tis I will speak: you ever hated me,
I bore it, — have insulted me, borne too —
Now you insult yourself ; and I remember
What I believed you, what you really are,
And cannot bear it. What ! My life has passed
Under your eye, tormented as you know, —
Your whole sagacities, one after one,
At leisure brought to play on me — to prove me
A fool, I thought and I submitted ; now
You'd prove . . . what would you prove me ?
    Vic.   This to me ?
I hardly know you !
    Cha.   Know me ? Oh indeed
You do not ! Wait till I complain next time
Of my simplicity ! — for here's a sage
Knows the world well, is not to be deceived,
And his experience and his Macchiavels,
D'Ormeas, teach him — what ? — that I this
    while
Have envied him his crown ! He has not smiled,
I warrant, — has not eaten, drunk, nor slept,
For I was plotting with my Princess yonder !
Who knows what we might do or might not do ?
Go now, be politic, astound the world !
That sentry in the antechamber — nay,

The varlet who disposed this precious trap
　　　　　　　[Pointing to the crown.
That was to take me — ask them if they think
Their own sons envy them their posts ! — Know
　me !
　Vic. But you know me, it seems : so, learn,
　in brief,
My pleasure. This assembly is convened . . .
　Cha. Tell me, that woman put it in your
　head !
You were not sole contriver of the scheme,
My father !
　Vic. Now observe me, sir ! I jest
Seldom — on these points, never. Here, I say,
The knights assemble to see me concede,
And you accept, Sardinia's crown.
　Cha. Farewell !
'T were vain to hope to change this : I can end it.
Not that I cease from being yours, when sunk
Into obscurity : I 'll die for you,
But not annoy you with my presence. Sir,
Farewell ! Farewell !
　　　　　　　(Enter D'ORMEA.)
　D'O. [*Aside.*] Ha, sure he 's changed again—
Means not to fall into the cunning trap !
Then, Victor, I shall yet escape you, Victor !
　Vic. [*Suddenly placing the crown upon the
　head of* CHARLES.] D'Ormea, your king !
[*To* CHA.] My son, obey me ! Charles,
Your father, clearer-sighted than yourself,
Decides it must be so. 'Faith, this looks real !
My reasons after ; reason upon reason
After : but now, obey me ! Trust in me !
By this, you save Sardinia, you save me !
Why, the boy swoons ! [*To D'O.*] Come this
　side !
　D'O. [*As* CHARLES *turns from him to* VIC-
TOR.] You persist ?
　Vic. Yes, I conceive the gesture's meaning.
'Faith,
He almost seems to hate you : how is that ?
Be reassured, my Charles ! Is 't over now ?
Then, Marquis, tell the new King what remains
To do ! A moment's work. Del Borgo reads
The Act of Abdication out, you sign it,
Then I sign ; after that, come back to me.
　D'O. Sir, for the last time, pause !
　Vic. Five minutes longer
I am your sovereign, Marquis. Hesitate —
And I 'll so turn those minutes to account
That . . . Ay, you recollect me ! [*Aside.*]
　　　　　Could I bring
My foolish mind to undergo the reading
That Act of Abdication !
　　　　[*As* CHARLES *motions* D'ORMEA *to precede him.*
Thanks, dear Charles !
　　　　　[CHARLES *and* D'ORMEA *retire.*
　Vic. A novel feature in the boy, — indeed
Just what I feared he wanted most. Quite
　right,
This earnest tone : your truth, now for effect !
It answers every purpose : with that look,
That voice, — I hear him : "I began no
　treaty,"
(He speaks to Spain,) "nor ever dreamed of
　this
You show me ; this I from my soul regret ;
But if my father signed it, bid not me

Dishonor him — who gave me all, beside : "
And, " true," says Spain, " 't were harsh to
　visit that
Upon the Prince." Then come the nobles
　trooping :
" I grieve at these exactions — I had cut
This hand off ere impose them ; but shall I
Undo my father's deed ? " — and they confer :
" Doubtless he was no party, after all ;
Give the Prince time ! "
　　　　　Ay, give us time, but time !
Only, he must not, when the dark day comes,
Refer our friends to me and frustrate all.
We 'll have no child's play, no desponding fits,
No Charles at each cross turn entreating Victor
To take his crown again. Guard against that !
　　　　　　　(Enter D'ORMEA.)
Long live King Charles !
　　　　　No — Charles's counsellor !
Well, is it over, Marquis ? Did I jest ?
　D'O. " King Charles ! " What then may
　you be ?
　Vic. Anything !
A country gentleman that, cured of bustle,
Now beats a quick retreat toward Chambery,
Would hunt and hawk and leave you noisy folk
To drive your trade without him. I 'm Count
　Remont —
Count Tende — any little place's Count !
　D'O. Then Victor, Captain against Catinat
At Staffarde, where the French beat you ; and
　Duke
At Turin, where you beat the French ; King
　late
Of Savoy, Piedmont, Montferrat, Sardinia,
— Now, " any little place's Count " —
　Vic. Proceed !
　D'O. Breaker of vows to God, who crowned
　you first ;
Breaker of vows to man, who kept you since ;
Most profligate to me who outraged God
And man to serve you, and am made pay crimes
I was but privy to, by passing thus
To your imbecile son — who, well you know,
Must — (when the people here, and nations
　there,
Clamor for you the main delinquent, slipped
From King to — " Count of any little place)"
Must needs surrender me, all in his reach, —
I, sir, forgive you : for I see the end —
See you on your return — (you will return) —
To him you trust, a moment . . .
　Vic. Trust him ? How ?
My poor man, merely a prime-minister,
Make me know where my trust errs !
　D'O. In his fear,
His love, his — but discover for yourself
What you are weakest, trusting in !
　Vic. Aha,
D'Ormea, not a shrewder scheme than this
In your repertory ? You know old Victor —
Vain, choleric, inconstant, rash — (I 've heard
Talkers who little thought the King so close) —
Felicitous now, were 't not, to provoke him
To clean forget, one minute afterward,
His solemn act, and call the nobles back
And pray them give again the very power
He has abjured ? — for the dear sake of what ?

Vengeance on you, D'Ormea ! No : such am I,
Count Tende or Count anything you please,
— Only, the same that did the things you say,
And, among other things you say not, used
Your finest fibre, meanest muscle, — you
I used, and now, since you will have it so,
Leave to your fate — mere lumber in the midst,
You and your works. Why, what on earth be-
    side
Are you made for, you sort of ministers ?
    D'O. Not left, though, to my fate ! Your
    witless son
Has more wit than to load himself with lumber :
He foils you that way, and I follow you.
    Vic. Stay with my son — protect the weaker
    side !
    D'O. Ay, to be tossed the people like a rag,
And flung by them for Spain and Austria's
    sport,
Abolishing the record of your part
In all this perfidy !
    Vic.   Prevent, beside,
My own return !
    D'O.   That 's half prevented now !
'T will go hard but you find a wondrous charm
In exile, to discredit me. The Alps,
Silk-mills to watch, vines asking vigilance —
Hounds open for the stag, your hawk 's
    a-wing —
Brave days that wait the Louis of the South,
Italy's Janus !
    Vic.   So, the lawyer's clerk
Won't tell me that I shall repent !
    D'O.   You give me
Full leave to ask if you repent ?
    Vic.   Whene'er
Sufficient time 's elapsed for that, you judge !
    [*Shouts inside,* " KING CHARLES ! "

    D'O. Do you repent ?
    Vic. [*After a slight pause.*] . . . I 've kept
    them waiting ?   Yes !
Come in, complete the Abdication, sir ! [*They
    go out.*

(*Enter* POLYXENA.)

    Pol. A shout ! The sycophants are free of
    Charles !
Oh, is not this like Italy ? No fruit
Of his or my distempered fancy, this,
But just an ordinary fact ! Beside,
Here they 've set forms for such proceedings ;
    Victor
Imprisoned his own mother : he should know,
If any, how a son 's to be deprived
Of a son's right. Our duty 's palpable.
Ne'er was my husband for the wily king
And the unworthy subjects : be it so !
Come you safe out of them, my Charles ! Our
    life
Grows not the broad and dazzling life, I
    dreamed
Might prove your lot ; for strength was shut in
    you
None guessed but I — strength which, untram-
    melled once,
Had little shamed your vaunted ancestry —
Patience and self-devotion, fortitude,
Simplicity and utter truthfulness
— All which, they shout to lose !

                  So, now my work
Begins — to save him from regret. Save
    Charles
Regret ? — the noble nature ! He 's not made
Like these Italians : 't is a German soul.
    (CHARLES *enters crowned.*)
Oh, where 's the King's heir ? Gone : — the
    Crown-prince ? Gone : —
Where 's Savoy ? Gone ! — Sardinia ? Gone !
    But Charles
Is left ! And when my Rhine-land bowers ar-
    rive,
If he looked almost handsome yester-twilight
As his gray eyes seemed widening into black
Because I praised him, then how will he look ?
Farewell, you stripped and whited mulberry-
    trees
Bound each to each by lazy ropes of vine !
Now I 'll teach you my language : I 'm not
    forced
To speak Italian now, Charles ?
[*She sees the crown.*]   What is this ?
Answer me — who has done this ? Answer !
    Cha.   He !
I am King now.
    Pol.   Oh worst, worst, worst of all !
Tell me ! What, Victor ? He has made you
    King ?
What 's he then ? What 's to follow this ? You,
    King ?
    Cha. Have I done wrong ? Yes, for you were
    not by !
    Pol. Tell me from first to last.
    Cha.   Hush — a new world
Brightens before me ; he is moved away
— The dark form that eclipsed it, he subsides
Into a shape supporting me like you,
And I, alone, tend upward, more and more
Tend upward : I am grown Sardinia's King.
    Pol. Now stop : was not this Victor, Duke
    of Savoy
At ten years old ?
    Cha.   He was.
    Pol.   And the Duke spent,
Since then, just four-and-fifty years in toil
To be — what ?
    Cha.   King.
    Pol.   Then why unking himself ?
    Cha. Those years are cause enough.
    Pol.   The only cause ?
    Cha. Some new perplexities.
    Pol.   Which you can solve
Although he cannot ?
    Cha.   He assures me so.
    Pol. And this he means shall last — how
    long ?
    Cha.   How long ?
Think you I fear the perils I confront ?
He 's praising me before the people's face —
My people !
    Pol. Then he 's changed — grown kind, the
    King ?
Where can the trap be ?
    Cha.   Heart and soul I pledge !
My father, could I guard the crown you gained
Transmit as I received it, — all good else
Would I surrender !
    Pol.   Ah, it opens then

Before you, all you dreaded formerly?
You are rejoiced to be a king, my Charles?
  Cha. So much to dare? The better, — much
    to dread;
The better. I 'll adventure though alone.
Triumph or die, there 's Victor still to witness
Who dies or triumphs — either way, alone!
  Pol. Once I had found my share in triumph,
    Charles,
Or death.
  Cha.   But you are I! But you I call
To take, Heaven's proxy, vows I tendered
    Heaven
A moment since. I will deserve the crown!
  Pol. You will. [*Aside.*] No doubt it were a
    glorious thing
For any people, if a heart like his
Ruled over it. I would I saw the trap.
        (*Enter* VICTOR.)
'T is he must show me.
  Vic.   So, the mask falls off
An old man's foolish love at last. Spare thanks!
I know you, and Polyxena I know.
Here 's Charles — I am his guest now — does he
    bid me
Be seated? And my light-haired blue-eyed
    child
Must not forget the old man far away
At Chambery, who dozes while she reigns.
  Pol. Most grateful shall we now be, talking
    least
Of gratitude — indeed of anything
That hinders what yourself must need to say
To Charles.
  Cha.   Pray speak, sir!
  Vic.   'Faith, not much to say:
Only what shows itself, you once i' the point
Of sight. You 're now the King: you 'll com-
    prehend
Much you may oft have wondered at — the
    shifts,
Dissimulation. wiliness I showed.
For what 's our post? Here 's Savoy and here 's
    Piedmont,
Here 's Montferrat — a breadth here, a space
    there —
To o'er-sweep all these, what 's one weapon
    worth?
I often think of how they fought in Greece
(Or Rome, which was it? You 're the scholar,
    Charles!)
You made a front-thrust? But if your shield
    too
Were not adroitly planted, some shrewd knave
Reached you behind; and him foiled, straight if
    thong
And handle of that shield were not cast loose,
And you enabled to outstrip the wind,
Fresh foes assailed you, either side; 'scape these,
And reach your place of refuge — e'en then,
    odds
If the gate opened unless breath enough
Were left in you to make its lord a speech.
Oh, you will see!
  Cha.   No: straight on shall I go,
Truth helping; win with it or die with it.
  Vic. 'Faith, Charles, you 're not made
    Europe's fighting-man!

The barrier-guarder, if you please. You clutch
Hold and consolidate, with envious France
This side, with Austria that, the territory
I held — ay, and will hold . . . which *you* sha'll
    hold
Despite the couple! But I 've surely earned
Exemption from these weary politics,
— The privilege to prattle with my son
And daughter here, though Europe wait the
    while.
  Pol. Nay, sir, — at Chambery, away forever,
As soon you will be, 't is farewell we bid you:
Turn these few fleeting moments to account!
'T is just as though it were a death.
  Vic.   Indeed!
  Pol. [*Aside.*] Is the trap there?
  Cha.   Ay, call this parting — death!
The sacreder your memory becomes.
If I misrule Sardinia, how bring back
My father?
  Vic.   I mean . . .
  Pol. [*who watches* VICTOR *narrowly this
    while*]. Your father does not mean
You should be ruling for your father's sake:
It is your people must concern you wholly
Instead of him. You mean this, sir? (He drops
My hand!)
  Cha.   That people is now part of me.
  Vic. About the people! I took certain
    measures
Some short time since . . . Oh, I know well,
    you know
But little of my measures! These affect
The nobles; we 've resumed some grants, im-
    posed
A tax or two: prepare yourself, in short,
For clamor on that score. Mark me: you yield
No jot of aught entrusted you!
  Pol.   No jot
You yield!
  Cha. My father, when I took the oath,
Although my eye might stray in search of yours,
I heard it, understood it, promised God
What you require. Till from this eminence
He move me, here I keep, nor shall concede
The meanest of my rights.
  Vic. [*Aside.*]   The boy 's a fool!
— Or rather, I 'm a fool: for, what 's wrong
    here?
To-day the sweets of reigning: let to-morrow
Be ready with its bitters.
      (*Enter* D'ORMEA.)
        There 's beside
Somewhat to press upon your notice first.
  Cha. Then why delay it for an instant, sir?
That Spanish claim perchance? And, now you
    speak,
— This morning, my opinion was mature,
Which, boy-like, I was bashful in producing
To one I ne'er am like to fear in future!
My thought is formed upon that Spanish claim.
  Vic. Betimes indeed. Not now, Charles!
    You require
A host of papers on it.
  D'O. [*Coming forward.*] Here they are.
[*To* CHA.] I, sir, was minister and much beside
Of the late monarch; to say little, him
I served: on you I have, to say e'en less,

No claim. This case contains those papers:
    with them
I tender you my office.
    Vic. [*Hastily.*]   Keep him, Charles!
There 's reason for it — many reasons: you
Distrust him, nor are so far wrong there, — but
He 's mixed up in this matter — he 'll desire
To quit you, for occasions known to me:
Do not accept those reasons: have him stay!
    Pol. [*Aside.*] His minister thrust on us!
    Cha. [*To D'O.*]   Sir, believe,
In justice to myself, you do not need
E'en this commending: howsoe'er might seem
My feelings toward you, as a private man,
They quit me in the vast and untried field
Of action. Though I shall myself (as late
In your own hearing I engaged to do)
Preside o'er my Sardinia, yet your help
Is necessary. Think the past forgotten
And serve me now!
    D'O.   I did not offer you
My service — would that I could serve you, sir!
As for the Spanish matter . . .
    Vic.   But dispatch
At least the dead, in my good daughter's phrase,
Before the living! Help to house me safe
Ere with D'Ormea you set the world agape!
Here is a paper — will you overlook
What I propose reserving for my needs?
I get as far from you as possible:
Here 's what I reckon my expenditure.
    Cha. [*Reading.*] A miserable fifty thousand
        crowns!
    Vic. Oh, quite enough for country gentle-
        men!
Beside, the exchequer happens . . . but find
    out
All that, yourself!
    Cha. [*Still reading.*] "Count Tende" —
        what means this?
    Vic. Me: you were but an infant when I
        burst
Through the defile of Tende upon France.
Had only my allies kept true to me!
No matter. Tende 's, then, a name I take
Just as . . .
    D'O. — The Marchioness Sebastian takes
The name of Spigno.
    Cha.   How, sir?
    Vic. [*To D'O.*]   Fool! All that
Was for my own detailing. [*To* CHA.] That
    anon!
    Cha. [*To D'O.*] Explain what you have
        said, sir!
    D'O.   I supposed
The marriage of the King to her I named,
Profoundly kept a secret these few weeks,
Was not to be one, now he 's Count.
    Pol. [*Aside.*]   With us
The minister — with him the mistress!
    Cha. [*To* VIC.]   No —
Tell me you have not taken her — that wo-
    man —
To live with, past recall!
    Vic.   And where 's the crime . . .
    Pol. [*To* CHA.] True, sir, this is a matter
        past recall
And past your cognizance. A day before,

And you had been compelled to note this —
    now
Why note it? The King saved his House
    from shame:
What the Count did, is no concern of yours.
    Cha. [*After a pause.*] The Spanish claim,
        D'Ormea!
    Vic.   Why, my son,
I took some ill-advised . . . one's age, in fact,
Spoils everything: though I was overreached,
A younger brain, we 'll trust, may extricate
Sardinia readily. To-morrow, D'Ormea,
Inform the King!
    D'O. [*Without regarding* VICTOR, *and
        leisurely.*]
            Thus stands the case with Spain:
When first the Infant Carlos claimed his proper
Succession to the throne of Tuscany . . .
    Vic. I tell you, that stands over! Let that
        rest!
There is the policy!
    Cha. [*To D'O.*] Thus much I know,
And more — too much. The remedy?
    D'O.   Of course!
No glimpse of one.
    Vic.   No remedy at all!
It makes the remedy itself — time makes it.
    D'O. [*To* CHA.] But if . . .
    Vic. [*Still more hastily.*] In fine, I shall
        take care of that:
And, with another project that I have . . .
    D'O. [*Turning on him.*] Oh, since Count
        Tende means to take again
King Victor's crown! —
    Pol. [*Throwing herself at* VICTOR'S *feet.*]
            E'en now retake it, sir!
Oh, speak! We are your subjects both, once
    more!
Say it — a word effects it! You meant not,
Nor do mean now, to take it: but you must!
'T is in you — in your nature — and the shame 's
Not half the shame 't would grow to afterwards!
    Cha. Polyxena!
    Pol.   A word recalls the knights —
Say it! — What 's promising and what 's the
    past?
Say you are still King Victor!
    D'O.   Better say
The Count repents, in brief!
            [VICTOR *rises.*
    Cha.   With such a crime
I have not charged you, sir!
    Pol.   Charles turns from me!

SECOND YEAR, 1731. — KING CHARLES

PART I

Enter QUEEN POLYXENA *and* D'ORMEA. — *A pause.*

    Pol. And now, sir, what have you to say?
    D'O.   Count Tende . . .
    Pol. Affirm not I betrayed you; you re
        solve
On uttering this strange intelligence
— Nay, post yourself to find me ere I reach
The capital, because you know King Charles
Tarries a day or two at Evian baths

Behind me : — but take warning, — here and
thus   [*Seating herself in the royal seat.*
I listen, if I listen — not your friend.
Explicitly the statement, if you still
Persist to urge it on me, must proceed :
I am not made for aught else.
D'O.   Good ! Count Tende . . .
Pol. I, who mistrust you, shall acquaint
     King Charles,
Who even more mistrusts you.
D'O.   Does he so ?
Pol. Why should he not ?
D'O.   Ay, why not ? Motives, seek
You virtuous people, motives ! Say, I serve
God at the devil's bidding — will that do ?
I 'm proud : our people have been pacified,
Really I know not how —
Pol.   By truthfulness.
D'O. Exactly ; that shows I had naught to
do
With pacifying them. Our foreign perils
Also exceed my means to stay : but here
'T is otherwise, and my pride 's piqued. Count
     Tende
Completes a full year's absence : would you,
     madam,
Have the old monarch back, his mistress back,
His measures back ? I pray you, act upon
My counsel, or they will be.
Pol.   When ?
D'O.   Let 's think.
Home-matters settled — Victor 's coming now ;
Let foreign matters settle — Victor 's here
Unless I stop him ; as I will, this way.
Pol. [*Reading the papers he presents.*] If this
should prove a plot 'twixt you and Victor ?
You seek annoyances to give the pretext
For what you say you fear !
D'O.   Oh, possibly !
I go for nothing. Only show King Charles
That thus Count Tende purposes return,
And style me his inviter, if you please !
Pol. Half of your tale is true ; most like,
     the Count
Seeks to return : but why stay you with us ?
To aid in such emergencies.
D'O.   Keep safe
Those papers : or, to serve me, leave no proof
I thus have counselled ! When the Count re-
     turns,
And the King abdicates, 't will stead me little
To have thus counselled.
Pol.   The King abdicate !
D'O. He 's good, we knew long since —
     wise, we discover —
Firm, let us hope : — but I 'd have gone to work
With him away. Well !
[CHARLES *without.*] In the Council Chamber ?
D'O. All 's lost !
Pol. Oh, surely not King Charles ! He 's
     changed —
That 's not this year's care-burdened voice and
     step :
'T is last year's step, the Prince's voice !
D'O.   I know.
(*Enter* CHARLES — D'ORMEA *retiring a little.*)
Cha. Now wish me joy, Polyxena ! Wish it
     me

The old way !   [*She embraces him.*
     There was too much cause for that !
But I have found myself again. What news
At Turin ? Oh, if you but felt the load
I 'm free of — free ! I said this year would
     end
Or it, or me — but I am free, thank God !
Pol. How, Charles ?
Cha. You do not guess ? The day I found
Sardinia's hideous coil, at home, abroad,
And how my father was involved in it, —
Of course, I vowed to rest and smile no more
Until I cleared his name from obloquy.
We did the people right — 't was much to
     gain
That point, redress our nobles' grievance, too —
But that took place here, was no crying shame :
All must be done abroad, — if I abroad
Appeased the justly-angered Powers, destroyed
The scandal, took down Victor's name at last
From a bad eminence, I then might breathe
And rest ! No moment was to lose. Behold
The proud result — a Treaty, Austria, Spain
Agree to —
D'O. [*Aside.*] I shall merely stipulate
For an experienced headsman.
Cha.   Not a soul
Is compromised : the blotted past 's a blank :
Even D'Ormea escapes unquestioned. See !
It reached me from Vienna ; I remained
At Evian to dispatch the Count his news ;
'T is gone to Chambery a week ago —
And here am I : do I deserve to feel
Your warm white arms around me ?
D'O. [*Coming forward.*] He knows that ?
Cha. What, in Heaven's name, means this ?
D'O.   He knows that matters
Are settled at Vienna ? Not too late !
Plainly, unless you post this very hour
Some man you trust (say, me) to Chambery
And take precautions I acquaint you with,
Your father will return here.
Cha.   Are you crazed,
D'Ormea ? Here ? For what ? As well re-
     turn
To take his crown !
D'O.   He will return for that.
Cha. [*To* POL.] You have not listened to
     this man ?
Pol.   He spoke
About your safety — and I listened.
     [*He disengages himself from her arms.*
Cha. [*To* D'O.]   What
Apprised you of the Count's intentions ?
D'O.   Me ?
His heart, sir ; you may not be used to read
Such evidence however ; therefore read
     [*Pointing to* POLYXENA's *papers.*
My evidence.
Cha. [*To* POL.] Oh, worthy this of you !
And of your speech I never have forgotten,
Though I professed forgetfulness ; which haunts
     me
As if I did not know how false it was ;
Which made me toil unconsciously thus long
That there might be no least occasion left
For aught of its prediction coming true !
And now, when there is left no least occasion

To instigate my father to such crime —
When I might venture to forget (I hoped)
That speech and recognize Polyxena —
Oh worthy, to revive, and tenfold worse,
That plague! D'Ormea at your ear, his slan-
    ders
Still in your hand! Silent?
    Pol.   As the wronged are.
    Cha. And you, D'Ormea, since when have
        you presumed
To spy upon my father? I conceive
What that wise paper shows, and easily.
Since when?
    D'O. The when and where and how belong
To me. 'T is sad work, but I deal in such.
You ofttimes serve yourself ; I 'd serve you here :
Use makes me not so squeamish. In a word,
Since the first hour he went to Chambery,
Of his seven servants, five have I suborned.
    Cha. You hate my father?
    D'O.   Oh, just as you will!
                        [*Looking at* POLYXENA.
A minute since, I loved him — hate him, now!
What matter? — if you ponder just one thing :
Has he that treaty? — he is setting forward
Already. Are your guards here?
    Cha.   Well for you
They are not! [*To* POL.] Him I knew of old,
    but you —
To hear that pickthank, further his designs!
                        [*To* D'O.
Guards? — were they here, I 'd bid them, for
    your trouble,
Arrest you.
    D'O.   Guards you shall not want. I lived
The servant of your choice, not of your need.
You never greatly needed me till now
That you discard me. This is my arrest.
Again I tender you my charge — its duty
Would bid me press you read those documents.
Here, sir!   [*Offering his badge of Office.*
    Cha. [*Taking it.*] The papers also! Do you
        think
I dare not read them?
    Pol.   Read them, sir!
    Cha.   They prove,
My father, still a month within the year
Since he so solemnly consigned it me,
Means to resume his crown? They shall prove
    that,
Or my best dungeon . . .
    D'O.   Even say, Chambery!
'T is vacant, I surmise, by this.
    Cha.   You prove
Your words or pay their forfeit, sir. Go there!
Polyxena, one chance to rend the veil
Thickening and blackening 'twixt us two! Do
    say,
You 'll see the falsehood of the charges proved!
Do say, at least, you wish to see them proved
False charges — my heart's love of other times!
    Pol. Ah, Charles!
    Cha. [*To* D'O.]   Precede me, sir!
    D'O.   And I 'm at length
A martyr for the truth! No end, they say,
Of miracles. My conscious innocence!
(*As they go out, enter — by the middle door, at which
        he pauses —* VICTOR.)

    Vic.   Sure I heard voices? No. Well, I
        do best
To make at once for this, the heart o' the place.
The old room! Nothing changed! So near my
    seat,
D'Ormea? [*Pushing away the stool which is by
    the* KING'S *chair.*
                I want that meeting over first,
I know not why. Tush, he, D'Ormea, slow
To hearten me, the supple knave? That burst
Of spite so eased him! He 'll inform me . . .
                                    What?
Why come I hither? All 's in rough : let all
Remain rough. There 's full time to draw back
    — nay,
There 's naught to draw back from, as yet ;
    whereas,
If reason should be, to arrest a course
Of error — reason good, to interpose
And save, as I have saved so many times,
Our House, admonish my son's giddy youth,
Relieve him of a weight that proves too much —
Now is the time, — or now, or never.
                                    'Faith,
This kind of step is pitiful, not due
To Charles, this stealing back — hither, be-
    cause
He 's from his capital! Oh Victor! Victor!
But thus it is. The age of crafty men
Is loathsome ; youth contrives to carry off
Dissimulation ; we may intersperse
Extenuating passages of strength,
Ardor, vivacity and wit — may turn
E'en guile into a voluntary grace :
But one's old age, when graces drop away
And leave guile the pure staple of our lives —
Ah, loathsome!
                Not so — or why pause I? Turin
Is mine to have, were I so minded, for
The asking ; all the army 's mine — I 've wit-
    nessed
Each private fight beneath me ; all the Court 's
Mine too ; and, best of all, D'Ormea's still
D'Ormea and mine. There 's some grace cling-
    ing yet.
Had I decided on this step, ere midnight
I 'd take the crown.
                No. Just this step to rise
Exhausts me. Here am I arrived : the rest
Must be done for me. Would I could sit here
And let things right themselves, the masque
    unmasque
Of the old King, crownless, gray hair and hot
    blood, —
The young King, crowned, but calm before his
    time,
They say, — the eager mistress with her
    taunts, —
And the sad earnest wife who motions me
Away — ay, there she knelt to me! E'en yet
I can return and sleep at Chambery
A dream out.
                Rather shake it off at Turin,
King Victor! Say : to Turin — yes, or no?
'T is this relentless noonday-lighted chamber,
Lighted like life but silent as the grave,
That disconcerts me. That 's the change must
    strike.

No silence last year! Some one flung doors wide
(Those two great doors which scrutinize me now)
And out I went 'mid crowds of men — men talking,
Men watching if my lip fell or brow knit,
Men saw me safe forth, put me on my road :
That makes the misery of this return.
Oh had a battle done it ! Had I dropped,
Haling some battle, three entire days old,
Hither and thither by the forehead — dropped
In Spain, in Austria, best of all, in France —
Spurned on its horns or underneath its hoofs,
When the spent monster went upon its knees
To pad and pash the prostrate wretch — I, Victor,
Sole to have stood up against France, beat down
By inches, brayed to pieces finally
In some vast unimaginable charge,
A flying hell of horse and foot and guns
Over me, and all 's lost, forever lost,
There 's no more Victor when the world wakes up !
Then silence, as of a raw battlefield,
Throughout the world. Then after (as whole days
After, you catch at intervals faint noise
Through the stiff crust of frozen blood) — there creeps
A rumor forth, so faint, no noise at all,
That a strange old man, with face outworn for wounds,
Is stumbling on from frontier town to town,
Begging a pittance that may help him find
His Turin out ; what scorn and laughter follow
The coin you fling into his cap ! And last,
Some bright morn, how men crowd about the midst
O' the market-place, where takes the old king breath
Ere with his crutch he strike the palace-gate
Wide ope !
           To Turin, yes or no — or no ?
        (*Re-enter* CHARLES *with papers.*)
Cha. Just as I thought ! A miserable falsehood
Of hirelings discontented with their pay
And longing for enfranchisement ! A few
Testy expressions of old age that thinks
To keep alive its dignity o'er slaves
By means that suit their natures !
    [*Tearing them.*]   Thus they shake
My faith in Victor !
        [*Turning, he discovers* VICTOR.]
Vic. [*After a pause.*] Not at Evian, Charles?
What 's this ? Why do you run to close the doors ?
No welcome for your father ?
Cha. [*Aside.*]   Not his voice !
What would I give for one imperious tone
Of the old sort ! That 's gone forever.
Vic.   Must
I ask once more . . .
Cha.   No — I concede it, sir !
You are returned for . . . true, your health declines ;
True, Chambery 's a bleak unkindly spot ;

You 'd choose one fitter for your final lodge —
Veneria, or Moncaglier — ay, that 's close
And I concede it.
Vic.   I received advices
Of the conclusion of the Spanish matter,
Dated from Evian Baths . . .
Cha.   And you forbore
To visit me at Evian, satisfied
The work I had to do would fully task
The little wit I have, and that your presence
Would only disconcert me —
Vic.   Charles ?
Cha.   — Me, set
Forever in a foreign course to yours,
And . . .
      Sir, this way of wile were good to catch,
But I have not the sleight of it. The truth !
Though I sink under it ! What brings you here ?
Vic. Not hope of this reception, certainly,
From one who 'd scarce assume a stranger mode
Of speech, did I return to bring about
Some awfullest calamity !
Cha.   — You mean,
Did you require your crown again ! Oh yes,
I should speak otherwise ! But turn not that
To jesting ! Sir, the truth ! Your health declines ?
Is aught deficient in your equipage ?
Wisely you seek myself to make complaint,
And foil the malice of the world which laughs
At petty discontents ; but I shall care
That not a soul knows of this visit. Speak !
Vic. [*Aside.*] Here is the grateful much-professing son
Prepared to worship me, for whose sole sake
I think to waive my plans of public good !
[*Aloud.*] Nay, Charles, if I did seek to take once more
My crown, were so disposed to plague myself,
What would be warrant for this bitterness ?
I gave it — grant I would resume it — well ?
Cha. I should say simply — leaving out the why
And how — you made me swear to keep that crown :
And as you then intended . . .
Vic.   Fool ! What way
Could I intend or not intend ? As man,
With a man's will, when I say " I intend,"
I can intend up to a certain point,
No farther. I intended to preserve
The crown of Savoy and Sardinia whole :
And if events arise demonstrating
The way, I hoped should guard it, rather like
To lose it . .
Cha. Keep within your sphere and mine !
It is God's province we usurp on, else.
Here, blindfold through the maze of things we walk
By a slight clue of false, true, right and wrong ;
All else is rambling and presumption. I
Have sworn to keep this kingdom : there 's my truth.
Vic. Truth, boy, is here, within my breast and in
Your recognition of it, truth is, too ;
And in the effect of all this tortuous dealing

With falsehood, used to carry out the truth,
— In its success, this falsehood turns, again,
Truth for the world! But you are right: these
    themes
Are over-subtle. I should rather say
In such a case, frankly, — it fails, my scheme:
I hoped to see you bring about, yourself,
What I must bring about. I interpose
On your behalf — with my son's good in sight —
To hold what he is nearly letting go,
Confirm his title, add a grace perhaps.
There's Sicily, for instance, — granted me
And taken back, some years since: till I give
That island with the rest, my work's half
    done.
For his sake, therefore, as of those he rules . . .
    Cha. Our sakes are one; and that, you could
        not say,
Because my answer would present itself
Forthwith: — a year has wrought an age's
    change.
This people's not the people now, you once
Could benefit; nor is my policy
Your policy.
    Vic. [*With an outburst.*] I know it! You undo
All I have done — my life of toil and care!
I left you this the absolutest rule
In Europe: do you think I sit and smile,
Bid you throw power to the populace —
See my Sardinia, that has kept apart,
Join in the mad and democratic whirl
Whereto I see all Europe haste full tide?
England casts off her kings; France mimics
    England:
This realm I hoped was safe! Yet here I talk,
When I can save it, not by force alone,
But bidding plagues, which follow sons like you,
Fasten upon my disobedient . . .
        [*Recollecting himself.*] Surely
I could say this — if minded so — my son?
    Cha. You could not. Bitterer curses than
        your curse
Have I long since denounced upon myself
If I misused my power. In fear of these
I entered on those measures — will abide
By them: so, I should say, Count Tende . . .
    Vic.   No!
But no! But if, my Charles, your — more than
    old —
Half-foolish father urged these arguments,
And then confessed them futile, but said plainly
That he forgot his promise, found his strength
Fail him, that thought at savage Chambery
Too much of brilliant Turin, Rivoli here,
And Susa, and Veneria, and Superga —
Pined for the pleasant places he had built
When he was fortunate and young —
    Cha.   My father!
    Vic. Stay yet! — and if he said he could not
        die
Deprived of baubles he had put aside,
He deemed, forever — of the Crown that binds
Your brain up, whole, sound and impregnable,
Creating kingliness — the Sceptre too,
Whose mere wind, should you wave it, back
    would beat
Invaders — and the golden Ball which throbs
As if you grasped the palpitating heart

Indeed o' the realm, to mould as choose you
    may!
— If I must totter up and down the streets
My sires built, where myself have introduced
And fostered laws and letters, sciences,
The civil and the military arts!
Stay, Charles! I see you letting me pretend
To live my former self once more — King Victor,
The venturous yet politic: they style me
Again, the Father of the Prince: friends wink
Good-humoredly at the delusion you
So sedulously guard from all rough truths
That else would break upon my dotage! —
    You —
Whom now I see preventing my old shame —
I tell not, point by cruel point, my tale —
For is 't not in your breast my brow is hid?
Is not your hand extended? Say you not . . .
    (*Enter* D'ORMEA, *leading in* POLYXENA.)
    Pol. [*Advancing and withdrawing* CHARLES
        — *to* VICTOR.]
In this conjuncture even, he would say
(Though with a moistened eye and quivering lip)
The suppliant is my father. I must save
A great man from himself, nor see him fling
His well-earned fame away: there must not
    follow
Ruin so utter, a break-down of worth
So absolute: no enemy shall learn,
He thrust his child 'twixt danger and himself,
And, when that child somehow stood danger
    out,
Stole back with serpent wiles to ruin Charles
— Body, that's much, — and soul, that's more
    — and realm,
That's most of all! No enemy shall say . . .
    D'O. Do you repent, sir?
    Vic. [*Resuming himself.*] D'Ormea? This is
        well!
Worthily done, King Charles, craftily done!
Judiciously you post these, to o'erhear
The little your importunate father thrusts
Himself on you to say! — Ah, they'll correct
The amiable blind facility
You show in answering his peevish suit.
What can he need to sue for? Thanks,
    D'Ormea!
You have fulfilled your office: but for you,
The old Count might have drawn some few
    more livres
To swell his income! Had you, lady, missed
The moment, a permission might be granted
To buttress up my ruinous old pile!
But you remember properly the list
Of wise precautions I took when I gave
Nearly as much away — to reap the fruits
I should have looked for!
    Cha.   Thanks, sir: degrade me,
So you remain yourself! Adieu!
    Vic.   I'll not
Forget it for the future, nor presume
Next time to slight such mediators! Nay —
Had I first moved them both to intercede,
I might secure a chamber in Moncaglier
— Who knows?
    Cha.   Adieu!
    Vic.   You bid me this adieu
With the old spirit?

Cha.   Adieu !
Vic.   Charles — Charles !
Cha.   Adieu !
                                   [VICTOR *goes.*

Cha. You were mistaken, Marquis, as you
   hear !
'T was for another purpose the Count came.
The Count desires Moncaglier. Give the order !
   D'O. [*Leisurely.*] Your minister has lost
your confidence,
Asserting late, for his own purposes,
Count Tende would . . .
   Cha. [*Flinging his badge back.*] Be still the
   minister !
And give a loose to your insulting joy ;
It irks me more thus stifled than expressed :
Loose it !
   D'O.   There 's none to loose, alas !   I see
I never am to die a martyr.
Pol.   Charles !
Cha. No praise, at least, Polyxena — no
   praise !

KING CHARLES

PART II

D'ORMEA seated, folding papers he has been examining.

This at the last effects it : now, King Charles
Or else King Victor — that 's a balance : but
   now,
D'Ormea the arch-culprit, either turn
O' the scale, — that 's sure enough. A point to
   solve,
My masters, moralists, whate'er your style !
When you discover why I push myself
Into a pitfall you 'd pass safely by,
Impart to me among the rest !   No matter.
Prompt are the righteous ever with their rede
To us the wrongful : lesson them this once !
For safe among the wicked are you set,
D'Ormea !   We lament life's brevity,
Yet quarter e'en the threescore years and ten,
Nor stick to call the quarter roundly " life."
D'Ormea was wicked, say, some twenty years ;
A tree so long was stunted ; afterward,
What if it grew, continued growing, till
No fellow of the forest equalled it ?
'T was a stump then ; a stump it still must be :
While forward saplings, at the outset checked,
In virtue of that first sprout keep their style
Amid the forest's green fraternity.
Thus I shoot up to surely get lopped down
And bound up for the burning. Now for it !
   (*Enter* CHARLES *and* POLYXENA *with* Attendants.)
   D'O. [*Rises.*] Sir, in the due discharge of
   this my office —
This enforced summons of yourself from Turin,
And the disclosure I am bound to make
To-night, — there must already be, I feel,
So much that wounds . . .
   Cha.   Well, sir ?
   D'O.   — That I, perchance,
May utter also what, another time,
Would irk much, — it may prove less irksome
   now.
   Cha. What would you utter ?

   D'O.   That I from my soul
Grieve at to-night's event : for you I grieve,
E'en grieve for . . .
   Cha.   Tush, another time for talk !
My kingdom is in imminent danger ?
   D'O.   Let
The Count communicate with France — il
   King,
His grandson, will have Fleury's aid for this,
Though for no other war.
   Cha.   First for the levies :
What forces can I muster presently ?
   [D'ORMEA *delivers papers which* CHARLES *inspects.*
   Cha. Good — very good.   Montorio . . .
   how is this ?
— Equips me double the old complement
Of soldiers ?
   D'O.   Since his land has been relieved
From double imposts, this he manages :
But under the late monarch . . .
   Cha.   Peace !   I know.
Count Spava has omitted mentioning
What proxy is to head these troops of his.
   D'O.   Count Spava means to head his troops
   himself.
Something to fight for now ; " Whereas," says
   he,
" Under the sovereign's father " . . .
   Cha.   It would seem
That all my people love me.
   D'O.   Yes.
[*To* POLYXENA *while* CHARLES *continues to inspect the*
   papers.
                              A temper
Like Victor's may avail to keep a state ;
He terrifies men and they fall not off ;
Good to restrain : best, if restraint were all.
But, with the silent circle round him, ends
Such sway : our King's begins precisely there.
For to suggest, impel and set at work,
Is quite another function.   Men may slight,
In time of peace, the King who brought them
   peace :
In war, — his voice, his eyes, help more than
   fear.
They love you, sir !
   Cha. [*To Attendants.*]   Bring the regalia
   forth !
Quit the room !   And now, Marquis, answer
   me !
Why should the King of France invade my
   realm ?
   D'O. Why ?   Did I not acquaint your Ma-
   jesty
An hour ago ?
   Cha.   I choose to hear again
What then I heard.
   D'O.   Because, sir, as I said,
Your father is resolved to have his crown
At any risk ; and, as I judge, calls in
The foreigner to aid him.
   Cha.   And your reason
For saying this ?
   D'O. [*Aside.*]   Ay, just his father's way !
   [*To* CHA.]   The Count wrote yesterday to your
   forces' Chief,
Rhebinder — made demand of help —
   Cha.   To try

Rhebinder — he 's of alien blood. Aught else ?

D'O. Receiving a refusal, — some hours
after,
The Count called on Del Borgo to deliver
The Act of Abdication : he refusing,
Or hesitating, rather —

Cha. What ensued ?

D'O. At midnight, only two hours since, at
Turin,
He rode in person to the citadel
With one attendant, to Soccorso gate,
And bade the governor, San Remi, open —
Admit him.

Cha. For a purpose I divine.
These three were faithful, then ?

D'O. They told it me :
And I —

Cha. Most faithful —

D'O. Tell it you — with this
Moreover of my own : if, an hour hence,
You have not interposed, the Count will be
O' the road to France for succor.

Cha. Very good !
You do your duty now to me your monarch
Fully, I warrant ? — have, that is, your project
For saving both of us disgrace, no doubt ?

D'O. I give my counsel, — and the only
one.
A month since, I besought you to employ
Restraints which had prevented many a pang :
But now the harsher course must be pursued.
These papers, made for the emergency,
Will pain you to subscribe : this is a list
Of those suspected merely — men to watch ;
This — of the few of the Count's very house-
hold
You must, however reluctantly, arrest ;
While here 's a method of remonstrance — sure
Not stronger than the case demands — to take
With the Count's self.

Cha. Deliver those three papers.

Pol. [*While* CHARLES *inspects them — to*
D'ORMEA.]
Your measures are not over-harsh, sir : France
Will hardly be deterred from her intents
By these.

D'O. If who proposes might dispose,
I could soon satisfy you. Even these,
Hear what he 'll say at my presenting !

Cha. [*who has signed them*]. There !
About the warrants ! You 've my signature.
What turns you pale ? I do my duty by you
In acting boldly thus on your advice.

D'O. [*Reading them separately.*] Arrest the
people I suspected merely ?

Cha. Did you suspect them ?

D'O. Doubtless : but — but — sir,
This Forquieri 's governor of Turin,
And Rivarol and he have influence over
Half of the capital ! Rabella, too ?
Why, sir —

Cha. Oh, leave the fear to me !

D'O. [*Still reading.*] You bid me
Incarcerate the people on this list ?
Sir —

Cha. But you never bade arrest those men,
So close related to my father too,
On trifling grounds ?

D'O. Oh, as for that, St. George
President of Chambery's senators,
Is hatching treason ! still —
[*More troubled.*] Sir, Count Cumiane
Is brother to your father's wife ! What 's
here ?
Arrest the wife herself ?

Cha. You seem to think
A venial crime this plot against me. Well ?

D'O. [*who has read the last paper*]. Where-
fore am I thus ruined ? Why not take
My life at once ? This poor formality
Is, let me say, unworthy you ! Prevent it
You, madam ! I have served you, am pre-
pared
For all disgraces : only, let disgrace
Be plain, be proper — proper for the world
To pass its judgment on 'twixt you and me !
Take back your warrant, I will none of it !

Cha. Here is a man to talk of fickleness !
He stakes his life upon my father's falsehood ;
I bid him . . .

D'O. Not you ! Were he trebly false,
You do not bid me . . .

Cha. Is 't not written there ?
I thought so : give — I 'll set it right.

D'O. Is it there ?
Oh yes, and plain — arrest him now — drag
here
Your father ! And were all six times as plain,
Do you suppose I trust it ?

Cha. Just one word !
You bring him, taken in the act of flight,
Or else your life is forfeit.

D'O. Ay, to Turin
I bring him, and to-morrow ?

Cha. Here and now !
The whole thing is a lie, a hateful lie,
As I believed and as my father said.
I knew it from the first, but was compelled
To circumvent you ; and the great D'Ormea,
That baffled Alberoni and tricked Coscia,
The miserable sower of such discord
'Twixt sire and son, is in the toils at last.
Oh I see ! you arrive — this plan of yours,
Weak as it is, torments sufficiently
A sick old peevish man — wrings hasty speech,
An ill-considered threat from him ; that 's
noted ;
Then out you ferret papers, his amusement
In lonely hours of lassitude — examine
The day-by-day report of your paid spies —
And back you come : all was not ripe, you find,
And, as you hope, may keep from ripening yet,
But you were in bare time ! Only, 't were best
I never saw my father — these old men
Are potent in excuses : and meanwhile,
D'Ormea 's the man I cannot do without !

Pol. Charles —

Cha. Ah, no question ! You against me too !
You 'd have me eat and drink and sleep, live,
die,
With this lie coiled about me, choking me !
No, no, D'Ormea ! You venture life, you say
Upon my father's perfidy : and I
Have, on the whole, no right to disregard
The chains of testimony you thus wind
About me ; though I do — do from my soul

Discredit them: still I must authorize
These measures, and I will.   Perugia!
[*Many* Officers *enter*.]   Count —
You and Solar, with all the force you have,
Stand at the Marquis' orders: what he bids,
Implicitly perform!   You are to bring
A traitor here; the man that 's likest one
At present, fronts me; you are at his beck
For a full hour!   he undertakes to show
A fouler than himself, — but, failing that,
Return with him, and, as my father lives,
He dies this night!   The clemency you blame
So oft, shall be revoked — rights exercised,
Too long abjured.
          [*To D'O.*]   Now, sir, about the work!
To save your king and country!   Take the
          warrant!
D'O.   You hear the sovereign's mandate,
          Count Perugia?
Obey me!   As your diligence, expect
Reward!   All follow to Montcaglier!
                                        [D'ORMEA *goes.*

Cha.   [*In great anguish.*] D'Ormea!
He goes, lit up with that appalling smile!
          [*To* POLYXENA *after a pause.*
At least you understand all this?
Pol.   These means
Of our defence — these measures of precaution?
Cha.   It must be the best way: I should
          have else
Withered beneath his scorn.
Pol.   What would you say?
Cha.   Why, do you think I mean to keep
          the crown, Polyxena?
Pol.   You then believe the story
In spite of all — that Victor comes?
Cha.   Believe it?
I know that he is coming — feel the strength
That has upheld me leave me at his coming!
'T was mine, and now he takes his own again.
Some kinds of strength are well enough to
          have;
But who 's to have that strength?   Let my
          crown go!
I meant to keep it; but I cannot — cannot!
Only, he shall not taunt me — he, the first . . .
See if he would not be the first to taunt me
With having left his kingdom at a word,
With letting it be conquered without stroke,
With . . . no — no — 't is no worse than when
          he left!
I 've just to bid him take it, and, that over,
We 'll fly away — fly. for I loathe this Turin,
This Rivoli, all titles loathe, all state.
We 'd best go to your country — unless God
Send I die now!
Pol.   Charles, hear me!
Cha.   And again
Shall you be my Polyxena — you 'll take me
Out of this woe!   Yes, do speak, and keep
          speaking!
I would not let you speak just now, for fear
You 'd counsel me against him: but talk, now,
As we two used to talk in blessed times:
Bid me endure all his caprices; take me
From this mad post above him!
Pol.   I believe
We are undone. but from a different cause.

All your resources, down to the least guard,
Are at D'Ormea's beck.   What if, the while,
He act in concert with your father?   We
Indeed were lost.   This lonely Rivoli —
Where find a better place for them?
     Cha. [*Pacing the room.*]   And why
Does Victor come?   To undo all that 's done,
Restore the past, prevent the future!   Seat
His mistress in your seat, and place in mine
. . . Oh, my own people, whom will you find
          there,
To ask of, to consult with, to care for,
To hold up with your hands?   Whom?   One
          that 's false —
False — from the head's crown to the foot's
          sole, false!
The best is, that I knew it in my heart
From the beginning, and expected this,
And hated you, Polyxena, because
You saw through him, though I too saw through
          him,
Saw that he meant this while he crowned me,
          while
He prayed for me, — nay, while he kissed my
          brow,
I saw —
     Pol.   But if your measures take effect,
D'Ormea true to you?
     Cha.   Then worst of all!
I shall have loosed that callous wretch on him!
Well may the woman taunt him with his child —
I, eating here his bread, clothed in his clothes,
Seated upon his seat, let slip D'Ormea
To outrage him!   We talk — perchance he
          tears
My father from his bed; the old hands feel
For one who is not, but who should be there:
He finds D'Ormea!   D'Ormea too finds him!
The crowded chamber when the lights go
          out —
Closed doors — the horrid scuffle in the dark —
The accursed prompting of the minute!   My
          guards!
To horse — and after, with me — and prevent!
     Pol. [*Seizing his hand.*]   King Charles!
          Pause here upon this strip of time
Allotted you out of eternity!
Crowns are from God: you in his name hold
          yours.
Your life 's no least thing, were it fit your life
Should be abjured along with rule; but now,
Keep both!   Your duty is to live and rule —
You, who would vulgarly look fine enough
In the world's eye, deserting your soul's
          charge, —
Ay, you would have men's praise, this Rivoli
Would be illumined!   While, as 't is, no doubt
Something of stain will ever rest on you;
No one will rightly know why you refused
To abdicate; they 'll talk of deeds you could
Have done, no doubt, — nor do I much expect
Future achievement will blot out the past,
Envelope it in haze — nor shall we two
Live happy any more.   'T will be, I feel,
Only in moments that the duty 's seen
As palpably as now: the months, the years
Of painful indistinctness are to come,
While daily must we tread these palace-rooms

Pregnant with memories of the past: your eye
May turn to mine and find no comfort there,
Through fancies that beset me, as yourself,
Of other courses, with far other issues,
We might have taken this great night: such
    bear,
As I will bear! What matters happiness?
Duty! There's man's one moment: this is
    yours!

[*Putting the crown on his head, and the sceptre in his
hand, she places him on his seat: a long pause and
silence.*

    (*Enter* D'ORMEA *and* VICTOR, *with* GUARDS.)

Vic. At last I speak; but once — that once,
    to you!
'T is you I ask, not these your varletry,
Who 's King of us?
Cha. [*From his seat.*]   Count Tende . . .
Vic.   What your spies
Assert I ponder in my soul, I say —
Here to your face, amid your guards! I choose
To take again the crown whose shadow I gave —
For still its potency surrounds the weak
White locks their felon hands have discomposed.
Or I 'll not ask who 's King, but simply, who
Withholds the crown I claim? Deliver it!
I have no friend in the wide world: nor France
Nor England cares for me: you see the sum
Of what I can avail. Deliver it!
Cha. Take it, my father!
                  And now say in turn,
Was it done well, my father — sure not well,
To try me thus! I might have seen much cause
For keeping it — too easily seen cause!
But, from that moment, e'en more woefully
My life had pined away, than pine it will.
Already you have much to answer for.
My life to pine is nothing, — her sunk eyes
Were happy once! No doubt, my people think
I am their King still . . . but I cannot strive!
Take it!
Vic. [*One hand on the crown* CHARLES *offers,
    the other on his neck.*] So few years give it
    quietly,
My son! It will drop from me. See you
    not?
A crown 's unlike a sword to give away —
That, let a strong hand to a weak hand give!
But crowns should slip from palsied brows to
    heads
Young as this head: yet mine is weak enough,
E'en weaker than I knew. I seek for phrases
To vindicate my right. 'T is of a piece!
All is alike gone by with me — who beat
Once D'Orleans in his lines — his very lines!
To have been Eugene's comrade, Louis's rival,
And now . . .
Cha. [*Putting the crown on him, to the rest.*]
    The King speaks, yet none kneels, I
    think!
Vic. I am then King! As I became a King

Despite the nations, kept myself a King,
So I die King, with Kingship dying too
Around me! I have lasted Europe's time!
What wants my story of completion? Where
Must needs the damning break show? Who
    mistrusts
My children here — tell they of any break
'Twixt my day's sunrise and its fiery fall?
And who were by me when I died but they?
D'Ormea there!
Cha.   What means he?
Vic.   Ever there!
Charles — how to save your story! Mine must
    go!
Say — say that you refused the crown to me!
Charles, yours shall be my story! You im-
    mured
Me, say, at Rivoli. A single year
I spend without a sight of you, then die.
That will serve every purpose — tell that tale
The world!
Cha. Mistrust me? Help!
Vic.   Past help, past reach!
'T is in the heart — you cannot reach the heart:
This broke mine, that I did believe, you,
    Charles,
Would have denied me and disgraced me.
Pol.   Charles
Has never ceased to be your subject, sir!
He reigned at first through setting up yourself
As pattern: if he e'er seemed harsh to you,
'T was from a too intense appreciation
Of your own character: he acted you —
Ne'er for an instant did I think it real,
Nor look for any other than this end.
I hold him worlds the worse on that account;
But so it was.
Cha. [*To* POL.] I love you now indeed!
[*To* VIC.] You never knew me!
Vic.   Hardly till this moment,
When I seem learning many other things
Because the time for using them is past.
If 't were to do again! That 's idly wished.
Truthfulness might prove policy as good
As guile. Is this my daughter's forehead?
    Yes:
I 've made it fitter now to be a queen's
Than formerly: I 've ploughed the deep lines
    there
Which keep too well a crown from slipping off.
No matter. Guile has made me King again.
Louis — 't was in King Victor's time: — long
    since,
When Louis reigned and, also, Victor reigned.
How the world talks already of us two!
God of eclipse and each discolored star,
Why do I linger then?
                  Ha! Where lurks he?
D'Ormea! Nearer to your King! Now stand!
    [*Collecting his strength as* D'ORMEA *approaches.*
You lied, D'Ormea! I do not repent.   [*Dies*

DRAMATIC LYRICS

THE third number of *Bells and Pomegranates*, published in 1842, contained a collection of short poems under the general head of *Dramatic Lyrics*. When Browning made his first collective edition, he redistributed all his groups of poems, retaining this title and making it cover some of the poems included in the original group, but many more first published under other headings. The arrangement here given is that adopted finally by Browning. "Such Poems," he says, "as the majority in this volume (*Dramatic Lyr*-ics) might also come properly enough, I suppose, under the head of *Dramatic Pieces;* being, though often Lyric in expression, always Dramatic in principle, and so many utterances of so many imaginary persons, not mine. Part of the Poems were inscribed to my dear friend, John Kenyon; I hope the whole may obtain the honor of an association with his memory."

The third of the *Cavalier Tunes* was originally entitled *My Wife Gertrude.* The three songs have been set to music by Dr. Villiers Stanford.

CAVALIER TUNES

I. MARCHING ALONG

KENTISH Sir Byng stood for his King,
Bidding the crop-headed Parliament swing:
And, pressing a troop unable to stoop
And see the rogues flourish and honest folk droop,
Marched them along, fifty-score strong,
Great-hearted gentlemen, singing this song.

God for King Charles! Pym and such carles
To the Devil that prompts 'em their treasonous parles!
Cavaliers, up! Lips from the cup,
Hands from the pasty, nor bite take nor sup
Till you 're —
  CHORUS. — Marching along, fifty-score strong,
      Great-hearted gentlemen, singing
      this song.

Hampden to hell, and his obsequies' knell.
Serve Hazelrig, Fiennes, and young Harry as well!
England, good cheer! Rupert is near!
Kentish and loyalists, keep we not here,
  CHO. — Marching along, fifty-score strong,
      Great-hearted gentlemen, singing this
      song?

Then, God for King Charles! Pym and his snarls
To the Devil that pricks on such pestilent carles!
Hold by the right, you double your might;
So, onward to Nottingham, fresh for the fight,
  CHO. — March we along, fifty-score strong,
      Great-hearted gentlemen, singing this
      song!

II. GIVE A ROUSE

King Charles, and who 'll do him right now?
King Charles, and who 's ripe for fight now?
Give a rouse: here 's, in hell's despite now,
King Charles!

Who gave me the goods that went since?
Who raised me the house that sank once?
Who helped me to gold I spent since?
Who found me in wine you drank once?
  CHO. — King Charles, and who 'll do him
      right now?
      King Charles, and who 's ripe for fight
      now?
      Give a rouse: here 's, in hell's de-
      spite now,
      King Charles!

To whom used my boy George quaff else,
By the old fool's side that begot him?
For whom did he cheer and laugh else,
While Noll's damned troopers shot him?
  CHO. — King Charles, and who 'll do him
      right now?
      King Charles, and who 's ripe for fight
      now?
      Give a rouse: here 's, in hell's de-
      spite now,
      King Charles!

III. BOOT AND SADDLE

Boot, saddle, to horse, and away!
Rescue my castle before the hot day
Brightens to blue from its silvery gray.
  CHO. — Boot, saddle, to horse, and away!

Ride past the suburbs, asleep as you 'd say;
Many 's the friend there, will listen and pray
" God's luck to gallants that strike up the lay —
  CHO. — Boot, saddle, to horse, and away!"

Forty miles off, like a roebuck at bay,
Flouts Castle Brancepeth the Roundheads' array:
Who laughs, " Good fellows ere this, by my fay,
  CHO. — Boot, saddle, to horse, and away!"

Who? My wife Gertrude; that, honest and gay,
Laughs when you talk of surrendering, " Nay!
I 've better counsellors; what counsel they?
  CHO. — Boot, saddle, to horse, and away!"

THE LOST LEADER

Browning was beset with questions by people asking if he referred to Wordsworth in this poem. He answered the question more than once, as an artist would : the following letter to Rev. A. B. Grosart, the editor of Wordsworth's *Prose Works*, sufficiently states his position.

" 19 Warwick-Crescent, W., *Feb.* 24, '75.

" DEAR MR. GROSART, — I have been asked the question you now address me with, and as duly answered it, I can't remember how many times ; there is no sort of objection to one more assurance or rather confession, on my part, that I *did* in my hasty youth presume to use the great and venerated personality of Wordsworth as a sort of painter's model ; one from which this or the other particular feature may be selected and turned to account ; had I intended more, above all, such a boldness as portraying the entire man, I should not have talked about ' handfuls of silver and bits of ribbon.' These never influenced the change of politics in the great poet, whose defection, nevertheless, accompanied as it was by a regular face-about of his special party, was to my juvenile apprehension, and even mature consideration, an event to deplore. But just as in the tapestry on my wall I can recognize figures which have *struck out* a fancy, on occasion, that though truly enough thus derived, yet would be preposterous as a copy, so, though I dare not deny the original of my little poem, I altogether refuse to have it considered as the ' very effigies ' of such a moral and intellectual superiority.

" Faithfully yours,
" ROBERT BROWNING."

Just for a handful of silver he left us,
　Just for a riband to stick in his coat —
Found the one gift of which fortune bereft us,
　Lost all the others she lets us devote ;
They, with the gold to give, doled him out silver,
　So much was theirs who so little allowed :
How all our copper had gone for his service !
　Rags — were they purple, his heart had been proud !
We that had loved him so, followed him, honored him,
　Lived in his mild and magnificent eye,
Learned his great language, caught his clear accents,
　Made him our pattern to live and to die !
Shakespeare was of us, Milton was for us,
　Burns, Shelley, were with us, — they watch from their graves !
He alone breaks from the van and the freemen,
　— He alone sinks to the rear and the slaves !

We shall march prospering, — not through his presence ;
Songs may inspirit us, — not from his lyre ;
Deeds will be done, — while he boasts his quiescence,
　Still bidding crouch whom the rest bade aspire :
Blot out his name, then, record one lost soul more,
　One task more declined, one more footpath untrod,
One more devils'-triumph and sorrow for angels,
　One wrong more to man, one more insult to God !
Life's night begins : let him never come back to us !
　There would be doubt, hesitation and pain,
Forced praise on our part — the glimmer of twilight,
　Never glad confident morning again !
Best fight on well, for we taught him — strike gallantly,
　Menace our heart ere we master his own ;
Then let him receive the new knowledge and wait us,
　Pardoned in heaven, the first by the throne !

"HOW THEY BROUGHT THE GOOD NEWS FROM GHENT TO AIX "

Browning wrote to an American inquirer about this poem : " There is no sort of historical foundation for the poem about ' Good News from Ghent.' I wrote it under the bulwark of a vessel, off the African coast, after I had been at sea long enough to appreciate even the fancy of a gallop on the back of a certain good horse ' York,' then in my stable at home. It was written in pencil on the fly-leaf of Bartoli's *Simboli*, I remember."

[16—]

I SPRANG to the stirrup, and Joris, and he ;
I galloped, Dirck galloped, we galloped all three ;
" Good speed ! " cried the watch, as the gate-bolts undrew ;
" Speed ! " echoed the wall to us galloping through ;
Behind shut the postern, the lights sank to rest,
And into the midnight we galloped abreast.

Not a word to each other ; we kept the great pace
Neck by neck, stride by stride, never changing our place ;
I turned in my saddle and made its girths tight,
Then shortened each stirrup, and set the pique right,
Rebuckled the cheek-strap, chained slacker the bit,
Nor galloped less steadily Roland a whit.

'T was moonset at starting ; but while we drew
　　near
Lokeren, the cocks crew and twilight dawned
　　clear ;
At Boom, a great yellow star came out to see ;
At Düffeld, 't was morning as plain as could
　　be ;
And from Mecheln church-steeple we heard the
　　half-chime,
So Joris broke silence with, "Yet there is
　　time ! "

At Aershot, up leaped of a sudden the sun,
And against him the cattle stood black every
　　one,
To stare through the mist at us galloping past,
And I saw my stout galloper Roland at last,
With resolute shoulders, each butting away
The haze, as some bluff river headland its spray :

And his low head and crest, just one sharp ear
　　bent back
For my voice, and the other pricked out on his
　　track ;
And one eye's black intelligence, — ever that
　　glance
O'er its white edge at me, his own master,
　　askance !
And the thick heavy spume-flakes which aye
　　and anon
His fierce lips shook upwards in galloping on.

By Hasselt, Dirck groaned ; and cried Joris,
　　"Stay spur !
Your Roos galloped bravely, the fault 's not in
　　her,
We 'll remember at Aix " — for one heard the
　　quick wheeze
Of her chest, saw the stretched neck and stag-
　　gering knees,
And sunk tail, and horrible heave of the flank,
As down on her haunches she shuddered and
　　sank.

So, we were left galloping, Joris and I,
Past Looz and past Tongres, no cloud in the sky ;
The broad sun above laughed a pitiless laugh,
'Neath our feet broke the brittle bright stubble
　　like chaff ;
Till over by Dalhem a dome-spire sprang white,
And "Gallop," gasped Joris, "for Aix is in
　　sight ! "

"How they 'll greet us ! " — and all in a moment
　　his roan
Rolled neck and croup over, lay dead as a stone ;
And there was my Roland to bear the whole
　　weight
Of the news which alone could save Aix from
　　her fate,
With his nostrils like pits full of blood to the
　　brim,
And with circles of red for his eye-sockets' rim.

Then I cast loose my buffcoat, each holster let
　　fall,
Shook off both my jack-boots, let go belt and all,

Stood up in the stirrup, leaned, patted his ear,
Called my Roland his pet-name, my horse with-
　　out peer ;
Clapped my hands, laughed and sang, any noise,
　　bad or good,
Till at length into Aix Roland galloped and
　　stood.

And all I remember is — friends flocking round
As I sat with his head 'twixt my knees on the
　　ground ;
And no voice but was praising this Roland of
　　mine,
As I poured down his throat our last measure
　　of wine,
Which (the burgesses voted by common consent)
Was no more than his due who brought good
　　news from Ghent.

THROUGH THE METIDJA TO ABD-EL-KADR

As I ride, as I ride,
With a full heart for my guide,
So its tide rocks my side,
As I ride, as I ride,
That, as I were double-eyed,
He, in whom our Tribes confide,
Is deseried, ways untried,
As I ride, as I ride.

As I ride, as I ride
To our Chief and his Allied,
Who dares chide my heart's pride
As I ride, as I ride ?
Or are witnesses denied —
Through the desert waste and wide
Do I glide unespied
As I ride, as I ride ?

As I ride, as I ride,
When an inner voice has cried,
The sands slide, nor abide
(As I ride, as I ride)
O'er each visioned homicide
That came vaunting (has he lied ?)
To reside — where he died,
As I ride, as I ride.

As I ride, as I ride,
Ne'er has spur my swift horse plied,
Yet his hide, streaked and pied,
As I ride, as I ride,
Shows where sweat has sprung and dried,
— Zebra-footed, ostrich-thighed —
How has vied stride with stride
As I ride, as I ride !

As I ride, as I ride,
Could I loose what Fate has tied,
Ere I pried, she should hide
(As I ride, as I ride)
All that 's meant me — satisfied
When the Prophet and the Bride
Stop veins I 'd have subside
As I ride, as I ride !

NATIONALITY IN DRINKS

The first two of this group, under the titles *Claret* and *Tokay*, were published in *Hood's Magazine*, June, 1844, at the request of Richard Monckton Milnes, who was editing the magazine during Hood's illness. The third, first entitled *Beer*, was called out by the description of Nelson's coat at Greenwich, given by the captain of the vessel in which Browning was sailing to Italy.

I

My heart sank with our Claret-flask,
    Just now, beneath the heavy sedges
That serve this pond's black face for mask ;
    And still at yonder broken edges
O' the hole, where up the bubbles glisten,
After my heart I look and listen.

Our laughing little flask, compelled
    Through depth to depth more bleak and
        shady ;
As when, both arms beside her held,
    Feet straightened out, some gay French lady
Is caught up from life's light and motion,
And dropped into death's silent ocean !

II

— Up jumped Tokay on our table,
Like a pygmy castle-warder,
Dwarfish to see, but stout and able,
Arms and accoutrements all in order ;
And fierce he looked North, then, wheeling
        South,
Blew with his bugle a challenge to Drouth,
Cocked his flap-hat with the tosspot-feather,
Twisted his thumb in his red moustache,
Jingled his huge brass spurs together,
Tightened his waist with its Buda sash,
And then, with an impudence naught could
        abash,
Shrugged his hump-shoulder, to tell the be-
        holder,
For twenty such knaves he should laugh but
        the bolder :
And so, with his sword-hilt gallantly jutting,
And dexter-hand on his haunch abutting,
Went the little man, Sir Ausbruch, strutting !

III

— Here 's to Nelson's memory !
'T is the second time that I, at sea,
Right off Cape Trafalgar here,
Have drunk it deep in British Beer.
Nelson forever — any time
Am I his to command in prose or rhyme !
Give me of Nelson only a touch,
And I save it, be it little or much :
Here 's one our Captain gives, and so
Down at the word, by George, shall it go !
He says that at Greenwich they point the be-
        holder
To Nelson's coat, "still with tar on the shoulder :

For he used to lean with one shoulder digging,
Jigging, as it were, and zig-zag-zigging
Up against the mizzen-rigging ! "

GARDEN FANCIES

These two poems also appeared in *Hood's Magazine*, July, 1844.

I. THE FLOWER'S NAME

Here 's the garden she walked across,
    Arm in my arm, such a short while since:
Hark, now I push its wicket, the moss
    Hinders the hinges and makes them wince !
She must have reached this shrub ere she turned,
    As back with that murmur the wicket swung ;
For she laid the poor snail, my chance foot
        spurned,
To feed and forget it the leaves among.

Down this side of the gravel-walk
    She went while her robe's edge brushed the
        box :
And here she paused in her gracious talk
    To point me a moth on the milk-white phlox.
Roses, ranged in valiant row,
    I will never think that she passed you by !
She loves you, noble roses, I know ;
    But yonder, see, where the rock-plants lie !

This flower she stopped at, finger on lip,
    Stooped over, in doubt, as settling its claim ;
Till she gave me, with pride to make no slip,
    Its soft meandering Spanish name :
What a name !   Was it love or praise ?
    Speech half-asleep or song half-awake ?
I must learn Spanish, one of these days,
    Only for that slow sweet name's sake.

Roses, if I live and do well,
    I may bring her, one of these days,
To fix you fast with as fine a spell,
    Fit you each with his Spanish phrase ;
But do not detain me now ; for she lingers
    There, like sunshine over the ground,
And ever I see her soft white fingers
    Searching after the bud she found.

Flower, you Spaniard, look that you grow not,
    Stay as you are and be loved forever !
Bud, if I kiss you 't is that you blow not,
    Mind, the shut pink mouth opens never !
For while it pouts, her fingers wrestle,
    Twinkling the audacious leaves between,
Till round they turn and down they nestle —
    Is not the dear mark still to be seen ?

Where I find her not, beauties vanish ;
    Whither I follow her, beauties flee ;
Is there no method to tell her in Spanish
    June 's twice June since she breathed it with
        me ?
Come, bud, show me the least of her traces,
    Treasure my lady's lightest footfall !
— Ah, you may flout and turn up your faces —
    Roses, you are not so fair after all !

II. SIBRANDUS SCHAFNABURGENSIS

Plague take all your pedants, say I !
  He who wrote what I hold in my hand,
Centuries back was so good as to die,
  Leaving this rubbish to cumber the land ;
This, that was a book in its time,
  Printed on paper and bound in leather,
Last month in the white of a matin-prime,
  Just when the birds sang all together.

Into the garden I brought it to read,
  And under the arbute and laurustine
Read it, so help me grace in my need,
  From title-page to closing line.
Chapter on chapter did I count,
  As a curious traveller counts Stonehenge ;
Added up the mortal amount ;
  And then proceeded to my revenge.

Yonder 's a plum-tree with a crevice
  An owl would build in, were he but sage ;
For a lap of moss, like a fine pont-levis
  In a castle of the Middle Age,
Joins to a lip of gum, pure amber ;
  When he 'd be private, there might he spend
Hours alone in his lady's chamber :
  Into this crevice I dropped our friend.

Splash, went he, as under he ducked,
  — At the bottom, I knew, rain-drippings
    stagnate ;
Next, a handful of blossoms I plucked
  To bury him with, my bookshelf's magnate ;
Then I went in-doors, brought out a loaf,
  Half a cheese, and a bottle of Chablis ;
Lay on the grass and forgot the oaf
  Over a jolly chapter of Rabelais.

Now, this morning, betwixt the moss
  And gum that locked our friend in limbo,
A spider had spun his web across,
  And sat in the midst with arms akimbo :
So, I took pity, for learning's sake,
  And, *de profundis, accentibus lætis,*
Cantate ! quoth I, as I got a rake ;
  And up I fished his delectable treatise.

Here you have it, dry in the sun,
  With all the binding all of a blister,
And great blue spots where the ink has run,
  And reddish streaks that wink and glister
O'er the page so beautifully yellow :
  Oh, well have the droppings played their
    tricks !
Did he guess how toadstools grow, this fel-
    low ?
  Here 's one stuck in his chapter six !

How did he like it when the live creatures
  Tickled and toused and browsed him all
    over,
And worm, slug, eft, with serious features,
  Came in, each one, for his right of trover ?
  When the water-beetle with great blind deaf
    face
Made of her eggs the stately deposit.

And the newt borrowed just so much of the
    preface
  As tiled in the top of his black wife's closet ?

All that life and fun and romping,
  All that frisking and twisting and coupling,
While slowly our poor friend's leaves were
    swamping
  And clasps were cracking and covers suppling !
As if you had carried sour John Knox
  To the play-house at Paris, Vienna or Munich,
Fastened him into a front-row box,
  And danced off the ballet with trousers and
    tunic.

Come, old martyr ! What, torment enough is it ?
  Back to my room shall you take your sweet
    self.
Good-bye, mother-beetle ; husband-eft, *sufficit !*
  See the snug niche I have made on my shelf !
A's book shall prop you up, B's shall cover you,
  Here 's C to be grave with, or D to be gay,
And with E on each side, and F right over you,
  Dry-rot at ease till the Judgment-day !

SOLILOQUY OF THE SPANISH CLOISTER

When first printed in *Bells and Pomegranates*, this poem was the second of a group of two bearing the general title *Camp and Cloister*, the first of the two being *Incident of the French Camp.*

GR-R-R — there go, my heart's abhorrence !
  Water your damned flower-pots, do !
If hate killed men, Brother Lawrence,
  God's blood, would not mine kill you !
What ? your myrtle-bush wants trimming ?
  Oh, that rose has prior claims —
Needs its leaden vase filled brimming ?
  Hell dry you up with its flames !

At the meal we sit together :
  Salve tibi ! I must hear
Wise talk of the kind of weather,
  Sort of season, time of year :
Not a plenteous cork-crop : scarcely
  Dare we hope oak-galls, I doubt :
What 's the Latin name for " parsley " ?
  What 's the Greek name for Swine's Snout ?

Whew ! We 'll have our platter burnished,
  Laid with care on our own shelf !
With a fire-new spoon we 're furnished,
  And a goblet for ourself,
Rinsed like something sacrificial
  Ere 't is fit to touch our chaps —
Marked with L for our initial !
  (He-he ! There his lily snaps !)

Saint, forsooth ! While brown Dolores
  Squats outside the Convent bank
With Sanchicha, telling stories,
  Steeping tresses in the tank,
Blue-black, lustrous, thick like horsehairs,
  — Can't I see his dead eye glow,

Bright as 't were a Barbary corsair's?
  (That is, if he 'd let it show !)

When he finishes refection,
  Knife and fork he never lays
Cross-wise, to my recollection,
  As do I, in Jesu's praise.
I the Trinity illustrate,
  Drinking watered orange-pulp —
In three sips the Arian frustrate;
  While he drains his at one gulp.

Oh, those melons ! If he 's able
  We 're to have a feast ! so nice !
One goes to the Abbot's table,
  All of us get each a slice.
How go on your flowers ? None double ?
  Not one fruit-sort can you spy ?
Strange ! — And I, too, at such trouble
  Keep them close-nipped on the sly !

There 's a great text in Galatians,
  Once you trip on it, entails
Twenty-nine distinct damnations,
  One sure, if another fails :
If I trip him just a-dying,
  Sure of heaven as sure can be,
Spin him round and send him flying
  Off to hell, a Manichee ?

Or, my scrofulous French novel
  On gray paper with blunt type !
Simply glance at it, you grovel
  Hand and foot in Belial's gripe :
If I double down its pages
  At the woeful sixteenth print,
When he gathers his greengages,
  Ope a sieve and slip it in 't ?

Or, there 's Satan ! — one might venture
  Pledge one's soul to him, yet leave
Such a flaw in the indenture
  As he 'd miss till, past retrieve,
Blasted lay that rose-acacia
  We 're so proud of ! *Hy, Zy, Hine* . . .
'St, there 's Vespers ! *Plena gratiâ,*
  Ave, Virgo ! Gr-r-r — you swine !

THE LABORATORY

ANCIEN RÉGIME

Published first in *Hood's Magazine*, June,
1844. In *Bells and Pomegranates* it was grouped
with *The Confessional* under the title *France
and Spain.*

Now that I, tying thy glass mask tightly,
May gaze through these faint smokes curling
        whitely,
As thou pliest thy trade in this devil's-smithy —
Which is the poison to poison her, prithee ?

He is with her, and they know that I know
Where they are, what they do : they believe
  my tears flow

While they laugh, laugh at me, at me fled to
  the drear
Empty church, to pray God in, for them ! — I
  am here.

Grind away, moisten and mash up thy paste,
Pound at thy powder, — I am not in haste !
Better sit thus, and observe thy strange things,
Than go where men wait me and dance at the
  King's.

That in the mortar — you call it a gum ?
Ah, the brave tree whence such gold oozings
  come !
And yonder soft phial, the exquisite blue,
Sure to taste sweetly, — is that poison too ?

Had I but all of them, thee and thy treasures,
What a wild crowd of invisible pleasures !
To carry pure death in an earring, a casket,
A signet, a fan-mount, a filigree basket !

Soon, at the King's, a mere lozenge to give,
And Pauline should have just thirty minutes to
  live !
But to light a pastile, and Elise, with her head
And her breast and her arms and her hands,
  should drop dead !

Quick — is it finished ? The color 's too grim !
Why not soft like the phial's, enticing and
  dim ?
Let it brighten her drink, let her turn it and
  stir,
And try it and taste, ere she fix and prefer !

What a drop ! She 's not little, no minion like
  me !
That 's why she ensnared him : this never will
  free
The soul from those masculine eyes, — say,
  "no !"
To that pulse's magnificent come-and-go.

For only last night, as they whispered, I brought
My own eyes to bear on her so, that I thought
Could I keep them one half minute fixed, she
  would fall
Shrivelled ; she fell not ; yet this does it all !

Not that I bid you spare her the pain ;
Let death be felt and the proof remain :
Brand, burn up, bite into its grace —
He is sure to remember her dying face !

Is it done ? Take my mask off ! Nay, be not
  morose ;
It kills her, and this prevents seeing it close :
The delicate droplet, my whole fortune's fee !
If it hurts her, beside, can it ever hurt me ?

Now, take all my jewels, gorge gold to your
  fill,
You may kiss me, old man, on my mouth if you
  will !
But brush this dust off me, lest horror it brings
Ere I know it — next moment I dance at the
  King's !

THE CONFESSIONAL

SPAIN

It is a lie — their Priests, their Pope,
Their Saints, their . . . all they fear or hope
Are lies, and lies — there ! through my door
And ceiling, there ! and walls and floor,
There, lies, they lie — shall still be hurled
Till spite of them I reach the world !

You think Priests just and holy men !
Before they put me in this den
I was a human creature too,
With flesh and blood like one of you,
A girl that laughed in beauty's pride
Like lilies in your world outside.

I had a lover — shame avaunt !
This poor wrenched body, grim and gaunt,
Was kissed all over till it burned,
By lips the truest, love e'er turned
His heart's own tint : one night they kissed
My soul out in a burning mist.

So, next day when the accustomed train
Of things grew round my sense again,
"That is a sin," I said : and slow
With downcast eyes to church I go,
And pass to the confession-chair,
And tell the old mild father there.

But when I falter Beltran's name,
"Ha!" quoth the father ; "much I blame
The sin ; yet wherefore idly grieve ?
Despair not — strenuously retrieve !
Nay, I will turn this love of thine
To lawful love, almost divine ;

"For he is young, and led astray,
This Beltran, and he schemes, men say,
To change the laws of church and state ;
So, thine shall be an angel's fate,
Who, ere the thunder breaks, should roll
Its cloud away and save his soul.

"For, when he lies upon thy breast,
Thou mayest demand and be possessed
Of all his plans, and next day steal
To me, and all those plans reveal,
That I and every priest, to purge
His soul, may fast and use the scourge."

That father's beard was long and white,
With love and truth his brow seemed bright ;
I went back, all on fire with joy,
And, that same evening, bade the boy
Tell me, as lovers should, heart-free,
Something to prove his love of me.

He told me what he would not tell
For hope of heaven or fear of hell ;
And I lay listening in such pride !
And, soon as he had left my side,
Tripped to the church by morning-light
To save his soul in his despite.

I told the father all his schemes,
Who were his comrades, what their dreams ;
"And now make haste," I said, " to pray
The one spot from his soul away ;
To-night he comes, but not the same
Will look ! " At night he never came.

Nor next night : on the after-morn,
I went forth with a strength new-born.
The church was empty ; something drew
My steps into the street ; I knew
It led me to the market-place :
Where, lo, on high, the father's face !

That horrible black scaffold dressed,
That stapled block . . . God sink the rest !
That head strapped back, that blinding vest,
Those knotted hands and naked breast,
Till near one busy hangman pressed,
And, on the neck these arms caressed . . .

No part in aught they hope or fear !
No heaven with them, no hell ! — and here,
No earth, not so much space as pens
My body in their worst of dens
But shall bear God and man my cry.
Lies — lies, again — and still, they lie !

CRISTINA

In *Bells and Pomegranates*, this poem was
the second of a group headed *Queen-Worship*,
the first being *Rudel and the Lady of Tripoli*.

She should never have looked at me
　If she meant I should not love her !
There are plenty . . . men, you call such,
　I suppose . . . she may discover
All her soul to, if she pleases,
　And yet leave much as she found them :
But I 'm not so, and she knew it
　When she fixed me, glancing round them.

What ? To fix me thus meant nothing ?
　But I can't tell (there 's my weakness)
What her look said ! — no vile cant, sure,
　About " need to strew the bleakness
Of some lone shore with its pearl-seed,
　That the sea feels " — no " strange yearning
That such souls have, most to lavish
　Where there 's chance of least returning."

Oh, we 're sunk enough here, God knows !
　But not quite so sunk that moments,
Sure though seldom, are denied us,
　When the spirit's true endowments
Stand out plainly from its false ones,
　And apprise it if pursuing
Or the right way or the wrong way,
　To its triumph or undoing.

There are flashes struck from midnights,
　There are fire-flames noondays kindle,
Whereby piled-up honors perish,
　Whereby swollen ambitions dwindle,

While just this or that poor impulse,
  Which for once had play unstifled,
Seems the sole work of a lifetime,
  That away the rest have trifled.

Doubt you if, in some such moment,
  As she fixed me, she felt clearly,
Ages past the soul existed,
  Here an age 't is resting merely,
And hence fleets again for ages,
  While the true end, sole and single,
It stops here for is, this love-way,
  With some other soul to mingle?

Else it loses what it lived for,
  And eternally must lose it ;
Better ends may be in prospect,
  Deeper blisses (if you choose it),
But this life's end and this love-bliss
  Have been lost here.   Doubt you whether
This she felt as, looking at me,
  Mine and her souls rushed together?

Oh, observe!   Of course, next moment,
  The world's honors, in derision,
Trampled out the light forever:
  Never fear but there 's provision
Of the devil's to quench knowledge
  Lest we walk the earth in rapture !
— Making those who catch God's secret
  Just so much more prize their capture !

Such am I : the secret 's mine now !
  She has lost me, I have gained her ;
Her soul 's mine : and thus, grown perfect,
  I shall pass my life's remainder.
Life will just hold out the proving
  Both our powers, alone and blended:
And then, come the next life quickly !
  This world's use will have been ended.

THE LOST MISTRESS

ALL 's over, then: does truth sound bitter
  As one at first believes ?
Hark, 't is the sparrows' good-night twitter
  About your cottage eaves !

And the leaf-buds on the vine are woolly,
  I noticed that, to-day ;
One day more bursts them open fully
  — You know the red turns gray.

To-morrow we meet the same then, dearest?
  May I take your hand in mine ?
Mere friends are we, — well, friends the merest
  Keep much that I resign :

For each glance of the eye so bright and black
  Though I keep with heart's endeavor, —
Your voice, when you wish the snowdrops back,
  Though it stay in my soul forever ! —

Yet I will but say what mere friends say,
  Or only a thought stronger ;
I will hold your hand but as long as all may,
  Or so very little longer !

EARTH'S IMMORTALITIES

FAME

SEE, as the prettiest graves will do in time,
Our poet's wants the freshness of its prime ;
Spite of the sexton's browsing horse, the sods
Have struggled through its binding osier rods
Headstone and half-sunk footstone lean awry,
Wanting the brick-work promised by-and-by ;
How the minute gray lichens, plate o'er plate,
Have softened down the crisp-cut name and
  date !

LOVE

So, the year 's done with !
  (Love me forever !)
All March begun with,
  April's endeavor ;
May-wreaths that bound me
  June needs must sever ;
Now snows fall round me,
  Quenching June's fever —
  (Love me forever !)

MEETING AT NIGHT

This and its companion piece were published
originally simply as Night and Morning.

THE gray sea and the long black land ;
And the yellow half-moon large and low ;
And the startled little waves that leap
In fiery ringlets from their sleep,
As I gain the cove with pushing prow,
And quench its speed i' the slushy sand.

Then a mile of warm sea-scented beach ;
Three fields to cross till a farm appears ;
A tap at the pane, the quick sharp scratch
And blue spurt of a lighted match,
And a voice less loud, through its joys and
  fears,
Than the two hearts beating each to each !

PARTING AT MORNING

ROUND the cape of a sudden came the sea,
And the sun looked over the mountain's rim :
And straight was a path of gold for him,
And the need of a world of men for me.

SONG

NAY but you, who do not love her,
  Is she not pure gold, my mistress ?
Holds earth aught — speak truth — above her
  Aught like this tress, see, and this tress,
And this last fairest tress of all,
So fair, see, ere I let it fall ?

Because you spend your lives in praising ;
  To praise, you search the wide world over :

Then why not witness, calmly gazing,
  If earth holds aught — speak truth — above
     her ?
Above this tress, and this, I touch
But cannot praise, I love so much !

A WOMAN'S LAST WORD

LET 's contend no more, Love,
  Strive nor weep :
All be as before, Love,
  — Only sleep !

What so wild as words are ?
  I and thou
In debate, as birds are,
  Hawk on bough !

See the creature stalking
  While we speak !
Hush and hide the talking,
  Cheek on cheek !

What so false as truth is,
  False to thee ?
Where the serpent's tooth is
  Shun the tree —

Where the apple reddens
  Never pry —
Lest we lose our Edens,
  Eve and I.

Be a god and hold me
  With a charm !
Be a man and fold me
  With thine arm !

Teach me, only teach, Love !
  As I ought
I will speak thy speech, Love,
  Think thy thought —

Meet, if thou require it,
  Both demands,
Laying flesh and spirit
  In thy hands.

That shall be to-morrow,
  Not to-night :
I must bury sorrow
  Out of sight :

— Must a little weep, Love,
  (Foolish me !)
And so fall asleep, Love,
  Loved by thee.

EVELYN HOPE

BEAUTIFUL Evelyn Hope is dead !
  Sit and watch by her side an hour.
That is her book-shelf, this her bed ;
  She plucked that piece of geranium-flower,
Beginning to die too, in the glass ;
  Little has yet been changed, I think :

The shutters are shut, no light may pass
  Save two long rays through the hinge's chink.

Sixteen years old when she died !
  Perhaps she had scarcely heard my name ;
It was not her time to love ; beside,
  Her life had many a hope and aim,
Duties enough and little cares,
  And now was quiet, now astir,
Till God's hand beckoned unawares, —
  And the sweet white brow is all of her.

Is it too late then, Evelyn Hope ?
  What, your soul was pure and true,
The good stars met in your horoscope,
  Made you of spirit, fire and dew —
And, just because I was thrice as old
  And our paths in the world diverged so wide,
Each was naught to each, must I be told ?
  We were fellow mortals, naught beside ?

No, indeed ! for God above
  Is great to grant, as mighty to make,
And creates the love to reward the love :
  I claim you still, for my own love's sake !
Delayed it may be for more lives yet,
  Through worlds I shall traverse, not a few :
Much is to learn, much to forget
  Ere the time be come for taking you.

But the time will come, — at last it will,
  When, Evelyn Hope, what meant (I shall say)
In the lower earth, in the years long still,
  That body and soul so pure and gay ?
Why your hair was amber, I shall divine,
  And your mouth of your own geranium's
    red —
And what you would do with me, in fine,
  In the new life come in the old one's stead.

I have lived (I shall say) so much since then,
  Given up myself so many times,
Gained me the gains of various men,
  Ransacked the ages, spoiled the climes ;
Yet one thing, one, in my soul's full scope,
  Either I missed or itself missed me :
And I want and find you, Evelyn Hope !
  What is the issue ? let us see !

I loved you, Evelyn, all the while !
  My heart seemed full as it could hold ;
There was place and to spare for the frank
    young smile,
  And the red young mouth, and the hair's
    young gold.
So, hush, — I will give you this leaf to keep :
  See, I shut it inside the sweet cold hand !
There, that is our secret : go to sleep !
  You will wake, and remember, and under-
    stand.

LOVE AMONG THE RUINS

WHERE the quiet-colored end of evening smiles
    Miles and miles
On the solitary pastures where our sheep
    Half-asleep

Tinkle homeward through the twilight, stray
or stop
    As they crop —
Was the site once of a city great and gay,
    (So they say)
Of our country's very capital, its prince
    Ages since
Held his court in, gathered councils, wielding far
    Peace or war.

Now, — the country does not even boast a tree,
    As you see,
To distinguish slopes of verdure, certain rills
    From the hills
Intersect and give a name to, (else they run
    Into one,)
Where the domed and daring palace shot its
spires
    Up like fires
O'er the hundred-gated circuit of a wall
    Bounding all,
Made of marble, men might march on nor be
pressed,
    Twelve abreast.

And such plenty and perfection, see, of grass
    Never was !
Such a carpet as, this summer-time, o'erspreads
    And embeds
Every vestige of the city, guessed alone,
    Stock or stone —
Where a multitude of men breathed joy and woe
    Long ago ;
Lust of glory pricked their hearts up, dread of
shame
    Struck them tame ;
And that glory and that shame alike, the gold
    Bought and sold.

Now, — the single little turret that remains
    On the plains,
By the caper overrooted, by the gourd
    Overscored,
While the patching houseleek's head of blos-
som winks
    Through the chinks —
Marks the basement whence a tower in ancient
time
    Sprang sublime,
And a burning ring, all round, the chariots
traced
    As they raced,
And the monarch and his minions and his
dames
    Viewed the games.

And I know, while thus the quiet-colored eve
    Smiles to leave
To their folding, all our many-tinkling fleece
    In such peace,
And the slopes and rills in undistinguished
gray
    Melt away —
That a girl with eager eyes and yellow hair
    Waits me there
In the turret whence the charioteers caught
soul
    For the goal,

When the king looked, where she looks now,
breathless, dumb
    Till I come.

But he looked upon the city, every side,
    Far and wide,
All the mountains topped with temples, all the
glades'
    Colonnades,
All the causeys, bridges, aqueducts, — and then,
    All the men !
When I do come, she will speak not, she will
stand,
    Either hand
On my shoulder, give her eyes the first embrace
    Of my face,
Ere we rush, ere we extinguish sight and speech
    Each on each.

In one year they sent a million fighters forth
    South and North,
And they built their gods a brazen pillar high
    As the sky,
Yet reserved a thousand chariots in full force —
    Gold, of course.
Oh heart ! oh blood that freezes, blood that
burns !
    Earth's returns
For whole centuries of folly, noise and sin !
    Shut them in,
With their triumphs and their glories and the
rest !
    Love is best.

A LOVERS' QUARREL

OH, what a dawn of day !
How the March sun feels like May !
    All is blue again
    After last night's rain,
And the South dries the hawthorn-spray.
    Only, my Love 's away !
I 'd as lief that the blue were gray.

Runnels, which rillets swell,
Must be dancing down the dell,
    With a foaming head
    On the beryl bed
Paven smooth as a hermit's cell ;
    Each with a tale to tell,
Could my Love but attend as well.

Dearest, three months ago !
When we lived blocked-up with snow, —
    When the wind would edge
    In and in his wedge,
In, as far as the point could go —
    Not to our ingle, though,
Where we loved each the other so !

Laughs with so little cause !
We devised games out of straws,
    We would try and trace
    One another's face
In the ash, as an artist draws ;
    Free on each other's flaws,
How we chattered like two church daws !

What 's in the " Times " ? — a scold
At the Emperor deep and cold ;
 He has taken a bride
 To his gruesome side,
That 's as fair as himself is bold :
 There they sit ermine-stoled,
And she powders her hair with gold.

Fancy the Pampas' sheen !
Miles and miles of gold and green
 Where the sunflowers blow
 In a solid glow,
And — to break now and then the screen —
 Black neck and eyeballs keen,
Up a wild horse leaps between !

Try, will our table turn ?
Lay your hands there light, and yearn
 Till the yearning slips
 Through the finger-tips
In a fire which a few discern,
 And a very few feel burn,
And the rest, they may live and learn !

Then we would up and pace,
For a change, about the place,
 Each with arm o'er neck :
 'T is our quarter-deck,
We are seamen in woeful case.
 Help in the ocean-space !
Or, if no help, we 'll embrace.

See, how she looks now, dressed
In a sledging-cap and vest !
 'T is a huge fur cloak —
 Like a reindeer's yoke
Falls the lappet along the breast :
 Sleeves for her arms to rest,
Or to hang, as my Love likes best.

Teach me to flirt a fan
As the Spanish ladies can,
 Or I tint your lip
 With a burnt stick's tip
And you turn into such a man !
 Just the two spots that span
Half the bill of the young male swan.

Dearest, three months ago
When the mesmerizer Snow
 With his hand's first sweep
 Put the earth to sleep :
'T was a time when the heart could show
 All — how was earth to know,
'Neath the mute hand's to-and-fro ?

Dearest, three months ago
When we loved each other so,
 Lived and loved the same
 Till an evening came
When a shaft from the devil's bow
 Pierced to our ingle-glow,
And the friends were friend and foe !

Not from the heart beneath —
'T was a bubble born of breath,
 Neither sneer nor vaunt,
 Nor reproach nor taunt.

See a word, how it severeth !
 Oh, power of life and death
In the tongue, as the Preacher saith !

Woman, and will you cast
For a word, quite off at last
 Me, your own, your You, —
 Since, as truth is true,
I was You all the happy past —
 Me do you leave aghast
With the memories We amassed ?

Love, if you knew the light
That your soul casts in my sight,
 How I look to you
 For the pure and true,
And the beauteous and the right, —
 Bear with a moment's spite
When a mere mote threats the white !

What of a hasty word ?
Is the fleshly heart not stirred
 By a worm's pin-prick
 Where its roots are quick ?
See the eye, by a fly's-foot blurred —
 Ear, when a straw is heard
Scratch the brain's coat of curd !

Foul be the world or fair
More or less, how can I care ?
 'T is the world the same
 For my praise or blame,
And endurance is easy there.
 Wrong in the one thing rare —
Oh, it is hard to bear !

Here 's the spring back or close,
When the almond-blossom blows ;
 We shall have the word
 In a minor third,
There is none but the cuckoo knows :
 Heaps of the guelder-rose !
I must bear with it, I suppose.

Could but November come,
Were the noisy birds struck dumb
 At the warning slash
 Of his driver's-lash —
I would laugh like the valiant Thumb
 Facing the castle glum
And the giant's fee-faw-fum !

Then, were the world well stripped
Of the gear wherein equipped
 We can stand apart,
 Heart dispense with heart
In the sun, with the flowers unnipped, —
 Oh, the world's hangings ripped,
We were both in a bare-walled crypt !

Each in the crypt would cry
" But one freezes here ! and why ?
 When a heart, as chill,
 At my own would thrill
Back to life, and its fires out-fly ?
 Heart, shall we live or die ?
The rest, . . . settle by and by ! "

So, she 'd efface the score,
And forgive me as before.
It is twelve o'clock :
I shall hear her knock
In the worst of a storm's uproar,
I shall pull her through the door,
I shall have her for evermore !

UP AT A VILLA — DOWN IN THE CITY

(AS DISTINGUISHED BY AN ITALIAN PERSON OF
QUALITY)

HAD I but plenty of money, money enough and
to spare,
The house for me, no doubt, were a house in the
city-square ;
Ah, such a life, such a life, as one leads at the
window there !

Something to see, by Bacchus, something to
hear, at least !
There, the whole day long, one's life is a perfect
feast ;
While up at a villa one lives, I maintain it, no
more than a beast.

Well now, look at our villa ! stuck like the horn
of a bull
Just on a mountain-edge as bare as the crea-
ture's skull,
Save a mere shag of a bush with hardly a leaf
to pull !
— I scratch my own, sometimes, to see if the
hair 's turned wool.

But the city, oh the city — the square with the
houses ! Why ?
They are stone-faced, white as a curd, there 's
something to take the eye !
Houses in four straight lines, not a single front
awry ;
You watch who crosses and gossips, who saun-
ters, who hurries by ;
Green blinds, as a matter of course, to draw
when the sun gets high ;
And the shops with fanciful signs which are
painted properly.

What of a villa ? Though winter be over in
March by rights,
'T is May perhaps ere the snow shall have with-
ered well off the heights :
You 've the brown ploughed land before, where
the oxen steam and wheeze,
And the hills over-smoked behind by the faint
gray olive-trees.

Is it better in May, I ask you ? You 've sum-
mer all at once ;
In a day he leaps complete with a few strong
April suns.
'Mid the sharp short emerald wheat, scarce
risen three fingers well,
The wild tulip, at end of its tube, blows out its
great red bell
Like a thin clear bubble of blood, for the
children to pick and sell.

Is it ever hot in the square ? There 's a foun-
tain to spout and splash !
In the shade it sings and springs ; in the shine
such foambows flash
On the horses with curling fish-tails, that prance
and paddle and pash
Round the lady atop in her conch — fifty gazers
do not abash,
Though all that she wears is some weeds round
her waist in a sort of sash.

All the year long at the villa, nothing to see
though you linger,
Except yon cypress that points like death's lean
lifted forefinger.
Some think fireflies pretty, when they mix i' the
corn and mingle,
Or thrid the stinking hemp till the stalks of it
seem a-tingle.
Late August or early September, the stunning
cicala is shrill,
And the bees keep their tiresome whine round
the resinous firs on the hill.
Enough of the seasons, — I spare you the
months of the fever and chill.

Ere you open your eyes in the city, the blessed
church-bells begin :
No sooner the bells leave off than the diligence
rattles in :
You get the pick of the news, and it costs you
never a pin.
By and by there 's the travelling doctor gives
pills, lets blood, draws teeth ;
Or the Pulcinello-trumpet breaks up the mar-
ket beneath.
At the post-office such a scene-picture — the
new play, piping hot !
And a notice how, only this morning, three
liberal thieves were shot.
Above it, behold the Archbishop's most fa-
therly of rebukes,
And beneath, with his crown and his lion, some
little new law of the Duke's !
Or a sonnet with flowery marge, to the Rever-
end Don So-and-so,
Who is Dante, Boccaccio, Petrarca, Saint Je-
rome, and Cicero,
"And moreover," (the sonnet goes rhyming,)
"the skirts of Saint Paul has reached,
Having preached us those six Lent-lectures more
unctuous than ever he preached."
Noon strikes, — here sweeps the procession !
our Lady borne smiling and smart
With a pink gauze gown all spangles, and seven
swords stuck in her heart !
Bang-whang-whang goes the drum, *tootle-te-
tootle* the fife ;
No keeping one's haunches still : it 's the great-
est pleasure in life.

But bless you, it 's dear — it 's dear ! fowls,
wine, at double the rate.
They have clapped a new tax upon salt, and
what oil pays passing the gate
It 's a horror to think of. And so, the villa for
me, not the city !

Beggars can scarcely be choosers: but still —
  ah, the pity, the pity!
Look, two and two go the priests, then the
  monks with cowls and sandals,
And the penitents dressed in white shirts,
  a-holding the yellow candles;
One, he carries a flag up straight, and another
  a cross with handles,
And the Duke's guard brings up the rear, for
  the better prevention of scandals:
Bang-whang-whang goes the drum, tootle-te-tootle
  the fife.
Oh, a day in the city-square, there is no such
  pleasure in life!

A TOCCATA OF GALUPPI'S

Published in *Men and Women* in 1855. An
American author, visiting Browning and his
wife at Casa Guidi in 1847, wrote of their occu-
pations: "Mrs. Browning," he said, "was still
too much of an invalid to walk, but she sat
under the great trees upon the lawn-like hill-
sides near the convent, or in the seats of the
dusky convent chapel, while Robert Browning
at the organ chased a fugue, or dreamed out
upon the twilight keys a faint throbbing *toccata*
of Galuppi."

Oh Galuppi, Baldassare, this is very sad to
  find!
I can hardly misconceive you; it would prove
  me deaf and blind;
But although I take your meaning, 't is with
  such a heavy mind!

Here you come with your old music, and here 's
  all the good it brings.
What, they lived once thus at Venice where
  the merchants were the kings,
Where St. Mark's is, where the Doges used to
  wed the sea with rings?

Ay, because the sea 's the street there; and
  't is arched by . . . what you call
. . . Shylock's bridge with houses on it, where
  they kept the carnival:
I was never out of England — it 's as if I saw it
  all.

Did young people take their pleasure when the
  sea was warm in May?
Balls and masks begun at midnight, burning
  ever to mid-day,
When they made up fresh adventures for the
  morrow, do you say?

Was a lady such a lady, cheeks so round and
  lips so red, —
On her neck the small face buoyant, like a bell-
  flower on its bed,
O'er the breast's superb abundance where a
  man might base his head?

Well, and it was graceful of them — they 'd
  break talk off and afford

— She, to bite her mask's black velvet — he, to
  finger on his sword,
While you sat and played Toccatas, stately at
  the clavichord?

What? Those lesser thirds so plaintive, sixths
  diminished, sigh on sigh,
Told them something? Those suspensions,
  those solutions — "Must we die?"
Those commiserating sevenths — "Life might
  last! we can but try!"

"Were you happy?" — "Yes." — "And are
  you still as happy?" — "Yes. And
  you?"
— "Then, more kisses!" — "Did *I* stop them,
  when a million seemed so few?"
Hark, the dominant's persistence till it must
  be answered to!

So, an octave struck the answer. Oh, they
  praised you, I dare say!
"Brave Galuppi! that was music! good alike
  at grave and gay!
I can always leave off talking when I hear a
  master play!"

Then they left you for their pleasure: till in
  due time, one by one,
Some with lives that came to nothing, some
  with deeds as well undone,
Death stepped tacitly and took them where
  they never see the sun.

But when I sit down to reason, think to take
  my stand nor swerve,
While I triumph o'er a secret wrung from na-
  ture's close reserve,
In you come with your cold music till I creep
  through every nerve.

Yes, you, like a ghostly cricket, creaking where
  a house was burned:
"Dust and ashes, dead and done with, Venice
  spent what Venice earned.
The soul, doubtless, is immortal — where a soul
  can be discerned.

"Yours for instance: you know physics, some-
  thing of geology,
Mathematics are your pastime; souls shall rise
  in their degree;
Butterflies may dread extinction, — you 'll not
  die, it cannot be!

"As for Venice and her people, merely born
  to bloom and drop,
Here on earth they bore their fruitage, mirth
  and folly were the crop:
What of soul was left, I wonder, when the kiss-
  ing had to stop?

"Dust and ashes!" So you creak it, and I
  want the heart to scold.
Dear dead women, with such hair, too — what 's
  become of all the gold
Used to hang and brush their bosoms? I feel
  chilly and grown old.

OLD PICTURES IN FLORENCE

The morn when first it thunders in March,
 The eel in the pond gives a leap, they say :
As I leaned and looked over the aloed arch
 Of the villa-gate this warm March day,
No flash snapped, no dumb thunder rolled
 In the valley beneath where, white and wide
And washed by the morning water-gold,
 Florence lay out on the mountain-side.

River and bridge and street and square
 Lay mine, as much at my beck and call,
Through the live translucent bath of air,
 As the sights in a magic crystal ball.
And of all I saw and of all I praised,
 The most to praise and the best to see,
Was the startling bell-tower Giotto raised :
 But why did it more than startle me ?

Giotto, how, with that soul of yours,
 Could you play me false who loved you so ?
Some slights if a certain heart endures
 Yet it feels, I would have your fellows know !
I' faith, I perceive not why I should care
 To break a silence that suits them best,
But the thing grows somewhat hard to bear
 When I find a Giotto join the rest.

On the arch where olives overhead
 Print the blue sky with twig and leaf,
(That sharp-curled leaf which they never shed)
 'Twixt the aloes, I used to lean in chief,
And mark through the winter afternoons,
 By a gift God grants me now and then,
In the mild decline of those suns like moons,
 Who walked in Florence, besides her men.

They might chirp and chaffer, come and go
 For pleasure or profit, her men alive —
My business was hardly with them, I trow,
 But with empty cells of the human hive ;
— With the chapter-room, the cloister-porch,
 The church's apsis, aisle or nave,
Its crypt, one fingers along with a torch,
 Its face set full for the sun to shave.

Wherever a fresco peels and drops,
 Wherever an outline weakens and wanes
Till the latest life in the painting stops,
 Stands One whom each fainter pulse-tick
  pains :
One, wishful each scrap should clutch the brick,
 Each tinge not wholly escape the plaster,
— A lion who dies of an ass's kick,
 The wronged great soul of an ancient Master.

For oh, this world and the wrong it does !
 They are safe in heaven with their backs to
  it,
The Michaels and Rafaels, you hum and buzz
 Round the works of, you of the little wit !
Do their eyes contract to the earth's old scope,
 Now that they see God face to face,
And have all attained to be poets, I hope ?
 'T is their holiday now, in any case.

Much they reck of your praise and you !
 But the wronged great souls — can they be
  quit
Of a world where their work is all to do,
 Where you style them, you of the little wit,
Old Master This and Early the Other,
 Not dreaming that Old and New are fellows :
A younger succeeds to an elder brother,
 Da Vincis derive in good time from Dellos.

And here where your praise might yield returns,
 And a handsome word or two give help,
Here, after your kind, the mastiff girns
 And the puppy pack of poodles yelp.
What, not a word for Stefano there,
 Of brow once prominent and starry,
Called Nature's Ape, and the world's despair
 For his peerless painting ? (See Vasari.)

There stands the Master. Study, my friends,
 What a man's work comes to ! So he plans
  it,
Performs it, perfects it, makes amends
 For the toiling and moiling, and then, sic
  transit !
Happier the thrifty blind-folk labor,
 With upturned eye while the hand is busy,
Not sidling a glance at the coin of their
  neighbor !
 'T is looking downward that makes one dizzy.

" If you knew their work you would deal your
  dole."
 May I take upon me to instruct you ?
When Greek Art ran and reached the goal,
 Thus much had the world to boast in fructu —
The Truth of Man, as by God first spoken,
 Which the actual generations garble,
Was re-uttered, and Soul (which Limbs betoken)
 And Limbs (Soul informs) made new in
  marble.

So you saw yourself as you wished you were,
 As you might have been, as you cannot be :
Earth here, rebuked by Olympus there :
 And grew content in your poor degree
With your little power, by those statues' god-
  head,
 And your little scope, by their eyes' full sway,
And your little grace, by their grace embodied,
 And your little date, by their forms that stay.

You would fain be kinglier, say, than I am ?
 Even so, you will not sit like Theseus.
You would prove a model ? The Son of Priam
 Has yet the advantage in arms' and knees'
  use.
You 're wroth — can you slay your snake like
  Apollo ?
 You 're grieved — still Niobe 's the grander !
You live — there 's the Racers' frieze to follow :
 You die — there 's the dying Alexander.

So, testing your weakness by their strength,
 Your meagre charms by their rounded beauty,
Measured by Art in your breadth and length,
 You learned — to submit is a mortal's duty.

—When I say " you " 't is the common soul,
  The collective, I mean : the race of Man
That receives life in parts to live in a whole,
  And grow here according to God's clear plan.

Growth came when, looking your last on them
    all,
  You turned your eyes inwardly one fine day
And cried with a start — What if we so small
  Be greater and grander the while than they ?
Are they perfect of lineament, perfect of stat-
    ure ?
  In both, of such lower types are we
Precisely because of our wider nature ;
  For time, theirs — ours, for eternity.

To-day's brief passion limits their range ;
  It seethes with the morrow for us and more.
They are perfect — how else ? they shall never
    change :
  We are faulty — why not ? we have time in
    store.
The Artificer's hand is not arrested
  With us ; we are rough-hewn, nowise pol-
    ished :
They stand for our copy, and, once invested
  With all they can teach, we shall see them
    abolished.

'T is a life-long toil till our lump be leaven —
  The better ! What 's come to perfection
    perishes.
Things learned on earth, we shall practise in
    heaven :
  Works done least rapidly, Art most cherishes.
Thyself shalt afford the example, Giotto !
  Thy one work, not to decrease or diminish,
Done at a stroke, was just (was it not ?) "O ! "
  Thy great Campanile is still to finish.

Is it true that we are now, and shall be here-
    after,
  But what and where depend on life's minute ?
Hails heavenly cheer or infernal laughter
  Our first step out of the gulf or in it ?
Shall Man, such step within his endeavor,
  Man's face, have no more play and action
Than joy which is crystallized forever,
  Or grief, an eternal petrifaction ?

On which I conclude, that the early painters,
  To cries of " Greek Art and what more wish
    you ? " —
Replied, " To become now self-acquainters,
  And paint man, man, whatever the issue !
Make new hopes shine through the flesh they
    fray,
  New fears aggrandize the rags and tatters :
To bring the invisible full into play !
  Let the visible go to the dogs — what mat-
    ters ? "

Give these, I exhort you, their guerdon and
    glory
  For daring so much, before they well did it.
The first of the new, in our race's story,
  Beats the last of the old ; 't is no idle quiddit.
The worthies began a revolution,

Which if on earth you intend to acknowledge,
Why, honor them now ! (ends my allocution)
  Nor confer your degree when the folk leave
    college.

There 's a fancy some lean to and others hate —
  That, when this life is ended, begins
New work for the soul in another state,
  Where it strives and gets weary, loses and
    wins :
Where the strong and the weak, this world's
    congeries,
  Repeat in large what they practised in small,
Through life after life in unlimited series ;
  Only the scale 's to be changed, that 's all.

Yet I hardly know. When a soul has seen
  By the means of Evil that Good is best,
And, through earth and its noise, what is
    heaven's serene, —
  When our faith in the same has stood the
    test —
Why, the child grown man, you burn the rod,
  The uses of labor are surely done ;
There remaineth a rest for the people of God :
  And I have had troubles enough, for one.

But at any rate I have loved the season
  Of Art's spring-birth so dim and dewy ;
My sculptor is Nicolo the Pisan,
  My painter — who but Cimabue ?
Nor ever was man of them all indeed,
  From these to Ghiberti and Ghirlandajo,
Could say that he missed my critic-meed.
  So, now to my special grievance — heigh-ho !

Their ghosts still stand, as I said before,
  Watching each fresco flaked and rasped,
Blocked up, knocked out, or whitewashed o'er :
  — No getting again what the church has
    grasped !
The works on the wall must take their chance ;
  " Works never conceded to England's thick
    clime ! "
(I hope they prefer their inheritance
  Of a bucketful of Italian quick-lime.)

When they go at length, with such a shaking
  Of heads o'er the old delusion, sadly
Each master his way through the black streets
    taking,
  Where many a lost work breathes though
    badly —
Why don't they bethink them of who has mer-
    ited ?
  Why not reveal, while their pictures dree
Such doom, how a captive might be out-ferreted ?
  Why is it they never remember me ?

Not that I expect the great Bigordi,
  Nor Sandro to hear me, chivalric, bellicose ;
Nor the wronged Lippino ; and not a word I
  Say of a scrap of Frà Angelico's :
But are you too fine, Taddeo Gaddi,
  To grant me a taste of your intonaco,
Some Jerome that seeks the heaven with a sad
    eye ?
  Not a churlish saint, Lorenzo Monaco ?

Could not the ghost with the close red cap,
  My Pollajolo, the twice a craftsman,
Save me a sample, give me the hap
  Of a muscular Christ that shows the draughts-
    man?
No Virgin by him the somewhat petty,
  Of finical touch and tempera crumbly —
Could not Alesso Baldovinetti
  Contribute so much, I ask him humbly?

Margheritone of Arezzo,
  With the grave-clothes garb and swaddling
    barret,
(Why purse up mouth and beak in a pet so,
  You bald old saturnine poll-clawed parrot?)
Not a poor glimmering Crucifixion,
  Where in the foreground kneels the donor?
If such remain, as is my conviction,
  The hoarding it does you but little honor.

They pass; for them the panels may thrill,
  The tempera grow alive and tinglish;
Their pictures are left to the mercies still
  Of dealers and stealers, Jews and the Eng-
    lish,
Who, seeing mere money's worth in their prize,
  Will sell it to somebody calm as Zeno
At naked High Art, and in ecstasies
  Before some clay-cold vile Carlino!

No matter for these! But Giotto, you,
  Have you allowed, as the town-tongues babble
    it, —
Oh, never! it shall not be counted true —
  That a certain precious little tablet
Which Buonarroti eyed like a lover —
  Was buried so long in oblivion's womb
And, left for another than I to discover,
  Turns up at last! and to whom? — to whom?

I, that have haunted the dim San Spirito,
  (Or was it rather the Ognissanti?)
Patient on altar-step planting a weary toe!
  Nay, I shall have it yet! *Detur amanti*!
My Koh-i-noor — or (if that's a platitude)
  Jewel of Giamschid, the Persian Sofi's eye;
So, in anticipative gratitude,
  What if I take up my hope and prophesy?

When the hour grows ripe, and a certain do-
    tard
  Is pitched, no parcel that needs invoicing,
To the worse side of the Mont St. Gothard,
  We shall begin by way of rejoicing;
None of that shooting the sky (blank cartridge),
  Nor a civic guard, all plumes and lacquer,
Hunting Radetzky's soul like a partridge
  Over Morello with squib and cracker.

This time we'll shoot better game and bag 'em
    hot —
  No mere display at the stone of Dante,
But a kind of sober Witanagemot
  (Ex: "Casa Guidi," *quod videas ante*)
Shall ponder, once Freedom restored to Florence,
  How Art may return that departed with her.
Go, hated house, go each trace of the Loraine's,
  And bring us the days of Orgagna hither!

How we shall prologuize, how we shall perorate,
  Utter fit things upon art and history,
Feel truth at blood-heat and falsehood at zero
    rate,
  Make of the want of the age no mystery;
Contrast the fructuous and sterile eras,
  Show — monarchy ever its uncouth cub licks
Out of the bear's shape into Chimæra's,
  While Pure Art's birth is still the republic's.

Then one shall propose in a speech (curt Tuscan,
  Expurgate and sober, with scarcely an
    "*issimo*,")
To end now our half-told tale of Cambuscan,
  And turn the bell-tower's *alt* to *altissimo*:
And fine as the beak of a young beccaccia
  The Campanile, the Duomo's fit ally,
Shall soar up in gold full fifty braccia,
  Completing Florence, as Florence Italy.

Shall I be alive that morning the scaffold
  Is broken away, and the long-pent fire,
Like the golden hope of the world, unbaffled
  Springs from its sleep, and up goes the spire
While "God and the People" plain for its
    motto,
  Thence the new tricolor flaps at the sky?
At least to foresee that glory of Giotto
  And Florence together, the first am I!

"DE GUSTIBUS — "

YOUR ghost will walk, you lover of trees,
    (If our loves remain)
      In an English lane,
By a cornfield-side a-flutter with poppies.
Hark, those two in the hazel coppice —
  A boy and a girl, if the good fates please,
    Making love, say, —
    The happier they!
Draw yourself up from the light of the moon,
And let them pass, as they will too soon,
    With the beanflowers' boon,
    And the blackbird's tune,
    And May, and June!

What I love best in all the world
Is a castle, precipice-encurled,
In a gash of the wind-grieved Apennine.
Or look for me, old fellow of mine,
  (If I get my head from out the mouth
  O' the grave, and loose my spirit's bands,
  And come again to the land of lands) —
In a sea-side house to the farther South,
Where the baked cicala dies of drouth,
And one sharp tree — 't is a cypress — stands
By the many hundred years red-rusted,
Rough iron-spiked, ripe fruit-o'ercrusted,
My sentinel to guard the sands
To the water's edge. For, what expands
Before the house, but the great opaque
Blue breadth of sea without a break?
While, in the house, forever crumbles
Some fragment of the frescoed walls,
From blisters where a scorpion sprawls.
A girl bare-footed brings, and tumbles
Down on the pavement, green-flesh melons,

And says there 's news to-day — the king
Was shot at, touched in the liver-wing,
Goes with his Bourbon arm in a sling:
— She hopes they have not caught the felons.
Italy, my Italy!
Queen Mary's saying serves for me —
    (When fortune's malice
      Lost her, Calais)
Open my heart and you will see
Graved inside of it, " Italy."
Such lovers old are I and she :
So it always was, so shall ever be !

HOME-THOUGHTS, FROM ABROAD

This and the following poem were first published along with *Beer*, which bore the name *Here 's to Nelson's Memory*, under the general reading *Home-Thoughts, from Abroad*. The final member of the group, *Home-Thoughts, from the Sea*, was written under the same circumstances as the poem, *How They brought the Good News from Ghent to Aix*.

Oh, to be in England
Now that April 's there,
And whoever wakes in England
Sees, some morning, unaware,
That the lowest boughs and the brush-wood
    sheaf
Round the elm-tree bole are in tiny leaf,
While the chaffinch sings on the orchard bough
In England — now !

And after April, when May follows,
And the whitethroat builds, and all the swallows !
Hark, where my blossomed pear-tree in the
    hedge
Leans to the field and scatters on the clover
Blossoms and dewdrops — at the bent spray's
    edge —
That 's the wise thrush ; he sings each song
    twice over,
Lest you should think he never could recapture
The first fine careless rapture !
And though the fields look rough with hoary
    dew,
All will be gay when noontide wakes anew
The buttercups, the little children's dower
— Far brighter than this gaudy melon-flower !

HOME-THOUGHTS, FROM THE SEA

Nobly, nobly Cape Saint Vincent to the Northwest died away ;
Sunset ran, one glorious blood-red, reeking into
    Cadiz Bay ;
Bluish 'mid the burning water, full in face Trafalgar lay ;
In the dimmest Northeast distance dawned
    Gibraltar grand and gray ;
" Here and here did England help me : how can
    I help England ? " — say,
Whoso turns as I, this evening, turn to God to
    praise and pray,
While Jove's planet rises yonder, silent over
    Africa.

SAUL

The first nine sections of this poem were printed under the same title in No. VII. of *Bells and Pomegranates*, in 1845. The poem as enlarged was published in *Men and Women* in 1855.

I

Said Abner, " At last thou art come ! Ere I
    tell, ere thou speak,
Kiss my cheek, wish me well ! " Then I wished
    it, and did kiss his cheek.
And he : " Since the King, O my friend, for thy
    countenance sent,
Neither drunken nor eaten have we ; nor until
    from his tent
Thou return with the joyful assurance the King
    liveth yet,
Shall our lip with the honey be bright, with the
    water be wet.
For out of the black mid-tent's silence, a space
    of three days,
Not a sound hath escaped to thy servants, of
    prayer nor of praise,
To betoken that Saul and the Spirit have ended
    their strife,
And that, faint in his triumph, the monarch
    sinks back upon life.

II

" Yet now my heart leaps, O beloved ! God's
    child with his dew
On thy gracious gold hair, and those lilies still
    living and blue
Just broken to twine round thy harp-strings, as
    if no wild heat
Were now raging to torture the desert ! "

III
                  Then I, as was meet,
Knelt down to the God of my fathers, and rose
    on my feet,
And ran o'er the sand burnt to powder. The
    tent was unlooped ;
I pulled up the spear that obstructed, and
    under I stooped ;
Hands and knees on the slippery grass-patch,
    all withered and gone,
That extends to the second enclosure, I groped
    my way on
Till I felt where the foldskirts fly open. Then
    once more I prayed,
And opened the foldskirts and entered, and was
    not afraid
But spoke, " Here is David, thy servant ! "
    And no voice replied.
At the first I saw naught but the blackness :
    but soon I descried
A something more black than the blackness —
    the vast, the upright
Main prop which sustains the pavilion : and slow
    into sight

Grew a figure against it, gigantic and blackest
    of all.
Then a sunbeam, that burst through the tent-
    roof, showed Saul.

IV

He stood as erect as that tent-prop, both arms
    stretched out wide
On the great cross-support in the centre, that
    goes to each side ;
He relaxed not a muscle, but hung there as,
    caught in his pangs
And waiting his change, the king-serpent all
    heavily hangs,
Far away from his kind, in the pine, till deliv-
    erance come
With the spring-time, — so agonized Saul, drear
    and stark, blind and dumb.

V

Then I tuned my harp, — took off the lilies we
    twine round its chords
Lest they snap 'neath the stress of the noontide
    — those sunbeams like swords !
And I first played the tune all our sheep know,
    as, one after one,
So docile they come to the pen-door till folding
    be done.
They are white and untorn by the bushes, for
    lo, they have fed
Where the long grasses stifle the water within
    the stream's bed ;
And now one after one seeks its lodging, as star
    follows star
Into eve and the blue far above us, — so blue
    and so far !

VI

— Then the tune for which quails on the corn-
    land will each leave his mate
To fly after the player ; then, what makes the
    crickets elate
Till for boldness they fight one another ; and
    then, what has weight
To set the quick jerboa a-musing outside his
    sand house —
There are none such as he for a wonder, half
    bird and half mouse !
God made all the creatures and gave them our
    love and our fear,
To give sign, we and they are his children, one
    family here.

VII

Then I played the help-tune of our reapers,
    their wine-song, when hand
Grasps at hand, eye lights eye in good friend-
    ship, and great hearts expand
And grow one in the sense of this world's life.
    — And then, the last song
When the dead man is praised on his journey —
    " Bear, bear him along,
With his few faults shut up like dead flowerets !
    Are balm seeds not here
To console us ? The land has none left such as
    he on the bier.
Oh, would we might keep thee, my brother ! "
    — And then, the glad chaunt

Of the marriage, — first go the young maidens
    next, she whom we vaunt
As the beauty, the pride of our dwelling. — And
    then, the great march
Wherein man runs to man to assist him and
    buttress an arch
Naught can break ; who shall harm them, our
    friends ? Then, the chorus intoned
As the Levites go up to the altar in glory en-
    throned.
But I stopped here : for here in the darkness
    Saul groaned.

VIII

And I paused, held my breath in such silence,
    and listened apart ;
And the tent shook, for mighty Saul shuddered :
    and sparkles 'gan dart
From the jewels that woke in his turban, at
    once with a start,
All its lordly male-sapphires, and rubies coura-
    geous at heart.
So the head : but the body still moved not, still
    hung there erect.
And I bent once again to my playing, pursued
    it unchecked,
As I sang : —

IX

" Oh, our manhood's prime vigor ! No spirit
    feels waste,
Not a muscle is stopped in its playing nor sinew
    unbraced.
Oh, the wild joys of living ! the leaping from
    rock up to rock,
The strong rending of boughs from the fir-tree,
    the cool silver shock
Of the plunge in a pool's living water, the hunt
    of the bear,
And the sultriness showing the lion is couched
    in his lair.
And the meal, the rich dates yellowed over with
    gold dust divine,
And the locust-flesh steeped in the pitcher, the
    full draught of wine,
And the sleep in the dried river-channel where
    bulrushes tell
That the water was wont to go warbling so
    softly and well.
How good is man's life, the mere living ! how
    fit to employ
All the heart and the soul and the senses for-
    ever in joy !
Hast thou loved the white locks of thy father,
    whose sword thou didst guard
When he trusted thee forth with the armies
    for glorious reward ?
Didst thou see the thin hands of thy mother,
    held up as men sung
The low song of the nearly-departed, and heard
    her faint tongue
Joining in while it could to the witness, ' Let
    one more attest,
I have lived, seen God's hand through a life-
    time, and all was for best ' ?
Then they sung through their tears in strong
    triumph, not much, but the rest.

And thy brothers, the help and the contest, the
 working whence grew
Such result as, from seething grape-bundles, the
 spirit strained true :
And the friends of thy boyhood — that boyhood
 of wonder and hope,
Present promise and wealth of the future beyond
 the eye's scope, —
Till lo, thou art grown to a monarch ; a people
 is thine ;
And all gifts, which the world offers singly, on
 one head combine !
On one head, all the beauty and strength, love
 and rage (like the throe
That, a-work in the rock, helps its labor and
 lets the gold go)
High ambition and deeds which surpass it, fame
 crowning them, — all
Brought to blaze on the head of one creature —
 King Saul ! "

X

And lo, with that leap of my spirit, — heart,
 hand, harp and voice,
Each lifting Saul's name out of sorrow, each
 bidding rejoice
Saul's fame in the light it was made for — as
 when, dare I say,
The Lord's army, in rapture of service, strains
 through its array,
And upsoareth the cherubim-chariot — " Saul ! "
 cried I, and stopped,
And waited the thing that should follow. Then
 Saul, who hung propped
By the tent's cross-support in the centre, was
 struck by his name.
Have ye seen when Spring's arrowy summons
 goes right to the aim,
And some mountain, the last to withstand her,
 that held (he alone,
While the vale laughed in freedom and flowers)
 on a broad bust of stone
A year's snow bound about for a breastplate, —
 leaves grasp of the sheet ?
Fold on fold all at once it crowds thunderously
 down to his feet,
And there fronts you, stark, black, but alive
 yet, your mountain of old,
With his rents, the successive bequeathings of
 ages untold —
Yea, each harm got in fighting your battles,
 each furrow and scar   .
Of his head thrust 'twixt you and the tempest
 — all hail, there they are !
— Now again to be softened with verdure, again
 hold the nest
Of the dove, tempt the goat and its young to
 the green on his crest
For their food in the ardors of summer. One
 long shudder thrilled
All the tent till the very air tingled, then sank
 and was stilled
At the King's self left standing before me, re-
 leased and aware.
What was gone, what remained ? All to tra-
 verse 'twixt hope and despair,
Death was past, life not come : so he waited.
 Awhile his right hand

Held the brow, helped the eyes left too vacant
 forthwith to remand
To their place what new objects should enter:
 't was Saul as before.
I looked up and dared gaze at those eyes, nor
 was hurt any more
Than by slow pallid sunsets in autumn, ye
 watch from the shore,
At their sad level gaze o'er the ocean — a sun's
 slow decline
Over hills which, resolved in stern silence, o'er-
 lap and entwine
Base with base to knit strength more intensely :
 so, arm folded arm
O'er the chest whose slow heavings subsided.

XI

What spell or what charm,
(For awhile there was trouble within me,) what
 next should I urge
To sustain him where song had restored him ?
 — Song filled to the verge
His cup with the wine of this life, pressing all
 that it yields
Of mere fruitage, the strength and the beauty:
 beyond, on what fields,
Glean a vintage more potent and perfect to
 brighten the eye
And bring blood to the lip, and commend them
 the cup they put by ?
He saith, " It is good ; " still he drinks not : he
 lets me praise life,
Gives assent, yet would die for his own part.

XII

Then fancies grew rife
Which had come long ago on the pasture, when
 round me the sheep
Fed in silence — above, the one eagle wheeled
 slow as in sleep ;
And I lay in my hollow and mused on the world
 that might lie
'Neath his ken, though I saw but the strip
 'twixt the hill and the sky:
And I laughed — " Since my days are ordained
 to be passed with my flocks,
Let me people at least, with my fancies, the
 plains and the rocks,
Dream the life I am never to mix with, and
 image the show
Of mankind as they live in those fashions I
 hardly shall know !
Schemes of life, its best rules and right uses,
 the courage that gains,
And the prudence that keeps what men strive
 for." And now these old trains
Of vague thought came again ; I grew surer ;
 so, once more the string
Of my harp made response to my spirit, as
 thus —

XIII

" Yea, my King,"
I began — " thou dost well in rejecting mere
 comforts that spring
From the mere mortal life held in common by
 man and by brute :
In our flesh grows the branch of this life, in our
 soul it bears fruit.

Thou hast marked the slow rise of the tree, —
  how its stem trembled first
Till it passed the kid's lip, the stag's antler;
  then safely outburst
The fan-branches all round ; and thou mindest
  when these too, in turn,
Broke a-bloom and the palm-tree seemed per-
  fect : yet more was to learn,
E'en the good that comes in with the palm-fruit.
  Our dates shall we slight,
When their juice brings a cure for all sorrow ?
  or care for the plight
Of the palm's self whose slow growth produced
  them ? Not so ! stem and branch
Shall decay, nor be known in their place, while
  the palm-wine shall stanch
Every wound of man's spirit in winter. I pour
  thee such wine.
Leave the flesh to the fate it was fit for ! the
  spirit be thine !
By the spirit, when age shall o'ercome thee,
  thou still shalt enjoy
More indeed, than at first when inconscious, the
  life of a boy.
Crush that life, and behold its wine running !
  Each deed thou hast done
Dies, revives, goes to work in the world ; until
  e'en as the sun
Looking down on the earth, though clouds
  spoil him, though tempests efface,
Can find nothing his own deed produced not,
  must everywhere trace
The results of his past summer-prime, — so,
  each ray of thy will,
Every flash of thy passion and prowess, long
  over, shall thrill
Thy whole people, the countless, with ardor,
  till they too give forth
A like cheer to their sons, who in turn, fill the
  South and the North
With the radiance thy deed was the germ cf.
  Carouse in the past !
But the license of age has its limit ; thou diest
  at last :
As the lion when age dims his eyeball, the rose
  at her height,
So with man — so his power and his beauty for-
  ever take flight.
No ! Again a long draught of my soul-wine !
  Look forth o'er the years !
Thou hast done now with eyes for the actual ;
  begin with the seer's !
Is Saul dead ? In the depth of the vale make
  his tomb — bid arise
A gray mountain of marble heaped four-square,
  till, built to the skies,
Let it mark where the great First King slum-
  bers : whose fame would ye know ?
Up above see the rock's naked face, where
  the record shall go
In great characters cut by the scribe, — Such
  was Saul, so he did ;
With the sages directing the work, by the popu-
  lace chid, —
For not half, they 'll affirm, is comprised there !
  Which fault to amend,
In the grove with his kind grows the cedar,
  whereon they shall spend

(See, in tablets 't is level before them) their
  praise, and record
With the gold of the graver, Saul's story, —
  the statesman's great word
Side by side with the poet's sweet comment.
  The river 's a-wave
With smooth paper-reeds grazing each other
  when prophet-winds rave :
So the pen gives unborn generations their due
  and their part
In thy being ! Then, first of the mighty,
  thank God that thou art ! "

XIV

And behold while I sang . . . but O Thou who
  didst grant me that day,
And before it not seldom hast granted thy help
  to essay,
Carry on and complete an adventure, — my
  shield and my sword
In that act where my soul was thy servant,
  thy word was my word, —
Still be with me, who then at the summit of
  human endeavor
And scaling the highest, man's thought could,
  gazed hopeless as ever
On the new stretch of heaven above me — till,
  mighty to save,
Just one lift of thy hand cleared that distance
  — God's throne from man's grave !
Let me tell out my tale to its ending — my
  voice to my heart
Which can scarce dare believe in what marvels
  last night I took part,
As this morning I gather the fragments, alone
  with my sheep,
And still fear lest the terrible glory evanish
  like sleep !
For I wake in the gray dewy covert, while
  Hebron upheaves
The dawn struggling with night on his shoulder,
  and Kidron retrieves
Slow the damage of yesterday's sunshine.

XV

      I say then, — my song
While I sang thus, assuring the monarch, and
  ever more strong
Made a proffer of good to console him — he
  slowly resumed
His old motions and habitudes kingly. The
  right hand replumed
His black locks to their wonted composure, ad
  justed the swathes
Of his turban, and see — the huge sweat that
  his countenance bathes,
He wipes off with the robe ; and he girds now
  his loins as of yore,
And feels slow for the armlets of price, with
  the clasp set before.
He is Saul, ye remember in glory, — ere error
  had bent
The broad brow from the daily communion ;
  and still, though much spent
Be the life and the bearing that front you, the
  same, God did choose,
To receive what a man may waste, desecrate,
  never quite lose.

So sank he along by the tent-prop till, stayed
    by the pile
Of his armor and war-cloak and garments, he
    leaned there awhile,
And sat out my singing, — one arm round the
    tent-prop, to raise
His bent head, and the other hung slack — till
    I touched on the praise
I foresaw from all men in all time, to the man
    patient there ;
And thus ended, the harp falling forward.
    Then first I was 'ware
That he sat, as I say, with my head just above
    his vast knees
Which were thrust out on each side around
    me, like oak roots which please
To encircle a lamb when it slumbers. I looked
    up to know
If the best I could do had brought solace : he
    spoke not, but slow
Lifted up the hand slack at his side, till he laid
    it with care
Soft and grave, but in mild settled will, on my
    brow : through my hair
The large fingers were pushed, and he bent
    back my head, with kind power —
All my face back, intent to peruse it, as men do
    a flower.
Thus held he me there with his great eyes that
    scrutinized mine —
And oh, all my heart how it loved him ! but
    where was the sign ?
I yearned — " Could I help thee, my father,
    inventing a bliss,
I would add, to that life of the past, both the
    future and this ;
I would give thee new life altogether, as good,
    ages hence,
As this moment, — had love but the warrant,
    love's heart to dispense ! "

XVI

Then the truth came upon me. No harp more
    — no song more ! outbroke —

XVII

" I have gone the whole round of creation : I
    saw and I spoke :
I, a work of God's hand for that purpose, re-
    ceived in my brain
And pronounced on the rest of his handwork —
    returned him again
His creation's approval or censure : I spoke as
    I saw —
I report, as a man may of God's work — all 's
    love, yet all 's law.
Now I lay down the judgeship he lent me.
    Each faculty tasked
To perceive him, has gained an abyss, where a
    dewdrop was asked.
Have I knowledge ? confounded it shrivels at
    Wisdom laid bare.
Have I forethought ? how purblind, how blank,
    to the Infinite Care !
Do I task any faculty highest, to image suc-
    cess ?
I but open my eyes, — and perfection, no more
    and no less,

In the kind I imagined, full-fronts me, and
    God is seen God
In the star, in the stone, in the flesh, in the
    soul and the clod.
And thus looking within and around me, I ever
    renew
(With that stoop of the soul which in bending
    upraises it too)
The submission of man's nothing-perfect to
    God's all-complete,
As by each new obeisance in spirit, I climb to
    his feet.
Yet with all this abounding experience, this
    deity known,
I shall dare to discover some province, some
    gift of my own.
There 's a faculty pleasant to exercise, hard to
    hoodwink,
I am fain to keep still in abeyance, (I laugh as
    I think)
Lest, insisting to claim and parade in it, wot ye,
    I worst
E'en the Giver in one gift. — Behold, I could
    love if I durst !
But I sink the pretension as fearing a man may
    o'ertake
God's own speed in the one way of love : I ab-
    stain for love's sake.
— What, my soul ? see thus far and no farther ?
    when doors great and small,
Nine-and-ninety flew ope at our touch, should
    the hundredth appall ?
In the least things have faith, yet distrust in
    the greatest of all ?
Do I find love so full in my nature, God's ulti-
    mate gift,
That I doubt his own love can compete with
    it ? Here, the parts shift ?
Here, the creature surpass the Creator, — the
    end, what Began ?
Would I fain in my impotent yearning do all
    for this man,
And dare doubt he alone shall not help him,
    who yet alone can ?
Would it ever have entered my mind, the bare
    will, much less power,
To bestow on this Saul what I sang of, the
    marvellous dower
Of the life he was gifted and filled with ? to
    make such a soul,
Such a body, and then such an earth for inspher-
    ing the whole ?
And doth it not enter my mind (as my warm
    tears attest)
These good things being given, to go on, and
    give one more, the best ?
Ay, to save and redeem and restore him, main-
    tain at the height
This perfection, — succeed with life's day-
    spring, death's minute of night ?
Interpose at the difficult minute, snatch Saul
    the mistake,
Saul the failure, the ruin he seems now, — and
    bid him awake
From the dream, the probation, the prelude, to
    find himself set
Clear and safe in new light and new life, — a
    new harmony yet

To be run, and continued, and ended — who
   knows ? — or endure !
The man taught enough by life's dream, of the
   rest to make sure ;
By the pain-throb, triumphantly winning inten-
   sified bliss,
And the next world's reward and repose, by the
   struggles in this.

XVIII

"I believe it ! 'T is thou, God, that givest,
   't is I who receive :
In the first is the last, in thy will is my power
   to believe.
All 's one gift : thou canst grant it moreover,
   as prompt to my prayer
As I breathe out this breath, as I open these
   arms to the air.
From thy will stream the worlds, life and na-
   ture, thy dread Sabaoth :
I will ? — the mere atoms despise me ! Why
   am I not loth
To look that, even that in the face too ? Why
   is it I dare
Think but lightly of such impuissance ? What
   stops my despair ?
This ; — 't is not what man Does which exalts
   him, but what man Would do !
See the King — I would help him but cannot,
   the wishes fall through.
Could I wrestle to raise him from sorrow, grow
   poor to enrich,
To fill up his life, starve my own out, I would —
   knowing which,
I know that my service is perfect. Oh, speak
   through me now !
Would I suffer for him that I love ? So wouldst
   thou — so wilt thou !
So shall crown thee the topmost, ineffablest,
   uttermost crown —
And thy love fill infinitude wholly, nor leave up
   nor down
One spot for the creature to stand in ! It is by
   no breath,
Turn of eye, wave of hand, that salvation joins
   issue with death !
As thy Love is discovered almighty, almighty
   be proved
Thy power, that exists with and for it, of being
   Beloved !
He who did most, shall bear most ; the strong-
   est shall stand the most weak.
'T is the weakness in strength, that I cry for !
   my flesh, that I seek
In the Godhead ! I seek and I find it. O Saul,
   it shall be
A Face like my face that receives thee ; a Man
   like to me,
Thou shalt love and be loved by, forever : a
   Hand like this hand
Shall throw open the gates of new life to thee !
   See the Christ stand ! "

XIX

I know not too well how I found my way home
   in the night.
There were witnesses, cohorts about me, to left
   and to right,

Angels, powers, the unuttered, unseen, the
   alive, the aware :
I repressed, I got through them as hardly, as
   strugglingly there,
As a runner beset by the populace famished
   for news —
Life or death. The whole earth was awakened,
   hell loosed with her crews ;
And the stars of night beat with emotion, and
   tingled and shot
Out in fire the strong pain of pent knowledge :
   but I fainted not,
For the Hand still impelled me at once and
   supported, suppressed
All the tumult, and quenched it with quiet,
   and holy behest,
Till the rapture was shut in itself, and the
   earth sank to rest.
Anon at the dawn, all that trouble had with-
   ered from earth —
Not so much, but I saw it die out in the day's
   tender birth ;
In the gathered intensity brought to the gray
   of the hills ;
In the shuddering forests' held breath ; in the
   sudden wind-thrills ;
In the startled wild beasts that bore off, each
   with eye sidling still
Though averted with wonder and dread ; in the
   birds stiff and chill
That rose heavily, as I approached them, made
   stupid with awe :
E'en the serpent that slid away silent, — he felt
   the new law.
The same stared in the white humid faces up-
   turned by the flowers ;
The same worked in the heart of the cedar and
   moved the vine-bowers :
And the little brooks witnessing murmured,
   persistent and low,
With their obstinate, all but hushed voices —
   " E'en so, it is so ! "

MY STAR

This poem has been held to refer pointedly to
Mrs. Browning. An inference to this end may
be drawn from the fact that it stands first in a
volume of *Selections from the Poetical Works of
Robert Browning*, published in 1872 and dedi-
cated to Alfred Tennyson. " In Poetry — Il-
lustrious and consummate : In Friendship —
Noble and sincere." The selection was made
under Browning's supervision and contains the
following preface : —

" In the present selection from my poetry,
there is an attempt to escape from the embar-
rassment of appearing to pronounce upon what
myself may consider the best of it. I adopt
another principle ; and by simply stringing to-
gether certain pieces on the thread of an ima-
gined personality, I present them in succession,
rather as the natural development of a particu-

lar experience than because I account them the most noteworthy portion of my work. Such an attempt was made in the volume of selections from the poetry of Elizabeth Barrett Browning: to which — in outward uniformity, at least — my own would venture to become a companion.

"A few years ago, had such an opportunity presented itself, I might have been tempted to say a word in reply to the objections my poetry was used to encounter. Time has kindly coöperated with my disinclination to write the poetry and the criticism besides. The readers I am at last privileged to expect, meet me fully halfway; and if, from the fitting stand-point, they must still ' censure me in their wisdom,' they have previously ' awakened their senses that they may the better judge.' Nor do I apprehend any more charges of being willfully obscure, unconscientiously careless, or perversely harsh. Having hitherto done my utmost in the art to which my life is a devotion, I cannot engage to increase the effort; but I conceive that there may be helpful light, as well as reassuring warmth, in the attention and sympathy I gratefully acknowledge.   R. B."

LONDON, *May* 14, 1872.

ALL that I know
    Of a certain star
Is, it can throw
    (Like the angled spar)
Now a dart of red,
    Now a dart of blue;
Till my friends have said
    They would fain see, too,
My star that dartles the red and the blue!
Then it stops like a bird; like a flower, hangs
        furled:
    They must solace themselves with the Saturn
        above it.
What matter to me if their star is a world?
    Mine has opened its soul to me; therefore I
        love it.

BY THE FIRESIDE

The scene of the declaration in this poem is laid in a little mountain gorge adjacent to the Baths of Lucca, where the Brownings spent the summer of 1853.

How well I know what I mean to do
    When the long dark autumn evenings come;
And where, my soul, is thy pleasant hue?
    With the music of all thy voices, dumb
In life's November too!

I shall be found by the fire, suppose,
    O'er a great wise book as beseemeth age,
While the shutters flap as the cross-wind blows,
    And I turn the page, and I turn the page,
Not verse now, only prose!

Till the young ones whisper, finger on lip,
    "There he is at it, deep in Greek:
Now then, or never, out we slip
    To cut from the hazels by the creek
A mainmast for our ship!"

I shall be at it indeed, my friends!
    Greek puts already on either side
Such a branch-work forth as soon extends
    To a vista opening far and wide,
And I pass out where it ends.

The outside-frame, like your hazel-trees —
    But the inside-archway widens fast,
And a rarer sort succeeds to these,
    And we slope to Italy at last
And youth, by green degrees.

I follow wherever I am led,
    Knowing so well the leader's hand:
Oh woman-country, wooed not wed,
    Loved all the more by earth's male-lands,
Laid to their hearts instead!

Look at the ruined chapel again
    Half-way up in the Alpine gorge!
Is that a tower, I point you plain,
    Or is it a mill, or an iron forge
Breaks solitude in vain?

A turn, and we stand in the heart of things;
    The woods are round us, heaped and dim;
From slab to slab how it slips and springs,
    The thread of water single and slim,
Through the ravage some torrent brings!

Does it feed the little lake below?
    That speck of white just on its marge
Is Pella; see, in the evening-glow,
    How sharp the silver spear-heads charge
When Alp meets heaven in snow!

On our other side is the straight-up rock;
    And a path is kept 'twixt the gorge and it
By boulder-stones where lichens mock
    The marks on a moth, and small ferns fit
Their teeth to the polished block.

Oh the sense of the yellow mountain-flowers,
    And thorny balls, each three in one,
The chestnuts throw on our path in showers!
    For the drop of the woodland fruit's begun,
These early November hours,

That crimson the creeper's leaf across
    Like a splash of blood, intense, abrupt,
O'er a shield else gold from rim to boss,
    And lay it for show on the fairy-cupped
Elf-needled mat of moss,

By the rose-flesh mushrooms, undivulged
    Last evening — nay, in to-day's first dew
Yon sudden coral nipple bulged,
    Where a freaked fawn-colored flaky crew
Of toad-stools peep indulged.

And yonder, at foot of the fronting ridge
    That takes the turn to a range beyond,

Is the chapel reached by the one-arched bridge,
　Where the water is stopped in a stagnant pond
Danced over by the midge.

The chapel and bridge are of stone alike,
　Blackish-gray and mostly wet ;
Cut hemp-stalks steep in the narrow dyke.
　See here again, how the lichens fret
And the roots of the ivy strike !

Poor little place, where its one priest comes
　On a festa-day, if he comes at all,
To the dozen folk from their scattered homes,
　Gathered within that precinct small
By the dozen ways one roams —

To drop from the charcoal-burners' huts,
　Or climb from the hemp-dressers' low shed,
Leave the grange where the woodman stores
　　his nuts,
Or the wattled cote where the fowlers spread
Their gear on the rock's bare juts.

It has some pretension too, this front,
　With its bit of fresco half-moon-wise
Set over the porch, Art's early wont :
　'T is John in the Desert, I surmise,
But has borne the weather's brunt —

Not from the fault of the builder, though,
　For a pent-house properly projects
Where three carved beams make a certain show,
　Dating — good thought of our architect's —
'Five, six, nine, he lets you know.

And all day long a bird sings there,
　And a stray sheep drinks at the pond at times ;
The place is silent and aware ;
　It has had its scenes, its joys and crimes,
But that is its own affair.

My perfect wife, my Leonor,
　Oh heart, my own, oh eyes, mine too,
Whom else could I dare look backward for,
　With whom beside should I dare pursue
The path gray heads abhor ?

For it leads to a crag's sheer edge with them ;
　Youth, flowery all the way, there stops —
Not they ; age threatens and they contemn,
　Till they reach the gulf wherein youth drops,
One inch from life's safe hem !

With me, youth led . . . I will speak now,
　No longer watch you as you sit
Reading by fire-light, that great brow
　And the spirit-small hand propping it,
Mutely, my heart knows how —

When, if I think but deep enough,
　You are wont to answer, prompt as rhyme ;
And you, too, find without rebuff
　Response your soul seeks many a time
Piercing its fine flesh-stuff.

My own, confirm me ! If I tread
　This path back, is it not in pride
To think how little I dreamed it led

To an age so blest that, by its side,
Youth seems the waste instead ?

My own, see where the years conduct !
　At first, 't was something our two souls
Should mix as mists do ; each is sucked
　In each now : on, the new stream rolls,
Whatever rocks obstruct.

Think, when our one soul understands
　The great Word which makes all things new,
When earth breaks up and heaven expands,
　How will the change strike me and you
In the house not made with hands ?

Oh, I must feel your brain prompt mine,
　Your heart anticipate my heart,
You must be just before, in fine,
　See and make me see, for your part,
New depths of the divine !

But who could have expected this
　When we two drew together first
Just for the obvious human bliss,
　To satisfy life's daily thirst
With a thing men seldom miss ?

Come back with me to the first of all,
　Let us lean and love it over again,
Let us now forget and now recall,
　Break the rosary in a pearly rain
And gather what we let fall !

What did I say ? — that a small bird sings
　All day long, save when a brown pair
Of hawks from the wood float with wide wings
　Strained to a bell : 'gainst noon-day glare
You count the streaks and rings.

But at afternoon or almost eve
　'T is better ; then the silence grows
To that degree, you half believe
　It must get rid of what it knows,
Its bosom does so heave.

Hither we walked then, side by side,
　Arm in arm and cheek to cheek,
And still I questioned or replied,
　While my heart, convulsed to really speak,
Lay choking in its pride.

Silent the crumbling bridge we cross,
　And pity and praise the chapel sweet,
And care about the fresco's loss,
　And wish for our souls a like retreat,
And wonder at the moss.

Stoop and kneel on the settle under,
　Look through the window's grated square :
Nothing to see ! For fear of plunder,
　The cross is down and the altar bare,
As if thieves don't fear thunder.

We stoop and look in through the grate,
　See the little porch and rustic door,
Read duly the dead builder's date ;
　Then cross the bridge that we crossed before,
Take the path again — but wait !

Oh moment, one and infinite !
  The water slips o'er stock and stone ;
The West is tender, hardly bright :
  How gray at once is the evening grown —
One star, its chrysolite !

We two stood there with never a third,
  But each by each, as each knew well :
The sights we saw and the sounds we heard,
  The lights and the shades made up a spell
Till the trouble grew and stirred.

Oh, the little more, and how much it is !
  And the little less, and what worlds away !
How a sound shall quicken content to bliss,
  Or a breath suspend the blood's best play,
And life be a proof of this !

Had she willed it, still had stood the screen
  So slight, so sure, 'twixt my love and her :
I could fix her face with a guard between,
  And find her soul as when friends confer,
Friends — lovers that might have been.

For my heart had a touch of the woodland-
    time,
  Wanting to sleep now over its best.
Shake the whole tree in the summer-prime,
  But bring to the last leaf no such test !
" Hold the last fast ! " runs the rhyme.

For a chance to make your little much,
  To gain a lover and lose a friend,
Venture the tree and a myriad such,
  When nothing you mar but the year can
    mend :
But a last leaf — fear to touch !

Yet should it unfasten itself and fall
  Eddying down till it find your face
At some slight wind — best chance of all !
  Be your heart henceforth its dwelling-place
You trembled to forestall !

Worth how well, those dark gray eyes,
  That hair so dark and dear, how worth
That a man should strive and agonize,
  And taste a veriest hell on earth
For the hope of such a prize !

You might have turned and tried a man,
  Set him a space to weary and wear,
And prove which suited more your plan,
  His best of hope or his worst despair,
Yet end as he began.

But you spared me this, like the heart you
    are,
  And filled my empty heart at a word.
If two lives join, there is oft a scar,
  They are one and one, with a shadowy third ;
One near one is too far.

A moment after, and hands unseen
  Were hanging the night around us fast ;
But we knew that a bar was broken between
  Life and life : we were mixed at last
In spite of the mortal screen.

The forests had done it ; there they stood ;
  We caught for a moment the powers at play.
They had mingled us so, for once and good,
  Their work was done — we might go or stay,
They relapsed to their ancient mood.

How the world is made for each of us !
  How all we perceive and know in it
Tends to some moment's product thus,
  When a soul declares itself — to wit,
By its fruit, the thing it does !

Be hate that fruit or love that fruit,
  It forwards the general deed of man,
And each of the Many helps to recruit
  The life of the race by a general plan ;
Each living his own, to boot.

I am named and known by that moment's feat
  There took my station and degree ;
So grew my own small life complete,
  As nature obtained her best of me —
One born to love you, sweet !

And to watch you sink by the fireside now
  Back again, as you mutely sit
Musing by fire-light, that great brow
  And the spirit-small hand propping it,
Yonder, my heart knows how !

So, earth has gained by one man the more,
  And the gain of earth must be heaven's gain
    too ;
And the whole is well worth thinking o'er
  When autumn comes : which I mean to do
One day, as I said before.

ANY WIFE TO ANY HUSBAND

My love, this is the bitterest, that thou —
Who art all truth, and who dost love me now
  As thine eyes say, as thy voice breaks to say —
Shouldst love so truly, and couldst love me still
A whole long life through, had but love its will,
  Would death that leads me from thee brook
    delay.

I have but to be by thee, and thy hand
Will never let mine go, nor heart withstand
  The beating of my heart to reach its place.
When shall I look for thee and feel thee gone ?
When cry for the old comfort and find none ?
  Never, I know ! Thy soul is in thy face.

Oh, I should fade — 't is willed so ! Might I
    save,
Gladly I would, whatever beauty gave
  Joy to thy sense, for that was precious too.
It is not to be granted. But the soul
Whence the love comes, all ravage leaves that
    whole ;
  Vainly the flesh fades ; soul makes all things
    new.

It would not be because my eye grew dim
Thou couldst not find the love there, thanks to
    Him

Who never is dishonored in the spark
He gave us from his fire of fires, and bade
Remember whence it sprang, nor be afraid
  While that burns on, though all the rest grow
    dark.

So, how thou wouldst be perfect, white and
    clean
Outside as inside, soul and soul's demesne
  Alike, this body given to show it by!
Oh, three-parts through the worst of life's
    abyss,
What plaudits from the next world after this,
  Couldst thou repeat a stroke and gain the
    sky!

And is it not the bitterer to think
That disengage our hands and thou wilt sink
  Although thy love was love in very deed?
I know that nature! Pass a festive day,
Thou dost not throw its relic-flower away
  Nor bid its music's loitering echo speed.

Thou let'st the stranger's glove lie where it fell;
If old things remain old things all is well,
  For thou art grateful as becomes man best:
And hadst thou only heard me play one tune,
Or viewed me from a window, not so soon
  With thee would such things fade as with the
    rest.

I seem to see! We meet and part; 't is brief;
The book I opened keeps a folded leaf,
  The very chair I sat on, breaks the rank;
That is a portrait of me on the wall —
Three lines, my face comes at so slight a call:
  And for all this, one little hour to thank!

But now, because the hour through years was
    fixed,
Because our inmost beings met and mixed,
  Because thou once hast loved me — wilt thou
    dare
Say to thy soul and Who may list beside,
"Therefore she is immortally my bride;
  Chance cannot change my love, nor time
    impair.

"So, what if in the dusk of life that's left,
I, a tired traveller of my sun bereft,
  Look from my path when, mimicking the
    same,
The fire-fly glimpses past me, come and gone?
— Where was it till the sunset? Where anon
  It will be at the sunrise! What's to
    blame?"

Is it so helpful to thee? Canst thou take
The mimic up, nor, for the true thing's sake,
  Put gently by such efforts at a beam?
Is the remainder of the way so long,
Thou need'st the little solace, thou the strong?
  Watch out thy watch, let weak ones doze and
    dream!

Ah, but the fresher faces! "Is it true,"
Thou 'lt ask, "some eyes are beautiful and
    new?

Some hair, — how can one choose but grasp
    such wealth?
And if a man would press his lips to lips
Fresh as the wilding hedge-rose-cup there slips
  The dewdrop out of, must it be by stealth?

"It cannot change the love still kept for Her,
More than if such a picture I prefer
  Passing a day with, to a room's bare side:
The painted form takes nothing she possessed,
Yet, while the Titian's Venus lies at rest,
  A man looks. Once more, what is there to
    chide?"

So must I see, from where I sit and watch,
My own self sell myself, my hand attach
  Its warrant to the very thefts from me —
Thy singleness of soul that made me proud,
Thy purity of heart I loved aloud,
  Thy man's-truth I was bold to bid God see!

Love so, then, if thou wilt! Give all thou canst
Away to the new faces — disentranced,
  (Say it and think it) obdurate no more:
Re-issue looks and words from the old mint,
Pass them afresh, no matter whose the print
  Image and superscription once they bore!

Re-coin thyself and give it them to spend, —
It all comes to the same thing at the end,
  Since mine thou wast, mine art and mine
    shalt be,
Faithful or faithless, sealing up the sum
Or lavish of my treasure, thou must come
  Back to the heart's place here I keep for
    thee!

Only, why should it be with stain at all?
Why must I, 'twixt the leaves of coronal,
  Put any kiss of pardon on thy brow?
Why need the other women know so much,
And talk together, "Such the look and such
  The smile he used to love with, then as now!"

Might I die last and show thee! Should I find
Such hardship in the few years left behind,
  If free to take and light my lamp, and go
Into thy tomb, and shut the door and sit,
Seeing thy face on those four sides of it
  The better that they are so blank, I know!

Why, time was what I wanted, to turn o'er
Within my mind each look, get more and more
  By heart each word, too much to learn at
    first:
And join thee all the fitter for the pause
'Neath the low doorway's lintel. That were
    cause
  For lingering, though thou calledst, if I
    durst!

And yet thou art the nobler of us two:
What dare I dream of, that thou canst not do,
  Outstripping my ten small steps with one
    stride?
I 'll say then, here 's a trial and a task —
Is it to bear? — if easy, I 'll not ask:
  Though love fail, I can trust on in thy pride.

Pride? — when those eyes forestall the life be-
   hind
The death I have to go through! — when I find,
  Now that I want thy help most, all of thee!
What did I fear? Thy love shall hold me fast
Until the little minute's sleep is past
  And I wake saved. — And yet it will not be!

TWO IN THE CAMPAGNA

I WONDER do you feel to-day
  As I have felt since, hand in hand,
We sat down on the grass, to stray
  In spirit better through the land,
This morn of Rome and May?

For me, I touched a thought, I know,
  Has tantalized me many times,
(Like turns of thread the spiders throw
  Mocking across our path) for rhymes
To catch at and let go.

Help me to hold it! First it left
  The yellowing fennel, run to seed
There, branching from the brickwork's cleft,
  Some old tomb's ruin: yonder weed
Took up the floating weft,

Where one small orange cup amassed
  Five beetles, — blind and green they grope
Among the honey-meal: and last,
  Everywhere on the grassy slope
I traced it. Hold it fast!

The champaign with its endless fleece
  Of feathery grasses everywhere!
Silence and passion, joy and peace,
  An everlasting wash of air —
Rome's ghost since her decease.

Such life here, through such lengths of hours,
  Such miracles performed in play,
Such primal naked forms of flowers,
  Such letting nature have her way
While heaven looks from its towers!

How say you? Let us, O my dove,
  Let us be unashamed of soul,
As earth lies bare to heaven above!
  How is it under our control
To love or not to love?

I would that you were all to me,
  You that are just so much, no more.
Nor yours nor mine, nor slave nor free!
  Where does the fault lie? What the core
O' the wound, since wound must be?

I would I could adopt your will,
  See with your eyes, and set my heart
Beating by yours, and drink my fill
  At your soul's springs, — your part my part
In life, for good and ill.

No. I yearn upward, touch you close,
  Then stand away. I kiss your cheek,

Catch your soul's warmth, — I pluck the rose
  And love it more than tongue can speak —
Then the good minute goes.

Already how am I so far
  Out of that minute? Must I go
Still like the thistle-ball, no bar,
  Onward, whenever light winds blow,
Fixed by no friendly star?

Just when I seemed about to learn!
  Where is the thread now? Off again!
The old trick! Only I discern —
  Infinite passion, and the pain
Of finite hearts that yearn.

MISCONCEPTIONS

THIS is a spray the Bird clung to,
  Making it blossom with pleasure,
Ere the high tree-top she sprung to,
  Fit for her nest and her treasure.
Oh, what a hope beyond measure
Was the poor spray's, which the flying feet
  hung to, —
So to be singled out, built in, and sung to!

This is a heart the Queen leant on,
  Thrilled in a minute erratic,
Ere the true bosom she bent on,
  Meet for love's regal dalmatic.
Oh, what a fancy ecstatic
Was the poor heart's, ere the wanderer went
  on—
Love to be saved for it, proffered to, spent on!

A SERENADE AT THE VILLA

THAT was I, you heard last night.
  When there rose no moon at all,
Nor, to pierce the strained and tight
  Tent of heaven, a planet small:
Life was dead and so was light.

Not a twinkle from the fly,
  Not a glimmer from the worm;
When the crickets stopped their cry,
  When the owls forebore a term,
You heard music; that was I.

Earth turned in her sleep with pain,
  Sultrily suspired for proof:
In at heaven and out again,
  Lightning! — where it broke the roof,
Bloodlike, some few drops of rain.

What they could my words expressed.
  O my love, my all, my one!
Singing helped the verses best,
  And when singing's best was done,
To my lute I left the rest.

So wore night; the East was gray,
  White the broad-faced hemlock-flowers:
There would be another day;

Ere its first of heavy hours
Found me, I had passed away.

What became of all the hopes,
  Words and song and lute as well ?
Say, this struck you — " When life gropes
  Feebly for the path where fell
Light last on the evening slopes,

' One friend in that path shall be,
  To secure my step from wrong ;
One to count night day for me,
  Patient through the watches long,
Serving most with none to see."

Never say — as something bodes —
  " So, the worst has yet a worse !
When life halts 'neath double loads,
  Better the task-master's curse
Than such music on the roads !

" When no moon succeeds the sun,
  Nor can pierce the midnight's tent
Any star, the smallest one,
  While some drops, where lightning rent,
Show the final storm begun —

" When the fire-fly hides its spot,
  When the garden-voices fail
In the darkness thick and hot, —
  Shall another voice avail,
That shape be where these are not ?

" Has some plague a longer lease,
  Proffering its help uncouth ?
Can't one even die in peace ?
  As one shuts one's eyes on youth,
Is that face the last one sees ? "

Oh, how dark your villa was,
  Windows fast and obdurate !
How the garden grudged me grass
  Where I stood — the iron gate
Ground its teeth to let me pass !

ONE WAY OF LOVE

ALL June I bound the rose in sheaves.
Now, rose by rose, I strip the leaves
And strew them where Pauline may pass.
She will not turn aside ? Alas !
Let them lie. Suppose they die ?
The chance was they might take her eye.

How many a month I strove to suit
These stubborn fingers to the lute !
To-day I venture all I know.
She will not hear my music ? So !
Break the string ; fold music's wing :
Suppose Pauline had bade me sing !

My whole life long I learned to love.
This hour my utmost art I prove
And speak my passion — heaven or hell ?
She will not give me heaven ? 'T is well !
Lose who may — I still can say,
Those who win heaven, blest are they !

ANOTHER WAY OF LOVE

JUNE was not over
  Though past the full,
And the best of her roses
  Had yet to blow,
  When a man I know
(But shall not discover,
  Since ears are dull,
  And time discloses)
Turned him and said with a man's true air,
Half sighing a smile in a yawn, as 't were, —
" If I tire of your June, will she greatly care ? "

Well, dear, in-doors with you !
  True ! serene deadness
Tries a man's temper.
  What 's in the blossom
  June wears on her bosom ?
Can it clear scores with you ?
  Sweetness and redness,
  Eadem semper !
Go, let me care for it greatly or slightly !
If June mend her bower now, your hand left
    unsightly
By plucking the roses, — my June will do
    rightly.

And after, for pastime,
  If June be refulgent
With flowers in completeness,
  All petals, no prickles,
  Delicious as trickles
Of wine poured at mass-time, —
  And choose One indulgent
  To redness and sweetness :
Or if, with experience of man and of spider,
June use my June-lightning, the strong insect-
    ridder,
And stop the fresh film-work, — why, June will
    consider.

A PRETTY WOMAN

THAT fawn-skin-dappled hair of hers,
  And the blue eye
  Dear and dewy,
And that infantine fresh air of hers !

To think men cannot take you, Sweet,
  And enfold you,
  Ay, and hold you,
And so keep you what they make you, Sweet !

You like us for a glance, you know —
  For a word's sake
  Or a sword's sake,
All 's the same, whate'er the chance, you know

And in turn we make you ours, we say —
  You and youth too,
  Eyes and mouth too,
All the face composed of flowers, we say.

All 's our own, to make the most of, Sweet —
  Sing and say for,

Watch and pray for,
Keep a secret or go boast of, Sweet!

But for loving, why, you would not, Sweet,
　　Though we prayed you,
　　Paid you, brayed you
In a mortar — for you could not, Sweet!

So, we leave the sweet face fondly there:
　　Be its beauty
　　Its sole duty!
Let all hope of grace beyond, lie there!

And while the face lies quiet there,
　　Who shall wonder
　　That I ponder
A conclusion?　I will try it there.

As, — why must one, for the love foregone,
　　Scout mere liking?
　　Thunder-striking
Earth, — the heaven, we looked above for, gone!

Why, with beauty, needs there money be,
　　Love with liking?
　　Crush the fly-king
In his gauze, because no honey-bee?

May not liking be so simple-sweet,
　　If love grew there
　　'T would undo there
All that breaks the cheek to dimples sweet?

Is the creature too imperfect, say?
　　Would you mend it
　　And so end it?
Since not all addition perfects aye!

Or is it of its kind, perhaps,
　　Just perfection —
　　Whence, rejection
Of a grace not to its mind, perhaps?

Shall we burn up, tread that face at once
　　Into tinder,
　　And so hinder
Sparks from kindling all the place at once?

Or else kiss away one's soul on her?
　　Your love-fancies!
　　— A sick man sees
Truer, when his hot eyes roll on her!

Thus the craftsman thinks to grace the rose, —
　　Plucks a mould-flower
　　For his gold flower,
Uses fine things that efface the rose:

Rosy rubies make its cup more rose,
　　Precious metals
　　Ape the petals, —
Last, some old king locks it up, morose!

Then how grace a rose?　I know a way!
　　Leave it, rather.
　　Must you gather?
Smell, kiss, wear it — at last, throw away!

RESPECTABILITY

DEAR, had the world in its caprice
　　Deigned to proclaim " I know you both.
　　Have recognized your plighted troth,
Am sponsor for you: live in peace!" —
How many precious months and years
　　Of youth had passed, that speed so fast,
　　Before we found it out at last,
The world, and what it fears!

How much of priceless life were spent
　　With men that every virtue decks,
　　And women models of their sex,
Society's true ornament, —
Ere we dared wander, nights like this,
　　Through wind and rain, and watch the Seine,
　　And feel the Boulevard break again
To warmth and light and bliss!

I know! the world proscribes not love;
　　Allows my finger to caress
　　Your lips' contour and downiness,
Provided it supply a glove.
The world's good word! — the Institute!
　　Guizot receives Montalembert!
　　Eh?　Down the court three lampions flare:
Put forward your best foot!

LOVE IN A LIFE

ROOM after room,
I hunt the house through
We inhabit together.
Heart, fear nothing, for, heart, thou shalt find
　　her —
Next time, herself! — not the trouble behind
　　her
Left in the curtain, the couch's perfume!
As she brushed it, the cornice-wreath blos-
　　somed anew:
Yon looking-glass gleamed at the wave of her
　　feather.

Yet the day wears,
And door succeeds door;
I try the fresh fortune —
Range the wide house from the wing to the
　　centre.
Still the same chance! she goes out as I enter.
Spend my whole day in the quest, — who cares?
But 't is twilight, you see, — with such suites to
　　explore,
Such closets to search, such alcoves to impor-
　　tune!

LIFE IN A LOVE

　　ESCAPE me?
　　Never —
　　Beloved!
While I am I, and you are you,
　　So long as the world contains us both,
　　Me the loving and you the loth,
While the one eludes, must the other pursue.

My life is a fault at last, I fear:
　It seems too much like a fate, indeed !
　Though I do my best I shall scarce succeed.
But what if I fail of my purpose here ?
It is but to keep the nerves at strain,
　To dry one's eyes and laugh at a fall,
And baffled, get up and begin again, —
　So the chase takes up one's life, that 's all.
While, look but once from your farthest bound
　At me so deep in the dust and dark,
No sooner the old hope goes to ground
　Than a new one, straight to the selfsame mark,
　I shape me —
　Ever
　Removed !

IN THREE DAYS

So, I shall see her in three days
And just one night, but nights are short,
Then two long hours, and that is morn.
See how I come, unchanged, unworn !
Feel, where my life broke off from thine,
How fresh the splinters keep and fine, —
Only a touch and we combine !

Too long, this time of year, the days !
But nights, at least the nights are short.
As night shows where her one moon is,
A hand's-breadth of pure light and bliss,
So life's night gives my lady birth
And my eyes hold her ! What is worth
The rest of heaven, the rest of earth ?

O loaded curls, release your store
Of warmth and scent, as once before
The tingling hair did, lights and darks
Outbreaking into fairy sparks,
When under curl and curl I pried
After the warmth and scent inside,
Through lights and darks how manifold —
The dark inspired, the light controlled !
As early Art embrowns the gold.

What great fear, should one say, " Three days
That change the world might change as well
Your fortune ; and if joy delays,
Be happy that no worse befell ! "
What small fear, if another says,
" Three days and one short night beside
May throw no shadow on your ways ;
But years must teem with change untried,
With chance not easily defied,
With an end somewhere undescried."
No fear ! — or if a fear be born
This minute, it dies out in scorn.
Fear ? I shall see her in three days
And one night, now the nights are short,
Then just two hours, and that is morn.

IN A YEAR

Never any more,
　While I live,
Need I hope to see his face
　As before.

Once his love grown chill,
　Mine may strive :
Bitterly we re-embrace,
　Single still.

Was it something said,
　Something done,
Vexed him ? Was it touch of hand
　Turn of head ?
Strange ! that very way
　Love begun :
I as little understand
　Love's decay.

When I sewed or drew,
　I recall
How he looked as if I sung,
　— Sweetly too.
If I spoke a word,
　First of all
Up his cheek the color sprung,
　Then he heard.

Sitting by my side,
　At my feet,
So he breathed but air I breathed,
　Satisfied !
I, too, at love's brim
　Touched the sweet :
I would die if death bequeathed
　Sweet to him.

" Speak, I love thee best ! "
　He exclaimed :
" Let thy love my own foretell ! "
　I confessed :
" Clasp my heart on thine
　Now unblamed,
Since upon thy soul as well
　Hangeth mine ! "

Was it wrong to own,
　Being truth ?
Why should all the giving prove
　His alone ?
I had wealth and ease,
　Beauty, youth :
Since my lover gave me love,
　I gave these.

That was all I meant,
　— To be just,
And the passion I had raised,
　To content.
Since he chose to change
　Gold for dust,
If I gave him what he praised
　Was it strange ?

Would he loved me yet,
　On and on,
While I found some way undreamed
　— Paid my debt !
Gave more life and more,
　Till, all gone,
He should smile " She never seemed
　Mine before.

" What, she felt the while,
    Must I think?
Love 's so different with us men ! "
    He should smile :
" Dying for my sake —
    White and pink !
Can't we touch these bubbles then
    But they break ? ''

Dear, the pang is brief,
    Do thy part,
Have thy pleasure !   How perplexed
    Grows belief !
Well, this cold clay clod
    Was man's heart :
Crumble it, and what comes next ?
    Is it God ?

WOMEN AND ROSES

Written on the suggestion of some roses sent
Mrs. Browning.   At the time of writing,
Browning was carrying out a resolve to write a
poem a day, a resolve which lasted a fortnight.

I

I DREAM of a red-rose tree.
And which of its roses three
Is the dearest rose to me ?

II

Round and round, like a dance of snow
In a dazzling drift, as its guardians, go
Floating the women faded for ages,
Sculptured in stone, on the poet's pages.
Then follow women fresh and gay,
Living and loving and loved to-day,
Last, in the rear, flee the multitude of maidens,
Beauties yet unborn.   And all, to one cadence,
They circle their rose on my rose tree.

III

Dear rose, thy term is reached,
Thy leaf hangs loose and bleached :
Bees pass it unimpeached.

IV

Stay then, stoop, since I cannot climb,
You, great shapes of the antique time !
How shall I fix you, fire you, freeze you,
Break my heart at your feet to please you ?
Oh, to possess and be possessed !
Hearts that beat 'neath each pallid breast !
Once but of love, the poesy, the passion,
Drink but once and die ! — In vain, the same
    fashion,
They circle their rose on my rose tree.

V

Dear rose, thy joy 's undimmed,
Thy cup is ruby-rimmed,
Thy cup's heart Lectar-brimmed.

VI

Deep, as drops from a statue's plinth
The bee sucked in by the hyacinth,

So will I bury me while burning,
Quench like him at a plunge my yearning,
Eyes in your eyes, lips on your lips !
Fold me fast where the cincture slips,
Prison all my soul in eternities of pleasure,
Girdle me for once !   But no — the old measure.
They circle their rose on my rose tree.

VII

Dear rose without a thorn,
Thy bud 's the babe unborn :
First streak of a new morn.

VIII

Wings, lend wings for the cold, the clear !
What is far conquers what is near.
Roses will bloom nor want beholders,
Sprung from the dust where our flesh moulders,
What shall arrive with the cycle's change ?
A novel grace and a beauty strange.
I will make an Eve, be the artist that began her,
Shaped her to his mind ! — Alas ! in like man-
    ner
They circle their rose on my rose tree.

BEFORE

LET them fight it out, friend ! things have gone
    too far.
God must judge the couple : leave them as they
    are
— Whichever one 's the guiltless, to his glory,
And whichever one the guilt 's with, to my
    story !

Why, you would not bid men, sunk in such a
    slough,
Strike no arm out further, stick and stink as
    now,
Leaving right and wrong to settle the embroil-
    ment,
Heaven with snaky hell, in torture and entoil-
    ment ?

Who 's the culprit of them ?   How must he
    conceive
God — the queen he caps to, laughing in his
    sleeve,
" 'T is but decent to profess one's self beneath
    her :
Still, one must not be too much in earnest,
    either ! ''

Better sin the whole sin, sure that God ob-
    serves ;
Then go live his life out !   Life will try his
    nerves,
When the sky, which noticed all, makes no dis-
    closure,
And the earth keeps up her terrible composure.

Let him pace at pleasure, past the walls of rose,
Pluck their fruits when grape-trees graze him
    as he goes !
For he 'gins to guess the purpose of the garden,
With the sly mute thing, beside there, for a
    warden.

What's the leopard-dog-thing, constant at his
    side,
A leer and lie in every eye of its obsequious hide?
When will come an end to all the mock obei-
    sance,
And the price appear that pays for the misfea-
    sance?

So much for the culprit.   Who's the martyred
    man?
Let him bear one stroke more, for be sure he can!
He that strove thus evil's lump with good to
    leaven,
Let him give his blood at last and get his
    heaven!

All or nothing, stake it! Trusts he God or no?
Thus far and no farther? farther? be it so!
Now, enough of your chicane of prudent pauses,
Sage provisos, sub-intents and saving-clauses!

Ah, "forgive" you bid him? While God's
    champion lives,
Wrong shall be resisted: dead, why, he forgives.
But you must not end my friend ere you begin
    him;
Evil stands not crowned on earth, while breath
    is in him.

Once more — Will the wronger, at this last of all,
Dare to say, "I did wrong," rising in his fall?
No? — Let go, then! Both the fighters to their
    places!
While I count three, step you back as many
    paces!

AFTER

Take the cloak from his face, and at first
    Let the corpse do its worst!

How he lies in his rights of a man!
    Death has done all death can.
And, absorbed in the new life he leads,
    He recks not, he heeds
Nor his wrong nor my vengeance; both strike
    On his senses alike,
And are lost in the solemn and strange
    Surprise of the change.

Ha, what avails death to erase
    His offence, my disgrace?
I would we were boys as of old
    In the field, by the fold:
His outrage, God's patience, man's scorn
    Were so easily borne!

I stand here now, he lies in his place:
    Cover the face!

THE GUARDIAN-ANGEL

A PICTURE AT FANO

Dear and great Angel, wouldst thou only leave
    That child, when thou hast done with him,
    for me!

Let me sit all the day here, that when eve
    Shall find performed thy special ministry,
And time come for departure, thou, suspending,
Thy flight, may'st see another child for tending,
    Another still, to quiet and retrieve.

Then I shall feel thee step one step, no more,
    From where thou standest now, to where I
    gaze,
— And suddenly my head is covered o'er
    With those wings, white above the child who
    prays
Now on that tomb — and I shall feel thee
    guarding
Me, out of all the world; for me, discarding
    Yon heaven thy home, that waits and opes its
    door.

I would not look up thither past thy head
    Because the door opes, like that child, I know,
For I should have thy gracious face instead,
    Thou bird of God! And wilt thou bend me
    low
Like him, and lay, like his, my hands together,
And lift them up to pray, and gently tether
    Me, as thy lamb there, with thy garment's
    spread?

If this was ever granted, I would rest
    My head beneath thine, while thy healing
    hands
Close-covered both my eyes beside thy breast,
    Pressing the brain, which too much thought
    expands,
Back to its proper size again, and smoothing
Distortion down till every nerve had soothing,
    And all lay quiet, happy and suppressed.

How soon all worldly wrong would be repaired!
    I think how I should view the earth and skies
And sea, when once again my brow was bared
    After thy healing, with such different eyes.
O world, as God has made it! All is beauty:
And knowing this, is love, and love is duty.
    What further may be sought for or declared?

Guercino drew this angel I saw teach
    (Alfred, dear friend!) — that little child to
    pray,
Holding the little hands up, each to each
    Pressed gently, — with his own head turned
    away
Over the earth where so much lay before him
Of work to do, though heaven was opening o'er
    him,
    And he was left at Fano by the beach.

We were at Fano, and three times we went
    To sit and see him in his chapel there,
And drink his beauty to our soul's content
    — My angel with me too: and since I care
For dear Guercino's fame (to which in power
And glory comes this picture for a dower,
    Fraught with a pathos so magnificent) —

And since he did not work thus earnestly
    At all times, and has else endured some
    wrong —

I took one thought his picture struck from
　me,
And spread it out, translating it to song.
My love is here. Where are you, dear old
　friend?
How rolls the Wairoa at your world's far end?
This is Ancona, yonder is the sea.

MEMORABILIA

AH, did you once see Shelley plain,
　And did he stop and speak to you,
And did you speak to him again?
　How strange it seems and new!

But you were living before that,
　And also you are living after;
And the memory I started at —
　My starting moves your laughter!

I crossed a moor, with a name of its own
　And a certain use in the world no doubt,
Yet a hand's-breadth of it shines alone
　'Mid the blank miles round about:

For there I picked up on the heather,
　And there I put inside my breast
A moulted feather, an eagle-feather!
　Well, I forget the rest.

POPULARITY

As the previous poem was an appreciation of
Shelley, so this, of Keats.

STAND still, true poet that you are!
　I know you; let me try and draw you.
Some night you 'll fail us: when afar
　You rise, remember one man saw you,
Knew you, and named a star!

My star, God's glow-worm! Why extend
　That loving hand of his which leads you,
Yet locks you safe from end to end
　Of this dark world, unless he needs you,
Just saves your light to spend?

His clenched hand shall unclose at last,
　I know, and let out all the beauty:
My poet holds the future fast,
　Accepts the coming ages' duty,
Their present for this past.

That day, the earth's feast-master's brow
　Shall clear, to God the chalice raising;
"Others give best at first, but thou
　Forever set'st our table praising,
Keep'st the good wine till now!"

Meantime, I 'll draw you as you stand,
　With few or none to watch and wonder:
I 'll say — a fisher, on the sand
　By Tyre the old, with ocean-plunder,
A netful, brought to land.

Who has not heard how Tyrian shells
　Enclosed the blue, that dye of dyes
Whereof one drop worked miracles,
　And colored like Astarte's eyes
Raw silk the merchant sells?

And each bystander of them all
　Could criticise, and quote tradition
How depths of blue sublimed some pall
　— To get which, pricked a king's ambition;
Worth sceptre, crown and ball.

Yet there 's the dye, in that rough mesh,
　The sea has only just o'er-whispered!
Live whelks, each lip's beard dripping fresh,
　As if they still the water's lisp heard
Through foam the rock-weeds thresh.

Enough to furnish Solomon
　Such hangings for his cedar-house,
That, when gold-robed he took the throne
　In that abyss of blue, the Spouse
Might swear his presence shone

Most like the centre-spike of gold
　Which burns deep in the bluebell's womb
What time, with ardors manifold,
　The bee goes singing to her groom,
Drunken and overbold.

Mere conchs! not fit for warp or woof!
　Till cunning come to pound and squeeze
And clarify, — refine to proof
　The liquor filtered by degrees,
While the world stands aloof.

And there 's the extract, flasked and fine,
　And priced and salable at last!
And Hobbs, Nobbs, Stokes and Nokes combine
　To paint the future from the past,
Put blue into their line.

Hobbs hints blue, — straight he turtle eats:
　Nobbs prints blue, — claret crowns his cup:
Nokes outdares Stokes in azure feats, —
　Both gorge. Who fished the murex up?
What porridge had John Keats?

MASTER HUGUES OF SAXE-GOTHA

Whomever Browning may have had in mind,
there was no historical figure with this name
and place.

HIST, but a word, fair and soft!
　Forth and be judged, Master Hugues!
Answer the question I 've put you so oft:
　What do you mean by your mountainous
　　fugues?
See, we 're alone in the loft, —

I, the poor organist here,
　Hugues, the composer of note,
Dead though, and done with, this many a year.
　Let 's have a colloquy, something to quote,
Make the world prick up its ear!

See, the church empties apace :
    Fast they extinguish the lights.
Hallo there, sacristan !   Five minutes' grace !
Here 's a crank pedal wants setting to rights,
Balks one of holding the base.

See, our huge house of the sounds,
    Hushing its hundreds at once
Bids the last loiterer back to his bounds !
    — O you may challenge them, not a response
Get the church-saints on their rounds !

(Saints go their rounds, who shall doubt ?
    — March, with the moon to admire,
Up nave, down chancel, turn transept about,
    Supervise all betwixt pavement and spire,
Put rats and mice to the rout —

Aloys and Jurien and Just —
    Order things back to their place,
Have a sharp eye lest the candlesticks rust,
    Rub the church-plate, darn the sacrament-
        lace,
Clear the desk-velvet of dust.)

Here 's your book, younger folks shelve !
    Played I not off-hand and runningly,
Just now, your masterpiece, hard number
        twelve ?
Here 's what should strike, could one handle
        it cunningly :
Help the axe, give it a helve !

Page after page as I played,
    Every bar's rest where one wipes
Sweat from one's brow, I looked up and sur-
        veyed,
O'er my three claviers, yon forest of pipes
Whence you still peeped in the shade.

Sure you were wishful to speak ?
    You, with brow ruled like a score,
Yes, and eyes buried in pits on each cheek,
    Like two great breves, as they wrote them
        of yore,
Each side that bar, your straight beak !

Sure you said — " Good, the mere notes !
    Still, couldst thou take my intent,
Know what procured me our Company's
        votes —
A master were lauded and sciolists shent,
Parted the sheep from the goats ! "

Well then, speak up, never flinch !
    Quick, ere my candle 's a snuff
— Burnt, do you see ? to its uttermost inch —
    I believe in you, but that 's not enough :
Give my conviction a clinch !

First you deliver your phrase
    — Nothing propound, that I see,
Fit in itself for much blame or much praise —
    Answered no less, where no answer needs be ;
Off start the Two on their ways.

Straight must a Third interpose,
    Volunteer needlessly help ;

In strikes a Fourth, a Fifth thrusts in his nose,
    So the cry 's open, the kennel 's a-yelp,
Argument 's hot to the close.

One dissertates, he is candid ;
    Two must discept, — has distinguished ;
Three helps the couple, if ever yet man did ;
    Four protests ; Five makes a dart at the
        thing wished :
Back to One, goes the case bandied.

One says his say with a difference ;
    More of expounding, explaining !
All now is wrangle, abuse and vociferance ;
    Now there 's a truce, all 's subdued, self-re-
        straining :
Five, though, stands out all the stiffer hence.

One is incisive, corrosive ;
    Two retorts, nettled, curt, crepitant ;
Three makes rejoinder, expansive, explosive ;
    Four overbears them all, strident and strepi-
        tant :
Five . . . O Danaides, O Sieve !

Now, they ply axes and crowbars ;
    Now, they prick pins at a tissue
Fine as a skein of the casuist Escobar's
    Worked on the bone of a lie.   To what issue ?
Where is our gain at the Two-bars ?

Est fuga, volvitur rota.
    On we drift : where looms the dim port ?
One, Two, Three, Four, Five, contribute their
        quota ;
    Something is gained, if one caught but the
        import —
Show it us, Hugues of Saxe-Gotha !

What with affirming, denying,
    Holding, risposting, subjoining,
All 's like . . . it 's like . . . for an instance
        I 'm trying . . .
    There ! See our roof, its gilt moulding and
        groining
Under those spider-webs lying !

So your fugue broadens and thickens,
    Greatens and deepens and lengthens,
Till we exclaim — " But where 's music, the
        dickens ?
    Blot ye the gold, while your spider-web
        strengthens
— Blacked to the stoutest of tickens ? "

I for man's effort am zealous :
    Prove me such censure unfounded !
Seems it surprising a lover grows jealous —
    Hopes 't was for something, his organ-pipes
        sounded,
Tiring three boys at the bellows ?

Is it your moral of Life ?
    Such a web, simple and subtle,
Weave we on earth here in impotent strife,
    Backward and forward each throwing his
        shuttle,
Death ending all with a knife ?

Over our heads truth and nature —
Still our life's zigzags and dodges,
Ins and outs, weaving a new legislature —
God's gold just shining its last where that
lodges,
Palled beneath man's usurpature.

So we o'ershroud stars and roses,
Cherub and trophy and garland ;
Nothings grow something which quietly closes
Heaven's earnest eye : not a glimpse of the
far land
Gets through our comments and glozes.

Ah, but traditions, inventions,
(Say we and make up a visage)
So many men with such various intentions,
Down the past ages, must know more than this
age !
Leave we the web its dimensions !

Who thinks Hugues wrote for the deaf,
Proved a mere mountain in labor ?
Better submit ; try again ; what 's the clef ?
'Faith, 't is no trifle for pipe and for tabor —
Four flats, the minor in F.

Friend, your fugue taxes the finger :
Learning it once, who would lose it ?
Yet all the while a misgiving will linger,
Truth 's golden o'er us although we refuse
it —
Nature, through cobwebs we string her.

Hugues ! I advise meâ pœnâ
(Counterpoint glares like a Gorgon)
Bid One, Two, Three, Four, Five, clear the
arena !
Say the word, straight I unstop the full or-
gan,
Blare out the mode Palestrina.

While in the roof, if I 'm right there,
. . . Lo you, the wick in the socket !
Hallo, you sacristan, show us a light there !
Down it dips, gone like a rocket.
What, you want, do you, to come unawares,
Sweeping the church up for first morning-
prayers,
And find a poor devil has ended his cares
At the foot of your rotten-runged rat-riddled
stairs ?
Do I carry the moon in my pocket ?

THE RETURN OF THE DRUSES

A TRAGEDY

Originally published as No. IV. of *Bells and Pomegranates* in 1843. The manuscript was first named *Mansoor the Hierophant.*

PERSONS

The Grand-Master's Prefect.
The Patriarch's Nuncio.
The Republic's Admiral.
Loys de Dreux, *Knight-Novice.*

Initiated Druses — Djabal, Khalil, Anael, Maani, Karshook, Raghib, Ayoob, and others.
Uninitiated Druses, Prefect's Guard, Nuncio's Attend-ants, Admiral's Force.

Time, 14—.

Place, *An Islet of the Southern Sporades, colonized by Druses of Lebanon, and garrisoned by the Knights-Hospitallers of Rhodes.*

Scene, *A Hall in the Prefect's Palace.*

ACT I

Enter stealthily Karshook, Raghib, Ayoob, *and other initiated* Druses, *each as he enters casting off a robe that conceals his distinctive black vest and white tur-ban ; then, as giving a loose to exultation, —*

Karshook. The moon is carried off in purple
fire :
Day breaks at last ! Break glory, with the day,
On Djabal's dread incarnate mystery
Now ready to resume its pristine shape
Of Hakeem, as the Khalif vanished erst
In what seemed death to uninstructed eyes,
On red Mokattam's verge — our Founder's flesh,
As he resumes our Founder's function !
    Raghib.   — Death
Sweep to the Christian Prefect that enslaved
So long us sad Druse exiles o'er the sea !
   Ayoob. — Most joy be thine, O Mother-mount !
   Thy brood

Returns to thee, no outcasts as we left,
But thus — but thus ! Behind, our Prefect's
corse ;
Before, a presence like the morning — thine,
Absolute Djabal late, — God Hakeem now
That day breaks !
   Kar.   Off then, with disguise at last !
As from our forms this hateful garb we strip,
Lose every tongue its glozing accent too,
Discard each limb the ignoble gesture ! Cry,
'T is the Druse Nation, warders on our Mount
Of the world's secret, since the birth of time,
— No kindred slips, no offsets from thy stock,
No spawn of Christians are we, Prefect, we
Who rise . . .
   Ay.   Who shout . . .
   Ragh.   Who seize, a first-fruits, ha —
Spoil of the spoiler ! Brave !
[They begin to tear down, and to dispute for, the decora-
tions of the hall.

Kar.   Hold !
Ay.   — Mine, I say ;
And mine shall it continue !
Kar.   Just this fringe !
Take anything beside ! Lo, spire on spire,
Curl serpentwise wreathed columns to the top
O' the roof, and hide themselves mysteriously
Among the twinkling lights and darks that
     haunt
Yon cornice ! Where the huge veil, they suspend
Before the Prefect's chamber of delight,
Floats wide, then falls again as if its slave,
The scented air, took heart now, and anon
Lost heart to buoy its breadths of gorgeous-
     ness
Above the gloom they droop in — all the porch
Is jewelled o'er with frostwork charactery ;
And, see, yon eight-point cross of white flame,
     winking
Hoar - silvery like some fresh - broke marble
     stone :
Raze out the Rhodian cross there, so thou leav'st
     me
This single fringe !
Ay.   Ha, wouldst thou, dog-fox ? Help !
— Three hand-breadths of gold fringe, my son
     was set
To twist, the night he died !
Kar.   Nay, hear the knave !
And I could witness my one daughter borne,
A week since, to the Prefect's couch, yet fold
These arms, be mute, lest word of mine should
     mar
Our Master's work, delay the Prefect here
A day, prevent his sailing hence for Rhodes —
How know I else ? — Hear me denied my right
By such a knave !
Ragh. [*Interposing.*] Each ravage for him-
     self !
Booty enough ! On, Druses ! Be there found
Blood and a heap behind us ; with us, Djabal
Turned Hakeem ; and before us, Lebanon !
Yields the porch ? Spare not ! There his min-
     ions dragged
Thy daughter, Karshook, to the Prefect's
     couch !
Ayoob ! Thy son, to soothe the Prefect's
     pride,
Bent o'er that task, the death-sweat on his
     brow,
Carving the spice-tree's heart in scroll-work
     there !
Onward in Djabal's name !
(*As the tumult is at height, enter* KHALIL. *A pause and
     silence.*)
Khalil.   Was it for this,
Djabal hath summoned you ? Deserve you
     thus
A portion in to-day's event ? What, here —
When most behoves your feet fall soft, your
     eyes
Sink low, your tongues lie still, — at Djabal's
     side,
Close in his very hearing, who, perchance,
Assumes e'en now God Hakeem's dreaded
     shape, —
Dispute you for these gauds ?
Ay.   How say'st thou, Khalil ?

Doubtless our Master prompts thee ! Take the
     fringe,
Old Karshook ! I supposed it was a day . . .
Kha. For pillage ?
Kar.   Hearken, Khalil ! Never spoke
A boy so like a song-bird ; we avouch thee
Prettiest of all our Master's instruments
Except thy bright twin-sister ; thou and Anael
Challenge his prime regard : but we may crave
(Such nothings as we be) a portion too
Of Djabal's favor ; in him we believed,
His bound ourselves, him moon by moon
     obeyed,
Kept silence till this daybreak — so, may claim
Reward : who grudges me my claim ?
Ay.   To-day
Is not as yesterday !
Ragh.   Stand off !
Kha.   Rebel you ?
Must I, the delegate of Djabal, draw
His wrath on you, the day of our Return ?
Other Druses. Wrench from their grasp the
     fringe ! Hounds ! must the earth
Vomit her plagues on us through thee ? — and
     thee ?
Plague me not, Khalil, for their fault !
Kha.   Oh, shame !
Thus breaks to-day on you, the mystic tribe
Who, flying the approach of Osman, bore
Our faith, a merest spark, from Syria's ridge,
Its birthplace, hither ! " Let the sea divide
These hunters from their prey," you said ;
     " and safe
In this dim islet's virgin solitude
Tend we our faith, the spark, till happier time
Fan it to fire ; till Hakeem rise again,
According to his word that, in the flesh
Which faded on Mokattam ages since,
He, at our extreme need, would interpose,
And, reinstating all in power and bliss,
Lead us himself to Lebanon once more."
Was 't not thus you departed years ago,
Ere I was born ?
Druses.   'T was even thus, years ago.
Kha. And did you call — (according to old
     laws
Which bid us, lest the sacred grow profane,
Assimilate ourselves in outward rites
With strangers fortune makes our lords, and
     live
As Christian with the Christian, Jew with Jew
Druse only with the Druses) — did you call
Or no, to stand 'twixt you and Osman's rage,
(Mad to pursue e'en hither through the sea
The remnant of our tribe,) a race self vowed
To endless warfare with his hordes and him,
The White-cross Knights of the adjacent Isle ?
Kar. And why else rend we down, wrench
     up, rase out ?
These Knights of Rhodes we thus solicited
For help, bestowed on us a fiercer pest
Than aught we fled — their Prefect ; who began
His promised mere paternal governance,
By a prompt massacre of all our Sheikhs
Able to thwart the Order in its scheme
Of crushing, with our nation's memory,
Each chance of our return, and taming us
Bondslaves to Rhodes forever — all, he thinks

To end by this day's treason.

Kha.   Say I not?
You, fitted to the Order's purposes,
Your Sheikhs cut off, your rights, your garb proscribed,
Must yet receive one degradation more;
The Knights at last throw off the mask — transfer,
As tributary now and appanage,
This islet they are but protectors of,
To their own ever-craving liege, the Church,
Who licenses all crimes that pay her thus.
You, from their Prefect, were to be consigned
(Pursuant of I know not what vile pact)
To the Knights' Patriarch, ardent to outvie
His predecessor in all wickedness.
When suddenly rose Djabal in the midst,
Djabal, the man in semblance, but our God
Confessed by signs and portents. Ye saw fire
Bicker round Djabal, heard strange music flit
Bird-like about his brow?
Druses.   We saw — we heard!
Djabal is Hakeem, the incarnate Dread,
The phantasm Khalif, King of Prodigies!
Kha. And as he said has not our Khalif done,
And so disposed events (from land to land
Passing invisibly) that when, this morn,
The pact of villany complete, there comes
This Patriarch's Nuncio with this Master's Prefect
Their treason to consummate, — each will face
For a crouching handful, an uplifted nation;
For simulated Christians, confessed Druses;
And, for slaves past hope of the Mother-mount,
Freedmen returning there 'neath Venice' flag;
That Venice which, the Hospitallers' foe,
Grants us from Candia escort home at price
Of our relinquished isle, Rhodes counts her own —
Venice, whose promised argosies should stand
Toward harbor: is it now that you, and you,
And you, selected from the rest to bear
The burden of the Khalif's secret, further
To-day's event, entitled by your wrongs,
And witness in the Prefect's hall his fate —
That you dare clutch these gauds? Ay, drop them!

Kar.   True,
Most true, all this; and yet, may one dare hint,
Thou art the youngest of us? — though employed
Abundantly as Djabal's confidant,
Transmitter of his mandates, even now.
Much less, whene'er beside him Anael graces
The cedar throne, his queen-bride, art thou like
To occupy its lowest step that day!
Now, Khalil, wert thou checked as thou aspirest,
Forbidden such or such an honor, — say,
Would silence serve so amply?
Kha.   Karshook thinks
I covet honors? Well, nor idly thinks!
Honors? I have demanded of them all
The greatest!
Kar.   I supposed so.
Kha.   Judge, yourselves!
Turn. thus: 't is in the alcove at the back

Of yonder columned porch, whose entrance now
The veil hides, that our Prefect holds his state,
Receives the Nuncio, when the one, from Rhodes,
The other lands from Syria; there they meet.
Now, I have sued with earnest prayers . . .
Kar.   For what
Shall the Bride's brother vainly sue?
Kha.   That mine—
Avenging in one blow a myriad wrongs
— Might be the hand to slay the Prefect there!
Djabal reserves that office for himself.
                              [*A silence.*
Thus far, as youngest of you all, I speak
— Scarce more enlightened than yourselves: since, near
As I approach him, nearer as I trust
Soon to approach our Master, he reveals
Only the God's power, not the glory yet.
Therefore I reasoned with you: now, as servant
To Djabal, bearing his authority,
Hear me appoint your several posts! Till noon
None see him save myself and Anael: once
The deed achieved, our Khalif, casting off
The embodied Awe's tremendous mystery,
The weakness of the flesh disguise, resumes
His proper glory, ne'er to fade again.
              (*Enter a* Druse.)
The Druse. Our Prefect lands from Rhodes!
              — without a sign
That he suspects aught since he left our Isle;
Nor in his train a single guard beyond
The few he sailed with hence: so have we learned
From Loys.
Kar.   Loys? Is not Loys gone
Forever?
Ay.   Loys, the Frank Knight, returned?
The Druse. Loys, the boy, stood on the leading prow
Conspicuous in his gay attire, and leapt
Into the surf the foremost. Since day-dawn
I kept watch to the Northward; take but note
Of my poor vigilance to Djabal!
Kha.   Peace!
Thou, Karshook, with thy company, receive
The Prefect as appointed: see, all keep
The wonted show of servitude: announce
His entry here by the accustomed peal
Of trumpets, then await the further pleasure
Of Djabal! (Loys back, whom Djabal sent
To Rhodes that we might spare the single Knight
Worth sparing!)
              (*Enter a second* Druse.)
The Druse.   I espied it first! Say, I
First spied the Nuncio's galley from the South!
Said'st thou a Crossed-keys' flag would flap the mast?
It nears apace! One galley and no more.
If Djabal chance to ask who spied the flag,
Forget not, I it was!
Kha.   Thou, Ayoob, bring
The Nuncio and his followers hither! Break
One rule prescribed, ye wither in your blood,
Die at your fault!
              (*Enter a third* Druse.)
The Druse.   I shall see home, see home!
— Shall banquet in the sombre groves again!

Hail to thee, Khalil! Venice looms afar;
The argosies of Venice, like a cloud,
Bear up from Candia in the distance!
Kha.   Joy!
Summon our people, Raghib! Bid all forth!
Tell them the long-kept secret, old and young!
Set free the captive, let the trampled raise
Their faces from the dust, because at length
The cycle is complete, God Hakeem's reign
Begins anew! Say, Venice for our guard,
Ere night we steer for Syria! Hear you, Druses?
Hear you this crowning witness to the claims
Of Djabal? Oh, I spoke of hope and fear,
Reward and punishment, because he bade
Who has the right: for me, what should I say
But, mar not those imperial lineaments,
No majesty of all that rapt regard
Vex by the least omission! Let him rise
Without a check from you!
Druses.   Let Djabal rise!
        (*Enter* Loys. — *The* Druses *are silent.*)
Loys. Who speaks of Djabal? — for I seek
        him, friends!
[*Aside.*] *Tu Dieu!* 'T is as our Isle broke out
        in song
For joy, its Prefect-incubus drops off
To-day, and I succeed him in his rule!
But no — they cannot dream of their good for-
        tune!
[*Aloud.*] Peace to you, Druses! I have tidings
        for you,
But first for Djabal: where 's your tall be-
        witcher,
With that small Arab thin-lipped silver-mouth?
Kha. [*Aside to* Kar.] Loys, in truth! Yet
        Djabal cannot err!
Kar. [*To* Kha.] And who takes charge of
        Loys? That 's forgotten,
Despite thy wariness! Will Loys stand
And see his comrades slaughtered?
Loys. [*Aside.*]   How they shrink
And whisper, with those rapid faces! What?
The sight of me in their oppressors' garb
Strikes terror to the simple tribe? God's
        shame
On those that bring our Order ill repute!
But all 's at end now; better days begin
For these mild mountaineers from over-sea:
The timidest shall have in me no Prefect
To cower at thus! [*Aloud.*] I asked for
        Djabal —
Kar. [*Aside.*]   Better
One lured him, ere he can suspect, inside
The corridor; 't were easy to dispatch
A youngster. [*To* Loys.] Djabal passed some
        minutes since
Through yonder porch, and . . .
Kha. [*Aside.*] Hold! What, him dispatch?
The only Christian of them all we charge
No tyranny upon? Who, — noblest Knight
Of all that learned from time to time their
        trade
Of lust and cruelty among us, — heir
To Europe's pomp, a truest child of pride, —
Yet stood between the Prefect and ourselves
From the beginning? Loys, Djabal makes
Account of, and precisely sent to Rhodes
For safety? I take charge of him!

        [*To* Loys.]   Sir Loys, —
Loys. There, cousins! Does Sir Loys strike
        you dead?
Kha. [*Advancing.*] Djabal has intercourse
        with few or none
Till noontide: but, your pleasure?
Loys.   " Intercourse
With few or none? " — (Ah, Khalil, when you
        spoke
I saw not your smooth face! All health! —
        and health
To Anael! How fares Anael?) — " Intercourse
With few or none? " Forget you, I 've been
        friendly
With Djabal long ere you or any Druse?
— Enough of him at Rennes, I think, beneath
The Duke my father's roof! He 'd tell by the
        hour,
With fixed white eyes beneath his swarthy brow
Plausiblest stories . . .
Kha.   Stories, say you? — Ah,
The quaint attire!
Loys.   My dress for the last time!
How sad I cannot make you understand,
This ermine, o'er a shield, betokens me
Of Bretagne, ancientest of provinces
And noblest; and, what 's best and oldest there,
See, Dreux', our house's blazon, which the
        Nuncio
Tacks to an Hospitaller's vest to-day!
Kha. The Nuncio we await? What brings
        you back
From Rhodes, Sir Loys?
Loys.   How you island-tribe
Forget the world 's awake while here you
        drowse!
What brings me back? What should not bring
        me, rather!
Our Patriarch's Nuncio visits you to-day —
Is not my year's probation out? I come
To take the knightly vows.
Kha.   What 's that you wear?
Loys. This Rhodian cross? The cross your
        Prefect wore.
You should have seen, as I saw, the full Chap-
        ter
Rise, to a man, while they transferred this cross
From that unworthy Prefect's neck to . . .
        (fool —
My secret will escape me!) In a word,
My year's probation passed, a Knight ere eve
Am I; bound, like the rest, to yield my wealth
To the common stock, to live in chastity,
(We Knights espouse alone our Order's fame)
— Change this gay weed for the black white-
        crossed gown,
And fight to death against the Infidel
— Not, therefore, against you, you Christians
        with
Such partial difference only as befits
The peacefullest of tribes. But Khalil, pri-
        thee,
Is not the Isle brighter than wont to-day?
Kha. Ah, the new sword!
Loys.   See now! You handle sword
As 't were a camel-staff! Pull! That 's my
        motto,
Annealed " *Pro fide,*" on the blade in blue.

Kha. No curve in it ? Surely a blade should
curve.
Loys. Straight from the wrist ! Loose — it
should poise itself !
Kha. [*Waving with irrepressible exultation the
sword.*] We are a nation, Loys, of old fame
Among the mountains ! Rights have we to
keep
With the sword too !
Remembering himself.] But I forget — you bid
me
Seek Djabal ?
Loys. What ! A sword's sight scares you
not ?
The People I will make of him and them !
Oh let my Prefect-sway begin at once !)
Bring Djabal — say, indeed, that come he must !
Kha. At noon seek Djabal in the Prefect's
Chamber,
And find . . . [*Aside.*] Nay, 't is thy cursed
race's token,
Frank pride, no special insolence of thine !
Aloud.] Tarry, and I will do your bidding,
Loys !
To the rest aside.] Now, forth you ! I pro-
ceed to Djabal straight.
Leave this poor boy, who knows not what he
says !
Oh will it not add joy to even thy joy,
Djabal, that I report all friends were true ?
[KHALIL *goes, followed by the* Druses.
Loys. Tu Dieu ! How happy I shall make
these Druses !
Was 't not surpassingly contrived of me
To get the long list of their wrongs by heart,
Then take the first pretence for stealing off
From these poor islanders, present myself
Sudden at Rhodes before the noble Chapter,
And (as best proof of ardor in its cause
Which ere to-night will have become, too, mine)
Acquaint it with this plague-sore in its body,
This Prefect and his villanous career ?
The princely Synod ! All I dared request
Was his dismissal ; and they graciously
Consigned his very office to myself —
Myself may cure the Isle diseased !
                                And well
For them, they did so ! Since I never felt
How lone a lot, though brilliant, I embrace,
Till now that, past retrieval, it is mine.
To live thus, and thus die ! Yet, as I leapt
On shore, so home a feeling greeted me
That I could half believe in Djabal's story,
He used to tempt my father with, at Rennes —
And me, too, since the story brought me here —
Of some Count Dreux and ancestor of ours
Who, sick of wandering from Bouillon's war,
Left his old name in Lebanon.
                              Long days
At least to spend in the Isle ! and, my news
known
An hour hence, what if Anael turn on me
The great black eyes I must forget ?
                                Why, fool,
Recall them, then ? My business is with Dja-
bal,
Not Anael ! Djabal tarries : if I seek him ? —
The Isle is brighter than its wont to-day !

ACT II

Enter DJABAL.

Dja. That a strong man should think him-
self a God !
I — Hakeem ? To have wandered through the
world,
Sown falsehood, and thence reaped now scorn,
now faith,
For my one chant with many a change, my
tale
Of outrage, and my prayer for vengeance — this
Required, forsooth, no mere man's faculty,
·Naught less than Hakeem's ? The persuading
Loys
To pass probation here : the getting access
By Loys to the Prefect ; worst of all,
The gaining my tribe's confidence by fraud
That would disgrace the very Frank, — a few
Of Europe's secrets which subdue the flame,
The wave, — to ply a simple tribe with these,
Took Hakeem ?
                And I feel this first to-day !
Does the day break, is the hour imminent
When one deed, when my whole life's deed, my
deed
Must be accomplished ? Hakeem ? Why the
God ?
Shout, rather, " Djabal, Youssof's child,
thought slain
With his whole race, the Druses' Sheikhs, this
Prefect
Endeavored to extirpate — saved, a child,
Returns from traversing the world, a man,
Able to take revenge, lead back the march
To Lebanon " — so shout, and who gainsays ?
But now, because delusion mixed itself
Insensibly with this career, all 's changed !
Have I brought Venice to afford us convoy ?
" True — but my jugglings wrought that ! "
                Put I heart
Into our people where no heart lurked ? — " Ah,
What cannot an impostor do ! "
                                Not this !
Not do this which I do ! Not bid avaunt
Falsehood ! Thou shalt not keep thy hold on
me !
— Nor even get a hold on me ! 'T is now —
This day — hour — minute — 't is as here I stand
On the accursed threshold of the Prefect,
That I am found deceiving and deceived !
And now what do I ? — hasten to the few
Deceived, ere they deceive the many — shout.
" As I professed, I did believe myself ! "
Say, Druses, had you seen a butchery —
If Ayoob, Karshook saw —— Maani there
Must tell you how I saw my father sink ;
My mother's arms twine still about my neck ;
I hear my brother shriek, here 's yet the scar
Of what was meant for my own death-blow —
say,
If you had woke like me, grown year by year
Out of the tumult in a far-off clime,
Would it be wondrous such delusion grew ?
I walked the world, asked help at every hand ;
Came help or no ? Not this and this ? Which
helps

When I returned with, found the Prefect here,
The Druses here, all here but Hakeem's self,
The Khalif of the thousand prophecies,
Reserved for such a juncture, — could I call
My mission aught but Hakeem's? Promised
  Hakeem
More than performs the Djabal — you absolve?
— Me, you will never shame before the crowd
Yet happily ignorant ? — Me, both throngs sur-
  round,
The few deceived, the many unabused,
— Who, thus surrounded, slay for you and them
The Prefect, lead to Lebanon ? No Khalif,
But Sheikh once more ! Mere Djabal — not " . . .
      (*Enter* KHALIL *hastily.*)
  Kha.   — God Hakeem !
'T is told ! The whole Druse nation knows thee,
  Hakeem,
As we ! and mothers lift on high their babes
Who seem aware, so glisten their great eyes,
Thou hast not failed us ; ancient brows are
  proud ;
Our elders could not earlier die, it seems,
Than at thy coming ! The Druse heart is thine !
Take it ! my lord and theirs, be thou adored !
  Dja. [*Aside.*] Adored ! — but I renounce
  it utterly !
  Kha. Already are they instituting choirs
And dances to the Khalif, as of old
'T is chronicled thou bad'st them.
  Dja. [*Aside.*]   I abjure it !
'T is not mine — not for me !
  Kha.   Why pour they wine
Flavored like honey and bruised mountain-
  herbs,
Or wear those strings of sun-dried cedar-fruit ?
Oh, let me tell thee — Esaad, we supposed
Doting, is carried forth, eager to see
The last sun rise on the Isle : he can see now !
The shamed Druse women never wept before :
They can look up when we reach home, they
  say.
Smell ! — sweet cane, saved in Lilith's breast
  thus long —
Sweet ! — it grows wild in Lebanon. And I
Alone do nothing for thee ! 'T is my office
Just to announce what well thou know'st — but
  thus
Thou bidst me. At this self-same moment tend
The Prefect, Nuncio and the Admiral
Hither by their three sea-paths : nor forget
Who were the trusty watchers ! — thou forget ?
Like me, who do forget that Anael bade . . .
  Dja. [*Aside*]. Ay, Anael, Anael — is that
  said at last ?
Louder than all, that would be said, I knew !
What does abjuring mean, confessing mean,
To the people ? Till that woman crossed my
  path,
On went I, solely for my people's sake :
I saw her, and I then first saw myself,
And slackened pace : " If I should prove indeed
Hakeem — with Anael by ! "
  Kha. [*Aside.*]   Ah, he is rapt !
Dare I at such a moment break on him
Even to do my sister's bidding ? Yes :
The eyes are Djabal's and not Hakeem's yet,
Though but till I have spoken this, perchance.

  Dja. [*Aside.*] To yearn to tell her, and ye
  have no one
Great heart's word that will tell her ! I could
  gasp
Doubtless one such word out, and die.
              [*Aloud.*]   You said
That Anael . . .
  Kha. . . . Fain would see thee, speak with
  thee,
Before thou change, discard this Djabal's shape
She knows, for Hakeem's shape she is to know
Something to say that will not from her mind
I know not what — " Let him but come ! " she
  said.
  Dja. [*Half apart.*] My nation — all my
  Druses — how fare they ?
Those I must save, and suffer thus to save,
Hold they their posts ? Wait they their Khalif
  too ?
  Kha. All at the signal pant to flock around
That banner of a brow !
  Dja. [*Aside.*]   And when they flock
Confess them this : and after, for reward,
Be chased with howlings to her feet perchance
— Have the poor outraged Druses, deaf and
  blind,
Precede me there, forestall my story there,
Tell it in mocks and jeers !
            I lose myself !
Who needs a Hakeem to direct him now ?
I need the veriest child — why not this child ?
        [*Turning abruptly to* KHALIL
You are a Druse too, Khalil ; you were nourished
Like Anael with our mysteries : if she
Could vow, so nourished, to love only one
Who should avenge the Druses, whence pro-
  ceeds
Your silence ? Wherefore made you no essay
Who thus implicitly can execute
My bidding ? What have I done, you could not ?
Who, knowing more than Anael the prostration
Of our once lofty tribe, the daily life
Of this detested . . .
        Does he come, you say,
This Prefect ? All 's in readiness ?
  Kha.   The sword
The sacred robe, the Khalif's mystic tiar,
Laid up so long, are all disposed beside
The Prefect's chamber.
  Dja.   — Why did you despair ?
  Kha. I know our nation's state ? Too surely
  know,
As thou who speak'st to prove me ! Wrongs
  like ours
Should wake revenge : but when I sought the
  wronged
And spoke, — " The Prefect stabbed your son —
  arise !
Your daughter, while you starve, eats shameless
  bread
In his pavilion — then arise ! " — my speech
Fell idly : 't was, " Be silent, or worse fare ! "
Endure till time's slow cycle prove complete ?
Who may'st thou be that takest on thee to
  thrust
Into this peril — art thou Hakeem ? " No !
Only a mission like thy mission renders
All these obedient at a breath, subdues

heir private passions, brings their wills to one!
Dja. You think so?
Kha. Even now — when they have witnessed
hy miracles — had I not threatened all
Vith Hakeem's vengeance, they would mar the
    work,
nd couch ere this, each with his special prize,
afe in his dwelling, leaving our main hope
o perish. No! When these have kissed thy
    feet
t Lebanon, the past purged off, the present
lear, — for the future, even Hakeem's mission
lay end, and I perchance, or any youth,
hall rule them thus renewed. — I tutor thee!
    Dja. And wisely. (He is Anael's brother,
    pure
s Anael's self.) Go say i come to her.
laste! I will follow you.   [KHALIL *goes.*
                        Oh, not confess
o these, the blinded multitude — confess,
efore at least the fortune of my deed
lalf authorize its means! Only to her
et me confess my fault, who in my path
urled up like incense from a Mage-king's
    tomb
Vhen he would have the wayfarer descend
hrough the earth's rift and bear hid treasure
    forth!
low should child's-carelessness prove man-
    hood's crime
ill now that I, whose lone youth hurried past,
etting each joy 'scape for the Druses' sake,
t length recover in one Druse all joy?
Vere her brow brighter, her eyes richer, still
Vould I confess! On the gulf's verge I pause.
low could I slay the Prefect, thus and thus?
nael, be mine to guard me, not destroy! [*Goes.*
Enter ANAEL, *and* MAANI *who is assisting to array her
    in the ancient dress of the Druses.*)
    Anael. Those saffron vestures of the tabret-
    girls!
omes Djabal, think you?
    Maani.   Doubtless Djabal comes.
    An. Dost thou snow-swathe thee kinglier,
    Lebanon,
han in my dreams? — Nay, all the tresses off
ly forehead! Look I lovely so? He says
hat I am lovely.
    Maa.   Lovely: nay, that hangs
wry.
    An. You tell me how a khandjar hangs?
he sharp side, thus, along the heart, see,
    marks
he maiden of our class. Are you content
or Djabal as for me?
    Maa.   Content, my child.
    An. Oh mother, tell me more of him! He
    comes
ven now — tell more, fill up my soul with him!
    Maa. And did I not . . . yes, surely . . .
    tell you all?
    An. What will be changed in Djabal when
    the Change
rrives? Which feature? Not his eyes!
    Maa.   'T is writ
ur Hakeem's eyes rolled fire and clove the
    dark
uperbly.

    An. Not his eyes! His voice perhaps?
Yet that's no change; for a grave current lived
— Grandly beneath the surface ever lived,
That, scattering, broke as in live silver spray
While . . . ah, the bliss . . . he would dis-
    course to me
In that enforced still fashion, word on word!
'T is the old current which must swell through
    that,
For what least tone, Maani, could I lose?
'T is surely not his voice will change!
                        — If Hakeem
Only stood by! If Djabal, somehow, passed
Out of the radiance as from out a robe;
Possessed, but was not it!
                        He lived with you?
Well — and that morning Djabal saw me first
And heard me vow never to wed but one
Who saved my People — on that day . . . pro-
    ceed!
    Maa. Once more, then: from the time of
    his return
In secret, changed so since he left the Isle
That I, who screened our Emir's last of sons,
This Djabal, from the Prefect's massacre
— Who bade him ne'er forget the child he was,
— Who dreamed so long the youth he might be-
    come —
I knew not in the man that child; the man
Who spoke alone of hope to save our tribe,
How he had gone from land to land to save
Our tribe — allies were sure, nor foes to dread;
And much he mused, days, nights, alone he
    mused:
But never till that day when, pale and worn
As by a persevering woe, he cried
"Is there not one Druse left me?" — and I
    showed
The way to Khalil's and your hiding-place
From the abhorred eye of the Prefect here,
So that he saw you, heard you speak — till then,
Never did he announce — (how the moon seemed
To ope and shut, the while, above us both!)
— His mission was the mission promised us;
The cycle had revolved; all things renewing,
He was lost Hakeem clothed in flesh to lead
His children home anon, now veiled to work
Great purposes: the Druses now would change!
    An. And they have changed! And obsta-
    cles did sink,
And furtherances rose! And round his form
Played fire, and music beat her angel wings!
My people, let me more rejoice, oh more
For you than for myself! Did I but watch
Afar the pageant, feel our Khalif pass,
One of the throng, how proud were I — though
    ne'er
Singled by Djabal's glance! But to be chosen
His own from all, the most his own of all,
To be exalted with him, side by side,
Lead the exulting Druses, meet . . . ah, how
Worthily meet the maidens who await
Ever beneath the cedars — how deserve
This honor, in their eyes? So bright are they
Who saffron-vested sound the tabret there,
The girls who throng there in my dream! One
    hour
And all is over: how shall I do aught

That may deserve next hour's exalting? —
How? —   [*Suddenly to* MAANI.
Mother, I am not worthy him! I read it
Still in his eyes! He stands as if to tell me
I am not, yet forbears. Why else revert
To one theme ever? — how mere human gifts
Suffice him in myself — whose worship fades,
Whose awe goes ever off at his approach,
As now, who when he comes . . .
(DJABAL *enters.*)
                         Oh why is it
I cannot kneel to you?
  Dja.   Rather, 't is I
Should kneel to you, my Anael!
  An.   Even so!
For never seem you — shall I speak the truth? —
Never a God to me! 'T is the Man's hand,
Eye, voice! Oh, do you veil these to our people,
Or but to me? To them, I think, to them!
And brightness is their veil, shadow — my truth!
You mean that I should never kneel to you
— So, thus I kneel!
  Dja. [*Preventing her.*] No — no!
    [*Feeling the khandjar as he raises her.*
        Ha, have you chosen . . .
  An. The khandjar with our ancient garb.
But, Djabal,
Change not, be not exalted yet! Give time
That I may plan more, perfect more! My blood
Beats, beats!
  [*Aside.*] Oh, must I then — since Loys leaves
us
Never to come again, renew in me
These doubts so near effaced already — must
I needs confess them now to Djabal? — own
That when I saw that stranger, heard his voice,
My faith fell, and the woeful thought flashed
first
That each effect of Djabal's presence, taken
For proof of more than human attributes
In him, by me whose heart at his approach
Beat fast, whose brain while he was by swam
round,
Whose soul at his departure died away,
— That every such effect might have been
wrought
In other frames, though not in mine, by Loys
Or any merely mortal presence? Doubt
Is fading fast: shall I reveal it now?
How shall I meet the rapture presently,
With doubt unexpiated, undisclosed?
  Dja. [*Aside.*] Avow the truth? I cannot!
In what words
Avow that all she loved in me was false?
— Which yet has served that flower-like love of
hers
To climb by, like the clinging gourd, and clasp
With its divinest wealth of leaf and bloom.
Could I take down the prop-work, in itself
So vile, yet interlaced and overlaid
With painted cups and fruitage — might these
still
Bask in the sun, unconscious their own strength
Of matted stalk and tendril had replaced
The old support thus silently withdrawn!
But no; the beauteous fabric crushes too.
'T is not for my sake but for Anael's sake
I leave her soul this Hakeem where it leans.

Oh could I vanish from her, quit the Isle!
And yet — a thought comes: here my work i
done
At every point; the Druses must return —
Have convoy to their birth-place back, whoe'e
The leader be, myself or any Druse —
Venice is pledged to that: 't is for myself,
For my own vengeance in the Prefect's death,
I stay now, not for them: to slay or spare
The Prefect, whom imports it save myself?
He cannot bar their passage from the Isle;
What would his death be but my own reward ?
Then, mine I will forego. It is foregone!
Let him escape with all my House's blood!
Ere he can reach land, Djabal disappears,
And Hakeem, Anael loved, shall, fresh as first
Live in her memory, keeping her sublime
Above the world. She cannot touch that world
By ever knowing what I truly am,
Since Loys, — of mankind the only one
Able to link my present with my past,
My life in Europe with my Island life,
Thence, able to unmask me, — I 've disposed
Safely at last at Rhodes, and . . .
          (*Enter* KHALIL.)
  Kha.   Loys greets thee !
  Dja. Loys? To drag me back? It cannot
be !
  An. [*Aside.*] Loys! Ah, doubt may not be
stifled so!
  Kha. Can I have erred that thou so gazest?
Yes,
I told thee not in the glad press of tidings
Of higher import, Loys is returned
Before the Prefect, with, if possible,
Twice the light-heartedness of old. As though
On some inauguration he expects,
To-day, the world's fate hung!
  Dja.   — And asks for me ?
  Kha. Thou knowest all things. Thee in
chief he greets,
But every Druse of us is to be happy
At his arrival, he declares: were Loys
Thou, Master, he could have no wider soul
To take us in with. How I love that Loys!
  Dja. [*Aside.*] Shame winds me with her
tether round and round !
  An. [*Aside.*] Loys? I take the trial! it
is meet,
The little I can do, be done; that faith,
All I can offer, want no perfecting
Which my own act may compass. Ay, this
way
All may go well, nor that ignoble doubt
Be chased by other aid than mine. Advance
Close to my fear, weigh Loys with my Lord,
The mortal with the more than mortal gifts!
  Dja. [*Aside.*] Before, there were so few
deceived! and now
There 's doubtless not one least Druse in the
Isle
But, having learned my superhuman claims,
And calling me his Khalif-God, will clash
The whole truth out from Loys at first word!
While Loys, for his part, will hold me up,
With a Frank's unimaginable scorn
Of such imposture, to my people's eyes!
Could I but keep him longer yet awhile

From them, amuse him here until I plan
How he and I at once may leave the Isle!
Khalil I cannot part with from my side —
My only help in this emergency:
There 's Anael!
  An.   Please you?
  Dja.   Anael — none but she!
  To ANAEL.] I pass some minutes in the cham-
      ber there,
Ere I see Loys: you shall speak with him
Until I join you. Khalil follows me.
  An. [*Aside.*] As I divined: he bids me
      save myself,
Offers me a probation — I accept!
Let me see Loys!
  Loys. [*Without.*] Djabal!
  An. [*Aside.*]   'T is his voice.
The smooth Frank trifler with our people's
      wrongs,
The self-complacent boy-inquirer, loud
On this and that inflicted tyranny,
— Aught serving to parade an ignorance
Of how wrong feels, inflicted! Let me close
With what I viewed at distance: let myself
Probe this delusion to the core!
  Dja.   He comes.
Khalil, along with me! while Anael waits
Till I return once more — and but once more!

ACT III

ANAEL *and* LOYS.

  An. Here leave me! Here I wait another.
      'T was
For no mad protestation of a love
Like this you say possesses you, I came.
  Loys. Love? how protest a love I dare not
      feel?
Mad words may doubtless have escaped me:
      you
Are here — I only feel you here!
  An.   No more!
  Loys. But once again, whom could you love?
      I dare,
Alas, say nothing of myself, who am
A Knight now, for when Knighthood we em-
      brace,
Love we abjure: so, speak on safely: speak,
Lest I speak, and betray my faith! And yet
To say your breathing passes through me,
      changes
My blood to spirit, and my spirit to you,
As Heaven the sacrificer's wine to it —
This is not to protest my love! You said
You could love one . . .
  An.   One only! We are bent
To earth — who raises up my tribe, I love;
The Prefect bows us — who removes him; we
Have ancient rights — who gives them back to
      us,
I love. Forbear me! Let my hand go!
  Loys.   Him
You could love only? Where is Djabal?
      Stay!
[*Aside.*] Yet wherefore stay? Who does this
      but myself?
Had I apprised her that I come to do

Just this, what more could she acknowledge?
      No,
She sees into my heart's core! What is it
Feeds either cheek with red, as June some
      rose?
Why turns she from me? Ah fool, over-fond
To dream I could call up . . .
                . . . What never dream
Yet feigned! 'T is love! Oh Anael, speak to
      me!
Djabal —
  An. Seek Djabal by the Prefect's chamber
At noon!   [*She paces the room.*
  Loys. [*Aside.*] And am I not the Prefect
      now?
Is it my fate to be the only one
Able to win her love, the only one
Unable to accept her love? The past
Breaks up beneath my footing: came I here
This morn as to a slave, to set her free
And take her thanks, and then spend day by
      day
Content beside her in the Isle? What works
This knowledge in me now? Her eye has
      broken
The faint disguise away: for Anael's sake
I left the Isle, for her espoused the cause
Of the Druses, all for her I thought, till now,
To live without!
              — As I must live! To-day
Ordains me Knight, forbids me . . . never shall
Forbid me to profess myself, heart, arm,
Thy soldier!
  An.   Djabal you demanded, comes!
  Loys. [*Aside.*] What wouldst thou, Loys?
      see him? Naught beside
Is wanting: I have felt his voice a spell
From first to last. He brought me here, made
      known
The Druses to me, drove me hence to seek
Redress for them; and shall I meet him now,
When naught is wanting but a word of his,
To — what? — induce me to spurn hope, faith,
      pride,
Honor away, — to cast my lot among
His tribe, become a proverb in men's mouths,
Breaking my high pact of companionship
With those who graciously bestowed on me
The very opportunities I turn
Against them! Let me not see Djabal now!
  An. The Prefect also comes!
  Loys. [*Aside.*]   Him let me see,
Not Djabal! Him, degraded at a word,
To soothe me, — to attest belief in me —
And after, Djabal! Yes, ere I return
To her, the Nuncio's vow shall have destroyed
This heart's rebellion, and coerced this will
Forever.
          Anael, not before the vows
Irrevocably fix me . . .
                  Let me fly!
The Prefect, or I lose myself forever!   [*Goes*
  An. Yes, I am calm now; just one way
      remains —
One, to attest my faith in him: for, see,
I were quite lost else: Loys, Djabal, stand
On either side — two men! I balance looks
And words, give Djabal a man's preference.

No more. In Djabal, Hakeem is absorbed !
And for a love like this, the God who saves
My race, selects me for his bride ? One way ! —
    (*Enter* DJABAL.)
 Dja. [*To himself.*] No moment is to waste
then ; 't is resolved.
If Khalil may be trusted to lead back
My Druses, and if Loys can be lured
Out of the Isle — if I procure his silence,
Or promise never to return at least, —
All 's over. Even now my bark awaits :
I reach the next wild islet and the next,
And lose myself beneath the sun forever.
And now, to Anael !
 An.   Djabal, I am thine !
 Dja. Mine ? Djabal's ? — As if Hakeem
  had not been ?
 An. Not Djabal's ? Say first, do you read
my thought ?
Why need I speak, if you can read my thought ?
 Dja. I do not, I have said a thousand times.
 An. (My secret 's safe, I shall surprise him
  yet !)
Djabal, I knew your secret from the first :
Djabal, when first I saw you . . . (by our porch
You leant, and pressed the tinkling veil away,
And one fringe fell behind your neck — I
 see !)
 . . . I knew you were not human, for I said
"This dim secluded house where the sea beats
Is heaven to me — my people's huts are hell
To them ; this august form will follow me,
Mix with the waves his voice will, — I have
 him ;
And they, the Prefect ! Oh, my happiness
Rounds to the full whether I choose or no !
His eyes met mine, he was about to speak,
His hand ' grew damp -- surely he meant to
 say
He let me love him : in that moment's bliss
I shall forget my people pine for home —
They pass and they repass with pallid eyes ! "
I vowed at once a certain vow ; this vow —
Not to embrace you till my tribe was saved.
Embrace me !
 Dja. [*Apart.*] And she loved me ! Naught
  remained
But that ! Nay, Anael, is the Prefect dead ?
 An. Ah, you reproach me ! True, his death
  crowns all,
I know — or should know : and I would do
 much,
Believe ! but, death ! Oh, you, who have
 known death,
Would never doom the Prefect, were death
 fearful
As we report !
    Death ! — a fire curls within us
From the foot's palm, and fills up to the brain,
Up, out, then shatters the whole bubble-shell
Of flesh, perchance !
    Death ! — witness, I would die,
Whate'er death be, would venture now to die
For Khalil, for Maani — what for thee ?
Nay, but embrace me, Djabal, in assurance
My vow will not be broken, for I must
Do something to attest my faith in you,
Be worthy you !

 Dja. [*Avoiding her.*] I come for that — t
  say
Such an occasion is at hand : 't is like
I leave you — that we part, my Anael, — part
Forever !
 An. We part ? Just so ! I have suc
  cumbed, —
I am, he thinks, unworthy — and naught less
Will serve than such approval of my faith.
Then, we part not ! Remains there no wa
 short
Of that ? Oh, not that !
    Death ! — yet a hurt bir
Died in my hands ; its eyes filmed — " Nay, i
 sleeps,"
I said, " will wake to-morrow well : " 't wa
 dead.
 Dja. I stand here and time fleets. Anae
 — I come
To bid a last farewell to you : perhaps
We never meet again. But, ere the Prefect
Arrive . . .
    (*Enter* KHALIL, *breathlessly.*)
 Kha. He 's here ! The Prefect ! Twent
  guards,
No more — no sign he dreams of danger. All
Awaits thee only. Ayoob, Karshook, keep
Their posts — wait but the deed's accomplish
 ment
To join us with thy Druses to a man.
Still holds his course the Nuncio — near an
 near
The fleet from Candia steering.
 Dja. [*Aside.*]   All is lost !
— Or won ?
 Kha. And I have laid the sacred robe,
The sword, the head-tiar, at the porch — th
 place
Commanded. Thou wilt hear the Prefect'
 trumpet.
 Dja. Then I keep Anael, — him then, pas
 recall,
I slay — 't is forced on me ! As I began
I must conclude — so be it !
 Kha.   For the rest,
Save Loys, our foe's solitary sword,
All is so safe that . . . I will ne'er entreat
Thy post again of thee : though danger none,
There must be glory only meet for thee
In slaying the Prefect !
 An. [*Aside.*] And 't is now that Djaba
Would leave me ! — in the glory meet for him
 Dja. As glory, I would yield the deed t
 you
Or any Druse ; what peril there may be,
I keep. [*Aside.*] All things conspire to hound
 me on !
Not now, my soul, draw back, at least ! No
 now !
The course is plain, howe'er obscure all else.
Once offer this tremendous sacrifice,
Prevent what else will be irreparable,
Secure these transcendental helps, regain
The Cedars — then let all dark clear itself !
I slay him !
 Kha. Anael, and no part for us !
[*To* DJA.] Hast thou possessed her with . . .
 Dja. [*To* AN.]   Whom speak you to ?

What is it you behold there? Nay, this smile
Turns stranger. Shudder you? The man
    must die,
As thousands of our race have died through
    him.
One blow, and I discharge his weary soul
From the flesh that pollutes it! Let him fill
Straight some new expiatory form, of earth
Or sea, the reptile or some aëry thing:
What is there in his death?

An.   My brother said,
Is there no part in it for us?

Dja.   For Khalil, —
The trumpet will announce the Nuncio's entry;
Here, I shall find the Prefect hastening
In the Pavilion to receive him — here
Slay the Prefect; meanwhile Ayoob leads
The Nuncio with his guards within: once these
Secured in the outer hall, bid Ayoob bar
Entry or egress till I give the sign
Which waits the landing of the argosies
You will announce to me: this double sign
That justice is performed and help arrived,
When Ayoob shall receive, but not before,
Let him throw ope the palace doors, admit
The Druses to behold their tyrant, ere
We leave forever this detested spot.
So, Khalil, hurry all! No pause, no pause!
Whirl on the dream, secure to wake anon!

Kha. What sign? and who the bearer?

Dja.   Who shall show
My ring, admit to Ayoob. How she stands!
Have I not . . . I must have some task for her.
Anael, not that way! 'T is the Prefect's
    chamber!
Anael, keep you the ring — give you the sign!
It holds her safe amid the stir.) You will
Be faithful?

An. [*Taking the ring.*] I would fain be wor-
    thy. Hark!   [*Trumpet without.*

Kha. He comes!

Dja.   And I too come.

An.   One word, but one!
Say, shall you be exalted at the deed?
Then? On the instant?

Dja.   I exalted? What?
He, there — we, thus — our wrongs revenged,
    our tribe
Set free? Oh, then shall I, assure yourself,
Shall you, shall each of us, be in his death
Exalted!

Kha.   He is here!

Dja.   Away — away! [*They go.*
    (*Enter the* PREFECT *with* GUARDS, *and* LOYS.)

The Prefect. [*To* Guards.] Back, I say, to
    the galley every guard!
That 's my sole care now; see each bench re-
    tains
Its complement of rowers; I embark
O' the instant, since this Knight will have it
    so.
Alas me! Could you have the heart, my Loys!
To a Guard *who whispers.*] Oh, bring the holy
    Nuncio here forthwith!   [*The* Guards *go.*
Loys, a rueful sight, confess, to see
The gray discarded Prefect leave his post,
With tears i' the eye! So, you are Prefect
    now?

You depose me — you succeed me? Ha, ha!

Loys. And dare you laugh, whom laughter
    less becomes
Than yesterday's forced meekness we be-
    held . . .

Pref. — When you so eloquently pleaded,
    Loys,
For my dismissal from the post? Ah, meek
With cause enough, consult the Nuncio else!
And wish him the like meekness: for,so stanch
A servant of the church can scarce have bought
His share in the Isle, and paid for it, hard
    pieces!
You 've my successor to condole with, Nuncio!
I shall be safe by then i' the galley, Loys!

Loys. You make as you would tell me you
    rejoice
To leave your scene of . . .

Pref.   Trade in the dear Druses?
Blood and sweat traffic? Spare what yesterday
We heard enough of! Drove I in the Isle
A profitable game? Learn wit, my son,
Which you 'll need shortly! Did it never
    breed
Suspicion in you, all was not pure profit,
When I, the insatiate . . . and so forth — was
    bent
On having a partaker in my rule?
Why did I yield this Nuncio half the gain,
If not that I might also shift — what on him?
Half of the peril, Loys!

Loys.   Peril?

Pref.   Hark you!
I 'd love you if you 'd let me —this for reason,
You save my life at price of . . . well, say risk
At least, of yours. I came a long time since
To the Isle; our Hospitallers bade me tame
These savage wizards, and reward myself —

Loys. The Knights who so repudiate your
    crime?

Pref. Loys, the Knights! we doubtless un-
    derstood
Each other; as for trusting to reward
From any friend beside myself . . . no, no!
I clutched mine on the spot, when it was sweet,
And I had taste for it. I felt these wizards
Alive — was sure they were not on me, only
When I was on them: but with age comes
    caution:
And stinging pleasures please less and sting
    more.
Year by year, fear by fear! The girls were
    brighter
Than ever ('faith, there 's yet one Anael left,
I set my heart upon — Oh, prithee, let
That brave new sword lie still!) — These joys
    looked brighter,
But silenter the town, too, as I passed.
With this alcove's delicious memories
Began to mingle visions of gaunt fathers,
Quick-eyed sons, fugitives from the mine, the
    oar,
Stealing to catch me. Brief, when I began
To quake with fear — (I think I hear the Chap-
    ter
Solicited to let me leave, now all
Worth staying for was gained and gone!) — I
    say,

Just when, for the remainder of my life,
All methods of escape seemed lost — that then
Up should a young hot-headed Loys spring,
Talk very long and loud, — in fine, compel
The Knights to break their whole arrangement,
    have me
Home for pure shame — from this safehold of
    mine
Where but ten thousand Druses seek my life,
To my wild place of banishment, San Gines
By Murcia, where my three fat manors lying,
Purchased by gains here and the Nuncio's gold,
Are all I have to guard me, — that such fortune
Should fall to me, I hardly could expect.
Therefore I say, I 'd love you.
 Loys.   Can it be?
I play into your hands then? Oh no, no!
The Venerable Chapter, the Great Order
Sunk o' the sudden into fiends of the pit?
But I will back — will yet unveil you!
 Pref.   Me?
To whom? — perhaps Sir Galeas, who in Chapter
Shook his white head thrice — and some dozen
    times
My hand next morning shook, for value paid!
To that Italian saint, Sir Cosimo? —
Indignant at my wringing year by year
A thousand bezants from the coral divers,
As you recounted; felt the saint aggrieved
Well might he — I allowed for his half-share
Merely one hundred! To Sir . . .
 Loys.   See! you dare
Inculpate the whole Order; yet should I,
A youth, a sole voice, have the power to change
Their evil way, had they been firm in it?
Answer me!
 Pref. Oh, the son of Bretagne's Duke,
And that son's wealth, the father's influence,
    too,
And the young arm, we 'll even say, my Loys,
— The fear of losing or diverting these
Into another channel, by gainsaying
A novice too abruptly, could not influence
The Order! You might join, for aught they
    cared, •
Their red-cross rivals ot the Temple! Well,
I thank you for my part, at all events.
Stay here till they withdraw you! You 'll in
    habit
My palace — sleep, perchance, in the alcove
Whither I go to meet our holy friend.
Good! and now disbelieve me if you can, —
This is the first time for long years I enter
Thus [*lifts the arras*] without feeling just as if
    I lifted
The lid up of my tomb.
 Loys.   They share his crime!
God's punishment will overtake you yet.
 Pref. Thank you it does not! Pardon this
    last flash:
I bear a sober visage presently
With the disinterested Nuncio here —
His purchase-money safe at Murcia, too!
Let me repeat — for the first time, no draught
Coming as from a sepulchre salutes me.
When we next meet, this folly may have passed,
We 'll hope. Ha, ha! [*Goes through the arras.*
 Loys.   Assure me but . . . he 's gone!

He could not lie. Then what have I escaped,
I, who had so nigh given up happiness
Forever, to be linked with him and them!
Oh, opportunest of discoveries! I
Their Knight? I utterly renounce them all!
Hark! What, he meets by this the Nuncio
 Yes,
The same hyæna groan-like laughter! Quick —
To Djabal! I am one of them at last,
These simple-hearted Druses — Anael's tribe!
Djabal! She 's mine at last. Djabal, I say!
            [*Goes*

ACT IV

Enter DJABAL.

 Dja. Let me out slay the Prefect. The en
    now!
To-morrow will be time enough to pry
Into the means I took: suffice, they served,
Ignoble as they were, to hurl revenge
True to its object. [*Seeing the robe, etc. disposed*
      Mine should never so
Have hurried to accomplishment! Thee
    Djabal,
Far other mood befitted! Calm the Robe
Should clothe this doom's awarder!
   [*Taking the robe.*] Shall I dar
Assume my nation's Robe? I am at least
A Druse again, chill Europe's policy
Drops from me: I dare take the Robe. Why
    not
The Tiar? I rule the Druses, and what more
Betokens it than rule? — yet — yet —
       [*Lays down the tiar*
 [*Footsteps in the alcove.*] He comes!
        [*Taking the sword*
If the Sword serve, let the Tiar lie! So, feet
Clogged with the blood of twenty years can
    fall
Thus lightly! Round me, all ye ghosts! He'll
    lift . . .
Which arm to push the arras wide? — or both
Stab from the neck down to the heart — there
    stay!
Near he comes — nearer — the next footstep
    Now!
 [*As he dashes aside the arras,* ANAEL *is discovered*
Ha' Anael! Nay, my Anael, can it be?
Heard you the trumpet? I must slay him
    here,
And here you ruin all. Why speak you not?
Anael, the Prefect comes! [ANAEL *screams.*
    So slow to feel
'T is not a sight for you to look upon?
A moment's work — but such work! Till you
    go,
I must be idle — idle, I risk all!
      [*Pointing to her hair.*
Those locks are well, and you are beauteous
    thus,
But with the dagger 't is, I have to do!
 An. With mine!
 Dja.   Blood — Anael?
 An.   Djabal, 't is thy deed
It must be! I had hoped to claim it mine —
Be worthy thee — but I must needs confess

T was not I, but thyself . . . not I have . . .
   Djabal!
Speak to me!
  Dja.   Oh my punishment!
  An.   Speak to me
While I can speak! touch me, despite the blood!
When the command passed from thy soul to
  mine,
I went, fire leading me, muttering of thee,
And the approaching exaltation, — "make
One sacrifice!" I said, — and he sat there,
Bade me approach; and, as I did approach,
Thy fire with music burst into my brain.
'T was but a moment's work, thou saidst — per-
  chance
it may have been so! Well, it is thy deed!
  Dja. It is my deed!
  An.   His blood all this! — this! and . . .
And more! Sustain me, Djabal! Wait not —
  now
Let flash thy glory! Change thyself and me!
It must be! Ere the Druses flock to us!
At least confirm me! Djabal, blood gushed
  forth —
He was our tyrant — but I looked he 'd fall
Prone as asleep — why else is death called sleep?
Sleep? He bent o'er his breast! 'T is sin, I
  know, —
Punish me, Djabal, but wilt thou let him?
Be it thou that punishest, not he — who creeps
On his red breast — is here! 'T is the small
  groan
Of a child — no worse! Bestow the new life,
  then!
Too swift it cannot be, too strange, surpassing!
             [Following him up as he retreats.
Now! Change us both! Change me and
  change thou!
  Dja. [*Sinks on his knees.*] Thus!
Behold my change! You have done nobly.
  I! —
  An. Can Hakeem kneel?
  Dja.   No Hakeem, and scarce Djabal!
I have dealt falsely, and this woe is come.
No — hear me ere scorn blast me! Once and
  ever,
The deed is mine! Oh think upon the past!
  An. [*To herself.*] Did I strike once, or twice,
  or many times?
  Dja. I came to lead my tribe where, bathed
  in glooms,
Doth Bahumid the Renovator sleep:
Anael, I saw my tribe: I said, "Without
A miracle this cannot be" — I said
"Be there a miracle!" — for I saw you!
  An. His head lies south the portal!
  Dja.   — Weighed with this
The general good, how could I choose my
  own?
What matter was my purity of soul?
Little by little I engaged myself —
Heaven would accept me for its instrument,
I hoped: I said Heaven had accepted me!
  An. Is it this blood breeds dreams in me?
  — Who said
You were not Hakeem? And your miracles —
The fire that plays innocuous round your form?
             [Again changing her whole manner.

Ah, thou wouldst try me — thou art Hakeem
  still!
  Dja. Woe — woe! As if the Druses of the
  Mount
(Scarce Arabs, even there, but here, in the Isle,
Beneath their former selves) should comprehend
The subtle lore of Europe! A few secrets
That would not easily affect the meanest
Of the crowd there, could wholly subjugate
The best of our poor tribe. Again that eye?
  An. [*After a pause springs to his neck.*] Djabal,
  in this there can be no deceit!
Why, Djabal, were you human only, — think,
Maani is but human, Khalil human,
Loys is human even — did their words
Haunt me, their looks pursue me? Shame on
  you
So to have tried me! Rather, shame on me
So to need trying! Could I, with the Prefect
And the blood, there — could I see only you?
— Hang by your neck over this gulf of blood?
Speak, I am saved! Speak, Djabal! Am I
  saved?
   [*As* Djabal *slowly unclasps her arms, and puts her
      silently from him.*
Hakeem would save me! Thou art Djabal!
  Crouch!
Bow to the dust, thou basest of our kind!
The pile of thee, I reared up to the cloud —
Full, midway, of our fathers' trophied tombs,
Based on the living rock, devoured not by
The unstable desert's jaws of sand, — falls
  prone!
Fire, music, quenched: and now thou liest there
A ruin, obscene creatures will moan through!
— Let us come, Djabal!
  Dja.   Whither come?
  An.   At once —
Lest so it grow intolerable. Come!
Will I not share it with thee? Best at once!
So, feel less pain! Let them deride, — thy tribe
Now trusting in thee, — Loys shall deride!
Come to them, hand in hand, with me!
  Dja.   Where come?
  An. Where? — to the Druses thou hast
  wronged! Confess,
Now that the end is gained — (I love thee now —)
That thou hast so deceived them — (perchance
  love thee
Better than ever!) Come, receive their doom
Of infamy! Oh, best of all I love thee!
Shame with the man, no triumph with the God,
Be mine! Come!
  Dja. Never! More shame yet? and why?
Why? You have called this deed mine — it is
  mine!
And with it I accept its circumstance.
How can I longer strive with fate? The past
Is past: my false life shall henceforth show
  true.
Hear me! The argosies touch land by this;
They bear us to fresh scenes and happier skies:
What if we reign together? — if we keep
Our secret for the Druses' good? — by means
Of even their superstition, plant in them
New life? I learn from Europe: all who seek
Man's good must awe man, by such means as
  these.

We two will be divine to them — we are!
All great works in this world spring from the
  ruins
Of greater projects — ever, on our earth,
Babels men block out, Babylons they build.
I wrest the weapon from your hand! I claim
The deed! Retire! You have my ring — you bar
All access to the Nuncio till the forces
From Venice land!
  An.   Thou wilt feign Hakeem then?
  Dja. [*Putting the Tiara of Hakeem on his
    head.*] And from this moment that I
    dare ope wide
Eyes that till now refused to see, begins
My true dominion: for I know myself,
And what am I to personate. No word?
                              [ANAEL *goes.*
'Tis come on me at last! His blood on her —
What memories will follow that! Her eye,
Her fierce distorted lip and ploughed black
  brow!
Ah, fool! Has Europe then so poorly tamed
The Syrian blood from out thee? Thou, pre-
  sume
To work in this foul earth by means not foul?
Scheme, as for heaven, — but, on the earth, be
  glad
If a least ray like heaven's be left thee!
                                        Thus
I shall be calm — in readiness — no way
Surprised.   [*A noise without.*
            This should be Khalil and my Druses.
Venice is come then! Thus I grasp thee, sword!
Druses, 't is Hakeem saves you! In! Behold
Your Prefect!
(*Enter* LOYS. DJABAL *hides the khandjar in his robe.*)
  Loys. Oh, well found, Djabal! — but no time
    for words.
You know who waits there?
                      [*Pointing to the alcove.*
            Well! — and that 't is there
He meets the Nuncio? Well? Now, a surprise —
He there —
  Dja.   I know —
  Loys.   — is now no mortal's lord,
Is absolutely powerless — call him, dead —
He is no longer Prefect — you are Prefect!
Oh, shrink not! I do nothing in the dark,
Nothing unworthy Breton blood, believe!
I understood at once your urgency
That I should leave this isle for Rhodes; I felt
What you were loath to speak — your need of
  help.
I have fulfilled the task, that earnestness
Imposed on me: have, face to face, confronted
The Prefect in full Chapter, charged on him
The enormities of his long rule; he stood
Mute, offered no defence, no crime denied.
On which, I spoke of you, and of your tribe,
Your faith so like our own, and all you urged
Of old to me — I spoke, too, of your goodness,
Your patience — brief, I hold henceforth the
  Isle
In charge, am nominally lord, — but you,
You are associated in my rule —
Are the true Prefect! Ay, such faith had they
In my assurance of your loyalty
(For who insults an imbecile old man?)

That we assume the Prefecture this hour!
You gaze at me? Hear greater wonders yet —
I cast down all the fabric I have built!
These Knights, I was prepared to worship . .
  but
Of that another time; what 's now to say,
Is — I shall never be a Knight! Oh, Djabal,
Here first I throw all prejudice aside,
And call you brother! I am Druse like you:
My wealth, my friends, my power, are wholly
  yours,
Your people's, which is now my people: for
There is a maiden of your tribe, I love —
She loves me — Khalil's sister —
  Dja.   Anael?
  Loys.   Start you
Seems what I say, unknightly? Thus it chanced
When first I came, a novice, to the isle . . .
  (*Enter one of the* NUNCIO'S *Guards from the alcove.*)
  Guard. Oh horrible! Sir Loys! Here is Loys
And here —   [*Others enter from the alcove*
[*Pointing to* DJABAL.] Secure him, bind him —
  this is he!   [*They surround* DJABAL
  Loys. Madmen — what is 't you do? Stand
    from my friend,
And tell me!
  Guard.   Thou canst have no part in this —
Surely no part! But slay him not! The Nuncio
Commanded, slay him not!
  Loys.   Speak, or . . .
  Guard.   The Prefect
Lies murdered there by him thou dost embrace
  Loys. By Djabal? Miserable fools! How
    Djabal?
[*A Guard lifts* DJABAL'S *robe;* DJABAL *flings down the
    khandjar.*
  Loys. [*After a pause.*] Thou hast received
    some insult worse than all,
Some outrage not to be endured —
                    [*To the* Guards.] Stand back!
He is my friend — more than my friend! Thou
  hast
Slain him upon that provocation!
  Guard.   No!
No provocation! 'T is a long devised
Conspiracy: the whole tribe is involved.
He is their Khalif — 't is on that pretence —
Their mighty Khalif who died long ago,
And now comes back to life and light again!
All is just now revealed, I know not how,
By one of his confederates — who, struck
With horror at this murder, first apprised
The Nuncio. As 't was said, we find this Djabal
Here where we take him.
  Dja. [*Aside.*] Who broke faith with me?
  Loys. [*To* DJABAL.] Hear'st thou? Speak!
    Till thou speak I keep off these,
Or die with thee. Deny this story! Thou
A Khalif, an impostor? Thou, my friend,
Whose tale was of an inoffensive tribe,
With . . . but thou know'st — on that tale's
    truth I pledged
My faith before the Chapter: what art thou?
  Dja. Loys, I am as thou hast heard. All 's
    true!
No more concealment! As these tell thee, all
Was long since planned. Our Druses are enough
To crush this handful: the Venetians land

Even now in our behalf. Loys, we part !
Thou, serving much, wouldst fain have served
  me more ;
It might not be. I thank thee. As thou hear-
  est,
We are a separated tribe : farewell !
  Loys. Oh, where will truth be found now ?
    Canst thou so
Belie the Druses ? Do they share thy crime ?
Those thou professest of our Breton stock,
Are partners with thee ? Why, I saw but
  now
Khalil, my friend — he spoke with me — no
  word
Of this ! and Anael — whom I love, and who
Loves me — she spoke no word of this !
  Dja.   Poor boy !
Anael, who loves thee ? Khalil, fast thy friend ?
We, offsets from a wandering Count of Dreux ?
No : older than the oldest, princelier
Than Europe's princeliest race, our tribe :
  enough
For thine, that on our simple faith we found
A monarchy to shame your monarchies
At their own trick and secret of success.
The child of this our tribe shall laugh upon
The palace-step of him whose life ere night
Is forfeit, as that child shall know, and yet
Shall laugh there ! What, we Druses wait for-
  sooth
The kind interposition of a boy
 — Can only save ourselves if thou concede ?
 — Khalil admire thee ? He is my right hand,
My delegate ! — Anael accept thy love ?
She is my bride !
  Loys.   Thy bride ? She one of them ?
  Dja. My bride !
  Loys.   And she retains her glorious eyes !
She, with those eyes, has shared this miscreant's
  guilt !
Ah — who but she directed me to find
Djabal within the Prefect's chamber ? Khalil
Bade me seek Djabal there, too ! All is truth !
What spoke the Prefect worse of them than
  this ?
Did the Church ill to institute long since
Perpetual warfare with such serpentry ?
And I — have I desired to shift my part,
Evade my share in her design ? 'T is well !
  Dja. Loys, I wronged thee — but unwittingly :
I never thought there was in thee a virtue
That could attach itself to what thou deem-
  est
A race below thine own. I wronged thee, Loys,
But that is over : all is over now,
Save the protection I ensure against
My people's anger. By their Khalif's side,
Thou art secure and may'st depart : so, come !
  Loys. Thy side ? I take protection at thy
  hand ?

         (*Enter other* Guards.)

  Guards. Fly with him ! Fly, Sir Loys ! 'T is
  too true !
And only by his side thou may'st escape !
The whole tribe is in full revolt : they flock
About the palace — will be here — on thee —
And there are twenty of us, we the Guards
O' the Nuncio, to withstand them ! Even we

Had stayed to meet our death in ignorance,
But that one Druse, a single faithful Druse,
Made known the horror to the Nuncio. Fly !
The Nuncio stands aghast. At least let us
Escape thy wrath, O Hakeem ! We are naught
In thy tribe's persecution ! [*To* Loys.] Keep
  by him !
They hail him Hakeem, their dead Prince re-
  turned :
He is their God, they shout, and at his beck
Are life and death !
  [Loys, *springing at the khandjar* Djabal *had thrown
    down, seizes him by the throat.*
                  Thus by his side am I !
Thus I resume my knighthood and its war-
  fare,
Thus end thee, miscreant, in thy pride of place !
Thus art thou caught. Without, thy dupes may
  cluster.
Friends aid thee, foes avoid thee, — thou art
  Hakeem,
How say they ? — God art thou ! but also here
Is the least, youngest, meanest the Church
  calls
Her servant, and his single arm avails
To aid her as she lists. I rise, and thou
Art crushed ! Hordes of thy Druses flock with-
  out :
Here thou hast me, who represent the Cross,
Honor and Faith, 'gainst Hell, Mahound and
  thee.
Die ! [Djabal *remains calm.*] Implore my
  mercy, Hakeem, that my scorn
May help me ! Nay, I cannot ply thy trade ;
I am no Druse, no stabber : and thine eye,
Thy form, are too much as they were — my
  friend
Had such ! Speak ! Beg for mercy at my foot !
                [Djabal *still silent.*
Heaven could not ask so much of me — not,
  sure,
So much ! I cannot kill him so !
         [*After a pause.*] Thou art
Strong in thy cause, then — dost outbrave us,
  then.
Heardst thou that one of thine accomplices,
Thy very people, has accused thee ? Meet
His charge ! Thou hast not even slain the Pre-
  fect
As thy own vile creed warrants. Meet that
  Druse !
Come with me and disprove him — be thou tried
By him, nor seek appeal ! Promise me this,
Or I will do God's office ! What, shalt thou
Boast of assassins at thy beck, yet truth
Want even an executioner ? Consent,
Or I will strike — look in my face — I will !
  Dja. Give me again my khandjar, if thou
  darest !   [Loys *gives it.*
Let but one Druse accuse me, and I plunge
This home. A Druse betray me ? Let us go !
[*Aside.*] Who has betrayed me ?
                  [*Shouts without.*
            Hearest thou ? I hear
No plainer than long years ago I heard
That shout — but in no dream now ! They re
  turn !
Wilt thou be leader with me, Loys ? Well !

ACT V

The uninitiated Druses, *filling the hall tumultuously, and speaking together.*

Here flock we, obeying the summons. Lo,
Hakeem hath appeared, and the Prefect is
dead, and we return to Lebanon! My manu-
facture of goats' f.eece must, I doubt, soon fall
away there. Come, old Nasif — link thine arm
in mine — we fight, if needs be. Come, what
is a great fight-word? — "Lebanon?" (My
daughter — my daughter!) — But is Khalil to
have the office of Hamza? — Nay, rather, if he
be wise, the monopoly of henna and cloves.
Where is Hakeem? — The only prophet I ever
saw, prophesied at Cairo once, in my youth: a
little black Copht, dressed all in black too,
with a great stripe of yellow cloth flapping
down behind him like the back-fin of a water-
serpent. Is this he? Biamrallah! Biamreh!
Hakeem!

> (*Enter the* Nuncio, *with* Guards.)

Nuncio. [*To his* Attendants.] Hold both, the
    sorcerer and this accomplice
Ye talk of, that accuseth him! And tell
Sir Loys he is mine, the Church's hope:
Bid him approve himself our Knight indeed!
Lo, this black disemboguing of the Isle!
[*To the* Druses.] Ah, children, what a sight for
    these old eyes
That kept themselves alive this voyage through
To smile their very last on you! I came
To gather one and all you wandering sheep
Into my fold, as though a father came . . .
As though, in coming, a father should . . .
        [*To his* Guards.] (Ten, twelve
— Twelve guards of you, and not an outlet?
    None?
The wizards stop each avenue? Keep close!)
[*To the* Druses.] As if one came to a son's house,
    I say,
So did I come — no guard with me — to find . . .
Alas — alas!

A Druse. Who is the old man?
Another.   Oh, ye are to shout!
Children, he styles you.
Druses.   Ay, the Prefect's slain!
Glory to the Khalif, our Father!
Nuncio.   Even so!
I find (ye prompt aright) your father slain!
While most he plotted for your good, that father
(Alas, how kind, ye never knew) — lies slain!
[*Aside.*] (And hell's worm gnaw the glozing
    knave — with me,
For being duped by his cajoleries!
Are these the Christians? These the docile
    crew
My bezants went to make me Bishop o'er?)
[*To his* Attendants, *who whisper.*] What say ye
    does this wizard style himself?
Hakeem? Biamrallah? The third Fatemite?
What is this jargon? He — the insane Khalif,
Dead near three hundred years ago, come back
In flesh and blood again?
Druses.   He mutters! Hear ye?
He is blaspheming Hakeem. The old man
Is our dead Prefect's friend. Tear him!

Nuncio.   Ye dare not.
I stand here with my five-and-seventy years,
The Patriarch's power behind me, God's above
Those years have witnessed sin enough ; ere now
Misguided men arose against their lords,
And found excuse ; but ye, to be enslaved
By sorceries, cheats — alas! the same tricks
    tried
On my poor children in this nook o' the earth,
Could triumph, that have been successively
Exploded, laughed to scorn, all nations through
"Romaioi, Ioudaioi te kai proselutoi,
Cretes and Arabians," — you are duped the
    last.
Said I, refrain from tearing me? I pray ye
Tear me! Shall I return to tell the Patriarch
That so much love was wasted — every gift
Rejected, from his benison I brought,
Down to the galley-full of bezants, sunk
An hour since at the harbor's mouth, by that . . .
That . . . never will I speak his hated name!
[*To his* Servants.] What was the name his fel-
    low slip-fetter
Called their arch-wizard by? [*They whisper.*]
    Oh, Djabal was 't?
Druses. But how a sorcerer? false wherein?
Nuncio.   (Ay, Djabal!)
How false? Ye know not, Djabal has con-
    fessed . . .
Nay, that by tokens found on him we learn . . .
What I sailed hither solely to divulge —
How by his spells the demons were allured
To seize you: not that these be aught save lies
And mere illusions. Is this clear? I say,
By measures such as these, he would have led
    you
Into a monstrous ruin: follow ye?
Say, shall ye perish for his sake, my sons?
Druses. Hark ye!
Nuncio.   — Be of one privilege amerced?
No! Infinite the Patriarch's mercies are!
No! With the Patriarch's license, still I bid
Tear him to pieces who misled you! Haste!
Druses.   The old man's beard shakes, and
his eyes are white fire! After all, I know no-
thing of Djabal beyond what Karshook says ;
he knows but what Khalil says, who knows
just what Djabal says himself. Now, the little
Copht Prophet, I saw at Cairo in my youth,
began by promising each bystander three full
measures of wheat . . .

> (*Enter* Khalil *and the initiated* Druses.)

Kha. Venice and her deliverance are at hand!
Their fleet stands through the harbor! Hath
    he slain
The Prefect yet? Is Djabal's change come yet?
Nuncio. [*To* Attendants.] What 's this of
    Venice? Who 's this boy?
        [*Attendants whisper.*]   One Khalil?
Djabal's accomplice, Loys called, but now,
The only Druse, save Djabal's self, to fear?
[*To the* Druses.] I cannot hear ye with these
    aged ears ;
Is it so? Ye would have my troops assist?
Doth he abet him in his sorceries?
Down with the cheat, guards, as my children
    bid!
    [*They spring at* Khalil ; *as he beats them back,*

Stay! No more bloodshed! Spare deluded
    youth!
Whom seek'st thou? (I will teach him) —
    whom, my child?
Thou know'st not what these know, what these
    declare.
I am an old man, as thou seest — have done
With life; and what should move me but the
    truth?
Art thou the only fond one of thy tribe?
'T is I interpret for thy tribe!
    Kha.   Oh, this
Is the expected Nuncio! Druses, hear —
Endure ye this? Unworthy to partake
The glory Hakeem gains you! While I speak,
The ships touch land: who makes for Lebanon?
They plant the wingèd lion in these halls!
    Nuncio. [*Aside.*] If it be true! Venice?
    Oh, never true!
Yet Venice would so gladly thwart our Knights,
So fain get footing here, stand close by Rhodes!
Oh, to be duped this way!
    Kha.   Ere he appear
And lead you gloriously, repent, I say!
    Nuncio. [*Aside.*] Nor any way to stretch
        the arch-wizard stark
Ere the Venetians come? Cut off the head,
The trunk were easily stilled. [*To the* Druses.]
    He? Bring him forth!
Since so you needs will have it, I assent!
You'd judge him, say you, on the spot? —
    confound
The sorcerer in his very circle? Where's
Our short black-bearded sallow friend who swore
He'd earn the Patriarch's guerdon by one stab!
Bring Djabal forth at once!
    Druses.   Ay, bring him forth!
The Patriarch drives a trade in oil and silk,
And we're the Patriarch's children — true
    men, we!
Where is the glory? Show us all the glory!
    Kha. You dare not so insult him! What,
        not see . . .
(I tell thee, Nuncio, these are uninstructed,
Untrusted — they know nothing of our Khalif!)
— Not see that if he lets a doubt arise
'T is but to give yourselves the chance of
    seeming
To have some influence in your own return!
That all may say ye would have trusted him
Without the all-convincing glory — ay,
And did! Embrace the occasion, friends! For,
    think —
What wonder when his change takes place?
    But now
For your sakes, he should not reveal himself.
No — could I ask and have, I would not ask
The change yet!
        (*Enter* DJABAL *and* LOYS.)
                    Spite of all, reveal thyself!
I had said, pardon them for me — for Anael —
For our sakes pardon these besotted men —
Ay, for thine own — they hurt not thee! Yet
    now
One thought swells in me and keeps down all
    else.
This Nuncio couples shame with thee, has called
Imposture thy whole course, all bitter things

Has said: he is but an old fretful man!
Hakeem — nay, I must call thee Hakeem now —
Reveal thyself! See! Where is Anael? See!
    Loys. [*To* DJA.] Here are thy people! Keep
        thy word to me!
    Dja. Who of my people hath accused me?
    Nuncio.   So!
So this is Djabal, Hakeem, and what not?
A fit deed, Loys, for thy first Knight's day!
May it be augury of thy after-life!
Ever prove truncheon of the Church as now
That, Nuncio of the Patriarch, having charge
Of the Isle here, I claim thee [*turning to* DJA.]
    as these bid me,
Forfeit for murder done thy lawful prince,
Thou conjurer that peep'st and mutterest!
Why should I hold thee from their hands?
    (Spells, children?
But hear how I dispose of all his spells!)
Thou art a prophet? — wouldst entice thy
    tribe
From me? — thou workest miracles? (Attend!
Let him but move me with his spells!) I,
    Nuncio . . .
    Dja. . . . Which how thou camest to be, I
        say not now,
Though I have also been at Stamboul, Luke!
Ply thee with spells, forsooth! What need of
    spells?
If Venice, in her Admiral's person, stoop
To ratify thy compact with her foe,
The Hospitallers, for this Isle — withdraw
Her warrant of the deed which reinstates
My people in their freedom, tricked away
By him I slew, — refuse to convoy us
To Lebanon and keep the Isle we leave —
Then will be time to try what spells can do!
Dost thou dispute the Republic's power?
    Nuncio.   Lo ye!
He tempts me too, the wily exorcist!
No! The renowned Republic was and is
The Patriarch's friend: 't is not for courting
    Venice
That I — that these implore thy blood of me!
Lo ye, the subtle miscreant! Ha, so subtle?
Ye Druses, hear him! Will ye be deceived?
How he evades me! Where's the miracle
He works? I bid him to the proof — fish up
Your galley full of bezants that he sank!
That were a miracle! One miracle!
Enough of trifling, for it chafes my years.
I am the Nuncio, Druses! I stand forth
To save you from the good Republic's rage
When she shall find her fleet was summoned here
To aid the mummeries of a knave like this!
    [*As the* Druses *hesitate, his* Attendants *whisper.*
Ah, well suggested! Why, we hold the while
One who, his close confederate till now,
Confesses Djabal at the last a cheat,
And every miracle a cheat! Who throws me
His head? I make three offers, once I offer, —
And twice . . .
    Dja. Let who moves perish at my foot!
    Kha. Thanks, Hakeem, thanks! Oh, Anael,
        Maani,
Why tarry they?
    Druses. [*To each other.*] He can! He can'
        Live fire —

[*To the* NUNCIO.] I say he can, old man!
    Thou know'st him not.
Live fire like that thou seest now in his eyes,
Plays fawning round him. See! The change
    begins!
All the brow lightens as he lifts his arm!
Look not at me! It was not I!
Dja.   What Druse
Accused me, as he saith? I bid each bone
Crumble within that Druse! None, Loys, none
Of my own people, as thou said'st, have raised
A voice against me.
    Nuncio. [*Aside.*] Venice to come! Death!
    Dja. [*Continuing.*] Confess and go unscathed,
        however false!
Seest thou my Druses, Luke? I would submit
To thy pure malice did one Druse confess!
How said I, Loys?
    Nuncio. [*To his* Attendants *who whisper.*] Ah,
ye counsel so?
[*Aloud.*] Bring in the witness, then, who, first
    of all,
Disclosed the treason! Now I have thee,
    wizard!
Ye hear that? If one speaks, he bids you tear
    him
Joint after joint: well then, one does speak!
    One,
Befooled by Djabal, even as yourselves,
But who hath voluntarily proposed
To expiate, by confessing thus, the fault
Of having trusted him.
                    [*They bring in a veiled* Druse.
Loys.   Now, Djabal, now!
Nuncio. Friend, Djabal fronts thee! Make
    a ring, sons. Speak!
Expose this Djabal — what he was, and how;
The wiles he used, the aims he cherished; all,
Explicitly as late 't was spoken to these
My servants: I absolve and pardon thee.
    Loys. Thou hast the dagger ready, Djabal?
Dja.   Speak,
Recreant!
    Druses. Stand back, fool! farther! Sud-
        denly
You shall see some huge serpent glide from
    under
The empty vest, or down will thunder crash!
Back, Khalil!
    Kha.   I go back? Thus go I back!
[*To* AN.] Unveil! Nay, thou shalt face the
    Khalif! Thus!

[*He tears away* ANAEL's *veil;* DJABAL *folds his arms
and bows his head; the* Druses *fall back;* LOYS
springs from the side of DJABAL *and the* NUNCIO.

    Loys. Then she was true — she only of them
        all!
True to her eyes — may keep those glorious
    eyes,
And now be mine, once again mine! Oh,
    Anael!
Dared I think thee a partner in his crime —
That blood could soil that hand? nay, 't is
    mine — Anael,
— Not mine? — Who offer thee before all these
My heart, my sword, my name — so thou wilt
    say
That Djabal, who affirms thou art his bride,

Lies — say but that he lies!
    Dja.   Thou, Anael?
    Loys. Nay, Djabal, nay, one chance for me
        — the last!
Thou hast had every other; thou hast spoken
Days, nights, what falsehood listed thee — let
    me
Speak first now; I will speak now!
    Nuncio.   Loys, pause!
Thou art the Duke's son, Bretagne's choicest
    stock,
Loys of Dreux, God's sepulchre's first sword:
This wilt thou spit on, this degrade, this tram-
    ple
To earth?
    Loys. [*To* AN.] Who had foreseen that one
        day, Loys
Would stake these gifts against some other good
In the whole world? I give them thee! I
    would
My strong will might bestow real shape on them,
That I might see, with my own eyes, thy foot
Tread on their very neck! 'T is not by gifts
I put aside this Djabal: we will stand —
We do stand, see, two men! Djabal, stand
    forth!
Who's worth her, I or thou? I — who for
    Anael
Uprightly, purely kept my way, the long
True way — left thee each by-path, boldly lived
Without the lies and blood, — or thou, or thou?
Me! love me, Anael! Leave the blood and
    him!
[*To* DJA.] Now speak — now, quick on this
    that I have said, —
Thou with the blood, speak if thou art a man!
    Dja. [*To* AN.] And was it thou betrayedst
        me? 'T is well!
I have deserved this of thee, and submit.
Nor 't is much evil thou inflictest: life
Ends here. The cedars shall not wave for us:
For there was crime, and must be punishment.
See fate! By thee I was seduced, by thee
I perish: yet do I — can I repent?
I with my Arab instinct, thwarted ever
By my Frank policy, — and with, in turn,
My Frank brain, thwarted by my Arab heart —
While these remained in equipoise, I lived
— Nothing; had either been predominant,
As a Frank schemer or an Arab mystic,
I had been something; — now, each has de-
    stroyed
The other — and behold, from out their crash,
A third and better nature rises up —
My mere man's-nature! And I yield to it:
I love thee, I who did not love before!
    An. Djabal!
    Dja.   It seemed love, but it was not love:
How could I love while thou adoredst me?
Now thou despisest, art above me so
Immeasurably! Thou, no other, doomest
My death now; this my steel shall execute
Thy judgment; I shall feel thy hand in it!
Oh, luxury to worship, to submit,
Transcended, doomed to death by thee!
    An.   My Djabal!
    Dja. Dost hesitate? I force thee then!
        Approach.

Druses ! for I am out of reach of fate ;
No further evil waits me. Speak the doom !
Hear, Druses, and hear, Nuncio, and hear,
   Loys !
An.   HAKEEM !   [*She falls dead.*
   [*The* Druses *scream, grovelling before him.*
Druses. Ah, Hakeem ! — not on me thy
   wrath !
Biamrallah, pardon ! never doubted I !
Ha, dog, how sayest thou ?
[*They surround and seize the* NUNCIO *and his* Guards.
   LOYS *flings himself upon the body of* ANAEL, *on
   which* DJABAL *continues to gaze as stupefied.*

Nuncio.   Caitiffs ! Have ye eyes ?
Whips, racks should teach you ! What, his
   fools ? his dupes ?
Leave me ! unhand me !
   Kha. [*Approaching* DJABAL *timidly.*] Save
   her for my sake !
She was already thine ; she would have shared
To-day thine exaltation : think, this day
Her hair was plaited thus because of thee !
Yes, feel the soft bright hair — feel !
   Nuncio. [*Struggling with those who have seized
   him.*] What, because
His leman dies for him ? You think it hard
To die ? Oh, would you were at Rhodes, and
   choice
Of deaths should suit you !
   Kha. [*Bending over* ANAEL'S *body.*] Just
   restore her life !
So little does it ! there — the eyelids tremble !
'T was not my breath that made them : and the
   lips
Move of themselves. I could restore her life !
Hakeem, we have forgotten — have presumed
On our free converse : we are better taught.
See, I kiss — how I kiss thy garment's hem
For her ! She kisses it — Oh, take her deed
In mine ! Thou dost believe now, Anael ? —
   See,
She smiles ! Were her lips open o'er the teeth
Thus, when I spoke first ? She believes in
   thee !
Go not without her to the cedars, lord !
Or leave us both — I cannot go alone !
I have obeyed thee, if I dare so speak :
Hath Hakeem thus forgot all Djabal knew ?
Thou feelest then my tears fall hot and fast
Upon thy hand, and yet thou speakest not ?
Ere the Venetian trumpet sound — ere thou
Exalt thyself, O Hakeem ! save thou her !
   Nuncio. And the accursed Republic will
   arrive
And find me in their toils — dead, very like,
Under their feet !
                  What way — not one way yet
To foil them ? None ? [*Observing* DJABAL'S
   face.] What ails the Khalif ? Ah,
That ghastly face ! A way to foil them yet !
   [*To the* Druses.] Look to your Khalif, Druses !
   Is that face
God Hakeem's ? Where is triumph, — where
   is . . . what
Said he of exaltation — hath he promised
So much to-day ? Why then, exalt thyself !
Cast off that husk, thy form, set free thy soul

In splendor ! Now, bear witness ! here I
   stand —
I challenge him exalt himself, and I
Become, for that, a Druse like all of you !
   The Druses. Exalt thyself ! Exalt thyself.
   O Hakeem !
   Dja. [*Advances.*] I can confess now all
   from first to last.
There is no longer shame for me. I am . . .
[*Here the Venetian trumpet sounds: the* Druses *shout,*
   DJABAL'S *eye catches the expression of those about
   him, and, as the old dream comes back, he is again
   confident and inspired.*
— Am I not Hakeem ? And ye would have
   crawled
But yesterday within these impure courts
Where now ye stand erect ! Not grand enough ?
— What more could be conceded to such beasts
As all of you, so sunk and base as you,
Than a mere man ? A man among such beasts
Was miracle enough : yet him you doubt,
Him you forsake, him fain would you destroy —
With the Venetians at your gate, the Nuncio
Thus — (see the baffled hypocrite !) and, best,
The Prefect there !
   Druses.   No, Hakeem, ever thine !
   Nuncio. He lies — and twice he lies — and
   thrice he lies !
Exalt thyself, Mahound ! Exalt thyself !
   Dja. Druses ! we shall henceforth be far
   away —
Out of mere mortal ken — above the cedars —
But we shall see ye go, hear ye return,
Repeopling the old solitudes, — through thee,
My Khalil ! Thou art full of me : I fill
Thee full — my hands thus fill thee ! Yester-
   eve,
— Nay, but this morn, I deemed thee igno-
   rant
Of all to do, requiring word of mine
To teach it : now, thou hast all gifts in one,
With truth and purity go other gifts,
All gifts come clustering to that. Go, lead
My people home whate'er betide !
                  [*Turning to the* Druses.] Ye take
This Khalil for my delegate ? To him
Bow as to me ? He leads to Lebanon —
Ye follow ?
   Druses. We follow ! Now exalt thyself !
   Dja. [*Raises* LOYS.] Then to thee, Loys !
   How I wronged thee, Loys !
Yet, wronged, no less thou shalt have full re-
   venge,
Fit for thy noble self, revenge — and thus.
Thou, loaded with such wrongs, the princely
   soul,
The first sword of Christ's sepulchre — thou
   shalt
Guard Khalil and my Druses home again !
Justice, no less, God's justice and no more,
For those I leave ! — to seeking this, devote
Some few days out of thy Knight's brilliant
   life :
And, this obtained them, leave their Lebanon,
My Druses' blessing in thine ears — (they shall
Bless thee with blessing sure to have its way)
— One cedar-blossom in thy ducal cap,
One thought of Anael in thy heart, — perchance

One thought of him who thus, to bid thee
    speed,
His last word to the living speaks! This done,
Resume thy course, and, first amidst the first
In Europe, take my heart along with thee!
Go boldly, go serenely, go augustly —
What shall withstand thee then?
    [*He bends over* ANAEL.] And last to thee!
Ah, did I dream I was to have, this day,
Exalted thee? A vain dream: hast thou not
Won greater exaltation? What remains
But press to thee, exalt myself to thee?

Thus I exalt myself, set free my soul!
    [*He stabs himself. As he falls, supported by* KHALIL
    and LOYS, *the* VENETIANS *enter; the* ADMIRAL *ad-*
    vances.

    Admiral. God and St. Mark for Venice!
      Plant the Lion!
    [*At the clash of the planted standard, the* Druses *shout,*
    and move tumultuously forward, LOYS *drawing his*
    sword.

    Dja. [*Leading them a few steps between* KHA-
      LIL *and* LOYS.] On to the Mountain!
      At the Mountain, Druses! [*Dies.*

A BLOT IN THE 'SCUTCHEON

A TRAGEDY

THIS play was written in 1843 at the request
of Macready, and very rapidly, in four or five
days. A misunderstanding with Macready,
fully related in Mrs. Orr's *Life and Letters of
Robert Browning*, I. 168–184, and in Mr. Gosse's
Personalia, led to a breach between the two
friends.

The play was received with great applause,
but circumstances prevented it from being kept
on the boards. It has, however, been repro-
duced both in England and in America, near the
close of Browning's life and after his death
Helen Faucit, afterward Lady Martin, took the
part of Mildred. The play was printed shortly
after it first appeared, as No. V. of *Bells and
Pomegranates*.

PERSONS

MILDRED TRESHAM.
GUENDOLEN TRESHAM.
THOROLD, Earl Tresham.
AUSTIN TRESHAM.
HENRY, Earl Mertoun.
GERARD, and other Retainers of Lord Tresham.

TIME, 17—

ACT I

SCENE I. *The interior of a lodge in* LORD TRESHAM'S
*park. Many Retainers crowded at the window, sup-
posed to command a view of the entrance to his man-
sion.* GERARD, *the Warrener, his back to a table on
which are flagons, etc.*

1st *Retainer.* Ay, do! push, friends, and
    then you 'll push down me!
— What for? Does any hear a runner's foot
Or a steed's trample or a coach-wheel's cry?
Is the Earl come or his least poursuivant?
But there 's no breeding in a man of you
Save Gerard yonder: here 's a half-place yet,
Old Gerard!
    Gerard. Save your courtesies, my friend.
Here is my place.
    2d *Ret.* Now, Gerard, out with it!
What makes you sullen, this of all the days
I' the year? To-day that young rich bountiful
Handsome Earl Mertoun, whom alone they
    match
With our Lord Tresham through the country-
    side,
Is coming here in utmost bravery

To ask our master's sister's hand?
    Ger. What then?
    2d *Ret.* What then? Why, you, she speaks
    to, if she meets
Your worship, smiles on as you hold apart
The boughs to let her through her forest walks,
You, always favorite for your no-deserts,
You 've heard, these three days, how Earl Mer-
    toun sues
To lay his heart and house and broad lands too
At Lady Mildred's feet: and while we squeeze
Ourselves into a mousehole lest we miss
One congee of the least page in his train,
You sit o' one side — "there 's the Earl," say
    I —
"What then?" say you!
    3d *Ret.* I 'll wager he has let
Both swans he tamed for Lady Mildred swim
Over the falls and gain the river!
    Ger. Ralph,
Is not to-morrow my inspecting-day
For you and for your hawks?
    4th *Ret.* Let Gerard be!
He 's coarse-grained, like his carved black
    cross-bow stock.
Ha, look now, while we squabble with him
    look!
Well done, now — is not this beginning, now,
To purpose?
    1st *Ret.* Our retainers look as fine —
That 's comfort. Lord, how Richard holds
    himself
With his white staff! Will not a knave behind
Prick him upright?

4th Ret. He 's only bowing, fool !
The Earl's man bent us lower by this much.
1st Ret. That 's comfort. Here 's a very cav-
alcade !
3d Ret. I don't see wherefore Richard, and
his troop
Of silk and silver varlets there, should find
Their perfumed selves so indispensable
On high days, holidays ! Would it so disgrace
Our family, if I, for instance, stood —
In my right hand a cast of Swedish hawks,
A leash of greyhounds in my left ? —
Ger. — With Hugh
The logman for supporter, in his right
The bill-hook, in his left the brushwood-shears !
3d Ret. Out on you, crab ! What next,
what next ? The Earl !
1st Ret. Oh Walter, groom, our horses, do
they match
The Earl's ? Alas, that first pair of the six —
They paw the ground — Ah, Walter ! and that
brute
Just on his haunches by the wheel !
6th Ret. Ay — Ay !
You, Philip, are a special hand, I hear,
At soups and sauces : what 's a horse to you ?
D' ye mark that beast they 've slid into the
midst
So cunningly ? — then, Philip, mark this fur-
ther ;
No leg has he to stand on !
1st Ret. No ? That 's comfort.
2d Ret. Peace, Cook ! The Earl descends.
— Well, Gerard, see
The Earl at least ! Come, there 's a proper
man,
I hope ! Why, Ralph, no falcon, Pole or
Swede,
Has got a starrier eye.
3d Ret. His eyes are blue —
But leave my hawks alone !
4th Ret. So young, and yet
So tall and shapely !
5th Ret. Here 's Lord Tresham's self !
There now — there 's what a nobleman should
be !
He 's older, graver, loftier, he 's more like
A House's head !
2d Ret. But you 'd not have a boy
— And what 's the Earl beside ? — possess too
soon
That stateliness ?
1st Ret. Our master takes his hand —
Richard and his white staff are on the move —
Back fall our people — (tsh ! — there 's Timo-
thy
Sure to get tangled in his ribbon-ties,
And Peter's cursed rosette 's a-coming off !)
— At last I see our lord's back and his friend's ;
And the whole beautiful bright company
Close round them : in they go ! [*Jumping down
from the window-bench, and making for the
table and its jugs.*] Good health, long life
Great joy to our Lord Tresham and his House !
6th Ret. My father drove his father first to
court,
After his marriage-day — ay, did he !
2d Ret. God bless

Lord Tresham, Lady Mildred, and the Earl !
Here, Gerard, reach your beaker !
Ger. Drink, my boys !
Don't mind me — all 's not right about me —
drink !
2d Ret. [*Aside.*] He 's vexed, now, that he
let the show escape !
[*To* GER.] Remember that the Earl returns
this way.
Ger. That way ?
2d Ret. Just so.
Ger. Then my way 's here. [*Goes.*
2d Ret. Old Gerard
Will die soon — mind, I said it ! He was used
To care about the pitifullest thing
That touched the House's honor, not an eye
But his could see wherein : and on a cause
Of scarce a quarter this importance, Gerard
Fairly had fretted flesh and bone away
In cares that this was right, nor that was
wrong,
Such point decorous, and such square by rule —
He knew such niceties, no herald more :
And now — you see his humor : die he will !
2d Ret. God help him ! Who 's for the
great servants'-hall
To hear what 's going on inside ? They 'd fol-
low
Lord Tresham into the saloon.
3d Ret. I ! —
4th Ret. I ! —
Leave Frank alone for catching, at the door,
Some hint of how the parley goes inside !
Prosperity to the great House once more !
Here 's the last drop !
1st Ret. Have at you ! Boys, hurrah !

SCENE II. *A saloon in the Mansion.*

Enter LORD TRESHAM, LORD MERTOUN, AUSTIN, *and*
GUENDOLEN.

Tresham. I welcome you, Lord Mertoun, yet
once more,
To this ancestral roof of mine. Your name
— Noble among the noblest in itself,
Yet taking in your person, fame avers,
New price and lustre, — (as that gem you wear,
Transmitted from a hundred knightly breasts,
Fresh chased and set and fixed by its last lord,
Seems to rekindle at the core) — your name
Would win you welcome !
Mertoun. Thanks !
Tresh. — But add to that,
The worthiness and grace and dignity
Of your proposal for uniting both
Our Houses even closer than respect
Unites them now — add these, and you must
grant
One favor more, nor that the least, — to think
The welcome I should give ; — 't is given ! My
lord,
My only brother, Austin — he 's the king's.
Our cousin, Lady Guendolen — betrothed
To Austin : all are yours.
Mer. I thank you — lest
For the expressed commendings which your seal
And only that, authenticates — forbids
My putting from me . . . to my heart I take

Your praise . . . but praise less claims my
    gratitude,
Than the indulgent insight it implies
Of what must needs be uppermost with one
Who comes, like me, with the bare leave to
    ask,
In weighed and measured unimpassioned words,
A gift, which, if as calmly 't is denied,
He must withdraw, content upon his cheek,
Despair within his soul.   That I dare ask
Firmly, near boldly, near with confidence
That gift, I have to thank you. Yes, Lord
    Tresham,
I love your sister — as you 'd have one love
That lady . . . oh more, more I love her!
    Wealth,
Rank, all the world thinks me, they 're yours,
    you know,
To hold or part with, at your choice — but grant
My true self, me without a rood of land,
A piece of gold, a name of yesterday,
Grant me that lady, and you . . . Death or
    life?
    Guendolen. [*Apart to* Aus.] Why, this is
    loving, Austin!
    Austin.   He 's so young!
    Guen. Young? Old enough, I think, to half
    surmise
He never had obtained an entrance here,
Were all this fear and trembling needed.
    Aus.   Hush!
He reddens.
    Guen. Mark him, Austin; that 's true love!
Ours must begin again.
    Tresh.   We 'll sit, my lord.
Ever with best desert goes diffidence.
I may speak plainly nor be misconceived.
That I am wholly satisfied with you
On this occasion, when a falcon's eye
Were dull compared with mine to search out
    faults,
Is somewhat.   Mildred's hand is hers to give
Or to refuse.
    Mer.   But you, you grant my suit?
I have your word if hers?
    Tresh.   My best of words
If hers encourage you.   I trust it will.
Have you seen Lady Mildred, by the way?
    Mer. I . . . I . . . our two demesnes, re-
    member, touch;
I have been used to wander carelessly
After my stricken game : the heron roused
Deep in my woods, has trailed its broken wing
Through thicks and glades a mile in yours, —
    or else
Some eyass ill-reclaimed has taken flight
And lured me after her from tree to tree,
I marked not whither.   I have come upon
The lady's wondrous beauty unaware,
And — and then . . . I have seen her.
    Guen. [*Aside to* Aus.]   Note that mode
Of faltering out that, when a lady passed,
He, having eyes, did see her!   You had said —
" On such a day I scanned her, head to foot ;
Observed a red, where red should not have
    been,
Outside her elbow ; but was pleased enough
Upon the whole."   Let such irreverent talk

Be lessoned for the future!
    Tresh.   What 's to say
May be said briefly.   She has never known
A mother's care ; I stand for father too.
Her beauty is not strange to you, it seems —
You cannot know the good and tender heart,
Its girl's trust and its woman's constancy,
How pure yet passionate, how calm yet kind,
How grave yet joyous, how reserved yet free
As light where friends are — how imbued with
    lore
The world most prizes, yet the simplest, yet
The . . . one might know I talked of Mildred
    — thus
We brothers talk !
    Mer.   I thank you.
    Tresh.   In a word,
Control 's not for this lady ; but her wish
To please me outstrips in its subtlety
My power of being pleased : herself creates
The want she means to satisfy.   My heart
Prefers your suit to her as 't were its own.
Can I say more?
    Mer. No more — thanks, thanks — no more!
    Tresh. This matter then discussed . . .
    Mer.   — We 'll waste no breath
On aught less precious.   I 'm beneath the roof
Which holds her : while I thought of that, my
    speech
To you would wander — as it must not do,
Since as you favor me I stand or fall.
I pray you suffer that I take my leave !
    Tresh. With less regret 't is suffered, that
    again
We meet, I hope, so shortly.
    Mer.   We ? again ? —
Ah yes, forgive me — when shall . . . you will
    crown
Your goodness by forthwith apprising me
When . . . if . . . the lady will appoint a day
For me to wait on you — and her.
    Tresh.   So soon
As I am made acquainted with her thoughts
On your proposal — howsoe'er they lean —
A messenger shall bring you the result.
    Mer. You cannot bind me more to you, my
    lord.
Farewell till we renew . . . I trust, renew
A converse ne'er to disunite again.
    Tresh. So may it prove !
    Mer.   You, lady, you, sir, take
My humble salutation !
    Guen. and Aus.   Thanks!
    Tresh.   Within there !
(Servants *enter.* Tresham *conducts* Mertoun *to the
    door. Meantime* Austin *remarks*)
                            Well,
Here I have an advantage of the Earl,
Confess now !   I 'd not think that all was safe
Because my lady's brother stood my friend !
Why, he makes sure of her — " do you say,
    yes —
She 'll not say, no," — what comes it to beside?
I should have prayed the brother, " speak this
    speech,
For Heaven's sake urge this on her — put in
    this —
Forget not, as you 'd save me, t' other thing, —

Then set down what she says, and how she looks,
And if she smiles, and " (in an under breath)
" Only let her accept me, and do you
And all the world refuse me, if you dare ! "
  Guen. That way you 'd take, friend Austin ?
      What a shame
I was your cousin, tamely from the first
Your bride, and all this fervor 's run to waste !
Do you know you speak sensibly to-day ?
The Earl 's a fool.
  Aus.   Here 's Thorold. Tell him so !
  Tresh. [*Returning.*] Now, voices, voices ! 'St !
      the lady 's first !
How seems he ? — seems he not . . . come,
      faith give fraud
The mercy-stroke whenever they engage !
Down with fraud, up with faith ! How seems
      the Earl ?
A name ! a blazon ! if you knew their worth,
As you will never ! come — the Earl ?
  Guen.   He 's young.
  Tresh. What 's she ? an infant save in heart
      and brain.
Young ! Mildred is fourteen, remark ! And
      you . . .
Austin, how old is she ?
  Guen.   There 's tact for you !
I meant that being young was good excuse
If one should tax him . . .
  Tresh.   Well ?
  Guen.   — With lacking wit.
  Tresh. He lacked wit ? Where might he
      lack wit, so please you ?
  Guen. In standing straighter than the stew-
      ard's rod
And making you the tiresomest harangue,
Instead of slipping over to my side
And softly whispering in my ear, " Sweet lady,
Your cousin there will do me detriment
He little dreams of : he 's absorbed, I see,
In my old name and fame — be sure he 'll leave
My Mildred, when his best account of me
Is ended, in full confidence I wear
My grandsire's periwig down either cheek.
I 'm lost unless your gentleness vouchsafes " . . .
  Tresh. . . . " To give a best of best accounts,
      yourself,
Of me and my demerits." You are right !
He should have said what now I say for him.
You golden creature, will you help us all ?
Here 's Austin means to vouch for much, but you
— You are . . . what Austin only knows !
      Come up,
All three of us : she 's in the library
No doubt, for the day 's wearing fast. Precede !
  Guen. Austin, how we must — !
  Tresh.   Must what ? Must speak truth,
Malignant tongue ! Detect one fault in him !
I challenge you !
  Guen.   Witchcraft 's a fault in him,
For you 're bewitched.
  Tresh.   What 's urgent we obtain
Is, that she soon receive him — say, to-morrow —
Next day at furthest.
  Guen.   Ne'er instruct me !
  Tresh.   Come !
— He 's out of your good graces, since forsooth,
He stood not as he 'd carry us by storm

With his perfections ! You 're for the com-
      posed
Manly assured becoming confidence !
— Get her to say, " To-morrow," and I 'll give
      you . . .
I 'll give you black Urganda, to be spoiled
With petting and snail-paces. Will you ?
      Come !

SCENE III. MILDRED'S *Chamber. A painted window
      overlooks the Park.* MILDRED *and* GUENDOLEN.

  Guen. Now, Mildred, spare those pains.
      have not left
Our talkers in the library, and climbed
The wearisome ascent to this your bower
In company with you, — I have not dared . . .
Nay, worked such prodigies as sparing you
Lord Mertoun's pedigree before the flood,
Which Thorold seemed in very act to tell
— Or bringing Austin to pluck up that most
Firm-rooted heresy — your suitor's eyes,
He would maintain, were gray instead of blue —
I think I brought him to contrition ! — Well,
I have not done such things, (all to deserve
A minute's quiet cousins' talk with you,)
To be dismissed so coolly !
  Mildred.   Guendolen !
What have I done ? what could suggest . . .
  Guen.   There, there !
Do I not comprehend you 'd be alone
To throw those testimonies in a heap,
Thorold's enlargings, Austin's brevities,
With that poor silly heartless Guendolen's
Ill-timed misplaced attempted smartnesses —
And sift their sense out ? now, I come to spare
      you
Nearly a whole night's labor. Ask and have !
Demand, be answered ! Lack I ears and eyes ?
Am I perplexed which side of the rock-table
The Conqueror dined on when he landed first,
Lord Mertoun's ancestor was bidden take —
The bow-hand or the arrow-hand's great meed ?
Mildred, the Earl has soft blue eyes !
  Mil.   My brother —
Did he . . . you said that he received him well ?
  Guen. If I said only " well " I said not much.
Oh, stay — which brother ?
  Mil.   Thorold ! who — who else ?
  Guen. Thorold (a secret) is too proud by
      half, —
Nay, hear me out — with us he 's even gentler
Than we are with our birds. Of this great
      House
The least retainer that e'er caught his glance
Would die for him, real dying — no mere talk :
And in the world, the court, if men would cite
The perfect spirit of honor, Thorold's name
Rises of its clear nature to their lips.
But he should take men's homage, trust in it,
And care no more about what drew it down.
He has desert, and that, acknowledgment ;
Is he content ?
  Mil.   You wrong him, Guendolen.
  Guen. He 's proud, confess ; so proud with
      brooding o'er
The light of his interminable line,
An ancestry with men all paladins,
And women all . . .

Mil.   Dear Guendolen, 't is late !
When yonder purple pane the climbing moon
Pierces, I know 't is midnight.
Guen.   Well, that Thorold
Should rise up from such musings, and receive
One come audaciously to graft himself
Into this peerless stock, yet find no flaw,
No slightest spot in such an one . . .
Mil.   Who finds
A spot in Mertoun ?
Guen.   Not your brother ; therefore,
Not the whole world.
Mil.   I am weary, Guendolen.
Bear with me !
Guen.   I am foolish.
Mil.   Oh no, kind !
But I would rest.
Guen.   Good night and rest to you !
I said how gracefully his mantle lay
Beneath the rings of his light hair ?
Mil.   Brown hair.
Guen. Brown ? why, it *is* brown : how could
   you know that ?
Mil. How ? did not you — Oh, Austin 't was
   declared
His hair was light, not brown — my head ! —
   and look,
The moon-beam purpling the dark chamber !
   Sweet,
Good night !
Guen. Forgive me — sleep the soundlier for
   me !   [*Going, she turns suddenly.*
                    Mildred !
Perdition ! all 's discovered ! Thorold finds
— That the Earl's greatest of all grandmothers
Was grander daughter still — to that fair dame
Whose garter slipped down at the famous dance !
                    [*Goes.*
Mil. Is she — can she be really gone at last ?
My heart ! I shall not reach the window.
   Needs
Must I have sinned much, so to suffer !
*She lifts the small lamp which is suspended before the
Virgin's image in the window, and places it by the
purple pane.*
                    There !
          [*She returns to the seat in front.*
Mildred and Mertoun ! Mildred, with consent
Of all the world and Thorold, Mertoun's bride !
Too late ! 'T is sweet to think of, sweeter
   still
To hope for, that this blessed end soothes up
The curse of the beginning ; but I know
It comes too late : 't will sweetest be of all
To dream my soul away and die upon.
                    [*A noise without.*
The voice ! Oh why, why glided sin the snake
Into the paradise Heaven meant us both ?
          [*The window opens softly. A low voice sings.*

There 's a woman like a dew-drop, she 's so purer
   than the purest ;
And her noble heart 's the noblest, yes, and her
   sure faith 's the surest :
And her eyes are dark and humid, like the depth
   on depth of lustre
Hid i' the harebell, while her tresses, sunnier than
   the wild-grape cluster,

Gush in golden-tinted plenty down her neck's rose
   misted marble :
Then her voice's music . . . call it the well's bub
   bling, the bird's warble !
          [*A figure wrapped in a mantle appears at the window.*

And this woman says, " My days were sunless
   and my nights were moonless,
Parched the pleasant April herbage, and the
   lark's heart's outbreak tuneless,
If you loved me not !" And I who — (ah, for
   words of flame !) adore her,
Who am mad to lay my spirit prostrate palpably
   before her —

          [*He enters, approaches her seat, and bends over her.*

I may enter at her portal soon, as now her lattice
   takes me,
And by noontide as by midnight make her mine,
   as hers she makes me !

          [*The EARL throws off his slouched hat and long cloak.*
My very heart sings, so I sing, Beloved !
Mil. Sit, Henry — do not take my hand !
Mer.   'T is mine.
The meeting that appalled us both so much
Is ended.
Mil.   What begins now ?
Mer.   Happiness
Such as the world contains not.
Mil.   That is it.
Our happiness would, as you say, exceed
The whole world's best of blisses : we — do we
Deserve that ? Utter to your soul, what mine
Long since, Beloved, has grown used to hear,
Like a death-knell, so much regarded once,
And so familiar now ; this will not be !
Mer. Oh, Mildred, have I met your brother's
   face ?
Compelled myself — if not to speak untruth,
Yet to disguise, to shun, to put aside
The truth, as — what had e'er prevailed on me
Save you, to venture ? Have I gained at last
Your brother, the one scarer of your dreams,
And waking thoughts' sole apprehension too ?
Does a new life, like a young sunrise, break
On the strange unrest of our night, confused
With rain and stormy flaw — and will you see
No dripping blossoms, no fire-tinted drops
On each live spray, no vapor steaming up,
And no expressless glory in the East ?
When I am by you, to be ever by you,
When I have won you and may worship you,
Oh, Mildred, can you say " this will not be " ?
Mil. Sin has surprised us, so will punishment.
Mer. No — me alone, who sinned alone !
Mil.   The night
You likened our past life to — was it storm
Throughout to you then, Henry ?
Mer.   Of your life
I spoke — what am I, what my life, to waste
A thought about when you are by me ? — you
It was, I said my folly called the storm
And pulled the night upon. 'T was day with
   me —
Perpetual dawn with me.
Mil.   Come what come will.
You have been happy · take my hand !

Mer. [*After a pause.*]   How good
Your brother is ! I figured him a cold —
Shall I say, haughty man ?
Mil.   They told me all.
I know all.
Mer.   It will soon be over.
Mil.   Over ?
Oh, what is over ? what must I live through
And say, " 't is over " ? Is our meeting over ?
Have I received in presence of them all
The partner of my guilty love — with brow
Trying to seem a maiden's brow — with lips
Which make believe that when they strive to
    form
Replies to you and tremble as they strive,
It is the nearest ever they approached
A stranger's . . . Henry, yours that stranger's
    . . . lip —
With cheek that looks a virgin's, and that is . . .
Ah God, some prodigy of thine will stop
This planned piece of deliberate wickedness
In its birth even ! some fierce leprous spot
Will mar the brow's dissimulating ! I
Shall murmur no smooth speeches got by heart,
But, frenzied, pour forth all our woeful story,
The love, the shame, and the despair — with
    them
Round me aghast as round some cursed fount
That should spirt water, and spouts blood. I 'll
    not
. . . Henry, you do not wish that I should
    draw
This vengeance down ? I 'll not affect a grace
That 's gone from me — gone once, and gone
    forever !
Mer. Mildred, my honor is your own. I 'll
    share
Disgrace I cannot suffer by myself.
A word informs your brother I retract
This morning's offer ; time will yet bring forth
Some better way of saving both of us.
Mil. I 'll meet their faces, Henry !
Mer.   When ? to-morrow !
Get done with it !
Mil.   Oh, Henry, not to-morrow !
Next day ! I never shall prepare my words
And looks and gestures sooner. — How you
    must
Despise me !
Mer.   Mildred, break it if you choose,
A heart the love of you uplifted — still
Uplifts, through this protracted agony,
To heaven ! but, Mildred, answer me, — first
    pace
The chamber with me — once again — now, say
Calmly the part, the . . . what it is of me
You see contempt (for you did say contempt)
— Contempt for you in ! I would pluck it off
And cast it from me ! — but no — no, you 'll not
Repeat that ? — will you, Mildred, repeat that ?
Mil. Dear Henry !
Mer.   I was scarce a boy — e'en now
What am I more ? And you were infantine
When first I met you ; why, your hair fell loose
On either side ! My fool's-cheek reddens now
Only in the recalling how it burned
That morn to see the shape of many a dream
— You know we boys are prodigal of charms

To her we dream of — I had heard of one,
Had dreamed of her, and I was close to her,
Might speak to her, might live and die her own,
Who knew ? I spoke. Oh, Mildred, feel you
    not
That now, while I remember every glance
Of yours, each word of yours, with power to test
And weigh them in the diamond scales of pride,
Resolved the treasure of a first and last
Heart's love shall have been bartered at its
    worth,
— That now I think upon your purity
And utter ignorance of guilt — your own
Or other's guilt — the girlish undisguised
Delight at a strange novel prize — (I talk
A silly language, but interpret, you !)
If I, with fancy at its full, and reason
Scarce in its germ, enjoined you secrecy,
If you had pity on my passion, pity
On my protested sickness of the soul
To sit beside you, hear you breathe, and watch
Your eyelids and the eyes beneath — if you
Accorded gifts and knew not they were gifts —
If I grew mad at last with enterprise
And must behold my beauty in her bower
Or perish — (I was ignorant of even
My own desires — what then were you ?) if sor-
    row —
Sin — if the end came — must I now renounce
My reason, blind myself to light, say truth
Is false and lie to God and my own soul ?
Contempt were all of this !
Mil.   Do you believe . . .
Or, Henry, I 'll not wrong you — you believe
That I was ignorant. I scarce grieve o'er
The past ! We 'll love on ; you will love me
    still !
Mer. Oh, to love less what one has injured !
    Dove,
Whose pinion I have rashly hurt, my breast —
Shall my heart's warmth not nurse thee into
    strength ?
Flower I have crushed, shall I not care for
    thee ?
Bloom o'er my crest, my fight-mark and device !
Mildred, I love you and you love me !
Mil.   Go !
Be that your last word. I shall sleep to-night.
Mer. This is not our last meeting ?
Mil.   One night more.
Mer. And then — think, then !
Mil.   Then, no sweet courtship-days,
No dawning consciousness of love for us,
No strange and palpitating births of sense
From words and looks, no innocent fears and
    hopes,
Reserves and confidences : morning's over !
Mer. How else should love's perfected noon-
    tide follow ?
All the dawn promised shall the day perform.
Mil. So may it be ! but —
                    You are cautious, Love ?
Are sure that unobserved you scaled the walls ?
Mer. Oh, trust me ! Then our final meet-
    ing 's fixed
To-morrow night ?
Mil. Farewell ! Stay, Henry . . . where-
    fore ?

His foot is on the yew-tree bough : the turf
Receives him : now the moonlight as he runs
Embraces him — but he must go — is gone.
Ah, once again he turns — thanks, thanks, my
　　Love !
He 's gone.　Oh, I 'll believe him every word !
I was so young, I loved him so, I had
No mother, God forgot me, and I fell.
There may be pardon yet : all 's doubt beyond.
Surely the bitterness of death is past !

ACT II

Scene.　*The Library.*

Enter Lord Tresham, *hastily.*

Tresh.　This way !　In, Gerard, quick !
　　[*As* Gerard *enters,* Tresham *secures the door.*
　　　　　　　Now speak ! or, wait —
I 'll bid you speak directly.　　[*Seats himself.*
　　　　　　　Now repeat
Firmly and circumstantially the tale
You just now told me ; it eludes me ; either
I did not listen, or the half is gone
Away from me.　How long have you lived
　　here ?
Here in my house, your father kept our woods
Before you ?
Ger.　　— As his father did, my lord.
I have been eating, sixty years almost,
Your bread.
Tresh.　　Yes, yes.　You ever were of all
The servant in my father's house, I know,
The trusted one.　You 'll speak the truth.
Ger.　　　　　　I 'll speak
God's truth.　Night after night . . .
Tresh.　　　　　　Since when ?
Ger.　　　　　　At least
A month — each midnight has some man access
To Lady Mildred's chamber.
Tresh.　　　　　Tush, "access " —
No wide words like " access " to me !
Ger.　　　　　　He runs
Along the woodside, crosses to the south,
Takes the left tree that ends the avenue . . .
Tresh.　The last great yew-tree ?
Ger.　　　　　You might stand upon
The main boughs like a platform.　Then
　　he . . .
Tresh.　　Quick !
Ger.　Climbs up, and, where they lessen at
　　the top,
— I cannot see distinctly, but he throws,
I think — for this I do not vouch — a line
That reaches to the lady's casement —
Tresh.　　　　　— Which
He enters not !　Gerard, some wretched fool
Dares pry into my sister's privacy !
When such are young, it seems a precious thing
To have approached, — to merely have ap-
　　proached,
Got sight of, the abode of her they set
Their frantic thoughts upon !　He does not
　　enter ?
Gerard ?
Ger.　There is a lamp that 's full i' the midst,
Under a red square in the painted glass

Of Lady Mildred's . . .
Tresh.　　　Leave that name out !　Well ?
That lamp ?
Ger.　　— Is moved at midnight higher up
To one pane — a small dark-blue pane : he waits
For that among the boughs : at sight of that,
I see him, plain as I see you, my lord,
Open the lady's casement, enter there . . .
Tresh. — And stay ?
Ger.　　　　An hour, two hours.
Tresh.　　　　　And this you saw
Once ? — twice ? — quick !
Ger.　　　Twenty times.
Tresh.　　　　And what brings you
Under the yew-trees ?
Ger.　　　　The first night I left
My range so far, to track the stranger stag
That broke the pale, I saw the man.
Tresh.　　　　　Yet sent
No cross-bow shaft through the marauder ?
Ger.　　　　　　But
He came, my lord, the first time he was seen,
In a great moonlight, light as any day,
From Lady Mildred's chamber.
Tresh.　[*After a pause.*]　You have no cause
— Who could have cause to do my sister wrong ?
Ger.　Oh, my lord, only once — let me this
　　once
Speak what is on my mind !　Since first I noted
All this, I 've groaned as if a fiery net
Plucked me this way and that — fire if I turned
To her, fire if I turned to you, and fire
If down I flung myself and strove to die.
The lady could not have been seven years old
When I was trusted to conduct her safe
Through the deer-herd to stroke the snow-white
　　fawn
I brought to eat bread from her tiny hand
Within a month.　She ever had a smile
To greet me with — she . . . if it could undo
What 's done, to lop each limb from off this
　　trunk . . .
All that is foolish talk, not fit for you —
I mean, I could not speak and bring her hurt
For Heaven's compelling.　But when I was
　　fixed
To hold my peace, each morsel of your food
Eaten beneath your roof, my birth-place too,
Choked me.　I wish I had grown mad in doubts
What it behoved me do.　This morn it seemed
Either I must confess to you, or die :
Now it is done, I seem the vilest worm
That crawls, to have betrayed my lady !
Tresh.　　　　　　No —
No, Gerard !
Ger.　　Let me go !
Tresh.　　　　A man, you say :
What man ?　Young ?　Not a vulgar hind ?
　　What dress ?
Ger.　A slouched hat and a large dark foreign
　　cloak
Wraps his whole form ; even his face is hid ;
But I should judge him young : no hind, be
　　sure !
Tresh.　Why ?
Ger.　He is ever armed : his sword projects
Beneath the cloak.
Tresh.　　　Gerard, — I will not say

No word, no breath of this!
Ger. Thanks, thanks, my lord! [*Goes.*
TRESHAM *paces the room. After a pause,*
Oh, thought's absurd! — as with some monstrous fact
Which, when ill thoughts beset us, seems to give
Merciful God that made the sun and stars,
The waters and the green delights of earth,
The lie! I apprehend the monstrous fact —
Yet know the maker of all worlds is good,
And yield my reason up inadequate
To reconcile what yet I do behold —
Blasting my sense! There's cheerful day outside:
This is my library, and this the chair
My father used to sit in carelessly
After his soldier-fashion, while I stood
Between his knees to question him : and here
GERARD our gray retainer, — as he says,
Fed with our food, from sire to son, an age —
Has told a story — I am to believe!
That Mildred . . . oh, no, no! both tales are true,
Her pure cheek's story and the forester's!
Would she, or could she, err — much less, confound
All guilts of treachery, of craft, of . . . Heaven
Keep me within its hand! — I will sit here
Until thought settle and I see my course.
Avert, O God, only this woe from me!
[*As he sinks his head between his arms on the table,*
GUENDOLEN's *voice is heard at the door.*
Lord Tresham! [*She knocks.*] Is Lord Tresham there?
[TRESHAM, *hastily turning, pulls down the first book above him and opens it.*
Tresh. Come in! [*She enters.*
Ha, Guendolen! — good morning.
Guen. Nothing more?
Tresh. What should I say more?
Guen. Pleasant question! more?
This more. Did I besiege poor Mildred's brain
Last night till close on morning with "the Earl,"
"The Earl" — whose worth did I asseverate
Till I am very fain to hope that . . . Thorold,
What is all this? You are not well!
Tresh. Who, I?
You laugh at me.
Guen. Has what I'm fain to hope,
Arrived then? Does that huge tome show some blot
In the Earl's 'scutcheon come no longer back
Than Arthur's time?
Tresh. When left you Mildred's chamber?
Guen. Oh, late enough, I told you! The main thing
To ask is, how I left her chamber, — sure,
Content yourself, she'll grant this paragon
Of Earls no such ungracious . . .
Tresh. Send her here!
Guen. Thorold?
Tresh. I mean — acquaint her, Guendolen,
— But mildly!
Guen. Mildly?
Tresh. Ah, you guessed aright!
I am not well : there is no hiding it.
But tell her I would see her at her leisure —

That is, at once! here in the library!
The passage in that old Italian book
We hunted for so long is found, say, found —
And if I let it slip again . . . you see,
That she must come — and instantly!
Guen. I'll die
Piecemeal, record that, if there have not gloomed
Some blot i' the 'scutcheon!
Tresh. Go! or, Guendolen
Be you at call, — with Austin, if you choose, —
In the adjoining gallery! There, go:
[GUENDOLEN *goes.*
Another lesson to me! You might bid
A child disguise his heart's sore, and conduct
Some sly investigation point by point
With a smooth brow, as well as bid me catch
The inquisitorial cleverness some praise!
If you had told me yesterday, "There's one
You needs must circumvent and practise with,
Entrap by policies, if you would worm
The truth out: and that one is — Mildred!'
There,
There — reasoning is thrown away on it!
Prove she's unchaste . . . why, you may after prove
That she's a poisoner, traitress, what you will!
Where I can comprehend naught, naught's to say,
Or do, or think! Force on me but the first
Abomination, — then outpour all plagues,
And I shall ne'er make count of them!
(*Enter* MILDRED.)
Mil. What book
Is it I wanted, Thorold? Guendolen
Thought you were pale; you are not pale.
That book?
That's Latin surely.
Tresh. Mildred, here's a line,
(Don't lean on me : I'll English it for you)
"Love conquers all things." What love conquers them?
What love should you esteem — best love?
Mil. True love.
Tresh. I mean, and should have said, whose love is best
Of all that love or that profess to love?
Mil. The list's so long: there's father's,
mother's, husband's . . .
Tresh. Mildred, I do believe a brother's love
For a sole sister must exceed them all.
For see now, only see! there's no alloy
Of earth that creeps into the perfect'st gold
Of other loves — no gratitude to claim;
You never gave her life, not even aught
That keeps life — never tended her, instructed,
Enriched her — so, your love can claim no right
O'er her save pure love's claim : that's what I call
Freedom from earthliness. You'll never hope
To be such friends, for instance, she and you,
As when you hunted cowslips in the woods
Or played together in the meadow hay.
Oh yes — with age, respect comes, and your worth
Is felt, there's growing sympathy of tastes,
There's ripened friendship, there's confirmed esteem :

—Much head these make against the new-
comer!
The startling apparition, the strange youth—
Whom one half-hour's conversing with, or, say,
Mere gazing at, shall change (beyond all change
This Ovid ever sang about) your soul
. . . Her soul, that is, — the sister's soul! With
her
'T was winter yesterday; now, all is warmth,
The green leaf 's springing and the turtle's voice,
" Arise and come away!" Come whither?—
far
Enough from the esteem, respect, and all
The brother's somewhat insignificant
Array of rights! All which he knows before,
Has calculated on so long ago!
I think such love, (apart from yours and mine,)
Contented with its little term of life,
Intending to retire betimes, aware
How soon the background must be place for it,
—I think, am sure, a brother's love exceeds
All the world's love in its unworldliness.
    Mil.   What is this for?
    Tresh.   This, Mildred, is it for!
Or, no, I cannot go to it so soon!
That 's one of many points my haste left out—
Each day, each hour throws forth its silk-slight
film
Between the being tied to you by birth,
And you, until those slender threads compose
A web that shrouds her daily life of hopes
And fears and fancies, all her life, from yours:
So close you live and yet so far apart!
And must I rend this web, tear up, break down
The sweet and palpitating mystery
That makes her sacred? You—for you I mean,
Shall I speak, shall I not speak?
    Mil.   Speak!
    Tresh.   I will,
Is there a story men could—any man
Could tell of you, you would conceal from me?
I 'll never think there 's falsehood on that lip.
Say " There is no such story men could tell,"
And I 'll believe you, though I disbelieve
The world—the world of better men than I,
And women such as I suppose you. Speak!
[*After a pause.*] Not speak? Explain then!
        Clear it up then! Move
Some of the miserable weight away
That presses lower than the grave! Not speak?
Some of the dead weight, Mildred! Ah, if I
Could bring myself to plainly make their charge
Against you! Must I, Mildred? Silent still?
[*After a pause.*] Is there a gallant that has
        night by night
Admittance to your chamber?
[*After a pause.*]   Then, his name!
Till now, I only had a thought for you:
But now, — his name!
    Mil.   Thorold, do you devise
Fit expiation for my guilt, if fit
There be! 'T is naught to say that I 'll endure
And bless you, —that my spirit yearns to purge
Her stains off in the fierce renewing fire:
But do not plunge me into other guilt!
Oh, guilt enough! I cannot tell his name.
    Tresh.   Then judge yourself! How should I
        act? Pronounce!

Mil. Oh, Thorold, you must never tempt me
        thus!
To die here in this chamber by that sword
Would seem like punishment: so should I glide,
Like an arch-cheat, into extremest bliss!
'T were easily arranged for me: but you—
What would become of you?
    Tresh.   And what will now
Become of me? I 'll hide your shame and mine
From every eye; the dead must heave their
        hearts
Under the marble of our chapel-floor;
They cannot rise and blast you. You may wed
Your paramour above our mother's tomb;
Our mother cannot move from 'neath your foot,
We too will somehow wear this one day out:
But with to-morrow hastens here—the Earl!
The youth without suspicion face can come
From heaven, and heart from . . . whence
        proceed such hearts?
I have dispatched last night at your command
A missive bidding him present himself
To-morrow—here—thus much is said; the
        rest
Is understood as if 't were written down—
" His suit finds favor in your eyes." Now
        dictate
This morning's letter that shall countermand
Last night's—do dictate that!
    Mil.   But, Thorold—if
I will receive him as I said?
    Tresh.   The Earl?
    Mil. I will receive him.
    Tresh. [*Starting up.*] Ho there! Guendolen!
            (GUENDOLEN *and* AUSTIN *enter.*)
And, Austin, you are welcome, too! Look
        there!
The woman there!
    Aus. and Guen. How? Mildred?
    Tresh.   Mildred once!
Now the receiver night by night, when sleep
Blesses the inmates of her father's house,
—I say, the soft sly wanton that receives
Her guilt's accomplice 'neath this roof which
        holds
You, Guendolen, you, Austin, and has held
A thousand Treshams—never one like her!
No lighter of the signal-lamp her quick
Foul breath near quenches in hot eagerness
To mix with breath as foul! no loosener
O' the lattice, practised in the stealthy tread,
The low voice and the noiseless come-and-go!
Not one composer of the bacchant's mien
Into—what you thought Mildred's, in a word!
Know her!
    Guen.   Oh, Mildred, look to me, at least!
Thorold—she 's dead, I 'd say, but that she
        stands
Rigid as stone and whiter!
    Tresh.   You have heard . . .
    Guen. Too much! You must proceed no
        further.
    Mil.   Yes—
Proceed! All 's truth. Go from me!
    Tresh.   All is truth,
She tells you! Well, you know, or ought to
        know,
All this I would forgive in her. I 'd con

Each precept the harsh world enjoins, I 'd take
Our ancestors' stern verdicts one by one,
I 'd bind myself before them to exact
The prescribed vengeance — and one word of
    hers,
The sight of her, the bare least memory
Of Mildred, my one sister, my heart's pride
Above all prides, my all in all so long,
Would scatter every trace of my resolve.
What were it silently to waste away
And see her waste away from this day forth,
Two scathèd things with leisure to repent,
And grow acquainted with the grave, and die
Tired out if not at peace, and be forgotten?
It were not so impossible to bear.
But this — that, fresh from last night's pledge
    renewed
Of love with the successful gallant there,
She calmly bids me help her to entice,
Inveigle an unconscious trusting youth
Who thinks her all that 's chaste and good and
    pure,
— Invites me to betray him . . . who so fit
As honor's self to cover shame's arch-deed?
— That she 'll receive Lord Mertoun — (her own
    phrase) —
This, who could bear? Why, you have heard
    of thieves,
Stabbers, the earth's disgrace, who yet have
    laughed,
"Talk not to me of torture — I 'll betray
No comrade I 've pledged faith to!" — you
    have heard
Of wretched women — all but Mildreds — tied
By wild illicit ties to losels vile
You 'd tempt them to forsake; and they 'll
    reply
" Gold, friends, repute, I left for him, I find
In him, why should I leave him then for gold,
Repute or friends?" — and you have felt your
    heart
Respond to such poor outcasts of the world
As to so many friends; bad as you please,
You 've felt they were God's men and women
    still,
So, not to be disowned by you. But she
That stands there, calmly gives her lover up
As means to wed the Earl that she may hide
Their intercourse the surelier: and, for this,
I curse her to her face before you all.
Shame hunt her from the earth! Then Heaven
    do right
To both! It hears me now — shall judge her
    then!

[As MILDRED *faints and falls,* TRESHAM *rushes out.*
Aus. Stay, Tresham, we 'll accompany you!
Guen.   We?
What, and leave Mildred? We? Why,
    where 's my place
But by her side, and where yours but by mine?
Mildred — one word! Only look at me, then!
Aus. No, Guendolen! I echo Thorold's
    voice.
She is unworthy to behold . . .
Guen.   Us two?
If you spoke on reflection, and if I
Approved your speech — if you (to put the thing
At lowest) you the soldier, bound to make

The king's cause yours and fight for it, and
    throw
Regard to others of its right or wrong,
— If with a death-white woman you can help,
Let alone sister, let alone a Mildred,
You left her — or if I, her cousin, friend
This morning, playfellow but yesterday,
Who said, or thought at least a thousand times,
"I 'd serve you if I could," should now face
    round
And say, "Ah, that 's to only signify
I 'd serve you while you 're fit to serve yourself,
So long as fifty eyes await the turn
Of yours to forestall its yet half-formed wish,
I 'll proffer my assistance you 'll not need —
When every tongue is praising you, I 'll join
The praisers' chorus — when you 're hemmed
    about
With lives between you and detraction — lives
To be laid down if a rude voice, rash eye,
Rough hand should violate the sacred ring
Their worship throws about you, — then indeed,
Who 'll stand up for you stout as I?" If so
We said, and so we did, — not Mildred there
Would be unworthy to behold us both,
But we should be unworthy, both of us,
To be beheld by — by — your meanest dog,
Which, if that sword were broken in your
    face
Before a crowd, that badge torn off your breast,
And you cast out with hooting and contempt,
— Would push his way through all the hooters,
    gain
Your side, go off with you and all your shame
To the next ditch you choose to die in! Austin,
Do you love me? Here 's Austin, Mildred, —
    here 's
Your brother says he does not believe half —
No, nor half that — of all he heard! He says,
Look up and take his hand!
Aus.   Look up and take
My hand, dear Mildred!
Mil.   I — I was so young!
Beside, I loved him, Thorold — and I had
No mother; God forgot me: so, I fell.
Guen. Mildred!
Mil.   Require no further! Did I dream
That I could palliate what is done? All 's true.
Now, punish me! A woman takes my hand?
Let go my hand! You do not know, I see.
I thought that Thorold told you.
Guen.   What is this?
Where start you to?
Mil.   Oh, Austin, loosen me!
You heard the whole of it — your eyes were
    worse,
In their surprise, than Thorold's! Oh, unless
You stay to execute his sentence, loose
My hand! Has Thorold gone, and are you here?
Guen. Here, Mildred, we two friends of yours
    will wait
Your bidding; be you silent, sleep or muse!
Only, when you shall want your bidding done,
How can we do it if we are not by?
Here 's Austin waiting patiently your will!
One spirit to command, and one to love
And to believe in it and do its best,
Poor as that is, to help it — why, the world

Has been won many a time, its length and
    breadth,
By just such a beginning!
Mil.   I believe
If once I threw my arms about your neck
And sunk my head upon your breast, that I
Should weep again.
Guen.   Let go her hand now, Austin!
Wait for me. Pace the gallery and think
On the world's seemings and realities,
Until I call you.   [*Austin goes.*
Mil.   No — I cannot weep.
No more tears from this brain — no sleep — no
    tears!
O Guendolen, I love you!
Guen.   Yes: and " love "
Is a short word that says so very much!
It says that you confide in me.
Mil.   Confide!
Guen. Your lover's name, then! I 've so
    much to learn,
Ere I can work in your behalf!
Mil.   My friend,
You know I cannot tell his name.
Guen.   At least
He is your lover? and you love him too?
Mil. Ah, do you ask me that? — but I am
    fallen
So low!
Guen. You love him still, then?
Mil.   My sole prop
Against the guilt that crushes me! I say,
Each night ere I lie down, " I was so young —
I had no mother, and I loved him so ! "
And then God seems indulgent, and I dare
Trust him my soul in sleep.
Guen.   How could you let us
E'en talk to you about Lord Mertoun then?
Mil. There is a cloud around me.
Guen.   But you said
You would receive his suit in spite of this?
Mil. I say there is a cloud . . .
Guen.   No cloud to me!
Lord Mertoun and your lover are the same!
Mil. What maddest fancy . . .
Guen. [*Calling aloud.*] Austin! (spare your
    pains —
When I have got a truth, that truth I keep) —
Mil. By all you love, sweet Guendolen, for-
    bear!
Have I confided in you . . .
Guen.   Just for this!
Austin! — Oh, not to guess it at the first!
But I did guess it — that is, I divined,
Felt by an instinct how it was: why else
Should I pronounce you free from all that heap
Of sins which had been irredeemable?
I felt they were not yours — what other way
Than this, not yours? The secret's wholly
    mine!
Mil. If you would see me die before his face . . .
Guen. I 'd hold my peace! And if the Earl
    returns
To-night?
Mil. Ah Heaven, he 's lost!
Guen.   I thought so. Austin!
        (*Enter* Austin.)
Oh, where have you been hiding?

Aus.   Thorold 's gone,
I know not how, across the meadow-land.
I watched him till I lost him in the skirts
O' the beech-wood.
Guen.   Gone? All thwarts us.
Mil.   Thorold too?
Guen. I have thought. First lead this Mil-
    dred to her room.
Go on the other side; and then we 'll seek
Your brother: and I 'll tell you, by the way,
The greatest comfort in the world. You said
There was a clue to all. Remember, Sweet,
He said there was a clue! I hold it. Come!

ACT III

Scene I. *The end of the Yew-tree Avenue under* Mil-
dred's *window. A light seen through a central red
pane.*

    Enter Tresham *through the trees.*

Tresh. Again here! But I cannot lose my-
    self.
The heath — the orchard — I have traversed
    glades
And dells and bosky paths which used to lead
Into green wild-wood depths, bewildering
My boy's adventurous step. And now they tend
Hither or soon or late; the blackest shade
Breaks up, the thronged trunks of the trees ope
    wide,
And the dim turret I have fled from, fronts
Again my step; the very river put
Its arm about me and conducted me
To this detested spot. Why then, I 'll shun
Their will no longer: do your will with me!
Oh, bitter! To have reared a towering scheme
Of happiness, and to behold it razed,
Were nothing; all men hope, and see their hopes
Frustrate, and grieve awhile, and hope anew.
But I . . . to hope that from a line like ours
No horrid prodigy like this would spring,
Were just as though I hoped that from these old
Confederates against the sovereign day,
Children of older and yet older sires,
Whose living coral berries dropped, as now
On me, on many a baron's surcoat once,
On many a beauty's wimple — would proceed
No poison-tree, to thrust, from hell its root,
Hither and thither its strange snaky arms.
Why came I here? What must I do? [*A bell
    strikes.*] A bell?
Midnight! and 't is at midnight . . . Ah, I catch
— Woods, river, plains, I catch your meaning
    now.
And I obey you! Hist! This tree will serve.
[*He retires behind one of the trees. After a pause,
    enter* Mertoun *cloaked as before.*

Mer. Not time! Beat out thy last voluptuous
    beat
Of hope and fear, my heart! I thought the
    clock
I' the chapel struck as I was pushing through
The ferns. And so I shall no more see rise
My love-star! Oh, no matter for the past!
So much the more delicious task to watch
Mildred revive: to pluck out, thorn by thorn,
All traces of the rough forbidden path

My rash love lured her to!   Each day must see
Some fear of hers effaced, some hope renewed:
Then there will be surprises, unforeseen
Delights in store.   I 'll not regret the past.
      [*The light is placed above in the purple pane.*
And see, my signal rises, Mildred's star!
I never saw it lovelier than now
It rises for the last time.   If it sets,
'T is that the reassuring sun may dawn.
[*As he prepares to ascend the last tree of the avenue,*
      TRESHAM *arrests his arm.*
Unhand me — peasant, by your grasp!   Here 's
      gold.
'T was a mad freak of mine.   I said I 'd pluck
A branch from the white-blossomed shrub be-
      neath
The casement there.   Take this, and hold your
      peace.
  Tresh.   Into the moonlight yonder, come with
      me!
Out of the shadow.
  Mer.   I am armed, fool!
  Tresh.   Yes,
Or no?   You 'll come into the light, or no?
My hand is on your throat — refuse! —
  Mer.   That voice!
Where have I heard . . . no — that was mild
      and slow.
I 'll come with you.   [*They advance.*
  Tresh.   You 're armed: that 's well.   Declare
Your name: who are you?
  Mer.   (Tresham! — she is lost!)
  Tresh. Oh, silent?   Do you know, you bear
      yourself
Exactly as, in curious dreams I 've had
How felons, this wild earth is full of, look
When they 're detected, still your kind has
      looked!
The bravo holds an assured countenance,
The thief is voluble and plausible,
But silently the slave of lust has crouched
When I have fancied it before a man.
Your name!
  Mer.   I do conjure Lord Tresham — ay,
Kissing his foot, if so I might prevail —
That he for his own sake forbear to ask
My name!   As heaven 's above, his future weal
Or woe depends upon my silence!   Vain!
I read your white inexorable face.
Know me, Lord Tresham!
          [*He throws off his disguises.*
  Tresh.   Mertoun!
      [*After a pause.*]   Draw now!
  Mer.   Hear me
But speak first!
  Tresh.   Not one least word on your life!
Be sure that I will strangle in your throat
The least word that informs me how you live
And yet seem what you seem!   No doubt 't was
      you
Taught Mildred still to keep that face and sin.
We should join hands in frantic sympathy
If you once taught me the unteachable,
Explained how you can live so, and so lie.
With God's help I retain, despite my sense,
The old belief — a life like yours is still
Impossible.   Now draw!
  Mer.   Not for my sake,

Do I entreat a hearing — for your sake,
And most, for her sake!
  Tresh.   Ha ha, what should I
Know of your ways?   A miscreant like yourself,
How must one rouse his ire?   A blow? — that 's
      pride
No doubt, to him!   One spurns him, does one
      not?
Or sets the foot upon his mouth, or spits
Into his face!   Come!   Which, or all of these?
  Mer. 'Twixt him and me and Mildred.
      Heaven be judge!
Can I avoid this?   Have your will, my lord!
      [*He draws and, after a few passes, falls.*
  Tresh.   You are not hurt?
  Mer.   You 'll hear me now!
  Tresh.   But rise!
  Mer.   Ah, Tresham, say I not " you 'll hear
      me now!' "
And what procures a man the right to speak
In his defence before his fellow man,
But — I suppose — the thought that presently
He may have leave to speak before his God
His whole defence?
  Tresh.   Not hurt?   It cannot be!
You made no effort to resist me.   Where
Did my sword reach you?   Why not have re-
      turned
My thrusts?   Hurt where?
  Mer.   My lord —
  Tresh.   How young he is!
  Mer.   Lord Tresham, I am very young, and
      yet
I have entangled other lives with mine.
Do let me speak, and do believe my speech!
That when I die before you presently, —
  Tresh.   Can you stay here till I return with
      help?
  Mer.   Oh, stay by me!   When I was less
      than boy
I did you grievous wrong and knew it not —
Upon my honor, knew it not!   Once known,
I could not find what seemed a better way
To right you than I took: my life — you feel
How less than nothing were the giving you
The life you 've taken!   But I thought my way
The better — only for your sake and hers:
And as you have decided otherwise,
Would I had an infinity of lives
To offer you!   Now say — instruct me — think!
Can you, from the brief minutes I have left,
Eke out my reparation?   Oh think — think!
For I must wring a partial — dare I say,
Forgiveness from you, ere I die?
  Tresh.   I do
Forgive you.
  Mer.   Wait and ponder that great word!
Because, if you forgive me, I shall hope
To speak to you of — Mildred!
  Tresh.   Mertoun, haste
And anger have undone us.   'T is not you
Should tell me for a novelty you 're young,
Thoughtless, unable to recall the past.
Be but your pardon ample as my own!
  Mer.   Ah, Tresham, that a sword-stroke and
      a drop
Of blood or two, should bring all this about!
Why, 't was my very fear of you, my love

Of you — (what passion like a boy's for one
Like you?) — that ruined me! I dreamed of
    you —
You, all accomplished, courted everywhere,
The scholar and the gentleman. I burned
To knit myself to you : but I was young,
And your surpassing reputation kept me
So far aloof ! Oh, wherefore all that love ?
With less of love, my glorious yesterday
Of praise and gentlest words and kindest looks,
Had taken place perchance six months ago.
Even now, how happy we had been ! And yet
I know the thought of this escaped you,
    Tresham !
Let me look up into your face ; I feel
'T is changed above me : yet my eyes are glazed.
Where ? where ?
[*As he endeavors to raise himself his eye catches the
    lamp.*
        Ah, Mildred ! What will Mildred do ?
Tresham, her life is bound up in the life
That 's bleeding fast away ! I 'll live — must
    live,
There, if you 'll only turn me I shall live
And save her ! Tresham — oh, had you but
    heard !
Had you but heard ! What right was yours to
    set
The thoughtless foot upon her life and mine,
And then say, as we perish, "Had I thought,
All had gone otherwise" ? We 've sinned and
    die —
Never you sin, Lord Tresham ! for you 'll die,
And God will judge you.
    Tresh.   Yes, be satisfied !
That process is begun.
    Mer.   And she sits there
Waiting for me ! Now, say you this to her —
You, not another — say, I saw him die
As he breathed this, "I love her" — you don't
    know
What those three small words mean ! Say, lov-
    ing her
Lowers me down the bloody slope to death
With memories . . . I speak to her, not you,
Who had no pity, will have no remorse,
Perchance intend her . . . Die along with me,
Dear Mildred ! 't is so easy, and you 'll 'scape
So much unkindness ! Can I lie at rest,
With rude speech spoken to you, ruder deeds
Done to you ? — heartless men shall have my
    heart,
And I tied down with grave-clothes and the
    worm,
Aware, perhaps, of every blow — oh God ! —
Upon those lips — yet of no power to tear
The felon stripe by stripe ! Die, Mildred !
    Leave
Their honorable world to them ! For God
We 're good enough, though the world casts us
    out.   [*A whistle is heard.*
    Tresh. Ho, Gerard !
(*Enter* GERARD, AUSTIN *and* GUENDOLEN, *with lights.*)
        No one speak ! You see what 's done.
I cannot bear another voice.
    Mer.   There 's light —
Light all about me, and I move to it.
Tresham, did I not tell you — did you not

Just promise to deliver words of mine
To Mildred ?
    Tresh. I will bear those words to her.
    Mer. Now ?
    Tresh. Now. Lift you the body, and leave
        me
The head.
[*As they have half raised* MERTOUN, *he turns suddenly.*
    Mer. I knew they turned me : turn me not
        from her !
There ! stay you ! there !   [*Dies*
    Guen. [*After a pause.*] Austin, remain you
        here
With Thorold until Gerard comes with help :
Then lead him to his chamber. I must go
To Mildred.
    Tresh.   Guendolen, I hear each word
You utter. Did you hear him bid me give
His message ? Did you hear my promise ? I,
And only I, see Mildred.
    Guen.   She will die.
    Tresh. Oh no, she will not die ! I dare not
        hope
She 'll die. What ground have you to think
        she 'll die ?
Why, Austin 's with you !
    Aus.   Had we but arrived
Before you fought !
    Tresh.   There was no fight at all.
He let me slaughter him — the boy ! I 'll trust
The body there to you and Gerard — thus !
Now bear him on before me.
    Aus.   Whither bear him ?
    Tresh. Oh, to my chamber ! When we meet
        there next,
We shall be friends.
        [*They bear out the body of* MERTOUN.
            Will she die, Guendolen ?
    Guen. Where are you taking me ?
    Tresh.   He fell just here.
Now answer me. Shall you in your whole life
— You who have naught to do with Mertoun's
        fate,
Now you have seen his breast upon the turf,
Shall you e'er walk this way if you can help ?
When you and Austin wander arm-in-arm
Through our ancestral grounds, will not a shade
Be ever on the meadow and the waste —
Another kind of shade than when the night
Shuts the woodside with all its whispers up ?
But will you ever so forget his breast
As carelessly to cross this bloody turf
Under the black yew avenue ? That 's well !
You turn your head : and I then ? —
    Guen.   What is done
Is done. My care is for the living. Thorold,
Bear up against this burden : more remains
To set the neck to !
    Tresh.   Dear and ancient trees
My fathers planted, and I loved so well !
What have I done that, like some fabled crime
Of yore, lets loose a Fury leading thus
Her miserable dance amidst you all ?
Oh, never more for me shall winds intone
With all your tops a vast antiphony,
Demanding and responding in God's praise !
Hers ye are now, not mine ! Farewell — fare-
    well !

SCENE II. MILDRED'S *Chamber*. MILDRED *alone*.

Mil. He comes not! I have heard of those
  who seemed
Resourceless in prosperity, — you thought
Sorrow might slay them when she listed; yet
Did they so gather up their diffused strength
At her first menace, that they bade her strike,
And stood and laughed her subtlest skill to
  scorn.
Oh, 't is not so with me! The first woe fell,
And the rest fall upon it, not on me:
Else should I bear that Henry comes not? —
  fails
Just this first night out of so many nights?
Loving is done with. Were he sitting now,
As so few hours since, on that seat, we 'd love
No more — contrive no thousand happy ways
To hide love from the loveless, any more.
I think I might have urged some little point
In my defence, to Thorold; he was breathless
For the least hint of a defence: but no,
The first shame over, all that would might fall.
No Henry! Yet I merely sit and think
The morn's deed o'er and o'er. I must have
  crept
Out of myself. A Mildred that has lost
Her lover — oh, I dare not look upon
Such woe! I crouch away from it! 'T is she,
Mildred, will break her heart, not I! The
  world
Forsakes me: only Henry 's left me — left?
When I have lost him, for he does not come,
And I sit stupidly . . . Oh Heaven, break up
This worse than anguish, this mad apathy,
By any means or any messenger!
Tresh. [*Without.*] Mildred!
Mil.   Come in! Heaven hears me!
  [*Enter* TRESHAM.] You? alone?
Oh, no more cursing!
Tresh.   Mildred, I must sit.
There — you sit!
Mil.   Say it, Thorold — do not look
The curse! deliver all you come to say!
What must become of me? Oh, speak that
  thought
Which makes your brow and cheeks so pale!
Tresh.   My thought?
Mil. All of it!
Tresh.   How we waded — years ago —
After those water-lilies, till the plash,
I know not how, surprised us; and you dared
Neither advance nor turn back: so, we stood
Laughing and crying until Gerard came —
Once safe upon the turf, the loudest too,
For once more reaching the relinquished prize!
How idle thoughts are, some men's, dying
  men's!
Mildred, —
Mil.   You call me kindlier by my name
Than even yesterday: what is in that?
Tresh. It weighs so much upon my mind
  that I
This morning took an office not my own!
I might . . . of course, I must be glad or
  grieved,
Content or not, at every little thing
That touches you. I may with a wrung heart

Even reprove you, Mildred; I did more:
Will you forgive me?
Mil.   Thorold? do you mock?
Or no . . . and yet you bid me . . . say that
  word!
Tresh. Forgive me, Mildred! — are you si-
  lent, Sweet?
Mil. [*Starting up.*] Why does not Henry
  Mertoun come to-night?
Are you, too, silent?
[*Dashing his mantle aside, and pointing to his scab-
  bard, which is empty.*
                  Ah, this speaks for you!
You 've murdered Henry Mertoun! Now pro-
  ceed!
What is it I must pardon? This and all?
Well, I do pardon you — I think I do.
Thorold, how very wretched you must be!
Tresh. He bade me tell you . . .
Mil.   What I do forbid
Your utterance of! So much that you may tell
And will not — how you murdered him . . .
  but, no!
You 'll tell me that he loved me, never more
Than bleeding out his life there: must I say
"Indeed," to that? Enough! I pardon you.
Tresh. You cannot, Mildred! for the harsh
  words, yes:
Of this last deed Another 's judge: whose doom
I wait in doubt, despondency and fear.
Mil. Oh, true! There 's naught for me to
  pardon! True!
You loose my soul of all its cares at once.
Death makes me sure of him forever! You
Tell me his last words? He shall tell me them,
And take my answer — not in words, but read-
  ing
Himself the heart I had to read him late,
Which death . . .
Tresh. Death? You are dying too? Well
  said
Of Guendolen! I dared not hope you 'd die:
But she was sure of it.
Mil.   Tell Guendolen
I loved her, and tell Austin . . .
Tresh.   Him you loved,
And me?
Mil. Ah, Thorold! Was 't not rashly done
To quench that blood, on fire with youth and
  hope
And love of me — whom you loved too, and yet
Suffered to sit here waiting his approach
While you were slaying him? Oh, doubtlessly
You let him speak his poor confused boy's-
  speech
— Do his poor utmost to disarm your wrath
And respite me! — you let him try to give
The story of our love and ignorance,
And the brief madness and the long despair —
You let him plead all this, because your code
Of honor bids you hear before you strike:
But at the end, as he looked up for life
Into your eyes — you struck him down!
Tresh.   No! No!
Had I but heard him — had I let him speak
Half the truth — less — had I looked long on
  him
I had desisted! Why, as he lay there,

The moon on his flushed cheek, I gathered all
The story ere he told it : I saw through
The troubled surface of his crime and yours
A depth of purity immovable ;
Had I but glanced, where all seemed turbidest
Had gleamed some inlet to the calm beneath ;
I would not glance : my punishment 's at hand.
There, Mildred, is the truth ! and you — say
    on —
You curse me ?
  Mil.   As I dare approach that Heaven
Which has not bade a living thing despair,
Which needs no code to keep its grace from
    stain,
But bids the vilest worm that turns on it
Desist and be forgiven, — I — forgive not,
But bless you, Thorold, from my soul of souls !
                [Falls on his neck.
There ! Do not think too much upon the past !
The cloud that 's broke was all the same a cloud
While it stood up between my friend and you ;
You hurt him 'neath its shadow : but is that
So past retrieve ? I have his heart, you know ;
I may dispose of it : I give it you !
It loves you as mine loves ! Confirm me,
    Henry !   *[Dies.*
  Tresh. I wish thee joy, Beloved ! I am glad
In thy full gladness !
  Guen. [*Without.*] Mildred ! Tresham !
  [*Entering with* AUSTIN.]   Thorold,
I could desist no longer. Ah, she swoons !
That 's well.
  Tresh.   Oh, better far than that !
  Guen.   She 's dead !
Let me unlock her arms !
  Tresh.   She threw them thus
About my neck, and blessed me, and then died :
You 'll let them stay now, Guendolen !
  Aus.   Leave her
And look to him ! What ails you, Thorold ?
  Guen.   White
As she, and whiter ! Austin ! quick — this
    side !

  Aus. A froth is oozing through his clenchèd
    teeth ;
Both lips, where they 're not bitten through,
    are black :
Speak, dearest Thorold !
  Tresh.   Something does weigh down
My neck beside her weight : thanks : I should
    fall
But for you, Austin, I believe ! — there, there,
'T will pass away soon ! — ah, — I had for-
    gotten :
I am dying.
  Guen. Thorold — Thorold — why was this ?
  Tresh. I said, just as I drank the poison off,
The earth would be no longer earth to me,
The life out of all life was gone from me.
There are blind ways provided, the foredone
Heart-weary player in this pageant-world
Drops out by, letting the main masque defile
By the conspicuous portal : I am through —
Just through !
  Guen. Don't leave him, Austin ! Death is
    close.
  Tresh. Already Mildred's face is peacefuller.
I see you, Austin — feel you : here 's my hand,
Put yours in it — you, Guendolen, yours too !
You 're lord and lady now — you 're Treshams ;
    name
And fame are yours : you hold our 'scutcheon
    up.
Austin, no blot on it ! You see how blood
Must wash one blot away : the first blot came
And the first blood came. To the vain world's
    eye
All 's gules again : no care to the vain world,
From whence the red was drawn !
  Aus.   No blot shall come !
  Tresh. I said that : yet it did come. Should
    it come,
Vengeance is God's, not man's. Remember me !
                      [Dies.
  Guen. [*Letting fall the pulseless arm.*] Ah,
Thorold, we can but — remember you !

COLOMBE'S BIRTHDAY

A PLAY

" Ivy and violet, what do ye here
  With blossom and shoot in the warm spring-weather,
  Hiding the arms of Monchenci and Vere ? "
                         HANMER.

NO ONE LOVES AND HONORS BARRY CORNWALL MORE THAN DOES
ROBERT BROWNING ;
WHO, HAVING NOTHING BETTER THAN THIS PLAY
TO GIVE HIM IN PROOF OF IT, MUST SAY SO.

BROWNING was stimulated by the enthusiastic reception of *A Blot in the 'Scutcheon* to write another play for the stage, but for some reason it was not performed for ten years or so. It was printed in 1844 as No. VI. of *Bells and Pomegranates*. Mr. Gosse in his *Personalia* says : —

"I have before me at the present moment a

copy of the first edition, marked for acting by
the author, who has written: 'I made the
alterations in this copy to suit some — I for-
get what — projected stage representation; not
that of Miss Faucit, which was carried into
effect long afterward.' The stage directions
are numerous and minute, showing the science
which the dramatist had gained since he first
essayed to put his creations on the boards.

PERSONS

COLOMBE OF RAVESTEIN, *Duchess of Juliers and Cleves.*
SABYNE, ADOLF, *her Attendants.*
GUIBERT, GAUCELME, MAUFROY, CLUGNET, *Courtiers.*
VALENCE, *Advocate of Cleves.*
PRINCE BERTHOLD, *Claimant of the Duchy.*
MELCHIOR, *his Confidant.*

PLACE, *The Palace at Juliers.*

TIME, 16—.

ACT I

Morning. SCENE. *A corridor leading to the Audience-
chamber.*
GAUCELME, CLUGNET, MAUFROY *and other* Courtiers,
round GUIBERT *who is silently reading a paper: as
he drops it at the end —*

 Guibert. That this should be her birthday;
  and the day
We all invested her, twelve months ago,
As the late Duke's true heiress and our liege ;
And that this also must become the day . . .
Oh, miserable lady !
 1st Courtier. Ay, indeed ?
 2d Court. Well, Guibert ?
 3d Court. But your news, my friend, your
  news !
The sooner, friend, one learns Prince Berthold's
  pleasure,
The better for us all : how writes the Prince ?
Give me ! I 'll read it for the common good.
 Gui. In time, sir, — but till time comes, par-
  don me !
Our old Duke just disclosed his child's re-
  treat,
Declared her true succession to his rule,
And died : this birthday was the day, last year,
We convoyed her from Castle Ravestein —
That sleeps out trustfully its extreme age
On the Meuse' quiet bank, where she lived
  queen
Over the water-buds, — to Juliers' court
With joy and bustle. Here again we stand ;
Sir Gaucelme's buckle 's constant to his cap:
To-day 's much such another sunny day !
 Gaucelme. Come, Guibert, this outgrows a
  jest, I think !
You 're hardly such a novice as to need
The lesson, you pretend.
 Gui. What lesson, sir ?
That everybody, if he 'd thrive at court,
Should, first and last of all, look to himself ?
Why, no : and therefore with your good ex-
  ample.

Some of the suggestions are characteristic
enough. For instance: 'Unless a very good
Valence is found, this extremely fine speech,
[in Act IV. where Valence describes Berthold
to Colombe], perhaps the jewel of the play, is
to be left out.' In the present editions the
verses run otherwise."

The play has recently [1895] been rearranged
in three acts and brought again on the stage.

 (— Ho, Master Adolf !) — to myself I 'll look.
    (*Enter* ADOLF.)
 Gui. The Prince's letter ; why, of all men
  else,
Comes it to me ?
 Adolf. By virtue of your place,
Sir Guibert ! 'T was the Prince's express
  charge,
His envoy told us, that the missive there
Should only reach our lady by the hand
Of whosoever held your place.
 Gui. Enough !
       [ADOLF *retires.*
Then, gentles, who 'll accept a certain poor
Indifferently honorable place,
My friends, I make no doubt, have gnashed
  their teeth
At leisure minutes these half-dozen years,
To find me never in the mood to quit ?
Who asks may have it, with my blessing, and —
This to present our lady. Who 'll accept ?
You, — you, — you ? There it lies, and may,
  for me !
 Maufroy. [*A youth, picking up the paper, reads
  aloud.*] "Prince Berthold, proved by
  titles following
Undoubted Lord of Juliers, comes this day
To claim his own, with license from the Pope,
The Emperor, the Kings of Spain and
  France " . . .
 Gau. Sufficient " titles following," I judge !
Don't read another ! Well, — " to claim his
  own ? "
 Mau. " — And take possession of the Duchy
  held
Since twelve months, to the true heir's preju-
  dice,
By " . . . . Colombe, Juliers' mistress, so she
  thinks,
And Ravestein's mere lady, as we find !
Who wants the place and paper ? Guibert 's
  right.
I hope to climb a little in the world, —
I 'd push my fortunes, — but, no more than
  he,
Could tell her on this happy day of days,
That, save the nosegay in her hand, perhaps,
There 's nothing left to call her own. Sir
  Clugnet,
You famish for promotion ; what say you ?
 Clugnet. [*An old man.*] To give this letter
  were a sort, I take it,
Of service : services ask recompense :
What kind of corner may be Ravestein ?
 Gui. The castle ? Oh, you 'd share her
  fortunes ? Good !

Three walls stand upright, full as good as four,
With no such bad remainder of a roof.
  Clug. Oh, — but the town?
  Gui.   Five houses, fifteen huts;
A church whereto was once a spire, 't is judged;
And half a dyke, except in time of thaw.
  Clug. Still there 's some revenue?
  Gui.   Else Heaven forfend!
You hang a beacon out, should fogs increase;
So, when the Autumn floats of pine-wood steer
Safe 'mid the white confusion, thanks to you,
Their grateful raftsman flings a guilder in;
— That 's if he mean to pass your way next
    time.
  Clug. If not?
  Gui.   Hang guilders, then! he blesses you.
  Clug. What man do you suppose me? Keep
    your paper!
And, let me say, it shows no handsome spirit
To dally with misfortune: keep your place!
  Gau. Some one must tell her.
  Gui.   Some one may: you may!
  Gau. Sir Guibert, 't is no trifle turns me sick
Of court-hypocrisy at years like mine,
But this goes near it.   Where 's there news at
    all?
Who 'll have the face, for instance, to affirm
He never heard, e'en while we crowned the
    girl,
That Juliers' tenure was by Salic law;
That one, confessed her father's cousin's child,
And, she away, indisputable heir,
Against our choice protesting and the Duke's,
Claimed Juliers? — nor, as he preferred his
    claim,
That first this, then another potentate,
Inclined to its allowance? — I or you,
Or any one except the lady's self?
Oh, it had been the direst cruelty
To break the business to her! Things might
    change:
At all events, we 'd see next masque at end,
Next mummery over first: and so the edge
Was taken off sharp tidings as they came,
Till here 's the Prince upon us, and there 's
    she
— Wreathing her hair, a song between her lips,
With just the faintest notion possible
That some such claimant earns a livelihood
About the world, by feigning grievances —
Few pay the story of, but grudge its price,
And fewer listen to, a second time.
Your method proves a failure; now try mine!
And, since this must be carried . . .
  Gui. [*Snatching the paper from him.*] By
    your leave!
Your zeal transports you! 'T will not serve
    the Prince
So much as you expect, this course you 'd take.
If she leaves quietly her palace, — well;
But if she died upon its threshold, — no:
He 'd have the trouble of removing her.
Come, gentles, we 're all — what the devil
    knows!
You, Gaucelme, won't lose character, beside —
You broke your father's heart superiorly
To gather his succession — never blush!
You 're from my province, and, be comforted,

They tell of it with wonder to this day.
You can afford to let your talent sleep.
We 'll take the very worst supposed, as true:
There, the old Duke knew, when he hid his
    child
Among the river-flowers at Ravestein,
With whom the right lay! Call the Prince our
    Duke!
There, she 's no Duchess, she 's no anything
More than a young maid with the bluest eyes:
And now, sirs, we 'll not break this young
    maid's heart
Coolly as Gaucelme could and would! No
    haste!
His talent 's full-blown, ours but in the bud:
We 'll not advance to his perfection yet —
Will we, Sir Maufroy? See, I 've ruined Man-
    froy
Forever as a courtier!
  Gau.   Here 's a coil!
And, count us, will you? Count its residue,
This boasted convoy, this day last year's crowd!
A birthday, too, a gratulation day!
I 'm dumb: bid that keep silence!
  Mau. and others.   Eh, Sir Guibert?
He 's right: that does say something: that 's
    bare truth.
Ten — twelve, I make: a perilous dropping off!
  Gui. Pooh — is it audience hour? The ves-
    tibule
Swarms too, I wager, with the common sort
That want our privilege of entry here.
  Gau. Adolf! [*Re-enter* ADOLF.] Who 's
    outside?
  Gui.   Oh, your looks suffice!
Nobody waiting?
  Mau. [*Looking through the door-folds.*] Scarce
    our number!
  Gui.   'Sdeath!
Nothing to beg for, to complain about?
It can't be! Ill news spreads, but not so fast
As thus to frighten all the world!
  Gau.   The world
Lives out of doors, sir — not with you and me
By presence-chamber porches, state-room stairs,
Wherever warmth 's perpetual: outside 's free
To every wind from every compass-point
And who may get nipped needs be weather-
    wise.
The Prince comes and the lady's People go;
The snow-goose settles down, the swallows
    flee —
Why should they wait for winter-time? 'T is
    instinct:
Don't you feel somewhat chilly?
  Gui.   That 's their craft?
And last year's crowders-round and criers-forth
That strewed the garlands, overarched the
    roads,
Lighted the bonfires, sang the loyal songs!
Well 't is my comfort, you could never call me
The People's Friend! The People keep their
    word —
I keep my place: don't doubt I 'll entertain
The People when the Prince comes, and the
    People
Are talked of! Then, their speeches — no one
    tongue

Found respite, not a pen had holiday
— For they wrote, too, as well as spoke, these
    knaves!
Now see : we tax and tithe them, pill and poll,
They wince and fret enough, but pay they must
— We manage that, — so, pay with a good grace
They might as well. it costs so little more.
But when we 've done with taxes, meet folk
    next
Outside the toll-booth and the rating-place,
In public — there they have us if they will,
We 're at their mercy after that, you see !
For one tax not ten devils could extort —
Over and above necessity, a grace ;
This prompt disbosoming of love, to wit —
Their vine-leaf wrappage of our tribute penny,
And crowning attestation, all works well.
Yet this precisely do they thrust on us !
These cappings quick, these crook-and-cringings
    low,
Hand to the heart, and forehead to the knee,
With grin that shuts the eyes and opes the
    mouth —
So tender they their love ; and, tender made,
Go home to curse us, the first doit we ask.
As if their souls were any longer theirs !
As if they had not given ample warrant
To who should clap a collar on their neck,
Rings in their nose, a goad to either flank,
And take them for the brute they boast them-
    selves !
Stay — there 's a bustle at the outer door —
And somebody entreating . . . that 's my name !
Adolf, — I heard my name !
    Adolf.   'T was probably
The suitor.
    Gui.   Oh, there is one ?
    Adolf.   With a suit
He 'd fain enforce in person.
    Gui.   The good heart
— And the great fool ! Just ope the mid-door's
    fold !
Is that a lappet of his cloak, I see ?
    Adolf. If it bear plenteous sign of travel
    . . . ay,
The very cloak my comrades tore !
    Gui.   Why tore ?
    Adolf. He seeks the Duchess' presence in
    that trim :
Since daybreak, was he posted hereabouts
Lest he should miss the moment.
    Gui.   Where 's he now ?
    Adolf. Gone for a minute possibly, not more :
They have ado enough to thrust him back.
    Gui. Ay — but my name, I caught ?
    Adolf.   Oh, sir — he said
— What was it ? — You had known him for-
    merly,
And, he believed, would help him did you
    guess
He waited now ; you promised him as much :
The old plea ! 'Faith, he 's back, — renews the
    charge !
[*Speaking at the door.*] So long as the man
    parleys, peace outside —
Nor be too ready with your halberts, there !
    Gau. My horse bespattered, as he blocked
    the path

A thin sour man, not unlike somebody.
    Adolf. He holds a paper in his breast,
    whereon
He glances when his cheeks flush and his brow
At each repulse —
    Gau.   I noticed he 'd a brow.
    Adolf. So glancing, he grows calmer, leans
    awhile
Over the balustrade, adjusts his dress,
And presently turns round, quiet again,
With some new pretext for admittance. —
    Back !
[*To* GUIBERT.] — Sir, he has seen you ! Now
    cross halberts ! Ha —
Pascal is prostrate — there lies Fabian too !
No passage ! Whither would the madman
    press ?
Close the doors quick on me !
    Gui.   Too late ! He 's here.
(*Enter, hastily and with discomposed dress,* VALENCE.)
    Valence. Sir Guibert, will you help me ? —
    Me, that come
Charged by your townsmen, all who starve at
    Cleves,
To represent their heights and depths of woe
Before our Duchess and obtain relief !
Such errands barricade such doors, it seems :
But not a common hindrance drives me back
On all the sad yet hopeful faces, lit
With hope for the first time, which sent me
    forth.
Cleves, speak for me ! Cleves' men and wo-
    men, speak !
Who followed me — your strongest — many a
    mile
That I might go the fresher from their ranks,
— Who sit — your weakest — by the city gates,
To take me fuller of what news I bring
As I return — for I must needs return !
— Can I ? 'T were hard, no listener for their
    wrongs,
To turn them back upon the old despair —
Harder, Sir Guibert, than imploring thus —
So, I do — any way you please — implore !
If you . . . but how should you remember
    Cleves ?
Yet they of Cleves remember you so well !
Ay, comment on each trait of you they keep,
Your words and deeds caught up at second
    hand, —
Proud, I believe, at bottom of their hearts,
O' the very levity and recklessness
Which only prove that you forget their wrongs,
Cleves, the grand town, whose men and women
    starve,
Is Cleves forgotten ? Then, remember me !
You promised me that you would help me once
For other purpose : will you keep your word ?
    Gui. And who may you be, friend ?
    Val.   Valence of Cleves.
    Gui. Valence of . . . not the advocate of
    Cleves,
I owed my whole estate to, three years back ?
Ay, well may you keep silence ! Why, my
    lords,
You 've heard, I 'm sure, how, Pentecost three
    years,
I was so nearly ousted of my land

By some knave's-pretext — (eh? when you re-
fused me
Your ugly daughter, Clugnet!) — and you 've
heard
How I recovered it by miracle
— (When I refused her!) Here 's the very
friend,
— Valence of Cleves, all parties have to
thank!
Nay, Valence, this procedure 's vile in you!
I 'm no more grateful than a courtier should,
But politic am I — I bear a brain,
Can cast about a little, might require
Your services a second time. I tried
To tempt you with advancement here to court
— "No!" — well, for curiosity at least
To view our life here — "No!" — our Duchess,
then, —
A pretty woman 's worth some pains to see,
Nor is she spoiled, I take it, if a crown
Complete the forehead pale and tresses
pure . . .
Val. Our city trusted me its miseries,
And I am come.
Gui. So much for taste! But "come," —
So may you be, for anything I know,
To beg the Pope's cross, or Sir Clugnet's
daughter,
And with an equal chance you get all three!
If it was ever worth your while to come,
Was not the proper way worth finding too?
Val. Straight to the palace-portal, sir, I
came —
Gui. — And said? —
Val. — That I had brought the miseries
Of a whole city to relieve.
Gui. — Which saying
Won your admittance? You saw me, indeed,
And here, no doubt, you stand: as certainly,
My intervention, I shall not dispute,
Procures you audience; which, if I procure, —
That paper 's closely written — by Saint Paul,
Here flock the Wrongs, follow the Remedies,
Chapter and verse, One, Two, A, B and C!
Perhaps you 'd enter, make a reverence,
And launch these "miseries" from first to
last?
Val. How should they let me pause or turn
aside?
Gau. [*To* VALENCE.] My worthy sir, one
question! You 've come straight
From Cleves, you tell us: heard you any talk
At Cleves about our lady?
Val. Much.
Gau. And what?
Val. Her wish was to redress all wrongs she
knew.
Gau. That, you believed?
Val. You see me, sir!
Gau. — Nor stopped
Upon the road from Cleves to Juliers here,
For any — rumors you might find afloat?
Val. I had my townsmen's wrongs to busy
me.
Gau. This is the lady's birthday, do you
know?
— Her day of pleasure?
Val. — That the great, I know,

For pleasure born, should still be on the watch
To exclude pleasure when a duty offers:
Even as, for duty born, the lowly too
May ever snatch a pleasure if in reach:
Both will have plenty of their birthright, sir!
Gau. [*Aside to* GUIBERT.] Sir Guibert,
here 's your man! No scruples now —
You 'll never find his like! Time presses hard
I 've seen your drift and Adolf's too, this while,
But you can't keep the hour of audience back
Much longer, and at noon the Prince arrives.
[*Pointing to* VALENCE.] Entrust him with it —
fool no chance away!
Gui. Him?
Gau. — With the missive! What 's the man
to her?
Gui. No bad thought! — Yet, 't is yours,
who ever played
The tempting serpent: else 't were no bad
thought!
I should — and do — mistrust it for your sake,
Or else . . .
(*Enter an* Official *who communicates with* ADOLF.)
Adolf. The Duchess will receive the court!
Gui. Give us a moment, Adolf! Valence,
friend,
I 'll help you. We of the service, you 're to
mark,
Have special entry, while the herd . . . the folk
Outside, get access through our help alone;
— Well, it is so, was so, and I suppose
So ever will be: your natural lot is, therefore,
To wait your turn and opportunity,
And probably miss both. Now, I engage
To set you, here and in a minute's space,
Before the lady, with full leave to plead
Chapter and verse, and A, and B, and C,
To heart's content.
Val. I grieve that I must ask, —
This being, yourself admit, the custom here, —
To what the price of such a favor mounts?
Gui. Just so! You 're not without a courtier's
tact.
Little at court, as your quick instinct prompts,
Do such as we without a recompense.
Val. Yours is?
Gui. A trifle: here 's a document
'T is some one's duty to present her Grace —
I say, not mine — these say, not theirs — such
points
Have weight at court. Will you relieve us all
And take it? Just say, "I am bidden lay
This paper at the Duchess' feet!"
Val. No more?
I thank you, sir!
Adolf. Her Grace receives the court!
Gui. [*Aside.*] Now, *sursum corda*, quoth
the mass-priest! Do —
Whoever 's my kind saint, do let alone
These pushings to and fro, and pullings back;
Peaceably let me hang o' the devil's arm
The downward path, if you can't pluck me off
Completely! Let me live quite his, or yours!
[*The* Courtiers *begin to range themselves, and move
toward the door.*
After me, Valence! So, our famous Cleves
Lacks bread? Yet don't we gallants buy their
lace?

And dear enough — it beggars me, I know,
To keep my very gloves fringed properly.
This, Valence, is our Great State Hall you cross;
Yon gray urn's veritable marcasite,
The Pope's gift : and those salvers testify
The Emperor. Presently you 'll set your foot
. . . But you don't speak, friend Valence!
   Val.   I shall speak.
   Gau. [*Aside to* GUIBERT.] Guibert — it were
no such ungraceful thing
If you and I, at first, seemed horror-struck
With the bad news. Look here, what you shall
do!
Suppose you, first, clap hand to sword and cry
" Yield strangers our allegiance? First I 'll
   perish
Beside your Grace ! " — and so give me the cue
To . . .
   Gui. — Clap your hand to note-book and jot
down
That to regale the Prince with ? I conceive.
[*To* VALENCE.] Do, Valence, speak, or I shall
   half suspect
You 're plotting to supplant us, me the first,
I' the lady's favor ! Is 't the grand harangue
You mean to make, that thus engrosses you ?
— Which of her virtues you 'll apostrophize ?
Or is 't the fashion you aspire to start,
Of that close-curled, not unbecoming hair ?
Or what else ponder you ?
   Val.   My townsmen's wrongs.

ACT II

Noon. SCENE. *The Presence-chamber.*

The DUCHESS *and* SABYNE.

Duchess. Announce that I am ready for the
   court !
   Sabyne. 'T is scarcely audience-hour, I think;
   your Grace
May best consult your own relief, no doubt,
And shun the crowd : but few can have arrived.
   Duch. Let those not yet arrived, then, keep
away !
'T was me, this day last year at Ravestein,
You hurried. It has been full time, beside,
This half-hour. Do you hesitate ? ·
   Sab.   Forgive me !
   Duch. Stay, Sabyne ; let me hasten to make
sure
Of one true thanker : here with you begins
My audience, claim you first its privilege !
It is my birth's event they celebrate :
You need not wish me more such happy days,
But — ask some favor ! Have you none to ask ?
Has Adolf none, then ? this was far from least
Of much I waited for impatiently,
Assure yourself ! It seemed so natural
Your gift, beside this bunch of river-bells,
Should be the power and leave of doing good
To you, and greater pleasure to myself.
You ask my leave to-day to marry Adolf ?
The rest is my concern.
   Sab.   Your Grace is ever
Our lady of dear Ravestein, — but, for
   Adolf . . .

   Duch. " But " ? You have not, sure, changed
   in your regard
And purpose towards him ?
   Sab.   We change ?
   Duch.   Well then ? Well ?
   Sab. How could we two be happy, and, most
like,
Leave   Juliers, when — when . . . but 't is
   audience-time !
   Duch. " When, if you left me, I were left
   indeed ! "
Would you subjoin that ? Bid the court
   approach !
— Why should we play thus with each other,
   Sabyne ?
Do I not know, if courtiers prove remiss,
If friends detain me, and get blame for it,
There is a cause ? Of last year's fervid throng
Scarce one half comes now.
   Sab. [*Aside.*]   One half ? No, alas !
   Duch. So can the mere suspicion of a cloud
Over my fortunes, strike each loyal heart.
They 've heard of this Prince Berthold ; and,
   forsooth,
Some foolish arrogant pretence he makes,
May grow more foolish and more arrogant,
They please to apprehend ! I thank their love.
Admit them !
   Sab. [*Aside.*] How much has she really
   learned ?
   Duch. Surely, whoever 's absent, Tristan
   waits ?
— Or at least Romuald, whom my father raised
From nothing — come, he 's faithful to me,
   come !
(Sabyne, I should but be the prouder — yes,
The fitter to comport myself aright)
Not Romuald ? Xavier — what said he to that ?
For Xavier hates a parasite, I know !
               [SABYNE *goes out.*
   Duch. Well, sunshine 's everywhere, and
   summer too.
Next year 't is the old place again, perhaps —
The water-breeze again, the birds again.
— It cannot be ! It is too late to be !
What part had I, or choice in all of it ?
Hither they brought me ; I had not to think
Nor care, concern myself with doing good
Or ill, my task was just — to live, — to live,
And, answering ends there was no need explain,
To render Juliers happy — so they said.
All could not have been falsehood : some was
   love,
And wonder and obedience. I did all
They looked for : why then cease to do it now ?
Yet this is to be calmly set aside,
And — ere next birthday's dawn, for aught I
   know,
Things change, a claimant may arrive, and
   I . . .
It cannot nor it shall not be ! His right ?
Well then, he has the right, and I have not,
— But who bade all of you surround my life
And close its growth up with your ducal crown
Which, plucked off rudely, leaves me perishing ?
I could have been like one of you, — loved, hoped,
Feared, lived and died like one of you — but
   you

Would take that life away and give me this,
And I will keep this ! I will face you ! Come !
    (*Enter the* Courtiers *and* VALENCE.)
The Courtiers. Many such happy mornings
    to your Grace !
Duch. [*Aside, as they pay their devoir.*] The
    same words, the same faces, — the same
    love !
I have been overfearful. These are few ;
But these, at least, stand firmly : these are
    mine.
As many come as may ; and if no more,
'T is that these few suffice — they do suffice !
What succor may not next year bring me ?
    Plainly,
I feared too soon. [*To the* Courtiers.] I thank
    you, sirs : all thanks !
Val. [*Aside, as the* DUCHESS *passes from one
    group to another, conversing.*] 'T is she —
    the vision this day last year brought,
When, for a golden moment at our Cleves,
She tarried in her progress hither.   Cleves
Chose me to speak its welcome, and I spoke
— Not that she could have noted the recluse
— Ungainly, old before his time — who gazed.
Well, Heaven's gifts are not wasted, and that
    gaze
Kept, and shall keep me to the end, her own !
She was above it — but so would not sink
My gaze to earth ! The People caught it, hers —
Thenceforward, mine ; but thus entirely mine,
Who shall affirm, had she not raised my soul
Ere she retired and left me — them ? She
    turns —
There 's all her wondrous face at once ! The
    ground
Reels and . . .
    [*Suddenly occupying himself with his paper.*]
    These wrongs of theirs I have to plead !
Duch. [*To the* Courtiers.] Nay, compliment
    enough ! and kindness' self
Should pause before it wish me more such years.
'T was fortunate that thus, ere youth escaped,
I tasted life's pure pleasure — one such, pure,
Is worth a thousand, mixed — and youth 's for
    pleasure :
Mine is received ; let my age pay for it.
Gau. So, pay, and pleasure paid for, thinks
    your Grace,
Should never go together ?
Gui.   How, Sir Gaucelme ?
Hurry one's feast down unenjoyingly
At the snatched breathing-intervals of work ?
As good you saved it till the dull day's-end
When, stiff and sleepy, appetite is gone.
Eat first, then work upon the strength of food !
Duch. True : you enable me to risk my
    future,
By giving me a past beyond recall.
I lived, a girl, one happy leisure year :
Let me endeavor to be the Duchess now !
And so, — what news, Sir Guibert, spoke you
    of ?
    [*As they advance a little, and* GUIBERT *speaks —*
— That gentleman ?
Val. [*Aside*].   I feel her eyes on me.
Gui. [*To* VALENCE.] The Duchess, sir,
    inclines to hear your suit.

Advance ! He is from Cleves.
Val. [*Coming forward.*] [*Aside.*] Their
    wrongs — their wrongs !
Duch. And you, sir, are from Cleves ? How
    fresh in mind,
The hour or two I passed at queenly Cleves !
She entertained me bravely, but the best
Of her good pageant seemed its standers-by
With insuppressive joy on every face !
What says my ancient famous happy Cleves ?
Val. Take the truth, lady — you are made
    for truth !
So think my friends : nor do they less deserve
The having you to take it, you shall think,
When you know all — nay, when you only know
How, on that day you recollect at Cleves,
When the poor acquiescing multitude
Who thrust themselves with all their woes apart
Into unnoticed corners, that the few,
Their means sufficed to muster trappings for,
Might fill the foreground, occupy your sight
With joyous faces fit to bear away
And boast of as a sample of all Cleves
— How, when to daylight these crept out once
    more,
Clutching, unconscious, each his empty rags
Whence the scant coin, which had not half
    bought bread,
That morn he shook forth, counted piece by
    piece,
And, well-advisedly, on perfumes spent them
To burn, or flowers to strew, before your path
— How, when the golden flood of music and bliss
Ebbed, as their moon retreated, and again
Left the sharp black-point rocks of misery bare
— Then I, their friend, had only to suggest
"Saw she the horror as she saw the pomp ! "
And as one man they cried, "He speaks the
    truth :
Show her the horror ! Take from our own
    mouths
Our wrongs and show them, she will see them
    too ! "
This they cried, lady ! I have brought the
    wrongs.
Duch. Wrongs ? Cleves has wrongs — ap-
    parent now and thus ?
I thank you ! In that paper ? Give it me !
Val. (There, Cleves !) In this ! (What did
    I promise, Cleves ?)
Our weavers, clothiers, spinners are reduced
Since . . . Oh, I crave your pardon ! I forget
I buy the privilege of this approach,
And promptly would discharge my debt. I lay
This paper humbly at the Duchess' feet.
    [*Presenting* GUIBERT'S *paper.*
Gui. Stay ! for the present . . .
Duch.   Stay, sir ? I take aught
That teaches me their wrongs with greater pride
Than this your ducal circlet. Thank you, sir !
[*The* DUCHESS *reads hastily ; then, turning to the* Cour-
    tiers —
What have I done to you ? Your deed or mine
Was it, this crowning me ? I gave myself
No more a title to your homage, no,
Than church-flowers, born this season, wrote
    the words
In the saint's-book that sanctified them first.

For such a flower, you plucked me ; well, you
    erred —
Well, 't was a weed ; remove the eye-sore
    quick !
But should you not remember it has lain
Steeped in the candles' glory, palely shrined,
Nearer God's Mother than most earthly things ?
— That if 't be faded 't is with prayer's sole
    breath —
That the one day it boasted was God's day ?
Still, I do thank you ! Had you used respect,
Here might I dwindle to my last white leaf,
Here lose life's latest freshness, which even yet
May yield some wandering insect rest and food :
So, fling me forth, and — all is best for all !
[*After a pause.*] Prince Berthold, who art
Juliers' Duke it seems —
The King's choice, and the Emperor's, and the
    Pope's —
Be mine, too ! Take this People ! Tell not me
Of rescripts, precedents, authorities,
— But take them, from a heart that yearns to
    give !
Find out their love, — I could not ; find their
    fear, —
I would not ; find their like, — I never shall,
Among the flowers !   [*Taking off her coronet.*
    Colombe of Ravestein
Thanks God she is no longer Duchess here !
  Val. [*Advancing to* GUIBERT.] Sir Guibert,
    knight, they call you — this of mine
Is the first step I ever set at court.
You dared make me your instrument, I find ;
For that, so sure as you and I are men,
We reckon to the utmost presently :
But as you are a courtier and I none,
Your knowledge may instruct me. I, already,
Have too far outraged, by my ignorance
Of courtier-ways, this lady, to proceed
A second step and risk addressing her :
— I am degraded — you let me address !
Out of her presence, all is plain enough
What I shall do — but in her presence, too,
Surely there 's something proper to be done.
[*To the others.*] You, gentles, tell me if I guess
    aright —
May I not strike this man to earth ?
  The Courtiers. [*As* GUIBERT *springs forward,
    withholding him.*]   Let go !
— The clothiers' spokesman, Guibert ? Grace a
    churl ?
  Duch. [*To* VALENCE.] Oh, be acquainted
    with your party, sir !
He 's of the oldest lineage Juliers boasts ;
A lion crests him for a cognizance ;
"Scorning to waver " — that 's his 'scutcheon's
    word ;
His office with the new Duke — probably
The same in honor as with me ; or more,
By so much as this gallant turn deserves.
He 's now, I dare say, of a thousand times
The rank and influence that remain with her
Whose part you take ! So, lest for taking it
You suffer . . .
  Val.   I may strike him then to earth ?
  Gui. [*Falling on his knee.*] Great and dear
    lady, pardon me ! Hear once !
Believe me and be merciful — be just !

I could not bring myself to give that paper
Without a keener pang than I dared meet
— And so felt Clugnet here, and Maufroy here
— No one dared meet it. Protestation's cheap,—
But, if to die for you did any good,
  [*To* GAUCELME.] Would not I die, sir ? Say
    your worst of me !
But it does no good, that 's the mournful truth.
And since the hint of a resistance, even,
Would just precipitate, on you the first,
A speedier ruin — I shall not deny,
Saving myself indubitable pain,
I thought to give you pleasure (who might say ?
By showing that your only subject found
To carry the sad notice was the man
Precisely ignorant of its contents ;
A nameless, mere provincial advocate ;
One whom 't was like you never saw before,
Never would see again. All has gone wrong :
But I meant right, God knows, and you, I trust !
  Duch. A nameless advocate, this gentleman ?
 — (I pardon you, Sir Guibert !)
  Gui. [*Rising, to* VALENCE.] Sir, and you ?
  Val. — Rejoice that you are lightened of a
    load.
Now, you have only me to reckon with.
  Duch. One I have never seen, much less
    obliged ?
  Val. Dare I speak, lady ?
  Duch.   Dare you ! Heard you not
I rule no longer ?
  Val.   Lady, if your rule
Were based alone on such a ground as these
        [*Pointing to the* Courtiers.
Could furnish you, — abjure it ! They have
    hidden
A source of true dominion from your sight.
  Duch. You hear them — no such source is
    left . . .
  Val.   Hear Cleves !
Whose haggard craftsmen rose to starve this
    day,
Starve now, and will lie down at night to starve,
Sure of a like to-morrow — but as sure
Of a most unlike morrow-after-that,
Since end things must, end howsoe'er things
    may.
What curbs the brute-force instinct in its hour ?
What makes — instead of rising, all as one,
And teaching fingers, so expert to wield
Their tool, the broadsword's play or carbine's
    trick,
— What makes that there 's an easier help, they
    think,
For you, whose name so few of them can spell,
Whose face scarce one in every hundred saw, —
You simply have to understand their wrongs,
And wrongs will vanish — so, still trades are
    plied,
And swords lie rusting and myself stand here ?
There is a vision in the heart of each
Of justice, mercy, wisdom, tenderness
To wrong and pain, and knowledge of its cure :
And these embodied in a woman's form
That best transmits them, pure as first received,
From God above her, to mankind below.
Will you derive your rule from such a ground,
Or rather hold it by the suffrage, say,

Of this man — this — and this ?
   Duch. [*After a pause.*] You come from Cleves :
How many are at Cleves of such a mind ?
   Val. [*From his paper.*] " We, all the manu-
    facturers of Cleves — "
   Duch.   Or stay, sir — lest I seem too cov-
    etous —
Are you my subject ? such as you describe,
Am I to you, though to no other man ?
   Val. [*From his paper.*] — " Valence, ordained
    your Advocate at Cleves " —
   Duch.   [*Replacing the coronet.*] Then I re-
main Cleves' Duchess ! Take you note,
While Cleves but yields one subject of this
    stamp,
I stand her lady till she waves me off !
For her sake, all the Prince claims I withhold ;
Laugh at each menace ; and, his power defy-
    ing,
Return his missive with its due contempt !
                      [*Casting it away.*
   Gui. [*Picking it up.*] — Which to the Prince
    I will deliver, lady,
(Note it down, Gaucelme) — with your message
    too !
   Duch.   I think the office is a subject's, sir !
— Either . . . how style you him ? — my special
    guarder
The Marshal's — for who knows but violence
May follow the delivery ? — Or, perhaps,
My Chancellor's — for law may be to urge
On its receipt ! — Or, even my Chamberlain's —
For I may violate established form !
[*To* VALENCE.] Sir, — for the half-hour till this
    service ends,
Will you become all these to me ?
   Val.   [*Falling on his knee.*]   My liege !
   Duch.   Give me !
        [*The* Courtiers *present their badges of office.*
[*Putting them by.*]   Whatever was their virtue
    once,
They need new consecration. [*Raising* VA-
    LENCE.]   Are you mine ?
I will be Duchess yet !   [*She retires.*
   The Courtiers.   Our Duchess yet !
A glorious lady ! Worthy love and dread !
I 'll stand by her, — and I, whate'er betide !
   Gui. [*To* VALENCE.] Well done, well done,
    sir ! I care not who knows,
You have done nobly and I envy you —
Though I am but unfairly used, I think :
For when one gets a place like this I hold,
One gets too the remark that its mere wages,
The pay and the preferment, make our prize.
Talk about zeal and faith apart from these,
We 're laughed at — much would zeal and faith
    subsist
Without these also ! Yet, let these be stopped,
Our wages discontinue, — then, indeed,
Our zeal and faith, (we hear on every side,)
Are not released — having been pledged away
I wonder, for what zeal and faith in turn ?
Hard money purchased me my place !   No,
    no —
I 'm right, sir — but your wrong is better still,
If I had time and skill to argue it.
Therefore, I say, I 'll serve you, how you
    please —

If you like, — fight you, as you seem to wish —
(The kinder of me that, in sober truth,
I never dreamed I did you any harm) . . .
   Gau. — Or, kinder still, you 'll introduce, no
    doubt,
His merits to the Prince who 's just at hand,
And let no hint drop he 's made Chancellor
And Chamberlain and Heaven knows what be-
    side !
   Clug. [*To* VALENCE.] You stare, young sir,
    and threaten ! Let me say,
That at your age, when first I came to court,
I was not much above a gentleman ;
While now . . .
   Val.   — You are Head-Lackey ? With your
    office
I have not yet been graced, sir !
   Other Courtiers. [*To* Clugnet.] Let him talk !
Fidelity, disinterestedness,
Excuse so much ! Men claim my worship ever
Who stanchly and steadfastly . . .
               (*Enter* ADOLF.)
   Adolf.   The Prince arrives.
   Courtiers.   Ha ?   How ?
   Adolf.   He leaves his guard a stage behind
At Aix, and enters almost by himself.
   1st Court.   The Prince ! This foolish busi-
    ness puts all out.
   2d Court.   Let Gaucelme speak first !
   3d Court.   Better I began
About the state of Juliers : should one say
All 's prosperous and inviting him ?
   4th Court.   — Or rather,
All 's prostrate and imploring him ?
   5th Court.   That 's best.
Where 's the Cleves' paper, by the way ?
   4th Court. [*To* VALENCE.]   Sir — sir —
If you 'll but lend that paper — trust it me,
I 'll warrant . . .
   5th Court.   Softly, sir — the Marshal's duty !
   Clug.   Has not the Chamberlain a hearing
    first
By virtue of his patent ?
   Gau.   Patents ? — Duties ?
All that, my masters, must begin again !
One word composes the whole controversy :
We 're simply now — the Prince's !
   The Others.   Ay — the Prince's !
             (*Enter* SABYNE.)
   Sab.   Adolf !   Bid . . . Oh, no time for
    ceremony !
Where 's whom our lady calls her only subject ?
She needs him. Who is here the Duchess's ?
   Val. [*Starting from his reverie.*] Most grate-
    fully I follow to her feet.

ACT III

Afternoon.   SCENE.   *The Vestibule.*

Enter PRINCE BERTHOLD *and* MELCHIOR.

   Berthold.   A thriving little burgh this Juliers
    looks.
[*Half-apart.*] Keep Juliers, and as good you
    kept Cologne :
Better try Aix, though ! —
   Melchior.   Please 't your Highness speak ?

Berth. [*As before.*] Aix, Cologne, Frankfort,
— Milan ; — Rome ! —
Mel.   The Grave.
More weary seems your Highness, I remark,
Than sundry conquerors whose path I 've
    watched
Through fire and blood to any prize they gain.
I could well wish you, for your proper sake,
Had met some shade of opposition here
— Found a blunt seneschal refuse unlock,
Or a scared usher lead your steps astray.
You must not look for next achievement's palm
So easily : this will hurt your conquering.
Berth. My next ? Ay, as you say, my next
    and next !
Well, I am tired, that 's truth, and moody too,
This quiet entrance-morning : listen why !
Our little burgh, now, Juliers — 't is indeed
One link, however insignificant,
Of the great chain by which I reach my hope,
— A link I must secure ; but otherwise,
You 'd wonder I esteem it worth my grasp.
Just see what life is, with its shifts and turns !
It happens now — this very nook — to be
A place that once . . . not a long while since,
    neither —
When I lived an ambiguous hanger-on
Of foreign courts, and bore my claims about,
Discarded by one kinsman, and the other
A poor priest merely, — then, I say, this place
Shone my ambition's object ; to be Duke —
Seemed then, what to be Emperor seems now.
My rights were far from judged as plain and
    sure
In those days as of late, I promise you :
And 't was my day-dream, Lady Colombe here
Might e'en compound the matter, pity me,
Be struck, say, with my chivalry and grace
(I was a boy !) — bestow her hand at length,
And make me Duke, in her right if not mine.
Here am I, Duke confessed, at Juliers now.
Hearken : if ever I be Emperor,
Remind me what I felt and said to-day !
Mel. All this consoles a bookish man like
    me.
— And so will weariness cling to you. Wrong,
Wrong ! Had you sought the lady's court your-
    self, —
Faced the redoubtables composing it,
Flattered this, threatened that man bribed the
    other, —
Pleaded by writ and word and deed, your
    cause, —
Conquered a footing inch by painful inch, —
And, after long years' struggle, pounced at last
On her for prize, — the right life had been lived,
And justice done to divers faculties
Shut in that brow. Yourself were visible
As you stood victor, then ; whom now — (your
    pardon !)
I am forced narrowly to search and see,
So are you hid by helps — this Pope, your
    uncle —
Your cousin, the other King ! You are a mind,—
They, body : too much of mere legs-and-arms
Obstructs the mind so ! Match these with their
    like :
Match mind with mind !

Berth.   And where 's your mind to match ?
They show me legs-and-arms to cope withal !
I 'd subjugate this city — where 's its mind ?
    (*The* Courtiers *enter slowly.*)
Mel. Got out of sight when you came troops
    and all !
And in its stead, here greets you flesh-and-blood :
A smug economy of both, this first !
    [*As* CLUGNET *bows obsequiously.*
Well done, gout, all considered ! — I may go ?
Berth. Help me receive them !
Mel.   Oh, they just will say
What yesterday at Aix their fellows said, —
At Treves, the day before ! Sir Prince, my
    friend,
Why do you let your life slip thus ? — Meantime
I have my little Juliers to achieve —
The understanding this tough Platonist,
Your holy uncle disinterred, Amelius :
Lend me a company of horse and foot,
To help me through his tractate — gain my
    Duchy !
Berth. And Empire, after that is gained, will
    be — ?
Mel. To help me through your uncle's com-
    ment, Prince !   [*Goes.*
Berth. Ah ? Well : he o'er-refines — the schol-
    ar's fault !
How do I let my life slip ? Say, this life,
I lead now, differs from the common life
Of other men in mere degree, not kind,
Of joys and griefs, — still there is such degree
Mere largeness in a life is something, sure, —
Enough to care about and struggle for,
In this world : for this world, the size of things ;
The sort of things, for that to come, no doubt.
A great is better than a little aim :
And when I wooed Priscilla's rosy mouth
And failed so, under that gray convent-wall,
Was I more happy than I should be now
    [*By this time, the* Courtiers *are ranged before him.*
If failing of my Empire ? Not a whit.
— Here comes the mind, it once had tasked me
    sore
To baffle, but for my advantages !
All 's best as 't is : these scholars talk and talk.
                            [*Seats himself.*
The Courtiers. Welcome our Prince to Juliers !
    — to his heritage !
Our dutifullest service proffer we !
Clug. I, please your Highness, having exer-
    cised
The function of Grand Chamberlain at court,
With much acceptance, as men testify . . .
Berth. I cannot greatly thank you, gentle-
    men !
The Pope declares my claim to the Duchy
    founded
On strictest justice — you concede it, therefore.
I do not wonder : and the kings my friends
Protest they mean to see such claim enforced, —
You easily may offer to assist.
But there 's a slight discretionary power
To serve me in the matter, you 've had long,
Though late you use it. This is well to say —
But could you not have said it months ago ?
I 'm not denied my own Duke's truncheon,
    true —

'T is flung me — I stoop down, and from the
    ground
Pick it, with all you placid standers-by:
And now I have it, gems and mire at once,
Grace go with it to my soiled hands, you say!
    Gui. (By Paul, the advocate our doughty
        friend
Cuts the best figure!)
    Gau.   If our ignorance
May have offended, sure our loyalty . . .
    Berth. Loyalty? Yours? Oh — of yourselves
        you speak!
I mean the Duchess all this time, I hope!
And since I have been forced repeat my claims
As if they never had been urged before,
As I began, so must I end, it seems.
The formal answer to the grave demand!
What says the lady?
    Courtiers. [*One to another.*] 1*st Court.* Mar-
        shal! 2*d Court.* Orator!
    Gui. A variation of our mistress' way!
Wipe off his boots' dust, Clugnet! — that, he
    waits!
    1*st Court.* Your place!
    2*d Court.* Just now it was your own!
    Gui.   The devil's!
    Berth. [*To* GUIBERT.] Come forward, friend
        — you with the paper, there!
Is Juliers the first city I 've obtained?
By this time, I may boast proficiency
In each decorum of the circumstance.
Give it me as she gave it — the petition,
Demand, you style it! What 's required, in
    brief?
What title's reservation, appanage's
Allowance? I heard all at Treves, last week.
    Gau. [*To* GUIBERT.] "Give it him as she
        gave it!"
    Gui.   And why not?
[*To* BERTHOLD.] The lady crushed your sum-
    mons thus together,
And bade me, with the very greatest scorn
So fair a frame could hold, inform you . . .
    Courtiers.   Stop —
Idiot!
    Gui. — Inform you she denied your claim,
Defied yourself! (I tread upon his heel,
The blustering advocate!)
    Berth.   By heaven and earth!
Dare you jest, sir?
    Gui.   Did they at Treves, last week?
    Berth. [*Starting up.*] Why then, I look much
        bolder than I knew,
And you prove better actors than I thought:
Since, as I live, I took you as you entered
For just so many dearest friends of mine,
Fled from the sinking to the rising power
— The sneaking'st crew, in short, I e'er de-
    spised!
Whereas, I am alone here for the moment,
With every soldier left behind at Aix!
Silence? That means the worst? I thought
    as much!
What follows next?
    Courtiers.   Gracious Prince — he raves!
    Gui. He asked the truth and why not get the
        truth?

Berth. Am I a prisoner? Speak, will some
    body?
— But why stand paltering with imbeciles?
Let me see her, or . . .
    Gui.   Her, without her leave,
Shall no one see: she 's Duchess yet!
    Courtiers. [*Footsteps without, as they are dis-
        puting.*] Good chance!
She 's here — the Lady Colombe's self!
    Berth.   'T is well!
[*Aside.*] Array a handful thus against my
    world?
Not ill done, truly! Were not this a mind
To match one's mind with? Colombe! Let
    us wait!
I failed so, under that gray convent wall!
She comes.
    Gui. The Duchess! Strangers, range your-
        selves!
[*As the* DUCHESS *enters in conversation with* VALENCE,
    BERTHOLD *and the* Courtiers *fall back a little.*
    Duch. Presagefully it beats, presagefully,
My heart: the right is Berthold's and not mine.
    Val. Grant that he has the right, dare I mis-
    trust
Your power to acquiesce so patiently
As you believe, in such a dream-like change
Of fortune — change abrupt, profound, com-
    plete?
    Duch. Ah, the first bitterness is over now!
Bitter I may have felt it to confront
The truth, and ascertain those natures' value
I had so counted on; that was a pang:
But I did bear it, and the worst is over.
Let the Prince take them!
    Val.   And take Juliers too?
— Your people without crosses, wands and
    chains —
Only with hearts?
    Duch.   There I feel guilty, sir!
I cannot give up what I never had:
For I ruled these, not them — these stood be-
    tween.
Shall I confess, sir? I have heard by stealth
Of Berthold from the first; more news and
    more:
Closer and closer swam the thunder cloud,
But I was safely housed with these, I knew.
At times when to the casement I would turn,
At a bird's passage or a flower-trail's play,
I caught the storm's red glimpses on its edge —
Yet I was sure some one of all these friends
Would interpose: I followed the bird's flight
Or plucked the flower — some one would inter-
    pose!
    Val. Not one thought on the People — and
        Cleves there!
    Duch. Now, sadly conscious my real sway
        was missed,
Its shadow goes without so much regret:
Else could I not again thus calmly bid you,
Answer Prince Berthold!
    Val.   Then you acquiesce?
    Duch. Remember over whom it was I ruled!
    Gui. [*Stepping forward.*] Prince Berthold,
        yonder, craves an audience, lady!
    Duch. [*To* VALENCE.] I only have to turn
        and I shall face

Prince Berthold! Oh, my very heart is sick!
It is the daughter of a line of Dukes
This scornful insolent adventurer
Will bid depart from my dead father's halls!
I shall not answer him — dispute with him —
But, as he bids, depart! Prevent it, sir!
Sir — but a mere day's respite! Urge for me
— What I shall call to mind I should have
    urged
When time's gone by — 't will all be mine, you
    urge!
A day — an hour — that I myself may lay
My rule down! 'T is too sudden — must not be!
The world's to hear of it! Once done — for-
    ever!
How will it read, sir? How be sung about?
Prevent it!
    Berth. [*Approaching.*] Your frank indigna-
        tion, lady,
Cannot escape me. Overbold I seem;
But somewhat should be pardoned my surprise
At this reception, — this defiance, rather.
And if, for their and your sake, I rejoice
Your virtues could inspire a trusty few
To make such gallant stand in your behalf,
I cannot but be sorry, for my own,
Your friends should force me to retrace my
    steps:
Since I no longer am permitted speak
After the pleasant peaceful course prescribed
No less by courtesy than relationship —
Which I remember, if you once forgot.
But never must attack pass unrepelled.
Suffer that, through you, I demand of these,
Who controverts my claim to Juliers?
    Duch.   — Me
You say, you do not speak to —
    Berth.   Of your subjects
I ask, then: whom do you accredit? Where
Stand those should answer?
    Val. [*Advancing.*]   The lady is alone.
    Berth. Alone, and thus? So weak and yet
        so bold?
    Val. I said she was alone —
    Berth.   And weak, I said.
    Val. When is man strong until he feels
        alone?
It was some lonely strength at first, be sure,
Created organs, such as those you seek,
By which to give its varied purpose shape:
And, naming the selected ministrants,
Took sword, and shield, and sceptre, — each, a
    man!
That strength performed its work and passed
    its way:
You see our lady: there, the old shapes stand!
— A Marshal, Chamberlain, and Chancellor —
" Be helped their way, into their death put life
And find advantage!" — so you counsel us.
But let strength feel alone, seek help itself, —
And, as the inland-hatched sea-creature hunts
The sea's breast out, — as, littered 'mid the
    waves
The desert-brute makes for the desert's joy,
So turns our lady to her true resource,
Passing o'er hollow fictions, worn-out types,
— And I am first her instinct fastens on.
And prompt I say, as clear as heart can speak,

The People will not have you; nor shall have
It is not merely I shall go bring Cleves
And fight you to the last, — though that does
    much,
And men and children, — ay, and women too,
Fighting for home, are rather to be feared
Than mercenaries fighting for their pay —
But, say you beat us, since such things have
    been,
And, where this Juliers laughed, you set your
    foot
Upon a steaming bloody plash — what then?
Stand you the more our lord that there you
    stand?
Lord it o'er troops whose force you concentrate,
A pillared flame whereto all ardors tend —
Lord it 'mid priests whose schemes you amplify,
A cloud of smoke 'neath which all shadows
    brood —
But never, in this gentle spot of earth,
Can you become our Colombe, our play-queen.
For whom, to furnish lilies for her hair,
We'd pour our veins forth to enrich the soil!
— Our conqueror? Yes! — Our despot? Yes:
    — Our Duke?
Know yourself, know us!
    Berth. [*Who has been in thought.*] Know your
        lady, also!
[*Very deferentially.*] — To whom I needs must
    exculpate myself
For having made a rash demand, at least.
Wherefore to you, sir, who appear to be
Her chief adviser, I submit my claims,
                                [*Giving papers.*
But, this step taken, take no further step,
Until the Duchess shall pronounce their worth.
Here be our meeting-place; at night, its time:
Till when I humbly take the lady's leave!
[*He withdraws. As the* DUCHESS *turns to* VALENCE,
    the Courtiers *interchange glances and come forward
    a little.*
    1st Court. So, this was their device!
    2d Court. No bad device!
    3d Court. You'd say they love each other,
        Guibert's friend
From Cleves, and she, the Duchess!
    4th Court.   — And moreover,
That all Prince Berthold comes for, is to help
Their loves!
    5th Court. Pray, Guibert, what is next to do?
    Gui. [*Advancing.*] I laid my office at the
        Duchess' foot —
    Others. And I — and I — and I!
    Duch.   I took them, sirs.
    Gui. [*Apart to* VALENCE.] And now, sir, I
        am simple knight again —
Guibert, of the great ancient house, as yet
That never bore affront; whate'er your birth, --
As things stand now, I recognize yourself
(If you'll accept experience of some date)
As like to be the leading man o' the time,
Therefore as much above me now, as I
Seemed above you this morning. Then, I of-
    fered
To fight you: will you be as generous
And now fight me?
    Val.   Ask when my life is mine!
    Gui. ('T is hers now!)

Clug. [*Apart to* VALENCE, *as* GUIBERT *turns
from him.*] You, sir, have insulted me
Grossly, — will grant me, too, the selfsame favor
You 've granted him, just now, I make no ques-
tion?
Val.   I promise you, as him, sir.
Clug.   Do you so?
Handsomely said! I hold you to it, sir.
You 'll get me reinstated in my office
As you will Guibert!
Duch.   I would be alone!
[*They begin to retire slowly: as* VALENCE *is about to
follow —*
Alone, sir — only with my heart : you stay!
Gau.   You hear that?   Ah, light breaks
upon me ! Cleves —
It was at Cleves some man harangued us all —
With great effect, — so those who listened said,
My thoughts being busy elsewhere : was this he?
Guibert, — your strange, disinterested man!
Your uncorrupted, if uncourtly friend!
The modest worth you mean to patronize!
He cares about no Duchesses, not he!
His sole concern is with the wrongs of Cleves!
What, Guibert?   What, it breaks on you at
last?
Gui.   Would this hall's floor were a mine's
roof ! I 'd back
And in her very face . . .
Gau.   Apply the match
That fired the train, — and where would you
be, pray?
Gui.   With him!
Gau.   Stand, rather, safe outside with me!
The mine 's charged : shall I furnish you the
match
And place you properly? To the antechamber!
Gui.   Can you?
Gau.   Try me! Your friend 's in fortune!
Gui.   Quick —
To the antechamber! He is pale with bliss!
Gau.   No wonder! Mark her eyes!
Gui.   To the antechamber!
[*The* Courtiers *retire.*
Duch.   Sir, could you know all you have done
for me
You were content! You spoke, and I am saved.
Val.   Be not too sanguine, lady! Ere you
dream,
That transient flush of generosity
Fades off, perchance! The man, beside, is
gone, —
Him we might bend ; but see, the papers here —
Inalterably his requirement stays,
And cold hard words have we to deal with now.
In that large eye there seemed a latent pride,
To self-denial not incompetent,
But very like to hold itself dispensed
From such a grace : however, let us hope!
He is a noble spirit in noble form.
I wish he less had bent that brow to smile
As with the fancy how he could subject
Himself upon occasion to — himself!
From rudeness, violence, you rest secure ;
But do not think your Duchy rescued yet!
Duch.   You, who have opened a new world
to me,
Will never take the faded language up

Of that I leave?   My Duchy — keeping it,
Or losing it — is that my sole world now?
Val.   Ill have I spoken if you thence despise
Juliers ; although the lowest, on true grounds,
Be worth more than the highest rule, on false :
Aspire to rule, on the true grounds!
Duch.   Nay, hear —
False, I will never — rash, I would not be !
This is indeed my birthday — soul and body,
Its hours have done on me the work of years.
You hold the requisition : ponder it !
If I have right, my duty's plain : if he —
Say so, nor ever change a tone of voice !
At night you meet the Prince ; meet me at eve?
Till when, farewell! This discomposes you?
Believe in your own nature, and its force
Of renovating mine ! I take my stand
Only as under me the earth is firm :
So, prove the first step stable, all will prove.
That first, I choose — [*Laying her hand on his*]
— the next to take, choose you !
[*She withdraws.*
Val. [*After a pause.*] What drew down
this on me? — on me, dead once,
She thus bids live, — since all I hitherto
Thought dead in me, youth's ardors and em-
prise,
Burst into life before her, as she bids
Who needs them. Whither will this reach,
where end?
Her hand's print burns on mine . . . Yet she 's
above —
So very far above me ! All 's too plain :
I served her when the others sank away,
And she rewards me as such souls reward —
The changed voice, the suffusion of the cheek,
The eye's acceptance, the expressive hand,
— Reward, that 's little, in her generous
thought,
Though all to me . . .
                   I cannot so disclaim
Heaven's gift, nor call it other than it is !
She loves me !
[*Looking at the* Prince's *papers.*] — Which love,
these, perchance, forbid.
Can I decide against myself — pronounce
She is the Duchess and no mate for me?
— Cleves, help me ! Teach me, — every hag-
gard face, —
To sorrow and endure ! I will do right
Whatever be the issue. Help me, Cleves !

ACT IV

Evening. SCENE. *An Antechamber.*

Enter the Courtiers.

Mau.   Now, then, that we may speak —
how spring this mine?
Gau.   Is Guibert ready for its match? He
cools!
Not so friend Valence with the Duchess there !
"Stay, Valence ! Are not you my better
self?"
And her cheek mantled —
Gui.   Well, she loves him, sir!
And more, — since you will have it I grow
cool. —

She's right : he's worth it.
Gau.   For his deeds to-day ?
Say so !
Gui. What should I say beside ?
Gau.   Not this —
For friendship's sake leave this for me to say —
That we 're the dupes of an egregious cheat !
This plain unpractised suitor, who found way
To the Duchess through the merest die's turn-
up,
A year ago had seen her and been seen,
Loved and been loved.
Gui.   Impossible !
Gau.   — Nor say,
How sly and exquisite a trick, moreover,
Was this which — taking not their stand on
facts
Boldly, for that had been endurable,
But worming on their way by craft, they
choose
Resort to, rather, — and which you and we,
Sheep-like, assist them in the playing-off !
The Duchess thus parades him as preferred,
Not on the honest ground of preference,
Seeing first, liking more, and there an end —
But as we all had started equally,
And at the close of a fair race he proved
The only valiant, sage and loyal man.
Herself, too, with the pretty fits and starts, —
The careless, winning, candid ignorance
Of what the Prince might challenge or forego —
She had a hero in reserve ! What risk
Ran she ? This deferential easy Prince
Who brings his claims for her to ratify
— He 's just her puppet for the nonce ! You 'll
see, —
Valence pronounces, as is equitable,
Against him : off goes the confederate :
As equitably, Valence takes her hand !
The Chancellor. You run too fast : her
hand, no subject takes.
Do not our archives hold her father's will ?
That will provides against such accident,
And gives next heir, Prince Berthold, the re-
version
Of Juliers, which she forfeits, wedding so.
Gau. I know that, well as you, — but does
the Prince ?
Knows Berthold, think you, that this plan, he
helps,
For Valence's ennoblement, — would end,
If crowned with the success which seems its due,
In making him the very thing he plays,
The actual Duke of Juliers ? All agree
That Colombe's title waived or set aside,
He is next heir.
The Chan.   Incontrovertibly.
Gau. Guibert, your match, now, to the
train !
Gui.   Enough !
I 'm with you : selfishness is best again.
I thought of turning honest — what a dream !
Let 's wake now !
Gau.   Selfish, friend, you never were :
'T was but a series of revenges taken
On your unselfishness for prospering ill.
But now that you 're grown wiser, what 's our
course ?

Gui. — Wait, I suppose, till Valence weds our
lady,
And then, if we must needs revenge ourselves,
Apprise the Prince.
Gau.   — The Prince, ere then dismissed
With thanks for playing his mock part so well ?
Tell the Prince now, sir ! Ay, this very night,
Ere he accepts his dole and goes his way,
Explain how such a marriage makes him Duke,
Then trust his gratitude for the surprise !
Gui. — Our lady wedding Valence all the
same
As if the penalty were undisclosed ?
Good ! If she loves, she 'll not disown her love,
Throw Valence up. I wonder you see that.
Gau. The shame of it — the suddenness and
shame !
Within her, the inclining heart — without,
A terrible array of witnesses —
And Valence by, to keep her to her word,
With Berthold's indignation or disgust !
We 'll try it ! — Not that we can venture much.
Her confidence we 've lost forever : Berthold's
Is all to gain.
Gui.   To-night, then, venture we !
Yet — if lost confidence might be renewed ?
Gau. Never in noble natures ! With the
base ones, —
Twist off the crab's claw, wait a smarting-
while,
And something grows and grows and gets to be
A mimic of the lost joint, just so like
As keeps in mind it never, never will
Replace its predecessor ! Crabs do that :
But lop the lion's foot — and . . .
Gui.   To the Prince !
Gau. [*Aside.*] And come what will to the
lion's foot, I pay you,
My cat's paw, as I long have yearned to pay !
[*Aloud.*] Footsteps ! Himself ! 'T is Valence
breaks on us,
Exulting that their scheme succeeds. We 'll
hence —
And perfect ours ! Consult the archives,
first —
Then, fortified with knowledge, seek the Hall !
Clug. [*To* GAUCELME *as they retire.*] You
have not smiled so since your father died !
(*As they retire, enter* VALENCE *with papers.*)
Val. So must it be ! I have examined these
With scarce a palpitating heart — so calm,
Keeping her image almost wholly off,
Setting upon myself determined watch,
Repelling to the uttermost his claims :
And the result is — all men would pronounce,
And not I, only, the result to be —
Berthold is heir ; she has no shade of right
To the distinction which divided us,
But, suffered to rule first, I know not why,
Her rule connived at by those Kings and Popes,
To serve some devil's-purpose, — now 't is
gained,
Whate'er it was, the rule expires as well.
— Valence, this rapture . . . selfish can it be ?
Eject it from your heart, her home ! — It stays !
Ah, the brave world that opens on us both !
— Do my poor townsmen so esteem it ?
Cleves, —

I need not your pale faces! This, reward
For service done to you? Too horrible!
I never served you: 't was myself I served —
Nay, served not — rather saved from punish-
　　ment
Which, had I failed you then, would plague me
　　now!
My life continues yours, and your life, mine.
But if, to take God's gift, I swerve no step —
Cleves! If I breathe no prayer for it — if she,
　　　　　　　　　　　　　[Footsteps without.
Colombe, that comes now, freely gives herself —
Will Cleves require, that, turning thus to her,
I . . .
　　　　　(Enter PRINCE BERTHOLD.)
　　　　Pardon, sir! I did not look for you
Till night, i' the Hall; nor have as yet declared
My judgment to the lady.
　Berth.　　　　　　So I hoped.
　Val. And yet I scarcely know why that
　　should check
The frank disclosure of it first to you —
What her right seems, and what, in conse-
　quence,
She will decide on.
　Berth.　　　That I need not ask.
　Val. You need not: I have proved the
　　lady's mind:
And, justice being to do, dare act for her.
　Berth. Doubtless she has a very noble mind.
　Val. Oh, never fear but she'll in each con-
　juncture
Bear herself bravely! She no whit depends
On circumstance; as she adorns a throne,
She had adorned . . .
　Berth.　　　A cottage — in what book
Have I read that, of every queen that lived?
A throne! You have not been instructed, sure,
To forestall my request?
　Val.　　　　　'T is granted, sir!
My heart instructs me. I have scrutinized
Your claims . . .
　Berth. Ah — claims, you mean, at first pre-
　ferred?
I come, before the hour appointed me,
To pray you let those claims at present rest,
In favor of a new and stronger one.
　Val. You shall not need a stronger: on the
　part
O' the lady, all you offer I accept,
Since one clear right suffices: yours is clear.
Propose!
　Berth. I offer her my hand.
　Val.　　　　　　Your hand?
　Berth. A Duke's, yourself say; and, at no
　far time,
Something here whispers me — an Emperor's.
The lady's mind is noble: which induced
This seizure of occasion: ere my claims
Were — settled, let us amicably say!
Val. Your hand!
　Berth. (He will fall down and kiss it next!)
Sir, this astonishment's too flattering,
Nor must you hold your mistress' worth so
　cheap.
Enhance it, rather, — urge that blood is blood —
The daughter of the Burgraves, Landgraves,
　Markgraves,

Remains their daughter! I shall scarce gain
　say.
Elsewhere, or here, the lady needs must rule:
Like the imperial crown's great chrysoprase,
They talk of — somewhat out of keeping there,
And yet no jewel for a meaner cap.
　Val. You wed the Duchess?
　Berth.　　　　Cry you mercy, friend!
Will the match also influence fortunes here?
A natural solicitude enough.
Be certain, no bad chance it proves for you!
However high you take your present stand,
There's prospect of a higher still remove —
For Juliers will not be my resting-place,
And, when I have to choose a substitute
To rule the little burgh, I'll think of you
Who need not give your mates a character.
And yet I doubt your fitness to supplant
The gray smooth Chamberlain: he'd hesitate
A doubt his lady could demean herself
So low as to accept me. Courage, sir!
I like your method better: feeling's play
Is franker much, and flatters me beside.
　Val. I am to say, you love her?
　Berth.　　　　　Say that too!
Love has no great concernment, thinks the
　world,
With a Duke's marriage. How go precedents
In Juliers' story — how use Juliers' Dukes?
I see you have them here in goodly row;
Yon must be Luitpold — ay, a stalwart sire!
Say, I have been arrested suddenly
In my ambition's course, its rocky course,
By this sweet flower: I fain would gather it
And then proceed: so say and speedily
— (Nor stand there like Duke Luitpold's brazen
　self!)
Enough, sir: you possess my mind, I think.
This is my claim, the others being withdrawn,
And to this be it that, i' the Hall to-night,
Your lady's answer comes; till when, farewell!
　　　　　　　　　　　　　[He retires.
　Val. [After a pause.] The heavens and
　　earth stay as they were; my heart
Beats as it beat: the truth remains the truth.
What falls away, then, if not faith in her?
Was it my faith, that she could estimate
Love's value, and, such faith still guiding me,
Dare I now test her? Or grew faith so strong
Solely because no power of test was mine?
　　　　　(Enter the DUCHESS.)
　Duch. My fate, sir! Ah, you turn away.
　　All's over.
But you are sorry for me? Be not so!
What I might have become, and never was,
Regret with me! What I have merely been,
Rejoice I am no longer! What I seem
Beginning now, in my new state, to be,
Hope that I am! — for, once my rights proved
　void,
This heavy roof seems easy to exchange
For the blue sky outside — my lot henceforth.
　Val. And what a lot is Berthold's!
　Duch.　　　　　　How of him?
　Val. He gathers earth's whole good into his
　arms;
Standing, as man now, stately, strong and wise,
Marching to fortune, not surprised by her.

One great aim, like a guiding-star, above —
Which tasks strength, wisdom, stateliness, to lift
His manhood to the height that takes the prize ;
A prize not near — lest overlooking earth
He rashly spring to seize it — nor remote,
So that he rest upon his path content :
But day by day, while shimmering grows shine,
And the faint circlet prophesies the orb,
He sees so much as, just evolving these,
The stateliness, the wisdom and the strength,
To due completion, will suffice this life,
And lead him at his grandest to the grave.
After this star, out of a night he springs ;
A beggar's cradle for the throne of thrones
He quits ; so, mounting, feels each step he
   mounts,
Nor, as from each to each exultingly
He passes, overleaps one grade of joy.
This, for his own good : — with the world, each
   gift
Of God and man, — reality, tradition,
Fancy and fact — so well environ him,
That as a mystic panoply they serve —
Of force, untenanted, to awe mankind,
And work his purpose out with half the world,
While he, their master, dexterously slipt
From such encumbrance, is meantime em-
   ployed
With his own prowess on the other half.
Thus shall he prosper, every day's success
Adding, to what is he, a solid strength —
An aëry might to what encircles him,
Till at the last, so life's routine lends help,
That as the Emperor only breathes and moves,
His shadow shall be watched, his step or stalk
Become a comfort or a portent, how
He trails his ermine take significance, —
Till even his power shall cease to be most
   power,
And men shall dread his weakness more, nor
   dare
Peril their earth its bravest, first and best,
Its typified invincibility.
Thus shall he go on, greatening, till he ends —
The man of men, the spirit of all flesh,
The fiery centre of an earthly world !
   Duch. Some such a fortune I had dreamed
      should rise
Out of my own — that is, above my power
Seemed other, greater potencies to stretch —
   Val. For you ?
   Duch.   It was not I moved there, I think :
But one I could, — though constantly beside,
And aye approaching, — still keep distant from,
And so adore. 'T was a man moved there.
   Val.   Who ?
   Duch. I felt the spirit, never saw the face.
   Val. See it ! 'T is Berthold's ! He enables
      you
To realize your vision.
   Duch.   Berthold ?
   Val.   Duke —
Emperor to be : he proffers you his hand.
   Duch. Generous and princely !
   Val.   He is all of this.
   Duch. Thanks, Berthold, for my father's
      sake. No hand
Degrades me !

   Val.   You accept the proffered hand ?
   Duch. That he should love me !
   Val.   " Loved " I did not say.
Had that been — love might so incline the
      Prince
To the world's good, the world that 's at his
      foot, —
I do not know, this moment, I should dare
Desire that you refused the world — and
      Cleves —
The sacrifice he asks.
   Duch.   Not love me, sir ?
   Val. He scarce affirmed it.
   Duch.   May not deeds affirm ?
   Val. What does he ? . . . Yes, yes, very
      much he does !
All the shame saved, he thinks, and sorrow
      saved —
Immitigable sorrow, so he thinks, —
Sorrow that 's deeper than we dream, per-
      chance !
   Duch. Is not this love ?
   Val.   So very much he does !
For look, you can descend now gracefully :
All doubts are banished, that the world might
      have,
Or worst, the doubts yourself, in after-time,
May call up of your heart's sincereness now.
To such, reply, " I could have kept my rule —
Increased it to the utmost of my dreams —
Yet I abjured it." This, he does for you :
It is munificently much.
   Duch.   Still " much ! "
But why is it not love, sir ? Answer me !
   Val. Because not one of Berthold's words
      and looks
Had gone with love's presentment of a flower
To the beloved : because bold confidence,
Open superiority, free pride —
Love owns not, yet were all that Berthold
      owned :
Because where reason, even, finds no flaw,
Unerringly a lover's instinct may.
   Duch. You reason, then, and doubt ?
   Val.   I love, and know.
   Duch. You love ? How strange ! I never
      cast a thought
On that ! Just see our selfishness ! You seemed
So much my own . . . I had no ground — and
      yet,
I never dreamed another might divide
My power with you, much less exceed it.
   Val.   Lady
I am yours wholly.
   Duch.   Oh, no, no, not mine !
'T is not the same now, never more can be.
— Your first love, doubtless. Well, what'
      gone from me ?
What have I lost in you ?
   Val.   My heart replies —
No loss there ! So, to Berthold back again :
This offer of his hand, he bids me make —
Its obvious magnitude is well to weigh.
   Duch. She 's . . . yes, she must be very fair
      for you !
   Val. I am a simple advocate of Cleves.
   Duch. You ! With the heart and brain that
      so helped me,

I fancied them exclusively my own,
Yet find are subject to a stronger sway!
She must be . . . tell me, is she very fair?
  Val. Most fair, beyond conception or belief.
  Duch. Black eyes? — no matter! Colombe,
    the world leads
Its life without you, whom your friends pro-
    fessed
The only woman — see how true they spoke!
One lived this while, who never saw your face,
Nor heard your voice — unless . . . Is she
    from Cleves?
  Val. Cleves knows her well.
  Duch.   Ah — just a fancy, now!
When you poured forth the wrongs of Cleves, —
    I said,
— Thought, that is, afterward . . .
  Val.   You thought of me?
  Duch. Of whom else? Only such great
    cause, I thought,
For such effect: see what true love can do!
Cleves is his love. I almost fear to ask
. . . And will not. This is idling: to our
    work!
Admit before the Prince, without reserve,
My claims misgrounded; then may follow
    better
. . . When you poured out Cleves' wrongs im-
    petuously,
Was she in your mind?
  Val.   All done was done for her
— To humble me!
  Duch.   She will be proud at least.
  Val. She?
  Duch.   When you tell her.
  Val.   That will never be.
  Duch. How — are there sweeter things you
    hope to tell?
No, sir! You counselled me, — I counsel you
In the one point I — any woman — can.
Your worth, the first thing; let her own come
    next —
Say what you did through her, and she through
    you —
The praises of her beauty afterward!
Will you?
  Val. I dare not.
  Duch.   Dare not?
  Val.   She I love
Suspects not such a love in me.
  Duch.   You jest.
  Val. The lady is above me and away.
Not only the brave form, and the bright mind,
And the great heart, combine to press me low —
But all the world calls rank divides us.
  Duch.   Rank!
Now grant me patience! Here's a man de-
    clares
Oracularly in another's case —
Sees the true value and the false, for them —
Nay, bids them see it, and they straight do see.
You called my court's love worthless — so it
    turned:
I threw away as dross my heap of wealth,
And here you stickle for a piece or two!
First — has she seen you?
  Val.   Yes.
  Duch.   She loves you, then

  Val. One flash of hope burst; then succeeded
    night:
And all's at darkest now. Impossible!
  Duch. We'll try: you are — so to speak —
    my subject yet?
  Val. As ever — to the death.
  Duch.   Obey me, then!
  Val. I must.
  Duch. Approach her, and . . . no! first of
    all
Get more assurance. "My instructress," say,
"Was great, descended from a line of kings,
And even fair" — (wait why I say this folly) —
"She said, of all men, none for eloquence,
Courage, and" (what cast even these to shade)
"The heart they sprung from, — none deserved
    like him
Who saved her at her need: if she said this,
What should not one I love, say?"
  Val.   Heaven — this hope —
Oh, lady, you are filling me with fire!
  Duch. Say this! — nor think I bid you cast
    aside
One touch of all the awe and reverence;
Nay, make her proud for once to heart's con-
    tent
That all this wealth of heart and soul's her
    own!
Think you are all of this, — and, thinking it.
    . . (Obey!)
  Val. I cannot choose.
  Duch.   Then, kneel to her
                  [VALENCE *sinks on his knee.*
I dream!
  Val. Have mercy! Yours, unto the death, —
I have obeyed. Despise, and let me die!
  Duch. Alas, sir, is it to be ever thus?
Even with you as with the world? I know
This morning's service was no vulgar deed
Whose motive, once it dares avow itself,
Explains all done and infinitely more,
So, takes the shelter of a nobler cause.
Your service named its true source, — loyalty!
The rest's unsaid again. The Duchess bids you.
Rise, sir! The Prince's words were in debate.
  Val. [*Rising.*] Rise? Truth, as ever, lady
    comes from you!
I should rise — I who spoke for Cleves, can
    speak
For Man — yet tremble now, who stood firm
    then.
I laughed — for 't was past tears — that Cleves
    should starve
With all hearts beating loud the infamy,
And no tongue daring trust as much to air:
Yet here, where all hearts speak, shall I be
    mute?
Oh, lady, for your own sake look on me!
On all I am, and have, and do — heart, brain,
Body and soul, — this Valence and his gifts!
I was proud once: I saw you, and they sank,
So that each, magnified a thousand times,
Were nothing to you — but such nothingness,
Would a crown gild it, or a sceptre prop,
A treasure speed, a laurel-wreath enhance?
What is my own desert? But should your love
Have . . . there's no language helps here . . .
    singled me, —

Then — oh, that wild word " then ! " — be just
to love,
In generosity its attribute !
Love, since you pleased to love ! All 's cleared
— a stage
For trial of the question kept so long :
Judge you — Is love or vanity the best ?
You, solve it for the world's sake — you, speak
first
What all will shout one day — you, vindicate
Our earth and be its angel ! All is said.
Lady, I offer nothing — I am yours :
But, for the cause' sake, look on me and him,
And speak !
    Duch. I have received the Prince's mes-
sage :
Say, I prepare my answer !
    Val.   Take me, Cleves !
                           [*He withdraws.*
    Duch. Mournful — that nothing 's what it
calls itself !
Devotion, zeal, faith, loyalty — mere love !
And, love in question, what may Berthold's be ?
I did ill to mistrust the world so soon :
Already was this Berthold at my side.
The valley-level has its hawks, no doubt :
May not the rock-top have its eagles, too ?
Yet Valence . . . let me see his rival then !

ACT V

Night. Scene. *The Hall.*

Enter BERTHOLD *and* MELCHIOR.

    Mel. And here you wait the matter's issue ?
    Berth.   Here.
    Mel. I don't regret I shut Amelius, then.
But tell me, on this grand disclosure, — how
Behaved our spokesman with the forehead ?
    Berth.   Oh,
Turned out no better than the foreheadless —
Was dazzled not so very soon, that 's all !
For my part, this is scarce the hasty showy
Chivalrous measure you give me credit of.
Perhaps I had a fancy, — but 't is gone.
— Let her commence the unfriended innocent
And carry wrongs about from court to court ?
No, truly ! The least shake of fortune's sand,
— My uncle-Pope chokes in a coughing fit,
King-cousin takes a fancy to blue eyes, —
And wondrously her claims would brighten
up ;
Forth comes a new gloss on the ancient law,
O'er-looked provisoes, o'er-past premises,
Follow in plenty. No : 't is the safe step.
The hour beneath the convent-wall is lost :
Juliers and she, once mine, are ever mine.
    Mel. Which is to say, you, losing heart
already,
Elude the adventure.
    Berth.   Not so — or, if so —
Why not confess at once that I advise
None of our kingly craft and guild just now
To lay, one moment, down their privilege
With the notion they can any time at pleasure
Retake it : that may turn out hazardous.
We seem, in Europe, pretty well at end

O' the night, with our great masque : those
favored few
Who keep the chamber's top, and honor's
chance
Of the early evening, may retain their place
And figure as they list till out of breath.
But it is growing late : and I observe
A dim grim kind of tipstaves at the doorway
Not only bar new-comers entering now,
But caution those who left, for any cause,
And would return, that morning draws too near :
The ball must die off, shut itself up. We —
I think, may dance lights out and sunshine in,
And sleep off headache on our frippery :
But friend the other, who cunningly stole out,
And, after breathing the fresh air outside,
Means to re-enter with a new costume,
Will be advised go back to bed, I fear.
I stick to privilege, on second thoughts.
    Mel. Yes — you evade the adventure : and
beside,
Give yourself out for colder than you are.
King Philip, only, notes the lady's eyes ?
Don't they come in for somewhat of the motive
With you too ?
    Berth.   Yes — no : I am past that now.
Gone 't is : I cannot shut my soul to fact.
Of course, I might by forethought and contri-
vance
Reason myself into a rapture. Gone :
And something better come instead, no doubt.
    Mel. So be it ! Yet, all the same, proceed
my way,
Though to your ends ; so shall you prosper best !
The lady — to be won for selfish ends —
Will be won easier my unselfish . . . call it,
Romantic way.
    Berth.   Won easier ?
    Mel.   Will not she ?
    Berth. There I profess humility without
bound :
Ill cannot speed — not I — the Emperor.
    Mel. And I should think the Emperor best
waived,
From your description of her mood and way.
You could look, if it pleased you, into hearts ;
But are too indolent and fond of watching
Your own — you know that, for you study it.
    Berth. Had you but seen the orator her
friend,
So bold and voluble an hour before,
Abashed to earth at aspect of the change !
Make her an Empress ? Ah, that changed the
case !
Oh, I read hearts ! 'T is for my own behoof,
I court her with my true worth : wait the event !
I learned my final lesson on that head
When years ago, — my first and last essay —
Before the priest my uncle could by help
Of his superior raise me from the dirt —
Priscilla left me for a Brabant lord
Whose cheek was like the topaz on his thumb.
I am past illusion on that score.
    Mel.   Here comes
The lady —
    Berth. — And there you go. But do not !
Give me
Another chance to please you ! Hear me plead !

Mel. You 'll keep, then, to the lover, to the man ?

[*Enter the* DUCHESS — *followed by* ADOLF *and* SABYNE, *and, after an interval, by the* Courtiers.)

Berth. Good auspice to our meeting !

Duch.   May it prove !
— And you, sir, will be Emperor one day ?

Berth. (Ay, that 's the point !) I may be Emperor.

Duch. 'T is not for my sake only, I am proud
Of this you offer : I am prouder far
That from the highest state should duly spring
The highest, since most generous, of deeds.

Berth. (Generous — still that !) You underrate yourself.
You are, what I, to be complete, must gain —
Find now, and may not find, another time.
While I career on all the world for stage,
There needs at home my representative.

Duch. — Such, rather, would some warriorwoman be —
One dowered with lands and gold, or rich in friends —
One like yourself.

Berth.   Lady, I am myself,
And have all these : I want what 's not myself,
Nor has all these. Why give one hand two swords ?
Here 's one already : be a friend's next gift
A silk glove, if you will — I have a sword.

Duch. You love me, then ?

Berth.   Your lineage I revere,
Honor your virtue, in your truth believe,
Do homage to your intellect, and bow
Before your peerless beauty.

Duch.   But, for love —

Berth. A further love I do not understand.
Our best course is to say these hideous truths,
And see them, once said, grow endurable :
Like waters shuddering from their central bed,
Black with the midnight bowels of the earth,
That, once up-spouted by an earthquake's throe,
A portent and a terror — soon subside,
Freshen apace, take gold and rainbow hues
In sunshine, sleep in shadow, and at last
Grow common to the earth as hills or trees —
Accepted by all things they came to scare.

Duch. You cannot love, then ?

Berth.   — Charlemagne, perhaps !
Are you not over-curious in love-lore ?

Duch. I have become so, very recently.
It seems, then, I shall best deserve esteem
Respect, and all your candor promises,
By putting on a calculating mood —
Asking the terms of my becoming yours ?

Berth. Let me not do myself injustice, neither.
Because I will not condescend to fictions
That promise what my soul can ne'er acquit,
It does not follow that my guarded phrase
May not include far more of what you seek,
Than wide profession of less scrupulous men.
You will be Empress, once for all : with me
The Pope disputes supremacy — you stand,
And none gainsays, the earth's first woman.

Duch.   That —
Or simple Lady of Ravestein again ?

Berth. The matter 's not in my arbitrament :

Now I have made my claims — which I regret —
Cede one, cede all.

Duch.   This claim then, you enforce ?

Berth. The world looks on.

Duch.   And when must I decide ?

Berth. When, lady ? Have I said thus much so promptly
For nothing ? — Poured out, with such pains, at once
What I might else have suffered to ooze forth
Droplet by droplet in a lifetime long —
For aught less than as prompt an answer, too ?
All 's fairly told now : who can teach you more ?

Duch. I do not see him.

Berth.   I shall ne'er deceive.
This offer should be made befittingly
Did time allow the better setting forth
The good of it, with what is not so good,
Advantage, and disparagement as well :
But as it is, the sum of both must serve.
I am already weary of this place ;
My thoughts are next stage on to Rome.
Decide !
The Empire — or, — not even Juliers now !
Hail to the Empress — farewell to the Duchess !

[*The* Courtiers, *who have been drawing nearer and nearer, interpose.*

Gau. — "Farewell," Prince ? when we break in at our risk —

Clug. Almost upon court-license trespassing —

Gau. — To point out how your claims are valid yet !
You know not, by the Duke her father's will,
The lady, if she weds beneath her rank,
Forfeits her Duchy in the next heir's favor —
So 't is expressly stipulate. And if
It can be shown 't is her intent to wed
A subject, then yourself, next heir, by right
Succeed to Juliers.

Berth.   What insanity ? —

Gui. Sir, there 's one Valence, the pale fiery man
You saw and heard this morning — thought, no doubt,
Was of considerable standing here :
I put it to your penetration, Prince,
If aught save love, the truest love for her
Could make him serve the lady as he did !
He 's simply a poor advocate of Cleves
— Creeps here with difficulty, finds a place
With danger, gets in by a miracle,
And for the first time meets the lady's face —
So runs the story : is that credible ?
For, first — no sooner in, than he 's apprised
Fortunes have changed ; you are all-powerful here,
The lady as powerless : he stands fast by her !

Duch. [*Aside.*] And do such deeds spring up from love alone ?

Gui. But here occurs the question, does the lady
Love him again ? I say, how else can she ?
Can she forget how he stood singly forth
In her defence, dared outrage all of us,
Insult yourself — for what, save love 's reward ?

Duch. [*Aside.*] And is love then the sole reward of love ?

Gui. But, love him as she may and must —
  you ask,
Means she to wed him? "Yes," both natures
  answer!
Both, in their pride, point out the sole result;
Naught less would he accept nor she propose.
For each conjecture was she great enough
— Will be, for this.
Clug.   Though, now that this is known,
Policy, doubtless, urges she deny . . .
Duch. — What, sir, and wherefore? — since I
  am not sure
That all is any other than you say!
You take this Valence, hold him close to me,
Him with his actions: can I choose but look?
I am not sure, love trulier shows itself
Than in this man, you hate and would degrade,
Yet, with your worst abatement, show me thus.
Nor am I — (thus made look within myself,
Ere I had dared) — now that the look is dared —
Sure that I do not love him!
Gui.   Hear you, Prince?
Berth. And what, sirs, please you, may this
  prattle mean
Unless to prove with what alacrity
You give your lady's secrets to the world?
How much indebted, for discovering
That quality, you make me, will be found
When there 's a keeper for my own to seek.
Courtiers. "Our lady?"
Berth.   — She assuredly remains.
Duch. Ah, Prince — and you too can be gen-
  erous?
You could renounce your power, if this were so,
And let me, as these phrase it, wed my love
Yet keep my Duchy? You perhaps exceed
Him, even, in disinterestedness!
Berth. How, lady, should all this affect my
  purpose?
Your will and choice are still as ever, free.
Say, you have known a worthier than myself
In mind and heart, of happier form and face —
Others must have their birthright: I have gifts,
To balance theirs, not blot them out of sight.
Against a hundred alien qualities,
I lay the prize I offer. I am nothing:
Wed you the Empire?
Duch.   And my heart away?
Berth. When have I made pretension to your
  heart?
I give none. I shall keep your honor safe;
With mine I trust you, as the sculptor trusts
Yon marble woman with the marble rose,
Loose on her hand, she never will let fall,
In graceful, slight, silent security.
You will be proud of my world-wide career,
And I content in you the fair and good.
What were the use of planting a few seeds
The thankless climate never would mature —
Affections all repelled by circumstance?
Enough: to these no credit I attach, —
To what you own, find nothing to object.
Write simply on my requisition's face
What shall content my friends — that you
  admit,
As Colombe of Ravestein, the claims therein,
Or never need admit them, as my wife —
And either way, all 's ended!

Duch.   Let all end!
Berth. The requisition!
Gui.   — Valence holds, of course!
Berth. Desire his presence!   [ADOLF *goes out.*
Courtiers. [*To each other.*] Out it all comes
  yet;
He 'll have his word against the bargain yet;
He 's not the man to tamely acquiesce.
One passionate appeal — upbraiding even,
May turn the tide again. Despair not yet!
                    [*They retire a little.*
Berth. [*To* MELCHIOR.] The Empire has its
  old success, my friend!
Mel. You 've had your way: before the
  spokesman speaks
Let me, but this once, work a problem out,
And ever more be dumb! The Empire wins?
To better purpose have I read my books!
                    (*Enter* VALENCE.)
Mel. [*To the* Courtiers.] Apart, my masters!
       [*To* VALENCE.] Sir, one word with you!
I am a poor dependant of the Prince's —
Pitched on to speak, as of slight consequence.
You are no higher, I find: in other words,
We two, as probably the wisest here,
Need not hold diplomatic talk like fools.
Suppose I speak, divesting the plain fact
Of all their tortuous phrases, fit for them?
Do you reply so, and what trouble saved!
The Prince, then — an embroiled strange heap
  of news
This moment reaches him — if true or false,
All dignity forbids he should inquire
In person, or by worthier deputy;
Yet somehow must inquire, lest slander come:
And so, 't is I am pitched on. You have heard
His offer to your lady?
Val.   Yes.
Mel.   — Conceive
Her joy thereat?
Val.   I cannot.
Mel.   No one can.
All draws to a conclusion, therefore.
Val. [*Aside.*]   So!
No after-judgment — no first thought revised —
Her first and last decision! — me, she leaves,
Takes him; a simple heart is flung aside,
The ermine o'er a heartless breast embraced.
Oh Heaven, this mockery has been played too
  oft!
Once, to surprise the angels — twice, that fiends,
Recording, might be proud they chose not so —
Thrice, many thousand times, to teach the world
All men should pause, misdoubt their strength,
  since men
Can have such chance yet fail so signally
— But ever, ever this farewell to Heaven,
Welcome to earth — this taking death for life —
This spurning love and kneeling to the world —
Oh Heaven, it is too often and too old!
Mel. Well, on this point, what but an absurd
  rumor
Arises — these, its source — its subject, you!
Your faith and loyalty misconstruing,
They say, your service claims the lady's hand:
Of course, nor Prince nor lady can respond:
Yet something must be said: for, were it true
You made such claim, the Prince would . .

Val. Well, sir, — would?

Mel. — Not only probably withdraw his suit,
But, very like, the lady might be forced
Accept your own. Oh, there are reasons why!
But you'll excuse at present all save one, —
I think so. What we want is, your own witness,
For, or against — her good, or yours: decide!

Val. [*Aside.*] Be it her good if she accounts
it so!
[*After a contest.*] For what am I but hers, to
choose as she?
Who knows how far, beside, the light from her
May reach, and dwell with, what she looks
upon?

Mel. [*To the Prince.*] Now to him, you!

Berth. [*To* VALENCE.] My friend acquaints
you, sir,
The noise runs . . .

Val. — Prince, how fortunate are you,
Wedding her as you will, in spite of noise,
To show belief in love! Let her but love you,
All else you disregard! What else can be?
You know how love is incompatible
With falsehood — purifies, assimilates
All other passions to itself.

Mel. Ay. sir:
But softly! Where, in the object we select,
Such love is, perchance, wanting?

Val. Then indeed,
What is it you can take?

Mel. Nay, ask the world!
Youth, beauty, virtue, an illustrious name,
An influence o'er mankind.

Val. When man perceives . . .
— Ah, I can only speak as for myself!

Duch. Speak for yourself!

Val. May I? — no, I have spoken,
And time's gone by. Had I seen such an one,
As I loved her — weighing thoroughly that
word —
So should my task be to evolve her love:
If for myself! — if for another — well.

Berth. Heroic truly! And your sole re-
ward, —
The secret pride in yielding up love's right?

Val. Who thought upon reward? And yet
how much
Comes after — oh, what amplest recompense!
Is the knowledge of her, naught? the memory,
naught?
— Lady, should such an one have looked on
you,
Ne'er wrong yourself so far as quote the world
And say, love can go unrequited here!
You will have blessed him to his whole life's
end —
Low passions hindered, baser cares kept back,
All goodness cherished where you dwelt — and
dwell.
What would he have? He holds you — you,
both form
And mind, in his, — where self-love makes such
room
For love of you, he would not serve you now
The vulgar way, — repulse your enemies,
Win you new realms, or best, to save the old
Die blissfully — that's past so long ago!
He wishes you no need, thought, care of him —

Your good, by any means, himself unseen,
Away, forgotten! — He gives that life's task
up,
As it were . . . but this charge which I re-
turn —
[*Offers the requisition, which she takes*
Wishing your good.

Duch. [*Having subscribed it.*] And oppor-
tunely, sir —
Since at a birthday's close, like this of mine,
Good wishes gentle deeds reciprocate.
Most on a wedding-day, as mine is too,
Should gifts be thought of: yours comes first
by right.
Ask of me!

Berth. He shall have whate'er he asks,
For your sake and his own.

Val. [*Aside.*] If I should ask —
The withered bunch of flowers she wears — per-
haps,
One last touch of her hand, I never more
Shall see!
[*After a pause, presenting his paper to the* Prince.
Cleves' Prince, redress the wrongs of Cleves!

Berth. I will, sir!

Duch. [*As* VALENCE *prepares to retire.*] —
Nay, do out your duty, first!
You bore this paper; I have registered
My answer to it: read it and have done!
[VALENCE *reads it.*
I take him — give up Juliers and the world.
This is my Birthday.

Mel. Berthold, my one hero
Of the world she gives up, one friend worth my
books,
Sole man I think it pays the pains to watch, —
Speak, for I know you through your Popes and
Kings!

Berth. [*After a pause.*] Lady, well rewarded!
Sir, as well deserved!
I could not imitate — I hardly envy —
I do admire you. All is for the best.
Too costly a flower were this, I see it now,
To pluck and set upon my barren helm
To wither — any garish plume will do.
I'll not insult you and refuse your Duchy —
You can so well afford to yield it me,
And I were left, without it, sadly lorn.
As it is — for me — if that will flatter you,
A somewhat wearier life seems to remain
Than I thought possible where . . . 'faith, their
life
Begins already! They're too occupied
To listen: and few words content me best.
[*Abruptly to the* Courtiers.] I am your Duke,
though! Who obey me here?

Duch. Adolf and Sabyne follow us —

Gui. [*Starting from the* Courtiers.] — And I!
Do I not follow them, if I may n't you?
Shall not I get some little duties up
At Ravestein and emulate the rest?
God save you, Gaucelme! 'T is my Birthday
too!

Berth. You happy handful that remain with
me
. . . That is, with Dietrich the black Barna-
bite
I shall leave over you — will earn your wages

Or Dietrich has forgot to ply his trade !
Meantime, — go copy me the precedents
Of every installation, proper styles
And pedigrees of all your Juliers' Dukes —
While I prepare to plod on my old way,

And somewhat wearily, I must confess !
    Duch. [*With a light joyous laugh as she turns
        from them.*] Come, Valence, to our friends,
        God's earth . . .
    Val. [*As she falls into his arms.*] — And thee !

DRAMATIC ROMANCES

THE seventh number of *Bells and Pomegranates* was entitled *Dramatic Romances and Lyrics.* In the redistribution of his shorter poems when he collected his writings, Browning having already a group of *Dramatic Lyrics* made a second of *Dramatic Romances*, taking the occasion to make a little nicer discrimination. Thus some of the poems originally included under the combined title were distributed among the *Lyrics*, and some at first grouped under *Lyrics* were transferred to this division of *Romances.* The first poem in the group was originally contained in *Dramatic Lyrics* along with *Soliloquy of the Spanish Cloister* under the general title of *Camp and Cloister*, this poem representing the camp.

INCIDENT OF THE FRENCH CAMP

You know, we French stormed Ratisbon :
    A mile or so away,
On a little mound, Napoleon
    Stood on our storming-day ;
With neck out-thrust, you fancy how,
    Legs wide, arms locked behind,
As if to balance the prone brow
    Oppressive with its mind.

Just as perhaps he mused " My plans
    That soar, to earth may fall,
Let once my army-leader Lannes
    Waver at yonder wall," —
Out 'twixt the battery-smokes there flew
    A rider, bound on bound
Full-galloping ; nor bridle drew
    Until he reached the mound.

Then off there flung in smiling joy,
    And held himself erect
By just his horse's mane, a boy :
    You hardly could suspect —
(So tight he kept his lips compressed,
    Scarce any blood came through)
You looked twice ere you saw his breast
    Was all but shot in two.

" Well," cried he, " Emperor, by God's grace
    We 've got you Ratisbon !
The Marshal 's in the market-place,
    And you 'll be there anon
To see your flag-bird flap his vans
    Where I, to heart's desire,
Perched him ! " The chief's eye flashed ; his
        plans
    Soared up again like fire.

The chief's eye flashed ; but presently
    Softened itself, as sheathes
A film the mother-eagle's eye
    When her bruised eaglet breathes ;

" You 're wounded ! " " Nay," the soldier's
        pride
    Touched to the quick, he said :
" I 'm killed, Sire ! " And his chief beside,
    Smiling the boy fell dead.

THE PATRIOT

AN OLD STORY

Mr. Browning has denied that this poem refers to Arnold of Brescia. It is imaginative, not historical in its dramatic action. It was possibly to relieve the poem of its apparent distinct reference to history that he removed the name of Brescia, which was used in the poem in its first form.

IT was roses, roses, all the way,
    With myrtle mixed in my path like mad :
The house-roofs seemed to heave and sway,
    The church-spires flamed, such flags they had,
A year ago on this very day.

The air broke into a mist with bells,
    The old walls rocked with the crowd and
        cries.
Had I said, " Good folk, mere noise repels —
    But give me your sun from yonder skies ! "
They had answered, " And afterward, what
        else ? "

Alack, it was I who leaped at the sun
    To give it my loving friends to keep !
Naught man could do, have I left undone :
    And you see my harvest, what I reap
This very day, now a year is run.

There 's nobody on the house-tops now —
    Just a palsied few at the windows set ;
For the best of the sight is, all allow.

At the Shambles' Gate — or, better yet,
By the very scaffold's foot, I trow.

I go in the rain, and, more than needs,
    A rope cuts both my wrists behind ;
And I think, by the feel, my forehead bleeds,
    For they fling, whoever has a mind,
Stones at me for my year's misdeeds.

Thus I entered, and thus I go !
    In triumphs, people have dropped down dead.
" Paid by the world, what dost thou owe
    Me ? " — God might question ; now instead,
'Tis God shall repay : I am safer so.

MY LAST DUCHESS

FERRARA

In *Dramatic Lyrics* this was entitled *Italy*, and
grouped with *Count Gismond* under the head
Italy and France.

THAT 's my last Duchess painted on the wall,
Looking as if she were alive. I call
That piece a wonder, now : Frà Pandolf's hands
Worked busily a day, and there she stands.
Will 't please you sit and look at her ? I said
" Frà Pandolf " by design, for never read
Strangers like you that pictured countenance,
The depth and passion of its earnest glance,
But to myself they turned (since none puts by
The curtain I have drawn for you, but I)
And seemed as they would ask me, if they
        durst,
How such a glance came there ; so, not the first
Are you to turn and ask thus. Sir, 't was not
Her husband's presence only, called that spot
Of joy into the Duchess' cheek : perhaps
Frà Pandolf chanced to say, " Her mantle laps
Over my lady's wrist too much," or " Paint
Must never hope to reproduce the faint
Half-flush that dies along her throat : " such
        stuff
Was courtesy, she thought, and cause enough
For calling up that spot of joy. She had
A heart — how shall I say ? — too soon made
        glad,
Too easily impressed : she liked whate'er
She looked on, and her looks went everywhere.
Sir, 't was all one ! My favor at her breast,
The dropping of the daylight in the West,
The bough of cherries some officious fool
Broke in the orchard for her, the white mule
She rode with round the terrace — all and each
Would draw from her alike the approving
        speech,
Or blush, at least. She thanked men, — good !
        but thanked
Somehow — I know not how — as if she ranked
My gift of a nine-hundred-years-old name
With anybody's gift. Who 'd stoop to blame
This sort of trifling ? Even had you skill
In speech — (which I have not) — to make your
        will
Quite clear to such an one, and say, " Just this
Or that in you disgusts me ; here you miss,

Or there exceed the mark " — and if she let
Herself be lessoned so, nor plainly set
Her wits to yours, forsooth, and made excuse,
— E'en then would be some stooping ; and I
        choose
Never to stoop. Oh sir, she smiled, no doubt,
Whene'er I passed her ; but who passed without
Much the same smile ? This grew ; I gave
        commands ;
Then all smiles stopped together. There she
        stands
As if alive. Will 't please you rise ? We 'll
        meet
The company below, then. I repeat,
The Count your master's known munificence
Is ample warrant that no just pretence
Of mine for dowry will be disallowed ;
Though his fair daughter's self, as I avowed
At starting, is my object. Nay, we 'll go
Together down, sir. Notice Neptune, though,
Taming a sea-horse, thought a rarity,
Which Claus of Innsbruck cast in bronze for
        me !

COUNT GISMOND

AIX IN PROVENCE

CHRIST GOD who savest man, save most
    Of men Count Gismond who saved me !
Count Gauthier, when he chose his post,
    Chose time and place and company
To suit it ; when he struck at length
My honor, 't was with all his strength.

And doubtlessly ere he could draw
    All points to one, he must have schemed !
That miserable morning saw
    Few half so happy as I seemed,
While being dressed in queen's array
To give our tourney prize away.

I thought they loved me, did me grace
    To please themselves ; 't was all their deed
God makes, or fair or foul, our face ;
    If showing mine so caused to bleed
My cousins' hearts, they should have dropped
A word, and straight the play had stopped.

They, too, so beauteous ! Each a queen
    By virtue of her brow and breast ;
Not needing to be crowned, I mean,
    As I do. E'en when I was dressed,
Had either of them spoke, instead
Of glancing sideways with still head !

But no : they let me laugh, and sing
    My birthday song quite through, adjust
The last rose in my garland, fling
    A last look on the mirror, trust
My arms to each an arm of theirs,
And so descend the castle-stairs —

And come out on the morning-troop
    Of merry friends who kissed my cheek,
And called me queen, and made me stoop
    Under the canopy — (a streak

That pierced it, of the outside sun,
Powdered with gold its gloom's soft dun) —

And they could let me take my state
And foolish throne amid applause
Of all come there to celebrate
My queen's-day — Oh I think the cause
Of much was, they forgot no crowd
Makes up for parents in their shroud !

Howe'er that be, all eyes were bent
Upon me, when my cousins cast
Theirs down ; 't was time I should present
The victor's crown, but . . . there, 't will last
No long time . . . the old mist again
Blinds me as then it did. How vain !

See ! Gismond 's at the gate, in talk
With his two boys : I can proceed.
Well, at that moment, who should stalk
Forth boldly — to my face, indeed —
But Gauthier, and he thundered, " Stay ! "
And all stayed. " Bring no crowns, I say !

" Bring torches ! Wind the penance-sheet
About her ! Let her shun the chaste,
Or lay herself before their feet !
Shall she whose body I embraced
A night long, queen it in the day ?
For honor's sake no crowns, I say ! "

I ? What I answered ? As I live,
I never fancied such a thing
As answer possible to give.
What says the body when they spring
Some monstrous torture-engine's whole
Strength on it ? No more says the soul.

Till out strode Gismond ; then I knew
That I was saved. I never met
His face before, but, at first view,
I felt quite sure that God had set
Himself to Satan ; who would spend
A minute's mistrust on the end ?

He strode to Gauthier, in his throat
Gave him the lie, then struck his mouth
With one back-handed blow that wrote *
In blood men's verdict there. North, South,
East, West, I looked. The lie was dead,
And damned, and truth stood up instead.

This glads me most, that I enjoyed
The heart of the joy, with my content
In watching Gismond unalloyed
By any doubt of the event :
God took that on him — I was bid
Watch Gismond for my part : I did.

Did I not watch him while he let
His armorer just brace his greaves,
Rivet his hauberk, on the fret
The while ! His foot . . . my memory leaves
No least stamp out, nor how anon
He pulled his ringing gauntlets on.

And e'en before the trumpet's sound
Was finished, prone lay the false knight,

Prone as his lie, upon the ground :
Gismond flew at him, used no sleight
O' the sword, but open-breasted drove,
Cleaving till out the truth he clove.

Which done, he dragged him to my feet
And said, " Here die, but end thy breath
In full confession, lest thou fleet
From my first, to God's second death !
Say, hast thou lied ? " And, " I have lied
To God and her," he said, and died.

Then Gismond, kneeling to me, asked
— What safe my heart holds, though no word
Could I repeat now, if I tasked
My powers forever, to a third
Dear even as you are. Pass the rest
Until I sank upon his breast.

Over my head his arm he flung
Against the world ; and scarce I felt
His sword (that dripped by me and swung)
A little shifted in its belt :
For he began to say the while
How South our home lay many a mile.

So 'mid the shouting multitude
We two walked forth to never more
Return. My cousins have pursued
Their life, untroubled as before
I vexed them. Gauthier's dwelling-place
God lighten ! May his soul find grace !

Our elder boy has got the clear
Great brow ; though when his brother's black
Full eye shows scorn, it . . . Gismond here ?
And have you brought my tercel back ?
I just was telling Adela
How many birds it struck since May.

THE BOY AND THE ANGEL

First published in *Hood's Magazine*, August,
1844. It was rewritten, with five new coup-
lets, and was published in 1845, in *Dramatic
Romances and Lyrics*, or No. VII. of *Bells and
Pomegranates*. When it appeared in the *Poeti-
cal Works* of 1868, a fresh verse was added.
In 1844 the poem ended as follows : —

" Go back and praise again
The early way, while I remain.

" Be again the boy all curl'd ;
I will finish with the world."

Theocrite grew old at home,
Gabriel dwelt in Peter's dome.

MORNING, evening, noon and night,
" Praise God ! " sang Theocrite.

Then to his poor trade he turned,
Whereby the daily meal was earned.

Hard he labored, long and well ;
O'er his work the boy's curls fell.

But ever, at each period,
He stopped and sang, " Praise God ! "

Then back again his curls he threw,
And cheerful turned to work anew.

Said Blaise, the listening monk, " Well done ;
I doubt not thou art heard, my son :

" As well as if thy voice to-day
Were praising God, the Pope's great way.

" This Easter Day, the Pope at Rome
Praises God from Peter's dome."

Said Theocrite, " Would God that I
Might praise him that great way, and die ! "

Night passed, day shone,
And Theocrite was gone.

With God a day endures alway,
A thousand years are but a day.

God said in heaven, " Nor day nor night
Now brings the voice of my delight."

Then Gabriel, like a rainbow's birth,
Spread his wings and sank to earth ;

Entered, in flesh, the empty cell,
Lived there, and played the craftsman well ;

And morning, evening, noon and night,
Praised God in place of Theocrite.

And from a boy, to youth he grew :
The man put off the stripling's hue :

The man matured and fell away
Into the season of decay :

And ever o'er the trade he bent,
And ever lived on earth content.

(He did God's will ; to him, all one
If on the earth or in the sun.)

God said, " A praise is in mine ear ;
There is no doubt in it, no fear :

"So sing old worlds, and so
New worlds that from my footstool go.

" Clearer loves sound other ways :
I miss my little human praise."

Then forth sprang Gabriel's wings, off fell
The flesh disguise, remained the cell.

'T was Easter Day : he flew to Rome,
And paused above Saint Peter's dome.

In the tiring-room close by
The great outer gallery,

With his holy vestments dight,
Stood the new Pope, Theocrite :

And all his past career
Came back upon him clear,

Since when, a boy, he plied his trade,
Till on his life the sickness weighed ;

And in his cell, when death drew near,
An angel in a dream brought cheer :

And rising from the sickness drear,
He grew a priest, and now stood here.

To the East with praise he turned,
And on his sight the angel burned.

" I bore thee from thy craftsman's cell,
And set thee here ; I did not well.

" Vainly I left my angel-sphere,
Vain was thy dream of many a year.

" Thy voice's praise seemed weak ; it
     dropped —
Creation's chorus stopped !

" Go back and praise again
The early way, while I remain.

" With that weak voice of our disdain,
Take up creation's pausing strain.

" Back to the cell and poor employ :
Resume the craftsman and the boy ! "

Theocrite grew old at home ;
A new Pope dwelt in Peter's dome.

One vanished as the other died :
They sought God side by side.

INSTANS TYRANNUS

I

OF the million or two, more or less,
I rule and possess,
One man, for some cause undefined,
Was least to my mind.

II

I struck him, he grovelled of course —
For, what was his force ?
I pinned him to earth with my weight
And persistence of hate :
And he lay, would not moan, would not curse
As his lot might be worse.

III

" Were the object less mean, would he stand
At the swing of my hand !
For obscurity helps him and blots
The hole where he squats."
So, I set my five wits on the stretch
To inveigle the wretch.
All in vain ! Gold and jewels I threw,
Still he couched there perdue ;
I tempted his blood and his flesh,
Hid in roses my mesh,

Choicest cates and the flagon's best spilth :
Still he kept to his filth.

IV

Had he kith now or kin, were access
To his heart, did I press :
Just a son or a mother to seize !
No such booty as these.
Were it simply a friend to pursue
'Mid my million or two,
Who could pay me in person or pelf
What he owes me himself !
No : I could not but smile through my chafe :
For the fellow lay safe
As his mates do, the midge and the nit,
— Through minuteness, to wit.

V

Then a humor more great took its place
At the thought of his face,
The droop, the low cares of the mouth,
The trouble uncouth
'Twixt the brows, all that air one is fain
To put out of its pain.
And, " no ! " I admonished myself,
" Is one mocked by an elf,
Is one baffled by toad or by rat ?
The gravamen 's in that !
How the lion, who crouches to suit
His back to my foot,
Would admire that I stand in debate !
But the small turns the great
If it vexes you, — that is the thing !
Toad or rat vex the king ?
Though I waste half my realm to unearth
Toad or rat, 't is well worth ! ' "

VI

So, I soberly laid my last plan
To extinguish the man.
Round his creep-hole, with never a break,
Ran my fires for his sake ;
Over-head, did my thunder combine
With my underground mine :
Till I looked from my labor content
To enjoy the event.

VII

When sudden . . . how think ye, the end ?
Did I say " without friend " ?
Say rather, from marge to blue marge
The whole sky grew his targe
With the sun's self for visible boss,
While an Arm ran across
Which the earth heaved beneath like a breast
Where the wretch was safe prest !
Do you see ? Just my vengeance complete,
The man sprang to his feet,
Stood erect, caught at God's skirts, and prayed !
—So, _I_ was afraid !

MESMERISM

ALL I believed is true !
I am able yet
All I want, to get

By a method as strange as new :
Dare I trust the same to you ?

If at night, when doors are shut,
And the wood-worm picks,
And the death-watch ticks,
And the bar has a flag of smut,
And a cat 's in the water-butt —

And the socket floats and flares,
And the house-beams groan,
And a foot unknown
Is surmised on the garret-stairs,
And the locks slip unawares —

And the spider, to serve his ends,
By a sudden thread,
Arms and legs outspread,
On the table's midst descends,
Comes to find, God knows what friends !

If since eve drew in, I say,
I have sat and brought
(So to speak) my thought
To bear on the woman away,
Till I felt my hair turn gray —

Till I seemed to have and hold,
In the vacancy
'Twixt the wall and me,
From the hair-plait's chestnut-gold
To the foot in its muslin fold —

Have and hold, then and there,
Her, from head to foot,
Breathing and mute,
Passive and yet aware,
In the grasp of my steady stare —

Hold and have, there and then,
All her body and soul
That completes my whole,
All that women add to men,
In the clutch of my steady ken —

Having and holding, till
I imprint her fast
On the void at last
As the sun does whom he will
By the calotypist's skill —

Then, — if my heart's strength serve,
And through all and each
Of the veils I reach
To her soul and never swerve,
Knitting an iron nerve —

Command her soul to advance
And inform the shape
Which has made escape
And before my countenance
Answers me glance for glance —

I, still with a gesture fit
Of my hands that best
Do my soul's behest,
Pointing the power from it,
While myself do steadfast sit

Steadfast and still the same
    On my object bent,
    While the hands give vent
To my ardor and my aim
And break into very flame —

Then I reach, I must believe,
    Not her soul in vain,
    For to me again
It reaches, and past retrieve
Is wound in the toils I weave;

And must follow as I require,
    As befits a thrall,
    Bringing flesh and all,
Essence and earth-attire,
To the source of the tractile fire:

Till the house called hers, not mine,
    With a growing weight
    Seems to suffocate
If she break not its leaden line
And escape from its close confine.

Out of doors into the night!
    On to the maze
    Of the wild wood-ways,
Not turning to left nor right
From the pathway, blind with sight —

Making through rain and wind
    O'er the broken shrubs,
    'Twixt the stems and stubs,
With a still, composed, strong mind,
Nor a care for the world behind —

Swifter and still more swift,
    As the crowding peace
    Doth to joy increase
In the wide blind eyes uplift
Through the darkness and the drift!

While I — to the shape, I too
    Feel my soul dilate
    Nor a whit abate,
And relax not a gesture due,
As I see my belief come true.

For, there! have I drawn or no
    Life to that lip?
    Do my fingers dip
In a flame which again they throw
On the cheek that breaks aglow?

Ha! was the hair so first?
    What, unfilleted,
    Made alive, and spread
Through the void with a rich outburst,
Chestnut gold-interspersed?

Like the doors of a casket-shrine,
    See, on either side,
    Her two arms divide
Till the heart betwixt makes sign,
Take me, for I am thine!

"Now — now "—the door is heard!
    Hark, the stairs! and near —

Nearer — and here —
"Now!" and at call the third
She enters without a word.

On doth she march and on
    To the fancied shape;
    It is, past escape,
Herself, now: the dream is done
And the shadow and she are one.

First I will pray. Do Thou
    That ownest the soul,
    Yet wilt grant control
To another, nor disallow
For a time, restrain me now!

I admonish me while I may,
    Not to squander guilt,
    Since require Thou wilt
At my hand its price one day!
What the price is, who can say?

THE GLOVE

(PETER RONSARD *loquitur*.)

"HEIGHO," yawned one day King Francis,
"Distance all value enhances!
When a man's busy, why, leisure
Strikes him as wonderful pleasure:
'Faith, and at leisure once is he?
Straightway he wants to be busy.
Here we 've got peace; and aghast I 'm
Caught thinking war the true pastime.
Is there a reason in metre?
Give us your speech, master Peter!"
I who, if mortal dare say so,
Ne'er am at loss with my Naso,
"Sire," I replied, "joys prove cloudlets:
Men are the merest Ixions "—
Here the King whistled aloud, "Let 's
— Heigho — go look at our lions!"
Such are the sorrowful chances
If you talk fine to King Francis.

And so, to the courtyard proceeding
Our company, Francis was leading,
Increased by new followers tenfold
Before he arrived at the penfold;
Lords, ladies, like clouds which bedizen
At sunset the western horizon.
And Sir De Lorge pressed 'mid the foremost
With the dame he professed to adore most.
Oh, what a face! One by fits eyed
Her, and the horrible pitside;
For the penfold surrounded a hollow
Which led where the eye scarce dared follow
And shelved to the chamber secluded
Where Bluebeard, the great lion, brooded.
The King hailed his keeper, an Arab
As glossy and black as a scarab,
And bade him make sport and at once stir
Up and out of his den the old monster.
They opened a hole in the wire-work
Across it, and dropped there a firework,
And fled: one's heart's beating redoubled:
A pause, while the pit's mouth was troubled,
The blackness and silence so utter,

By the firework's slow sparkling and sputter ;
Then earth in a sudden contortion
Gave out to our gaze her abortion.
Such a brute ! Were I friend Clement Marot
(Whose experience of nature 's but narrow,
And whose faculties move in no small mist
When he versifies David the Psalmist)
I should study that brute to describe you
Illum Juda Leonem de Tribu.

One's whole blood grew curdling and creepy
To see the black mane, vast and heapy,
The tail in the air stiff and straining,
The wide eyes, nor waxing nor waning,
As over the barrier which bounded
His platform, and us who surrounded
The barrier, they reached and they rested
On space that might stand him in best stead :
For who knew, he thought, what the amazement,
The eruption of clatter and blaze meant,
And if, in this minute of wonder,
No outlet, 'mid lightning and thunder,
Lay broad, and, his shackles all shivered,
The lion at last was delivered ?
Ay, that was the open sky o'erhead !
And you saw by the flash on his forehead,
By the hope in those eyes wide and steady,
He was leagues in the desert already,
Driving the flocks up the mountain,
Or catlike couched hard by the fountain
To waylay the date-gathering negress :
So guarded he entrance or egress.
"How he stands !" quoth the King : "we may
      well swear,
(No novice, we 've won our spurs elsewhere
And so can afford the confession,)
We exercise wholesome discretion
In keeping aloof from his threshold,
Once hold you, those jaws want no fresh hold,
Their first would too pleasantly purloin
The visitor's brisket or surloin :
But who 's he would prove so fool-hardy ?
Not the best man of Marignan, pardie !"

The sentence no sooner was uttered,
Than over the rails a glove fluttered,
Fell close to the lion, and rested :
The dame 't was, who flung it and jested
With life so, De Lorge had been wooing
For months past ; he sat there pursuing
His suit, weighing out with nonchalance
Fine speeches like gold from a balance.

Sound the trumpet, no true knight 's a tarrier !
De Lorge made one leap at the barrier,
Walked straight to the glove, — while the lion
Ne'er moved, kept his far-reaching eye on
The palm-tree-edged desert-spring's sapphire,
And the musky oiled skin of the Kaffir, —
Picked it up, and as calmly retreated,
Leaped back where the lady was seated,
And full in the face of its owner
Flung the glove.

      "Your heart's queen, you dethrone her ?
So should I !" — cried the King — "'t was mere
      vanity,
Not love, set that task to humanity !"

Lords and ladies alike turned with loathing
From such a proved wolf in sheep's clothing.

Not so, I ; for I caught an expression
In her brow's undisturbed self-possession
Amid the Court's scoffing and merriment, —
As if from no pleasing experiment
She rose, yet of pain not much heedful
So long as the process was needful, —
As if she had tried in a crucible,
To what "speeches like gold" were reducible
And, finding the finest prove copper,
Felt the smoke in her face was but proper ;
To know what she had *not* to trust to,
Was worth all the ashes and dust too.
She went out 'mid hooting and laughter ;
Clement Marot stayed ; I followed after,
And asked, as a grace, what it all meant ?
If she wished not the rash deed's recallment ?
" For I " — so I spoke — " am a poet :
Human nature, — behooves that I know it ! "

She told me, " Too long had I heard
Of the deed proved alone by the word :
For my love — what De Lorge would not dare !
With my scorn — what De Lorge could com
      pare !
And the endless descriptions of death
He would brave when my lip formed a breath,
I must reckon as braved, or, of course,
Doubt his word — and moreover, perforce,
For such gifts as no lady could spurn,
Must offer my love in return.
When I looked on your lion, it brought
All the dangers at once to my thought,
Encountered by all sorts of men,
Before he was lodged in his den, —
From the poor slave whose club or bare hands
Dug the trap, set the snare on the sands,
With no King and no Court to applaud,
By no shame, should he shrink, overawed,
Yet to capture the creature made shift,
That his rude boys might laugh at the gift,
— To the page who last leaped o'er the fence
Of the pit, on no greater pretence
Than to get back the bonnet he dropped,
Lest his pay for a week should be stopped.
So, wiser I judged it to make
One trial what ' death for my sake '
Really meant, while the power was yet mine
Than to wait until time should define
Such a phrase not so simply as I,
Who took it to mean just ' to die.'
The blow a glove gives is but weak :
Does the mark yet discolor my cheek ?
But when the heart suffers a blow,
Will the pain pass so soon, do you know ? "

I looked, as away she was sweeping,
And saw a youth eagerly keeping
As close as he dared to the doorway.
No doubt that a noble should more weigh
His life than befits a plebeian ;
And yet, had our brute been Nemean —
(I judge by a certain calm fervor
The youth stepped with, forward to serve her)
— He 'd have scarce thought you did him the
      worst turn

If you whispered, "Friend, what you'd get,
    first earn!"
And when, shortly after, she carried
Her shame from the Court, and they married,
To that marriage some happiness, maugre
The voice of the Court, I dared augur.

For De Lorge, he made women with men vie,
Those in wonder and praise, these in envy;
And in short stood so plain a head taller
That he wooed and won . . . how do you call
    her?
The beauty, that rose in the sequel
To the King's love, who loved her a week well.
And 't was noticed he never would honor
De Lorge (who looked daggers upon her)
With the easy commission of stretching
His legs in the service, and fetching
His wife, from her chamber, those straying
Sad gloves she was always mislaying,
While the King took the closet to chat in, —
But of course this adventure came pat in.
And never the King told the story,
How bringing a glove brought such glory,
But the wife smiled — "His nerves are grown
    firmer:
Mine he brings now and utters no murmur."

Venienti occurrite morbo!
With which moral I drop my theorbo.

TIME'S REVENGES

I 've a Friend, over the sea;
I like him, but he loves me.
It all grew out of the books I write;
They find such favor in his sight
That he slaughters you with savage looks
Because you don't admire my books.
He does himself though, — and if some vein
Were to snap to-night in this heavy brain,
To-morrow month, if I lived to try,
Round should I just turn quietly,
Or out of the bedclothes stretch my hand
Till I found him, come from his foreign land
To be my nurse in this poor place,
And make my broth and wash my face
And light my fire and, all the while,
Bear with his old good-humored smile
That I told him "Better have kept away
Than come and kill me, night and day,
With, worse than fever throbs and shoots,
The creaking of his clumsy boots."
I am as sure that this he would do,
As that Saint Paul's is striking two.
And I think I rather . . . woe is me!

— Yes, rather should see him than not see,
If lifting a hand could seat him there
Before me in the empty chair
To-night, when my head aches indeed,
And I can neither think nor read,
Nor make these purple fingers hold
The pen; this garret's freezing cold!

And I 've a Lady — there he wakes,
The laughing fiend and prince of snakes

Within me, at her name, to pray
Fate send some creature in the way
Of my love for her, to be down-torn,
Upthrust and outward-borne,
So I might prove myself that sea
Of passion which I needs must be!
Call my thoughts false and my fancies quaint
And my style infirm and its figures faint,
All the critics say, and more blame yet,
And not one angry word you get.
But, please you, wonder I would put
My cheek beneath that lady's foot
Rather than trample under mine
The laurels of the Florentine,
And you shall see how the devil spends
A fire God gave for other ends!
I tell you, I stride up and down
This garret, crowned with love's best crown,
And feasted with love's perfect feast,
To think I kill for her, at least,
Body and soul and peace and fame,
Alike youth's end and manhood's aim,
— So is my spirit, as flesh with sin,
Filled full, eaten out and in
With the face of her, the eyes of her,
The lips, the little chin, the stir
Of shadow round her mouth; and she
— I 'll tell you — calmly would decree
That I should roast at a slow fire,
If that would compass her desire
And make her one whom they invite
To the famous ball to-morrow night.

There may be heaven; there must be hell;
Meantime, there is our earth here — well!

THE ITALIAN IN ENGLAND

Both this poem and the following were writ-
ten after Browning's visit to Italy in 1844. As
originally published they were entitled *Italy
in England* and *England in Italy*. The dra-
matic incident in the former poem was not a
rescript of a particular historic incident.

THAT second time they hunted me
From hill to plain, from shore to sea,
And Austria, hounding far and wide
Her blood-hounds through the country-side,
Breathed hot and instant on my trace, —
I made six days a hiding-place
Of that dry green old aqueduct
Where I and Charles, when boys, have plucked
The fire-flies from the roof above,
Bright creeping through the moss they love:
— How long it seems since Charles was lost!
Six days the soldiers crossed and crossed
The country in my very sight;
And when that peril ceased at night,
The sky broke out in red dismay
With signal fires; well, there I lay
Close covered o'er in my recess,
Up to the neck in ferns and cress,
Thinking on Metternich our friend,
And Charles's miserable end,
And much beside, two days; the third,

Hunger o'ercame me when I heard
The peasants from the village go
To work among the maize ; you know,
With us in Lombardy, they bring
Provisions packed on mules, a string
With little bells that cheer their task,
And casks, and boughs on every cask
To keep the sun's heat from the wine ;
These I let pass in jingling line,
And, close on them, dear noisy crew,
The peasants from the village, too ;
For at the very rear would troop
Their wives and sisters in a group
To help, I knew. When these had passed,
I threw my glove to strike the last,
Taking the chance : she did not start,
Much less cry out, but stooped apart,
One instant rapidly glanced round,
And saw me beckon from the ground ;
A wild bush grows and hides my crypt ;
She picked my glove up while she stripped
A branch off, then rejoined the rest
With that ; my glove lay in her breast.
Then I drew breath : they disappeared :
It was for Italy I feared.

An hour, and she returned alone
Exactly where my glove was thrown.
Meanwhile came many thoughts ; on me
Rested the hopes of Italy ;
I had devised a certain tale
Which, when 't was told her, could not fail
Persuade a peasant of its truth ;
I meant to call a freak of youth
This hiding, and give hopes of pay,
And no temptation to betray.
But when I saw that woman's face,
Its calm simplicity of grace,
Our Italy's own attitude
In which she walked thus far, and stood,
Planting each naked foot so firm,
To crush the snake and spare the worm —
At first sight of her eyes, I said,
" I am that man upon whose head
They fix the price, because I hate
The Austrians over us : the State
Will give you gold — oh, gold so much ! —
If you betray me to their clutch,
And be your death, for aught I know,
If once they find you saved their foe.
Now, you must bring me food and drink,
And also paper, pen and ink,
And carry safe what I shall write
To Padua, which you 'll reach at night
Before the duomo shuts ; go in,
And wait till Tenebræ begin ;
Walk to the third confessional,
Between the pillar and the wall,
And kneeling whisper, *Whence comes peace ?*
Say it a second time, then cease ;
And if the voice inside returns,
From Christ and Freedom ; what concerns
The cause of Peace ? — for answer, slip
My letter where you placed your lip ;
Then come back happy we have done
Our mother service — I, the son,
As you the daughter of our land ! "

Three mornings more, she took her stand
In the same place, with the same eyes :
I was no surer of sunrise
Than of her coming. We conferred
Of her own prospects, and I heard
She had a lover — stout and tall,
She said — then let her eyelids fall,
" He could do much " — as if some doubt
Entered her heart, — then, passing out,
" She could not speak for others, who
Had other thoughts ; herself she knew : "
And so she brought me drink and food.
After four days, the scouts pursued
Another path ; at last arrived
The help my Paduan friends contrived
To furnish me : she brought the news.
For the first time I could not choose
But kiss her hand, and lay my own
Upon her head — " This faith was shown
To Italy, our mother ; she
Uses my hand and blesses thee."
She followed down to the sea-shore ;
I left and never saw her more.

How very long since I have thought
Concerning — much less wished for — aught
Beside the good of Italy,
For which I live and mean to die !
I never was in love ; and since
Charles proved false, what shall now convince
My inmost heart I have a friend ?
However, if I pleased to spend
Real wishes on myself — say, three —
I know at least what one should be.
I would grasp Metternich until
I felt his red wet throat distil
In blood through these two hands. And next
— Nor much for that am I perplexed —
Charles, perjured traitor, for his part,
Should die slow of a broken heart
Under his new employers. Last
— Ah, there, what should I wish ? For fast
Do I grow old and out of strength.
If I resolved to seek at length
My father's house again, how scared
They all would look, and unprepared !
My brothers live in Austria's pay
— Disowned me long ago, men say ;
And all my early mates who used
To praise me so — perhaps induced
More than one early step of mine —
Are turning wise : while some opine
" Freedom grows license," some suspect
" Haste breeds delay," and recollect
They always said, such premature
Beginnings never could endure !
So, with a sullen " All 's for best,"
The land seems settling to its rest.
I think then, I should wish to stand
This evening in that dear, lost land,
Over the sea the thousand miles,
And know if yet that woman smiles
With the calm smile ; some little farm
She lives in there, no doubt : what harm
If I sat on the door-side bench,
And, while her spindle made a trench
Fantastically in the dust,
Inquired of all her fortunes — just

Her children's ages and their names,
And what may be the husband's aims
For each of them.   I 'd talk this out,
And sit there, for an hour about,
Then kiss her hand once more, and lay
Mine on her head, and go my way.

So much for idle wishing — how
It steals the time !   To business now.

THE ENGLISHMAN IN ITALY

PIANO DI SORRENTO

FORTÙ, Fortù, my beloved one,
Sit here by my side,
On my knees put up both little feet !
I was sure, if I tried,
I could make you laugh spite of Scirocco.
Now, open your eyes,
Let me keep you amused till he vanish
In black from the skies,
With telling my memories over
As you tell your beads ;
All the Plain saw me gather, I garland
— The flowers or the weeds.
Time for rain ! for your long hot dry Autumn
Had net-worked with brown
The white skin of each grape on the bunches,
Marked like a quail's crown,
Those creatures you make such account of,
Whose heads, — speckled white
Over brown like a great spider's back,
As I told you last night, —
Your mother bites off for her supper.
Red-ripe as could be,
Pomegranates were chapping and splitting
In halves on the tree :
And betwixt the loose walls of great flintstone,
Or in the thick dust
On the path, or straight out of the rock-side,
Wherever could thrust
Some burnt sprig of bold hardy rock-flower
Its yellow face up,
For the prize were great butterflies fighting,
Some five for one cup.
So, I guessed, ere I got up this morning,
What change was in store,
By the quick rustle-down of the quail-nets
Which woke me before
I could open my shutter, made fast
With a bough and a stone,
And look through the twisted dead vine-twigs,
Sole lattice that 's known.
Quick and sharp rang the rings down the net-
poles,
While, busy beneath,
Your priest and his brother tugged at them,
The rain in their teeth.
And out upon all the flat house-roofs
Where split figs lay drying,
The girls took the frails under cover :
Nor use seemed in trying
To get out the boats and go fishing,
For, under the cliff,
Fierce the black water frothed o'er the blind-
rock,
No seeing our skiff

Arrive about noon from Amalfi,
— Our fisher arrive,
And pitch down his basket before us,
All trembling alive
With pink and gray jellies, your sea-fruit ;
You touch the strange lumps,
And mouths gape there, eyes open, all manner
Of horns and of humps,
Which only the fisher looks grave at,
While round him like imps
Cling screaming the children as naked
And brown as his shrimps ;
Himself too as bare to the middle
— You see round his neck
The string and its brass coin suspended,
That saves him from wreck.
But to-day not a boat reached Salerno,
So back, to a man,
Came our friends, with whose help in the vine
yards
Grape-harvest began.
In the vat, halfway up in our house-side,
Like blood the juice spins,
While your brother all bare-legged is dancing
Till breathless he grins
Dead-beaten in effort on effort
To keep the grapes under,
Since still when he seems all but master,
In pours the fresh plunder
From girls who keep coming and going
With basket on shoulder,
And eyes shut against the rain's driving ;
Your girls that are older, —
For under the hedges of aloe,
And where, on its bed
Of the orchard's black mould, the love-apple
Lies pulpy and red,
All the young ones are kneeling and filling
Their laps with the snails
Tempted out by this first rainy weather, —
Your best of regales,
As to-night will be proved to my sorrow,
When, supping in state,
We shall feast our grape-gleaners (two dozen,
Three over one plate)
With lasagne so tempting to swallow
In slippery ropes,
And gourds fried in great purple slices,
That color of popes.
Meantime, see the grape bunch they 've brought
you :
The rain-water slips
O'er the heavy blue bloom on each globe
Which the wasp to your lips
Still follows with fretful persistence :
Nay, taste, while awake,
This half of a curd-white smooth cheese-ball
That peels, flake by flake,
Like an onion, each smoother and whiter ;
Next, sip this weak wine
From the thin green glass flask, with its stop
per,
A leaf of the vine ;
And end with the prickly-pear's red flesh
That leaves through its juice
The stony black seeds on your pearl-teeth.
Scirocco is loose !
Hark, the quick, whistling pelt of the olives

Which, thick in one's track,
Tempt the stranger to pick up and bite them,
    Though not yet half black !
How the old twisted olive trunks shudder,
    The medlars let fall
Their hard fruit, and the brittle great fig-
        trees
    Snap off, figs and all,
For here comes the whole of the tempest !
    No refuge, but creep
Back again to my side and my shoulder,
    And listen or sleep.

Oh, how will your country show next week,
    When all the vine-boughs
Have been stripped of their foliage to pasture
    The mules and the cows ?
Last eve, I rode over the mountains ;
    Your brother, my guide,
Soon left me, to feast on the myrtles
    That offered, each side,
Their fruit-balls, black, glossy and luscious, —
    Or strip from the sorbs
A treasure, or, rosy and wondrous,
    Those hairy gold orbs !
But my mule picked his sure sober path out,
    Just stopping to neigh
When he recognized down in the valley
    His mates on their way
With the faggots and barrels of water ;
    And soon we emerged
From the plain, where the woods could scarce
        follow ;
    And still as we urged
Our way, the woods wondered, and left us,
    As up still we trudged,
Though the wild path grew wilder each instant,
    And place was e'en grudged
'Mid the rock-chasms and piles of loose stones
    Like the loose broken teeth
Of some monster which climbed there to die
    From the ocean beneath —
Place was grudged to the silver-gray fume-weed
    That clung to the path,
And dark rosemary ever a-dying
    That, 'spite the wind's wrath,
So loves the salt rock's face to seaward,
    And lentisks as stanch
To the stone where they root and bear berries,
    And . . . what shows a branch
Coral-colored, transparent, with circlets
    Of pale seagreen leaves ;
Over all trod my mule with the caution
    Of gleaners o'er sheaves,
Still, foot after foot like a lady,
    Till, round after round,
He climbed to the top of Calvano,
    And God's own profound
Was above me, and round me the mountains,
    And under, the sea,
And within me my heart to bear witness
    What was and shall be.
Oh, heaven and the terrible crystal !
    No rampart excludes
Your eye from the life to be lived
    In the blue solitudes.
Oh, those mountains, their infinite movement !
    Still moving with you ;

For, ever some new head and breast of them
    Thrusts into view
To observe the intruder ; you see it
    If quickly you turn
And, before they escape you, surprise them.
    They grudge you should learn
How the soft plains they look on, lean over
    And love (they pretend)
— Cower beneath them, the flat sea-pine
        crouches,
    The wild fruit-trees bend,
E'en the myrtle-leaves curl, shrink and shut :
    All is silent and grave :
'T is a sensual and timorous beauty,
    How fair ! but a slave.
So, I turned to the sea ; and there slumbered
    As greenly as ever
Those isles of the siren, your Galli ;
    No ages can sever
The Three, nor enable their sister
    To join them, — halfway
On the voyage, she looked at Ulysses —
    No farther to-day,
Though the small one, just launched in the wave
    Watches breast-high and steady
From under the rock, her bold sister
    Swum halfway already.
Forth, shall we sail there together
    And see from the sides
Quite new rocks show their faces, new haunts
    Where the siren abides ?
Shall we sail round and round them, close over
    The rocks, though unseen,
That ruffle the gray glassy water
    To glorious green ?
Then scramble from splinter to splinter,
    Reach land and explore,
On the largest, the strange square black turret
    With never a door,
Just a loop to admit the quick lizards ;
    Then, stand there and hear
The birds' quiet singing, that tells us
    What life is, so clear ?
— The secret they sang to Ulysses
    When, ages ago,
He heard and he knew this life's secret
    I hear and I know.

Ah, see ! The sun breaks o'er Calvano ;
    He strikes the great gloom
And flutters it o'er the mount's summit
    In airy gold fume.
All is over. Look out, see the gypsy,
    Our tinker and smith,
Has arrived, set up bellows and forge,
    And down-squatted forthwith
To his hammering, under the wall there ;
    One eye keeps aloof
The urchins that itch to be putting
    His jews'-harps to proof,
While the other, through locks of curled wire
    Is watching how sleek
Shines the hog, come to share in the windfall
    — Chew abbot's own cheek !
All is over. Wake up and come out now
    And down let us go,
And see the fine things got in order
    At church for the show

Of the Sacrament, set forth this evening ;
  To-morrow 's the Feast
Of the Rosary's Virgin, by no means
  Of Virgins the least,
As you 'll hear in the off-hand discourse
  Which (all nature, no art)
The Dominican brother, these three weeks,
  Was getting by heart.
Not a pillar nor post but is dizened
  With red and blue papers ;
All the roof waves with ribbons, each altar
  Ablaze with long tapers ;
But the great masterpiece is the scaffold
  Rigged glorious to hold
All the fiddlers and fifers and drummers
  And trumpeters bold,
Not afraid of Bellini nor Auber,
  Who, when the priest 's hoarse,
Will strike us up something that 's brisk
  For the feast's second course.
And then will the flaxen-wigged Image
  Be carried in pomp
Through the plain, while in gallant proces-
  sion
  The priests mean to stomp.
All round the glad church lie old bottles
  With gunpowder stopped,
Which will be, when the Image re-enters,
  Religiously popped ;
And at night from the crest of Calvano
  Great bonfires will hang,
On the plain will the trumpets join chorus,
  And more poppers bang.
At all events, come — to the garden
  As far as the wall ;
See me tap with a hoe on the plaster
  Till out there shall fall
A scorpion with wide angry nippers !

— "Such trifles !" you say ?
Fortù, in my England at home,
  Men meet gravely to-day
And debate, if abolishing Corn-laws
  Be righteous and wise
— If 't were proper, Scirocco should vanish
  In black from the skies !

IN A GONDOLA

In a letter to Miss Haworth, Browning writes,
"I am getting to love painting as I did once.
. . . I chanced to call on Forster the other day,
and he pressed me into committing verse on the
instant, not the minute, in Maclise's behalf, who
has wrought a divine Venetian work, it seems,
for the British Institution. Forster described
it well — but I could do nothing better than
this wooden ware — (all the ' properties,' as
we say, were given and the problem was how
to catalogue them in rhyme and unreason.)"
Thereupon followed the first stanza of the
following poem ; but after seeing the picture he
was moved to go on and carry the poem through
to a real end.

He sings.

I SEND my heart up to thee, all my heart
  In this my singing.
For the stars help me, and the sea bears part;
  The very night is clinging
Closer to Venice' streets to leave one space
  Above me, whence thy face
May light my joyous heart to thee its dwelling
  place.

She speaks.

Say after me, and try to say
My very words, as if each word
Came from you of your own accord,
In your own voice, in your own way :
"This woman's heart and soul and brain
Are mine as much as this gold chain
She bids me wear ; which " (say again)
" I choose to make by cherishing
A precious thing, or choose to fling
Over the boat-side, ring by ring."
And yet once more say . . . no word more
Since words are only words. Give o'er !

Unless you call me, all the same,
Familiarly by my pet name,
Which if the Three should hear you call.
And me reply to, would proclaim
At once our secret to them all.
Ask of me, too, command me, blame —
Do, break down the partition-wall
'Twixt us, the daylight world beholds
Curtained in dusk and splendid folds !
What 's left but — all of me to take ?
I am the Three's : prevent them, slake
Your thirst ! 'T is said, the Arab sage.
In practising with gems, can loose
Their subtle spirit in his cruce
And leave but ashes : so, sweet mage,
Leave them my ashes when thy use
Sucks out my soul, thy heritage !

He sings.

Past we glide, and past, and past !
  What 's that poor Agnese doing
Where they make the shutters fast ?
  Gray Zanobi 's just a-wooing
To his couch the purchased bride :
  Past we glide !

Past we glide, and past, and past !
  Why 's the Pucci Palace flaring
Like a beacon to the blast ?
  Guests by hundreds, not one caring
If the dear host's neck were wried :
  Past we glide !

She sings.

The moth's kiss, first !
Kiss me as if you made believe
You were not sure, this eve,
How my face, your flower, had pursed
Its petals up ; so, here and there
You brush it, till I grow aware
Who wants me, and wide ope I burst.

The bee's kiss, now !
Kiss me as if you entered gay

My heart at some noonday,
A bud that dares not disallow
The claim, so all is rendered up,
And passively its shattered cup
Over your head to sleep I bow.

He sings.

What are we two?
I am a Jew,
And carry thee, farther than friends can pursue,
To a feast of our tribe;
Where they need thee to bribe
The devil that blasts them unless he imbibe
Thy . . . Scatter the vision forever! And now,
As of old, I am I, thou art thou!

Say again, what we are?
The sprite of a star,
I lure thee above where the destinies bar
My plumes their full play
Till a ruddier ray
Than my pale one announce there is withering away
Some . . . Scatter the vision forever! And now,
As of old, I am I, thou art thou!

He muses.

Oh, which were best, to roam or rest?
The land's lap or the water's breast?
To sleep on yellow millet-sheaves,
Or swim in lucid shallows just
Eluding water-lily leaves,
An inch from Death's black fingers, thrust
To lock you, whom release he must;
Which life were best on Summer eves?

He speaks, musing.

Lie back; could thought of mine improve you?
From this shoulder let there spring
A wing; from this, another wing;
Wings, not legs and feet, shall move you!
Snow-white must they spring, to blend
With your flesh, but I intend
They shall deepen to the end,
Broader, into burning gold,
Till both wings crescent-wise enfold
Your perfect self, from 'neath your feet
To o'er your head, where, lo, they meet
As if a million sword-blades hurled
Defiance from you to the world!

Rescue me thou, the only real!
And scare away this mad ideal
That came, nor motions to depart!
Thanks! Now, stay ever as thou art!

Still he muses.

What if the Three should catch at last
Thy serenader? While there 's cast
Paul's cloak about my head, and fast
Gian pinions me, Himself has past
His stylet through my back; I reel;
And . . . is it thou I feel?

They trail me, these three godless knaves,
Past every church that saints and saves,

Nor stop till, where the cold sea raves
By Lido's wet accursed graves,
They scoop mine, roll me to its brink,
And . . . on thy breast I sink!

She replies, musing.

Dip your arm o'er the boat-side, elbow-deep,
As I do: thus: were death so unlike sleep,
Caught this way? Death 's to fear from flame
or steel,
Or poison doubtless; but from water — feel!

Go find the bottom! Would you stay me?
There!
Now pluck a great blade of that ribbon-grass
To plait in where the foolish jewel was,
I flung away: since you have praised my hair,
'T is proper to be choice in what I wear.

He speaks.

Row home? must we row home? Too surely
Know I where its front 's demurely
Over the Giudecca piled;
Window just with window mating,
Door on door exactly waiting,
All 's the set face of a child:
But behind it, where 's a trace
Of the staidness and reserve,
And formal lines without a curve,
In the same child's playing-face?
No two windows look one way
O'er the small sea-water thread
Below them. Ah, the autumn day
I, passing, saw you overhead!
First, out a cloud of curtain blew,
Then a sweet cry, and last came you —
To catch your lory that must needs
Escape just then, of all times then,
To peck a tall plant's fleecy seeds,
And make me happiest of men.
I scarce could breathe to see you reach
So far back o'er the balcony
To catch him ere he climbed too high
Above you in the Smyrna peach,
That quick the round smooth cord of gold,
This coiled hair on your head, unrolled,
Fell down you like a gorgeous snake
The Roman girls were wont, of old,
When Rome there was, for coolness' sake
To let live curling o'er their bosoms.
Dear lory, may his beak retain
Ever its delicate rose stain
As if the wounded lotus-blossoms
Had marked their thief to know again!

Stay longer yet, for others' sake
Than mine! What should your chamber do?
— With all its rarities that ache
In silence while day lasts, but wake
At night-time and their life renew,
Suspended just to pleasure you
Who brought against their will together
These objects, and, while day lasts, weave
Around them such a magic tether
That dumb they look: your harp, believe.
With all the sensitive tight strings
Which dare not speak, now to itself
Breathes slumberously, as if some elf

Went in and out the chords, his wings
Make murmur wheresoe'er they graze,
As an angel may, between the maze
Of midnight palace-pillars, on
And on, to sow God's plagues, have gone
Through guilty glorious Babylon.
And while such murmurs flow, the nymph
Bends o'er the harp-top from her shell
As the dry limpet for the lymph
Come with a tune he knows so well.
And how your statues' hearts must swell !
And how your pictures must descend
To see each other, friend with friend !
Oh, could you take them by surprise,
You 'd find Schidone's eager Duke
Doing the quaintest courtesies
To that prim saint by Haste-thee-Luke !
And, deeper into her rock den,
Bold Castelfranco's Magdalen
You 'd find retreated from the ken
Of that robed counsel-keeping Ser —
As if the Tizian thinks of her,
And is not, rather, gravely bent
On seeing for himself what toys
Are these, his progeny invent,
What litter now the board employs
Whereon he signed a document
That got him murdered !   Each enjoys
Its night so well, you cannot break
The sport up, so, indeed must make
More stay with me, for others' sake.

She speaks.

To-morrow, if a harp-string, say,
Is used to tie the jasmine back
That overfloods my room with sweets,
Contrive your Zorzi somehow meets
My Zanze ! If the ribbon 's black,
The Three are watching : keep away !

Your gondola — let Zorzi wreathe
A mesh of water-weeds about
Its prow, as if he unaware
Had struck some quay or bridge-foot stair !
That I may throw a paper out
As you and he go underneath.

There 's Zanze 's vigilant taper ; safe are we.
Only one minute more to-night with me ?
Resume your past self of a month ago !
Be you the bashful gallant, I will be
The lady with the colder breast than snow.
Now bow you, as becomes, nor touch my hand
More than I touch yours when I step to land,
And say, " All thanks, Siora ! " —
                          Heart to heart
And lips to lips ! Yet once more, ere we part,
Clasp me and make me thine, as mine thou art !
He is surprised, and stabbed.
It was ordained to be so, sweet ! — and best
Comes now, beneath thine eyes, upon thy
       breast.
Still kiss me ! Care not for the cowards ! Care
Only to put aside thy beauteous hair
My blood will hurt ! The Three, I do not scorn
To death, because they never lived : but I
Have lived indeed, and so — (yet one more
       kiss) — can die !

WARING

An account of Alfred Domett, Browning's
early friend, who was the occasion of this poem
will be found in the notes.

I

I

WHAT 's become of Waring
Since he gave us all the slip,
Chose land-travel or seafaring,
Boots and chest or staff and scrip,
Rather than pace up and down
Any longer London town ?

II

Who 'd have guessed it from his lip
Or his brow's accustomed bearing,
On the night he thus took ship
Or started landward ? — little caring
For us, it seems, who supped together
(Friends of his too, I remember)
And walked home through the merry weather,
The snowiest in all December.
I left his arm that night myself
For what 's-his-name's, the new prose-poet
Who wrote the book there, on the shelf —
How, forsooth, was I to know it
If Waring meant to glide away
Like a ghost at break of day ?
Never looked he half so gay !

III

He was prouder than the devil :
How he must have cursed our revel !
Ay and many other meetings,
Indoor visits, outdoor greetings,
As up and down he paced this London,
With no work done, but great works undone,
Where scarce twenty knew his name.
Why not, then, have earlier spoken,
Written, bustled ? Who 's to blame
If your silence kept unbroken ?
" True, but there were sundry jottings,
Stray-leaves, fragments, blurs and blottings,
Certain first steps were achieved
Already which " — (is that your meaning ?)
" Had well borne out whoe'er believed
In more to come ! " But who goes gleaning
Hedgeside chance-blades, while full-sheaved
Stand cornfields by him ? Pride, o'erweening
Pride alone, puts forth such claims
O'er the day's distinguished names.

IV

Meantime, how much I loved him,
I find out now I 've lost him.
I who cared not if I moved him,
Who could so carelessly accost him,
Henceforth never shall get free
Of his ghostly company.
His eyes that just a little wink
As deep I go into the merit
Of this and that distinguished spirit —
His cheeks' raised color, soon to sink,

As long I dwell on some stupendous
And tremendous (Heaven defend us !)
Monstr'-inform'-ingens-horrend-ous
Demoniaco-seraphic
Penman's latest piece of graphic.
Nay, my very wrist grows warm
With his dragging weight of arm.
E'en so, swimmingly appears,
Through one's after-supper musings,
Some lost lady of old years
With her beauteous vain endeavor
And goodness unrepaid as ever ;
The face, accustomed to refusings,
We, puppies that we were . . . Oh never
Surely, nice of conscience, scrupled
Being aught like false, forsooth, to ?
Telling aught but honest truth to ?
What a sin, had we centupled
Its possessor's grace and sweetness !
No ! she heard in its completeness
Truth, for truth 's a weighty matter,
And truth, at issue, we can't flatter !
Well, 't is done with ; she 's exempt
From damning us through such a sally ;
And so she glides, as down a valley,
Taking up with her contempt,
Past our reach ; and in, the flowers
Shut her unregarded hours.

V

Oh, could I have him back once more,
This Waring, but one half-day more !
Back, with the quiet face of yore,
So hungry for acknowledgment
Like mine ! I 'd fool him to his bent.
Feed, should not he, to heart's content ?
I 'd say, " to only have conceived,
Planned your great works, apart from progress,
Surpasses little works achieved ! "
I 'd lie so, I should be believed.
I 'd make such havoc of the claims
Of the day's distinguished names
To feast him with, as feasts an ogress
Her feverish sharp-toothed gold-crowned child !
Or as one feasts a creature rarely
Captured here, unreconciled
To capture ; and completely gives
Its pettish humors license, barely
Requiring that it lives.

VI

Ichabod, Ichabod,
The glory is departed !
Travels Waring East away ?
Who, of knowledge, by hearsay,
Reports a man upstarted
Somewhere as a god,
Hordes grown European-hearted,
Millions of the wild made tame
On a sudden at his fame ?
In Vishnu-land what Avatar ?
Or who in Moscow, toward the Czar,
With the demurest of footfalls
Over the Kremlin's pavement bright
With serpentine and syenite,
Steps, with five other Generals
That simultaneously take snuff,
For each to have pretext enough

And kerchiefwise unfold his sash
Which, softness' self, is yet the stuff
To hold fast where a steel chain snaps,
And leave the grand white neck no gash ?
Waring in Moscow, to those rough
Cold northern natures born perhaps,
Like the lambwhite maiden dear
From the circle of mute kings
Unable to repress the tear,
Each as his sceptre down he flings,
To Dian's fane at Taurica,
Where now a captive priestess, she alway
Mingles her tender grave Hellenic speech
With theirs, tuned to the hailstone-beaten beach
As pours some pigeon, from the myrrhy lands
Rapt by the whirlblast to fierce Scythian
     strands
Where breed the swallows, her melodious cry
Amid their barbarous twitter !
In Russia ? Never ! Spain were fitter !
Ay, most likely 't is in Spain
That we and Waring meet again
Now, while he turns down that cool narrow lane
Into the blackness, out of grave Madrid
All fire and shine, abrupt as when there 's slid
Its stiff gold blazing pall
From some black coffin-lid.
Or, best of all,
I love to think
The leaving us was just a feint ;
Back here to London did he slink,
And now works on without a wink
Of sleep, and we are on the brink
Of something great in fresco-paint :
Some garret's ceiling, walls and floor,
Up and down and o'er and o'er
He splashes, as none splashed before
Since great Caldara Polidore.
Or Music means this land of ours
Some favor yet, to pity won
By Purcell from his Rosy Bowers, —
" Give me my so-long promised son,
Let Waring end what I begun ! "
Then down he creeps and out he steals
Only when the night conceals
His face ; in Kent 't is cherry-time,
Or hops are picking : or at prime
Of March he wanders as, too happy,
Years ago when he was young,
Some mild eve when woods grew sappy
And the early moths had sprung
To life from many a trembling sheath
Woven the warm boughs beneath ;
While small birds said to themselves
What should soon be actual song,
And young gnats, by tens and twelves,
Made as if they were the throng
That crowd around and carry aloft
The sound they have nursed, so sweet and pure,
Out of a myriad noises soft,
Into a tone that can endure
Amid the noise of a July noon
When all God's creatures crave their boon,
All at once and all in tune,
And get it, happy as Waring then,
Having first within his ken
What a man might do with men :
And far too glad, in the even-glow.

To mix with the world he meant to take
Into his hand, he told you, so —
And out of it his world to make,
To contract and to expand
As he shut or oped his hand.
O Waring, what 's to really be?
A clear stage and a crowd to see!
Some Garrick, say, out shall not he
The heart of Hamlet's mystery pluck?
Or, where most unclean beasts are rife,
Some Junius — am I right? — shall tuck
His sleeve, and forth with flaying-knife!
Some Chatterton shall have the luck
Of calling Rowley into life!
Some one shall somehow run a-muck
With this old world for want of strife
Sound asleep.   Contrive, contrive
To rouse us, Waring! Who 's alive?
Our men scarce seem in earnest now.
Distinguished names! — but 't is, somehow,
As if they played at being names
Still more distinguished, like the games
Of children.   Turn our sport to earnest
With a visage of the sternest!
Bring the real times back, confessed
Still better than our very best!

II

I

" When I last saw Waring . . . "
(How all turned to him who spoke!
You saw Waring? Truth or joke?
In land-travel or sea-faring?)

II

" We were sailing by Triest
Where a day or two we harbored :
A sunset was in the West,
When, looking over the vessel's side,
One of our company espied
A sudden speck to larboard.
And as a sea-duck flies and swims
At once, so came the light craft up,
With its sole lateen sail that trims
And turns (the water round its rims
Dancing, as round a sinking cup)
And by us like a fish it curled,
And drew itself up close beside,
Its great sail on the instant furled,
And o'er its thwarts a shrill voice cried,
(A neck as bronzed as a Lascar's)
' Buy wine of us, you English brig?
Or fruit, tobacco and cigars?
A pilot for you to Triest?
Without one, look you ne'er so big,
They 'll never let you up the bay!
We natives should know best.'
I turned, and ' just those fellows' way,'
Our captain said, ' The 'long-shore thieves
Are laughing at us in their sleeves.'

III

" In truth, the boy leaned laughing back;
And one, half-hidden by his side
Under the furled sail, soon I spied,
With great grass hat and kerchief black,

Who looked up with his kingly throat
Said somewhat, while the other shook
His hair back from his eyes to look
Their longest at us; then the boat,
I know not how, turned sharply round,
Laying her whole side on the sea
As a leaping fish does; from the lee
Into the weather, cut somehow
Her sparkling path beneath our bow
And so went off, as with a bound,
Into the rosy and golden half
O' the sky, to overtake the sun
And reach the shore, like the sea-calf
Its singing cave; yet I caught one
Glance ere away the boat quite passed,
And neither time nor toil could mar
Those features : so I saw the last
Of Waring!" — You? Oh, never star
Was lost here but it rose afar!
Look East, where whole new thousands are!
In Vishnu-land what Avatar?

THE TWINS

" Give " and " It-shall-be-given-unto-you "

Originally published in 1854, in connection
with a poem by Mrs. Browning, *A Plea for the
Ragged Schools of London*, in a volume issued
for a bazaar to benefit the " Refuge for Young
Destitute Girls."

GRAND rough old Martin Luther
    Bloomed fables — flowers on furze,
The better the uncouther :
    Do roses stick like burrs?

A beggar asked an alms
    One day at an abbey-door,
Said Luther; but, seized with qualms,
    The Abbot replied, " We 're poor!

" Poor, who had plenty once,
    When gifts fell thick as rain :
But they give us naught, for the nonce,
    And how should we give again? "

Then the beggar, " See your sins!
    Of old, unless I err,
Ye had brothers for inmates, twins,
    Date and Dabitur.

" While Date was in good case
    Dabitur flourished too :
For Dabitur's lenten face
    No wonder if Date rue.

" Would ye retrieve the one?
    Try and make plump the other!
When Date's penance is done,
    Dabitur helps his brother.

" Only, beware relapse! "
    The Abbot hung his head.
This beggar might be perhaps
    An angel, Luther said.

A LIGHT WOMAN

So far as our story approaches the end,
  Which do you pity the most of us three? —
My friend, or the mistress of my friend
  With her wanton eyes, or me?

My friend was already too good to lose,
  And seemed in the way of improvement
    yet,
When she crossed his path with her hunting-
    noose,
  And over him drew her net.

When I saw him tangled in her toils,
  A shame, said I, if she adds just him
To her nine-and-ninety other spoils,
  The hundredth for a whim!

And before my friend be wholly hers,
  How easy to prove to him, I said,
An eagle's the game her pride prefers,
  Though she snaps at a wren instead!

So, I gave her eyes my own eyes to take,
  My hand sought hers as in earnest need,
And round she turned for my noble sake,
  And gave me herself indeed.

The eagle am I, with my fame in the world,
  The wren is he, with his maiden face.
— You look away and your lip is curled?
  Patience, a moment's space!

For see, my friend goes shaking and white;
  He eyes me as the basilisk:
I have turned, it appears, his day to night,
  Eclipsing his sun's disk.

And I did it, he thinks, as a very thief:
  " Though I love her — that, he compre-
    hends —
One should master one's passions, (love, in chief)
  And be loyal to one's friends!"

And she, — she lies in my hand as tame
  As a pear late basking over a wall;
Just a touch to try and off it came;
  'T is mine, — can I let it fall?

With no mind to eat it, that's the worst!
  Were it thrown in the road, would the case
    assist?
'T was quenching a dozen blue-flies' thirst
  When I gave its stalk a twist.

And I, — what I seem to my friend, you see:
  What I soon shall seem to his love, you
    guess:
What I seem to myself, do you ask of me?
  No hero, I confess.

'T is an awkward thing to play with souls,
  And matter enough to save one's own:
Yet think of my friend, and the burning coals
  He played with for bits of stone!

One likes to show the truth for the truth;
  That the woman was light is very true:
But suppose she says, — Never mind that
    youth!
  What wrong have I done to you?

Well, anyhow, here the story stays,
  So far at least as I understand;
And, Robert Browning, you writer of plays,
  Here's a subject made to your hand!

THE LAST RIDE TOGETHER

I SAID — Then, dearest, since 't is so,
Since now at length my fate I know,
Since nothing all my love avails,
Since all, my life seemed meant for, fails,
  Since this was written and needs must be —
My whole heart rises up to bless
Your name in pride and thankfulness!
Take back the hope you gave, — I claim
Only a memory of the same,
  — And this beside, if you will not blame,
  Your leave for one more last ride with me.

My mistress bent that brow of hers;
Those deep dark eyes where pride demurs
When pity would be softening through,
Fixed me a breathing-while or two
  With life or death in the balance: right!
The blood replenished me again;
My last thought was at least not vain:
I and my mistress, side by side
Shall be together, breathe and ride,
So, one day more am I deified.
  Who knows but the world may end to-night!

Hush! if you saw some western cloud
All billowy-bosomed, over-bowed
By many benedictions — sun's
And moon's and evening-star's at once —
  And so, you, looking and loving best,
Conscious grew, your passion drew
Cloud, sunset, moonrise, star-shine too,
Down on you, near and yet more near,
Till flesh must fade for heaven was here! —
Thus leant she and lingered — joy and fear!
  Thus lay she a moment on my breast.

Then we began to ride. My soul
Smoothed itself out, a long-cramped scroll
Freshening and fluttering in the wind.
Past hopes already lay behind.
  What need to strive with a life awry?
Had I said that, had I done this,
So might I gain, so might I miss.
Might she have loved me? just as well
She might have hated, who can tell!
Where had I been now if the worst befell'
  And here we are riding, she and I.

Fail I alone, in words and deeds?
Why, all men strive, and who succeeds?
We rode; it seemed my spirit flew,
Saw other regions, cities new,
  As the world rushed by on either side.

I thought, — All labor, yet no less
Bear up beneath their unsuccess.
Look at the end of work, contrast
The petty done, the undone vast,
    This present of theirs with the hopeful past !
    I hoped she would love me ; here we ride.

What hand and brain went ever paired ?
What heart alike conceived and dared ?
What act proved all its thought had been ?
What will but felt the fleshly screen ?
    We ride and I see her bosom heave.
There 's many a crown for who can reach.
Ten lines, a statesman's life in each !
The flag stuck on a heap of bones,
A soldier's doing ! what atones ?
    They scratch his name on the Abbey-stones.
    My riding is better, by their leave.

What does it all mean, poet ? Well,
Your brains beat into rhythm, you tell
What we felt only ; you expressed
You hold things beautiful the best,
    And place them in rhyme so, side by side.
'T is something, nay 't is much : but then,
Have you yourself what 's best for men ?
Are you — poor, sick, old ere your time —
Nearer one whit your own sublime
    Than we who never have turned a rhyme ?
    Sing, riding 's a joy ! For me, I ride.

And you, great sculptor — so, you gave
A score of years to Art, her slave,
And that 's your Venus, whence we turn
To yonder girl that fords the burn !
    You acquiesce, and shall I repine ?
What, man of music, you grown gray
With notes and nothing else to say,
Is this your sole praise from a friend,
" Greatly his opera's strains intend,
    But in music we know how fashions end ! "
    I gave my youth ; but we ride, in fine.

Who knows what 's fit for us ? Had fate
Proposed bliss here should sublimate
My being — had I signed the bond —
Still one must lead some life beyond,
    Have a bliss to die with, dim-descried.
This foot once planted on the goal,
This glory-garland round my soul,
Could I descry such ? Try and test !
I sink back shuddering from the quest.
    Earth being so good, would heaven seem best ?
    Now, heaven and she are beyond this ride.

And yet — she has not spoke so long !
What if heaven be that, fair and strong
At life's best, with our eyes upturned
Whither life's flower is first discerned,
    We, fixed so, ever should so abide ?
What if we still ride on, we two,
With life forever old yet new,
Changed not in kind but in degree,
The instant made eternity, —
    And heaven just prove that I and she
    Ride, ride together, forever ride ?

THE PIED PIPER OF HAMELIN

A CHILD'S STORY

(*Written for, and inscribed to, W. M. the Younger*)

Macready's eldest son when a child was con-
fined to the house by illness, and Browning
wrote this *jeu d'esprit* to amuse the child and
give him a subject for illustrative drawings.

I

HAMELIN Town 's in Brunswick,
By famous Hanover city ;
    The river Weser, deep and wide,
    Washes its wall on the southern side ;
    A pleasanter spot you never spied ;
But, when begins my ditty,
    Almost five hundred years ago,
    To see the townsfolk suffer so
      From vermin, was a pity.

II

Rats !
They fought the dogs and killed the cats,
    And bit the babies in the cradles,
And ate the cheeses out of the vats,
    And licked the soup from the cooks' own
      ladles,
Split open the kegs of salted sprats,
Made nests inside men's Sunday hats,
And even spoiled the women's chats
    By drowning their speaking
    With shrieking and squeaking
In fifty different sharps and flats.

III

At last the people in a body
    To the Town Hall came flocking :
" 'T is clear," cried they, " our Mayor 's a
      noddy ;
And as for our Corporation — shocking
To think we buy gowns lined with ermine
For dolts that can't or won't determine
What 's best to rid us of our vermin !
You hope, because you 're old and obese,
To find in the furry civic robe ease ?
Rouse up, sirs ! Give your brains a racking
To find the remedy we 're lacking,
Or, sure as fate, we 'll send you packing ! "
At this the Mayor and Corporation
Quaked with a mighty consternation.

IV

An hour they sat in council ;
    At length the Mayor broke silence :
" For a guilder I 'd my ermine gown sell,
    I wish I were a mile hence !
It 's easy to bid one rack one's brain —
I 'm sure my poor head aches again,
I 've scratched it so, and all in vain.
Oh for a trap, a trap, a trap ! "
Just as he said this, what should hap
At the chamber-door but a gentle tap ?
" Bless us," cried the Mayor, " what 's that ?
(With the Corporation as he sat,

Looking little though wondrous fat ;
Nor brighter was his eye, nor moister
Than a too-long-opened oyster,
Save when at noon his paunch grew mutinous
For a plate of turtle green and glutinous)
" Only a scraping of shoes on the mat ?
Anything like the sound of a rat
Makes my heart go pit-a-pat ! "

V

" Come in ! " — the Mayor cried, looking
        bigger :
And in did come the strangest figure !
His queer long coat from heel to head
Was half of yellow and half of red,
And he himself was tall and thin,
With sharp blue eyes, each like a pin,
And light loose hair, yet swarthy skin,
No tuft on cheek nor beard on chin,
But lips where smiles went out and in ;
There was no guessing his kith and kin :
And nobody could enough admire
The tall man and his quaint attire.
Quoth one : " It 's as my great-grandsire,
Starting up at the Trump of Doom's tone,
Had walked this way from his painted tomb-
        stone ! "

VI

He advanced to the council-table :
And, " Please your honors," said he, " I 'm
        able,
By means of a secret charm, to draw
All creatures living beneath the sun,
That creep or swim or fly or run,
After me so as you never saw !
And I chiefly use my charm
On creatures that do people harm,
The mole and toad and newt and viper ;
And people call me the Pied Piper."
(And here they noticed round his neck
A scarf of red and yellow stripe,
To match with his coat of the self-same cheque ;
And at the scarf's end hung a pipe ;
And his fingers, they noticed, were ever stray-
        ing
As if impatient to be playing
Upon this pipe, as low it dangled
Over his vesture so old-fangled.)
" Yet," said he, " poor piper as I am,
In Tartary I freed the Cham,
Last June, from his huge swarms of gnats ;
I eased in Asia the Nizam
Of a monstrous brood of vampire-bats :
And as for what your brain bewilders,
If I can rid your town of rats
Will you give me a thousand guilders ? "
" One ? fifty thousand ! " — was the exclama-
        tion
Of the astonished Mayor and Corporation.

VII

Into the street the Piper stept,
        Smiling first a little smile,
As if he knew what magic slept
        In his quiet pipe the while ;
Then, like a musical adept,
To blow the pipe his lips he wrinkled,

And green and blue his sharp eyes twinkled,
Like a candle-flame where salt is sprinkled ;
And ere three shrill notes the pipe uttered,
You heard as if an army muttered ;
And the muttering grew to a grumbling ;
And the grumbling grew to a mighty rumbling ;
And out of the houses the rats came tumbling.
Great rats, small rats, lean rats, brawny rats,
Brown rats, black rats, gray rats, tawny rats,
Grave old plodders, gay young friskers,
        Fathers, mothers, uncles, cousins,
Cocking tails and pricking whiskers,
        Families by tens and dozens,
Brothers, sisters, husbands, wives —
Followed the Piper for their lives.
From street to street he piped advancing,
And step for step they followed dancing,
Until they came to the river Weser,
Wherein all plunged and perished !
— Save one who, stout as Julius Cæsar,
Swam across and lived to carry
(As he, the manuscript he cherished)
To Rat-land home his commentary :
Which was, " At the first shrill notes of the
        pipe,
I heard a sound as of scraping tripe,
And putting apples, wondrous ripe,
Into a cider-press's gripe :
And a moving away of pickle-tub-boards,
And a leaving ajar of conserve-cupboards,
And a drawing the corks of train-oil-flasks,
And a breaking the hoops of butter-casks :
And it seemed as if a voice
(Sweeter far than by harp or by psaltery
Is breathed) called out, ' Oh rats, rejoice !
The world is grown to one vast drysaltery !
So munch on, crunch on, take your nuncheon,
Breakfast, supper, dinner, luncheon ! '
And just as a bulky sugar-puncheon,
All ready staved, like a great sun shone
Glorious scarce an inch before me,
Just as methought it said, ' Come, bore me ! '
— I found the Weser rolling o'er me."

VIII

You should have heard the Hamelin people
Ringing the bells till they rocked the steeple.
" Go," cried the Mayor, " and get long poles,
Poke out the nests and block up the holes !
Consult with carpenters and builders,
And leave in our town not even a trace
Of the rats ! " — when suddenly, up the face
Of the Piper perked in the market-place,
With a, " First, if you please, my thousand
        guilders ! "

IX

A thousand guilders ! The Mayor looked blue ;
So did the Corporation too.
For council dinners made rare havoc
With Claret, Moselle, Vin-de-Grave, Hock :
And half the money would replenish
Their cellar's biggest butt with Rhenish.
To pay this sum to a wandering fellow
With a gypsy coat of red and yellow !
" Beside," quoth the Mayor with a knowing
        wink,
" Our business was done at the river's brink ;

We saw with our eyes the vermin sink,
And what 's dead can't come to life, I think.
So, friend, we 're not the folks to shrink
From the duty of giving you something for drink,
And a matter of money to put in your poke ;
But as for the guilders, what we spoke
Of them, as you very well know, was in joke.
Beside, our losses have made us thrifty.
A thousand guilders ! Come, take fifty ! ''

X

The Piper's face fell, and he cried,
" No trifling ! I can't wait, beside !
I 've promised to visit by dinner time
Bagdat, and accept the prime
Of the Head-Cook's pottage, all he 's rich in,
For having left, in the Caliph's kitchen,
Of a nest of scorpions no survivor :
With him I proved no bargain-driver,
With you, don't think I 'll bate a stiver !
And folks who put me in a passion
May find me pipe after another fashion.''

XI

" How ? '' cried the Mayor, " d' ye think I brook
Being worse treated than a Cook ?
Insulted by a lazy ribald
With idle pipe and vesture piebald ?
You threaten us, fellow ? Do your worst,
Blow your pipe there till you burst ! ''

XII

Once more he stept into the street,
   And to his lips again
Laid his long pipe of smooth straight cane ;
   And ere he blew three notes (such sweet
Soft notes as yet musician's cunning
   Never gave the enraptured air)
There was a rustling that seemed like a bustling
Of merry crowds justling at pitching and hustling ;
Small feet were pattering, wooden shoes clattering,
Little hands clapping and little tongues chattering,
And, like fowls in a farm-yard when barley is scattering,
Out came the children running.
All the little boys and girls,
With rosy cheeks and flaxen curls,
And sparkling eyes and teeth like pearls,
Tripping and skipping, ran merrily after
The wonderful music with shouting and laughter.

XIII

The Mayor was dumb, and the Council stood
As if they were changed into blocks of wood,
Unable to move a step, or cry
To the children merrily skipping by,
— Could only follow with the eye
That joyous crowd at the Piper's back.
But how the Mayor was on the rack,
And the wretched Council's bosoms beat,
As the Piper turned from the High Street
To where the Weser rolled its waters
Right in the way of their sons and daughters !
However, he turned from South to West,

And to Koppelberg Hill his steps addressed,
And after him the children pressed ;
Great was the joy in every breast.
" He never can cross that mighty top !
He 's forced to let the piping drop,
And we shall see our children stop ! ''
When, lo, as they reached the mountain-side,
A wondrous portal opened wide,
As if a cavern was suddenly hollowed ;
And the Piper advanced and the children followed,
And when all were in to the very last,
The door in the mountain-side shut fast.
Did I say, all ? No ! One was lame,
And could not dance the whole of the way ;
And in after years, if you would blame
His sadness, he was used to say, —
" It 's dull in our town since my playmates left :
I can't forget that I 'm bereft
Of all the pleasant sights they see,
Which the Piper also promised me.
For he led us, he said, to a joyous land,
Joining the town and just at hand,
Where waters gushed and fruit-trees grew
And flowers put forth a fairer hue,
And everything was strange and new ;
The sparrows were brighter than peacocks here,
And their dogs outran our fallow deer,
And honey-bees had lost their stings,
And horses were born with eagles' wings :
And just as I became assured
My lame foot would be speedily cured,
The music stopped and I stood still,
And found myself outside the hill,
Left alone against my will,
To go now limping as before,
And never hear of that country more ! ''

XIV

Alas, alas for Hamelin !
   There came into many a burgher's pate
   A text which says that heaven's gate
Opes to the rich at as easy rate
As the needle's eye takes a camel in !
The Mayor sent East, West, North and South
To offer the Piper, by word of mouth,
   Wherever it was men's lot to find him,
Silver and gold to his heart's content,
If he 'd only return the way he went,
   And bring the children behind him.
But when they saw 't was a lost endeavor,
And Piper and dancers were gone forever,
They made a decree that lawyers never
   Should think their records dated duly
If, after the day of the month and year,
These words did not as well appear,
" And so long after what happened here
   On the Twenty-second of July,
Thirteen hundred and seventy-six : ''
And the better in memory to fix
The place of the children's last retreat,
They called it, the Pied Piper's Street —
Where any one playing on pipe or tabor
Was sure for the future to lose his labor.
Nor suffered they hostelry or tavern
   To shock with mirth a street so solemn
But opposite the place of the cavern
   They wrote the story on a column.

And on the great church-window painted
The same, to make the world acquainted
How their children were stolen away,
And there it stands to this very day.
And I must not omit to say
That in Transylvania there 's a tribe
Of alien people who ascribe
The outlandish ways and dress
On which their neighbors lay such stress,
To their fathers and mothers having risen
Out of some subterraneous prison
Into which they were trepanned
Long time ago in a mighty band
Out of Hamelin town in Brunswick land,
But how or why, they don't understand.

                    XV

So, Willy, let me and you be wipers
Of scores out with all men — especially pipers !
And, whether they pipe us free fróm rats or
    fróm mice,
If we 've promised them aught, let us keep our
    promise !

THE FLIGHT OF THE DUCHESS

The first nine sections of this poem were
printed in *Hood's Magazine* for April, 1845.

The poem took its rise from a line — "Fol-
lowing the Queen of the Gypsies, O !" the bur-
den of a song which the poet, when a boy, heard
a woman singing on a Guy Fawkes' Day. As
Browning was writing it, he was interrupted by
the arrival of a friend on some important busi-
ness, which drove all thoughts of the Duchess,
and the scheme of her story, out of the poet's
head. But some months after the publication
of the first part, when he was staying at Bettis-
field Park, in Shropshire, a guest, speaking of
early winter, said, "The deer had already to
break the ice in the pond." On this a fancy
struck the poet, and, returning home, he worked
it up into the conclusion of the poem as it now
stands.

                    I

You 're my friend :
I was the man the Duke spoke to ;
I helped the Duchess to cast off his yoke, too ;
So, here 's the tale from beginning to end,
My friend !

                    II

Ours is a great wild country :
If you climb to our castle's top,
I don't see where your eye can stop ;
For when you 've passed the cornfield country,
Where vineyards leave off, flocks are packed,
And sheep-range leads to cattle-tract,
And cattle-tract to open-chase,
And open-chase to the very base
Of the mountain where, at a funeral pace,
Round about, solemn and slow,
One by one, row after row,

Up and up the pine-trees go,
So, like black priests up, and so
Down the other side again
To another greater, wilder country,
That 's one vast red drear burnt-up plain,
Branched through and through with many a
    vein
Whence iron 's dug, and copper 's dealt ;
Look right, look left, look straight before, —
Beneath they mine, above they smelt,
Copper-ore and iron-ore,
And forge and furnace mould and melt,
And so on, more and ever more,
Till at the last, for a bounding belt,
Comes the salt sand hoar of the great sea-shore
— And the whole is our Duke's country.

                    III

I was born the day this present Duke was —
(And O, says the song, ere I was old !)
In the castle where the other Duke was —
(When I was happy and young, not old !)
I in the kennel, he in the bower :
We are of like age to an hour.
My father was huntsman in that day ;
Who has not heard my father say
That, when a boar was brought to bay,
Three times, four times out of five,
With his huntspear he 'd contrive
To get the killing-place transfixed,
And pin him true, both eyes betwixt ?
And that 's why the old Duke would rather
He lost a salt-pit than my father,
And loved to have him ever in call ;
That 's why my father stood in the hall
When the old Duke brought his infant out
To show the people, and while they passed
The wondrous bantling round about,
Was first to start at the outside blast
As the Kaiser's courier blew his horn,
Just a month after the babe was born.
" And," quoth the Kaiser's courier, " since
The Duke has got an heir, our Prince
Needs the Duke's self at his side : "
The Duke looked down and seemed to wince,
But he thought of wars o'er the world wide,
Castles a-fire, men on their march,
The toppling tower, the crashing arch ;
And up he looked, and awhile he eyed
The row of crests and shields and banners
Of all achievements after all manners,
And " ay," said the Duke with a surly pride.
The more was his comfort when he died
At next year's end, in a velvet suit,
With a gilt glove on his hand, his foot
In a silken shoe for a leather boot,
Petticoated like a herald,
In a chamber next to an ante-room,
Where he breathed the breath of page and
    groom
What he called stink, and they, perfume :
— They should have set him on red Berold
Mad with pride, like fire to manage !
They should have got his cheek fresh tannage
Such a day as to-day in the merry sunshine !
Had they stuck on his fist a rough-foot merlin !
(Hark, the wind's on the heath at its game !
Oh for a noble falcon-lanner

To flap each broad wing like a banner,
And turn in the wind, and dance like flame !)
Had they broached a white-beer cask from
    Berlin
— Or if you incline to prescribe mere wine
Put to his lips, when they saw him pine,
A cup of our own Moldavia fine,
Cotnar for instance, green as May sorrel
And ropy with sweet, — we shall not quarrel.

IV

So, at home, the sick tall yellow Duchess
Was left with the infant in her clutches,
She being the daughter of God knows who :
And now was the time to revisit her tribe.
Abroad and afar they went, the two,
And let our people rail and gibe
At the empty hall and extinguished fire,
As loud as we liked, but ever in vain,
Till after long years we had our desire,
And back came the Duke and his mother again.

V

And he came back the pertest little ape
That ever affronted human shape ;
Full of his travel, struck at himself.
You 'd say, he despised our bluff old ways ?
— Not he ! For in Paris they told the elf
Our rough North land was the Land of Lays,
The one good thing left in evil days ;
Since the Mid-Age was the Heroic Time,
And only in wild nooks like ours
Could you taste of it yet as in its prime,
And see true castles, with proper towers,
Young-hearted women, old-minded men,
And manners now as manners were then.
So, all that the old Dukes had been, without
    knowing it,
This Duke would fain know he was, without
    being it ;
'T was not for the joy's self, but the joy of his
    showing it,
Nor for the pride's self, but the pride of our
    seeing it,
He revived all usages thoroughly worn-out,
The souls of them fumed-forth, the hearts of
    them torn-out :
And chief in the chase his neck he perilled,
On a lathy horse, all legs and length,
With blood for bone, all speed, no strength ;
— They should have set him on red Berold
With the red eye slow consuming in fire,
And the thin stiff ear like an abbey spire !

VI

Well, such as he was, he must marry, we heard :
And out of a convent, at the word,
Came the lady, in time of spring.
— Oh, old thoughts they cling, they cling !
That day, I know, with a dozen oaths
I clad myself in thick hunting-clothes
Fit for the chase of urochs or buffle
In winter-time when you need to muffle.
But the Duke had a mind we should cut a
    figure,
And so we saw the lady arrive :
My friend, I have seen a white crane bigger !
She was the smallest lady alive,

Made in a piece of nature's madness,
Too small, almost, for the life and gladness
That over-filled her, as some hive
Out of the bears' reach on the high trees
Is crowded with its safe merry bees :
In truth, she was not hard to please !
Up she looked, down she looked, round at the
    mead,
Straight at the castle, that 's best indeed
To look at from outside the walls :
As for us, styled the " serfs and thralls,"
She as much thanked me as if she had said it,
(With her eyes, do you understand ?)
Because I patted her horse while I led it ;
And Max, who rode on her other hand,
Said, no bird flew past but she inquired
What its true name was, nor ever seemed
    tired —
If that was an eagle she saw hover,
And the green and gray bird on the field was
    the plover.
When suddenly appeared the Duke :
And as down she sprung, the small foot pointed
On to my hand, — as with a rebuke,
And as if his backbone were not jointed,
The Duke stepped rather aside than forward,
And welcomed her with his grandest smile ;
And, mind you, his mother all the while
Chilled in the rear, like a wind to Nor'ward ;
And up, like a weary yawn, with its pulleys
Went, in a shriek, the rusty portcullis ;
And, like a glad sky the north-wind sullies,
The lady's face stopped its play,
As if her first hair had grown gray ;
For such things must begin some one day.

VII

In a day or two she was well again ;
As who should say, " You labor in vain !
This is all a jest against God, who meant
I should ever be, as I am, content
And glad in his sight ; therefore, glad I will
    be."
So, smiling as at first went she.

VIII

She was active, stirring, all fire —
Could not rest, could not tire —
To a stone she might have given life !
(I myself loved once, in my day)
— For a shepherd's, miner's, huntsman's wife,
(I had a wife, I know what I say)
Never in all the world such an one !
And here was plenty to be done,
And she that could do it, great or small,
She was to do nothing at all.
There was already this man in his post,
This in his station, and that in his office,
And the Duke's plan admitted a wife, at most
To meet his eye, with the other trophies,
Now outside the hall, now in it,
To sit thus, stand thus, see and be seen,
At the proper place in the proper minute,
And die away the life between.
And it was amusing enough, each infraction
Of rule — (but for after-sadness that came)
To hear the consummate self-satisfaction
With which the young Duke and the old dame

Would let her advise, and criticise,
And, being a fool, instruct the wise,
And, child-like, parcel out praise or blame :
They bore it all in complacent guise,
As though an artificer, after contriving
A wheel-work image as if it were living,
Should find with delight it could motion to
strike him !
So found the Duke, and his mother like him :
The lady hardly got a rebuff —
That had not been contemptuous enough,
With his cursed smirk, as he nodded applause,
And kept off the old mother-cat's claws.

IX

So, the little lady grew silent and thin,
Paling and ever paling,
As the way is with a hid chagrin ;
And the Duke perceived that she was ailing,
And said in his heart, " 'T is done to spite me,
But I shall find in my power to right me ! "
Don't swear, friend ! The old one, many a
year,
Is in hell, and the Duke's self . . . you shall
hear.

X

Well, early in autumn, at first winter-warning,
When the stag had to break with his foot, of a
morning,
A drinking-hole out of the fresh tender ice
That covered the pond till the sun, in a trice,
Loosening it, let out a ripple of gold,
And another and another, and faster and faster,
Till, dimpling to blindness, the wide water
rolled :
Then it so chanced that the Duke our master
Asked himself what were the pleasures in
season,
And found, since the calendar bade him be
hearty,
He should do the Middle Age no treason
In resolving on a hunting-party.
Always provided, old books showed the way of
it !
What meant old poets by their strictures ?
And when old poets had said their say of it,
How taught old painters in their pictures ?
We must revert to the proper channels,
Workings in tapestry, paintings on panels,
And gather up woodcraft's authentic tradi-
tions :
Here was food for our various ambitions,
As on each case, exactly stated —
To encourage your dog, now, the properest
chirrup,
Or best prayer to Saint Hubert on mounting
your stirrup —
We of the household took thought and de-
bated.
Blessed was he whose back ached with the jerkin
His sire was wont to do forest-work in ;
Blesseder he who nobly sunk " ohs "
And " ahs " while he tugged on his grandsire's
trunk-hose ;
What signified hats if they had no rims on,
Each slouching before and behind like the scal-
lop,

And able to serve at sea for a shallop,
Loaded with lacquer and looped with crimson ?
So that the deer now, to make a short rhyme
on 't,
What with our Venerers, Prickers and Verder-
ers,
Might hope for real hunters at length and not
murderers,
And oh the Duke's tailor, he had a hot time
on 't !

XI

Now you must know that when the first dizzi-
ness
Of flap-hats and buff-coats and jack-boots sub-
sided,
The Duke put this question, " The Duke's
part provided,
Had not the Duchess some share in the busi-
ness ? "
For out of the mouth of two or three witnesses
Did he establish all fit-or-unfitnesses :
And, after much laying of heads together,
Somebody's cap got a notable feather
By the announcement with proper unction
That he had discovered the lady's function ;
Since ancient authors gave this tenet,
" When horns wind a mort and the deer is at
siege,
Let the dame of the castle prick forth on her
jennet.
And, with water to wash the hands of her liege
In a clean ewer with a fair towelling,
Let her preside at the disembowelling."
Now, my friend, if you had so little religion
As to catch a hawk, some falcon-lanner,
And thrust her broad wings like a banner
Into a coop for a vulgar pigeon ;
And if day by day and week by week
You cut her claws, and sealed her eyes,
And clipped her wings, and tied her beak,
Would it cause you any great surprise
If, when you decided to give her an airing,
You found she needed a little preparing ?
— I say, should you be such a curmudgeon,
If she clung to the perch, as to take it in dud-
geon ?
Yet when the Duke to his lady signified,
Just a day before, as he judged most dignified,
In what a pleasure she was to participate, —
And, instead of leaping wide in flashes,
Her eyes just lifted their long lashes,
As if pressed by fatigue even he could not dissi-
pate,
And duly acknowledged the Duke's fore-
thought,
But spoke of her health, if her health were
worth aught,
Of the weight by day and the watch by night,
And much wrong now that used to be right,
So, thanking him, declined the hunting, —
Was conduct ever more affronting ?
With all the ceremony settled —
With the towel ready, and the sewer
Polishing up his oldest ewer,
And the jennet pitched upon, a piebald,
Black-barred, cream-coated and pink eye-
balled, —

No wonder if the Duke was nettled!
And when she persisted nevertheless, —
Well, I suppose here 's the time to confess
That there ran half round our lady's chamber
A balcony none of the hardest to clamber;
And that Jacynth the tire-woman, ready in
waiting,
Stayed in call outside, what need of relating?
And since Jacynth was like a June rose, why, a
fervent
Adorer of Jacynth of course was your servant;
And if she had the habit to peep through the
casement,
How could I keep at any vast distance?
And so, as I say, on the lady's persistence,
The Duke, dumb-stricken with amazement,
Stood for a while in a sultry smother,
And then, with a smile that partook of the aw-
ful,
Turned her over to his yellow mother
To learn what was held decorous and lawful;
And the mother smelt blood with a cat-like
instinct,
As her cheek quick whitened through all its
quince-tinct.
Oh, but the lady heard the whole truth at once!
What meant she? — Who was she? — Her
duty and station,
The wisdom of age and the folly of youth, at
once,
Its decent regard and its fitting relation —
In brief, my friend, set all the devils in hell
free
And turn them out to carouse in a belfry
And treat the priests to a fifty-part canon,
And then you may guess how that tongue of
hers ran on!
Well, somehow or other it ended at last
And, licking her whiskers, out she passed;
And after her, — making (he hoped) a face
Like Emperor Nero or Sultan Saladin,
Stalked the Duke's self with the austere grace
Of ancient hero or modern paladin,
From door to staircase — oh such a solemn
Unbending of the vertebral column!

XII

However, at sunrise our company mustered;
And here was the huntsman bidding unken-
nel,
And there 'neath his bonnet the pricker blus-
tered,
With feather dank as a bough of wet fennel;
For the court-yard walls were filled with fog
You might have cut as an axe chops a log —
Like so much wool for color and bulkiness;
And out rode the Duke in a perfect sulkiness,
Since, before breakfast, a man feels but queasily,
And a sinking at the lower abdomen
Begins the day with indifferent omen.
And lo, as he looked around uneasily,
The sun ploughed the fog up and drove it asun-
der
This way and that from the valley under;
And, looking through the court-yard arch,
Down in the valley, what should meet him
But a troop of Gypsies on their march?
No doubt with the annual gifts to greet him.

XIII

Now, in your land, Gypsies reach you, only
After reaching all lands beside;
North they go, South they go, trooping or
lonely,
And still, as they travel far and wide,
Catch they and keep now a trace here, a trace
there,
That puts you in mind of a place here, a place
there.
But with us, I believe they rise out of the
ground,
And nowhere else, I take it, are found
With the earth-tint yet so freshly embrowned:
Born, no doubt, like insects which breed on
The very fruit they are meant to feed on.
For the earth — not a use to which they don't
turn it,
The ore that grows in the mountain's womb,
Or the sand in the pits like a honeycomb,
They sift and soften it, bake it and burn it —
Whether they weld you, for instance, a snaffle
With side-bars never a brute can baffle;
Or a lock that 's a puzzle of wards within wards;
Or, if your colt's forefoot inclines to curve in-
wards,
Horseshoes they hammer which turn on a swivel
And won't allow the hoof to shrivel.
Then they cast bells like the shell of the winkle
That keep a stout heart in the ram with their
tinkle;
But the sand — they pinch and pound it like
otters;
Commend me to Gypsy glass-makers and pot-
ters!
Glasses they 'll blow you, crystal-clear,
Where just a faint cloud of rose shall appear,
As if in pure water you dropped and let die
A bruised black-blooded mulberry;
And that other sort, their crowning pride,
With long white threads distinct inside,
Like the lake-flower's fibrous roots which dangle
Loose such a length and never tangle,
Where the bold sword-lily cuts the clear waters,
And the cup-lily couches with all the white
daughters:
Such are the works they put their hand to,
The uses they turn and twist iron and sand to.
And these made the troop, which our Duke saw
sally
Toward his castle from out of the valley,
Men and women, like new-hatched spiders,
Come out with the morning to greet our riders.
And up they wound till they reached the ditch,
Whereat all stopped save one, a witch
That I knew, as she hobbled from the group,
By her gait directly and her stoop,
I, whom Jacynth was used to importune
To let that same witch tell us our fortune,
The oldest Gypsy then above ground;
And, sure as the autumn season came round,
She paid us a visit for profit or pastime,
And every time, as she swore, for the last time
And presently she was seen to sidle
Up to the Duke till she touched his bridle,
So that the horse of a sudden reared up
As under its nose the old witch peered up

With her worn-out eyes, or rather eye-holes
Of no use now but to gather brine,
And began a kind of level whine
Such as they use to sing to their viols
When their ditties they go grinding
Up and down with nobody minding:
And then, as of old, at the end of the humming
Her usual presents were forthcoming
— A dog-whistle blowing the fiercest of trebles,
(Just a sea-shore stone holding a dozen fine
    pebbles,)
Or a porcelain mouthpiece to screw on a pipe-
    end, —
And so she awaited her annual stipend.
But this time, the Duke would scarcely vouch-
    safe
A word in reply ; and in vain she felt
With twitching fingers at her belt
For the purse of sleek pine-marten pelt,
Ready to put what he gave in her pouch safe, —
Till, either to quicken his apprehension,
Or possibly with an after-intention,
She was come, she said, to pay her duty
To the new Duchess, the youthful beauty.
No sooner had she named his lady,
Than a shine lit up the face so shady,
And its smirk returned with a novel meaning —
For it struck him, the babe just wanted wean-
    ing ;
If one gave her a taste of what life was and
    sorrow,
She, foolish to-day, would be wiser to-morrow ;
And who so fit a teacher of trouble
As this sordid crone bent well-nigh double ?
So, glancing at her wolf-skin vesture,
(If such it was, for they grow so hirsute
That their own fleece serves for natural fur-
    suit)
He was contrasting, 't was plain from his ges-
    ture,
The life of the lady so flower-like and delicate
With the loathsome squalor of this helicat.
I, in brief, was the man the Duke beckoned
From out of the throng, and while I drew near
He told the crone — as I since have reckoned
By the way he bent and spoke into her ear
With circumspection and mystery —
The main of the lady's history,
Her frowardness and ingratitude :
And for all the crone's submissive attitude
I could see round her mouth the loose plaits
    tightening,
And her brow with assenting intelligence
    brightening,
As though she engaged with hearty goodwill
Whatever he now might enjoin to fulfil,
And promised the lady a thorough frightening.
And so, just giving her a glimpse
Of a purse, with the air of a man who imps
The wing of the hawk that shall fetch the hern-
    shaw,
He bade me take the Gypsy mother
And set her telling some story or other
Of hill or dale, oak-wood or fernshaw,
To while away a weary hour
For the lady left alone in her bower,
Whose mind and body craved exertion
And yet shrank from all better diversion.

XIV

Then clapping heel to his horse, the mere
    curveter,
Out rode the Duke, and after his hollo
Horses and hounds swept, huntsman and servi
    tor,
And back I turned and bade the crone follow.
And what makes me confident what 's to be
    told you
Had all along been of this crone's devising,
Is, that, on looking round sharply, behold you,
There was a novelty quick as surprising :
For first, she had shot up a full head in stature,
And her step kept pace with mine nor faltered,
As if age had foregone its usurpature,
And the ignoble mien was wholly altered,
And the face looked quite of another nature,
And the change reached too, whatever the
    change meant,
Her shaggy wolf-skin cloak's arrangement :
For where its tatters hung loose like sedges,
Gold coins were glittering on the edges,
Like the band-roll strung with tomans
Which proves the veil a Persian woman's :
And under her brow, like a snail's horns newly
Come out as after the rain he paces,
Two unmistakable eye-points duly
Live and aware looked out of their places.
So, we went and found Jacynth at the entry
Of the lady's chamber standing sentry ;
I told the command and produced my com-
    panion,
And Jacynth rejoiced to admit any one,
For since last night, by the same token,
Not a single word had the lady spoken :
They went in both to the presence together,
While I in the balcony watched the weather.

XV

And now, what took place at the very first of all
I cannot tell, as I never could learn it :
Jacynth constantly wished a curse to fall
On that little head of hers and burn it,
If she knew how she came to drop so soundly
Asleep of a sudden and there continue
The whole time sleeping as profoundly
As one of the boars my father would pin you
'Twixt the eyes where life holds garrison,
— Jacynth forgive me the comparison !
But where I begin my own narration
Is a little after I took my station
To breathe the fresh air from the balcony,
And, having in those days a falcon eye,
To follow the hunt through the open country,
From where the bushes thinlier crested
The hillocks, to a plain where 's not one tree.
When, in a moment, my ear was arrested
By — was it singing, or was it saying,
Or a strange musical instrument playing
In the chamber ? — and to be certain
I pushed the lattice, pulled the curtain,
And there lay Jacynth asleep,
Yet as if a watch she tried to keep,
In a rosy sleep along the floor
With her head against the door ;
While in the midst, on the seat of state,
Was a queen — the Gypsy woman late,

With head and face downbent
On the lady's head and face intent :
For, coiled at her feet like a child at ease,
The lady sat between her knees,
And o'er them the lady's clasped hands met,
And on those hands her chin was set,
And her upturned face met the face of the crone
Wherein the eyes had grown and grown
As if she could double and quadruple
At pleasure the play of either pupil
— Very like, by her hands' slow fanning,
As up and down like a gor-crow's flappers
They moved to measure, or bell clappers.
I said, " Is it blessing, is it banning,
Do they applaud you or burlesque you —
Those hands and fingers with no flesh on ? "
But, just as I thought to spring in to the rescue,
At once I was stopped by the lady's expression :
For it was life her eyes were drinking
From the crone's wide pair above unwinking,
— Life's pure fire received without shrinking,
Into the heart and breast whose heaving
Told you no single drop they were leaving,
— Life, that filling her, passed redundant
Into her very hair, back swerving
Over each shoulder, loose and abundant,
As her head thrown back showed the white
            throat curving ;
And the very tresses shared in the pleasure,
Moving to the mystic measure,
Bounding as the bosom bounded.
I stopped short, more and more confounded,
As still her cheeks burned and eyes glistened,
As she listened and she listened :
When all at once a hand detained me,
The selfsame contagion gained me,
And I kept time to the wondrous chime,
Making out words and prose and rhyme,
Till it seemed that the music furled
Its wings like a task fulfilled, and dropped
From under the words it first had propped,
And left them midway in the world :
Word took word as hand takes hand,
I could hear at last, and understand,
And when I held the unbroken thread,
The Gypsy said : —

" And so at last we find my tribe.
And so I set thee in the midst,
And to one and all of them describe
What thou saidst and what thou didst,
Our long and terrible journey through,
And all thou art ready to say and do
In the trials that remain :
I trace them the vein and the other vein
That meet on thy brow and part again,
Making our rapid mystic mark ;
And I bid my people prove and probe
Each eye's profound and glorious globe
Till they detect the kindred spark
In those depths so dear and dark,
Like the spots that snap and burst and flee,
Circling over the midnight sea.
And on that round young cheek of thine
I make them recognize the tinge,
As when of the costly scarlet wine
They drip so much as will impinge
And spread in a thinnest scale afloat

One thick gold drop from the olive's coat
Over a silver plate whose sheen
Still through the mixture shall be seen.
For so I prove thee, to one and all,
Fit, when my people ope their breast,
To see the sign, and hear the call,
And take the vow, and stand the test
Which adds one more child to the rest —
When the breast is bare and the arms are wide
And the world is left outside.
For there is probation to decree,
And many and long must the trials be
Thou shalt victoriously endure,
If that brow is true and those eyes are sure ;
Like a jewel-finder's fierce assay
Of the prize he dug from its mountain tomb
Let once the vindicating ray
Leap out amid the anxious gloom,
And steel and fire have done their part
And the prize falls on its finder's heart ;
So, trial after trial past,
Wilt thou fall at the very last
Breathless, half in trance
With the thrill of the great deliverance,
Into our arms forevermore ;
And thou shalt know, those arms once curled
About thee, what we knew before,
How love is the only good in the world.
Henceforth be loved as heart can love,
Or brain devise, or hand approve !
Stand up, look below,
It is our life at thy feet we throw
To step with into light and joy ;
Not a power of life but we employ
To satisfy thy nature's want ;
Art thou the tree that props the plant,
Or the climbing plant that seeks the tree —
Canst thou help us, must we help thee ?
If any two creatures grew into one,
They would do more than the world has done :
Though each apart were never so weak,
Ye vainly through the world should seek
For the knowledge and the might
Which in such union grew their right :
So, to approach at least that end,
And blend, — as much as may be, blend
Thee with us or us with thee, —
As climbing plant or propping tree,
Shall some one deck thee, over and down,
Up and about, with blossoms and leaves ?
Fix his heart's fruit for thy garland-crown,
Cling with his soul as the gourd-vine cleaves
Die on thy boughs and disappear
While not a leaf of thine is sere ?
Or is the other fate in store,
And art thou fitted to adore,
To give thy wondrous self away,
And take a stronger nature's sway ?
I foresee and could foretell
Thy future portion, sure and well :
But those passionate eyes speak true, speak
            true,
Let them say what thou shalt do !
Only be sure thy daily life,
In its peace or in its strife,
Never shall be unobserved ;
We pursue thy whole career,
And hope for it, or doubt, or fear.

Lo, hast thou kept thy path or swerved,
We are beside thee in all thy ways,
With our blame, with our praise,
Our shame to feel, our pride to show,
Glad, angry — but indifferent, no !
Whether it be thy lot to go,
For the good of us all, where the haters meet
In the crowded city's horrible street ;
Or thou step alone through the morass
Where never sound yet was
Save the dry quick clap of the stork's bill,
For the air is still, and the water still,
When the blue breast of the dipping coot
Dives under, and all is mute.
So, at the last shall come old age,
Decrepit as befits that stage ;
How else wouldst thou retire apart
With the hoarded memories of thy heart,
And gather all to the very least
Of the fragments of life's earlier feast,
Let fall through eagerness to find
The crowning dainties yet behind ?
Ponder on the entire past
Laid together thus at last,
When the twilight helps to fuse
The first fresh with the faded hues,
And the outline of the whole,
As round eve's shades their framework roll,
Grandly fronts for once thy soul.
And then as, 'mid the dark, a gleam
Of yet another morning breaks,
And like the hand which ends a dream,
Death, with the might of his sunbeam,
Touches the flesh and the soul awakes,
Then " —
   Ay, then indeed something would happen !
But what ?   For here her voice changed like a
      bird's ;
There grew more of the music and less of the
      words ;
Had Jacynth only been by me to clap pen
To paper and put you down every syllable
With those clever clerkly fingers,
All I 've forgotten as well as what lingers
In this old brain of mine that 's but ill able
To give you even this poor version
Of the speech I spoil, as it were, with stammer-
      ing
— More fault of those who had the hammering
Of prosody into me and syntax,
And did it, not with hobnails but tintacks !
But to return from this excursion, —
Just, do you mark, when the song was sweetest,
The peace most deep and the charm completest,
There came, shall I say, a snap —
And the charm vanished !
And my sense returned, so strangely banished,
And, starting as from a nap,
I knew the crone was bewitching my lady,
With Jacynth asleep ; and but one spring made I
Down from the casement, round to the portal,
Another minute and I had entered, —
When the door opened, and more than mortal
Stood, with a face where to my mind centred
All beauties I ever saw or shall see,
The Duchess : I stopped as if struck by palsy.
She was so different, happy and beautiful,
I felt at once that all was best,

And that I had nothing to do, for the rest,
But wait her commands, obey and be dutiful.
Not that, in fact, there was any commanding ;
I saw the glory of her eye,
And the brow's height and the breast's expand
      ing,
And I was hers to live or to die.
As for finding what she wanted,
You know God Almighty granted
Such little signs should serve wild creatures
To tell one another all their desires,
So that each knows what his friend requires,
And does its bidding without teachers.
I preceded her ; the crone
Followed silent and alone ;
I spoke to her, but she merely jabbered
In the old style ; both her eyes had slunk
Back to their pits ; her stature shrunk ;
In short, the soul in its body sunk
Like a blade sent home to its scabbard.
We descended, I preceding ;
Crossed the court with nobody heeding ;
All the world was at the chase,
The court-yard like a desert-place,
The stable emptied of its small fry ;
I saddled myself the very palfrey
I remember patting while it carried her,
The day she arrived and the Duke married her.
And, do you know, though it 's easy deceiving
One's self in such matters, I can't help believing
The lady had not forgotten it either,
And knew the poor devil so much beneath her
Would have been only too glad for her service
To dance on hot ploughshares like a Turk der-
      vise,
But, unable to pay proper duty where owing it,
Was reduced to that pitiful method of showing
      it :
For though the moment I began setting
His saddle on my own nag of Berold's begetting,
(Not that I meant to be obtrusive)
She stopped me, while his rug was shifting,
By a single rapid finger's lifting,
And, with a gesture kind but conclusive,
And a little shake of the head, refused me, —
I say, although she never used me,
Yet when she was mounted, the Gypsy behind
      her,
And I ventured to remind her,
I suppose with a voice of less steadiness
Than usual, for my feeling exceeded me,
— Something to the effect that I was in readiness
Whenever God should please she needed me, —
Then, do you know, her face looked down on me
With a look that placed a crown on me,
And she felt in her bosom, — mark, her bosom —
And, as a flower-tree drops its blossom,
Dropped me . . . ah, had it been a purse
Of silver, my friend, or gold that 's worse,
Why, you see, as soon as I found myself
So understood, — that a true heart so may gain
Such a reward, — I should have gone home
      again,
Kissed Jacynth, and soberly drowned myself !
It was a little plait of hair
Such as friends in a convent make
To wear, each for the other's sake, —
This, see, which at my breast I wear.

Ever did (rather to Jacynth's grudgment),
And ever shall, till the Day of Judgment.
And then, — and then, — to cut short, — this is
    idle,
These are feelings it is not good to foster, —
I pushed the gate wide, she shook the bridle,
And the palfrey bounded, — and so we lost her.

XVI

When the liquor 's out why clink the cannikin?
I did think to describe you the panic in
The redoubtable breast of our master the man-
    nikin,
And what was the pitch of his mother's yellow-
    ness,
How she turned as a shark to snap the spare-
    rib
Clean off, sailors say, from a pearl-diving Carib,
When she heard, what she called the flight of
    the feloness
— But it seems such child's play,
What they said and did with the lady away!
And to dance on, when we 've lost the music,
Always made me — and no doubt makes you —
    sick.
Nay, to my mind, the world's face looked so
    stern
As that sweet form disappeared through the
    postern,
She that kept it in constant good-humor,
It ought to have stopped ; there seemed nothing
    to do more.
But the world thought otherwise and went on,
And my head 's one that its spite was spent on :
Thirty years are fled since that morning,
And with them all my head's adorning,
Nor did the old Duchess die outright,
As you expect, of suppressed spite,
The natural end of every adder
Not suffered to empty its poison-bladder :
But she and her son agreed, I take it,
That no one should touch on the story to wake
    it,
For the wound in the Duke's pride rankled fiery,
So, they made no search and small inquiry —
And when fresh Gypsies have paid us a visit,
    I 've
Noticed the couple were never inquisitive,
But told them they 're folks the Duke don't
    want here,
And bade them make haste and cross the fron-
    tier.
Brief, the Duchess was gone and the Duke was
    glad of it,
And the old one was in the young one's stead,
And took, in her place, the household's head,
And a blessed time the household had of it !
And were I not, as a man may say, cautious
How I trench, more than needs, on the nauseous,
I could favor you with sundry touches
Of the paint-smutches with which the Duchess
Heightened the mellowness of her cheek's yel-
    lowness
(To get on faster) until at last her
Cheek grew to be one master-plaster
Of mucus and fucus from mere use of ceruse :
In short, she grew from scalp to udder
Just the object to make you shudder.

XVII

You 're my friend —
What a thing friendship is, world without end!
How it gives the heart and soul a stir-up
As if somebody broached you a glorious runlet,
And poured out, all lovelily, sparklingly, sunlit,
Our green Moldavia, the streaky syrup,
Cotnar as old as the time of the Druids —
Friendship may match with that monarch of
    fluids ;
Each supples a dry brain, fills you its ins-and-
    outs,
Gives your life's hour-glass a shake when the
    thin sand doubts
Whether to run on or stop short, and guarantees
Age is not all made of stark sloth and arrant
    ease.
I have seen my little lady once more,
Jacynth, the Gypsy, Berold, and the rest of it,
For to me spoke the Duke, as I told you before ;
I always wanted to make a clean breast of it :
And now it is made — why, my heart's blood,
    that went trickle,
Trickle, but anon, in such muddy driblets,
Is pumped up brisk now, through the main ven-
    tricle,
And genially floats me about the giblets.
I 'll tell you what I intend to do :
I must see this fellow his sad life through —
He is our Duke, after all,
And I, as he says, but a serf and thrall.
My father was born here, and I inherit
His fame, a chain he bound his son with ;
Could I pay in a lump I should prefer it,
But there 's no mine to blow up and get done
    with :
So, I must stay till the end of the chapter,
For, as to our middle-age-manners-adapter,
Be it a thing to be glad on or sorry on,
Some day or other, his head in a morion
And breast in a hauberk, his heels he 'll kick up
Slain by an onslaught fierce of hiccup.
And then, when red doth the sword of our
    Luke rust,
And its leathern sheath lie o'ergrown with a
    blue crust,
Then I shall scrape together my earnings ;
For, you see, in the churchyard Jacynth reposes,
And our children all went the way of the roses :
It 's a long lane that knows no turnings.
One needs but little tackle to travel in ;
So, just one stout cloak shall I indue :
And for a staff, what beats the javelin
With which his boars my father pinned you ?
And then, for a purpose you shall hear presently,
Taking some Cotnar, a tight plump skinful,
I shall go journeying, who but I, pleasantly !
Sorrow is vain and despondency sinful.
What 's a man's age ? He must hurry more,
    that 's all ;
Cram in a day, what his youth took a year to
    hold :
When we mind labor, then only, we 're too old —
What age had Methusalem when he begat Saul ?
And at last, as its haven some buffeted ship sees,
(Come all the way from the north-parts with
    sperm oil)

I hope to get safely out of the turmoil
And arrive one day at the land of the Gypsies,
And find my lady, or hear the last news of her
From some old thief and son of Lucifer,
His forehead chapleted green with wreathy hop,
Sunburned all over like an Æthiop.
And when my Cotnar begins to operate
And the tongue of the rogue to run at a proper
  rate,
And our wine-skin, tight once, shows each flac-
  cid dent,
I shall drop in with — as if by accident —
" You never knew, then, how it all ended,
What fortune good or bad attended
The little lady your Queen befriended ? "
— And when that 's told me, what 's remaining ?
This world 's too hard for my explaining.
The same wise judge of matters equine
Who still preferred some slim four-year-old
To the big-boned stock of mighty Berold,
And, for strong Cotnar, drank French weak
  wine,
He also must be such a lady's scorner !
Smooth Jacob still robs homely Esau:
Now up, now down, the world's one see-saw.
— So, I shall find out some snug corner
Under a hedge, like Orson the wood-knight,
Turn myself round and bid the world good-
  night ;
And sleep a sound sleep till the trumpet's blow-
  ing
Wakes me (unless priests cheat us laymen)
To a world where will be no further throwing
Pearls before swine that can't value them.
  Amen !

A GRAMMARIAN'S FUNERAL

SHORTLY AFTER THE REVIVAL OF LEARNING IN EUROPE

LET us begin and carry up this corpse,
  Singing together.
Leave we the common crofts, the vulgar
  thorpes
  Each in its tether
Sleeping safe on the bosom of the plain,
  Cared-for till cock-crow:
Look out if yonder be not day again
  Rimming the rock-row !
That 's the appropriate country ; there, man's
  thought,
  Rarer, intenser,
Self-gathered for an outbreak, as it ought,
  Chafes in the censer.
Leave we the unlettered plain its herd and crop ;
  Seek we sepulture
On a tall mountain, citied to the top,
  Crowded with culture !
All the peaks soar, but one the rest excels ;
  Clouds overcome it ;
No ! yonder sparkle is the citadel's
  Circling its summit.
Thither our path lies ; wind we up the heights ;
  Wait ye the warning ?
Our low life was the level's and the night's ;
  He 's for the morning.

Step to a tune, square chests, erect each head,
  'Ware the beholders !
This is our master, famous, calm and dead,
  Borne on our shoulders.

Sleep, crop and herd ! sleep, darkling thorpe
  and croft,
  Safe from the weather !
He, whom we convoy to his grave aloft,
  Singing together,
He was a man born with thy face and throat,
  Lyric Apollo !
Long he lived nameless : how should Spring
  take note
  Winter would follow ?
Till lo, the little touch, and youth was gone !
  Cramped and diminished,
Moaned he, " New measures, other feet anon !
  My dance is finished " ?
No, that 's the world's way : (keep the moun-
  tain-side,
  Make for the city !)
He knew the signal, and stepped on with pride
  Over men 's pity ;
Left play for work, and grappled with the
  world
  Bent on escaping :
" What 's in the scroll," quoth he, " thou
  keepest furled ?
  Show me their shaping,
Theirs who most studied man, the bard and
  sage, —
  Give ! " — So, he gowned him,
Straight got by heart that book to its last page :
  Learned, we found him.
Yea, but we found him bald too, eyes like lead,
  Accents uncertain :
" Time to taste life," another would have said,
  " Up with the curtain ! "
This man said rather, " Actual life comes next ?
  Patience a moment !
Grant I have mastered learning's crabbed text,
  Still there 's the comment.
Let me know all ! Prate not of most or least,
  Painful or easy !
Even to the crumbs I 'd fain eat up the feast,
  Ay, nor feel queasy."
Oh, such a life as he resolved to live,
  When he had learned it,
When he had gathered all books had to give !
  Sooner, he spurned it.
Image the whole, then execute the parts —
  Fancy the fabric
Quite, ere you build, ere steel strike fire from
  quartz,
  Ere mortar dab brick !

(Here 's the town-gate reached : there 's the
  market-place
  Gaping before us.)
Yea, this in him was the peculiar grace
  (Hearten our chorus !)
That before living he 'd learn how to live —
  No end to learning :
Earn the means first — God surely will contrive
  Use for our earning.
Others mistrust and say, " But time escapes ·
  Live now or never ! "

He said, " What 's time ? Leave Now for dogs
    and apes !
    Man has Forever."
Back to his book then : deeper drooped his head :
    Calculus racked him :
Leaden before, his eyes grew dross of lead :
    Tussis attacked him.
" Now, master, take a little rest ! " — not he !
    (Caution redoubled,
Step two abreast, the way winds narrowly !)
    Not a whit troubled,
Back to his studies, fresher than at first,
    Fierce as a dragon
He (soul-hydroptic with a sacred thirst)
    Sucked at the flagon.
Oh, if we draw a circle premature,
    Heedless of far gain,
Greedy for quick returns of profit, sure
    Bad is our bargain !
Was it not great ? did not he throw on God,
    (He loves the burthen) —
God's task to make the heavenly period
    Perfect the earthen ?
Did not he magnify the mind, show clear
    Just what it all meant ?
He would not discount life, as fools do here,
    Paid by instalment.
He ventured neck or nothing — heaven's success
    Found, or earth's failure :
" Wilt thou trust death or not ? " He answered
       " Yes !
Hence with life's pale lure ! "
That low man seeks a little thing to do,
    Sees it and does it :
This high man, with a great thing to pursue,
    Dies ere he knows it.
That low man goes on adding one to one,
    His hundred 's soon hit :
This high man, aiming at a million,
    Misses an unit.
That, has the world here — should he need the
    next,
    Let the world mind him !
This, throws himself on God, and unperplexed
    Seeking shall find him.
So, with the throttling hands of death at strife,
    Ground he at grammar ;
Still, through the rattle, parts of speech were
    rife :
    While he could stammer
He settled *Hoti*'s business — let it be ! —
    Properly based *Oun* —
Gave us the doctrine of the enclitic *De*,
    Dead from the waist down.
Well, here 's the platform, here 's the proper
    place :
    Hail to your purlieus,
All ye highfliers of the feathered race,
    Swallows and curlews !
Here 's the top-peak ; the multitude below
    Live, for they can, there :
This man decided not to Live but Know —
    Bury this man there ?
Here — here 's his place, where meteors shoot,
    clouds form,
    Lightnings are loosened,
Stars come and go ! Let joy break with the
    storm,

    Peace let the dew send !
Lofty designs must close in like effects :
    Loftily lying,
Leave him — still loftier than the world suspects,
    Living and dying.

THE HERETIC'S TRAGEDY

A MIDDLE-AGE INTERLUDE

*Rosa Mundi ; seu, fulcite me Floribus. A Conceit of
Master Gysbrecht, Canon-Regular of Saint Jodocus-
by-the-Bar, Ypres City. Cantuque, Virgilius. And
hath often been sung at Hock-tide and Festivals.
Gavisus eram, Jessides.*

(It would seem to be a glimpse from the
burning of Jacques du Bourg-Molay, at Paris,
A. D. 1314 ; as distorted by the refraction from
Flemish brain to brain, during the course of a
couple of centuries. R. B.)

PREADMONISHETH THE ABBOT DEODAET

THE Lord, we look to once for all,
    Is the Lord we should look at, all at once :
He knows not to vary, saith Saint Paul,
    Nor the shadow of turning, for the nonce.
See him no other than as he is !
    Give both the infinitudes their due —
Infinite mercy, but, I wis,
    As infinite a justice too.
            [*Organ : plagal-cadence*
    As infinite a justice too.

ONE SINGETH

John, Master of the Temple of God,
    Falling to sin the Unknown Sin,
What he bought of Emperor Aldabrod,
    He sold it to Sultan Saladin :
Till, caught by Pope Clement, a-buzzing there,
    Hornet-prince of the mad wasps' hive,
And clipt of his wings in Paris square,
    They bring him now to be burned alive.
[*And wanteth there grace of lute or clavicithern, ye
    shall say to confirm him who singeth —*
We bring John now to be burned alive.

In the midst is a goodly gallows built ;
    'Twixt fork and fork, a stake is stuck ;
But first they set divers tumbrils a-tilt,
    Make a trench all round with the city muck ;
Inside they pile log upon log, good store ;
    Fagots not few, blocks great and small,
Reach a man's mid-thigh, no less, no more, —
    For they mean he should roast in the sight of
    all.
CHO. — We mean he should roast in the sight
    of all.

Good sappy bavins that kindle forthwith ;
    Billets that blaze substantial and slow ;
Pine-stump split deftly, dry as pith ;
    Larch-heart that chars to a chalk-white glow
Then up they hoist me John in a chafe,

Sling him fast like a hog to scorch,
Spit in his face, then leap back safe,
  Sing " Laudes " and bid clap-to the torch.
CHO. — *Laus Deo* — who bids clap-to the torch.

John of the Temple, whose fame so bragged,
  Is burning alive in Paris square !
How can he curse, if his mouth is gagged ?
  Or wriggle his neck, with a collar there ?
Or heave his chest, which a band goes round ?
  Or threat with his fist, since his arms are
     spliced ?
Or kick with his feet, now his legs are bound ?
  — Thinks John, I will call upon Jesus Christ.
         [*Here one crosseth himself.*

Jesus Christ — John had bought and sold,
  Jesus Christ — John had eaten and drunk ;
To him, the Flesh meant silver and gold.
  (*Salva reverentia.*)
Now it was, " Saviour, bountiful lamb,
  I have roasted thee Turks, though men roast
     me !
See thy servant, the plight wherein I am !
  Art thou a saviour ? Save thou me ! "
CHO. — 'T is John the mocker cries, " Save thou
    me ! "

Who maketh God's menace an idle word ?
  — Saith, it no more means what it proclaims,
Than a damsel's threat to her wanton bird ? —
  For she too prattles of ugly names.
— Saith, he knoweth but one thing, — what he
    knows ?
  That God is good and the rest is breath ;
Why else is the same styled Sharon's rose ?
  Once a rose, ever a rose, he saith.
CHO. — Oh, John shall yet find a rose, he saith !

Alack, there be roses and roses, John !
  Some, honeyed of taste like your leman's
    tongue :
Some, bitter ; for why ? (roast gayly on !)
  Their tree struck root in devil's dung.
When Paul once reasoned of righteousness
  And of temperance and of judgment to come,
Good Felix trembled, he could no less :
  John, snickering, crook'd his wicked thumb.
CHO. — What cometh to John of the wicked
    thumb ?

Ha ha, John plucketh now at his rose
  To rid himself of a sorrow at heart !
Lo, — petal on petal, fierce rays unclose ;
  Anther on anther, sharp spikes outstart ;
And with blood for dew, the bosom boils ;
  And a gust of sulphur is all its smell ;
And lo, he is horribly in the toils
  Of a coal-black giant flower of hell !
CHO. — What maketh heaven, That maketh hell.

So, as John called now, through the fire amain,
  On the Name, he had cursed with, all his
    life —
To the Person, he bought and sold again —
  For the Face, with his daily buffets rife —
Feature by feature It took its place :
  And his voice, like a mad dog's choking bark,

At the steady whole of the Judge's face —
  Died. Forth John's soul flared into the dark

SUBJOINETH THE ABBOT DEODAET

God help all poor souls lost in the dark !

HOLY-CROSS DAY

ON WHICH THE JEWS WERE FORCED TO ATTEND
AN ANNUAL CHRISTIAN SERMON IN ROME

The passage from a mock-historic Diary which
follows is by Browning himself.

" Now was come about Holy-Cross Day, and
now must my lord preach his first sermon to the
Jews : as it was of old cared for in the merciful
bowels of the Church, that, so to speak, a crumb
at least from her conspicuous table here in
Rome should be, though but once yearly, cast
to the famishing dogs, under-trampled and be-
spitten-upon beneath the feet of the guests.
And a moving sight in truth, this, of so many
of the besotted blind restif and ready-to-perish
Hebrews ! now maternally brought — nay, (for
He saith, ' Compel them to come in ') haled, as
it were, by the head and hair, and against their
obstinate hearts, to partake of the heavenly
grace. What awakening, what striving with
tears, what working of a yeasty conscience !
Nor was my lord wanting to himself on so apt
an occasion ; witness the abundance of conver-
sions which did incontinently reward him :
though not to my lord be altogether the glory."
— *Diary by the Bishop's Secretary,* 1600.

What the Jews really said, on thus being
driven to church, was rather to this effect : —

FEE, faw, fum ! bubble and squeak !
Blessedest Thursday 's the fat of the week.
Rumble and tumble, sleek and rough,
Stinking and savory, smug and gruff,
Take the church-road, for the bell's due chime
Gives us the summons — 't is sermon-time !

Boh, here 's Barnabas ! Job, that 's you ?
Up stumps Solomon — bustling too ?
Shame, man ! greedy beyond your years
To handsel the bishop's shaving-shears ?
Fair play 's a jewel ! Leave friends in the
  lurch ?
Stand on a line ere you start for the church !

Higgledy piggledy, packed we lie,
Rats in a hamper, swine in a sty,
Wasps in a bottle, frogs in a sieve,
Worms in a carcass, fleas in a sleeve,
Hist ! square shoulders, settle your thumbs
And buzz for the bishop — here he comes.

Bow, wow, wow — a bone for the dog !
I liken his Grace to an acorned hog.

What, a boy at his side, with the bloom of a
    lass,
To help and handle my lord's hour-glass !
Didst ever behold so lithe a chine ?
His cheek hath laps like a fresh-singed swine.

Aaron's asleep — shove hip to haunch,
Or somebody deal him a dig in the paunch !
Look at the purse with the tassel and knob,
And the gown with the angel and thingum-
    bob !
What's he at, quotha ? reading his text !
Now you've his curtsey — and what comes
    next ?

See to our converts — you doomed black dozen —
No stealing away — nor cog nor cozen !
You five, that were thieves, deserve it fairly ;
You seven, that were beggars, will live less
    sparely ;
You took your turn and dipped in the hat,
Got fortune — and fortune gets you ; mind that !

Give your first groan — compunction's at work ;
And soft ! from a Jew you mount to a Turk.
Lo, Micah, — the selfsame beard on chin
He was four times already converted in !
Here's a knife, clip quick — it's a sign of
    grace —
Or he ruins us all with his hanging-face.

Whom now is the bishop a-leering at ?
I know a point where his text falls pat.
I'll tell him to-morrow, a word just now
Went to my heart and made me vow
I meddle no more with the worst of trades —
Let somebody else pay his serenades.

Groan all together now, whee — hee — hee !
It's a-work, it's a-work, ah, woe is me !
It began, when a herd of us, picked and placed,
Were spurred through the Corso, stripped to
    the waist ;
Jew brutes, with sweat and blood well spent
To usher in worthily Christian Lent.

It grew, when the hangman entered our bounds,
Yelled, pricked us out to his church like
    hounds :
It got to a pitch, when the hand indeed
Which gutted my purse would throttle my
    creed :
And it overflows, when, to even the odd,
Men I helped to their sins help me to their
    God.

But now, while the scapegoats leave our flock,
And the rest sit silent and count the clock,
Since forced to muse the appointed time
On these precious facts and truths sublime, —
Let us fitly employ it, under our breath,
In saying Ben Ezra's Song of Death.

For Rabbi Ben Ezra, the night he died,
Called sons and sons' sons to his side,
And spoke, "This world has been harsh and
    strange ;
Something is wrong : there needeth a change.

But what, or where ? at the last or first ?
In one point only we sinned, at worst.

" The Lord will have mercy on Jacob yet,
And again in his border see Israel set.
When Judah beholds Jerusalem,
The stranger-seed shall be joined to them :
To Jacob's House shall the Gentiles cleave.
So the Prophet saith and his sons believe.

" Ay, the children of the chosen race
Shall carry and bring them to their place :
In the land of the Lord shall lead the same,
Bondsmen and handmaids.   Who shall blame,
When the slaves enslave, the oppressed ones o'er
The oppressor triumph forevermore ?

" God spoke, and gave us the word to keep :
Bade never fold the hands nor sleep
'Mid a faithless world, — at watch and ward,
Till Christ at the end relieve our guard.
By his servant Moses the watch was set :
Though near upon cock-crow, we keep it yet.

" Thou ! if thou wast he, who at mid-watch
    came,
By the starlight, naming a dubious name !
And if, too heavy with sleep — too rash
With fear — O thou, if that martyr-gash
Fell on thee coming to take thine own,
And we gave the Cross, when we owed the
    Throne —

" Thou art the Judge.   We are bruisèd thus.
But, the Judgment over, join sides with us !
Thine too is the cause ! and not more thine
Than ours, is the work of these dogs and swine,
Whose life laughs through and spits at their
    creed,
Who maintain thee in word, and defy thee in
    deed !

" We withstood Christ then ? Be mindful how
At least we withstand Barabbas now !
Was our outrage sore ? But the worst we
    spared,
To have called these — Christians, had we
    dared !
Let defiance to them pay mistrust of thee,
And Rome make amends for Calvary !

" By the torture, prolonged from age to age,
By the infamy, Israel's heritage,
By the Ghetto's plague, by the garb's disgrace,
By the badge of shame, by the felon's place,
By the branding-tool, the bloody whip,
And the summons to Christian fellowship, —

" We boast our proof that at least the Jew
Would wrest Christ's name from the Devil's
    crew.
Thy face took never so deep a shade
But we fought them in it, God our aid !
A trophy to bear, as we march, thy band,
South, East, and on to the Pleasant Land ! " [1]

[1] Pope Gregory XVI. abolished this bad business of
the Sermon. — R. B.

PROTUS

AMONG these latter busts we count by scores,
Half-emperors and quarter-emperors,
Each with his bay-leaf fillet, loose-thonged
    vest,
Loric and low-browed Gorgon on the breast, —
One loves a baby face, with violets there,
Violets instead of laurel in the hair,
As those were all the little locks could bear.

Now read here. " Protus ends a period
Of empery beginning with a god ;
Born in the porphyry chamber at Byzant,
Queens by his cradle, proud and ministrant :
And if he quickened breath there, 't would like
    fire
Pantingly through the dim vast realm transpire.
A fame that he was missing spread afar :
The world, from its four corners, rose in war,
Till he was borne out on a balcony
To pacify the world when it should see.
The captains ranged before him, one, his hand
Made baby points at, gained the chief command.
And day by day more beautiful he grew
In shape, all said, in feature and in hue,
While young Greek sculptors, gazing on the
    child,
Became with old Greek sculpture reconciled.
Already sages labored to condense
In easy tomes a life's experience :
And artists took grave counsel to impart
In one breath and one hand-sweep, all their
    art —
To make his graces prompt as blossoming
Of plentifully-watered palms in spring :
Since well beseems it, whoso mounts the throne,
For beauty, knowledge, strength, should stand
    alone,
And mortals love the letters of his name."

— Stop ! Have you turned two pages ? Still
    the same
New reign, same date. The scribe goes on to
    say
How that same year, on such a month and day,
" John the Pannonian, groundedly believed
A blacksmith's bastard, whose hard hand re-
    prieved
The Empire from its fate the year before, —
Came, had a mind to take the crown, and wore
The same for six years (during which the Huns
Kept off their fingers from us), till his sons
Put something in his liquor " — and so forth.
Then a new reign. Stay — " Take at its just
    worth "
(Subjoins an annotator) " what I give
As hearsay. Some think, John let Protus live
And slip away. 'T is said, he reached man's age
At some blind northern court ; made, first a
    page,
Then tutor to the children ; last, of use
About the hunting-stables. I deduce
He wrote the little tract ' On worming dogs,'
Whereof the name in sundry catalogues
Is extant yet. A Protus of the race
Is rumored to have died a monk in Thrace, —

And if the same, he reached senility."
Here 's John the Smith's rough - hammered
    head. Great eye,
Gross jaw and griped lips do what granite can
To give you the crown-grasper. What a man !

THE STATUE AND THE BUST

This poem was published first in 1855 as an
independent issue. A correspondent of an
American paper once asked the following ques-
tions respecting this poem : —

" 1. When, how, and where did it happen ?
Browning's divine vagueness lets one gather
only that the lady's husband was a Riccardi.
2. Who was the lady ? who the duke ? 3. The
magnificent house wherein Florence lodges her
préfet is known to all Florentine ball-goers as
the Palazzo Riccardi. It was bought by the
Riccardi from the Medici in 1659. From none
of its windows did the lady gaze at her more
than royal lover. From what window, then, if
from any ? Are the statue and the bust still in
their original positions ? "

The letter fell into the hands of Mr. Thomas
J. Wise, who sent it to Mr. Browning, and re-
ceived the following answer.

Jan. 8, 1887.

" DEAR MR. WISE, — I have seldom met with
such a strange inability to understand what
seems the plainest matter possible : ' ball-
goers ' are probably not history-readers, but
any guide-book would confirm what is suffi-
ciently stated in the poem. I will append a note
or two, however. 1. ' This story the townsmen
tell ; ' ' when, how, and where,' constitutes the
subject of the poem. 2. The lady was the wife
of Riccardi ; and the duke, Ferdinand, just as
the poem says. 3. As it was built by, and in-
habited by, the Medici till sold, long after, to
the Riccardi, it was not from the duke's pal-
ace, but a window in that of the Riccardi,
that the lady gazed at her lover riding by.
The statue is still in its place, looking at the
window under which ' now is the empty shrine.'
Can anything be clearer ? My ' vagueness '
leaves what to be ' gathered ' when all these
things are put down in black and white ? Oh,
' ball-goers ' ! "

THERE 's a palace in Florence, the world knows
    well,
And a statue watches it from the square,
And this story of both do our townsmen tell.

Ages ago, a lady there,
At the farthest window facing the East
Asked, " Who rides by with the royal air ? "

The bridesmaids' prattle around her ceased ;
She leaned forth, one on either hand ;
They saw how the blush of the bride increased —

They felt by its beats her heart expand —
As one at each ear and both in a breath
Whispered, " The Great-Duke Ferdinand."

That selfsame instant, underneath,
The Duke rode past in his idle way,
Empty and fine like a swordless sheath.

Gay he rode, with a friend as gay,
Till he threw his head back — " Who is she ? "
— " A bride the Riccardi brings home to-day."

Hair in heaps lay heavily
Over a pale brow spirit-pure —
Carved like the heart of the coal-black tree,

Crisped like a war-steed's encolure —
And vainly sought to dissemble her eyes
Of the blackest black our eyes endure,

And lo, a blade for a knight's emprise
Filled the fine empty sheath of a man, —
The Duke grew straightway brave and wise.

He looked at her, as a lover can ;
She looked at him, as one who awakes :
The past was a sleep, and her life began.

Now, love so ordered for both their sakes,
A feast was held that selfsame night
In the pile which the mighty shadow makes.

(For Via Larga is three-parts light,
But the palace overshadows one,
Because of a crime, which may God requite !

To Florence and God the wrong was done,
Through the first republic's murder there
By Cosimo and his cursed son.)

The Duke (with the statue's face in the square)
Turned in the midst of his multitude
At the bright approach of the bridal pair.

Face to face the lovers stood
A single minute and no more,
While the bridegroom bent as a man subdued —

Bowed till his bonnet brushed the floor —
For the Duke on the lady a kiss conferred,
As the courtly custom was of yore.

In a minute can lovers exchange a word ?
If a word did pass, which I do not think,
Only one out of a thousand heard.

That was the bridegroom. At day's brink
He and his bride were alone at last
In a bed chamber by a taper's blink.

Calmly he said that her lot was cast,
That the door she had passed was shut on
        her
Till the final catafalk repassed.

The world meanwhile, its noise and stir,
Through a certain window facing the East
She could watch like a convent's chronicler.

Since passing the door might lead to a feast,
And a feast might lead to so much beside,
He, of many evils, chose the least.

" Freely I choose too," said the bride —
" Your window and its world suffice,"
Replied the tongue, while the heart replied -

" If I spend the night with that devil twice,
May his window serve as my loop of hell
Whence a damned soul looks on paradise !

" I fly to the Duke who loves me well,
Sit by his side and laugh at sorrow
Ere I count another ave-bell.

" 'T is only the coat of a page to borrow,
And tie my hair in a horse-boy's trim,
And I save my soul — but not to-morrow " —

(She checked herself and her eye grew dim)
" My father tarries to bless my state :
I must keep it one day more for him.

" Is one day more so long to wait ?
Moreover the Duke rides past, I know ;
We shall see each other, sure as fate."

She turned on her side and slept.   Just so !
So we resolve on a thing and sleep :
So did the lady, ages ago.

That night the Duke said, " Dear or cheap
As the cost of this cup of bliss may prove
To body or soul, I will drain it deep."

And on the morrow, bold with love,
He beckoned the bridegroom (close on call,
As his duty bade, by the Duke's alcove)

And smiled " 'T was a very funeral,
Your lady will think, this feast of ours, —
A shame to efface, whate'er befall !

" What if we break from the Arno bowers,
And try if Petraja, cool and green,
Cure last night's fault with this morning
        flowers ? "

The bridegroom, not a thought to be seen
On his steady brow and quiet mouth,
Said, " Too much favor for me so mean !

" But, alas ! my lady leaves the South ;
Each wind that comes from the Apennine
Is a menace to her tender youth :

" Nor a way exists, the wise opine,
If she quits her palace twice this year,
To avert the flower of life's decline."

Quoth the Duke, " A sage and a kindly fear
Moreover Petraja is cold this spring :
Be our feast to-night as usual here ! "

And then to himself — " Which night shall bring
Thy bride to her lover's embraces, fool —
Or I am the fool, and thou art the king !

" Yet my passion must wait a night, nor cool —
For to-night the Envoy arrives from France
Whose heart I unlock with thyself, my tool.

" I need thee still and might miss perchance.
To-day is not wholly lost, beside,
With its hope of my lady's countenance :

" For I ride — what should I do but ride ?
And passing her palace, if I list,
May glance at its window — well betide ! "

So said, so done : nor the lady missed
One ray that broke from the ardent brow,
Nor a curl of the lips where the spirit kissed.

Be sure that each renewed the vow,
No morrow's sun should arise and set
And leave them then as it left them now.

But next day passed, and next day yet,
With still fresh cause to wait one day more
Ere each leaped over the parapet.

And still, as love's brief morning wore,
With a gentle start, half smile, half sigh,
They found love not as it seemed before.

They thought it would work infallibly,
But not in despite of heaven and earth :
The rose would blow when the storm passed
by.

Meantime they could profit in winter's dearth
By store of fruits that supplant the rose :
The world and its ways have a certain worth :

And to press a point while these oppose
Were simple policy ; better wait :
We lose no friends and we gain no foes.

Meantime, worse fates than a lover's fate,
Who daily may ride and pass and look
Where his lady watches behind the grate !

And she — she watched the square like a
book
Holding one picture and only one,
Which daily to find she undertook :

When the picture was reached the book was
done,
And she turned from the picture at night to
scheme
Of tearing it out for herself next sun.

So weeks grew months, years ; gleam by gleam
The glory dropped from their youth and love,
And both perceived they had dreamed a dream ;

Which hovered as dreams do, still above :
But who can take a dream for a truth ?
Oh, hide our eyes from the next remove !

One day as the lady saw her youth
Depart, and the silver thread that streaked
Her hair, and, worn by the serpent's tooth,

The brow so puckered, the chin so peaked, —
And wondered who the woman was,
Hollow-eyed and haggard-cheeked,

Fronting her silent in the glass —
" Summon here," she suddenly said,
" Before the rest of my old self pass,

" Him, the Carver, a hand to aid,
Who fashions the clay no love will change,
And fixes a beauty never to fade.

" Let Robbia's craft so apt and strange
Arrest the remains of young and fair,
And rivet them while the seasons range.

" Make me a face on the window there,
Waiting as ever, mute the while,
My love to pass below in the square !

" And let me think that it may beguile
Dreary days which the dead must spend
Down in their darkness under the aisle,

" To say, ' What matters it at the end ?
I did no more while my heart was warm
Than does that image, my pale-faced friend.

" Where is the use of the lip's red charm,
The heaven of hair, the pride of the brow,
And the blood that blues the inside arm —

" Unless we turn, as the soul knows how,
The earthly gift to an end divine ?
A lady of clay is as good, I trow."

But long ere Robbia's cornice, fine,
With flowers and fruits which leaves enlace,
Was set where now is the empty shrine —

(And, leaning out of a bright blue space,
As a ghost might lean from a chink of sky,
The passionate pale lady's face —

Eying ever, with earnest eye
And quick-turned neck at its breathless stretch
Some one who ever is passing by —)

The Duke had sighed like the simplest wretch
In Florence, " Youth — my dream escapes !
Will its record stay ? " And he bade them fetch

Some subtle moulder of brazen shapes —
" Can the soul, the will, die out of a man
Ere his body find the grave that gapes ?

" John of Douay shall effect my plan,
Set me on horseback here aloft,
Alive, as the crafty sculptor can,

" In the very square I have crossed so oft :
That men may admire, when future suns
Shall touch the eyes to a purpose soft,

" While the mouth and the brow stay brave in
    bronze —
Admire and say, ' When he was alive
How he would take his pleasure once ! '

" And it shall go hard but I contrive
To listen the while, and laugh in my tomb
At idleness which aspires to strive."

So ! While these wait the trump of doom,
How do their spirits pass, I wonder,
Nights and days in the narrow room ?

Still, I suppose, they sit and ponder
What a gift life was, ages ago,
Six steps out of the chapel yonder.

Only they see not God, I know,
Nor all that chivalry of his,
The soldier-saints who, row on row,

Burn upward each to his point of bliss —
Since, the end of life being manifest,
He had burned his way through the world to
    this.

I hear you reproach, " But delay was best,
For their end was a crime." — Oh, a crime will
    do
As well, I reply, to serve for a test,

As a virtue golden through and through,
Sufficient to vindicate itself
And prove its worth at a moment's view !

Must a game be played for the sake of pelf ?
Where a button goes, 't were an epigram
To offer the stamp of the very Guelph.

The true has no value beyond the sham :
As well the counter as coin, I submit,
When your table 's a hat, and your prize, a
    dram.

Stake your counter as boldly every whit,
Venture as warily, use the same skill,
Do your best, whether winning or losing it,

If you choose to play ! — is my principle.
Let a man contend to the uttermost
For his life's set prize, be it what it will !

The counter our lovers staked was lost
As surely as if it were lawful coin :
And the sin I impute to each frustrate ghost

Is — the unlit lamp and the ungirt loin,
Though the end in sight was a vice, I say.
You of the virtue (we issue join)
How strive you ? *De te, fabula !*

PORPHYRIA'S LOVER

First printed in Mr. Fox's *Monthly Repository*
in 1836, under the signature Z. When issued in
Bells and Pomegranates it was grouped with
Johannes Agricola in Meditation as No. II. of
Madhouse Cells. The poem has an interest as
the earliest, apparently, of Browning's mono-
logues.

THE rain set early in to-night,
    The sullen wind was soon awake,
It tore the elm-tops down for spite,
    And did its worst to vex the lake :
I listened with heart fit to break.
When glided in Porphyria ; straight
    She shut the cold out and the storm,
And kneeled and made the cheerless grate
    Blaze up, and all the cottage warm ;
Which done, she rose, and from her form
Withdrew the dripping cloak and shawl,
    And laid her soiled gloves by, untied
Her hat and let the damp hair fall,
    And, last, she sat down by my side
And called me. When no voice replied,
She put my arm about her waist,
    And made her smooth white shoulder bare
And all her yellow hair displaced,
    And, stooping, made my cheek lie there,
And spread, o'er all, her yellow hair,
Murmuring how she loved me — she
    Too weak, for all her heart's endeavor,
To set its struggling passion free
    From pride, and vainer ties dissever,
And give herself to me forever.
But passion sometimes would prevail,
    Nor could to-night's gay feast restrain
A sudden thought of one so pale
    For love of her, and all in vain :
So, she was come through wind and rain.
Be sure I looked up at her eyes
    Happy and proud ; at last I knew
Porphyria worshipped me ; surprise
    Made my heart swell, and still it grew
While I debated what to do.
That moment she was mine, mine, fair,
    Perfectly pure and good : I found
A thing to do, and all her hair
    In one long yellow string I wound
Three times her little throat around,
And strangled her. No pain felt she ;
    I am quite sure she felt no pain.
As a shut bud that holds a bee,
    I warily oped her lids : again
Laughed the blue eyes without a stain.
And I untightened next the tress
    About her neck ; her cheek once more
Blushed bright beneath my burning kiss :
    I propped her head up as before,
Only, this time my shoulder bore
Her head, which droops upon it still :
    The smiling rosy little head,
So glad it has its utmost will,
    That all it scorned at once is fled,
And I, its love, am gained instead !
Porphyria's love : she guessed not how
    Her darling one wish would be heard.
And thus we sit together now,
    And all night long we have not stirred,
And yet God has not said a word !

"CHILDE ROLAND TO THE DARK TOWER CAME"

See Edgar's song in *Lear*.

My first thought was, he lied in every word,
  That hoary cripple, with malicious eye
  Askance to watch the working of his lie
On mine, and mouth scarce able to afford
Suppression of the glee, that pursed and scored
  Its edge, at one more victim gained thereby.

What else should he be set for, with his staff?
  What, save to waylay with his lies, ensnare
  All travellers who might find him posted
    there,
And ask the road? I guessed what skull-like
    laugh
  Would break, what crutch 'gin write my epitaph
  For pastime in the dusty thoroughfare,

If at his counsel I should turn aside
  Into that ominous tract which, all agree,
  Hides the Dark Tower. Yet acquiescingly
I did turn as he pointed: neither pride
Nor hope rekindling at the end descried,
  So much as gladness that some end might be.

For, what with my whole world-wide wander-
    ing,
  What with my search drawn out through
    years, my hope
  Dwindled into a ghost not fit to cope
With that obstreperous joy success would
    bring, —
I hardly tried now to rebuke the spring
  My heart made, finding failure in its scope.

As when a sick man very near to death
  Seems dead indeed, and feels begin and end
  The tears, and takes the farewell of each
    friend,
And hears one bid the other go, draw breath
Freelier outside, ("since all is o'er," he saith,
  "And the blow fallen no grieving can
    amend;")

While some discuss if near the other graves
  Be room enough for this, and when a day
  Suits best for carrying the corpse away,
With care about the banners, scarves and
    staves:
And still the man hears all, and only craves
  He may not shame such tender love and stay.

Thus, I had so long suffered in this quest,
  Heard failure prophesied so oft, been writ
  So many times among "The Band"—to wit,
The knights who to the Dark Tower's search
    addressed
Their steps—that just to fail as they, seemed
    best,
  And all the doubt was now—should I be fit?

So, quiet as despair, I turned from him,
  That hateful cripple, out of his highway
  Into the path he pointed. All the day

Had been a dreary one at best, and dim
Was settling to its close, yet shot one grim
  Red leer to see the plain catch its estray.

For mark! no sooner was I fairly found
  Pledged to the plain, after a pace or two,
  Than, pausing to throw backward a last view
O'er the safe road, 't was gone; gray plain all
    round:
Nothing but plain to the horizon's bound.
  I might go on; naught else remained to do.

So, on I went. I think I never saw
  Such starved ignoble nature; nothing throve:
  For flowers—as well expect a cedar grove!
But cockle, spurge, according to their law
Might propagate their kind, with none to awe,
  You 'd think: a burr had been a treasure
    trove.

No! penury, inertness and grimace,
  In some strange sort, were the land's portion.
    "See
  Or shut your eyes," said Nature peevishly,
"It nothing skills: I cannot help my case:
'T is the Last Judgment's fire must cure this
    place,
  Calcine its clods and set my prisoners free."

If there pushed any ragged thistle-stalk
  Above its mates, the head was chopped; the
    bents
  Were jealous else. What made those holes
    and rents
In the dock's harsh swarth leaves, bruised as to
    balk
All hope of greenness? 't is a brute must walk
  Pashing their life out, with a brute's intents.

As for the grass, it grew as scant as hair
  In leprosy; thin-dry blades pricked the mud
  Which underneath looked kneaded up with
    blood.
One stiff blind horse, his every bone a-stare,
Stood stupefied, however he came there:
  Thrust out past service from the devil's stud!

Alive? he might be dead for aught I know,
  With that red gaunt and colloped neck
    a-strain,
  And shut eyes underneath the rusty mane;
Seldom went such grotesqueness with such woe;
I never saw a brute I hated so;
  He must be wicked to deserve such pain.

I shut my eyes and turned them on my heart.
  As a man calls for wine before he fights,
  I asked one draught of earlier, happier sights,
Ere fitly I could hope to play my part.
Think first, fight afterwards—the soldier's art:
  One taste of the old time sets all to rights.

Not it! I fancied Cuthbert's reddening face
  Beneath its garniture of curly gold,
  Dear fellow, till I almost felt him fold
An arm in mine to fix me to the place,
That way he used. Alas, one night's disgrace!
  Out went my heart's new fire and left it cold.

Giles then, the soul of honor — there he stands
  Frank as ten years ago when knighted first.
  What honest man should dare (he said) he
    durst.
Good — but the scene shifts — faugh ! what
    hangman hands
Pin to his breast a parchment ? His own bands
Read it. Poor traitor, spit upon and curst !

Better this present than a past like that ;
  Back therefore to my darkening path again !
  No sound, no sight as far as eye could strain.
Will the night send a howlet or a bat ?
I asked : when something on the dismal flat
  Came to arrest my thoughts and change their
    train.

A sudden little river crossed my path
  As unexpected as a serpent comes.
  No sluggish tide congenial to the glooms ;
This, as it frothed by, might have been a bath
For the fiend's glowing hoof — to see the wrath
  Of its black eddy bespate with flakes and
    spumes.

So petty yet so spiteful ! All along,
  Low scrubby alders kneeled down over it ;
  Drenched willows flung them headlong in a
    fit
Of mute despair, a suicidal throng :
The river which had done them all the wrong,
  Whate'er that was, rolled by, deterred no
    whit.

Which, while I forded, — good saints, how I
    feared
  To set my foot upon a dead man's cheek,
  Each step, or feel the spear I thrust to seek
For hollows, tangled in his hair or beard !
— It may have been a water-rat I speared,
  But, ugh ! it sounded like a baby's shriek.

Glad was I when I reached the other bank.
  Now for a better country. Vain presage !
  Who were the strugglers, what war did they
    wage,
Whose savage trample thus could pad the dank
Soil to a plash ? Toads in a poisoned tank,
  Or wild cats in a red-hot iron cage —

The fight must so have seemed in that fell
    cirque.
  What penned them there, with all the plain
    to choose ?
  No footprint leading to that horrid mews,
None out of it. Mad brewage set to work
Their brains, no doubt, like galley-slaves the
    Turk
  Pits for his pastime, Christians against Jews.

And more than that — a furlong on — why,
    there !
  What bad use was that engine for, that wheel,
  Or brake, not wheel — that harrow fit to reel
Men's bodies out like silk ? with all the air
Of Tophet's tool. on earth left unaware,
  Or brought to sharpen its rusty teeth of steel.

Then came a bit of stubbed ground, once a
    wood,
  Next a marsh, it would seem, and now mere
    earth
  Desperate and done with : (so a fool finds
    mirth,
Makes a thing and then mars it, till his mood
Changes and off he goes !) within a rood —
  Bog, clay and rubble, sand and stark black
    dearth.

Now blotches rankling, colored gay and grim,
  Now patches where some leanness of the
    soil's
  Broke into moss or substances like boils ;
Then came some palsied oak, a cleft in him
Like a distorted mouth that splits its rim
  Gaping at death, and dies while it recoils.

And just as far as ever from the end !
  Naught in the distance but the evening,
    naught
  To point my footstep further ! At the
    thought,
A great black bird, Apollyon's bosom-friend,
Sailed past, nor beat his wide wing dragon-
    penned
  That brushed my cap — perchance the guide
    I sought.

For, looking up, aware I somehow grew,
  'Spite of the dusk, the plain had given place
  All round to mountains — with such name to
    grace
Mere ugly heights and heaps now stolen in
    view.
How thus they had surprised me, — solve it,
    you !
  How to get from them was no clearer case.

Yet half I seemed to recognize some trick
  Of mischief happened to me, God knows
    when —
  In a bad dream perhaps. Here ended, then,
Progress this way. When, in the very nick
Of giving up, one time more, came a click
  As when a trap shuts — you 're inside the
    den !

Burningly it came on me all at once,
  This was the place ! those two hills on the
    right,
  Crouched like two bulls locked horn in horn
    in fight ;
While to the left, a tall scalped mountain . . .
    Dunce,
Dotard, a-dozing at the very nonce,
  After a life spent training for the sight !

What in the midst lay but the Tower itself ?
  The round squat turret, blind as the fool's
    heart,
  Built of brown stone, without a counterpart
In the whole world. The tempest's mocking
    elf
Points to the shipman thus the unseen shelf
  He strikes on, only when the timbers start.

Not see ? because of night perhaps ? — why, day
  Came back again for that ! before it left,
  The dying sunset kindled through a cleft:
The hills, like giants at a hunting, lay,
Chin upon hand, to see the game at bay, —
  " Now stab and end the creature — to the
    heft ! "

Not hear ? when noise was everywhere ! it tolled
  Increasing like a bell.   Names in my ears,
  Of all the lost adventurers my peers, —
How such a one was strong, and such was bold,

And such was fortunate, yet each of old
  Lost, lost ! one moment knelled the woe of
    years.

There they stood, ranged along the hillsides,
    met
  To view the last of me, a living frame
  For one more picture ! in a sheet of flame
I saw them and I knew them all.   And yet
Dauntless the slug-horn to my lips I set,
  And blew.   " *Childe Roland to the Dark
    Tower came.*"

A SOUL'S TRAGEDY

ACT FIRST, BEING WHAT WAS CALLED THE POETRY OF CHIAPPINO'S LIFE; AND ACT SECOND, ITS PROSE

THIS drama was first printed with *Luria* as
the concluding number of *Bells and Pomegran-
ates* in April, 1846.

PERSONS

LUITOLFO and EULALIA, betrothed lovers.
CHIAPPINO, their friend.
OGNIBEN, the Pope's Legate.
Citizens of Faenza.

TIME, 15—.   Place, FAENZA.

ACT I

Inside LUITOLFO'S *house.*   CHIAPPINO, EULALIA.
Eulalia.   What is it keeps Luitolfo ?   Night 's
    fast falling,
And 't was scarce sunset . . . had the ave-bell
Sounded before he sought the Provost's house ?
I think not: all he had to say would take
Few minutes, such a very few, to say !
How do you think, Chiappino ?   If our lord
The Provost were less friendly to your friend
Than everybody here professes him,
I should begin to tremble — should not you ?
Why are you silent when so many times
I turn and speak to you ?
  Chiappino.   That 's good !
  Eu.   You laugh !
  Ch.   Yes.   I had fancied nothing that bears
      price
In the whole world was left to call my own ;
And, maybe, felt a little pride thereat.
Up to a single man's or woman's love,
Down to the right in my own flesh and blood,
There 's nothing mine, I fancied, — till you
    spoke :
— Counting, you see, as " nothing " the permis-
    sion
To study this peculiar lot of mine
In silence: well, go silence with the rest
Of the world's good !   What can I say, shall
    serve ?

  Eu.   This, — lest you, even more than needs,
      embitter
Our parting : say your wrongs have cast, for
    once,
A cloud across your spirit !
  Ch.   How a cloud ?
  Eu.   No man nor woman loves you, did you
      say ?
  Ch.   My God, were 't not for thee !
  Eu.   Ay, God remains,
Even did men forsake you.
  Ch.   Oh, not so !
Were 't not for God, I mean, what hope of
    truth —
Speaking truth, hearing truth, would stay with
    man ?
I, now — the homeless friendless penniless
Proscribed and exiled wretch who speak to
    you, —
Ought to speak truth, yet could not, for my
    death,
(The thing that tempts me most) help speaking
    lies
About your friendship and Luitolfo's courage
And all our townsfolk's equanimity —
Through sheer incompetence to rid myself
Of the old miserable lying trick
Caught from the liars I have lived with, — God
Did I not turn to thee !   It is thy prompting
I dare to be ashamed of, and thy counsel
Would die along my coward lip, I know.
But I do turn to thee.   This craven tongue,
These features which refuse the soul its way,
Reclaim thou !   Give me truth — truth, power
    to speak
— And after be sole present to approve
The spoken truth !   Or, stay, that spoken truth,
Who knows but you, too, may approve ?
  Eu.   Ah, well —
Keep silence then, Chiappino !
  Ch.   You would hear, —
You shall now, — why the thing we please to
    style
My gratitude to you and all your friends

For service done me, is just gratitude
So much as yours was service : no whit more.
I was born here, so was Luitolfo ; both
At one time, much with the same circumstance
Of rank and wealth ; and both, up to this night
Of parting company, have side by side
Still fared, he in the sunshine — I, the shadow.
" Why ? " asks the world. " Because," replies
　　the world
To its complacent self, " these playfellows,
Who took at church the holy-water drop
Each from the other's finger, and so forth, —
Were of two moods : Luitolfo was the proper
Friend-making, everywhere friend-finding soul,
Fit for the sunshine, so, it followed him.
A happy-tempered bringer of the best
Out of the worst ; who bears with what 's past
　　cure,
And puts so good a face on 't — wisely passive
Where action 's fruitless, while he remedies
In silence what the foolish rail against ;
A man to smooth such natures as parade
Of opposition must exasperate ;
No general gauntlet-gatherer for the weak
Against the strong, yet over-scrupulous
At lucky junctures ; one who won't forego
The after-battle work of binding wounds,
Because, forsooth he 'd have to bring himself
To side with wound-inflictors for their leave ! "
— Why do you gaze, nor help me to repeat
What comes so glibly from the common mouth,
About Luitolfo and his so-styled friend ?
　　Eu.　Because, that friend's sense is ob-
　　　　scured . . .
　　Ch.　　　　　I thought
You would be readier with the other half
Of the world's story, my half ! Yet, 't is true.
For all the world does say it. Say your worst !
True, I thank God, I ever said " you sin,"
When a man did sin : if I could not say it,
I glared it at him ; if I could not glare it,
I prayed against him ; then my part seemed over.
God's may begin yet : so it will, I trust.
　　Eu.　If the world outraged you, did we ?
　　Ch.　　　　　What 's " me "
That you use well or ill ? It 's man, in me,
All your successes are an outrage to,
You all, whom sunshine follows, as you say !
Here 's our Faenza birthplace ; they send here
A provost from Ravenna : how he rules,
You can at times be eloquent about.
" Then, end his rule ! " — " Ah yes, one stroke
　　does that !
But patience under wrong works slow and sure.
Must violence still bring peace forth ? He,
　　beside,
Returns so blandly one's obeisance ! ah —
Some latent virtue may be lingering yet,
Some human sympathy which, once excite,
And all the lump were leavened quietly :
So, no more talk of striking, for this time ! "
But I, as one of those he rules, won't bear
These pretty takings-up and layings-down
Our cause, just as you think occasion suits.
Enough of earnest, is there ? You 'll play, will
　　you ?
Diversify your tactics, give submission,
Obsequiousness and flattery a turn,

While we die in our misery patient deaths ?
We all are outraged then, and I the first :
I, for mankind, resent each shrug and smirk,
Each beck and bend, each . . . all you do an[
　　are,
I hate !
　　Eu.　We share a common censure, then.
'T is well you have not poor Luitolfo's part
Nor mine to point out in the wide offence.
　　Ch.　Oh, shall I let you so escape me, lady ?
Come, on your own ground, lady, — from your
　　self,
(Leaving the people's wrong, which most i[
　　mine)
What have I got to be so grateful for ?
These three last fines, no doubt, one on the
　　other
Paid by Luitolfo ?
　　Eu.　　　　Shame, Chiappino !
　　Ch.　　　　　　　Shame
Fall presently on who deserves it most !
— Which is to see. He paid my fines — my
　　friend,
Your prosperous smooth lover presently,
Then, scarce your wooer, — soon, your hus-
　　band : well —
I loved you.
　　Eu.　　Hold !
　　Ch.　　　　You knew it, years ago.
When my voice faltered and my eye grew dim
Because you gave me your silk mask to hold —
My voice that greatens when there 's need to
　　curse
The people's Provost to their heart's content.
— My eye, the Provost, who bears all men's
　　eyes,
Banishes now because he cannot bear, —
You knew . . . but you do your parts — my
　　part, I :
So be it ! You flourish, I decay : all 's well.
　　Eu.　I hear this for the first time.
　　Ch.　　　　　The fault 's there ?
Then my days spoke not, and my nights of fire
Were voiceless ? Then the very heart may
　　burst.
Yet all prove naught, because no mincing
　　speech
Tells leisurely that thus it is and thus ?
Eulalia, truce with toying for this once !
A banished fool, who troubles you to-night
For the last time — why, what 's to fear from
　　me ?
You knew I loved you !
　　Eu.　　　　Not so, on my faith !
You were my now-affianced lover's friend —
Came in, went out with him, could speak as he.
All praise your ready parts and pregnant wit ;
See how your words come from you in a crowd [
Luitolfo 's first to place you o'er himself
In all that challenges respect and love :
Yet you were silent then, who blame me now.
I say all this by fascination, sure :
I, all but wed to one I love, yet listen !
It must be, you are wronged, and that the
　　wrongs
Luitolfo pities . . .
　　Ch.　　　— You too pity ? Do !
But hear first what my wrongs are ; so began

This talk and so shall end this talk. I say,
Was 't not enough that I must strive (I saw)
To grow so far familiar with your charms
As next contrive some way to win them — which
To do, an age seemed far too brief — for, see!
We all aspire to heaven ; and there lies heaven
Above us : go there ! Dare we go ? no, surely !
How dare we go without a reverent pause,
A growing less unfit for heaven ? Just so,
I dared not speak : the greater fool, it seems!
Was 't not enough to struggle with such folly,
But I must have, beside, the very man
Whose slight free loose and incapacious soul
Gave his tongue scope to say whate'er he would
— Must have him load me with his benefits
— For fortune's fiercest stroke ?
Eu.   Justice to him
That 's now entreating, at his risk perhaps,
Justice for you ! Did he once call those acts
Of simple friendship — bounties, benefits ?
   Ch. No : the straight course had been to call
      them thus.
Then, I had flung them back, and kept myself
Unhampered, free as he to win the prize
We both sought. But " the gold was dross,"
      he said :
" He loved me, and I loved him not : why
      spurn
A trifle out of superfluity ?
He had forgotten he had done as much."
So had not I ! Henceforth, try as I could
To take him at his word, there stood by you
My benefactor ; who might speak and laugh
And urge his nothings, even banter me
Before you — but my tongue was tied. A
      dream !
Let 's wake : your husband . . . how you shake
      at that !
Good — my revenge !
   Eu.   Why should I shake ? What forced
Or forces me to be Luitolfo's bride ?
   Ch. There 's my revenge, that nothing
      forces you.
No gratitude, no liking of the eye
Nor longing of the heart, but the poor bond
Of habit — here so many times he came,
So much he spoke, — all these compose the tie
That pulls you from me. Well, he paid my
      fines,
Nor missed a cloak from wardrobe, dish from
      table ;
He spoke a good word to the Provost here,
Held me up when my fortunes fell away,
— It had not looked so well to let me drop, —
Men take pains to preserve a tree-stump, even,
Whose boughs they played beneath — much
      more a friend.
But one grows tired of seeing, after the first,
Pains spent upon impracticable stuff
Like me. I could not change : you know the
      rest.
I 've spoke my mind too fully out, by chance,
This morning to our Provost ; so, ere night
I leave the city on pain of death. And now
On my account there 's gallant intercession
Goes forward — that 's so graceful ! — and anon
He 'll noisily come back : " the intercession
Was made and fails : all 's over for us both ;

'T is vain contending ; I would better go."
And I do go — and straight to you he turns
Light of a load ; and ease of that permits
His visage to repair the natural bland
Œconomy, sore broken late to suit
My discontent. Thus, all are pleased — you,
      with him,
He with himself, and all of you with me
— " Who," say the citizens, " had done far
      better
In letting people sleep upon their woes,
If not possessed with talent to relieve them
When once awake ; — but then I had," they 'll
      say,
" Doubtless some unknown compensating pride
In what I did ; and as I seem content
With ruining myself, why, so should they be."
And so they are, and so be with his prize
The devil, when he gets them speedily !
Why does not your Luitolfo come ? I long
To don this cloak and take the Lugo path.
It seems you never loved me, then ?
   Eu.   Chiappino !
   Ch. Never ?
   Eu.   Never.
   Ch.   That 's sad. Say what I might,
There was no help from being sure this while
You loved me. Love like mine must have
      return,
I thought : no river starts but to some sea.
And had you loved me, I could soon devise
Some specious reason why you stifled love,
Some fancied self-denial on your part,
Which made you choose Luitolfo ; so, except-
      ing
From the wide condemnation of all here,
One woman. Well, the other dream may
      break !
If I knew any heart, as mine loved you,
Loved me, though in the vilest breast 't were
      lodged,
I should, I think, be forced to love again :
Else there 's no right nor reason in the world.
   Eu. " If you knew," say you, — but I did
      not know.
That 's where you 're blind, Chiappino ! — a
      disease
Which if I may remove, I 'll not repent
The listening to. You cannot, will not, see
How, place you but in every circumstance
Of us, you are just now indignant at,
You 'd be as we.
   Ch.   I should be ? . . . that ; again !
I, to my friend, my country and my love,
Be as Luitolfo and these Faentines ?
   Eu. As we.
   Ch. Now, I 'll say something to remember
I trust in nature for the stable laws
Of beauty and utility. — Spring shall plant,
And Autumn garner to the end of time :
I trust in God — the right shall be the right
And other than the wrong, while he endures :
I trust in my own soul, that can perceive
The outward and the inward, nature's good
And God's : so, seeing these men and myself,
Having a right to speak, thus do I speak.
I 'll not curse — God bears with them, well
      may I —

But I — protest against their claiming me.
I simply say, if that 's allowable,
I would not (broadly) do as they have done.
— God curse this townful of born slaves, bred slaves,
Branded into the blood and bone, slaves!
Curse
Whoever loves, above his liberty,
House, land or life! and . . .
                    [A knocking without.
                    — bless my hero-friend,
Luitolfo!
Eu.   How he knocks!
Ch.   The peril, lady!
" Chiappino, I have run a risk — a risk!
For when I prayed the Provost (he 's my friend)
To grant you a week's respite of the sentence
That confiscates your goods, exiles yourself,
He shrugged his shoulder — I say, shrugged it!
    Yes,
And fright of that drove all else from my head.
Here 's a good purse of *scudi:* off with you,
Lest of that shrug come what God only knows!
The *scudi* — friend, they 're trash — no thanks,
    I beg!
Take the north gate, — for San Vitale's suburb,
Whose double taxes you appealed against,
In discomposure at your ill-success
Is apt to stone you: there, there — only go!
Beside, Eulalia here looks sleepily.
Shake . . . oh, you hurt me, so you squeeze
    my wrist!"
— Is it not thus you 'll speak, adventurous
    friend?
[As he opens the door, LUITOLFO rushes in, his gar-
    ments disordered.
Eu. Luitolfo! Blood?
Luitolfo.   There 's more — and more of it!
Eulalia — take the garment! No —you, friend!
You take it and the blood from me — you dare!
Eu. Oh, who has hurt you? where 's the
    wound?
Ch.   " Who," say you?
The man with many a touch of virtue yet!
The Provost's friend has proved too frank of
    speech,
And this comes of it. Miserable hound!
This comes of temporizing, as I said!
Here 's fruit of your smooth speeches and soft
    looks!
Now see my way! As God lives, I go straight
To the palace and do justice, once for all!
Luit. What says he?
Ch.   I 'll do justice on him.
Luit.   Him?
Ch. The Provost.
Luit.   I 've just killed him.
Eu.   Oh, my God!
Luit. My friend, they 're on my trace;
    they 'll have me — now!
They 're round him, busy with him: soon
    they 'll find
He 's past their help, and then they 'll be on
    me!
Chiappino, save Eulalia! I forget . . .
Were you not bound for . . .
Ch.   Lugo?
Luit.   Ah — yes — yes!

That was the point I prayed of him to change.
Well, go — be happy! Is Eulalia safe?
They 're on me!
Ch. 'T is through me they reach you, then!
Friend, seem the man you are! Lock arms —
    that 's right!
Now tell me what you 've done; explain how
    you,
That still professed forbearance, still preached
    peace,
Could bring yourself . . .
Luit.   What was peace for, Chiappino?
I tried peace: did that promise, when peace
    failed,
Strife should not follow? All my peaceful
    days
Were just the prelude to a day like this.
I cried " You call me ' friend ': save my true
    friend!
Save him, or lose me!"
Ch.   But you never said
You meant to tell the Provost thus and thus.
Luit. Why should I say it? What else did
    I mean?
Ch. Well? He persisted?
Luit.   — " Would so order it
You should not trouble him too soon again."
I saw a meaning in his eye and lip;
I poured my heart's store of indignant words
Out on him: then — I know not! He retorted,
And I . . . some staff lay there to hand — I
    think
He bade his servants thrust me out — I
    struck . . .
Ah, they come! Fly you, save yourselves, you
    two!
The dead back-weight of the beheading axe!
The glowing trip-hook, thumbscrews and the
    gadge!
Eu. They do come! Torches in the Place!
    Farewell,
Chiappino! You can work no good to us —
Much to yourself; believe not, all the world
Must needs be cursed henceforth!
Ch.   And you?
Eu.   I stay.
Ch. Ha, ha! Now, listen! I am master
    here!
This was my coarse disguise; this paper shows
My path of flight and place of refuge — see —
Lugo, Argenta, past San Nicolo,
Ferrara, then to Venice and all 's safe!
Put on the cloak! His people have to fetch
A compass round about. There 's time enough
Ere they can reach us, so you straightway make
For Lugo . . . nay, he hears not! On with
    it —
The cloak, Luitolfo, do you hear me? See —
He obeys he knows not how. Then, if I must —
Answer me! Do you know the Lugo gate?
Eu. The northwest gate, over the bridge?
Luit.   I know.
Ch. Well, there — you are not frightened?
    all my route
Is traced in that: at Venice you escape
Their power. Eulalia, I am master here!
[Shouts from without. He pushes out LUITOLFO, who
        complies mechanically.

in time! Nay, help me with him — so! He's
gone.
Eu. What have you done? On you, per-
chance, all know
The Provost's hater, will men's vengeance fall
As our accomplice.
Ch. Mere accomplice? See!
[Putting on LUITOLFO's *vest.*
Now, lady, am I true to my profession,
Or one of these?
Eu. You take Luitolfo's place?
Ch. Die for him.
Eu. Well done!
[Shouts increase.
Ch. How the people tarry!
I can't be silent; I must speak : or sing —
How natural to sing now!
Eu. Hush and pray!
We are to die ; but even I perceive
'T is not a very hard thing so to die.
My cousin of the pale-blue tearful eyes,
Poor Cesca, suffers more from one day's life
With the stern husband ; Tisbe's heart goes
forth
Each evening after that wild son of hers,
To track his thoughtless footstep through the
streets :
How easy for them both to die like this!
I am not sure that I could live as they.
Ch. Here they come, crowds! they pass
the gate? Yes! — No! —
One torch is in the courtyard. Here flock all.
Eu. At least Luitolfo has escaped. What
cries!
Ch. If they would drag one to the market-
place,
One might speak there!
Eu. List, list!
Ch. They mount the steps.
(Enter the Populace.)
Ch. I killed the Provost!
The Populace. [Speaking together.] 'T was
Chiappino, friends!
Our savior! The best man at last as first!
He who first made us feel what chains we wore,
He also strikes the blow that shatters them,
He at last saves us — our best citizen!
— Oh, have you only courage to speak now?
My eldest son was christened a year since
"Cino" to keep Chiappino's name in mind —
Cino, for shortness merely, you observe!
The city's in our hands. The guards are fled.
Do you, the cause of all, come down — come
up —
Come out to counsel us, our chief, our king,
Whate'er rewards you! Choose your own re-
ward!
The peril over, its reward begins!
Come and harangue us in the market-place!
Eu. Chiappino?
Ch. Yes — I understand your eyes!
You think I should have promptlier disowned
This deed with its strange unforeseen success,
In favor of Luitolfo. But the peril,
So far from ended, hardly seems begun.
To-morrow, rather, when a calm succeeds,
We easily shall make him full amends :
And meantime — if we save them as they pray.

And justify the deed by its effects?
Eu. You would, for worlds, you had denied
at once.
Ch. I know my own intention, be assured!
All 's well. Precede us, fellow-citizens!

ACT II

The Market-place. LUITOLFO *in disguise mingling with
the* Populace *assembled opposite the* Provost's *Palace.*

1st Bystander. [To LUIT.] You, a friend of
Luitolfo's? Then, your friend is vanished, —
in all probability killed on the night that his
patron the tyrannical Provost was loyally sup-
pressed here, exactly a month ago, by our illus-
trious fellow-citizen, thrice-noble savior, and
new Provost that is like to be, this very morn-
ing, — Chiappino!
Luit. He the new Provost?
2d By. Up those steps will he go, and beneath
yonder pillar stand, while Ogniben, the Pope's
Legate from Ravenna, reads the new digni-
tary's title to the people, according to established
custom : for which reason, there is the assem-
blage you inquire about.
Luit. Chiappino — the late Provost's suc-
cessor? Impossible! But tell me of that
presently. What I would know first of all is,
wherefore Luitolfo must so necessarily have
been killed on that memorable night?
3d By. You were Luitolfo's friend? So was
I. Never, if you will credit me, did there exist
so poor-spirited a milk-sop. He, with all the
opportunities in the world, furnished by daily
converse with our oppressor, would not stir a
finger to help us : and, when Chiappino rose
in solitary majesty and . . . how does one go
on saying? . . . dealt the godlike blow, — this
Luitolfo, not unreasonably fearing the indigna-
tion of an aroused and liberated people, fled
precipitately. He may have got trodden to
death in the press at the southeast gate, when
the Provost's guards fled through it to Ravenna,
with their wounded master, — if he did not
rather hang himself under some hedge.
Luit. Or why not simply have lain perdue
in some quiet corner, — such as San Cassiano,
where his estate was, — receiving daily intelli-
gence from some sure friend, meanwhile, as to
the turn matters were taking here — how, for
instance, the Provost was not dead, after all,
only wounded — or, as to-day's news would
seem to prove, how Chiappino was not Brutus
the Elder, after all, only the new Provost — and
thus Luitolfo be enabled to watch a favorable
opportunity for returning? Might it not have
been so?
3d By. Why, he may have taken that care of
himself, certainly, for he came of a cautious
stock. I'll tell you how his uncle, just such
another gingerly treader on tiptoes with finger
on lip, — how he met his death in the great
plague-year : *dico vobis!* Hearing that the
seventeenth house in a certain street was in-
fected, he calculates to pass it in safety by
taking plentiful breath, say, when he shall
arrive at the eleventh house ; then scouring by,

holding that breath, till he be got so far on the other side as number twenty-three, and thus elude the danger. — And so did he begin ; but, as he arrived at thirteen, we will say, — thinking to improve on his precaution by putting up a little prayer to Saint Nepomucene of Prague, this exhausted so much of his lungs' reserve, that at sixteen it was clean spent, — consequently at the fatal seventeen he inhaled with a vigor and persistence enough to suck you any latent venom out of the heart of a stone — Ha, ha!

Luit. [*Aside.*] (If I had **not** lent that man the money he wanted last spring, I should fear this bitterness was attributable to me.) Luitolfo is dead then, one may conclude ?

3d By. Why, he had a house here, and a woman to whom he was affianced ; and as they both pass naturally to the new Provost, his friend and heir . . .

Luit. Ah, I suspected you of imposing on me with your pleasantry ! I know Chiappino better.

1st By. (Our friend has the bile ! After all, I do not dislike finding somebody vary a little this general gape of admiration at Chiappino's glorious qualities.) Pray, how much may you know of what has taken place in Faenza since that memorable night ?

Luit. It is most to the purpose, that I know Chiappino to have been by profession a hater of that very office of Provost, you now charge him with proposing to accept.

1st By. Sir, I 'll tell you. That night was indeed memorable. Up we rose, a mass of us, men, women, children ; out fled the guards with the body of the tyrant ; we were to defy the world : but, next gray morning, " What will Rome say ? " began everybody. You know we are governed by Ravenna, which is governed by Rome. And quietly into the town, by the Ravenna road, comes on muleback a portly personage, Ogniben by name, with the quality of Pontifical Legate ; trots briskly through the streets humming a " *Cur fremuere gentes,*" and makes directly for the Provost's Palace — there it faces you. " One Messer Chiappino is your leader ? I have known three-and-twenty leaders of revolts ! " (laughing gently to himself) — " Give me the help of your arm from my mule to yonder steps under the pillar — So ! And now, my revolters and good friends, what do you want ? The guards burst into Ravenna last night bearing your wounded Provost ; and, having had a little talk with him, I take on myself to come and try appease the disorderliness, before Rome, hearing of it, resort to another method : 't is I come, and not another, from a certain love I confess to, of composing differences. So, do you understand, you are about to experience this unheard-of tyranny from me, that there shall be no heading nor hanging, nor confiscation nor exile : I insist on your simply pleasing yourselves. And now, pray, what does please you ? To live without any government at all ? Or having decided for one, to see its minister murdered by the first of your body that chooses to find himself

wronged, or disposed for reverting to first principles and a justice anterior to all institutions, — and so will you carry matters, that the rest of the world must at length unite and put down such a den of wild beasts ? As for vengeance on what has just taken place, — once for all, the wounded man assures me he cannot conjecture who struck him ; and this so earnestly, that one may be sure he knows perfectly well what intimate acquaintance could find admission to speak with him late last evening. I come not for vengeance therefore, but from pure curiosity to hear what you will do next." And thus he ran on, on, easily and volubly, till he seemed to arrive quite naturally at the praise of law, order, and paternal government by somebody from rather a distance. All our citizens were in the snare, and about to be friends with so congenial an adviser ; but that Chiappino suddenly stood forth, spoke out in dignantly, and set things right again.

Luit. Do you see ? I recognize him there !

3d By. Ay, but, mark you, at the end of Chiappino's longest period in praise of a pure republic, — " And by whom do I desire such a government should be administered, perhaps, but by one like yourself ? " returns the Legate : thereupon speaking for a quarter of an hour together, on the natural and only legitimate government by the best and wisest. And it should seem there was soon discovered to be no such vast discrepancy at bottom between this and Chiappino's theory, place but each in its proper light. " Oh, are you there ? " quoth Chiappino : " Ay, in that, I agree," returns Chiappino : and so on.

Luit. But did Chiappino cede at once to this ?

1st By. Why, not altogether at once. For instance, he said that the difference between him and all his fellows was, that they seemed all wishing to be kings in one or another way, — " whereas what right," asked he, " has any man to wish to be superior to another ? " — whereat, " Ah, sir," answers the Legate, " this is the death of me, so often **as** I expect something is really going to be revealed to us by you clearer-seers, deeper-thinkers — this — that your right-hand (to speak by a figure) should be found taking up the weapon it displayed so ostentatiously, not to destroy any dragon in our path, as was prophesied, but simply to cut off its own fellow left-hand : yourself set about attacking yourself. For see now ! Here are you who, I make sure, glory exceedingly in knowing the noble nature of the soul, its divine impulses, and so forth ; and with such a knowledge you stand, as it were, armed to encounter the natural doubts and fears as to that same inherent nobility, which are apt to waylay us, the weaker ones, in the road of life. And when we look eagerly to see them fall before you, lo, round you wheel, only the left-hand gets the blow ; one proof of the soul's nobility destroys simply another proof, quite as good, of the same, for you are found delivering an opinion like this ! Why, what is this perpetual yearning to exceed, to subdue, to be better than, and a king over, one's fellows, — all that you so disclaim, — but the very tendency yourself are most proud of, and under another form, would oppose to it, — only in a lower stage of manifestation? You don't want to be vulgarly superior to your fellows after their poor fashion — to have me hold solemnly up your gown's tail, or hand you an express of the last importance from the Pope, with all these bystanders noticing how unconcerned you look the while: but neither does our gaping friend, the burgess yonder, want the other kind of kingship, that consists in understanding better than his fellows this and similar points of human nature, nor to roll under his tongue this sweeter morsel still, — the feeling that, through immense philosophy, he does *not* feel, he rather thinks, above you and me!" And so chatting, they glided off arm-in-arm.

Luit. And the result is . . .

1st By. Why that, a month having gone by, the indomitable Chiappino, marrying as he will Luitolfo's love — at all events succeeding to Luitolfo's wealth — becomes the first inhabitant of Faenza, and a proper aspirant to the Provost-ship; which we assemble here to see conferred on him this morning. The Legate's Guard to clear the way! ·He will follow presently.

Luit. [*Withdrawing a little.*] I understand the drift of Eulalia's communications less than ever. Yet she surely said, in so many words, that Chiappino was in urgent danger: wherefore, disregarding her injunction to continue in my retreat and await the result of — what she called, some experiment yet in process — I hastened here without her leave or knowledge: how could I else? But if this they say be true — if it were for such a purpose, she and Chiappino kept me away . . . Oh, no, no! I must confront him and her before I believe this of them. And at the word, see!

(*Enter* CHIAPPINO *and* EULALIA.)

Eu. We part here, then? The change in your principles would seem to be complete.

Ch. Now, why refuse to see that in my present course I change no principles, only re-adapt them and more adroitly? I had despaired of what you may call the material instrumentality of life; of ever being able to rightly operate on mankind through such a deranged machinery as the existing modes of government: but now, if I suddenly discover how to inform these perverted institutions with fresh purpose, bring the functionary limbs once more into immediate communication with, and subjection to, the soul I am about to bestow on them — do you see? Why should one desire to invent, as long as it remains possible to renew and transform? When all further hope of the old organization shall be extinct, then, I grant you, it may be time to try and create another.

Eu. And there being discoverable some hope yet in the hitherto much-abused old system of absolute government by a Provost here, you mean to take your time about endeavoring to realize those visions of a perfect State we once heard of?

Ch. Say, I would fain realize my conception of a palace, for instance, and that there is, abstractedly, but a single way of erecting one perfectly. Here, in the market-place is my allotted building-ground; here I stand without a stone to lay, or a laborer to help me, — stand, too, during a short day of life, close on which the night comes. On the other hand, circumstances suddenly offer me (turn and see it!) the old Provost's house to experiment upon — ruinous, if you please, wrongly constructed at the beginning, and ready to tumble now. But materials abound, a crowd of workmen offer their services; here exists yet a Hall of Audience of originally noble proportions, there a Guest-chamber of symmetrical design enough: and I may restore, enlarge, abolish or unite these to heart's content. Ought I not make the best of such an opportunity, rather than continue to gaze disconsolately with folded arms on the flat pavement here, while the sun goes slowly down, never to rise again? Since you cannot understand this nor me, it is better we should part as you desire.

Eu. So, the love breaks away too!

Ch. No, rather my soul's capacity for love widens — needs more than one object to content it, — and, being better instructed, will not persist in seeing all the component parts of love in what is only a single part, — nor in finding that so many and so various loves are all united in the love of a woman, — manifold uses in one instrument, as the savage has his sword, staff, sceptre and idol, all in one club-stick. Love is a very compound thing. The intellectual part of my love I shall give to men, the mighty dead or the illustrious living; and determine to call a mere sensual instinct by as few fine names as possible. What do I lose?

Eu. Nay, I only think, what do I lose? and, one more word — which shall complete my instruction — does friendship go too? What of Luitolfo, the author of your present prosperity?

Ch. How the author?

Eu. That blow not called yours . . .

Ch. Struck without principle or purpose, as by a blind natural operation: yet to which all my thought and life directly and advisedly tended. I would have struck it, and could not: he would have done his utmost to avoid striking it, yet did so. I dispute his right to that deed of mine — a final action with him, from the first effect of which he fled away, — a mere first step with me, on which I base a whole mighty superstructure of good to follow. Could he get good from it?

Eu. So we profess, so we perform!

(*Enter* OGNIBEN. EULALIA *stands apart.*)

Ogniben. I have seen three-and-twenty leaders of revolts. By your leave, sir! Perform? What does the lady say of performing?

Ch. Only the trite saying, that we must not trust profession, only performance.

Ogni. She'll not say that, sir, when she knows you longer; you'll instruct her better. Ever judge of men by their professions! For though the bright moment of promising is but a moment and cannot be prolonged, yet, if sincere in its moment's extravagant goodness, why, trust it and know the man by it, I say — not by his performance; which is half the world's work, interfere as the world needs must, with its accidents and circumstances: the profession was purely the man's own. I judge people by what they might be, — not are, nor will be.

Ch. But have there not been found, too, performing natures, not merely promising?

Ogni. Plenty. Little Bindo of our town, for instance, promised his friend, great ugly Masaccio, once, "I will repay you!" — for a favor done him. So, when his father came to die, and Bindo succeeded to the inheritance, he sends straightway for Masaccio and shares all with him — gives him half the land, half the money, half the kegs of wine in the cellar. "Good," say you: and it is good. But had little Bindo found himself possessor of all this wealth some five years before — on the happy night when Masaccio procured him that interview in the garden with his pretty cousin Lisa — instead of being the beggar he then was, — I am bound to believe that in the warm moment of promise he would have given away all the wine-kegs and all the money and all the land, and only reserved to himself some hut on a hilltop hard by, whence he might spend his life in looking and seeing his friend enjoy himself: he meant fully that much, but the world interfered. — To our business! Did I understand you just now within-doors? You are not going to marry your old friend's love, after all?

Ch. I must have a woman that can sympathize with, and appreciate me, I told you.

Ogni. Oh, I remember! You, the greater nature, needs must have a lesser one (— avowedly lesser — contest with you on that score would never do) — such a nature must comprehend you, as the phrase is, accompany and testify of your greatness from point to point onward. Why, that were being not merely as great as yourself, but greater considerably! Meantime, might not the more bounded nature as reasonably count on your appreciation of it, rather? — on your keeping close by it, so far as you both go together, and then going on by yourself as far as you please? Thus God serves us.

Ch. And yet a woman that could understand the whole of me, to whom I could reveal alike the strength and the weakness —

Ogni. Ah, my friend, wish for nothing so foolish! Worship your love, give her the best of you to see; be to her like the western lands (they bring us such strange news of) to the Spanish Court; send her only your lumps of gold, fans of feathers, your spirit-like birds, and fruits and gems! So shall you, what is unseen of you, be supposed altogether a paradise by her, — as these western lands by Spain: though I warrant there is filth, red baboons, ugly reptiles and squalor enough, which they bring Spain as few samples of as possible. Do you want your mistress to respect your body generally? Offer her your mouth to kiss: don't strip off your boot and put your foot to her lips! You understand my humor by this time? I help men to carry out their own prin-

ciples: if they please to say two and two make five, I assent, so they will but go on and say, four and four make ten.

Ch. But these are my private affairs; what I desire you to occupy yourself about, is my public appearance presently: for when the people hear that I am appointed Provost, though you and I may thoroughly discern — and easily, too — the right principle at bottom of such a movement, and how my republicanism remains thoroughly unaltered, only takes a form of expression hitherto commonly judged (and heretofore by myself) incompatible with its existence, — when thus I reconcile myself to an old form of government instead of proposing a new one —

Ogni. Why, you must deal with people broadly. Begin at a distance from this matter and say, — New truths, old truths! sirs, there is nothing new possible to be revealed to us in the moral world; we know all we shall ever know: and it is for simply reminding us, by their various respective expedients, how we do know this and the other matter, that men get called prophets, poets and the like. A philosopher's life is spent in discovering that, of the half-dozen truths he knew when a child, such an one is a lie, as the world states it in set terms; and then, after a weary lapse of years, and plenty of hard thinking, it becomes a truth again after all, as he happens to newly consider it and view it in a different relation with the others: and so he re-states it, to the confusion of somebody else in good time. As for adding to the original stock of truths, — impossible! Thus, you see the expression of them is the grand business: — you have got a truth in your head about the right way of governing people, and you took a mode of expressing it which now you confess to be imperfect. But what then? There is truth in falsehood, falsehood in truth. No man ever told one great truth, that I know, without the help of a good dozen of lies at least, generally unconscious ones. And as when a child comes in breathlessly and relates a strange story, you try to conjecture from the very falsities in it what the reality was, — do not conclude that he saw nothing in the sky, because he assuredly did not see a flying horse there as he says, — so, through the contradictory expression, do you see, men should look painfully for, and trust to arrive eventually at, what you call the true principle at bottom. Ah, what an answer is there! to what will it not prove applicable? — "Contradictions? Of course there were," say you!

Ch. Still, the world at large may call it inconsistency, and what shall I urge in reply?

Ogni. Why, look you, when they tax you with tergiversation or duplicity, you may answer — you begin to perceive that, when all 's done and said, both great parties in the State, the advocators of change in the present system of things, and the opponents of it, patriot and anti-patriot, are found working together for the common good; and that in the midst of their efforts for and against its progress, the world somehow or other still advances: to which result they contribute in equal proportions, those who spend their life in pushing it onward, as those who give theirs to the business of pulling it back. Now, if you found the world stand still between the opposite forces, and were glad, I should conceive you: but it steadily advances, you rejoice to see! By the side of such a rejoicer, the man who only winks as he keeps cunning and quiet, and says, "Let yonder hot-headed fellow fight out my battle! I, for one, shall win in the end by the blows he gives, and which I ought to be giving," — even he seems graceful in his avowal, when one considers that he might say, "I shall win quite as much by the blows our antagonist gives him, blows from which he saves me — I thank the antagonist equally!" Moreover, you may enlarge on the loss of the edge of party-animosity with age and experience . . .

Ch. And naturally time must wear off such asperities : the bitterest adversaries get to discover certain points of similarity between each other, common sympathies — do they not ?

Ogni. Ay, had the young David but sat first to dine on his cheeses with the Philistine, he had soon discovered an abundance of such common sympathies. He of Gath, it is recorded, was born of a father and mother, had brothers and sisters like another man, — they, no more than the sons of Jesse, were used to eat each other. But, for the sake of one broad antipathy that had existed from the beginning, David slung the stone, cut off the giant's head, made a spoil of it, and after ate his cheeses alone, with the better appetite, for all I can learn. My friend, as you, with a quickened eyesight, go on discovering much good on the worse side, remember that the same process should proportionably magnify and demonstrate to you the much more good on the better side! And when I profess no sympathy for the Goliaths of our time, and you object that a large nature should sympathize with every form of intelligence, and see the good in it, however limited, — I answer, "So I do; but preserve the proportions of my sympathy, however finelier or widelier I may extend its action." I desire to be able, with a quickened eyesight, to descry beauty in corruption where others see foulness only ; but I hope I shall also continue to see a redoubled beauty in the higher forms of matter, where already everybody sees no foulness at all. I must retain, too, my old power of selection, and choice of appropriation, to apply to such new gifts ; else they only dazzle instead of enlightening me. God has his archangels and consorts with them: though he made too, and intimately sees what is good in, the worm. Observe, I speak only as you profess to think and so ought to speak : I do justice to your own principles, that is all.

Ch. But you very well know that the two parties do, on occasion, assume each other's characteristics. What more disgusting, for instance, than to see how promptly the newly emancipated slave will adopt, in his own favor, the very measures of precaution, which pressed soreliest on himself as institutions of the tyranny he has just escaped from ? Do the classes, hitherto without opinion, get leave to express it ? there follows a confederacy immediately, from which — exercise your individual right and dissent, and woe be to you !

Ogni. And a journey over the sea to you ! That is the generous way. Cry — "Emancipated slaves, the first excess, and off I go !" The first time a poor devil, who has been bastinadoed steadily his whole life long, finds himself let alone and able to legislate, so, begins pettishly, while he rubs his soles, "Woe be to whoever brings anything in the shape of a stick this way ! " — you, rather than give up the very innocent pleasure of carrying one to switch flies with, — you go away, to everybody's sorrow. Yet you were quite reconciled to staying at home while the governors used to pass, every now and then, some such edict as, "Let no man indulge in owning a stick which is not thick enough to chastise our slaves, if need require ! " Well, there are pre-ordained hierarchies among us, and a profane vulgar subjected to a different law altogether ; yet I am rather sorry you should see it so clearly : for, do you know what is to — all but save you at the Day of Judgment, all you men of genius ? It is this: that, while you generally began by pulling down God, and went on to the end of your life in one effort at setting up your own genius in his place, — still, the last, bitterest concession wrung with the utmost unwillingness from the experience of the very loftiest of you, was invariably — would one think it ? — that the rest of mankind, down to the lowest of the mass, stood not, nor ever could stand, just on a level and equality with yourselves. That will be a point in the favor of all such, I hope and believe.

Ch. Why, men of genius are usually charged, I think, with doing just the reverse ; and at once acknowledging the natural inequality of mankind, by themselves participating in the universal craving after, and deference to, the civil distinctions which represent it. You wonder they pay such undue respect to titles and badges of superior rank.

Ogni. Not I (always on your own ground and showing, be it noted !) Who doubts that, with a weapon to brandish, a man is the more formidable ? Titles and badges are exercised as such a weapon, to which you and I look up wistfully. We could pin lions with it moreover, while in its present owner's hands it hardly prods rats. Nay, better than a mere weapon of easy mastery and obvious use, it is a mysterious divining-rod that may serve us in undreamed-of ways. Beauty, strength, intellect — men often have none of these, and yet conceive pretty accurately what kind of advantages they would bestow on the possessor. We know at least what it is we make up our mind to forego, and so can apply the fittest substitute in our power. Wanting beauty, we cultivate good-humor ; missing wit, we get riches: but the mystic unimaginable operation of that gold collar and string of Latin names which suddenly turned poor stupid little peevish Cecco of our town into natural lord of the best of us — a Duke, he is now — there indeed is a virtue to be reverenced !

Ch. Ay, by the vulgar : not by Messere Stiatta the poet, who pays more assiduous court to him than anybody.

Ogni. What else should Stiatta pay court to ? He has talent, not honor and riches : men naturally covet what they have not.

Ch. No ; or Cecco would covet talent, which he has not, whereas he covets more riches, of which he has plenty, already.

Ogni. Because a purse added to a purse makes the holder twice as rich : but just such another talent as Stiatta's, added to what he now possesses, what would that profit him ? Give the talent a purse indeed, to do something with ! But lo, how we keep the good people waiting ! I only desired to do justice to the noble sentiments which animate you, and which you are too modest to duly enforce. Come, to our main business : shall we ascend the steps ? I am going to propose you for Provost to the people ; they know your antecedents, and will accept you with a joyful unanimity : whereon I confirm their choice. Rouse up ! Are you nerving yourself to an effort ? Beware the disaster of Messere Stiatta we were talking of ! who, determining to keep an equal mind and constant face on whatever might be the fortune of his last new poem with our townsmen, heard too plainly "hiss, hiss, hiss," increase every moment. Till at last the man fell senseless : not perceiving that the portentous sounds had all the while been issuing from between his own nobly clenched teeth, and nostrils narrowed by resolve.

Ch. Do you begin to throw off the mask ? — to jest with me, having got me effectually into your trap ?

Ogni. Where is the trap, my friend ? You hear what I engage to do, for my part : you, for yours, have only to fulfil your promise made just now within doors, of professing unlimited obedience to Rome's authority in my person. And I shall authorize no more than the simple re-establishment of the Provostship and the conferment of its privileges upon yourself : the only novel stipulation being a birth of the peculiar circumstances of the time.

Ch. And that stipulation ?

Ogni. Just the obvious one — that in the event of the discovery of the actual assailant of the late Provost . . .

Ch. Ha !

Ogni. Why, he shall suffer the proper penalty, of course ; what did you expect ?

Ch. Who heard of this ?

Ogni. Rather, who needed to hear of this ?

Ch. Can it be, the popular rumor never reached you . . .

Ogni. Many more such rumors reach me, friend, than I choose to receive : those which wait longest have best chance. Has the present one sufficiently waited ? Now is its time for entry with effect. See the good people crowding about yonder palace-steps — which we may not have to ascend, after all ! My good friends ! (nay, two or three of you will answer every purpose) — who was it fell upon and proved nearly the death of your late Provost ? His successor desires to hear, that his day of inau-

guration may be graced by the act of prompt, bare justice we all anticipate. Who dealt the blow that night, does anybody know ?

Luit. [*Coming forward*]. I !

All. Luitolfo !

Luit. I avow the deed, justify and approve it, and stand forth now, to relieve my friend of an unearned responsibility. Having taken thought, I am grown stronger : I shall shrink from nothing that awaits me. Nay, Chiappino — we are friends still : I dare say there is some proof of your superior nature in this starting aside, strange as it seemed at first. So, they tell me, my horse is of the right stock, because a shadow in the path frightens him into a frenzy, makes him dash my brains out. I understand only the dull mule's way of standing stockishly, plodding soberly, suffering on occasion a blow or two with due patience.

Eu. I was determined to justify my choice, Chiappino ; to let Luitolfo's nature vindicate itself. Henceforth we are undivided, whatever be our fortune.

Ogni. Now, in these last ten minutes of silence, what have I been doing, deem you ? Putting the finishing stroke to a homily of mine, I have long taken thought to perfect, on the text, "Let whoso thinketh he standeth, take heed lest he fall." To your house, Luitolfo ! Still silent, my patriotic friend ? Well, that is a good sign however. And you will go aside for a time ? That is better still. I understand : it would be easy for you to die of remorse here on the spot and shock us all, but you mean to live and grow worthy of coming back to us one day. There, I will tell everybody ; and you only do right to believe you must get better as you get older. All men do so : they are worst in childhood, improve in manhood, and get ready in old age for another world. Youth, with its beauty and grace, would seem bestowed on us for some such reason as to make us partly endurable till we have time for really becoming so of ourselves, without their aid ; when they leave us. The sweetest child we all smile on for his pleasant want of the whole world to break up, or suck in his mouth, seeing no other good in it — would be rudely handled by that world's inhabitants, if he retained those angelic infantine desires when he had grown six feet high, black and bearded. But, little by little, he sees fit to forego claim after claim on the world, puts up with a less and less share of its good as his proper portion ; and when the octogenarian asks barely a sup of gruel and a fire of dry sticks, and thanks you as for his full allowance and right in the common good of life, — hoping nobody may murder him, — he who began by asking and expecting the whole of us to bow down in worship to him, — why, I say he is advanced, far onward, very far, nearly out of sight like our friend Chiappino yonder. And now — (ay, good-by to you ! He turns round the northwest gate : going to Lugo again ? Good-by !) — And now give thanks to God, the keys of the Provost's palace to me, and yourselves to profitable meditation at home ! I have known *Four*-and-twenty leaders of revolts.

LURIA

A TRAGEDY

I DEDICATE THIS LAST ATTEMPT FOR THE PRESENT AT DRAMATIC POETRY
TO A GREAT DRAMATIC POET;
" WISHING WHAT I WRITE MAY BE READ BY HIS LIGHT:"
IF A PHRASE ORIGINALLY ADDRESSED, BY NOT THE LEAST WORTHY OF HIS CONTEMPORARIES
TO SHAKESPEARE,
MAY BE APPLIED HERE, BY ONE WHOSE SOLE PRIVILEGE IS IN A GRATEFUL ADMIRATION,
To WALTER SAVAGE LANDOR
London, 1846.

PERSONS

LURIA, a Moor, Commander of the Florentine Forces.
HUSAIN, a Moor, his friend.
PUCCIO, the old Florentine Commander, now LURIA's Chief Officer.
BRACCIO, Commissary of the Republic of Florence.
JACOPO (LAPO), his Secretary.
TIBURZIO, Commander of the Pisans.
DOMIZIA, a noble Florentine Lady.

TIME, 14—.

SCENE. LURIA's *Camp between Florence and Pisa.*

ACT I

MORNING

BRACCIO, *as dictating to his* Secretary ; PUCCIO *standing by.*

Braccio.[*To* PUCCIO.] Then, you join battle in an hour ?
Puccio.   Not I ;
Luria, the captain.
Brac. [*To the* Sec.] " In an hour, the battle."
[*To* PUC.] Sir, let your eye run o'er this loose digest,
And see if very much of your report
Have slipped away through my civilian phrase.
Does this instruct the Signory aright
How army stands with army ?
 Puc. [*Taking the paper.*] All seems here :
— That Luria, seizing with our city's force
The several points of vantage, hill and plain,
Shuts Pisa safe from help on every side,
And, baffling the Lucchese arrived too late,
Must, in the battle he delivers now,
Beat her best troops and first of chiefs.
Brac.   So sure ?
Tiburzio 's a consummate captain too !
Puc. Luria holds Pisa's fortune in his hand.
Brac. [*To the* Sec.] " The Signory hold Pisa in their hand."
Your own proved soldiership 's our warrant, sir :
So, while my secretary ends his task,
Have out two horsemen, by the open roads,
To post with it to Florence !
Puc. [*Returning the paper.*] All seems here ;
Unless . . . Ser Braccio, 't is my last report !
Since Pisa's outbreak, and my overthrow,
And Luria's hastening at the city's call
To save her, as he only could, no doubt ;
Till now that she is saved or sure to be, —
Whatever you tell Florence, I tell you :
Each day's note you, her Commissary, make
Of Luria's movements, I myself supply.
No youngster am I longer, to my cost ;
Therefore while Florence gloried in her choice
And vaunted Luria, whom but Luria, still,
As if zeal, courage, prudence, conduct, faith,
Had never met in any man before,
I saw no pressing need to swell the cry.
But now, this last report and I have done :
So, ere to-night comes with its roar of praise,
'T were not amiss if some one old i' the trade
Subscribed with, " True, for once rash counsel 's best.
This Moor of the bad faith and doubtful race,
This boy to whose untried sagacity,
Raw valor, Florence trusts without reserve
The charge to save her, — justifies her choice ;
In no point has this stranger failed his friends.
Now praise ! " I say this, and it is not here.
Brac. [*To the* Sec.] Write, " Puccio, super-seded in the charge,
By Luria, bears full witness to his worth,
And no reward our Signory can give
Their champion but he 'll back it cheerfully."
Aught more ? Five minutes hence, both mes-sengers !   [PUCCIO *goes.*
Brac. [*After a pause, and while he slowly tears the paper into shreds.*] I think . . . (pray God, I hold in fit contempt
This warfare's noble art and ordering,
And, — once the brace of prizers fairly matched,
Poleaxe with poleaxe, knife with knife as good, —
Spit properly at what men term their skill ! —)
Yet here I think our fighter has the odds.
With Pisa's strength diminished thus and thus,
Such points of vantage in our hands and such,
Lucca still off the stage, too, — all 's assured :
Luria must win this battle. Write the Court,
That Luria's trial end and sentence pass !
Secretary. Patron, —
Brac.   Ay, Lapo ?
Sec.   If you trip, I fall ;
'T is in self-interest I speak —
Brac.   Nay, nay,
You overshoot the mark, my Lapo ! Nay !
When did I say pure love 's impossible ?

I make you daily write those red cheeks thin,
Load your young brow with what concerns it
    least,
And, when we visit Florence, let you pace
The Piazza by my side as if we talked,
Where all your old acquaintances may see:
You 'd die for me, I should not be surprised.
Now then!
    Sec.   Sir, look about and love yourself!
Step after step, the Signory and you
Tread gay till this tremendous point 's to pass;
Which pass not, pass not, ere you ask your-
    self, —
Bears the brain steadily such draughts of fire,
Or too delicious may not prove the pride
Of this long secret trial you dared plan,
Dare execute, you solitary here,
With the gray-headed toothless fools at home,
Who think themselves your lords, such slaves
    are they?
If they pronounce this sentence as you bid,
Declare the treason, claim its penalty, —
And sudden out of all the blaze of life,
On the best minute of his brightest day,
From that adoring army at his back,
Through Florence' joyous crowds before his
    face,
Into the dark you beckon Luria . . .
    Brac.   Then —
Why, Lapo, when the fighting-people vaunt,
We of the other craft and mystery,
May we not smile demure, the danger past?
    Sec. Sir, no, no, no, — the danger, and your
    spirit
At watch and ward? Where 's danger on your
    part,
With that thin flitting instantaneous steel
'Gainst the blind bull-front of a brute-force
    world?
If Luria, that 's to perish sure as fate,
Should have been really guiltless after all?
    Brac. Ah, you have thought that?
    Sec.   Here I sit, your scribe,
And in and out goes Luria, days and nights;
This Puccio comes; the Moor his other friend,
Husain; they talk — that 's all feigned easily;
He speaks (I would not listen if I could),
Reads, orders, counsels: — but he rests some-
    times, —
I see him stand and eat, sleep stretched an
    hour
On the lynx-skins yonder; hold his bared black
    arms
Into the sun from the tent-opening; laugh
When his horse drops the forage from his teeth
And neighs to hear him hum his Moorish songs.
That man believes in Florence, as the saint
Tied to the wheel believes in God.
    Brac.   How strange!
You too have thought that!
    Sec.   Do but you think too,
And all is saved! I only have to write,
" The man seemed false awhile, proves true at
    last;
Bury it " — so I write the Signory —
" Bury this trial in your breast forever,
Blot it from things or done or dreamed about!
So Luria shall receive his meed to-day

With no suspicion what reverse was near, —
As if no meteoric finger hushed
The doom-word just on the destroyer's lip,
Motioned him off, and let life's sun fall straight."
    Brac. [*Looks to the wall of the tent.*] Did he
        draw that?
    Sec.   With charcoal, when the watch
Made the report at midnight; Lady Domizia
Spoke of the unfinished Duomo, you remember;
That is his fancy how a Moorish front
Might join to, and complete, the body, — a
    sketch, —
And again where the cloak hangs, yonder in the
    shadow.
    Brac. He loves that woman.
    Sec.   She is sent the spy
Of Florence, — spies on you as you on him:
Florence, if only for Domizia's sake,
Is surely safe. What shall I write?
    Brac.   I see —
A Moorish front, nor of such ill design!
Lapo, there 's one thing plain and positive;
Man seeks his own good at the whole world's
    cost.
What? If to lead our troops, stand forth our
    chiefs,
And hold our fate, and see us at their beck,
Yet render up the charge when peace return,
Have ever proved too much for Florentines,
Even for the best and bravest of ourselves —
If in the struggle when the soldier's sword
Should sink its point before the statist's pen,
And the calm head replace the violent hand,
Virtue on virtue still have fallen away
Before ambition with unvarying fate,
Till Florence' self at last in bitterness
Be forced to own such falls the natural end,
And, sparing further to expose her sons
To a vain strife and profitless disgrace,
Declare, " The foreigner, one not my child,
Shall henceforth lead my troops, reach height
    by height
The glory, then descend into the shame;
So shall rebellion be less guilt in him,
And punishment the easier task for me: "
— If on the best of us such brand she set,
Can I suppose an utter alien here,
This Luria, our inevitable foe,
Confessed a mercenary and a Moor,
Born free from many ties that bind the rest
Of common faith in Heaven or hope on earth,
No past with us, no future, — such a spirit
Shall hold the path from which our staunchest
    broke,
Stand firm where every famed precursor fell?
My Lapo, I will frankly say, these proofs
So duly noted of the man's intent,
Are for the doting fools at home, not me.
The charges here, they may be true or false:
— What is set down? Errors and oversights,
A dallying interchange of courtesies
With Pisa's General, — all that, hour by hour,
Puccio's pale discontent has furnished us,
Of petulant speeches, inconsiderate acts,
Now overhazard, overcaution now;
Even that he loves this lady who believes
She outwits Florence, and whom Florence
    posted

By my procurement here, to spy on me,
Lest I one minute lose her from my sight —
She who remembering her whole House's fall,
That nest of traitors strangled in the birth,
Now labors to make Luria (poor device
As plain) the instrument of her revenge!
— That she is ever at his ear to prompt
Inordinate conceptions of his worth,
Exorbitant belief in worth's reward,
And after, when sure disappointment follows,
Proportionable rage at such a wrong —
Why, all these reasons, while I urge them
        most,
Weigh with me less than least; as nothing
        weigh.
Upon that broad man's-heart of his, I go:
On what I know must be, yet while I live
Shall never be, because I live and know.
Brute-force shall not rule Florence! Intellect
May rule her, bad or good as chance supplies:
But intellect it shall be, pure if bad,
And intellect's tradition so kept up!
Till the good come — 't was intellect that ruled,
Not brute-force bringing from the battlefield
The attributes of wisdom, foresight's graces
We lent it there to lure its grossness on;
All which it took for earnest and kept safe
To show against us in our market-place,
Just as the plumes and tags and swordsman's-
        gear
(Fetched from the camp where, at their foolish
        best,
When all was done they frightened nobody)
Perk in our faces in the street, forsooth,
With our own warrant and allowance. No!
The whole procedure 's overcharged, — its end
In too strict keeping with the bad first step.
To conquer Pisa was sheer inspiration?
Well then, to perish for a single fault,
Let that be simple justice! There, my Lapo!
A Moorish front ill suits our Duomo's body:
Blot it out — and bid Luria's sentence come!
(LURIA, *who, with* DOMIZIA, *has entered unobserved at
        the close of the last phrase, now advances.*)
  Luria. And Luria, Luria, what of Luria
        now?
  Brac. Ah, you so close, sir? Lady Domizia
        too?
I said it needs must be a busy moment
For one like you; that you were now i' the
        thick
Of your duties, doubtless, while we idlers sat ...
  Lur. No — in that paper, — it was in that
        paper
What you were saying!
  Brac.   Oh — my day's despatch!
I censure you to Florence: will you see?
  Lur. See your despatch, your last, for the
        first time?
Well, if I should, now? For in truth, Domizia,
He would be forced to set about another,
In his sly cool way, the true Florentine,
To mention that important circumstance.
So, while he wrote I should gain time, such
        time!
Do not send this!
  Brac.   And wherefore?
  Lur.   These Lucchese

Are not arrived — they never will arrive!
And I must fight to-day, arrived or not,
And I shall beat Tiburzio, that is sure:
And then will be arriving his Lucchese,
But slowly, oh so slowly, just in time
To look upon my battle from the hills,
Like a late moon, of use to nobody!
And I must break my battle up, send forth,
Surround on this side, hold in check on that.
Then comes to-morrow, we negotiate,
You make me send for fresh instructions home
— Incompleteness, incompleteness!
  Brac.   Ah, we scribes
Why, I had registered that very point,
The non-appearance of our foes' ally,
As a most happy fortune; both at once
Were formidable : singly faced, each falls.
  Lur. So, no great battle for my Florentines
No crowning deed, decisive and complete,
For all of them, the simple as the wise,
Old, young, alike, that do not understand
Our wearisome pedantic art of war,
By which we prove retreat may be success,
Delay — best speed, — half loss, at times,—
        whole gain:
They want results : as if it were their fault!
And you, with warmest wish to be my friend,
Will not be able now to simply say
"Your servant has performed his task—
        enough!
You ordered, he has executed : good!
Now walk the streets in holiday attire,
Congratulate your friends, till noon strikes
        fierce,
Then form bright groups beneath the Duomo's
        shade!"
No, you will have to argue and explain,
Persuade them, all is not so ill in the end,
Tease, tire them out! Arrive, arrive, Lucchese!
  Domizia. Well, you will triumph for the past
        enough,
Whatever be the present chance; no service
Falls to the ground with Florence: she awaits
Her savior, will receive him fittingly.
  Lur. Ah, Braccio, you know Florence! Will
        she, think you,
Receive one . . . what means "fittingly re-
        ceive"?
— Receive compatriots, doubtless — I am none:
And yet Domizia promises so much!
  Brac. Kind women still give men a woman's
        prize.
I know not o'er which gate most boughs will
        arch,
Nor if the Square will wave red flags or blue.
I should have judged, the fullest of rewards
Our state gave Luria, when she made him chief
Of her whole force, in her best captain's place.
  Lur. That, my reward? Florence on my
        account
Relieved Ser Puccio? — mark you, my reward!
And Puccio 's having all the fight's true joy —
Goes here and there, gets close, may fight, him-
        self,
While I must order, stand aloof, o'ersee.
That was my calling, there was my true place!
I should have felt, in some one over me,
Florence impersonate, my visible head.

As I am over Puccio, — taking life
Directly from her eye! They give me you:
But do you cross me, set me half to work?
I enjoy nothing — though I will, for once!
Decide, shall we join battle? may I wait?
   Brac. Let us compound the matter; wait
    till noon:
Then, no arrival, —
   Lur.   Ah, noon comes too fast!
I wonder, do you guess why I delay
Involuntarily the final blow
As long as possible? Peace follows it!
Florence at peace, and the calm studious heads
Come out again, the penetrating eyes;
As if a spell broke, all 's resumed, each art
You boast, more vivid that it slept awhile.
'Gainst the glad heaven, o'er the white palace-
    front
The interrupted scaffold climbs anew;
The walls are peopled by the painter's brush;
The statue to its niche ascends to dwell.
The present noise and trouble have retired
And left the eternal past to rule once more;
You speak its speech and read its records plain,
Greece lives with you, each Roman breathes
    your friend:
But Luria — where will then be Luria's place?
   Dom. Highest in honor, for that past's own
    sake,
Of which his actions, sealing up the sum
By saving all that went before from wreck,
Will range as part, with which be worshipped too.
   Lur. Then I may walk and watch you in
    your streets,
Lead the smooth life my rough life helps no
    more,
So different, so new, so beautiful —
Nor fear that you will tire to see parade
The club that slew the lion, now that crooks
And shepherd-pipes come into use again?
For very lone and silent seems my East
In its drear vastness: still it spreads, and still
No Braccios, no Domizias anywhere —
Not ever more! Well, well, to-day is ours!
   Dom. [*To* BRAC.] Should he not have been
    one of us?
   Lur.   Oh, no!
Not one of you, and so escape the thrill
Of coming into you, of changing thus, —
Feeling a soul grow on me that restricts
The boundless unrest of the savage heart!
The sea heaves up, hangs loaded o'er the land,
Breaks there and buries its tumultuous
    strength;
Horror, and silence, and a pause awhile:
Lo, inland glides the gulf-stream, miles away,
In rapture of assent, subdued and still,
'Neath those strange banks, those unimagined
    skies.
Well, 't is not sure the quiet lasts forever!
Your placid heads still find rough hands new
    work;
Some minute's chance — there comes the need
    of mine.
And, all resolved on, I too hear at last.
Oh, you must find some use for me, Ser Braccio!
You hold my strength; 't were best dispose of
    it:

What you created, see that you find food for —
I shall be dangerous else!
   Brac.   How dangerous, sir?
   Lur. There are so many ways, Domizia
    warns me,
And one with half the power that I possess,
— Grows very formidable! Do you doubt?
Why, first, who holds the army . . .
   Dom.   While we talk.
Morn wears; we keep you from your proper
    place,
The field.
   Lur. Nay, to the field I move no more;
My part is done, and Puccio's may begin:
I cannot trench upon his province longer
With any face. — You think yourselves so safe?
Why, see — in concert with Tiburzio, now —
One could . . .
   Dom.   A trumpet!
   Lur.   My Lucchese at last!
Arrived, as sure as Florence stands! Your
    leave!   [*Springs out.*
   Dom. How plainly is true greatness charac-
    tered
By such unconscious sport as Luria's here,
Strength sharing least the secret of itself!
Be it with head that schemes or hand that acts,
Such save the world which none but they could
    save,
Yet think whate'er they did, that world could
    do.
   Brac. Yes: and how worthy note, that these
    same great ones
In hand or head, with such unconsciousness
And all its due entailed humility,
Should never shrink, so far as I perceive,
From taking up whatever tool there be
Effects the whole world's safety or mishap,
Into their mild hands as a thing of course!
The statist finds it natural to lead
The mob who might as easily lead him —
The captain marshals troops born skilled in
    war —
Statist and captain verily believe!
While we poor scribes . . . you catch me think
    ing now,
That I shall in this very letter write
What none of you are able! To it, Lapo!
               [DOMIZIA *goes*
This last worst all-affected childish fit
Of Luria's, this be-praised unconsciousness,
Convinces me; the past was no child's play:
It was a man beat Pisa, — not a child.
All 's mere dissimulation — to remove
The fear, he best knows we should entertain.
The utmost danger was at hand. Is 't written?
Now make a duplicate, lest this should fail,
And speak your fullest on the other side.
   Sec. I noticed he was busily repairing
My half-effacement of his Duomo sketch,
And, while he spoke of Florence, turned to it,
As the Mage Negro king to Christ the babe.
I judge his childishness the mere relapse
To boyhood of a man who has worked lately,
And presently will work, so, meantime, plays:
Whence, more than ever I believe in him.
   Brac. [*After a pause.*] The sword! At best,
    the soldier, as he says,

In Florence — the black face, the barbarous
  name,
For Italy to boast her show of the age,
Her man of men! — To Florence with each
  letter!

ACT II

NOON

Dom. Well, Florence, shall I reach thee,
  pierce thy heart
Through all its safeguards? Hate is said to
  help —
Quicken the eye, invigorate the arm;
And this my hate, made up of many hates,
Might stand in scorn of visible instrument,
And will thee dead: yet do I trust it not.
Nor man's devices nor Heaven's memory
Of wickedness forgot on earth so soon,
But thy own nature, — hell and thee I trust,
To keep thee constant in that wickedness,
Where my revenge may meet thee. Turn aside
A single step, for gratitude or shame, —
Grace but this Luria, — this wild mass of rage
I have prepared to launch against thee now, —
With other payment than thy noblest found, —
Give his desert for once its due reward, —
And past thee would my sure destruction roll.
But thou, who mad'st our House thy sacrifice,
It cannot be thou wilt except this Moor
From the accustomed fate of zeal and truth:
Thou wilt deny his looked-for recompense,
And then — I reach thee. Old and trained, my
  sire
Could bow down on his quiet broken heart,
Die awe-struck and submissive, when at last
The strange blow came for the expected wreath;
And Porzio passed in blind bewilderment
To exile, never to return, — they say,
Perplexed in his frank simple honest soul,
As if some natural law had changed, — how
  else
Could Florence, on plain fact pronouncing thus,
Judge Porzio's actions worthy such reward?
But Berto, with the ever-passionate pulse,
— Oh that long night, its dreadful hour on hour,
In which no way of getting his fair fame
From their inexplicable charges free,
Was found, save pouring forth the impatient
  blood
To show its color whether false or no!
My brothers never had a friend like me
Close in their need to watch the time, then
  speak,
— Burst with a wakening laughter on their
  dream,
Cry, "Florence was all falseness, so, false
  here!"
And show them what a simple task remained —
To leave dreams, rise, and punish in God's name
The city wedded to the wickedness.
None stood by them as I by Luria stand.
So, when the stranger cheated of his due
Turns on thee as his rapid nature bids,
Then, Florence, think, a hireling at thy throat
For the first outrage, think who bore thy last,
Yet mutely in forlorn obedience died!

He comes — his friend — black faces in the
  camp
Where moved those peerless brows and eyes of
  old.
          (*Enter* LURIA *and* HUSAIN.)
  Well, and the movement — is it as you hope?
'T is Lucca?
  Lur.   Ah, the Pisan trumpet merely!
Tiburzio's envoy, I must needs receive.
  Dom. Whom I withdraw before; though if
  I lingered
You could not wonder, for my time fleets fast.
The overtaking night brings such reward!
And where will then be room for me? Yet
  praised,
Remember who was first to promise praise,
And envy those who also can perform!   [*Goes.*
  Lur. This trumpet from the Pisans? —
  Husain.   In the camp,
A very noble presence — Braccio's visage
On Puccio's body — calm and fixed and good;
A man I seem as I had seen before:
Most like, it was some statue had the face.
  Lur. Admit him! This will prove the last
  delay.
  Hus. Ay, friend, go on, and die thou going
  on!
Thou heard'st what the grave woman said but
  now:
To-night rewards thee. That is well to hear;
But stop not therefore: hear it, and go on!
  Lur. Oh, their reward and triumph and the
  rest
They round me in the ears with, all day long?
All that, I never take for earnest, friend!
Well would it suit us, — their triumphal arch
Or storied pillar, — thee and me, the Moors!
But gratitude in those Italian eyes —
That, we shall get?
  Hus.   It is too cold an air.
Our sun rose out of yonder mound of mist:
Where is he now? So, I trust none of them.
  Lur. Truly?
  Hus. I doubt and fear. There stands a wall
'Twixt our expansive and explosive race
And those absorbing, concentrating men.
They use thee.
  Lur.   And I feel it, Husain! yes,
And care not — yes, an alien force like mine
Is only called to play its part outside
Their different nature; where its sole use seems
To fight with and keep off an adverse force,
As alien, — which repelled, mine too withdraws:
Inside, they know not what to do with me.
Thus I have told them laughingly and oft,
But long since am prepared to learn the worst.
  Hus. What is the worst?
  Lur.   I will forestall them, Husain,
Will speak the destiny they dare not speak —
Banish myself before they find the heart.
I will be first to say, "The work rewards!
I know, for all your praise, my use is over,
So may it prove! — meanwhile 't is best I go,
Go carry safe my memories of you all
To other scenes of action, newer lands." —
Thus leaving them confirmed in their belief
They would not easily have tired of me.
You think this hard to say?

Hus.   Say or not say,
So thou but go, so they but let thee go!
This hating people, that hate each the other,
And in one blandness to us Moors unite —
Locked each to each like slippery snakes, I say,
Which still in all their tangles, hissing tongue
And threatening tail, ne'er do each other harm ;
While any creature of a better blood,
They seem to fight for, while they circle safe
And never touch it, — pines without a wound,
Withers away beside their eyes and breath.
See thou, if Puccio come not safely out
Of Braccio's grasp, this Braccio sworn his foe,
As Braccio safely from Domizia's toils
Who hates him most! But thou, the friend of all,
. . . Come out of them!
Lur.   The Pisan trumpet now!
Hus.   Breathe free — it is an enemy, no
friend!   [*Goes.*
Lur.   He keeps his instincts, no new culture
mars
Their perfect use in him ; just so the brutes
Rest not, are anxious without visible cause,
When change is in the elements at work,
Which man's trained senses fail to apprehend.
But here, — he takes the distant chariot-wheel
For thunder, festal flame for lightning's flash,
The finer traits of cultivated life
For treachery and malevolence: I see!
              (*Enter* TIBURZIO.)
Lur.   Quick, sir, your message! I but wait
your message
To sound the charge. You bring no overture
For truce? — I would not, for your General's
sake,
You spoke of truce: a time to fight is come,
And, whatsoe'er the fight's event, he keeps
His honest soldier's-name to beat me with,
Or leaves me all himself to beat, I trust!
Tiburzio.   I am Tiburzio.
Lur.   You? 'T is — yes . . . Tiburzio!
You were the last to keep the ford i' the valley
From Puccio, when I threw in succors there !
Why, I was on the heights — through the defile
Ten minutes after, when the prey was lost!
You wore an open skull-cap with a twist
Of water-reeds — the plume being hewn away ;
While I drove down my battle from the heights,
I saw with my own eyes !
Tib.   And you are Luria
Who sent my cohort, that laid down its arms
In error of the battle-signal's sense,
Back safely to me at the critical time —
One of a hundred deeds. I know you! There-
fore
To none but you could I . . .
Lur.   No truce, Tiburzio !
Tib.   Luria, you know the peril imminent
On Pisa, — that you have us in the toils,
Us her last safeguard, all that intercepts
The rage of her implacablest of foes
From Pisa: if we fall to-day, she falls.
Though Lucca will arrive, yet, 't is too late.
You have so plainly here the best of it,
That you must feel, brave soldier as you are,
How dangerous we grow in this extreme,
How truly formidable by despair.

Still, probabilities should have their weight:
The extreme chance is ours, but, that chance
failing,
You win this battle. Wherefore say I this?
To be well apprehended when I add,
This danger absolutely comes from you.
Were you, who threaten thus, a Florentine . . .
Lur.   Sir, I am nearer Florence than her sons
I can, and have perhaps obliged the State,
Nor paid a mere son's duty.
Tib.   Even so.
Were you the son of Florence, yet endued
With all your present nobleness of soul,
No question, what I must communicate
Would not detach you from her.
Lur.   Me, detach !
Tib.   Time urges. You will ruin presently
Pisa, you never knew, for Florence' sake
You think you know. I have from time to
time
Made prize of certain secret missives sent
From Braccio here, the Commissary, home :
And knowing Florence otherwise, I piece
The entire chain out, from these its scattered
links.
Your trial occupies the Signory ;
They sit in judgment on your conduct now.
When men at home inquire into the acts
Which in the field e'en foes appreciate . . .
Brief, they are Florentines! You, saving
them,
Seek but the sure destruction saviors find.
Lur.   Tiburzio !
Tib.   All the wonder is of course
I am not here to teach you, nor direct,
Only to loyally apprise — scarce that.
This is the latest letter, sealed and safe,
As it left here an hour ago. One way
Of two thought free to Florence, I command.
The duplicate is on its road ; but this, —
Read it, and then I shall have more to say.
Lur.   Florence !
Tib.   Now, were yourself a Florentine,
This letter, let it hold the worst it can,
Would be no reason you should fall away.
The mother city is the mother still,
And recognition of the children's service
Her own affair ; reward — there 's no reward !
But you are bound by quite another tie.
Nor nature shows, nor reason, why at first
A foreigner, born friend to all alike,
Should give himself to any special State
More than another, stand by Florence' side
Rather than Pisa ; 't is as fair a city
You war against, as that you fight for — famed
As well as she in story, graced no less
With noble heads and patriotic hearts :
Nor to a stranger's eye would either cause,
Stripped of the cumulative loves and hates
Which take importance from familiar view,
Stand as the right and sole to be upheld.
Therefore, should the preponderating gift
Of love and trust, Florence was first to throw,
Which made you hers, not Pisa's, void the
scale, —
Old ties dissolving, things resume their place,
And all begins again. Break seal and read !
At least let Pisa offer for you now !

And I, as a good Pisan, shall rejoice,
Though for myself I lose, in gaining you,
This last fight and its opportunity;
The chance it brings of saving Pisa yet,
Or in the turn of battle dying so
That shame should want its extreme bitterness.
   Lur. Tiburzio, you that fight for Pisa now
As I for Florence . . . say my chance were
     yours!
You read this letter, and you find . . . no, no!
Too mad!
   Tib.   I read the letter, find they purpose
When I have crushed their foe, to crush me:
     well?
   Lur. You, being their captain, what is it you
     do?
   Tib. Why, as it is, all cities are alike;
As Florence pays you, Pisa will pay me.
I shall be as belied, whate'er the event,
As you, or more: my weak head, they will say
Prompted this last expedient, my faint heart
Entailed on them indelible disgrace,
Both which defects ask proper punishment.
Another tenure of obedience, mine!
You are no son of Pisa's: break and read!
   Lur. And act on what I read? What act
     were fit?
If the firm-fixed foundation of my faith
In Florence, who to me stands for mankind,
— If that break up and, disimprisoning
From the abyss . . . Ah friend, it cannot be!
You may be very sage, yet — all the world
Having to fail, or your sagacity,
You do not wish to find yourself alone!
What would the world be worth? Whose love
     be sure?
The world remains: you are deceived!
   Tib.   Your hand!
I lead the vanguard. — If you fall, beside,
The better: I am left to speak! For me,
This was my duty, nor would I rejoice
If I could help, it misses its effect;
And after all you will look gallantly
Found dead here with that letter in your breast.
   Lur. Tiburzio — I would see these people
     once
And test them ere I answer finally!
At your arrival let the trumpet sound:
If mine return not then the wonted cry
It means that I believe — am Pisa's!
   Tib.   Well!
                 [Goes.
   Lur. My heart will have it he speaks true!
     My blood
Beats close to this Tiburzio as a friend.
If he had stept into my watch-tent, night
And the wild desert full of foes around,
I should have broke the bread and given the
     salt
Secure, and, when my hour of watch was done,
Taken my turn to sleep between his knees
Safe in the untroubled brow and honest cheek.
Oh world, where all things pass and naught
     abides,
Oh life, the long mutation — is it so?
Is it with life as with the body's change?
— Where, e'en though better follow, good must
     pass,

Nor manhood's strength can mate with boy-
     hood's grace,
Nor age's wisdom, in its turn, find strength,
But silently the first gift dies away,
And though the new stays, never both at once.
Life's time of savage instinct o'er with me,
It fades and dies away, past trusting more,
As if to punish the ingratitude
With which I turned to grow in these new
     lights,
And learned to look with European eyes.
Yet it is better, this cold certain way,
Where Braccio's brow tells nothing, Puccio's
     mouth,
Domizia's eyes reject the searcher: yes!
For on their calm sagacity I lean,
Their sense of right, deliberate choice of good,
Sure, as they know my deeds, they deal with
     me.
Yes, that is better — that is best of all!
Such faith stays when mere wild belief would
     go.
Yes — when the desert creature's heart, at fault
Amid the scattering tempest's pillared sands,
Betrays its step into the pathless drift —
The calm instructed eye of man holds fast
By the sole bearing of the visible star,
Sure that when slow the whirling wreck subside,
The boundaries, lost now, shall be found
     again, —
The palm-trees and the pyramid over all.
Yes: I trust Florence: Pisa is deceived.
     (*Enter* Braccio, Puccio, *and* Domizia.)
   Brac. Noon's at an end: no Lucca? You
     must fight.
   Lur. Do you remember ever, gentle friends,
I am no Florentine?
   Dom.   It is yourself
Who still are forcing us, importunately,
To bear in mind what else we should forget.
   Lur. For loss! — for what I lose in being
     none!
No shrewd man, such as you yourselves respect,
But would remind you of the stranger's loss
In natural friends and advocates at home,
Hereditary loves, even rivalships
With precedent for honor and reward.
Still, there's a gain, too! If you take it so,
The stranger's lot has special gain as well.
Do you forget there was my own far East
I might have given away myself to, once,
As now to Florence, and for such a gift,
Stood there like a descended deity?
There, worship waits us: what is it waits here?
                [Shows the letter.
See! Chance has put into my hand the means
Of knowing what I earn, before I work.
Should I fight better, should I fight the worse,
With payment palpably before me? See!
Here lies my whole reward! Best learn it now
Or keep it for the end's entire delight?
   Brac. If you serve Florence as the vulgar
     serve,
For swordsman's-pay alone, — break seal and
     read!
In that case, you will find your full desert.
   Lur. Give me my one last happy moment,
     friends!

You need me now, and all the graciousness
This letter can contain will hardly balance
The after-feeling that you need no more.
This moment . . . oh, the East has use with
    you !
Its sword still flashes — is not flung aside
With the past praise, in a dark corner yet !
How say you ?   'T is not so with Florentines —
Captains of yours : for them, the ended war
Is but a first step to the peace begun :
He who did well in war, just earns the right
To begin doing well in peace, you know :
And certain my precursors, — would not such
Look to themselves in such a chance as mine,
Secure the ground they trod upon, perhaps ?
For I have heard, by fits, or seemed to hear,
Of strange mishap, mistake, ingratitude,
Treachery even.   Say that one of you
Surmised this letter carried what might turn
To harm hereafter, cause him prejudice :
What would he do ?
    Dom. [*Hastily.*]   Thank God and take re-
venge !
Hurl her own force against the city straight !
And, even at the moment when the foe
Sounded defiance . . .
    (Tiburzio's *trumpet sounds in the distance.*
    Lur.   Ah, you Florentines !
So would you do ?   Wisely for you, no doubt !
My simple Moorish instinct bids me clench
The obligation you relieve me from,
Still deeper ! [*To* Puc.]   Sound our answer, I
    should say,
And thus : — [*Tearing the paper.*] — The battle !
    That solves every doubt.

ACT III

AFTERNOON

Puccio, *as making a report to* Jacopo.

    Puc. And here, your captain must report
    the rest ;
For, as I say, the main engagement over
And Luria's special part in it performed,
How could a subaltern like me expect
Leisure or leave to occupy the field
And glean what dropped from his wide harvest-
    ing ?
I thought, when Lucca at the battle's end
Came up, just as the Pisan centre broke,
That Luria would detach me and prevent
The flying Pisans seeking what they found,
Friends in the rear, a point to rally by.
But no, more honorable proved my post !
I had the august captive to escort
Safe to our camp ; some other could pursue,
Fight, and be famous ; gentler chance was
    mine —
Tiburzio's wounded spirit must be soothed !
He 's in the tent there.
    Jacopo.   Is the substance down ?
I write — " The vanguard beaten and both
    wings
In full retreat, Tiburzio prisoner " —
And now, — " That they fell back and formed
    again

On Lucca's coming."   Why then, after all,
'T is half a victory, no conclusive one ?
    Puc. Two operations where a sole had
    served.
    Jac. And Luria's fault was — ?
    Puc.   Oh, for fault — not much !
He led the attack, a thought impetuously,
— There 's commonly more prudence ; now, he
    seemed
To hurry measures, otherwise well judged.
By over-concentrating strength at first
Against the enemy's van, both wings escaped :
That 's reparable, yet it is a fault.
    (*Enter* Braccio.)
    Jac. As good as a full victory to Florence,
With the advantage of a fault beside —
What is it, Puccio ? — that by pressing forward
With too impetuous . . .
    Brac.   The report anon !
Thanks, sir — you have elsewhere a charge, I
    know.   [Puccio *goes ;*
There 's nothing done but I would do again ;
Yet, Lapo, it may be the past proves nothing,
And Luria has kept faithful to the close.
    Jac. I was for waiting.
    Brac.   Yes : so was not I.
He could not choose but tear that letter — true !
Still, certain of his tones, I mind, and looks : —
You saw, too, with a fresher soul than I.
So, Porzio seemed an injured man, they say !
Well, I have gone upon the broad, sure ground.
    (*Enter* Luria, Puccio, *and* Domizia.)
    Lur. [*To* Puc.]   Say, at his pleasure I will
    see Tiburzio !
All 's at his pleasure.
    Dom. [*To* Lur.]   Were I not forewarned
You would reject, as you do constantly,
Praise, — I might tell you how you have de-
    served
Of Florence by this last and crowning feat :
But words offend.
    Lur.   Nay, you may praise me now.
I want instruction every hour, I find,
On points where once I saw least need of it ;
And praise, I have been used to slight per-
    haps,
Seems scarce so easily dispensed with now.
After a battle, half one's strength is gone ;
The glorious passion in us once appeased,
Our reason's calm cold dreadful voice begins.
All justice, power and beauty scarce appear
Monopolized by Florence, as of late,
To me, the stranger : you, no doubt, may
    know
Why Pisa needs must bear her rival's yoke.
And peradventure I grow nearer you,
For I, too, want to know and be assured.
When a cause ceases to reward itself,
Its friend seeks fresh sustainments ; praise is
    one,
And here stand you — you, lady, praise me
    well.
But yours — (your pardon) — is unlearnèd
    praise.
To the motive, the endeavor, the heart's self,
Your quick sense looks : you crown and call
    aright
The soul o' the purpose, ere 't is shaped as act.

Takes flesh i' the world, and clothes itself a
 king.
But when the act comes, stands for what 't is
 worth,
— Here 's Puccio, the skilled soldier, he 's my
 judge !
Was all well, Puccio?
 Puc.   All was . . . must be well :
If we beat Lucca presently, as doubtless . . .
— No, there 's no doubt, we must — all was well
 done.
 Lur. In truth ? Still you are of the trade,
 my Puccio !
You have the fellow-craftsman's sympathy.
There 's none cares, like a fellow of the craft,
For the all unestimated sum of pains
That go to a success the world can see :
They praise then, but the best they never know
— While you know ! So, if envy mix with it,
Hate even, still the bottom-praise of all,
Whatever be the dregs, that drop 's pure gold !
— For nothing 's like it ; nothing else records
Those daily, nightly drippings in the dark
Of the heart's blood, the world lets drop away
Forever — so, pure gold that praise must be !
And I have yours, my soldier ! yet the best
Is still to come. There 's one looks on apart
Whom all refers to, failure or success ;
What 's done might be our best, our utmost
 work,
And yet inadequate to serve his need.
Here 's Braccio now, for Florence — here 's our
 service —
Well done for us, seems it well done for him ?
His chosen engine, tasked to its full strength
Answers the end ? Should he have chosen
 higher ?
Do we help Florence, now our best is wrought ?
 Brac. This battle, with the foregone services,
Saves Florence.
 Lur.   Why then, all is very well !
Here am I in the middle of my friends,
Who know me and who love me, one and all.
And yet . . . 't is like . . . this instant while
 I speak
Is like the turning-moment of a dream
When . . . Ah, you are not foreigners like
 me !
Well then, one always dreams of friends at
 home ;
And always comes, I say, the turning-point
When something changes in the friendly eyes
That love and look on you . . . so slight, so
 slight . . .
And yet it tells you they are dead and gone,
Or changed and enemies, for all their words,
And all is mockery and a maddening show.
You now, so kind here, all you Florentines,
What is it in your eyes . . . those lips, those
 brows . . .
Nobody spoke it, yet I know it well !
Come now — this battle saves you, all 's at end,
Your use of me is o'er, for good, for ill, —
Come now, what 's done against me, while I
 speak,
In Florence ? Come ! I feel it in my blood,
My eyes, my hair, a voice is in my ears
That spite of all this smiling and soft speech

You are betraying me ! What is it you do ?
Have it your way, and think my use is over —
Think you are saved and may throw off the
 mask —
Have it my way, and think more work remains
Which I could do, — so, show you fear me not !
Or prudent be, or daring, as you choose,
But tell me — tell what I refused to know
At noon, lest heart should fail me ! Well ?
 That letter ?
My fate is sealed at Florence ! What is it ?
 Brac. Sir, I shall not deny what you divine.
It is no novelty for innocence
To be suspected, but a privilege :
The after certain compensation comes.
Charges, I say not whether false or true,
Have been preferred against you some time
 since,
Which Florence was bound, plainly, to receive
And which are therefore undergoing now
The due investigation. That is all.
I doubt not but your innocence will prove
Apparent and illustrious, as to me,
To them this evening, when the trial ends.
 Lur. My trial ?
 Dom.   Florence, Florence to the end,
My whole heart thanks thee !
 Puc. [*To* BRAC.] What is " trial," sir ?
It was not for a trial, — surely, no —
I furnished you those notes from time to time ?
I held myself aggrieved — I am a man —
And I might speak, — ay, and speak mere
 truth, too,
And yet not mean at bottom of my heart
What should assist a — trial, do you say ?
You should have told me !
 Dom.   Nay, go on, go on !
His sentence ! Do they sentence him ? What
 is it ?
The block — wheel ?
 Brac.   Sentence there is none as yet,
Nor shall I give my own opinion now
Of what it should be, or is like to be.
When it is passed, applaud or disapprove !
Up to that point, what is there to impugn ?
 Lur. They are right, then, to try me ?
 Brac.   I assert,
Maintain and justify the absolute right
Of Florence to do all she can have done
In this procedure, — standing on her guard,
Receiving even services like yours
With utmost fit suspicious wariness.
In other matters, keep the mummery up !
Take all the experiences of all the world,
Each knowledge that broke through a heart to
 life,
Each reasoning which, to reach, burnt out a
 brain,
— In other cases, know these, warrant these,
And then dispense with these — 't is very well !
Let friend trust friend, and love demand love's
 like,
And gratitude be claimed for benefits, —
There 's grace in that, — and when the fresh
 heart breaks,
The new brain proves a ruin, what of them ?
Where is the matter of one moth the more
Singed in the candle, at a summer's end ?

But Florence is no simple John or James
To have his toy, his fancy, his conceit
That he 's the one excepted man by fate,
And, when fate shows him he 's mistaken
　　there,
Die with all good men's praise, and yield his
　　place
To Paul and George intent to try their chance !
Florence exists because these pass away.
She 's a contrivance to supply a type
Of man, which men's deficiencies refuse ;
She binds so many, that she grows out of
　　them —
Stands steady o'er their numbers, though they
　　change
And pass away — there 's always what upholds,
Always enough to fashion the great show.
As see, yon hanging city, in the sun,
Of shapely cloud substantially the same !
A thousand vapors rise and sink again,
Are interfused, and live their life and die, —
Yet ever hangs the steady show i' the air,
Under the sun's straight influence : that is
　　well,
That is worth heaven should hold, and God
　　should bless !
And so is Florence, — the unseen sun above,
Which draws and holds suspended all of us,
Binds transient vapors into a single cloud
Differing from each and better than they all.
And shall she dare to stake this permanence
On any one man's faith ?　Man's heart is weak,
And its temptations many : let her prove
Each servant to the very uttermost
Before she grant him her reward, I say !
　　Dom.　And as for hearts she chances to mis-
　　take,
Wronged hearts, not destined to receive re-
　　ward,
Though they deserve it, did she only know,
— What should she do for these ?
　　Brac.　　　　　　What does she not ?
Say, that she gives them but herself to serve !
Here 's Luria — what had profited his strength,
When half an hour of sober fancying
Had shown him step by step the uselessness
Of strength exerted for strength's proper sake ?
But the truth is, she did create that strength,
Draw to the end the corresponding means.
The world is wide — are we the only men ?
Oh, for the time, the social purpose' sake,
Use words agreed on, bandy epithets,
Call any man the sole great wise and good !
But shall we therefore, standing by ourselves,
Insult our souls and God with the same speech ?
There, swarm the ignoble thousands under
　　him :
What marks us from the hundreds and the
　　tens ?
Florence took up, turned all one way the soul
Of Luria with its fires, and here he glows !
She takes me out of all the world as him,
Fixing my coldness till like ice it checks
The fire !　So, Braccio, Luria, which is best ?
　　Lur.　Ah, brave me ?　And is this indeed the
　　way
To gain your good word and sincere esteem ?
Am I the baited animal that must turn

And fight his baiters to deserve their praise ?
Obedience is mistake then ?　Be it so !
Do you indeed remember I stand here
The captain of the conquering army, — mine —
With all your tokens, praise and promise, ready
To show for what their names meant when you
　　gave,
Not what you style them now you take away ?
If I call in my troops to arbitrate,
And dash the first enthusiastic thrill
Of victory with this you menace now —
Commend to the instinctive popular sense,
My story first, your comment afterward, —
Will they take, think you, part with you or me ?
If I say — I, the laborer they saw work,
Ending my work, ask pay, and find my lords
Have all this while provided silently
Against the day of pay and proving faith,
By what you call my sentence that 's to come
Will friends advise I wait complacently ?
If I meet Florence half-way at their head,
What will you do, my mild antagonist ?
　　Brac.　I will rise up like fire, proud and
　　triumphant
That Florence knew you thoroughly and by
　　me,
And so was saved.　"See, Italy," I 'll say,
"The crown of our precautions !　Here 's a
　　man
Was far advanced, just touched on the belief
Less subtle cities had accorded long ;
But we were wiser : at the end comes this ! "
And from that minute, where is Luria ?　Lost !
The very stones of Florence cry against
The all-exacting, naught-enduring fool,
Who thus resents her first probation, flouts
As if he, only, shone and cast no shade,
He, only, walked the earth with privilege
Against suspicion, free where angels fear :
He, for the first inquisitive mother's-word,
Must turn, and stand on his defence, forsooth !
Reward ?　You will not be worth punishment !
　　Lur.　And Florence knew me thus !　Thus I
　　have lived, —
And thus you, with the clear fine intellect,
Braccio, the cold acute instructed mind,
Out of the stir, so calm and unconfused,
Reported me — how could you otherwise !
Ay ? — and what dropped from you, just now
　　moreover ?
Your information, Puccio ? — Did your skill,
Your understanding sympathy approve
Such a report of me ?　Was this the end ?
Or is even this the end ?　Can I stop here ?
You, lady, with the woman's stand apart,
The heart to see with, past man's brain and
　　eyes,
. . . I cannot fathom why you should destroy
The unoffending one, you call your friend —
Still, lessoned by the good examples here
Of friendship, 't is but natural I ask —
Had you a further aim, in aught you urged,
Than your friend's profit — in all those in-
　　stances
Of perfidy, all Florence wrought of wrong —
All I remember now for the first time ?
　　Dom.　I am a daughter of the Traversari,
Sister of Porzio and of Berto both.

So, have foreseen all that has come to pass.
I knew the Florence that could doubt their
    faith,
Must needs mistrust a stranger's — dealing
    them
Punishment, would deny him his reward.
And I believed, the shame they bore and died,
He would not bear, but live and fight against —
Seeing he was of other stuff than they.
    Lur. Hear them! All these against one
    foreigner!
And all this while, where is, in the whole world,
To his good faith a single witness?
    Tib. [*Who has entered unseen during the pre-
    ceding dialogue.*]   Here!
Thus I bear witness, not in word but deed.
I live for Pisa; she's not lost to-day
By many chances — much prevents from that!
Her army has been beaten, I am here,
But Lucca comes at last, one happy chance!
I rather would see Pisa three times lost
Than saved by any traitor, even by you;
The example of a traitor's happy fortune
Would bring more evil in the end than good; —
Pisa rejects the traitor, craves yourself!
I, in her name, resign forthwith to you
My charge, — the highest office, sword and
    shield!
You shall not, by my counsel, turn on Flor-
    ence
Your army, give her calumny that ground —
Nor bring one soldier: be you all we gain!
And all she'll lose, — a head to deck some
    bridge,
And save the cost o' the crown should deck the
    head.
Leave her to perish in her perfidy,
Plague-stricken and stripped naked to all eyes,
A proverb and a by-word in all mouths!
Go you to Pisa! Florence is my place —
Leave me to tell her of the rectitude,
I, from the first, told Pisa, knowing it.
To Pisa!
    Dom. Ah my Braccio, are you caught?
    Brac. Puccio, good soldier and good citi-
    zen,
Whom I have ever kept beneath my eye,
Ready as fit, to serve in this event
Florence, who clear foretold it from the first —
Through me, she gives you the command and
    charge
She takes, through me, from him who held it
    late!
A painful trial, very sore, was yours:
All that could draw out, marshal in array
The selfish passions 'gainst the public good —
Slights, scorns, neglects, were heaped on you to
    bear:
And ever you did bear and bow the head!
It had been sorry trial, to precede
Your feet, hold up the promise of reward
For luring gleam; your footsteps kept the
    track
Through dark and doubt: take all the light at
    once!
Trial is over, consummation shines;
Well have you served, as well henceforth com-
    mand!

    Puc. No, no . . . I dare not! I am grate-
    ful, glad;
But Luria — you shall understand he's
    wronged:
And he's my captain — this is not the way
We soldiers climb to fortune: think again!
The sentence is not even passed, beside!
I dare not: where's the soldier could?
    Lur.   Now, Florence —
Is it to be? You will know all the strength
O' the savage — to your neck the proof must
    go?
You will prove the brute nature? Ah, I see!
The savage plainly is impassible —
He keeps his calm way through insulting words,
Sarcastic looks, sharp gestures — one of which
Would stop you, fatal to your finer sense,
But if he stolidly advance, march mute
Without a mark upon his callous hide,
Through the mere brushwood you grow angry
    with,
And leave the tatters of your flesh upon,
— You have to learn that when the true bar
    comes,
The murk mid-forest, the grand obstacle,
Which when you reach, you give the labor up,
Nor dash on, but lie down composed before,
— He goes against it, like the brute he is:
It falls before him, or he dies in his course.
I kept my course through past ingratitude:
I saw — it does seem, now, as if I saw,
Could not but see, those insults as they fell,
— Ay, let them glance from off me, very like,
Laughing, perhaps, to think the quality
You grew so bold on, while you so despised
The Moor's dull mute inapprehensive mood,
Was saving you: I bore and kept my course.
Now real wrong fronts me: see if I succumb!
Florence withstands me? I will punish her.

At night my sentence will arrive, you say.
Till then I cannot, if I would, rebel
— Unauthorized to lay my office down,
Retaining my full power to will and do:
After — it is to see. Tiburzio, thanks!
Go; you are free: join Lucca! I suspend
All further operations till to-night.
Thank you, and for the silence most of all!
[*To* Brac.] Let my complacent bland accuser
    go
Carry his self-approving head and heart
Safe through the army which would trample
    him
Dead in a moment at my word or sign!
Go, sir, to Florence; tell friends what I say —
That, while I wait my sentence, theirs waits
    them!
[*To* Dom.] You, lady, — you have black
    Italian eyes!
I would be generous if I might: oh, yes —
For I remember how so oft you seemed
Inclined at heart to break the barrier down
Which Florence finds God built between us
    both.
Alas, for generosity! this hour
Asks retribution: bear it as you may,
I must — the Moor — the savage, — pardon you!
Puccio, my trusty soldier, see them forth!

ACT IV

EVENING

Enter Puccio *and* Jacopo.

Puc.   What Luria will do ?   Ah, 't is yours,
    fair sir,
Your and your subtle-witted master's part,
To tell me that ; I tell you what he can.
Jac.   Friend, you mistake my station : I ob-
    serve
The game, watch how my betters play, no
    more.
Puc.   But mankind are not pieces — there 's
    your fault !
You cannot push them, and, the first move
    made,
Lean back and study what the next shall be,
In confidence that, when 't is fixed upon,
You find just where you left them, blacks and
    whites :
Men go on moving when your hand 's away.
You build, I notice, firm on Luria's faith
This whole time, — firmlier than I choose to
    build,
Who never doubted it — of old, that is —
With Luria in his ordinary mind.
But now, oppression makes the wise man mad :
How do I know he will not turn and stand
And hold his own against you, as he may ?
Suppose he but withdraw to Pisa — well, —
Then, even if all happen to your wish,
Which is a chance . . .
Jac.   Nay — 't was an oversight,
Not waiting till the proper warrant came :
You could not take what was not ours to give.
But when at night the sentence really comes,
Our city authorizes past dispute
Luria's removal and transfers the charge,
You will perceive your duty and accept ?
Puc.   Accept what ? muster-rolls of soldiers'
    names ?
An army upon paper ?   I want men,
The hearts as well as hands — and where 's a
    heart
But beats with Luria, in the multitude
I come from walking through by Luria's side ?
You gave them Luria, set him thus to grow,
Head-like, upon their trunk ; one heart feeds
    both,
They feel him there, live twice, and well know
    why.
— For they do know, if you are ignorant,
Who kept his own place and respected theirs,
Managed their sweat, yet never spared his blood.
All was your act : another might have served —
There 's peradventure no such dearth of heads —
But you chose Luria : so, they grew one flesh,
And now, for nothing they can understand,
Luria removed, off is to roll the head ;
The body 's mine — much I shall do with it !
Jac.   That 's at the worst.
Puc.   No — at the best, it is !
Best, do you hear ?   I saw them by his side.
Only we two with Luria in the camp
Are left that keep the secret ?   You think that ?
Hear what I know : from rear to van, no heart

But felt the quiet patient hero there
Was wronged, nor in the moveless ranks an eye
But glancing told its fellow the whole story
Of that convicted silent knot of spies
Who passed through them to Florence ; they
    might pass —
No breast but gladlier beat when free of such !
Our troops will catch up Luria, close him round,
Bear him to Florence as their natural lord,
Partake his fortune, live or die with him.
Jac.   And by mistake catch up along with
    him
Puccio, no doubt, compelled in self despite
To still continue second in command !
Puc.   No, sir, no second nor so fortunate !
Your tricks succeed with me too well for that !
I am as you have made me, live and die
To serve your end — a mere trained fighting-
    hack,
With words, you laugh at while they leave your
    mouth,
For my life's rule and ordinance of God !
I have to do my duty, keep my faith,
And earn my praise, and guard against my
    blame,
As I was trained.   I shall accept your charge,
And fight against one better than myself,
Spite of my heart's conviction of his worth —
That, you may count on ! — just as hitherto
I have gone on, persuaded I was wronged,
Slighted, insulted, terms we learn by rote, —
All because Luria superseded me —
Because the better nature, fresh-inspired,
Mounted above me to its proper place !
What mattered all the kindly graciousness,
The cordial brother's-bearing ?   This was
    clear —
I, once the captain, now was subaltern,
And so must keep complaining like a fool !
Go, take the curse of a lost soul, I say !
You neither play your puppets to the end,
Nor treat the real man, — for his realness' sake
Thrust rudely in their place, — with such re-
    gard
As might console them for their altered rank.
Me, the mere steady soldier, you depose
For Luria, and here 's all your pet deserves !
Of what account, then, is your laughing-stock ?
One word for all : whatever Luria does,
— If backed by his indignant troops he turn,
Revenge himself, and Florence go to ground, —
Or, for a signal everlasting shame,
He pardon you, simply seek better friends,
Side with the Pisans and Lucchese for change
— And if I, pledged to ingrates past belief,
Dare fight against a man such fools call false,
Who, inasmuch as he was true, fights me, —
Whichever way he win, he wins for worth,
For every soldier, for all true and good !
Sir, chronicling the rest, omit not this !
    (*As they go, enter* Luria *and* Husain.)
Hus.   Saw'st thou ? — For they are gone
    The world lies bare
Before thee, to be tasted, felt and seen
Like what it is, now Florence goes away !
Thou livest now, with men art man again !
Those Florentines were all to thee of old ;
But Braccio, but Domizia, gone is each,

There lie beneath thee thine own multitudes !
Saw'st thou ?
   Lur.   I saw.
   Hus.   Then, hold thy course, my king !
The years return. Let thy heart have its way :
Ah, they would play with thee as with all else,
Turn thee to use, and fashion thee anew,
Find out God's fault in thee as in the rest ?
Oh watch, oh listen only to these fiends
Once at their occupation ! Ere we know,
The free great heaven is shut, their stifling pall
Drops till it frets the very tingling hair,
So weighs it on our head, — and, for the earth,
Our common earth is tethered up and down,
Over and across — " here shalt thou move,"
    they cry !
   Lur.   Ay, Husain ?
   Hus.   So have they spoiled all beside !
So stands a man girt round with Florentines,
Priests, graybeards, Braccios, women, boys and
    spies,
All in one tale, all singing the same song,
How thou must house, and live at bed and
    board,
Take pledge and give it, go their every way,
Breathe to their measure, make thy blood beat
    time
With theirs — or, all is nothing — thou art
    lost —
A savage, how shouldst thou perceive as they ?
Feel glad to stand 'neath God's close naked
    hand !
Look up to it ! Why, down they pull thy neck,
Lest it crush thee, who feel'st it and wouldst
    kiss,
Without their priests that needs must glove it
    first,
Lest peradventure flesh offend thy lip.
Love woman ! Why, a very beast thou art !
Thou must . . .
   Lur.   Peace, Husain !
   Hus.   Ay, but, spoiling all,
For all, else true things, substituting false,
That they should dare spoil, of all instincts,
    thine !
Should dare to take thee with thine instincts up,
Thy battle-ardors, like a ball of fire,
And class them and allow them place and play
So far, no farther — unabashed the while !
Thou with the soul that never can take rest —
Thou born to do, undo, and do again,
And never to be still, — wouldst thou make war ?
Oh, that is commendable, just and right !
" Come over," say they, " have the honor due
In living out thy nature ! Fight thy best :
It is to be for Florence, not thyself !
For thee, it were a horror and a plague ;
For us, when war is made for Florence, see,
How all is changed : the fire that fed on earth
Now towers to heaven ! " —
   Lur.   And what sealed up so long
My Husain's mouth ?
   Hus.   Oh friend, oh lord — for me,
What am I ? — I was silent at thy side,
Who am a part of thee. It is thy hand,
Thy foot that glows when in the heart fresh
    blood
Boils up, thou heart of me ! Now, live again,

Again love as thou likest, hate as free !
Turn to no Braccios nor Domizias now,
To ask, before thy very limbs dare move,
If Florence' welfare be concerned thereby !
   Lur.   So clear what Florence must expect of
    me ?
   Hus.   Both armies against Florence ! Take
    revenge !
Wide, deep — to live upon, in feeling now, —
And, after live, in memory, year by year —
And, with the dear conviction, die at last !
She lies now at thy pleasure : pleasure have !
Their vaunted intellect that gilds our sense,
And blends with life, to show it better by,
— How think'st thou ? — I have turned that
    light on them !
They called our thirst of war a transient thing ;
" The battle-element must pass away
From life," they said, " and leave a tranquil
    world."
— Master, I took their light and turned it full
On that dull turgid vein they said would burst
And pass away ; and as I looked on life,
Still everywhere I tracked this, though it hid
And shifted, lay so silent as it thought,
Changed shape and hue yet ever was the same.
Why, 't was all fighting, all their nobler life !
All work was fighting, every harm — defeat,
And every joy obtained — a victory !
Be not their dupe !
    — Their dupe ? That hour is past !
Here stand'st thou in the glory and the calm :
All is determined. Silence for me now !
                       [HUSAIN *goes.*

   Lur.   Have I heard all ?
   Dom.   [*Advancing from the background.*] No,
    Luria, I remain !
Not from the motives these have urged on thee,
Ignoble, insufficient, incomplete,
And pregnant each with sure seeds of decay,
As failing of sustainment from thyself,
— Neither from low revenge, nor selfishness,
Nor savage lust of power, nor one, nor all,
Shalt thou abolish Florence ! I proclaim
The angel in thee, and reject the sprites
Which ineffectual crowd about his strength,
And mingle with his work and claim a share !
Inconsciously to the augustest end
Thou hast arisen : second not in rank
So much as time, to him who first ordained
That Florence, thou art to destroy, should be.
Yet him a star, too, guided, who broke first
The pride of lonely power, the life apart,
And made the eminences, each to each,
Lean o'er the level world and let it lie
Safe from the thunder henceforth 'neath their
    tops ;
So the few famous men of old combined,
And let the multitude rise underneath,
And reach them and unite — so Florence grew :
Braccio speaks true, it was well worth the price.
But when the sheltered many grew in pride
And grudged the station of the elected ones,
Who, greater than their kind, are truly great
Only in voluntary servitude —
Time was for thee to rise, and thou art here.
Such plague possessed this Florence : who can
    tell

The mighty girth and greatness at the heart
Of those so perfect pillars of the grove
She pulled down in her envy? Who as I,
The light weak parasite born but to twine
Round each of them and, measuring them, live?
My light love keeps the matchless circle safe,
My slender life proves what has passed away.
I lived when they departed ; lived to cling
To thee, the mighty stranger ; thou wouldst rise
And burst the thraldom, and avenge, I knew.
I have done nothing ; all was thy strong bole.
But a bird's weight can break the infant tree
Which after holds an aery in its arms,
And 't was my care that naught should warp
    thy spire
From rising to the height ; the roof is reached
O' the forest, break through, see extend the
    sky !
Go on to Florence, Luria ! 'T is man's cause !
Fail thou, and thine own fall were least to
    dread :
Thou keepest Florence in her evil way,
Encouragest her sin so much the more —
And while the ignoble past is justified,
Thou all the surelier warp'st the future growth,
The chiefs to come, the Lurias yet unborn,
That, greater than thyself, are reached o'er thee
Who giv'st the vantage-ground their foes re-
    quire,
As o'er my prostrate House thyself wast
    reached !
Man calls thee, God requites thee ! All is said,
The mission of my House fulfilled at last :
And the mere woman, speaking for herself,
Reserves speech — it is now no woman's time.
                                    [DOMIZIA goes.

Lur. Thus at the last must figure Luria,
    then !
Doing the various work of all his friends,
And answering every purpose save his own.
No doubt, 't is well for them to wish ; but him —
After the exploit what were left ? Perchance
A little pride upon the swarthy brow,
At having brought successfully to bear
'Gainst Florence' self her own especial arms, —
Her craftiness, impelled by fiercer strength
From Moorish blood than feeds the northern wit.
But after ! — once the easy vengeance willed,
Beautiful Florence at a word laid low
— (Not in her domes and towers and palaces,
Not even in a dream, that outrage !) — low,
As shamed in her own eyes henceforth forever,
Low, for the rival cities round to laugh,
Conquered and pardoned by a hireling Moor !
— For him, who did the irreparable wrong,
What would be left, his life's illusion fled, —
What hope or trust in the forlorn wide world ?
How strange that Florence should mistake me
    so !
Whence grew this ? What withdrew her faith
    from me ?
Some cause ! These fretful-blooded children
    talk
Against their mother, — they are wronged, they
    say —
Notable wrongs her smile makes up again !
So, taking fire at each supposed offence,
They may speak rashly, suffer for their speech :

But what could it have been in word or deed
Thus injured me ? Some one word spoken
    more
Out of my heart, and all had changed perhaps.
My fault, it must have been, — for, what gain
    they ?
Why risk the danger ? See, what I could do !
And my fault, wherefore visit upon them,
My Florentines ? The notable revenge
I meditated ! To stay passively,
Attend their summons, be as they dispose !
Why, if my very soldiers keep the rank,
And if my chieftains acquiesce, what then ?
I ruin Florence, teach her friends mistrust,
Confirm her enemies in harsh belief,
And when she finds one day, as find she must,
The strange mistake, and how my heart was
    hers,
Shall it console me, that my Florentines
Walk with a sadder step, in graver guise,
Who took me with such frankness, praised me
    so,
At the glad outset ? Had they loved me less,
They had less feared what seemed a change in
    me.
And after all, who did the harm ? Not they !
How could they interpose with those old fools
I' the council ? Suffer for those old fools'
    sake —
They, who made pictures of me, sang the songs
About my battles ? Ah, we Moors get blind
Out of our proper world, where we can see !
The sun that guides is closer to us ! There —
There, my own orb ! He sinks from out the
    sky !
Why, there ! a whole day has he blessed the
    land,
My land, our Florence all about the hills,
The fields and gardens, vineyards, olive-
    grounds,
All have been blest — and yet we Florentines,
With souls intent upon our battle here,
Found that he rose too soon, or set too late,
Gave us no vantage, or gave Pisa much —
Therefore we wronged him ! Does he turn in
    ire
To burn the earth that cannot understand ?
Or drop out quietly, and leave the sky,
His task once ended ? Night wipes blame
    away.
Another morning from my East shall spring
And find all eyes at leisure, all disposed
To watch and understand its work, no doubt.
So, praise the new sun, the successor praise,
Praise the new Luria and forget the old !
                    [*Taking a phial from his breast.*
— Strange ! This is all I brought from my own
    land
To help me : Europe would supply the rest,
All needs beside, all other helps save one !
I thought of adverse fortune, battle lost,
The natural upbraiding of the loser,
And then this quiet remedy to seek
At end of the disastrous day.   [*He drinks.*
                            'T is sought !
This was my happy triumph-morning : Florence
Is saved : I drink this, and ere night, — die !
    Strange !

ACT V

NIGHT

LURIA *and* PUCCIO

Lur. I thought to do this, not to talk this: well,
Such were my projects for the city's good,
To help her in attack or by defence.
Time, here as elsewhere, soon or late may take
Our foresight by surprise through chance and change ;
But not a little we provide against
— If you see clear on every point.
Puc. Most clear.
Lur. Then all is said — not much, if you count words,
Yet to an understanding ear enough ;
And all that my brief stay permits, beside.
Nor must you blame me, as I sought to teach
My elder in command, or threw a doubt
Upon the very skill, it comforts me
To know I leave, — your steady soldiership
Which never failed me : yet, because it seemed
A stranger's eye might haply note defect
That skill, through use and custom, over-looks —
I have gone into the old cares once more,
As if I had to come and save again
Florence — that May — that morning ! 'T is night now.
Well — I broke off with ? . . .
Puc. Of the past campaign
You spoke — of measures to be kept in mind
For future use.
Lur. True, so . . . but, time — no time !
As well end here : remember this, and me !
Farewell now !
Puc. Dare I speak ?
Lur. South o' the river —
How is the second stream called . . . no, — the third ?
Puc. Pesa.
Lur. And a stone's-cast from the fording-place,
To the east, — the little mount's name ?
Puc. Lupo.
Lur. Ay !
Ay — there the tower, and all that side is safe !
With San Romano, west of Evola,
San Miniato, Scala, Empoli,
Five towers in all, — forget not !
Puc. Fear not me !
Lur. — Nor to memorialize the Council now,
I' the easy hour, on those battalions' claim,
Who forced a pass by Staggia on the hills,
And kept the Sienese at check !
Puc. One word —
Sir, I must speak ! That you submit yourself
To Florence' bidding, howsoe'er it prove,
And give up the command to me — is much,
Too much, perhaps : but what you tell me now,
Even will affect the other course you choose —
Poor as it may be, perils even that !
Refuge you seek at Pisa : yet these plans
All militate for Florence, all conclude
Your formidable work to make her queen

O' the country, — which her rivals rose against
When you began it, — which to interrupt,
Pisa would buy you off at any price !
You cannot mean to sue for Pisa's help,
With this made perfect and on record ?
Lur. I—
At Pisa, and for refuge, do you say ?
Puc. Where are you going, then ? You must decide
On leaving us, a silent fugitive,
Alone, at night — you, stealing through our lines,
Who were this morning's Luria, — you escape
To painfully begin the world once more,
With such a past, as it had never been !
Where are you going ?
Lur. Not so far, my Puccio,
But that I hope to hear, enjoy and praise
(If you mind praise from your old captain yet)
Each happy blow you strike for Florence !
Puc. Ay,
But ere you gain your shelter, what may come ?
For see — though nothing 's surely known as yet,
Still — truth must out — I apprehend the worst.
If mere suspicion stood for certainty
Before, there 's nothing can arrest the step
Of Florence toward your ruin, once on foot.
Forgive her fifty times, it matters not !
And having disbelieved your innocence,
How can she trust your magnanimity ?
You may do harm to her — why then, you will !
And Florence is sagacious in pursuit.
Have you a friend to count on ?
Lur. One sure friend.
Puc. Potent ?
Lur. All-potent.
Puc. And he is apprised ?
Lur. He waits me.
Puc. So ! — Then I, put in your place,
Making my profit of all done by you,
Calling your labors mine, reaping their fruit,
To this, the State's gift, now add yours beside —
That I may take as my peculiar store
These your instructions to work Florence good.
And if, by putting some few happily
In practice, I should both advantage her
And draw down honor on myself, — what then ?
Lur. Do it, my Puccio ! I shall know and praise !
Puc. Though so, men say, " mark what we gain by change
— A Puccio for a Luria ! "
Lur. Even so !
Puc. Then, not for fifty hundred Florences
Would I accept one office save my own,
Fill any other than my rightful post
Here at your feet, my captain and my lord !
That such a cloud should break, such trouble be,
Ere a man settle, soul and body, down
Into his true place and take rest forever !
Here were my wise eyes fixed on your right hand,
And so the bad thoughts came and the worse words,
And all went wrong and painfully enough, —

No wonder, — till, the right spot stumbled on,
All the jar stops, and there is peace at once!
I am yours now, — a tool your right hand
    wields!
God's love, that I should live, the man I am,
On orders, warrants, patents and the like,
As if there were no glowing eye i' the world
To glance straight inspiration to my brain,
No glorious heart to give mine twice the beats!
For, see — my doubt, where is it? — fear? 't is
    flown!
And Florence and her anger are a tale
To scare a child! Why, half-a-dozen words
Will tell her, spoken as I now can speak,
Her error, my past folly — and all 's right,
And you are Luria, our great chief again!
Or at the worst — which worst were best of
    all —
To exile or to death I follow you!
    Lur.   Thanks, Puccio! Let me use the
    privilege
You grant me: if I still command you, — stay!
Remain here, my vicegerent, it shall be,
And not successor: let me, as of old,
Still serve the State, my spirit prompting
    yours —
Still triumph, one for both. There! Leave
    me now!
You cannot disobey my first command?
Remember what I spoke of Jacopo,
And what you promised to concert with him!
Send him to speak with me — nay, no farewell!
You shall be by me when the sentence comes.
                      [*Puccio goes.*
So, there 's one Florentine returns again!
Out of the genial morning company,
One face is left to take into the night.
             (*Enter* JACOPO.)
    Jac.   I wait for your command, sir.
    Lur.   What, so soon?
I thank your ready presence and fair word.
I used to notice you in early days
As of the other species, so to speak,
Those watchers of the lives of us who act —
That weigh our motives, scrutinize our thoughts.
So, I propound this to your faculty
As you would tell me, was a town to take
. . . That is, of old. I am departing hence
Under these imputations; that is naught —
I leave no friend on whom they may rebound,
Hardly a name behind me in the land,
Being a stranger: all the more behoves
That I regard how altered were the case
With natives of the country, Florentines
On whom the like mischance should fall: the
    roots
O' the tree survive the ruin of the trunk —
No root of mine will throb, you understand.
But I had predecessors, Florentines,
Accused as I am now, and punished so —
The Traversari: you know more than I
How stigmatized they are and lost in shame.
Now Puccio, who succeeds me in command,
Both served them and succeeded, in due time;
He knows the way, holds proper documents,
And has the power to lay the simple truth
Before an active spirit, as I count yours:
And also there 's Tiburzio, my new friend,

Will, at a word, confirm such evidence,
He being the great chivalric soul we know.
I put it to your tact, sir — were 't not well,
— A grace, though but for contrast's sake, no
    more, —
If you who witness, and have borne a share
Involuntarily in my mischance,
Should, of your proper motion, set your skill
To indicate — that is, investigate
The right or wrong of what mischance befell
Those famous citizens, your countrymen?
Nay, you shall promise nothing: but reflect,
And if your sense of justice prompt you —
    good!
    Jac.   And if, the trial past, their fame stand
    clear
To all men's eyes, as yours, my lord, to mine —
Their ghosts may sleep in quiet satisfied!
For me, a straw thrown up into the air,
My testimony goes for a straw's worth.
I used to hold by the instructed brain,
And move with Braccio as my master-wind;
The heart leads surelier: I must move with
    you —
As greatest now, who ever were the best.
So, let the last and humblest of your servants
Accept your charge, as Braccio's heretofore,
And tender homage by obeying you!
                    [JACOPO *goes.*
    Lur.   Another! — Luria goes not poorly forth.
If we could wait! The only fault 's with time;
All men become good creatures: but so slow!
        (*Enter* DOMIZIA.)
    Lur.   Ah, you once more?
    Dom.   Domizia, whom you knew,
Performed her task, and died with it. 'T is I,
Another woman, you have never known.
Let the past sleep now!
    Lur.   I have done with it.
    Dom.   How inexhaustibly the spirit grows!
One object, she seemed erewhile born to reach
With her whole energies and die content, —
So like a wall at the world's edge it stood,
With naught beyond to live for, — is that
    reached? —
Already are new undreamed energies
Outgrowing under, and extending farther
To a new object; there 's another world.
See! I have told the purpose of my life;
'T is gained: you are decided, well or ill —
You march on Florence, or submit to her —
My work is done with you, your brow declares.
But — leave you? — More of you seems yet to
    reach:
I stay for what I just begin to see.
    Lur.   So that you turn not to the past!
    Dom.   You trace
Nothing but ill in it — my selfish impulse,
Which sought its end and disregarded yours?
    Lur.   Speak not against your nature: best,
    each keep
His own — you, yours — most, now that I keep
    mine,
— At least, fall by it, having too weakly stood
God's finger marks distinctions, all so fine,
We would confound: the lesser has its use,
Which, when it apes the greater, is foregone.
I, born a Moor, lived half a Florentine;

But, punished properly, can end, a Moor.
Beside, there 's something makes me understand
Your nature : I have seen it.
   Dom.   Aught like mine ?
   Lur. In my own East . . . if you would
     stoop and help
My barbarous illustration ! It sounds ill ;
Yet there 's no wrong at bottom : rather, praise.
   Dom. Well ?
   Lur.   We have creatures there, which if you
     saw
The first time, you would doubtless marvel at
For their surpassing beauty, craft and strength.
And though it were a lively moment's shock
When you first found the purpose of forked
     tongues
That seem innocuous in their lambent play,
Yet, once made know such grace requires such
     guard,
Your reason soon would acquiesce, I think,
In wisdom which made all things for the best —
So, take them, good with ill, contentedly,
The prominent beauty with the latent sting.
I am glad to have seen you wondrous Flor-
     entines :
Yet . . .
   Dom. I am here to listen.
   Lur.   My own East !
How nearer God we were ! He glows above
With scarce an intervention, presses close
And palpitatingly, his soul o'er ours :
We feel him, nor by painful reason know !
The everlasting minute of creation
Is felt there ; now it is, as it was then ;
All changes at his instantaneous will,
Not by the operation of a law
Whose maker is elsewhere at other work.
His hand is still engaged upon his world —
Man's praise can forward it, man's prayer
     suspend,
For is not God all-mighty ? To recast
The world, erase old things and make them new.
What costs it Him ? So, man breathes nobly
     there.
And inasmuch as feeling, the East's gift,
Is quick and transient — comes, and lo, is
     gone —
While Northern thought is slow and durable,
Surely a mission was reserved for me,
Who, born with a perception of the power
And use of the North's thought for us of the
     East,
Should have remained, turned knowledge to
     account,
Giving thought's character and permanence
To the too transitory feeling there —
Writing God's message plain in mortal words.
Instead of which, I leave my fated field
For this where such a task is needed least,
Where all are born consummate in the art
I just perceive a chance of making mine, —
And then, deserting thus my early post,
I wonder that the men I come among
Mistake me ! There, how all had understood.
Still brought fresh stuff for me to stamp and
     keep,
Fresh instinct to translate them into law !
Me, who . . .

   Dom.   Who here the greater task achieve,
More needful even : who have brought fresh
     stuff
For us to mould, interpret and prove right, —
New feeling fresh from God, which, could we
     know
O' the instant, where had been our need of it ?
— Whose life re-teaches us what life should
     be,
What faith is, loyalty and simpleness,
All, once revealed but taught us so long since
That, having mere tradition of the fact, —
Truth copied falteringly from copies faint,
The early traits all dropped away, — we said
On sight of faith like yours, " So looks not
     faith
We understand, described and praised before."
But still, the feat was dared ; and though at
     first
It suffered from our haste, yet trace by trace
Old memories reappear, old truth returns,
Our slow thought does its work, and all 's re-
     known.
Oh noble Luria ! What you have decreed
I see not, but no animal revenge,
No brute-like punishment of bad by worse —
It cannot be, the gross and vulgar way
Traced for me by convention and mistake,
Has gained that calm approving eye and brow !
Spare Florence, after all ! Let Luria trust
To his own soul, he whom I trust with mine !
   Lur. In time !
   Dom.   How, Luria ?
   Lur.   It is midnight now,
And they arrive from Florence with my fate.
   Dom. I hear no step.
   Lur.   I feel one, as you say.
             (*Enter* HUSAIN.)
   Hus. The man returned from Florence !
   Lur.   As I knew.
   Hus. He seeks thee.
   Lur.   And I only wait for him.
Aught else ?
   Hus.   A movement of the Lucchese troops
Southward —
   Lur. Toward Florence ? Have out in-
     stantly . . .
Ah, old use clings ! Puccio must care hence-
     forth.
In — quick — 't is nearly midnight ! Bid him
     come !
      (*Enter* TIBURZIO, BRACCIO, *and* PUCCIO.)
   Lur. Tiburzio ? — not at Pisa ?
   Tib.   I return
From Florence : I serve Pisa, and must think
By such procedure I have served her best.
A people is but the attempt of many
To rise to the completer life of one ;
And those who live as models for the mass
Are singly of more value than they all.
Such man are you, and such a time is this,
That your sole fate concerns a nation more
Than much apparent welfare : that to prove
Your rectitude, and duly crown the same,
Imports us far beyond to-day's event,
A battle's loss or gain : man's mass re
     mains, —
Keep but God's model safe, new men will rise

To take its mould, and other days to prove
How great a good was Luria's glory. True —
I might go try my fortune as you urged,
And, joining Lucca, helped by your disgrace,
Repair our harm — so were to-day's work done ;
But where leave Luria for our sons to see ?
No, I look farther. I have testified
(Declaring my submission to your arms)
Her full success to Florence, making clear
Your probity, as none else could : I spoke,
And out it shone !
    Lur.   Ah — until Braccio spoke !
    Brac. Till Braccio told in just a word the
      whole —
His lapse to error, his return to knowledge:
Which told . . . Nay, Luria, *I* should droop
    the head,
I whom shame rests with ! Yet I dare look
up,

Sure of your pardon how I sue for it,
Knowing you wholly. Let the midnight end !
'T is morn approaches !   Still you answer
    not ?
Sunshine succeeds the shadow passed away ;
Our faces, which phantasmal grew and false,
Are all that felt it : they change round you,
    turn
Truly themselves now in its vanishing.
Speak, Luria ! Here begins your true career :
Look up, advance !   All now is possible,
Fact's grandeur, no false dreaming !   Dare and
    do !
And every prophecy shall be fulfilled
Save one — (nay, now your word must come at
    last)
— That you would punish Florence !
    Hus. [*Pointing to* LURIA'S *dead body.*] That
    is done.

CHRISTMAS-EVE AND EASTER-DAY

FLORENCE, 1850

CHRISTMAS-EVE

I

OUT of the little chapel I burst
Into the fresh night-air again.
Five minutes full, I waited first
In the doorway, to escape the rain
That drove in gusts down the common's centre
At the edge of which the chapel stands,
Before I plucked up heart to enter.
Heaven knows how many sorts of hands
Reached past me, groping for the latch
Of the inner door that hung on catch
More obstinate the more they fumbled,
Till, giving way at last with a scold
Of the crazy hinge, in squeezed or tumbled
One sheep more to the rest in fold,
And left me irresolute, standing sentry
In the sheepfold's lath-and-plaster entry,
Six feet long by three feet wide,
Partitioned off from the vast inside —
I blocked up half of it at least.
No remedy ; the rain kept driving.
They eyed me much as some wild beast,
That congregation, still arriving,
Some of them by the main road, white
A long way past me into the night.
Skirting the common, then diverging ;
Not a few suddenly emerging
From the common's self through the paling-
    gaps,
— They house in the gravel-pits perhaps,
Where the road stops short with its safeguard
    border
Of lamps, as tired of such disorder ; —
But the most turned in yet more abruptly
From a certain squalid knot of alleys,
Where the town's bad blood once slept cor-
    ruptly,

Which now the little chapel rallies
And leads into day again, — its priestliness
Lending itself to hide their beastliness
So cleverly (thanks in part to the mason),
And putting so cheery a whitewashed face on
Those neophytes too much in lack of it,
That, where you cross the common as I did,
And meet the party thus presided,
" Mount Zion " with Love-lane at the back of
    it,
They front you as little disconcerted
As, bound for the hills, her fate averted,
And her wicked people made to mind him,
Lot might have marched with Gomorrah behind
    him.

II

Well, from the road, the lanes or the common,
In came the flock : the fat weary woman,
Panting and bewildered, down-clapping
Her umbrella with a mighty report,
Grounded it by me, wry and flapping,
A wreck of whalebones ; then, with a snort,
Like a startled horse, at the interloper
(Who humbly knew himself improper,
But could not shrink up small enough)
— Round to the door, and in, — the gruff
Hinge's invariable scold
Making my very blood run cold.
Prompt in the wake of her, up-pattered
On broken clogs, the many-tattered
Little old-faced peaking sister-turned-mother
Of the sickly babe she tried to smother
Somehow up, with its spotted face,
From the cold, on her breast, the one warm
    place ;
She too must stop, wring the poor ends dry
Of a draggled shawl, and add thereby
Her tribute to the door-mat, sopping
Already from my own clothes' dropping,

Which yet she seemed to grudge I should stand
    on :
Then, stooping down to take off her pattens,
She bore them defiantly, in each hand one,
Planted together before her breast
And its babe, as good as a lance in rest.
Close on her heels, the dingy satins
Of a female something past me flitted,
With lips as much too white, as a streak
Lay far too red on each hollow cheek ;
And it seemed the very door-hinge pitied
All that was left of a woman once,
Holding at least its tongue for the nonce.
Then a tall yellow man, like the Penitent Thief,
With his jaw bound up in a handkerchief,
And eyelids screwed together tight,
Led himself in by some inner light.
And, except from him, from each that entered,
I got the same interrogation —
" What, you the alien, you have ventured
To take with us, the elect, your station ?
A carer for none of it, a Gallio ! " —
Thus, plain as print, I read the glance
At a common prey, in each countenance
As of huntsman giving his hounds the tallyho.
And, when the door's cry drowned their won-
    der,
The draught, it always sent in shutting,
Made the flame of the single tallow candle
In the cracked square lantern I stood under,
Shoot its blue lip at me, rebutting
As it were, the luckless cause of scandal :
I verily fancied the zealous light
(In the chapel's secret, too !) for spite
Would shudder itself clean off the wick,
With the airs of a Saint John's Candlestick.
There was no standing it much longer.
" Good folks," thought I, as resolve grew
    stronger,
" This way you perform the Grand-Inquisitor
When the weather sends you a chance visitor ?
You are the men, and wisdom shall die with
    you,
And none of the old Seven Churches vie with
    you !
But still, despite the pretty perfection
To which you carry your trick of exclusive-
    ness,
And, taking God's word under wise protec-
    tion,
Correct its tendency to diffusiveness,
And bid one reach it over hot ploughshares, —
Still, as I say, though you 've found salvation,
If I should choose to cry, as now, ' Shares ! ' —
See if the best of you bars me my ration !
I prefer, if you please, for my expounder
Of the laws of the feast, the feast's own Foun-
    der ;
Mine 's the same right with your poorest and
    sickliest,
Supposing I don the marriage vestiment :
So, shut your mouth and open your Testament,
And carve me my portion at your quickliest ! "
Accordingly, as a shoemaker's lad
With wizened face in want of soap,
And wet apron wound round his waist like a
    rope,
(After stopping outside, for his cough was bad,

To get the fit over, poor gentle creature,
And so avoid disturbing the preacher)
— Passed in, I sent my elbow spikewise
At the shutting door, and entered likewise,
Received the hinge's accustomed greeting,
And crossed the threshold's magic pentacle,
And found myself in full conventicle,
— To wit, in Zion Chapel Meeting,
On the Christmas-Eve of 'Forty-nine,
Which, calling its flock to their special clover,
Found all assembled and one sheep over,
Whose lot, as the weather pleased, was mine.

III

I very soon had enough of it.
The hot smell and the human noises,
And my neighbor's coat, the greasy cuff of it,
Were a pebble-stone that a child's hand poises,
Compared with the pig-of-lead-like pressure
Of the preaching man's immense stupidity,
As he poured his doctrine forth, full measure,
To meet his audience's avidity.
You needed not the wit of the Sibyl
To guess the cause of it all, in a twinkling :
No sooner our friend had got an inkling
Of treasure hid in the Holy Bible,
(Whene'er 't was the thought first struck him,
How death, at unawares, might duck him
Deeper than the grave, and quench
The gin-shop's light in hell's grim drench)
Than he handled it so, in fine irreverence,
As to hug the book of books to pieces :
And, a patchwork of chapters and texts in sev-
    erance,
Not improved by the private dog's-ears and
    creases,
Having clothed his own soul with, he 'd fain
    see equipt yours, —
So tossed you again your Holy Scriptures.
And you picked them up, in a sense, no doubt :
Nay, had but a single face of my neighbors
Appeared to suspect that the preacher's la-
    bors
Were help which the world could be saved with-
    out,
'T is odds but I might have borne in quiet
A qualm or two at my spiritual diet,
Or (who can tell ?) perchance even mustered
Somewhat to urge in behalf of the sermon :
But the flock sat on, divinely flustered,
Sniffing, methought, its dew of Hermon
With such content in every snuffle,
As the devil inside us loves to ruffle.
My old fat woman purred with pleasure,
And thumb round thumb went twirling faster,
While she, to his periods keeping measure,
Maternally devoured the pastor.
The man with the handkerchief untied it,
Showed us a horrible wen inside it,
Gave his eyelids yet another screwing,
And rocked himself as the woman was doing.
The shoemaker's lad, discreetly choking,
Kept down his cough. 'T was too provoking !
My gorge rose at the nonsense and stuff of it ;
So, saying like Eve when she plucked the apple,
" I wanted a taste, and now there 's enough of
    it,"
I flung out of the little chapel.

IV

There was a lull in the rain, a lull
In the wind too; the moon was risen,
And would have shone out pure and full,
But for the ramparted cloud-prison,
Block on block built up in the West,
For what purpose the wind knows best,
Who changes his mind continually.
And the empty other half of the sky
Seemed in its silence as if it knew
What, any moment, might look through
A chance gap in that fortress massy: —
Through its fissures you got hints
Of the flying moon, by the shifting tints,
Now, a dull lion-color, now, brassy
Burning to yellow, and whitest yellow,
Like furnace-smoke just ere flames bellow,
All a-simmer with intense strain
To let her through, — then blank again,
At the hope of her appearance failing.
Just by the chapel a break in the railing
Shows a narrow path directly across;
'T is ever dry walking there, on the moss —
Besides, you go gently all the way up-hill.
I stooped under and soon felt better;
My head grew lighter, my limbs more supple,
As I walked on, glad to have slipt the fetter.
My mind was full of the scene I had left,
That placid flock, that pastor vociferant,
— How this outside was pure and different!
The sermon, now — what a mingled weft
Of good and ill! Were either less,
Its fellow had colored the whole distinctly;
But alas for the excellent earnestness,
And the truths, quite true if stated succinctly,
But as surely false, in their quaint presentment,
However to pastor and flock's contentment!
Say rather, such truths looked false to your
    eyes,
With his provings and parallels twisted and
    twined,
Till how could you know them, grown double
    their size
In the natural fog of the good man's mind,
Like yonder spots of our roadside lamps,
Haloed about with the common's damps?
Truth remains true, the fault 's in the prover;
The zeal was good, and the aspiration;
And yet, and yet, yet, fifty times over,
Pharaoh received no demonstration,
By his Baker's dream of Baskets Three,
Of the doctrine of the Trinity, —
Although, as our preacher thus embellished it,
Apparently his hearers relished it
With so unfeigned a gust — who knows if
They did not prefer our friend to Joseph?
But so it is everywhere, one way with all of
    them!
These people have really felt, no doubt,
A something, the motion they style the Call of
    them;
And this is their method of bringing about,
By a mechanism of words and tones,
(So many texts in so many groans)
A sort of reviving and reproducing,
More or less perfectly, (who can tell?)
The mood itself, which strengthens by using;

And how that happens, I understand well.
A tune was born in my head last week,
Out of the thump-thump and shriek-shriek
Of the train, as I came by it, up from Manches
    ter;
And when, next week, I take it back again,
My head will sing to the engine's clack again,
While it only makes my neighbor's haunches
    stir,
—Finding no dormant musical sprout
In him, as in me, to be jolted out.
'T is the taught already that profits by teach
    ing;
He gets no more from the railway's preaching
Than, from this preacher who does the rail's
    office, I:
Whom therefore the flock cast a jealous eye on.
Still, why paint over their door "Mount Zion,"
To which all flesh shall come, saith the pro
    phecy?

V

But wherefore be harsh on a single case?
After how many modes, this Christmas-Eve,
Does the self-same weary thing take place?
The same endeavor to make you believe,
And with much the same effect, no more:
Each method abundantly convincing,
As I say, to those convinced before,
But scarce to be swallowed without wincing
By the not-as-yet-convinced. For me,
I have my own church equally:
And in this church my faith sprang first!
(I said, as I reached the rising ground,
And the wind began again, with a burst
Of rain in my face, and a glad rebound
From the heart beneath, as if, God speeding me,
I entered his church-door, nature leading me)
— In youth I looked to these very skies,
And probing their immensities,
I found God there, his visible power;
Yet felt in my heart, amid all its sense
Of the power, an equal evidence
That his love, there too, was the nobler dower.
For the loving worm within its clod
Were diviner than a loveless god
Amid his worlds, I will dare to say.
You know what I mean: God 's all man 's
    naught:
But also, God, whose pleasure brought
Man into being, stands away
As it were a handbreadth off, to give
Room for the newly-made to live,
And look at him from a place apart,
And use his gifts of brain and heart,
Given, indeed, but to keep forever.
Who speaks of man, then, must not sever
Man's very elements from man,
Saying, "But all is God's" — whose plan
Was to create man and then leave him
Able, his own word saith, to grieve him,
But able to glorify him too,
As a mere machine could never do,
That prayed or praised, all unaware
Of its fitness for aught but praise and prayer,
Made perfect as a thing of course.
Man, therefore, stands on his own stock
Of love and power as a pin-point rock:

And, looking to God who ordained divorce
Of the rock from his boundless continent,
Sees, in his power made evident,
Only excess by a million-fold
O'er the power God gave man in the mould.
For, note: man's hand, first formed to carry
A few pounds' weight, when taught to marry
Its strength with an engine's, lifts a mountain,
— Advancing in power by one degree;
And why count steps through eternity?
But love is the ever-springing fountain:
Man may enlarge or narrow his bed
For the water's play, but the water-head —
How can he multiply or reduce it?
As easy create it, as cause it to cease;
He may profit by it, or abuse it,
But 't is not a thing to bear increase
As power does: be love less or more
In the heart of man, he keeps it shut
Or opes it wide, as he pleases, but
Love's sum remains what it was before.
So, gazing up, in my youth, at love
As seen through power, ever above
All modes which make it manifest,
My soul brought all to a single test —
That he, the Eternal First and Last,
Who, in his power, had so surpassed
All man conceives of what is might, —
Whose wisdom, too, showed infinite,
— Would prove as infinitely good;
Would never, (my soul understood,)
With power to work all love desires,
Bestow e'en less than man requires;
That he who endlessly was teaching,
Above my spirit's utmost reaching,
What love can do in the leaf or stone,
(So that to master this alone,
This done in the stone or leaf for me,
I must go on learning endlessly)
Would never need that I, in turn,
Should point him out defect unheeded,
And show that God had yet to learn
What the meanest human creature needed,
— Not life, to wit, for a few short years,
Tracking his way through doubts and fears,
While the stupid earth on which I stay
Suffers no change, but passive adds
Its myriad years to myriads,
Though I, he gave it to, decay,
Seeing death come and choose about me,
And my dearest ones depart without me.
No: love which, on earth, amid all the shows
    of it,
Has ever been seen the sole good of life in it,
The love, ever growing there, spite of the strife
    in it,
Shall arise, made perfect, from death's repose
    of it.
And I shall behold thee, face to face,
O God, and in thy light retrace
How in all I loved here, still wast thou!
Whom pressing to, then, as I fain would now,
I shall find as able to satiate
The love, thy gift, as my spirit's wonder
Thou art able to quicken and sublimate,
With this sky of thine, that I now walk under
And glory in thee for, as I gaze
Thus, thus! Oh, let men keep their ways

Of seeking thee in a narrow shrine —
Be this my way! And this is mine!

VI

For lo, what think you? suddenly
The rain and the wind ceased, and the sky
Received at once the full fruition
Of the moon's consummate apparition.
The black cloud-barricade was riven,
Ruined beneath her feet, and driven
Deep in the West; while, bare and breathless,
North and South and East lay ready
For a glorious thing that, dauntless, deathless,
Sprang across them and stood steady.
'T was a moon-rainbow, vast and perfect,
From heaven to heaven extending, perfect
As the mother-moon's self, full in face.
It rose, distinctly at the base
With its seven proper colors chorded,
Which still, in the rising, were compressed,
Until at last they coalesced,
And supreme the spectral creature lorded
In a triumph of whitest white, —
Above which intervened the night.
But above night too, like only the next,
The second of a wondrous sequence,
Reaching in rare and rarer frequence,
Till the heaven of heavens were circumflexed,
Another rainbow rose, a mightier,
Fainter, flushier and flightier, —
Rapture dying along its verge.
Oh, whose foot shall I see emerge,
Whose, from the straining topmost dark,
On to the keystone of that arc?

VII

This sight was shown me, there and then, —
Me, one out of a world of men,
Singled forth, as the chance might hap
To another if, in a thunderclap
Where I heard noise and you saw flame,
Some one man knew God called his name.
For me, I think I said, "Appear!
Good were it to be ever here.
If thou wilt, let me build to thee
Service-tabernacles three,
Where, forever in thy presence,
In ecstatic acquiescence,
Far alike from thriftless learning
And ignorance's undiscerning,
I may worship and remain!"
Thus at the show above me, gazing
With upturned eyes, I felt my brain
Glutted with the glory, blazing
Throughout its whole mass, over and under,
Until at length it burst asunder
And out of it bodily there streamed,
The too-much glory, as it seemed,
Passing from out me to the ground,
Then palely serpentining round
Into the dark with mazy error.

VIII

All at once I looked up with terror.
He was there.
He himself with his human air,
On the narrow pathway, just before.
I saw the back of him, no more —

He had left the chapel, then, as I.
I forgot all about the sky.
No face: only the sight
Of a sweepy garment, vast and white,
With a hem that I could recognize.
I felt terror, no surprise;
My mind filled with the cataract
At one bound of the mighty fact.
" I remember, he did say
Doubtless that, to this world's end,
Where two or three should meet and pray,
He would be in the midst, their friend;
Certainly he was there with them ! "
And my pulses leaped for joy
Of the golden thought without alloy,
That I saw his very vesture's hem.
Then rushed the blood back, cold and clear,
With a fresh enhancing shiver of fear;
And I hastened, cried out while I pressed
To the salvation of the vest,
" But not so, Lord ! It cannot be
That thou, indeed, art leaving me —
Me, that have despised thy friends !
Did my heart make no amends ?
Thou art the love of God — above
His power, didst hear me place his love,
And that was leaving the world for thee.
Therefore thou must not turn from me
As I had chosen the other part !
Folly and pride o'ercame my heart.
Our best is bad, nor bears thy test;
Still, it should be our very best.
I thought it best that thou, the spirit,
Be worshipped in spirit and in truth,
And in beauty, as even we require it —
Not in the forms burlesque, uncouth,
I left but now, as scarcely fitted
For thee : I knew not what I pitied.
But, all I felt there, right or wrong,
What is it to thee, who curest sinning ?
Am I not weak as thou art strong ?
I have looked to thee from the beginning,
Straight up to thee through all the world
Which, like an idle scroll, lay furled
To nothingness on either side :
And since the time thou wast descried,
Spite of the weak heart, so have I
Lived ever, and so fain would die,
Living and dying, thee before !
But if thou leavest me " —

IX

Less or more,
I suppose that I spoke thus.
When, — have mercy, Lord, on us !
The whole face turned upon me full.
And I spread myself beneath it,
As when the bleacher spreads, to seethe it
In the cleansing sun, his wool, —
Steeps in the flood of noontide whiteness
Some defiled, discolored web —
So lay I, saturate with brightness,
And when the flood appeared to ebb,
Lo, I was walking, light and swift,
With my senses settling fast and steadying,
But my body caught up in the whirl and drift
Of the vesture's amplitude, still eddying
On, just before me, still to be followed,

As it carried me after with its motion :
What shall I say ? — as a path were hollowed
And a man went weltering through the ocean,
Sucked along in the flying wake
Of the luminous water-snake.
Darkness and cold were cloven, as through
I passed, upborne yet walking too.
And I turned to myself at intervals, —
" So he said, so it befalls.
God who registers the cup
Of mere cold water, for his sake
To a disciple rendered up,
Disdains not his own thirst to slake
At the poorest love was ever offered:
And because my heart I proffered,
With true love trembling at the brim,
He suffers me to follow him
Forever, my own way, — dispensed
From seeking to be influenced
By all the less immediate ways
That earth, in worships manifold,
Adopts to reach, by prayer and praise,
The garment's hem, which, lo, I hold ! "

X

And so we crossed the world and stopped.
For where am I, in city or plain,
Since I am 'ware of the world again ?
And what is this that rises propped
With pillars of prodigious girth ?
Is it really on the earth,
This miraculous Dome of God ?
Has the angel's measuring-rod
Which numbered cubits, gem from gem,
'Twixt the gates of the New Jerusalem,
Meted it out, — and what he meted,
Have the sons of men completed ?
— Binding, ever as he bade,
Columns in the colonnade
With arms wide open to embrace
The entry of the human race
To the breast of . . . what is it, yon building.
Ablaze in front, all paint and gilding,
With marble for brick, and stones of price
For garniture of the edifice ?
Now I see ; it is no dream :
It stands there and it does not seem :
Forever, in pictures, thus it looks,
And thus I have read of it in books
Often in England, leagues away,
And wondered how these fountains play,
Growing up eternally
Each to a musical water-tree,
Whose blossoms drop, a glittering boon,
Before my eyes, in the light of the moon,
To the granite lavers underneath.
Liar and dreamer in your teeth !
I, the sinner that speak to you,
Was in Rome this night, and stood, and knew
Both this and more. For see, for see,
The dark is rent, mine eye is free
To pierce the crust of the outer wall,
And I view inside, and all there, all,
As the swarming hollow of a hive,
The whole Basilica alive !
Men in the chancel, body and nave,
Men on the pillars' architrave,
Men on the statues, men on the tombs

With popes and kings in their porphyry
    wombs,
All famishing in expectation
Of the main altar's consummation.
For see, for see, the rapturous moment
Approaches, and earth's best endowment
Blends with heaven's ; the taper-fires
Pant up, the winding brazen spires
Heave loftier yet the baldachin ;
The incense-gaspings, long kept in,
Suspire in clouds ; the organ blatant
Holds his breath and grovels latent,
As if God's hushing finger grazed him,
(Like Behemoth when he praised him)
At the silver bell's shrill tinkling,
Quick cold drops of terror sprinkling
On the sudden pavement strewed
With faces of the multitude.
Earth breaks up, time drops away,
In flows heaven, with its new day
Of endless life, when He who trod,
Very man and very God,
This earth in weakness, shame and pain,
Dying the death whose signs remain
Up yonder on the accursed tree, —
Shall come again, no more to be
Of captivity the thrall,
But the one God, All in all,
King of kings, Lord of lords,
As His servant John received the words,
" I died, and live forevermore ! "

XI

Yet I was left outside the door.
" Why sit I here on the threshold-stone,
Left till He return, alone
Save for the garment's extreme fold
Abandoned still to bless my hold ? "
My reason, to my doubt, replied,
As if a book were opened wide,
And at a certain page I traced
Every record undefaced,
Added by successive years, —
The harvestings of truth's stray ears
Singly gleaned, and in one sheaf
Bound together for belief.
Yes, I said — that he will go
And sit with these in turn, I know.
Their faith's heart beats, though her head
    swims
Too giddily to guide her limbs,
Disabled by their palsy-stroke
From propping mine. Though Rome's gross
    yoke
Drops off, no more to be endured,
Her teaching is not so obscured
By errors and perversities,
That no truth shines athwart the lies :
And he, whose eye detects a spark
Even where, to man's, the whole seems dark,
May well see flame where each beholder
Acknowledges the embers smoulder.
But I, a mere man, fear to quit
The clue God gave me as most fit
To guide my footsteps through life's maze,
Because himself discerns all ways
Open to reach him : I, a man
Able to mark where faith began

To swerve aside, till from its summit
Judgment drops her damning plummet,
Pronouncing such a fatal space
Departed from the founder's base ·
He will not bid me enter too,
But rather sit, as now I do,
Awaiting his return outside.
— 'T was thus my reason straight replied
And joyously I turned, and pressed
The garment's skirt upon my breast,
Until, afresh its light suffusing me,
My heart cried — " What has been abusing
    me
That I should wait here lonely and coldly,
Instead of rising, entering boldly,
Baring truth's face, and letting drift
Her veils of lies as they choose to shift ?
Do these men praise him ? I will raise
My voice up to their point of praise !
I see the error ; but above
The scope of error, see the love. —
Oh, love of those first Christian days !
— Fanned so soon into a blaze,
From the spark preserved by the trampled sect,
That the antique sovereign Intellect
Which then sat ruling in the world,
Like a change in dreams, was hurled
From the throne he reigned upon :
You looked up and he was gone.
Gone, his glory of the pen !
— Love, with Greece and Rome in ken,
Bade her scribes abhor the trick
Of poetry and rhetoric,
And exult with hearts set free,
In blessed imbecility
Scrawled, perchance, on some torn sheet
Leaving Sallust incomplete.
Gone, his pride of sculptor, painter !
— Love, while able to acquaint her
While the thousand statues yet
Fresh from chisel, pictures wet
From brush, she saw on every side,
Chose rather with an infant's pride
To frame those portents which impart
Such unction to true Christian Art.
Gone, music too ! The air was stirred
By happy wings : Terpander's bird
(That, when the cold came, fled away)
Would tarry not the wintry day, —
As more-enduring sculpture must,
Till filthy saints rebuked the gust
With which they chanced to get a sight
Of some dear naked Aphrodite
They glanced a thought above the toes of,
By breaking zealously her nose off.
Love, surely, from that music's lingering,
Might have filched her organ-fingering,
Nor chosen rather to set prayings
To hog-grunts, praises to horse-neighings.
Love was the startling thing, the new :
Love was the all-sufficient too ;
And seeing that, you see the rest :
As a babe can find its mother's breast
As well in darkness as in light,
Love shut our eyes, and all seemed right.
True, the world's eyes are open now :
— Less need for me to disallow
Some few that keep Love's zone unbuckled,

Peevish as ever to be suckled,
Lulled by the same old baby-prattle
With intermixture of the rattle,
When she would have them creep, stand steady
Upon their feet, or walk already,
Not to speak of trying to climb.
I will be wise another time,
And not desire a wall between us,
When next I see a church-roof cover
So many species of one genus,
All with foreheads bearing *lover*
Written above the earnest eyes of them ;
All with breasts that beat for beauty,
Whether sublimed, to the surprise of them,
In noble daring, steadfast duty,
The heroic in passion, or in action, —
Or, lowered for sense's satisfaction,
To the mere outside of human creatures,
Mere perfect form and faultless features.
What ? with all Rome here, whence to levy
Such contributions to their appetite,
With women and men in a gorgeous bevy,
They take, as it were, a padlock, clap it tight
On their southern eyes, restrained from feed-
    ing
On the glories of their ancient reading,
On the beauties of their modern singing,
On the wonders of the builder's bringing,
On the majesties of Art around them, —
And, all these loves, late struggling incessant,
When faith has at last united and bound them,
They offer up to God for a present ?
Why, I will, on the whole, be rather proud of
    it, —
And, only taking the act in reference
To the other recipients who might have allowed
    it,
I will rejoice that God had the preference."

XII

So I summed up my new resolves:
Too much love there can never be.
And where the intellect devolves
Its function on love exclusively,
I, a man who possesses both,
Will accept the provision, nothing loth,
— Will feast my love, then depart elsewhere,
That my intellect may find its share.
And ponder, O soul, the while thou departest,
And see thou applaud the great heart of the
    artist,
Who, examining the capabilities
Of the block of marble he has to fashion
Into a type of thought or passion, —
Not always, using obvious facilities,
Shapes it, as any artist can,
Into a perfect symmetrical man,
Complete from head to foot of the life-size,
Such as old Adam stood in his wife's eyes, —
But, now and then, bravely aspires to consum-
    mate
A Colossus by no means so easy to come at,
And uses the whole of his block for the bust,
Leaving the mind of the public to finish it,
Since cut it ruefully short he must :
On the face alone he expends his devotion,
He rather would mar than resolve to diminish
    it,

—Saying, " Applaud me for this grand notion
Of what a face may be ! As for completing it
In breast and body and limbs, do that, you ! "
All hail ! I fancy how, happily meeting it,
A trunk and legs would perfect the statue,
Could man carve so as to answer volition.
And how much nobler than petty cavils,
Were a hope to find, in my spirit-travels,
Some artist of another ambition,
Who having a block to carve, no bigger,
Has spent his power on the opposite quest,
And believed to begin at the feet was best —
For so may I see, ere I die, the whole figure !

XIII

No sooner said than out in the night !
My heart beat lighter and more light :
And still, as before, I was walking swift,
With my senses settling fast and steadying,
But my body caught up in the whirl and drift
Of the vesture's amplitude, still eddying
On, just before me, still to be followed,
As it carried me after with its motion :
What shall I say ? — as a path were hollowed,
And a man went weltering through the ocean,
Sucked along in the flying wake
Of the luminous water-snake.

XIV

Alone ! I am left alone once more —
(Save for the garment's extreme fold
Abandoned still to bless my hold)
Alone, beside the entrance-door
Of a sort of temple — perhaps a college,
— Like nothing I ever saw before
At home in England, to my knowledge.
The tall old quaint irregular town !
It may be . . . though which, I can't affirm
    . . . any
Of the famous middle-age towns of Germany ;
And this flight of stairs where I sit down,
Is it Halle, Weimar, Cassel, Frankfort,
Or Göttingen, I have to thank for 't ?
It may be Göttingen, — most likely.
Through the open door I catch obliquely
Glimpses of a lecture-hall ;
And not a bad assembly neither,
Ranged decent and symmetrical
On benches, waiting what 's to see there ;
Which, holding still by the vesture's hem,
I also resolve to see with them,
Cautious this time how I suffer to slip
The chance of joining in fellowship
With any that call themselves his friends ;
As these folks do, I have a notion.
But hist — a buzzing and emotion !
All settle themselves, the while ascends
By the creaking rail to the lecture-desk,
Step by step, deliberate
Because of his cranium's over-freight,
Three parts sublime to one grotesque,
If I have proved an accurate guesser,
The hawk-nosed, high-cheekboned Professor.
I felt at once as if there ran
A shoot of love from my heart to the man —
That sallow virgin-minded studious
Martyr to mild enthusiasm,
As he uttered a kind of cough-preludious

That woke my sympathetic spasm,
(Beside some spitting that made me sorry)
And stood, surveying his auditory
With a wan pure look, wellnigh celestial, —
Those blue eyes had survived so much !
While, under the foot they could not smutch,
Lay all the fleshly and the bestial.
Over he bowed, and arranged his notes,
Till the auditory's clearing of throats
Was done with, died into a silence ;
And, when each glance was upward sent,
Each bearded mouth composed intent,
And a pin might be heard drop half a mile
    hence, —
He pushed back higher his spectacles,
Let the eyes stream out like lamps from cells.
And giving his head of hair — a hake
Of undressed tow, for color and quantity —
One rapid and impatient shake,
(As our own young England adjusts a jaunty tie
When about to impart, on mature digestion,
Some thrilling view of the surplice-question)
— The Professor's grave voice, sweet though
    hoarse,
Broke into his Christmas-Eve discourse.

XV

And he began it by observing
How reason dictated that men
Should rectify the natural swerving,
By a reversion, now and then,
To the well-heads of knowledge, few
And far away, whence rolling grew
The life-stream wide whereat we drink,
Commingled, as we needs must think,
With waters alien to the source ;
To do which, aimed this eve's discourse ;
Since, where could be a fitter time
For tracing backward to its prime,
This Christianity, this lake,
This reservoir, whereat we slake,
From one or other bank, our thirst ?
So, he proposed inquiring first
Into the various sources whence
This Myth of Christ is derivable ;
Demanding from the evidence,
(Since plainly no such life was livable)
How these phenomena should class ?
Whether 't were best opine Christ was,
Or never was at all, or whether
He was and was not, both together —
It matters little for the name,
So the idea be left the same.
Only, for practical purpose' sake,
'T was obviously as well to take
The popular story, — understanding
How the ineptitude of the time,
And the penman's prejudice, expanding
Fact into fable fit for the clime,
Had, by slow and sure degrees, translated it
Into this myth, this Individuum, —
Which when reason had strained and abated it
Of foreign matter, left, for residuum,
A Man ! — a right true man, however,
Whose work was worthy a man's endeavor :
Work, that gave warrant almost sufficient
To his disciples, for rather believing
He was just omnipotent and omniscient,

As it gives to us, for as frankly receiving
His word, their tradition, — which, though it
    meant
Something entirely different
From all that those who only heard it,
In their simplicity thought and averred it,
Had yet a meaning quite as respectable :
For, among other doctrines delectable,
Was he not surely the first to insist on
The natural sovereignty of our race ? —
Here the lecturer came to a pausing-place.
And while his cough, like a droughty piston,
Tried to dislodge the husk that grew to him,
I seized the occasion of bidding adieu to him,
The vesture still within my hand.

XVI

I could interpret its command.
This time he would not bid me enter
The exhausted air-bell of the Critic.
Truth's atmosphere may grow mephitic
When Papist struggles with Dissenter,
Impregnating its pristine clarity,
— One, by his daily fare's vulgarity,
Its gust of broken meat and garlic ;
— One, by his soul's too-much presuming
To turn the frankincense's fuming
And vapors of the candle starlike
Into the cloud her wings she buoys on.
Each, that thus sets the pure air seething,
May poison it for healthy breathing —
But the Critic leaves no air to poison ;
Pumps out with ruthless ingenuity
Atom by atom, and leaves you — vacuity.
Thus much of Christ does he reject ?
And what retain ? His intellect ?
What is it I must reverence duly ?
Poor intellect for worship, truly,
Which tells me simply what was told
(If mere morality, bereft
Of the God in Christ, be all that 's left)
Elsewhere by voices manifold ;
With this advantage, that the stater
Made nowise the important stumble
Of adding, he, the sage and humble,
Was also one with the Creator.
You urge Christ's followers' simplicity :
But how does shifting blame evade it ?
Have wisdom's words no more felicity ?
The stumbling-block, his speech — who laid it ?
How comes it that for one found able
To sift the truth of it from fable,
Millions believe it to the letter ?
Christ's goodness, then — does that fare better ?
Strange goodness, which upon the score
Of being goodness, the mere due
Of man to fellow-man, much more
To God — should take another view
Of its possessor's privilege,
And bid him rule his race ! You pledge
Your fealty to such rule ? What, all —
From heavenly John and Attic Paul,
And that brave weather-battered Peter,
Whose stout faith only stood completer
For buffets, sinning to be pardoned,
As, more his hands hauled nets, they hard
    ened, —
All, down to you, the man of men.

Professing here at Göttingen,
Compose Christ's flock ! They, you and I,
Are sheep of a good man ! And why ?
The goodness, — how did he acquire it ?
Was it self-gained, did God inspire it ?
Choose which ; then tell me, on what ground
Should its possessor dare propound
His claim to rise o'er us an inch ?
Were goodness all some man's invention,
Who arbitrarily made mention
What we should follow, and whence flinch, —
What qualities might take the style
Of right and wrong, — and had such guessing
Met with as general acquiescing
As graced the alphabet erewhile,
When A got leave an Ox to be,
No Camel (quoth the Jews) like G, —
For thus inventing thing and title
Worship were that man's fit requital.
But if the common conscience must
Be ultimately judge, adjust
Its apt name to each quality
Already known, — I would decree
Worship for such mere demonstration
And simple work of nomenclature,
Only the day I praised, not nature,
But Harvey, for the circulation.
I would praise such a Christ, with pride
And joy, that he, as none beside,
Had taught us how to keep the mind
God gave him, as God gave his kind,
Freer than they from fleshly taint :
I would call such a Christ our Saint,
As I declare our Poet, him
Whose insight makes all others dim :
A thousand poets pried at life,
And only one amid the strife
Rose to be Shakespeare : each shall take
His crown, I'd say, for the world's sake —
Though some objected — " Had we seen
The heart and head of each, what screen
Was broken there to give them light,
While in ourselves it shuts the sight,
We should no more admire, perchance,
That these found truth out at a glance,
Than marvel how the bat discerns
Some pitch-dark cavern's fifty turns,
Led by a finer tact, a gift
He boasts, which other birds must shift
Without, and grope as best they can."
No, freely I would praise the man, —
Nor one whit more, if he contended
That gift of his from God descended.
Ah friend, what gift of man's does not ?
No nearer something, by a jot,
Rise an infinity of nothings
Than one : take Euclid for your teacher :
Distinguish kinds : do crownings, clothings,
Make that creator which was creature ?
Multiply gifts upon man's head,
And what, when all 's done, shall be said
But — the more gifted he, I ween !
That one 's made Christ, this other, Pilate,
And this might be all that has been, —
So what is there to frown or smile at ?
What is left for us, save, in growth
Of soul, to rise up, far past both,
From the gift looking to the giver,

And from the cistern to the river,
And from the finite to infinity,
And from man's dust to God's divinity ?

XVII

Take all in a word : the truth in God's breast
Lies trace for trace upon ours impressed :
Though he is so bright and we so dim,
We are made in his image to witness him :
And were no eye in us to tell,
Instructed by no inner sense,
The light of heaven from the dark of hell,
That light would want its evidence, —
Though justice, good and truth were still
Divine, if, by some demon's will,
Hatred and wrong had been proclaimed
Law through the worlds, and right misnamed.
No mere exposition of morality
Made or in part or in totality,
Should win you to give it worship, therefore :
And, if no better proof you will care for,
— Whom do you count the worst man upor
    earth ?
Be sure, he knows, in his conscience, more
Of what right is, than arrives at birth
In the best man's acts that we bow before :
This last knows better — true, but my fact is,
'T is one thing to know, and another to practice.
And thence I conclude that the real God-func-
    tion
Is to furnish a motive and injunction
For practising what we know already.
And such an injunction and such a motive
As the God in Christ, do you waive, and
    " heady,
High-minded," hang your tablet-votive
Outside the fane on a finger-post ?
Morality to the uttermost,
Supreme in Christ as we all confess,
Why need we prove would avail no jot
To make him God, if God he were not ?
What is the point where himself lays stress ?
Does the precept run " Believe in good,
In justice, truth, now understood
For the first time " ? — or, " Believe in me,
Who lived and died, yet essentially
Am Lord of Life " ? Whoever can take
The same to his heart and for mere love's sake
Conceive of the love, — that man obtains
A new truth ; no conviction gains
Of an old one only, made intense
By a fresh appeal to his faded sense.

XVIII

Can it be that he stays inside ?
Is the vesture left me to commune with ?
Could my soul find aught to sing in tune with
Even at this lecture, if she tried ?
Oh, let me at lowest sympathize
With the lurking drop of blood that lies
In the desiccated brain's white roots
Without throb for Christ's attributes,
As the lecturer makes his special boast !
If love 's dead there, it has left a ghost.
Admire we, how from heart to brain
(Though to say so strike the doctors dumb)
One instinct rises and falls again,
Restoring the equilibrium.

And how when the Critic had done his best,
And the pearl of price, at reason's test,
Lay dust and ashes levigable
On the Professor's lecture-table, —
When we looked for the inference and monition
That our faith, reduced to such condition,
Be swept forthwith to its natural dust-hole, —
He bids us, when we least expect it,
Take back our faith, — if it be not just whole,
Yet a pearl indeed, as his tests affect it,
Which fact pays damage done rewardingly,
So, prize we our dust and ashes accordingly!
" Go home and venerate the myth
I thus have experimented with —
This man, continue to adore him
Rather than all who went before him,
And all who ever followed after ! " —
Surely for this I may praise you, my brother !
Will you take the praise in tears or laughter ?
That 's one point gained : can I compass another ?
Unlearnèd love was safe from spurning —
Can't we respect your loveless learning ?
Let us at least give learning honor !
What laurels had we showered upon her,
Girding her loins up to perturb
Our theory of the Middle Verb ;
Or Turk-like brandishing a scimitar
O'er anapæsts in comic-trimeter ;
Or curing the halt and maimed " Iketides,"
While we lounged on at our indebted ease :
Instead of which, a tricksy demon
Sets her at Titus or Philemon !
When ignorance wags his ears of leather
And hates God's word, 't is altogether ;
Nor leaves he his congenial thistles
To go and browse on Paul's Epistles.
— And you, the audience, who might ravage
The world wide, enviably savage,
Nor heed the cry of the retriever,
More than Herr Heine (before his fever), —
I do not tell a lie so arrant
As say my passion's wings are furled up,
And, without plainest heavenly warrant,
I were ready and glad to give the world up —
But still, when you rub brow meticulous,
And ponder the profit of turning holy
If not for God's, for your own sake solely,
— God forbid I should find you ridiculous !
Deduce from this lecture all that eases you,
Nay, call yourselves, if the calling pleases you,
" Christians," — abhor the deist's pravity, —
Go on, you shall no more move my gravity
Than, when I see boys ride a-cockhorse,
I find it in my heart to embarrass them
By hinting that their stick 's a mock horse,
And they really carry what they say carries
          them.

XIX

So sat I talking with my mind.
I did not long to leave the door
And find a new church, as before,
But rather was quiet and inclined
To prolong and enjoy the gentle resting
From further tracking and trying and testing.
" This tolerance is a genial mood ! "
(Said I, and a little pause ensued.)
" One trims the bark 'twixt shoal and shelf,

And sees, each side, the good effects of it,
A value for religion's self,
A carelessness about the sects of it.
Let me enjoy my own conviction,
Not watch my neighbor's faith with fretfulness
Still spying there some dereliction
Of truth, perversity, forgetfulness !
Better a mild indifferentism,
Teaching that both our faiths (though duller
His shine through a dull spirit's prism)
Originally had one color !
Better pursue a pilgrimage
Through ancient and through modern times
To many peoples, various climes,
Where I may see saint, savage, sage
Fuse their respective creeds in one
Before the general Father's throne ! "

XX

— 'T was the horrible storm began afresh !
The black night caught me in his mesh,
Whirled me up, and flung me prone.
I was left on the college-step alone.
I looked, and far there, ever fleeting
Far, far away, the receding gesture,
And looming of the lessening vesture ! —
Swept forward from my stupid hand,
While I watched my foolish heart expand
In the lazy glow of benevolence,
O'er the various modes of man's belief.
I sprang up with fear's vehemence,
Needs must there be one way, our chief
Best way of worship : let me strive
To find it, and when found, contrive
My fellows also take their share !
This constitutes my earthly care :
God's is above it and distinct,
For I, a man, with men am linked
And not a brute with brutes ; no gain
That I experience, must remain
Unshared : but should my best endeavor
To share it, fail — subsisteth ever
God's care above, and I exult
That God, by God's own ways occult,
May — doth, I will believe — bring back
All wanderers to a single track.
Meantime, I can but testify
God's care for me — no more, can I —
It is but for myself I know ;
The world rolls witnessing around me
Only to leave me as it found me ;
Men cry there, but my ear is slow :
Their races flourish or decay
— What boots it ; while you lucid way
Loaded with stars divides the vault ?
But soon my soul repairs its fault
When, sharpening sense's hebetude,
She turns on my own life ! So viewed,
No mere mote's-breadth but teems immense
With witnessings of providence :
And woe to me if when I look
Upon that record, the sole book
Unsealed to me, I take no heed
Of any warning that I read !
Have I been sure, this Christmas-Eve,
God's own hand did the rainbow weave,
Whereby the truth from heaven slid
Into my soul ? — I cannot bid

The world admit he stooped to heal
My soul, as if in a thunder-peal
Where one heard noise, and one saw flame,
I only knew he named my name :
But what is the world to me, for sorrow
Or joy in its censure, when to-morrow
It drops the remark, with just-turned head,
Then, on again, " That man is dead " ?
Yes, but for me — my name called, — drawn
As a conscript's lot from the lap's black yawn,
He has dipt into on a battle-dawn :
Bid out of life by a nod, a glance, —
Stumbling, mute-mazed, at nature's chance, —
With a rapid finger circled round,
Fixed to the first poor inch of ground
To fight from, where his foot was found ;
Whose ear but a minute since lay free
To the wide camp's buzz and gossipry —
Summoned, a solitary man,
To end his life where his life began,
From the safe glad rear, to the dreadful van !
Soul of mine, hadst thou caught and held
By the hem of the vesture ! —

XXI

                               And I caught
At the flying robe, and unrepelled
Was lapped again in its folds full-fraught
With warmth and wonder and delight,
God's mercy being infinite.
For scarce had the words escaped my tongue,
When, at a passionate bound, I sprung
Out of the wondering world of rain,
Into the little chapel again.

XXII

How else was I found there, bolt upright
On my bench, as if I had never left it ?
— Never flung out on the common at night,
Nor met the storm and wedge-like cleft it,
Seen the raree-show of Peter's successor,
Or the laboratory of the Professor !
For the Vision, that was true, I wist,
True as that heaven and earth exist.
There sat my friend, the yellow and tall,
With his neck and its wen in the selfsame place ;
Yet my nearest neighbor's cheek showed gall.
She had slid away a contemptuous space :
And the old fat woman, late so placable,
Eyed me with symptoms, hardly mistakable,
Of her milk of kindness turning rancid,
In short, a spectator might have fancied
That I had nodded, betrayed by slumber,
Yet kept my seat, a warning ghastly,
Through the heads of the sermon, nine in number,
And woke up now at the tenth and lastly.
But again, could such disgrace have happened ?
Each friend at my elbow had surely nudged it ;
And, as for the sermon, where did my nap end ?
Unless I heard it, could I have judged it ?
Could I report as I do at the close,
First, the preacher speaks through his nose :
Second, his gesture is too emphatic :
Thirdly, to waive what 's pedagogic,
The subject-matter itself lacks logic :
Fourthly, the English is ungrammatic.
Great news ! the preacher is found no Pascal,

Whom, if I pleased, I might to the task call
Of making square to a finite eye
The circle of infinity,
And find so all-but-just-succeeding !
Great news ! the sermon proves no reading
Where bee-like in the flowers I bury me,
Like Taylor's, the immortal Jeremy !
And now that I know the very worst of him,
What was it I thought to obtain at first of him !
Ha ! Is God mocked, as he asks ?
Shall I take on me to change his tasks,
And dare, dispatched to a river-head
For a simple draught of the element,
Neglect the thing for which he sent,
And return with another thing instead ? —
Saying, " Because the water found
Welling up from underground,
Is mingled with the taints of earth,
While thou, I know, dost laugh at dearth,
And couldst, at wink or word, convulse
The world with the leap of a river-pulse, —
Therefore I turned from the oozings muddy,
And bring thee a chalice I found, instead :
See the brave veins in the breccia ruddy !
One would suppose that the marble bled.
What matters the water ? A hope I have
                                                   nursed :
The waterless cup will quench my thirst."
— Better have knelt at the poorest stream
That trickles in pain from the straitest rift !
For the less or the more is all God's gift,
Who blocks up or breaks wide the granite-seam
And here, is there water or not, to drink ?
I then, in ignorance and weakness,
Taking God's help, have attained to think
My heart does best to receive in meekness
That mode of worship, as most to his mind,
Where earthly aids being cast behind,
His All in All appears serene
With the thinnest human veil between,
Letting the mystic lamps, the seven,
The many motions of his spirit,
Pass, as they list, to earth from heaven.
For the preacher's merit or demerit,
It were to be wished the flaws were fewer
In the earthen vessel, holding treasure
Which lies as safe in a golden ewer ;
But the main thing is, does it hold good meas
                                                        ure ?
Heaven soon sets right all other matters ! —
Ask, else, these ruins of humanity,
This flesh worn out to rags and tatters,
This soul at struggle with insanity,
Who thence take comfort — can I doubt ? —
Which an empire gained, were a loss without.
May it be mine ! And let us hope
That no worse blessing befall the Pope,
Turned sick at last of to-day's buffoonery,
Of posturings and petticoatings,
Beside his Bourbon bully's gloatings
In the bloody orgies of drunk poltroonery !
Nor may the Professor forego its peace
At Göttingen presently, when, in the dusk
Of his life, if his cough, as I fear, should in
                                                      crease,
Prophesied of by that horrible husk —
When thicker and thicker the darkness fills
The world through his misty spectacles,

And he gropes for something more substantial
Than a fable, myth or personification, —
May Christ do for him what no mere man shall,
And stand confessed as the God of salvation!
Meantime, in the still recurring fear
Lest myself, at unawares, be found,
While attacking the choice of my neighbors
    round,
With none of my own made — I choose here!
The giving out of the hymn reclaims me;
I have done: and if any blames me,
Thinking that merely to touch in brevity
The topics I dwell on, were unlawful, —
Or worse, that I trench, with undue levity,
On the bounds of the holy and the awful, —
I praise the heart, and pity the head of him,
And refer myself to THEE, instead of him,
Who head and heart alike discernest,
Looking below light speech we utter,
When frothy spume and frequent sputter
Prove that the soul's depths boil in earnest!
May truth shine out, stand ever before us!
I put up pencil and join chorus
To Hepzibah Tune, without further apology,
The last five verses of the third section
Of the seventeenth hymn of Whitefield's Col-
    lection,
To conclude with the doxology.

EASTER-DAY

I

How very hard it is to be
A Christian! Hard for you and me,
— Not the mere task of making real
That duty up to its ideal,
Effecting thus, complete and whole,
A purpose of the human soul —
For that is always hard to do;
But hard, I mean, for me and you
To realize it, more or less,
With even the moderate success
Which commonly repays our strife
To carry out the aims of life.
"This aim is greater," you will say,
"And so more arduous every way."
— But the importance of their fruits
Still proves to man, in all pursuits,
Proportional encouragement.
"Then, what if it be God's intent
That labor to this one result
Should seem unduly difficult?"
Ah, that's a question in the dark —
And the sole thing that I remark
Upon the difficulty, this:
We do not see it where it is,
At the beginning of the race:
As we proceed, it shifts its place,
And where we looked for crowns to fall,
We find the tug 's to come, — that 's all.

II

At first you say, "The whole, or chief
Of difficulties, is belief.
Could I believe once thoroughly,
The rest were simple. What? Am I
An idiot, do you think, — a beast?

Prove to me, only that the least
Command of God is God's indeed,
And what injunction shall I need
To pay obedience? Death so nigh,
When time must end, eternity
Begin, — and cannot I compute,
Weigh loss and gain together, suit
My actions to the balance drawn,
And give my body to be sawn
Asunder, hacked in pieces, tied
To horses, stoned, burned, crucified,
Like any martyr of the list?
How gladly! — if I make acquist,
Through the brief minute's fierce annoy,
Of God's eternity of joy."

III

— And certainly you name the point
Whereon all turns: for could you joint
This flexile finite life once tight
Into the fixed and infinite,
You, safe inside, would spurn what 's out,
With carelessness enough, no doubt —
Would spurn mere life: but when time brings
To their next stage your reasonings,
Your eyes, late wide, begin to wink
Nor see the path so well, I think.

IV

You say, "Faith may be, one agrees,
A touchstone for God's purposes,
Even as ourselves conceive of them.
Could he acquit us or condemn
For holding what no hand can loose,
Rejecting when we can't but choose?
As well award the victor's wreath
To whosoever should take breath
Duly each minute while he lived —
Grant heaven, because a man contrived
To see its sunlight every day
He walked forth on the public way.
You must mix some uncertainty
With faith, if you would have faith be.
Why, what but faith, do we abhor
And idolize each other for —
Faith in our evil or our good,
Which is or is not understood
Aright by those we love or those
We hate, thence called our friends or foes?
Your mistress saw your spirit's grace,
When, turning from the ugly face,
I found belief in it too hard;
And she and I have our reward.
— Yet here a doubt peeps: well for us
Weak beings, to go using thus
A touchstone for our little ends,
Trying with faith the foes and friends;
— But God, bethink you! I would fain
Conceive of the Creator's reign
As based upon exacter laws
Than creatures build by with applause.
In all God's acts — (as Plato cries
He doth) — he should geometrize.
Whence, I desiderate" . . .

V

              I see!
You would grow as a natural tree,

Stand as a rock, soar up like fire.
The world 's so perfect and entire,
Quite above faith, so right and fit!
Go there, walk up and down in it !
No.   The creation travails, groans —
Contrive your music from its moans,
Without or let or hindrance, friend !
That 's an old story, and its end
As old — you come back (be sincere)
With every question you put here
(Here where there once was, and is still,
We think, a living oracle,
Whose answers you stand carping at)
This time flung back unanswered flat, —
Beside, perhaps, as many more
As those that drove you out before,
Now added, where was little need.
Questions impossible, indeed,
To us who sat still, all and each
Persuaded that our earth had speech,
Of God's, writ down, no matter if
In cursive type or hieroglyph, —
Which one fact freed us from the yoke
Of guessing why He never spoke.
You come back in no better plight
Than when you left us, — am I right ?

VI

So, the old process, I conclude,
Goes on, the reasoning 's pursued
Further.   You own, " 'T is well averred,
A scientific faith 's absurd,
— Frustrates the very end 't was meant
To serve. So, I would rest content
With a mere probability,
But, probable ; the chance must lie
Clear on one side, — lie all in rough,
So long as there be just enough
To pin my faith to, though it hap
Only at points : from gap to gap
One hangs up a huge curtain so,
Grandly, nor seeks to have it go
Foldless and flat along the wall.
What care I if some interval
Of life less plainly may depend
On God ? I 'd hang there to the end ;
And thus I should not find it hard
To be a Christian and debarred
From trailing on the earth, till furled
Away by death. — Renounce the world !
Were that a mighty hardship ? Plan
A pleasant life, and straight some man
Beside you, with, if he thought fit,
Abundant means to compass it,
Shall turn deliberate aside
To try and live as, if you tried
You clearly might, yet most despise.
One friend of mine wears out his eyes,
Slighting the stupid joys of sense,
In patient hope that, ten years hence,
'Somewhat completer,' he may say,
' My list of *coleoptera!* '
While just the other who most laughs
At him, above all epitaphs
Aspires to have his tomb describe
Himself as sole among the tribe
Of snuffbox-fanciers, who possessed
A Grignon with the Regent's crest.

So that, subduing, as you want,
Whatever stands predominant
Among my earthly appetites
For tastes and smells and sounds and sights,
I shall be doing that alone,
To gain a palm-branch and a throne,
Which fifty people undertake
To do, and gladly, for the sake
Of giving a Semitic guess,
Or playing pawns at blindfold chess."

VII

Good : and the next thing is, — look round
For evidence enough ! 'T is found,
No doubt : as is your sort of mind,
So is your sort of search : you 'll find
What you desire, and that 's to be
A Christian.   What says history ?
How comforting a point it were
To find some mummy-scrap declare
There lived a Moses ! Better still,
Prove Jonah's whale translatable
Into some quicksand of the seas,
Isle, cavern, rock, or what you please,
That faith might flap her wings and crow
From such an eminence ! Or, no —
The human heart 's best ; you prefer
Making that prove the minister
To truth ; you probe its wants and needs,
And hopes and fears, then try what creeds
Meet these most aptly, — resolute
That faith plucks such substantial fruit
Wherever these two correspond,
She little needs to look beyond
And puzzle out who Orpheus was,
Or Dionysius Zagrias.
You 'll find sufficient, as I say,
To satisfy you either way ;
You wanted to believe ; your pains
Are crowned — you do : and what remains ?
" Renounce the world ! " — Ah, were it done
By merely cutting one by one
Your limbs off, with your wise head last,
How easy were it ! — how soon past,
If once in the believing mood !
" Such is man's usual gratitude,
Such thanks to God do we return,
For not exacting that we spurn
A single gift of life, forego
One real gain, — only taste them so
With gravity and temperance,
That those mild virtues may enhance
Such pleasures, rather than abstract —
Last spice of which, will be the fact
Of love discerned in every gift ;
While, when the scene of life shall shift,
And the gay heart be taught to ache,
As sorrows and privations take
The place of joy, — the thing that seems
Mere misery, under human schemes,
Becomes, regarded by the light
Of love, as very near or quite
As good a gift as joy before.
So plain is it that, all the more
A dispensation 's merciful,
More pettishly we try and cull
Briers, thistles, from our private plot,
To mar God's ground where thorns are not ! "

VIII

Do you say this, or I ? — Oh, you !
Then, what, my friend ? — (thus I pursue
Our parley) — you indeed opine
That the Eternal and Divine
Did, eighteen centuries ago,
In very truth . . . Enough ! you know
The all-stupendous tale, — that Birth,
That Life, that Death ! And all, the earth
Shuddered at, — all, the heavens grew black
Rather than see ; all, nature's rack
And throe at dissolution's brink
Attested, — all took place, you think,
Only to give our joys a zest,
And prove our sorrows for the best ?
We differ, then ! Were I, still pale
And heartstruck at the dreadful tale,
Waiting to hear God's voice declare
What horror followed for my share,
As implicated in the deed,
Apart from other sins, — concede
That if He blacked out in a blot
My brief life's pleasantness, 't were not
So very disproportionate !
Or there might be another fate —
I certainly could understand
(If fancies were the thing in hand)
How God might save, at that day's price,
The impure in their impurities,
Give license formal and complete
To choose the fair and pick the sweet.
But there be certain words, broad, plain,
Uttered again and yet again,
Hard to mistake or overgloss —
Announcing this world's gain for loss,
And bidding us reject the same :
The whole world lieth (they proclaim)
In wickedness, — come out of it !
Turn a deaf ear, if you think fit,
But I who thrill through every nerve
At thought of what deaf ears deserve —
How do you counsel in the case ?

IX

" I 'd take, by all means, in your place,
The safe side, since it so appears :
Deny myself, a few brief years,
The natural pleasure, leave the fruit
Or cut the plant up by the root.
Remember what a martyr said
On the rude tablet overhead !
' I was born sickly, poor and mean,
A slave : no misery could screen
The holders of the pearl of price
From Cæsar's envy ; therefore twice
I fought with beasts, and three times saw
My children suffer by his law ;
At last my own release was earned :
I was some time in being burned,
But at the close a Hand came through
The fire above my head, and drew
My soul to Christ, whom now I see.
Sergius, a brother, writes for me
This testimony on the wall —
For me, I have forgot it all.'
You say right ; this were not so hard !
And since one nowise is debarred

From this, why not escape some sins
By such a method ? "

X

Then begins
To the old point revulsion new —
(For 't is just this I bring you to) —
If after all we should mistake,
And so renounce life for the sake
Of death and nothing else ? You hear
Each friend we jeered at, send the jeer
Back to ourselves with good effect —
" There were my beetles to collect !
My box — a trifle, I confess,
But here I hold it, ne'ertheless ! "
Poor idiots, (let us pluck up heart
And answer) we, the better part
Have chosen, though 't were only hope, -
Nor envy moles like you that grope
Amid your veritable muck,
More than the grasshoppers would truck
For yours, their passionate life away,
That spends itself in leaps all day
To reach the sun, you want the eyes
To see, as they the wings to rise
And match the noble hearts of them !
Thus the contemner we contemn, —
And, when doubt strikes us, thus we ward
Its stroke off, caught upon our guard,
— Not struck enough to overturn
Our faith, but shake it — make us learn
What I began with, and, I wis,
End, having proved, — how hard it is
To be a Christian !

XI

" Proved, or not,
Howe'er you wis, small thanks, I wot,
You get of mine, for taking pains
To make it hard to me. Who gains
By that, I wonder ? Here I live
In trusting ease ; and here you drive
At causing me to lose what most
Yourself would mourn for had you lost ! "

XII

But, do you see, my friend, that thus
You leave Saint Paul for Æschylus ?
— Who made his Titan's arch-device
The giving men *blind hopes* to spice
The meal of life with, else devoured
In bitter haste, while lo, death loured
Before them at the platter's edge !
If faith should be, as I allege,
Quite other than a condiment
To heighten flavors with, or meant
(Like that brave curry of his Grace)
To take at need the victuals' place ?
If, having dined, you would digest
Besides, and turning to your rest
Should find instead . . .

XIII

Now, you shall see
And judge if a mere foppery
Pricks on my speaking ! I resolve
To utter — yes, it shall devolve
On you to hear as solemn, strange
And dread a thing as in the range

Of facts, — or fancies, if God will —
E'er happened to our kind !   I still
Stand in the cloud and, while it wraps
My face, ought not to speak perhaps ;
Seeing that if I carry through
My purpose, if my words in you
Find a live actual listener,
My story, reason must aver
False after all — the happy chance !
While, if each human countenance
I meet in London day by day,
Be what I fear, — my warnings fray
No one, and no one they convert,
And no one helps me to assert
How hard it is to really be
A Christian, and in vacancy
I pour this story !

XIV

                        I commence
By trying to inform you, whence
It comes that every Easter-night
As now, I sit up, watch, till light,
Upon those chimney-stacks and roofs,
Give, through my window-pane, gray proofs
That Easter-Day is breaking slow.
On such a night, three years ago,
It chanced that I had cause to cross
The common, where the chapel was,
Our friend spoke of, the other day —
You 've not forgotten, I dare say.
I fell to musing of the time
So close, the blessed matin-prime
All hearts leap up at, in some guise —
One could not well do otherwise.
Insensibly my thoughts were bent
Toward the main point ; I overwent
Much the same ground of reasoning
As you and I just now.   One thing
Remained, however — one that tasked
My soul to answer ; and I asked,
Fairly and frankly, what might be
That History, that Faith, to me
— Me there — not me in some domain
Built up and peopled by my brain,
Weighing its merits as one weighs
Mere theories for blame or praise,
— The kingcraft of the Lucumons,
Or Fourier's scheme, its pros and cons, —
But my faith there, or none at all.
" How were my case, now, did I fall
Dead here, this minute — should I lie
Faithful or faithless ? "   Note that I
Inclined thus ever ! — little prone
For instance, when I lay alone
In childhood, to go calm to sleep
And leave a closet where might keep
His watch perdue some murderer
Waiting till twelve o'clock to stir,
As good authentic legends tell :
" He might : but how improbable !
How little likely to deserve
The pains and trial to the nerve
Of thrusting head into the dark ! " —
Urged my old nurse, and bade me mark
Beside, that, should the dreadful scout
Really lie hid there, and leap out
At first turn of the rusty key,

Mine were small gain that she could see,
Killed not in bed but on the floor,
And losing one night's sleep the more.
I tell you, I would always burst
The door ope, know my fate at first.
This time, indeed, the closet penned
No such assassin : but a friend
Rather, peeped out to guard me, fit
For counsel, Common Sense, to wit,
Who said a good deal that might pass, —
Heartening, impartial too, it was,
Judge else : " For, soberly now, — who
Should be a Christian if not you ? "
(Hear how he smoothed me down.) " One takes
A whole life, sees what course it makes
Mainly, and not by fits and starts —
In spite of stoppage which imparts
Fresh value to the general speed.
A life, with none, would fly indeed :
Your progressing is slower — right !
We deal with progress and not flight.
Through baffling senses passionate,
Fancies as restless, — with a freight
Of knowledge cumbersome enough
To sink your ship when waves grow rough,
Though meant for ballast in the hold, —
I find, 'mid dangers manifold,
The good bark answers to the helm
Where faith sits, easier to o'erwhelm
Than some stout peasant's heavenly guide,
Whose hard head could not, if it tried,
Conceive a doubt, nor understand
How senses hornier than his hand
Should 'tice the Christian off his guard.
More happy !   But shall we award
Less honor to the hull which, dogged
By storms, a mere wreck, waterlogged,
Masts by the board, her bulwarks gone
And stanchions going, yet bears on, —
Than to mere lifeboats, built to save,
And triumph o'er the breaking wave ?
Make perfect your good ship as these,
And what were her performances ! "
I added — " Would the ship reach home !
I wish indeed ' God's kingdom come ' —
The day when I shall see appear
His bidding, as my duty, clear
From doubt !   And it shall dawn, that day,
Some future season ; Easter may
Prove, not impossibly, the time —
Yes, that were striking — fates would chime
So aptly !   Easter-morn, to bring
The Judgment ! — deeper in the spring
Than now, however, when there 's snow
Capping the hills ; for earth must show
All signs of meaning to pursue
Her tasks as she was wont to do
— The skylark, taken by surprise
As we ourselves, shall recognize
Sudden the end.   For suddenly
It comes ; the dreadfulness must be
In that ; all warrants the belief —
' At night it cometh like a thief.'
I fancy why the trumpet blows ;
— Plainly, to wake one.   From repose
We shall start up, at last awake
From life, that insane dream we take
For waking now, because it seems.

And as, when now we wake from dreams,
We laugh, while we recall them, 'Fool,
To let the chance slip, linger cool
When such adventure offered ! Just
A bridge to cross, a dwarf to thrust
Aside, a wicked mage to stab —
And, lo ye, I had kissed Queen Mab !'
So shall we marvel why we grudged
Our labor here, and idly judged
Of heaven, we might have gained, but lose !
Lose ? Talk of loss, and I refuse
To plead at all ! You speak no worse
Nor better than my ancient nurse
When she would tell me in my youth
I well deserved that shapes uncouth
Frighted and teased me in my sleep :
Why could I not in memory keep
Her precept for the evil's cure ?
' Pinch your own arm, boy, and be sure
You 'll wake forthwith ! ' "

XV

                And as I said
This nonsense, throwing back my head
With light complacent laugh, I found
Suddenly all the midnight round
One fire. The dome of heaven had stood
As made up of a multitude
Of handbreadth cloudlets, one vast rack
Of ripples infinite and black,
From sky to sky. Sudden there went,
Like horror and astonishment,
A fierce vindictive scribble of red
Quick flame across, as if one said
(The angry scribe of Judgment) "There —
Burn it !" And straight I was aware
That the whole ribwork round, minute
Cloud touching cloud beyond compute,
Was tinted, each with its own spot
Of burning at the core, till clot
Jammed against clot, and spilt its fire
Over all heaven, which 'gan suspire
As fanned to measure equable, —
Just so great conflagrations kill
Night overhead, and rise and sink,
Reflected. Now the fire would shrink
And wither off the blasted face
Of heaven, and I distinct might trace
The sharp black ridgy outlines left
Unburned like network — then, each cleft
The fire had been sucked back into,
Regorged, and out it surging flew
Furiously, and night writhed inflamed,
Till, tolerating to be tamed
No longer, certain rays world-wide
Shot downwardly. On every side
Caught past escape, the earth was lit ;
As if a dragon's nostril split
And all his famished ire o'erflowed ;
Then, as he winced at his lord's goad,
Back he inhaled : whereat I found
The clouds into vast pillars bound,
Based on the corners of the earth,
Propping the skies at top : a dearth
Of fire i' the violet intervals,
Leaving exposed the utmost walls
Of time, about to tumble in
And end the world.

XVI

                I felt begin
The Judgment-Day : to retrocede
Was too late now. "In very deed,"
(I uttered to myself) "that Day !"
The intuition burned away
All darkness from my spirit too :
There, stood I, found and fixed, I knew,
Choosing the world. The choice was made ;
And naked and disguiseless stayed,
And unevadable, the fact.
My brain held all the same compact
Its senses, nor my heart declined
Its office ; rather, both combined
To help me in this juncture. I
Lost not a second, — agony
Gave boldness : since my life had end
And my choice with it — best defend,
Applaud both ! I resolved to say,
"So was I framed by thee, such way
I put to use thy senses here !
It was so beautiful, so near,
Thy world, — what could I then but choose
My part there ? Nor did I refuse
To look above the transient boon
Of time ; but it was hard so soon
As in a short life, to give up
Such beauty : I could put the cup,
Undrained of half its fulness, by ;
But, to renounce it utterly,
— That was too hard ! Nor did the cry
Which bade renounce it, touch my brain
Authentically deep and plain
Enough to make my lips let go.
But thou, who knowest all, dost know
Whether I was not, life's brief while,
Endeavoring to reconcile
Those lips (too tardily, alas !)
To letting the dear remnant pass,
One day, — some drops of earthly good
Untasted ! Is it for this mood,
That thou, whose earth delights so well,
Hast made its complement a hell ? "

XVII

A final belch of fire like blood,
Overbroke all heaven in one flood
Of doom. Then fire was sky, and sky
Fire, and both, one brief ecstasy,
Then ashes. But I heard no noise
(Whatever was) because a voice
Beside me spoke thus, "Life is done,
Time ends, Eternity 's begun,
And thou art judged forevermore."

XVIII

I looked up ; all seemed as before ;
Of that cloud-Tophet overhead
No trace was left : I saw instead
The common round me, and the sky
Above, stretched drear and emptily
Of life. 'T was the last watch of night,
Except what brings the morning quite ;
When the armed angel, conscience-clear,
His task nigh done, leans o'er his spear
And gazes on the earth he guards,
Safe one night more through all its wards,

Till God relieve him at his post.
" A dream — a waking dream at most ! "
(I spoke out quick, that I might shake
The horrid nightmare off, and wake.)
" The world gone, yet the world is here ?
Are not all things as they appear ?
Is Judgment past for me alone ?
— And where had place the great white
    throne ?
The rising of the quick and dead ?
Where stood they, small and great ? Who
    read
The sentence from the opened book ? "
So, by degrees, the blood forsook
My heart, and let it beat afresh ;
I knew I should break through the mesh
Of horror, and breathe presently :
When, lo, again, the voice by me !

XIX

I saw . . . O brother, 'mid far sands
The palm-tree-cinctured city stands,
Bright-white beneath, as heaven, bright-blue,
Leans o'er it, while the years pursue
Their course, unable to abate
Its paradisal laugh at fate !
One morn, — the Arab staggers blind
O'er a new tract of death, calcined
To ashes, silence, nothingness, —
And strives, with dizzy wits, to guess
Whence fell the blow. What if, 'twixt skies
And prostrate earth, he should surprise
The imaged vapor, head to foot,
Surveying, motionless and mute,
Its work, ere, in a whirlwind rapt
It vanish up again ? — So hapt
My chance. HE stood there. Like the smoke
Pillared o'er Sodom, when day broke, —
I saw him. One magnific pall
Mantled in massive fold and fall
His head, and coiled in snaky swathes
About his feet : night's black, that bathes
All else, broke, grizzled with despair,
Against the soul of blackness there.
A gesture told the mood within —
That wrapped right hand which based the chin,
That intense meditation fixed
On his procedure, — pity mixed
With the fulfilment of decree.
Motionless, thus, he spoke to me,
Who fell before his feet, a mass,
No man now.

XX

    " All is come to pass.
Such shows are over for each soul
They had respect to. In the roll
Of Judgment which convinced mankind
Of sin, stood many, bold and blind,
Terror must burn the truth into :
Their fate for them ! — thou hadst to do
With absolute omnipotence,
Able its judgments to dispense
To the whole race, as every one
Were its sole object. Judgment done,
God is, thou art, — the rest is hurled
To nothingness for thee. This world,
This finite life, thou hast preferred,
In disbelief of God's plain word,

To heaven and to infinity.
Here the probation was for thee,
To show thy soul the earthly mixed
With heavenly, it must choose betwixt.
The earthly joys lay palpable, —
A taint, in each, distinct as well ;
The heavenly flitted, faint and rare,
Above them, but as truly were
Taintless, so, in their nature, best.
Thy choice was earth : thou didst attest
'T was fitter spirit should subserve
The flesh, than flesh refine to nerve
Beneath the spirit's play. Advance
No claim to their inheritance
Who chose the spirit's fugitive
Brief gleams, and yearned, ' This were to live
Indeed, if rays, completely pure
From flesh that dulls them, could endure, —
Not shoot in meteor-light athwart
Our earth, to show how cold and swart
It lies beneath their fire, but stand
As stars do, destined to expand,
Prove veritable worlds, our home ! '
Thou saidst, — 'Let spirit star the dome
Of sky, that flesh may miss no peak,
No nook of earth, — I shall not seek
Its service further ! ' Thou art shut
Out of the heaven of spirit ; glut
Thy sense upon the world : 't is thine
Forever — take it ! "

XXI

      " How ? Is mine,
The world ? " (I cried, while my soul broke
Out in a transport.) " Hast thou spoke
Plainly in that ? Earth's exquisite
Treasures of wonder and delight
For me ? "

XXII

    The austere voice returned, —
" So soon made happy ? Hadst thou learned
What God accounteth happiness,
Thou wouldst not find it hard to guess
What hell may be his punishment
For those who doubt if God invent
Better than they. Let such men rest
Content with what they judged the best.
Let the unjust usurp at will :
The filthy shall be filthy still :
Miser, there waits the gold for thee !
Hater, indulge thine enmity !
And thou, whose heaven self-ordained
Was, to enjoy earth unrestrained,
Do it ! Take all the ancient show !
The woods shall wave, the rivers flow,
And men apparently pursue
Their works, as they were wont to do,
While living in probation yet.
I promise not thou shalt forget
The past, now gone to its account ;
But leave thee with the old amount
Of faculties, nor less nor more,
Unvisited, as heretofore,
By God's free spirit, that makes an end.
So, once more, take thy world ! Expend
Eternity upon its shows
Flung thee as freely as one rose
Out of a summer's opulence,

Over the Eden-barrier whence
Thou art excluded.   Knock in vain ! "

XXIII

I sat up.   All was still again.
I breathed free : to my heart, back fled
The warmth.   " But, all the world ! " — I said.
I stooped and picked a leaf of fern,
And recollected I might learn
From books, how many myriad sorts
Of fern exist, to trust reports,
Each as distinct and beautiful
As this, the very first I cull.
Think, from the first leaf to the last !
Conceive, then, earth's resources !   Vast
Exhaustless beauty, endless change
Of wonder !   And this foot shall range
Alps, Andes, — and this eye devour
The bee-bird and the aloe-flower ?

XXIV

Then the voice : " Welcome so to rate
The arras-folds that variegate
The earth, God's antechamber, well !
The wise, who waited there, could tell
By these, what royalties in store
Lay one step past the entrance-door.
For whom, was reckoned, not too much,
This life's munificence ?   For such
As thou, — a race, whereof scarce one
Was able, in a million,
To feel that any marvel lay
In objects round his feet all day ;
Scarce one, in many millions more,
Willing, if able, to explore
The secreter, minuter charm !
— Brave souls, a fern-leaf could disarm
Of power to cope with God's intent, —
Or scared if the south firmament
With north-fire did its wings refledge !
All partial beauty was a pledge
Of beauty in its plenitude :
But since the pledge sufficed thy mood,
Retain it ! plenitude be theirs
Who looked above ! "

XXV

Though sharp despairs
Shot through me, I held up, bore on.
" What matter though my trust were gone
From natural things ?   Henceforth my part
Be less with nature than with art !
For art supplants, gives mainly worth
To nature ; 't is man stamps the earth —
And I will seek his impress, seek
The statuary of the Greek,
Italy's painting — there my choice
Shall fix ! "

XXVI

" Obtain it ! " said the voice,
" The one form with its single act,
Which sculptors labored to abstract,
The one face, painters tried to draw,
With its one look, from throngs they saw
And that perfection in their soul,
These only hinted at ?   The whole,
They were but parts of ?   What each laid

His claim to glory on ? —afraid
His fellow-men should give him rank
By mere tentatives which he shrank
Smitten at heart from, all the more,
That gazers pressed in to adore !
' Shall I be judged by only these ? '
If such his soul's capacities,
Even while he trod the earth, — think, now,
What pomp in Buonarroti's brow,
With its new palace-brain where dwells
Superb the soul, unvexed by cells
That crumbled with the transient clay !
What visions will his right hand's sway
Still turn to forms, as still they burst
Upon him ?   How will he quench thirst,
Titanically infantine,
Laid at the breast of the Divine ?
Does it confound thee, — this first page
Emblazoning man's heritage ? —
Can this alone absorb thy sight,
As pages were not infinite, —
Like the omnipotence which tasks
Itself to furnish all that asks
The soul it means to satiate ?
What was the world, the starry state
Of the broad skies, — what, all displays
Of power and beauty intermixed,
Which now thy soul is chained betwixt, —
What else than needful furniture
For life's first stage ?   God's work, be sure
No more spreads wasted, than falls scant !
He filled, did not exceed, man's want
Of beauty in this life.   But through
Life pierce, — and what has earth to do,
Its utmost beauty's appanage,
With the requirement of next stage ?
Did God pronounce earth ' very good ' ?
Needs must it be, while understood
For man's preparatory state ;
Naught here to heighten nor abate ;
Transfer the same completeness here,
To serve a new state's use, — and drear
Deficiency gapes every side !
The good, tried once, were bad, retried.
See the enwrapping rocky niche,
Sufficient for the sleep in which
The lizard breathes for ages safe :
Split the mould — and as light would chafe
The creature's new world-widened sense,
Dazzled to death at evidence
Of all the sounds and sights that broke
Innumerous at the chisel's stroke, —
So, in God's eye, the earth's first stuff
Was, neither more nor less, enough
To house man's soul, man's need fulfil.
Man reckoned it immeasurable ?
So thinks the lizard of his vault !
Could God be taken in default,
Short of contrivances, by you, —
Or reached, ere ready to pursue
His progress through eternity ?
That chambered rock, the lizard's world.
Your easy mallet's blow has hurled
To nothingness forever ; so,
Has God abolished at a blow
This world, wherein his saints were pent,
Who, though found grateful and content,
With the provision there, as thou,

Yet knew he would not disallow
Their spirit's hunger, felt as well, —
Unsated, — not unsatable,
As paradise gives proof.   Deride
Their choice now, thou who sit'st outside ! "

XXVII

I cried in anguish : " Mind, the mind,
So miserably cast behind,
To gain what had been wisely lost !
Oh, let me strive to make the most
Of the poor stinted soul, I nipped
Of budding wings, else now equipped
For voyage from summer isle to isle !
And though she needs must reconcile
Ambition to the life on ground,
Still, I can profit by late found
But precious knowledge.   Mind is best —
I will seize mind, forego the rest,
And try how far my tethered strength
May crawl in this poor breadth and length.
Let me, since I can fly no more,
At least spin dervish-like about
(Till giddy rapture almost doubt
I fly) through circling sciences,
Philosophies and histories !
Should the whirl slacken there, then verse,
Fining to music, shall asperse
Fresh and fresh fire-dew, till I strain
Intoxicate, half-break my chain !
Not joyless, though more favored feet
Stand calm, where I want wings to beat
The floor.   At least earth's bond is broke ! "

XXVIII

Then (sickening even while I spoke) :
" Let me alone ! No answer, pray,
To this ! I know what thou wilt say !
All still is earth's, — to know, as much
As feel its truths, which if we touch
With sense, or apprehend in soul,
What matter ? I have reached the goal —
' Whereto does knowledge serve ! ' will burn
My eyes, too sure, at every turn !
I cannot look back now, nor stake
Bliss on the race, for running's sake.
The goal 's a ruin like the rest ! "
" And so much worse thy latter quest,"
(Added the voice,) " that even on earth —
Whenever, in man's soul, had birth
Those intuitions, grasps of guess,
Which pull the more into the less,
Making the finite comprehend
Infinity, — the bard would spend
Such praise alone, upon his craft,
As, when wind-lyres obey the waft,
Goes to the craftsman who arranged
The seven strings, changed them and re-
          changed —
Knowing it was the South that harped.
He felt his song, in singing, warped ;
Distinguished his and God's part : whence
A world of spirit as of sense
Was plain to him, yet not too plain,
Which he could traverse, not remain
A guest in : — else were permanent
Heaven on the earth its gleams were meant
To sting with hunger for full light, —

Made visible in verse, despite
The veiling weakness, — truth by means
Of fable, showing while it screens, —
Since highest truth, man e'er supplied,
Was ever fable on outside.
Such gleams made bright the earth an age ;
Now the whole sun 's his heritage !
Take up thy world, it is allowed,
Thou who hast entered in the cloud ! "

XXIX

Then I — " Behold, my spirit bleeds,
Catches no more at broken reeds, —
But lilies flower those reeds above :
I let the world go, and take love !
Love survives in me, albeit those
I love be henceforth masks and shows,
Not living men and women : still
I mind how love repaired all ill,
Cured wrong, soothed grief, made earth amend
With parents, brothers, children, friends !
Some semblance of a woman yet
With eyes to help me to forget,
Shall look on me ; and I will match
Departed love with love, attach
Old memories to new dreams, nor scorn
The poorest of the grains of corn
I save from shipwreck on this isle,
Trusting its barrenness may smile
With happy foodful green one day,
More precious for the pains.   I pray, —
Leave to love, only ! "

XXX

                    At the word,
The form, I looked to have been stirred
With pity and approval, rose
O'er me, as when the headsman throws
Axe over shoulder to make end —
I fell prone, letting him expend
His wrath, while thus the inflicting voice
Smote me.   " Is this thy final choice ?
Love is the best ? 'T is somewhat late !
And all thou dost enumerate
Of power and beauty in the world,
The mightiness of love was curled
Inextricably round about.
Love lay within it and without,
To clasp thee, — but in vain ! Thy soul
Still shrunk from him who made the whole
Still set deliberate aside
His love ! — Now take love ! Well betide
Thy tardy conscience ! Haste to take
The show of love for the name's sake,
Remembering every moment who,
Beside creating thee unto
These ends, and these for thee, was said
To undergo death in thy stead
In flesh like thine : so ran the tale.
What doubt in thee could countervail
Belief in it ? Upon the ground
' That in the story had been found
Too much love ! How could God love so ?
He who in all his works below
Adapted to the needs of man,
Made love the basis of the plan, —
Did love, as was demonstrated :
While man, who was so fit instead

To hate, as every day gave proof, —
Man thought man, for his kind's behoof,
Both could and did invent that scheme
Of perfect love: 't would well beseem
Cain's nature thou wast wont to praise,
Not tally with God's usual ways!"

XXXI

And I cowered deprecatingly —
"Thou Love of God! Or let me die,
Or grant what shall seem heaven almost!
Let me not know that all is lost,
Though lost it be — leave me not tied
To this despair, this corpse-like bride!
Let that old life seem mine — no more —
With limitation as before,
With darkness, hunger, toil, distress:
Be all the earth a wilderness!
Only let me go on, go on,
Still hoping ever and anon
To reach one eve the Better Land!"

XXXII

Then did the form expand, expand —
I knew him through the dread disguise
As the whole God within his eyes
Embraced me.

XXXIII

When I lived again,
The day was breaking, — the gray plain
I rose from, silvered thick with dew.

Was this a vision? False or true?
Since then, three varied years are spent,
And commonly my mind is bent
To think it was a dream — be sure
A mere dream and distemperature —
The last day's watching: then the night, —
The shock of that strange Northern Light
Set my head swimming, bred in me
A dream. And so I live, you see,
Go through the world, try, prove, reject,
Prefer, still struggling to effect
My warfare; happy that I can
Be crossed and thwarted as a man,
Not left in God's contempt apart,
With ghastly smooth life, dead at heart,
Tame in earth's paddock as her prize.
Thank God, she still each method tries
To catch me, who may yet escape,
She knows, — the fiend in angel's shape!
Thank God, no paradise stands barred
To entry, and I find it hard
To be a Christian, as I said!
Still every now and then my head
Raised glad, sinks mournful — all grows drear
Spite of the sunshine, while I fear
And think, "How dreadful to be grudged
No ease henceforth, as one that's judged,
Condemned to earth forever, shut
From heaven!"
                          But Easter-Day breaks! But
Christ rises! Mercy every way
Is infinite, — and who can say?

MEN AND WOMEN

LONDON AND FLORENCE, 184– 185–

In making his final distribution of poems
Browning gave the above title and dates to the
thirteen poems which follow, but the title was
originally given by him to two volumes pub-
lished in 1855. The other poems are dispersed
among the several groups already named, with
the exception of *In a Balcony*, which appeared
by itself.

"TRANSCENDENTALISM: A POEM IN TWELVE BOOKS"

Stop playing, poet! May a brother speak?
'T is you speak, that's your error. Song's our
    art:
Whereas you please to speak these naked
    thoughts
Instead of draping them in sights and sounds.
— True thoughts, good thoughts, thoughts fit
    to treasure up!
But why such long prolusion and display,
Such turning and adjustment of the harp,
And taking it upon your breast, at length,
Only to speak dry words across its strings?
Stark-naked thought is in request enough:
Speak prose and hollo it till Europe hears!

The six-foot Swiss tube, braced about with
    bark,
Which helps the hunter's voice from Alp to
    Alp —
Exchange our harp for that, — who hinders
    you?

    But here's your fault; grown men want
        thought, you think;
Thought's what they mean by verse, and seek
    in verse:
Boys seek for images and melody,
Men must have reason — so, you aim at men.
Quite otherwise! Objects throng our youth
    't is true;
We see and hear and do not wonder much:
If you could tell us what they mean, indeed!

As German Boehme never cared for plants
Until it happed, a-walking in the fields,
He noticed all at once that plants could speak,
Nay, turned with loosened tongue to talk with
    him.
That day the daisy had an eye indeed —
Colloquized with the cowslip on such themes !
We find them extant yet in Jacob's prose.
But by the time youth slips a stage or two
While reading prose in that tough book he
    wrote
(Collating and emendating the same
And settling on the sense most to our mind),
We shut the clasps and find life's summer past.
Then, who helps more, pray, to repair our
    loss —
Another Boehme with a tougher book
And subtler meanings of what roses say, —
Or some stout Mage like him of Halberstadt,
John, who made things Boehme wrote thoughts
    about ?
He with a " look you ! " vents a brace of
    rhymes,
And in there breaks the sudden rose herself,
Over us, under, round us every side,
Nay, in and out the tables and the chairs
And musty volumes, Boehme's book and all, —
Buries us with a glory; young once more,
Pouring heaven into this shut house of life.

So come, the harp back to your heart again !
You are a poem, though your poem 's naught.
The best of all you showed before, believe,
Was your own boy-face o'er the finer chords
Bent, following the cherub at the top
That points to God with his paired half-moon
    wings.

HOW IT STRIKES A CONTEMPORARY

I ONLY knew one poet in my life :
And this, or something like it, was his way.

You saw go up and down Valladolid,
A man of mark, to know next time you saw.
His very serviceable suit of black
Was courtly once and conscientious still,
And many might have worn it, though none
    did :
The cloak, that somewhat shone and showed
    the threads,
Had purpose, and the ruff, significance.
He walked and tapped the pavement with his
    cane,
Scenting the world, looking it full in face,
An old dog, bald and blindish, at his heels.
They turned up, now, the alley by the church,
That leads nowhither ; now, they breathed
    themselves
On the main promenade just at the wrong time :
You 'd come upon his scrutinizing hat,
Making a peaked shade blacker than itself
Against the single window spared some house
Intact yet with its mouldered Moorish work, —
Or else surprise the ferrel of his stick
Trying the mortar's temper 'tween the chinks
Of some new shop a-building, French and fine.

He stood and watched the cobbler at his trade,
The man who slices lemons into drink,
The coffee-roaster's brazier, and the boys
That volunteer to help him turn its winch.
He glanced o'er books on stalls with half an
    eye,
And fly-leaf ballads on the vender's string,
And broad-edge bold-print posters by the wall.
He took such cognizance of men and things,
If any beat a horse, you felt he saw ;
If any cursed a woman, he took note ;
Yet stared at nobody, — you stared at him,
And found, less to your pleasure than surprise,
He seemed to know you and expect as much.
So, next time that a neighbor's tongue was
    loosed,
It-marked the shameful and notorious fact,
We had among us, not so much a spy,
As a recording chief-inquisitor,
The town's true master if the town but knew !
We merely kept a governor for form,
While this man walked about and took account
Of all thought, said and acted, then went home,
And wrote it fully to our Lord the King
Who has an itch to know things, he knows why,
And reads them in his bedroom of a night.
Oh, you might smile ! there wanted not a touch,
A tang of . . . well, it was not wholly ease
As back into your mind the man's look came.
Stricken in years a little, — such a brow
His eyes had to live under ! — clear as flint
On either side the formidable nose
Curved, cut and colored like an eagle's claw.
Had he to do with A 's surprising fate ?
When altogether old B disappeared
And young C got his mistress, — was 't our
    friend,
His letter to the King, that did it all ?
What paid the bloodless man for so much
    pains ?
Our Lord the King has favorites manifold,
And shifts his ministry some once a month ;
Our city gets new governors at whiles, —
But never word or sign, that I could hear,
Notified to this man about the streets
The King's approval of those letters conned
The last thing duly at the dead of night.
Did the man love his office ? Frowned our
    Lord,
Exhorting when none heard — " Beseech me
    not !
Too far above my people, — beneath me !
I set the watch, —how should the people know ?
Forget them, keep me all the more in mind ! "
Was some such understanding 'twixt the two ?

I found no truth in one report at least —
That if you tracked him to his home, down
    lanes
Beyond the Jewry, and as clean to pace,
You found he ate his supper in a room
Blazing with lights, four Titians on the wall,
And twenty naked girls to change his plate !
Poor man, he lived another kind of life
In that new stuccoed third house by the bridge,
Fresh-painted, rather smart than otherwise !
The whole street might o'erlook him as he sat,
Leg crossing leg, one foot on the dog's back,

Playing a decent cribbage with his maid
(Jacynth, you 're sure her name was) o'er the
cheese
And fruit, three red halves of starved winter-
pears,
Or treat of radishes in April. Nine,
Ten, struck the church clock, straight to bed
went he.

My father, like the man of sense he was,
Would point him out to me a dozen times ;
" 'St — 'St," he 'd whisper, " the Corregidor ! "
I had been used to think that personage
Was one with lacquered breeches, lustrous belt,
And feathers like a forest in his hat,
Who blew a trumpet and proclaimed the news,
Announced the bull-fights, gave each church
its turn,
And memorized the miracle in vogue !
He had a great observance from us boys ;
We were in error ; that was not the man.

I 'd like now, yet had haply been afraid,
To have just looked, when this man came to
die,
And seen who lined the clean gay garret-sides
And stood about the neat low truckle-bed,
With the heavenly manner of relieving guard.
Here had been, mark, the general-in-chief,
Through a whole campaign of the world's life
and death,
Doing the King's work all the dim day long,
In his old coat and up to knees in mud,
Smoked like a herring, dining on a crust, —
And, now the day was won, relieved at once !
No further show or need for that old coat,
You are sure, for one thing ! Bless us, all the
while
How sprucely we are dressed out, you and I !
A second, and the angels alter that.
Well, I could never write a verse, — could you ?
Let 's to the Prado and make the most of time.

ARTEMIS PROLOGIZES

Upon the first proof of this poem Browning
wrote : " I had better say perhaps that the
above is nearly all retained of a tragedy I com-
posed much against my endeavor, while in bed
with a fever two years ago — it went farther
into the story of Hippolytus and Aricia ; but
when I got well, putting only thus much down
at once, I soon forgot the remainder." The
notes contain an interesting defence by Brown-
ing of the form of his Greek names.

I AM a goddess of the ambrosial courts,
And save by Here, Queen of Pride, surpassed
By none whose temples whiten this the world.
Through heaven I roll my lucid moon along ;
I shed in hell o'er my pale people peace ;
On earth I, caring for the creatures, guard
Each pregnant yellow wolf and fox-bitch sleek,
And every feathered mother's callow brood,
And all that love green haunts and loneliness.

Of men, the chaste adore me, hanging crowns
Of poppies red to blackness, bell and stem,
Upon my image at Athenai here ;
And this dead Youth, Asclepios bends above,
Was dearest to me. He, my buskined step
To follow through the wild-wood leafy ways,
And chase the panting stag, or swift with darts
Stop the swift ounce, or lay the leopard low,
Neglected homage to another god :
Whence Aphrodite, by no midnight smoke
Of tapers lulled, in jealousy dispatched
A noisome lust that, as the gadbee stings,
Possessed his stepdame Phaidra for himself
The son of Theseus her great absent spouse.
Hippolutos exclaiming in his rage
Against the fury of the Queen, she judged
Life insupportable ; and, pricked at heart
An Amazonian stranger's race should dare
To scorn her, perished by the murderous cord :
Yet, ere she perished, blasted in a scroll
The fame of him her swerving made not
swerve.
And Theseus read, returning, and believed,
And exiled, in the blindness of his wrath,
The man without a crime who, last as first,
Loyal, divulged not to his sire the truth.
Now Theseus from Poseidon had obtained
That of his wishes should be granted three,
And one he imprecated straight — " Alive
May ne'er Hippolutos reach other lands ! "
Poseidon heard, ai ai ! And scarce the prince
Had stepped into the fixed boots of the car
That give the feet a stay against the strength
Of the Henetian horses, and around
His body flung the rein, and urged their speed
Along the rocks and shingles of the shore,
When from the gaping wave a monster flung
His obscene body in the coursers' path.
These, mad with terror, as the sea-bull sprawled
Wallowing about their feet, lost care of him
That reared them ; and the master-chariot-pole
Snapping beneath their plunges like a reed,
Hippolutos, whose feet were trammelled fast,
Was yet dragged forward by the circling rein
Which either hand directed ; nor they quenched
The frenzy of their flight before each trace,
Wheel-spoke and splinter of the woeful car,
Each boulder-stone, sharp stub and spiny shell,
Huge fish-bone wrecked and wreathed amid the
sands
On that detested beach, was bright with blood
And morsels of his flesh : then fell the steeds
Head-foremost, crashing in their mooned fronts,
Shivering with sweat, each white eye horror-
fixed.
His people, who had witnessed all afar,
Bore back the ruins of Hippolutos.
But when his sire, too swoln with pride, rejoiced
(Indomitable as a man foredoomed)
That vast Poseidon had fulfilled his prayer,
I, in a flood of glory visible,
Stood o'er my dying votary and, deed
By deed, revealed, as all took place, the truth.
Then Theseus lay the woefullest of men,
And worthily ; but ere the death-veils hid
His face, the murdered prince full pardon
breathed
To his rash sire. Whereat Athenai wails.

So I, who ne'er forsake my votaries,
Lest in the cross-way none the honey-cake
Should tender, nor pour out the dog's hot life ;
Lest at my fane the priests disconsolate
Should dress my image with some faded poor
Few crowns, made favors of, nor dare object
Such slackness to my worshippers who turn
Elsewhere the trusting heart and loaded hand,
As they had climbed Olumpos to report
Of Artemis and nowhere found her throne —
I interposed : and, this eventful night, —
(While round the funeral pyre the populace
Stood with fierce light on their black robes
     which bound
Each sobbing head, while yet their hair they
     clipped
O'er the dead body of their withered prince,
And, in his palace, Theseus prostrated
On the cold hearth, his brow cold as the slab
'T was bruised on, groaned away the heavy
     grief —
As the pyre fell, and down the cross logs crashed
Sending a crowd of sparkles through the night,
And the gay fire, elate with mastery,
Towered like a serpent o'er the clotted jars
Of wine, dissolving oils and frankincense,
And splendid gums like gold,) — my potency
Conveyed the perished man to my retreat
In the thrice-venerable forest here.
And this white-bearded sage who squeezes now
The berried plant, is Phoibos' son of fame,
Asclepios, whom my radiant brother taught
The doctrine of each herb and flower and root,
To know their secret'st virtue and express
The saving soul of all : who so has soothed
With lavers the torn brow and murdered cheeks,
Composed the hair and brought its gloss again,
And called the red bloom to the pale skin back,
And laid the strips and jagged ends of flesh
Even once more, and slacked the sinew's knot
Of every tortured limb — that now he lies
As if mere sleep possessed him underneath
These interwoven oaks and pines. Oh cheer,
Divine presenter of the healing rod,
Thy snake, with ardent throat and lulling eye,
Twines his lithe spires around ! I say, much
     cheer !
Proceed thou with thy wisest pharmacies !
And ye, white crowd of woodland sister-nymphs,
Ply, as the sage directs, these buds and leaves
That strew the turf around the twain ! While I
Await, in fitting silence, the event.

AN EPISTLE

CONTAINING THE STRANGE MEDICAL EXPERI-
ENCE OF KARSHISH, THE ARAB PHYSICIAN

KARSHISH, the picker-up of learning's crumbs,
The not-incurious in God's handiwork
(This man's-flesh he hath admirably made,
Blown like a bubble, kneaded like a paste,
To coop up and keep down on earth a space
That puff of vapor from his mouth, man's soul)
— To Abib, all-sagacious in our art,
Breeder in me of what poor skill I boast,
Like me inquisitive how pricks and cracks

Befall the flesh through too much stress and
     strain,
Whereby the wily vapor fain would slip
Back and rejoin its source before the term, —
And aptest in contrivance (under God)
To baffle it by deftly stopping such : —
The vagrant Scholar to his Sage at home
Sends greeting (health and knowledge, fame
     with peace)
Three samples of true snake-stone — rarer still,
One of the other sort, the melon-shaped,
(But fitter, pounded fine, for charms than drugs)
And writeth now the twenty-second time.

My journeyings were brought to Jericho :
Thus I resume. Who studious in our art
Shall count a little labor unrepaid ?
I have shed sweat enough, left flesh and bone
On many a flinty furlong of this land.
Also, the country-side is all on fire
With rumors of a marching hitherward :
Some say Vespasian cometh, some, his son.
A black lynx snarled and pricked a tufted ear ;
Lust of my blood inflamed his yellow balls :
I cried and threw my staff and he was gone.
Twice have the robbers stripped and beaten me,
And once a town declared me for a spy ;
But at the end, I reach Jerusalem,
Since this poor covert where I pass the night,
This Bethany, lies scarce the distance thence
A man with plague-sores at the third degree
Runs till he drops down dead. Thou laughest
     here !
'Sooth, it elates me, thus reposed and safe,
To void the stuffing of my travel-scrip
And share with thee whatever Jewry yields.
A viscid choler is observable
In tertians, I was nearly bold to say ;
And falling-sickness hath a happier cure
Than our school wots of : there 's a spider
     here
Weaves no web, watches on the ledge of tombs,
Sprinkled with mottles on an ash-gray back ;
Take five and drop them . . . but who knows
     his mind,
The Syrian runagate I trust this to ?
His service payeth me a sublimate
Blown up his nose to help the ailing eye.
Best wait : I reach Jerusalem at morn,
There set in order my experiences,
Gather what most deserves, and give thee
     all —
Or I might add, Judæa's gum-tragacanth
Scales off in purer flakes, shines clearer-grained,
Cracks 'twixt the pestle and the porphyry,
In fine exceeds our produce. Scalp-disease
Confounds me, crossing so with leprosy —
Thou hadst admired one sort I gained at
     Zoar —
But zeal outruns discretion. Here I end.

Yet stay : my Syrian blinketh gratefully,
Protesteth his devotion is my price —
Suppose I write what harms not, though he
     steal ?
I half resolve to tell thee, yet I blush,
What set me off a-writing first of all.
An itch I had, a sting to write, a tang !

For, be it this town's barrenness — or else
The Man had something in the look of him —
His case has struck me far more than 't is
worth.
So, pardon if — (lest presently I lose
In the great press of novelty at hand
The care and pains this somehow stole from
me)
I bid thee take the thing while fresh in mind,
Almost in sight — for, wilt thou have the truth ?
The very man is gone from me but now,
Whose ailment is the subject of discourse.
Thus then, and let thy better wit help all !

'T is but a case of mania — subinduced
By epilepsy, at the turning-point
Of trance prolonged unduly some three days :
When, by the exhibition of some drug
Or spell, exorcization, stroke of art
Unknown to me and which 't were well to
know,
The evil thing out-breaking all at once
Left the man whole and sound of body indeed, —
But, flinging (so to speak) life's gates too wide,
Making a clear house of it too suddenly,
The first conceit that entered might inscribe
Whatever it was minded on the wall
So plainly at that vantage, as it were,
(First come, first served) that nothing subse-
quent
Attaineth to erase those fancy-scrawls
The just-returned and new-established soul
Hath gotten now so thoroughly by heart
That henceforth she will read or these or none.
And first — the man's own firm conviction rests
That he was dead (in fact they buried him)
— That he was dead and then restored to life
By a Nazarene physician of his tribe :
— 'Sayeth, the same bade " Rise," and he did
rise.
" Such cases are diurnal," thou wilt cry.
Not so this figment ! — not, that such a fume,
Instead of giving way to time and health,
Should eat itself into the life of life,
As saffron tingeth flesh, blood, bones and all !
For see, how he takes up the after-life.
The man — it is one Lazarus a Jew,
Sanguine, proportioned, fifty years of age,
The body's habit wholly laudable,
As much, indeed, beyond the common health
As he were made and put aside to show.
Think, could we penetrate by any drug
And bathe the wearied soul and worried flesh,
And bring it clear and fair, by three days'
sleep !
Whence has the man the balm that brightens
all ?
This grown man eyes the world now like a
child.
Some elders of his tribe, I should premise,
Led in their friend, obedient as a sheep,
To bear my inquisition. While they spoke,
Now sharply, now with sorrow, — told the
case, —
He listened not except I spoke to him,
But folded his two hands and let them talk,
Watching the flies that buzzed : and yet no
fool.

And that 's a sample how his years must go.
Look, if a beggar, in fixed middle-life,
Should find a treasure, — can he use the same
With straitened habits and with tastes starved
small,
And take at once to his impoverished brain
The sudden element that changes things,
That sets the undreamed-of rapture at his hand
And puts the cheap old joy in the scorned dust ?
Is he not such an one as moves to mirth —
Warily parsimonious, when no need,
Wasteful as drunkenness at undue times ?
All prudent counsel as to what befits
The golden mean, is lost on such an one :
The man's fantastic will is the man's law.
So here — we call the treasure knowledge, say,
Increased beyond the fleshly faculty —
Heaven opened to a soul while yet on earth,
Earth forced on a soul's use while seeing hea-
ven :
The man is witless of the size, the sum,
The value in proportion of all things,
Or whether it be little or be much.
Discourse to him of prodigious armaments
Assembled to besiege his city now,
And of the passing of a mule with gourds —
'T is one ! Then take it on the other side,
Speak of some trifling fact, — he will gaze rapt
With stupor at its very littleness,
(Far as I see) as if in that indeed
He caught prodigious import, whole results ;
And so will turn to us the bystanders
In ever the same stupor (note this point)
That we too see not with his opened eyes.
Wonder and doubt come wrongly into play,
Preposterously, at cross purposes.
Should his child sicken unto death, — why, look
For scarce abatement of his cheerfulness,
Or pretermission of the daily craft !
While a word, gesture, glance from that same
child
At play or in the school or laid asleep
Will startle him to an agony of fear,
Exasperation, just as like. Demand
The reason why — " 't is but a word," object —
" A gesture " — he regards thee as our lord
Who lived there in the pyramid alone,
Looked at us (dost thou mind ?) when, being
young,
We both would unadvisedly recite
Some charm's beginning, from that book of his,
Able to bid the sun throb wide and burst
All into stars, as suns grown old are wont.
Thou and the child have each a veil alike
Thrown o'er your heads, from under which ye
both
Stretch your blind hands and trifle with a
match
Over a mine of Greek fire, did ye know !
He holds on firmly to some thread of life —
(It is the life to lead perforcedly)
Which runs across some vast distracting orb
Of glory on either side that meagre thread,
Which, conscious of, he must not enter yet —
The spiritual life around the earthly life :
The law of that is known to him as this,
His heart and brain move there, his feet stay
here.

So is the man perplext with impulses
Sudden to start off crosswise, not straight on,
Proclaiming what is right and wrong across,
And not along, this black thread through the
    blaze —
" It should be " balked by " here it cannot
    be."
And oft the man's soul springs into his face
As if he saw again and heard again
His sage that bade him " Rise " and he did
    rise.
Something, a word, a tick o' the blood within
Admonishes: then back he sinks at once
To ashes, who was very fire before,
In sedulous recurrence to his trade
Whereby he earneth him the daily bread;
And studiously the humbler for that pride,
Professedly the faultier that he knows
God's secret, while he holds the thread of life.
Indeed the especial marking of the man
Is prone submission to the heavenly will —
Seeing it, what it is, and why it is.
'Sayeth, he will wait patient to the last
For that same death which must restore his
    being
To equilibrium, body loosening soul
Divorced even now by premature full growth:
He will live, nay, it pleaseth him to live
So long as God please, and just how God please.
He even seeketh not to please God more
(Which meaneth, otherwise) than as God please.
Hence, I perceive not he affects to preach
The doctrine of his sect whate'er it be,
Make proselytes as madmen thirst to do:
How can he give his neighbor the real ground,
His own conviction? Ardent as he is —
Call his great truth a lie, why, still the old
" Be it as God please " reassureth him.
I probed the sore as thy disciple should:
" How, beast," said I, " this stolid carelessness
Sufficeth thee, when Rome is on her march
To stamp out like a little spark thy town,
Thy tribe, thy crazy tale and thee at once? "
He merely looked with his large eyes on me.
The man is apathetic, you deduce?
Contrariwise, he loves both old and young,
Able and weak, affects the very brutes
And birds — how say I? flowers of the field —
As a wise workman recognizes tools
In a master's workshop, loving what they
    make.
Thus is the man as harmless as a lamb:
Only impatient, let him do his best,
At ignorance and carelessness and sin —
An indignation which is promptly curbed:
As when in certain travel I have feigned
To be an ignoramus in our art
According to some preconceived design,
And happed to hear the land's practitioners,
Steeped in conceit sublimed by ignorance,
Prattle fantastically on disease,
Its cause and cure — and I must hold my peace!

Thou wilt object — Why have I not ere this
Sought out the sage himself, the Nazarene
Who wrought this cure, inquiring at the
    source,
Conferring with the frankness that befits?

Alas! it grieveth me, the learned leech
Perished in a tumult many years ago,
Accused — our learning's fate — of wizardry,
Rebellion, to the setting up a rule
And creed prodigious as described to me.
His death, which happened when the earth
    quake fell
(Prefiguring, as soon appeared, the loss
To occult learning in our lord the sage
Who lived there in the pyramid alone)
Was wrought by the mad people — that 's their
    wont!
On vain recourse, as I conjecture it,
To his tried virtue, for miraculous help —
How could he stop the earthquake? That 's
    their way!
The other imputations must be lies:
But take one, though I loathe to give it thee,
In mere respect for any good man's fame.
(And after all, our patient Lazarus
Is stark mad; should we count on what he
    says?
Perhaps not: though in writing to a leech
'T is well to keep back nothing of a case.)
This man so cured regards the curer, then,
As — God forgive me! who but God himself,
Creator and sustainer of the world,
That came and dwelt in flesh on it awhile!
— 'Sayeth that such an one was born and lived,
Taught, healed the sick, broke bread at his
    own house,
Then died, with Lazarus by, for aught I know,
And yet was . . . what I said nor choose re
    peat,
And must have so avouched himself, in fact,
In hearing of this very Lazarus
Who saith — but why all this of what he saith?
Why write of trivial matters, things of price
Calling at every moment for remark?
I noticed on the margin of a pool
Blue-flowering borage, the Aleppo sort,
Aboundeth, very nitrous. It is strange!

Thy pardon for this long and tedious case,
Which, now that I review it, needs must seem
Unduly dwelt on, prolixly set forth!
Nor I myself discern in what is writ
Good cause for the peculiar interest
And awe indeed this man has touched me with.
Perhaps the journey's end, the weariness
Had wrought upon me first. I met him thus:
I crossed a ridge of short sharp broken hills
Like an old lion's cheek teeth. Out there came
A moon made like a face with certain spots
Multiform, manifold, and menacing:
Then a wind rose behind me. So we met
In this old sleepy town at unaware,
The man and I. I send thee what is writ.
Regard it as a chance, a matter risked
To this ambiguous Syrian — he may lose,
Or steal, or give it thee with equal good.
Jerusalem's repose shall make amends
For time this letter wastes, thy time and mine;
Till when, once more thy pardon and fare
    well!

The very God! think, Abib; dost thou think?
So, the All-Great, were the All-Loving too —

So, through the thunder comes a human voice
Saying, "O heart I made, a heart beats here!
Face, my hands fashioned, see it in myself!
Thou hast no power nor mayst conceive of
        mine,
But love I gave thee, with myself to love,
And thou must love me who have died for
        thee!"
The madman saith He said so: it is strange.

JOHANNES AGRICOLA IN MEDITATION

First published with the signature Z in *The
Monthly Repository* in 1836. A quotation from
a *Dictionary of all Religions* followed the title
on the first publication, but is here transferred
to the notes.

THERE's heaven above, and night by night
  I look right through its gorgeous roof;
No suns and moons though e'er so bright
  Avail to stop me; splendor-proof
  I keep the broods of stars aloof:
For I intend to get to God,
  For 't is to God I speed so fast,
For in God's breast, my own abode,
  Those shoals of dazzling glory, passed,
  I lay my spirit down at last.
I lie where I have always lain,
  God smiles as he has always smiled;
Ere suns and moons could wax and wane,
  Ere stars were thundergirt, or piled
  The heavens, God thought on me his child;
Ordained a life for me, arrayed
  Its circumstances every one
To the minutest; ay, God said
  This head this hand should rest upon
  Thus, ere he fashioned star or sun.
And having thus created me,
  Thus rooted me, he bade me grow,
Guiltless forever, like a tree
  That buds and blooms, nor seeks to know
  The law by which it prospers so:
But sure that thought and word and deed
  All go to swell his love for me,'
Me, made because that love had need
  Of something irreversibly
  Pledged solely its content to be.
Yes, yes, a tree which must ascend,
  No poison-gourd foredoomed to stoop!
I have God's warrant, could I blend
  All hideous sins, as in a cup,
  To drink the mingled venoms up;
Secure my nature will convert
  The draught to blossoming gladness fast:
While sweet dews turn to the gourd's hurt,
  And bloat, and while they bloat it, blast,
  As from the first its lot was cast.
For as I lie, smiled on, full-fed
  By unexhausted power to bless,
I gaze below on hell's fierce bed,
  And those its waves of flame oppress,
  Swarming in ghastly wretchedness;
Whose life on earth aspired to be
  One altar-smoke, so pure! — to win
If not love like God's love for me,

At least to keep his anger in;
  And all their striving turned to sin.
Priest, doctor, hermit, monk grown white
  With prayer, the broken-hearted nun,
The martyr, the wan acolyte,
  The incense-swinging child, — undone
  Before God fashioned star or sun!
God, whom I praise; how could I praise,
  If such as I might understand,
Make out and reckon on his ways,
  And bargain for his love, and stand,
  Paying a price, at his right hand?

PICTOR IGNOTUS

FLORENCE, 15—

I COULD have painted pictures like that youth's
  Ye praise so. How my soul springs up! No
    bar
Stayed me — ah, thought which saddens while
    it soothes!
  — Never did fate forbid me, star by star,
To outburst on your night with all my gift
  Of fires from God: nor would my flesh have
    shrunk
From seconding my soul, with eyes uplift
  And wide to heaven, or, straight like thun-
    der, sunk
To the centre, of an instant; or around
  Turned calmly and inquisitive, to scan
The license and the limit, space and bound,
  Allowed to truth made visible in man.
And, like that youth ye praise so, all I saw,
  Over the canvas could my hand have flung,
Each face obedient to its passion's law,
  Each passion clear proclaimed without a
    tongue;
Whether Hope rose at once in all the blood,
  A-tiptoe for the blessing of embrace,
Or Rapture drooped the eyes, as when her brood
  Pull down the nesting dove's heart to its
    place;
Or Confidence lit swift the forehead up,
  And locked the mouth fast, like a castle
    braved, —
O human faces, hath it spilt, my cup?
  What did ye give me that I have not saved?
Nor will I say I have not dreamed (how well!)
  Of going — I, in each new picture, — forth,
As, making new hearts beat and bosoms swell.
  To Pope or Kaiser, East, West, South, or
    North,
Bound for the calmly satisfied great State,
  Or glad aspiring little burgh, it went,
Flowers cast upon the car which bore the
    freight,
  Through old streets named afresh from the
    event,
Till it reached home, where learned age should
    greet
  My face, and youth, the star not yet distinct
Above his hair, lie learning at my feet! —
  Oh, thus to live, I and my picture, linked
With love about, and praise, till life should
    end,
  And then not go to heaven, but linger here,

Here on my earth, earth's every man my
    friend, —
    The thought grew frightful, 't was so wildly
        dear !
But a voice changed it. Glimpses of such
        sights
    Have scared me, like the revels through a
        door
Of some strange house of idols at its rites !
    This world seemed not the world it was be-
        fore :
Mixed with my loving trusting ones, there
        trooped
    . . . Who summoned those cold faces that
        begun
To press on me and judge me ? Though I
        stooped
    Shrinking, as from the soldiery a nun,
They drew me forth, and spite of me . . .
        enough !
    These buy and sell our pictures, take and
        give,
Count them for garniture and household-stuff,
    And where they live needs must our pictures
        live
And see their faces, listen to their prate,
    Partakers of their daily pettiness,
Discussed of, — " This I love, or this I hate,
    This likes me more, and this affects me less ! "
Wherefore I chose my portion. If at whiles
    My heart sinks, as monotonous I paint
These endless cloisters and eternal aisles
    With the same series, Virgin, Babe and
        Saint,
With the same cold calm beautiful regard, —
    At least no merchant traffics in my heart ;
The sanctuary's gloom at least shall ward
    Vain tongues from where my pictures stand
        apart :
Only prayer breaks the silence of the shrine
    While, blackening in the daily candle-smoke,
They moulder on the damp wall's travertine,
    'Mid echoes the light footstep never woke.
So, die my pictures ! surely, gently die !
    O youth, men praise so, — holds their praise its
        worth ?
Blown harshly, keeps the trump its golden cry ?
    Tastes sweet the water with such specks of
        earth ?

FRA LIPPO LIPPI

I AM poor brother Lippo, by your leave !
You need not clap your torches to my face.
Zooks, what 's to blame ? you think you see a
        monk !
What, 't is past midnight, and you go the
        rounds,
And here you catch me at an alley's end
Where sportive ladies leave their doors ajar ?
The Carmine 's my cloister : hunt it up,
Do, — harry out, if you must show your zeal,
Whatever rat, there, haps on his wrong hole,
And nip each softling of a wee white mouse,
Weke, weke, that 's crept to keep him company !
Aha, you know your betters ! Then, you 'll
        take

Your hand away that 's fiddling on my throat,
And please to know me likewise. Who am I ?
Why, one, sir, who is lodging with a friend
Three streets off — he 's a certain . . . how d'
        ye call ?
Master — a . . . Cosimo of the Medici,
I ' the house that caps the corner. Boh ! you
        were best !
Remember and tell me, the day you 're hanged,
How you affected such a gullet's-gripe !
But you, sir, it concerns you that your knaves
Pick up a manner nor discredit you :
Zooks, are we pilchards, that they sweep the
        streets
And count fair prize what comes into their net ?
He 's Judas to a tittle, that man is !
Just such a face ! Why, sir, you make amends.
Lord, I 'm not angry ! Bid your hangdogs go
Drink out this quarter-florin to the health
Of the munificent House that harbors me
(And many more beside, lads ! more beside !)
And all 's come square again. I 'd like his
        face —
His, elbowing on his comrade in the door
With the pike and lantern, — for the slave that
        holds
John Baptist's head a-dangle by the hair
With one hand (" Look you, now," as who
        should say)
And his weapon in the other, yet unwiped !
It 's not your chance to have a bit of chalk,
A wood-coal or the like ? or you should see !
Yes, I 'm the painter, since you style me so.
What, brother Lippo's doings, up and down,
You know them and they take you ? like
        enough !
I saw the proper twinkle in your eye —
'Tell you, I liked your looks at very first.
Let 's sit and set things straight now, hip to
        haunch.
Here 's spring come, and the nights one makes
        up bands
To roam the town and sing out carnival,
And I 've been three weeks shut within my
        mew,
A-painting for the great man, saints and saints
And saints again. I could not paint all night —
Ouf ! I leaned out of window for fresh air.
There came a hurry of feet and little feet,
A sweep of lute-strings, laughs, and whiffs of
        song, —
Flower o' the broom,
Take away love, and our earth is a tomb !
Flower o' the quince,
I let Lisa go, and what good in life since ?
Flower o' the thyme — and so on. Round they
        went.
Scarce had they turned the corner when a titter
Like the skipping of rabbits by moonlight, --
        three slim shapes,
And a face that looked up . . . zooks, sir,
        flesh and blood,
That 's all I 'm made of ! Into shreds it went,
Curtain and counterpane and coverlet,
All the bed-furniture — a dozen knots,
There was a ladder ! Down I let myself,
Hands and feet, scrambling somehow, and so
        dropped,

And after them. I came up with the fun
Hard by Saint Laurence, hail fellow, well
     met, —
Flower o' the rose,
If I 've been merry, what matter who knows ?
And so as I was stealing back again
To get to bed and have a bit of sleep
Ere I rise up to-morrow and go work
On Jerome knocking at his poor old breast
With his great round stone to subdue the flesh,
You snap me of the sudden. Ah, I see !
Though your eye twinkles still, you shake your
     head —
Mine 's shaved — a monk, you say — the sting 's
     in that !
If Master Cosimo announced himself,
Mum 's the word naturally ; but a monk !
Come, what am I a beast for ? tell us, now !
I was a baby when my mother died
And father died and left me in the street.
I starved there, God knows how, a year or two
On fig-skins, melon-parings, rinds and shucks,
Refuse and rubbish. One fine frosty day,
My stomach being empty as your hat,
The wind doubled me up and down I went.
Old Aunt Lapaccia trussed me with one hand,
(Its fellow was a stinger as I knew)
And so along the wall, over the bridge,
By the straight cut to the convent. Six words
     there,
While I stood munching my first bread that
     month :
" So, boy, you 're minded," quoth the good fat
     father,
Wiping his own mouth, 't was refection-time, —
" To quit this very miserable world ?
Will you renounce " . . . " the mouthful of
     bread ? " thought I ;
By no means ! Brief, they made a monk of
     me ;
I did renounce the world, its pride and greed,
Palace, farm, villa, shop, and banking-house,
Trash, such as these poor devils of Medici
Have given their hearts to — all at eight years
     old.
Well, sir, I found in time, you may be sure,
'T was not for nothing — the good bellyful,
The warm serge and the rope that goes all
     round,
And day-long blessed idleness beside !
" Let 's see what the urchin 's fit for " — that
     came next.
Not overmuch their way, I must confess.
Such a to-do ! They tried me with their books ;
Lord, they 'd have taught me Latin in pure
     waste !
Flower o' the clove,
All the Latin I construe is " amo," I love !
But, mind you, when a boy starves in the streets
Eight years together, as my fortune was,
Watching folk's faces to know who will fling
The bit of half-stripped grape-bunch he desires,
And who will curse or kick him for his pains, —
Which gentleman processional and fine,
Holding a candle to the Sacrament,
Will wink and let him lift a plate and catch
The droppings of the wax to sell again,
Or holla for the Eight and have him whipped, —

How say I ? — nay, which dog bites, which lets
     drop
His bone from the heap of offal in the street, —
Why, soul and sense of him grow sharp alike,
He learns the look of things, and none the less
For admonition from the hunger-pinch.
I had a store of such remarks, be sure,
Which, after I found leisure, turned to use.
I drew men's faces on my copy-books,
Scrawled them within the antiphonary's marge,
Joined legs and arms to the long music-notes,
Found eyes and nose and chin for A's and B's,
And made a string of pictures of the world
Betwixt the ins and outs of verb and noun,
On the wall, the bench, the door. The monks
     looked black.
" Nay," quoth the Prior, " turn him out, d' ye
     say ?
In no wise. Lose a crow and catch a lark.
What if at last we get our man of parts,
We Carmelites, like those Camaldolese
And Preaching Friars, to do our church up fine
And put the front on it that ought to be ! "
And hereupon he bade me daub away.
Thank you ! my head being crammed, the walls
     a blank,
Never was such prompt disemburdening.
First, every sort of monk, the black and white,
I drew them, fat and lean : then, folk at church,
From good old gossips waiting to confess
Their cribs of barrel-droppings, candle-ends, —
To the breathless fellow at the altar-foot,
Fresh from his murder, safe and sitting there
With the little children round him in a row
Of admiration, half for his beard and half
For that white anger of his victim's son
Shaking a fist at him with one fierce arm,
Signing himself with the other because of Christ
(Whose sad face on the cross sees only this
After the passion of a thousand years)
Till some poor girl, her apron o'er her head,
(Which the intense eyes looked through) came
     at eve
On tiptoe, said a word, dropped in a loaf,
Her pair of earrings and a bunch of flowers
(The brute took growling), prayed, and so was
     gone.
I painted all, then cried " 'T is ask and have ;
Choose, for more 's ready ! " — laid the ladder
     flat,
And showed my covered bit of cloister-wall.
The monks closed in a circle and praised loud
Till checked, taught what to see and not to see,
Being simple bodies, — " That 's the very man !
Look at the boy who stoops to pat the dog !
That woman 's like the Prior's niece who comes
To care about his asthma : it 's the life ! "
But there my triumph's straw-fire flared and
     funked ;
Their betters took their turn to see and say :
The Prior and the learned pulled a face
And stopped all that in no time. " How ?
     what 's here ?
Quite from the mark of painting, bless us all !
Faces, arms, legs, and bodies like the true
As much as pea and pea ! it 's devil's-game !
Your business is not to catch men with show
With homage to the perishable clay,

But lift them over it, ignore it all,
Make them forget there's such a thing as flesh.
Your business is to paint the souls of men —
Man's soul, and it's a fire, smoke . . . no, it's
    not . . .
It's vapor done up like a new-born babe —
(In that shape when you die it leaves your
    mouth)
It's . . . well, what matters talking, it's the
    soul!
Give us no more of body than shows soul!
Here's Giotto, with his Saint a-praising God,
That sets us praising, — why not stop with him?
Why put all thoughts of praise out of our head
With wonder at lines, colors, and what not?
Paint the soul, never mind the legs and arms!
Rub all out, try at it a second time.
Oh, that white smallish female with the breasts,
She's just my niece . . . Herodias, I would
    say, —
Who went and danced and got men's heads cut
    off!
Have it all out!" Now, is this sense, I ask?
A fine way to paint soul, by painting body
So ill, the eye can't stop there, must go further
And can't fare worse! Thus, yellow does for
    white
When what you put for yellow's simply black,
And any sort of meaning looks intense
When all beside itself means and looks naught.
Why can't a painter lift each foot in turn,
Left foot and right foot, go a double step,
Make his flesh liker and his soul more like,
Both in their order? Take the prettiest face,
The Prior's niece . . . patron-saint — is it so
    pretty
You can't discover if it means hope, fear,
Sorrow or joy? won't beauty go with these?
Suppose I've made her eyes all right and blue,
Can't I take breath and try to add life's flash,
And then add soul and heighten them three-
    fold?
Or say there's beauty with no soul at all —
(I never saw it — put the case the same —)
If you get simple beauty and naught else,
You get about the best thing God invents:
That's somewhat: and you'll find the soul you
    have missed,
Within yourself, when you return him thanks.
"Rub all out!" Well, well, there's my life,
    in short,
And so the thing has gone on ever since.
I'm grown a man no doubt, I've broken
    bounds:
You should not take a fellow eight years old
And make him swear to never kiss the girls.
I'm my own master, paint now as I please —
Having a friend, you see, in the Corner-house!
Lord, it's fast holding by the rings in front —
Those great rings serve more purposes than just
To plant a flag in, or tie up a horse!
And yet the old schooling sticks, the old grave
    eyes
Are peeping o'er my shoulder as I work,
The heads shake still — "It's art's decline, my
    son!
You're not of the true painters, great and old;
Brother Angelico's the man, you'll find;

Brother Lorenzo stands his single peer:
Fag on at flesh, you'll never make the third!"
Flower o' the pine,
You keep your mistr . . . manners, and I'll
    stick to mine!
I'm not the third, then: bless us, they must
    know!
Don't you think they're the likeliest to know,
They with their Latin? So, I swallow my
    rage,
Clench my teeth, suck my lips in tight, and
    paint
To please them — sometimes do and sometimes
    don't;
For, doing most, there's pretty sure to come
A turn, some warm eve finds me at my saints —
A laugh, a cry, the business of the world —
(*Flower o' the peach,*
Death for us all, and his own life for each!)
And my whole soul revolves, the cup runs over,
The world and life's too big to pass for a dream,
And I do these wild things in sheer despite,
And play the fooleries you catch me at,
In pure rage! The old mill-horse, out at grass
After hard years, throws up his stiff heels so,
Although the miller does not preach to him
The only good of grass is to make chaff.
What would men have? Do they like grass or
    no —
May they or may n't they? all I want's the
    thing
Settled forever one way. As it is,
You tell too many lies and hurt yourself:
You don't like what you only like too much,
You do like what, if given you at your word,
You find abundantly detestable.
For me, I think I speak as I was taught;
I always see the garden and God there
A-making man's wife: and, my lesson learned,
The value and significance of flesh,
I can't unlearn ten minutes afterwards.

You understand me: I'm a beast, I know.
But see, now — why, I see as certainly
As that the morning-star's about to shine,
What will hap some day. We've a youngster
    here
Comes to our convent, studies what I do,
Slouches and stares and lets no atom drop:
His name is Guidi — he'll not mind the
    monks —
They call him Hulking Tom, he lets them
    talk —
He picks my practice up — he'll paint apace,
I hope so — though I never live so long,
I know what's sure to follow. You be judge!
You speak no Latin more than I, belike;
However, you're my man, you've seen the
    world
— The beauty and the wonder and the power,
The shapes of things, their colors, lights and
    shades,
Changes, surprises, — and God made it all!
— For what? Do you feel thankful, ay or
    no,
For this fair town's face, yonder river's line,
The mountain round it and the sky above,
Much more the figures of man, woman, child,

These are the frame to? What's it all about?
To be passed over, despised? or dwelt upon,
Wondered at? oh, this last of course! — you
  say.
But why not do as well as say, — paint these
Just as they are, careless what comes of it?
God's works — paint any one, and count it crime
To let a truth slip. Don't object, "His works
Are here already; nature is complete:
Suppose you reproduce her — (which you can't)
There's no advantage! you must beat her,
  then."
For, don't you mark? we're made so that we
  love
First when we see them painted, things we
  have passed
Perhaps a hundred times nor cared to see;
And so they are better, painted — better to us,
Which is the same thing. Art was given for
  that;
God uses us to help each other so,
Lending our minds out. Have you noticed,
  now,
Your cullion's hanging face? A bit of chalk,
And trust me but you should, though! How
  much more,
If I drew higher things with the same truth!
That were to take the Prior's pulpit-place,
Interpret God to all of you! Oh, oh,
It makes me mad to see what men shall do
And we in our graves! This world's no blot
  for us,
Nor blank; it means intensely, and means
  good:
To find its meaning is my meat and drink.
"Ay, but you don't so instigate to prayer!"
Strikes in the Prior: "when your meaning's
  plain
It does not say to folk — remember matins,
Or, mind you fast next Friday!" Why, for
  this
What need of art at all? A skull and bones,
Two bits of stick nailed crosswise, or, what's
  best,
A bell to chime the hour with, does as well.
I painted a Saint Laurence six months since
At Prato, splashed the fresco in fine style:
"How looks my painting, now the scaffold's
  down?"
I ask a brother: "Hugely," he returns —
"Already not one phiz of your three slaves
Who turn the Deacon off his toasted side,
But's scratched and prodded to our heart's con-
  tent,
The pious people have so eased their own
With coming to say prayers there in a rage:
We get on fast to see the bricks beneath.
Expect another job this time next year,
For pity and religion grow i' the crowd —
Your painting serves its purpose!" Hang the
  fools!

  — That is — you'll not mistake an idle word
Spoke in a huff by a poor monk, God wot,
Tasting the air this spicy night which turns
The unaccustomed head like Chianti wine!
Oh, the church knows! don't misreport me,
  now!

It's natural a poor monk out of bounds
Should have his apt word to excuse himself:
And hearken how I plot to make amends.
I have bethought me: I shall paint a piece
. . . There's for you! Give me six months,
  then go, see
Something in Sant' Ambrogio's! Bless the
  nuns!
They want a cast o' my office. I shall paint
God in the midst, Madonna and her babe,
Ringed by a bowery, flowery angel-brood,
Lilies and vestments and white faces, sweet
As puff on puff of grated orris-root
When ladies crowd to Church at midsummer.
And then i' the front, of course a saint or
  two —
Saint John, because he saves the Florentines,
Saint Ambrose, who puts down in black and
  white
The convent's friends and gives them a long
  day,
And Job, I must have him there past mis-
  take,
The man of Uz (and Us without the z,
Painters who need his patience). Well, all
  these
Secured at their devotion, up shall come
Out of a corner when you least expect,
As one by a dark stair into a great light,
Music and talking, who but Lippo! I! —
Mazed, motionless, and moonstruck — I'm the
  man!
Back I shrink — what is this I see and hear?
I, caught up with my monk's-things by mis-
  take,
My old serge gown and rope that goes all round,
I, in this presence, this pure company!
Where's a hole, where's a corner for escape?
Then steps a sweet angelic slip of a thing
Forward, puts out a soft palm — "Not so
  fast!"
— Addresses the celestial presence, "nay —
He made you and devised you, after all,
Though he's none of you! Could Saint John
  there draw —
His camel-hair make up a painting-brush?
We come to brother Lippo for all that,
Iste perfecit opus!" So, all smile —
I shuffle sideways with my blushing face
Under the cover of a hundred wings
Thrown like a spread of kirtles when you're
  gay
And play hot cockles, all the doors being shut,
Till, wholly unexpected, in there pops
The hothead husband! Thus I scuttle off
To some safe bench behind, not letting go
The palm of her, the little lily thing
That spoke the good word for me in the nick,
Like the Prior's niece . . . Saint Lucy, I would
  say.
And so all's saved for me, and for the church
A pretty picture gained. Go, six months hence!
Your hand, sir, and good-by: no lights, no
  lights!
The street's hushed, and I know my own way
  back,
Don't fear me! There's the gray beginning.
  Zooks!

ANDREA DEL SARTO

CALLED "THE FAULTLESS PAINTER"

BUT do not let us quarrel any more,
No, my Lucrezia ; bear with me for once :
Sit down and all shall happen as you wish.
You turn your face, but does it bring your
    heart ?
I 'll work then for your friend's friend, never
    fear,
Treat his own subject after his own way,
Fix his own time, accept too his own price,
And shut the money into this small hand
When next it takes mine. Will it ? tenderly ?
Oh, I 'll content him, — but to-morrow, Love !
I often am much wearier than you think,
This evening more than usual, and it seems
As if — forgive now — should you let me sit
Here by the window with your hand in mine
And look a half-hour forth on Fiesole,
Both of one mind, as married people use,
Quietly, quietly the evening through,
I might get up to-morrow to my work
Cheerful and fresh as ever. Let us try.
To-morrow, how you shall be glad for this !
Your soft hand is a woman of itself,
And mine the man's bared breast she curls in-
    side.
Don't count the time lost, neither ; you must
    serve
For each of the five pictures we require :
It saves a model. So ! keep looking so —
My serpentining beauty, rounds on rounds !
— How could you ever prick those perfect ears,
Even to put the pearl there ! oh, so sweet —
My face, my moon, my everybody's moon,
Which everybody looks on and calls his,
And, I suppose, is looked on by in turn,
While she looks — no one's : very dear, no less.
You smile ? why, there 's my picture ready
    made,
There 's what we painters call our harmony !
A common grayness silvers everything, —
All in a twilight, you and I alike
— You, at the point of your first pride in me
(That 's gone you know), — but I, at every
    point ;
My youth, my hope, my art, being all toned
    down
To yonder sober pleasant Fiesole.
There 's the bell clinking from the chapel-top ;
That length of convent-wall across the way
Holds the trees safer, huddled more inside ;
The last monk leaves the garden ; days de-
    crease,
And autumn grows, autumn in everything.
Eh ? the whole seems to fall into a shape
As if I saw alike my work and self
And all that I was born to be and do,
A twilight-piece. Love, we are in God's hand.
How strange now looks the life he makes us
    lead ;
So free we seem, so fettered fast we are !
I feel he laid the fetter : let it lie !
This chamber for example — turn your head —
All that 's behind us ! You don't understand

Nor care to understand about my art,
But you can hear at least when people speak :
And that cartoon, the second from the door
— It is the thing, Love ! so such thing should
    be —
Behold Madonna ! — I am bold to say.
I can do with my pencil what I know,
What I see, what at bottom of my heart
I wish for, if I ever wish so deep —
Do easily, too — when I say, perfectly,
I do not boast, perhaps : yourself are judge,
Who listened to the Legate's talk last week,
And just as much they used to say in France.
At any rate 't is easy, all of it !
No sketches first, no studies, that 's long past :
I do what many dream of all their lives,
— Dream ? strive to do, and agonize to do,
And fail in doing. I could count twenty such
On twice your fingers, and not leave this town,
Who strive — you don't know how the others
    strive
To paint a little thing like that you smeared
Carelessly passing with your robes afloat, —
Yet do much less, so much less, Someone says,
(I know his name, no matter) — so much less !
Well, less is more, Lucrezia : I am judged.
There burns a truer light of God in them,
In their vexed beating stuffed and stopped-up
    brain,
Heart, or whate'er else, than goes on to prompt
This low-pulsed forthright craftsman's hand of
    mine.
Their works drop groundward, but themselves,
    I know,
Reach many a time a heaven that 's shut to me,
Enter and take their place there sure enough,
Though they come back and cannot tell the
    world.
My works are nearer heaven, but I sit here.
The sudden blood of these men ! at a word —
Praise them, it boils, or blame them, it boils
    too.
I, painting from myself and to myself,
Know what I do, am unmoved by men's blame
Or their praise either. Somebody remarks
Morello's outline there is wrongly traced,
His hue mistaken ; what of that ? or else,
Rightly traced and well ordered ; what of that ?
Speak as they please, what does the mountain
    care ?
Ah, but a man's reach should exceed his grasp,
Or what 's a heaven for ? All is silver-gray
Placid and perfect with my art : the worse !
I know both what I want and what might gain,
And yet how profitless to know, to sigh
" Had I been two, another and myself,
Our head would have o'erlooked the world ! "
    No doubt.
Yonder 's a work now, of that famous youth
The Urbinate who died five years ago.
('T is copied, George Vasari sent it me.)
Well, I can fancy how he did it all,
Pouring his soul, with kings and popes to see,
Reaching, that heaven might so replenish him,
Above and through his art — for it gives way ;
That arm is wrongly put — and there again —
A fault to pardon in the drawing's lines,
Its body, so to speak : its soul is right,

He means right — that, a child may understand.
Still, what an arm! and I could alter it:
But all the play, the insight and the stretch —
Out of me, out of me! And wherefore out?
Had you enjoined them on me, given me soul,
We might have risen to Rafael, I and you!
Nay, Love, you did give all I asked, I think —
More than I merit, yes, by many times.
But had you — oh, with the same perfect brow,
And perfect eyes, and more than perfect mouth,
And the low voice my soul hears, as a bird
The fowler's pipe, and follows to the snare —
Had you, with these the same, but brought a
    mind!
Some women do so. Had the mouth there urged
"God and the glory! never care for gain.
The present by the future, what is that?
Live for fame, side by side with Agnolo!
Rafael is waiting: up to God, all three!"
I might have done it for you. So it seems:
Perhaps not. All is as God overrules.
Beside, incentives come from the soul's self;
The rest avail not. Why do I need you?
What wife had Rafael, or has Agnolo?
In this world, who can do a thing, will not;
And who would do it, cannot, I perceive:
Yet the will 's somewhat — somewhat, too, the
    power —
And thus we half-men struggle. At the end,
God, I conclude, compensates, punishes.
'T is safer for me, if the award be strict,
That I am something underrated here,
Poor this long while, despised, to speak the
    truth.
I dared not, do you know, leave home all day,
For fear of chancing on the Paris lords.
The best is when they pass and look aside;
But they speak sometimes; I must bear it all.
Well may they speak! That Francis, that first
    time,
And that long festal year at Fontainebleau!
I surely then could sometimes leave the ground,
Put on the glory, Rafael's daily wear,
In that humane great monarch's golden look, —
One finger in his beard or twisted curl
Over his mouth's good mark that made the
    smile,
One arm about my shoulder, round my neck,
The jingle of his gold chain in my ear,
I painting proudly with his breath on me,
All his court round him, seeing with his eyes,
Such frank French eyes, and such a fire of souls
Profuse, my hand kept plying by those
    hearts, —
And, best of all, this, this, this face beyond,
This in the background, waiting on my work,
To crown the issue with a last reward!
A good time, was it not, my kingly days?
And had you not grown restless . . . but I
    know —
'T is done and past; 't was right, my instinct
    said;
Too live the life grew, golden and not gray,
And I 'm the weak-eyed bat no sun should
    tempt
Out of the grange whose four walls make his
    world.
How could it end in any other way?

You called me, and I came home to your heart.
The triumph was — to reach and stay there;
    since
I reached it ere the triumph, what is lost?
Let my hands frame your face in your hair's
    gold,
You beautiful Lucrezia that are mine!
" Rafael did this, Andrea painted that;
The Roman's is the better when you pray,
But still the other's Virgin was his wife " —
Men will excuse me. I am glad to judge
Both pictures in your presence; clearer grows
My better fortune, I resolve to think.
For, do you know, Lucrezia, as God lives,
Said one day Agnolo, his very self,
To Rafael . . . I have known it all these
    years . . .
(When the young man was flaming out his
    thoughts
Upon a palace-wall for Rome to see,
Too lifted up in heart because of it)
" Friend, there 's a certain sorry little scrub
Goes up and down our Florence, none cares how,
Who, were he set to plan and execute
As you are, pricked on by your popes and kings,
Would bring the sweat into that brow of yours!"
To Rafael's! — And indeed the arm is wrong.
I hardly dare . . . yet, only you to see,
Give the chalk here — quick, thus the line
    should go!
Ay, but the soul! he 's Rafael! rub it out!
Still, all I care for, if he spoke the truth,
(What he? why, who but Michel Agnolo?
Do you forget already words like those?)
If really there was such a chance, so lost, —
Is, whether you 're — not grateful — but more
    pleased.
Well, let me think so. And you smile indeed!
This hour has been an hour! Another smile?
If you would sit thus by me every night
I should work better, do you comprehend?
I mean that I should earn more, give you more.
See, it is settled dusk now; there 's a star;
Morello's gone, the watch-lights show the wall,
The cue-owls speak the name we call them by.
Come from the window, love, — come in, at last,
Inside the melancholy little house
We built to be so gay with. God is just.
King Francis may forgive me: oft at nights
When I look up from painting, eyes tired out,
The walls become illumined, brick from brick
Distinct, instead of mortar, fierce bright gold,
That gold of his I did cement them with!
Let us but love each other. Must you go?
That Cousin here again? he waits outside?
Must see you — you, and not with me? Those
    loans?
More gaming debts to pay? you smiled for that?
Well, let smiles buy me! have you more to
    spend?
While hand and eye and something of a heart
Are left me, work 's my ware, and what 's it
    worth?
I 'll pay my fancy. Only let me sit
The gray remainder of the evening out,
Idle, you call it, and muse perfectly
How I could paint, were I but back in France,
One picture, just one more — the Virgin's face

Not yours this time ! I want you at my side
To hear them — that is, Michel Agnolo —
Judge all I do and tell you of its worth.
Will you ? To-morrow, satisfy your friend.
I take the subjects for his corridor,
Finish the portrait out of hand — there, there,
And throw him in another thing or two
If he demurs ; the whole should prove enough
To pay for this same Cousin's freak. Beside,
What 's better and what 's all I care about,
Get you the thirteen scudi for the ruff !
Love, does that please you ? Ah, but what does
   he,
The Cousin ! what does he to please you more ?

I am grown peaceful as old age to-night.
I regret little, I would change still less.
Since there my past life lies, why alter it ?
The very wrong to Francis ! — it is true
I took his coin, was tempted and complied,
And built this house and sinned, and all is said.
My father and my mother died of want.
Well, had I riches of my own ? you see
How one gets rich ! Let each one bear his lot.
They were born poor, lived poor, and poor they
   died :
And I have labored somewhat in my time
And not been paid profusely. Some good son
Paint my two hundred pictures — let him try !
No doubt, there 's something strikes a balance.
   Yes,
You loved me quite enough, it seems to-night.
This must suffice me here. What would one
   have ?
In heaven, perhaps, new chances, one more
   chance —
Four great walls in the New Jerusalem,
Meted on each side by the angel's reed,
For Leonard, Rafael, Agnolo and me
To cover — the three first without a wife,
While I have mine ! So — still they overcome
Because there 's still Lucrezia, — as I choose.

Again the Cousin's whistle ! Go, my Love.

THE BISHOP ORDERS HIS TOMB AT
SAINT PRAXED'S CHURCH

ROME, 15—

This poem was first published in *Hood's
Magazine*, March, 1845, with the title *The Tomb
at Saint Praxed's* (Rome, 15—).

VANITY, saith the preacher, vanity !
Draw round my bed : is Anselm keeping back ?
Nephews — sons mine . . . ah God, I know not !
   Well —
She, men would have to be your mother once,
Old Gandolf envied me, so fair she was !
What 's done is done, and she is dead beside,
Dead long ago, and I am Bishop since,
And as she died so must we die ourselves,
And thence ye may perceive the world 's a dream.
Life, how and what is it ? As here I lie
In this state-chamber, dying by degrees,

Hours and long hours in the dead night, I ask
" Do I live, am I dead ? " Peace, peace seem
   all.
Saint Praxed's ever was the church for peace ;
And so, about this tomb of mine. I fought
With tooth and nail to save my niche, ye know :
— Old Gandolf cozened me, despite my care ;
Shrewd was that snatch from out the corner
   South
He graced his carrion with, God curse the same !
Yet still my niche is not so cramped but thence
One sees the pulpit o' the epistle-side,
And somewhat of the choir, those silent seats,
And up into the aery dome where live
The angels, and a sunbeam 's sure to lurk :
And I shall fill my slab of basalt there,
And 'neath my tabernacle take my rest,
With those nine columns round me, two and two,
The odd one at my feet where Anselm stands :
Peach-blossom marble all, the rare, the ripe
As fresh-poured red wine of a mighty pulse.
— Old Gandolf with his paltry onion-stone,
Put me where I may look at him ! True peach,
Rosy and flawless : how I earned the prize !
Draw close : that conflagration of my church
— What then ? So much was saved if aught
   were missed !
My sons, ye would not be my death ? Go dig
The white-grape vineyard where the oil-press
   stood,
Drop water gently till the surface sink,
And if ye find . . . Ah God, I know not, I ! . .
Bedded in store of rotten fig-leaves soft,
And corded up in a tight olive-frail,
Some lump, ah God, of *lapis lazuli*,
Big as a Jew's head cut off at the nape,
Blue as a vein o'er the Madonna's breast . . .
Sons, all have I bequeathed you, villas, all,
That brave Frascati villa with its bath,
So, let the blue lump poise between my knees,
Like God the Father's globe on both his hands
Ye worship in the Jesu Church so gay,
For Gandolf shall not choose but see and burst !
Swift as a weaver's shuttle fleet our years :
Man goeth to the grave, and where is he ?
Did I say basalt for my slab, sons ? Black —
'T was ever antique-black I meant ! How else
Shall ye contrast my frieze to come beneath ?
The bas-relief in bronze ye promised me,
Those Pans and Nymphs ye wot of, and per-
   chance
Some tripod, thyrsus, with a vase or so,
The Saviour at his sermon on the mount,
Saint Praxed in a glory, and one Pan
Ready to twitch the Nymph's last garment off,
And Moses with the tables . . . but I know
Ye mark me not ! What do they whisper thee,
Child of my bowels, Anselm ? Ah, ye hope
To revel down my villas while I gasp
Bricked o'er with beggar's mouldy travertine
Which Gandolf from his tomb-top chuckles at !
Nay, boys, ye love me — all of jasper, then !
'T is jasper ye stand pledged to, lest I grieve
My bath must needs be left behind, alas !
One block, pure green as a pistachio-nut,
There 's plenty jasper somewhere in the world —
And have I not Saint Praxed's ear to pray
Horses for ye, and brown Greek manuscripts

And mistresses with great smooth marbly limbs?
— That's if ye carve my epitaph aright,
Choice Latin, picked phrase, Tully's every word,
No gaudy ware like Gandolf's second line —
Tully, my masters? Ulpian serves his need!
And then how I shall lie through centuries,
And hear the blessed mutter of the mass,
And see God made and eaten all day long,
And feel the steady candle-flame, and taste
Good strong thick stupefying incense-smoke!
For as I lie here, hours of the dead night,
Dying in state and by such slow degrees,
I fold my arms as if they clasped a crook,
And stretch my feet forth straight as stone can
   point,
And let the bedclothes, for a mortcloth, drop
Into great laps and folds of sculptor's-work:
And as yon tapers dwindle, and strange thoughts
Grow, with a certain humming in my ears,
About the life before I lived this life,
And this life too, popes, cardinals and priests,
Saint Praxed at his sermon on the mount,
Your tall pale mother with her talking eyes,
And new-found agate urns as fresh as day,
And marble's language, Latin pure, discreet,
— Aha, ELUCESCEBAT quoth our friend?
No Tully, said I, Ulpian at the best!
Evil and brief hath been my pilgrimage.
All *lapis*, all, sons! Else I give the Pope
My villas! Will ye ever eat my heart?
Ever your eyes were as a lizard's quick,
They glitter like your mother's for my soul,
Or ye would heighten my impoverished frieze,
Piece out its starved design, and fill my vase
With grapes, and add a visor and a Term,
And to the tripod ye would tie a lynx
That in his struggle throws the thyrsus down,
To comfort me on my entablature
Whereon I am to lie till I must ask
"Do I live, am I dead?" There, leave me,
   there!
For ye have stabbed me with ingratitude
To death — ye wish it — God, ye wish it!
   Stone —
Gritstone, a-crumble! Clammy squares which
   sweat
As if the corpse they keep . were oozing
   through —
And no more *lapis* to delight the world!
Well, go! I bless ye. Fewer tapers there,
But in a row: and, going, turn your backs
— Ay, like departing altar-ministrants,
And leave me in my church, the church for
   peace,
That I may watch at leisure if he leers —
Old Gandolf — at me, from his onion-stone,
As still he envied me, so fair she was!

BISHOP BLOUGRAM'S APOLOGY

No more wine? then we 'll push back chairs
   and talk.
A final glass for me, though: cool, i' faith!
We ought to have our Abbey back, you see.
It 's different, preaching in basilicas,
And doing duty in some masterpiece
Like this of brother Pugin's, bless his heart!

I doubt if they 're half baked, those chalk
   rosettes,
Ciphers and stucco-twiddlings everywhere;
It 's just like breathing in a lime-kiln: eh?
These hot long ceremonies of our church
Cost us a little — oh, they pay the price,
You take me — amply pay it! Now, we 'll talk.

So, you despise me, Mr. Gigadibs.
No deprecation, — nay, I beg you, sir!
Beside 't is our engagement: don't you know,
I promised, if you 'd watch a dinner out,
We 'd see truth dawn together? — truth that
   peeps
Over the glasses' edge when dinner 's done,
And body gets its sop and holds its noise
And leaves soul free a little. Now 's the time:
Truth's break of day! You do despise me then.
And if I say, "despise me," — never fear!
I know you do not in a certain sense —
Not in my arm-chair, for example: here,
I well imagine you respect my place
(*Status*, *entourage*, worldly circumstance)
Quite to its value — very much indeed:
— Are up to the protesting eyes of you
In pride at being seated here for once —
You 'll turn it to such capital account!
When somebody, through years and years to
   come,
Hints of the bishop, — names me — that 's
   enough:
"Blougram? I knew him" — (into it you
   slide)
"Dined with him once, a Corpus Christi Day,
All alone, we two; he 's a clever man:
And after dinner, — why, the wine you
   know, —
Oh, there was wine, and good! — what with the
   wine . . .
'Faith, we began upon all sorts of talk!
He 's no bad fellow, Blougram; he had seen
Something of mine he relished, some review:
He 's quite above their humbug in his heart,
Half-said as much, indeed — the thing 's his
   trade.
I warrant, Blougram 's skeptical at times:
How otherwise? I liked him, I confess!"
Che che, my dear sir, as we say at Rome,
Don't you protest now! It 's fair give and
   take;
You have had your turn and spoken your home-
   truths:
The hand 's mine now, and here you follow suit.

Thus much conceded, still the first fact
   stays —
You do despise me; your ideal of life
Is not the bishop's; you would not be I.
You would like better to be Goethe, now,
Or Buonaparte, or, bless me, lower still,
Count D'Orsay, — so you did what you pre-
   ferred,
Spoke as you thought, and, as you cannot help,
Believed or disbelieved, no matter what,
So long as on that point, whate'er it was,
You loosed your mind, were whole and sole
   yourself.
— That, my ideal never can include,

Upon that element of truth and worth
Never be based ! for say they make me Pope —
(They can't — suppose it for our argument !)
Why, there I 'm at my tether's end, I 've reached
My height, and not a height which pleases you :
An unbelieving Pope won't do, you say.
It 's like those eerie stories nurses tell,
Of how some actor on a stage played Death,
With pasteboard crown, sham orb and tinselled dart,
And called himself the monarch of the world ;
Then, going in the tire-room afterward,
Because the play was done, to shift himself,
Got touched upon the sleeve familiarly,
The moment he had shut the closet door,
By Death himself.   Thus God might touch a Pope
At unawares, ask what his baubles mean,
And whose part he presumed to play just now.
Best be yourself, imperial, plain and true !

So, drawing comfortable breath again,
You weigh and find, whatever more or less
I boast of my ideal realized
Is nothing in the balance when opposed
To your ideal, your grand simple life,
Of which you will not realize one jot.
I am much, you are nothing ; you would be all,
I would be merely much : you beat me there.

No, friend, you do not beat me : hearken why !
The common problem, yours, mine, every one's,
Is — not to fancy what were fair in life
Provided it could be, — but, finding first
What may be, then find how to make it fair
Up to our means : a very different thing !
No abstract intellectual plan of life
Quite irrespective of life's plainest laws,
But one, a man, who is man and nothing more,
May lead within a world which (by your leave)
Is Rome or London, not Fool's-paradise.
Embellish Rome, idealize away,
Make paradise of London if you can,
You 're welcome, nay, you 're wise.

A simile !
We mortals cross the ocean of this world
Each in his average cabin of a life ;
The best 's not big, the worst yields elbow-room.
Now for our six months' voyage — how prepare ?
You come on shipboard with a landsman's list
Of things he calls convenient : so they are !
An India screen is pretty furniture,
A piano-forte is a fine resource,
All Balzac's novels occupy one shelf,
The new edition fifty volumes long ;
And little Greek books, with the funny type
They get up well at Leipsic, fill the next :
Go on ! slabbed marble, what a bath it makes !
And Parma's pride, the Jerome, let us add !
'T were pleasant could Correggio's fleeting glow
Hang full in face of one where'er one roams,
Since he more than the others brings with him
Italy's self, — the marvellous Modenese ! —
Yet was not on your list before, perhaps.

— Alas, friend, here 's the agent . . . is 't the name ?
The captain, or whoever 's master here —
You see him screw his face up ; what 's his cry
Ere you set foot on shipboard ?   "Six feet square ! "
If you won't understand what six feet mean,
Compute and purchase stores accordingly —
And if, in pique because he overhauls
Your Jerome, piano, bath, you come on board
Bare — why, you cut a figure at the first
While sympathetic landsmen see you off ;
Not afterward, when long ere half seas over,
You peep up from your utterly naked boards
Into some snug and well-appointed berth,
Like mine for instance (try the cooler jug —
Put back the other, but don't jog the ice !)
And mortified you mutter, "Well and good ;
He sits enjoying his sea-furniture ;
'T is stout and proper, and there 's store of it :
Though I 've the better notion, all agree,
Of fitting rooms up.   Hang the carpenter,
Neat ship-shape fixings and contrivances —
I would have brought my Jerome, frame and all ! "
And meantime you bring nothing : never mind —
You 've proved your artist-nature : what you don't
You might bring, so despise me, as I say.

Now come, let 's backward to the starting-place.
See my way : we 're two college friends, suppose.
Prepare together for our voyage, then ;
Each note and check the other in his work, —
Here 's mine, a bishop's outfit ; criticise !
What 's wrong ? why won't you be a bishop too ?

Why first, you don't believe, you don't and can't,
(Not stately, that is, and fixedly
And absolutely and exclusively)
In any revelation called divine.
No dogmas nail your faith ; and what remains
But say so, like the honest man you are ?
First, therefore, overhaul theology !
Nay, I too, not a fool, you please to think,
Must find believing every whit as hard :
And if I do not frankly say as much,
The ugly consequence is clear enough.

Now wait, my friend : well, I do not believe —
If you 'll accept no faith that is not fixed,
Absolute and exclusive, as you say.
You 're wrong — I mean to prove it in due time.
Meanwhile, I know where difficulties lie
I could not, cannot solve, nor ever shall,
So give up hope accordingly to solve —
(To you, and over the wine).   Our dogmas then
With both of us, though in unlike degree,
Missing full credence — overboard with them !
I mean to meet you on your own premise :
Good, there go mine in company with yours !

And now what are we? unbelievers both,
Calm and complete, determinately fixed
To-day, to-morrow, and forever, pray?
You 'll guarantee me that? Not so, I think!
In no wise! all we 've gained is, that belief,
As unbelief before, shakes us by fits,
Confounds us like its predecessor. Where 's
The gain? how can we guard our unbelief,
Make it bear fruit to us? — the problem here.
Just when we are safest, there 's a sunset-touch,
A fancy from a flower-bell, some one's death,
A chorus-ending from Euripides, —
And that 's enough for fifty hopes and fears
As old and new at once as nature's self,
To rap and knock and enter in our soul,
Take hands and dance there, a fantastic ring,
Round the ancient idol, on his base again, —
The grand Perhaps! We look on helplessly.
There the old misgivings, crooked questions
are —
This good God, — what he could do, if he would,
Would, if he could — then must have done long
since:
If so, when, where and how? some way must
be, —
Once feel about, and soon or late you hit
Some sense, in which it might be, after all.
Why not, "The Way, the Truth, the Life?"

— That way
Over the mountain, which who stands upon
Is apt to doubt if it be meant for a road;
While, if he views it from the waste itself,
Up goes the line there, plain from base to brow,
Not vague, mistakable! what 's a break or two
Seen from the unbroken desert either side?
And then (to bring in fresh philosophy)
What if the breaks themselves should prove at
last
The most consummate of contrivances
To train a man's eye, teach him what is faith?
And so we stumble at truth's very test!
All we have gained then by our unbelief
Is a life of doubt diversified by faith,
For one of faith diversified by doubt:
We called the chess-board white, — we call it
black.

"Well," you rejoin, "the end 's no worse, at
least!
We 've reason for both colors on the board:
Why not confess then, where I drop the faith
And you the doubt, that I 'm as right as you?"

Because, friend, in the next place, this being
so,
And both things even, — faith and unbelief
Left to a man's choice, — we 'll proceed a step,
Returning to our image, which I like.

A man's choice, yes — but a cabin-passen-
ger's —
The man made for the special life o' the
world —
Do you forget him? I remember though!
Consult our ship's conditions and you find
One and but one choice suitable to all;
The choice, that you unluckily prefer,

Turning things topsy-turvy — they or it
Going to the ground. Belief or unbelief
Bears upon life, determines its whole course,
Begins at its beginning. See the world
Such as it is, — you made it not, nor I;
I mean to take it as it is, — and you,
Not so you 'll take it, — though you get naught
else.
I know the special kind of life I like,
What suits the most my idiosyncrasy,
Brings out the best of me and bears me fruit
In power, peace, pleasantness and length of
days.
I find that positive belief does this
For me, and unbelief, no whit of this.
— For you, it does, however? — that, we 'll try!
'T is clear, I cannot lead my life, at least,
Induce the world to let me peaceably,
Without declaring at the outset, "Friends,
I absolutely and peremptorily
Believe!" — I say, faith is my waking life:
One sleeps, indeed, and dreams at intervals,
We know, but waking 's the main point with
us,
And my provision 's for life's waking part.
Accordingly, I use heart, head and hand
All day, I build, scheme, study, and make
friends;
And when night overtakes me, down I lie,
Sleep, dream a little, and get done with it,
The sooner the better, to begin afresh.
What 's midnight doubt before the dayspring's
faith?
You, the philosopher, that disbelieve,
That recognize the night, give dreams their
weight —
To be consistent you should keep your bed,
Abstain from healthy acts that prove you man,
For fear you drowse perhaps at unawares!
And certainly at night you 'll sleep and dream,
Live through the day and bustle as you please.
And so you live to sleep as I to wake,
To unbelieve as I to still believe?
Well, and the common sense o' the world calls
you
Bed-ridden, — and its good things come to me.
Its estimation, which is half the fight,
That 's the first-cabin comfort I secure:
The next . . . but you perceive with half an
eye!
Come, come, it 's best believing, if we may;
You can't but own that!

Next, concede again,
If once we choose belief, on all accounts
We can't be too decisive in our faith,
Conclusive and exclusive in its terms,
To suit the world which gives us the good
things.
In every man's career are certain points
Whereon he dares not be indifferent;
The world detects him clearly, if he dare,
As baffled at the game, and losing life.
He may care little or he may care much
For riches, honor, pleasure, work, repose.
Since various theories of life and life's
Success are extant which might easily
Comport with either estimate of these:

And whoso chooses wealth or poverty,
Labor or quiet, is not judged a fool
Because his fellow would choose otherwise :
We let him choose upon his own account
So long as he 's consistent with his choice.
But certain points, left wholly to himself,
When once a man has arbitrated on,
We say he must succeed there or go hang.
Thus, he should wed the woman he loves most
Or needs most, whatsoe'er the love or need —
For he can't wed twice. Then, he must avouch,
Or follow, at the least, sufficiently,
The form of faith his conscience holds the best,
Whate'er the process of conviction was :
For nothing can compensate his mistake
On such a point, the man himself being judge :
He cannot wed twice, nor twice lose his soul.

Well now, there 's one great form of Christian
     faith
I happened to be born in — which to teach
Was given me as I grew up, on all hands,
As best and readiest means of living by ;
The same on examination being proved
The most pronounced moreover, fixed, precise
And absolute form of faith in the whole world —
Accordingly, most potent of all forms
For working on the world. Observe, my
     friend !
Such as you know me, I am free to say,
In these hard latter days which hamper one,
Myself — by no immoderate exercise
Of intellect and learning, but the tact
To let external forces work for me,
— Bid the street's stones be bread and they are
     bread ;
Bid Peter's creed, or rather, Hildebrand's,
Exalt me o'er my fellows in the world
And make my life an ease and joy and pride ;
It does so, — which for me 's a great point
     gained,
Who have a soul and body that exact
A comfortable care in many ways.
There 's power in me and will to dominate
Which I must exercise, they hurt me else :
In many ways I need mankind's respect,
Obedience, and the love that 's born of fear :
While at the same time, there 's a taste I have,
A toy of soul, a titillating thing,
Refuses to digest these dainties crude.
The naked life is gross till clothed upon :
I must take what men offer, with a grace
As though I would not, could I help it, take !
An uniform I wear though over-rich —
Something imposed on me, no choice of mine ;
No fancy-dress worn for pure fancy's sake
And despicable therefore ! now folk kneel
And kiss my hand — of course the Church's
     hand.
Thus I am made, thus life is best for me,
And thus that it should be I have procured ;
And thus it could not be another way,
I venture to imagine.

               You 'll reply,
So far my choice, no doubt, is a success ;
But were I made of better elements,
With nobler instincts, purer tastes, like you,

I hardly would account the thing success
Though it did all for me I say.

               But, friend,
We speak of what is ; not of what might be,
And how 't were better if 't were otherwise.
I am the man you see here plain enough :
Grant I 'm a beast, why, beasts must lead
     beasts' lives !
Suppose I own at once to tail and claws ;
The tailless man exceeds me : but being tailed
I 'll lash out lion fashion, and leave apes
To dock their stump and dress their haunches
     up.
My business is not to remake myself,
But make the absolute best of what God made.
Or — our first simile — though you prove me
     doomed
To a viler berth still, to the steerage-hole,
The sheep-pen or the pig-sty, I should strive
To make what use of each were possible ;
And as this cabin gets upholstery,
That hutch should rustle with sufficient straw.

But, friend, I don't acknowledge quite so fast
I fail of all your manhood's lofty tastes
Enumerated so complacently,
On the mere ground that you forsooth can find
In this particular life I choose to lead
No fit provision for them. Can you not ?
Say you, my fault is I address myself
To grosser estimators than should judge ?
And that 's no way of holding up the soul,
Which, nobler, needs men's praise perhaps, yet
     knows
One wise man's verdict outweighs all the
     fools' —
Would like the two, but, forced to choose,
     takes that.
I pine among my million imbeciles
(You think) aware some dozen men of sense
Eye me and know me, whether I believe
In the last winking Virgin, as I vow,
And am a fool, or disbelieve in her
And am a knave, — approve in neither case,
Withhold their voices though I look their way :
Like Verdi when, at his worst opera's end
(The thing they gave at Florence, — what 's its
     name ?)
While the mad houseful's plaudits near out
     bang
His orchestra of salt-box, tongs, and bones,
He looks through all the roaring and the
     wreaths
Where sits Rossini patient in his stall.

Nay, friend, I meet you with an answer
     here —
That even your prime men who appraise their
     kind
Are men still, catch a wheel within a wheel,
See more in a truth than the truth's simple self,
Confuse themselves. You see lads walk the
     street
Sixty the minute ; what 's to note in that ?
You see one lad o'erstride a chimney-stack ;
Him you must watch — he 's sure to fall, yet
     stands !

Our interest 's on the dangerous edge of things.
The honest thief, the tender murderer,
The superstitious atheist, demirep
That loves and saves her soul in new French
     books —
We watch while these in equilibrium keep
The giddy line midway : one step aside,
They 're classed and done with. I, then, keep
     the line
Before your sages, — just the men to shrink
From the gross weights, coarse scales and
     labels broad
You offer their refinement. Fool or knave ?
Why needs a bishop be a fool or knave
When there 's a thousand diamond weights
     between ?
So, I enlist them. Your picked twelve, you 'll
     find,
Profess themselves indignant, scandalized
At thus being held unable to explain
How a superior man who disbelieves
May not believe as well : that 's Schelling's
     way !
It 's through my coming in the tail of time,
Nicking the minute with a happy tact.
Had I been born three hundred years ago
They 'd say, " What 's strange ? Blougram of
     course believes ; "
And, seventy years since, " disbelieves of
     course."
But now, " He may believe ; and yet, and yet
How can he ? " All eyes turn with interest.
Whereas, step off the line on either side —
You, for example, clever to a fault,
The rough and ready man who write apace,
Read somewhat seldomer, think perhaps even
     less —
You disbelieve ! Who wonders and who cares ?
Lord So-and-So — his coat bedropped with
     wax,
All Peter's chains about his waist, his back
Brave with the needlework of Noodledom —
Believes ! Again, who wonders and who cares ?
But I, the man of sense and learning too,
The able to think yet act, the this, the that,
I, to believe at this late time of day !
Enough ; you see, I need not fear contempt.

     — Except it 's yours ! Admire me as these
     may,
You don't. But whom at least do you admire ?
Present your own perfection, your ideal,
Your pattern man for a minute — oh, make
     haste !
Is it Napoleon you would have us grow ?
Concede the means ; allow his head and hand,
(A large concession, clever as you are)
Good ! In our common primal element
Of unbelief (we can't believe, you know —
We 're still at that admission, recollect !)
Where do you find — apart from, towering o'er
The secondary temporary aims
Which satisfy the gross taste you despise —
Where do you find his star ? — his crazy trust
God knows through what or in what ? it 's alive
And shines and leads him, and that 's all we
     want.
Have we aught in our sober night shall point

Such ends as his were, and direct the means
Of working out our purpose straight as his,
Nor bring a moment's trouble on success
With after-care to justify the same ?
— Be a Napoleon, and yet disbelieve —
Why, the man 's mad, friend, take his light
     away !
What 's the vague good o' the world, for which
     you dare
With comfort to yourself blow millions up ?
We neither of us see it ! we do see
The blown-up millions — spatter of their brains
And writhing of their bowels and so forth,
In that bewildering entanglement
Of horrible eventualities
Past calculation to the end of time !
Can I mistake for some clear word of God
(Which were my ample warrant for it all)
His puff of hazy instinct, idle talk,
" The State, that 's I," quack-nonsense about
     crowns,
And (when one beats the man to his last hold)
A vague idea of setting things to rights,
Policing people efficaciously,
More to their profit, most of all to his own ;
The whole to end that dismallest of ends
By an Austrian marriage, cant to us the Church,
And resurrection of the old régime ?
Would I, who hope to live a dozen years,
Fight Austerlitz for reasons such and such ?
No : for, concede me but the merest chance
Doubt may be wrong — there 's judgment, life
     to come !
With just that chance, I dare not. Doubt
     proves right ?
This present life is all ? — you offer me
Its dozen noisy years, without a chance
That wedding an archduchess, wearing lace,
And getting called by divers new-coined names
Will drive off ugly thoughts and let me dine,
Sleep, read and chat in quiet as I like !
Therefore I will not.

                    Take another case ;
Fit up the cabin yet another way.
What say you to the poets ? shall we write
Hamlet, Othello — make the world our own,
Without a risk to run of either sort ?
I can't ! — to put the strongest reason first.
" But try," you urge, " the trying shall suffice ;
The aim, if reached or not, makes great the
     life :
Try to be Shakespeare, leave the rest to fate ! "
Spare my self-knowledge — there 's no fooling
     me !
If I prefer remaining my poor self.
I say so not in self-dispraise but praise.
If I 'm a Shakespeare, let the well alone ;
Why should I try to be what now I am ?
If I 'm no Shakespeare, as too probable, —
His power and consciousness and self-delight
And all we want in common, shall I find —
Trying forever ? while on points of taste
Wherewith, to speak it humbly, he and I
Are dowered alike — I 'll ask you, I or he,
Which in our two lives realizes most ?
Much, he imagined — somewhat, I possess.
He had the imagination ; stick to that !

Let him say, " In the face of my soul's works
Your world is worthless and I touch it not
Lest I should wrong them " — I 'll withdraw
    my plea.
But does he say so ? look upon his life !
Himself, who only can, gives judgment there.
He leaves his towers and gorgeous palaces
To build the trimmest house in Stratford town ;
Saves money, spends it, owns the worth of
    things,
Giulio Romano's pictures, Dowland's lute ;
Enjoys a show, respects the puppets, too,
And none more, had he seen its entry once,
Than " Pandulph, of fair Milan cardinal."
Why then should I who play that personage,
The very Pandulph Shakespeare's fancy made,
Be told that had the poet chanced to start
From where I stand now (some degree like
    mine
Being just the goal he ran his race to reach)
He would have run the whole race back, for-
    sooth,
And left being Pandulph, to begin write plays ?
Ah, the earth's best can be but the earth's best !
Did Shakespeare live, he could but sit at home
And get himself in dreams the Vatican,
Greek busts, Venetian paintings, Roman walls,
And English books, none equal to his own,
Which I read, bound in gold (he never did).
— Terni's fall, Naples' bay, and Gothard's
    top —
Eh, friend ? I could not fancy one of these ;
But, as I pour this claret, there they are :
I 've gained them — crossed Saint Gothard last
    July
With ten mules to the carriage and a bed
Slung inside ; is my hap the worse for that ?
We want the same things, Shakespeare and my-
    self,
And what I want, I have : he, gifted more,
Could fancy he too had them when he liked,
But not so thoroughly that, if fate allowed,
He would not have them also in my sense.
We play one game ; I send the ball aloft
No less adroitly that of fifty strokes
Scarce five go o'er the wall so wide and high
Which sends them back to me : I wish and get.
He struck balls higher and with better skill,
But at a poor fence level with his head,
And hit — his Stratford house, a coat of arms,
Successful dealings in his grain and wool, —
While I receive heaven's incense in my nose
And style myself the cousin of Queen Bess.
Ask him, if this life 's all, who wins the game ?

Believe — and our whole argument breaks up.
Enthusiasm 's the best thing, I repeat ;
Only, we can't command it ; fire and life
Are all, dead matter 's nothing, we agree :
And be it a mad dream or God's very breath,
The fact 's the same, — belief's fire, once in us,
Makes of all else mere stuff to show itself :
We penetrate our life with such a glow
As fire lends wood and iron — this turns steel,
That burns to ash — all 's one, fire proves its
    power
For good or ill, since men call flare success.
But paint a fire, it will not therefore burn.

Light one in me, I 'll find it food enough !
Why, to be Luther — that 's a life to lead,
Incomparably better than my own.
He comes, reclaims God's earth for God, he
    says,
Sets up God's rule again by simple means,
Reopens a shut book, and all is done.
He flared out in the flaring of mankind ;
Such Luther's luck was : how shall such be
    mine ?
If he succeeded, nothing 's left to do :
And if he did not altogether — well,
Strauss is the next advance. All Strauss
    should be
I might be also. But to what result ?
He looks upon no future : Luther did.
What can I gain on the denying side ?
Ice makes no conflagration. State the facts,
Read the text right, emancipate the world —
The emancipated world enjoys itself
With scarce a thank-you : Blougram told it first
It could not owe a farthing, — not to him
More than Saint Paul ! 't would press its pay,
    you think ?
Then add there 's still that plaguy hundredth
    chance
Strauss may be wrong. And so a risk is run —
For what gain ? not for Luther's, who secured
A real heaven in his heart throughout his life,
Supposing death a little altered things.

" Ay, but since really you lack faith," you
    cry,
" You run the same risk really on all sides,
In cool indifference as bold unbelief.
As well be Strauss as swing 'twixt Paul and
    him.
It 's not worth having, such imperfect faith,
No more available to do faith's work
Than unbelief like mine. Whole faith, or
    none ! "

Softly, my friend ! I must dispute that
    point.
Once own the use of faith, I 'll find you faith.
We 're back on Christian ground. You call for
    faith :
I show you doubt, to prove that faith exists.
The more of doubt, the stronger faith, I say,
If faith o'ercomes doubt. How I know it does
By life and man's free will, God gave for that
To mould life as we choose it, shows our
    choice :
That 's our one act, the previous work 's his
    own.
You criticise the soul ? it reared this tree —
This broad life and whatever fruit it bears !
What matter though I doubt at every pore,
Head-doubts, heart-doubts, doubts at my fin-
    gers' ends,
Doubts in the trivial work of every day,
Doubts at the very bases of my soul
In the grand moments when she probes her
    self —
If finally I have a life to show,
The thing I did, brought out in evidence
Against the thing done to me underground
By hell and all its brood, for aught I know ?

I say, whence sprang this? shows it faith or
  doubt?
All 's doubt in me; where 's break of faith in
  this?
It is the idea, the feeling and the love,
God means mankind should strive for and show
  forth
Whatever be the process to that end, —
And not historic knowledge, logic sound,
And metaphysical acumen, sure!
" What think ye of Christ," friend? when all 's
  done and said,
Like you this Christianity or not?
It may be false, but will you wish it true?
Has it your vote to be so if it can?
Trust you an instinct silenced long ago
That will break silence and enjoin you love
What mortified philosophy is hoarse,
And all in vain, with bidding you despise?
If you desire faith — then you 've faith enough:
What else seeks God — nay, what else seek our-
  selves?
You form a notion of me, we 'll suppose,
On hearsay; it 's a favorable one:
"But still" (you add), " there was no such
  good man,
Because of contradiction in the facts.
One proves, for instance, he was born in Rome,
This Blougram; yet throughout the tales of him
I see he figures as an Englishman."
Well, the two things are reconcilable.
But would I rather you discovered that,
Subjoining — " Still, what matter though they
  be?
Blougram concerns me naught, born here or
  there."

  Pure faith indeed — you know not what you
  ask!
Naked belief in God the Omnipotent,
Omniscient, Omnipresent, sears too much
The sense of conscious creatures to be borne.
It were the seeing him, no flesh shall dare.
Some think, Creation 's meant to show him
  forth:
I say it 's meant to hide him all it can,
And that 's what all the blessed evil 's for.
Its use in Time is to environ us,
Our breath, our drop of dew, with shield
  enough
Against that sight till we can bear its stress.
Under a vertical sun, the exposed brain
And lidless eye and disemprisoned heart
Less certainly would wither up at once
Than mind, confronted with the truth of him.
But time and earth case-harden us to live;
The feeblest sense is trusted most; the child
Feels God a moment, ichors o'er the place,
Plays on and grows to be a man like us.
With me, faith means perpetual unbelief
Kept quiet like the snake 'neath Michael's foot
Who stands calm just because he feels it
  writhe.
Or, if that 's too ambitious, — here 's my box —
I need the excitation of a pinch
Threatening the torpor of the inside-nose
Nigh on the imminent sneeze that never comes.
" Leave it in peace," advise the simple folk:

Make it aware of peace by itching-fits,
Say I — let doubt occasion still more faith!

  You 'll say, once all believed, man, woman
  child,
In that dear middle-age these noodles praise.
How you 'd exult if I could put you back
Six hundred years, blot out cosmogony,
Geology, ethnology, what not,
(Greek endings, each the little passing-bell
That signifies some faith 's about to die),
And set you square with Genesis again, —
When such a traveller told you his last news,
He saw the ark a-top of Ararat
But did not climb there since 't was getting
  dusk
And robber-bands infest the mountain's foot!
How should you feel, I ask, in such an age,
How act? As other people felt and did;
With soul more blank than this decanter'
  knob,
Believe — and yet lie, kill, rob, fornicate,
Full in belief's face, like the beast you 'd be!

  No, when the fight begins within himself,
A man 's worth something. God stoops o'er his
  head,
Satan looks up between his feet — both tug —
He 's left, himself, i' the middle: the soul
  wakes
And grows. Prolong that battle through his
  life!
Never leave growing till the life to come!
Here, we 've got callous to the Virgin's winks
That used to puzzle people wholesomely:
Men have outgrown the shame of being fools.
What are the laws of nature, not to bend
If the Church bid them? — brother Newman
  asks.
Up with the Immaculate Conception, then —
On to the rack with faith! — is my advice.
Will not that hurry us upon our knees,
Knocking our breasts, "It can't be — yet it
  shall!
Who am I, the worm, to argue with my Pope?
Low things confound the high things!" and so
  forth.
That 's better than acquitting God with grace
As some folk do. He 's tried — no case is
  proved,
Philosophy is lenient — he may go!

  You 'll say, the old system 's not so obsolete
But men believe still: ay, but who and where?
King Bomba's lazzaroni foster yet
The sacred flame, so Antonelli writes;
But even of these, what ragamuffin-saint
Believes God watches him continually,
As he believes in fire that it will burn,
Or rain that it will drench him? Break fire's
  law,
Sin against rain, although the penalty
Be just a singe or soaking? "No," he smiles;
" Those laws are laws that can enforce them-
  selves."

  The sum of all is — yes, my doubt is great,
My faith 's still greater, then my faith 's enough

I have read much, thought much, experienced
   much,
Yet would die rather than avow my fear
The Naples' liquefaction may be false,
When set to happen by the palace-clock
According to the clouds or dinner-time.
I hear you recommend, I might at least
Eliminate, decrassify my faith
Since I adopt it; keeping what I must
And leaving what I can — such points as this.
I won't — that is, I can't throw one away.
Supposing there 's no truth in what I hold
About the need of trial to man's faith,
Still, when you bid me purify the same,
To such a process I discern no end.
Clearing off one excrescence to see two,
There 's ever a next in size, now grown as big,
That meets the knife: I cut and cut again!
First cut the Liquefaction, what comes last
But Fichte's clever cut at God himself?
Experimentalize on sacred things!
I trust nor hand nor eye nor heart nor brain
To stop betimes: they all get drunk alike.
The first step, I am master not to take.

You 'd find the cutting-process to your taste
As much as leaving growths of lies unpruned,
Nor see more danger in it, — you retort.
Your taste 's worth mine; but my taste proves
   more wise
When we consider that the steadfast hold
On the extreme end of the chain of faith
Gives all the advantage, makes the difference
With the rough purblind mass we seek to rule:
We are their lords, or they are free of us,
Just as we tighten or relax our hold.
So, other matters equal, we 'll revert
To the first problem — which, if solved my way
And thrown into the balance, turns the scale —
How we may lead a comfortable life,
How suit our luggage to the cabin's size.

Of course you are remarking all this time
How narrowly and grossly I view life,
Respect the creature-comforts, care to rule
The masses, and regard complacently
"The cabin," in our old phrase. Well, I do.
I act for, talk for, live for this world now,
As this world prizes action, life and talk:
No prejudice to what next world may prove,
Whose new laws and requirements, my best
   pledge
To observe then, is that I observe these now,
Shall do hereafter what I do meanwhile.
Let us concede (gratuitously though)
Next life relieves the soul of body, yields
Pure spiritual enjoyment: well, my friend,
Why lose this life i' the meantime, since its use
May be to make the next life more intense?

Do you know, I have often had a dream
(Work it up in your next month's article)
Of man's poor spirit in its progress, still
Losing true life forever and a day
Through ever trying to be and ever being —
In the evolution of successive spheres —
Before its actual sphere and place of life,
Halfway into the next, which having reached,

It shoots with corresponding foolery
Halfway into the next still, on and off!
As when a traveller, bound from North to
   South,
Scouts fur in Russia: what 's its use in France?
In France spurns flannel: where 's its need in
   Spain?
In Spain drops cloth, too cumbrous for Algiers!
Linen goes next, and last the skin itself,
A superfluity at Timbuctoo.
When, through his journey, was the fool at
   ease?
I'm at ease now, friend; worldly in this world,
I take and like its way of life; I think
My brothers, who administer the means,
Live better for my comfort — that 's good too;
And God, if he pronounce upon such life,
Approves my service, which is better still.
If he keep silence, — why, for you or me
Or that brute beast pulled-up in to-day's
   " Times,"
What odds is 't, save to ourselves, what life we
   lead?

You meet me at this issue: you declare, —
All special-pleading done with — truth is truth,
And justifies itself by undreamed ways.
You don't fear but it 's better, if we doubt,
To say so, act up to our truth perceived
However feebly. Do then, — act away!
'T is there I 'm on the watch for you. How
   one acts
Is, both of us agree, our chief concern:
And how you 'll act is what I fain would see
If, like the candid person you appear,
You dare to make the most of your life's
   scheme
As I of mine, live up to its full law
Since there 's no higher law that counterchecks.
Put natural religion to the test
You 've just demolished the revealed with —
   quick,
Down to the root of all that checks your will,
All prohibition to lie, kill and thieve,
Or even to be an atheistic priest!
Suppose a pricking to incontinence —
Philosophers deduce you chastity
Or shame, from just the fact that at the first
Whoso embraced a woman in the field,
Threw club down and forewent his brains be-
   side,
So, stood a ready victim in the reach
Of any brother savage, club in hand;
Hence saw the use of going out of sight
In wood or cave to prosecute his loves:
I read this in a French book t'other day.
Does law so analyzed coerce you much?
Oh, men spin clouds of fuzz where matters end,
But you who reach where the first thread be-
   gins,
You 'll soon cut that! — which means you can,
   but won't,
Through certain instincts. blind. unreasoned
   out,
You dare not set aside, you can't tell why,
But there they are, and so you let them rule.
Then, friend, you seem as much a slave as I,
A liar, conscious coward and hypocrite,

Without the good the slave expects to get,
In case he has a master after all!
You own your instincts? why, what else do I,
Who want, am made for, and must have a God
Ere I can be aught, do aught? — no mere name
Want, but the true thing with what proves its
    truth,
To wit, a relation from that thing to me,
Touching from head to foot — which touch I
    feel,
And with it take the rest, this life of ours!
I live my life here; yours you dare not live.

— Not as I state it, who (you please subjoin)
Disfigure such a life and call it names,
While, to your mind, remains another way
For simple men: knowledge and power have
    rights,
But ignorance and weakness have rights too.
There needs no crucial effort to find truth
If here or there or anywhere about:
We ought to turn each side, try hard and see,
And if we can't, be glad we 've earned at least
The right, by one laborious proof the more,
To graze in peace earth's pleasant pasturage.
Men are not angels, neither are they brutes:
Something we may see, all we cannot see.
What need of lying? I say, I see all,
And swear to each detail the most minute
In what I think a Pan's face — you, mere cloud:
I swear I hear him speak and see him wink,
For fear, if once I drop the emphasis,
Mankind may doubt there 's any cloud at all.
You take the simple life — ready to see,
Willing to see (for no cloud 's worth a face) —
And leaving quiet what no strength can move,
And which, who bids you move? who has the
    right?
I bid you; but you are God's sheep, not mine:
" Pastor est tui Dominus." You find
In this the pleasant pasture of our life
Much you may eat without the least offence,
Much you don't eat because your maw objects,
Much you would eat but that your fellow-flock
Open great eyes at you and even butt,
And thereupon you like your mates so well
You cannot please yourself, offending them;
Though when they seem exorbitantly sheep,
You weigh your pleasure with their butts and
    bleats
And strike the balance. Sometimes certain
    fears
Restrain you, real checks since you find them
    so;
Sometimes you please yourself and nothing
    checks:
And th is you graze through life with not one
    lie,
And like it best.

            But do you, in truth's name?
If so, you beat — which means you are not I —
Who needs must make earth mine and feed my
    fill
Not simply unbutted at, unbickered with,
But motioned to the velvet of the sward
By those obsequious wethers' very selves.
Look at me, sir; my age is double yours:

At yours, I knew beforehand, so enjoyed,
What now I should be — as, permit the word,
I pretty well imagine your whole range
And stretch of tether twenty years to come.
We both have minds and bodies much alike.
In truth's name, don't you want my bishopric,
My daily bread, my influence, and my state?
You 're young. I 'm old; you must be old one
    day;
Will you find then, as I do hour by hour,
Women their lovers kneel to, who cut curls
From your fat lap-dog's ear to grace a brooch —
Dukes, who petition just to kiss your ring —
With much beside you know or may conceive?
Suppose we die to-night: well, here am I,
Such were my gains, life bore this fruit to
    me,
While writing all the same my articles
On music, poetry, the fictile vase
Found at Albano, chess, Anacreon's Greek.
But you — the highest honor in your life,
The thing you 'll crown yourself with, all your
    days,
Is — dining here and drinking this last glass
I pour you out in sign of amity
Before we part forever. Of your power
And social influence, worldly worth in short,
Judge what 's my estimation by the fact,
I do not condescend to enjoin, beseech,
Hint secrecy on one of all these words!
You 're shrewd and know that should you pub-
    lish one
The world would brand the lie — my enemies
    first,
Who 'd sneer — " the bishop 's an arch-hypo-
    crite
And knave perhaps, but not so frank a fool."
Whereas I should not dare for both my ears
Breathe one such syllable, smile one such smile,
Before the chaplain who reflects myself —
My shade 's so much more potent than your
    flesh.
What 's your reward, self-abnegating friend?
Stood you confessed of those exceptional
And privileged great natures that dwarf mine —
A zealot with a mad ideal in reach,
A poet just about to print his ode,
A statesman with a scheme to stop this war,
An artist whose religion is his art —
I should have nothing to object: such men
Carry the fire, all things grow warm to them,
Their drugget 's worth my purple, they beat
    me.
But you, — you 're just as little those as I —
You, Gigadibs, who, thirty years of age,
Write statedly for Blackwood's Magazine,
Believe you see two points in Hamlet's soul
Unseized by the Germans yet — which view
    you 'll print —
Meantime the best you have to show being still
That lively lightsome article we took
Almost for the true Dickens, — what 's its
    name?
" The Slum and Cellar, or Whitechapel life
Limned after dark!" it made me laugh, I know,
And pleased a month, and brought you in ten
    pounds.
— Success I recognize and compliment,

And therefore give you, if you choose, three
    words
(The card and pencil-scratch is quite enough)
Which whether here, in Dublin or New York,
Will get you, prompt as at my eyebrow's wink,
Such terms as never you aspired to get
In all our own reviews and some not ours.
Go write your lively sketches ! be the first
"Blougram, or The Eccentric Confidence" —
Or better simply say, "The Outward-bound."
Why, men as soon would throw it in my teeth
As copy and quote the infamy chalked broad
About me on the church-door opposite.
You will not wait for that experience though,
I fancy, howsoever you decide,
To discontinue — not detesting, not
Defaming, but at least — despising me !

Over his wine so smiled and talked his hour
Sylvester Blougram, styled *in partibus
Episcopus, nec non* — (the deuce knows what
It 's changed to by our novel hierarchy)
With Gigadibs the literary man,
Who played with spoons, explored his plate's
    design,
And ranged the olive-stones about its edge,
While the great bishop rolled him out a mind
Long crumpled, till creased consciousness lay
    smooth.

For Blougram, he believed, say, half he spoke.
The other portion, as he shaped it thus
For argumentatory purposes,
He felt his foe was foolish to dispute,
Some arbitrary accidental thoughts
That crossed his mind, amusing because new,
He chose to represent as fixtures there,
Invariable convictions (such they seemed
Beside his interlocutor's loose cards
Flung daily down, and not the same way twice),
While certain hell-deep instincts, man's weak
    tongue
Is never bold to utter in their truth
Because styled hell-deep ('t is an old mistake
To place hell at the bottom of the earth),
He ignored these, — not having in readiness
Their nomenclature and philosophy:
He said true things, but called them by wrong
    names.
"On the whole," he thought, "I justify myself
On every point where cavillers like this
Oppugn my life : he tries one kind of fence,
I close, he 's worsted, that 's enough for him.
He 's on the ground : if ground should break
    away
I take my stand on, there 's a firmer yet
Beneath it, both of us may sink and reach.
His ground was over mine and broke the first :
So, let him sit with me this many a year ! "

He did not sit five minutes. Just a week
Sufficed his sudden healthy vehemence.
Something had struck him in the "Outward-
    bound "
Another way than Blougram's purpose was :
And having bought, not cabin-furniture

But settler's-implements (enough for three)
And started for Australia — there, I hope,
By this time he has tested his first plough,
And studied his last chapter of Saint John.

CLEON

" As certain also of your own poets have said " —

CLEON the poet (from the sprinkled isles,
Lily on lily, that o'erlace the sea,
And laugh their pride when the light wave lisps
    " Greece ") —
To Protus in his Tyranny : much health !

They give thy letter to me, even now :
I read and seem as if I heard thee speak.
The master of thy galley still unlades
Gift after gift ; they block my court at last
And pile themselves along its portico
Royal with sunset, like a thought of thee :
And one white she-slave from the group dis-
    persed
Of black and white slaves (like the chequer-
    work
Pavement, at once my nation's work and gift,
Now covered with this settle-down of doves),
One lyric woman, in her crocus vest
Woven of sea-wools, with her two white hands
Commends to me the strainer and the cup
Thy lip hath bettered ere it blesses mine.

Well-counselled, king, in thy munificence !
For so shall men remark, in such an act
Of love for him whose song gives life its joy,
Thy recognition of the use of life ;
Nor call thy spirit barely adequate
To help on life in straight ways, broad enough
For vulgar souls, by ruling and the rest.
Thou, in the daily building of thy tower, —
Whether in fierce and sudden spasms of toil,
Or through dim lulls of unapparent growth,
Or when the general work 'mid good acclaim
Climbed with the eye to cheer the architect, —
Didst ne'er engage in work for mere work's
    sake —
Hadst ever in thy heart the luring hope
Of some eventual rest a-top of it,
Whence, all the tumult of the building hushed,
Thou first of men mightst look out to the East :
The vulgar saw thy tower, thou sawest the
    sun.
For this, I promise on thy festival
To pour libation, looking o'er the sea,
Making this slave narrate thy fortunes, speak
Thy great words, and describe thy royal face —
Wishing thee wholly where Zeus lives the most,
Within the eventual element of calm.

Thy letter's first requirement meets me here
It is as thou hast heard : in one short life
I, Cleon, have effected all those things
Thou wonderingly dost enumerate.
That epos on thy hundred plates of gold
Is mine, — and also mine the little chant,
So sure to rise from every fishing-bark
When, lights at prow, the seamen haul their net

The image of the sun-god on the phare,
Men turn from the sun's self to see, is mine ;
The Pœcile, o'er-storied its whole length,
As thou didst hear, with painting, is mine too.
I know the true proportions of a man
And woman also, not observed before ;
And I have written three books on the soul,
Proving absurd all written hitherto,
And putting us to ignorance again.
For music, — why, I have combined the moods,
Inventing one. In brief, all arts are mine ;
Thus much the people know and recognize,
Throughout our seventeen islands. Marvel not.
We of these latter days, with greater mind
Than our forerunners, since more composite,
Look not so great, beside their simple way,
To a judge who only sees one way at once,
One mind-point and no other at a time, —
Compares the small part of a man of us
With some whole man of the heroic age,
Great in his way — not ours, nor meant for ours.
And ours is greater, had we skill to know :
For, what we call this life of men on earth,
This sequence of the soul's achievements here
Being, as I find much reason to conceive,
Intended to be viewed eventually
As a great whole, not analyzed to parts,
But each part having reference to all, —
How shall a certain part, pronounced complete,
Endure effacement by another part ?
Was the thing done ? — then, what 's to do
    again ?
See, in the chequered pavement opposite,
Suppose the artist made a perfect rhomb,
And next a lozenge, then a trapezoid —
He did not overlay them, superimpose
The new upon the old and blot it out,
But laid them on a level in his work,
Making at last a picture ; there it lies.
So, first the perfect separate forms were made,
The portions of mankind ; and after, so,
Occurred the combination of the same.
For where had been a progress, otherwise ?
Mankind, made up of all the single men, —
In such a synthesis the labor ends.
Now mark me ! those divine men of old time
Have reached, thou sayest well, each at one
    point
The outside verge that rounds our faculty ;
And where they reached, who can do more than
    reach ?
It takes but little water just to touch
At some one point the inside of a sphere,
And, as we turn the sphere, touch all the rest
In due succession : but the finer air
Which not so palpably nor obviously,
Though no less universally, can touch
The whole circumference of that emptied sphere
Fills it more fully than the water did ;
Holds thrice the weight of water in itself
Resolved into a subtler element.
And yet the vulgar call the sphere first full
Up to the visible height — and after, void ;
Not knowing air's more hidden properties.
And thus our soul, misknown, cries out to Zeus
To vindicate his purpose in our life :
Why stay we on the earth unless to grow ?
Long since, I imaged, wrote the fiction out,

That he or other god descended here
And, once for all, showed simultaneously
What, in its nature, never can be shown,
Piecemeal or in succession ; — showed, I say,
The worth both absolute and relative
Of all his children from the birth of time,
His instruments for all appointed work.
I now go on to image, — might we hear
The judgment which should give the due to
    each,
Show where the labor lay and where the ease,
And prove Zeus' self, the latent everywhere !
This is a dream : — but no dream, let us hope,
That years and days, the summers and the
    springs,
Follow each other with unwaning powers.
The grapes which dye thy wine are richer far,
Through culture, than the wild wealth of the
    rock ;
The suave plum than the savage-tasted drupe ;
The pastured honey-bee drops choicer sweet ;
The flowers turn double, and the leaves turn
    flowers ;
That young and tender crescent-moon, thy
    slave,
Sleeping above her robe as buoyed by clouds,
Refines upon the women of my youth.
What, and the soul alone deteriorates ?
I have not chanted verse like Homer, no —
Nor swept string like Terpander, no — no
    carved
And painted men like Phidias and his friend :
I am not great as they are, point by point.
But I have entered into sympathy
With these four, running these into one soul,
Who, separate, ignored each other's art.
Say, is it nothing that I know them all ?
The wild flower was the larger ; I have dashed
Rose-blood upon its petals, pricked its cup's
Honey with wine, and driven its seed to fruit,
And show a better flower if not so large :
I stand myself. Refer this to the gods
Whose gift alone it is ! which, shall I dare
(All pride apart) upon the absurd pretext
That such a gift by chance lay in my hand,
Discourse of lightly or depreciate ?
It might have fallen to another's hand : what
    then ?
I pass too surely : let at least truth stay !

And next, of what thou followest on to ask.
This being with me as I declare, O king,
My works, in all these varicolored kinds,
So done by me, accepted so by men —
Thou askest, if (my soul thus in men's hearts)
I must not be accounted to attain
The very crown and proper end of life ?
Inquiring thence how, now life closeth up,
I face death with success in my right hand :
Whether I fear death less than dost thyself
The fortunate of men ? "For" (writest thou)
"Thou leavest much behind, while I leave
    naught.
Thy life stays in the poems men shall sing,
The pictures men shall study ; while my life,
Complete and whole now in its power and joy,
Dies altogether with my brain and arm,
Is lost indeed ; since, what survives myself ?

The brazen statue to o'erlook my grave,
Set on the promontory which I named.
And that — some supple courtier of my heir
Shall use its robed and sceptred arm, perhaps,
To fix the rope to, which best drags it down.
I go then: triumph thou, who dost not go!"

Nay, thou art worthy of hearing my whole
       mind.
Is this apparent, when thou turn'st to muse
Upon the scheme of earth and man in chief,
That admiration grows as knowledge grows?
That imperfection means perfection hid,
Reserved in part, to grace the after-time?
If, in the morning of philosophy,
Ere aught had been recorded, nay perceived,
Thou, with the light now in thee, couldst have
       looked
On all earth's tenantry, from worm to bird,
Ere man, her last, appeared upon the stage —
Thou wouldst have seen them perfect, and de-
       duced
The perfectness of others yet unseen.
Conceding which, — had Zeus then questioned
       thee,
"Shall I go on a step, improve on this,
Do more for visible creatures than is done?"
Thou wouldst have answered, "Ay, by making
       each
Grow conscious in himself — by that alone.
All's perfect else: the shell sucks fast the rock,
The fish strikes through the sea, the snake both
       swims
And slides, forth range the beasts, the birds
       take flight,
Till life's mechanics can no further go —
And all this joy in natural life is put
Like fire from off thy finger into each,
So exquisitely perfect is the same.
But 't is pure fire, and they mere matter are;
It has them, not they it: and so I choose
For man, thy last premeditated work
(If I might add a glory to the scheme),
That a third thing should stand apart from
       both,
A quality arise within his soul,
Which, intro-active, made to supervise
And feel the force it has, may view itself,
And so be happy." Man might live at first
The animal life: but is there nothing more?
In due time, let him critically learn
How he lives; and, the more he gets to know
Of his own life's adaptabilities,
The more joy-giving will his life become.
Thus man, who hath this quality, is best.

But thou, king, hadst more reasonably said:
"Let progress end at once, — man make no step
Beyond the natural man, the better beast,
Using his senses, not the sense of sense."
In man there's failure, only since he left
The lower and inconscious forms of life.
We called it an advance, the rendering plain
Man's spirit might grow conscious of man's life,
And, by new lore so added to the old,
Take each step higher over the brute's head.
This grew the only life, the pleasure-house,
Watch-tower and treasure-fortress of the soul,

Which whole surrounding flats of natural life
Seemed only fit to yield subsistence to;
A tower that crowns a country. But alas,
The soul now climbs it just to perish there!
For thence we have discovered ('t is no dream —
We know this, which we had not else perceived)
That there's a world of capability
For joy, spread round about us, meant for us,
Inviting us; and still the soul craves all,
And still the flesh replies, "Take no jot more
Than ere thou clombst the tower to look abroad!
Nay, so much less as that fatigue has brought
Deduction to it." We struggle, fain to enlarge
Our bounded physical recipiency,
Increase our power, supply fresh oil to life,
Repair the waste of age and sickness: no,
It skills not! life's inadequate to joy,
As the soul sees joy, tempting life to take.
They praise a fountain in my garden here
Wherein a Naiad sends the water-bow
Thin from her tube; she smiles to see it rise.
What if I told her, it is just a thread
From that great river which the hills shut up,
And mock her with my leave to take the same?
The artificer has given her one small tube
Past power to widen or exchange — what boots
To know she might spout oceans if she could?
She cannot lift beyond her first thin thread:
And so a man can use but a man's joy
While he sees God's. Is it for Zeus to boast,
"See, man, how happy I live, and despair —
That I may be still happier — for thy use!"
If this were so, we could not thank our lord,
As hearts beat on to doing; 't is not so —
Malice it is not. Is it carelessness?
Still, no. If care — where is the sign? I ask,
And get no answer, and agree in sum,
O king, with thy profound discouragement,
Who seest the wider but to sigh the more.
Most progress is most failure: thou sayest well.

The last point now: — thou dost except a
       case —
Holding joy not impossible to one
With artist-gifts — to such a man as I
Who leave behind me living works indeed;
For, such a poem, such a painting lives.
What? dost thou verily trip upon a word,
Confound the accurate view of what joy is
(Caught somewhat clearer by my eyes than
       thine)
With feeling joy? confound the knowing how
And showing how to live (my faculty)
With actually living? — Otherwise
Where is the artist's vantage o'er the king?
Because in my great epos I display
How divers men young, strong, fair, wise, can
       act —
Is this as though I acted? if I paint,
Carve the young Phœbus, am I therefore young?
Methinks I'm older that I bowed myself
The many years of pain that taught me art!
Indeed, to know is something, and to prove
How all this beauty might be enjoyed, is more:
But, knowing naught, to enjoy is something
       too.
Yon rower, with the moulded muscles there,
Lowering the sail, is nearer it than I.

I can write love-odes: thy fair slave 's an ode.
I get to sing of love, when grown too gray
For being beloved: she turns to that young
man,
The muscles all a-ripple on his back.
I know the joy of kingship: well, thou art king!

" But," sayest thou — (and I marvel, I repeat,
To find thee trip on such a mere word) " what
Thou writest, paintest, stays; that does not
die:
Sappho survives, because we sing her songs,
And Æschylus, because we read his plays ! "
Why, if they live still, let them come and take
Thy slave in my despite, drink from thy cup,
Speak in my place. Thou diest while I
survive ?
Say rather that my fate is deadlier still,
In this, that every day my sense of joy
Grows more acute, my soul (intensified
By power and insight) more enlarged, more
keen ;
While every day my hairs fall more and more,
My hand shakes, and the heavy years increase —
The horror quickening still from year to year,
The consummation coming past escape,
When I shall know most, and yet least en-
joy —
When all my works wherein I prove my worth,
Being present still to mock me in men's mouths,
Alive still, in the praise of such as thou,
I, I the feeling, thinking, acting man,
The man who loved his life so over-much,
Sleep in my urn. It is so horrible,
I dare at times imagine to my need
Some future state revealed to us by Zeus,
Unlimited in capability
For joy, as this is in desire for joy,
— To seek which, the joy-hunger forces us :
That, stung by straitness of our life, made strait
On purpose to make prized the life at large —
Freed by the throbbing impulse we call death,
We burst there as the worm into the fly,
Who, while a worm still, wants his wings. But
no !
Zeus has not yet revealed it ; and alas,
He must have done so, were it possible !

Live long and happy, and in that thought
die:
Glad for what was ! Farewell. And for the
rest,
I cannot tell thy messenger aright
Where to deliver what he bears of thine
To one called Paulus ; we have heard his fame
Indeed, if Christus be not one with him —
I know not, nor am I troubled much to know.
Thou canst not think a mere barbarian Jew,
As Paulus proves to be, one circumcised,
Hath access to a secret shut from us ?
Thou wrongest our philosophy, O king,
In stooping to inquire of such an one,
As if his answer could impose at all !
He writeth, doth he ? well, and he may write.
Oh, the Jew findeth scholars ! certain slaves
Who touched on this same isle, preached him
and Christ ;
And (as I gathered from a bystander)
Their doctrine could be held by no sane man.

RUDEL TO THE LADY OF TRIPOLI

Originally published in *Bells and Pomegran-
ates* as the first of two poems, *Cristina* being
the other, under the title *Queen Worship.*

I

I KNOW a Mount, the gracious Sun perceives
First, when he visits, last, too, when he leaves
The world ; and, vainly favored, it repays
The day-long glory of his steadfast gaze
By no change of its large calm front of snow.
And underneath the Mount, a Flower I know,
He cannot have perceived, that changes ever
At his approach ; and, in the lost endeavor
To live his life, has parted, one by one,
With all a flower's true graces, for the grace
Of being but a foolish mimic sun,
With ray-like florets round a disk-like face.
Men nobly call by many a name the Mount
As over many a land of theirs its large
Calm front of snow like a triumphal targe
Is reared, and still with old names, fresh names
vie,
Each to its proper praise and own account :
Men call the Flower the Sunflower, sportively.

II

Oh, Angel of the East, one, one gold look
Across the waters to this twilight nook,
— The far sad waters, Angel, to this nook !

III

Dear Pilgrim, art thou for the East indeed ?
Go ! — saying ever as thou dost proceed,
That I, French Rudel, choose for my device
A sunflower outspread like a sacrifice
Before its idol. See ! These inexpert
And hurried fingers could not fail to hurt
The woven picture ; 't is a woman's skill
Indeed ; but nothing baffled me, so, ill
Or well, the work is finished. Say, men feed
On songs I sing, and therefore bask the bees
On my flower's breast as on a platform broad :
But, as the flower's concern is not for these
But solely for the sun, so men applaud
In vain this Rudel, he not looking here
But to the East — the East ! Go, say this,
Pilgrim dear !

ONE WORD MORE

TO E. B. B.

London, September, 1855

Originally appended to the collection of Poems
called *Men and Women,* the greater portion of
which has now been, more correctly, distributed
under the other titles of this edition. R. B.

I

THERE they are, my fifty men and women
Naming me the fifty poems finished !
Take them, Love, the book and me together:
Where the heart lies, let the brain lie also.

II

Rafael made a century of sonnets,
Made and wrote them in a certain volume
Dinted with the silver-pointed pencil
Else he only used to draw Madonnas :
These, the world might view — but one, the
　　volume.
Who that one, you ask ?　Your heart instructs
　　you.
Did she live and love it all her lifetime ?
Did she drop, his lady of the sonnets,
Die, and let it drop beside her pillow
Where it lay in place of Rafael's glory,
Rafael's cheek so duteous and so loving —
Cheek, the world was wont to hail a painter's,
Rafael's cheek, her love had turned a poet's ?

III

You and I would rather read that volume,
(Taken to his beating bosom by it)
Lean and list the bosom-beats of Rafael,
Would we not ? than wonder at Madonnas —
Her, San Sisto names, and Her, Foligno,
Her, that visits Florence in a vision,
Her, that 's left with lilies in the Louvre —
Seen by us and all the world in circle.

IV

You and I will never read that volume.
Guido Reni, like his own eye's apple
Guarded long the treasure-book and loved it.
Guido Reni dying, all Bologna
Cried, and the world cried too, " Ours. the
　　treasure ! "
Suddenly, as rare things will, it vanished.

V

Dante once prepared to paint an angel :
Whom to please ? You whisper " Beatrice."
While he mused and traced it and retraced it,
(Peradventure with a pen corroded
Still by drops of that hot ink he dipped for,
When, his left-hand i' the hair o' the wicked,
Back he held the brow and pricked its stigma,
Bit into the live man's flesh for parchment,
Loosed him, laughed to see the writing rankle,
Let the wretch go festering through Florence) —
Dante, who loved well because he hated,
Hated wickedness that hinders loving,
Dante standing, studying his angel, —
In there broke the folk of his Inferno.
Says he — " Certain people of importance "
(Such he gave his daily dreadful line to)
" Entered and would seize, forsooth, the poet."
Says the poet — " Then I stopped my paint-
　　ing."

VI

You and I would rather see that angel,
Painted by the tenderness of Dante,
Would we not ? — than read a fresh Inferno.

VII

You and I will never see that picture.
While he mused on love and Beatrice,
While he softened o'er his outlined angel,
In they broke, those " people of importance : "
We and Bice bear the loss forever.

VIII

What of Rafael's sonnets, Dante's picture ?
This : no artist lives and loves, that longs not
Once, and only once, and for one only,
(Ah, the prize !) to find his love a language
Fit and fair and simple and sufficient —
Using nature that's an art to others,
Not, this one time, art that 's turned his na
　　ture.
Ay, of all the artists living, loving,
None but would forego his proper dowry, —
Does he paint ? he fain would write a poem, —
Does he write ? he fain would paint a picture,
Put to proof art alien to the artist's,
Once, and only once, and for one only,
So to be the man and leave the artist,
Gain the man's joy, miss the artist's sorrow。

IX

Wherefore ? Heaven's gift takes earth's abate-
　　ment !
He who smites the rock and spreads the water,
Bidding drink and live a crowd beneath him,
Even he, the minute makes immortal,
Proves, perchance, but mortal in the minute,
Desecrates, belike, the deed in doing.
While he smites, how can he but remember,
So he smote before, in such a peril,
When they stood and mocked — " Shall smiting
　　help us ? "
When they drank and sneered — " A stroke is
　　easy ! "
When they wiped their mouths and went their
　　journey,
Throwing him for thanks — " But drought was
　　pleasant."
Thus old memories mar the actual triumph ;
Thus the doing savors of disrelish ;
Thus achievement lacks a gracious somewhat ;
O'er-importuned brows becloud the mandate,
Carelessness or consciousness — the gesture.
For he bears an ancient wrong about him,
Sees and knows again those phalanxed faces,
Hears, yet one time more, the 'customed pre-
　　lude —
" How shouldst thou, of all men, smite, and
　　save us ? "
Guesses what is like to prove the sequel —
" Egypt's flesh-pots — nay, the drought was
　　better."

X

Oh, the crowd must have emphatic warrant !
Theirs, the Sinai-forehead's cloven brilliance,
Right-arm's rod-sweep, tongue's imperial fiat.
Never dares the man put off the prophet.

XI

Did he love one face from out the thousands,
(Were she Jethro's daughter, white and wifely
Were she but the Æthiopian bondslave,)
He would envy yon dumb patient camel,
Keeping a reserve of scanty water
Meant to save his own life in the desert ;
Ready in the desert to deliver
(Kneeling down to let his breast be opened)
Hoard and life together for his mistress.

XII

I shall never, in the years remaining,
Paint you pictures, no, nor carve you statues,
Make you music that should all-express me;
So it seems: I stand on my attainment.
This of verse alone, one life allows me ;
Verse and nothing else have I to give you.
Other heights in other lives, God willing :
All the gifts from all the heights, your own,
  Love !

XIII

Yet a semblance of resource avails us —
Shade so finely touched, love's sense must seize
  it.
Take these lines, look lovingly and nearly,
Lines I write the first time and the last time.
He who works in fresco, steals a hair-brush,
Curbs the liberal hand, subservient proudly,
Cramps his spirit, crowds its all in little,
Makes a strange art of an art familiar,
Fills his lady's missal-marge with flowerets.
He who blows through bronze, may breathe
  through silver,
Fitly serenade a slumbrous princess.
He who writes, may write for once as I do.

XIV

Love, you saw me gather men and women,
Live or dead or fashioned by my fancy,
Enter each and all, and use their service,
Speak from every mouth, — the speech, a poem.
Hardly shall I tell my joys and sorrows,
Hopes and fears, belief and disbelieving:
I am mine and yours — the rest be all men's,
Karshish, Cleon, Norbert, and the fifty.
Let me speak this once in my true person,
Not as Lippo, Roland, or Andrea,
Though the fruit of speech be just this sentence :
Pray you, look on these my men and women,
Take and keep my fifty poems finished ;
Where my heart lies, let my brain lie also !
Poor the speech ; be how I speak, for all things.

XV

Not but that you know me ! Lo, the moon's
  self !
Here in London, yonder late in Florence,
Still we find her face, the thrice-transfigured.
Curving on a sky imbrued with color,
Drifted over Fiesole by twilight,
Came she, our new crescent of a hair's-breadth.
Full she flared it, lamping Samminiato,
Rounder 'twixt the cypresses and rounder,
Perfect till the nightingales applauded.
Now, a piece of her old self, impoverished,
Hard to greet, she traverses the house-roofs,
Hurries with unhandsome thrift of silver,
Goes dispiritedly, glad to finish.

XVI

What, there's nothing in the moon note-
  worthy ?
Nay : for if that moon could love a mortal,

Use, to charm him (so to fit a fancy),
All her magic ('t is the old sweet mythos),
She would turn a new side to her mortal,
Side unseen of herdsman, huntsman, steers
  man —
Blank to Zoroaster on his terrace,
Blind to Galileo on his turret,
Dumb to Homer, dumb to Keats — him, even !
Think, the wonder of the moonstruck mor-
  tal —
When she turns round, comes again in heaven,
Opens out anew for worse or better !
Proves she like some portent of an iceberg
Swimming full upon the ship it founders,
Hungry with huge teeth of splintered crys-
  tals ?
Proves she as the paved work of a sapphire
Seen by Moses when he climbed the moun-
  tain ?
Moses, Aaron, Nadab and Abihu
Climbed and saw the very God, the Highest,
Stand upon the paved work of a sapphire.
Like the bodied heaven in his clearness
Shone the stone, the sapphire of that paved
  work,
When they ate and drank and saw God also !

XVII

What were seen ? None knows, none ever shall
  know.
Only this is sure — the sight were other,
Not the moon's same side, born late in Flor-
  ence,
Dying now impoverished here in London.
God be thanked, the meanest of his creatures
Boasts two soul-sides, one to face the world
  with,
One to show a woman when he loves her !

XVIII

This I say of me, but think of you, Love !
This to you — yourself my moon of poets !
Ah, but that's the world's side, there's the
  wonder,
Thus they see you, praise you, think they know
  you !
There, in turn I stand with them and praise
  you —
Out of my own self, I dare to phrase it.
But the best is when I glide from out them,
Cross a step or two of dubious twilight,
Come out on the other side, the novel
Silent silver lights and darks undreamed of,
Where I hush and bless myself with silence.

XIX

Oh, their Rafael of the dear Madonnas,
Oh, their Dante of the dread Inferno,
Wrote one song — and in my brain I sing it,
Drew one angel — borne, see, on my bosom !
                                        R. B.

IN A BALCONY

WRITTEN in 1853, partly at Bagni di Lucca, partly at Rome. It was included in the original series of *Men and Women* and there divided into three parts.

PERSONS

NORBERT.
CONSTANCE.
THE QUEEN.

CONSTANCE *and* NORBERT.

Norbert. Now!
Constance.   Not now!
Nor.   Give me them again, those hands :
Put them upon my forehead, how it throbs !
Press them before my eyes, the fire comes
    through !
You cruellest, you dearest in the world,
Let me ! The Queen must grant whate'er I
    ask —
How can I gain you and not ask the Queen ?
There she stays waiting for me, here stand you ;
Some time or other this was to be asked ;
Now is the one time — what I ask, I gain :
Let me ask now, Love !
Con.   Do, and ruin us !
Nor. Let it be now, Love ! All my soul
    breaks forth.
How I do love you ! Give my love its way !
A man can have but one life and one death,
One heaven, one hell. Let me fulfil my fate —
Grant me my heaven now ! Let me know you
    mine,
Prove you mine, write my name upon your
    brow,
Hold you and have you, and then die away,
If God please, with completion in my soul !
Con. I am not yours then ? How content
    this man !
I am not his — who change into himself,
Have passed into his heart and beat its beats,
Who give my hands to him, my eyes, my hair,
Give all that was of me away to him —
So well, that now, my spirit turned his own,
Takes part with him against the woman here,
Bids him not stumble at so mere a straw
As caring that the world be cognizant
How he loves her and how she worships him.
You have this woman, not as yet that world.
Go on, I bid, nor stop to care for me
By saving what I cease to care about,
The courtly name and pride of circumstance —
The name you 'll pick up and be cumbered with
Just for the poor parade's sake, nothing more ;
Just that the world may slip from under you —
Just that the world may cry, " So much for
    him —
The man predestined to the heap of crowns :
There goes his chance of winning one, at least ! "
Nor. The world !
Con. You love it ! Love me quite as well,
And see if I shall pray for this in vain !
Why must you ponder what it knows or thinks ?
Nor. You pray for — what, in vain ?
Con.   Oh my heart's heart,

How I do love you, Norbert ! That is right :
But listen, or I take my hands away !
You say, " let it be now : " you would go now
And tell the Queen, perhaps six steps from us,
You love me — so you do, thank God !
Nor.   Thank God !
Con. Yes, Norbert, — but you fain would
    tell your love,
And, what succeeds the telling, ask of her
My hand. Now take this rose and look at it,
Listening to me. You are the minister,
The Queen's first favorite, nor without a cause.
To-night completes your wonderful year's-work
(This palace-feast is held to celebrate)
Made memorable by her life's success,
The junction of two crowns, on her sole head,
Her house had only dreamed of anciently :
That this mere dream is grown a stable truth,
To-night's feast makes authentic. Whose the
    praise ?
Whose genius, patience, energy, achieved
What turned the many heads and broke the
    hearts ?
You are the fate, your minute 's in the heaven.
Next comes the Queen's turn. " Name your
    own reward ! "
With leave to clench the past, chain the to-
    come,
Put out an arm and touch and take the sun
And fix it ever full-faced on your earth,
Possess yourself supremely of her life, —
You choose the single thing she will not grant ;
Nay, very declaration of which choice
Will turn the scale and neutralize your work :
At best she will forgive you, if she can.
You think I 'll let you choose — her cousin's
    hand ?
Nor. Wait. First, do you retain your old
    belief
The Queen is generous, — nay, is just ?
Con.   There, there !
So men make women love them, while they
    know
No more of women's hearts than . . . look you
    here,
You that are just and generous beside.
Make it your own case ! For example now,
I 'll say — I let you kiss me, hold my hands —
Why ? do you know why ? I 'll instruct you,
    then —
The kiss, because you have a name at court ;
This hand and this, that you may shut in each
A jewel, if you please to pick up such.
That 's horrible ? Apply it to the Queen —
Suppose I am the Queen to whom you speak.
" I was a nameless man ; you needed me :
Why did I proffer you my aid ? there stood
A certain pretty cousin at your side.
Why did I make such common cause with you ?
Access to her had not been easy else.

You give my labor here abundant praise ?
'Faith, labor, which she overlooked, grew
    play.
How shall your gratitude discharge itself ?
Give me her hand ! ''
  Nor.   And still I urge the same.
Is the Queen just ? just — generous or no !
  Con. Yes, just. You love a rose : no harm
    in that :
But was it for the rose's sake or mine
You put it in your bosom ? mine, you said —
Then, mine you still must say or else be false.
You told the Queen you served her for herself ;
If so, to serve her was to serve yourself,
She thinks, for all your unbelieving face !
I know her. In the hall, six steps from us,
One sees the twenty pictures : there 's a life
Better than life, and yet no life at all.
Conceive her born in such a magic dome,
Pictures all round her ! why, she sees the world,
Can recognize its given things and facts,
The fight of giants or the feast of gods,
Sages in senate, beauties at the bath,
Chases and battles, the whole earth's display,
Landscape and sea-piece, down to flowers and
    fruit —
And who shall question that she knows them all,
In better semblance than the things outside ?
Yet bring into the silent gallery
Some live thing to contrast in breath and blood,
Some lion, with the painted lion there —
You think she 'll understand composedly ?
— Say, " that 's his fellow in the hunting-piece
Yonder, I 've turned to praise a hundred
    times ? ''
Not so. Her knowledge of our actual earth,
Its hopes and fears, concerns and sympathies,
Must be too far, too mediate, too unreal.
The real exists for us outside, not her :
How should it, with that life in these four
    walls,
That father and that mother, first to last
No father and no mother — friends, a heap,
Lovers, no lack — a husband in due time,
And every one of them alike a lie !
Things painted by a Rubens out of naught
Into what kindness, friendship, love should be ;
All better, all more grandiose than the life,
Only no life ; mere cloth and surface-paint,
You feel, while you admire. How should she
    feel ?
Yet now that she has stood thus fifty years
The sole spectator in that gallery,
You think to bring this warm real struggling
    love
In to her of a sudden, and suppose
She 'll keep her state untroubled ? Here 's the
    truth —
She 'll apprehend truth's value at a glance,
Prefer it to the pictured loyalty ?
You only have to say, " So men are made,
For this they act ; the thing has many names,
But this the right one : and now, Queen, be
    just ! ''
Your life slips back ; you lose her at the word :
You do not even for amends gain me.
He will not understand ! oh, Norbert, Norbert,
Do you not understand ?

  Nor.   The Queen 's the Queen,
I am myself — no picture, but alive
In every nerve and every muscle, here
At the palace-window o'er the people's street,
As she in the gallery where the pictures glow :
The good of life is precious to us both.
She cannot love ; what do I want with rule ?
When first I saw your face a year ago
I knew my life's good, my soul heard one
    voice —
" The woman yonder, there 's no use of life
But just to obtain her ! heap earth's woes in one
And bear them — make a pile of all earth's
    joys
And spurn them, as they help or help not this ;
Only, obtain her ! '' How was it to be ?
I found you were the cousin of the Queen ;
I must then serve the Queen to get to you.
No other way. Suppose there had been one,
And I, by saying prayers to some white star
With promise of my body and my soul,
Might gain you, — should I pray the star or no ?
Instead, there was the Queen to serve ! I
    served,
Helped, did what other servants failed to do.
Neither she sought nor I declared my end.
Her good is hers, my recompense be mine, —
I therefore name you as that recompense.
She dreamed that such a thing could never be ?
Let her wake now. She thinks there was
    more cause
In love of power, high fame, pure loyalty ?
Perhaps she fancies men wear out their lives
Chasing such shades. Then, I 've a fancy too ;
I worked because I want you with my soul :
I therefore ask your hand. Let it be now !
  Con. Had I not loved you from the very
    first,
Were I not yours, could we not steal out thus
So wickedly, so wildly, and so well,
You might become impatient. What 's con-
    ceived
Of us without here, by the folk within ?
Where are you now ? immersed in cares of
    state —
Where am I now ? intent on festal robes —
We two, embracing under death's spread hand !
What was this thought for, what that scruple
    of yours
Which broke the council up ? — to bring about
One minute's meeting in the corridor !
And then the sudden sleights, strange secrecies,
Complots inscrutable, deep telegraphs,
Long-planned chance-meetings, hazards of a
    look,
" Does she know ? does she not know ? saved
    or lost ? ''
A year of this compression's ecstasy
All goes for nothing ! you would give this up
For the old way, the open way, the world's,
His way who beats, and his who sells his wife !
What tempts you ? — their notorious happiness
Makes you ashamed of ours ? The best you 'll
    gain
Will be — the Queen grants all that you require,
Concedes the cousin, rids herself of you
And me at once, and gives us ample leave
To live like our five hundred happy friends.

The world will show us with officious hand
Our chamber-entry, and stand sentinel
Where we so oft have stolen across its traps !
Get the world's warrant, ring the falcons' feet,
And make it duty to be bold and swift,
Which long ago was nature. Have it so !
We never hawked by rights till flung from
    fist ?
Oh, the man's thought ! no woman 's such a
    fool.
    Nor. Yes, the man's thought and my
    thought, which is more —
One made to love you, let the world take note !
Have I done worthy work ? be love's the
    praise,
Though hampered by restrictions, barred
    against
By set forms, blinded by forced secrecies !
Set free my love, and see what love can do
Shown in my life — what work will spring
    from that !
The world is used to have its business done
On other grounds, find great effects produced
For power's sake, fame's sake, motives in men's
    mouth.
So, good : but let my low ground shame their
    high !
Truth is the strong thing. Let man's life be
    true !
And love 's the truth of mine. Time prove the
    rest !
I choose to wear you stamped all over me,
Your name upon my forehead and my breast,
You, from the sword's blade to the ribbon's edge,
That men may see, all over, you in me —
That pale loves may die out of their pretence
In face of mine, shames thrown on love fall
    off.
Permit this, Constance ! Love has been so
    long
Subdued in me, eating me through and through,
That now 't is all of me and must have way.
Think of my work, that chaos of intrigues,
Those hopes and fears, surprises and delays,
That long endeavor, earnest, patient, slow,
Trembling at last to its assured result :
Then think of this revulsion ! I resume
Life after death, (it is no less than life,
After such long unlovely laboring days,)
And liberate to beauty life's great need
O' the beautiful, which, while it prompted work,
Suppressed itself erewhile. This eve 's the
    time,
This eve intense with yon first trembling star
We seem to pant and reach ; scarce aught be-
    tween
The earth that rises and the heaven that bends ;
All nature self-abandoned, every tree
Flung as it will, pursuing its own thoughts
And fixed so, every flower and every weed,
No pride, no shame, no victory, no defeat ;
All under God, each measured by itself.
These statues round us stand abrupt, distinct,
The strong in strength, the weak in weakness
    fixed,
The Muse forever wedded to her lyre,
Nymph to her fawn, and Silence to her rose :
See God's approval on his universe !

Let us do so — aspire to live as these
In harmony with truth, ourselves being true !
Take the first way, and let the second come !
My first is to possess myself of you ;
The music sets the march-step — forward, then :
And there 's the Queen, I go to claim you of,
The world to witness, wonder and applaud.
Our flower of life breaks open. No delay !
    Con. And so shall we be ruined, both of us
Norbert, I know her to the skin and bone :
You do not know her, were not born to it,
To feel what she can see or cannot see.
Love, she is generous, — ay, despite your
    smile,
Generous as you are : for, in that thin frame
Pain-twisted, punctured through and through
    with cares,
There lived a lavish soul until it starved,
Debarred of healthy food. Look to the soul —
Pity that, stoop to that, ere you begin
(The true man's - way) on justice and your
    rights,
Exactions and acquittance of the past !
Begin so — see what justice she will deal !
We women hate a debt as men a gift.
Suppose her some poor keeper of a school
Whose business is to sit through summer
    months
And dole out children leave to go and play,
Herself superior to such lightness — she
In the arm-chair's state and pædagogic pomp —
To the life, the laughter, sun and youth out
    side :
We wonder such a face looks black on us ?
I do not bid you wake her tenderness,
(That were vain truly — none is left to wake,)
But, let her think her justice is engaged
To take the shape of tenderness, and mark
If she 'll not coldly pay its warmest debt !
Does she love me, I ask you ? not a whit :
Yet, thinking that her justice was engaged
To help a kinswoman, she took me up —
Did more on that bare ground than other love'
Would do on greater argument. For me,
I have no equivalent of such cold kind
To pay her with, but love alone to give
If I give anything. I give her love :
I feel I ought to help her, and I will.
So, for her sake, as yours, I tell you twice
That women hate a debt as men a gift.
If I were you, I could obtain this grace —
Could lay the whole I did to love's account,
Nor yet be very false as courtiers go —
Declaring my success was recompense ;
It would be so, in fact : what were it else ?
And then, once loose her generosity, —
Oh, how I see it ! then, were I but you
To turn it, let it seem to move itself,
And make it offer what I really take,
Accepting just, in the poor cousin's hand,
Her value as the next thing to the Queen's —
Since none love Queens directly, none dare that
And a thing's shadow or a name's mere echo
Suffices those who miss the name and thing !
You pick up just a ribbon she has worn,
To keep in proof how near her breath you
    came.
Say, I 'm so near I seem a piece of her —

Ask for me that way — (oh, you understand,)
You 'd find the same gift yielded with a grace,
Which, if you make the least show to ex-
    tort . . .
— You 'll see! and when you have ruined both
    of us,
Dissertate on the Queen's ingratitude!
Nor. Then, if I turn it that way, you con-
    sent?
'T is not my way; I have more hope in truth:
Still, if you won't have truth — why, this in-
    deed,
Were scarcely false, as I 'd express the sense.
Will you remain here?
Con.   O best heart of mine,
How I have loved you! then, you take my way?
Are mine as you have been her minister,
Work out my thought, give it effect for me,
Paint plain my poor conceit and make it serve?
I owe that withered woman everything —
Life, fortune, you, remember! Take my
    part —
Help me to pay her! Stand upon your rights?
You, with my rose, my hands, my heart on
    you?
Your rights are mine — you have no rights but
    mine.
Nor. Remain here. How you know me!
Con.   Ah, but still —
[*He breaks from her; she remains. Dance-music from
    within.*
        (*Enter the* QUEEN.)
Queen. Constance? She is here as he said.
Speak quick!
Is it so? Is it true or false? One word!
Con. True.
Queen. Mercifullest Mother, thanks to thee!
Con. Madam?
Queen. I love you, Constance, from my soul.
Now say once more, with any words you will,
'T is true, all true, as true as that I speak.
Con. Why should you doubt it?
Queen.   Ah, why doubt? why doubt?
Dear, make me see it! Do you see it so?
None see themselves; another sees them best.
You say "why doubt it?" — you see him and
    me.
It is because the Mother has such grace
That if we had but faith — wherein we fail —
Whate'er we yearn for would be granted us;
Yet still we let our whims prescribe despair,
Our fancies thwart and cramp our will and
    power,
And while accepting life, abjure its use.
Constance, I had abjured the hope of love
And being loved, as truly as yon palm
The hope of seeing Egypt from that plot.
Con. Heaven!
Queen. But it was so, Constance, it was so!
Men say — or do men say it? fancies say —
"Stop here, your life is set, you are grown
    old.
Too late — no love for you, too late for love —
Leave love to girls. Be queen: let Constance
    love!"
One takes the hint — half meets it like a child,
Ashamed at any feelings that oppose.
"Oh love, true, never think of love again!

I am a queen: I rule, not love, forsooth."
So it goes on; so a face grows like this,
Hair like this hair, poor arms as lean as these,
Till, — nay, it does not end so, I thank God!
Con. I cannot understand —
Queen.   The happier you!
Constance, I know not how it is with men:
For women (I am a woman now like you)
There is no good of life but love — but love!
What else looks good, is some shade flung from
    love;
Love gilds it, gives it worth. Be warned by
    me,
Never you cheat yourself one instant! Love,
Give love, ask only love, and leave the rest!
O Constance, how I love you!
Con.   I love you.
Queen. I do believe that all is come through
    you.
I took you to my heart to keep it warm
When the last chance of love seemed dead in
    me;
I thought your fresh youth warmed my with-
    ered heart.
Oh, I am very old now, am I not?
Not so! it is true and it shall be true!
Con. Tell it me: let me judge if true or
    false.
Queen. Ah, but I fear you! you will look at
    me
And say, "she 's old, she 's grown unlovely
    quite
Who ne'er was beauteous: men want beauty
    still."
Well, so I feared — the curse! so I felt sure!
Con. Be calm. And now you feel not sure,
    you say?
Queen. Constance, he came, — the coming
    was not strange —
Do not I stand and see men come and go?
I turned a half-look from my pedestal
Where I grow marble — "one young man the
    more!
He will love some one; that is naught to me:
What would he with my marble stateliness?"
Yet this seemed somewhat worse than hereto-
    fore;
The man more gracious, youthful, like a god,
And I still elder, with less flesh to change —
We two those dear extremes that long to touch.
It seemed still harder when he first began
To labor at those state-affairs, absorbed
The old way for the old end — interest.
Oh, to live with a thousand beating hearts
Around you, swift eyes, serviceable hands,
Professing they 've no care but for your cause,
Thought but to help you, love but for your-
    self, —
And you the marble statue all the time
They praise and point at as preferred to life,
Yet leave for the first breathing woman's smile,
First dancer's, gypsy's, or street baladine's!
Why, how I have ground my teeth to hear
    men's speech
Stifled for fear it should alarm my ear,
Their gait subdued lest step should startle me,
Their eyes declined, such queendom to respect,
Their hands alert, such treasure to preserve,

While not a man of them broke rank and spoke,
Wrote me a vulgar letter all of love,
Or caught my hand and pressed it like a hand !
There have been moments, if the sentinel
Lowering his halbert to salute the queen,
Had flung it brutally and clasped my knees,
I would have stooped and kissed him with my
    soul.
    Con. Who could have comprehended ?
    Queen.   Ay, who — who ?
Why, no one, Constance, but this one who did.
Not they, not you, not I. Even now perhaps
It comes too late — would you but tell the truth.
    Con. I wait to tell it.
    Queen.   Well, you see, he came,
Outfaced the others, did a work this year
Exceeds in value all was ever done,
You know — it is not I who say it — all
Say it. And so (a second pang and worse)
I grew aware not only of what he did,
But why so wondrously. Oh, never work
Like his was done for work's ignoble sake —
Souls need a finer aim to light and lure !
I felt, I saw, he loved — loved somebody.
And Constance, my dear Constance, do you
    know,
I did believe this while 't was you he loved.
    Con. Me, madam ?
    Queen.   It did seem to me, your face
Met him where'er he looked : and whom but
    you
Was such a man to love ? It seemed to me,
You saw he loved you, and approved his love,
And both of you were in intelligence.
You could not loiter in that garden, step
Into this balcony, but I straight was stung
And forced to understand. It seemed so true,
So right, so beautiful, so like you both,
That all this work should have been done by
    him
Not for the vulgar hope of recompense,
But that at last — suppose, some night like
    this —
Borne on to claim his due reward of me,
He might say, " Give her hand and pay me
    so."
And I (O Constance, you shall love me now !)
I thought, surmounting all the bitterness,
- - " And he shall have it. I will make her
    blest,
My flower of youth, my woman's self that was,
My happiest woman's self that might have been!
These two shall have their joy and leave me
    here."
Yes — yes !
    Con. Thanks !
    Queen.   And the word was on my lips
When he burst in upon me. I looked to hear
A mere calm statement of his just desire
For payment of his labor. When — O heaven,
How can I tell you ? lightning on my eyes
And thunder in my ears proved that first word
Which told 't was love of me, of me, did all —
He loved me — from the first step to the last,
Loved me !
    Con. You hardly saw. scarce heard him
    speak
Of love : what if you should mistake ?

    Queen.   No, no --
No mistake ! Ha, there shall be no mistake !
He had not dared to hint the love he felt —
You were my reflex — (how I understood !)
He said you were the ribbon I had worn,
He kissed my hand, he looked into my eyes,
And love, love came at end of every phrase.
Love is begun ; this much is come to pass :
The rest is easy. Constance, I am yours !
I will learn, I will place my life on you,
Teach me but how to keep what I have won !
Am I so old ? This hair was early gray ;
But joy ere now has brought hair brown again,
And joy will bring the cheek's red back, I feel.
I could sing once too ; that was in my youth.
Still, when men paint me, they declare me . . .
    yes,
Beautiful — for the last French painter did !
I know they flatter somewhat ; you are frank —
I trust you. How I loved you from the
    first !
Some queens would hardly seek a cousin out
And set her by their side to take the eye :
I must have felt that good would come from
    you.
I am not generous — like him — like you !
But he is not your lover after all :
It was not you he looked at. Saw you him ?
You have not been mistaking words or looks ?
He said you were the reflex of myself.
And yet he is not such a paragon
To you, to younger women who may choose
Among a thousand Norberts. Speak the
    truth !
You know you never named his name to me :
You know, I cannot give him up — ah God,
Not up now, even to you !
    Con.   Then calm yourself.
    Queen. See, I am old — look here, you happy
    girl !
I will not play the fool, deceive — ah, whom ?
'T is all gone : put your cheek beside my cheek
And what a contrast does the moon behold !
But then I set my life upon one chance,
The last chance and the best — am I not left,
My soul, myself ? All women love great men
If young or old ; it is in all the tales :
Young beauties love old poets who can love —
Why should not he, the poems in my soul,
The passionate faith, the pride of sacrifice,
Life-long, death-long ? I throw them at his
    feet.
Who cares to see the fountain's very shape,
Whether it be a Triton's or a Nymph's
That pours the foam, makes rainbows all
    around ?
You could not praise indeed the empty conch ;
But I 'll pour floods of love and hide myself.
How I will love him ! Cannot men love love ?
Who was a queen and loved a poet once
Humpbacked, a dwarf ? ah, women can do
    that !
Well, but men too ; at least, they tell you so.
They love so many women in their youth,
And even in age they all love whom they please ;
And yet the best of them confide to friends
That 't is not beauty makes the lasting love —
They spend a day with such and tire the next

They like soul,— well then, they like phantasy,
Novelty even. Let us confess the truth,
Horrible though it be, that prejudice,
Prescription . . . curses ! they will love a queen.
They will, they do : and will not, does not — he ?
 Con. How can he ? You are wedded : 't is
  a name
We know, but still a bond. Your rank remains,
His rank remains. How can he, nobly souled
As you believe and I incline to think,
Aspire to be your favorite, shame and all ?
 Queen. Hear her ! There, there now — could
  she love like me ?
What did I say of smooth-cheeked youth and
 grace ?
See all it does or could do ! so youth loves !
Oh, tell him, Constance, you could never do
What I will — you, it was not born in ! I
Will drive these difficulties far and fast
As yonder mists curdling before the moon.
I 'll use my light too, gloriously retrieve
My youth from its enforced calamity,
Dissolve that hateful marriage, and be his,
His own in the eyes alike of God and man.
 Con. You will do — dare do . . . pause on
  what you say !
 Queen. Hear her ! I thank you, sweet, for
  that surprise.
You have the fair face : for the soul, see mine !
I have the strong soul : let me teach you, here.
I think I have borne enough and long enough,
And patiently enough, the world remarks,
To have my own way now, unblamed by all.
It does so happen (I rejoice for it)
This most unhoped-for issue cuts the knot.
There 's not a better way of settling claims
Than this ; God sends the accident express :
And were it for my subjects' good, no more,
'T were best thus ordered. I am thankful now,
Mute, passive, acquiescent. I receive,
And bless God simply, or should almost fear
To walk so smoothly to my ends at last.
Why, how I baffle obstacles, spurn fate !
How strong I am ! Could Norbert see me now !
 Con. Let me consider. It is all too strange.
 Queen. You, Constance, learn of me ; do you,
  like me !
You are young, beautiful : my own, best girl,
You will have many lovers, and love one —
Light hair, not hair like Norbert's, to suit
 yours,
Taller than he is, since yourself are tall.
Love him, like me ! Give all away to him ;
Think never of yourself ; throw by your pride,
Hope, fear, — your own good as you saw it once,
And love him simply for his very self.
Remember, I (and what am I to you ?)
Would give up all for one, leave throne, lose life,
Do all but just unlove him ! He loves me.
 Con. He shall.
 Queen. You, step inside my inmost heart !
Give me your own heart : let us have one heart !
I 'll come to you for counsel ; "this he says,
This he does ; what should this amount to,
 pray ?
Beseech you, change it into current coin !
Is that worth kisses ? Shall I please him
 there ? "

And then we 'll speak in turn of you — what
 else ?
Your love, according to your beauty's worth,
For you shall have some noble love, all gold :
Whom choose you ? we will get him at your
 choice.
— Constance, I leave you. Just a minute since,
I felt as I must die or be alone
Breathing my soul into an ear like yours :
Now, I would face the world with my new life,
Wear my new crown. I 'll walk around the
 rooms,
And then come back and tell you how it feels.
How soon a smile of God can change the world !
How we are made for happiness — how work
Grows play, adversity a winning fight !
True, I have lost so many years : what then ?
Many remain : God has been very good.
You, stay here ! 'T is as different from dreams,
From the mind's cold calm estimate of bliss,
As these stone statues from the flesh and
 blood.
The comfort thou hast caused mankind, God's
 moon !
[*She goes out, leaving* CONSTANCE. *Dance-music from*
  within.
  (NORBERT *enters.*)
 Nor. Well ? we have but one minute and one
  word !
 Con. I am yours, Norbert !
 Nor.   Yes, mine.
 Con.   Not till now !
You were mine. Now I give myself to you.
 Nor. Constance ?
 Con. Your own ! I know the thriftier way
Of giving — haply, 't is the wiser way.
Meaning to give a treasure, I might dole
Coin after coin out (each, as that were all,
With a new largess still at each despair)
And force you keep in sight the deed, preserve
Exhaustless till the end my part and yours,
My giving and your taking ; both our joys
Dying together. Is it the wiser way ?
I choose the simpler ; I give all at once.
Know what you have to trust to, trade upon !
Use it, abuse it, — anything but think
Hereafter, "Had I known she loved me so,
And what my means, I might have thriven with
 it."
This is your means. I give you all myself.
 Nor. I take you and thank God.
 Con.   Look on through years !
We cannot kiss, a second day like this ;
Else were this earth no earth.
 Nor.   With this day's heat
We shall go on through years of cold.
 Con.   So, best !
— I try to see those years — I think I see.
You walk quick and new warmth comes ; you
 look back
And lay all to the first glow — not sit down
Forever brooding on a day like this
While seeing embers whiten and love die.
Yes, love lives best in its effect ; and mine,
Full in its own life, yearns to live in yours.
 Nor. Just so. I take and know you all at
 once.
Your soul is disengaged so easily.

Your face is there, I know you ; give me time,
Let me be proud and think you shall know me.
My soul is slower : in a life I roll
The minute out whereto you condense yours —
The whole slow circle round you I must move,
To be just you. I look to a long life
To decompose this minute, prove its worth.
'T is the sparks' long succession one by one
Shall show you, in the end, what fire was
    crammed
In that mere stone you struck : how could you
    know,
If it lay ever unproved in your sight,
As now my heart lies ? your own warmth would
    hide
Its coldness, were it cold.
    Con.   But how prove, how ?
    Nor.   Prove in my life, you ask ?
    Con.   Quick, Norbert — how ?
    Nor.   That 's easy told. I count life just a
    stuff
To try the soul's strength on, educe the man.
Who keeps one end in view makes all things
    serve
As with the body — he who hurls a lance
Or heaps up stone on stone, shows strength
    alike :
So must I seize and task all means to prove
And show this soul of mine, you crown as yours,
And justify us both.
    Con.   Could you write books,
Paint pictures ! One sits down in poverty
And writes or paints, with pity for the rich.
    Nor.   And loves one's painting and one's
    writing, then.
And not one's mistress ! All is best, believe,
And we best as no other than we are.
We live, and they experiment on life —
Those poets, painters, all who stand aloof
To overlook the farther. Let us be
The thing they look at ! I might take your
    face
And write of it and paint it — to what end ?
For whom ? what pale dictatress in the air
Feeds, smiling sadly, her fine ghost-like form
With earth's real blood and breath, the beaute-
    ous life
She makes despised forever ? You are mine,
Made for me, not for others in the world,
Nor yet for that which I should call my art,
The cold calm power to see how fair you look.
I come to you ; I leave you not, to write
Or paint. You are, I am : let Rubens there
Paint us !
    Con.   So, best !
    Nor.   I understand your soul,
You live, and rightly sympathize with life,
With action, power, success. This way is
    straight ;
And time were short beside, to let me change
The craft my childhood learnt : my craft
    shall serve.
Men set me here to subjugate, enclose,
Manure their barren lives, and force thence
    fruit
First for themselves, and afterward for me
In the due tithe ; the task of some one soul,
Through ways of work appointed by the world.

I am not bid create — men see no star
Transfiguring my brow to warrant that —
But find and bind and bring to bear their wills
So I began : to-night sees how I end.
What if it see, too, power's first outbreak here
Amid the warmth, surprise and sympathy,
And instincts of the heart that teach the head ?
What if the people have discerned at length
The dawn of the next nature, novel brain
Whose will they venture in the place of theirs,
Whose work, they trust, shall find them as
    novel ways
To untried heights which yet he only sees ?
I felt it when you kissed me. See this Queen,
This people — in our phrase this mass of
    men —
See how the mass lies passive to my hand
Now that my hand is plastic, with you by
To make the muscles iron ! Oh, an end
Shall crown this issue as this crowns the first !
My will be on the people ! then, the strain,
The grappling of the potter with his clay,
The long uncertain struggle, — the success
And consummation of the spirit-work,
Some vase shape to the curl of the god's lip,
While rounded fair for human sense to see
The Graces in a dance men recognize
With turbulent applause and laughs of heart !
So triumph ever shall renew itself ;
Ever shall end in efforts higher yet,
Ever begin . . .
    Con.   I ever helping ?
    Nor.   Thus !
    (*As he embraces her, the* QUEEN *enters.*)
    Con.   Hist, madam ! So have I performed
    my part.
You see your gratitude's true decency,
Norbert ? A little slow in seeing it !
Begin, to end the sooner ! What 's a kiss ?
    Nor.   Constance ?
    Con.   Why, must I teach it you again ?
You want a witness to your dulness, sir ?
What was I saying these ten minutes long ?
Then I repeat — when some young handsome
    man
Like you has acted out a part like yours,
Is pleased to fall in love with one beyond,
So very far beyond him, as he says —
So hopelessly in love that but to speak
Would prove him mad, — he thinks judiciously,
And makes some insignificant good soul,
Like me, his friend, adviser, confidant,
And very stalking-horse to cover him
In following after what he dares not face —
When his end 's gained — (sir, do you under-
    stand ?)
When she, he dares not face, has loved him
    first,
— May I not say so, madam ? — tops his hope,
And overpasses so his wildest dream,
With glad consent of all, and most of her
The confidant who brought the same about —
Why, in the moment when such joy explodes,
I do hold that the merest gentleman
Will not start rudely from the stalking-horse,
Dismiss it with a " There, enough of you ! "
Forget it, show his back unmannerly ;
But like a liberal heart will rather turn

And say, " A tingling time of hope was ours ;
Betwixt the fears and falterings, we two lived
A chanceful time in waiting for the prize :
The confidant, the Constance, served not ill.
And though I shall forget her in good time,
Her use being answered now, as reason bids,
Nay as herself bids from her heart of hearts, —
Still, she has rights, the first thanks go to her,
The first good praise goes to the prosperous
     tool,
And the first — which is the last — rewarding
     kiss."
     Nor. Constance, it is a dream — ah, see,
     you smile !
     Con. So, now his part being properly per-
     formed,
Madam, I turn to you and finish mine
As duly ; I do justice in my turn.
Yes, madam, he has loved you — long and
     well ;
He could not hope to tell you so — 't was I
Who served to prove your soul accessible,
I led his thoughts on, drew them to their place
When they had wandered else into despair,
And kept love constant toward its natural aim.
Enough, my part is played ; you stoop half-way
And meet us royally and spare our fears :
'T is like yourself. He thanks you, so do I.
Take him — with my full heart ! my work is
     praised
By what comes of it. Be you happy, both !
Yourself — the only one on earth who can —
Do all for him, much more than a mere heart
Which though warm is not useful in its warmth
As the silk vesture of a queen ! fold that
Around him gently, tenderly. For him —
For him, — he knows his own part !
     Nor.   Have you done ?
I take the jest at last. Should I speak now ?
Was yours the wager, Constance, foolish child,
Or did you but accept it ? Well — at least
You lose by it.
     Con.   Nay, madam, 't is your turn !
Restrain him still from speech a little more,
And make him happier as more confident !
Pity him, madam, he is timid yet !
Mark, Norbert ! Do not shrink how ! Here I
     yield
My whole right in you to the Queen, observe !
With her go put in practice the great schemes
You teem with, follow the career else closed —
Be all you cannot be except by her !
Behold her ! — Madam, say for pity's sake
Anything — frankly say you love him ! Else
He 'll not believe it : there 's more earnest in
His fear than you conceive : I know the man !
     Nor. I know the woman somewhat, and
     confess
I thought she had jested better : she begins
To overcharge her part. I gravely wait
Your pleasure, madam : where is my reward ?
     Queen. Norbert, this wild girl (whom I
     recognize
Scarce more than you do, in her fancy-fit,
Eccentric speech and variable mirth,
Not very wise perhaps and somewhat bold,
Yet suitable, the whole night's work being
     strange)

— May still be right : I may do well to speak
And make authentic what appears a dream
To even myself. For, what she says is true :
Yes, Norbert — what you spoke just now of love,
Devotion, stirred no novel sense in me,
But justified a warmth felt long before.
Yes, from the first — I loved you, I shall say :
Strange ! but I do grow stronger, now 't is said.
Your courage helps mine : you did well to speak
To-night, the night that crowns your twelve-
     months' toil :
But still I had not waited to discern
Your heart so long, believe me ! From the first
The source of so much zeal was almost plain,
In absence even of your own words just now
Which hazarded the truth. 'T is very strange,
But takes a happy ending — in your love
Which mine meets : be it so ! as you choose me,
So I choose you.
     Nor.   And worthily you choose.
I will not be unworthy your esteem,
No, madam. I do love you ; I will meet
Your nature, now I know it. This was well.
I see, — you dare and you are justified :
But none had ventured such experiment,
Less versed than you in nobleness of heart,
Less confident of finding such in me.
I joy that thus you test me ere you grant
The dearest, richest, beauteousest and best
Of women to my arms : 't is like yourself.
So — back again into my part's set words —
Devotion to the uttermost is yours,
But no, you cannot, madam, even you,
Create in me the love our Constance does.
Or — something truer to the tragic phrase —
Not yon magnolia-bell superb with scent
Invites a certain insect — that 's myself —
But the small eye-flower nearer to the ground.
I take this lady.
     Con.   Stay — not hers, the trap —
Stay, Norbert — that mistake were worst of all !
He is too cunning, madam ! It was I,
I, Norbert, who . . .
     Nor.   You, was it, Constance ? Then,
But for the grace of this divinest hour
Which gives me you, I might not pardon here !
I am the Queen's ; she only knows my brain :
She may experiment upon my heart
And I instruct her too by the result.
But you, Sweet, you who know me, who so long
Have told my heartbeats over, held my life
In those white hands of yours, — it is not well !
     Con. Tush ! I have said it, did I not say it
     all ?
The life, for her — the heartbeats, for her sake !
     Nor. Enough ! my cheek grows red, I think.
     Your test ?
There 's not the meanest woman in the world,
Not she I least could love in all the world,
Whom, did she love me, had love proved itself,
I dare insult as you insult me now.
Constance, I could say, if it must be said,
" Take back the soul you offer, I keep mine ! "
But — " Take the soul still quivering on your
     hand,
The soul so offered, which I cannot use,
And, please you, give it to some playful friend,
For — what 's the trifle he requites me with ? "

I, tempt a woman, to amuse a man,
That two may mock her heart if it succumb ?
No : fearing God and standing 'neath his
　　heaven,
I would not dare insult a woman so,
Were she the meanest woman in the world,
And he, I cared to please, ten emperors !
　　Con.　Norbert !
　　Nor.　　　　I love once as I live but once.
What case is this to think or talk about ?
I love you.　Would it mend the case at all
If such a step as this killed love in me ?
Your part were done : account to God for it !
But mine — could murdered love get up again,
And kneel to whom you please to designate,
And make you mirth ?　It is too horrible.
You did not know this, Constance ? now you
　　know
That body and soul have each one life, but
　　one :
And here 's my love, here, living, at your feet.
　　Con.　See the Queen !　Norbert — this one
　　more last word —
If thus you have taken jest for earnest — thus
Loved me in earnest . . .
　　Nor.　　　　　　Ah, no jest holds here !
Where is the laughter in which jests break up,
And what this horror that grows palpable ?
Madam — why grasp you thus the balcony ?
Have I done ill ?　Have I not spoken truth ?
How could I other ?　Was it not your test,
To try me, what my love for Constance meant ?
Madam, your royal soul itself approves,
The first, that I should choose thus ! so one takes
A beggar, — asks him, what would buy his
　　child ?
And then approves the expected laugh of scorn
Returned as something noble from the rags.
Speak, Constance, I 'm the beggar !　Ha,
　　what 's this ?
You two glare each at each like panthers now.
Constance, the world fades ; only you stand
　　there !
You did not, in to-night's wild whirl of things,
Sell me — your soul of souls, for any price ?
No — no — 't is easy to believe in you !
Was it your love's mad trial to o'ertop
Mine by this vain self-sacrifice ? well, still —
Though I might curse, I love you.　I am love
And cannot change : love 's self is at your feet !
　　　　　　　　　　[*The* QUEEN *goes out.*
　　Con.　Feel my heart ; let it die against your
　　own !
　　Nor.　Against my own.　Explain not ; let this
　　be !
This is life's height.
　　Con.　　　　Yours, yours, yours !
　　Nor.　　　　　　　　You and I —
Why care by what meanders we are here
I' the centre of the labyrinth ?　Men have died
Trying to find this place, which we have found.
　　Con.　Found, found !
　　Nor.　　Sweet, never fear what she can do !
We are past harm now.

　　Con.　　　　　On the breast of God.
I thought of men — as if you were a man.
Tempting him with a crown !
　　Nor.　　　　　　This must end here :
It is too perfect.
　　Con.　　　There 's the music stopped.
What measured heavy tread ?　It is one blaze
About me and within me.
　　Nor.　　　　　Oh, some death
Will run its sudden finger round this spark
And sever us from the rest !
　　Con.　　　　　And so do well.
Now the doors open,
　　Nor.　　　　'T is the guard comes.
　　Con.　　　　　　　　　Kiss !

BEN KARSHOOK'S WISDOM

The eighth line of the fourteenth section of
One Word More reads,

　"Karshish, Cleon, Norbert and the fifty."

Originally it read,

　"Karshook, Cleon, Norbert and the fifty."

The reference apparently was to the poem writ-
ten in April, 1854, and printed in *The Keep-
sake*, an annual edited by Miss Power, a niece of
Lady Blessington, in whom Dickens also took
an interest.　It may have been Browning's
intention to include this poem in *Men and Wo-
men*, but he never did place it there, and finally
dropped Karshook and substituted Karshish,
who narrates his medical experience.

I

"WOULD a man 'scape the rod ? "
　　Rabbi Ben Karshook saith,
"See that he turn to God
　　The day before his death."

"Ay, could a man inquire
　　When it shall come ! " I say.
The Rabbi's eye shoots fire —
　　"Then let him turn to-day ! "

II

Quoth a young Sadducee :
　"Reader of many rolls,
Is it so certain we
　　Have, as they tell us, souls ? "

"Son, there is no reply ! "
　　The Rabbi bit his beard :
"Certain, a soul have *I* —
　We may have none," he sneered.

Thus Karshook, the Hiram's-Hammer,
　　The Right-hand Temple-column,
Taught babes in grace their grammar,
　　And struck the simple, solemn.

DRAMATIS PERSONÆ

THE volume bearing the title *Dramatis Personæ* was published in 1864 and the contents remained unchanged in subsequent editions except that two short poems were added in the edition of 1868. The first poem was however originally entitled *James Lee*. The first six stanzas of the sixth section of the poem were first printed in 1836 in Mr. Fox's *The Monthly Repository*, and bore the title merely *Lines*, with the signature Z.

JAMES LEE'S WIFE

I

JAMES LEE'S WIFE SPEAKS AT THE WINDOW

AH, Love, but a day
    And the world has changed!
The sun's away,
    And the bird estranged;
The wind has dropped,
    And the sky's deranged:
Summer has stopped.

Look in my eyes!
    Wilt thou change too?
Should I fear surprise?
    Shall I find aught new
In the old and dear,
    In the good and true,
With the changing year?

Thou art a man,
    But I am thy love.
For the lake, its swan;
    For the dell its dove;
And for thee — (oh, haste!)
    Me, to bend above,
Me, to hold embraced.

II

BY THE FIRESIDE

Is all our fire of shipwreck wood,
    Oak and pine?
Oh, for the ills half-understood,
    The dim dead woe
    Long ago
Befallen this bitter coast of France!
Well, poor sailors took their chance;
    I take mine.

A ruddy shaft our fire must shoot
    O'er the sea:
Do sailors eye the casement — mute
    Drenched and stark,
    From their bark —
And envy, gnash their teeth for hate
O' the warm safe house and happy freight
    — Thee and me?

God help you, sailors, at your need!
    Spare the curse!
For some ships, safe in port indeed,
    Rot and rust,
    Run to dust,
All through worms i' the wood, which crept,
Gnawed our hearts out while we slept:
    That is worse.

Who lived here before us two?
    Old-world pairs.
Did a woman ever — would I knew! —
    Watch the man
    With whom began
Love's voyage full-sail,—(now gnash your teeth!)
When planks start, open hell beneath
    Unawares?

III

IN THE DOORWAY

The swallow has set her six young on the rail,
    And looks seaward:
The water's in stripes like a snake, olive-pale
    To the leeward, —
On the weather-side, black, spotted white with
        the wind.
"Good fortune departs, and disaster's be
        hind," —
Hark, the wind with its wants and its infinite
        wail!

Our fig-tree, that leaned for the saltness, has
        furled
    Her five fingers,
Each leaf like a hand opened wide to the world
        Where there lingers
No glint of the gold, Summer sent for her sake:
How the vines writhe in rows, each impaled on
        its stake!
My heart shrivels up and my spirit shrinks
        curled.

Yet here are we two; we have love, house
        enough,
    With the field there,
This house of four rooms, that field red and
        rough,
        Though it yield there,
For the rabbit that robs, scarce a blade or a
        bent;
If a magpie alight now, it seems an event;
And they both will be gone at November's re-
        buff.

But why must cold spread? but wherefore bring
        change
    To the spirit.

God meant should mate his with an infinite
    range,
    And inherit
His power to put life in the darkness and cold ?
Oh, live and love worthily, bear and be bold !
Whom Summer made friends of, let Winter
    estrange !

IV

ALONG THE BEACH

I will be quiet and talk with you,
    And reason why you are wrong.
You wanted my love — is that much true ?
    And so I did love, so I do :
    What has come of it all along ?

I took you — how could I otherwise ?
    For a world to me, and more ;
For all, love greatens and glorifies
Till God 's aglow, to the loving eyes,
    In what was mere earth before.

Yes, earth — yes, mere ignoble earth !
    Now do I mis-state, mistake ?
Do I wrong your weakness and call it worth ?
Expect all harvest, dread no dearth,
    Seal my sense up for your sake ?

Oh, Love, Love, no, Love ! not so, indeed !
    You were just weak earth, I knew :
With much in you waste, with many a weed,
And plenty of passions run to seed,
    But a little good grain too.

And such as you were, I took you for mine :
    Did not you find me yours,
To watch the olive and wait the vine,
And wonder when rivers of oil and wine
    Would flow, as the Book assures ?

Well, and if none of these good things came,
    What did the failure prove ?
The man was my whole world, all the same,
With his flowers to praise or his weeds to blame,
    And, either or both, to love.

Yet this turns now to a fault — there ! there !
    That I do love, watch too long,
And wait too well, and weary and wear ;
And 't is all an old story, and my despair
    Fit subject for some new song :

"How the light, light love, he has wings to fly
    At suspicion of a bond :
My wisdom has bidden your pleasure good-by,
Which will turn up next in a laughing eye,
    And why should you look beyond ? "

V

ON THE CLIFF

I leaned on the turf,
I looked at a rock
Left dry by the surf ;

For the turf, to call it grass were to mock :
Dead to the roots, so deep was done
The work of the summer sun.

And the rock lay flat
As an anvil's face :
No iron like that !
Baked dry ; of a weed, of a shell, no trace
Sunshine outside, but ice at the core,
Death's altar by the lone shore.

On the turf, sprang gay
With his films of blue,
No cricket, I 'll say,
But a warhorse, barded and chanfroned too,
The gift of a quixote-mage to his knight,
Real fairy, with wings all right.

On the rock, they scorch
Like a drop of fire
From a brandished torch,
Fall two red fans of a butterfly :
No turf, no rock : in their ugly stead,
See, wonderful blue and red !

Is it not so
With the minds of men ?
The level and low,
The burnt and bare, in themselves ; but then
With such a blue and red grace, not theirs, —
Love settling unawares !

VI

READING A BOOK, UNDER THE CLIFF

"Still ailing, Wind ? Wilt be appeased or
    no ?
    Which needs the other's office, thou or I ?
Dost want to be disburdened of a woe,
    And can, in truth, my voice untie
Its links, and let it go ?

"Art thou a dumb, wronged thing that would
    be righted,
    Entrusting thus thy cause to me ? Forbear !
No tongue can mend such pleadings ; faith, re-
    quited
    With falsehood, — love, at last aware
Of scorn, — hopes, early blighted, —

"We have them ; but I know not any tone
    So fit as thine to falter forth a sorrow :
Dost think men would go mad without a moan,
    If they knew any way to borrow
A pathos like thy own ?

"Which sigh wouldst mock, of all the sighs ?
    The one
    So long escaping from lips starved and blue,
That lasts while on her pallet-bed the nun
    Stretches her length ; her foot comes through
The straw she shivers on ;

"You had not thought she was so tall, and
    spent,
    Her shrunk lids open, her lean fingers shut

Close, close, their sharp and livid nails indent
  The clammy palm; then all is mute:
That way, the spirit went.

" Or wouldst thou rather that I understand
  Thy will to help me? — like the dog I found
Once, pacing sad this solitary strand,
  Who would not take my food, poor hound,
But whined and licked my hand."

All this, and more, comes from some young
    man's pride
Of power to see, — in failure and mistake,
Relinquishment, disgrace, on every side, —
  Merely examples for his sake,
Helps to his path untried:

Instances he must — simply recognize?
  Oh, more than so! — must, with a learner's
    zeal,
Make doubly prominent, twice emphasize,
  By added touches that reveal
The god in babe's disguise.

Oh, he knows what defeat means, and the
    rest!
  Himself the undefeated that shall be:
Failure, disgrace, he flings them you to test, —
  His triumph, in eternity
Too plainly manifest!

Whence, judge if he learn forthwith what the
    wind
  Means in its moaning — by the happy prompt
Instinctive way of youth, I mean; for kind
  Calm years, exacting their accompt
Of pain, mature the mind:

And some midsummer morning, at the lull
  Just about daybreak, as he looks across
A sparkling foreign country, wonderful
  To the sea's edge for gloom and gloss,
Next minute must annul, —

Then, when the wind begins among the vines,
  So low, so low, what shall it say but this?
" Here is the change beginning, here the lines
  Circumscribe beauty, set to bliss
The limit time assigns."

Nothing can be as it has been before;
  Better, so call it, only not the same.
To draw one beauty into our hearts' core,
  And keep it changeless! such our claim;
So answered, — Nevermore!

Simple? Why this is the old woe o' the world;
  Tune, to whose rise and fall we live and
    die.
Rise with it, then! Rejoice that man is hurled
  From change to change unceasingly,
His soul's wings never furled!

That 's a new question; still replies the fact,
  Nothing endures: the wind moans, saying
    so;

We moan in acquiescence: there 's life's pact.
  Perhaps probation — do *I* know?
God does: endure his act!

Only, for man, how bitter not to grave
  On his soul's hands' palms one fair good wise
    thing
Just as he grasped it! For himself, death's
    wave;
  While time first washes — ah, the sting! —
O'er all he 'd sink to save.

VII

AMONG THE ROCKS

Oh, good gigantic smile o' the brown old earth,
  This autumn morning! How he sets his
    bones
To bask i' the sun, and thrusts out knees and
    feet
For the ripple to run over in its mirth;
  Listening the while, where on the heap of
    stones
The white breast of the sea-lark twitters sweet.

That is the doctrine, simple, ancient, true;
  Such is life's trial, as old earth smiles and
    knows.
If you loved only what were worth your love,
Love were clear gain, and wholly well for
    you:
  Make the low nature better by your throes!
Give earth yourself, go up for gain above!

VIII

BESIDE THE DRAWING-BOARD

I

" As like as a Hand to another Hand! "
  Whoever said that foolish thing,
Could not have studied to understand
  The councils of God in fashioning,
Out of the infinite love of his heart,
This Hand, whose beauty I praise, apart
From the world of wonder left to praise,
If I tried to learn the other ways
Of love in its skill, or love in its power.
  " As like as a Hand to another Hand: "
  Who said that, never took his stand,
Found and followed, like me, an hour,
The beauty in this, — how free, how fine
To fear, almost, — of the limit-line!
As I looked at this, and learned and drew,
  Drew and learned, and looked again,
While fast the happy minutes flew,
  Its beauty mounted into my brain,
  And a fancy seized me; I was fain
To efface my work, begin anew,
Kiss what before I only drew;
Ay, laying the red chalk 'twixt my lips,
  With soul to help if the mere lips failed,
  I kissed all right where the drawing ailed,
Kissed fast the grace that somehow slips
Still from one's soulless finger-tips.

II

'Tis a clay cast, the perfect thing,
  From Hand live once, dead long ago:
Princess-like it wears the ring
  To fancy's eye, by which we know
That here at length a master found
  His match, a proud lone soul its mate,
As soaring genius sank to ground,
  And pencil could not emulate
The beauty in this, — how free, how fine
To fear almost ! — of the limit-line.
Long ago the god, like me
The worm, learned, each in our degree:
Looked and loved, learned and drew,
  Drew and learned and loved again,
While fast the happy minutes flew,
  Till beauty mounted into his brain
And on the finger which outvied
  His art he placed the ring that 's there,
Still by fancy's eye descried,
  In token of a marriage rare:
For him on earth, his art's despair,
For him in heaven, his soul's fit bride.

III

Little girl with the poor coarse hand
  I turned from to a cold clay cast —
I have my lesson, understand
  The worth of flesh and blood at last !
Nothing but beauty in a Hand?
  Because he could not change the hue,
  Mend the lines and make them true
To this which met his soul's demand, —
  Would Da Vinci turn from you ?
I hear him laugh my woes to scorn —
" The fool forsooth is all forlorn
Because the beauty, she thinks best,
Lived long ago or was never born, —
Because no beauty bears the test
In this rough peasant Hand ! Confessed
'Art is null and study void !'
So sayest thou? So said not I,
Who threw the faulty pencil by,
And years instead of hours employed,
Learning the veritable use
Of flesh and bone and nerve beneath
Lines and hue of the outer sheath,
If haply I might reproduce
One motive of the powers profuse,
Flesh and bone and nerve that make
The poorest coarsest human hand
An object worthy to be scanned
A whole life long for their sole sake.
Shall earth and the cramped moment-space
Yield the heavenly crowning grace ?
Now the parts and then the whole !
Who art thou, with stinted soul
And stunted body, thus to cry,
'I love, — shall that be life's strait dole ?
I must live beloved or die !'
This peasant hand that spins the wool
And bakes the bread, why lives it on,
Poor and coarse with beauty gone, —
What use survives the beauty ? " Fool !

Go, little girl with the poor coarse hand !
I have my lesson, shall understand.

IX

ON DECK

There is nothing to remember in me,
  Nothing I ever said with a grace,
Nothing I did that you care to see,
  Nothing I was that deserves a place
In your mind, now I leave you, set you free.

Conceded ! In turn, concede to me,
  Such things have been as a mutual flame.
Your soul 's locked fast ; but, love for a key,
  You might let it loose, till I grew the same
In your eyes, as in mine you stand: strange
    plea !

For then, then, what would it matter to me
  That I was the harsh, ill-favored one ?
We both should be like as pea and pea ;
  It was ever so since the world begun :
So, let me proceed with my reverie.

How strange it were if you had all me,
  As I have all you in my heart and brain,
You, whose least word brought gloom or glee,
  Who never lifted the hand in vain —
Will hold mine yet, from over the sea !

Strange, if a face, when you thought of me,
  Rose like your own face present now,
With eyes as dear in their due degree,
  Much such a mouth, and as bright a brow,
Till you saw yourself, while you cried "'T is
    She ! "

Well, you may, you must, set down to me
  Love that was life, life that was love ;
A tenure of breath at your lips' decree,
  A passion to stand as your thoughts approve,
A rapture to fall where your foot might be.

But did one touch of such love for me
  Come in a word or a look of yours,
Whose words and looks will, circling, flee
  Round me and round while life endures, —
Could I fancy " As I feel, thus feels He ; "

Why, fade you might to a thing like me,
  And your hair grow these coarse hanks of
    hair,
Your skin, this bark of a gnarled tree, —
  You might turn myself ! — should I know or
    care,
When I should be dead of joy, James Lee ?

GOLD HAIR

A STORY OF PORNIC

  This poem was issued by itself as well as
included later in *Dramatis Personæ*, and si-
multaneously with its appearance in England it
was printed in *The Atlantic Monthly*. It was
written in Normandy, and in a letter printed in

Mrs. Orr's *Life*, II. 395, there is an account of the destruction of the church referred to in the poem.

Oh, the beautiful girl, too white,
  Who lived at Pornic, down by the sea,
Just where the sea and the Loire unite!
  And a boasted name in Brittany
She bore, which I will not write.

Too white, for the flower of life is red:
  Her flesh was the soft seraphic screen
Of a soul that is meant (her parents said)
  To just see earth, and hardly be seen,
And blossom in heaven instead.

Yet earth saw one thing, one how fair!
  One grace that grew to its full on earth:
Smiles might be sparse on her cheek so spare,
  And her waist want half a girdle's girth,
But she had her great gold hair.

Hair, such a wonder of flix and floss,
  Freshness and fragrance — floods of it, too!
Gold, did I say? Nay, gold's mere dross:
  Here, Life smiled, "Think what I meant to do!"
And Love sighed, "Fancy my loss!"

So, when she died, it was scarce more strange
  Than that, when delicate evening dies,
And you follow its spent sun's pallid range,
  There's a shoot of color startles the skies
With sudden, violent change, —

That, while the breath was nearly to seek,
  As they put the little cross to her lips,
She changed; a spot came out on her cheek,
  A spark from her eye in mid-eclipse,
And she broke forth, "I must speak!"

"Not my hair!" made the girl her moan —
  "All the rest is gone or to go;
But the last, last grace, my all, my own,
  Let it stay in the grave, that the ghosts may know!
Leave my poor gold hair alone!"

The passion thus vented, dead lay she;
  Her parents sobbed their worst on that;
All friends joined in, nor observed degree:
  For indeed the hair was to wonder at,
As it spread — not flowing free,

But curled around her brow, like a crown,
  And coiled beside her cheeks, like a cap,
And calmed about her neck — ay, down
  To her breast, pressed flat, without a gap
I' the gold, it reached her gown.

All kissed that face, like a silver wedge
  'Mid the yellow wealth, nor disturbed its hair:
E'en the priest allowed death's privilege,
  As he planted the crucifix with care
On her breast, 'twixt edge and edge.

And thus was she buried, inviolate
  Of body and soul, in the very space

By the altar; keeping saintly state
  In Pornic church, for her pride of race,
Pure life and piteous fate.

And in after-time would your fresh tear fall,
  Though your mouth might twitch with a dubious smile,
As they told you of gold, both robe and pall,
  How she prayed them leave it alone awhile,
So it never was touched at all.

Years flew; this legend grew at last
  The life of the lady; all she had done,
All been, in the memories fading fast
  Of lover and friend, was summed in one
Sentence survivors passed:

To wit, she was meant for heaven, not earth;
  Had turned an angel before the time:
Yet, since she was mortal, in such dearth
  Of frailty, all you could count a crime
Was — she knew her gold hair's worth.

At little pleasant Pornic church,
  It chanced, the pavement wanted repair,
Was taken to pieces: left in the lurch,
  A certain sacred space lay bare,
And the boys began research.

'Twas the space where our sires would lay saint,
  A benefactor, — a bishop, suppose,
A baron with armor-adornments quaint,
  Dame with chased ring and jewelled rose,
Things sanctity saves from taint;

So we come to find them in after-days
  When the corpse is presumed to have done with gauds
Of use to the living, in many ways:
  For the boys get pelf, and the town applauds,
And the church deserves the praise.

They grubbed with a will: and at length — *O cor
  Humanum, pectora cœca*, and the rest! —
They found — no gaud they were prying for,
  No ring, no rose, but — who would have guessed? —
A double Louis-d'or!

Here was a case for the priest: he heard,
  Marked, inwardly digested, laid
Finger on nose, smiled, "There's a bird
  Chirps in my ear:" then, "Bring a spade,
Dig deeper!" — he gave the word.

And lo, when they came to the coffin-lid,
  Or rotten planks which composed it once,
Why, there lay the girl's skull wedged amid
  A mint of money, it served for the nonce
To hold in its hair-heaps hid!

Hid there? Why? Could the girl be wont
  (She the stainless soul) to treasure up

Money, earth's trash and heaven's affront?
  Had a spider found out the communion-cup,
Was a toad in the christening-font?

Truth is truth: too true it was.
  Gold! She hoarded and hugged it first,
Longed for it, leaned o'er it, loved it — alas —
  Till the humor grew to a head and burst,
And she cried, at the final pass, —

" Talk not of God, my heart is stone!
  Nor lover nor friend — be gold for both!
Gold I lack; and, my all, my own,
  It shall hide in my hair. I scarce die loth
If they let my hair alone!"

Louis-d'or, some six times five,
  And duly double, every piece.
Now, do you see? With the priest to shrive,
  With parents preventing her soul's release
By kisses that kept alive, —

With heaven's gold gates about to ope,
  With friends' praise, gold-like, lingering still,
An instinct had bidden the girl's hand grope
  For gold, the true sort — " Gold in heaven, if
    you will;
But I keep earth's too, I hope."

Enough! The priest took the grave's grim
    yield:
The parents, they eyed that price of sin
As if *thirty pieces* lay revealed
  On the place *to bury strangers in*,
The hideous Potter's Field.

But the priest bethought him: " 'Milk that's
    spilt'
  — You know the adage! Watch and pray!
Saints tumble to earth with so slight a tilt!
  It would build a new altar; that, we may!"
And the altar therewith was built.

Why I deliver this horrible verse?
  As the text of a sermon, which now I preach:
Evil or good may be better or worse
  In the human heart, but the mixture of each
Is a marvel and a curse.

The candid incline to surmise of late
  That the Christian faith proves false, I find;
For our Essays-and-Reviews' debate
  Begins to tell on the public mind,
And Colenso's words have weight:

I still, to suppose it true, for my part,
  See reasons and reasons; this, to begin:
'T is the faith that launched point-blank her dart
  At the head of a lie — taught Original Sin,
The Corruption of Man's Heart.

THE WORST OF IT

Would it were I had been false, not you!
  I that am nothing, not you that are all:
I, never the worse for a touch or two
  On my speckled hide; not you, the pride

Of the day, my swan, that a first fleck's fall
  On her wonder of white must unswan, undo!

I had dipped in life's struggle and, out again,
  Bore specks of it here, there, easy to see,
When I found my swan and the cure was plain;
  The dull turned bright as I caught your white
On my bosom: you saved me — saved in vain
  If you ruined yourself, and all through me!

Yes, all through the speckled beast that I am,
  Who taught you to stoop; you gave me your-
    self,
And bound your soul by the vows that damn:
  Since on better thought you break, as you
    ought,
Vows — words, no angel set down, some elf
  Mistook, — for an oath, an epigram!

Yes, might I judge you, here were my heart,
  And a hundred its like, to treat as you
    pleased!
I choose to be yours, for my proper part,
  Yours, leave or take, or mar me or make;
If I acquiesce, why should you be teased
  With the conscience-prick and the memory-
    smart?

But what will God say? Oh, my sweet,
  Think, and be sorry you did this thing!
Though earth were unworthy to feel your feet,
  There's a heaven above may deserve your
    love:
Should you forfeit heaven for a snapt gold ring
  And a promise broke, were it just or meet?

And I to have tempted you! I, who tried
  Your soul, no doubt, till it sank! Unwise,
I loved, and was lowly, loved and aspired,
  Loved, grieving or glad, till I made you mad,
And you meant to have hated and despised —
  Whereas, you deceived me nor inquired!

She, ruined? How? No heaven for her?
  Crowns to give, and none for the brow
That looked like marble and smelt like myrrh?
  Shall the robe be worn, and the palm-branch
    borne,
And she go graceless, she graced now
  Beyond all saints, as themselves aver?

Hardly! That must be understood!
  The earth is your place of penance, then;
And what will it prove? I desire your good,
  But, plot as I may, I can find no way
How a blow should fall, such as falls on men,
  Nor prove too much for your womanhood.

It will come, I suspect, at the end of life,
  When you walk alone, and review the past;
And I, who so long shall have done with strife,
  And journeyed my stage and earned my wage
And retired as was right, — I am called at
    last
When the devil stabs you, to lend the knife.

He stabs for the minute of trivial wrong,
  Nor the other hours are able to save,

The happy, that lasted my whole life long :
For a promise broke, not for first words spoke,
The true, the only, that turn my grave
To a blaze of joy and a crash of song.

Witness beforehand ! Off I trip
On a safe path gay through the flowers you
flung :
My very name made great by your lip,
And my heart aglow with the good I know
Of a perfect year when we both were young,
And I tasted the angels' fellowship.

And witness, moreover . . . Ah, but wait !
I spy the loop whence an arrow shoots !
It may be for yourself, when you meditate,
That you grieve — for slain ruth, murdered
truth :
"Though falsehood escape in the end, what
boots ?
How truth would have triumphed ! " — you
sigh too late.

Ay, who would have triumphed like you, I
say !
Well, it is lost now ; well, you must bear,
Abide and grow fit for a better day :
You should hardly grudge, could I be your
judge !
But hush ! For you, can be no despair :
There 's amends : 't is a secret : hope and pray !

For I was true at least — oh, true enough !
And, Dear, truth is not as good as it seems !
Commend me to conscience ! Idle stuff !
Much help is in mine, as I mope and pine,
And skulk through day, and scowl in my dreams
At my swan's obtaining the crow's rebuff.

Men tell me of truth now — " False ! " I cry :
Of beauty — " A mask, friend ! Look be-
neath ! "
We take our own method, the devil and I,
With pleasant and fair and wise and rare :
And the best we wish to what lives, is — death ;
Which even in wishing, perhaps we lie !

Far better commit a fault and have done —
As you, Dear ! — forever ; and choose the
pure,
And look where the healing waters run,
And strive and strain to be good again,
And a place in the other world ensure,
All glass and gold, with God for its sun.

Misery ! What shall I say or do ?
I cannot advise, or, at least, persuade :
Most like, you are glad you deceived me —
rue
No whit of the wrong : you endured too long,
Have done no evil and want no aid,
Will live the old life out and chance the
new.

And your sentence is written all the same,
And I can do nothing, — pray, perhaps :
But somehow the world pursues its game, —
If I pray, if I curse, — for better or worse ·

And my faith is torn to a thousand scraps,
And my heart feels ice while my words
breathe flame.

Dear, I look from my hiding-place.
Are you still so fair ? Have you still the eyes ?
Be happy ! Add but the other grace,
Be good ! Why want what the angels vaunt ?
I knew you once : but in Paradise,
If we meet, I will pass nor turn my face

DÎS ALITER VISUM ;

OR, LE BYRON DE NOS JOURS

STOP, let me have the truth of that !
Is that all true ? I say, the day
Ten years ago when both of us
Met on a morning, friends — as thus
We meet this evening, friends or what ? —

Did you — because I took your arm
And sillily smiled, " A mass of brass
That sea looks, blazing underneath ! "
While up the cliff-road edged with heath,
We took the turns nor came to harm —

Did you consider, " Now makes twice
That I have seen her, walked and talked
With this poor pretty thoughtful thing,
Whose worth I weigh : she tries to sing ;
Draws, hopes in time the eye grows nice ;

" Reads verse and thinks she understands ;
Loves all, at any rate, that 's great,
Good, beautiful ; but much as we
Down at the bath-house love the sea,
Who breathe its salt and bruise its sands :

" While . . . do but follow the fishing-gull
That flaps and floats from wave to cave !
There 's the sea-lover, fair my friend !
What then ? Be patient, mark and mend !
Had you the making of your skull ? "

And did you, when we faced the church
With spire and sad slate roof, aloof
From human fellowship so far,
Where a few graveyard crosses are,
And garlands for the swallows' perch, —

Did you determine, as we stepped
O'er the lone stone fence, " Let me get
Her for myself, and what 's the earth
With all its art, verse, music, worth —
Compared with love, found, gained, and kept ?

" Schumann 's our music-maker now ;
Has his march-movement youth and mouth ?
Ingres 's the modern man that paints ;
Which will lean on me, of his saints ?
Heine for songs ; for kisses, how ? "

And did you, when we entered, reached
The votive frigate, soft aloft
Riding on air this hundred years,
Safe-smiling at old hopes and fears, —
Did you draw profit while she preached ?

Resolving, "Fools we wise men grow!
　Yes, I could easily blurt out curt
Some question that might find reply
　As prompt in her stopped lips, dropped eye,
And rush of red to cheek and brow :

"Thus were a match made, sure and fast,
　'Mid the blue weed-flowers round the mound
Where, issuing, we shall stand and stay
　For one more look at baths and bay,
Sands, sea-gulls, and the old church last —

"A match 'twixt me, bent, wigged and lamed,
　Famous, however, for verse and worse,
Sure of the Fortieth spare Arm-chair
　When gout and glory seat me there,
So, one whose love-freaks pass unblamed, —

"And this young beauty, round and sound
　As a mountain-apple, youth and truth
With loves and doves, at all events
　With money in the Three per Cents ;
Whose choice of me would seem profound : —

"She might take me as I take her.
　Perfect the hour would pass, alas !
Climb high, love high, what matter ? Still,
　Feet, feelings, must descend the hill :
An hour's perfection can't recur.

"Then follows Paris and full time
　For both to reason : ' Thus with us ! '
She 'll sigh, ' Thus girls give body and soul
　At first word, think they gain the goal,
When 't is the starting-place they climb !

"' My friend makes verse and gets renown ;
　Have they all fifty years, his peers ?
He knows the world, firm, quiet and gay ;
　Boys will become as much one day :
They 're fools ; he cheats, with beard less
　brown.

"' For boys say, Love me or I die !
　He did not say, The truth is, youth
I want, who am old and know too much ;
　I 'd catch youth : lend me sight and touch !
Drop heart's blood where life's wheels grate dry ! '

"While I should make rejoinder " — (then
　It was no doubt, you ceased that least
Light pressure of my arm in yours) —
"' I can conceive of cheaper cures
For a yawning-fit o'er books and men.

"' What ? All I am, was, and might be,
　All, books taught, art brought, life's whole
　strife,
Painful results since precious, just
　Were fitly exchanged, in wise disgust,
For two cheeks freshened by youth and sea ?

"' All for a nosegay ! — what came first ;
　With fields on flower, untried each side ;
I rally, need my books and men,
　And find a nosegay : ' drop it, then,
No match yet made for best or worst ! "

That ended me. You judged the porch
　We left by, Norman ; took our look
At sea and sky ; wondered so few
　Find out the place for air and view ;
Remarked the sun began to scorch ;

Descended, soon regained the baths,
　And then, good-by ! Years ten since then :
Ten years ! We meet : you tell me, now,
　By a window-seat for that cliff-brow,
On carpet-stripes for those sand-paths.

Now I may speak : you fool, for all
　Your lore ! WHO made things plain in vain ?
What was the sea for ? What, the gray
　Sad church, that solitary day,
Crosses and graves and swallows' call ?

Was there naught better than to enjoy ?
　No feat which, done, would make time break
And let us pent-up creatures through
　Into eternity, our due ?
No forcing earth teach heaven's employ ?

No wise beginning, here and now,
　What cannot grow complete (earth's feat)
And heaven must finish, there and then ?
　No tasting earth's true food for men,
Its sweet in sad, its sad in sweet ?

No grasping at love, gaining a share
　O' the sole spark from God's life at strife
With death, so, sure of range above
　The limits here ? For us and love,
Failure ; but, when God fails, despair.

This you call wisdom ? Thus you add
　Good unto good again, in vain ?
You loved, with body worn and weak ;
　I loved, with faculties to seek :
Were both loves worthless since ill-clad ?

Let the mere star-fish in his vault
　Crawl in a wash of weed, indeed,
Rose-jacynth to the finger-tips :
　He, whole in body and soul, outstrips
Man, found with either in default.

But what 's whole can increase no more,
　Is dwarfed and dies, since here 's its sphere
The devil laughed at you in his sleeve !
　You know not ? That I well believe ;
Or you had saved two souls : nay, four.

For Stephanie sprained last night her wrist,
　Ankle or something. "Pooh," cry you ?
At any rate she danced, all say,
　Vilely ; her vogue has had its day.
Here comes my husband from his whist.

TOO LATE

HERE was I with my arm and heart
　And brain, all yours for a word, a want
Put into a look — just a look, your part, —
　While mine, to repay it . . . vainest vaunt

Were the woman, that's dead, alive to hear,
  Had her lover, that's lost, love's proof to
    show!
But I cannot show it; you cannot speak
  From the churchyard neither, miles removed,
Though I feel by a pulse within my cheek,
  Which stabs and stops, that the woman I
    loved
Needs help in her grave and finds none near,
  Wants warmth from the heart which sends it
    — so!

Did I speak once angrily, all the drear days
  You lived, you woman I loved so well,
Who married the other? Blame or praise,
  Where was the use then? Time would tell,
And the end declare what man for you,
  What woman for me, was the choice of God.
But, Edith dead! no doubting more!
  I used to sit and look at my life
As it rippled and ran till, right before,
  A great stone stopped it: oh, the strife
Of waves at the stone some devil threw
In my life's midcurrent, thwarting God!

But either I thought, "They may churn and
    chide
Awhile, my waves which came for their joy
And found this horrible stone full-tide:
  Yet I see just a thread escape, deploy
Through the evening-country, silent and safe,
  And it suffers no more till it finds the sea."
Or else I would think, "Perhaps some night
  When new things happen, a meteor-ball
May slip through the sky in a line of light,
  And earth breathe hard, and landmarks fall,
And my waves no longer champ nor chafe,
  Since a stone will have rolled from its place:
    let be!'"

But, dead! All's done with: wait who may,
  Watch and wear and wonder who will.
Oh, my whole life that ends to-day!
  Oh, my soul's sentence, sounding still,
"The woman is dead that was none of his;
  And the man that was none of hers may go!"
There's only the past left: worry that!
  Wreak, like a bull, on the empty coat,
Rage, its late wearer is laughing at!
  Tear the collar to rags, having missed his
    throat;
Strike stupidly on — "This, this and this,
  Where I would that a bosom received the
    blow!"

I ought to have done more: once my speech,
  And once your answer, and there, the end,
And Edith was henceforth out of reach!
  Why, men do more to deserve a friend,
Be rid of a foe, get rich, grow wise,
  Nor, folding their arms, stare fate in the face.
Why, better even have burst like a thief
  And borne you away to a rock for us two,
In a moment's horror, bright, bloody and brief,
  Then changed to myself again — "I slew
Myself in that moment; a ruffian lies
  Somewhere: your slave, see, born in his
    place!"

What did the other do? You be judge!
  Look at us, Edith! Here are we both!
Give him his six whole years: I grudge
  None of the life with you, nay, loathe
Myself that I grudged his start in advance
  Of me who could overtake and pass.
But, as if he loved you! No, not he,
  Nor any one else in the world, 't is plain:
Who ever heard that another, free
  As I, young, prosperous, sound and sane,
Poured life out, proffered it — "Half a glance
  Of those eyes of yours and I drop the glass!"

Handsome, were you? 'T is more than they
    held,
  More than they said; I was 'ware and
    watched:
I was the scapegrace, this rat belled
  The cat, this fool got his whiskers scratched:
The others? No head that was turned, no heart
  Broken, my lady, assure yourself!
Each soon made his mind up; so and so
  Married a dancer, such and such
Stole his friend's wife, stagnated slow,
  Or maundered, unable to do as much,
And muttered of peace where he had no part:
  While, hid in the closet, laid on the shelf, —

On the whole, you were let alone, I think!
  So, you looked to the other, who acquiesced;
My rival, the proud man, — prize your pink
  Of poets! A poet he was! I 've guessed:
He rhymed you his rubbish nobody read,
  Loved you and doved you — did not I laugh!
There was a prize! But we both were tried.
  Oh, heart of mine, marked broad with her
    mark,
Tekel, found wanting, set aside,
  Scorned! See, I bleed these tears in the dark
Till comfort come and the last be bled:
  He? He is tagging your epitaph.

If it would only come over again!
  — Time to be patient with me, and probe
This heart till you punctured the proper vein,
  Just to learn what blood is: twitch the robe
From that blank lay-figure your fancy draped,
  Prick the leathern heart till the — verses
    spirt!
And late it was easy; late, you walked
  Where a friend might meet you; Edith's
    name
Arose to one's lip if one laughed or talked;
  If I heard good news, you heard the same;
When I woke, I knew that your breath escaped;
  I could bide my time, keep alive, alert.

And alive I shall keep and long, you will see!
  I knew a man, was kicked like a dog
From gutter to cesspool; what cared he
  So long as he picked from the filth his prog?
He saw youth, beauty and genius die,
  And jollily lived to his hundredth year.
But I will live otherwise: none of such life!
  At once I begin as I mean to end.
Go on with the world, get gold in its strife,
  Give your spouse the slip and betray your
    friend!

There are two who decline, a woman and I,
  And enjoy our death in the darkness here.

I liked that way you had with your curls
  Wound to a ball in a net behind :
Your cheek was chaste as a Quaker-girl's,
  And your mouth — there was never, to my
      mind,
Such a funny mouth, for it would not shut ;
  And the dented chin too — what a chin !
There were certain ways when you spoke, some
      words
  That you know you never could pronounce :
You were thin, however ; like a bird's
  Your hand seemed — some would say, the
      pounce
Of a scaly-footed hawk — all but !
  The world was right when it called you thin.

But I turn my back on the world : I take
  Your hand, and kneel, and lay to my lips.
Bid me live, Edith ! Let me slake
  Thirst at your presence ! Fear no slips :
'T is your slave shall pay, while his soul en-
      dures,
  Full due, love's whole debt, *summum jus*.
My queen shall have high observance, planned
  Courtship made perfect, no least line
Crossed without warrant. There you stand,
  Warm too, and white too : would this wine
Had washed all over that body of yours.
  Ere I drank it, and you down with it, thus !

ABT VOGLER

(AFTER HE HAS BEEN EXTEMPORIZING UPON
THE MUSICAL INSTRUMENT OF HIS INVENTION)

WOULD that the structure brave, the manifold
      music I build,
  Bidding my organ obey, calling its keys to
      their work,
Claiming each slave of the sound, at a touch, as
      when Solomon willed
  Armies of angels that soar, legions of demons
      that lurk,
Man, brute, reptile, fly, — alien of end and of
      aim,
  Adverse, each from the other heaven-high,
      hell-deep removed, —
Should rush into sight at once as he named the
      ineffable Name,
  And pile him a palace straight, to pleasure
      the princess he loved !

Would it might tarry like his, the beautiful
      building of mine,
  This which my keys in a crowd pressed and
      importuned to raise !
Ah, one and all, how they helped, would dispart
      now and now combine,
  Zealous to hasten the work, heighten their
      master his praise !
And one would bury his brow with a blind
      plunge down to hell,
  Burrow awhile and build, broad on the roots
      of things,

Then up again swim into sight, having based
      me my palace well,
  Founded it, fearless of flame, flat on the
      nether springs.

And another would mount and march, like the
      excellent minion he was,
  Ay, another and yet another, one crowd but
      with many a crest,
Raising my rampired walls of gold as transpar-
      ent as glass,
  Eager to do and die, yield each his place to
      the rest :
For higher still and higher (as a runner tips
      with fire,
  When a great illumination surprises a festal
      night —
Outlined round and round Rome's dome from
      space to spire)
  Up, the pinnacled glory reached, and the
      pride of my soul was in sight.

In sight ? Not half ! for it seemed, it was
      certain, to match man's birth,
  Nature in turn conceived, obeying an impulse
      as I ;
And the emulous heaven yearned down, made
      effort to reach the earth,
  As the earth had done her best, in my passion,
      to scale the sky :
Novel splendors burst forth, grew familiar and
      dwelt with mine,
  Not a point nor peak but found and fixed its
      wandering star ;
Meteor-moons, balls of blaze : and they did not
      pale nor pine,
  For earth had attained to heaven, there was
      no more near nor far.

Nay more ; for there wanted not who walked
      in the glare and glow,
  Presences plain in the place ; or, fresh from
      the Protoplast,
Furnished for ages to come, when a kindlier
      wind should blow,
  Lured now to begin and live, in a house to
      their liking at last ;
Or else the wonderful Dead who have passed
      through the body and gone,
  But were back once more to breathe in an old
      world worth their new :
What never had been, was now ; what was, as
      it shall be anon ;
  And what is, — shall I say, matched both ? for
      I was made perfect too.

All through my keys that gave their sounds to
      a wish of my soul,
  All through my soul that praised as its wish
      flowed visibly forth,
All through music and me ! For think, had I
      painted the whole,
  Why, there it had stood, to see, nor the pro-
      cess so wonder-worth :
Had I written the same, made verse — still,
      effect proceeds from cause,
  Ye know why the forms are fair, ye hear how
      the tale is told ;

It is all triumphant art, but art in obedience to
      laws,
  Painter and poet are proud in the artist-list
      enrolled : —

But here is the finger of God, a flash of the will
      that can,
  Existent behind all laws, that made them
      and, lo, they are !
And I know not if, save in this, such gift be
      allowed to man,
  That out of three sounds he frame, not a
      fourth sound, but a star.
Consider it well : each tone of our scale in itself
      is naught :
  It is everywhere in the world — loud, soft,
      and all is said :
Give it to me to use ! I mix it with two in my
      thought :
  And there ! Ye have heard and seen : con-
      sider and bow the head !

Well, it is gone at last, the palace of music I
      reared ;
  Gone ! and the good tears start, the praises
      that come too slow ;
For one is assured at first, one scarce can say
      that he feared,
  That he even gave it a thought, the gone
      thing was to go.
Never to be again ! But many more of the
      kind
  As good, nay, better perchance : is this your
      comfort to me ?
To me, who must be saved because I cling with
      my mind
  To the same, same self, same love, same God :
      ay, what was, shall be

Therefore to whom turn I but to thee, the
      ineffable Name ?
  Builder and maker, thou, of houses not
      made with hands !
What, have fear of change from thee who art
      ever the same ?
  Doubt that thy power can fill the heart that
      thy power expands ?
There shall never be one lost good ! What was,
      shall live as before ;
  The evil is null, is naught, is silence implying
      sound ;
What was good shall be good, with, for evil,
      so much good more ;
  On the earth the broken arcs ; in the heaven
      a perfect round.

All we have willed or hoped or dreamed of good
      shall exist ;
  Not its semblance, but itself ; no beauty, nor
      good, nor power
Whose voice has gone forth, but each survives
      for the melodist
  When eternity affirms the conception of an
      hour.
The high that proved too high, the heroic for
      earth too hard,
  The passion that left the ground to lose itself
      in the sky,

Are music sent up to God by the lover and the
      bard ;
  Enough that he heard it once : we shall hear
      it by and by.

And what is our failure here but a triumph's
      evidence
  For the fulness of the days ? Have we with-
      ered or agonized ?
Why else was the pause prolonged but that
      singing might issue thence ?
  Why rushed the discords in, but that harmony
      should be prized ?
Sorrow is hard to bear, and doubt is slow to
      clear,
  Each sufferer says his say, his scheme of the
      weal and woe :
But God has a few of us whom he whispers in
      the ear ;
  The rest may reason and welcome : 't is we
      musicians know.

Well, it is earth with me ; silence resumes her
      reign :
  I will be patient and proud, and soberly
      acquiesce.
Give me the keys. I feel for the common chord
      again,
  Sliding by semitones till I sink to the minor,
      — yes,
And I blunt it into a ninth, and I stand on
      alien ground,
  Surveying awhile the heights I rolled from
      into the deep ;
Which, hark, I have dared and done, for my
      resting-place is found,
  The C Major of this life : so, now I will try
      to sleep.

RABBI BEN EZRA

Grow old along with me !
The best is yet to be,
The last of life, for which the first was made :
Our times are in his hand
Who saith, " A whole I planned,
Youth shows but half ; trust God : see all, nor
      be afraid ! "

Not that, amassing flowers,
Youth sighed, " Which rose make ours,
Which lily leave and then as best recall ? "
Not that, admiring stars,
It yearned, " Nor Jove, nor Mars ;
Mine be some figured flame which blends, tran-
      scends them all ! "

Not for such hopes and fears
Annulling youth's brief years,
Do I remonstrate : folly wide the mark !
Rather I prize the doubt
Low kinds exist without,
Finished and finite clods, untroubled by a spark.

Poor vaunt of life indeed,
Were man but formed to feed
On joy, to solely seek and find and feast :

Such feasting ended, then
As sure an end to men ;
Irks care the crop full bird ? Frets doubt the
    maw-crammed beast ?

Rejoice we are allied
To that which doth provide
And not partake, effect and not receive !
A spark disturbs our clod ;
Nearer we hold of God
Who gives, than of his tribes that take, I must
    believe.

Then, welcome each rebuff
That turns earth's smoothness rough,
Each sting that bids nor sit nor stand but go !
Be our joys three-parts pain !
Strive, and hold cheap the strain ;
Learn, nor account the pang ; dare, never
    grudge the throe !

For thence, — a paradox
Which comforts while it mocks, —
Shall life succeed in that it seems to fail :
What I aspired to be,
And was not, comforts me :
A brute I might have been, but would not sink
    i' the scale.

What is he but a brute
Whose flesh has soul to suit,
Whose spirit works lest arms and legs want
    play ?
To man, propose this test —
Thy body at its best,
How far can that project thy soul on its lone
    way ?

Yet gifts should prove their use :
I own the Past profuse
Of power each side, perfection every turn :
Eyes, ears took in their dole,
Brain treasured up the whole ;
Should not the heart beat once " How good to
    live and learn" ?

Not once beat " Praise be thine !
I see the whole design,
I, who saw power, see now Love perfect
    too :
Perfect I call thy plan :
Thanks that I was a man !
Maker, remake, complete, — I trust what thou
    shalt do ! ''

For pleasant is this flesh ;
Our soul, in its rose-mesh
Pulled ever to the earth, still yearns for rest :
Would we some prize might hold
To match those manifold
Possessions of the brute, — gain most, as we
    did best !

Let us not always say,
" Spite of this flesh to-day
I strove, made head, gained ground upon the
    whole ! ''
As the bird wings and sings,

Let us cry, " All good things
Are ours, nor soul helps flesh more, now, than
    flesh helps soul ! ''

Therefore I summon age
To grant youth's heritage,
Life's struggle having so far reached its term :
Thence shall I pass, approved
A man, for aye removed
From the developed brute ; a God though in
    the germ.

And I shall thereupon
Take rest, ere I be gone
Once more on my adventure brave and new :
Fearless and unperplexed,
When I wage battle next,
What weapons to select, what armor to indue.

Youth ended, I shall try
My gain or loss thereby ;
Leave the fire ashes, what survives is gold :
And I shall weigh the same,
Give life its praise or blame :
Young, all lay in dispute ; I shall know, being
    old.

For note, when evening shuts,
A certain moment cuts
The deed off, calls the glory from the gray :
A whisper from the west
Shoots — " Add this to the rest,
Take it and try its worth : here dies another
    day.''

So, still within this life,
Though lifted o'er its strife,
Let me discern, compare, pronounce at last,
" This rage was right i' the main,
That acquiescence vain :
The Future I may face now I have proved the
    Past.''

For more is not reserved
To man, with soul just nerved
To act to-morrow what he learns to-day :
Here, work enough to watch
The Master work, and catch
Hints of the proper craft, tricks of the tool's true
    play.

As it was better, youth
Should strive, through acts uncouth,
Toward making, than repose on aught found
    made :
So, better, age, exempt
From strife, should know, than tempt
Further. Thou waitedst age : wait death nor
    be afraid !

Enough now, if the Right
And Good and Infinite
Be named here, as thou callest thy hand
    thine own,
With knowledge absolute,
Subject to no dispute
From fools that crowded youth, nor let thee
    feel alone.

Be there, for once and all,
Severed great minds from small,
Announced to each his station in the Past !
Was I, the world arraigned,
Were they, my soul disdained,
Right ?   Let age speak the truth and give us
      peace at last !

Now, who shall arbitrate ?
Ten men love what I hate,
Shun what I follow, slight what I receive ;
Ten, who in ears and eyes
Match me : we all surmise,
They this thing, and I that : whom shall my
      soul believe ?

Not on the vulgar mass
Called " work," must sentence pass,
Things done, that took the eye and had the
      price ;
O'er which, from level stand,
The low world laid its hand,
Found straightway to its mind, could value in
      a trice :

But all, the world's coarse thumb
And finger failed to plumb,
So passed in making up the main account ;
All instincts immature,
All purposes unsure,
That weighed not as his work, yet swelled the
      man's amount :

Thoughts hardly to be packed
Into a narrow act,
Fancies that broke through language and
      escaped ;
All I could never be,
All, men ignored in me,
This, I was worth to God, whose wheel the
      pitcher shaped.

Ay, note that Potter's wheel,
That metaphor ! and feel
Why time spins fast, why passive lies our
      clay, —
Thou, to whom fools propound,
When the wine makes its round,
" Since life fleets, all is change ; the Past gone,
      seize to-day ! "

Fool !   All that is, at all,
Lasts ever, past recall ;
Earth changes, but thy soul and God stand
      sure :
What entered into thee,
That was, is, and shall be :
Time's wheel runs back or stops : Potter and
      clay endure.

He fixed thee 'mid this dance
Of plastic circumstance,
This Present, thou, forsooth, would fain ar-
      rest :
Machinery just meant
To give thy soul its bent,
Try thee and turn thee forth, sufficiently im-
      pressed.

What though the earlier grooves,
Which ran the laughing loves
Around thy base, no longer pause and press ?
What though, about thy rim,
Skull-things in order grim
Grow out, in graver mood, obey the sterner
      stress ?

Look not thou down but up !
To uses of a cup,
The festal board, lamp's flash and trumpet's
      peal,
The new wine's foaming flow,
The Master's lips aglow !
Thou, heaven's consummate cup, what needst
      thou with earth's wheel ?

But I need, now as then,
Thee, God, who mouldest men ;
And since, not even while the whirl was worst,
Did I — to the wheel of life
With shapes and colors rife,
Bound dizzily — mistake my end, to slake thy
      thirst :

So, take and use thy work :
Amend what flaws may lurk,
What strain o' the stuff, what warpings past the
      aim !
My times be in thy hand !
Perfect the cup as planned !
Let age approve of youth, and death complete
      the same !

A DEATH IN THE DESERT

[SUPPOSED of Pamphylax the Antiochene :
It is a parchment, of my rolls the fifth,
Hath three skins glued together, is all Greek,
And goeth from *Epsilon* down to *Mu* :
Lies second in the surnamed Chosen Chest,
Stained and conserved with juice of terebinth,
Covered with cloth of hair, and lettered *Xi*,
From Xanthus, my wife's uncle now at peace :
Mu and *Epsilon* stand for my own name.
I may not write it, but I make a cross
To show I wait His coming, with the rest,
And leave off here : beginneth Pamphylax.]

I said, " If one should wet his lips with wine,
And slip the broadest plantain-leaf we find,
Or else the lappet of a linen robe,
Into the water-vessel, lay it right,
And cool his forehead just above the eyes,
The while a brother, kneeling either side,
Should chafe each hand and try to make it
      warm, —
He is not so far gone but he might speak."

This did not happen in the outer cave,
Nor in the secret chamber of the rock,
Where, sixty days since the decree was out,
We had him, bedded on a camel-skin,
And waited for his dying all the while ;
But in the midmost grotto : since noon's light
Reached there a little, and we would not lose
The last of what might happen on his face.

I at the head, and Xanthus at the feet,
With Valens and the Boy, had lifted him,
And brought him from the chamber in the
   depths,
And laid him in the light where we might see:
For certain smiles began about his mouth,
And his lids moved, presageful of the end.

Beyond, and halfway up the mouth o' the cave,
The Bactrian convert, having his desire,
Kept watch, and made pretence to graze a goat
That gave us milk, on rags of various herb,
Plantain and quitch, the rocks' shade keeps
   alive:
So that if any thief or soldier passed,
(Because the persecution was aware,)
Yielding the goat up promptly with his life,
Such man might pass on, joyful at a prize,
Nor care to pry into the cool o' the cave.
Outside was all noon and the burning blue.

" Here is wine," answered Xanthus, — dropped
   a drop;
I stooped and placed the lap of cloth aright,
Then chafed his right hand. and the Boy his left:
But Valens had bethought him, and produced
And broke a ball of nard, and made perfume.
Only, he did — not so much wake, as — turn
And smile a little, as a sleeper does
If any dear one call him, touch his face —
And smiles and loves, but will not be disturbed.

Then Xanthus said a prayer, but still he slept:
It is the Xanthus that escaped to Rome,
Was burned, and could not write the chronicle.

Then the Boy sprang up from his knees, and
   ran,
Stung by the splendor of a sudden thought,
And fetched the seventh plate of graven lead
Out of the secret chamber, found a place,
Pressing with finger on the deeper dints,
And spoke, as 't were his mouth proclaiming
   first,
" I am the Resurrection and the Life."

Whereat he opened his eyes wide at once,
And sat up of himself, and looked at us;
And thenceforth nobody pronounced a word:
Only, outside, the Bactrian cried his cry
Like the lone desert-bird that wears the ruff,
As signal we were safe, from time to time.

First he said, " If a friend declared to me,
This my son Valens, this my other son,
Were James and Peter, — nay, declared as well
This lad was very John, — I could believe!
— Could, for a moment, doubtlessly believe:
So is myself withdrawn into my depths,
The soul retreated from the perished brain
Whence it was wont to feel and use the world
Through these dull members, done with long
   ago.
Yet I myself remain; I feel myself:
And there is nothing lost. Let be, awhile!"

[This is the doctrine he was wont to teach,
How divers persons witness in each man,
Three souls which make up one soul: first, to
   wit,
A soul of each and all the bodily parts,
Seated therein, which works, and is what Does,
And has the use of earth, and ends the man
Downward: but, tending upward for advice,
Grows into, and again is grown into
By the next soul, which, seated in the brain,
Useth the first with its collected use,
And feeleth, thinketh, willeth, — is what
   Knows:
Which, duly tending upward in its turn,
Grows into, and again is grown into
By the last soul, that uses both the first,
Subsisting whether they assist or no,
And, constituting man's self, is what Is —
And leans upon the former, makes it play,
As that played off the first: and, tending up,
Holds, is upheld by, God, and ends the man
Upward in that dread point of intercourse,
Nor needs a place, for it returns to Him.
What Does, what Knows, what Is; three souls,
   one man.
I give the glossa as Theotypas.]

And then, " A stick, once fire from end to
   end;
Now, ashes save the tip that holds a spark!
Yet, blow the spark, it runs back, spreads it-
   self
A little where the fire was: thus I urge
The soul that served me, till it task once more
What ashes of my brain have kept their shape,
And these make effort on the last o' the flesh,
Trying to taste again the truth of things " —
(He smiled) — " their very superficial truth;
As that ye are my sons, that it is long
Since James and Peter had release by death,
And I am only he, your brother John,
Who saw and heard, and could remember all.
Remember all! It is not much to say.
What if the truth broke on me from above
As once and ofttimes? Such might hap again:
Doubtlessly He might stand in presence here,
With head wool-white, eyes flame, and feet like
   brass,
The sword and the seven stars, as I have seen —
I who now shudder only and surmise
'How did your brother bear that sight and
   live?'

" If I live yet, it is for good, more love
Through me to men: be naught but ashes here
That keep awhile my semblance, who was
   John, —
Still, when they scatter, there is left on earth
No one alive who knew (consider this!)
—Saw with his eyes and handled with his
   hands
That which was from the first, the Word of
   Life.
How will it be when none more saith 'I saw'?

" Such ever was love's way: to rise, it stoops.
Since I, whom Christ's mouth taught, was bid-
   den teach,
I went, for many years, about the world,
Saying 'It was so; so I heard and saw,'

Speaking as the case asked : and men believed.
Afterward came the message to myself
In Patmos isle ; I was not bidden teach,
But simply listen, take a book and write,
Nor set down other than the given word,
With nothing left to my arbitrament
To choose or change : I wrote, and men be-
    lieved,
Then, for my time grew brief, no message
    more,
No call to write again, I found a way,
And, reasoning from my knowledge, merely
    taught
Men should, for love's sake, in love's strength
    believe ;
Or I would pen a letter to a friend
And urge the same as friend, nor less nor
    more :
Friends said I reasoned rightly, and believed.
But at the last, why, I seemed left alive
Like a sea-jelly weak on Patmos strand,
To tell dry sea-beach gazers how I fared
When there was mid-sea, and the mighty
    things ;
Left to repeat, 'I saw, I heard, I knew,'
And go all over the old ground again,
With Antichrist already in the world,
And many Antichrists, who answered prompt,
'Am I not Jasper as thyself art John ?
Nay, young, whereas through age thou mayest
    forget :
Wherefore, explain, or how shall we believe ? '
I never thought to call down fire on such,
Or, as in wonderful and early days,
Pick up the scorpion, tread the serpent dumb ;
But patient stated much of the Lord's life
Forgotten or misdelivered, and let it work :
Since much that at the first, in deed and word,
Lay simply and sufficiently exposed,
Had grown (or else my soul was grown to
    match,
Fed through such years, familiar with such
    light,
Guarded and guided still to see and speak)
Of new significance and fresh result ;
What first were guessed as points, I now knew
    stars,
And named them in the Gospel I have writ.
For men said, ' It is getting long ago :
Where is the promise of his coming ? ' — asked
These young ones in their strength, as loth to
    wait,
Of me who, when their sires were born, was old.
I, for I loved them, answered, joyfully,
Since I was there, and helpful in my age ;
And, in the main, I think such men believed.
Finally, thus endeavoring, I fell sick,
Ye brought me here, and I supposed the end,
And went to sleep with one thought that, at
    least,
Though the whole earth should lie in wicked-
    ness,
We had the truth, might leave the rest to God.
Yet now I wake in such decrepitude
As I had slidden down and fallen afar,
Past even the presence of my former self,
Grasping the while for stay at facts which snap,
Till I am found away from my own world,

Feeling for foothold through a blank profound,
Along with unborn people in strange lands,
Who say — I hear said or conceive they say —
' Was John at all, and did he say he saw ?
Assure us, ere we ask what he might see ! '

" And how shall I assure them ? Can they
    share
— They, who have flesh, a veil of youth and
    strength
About each spirit, that needs must bide its time,
Living and learning still as years assist
Which wear the thickness thin, and let man
    see —
With me who hardly am withheld at all,
But shudderingly, scarce a shred between,
Lie bare to the universal prick of light ,
Is it for nothing we grow old and weak,
We whom God loves ? When pain ends, gain
    ends too.
To me, that story — ay, that Life and Death
Of which I wrote ' it was ' — to me, it is ;
— Is, here and now : I apprehend naught else.
Is not God now i' the world his power first
    made ?
Is not his love at issue still with sin,
Visibly when a wrong is done on earth ?
Love, wrong, and pain, what see I else around ?
Yea, and the Resurrection and Uprise
To the right hand of the throne — what is it
    beside,
When such truth, breaking bounds, o'erfloods
    my soul,
And, as I saw the sin and death, even so
See I the need yet transiency of both,
The good and glory consummated thence ?
I saw the power ; I see the Love, once weak,
Resume the Power : and in this word ' I see,'
Lo, there is recognized the Spirit of both
That moving o'er the spirit of man, unblinds
His eye and bids him look. These are, I see ;
But ye, the children, his beloved ones too,
Ye need, — as I should use an optic glass
I wondered at erewhile, somewhere i' the world,
It had been given a crafty smith to make ;
A tube, he turned on objects brought too close,
Lying confusedly insubordinate
For the unassisted eye to master once :
Look through his tube, at distance now they lay,
Become succinct, distinct, so small, so clear !
Just thus, ye needs must apprehend what truth
I see, reduced to plain historic fact,
Diminished into clearness, proved a point
And far away : ye would withdraw your sense
From out eternity, strain it upon time,
Then stand before that fact, that Life and
    Death,
Stay there at gaze, till it dispart, dispread,
As though a star should open out, all sides,
Grow the world on you, as it is my world.

" For life, with all it yields of joy and woe,
And hope and fear, — believe the aged
    friend, —
Is just our chance o' the prize of learning love,
How love might be, hath been indeed, and is ;
And that we hold thenceforth to the uttermost
Such prize despite the envy of the world.

And, having gained truth, keep truth: that is
all.
But see the double way wherein we are led,
How the soul learns diversely from the flesh!
With flesh, that hath so little time to stay,
And yields mere basement for the soul's em-
prise,
Expect prompt teaching. Helpful was the light,
And warmth was cherishing and food was
choice
To every man's flesh, thousand years ago,
As now to yours and mine; the body sprang
At once to the height, and stayed: but the
soul, — no!
Since sages who, this noontide, meditate
In Rome or Athens, may descry some point
Of the eternal power, hid yestereve;
And, as thereby the power's whole mass ex-
tends,
So much extends the æther floating o'er
The love that tops the might, the Christ in God.
Then, as new lessons shall be learned in these
Till earth's work stop and useless time run out,
So duly, daily, needs provision be
For keeping the soul's prowess possible,
Building new barriers as the old decay,
Saving us from evasion of life's proof,
Putting the question ever, 'Does God love,
And will ye hold that truth against the world?'
Ye know there needs no second proof with good
Gained for our flesh from any earthly source:
We might go freezing, ages, — give us fire,
Thereafter we judge fire at its full worth,
And guard it safe through every chance, ye
know!
That fable of Prometheus and his theft,
How mortals gained Jove's fiery flower, grows
old
(I have been used to hear the pagans own)
And out of mind; but fire, howe'er its birth,
Here is it, precious to the sophist now
Who laughs the myth of Æschylus to scorn,
As precious to those satyrs of his play,
Who touched it in gay wonder at the thing.
While were it so with the soul, — this gift of
truth
Once grasped, were this our soul's gain safe, and
sure
To prosper as the body's gain is wont, —
Why, man's probation would conclude, his
earth
Crumble; for he both reasons and decides,
Weighs first, then chooses: will he give up fire
For gold or purple once he knows its worth?
Could he give Christ up were his worth as
plain?
Therefore, I say, to test man, the proofs shift,
Nor may he grasp that fact like other fact,
And straightway in his life acknowledge it,
As, say, the indubitable bliss of fire.
Sigh ye, 'It had been easier once than now'?
To give you answer I am left alive;
Look at me who was present from the first!
Ye know what things I saw; then came a test,
My first, befitting me who so had seen:
'Forsake the Christ thou sawest transfigured,
him
Who trod the sea and brought the dead to life?

What should wring this from thee!' — ye laugh
and ask.
What wrung it? Even a torchlight and a
noise,
The sudden Roman faces, violent hands,
And fear of what the Jews might do! Just that.
And it is written, 'I forsook and fled:'
There was my trial, and it ended thus.
Ay, but my soul had gained its truth, could
grow:
Another year or two, — what little child,
What tender woman that had seen no least
Of all my sights, but barely heard them told,
Who did not clasp the cross with a light laugh.
Or wrap the burning robe round, thanking God?
Well, was truth safe forever, then? Not so.
Already had begun the silent work
Whereby truth, deadened of its absolute blaze,
Might need love's eye to pierce the o'erstretched
doubt.
Teachers were busy, whispering 'All is true
As the aged ones report: but youth can reach
Where age gropes dimly, weak with stir and
strain,
And the full doctrine slumbers till to-day.'
Thus, what the Roman's lowered spear was
found,
A bar to me who touched and handled truth,
Now proved the glozing of some new shrewd
tongue,
This Ebion, this Cerinthus or their mates,
Till imminent was the outcry 'Save our
Christ!'
Whereon I stated much of the Lord's life
Forgotten or misdelivered, and let it work.
Such work done, as it will be, what come,
next?
What do I hear say, or conceive men say,
'Was John at all, and did he say he saw?
Assure us, ere we ask what he might see!'

"Is this indeed a burden for late days,
And may I help to bear it with you all,
Using my weakness which becomes your
strength?
For if a babe were born inside this grot,
Grew to a boy here, heard us praise the sun,
Yet had but yon sole glimmer in light's place, —
One loving him and wishful he should learn,
Would much rejoice himself was blinded first
Month by month here, so made to understand
How eyes, born darkling, apprehend amiss:
I think I could explain to such a child
There was more glow outside than gleams he
caught,
Ay, nor need urge 'I saw it, so believe!'
It is a heavy burden you shall bear
In latter days, new lands, or old grown strange,
Left without me, which must be very soon.
What is the doubt, my brothers? Quick with
it!
I see you stand conversing, each new face,
Either in fields, of yellow summer eves,
On islets yet unnamed amid the sea;
Or pace for shelter 'neath a portico
Out of the crowd in some enormous town
Where now the larks sing in a solitude;
Or muse upon blank heaps of stone and sand

ldly conjectured to be Ephesus :
And no one asks his fellow any more
  Where is the promise of his coming ? ' but
' Was he revealed in any of his lives,
As Power, as Love, as Influencing Soul ? '

" Quick, for time presses, tell the whole mind
    out,
And let us ask and answer and be saved !
My book speaks on, because it cannot pass ;
One listens quietly, nor scoffs but pleads,
' Here is a tale of things done ages since ;
What truth was ever told the second day ?
Wonders, that would prove doctrine, go for
    naught.
Remains the doctrine, love ; well, we must love,
And what we love most, power and love in one,
Let us acknowledge on the record here,
Accepting these in Christ : must Christ then be ?
Has he been ? Did not we ourselves make him ?
Our mind receives but what it holds, no more.
First of the love, then ; we acknowledge
    Christ —
A proof we comprehend his love, a proof
We had such love already in ourselves,
Knew first what else we should not recognize.
'T is mere projection from man's inmost mind,
And, what he loves, thus falls reflected back,
Becomes accounted somewhat out of him ;
He throws it up in air, it drops down earth's,
With shape, name, story added, man's old way.
How prove you Christ came otherwise at least ?
Next try the power : he made and rules the
    world :
Certes there is a world once made, now ruled,
Unless things have been ever as we see.
Our sires declared a charioteer's yoked steeds
Brought the sun up the east and down the west,
Which only of itself now rises, sets,
As if a hand impelled it and a will, —
Thus they long thought, they who had will and
    hands :
But the new question's whisper is distinct,
Wherefore must all force needs be like our-
    selves ?
We have the hands, the will ; what made and
    drives
The sun is force, is law, is named, not known,
While will and love we do know ; marks of
    these,
Eye-witnesses attest, so books declare —
As that, to punish or reward our race,
The sun at undue times arose or set
Or else stood still : what do not men affirm ?
But earth requires as urgently reward
Or punishment to-day as years ago,
And none expects the sun will interpose :
Therefore it was mere passion and mistake,
Or erring zeal for right, which changed the
    truth.
Go back, far, farther, to the birth of things ;
Ever the will, the intelligence, the love,
Man's ! — which he gives, supposing he but
    finds,
As late he gave head, body, hands and feet,
To help these in what forms he called his gods.
First, Jove's brow, Juno's eyes were swept
    away,

But Jove's wrath, Juno's pride continued long :
As last, will, power, and love discarded these.
So law in turn discards power, love, and will.
What proveth God is otherwise at least ?
All else, projection from the mind of man ! '

" Nay, do not give me wine, for I am strong,
But place my gospel where I put my hands.

" I say that man was made to grow, not stop ;
That help, he needed once, and needs no more,
Having grown but an inch by, is withdrawn :
For he hath new needs, and new helps to these.
This imports solely, man should mount on each
New height in view ; the help whereby he
    mounts,
The ladder-rung his foot has left, may fall,
Since all things suffer change save God the
    Truth.
Man apprehends him newly at each stage
Whereat earth's ladder drops, its service done ;
And nothing shall prove twice what once was
    proved.
You stick a garden-plot with ordered twigs
To show inside lie germs of herbs unborn,
And check the careless step would spoil their
    birth ;
But when herbs wave, the guardian twigs may
    go,
Since should ye doubt of virtues, question kinds,
It is no longer for old twigs ye look,
Which proved once underneath lay store of
    seed,
But to the herb's self, by what light ye boast,
For what fruit's signs are. This book's fruit is
    plain,
Nor miracles need prove it any more.
Doth the fruit show ? Then miracles bade
    'ware
At first of root and stem, saved both till now
From trampling ox, rough boar and wanton
    goat.
What ? Was man made a wheelwork to wind
    up,
And be discharged, and straight wound up
    anew ?
No ! — grown, his growth lasts ; taught, he
    ne'er forgets :
May learn a thousand things, not twice the
    same.

" This might be pagan teaching : now hear
    mine.

" I say, that as the babe, you feed awhile,
Becomes a boy and fit to feed himself,
So, minds at first must be spoon-fed with truth :
When they can eat, babe's nurture is with-
    drawn.
I fed the babe whether it would or no :
I bid the boy or feed himself or starve.
I cried once, ' That ye may believe in Christ,
Behold this blind man shall receive his sight !
I cry now, ' Urgest thou, *for I am shrewd*
And smile at stories how John's word could
    cure —
Repeat that miracle and take my faith ? '
I say, that miracle was duly wrought

When, save for it, no faith was possible.
Whether a change were wrought i' the shows
    o' the world,
Whether the change came from our minds
    which see
Of shows o' the world so much as and no more
Than God wills for his purpose, — (what do I
See now, suppose you, there where you see rock
Round us ?) — I know not ; such was the effect,
So faith grew, making void more miracles
Because too much : they would compel, not
    help.
I say, the acknowledgment of God in Christ
Accepted by thy reason, solves for thee
All questions in the earth and out of it,
And has so far advanced thee to be wise.
Wouldst thou unprove this to re-prove the
    proved ?
In life's mere minute, with power to use that
    proof,
Leave knowledge and revert to how it sprung ?
Thou hast it ; use it and forthwith, or die !

" For I say, this is death and the sole death,
When a man's loss comes to him from his
    gain,
Darkness from light, from knowledge ignorance,
And lack of love from love made manifest ;
A lamp's death when, replete with oil, it
    chokes ;
A stomach's when, surcharged with food, it
    starves.
With ignorance was surety of a cure.
When man, appalled at nature, questioned first,
' What if there lurk a might behind this might ?'
He needed satisfaction God could give,
And did give, as ye have the written word :
But when he finds might still redouble might,
Yet asks, ' Since all is might, what use of will ? '
— Will, the one source of might, — he being
    man
With a man's will and a man's might, to teach
In little how the two combine in large, —
That man has turned round on himself and
    stands,
Which in the course of nature is, to die.

" And when man questioned, ' What if there
    be love
Behind the will and might, as real as they ? ' —
He needed satisfaction God could give,
And did give, as ye have the written word :
But when, beholding that love everywhere,
He reasons, ' Since such love is everywhere,
And since ourselves can love and would be loved,
We ourselves make the love, and Christ was
    not,' —
How shall ye help this man who knows him-
    self,
That he must love and would be loved again,
Yet, owning his own love that proveth Christ,
Rejecteth Christ through very need of him ?
The lamp o'erswims with oil, the stomach flags
Loaded with nurture, and that man's soul dies.

" If he rejoin, ' But this was all the while
A trick ; the fault was, first of all, in thee,
Thy story of the places, names and dates,

Where, when and how the ultimate truth had
    rise,
— Thy prior truth, at last discovered none,
Whence now the second suffers detriment.
What good of giving knowledge if, because
O' the manner of the gift, its profit fail ?
And why refuse what modicum of help
Had stopped the after-doubt, impossible
I' the face of truth — truth absolute, uniform?
Why must I hit of this and miss of that,
Distinguish just as I be weak or strong,
And not ask of thee and have answer prompt,
Was this once, was it not once ? — then and
    now
And evermore, plain truth from man to man.
Is John's procedure just the heathen bard's ?
Put question of his famous play again
How for the ephemerals' sake, Jove's fire was
    filched,
And carried in a cane and brought to earth :
The fact is in the fable, cry the wise,
Mortals obtained the boon, so much is fact,
Though fire be spirit and produced on earth.
As with the Titan's, so now with thy tale :
Why breed in us perplexity, mistake,
Nor tell the whole truth in the proper words ? '

" I answer, Have ye yet to argue out
The very primal thesis, plainest law,
— Man is not God but hath God's end to serve,
A master to obey, a course to take,
Somewhat to cast off, somewhat to become ?
Grant this, then man must pass from old to
    new,
From vain to real, from mistake to fact,
From what once seemed good, to what now
    proves best.
How could man have progression otherwise ?
Before the point was mooted ' What is God ? '
No savage man inquired ' What am myself ? '
Much less replied, ' First, last, and best of
    things.'
Man takes that title now if he believes
Might can exist with neither will nor love,
In God's case — what he names now Nature's
    Law —
While in himself he recognizes love
No less than might and will : and rightly takes.
Since if man prove the sole existent thing
Where these combine, whatever their degree
However weak the might or will or love,
So they be found there, put in evidence, —
He is as surely higher in the scale
Than any might with neither love nor will,
As life, apparent in the poorest midge,
(When the faint dust-speck flits, ye guess its
    wing,)
Is marvellous beyond dead Atlas' self —
Given to the nobler midge for resting-place !
Thus, man proves best and highest — God, in
    fine,
And thus the victory leads but to defeat,
The gain to loss, best rise to the worst fall,
His life becomes impossible, which is death.

" But if, appealing thence, he cower, avouch
He is mere man, and in humility
Neither may know God nor mistake himself ;

I point to the immediate consequence
And say, by such confession straight he falls
Into man's place, a thing nor God nor beast,
Made to know that he can know and not more :
Lower than God who knows all and can all,
Higher than beasts which know and can so far
As each beast's limit, perfect to an end,
Nor conscious that they know, nor craving
    more ;
While man knows partly but conceives beside,
Creeps ever on from fancies to the fact,
And in this striving, this converting air
Into a solid he may grasp and use,
Finds progress, man's distinctive mark alone,
Not God's, and not the beasts': God is, they
    are,
Man partly is and wholly hopes to be.
Such progress could no more attend his soul
Were all it struggles after found at first
And guesses changed to knowledge absolute,
Than motion wait his body, were all else
Than it the solid earth on every side,
Where now through space he moves from rest
    to rest.
Man, therefore, thus conditioned, must expect
He could not, what he knows now, know at
    first ;
What he considers that he knows to-day,
Come but to-morrow, he will find misknown ;
Getting increase of knowledge, since he learns
Because he lives, which is to be a man,
Set to instruct himself by his past self :
First, like the brute, obliged by facts to learn,
Next, as man may, obliged by his own mind,
Bent, habit, nature, knowledge turned to law.
God's gift was that man should conceive of
    truth
And yearn to gain it, catching at mistake,
As midway help till he reach fact indeed.
The statuary ere he mould a shape
Boasts a like gift, the shape's idea, and next
The aspiration to produce the same ;
So, taking clay, he calls his shape thereout,
Cries ever ' Now I have the thing I see :'
Yet all the while goes changing what was
    wrought,
From falsehood like the truth, to truth itself.
How were it had he cried, ' I see no face,
No breast, no feet i' the ineffectual clay ' ?
Rather commend him that he clapped his hands,
And laughed ' It is my shape and lives again ! '
Enjoyed the falsehood, touched it on to truth,
Until yourselves applaud the flesh indeed
In what is still flesh-imitating clay.
Right in you, right in him, such way be man's !
God only makes the live shape at a jet.
Will ye renounce this pact of creatureship ?
The pattern on the Mount subsists no more,
Seemed awhile, then returned to nothingness ;
But copies, Moses strove to make thereby,
Serve still and are replaced as time requires :
By these, make newest vessels, reach the type !
If ye demur, this judgment on your head,
Never to reach the ultimate, angels' law,
Indulging every instinct of the soul
There where law, life, joy, impulse are one
    thing !

" Such is the burden of the latest time.
I have survived to hear it with my ears,
Answer it with my lips : does this suffice ?
For if there be a further woe than such,
Wherein my brothers struggling need a hand,
So long as any pulse is left in mine,
May I be absent even longer yet,
Plucking the blind ones back from the abyss,
Though I should tarry a new hundred years ! ''

But he was dead : 't was about noon, the day
Somewhat declining : we five buried him
That eve, and then, dividing, went five ways,
And I, disguised, returned to Ephesus.

By this, the cave's mouth must be filled with
    sand.
Valens is lost, I know not of his trace ;
The Bactrian was but a wild childish man,
And could not write nor speak, but only loved :
So, lest the memory of this go quite,
Seeing that I to-morrow fight the beasts,
I tell the same to Phœbas, whom believe !
For many look again to find that face,
Beloved John's to whom I ministered,
Somewhere in life about the world ; they err :
Either mistaking what was darkly spoke
At ending of his book, as he relates,
Or misconceiving somewhat of this speech
Scattered from mouth to mouth, as I suppose.
Believe ye will not see him any more
About the world with his divine regard !
For all was as I say, and now the man
Lies as he lay once, breast to breast with God.

[Cerinthus read and mused ; one added this :

" If Christ, as thou affirmest, be of men
Mere man, the first and best but nothing
    more, —
Account him, for reward of what he was,
Now and forever, wretchedest of all.
For see ; himself conceived of life as love,
Conceived of love as what must enter in,
Fill up, make one with his each soul he loved :
Thus much for man's joy, all men's joy for him.
Well, he is gone, thou sayest, to fit reward.
But by this time are many souls set free,
And very many still retained alive :
Nay, should his coming be delayed awhile,
Say, ten years longer (twelve years, some com
    pute),
See if, for every finger of thy hands,
There be not found, that day the world shall
    end,
Hundreds of souls, each holding by Christ's
    word
That he will grow incorporate with all,
With me as Pamphylax, with him as John,
Groom for each bride ! Can a mere man do
    this ?
Yet Christ saith, this he lived and died to do.
Call Christ, then, the illimitable God,
Or lost ! "

    But 't was Cerinthus that is lost.]

CALIBAN UPON SETEBOS;

OR, NATURAL THEOLOGY IN THE ISLAND

" Thou thoughtest that I was altogether such an one as
thyself."

['WILL sprawl, now that the heat of day is best,
Flat on his belly in the pit's much mire,
With elbows wide, fists clenched to prop his
chin.
And, while he kicks both feet in the cool slush,
And feels about his spine small eft-things course,
Run in and out each arm, and make him laugh:
And while above his head a pompion-plant,
Coating the cave-top as a brow its eye,
Creeps down to touch and tickle hair and beard,
And now a flower drops with a bee inside,
And now a fruit to snap at, catch and crunch, —
He looks out o'er yon sea which sunbeams cross
And recross till they weave a spider-web,
(Meshes of fire, some great fish breaks at times,)
And talks to his own self, howe'er he please,
Touching that other, whom his dam called God.
Because to talk about Him, vexes — ha,
Could He but know! and time to vex is now,
When talk is safer than in winter-time.
Moreover Prosper and Miranda sleep
In confidence he drudges at their task,
And it is good to cheat the pair, and gibe,
Letting the rank tongue blossom into speech.]

Setebos, Setebos, and Setebos!
'Thinketh, He dwelleth i' the cold o' the moon.

'Thinketh He made it, with the sun to match,
But not the stars; the stars came otherwise;
Only made clouds, winds, meteors, such as that:
Also this isle, what lives and grows thereon,
And snaky sea which rounds and ends the same.

'Thinketh, it came of being ill at ease:
He hated that He cannot change His cold,
Nor cure its ache. 'Hath spied an icy fish
That longed to 'scape the rock-stream where she
lived,
And thaw herself within the lukewarm brine
O' the lazy sea her stream thrusts far amid,
A crystal spike 'twixt two warm walls of wave;
Only, she ever sickened, found repulse
At the other kind of water, not her life,
(Green-dense and dim-delicious, bred o' the sun,)
Flounced back from bliss she was not born to
breathe,
And in her old bounds buried her despair,
Hating and loving warmth alike: so He.

'Thinketh, He made thereat the sun, this isle,
Trees and the fowls here, beast and creeping
thing.
Yon otter, sleek-wet, black, lithe as a leech;
Yon auk, one fire-eye in a ball of foam,
That floats and feeds; a certain badger brown
He hath watched hunt with that slant white-
wedge eye
By moonlight; and the pie with the long tongue
That pricks deep into oakwarts for a worm,
And says a plain word when she finds her prize,
But will not eat the ants; the ants themselves
That build a wall of seeds and settled stalks
About their hole — He made all these and more,
Made all we see, and us, in spite: how else?
He could not, Himself, make a second self
To be His mate; as well have made Himself:
He would not make what He mislikes or slights,
An eyesore to Him, or not worth His pains:
But did, in envy, listlessness or sport,
Make what Himself would fain, in a manner,
be —
Weaker in most points, stronger in a few,
Worthy, and yet mere playthings all the while
Things He admires and mocks too, — that is it.
Because, so brave, so better though they be,
It nothing skills if He begin to plague.
Look now, I melt a gourd-fruit into mash,
Add honeycomb and pods, I have perceived,
Which bite like finches when they bill and
kiss, —
Then, when froth rises bladdery, drink up all,
Quick, quick, till maggots scamper through my
brain;
Last, throw me on my back i' the seeded thyme,
And wanton, wishing I were born a bird.
Put case, unable to be what I wish,
I yet could make a live bird out of clay:
Would not I take clay, pinch my Caliban
Able to fly? — for, there, see, he hath wings,
And great comb like the hoopoe's to admire,
And there, a sting to do his foes offence,
There, and I will that he begin to live,
Fly to yon rock-top, nip me off the horns
Of grigs high up that make the merry din,
Saucy through their veined wings, and mind me
not.
In which feat, if his leg snapped, brittle clay,
And he lay stupid-like, — why, I should laugh;
And if he, spying me, should fall to weep,
Beseech me to be good, repair his wrong,
Bid his poor leg smart less or grow again, —
Well, as the chance were, this might take or
else
Not take my fancy: I might hear his cry,
And give the manikin three sound legs for one,
Or pluck the other off, leave him like an egg,
And lessoned he was mine and merely clay.
Were this no pleasure, lying in the thyme,
Drinking the mash, with brain become alive,
Making and marring clay at will? So He.

'Thinketh, such shows nor right nor wrong in
Him,
Nor kind, nor cruel: He is strong and Lord.
'Am strong myself compared to yonder crabs
That march now from the mountain to the
sea;
'Let twenty pass, and stone the twenty-first,
Loving not, hating not, just choosing so.
'Say, the first straggler that boasts purple spots
Shall join the file, one pincer twisted off;
'Say, this bruised fellow shall receive a worm,
And two worms he whose nippers end in red;
As it likes me each time, I do: so He.

Well then, 'supposeth He is good i' the main,
Placable if His mind and ways were guessed,
But rougher than His handiwork, be sure!

Oh, He hath made things worthier than Him-
    self,
And envieth that, so helped, such things do
    more
Than He who made them! What consoles but
    this?
That they, unless through Him, do naught at
    all,
And must submit: what other use in things?
'Hath cut a pipe of pithless elder-joint
That, blown through, gives exact the scream o'
    the jay
When from her wing you twitch the feathers
    blue:
Sound this, and little birds that hate the jay
Flock within stone's throw, glad their foe is
    hurt:
Put case such pipe could prattle and boast for-
    sooth,
" I catch the birds, I am the crafty thing,
I make the cry my maker cannot make
With his great round mouth; he must blow
    through mine! "
Would not I smash it with my foot? So He.

But wherefore rough, why cold and ill at ease?
Aha, that is a question! Ask, for that,
What knows, — the something over Setebos
That made Him, or He, may be, found and
    fought,
Worsted, drove off and did to nothing, per-
    chance.
There may be something quiet o'er His head,
Out of His reach, that feels nor joy nor grief,
Since both derive from weakness in some way.
I joy because the quails come; would not joy
Could I bring quails here when I have a mind:
This Quiet, all it hath a mind to, doth.
'Esteemeth stars the outposts of its couch,
But never spends much thought nor care that
    way.
It may look up, work up, — the worse for those
It works on! 'Careth but for Setebos
The many-handed as a cuttle-fish,
Who, making Himself feared through what He
    does,
Looks up, first, and perceives he cannot soar
To what is quiet and hath happy life;
Next looks down here, and out of very spite
Makes this a bauble-world to ape yon real,
These good things to match those as hips do
    grapes.
'T is solace making baubles, ay, and sport.
Himself peeped late, eyed Prosper at his books
Careless and lofty, lord now of the isle:
Vexed, 'stitched a book of broad leaves, arrow-
    shaped,
Wrote thereon, he knows what, prodigious
    words;
Has peeled a wand and called it by a name;
Weareth at whiles for an enchanter's robe
The eyed skin of a supple oncelot;
And hath an ounce sleeker than youngling mole,
A four-legged serpent he makes cower and
    couch,
Now snarl, now hold its breath and mind his
    eye,
And saith she is Miranda and my wife:

'Keeps for his Ariel a tall pouch-bill crane
He bids go wade for fish and straight disgorge;
Also a sea-beast, lumpish, which he snared,
Blinded the eyes of, and brought somewhat
    tame,
And split its toe-webs, and now pens the drudge
In a hole o' the rock and calls him Caliban;
A bitter heart that bides its time and bites.
'Plays thus at being Prosper in a way,
Taketh his mirth with make-believes: so He.

His dam held that the Quiet made all things
Which Setebos vexed only: 'holds not so.
Who made them weak, meant weakness He
    might vex.
Had He meant other, while His hand was in,
Why not make horny eyes no thorn could prick,
Or plate my scalp with bone against the snow,
Or overscale my flesh 'neath joint and joint,
Like an orc's armor? Ay, — so spoil His sport!
He is the One now: only He doth all.

'Saith, He may like, perchance, what profits
    Him.
Ay, himself loves what does him good; but
    why?
'Gets good no otherwise. This blinded beast
Loves whoso places flesh-meat on his nose,
But, had he eyes, would want no help, but hate
Or love, just as it liked him: He hath eyes.
Also it pleaseth Setebos to work,
Use all His hands, and exercise much craft,
By no means for the love of what is worked.
'Tasteth, himself, no finer good i' the world
When all goes right, in this safe summer-time,
And he wants little, hungers, aches not much,
Than trying what to do with wit and strength.
'Falls to make something: 'piled yon pile of
    turfs,
And squared and stuck there squares of soft
    white chalk,
And, with a fish-tooth, scratched a moon on
    each,
And set up endwise certain spikes of tree,
And crowned the whole with a sloth's skull
    a-top,
Found dead i' the woods, too hard for one to
    kill.
No use at all i' the work, for work's sole sake;
'Shall some day knock it down again: so He.

'Saith He is terrible: watch His feats in proof!
One hurricane will spoil six good months' hope.
He hath a spite against me, that I know,
Just as He favors Prosper, who knows why?
So it is, all the same, as well I find.
'Wove wattles half the winter, fenced them firm
With stone and stake to stop she-tortoises
Crawling to lay their eggs here: well, one wave,
Feeling the foot of Him upon its neck,
Gaped as a snake does, lolled out its large
    tongue,
And licked the whole labor flat: so much for
    spite.

'Saw a ball flame down late (yonder it lies)
Where, half an hour before, I slept i' the shade:
Often they scatter sparkles: there is force!

'Dug up a newt He may have envied once
And turned to stone, shut up inside a stone.
Please Him and hinder this? — What Prosper
    does?
Aha, if He would tell me how! Not He!
There is the sport: discover how or die!
All need not die, for of the things o' the isle
Some flee afar, some dive, some run up trees;
Those at His mercy, — why, they please Him
    most
When . . . when . . . well, never try the same
    way twice!
Repeat what act has pleased, He may grow
    wroth.
You must not know His ways, and play Him off,
Sure of the issue. 'Doth the like himself:
'Spareth a squirrel that it nothing fears
But steals the nut from underneath my thumb,
And when I threat, bites stoutly in defence:
'Spareth an urchin that contrariwise,
Curls up into a ball, pretending death
For fright at my approach: the two ways please.
But what would move my choler more than this,
That either creature counted on its life
To-morrow and next day and all days to come,
Saying, forsooth, in the inmost of its heart,
" Because he did so yesterday with me,
And otherwise with such another brute,
So must he do henceforth and always." — Ay?
Would teach the reasoning couple what "must"
    means!
'Doth as he likes, or wherefore Lord? So He.

'Conceiveth all things will continue thus,
And we shall have to live in fear of Him
So long as He lives, keeps His strength: no
    change,
If He have done His best, make no new world
To please Him more, so leave off watching
    this, —
If He surprise not even the Quiet's self
Some strange day, — or, suppose, grow into it
As grubs grow butterflies: else, here we are,
And there is He, and nowhere help at all.

'Believeth with the life, the pain shall stop.
His dam held different, that after death
He both plagued enemies and feasted friends:
Idly! He doth His worst in this our life,
Giving just respite lest we die through pain,
Saving last pain for worst, — with which, an
    end.
Meanwhile, the best way to escape His ire
Is, not to seem too happy. 'Sees, himself,
Yonder two flies, with purple films and pink,
Bask on the pompion-bell above: kills both.
'Sees two black painful beetles roll their ball
On head and tail as if to save their lives:
Moves them the stick away they strive to clear.

Even so, 'would have Him misconceive, suppose
This Caliban strives hard and ails no less,
And always, above all else, envies Him;
Wherefore he mainly dances on dark nights,
Moans in the sun, gets under holes to laugh,
And never speaks his mind save housed as now:
Outside, 'groans, curses. If He caught me here,

O'erheard this speech, and asked "What
    chucklest at?"
'Would, to appease Him, cut a finger off,
Or of my three kid yearlings burn the best,
Or let the toothsome apples rot on tree,
Or push my tame beast for the orc to taste:
While myself lit a fire, and made a song
And sung it, " What I hate, be consecrate
To celebrate Thee and Thy state, no mate
For Thee; what see for envy in poor me?"
Hoping the while, since evils sometimes mend,
Warts rub away and sores are cured with slime,
That some strange day, will either the Quiet
    catch
And conquer Setebos, or likelier He
Decrepit may doze, doze, as good as die.

[What, what? A curtain o'er the world at
    once!
Crickets stop hissing; not a bird — or, yes,
There scuds His raven that has told Him all!
It was fool's play, this prattling! Ha! The
    wind
Shoulders the pillared dust, death's house o'
    the move,
And fast invading fires begin! White blaze —
A tree's head snaps — and there, there, there,
    there, there,
His thunder follows! Fool to gibe at Him!
Lo! 'Lieth flat and loveth Setebos!
'Maketh his teeth meet through his upper lip,
Will let those quails fly, will not eat this month
One little mess of whelks, so he may 'scape!]

CONFESSIONS

What is he buzzing in my ears?
    " Now that I come to die,
Do I view the world as a vale of tears?"
    Ah, reverend sir, not I!

What I viewed there once, what I view again
    Where the physic bottles stand
On the table's edge, — is a suburb lane,
    With a wall to my bedside hand.

That lane sloped, much as the bottles do,
    From a house you could descry
O'er the garden-wall; is the curtain blue
    Or green to a healthy eye?

To mine, it serves for the old June weather
    Blue above lane and wall;
And that farthest bottle labelled " Ether "
    Is the house o'ertopping all.

At a terrace, somewhere near the stopper,
    There watched for me, one June,
A girl: I know, sir, it 's improper,
    My poor mind 's out of tune.

Only, there was a way . . . you crept
    Close by the side, to dodge
Eyes in the house, two eyes except:
    They styled their house " The Lodge."

What right had a lounger up their lane?
  But, by creeping very close,
With the good wall's help, — their eyes might
      strain
  And stretch themselves to Oes,

Yet never catch her and me together,
  As she left the attic, there,
By the rim of the bottle labelled " Ether,"
  And stole from stair to stair,

And stood by the rose-wreathed gate. Alas,
  We loved, sir — used to meet:
How sad and bad and mad it was —
  But then, how it was sweet !

MAY AND DEATH

Among Browning's companions in boyhood
were three Silverthornes, cousins on his mo-
ther's side. The name of Charles in the poem
stands for the more familiar Jim, and it was in
remembrance of him, the eldest and most tal-
ented of the three, that this poem was written.
First published in *The Keepsake*, 1857.

I WISH that when you died last May,
  Charles, there had died along with you
Three parts of spring's delightful things ;
  Ay, and, for me, the fourth part too.

A foolish thought, and worse, perhaps !
  There must be many a pair of friends
Who, arm in arm, deserve the warm
  Moon-births and the long evening-ends.

So, for their sake, be May still May !
  Let their new time, as mine of old,
Do all it did for me: I bid
  Sweet sights and sounds throng manifold.

Only, one little sight, one plant,
  Woods have in May, that starts up green
Save a sole streak which, so to speak,
  Is spring's blood, spilt its leaves between, —

That, they might spare ; a certain wood
  Might miss the plant; their loss were small:
But I, — whene'er the leaf grows there,
  Its drop comes from my heart, that 's all.

DEAF AND DUMB

A GROUP BY WOOLNER

ONLY the prism's obstruction shows aright
The secret of a sunbeam, breaks its light
Into the jewelled bow from blankest white ;
  So may a glory from defect arise :
Only by Deafness may the vexed Love wreak
Its insuppressive sense on brow and cheek,
Only by Dumbness adequately speak
  As favored mouth could never, through the
      eyes.

PROSPICE

Written in the autumn following Mrs. Brown-
ing's death. The closing lines intensify the asso-
ciation.

FEAR death ? — to feel the fog in my throat,
  The mist in my face,
When the snows begin, and the blasts denote
  I am nearing the place,
The power of the night, the press of the storm,
  The post of the foe ;
Where he stands, the Arch Fear in a visible
      form,
  Yet the strong man must go :
For the journey is done and the summit at-
      tained,
  And the barriers fall,
Though a battle 's to fight ere the guerdon be
      gained,
  The reward of it all.
I was ever a fighter, so — one fight more,
  The best and the last !
I would hate that death bandaged my eyes, and
      forbore,
  And bade me creep past.
No ! let me taste the whole of it, fare like my
      peers
  The heroes of old,
Bear the brunt, in a minute pay glad life's
      arrears
  Of pain, darkness and cold.
For sudden the worst turns the best to the
      brave,
  The black minute 's at end,
And the elements' rage, the fiend-voices that
      rave,
  Shall dwindle, shall blend,
Shall change, shall become first a peace out of
      pain,
  Then a light, then thy breast,
O thou soul of my soul ! I shall clasp thee
      again,
  And with God be the rest !

EURYDICE TO ORPHEUS

A PICTURE BY LEIGHTON

First published, without metrical divisions, in
the *Royal Academy Catalogue*, 1864.

BUT give them me, the mouth, the eyes, the
      brow !
Let them once more absorb me ! One look
      now
  Will lap me round forever, not to pass
Out of its light, though darkness lie beyond :
Hold me but safe again within the bond
  Of one immortal look ! All woe that was,
Forgotten, and all terror that may be,
Defied, — no past is mine, no future : look at
      me !

YOUTH AND ART

IT once might have been, once only :
  We lodged in a street together,
You, a sparrow on the housetop lonely,
  I, a lone she-bird of his feather.

Your trade was with sticks and clay,
  You thumbed, thrust, patted and polished,
Then laughed " They will see some day
  Smith made, and Gibson demolished."

My business was song, song, song ;
  I chirped, cheeped, trilled and twittered,
" Kate Brown 's on the boards ere long,
  And Grisi's existence embittered ! "

I earned no more by a warble
  Than you by a sketch in plaster ;
You wanted a piece of marble,
  I needed a music-master.

We studied hard in our styles,
  Chipped each at a crust like Hindoos,
For air, looked out on the tiles,
  For fun, watched each other's windows.

You lounged, like a boy of the South,
  Cap and blouse — nay, a bit of beard too ;
Or you got it, rubbing your mouth
  With fingers the clay adhered to.

And I — soon managed to find
  Weak points in the flower-fence facing,
Was forced to put up a blind
  And be safe in my corset-lacing.

No harm ! It was not my fault
  If you never turned your eye's tail up
As I shook upon E in alt.,
  Or ran the chromatic scale up :

For spring bade the sparrows pair,
  And the boys and girls gave guesses,
And stalls in our street looked rare
  With bulrush and watercresses.

Why did not you pinch a flower
  In a pellet of clay and fling it ?
Why did not I put a power
  Of thanks in a look, or sing it ?

I did look, sharp as a lynx,
  (And yet the memory rankles,)
When models arrived, some minx
  Tripped up-stairs, she and her ankles.

But I think I gave you as good !
  " That foreign fellow, — who can know
How she pays, in a playful mood,
  For his tuning her that piano ? "

Could you say so, and never say,
  " Suppose we join hands and fortunes,
And I fetch her from over the way,
  Her, piano, and long tunes and short tunes " ?

No, no : you would not be rash,
  Nor I rasher and something over :
You 've to settle yet Gibson's hash,
  And Grisi yet lives in clover.

But you meet the Prince at the Board,
  I 'm queen myself at bals-paré,
I 've married a rich old lord,
  And you 're dubbed knight and an R. A.

Each life unfulfilled, you see ;
  It hangs still, patchy and scrappy :
We have not sighed deep, laughed free,
  Starved, feasted, despaired, — been happy

And nobody calls you a dunce,
  And people suppose me clever :
This could but have happened once,
  And we missed it, lost it forever.

A FACE

IF one could have that little head of hers
Painted upon a background of pale gold,
Such as the Tuscan's early art prefers !
No shade encroaching on the matchless mould
Of those two lips, which should be opening soft
In the pure profile ; not as when she laughs,
For that spoils all : but rather as if aloft
Yon hyacinth, she loves so, leaned its staff's
Burden of honey-colored buds to kiss
And capture 'twixt the lips apart for this.
Then her lithe neck, three fingers might sur-
        round,
How it should waver on the pale gold ground
Up to the fruit-shaped, perfect chin it lifts !
I know, Correggio loves to mass, in rifts
Of heaven, his angel faces, orb on orb
Breaking its outline, burning shades absorb :
But these are only massed there, I should think
Waiting to see some wonder momently
Grow out, stand full, fade slow against the sky
(That 's the pale ground you 'd see this sweet
        face by),
All heaven, meanwhile, condensed into one eye
Which fears to lose the wonder, should it wink.

A LIKENESS

SOME people hang portraits up
In a room where they dine or sup :
And the wife clinks tea-things under,
And her cousin, he stirs his cup,
Asks, " Who was the lady, I wonder ? "
" 'T is a daub John bought at a sale,"
Quoth the wife, — looks black as thunder.
" What a shade beneath her nose !
Snuff-taking, I suppose," —
Adds the cousin, while John's corns ail.

Or else, there 's no wife in the case,
But the portrait 's queen of the place,
Alone 'mid the other spoils
Of youth, — masks, gloves and foils,
And pipe-sticks, rose, cherry-tree, jasmine,
And the long whip, the tandem-lasher,

And the cast from a fist (" not, alas ! mine,
But my master's, the Tipton Slasher "),
And the cards where pistol-balls mark ace,
And a satin shoe uses for cigar-case,
And the chamois-horns (" shot in the Chab-
   lais "),
And prints — Rarey drumming on Cruiser,
And Sayers, our champion, the bruiser,
And the little edition of Rabelais:
Where a friend, with both hands in his pockets,
May saunter up close to examine it,
And remark a good deal of Jane Lamb in it,
" But the eyes are half out of their sockets ;
That hair 's not so bad, where the gloss is,
But they 've made the girl's nose a proboscis :
Jane Lamb, that we danced with at Vichy !
What, is not she Jane ?   Then, who is she ? "

All that I own is a print,
An etching, a mezzotint ;
'T is a study, a fancy, a fiction,
Yet a fact (take my conviction)
Because it has more than a hint
Of a certain face, I never
Saw elsewhere touch or trace of
In women I 've seen the face of :
Just an etching, and, so far, clever.

I keep my prints, an imbroglio,
Fifty in one portfolio.
When somebody tries my claret,
We turn round chairs to the fire,
Chirp over days in a garret,
Chuckle o'er increase of salary,
Taste the good fruits of our leisure,
Talk about pencil and lyre,
And the National Portrait Gallery :
Then I exhibit my treasure.
After we 've turned over twenty,
And the debt of wonder my crony owes
Is paid to my Marc Antonios,
He stops me — " *Festina lentè !*
What 's that sweet thing there, the etching ? "
How my waistcoat-strings want stretching,
How my cheeks grow red as tomatoes,
How my heart leaps !   But hearts, after leaps,
   ache.

" By the by, you must take, for a keepsake,
That other, you praised, of Volpato's."
The fool ! would he try a flight further and
   say —
He never saw, never before to-day,
What was able to take his breath away,
A face to lose youth for, to occupy age
With the dream of, meet death with, — why,
   I 'll not engage
But that, half in a rapture and half in a rage,
I should toss him the thing's self — " 'T is only
   a duplicate,
A thing of no value !   Take it, I supplicate ! "

MR. SLUDGE, " THE MEDIUM "

Mr. D. D. Home, an American spiritualist,
attracted much attention in the circle in which
Mr. and Mrs. Browning lived in Florence.

Now, don't, sir !   Don't expose me !   Just this
   once !
This was the first and only time, I 'll swear, —
Look at me, — see, I kneel, — the only time,
I swear, I ever cheated, — yes, by the soul
Of Her who hears — (your sainted mother, sir !)
All, except this last accident, was truth —
This little kind of slip ! — and even this,
It was your own wine, sir, the good champagne,
(I took it for Catawba, you 're so kind,)
Which put the folly in my head !

                              " Get up ? "
You still inflict on me that terrible face ?
You show no mercy ? — Not for Her dear sake,
The sainted spirit's, whose soft breath even
   now
Blows on my cheek — (don't you feel something,
   sir ?)
You 'll tell ?

                        Go tell, then !   Who the devil cares
What such a rowdy chooses to . . .
                              Aie — aie — aie !
Please, sir ! your thumbs are through my wind-
   pipe, sir !
Ch—ch !

                        Well, sir, I hope you 've done it now !
Oh Lord !   I little thought, sir, yesterday,
When your departed mother spoke those words
Of peace through me, and moved you, sir, so
   much,
You gave me — (very kind it was of you)
These shirt-studs — (better take them back
   again,
Please, sir) — yes, little did I think so soon
A trifle of trick, all through a glass too much
Of his own champagne, would change my best
   of friends
Into an angry gentleman !

                        Though, 't was wrong.
I don't contest the point ; your anger 's just :
Whatever put such folly in my head,
I know 't was wicked of me.   There 's a thick
Dusk undeveloped spirit (I 've observed)
Owes me a grudge — a negro's, I should say,
Or else an Irish emigrant's ;   yourself
Explained the case so well last Sunday, sir,
When we had summoned Franklin to clear up
A point about those shares i' the telegraph :
Ay, and he swore . . . or might it be Tom
   Paine ? . . .
Thumping the table close by where I crouched,
He 'd do me soon a mischief : that 's come
   true !
Why, now your face clears !   I was sure it
   would !
Then, this one time . . . don't take your hand
   away,
Through yours I surely kiss your mother's
   hand . . .
You 'll promise to forgive me ? — or, at least,
Tell nobody of this ?   Consider, sir !
What harm can mercy do ?   Would but the
   shade
Of the venerable dead-one just vouchsafe

A rap or tip! What bit of paper 's here?
Suppose we take a pencil, let her write,
Make the least sign, she urges on her child
Forgiveness? There now! Eh? Oh! 'T was
    your foot,
And not a natural creak, sir?

                            Answer, then!
Once, twice, thrice . . . see, I 'm waiting to
    say "thrice!"
All to no use? No sort of hope for me?
It 's all to post to Greeley's newspaper?

What? If I told you all about the tricks?
Upon my soul! — the whole truth, and naught
    else.
And how there 's been some falsehood — for
    your part,
Will you engage to pay my passage out,
And hold your tongue until I 'm safe on board?
England 's the place, not Boston — no offence!
I see what makes you hesitate: don't fear!
I mean to change my trade and cheat no more,
Yes, this time really it 's upon my soul!
Be my salvation! — under Heaven, of course.
I 'll tell some queer things. Sixty V's must do.
A trifle, though, to start with! We 'll refer
The question to this table?

                        How you 're changed!
Then split the difference; thirty more, we 'll say.
Ay, but you leave my presents! Else I 'll
    swear
'T was all through those: you wanted yours
    again,
So, picked a quarrel with me, to get them
    back!
Tread on a worm, it turns, sir! If I turn,
Your fault! 'T is you 'll have forced me!
    Who 's obliged
To give up life yet try no self-defence?
At all events, I 'll run the risk. Eh?

                                Done!
May I sit, sir? This dear old table, now!
Please, sir, a parting eggnog and cigar!
I 've been so happy with you! Nice stuffed
    chairs,
And sympathetic sideboards; what an end
To all the instructive evenings! (It 's alight.)
Well, nothing lasts, as Bacon came and said.
Here goes, — but keep your temper, or I 'll
    scream!

Fol-lol-the-rido-liddle-iddle-ol!
You see, sir, it 's your own fault more than
    mine;
It 's all your fault, you curious gentlefolk!
You 're prigs, — excuse me, — like to look so
    spry,
So clever, while you cling by half a claw
To the perch whereon you puff yourselves at
    roost,
Such piece of self-conceit as serves for perch
Because you chose it, so it must be safe.
Oh, otherwise you 're sharp enough! You spy
Who slips, who slides, who holds by help of
    wing,

Wanting real foothold, — who can't keep up
    right
On the other perch, your neighbor chose, not
    you:
There 's no outwitting you respecting him!
For instance, men love money — that, you
    know —
And what men do to gain it: well, suppose
A poor lad, say a help's son in your house,
Listening at keyholes, hears the company
Talk grand of dollars, V-notes, and so forth,
How hard they are to get, how good to hold,
How much they buy, — if, suddenly, in pops
    he —
"*I* 've got a V-note!" — what do you say to
    him?
What 's your first word which follows your last
    kick?
"Where did you steal it, rascal?" That 's be-
    cause
He finds you, fain would fool you, off your
    perch,
Not on the special piece of nonsense, sir,
Elected your parade-ground: let him try
Lies to the end of the list, — "He picked it
    up,
His cousin died and left it him by will,
The President flung it to him, riding by,
An actress trucked it for a curl of his hair,
He dreamed of luck and found his shoe en-
    riched,
He dug up clay, and out of clay made gold" —
How would you treat such possibilities!
Would not you, prompt, investigate the case
With cowhide? "Lies, lies, lies," you 'd shout:
    and why?
Which of the stories might not prove mere
    truth?
This last, perhaps, that clay was turned to
    coin!
Let 's see, now, give him me to speak for him!
How many of your rare philosophers,
In plaguy books I 've had to dip into,
Believed gold could be made thus, saw it
    made,
And made it? Oh, with such philosophers
You 're on your best behavior! While the
    lad —
With him, in a trice, you settle likelihoods,
Nor doubt a moment how he got his prize:
In his case, you hear, judge and execute,
All in a breath: so would most men of sense.

But let the same lad hear you talk as grand
At the same keyhole, you and company,
Of signs and wonders, the invisible world;
How wisdom scouts our vulgar unbelief
More than our vulgarest credulity;
How good men have desired to see a ghost,
What Johnson used to say, what Wesley did,
Mother Goose thought, and fiddle-diddle-
    dee: —
If he break in with, "Sir, *I* saw a ghost!"
Ah, the ways change! He finds you perched
    and prim;
It 's a conceit of yours that ghosts may be:
There 's no talk now of cowhide. "Tell it out!
Don't fear us! Take your time and recollect!

Sit down first: try a glass of wine, my boy!
And, David, (is not that your Christian name?)
Of all things, should this happen twice — it
    may —
Be sure, while fresh in mind, you let us
    know!"
Does the boy blunder, blurt out this, blab that,
Break down in the other, as beginners will?
All 's candor, all 's considerateness — " No
    haste!
Pause and collect yourself! We understand!
That 's the bad memory, or the natural shock,
Or the unexplained *phenomena!*"

                                     Egad,
The boy takes heart of grace; finds, never
    fear,
The readiest way to ope your own heart wide,
Show — what I call your peacock-perch, pet
    post
To strut, and spread the tail, and squawk
    upon!
"Just as you thought, much as you might
    expect!
There be more things in heaven and earth,
    Horatio," . . .
And so on. Shall not David take the hint,
Grow bolder, stroke you down at quickened
    rate?
If he ruffle a feather, it 's "Gently, patiently!
Manifestations are so weak at first!
Doubting, moreover, kills them, cuts all short,
Cures with a vengeance!"

                     There, sir, that 's your style!
You and your boy — such pains bestowed on
    him,
Or any headpiece of the average worth,
To teach, say, Greek, would perfect him apace,
Make him a Person ("Porson?" thank you,
    sir!)
Much more, proficient in the art of lies.
You never leave the lesson! Fire alight,
Catch you permitting it to die! You 've
    friends;
There 's no withholding knowledge, — least from
    those
Apt to look elsewhere for their souls' supply:
Why should not you parade your lawful prize?
Who finds a picture, digs a medal up,
Hits on a first edition, — he henceforth
Gives it his name, grows notable: how much
    more,
Who ferrets out a "medium"? "David 's
    yours,
You highly-favored man? Then, pity souls
Less privileged! Allow us share your luck!"
So, David holds the circle, rules the roast,
Narrates the vision, peeps in the glass ball,
Sets-to the spirit-writing, hears the raps,
As the case may be.

                     Now mark! To be precise —
Though I say, "lies" all these, at this first
    stage,
'T is just for science' sake: I call such grubs
By the name of what they 'll turn to, dragon-
    flies.

Strictly it 's what good people style untruth;
But yet, so far, not quite the full-grown thing:
It 's fancying, fable-making, nonsense-work —
What never meant to be so very bad —
The knack of story-telling, brightening up
Each dull old bit of fact that drops its shine.
One does see somewhat when one shuts one 's
    eyes,
If only spots and streaks; tables do tip
In the oddest way of themselves: and pens,
    good Lord,
Who knows if you drive them or they drive
    you?
'T is but a foot in the water and out again;
Not that duck-under which decides your dive.
Note this, for it 's important: listen why.

I 'll prove, you push on David till he dives
And ends the shivering. Here 's your circle,
    now:
Two-thirds of them, with heads like you their
    host,
Turn up their eyes, and cry, as you expect,
"Lord, who 'd have thought it!" But there 's
    always one
Looks wise, compassionately smiles, submits,
" Of your veracity no kind of doubt,
But — do you feel so certain of that boy's?
Really, I wonder! I confess myself
More chary of my faith!" That 's galling
    sir!
What, he the investigator, he the sage,
When all 's done? Then, you just have shut
    your eyes,
Opened your mouth, and gulped down David
    whole,
You! Terrible were such catastrophe!
So, evidence is redoubled, doubled again,
And doubled besides; once more, "He heard,
    we heard,
You and they heard, your mother and your
    wife,
Your children and the stranger in your gates:
Did they or did they not?" So much for
    him,
The black sheep, guest without the wedding-
    garb,
The doubting Thomas! Now 's your turn to
    crow:
" He 's kind to think you such a fool: Sludge
    cheats?
Leave you alone to take precautions!"

                                     Straight
The rest join chorus. Thomas stands abashed,
Sips silent some such beverage as this,
Considers if it be harder, shutting eyes
And gulping David in good fellowship,
Than going elsewhere, getting, in exchange,
With no eggnog to lubricate the food,
Some just as tough a morsel. Over the way,
Holds Captain Sparks his court: is it better
    there?
Have not you hunting-stories, scalping scenes,
And Mexican War exploits to swallow plump
If you 'd be free o' the stove-side, rocking-
    chair,
And trio of affable daughters?

Doubt succumbs !
Victory !   All your circle 's yours again !
Out of the clubbing of submissive wits,
David's performance rounds, each chink gets
    patched,
Every protrusion of a point 's filed fine,
All 's fit to set a-rolling round the world,
And then return to David finally,
Lies seven feet thick about his first half-inch.
Here 's a choice birth o' the supernatural,
Poor David 's pledged to !   You 've employed
    no tool
That law exclaims at, save the devil's own,
Yet screwed him into henceforth gulling you
To the top o' your bent, — all out of one half-
    lie !

You hold, if there 's one half or a hundredth
    part
Of a lie, that 's his fault, — his be the penalty !
I dare say !   You 'd prove firmer in his place ?
You 'd find the courage, — that first flurry
    over,
That mild bit of romancing-work at end, —
To interpose with " It gets serious, this ;
Must stop here.   Sir, I saw no ghost at all.
Inform your friends I made . . . well, fools
    of them,
And found you ready made.   I 've lived in
    clover
These three weeks : take it out in kicks of
    me ! "
I doubt it.   Ask your conscience !   Let me
    know,
Twelve months hence, with how few embellish-
    ments
You 've told almighty Boston of this passage
Of arms between us, your first taste o' the foil
From Sludge who could not fence, sir !   Sludge,
    your boy !
I lied, sir, — there !   I got up from my gorge
On offal in the gutter, and preferred
Your canvas-backs : I took their carver's size,
Measured his modicum of intelligence,
Tickled him on the cockles of his heart
With a raven feather, and next week found
    myself
Sweet and clean, dining daintily, dizened
    smart,
Set on a stool buttressed by ladies' knees,
Every soft smiler calling me her pet,
Encouraging my story to uncoil
And creep out from its hole, inch after inch,
" How last night, I no sooner snug in bed,
Tucked up, just as they left me, — than came
    raps !
While a light whisked " . . . " Shaped some-
    what like a star ? "
" Well, like some sort of stars, ma'am." — " So
    we thought !
And any voice ?   Not yet ?   Try hard, next
    time,
If you can't hear a voice ; we think you may :
At least, the Pennsylvanian ' mediums ' did."
Oh, next time comes the voice !   " Just as we
    hoped ! "
Are not the hopers proud now, pleased, profuse
O' the natural acknowledgment ?

Of course !
So, off we push, illy-oh-yo, trim the boat,
On we sweep with a cataract ahead,
We 're midway to the Horse-shoe : stop, who
    can.
The dance of bubbles gay about our prow !
Experiences become worth waiting for,
Spirits now speak up, tell their inmost mind,
And compliment the " medium " properly,
Concern themselves about his Sunday coat,
See rings on his hand with pleasure.   Ask
    yourself
How you 'd receive a course of treats like these !
Why, take the quietest hack and stall him up,
Cram him with corn a month, then out with
    him
Among his mates on a bright April morn,
With the turf to tread ; see if you find or no
A caper in him, if he bucks or bolts !
Much more a youth whose fancies sprout as
    rank
As toadstool-clump from melon-bed.   'T is
    soon,
" Sirrah, you spirit, come, go, fetch and carry,
Read, write, rap, rub-a-dub, and hang your-
    self ! "
I 'm spared all further trouble ; all 's arranged ;
Your circle does my business ; I may rave
Like an epileptic dervish in the books,
Foam, fling myself flat, rend my clothes to
    shreds ;
No matter : lovers, friends and countrymen
Will lay down spiritual laws, read wrong things
    right
By the rule o' reverse.   If Francis Verulam
Styles himself Bacon, spells the name beside
With a y and a k, says he drew breath in York,
Gave up the ghost in Wales when Cromwell
    reigned,
(As, sir, we somewhat fear he was apt to say,
Before I found the useful book that knows) —
Why, what harm 's done ?   The circle smiles
    apace,
" It was not Bacon, after all, you see !
We understand ; the trick 's but natural :
Such spirits' individuality
Is hard to put in evidence : they incline
To gibe and jeer, these undeveloped sorts.
You see, their world 's much like a jail broke
    loose,
While this of ours remains shut, bolted, barred,
With a single window to it.   Sludge, our friend,
Serves as this window, whether thin or thick,
Or stained or stainless ; he 's the medium-pane
Through which, to see us and be seen, they
    peep :
They crowd each other, hustle for a chance,
Tread on their neighbor's kibes, play tricks
    enough !
Does Bacon, tired of waiting, swerve aside ?
Up in his place jumps Barnum — ' I 'm your
    man,
I 'll answer you for Bacon ! '   Try once more ! '

Or else it 's — " What 's a ' medium ' ?   He 's
    a means,
Good, bad, indifferent, still the only means
Spirits can speak by ; he may misconceive,

Stutter and stammer, — he's their Sludge and
    drudge,
Take him or leave him ; they must hold their
    peace,
Or else, put up with having knowledge strained
To half-expression through his ignorance.
Suppose, the spirit Beethoven wants to shed
New music he's brimful of ; why, he turns
The handle of this organ, grinds with Sludge,
And what he poured in at the mouth o' the
    mill
As a Thirty-third Sonata, (fancy now !)
Comes from the hopper as bran-new Sludge,
    naught else,
The Shakers' Hymn in G, with a natural F,
Or the 'Stars and Stripes' set to consecutive
    fourths."

Sir, where's the scrape you did not help me
    through,
You that are wise ? And for the fools, the
    folk
Who came to see, — the guests, (observe that
    word !)
Pray do you find guests criticise your wine,
Your furniture, your grammar, or your nose ?
Then, why your "medium" ? What's the
    difference ?
Prove your madeira red-ink and gamboge, —
Your Sludge a cheat — then, somebody's a
    goose
For vaunting both as genuine. "Guests !"
    Don't fear !
They'll make a wry face, nor too much of
    that,
And leave you in your glory.

                    " No, sometimes
They doubt and say as much !" Ay, doubt
    they do !
And what's the consequence ? "Of course
    they doubt " —
(You triumph) — " that explains the hitch at
    once !
Doubt posed our ' medium,' puddled his pure
    mind ;
He gave them back their rubbish : pitch chaff
    in,
Could flour come out o' the honest mill ? " So,
    prompt
Applaud the faithful : cases flock in point,
" How, when a mocker willed a ' medium ' once
Should name a spirit James whose name was
    George,
' James,' cried the ' medium,' — 't was the test
    of truth ! "
In short, a hit proves much, a miss proves more.
Does this convince ? The better : does it fail ?
Time for the double-shotted broadside, then —
The grand means, last resource. Look black
    and big !
"You style us idiots, therefore — why stop
    short ?
Accomplices in rascality : this we hear
In our own house, from our invited guest
Found brave enough to outrage a poor boy
Exposed by our good faith ! Have you been
    heard ?

Now, then, hear us ; one man 's not quite worth
    twelve.
You see a cheat ? Here's some twelve see an
    ass :
Excuse me if I calculate : good day ! "
Out slinks the skeptic, all the laughs explode,
Sludge waves his hat in triumph !

                            Or — he don't.
There's something in real truth (explain who
    can !)
One casts a wistful eye at, like the horse
Who mopes beneath stuffed hay-racks and
    won't munch
Because he spies a corn-bag : hang that truth,
It spoils all dainties proffered in its place !
I 've felt at times when, cockered, cosseted
And coddled by the aforesaid company,
Bidden enjoy their bullying, — never fear,
But o'er their shoulders spit at the flying man, —
I 've felt a child ; only, a fractious child
That, dandled soft by nurse, aunt, grandmother,
Who keep him from the kennel, sun and wind,
Good fun and wholesome mud, — enjoined be
    sweet,
And comely and superior, — eyes askance
The ragged sons o' the gutter at their game,
Fain would be down with them i' the thick o'
    the filth,
Making dirt-pies, laughing free, speaking plain,
And calling granny the gray old cat she is.
I 've felt a spite, I say, at you, at them,
Huggings and humbug — gnashed my teeth to
    mark
A decent dog pass ! It 's too bad, I say,
Ruining a soul so !

                    But what 's " so," what 's fixed,
Where may one stop ? Nowhere ! The cheat-
    ing 's nursed
Out of the lying, softly and surely spun
To just your length, sir ! I 'd stop soon enough :
But you 're for progress. " All old, nothing
    new ?
Only the usual talking through the mouth,
Or writing by the hand ? I own, I thought
This would develop, grow demonstrable,
Make doubt absurd, give figures we might see,
Flowers we might touch. There 's no one
    doubts you, Sludge !
You dream the dreams, you see the spiritual
    sights,
The speeches come in your head, beyond dis-
    pute.
Still, for the skeptics' sake, to stop all mouths,
We want some outward manifestation ! — well,
The Pennsylvanians gained such ; why not
    Sludge ?
He may improve with time ! "

                            Ay, that he may !
He sees his lot : there 's no avoiding fate.
'T is a trifle at first. " Eh, David ? Did you
    hear ?
You jogged the table, your foot caused the
    squeak,
This time you 're . . . joking, are you not. my
    boy ? "

" N-n-no ! " — and I 'm done for, bought and
    sold henceforth
The old good easy jog-trot way, the . . . eh ?
The . . . not so very false, as falsehood goes,
The spinning out and drawing fine, you know, —
Really mere novel-writing of a sort,
Acting, or improvising, make-believe,
Surely not downright cheatery, — anyhow,
'T is done with and my lot cast ; Cheat 's my
    name :
The fatal dash of brandy in your tea
Has settled what you 'll have the souchong's
    smack :
The caddy gives way to the dram-bottle.

Then, it 's so cruel easy ! Oh, those tricks
That can't be tricks, those feats by sleight of
    hand,
Clearly no common conjurer's ! — no, indeed !
A conjurer ? Choose me any craft i' the world
A man puts hand to ; and with six months'
    pains,
I 'll play you twenty tricks miraculous
To people untaught the trade : have you seen
    glass blown,
Pipes pierced ? Why, just this biscuit that I
    chip,
Did you ever watch a baker toss one flat
To the oven ? Try and do it ! Take my word,
Practice but half as much, while limbs are
    lithe,
To turn, shove, tilt a table, crack your joints,
Manage your feet, dispose your hands aright,
Work wires that twitch the curtains, play the
    glove
At end o' your slipper, — then put out the lights
And . . . there, there, all you want you 'll get,
    I hope !
I found it slip, easy as an old shoe.

Now, lights on table again ! I 've done my part,
You take my place while I give thanks and
    rest.
" Well, Judge Humgruffin, what 's your verdict,
    sir ?
You, hardest head in the United States, —
Did you detect a cheat here ? Wait ! Let 's
    see !
Just an experiment first, for candor's sake !
I 'll try and cheat you, Judge ! the table tilts :
Is it I that move it ? Write ! I 'll press your
    hand :
Cry when I push, or guide your pencil, Judge ! "
Sludge still triumphant ! " That a rap, indeed ?
That, the real writing ? Very like a whale !
Then, if, sir, you — a most distinguished man,
And, were the Judge not here, I 'd say, . . .
    no matter !
Well, sir, if you fail, you can't take us in, —
There 's little fear that Sludge will ! "

                  Won't he, ma'am ?
But what if our distinguished host, like Sludge,
Bade God bear witness that he played no trick,
While you believed that what produced the raps
Was just a certain child who died, you know,
And whose last breath you thought your lips had
    felt ?

Eh ? That 's a capital point, ma'am : Sludge
    begins
At your entreaty with your dearest dead,
The little voice set lisping once again,
The tiny hand made feel for yours once more,
The poor lost image brought back, plain as
    dreams,
Which image, if a word had chanced recall,
The customary cloud would cross your eyes,
Your heart return the old tick, pay its pang !
A right mood for investigation, this !
One 's at one's ease with Saul and Jonathan,
Pompey and Cæsar : but one's own lost
    child . . .
I wonder, when you heard the first clod drop
From the spadeful at the grave-side, felt you free
To investigate who twitched your funeral scarf
Or brushed your flounces ? Then, it came of
    course,
You should be stunned and stupid ; then (how
    else ?)
Your breath stopped with your blood, your
    brain struck work.
But now, such causes fail of such effects,
All 's changed, — the little voice begins afresh,
Yet you, calm, consequent, can test and try
And touch the truth. " Tests ? Did n't the
    creature tell
Its nurse's name, and say it lived six years,
And rode a rocking-horse ? Enough of tests !
Sludge never could learn that ! "

                He could not, eh ?
You compliment him. " Could not ? " Speak
    for yourself !
I 'd like to know the man I ever saw
Once, — never mind where, how, why, when, —
    once saw,
Of whom I do not keep some matter in mind
He 'd swear I " could not " know, sagacious
    soul !
What ? Do you live in this world's blow of
    blacks,
Palaver, gossipry, a single hour
Nor find one smut has settled on your nose,
Of a smut's worth, no more, no less ? — one fact
Out of the drift of facts, whereby you learn
What some one was, somewhere, somewhen,
    somewhy ?
You don't tell folk — " See what has stuck to
    me !
Judge Humgruffin, our most distinguished man,
Your uncle was a tailor, and your wife
Thought to have married Miggs, missed him,
    hit you ! " —
Do you, sir, though you see him twice a-week ?
" No," you repiy, " what use retailing it ?
Why should I ? " But, you see, one day you
    should,
Because one day there 's much use, — when
    this fact
Brings you the Judge upon both gouty knees
Before the supernatural ; proves that Sludge
Knows, as you say, a thing he " could not "
    know :
Will not Sludge thenceforth keep an out-
    stretched face,
The way the wind drives ?

" Could not ! " Look you now,
I 'll tell you a story ! There 's a whiskered
  chap,
A foreigner, that teaches music here
And gets his bread, — knowing no better way :
He says, the fellow who informed of him
And made him fly his country and fall West,
Was a hunchback cobbler, sat, stitched soles
  and sang,
In some outlandish place, the city Rome,
In a cellar by their Broadway, all day long ;
Never asked questions, stopped to listen or look,
Nor lifted nose from lapstone ; let the world
Roll round his three-legged stool, and news run
  in
The ears he hardly seemed to keep pricked up.
Well, that man went on Sundays, touched his
  pay,
And took his praise from government, you see ;
For something like two dollars every week,
He 'd engage tell you some one little thing
Of some one man, which led to many more,
(Because one truth leads right to the world's
  end,)
And make you that man's master — when he
  dined
And on what dish, where walked to keep his
  health
And to what street. His trade was, throwing
  thus
His sense out, like an ant-eater's long tongue,
Soft, innocent, warm, moist, impassible,
And when 't was crusted o'er with creatures —
  slick,
Their juice enriched his palate. " Could not
  Sludge ! "

I 'll go yet a step further, and maintain,
Once the imposture plunged its proper depth
I' the rotten of your natures, all of you, —
(If one 's not mad nor drunk, and hardly then)
It 's impossible to cheat — that 's, be found out !
Go tell your brotherhood this first slip of mine,
All to-day's tale, how you detected Sludge,
Behaved unpleasantly, till he was fain confess,
And so has come to grief ! You 'll find, I think,
Why Sludge still snaps his fingers in your face.
There now, you 've told them ! What 's their
  prompt reply ?
"Sir, did that youth confess he had cheated
  me,
I 'd disbelieve him. He may cheat at times ;
That 's in the 'medium'-nature, thus they 're
  made,
Vain and vindictive, cowards, prone to scratch.
And so all cats are ; still, a cat 's the beast
You coax the strange electric sparks from out,
By rubbing back its fur ; not so a dog,
Nor lion, nor lamb : 't is the cat's nature, sir !
Why not the dog's ? Ask God, who made them
  beasts !
D' ye think the sound, the nicely-balanced man
(Like me " — aside) — "like you yourself," —
  (aloud)
" — He 's stuff to make a 'medium'? Bless
  your soul,
'T is these hysteric, hybrid half-and-halfs,
Equivocal, worthless vermin yield the fire !

We take such as we find them, 'ware their
  tricks,
Wanting their service. Sir, Sludge took in
  you —
How, I can't say, not being there to watch :
He was tried, was tempted by your easiness, —
He did not take in me ! "

Thank you for Sludge !
I 'm to be grateful to such patrons, eh,
When what you hear 's my best word ? 'T is a
  challenge,
"Snap at all strangers, half-tamed prairie-dog,
So you cower duly at your keeper's beck !
Cat, show what claws were made for, muffling
  them
Only to me ! Cheat others if you can,
Me, if you dare ! " And, my wise sir, I dared -
Did cheat you first, made you cheat others next
And had the help o' your vaunted manliness
To bully the incredulous. You used me ?
Have not I used you, taken full revenge,
Persuaded folk they knew not their own name,
And straight they 'd own the error ! Who was
  the fool
When, to an awe-struck wide-eyed open-mouthed
Circle of sages, Sludge would introduce
Milton composing baby-rhymes, and Locke
Reasoning in gibberish, Homer writing Greek
In naughts and crosses, Asaph setting psalms
To crotchet and quaver ? I 've made a spirit
  squeak
In sham voice for a minute, then outbroke
Bold in my own, defying the imbeciles —
Have copied some ghost's pothooks, half a page,
Then ended with my own scrawl undisguised.
" All right ! The ghost was merely using
  Sludge,
Suiting itself from his imperfect stock ! "
Don't talk of gratitude to me ! For what ?
For being treated as a showman's ape,
Encouraged to be wicked and make sport,
Fret or sulk, grin or whimper, any mood
So long as the ape be in it and no man —
Because a nut pays every mood alike.
Curse your superior, superintending sort,
Who, since you hate smoke, send up boys that
  climb
To cure your chimney, bid a "medium" lie
To sweep you truth down ! Curse your women
  too,
Your insolent wives and daughters, that fire up
Or faint away if a male hand squeeze theirs,
Yet, to encourage Sludge, may play with Sludge
As only a "medium," only the kind of thing
They must humor, fondle . . . oh, to miscon-
  ceive
Were too preposterous ! But I 've paid them
  out !
They 've had their wish — called for the naked
  truth,
And in she tripped, sat down and bade them
  stare :
They had to blush a little and forgive !
" The fact is, children talk so ; in next world
All our conventions are reversed, — perhaps
Made light of : something like old prints, my
  dear !

The Judge has one, he brought from Italy,
A metropolis in the background, — o'er a bridge,
A team of trotting roadsters, — cheerful groups
Of wayside travellers, peasants at their work,
And, full in front, quite unconcerned, why not?
Three nymphs conversing with a cavalier,
And never a rag among them : ' fine,' folk cry —
And heavenly manners seem not much unlike !
Let Sludge go on ; we 'll fancy it 's in print ! ''
If such as came for wool, sir, went home shorn,
Where is the wrong I did them ? 'T was their
        choice ;
They tried the adventure, ran the risk, tossed
        up
And lost, as some one 's sure to do in games ;
They fancied I was made to lose, — smoked
        glass
Useful to spy the sun through, spare their eyes :
And had I proved a red-hot iron plate
They thought to pierce, and, for their pains,
        grew blind,
Whose were the fault but theirs ? While, as
        things go,
Their loss amounts to gain, the more 's the
        shame !
They 've had their peep into the spirit-world,
And all this world may know it ! They 've fed
        fat
Their self-conceit which else had starved : what
        chance
Save this, of cackling o'er a golden egg
And compassing distinction from the flock,
Friends of a feather ? Well, they paid for it,
And not prodigiously ; the price o' the play,
Not counting certain pleasant interludes,
Was scarce a vulgar play's worth. When you
        buy
The actor's talent, do you dare propose
For his soul beside ? Whereas, my soul you
        buy !
Sludge acts Macbeth, obliged to be Macbeth,
Or you 'll not hear his first word ! Just go
        through
That slight formality, swear himself 's the
        Thane,
And thenceforth he may strut and fret his hour,
Spout, spawl, or spin his target, no one cares !
Why had n't I leave to play tricks, Sludge as
        Sludge ?
Enough of it all ! I 've wiped out scores with
        you —
Vented your fustian, let myself be streaked
Like tom-fool with your ochre and carmine,
Worn patchwork your respectable fingers sewed
To metamorphose somebody, — yes, I 've earned
My wages, swallowed down my bread of shame,
And shake the crumbs off — where but in your
        face ?

As for religion — why, I served it, sir !
I 'll stick to that ! With my *phenomena*
I laid the atheist sprawling on his back,
Propped up Saint Paul, or, at least, Sweden-
        borg !
In fact, it 's just the proper way to balk
These troublesome fellows — liars, one and all,
Are not these skeptics ? Well, to baffle them,
No use in being squeamish : lie yourself !

Erect your buttress just as wide o' the line,
Your side, as they build up the wall on theirs ;
Where both meet, midway in a point, is truth.
High overhead : so, take your room, pile bricks,
Lie ! Oh, there 's titillation in all shame !
What snow may lose in white, snow gains in
        rose !
Miss Stokes turns — Rahab, — nor a bad ex-
        change !
Glory be on her, for the good she wrought,
Breeding belief anew 'neath ribs of death,
Browbeating now the unabashed before,
Ridding us of their whole life's gathered straw
By a live coal from the altar ! Why, of old,
Great men spent years and years in writing
        books
To prove we 've souls, and hardly proved it
        then :
Miss Stokes with her live coal, for you and me !
Surely, to this good issue, all was fair —
Not only fondling Sludge, but, even suppose
He let escape some spice of knavery, — well,
In wisely being blind to it ! Don't you praise
Nelson for setting spy-glass to blind eye
And saying . . . what was it — that he could
        not see
The signal he was bothered with ? Ay, indeed !

I 'll go beyond : there 's a real love of a lie,
Liars find ready-made for lies they make,
As hand for glove, or tongue for sugar-plum.
At bes , 't is never pure and full belief ;
Those f rthest in the quagmire, — don't suppose
They strayed there with no warning, got no
        chance
Of a filth-speck in their face, which they
        clenched teeth,
Bent brow against ! Be sure they had their
        doubts,
And fears, and fairest challenges to try
The floor o' the seeming solid sand ! But no !
Their faith was pledged, acquaintance too ap-
        prised,
All but the last step ventured, kerchiefs waved,
And Sludge called " pet : " 't was easier march-
        ing on
To the promised land ; join those who, Thurs-
        day next,
Meant to meet Shakespeare ; better follow
        Sludge —
Prudent, oh sure ! — on the alert, how else ?
But making for the mid-bog, all the same !
To hear your outcries, one would think I caught
Miss Stokes by the scruff o' the neck, and
        pitched her flat,
Foolish-face-foremost ! Hear these simpletons,
That 's all I beg, before my work 's begun,
Before I 've touched them with my finger-tip !
Thus they await me (do but listen, now !
It 's reasoning, this is, — I can't imitate
The baby voice, though), — " In so many tales
Must be some truth, truth though a pin-point big,
Yet, some : a single man 's deceived, perhaps —
Hardly, a thousand : to suppose one cheat
Can gull all these, were more miraculous far
Than aught we should confess a miracle," —
And so on. Then the Judge sums up — (it 's
        rare)

Bids you respect the authorities that leap
To the judgment-seat at once, — why don't you
　　note
The limpid nature, the unblemished life,
The spotless honor, indisputable sense
Of the first upstart with his story? What —
Outrage a boy on whom you ne'er till now
Set eyes, because he finds raps trouble him?

Fools, these are: ay, and how of their opposites
Who never did, at bottom of their hearts,
Believe for a moment? — Men emasculate,
Blank of belief, who played, as eunuchs use,
With superstition safely, — cold of blood,
Who saw what made for them i' the mystery,
Took their occasion, and supported Sludge
— As proselytes? No, thank you, far too
　　shrewd!
— But promisers of fair play, encouragers
O' the claimant; who in candor needs must
　　hoist
Sludge upon Mars' Hill, get speech out of Sludge
To carry off, criticise, and cant about!
Did n't Athens treat Saint Paul so? — at any
　　rate,
It's "a new thing" philosophy fumbles at.
Then there's the other picker-out of pearl
From dungheaps, — ay, your literary man,
Who draws on his kid gloves to deal with Sludge
Daintily and discreetly, — shakes a dust
O' the doctrine, flavors thence, he well knows
　　how,
The narrative or the novel, — half-believes,
All for the book's sake, and the public's stare,
And the cash that's God's sole solid in this
　　world!
Look at him! Try to be too bold, too gross
For the master! Not you! He's the man for
　　muck;
Shovel it forth, full-splash, he'll smooth your
　　brown
Into artistic richness, never fear!
Find him the crude stuff; when you recognize
Your lie again, you'll doff your hat to it,
Dressed out for company! "For company,"
I say, since there's the relish of success:
Let all pay due respect, call the lie truth,
Save the soft silent smirking gentleman
Who ushered in the stranger: you must sigh
"How melancholy, he, the only one,
Fails to perceive the bearing of the truth
Himself gave birth to!" — There's the tri-
　　umph's smack!
That man would choose to see the whole world
　　roll
I' the slime o' the slough, so he might touch the
　　tip
Of his brush with what I call the best of
　　browns —
Tint ghost-tales, spirit-stories, past the power
Of the outworn umber and bistre!

　　　　　　　　　　　　　Yet I think
There's a more hateful form of foolery —
The social sage's, Solomon of saloons
And philosophic diner-out, the fribble
Who wants a doctrine for a chopping-block
To try the edge of his faculty upon,

Prove how much common sense he'll hack and
　　hew
I' the critical moment 'twixt the soup and fish!
These were my patrons: these, and the like of
　　them
Who, rising in my soul now, sicken it, —
These I have injured! Gratitude to these?
The gratitude, forsooth, of a prostitute
To the greenhorn and the bully — friends of
　　hers,
From the wag that wants the queer jokes for
　　his club,
To the snuffbox-decorator, honest man,
Who just was at his wits' end where to find
So genial a Pasiphae! All and each
Pay, compliment, protect from the police:
And how she hates them for their pains, like
　　me!
So much for my remorse at thanklessness
Toward a deserving public!

　　　　　　　　　　　　　But, for God?
Ay, that's a question! Well, sir, since you
　　press —
(How you do tease the whole thing out of me!
I don't mean you, you know, when I say
　　"them:")
Hate you, indeed! But that Miss Stokes, that
　　Judge!
Enough, enough — with sugar: thank you, sir!)
Now for it, then! Will you believe me, though?
You've heard what I confess; I don't unsay
A single word: I cheated when I could,
Rapped with my toe-joints, set sham hands at
　　work,
Wrote down names weak in sympathetic ink,
Rubbed odic lights with ends of phosphor-match,
And all the rest; believe that: believe this,
By the same token, though it seem to set
The crooked straight again, unsay the said,
Stick up what I've knocked down; I can't help
　　that
It's truth! I somehow vomit truth to-day.
This trade of mine — I don't know, can't be
　　sure
But there was something in it, tricks and all!
Really, I want to light up my own mind.
They were tricks, — true, but what I mean to
　　add
Is also true. First, — don't it strike you, sir?
Go back to the beginning, — the first fact
We're taught is, there's a world beside this
　　world,
With spirits, not mankind, for tenantry;
That much within that world once sojourned
　　here,
That all upon this world will visit there,
And therefore that we, bodily here below,
Must have exactly such an interest
In learning what may be the ways o' the world
Above us, as the disembodied folk
Have (by all analogic likelihood)
In watching how things go in the old home
With us, their sons, successors, and what not.
Oh, yes, with added powers probably,
Fit for the novel state, — old loves grown pure,
Old interests understood aright, — they watch!
Eyes to see, ears to hear, and hands to help,

Proportionate to advancement : they 're ahead,
That 's all — do what we do, but nobler done —
Use plate, whereas we eat our meals off delf,
(To use a figure.)

Concede that, and I ask
Next what may be the mode of intercourse
Between us men here, and those once-men
there ?
First comes the Bible's speech ; then, history
With the supernatural element, — you know —
All that we sucked in with our mothers' milk,
Grew up with, got inside of us at last,
Till it 's found bone of bone and flesh of flesh.
See now, we start with the miraculous,
And know it used to be, at all events :
What 's the first step we take, and can't but
take,
In arguing from the known to the obscure ?
Why this : " What was before, may be to-day.
Since Samuel's ghost appeared to Saul, — of
course
My brother's spirit may appear to me."
Go tell your teacher that ! What 's his reply ?
What brings a shade of doubt for the first time
O'er his brow late so luminous with faith ?
" Such things have been," says he, " and there 's
no doubt
Such things may be : but I advise mistrust
Of eyes, ears, stomach, and, more than all, your
brain,
Unless it be of your great-grandmother,
Whenever they propose a ghost to you ! "
The end is, there 's a composition struck ;
'T is settled, we 've some way of intercourse
Just as in Saul's time ; only, different :
How, when and where, precisely, — find it out !
I want to know, then, what 's so natural
As that a person born into this world
And seized on by such teaching, should begin
With firm expectancy and a frank look-out
For his own allotment, his especial share
I' the secret, — his particular ghost, in fine ?
I mean, a person born to look that way,
Since natures differ : take the painter-sort,
One man lives fifty years in ignorance
Whether grass be green or red, — " No kind of
eye
For color," say you ; while another picks
And puts away even pebbles, when a child,
Because of bluish spots and pinky veins —
" Give him forthwith a paint-box ! " Just the
same
Was I born . . . " medium," you won't let me
say, —
Well, seer of the supernatural
Everywhen, everyhow, and everywhere, —
Will that do ?

I and all such boys of course
Started with the same stock of Bible-truth ;
Only, — what in the rest you style their sense,
Instinct, blind reasoning but imperative,
This, betimes, taught them the old world had
one law
And ours another : " New world, new laws,"
cried they :
" None but old laws, seen everywhere at work,"

Cried I, and by their help explained my life
The Jews' way, still a working way to me.
Ghosts made the noises, fairies waved the lights,
Or Santa Claus slid down on New Year's Eve
And stuffed with cakes the stocking at my bed,
Changed the worn shoes, rubbed clean the
fingered slate
O' the sum that came to grief the day before.

This could not last long : soon enough I found
Who had worked wonders thus, and to what
end :
But did I find all easy, like my mates ?
Henceforth no supernatural any more ?
Not a whit : what projects the billiard-balls ?
" A cue," you answer. " Yes, a cue," said I ;
" But what hand, off the cushion, moved the
cue ?
What unseen agency, outside the world,
Prompted its puppets to do this and that,
Put cakes and shoes and slates into their mind,
These mothers and aunts, nay even school-
masters ? "
Thus high I sprang, and there have settled since.
Just so I reason, in sober earnest still,
About the greater godsends, what you call
The serious gains and losses of my life.
What do I know or care about your world
Which either is or seems to be ? This snap
O' my fingers, sir ! My care is for myself ;
Myself am whole and sole reality
Inside a raree-show and a market-mob
Gathered about it : that 's the use of things.
'T is easy saying they serve vast purposes,
Advantage their grand selves : be it true or
false,
Each thing may have two uses. What 's a star ?
A world, or a world's sun : does n't it serve
As taper also, timepiece. weather-glass,
And almanac ? Are stars not set for signs
When we should shear our sheep, sow corn,
prune trees ?
The Bible says so.

Well, I add one use
To all the acknowledged uses, and declare
If I spy Charles's Wain at twelve to-night,
It warns me, " Go, nor lose another day,
And have your hair cut, Sludge ! " You
laugh : and why ?
Were such a sign too hard for God to give ?
No : but Sludge seems too little for such grace :
Thank you, sir ! So you think, so does not
Sludge !
When you and good men gape at Providence,
Go into history and bid us mark
Not merely powder-plots prevented, crowns
Kept on kings' heads by miracle enough,
But private mercies — oh, you 've told me, sir,
Of such interpositions ! How yourself
Once, missing on a memorable day
Your handkerchief — just setting out, you
know, —
You must return to fetch it, lost the train,
And saved your precious self from what be-
fell
The thirty-three whom Providence forgot.
You tell, and ask me what I think of this ?

Well, sir, I think then, since you needs must
      know,
What matter had you and Boston city to boot
Sailed skyward, like burnt onion-peelings?
      Much
To you, no doubt: for me — undoubtedly
The cutting of my hair concerns me more,
Because, however sad the truth may seem,
Sludge is of all-importance to himself.
You set apart that day in every year
For special thanksgiving, were a heathen else:
Well, I who cannot boast the like escape,
Suppose I said, " I don't thank Providence
For my part, owing it no gratitude " ?
"Nay, but you owe as much,"—you 'd tutor me,
"You, every man alive, for blessings gained
In every hour o' the day, could you but know!
I saw my crowning mercy: all have such,
Could they but see!" Well, sir, why don't
      they see?
" Because they won't look, — or perhaps, they
      can't."
Then, sir, suppose I can, and will, and do
Look, microscopically as is right,
Into each hour with its infinitude
Of influences at work to profit Sludge?
For that 's the case: I 've sharpened up my
      sight
To spy a providence in the fire's going out,
The kettle's boiling, the dime's sticking fast
Despite the hole i' the pocket. Call such facts
Fancies, too petty a work for Providence,
And those same thanks which you exact from
      me
Prove too prodigious payment: thanks for
      what,
If nothing guards and guides us little men?
No, no, sir! You must put away your pride,
Resolve to let Sludge into partnership!
I live by signs and omens: looked at the roof
Where the pigeons settle—"If the further
      bird,
The white, takes wing first, I 'll confess when
      thrashed;
Not, if the blue does," — so I said to myself
Last week, lest you should take me by sur-
      prise:
Off flapped the white, — and I 'm confessing,
      sir!
Perhaps 't is Providence's whim and way
With only me, i' the world: how can you tell?
" Because unlikely!" Was it likelier, now,
That this our one out of all worlds beside,
The what-d'-you-call-'em millions, should be
      just
Precisely chosen to make Adam for,
And the rest o' the tale? Yet the tale 's true,
      you know:
Such undeserving clod was graced so once;
Why not graced likewise undeserving Sludge?
Are we merit-mongers, flaunt we filthy rags?
All you can bring against my privilege
Is, that another way was taken with you, —
Which I don't question. It 's pure grace, my
      luck:
I 'm broken to the way of nods and winks,
And need no formal summoning. You 've a
      help;

Holloa his name or whistle, clap your hands,
Stamp with your foot or pull the bell: all 's
      one,
He understands you want him, here he comes.
Just so, I come at the knocking: you, sir, wait
The tongue o' the bell, nor stir before you
      catch
Reason's clear tingle, nature's clapper brisk,
Or that traditional peal was wont to cheer
Your mother's face turned heavenward: short
      of these
There 's no authentic intimation, eh?
Well, when you hear, you 'll answer them,
      start up
And stride into the presence, top of toe,
And there find Sludge beforehand, Sludge that
      sprang
At noise o' the knuckle on the partition-wall!
I think myself the more religious man.
Religion 's all or nothing; it 's no mere smile
O' contentment, sigh of aspiration, sir —
No quality o' the finelier-tempered clay
Like its whiteness or its lightness; rather, stuff
O' the very stuff, life of life, and self of self.
I tell you, men won't notice; when they do,
They 'll understand. I notice nothing else:
I 'm eyes, ears, mouth of me, one gaze and
      gape,
Nothing eludes me, everything 's a hint,
Handle and help. It 's all absurd, and yet
There 's something in it all, I know: how
      much?
No answer! What does that prove? Man 's
      still man,
Still meant for a poor blundering piece of work
When all 's done; but, if somewhat 's done, like
      this,
Or not done, is the case the same? Suppose
I blunder in my guess at the true sense
O' the knuckle-summons, nine times out of
      ten, —
What if the tenth guess happen to be right?
If the tenth shovel-load of powdered quartz
Yield me the nugget? I gather, crush, sift all,
Pass o'er the failure, pounce on the success.
To give you a notion, now — (let who wins,
      laugh!)
When first I see a man, what do I first?
Why, count the letters which make up his
      name,
And as their number chances, even or odd,
Arrive at my conclusion, trim my course:
Hiram H. Horsefall is your honored name,
And have n't I found a patron, sir, in you?
"Shall I cheat this stranger?" I take apple-
      pips,
Stick one in either canthus of my eye,
And if the left drops first — (your left, sir,
      stuck)
I 'm warned, I let the trick alone this time.
You, sir, who smile, superior to such trash,
You judge of character by other rules:
Don't your rules sometimes fail you? Pray,
      what rule
Have you judged Sludge by hitherto?

                                        Oh, be sure
You, everybody blunders, just as I.

In simpler things than these by far ! For see :
I knew two farmers, — one, a wiseacre
Who studied seasons, rummaged almanacs,
Quoted the dew-point, registered the frost,
And then declared, for outcome of his pains,
Next summer must be dampish : 't was a
    drought.
His neighbor prophesied such drought would
    fall,
Saved hay and corn, made cent. per cent.
    thereby,
And proved a sage indeed : how came his lore ?
Because one brindled heifer, late in March,
Stiffened her tail of evenings, and somehow
He got into his head that drought was meant !
I don't expect all men can do as much :
Such kissing goes by favor. You must take
A certain turn of mind for this, — a twist
I' the flesh, as well. Be lazily alive,
Open-mouthed, like my friend the ant-eater,
Letting all nature's loosely-guarded motes
Settle and, slick, be swallowed ! Think your-
    self
The one i' the world, the one for whom the
    world
Was made, expect it tickling at your mouth !
Then will the swarm of busy buzzing flies,
Clouds of coincidence, break egg-shell, thrive,
Breed, multiply, and bring you food enough.

I can't pretend to mind your smiling, sir !
Oh, what you mean is this ! Such intimate way,
Close converse, frank exchange of offices,
Strict sympathy of the immeasurably great
With the infinitely small, betokened here
By a course of signs and omens, raps and
    sparks, —
How does it suit the dread traditional text
O' the " Great and Terrible Name " ? Shall
    the Heaven of Heavens
Stoop to such child's play ?

Please, sir, go with me
A moment, and I 'll try to answer you.
The " Magnum et terribile " (is that right ?)
Well, folk began with this in the early day ;
And all the acts they recognized in proof
Were thunders, lightnings, earthquakes, whirl-
    winds, dealt
Indisputably on men whose death they caused,
There, and there only, folk saw Providence
At work, — and seeing it, 't was right enough
All heads should tremble, hands wring hands
    amain,
And knees knock hard together at the breath
O' the Name's first letter ; why, the Jews, I 'm
    told,
Won't write it down, no, to this very hour,
Nor speak aloud : you know best if 't be so.
Each ague-fit of fear at end, they crept
(Because somehow people once born must live)
Out of the sound, sight, swing and sway o' the
    Name,
Into a corner, the dark rest of the world,
And safe space where as yet no fear had
    reached ;
'T was there they looked about them, breathed
    again,

And felt indeed at home, as we might say.
The current o' common things, the daily life,
This had their due contempt ; no Name pur
    sued
Man from the mountain-top where fires abide
To his particular mouse-hole at its foot
Where he ate, drank, digested, lived in short :
Such was man's vulgar business, far too small
To be worth thunder : " small," folk kept on,
    " small,"
With much complacency in those great days !
A mote of sand, you know, a blade of grass —
What was so despicable as mere grass,
Except perhaps the life o' the worm or fly
Which fed there ? These were " small " and
    men were great.
Well, sir, the old way 's altered somewhat
    since,
And the world wears another aspect now :
Somebody turns our spyglass round, or else
Puts a new lens in it : grass, worm, fly grow
    big :
We find great things are made of little things,
And little things go lessening till at last
Comes God behind them.   Talk of mountains
    now ?
We talk of mould that heaps the mountain,
    mites
That throng the mould, and God that makes
    the mites.
The Name comes close behind a stomach-cyst,
The simplest of creations, just a sac
That 's mouth, heart, legs and belly at once,
    yet lives
And feels, and could do neither, we conclude,
If simplified still further one degree :
The small becomes the dreadful and immense !
Lightning, forsooth ? No word more upon
    that !
A tin-foil bottle, a strip of greasy silk,
With a bit of wire and knob of brass, and
    there 's
Your dollar's-worth of lightning !   But the
    cyst —
The life of the least of the little things ?

No, no !
Preachers and teachers try another tack,
Come near the truth this time : they put aside
Thunder and lightning.   " That 's mistake,"
    they cry ;
" Thunderbolts fall for neither fright nor sport,
But do appreciable good, like tides,
Changes o' the wind, and other natural facts —
' Good ' meaning good to man, his body or soul.
Mediate, immediate, all things minister
To man, — that 's settled : be our future text
' We are His children ! ' " So, they now ha-
    rangue
About the intention, the contrivance, all
That keeps up an incessant play of love, —
See the Bridgewater book.

Amen to it !
Well, sir, I put this question : I 'm a child ?
I lose no time, but take you at your word :
How shall I act a child's part properly ?
Your sainted mother, sir, — used you to live

With such a thought as this a-worrying you?
"She has it in her power to throttle me,
Or stab or poison: she may turn me out,
Or lock me in, — nor stop at this to-day,
But cut me off to-morrow from the estate
I look for" — (long may you enjoy it, sir!)
"In brief, she may unchild the child I am."
You never had such crotchets? Nor have I!
Who, frank confessing childship from the first,
Cannot both fear and take my ease at once,
So, don't fear, — know what might be, well
    enough,
But know too, child-like, that it will not be,
At least in my case, mine, the son and heir
O' the kingdom, as yourself proclaim my style.
But do you fancy I stop short at this?
Wonder if suit and service, son and heir
Needs must expect, I dare pretend to find?
If, looking for signs proper to such an one,
I straight perceive them irresistible,
Concede that homage is a son's plain right,
And, never mind the nods and raps and winks,
'T is the pure obvious supernatural
Steps forward, does its duty: why, of course!
I have presentiments: my dreams come true:
I fancy a friend stands whistling all in white
Blithe as a boblink, and he's dead I learn.
I take dislike to a dog my favorite long,
And sell him; he goes mad next week and
    snaps.
I guess that stranger will turn up to-day
I have not seen these three years; there's his
    knock.
I wager "sixty peaches on that tree!"—
That I pick up a dollar in my walk,
That your wife's brother's cousin's name was
    George —
And win on all points. Oh, you wince at
    this?
You'd fain distinguish between gift and gift,
Washington's oracle and Sludge's itch
O' the elbow when at whist he ought to trump?
With Sludge it's too absurd? *Fine, draw the
    line
Somewhere, but, sir, your somewhere is not mine!*

Bless us, I'm turning poet! It's time to end.
How you have drawn me out, sir! All I ask
Is — am I heir or not heir? If I'm he,
Then, sir, remember, that same personage
(To judge by what we read i' the newspaper)
Requires, beside one nobleman in gold
To carry up and down his coronet,
Another servant, probably a duke,
To hold eggnog in readiness: why want
Attendance, sir, when helps in his father's
    house
Abound, I'd like to know?

                    Enough of talk!
My fault is that I tell too plain a truth.
Why, which of those who say they disbelieve,
Your clever people, but has dreamed his
    dream,
Caught his coincidence, stumbled on his fact
He can't explain, (he'll tell you smilingly,)
Which he's too much of a philosopher
To count as supernatural, indeed,

So calls a puzzle and problem, proud of it:
Bidding you still be on your guard, you know,
Because one fact don't make a system stand,
Nor prove this an occasional escape
Of spirit beneath the matter: that's the way!
Just so wild Indians picked up, piece by piece,
The fact in California, the fine gold
That underlay the gravel — hoarded these,
But never made a system stand, nor dug!
So wise men hold out in each hollowed palm
A handful of experience, sparkling fact
They can't explain; and since their rest of life
Is all explainable, what proof in this?
Whereas I take the fact, the grain of gold,
And fling away the dirty rest of life,
And add this grain to the grain each fool has
    found
O' the million other such philosophers, —
Till I see gold, all gold and only gold,
Truth questionless though unexplainable,
And the miraculous proved the commonplace!
The other fools believed in mud, no doubt —
Failed to know gold they saw: was that so
    strange?
Are all men born to play Bach's fiddle-fugues,
"Time" with the foil in carte, jump their own
    height,
Cut the mutton with the broadsword, skate a
    five,
Make the red hazard with the cue, clip nails
While swimming, in five minutes row a mile,
Pull themselves three feet up with the left arm,
Do sums of fifty figures in their head,
And so on, by the scores of instances?
The Sludge with luck, who sees the spiritual
    facts,
His fellows strive and fail to see, may rank
With these, and share the advantage.

                    Ay, but share
The drawback! Think it over by yourself;
I have not heart, sir, and the fire's gone gray.
Defect somewhere compensates for success,
Every one knows that. Oh, we're equals, sir!
The big-legged fellow has a little arm
And a less brain, though big legs win the race:
Do you suppose I 'scape the common lot?
Say, I was born with flesh so sensitive,
Soul so alert, that, practice helping both,
I guess what's going on outside the veil,
Just as a prisoned crane feels pairing-time
In the islands where his kind are, so must fall
To capering by himself some shiny night,
As if your back-yard were a plot of spice —
Thus am I 'ware o' the spirit-world: while
    you,
Blind as a beetle that way, — for amends,
Why, you can double fist and floor me, sir!
Ride that hot hardmouthed horrid horse of
    yours,
Laugh while it lightens, play with the great
    dog,
Speak your mind though it vex some friend to
    hear,
Never brag, never bluster, never blush, —
In short, you've pluck, when I'm a coward -
    there!
I know it, I can't help it, — folly or no.

I 'm paralyzed, my hand 's no more a hand,
Nor my head a head, in danger : you can smile
And change the pipe in your cheek. Your gift 's
    not mine.
Would you swap for mine ? No ! but you 'd
    add my gift
To yours : I dare say ! I too sigh at times,
Wish I were stouter, could tell truth nor flinch,
Kept cool when threatened, did not mind so
    much
Being dressed gayly, making strangers stare,
Eating nice things ; when I 'd amuse myself,
I shut my eyes and fancy in my brain,
I 'm — now the President, now Jenny Lind,
Now Emerson, now the Benicia Boy —
With all the civilized world a-wondering
And worshipping. I know it 's folly and worse;
I feel such tricks sap, honeycomb the soul,
But I can't cure myself, — despond, despair,
And then, hey, presto, there 's a turn o' the
    wheel,
Under comes uppermost, fate makes full
    amends ;
Sludge knows and sees and hears a hundred
    things
You all are blind to, — I 've my taste of truth,
Likewise my touch of falsehood, — vice no
    doubt,
But you 've your vices also : I 'm content.

What, sir ? You won't shake hands ? " Be-
    cause I cheat ! "
" You 've found me out in cheating ! " That 's
    enough
To make an apostle swear ! Why, when I
    cheat,
Mean to cheat, do cheat, and am caught in the
    act,
Are you, or rather, am I sure o' the fact ?
(There 's verse again, but I 'm inspired some-
    how.)
Well then I 'm not sure ! I may be, perhaps,
Free as a babe from cheating : how it began,
My gift, — no matter ; what 't is got to be
In the end now, that 's the question ; answer
    that !
Had I seen, perhaps, what hand was holding
    mine,
Leading me whither, I had died of fright :
So, I was made believe I led myself.
If I should lay a six-inch plank from roof
To roof, you would not cross the street, one step,
Even at your mother's summons: but, being
    shrewd,
If I paste paper on each side the plank
And swear 't is solid pavement, why, you 'll
    cross
Humming a tune the while, in ignorance
Beacon Street stretches a hundred feet below:
I walked thus, took the paper-cheat for stone.
Some impulse made me set a thing o' the move
Which, started once, ran really by itself ;
Beer flows thus, suck the siphon ; toss the kite,
It takes the wind and floats of its own force.
Don't let truth's lump rot stagnant for the lack
Of a timely helpful lie to leaven it !
Put a chalk-egg beneath the clucking hen,
She 'll lay a real one, laudably deceived,

Daily for weeks to come. I 've told my lie,
And seen truth follow, marvels none of mine ;
All was not cheating, sir, I 'm positive !
I don't know if I move your hand sometimes
When the spontaneous writing spreads so far,
If my knee lifts the table all that height,
Why the inkstand don't fall off the desk a-tilt,
Why the accordion plays a prettier waltz
Than I can pick out on the pianoforte,
Why I speak so much more than I intend,
Describe so many things I never saw.
I tell you, sir, in one sense, I believe
Nothing at all, — that everybody can,
Will, and does cheat : but in another sense
I 'm ready to believe my very self —
That every cheat 's inspired, and every lie
Quick with a germ of truth.

                 You ask perhaps
Why I should condescend to trick at all
If I know a way without it ? This is why !
There 's a strange secret sweet self-sacrifice
In any desecration of one's soul
To a worthy end, — is n't it Herodotus
(I wish I could read Latin !) who describes
The single gift o' the land's virginity,
Demanded in those old Egyptian rites,
(I 've but a hazy notion — help me, sir !)
For one purpose in the world, one day in a life,
One hour in a day — thereafter, purity,
And a veil thrown o'er the past forevermore !
Well now, they understood a many things
Down by Nile city, or wherever it was !
I 've always vowed, after the minute's lie,
And the end's gain, — truth should be mine
    henceforth.
This goes to the root o' the matter, sir, — this
    plain
Plump fact: accept it and unlock with it
The wards of many a puzzle !

                 Or, finally,
Why should I set so fine a gloss on things ?
What need I care ? I cheat in self-defence,
And there 's my answer to a world of cheats !
Cheat ? To be sure, sir ! What 's the world
    worth else ?
Who takes it as he finds, and thanks his stars ?
Don't it want trimming, turning, furbishing up
And polishing over ? Your so-styled great
    men,
Do they accept one truth as truth is found,
Or try their skill at tinkering ? What 's your
    world ?
Here are you born, who are, I 'll say at once,
Of the luckiest kind, whether in head and
    heart,
Body and soul, or all that helps them both.
Well, now, look back : what faculty of yours
Came to its full, had ample justice done
By growing when rain fell, biding its time,
Solidifying growth when earth was dead,
Spiring up, broadening wide, in seasons due ?
Never ! You shot up and frost nipped you off,
Settled to sleep when sunshine bade you sprout;
One faculty thwarted its fellow : at the end,
All you boast is, " I had proved a topping tree
In other climes," — yet this was the right clime

Had you foreknown the seasons. Young,
     you 've force
Wasted like well-streams: old, — oh, then in-
     deed,
Behold a labyrinth of hydraulic pipes
Through which you 'd play off wondrous water-
     work ;
Only, no water 's left to feed their play.
Young, — you 've a hope, an aim, a love ; it 's
     tossed
And crossed and lost : you struggle on, some
     spark
Shut in your heart against the puffs around,
Through cold and pain ; these in due time sub-
     side,
Now then for age's triumph, the hoarded light
You mean to loose on the altered face of
     things, —
Up with it on the tripod ! It 's extinct.
Spend your life's remnant asking, which was
     best,
Light smothered up that never peeped forth
     once,
Or the cold cresset with full leave to shine ?
Well, accept this too, — seek the fruit of it
Not in enjoyment, proved a dream on earth,
But knowledge, useful for a second chance,
Another life, — you 've lost this world — you 've
     gained
Its knowledge for the next. — What knowledge,
     sir,
Except that you know nothing ? Nay, you
     doubt
Whether 't were better have made you man or
     brute,
If aught be true, if good and evil clash.
No foul, no fair, no inside, no outside,
There 's your world !

                         Give it me ! I slap it brisk
With harlequin's pasteboard sceptre : what 's it
     now ?
Changed like a rock-flat, rough with rusty
     weed,
At first wash-over o' the returning wave !
All the dry dead impracticable stuff
Starts into life and light again ; this world
Pervaded by the influx from the next.
I cheat, and what 's the happy consequence ?
You find full justice straightway dealt you out,
Each want supplied, each ignorance set at ease,
Each folly fooled. No life-long labor now
As the price of worse than nothing ! No mere
     film
Holding you chained in iron, as it seems,
Against the outstretch of your very arms
And legs i' the sunshine moralists forbid !
What would you have ? Just speak and, there,
     you see !
You 're supplemented, made a whole at last,
Bacon advises, Shakespeare writes you songs,
And Mary Queen of Scots embraces you.
Thus it goes on, not quite like life perhaps,
But so near, that the very difference piques,
Shows that e'en better than this best will be —
This passing entertainment in a hut
Whose bare walls take your taste since, one
     stage more,

And you arrive at the palace : all half real,
And you, to suit it, less than real beside,
In a dream, lethargic kind of death in life,
That helps the interchange of natures, flesh
Transfused by souls, and such souls ! Oh, 't is
     choice !
And if at whiles the bubble, blown too thin,
Seem nigh on bursting, — if you nearly see
The real world through the false, — what *do*
     you see ?
Is the old so ruined ? You find you 're in a flock
O' the youthful, earnest, passionate — genius,
     beauty,
Rank and wealth also, if you care for these :
And all depose their natural rights, hail you
(That 's me, sir) as their mate and yoke-fellow,
Participate in Sludgehood — nay, grow mine,
I veritably possess them — banish doubt,
And reticence and modesty alike !
Why, here 's the Golden Age, old Paradise
Or new Utopia ! Here 's true life indeed,
And the world well won now, mine for the first
     time !

And all this might be, may be, and with good
     help
Of a little lying shall be : so, Sludge lies !
Why, he 's at worst your poet who sings how
     Greeks
That never were, in Troy which never was,
Did this or the other impossible great thing !
He 's Lowell — it 's a world (you smile applause)
Of his own invention — wondrous Longfellow,
Surprising Hawthorne ! Sludge does more than
     they,
And acts the books they write : the more his
     praise !

But why do I mount to poets ? Take plain
     prose —
Dealers in common sense, set these at work,
What can they do without their helpful lies ?
Each states the law and fact and face o' the
     thing
Just as he 'd have them, finds what he thinks
     fit,
Is blind to what missuits him, just records
What makes his case out, quite ignores the rest.
It 's a History of the World, the Lizard Age,
The Early Indians, the Old Country War,
Jerome Napoleon, whatsoever you please,
All as the author wants it. Such a scribe
You pay and praise for putting life in stones,
Fire into fog, making the past your world.
There 's plenty of " How did you contrive to
     grasp
The thread which led you through this laby-
     rinth ?
How build such solid fabric out of air ?
How on so slight foundation found this tale,
Biography, narrative ? " or, in other words,
" How many lies did it require to make
The portly truth you here present us with ? "
" Oh," quoth the penman, purring at your
     praise,
" 'T is fancy all ; no particle of fact :
I was poor and threadbare when I wrote that
     book

'Bliss in the Golden City.' I, at Thebes?
We writers paint out of our heads, you see!"
" — Ah, the more wonderful the gift in you,
The more creativeness and godlike craft!"
But I, do I present you with my piece,
It's "What, Sludge? When my sainted mo-
   ther spoke
The verses Lady Jane Grey last composed
About the rosy bower in the seventh heaven
Where she and Queen Elizabeth keep house, —
You made the raps? 'T was your invention
   that?
Cur, slave, and devil!" — eight fingers and two
   thumbs
Stuck in my throat!

      Well, if the marks seem gone,
'T is because stiffish cocktail, taken in time,
Is better for a bruise than arnica.
There, sir! I bear no malice: 't is n't in me.
I know I acted wrongly: still, I 've tried
What I could say in my excuse, — to show
The devil's not all devil . . . I don't pretend
He 's angel, much less such a gentleman
As you, sir! And I 've lost you, lost myself,
Lost all-l-l-l- . . .

      No — are you in earnest, sir?
Oh, yours, sir, is an angel's part! I know
What prejudice prompts, and what 's the com-
   mon course
Men take to soothe their ruffled self-conceit:
Only you rise superior to it all!
No, sir, it don't hurt much; it 's speaking
   long
That makes me choke a little : the marks will
   go!
What? Twenty V-notes more, and outfit too,
And not a word to Greeley? One — one kiss
O' the hand that saves me! You 'll not let me
   speak,
I well know, and I 've lost the right, too true!
But I must say, sir, if She hears (she does)
Your sainted . . . Well, sir, — be it so! That 's,
   I think,
My bedroom candle. Good-night! Bl-l-less
   you, sir!

R-r-r, you brute-beast and blackguard! Cow-
   ardly scamp!
I only wish I dared burn down the house
And spoil your sniggering! Oh, what, you 're
   the man?
You 're satisfied at last? You 've found out
   Sludge?
We 'll see that presently : my turn, sir, next!
I too can tell my story : brute, — do you
   hear? —
You throttled your sainted mother, that old
   hag,
In just such a fit of passion : no, it was . . .
To get this house of hers, and many a note
Like these . . . I 'll pocket them, however . . .
   five,
Ten, fifteen . . . ay, you gave her throat the
   twist,

Or else you poisoned her! Confound the cuss!
Where was my head? I ought to have prophe-
   sied
He 'll die in a year and join her : that 's the way.

I don't know where my head is: what had I
   done?
How did it all go? I said he poisoned her,
And hoped he 'd have grace given him to repent,
Whereon he picked this quarrel, bullied me
And called me cheat: I thrashed him, — who
   could help?
He howled for mercy, prayed me on his knees
To cut and run and save him from disgrace :
I do so, and once off, he slanders me.
An end of him! Begin elsewhere anew!
Boston 's a hole, the herring-pond is wide,
V-notes are something, liberty still more.
Beside, is he the only fool in the world?

APPARENT FAILURE

" We shall soon lose a celebrated building."
           Paris Newspaper

No, for I 'll save it! Seven years since,
  I passed through Paris, stopped a day
To see the baptism of your Prince ;
  Saw, made my bow, and went my way:
Walking the heat and headache off,
  I took the Seine-side, you surmise,
Thought of the Congress, Gortschakoff,
  Cavour's appeal and Buol's replies,
So sauntered till — what met my eyes?

Only the Doric little Morgue!
  The dead - house where you show your
   drowned :
Petrarch's Vaucluse makes proud the Sorgue,
  Your Morgue has made the Seine renowned.
One pays one's debt in such a case ;
  I plucked up heart and entered, — stalked,
Keeping a tolerable face
  Compared with some whose cheeks were
   chalked :
Let them! No Briton 's to be balked!

First came the silent gazers ; next,
  A screen of glass, we 're thankful for;
Last, the sight's self, the sermon's text,
  The three men who did most abhor
Their life in Paris yesterday,
  So killed themselves : and now, enthroned
Each on his copper couch, they lay
  Fronting me, waiting to be owned.
I thought, and think, their sin 's atoned.

Poor men, God made, and all for that!
  The reverence struck me ; o'er each head
Religiously was hung its hat,
  Each coat dripped by the owner's bed,
Sacred from touch : each had his berth,
  His bounds, his proper place of rest,
Who last night tenanted on earth
  Some arch, where twelve such slept
   abreast, —
Unless the plain asphalt seemed best.

How did it happen, my poor boy?
　You wanted to be Buonaparte
And have the Tuileries for toy,
　And could not, so it broke your heart?
You, old one by his side, I judge,
　Were, red as blood, a socialist,
A leveller! Does the Empire grudge
You 've gained what no Republic missed?
　Be quiet, and unclench your fist!

And this — why, he was red in vain,
　Or black, — poor fellow that is blue!
What fancy was it, turned your brain?
　Oh, women were the prize for you!
Money gets women, cards and dice
　Get money, and ill-luck gets just
The copper couch and one clear nice
　Cool squirt of water o'er your bust,
The right thing to extinguish lust!

It 's wiser being good than bad;
　It 's safer being meek than fierce:
It 's fitter being sane than mad.
　My own hope is, a sun will pierce
The thickest cloud earth ever stretched;
　That, after Last, returns the First,
Though a wide compass round be fetched;
　That what began best, can't end worst,
Nor what God blessed once, prove accurst.

EPILOGUE

FIRST SPEAKER, *as David*

ON the first of the Feast of Feasts,
　The Dedication Day,
When the Levites joined the Priests
　At the Altar in robed array,
Gave signal to sound and say, —

When the thousands, rear and van,
　Swarming with one accord,
Became as a single man
　(Look, gesture, thought and word)
In praising and thanking the Lord, —

When the singers lift up their voice,
　And the trumpets made endeavor,
Sounding, "In God rejoice!"
　Saying, "In Him rejoice
Whose mercy endureth forever!" —

Then the Temple filled with a cloud,
　Even the House of the Lord;
Porch bent and pillar bowed:
　For the presence of the Lord,
In the glory of his cloud,
　Had filled the House of the Lord.

SECOND SPEAKER, *as Renan*

Gone now! All gone across the dark so far,
　Sharpening fast, shuddering ever, shutting
　　still,
Dwindling into the distance, dies that star
　Which came, stood, opened once! We gazed
　　our fill

With upturned faces on as real a Face
　That, stooping from grave music and mild
　　fire,
Took in our homage, made a visible place
　Through many a depth of glory, gyre on
　　gyre,
For the dim human tribute. Was this true?
　Could man indeed avail, mere praise of his,
To help by rapture God's own rapture too,
　Thrill with a heart's red tinge that pure pale
　　bliss?
Why did it end? Who failed to beat the
　breast,
And shriek, and throw the arms protesting
　wide,
When a first shadow showed the star addressed
　Itself to motion, and on either side
The rims contracted as the rays retired;
　The music, like a fountain's sickening pulse,
Subsided on itself; awhile transpired
　Some vestige of a Face no pangs convulse,
No prayers retard; then even this was gone,
　Lost in the night at last. We, lone and
　　left
Silent through centuries, ever and anon
　Venture to probe again the vault bereft
Of all now save the lesser lights, a mist
　Of multitudinous points, yet suns, men say —
And this leaps ruby, this lurks amethyst,
　But where may hide what came and loved
　　our clay?
How shall the sage detect in yon expanse
　The star which chose to stoop and stay for us?
Unroll the records! Hailed ye such advance
　Indeed, and did your hope evanish thus?
Watchers of twilight, is the worst averred?
　We shall not look up, know ourselves are
　　seen,
Speak, and be sure that we again are heard,
　Acting or suffering, have the disk's serene
Reflect our life, absorb an earthly flame,
　Nor doubt that, were mankind inert and
　　numb,
Its core had never crimsoned all the same,
　Nor, missing ours, its music fallen dumb?
Oh, dread succession to a dizzy post,
　Sad sway of sceptre whose mere touch ap-
　　palls,
Ghastly dethronement, cursed by those the
　　most
On whose repugnant brow the crown next falls!

THIRD SPEAKER

Witless alike of will and way divine,
How heaven's high with earth's low should
　intertwine!
Friends, I have seen through your eyes: now
　use mine!

Take the least man of all mankind, as I;
Look at his head and heart, find how and
　why
He differs from his fellows utterly:

Then, like me, watch when nature by degrees
Grows alive round him, as in Arctic seas
(They said of old) the instinctive water flees

Toward some elected point of central rock,
As though, for its sake only, roamed the flock
Of waves about the waste : awhile they mock

With radiance caught for the occasion, — hues
Of blackest hell now, now such reds and blues
As only heaven could fitly interfuse, —

The mimic monarch of the whirlpool, king
O' the current for a minute : then they wring
Up by the roots and oversweep the thing,

And hasten off, to play again elsewhere
The same part, choose another peak as bare,
They find and flatter, feast and finish there.

When you see what I tell you, — nature dance
About each man of us, retire, advance,
As though the pageant's end were to enhance

His worth, and — once the life, his product, gained —
Roll away elsewhere, keep the strife sustained,
And show thus real, a thing the North but feigned —

When you acknowledge that one world could do
All the diverse work, old yet ever new,
Divide us, each from other, me from you, —

Why, where 's the need of Temple, when the walls
O' the world are that ?   What use of swells and falls
From Levites' choir, Priests' cries, and trumpet-calls ?

That one Face, far from vanish, rather grows,
Or decomposes but to recompose,
Become my universe that feels and knows !

THE RING AND THE BOOK

THIS, the most long sustained of Browning's writings, was published originally in four volumes, successively in November, December, 1868, January, February, 1869. Mrs. Orr has given so circumstantial an account of the inception of the work, that the main facts are here reproduced from her *Hand-Book*.

"Mr. Browning was strolling one day through a square in Florence, the Piazza San Lorenzo, which is a standing market for old clothes, old furniture, and old curiosities of every kind, when a parchment-covered book attracted his eye, from amidst the artistic or nondescript rubbish of one of the stalls. It was the record of a murder which had taken place in Rome, and bore inside it an inscription [in Latin] which Mr. Browning transcribes [on p. 415].

"The book proved, on examination, to contain the whole history of the case, as carried on in writing, after the fashion of those days :

pleadings and counter-pleadings, the depositions of defendants and witnesses ; manuscript letters announcing the execution of the murderer, and the ' instrument of the Definitive Sentence ' which established the perfect innocence of the murdered wife : these various documents having been collected and bound together by some person interested in the trial, possibly the very Cencini, friend of the Franceschini family, to whom the manuscript letters are addressed. Mr. Browning bought the whole for the value of eightpence, and it became the raw material of what appeared four years later as *The Ring and the Book*."

In another place Mrs. Orr states that the subject was conceived about four years before the poet took it actually in hand, and that, before he wrote it himself, he offered the theme for prose treatment to Miss Ogle, the author of *A Lost Love*.

I

THE RING AND THE BOOK

Do you see this Ring ?
          'T is Rome-work, made to match
(By Castellani's imitative craft)
Etrurian circlets found, some happy morn,
After a dropping April ; found alive
Spark-like 'mid unearthed slope-side figtree-roots
That roof old tombs at Chiusi : soft, you see,
Yet crisp as jewel-cutting. There 's one trick,
(Craftsmen instruct me) one approved device
And but one, fits such slivers of pure gold

As this was, — such mere oozings from the mine,
Virgin as oval tawny pendent tear
At beehive-edge when ripened combs o'erflow, —
To bear the file's tooth and the hammer's tap :
Since hammer needs must widen out the round,
And file emboss it fine with lily-flowers,
Ere the stuff grow a ring-thing right to wear.
That trick is, the artificer melts up wax
With honey, so to speak ; he mingles gold
With gold's alloy, and, duly tempering both,
Effects a manageable mass, then works :
But his work ended, once the thing a ring,
Oh, there 's repristination ! Just a spirt
O' the proper fiery acid o'er its face,
And forth the alloy unfastened flies in fume;

While, self-sufficient now, the shape remains,
The rondure brave, the lilied loveliness,
Gold as it was, is, shall be evermore:
Prime nature with an added artistry —
No carat lost, and you have gained a ring.
What of it? 'T is a figure, a symbol, say;
A thing's sign: now for the thing signified.

Do you see this square old yellow Book, I
    toss
I' the air, and catch again, and twirl about
By the crumpled vellum covers, — pure crude
    fact
Secreted from man's life when hearts beat hard,
And brains, high-blooded, ticked two centuries
    since?
Examine it yourselves! I found this book,
Gave a *lira* for it, eightpence English just,
(Mark the predestination!) when a Hand,
Always above my shoulder, pushed me once,
One day still fierce 'mid many a day struck
    calm,
Across a Square in Florence, crammed with
    booths,
Buzzing and blaze, noontide and market-time,
Toward Baccio's marble, — ay, the basement-
    ledge
O' the pedestal where sits and menaces
John of the Black Bands with the upright spear,
'Twixt palace and church, — Riccardi where
    they lived,
His race, and San Lorenzo where they lie.
This book, — precisely on that palace-step
Which, meant for lounging knaves o' the Me-
    dici,
Now serves re-venders to display their ware, —
'Mongst odds and ends of ravage, picture-frames
White through the worn gilt, mirror-sconces
    chipped,
Bronze angel-heads once knobs attached to
    chests
(Handled when ancient dames chose forth bro-
    cade),
Modern chalk drawings, studies from the nude,
Samples of stone, jet, breccia, porphyry
Polished and rough, sundry amazing busts
In baked earth (broken, Providence be praised!)
A wreck of tapestry, proudly-purposed web
When reds and blues were indeed red and blue,
Now offered as a mat to save bare feet
(Since carpets constitute a cruel cost)
Treading the chill scagliola bedward; then
A pile of brown-etched prints, two *crazie* each,
Stopped by a conch a-top from fluttering forth
— Sowing the Square with works of one and
    the same
Master, the imaginative Sienese
Great in the scenic backgrounds — (name and
    fame
None of you know, nor does he fare the worse:)
From these . . . Oh, with a Lionard going cheap
If it should prove, as promised, that Joconde
Whereof a copy contents the Louvre! — these
I picked this book from. Five compeers in
    flank
Stood left and right of it as tempting more —
A dogs-eared Spicilegium, the fond tale

O' the Frail One of the Flower, by young Du-
    mas,
Vulgarized Horace for the use of schools,
The Life, Death, Miracles of Saint Somebody,
Saint Somebody Else, his Miracles, Death and
    Life, —
With this, one glance at the lettered back of
    which,
And "Stall!" cried I: a *lira* made it mine.

Here it is, this I toss and take again;
Small-quarto size, part print, part manuscript:
A book in shape but, really, pure crude fact
Secreted from man's life when hearts beat
    hard,
And brains, high-blooded, ticked two centuries
    since.
Give it me back! The thing's restorative
I' the touch and sight.

               That memorable day,
(June was the month, Lorenzo named the
    Square),
I leaned a little and overlooked my prize
By the low railing round the fountain-source
Close to the statue, where a step descends:
While clinked the cans of copper, as stooped
    and rose
Thick-ankled girls who brimmed them, and
    made place
For marketmen glad to pitch basket down,
Dip a broad melon-leaf that holds the wet,
And whisk their faded fresh. And on I read
Presently, though my path grew perilous
Between the outspread straw-work, piles of
    plait
Soon to be flapping, each o'er two black eyes
And swathe of Tuscan hair, on festas fine:
Through fire-irons, tribes of tongs, shovels in
    sheaves,
Skeleton bedsteads, wardrobe-drawers agape,
Rows of tall slim brass lamps with dangling
    gear, —
And worse, cast clothes a-sweetening in the
    sun:
None of them took my eye from off my prize.
Still read I on, from written title-page
To written index, on, through street and street,
At the Strozzi, at the Pillar, at the Bridge;
Till, by the time I stood at home again
In Casa Guidi by Felice Church,
Under the doorway where the black begins
With the first stone-slab of the staircase cold,
I had mastered the contents, knew the whole
    truth
Gathered together, bound up in this book,
Print three-fifths, written supplement the rest.
"*Romana Homicidiorum*" — nay,
Better translate — "A Roman murder-case:
Position of the entire criminal cause
Of Guido Franceschini, nobleman,
With certain Four the cutthroats in his pay,
Tried, all five, and found guilty and put to
    death
By heading or hanging as befitted ranks,
At Rome on February Twenty Two,
Since our salvation Sixteen Ninety Eight:

Wherein it is disputed if, and when,
Husbands may kill adulterous wives, yet 'scape
The customary forfeit."

               Word for word,
So ran the title-page: murder, or else
Legitimate punishment of the other crime,
Accounted murder by mistake, — just that
And no more, in a Latin cramp enough
When the law had her eloquence to launch,
But interfilleted with Italian streaks
When testimony stooped to mother-tongue, —
That, was this old square yellow book about.

Now, as the ingot, ere the ring was forged,
Lay gold, (beseech you, hold that figure fast!)
So, in this book lay absolutely truth,
Fanciless fact, the documents indeed,
Primary lawyer-pleadings for, against,
The aforesaid Five; real summed-up circum-
    stance
Adduced in proof of these on either side,
Put forth and printed, as the practice was,
At Rome, in the Apostolic Chamber's type,
And so submitted to the eye o' the Court
Presided over by His Reverence
Rome's Governor and Criminal Judge, — the
    trial
Itself, to all intents, being then as now
Here in the book and nowise out of it;
Seeing, there properly was no judgment-bar,
No bringing of accuser and accused,
And whoso judged both parties, face to face
Before some court, as we conceive of courts.
There was a Hall of Justice; that came last:
For Justice had a chamber by the hall
Where she took evidence first, summed up the
    same,
Then sent accuser and accused alike,
In person of the advocate of each,
To weigh its worth, thereby arrange, array
The battle. 'T was the so-styled Fisc began,
Pleaded (and since he only spoke in print
The printed voice of him lives now as then)
The public Prosecutor — " Murder 's proved;
With five . . . what we call qualities of bad,
Worse, worst, and yet worse still, and still
    worse yet;
Crest over crest crowning the cockatrice,
That beggar hell's regalia to enrich
Count Guido Franceschini: punish him!"
Thus was the paper put before the court
In the next stage, (no noisy work at all,)
To study at ease. In due time like reply
Came from the so-styled Patron of the Poor,
Official mouthpiece of the five accused
Too poor to fee a better, — Guido's luck
Or else his fellows', — which, I hardly know, —
An outbreak as of wonder at the world,
A fury-fit of outraged innocence,
A passion of betrayed simplicity:
" Punish Count Guido? For what crime, what
    hint
O' the color of a crime, inform us first!
Reward him rather! Recognize, we say,
In the deed done, a righteous judgment dealt!
All conscience and all courage, — there 's our
    Count

Charactered in a word; and, what 's more
    strange,
He had companionship in privilege,
Found four courageous conscientious friends:
Absolve, applaud all five, as props of law,
Sustainers of society! — perchance
A trifle over-hasty with the hand
To hold her tottering ark, had tumbled else;
But that 's a splendid fault whereat we wink,
Wishing your cold correctness sparkled so!"
Thus paper second followed paper first,
Thus did the two join issue — nay, the four,
Each pleader having an adjunct. " True, ho
    killed
— So to speak — in a certain sort — his wife,
But laudably, since thus it happed!" quoth
    one:
Whereat, more witness and the case postponed.
" Thus it happed not, since thus he did the
    deed,
And proved himself thereby portentousest
Of cutthroats and a prodigy of crime,
As the woman that he slaughtered was a
    saint,
Martyr and miracle!" quoth the other to
    match:
Again, more witness and the case postponed.
" A miracle, ay — of lust and impudence;
Hear my new reasons!" interposed the first:
" — Coupled with more of mine!" pursued his
    peer.
" Beside, the precedents, the authorities!"
From both at once a cry with an echo, that!
That was a firebrand at each fox's tail
Unleashed in a cornfield: soon spread flare
    enough,
As hurtled thither and there heaped them-
    selves
From earth's four corners, all authority
And precedent for putting wives to death,
Or letting wives live, sinful as they seem.
How legislated, now, in this respect,
Solon and his Athenians? Quote the code
Of Romulus and Rome! Justinian speak!
Nor modern Baldo, Bartolo be dumb!
The Roman voice was potent, plentiful;
Cornelia de Sicariis hurried to help
Pompeia de Parricidiis; Julia de
Something-or-other jostled *Lex* this-and-that;
King Solomon confirmed Apostle Paul:
That nice decision of Dolabella, eh?
That pregnant instance of Theodoric, oh!
Down to that choice example Ælian gives
(An instance I find much insisted on)
Of the elephant who, brute-beast though he
    were,
Yet understood and punished on the spot
His master's naughty spouse and faithless
    friend;
A true tale which has edified each child,
Much more shall flourish favored by our court!
Pages of proof this way, and that way proof,
And always — once again the case postponed.

Thus wrangled, brangled, jangled they a
    month,
— Only on paper, pleadings all in print,
Nor ever was, except i' the brains of men,

More noise by word of mouth than you hear
now —
Till the court cut all short with "Judged, your
cause.
Receive our sentence! Praise God! We pro-
nounce
Count Guido devilish and damnable:
His wife Pompilia in thought, word and deed,
Was perfect pure, he murdered her for that:
As for the Four who helped the One, all Five —
Why, let employer and hirelings share alike
In guilt and guilt's reward, the death their
due!"

So was the trial at end, do you suppose?
"Guilty you find him, death you doom him to?
Ay, were not Guido, more than needs, a priest,
Priest and to spare!"—this was a shot re-
served;
I learn this from epistles which begin
Here where the print ends, — see the pen and
ink
Of the advocate, the ready at a pinch!—
"My client boasts the clerkly privilege,
Has taken minor orders many enough,
Shows still sufficient chrism upon his pate
To neutralize a blood-stain: *presbyter*,
Primæ tonsuræ, subdiaconus,
Sacerdos, so he slips from underneath
Your power, the temporal, slides inside the
robe
Of mother Church: to her we make appeal
By the Pope, the Church's head!"

A parlous plea,
Put in with noticeable effect, it seems;
"Since straight," — resumes the zealous orator,
Making a friend acquainted with the facts, —
"Once the word ' clericality ' let fall,
Procedure stopped and freer breath was drawn
By all considerate and responsible Rome."
Quality took the decent part, of course;
Held by the husband, who was noble too:
Or, for the matter of that, a churl would side
With too-refined susceptibility,
And honor which, tender in the extreme,
Stung to the quick, must roughly right itself
At all risks, not sit still and whine for law
As a Jew would, if you squeezed him to the
wall,
Brisk-trotting through the Ghetto. Nay, it
seems,
Even the Emperor's Envoy had his say
To say on the subject; might not see, un-
moved,
Civility menaced throughout Christendom
By too harsh measure dealt her champion here.
Lastly, what made all safe, the Pope was kind,
From his youth up, reluctant to take life,
If mercy might be just and yet show grace;
Much more unlikely then, in extreme age,
To take a life the general sense bade spare.
'T was plain that Guido would go scatheless yet.

But human promise, oh, how short of shine!
How topple down the piles of hope we rear!
How history proves . . . nay, read Herodotus!
Suddenly starting from a nap, as it were,

A dog-sleep with one shut, one open orb,
Cried the Pope's great self, — Innocent by
name
And nature too, and eighty-six years old,
Antonio Pignatelli of Naples, Pope
Who had trod many lands, known many deeds,
Probed many hearts, beginning with his own,
And now was far in readiness for God, —
'T was he who first bade leave those souls in
peace,
Those Jansenists, re-nicknamed Molinists,
('Gainst whom the cry went, like a frowsy tune,
Tickling men's ears — the sect for a quarter of
an hour
I' the teeth of the world which, clown-like,
loves to chew
Be it but a straw 'twixt work and whistling-
while,
Taste some vituperation, bite away,
Whether at marjoram-sprig or garlic-clove,
Aught it may sport with, spoil, and then spit
forth,)
"Leave them alone," bade he, "those Moli-
nists!
Who may have other light than we perceive,
Or why is it the whole world hates them thus?"
Also he peeled off that last scandal-rag
Of Nepotism; and so observed the poor
That men would merrily say, "Halt, deaf and
blind,
Who feed on fat things, leave the master's self
To gather up the fragments of his feast,
These be the nephews of Pope Innocent!—
His own meal costs but five carlines a day,
Poor-priest's allowance, for he claims no more."
— He cried of a sudden, this great good old
Pope,
When they appealed in last resort to him,
"I have mastered the whole matter: I nothing
doubt.
Though Guido stood forth priest from head to
heel,
Instead of, as alleged, a piece of one, —
And further, were he, from the tonsured scalp
To the sandaled sole of him, my son and
Christ's,
Instead of touching us by finger-tip
As you assert, and pressing up so close
Only to set a blood-smutch on our robe, —
I and Christ would renounce all right in him.
Am I not Pope, and presently to die,
And busied how to render my account,
And shall I wait a day ere I decide
On doing or not doing justice here?
Cut off his head to-morrow by this time,
Hang up his four mates, two on either hand,
And end one business more!"

So said, so done –
Rather so writ, for the old Pope bade this,
I find, with his particular chirograph,
His own no such infirm hand, Friday night;
And next day, February Twenty Two,
Since our salvation Sixteen Ninety Eight,
— Not at the proper head-and-hanging-place
On bridge-foot close by Castle Angelo,
Where custom somewhat staled the spectacle,
('T was not so well i' the way of Rome, beside,

The noble Rome, the Rome of Guido's rank)
But at the city's newer gayer end, —
The cavalcading promenading place
Beside the gate and opposite the church
Under the Pincian gardens green with Spring,
'Neath the obelisk 'twixt the fountains in the
  Square,
Did Guido and his fellows find their fate,
All Rome for witness, and — my writer adds —
Remonstrant in its universal grief,
Since Guido had the suffrage of all Rome.

This is the bookful; thus far take the truth,
The untempered gold, the fact untampered
  with,
The mere ring-metal ere the ring be made!
And what has hitherto come of it? Who pre-
  serves
The memory of this Guido, and his wife
Pompilia, more than Ademollo's name,
The etcher of those prints, two *crazie* each,
Saved by a stone from snowing broad the
  Square
With scenic backgrounds? Was this truth of
  force?
Able to take its own part as truth should,
Sufficient, self-sustaining? Why, if so —
Yonder's a fire, into it goes my book,
As who shall say me nay, and what the loss?
You know the tale already: I may ask,
Rather than think to tell you, more thereof, —
Ask you not merely who were he and she,
Husband and wife, what manner of mankind,
But how you hold concerning this and that
Other yet-unnamed actor in the piece.
The young frank handsome courtly Canon, now,
The priest, declared the lover of the wife,
He who, no question, did elope with her,
For certain bring the tragedy about,
Giuseppe Caponsacchi; — his strange course
I' the matter, was it right or wrong or both?
Then the old couple, slaughtered with the wife
By the husband as accomplices in crime,
Those Comparini, Pietro and his spouse, —
What say you to the right or wrong of that,
When, at a known name whispered through the
  door
Of a lone villa on a Christmas night,
It opened that the joyous hearts inside
Might welcome as it were an angel-guest
Come in Christ's name to knock and enter, sup
And satisfy the loving ones he saved;
And so did welcome devils and their death?
I have been silent on that circumstance
Although the couple passed for close of kin
To wife and husband, were by some accounts
Pompilia's very parents: you know best.
Also that infant the great joy was for,
That Gaetano, the wife's two-weeks' babe,
The husband's first-born child, his son and heir,
Whose birth and being turned his night to
  day —
Why must the father kill the mother thus
Because she bore his son and saved himself?

Well, British Public, ye who like me not,
(God love you!) and will have your proper
  laugh

At the dark question, laugh it! I laugh first.
Truth must prevail, the proverb vows; and
  truth
— Here is it all i' the book at last, as first
There it was all i' the heads and hearts of
  Rome
Gentle and simple, never to fall nor fade
Nor be forgotten. Yet, a little while,
The passage of a century or so,
Decads thrice five, and here's time paid his
  tax,
Oblivion gone home with her harvesting,
And all left smooth again as scythe could
  shave.
Far from beginning with you London folk,
I took my book to Rome first, tried truth's
  power
On likely people. "Have you met such
  names?
Is a tradition extant of such facts?
Your law-courts stand, your records frown
  a-row:
What if I rove and rummage?" " — Why,
  you'll waste
Your pains and end as wise as you began!"
Every one snickered: "names and facts thus
  old
Are newer much than Europe news we find
Down in to-day's *Diario*. Records, quotha?
Why, the French burned them, what else do
  the French?
The rap-and-rending nation! And it tells
Against the Church, no doubt, — another gird
At the Temporality, your Trial, of course?"
" — Quite otherwise this time," submitted I;
"Clean for the Church and dead against the
  world,
The flesh and the devil, does it tell for once."
" — The rarer and the happier! All the same,
Content you with your treasure of a book,
And waive what's wanting! Take a friend's
  advice!
It's not the custom of the country. Mend
Your ways indeed and we may stretch a point:
Go get you manned by Manning and new-
  manned
By Newman and, mayhap, wise-manned to boot
By Wiseman, and we'll see or else we won't!
Thanks meantime for the story, long and strong,
A pretty piece of narrative enough,
Which scarce ought so to drop out, one would
  think,
From the more curious annals of our kind.
Do you tell the story, now, in off-hand style,
Straight from the book? Or simply here and
  there,
(The while you vault it through the loose and
  large)
Hang to a hint? Or is there book at all,
And don't you deal in poetry, make-believe,
And the white lies it sounds like?"

                        Yes and no!
From the book, yes; thence bit by bit I dug
The lingot truth, that memorable day,
Assayed and knew my piecemeal gain was
  gold, —
Yes; but from something else surpassing that,

Something of mine which, mixed up with the mass,
Made it bear hammer and be firm to file.
Fancy with fact is just one fact the more ;
To wit, that fancy has informed, transpierced,
Thridded and so thrown fast the facts else free,
As right through ring and ring runs the djereed
And binds the loose, one bar without a break.
I fused my live soul and that inert stuff,
Before attempting smithcraft, on the night
After the day when — truth thus grasped and gained —
The book was shut and done with and laid by
On the cream-colored massive agate, broad
'Neath the twin cherubs in the tarnished frame
O' the mirror, tall thence to the ceiling-top.
And from the reading, and that slab I leant
My elbow on, the while I read and read,
I turned, to free myself and find the world,
And stepped out on the narrow terrace, built
Over the street and opposite the church,
And paced its lozenge-brickwork sprinkled cool —
Because Felice-church-side stretched, aglow
Through each square window fringed for festival,
Whence came the clear voice of the cloistered ones
Chanting a chant made for midsummer nights —
I know not what particular praise of God,
It always came and went with June. Beneath
I' the street, quick shown by openings of the sky
When flame fell silently from cloud to cloud,
Richer than that gold snow Jove rained on Rhodes,
The townsmen walked by twos and threes, and talked,
Drinking the blackness in default of air —
A busy human sense beneath my feet :
While in and out the terrace-plants, and round
One branch of tall datura, waxed and waned
The lamp-fly lured there, wanting the white flower.
Over the roof o' the lighted church I looked
A bowshot to the street's end, north away
Out of the Roman gate to the Roman road
By the river, till I felt the Apennine.
And there would lie Arezzo, the man's town,
The woman's trap and cage and torture-place,
Also the stage where the priest played his part,
A spectacle for angels, — ay, indeed,
There lay Arezzo ! Farther then I fared,
Feeling my way on through the hot and dense,
Romeward, until I found the wayside inn
By Castelnuovo's few mean hut-like homes
Huddled together on the hill-foot bleak,
Bare, broken only by that tree or two
Against the sudden bloody splendor poured
Cursewise in day's departure by the sun
O'er the low house-roof of that squalid inn
Where they three, for the first time and the last,
Husband and wife and priest, met face to face.
Whence I went on again, the end was near,
Step by step, missing none and marking all,
Till Rome itself, the ghastly goal, I reached.
Why, all the while, — how could it otherwise ? —
The life in me abolished the death of things,

Deep calling unto deep : as then and there
Acted itself over again once more
The tragic piece. I saw with my own eyes
In Florence as I trod the terrace, breathed
The beauty and the fearfulness of night,
How it had run, this round from Rome to Rome —
Because, you are to know, they lived at Rome,
Pompilia's parents, as they thought themselves,
Two poor ignoble hearts who did their best
Part God's way, part the other way than God's,
To somehow make a shift and scramble through
The world's mud, careless if it splashed and spoiled,
Provided they might so hold high, keep clean
Their child's soul, one soul white enough for three,
And lift it to whatever star should stoop,
What possible sphere of purer life than theirs
Should come in aid of whiteness hard to save.
I saw the star stoop, that they strained to touch,
And did touch and depose their treasure on,
As Guido Franceschini took away
Pompilia to be his forevermore,
While they sang " Now let us depart in peace,
Having beheld thy glory, Guido's wife ! "
I saw the star supposed, but fog o' the fen,
Gilded star-fashion by a glint from hell ;
Having been heaved up, haled on its gross way,
By hands unguessed before, invisible help
From a dark brotherhood, and specially
Two obscure goblin creatures, fox-faced this,
Cat-clawed the other, called his next of kin
By Guido the main monster, — cloaked and caped,
Making as they were priests, to mock God more, —
Abate Paul, Canon Girolamo.
These who had rolled the starlike pest to Rome
And stationed it to suck up and absorb
The sweetness of Pompilia, rolled again
That bloated bubble, with her soul inside,
Back to Arezzo and a palace there —
Or say, a fissure in the honest earth
Whence long ago had curled the vapor first,
Blown big by nether fires to appall day :
It touched home, broke, and blasted far and wide.
I saw the cheated couple find the cheat
And guess what foul rite they were captured for, —
Too fain to follow over hill and dale
That child of theirs caught up thus in the cloud
And carried by the Prince o' the Power of the Air
Whither he would, to wilderness or sea.
I saw them, in the potency of fear,
Break somehow through the satyr-family
(For a gray mother with a monkey-mien,
Mopping and mowing, was apparent too,
As, confident of capture, all took hands
And danced about the captives in a ring)
— Saw them break through, breathe safe, at Rome again,
Saved by the selfish instinct, losing so
Their loved one left with haters. These I saw,
In recrudescency of baffled hate,
Prepare to wring the uttermost revenge

From body and soul thus left them : all was
    sure,
Fire laid and caldron set, the obscene ring
    traced,
The victim stripped and prostrate : what of
    God ?
The cleaving of a cloud, a cry, a crash,
Quenched lay their caldron, cowered i' the dust
    the crew,
As, in a glory of armor like Saint George,
Out again sprang the young good beauteous
    priest
Bearing away the lady in his arms,
Saved for a splendid minute and no more.
For, whom i' the path did that priest come
    upon,
He and the poor lost lady borne so brave,
— Checking the song of praise in me, had else
Swelled to the full for God's will done on earth —
Whom but a dusk misfeatured messenger,
No other than the angel of this life,
Whose care is lest men see too much at once.
He made the sign, such God-glimpse must
    suffice,
Nor prejudice the Prince o' the Power of the
    Air,
Whose ministration piles us overhead
What we call, first, earth's roof and, last,
    heaven's floor,
Now grate o' the trap, then outlet of the cage :
So took the lady, left the priest alone,
And once more canopied the world with black.
But through the blackness I saw Rome again,
And where a solitary villa stood
In a lone garden-quarter : it was eve,
The second of the year, and oh so cold !
Ever and anon there flittered through the air
A snow-flake, and a scanty couch of snow
Crusted the grass-walk and the garden-mould.
All was grave, silent, sinister, — when, ha ?
Glimmeringly did a pack of were-wolves pad
The snow, those flames were Guido's eyes in
    front,
And all five found and footed it, the track,
To where a threshold-streak of warmth and
    light
Betrayed the villa-door with life inside,
While an inch outside were those blood-bright
    eyes,
And black lips wrinkling o'er the flash of teeth,
And tongues that lolled — O God that madest
    man !
They parleyed in their language. Then one
    whined —
That was the policy and master-stroke —
Deep in his throat whispered what seemed a
    name —
"Open to Caponsacchi !" Guido cried :
"Gabriel !" cried Lucifer at Eden-gate.
Wide as a heart, opened the door at once,
Showing the joyous couple, and their child
The two-weeks' mother, to the wolves, the
    wolves
To them. Close eyes ! And when the corpses
    lay
Stark-stretched, and those the wolves, their
    wolf-work done.
Were safe-embosomed by the night again,

I knew a necessary change in things ;
As when the worst watch of the night gives
    way,
And there comes duly, to take cognizance,
The scrutinizing eye-point of some star —
And who despairs of a new daybreak now ?
Lo, the first ray protruded on those five !
It reached them, and each felon writhed trans-
    fixed.
Awhile they palpitated on the spear
Motionless over Tophet : stand or fall ?
"I say, the spear should fall — should stand, I
    say ! "
Cried the world come to judgment, granting
    grace
Or dealing doom according to world's wont,
Those world's-bystanders grouped on Rome's
    cross-road
At prick and summons of the primal curse
Which bids man love as well as make a lie.
There prattled they, discoursed the right and
    wrong,
Turned wrong to right, proved wolves sheep and
    sheep wolves,
So that you scarce distinguished fell from
    fleece ;
Till out spoke a great guardian of the fold,
Stood up, put forth his hand that held the
    crook,
And motioned that the arrested point decline :
Horribly off, the wriggling dead-weight reeled,
Rushed to the bottom and lay ruined there.
Though still at the pit's mouth, despite the
    smoke
O' the burning, tarriers turned again to talk
And trim the balance, and detect at least
A touch of wolf in what showed whitest sheep,
A cross of sheep redeeming the whole wolf, —
Vex truth a little longer : — less and less,
Because years came and went, and more and
    more
Brought new lies with them to be loved in turn.
Till all at once the memory of the thing, —
The fact that, wolves or sheep, such creatures
    were, —
Which hitherto, however men supposed,
Had somehow plain and pillar-like prevailed
I' the midst of them, indisputably fact,
Granite, time's tooth should grate against, not
    graze, —
Why, this proved sandstone, friable, fast to fly
And give its grain away at wish o' the wind.
Ever and ever more diminutive,
Base gone, shaft lost, only entablature,
Dwindled into no bigger than a book,
Lay of the column ; and that little, left
By the roadside 'mid the ordure, shards and
    weeds.
Until I haply, wandering that lone way,
Kicked it up, turned it over, and recognized,
For all the crumblement, this abacus,
This square old yellow book, — could calculate
By this the lost proportions of the style.

This was it from, my fancy with those facts,
I used to tell the tale, turned gay to grave,
But lacked a listener seldom ; such alloy,
Such substance of me interfused the gold

Which, wrought into a shapely ring therewith,
Hammered and filed, fingered and favored, last
Lay ready for the renovating wash
O' the water. "How much of the tale was
    true?"
I disappeared; the book grew all in all;
The lawyers' pleadings swelled back to their
    size, —
Doubled in two, the crease upon them yet,
For more commodity of carriage, see! —
And these are letters, veritable sheets
That brought post-haste the news to Florence,
    writ
At Rome the day Count Guido died, we find,
To stay the craving of a client there,
Who bound the same and so produced my book.
Lovers of dead truth, did ye fare the worse?
Lovers of live truth, found ye false my tale?

Well, now; there's nothing in nor out o' the
    world
Good except truth: yet this, the something else,
What's this then, which proves good yet seems
    untrue?
This that I mixed with truth, motions of mine
That quickened, made the inertness malleola-
    ble
O' the gold was not mine, — what's your name
    for this?
Are means to the end, themselves in part the
    end?
Is fiction which makes fact alive, fact too?
The somehow may be thishow.

                        I find first
Writ down for very A B C of fact.
"In the beginning God made heaven and
    earth;"
From which, no matter with what lisp, I spell
And speak you out a consequence — that man,
Man, — as befits the made, the inferior thing, —
Purposed, since made, to grow, not make in
    turn,
Yet forced to try and make, else fail to grow, —
Formed to rise, reach at, if not grasp and gain
The good beyond him, — which attempt is
    growth, —
Repeats God's process in man's due degree,
Attaining man's proportionate result, —
Creates, no, but resuscitates, perhaps.
Inalienable, the arch-prerogative
Which turns thought, act — conceives, expresses
    too!
No less, man, bounded, yearning to be free,
May so project his surplusage of soul
In search of body, so add self to self
By owning what lay ownerless before, —
So find, so fill full, so appropriate forms —
That, although nothing which had never life
Shall get life from him, be, not having been,
Yet, something dead may get to live again,
Something with too much life or not enough,
Which, either way imperfect, ended once:
An end whereat man's impulse intervenes,
Makes new beginning, starts the dead alive,
Completes the incomplete and saves the thing.
Man's breath were vain to light a virgin
    wick, —

Half-burned-out, all but quite-quenched wicks
    o' the lamp
Stationed for temple-service on this earth,
These indeed let him breathe on and relume!
For such man's feat is, in the due degree,
— Mimic creation, galvanism for life,
But still a glory portioned in the scale.
Why did the mage say — feeling as we are wont
For truth, and stopping midway short of truth,
And resting on a lie — "I raise a ghost"?
"Because," he taught adepts, "man makes
    not man.
Yet by a special gift, an art of arts,
More insight and more outsight and much more
Will to use both of these than boast my mates,
I can detach from me, commission forth
Half of my soul; which in its pilgrimage
O'er old unwandered waste ways of the world,
May chance upon some fragment of a whole,
Rag of flesh, scrap of bone in dim disuse,
Smoking flax that fed fire once: prompt therein
I enter, spark-like, put old powers to play,
Push lines out to the limit, lead forth last
(By a moonrise through a ruin of a crypt)
What shall be mistily seen, murmuringly heard,
Mistakenly felt: then write my name with
    Faust's!"
Oh, Faust, why Faust? Was not Elisha
    once? —
Who bade them lay his staff on a corpse-face.
There was no voice, no hearing: he went in
Therefore, and shut the door upon them twain,
And prayed unto the Lord: and he went up
And lay upon the corpse, dead on the couch,
And put his mouth upon its mouth, his eyes
Upon its eyes, his hands upon its hands,
And stretched him on the flesh; the flesh waxed
    warm:
And he returned, walked to and fro the house,
And went up, stretched him on the flesh again,
And the eyes opened. 'T is a credible feat
With the right man and way.

                        Enough of me!
The Book! I turn its medicinable leaves
In London now till, as in Florence erst,
A spirit laughs and leaps through every limb,
And lights my eye, and lifts me by the hair,
Letting me have my will again with these
— How title I the dead alive once more?

Count Guido Franceschini the Aretine,
Descended of an ancient house, though poor,
A beak-nosed bushy-bearded black-haired lord,
Lean, pallid, low of stature yet robust,
Fifty years old, — having four years ago
Married Pompilia Comparini, young,
Good, beautiful, at Rome, where she was born,
And brought her to Arezzo, where they lived
Unhappy lives, whatever curse the cause, —
This husband, taking four accomplices,
Followed this wife to Rome, where she was fled
From their Arezzo to find peace again,
In convoy, eight months earlier, of a priest,
Aretine also, of still nobler birth,
Giuseppe Caponsacchi, — caught her there
Quiet in a villa on a Christmas night,
With only Pietro and Violante by.

Both her putative parents ; killed the three,
Aged they, seventy each, and she, seventeen,
And, two weeks since, the mother of his babe
First-born and heir to what the style was
        worth
O' the Guido who determined, dared and did
This deed just as he purposed point by point.
Then, bent upon escape, but hotly pressed,
And captured with his co-mates that same
        night,
He, brought to trial, stood on this defence —
Injury to his honor caused the act ;
And since his wife was false, (as manifest
By flight from home in such companionship,)
Death, punishment deserved of the false wife
And faithless parents who abetted her
I' the flight aforesaid, wronged nor God nor
        man.
" Nor false she, nor yet faithless they," replied
The accuser ; "cloaked and masked this
        murder glooms ;
True was Pompilia, loyal too the pair ;
Out of the man's own heart a monster curled,
Which — crime coiled with connivancy at
        crime —
His victim's breast, he tells you, hatched and
        reared ;
Uncoil we and stretch stark the worm of hell ! "
A month the trial swayed this way and that
Ere judgment settled down on Guido's guilt ;
Then was the Pope, that good Twelfth Innocent,
Appealed to : who well weighed what went be-
        fore,
Affirmed the guilt and gave the guilty doom.

Let this old woe step on the stage again !
Act itself o'er anew for men to judge,
Not by the very sense and sight indeed —
(Which take at best imperfect cognizance,
Since, how heart moves brain, and how both
        move hand,
What mortal ever in entirety saw ?)
— No dose of purer truth than man digests,
But truth with falsehood, milk that feeds him
        now,
Not strong meat he may get to bear some
        day —
To wit, by voices we call evidence,
Uproar in the echo, live fact deadened down,
Talked over, bruited abroad, whispered away,
Yet helping us to all we seem to hear :
For how else know we save by worth of word ?

Here are the voices presently shall sound
In due succession. First, the world's outcry
Around the rush and ripple of any fact
Fallen stonewise, plumb on the smooth face of
        things ;
The world's guess, as it crowds the bank o' the
        pool,
At what were figure and substance, by their
        splash :
Then, by vibrations in the general mind,
At depth of deed already out of reach.
This threefold murder of the day before, —
Say, Half - Rome's feel after the vanished
        truth ;
Honest enough, as the way is : all the same,

Harboring in the centre of its sense
A hidden germ of failure, shy but sure,
To neutralize that honesty and leave
That feel for truth at fault, as the way is too.
Some prepossession such as starts amiss,
By but a hair's breadth at the shoulder-blade,
The arm o' the feeler, dip he ne'er so bold ;
So leads arm waveringly, lets fall wide
O' the mark its finger, sent to find and fix
Truth at the bottom, that deceptive speck.
With this Half-Rome, — the source of swerving,
        call
Over-belief in Guido's right and wrong
Rather than in Pompilia's wrong and right :
Who shall say how, who shall say why ?   'T is
        there —
The instinctive theorizing whence a fact
Looks to the eye as the eye likes the look.
Gossip in a public place, a sample-speech.
Some worthy, with his previous hint to find
A husband's side the safer, and no whit
Aware he is not Æacus the while, —
How such an one supposes and states fact
To whosoever of a multitude
Will listen, and perhaps prolong thereby
The not-unpleasant flutter at the breast,
Born of a certain spectacle shut in
By the church Lorenzo opposite. So, they
        lounge
Midway the mouth o' the street, on Corso side,
'Twixt palace Fiano and palace Ruspoli,
Linger and listen ; keeping clear o' the crowd,
Yet wishful one could lend that crowd one's
        eyes,
(So universal is its plague of squint)
And make hearts beat our time that flutter
        false :
— All for the truth's sake, mere truth, nothing
        else !
How Half-Rome found for Guido much ex-
        cuse.

Next, from Rome's other half, the opposite
        feel
For truth with a like swerve, like unsuccess, —
Or if success, by no skill but more luck,
This time, through siding rather with the wife
Because a fancy-fit inclined that way,
Than with the husband. One wears drab, one
        pink ;
Who wears pink, ask him "Which shall win
        the race,
Of coupled runners like as egg and egg ?"
" — Why, if I must choose, he with the pink
        scarf."
Doubtless for some such reason choice fell here.
A piece of public talk to correspond
At the next stage of the story ; just a day
Let pass and new day brings the proper change.
Another sample-speech i' the market-place
O' the Barberini by the Capucins ;
Where the old Triton, at his fountain-sport,
Bernini's creature plated to the paps,
Puffs up steel sleet which breaks to diamond
        dust,
A spray of sparkles snorted from his conch,
High over the caritellas, out o' the way
O' the motley merchandising multitude.

Our murder has been done three days ago,
The frost is over and gone, the south wind
    laughs,
And, to the very tiles of each red roof
A-smoke i' the sunshine, Rome lies gold and
    glad :
So, listen how, to the other half of Rome,
Pompilia seemed a saint and martyr both !

Then, yet another day let come and go,
With pause prelusive still of novelty,
Hear a fresh speaker ! — neither this nor that
Half-Rome aforesaid ; something bred of both :
One and one breed the inevitable three.
Such is the personage harangues you next ;
The elaborated product, *tertium quid* :
Rome's first commotion in subsidence gives
The curd o' the cream, flower o' the wheat, as
    it were,
And finer sense o' the city. Is this plain ?
You get a reasoned statement of the case,
Eventual verdict of the curious few
Who care to sift a business to the bran
Nor coarsely bolt it like the simpler sort.
Here, after ignorance, instruction speaks ;
Here, clarity of candor, history's soul,
The critical mind, in short : no gossip-guess.
What the superior social section thinks,
In person of some man of quality
Who — breathing musk from lace-work and
    brocade,
His solitaire amid the flow of frill,
Powdered peruke on nose, and bag at back,
And cane dependent from the ruffled wrist —
Harangues in silvery and selectest phrase
'Neath waxlight in a glorified saloon
Where mirrors multiply the girandole :
Courting the approbation of no mob,
But Eminence This and All-Illustrious That
Who take snuff softly, range in well-bred ring,
Card-table-quitters for observance' sake,
Around the argument, the rational word —
Still, spite its weight and worth, a sample-
    speech.
How Quality dissertated on the case.

So much for Rome and rumor ; smoke comes
    first :
Once let smoke rise untroubled, we descry
Clearlier what tongues of flame may spire and
    spit
To eye and ear, each with appropriate tinge
According to its food, or pure or foul.
The actors, no mere rumors of the act,
Intervene. First you hear Count Guido's voice,
In a small chamber that adjoins the court,
Where Governor and Judges, summoned thence,
Tommati, Venturini and the rest,
Find the accused ripe for declaring truth.
Soft-cushioned sits he ; yet shifts seat, shirks
    touch,
As, with a twitchy brow and wincing lip
And cheek that changes to all kinds of white,
He proffers his defence, in tones subdued
Near to mock-mildness now, so mournful seems
The obtuser sense truth fails to satisfy ;
Now, moved, from pathos at the wrong endured,
To passion ; for the natural man is roused

At fools who first do wrong, then pour the blame
Of their wrong-doing, Satan-like, on Job.
Also his tongue at times is hard to curb ;
Incisive, nigh satiric bites the phrase,
Rough-raw, yet somehow claiming privilege
— It is so hard for shrewdness to admit
Folly means no harm when she calls black
    white !
— Eruption momentary at the most,
Modified forthwith by a fall o' the fire,
Sage acquiescence ; for the world 's the world,
And, what it errs in, Judges rectify :
He feels he has a fist, then folds his arms
Crosswise and makes his mind up to be meek,
And never once does he detach his eye
From those ranged there to slay him or to save,
But does his best man's-service for himself,
Despite, — what twitches brow and makes lip
    wince, —
His limbs' late taste of what was called the
    Cord,
Or Vigil-torture more facetiously.
Even so ; they were wont to tease the truth
Out of loth witness (toying, trifling time)
By torture : 't was a trick, a vice of the age,
Here, there and everywhere, what would you
    have ?
Religion used to tell Humanity
She gave him warrant or denied him course.
And since the course was much to his own mind,
Of pinching flesh and pulling bone from bone
To unhusk truth a-hiding in its hulls,
Nor whisper of a warning stopped the way,
He, in their joint behalf, the burly slave,
Bestirred him, mauled and maimed all recusants,
While, prim in place, Religion overlooked ;
And so had done till doomsday, never a sign
Nor sound of interference from her mouth,
But that at last the burly slave wiped brow,
Let eye give notice as if soul were there,
Muttered " 'T is a vile trick, foolish more than
    vile,
Should have been counted sin ; I make it so :
At any rate no more of it for me —
Nay, for I break the torture-engine thus ! "
Then did Religion start up, stare amain,
Look round for help and see none, smile and
    say
" What, broken is the rack ? Well done of
    thee !
Did I forget to abrogate its use ?
Be the mistake in common with us both !
— One more fault our blind age shall answer for,
Down in my book denounced though it must be
Somewhere. Henceforth find truth by milder
    means ! "
Ah but, Religion, did we wait for thee
To ope the book, that serves to sit upon,
And pick such place out, we should wait indeed !
That is all history : and what is not now,
Was then, defendants found it to their cost.
How Guido, after being tortured, spoke.

Also hear Caponsacchi who comes next,
Man and priest — could you comprehend the
    coil ! —
In days when that was rife which now is rare.
How, mingling each its multifarious wires,

Now heaven, now earth, now heaven and earth
  at once,
Had plucked at and perplexed their puppet
  here,
Played off the young frank personable priest ;
Sworn fast and tonsured plain heaven's celibate,
And yet earth's clear-accepted servitor,
A courtly spiritual Cupid, squire of dames
By law of love and mandate of the mode.
The Church's own, or why parade her seal,
Wherefore that chrism and consecrative work ?
Yet verily the world's, or why go badged
A prince of sonneteers and lutanists,
Show color of each vanity in vogue
Borne with decorum due on blameless breast ?
All that is changed now, as he tells the court
How he had played the part excepted at ;
Tells it, moreover, now the second time :
Since, for his cause of scandal, his own share
I' the flight from home and husband of the wife,
He has been censured, punished in a sort
By relegation, — exile, we should say,
To a short distance for a little time, —
Whence he is summoned on a sudden now,
Informed that she, he thought to save, is lost,
And, in a breath, bidden re-tell his tale,
Since the first telling somehow missed effect,
And then advise in the matter. There stands he,
While the same grim black-panelled chamber
  blinks
As though rubbed shiny with the sins of Rome
Told the same oak for ages — wave-washed wall
Against which sets a sea of wickedness.
There, where you yesterday heard Guido speak,
Speaks Caponsacchi ; and there face him too
Tommati, Venturini and the rest
Who, eight months earlier, scarce repressed the
  smile,
Forewent the wink ; waived recognition so
Of peccadillos incident to youth,
Especially youth high-born ; for youth means
  love,
Vows can't change nature, priests are only men,
And love likes stratagem and subterfuge :
Which age, that once was youth, should recog-
  nize,
May blame, but needs not press too hard upon.
Here sit the old Judges then, but with no grace
Of reverend carriage, magisterial port.
For why ?   The accused of eight months since,
  — the same
Who cut the conscious figure of a fool,
Changed countenance, dropped bashful gaze to
  ground,
While hesitating for an answer then, —
Now is grown judge himself, terrifies now
This, now the other culprit called a judge,
Whose turn it is to stammer and look strange,
As he speaks rapidly, angrily, speech that
  smites :
And they keep silence, bear blow after blow,
Because the seeming-solitary man,
Speaking for God, may have an audience too,
Invisible, no discreet judge provokes.
How the priest Caponsacchi said his say.

Then a soul sighs its lowest and its last
After the loud ones, — so much breath remains

Unused by the four-days'-dying ; for she lived
Thus long, miraculously long, 't was thought,
Just that Pompilia might defend herself.
How, while the hireling and the alien stoop,
Comfort, yet question, — since the time is brief,
And folk, allowably inquisitive,
Encircle the low pallet where she lies
In the good house that helps the poor to die, —
Pompilia tells the story of her life.
For friend and lover, — leech and man of law
Do service ; busy helpful ministrants
As varied in their calling as their mind,
Temper and age : and yet from all of these,
About the white bed under the arched roof,
Is somehow, as it were, evolved a one, —
Small separate sympathies combined and large
Nothings that were, grown something very
  much :
As if the bystanders gave each his straw,
All he had, though a trifle in itself,
Which, plaited all together, made a Cross
Fit to die looking on and praying with,
Just as well as if ivory or gold.
So, to the common kindliness she speaks,
There being scarce more privacy at the last
For mind than body : but she is used to bear,
And only unused to the brotherly look,
How she endeavored to explain her life.

Then, since a Trial ensued, a touch o' the same
To sober us, flustered with frothy talk,
And teach our common sense its helplessness.
For why deal simply with divining-rod,
Scrape where we fancy secret sources flow,
And ignore law, the recognized machine,
Elaborate display of pipe and wheel
Framed to unchoke, pump up and pour apace
Truth till a flowery foam shall wash the world ?
The patent truth-extracting process, — ha ?
Let us make that grave mystery turn one wheel,
Give you a single grind of law at least !
One orator, of two on either side,
Shall teach us the puissance of the tongue
  — That is, o' the pen which simulated tongue
On paper and saved all except the sound
Which never was.   Law's speech beside law's
  thought ?
That were too stunning, too immense an odds :
That point of vantage law lets nobly pass.
One lawyer shall admit us to behold
The manner of the making out a case,
First fashion of a speech ; the chick in egg,
The masterpiece law's bosom incubates.
How Don Giacinto of the Arcangeli,
Called Procurator of the Poor at Rome,
Now advocate for Guido and his mates, —
The jolly learned man of middle age,
Cheek and jowl all in laps with fat and law,
Mirthful as mighty, yet, as great hearts use,
Despite the name and fame that tempt our flesh
Constant to that devotion of the hearth,
Still captive in those dear domestic ties ! —
How he, — having a cause to triumph with,
All kind of interests to keep intact,
More than one efficacious personage
To tranquillize, conciliate and secure,
And above all, public anxiety
To quiet, show its Guido in good hands,

Also, as if such burdens were too light,
A certain family-feast to claim his care,
The birthday-banquet for the only son —
Paternity at smiling strife with law —
How he brings both to buckle in one bond ;
And, thick at throat, with waterish under-eye,
Turns to his task and settles in his seat
And puts his utmost means in practice now :
Wheezes out law-phrase, whiffles Latin forth,
And, just as though roast lamb would never be,
Makes logic levigate the big crime small :
Rubs palm on palm, rakes foot with itchy foot,
Conceives and inchoates the argument,
Sprinkling each flower appropriate to the time,
— Ovidian quip or Ciceronian crank,
A-bubble in the larynx while he laughs,
As he had fritters deep down frying there.
How he turns, twists, and tries the oily thing
Shall be — first speech for Guido 'gainst the Fisc.
Then with a skip as it were from heel to head,
Leaving yourselves fill up the middle bulk
O' the Trial, reconstruct its shape august,
From such exordium clap we to the close ;
Give you, if we dare wing to such a height,
The absolute glory in some full-grown speech
On the other side, some finished butterfly,
Some breathing diamond-flake with leaf-gold fans,
That takes the air, no trace of worm it was,
Or cabbage-bed it had production from.
Giovambattista o' the Bottini, Fisc,
Pompilia's patron by the chance of the hour,
To-morrow her persecutor, — composite, he,
As becomes who must meet such various calls —
Odds of age joined in him with ends of youth.
A man of ready smile and facile tear,
Improvised hopes, despairs at nod and beck,
And language — ah, the gift of eloquence !
Language that goes, goes, easy as a glove,
O'er good and evil, smoothens both to one.
Rashness helps caution with him, fires the straw,
In free enthusiastic careless fit,
On the first proper pinnacle of rock
Which offers, as reward for all that zeal,
To lure some bark to founder and bring gain :
While calm sits Caution, rapt with heavenward eye,
A true confessor's gaze, amid the glare
Beaconing to the breaker, death and hell.
" Well done, thou good and faithful ! " she approves :
" Hadst thou let slip a fagot to the beach,
The crew might surely spy thy precipice
And save their boat ; the simple and the slow
Might so, forsooth, forestall the wrecker's fee !
Let the next crew be wise and hail in time ! "
Just so compounded is the outside man,
Blue juvenile pure eye and pippin cheek,
And brow all prematurely soiled and seamed
With sudden age, bright devastated hair.
Ah, but you miss the very tones o' the voice,
The scrannel pipe that screams in heights of head,
As, in his modest studio, all alone,
The tall wight stands a-tiptoe, strives and strains,

Both eyes shut, like the cockerel that would crow,
Tries to his own self amorously o'er
What never will be uttered else than so —
Since to the four walls, Forum and Mars' Hill,
Speaks out the poesy which, penned, turns prose.
Clavecinist debarred his instrument,
He yet thrums — shirking neither turn nor trill,
With desperate finger on dumb table-edge —
The sovereign rondo, shall conclude his *Suite*,
Charm an imaginary audience there,
From old Corelli to young Haendel, both
I' the flesh at Rome, ere he perforce go print
The cold black score, mere music for the mind —
The last speech against Guido and his gang,
With special end to prove Pompilia pure,
How the Fisc vindicates Pompilia's fame.

Then comes the all but end, the ultimate
Judgment save yours. Pope Innocent the Twelfth,
Simple, sagacious, mild yet resolute,
With prudence, probity and — what beside
From the other world he feels impress at times,
Having attained to fourscore years and six, —
How, when the court found Guido and the rest
Guilty, but law supplied a subterfuge
And passed the final sentence to the Pope,
He, bringing his intelligence to bear
This last time on what ball behoves him drop
In the urn, or white or black, does drop a black,
Send five souls more to just precede his own,
Stand him in stead and witness, if need were,
How he is wont to do God's work on earth.
The manner of his sitting out the dim
Droop of a sombre February day
In the plain closet where he does such work,
With, from all Peter's treasury, one stool,
One table and one lathen crucifix.
There sits the Pope, his thoughts for company ;
Grave but not sad, — nay, something like a cheer
Leaves the lips free to be benevolent,
Which, all day long, did duty firm and fast.
A cherishing there is of foot and knee,
A chafing loose-skinned large-veined hand with hand, —
What steward but knows when stewardship earns its wage,
May levy praise, anticipate the lord ?
He reads, notes, lays the papers down at last,
Muses, then takes a turn about the room ;
Unclasps a huge tome in an antique guise,
Primitive print and tongue half obsolete,
That stands him in diurnal stead ; opes page,
Finds place where falls the passage to be conned
According to an order long in use :
And, as he comes upon the evening's chance,
Starts somewhat, solemnizes straight his smile,
Then reads aloud that portion first to last,
And at the end lets flow his own thoughts forth
Likewise aloud, for respite and relief,
Till by the dreary relics of the west
Wan through the half-moon window, all his light,
He bows the head while the lips move in prayer.

Writes some three brief lines, signs and seals
   the same,
Tinkles a hand-bell, bids the obsequious Sir
Who puts foot presently o' the closet-sill
He watched outside of, bear as superscribed
That mandate to the Governor forthwith :
Then heaves abroad his cares in one good sigh,
Traverses corridor with no arm's help,
And so to sup as a clear conscience should.
The manner of the judgment of the Pope.

Then must speak Guido yet a second time,
Satan's old saw being apt here — skin for skin,
All a man hath that will he give for life.
While life was graspable and gainable,
And bird-like buzzed her wings round Guido's
   brow,
Not much truth stiffened out the web of words
He wove to catch her : when away she flew
And death came, death's breath rivelled up the
   lies,
Left bare the metal thread, the fibre fine
Of truth, i' the spinning : the true words shone
   last.
How Guido, to another purpose quite,
Speaks and despairs, the last night of his life,
In that New Prison by Castle Angelo
At the bridge-foot : the same man, another
   voice.
On a stone bench in a close fetid cell,
Where the hot vapor of an agony,
Struck into drops on the cold wall, runs down —
Horrible worms made out of sweat and tears —
There crouch, wellnigh to the knees in dungeon-
   straw,
Lit by the sole lamp suffered for their sake,
Two awe-struck figures, this a Cardinal,
That an Abate, both of old styled friends
O' the thing part man, part monster in the midst,
So changed is Franceschini's gentle blood.
The tiger-cat screams now, that whined before,
That pried and tried and trod so gingerly,
Till in its silkiness the trap-teeth joined ;
Then you know how the bristling fury foams.
They listen, this wrapped in his folds of red,
While his feet fumble for the filth below ;
The other, as beseems a stouter heart,
Working his best with beads and cross to ban
The enemy that comes in like a flood
Spite of the standard set up, verily
And in no trope at all, against him there :
For at the prison-gate, just a few steps
Outside, already, in the doubtful dawn,
Thither, from this side and from that, slow
   sweep
And settle down in silence solidly,
Crow-wise, the frightful Brotherhood of Death.
Black-hatted and black-hooded huddle they,
Black rosaries a-dangling from each waist ;
So take they their grim station at the door,
Torches lit, skull-and-crossbones-banner spread,
And that gigantic Christ with open arms,
Grounded.   Nor lacks there aught but that the
   group
Break forth, intone the lamentable psalm,
" Out of the deeps, Lord, have I cried to
   thee ! " —
When inside, from the true profound, a sign

Shall bear intelligence that the foe is foiled,
Count Guido Franceschini has confessed,
And is absolved and reconciled with God.
Then they, intoning, may begin their march,
Make by the longest way for the People's
   Square,
Carry the criminal to his crime's award :
A mob to cleave, a scaffolding to reach,
Two gallows and Mannaia crowning all.
How Guido made defence a second time.

Finally, even as thus by step and step
I led you from the level of to-day
Up to the summit of so long ago,
Here, whence I point you the wide prospect
   round —
Let me, by like steps, slope you back to smooth,
Land you on mother-earth, no whit the worse,
To feed o' the fat o' the furrow : free to dwell,
Taste our time's better things profusely spread
For all who love the level, corn and wine,
Much cattle and the many-folded fleece.
Shall not my friends go feast again on sward,
Though cognizant of country in the clouds
Higher than wistful eagle's horny eye
Ever unclosed for, 'mid ancestral crags,
When morning broke and Spring was back once
   more,
And he died, heaven, save by his heart, un-
   reached ?
Yet heaven my fancy lifts to, ladder-like, —
As Jack reached, holpen of his beanstalk-
   rungs !

A novel country : I might make it mine
By chosing which one aspect of the year
Suited mood best, and putting solely that
On panel somewhere in the House of Fame,
Landscaping what I saved, not what I saw :
— Might fix you, whether frost in goblin-time
Startled the moon with his abrupt bright laugh,
Or, August's hair afloat in filmy fire,
She fell, arms wide, face foremost on the world,
Swooned there and so singed out the strength
   of things.
Thus were abolished Spring and Autumn both,
The land dwarfed to one likeness of the land,
Life cramped corpse-fashion.   Rather learn
   and love
Each facet-flash of the revolving year ! —
Red, green and blue that whirl into a white,
The variance now, the eventual unity,
Which make the miracle.   See it for your-
   selves,
This man's act, changeable because alive !
Action now shrouds, nor shows the informing
   thought ;
Man, like a glass ball with a spark a-top,
Out of the magic fire that lurks inside,
Shows one tint at a time to take the eye :
Which, let a finger touch the silent sleep,
Shifted a hair's-breadth shoots you dark for
   bright,
Suffuses bright with dark, and baffles so
Your sentence absolute for shine or shade.
Once set such orbs, — white styled, black stig-
   matized, —
A-rolling, see them once on the other side

Your good men and your bad men every one,
From Guido Franceschini to Guy Faux,
Oft would you rub your eyes and change your
names.

Such, British Public, ye who like me not,
(God love you!) — whom I yet have labored for,
Perchance more careful whoso runs may read
Than erst when all, it seemed, could read who
ran, —
Perchance more careless whoso reads may
praise
Than late when he who praised and read and
wrote
Was apt to find himself the selfsame me, —
Such labor had such issue, so I wrought
This arc, by furtherance of such alloy,
And so, by one spirt, take away its trace
Till, justifiably golden, rounds my ring.

A ring without a posy, and that ring mine?

O lyric Love, half angel and half bird,
And all a wonder and a wild desire, —
Boldest of hearts that ever braved the sun,
Took sanctuary within the holier blue,
And sang a kindred soul out to his face, —
Yet human at the red-ripe of the heart —
When the first summons from the darkling
earth
Reached thee amid thy chambers, blanched
their blue,
And bared them of the glory — to drop down,
To toil for man, to suffer or to die, —
This is the same voice: can thy soul know
change?
Hail then, and hearken from the realms of help!
Never may I commence my song, my due
To God who best taught song by gift of thee,
Except with bent head and beseeching hand —
That still, despite the distance and the dark,
What was, again may be; some interchange
Of grace, some splendor once thy very thought,
Some benediction anciently thy smile:
— Never conclude, but raising hand and head
Thither where eyes, that cannot reach, yet
yearn
For all hope, all sustainment, all reward,
Their utmost up and on, — so blessing back
In those thy realms of help, that heaven thy
home,
Some whiteness which, I judge, thy face makes
proud,
Some wanness where, I think, thy foot may
fall!

II

HALF-ROME

What, you, Sir, come too? (Just the man I'd
meet.)
Be ruled by me and have a care o' the crowd:
This way, while fresh folk go and get their
gaze:
I'll tell you like a book and save your shins.
Fie, what a roaring day we've had! Whose
fault?

Lorenzo in Lucina, — here's a church
To hold a crowd at need, accommodate
All comers from the Corso! If this crush
Make not its priests ashamed of what they
show
For temple-room, don't prick them to draw
purse
And down with bricks and mortar, eke us out
The beggarly transept with its bit of apse
Into a decent space for Christian ease,
Why, to-day's lucky pearl is cast to swine.
Listen and estimate the luck they've had!
(The right man, and I hold him.)

                    Sir, do you see
They laid both bodies in the church, this morn
The first thing, on the chancel two steps up,
Behind the little marble balustrade;
Disposed them, Pietro the old murdered fool
To the right of the altar, and his wretched wife
On the other side. In trying to count stabs,
People supposed Violante showed the most,
Till somebody explained us that mistake;
His wounds had been dealt out indifferent
where,
But she took all her stabbings in the face,
Since punished thus solely for honor's sake,
Honoris causâ, that's the proper term.
A delicacy there is, our gallants hold,
When you avenge your honor and only then,
That you disfigure the subject, fray the face,
Not just take life and end, in clownish guise.
It was Violante gave the first offence,
Got therefore the conspicuous punishment:
While Pietro, who helped merely, his mere
death
Answered the purpose, so his face went free.
We fancied even, free as you please, that face
Showed itself still intolerably wronged;
Was wrinkled over with resentment yet,
Nor calm at all, as murdered faces use,
Once the worst ended: an indignant air
O' the head there was — 't is said the body
turned
Round and away, rolled from Violante's side
Where they had laid it loving-husband-like.
If so, if corpses can be sensitive,
Why did not he roll right down altar-step,
Roll on through nave, roll fairly out of church,
Deprive Lorenzo of the spectacle,
Pay back thus the succession of affronts
Whereto this church had served as theatre?
For see: at that same altar where he lies,
To that same inch of step, was brought the babe
For blessing after baptism, and there styled
Pompilia, and a string of names beside,
By his bad wife, some seventeen years ago,
Who purchased her simply to palm on him,
Flatter his dotage and defraud the heirs.
Wait awhile! Also to this very step
Did this Violante, twelve years afterward,
Bring, the mock-mother, that child-cheat full
grown,
Pompilia, in pursuance of her plot,
And there brave God and man a second time
By linking a new victim to the lie.
There, having made a match unknown to him
She, still unknown to Pietro, tied the knot

Which nothing cuts except this kind of knife;
Yes, made her daughter, as the girl was held,
Marry a man, and honest man beside,
And man of birth to boot, — clandestinely
Because of this, because of that, because
O' the devil's will to work his worst for
   once, —
Confident she could top her part at need
And, when her husband must be told in turn,
Ply the wife's trade, play off the sex's trick
And, alternating worry with quiet qualms,
Bravado with submissiveness, prettily fool
Her Pietro into patience: so it proved.
Ay, 'tis four years since man and wife they
   grew,
This Guido Franceschini and this same
Pompilia, foolishly thought, falsely declared
A Comparini and the couple's child:
Just at this altar where, beneath the piece
Of Master Guido Reni, Christ on cross,
Second to naught observable in Rome,
That couple lie now, murdered yestereve.
Even the blind can see a providence here.

From dawn till now that it is growing dusk,
A multitude has flocked and filled the church,
Coming and going, coming back again,
Till to count crazed one. Rome was at the
   show.
People climbed up the columns, fought for
   spikes
O' the chapel-rail to perch themselves upon,
Jumped over and so broke the wooden work
Painted like porphyry to deceive the eye;
Serve the priests right! The organ-loft was
   crammed,
Women were fainting, no few fights ensued,
In short, it was a show repaid your pains:
For, though their room was scant undoubtedly,
Yet they did manage matters, to be just,
A little at this Lorenzo. Body o' me!
I saw a body exposed once . . . never mind!
Enough that here the bodies had their due.
No stinginess in wax, a row all round,
And one big taper at each head and foot.

So, people pushed their way, and took their turn,
Saw, threw their eyes up, crossed themselves,
   gave place
To pressure from behind, since all the world
Knew the old pair, could talk the tragedy
Over from first to last: Pompilia too,
Those who had known her — what 't was
   worth to them!
Guido's acquaintance was in less request;
The Count had lounged somewhat too long in
   Rome,
Made himself cheap; with him were hand and
   glove
Barbers and blear-eyed, as the ancient sings.
Also he is alive and like to be:
Had he considerately died, — aha!
I jostled Luca Cini on his staff,
Mute in the midst, the whole man one amaze,
Staring amain and crossing brow and breast.
"How now?" asked I. "'T is seventy years,"
   quoth he,
'Since I first saw, holding my father's hand,

Bodies set forth: a many have I seen,
Yet all was poor to this I live and see.
Here the world 's wickedness seals up the sum:
What with Molinos' doctrine and this deed,
Antichrist surely comes and doomsday 's near.
May I depart in peace, I have seen my see."
"Depart then," I advised, "nor block the road
For youngsters still behindhand with such
   sights!"
"Why no," rejoins the venerable sire,
"I know it 's horrid, hideous past belief,
Burdensome far beyond what eye can bear;
But they do promise, when Pompilia dies
I' the course o' the day, — and she can't outlive
   night, —
They 'll bring her body also to expose
Beside the parents, one, two, three abreast;
That were indeed a sight which, might I see,
I trust I should not last to see the like!"
Whereat I bade the senior spare his shanks,
Since doctors give her till to-night to live,
And tell us how the butchery happened. "Ah,
But you can't know!" sighs he, "I 'll not de-
   spair:
Beside I 'm useful at explaining things —
As, how the dagger laid there at the feet,
Caused the peculiar cuts; I mind its make,
Triangular i' the blade, a Genoese,
Armed with those little hook-teeth on the edge
To open in the flesh nor shut again:
I like to teach a novice: I shall stay!"
And stay he did, and stay be sure he will.

A personage came by the private door
At noon to have his look: I name no names:
Well then, His Eminence the Cardinal,
Whose servitor in honorable sort
Guido was once, the same who made the
   match,
(Will you have the truth?) whereof we see
   effect.
No sooner whisper ran he was arrived
Than up pops Curate Carlo, a brisk lad,
Who never lets a good occasion slip,
And volunteers improving the event.
We looked he 'd give the history's self some
   help,
Treat us to how the wife's confession went
(This morning she confessed her crime, we
   know)
And, maybe, throw in something of the
   Priest —
If he 's not ordered back, punished anew,
The gallant, Caponsacchi, Lucifer
I' the garden where Pompilia, Eve-like, lured
Her Adam Guido to his fault and fall.
Think you we got a sprig of speech akin
To this from Carlo, with the Cardinal there?
Too wary he was, too widely awake, I trow.
He did the murder in a dozen words;
Then said that all such outrages crop forth
I' the course of nature, when Molinos' tares
Are sown for wheat, flourish and choke the
   Church:
So slid on to the abominable sect
And the philosophic sin — we 've heard all that,
And the Cardinal too, (who book-made on the
   same)

But, for the murder, left it where he found.
Oh but he 's quick, the Curate, minds his
    game !
And, after all, we have the main o' the fact :
Case could not well be simpler, — mapped, as it
    were,
We follow the murder's maze from source to
    sea,
By the red line, past mistake : one sees indeed
Not only how all was and must have been,
But cannot other than be to the end of time.
Turn out here by the Ruspoli ! Do you hold
Guido was so prodigiously to blame ?
A certain cousin of yours has told you so ?
Exactly ! Here 's a friend shall set you right,
Let him but have the handsel of your ear.

These wretched Comparini were once gay
And galliard, of the modest middle class :
Born in this quarter seventy years ago,
And married young, they lived the accustomed
    life,
Citizens as they were of good repute :
And, childless, naturally took their ease
With only their two selves to care about
And use the wealth for : wealthy is the word,
Since Pietro was possessed of house and land —
And specially one house, when good days
    smiled,
In Via Vittoria, the aspectable street
Where he lived mainly ; but another house
Of less pretension did he buy betimes,
The villa, meant for jaunts and jollity,
I' the Pauline district, to be private there —
Just what puts murder in an enemy's head.
Moreover, — here 's the worm i' the core, the
    germ
O' the rottenness and ruin which arrived, —
He owned some usufruct, had moneys' use
Lifelong, but to determine with his life
In heirs' default : so, Pietro craved an heir,
(The story always old and always new)
Shut his fool's-eyes fast on the visible good
And wealth for certain, opened them owl-wide
On fortune's sole piece of forgetfulness,
The child that should have been and would not
    be.

Hence, seventeen years ago, conceive his glee
When first Violante, 'twixt a smile and blush,
With touch of agitation proper too,
Announced that, spite of her unpromising age,
The miracle would in time be manifest,
An heir's birth was to happen : and it did.
Somehow or other, — how, all in good time !
By a trick, a sleight of hand you are to hear, —
A child was born, Pompilia, for his joy,
Plaything at once and prop, a fairy-gift,
A saints' grace or, say, grant of the good
    God, —
A fiddle-pin's end ! What imbeciles are we !
Look now : if some one could have prophesied,
" For love of you, for liking to your wife,
I undertake to crush a snake I spy
Settling itself i' the soft of both your breasts.
Give me yon babe to strangle painlessly !
She 'll soar to the safe : you 'll have your cry-
    ing out,

Then sleep, then wake, then sleep, then end
    your days
In peace and plenty, mixed with mild regret,
Thirty years hence when Christmas takes old
    folk " —
How had old Pietro sprung up, crossed himself,
And kicked the conjurer ! Whereas you and I,
Being wise with after-wit, had clapped our
    hands ;
Nay, added, in the old fool's interest,
" Strangle the black-eyed babe, so far so good,
But on condition you relieve the man
O' the wife and throttle him Violante too —
She is the mischief ! "

                    We had hit the mark.
She, whose trick brought the babe into the
    world,
She it was, when the babe was grown a girl,
Judged a new trick should reinforce the old,
Send vigor to the lie now somewhat spent
By twelve years' service ; lest Eve's rule de-
    cline
Over this Adam of hers, whose cabbage-plot
Throve dubiously since turned fools'-paradise,
Spite of a nightingale on every stump.
Pietro's estate was dwindling day by day,
While he, rapt far above such mundane care,
Crawled all-fours with his baby pick-a-back,
Sat at serene cats'-cradle with his child,
Or took the measured tallness, top to toe,
Of what was grown a great girl twelve years
    old :
Till sudden at the door a tap discreet,
A visitor's premonitory cough,
And poverty had reached him in her rounds.

This came when he was past the working-time,
Had learned to dandle and forgot to dig,
And who must but Violante cast about,
Contrive and task that head of hers again ?
She who had caught one fish could make that
    catch
A bigger still, in angler's policy :
So, with an angler's mercy for the bait,
Her minnow was set wriggling on its barb
And tossed to mid-stream ; which means, this
    grown girl
With the great eyes and bounty of black hair
And first crisp youth that tempts a jaded taste,
Was whisked i' the way of a certain man, who
    snapped.

Count Guido Franceschini the Aretine
Was head of an old noble house enough,
Not over-rich, you can't have everything,
But such a man as riches rub against,
Readily stick to, — one with a right to them
Born in the blood : 't was in his very brow
Always to knit itself against the world,
Beforehand so, when that world stinted due
Service and suit : the world ducks and defers.
As such folks do, he had come up to Rome
To better his fortune, and, since many years,
Was friend and follower of a cardinal ;
Waiting the rather thus on providence,
That a shrewd younger poorer brother yet,
The Abate Paolo, a regular priest,

Had long since tried his powers and found he
    swam
With the deftest on the Galilean pool:
But then he was a web-foot, free o' the wave,
And no ambiguous dab-chick hatched to strut,
Humbled by any fond attempt to swim
When fiercer fowl usurped his dunghill-top —
A whole priest, Paolo, no mere piece of one,
Like Guido tacked thus to the Church's tail!
Guido moreover, as the head o' the house,
Claiming the main prize, not the lesser luck,
The centre lily, no mere chickweed fringe.

He waited and learned waiting, thirty years;
Got promise, missed performance — what would
    you have?
No petty post rewards a nobleman
For spending youth in splendid lackey-work,
And there 's concurrence for each rarer prize;
When that falls, rougher hand and readier foot
Push aside Guido spite of his black looks.
The end was, Guido, when the warning showed,
The first white hair i' the glass, gave up the
    game,
Determined on returning to his town,
Making the best of bad incurable,
Patching the old palace up and lingering there
The customary life out with his kin,
Where honor helps to spice the scanty bread.

Just as he trimmed his lamp and girt his loins
To go his journey and be wise at home,
In the right mood of disappointed worth,
Who but Violante sudden spied her prey
(Where was I with that angler-simile?)
And threw her bait, Pompilia, where he
    sulked —
A gleam i' the gloom!

                What if he gained thus much,
Wrung out this sweet drop from the bitter
    Past,
Bore off this rose-bud from the prickly brake
To justify such torn clothes and scratched
    hands,
And, after all, brought something back from
    Rome?
Would not a wife serve at Arezzo well
To light the dark house, lend a look of youth
To the mother's face grown meagre, left alone
And famished with the emptiness of hope,
Old Donna Beatrice? Wife you want
Would you play family-representative,
Carry you elder-brotherly, high and right
O'er what may prove the natural petulance
Of the third brother, younger, greedier still,
Girolamo, also a fledgeling priest,
Beginning life in turn with callow beak
Agape for luck, no luck had stopped and
    stilled.
Such were the pinks and grays about the bait
Persuaded Guido gulp down hook and all.

What constituted him so choice a catch,
You question? Past his prime and poor beside!
Ask that of any she who knows the trade.
Why first, here was a nobleman with friends,
A palace one might run to and be safe

When presently the threatened fate should fall,
A big-browed master to block doorway up,
Parley with people bent on pushing by,
And praying the mild Pietro quick clear
    scores:
Is birth a privilege and power or no?
Also — but judge of the result desired,
By the price paid and manner of the sale.
The Count was made woo, win and wed at
    once:
Asked, and was haled for answer, lest the heat
Should cool, to San Lorenzo, one blind eve,
And had Pompilia put into his arms
O' the sly there, by a hasty candle-blink,
With sanction of some priest-confederate
Properly paid to make short work and sure.

So did old Pietro's daughter change her style
For Guido Franceschini's lady-wife
Ere Guido knew it well; and why this haste
And scramble and indecent secrecy?
" Lest Pietro, all the while in ignorance,
Should get to learn, gainsay and break the
    match:
His peevishness had promptly put aside
Such honor and refused the proffered boon,
Pleased to become authoritative once.
She remedied the wilful man's mistake — "
Did our discreet Violante. Rather say,
Thus did she lest the object of her game,
Guido the gulled one, give him but a chance,
A moment's respite, time for thinking twice,
Might count the cost before he sold himself,
And try the clink of coin they paid him with.

But coin paid, bargain struck and business
    done,
Once the clandestine marriage over thus,
All parties made perforce the best o' the fact:
Pietro could play vast indignation off,
Be ignorant and astounded, dupe, poor soul,
Please you, of daughter, wife and son-in-law,
While Guido found himself in flagrant fault,
Must e'en do suit and service, soothe, subdue
A father not unreasonably chafed,
Bring him to terms by paying son's devoir.
Pleasant initiation!

                The end, this:
Guido's broad back was saddled to bear all —
Pietro, Violante, and Pompilia too, —
Three lots cast confidently in one lap,
Three dead-weights with one arm to lift the
    three
Out of their limbo up to life again.
The Roman household was to strike fresh root
In a new soil, graced with a novel name,
Gilt with an alien glory, Aretine
Henceforth and never Roman any more,
By treaty and engagement; thus it ran:
Pompilia's dowry for Pompilia's self
As a thing of course, — she paid her own ex-
    pense;
No loss nor gain there: but the couple, you see,
They, for their part, turned over first of all
Their fortune in its rags and rottenness
To Guido, fusion and confusion, he
And his with them and theirs, — whatever rag

With coin residuary fell on floor
When Brother Paolo's energetic shake
Should do the relics justice: since 't was
　　thought,
Once vulnerable Pietro out of reach,
That, left at Rome as representative,
The Abate, backed by a potent patron here,
And otherwise with purple flushing him,
Might play a good game with the creditor,
Make up a moiety which, great or small,
Should go to the common stock - if anything,
Guido's, so far repayment of the cost
About to be, — and if, as looked more like,
Nothing, — why, all the nobler cost were his
Who guaranteed, for better or for worse,
To Pietro and Violante, house and home,
Kith and kin, with the pick of company
And life o' the fat o' the land while life should
　　last.
How say you to the bargain at first blush?
Why did a middle-aged not-silly man
Show himself thus besotted all at once?
Quoth Solomon, one black eye does it all.

They went to Arezzo, — Pietro and his spouse,
With just the dusk o' the day of life to spend,
Eager to use the twilight, taste a treat,
Enjoy for once with neither stay nor stint
The luxury of lord-and-lady-ship,
And realize the stuff and nonsense long
A-simmer in their noddles; vent the fume
Born there and bred, the citizen's conceit
How fares nobility while crossing earth,
What rampart or invisible body-guard
Keeps off the taint of common life from such.
They had not fed for nothing on the tales
Of grandees who give banquets worthy Jove,
Spending gold as if Plutus paid a whim,
Served with obeisances as when . . . what God?
I 'm at the end of my tether; 't is enough
You understand what they came primed to see:
While Guido who should minister the sight,
Stay all this qualmish greediness of soul
With apples and with flagons — for his part,
Was set on life diverse as pole from pole :
Lust of the flesh, lust of the eye, — what else
Was he just now awake from, sick and sage,
After the very debauch they would begin? —
Suppose such stuff and nonsense really were.
That bubble, they were bent on blowing big,
He had blown already till he burst his cheeks,
And hence found soapsuds bitter to the tongue.
He hoped now to walk softly all his days
In soberness of spirit, if haply so,
Pinching and paring he might furnish forth
A frugal board, bare sustenance, no more,
Till times, that could not well grow worse,
　　should mend.

Thus minded then, two parties mean to meet
And make each other happy. The first week,
And fancy strikes fact and explodes in full.
"This," shrieked the Comparini, "this the
　　Count,
The palace, the signorial privilege,
The pomp and pageantry were promised us?
For this have we exchanged our liberty,
Our competence, our darling of a child?

To house as spectres in a sepulchre
Under this black stone heap, the street's dis-
　　grace,
Grimmest as that is of the gruesome town,
And here pick garbage on a pewter plate,
Or cough at verjuice dripped from earthen-
　　ware?
Oh Via Vittoria, oh the other place
I' the Pauline, did we give you up for this?
Where 's the foregone housekeeping good and
　　gay,
The neighborliness, the companionship,
The treat and feast when holidays came round,
The daily feast that seemed no treat at all,
Called common by the uncommon fools we
　　were!
Even the sun that used to shine at Rome,
Where is it? Robbed and starved and frozen
　　too,
We will have justice, justice if there be!"
Did not they shout, did not the town resound!
Guido's old lady-mother Beatrice,
Who since her husband, Count Tommaso's
　　death,
Had held sole sway i' the house, — the doited
　　crone
Slow to acknowledge, curtsey and abdicate, —
Was recognized of true novercal type,
Dragon and devil. His brother Girolamo
Came next in order: priest was he? The
　　worse!
No way of winning him to leave his mumps
And help the laugh against old ancestry
And formal habits long since out of date,
Letting his youth be patterned on the mode
Approved of where Violante laid down law.
Or did he brighten up by way of change,
Dispose himself for affability?
The malapert, too complaisant by half
To the alarmed young novice of a bride!
Let him go buzz, betake himself elsewhere,
Nor singe his fly-wings in the candle-flame!

Four months' probation of this purgatory,
Dog-snap and cat-claw, curse and counterblast,
The devil's self were sick of his own din;
And Pietro, after trumpeting huge wrongs
At church and market-place, pillar and post,
Square's corner, street's end, now the palace-
　　step
And now the wine-house bench — while, on her
　　side,
Violante up and down was voluble
In whatsoever pair of ears would perk
From goody, gossip, cater-cousin and sib,
Curious to peep at the inside of things
And catch in the act pretentious poverty
At its wits' end to keep appearance up,
Make both ends meet, — nothing the vulgar
　　loves
Like what this couple pitched them right and
　　left.
Then, their worst done that way, both struck
　　tent, marched
— Renounced their share o' the bargain, flung
　　what dues
Guido was bound to pay, in Guido's face,
Left their hearts'-darling, treasure of the twain

And so forth, the poor inexperienced bride,
To her own devices, bade Arezzo rot,
Cursed life signorial, and sought Rome once
    more.

I see the comment ready on your lip,
" The better fortune, Guido's — free at least
By this defection of the foolish pair,
He could begin make profit in some sort
Of the young bride and the new quietness,
Lead his own life now, henceforth breathe un-
    plagued."
Could he ? You know the sex like Guido's
    self.
Learn the Violante-nature !

                        Once in Rome,
By way of helping Guido lead such life,
Her first act to inaugurate return
Was, she got pricked in conscience : Jubilee
Gave her the hint. Our Pope, as kind as just,
Attained his eighty years, announced a boon
Should make us bless the fact, held Jubilee —
Short shrift, prompt pardon for the light
    offence,
And no rough dealing with the regular crime
So this occasion were not suffered slip —
Otherwise, sins commuted as before,
Without the least abatement in the price.
Now, who had thought it ? All this while, it
    seems,
Our sage Violante had a sin of a sort
She must compound for now or not at all.
Now be the ready riddance ! She confessed
Pompilia was a fable, not a fact :
She never bore a child in her whole life.
Had this child been a changeling, that were
    grace
In some degree, exchange is hardly theft ;
You take your stand on truth ere leap your
    lie :
Here was all lie, no touch of truth at all,
All the lie hers — not even Pietro guessed
He was as childless still as twelve years since.
The babe had been a find i' the filth-heap, Sir,
Catch from the kennel ! There was found at
    Rome,
Down in the deepest of our social dregs,
A woman who professed the wanton's trade
Under the requisite thin coverture,
Communis meretrix and washer-wife :
The creature thus conditioned found by chance
Motherhood like a jewel in the muck,
And straightway either trafficked with her
    prize
Or listened to the tempter and let be, —
Made pact abolishing her place and part
In womankind, beast-fellowship indeed.
She sold this babe eight months before its birth
To our Violante, Pietro's honest spouse,
Well-famed and widely-instanced as that crown
To the husband, virtue in a woman's shape.
She it was, bought, paid for, passed off the
    thing
As very flesh and blood and child of her
Despite the flagrant fifty years, — and why ?
Partly to please old Pietro, fill his cup
With wine at the late hour when lees are left,

And send him from life's feast rejoicingly, —
Partly to cheat the rightful heirs, agape,
Each uncle's cousin's brother's son of him,
For that same principal of the usufruct
It vext him he must die and leave behind.

Such was the sin had come to be confessed.
Which of the tales, the first or last, was true ?
Did she so sin once, or, confessing now,
Sin for the first time ? Either way you will.
One sees a reason for the cheat : one sees
A reason for a cheat in owning cheat,
Where no cheat had been. What of the revenge ?
What prompted the contrition all at once,
Made the avowal easy, the shame slight ?
Why, prove they but Pompilia not their child,
No child, no dowry ! this, supposed their child,
Had claimed what this, shown alien to their
    blood,
Claimed nowise : Guido's claim was through his
    wife,
Null then and void with hers. The biter bit,
Do you see ! For such repayment of the past,
One might conceive the penitential pair
Ready to bring their case before the courts,
Publish their infamy to all the world
And, arm in arm, go chuckling thence content.

Is this your view ? 'T was Guido's anyhow,
And colorable : he came forward then,
Protested in his very bride's behalf
Against this lie and all it led to, least
Of all the loss o' the dowry ; no ! From her
And him alike he would expunge the blot,
Erase the brand of such a bestial birth,
Participate in no hideous heritage
Gathered from the gutter to be garnered up
And glorified in a palace. Peter and Paul !
But that who likes may look upon the pair
Exposed in yonder church, and show his skill
By saying which is eye and which is mouth
Through those stabs thick and threefold, — but
    for that —
A strong word on the liars and their lie
Might crave expression and obtain it, Sir !
— Though prematurely, since there 's more to
    come,
More that will shake your confidence in things
Your cousin tells you, — may I be so bold ?

This makes the first act of the farce, — anon
The sombre element comes stealing in
Till all is black or blood-red in the piece.
Guido, thus made a laughing-stock abroad,
A proverb for the market-place at home,
Left alone with Pompilia now, this graft
So reputable on his ancient stock,
This plague-seed set to fester his sound flesh,
What does the Count ? Revenge him on his
    wife ?
Unfasten at all risks to rid himself
The noisome lazar-badge, fall foul of fate,
And, careless whether the poor rag was ware
O' the part it played, or helped unwittingly,
Bid it go burn and leave his frayed flesh free ?
Plainly, did Guido open both doors wide,
Spurn thence the cur-cast creature and clear
    scores

As man might, tempted in extreme like this?
No, birth and breeding, and compassion too
Saved her such scandal. She was young, he
　thought,
Not privy to the treason, punished most
I' the proclamation of it; why make her
A party to the crime she suffered by?
Then the black eyes were now her very own,
Not any more Violante's: let her live,
Lose in a new air, under a new sun,
The taint of the imputed parentage
Truly or falsely, take no more the touch
Of Pietro and his partner anyhow!
All might go well yet.

　　　　　　So she thought, herself,
It seems, since what was her first act and deed
When news came how these kindly ones at
　Rome
Had stripped her naked to amuse the world,
With spots here, spots there and spots every-
　where?
— For I should tell you that they noised abroad
Not merely the main scandal of her birth,
But slanders written, printed, published wide,
Pamphlets which set forth all the pleasantry
Of how the promised glory was a dream,
The power a bubble, and the wealth — why,
　dust.
There was a picture, painted to the life,
Of those rare doings, that superlative
Initiation in magnificence
Conferred on a poor Roman family
By favor of Arezzo and her first
And famousest, the Franceschini there.
You had the Countship holding head aloft
Bravely although bespattered, shifts and straits
In keeping out o' the way o' the wheels o' the
　world,
The comic of those home-contrivances
When the old lady-mother's wit was taxed
To find six clamorous mouths in food more
　real
Than fruit plucked off the cobwebbed family-
　tree,
Or acorns shed from its gilt mouldered frame —
Cold glories served up with stale fame for sauce.
What, I ask, — when the drunkenness of hate
Hiccuped return for hospitality,
Befouled the table they had feasted on,
Or say, — God knows I'll not prejudge the
　case, —
Grievances thus distorted, magnified,
Colored by quarrel into calumny, —
What side did our Pompilia first espouse?
Her first deliberate measure was, she wrote,
Pricked by some loyal impulse, straight to
　Rome
And her husband's brother the Abate there,
Who, having managed to effect the match,
Might take men's censure for its ill success.
She made a clean breast also in her turn,
And qualified the couple properly,
Since whose departure, hell, she said, was
　heaven,
And the house, late distracted by their peals,
Quiet as Carmel where the lilies live.
Herself had oftentimes complained: but why?

All her complaints had been their prompting,
　tales
Trumped up, devices to this very end,
Their game had been to thwart her husband's
　love
And cross his will, malign his words and ways,
To reach this issue, furnish this pretence
For impudent withdrawal from their bond, —
Theft, indeed murder, since they meant no less
Whose last injunction to her simple self
Had been — what parents' - precept do you
　think?
That she should follow after with all speed,
Fly from her husband's house clandestinely,
Join them at Rome again, but first of all
Pick up a fresh companion in her flight,
So putting youth and beauty to fit use, —
Some gay dare-devil cloak-and-rapier spark
Capable of adventure, — helped by whom
She, some fine eve when lutes were in the air,
Having put poison in the posset-cup,
Laid hands on money, jewels and the like,
And, to conceal the thing with more effect,
By way of parting benediction too,
Fired the house, — one would finish famously
I' the tumult, slip out, scurry off and away
And turn up merrily at home once more.
Fact this, and not a dream o' the devil, Sir!
And more than this, a fact none dare dispute,
Word for word, such a letter did she write,
And such the Abate read, nor simply read
But gave all Rome to ruminate upon,
In answer to such charges as, I say,
The couple sought to be beforehand with.

The cause thus carried to the courts at Rome,
Guido away, the Abate had no choice
But stand forth, take his absent brother's part,
Defend the honor of himself beside,
He made what head he might against the pair,
Maintained Pompilia's birth legitimate
And all her rights intact — hers, Guido's now:
And so far by his policy turned their flank,
(The enemy being beforehand in the place)
That, — though the courts allowed the cheat for
　fact,
Suffered Violante to parade her shame,
Publish her infamy to heart's content,
And let the tale o' the feigned birth pass for
　proved, —
Yet they stopped there, refused to intervene
And dispossess the innocents, befooled
By gifts o' the guilty, at guilt's new caprice.
They would not take away the dowry now
Wrongfully given at first, nor bar at all
Succession to the aforesaid usufruct,
Established on a fraud, nor play the game
Of Pietro's child and now not Pietro's child
As it might suit the gamester's purpose. Thus
Was justice ever ridiculed in Rome:
Such be the double verdicts favored here
Which send away both parties to a suit
Nor puffed up nor cast down, — for each a
　crumb
Of right, for neither of them the whole loaf.
Whence, on the Comparini's part, appeal —
Counter-appeal on Guido's, — that's the game:
And so the matter stands, even to this hour,

Bandied as balls are in a tennis-court,
And so might stand, unless some heart broke
    first,
Till doomsday.

                    Leave it thus, and now revert
To the old Arezzo whence we moved to Rome.
We 've had enough o' the parents, false or true,
Now for a touch o' the daughter's quality.
The start 's fair henceforth, every obstacle
Out of the young wife's footpath, she 's alone,
Left to walk warily now : how does she walk ?
Why, once a dwelling's threshold marked and
    crossed
In rubric by the enemy on his rounds
As eligible, as fit place of prey,
Baffle him henceforth, keep him out who can !
Stop up the door at the first hint of hoof,
Presently at the window taps a horn,
And Satan 's by your fireside, never fear !
Pompilia, left alone now, found herself ;
Found herself young too, sprightly, fair enough,
Matched with a husband old beyond his age
(Though that was something like four times
    her own)
Because of cares past, present and to come :
Found too the house dull and its inmates dead,
So, looked outside for light and life.
                                    And love
Did in a trice turn up with life and light, —
The man with the aureole, sympathy made
    flesh,
The all-consoling Caponsacchi, Sir !
A priest — what else should the consoler be ?
With goodly shoulder-blade and proper leg,
A portly make and a symmetric shape,
And curls that clustered to the tonsure quite.
This was a bishop in the bud, and now
A canon full-blown so far : priest, and priest
Nowise exorbitantly overworked,
The courtly Christian, not so much Saint Paul
As a saint of Cæsar's household : there posed he
Sending his god-glance after his shot shaft,
Apollos turned Apollo, while the snake
Pompilia writhed transfixed through all her
    spires.
He, not a visitor at Guido's house,
Scarce an acquaintance, but in prime request
With the magnates of Arezzo, was seen here,
Heard there, felt everywhere in Guido's path
If Guido's wife's path be her husband's too.
Now he threw comfits at the theatre
Into her lap, — what harm in Carnival ?
Now he pressed close till his foot touched her
    gown,
His hand brushed hers, — how help on prom-
    enade ?
And, ever on weighty business, found his steps
Incline to a certain haunt of doubtful fame
Which fronted Guido's palace by mere chance ;
While — how do accidents sometimes com-
    bine ! —
Pompilia chose to cloister up her charms
Just in a chamber that o'erlooked the street,
Sat there to pray, or peep thence at mankind.

This passage of arms and wits amused the town.
At last the husband lifted eyebrow, — bent

On day-book and the study how to wring
Half the due vintage from the worn-out vines
At the villa, tease a quarter the old rent
From the farmstead, tenants swore would
    tumble soon, —
Pricked up his ear a-singing day and night
With "ruin, ruin ; " — and so surprised at
    last —
Why, what else but a titter ? Up he jumps.
Back to mind come those scratchings at the
    grange,
Prints of the paw about the outhouse ; rife
In his head at once again are word and wink,
Mum here and *budget* there, the smell o' the fox.
The musk o' the gallant. "Friends, there 'a
    falseness here ! "

The proper help of friends in such a strait
Is waggery, the world over. Laugh him free
O' the regular jealous-fit that 's incident
To all old husbands that wed brisk young wives,
And he 'll go duly docile all his days.
"Somebody courts your wife, Count ? Where
    and when ?
How and why ? Mere horn-madness : have a
    care !
Your lady loves her own room, sticks to it,
Locks herself in for hours, you say yourself.
And — what, it 's Caponsacchi means you
    harm ?
The Canon ? We caress him, he 's the world's,
A man of such acceptance, — never dream,
Though he were fifty times the fox you fear,
He 'd risk his brush for your particular chick,
When the wide town 's his hen-roost ! Fie o'
    the fool ! "
So they dispensed their comfort of a kind.
Guido at last cried, "Something is in the air,
Under the earth, some plot against my peace.
The trouble of eclipse hangs overhead ;
How it should come of that officious orb
Your Canon in my system, you must say :
I say — that from the pressure of this spring
Began the chime and interchange of bells,
Ever one whisper, and one whisper more,
And just one whisper for the silvery last,
Till all at once a-row the bronze-throats burst
Into a larum both significant
And sinister : stop it I must and will.
Let Caponsacchi take his hand away
From the wire ! — disport himself in other paths
Than lead precisely to my palace-gate, —
Look where he likes except one window's way
Where, cheek on hand, and elbow set on sill,
Happens to lean and say her litanies
Every day and all day long, just my wife —
Or wife and Caponsacchi may fare the worse ! "

Admire the man's simplicity. "I 'll do this,
I 'll not have that, I 'll punish and prevent ! " —
'T is easy saying. But to a fray, you see,
Two parties go. The badger shows his teeth :
The fox nor lies down sheep-like nor dares fight.
Oh, the wife knew the appropriate warfare well,
The way to put suspicion to the blush !
At first hint of remonstrance, up and out
I' the face of the world, you found her : she
    could speak,

State her case, — Franceschini was a name,
Guido had his full share of foes and friends —
Why should not she call these to arbitrate ?
She bade the Governor do governance,
Cried out on the Archbishop, — why, there
    now,
Take him for sample ! Three successive times
Had he to reconduct her by main force
From where she took her station opposite
His shut door, — on the public steps thereto,
Wringing her hands, when he came out to see,
And shrieking all her wrongs forth at his foot, —
Back to the husband and the house she fled :
Judge if that husband warmed him in the face
Of friends or frowned on foes as heretofore !
Judge if he missed the natural grin of folk,
Or lacked the customary compliment
Of cap and bells, the luckless husband's fit !

So it went on and on till — who was right ?
One merry April morning, Guido woke
After the cuckoo, so late, near noonday,
With an inordinate yawning of the jaws,
Ears plugged, eyes gummed together, palate,
    tongue
And teeth one mud-paste made of poppy-milk ;
And found his wife flown, his scritoire the
    worse
For a rummage, — jewelry that was, was not,
Some money there had made itself wings too, —
The door lay wide and yet the servants slept
Sound as the dead, or dozed, which does as well.
In short, Pompilia, she who, candid soul,
Had not so much as spoken all her life
To the Canon, nay, so much as peeped at him
Between her fingers while she prayed in
    church, —
This lamb-like innocent of fifteen years
(Such she was grown to by this time of day)
Had simply put an opiate in the drink
Of the whole household overnight, and then
Got up and gone about her work secure,
Laid hand on this waif and the other stray,
Spoiled the Philistine and marched out of doors
In company of the Canon, who, Lord's love,
What with his daily duty at the church,
Nightly devoir where ladies congregate,
Had something else to mind, assure yourself,
Beside Pompilia, paragon though she be,
Or notice if her nose were sharp or blunt !
Well, anyhow, albeit impossible,
Both of them were together jollily
Jaunting it Rome-ward, half-way there by this,
While Guido was left go and get undrugged,
Gather his wits up, groaningly give thanks
When neighbors crowded round him to condole.
" Ah," quoth a gossip, " well I mind me now,
The Count did always say he thought he felt
He feared as if this very chance might fall !
And when a man of fifty finds his corns
Ache and his joints throb, and foresees a storm,
Though neighbors laugh and say the sky is
    clear,
Let us henceforth believe him weatherwise ! "
Then was the story told, I 'll cut you short :
All neighbors knew : no mystery in the world.
The lovers left at nightfall — overnight
Had Caponsacchi come to carry off

Pompilia, — not alone, a friend of his,
One Guillichini, the more conversant
With Guido's housekeeping that he was just
A cousin of Guido's and might play a prank —
(Have not you too a cousin that 's a wag ?)
— Lord and a Canon also, — what would you
    have ?
Such are the red-clothed milk-swollen poppy-
    heads
That stand and stiffen 'mid the wheat o' the
    Church ! —
This worthy came to aid, abet his best.
And so the house was ransacked, booty bagged,
The lady led downstairs and out of doors
Guided and guarded till, the city passed,
A carriage lay convenient at the gate.
Good-by to the friendly Canon ; the loving one
Could peradventure do the rest himself.
In jumps Pompilia, after her the priest,
" Whip, driver ! Money makes the mare to go,
And we 've a bagful. Take the Roman road ! "
So said the neighbors. This was eight hours
    since.

Guido heard all, swore the befitting oaths,
Shook off the relics of his poison-drench,
Got horse, was fairly started in pursuit
With never a friend to follow, found the track
Fast enough, 't was the straight Perugia way,
Trod soon upon their very heels, too late
By a minute only at Camoscia, reached
Chiusi, Foligno, ever the fugitives
Just ahead, just out as he galloped in,
Getting the good news ever fresh and fresh,
Till, lo, at the last stage of all, last post
Before Rome, — as we say, in sight of Rome
And safety (there 's impunity at Rome
For priests you know) at — what 's the little
    place ? —
What some call Castelnuovo, some just call
The Osteria, because o' the post-house inn, —
There, at the journey's all but end, it seems,
Triumph deceived them and undid them both,
Secure they might foretaste felicity
Nor fear surprisal : so, they were surprised.
There did they halt at early evening, there
Did Guido overtake them : 't was daybreak ;
He came in time enough, not time too much,
Since in the courtyard stood the Canon's self
Urging the drowsy stable-grooms to haste
Harness the horses, have the journey end,
The trifling four-hours' running, so reach
    Rome.
And the other runaway, the wife ? Upstairs,
Still on the couch where she had spent the
    night,
One couch in one room, and one room for both.
So gained they six hours, so were lost there-
    by.

Sir, what 's the sequel ? Lover and beloved
Fall on their knees ? No impudence serves
    here ?
They beat their breasts and beg for easy death,
Confess this, that and the other ? — anyhow
Confess there wanted not some likelihood
To the supposition so preposterous,
That, O Pompilia, thy sequestered eyes

Had noticed, straying o'er the prayer-book's
    edge,
More of the Canon than that black his coat,
Buckled his shoes were, broad his hat of brim :
And that, O Canon, thy religious care
Had breathed too soft a *benedicite*
To banish trouble from a lady's breast
So lonely and so lovely, nor so lean !
This you expect ? Indeed, then, much you err.
Not to such ordinary end as this
Had Caponsacchi flung the cassock far,
Doffed the priest, donned the perfect cavalier.
The die was cast : over shoes over boots :
And just as she, I presently shall show,
Pompilia, soon looked Helen to the life,
Recumbent upstairs in her pink and white,
So, in the inn-yard, bold as 't were Troy-town,
There strutted Paris in correct costume,
Cloak, cap and feather, no appointment
    missed,
Even to a wicked-looking sword at side,
He seemed to find and feel familiar at.
Nor wanted words as ready and as big
As the part he played, the bold abashless one.
" I interposed to save your wife from death,
Yourself from shame, the true and only shame :
Ask your own conscience else ! — or, failing
    that,
What I have done I answer, anywhere,
Here, if you will ; you see I have a sword :
Or, since I have a tonsure as you taunt,
At Rome, by all means, — priests to try a
    priest.
Only, speak where your wife's voice can reply ! "
And then he fingered at the sword again.
So, Guido called, in aid and witness both,
The Public Force. The Commissary came,
Officers also ; they secured the priest :
Then, for his more confusion, mounted up
With him, a guard on either side, the stair
To the bedroom where still slept or feigned a
    sleep
His paramour and Guido's wife : in burst
The company and bade her wake and rise.

Her defence? This. She woke, saw, sprang
    upright
I' the midst and stood as terrible as truth,
Sprang to her husband's side, caught at the
    sword
That hung there useless, — since they held each
    hand
O' the lover, had disarmed him properly, —
And in a moment out flew the bright thing
Full in the face of Guido : but for help
O' the guards, who held her back and pinioned
    her
With pains enough, she had finished you my
    tale
With a flourish of red all round it, pinked her
    man
Prettily ; but she fought them one to six.
They stopped that, — but her tongue continued
    free :
She spat forth such invective at her spouse,
O'erfrothed him with such foam of murderer,
Thief, pandar — that the popular tide scon
    turned,

The favor of the very *sbirri*, straight
Ebbed from the husband, set towards his wife ;
People cried " Hands off, pay a priest re-
    spect ! "
And " persecuting fiend " and " martyred
    saint "
Began to lead a measure from lip to lip.

But facts are facts and flinch not ; stubborn
    things,
And the question " Prithee, friend, how comes
    my purse
I' the poke of you ? " — admits of no reply.
Here was a priest found out in masquerade,
A wife caught playing truant if no more ;
While the Count, mortified in mien enough,
And, nose to face, an added palm in length,
Was plain writ " husband " every piece of him :
Capture once made, release could hardly be.
Beside, the prisoners both made appeal,
" Take us to Rome ! "

               Taken to Rome they were ;
The husband trooping after, piteously,
Tail between legs, no talk of triumph now —
No honor set firm on its feet once more
On two dead bodies of the guilty, — nay,
No dubious salve to honor's broken pate
From chance that, after all, the hurt might
    seem
A skin-deep matter, scratch that leaves no
    scar :
For Guido's first search, — ferreting, poor soul,
Here, there and everywhere in the vile place
Abandoned to him when their backs were
    turned,
Found — furnishing a last and best regale —
All the love-letters bandied 'twixt the pair
Since the first timid trembling into life
O' the love-star till its stand at fiery full,
Mad prose, mad verse, fears, hopes, triumph,
    despair,
Avowal, disclaimer, plans, dates, names, — was
    naught
Wanting to prove, if proof consoles at all,
That this had been but the fifth act o' the piece
Whereof the due proemium, months ago,
These playwrights had put forth, and ever
    since
Matured the middle, added 'neath his nose.
He might go cross himself : the case was
    clear.

Therefore to Rome with the clear case ; there
    plead
Each party its best, and leave law do each
    right,
Let law shine forth and show, as God in heaven,
Vice prostrate, virtue pedestalled at last,
The triumph of truth ! What else shall glad
    our gaze
When once authority has knit the brow
And set the brain behind it to decide
Between the wolf and sheep turned litigants ?
" This is indeed a business," law shook head :
" A husband charges hard things on a wife,
The wife as hard o' the husband : whose fault
    here ?

A wife that flies her husband's house, does
    wrong :
The male friend's interference looks amiss,
Lends a suspicion : but suppose the wife,
On the other hand, be jeopardized at home —
Nay, that she simply hold, ill-groundedly,
An apprehension she is jeopardized, —
And further, if the friend partake the fear,
And, in a commendable charity
Which trusteth all, trust her that she mis-
    trusts, —
What do they but obey law — natural law ?
Pretence may this be and a cloak for sin,
And circumstances that concur i' the close
Hint as much, loudly — yet scarce loud enough
To drown the answer 'strange may yet be
    true ':
Innocence often looks like guiltiness.
The accused declare that in thought, word and
    deed,
Innocent were they both from first to last
As male-babe haply laid by female-babe
At church on edge of the baptismal font
Together for a minute, perfect-pure.
Difficult to believe, yet possible,
As witness Joseph, the friend's patron-saint.
The night at the inn — there charity nigh
    chokes
Ere swallow what they both asseverate ;
Though down the gullet faith may feel it go,
When mindful of what flight fatigued the
    flesh
Out of its faculty and fleshliness,
Subdued it to the soul, as saints assure :
So long a flight necessitates a fall
On the first bed, though in a lion's den,
And the first pillow, though the lion's back :
Difficult to believe, yet possible.
Last come the letters' bundled beastliness —
Authority repugns give glance to — nay,
Turns head, and almost lets her whip-lash fall ;
Yet here a voice cries ' Respite ! ' from the
    clouds —
The accused, both in a tale, protest, disclaim,
Abominate the horror : ' Not my hand '
Asserts the friend — ' Nor mine ' chimes in the
    wife,
' Seeing I have no hand, nor write at all.'
Illiterate — for she goes on to ask,
What if the friend did pen now verse now
    prose,
Commend it to her notice now and then ?
'T was pearls to swine : she read no more than
    wrote,
And kept no more than read, for as they fell
She ever brushed the burr-like things away,
Or, better, burned them, quenched the fire in
    smoke.
As for this fardel, filth and foolishness,
She sees it now the first time : burn it too !
While for his part the friend vows ignorance
Alike of what bears his name and bears hers :
'Tis forgery, a felon's masterpiece,
And, as 'tis said the fox still finds the stench,
Home-manufacture and the husband's work.
Though he confesses, the ingenuous friend,
That certain missives, letters of a sort,
Flighty and feeble, which assigned themselves

To the wife, no less have fallen, far too oft,
In his path : wherefrom he understood just
    this —
That were they verily the lady's own,
Why, she who penned them, since he never saw
Save for one minute the mere face of her,
Since never had there been the interchange
Of word with word between them all their life,
Why, she must be the fondest of the frail,
And fit, she for the ' apage ' he flung,
Her letters for the flame they went to feed !
But, now he sees her face and hears her speech,
Much he repents him if, in fancy-freak
For a moment the minutest measurable,
He coupled her with the first flimsy word
O' the self-spun fabric some mean spider-soul
Furnished forth : stop his films and stamp or
    him !
Never was such a tangled knottiness,
But thus authority cuts the Gordian through,
And mark how her decision suits the need !
Here 's troublesomeness, scandal on both sides,
Plenty of fault to find, no absolute crime :
Let each side own its fault and make amends !
What does a priest in cavalier's attire
Consorting publicly with vagrant wives
In quarters close as the confessional,
Though innocent of harm ? 'T is harm enough :
Let him pay it, — say, be relegate a good
Three years, to spend in some place not too far
Nor yet too near, midway 'twixt near and far,
Rome and Arezzo, — Civita we choose,
Where he may lounge away time, live at large,
Find out the proper function of a priest,
Nowise an exile, — that were punishment, —
But one our love thus keeps out of harm's way
Not more from the husband's anger than, may-
    hap,
His own . . . say, indiscretion, waywardness,
And wanderings when Easter eves grow warm.
For the wife, — well, our best step to take with
    her,
On her own showing, were to shift her root
From the old cold shade and unhappy soil
Into a generous ground that fronts the south :
Where, since her callow soul, a-shiver late,
Craved simply warmth and called mere pass
    ers-by
To the rescue, she should have her fill of shine
Do house and husband hinder and not help ?
Why then, forget both and stay here at peace,
Come into our community, enroll
Herself along with those good Convertites,
Those sinners saved, those Magdalens re-made
Accept their ministration, well bestow
Her body and patiently possess her soul,
Until we see what better can be done.
Last for the husband : if his tale prove true,
Well is he rid of two domestic plagues —
Both wife that ailed, do whatsoever he would
And friend of hers that undertook the cure.
See, what a double load we lift from breast !
Off he may go, return, resume old life,
Laugh at the priest here and Pompilia there
In limbo each and punished for their pains,
And grateful tell the inquiring neighborhood —
In Rome, no wrong but has its remedy."
The case was closed. Now, am I fair or no

In what I utter? Do I state the facts,
Having forechosen a side? I promised you!

The Canon Caponsacchi, then, was sent
To change his garb, re-trim his tonsure, tie
The clerkly silk round, every plait correct,
Make the impressive entry on his place
Of relegation, thrill his Civita,
As Ovid, a like sufferer in the cause,
Planted a primrose-patch by Pontus: where, —
What with much culture of the sonnet-stave
And converse with the aborigines,
Soft savagery of eyes unused to roll,
And hearts that all awry went pit-a-pat
And wanted setting right in charity, —
What were a couple of years to while away?
Pompilia, as enjoined, betook herself
To the aforesaid Convertites, soft sisterhood
In Via Lungara, where the light ones live,
Spin, pray, then sing like linnets o'er the flax.
"Anywhere, anyhow, out of my husband's
        house
Is heaven," cried she, — was therefore suited so.
But for Count Guido Franceschini, he —
The injured man thus righted — found no hea-
        ven
I' the house when he returned there, I engage,
Was welcomed by the city turned upside down
In a chorus of inquiry. "What, back — you?
And no wife? Left her with the Penitents?
Ah, being young and pretty, 't were a shame
To have her whipped in public: leave the job
To the priests who understand! Such priests
        as yours —
(Pontifex Maximus whipped Vestals once)
Our madcap Caponsacchi: think of him!
So, he fired up, showed fight and skill of fence?
Ay, you drew also, but you did not fight!
The wiser, 't is a word and a blow with him,
True Caponsacchi, of old Head-i'-the-Sack
That fought at Fiesole ere Florence was:
He had done enough, to firk you were too much.
And did the little lady menace you,
Make at your breast with your own harmless
        sword?
The spitfire! Well, thank God you 're safe and
        sound,
Have kept the sixth commandment whether or
        no
The lady broke the seventh: I only wish
I were as saint-like, could contain me so.
I, the poor sinner, fear I should have left
Sir Priest no nose-tip to turn up at me!"
You, Sir, who listen but interpose no word,
Ask yourself, had you borne a baiting thus?
Was it enough to make a wise man mad?
Oh, but I 'll have your verdict at the end!

Well, not enough, it seems: such mere hurt
        falls,
Frets awhile, aches long, then grows less and
        less,
And so gets done with. Such was not the
        scheme
O' the pleasant Comparini: on Guido's wound
Ever in due succession, drop by drop,
Came slow distilment from the alembic here
Set on to simmer by Canidian hate,

Corrosives keeping the man's misery raw.
First fire-drop, — when he thought to make the
        best
O' the bad, to wring from out the sentence
        passed,
Poor, pitiful, absurd although it were,
Yet what might eke him out result enough
And make it worth while to have had the right
And not the wrong i' the matter judged at
        Rome.
Inadequate her punishment, no less
Punished in some slight sort his wife had been;
Then, punished for adultery, what else?
On such admitted crime he thought to seize,
And institute procedure in the courts
Which cut corruption of this kind from man,
Cast loose a wife proved loose and castaway:
He claimed in due form a divorce at least.

This claim was met now by a counterclaim:
Pompilia sought divorce from bed and board
Of Guido, whose outrageous cruelty,
Whose mother's malice and whose brother's hate
Were just the white o' the charge, such dread-
        ful depths
Blackened its centre, — hints of worse than
        hate,
Love from that brother, by that Guido's guile,
That mother's prompting. Such reply was
        made,
So was the engine loaded, wound up, sprung
On Guido, who received bolt full in breast;
But no less bore up, giddily perhaps.
He had the Abate Paolo still in Rome,
Brother and friend and fighter on his side:
They rallied in a measure, met the foe
Manlike, joined battle in the public courts,
As if to shame supine law from her sloth:
And waiting her award, let beat the while
Arezzo's banter, Rome's buffoonery,
On this ear and on that ear, deaf alike,
Safe from worse outrage. Let a scorpion nip,
And never mind till he contorts his tail!
But there was sting i' the creature; thus it
        struck.
Guido had thought in his simplicity —
That lying declaration of remorse,
That story of the child which was no child
And motherhood no motherhood at all,
— That even this sin might have its sort of good
Inasmuch as no question more could be, —
Call it false, call the story true, — no claim
Of further parentage pretended now:
The parents had abjured all right, at least,
I' the woman owned his wife: to plead right
        still
Were to declare the abjuration false:
He was relieved from any fear henceforth
Their hands might touch, their breath defile
        again
Pompilia with his name upon her yet.
Well, no: the next news was, Pompilia's health
Demanded change after full three long weeks
Spent in devotion with the Sisterhood, —
Which rendered sojourn — so the court opined —
Too irksome, since the convent's walls were high
And windows narrow, nor was air enough
Nor light enough, but all looked prison-like

The last thing which had come in the court's head.
Propose a new expedient therefore, — this!
She had demanded — had obtained indeed,
By intervention of her pitying friends
Or perhaps lovers — (beauty in distress,
Beauty whose tale is the town-talk beside,
Never lacks friendship's arm about her neck) —
Obtained remission of the penalty,
Permitted transfer to some private place
Where better air, more light, new food might soothe —
Incarcerated (call it, all the same)
At some sure friend's house she must keep inside,
Be found in at requirement fast enough, —
Domus pro carcere, in Roman style.
You keep the house i' the main, as most men do,
And all good women: but free otherwise,
Should friends arrive, to lodge them and what not?
And such a *domum*, such a dwelling-place,
Having all Rome to choose from, where chose she?
What house obtained Pompilia's preference?
Why, just the Comparini's — just, do you mark,
Theirs who renounced all part and lot in her
So long as Guido could be robbed thereby,
And only fell back on relationship
And found their daughter safe and sound again
When that might surelier stab him: yes, the pair
Who, as I told you, first had baited hook
With this poor gilded fly Pompilia-thing,
Then caught the fish, pulled Guido to the shore
And gutted him, — now found a further use
For the bait, would trail the gauze wings yet again
I' the way of what new swimmer passed their stand.
They took Pompilia to their hiding-place —
Not in the heart of Rome as formerly,
Under observance, subject to control —
But out o' the way, — or in the way, who knows?
That blind mute villa lurking by the gate
At Via Paulina, not so hard to miss
By the honest eye, easy enough to find
In twilight by marauders: where perchance
Some muffled Caponsacchi might repair,
Employ odd moments when he too tried change,
Found that a friend's abode was pleasanter
Than relegation, penance and the rest.

Come, here's the last drop does its worst to wound,
Here's Guido poisoned to the bone, you say,
Your boasted still's full strain and strength: not so!
One master-squeeze from screw shall bring to birth
The hoard i' the heart o' the toad, hell's quintessence.
He learned the true convenience of the change,
And why a convent lacks the cheerful hearts

And helpful hands which female straits require,
When, in the blind mute villa by the gate,
Pompilia — what? sang, danced, saw company?
— Gave birth, Sir, to a child, his son and heir,
Or Guido's heir and Caponsacchi's son.
I want your word now: what do you say to this?
What would say little Arezzo and great Rome,
And what did God say and the devil say,
One at each ear o' the man, the husband, now
The father? Why, the overburdened mind
Broke down, what was a brain became a blaze.
In fury of the moment — (that first news
Fell on the Count among his vines, it seems,
Doing his farm-work,) — why, he summoned steward,
Called in the first four hard hands and stout hearts
From field and furrow, poured forth his appeal,
Not to Rome's law and gospel any more,
But this clown with a mother or a wife,
That clodpole with a sister or a son:
And, whereas law and gospel held their peace,
What wonder if the sticks and stones cried out?

All five soon somehow found themselves at Rome,
At the villa door: there was the warmth and light —
The sense of life so just an inch inside —
Some angel must have whispered "One more chance!"

He gave it: bade the others stand aside:
Knocked at the door, — "Who is it knocks?" cried one.
"I will make," surely Guido's angel urged,
"One final essay, last experiment,
Speak the word, name the name from out all names,
Which, if, — as doubtless strong illusions are,
And strange disguisings whereby truth seems false,
And, since I am but man, I dare not do
God's work until assured I see with God, —
If I should bring my lips to breathe that name
And they be innocent, — nay, by one mere touch
Of innocence redeemed from utter guilt, —
That name will bar the door and bid fate pass.
I will not say ' It is a messenger,
A neighbor, even a belated man,
Much less your husband's friend, your husband's self:'
At such appeal the door is bound to ope.
But I will say" — here's rhetoric and to spare!
Why, Sir, the stumbling-block is cursed and kicked,
Block though it be; the name that brought offence
Will bring offence: the burnt child dreads the fire
Although that fire feed on some taper-wick
Which never left the altar nor singed a fly:
And had a harmless man tripped you by chance,

How would you wait him, stand or step aside,
When next you heard he rolled your way?
  Enough.

" Giuseppe Caponsacchi ! " Guido cried ;
And open flew the door : enough again.
Vengeance, you know, burst, like a mountain-
  wave
That holds a monster in it, over the house,
And wiped its filthy four walls free at last
With a wash of hell-fire, — father, mother,
  wife,
Killed them all, bathed his name clean in their
  blood,
And, reeking so, was caught, his friends and he,
Haled hither and imprisoned yesternight
O' the day all this was.
                    Now, Sir, tale is told,
Of how the old couple come to lie in state
Though hacked to pieces, — never, the expert
  say,
So thorough a study of stabbing — while the
  wife
(Viper-like, very difficult to slay)
Writhes still through every ring of her, poor
  wretch,
At the Hospital hard by — survives, we 'll
  hope,
To somewhat purify her putrid soul
By full confession, make so much amends
While time lasts ; since at day's end die she
  must.

For Caponsacchi, — why, they 'll have him
  here,
As hero of the adventure, who so fit
To figure in the coming Carnival ?
'T will make the fortune of whate'er saloon
Hears him recount, with helpful cheek, and eye
Hotly indignant now, now dewy-dimmed,
The incidents of flight, pursuit, surprise,
Capture, with hints of kisses all between —
While Guido, wholly unromantic spouse,
No longer fit to laugh at since the blood
Gave the broad farce an all too brutal air,
Why, he and those four luckless friends of his
May tumble in the straw this bitter day —
Laid by the heels i' the New Prison, I hear,
To bide their trial, since trial, and for the life,
Follows if but for form's sake : yes, indeed !

But with a certain issue : no dispute,
" Try him," bids law : formalities oblige :
But as to the issue, — look me in the face ! —
If the law thinks to find them guilty, Sir,
Master or men — touch one hair of the five,
Then I say in the name of all that 's left
Of honor in Rome, civility i' the world
Whereof Rome boasts herself the central
  source, —
There 's an end to all hope of justice more.
Astræa 's gone indeed, let hope go too !
Who is it dares impugn the natural law,
Deny God's word " the faithless wife shall
  die " ?
What, are we blind ? How can we fail to
  learn
This crowd of miseries make the man a mark,

Accumulate on one devoted head
For our example ? — yours and mine who read
Its lesson thus — " Henceforward let none dare
Stand, like a natural in the public way,
Letting the very urchins twitch his beard
And tweak his nose, to earn a nickname so,
Be styled male-Grissel or else modern Job ! "
Had Guido, in the twinkling of an eye,
Summed up the reckoning, promptly paid him-
  self,
That morning when he came up with the pair
At the wayside inn, — exacted his just debt
By aid of what first mattock, pitchfork, axe
Came to hand in the helpful stable-yard,
And with that axe, if providence so pleased,
Cloven each head, by some Rolando-stroke,
In one clean cut from crown to clavicle,
— Slain the priest-gallant, the wife-paramour,
Sticking, for all defence, in each skull's cleft
The rhyme and reason of the stroke thus dealt,
To wit, those letters and last evidence
Of shame, each package in its proper place, —
Bidding, who pitied, undistend the skulls, —
I say, the world had praised the man. But no !
That were too plain, too straight, too simply
  just !
He hesitates, calls law forsooth to help.
And law, distasteful to who calls in law
When honor is beforehand and would serve,
What wonder if law hesitate in turn,
Plead her disuse to calls o' the kind, reply
(Smiling a little), " 'T is yourself assess
The worth of what 's lost, sum of damage done.
What you touched with so light a finger-tip,
You whose concern it was to grasp the thing,
Why must law gird herself and grapple with ?
Law, alien to the actor whose warm blood
Asks heat from law whose veins run lukewarm
  milk, —
What you dealt lightly with, shall law make out
Heinous forsooth ? "
                    Sir, what 's the good of law
In a case o' the kind ? None, as she all but says.
Call in law when a neighbor breaks your fence,
Cribs from your field, tampers with rent or
  lease,
Touches the purse or pocket, — but wooes your
  wife ?
No : take the old way trod when men were
  men !
Guido preferred the new path, — for his pains,
Stuck in a quagmire, floundered worse and
  worse
Until he managed somehow scramble back
Into the safe sure rutted road once more,
Revenged his own wrong like a gentleman.
Once back 'mid the familiar prints, no doubt
He made too rash amends for his first fault,
Vaulted too loftily over what barred him late,
And lit i' the mire again, — the common
  chance,
The natural over-energy : the deed
Maladroit yields three deaths instead of one,
And one life left : for where 's the Canon's
  corpse ?
All which is the worse for Guido, but, be
  frank —
The better for you and me and all the world,

Husbands of wives, especially in Rome.
The thing is put right, in the old place, — ay,
The rod hangs on its nail behind the door,
Fresh from the brine : a matter I commend
To the notice, during Carnival that 's near,
Of a certain what 's-his-name and jackanapes
Somewhat too civil of eves with lute and song
About a house here, where I keep a wife.
(You, being his cousin, may go tell him so.)

III

THE OTHER HALF-ROME

Another day that finds her living yet,
Little Pompilia, with the patient brow
And lamentable smile on those poor lips,
And, under the white hospital-array,
A flower-like body, to frighten at a bruise
You 'd think, yet now, stabbed through and
    through again,
Alive i' the ruins. 'T is a miracle.
It seems that, when her husband struck her
    first,
She prayed Madonna just that she might live
So long as to confess and be absolved ;
And whether it was that, all her sad life long
Never before successful in a prayer,
This prayer rose with authority too dread, —
Or whether, because earth was hell to her,
By compensation, when the blackness broke
She got one glimpse of quiet and the cool blue,
To show her for a moment such things were, —
Or else, — as the Augustinian Brother thinks,
The friar who took confession from her lip, —
When a probationary soul that moved
From nobleness to nobleness, as she,
Over the rough way of the world, succumbs,
Bloodies its last thorn with unflinching foot,
The angels love to do their work betimes,
Stanch some wounds here nor leave so much
    for God.
Who knows ? However it be, confessed, ab-
    solved,
She lies, with overplus of life beside
To speak and right herself from first to last,
Right the friend also, lamb-pure, lion-brave,
Care for the boy's concerns, to save the son
From the sire, her two-weeks' infant orphaned
    thus,
And — with best smile of all reserved for him —
Pardon that sire and husband from the heart.
A miracle, so tell your Molinists !

There she lies in the long white lazar-house.
Rome has besieged, these two days, never
    doubt,
Saint Anna's where she waits her death, to
    hear
Though but the chink o' the bell, turn o' the
    hinge
When the reluctant wicket opes at last,
Lets in, on now this and now that pretence,
Too many by half, — complain the men of
    art, —
For a patient in such plight. The lawyers first
Paid the due visit — justice must be done :

They took her witness, why the murder was.
Then the priests followed properly, — a soul
To shrive ; 't was Brother Celestine's own
    right,
The same who noises thus her gifts abroad.
But many more, who found they were old
    friends,
Pushed in to have their stare and take their talk
And go forth boasting of it and to boast.
Old Monna Baldi chatters like a jay,
Swears — but that, prematurely trundled out
Just as she felt the benefit begin,
The miracle was snapped up by somebody, —
Her palsied limb 'gan prick and promise life
At touch o' the bedclothes merely, — how much
    more
Had she but brushed the body as she tried !
Cavalier Carlo — well, there 's some excuse
For him — Maratta who paints Virgins so —
He too must fee the porter and slip by
With pencil cut and paper squared, and straight
There was he figuring away at face :
" A lovelier face is not in Rome," cried he,
" Shaped like a peacock's egg, the pure as
    pearl,
That hatches you anon a snow-white chick."
Then, oh that pair of eyes, that pendent hair,
Black this and black the other ! Mighty fine —
But nobody cared ask to paint the same,
Nor grew a poet over hair and eyes
Four little years ago, when, ask and have,
The woman who wakes all this rapture leaned
Flower-like from out her window long enough,
As much uncomplimented as uncropped
By comers and goers in Via Vittoria : eh ?
'T is just a flower's fate : past parterre we trip,
Till peradventure some one plucks our
    sleeve —
" Yon blossom at the brier's end, that 's the
    rose
Two jealous people fought for yesterday
And killed each other : see, there 's undis-
    turbed
A pretty pool at the root, of rival red ! "
Then cry we, " Ah, the perfect paragon ! "
Then crave we, " Just one keepsake-leaf for
    us ! "

Truth lies between : there 's anyhow a child
Of seventeen years, whether a flower or weed,
Ruined : who did it shall account to Christ —
Having no pity on the harmless life
And gentle face and girlish form he found,
And thus flings back. Go practise if you
    please
With men and women : leave a child alone
For Christ's particular love's sake ! — so I say.

Somebody at the bedside said much more,
Took on him to explain the secret cause
O' the crime : quoth he, " Such crimes are very
    rife,
Explode nor make us wonder nowadays,
Seeing that Antichrist disseminates
That doctrine of the Philosophic Sin :
Molinos' sect will soon make earth too hot ! "
" Nay," groaned the Augustinian, " what 's
    there new ?

Crime will not fail to flare up from men's
    hearts
While hearts are men's and so born criminal ;
Which one fact, always old yet ever new,
Accounts for so much crime that, for my part,
Molinos may go whistle to the wind
That waits outside a certain church, you
    know ! "

Though really it does seem as if she here,
Pompilia, living so and dying thus,
Has had undue experience how much crime
A heart can hatch. Why was she made to
    learn
— Not you, not I, not even Molinos' self —
What Guido Franceschini's heart could hold ?
Thus saintship is effected probably ;
No sparing saints the process ! — which the more
Tends to the reconciling us, no saints,
To sinnership, immunity and all.

For see now: Pietro and Violante's life
Till seventeen years ago, all Rome might note
And quote for happy - see the signs distinct
Of happiness as we yon Triton s trump.
What could they be but happy ? — balanced so,
Nor low i' the social scale nor yet too high,
Nor poor nor richer than comports with ease,
Nor bright and envied, nor obscure and
    scorned,
Nor so young that their pleasures fell too thick,
Nor old past catching pleasure when it fell,
Nothing above, below the just degree,
All at the mean where joy's components mix.
So again, in the couple's very souls
You saw the adequate half with half to match,
Each having and each lacking somewhat, both
Making a whole that had all and lacked
    naught.
The round and sound, in whose composure just
The acquiescent and recipient side
Was Pietro's, and the stirring striving one
Violante's: both in union gave the due
Quietude, enterprise, craving and content,
Which go to bodily health and peace of mind.
But as 't is said a body, rightly mixed,
Each element in equipoise, would last
Too long and live forever, — accordingly
Holds a germ — sand-grain weight too much i'
    the scale —
Ordained to get predominance one day
And so bring all to ruin and release, —
Not otherwise a fatal germ lurked here :
" With mortals much must go, but something
    stays ;
Nothing will stay of our so happy selves."
Out of the very ripeness of life's core
A worm was bred — " Our life shall leave no
    fruit."
Enough of bliss, they thought, could bliss bear
    seed,
Yield its like, propagate a bliss in turn
And keep the kind up ; not supplant themselves
But put in evidence, record they were,
Show them, when done with, i' the shape of a
    child.
" 'T is in a child, man and wife grow complete,
One flesh : God says so : let him do his work ! ' "

Now, one reminder of this gnawing want,
One special prick o' the maggot at the core,
Always befell when, as the day came round,
A certain yearly sum, — our Pietro being,
As the long name runs, an usufructuary, —
Dropped in the common bag as interest
Of money, his till death, not afterward,
Failing an heir : an heir would take and take,
A child of theirs be wealthy in their place
To nobody's hurt — the stranger else seized all
Prosperity rolled river-like and stopped,
Making their mill go ; but when wheel wore out,
The wave would find a space and sweep on free
And, half-a-mile off, grind some neighbor's
    corn.

Adam-like, Pietro sighed and said no more :
Eve saw the apple was fair and good to taste,
So, plucked it, having asked the snake advice.
She told her husband God was merciful,
And his and her prayer granted at the last:
Let the old mill-stone moulder, — wheel un-
    worn,
Quartz from the quarry, shot into the stream
Adroitly, as before should go bring grist —
Their house continued to them by an heir,
Their vacant heart replenished with a child.
We have her own confession at full length
Made in the first remorse : 't was Jubilee
Pealed in the ear o' the conscience and it woke.
She found she had offended God no doubt,
So much was plain from what had happened
    since,
Misfortune on misfortune ; but she harmed
No one i' the world, so far as she could see.
The act had gladdened Pietro to the height,
Her spouse whom God himself must gladden so
Or not at all : thus much seems probable
From the implicit faith, or rather say
Stupid credulity of the foolish man
Who swallowed such a tale nor strained a whit
Even at his wife's far-over-fifty years
Matching his sixty - and - under. Him she
    blessed ;
And as for doing any detriment
To the veritable heir, — why, tell her first
Who was he ? Which of all the hands held up
I' the crowd, one day would gather round their
    gate
Did she so wrong by intercepting thus
The ducat, spendthrift fortune thought to fling
For a scramble just to make the mob break
    shins ?
She kept it, saved them kicks and cuffs thereby.
While at the least one good work had she
    wrought,
Good, clearly and incontestably ! Her cheat —
What was it to its subject, the child's self,
But charity and religion ? See the girl !
A body most like — a soul too probably —
Doomed to death, such a double death as waits
The illicit offspring of a common trull,
Sure to resent and forthwith rid herself
Of a mere interruption to sin's trade,
In the efficacious way old Tiber knows.
Was not so much proved by the ready sale
O' the child, glad transfer of this irksome
    chance ?

Well then, she had caught up this castaway :
This fragile egg, some careless wild bird
    dropped,
She had picked from where it waited the foot-
    fall,
And put in her own breast till forth broke finch
Able to sing God praise on mornings now.
What so excessive harm was done ? — she
    asked.

To which demand the dreadful answer comes —
For that same deed, now at Lorenzo's church,
Both agents, conscious and inconscious, lie ;
While she, the deed was done to benefit,
Lies also, the most lamentable of things,
Yonder where curious people count her breaths,
Calculate how long yet the little life
Unspilt may serve their turn nor spoil the show,
Give them their story, then the church its
    group.

Well, having gained Pompilia, the girl grew
I' the midst of Pietro here, Violante there,
Each, like a semicircle with stretched arms,
Joining the other round her preciousness —
Two walls that go about a garden-plot
Where a chance sliver, branchlet slipt from bole
Of some tongue-leaved eye-figured Eden tree,
Filched by two exiles and borne far away,
Patiently glorifies their solitude, —
Year by year mounting, grade by grade sur-
    mount
The builded brick-work, yet is compassed still,
Still hidden happily and shielded safe, —
Else why should miracle have graced the
    ground ?
But on the twelfth sun that brought April
    there
What meant that laugh ?   The coping-stone
    was reached ;
Nay, above towered a light tuft of bloom
To be toyed with by butterfly or bee,
Done good to or else harm to from outside :
Pompilia's root, stalk and a branch or two
Home enclosed still, the rest would be the
    world's.
All which was taught our couple though ob-
    tuse,
Since walls have ears, when one day brought a
    priest,
Smooth-mannered soft-speeched sleek-cheeked
    visitor,
The notable Abate Paolo — known
As younger brother of a Tuscan house
Whereof the actual representative,
Count Guido, had employed his youth and age
In culture of Rome's most productive plant —
A cardinal : but years pass and change comes,
In token of which, here was our Paolo brought
To broach a weighty business. Might he speak ?
Yes — to Violante somehow caught alone
While Pietro took his after-dinner doze,
And the young maiden, busily as befits,
Minded her broider-frame three chambers off.

So — giving now his great flap-hat a gloss
With flat o' the hand between-whiles, soothing
    now

The silk from out its creases o'er the calf,
Setting the stocking clerical again,
But never disengaging, once engaged,
The thin clear gray hold of his eyes on her —
He dissertated on that Tuscan house,
Those Franceschini, — very old they were —
Not rich however — oh, not rich, at least,
As people look to be who, low i' the scale
One way, have reason, rising all they can
By favor of the money-bag ! 't is fair —
Do all gifts go together ?   But don't suppose
That being not so rich means all so poor !
Say rather, well enough — i' the way, indeed,
Ha, ha, to fortune better than the best :
Since if his brother's patron-friend kept faith,
Put into promised play the Cardinalate,
Their house might wear the red cloth that keeps
    warm,
Would but the Count have patience — there 's
    the point !
For he was slipping into years apace,
And years make men restless — they needs
    must spy
Some certainty, some sort of end assured,
Some sparkle, though from topmost beacon-tip,
That warrants life a harbor through the haze.
In short, call him fantastic as you choose,
Guido was home-sick, yearned for the old sights
And usual faces, — fain would settle himself
And have the patron's bounty when it fell
Irrigate far rather than deluge near,
Go fertilize Arezzo, not flood Rome.
Sooth to say, 't was the wiser wish : the Count
Proved wanting in ambition, — let us avouch,
Since truth is best, — in callousness of heart,
And winced at pin-pricks whereby honors hang
A ribbon o'er each puncture : his — no soul
Ecclesiastic (here the hat was brushed),
Humble but self-sustaining, calm and cold,
Having, as one who puts his hand to the plough,
Renounced the over-vivid family-feel —
Poor brother Guido !   All too plain, he pined
Amid Rome's pomp and glare for dinginess
And that dilapidated palace-shell
Vast as a quarry and, very like, as bare —
Since to this comes old grandeur nowadays —
Or that absurd wild villa in the waste
O' the hillside, breezy though, for who likes air,
Vittiano, nor unpleasant with its vines,
Outside the city and the summer heats.
And now his harping on this one tense chord
The villa and the palace, palace this
And villa the other, all day and all night
Creaked like the implacable cicala's cry
And made one's ear-drum ache : naught else
    would serve
But that, to light his mother's visage up
With second youth, hope, gayety again,
He must find straightway, woo and haply win
And bear away triumphant back, some wife.
Well now, the man was rational in his way :
He, the Abate, — ought he to interpose ?
Unless by straining still his tutelage
(Priesthood leaps over elder-brothership)
Across this difficulty : then let go,
Leave the poor fellow in peace !   Would that
    be wrong ?
There was no making Guido great, it seems,

Spite of himself: then happy be his dole!
Indeed, the Abate's little interest
Was somewhat nearly touched i' the case, they
　　saw:
Since if his simple kinsman so were bent,
Began his rounds in Rome to catch a wife,
Full soon would such unworldliness surprise
The rare bird, sprinkle salt on phœnix' tail,
And so secure the nest a sparrow-hawk.
No lack of mothers here in Rome, — no dread
Of daughters lured as larks by looking-glass!
The first name-peeking credit-scratching fowl
Would drop her unfledged cuckoo in our nest
To gather grayness there, give voice at length
And shame the brood . . . but it was long ago
When crusades were, and we sent eagles forth!
No, that at least the Abate could forestall.
He read the thought within his brother's word,
Knew what he purposed better than himself.
We want no name and fame — having our own:
No worldly aggrandizement — such we fly:
But if some wonder of a woman's-heart
Were yet untainted on this grimy earth,
Tender and true — tradition tells of such —
Prepared to pant in time and tune with ours —
If some good girl (a girl, since she must take
The new bent, live new life, adopt new modes)
Not wealthy (Guido for his rank was poor)
But with whatever dowry came to hand, —
There were the lady-love predestinate!
And somehow the Abate's guardian eye —
Scintillant, rutilant, fraternal fire, —
Roving round every way had seized the prize
— The instinct of us, we, the spiritualty!
Come, cards on table; was it true or false
That here — here in this very tenement —
Yea, Via Vittoria did a marvel hide,
Lily of a maiden, white with intact leaf
Guessed through the sheath that saved it from
　　the sun?
A daughter with the mother's hands still clasped
Over her head for fillet virginal,
A wife worth Guido's house and hand and
　　heart?
He came to see; had spoken, he could no less —
(A final cherish of the stockinged calf)
If harm were, — well, the matter was off his
　　mind.

Then with the great air did he kiss, devout,
Violante's hand, and rise up his whole height
(A certain purple gleam about the black)
And go forth grandly, — as if the Pope came
　　next.
And so Violante rubbed her eyes awhile,
Got up too, walked to wake her Pietro soon
And pour into his ear the mighty news
How somebody had somehow somewhere seen
Their treetop-tuft of bloom above the wall,
And came now to apprise them the tree's self
Was no such crab-sort as should go feed swine,
But veritable gold, the Hesperian ball
Ordained for Hercules to haste and pluck,
And bear and give the Gods to banquet with —
Hercules standing ready at the door.
Whereon did Pietro rub his eyes in turn,
Look very wise, a little woeful too,
Then, periwig on head, and cane in hand,

Sally forth dignifiedly into the Square
Of Spain across Babbuino the six steps,
Toward the Boat-fountain where our idler.
　　lounge, —
Ask, for form's sake, who Hercules might be,
And have congratulation from the world.

Heartily laughed the world in his fool's-face
And told him Hercules was just the heir
To the stubble once a cornfield, and brick-hea;
Where used to be a dwelling-place now burned
Guido and Franceschini; a Count, — ay:
But a cross i' the poke to bless the Countship?
　　No!
All gone except sloth, pride, rapacity,
Humors of the imposthume incident
To rich blood that runs thin, — nursed to a
　　head
By the rankly-salted soil — a cardinal's court
Where, parasite and picker-up of crumbs,
He had hung on long, and now, let go, said
　　some,
Shaken off, said others, — but in any case
Tired of the trade and something worse for
　　wear,
Was wanting to change town for country quick,
Go home again: let Pietro help him home!
The brother, Abate Paolo, shrewder mouse,
Had pricked for comfortable quarters, inched
Into the core of Rome, and fattened so;
But Guido, over-burly for rat's hole
Suited to clerical slimness, starved outside,
Must shift for himself: and so the shift was
　　this!
What, was the snug retreat of Pietro tracked,
The little provision for his old age snuffed?
"Oh, make your girl a lady, an you list,
But have more mercy on our wit than vaunt
Your bargain as we burgesses who brag!
Why, Goodman Dullard, if a friend must speak,
Would the Count, think you, stoop to you and
　　yours
Were there the value of one penny-piece
To rattle 'twixt his palms — or likelier laugh,
Bid your Pompilia help you black his shoe?"

Home again, shaking oft the puzzled pate,
Went Pietro to announce a change indeed,
Yet point Violante where some solace lay
Of a rueful sort, — the taper, quenched so soon,
Had ended merely in a snuff, not stink —
Congratulate there was one hope the less,
Not misery the more: and so an end.

The marriage thus impossible, the rest
Followed: our spokesman, Paolo, heard his
　　fate,
Resignedly Count Guido bore the blow:
Violante wiped away the transient tear,
Renounced the playing Danae to gold dreams,
Praised much her Pietro's prompt sagacious-
　　ness,
Found neighbors' envy natural, lightly laughed
At gossips' malice, fairly wrapped herself
In her integrity three folds about,
And, letting pass a little day or two,
Threw, even over that integrity,
Another wrappage, namely one thick veil

That hid her, matron-wise, from head to foot,
And, by the hand holding a girl veiled too,
Stood, one dim end of a December day,
In Saint Lorenzo on the altar-step —
Just where she lies now and that girl will lie —
Only with fifty candles' company
Now, in the place of the poor winking one
Which saw — doors shut and sacristan made
    sure —
A priest — perhaps Abate Paolo — wed
Guido clandestinely, irrevocably
To his Pompilia aged thirteen years
And five months, — witness the church regis-
    ter, —
Pompilia, (thus become Count Guido's wife
Clandestinely, irrevocably his,)
Who all the while had borne, from first to last,
As brisk a part i' the bargain, as yon lamb,
Brought forth from basket and set out for
    sale,
Bears while they chaffer, wary market-man
And voluble housewife, o'er it, — each in turn
Patting the curly calm inconscious head,
With the shambles ready round the corner
    there,
When the talk's talked out and a bargain
    struck.

Transfer complete, why, Pietro was apprised.
Violante sobbed the sobs and prayed the
    prayers,
And said the serpent temp'ed so she fell,
Till Pietro had to clear his brow apace
And make the best of matters: wrath at first, —
How else? pacification presently,
Why not? — could flesh withstand the impur-
    pled one,
The very Cardinal, Paolo's patron-friend?
Who, justifiably surnamed "a hinge,"
Knew where the mollifying oil should drop
To cure the creak o' the valve, — considerate
For frailty, patient in a naughty world.
He even volunteered to supervise
The rough draught of those marriage-articles
Signed in a hurry by Pietro, since revoked:
Trust's politic, suspicion does the harm,
There is but one way to browbeat this world,
Dumb - founder doubt, and repay scorn in
    kind, —
To go on trusting, namely, till faith move
Mountains.

    And faith here made the mountains move.
Why, friends whose zeal cried "Caution ere
    too late!" —
Bade "Pause ere jump, with both feet joined,
    on slough!" —
Counselled "If rashness then, now temper-
    ance!" —
Heard for their pains that Pietro had closed
    eyes,
Jumped and was in the middle of the mire,
Money and all, just what might sink a man.
By the mere marriage, Guido gained forthwith
Dowry, his wife's right; no rescinding there:
But Pietro, why must he needs ratify
One gift Violante gave, pay down one doit
Promised in first fool's-flurry? Grasp the bag

Lest the son's service flag, — is reason and
    rhyme,
Above all when the son's a son-in-law.
Words to the wind! The parents cast their
    lot
Into the lap o' the daughter: and the son
Now with a right to lie there, took what fell,
Pietro's whole having and holding, house and
    field,
Goods, chattels and effects, his worldly worth
Present and in perspective, all renounced
In favor of Guido. As for the usufruct —
The interest now, the principal anon,
Would Guido please to wait, at Pietro's death:
Till when, he must support the couple's charge,
Bear with them, housemates, pensionaries,
    pawned
To an alien for fulfilment of their pact.
Guido should at discretion deal them orts,
Bread-bounty in Arezzo the strange place, —
They who had lived deliciously and rolled
Rome's choicest comfit 'neath the tongue before.
Into this quag, "jump" bade the Cardinal!
And neck-deep in a minute there flounced they.

But they touched bottom at Arezzo: there —
Four months' experience of how craft and
    greed,
Quickened by penury and pretentious hate
Of plain truth, brutify and bestialize, —
Four months' taste of apportioned insolence,
Cruelty graduated, dose by dose
Of ruffianism dealt out at bed and board,
And lo, the work was done, success clapped
    hands.
The starved, stripped, beaten brace of stupid
    dupes
Broke at last in their desperation loose,
Fled away for their lives, and lucky so;
Found their account in casting coat afar
And bearing off a shred of skin at least:
Left Guido lord o' the prey, as the lion is,
And, careless what came after, carried their
    wrongs
To Rome, — I nothing doubt, with such remorse
As folly feels, since pain can make it wise,
But crime, past wisdom, which is innocence,
Needs not be plagued with till a later day.

Pietro went back to beg from door to door,
In hope that memory not quite extinct
Of cheery days and festive nights would move
Friends and acquaintance — after the natural
    laugh,
And tributary "Just as we foretold —"
To show some bowels, give the dregs o' the cup
Scraps of the trencher, to their host that was,
Or let him share the mat with the mastiff, he
Who lived large and kept open house so long.
Not so Violante: ever ahead i' the march,
Quick at the by-road and the cut-across,
She went first to the best adviser, God —
Whose finger unmistakably was felt
In all this retribution of the past.
Here was the prize of sin, luck of a lie!
But here too was what Holy Year would help,
Bound to rid sinners of sin vulgar, sin
Abnormal, sin prodigious, up to sin

Impossible and supposed for Jubilee' sake:
To lift the leadenest of lies, let soar
The soul unhampered by a feather-weight.
" I will," said she, " go burn out this bad hole
That breeds the scorpion, balk the plague at
        least
Of hope to further plague by progeny:
I will confess my fault, be punished, yes,
But pardoned too: Saint Peter pays for all."

So, with the crowd she mixed, made for the
        dome,
Through the great door new-broken for the
        nonce
Marched, muffled more than ever matron-wise,
Up the left nave to the formidable throne,
Fell into file with this the poisoner
And that the parricide, and reached in turn
The poor repugnant Penitentiary
Set at this gully-hole o' the world's discharge
To help the frightfullest of filth have vent,
And then knelt down and whispered in his ear
How she had bought Pompilia, palmed the
        babe
On Pietro, passed the girl off as their child
To Guido, and defrauded of his due
This one and that one, — more than she could
        name,
Until her solid piece of wickedness
Happened to split and spread woe far and wide:
Contritely now she brought the case for cure.

Replied the throne — " Ere God forgive the
        guilt,
Make man some restitution! Do your part!
The owners of your husband's heritage,
Barred thence by this pretended birth and
        heir, —
Tell them, the bar came so, is broken so,
Theirs be the due reversion as before!
Your husband who, no partner in the guilt,
Suffers the penalty, led blindfold thus
By love of what he thought his flesh and blood
To alienate his all in her behalf, —
Tell him too such contract is null and void!
Last, he who personates your son-in-law,
Who with sealed eyes and stopped ears, tame
        and mute,
Took at your hand that bastard of a whore
You called your daughter and he calls his
        wife, --
Tell him, and bear the anger which is just!
Then, penance so performed, may pardon be!"

Who could gainsay this just and right award?
Nobody in the world: but, out o' the world,
Who knows? — might timid intervention be
From any makeshift of an angel-guide,
Substitute for celestial guardianship,
Pretending to take care of the girl's self:
" Woman, confessing crime is healthy work,
And telling truth relieves a liar like you,
But how of my quite unconsidered charge?
No thought if, while this good befalls yourself,
Aught in the way of harm may find out her?"
No least thought, I assure you: truth being
        truth,
Tell it and shame the devil!

Said and done:
Home went Violante, and disbosomed all:
And Pietro who, six months before, had borne
Word after word of such a piece of news
Like so much cold steel inched through his
        breast-blade,
Now at its entry gave a leap for joy,
As who — what did I say of one in a quag? —
Should catch a hand from heaven and spring
        thereby
Out of the mud, on ten toes stand once more.
" What? All that used to be, may be again?
My money mine again, my house, my land,
My chairs and tables, all mine evermore?
What, the girl's dowry never was the girl's,
And, unpaid yet, is never now to pay?
Then the girl's self, my pale Pompilia child
That used to be my own with her great eyes —
He who drove us forth, why should he keep her
When proved as very a pauper as himself?
Will she come back, with nothing changed at
        all,
And laugh, ' But how you dreamed uneasily!
I saw the great drops stand here on your
        brow —
Did I do wrong to wake you with a kiss?'
No, indeed, darling! No, for wide awake
I see another outburst of surprise:
The lout-lord, bully-beggar, braggart-sneak,
Who, not content with cutting purse, crops
        ear —
Assuredly it shall be salve to mine
When this great news red-letters him, the
        rogue!
Ay, let him taste the teeth o' the trap, this fox,
Give us our lamb back, golden fleece and all,
Let her creep in and warm our breasts again!
Why care for the past? — we three are our old
        selves,
And know now what the outside world is
        worth."

And so, he carried case before the courts;
And there Violante, blushing to the bone,
Made public declaration of her fault,
Renounced her motherhood, and prayed the law
To interpose, frustrate of its effect
Her folly, and redress the injury done.

Whereof was the disastrous consequence,
That though indisputably clear the case
(For thirteen years are not so large a lapse,
And still six witnesses survived in Rome
To prove the truth o' the tale) — yet, patent
        wrong
Seemed Guido's; the first cheat had chanced
        on him:
Here was the pity that, deciding right,
Those who began the wrong would gain the
        prize.
Guido pronounced the story one long lie
Lied to do robbery and take revenge:
Or say it were no lie at all but truth,
Then, it both robbed the right heirs and shamed
        him
Without revenge to humanize the deed:
What had he done when first they shamed him
        thus?
But that were too fantastic: losels they.

And leasing this world's-wonder of a lie,
They lied to blot him though it brand them-
  selves.

So answered Guido through the Abate's mouth.
Wherefore the court, its customary way,
Inclined to the middle course the sage affect.
They held the child to be a changeling, — good :
But, lest the husband got no good thereby,
They willed the dowry, though not hers at all,
Should yet be his, if not by right then grace —
Part-payment for the plain injustice done.
As for that other contract, Pietro's work,
Renunciation of his own estate,
That must be cancelled — give him back his
  gifts,
He was no party to the cheat at least !
So ran the judgment : — whence a prompt ap-
  peal
On both sides, seeing right is absolute.
Cried Pietro, " Is the child no child of mine ?
Why give her a child's dowry ? " — " Have I
  right
To the dowry, why not to the rest as well ? "
Cried Guido, or cried Paolo in his name :
Till law said, " Reinvestigate the case ! "
And so the matter pends, to this same day.

Hence new disaster — here no outlet seemed :
Whatever the fortune of the battlefield,
No path whereby the fatal man might march
Victorious, wreath on head and spoils in hand,
And back turned full upon the baffled foe, —
Nor cranny whence, desperate and disgraced,
Stripped to the skin, he might be fain to crawl
Worm-like, and so away with his defeat
To other fortune and a novel prey.
No, he was pinned to the place there, left alone
With his immense hate and, the solitary
Subject to satisfy that hate, his wife.
" Cast her off ? Turn her naked out of doors ?
Easily said ! But still the action pends,
Still dowry, principal and interest,
Pietro's possessions, all I bargained for, —
Any good day, be but my friends alert,
May give them me if she continue mine.
Yet, keep her ? Keep the puppet of my foes —
Her voice that lisps me back their curse — her
  eye
They lend their leer of triumph to — her lip
I touch and taste their very filth upon ? "

In short, he also took the middle course
Rome taught him — did at last excogitate
How he might keep the good and leave the
  bad
Twined in revenge, yet extricable, — nay
Make the very hate's eruption, very rush
Of the unpent sluice of cruelty relieve
His heart first, then go fertilize his field.
What if the girl-wife, tortured with due care,
Should take, as though spontaneously, the road
It were impolitic to thrust her on ?
If, goaded, she broke out in full revolt,
Followed her parents i' the face o' the world,
Branded as runaway, not castaway,
Self-sentenced and self-punished in the act ?
So should the loathed form and detested face

Launch themselves into hell and there be lost
While he looked o'er the brink with folded
  arms ;
So should the heaped-up shames go shuddering
  back
O' the head o' the heapers, Pietro and his wife,
And bury in the breakage three at once :
While Guido, left free, no one right renounced,
Gain present, gain prospective, all the gain,
None of the wife except her rights absorbed,
Should ask law what it was law paused about —
If law were dubious still whose word to take,
The husband's — dignified and derelict,
Or the wife's — the . . . what I tell you. It
  should be.

Guido's first step was to take pen, indite
A letter to the Abate, — not his own,
His wife's, — she should re-write, sign, seal and
  send.
She liberally told the household-news,
Rejoiced her vile progenitors were gone,
Revealed their malice — how they even laid
A last injunction on her, when they fled,
That she should forthwith find a paramour,
Complot with him to gather spoil enough,
Then burn the house down, — taking previous
  care
To poison all its inmates overnight, —
And so companioned, so provisioned too,
Follow to Rome and there join fortunes gay.
This letter, traced in pencil-characters,
Guido as easily got retraced in ink
By his wife's pen, guided from end to end,
As if it had been just so much Chinese.
For why ? That wife could broider, sing per-
  haps,
Pray certainly, but no more read than write
This letter, " which yet write she must," he
  said,
" Being half courtesy and compliment,
Half sisterliness : take the thing on trust ! "
She had as readily retraced the words
Of her own death-warrant, — in some sort
  't was so.
This letter the Abate in due course
Communicated to such curious souls
In Rome as needs must pry into the cause
Of quarrel, why the Comparini fled
The Franceschini, whence the grievance grew,
What the hubbub meant : " Nay, — see the
  wife's own word,
Authentic answer ! Tell detractors too
There 's a plan formed, a programme figured
  here
— Pray God no after-practice put to proof,
This letter cast no light upon, one day ! "

So much for what should work in Rome : back
  now
To Arezzo, follow up the project there,
Forward the next step with as bold a foot,
And plague Pompilia to the height, you see !
Accordingly did Guido set himself
To worry up and down, across, around,
The woman, hemmed in by her household
  bars,
Chase her about the coop of daily life,

Having first stopped each outlet thence save one
Which, like bird with a ferret in her haunt,
She needs must seize as sole way of escape
Though there was tied and twittering a decoy
To seem as if it tempted, — just the plume
O' the popinjay, not a real respite there
From tooth and claw of something in the
    dark, —
Giuseppe Caponsacchi.
                                    Now begins
The tenebrific passage of the tale:
How hold a light, display the cavern's gorge?
How, in this phase of the affair, show truth?
Here is the dying wife who smiles and says,
"So it was, — so it was not, — how it was,
I never knew nor ever care to know — "
Till they all weep, physican, man of law,
Even that poor old bit of battered brass
Beaten out of all shape by the world's sins,
Common utensil of the lazar-house —
Confessor Celestino groans, " 'T is truth,
All truth and only truth: there 's something
    here,
Some presence in the room beside us all,
Something that every lie expires before:
No question she was pure from first to last."
So far is well and helps us to believe:
But beyond, she the helpless, simple-sweet
Or silly-sooth, unskilled to break one blow
At her good fame by putting finger forth, —
How can she render service to the truth?
The bird says, " So I fluttered where a springe
Caught me : the springe did not contrive itself,
That I know: who contrived it, God forgive! "
But we, who hear no voice and have dry eyes,
Must ask, — we cannot else, absolving her, —
How of the part played by that same decoy
I' the catching, caging? Was himself caught
    first?
We deal here with no innocent at least,
No witless victim, — he 's a man of the age
And priest beside, — persuade the mocking
    world
Mere charity boiled over in this sort!
He whose own safety too, — (the Pope 's ap-
    prised —
Good-natured with the secular offence,
The Pope looks grave on priesthood in a
    scrape) —
Our priest's own safety therefore, maybe life,
Hangs on the issue ! You will find it hard.
Guido is here to meet you with fixed foot,·
Stiff like a statue — " Leave what went before !
My wife fled i' the company of a priest,
Spent two days and two nights alone with him :
Leave what came after ! " He stands hard to
    throw.
Moreover priests are merely flesh and blood ;
When we get weakness, and no guilt beside,
'T is no such great ill-fortune: finding gray,
We gladly call that white which might be
    black,
Too used to the double-dye. So, if the priest,
Moved by Pompilia's youth and beauty, gave
Way to the natural weakness . . . Anyhow,
Here be facts, charactery ; what they spell
Determine, and thence pick what sense you
    may !

There was a certain young bold handsome priest
Popular in the city, far and wide
Famed, since Arezzo 's but a little place,
As the best of good companions, gay and grave
At the decent minute ; settled in his stall,
Or sidling, lute on lap, by lady's couch,
Ever the courtly Canon : see in him
A proper star to climb and culminate,
Have its due handbreadth of the heaven at
    Rome,
Though meanwhile pausing on Arezzo's edge,
As modest candle does 'mid mountain fog,
To rub off redness and rusticity
Ere it sweep chastened, gain the silver-sphere !
Whether through Guido's absence or what else,
This Caponsacchi, favorite of the town,
Was yet no friend of his nor free o' the house,
Though both moved in the regular magnates'
    march :
Each must observe the other's tread and halt
At church, saloon, theatre, house of play.
Who could help noticing the husband's slouch,
The black of his brow — or miss the news that
    buzzed
Of how the little solitary wife
Wept and looked out of window all day long ?
What need of minute search into such springs
As start men, set o' the move ? — machinery
Old as earth, obvious as the noonday sun.
Why, take men as they come, — an instance
    now, —
Of all those who have simply gone to see
Pompilia on her deathbed since four days,
Half at the least are, call it how you please,
In love with her — I don't except the priests
Nor even the old confessor whose eyes run
Over at what he styles his sister's voice
Who died so early and weaned him from the
    world.
Well, had they viewed her ere the paleness
    pushed
The last o' the red o' the rose away, while yet
Some hand, adventurous 'twixt the wind and
    her,
Might let shy life run back and raise the flower
Rich with reward up to the guardian's face, —
Would they have kept that hand employed all
    day
At fumbling on with prayer-book pages? No!
Men are men : why then need I say one word
More than that our mere man the Canon here
Saw, pitied, loved Pompilia ?

                                This is why;
This startling why: that Caponsacchi's self —
Whom foes and friends alike avouch, for good
Or ill, a man of truth whate'er betide,
Intrepid altogether, reckless too
How his own fame and fortune, tossed to the
    winds,
Suffer by any turn the adventure take,
Nay, more — not thrusting, like a badge to hide,
'Twixt shirt and skin a joy which shown is
    shame —
But flirting flag-like i' the face o' the world
This tell-tale kerchief, this conspicuous love
For the lady, — oh, called innocent love, I
    know !

Only, such scarlet fiery innocence
As most folk would try muffle up in shade, —
— 'T is strange then that this else abashless
   mouth
Should yet maintain, for truth's sake which is
   God's,
That it was not he made the first advance,
That, even ere word had passed between the
   two,
Pompilia penned him letters, passionate prayers
If not love, then so simulating love
That he, no novice to the taste of thyme,
Turned from such over-luscious honey-clot
At end o' the flower, and would not lend his lip
Till . . . but the tale here frankly outsoars
   faith :
There must be falsehood somewhere. For her
   part,
Pompilia quietly constantly avers
She never penned a letter in her life
Nor to the Canon nor any other man,
Being incompetent to write and read :
Nor had she ever uttered word to him, nor he
To her till that same evening when they met,
She on her window-terrace, he beneath
I' the public street, as was their fateful chance,
And she adjured him in the name of God
To find out, bring to pass where, when and how
Escape with him to Rome might be contrived.
Means were found, plan laid, time fixed, she
   avers,
And heart assured to heart in loyalty,
All at an impulse ! All extemporized
As in romance-books ! Is that credible ?
Well, yes : as she avers this with calm mouth
Dying, I do think " Credible ! " you 'd cry —
Did not the priest's voice come to break the
   spell.
They questioned him apart, as the custom is,
When first the matter made a noise at Rome,
And he, calm, constant then as she is now,
For truth's sake did assert and reassert
Those letters called him to her and he came,
— Which damns the story credible otherwise.
Why should this man — mad to devote himself,
Careless what comes of his own fame, the first—
Be studious thus to publish and declare
Just what the lightest nature loves to hide,
So screening lady from the byword's laugh
" First spoke the lady, last the cavalier ! ' "
— I say, — why should the man tell truth just
   now
When graceful lying meets such ready shrift ?
Or is there a first moment for a priest
As for a woman, when invaded shame
Must have its first and last excuse to show ?
Do both contrive love's entry in the mind
Shall look. i' the manner of it, a surprise,
That after, once the flag o' the fort hauled
   down,
Effrontery may sink drawbridge, open gate,
Welcome and entertain the conqueror ?
Or what do you say to a touch of the devil's
   worst ?
Can it be that the husband, he who wrote
The letter to his brother I told you of,
I' the name of her it meant to criminate, —
What if he wrote those letters to the priest ?

Further the priest says, when it first befell,
This folly o' the letters, that he checked the
   flow,
Put them back lightly each with its reply.
Here again vexes new discrepancy :
There never reached her eye a word from him ;
He did write but she could not read — could
   just
Burn the offence to wifehood, womanhood,
So did burn : never bade him come to her,
Yet when it proved he must come, let him come,
And when he did come though uncalled, — why,
   spoke
Prompt by an inspiration : thus it chanced,
Will you go somewhat back to understand ?

When first, pursuant to his plan, there sprang,
Like an uncaged beast, Guido's cruelty
On soul and body of his wife, she cried
To those whom law appoints resource for such,
The secular guardian, — that 's the Governor,
And the Archbishop, — that 's the spiritual
   guide,
And prayed them take the claws from out her
   flesh.
Now, this is ever the ill consequence
Of being noble, poor and difficult,
Ungainly, yet too great to disregard, —
This — that born peers and friends hereditary,—
Though disinclined to help from their own store
The opprobrious wight, put penny in his poke
From private purse or leave the door ajar
When he goes wistful by at dinner-time, —
Yet, if his needs conduct him where they sit
Smugly in office, judge this, bishop that,
Dispensers of the shine and shade o' the place —
And if, friend's door shut and friend's purse
   undrawn,
Still potentates may find the office-seat
Do as good service at no cost — give help
By-the-bye, pay up traditional dues at once
Just through a feather-weight too much i' the
   scale,
Or finger-tip forgot at the balance-tongue, —
Why, only churls refuse, or Molinists.
Thus when, in the first roughness of surprise
At Guido's wolf-face whence the sheepskin fell,
The frightened couple, all bewilderment,
Rushed to the Governor, — who else rights
   wrong ?
Told him their tale of wrong and craved re-
   dress —
Why, then the Governor woke up to the fact
That Guido was a friend of old, poor Count ! —
So, promptly paid his tribute, promised the pair
Wholesome chastisement should soon cure their
   qualms
Next time they came, wept, prated and told
   lies :
So stopped all prating, sent them dumb to Rome.
Well, now it was Pompilia's turn to try :
The troubles pressing on her, as I said,
Three times she rushed, maddened by misery,
To the other mighty man, sobbed out her prayer
At footstool of the Archbishop — fast the friend
Of her husband also ! Oh, good friends of yore !
So, the Archbishop, not to be outdone
By the Governor, break custom more than he.

Thrice bade the foolish woman stop her tongue,
Unloosed her hands from harassing his gout,
Coached her and carried her to the Count again,
— His old friend should be master in his house,
Rule his wife and correct her faults at need !
Well, driven from post to pillar in this wise,
She, as a last resource, betook herself
To one, should be no family-friend at least,
A simple friar o' the city ; confessed to him,
Then told how fierce temptation of release
By self-dealt death was busy with her soul,
And urged that he put this in words, write plain
For one who could not write, set down her prayer
That Pietro and Violante, parent-like
If somehow not her parents, should for love
Come save her, pluck from out the flame the
        brand
Themselves had thoughtlessly thrust in so deep
To send gay-colored sparkles up and cheer
Their seat at the chimney-corner. The good
        friar
Promised as much at the moment ; but, alack,
Night brings discretion: he was no one's
        friend,
Yet presently found he could not turn about
Nor take a step i' the case and fail to tread
On some one's toe who either was a friend,
Or a friend's friend, or friend's friend thrice-
        removed,
And woe to friar by whom offences come !
So, the course being plain, — with a general
        sigh
At matrimony the profound mistake, —
He threw reluctantly the business up,
Having his other penitents to mind.

If then, all outlets thus secured save one,
At last she took to the open, stood and stared
With her wan face to see where God might
        wait —
And there found Caponsacchi wait as well
For the precious something at perdition's edge,
He only was predestinate to save, —
And if they recognized in a critical flash
From the zenith, each the other, her need of
        him,
His need of . . . say, a woman to perish for,
The regular way o' the world, yet break no
        vow,
Do no harm save to himself, — if this were
        thus ?
How do you say ? It were improbable ;
So is the legend of my patron-saint.

Anyhow, whether, as Guido states the case,
Pompilia — like a starving wretch i' the street
Who stops and rifles the first passenger
In the great right of an excessive wrong —
Did somehow call this stranger and he came, —
Or whether the strange sudden interview
Blazed as when star and star must needs go
        close
Till each hurts each and there is loss in
        heaven —
Whatever way in this strange world it was, —
Pompilia and Caponsacchi met, in fine,
She at her window, he i' the street beneath,
And understood each other at first look.

All was determined and performed at once.
And on a certain April evening, late
I' the month, this girl of sixteen, bride and
        wife
Three years and over, — she who hitherto
Had never taken twenty steps in Rome
Beyond the church, pinned to her mother's
        gown,
Nor, in Arezzo, knew her way through street
Except what led to the Archbishop's door, —
Such an one rose up in the dark, laid hand
On what came first, clothes and a trinket or
        two,
Belongings of her own in the old day, —
Stole from the side o' the sleeping spouse —
        who knows ?
Sleeping perhaps, silent for certain, — slid
Ghost-like from great dark room to great dark
        room,
In through the tapestries and out again
And onward, unembarrassed as a fate,
Descended staircase, gained last door of all,
Sent it wide open at first push of palm,
And there stood, first time, last and only time,
At liberty, alone in the open street, —
Unquestioned, unmolested found herself
At the city gate, by Caponsacchi's side,
Hope there, joy there, life and all good again,
The carriage there, the convoy there, light
        there
Broadening ever into blaze at Rome
And breaking small what long miles lay be-
        tween ;
Up she sprang, in he followed, they were safe.

The husband quotes this for incredible,
All of the story from first word to last :
Sees the priest's hand throughout upholding
        hers,
Traces his foot to the alcove, that night,
Whither and whence blindfold he knew the
        way,
Proficient in all craft and stealthiness ;
And cites for proof a servant, eye that watched
And ear that opened to purse secrets up,
A woman-spy, — suborned to give and take
Letters and tokens, do the work of shame
The more adroitly that herself, who helped
Communion thus between a tainted pair,
Had long since been a leper thick in spot,
A common trull o' the town : she witnessed
        all,
Helped many meetings, partings, took her wage
And then told Guido the whole matter. Lies !
The woman's life confutes her word, — her
        word
Confutes itself : " Thus, thus and thus I lied."
" And thus, no question, still you lie," we say.

" Ay, but at last, e'en have it how you will,
Whatever the means, whatever the way, ex-
        plodes
The consummation " — the accusers shriek :
" Here is the wife avowedly found in flight,
And the companion of her flight, a priest ;
She flies her husband, he the church his
        spouse :
What is this ? "

Wife and priest alike reply,
" This is the simple thing it claims to be,
A course we took for life and honor's sake,
Very strange, very justifiable."
She says, " God put it in my head to fly,
As when the martin migrates : autumn claps
Her hands, cries ' Winter 's coming, will be
    here,
Off with you ere the white teeth overtake !
Flee !' So I fled : this friend was the warm
    day,
The south wind and whatever favors flight ;
I took the favor, had the help, how else ?
And so we did fly rapidly all night,
All day, all night — a longer night — again,
And then another day, longest of days,
And all the while, whether we fled or stopped,
I scarce know how or why, one thought filled
    both,
' Fly and arrive !' So long as I found strength
I talked with my companion, told him much,
Knowing that he knew more, knew me, knew
    God
And God's disposal of me, — but the sense
O' the blessed flight absorbed me in the main,
And speech became mere talking through a
    sleep,
Till at the end of that last longest night
In a red daybreak, when we reached an inn
And my companion whispered ' Next stage —
    Rome !'
Sudden the weak flesh fell like piled-up cards,
All the frail fabric at a finger's touch,
And prostrate the poor soul too, and I said,
' But though Count Guido were a furlong off,
Just on me, I must stop and rest awhile !'
Then something like a huge white wave o' the
    sea
Broke o'er my brain and buried me in sleep
Blessedly, till it ebbed and left me loose,
And where was I found but on a strange bed
In a strange room like hell, roaring with noise,
Ruddy with flame, and filled with men, in front
Who but the man you call my husband ? ay —
Count Guido once more between heaven and
    me,
For there my heaven stood, my salvation, yes —
That Caponsacchi all my heaven of help,
Helpless himself, held prisoner in the hands
Of men who looked up in my husband's face
To take the fate thence he should signify,
Just as the way was at Arezzo. Then,
Not for my sake but his who had helped me —
I sprang up, reached him with one bound, and
    seized
The sword o' the felon, trembling at his side,
Fit creature of a coward, unsheathed the thing
And would have pinned him through the
    poison-bag
To the wall and left him there to palpitate,
As you serve scorpions, but men interposed —
Disarmed me, gave his life to him again
That he might take mine and the other lives ;
And he has done so. I submit myself !"

The priest says — oh, and in the main result
The facts asseverate, he truly says,
As to the very act and deed of him,

However you mistrust the mind o' the man —
The flight was just for flight's sake, no pretext
For aught except to set Pompilia free.
He says, " I cite the husband's self's worst
    charge
In proof of my best word for both of us.
Be it conceded that so many times
We took our pleasure in his palace : then,
What need to fly at all ? — or flying no less,
What need to outrage the lips sick and white
Of a woman, and bring ruin down beside,
By halting when Rome lay one stage beyond ? "
So does he vindicate Pompilia's fame,
Confirm her story in all points but one —
This ; that, so fleeing and so breathing forth
Her last strength in the prayer to halt a while,
She makes confusion of the reddening white
Which was the sunset when her strength gave
    way,
And the next sunrise and its whitening red
Which she revived in when her husband came :
She mixes both times, morn and eve, in one,
Having lived through a blank of night 'twixt
    each
Though dead-asleep, unaware as a corpse,
She on the bed above ; her friend below
Watched in the doorway of the inn the while,
Stood i' the red o' the morn, that she mistakes,
In act to rouse and quicken the tardy crew
And hurry out the horses, have the stage
Over, the last league, reach Rome and be safe :
When up came Guido.
                        Guido's tale begins —
How he and his whole household, drunk to
    death
By some enchanted potion, poppied drugs
Plied by the wife, lay powerless in gross sleep
And left the spoilers unimpeded way,
Could not shake off their poison and pursue,
Till noontide, then made shift to get on horse
And did pursue : which means he took his
    time,
Pressed on no more than lingered after, step
By step, just making sure o' the fugitives,
Till at the nick of time, he saw his chance,
Seized it, came up with and surprised the pair.
How he must needs have gnawn lip and gnashed
    teeth,
Taking successively at tower and town,
Village and roadside, still the same report :
" Yes, such a pair arrived an hour ago,
Sat in the carriage just where now you stand,
While we got horses ready, — turned deaf ear
To all entreaty they would even alight ;
Counted the minutes and resumed their
    course."
Would they indeed escape, arrive at Rome,
Leave no least loop-hole to let murder through,
But foil him of his captured infamy,
Prize of guilt proved and perfect ? So it
    seemed :
Till, oh the happy chance, at last stage, Rome
But two short hours off, Castelnuovo reached,
The guardian angel gave reluctant place,
Satan stepped forward with alacrity,
Pompilia's flesh and blood succumbed, perforce
A halt was, and her husband had his will.
Perdue he couched, counted out hour by hour

Till he should spy in the east a signal-streak —
Night had been, morrow was, triumph would
be.
Do you see the plan deliciously complete?
The rush upon the unsuspecting sleep,
The easy execution, the outcry
Over the deed, "Take notice all the world!
These two dead bodies, locked still in em-
brace, —
The man is Caponsacchi and a priest,
The woman is my wife: they fled me late,
Thus have I found and you behold them thus,
And may judge me: do you approve or no?"

Success did seem not so improbable,
But that already Satan's laugh was heard,
His black back turned on Guido — left i' the
lurch
Or rather, balked of suit and service now,
Left to improve on both by one deed more,
Burn up the better at no distant day,
Body and soul one holocaust to hell.
Anyhow, of this natural consequence
Did just the last link of the long chain snap:
For an eruption was o' the priest, alive
And alert, calm, resolute and formidable,
Not the least look of fear in that broad brow —
One not to be disposed of by surprise,
And armed moreover — who had guessed as
much?
Yes, there stood he in secular costume
Complete from head to heel, with sword at
side,
He seemed to know the trick of perfectly.
There was no prompt suppression of the man
As he said calmly, "I have saved your wife
From death; there was no other way but this;
Of what do I defraud you except death?
Charge any wrong beyond, I answer it."
Guido, the valorous, had met his match,
Was forced to demand help instead of flight,
Bid the authorities o' the place lend aid
And make the best of a broken matter so.
They soon obeyed the summons — I suppose,
Apprised and ready, or not far to seek —
Laid hands on Caponsacchi, found in fault,
A priest yet flagrantly accoutred thus, —
Then, to make good Count Guido's further
charge,
Proceeded, prisoner made lead the way,
In a crowd, upstairs to the chamber-door,
Where wax-white, dead asleep, deep beyond
dream,
As the priest laid her, lay Pompilia yet.

And as he mounted step and step with the
crowd
How I see Guido taking heart again!
He knew his wife so well and the way of her —
How at the outbreak she would shroud her
shame
In hell's heart, would it mercifully yawn —
How, failing that, her forehead to his foot,
She would crouch silent till the great doom
fell,
Leave him triumphant with the crowd to see
Guilt motionless or writhing like a worm!
No! Second misadventure, this worm turned.

I told you: would have slain him on the spot
With his own weapon, but they seized her
hands:
Leaving her tongue free, as it tolled the knell
Of Guido's hope so lively late. The past
Took quite another shape now. She who
shrieked,
"At least and forever I am mine and God's,
Thanks to his liberating angel Death —
Never again degraded to be yours
The ignoble noble, the unmanly man,
The beast below the beast in brutishness!" —
This was the froward child, "the restif lamb
Used to be cherished in his breast," he
groaned —
"Eat from his hand and drink from out his
cup,
The while his fingers pushed their loving way
Through curl on curl of that soft coat —
alas,
And she all silverly baaed gratitude
While meditating mischief!" — and so forth.
He must invent another story now!'
The ins and outs o' the rooms were searched:
he found
Or showed for found the abominable prize —
Love-letters from his wife who cannot write,
Love-letters in reply o' the priest — thank
God! —
Who can write and confront his character
With this, and prove the false thing forged
throughout:
Spitting whereat, he needs must spatter whom
But Guido's self? — that forged and falsified
One letter called Pompilia's, past dispute:
Then why not these to make sure still more
sure?

So was the case concluded then and there:
Guido preferred his charges in due form,
Called on the law to adjudicate, consigned
The accused ones to the Prefect of the place.
(Oh mouse-birth of that mountain-like re-
venge!)
And so to his own place betook himself
After the spring that failed, — the wildcat's
way.
The captured parties were conveyed to Rome;
Investigation followed here i' the court—
Soon to review the fruit of its own work,
From then to now being eight months and no
more.
Guido kept out of sight and safe at home:
The Abate, brother Paolo, helped most
At words when deeds were out of question,
pushed
Nearest the purple, best played deputy,
So, pleaded, Guido's representative
At the court shall soon try Guido's self, —
what 's more,
The court that also took — I told you, Sir —
That statement of that couple, how a cheat
Had been i' the birth of the babe, no child of
theirs.
That was the prelude; this, the play's first
act:
Whereof we wait what comes, crown, close of
all.

Well, the result was something of a shade
On the parties thus accused, — how otherwise?
Shade, but with shine as unmistakable.
Each had a prompt defence : Pompilia first —
"Earth was made hell to me who did no harm :
I only could emerge one way from hell
By catching at the one hand held me, so
I caught at it and thereby stepped to heaven :
If that be wrong, do with me what you will !"
Then Caponsacchi with a grave grand sweep
O' the arm as though his soul warned baseness
    off —
" If as a man, then much more as a priest
I hold me bound to help weak innocence :
If so my worldly reputation burst,
Being the bubble it is, why, burst it may :
Blame I can bear though not blameworthiness.
But use your sense first, see if the miscreant
    proved,
The man who tortured thus the woman, thus
Have not both laid the trap and fixed the lure
Over the pit should bury body and soul !
His facts are lies : his letters are the fact —
An infiltration flavored with himself !
As for the fancies — whether . . . what is it
    you say ?
The lady loves me, whether I love her
In the forbidden sense of your surmise, —
If, with the midday blaze of truth above,
The unlidded eye of God awake, aware,
You needs must pry about and trace the birth
Of each stray beam of light may traverse night,
To the night's sun that 's Lucifer himself,
Do so, at other time, in other place,
Not now nor here ! Enough that first to last
I never touched her lip nor she my hand,
Nor either of us thought a thought, much less
Spoke a word which the Virgin might not
    hear.
Be such your question, thus I answer it."

Then the court had to make its mind up, spoke.
" It is a thorny question, yea, a tale
Hard to believe, but not impossible :
Who can be absolute for either side ?
A middle course is happily open yet.
Here has a blot surprised the social blank, —
Whether through favor, feebleness or fault,
No matter, leprosy has touched our robe
And we unclean must needs be purified.
Here is a wife makes holiday from home,
A priest caught playing truant to his church,
In masquerade moreover : both allege
Enough excuse to stop our lifted scourge
Which else would heavily fall. On the other
    hand,
Here is a husband, ay and man of mark,
Who comes complaining here, demands redress
As if he were the pattern of desert —
The while those plaguy allegations frown,
Forbid we grant him the redress he seeks.
To all men be our moderation known !
Rewarding none while compensating each,
Hurting all round though harming nobody,
Husband, wife, priest, scot-free not one shall
    'scape,
Yet priest, wife, husband, boast the unbroken
    head

From application of our excellent oil :
So that, whatever be the fact, in fine,
We make no miss of justice in a sort.
First, let the husband stomach as he may,
His wife shall neither be returned him, no —
Nor branded, whipped and caged, but just con
    signed
To a convent and the quietude she craves ;
So is he rid of his domestic plague :
What better thing can happen to a man ?
Next, let the priest retire — unshent, unshamed
Unpunished as for perpetrating crime,
But relegated (not imprisoned, Sirs !)
Sent for three years to clarify his youth
At Civita, a rest by the way to Rome :
There let his life skim off its last of lees
Nor keep this dubious color. Judged the
    cause :
All parties may retire, content, we hope."
That 's Rome's way, the traditional road of law ;
Whither it leads is what remains to tell.

The priest went to his relegation-place,
The wife to her convent, brother Paolo
To the arms of brother Guido with the news
And this beside — his charge was counter-
    charged ;
The Comparini, his old brace of hates,
Were breathed and vigilant and venomous
    now —
Had shot a second bolt where the first stuck,
And followed up the pending dowry-suit
By a procedure should release the wife
From so much of the marriage-bond as barred
Escape when Guido turned the screw too much
On his wife's flesh and blood, as husband may.
No more defence, she turned and made attack,
Claimed now divorce from bed and board, in
    short :
Pleaded such subtle strokes of cruelty,
Such slow sure siege laid to her body and soul,
As, proved, — and proofs seemed coming thick
    and fast, —
Would gain both freedom and the dowry back
Even should the first suit leave them in his
    grasp :
So urged the Comparini for the wife.
Guido had gained not one of the good things
He grasped at by his creditable plan
O' the flight and following and the rest : the suit
That smouldered late was fanned to fury new,
This adjunct came to help with fiercer fire,
While he had got himself a quite new plague —
Found the world's face an universal grin
At this last best of the Hundred Merry Tales
Of how a young and spritely clerk devised
To carry off a spouse that moped too much,
And cured her of the vapors in a trice :
And how the husband, playing Vulcan's part,
Told by the Sun, started in hot pursuit
To catch the lovers, and came halting up,
Cast his net, and then called the Gods to see
The convicts in their rosy impudence —
Whereat said Mercury, " Would that I were
    Mars !"
Oh it was rare, and naughty all the same !
Brief, the wife's courage and cunning, — the
    priest's show

Of chivalry and adroitness, — last not least,
The husband — how he ne'er showed teeth at
      all,
Whose bark had promised biting; but just
      sneaked
Back to his kennel, tail 'twixt legs, as 't
      were, —
All this was hard to gulp down and digest.
So pays the devil his liegeman, brass for gold.
But this was at Arezzo: here in Rome
Brave Paolo bore up against it all —
Battled it out, nor wanting to himself
Nor Guido nor the House whose weight he bore
Pillar-like, by no force of arm but brain.
He knew his Rome, what wheels to set to
      work;
Plied influential folk, pressed to the ear
Of the efficacious purple, pushed his way
To the old Pope's self, — past decency indeed, —
Praying him take the matter in his hands
Out of the regular court's incompetence.
But times are changed and nephews out of date
And favoritism unfashionable: the Pope
Said, " Render Cæsar what is Cæsar's due ! "
As for the Comparini's counter-plea,
He met that by a counter-plea again,
Made Guido claim divorce — with help so far
By the trial's issue : for, why punishment
However slight unless for guiltiness
However slender ? — and a molehill serves
Much as a mountain of offence this way.
So was he gathering strength on every side
And growing more and more to menace — when
All of a terrible moment came the blow
That beat down Paolo's fence, ended the play
O' the foil and brought Mannaia on the stage.

Five months had passed now since Pompilia's
      flight,
Months spent in peace among the Convert
      nuns :
This, — being, as it seemed, for Guido's sake
Solely, what pride might call imprisonment
And quote as something gained, to friends at
      home, —
This naturally was at Guido's charge :
Grudge it he might, but penitential fare,
Prayers, preachings, who but he defrayed the
      cost ?
So, Paolo dropped, as proxy, doit by doit
Like heart's blood, till — what's here ? What
      notice comes ?
The convent's self makes application bland
That, since Pompilia's health is fast o' the
      wane,
She may have leave to go combine her cure
Of soul with cure of body, mend her mind
Together with her thin arms and sunk eyes
That want fresh air outside the convent-wall,
Say in a friendly house, — and which so fit
As a certain villa in the Pauline way,
That happens to hold Pietro and his wife,
The natural guardians ? " Oh, and shift the
      care
You shift the cost, too ; Pietro pays in turn,
And lightens Guido of a load ! And then,
Villa or convent, two names for one thing,
Always the sojourn means imprisonment,

Domus pro carcere — nowise we relax,
Nothing abate : how answers Paolo ? "
                                    You,
What would you answer ? All so smooth and
      fair,
Even Paul's astuteness sniffed no harm i' the
      world.
He authorized the transfer, saw it made
And, two months after, reaped the fruit of the
      same,
Having to sit down, rack his brain and find
What phrase should serve him best to notify
Our Guido that by happy providence
A son and heir, a babe was born to him
I' the villa, — go tell sympathizing friends !
Yes, such had been Pompilia's privilege :
She, when she fled, was one month gone with
      child,
Known to herself or unknown, either way
Availing to explain (say men of art)
The strange and passionate precipitance
Of maiden startled into motherhood
Which changes body and soul by nature's law.
So when the she-dove breeds, strange yearnings
      come
For the unknown shelter by undreamed-of
      shores,
And there is born a blood-pulse in her heart
To fight if needs be, though with flap of wing,
For the wool-flock or the fur-tuft, though a
      hawk
Contest the prize, — wherefore, she knows not
      yet.
Anyhow, thus to Guido came the news.
" I shall have quitted Rome ere you arrive
To take the one step left," — wrote Paolo.
Then did the winch o' the winepress of all hate,
Vanity, disappointment, grudge and greed,
Take the last turn that screws out pure revenge
With a bright bubble at the brim beside —
By an heir's birth he was assured at once
O' the main prize, all the money in dispute :
Pompilia's dowry might revert to her
Or stay with him as law's caprice should
      point, —
But now — now — what was Pietro's shall be
      hers,
What was hers shall remain her own. — if hers,
Why then, — oh, not her husband's, but — her
      heir's !
That heir being his too, all grew his at last
By this road or by that road, since they join.
Before, why, push he Pietro out o' the world, —
The current of the money stopped, you see,
Pompilia being proved no Pietro's child :
Or let it be Pompilia's life he quenched,
Again the current of the money stopped, —
Guido debarred his rights as husband soon,
So the new process threatened ; — now, the
      chance,
Now, the resplendent minute ! Clear the earth
Cleanse the house, let the three but disappear,
A child remains, depositary of all,
That Guido may enjoy his own again,
Repair all losses by a master-stroke,
Wipe out the past, all done all left undone,
Swell the good present to best evermore,
Die into new life, which let blood baptize !

So, i' the blue of a sudden sulphur-blaze,
Both why there was one step to take at Rome,
And why he should not meet with Paolo there,
He saw — the ins and outs to the heart of hell —
And took the straight line thither swift and
    sure.
He rushed to Vittiano, found four sons o' the
    soil,
Brutes of his breeding, with one spark i' the
    clod
That served for a soul, the looking up to him
Or aught called Franceschini as life, death,
Heaven, hell, — lord paramount, assembled
    these,
Harangued, equipped, instructed, pressed each
    clod
With his will's imprint; then took horse, plied
    spur,
And so arrived, all five of them, at Rome
On Christmas-Eve, and forthwith found them-
    selves
Installed i' the vacancy and solitude
Left them by Paolo, the considerate man
Who, good as his word, had disappeared at once
As if to leave the stage free. A whole week
Did Guido spend in study of his part,
Then played it fearless of a failure. One,
Struck the year's clock whereof the hours are
    days,
And off was rung o' the little wheels the chime
" Good will on earth and peace to man: " but,
    two,
Proceeded the same bell, and, evening come,
The dreadful five felt finger-wise their way
Across the town by blind cuts and black turns
To the little lone suburban villa; knocked —
" Who may be outside? " called a well-known
    voice.
" A friend of Caponsacchi's bringing friends
A letter."
              That 's a test, the excusers say:
Ay, and a test conclusive, I return.
What? Had that name brought touch of guilt
    or taste
Of fear with it, aught to dash the present joy
With memory of the sorrow just at end, —
She, happy in her parents' arms at length,
With the new blessing of the two-weeks'
    babe, —
How had that name's announcement moved the
    wife?
Or, as the other slanders circulate,
Were Caponsacchi no rare visitant
On nights and days whither safe harbor lured,
What bait had been i' the name to ope the
    door?
The promise of a letter? Stealthy guests
Have secret watchwords, private entrances:
The man's own self might have been found in-
    side
And all the scheme made frustrate by a word.
No: but since Guido knew, none knew so well,
The man had never since returned to Rome
Nor seen the wife's face more than villa's front,
So, could not be at hand to warn or save, —
For that, he took this sure way to the end.

" Come in," bade poor Violante cheerfully,

Drawing the door-bolt: that death was the first,
Stabbed through and through. Pietro, close on
    her heels,
Set up a cry — " Let me confess myself!
Grant but confession! " Cold steel was the
    grant.
Then came Pompilia's turn.
                Then they escaped.
The noise o' the slaughter roused the neighbor-
    hood.
They had forgotten just the one thing more
Which saves i' the circumstance, the ticket, to
    wit,
Which puts post-horses at a traveller's use:
So, all on foot, desperate through the dark
Reeled they like drunkards along open road,
Accomplished a prodigious twenty miles
Homeward, and gained Baccano very near,
Stumbled at last, deaf, dumb, blind through the
    feat,
Into a grange and, one dead heap, slept there
Till the pursuers hard upon their trace
Reached them and took them, red from head to
    heel,
And brought them to the prison where they lie.
The couple were laid i' the church two days ago,
And the wife lives yet by miracle.

                        All is told.
You hardly need ask what Count Guido says,
Since something he must say. " I own the
    deed — "
(He cannot choose, — but —) " I declare the
    same
Just and inevitable, — since no way else
Was left me, but by this of taking life,
To save my honor which is more than life.
I exercised a husband's rights." To which
The answer is as prompt — " There was no fault
In any one o' the three to punish thus:
Neither i' the wife, who kept all faith to you,
Nor in the parents, whom yourself first duped,
Robbed and maltreated, then turned out of
    doors.
You wronged and they endured wrong; yours
    the fault.
Next, had endurance overpassed the mark
And turned resentment needing remedy, —
Nay, put the absurd impossible case, for once —
You were all blameless of the blame alleged
And they blameworthy where you fix all blame,
Still, why this violation of the law?
Yourself elected law should take its course,
Avenge wrong, or show vengeance not your
    right;
Why, only when the balance in law's hand
Trembles against you and inclines the way
O' the other party, do you make protest,
Renounce arbitrament, flying out of court,
And crying ' Honor's hurt the sword must
    cure '?
Aha, and so i' the middle of each suit
Trying i' the courts, — and you had three in
    play
With an appeal to the Pope's self beside, —
What, you may chop and change and right your
    wrongs,
Leaving the law to lag as she thinks fit? "

That were too temptingly commodious, Count!
One would have still a remedy in reserve
Should reach the safest oldest sinner, you see!
One's honor forsooth? Does that take hurt
alone
From the extreme outrage? I who have no
wife,
Being yet sensitive in my degree
As Guido, — must discover hurt elsewhere
Which, half compounded for in days gone by,
May profitably break out now afresh,
Need cure from my own expeditious hands.
The lie that was, as it were, imputed me
When you objected to my contract's clause, —
The theft as good as, one may say, alleged,
When you, co-heir in a will, excepted, Sir,
To my administration of effects,
— Aha, do you think law disposed of these?
My honor's touched and shall deal death
around!
Count, that were too commodious, I repeat!
If any law be imperative on us all,
Of all are you the enemy: out with you
From the common light and air and life of man!

IV

TERTIUM QUID

True, Excellency — as his Highness says,
Though she's not dead yet, she's as good as
stretched
Symmetrical beside the other two;
Though he's not judged yet, he's the same as
judged,
So do the facts abound and superabound:
And nothing hinders that we lift the case
Out of the shade into the shine, allow
Qualified persons to pronounce at last,
Nay, edge in an authoritative word
Between this rabble's-brabble of dolts and fools
Who make up reasonless unreasoning Rome.
"Now for the Trial!" they roar: "the Trial
to test
The truth, weigh husband and weigh wife alike
I' the scales of law, make one scale kick the
beam!"
Law's a machine from which, to please the
mob,
Truth the divinity must needs descend
And clear things at the play's fifth act — aha!
Hammer into their noddles who was who
And what was what. I tell the simpletons,
"Could law be competent to such a feat
'T were done already: what begins next week
Is end o' the Trial, last link of a chain
Whereof the first was forged three years ago
When law addressed herself to set wrong right,
And proved so slow in taking the first step
That ever some new grievance, — tort, retort,
On one or the other side, — o'ertook i' the
game,
Retarded sentence, till this deed of death
Is thrown in, as it were, last bale to boat
Crammed to the edge with cargo — or passen-
gers?
Trecentos inseris: ohe, jam satis est!

Huc appelle!' — passengers, the word must be."
Long since, the boat was loaded to my eyes.
To hear the rabble and brabble, you'd call the
case
Fused and confused past human finding out.
One calls the square round, t' other the round
square —
And pardonably in that first surprise
O' the blood that fell and splashed the dia-
gram:
But now we've used our eyes to the violent
hue
Can't we look through the crimson and trace
lines?
It makes a man despair of history,
Eusebius and the established fact — fig's end!
Oh, give the fools their Trial, rattle away
With the leash of lawyers, two on either side —
One barks, one bites, — Masters Arcangeli
And Spreti, — that's the husband's ultimate
hope
Against the Fisc and the other kind of Fisc,
Bound to do barking for the wife: bow — wow!
Why, Excellency, we and his Highness here
Would settle the matter as sufficiently
As ever will Advocate This and Fiscal That
And Judge the Other, with even — a word and
a wink —
We well know who for ultimate arbiter.
Let us beware o' the basset-table — lest
We jog the elbow of Her Eminence,
Jostle his cards, — he'll rap you out a . . . st!
By the window-seat! And here's the Marquis
too!
Indulge me but a moment: if I fail
— Favored with such an audience, under-
stand! —
To set things right, why, class me with the
mob
As understander of the mind of man!

The mob, — now, that's just how the error
comes!
Bethink you that you have to deal with *plebs*,
The commonalty; this is an episode
In burgess-life, — why seek to aggrandize,
Idealize, denaturalize the class?
People talk just as if they had to do
With a noble pair that . . . Excellency, your
ear!
Stoop to me, Highness, — listen and look your-
selves!

This Pietro, this Violante, live their life
At Rome in the easy way that's far from worst
Even for their betters, — themselves love them-
selves,
Spend their own oil in feeding their own lamp
That their own faces may grow bright thereby.
They get to fifty and over: how's the lamp?
Full to the depth o' the wick, — moneys so
much;
And also with a remnant, — so much more
Of moneys, — which there's no consuming now,
But, when the wick shall moulder out some day,
Failing fresh twist of tow to use up dregs,
Will lie a prize for the passer-by, — to wit,
Any one that can prove himself the heir,

Seeing, the couple are wanting in a child:
Meantime their wick swims in the safe broad
 bowl
O' the middle rank, — not raised a beacon's
 height
For wind to ravage, nor dropped till lamp
 graze ground
Like cresset, mudlarks poke now here now
 there,
Doing their rounds to probe the ruts i' the road
Or fish the luck o' the puddle. Pietro's soul
Was satisfied when crony smirked, "No wine
Like Pietro's, and he drinks it every day!"
His wife's heart swelled her bodice, joyed its
 fill
When neighbors turned heads wistfully at
 church,
Sighed at the load of lace that came to pray.
Well, having got through fifty years of flare,
They burn out so, indulge so their dear selves,
That Pietro finds himself in debt at last,
As he were any lordling of us all:
And, now that dark begins to creep on day,
Creditors grow uneasy, talk aside,
Take counsel, then importune all at once.
For if the good fat rosy careless man,
Who has not laid a ducat by, decease —
Let the lamp fall, no heir at hand to catch —
Why, being childless, there's a spilth i' the
 street
O' the remnant, there's a scramble for the
 dregs
By the stranger: so, they grant him no long
 day
But come in a body, clamor to be paid.

What's his resource? He asks and straight
 obtains
The customary largess, dole dealt out
To, what we call our "poor dear shamefaced
 ones,"
In secret once a month to spare the shame
O' the slothful and the spendthrift, — pauper-
 saints
The Pope puts meat i' the mouth of, ravens
 they,
And providence he — just what the mob ad-
 mires!
That is, instead of putting a prompt foot
On selfish worthless human slugs whose slime
Has failed to lubricate their path in life,
Why, the Pope picks the first ripe fruit that
 falls
And gracious puts it in the vermin's way.
Pietro could never save a dollar? Straight
He must be subsidized at our expense:
And for his wife — the harmless household
 sheep
One ought not to see harassed in her age —
Judge, by the way she bore adversity,
O' the patient nature you ask pity for!
How long, now, would the roughest market-
 man,
Handling the creatures huddled to the knife,
Harass a mutton ere she made a mouth
Or menaced biting? Yet the poor sheep here,
Violante, the old innocent burgess-wife,
in her first difficulty showed great teeth

Fit to crunch up and swallow a good round
 crime.
She meditates the tenure of the Trust,
Fidei commissum is the lawyer-phrase,
These funds that only want an heir to take
Goes o'er the gamut o' the creditor's cry
By semitones from whine to snarl high up
And growl down low, one scale in sundry
 keys, —
Pauses with a little compunction for the face
Of Pietro frustrate of its ancient cheer, —
Never a bottle now for friend at need, —
Comes to a stop on her own frittered lace
And neighborly condolences thereat,
Then makes her mind up, sees the thing to do:
And so, deliberate, snaps house-book clasp,
Posts off to vespers, missal beneath arm,
Passes the proper San Lorenzo by,
Dives down a little lane to the left, is lost
In a labyrinth of dwellings best unnamed,
Selects a certain blind one, black at base,
Blinking at top, — the sign of we know
 what, —
One candle in a casement set to wink
Streetward, do service to no shrine inside, —
Mounts thither by the filthy flight of stairs,
Holding the cord by the wall, to the tip-top,
Gropes for the door i' the dark, ajar of course,
Raps, opens, enters in: up starts a thing
Naked as needs be — "What, you rogue, 't is
 you?
Back, — how can I have taken a farthing yet?
Mercy on me, poor sinner that I am!
Here's . . . why, I took you for Madonna's self
With all that sudden swirl of silk i' the place!
What may your pleasure be, my bonny
 dame?"
Your Excellency supplies aught left obscure?
One of those women that abound in Rome,
Whose needs oblige them eke out one poor trade
By another vile one: her ostensible work
Was washing clothes, out in the open air
At the cistern by Citorio; her true trade —
Whispering to idlers, when they stopped and
 praised
The ankles she let liberally shine
In kneeling at the slab by the fountain-side,
That there was plenty more to criticise
At home, that eve, i' the house where candle
 blinked
Decorously above, and all was done
I' the holy fear of God and cheap beside.
Violante, now, had seen this woman wash,
Noticed and envied her propitious shape,
Tracked her home to her house-top, noted too,
And now was come to tempt her and propose
A bargain far more shameful than the first
Which trafficked her virginity away
For a melon and three pauls at twelve years
 old.
Five minutes' talk with this poor child of Eve,
Struck was the bargain, business at an end —
"Then, six months hence, that person whom
 you trust,
Comes, fetches whatsoever babe it be;
I keep the price and secret, you the babe,
Paying beside for mass to make all straight:
Meantime, I pouch the earnest-money-piece."

Down-stairs again goes fumbling by the rope
Violante, triumphing in a flourish of fire
From her own brain, self-lit by such success, —
Gains church in time for the *Magnificat,*
And gives forth "My reproof is taken away,
And blessed shall mankind proclaim me now,"
So that the officiating priest turns round
To see who proffers the obstreperous praise :
Then home to Pietro, the enraptured-much
But puzzled-more when told the wondrous
    news —
How orisons and works of charity,
(Beside that pair of pinners and a coif,
Birthday surprise last Wednesday was five
    weeks)
Had borne fruit in the autumn of his life, —
They, or the Orvieto in a double dose.
Anyhow, she must keep house next six months,
Lie on the settle, avoid the three-legged stool,
And, chiefly, not be crossed in wish or whim,
And the result was like to be an heir.

Accordingly, when time was come about,
He found himself the sire indeed of this
Francesca Vittoria Pompilia and the rest
O' the names whereby he sealed her his, next
    day.
A crime complete in its way is here, I hope ?
Lies to God, lies to man, every way lies
To nature and civility and the mode :
Flat robbery of the proper heirs thus foiled
O' the due succession, — and, what followed
    thence,
Robbery of God, through the confessor's ear
Debarred the most noteworthy incident
When all else done and undone twelvemonth
    through
Was put in evidence at Easter-time.
All other peccadillos ! — but this one
To the priest who comes next day to dine with
    us ?
'T were inexpedient ; decency forbade.

Is so far clear ? You know Violante now,
Compute her capability of crime
By this authentic instance ? Black hard cold
Crime like a stone you kick up with your foot
I' the middle of a field ?

                    I thought as much.
But now, a question, — how long does it lie,
The bad and barren bit of stuff you kick,
Before encroached on and encompassed round
With minute moss, weed, wild-flower — made
    alive
By worm, and fly, and foot of the free bird ?
Your Highness, — healthy minds let bygones
    be,
Leave old crimes to grow young and virtuous-
    like
I' the sun and air ; so time treats ugly deeds :
They take the natural blessing of all change.
There was the joy o' the husband silly-sooth,
The softening of the wife's old wicked heart,
Virtues to right and left, profusely paid
If so they might compensate the saved sin.
And then the sudden existence, dewy-dear,
O' the rose above the dungheap, the pure child

As good as new created, since withdrawn
From the horror of the pre-appointed lot
With the unknown father and the mother
    known
Too well, — some fourteen years of squalid
    youth,
And then libertinage, disease, the grave —
Hell in life here, hereafter life in hell :
Look at that horror and this soft repose !
Why, moralist, the sin has saved a soul !
Then, even the palpable grievance to the
    heirs —
'Faith, this was no frank setting hand to throat
And robbing a man, but . . . Excellency, by
    your leave,
How did you get that marvel of a gem,
The sapphire with the Graces grand and Greek ?
The story is, stooping to pick a stone
From the pathway through a vineyard — no-
    man's-land —
To pelt a sparrow with, you chanced on this :
Why now, do those five clowns o' the family
O' the vinedresser digest their porridge worse
That not one keeps it in his goatskin pouch
To do flint's-service with the tinder-box ?
Don't cheat me, don't cheat you, don't cheat a
    friend !
But are you so hard on who jostles just
A stranger with no natural sort of claim
To the havings and the holdings (here 's the
    point)
Unless by misadventure, and defect
Of that which ought to be — nay, which there 's
    none
Would dare so much as wish to profit by —
Since who dares put in just so many words
" May Pietro fail to have a child, please God !
So shall his house and goods belong to me,
The sooner that his heart will pine betimes " ?
Well then, God does n't please, nor heart shall
    pine !
Because he has a child at last, you see,
Or selfsame thing as though a child it were,
He thinks, whose sole concern it is to think :
If he accepts it why should you demur ?

Moreover, say that certain sin there seem,
The proper process of unsinning sin
Is to begin well-doing somehow else.
Pietro, — remember, with no sin at all
I' the substitution, — why, this gift of God
Flung in his lap from over Paradise
Steadied him in a moment, set him straight
On the good path he had been straying from.
Henceforward no more wilfulness and waste,
Cuppings, carousings, — these a sponge wiped
    out.
All sort of self-denial was easy now
For the child's sake, the chatelaine to be,
Who must want much and might want who
    knows what ?
And so, the debts were paid, habits reformed.
Expense curtailed, the dowry set to grow.
As for the wife, — I said, hers the whole sin :
So, hers the exemplary penance. 'T was a text
Whereon folk preached and praised, the district
    through :
" Oh, make us happy and you make us good !

It all comes of God giving her a child :
Such graces follow God's best earthly gift ! "

Here you put by my guard, pass to my heart
By the home-thrust — " There 's a lie at base
   of all."
Why, thou exact Prince, is it a pearl or no,
Yon globe upon the Principessa's neck ?
That great round glory of pellucid stuff,
A fish secreted round a grain of grit !
Do you call it worthless for the worthless core ?
(She does n't, who well knows what she changed
   for it.)
So, to our brace of burgesses again !
You see so far i' the story, who was right,
Who wrong, who neither, don't you ? What,
   you don't ?
Eh ? Well, admit there 's somewhat dark i'
   the case,
Let 's on — the rest shall clear, I promise you.
Leap over a dozen years : you find, these passed,
An old good easy creditable sire,
A careful housewife's beaming bustling face,
Both wrapped up in the love of their one child,
The strange tall pale beautiful creature grown
Lily-like out o' the cleft i' the sun-smit rock
To bow its white miraculous birth of buds
I' the way of wandering Joseph and his
   spouse, —
So painters fancy : here it was a fact.
And this their lily, — could they but transplant
And set in vase to stand by Solomon's porch
'Twixt lion and lion ! — this Pompilia of theirs,
Could they see worthily married, well bestowed,
In house and home ! And why despair of this
With Rome to choose from, save the topmost
   rank ?
Themselves would help the choice with heart
   and soul,
Throw their late savings in a common heap
To go with the dowry, and be followed in time
By the heritage legitimately hers :
And when such paragon was found and fixed,
Why, they might chant their " Nunc di-
   mittis " straight.

Indeed the prize was simply full to a fault,
Exorbitant for the suitor they should seek,
And social class should choose among, these
   cits.
Yet there 's a latitude : exceptional white
Amid the general brown o' the species, lurks
A burgess nearly an aristocrat,
Legitimately in reach : look out for him !
What banker, merchant, has seen better days,
What second rate painter a-pushing up,
Poet a-slipping down, shall bid the best
For this young beauty with the thumping purse ?
Alack, were it but one of such as these
So like the real thing that they pass for it,
All had gone well ! Unluckily, poor souls,
It proved to be the impossible thing itself ;
Truth and not sham : hence ruin to them all.

For, Guido Franceschini was the head
Of an old family in Arezzo, old
To that degree they could afford be poor
Better than most : the case is common too.

Out of the vast door 'scutcheoned overhead,
Creeps out a serving-man on Saturdays
To cater for the week, — turns up anon
I' the market, chaffering for the lamb's least
   leg,
Or the quarter-fowl, less entrails, claws and
   comb :
Then back again with prize, — a liver begged
Into the bargain, gizzard overlooked.
He 's mincing these to give the beans a taste,
When, at your knock, he leaves the simmering
   soup,
Waits on the curious stranger-visitant,
Napkin in half-wiped hand, to show the rooms,
Point pictures out have hung their hundred
   years,
" Priceless," he tells you, — puts in his place at
   once
The man of money : yes, you 're banker-king
Or merchant-kaiser, wallow in your wealth
While patron, the house-master, can't afford
To stop our ceiling-hole that rain so rots :
But he 's the man of mark, and there 's his
   shield,
And yonder 's the famed Rafael, first in kind,
The painter painted for his grandfather,
And you have paid to see : " Good morning,
   Sir ! "
Such is the law of compensation. Still
The poverty was getting nigh acute ;
There gaped so many noble mouths to feed,
Beans must suffice unflavored of the fowl.
The mother, — hers would be a spun-out life
I' the nature of things ; the sisters had done
   well
And married men of reasonable rank :
But that sort of illumination stops,
Throws back no heat upon the parent-hearth.
The family instinct felt out for its fire
To the Church, — the Church traditionally helps
A second son : and such was Paolo,
Established here at Rome these thirty years,
Who played the regular game, — priest and
   Abate,
Made friends, owned house and land, became of
   use
To a personage : his course lay clear enough.
The youngest caught the sympathetic flame,
And, though unfledged wings kept him still i'
   the cage,
Yet he shot up to be a Canon, so
Clung to the higher perch and crowed in hope.
Even our Guido, eldest brother, went
As far i' the way o' the Church as safety seemed,
He being Head o' the House, ordained to wive, —
So, could but dally with an Order or two
And testify good-will i' the cause : he clipt
His top-hair and thus far affected Christ.
But main promotion must fall otherwise,
Though still from the side o' the Church : and
   here was he
At Rome, since first youth, worn threadbare of
   soul
By forty-six years' rubbing on hard life,
Getting fast tired o' the game whose word is —
   " Wait ! "
When one day, — he too having his Cardinal
To serve in some ambiguous sort, as serve

To draw the coach the plumes o' the horses'
      heads, —
The Cardinal saw fit to dispense with him,
Ride with one plume the less ; and off it
      dropped.

Guido thus left, — with a youth spent in vain
And not a penny in purse to show for it, —
Advised with Paolo, bent no doubt in chafe
The black brows somewhat formidably, growled
" Where is the good I came to get at Rome ?
Where the repayment of the servitude
To a purple popinjay, whose feet I kiss,
Knowing his father wiped the shoes of mine ? "

" Patience," pats Paolo the recalcitrant —
" You have not had, so far, the proper luck,
Nor do my gains suffice to keep us both :
A modest competency is mine, not more.
You are the Count however, yours the style,
Heirdom and state, — you can't expect all good.
Had I, now, held your hand of cards . . . well,
      well —
What 's yet unplayed, I 'll look at, by your
      leave,
Over your shoulder, — I who made my game,
Let 's see, if I can't help to handle yours.
Fie on you, all the Honors in your fist,
Countship, Householdship, — how have you
      misdealt !
Why, in the first place, these will marry a man !
Notum tonsoribus ! To the Tonsor then !
Come, clear your looks, and choose your fresh-
      est suit,
And, after function 's done with, down we go
To the woman-dealer in perukes, a wench
I and some others settled in the shop
At Place Colonna : she 's an oracle. Hmm !
' Dear, 't is my brother : brother, 't is my dear.
Dear, give us counsel ! Whom do you suggest
As properest party in the quarter round
For the Count here ? — he is minded to take
      wife,
And further tells me he intends to slip
Twenty zecchines under the bottom-scalp
Of his old wig when he sends it to revive
For the wedding : and I add a trifle too.
You know what personage I 'm potent with.' "
And so plumped out Pompilia's name the first.
She told them of the household and its ways,
The easy husband and the shrewder wife
In Via Vittoria, — how the tall young girl,
With hair black as yon patch and eyes as big
As yon pomander to make freckles fly,
Would have so much for certain, and so much
      more
In likelihood, — why, it suited, slipt as smooth
As the Pope's pantoufle does on the Pope's foot.
" I 'll to the husband ! " Guido ups and cries.
" Ay, so you 'd play your last court-card, no
      doubt ! "
Puts Paolo in with a groan — " Only, you see,
'T is I, this time, that supervise your lead.
Priests play with women, maids, wives, mothers
      — why ?
These play with men and take them off our
      hands.
Did I come, counsel with some cut-beard gruff

Or rather this sleek young-old barberess ?
Go, brother, stand you rapt in the ante-room
Of Her Efficacity my Cardinal
For an hour, — he likes to have lord-suitor
      lounge, —
While I betake myself to the gray mare,
The better horse, — how wise the people'
      word ! —
And wait on Madam Violante."

                              Said and done
He was at Via Vittoria in three skips :
Proposed at once to fill up the one want
O' the burgess-family which, wealthy enough,
And comfortable to heart's desire, yet crouche
Outside a gate to heaven, — locked, bolted
      barred,
Whereof Count Guido had a key he kept
Under his pillow, but Pompilia's hand
Might slide behind his neck and pilfer thence.
The key was fairy ; its mere mention made
Violante feel the thing shoot one sharp ray
That reached the womanly heart : so — " I as
      sent !
Yours be Pompilia, hers and ours that key
To all the glories of the greater life !
There 's Pietro to convince : leave that to me ! "

Then was the matter broached to Pietro ; then
Did Pietro make demand and get response
That in the Countship was a truth, but in
The counting up of the Count's cash, a lie.
He thereupon stroked grave his chin, looke
      great,
Declined the honor.   Then the wife wiped tea
Winked with the other eye turned Paolo-ward
Whispered Pompilia, stole to church at eve,
Found Guido there and got the marriage done,
And finally begged pardon at the feet
Of her dear lord and master.   Whereupon
Quoth Pietro — " Let us make the best o
      things ! "
" I knew your love would license us," quoth
      she :
Quoth Paolo once more, " Mothers, wives and
      maids,
These be the tools wherewith priests manag
      men."

Now, here take breath and ask, — which bir
      o' the brace
Decoyed the other into clapnet ? Who
Was fool, who knave ? Neither and both, per
      chance.
There was a bargain mentally proposed
On each side, straight and plain and fai
      enough ;
Mind knew its own mind : but when mind mus
      speak,
The bargain have expression in plain terms,
There came the blunder incident to words,
And in the clumsy process, fair turned foul.
The straight backbone-thought of the crooke
      speech
Were just — " I Guido truck my name and rank
For so much money and youth and female
      charms. —
We Pietro and Violante give our child

And wealth to you for a rise i' the world
    thereby."
Such naked truth while chambered in the brain
Shocks nowise : walk it forth by way of
    tongue, —
Out on the cynical unseemliness !
Hence was the need, on either side, of a lie
To serve as decent wrappage : so, Guido gives
Money for money, — and they, bride for groom,
Having, he, not a doit, they, not a child
Honestly theirs, but this poor waif and stray.
According to the words, each cheated each ;
But in the inexpressive barter of thoughts,
Each did give and did take the thing designed,
The rank on this side and the cash on that —
Attained the object of the traffic, so.
The way of the world, the daily bargain struck
In the first market ! Why sells Jack his ware ?
" For the sake of serving an old customer."
Why does Jill buy it ? " Simply not to break
A custom, pass the old stall the first time."
Why, you know where the gist is of the ex-
    change :
Each sees a profit, throws the fine words in.
Don't be too hard o' the pair ! Had each pre-
    tence
Been simultaneously discovered, stript
From off the body o' the transaction, just
As when a cook (will Excellency forgive ?)
Strips away those long rough superfluous legs
From either side the crayfish, leaving folk
A meal all meat henceforth, no garnishry,
(With your respect, Prince !) — balance had
    been kept,
No party blamed the other, — so, starting fair,
All subsequent fence of wrong returned by
    wrong
I' the matrimonial thrust and parry, at least
Had followed on equal terms. But, as it
    chanced,
One party had the advantage, saw the cheat
Of the other first and kept its own concealed :
And the luck o' the first discovery fell, beside,
To the least adroit and self-possessed o' the pair.
'T was foolish Pietro and his wife saw first
The nobleman was penniless, and screamed
" We are cheated ! "

           Such unprofitable noise
Angers at all times : but when those who plague,
Do it from inside your own house and home,
Gnats which yourself have closed the curtain
    round,
Noise goes too near the brain and makes you
    mad.
The gnats say, Guido used the candle-flame
Unfairly, — worsened that first bad of his,
By practising all kinds of cruelty
To oust them and suppress the wail and whine,—
That speedily he so scared and bullied them,
Fain were they, long before five months had
    passed,
To beg him grant, from what was once their
    wealth,
Just so much as would help them back to Rome,
Where, when they finished paying the last doit
O' the dowry, they might beg from door to door.
So say the Comparini — as if it came

Of pure resentment for this worse than bad,
That then Violante, feeling conscience prick,
Confessed her substitution of the child
Whence all the harm fell, — and that Pietro
    first
Bethought him of advantage to himself
I' the deed, as part revenge, part remedy
For all miscalculation in the pact.

On the other hand, " Not so ! " Guido retorts —
" I am the wronged, solely, from first to last,
Who gave the dignity I engaged to give,
Which was, is, cannot but continue gain.
My being poor was a by-circumstance,
Miscalculated piece of untowardness,
Might end to-morrow did heaven's windows
    ope,
Or uncle die and leave me his estate.
You should have put up with the minor flaw,
Getting the main prize of the jewel. If wealth,
Not rank, had been prime object in your
    thoughts,
Why not have taken the butcher's son, the boy
O' the baker or candlestick-maker ? In all the
    rest,
It was yourselves broke compact and played
    false,
And made a life in common impossible.
Show me the stipulation of our bond
That you should make your profit of being in-
    side
My house, to hustle and edge me out o' the
    same,
First make a laughing-stock of mine and me,
Then round us in the ears from morn to night
(Because we show wry faces at your mirth)
That you are robbed, starved, beaten and what
    not !
You fled a hell of your own lighting-up,
Pay for your own miscalculation too :
You thought nobility, gained at any price,
Would suit and satisfy, — find the mistake,
And now retaliate, not on yourselves, but me.
And how ? By telling me, i' the face of the
    world,
I it is have been cheated all this while,
Abominably and irreparably, — my name
Given to a cur-cast mongrel, a drab's brat,
A beggar's by-blow, — thus depriving me
Of what yourselves allege the whole and sole
Aim on my part i' the marriage, — money, to
    wit.
This thrust I have to parry by a guard
Which leaves me open to a counter-thrust
On the other side, — no way but there 's a pass
Clean through me. If I prove, as I hope to do,
There 's not one truth in this your odious tale
O' the buying, selling, substituting — prove
Your daughter was and is your daughter, —
    well,
And her dowry hers and therefore mine, — what
    then ?
Why, where 's the appropriate punishment for
    this
Enormous lie hatched for mere malice' sake
To ruin me ? Is that a wrong or no ?
And if I try revenge for remedy,
Can I well make it strong and bitter enough ? "

I anticipate however — only ask,
Which of the two here sinned most? A nice
     point!
Which brownness is least black, — decide who
     can,
Wager-by-battle-of-cheating! What do you say,
Highness? Suppose, your Excellency, we leave
The question at this stage, proceed to the next,
Both parties step out, fight their prize upon,
In the eye o' the world?

               They brandish law 'gainst law;
The grinding of such blades, each parry of each,
Throws terrible sparks off, over and above the
     thrusts,
And makes more sinister the fight, to the eye,
Than the very wounds that follow. Beside the
     tale
Which the Comparini have to re-assert,
They needs must write, print, publish all abroad
The straitnesses of Guido's household life —
The petty nothings we bear privately
But break down under when fools flock to jeer.
What is it all to the facts o' the couple's case,
How helps it prove Pompilia not their child,
If Guido's mother, brother, kith and kin
Fare ill, lie hard, lack clothes, lack fire, lack
     food?
That's one more wrong than needs.

               On the other hand,
Guido, — whose cue is to dispute the truth
O' the tale, reject the shame it throws on
     him, —
He may retaliate, fight his foe in turn
And welcome, we allow. Ay, but he can't!
He's at home, only acts by proxy here;
Law may meet law, — but all the gibes and
     jeers,
The superfluity of naughtiness,
Those libels on his House, — how reach at
     them?
Two hateful faces. grinning all aglow,
Not only make parade of spoil they filched,
But foul him from the height of a tower, you
     see.
Unluckily temptation is at hand —
To take revenge on a trifle overlooked,
A pet lamb they have left in reach outside,
Whose first bleat, when he plucks the wool
     away,
Will strike the grinners grave: his wife re-
     mains,
Who, four months earlier, some thirteen years
     old,
Never a mile away from mother's house
And petted to the height of her desire,
Was told one morning that her fate had come,
She must be married — just as, a month before,
Her mother told her she must comb her hair
And twist her curls into one knot behind.
These fools forgot their pet lamb, fed with
     flowers,
Then 'ticed as usual by the bit of cake,
Out of the bower into the butchery.
Plague her, he plagues them threefold: but
     how plague?
The world may have its word to say to that:

You can't do some things with impunity.
What remains . . . well, it is an ugly thought . .
But that he drive herself to plague herself —
Herself disgrace herself and so disgrace
Who seek to disgrace Guido?

               There's the clue
To what else seems gratuitously vile,
If, as is said, from this time forth the rack
Was tried upon Pompilia: 't was to wrench
Her limbs into exposure that brings shame.
The aim o' the cruelty being so crueller still,
That cruelty almost grows compassion's self
Could one attribute it to mere return
O' the parents' outrage, wrong avenging wrong.
They see in this a deeper deadlier aim,
Not to vex just a body they held dear,
But blacken too a soul they boasted white,
And show the world their saint in a lover's
     arms,
No matter how driven thither, — so they say.

On the other hand, so much is easily said,
And Guido lacks not an apologist.
The pair had nobody but themselves to blame,
Being selfish beasts throughout no less, no
     more:
— Cared for themselves, their supposed good,
     nought else,
And brought about the marriage; good proved
     bad,
As little they cared for her its victim — nay,
Meant she should stay behind and take the
     chance,
If haply they might wriggle themselves free.
They baited their own hook to catch a fish
With this poor worm, failed o' the prize, and
     then
Sought how to unbait tackle, let worm float
Or sink, amuse the monster while they 'scaped.
Under the best stars Hymen brings above,
Had all been honesty on either side,
A common sincere effort to good end,
Still, this would prove a difficult problem,
     Prince!
— Given, a fair wife, aged thirteen years,
A husband poor, care-bitten, sorrow-sunk,
Little, long - nosed, bush - bearded, lantern
     jawed,
Forty-six years old, — place the two grown one
She, cut off sheer from every natural aid,
In a strange town with no familiar face —
He, in his own parade-ground or retreat
If need were, free from challenge, much less
     check
To an irritated, disappointed will —
How evolve happiness from such a match?
'T were hard to serve up a congenial dish
Out of these ill-agreeing morsels, Duke,
By the best exercise of the cook's craft,
Best interspersion of spice, salt and sweet!
But let two ghastly scullions concoct mess
With brimstone, pitch, vitriol and devil's
     dung —
Throw in abuse o' the man, his body and soul,
Kith, kin and generation, shake all slab
At Rome, Arezzo, for the world to nose,
Then end by publishing, for fiend's arch-prank

That, over and above sauce to the meat's self,
Why, even the meat, bedevilled thus in dish,
Was never a pheasant but a carrion-crow —
Prince, what will then the natural loathing
  be ?
What wonder if this ? — the compound plague
  o' the pair
Pricked Guido, — not to take the course they
  hoped,
That is, submit him to their statement's truth,
Accept its obvious promise of relief,
And thrust them out of doors the girl again
Sinoe the girl's dowry would not enter there,
— Quit of the one if balked of the other : no !
Rather did rage and hate so work in him,
Their product proved the horrible conceit
That he should plot and plan and bring to pass
His wife might, of her own free will and deed,
Relieve him of her presence, get her gone,
And yet leave all the dowry safe behind,
Confirmed his own henceforward past dispute,
While blotting out, as by a belch of hell,
Their triumph in her misery and death.

You see, the man was Aretine, had touch
O' the subtle air that breeds the subtle wit ;
Was noble too, of old blood thrice-refined
That shrinks from clownish coarseness in dis-
  gust :
Allow that such an one may take revenge,
You don't expect he 'll catch up stone and fling,
Or try cross-buttock, or whirl quarter-staff ?
Instead of the honest drubbing clowns bestow,
When out of temper at the dinner spoilt,
On meddling mother - in - law and tiresome
  wife, —
Substitute for the clown a nobleman,
And you have Guido, practising, 't is said,
Immitigably from the very first,
The finer vengeance : this, they say, the fact
O' the famous letter shows — the writing
  traced
At Guido's instance by the timid wife
Over the pencilled words himself writ first —
Wherein she, who could neither write nor read,
Was made unblushingly declare a tale
To the brother, the Abate then in Rome,
How her putative parents had impressed,
On their departure, their enjoinment ; bade
" We being safely arrived here, follow, you !
Poison your husband, rob, set fire to all,
And then by means o' the gallant you procure
With ease, by helpful eye and ready tongue,
Some brave youth ready to dare, do and die,
You shall run off and merrily reach Rome
Where we may live like flies in honey-pot : " —
Such being exact the programme of the course
Imputed her as carried to effect.

They also say, — to keep her straight therein,
All sort of torture was piled, pain on pain,
On either side Pompilia's path of life,
Btuilt round about and over against by fear,
Circumvallated month by month, and week
By week, and day by day, and hour by hour,
Close, closer and yet closer still with pain,
No outlet from the encroaching pain save just
Where stood one savior like a piece of heaven,

Hell's arms would strain round but for this
  blue gap.
She, they say further, first tried every chink,
Every imaginable break i' the fire,
As way of escape : ran to the Commissary,
Who bade her not malign his friend her spouse ;
Flung herself thrice at the Archbishop's feet,
Where three times the Archbishop let her lie,
Spend her whole sorrow and sob full heart
  forth,
And then took up the slight load from the
  ground
And bore it back for husband to chastise, —
Mildly of course, — but natural right is right.
So went she slipping ever yet catching at help,
Missing the high till come to lowest and last,
To wit, a certain friar of mean degree,
Who heard her story in confession, wept,
Crossed himself, showed the man within the
  monk.
" Then, will you save me, you the one i' the
  world ?
I cannot even write my woes, nor put
My prayer for help in words a friend may
  read, —
I no more own a coin than have an hour
Free of observance, — I was watched to church,
Am watched now, shall be watched back pres-
  ently, —
How buy the skill of scribe i' the market-
  place ?
Pray you, write down and send whatever I say
O' the need I have my parents take me hence ! "
The good man rubbed his eyes and could not
  choose —
Let her dictate her letter in sueh a sense
That parents, to save breaking down a wall,
Might lift her over : she went back, heaven in
  heart.
Then the good man took counsel of his couch,
Woke and thought twice, the second thought
  the best :
" Here am I, foolish body that I be,
Caught all but pushing, teaching, who but I,
My betters their plain duty, — what, I dare
Help a case the Archbishop would not help,
Mend matters, peradventure, God loves mar ?
What hath the married life but strifes and
  plagues
For proper dispensation ? So a fool
Once touched the ark, — poor Uzzah that I
  am !
Oh married ones, much rather should I bid,
In patience all of ye possess your souls !
This life is brief and troubles die with it :
Where were the prick to soar up homeward
  else ? "
So saying, he burnt the letter he had writ,
Said *Ave* for her intention, in its place,
Took snuff and comfort, and had done with
  all.
Then the grim arms stretched yet a little more
And each touched each, all but one streak i'
  the midst,
Whereat stood Caponsacchi, who cried, " This
  way,
Out by me ! Hesitate one moment more
And the fire shuts out me and shuts in you !

Here my hand holds you life out! " Where-
    upon
She clasped the hand, which closed on hers and
    drew
Pompilia out o' the circle now complete.
Whose fault or shame but Guido's? — ask her
    friends.

But then this is the wife's — Pompilia's tale —
Eve's . . . no, not Eve's, since Eve, to speak
    the truth,
Was hardly fallen (our candor might pro-
    nounce)
When simply saying in her own defence
" The serpent tempted me and I did eat."
So much of paradisal nature, Eve's!
Her daughters ever since prefer to urge
" Adam so starved me I was fain accept
The apple any serpent pushed my way."
What an elaborate theory have we here,
Ingeniously nursed up, pretentiously
Brought forth, pushed forward amid trumpet-
    blast,
To account for the thawing of an icicle,
Show us there needed Ætna vomit flame
Ere run the crystal into dewdrops! Else,
How, unless hell broke loose to cause the step,
How could a married lady go astray?
Bless the fools!   And 't is just this way they
    are blessed,
And the world wags still, — because fools are
    sure
— Oh, not of my wife nor your daughter! No!
But of their own: the case is altered quite.
Look now, — last week, the lady we all love, —
Daughter o' the couple we all venerate,
Wife of the husband we all cap before,
Mother o' the babes we all breathe blessings
    on, —
Was caught in converse with a negro page.
Hell thawed that icicle, else " Why was it —
Why? " asked and echoed the fools.   " Be-
    cause, you fools, — "
So did the dame's self answer, she who could,
With that fine candor only forthcoming
When 't is no odds whether withheld or no —
" Because my husband was the saint you say,
And, — with that childish goodness, absurd
    faith,
Stupid self-satisfaction, you so praise, —
Saint to you, insupportable to me.
Had he, — instead of calling me fine names,
Lucretia and Susanna and so forth,
And curtaining Correggio carefully
Lest I be taught that Leda had two legs, —
— But once never so little tweaked my nose
For peeping through my fan at Carnival,
Confessing thereby, ' I have no easy task —
I need use all my powers to hold you mine,
And then, — why 't is so doubtful if they serve,
That — take this, as an earnest of despair!'
Why, we were quits: I had wiped the harm
    away,
Thought, ' The man fears me!' and foregone
    revenge."
We must not want all this elaborate work
To solve the problem why young Fancy-and-
    flesh

Slips from the dull side of a spouse in years,
Betakes it to the breast of Brisk-and-bold
Whose love-scrapes furnish talk for all the
    town!

Accordingly, one word on the other side
Tips over the piled-up fabric of a tale.
Guido says — that is, always, his friends say —
It is unlikely, from the wickedness,
That any man treat any woman so.
The letter in question was her very own,
Unprompted and unaided: she could write —
As able to write as ready to sin, or free,
When there was danger, to deny both facts.
He bids you mark, herself from first to last
Attributes all the so-styled torture just
To jealousy, — jealousy of whom but just
This very Caponsacchi! How suits here
This with the other alleged motive, Prince?
Would Guido make a terror of the man
He meant should tempt the woman, as they
    charge?
Do you fright your hare that you may catch
    your hare?
Consider too, the charge was made and met
At the proper time and place where proofs were
    plain —
Heard patiently and disposed of thoroughly
By the highest powers, possessors of most light,
The Governor for the law and the Archbishop
For the gospel: which acknowledged primacies,
'T is impudently pleaded, he could warp
Into a tacit partnership with crime —
He being the while, believe their own account,
Impotent, penniless and miserable!
He further asks — Duke, note the knotty
    point! —
How he — concede him skill to play such part
And drive his wife into a gallant's arms —
Could bring the gallant to play his part too
And stand with arms so opportunely wide?
How bring this Caponsacchi, — with whom,
    friends
And foes alike agree, throughout his life
He never interchanged a civil word
Nor lifted courteous cap to — him, how bend
To such observancy of beck and call,
— To undertake this strange and perilous
    feat
For the good of Guido, using, as the lure,
Pompilia whom, himself and she avouch,
He had nor spoken with nor seen, indeed,
Beyond sight in a public theatre,
When she wrote letters (she that could not
    write!)
The importunate shamelessly-protested love
Which brought him, though reluctant, to her
    feet,
And forced on him the plunge which, howsoe'er
She might swim up i' the whirl, must bury
    him
Under abysmal black: a priest contrive
No better, no amour to be hushed up,
But open flight and noonday infamy?
Try and concoct defence for such revolt!
Take the wife's tale as true, say she was
    wronged, —
Pray, in what rubric of the breviary

Do you find it registered — the part of a priest
Is — that to right wrongs from the church he
    skip,
Go journeying with a woman that 's a wife,
And be pursued, o 'ertaken and captured . . .
    how ?
In a lay-dress, playing the kind sentinel
Where the wife sleeps (says he who best should
    know)
And sleeping, sleepless, both have spent the
    night !
Could no one else be found to serve at need —
No woman — or if man, no safer sort
Than this not well-reputed turbulence ?

Then, look into his own account o' the case !
He, being the stranger and astonished one,
Yet received protestations of her love
From lady neither known nor cared about :
Love, so protested, bred in him disgust
After the wonder, — or incredulity,
Such impudence seeming impossible.
But, soon assured such impudence might be,
When he had seen with his own eyes at last
Letters thrown down to him i' the very street
From behind lattice where the lady lurked,
And read their passionate summons to her
    side —
Why then, a thousand thoughts swarmed up
    and in, —
How he had seen her once, a moment's space,
Observed she was both young and beautiful,
Heard everywhere report she suffered much
From a jealous husband thrice her age, — in
    short,
There flashed the propriety, expediency
Of treating, trying might they come to terms,
— At all events, granting the interview
Prayed for, one so adapted to assist
Decision as to whether he advance,
Stand or retire, in his benevolent mood !
Therefore the interview befell at length ;
And at this one and only interview,
He saw the sole and single course to take —
Bade her dispose of him, head, heart and hand,
Did her behest and braved the consequence,
Not for the natural end, the love of man
For woman whether love be virtue or vice,
But, please you, altogether for pity's sake —
Pity of innocence and helplessness !
And how did he assure himself of both ?
Had he been the house-inmate, visitor,
Eye-witness of the described martyrdom,
So, competent to pronounce its remedy
Ere rush on such extreme and desperate
    course —
Involving such enormity of harm,
Moreover, to the husband judged thus, doomed
And damned without a word in his defence ?
Not he ! the truth was felt by instinct here,
— Process which saves a world of trouble and
    time.
There 's the priest's story : what do you say
    to it,
Trying its truth by your own instinct too,
Since that 's to be the expeditious mode ?
" And now, do hear my version," Guido cries :
    " I accept argument and inference both.

It would indeed have been miraculous
Had such a confidency sprung to birth
With no more fanning from acquaintanceship
Than here avowed by my wife and this priest
Only, it did not : you must substitute
The old stale unromantic way of fault,
The commonplace adventure, mere intrigue
In prose form with the unpoetic tricks,
Cheatings and lies : they used the hackney
    chair
Satan jaunts forth with, shabby and service-
    able,
No gilded jimcrack-novelty from below,
To bowl you along thither, swift and sure.
That same officious go-between, the wench
Who gave and took the letters of the two,
Now offers self and service back to me :
Bears testimony to visits night by night
When all was safe, the husband far and
    away, —
To many a timely slipping out at large
By light o' the morning-star, ere he should
    wake.
And when the fugitives were found at last,
Why, with them were found also, to belie
What protest they might make of innocence,
All documents yet wanting, if need were,
To establish guilt in them, disgrace in me —
The chronicle o' the converse from its rise
To culmination in this outrage : read !
Letters from wife to priest, from priest to
    wife, —
Here they are, read and say where they chime
    in
With the other tale, superlative purity
O' the pair of saints ! I stand or fall by
    these."

But then on the other side again, — how say
The pair of saints ? That not one word is
    theirs —
No syllable o' the batch or writ or sent
Or yet received by either of the two.
" Found," says the priest, " because he needed
    them,
Failing all other proofs, to prove our fault :
So, here they are, just as is natural.
Oh yes — we had our missives, each of us !
Not these, but to the full as vile, no doubt :
Hers as from me, — she could not read, so
    burnt, —
Mine as from her, — I burnt because I read.
Who forged and found them ? *Cui profue-
    rint !* "
(I take the phrase out of your Highness'
    mouth)
" He who would gain by her fault and my
    fall,
The trickster, schemer and pretender — he
Whose whole career was lie entailing lie
Sought to be sealed truth by the worst lie
    last ! "

Guido rejoins — " Did the other end o' the
    tale
Match this beginning ! 'T is alleged I prove
A murderer at the end, a man of force
Prompt, indiscriminate, effectual : good !

Then what need all this trifling woman's-work,
Letters and embassies and weak intrigue,
When will and power were mine to end at once
Safely and surely? Murder had come first
Not last with such a man, assure yourselves!
The silent *acquetta*, stilling at command—
A drop a day i' the wine or soup, the dose, —
The shattering beam that breaks above the
    bed
And beats out brains, with nobody to blame
Except the wormy age which eats even oak, —
Nay, the stanch steel or trusty cord, — who
    cares
I' the blind old palace, a pitfall at each step,
With none to see, much more to interpose
O' the two, three, creeping-house-dog-servant-
    things
Born mine and bred mine? Had I willed
    gross death,
I had found nearer paths to thrust him prey
Than this that goes meandering here and there
Through half the world and calls down in its
    course
Notice and noise, — hate, vengeance, should it
    fail,
Derision and contempt though it succeed!
Moreover, what o' the future son and heir?
The unborn babe about to be called mine, —
What end in heaping all this shame on him,
Were I indifferent to my own black share?
Would I have tried these crookednesses, say,
Willing and able to effect the straight? "

" Ay, would you! " — one may hear the priest
    retort,
" Being as you are, i' the stock, a man of guile,
And ruffianism but an added graft.
You, a born coward, try a coward's arms,
Trick and chicane, — and only when these fail
Does violence follow, and like fox you bite
Caught out in stealing. Also, the disgrace
You hardly shrunk at, wholly shrivelled her:
You plunged her thin white delicate hand i'
    the flame
Along with your coarse horny brutish fist,
Held them a second there, then drew out both
— Yours roughed a little, hers ruined through
    and through.
Your hurt would heal forthwith at ointment's
    touch —
Namely, succession to the inheritance
Which bolder crime had lost you: let things
    change,
The birth o' the boy warrant the bolder crime,
Why, murder was determined, dared and done.
For me," the priest proceeds with his reply,
" The look o' the thing, the chances of mistake,
All were against me, — that, I knew the first:
But, knowing also what my duty was,
I did it : I must look to men more skilled
In reading hearts than ever was the world."

Highness, decide! Pronounce, Her Excellency!
Or . . . even leave this argument in doubt,
Account it a fit matter, taken up
With all its faces, manifold enough,
To ponder on — what fronts us, the next stage,
Next legal process? Guido, in pursuit,

Coming up with the fugitives at the inn,
Caused both to be arrested then and there
And sent to Rome for judgment on the case —
Thither, with all his armory of proofs,
Betook himself : 't is there we 'll meet him now,
Waiting the further issue.
                        Here you smile:
" And never let him henceforth dare to plead —
Of all pleas and excuses in the world
For any deed hereafter to be done —
His irrepressible wrath at honor's wound!
Passion and madness irrepressible?
Why, Count and cavalier, the husband comes
And catches foe i' the very act of shame!
There 's man to man, — nature must have her
    way, —
We look he should have cleared things on the
    spot.
Yes, then, indeed — even though it prove he
    erred —
Though the ambiguous first appearance, mount
Of solid injury, melt soon to mist,
Still, — had he slain the lover and the wife —
Or, since she was a woman and his wife,
Slain him, but stript her naked to the skin,
Or at best left no more of an attire
Than patch sufficient to pin paper to,
Some one love-letter, infamy and all,
As passport to the Paphos fit for such,
Safe-conduct to her natural home the stews, —
Good! One had recognized the power o' the
    pulse.
But when he stands, the stock-fish, — sticks to
    law —
Offers the hole in his heart, all fresh and warm,
For scrivener's pen to poke and play about —
Can stand, can stare, can tell his beads per-
    haps,
Oh, let us hear no syllable o' the rage!
Such rage were a convenient afterthought
For one who would have shown his teeth be-
    like,
Exhibited unbridled rage enough,
Had but the priest been found, as was to hope,
In serge, not silk, with crucifix, not sword:
Whereas the gray innocuous grub, of yore,
Had hatched a hornet, tickle to the touch,
The priest was metamorphosed into knight.
And even the timid wife, whose cue was —
    shriek,
Bury her brow beneath his trampling foot, —
She too sprang at him like a pythoness:
So, gulp down rage, passion must be postponed,
Calm be the word! Well, our word is — we
    brand
This part o' the business, howsoever the rest
Befall."
            " Nay," interpose as prompt his friends —
" This is the world's way! So you adjudge re
    ward
To the forbearance and legality
Yourselves begin by inculcating — ay,
Exacting from us all with knife at throat!
This one wrong more you add to wrong's
    amount, —
You publish all, with the kind comment here,
' Its victim was too cowardly for revenge.' "
Make it your own case, — you who stand apart!

The husband wakes one morn from heavy
   sleep,
With a taste of poppy in his mouth, — rubs eyes,
Finds his wife flown, his strong-box ransacked
   too,
Follows as he best can, overtakes i' the end.
You bid him use his privilege : well, it seems
He 's scarce cool-blooded enough for the right
   move —
Does not shoot when the game were sure, but
   stands
Bewildered at the critical minute, — since
He has the first flash of the fact alone
To judge from, act with, not the steady lights
Of after-knowledge, — yours who stand at ease
To try conclusions : he 's in smother and smoke,
You outside, with explosion at an end :
The sulphur may be lightning or a squib —
He 'll know in a minute, but till then, he doubts.
Back from what you know to what he knew not !
Hear the priest's lofty " I am innocent,"
The wife's as resolute " You are guilty ! "
Come !
Are you not staggered ? — pause, and you lose
   the move !
Naught left you but a low appeal to law,
" Coward " tied to your tail for compliment !
Another consideration : have it your way !
Admit the worst : his courage failed the Count,
He 's cowardly like the best o' the burgesses
He 's grown incorporate with, — a very cur,
Kick him from out your circle by all means !
Why, trundled down this reputable stair,
Still, the church-door lies wide to take him in,
And the court-porch also : in he sneaks to
   each,
" Yes, I have lost my honor and my wife,
And, being moreover an ignoble hound,
I dare not jeopardize my life for them ! "
Religion and Law lean forward from their
   chairs,
" Well done, thou good and faithful servant ! "
   Ay,
Not only applaud him that he scorned the world,
But punish should he dare do otherwise.
If the case be clear or turbid, — you must say !

Thus, anyhow, it mounted to the stage
In the law-courts, — let 's see clearly from this
   point ! —
Where the priest tells his story true or false,
And the wife her story, and the husband his,
All with result as happy as before.
The courts would nor condemn nor yet acquit
This, that or the other, in so distinct a sense
As end the strife to either's absolute loss :
Pronounced, in place of something definite,
" Each of the parties, whether goat or sheep
I' the main, has wool to show and hair to hide.
Each has brought somehow trouble, is somehow
   cause
Of pains enough, — even though no worse were
   proved.
Here is a husband, cannot rule his wife
Without provoking her to scream and scratch
And scour the fields, — causelessly, it may be :
Here is that wife, — who makes her sex our
   plague,

Wedlock, our bugbear, — perhaps with cause
   enough :
And here is the truant priest o' the trio, worst
Or best — each quality being conceivable.
Let us impose a little mulct on each.
We punish youth in state of pupilage
Who talk at hours when youth is bound to
   sleep,
Whether the prattle turn upon Saint Rose
Or Donna Olimpia of the Vatican :
'T is talk, talked wisely or unwisely talked,
I' the dormitory where to talk at all
Transgresses, and is mulct : as here we mean.
For the wife, — let her betake herself, for rest
After her run, to a House of Convertites —
Keep there, as good as real imprisonment :
Being sick and tired, she will recover so.
For the priest, spritely strayer out of bounds,
Who made Arezzo hot to hold him, — Rome
Profits by his withdrawal from the scene.
Let him be relegate to Civita,
Circumscribed by its bounds till matters mend :
There be at least lies out o' the way of harm
From foes — perhaps from the too friendly fair.
And finally for the husband, whose rash rule
Has but itself to blame for this ado, —
If he be vexed that, in our judgments dealt,
He fails obtain what he accounts his right,
Let him go comforted with the thought, no less,
That, turn each sentence howsoever he may,
There 's satisfaction to extract therefrom.
For, does he wish his wife proved innocent ?
Well, she 's not guilty, he may safely urge,
Has missed the stripes dishonest wives en-
   dure —
This being a fatherly pat o' the cheek, no more.
Does he wish her guilty ? Were she otherwise
Would she be locked up, set to say her prayers,
Prevented intercourse with the outside world,
And that suspected priest in banishment,
Whose portion is a further help i' the case ?
Oh, ay, you all of you want the other thing,
The extreme of law, some verdict neat, com-
   plete, —
Either, the whole o' the dowry in your poke
With full release from the false wife, to boot,
And heading, hanging for the priest, beside —
Or, contrary, claim freedom for the wife,
Repayment of each penny paid her spouse,
Amends for the past, release for the future :
   Such
Is wisdom to the children of this world ;
But we 've no mind, we children of the light,
To miss the advantage of the golden mean,
And push things to the steel point." Thus the
   courts.

Is it settled so far ? Settled or disturbed,
Console yourselves : 't is like . . . an instance,
   now !
You 've seen the puppets, of Place Navona,
   play, —
Punch and his mate, — how threats pass, blows
   are dealt,
And a crisis comes : the crowd or clap or hiss
Accordingly as disposed for man or wife —
When down the actors duck awhile perdue,
Donning what novel rag-and-feather trim

Best suits the next adventure, new effect :
And, — by the time the mob is on the move,
With something like a judgment *pro* and *con*, —
There 's a whistle, up again the actors pop
In t' other tatter with fresh-tinselled staves,
To re-engage in one last worst fight more
Shall show, what you thought tragedy was farce.
Note, that the climax and the crown of things
Invariably is, the devil appears himself,
Armed and accoutred, horns and hoofs and
    tail !
Just so, nor otherwise it proved — you 'll see :
Move to the murder, never mind the rest !

Guido, at such a general duck-down,
I' the breathing-space, — of wife to convent
    here,
Priest to his relegation, and himself
To Arezzo, — had resigned his part perforce
To brother Abate, who bustled, did his best,
Retrieved things somewhat, managed the three
    suits —
Since, it should seem, there were three suits-at-
    law
Behoved him look to, still, lest bad grow worse :
First civil suit, — the one the parents brought,
Impugning the legitimacy of his wife,
Affirming thence the nullity of her rights :
This was before the Rota, — Molinès,
That 's judge there, made that notable decree
Which partly leaned to Guido, as I said, —
But Pietro had appealed against the same
To the very court will judge what we judge
    now —
Tommati and his fellows, — Suit the first.
Next civil suit, — demand on the wife's part
Of separation from the husband's bed
On plea of cruelty and risk to life —
Claims restitution of the dowry paid,
Immunity from paying any more :
This second, the Vicegerent has to judge.
Third and last suit, — this time, a criminal
    one, —
Answer to, and protection from, both these, —
Guido's complaint of guilt against his wife
In the Tribunal of the Governor,
Venturini, also judge of the present cause.
Three suits of all importance plaguing him
Beside a little private enterprise
Of Guido's, — essay at a shorter cut.
For Paolo, knowing the right way at Rome,
Had, even while superintending these three
    suits
I' the regular way, each at its proper court,
Ingeniously made interest with the Pope
To set such tedious regular forms aside,
And, acting the supreme and ultimate judge,
Declare for the husband and against the wife.
Well, at such crisis and extreme of straits, —
The man at bay, buffeted in this wise, —
Happened the strangest accident of all.
"Then," sigh friends, " the last feather broke
    his back,
Made him forget all possible remedies
Save one — he rushed to, as the sole relief
From horror and the abominable thing."
" Or rather," laugh foes, " then did there be-
    fall

The luckiest of conceivable events,
Most pregnant with impunity for him,
Which henceforth turned the flank of all at
    tack,
And bade him do his wickedest and worst."
— The wife's withdrawal from the Convertites,
Visit to the villa where her parents lived,
And birth there of his babe.   Divergence here
I simply take the facts, ask what they show.

First comes this thunderclap of a surprise :
Then follow all the signs and silences
Premonitory of earthquake.   Paolo first
Vanished, was swept off somewhere, lost to
    Rome :
(Wells dry up, while the sky is sunny and blue.)
Then Guido girds himself for enterprise,
Hies to Vittiano, counsels with his steward,
Comes to terms with four peasants young and
    bold,
And starts for Rome the Holy, reaches her
At very holiest, for 't is Christmas Eve,
And makes straight for the Abate's dried-up
    font,
The lodge where Paolo ceased to work the
    pipes.
And then, rest taken, observation made
And plan completed, all in a grim week,
The five proceed in a body, reach the place,
— Pietro's, at the Paolina, silent, lone,
And stupefied by the propitious snow.
'T is one i' the evening : knock : a voice,
    " Who 's there ? "
" Friends with a letter from the priest your
    friend."
At the door, straight smiles old Violante's self.
She falls, — her son-in-law stabs through and
    through,
Reaches through her at Pietro — " With your
    son
This is the way to settle suits, good sire ! "
He bellows, " Mercy for heaven, not for earth !
Leave to confess and save my sinful soul,
Then do your pleasure on the body of me ! "
— " Nay, father, soul with body must take its
    chance ! "
He presently got his portion and lay still.
And last, Pompilia rushes here and there
Like a dove among the lightnings in her brake,
Falls also : Guido's, this last husband's-act.
He lifts her by the long dishevelled hair,
Holds her away at arm's length with one hand,
While the other tries if life come from the
    mouth —
Looks out his whole heart's hate on the shut
    eyes,
Draws a deep satisfied breath, "So — dead at
    last ! "
Throws down the burden on dead Pietro's
    knees,
And ends all with " Let us away, my boys ! "

And, as they left by one door, in at the other
Tumbled the neighbors — for the shrieks had
    pierced
To the mill and the grange, this cottage and
    that shed.
Soon followed the Public Force ; pursuit began

Though Guido had the start and chose the
 road :
So, that same night was he, with the other
 four,
Overtaken near Baccano, — where they sank
By the wayside, in some shelter meant for
 beasts,
And now lay heaped together, nuzzling swine,
Each wrapped in bloody cloak, each grasping
 still
His unwiped weapon, sleeping all the same
The sleep o' the just, — a journey of twenty
 miles
Brought just and unjust to a level, you see.
The only one i' the world that suffered aught
By the whole night's toil and trouble, flight and
 chase,
Was just the officer who took them, Head
O' the Public Force, — Patrizj, zealous soul,
Who, having but duty to sustain weak flesh,
Got heated, caught a fever and so died :
A warning to the over-vigilant,
— Virtue in a chafe should change her linen
 quick,
Lest pleurisy get start of providence.
(That 's for the Cardinal, and told, I think !)

Well, they bring back the company to Rome.
Says Guido, " By your leave, I fain would ask
How you found out 't was I who did the deed ?
What put you on my trace, a foreigner,
Supposed in Arezzo, — and assuredly safe
Except for an oversight : who told you, pray ? "
" Why, naturally your wife ! " Down Guido
 drops
O' the horse he rode, — they have to steady
 and stay
At either side the brute that bore him bound,
So strange it seemed his wife should live and
 speak !
She had prayed — at least so people tell you
 now —
For but one thing to the Virgin for herself,
Not simply, as did Pietro 'mid the stabs, —
Time to confess and get her own soul saved, —
But time to make the truth apparent, truth
For God's sake, lest men should believe a lie :
Which seems to have been about the single
 prayer
She ever put up, that was granted her.
With this hope in her head, of telling truth, —
Being familiarized with pain, beside, —
She bore the stabbing to a certain pitch
Without a useless cry, was flung for dead
On Pietro's lap, and so attained her point.
Her friends subjoin this — have I done with
 them ? —
And cite the miracle of continued life
(She was not dead when I arrived just now)
As attestation to her probity.

Does it strike your Excellency ? Why, your
 Highness,
The self-command and even the final prayer,
Our candor must acknowledge explicable
As easily by the consciousness of guilt.
So, when they add that her confession runs
She was of wifehood one white innocence

In thought, word, act, from first of her short
 life
To last of it ; praying, i' the face of death,
That God forgive her other sins — not this,
She is charged with and must die for, that she
 failed
Anyway to her husband : while thereon
Comments the old Religious — " So much good,
Patience beneath enormity of ill,
I hear to my confusion, woe is me,
Sinner that I stand, shamed in the walk and
 gait
I have practised and grown old in, by a
 child ! " —
Guido's friends shrug the shoulder, " Just the
 same
Prodigious absolute calm in the last hour
Confirms us, — being the natural result
Of a life which proves consistent to the close.
Having braved heaven and deceived earth
 throughout,
She braves still and deceives still, gains thereby
Two ends, she prizes beyond earth or heaven :
First sets her lover free, imperilled sore
By the new turn things take : he answers yet
For the part he played : they have summoned
 him indeed :
The past ripped up, he may be punished still :
What better way of saving him than this ?
Then, — thus she dies revenged to the utter-
 most
On Guido, drags him with her in the dark,
The lower still the better, do you doubt ?
Thus, two ways, does she love her love to the
 end,
And hate her hate, — death, hell is no such
 price
To pay for these, — lovers and haters hold."

But there 's another parry for the thrust.
"Confession," cry folks — "a confession,
 think !
Confession of the moribund is true ! "
Which of them, my wise friends ? This public
 one,
Or the private other we shall never know ?
The private may contain — your casuists
 teach —
The acknowledgment of, and the penitence for,
That other public one, so people say.
However it be, — we trench on delicate ground,
Her Eminence is peeping o'er the cards, —
Can one find nothing in behalf of this
Catastrophe ? Deaf folks accuse the dumb !
You criticise the drunken reel, fool's-speech,
Maniacal gesture of the man, — we grant !
But who poured poison in his cup, we ask ?
Recall the list of his excessive wrongs,
First cheated in his wife, robbed by her kin,
Rendered anon the laughing-stock o' the world
By the story, true or false, of his wife's birth, —
The last seal publicly apposed to shame
By the open flight of wife and priest, — why,
 Sirs,
Step out of Rome a furlong, would you know
What anotherguess tribunal than ours here,
Mere worldly Court without the help of grace,
Thinks of just that one incident o' the flight ?

Guido preferred the same complaint before
The court at Arezzo, bar of the Granduke, —
In virtue of it being Tuscany
Where the offence had rise and flight began, —
Selfsame complaint he made in the sequel here
Where the offence grew to the full, the flight
Ended : offence and flight, one fact judged
    twice
By two distinct tribunals, — what result ?
There was a sentence passed at the same time
By Arezzo and confirmed by the Granduke,
Which nothing balks of swift and sure effect
But absence of the guilty, (flight to Rome
Frees them from Tuscan jurisdiction now)
— Condemns the wife to the opprobrious doom
Of all whom law just lets escape from death.
The Stinche, House of Punishment, for life, —
That's what the wife deserves in Tuscany :
Here, she deserves — remitting with a smile
To her father's house, main object of the flight!
The thief presented with the thing he steals !

At this discrepancy of judgments — mad,
The man took on himself the office, judged ;
And the only argument against the use
O' the law he thus took into his own hands
Is . . . what, I ask you ? — that, revenging
    wrong,
He did not revenge sooner, kill at first
Whom he killed last ! That is the final charge.
Sooner ? What's soon or late i' the case ? —
    ask we.
A wound i' the flesh no doubt wants prompt re-
    dress ;
It smarts a little to-day, well in a week,
Forgotten in a month ; or never, or now, re-
    venge !
But a wound to the soul ? That rankles worse
    and worse.
Shall I comfort you, explaining — " Not this
    once
But now it may be some five hundred times
I called you ruffian, pandar, liar and rogue :
The injury must be less by lapse of time ? "
The wrong is a wrong, one and immortal too,
And that you bore it those five hundred times,
Let it rankle unrevenged five hundred years,
Is just five hundred wrongs the more and
    worse !
Men, plagued this fashion, get to explode this
    way,
If left no other.

                " But we left this man
Many another way, and there's his fault,"
'T is answered — " He himself preferred our
    arm
O' the law to fight his battle with. No doubt
We did not open him an armory
To pick and choose from, use, and then reject.
He tries one weapon and fails, — he tries the
    next
And next : he flourishes wit and common
    sense,
They fail him, — he plies logic doughtily,
It fails him too, — thereon, discovers last
He has been blind to the combustibles —
That all the while he is aglow with ire,

Boiling with irrepressible rage, and so
May try explosives and discard cold steel, —
So hires assassins, plots, plans, executes !
Is this the honest self-forgetting rage
We are called to pardon ? Does the furious
    bull
Pick out four help-mates from the grazing herd
And journey with them over hill and dale
Till he find his enemy ? "

                What rejoinder ? save
That friends accept our bull-similitude.
Bull-like, — the indiscriminate slaughter, rude
And reckless aggravation of revenge,
Were all i' the way o' the brute who never
    once
Ceases, amid all provocation more,
To bear in mind the first tormentor, first
Giver o' the wound that goaded him to fight :
And, though a dozen follow and reinforce
The aggressor, wound in front and wound in
    flank,
Continues undisturbedly pursuit,
And only after prostrating his prize
Turns on the pettier, makes a general prey.
So Guido rushed against Violante, first
Author of all his wrongs, *fons et origo*
Malorum — drops first, deluge since, — which
    done,
He finished with the rest. Do you blame a
    bull ?

In truth you look as puzzled as ere I preached !
How is that ? There are difficulties perhaps
On any supposition, and either side.
Each party wants too much, claims sympathy
For its object of compassion, more than just.
Cry the wife's friends, " Oh, the enormous crime
Caused by no provocation in the world ! "
" Was not the wife a little weak ? " — inquire —
" Punished extravagantly, if you please,
But meriting a little punishment ?
One treated inconsiderately, say,
Rather than one deserving not at all
Treatment and discipline o' the harsher sort ? "
No, they must have her purity itself,
Quite angel, — and her parents angels too
Of an aged sort, immaculate, word and deed :
At all events, so seeming, till the fiend,
Even Guido, by his folly, forced from them
The untoward avowal of the trick o' the birth,
Which otherwise were safe and secret now.
Why, here you have the awfullest of crimes
For nothing ! Hell broke loose on a butterfly !
A dragon born of rose-dew and the moon !
Yet here is the monster ! Why he's a mere
    man —
Born, bred and brought up in the usual way,
His mother loves him, still his brothers stick
To the good fellow of the boyish games ;
The Governor of his town knows and approves,
The Archbishop of the place knows and assists :
Here he has Cardinal This to vouch for the
    past,
Cardinal That to trust for the future, — match
And marriage were a Cardinal's making, -- in
    short.
What if a tragedy be acted here

Impossible for malice to improve,
And innocent Guido with his innocent four
Be added, all five, to the guilty three,
That we of these last days be edified
With one full taste o' the justice of the world ?

The long and the short is, truth seems what I
    show : —
Undoubtedly no pains ought to be spared
To give the mob an inkling of our lights.
It seems unduly harsh to put the man
To the torture, as I hear the court intends,
Though readiest way of twisting out the truth ;
He is noble, and he may be innocent.
On the other hand, if they exempt the man
(As it is also said they hesitate
On the fair ground, presumptive guilt is weak
I' the case of nobility and privilege), —
What crime that ever was, ever will be,
Deserves the torture ?   Then abolish it !
You see the reduction *ad absurdum*, Sirs ?

Her Excellency must pronounce, in fine !
What, she prefers going and joining play ?
Her Highness finds it late, intends retire ?
I am of their mind : only, all this talk talked,
'T was not for nothing that we talked, I hope ?
Both know as much about it, now, at least,
As all Rome : no particular thanks, I beg !
(You 'll see, I have not so advanced myself,
After my teaching the two idiots here !)

V

COUNT GUIDO FRANCESCHINI

Thanks, Sir, but, should it please the reverend
    Court,
I feel I can stand somehow, half sit down
Without help, make shift to even speak, you
    see,
Fortified by the sip of . . . why, 't is wine,
Velletri, — and not vinegar and gall,
So changed and good the times grow ! Thanks,
    kind Sir !
Oh, but one sip 's enough ! I want my head
To save my neck, there 's work awaits me still.
How cautious and considerate . . . aie, aie,
    aie,
Nor your fault, sweet Sir ! Come, you take to
    heart
An ordinary matter. Law is law.
Noblemen were exempt, the vulgar thought,
From racking ; but, since law thinks otherwise,
I have been put to the rack : all 's over now,
And neither wrist — what men style, out of
    joint :
If any harm be, 't is the shoulder-blade,
The left one, that seems wrong i' the socket, —
    Sirs,
Much could not happen, I was quick to faint,
Being past my prime of life, and out of health.
In short, I thank you, — yes, and mean the
    word.
Needs must the Court be slow to understand
How this quite novel form of taking pain,
This getting tortured merely in the flesh,

Amounts to almost an agreeable change
In my case, me fastidious, plied too much
With opposite treatment, used (forgive the
    joke)
To the rasp-tooth toying with this brain of
    mine,
And, in and out my heart, the play o' th,
    probe.
Four years have I been operated on
I' the soul, do you see — its tense or tremulous
    part —
My self-respect, my care for a good name,
Pride in an old one, love of kindred — just
A mother, brothers, sisters, and the like,
That looked up to my face when days were
    dim,
And fancied they found light there — no one
    spot,
Foppishly sensitive, but has paid its pang.
That, and not this you now oblige me with,
That was the Vigil-torment, if you please !
The poor old noble House that drew the rags
O' the Franceschini's once superb array
Close round her, hoped to slink unchallenged
    by, —
Pluck off these ! Turn the drapery inside out
And teach the tittering town how scarlet
    wears !
Show men the lucklessness, the improvidence
Of the easy-natured Count before this Count,
The father I have some slight feeling for,
Who let the world slide, nor foresaw that
    friends
Then proud to cap and kiss their patron's shoe,
Would, when the purse he left held spider-
    webs,
Properly push his child to wall one day !
Mimic the tetchy humor, furtive glance,
And brow where half was furious, half fa
    tigued,
O' the same son got to be of middle age,
Sour, saturnine, — your humble servant here, —
When things grow cross and the young wife, he
    finds
Take to the window at a whistle's bid,
And yet demurs thereon, preposterous fool ! —
Whereat the worthies judge he wants advice
And beg to civilly ask what 's evil here,
Perhaps remonstrate on the habit they deem
He 's given unduly to, of beating her :
. . . Oh, sure he beats her — why says John so
    else,
Who is cousin to George who is sib to Tecla's
    self
Who cooks the meal and combs the lady's
    hair ?
What ! 'T is my wrist you merely dislocate
For the future when you mean me martyrdom ?
— Let the old mother's economy alone,
How the brocade-strips saved o' the seamy side
O' the wedding-gown buy raiment for a year ?
— How she can dress and dish up — lordly dish
Fit for a duke, lamb's head and purtenance —
With her proud hands, feast household so a
    week ?
No word o' the wine rejoicing God and man,
The less when three-parts water ? Then, I
    say,

A trifle of torture to the flesh, like yours,
While soul is spared such foretaste of hell-fire,
Is naught. But I curtail the catalogue
Through policy, — a rhetorician's trick, —
Because I would reserve some choicer points
O' the practice, more exactly parallel
(Having an eye to climax) with what gift,
Eventual grace the Court may have in store
I' the way of plague — what crown of punish-
ments.
When I am hanged or headed, time enough
To prove the tenderness of only that,
Mere heading, hanging, — not their counter-
part,
Not demonstration public and precise
That I, having married the mongrel of a drab,
Am bound to grant that mongrel-brat, my
wife,
Her mother's birthright-license as is just, —
Let her sleep undisturbed, i' the family style,
Her sleep out in the embraces of a priest,
Nor disallow their bastard as my heir!
Your sole mistake — dare I submit so much
To the reverend Court ? — has been in all this
pains
To make a stone roll down hill, — rack and
wrench
And rend a man to pieces, all for what ?
Why — make him ope mouth in his own defence,
Show cause for what he has done, the irregular
deed,
(Since that he did it, scarce dispute can be)
And clear his fame a little, beside the luck
Of stopping even yet, if possible,
Discomfort to his flesh from noose or axe —
For that, out come the implements of law !
May it content my lords the gracious Court
To listen only half so patient-long
As I will in that sense profusely speak,
And — fie, they shall not call in screws to
help !
I killed Pompilia Franceschini, Sirs ;
Killed too the Comparini, husband, wife,
Who called themselves, by a notorious lie,
Her father and her mother to ruin me.
There 's the irregular deed : you want no more
Than right interpretation of the same,
And truth so far — am I to understand ?
To that then, with convenient speed, — because
Now I consider, — yes, despite my boast,
There is an ailing in this omoplate
May clip my speech all too abruptly short,
Whatever the good-will in me. Now for truth !

I' the name of the indivisible Trinity !
Will my lords, in the plentitude of their light,
Weigh well that all this trouble has come on
me
Through my persistent treading in the paths
Where I was trained to go, — wearing that
yoke
My shoulder was predestined to receive,
Born to the hereditary stoop and crease ?
Noble, I recognized my nobler still,
The Church, my suzerain ; no mock-mistress,
she ;
The secular owned the spiritual : mates of
mine

Have thrown their careless hoofs up at her call
" Forsake the clover and come drag my wain ! "
There they go cropping : I protruded nose
To halter, bent my back of docile beast,
And now am whealed, one wide wound all of
me,
For being found at the eleventh hour o' the day
Padding the mill-track, not neck-deep in grass :
— My one fault, I am stiffened by my work,
— My one reward, I help the Court to smile !

I am representative of a great line,
One of the first of the old families
In Arezzo, ancientest of Tuscan towns.
When my worst foe is fain to challenge this,
His worst exception runs — not first in rank
But second, noble in the next degree
Only ; not malice' self maligns me more.
So, my lord opposite has composed, we know,
A marvel of a book, sustains the point
That Francis boasts the primacy 'mid saints ;
Yet not inaptly hath his argument
Obtained response from yon my other lord
In thesis published with the world's applause
— Rather 't is Dominic such post befits :
Why, at the worst, Francis stays Francis still,
Second in rank to Dominic it may be,
Still, very saintly, very like our Lord ;
And I at least descend from Guido once
Homager to the Empire, naught below —
Of which account as proof that, none o' the line
Having a single gift beyond brave blood,
Or able to do aught but give, give, give
In blood and brain, in house and land and cash,
Not get and garner as the vulgar may,
We became poor as Francis or our Lord.
Be that as it likes you, Sirs, — whenever it
chanced
Myself grew capable anyway of remark,
(Which was soon — penury makes wit pre-
mature)
This struck me, I was poor who should be rich
Or pay that fault to the world which trifles not
When lineage lacks the flag yet lifts the pole :
On, therefore, I must move forthwith, transfer
My stranded self, born fish with gill and fin
Fit for the deep sea, now left flap bare-backed
In slush and sand, a show to crawlers vile
Reared of the low-tide and aright therein.
The enviable youth with the old name,
Wide chest, stout arms, sound brow and prick-
ing veins,
A heartful of desire, man's natural load,
A brainful of belief, the noble's lot, —
All this life, cramped and gasping, high and dry
I' the wave's retreat, — the misery, good my
lords,
Which made you merriment at Rome of late, —
It made me reason, rather — muse, demand
— Why our bare dropping palace, in the street
Where such-an-one whose grandfather sold tripe
Was adding to his purchased pile a fourth
Tall tower, could hardly show a turret sound ?
Why Countess Beatrice, whose son I am,
Cowered in the winter-time as she spun flax,
Blew on the earthen basket of live ash,
Instead of jaunting forth in coach and six
Like such-another widow who ne'er was wed ?

I asked my fellows, how came this about?
"Why, Jack, the sutler's child, perhaps the
    camp's,
Went to the wars, fought sturdily, took a town
And got rewarded as was natural.
She of the coach and six — excuse me there !
Why, don't you know the story of her friend ?
A clown dressed vines on somebody's estate,
His boy recoiled from muck, liked Latin more,
Stuck to his pen and got to be a priest,
Till one day . . . don't you mind that telling
    tract
Against Molinos, the old Cardinal wrote ?
He penned and dropped it in the patron's desk,
Who, deep in thought and absent much of mind,
Licensed the thing, allowed it for his own ;
Quick came promotion, — *suum cuique*, Count !
Oh, he can pay for coach and six, be sure ! ' "
" — Well, let me go, do likewise : war 's the
    word —
That way the Franceschini worked at first,
I 'll take my turn, try soldiership." — " What,
    you ?
The eldest son and heir and prop o' the house,
So do you see your duty ? Here 's your post,
Hard by the hearth and altar. (Roam from
    roof,
This youngster, play the gypsy out of doors,
And who keeps kith and kin that fall on us ?)
Stand fast, stick tight, conserve your gods at
    home ! "
" — Well then, the quiet course, the contrary
    trade !
We had a cousin amongst us once was Pope,
And minor glories manifold. Try the Church,
The tonsure, and, — since heresy 's but half-slain
Even by the Cardinal's tract he thought he
    wrote, —
Have at Molinos ! " — " Have at a fool's head !
You a priest ? How were marriage possible ?
There must be Franceschini till time ends —
That 's your vocation. Make your brothers
    priests,
Paul shall be porporate, and Girolamo step
Red-stockinged in the presence when you choose,
But save one Franceschini for the age !
Be not the vine but dig and dung its root,
Be not a priest but gird up priesthood's loins,
With one foot in Arezzo stride to Rome,
Spend yourself there and bring the purchase
    back !
Go hence to Rome, be guided ! "

                    So I was.
I turned alike from the hillside zigzag thread
Of way to the table-land a soldier takes,
Alike from the low-lying pasture-place
Where churchmen graze, recline and ruminate,
— Ventured to mount no platform like my lords
Who judge the world, bear brain I dare not
    brag —
But stationed me, might thus the expression
    serve,
As who should fetch and carry, come and go,
Meddle and make i' the cause my lords love
    most —
The public weal, which hangs to the law, which
    holds

By the Church, which happens to be through
    God himself.
Humbly I helped the Church till here I stand, —
Or would stand but for the omoplate, you see !
Bidden qualify for Rome, I, having a field,
Went, sold it, laid the sum at Peter's foot :
Which means — I settled home-accounts with
    speed,
Set apart just a modicum should suffice
To rule the villa's head above the waves
Of weed inundating its oil and wine,
And prop roof, stanchion wall o' the palace so
As to keep breath i' the body, out of heart
Amid the advance of neighboring loftiness —
(People like building where they used to beg) —
Till succored one day, — shared the residue
Between my mother and brothers and sisters
    there,
Black-eyed babe Donna This and Donna That,
As near to starving as might decently be,
— Left myself journey-charges, change of suit,
A purse to put i' the pocket of the Groom
O' the Chamber of the patron, and a glove
With a ring to it for the digits of the niece
Sure to be helpful in his household, — then
Started for Rome, and led the life prescribed.
Close to the Church, though clean of it, I as-
    sumed
Three or four orders of no consequence,
— They cast out evil spirits and exorcise,
For example ; bind a man to nothing more,
Give clerical savor to his layman's-salt,
Facilitate his claim to loaf and fish
Should miracle leave, beyond what feeds the
    flock,
Fragments to brim the basket of a friend —
While, for the world's sake, I rode, danced and
    gamed,
Quitted me like a courtier, measured mine
With whatsoever blade had fame in fence,
— Ready to let the basket go its round
Even though my turn was come to help myself,
Should Dives count on me at dinner-time
As just the understander of a joke
And not immoderate in repartee.
Utrique sic paratus, Sirs, I said,
" Here," (in the fortitude of years fifteen,
So good a pedagogue is penury)
" Here wait, do service, — serving and to serve !
And, in due time, I nowise doubt at all,
The recognition of my service comes.
Next year I 'm only sixteen. I can wait."

I waited thirty years, may it please the Court :
Saw meanwhile many a denizen o' the dung
Hop, skip, jump o'er my shoulder, make him
    wings
And fly aloft, — succeed, in the usual phrase.
Every one soon or late comes round by Rome :
Stand still here, you 'll see all in turn succeed.
Why, look you, so and so, the physician here,
My father's lacquey's son we sent to school,
Doctored and dosed this Eminence and that,
Salved the last Pope his certain obstinate sore,
Soon bought land as became him, names it now :
I grasp bell at his griffin-guarded gate,
Traverse the half-mile avenue, — a term,
A cypress, and a statue, three and three —

Deliver message from my Monsignor,
With varletry at lounge i' the vestibule
I 'm barred from, who bear mud upon my shoe.
My father's chaplain's nephew, Chamberlain, —
Nothing less, please you ! — courteous all the
    same,
— He does not see me though I wait an hour
At his staircase-landing 'twixt the brace of
    busts,
A noseless Sylla, Marius maimed to match,
My father gave him for a hexastich
Made on my birthday, — but he sends me down,
To make amends, that relic I prize most —
The unburnt end o' the very candle, Sirs,
Purfled with paint so prettily round and round,
He carried in such state last Peter's-day, —
In token I, his gentleman and squire,
Had held the bridle, walked his managed mule
Without a tittup the procession through.
Nay, the official, — one you know, sweet
    lords ! —
Who drew the warrant for my transfer late
To the New Prisons from Tordinona, — he
Graciously had remembrance — " Francesc . . .
    ha ?
His sire, now — how a thing shall come
    about ! —
Paid me a dozen florins above the fee,
For drawing deftly up a deed of sale
When troubles fell so thick on him, good heart,
And I was prompt and pushing ! By all means !
At the New Prisons be it his son shall lie, —
Anything for an old friend ! " and thereat
Signed name with triple flourish underneath.
These were my fellows, such their fortunes now,
While I — kept fasts and feasts innumerable,
Matins and vespers, functions to no end
I' the train of Monsignor and Eminence,
As gentleman-squire, and for my zeal's reward
Have rarely missed a place at the table-foot
Except when some Ambassador, or such like,
Brought his own people. Brief, one day I felt
The tick of time inside me, turning-point
And slight sense there was now enough of this :
That I was near my seventh climacteric,
Hard upon, if not over, the middle life,
And, although fed by the east-wind, fulsome-
    fine
With foretaste of the Land of Promise, still
My gorge gave symptom it might play me false ;
Better not press it further, — be content
With living and dying only a nobleman,
Who merely had a father great and rich,
Who simply had one greater and richer yet,
And so on back and back till first and best
Began i' the night : I finish in the day.
" The mother must be getting old," I said ;
" The sisters are well wedded away, our name
Can manage to pass a sister off, at need,
And do for dowry : both my brothers thrive —
Regular priests they are, nor, bat-like, 'bide
'Twixt flesh and fowl with neither privilege.
My spare revenue must keep me and mine.
I am tired : Arezzo's air is good to breathe ;
Vittiano, — one limes flocks of thrushes there ;
A leathern coat costs little and lasts long :
Let me bid hope good-by, content at home ! "
Thus, one day, I disbosomed me and bowed.

Whereat began the little buzz and thrill
O' the gazers round me ; each face brightened
    up :
As when at your Casino, deep in dawn,
A gamester says at last, " I play no more,
Forego gain, acquiesce in loss, withdraw
Anyhow : " and the watchers of his ways,
A trifle struck compunctious at the word,
Yet sensible of relief, breathe free once more,
Break up the ring, venture polite advice —
" How, Sir ? So scant of heart and hope indeed ?
Retire with neither cross nor pile from play ? —
So incurious, so short-casting ? — give your
    chance
To a younger, stronger, bolder spirit belike,
Just when luck turns and the fine throw sweeps
    all ? "
Such was the chorus : and its goodwill meant —
" See that the loser leave door handsomely !
There 's an ill look, — it 's sinister, spoils sport,
When an old bruised and battered year-by-year
Fighter with fortune, not a penny in poke,
Reels down the steps of our establishment
And staggers on broad daylight and the world,
In shagrag beard and doleful doublet, drops
And breaks his heart on the outside : people
    prate
' Such is the profit of a trip upstairs ! '
Contrive he sidle forth, balked of the blow
Best dealt by way of moral, bidding down
No curse but blessings rather on our heads
For some poor prize he bears at tattered breast,
Some palpable sort of kind of good to set
Over and against the grievance : give him
    quick ! "
Whereon protested Paul, " Go hang yourselves !
Leave him to me. Count Guido and brother of
    mine,
A word in your ear ! Take courage, since
    faint heart
Ne'er won . . . aha, fair lady, don't men say ?
There 's a *sors*, there 's a right Virgilian dip !
Do you see the happiness o' the hint ? At worst,
If the Church want no more of you, the Court
No more, and the Camp as little, the ingrates, —
    come,
Count you are counted : still you 've coat to back,
Not cloth of gold and tissue, as we hoped,
But cloth with sparks and spangles on its frieze
From Camp, Court, Church, enough to make a
    shine,
Entitle you to carry home a wife
With the proper dowry, let the worst betide !
Why, it was just a wife you meant to take ! "

Now, Paul's advice was weighty : priests should
    know :
And Paul apprised me, ere the week was out,
That Pietro and Violante, the easy pair,
The cits enough, with stomach to be more,
Had just the daughter and exact the sum
To truck for the quality of myself : " She 's
    young,
Pretty and rich : you 're noble, classic, choice.
Is it to be a match ? " " A match," said I.
Done ! He proposed all, I accepted all,
And we performed all. So I said and did
Simply. As simply followed, not at first,

But with the outbreak of misfortune, still
One comment on the saying and doing —
" What ?
No blush at the avowal you dared buy
A girl of age beseems your granddaughter,
Like ox or ass ?   Are flesh and blood a ware ?
Are heart and soul a chattel ? "
                                         Softly, Sirs !
Will the Court of its charity teach poor me
Anxious to learn, of any way i' the world,
Allowed by custom and convenience, save
This same which, taught from my youth up, I
    trod ?
Take me along with you ; where was the wrong
    step ?
If what I gave in barter, style and state
And all that hangs to Franceschinihood,
Were worthless, — why, society goes to ground,
Its rules are idiot's - rambling. Honor of
    birth, —
If that thing has no value, cannot buy
Something with value of another sort,
You 've no reward nor punishment to give
I' the giving or the taking honor ; straight
Your social fabric, pinnacle to base,
Comes down a-clatter like a house of cards.
Get honor, and keep honor free from flaw,
Aim at still higher honor, — gabble o' the
    goose !
Go bid a second blockhead like myself
Spend fifty years in guarding bubbles of breath,
Soapsuds with air i' the belly, gilded brave,
Guarded and guided, all to break at touch
O' the first young girl's hand and first old fool's
    purse !
All my privation and endurance, all
Love, loyalty and labor dared and did,
Fiddle-de-dee ! — why, doer and darer both, —
Count Guido Franceschini had hit the mark
Far better, spent his life with more effect,
As a dancer or a prizer, trades that pay !
On the other hand, bid this buffoonery cease,
Admit that honor is a privilege,
The question follows, privilege worth what ?
Why, worth the market-price, — now up, now
    down,
Just so with this as with all other ware :
Therefore essay the market, sell your name,
Style and condition to who buys them best !
" Does my name purchase," had I dared in-
    quire,
" Your niece, my lord ? " there would have been
    rebuff
Though courtesy, your Lordship cannot else —
" Not altogether ! Rank for rank may stand :
But I have wealth beside, you — poverty ;
Your scale flies up there :. bid a second bid,
Rank too and wealth too ! " Reasoned like
    yourself !
But was it to you I went with goods to sell ?
This time 't was my scale quietly kissed the
    ground,
Mere rank against mere wealth — some youth
    beside,
Some beauty too, thrown into the bargain, just
As the buyer likes or lets alone. I thought
To deal o' the square : others find fault, it
    seems :

The thing is, those my offer most concerned,
Pietro, Violante, cried they fair or foul ?
What did they make o' the terms ? Prepos-
    terous terms ?
Why then accede so promptly, close with such
Nor take a minute to chaffer ? Bargain
    struck,
They straight grew bilious, wished their money
    back,
Repented them, no doubt : why, so did I,
So did your Lordship, if town-talk be true,
Of paying a full farm's worth for that piece
By Pietro of Cortona — probably
His scholar Ciro Ferri may have retouched —
You caring more for color than design —
Getting a little tired of cupids too.
That 's incident to all the folk who buy !
I am charged, I know, with gilding fact by
    fraud ;
I falsified and fabricated, wrote
Myself down roughly richer than I prove,
Rendered a wrong revenue, — grant it all !
Mere grace, mere coquetry such fraud, I say :
A flourish round the figures of a sum
For fashion's sake, that deceives nobody.
The veritable back-bone, understood
Essence of this same bargain, blank and bare,
Being the exchange of quality for wealth, —
What may such fancy-flights be ? Flecks of
    oil
Flirted by chapmen where plain dealing grates.
I may have dripped a drop — " My name I
    sell ;
Not but that I too boast my wealth " — as they,
" — We bring you riches ; still our ancestor
Was hardly the rapscallion, folk saw flogged,
But heir to we know who, were rights of force ! "
They knew and I knew where the back-bone
    lurked
I' the writhings of the bargain, lords, believe !
I paid down all engaged for, to a doit,
Delivered them just that which, their life long,
They hungered in the hearts of them to gain —
Incorporation with nobility thus
In word and deed : for that they gave me
    wealth.
But when they came to try their gain, my
    gift,
Quit Rome and qualify for Arezzo, take
The tone o' the new sphere that absorbed the
    old,
Put away gossip Jack and goody Joan
And go become familiar with the Great,
Greatness to touch and taste and handle
    now, —
Why, then, — they found that all was vanity,
Vexation, and what Solomon describes !
The old abundant city-fare was best,
The kindly warmth o' the commons, the glad
    clap
Of the equal on the shoulder, the frank grin
Of the underling at all so many spoons
Fire-new at neighborly treat, — best, best and
    best
Beyond compare ! — down to the loll itself
O' the pot-house settle, — better such a bench
Than the stiff crucifixion by my dais
Under the piecemeal damask canopy

With the coroneted coat-of-arms a-top !
Poverty and privation for pride's sake,
All they engaged to easily brave and bear, —
With the fit upon them and their brains
    a-work, —
Proved unendurable to the sobered sots.
A banished prince, now, will exude a juice
And salamander-like support the flame :
He dines on chestnuts, chucks the husks to
    help
The broil o' the brazier, pays the due baioc,
Goes off light-hearted : his grimace begins
At the funny humors of the christening-feast
Of friend the money - lender, — then he 's
    touched
By the flame and frizzles at the babe to kiss !
Here was the converse trial, opposite mind :
Here did a petty nature split on rock
Of vulgar wants predestinate for such —
One dish at supper and weak wine to boot !
The prince had grinned and borne : the citizen
    shrieked,
Summoned the neighborhood to attest the
    wrong,
Made noisy protest he was murdered, — stoned
And burned and drowned and hanged, — then
    broke away,
He and his wife, to tell their Rome the rest.
And this you admire, you men o' the world,
    my lords ?
This moves compassion, makes you doubt my
    faith ?
Why, I appeal to . . . sun and moon ? Not I !
Rather to Plautus, Terence, Boccaccio's Book,
My townsman, frank Ser Franco's merry
    Tales, —
To all who strip a vizard from a face,
A body from its padding, and a soul
From froth and ignorance it styles itself, —
If this be other than the daily hap
Of purblind greed that dog-like still drops bone,
Grasps shadow, and then howls the case is
    hard !

So much for them so far : now for myself,
My profit or loss i' the matter : married am I :
Text whereon friendly censors burst to preach.
Ay, at Rome even, long ere I was left
To regulate her life for my young bride
Alone at Arezzo, friendliness outbroke
(Sifting my future to predict its fault)
" Purchase and sale being thus so plain a point,
How of a certain soul bound up, maybe,
I' the barter with the body and money-bags ?
From the bride's soul what is it you expect ? "
Why, loyalty and obedience, — wish and will
To settle and suit her fresh and plastic mind
To the novel, not disadvantageous mould !
Father and mother shall the woman leave,
Cleave to the husband, be it for weal or woe :
There is the law : what sets this law aside
In my particular case ? My friends submit
" Guide, guardian, benefactor, — fee, faw, fum,
The fact is you are forty-five years old,
Nor very comely even for that age :
Girls must have boys." Why, let girls say so
    then,
Nor call the boys and men, who say the same.

Brute this and beast the other as they do !
Come, cards on table ! When you chant us
    next
Epithalamium full to overflow
With praise and glory of white womanhood,
The chaste and pure — troll no such lies o'er
    lip !
Put in their stead a crudity or two,
Such short and simple statement of the case
As youth chalks on our walls at spring of
    year !
No ! I shall still think nobler of the sex,
Believe a woman still may take a man
For the short period that his soul wears flesh,
And, for the soul's sake, understand the fault
Of armor frayed by fighting. Tush, it tempts
One's tongue too much ! I 'll say — the law 'i
    the law :
With a wife I look to find all wifeliness,
As when I buy, timber and twig, a tree —
I buy the song o' the nightingale inside.

Such was the pact : Pompilia from the first
Broke it, refused from the beginning day
Either in body or soul to cleave to mine,
And published it forthwith to all the world.
No rupture, — you must join ere you can
    break, —
Before we had cohabited a month
She found I was a devil and no man, —
Made common cause with those who found as
    much,
Her parents, Pietro and Violante, — moved
Heaven and earth to the rescue of all three.
In four months' time, the time o' the parents'
    stay,
Arezzo was a-ringing, bells in a blaze,
With the unimaginable story rife
I' the mouth of man, woman and child — to
    wit
My misdemeanor. First the lighter side,
Ludicrous face of things, — how very poor
The Franceschini had become at last,
The meanness and the misery of each shift
To save a soldo, stretch and make ends meet.
Next, the more hateful aspect, — how myself
With cruelty beyond Caligula's
Had stripped and beaten, robbed and murdered
    them,
The good old couple, I decoyed, abused,
Plundered and then cast out, and happily so,
Since, — in due course the abominable comes, —
Woe worth the poor young wife left lonely here !
Repugnant in my person as my mind,
I sought, — was ever heard of such revenge ?
— To lure and bind her to so cursed a couch,
Such co-embrace with sulphur, snake and toad,
That she was fain to rush forth, call the stones
O' the common street to save her, not from hate
Of mine merely, but . . . must I burn my lips
With the blister of the lie ? . . . the satyr-love
Of who but my own brother, the young priest,
Too long enforced to lenten fare belike,
Now tempted by the morsel tossed him full
I' the trencher where lay bread and herbs at
    best.
Mark, this yourselves say ! — this, none disal
    lows,

Was charged to me by the universal voice
At the instigation of my four-months' wife! —
And then you ask, "Such charges so preferred,
(Truly or falsely, here concerns us not)
Pricked you to punish now if not before? —
Did not the harshness double itself, the hate
Harden?" I answer, "Have it your way and
    will!"
Say my resentment grew apace: what then?
Do you cry out on the marvel? When I find
That pure smooth egg which, laid within my
    nest,
Could not but hatch a comfort to us all,
Issues a cockatrice for me and mine,
Do you stare to see me stamp on it? Swans
    are soft:
Is it not clear that she you call my wife,
That any wife of any husband, caught
Whetting a sting like this against his breast, —
Speckled with fragments of the fresh - broke
    shell,
Married a month and making outcry thus, —
Proves a plague-prodigy to God and man?
She married: what was it she married for,
Counted upon and meant to meet thereby?
"Love," suggests some one, "love, a little word
Whereof we have not heard one syllable."
So, the Pompilia, child, girl, wife, in one,
Wanted the beating pulse, the rolling eye,
The frantic gesture, the devotion due
From Thyrsis to Neæra! Guido's love —
Why not Provençal roses in his shoe,
Plume to his cap, and trio of guitars
At casement, with a bravo close beside?
Good things all these are, clearly claimable
When the fit price is paid the proper way.
Had it been some friend's wife, now, threw her
    fan
At my foot, with just this pretty scrap attached.
"Shame, death, damnation — fall these as they
    may,
So I find you, for a minute! Come this eve!"
— Why, at such sweet self-sacrifice, — who
    knows?
I might have fired up, found me at my post,
Ardent from head to heel, nor feared catch
    cough.
Nay, had some other friend's . . . say, daugh-
    ter, tripped
Upstairs and tumbled flat and frank on me,
Bareheaded and barefooted, with loose hair
And garments all at large, — cried "Take me
    thus!
Duke So-and-So, the greatest man in Rome —
To escape his hand and heart have I broke
    bounds,
Traversed the town and reached you!" — Then,
    indeed,
The lady had not reached a man of ice!
I would have rummaged, ransacked at the word
Those old odd corners of an empty heart
For remnants of dim love the long disused,
And dusty crumblings of romance! But here,
We talk of just a marriage, if you please —
The every-day conditions and no more;
Where do these bind me to bestow one drop
Of blood shall dye my wife's true-love-knot
    pink?

Pompilia was no pigeon, Venus' pet,
That shuffled from between her pressing paps
To sit on my rough shoulder, — but a hawk,
I bought at a hawk's price and carried home
To do hawk's service — at the Rotunda, say,
Where, six o' the callow nestlings in a row,
You pick and choose and pay the price for such.
I have paid my pound, await my penny's worth,
So, hoodwink, starve and properly train my bird,
And, should she prove a haggard, — twist her
    neck!
Did I not pay my name and style, my hope
And trust, my all? Through spending these
    amiss
I am here! 'T is scarce the gravity of the Court
Will blame me that I never piped a tune,
Treated my falcon-gentle like my finch.
The obligation I incurred was just
To practise mastery, prove my mastership: —
Pompilia's duty was — submit herself,
Afford me pleasure, perhaps cure my bile.
Am I to teach my lords what marriage means,
What God ordains thereby and man fulfils
Who, docile to the dictate, treads the house?
My lords have chosen the happier part with Paul
And neither marry nor burn, — yet priestliness
Can find a parallel to the marriage-bond
In its own blessed special ordinance
Whereof indeed was marriage made the type:
The Church may show her insubordinate,
As marriage her refractory. How of the Monk
Who finds the claustral regimen too sharp
After the first month's essay? What's the
    mode
With the Deacon who supports indifferently
The rod o' the Bishop when he tastes its smart
Full four weeks? Do you straightway slacken
    hold
Of the innocents, the all-unwary ones
Who, eager to profess, mistook their mind? —
Remit a fast-day's rigor to the Monk
Who fancied Francis' manna meant roast
    quails, —
Concede the Deacon sweet society,
He never thought the Levite-rule renounced, —
Or rather prescribe short chain and sharp
    scourge
Corrective of such peccant humors? This —
I take to be the Church's mode, and mine.
If I was over-harsh, — the worse i' the wife
Who did not win from harshness as she ought,
Wanted the patience and persuasion, lore
Of love, should cure me and console herself.
Put case that I mishandle, flurry and fright
My hawk through clumsiness in sportsmanship,
Twitch out five pens where plucking one would
    serve —
What, shall she bite and claw to mend the case?
And, if you find I pluck five more for that,
Shall you weep "How he roughs the turtle
    there"?

Such was the starting; now of the further step.
In lieu of taking penance in good part,
The Monk, with hue and cry, summons a mob
To make a bonfire of the convent, say, —
And the Deacon's pretty piece of virtue (save
The ears o' the Court! I try to save my head)

Instructed by the ingenuous postulant,
Taxes the Bishop with adultery, (mud
Needs must pair off with mud, and filth with
  filth) —
Such being my next experience. Who knows
  not —
The couple, father and mother of my wife,
Returned to Rome, published before my lords,
Put into print, made circulate far and wide
That they had cheated me who cheated them?
Pompilia, I supposed their daughter, drew
Breath first 'mid Rome's worst rankness,
  through the deed
Of a drab and a rogue, was by-blow bastard-babe
Of a nameless strumpet, passed off, palmed on
  me
As the daughter with the dowry. Daughter?
  Dirt
O' the kennel! Dowry? Dust o' the street!
  Naught more
Naught less, naught else but — oh — ah — as-
  suredly
A Franceschini and my very wife!
Now take this charge as you will, for false or
  true, —
This charge, preferred before your very selves
Who judge me now, — I pray you, adjudge
  again,
Classing it with the cheats or with the lies,
By which category I suffer most!
But of their reckoning, theirs who dealt with me
In either fashion, — I reserve my word,
Justify that in its place ; I am now to say,
Whichever· point o' the charge might poison
  most,
Pompilia's duty was no doubtful one.
You put the protestation in her mouth,
"Henceforward and forevermore, avaunt
Ye fiends, who drop disguise and glare revealed
In your own shape, no longer father mine
Nor mother mine! Too nakedly you hate
Me whom you looked as if you loved once, — me
Whom, whether true or false, your tale now
  damns,
Divulged thus to my public infamy,
Private perdition, absolute overthrow.
For, hate my husband to your hearts' content,
I, spoil and prey of you from first to last,
I who have done you the blind service, lured
The lion to your pitfall, — I, thus left
To answer for my ignorant bleating there,
I should have been remembered and withdrawn
From the first o' the natural fury, not flung loose
A proverb and a byword men will mouth
At the cross-way, in the corner, up and down
Rome and Arezzo, — there, full in my face,
If my lord, missing them and finding me,
Content himself with casting his reproach
To drop i' the street where such impostors die.
Ah, but — that husband, what the wonder
  were! —
If, far from casting thus away the rag
Smeared with the plague, his hand had chanced
  upon,
Sewn to his pillow by Locusta's wile, —
Far from abolishing, root, stem and branch,
The misgrowth of infectious mistletoe
Foisted into his stock for honest graft, —

If he repudiate not, renounce nowise,
But, guarding, guiding me, maintain my cause
By making it his own, (what other way?)
— To keep my name for me, he call it his,
Claim it of who would take it by their lie, —
To save my wealth for me — or babe of mine
Their lie was framed to beggar at the birth —
He bid them loose grasp, give our gold again :
If he become no partner with the pair
Even in a game which, played adroitly, gives
Its winner life's great wonderful new chance, —
Of marrying, to wit, a second time, —
Ah. if he did thus, what a friend were he!
Anger he might show, — who can stamp out
  flame
Yet spread no black o' the brand? — yet, rough
  albeit
In the act, as whose bare feet feel embers
  scorch,
What grace were his, what gratitude were
  mine ! "
Such protestation should have been my wife's.
Looking for this, do I exact too much?
Why, here 's the — word for word so much, no
  more —
Avowal she made, her pure spontaneous speech
To my brother the Abate at first blush,
Ere the good impulse had begun to fade :
So did she make confession for the pair,
So pour forth praises in her own behalf.
"Ay, the false letter," interpose my lords —
"The simulated writing, — 't was a trick :
You traced the signs, she merely marked the
  same,
The product was not hers but yours."   Alack,
I want no more impulsion to tell truth
From the other trick, the torture inside there!
I confess all — let it be understood —
And deny nothing! If I baffle you so,
Can so fence, in the plentitude of right,
That my poor lathen dagger puts aside
Each pass o' the Bilboa, beats you all the
  same, —
What matters inefficiency of blade?
Mine and not hers the letter, — conceded, lords!
Impute to me that practice ! — take as proved
I taught my wife her duty, made her see
What it behoved her see and say and do,
Feel in her heart and with her tongue declare,
And, whether sluggish or recalcitrant,
Forced her to take the right step, I myself
Was marching in marital rectitude!
Why, who finds fault here, say the tale be true?
Would not my lords commend the priest whose
  zeal
Seized on the sick, morose or moribund,
By the palsy-smitten finger, made it cross
His brow correctly at the critical time?
— Or answered for the inarticulate babe
At baptism, in its stead declared the faith,
And saved what else would perish unprofessed?
True, the incapable hand may rally yet,
Renounce the sign with renovated strength, —
The babe may grow up man and Molinist, —
And so Pompilia, set in the good path
And left to go alone there, soon might see
That too frank-forward, all too simple-straight
Her step was, and decline to tread the rough,

When here lay, tempting foot, the meadow-side,
And there the coppice rang with singing-birds!
Soon she discovered she was young and fair,
That many in Arezzo knew as much, —
Yes, this next cup of bitterness, my lords,
Had to begin go filling, drop by drop,
Its measure up of full disgust for me,
Filtered into by every noisome drain —
Society's sink toward which all moisture runs.
Would not you prophesy — "She on whose
    brow is stamped
The note of the imputation that we know, —
Rightly or wrongly mothered with a whore, —
Such an one, to disprove the frightful charge,
What will she but exaggerate chastity,
Err in excess of wifehood, as it were,
Renounce even levities permitted youth,
Though not youth struck to age by a thunder-
    bolt?
Cry 'wolf' i' the sheepfold, where's the sheep
    dares bleat,
Knowing the shepherd listens for a growl?"
So you expect. How did the devil decree?
Why, my lords, just the contrary of course!
It was in the house from the window, at the
    church
From the hassock, — where the theatre lent its
    lodge,
Or staging for the public show left space, —
That still Pompilia needs must find herself
Launching her looks forth, letting looks reply
As arrows to a challenge; on all sides
Ever new contribution to her lap,
Till one day, what is it knocks at my clenched
    teeth
But the cup full, curse-collected all for me?
And I must needs drink, drink this gallant's
    praise,
That minion's prayer, the other fop's reproach,
And come at the dregs to — Caponsacchi!
    Sirs,
I, — chin deep in a marsh of misery,
Struggling to extricate my name and fame
And fortune from the marsh would drown them
    all,
My face the sole unstrangled part of me, —
I must have this new gad-fly in that face,
Must free me from the attacking lover too!
Men say I battled ungracefully enough —
Was harsh, uncouth and ludicrous beyond
The proper part o' the husband: have it so!
Your lordships are considerate at least —
You order me to speak in my defence
Plainly, expect no quavering tuneful trills
As when you bid a singer solace you, —
Nor look that I shall give it, for a grace,
Stans pede in uno: — you remember well
In the one case, 't is a plainsong too severe,
This story of my wrongs, — and that I ache
And need a chair, in the other. Ask you me
Why, when I felt this trouble flap my face,
Already pricked with every shame could
    perch, —
When, with her parents, my wife plagued me
    too, —
Why I enforced not exhortation mild
To leave whore's-tricks and let my brows alone,
With mulct of comfits, promise of perfume?

"Far from that! No, you took the opposite
    course,
Breathed threatenings, rage and slaughter!"
    What you will!
And the end has come, the doom is verily
    here,
Unhindered by the threatening. See fate's
    flare
Full on each face of the dead guilty three!
Look at them well, and now, lords, look at
    this!
Tell me: if on that day when I found first
That Caponsacchi thought the nearest way
To his church was some half-mile round by my
    door,
And that he so admired, shall I suppose,
The manner of the swallows' come-and-go
Between the props o' the window overhead, —
That window happening to be my wife's, —
As to stand gazing by the hour on high,
Of May-eves, while she sat and let him smile, —
If I, — instead of threatening, talking big,
Showing hair-powder, a prodigious pinch,
For poison in a bottle, — making believe
At desperate doings with a bauble-sword,
And other bugaboo-and-baby-work, —
Had, with the vulgarest household implement,
Calmly and quietly cut off, clean through bone,
But one joint of one finger of my wife,
Saying, "For listening to the serenade,
Here's your ring-finger shorter a full third:
Be certain I will slice away next joint,
Next time that anybody underneath
Seems somehow to be sauntering as he hoped
A flower would eddy out of your hand to his,
While you please fidget with the branch above
O' the rose-tree in the terrace!" — had I done
    so,
Why, there had followed a quick sharp scream,
    some pain,
Much calling for plaister, damage to the dress,
A somewhat sulky countenance next day,
Perhaps reproaches, — but reflections too!
I don't hear much of harm that Malchus did
After the incident of the ear, my lords!
Saint Peter took the efficacious way;
Malchus was sore but silenced for his life:
He did not hang himself i' the Potter's Field
Like Judas, who was trusted with the bag
And treated to sops after he proved a thief.
So, by this time, my true and obedient wife
Might have been telling beads with a gloved
    hand;
Awkward a little at pricking hearts and darts
On sampler possibly, but well otherwise:
Not where Rome shudders now to see her lie.
I give that for the course a wise man takes;
I took the other however, tried the fool's,
The lighter remedy, brandished rapier dread
With cork-ball at the tip, boxed Malchus' ear
Instead of severing the cartilage,
Called her a terrible nickname and the like,
And there an end: and what was the end of
    that?
What was the good effect o' the gentle course?
Why, one night I went drowsily to bed,
Dropped asleep suddenly, not suddenly woke,
But did wake with rough rousing and loud cry.

To find noon in my face, a crowd in my room,
Fumes in my brain, fire in my throat, my wife
Gone God knows whither, — rifled vesture-
chest,
And ransacked money-coffer.   "What does it
mean ? "
The servants had been drugged too, stared and
yawned,
" It must be that our lady has eloped ! "
— " Whither and with whom ? " — " With
whom but the Canon's self ?
One recognizes Caponsacchi there ! " —
(By this time the admiring neighborhood
Joined chorus round me while I rubbed my
eyes)
" 'T is months since their intelligence began, —
A comedy the town was privy to, —
He wrote and she wrote, she spoke, he re-
plied,
And going in and out your house last night
Was easy work for one . . . to be plain with
you . . .
Accustomed to do both, at dusk and dawn
When you were absent, — at the villa, you
know,
Where husbandry required the master-mind.
Did not you know ? Why, we all knew, you
see ! "
And presently, bit by bit, the full and true
Particulars of the tale were volunteered
With all the breathless zeal of friendship —
" Thus
Matters were managed : at the seventh hour of
night " . . .
— " Later, at daybreak " . . . " Caponsacchi
came " . . .
— " While you and all your household slept like
death,
Drugged as your supper was with drowsy
stuff " . . .
— " And your own cousin Guillichini too —
Either or both entered your dwelling-place,
Plundered it at their pleasure, made prize of
all,
Including your wife " . . . — " Oh, your wife
led the way,
Out of doors, on to the gate " . . . — " But
gates are shut,
In a decent town, to darkness and such deeds :
They climbed the wall — your lady must be
lithe —
At the gap, the broken bit " . . . — " Torrione,
true !
To escape the questioning guard at the proper
gate,
Clemente, where at the inn, hard by, 'the
Horse,'
Just outside, a calash in readiness
Took the two principals, all alone at last,
To gate San Spirito, which o'erlooks the road,
Leads to Perugia, Rome and liberty."
Bit by bit thus made-up mosaic-wise,
Flat lay my fortune, — tessellated floor,
Imperishable tracery devils should foot
And frolic it on, around my broken gods,
Over my desecrated hearth.
                              So much
For the terrible effect of threatening, Sirs !

Well, this way I was shaken wide awake,
Doctored and drenched, somewhat unpoisoned
so.
Then, set on horseback and bid seek the lost,
I started alone, head of me, heart of me
Fire, and each limb as languid . . . ah, sweet
lords,
Bethink you ! — poison-torture, try persuade
The next refractory Molinist with that ! . . .
Floundered through day and night, another day
And yet another night, and so at last,
As Lucifer kept falling to find hell,
Tumbled into the court-yard of an inn
At the end, and fell on whom I thought to
find,
Even Caponsacchi, — what part once was priest.
Cast to the winds now with the cassock-rags :
In cape and sword a cavalier confessed,
There stood he chiding dilatory grooms,
Chafing that only horseflesh and no team
Of eagles would supply the last relay,
Whirl him along the league, the one post more
Between the couple and Rome and liberty.
'T was dawn, the couple were rested in a sort,
And though the lady, tired, — the tenderer
sex, —
Still lingered in her chamber, — to adjust
The limp hair, look for any blush astray, —
She would descend in a twinkling, — " Have
you out
The horses therefore ! "
                          So did I find my wife.
Is the case complete ?   Do your eyes here see
with mine ?
Even the parties dared deny no one
Point out of all these points.
                               What follows next ?
" Why, that then was the time," you interpose,
" Or then or never, while the fact was fresh,
To take the natural vengeance : there and thus
They and you, — somebody had stuck a sword
Beside you while he pushed you on your
horse, —
'T was requisite to slay the couple, Count ! "
Just so my friends say — " Kill ! " they cry in
a breath,
Who presently, when matters grow to a head
And I do kill the offending ones indeed, —
When crime of theirs, only surmised before,
Is patent, proved indisputably now, —
When remedy for wrong, untried at the time,
Which law professes shall not fail a friend,
Is thrice tried now, found threefold worse than
null, —
When what might turn to transient shade, who
knows ?
Solidifies into a blot which breaks
Hell's black off in pale flakes for fear of
mine, —
Then, when I claim and take revenge — " So
rash ? "
They cry — " so little reverence for the law ? "

Listen, my masters, and distinguish here !
At first, I called in law to act and help :
Seeing I did so, " Why, 't is clear," they cry,
" You shrank from gallant readiness and risk,
Were coward : the thing 's inexplicable else."

Sweet my lords, let the thing be ! I fall flat,
Play the reed, not the oak, to breath of man.
Only, inform my ignorance ! Say I stand
Convicted of the having been afraid,
Proved a poltroon, no lion but a lamb, —
Does that deprive me of my right of lamb
And give my fleece and flesh to the first wolf ?
Are eunuchs, women, children, shieldless quite
Against attack their own timidity tempts ?
Cowardice were misfortune and no crime !
— Take it that way, since I am fallen so low
I scarce dare brush the fly that blows my face,
And thank the man who simply spits not
      there, —
Unless the Court be generous, comprehend
How one brought up at the very feet of law
As I, awaits the grave Gamaliel's nod
Ere he clench fist at outrage, — much less,
      stab !
— How, ready enough to rise at the right time,
I still could recognize no time mature
Unsanctioned by a move o' the judgment-seat,
So, mute in misery, eyed my masters here
Motionless till the authoritative word
Pronounced amercement.   There 's the riddle
      solved :
This is just why I slew nor her nor him,
But called in law, law's delegate in the place,
And bade arrest the guilty couple, Sirs !
We had some trouble to do so — you have
      heard
They braved me, — he with arrogance and
      scorn,
She, with a volubility of curse,
A conversancy in the skill of tooth
And claw to make suspicion seem absurd,
Nay, an alacrity to put to proof
At my own throat my own sword, teach me so
To try conclusions better the next time, —
Which did the proper service with the mob.
They never tried to put on mask at all :
Two avowed lovers forcibly torn apart,
Upbraid the tyrant as in a playhouse scene,
Ay, and with proper clapping and applause
From the audience that enjoys the bold and
      free.
I kept still, said to myself, " There 's law ! "
      Anon
We searched the chamber where they passed
      the night,
Found what confirmed the worst was feared be-
      fore,
However needless confirmation now —
The witches' circle intact, charms undisturbed
That raised the spirit and succubus, — letters,
      to wit,
Love-laden, each the bag o' the bee that bore
Honey from lily and rose to Cupid's hive, —
Now, poetry in some rank blossom-burst,
Now, prose, — " Come here, go there, wait such
      a while,
He 's at the villa, now he 's back again :
We are saved, we are lost, we are lovers all the
      same ! "
All in order, all complete, — even to a clue
To the drowsiness that happed so opportune —
No mystery, when I read, " Of all things, find
What wine Sir Jealousy decides to drink —

Red wine ?   Because a sleeping-potion, dust
Dropped into white, discolors wine and shows."

— " Oh, but we did not write a single word !
Somebody forged the letters in our name ! — "
Both in a breath protested presently.
Aha, Sacchetti again ! — " Dame," — quoth the
      Duke,
" What meaneth this epistle, counsel me,
I pick from out thy placket and peruse,
Wherein my page averreth thou art white
And warm and wonderful 'twixt pap and
      pap ? "
" Sir," laughed the Lady, " 't is a counterfeit !
Thy page did never stroke but Dian's breast,
The pretty hound I nurture for thy sake :
To lie were losel, — by my fay, no more ! "
And no more say I too, and spare the Court.

Ah, the Court ! yes, I come to the Court's self ;
Such the case, so complete in fact and proof,
I laid at the feet of law, — there sat my lords,
Here sit they now, so may they ever sit
In easier attitude than suits my haunch !
In this same chamber did I bare my sores
O' the soul and not the body, — shun no shame,
Shrink from no probing of the ulcerous part,
Since confident in Nature, — which is God, —
That she who, for wise ends, concocts a plague,
Curbs, at the right time, the plague's virulence
      too :
Law renovates even Lazarus, — cures me !
Cæsar thou seekest ?   To Cæsar thou shalt go !
Cæsar 's at Rome : to Rome accordingly !

The case was soon decided : both weights, cast
I' the balance, vibrate, neither kicks the beam.
Here away, there away, this now and now that.
To every one o' my grievances law gave
Redress, could purblind eye but see the point.
The wife stood a convicted runagate
From house and husband, — driven to such a
      course
By what she somehow took for cruelty,
Oppression and imperilment of life —
Not that such things were, but that so they
      seemed :
Therefore, the end conceded lawful, (since
To save life there 's no risk should stay our
      leap)
It follows that all means to the lawful end
Are lawful likewise, — poison, theft and flight.
As for the priest's part, did he meddle or make,
Enough that he too thought life jeopardized ;
Concede him then the color charity
Casts on a doubtful course, — if blackish white
Or whitish black, will charity hesitate ?
What did he else but act the precept out,
Leave, like a provident shepherd, his safe flock
To follow the single lamb and strayaway ?
Best hope so and think so, — that the ticklish
      time
I' the carriage, the tempting privacy, the last
Somewhat ambiguous accident at the inn,
— All may bear explanation : may ? then,
      must !
The letters, — do they so incriminate ?
But what if the whole prove a prank o' the pen,

Flight of the fancy, none of theirs at all,
Bred of the vapors of my brain belike,
Or at worst mere exercise of scholar's-wit
In the courtly Caponsacchi: verse, convict?
Did not Catullus write less seemly once?
Yet *doctus* and unblemished he abides.
Wherefore so ready to infer the worst?
Still, I did righteously in bringing doubts
For the law to solve, — take the solution now!
"Seeing that the said associates, wife and
   priest,
Bear themselves not without some touch of
   blame
— Else why the pother, scandal and outcry
Which trouble our peace and require chastise-
   ment?
We, for complicity in Pompilia's flight
And deviation, and carnal intercourse
With the same, do set aside and relegate
The Canon Caponsacchi for three years
At Civita in the neighborhood of Rome:
And we consign Pompilia to the care
Of a certain Sisterhood of penitents
I' the city's self, expert to deal with such."
Word for word, there's your judgment! Read
   it, lords,
Re-utter your deliberate penalty
For the crime yourselves establish! Your
   award —
Who chop a man's right-hand off at the wrist
For tracing with forefinger words in wine
O' the table of a drinking-booth that bear
Interpretation as they mocked the Church!
— Who brand a woman black between the
   breasts
For sinning by connection with a Jew:
While for the Jew's self — pudency be dumb! —
You mete out punishment such and such, yet so
Punish the adultery of wife and priest!
Take note of that, before the Molinists do,
And read me right the riddle, since right must
   be!
While I stood rapt away with wonderment,
Voices broke in upon my mood and muse.
"Do you sleep?" began the friends at either
   ear,
"The case is settled, — you willed it should be
   so —
None of our counsel, always recollect!
With law's award, budge! Back into your
   place!
Your betters shall arrange the rest for you.
We'll enter a new action, claim divorce:
Your marriage was a cheat themselves allow:
You erred i' the person, — might have married
   thus
Your sister or your daughter unaware.
We'll gain you, that way, liberty at least,
Sure of so much by law's own showing. Up
And off with you and your unluckiness —
Leave us to bury the blunder, sweep things
   smooth!"
I was in humble frame of mind, be sure!
I bowed, betook me to my place again.
Station by station I retraced the road,
Touched at this hostel, passed this post-house by,
Where, fresh-remembered yet, the fugitives
Had risen to the heroic stature: still —

"That was the bench they sat on, — there's
   the board
They took the meal at, — yonder garden-ground
They leaned across the gate of," — ever a word
O' the Helen and the Paris, with "Ha! you're
   he,
The . . . much-commiserated husband?"
   Step
By step, across the pelting, did I reach
Arezzo, underwent the archway's grin,
Traversed the length of sarcasm in the street,
Found myself in my horrible house once more,
And after a colloquy . . . no word assists!
With the mother and the brothers, stiffened me
Straight out from head to foot as dead man
   does,
And, thus prepared for life as he for hell,
Marched to the public Square and met the
   world.
Apologize for the pincers, palliate screws?
Ply me with such toy-trifles, I entreat!
Trust who has tried both sulphur and sops-in-
   wine!

I played the man as I best might, bade friends
Put non-essentials by and face the fact.
"What need to hang myself as you advise?
The paramour is banished, — the ocean's width,
Or the suburb's length, — to Ultima Thule, say,
Or Proxima Civitas, what's the odds of name
And place? He's banished, and the fact's the
   thing.
Why should law banish innocence an inch?
Here's guilt then, what else do I care to know?
The adulteress lies imprisoned, — whether in a
   well
With bricks above and a snake for company,
Or tied by a garter to a bedpost, — much
I mind what's little, — least's enough and to
   spare!
The little fillip on the coward's cheek
Serves as though crab-tree cudgel broke his
   pate.
Law has pronounced there's punishment, less
   or more:
And I take note o' the fact and use it thus —
For the first flaw in the original bond,
I claim release. My contract was to wed
The daughter of Pietro and Violante. Both
Protest they never had a child at all.
Then I have never made a contract: good!
Cancel me quick the thing pretended one.
I shall be free. What matter if hurried over
The harbor-boom by a great favoring tide,
Or the last of a spent ripple that lifts and
   leaves?
The Abate is about it. Laugh who wins!
You shall not laugh me out of faith in law!
I listen, through all your noise, to Rome!"
       Rome spoke.
In three months letters thence admonished me,
"Your plan for the divorce is all mistake.
It would hold, now, had you, taking thought to
   wed
Rachel of the blue eye and golden hair,
Found swarth-skinned Leah cumber couch
   next day:
But Rachel, blue-eyed golden-haired aright,

Proving to be only Laban's child, not Lot's,
Remains yours all the same forevermore.
No whit to the purpose is your plea : you err
I' the person and the quality — nowise
In the individual, — that 's the case in point !
You go to the ground, — are met by a cross-suit
For separation, of the Rachel here,
From bed and board, — she is the injured one,
You did the wrong and have to answer it.
As for the circumstance of imprisonment
And color it lends to this your new attack,
Never fear, that point is considered too !
The durance is already at an end ;
The convent-quiet preyed upon her health,
She is transferred now to her parents' house
— No-parents, when that cheats and plunders you,
But parentage again confessed in full,
When such confession pricks and plagues you more —
As now — for, this their house is not the house
In Via Vittoria wherein neighbors' watch
Might incommode the freedom of your wife,
But a certain villa smothered up in vines
At the town's edge by the gate i' the Pauline way,
Out of eye-reach, out of ear-shot, little and lone,
Whither a friend, — at Civita, we hope,
A good half-dozen-hours' ride off, — might, some eve,
Betake himself, and whence ride back, some morn,
Nobody the wiser : but be that as it may,
Do not afflict your brains with trifles now.
You have still three suits to manage, all and each
Ruinous truly should the event play false.
It is indeed the likelier so to do,
That brother Paul, your single prop and stay,
After a vain attempt to bring the Pope
To set aside procedures, sit himself
And summarily use prerogative,
Afford us the infallible finger's tact
To disentwine your tangle of affairs,
Paul, — finding it moreover past his strength
To stem the irruption, bear Rome's ridicule
Of . . . since friends must speak . . . to be round with you . . .
Of the old outwitted husband, wronged and wroth,
Pitted against a brace of juveniles —
A brisk priest who is versed in Ovid's art
More than his ' Summa,' and a gamesome wife
Able to act Corinna without book,
Beside the waggish parents who played dupes
To dupe the duper — (and truly divers scenes
Of the Arezzo palace, tickle rib
And tease eye till the tears come, so we laugh !
Nor wants the shock at the inn its comic force,
And then the letters and poetry — *merum sal !*)
— Paul, finally, in such a state of things,
After a brief temptation to go jump
And join the fishes in the Tiber, drowns
Sorrow another and a wiser way :
House and goods, he has sold all off, is gone,
Leaves Rome, — whether for France or Spain, who knows ?
Or Britain almost divided from our orb.

You have lost him anyhow."
          Now, — I see my lords
Shift in their seat, — would I could do the same !
They probably please expect my bile was moved
To purpose, nor much blame me : now, they judge,
The fiery titillation urged my flesh
Break through the bonds. By your pardon, no, sweet Sirs !
I got such missives in the public place ;
When I sought home, — with such news, mounted stair
And sat at last in the sombre gallery,
('T was Autumn, the old mother in bed betimes,
Having to bear that cold, the finer frame
Of her daughter-in-law had found intolerable —
The brother, walking misery away
O' the mountain-side with dog and gun belike,)
As I supped, ate the coarse bread, drank the wine
Weak once, now acrid with the toad's-head-squeeze,
My wife's bestowment, — I broke silence thus :
" Let me, a man, manfully meet the fact,
Confront the worst o' the truth, end, and have peace !
I am irremediably beaten here, —
The gross illiterate vulgar couple, — bah !
Why, they have measured forces, mastered mine,
Made me their spoil and prey from first to last.
They have got my name, — 't is nailed now fast to theirs,
The child or changeling is anyway my wife ;
Point by point as they plan they execute,
They gain all, and I lose all — even to the lure
That led to loss, — they have the wealth again
They hazarded awhile to hook me with,
Have caught the fish and find the bait entire :
They even have their child or changeling back
To trade with, turn to account a second time.
The brother, presumably might tell a tale
Or give a warning, — he, too, flies the field,
And with him vanish help and hope of help.
They have caught me in the cavern where I fell,
Covered my loudest cry for human aid
With this enormous paving-stone of shame.
Well, are we demigods or merely clay ?
Is success still attendant on desert ?
Is this, we live on, heaven and the final state,
Or earth which means probation to the end ?
Why claim escape from man's predestined lot
Of being beaten and baffled ? — God's decree,
In which I, bowing bruised head, acquiesce.
One of us Franceschini fell long since
I' the Holy Land, betrayed, tradition runs,
To Paynims by the feigning of a girl
He rushed to free from ravisher, and found
Lay safe enough with friends in ambuscade
Who flayed him while she clapped her hands
and laughed :
Let me end, falling by a like device.
It will not be so hard. I am the last
O' my line which will not suffer any more
I have attained to my full fifty years.

(About the average of us all, 't is said,
Though it seems longer to the unlucky man)
— Lived through my share of life; let all end
    here,
Me and the house and grief and shame at once.
Friends my informants, — I can bear your
    blow!"
And I believe 't was in no unmeet match
For the stoic's mood, with something like a
    smile,
That, when morose December roused me next,
I took into my hand, broke seal to read
The new epistle from Rome. "All to no use!
Whate'er the turn next injury take," smiled I,
"Here's one has chosen his part and knows
    his cue.
I am done with, dead now; strike away, good
    friends!
Are the three suits decided in a trice?
Against me, — there's no question! How does
    it go?
Is the parentage of my wife demonstrated
Infamous to her wish? Parades she now
Loosed of the cincture that so irked the loin?
Is the last penny extracted from my purse
To mulct me for demanding the first pound
Was promised in return for value paid?
Has the priest, with nobody to court beside,
Courted the Muse in exile, hitched my hap
Into a rattling ballad-rhyme which, bawled
At tavern-doors, wakes rapture everywhere,
And helps cheap wine down throat this Christ-
    mas time,
Beating the bagpipes? Any or all of these!
As well, good friends, you cursed my palace
    here
To its old cold stone face, — stuck your cap for
    crest
Over the shield that's extant in the Square, —
Or spat on the statue's cheek, the impatient
    world
Sees cumber tomb-top in our family church:
Let him creep under covert as I shall do,
Half below-ground already indeed. Good-by!
My brothers are priests, and childless so; that's
    well —
And, thank God most for this, no child leave
    I —
None after me to bear till his heart break
The being a Franceschini and my son!"

"Nay," said the letter, "but you have just
    that!
A babe, your veritable son and heir —
Lawful, — 't is only eight months since your
    wife
Left you, — so, son and heir, your babe was
    born
Last Wednesday in the villa, — you see the
    cause
For quitting Convent without beat of drum,
Stealing a hurried march to this retreat
That's not so savage as the Sisterhood
To slips and stumbles: Pietro's heart is soft,
Violante leans to pity's side, — the pair
Ushered you into life a bouncing boy:
And he's already hidden away and safe
From any claim on him you mean to make —

They need him for themselves, — don't fear,
    they know
The use o' the bantling, — the nerve thus laid
    bare
To nip at, new and nice, with finger-nail!"

Then I rose up like fire, and fire-like roared.
What, all is only beginning not ending now?
The worm which wormed its way from skin
    through flesh
To the bone and there lay biting, did its best, —
What, it goes on to scrape at the bone's self,
Will wind to inmost marrow and madden me?
There's to be yet my representative,
Another of the name shall keep displayed
The flag with the ordure on it, brandish still
The broken sword has served to stir a jakes?
Who will he be, how will you call the man?
A Franceschini, — when who cut my purse,
Filched my name, hemmed me round, hustled
    me hard
As rogues at a fair some fool they strip i' the
    midst,
When these count gains, vaunt pillage pres-
    ently: —
But a Caponsacchi, oh, be very sure!
When what demands its tribute of applause
Is the cunning and impudence o' the pair of
    cheats,
The lies and lust o' the mother, and the brave
Bold carriage of the priest, worthily crowned
By a witness to his feat i' the following age, —
And how this threefold cord could hook and
    fetch
And land leviathan that king of pride!
Or say, by some mad miracle of chance,
Is he indeed my flesh and blood, this babe?
Was it because fate forged a link at last
Betwixt my wife and me, and both alike
Found we had henceforth some one thing to
    love,
Was it when she could damn my soul indeed
She unlatched door, let all the devils o' the
    dark
Dance in on me to cover her escape?
Why then, the surplusage of disgrace, the
    spilth
Over and above the measure of infamy,
Failing to take effect on my coarse flesh
Seasoned with scorn now, saturate with
    shame, —
Is saved to instil on and corrode the brow,
The baby-softness of my first-born child —
The child I had died to see though in a dream,
The child I was bid strike out for, beat the
    wave
And baffle the tide of troubles where I swam,
So I might touch shore, lay down life at last
At the feet so dim and distant and divine
Of the apparition, as 't were Mary's babe
Had held, through night and storm, the torch
    aloft, —
Born now in very deed to bear this brand
On forehead and curse me who could not save!
Rather be the town-talk true, Square's jest,
    street's jeer
True, my own inmost heart's confession true,
And he the priest's bastard and none of mine!

Ay, there was cause for flight, swift flight and
    sure !
The husband gets unruly, breaks all bounds
When he encounters some familiar face,
Fashion of feature, brow and eyes and lips
Where he least looked to find them, — time to
    fly !
This bastard then, a nest for him is made,
As the manner is of vermin, in my flesh —
Shall I let the filthy pest buzz, flap and sting,
Busy at my vitals and, nor hand nor foot
Lift, but let be, lie still and rot resigned ?
No, I appeal to God, — what says himself,
How lessons Nature when I look to learn ?
Why, that I am alive, am still a man
With brain and heart and tongue and right-
    hand too —
Nay, even with friends, in such a cause as this,
To right me if I fail to take my right.
No more of law ; a voice beyond the law
Enters my heart, *Quis est pro Domino ?*

Myself, in my own Vittiano, told the tale
To my own serving-people summoned there :
Told the first half of it, scarce heard to end
By judges who got done with judgment quick
And clamored to go execute her 'hest —
Who cried, " Not one of us that dig your soil
And dress your vineyard, prune your olive-
    trees,
But would have brained the man debauched
    our wife,
And staked the wife whose lust allured the man,
And paunched the Duke, had it been possible,
Who ruled the land, yet barred us such re-
    venge ! "
I fixed on the first whose eyes caught mine,
    some four
Resolute youngsters with the heart still fresh,
Filled my purse with the residue o' the coin
Uncaught-up by my wife whom haste made
    blind,
Donned the first rough and rural garb I found,
Took whatsoever weapon came to hand,
And out we flung and on we ran or reeled
Romeward.   I have no memory of our way,
Only that, when at intervals the cloud
Of horror about me opened to let in life,
I listened to some song in the ear, some snatch
Of a legend, relic of religion, stray
Fragment of record very strong and old
Of the first conscience, the anterior right,
The God's-gift to mankind, impulse to quench
The antagonistic spark of hell and tread
Satan and all his malice into dust,
Declare to the world the one law, right is right.
Then the cloud re-encompassed me, and so
I found myself, as on the wings of winds,
Arrived : I was at Rome on Christmas Eve.

Festive bells — everywhere the Feast o' the
    Babe,
Joy upon earth, peace and good will to man !
I am baptized.   I started and let drop
The dagger.   " Where is it, his promised
    peace ? "
Nine days o' the Birth-Feast did I pause and
    pray

To enter into no temptation more.
I bore the hateful house, my brother's once,
Deserted, — let the ghost of social joy
Mock and make mouths at me from empty
    room
And idle door that missed the master's step, —
Bore the frank wonder of incredulous eyes,
As my own people watched without a word,
Waited, from where they huddled round the
    hearth
Black like all else, that nod so slow to come.
I stopped my ears even to the inner call
Of the dread duty, only heard the song
" Peace upon earth," saw nothing but the face
O' the Holy Infant and the halo there
Able to cover yet another face
Behind it, Satan's which I else should see.
But, day by day, joy waned and withered off :
The Babe's face, premature with peak and
    pine,
Sank into wrinkled ruinous old age,
Suffering and death, then mist-like disap-
    peared,
And showed only the Cross at end of all,
Left nothing more to interpose 'twixt me
And the dread duty, — for the angels' song,
" Peace upon earth," louder and louder pealed,
" O Lord, how long, how long be unavenged ? "
On the ninth day, this grew too much for man.
I started up — " Some end must be ! "   At
    once,
Silence : then, scratching like a death-watch-
    tick,
Slowly within my brain was syllabled,
" One more concession, one decisive way
And but one, to determine thee the truth, —
This way, in fine, I whisper in thy ear :
Now doubt, anon decide, thereupon act ! "

" That is a way, thou whisperest in my ear !
I doubt, I will decide, then act," said I —
Then beckoned my companions : " Time is
    come ! "

And so, all yet uncertain save the will
To do right, and the daring aught save leave
Right undone, I did find myself at last
I' the dark before the villa with my friends,
And made the experiment, the final test,
Ultimate chance that ever was to be
For the wretchedness inside.   I knocked — pro-
    nounced
The name, the predetermined touch for truth,
" What welcome for the wanderer ?   Open
    straight — "
To the friend, physician, friar upon his rounds,
Traveller belated, beggar lame and blind ?
No, but — " to Caponsacchi ! "   And the door
Opened.
          And then, — why, even then, I think,
I' the minute that confirmed my worst of
    fears,
Surely, — I pray God that I think aright ! —
Had but Pompilia's self, the tender thing
Who once was good and pure, was once my
    lamb
And lay in my bosom, had the well-known
    shape

Fronted me in the doorway, — stood there faint
With the recent pang, perhaps, of giving birth
To what might, though by miracle, seem my
    child, —
Nay more, I will say, had even the aged fool
Pietro, the dotard, in whom folly and age
Wrought, more than enmity or malevolence,
To practise and conspire against my peace, —
Had either of these but opened, I had paused.
But it was she the hag, she that brought hell
For a dowry with her to her husband's house,
She the mock-mother, she that made the
    match
And married me to perdition, spring and
    source
O' the fire inside me that boiled up from heart
To brain and hailed the Fury gave it birth, —
Violante Comparini, she it was,
With the old grin amid the wrinkles yet,
Opened : as if in turning from the Cross,
With trust to keep the sight and save my soul,
I had stumbled, first thing, on the serpent's
    head
Coiled with a leer at foot of it.
                            There was the end !
Then was I rapt away by the impulse, one
Immeasurable everlasting wave of a need
To abolish that detested life. 'T was done :
You know the rest and how the folds o' the
    thing,
Twisting for help, involved the other two
More or less serpent-like : how I was mad,
Blind, stamped on all, the earth-worms with
    the asp,
And ended so.
                    You came on me that night,
Your officers of justice, — caught the crime
In the first natural frenzy of remorse ?
Twenty miles off, sound sleeping as a child
On a cloak i' the straw which promised shelter
    first,
With the bloody arms beside me, — was it not
    so ?
Wherefore not ? Why, how else should I be
    found ?
I was my own self, had my sense again,
My soul safe from the serpents. I could sleep :
Indeed and, dear my lords, I shall sleep now,
Spite of my shoulder, in five minutes' space,
When you dismiss me, having truth enough !
It is but a few days are passed, I find,
Since this adventure. Do you tell me, four ?
Then the dead are scarce quiet where they lie,
Old Pietro, old Violante, side by side
At the church Lorenzo, — oh, they know it
    well !
So do I. But my wife is still alive,
Has breath enough to tell her story yet,
Her way, which is not mine, no doubt at all.
And Caponsacchi, you have summoned him, —
Was he so far to send for ? Not at hand ?
I thought some few o' the stabs were in his
    heart,
Or had not been so lavish : less had served.
Well, he too tells his story, — florid prose
As smooth as mine is rough. You see, my
    lords,
There will be a lying intoxicating smoke

Born of the blood, — confusion probably, —
For lies breed lies — but all that rests with
    you !
The trial is no concern of mine ; with me
The main of the care is over : I at least
Recognize who took that huge burden off,
Let me begin to live again. I did
God's bidding and man's duty, so, breathe
    free ;
Look you to the rest ! I heard Himself pre-
    scribe,
That great Physician, and dared lance the core
Of the bad ulcer ; and the rage abates,
I am myself and whole now : I proved cured
By the eyes that see, the ears that hear again,
The limbs that have relearned their youthful
    play,
The healthy taste of food and feel of clothes
And taking to our common life once more,
All that now urges my defence from death.
The willingness to live, what means it else ?
Before, — but let the very action speak !
Judge for yourselves, what life seemed worth
    to me
Who, not by proxy but in person, pitched
Head-foremost into danger as a fool
That never cares if he can swim or no —
So he but find the bottom, braves the brook.
No man omits precaution, quite neglects
Secrecy, safety, schemes not how retreat,
Having schemed he might advance. Did I so
    scheme ?
Why, with a warrant which 't is ask and have,
With horse thereby made mine without a word,
I had gained the frontier and slept safe that
    night.
Then, my companions, — call them what you
    please,
Slave or stipendiary, — what need of one
To me whose right-hand did its owner's work ?
Hire an assassin yet expose yourself ?
As well buy glove and then thrust naked hand
I' the thorn-bush. No, the wise man stays at
    home,
Sends only agents out, with pay to earn :
At home, when they come back, — he straight
    discards
Or else disowns. Why use such tools at all
When a man's foes are of his house, like mine,
Sit at his board, sleep in his bed ? Why noise,
When there 's the *acquetta* and the silent way ?
Clearly my life was valueless.

                            But now
Health is returned, and sanity of soul
Nowise indifferent to the body's harm.
I find the instinct bids me save my life ;
My wits, too, rally round me ; I pick up
And use the arms that strewed the ground be-
    fore,
Unnoticed or spurned aside : I take my stand,
Make my defence. God shall not lose a life
May do him further service, while I speak
And you hear, you my judges and last hope !
You are the law : 't is to the law I look.
I began life by hanging to the law,
To the law it is I hang till life shall end.
My brother made appeal to the Pope, 't is true

To stay proceedings, judge my cause himself
Nor trouble law, — some fondness of conceit
That rectitude, sagacity sufficed
The investigator in a case like mine,
Dispensed with the machine of law. The Pope
Knew better, set aside my brother's plea
And put me back to law, — referred the cause
Ad judices meos, — doubtlessly did well.
Here, then, I clutch my judges, — I claim law —
Cry, by the higher law whereof your law
O' the land is humbly representative, —
Cry, on what point is it, where either accuse,
I fail to furnish you defence? I stand
Acquitted, actually or virtually,
By every intermediate kind of court
That takes account of right or wrong in man,
Each unit in the series that begins
With God's throne, ends with the tribunal here.
God breathes, not speaks, his verdicts, felt not heard,
Passed on successively to each court I call
Man's conscience, custom, manners, all that make
More and more effort to promulgate, mark
God's verdict in determinable words,
Till last come human jurists — solidify
Fluid result, — what 's fixable lies forged,
Statute, — the residue escapes in fume,
Yet hangs aloft, a cloud, as palpable
To the finer sense as word the legist welds.
Justinian's Pandects only make precise
What simply sparkled in men's eyes before,
Twitched in their brow or quivered on their lip,
Waited the speech they called but would not come.
These courts then, whose decree your own confirms, —
Take my whole life, not this last act alone,
Look on it by the light reflected thence !
What has Society to charge me with ?
Come, unreservedly, — favor none nor fear, —
I am Guido Franceschini, am I not ?
You know the courses I was free to take ?
I took just that which let me serve the Church,
I gave it all my labor in body and soul
Till these broke down i' the service. "Specify ? "
Well, my last patron was a Cardinal.
I left him unconvicted of a fault —
Was even helped, by way of gratitude,
Into the new life that I left him for,
This very misery of the marriage, — he
Made it, kind soul, so far as in him lay —
Signed the deed where you yet may see his name.
He is gone to his reward, — dead, being my friend
Who could have helped here also, — that, of course !
So far, there 's my acquittal, I suppose.
Then comes the marriage itself — no question, lords,
Of the entire validity of that !
In the extremity of distress, 't is true,
For after-reasons, furnished abundantly,
I wished the thing invalid, went to you
Only some months since, set you duly forth

My wrong and prayed your remedy, that a cheat
Should not have force to cheat my whole life long.
"Annul a marriage? 'T is impossible !
Though ring about your neck be brass not gold,
Needs must it clasp, gangrene you all the same ! "
Well, let me have the benefit, just so far,
O' the fact announced, — my wife then is my wife,
I have allowance for a husband's right.
I am charged with passing right's due bound, — such acts
As I thought just, my wife called cruelty,
Complained of in due form, — convoked no court
Of common gossipry, but took her wrongs —
And not once, but so long as patience served —
To the town's top, jurisdiction's pride of place,
To the Archbishop and the Governor.
These heard her charge with my reply, and found
That futile, this sufficient : they dismissed
The hysteric querulous rebel, and confirmed
Authority in its wholesome exercise,
They, with directest access to the facts.
" — Ay, for it was their friendship favored you,
Hereditary alliance against a breach
I' the social order : prejudice for the name
Of Franceschini ! " — So I hear it said :
But not here. You, lords, never will you say
"Such is the nullity of grace and truth,
Such the corruption of the faith, such lapse
Of law, such warrant have the Molinists
For daring reprehend us as they do, —
That we pronounce it just a common case,
Two dignitaries, each in his degree
First, foremost, this the spiritual head, and that
The secular arm o' the body politic,
Should, for mere wrongs' love and injustice' sake,
Side with, aid and abet in cruelty
This broken beggarly noble, — bribed perhaps
By his watered wine and mouldy crust of bread —
Rather than that sweet tremulous flower-like wife
Who kissed their hands and curled about their feet
Looking the irresistible loveliness
In tears that takes man captive, turns " . . . enough !
Do you blast your predecessors ? What forbids
Posterity to trebly blast yourselves
Who set the example and instruct their tongue ?
You dreaded the crowd, succumbed to the popular cry,
Or else, would nowise seem defer thereto
And yield to public clamor though i' the right !
You ridded your eye of my unseemliness,
The noble whose misfortune wearied you, —
Or, what 's more probable, made common cause
With the cleric section, punished in myself
Maladroit uncomplaisant laity,
Defective in behavior to a priest
Who claimed the customary partnership
I' the house and the wife. Lords, any lie will serve !
Look to it, — or allow me freed so far !

Then I proceed a step, come with clean hands
Thus far, re-tell the tale told eight months since.
The wife, you allow so far, I have not wronged,
Has fled my roof, plundered me and decamped
In company with the priest her paramour :
And I gave chase, came up with, caught the two
At the wayside inn where both had spent the
     night,
Found them in flagrant fault, and found as well,
By documents with name and plan and date,
The fault was furtive then that 's flagrant now,
Their intercourse a long established crime.
I did not take the license law's self gives
To slay both criminals o' the spot at the time,
But held my hand, — preferred play prodigy
Of patience which the world calls cowardice,
Rather than seem anticipate the law
And cast discredit on its organs, — you.
So, to your bar I brought both criminals,
And made my statement : heard their counter-
     charge,
Nay, — their corroboration of my tale,
Nowise disputing its allegements, not
I' the main, not more than nature's decency
Compels men to keep silence in this kind, —
Only contending that the deeds avowed
Would take another color and bear excuse.
You were to judge between us ; so you did.
You disregard the excuse, you breathe away
The color of innocence and leave guilt black ;
" Guilty " is the decision of the court,
And that I stand in consequence untouched,
One white integrity from head to heel.
Not guilty ? Why then did you punish them ?
True, punishment has been inadequate —
'T is not I only, not my friends that joke,
My foes that jeer, who echo " inadequate " —
For, by a chance that comes to help for once,
The same case simultaneously was judged
At Arezzo, in the province of the Court
Where the crime had its beginning but not end.
They then, deciding on but half o' the crime,
The effraction, robbery, — features of the fault
I never cared to dwell upon at Rome, —
What was it they adjudged as penalty
To Pompilia, — the one criminal o' the pair
Amenable to their judgment, not the priest
Who is Rome's ? Why, just imprisonment for
     life
I' the Stinche. There was Tuscany's award
To a wife that robs her husband : you at
     Rome —
Having to deal with adultery in a wife
And, in a priest, breach of the priestly vow —
Give gentle sequestration for a month
In a manageable Convent, then release,
You call imprisonment, in the very house
O' the very couple, which the aim and end
Of the culprits' crime was — just to reach and
     rest
And there take solace and defy me : well, —
This difference 'twixt their penalty and yours
Is immaterial : make your penalty less —
Merely that she should henceforth wear black
     gloves
And white fan, she who wore the opposite —
Why, all the same the fact o' the thing sub-
     sists.

Reconcile to your conscience as you may,
Be it on your own heads, you pronounced but
     half
O' the penalty for heinousness like hers
And his, that pays a fault at Carnival
Of comfit-pelting past discretion's law,
Or accident to handkerchief in Lent
Which falls perversely as a lady kneels
Abruptly, and but half conceals her neck !
I acquiesce for my part : punished, though
By a pin-point scratch, means guilty : guilty
     means
— What have I been but innocent hitherto ?
Anyhow, here the offence, being punished
     ends.

Ends ? — for you deemed so, did you not, sweet
     lords ?
That was throughout the veritable aim
O' the sentence light or heavy, — to redress
Recognized wrong ? You righted me, I think ?
Well then, — what if I, at this last of all,
Demonstrate you, as my whole pleading proves
No particle of wrong received thereby
One atom of right ? — that cure grew worse dis-
     ease ?
That in the process you call " justice done "
All along you have nipped away just inch
By inch the creeping climbing length of plague
Breaking my tree of life from root to branch,
And left me, after all and every act
Of your interference, — lightened of what load
At liberty wherein ? Mere words and wind !
" Now I was saved, now I should feel no more
The hot breath, find a respite from fixed eye
And vibrant tongue ! " Why, scarce your back
     was turned,
There was the reptile, that feigned death at
     first,
Renewing its detested spire and spire
Around me, rising to such heights of hate
That, so far from mere purpose now to crush
And coil itself on the remains of me,
Body and mind, and there flesh fang content,
Its aim is now to evoke life from death,
Make me anew, satisfy in my son
The hunger I may feed but never sate,
Tormented on to perpetuity —
My son, whom dead, I shall know, understand,
Feel, hear, see, never more escape the sight
In heaven that 's turned to hell, or hell re-
     turned
(So rather say) to this same earth again, —
Moulded into the image and made one,
Fashioned of soul as featured like in face,
First taught to laugh and lisp and stand and
     go
By that thief, poisoner and adulteress
I call Pompilia, he calls . . . sacred name,
Be unpronounced, be unpolluted here !
And last led up to the glory and prize of hate
By his . . . foster-father, Caponsacchi's self,
The perjured priest, pink of conspirators,
Tricksters and knaves, yet polished, superfine,
Manhood to model adolescence by !
Lords, look on me, declare, — when, what I
     show,
Is nothing more nor less than what you deemed

And doled me out for justice, — what did you
  say ?
For reparation, restitution and more, —
Will you not thank, praise, bid me to your
  breasts
For having done the thing you thought to do,
And thoroughly trampled out sin's life at last ?
I have heightened phrase to make your soft
  speech serve,
Doubled the blow you but essayed to strike,
Carried into effect your mandate here
That else had fallen to ground : mere duty
  done,
Oversight of the master just supplied
By zeal i' the servant. I, being used to serve,
Have simply . . . what is it they charge me
  with ?
Blackened again, made legible once more
Your own decree, not permanently writ,
Rightly conceived but all too faintly traced.
It reads efficient, now, comminatory,
A terror to the wicked, answers so
The mood o' the magistrate, the mind of law.
Absolve, then, me, law's mere executant !
Protect your own defender, — save me, Sirs !
Give me my life, give me my liberty,
My good name and my civic rights again !
It would be too fond, too complacent play
Into the hands o' the devil, should we lose
The game here, I for God : a soldier-bee
That yields his life, exenterate with the stroke
O' the sting that saves the hive. I need that
  life.
Oh, never fear ! I 'll find life plenty use
Though it should last five years more, aches
  and all !
For, first thing, there 's the mother's age to
  help —
Let her come break her heart upon my breast,
Not on the blank stone of my nameless tomb !
The fugitive brother has to be bidden back
To the old routine, repugnant to the tread,
Of daily suit and service to the Church, —
Through gibe and jest, those stones that Shi-
  mei flung !
Ay, and the spirit-broken youth at home,
The awe-struck altar-ministrant, shall make
Amends for faith now palsied at the source,
Shall see truth yet triumphant, justice yet
A victor in the battle of this world !
Give me — for last, best gift — my son again,
Whom law makes mine, — I take him at your
  word,
Mine be he, by miraculous mercy, lords !
Let me lift up his youth and innocence
To purify my palace, room by room
Purged of the memories, lend from his bright
  brow
Light to the old proud paladin my sire
Shrunk now for shame into the darkest shade
O' the tapestry, showed him once and shrouds
  him now !
Then may we, — strong from that rekindled
  smile, —
Go forward, face new times, the better day.
And when, in times made better through your
  brave
Decision now, — might but Utopia be ! —

Rome rife with honest women and strong men,
Manners reformed, old habits back once more,
Customs that recognize the standard worth, —
The wholesome household rule in force again, —
Husbands once more God's representative,
Wives like the typical Spouse once more, and
  Priests
No longer men of Belial, with no aim
At leading silly women captive, but
Of rising to such duties as yours now, —
Then will I set my son at my right-hand
And tell his father's story to this point,
Adding, " The task seemed superhuman, still
I dared and did it, trusting God and law :
And they approved of me : give praise to
  both ! "
And if, for answer, he shall stoop to kiss
My hand, and peradventure start thereat, —
I engage to smile, " That was an accident
I' the necessary process, — just a trip
O' the torture-irons in their search for truth, —
Hardly misfortune, and no fault at all."

VI

GIUSEPPE CAPONSACCHI

Answer you, Sirs ? Do I understand aright ?
Have patience ! In this sudden smoke from
  hell, —
So things disguise themselves. — I cannot see
My own hand held thus broad before my face
And know it again. Answer you ? Then that
  means
Tell over twice what I, the first time, told
Six months ago : 't was here, I do believe,
Fronting you same three in this very room,
I stood and told you : yet now no one laughs,
Who then . . . nay, dear my lords, but laugh
  you did,
As good as laugh, what in a judge we style
Laughter — no levity, nothing indecorous, lords !
Only, — I think I apprehend the mood :
There was the blameless shrug, permissible
  smirk,
The pen's pretence at play with the pursed
  mouth,
The titter stifled in the hollow palm
Which rubbed the eyebrow and caressed the
  nose,
When I first told my tale : they meant, you
  know,
" The sly one, all this we are bound believe !
Well, he can say no other than what he says.
We have been young, too, — come, there 's
  greater guilt !
Let him but decently disembroil himself,
Scramble from out the scrape nor move the
  mud, —
We solid ones may risk a finger-stretch ! "
And now you sit as grave, stare as aghast
As if I were a phantom : now 't is — " Friend,
Collect yourself!" —no laughing matter more —
" Counsel the Court in this extremity,
Tell us again ! " — tell that, for telling which,
I got the jocular piece of punishment,
Was sent to lounge a little in the place

Whence now of a sudden here you summon me
To take the intelligence from just — your lips !
You, Judge Tommati, who then tittered most, —
That she I helped eight months since to escape
Her husband, was retaken by the same,
Three days ago, if I have seized your sense, —
(I being disallowed to interfere,
Meddle or make in a matter none of mine,
For you and law were guardians quite enough
O' the innocent, without a pert priest's help) —
And that he has butchered her accordingly,
As she foretold and as myself believed, —
And, so foretelling and believing so,
We were punished, both of us, the merry way:
Therefore, tell once again the tale ! For what ?
Pompilia is only dying while I speak !
Why does the mirth hang fire and miss the
    smile ?
My masters, there 's an old book, you should con
For strange adventures, applicable yet,
'T is stuffed with. Do you know that there was
    once
This thing : a multitude of worthy folk
Took recreation, watched a certain group
Of soldiery intent upon a game, —
How first they wrangled, but soon fell to play,
Threw dice, — the best diversion in the world.
A word in your ear, — they are now casting lots,
Ay, with that gesture quaint and cry uncouth,
For the coat of One murdered an hour ago !
I am a priest, — talk of what I have learned.
Pompilia is bleeding out her life belike,
Gasping away the latest breath of all,
This minute, while I talk — not while you
    laugh.

Yet, being sobered now, what is it you ask
By way of explanation ? There 's the fact !
It seems to fill the universe with sight
And sound, — from the four corners of this
    earth
Tells itself over, to my sense at least.
But you may want it lower set i' the scale, —
Too vast, too close it clangs in the ear, perhaps ;
You 'd stand back just to comprehend it more.
Well then, let me, the hollow rock, condense
The voice o' the sea and wind, interpret you
The mystery of this murder. God above !
It is too paltry, such a transference
O' the storm's roar to the cranny of the stone !

This deed, you saw begin — why does its end
Surprise you ? Why should the event enforce
The lesson, we ourselves learned, she and I,
From the first o' the fact, and taught you, all
    in vain ?
This Guido from whose throat you took my
    grasp,
Was this man to be favored, now, or feared,
Let do his will, or have his will restrained,
In the relation with Pompilia ? — say !
Did any other man need interpose
— Oh, though first comer, though as strange at
    the work
As fribble must be, coxcomb, fool that 's near
To knave as, say, a priest who fears the world —
Was he bound brave the peril, save the doomed,
Or go on, sing his snatch and pluck his flower,

Keep the straight path and let the victim die ?
I held so ; you decided otherwise,
Saw no such peril, therefore no such need
To stop song, loosen flower, and leave path.
    Law,
Law was aware and watching, would suffice,
Wanted no priest's intrusion, palpably
Pretence, too manifest a subterfuge !
Whereupon I, priest, coxcomb, fribble and fool,
Ensconced me in my corner, thus rebuked,
A kind of culprit, over-zealous hound
Kicked for his pains to kennel ; I gave place
To you, and let the law reign paramount :
I left Pompilia to your watch and ward,
And now you point me — there and thus she
    lies !

Men, for the last time, what do you want with
    me ?
Is it, — you acknowledge, as it were, a use,
A profit in employing me ? — at length
I may conceivably help the august law ?
I am free to break the blow, next hawk that
    swoops
On next dove, nor miss much of good repute ?
Or what if this your summons, after all,
Be but the form of mere release, no more,
Which turns the key and lets the captive go ?
I have paid enough in person at Civita,
Am free, — what more need I concern me with ?
Thank you ! I am rehabilitated then,
A very reputable priest. But she —
The glory of life, the beauty of the world,
The splendor of heaven, . . . well, Sirs, does
    no one move ?
Do I speak ambiguously ? The glory, I say,
And the beauty, I say, and splendor, still say I,
Who, priest and trained to live my whole life
    long
On beauty and splendor, solely at their source,
God, — have thus recognized my food in her,
You tell me, that 's fast dying while we talk,
Pompilia ! How does lenity to me
Remit one death-bed pang to her ? Come,
    smile !
The proper wink at the hot-headed youth
Who lets his soul show, through transparent
    words,
The mundane love that 's sin and scandal too !
You are all struck acquiescent now, it seems :
It seems the oldest, gravest signor here,
Even the redoubtable Tommati, sits
Chopfallen, — understands how law might take
Service like mine, of brain and heart and hand,
In good part. Better late than never, law !
You understand of a sudden, gospel too
Has a claim here, may possibly pronounce
Consistent with my priesthood, worthy Christ,
That I endeavored to save Pompilia ?

                                Then,
You were wrong, you see: that 's well to see,
    though late :
That 's all we may expect of man, this side
The grave: his good is — knowing he is bad:
Thus will it be with us when the books ope
And we stand at the bar on judgment-day.
Well then, I have a mind to speak, see cause

To relume the quenched flax by this dreadful
        light,
Burn my soul out in showing you the truth.
I heard, last time I stood here to be judged,
What is priest's-duty, — labor to pluck tares
And weed the corn of Molinism; let me
Make you hear, this time, how, in such a case,
Man, be he in the priesthood or at plough,
Mindful of Christ or marching step by step
With . . . what 's his style, the other potentate
Who bids have courage and keep honor safe,
Nor let minuter admonition tease ? —
How he is bound, better or worse, to act.
Earth will not end through this misjudgment,
        no !
For you and the others like you sure to come,
Fresh work is sure to follow, — wickedness
That wants withstanding. Many a man of blood,
Many a man of guile will clamor yet,
Bid you redress his grievance, — as he clutched
The prey, forsooth a stranger stepped between,
And there 's the good gripe in pure waste ! My
        part
Is done ; i' the doing it, I pass away
Out of the world. I want no more with earth.
Let me, in heaven's name, use the very snuff
O' the taper in one last spark shall show truth
For a moment, show Pompilia who was true !
Not for her sake, but yours : if she is dead,
Oh, Sirs, she can be loved by none of you
Most or least priestly ! Saints, to do us good,
Must be in heaven, I seem to understand :
We never find them saints before, at least.
Be her first prayer then presently for you —
She has done the good to me . . .
                        What is all this ?
There, I was born, have lived, shall die, a fool !
This is a foolish outset : — might with cause
Give color to the very lie o' the man,
The murderer, — make as if I loved his wife
In the way he called love. He is the fool
        there !
Why, had there been in me the touch of taint,
I had picked up so much of knaves'-policy
As hide it, keep one hand pressed on the place
Suspected of a spot would damn us both.
Or no, not her ! — not even if any of you
Dares think that I, i' the face of death, her
        death
That 's in my eyes and ears and brain and heart,
Lie, — if he does, let him ! I mean to say,
So he stop there, stay thought from smirching
        her
The snow-white soul that angels fear to take
Untenderly. But, all the same, I know
I too am taintless, and I bare my breast.
You can't think, men as you are, all of you,
But that, to hear thus suddenly such an end
Of such a wonderful white soul, that comes
Of a man and murderer calling the white black,
Must shake me, trouble and disadvantage.
        Sirs,
Only seventeen !

        Why, good and wise you are !
You might at the beginning stop my mouth :
So, none would be to speak for her, that knew.
I talk impertinently, and you bear,

All the same. This it is to have to do
With honest hearts : they easily may err,
But in the main they wish well to the truth.
You are Christians ; somehow, no one ever
        plucked
A rag, even, from the body of the Lord,
To wear and mock with, but, despite himself,
He looked the greater and was the better.
        Yes,
I shall go on now. Does she need or not
I keep calm ? Calm I 'll keep as monk that
        croons
Transcribing battle, earthquake, famine,
        plague,
From parchment to his cloister's chronicle.
Not one word more from the point now !

                        I begin.
Yes, I am one of your body and a priest.
Also I am a younger son o' the House
Oldest now, greatest once, in my birth-town
Arezzo, I recognize no equal there —
(I want all arguments, all sorts of arms
That seem to serve, — use this for a reason,
        wait !)
Not therefore thrust into the Church, because
O' the piece of bread one gets there. We were
        first
Of Fiesole, that rings still with the fame
Of Capo-in-Sacco our progenitor :
When Florence ruined Fiesole, our folk
Migrated to the victor-city, and there
Flourished, — our palace and our tower attest,
In the Old Mercato, — this was years ago,
Four hundred, full, — no, it wants fourteen just.
Our arms are those of Fiesole itself,
The shield quartered with white and red : a
        branch
Are the Salviati of us, nothing more.
That were good help to the Church ? But
        better still —
Not simply for the advantage of my birth
I' the way of the world, was I proposed for
        priest ;
But because there 's an illustration, late
I' the day, that 's loved and looked to as a
        saint
Still in Arezzo, he was bishop of,
Sixty years since : he spent to the last doit
His bishop's-revenue among the poor,
And used to tend the needy and the sick,
Barefoot, because of his humility.
He it was, — when the Granduke Ferdinand
Swore he would raze our city, plough the place
And sow it with salt, because we Aretines
Had tied a rope about the neck, to hale
The statue of his father from its base
For hate's sake, — he availed by prayers and
        tears
To pacify the Duke and save the town.
This was my father's father's brother. You see,
For his sake, how it was I had a right
To the selfsame office, bishop in the egg,
So, grew i' the garb and prattled in the school,
Was made expect, from infancy almost,
The proper mood o' the priest ; till time ran by
And brought the day when I must read the
        vows.

Declare the world renounced, and undertake
To become priest and leave probation, — leap
Over the ledge into the other life,
Having gone trippingly hitherto up to the height
O'er the wan water. Just a vow to read !

I stopped short awe-struck. " How shall holiest
    flesh
Engage to keep such vow inviolate,
How much less mine ? I know myself too
    weak,
Unworthy ! Choose a worthier stronger man ! "
And the very Bishop smiled and stopped my
    mouth
In its mid-protestation. " Incapable ?
Qualmish of conscience ? Thou ingenuous boy !
Clear up the clouds and cast thy scruples far !
I satisfy thee there 's an easier sense
Wherein to take such vow than suits the first
Rough rigid reading. Mark what makes all
    smooth,
Nay, has been even a solace to myself !
The Jews who needs must, in their synagogue,
Utter sometimes the holy name of God,
A thing their superstition boggles at,
Pronounce aloud the ineffable sacrosanct, —
How does their shrewdness help them ? In this
    wise ;
Another set of sounds they substitute,
Jumble so consonants and vowels — how
Should I know ? — that there grows from out
    the old
Quite a new word that means the very same —
And o'er the hard place slide they with a smile.
Giuseppe Maria Caponsacchi mine,
Nobody wants you in these latter days
To prop the Church by breaking your back-
    bone, —
As the necessary way was once, we know,
When Diocletian flourished and his like.
That building of the buttress-work was done
By martyrs and confessors : let it bide,
Add not a brick, but, where you see a chink,
Stick in a sprig of ivy or root a rose
Shall make amends and beautify the pile !
We profit as you were the painfullest
O' the martyrs, and you prove yourself a match
For the cruellest confessor ever was,
If you march boldly up and take your stand
Where their blood soaks, their bones yet strew
    the soil,
And cry ' Take notice, I the young and free
And well-to-do i' the world, thus leave the
    world,
Cast in my lot thus with no gay young world
But the grand old Church : she tempts me of
    the two ! '
Renounce the world ? Nay, keep and give it us !
Let us have you, and boast of what you bring.
We want the pick o' the earth to practise with,
Not its offscouring, halt and deaf and blind
In soul and body. There 's a rubble-stone
Unfit for the front o' the building, stuff to stow
In a gap behind and keep us weather-tight ;
There 's porphyry for the prominent place.
    Good lack !
Saint Paul has had enough and to spare, I trow,
Of ragged runaway Onesimus :

He wants the right-hand with the signet-ring
Of King Agrippa, now, to shake and use.
I have a heavy scholar cloistered up,
Close under lock and key, kept at his task
Of letting Fénelon know the fool he is,
In a book I promise Christendom next Spring.
Why, if he covets so much meat, the clown,
As a lark's wing next Friday, or, any day,
Diversion beyond catching his own fleas,
He shall be properly swinged, I promise him.
But you, who are so quite another paste
Of a man, — do you obey me ? Cultivate
Assiduous that superior gift you have
Of making madrigals — (who told me ? Ah !)
Get done a Marinesque Adoniad straight
With a pulse o' the blood a-pricking, here and
    there,
That I may tell the lady, ' And he 's ours ! ' "

So I became a priest : those terms changed all,
I was good enough for that, nor cheated so ;
I could live thus and still hold head erect.
Now you see why I may have been before
A fribble and coxcomb, yet, as priest, break
    word
Nowise, to make you disbelieve me now.
I need that you should know my truth. Well,
    then,
According to prescription did I live,
— Conformed myself, both read the breviary
And wrote the rhymes, was punctual to my
    place
I' the Pieve, and as diligent at my post
Where beauty and fashion rule. I throve apace,
Sub-deacon, Canon, the authority
For delicate play at tarocs, and arbiter
O' the magnitude of fan-mounts : all the while
Wanting no whit the advantage of a hint
Benignant to the promising pupil, — thus :
" Enough attention to the Countess now,
The young one ; 't is her mother rules the roast,
We know where, and puts in a word : go pay
Devoir to-morrow morning after mass !
Break that rash promise to preach, Passion-
    week !
Has it escaped you the Archbishop grunts
And snuffles when one grieves to tell his
    Grace
No soul dares treat the subject of the day
Since his own masterly handling it (ha, ha !)
Five years ago, — when somebody could help
And touch up an odd phrase in time of need,
(He, he !) — and somebody helps you, my son !
Therefore, don't prove so indispensable
At the Pieve, sit more loose i' the seat, nor
    grow
A fixture by attendance morn and eve !
Arezzo 's just a haven midway Rome —
Rome 's the eventual harbor, — make for port,
Crowd sail, crack cordage ! And your cargo
    be
A polished presence, a genteel manner, wit
At will, and tact at every pore of you !
I sent our lump of learning, Brother Clout,
And Father Slouch, our piece of piety,
To see Rome and try suit the Cardinal.
Thither they clump-clumped, beads and book
    in hand,

And ever since 't is meat for man and maid
How both flopped down, prayed blessing on
    bent pate
Bald many an inch beyond the tonsure's need,
Never once dreaming, the two moony dolts,
There 's nothing moves his Eminence so much
As — far from all this awe at sanctitude —
Heads that wag, eyes that twinkle, modified
    mirth
At the closet-lectures on the Latin tongue
A lady learns so much by, we know where.
Why, body o' Bacchus, you should crave his
    rule
For pauses in the elegiac couplet, chasms
Permissible only to Catullus! There!
Now go to duty : brisk, break Priscian's head
By reading the day's office — there 's no help.
You 've Ovid in your poke to plaster that ;
Amen 's at the end of all : then sup with me ! "

Well, after three or four years of this life,
In prosecution of my calling, I
Found myself at the theatre one night
With a brother Canon, in a mood and mind
Proper enough for the place, amused or no :
When I saw enter, stand, and seat herself
A lady, young, tall, beautiful, strange and sad.
It was as when, in our cathedral once,
As I got yawningly through matin-song,
I saw *facchini* bear a burden up,
Base it on the high-altar, break away
A board or two, and leave the thing inside
Lofty and lone : and lo, when next I looked,
There was the Rafael ! I was still one stare,
When — " Nay, I 'll make her give you back
    your gaze " —
Said Canon Conti ; and at the word he tossed
A paper-twist of comfits to her lap,
And dodged and in a trice was at my back
Nodding from over my shoulder. Then she
    turned,
Looked our way, smiled the beautiful sad
    strange smile.
" Is not she fair ? 'T is my new cousin," said
    he :
" The fellow lurking there i' the black o' the
    box
Is Guido, the old scapegrace : she 's his wife,
Married three years since : how his Countship
    sulks !
He has brought little back from Rome beside,
After the bragging, bullying. A fair face,
And — they do say — a pocketful of gold
When he can worry both her parents dead.
I don't go much there, for the chamber 's cold
And the coffee pale. I got a turn at first
Paying my duty : I observed they crouched
— The two old frightened family spectres —
    close
In a corner, each on each like mouse on mouse
I' the cat's cage : ever since, I stay at home.
Hallo, there 's Guido, the black, mean and
    small,
Bends his brows on us — please to bend your
    own
On the shapely nether limbs of Light-skirts
    there
By way of a diversion ! I was a fool

To fling the sweetmeats. Prudence, for God's
    love !
To-morrow I 'll make my peace, c'en tell some
    fib,
Try if I can't find means to take you there."

That night and next day did the gaze endure,
Burnt to my brain, as sunbeam through shut
    eyes,
And not once changed the beautiful sad strange
    smile.
At vespers Conti leaned beside my seat
I' the choir, — part said, part sung — " *In ex-cel
sis* —
All 's to no purpose ; I have louted low,
But he saw you staring — *quia sub* — don't in
    cline
To know you nearer ; him we would not hold
For Hercules, — the man would lick your shoe
If you and certain efficacious friends
Managed him warily, — but there 's the wife :
Spare her, because he beats her, as it is,
She 's breaking her heart quite fast enough —
    jam tu —
So, be you rational and make amends
With little Light-skirts yonder — *in secula
Secu-lo-o-o-rum*. Ah, you rogue ! Every one
    knows
What great dame she makes jealous : one
    against one,
Play, and win both ! "
        Sirs, ere the week was out,
I saw and said to myself, " Light-skirts hides
    teeth
Would make a dog sick, — the great dame
    shows spite
Should drive a cat mad : 't is but poor work
    this —
Counting one's fingers till the sonnet 's crowned.
I doubt much if Marino really be
A better bard than Dante after all.
'T is more amusing to go pace at eve
I' the Duomo, — watch the day's last gleam
    outside
Turn, as into a skirt of God's own robe,
Those lancet-windows' jewelled miracle, —
Than go eat the Archbishop's ortolans,
Digest his jokes. Luckily Lent is near :
Who cares to look will find me in my stall
At the Pieve, constant to this faith at least —
Never to write a canzonet any more."

So, next week, 't was my patron spoke abrupt,
In altered guise, " Young man, can it be true
That after all your promise of sound fruit,
You have kept away from Countess young or
    old
And gone play truant in church all day long ?
Are you turning Molinist ? " I answered
    quick :
" Sir, what if I turned Christian ? It might be.
The fact is, I am troubled in my mind,
Beset and pressed hard by some novel thoughts.
This your Arezzo is a limited world ;
There 's a strange Pope, — 't is said, a priest
    who thinks.
Rome is the port, you say : to Rome I go.
I will live alone, one does so in a crowd,

And look into my heart a little." "Lent
Ended," — I told friends, — "I shall go to
Rome."

One evening I was sitting in a muse
Over the opened "Summa," darkened round
By the mid-March twilight, thinking how my
life
Had shaken under me, — broke short indeed
And showed the gap 'twixt what is, what
should be, —
And into what abysm the soul may slip,
Leave aspiration here, achievement there,
Lacking omnipotence to connect extremes —
Thinking moreover . . . oh, thinking, if you
like,
How utterly dissociated was I
A priest and celibate, from the sad strange
wife
Of Guido, — just as an instance to the point,
Naught more, — how I had a whole store of
strengths
Eating into my heart, which craved employ,
And she, perhaps, need of a finger's help, —
And yet there was no way in the wide world
To stretch out mine and so relieve myself, —
How when the page o' the "Summa" preached
its best,
Her smile kept glowing out of it, as to mock
The silence we could break by no one word, —
There came a tap without the chamber-door,
And a whisper, when I bade who tapped speak
out,
And, in obedience to my summons, last
In glided a masked muffled mystery,
Laid lightly a letter on the opened book,
Then stood with folded arms and foot demure,
Pointing as if to mark the minutes' flight.

I took the letter, read to the effect
That she, I lately flung the comfits to,
Had a warm heart to give me in exchange,
And gave it, — loved me and confessed it thus,
And bade me render thanks by word of mouth,
Going that night to such a side o' the house
Where the small terrace overhangs a street
Blind and deserted, not the street in front:
Her husband being away, the surly patch,
At his villa of Vittiano.

                    " And you ? " — I asked:
" What may you be ? " " Count Guido's kind of
maid —
Most of us have two functions in his house.
We all hate him, the lady suffers much,
'T is just we show compassion, furnish help,
Specially since her choice is fixed so well.
What answer may I bring to cheer the sweet
Pompilia ? "

                    Then I took a pen and wrote:
" No more of this ! That you are fair, I know:
But other thoughts now occupy my mind.
I should not thus have played the insensible
Once on a time. What made you — may one
ask —
Marry your hideous husband ? 'T was a fault,
And now you taste the fruit of it. Farewell."

" There ! " smiled I as she snatched it and was
gone —
" There, let the jealous miscreant, — Guido's
self,
Whose mean soul grins through this transparent
trick, —
Be balked so far, defrauded of his aim !
What fund of satisfaction to the knave,
Had I kicked this his messenger down stairs,
Trussed to the middle of her impudence,
And set his heart at ease so ! No, indeed !
There 's the reply which he shall turn and twist
At pleasure, snuff at till his brain grow drunk,
As the bear does when he finds a scented glove
That puzzles him, — a hand and yet no hand,
Of other perfume than his own foul paw !
Last month, I had doubtless chosen to play the
dupe,
Accepted the mock-invitation, kept
The sham appointment, cudgel beneath cloak,
Prepared myself to pull the appointer's self
Out of the window from his hiding-place
Behind the gown of this part-messenger
Part-mistress who would personate the wife.
Such had seemed once a jest permissible :
Now, I am not i' the mood."

                    Back next morn brought
The messenger, a second letter in hand.
"You are cruel, Thyrsis, and Myrtilla moans
Neglected but adores you, makes request
For mercy : why is it you dare not come ?
Such virtue is scarce natural to your age :
You must love some one else ; I hear you do,
The Baron's daughter or the Advocate's wife,
Or both, — all 's one, would you make me the
third —
I take the crumbs from table gratefully
Nor grudge who feasts there. 'Faith, I blush
and blaze !
Yet if I break all bounds, there 's reason sure.
Are you determinedly bent on Rome ?
I am wretched here, a monster tortures me :
Carry me with you ! Come and say you will !
Concert this very evening ! Do not write !
I am ever at the window of my room
Over the terrace, at the *Ave*. Come ! "

I questioned — lifting half the woman's mask
To let her smile loose. " So, you gave my
line
To the merry lady ? " "She kissed off the
wax,
And put what paper was not kissed away
In her bosom to go burn: but merry, no !
She wept all night when evening brought no
friend,
Alone, the unkind missive at her breast ;
Thus Philomel, the thorn at her breast too,
Sings " . . . " Writes this second letter ? "
" Even so !
Then she may peep at vespers forth ? " —
" What risk
Do we run o' the husband ? " — " Ah, — no
risk at all !
He is more stupid even than jealous. Ah —
That was the reason ? Why, the man 's away !
Beside, his bugbear is that friend of yours,
Fat little Canon Conti. He fears him

How should he dream of you? I told you
    truth:
He goes to the villa at Vittiano — 't is
The time when Spring-sap rises in the vine —
Spends the night there. And then his wife 's a
    child:
Does he think a child outwits him? A mere
    child:
Yet so full-grown, a dish for any duke.
Don't quarrel longer with such cates, but
    come! "

I wrote, " In vain do you solicit me.
I am a priest: and you are wedded wife,
Whatever kind of brute your husband prove.
I have scruples, in short. Yet should you
    really show
Sign at the window . . . but nay, best be
    good!
My thoughts are elsewhere." — " Take her
    that! "
                   — " Again
Let the incarnate meanness, cheat and spy,
Mean to the marrow of him, make his heart
His food, anticipate hell's worm once more!
Let him watch shivering at the window — ay,
And let this hybrid, this his light-of-love
And lackey-of-lies, — a sage economy, —
Paid with embracings for the rank brass
    coin, —
Let her report and make him chuckle o'er
The breakdown of my resolution now,
And lour at disappointment in good time!
— So tantalize and so enrage by turns,
Until the two fall each on the other like
Two famished spiders, as the coveted fly.
That toys long, leaves their net and them at
    last! "

And so the missives followed thick and fast
For a month, say, — I still came at every turn
On the soft sly adder, endlong 'neath my tread.
I was met i' the street, made sign to in the
    church,
A slip was found i' the door-sill, scribbled word
'Twixt page and page o' the prayer-book in my
    place.
A crumpled thing dropped even before my feet,
Pushed through the blind, above the terrace-
    rail,
As I passed, by day, the very window once.
And ever from corners would be peering up
The messenger, with the selfsame demand,
"Obdurate still, no flesh but adamant?
Nothing to cure the wound, assuage the throe
O' the sweetest lamb that ever loved a bear? "
And ever my one answer in one tone —
"Go your ways, temptress! Let a priest read,
    pray,
Unplagued of vain talk, visions not for him!
In the end, you'll have your will and ruin
    me! "

One day, a variation: thus I read:
" You have gained little by timidity.
My husband has found out my love at length,
Sees cousin Conti was the stalking-horse,
And you the game he covered, poor fat soul!

My husband is a formidable foe,
Will stick at nothing to destroy you. Stand
Prepared, or better, run till you reach Rome!
I bade you visit me, when the last place
My tyrant would have turned suspicious at,
Or cared to seek you in, was . . . why say,
    where?
But now all 's changed: beside, the season 's
    past
At the villa, — wants the master's eye no more.
Anyhow, I beseech you, stay away
From the window! He might well be posted
    there."

I wrote — " You raise my courage, or call up
My curiosity, who am but man.
Tell him he owns the palace, not the street
Under — that 's his and yours and mine alike,
If it should please me pad the path this eve,
Guido will have two troubles, first to get
Into a rage and then get out again.
Be cautious, though: at the *Ave!* "
                   You of the court
When I stood question here and reached this
    point
O' the narrative, — search notes and see and say
If some one did not interpose with smile
And sneer, " And prithee why so confident
That the husband must, of all needs, not the
    wife,
Fabricate thus, — what if the lady loved?
What if she wrote the letters? "
                   Learned Sir,
I told you there 's a picture in our church.
Well, if a low-browed verger sidled up
Bringing me, like a blotch, on his prod's point,
A transfixed scorpion, let the reptile writhe,
And then said, " See a thing that Rafael
    made —
This venom issued from Madonna's mouth! "
I should reply, " Rather, the soul of you
Has issued from your body, like from like,
By way of the ordure-corner! "
                   But no less,
I tired of the same long black teasing lie
Obtruded thus at every turn; the pest
Was far too near the picture, anyhow:
One does Madonna service, making clowns
Remove their dung-heap from the sacristy.
" I will to the window, as he tempts," said I:
" Yes, whom the easy love has failed allure,
This new bait of adventure tempts, — thinks
    he.
Though the imprisoned lady keeps afar,
There will they lie in ambush, heads alert,
Kith, kin, and Count mustered to bite my heel.
No mother nor brother viper of the brood
Shall scuttle off without the instructive
    bruise! "

So I went: crossed street and street: " The
    next street's turn,
I stand beneath the terrace, see, above,
The black of the ambush-window. Then, in
    place
Of hand's throw of soft prelude over lute,
And cough that clears way for the ditty
    last," --

I began to laugh already — " he will have
' Out of the hole you hide in, on to the front,
Count Guido Franceschini, show yourself!
Hear what a man thinks of a thing like you,
And after, take this foulness in your face ! ' "

The words lay living on my lip, I made
The one turn more — and there at the window
 stood,
Framed in its black square length, with lamp
 in hand,
Pompilia ; the same great, grave, griefful air
As stands i' the dusk, on altar that I know,
Left alone with one moonbeam in her cell,
Our Lady of all the Sorrows. Ere I knelt —
Assured myself that she was flesh and blood —
She had looked one look and vanished.
     I thought — " Just so :
It was herself, they have set her there to
 watch —
Stationed to see some wedding-band go by,
On fair pretence that she must bless the bride,
Or wait some funeral with friends wind past,
And crave peace for the corpse that claims its
 due.
She never dreams they used her for a snare,
And now withdraw the bait has served its turn.
Well done, the husband, who shall fare the
 worse ! "
And on my lip again was — " Out with thee,
Guido ! " When all at once she reappeared ;
But, this time, on the terrace overhead,
So close above me, she could almost touch
My head if she bent down ; and she did bend,
While I stood still as stone, all eye, all ear.

She began — " You have sent me letters, Sir :
I have read none, I can neither read nor write ;
But she you gave them to, a woman here,
One of the people in whose power I am,
Partly explained their sense, I think, to me
Obliged to listen while she inculcates
That you, a priest, can dare love me, a wife,
Desire to live or die as I shall bid,
(She makes me listen,if I will or no)
Because you saw my face a single time.
It cannot be she says the thing you mean ;
Such wickedness were deadly to us both :
But good true love would help me now so
 much —
I tell myself, you may mean good and true.
You offer me, I seem to understand,
Because I am in poverty and starve,
Much money, where one piece would save my
 life.
The silver cup upon the altar-cloth
Is neither yours to give nor mine to take ;
But I might take one bit of bread therefrom,
Since I am starving, and return the rest,
Yet do no harm : this is my very case.
I am in that strait, I may not dare abstain
From so much of assistance as would bring
The guilt of theft on neither you nor me ;
But no superfluous particle of aid.
I think, if you will let me state my case,
Even had you been so fancy-fevered here,
Not your sound self, you must grow healthy
 now —

Care only to bestow what I can take.
That it is only you in the wide world,
Knowing me nor in thought nor word nor deed,
Who, all unprompted save by your own heart,
Come proffering assistance now, — were strange
But that my whole life is so strange : as strange
It is, my husband whom I have not wronged
Should hate and harm me. For his own soul's
 sake,
Hinder the harm ! But there is something
 more,
And that the strangest : it has got to be
Somehow for my sake too, and yet not mine,
— This is a riddle — for some kind of sake
Not any clearer to myself than you,
And yet as certain as that I draw breath, —
I would fain live, not die — oh no, not die !
My case is, I was dwelling happily
At Rome with those dear Comparini, called
Father and mother to me ; when at once
I found I had become Count Guido's wife :
Who then, not waiting for a moment, changed
Into a fury of fire, if once he was
Merely a man : his face threw fire at mine,
He laid a hand on me that burned all peace,
All joy, all hope, and last all fear away,
Dipping the bough of life, so pleasant once,
In fire which shrivelled leaf and bud alike,
Burning not only present life but past,
Which you might think was safe beyond his
 reach.
He reached it, though, since that beloved pair,
My father once, my mother all those years,
That loved me so, now say I dreamed a dream
And bid me wake, henceforth no child of theirs,
Never in all the time their child at all.
Do you understand ? I cannot : yet so it is.
Just so I say of you that proffer help :
I cannot understand what prompts your soul,
I simply needs must see that it is so,
Only one strange and wonderful thing more.
They came here with me, those two dear ones,
 kept
All the old love up, till my husband, till
His people here so tortured them, they fled.
And now, is it because I grow in flesh
And spirit one with him their torturer,
That they, renouncing him, must cast off me ?
If I were graced by God to have a child,
Could I one day deny God graced me so ?
Then, since my husband hates me, I shall break
No law that reigns in this fell house of hate,
By using — letting have effect so much
Of hate as hides me from that whole of hate
Would take my life which I want and must
 have —
Just as I take from your excess of love
Enough to save my life with, all I need.
The Archbishop said to murder me were sin :
My leaving Guido were a kind of death
With no sin, — more death, he must answer for.
Hear now what death to him and life to you
I wish to pay and owe. Take me to Rome !
You go to Rome, the servant makes me hear.
Take me as you would take a dog, I think,
Masterless left for strangers to maltreat :
Take me home like that — leave me in the
 house

Where the father and the mother are ; and soon
They 'll come to know and call me by my name,
Their child once more, since child I am, for
  all
They now forget me, which is the worst o' the
  dream —
And the way to end dreams is to break them,
  stand,
Walk, go : then help me to stand, walk, and go !
The Governor said the strong should help the
  weak :
You know how weak the strongest women are.
How could I find my way there by myself ?
I cannot even call out, make them hear —
Just as in dreams : I have tried and proved the
  fact.
I have told this story and more to good great
  men,
The Archbishop and the Governor : they smiled.
'Stop your mouth, fair one ! ' — presently they
  frowned,
' Get you gone, disengage you from our feet ! '
I went in my despair to an old priest,
Only a friar, no great man like these two,
But good, the Augustinian, people name
Romano, — he confessed me two months since :
He fears God, why then needs he fear the
  world ?
And when he questioned how it came about
That I was found in danger of a sin —
Despair of any help from providence, —
'Since, though your husband outrage you,' said
  he,
' That is a case too common, the wives die
Or live, but do not sin so deep as this ' —
Then I told — what I never will tell you —
How, worse than husband's hate, I had to bear
The love — soliciting to shame called love —
Of his brother, — the young idle priest i' the
  house
With only the devil to meet there. ' This is
  grave —
Yes, we must interfere : I counsel, — write
To those who used to be your parents once,
Of dangers here, bid them convey you hence ! '
' But,' said I, ' when I neither read nor write ? '
Then he took pity and promised ' I will write.'
If he did so, — why, they are dumb or dead :
Either they give no credit to the tale,
Or else, wrapped wholly up in their own joy
Of such escape, they care not who cries, still
I' the clutches. Anyhow, no word arrives.
All such extravagance and dreadfulness
Seems incident to dreaming, cured one way, —
Wake me ! The letter I received this morn,
Said — if the woman spoke your very sense —
' You would die for me : ' I can believe it now :
For now the dream gets to involve yourself.
First of all, you seemed wicked and not good,
In writing me those letters : you came in
Like a thief upon me. I this morning said
In my extremity, entreat the thief !
Try if he have in him no honest touch !
A thief might save me from a murderer.
'T was a thief said the last kind word to Christ :
Christ took the kindness and forgave the theft :
And so did I prepare what I now say.
But now, that you stand and I see your face,

Though you have never uttered word yet, —
  well, I know,
Here too has been dream-work, delusion too,
And that at no time, you with the eyes here,
Ever intended to do wrong by me,
Nor wrote such letters therefore. It is false,
And you are true, have been true, will be true.
To Rome then, — when is it you take me there ?
Each minute lost is mortal. When ? — I ask.'

I answered, " It shall be when it can be.
I will go hence and do your pleasure, find
The sure and speedy means of travel, then
Come back and take you to your friends in
  Rome.
There wants a carriage, money and the rest, —
A day's work by to-morrow at this time.
How shall I see you and assure escape ? "

She replied, " Pass, to-morrow at this hour.
If I am at the open window, well :
If I am absent, drop a handkerchief
And walk by ! I shall see from where I watch,
And know that all is done. Return next eve,
And next, and so till we can meet and speak ! "
" To-morrow at this hour I pass," said I.
She was withdrawn.
                        Here is another point
I bid you pause at. When I told thus far,
Some one said, subtly, " Here at least was found
Your confidence in error, — you perceived
The spirit of the letters, in a sort,
Had been the lady's, if the body should be
Supplied by Guido : say, he forged them all !
Here was the unforged fact — she sent for you.
Spontaneously elected you to help,
— What men call, loved you : Guido read her
  mind,
Gave it expression to assure the world
The case was just as he foresaw : he wrote,
She spoke."
              Sirs, that first simile serves still, —
That falsehood of a scorpion hatched, I say,
Nowhere i' the world but in Madonna's mouth.
Go on ! Suppose, that falsehood foiled, next
  eve
Pictured Madonna raised her painted hand,
Fixed the face Rafael bent above the Babe,
On my face as I flung me at her feet :
Such miracle vouchsafed and manifest,
Would that prove the first lying tale was true ?
Pompilia spoke, and I at once received,
Accepted my own fact, my miracle
Self-authorized and self-explained, — she chose
To summon me and signify her choice.
Afterward, — oh ! I gave a passing glance
To a certain ugly cloud-shape, goblin-shred
Of hell-smoke hurrying past the splendid moon
Out now to tolerate no darkness more,
And saw right through the thing that tried to
  pass
For truth and solid, not an empty lie :
" So, he not only forged the words for her
But words for me, made letters he called mine :
What I sent, he retained, gave these in place,
All by the mistress-messenger ! As I
Recognized her, at potency of truth,
So she, by the crystalline soul, knew me.

Never mistook the signs.   Enough of this —
Let the wraith go to nothingness again,
Here is the orb, have only thought for her ! "

" Thought ? " nay, Sirs, what shall follow was
        not thought :
I have thought sometimes, and thought long
        and hard.
I have stood before, gone round a serious thing,
Tasked my whole mind to touch and clasp it
        close,
As I stretch forth my arm to touch this bar.
God and man, and what duty I owe both, —
I dare to say I have confronted these
In thought : but no such faculty helped here.
I put forth no thought, — powerless, all that
        night
I paced the city : it was the first Spring.
By the invasion I lay passive to,
In rushed new things, the old were rapt away ;
Alike abolished — the imprisonment
Of the outside air, the inside weight o' the
        world
That pulled me down.   Death meant, to spurn
        the ground,
Soar to the sky, — die well and you do that.
The very immolation made the bliss ;
Death was the heart of life, and all the harm
My folly had crouched to avoid, now proved a
        veil
Hiding all gain my wisdom strove to grasp:
As if the intense centre of the flame
Should turn a heaven to that devoted fly
Which hitherto, sophist alike and sage,
Saint Thomas with his sober gray goose-quill,
And sinner Plato by Cephisian reed,
Would fain, pretending just the insect's good,
Whisk off, drive back, consign to shade again.
Into another state, under new rule
I knew myself was passing swift and sure ;
Whereof the initiatory pang approached,
Felicitous annoy, as bitter-sweet
As when the virgin-band, the victors chaste,
Feel at the end the earthly garments drop,
And rise with something of a rosy shame
Into immortal nakedness: so I
Lay, and let come the proper throe would thrill
Into the ecstasy and outthrob pain.

I' the gray of dawn it was I found myself
Facing the pillared front o' the Pieve — mine,
My church : it seemed to say for the first time,
" But am not I the Bride, the mystic love
O' the Lamb, who took thy plighted troth, my
        priest,
To fold thy warm heart on my heart of stone
And freeze thee nor unfasten any more ?
This is a fleshly woman, — let the free
Bestow their life - blood, thou art pulseless
        now ! "
See !   Day by day I had risen and left this
        church
At the signal waved me by some foolish fan,
With half a curse and half a pitying smile
For the monk I stumbled over in my haste,
Prostrate and corpse-like at the altar-foot
Intent on his *corona*: then the church
Was ready with her quip, if word conduced,

To quicken my pace nor stop for prating —
        " There !
Be thankful you are no such ninny, go
Rather to teach a black-eyed novice cards
Than gabble Latin and protrude that nose
Smooth to a sheep's through no brains and much
        faith ! "
That sort of incentive !   Now the church
        changed tone —
Now, when I found out first that life and
        death
Are means to an end, that passion uses both,
Indisputably mistress of the man
Whose form of worship is self-sacrifice :
Now, from the stone lungs sighed the scrannel
        voice,
" Leave that live passion, come be dead with
        me ! "
As if, i' the fabled garden, I had gone
On great adventure, plucked in ignorance
Hedge-fruit, and feasted to satiety,
Laughing at such high fame for hips and haws,
And scorned the achievement: then come all at
        once
O' the prize o' the place, the thing of perfect
        gold,
The apple's self : and, scarce my eye on that,
Was 'ware as well o' the seven-fold dragon's
        watch.

Sirs, I obeyed.   Obedience was too strange, —
This new thing that had been struck into me
By the look o' the lady, — to dare disobey
The first authoritative word.   'T was God's.
I had been lifted to the level of her,
Could take such sounds into my sense.   I said,
" We two are cognizant o' the Master now ;
She it is bids me bow the head: how true,
I am a priest !   I see the function here ;
I thought the other way self-sacrifice :
This is the true, seals up the perfect sum.
I pay it, sit down, silently obey."

So, I went home.   Dawn broke, noon broadened,
        I —
I sat stone-still, let time run over me.
The sun slanted into my room, had reached
The west.   I opened book, — Aquinas blazed
With one black name only on the white page.
I looked up, saw the sunset : vespers rang :
" She counts the minutes till I keep my word
And come say all is ready.   I am a priest.
Duty to God is duty to her : I think
God, who created her, will save her too
Some new way, by one miracle the more,
Without me.   Then, prayer may avail perhaps."
I went to my own place i' the Pieve, read
The office : I was back at home again
Sitting i' the dark.   " Could she but know —
        but know
That, were there good in this distinct from
        God's,
Really good as it reached her, though procured
By a sin of mine, — I should sin : God forgives.
She knows it is no fear withholds me : fear ?
Of what ?   Suspense here is the terrible thing.
If she should, as she counts the minutes, come
On the fantastic notion that I fear

The world now, fear the Archbishop, fear
    perhaps
Count Guido, he who, having forged the lies,
May wait the work, attend the effect, — I fear
The sword of Guido! Let God see to that —
Hating lies, let not her believe a lie!"

Again the morning found me. "I will work,
Tie down my foolish thoughts. Thank God so
    far!
I have saved her from a scandal, stopped the
    tongues
Had broken else into a cackle and hiss
Around the noble name. Duty is still
Wisdom: I have been wise." So the day wore.

At evening — "But, achieving victory,
I must not blink the priest's peculiar part,
Nor shrink to counsel, comfort: priest and
    friend —
How do we discontinue to be friends?
I will go minister, advise her seek
Help at the source, — above all, not despair:
There may be other happier help at hand.
I hope it, — wherefore then neglect to say?"

There she stood — leaned there, for the second
    time,
Over the terrace, looked at me, then spoke :
"Why is it you have suffered me to stay
Breaking my heart two days more than was
    need?
Why delay help, your own heart yearns to
    give?
You are again here, in the selfsame mind,
I see here, steadfast in the face of you, —
You grudge to do no one thing that I ask.
Why then is nothing done? You know my
    need.
Still, through God's pity on me, there is time
And one day more : shall I be saved or no?"
I answered — "Lady, waste no thought, no
    word
Even to forgive me! Care for what I care —
Only! Now follow me as I were fate!
Leave this house in the dark to-morrow night,
Just before daybreak : — there 's new moon
    this eve —
It sets, and then begins the solid black.
Descend, proceed to the Torrione, step
Over the low dilapidated wall,
Take San Clemente, there 's no other gate
Unguarded at the hour: some paces thence
An inn stands ; cross to it ; I shall be there."

She answered, "If I can but find the way.
But I shall find it. Go now!"

                  I did go,
Took rapidly the route myself prescribed,
Stopped at Torrione, climbed the ruined place,
Proved that the gate was practicable, reached
The inn, no eye, despite the dark, could miss,
Knocked there and entered, made the host se-
    cure :
"With Caponsacchi it is ask and have ;
I know my betters. Are you bound for Rome?
I get swift horse and trusty man," said he.

Then I retraced my steps, was found once more
In my own house for the last time : there lay
The broad pale opened "Summa." "Shut his
    book,
There 's other showing! 'T was a Thomas too
Obtained — more favored than his namesake
    here —
A gift, tied faith fast, foiled the tug of doubt, —
Our Lady's girdle ; down he saw it drop
As she ascended into heaven, they say :
He kept that safe and bade all doubt adieu.
I too have seen a lady and hold a grace."

I know not how the night passed : morning
    broke,
Presently came my servant. "Sir, this eve —
Do you forget?" I started. "How forget?
What is it you know?" "With due submis-
    sion, Sir,
This being last Monday in the month but one,
And a vigil, since to-morrow is Saint George,
And feast-day, and moreover day for copes,
And Canon Conti now away a month,
And Canon Crispi sour because, forsooth,
You let him sulk in stall and bear the brunt
Of the octave . . . Well, Sir, 't is important!"
                        "True!
Hearken, I have to start for Rome this night.
No word, lest Crispi overboil and burst!
Provide me with a laic dress! Throw dust
I' the Canon's eye, stop his tongue's scandal so!
See there 's a sword in case of accident."
I knew the knave, the knave knew me.

                         And thus
Through each familiar hindrance of the day
Did I make steadily for its hour and end, —
Felt time's old barrier-growth of right and fit
Give way through all its twines, and let me
    go.
Use and wont recognized the excepted man,
Let speed the special service, — and I sped
Till, at the dead between midnight and morn,
There was I at the goal, before the gate,
With a tune in the ears, low leading up to loud,
A light in the eyes, faint that would soon be
    flare,
Ever some spiritual witness new and new
In faster frequence, crowding solitude
To watch the way o' the warfare, — till, at last
When the ecstatic minute must bring birth,
Began a whiteness in the distance, waxed
Whiter and whiter, near grew and more near,
Till it was she : there did Pompilia come :
The white I saw shine through her was her
    soul's,
Certainly, for the body was one black,
Black from head down to foot. She did not
    speak,
Glided into the carriage, — so a cloud
Gathers the moon up. "By San Spirito,
To Rome, as if the road burned underneath!
Reach Rome, then hold my head in pledge, I
    pay
The run and the risk to heart's content!'
    Just that,
I said, — then, in another tick of time,
Sprang, was beside her, she and I alone.

So it began, our flight through dusk to clear,
Through day and night and day again to night
Once more, and to last dreadful dawn of all.
Sirs, how should I lie quiet in my grave
Unless you suffer me wring, drop by drop,
My brain dry, make a riddance of the drench
Of minutes with a memory in each,
Recorded motion, breath or look of hers,
Which poured forth would present you one pure
glass,
Mirror you plain — as God's sea, glassed in gold,
His saints — the perfect soul Pompilia? Men,
You must know that a man gets drunk with
truth
Stagnant inside him! Oh, they 've killed her,
Sirs!
Can I be calm?
                    Calmly! Each incident
Proves, I maintain, that action of the flight
For the true thing it was. The first faint scratch
O' the stone will test its nature, teach its worth
To idiots who name Parian — coprolite.
After all, I shall give no glare — at best
Only display you certain scattered lights
Lamping the rush and roll of the abyss:
Nothing but here and there a fire-point pricks
Wavelet from wavelet: well!
                    For the first hour
We both were silent in the night, I know:
Sometimes I did not see nor understand.
Blackness engulfed me, — partial stupor, say —
Then I would break way, breathe through the
surprise,
And be aware again, and see who sat
In the dark vest with the white face and hands.
I said to myself — " I have caught it, I con-
ceive
The mind o' the mystery : 't is the way they
wake
And wait, two martyrs somewhere in a tomb
Each by each as their blessing was to die ;
Some signal they are promised and expect, —
When to arise before the trumpet scares:
So, through the whole course of the world they
wait
The last day, but so fearless and so safe !
No otherwise, in safety and not fear,
I lie, because she lies too by my side."
You know this is not love, Sirs, — it is faith,
The feeling that there 's God, he reigns and
rules
Out of this low world : that is all ; no harm !
At times she drew a soft sigh — music seemed
Always to hover just above her lips,
Not settle, — break a silence music too.

In the determined morning, I first found
Her head erect, her face turned full to me,
Her soul intent on mine through two wide eyes.
I answered them. " You are saved hitherto.
We have passed Perugia, — gone round by the
wood,
Not through, I seem to think, — and opposite
I know Assisi ; this is holy ground."
Then she resumed. " How long since we both
left
Arezzo ? " — " Years — and certain hours be-
side."

It was at . . . ah, but I forget the names !
'T is a mere post-house and a hovel or two ;
I left the carriage and got bread and wine
And brought it her. — " Does it detain to eat ? "
" — They stay perforce, change horses, — there-
fore eat !
We lose no minute : we arrive, be sure ! "
This was — I know not where — there 's a great
hill
Close over, and the stream has lost its bridge,
One fords it. She began — " I have heard say
Of some sick body that my mother knew,
'T was no good sign when in a limb diseased
All the pain suddenly departs, — as if
The guardian angel discontinued pain
Because the hope of cure was gone at last :
The limb will not again exert itself,
It needs be pained no longer : so with me,
— My soul whence all the pain is past at once :
All pain must be to work some good in the end.
True, this I feel now, this may be that good,
Pain was because of, — otherwise, I fear ! "

She said, — a long while later in the day,
When I had let the silence be, — abrupt —
" Have you a mother ? " " She died, I was
born."
" A sister then ? " " No sister." " Who was
it —
What woman were you used to serve this way,
Be kind to, till I called you and you came ? "
I did not like that word. Soon afterward —
" Tell me, are men unhappy, in some kind
Of mere unhappiness at being men,
As women suffer, being womanish ?
Have you, now, some unhappiness, I mean,
Born of what may be man's strength overmuch,
To match the undue susceptibility,
The sense at every pore when hate is close ?
It hurts us if a baby hides its face
Or child strikes at us punily, calls names
Or makes a mouth, — much more if stranger
men
Laugh or frown, — just as that were much to
bear !
Yet rocks split, — and the blow-ball does no
more,
Quivers to feathery nothing at a touch ;
And strength may have its drawback, weakness
'scapes."

Once she asked, " What is it that made you
smile,
At the great gate with the eagles and the
snakes,
Where the company entered, 't is a long time
since ? "
" — Forgive — I think you would not under-
stand :
Ah, but you ask me, — therefore, it was this.
That was a certain bishop's villa-gate,
I knew it by the eagles, — and at once
Remember this same bishop was just he
People of old were wont to bid me please
If I would catch preferment : so, I smiled
Because an impulse came to me, a whim —
What if I prayed the prelate leave to speak,
Began upon him in his presence-hall

— ' What, still at work so gray and obsolete?
Still rocheted and mitred more or less?
Don't you feel all that out of fashion now?
I find out when the day of things is done ! ' "

At eve we heard the *angelus:* she turned —
" I told you I can neither read nor write.
My life stopped with the play-time ; I will
learn,
If I begin to live again : but you —
Who are a priest — wherefore do you not read
The service at this hour?   Read Gabriel's song,
The lesson, and then read the little prayer
To Raphael, proper for us travellers ! "
I did not like that, neither, but I read.

When we stopped at Foligno it was dark.
The people of the post came out with lights :
The driver said, " This time to-morrow, may
Saints only help, relays continue good,
Nor robbers hinder, we arrive at Rome.
I urged, — " Why tax your strength a second
night?
Trust me, alight here and take brief repose !
We are out of harm's reach, past pursuit : go
sleep
If but an hour ! I keep watch, guard the while
Here in the doorway." But her whole face
changed,
The misery grew again about her mouth,
The eyes burned up from faintness, like the
fawn's
Tired to death in the thicket, when she feels
The probing spear o' the huntsman.   " Oh, no
stay ! "
She cried, in the fawn's cry, " On to Rome, on,
on —
Unless 't is you who fear, — which cannot
be ! "

We did go on all night ; but at its close
She was troubled, restless, moaned low, talked
at whiles
To herself, her brow on quiver with the dream :
Once, wide awake, she menaced, at arms'
length
Waved away something — " Never again with
you !
My soul is mine, my body is my soul's :
You and I are divided ever more
In soul and body : get you gone ! "   Then I —
" Why, in my whole life I have never prayed !
Oh, if the God, that only can, would help !
Am I his priest with power to cast out fiends?
Let God arise and all his enemies
Be scattered ! "   By morn, there was peace, no
sigh
Out of the deep sleep.

When she woke at last,
I answered the first look — " Scarce twelve
hours more,
Then, Rome !   There probably was no pursuit,
There cannot now be peril : bear up brave !
Just some twelve hours to press through to the
prize :
Then, no more of the terrible journey ! "
" Then,

No more o' the journey : if it might but last !
Always, my life long, thus to journey still !
It is the interruption that I dread, —
With no dread, ever to be here and thus !
Never to see a face nor hear a voice !
Yours is no voice ; you speak when you are
dumb ;
Nor face, I see it in the dark.   I want
No face nor voice that change and grow
unkind."
That I liked, that was the best thing she said.

In the broad day, I dared entreat, " Descend ! "
I told a woman, at the garden-gate
By the post-house, white and pleasant in the
sun,
" It is my sister, — talk with her apart !
She is married and unhappy, you perceive ;
I take her home because her head is hurt ;
Comfort her as you women understand ! "
So, there I left them by the garden-wall,
Paced the road, then bade put the horses to,
Came back, and there she sat : close to her
knee,
A black-eyed child still held the bowl of milk,
Wondered to see how little she could drink,
And in her arms the woman's infant lay.
She smiled at me, " How much good this has
done !
This is a whole night's rest and how much
more !
I can proceed now, though I wish to stay.
How do you call that tree with the thick top
That holds in all its leafy green and gold
The sun now like an immense egg of fire ? "
(It was a million-leaved mimosa.)   " Take
The babe away from me and let me go ! "
And in the carriage, " Still a day, my friend !
And perhaps half a night, the woman fears.
I pray it finish since it cannot last.
There may be more misfortune at the close,
And where will you be?   God suffice me
then ! "
And presently — for there was a roadside-
shrine —
" When I was taken first to my own church
Lorenzo in Lucina, being a girl,
And bid confess my faults, I interposed,
' But teach me what fault to confess and
know ! '
So, the priest said — ' You should bethink
yourself :
Each human being needs must have done
wrong ! '
Now, be you candid and no priest but friend —
Were I surprised and killed here on the spot,
A runaway from husband and his home,
Do you account it were in sin I died ?
My husband used to seem to harm me, not . . .
Not on pretence he punished sin of mine,
Nor for sin's sake and lust of cruelty,
But as I heard him bid a farming-man
At the villa take a lamb once to the wood
And there ill-treat it, meaning that the wolf
Should hear its cries, and so come, quick be
caught,
Enticed to the trap : he practised thus with me
That so, whatever were his gain thereby,

Others than I might become prey and spoil.
Had it been only between our two selves, —
His pleasure and my pain, — why, pleasure him
By dying, nor such need to make a coil !
But this was worth an effort, that my pain
Should not become a snare, prove pain three-
    fold
To other people — strangers — or unborn —
How should I know ? I sought release from
    that —
I think, or else from, — dare I say, some cause
Such as is put into a tree, which turns
Away from the north wind with what nest it
    holds, —
The woman said that trees so turn : now,
    friend,
Tell me, because I cannot trust myself !
You are a man : what have I done amiss ? ''
You must conceive my answer, — I forget —
Taken up wholly with the thought, perhaps,
This time she might have said, — might, did
    not say —
'' You are a priest.'' She said, '' my friend.''
                              Day wore,
We passed the places, somehow the calm went,
Again the restless eyes began to rove
In new fear of the foe mine could not see.
She wandered in her mind, — addressed me
    once
'' Gaetano ! '' — that is not my name : whose
    name ?
I grew alarmed, my head seemed turning too.
I quickened pace with promise now, now
    threat :
Bade drive and drive, nor any stopping more.
'' Too deep i' the thick of the struggle, struggle
    through !
Then drench her in repose though death's self
    pour
The plenitude of quiet, — help us, God,
Whom the winds carry ! ''

                        Suddenly I saw
The old tower, and the little white-walled
    clump
Of buildings and the cypress-tree or two, —
'' Already Castelnuovo — Rome ! '' I cried,
'' As good as Rome, — Rome is the next stage,
    think !
This is where travellers' hearts are wont to
    beat.
Say you are saved, sweet lady ! '' Up she
    woke.
The sky was fierce with color from the sun
Setting. She screamed out, '' No, I must not
    die !
Take me no farther, I should die : stay here !
I have more life to save than mine ! ''
                              She swooned.
We seemed safe : what was it foreboded so ?
Out of the coach into the inn I bore
The motionless and breathless pure and pale
Pompilia, — bore her through a pitying group
And laid her on a couch, still calm and cured
By deep sleep of all woes at once. The host
Was urgent, '' Let her stay an hour or two !
Leave her to us, all will be right by morn ! ''
Oh, my foreboding ! But I could not choose.

I paced the passage, kept watch all night long.
I listened, — not one movement, not one sigh.
'' Fear not : she sleeps so sound ! '' they said :
    but I
Feared, all the same, kept fearing more and
    more,
Found myself throb with fear from head to foot,
Filled with a sense of such impending woe,
That, at first pause of night, pretence of gray,
I made my mind up it was morn. — '' Reach
    Rome,
Lest hell reach her ! A dozen miles to make,
Another long breath, and we emerge ! '' I stood
I' the courtyard, roused the sleepy grooms.
    '' Have out
Carriage and horse, give haste, take gold ! ''
    said I.
While they made ready in the doubtful morn, —
'T was the last minute, — needs must I ascend
And break her sleep ; I turned to go.
                              And there
Faced me Count Guido, there posed the mean
    man
As master, — took the field, encamped his
    rights,
Challenged the world : there leered new tri-
    umph, there
Scowled the old malice in the visage bad
And black o' the scamp. Soon triumph suppled
    the tongue
A little, malice glued to his dry throat,
And he part howled, part hissed . . . oh, how
    he kept
Well out o' the way, at arm's length and to
    spare ! —
'' My salutation to your priestship ! What ?
Matutinal, busy with book so soon
Of an April day that 's damp as tears that now
Deluge Arezzo at its darling's flight ? —
'T is unfair, wrongs femini'y at large,
To let a single dame monopolize
A heart the whole sex claims, should share alike :
Therefore I overtake you, Canon ! Come !
The lady, — could you leave her side so soon ?
You have not yet experienced at her hands
My treatment, you lay down undrugged, I see !
Hence this alertness — hence no death-in-life
Like what held arms fast when she stole from
    mine.
To be sure, you took the solace and repose
That first night at Foligno ! — news abound
O' the road by this time, — men regaled me
    much,
As past them I came halting after you,
Vulcan pursuing Mars, as poets sing, —
Still at the last here pant I, but arrive,
Vulcan — and not without my Cyclops too,
The Commissary and the unpoisoned arm
O' the Civil Force, should Mars turn mutineer.
Enough of fooling : capture the culprits, friend !
Here is the lover in the smart disguise
With the sword, — he is a priest, so mine lies
    still.
There upstairs hides my wife the runaway,
His leman : the two plotted, poisoned first,
Plundered me after, and eloped thus far
Where now you find them. Do your duty
    quick ! ''

Arrest and hold him! That's done: now catch
her!"
During this speech of that man, — well, I stood
Away, as he managed, — still, I stood as near
The throat of him, — with these two hands, my
own, —
As now I stand near yours, Sir, — one quick
spring,
One great good satisfying gripe, and lo!
There had he lain abolished with his lie,
Creation purged o' the miscreate, man re-
deemed,
A spittle wiped off from the face of God!
I, in some measure, seek a poor excuse
For what I left undone, in just this fact
That my first feeling at the speech I quote
Was — not of what a blasphemy was dared,
Not what a bag of venomed purulence
Was split and noisome, — but how splendidly
Mirthful, how ludicrous a lie was launched!
Would Molière's self wish more than hear such
man
Call, claim such woman for his own, his wife,
Even though, in due amazement at the boast,
He had stammered, she moreover was divine?
She to be his, — were hardly less absurd
Than that he took her name into his mouth,
Licked, and then let it go again, the beast,
Signed with his slaver. Oh, she poisoned him,
Plundered him, and the rest! Well, what I
wished
Was, that he would but go on, say once more
So to the world, and get his meed of men,
The fist's reply to the filth. And while I mused,
The minute, oh the misery, was gone!
On either idle hand of me there stood
Really an officer, nor laughed i' the least:
Nay, rendered justice to his reason, laid
Logic to heart, as 't were submitted them
"Twice two makes four."
            "And now, catch her!" he cried.
That sobered me. "Let myself lead the way —
Ere you arrest me, who am somebody,
Being, as you hear, a priest and privileged, —
To the lady's chamber! I presume you — men
Expert, instructed how to find out truth,
Familiar with the guise of guilt. Detect
Guilt on her face when it meets mine, then judge
Between us and the mad dog howling there!"
Up we all went together, in they broke
O' the chamber late my chapel. There she lay,
Composed as when I laid her, that last eve,
O' the couch, still breathless, motionless, sleep's
self,
Wax-white, seraphic, saturate with the sun
O' the morning that now flooded from the front
And filled the window with a light like blood.
"Behold the poisoner, the adulteress,
— And feigning sleep too! Seize, bind!" Guido
hissed.

She started up, stood erect, face to face
With the husband: back he fell, was buttressed
there
By the window all aflame with morning-red,
He the black figure, the opprobrious blur
Against all peace and joy and light and life.
"Away from between me and hell!" she cried:

"Hell for me, no embracing any more!
I am God's, I love God, God — whose knees I
clasp,
Whose utterly most just award I take,
But bear no more love-making devils: hence!"
I may have made an effort to reach her side
From where I stood i' the doorway, — anyhow
I found the arms, I wanted, pinioned fast,
Was powerless in the clutch to left and right
O' the rabble pouring in, rascality
Enlisted, rampant on the side of hearth,
Home and the husband, — pay in prospect too!
They heaped themselves upon me. "Ha! —
and him
Also you outrage? Him, too, my sole friend,
Guardian and savior? That I balk you of,
Since — see how God can help at last and
worst!"
She sprang at the sword that hung beside him,
seized,
Drew, brandished it, the sunrise burned for joy
O' the blade, "Die," cried she, "devil, in
God's name!"
Ah, but they all closed round her, twelve to one
— The unmanly men, no woman-mother made,
Spawned somehow! Dead-white and disarmed
she lay.
No matter for the sword, her word sufficed
To spike the coward through and through: he
shook,
Could only spit between the teeth — "You see?
You hear? Bear witness, then! Write down
. . . but no —
Carry these criminals to the prison-house,
For first thing! I begin my search meanwhile
After the stolen effects, gold, jewels, plate,
Money and clothes, they robbed me of and fled,
With no few amorous pieces, verse and prose,
I have much reason to expect to find."

When I saw that — no more than the first mad
speech,
Made out the speaker mad and a laughing-stock,
So neither did this next device explode
One listener's indignation, — that a scribe
Did sit down; set himself to write indeed,
While sundry knaves began to peer and pry
In corner and hole, — that Guido, wiping brow
And getting him a countenance, was fast
Losing his fear, beginning to strut free
O' the stage of his exploit, snuff here, sniff
there, —
Then I took truth in, guessed sufficiently
The service for the moment. "What I say,
Slight at your peril! We are aliens here,
My adversary and I, called noble both;
I am the nobler, and a name men know.
I could refer our cause to our own court
In our own country, but prefer appeal
To the nearer jurisdiction. Being a priest,
Though in a secular garb, — for reasons good
I shall adduce in due time to my peers, —
I demand that the Church I serve, decide
Between us, right the slandered lady there.
A Tuscan noble, I might claim the Duke:
A priest, I rather choose the Church, — bid
Rome
Cover the wronged with her inviolate shield."

There was no refusing this: they bore me off,
They bore her off, to separate cells o' the same
Ignoble prison, and, separate, thence to Rome.
Pompilia's face, then and thus, looked on me
The last time in this life : not one sight since,
Never another sight to be ! And yet
I thought I had saved her. I appealed to
    Rome :
It seems I simply sent her to her death.
You tell me she is dying now, or dead ;
I cannot bring myself to quite believe
This is a place you torture people in :
What if this your intelligence were just
A subtlety, an honest wile to work
On a man at unawares ? 'T were worthy you.
No, Sirs, I cannot have the lady dead !
That erect form, flashing brow, fulgurant eye,
That voice immortal (oh, that voice of hers !)
That vision in the blood-red daybreak — that
Leap to life of the pale electric sword
Angels go armed with, — that was not the last
O' the lady ! Come, I see through it, you find —
Know the manœuvre ! Also herself said
I had saved her : do you dare say she spoke
    false ?
Let me see for myself if it be so !
Though she were dying, a Priest might be of
    use,
The more when he 's a friend too, — she called
    me
Far beyond " friend." Come, let me see her —
    indeed
It is my duty, being a priest : I hope
I stand confessed, established, proved a priest ?
My punishment had motive that, a priest
I, in a laic garb, a mundane mode,
Did what were harmlessly done otherwise.
I never touched her with my finger-tip
Except to carry her to the couch, that eve,
Against my heart, beneath my head, bowed
    low,
As we priests carry the paten: that is why
— To get leave and go see her of your grace —
I have told you this whole story over again.
Do I deserve grace ? For I might lock lips,
Laugh at your jurisdiction: what have you
To do with me in the matter ? I suppose
You hardly think I donned a bravo's dress
To have a hand in the new crime ; on the old,
Judgment's delivered, penalty imposed,
I was chained fast at Civita hand and foot —
She had only you to trust to, you and Rome,
Rome and the Church, and no pert meddling
    priest
Two days ago, when Guido, with the right,
Hacked her to pieces. One might well be
    wroth ;
I have been patient, done my best to help :
I come from Civita and punishment
As friend of the court — and for pure friend-
    ship's sake
Have told my tale to the end, — nay, not the
    end —
For, wait — I 'll end — not leave you that excuse !

When we were parted, — shall I go on there ?
I was presently brought to Rome — yes, here I
    stood

Opposite yonder very crucifix —
And there sat you and you, Sirs, quite the
    same.
I heard charge, and bore question, and told tale
Noted down in the book there, — turn and see
If, by one jot or tittle, I vary now !
I' the color the tale takes, there 's change per-
    haps ;
'T is natural, since the sky is different,
Eclipse in the air now ; still, the outline stays.
I showed you how it came to be my part
To save the lady. Then your clerk produced
Papers, a pack of stupid and impure
Banalities called letters about love —
Love, indeed, — I could teach who styled them
    so,
Better, I think, though priest and loveless both !
" — How was it that a wife, young, innocent,
And stranger to your person, wrote this
    page ? " —
" — She wrote it when the Holy Father wrote
The bestiality that posts through Rome,
Put in his mouth by Pasquin." " Nor per-
    haps
Did you return these answers, verse and prose,
Signed, sealed and sent the lady ? There 's
    your hand ! "
" — This precious piece of verse, I really judge,
Is meant to copy my own character,
A clumsy mimic ; and this other prose,
Not so much even ; both rank forgery :
Verse, quotha ? Bembo's verse ! When Saint
    John wrote
The tract ' De Tribus,' I wrote this to match."
" — How came it, then, the documents were
    found
At the inn on your departure ? " — " I opine,
Because there were no documents to find
In my presence, — you must hide before you
    find.
Who forged them hardly practised in my view ;
Who found them waited till I turned my
    back."
" — And what of the clandestine visits paid,
Nocturnal passage in and out the house
With its lord absent ? 'T is alleged you
    climbed " —
" — Flew on a broomstick to the man i' the
    moon !
Who witnessed or will testify this trash ? "
" — The trusty servant, Margherita's self,
Even she who brought you letters, you con-
    fess,
And, you confess, took letters in reply :
Forget not we have knowledge of the facts ! "
" — Sirs, who have knowledge of the facts, de-
    fray
The expenditure of wit I waste in vain,
Trying to find out just one fact of all !
She who brought letters from who could not
    write,
And took back letters to who could not read, —
Who was that messenger, of your charity ? "
" — Well, so far favors you the circumstance
That this same messenger . . . how shall we
    say ? . . .
Sub imputatione meretricis
Laborat, — which makes accusation null :

We waive this woman's: — naught makes void
   the next.
Borsi, called Venerino, he who drove,
O' the first night when you fled away, at length
Deposes to your kissings in the coach,
— Frequent, frenetic " . . . " When deposed
   he so? "
" After some weeks of sharp imprison-
   ment " . . .
" Granted by friend the Governor, I engage " —
" — For his participation in your flight !
At length his obduracy melting made
The avowal mentioned " . . . " Was dismissed
   forthwith
To liberty, poor knave, for recompense.
Sirs, give what credit to the lie you can !
For me, no word in my defence I speak,
And God shall argue for the lady ! "
                                  So
Did I stand question, and make answer, still
With the same result of smiling disbelief,
Polite impossibility of faith
In such affected virtue in a priest ;
But a showing fair play, an indulgence, even,
To one no worse than others after all —
Who had not brought disgrace to the order,
   played
Discreetly, ruffled gown nor ripped the cloth
In a bungling game at romps : I have told you,
   Sirs —
If I pretended simply to be pure
Honest and Christian in the case, — absurd !
As well go boast myself above the needs
O' the human nature, careless how meat smells,
Wine tastes, — a saint above the smack ! But
   once
Abate my crest, own flaws i' the flesh, agree
To go with the herd, be hog no more nor less,
Why, hogs in common herd have common
   rights :
I must not be unduly borne upon,
Who just romanced a little, sowed wild oats,
But 'scaped without a scandal, flagrant fault.
My name helped to a mirthful circumstance :
" Joseph " would do well to amend his plea :
Undoubtedly — some toying with the wife,
But as for ruffian violence and rape,
Potiphar pressed too much on the other side !
The intrigue, the elopement, the disguise, —
   well charged !
The letters and verse looked hardly like the
   truth.
Your apprehension was — of guilt enough
To be compatible with innocence,
So, punished best a little and not too much.
Had I struck Guido Franceschini's face,
You had counselled me withdraw for my own
   sake,
Balk him of bravo-hiring. Friends came
   round,
Congratulated, " Nobody mistakes !
The pettiness o' the forfeiture defines
The peccadillo : Guido gets his share :
His wife is free of husband and hook-nose,
The mouldy viands and the mother-in-law.
To Civita with you and amuse the time,
Travesty us ' De Raptu Helenæ ! '
A funny figure must the husband cut

When the wife makes him skip, — too ticklish,
   eh ?
Do it in Latin, not the Vulgar, then !
Scazons — we 'll copy and send his Eminence.
Mind — one iambus in the final foot !
He 'll rectify it, be your friend for life ! "
Oh, Sirs, depend on me for much new light
Thrown on the justice and religion here
By this proceeding, much fresh food for
   thought !

And I was just set down to study these
In relegation, two short days ago,
Admiring how you read the rules, when, clap,
A thunder comes into my solitude —
I am caught up in a whirlwind and cast here,
Told of a sudden, in this room where so late
You dealt out law adroitly, that those scales,
I meekly bowed to, took my allotment from,
Guido has snatched at, broken in your hands,
Metes to himself the murder of his wife,
Full measure, pressed down, running over now !
Can I assist to an explanation ? — Yes,
I rise in your esteem, sagacious Sirs,
Stand up a renderer of reasons, not
The officious priest would personate Saint
   George
For a mock Princess in undragoned days.
What, the blood startles you ? What, after all
The priest who needs must carry sword on
   thigh
May find imperative use for it ? Then, there
   was
A Princess, was a dragon belching flame,
And should have been a Saint George also ?
   Then,
There might be worse schemes than to break
   the bonds
At Arezzo, lead her by the little hand,
Till she reached Rome, and let her try to live ?
But you were law and gospel, — would one
   please
Stand back, allow your faculty elbow-room ?
You blind guides who must needs lead eyes
   that see !
Fools, alike ignorant of man and God !
What was there here should have perplexed
   your wit
For a wink of the owl-eyes of you ? How miss,
   then,
What 's now forced on you by this flare of
   fact —
As if Saint Peter failed to recognize
Nero as no apostle, John or James,
Till some one burned a martyr, made a torch
O' the blood and fat to show his features by !
Could you fail read this cartulary aright
On head and front of Franceschini there, —
Large - lettered like hell's masterpiece of
   print, —
That he, from the beginning pricked at heart
By some lust, letch of hate against his wife,
Plotted to plague her into overt sin
And shame, would slay Pompilia body and
   soul,
And save his mean self — miserably caught
I' the quagmire of his own tricks, cheats and
   lies ?

—That himself wrote those papers,—from
  himself
To himself,—which, i' the name of me and
  her,
His mistress-messenger gave her and me,
Touching us with such pustules of the soul
That she and I might take the taint, be shown
To the world and shuddered over, speckled so ?
— That the agent put her sense into my words,
Made substitution of the thing she hoped,
For the thing she had and held, its opposite,
While the husband in the background bit his
  lips
At each fresh failure of his precious plot ?
— That when at the last we did rush each on
  each,
By no chance but because God willed it so —
The spark of truth was struck from out our
  souls —
Made all of me, descried in the first glance,
Seem fair and honest and permissible love
O' the good and true — as the first glance told
  me
There was no duty patent in the world
Like daring try be good and true myself,
Leaving the shows of things to the Lord of
  Show
And Prince o' the Power of the Air. Our very
  flight,
Even to its most ambiguous circumstance,
Irrefragably proved how futile, false . . .
Why, men — men and not boys — boys and not
  babes —
Babes and not beasts —beasts and not stocks
  and stones ! —
Had the liar's lie been true one pin - point
  speck,
Were I the accepted suitor, free o' the place,
Disposer of the time, to come at a call
And go at a wink as who should say me nay, —
What need of flight, what were the gain there-
  from
But just damnation, failure or success ?
Damnation pure and simple to her the wife
And me the priest — who bartered private bliss
For public reprobation, the safe shade
For the sunshine which men see to pelt me by :
What other advantage — we who led the days
And nights alone i' the house — was flight to
  find ?
In our whole journey did we stop an hour,
Diverge a foot from strait road till we reached
Or would have reached — but for that fate of
  ours —
The father and mother, in the eye of Rome,
The eye of yourselves we made aware of us
At the first fall of misfortune ? And indeed
You did so far give sanction to our flight,
Confirm its purpose, as lend helping hand,
Deliver up Pompilia not to him
She fled, but those the flight was ventured for.
Why then could you, who stopped short, not
  go on
One poor step more, and justify the means,
Having allowed the end ? — not see and say,
" Here 's the exceptional conduct that should
  claim
To be exceptionally judged on rules

Which, understood, make no exception here "
Why play instead into the devil's hands
By dealing so ambiguously as gave
Guido the power to intervene like me,
Prove one exception more ? I saved his wife
Against law : against law he slays her now :
Deal with him !

          I have done with being judged.
I stand here guiltless in thought, word and
  deed,
To the point that I apprise you, — in contempt
For all misapprehending ignorance
O' the human heart, much more the mind of
  Christ, —
That I assuredly did bow, was blessed
By the revelation of Pompilia. There !
Such is the final fact I fling you, Sirs,
To mouth and mumble and misinterpret :
  there !
" The priest 's in love," have it the vulgar
  way !
Unpriest me, rend the rags o' the vestment,
  do —
Degrade deep, disenfranchise all you dare —
Remove me from the midst, no longer priest
And fit companion for the like of you —
Your gay Abati with the well-turned leg
And rose i' the hat-rim, Canons, cross at neck
And silk mask in the pocket of the gown,
Brisk bishops with the world's musk still un-
  brushed
From the rochet ; I 'll no more of these good
  things :
There 's a crack somewhere, something that 's
  unsound
I' the rattle !

          For Pompilia — be advised,
Build churches, go pray ! You will find me
  there,
I know, if you come, — and you will come, I
  know.
Why, there 's a Judge weeping ! Did not I
  say
You were good and true at bottom ? You see
  the truth—
I am glad I helped you : she helped me just so.

But for Count Guido, — you must counsel
  there !
I bow my head, bend to the very dust,
Break myself up in shame of faultiness.
I had him one whole moment, as I said —
As I remember, as will never out
O' the thoughts of me, — I had him in arm's
  reach
There, — as you stand, Sir, now you cease to
  sit, —
I could have killed him ere he killed his wife,
And did not : he went off alive and well
And then effected this last feat — through me !
Me — not through you — dismiss that fear !
  'T was you
Hindered me staying here to save her,— not
From leaving you and going back to him
And doing service in Arezzo. Come,
Instruct me in procedure ! I conceive —

In all due self-abasement might I speak —
How you will deal with Guido: oh, not
    death!
Death, if it let her life be: otherwise
Not death, — your lights will teach you clear-
    er! I
Certainly have an instinct of my own
I' the matter: bear with me and weigh its
    worth!
Let us go away — leave Guido all alone
Back on the world again that knows him now!
I think he will be found (indulge so far!)
Not to die so much as slide out of life,
Pushed by the general horror and common hate
Low, lower, — left o' the very ledge of things,
I seem to see him catch convulsively
One by one at all honest forms of life,
At reason, order, decency and use —
To cramp him and get foothold by at least;
And still they disengage them from his clutch.
" What, you are he, then, had Pompilia once
And so forwent her? Take not up with us!"
And thus I see him slowly and surely edged
Off all the table-land whence life upsprings
Aspiring to be immortality,
As the snake, hatched on hill-top by mischance,
Despite his wriggling, slips, slides, slidders down
Hillside, lies low and prostrate on the smooth
Level of the outer place, lapsed in the vale:
So I lose Guido in the loneliness,
Silence and dusk, till at the doleful end,
At the horizontal line, creation's verge,
From what just is to absolute nothingness —
Whom is it, straining onward still, he meets?
What other man deep further in the fate,
Who, turning at the prize of a footfall
To flatter him and promise fellowship,
Discovers in the act a frightful face —
Judas, made monstrous by much solitude!
The two are at one now! Let them love their
    love
That bites and claws like hate, or hate their
    hate
That mops and mows and makes as it were
    love!
There, let them each tear each in devil's-fun,
Or fondle this the other while malice aches —
Both teach, both learn detestability!
Kiss him the kiss, Iscariot! Pay that back,
That smatch o' the slaver blistering on your
    lip,
By the better trick, the insult he spared
    Christ —
Lure him the lure o' the letters, Aretine!
Lick him o'er slimy-smooth with jelly-filth
O' the verse-and-prose pollution in love's guise!
The cockatrice is with the basilisk!
There let them grapple, denizens o' the dark,
Foes or friends, but indissolubly bound,
In their one spot out of the ken of God
Or care of man, forever and evermore!

Why, Sirs, what 's this? Why, this is sorry
    and strange!
Futility, divagation: this from me
Bound to be rational, justify an act
Of sober man! — whereas, being moved so
    much,

I give you cause to doubt the lady's mind:
A pretty sarcasm for the world! I fear
You do her wit injustice, — all through me!
Like my fate all through, — ineffective help!
A poor rash advocate I prove myself.
You might be angry with good cause: but sure
At the advocate, — only at the undue zeal
That spoils the force of his own plea, I think?
My part was just to tell you how things stand,
State facts and not be flustered at their fume.
But then 't is a priest speaks: as for love, —
    no!
If you let buzz a vulgar fly like that
About your brains, as if I loved, forsooth,
Indeed, Sirs, you do wrong! We had no
    thought
Of such infatuation, she and I:
There are many points that prove it: do be
    just!
I told you, — at one little roadside-place
I spent a good half-hour, paced to and fro
The garden; just to leave her free awhile,
I plucked a handful of Spring herb and bloom:
I might have sat beside her on the bench
Where the children were: I wish the thing had
    been,
Indeed: the event could not be worse, you
    know:
One more half-hour of her saved! She 's dead
    now, Sirs!
While I was running on at such a rate,
Friends should have plucked me by the sleeve:
    I went
Too much o' the trivial outside of her face
And the purity that shone there — plain to me,
Not to you, what more natural? Nor am I
Infatuated, — oh, I saw, be sure!
Her brow had not the right line, leaned too
    much,
Painters would say; they like the straight-up
    Greek:
This seemed bent somewhat with an invisible
    crown
Of martyr and saint, not such as art approves.
And how the dark orbs dwelt deep underneath,
Looked out of such a sad sweet heaven on me!
The lips, compressed a little, came forward too,
Careful for a whole world of sin and pain.
That was the face, her husband makes his plea,
He sought just to disfigure, — no offence
Beyond that! Sirs, let us be rational!
He needs must vindicate his honor, — ay,
Yet shirks, the coward, in a clown's disguise,
Away from the scene, endeavors to escape.
Now, had he done so, slain and left no trace
O' the slayer, — what were vindicated, pray?
You had found his wife disfigured or a corpse,
For what and by whom? It is too palpable!
Then, here 's another point involving law:
I use this argument to show you meant
No calumny against us by that title
O' the sentence, — liars try to twist it so:
What penalty it bore, I had to pay
Till further proof should follow of innocence —
Probationis ob defectum, — proof?
How could you get proof without trying us?
You went through the preliminary form,
Stopped there, contrived this sentence to amuse

The adversary. If the title ran
For more than fault imputed and not proved,
That was a simple penman's error, else
A slip i' the phrase, — as when we say of you
"Charged with injustice" — which may either be
Or not be, — 't is a name that sticks meanwhile.
Another relevant matter: fool that I am!
Not what I wish true, yet a point friends urge:
It is not true, — yet, since friends think it helps, —
She only tried me when some others failed —
Began with Conti, whom I told you of,
And Guillichini, Guido's kinsfolk both,
And when abandoned by them, not before,
Turned to me. That 's conclusive why she turned.
Much good they got by the happy cowardice!
Conti is dead, poisoned a month ago:
Does that much strike you as a sin? Not much,
After the present murder, — one mark more
On the Moor's skin, — what is black by blacker still?
Conti had come here and told truth. And so
With Guillichini; he 's condemned of course
To the galleys, as a friend in this affair,
Tried and condemned for no one thing i' the world,
A fortnight since by who but the Governor? —
The just judge, who refused Pompilia help
At first blush, being her husband's friend, you know.
There are two tales to suit the separate courts,
Arezzo and Rome: he tells you here, we fled
Alone, unhelped, — lays stress on the main fault,
The spiritual sin, Rome looks to: but elsewhere
He likes best we should break in, steal, bear off,
Be fit to brand and pillory and flog —
That 's the charge goes to the heart of the Governor:
If these unpriest me, you and I may yet
Converse, Vincenzo Marzi-Medici!
Oh, Sirs, there are worse men than you, I say!
More easily duped, I mean; this stupid lie,
Its liar never dared propound in Rome,
He gets Arezzo to receive, — nay more,
Gets Florence and the Duke to authorize!
This is their Rota's sentence, their Granduke
Signs and seals! Rome for me henceforward
— Rome,
Where better men are, — most of all, that man
The Augustinian of the Hospital,
Who writes the letter, — he confessed, he says,
Many a dying person, never one
So sweet and true and pure and beautiful.
A good man! Will you make him Pope one day?
Not that he is not good too, this we have —
But old, — else he would have his word to speak,
His truth to teach the world: I thirst for truth,
But shall not drink it till I reach the source.

Sirs, I am quiet again. You see, we are
So very pitiable, she and I,

Who had conceivably been otherwise.
Forget distemperature and idle heat!
Apart from truth's sake, what 's to move so much?
Pompilia will be presently with God;
I am, on earth, as good as out of it,
A relegated priest; when exile ends,
I mean to do my duty and live long.
She and I are mere strangers now: but priests
Should study passion; how else cure mankind,
Who come for help in passionate extremes?
I do but play with an imagined life
Of who, unfettered by a vow, unblessed
By the higher call, — since you will have it so, —
Leads it companioned by the woman there.
To live, and see her learn, and learn by her,
Out of the low obscure and petty world —
Or only see one purpose and one will
Evolve themselves i' the world, change wrong to right:
To have to do with nothing but the true,
The good, the eternal — and these, not alone
In the main current of the general life,
But small experiences of every day,
Concerns of the particular hearth and home:
To learn not only by a comet's rush
But a rose's birth, — not by the grandeur, God, —
But the comfort, Christ. All this, how far away!
Mere delectation, meet for a minute's dream! —
Just as a drudging student trims his lamp,
Opens his Plutarch, puts him in the place
Of Roman, Grecian; draws the patched gown close,
Dreams, "Thus should I fight, save or rule the world!" —
Then smilingly, contentedly, awakes
To the old solitary nothingness.
So I, from such communion, pass content . . .

O great, just, good God! Miserable me!

VII

POMPILIA

I am just seventeen years and five months old,
And, if I lived one day more, three full weeks
'T is writ so in the church's register,
Lorenzo in Lucina, all my names
At length, so many names for one poor child,
— Francesca Camilla Vittoria Angela
Pompilia Comparini, — laughable!
Also 't is writ that I was married there
Four years ago: and they will add, I hope,
When they insert my death, a word or two, —
Omitting all about the mode of death, —
This, in its place, this which one cares to know
That I had been a mother of a son
Exactly two weeks. It will be through grace
O' the Curate, not through any claim I have;
Because the boy was born at, so baptized
Close to, the Villa, in the proper church:
A pretty church, I say no word against,
Yet stranger-like, — while this Lorenzo seems

My own particular place, I always say.
I used to wonder, when I stood scarce high
As the bed here, what the marble lion meant,
With half his body rushing from the wall,
Eating the figure of a prostrate man —
(To the right, it is, of entry by the door) —
An ominous sign to one baptized like me,
Married, and to be buried there, I hope.
And they should add, to have my life complete,
He is a boy and Gaetan by name —
Gaetano, for a reason, — if the friar
Don Celestine will ask this grace for me
Of Curate Ottoboni: he it was
Baptized me: he remembers my whole life
As I do his gray hair.

        All these few things
I know are true, — will you remember them?
Because time flies. The surgeon cared for me,
To count my wounds, — twenty-two dagger-
    wounds,
Five deadly, but I do not suffer much —
Or too much pain, — and am to die to-night.

Oh how good God is that my babe was born,
— Better than born, baptized and hid away
Before this happened, safe from being hurt!
That had been sin God could not well forgive:
He was too young to smile and save himself.
When they took, two days after he was born,
My babe away from me to be baptized
And hidden awhile, for fear his foe should
    find, —
The country-woman, used to nursing babes,
Said, " Why take on so? where is the great loss?
These next three weeks he will but sleep and
    feed,
Only begin to smile at the month's end;
He would not know you, if you kept him here,
Sooner than that; so, spend three merry weeks
Snug in the Villa, getting strong and stout,
And then I bring him back to be your own,
And both of you may steal to — we know
    where!"
The month — there wants of it two weeks this
    day!
Still, I half fancied when I heard the knock
At the Villa in the dusk, it might prove she —
Come to say, " Since he smiles before the time,
Why should I cheat you out of one good hour?
Back I have brought him; speak to him and
    judge!"
Now I shall never see him; what is worse,
When he grows up and gets to be my age,
He will seem hardly more than a great boy;
And if he asks, " What was my mother like?"
People may answer, " Like girls of seven-
    teen" —
And how can he but think of this and that,
Lucias, Marias, Sofias, who titter or blush
When he regards them as such boys may do?
Therefore I wish some one will please to say
I looked already old though I was young;
Do I not . . . say, if you are by to speak . . .
Look nearer twenty? No more like, at least,
Girls who look arch or redden when boys laugh,
Than the poor Virgin that I used to know
At our street-corner in a lonely niche, —

The babe, that sat upon her knees, broke off, —
Thin white glazed clay, you pitied her the
    more:
She, not the gay ones, always got my rose.

How happy those are who know how to write!
Such could write what their son should read in
    time,
Had they a whole day to live out like me.
Also my name is not a common name,
" Pompilia," and may help to keep apart
A little the thing I am from what girls are.
But then how far away, how hard to find
Will anything about me have become,
Even if the boy bethink himself and ask!
No father that ever knew at all,
Nor ever had — no, never had, I say!
That is the truth, — nor any mother left,
Out of the little two weeks that she lived,
Fit for such memory as might assist:
As good too as no family, no name,
Not even poor old Pietro's name, nor hers,
Poor kind unwise Violante, since it seems
They must not be my parents any more.
That is why something put it in my head
To call the boy " Gaetano " — no old name
For sorrow's sake; I looked up to the sky
And took a new saint to begin anew.
One who has only been made saint — how long?
Twenty-five years: so, carefuller, perhaps,
To guard a namesake than those old saints grow,
Tired out by this time, — see my own five
    saints!

On second thoughts, I hope he will regard
The history of me as what some one dreamed,
And get to disbelieve it at the last:
Since to myself it dwindles fast to that,
Sheer dreaming and impossibility, —
Just in four days too! All the seventeen years,
Not once did a suspicion visit me
How very different a lot is mine
From any other woman's in the world.
The reason must be, 't was by step and step
It got to grow so terrible and strange.
These strange woes stole on tiptoe, as it were,
Into my neighborhood and privacy,
Sat down where I sat, laid them where I lay;
And I was found familiarized with fear,
When friends broke in, held up a torch and
    cried,
" Why, you Pompilia in the cavern thus,
How comes that arm of yours about a wolf?
And the soft length, — lies in and out your feet
And laps you round the knee, — a snake it is!"
And so on.

        Well, and they are right enough,
By the torch they hold up now: for first,
    observe,
I never had a father, — no, nor yet
A mother: my own boy can say at least,
" I had a mother whom I kept two weeks!"
Not I, who little used to doubt . . . I doubt
Good Pietro, kind Violante, gave me birth?
They loved me always as I love my babe
(— Nearly so, that is — quite so could not
    be —)

Did for me all I meant to do for him,
Till one surprising day, three years ago,
They both declared, at Rome, before some
    judge
In some court where the people flocked to hear,
That really I had never been their child,
Was a mere castaway, the careless crime
Of an unknown man, the crime and care too
    much
Of a woman known too well, — little to these,
Therefore, of whom I was the flesh and blood :
What then to Pietro and Violante, both
No more my relatives than you or you ?
Nothing to them ! You know what they de-
    clared.

So with my husband, — just such a surprise,
Such a mistake, in that relationship !
Every one says that husbands love their wives,
Guard them and guide them, give them
    happiness ;
'T is duty, law, pleasure, religion : well,
You see how much of this comes true in mine !
People indeed would fain have somehow proved
He was no husband : but he did not hear,
Or would not wait, and so has killed us all.
Then there is . . . only let me name one more !
There is the friend, — men will not ask about,
But tell untruths of, and give nicknames to,
And think my lover, most surprise of all !
Do only hear, it is the priest they mean,
Giuseppe Caponsacchi : a priest — love,
And love me ! Well, yet people think he did.
I am married, he has taken priestly vows,
They know that, and yet go on, say, the same,
"Yes, how he loves you !" "That was love"
    — they say,
When anything is answered that they ask :
Or else "No wonder you love him " — they say.
Then they shake heads, pity much, scarcely
    blame —
As if we neither of us lacked excuse,
And anyhow are punished to the full,
And downright love atones for everything !
Nay, I heard read out in the public court
Before the judge, in presence of my friends,
Letters 't was said the priest had sent to me,
And other letters sent him by myself,
We being lovers !

                Listen what this is like !
When I was a mere child, my mother . . .
    that 's
Violante, you must let me call her so,
Nor waste time, trying to unlearn the word, . . .
She brought a neighbor's child of my own age
To play with me of rainy afternoons :
And, since there hung a tapestry on the wall,
We two agreed to find each other out
Among the figures. "Tisbe, that is you,
With half-moon on your hair-knot, spear in
    hand,
Flying, but no wings, only the great scarf
Blown to a bluish rainbow at your back :
Call off your hound and leave the stag
    alone !"
"— And there are you, Pompilia, such green
    leaves

Flourishing out of your five finger-ends,
And all the rest of you so brown and rough :
Why is it you are turned a sort of tree ? "
You know the figures never were ourselves
Though we nicknamed them so. Thus, all my
    life, —
As well what was, as what, like this, was
    not, —
Looks old, fantastic and impossible :
I touch a fairy thing that fades and fades.
— Even to my babe ! I thought, when he was
    born,
Something began for once that would not end,
Nor change into a laugh at me, but stay
Forevermore, eternally quite mine.
Well, so he is, — but yet they bore him off,
The third day, lest my husband should lay
    traps
And catch him, and by means of him catch me.
Since they have saved him so, it was well done:
Yet thence comes such confusion of what was
With what will be, — that late seems long ago,
And, what years should bring round, already
    come,
Till even he withdraws into a dream
As the rest do : I fancy him grown great,
Strong, stern, a tall young man who tutors me,
Frowns with the others, "Poor imprudent
    child !
Why did you venture out of the safe street ?
Why go so far from help to that lone house ?
Why open at the whisper and the knock ? "

Six days ago when it was New Year's day,
We bent above the fire and talked of him,
What he should do when he was grown and
    great.
Violante, Pietro, each had given the arm
I leant on, to walk by, from couch to chair
And fireside, — laughed, as I lay safe at last,
"Pompilia's march from bed to board is made,
Pompilia back again and with a babe,
Shall one day lend his arm and help her
    walk !"
Then we all wished each other more New
    Years.
Pietro began to scheme — "Our cause is
    gained ;
The law is stronger than a wicked man :
Let him henceforth go his way, leave us ours !
We will avoid the city, tempt no more
The greedy ones by feasting and parade, —
Live at the other villa, we know where,
Still farther off, and we can watch the babe
Grow fast in the good air ; and wood is cheap
And wine sincere outside the city gate.
I still have two or three old friends will grope
Their way along the mere half-mile of road,
With staff and lantern on a moonless night
When one needs talk : they 'll find me, never
    fear,
And I 'll find them a flask of the old sort
    yet !"
Violante said, "You chatter like a crow :
Pompilia tires o' the tattle, and shall to bed :
Do not too much the first day, — somewhat
    more
To-morrow, and, the next, begin the cape

And hood and coat! I have spun wool
  enough."
Oh what a happy friendly eve was that!

And, next day, about noon, out Pietro went —
He was so happy and would talk so much,
Until Violante pushed and laughed him forth
Sight-seeing in the cold, — " So much to see
I' the churches! Swathe your throat three
  times! " she cried,
" And, above all, beware the slippery ways,
And bring us all the news by supper-time! "
He came back late, laid by cloak, staff and hat,
Powdered so thick with snow it made us laugh,
Rolled a great log upon the ash o' the hearth,
And bade Violante treat us to a flask,
Because he had obeyed her faithfully,
Gone sight-see through the seven, and found no
  church
To his mind like San Giovanni — "There's the
  fold,
And all the sheep together, big as cats!
And such a shepherd, half the size of life,
Starts up and hears the angel " — when, at the
  door,
A tap: we started up: you know the rest.

Pietro at least had done no harm, I know;
Nor even Violante, so much harm as makes
Such revenge lawful. Certainly she erred —
Did wrong, how shall I dare say otherwise? —
In telling that first falsehood, buying me
From my poor faulty mother at a price,
To pass off upon Pietro as his child.
If one should take my babe, give him a name,
Say he was not Gaetano and my own,
But that some other woman made his mouth
And hands and feet, — how very false were that!
No good could come of that; and all harm did.
Yet if a stranger were to represent
" Needs must you either give your babe to me
And let me call him mine forevermore,
Or let your husband get him " — ah, my God,
That were a trial I refuse to face!
Well, just so here: it proved wrong but seemed
  right
To poor Violante — for there lay, she said,
My poor real dying mother in her rags,
Who put me from her with the life and all,
Poverty, pain, shame and disease at once,
To die the easier by what price I fetched —
Also (I hope) because I should be spared
Sorrow and sin, — why may not that have
  helped?
My father, — he was no one, any one, —
The worse, the likelier, — call him, — he who
  came,
Was wicked for his pleasure, went his way,
And left no trace to track by; there remained
Nothing but me, the unnecessary life,
To catch up or let fall, — and yet a thing
She could make happy, be made happy with,
This poor Violante, — who would frown there-
  at?

Well, God, you see! God plants us where we
  grow.
It is not that, because a bud is born

At a wild brier's end, full i' the wild beast's
  way,
We ought to pluck and put it out of reach
On the oak-tree top, — say, " There the bud
  belongs! "
She thought, moreover, real lies were lies told
For harm's sake; whereas this had good at
  heart,
Good for my mother, good for me, and good
For Pietro who was meant to love a babe,
And needed one to make his life of use,
Receive his house and land when he should
  die.
Wrong, wrong, and always wrong! how plainly
  wrong!
For see, this fault kept pricking, as faults do,
All the same at her heart: this falsehood
  hatched,
She could not let it go nor keep it fast.
She told me so, — the first time I was found
Locked in her arms once more after the pain,
When the nuns let me leave them and go
  home,
And both of us cried all the cares away, —
This it was set her on to make amends,
This brought about the marriage — simply
  this!
Do let me speak for her you blame so much!
When Paul, my husband's brother, found me
  out,
Heard there was wealth for who should marry
  me,
So, came and made a speech to ask my hand
For Guido, — she, instead of piercing straight
Through the pretence to the ignoble truth,
Fancied she saw God's very finger point,
Designate just the time for planting me
(The wild-brier slip she plucked to love and
  wear)
In soil where I could strike real root, and grow,
And get to be the thing I called myself:
For, wife and husband are one flesh, God says,
And I, whose parents seemed such and were
  none,
Should in a husband have a husband now,
Find nothing, this time, but was what it
  seemed,
— All truth and no confusion any more.
I know she meant all good to me, all pain
To herself, — since how could it be aught but
  pain
To give me up, so, from her very breast,
The wilding flower-tree-branch that, all those
  years,
She had got used to feel for and find fixed?
She meant well: has it been so ill i' the main?
That is but fair to ask: one cannot judge
Of what has been the ill or well of life,
The day that one is dying, —sorrows change
Into not altogether sorrow-like;
I do see strangeness but scarce misery,
Now it is over, and no danger more.
My child is safe; there seems not so much pain.
It comes, most like, that I am just absolved,
Purged of the past, the foul in me, washed
  fair, —
One cannot both have and not have, you
  know. —

Being right now, I am happy and color things.
Yes, everybody that leaves life sees all
Softened and bettered : so with other sights :
To me at least was never evening yet
But seemed far beautifuller than its day,
For past is past.

            There was a fancy came,
When somewhere, in the journey with my
    friend,
We stepped into a hovel to get food ;
And there began a yelp here, a bark there, —
Misunderstanding creatures that were wroth
And vexed themselves and us till we retired.
The hovel is life : no matter what dogs bit
Or cat scratched in the hovel I break from,
All outside is lone field, moon and such peace —
Flowing in, filling up as with a sea
Whereon comes Someone, walks fast on the
    white,
Jesus Christ's self, Don Celestine declares,
To meet me and calm all things back again.

Beside, up to my marriage, thirteen years
Were, each day, happy as the day was long :
This may have made the change too terrible.
I know that when Violante told me first
The cavalier — she meant to bring next morn,
Whom I must also let take, kiss my hand —
Would be at San Lorenzo the same eve
And marry me, — which over, we should go
Home both of us without him as before,
And, till she bade speak, I must hold my
    tongue,
Such being the correct way with girl-brides,
From whom one word would make a father
    blush, —
I know, I say, that when she told me this,
— Well, I no more saw sense in what she said
Than a lamb does in people clipping wool ;
Only lay down and let myself be clipped.
And when next day the cavalier who came —
(Tisbe had told me that the slim young man
With wings at head, and wings at feet, and
    sword
Threatening a monster, in our tapestry,
Would eat a girl else, — was a cavalier) —
When he proved Guido Franceschini, — old
And nothing like so tall as I myself,
Hook-nosed and yellow in a bush of beard,
Much like a thing I saw on a boy's wrist,
He called an owl and used for catching birds, —
And when he took my hand and made a smile —
Why, the uncomfortableness of it all
Seemed hardly more important in the case
Than — when one gives you, say, a coin to
    spend —
Its newness or its oldness ; if the piece
Weigh properly and buy you what you wish,
No matter whether you get grime or glare !
Men take the coin, return you grapes and figs.
Here, marriage was the coin, a dirty piece
Would purchase me the praise of those I loved :
About what else should I concern myself ?

So, hardly knowing what a husband meant,
I supposed this or any man would serve,
No whit the worse for being so uncouth :

For I was ill once and a doctor came
With a great ugly hat, no plume thereto,
Black jerkin and black buckles and black
    sword,
And white sharp beard over the ruff in front,
And oh so lean, so sour-faced and austere ! —
Who felt my pulse, made me put out my tongue,
Then oped a phial, dripped a drop or two
Of a black bitter something, — I was cured !
What mattered the fierce beard or the grim
    face ?
It was the physic beautified the man,
Master Malpichi, — never met his match
In Rome, they said, — so ugly all the same !

However, I was hurried through a storm,
Next dark eve of December's deadest day —
How it rained ! — through our street and the
    Lion's-mouth
And the bit of Corso, — cloaked round, covered
    close,
I was like something strange or contraband, —
Into blank San Lorenzo, up the aisle,
My mother keeping hold of me so tight,
I fancied we were come to see a corpse
Before the altar which she pulled me toward.
There we found waiting an unpleasant priest
Who proved the brother, not our parish friend,
But one with mischief-making mouth and eye,
Paul, whom I know since to my cost. And then
I heard the heavy church-door lock out help
Behind us : for the customary warmth,
Two tapers shivered on the altar. "Quick —
Lose no time ! " cried the priest. And straight-
    way down
From . . . what 's behind the altar where he
    hid —
Hawk-nose and yellowness and bush and all,
Stepped Guido, caught my hand, and there
    was I
O' the chancel, and the priest had opened book,
Read here and there, made me say that and
    this,
And after, told me I was now a wife,
Honored indeed, since Christ thus weds the
    Church,
And therefore turned he water into wine,
To show I should obey my spouse like Christ.
Then the two slipped aside and talked apart,
And I, silent and scared, got down again
And joined my mother, who was weeping now.
Nobody seemed to mind us any more,
And both of us on tiptoe found our way
To the door which was unlocked by this, and
    wide.
When we were in the street, the rain had
    stopped,
All things looked better. At our own house-
    door,
Violante whispered, " No one syllable
To Pietro ! Girl-brides never breathe a word ! "
" — Well treated to a wetting, draggle-tails ! "
Laughed Pietro as he opened — " Very near
You made me brave the gutter's roaring sea
To carry off from roost old dove and young,
Trussed up in church, the cote, by me, the kite !
What do these priests mean, praying folk to
    death

On stormy afternoons, with Christmas close
To wash our sins off nor require the rain?"
Violante gave my hand a timely squeeze,
Madonna saved me from immodest speech,
I kissed him and was quiet, being a bride.

When I saw nothing more, the next three weeks,
Of Guido — "Nor the Church sees Christ"
  thought I:
"Nothing is changed however, wine is wine
And water only water in our house.
Nor did I see that ugly doctor since
That cure of the illness : just as I was cured,
I am married, — neither scarecrow will return."

Three weeks, I chuckled — "How would Giulia
  stare,
And Tecla smile and Tisbe laugh outright,
Were it not impudent for brides to talk !"—
Until one morning, as I sat and sang
At the broidery-frame alone i' the chamber, —
  loud
Voices, two, three together, sobbings too,
And my name, "Guido," "Paolo," flung like
  stones
From each to the other ! In I ran to see.
There stood the very Guido and the priest
With sly face, — formal but nowise afraid, —
While Pietro seemed all red and angry, scarce
Able to stutter out his wrath in words ;
And this it was that made my mother sob,
As he reproached her — "You have murdered
  us,
Me and yourself and this our child beside !"
Then Guido interposed, "Murdered or not,
Be it enough your child is now my wife !
I claim and come to take her." Paul put in,
"Consider — kinsman, dare I term you so ? —
What is the good of your sagacity
Except to counsel in a strait like this ?
I guarantee the parties man and wife
Whether you like or loathe it, bless or ban.
May spilt milk be put back within the bowl —
The done thing, undone ? You, it is, we look
For counsel to, you fitliest will advise !
Since milk, though spilt and spoilt, does marble
  good,
Better we down on knees and scrub the floor,
Than sigh, ' the waste would make a syllabub !'
Help us so turn disaster to account,
So predispose the groom, he needs shall grace
The bride with favor from the very first,
Not begin marriage an embittered man !"
He smiled, — the game so wholly in his hands !
While fast and faster sobbed Violante — "Ay,
All of us murdered, past averting now !
O my sin, O my secret !" and such like.

Then I began to half surmise the truth ;
Something had happened, low, mean, under-
  hand,
False, and my mother was to blame, and I
To pity, whom all spoke of, none addressed :
I was the chattel that had caused a crime.
I stood mute, — those who tangled must untie
The embroilment. Pietro cried, "Withdraw,
  my child !
She is not helpful to the sacrifice

At this stage, — do you want the victim by
While you discuss the value of her blood ?
For her sake, I consent to hear you talk :
Go, child, and pray God help the innocent !"

I did go and was praying God, when came
Violante, with eyes swollen and red enough,
But movement on her mouth for make-believe
Matters were somehow getting right again.
She bade me sit down by her side and hear.
"You are too young and cannot understand,
Nor did your father understand at first.
I wished to benefit all three of us,
And when he failed to take my meaning —
  why,
I tried to have my way at unaware —
Obtained him the advantage he refused.
As if I put before him wholesome food
Instead of broken victual, — he finds change
I' the viands, never cares to reason why,
But falls to blaming me, would fling the plate
From window, scandalize the neighborhood,
Even while he smacks his lips, — men's way
  my child !
But either you have prayed him unperverse
Or I have talked him back into his wits :
And Paolo was a help in time of need, —
Guido, not much — my child, the way of men !
A priest is more a woman than a man,
And Paul did wonders to persuade. In short,
Yes, he was wrong, your father sees and says ;
My scheme was worth attempting : and bears
  fruit,
Gives you a husband and a noble name,
A palace and no end of pleasant things.
What do you care about a handsome youth ?
They are so volatile, and tease their wives !
This is the kind of man to keep the house.
We lose no daughter, — gain a son, that 's all :
For 't is arranged we never separate,
Nor miss, in our gray time of life, the tints
Of you that color eve to match with morn.
In good or ill, we share and share alike,
And cast our lots into a common lap,
And all three die together as we lived !
Only, at Arezzo, — that 's a Tuscan town,
Not so large as this noisy Rome, no doubt,
But older far and finer much, say folk, —
In a great palace where you will be queen,
Know the Archbishop and the Governor,
And we see homage done you ere we die.
Therefore, be good and pardon !" — "Pardon
  what ?
You know things, I am very ignorant :
All is right if you only will not cry !"

And so an end ! Because a blank begins
From when, at the word, she kissed me hard
  and hot,
And took me back to where my father leaned
Opposite Guido — who stood eying him,
As eyes the butcher the cast panting ox
That feels his fate is come, nor struggles
  more, —
While Paul looked archly on, pricked brow at
  whiles
With the pen-point as to punish triumph
  there. —

And said, "Count Guido, take your lawful
    wife
Until death part you!"

                    All since is one blank,
Over and ended ; a terrific dream.
It is the good of dreams — so soon they go!
Wake in a horror of heart-beats, you may —
Cry, "The dread thing will never from my
    thoughts!"
Still, a few daylight doses of plain life,
Cock-crow and sparrow-chirp, or bleat and bell
Of goats that trot by, tinkling, to be milked;
And when you rub your eyes awake and wide,
Where is the harm o' the horror? Gone! So
    here.
I know I wake, — but from what? Blank, I
    say!
This is the note of evil : for good lasts.
Even when Don Celestine bade "Search and
    find!
For your soul's sake, remember what is past,
The better to forgive it," — all in vain!
What was fast getting indistinct before,
Vanished outright. By special grace perhaps,
Between that first calm and this last, four
    years
Vanish, — one quarter of my life, you know.
I am held up, amid the nothingness,
By one or two truths only — thence I hang,
And there I live, — the rest is death or dream,
All but those points of my support. I think
Of what I saw at Rome once in the Square
O' the Spaniards, opposite the Spanish House :
There was a foreigner had trained a goat,
A shuddering white woman of a beast,
To climb up, stand straight on a pile of sticks
Put close, which gave the creature room
    enough:
When she was settled there, he, one by one,
Took away all the sticks, left just the four
Whereon the little hoofs did really rest,
There she kept firm, all underneath was air.
So, what I hold by, are my prayer to God,
My hope, that came in answer to the prayer,
Some hand would interpose and save me —
    hand
Which proved to be my friend's hand : and, —
    blest bliss, —
That fancy which began so faint at first,
That thrill of dawn's suffusion through my
    dark,
Which I perceive was promise of my child,
The light his unborn face sent long before, —
God's way of breaking the good news to flesh.
That is all left now of those four bad years.
Don Celestine urged, "But remember more!
Other men's faults may help me find your own.
I need the cruelty exposed, explained,
Or how can I advise you to forgive ? "
He thought I could not properly forgive
Unless I ceased forgetting, — which is true:
For, bringing back reluctantly to mind
My husband's treatment of me, — by a light
That's later than my lifetime, I review
And comprehend much and imagine more,
And have but little to forgive at last.
For now, — be fair and say, — is it not true

He was ill-used and cheated of his hope
To get enriched by marriage ?   Marriage gave
Me and no money, broke the compact so :
He had a right to ask me on those terms,
As Pietro and Violante to declare
They would not give me : so the bargain stood
They broke it, and he felt himself aggrieved,
Became unkind with me to punish them.
They said 't was he began deception first,
Nor, in one point whereto he pledged himself,
Kept promise : what of that, suppose it were ?
Echoes die off, scarcely reverberate
Forever, — why should ill keep echoing ill,
And never let our ears have done with noise ?
Then my poor parents took the violent way
To thwart him, — he must needs retaliate, —
    wrong,
Wrong, and all wrong, — better say, all blind!
As I myself was, that is sure, who else
Had understood the mystery : for his wife
Was bound in some sort to help somehow
    there.
It seems as if I might have interposed,
Blunted the edge of their resentment so,
Since he vexed me because they first vexed
    him ;
"I will entreat them to desist, submit,
Give him the money and be poor in peace, —
Certainly not go tell the world : perhaps
He will grow quiet with his gains."
                    Yes, say
Something to this effect and you do well !
But then you have to see first : I was blind.
That is the fruit of all such wormy ways,
The indirect, the unapproved of God :
You cannot find their author's end and aim,
Not even to substitute your good for bad,
Your straight for the irregular ; you stand
Stupefied, profitless, as cow or sheep
That miss a man's mind ; anger him just twice
By trial at repairing the first fault.
Thus, when he blamed me, "You are a co-
    quette,
A lure-owl posturing to attract birds,
You look love-lures at theatre and church,
In walk, at window ! " — that, I knew, was
    false :
But why he charged me falsely, whither sought
To drive me by such charge, — how could I
    know ?
So, unaware, I only made things worse.
I tried to soothe him by abjuring walk,
Window, church, theatre, for good and all,
As if he had been in earnest : that, you know,
Was nothing like the object of his charge.
Yes, when I got my maid to supplicate
The priest, whose name she read when she
    would read
Those feigned false letters I was forced to hear
Though I could read no word of, — he should
    cease
Writing, — nay, if he minded prayer of mine,
Cease from so much as even pass the street
Whereon our house looked, — in my ignorance
I was just thwarting Guido's true intent ;
Which was, to bring about a wicked change
Of sport to earnest, tempt a thoughtless man
To write indeed, and pass the house, and more,

Till both of us were taken in a crime.
He ought not to have wished me thus act lies,
Simulate folly: but — wrong or right, the
wish —
I failed to apprehend its drift. How plain
It follows, — if I fell into such fault,
He also may have overreached the mark,
Made mistake, by perversity of brain,
I' the whole sad strange plot, the grotesque in-
trigue
To make me and my friend unself ourselves,
Be other man and woman than we were!
Think it out, you who have the time! for
me, —
I cannot say less; more I will not say.
Leave it to God to cover and undo!
Only, my dulness should not prove too much!
— Not prove that in a certain other point
Wherein my husband blamed me, — and you
blame,
If I interpret smiles and shakes of head, —
I was dull too. Oh, if I dared but speak!
Must I speak? I am blamed that I forwent
A way to make my husband's favor come.
That is true: I was firm, withstood, refused . . .
— Women as you are, how can I find the words?

I felt there was just one thing Guido claimed
I had no right to give nor he to take;
We being in estrangement, soul from soul:
Till, when I sought help, the Archbishop smiled,
Inquiring into privacies of life,
— Said I was blamable — (he stands for God)
Nowise entitled to exemption there.
Then I obeyed, — as surely had obeyed
Were the injunction "Since your husband bids,
Swallow the burning coal he proffers you!"
But I did wrong, and he gave wrong advice
Though he were thrice Archbishop, — that, I
know! —
Now I have got to die and see things clear.
Remember I was barely twelve years old —
A child at marriage: I was let alone
For weeks, I told you, lived my child-life still
Even at Arezzo, when I woke and found
First . . . but I need not think of that again —
Over and ended! Try and take the sense
Of what I signify, if it must be so.
After the first, my husband, for hate's sake,
Said one eve, when the simpler cruelty
Seemed somewhat dull at edge and fit to bear,
"We have been man and wife six months al-
most:
How long is this your comedy to last?
Go this night to my chamber, not your own!"
At which word, I did rush — most true the
charge —
And gain the Archbishop's house — he stands
for God —
And fall upon my knees and clasp his feet,
Praying him hinder what my estranged soul
Refused to bear, though patient of the rest:
"Place me within a convent," I implored —
"Let me henceforward lead the virgin life
You praise in her you bid me imitate!"
What did he answer? "Folly of ignorance!
Know, daughter, circumstances make or mar
Virginity, — 't is virtue or 't is vice.

That which was glory in the Mother of God
Had been, for instance, damnable in Eve
Created to be mother of mankind.
Had Eve, in answer to her Maker's speech
' Be fruitful, multiply, replenish earth ' —
Pouted ' But I choose rather to remain
Single ' — why, she had spared herself forthwith
Further probation by the apple and snake,
Been pushed straight out of Paradise! For
see —
If motherhood be qualified impure,
I catch you making God command Eve sin!
— A blasphemy so like these Molinists',
I must suspect you dip into their books."
Then he pursued " 'T was in your covenant!"

No! There my husband never used deceit.
He never did by speech nor act imply
"Because of our souls' yearning that we meet
And mix in soul through flesh, which yours and
mine
Wear and impress, and make their visible
selves,
— All which means, for the love of you and me,
Let us become one flesh, being one soul!"
He only stipulated for the wealth;
Honest so far. But when he spoke as plain —
Dreadfully honest also — "Since our souls
Stand each from each, a whole world's width
between,
Give me the fleshly vesture I can reach
And rend and leave just fit for hell to burn!" —
Why, in God's name, for Guido's soul's own sake
Imperilled by polluting mine, — I say,
I did resist; would I had overcome!

My heart died out at the Archbishop's smile;
— It seemed so stale and worn a way o' the
world,
As though 't were nature frowning — "Here is
Spring,
The sun shines as he shone at Adam's fall,
The earth requires that warmth reach every-
where:
What, must your patch of snow be saved for-
sooth
Because you rather fancy snow than flowers?"
Something in this style he began with me.
Last he said, savagely for a good man,
"This explains why you call your husband
harsh,
Harsh to you, harsh to whom you love. God's
Bread!
The poor Count has to manage a mere child
Whose parents leave untaught the simplest
things
Their duty was and privilege to teach, —
Goodwives' instruction, gossips' lore: they laugh
And leave the Count the task, — or leave it
me!"
Then I resolved to tell a frightful thing.
"I am not ignorant, — know what I say,
Declaring this is sought for hate, not love.
Sir, you may hear things like almighty God.
I tell you that my housemate, yes — the priest
My husband's brother, Canon Girolamo —
Has taught me what depraved and misnamed
love

Means, and what outward signs denote the sin,
For he solicits me and says he loves,
The idle young priest with naught else to do.
My husband sees this, knows this, and lets be.
Is it your counsel I bear this beside ? "
" — More scandal, and against a priest this
    time !
What, 't is the Canon now ? " — less snap-
    pishly —
" Rise up, my child, for such a child you are,
The rod were too advanced a punishment !
Let 's try the honeyed cake.   A parable !
' Without a parable spake he not to them.'
There was a ripe round long black toothsome
    fruit,
Even a flower-fig, the prime boast of May ;
And, to the tree, said . . . either the spirit o'
    the fig,
Or, if we bring in men, the gardener,
Archbishop of the orchard — had I time
To try o' the two which fits in best : indeed
It might be the Creator's self, but then
The tree should bear an apple, I suppose, —
Well, anyhow, one with authority said,
' Ripe fig, burst skin, regale the fig-pecker —
The bird whereof thou art a perquisite ! '
' Nay,' with a flounce, replied the restif fig,
' I much prefer to keep my pulp myself :
He may go breakfastless and dinnerless,
Supperless of one crimson seed, for me ! '
So, back she flopped into her bunch of leaves.
He flew off, left her, — did the natural lord, —
And lo, three hundred thousand bees and wasps
Found her out, feasted on her to the shuck :
Such gain the fig's that gave its bird no bite !
The moral, — fools elude their proper lot,
Tempt other fools, get ruined all alike.
Therefore go home, embrace your husband
    quick !
Which if his Canon brother chance to see,
He will the sooner back to book again."

So, home I did go ; so, the worst befell :
So, I had proof the Archbishop was just man,
And hardly that, and certainly no more.
For, miserable consequence to me,
My husband's hatred waxed nor waned at all,
His brother's boldness grew effrontery soon,
And my last stay and comfort in myself
Was forced from me : henceforth I looked to
God
Only, nor cared my desecrated soul
Should have fair walls, gay windows for the
    world.
God's glimmer, that came through the ruin-top,
Was witness why all lights were quenched in-
    side :
Henceforth I asked God counsel, not mankind.

So, when I made the effort, freed myself,
They said — " No care to save appearance here !
How cynic, — when, how wanton, were
    enough ! "
— Adding, it all came of my mother's life —
My own real mother, whom I never knew,
Who did wrong (if she needs must have done
    wrong)
Through being all her life, not my four years,

At mercy of the hateful : every beast
O' the field was wont to break that fountain
    fence,
Trample the silver into mud so murk
Heaven could not find itself reflected there.
Now they cry, " Out on her, who, plashy pool,
Bequeathed turbidity and bitterness
To the daughter-stream where Guido dipt and
    drank ! "

Well, since she had to bear this brand — let me !
The rather do I understand her now, —
From my experience of what hate calls love, —
Much love might be in what their love called
    hate.
If she sold . . . what they call, sold . . . me,
    her child —
I shall believe she hoped in her poor heart
That I at least might try be good and pure,
Begin to live untempted, not go doomed
And done with ere once found in fault, as she.
Oh and, my mother, it all came to this ?
Why should I trust those that speak ill of you,
When I mistrust who speaks even well of them ?
Why, since all bound to do me good, did harm,
May not you, seeming as you harmed me most,
Have meant to do most good — and feed your
    child
From bramble-bush, whom not one orchard-tree
But drew bough back from, nor let one fruit
    fall ?
This it was for you sacrificed your babe ?
Gained just this, giving your heart's hope away
As I might give mine, loving it as you,
If . . . but that never could be asked of me !

There, enough !   I have my support again,
Again the knowledge that my babe was, is,
Will be mine only.   Him, by death, I give
Outright to God, without a further care, —
But not to any parent in the world, —
So to be safe : why is it we repine ?
What guardianship were safer could we choose ?
All human plans and projects come to naught :
My life, and what I know of other lives,
Prove that : no plan nor project !   God shall
    care !

And now you are not tired ?   How patient then
All of you, — oh yes, patient this long while
Listening, and understanding, I am sure !
Four days ago, when I was sound and well
And like to live, no one would understand.
People were kind, but smiled, " And what of
    him,
Your friend, whose tonsure the rich dark-brown
    hides ?
There, there ! — your lover, do we dream he
    was ?
A priest too — never were such naughtiness !
Still, he thinks many a long think, never fear,
After the shy pale lady, — lay so light
For a moment in his arms, the lucky one ! "
And so on : wherefore should I blame you
    much ?
So we are made, such difference in minds,
Such difference too in eyes that see the minds !
That man, you misinterpret and misprise —

The glory of his nature, I had thought,
Shot itself out in white light, blazed the truth
Through every atom of his act with me :
Yet where I point you, through the crystal
      shrine,
Purity in quintessence, one dew-drop,
You all descry a spider in the midst.
One says, " The head of it is plain to see,"
And one, " They are the feet by which I judge,"
All say, " Those films were spun by nothing
      else."

Then, I must lay my babe away with God,
Nor think of him again for gratitude.
Yes, my last breath shall wholly spend itself
In one attempt more to disperse the stain,
The mist from other breath fond mouths have
      made,
About a lustrous and pellucid soul :
So that, when I am gone but sorrow stays,
And people need assurance in their doubt
If God yet have a servant, man a friend,
The weak a savior, and the vile a foe, —
Let him be present, by the name invoked,
Giuseppe-Maria Caponsacchi !

                              There,
Strength comes already with the utterance !
I will remember once more for his sake
The sorrow : for he lives and is belied.
Could he be here, how he would speak for me !

I had been miserable three drear years
In that dread palace and lay passive now,
When I first learned there could be such a man.
Thus it fell : I was at a public play,
In the last days of Carnival last March,
Brought there I knew not why, but now know
      well.
My husband put me where I sat, in front ;
Then crouched down, breathed cold through
      me from behind,
Stationed i' the shadow, — none in front could
      see, —
I, it was, faced the stranger-throng beneath,
The crowd with upturned faces, eyes one stare,
Voices one buzz. I looked but to the stage,
Whereon two lovers sang and interchanged
" True life is only love, love only bliss :
I love thee — thee I love ! " then they em-
      braced.
I looked thence to the ceiling and the walls, —
Over the crowd, those voices and those eyes, —
My thoughts went through the roof and out, to
      Rome
On wings of music, waft of measured words, —
Set me down there, a happy child again,
Sure that to-morrow would be festa-day,
Hearing my parents praise past festas more,
And seeing they were old if I was young,
Yet wondering why they still would end dis-
      course
With " We must soon go, you abide your time,
And, — might we haply see the proper friend
Throw his arm over you and make you safe ! "

Sudden I saw him ; into my lap there fell
A foolish twist of comfits. broke my dream

And brought me from the air and laid me low,
As ruined as the soaring bee that 's reached
(So Pietro told me at the Villa once)
By the dust-handful. There the comfits lay :
I looked to see who flung them, and I faced
This Caponsacchi, looking up in turn.
Ere I could reason out why, I felt sure,
Whoever flung them, his was not the hand, —
Up rose the round face and good-natured grin
Of one who, in effect, had played the prank,
From covert close beside the earnest face, —
Fat waggish Conti, friend of all the world.
He was my husband's cousin, privileged
To throw the thing : the other, silent, grave,
Solemn almost, saw me, as I saw him.

There is a psalm Don Celestine recites,
" Had I a dove's wings, how I fain would
      flee ! "
The psalm runs not " I hope, I pray for
      wings," —
Not " If wings fall from heaven, I fix them
      fast," —
Simply " How good it were to fly and rest,
Have hope now, and one day expect content !
How well to do what I shall never do ! "
So I said, " Had there been a man like that,
To lift me with his strength out of all strife
Into the calm, how I could fly and rest !
I have a keeper in the garden here
Whose sole employment is to strike me low
If ever I, for solace, seek the sun.
Life means with me successful feigning death,
Lying stone-like, eluding notice so,
Foregoing here the turf and there the sky.
Suppose that man had been instead of this ! "

Presently Conti laughed into my ear,
— Had tripped up to the raised place where I
      sat —
" Cousin, I flung them brutishly and hard !
Because you must be hurt, to look austere
As Caponsacchi yonder, my tall friend
A-gazing now. Ah, Guido, you so close ?
Keep on your knees, do ! Beg her to forgive !
My cornet battered like a cannon-ball.
Good-by, I 'm gone ! " — nor waited the reply.

That night at supper, out my husband broke,
" Why was that throwing, that buffoonery ?
Do you think I am your dupe ? What man
      would dare
Throw comfits in a stranger lady's lap ?
'T was knowledge of you bred such insolence
In Caponsacchi ; he dared shoot the bolt,
Using that Conti for his stalking-horse.
How could you see him this once and no more,
When he is always haunting hereabout
At the street-corner or the palace-side,
Publishing my shame and your impudence ?
You are a wanton, — I a dupe, you think ?
O Christ, what hinders that I kill her quick ? "
Whereat he drew his sword and feigned a
      thrust.

All this, now, — being not so strange to me,
Used to such misconception day by day
And broken-in to bear, — I bore, this time.

More quietly than woman should perhaps ;
Repeated the mere truth and held my tongue.

Then he said, "Since you play the ignorant,
I shall instruct you. This amour, — com-
    menced
Or finished or midway in act, all 's one, —
'T is the town-talk ; so my revenge shall be.
Does he presume because he is a priest ?
I warn him that the sword I wear shall pink
His lily-scented cassock through and through,
Next time I catch him underneath your eaves ! "
But he had threatened with the sword so oft
And, after all, not kept his promise. All
I said was, " Let God save the innocent !
Moreover, death is far from a bad fate.
I shall go pray for you and me, not him ;
And then I look to sleep, come death or, worse,
Life." So, I slept.

                    There may have elapsed a week,
When Margherita, — called my waiting-maid,
Whom it is said my husband found too fair —
Who stood and heard the charge and the reply,
Who never once would let the matter rest
From that night forward, but rang changes
    still
On this the thrust and that the shame, and how
Good cause for jealousy cures jealous fools,
And what a paragon was this same priest
She talked about until I stopped my ears, —
She said, " A week is gone ; you comb your
    hair,
Then go mope in a corner, cheek on palm,
Till night comes round again, — so, waste a
    week
As if your husband menaced you in sport.
Have not I some acquaintance with his tricks ?
Oh no, he did not stab the serving-man
Who made and sang the rhymes about me
    once !
For why ? They sent him to the wars next
    day.
Nor poisoned he the foreigner, my friend,
Who wagered on the whiteness of my breast, —
The swarth skins of our city in dispute :
For, though he paid me proper compliment,
The Count well knew he was besotted with
Somebody else, a skin as black as ink,
(As all the town knew save my foreigner) —
He found and wedded presently, — ' Why need
Better revenge ? ' — the Count asked. But
    what 's here ?
A priest that does not fight, and cannot wed,
Yet must be dealt with ! If the Count took fire
For the poor pastime of a minute, — me —
What were the conflagration for yourself,
Countess and lady-wife and all the rest ?
The priest will perish ; you will grieve too late :
So shall the city-ladies' handsomest
Frankest and liberalest gentleman
Die for you, to appease a scurvy dog
Hanging 's too good for. Is there no escape ?
Were it not simple Christian charity
To warn the priest be on his guard, — save him
Assured death, save yourself from causing it ?
I meet him in the street. Give me a glove,
A ring to show for token ! Mum 's the word ! "

I answered, " If you were, as styled, my maid
I would command you : as you are, you say,
My husband's intimate, — assist his wife
Who can do nothing but entreat ' Be still ! '
Even if you speak truth and a crime is planned,
Leave help to God as I am forced to do !
There is no other help, or we should craze,
Seeing such evil with no human cure.
Reflect that God, who makes the storm desist,
Can make an angry violent heart subside.
Why should we venture teach him governance ?
Never address me on this subject more ! "

Next night she said, " But I went, all the same,
— Ay, saw your Caponsacchi in his house,
And come back stuffed with news I must out-
    pour.
I told him, ' Sir, my mistress is a stone :
Why should you harm her for no good you
    get ?
For you do harm her — prowl about our place
With the Count never distant half the street,
Lurking at every corner, would you look !
'T is certain she has witched you with a spell.
Are there not other beauties at your beck ?
We all know, Donna This and Monna That
Die for a glance of yours, yet here you gaze !
Go make them grateful, leave the stone its
    cold ! '
And he — oh, he turned first white and then
    red,
And then — ' To her behest I bow myself,
Whom I love with my body and my soul :
Only a word i' the bowing ! See, I write
One little word, no harm to see or hear !
Then, fear no further ! ' This is what he
    wrote.
I know you cannot read, — therefore, let me !
' My idol ! ' " . . .

                    But I took it from her hand
And tore it into shreds. " Why, join the rest
Who harm me ? Have I ever done you
    wrong ?
People have told me 't is you wrong myself :
Let it suffice I either feel no wrong
Or else forgive it, — yet you turn my foe !
The others hunt me and you throw a noose ! "

She muttered, " Have your wilful way ! " I
    slept.

Whereupon . . . no, I leave my husband out,
It is not to do him more hurt, I speak.
Let it suffice, when misery was most,
One day, I swooned and got a respite so.
She stooped as I was slowly coming to,
This Margherita, ever on my trace,
And whispered — " Caponsacchi ! "

                    If I drowned,
But woke afloat i' the wave with upturned
    eyes,
And found their first sight was a star ! I
    turned —
For the first time, I let her have her will,
Heard passively, — " The imposthume at such
    head,

One touch, one lancet - puncture would re-
lieve, —
And still no glance the good physician's way
Who rids you of the torment in a trice !
Still he writes letters you refuse to hear.
He may prevent your husband, kill himself,
So desperate and all fordone is he !
Just hear the pretty verse he made to-day !
A sonnet from Mirtillo. ' *Peerless fair.* . . . '
All poetry is difficult to read,
— The sense of it is, anyhow, he seeks
Leave to contrive you an escape from hell,
And for that purpose asks an interview.
I can write, I can grant it in your name,
Or, what is better, lead you to his house.
Your husband dashes you against the stones ;
This man would place each fragment in a
shrine :
You hate him, love your husband ! "

                     I returned,
" It is not true I love my husband, — no,
Nor hate this man. I listen while you speak,
— Assured that what you say is false, the
same :
Much as when once, to me a little child,
A rough gaunt man in rags, with eyes on fire,
A crowd of boys and idlers at his heels,
Rushed as I crossed the Square, and held my
head
In his two hands, ' Here 's she will let me
speak !
You little girl, whose eyes do good to mine,
I am the Pope, am Sextus, now the Sixth ;
And that Twelfth Innocent, proclaimed to-day,
Is Lucifer disguised in human flesh !
The angels, met in conclave, crowned me ! ' —
thus
He gibbered and I listened ; but I knew
All was delusion, ere folk interposed,
' Unfasten him, the maniac ! ' Thus I know
All your report of Caponsacchi false,
Folly or dreaming : I have seen so much
By that adventure at the spectacle,
The face I fronted that one first, last time :
He would belie it by such words and thoughts.
Therefore while you profess to show him me,
I ever see his own face. Get you gone ! "

" — That will I, nor once open mouth again, —
No, by Saint Joseph and the Holy Ghost !
On your head be the damage, so adieu ! "

And so more days, more deeds I must forget,
Till . . . what a strange thing now is to de-
clare !
Since I say anything, say all if true !
And how my life seems lengthened as to serve !
It may be idle or inopportune,
But, true ? — why, what was all I said but
truth,
Even when I found that such as are untrue
Could only take the truth in through a lie ?
Now — I am speaking truth to the Truth's self :
God will lend credit to my words this time.

It had got half through April. I arose
One vivid daybreak, — who had gone to bed

In the old way my wont those last three years,
Careless until, the cup drained, I should die.
The last sound in my ear, the over-night,
Had been a something let drop on the sly
In prattle by Margherita, " Soon enough
Gayeties end, now Easter 's past : a week,
And the Archbishop gets him back to
Rome, —
Every one leaves the town for Rome, this
Spring, —
Even Caponsacchi, out of heart and hope,
Resigns himself and follows with the flock."
I heard this drop and drop like rain outside
Fast-falling through the darkness while she
spoke :
So had I heard with like indifference,
" And Michael's pair of wings will arrive first
At Rome, to introduce the company,
And bear him from our picture where he fights
Satan, — expect to have that dragon loose
And never a defender ! " — my sole thought
Being still, as night came, " Done, another
day !
How good to sleep and so get nearer death ! " —
When, what, first thing at daybreak, pierced
the sleep
With a summons to me ? Up I sprang alive,
Light in me, light without me, everywhere
Change ! A broad yellow sunbeam was let
fall
From heaven to earth, — a sudden drawbridge
lay,
Along which marched a myriad merry motes,
Mocking the flies that crossed them and re-
crossed
In rival dance, companions new-born too.
On the house-eaves, a dripping shag of weed
Shook diamonds on each dull gray lattice-
square,
As first one, then another bird leapt by,
And light was off, and lo was back again,
Always with one voice, — where are two such
joys ? —
The blessed building - sparrow ! I stepped
forth,
Stood on the terrace, — o'er the roofs, such
sky !
My heart sang, " I too am to go away,
I too have something I must care about,
Carry away with me to Rome, to Rome !
The bird brings hither sticks and hairs and
wool,
And nowhere else i' the world ; what fly breaks
rank,
Falls out of the procession that befits,
From window here to window there, with all
The world to choose, — so well he knows his
course ?
I have my purpose and my motive too,
My march to Rome, like any bird or fly !
Had I been dead ! How right to be alive !
Last night I almost prayed for leave to die,
Wished Guido all his pleasure with the sword
Or the poison, — poison, sword, was but a trick,
Harmless, may God forgive him the poor jest !
My life is charmed, will last till I reach Rome !
Yesterday, but for the sin, — ah, nameless be
The deed I could have dared against myself !

Now — see if I will touch an unripe fruit,
And risk the health I want to have and use !
Not to live, now, would be the wickedness, —
For life means to make haste and go to Rome
And leave Arezzo, leave all woes at once ! "

Now, understand here, by no means mistake !
Long ago had I tried to leave that house
When it seemed such procedure would stop
    sin ;
And still failed more the more I tried — at
    first
The Archbishop, as I told you, — next, our
    lord
The Governor, — indeed I found my way,
I went to the great palace where he rules,
Though I knew well 't was he who, — when I
    gave
A jewel or two, themselves had given me,
Back to my parents, — since they wanted bread,
They who had never let me want a nosegay, —
    he
Spoke of the jail for felons, if they kept
What was first theirs, then mine, so doubly
    theirs,
Though all the while my husband's most of all !
I knew well who had spoke the word wrought
    this :
Yet, being in extremity, I fled
To the Governor, as I say, — scarce opened
    lip
When — the cold cruel snicker close behind —
Guido was on my trace, already there,
Exchanging nod and wink for shrug and smile,
And I — pushed back to him and, for my pains,
Paid with . . . but why remember what is
    past ?
I sought out a poor friar the people call
The Roman, and confessed my sin which came
Of their sin, — that fact could not be re-
    pressed, —
The frightfulness of my despair in God :
And feeling, through the grate, his horror
    shake,
Implored him, " Write for me who cannot
    write,
Apprise my parents, make them rescue me !
You bid me be courageous and trust God :
Do you in turn dare somewhat, trust and
    write,
' Dear friends, who used to be my parents once,
And now declare you have no part in me,
This is some riddle I want wit to solve,
Since you must love me with no difference.
Even suppose you altered, — there 's your hate,
To ask for : hate of you two dearest ones
I shall find liker love than love found here,
If husbands love their wives. Take me away
And hate me as you do the gnats and fleas,
Even the scorpions ! How I shall rejoice ! '
Write that and save me ! " And he promised
    — wrote
Or did not write ; things never changed at all :
He was not like the Augustinian here !
Last, in a desperation I appealed
To friends, whoever wished me better days,
To Guillichini, that 's of kin, — " What, I —
Travel to Rome with you ? A flying gout

Bids me deny my heart and mind my leg ! "
Then I tried Conti, used to brave — laugh back
The louring thunder when his cousin scowled
At me protected by his presence : " You —
Who well know what you cannot save me
    from, —
Carry me off ! What frightens you, a priest ? "
He shook his head, looked grave — " Above my
    strength !
Guido has claws that scratch, shows feline
    teeth ;
A formidabler foe than I dare fret :
Give me a dog to deal with, twice the size !
Of course I am a priest and Canon too,
But . . . by the bye . . . though both, not
    quite so bold
As he, my fellow-Canon, brother-priest,
The personage in such ill odor here
Because of the reports — pure birth o' the
    brain !
Our Caponsacchi, he 's your true Saint George
To slay the monster, set the Princess free,
And have the whole High-Altar to himself :
I always think so when I see that piece
I' the Pieve, that 's his church and mine, you
    know :
Though you drop eyes at mention of his name ! "

That name had got to take a half-grotesque
Half-ominous, wholly enigmatic sense,
Like any by-word, broken bit of song
Born with a meaning, changed by mouth and
    mouth
That mix it in a sneer or smile, as chance
Bids, till it now means naught but ugliness
And perhaps shame.

                    — All this intends to say,
That, over-night, the notion of escape
Had seemed distemper, dreaming ; and the
    name,
Not the man, but the name of him, thus made
Into a mockery and disgrace, — why, she
Who uttered it persistently, had laughed,
" I name his name, and there you start and
    wince
As criminal from the red tongs' touch ! " — yet
    now,
Now, as I stood letting morn bathe me bright,
Choosing which butterfly should bear my
    news, —
The white, the brown one, or that tinier blue, —
The Margherita, I detested so,
In she came — " The fine day, the good Spring
    time !
What, up and out at window ? That is best.
No thought of Caponsacchi ? — who stood
    there
All night on one leg, like the sentry crane,
Under the pelting of your water-spout —
Looked last look at your lattice ere he leave
Our city, bury his dead hope at Rome.
Ay, go to looking-glass and make you fine,
While he may die ere touch one least loose
    hair
You drag at with the comb in such a rage ! "

I turned — " Tell Caponsacchi he may come ! '

" Tell him to come? Ah, but, for charity,
A truce to fooling! Come? What, — come
        this eve?
Peter and Paul ! But I see through the trick !
Yes, come, and take a flower-pot on his head.
Flung from your terrace ! No joke, sincere
        truth ? ”

How plainly I perceived hell flash and fade
O' the face of her, — the doubt that first paled
        joy,
Then, final reassurance I indeed
Was caught now, never to be free again !
What did I care ? — who felt myself of force
To play with silk, and spurn the horsehair-
        springe.

" But — do you know that I have bade him
        come,
And in your own name? I presumed so much,
Knowing the thing you needed in your heart.
But somehow — what had I to show in proof?
He would not come : half-promised, that was
        all,
And wrote the letters you refused to read.
What is the message that shall move him
        now ? ”

" After the Ave Maria, at first dark,
I will be standing on the terrace, say ! ”

" I would I had a good long lock of hair
Should prove I was not lying ! Never mind ! ”

Off she went — " May he not refuse, that 's
        all —
Fearing a trick ! ”

                I answered, " He will come."
And, all day, I sent prayer like incense up
To God the strong, God the beneficent,
God ever mindful in all strife and strait,
Who, for our own good, makes the need ex-
        treme,
Till at the last he puts forth might and saves.
An old rhyme came into my head and rang
Of how a virgin, for the faith of God,
Hid herself, from the Paynims that pursued,
In a cave's heart ; until a thunderstone,
Wrapped in a flame, revealed the couch and
        prey :
And they laughed — " Thanks to lightning,
        ours at last ! ”
And she cried, " Wrath of God, assert his
        love !
Servant of God, thou fire, befriend his child ! ”
And lo, the fire she grasped at, fixed its flash,
Lay in her hand a calm cold dreadful sword
She brandished till pursuers strewed the
        ground,
So did the souls within them die away,
As o'er the prostrate bodies, sworded, safe,
She walked forth to the solitudes and Christ :
So should I grasp the lightning and be saved !

And still, as the day wore, the trouble grew
Whereby I guessed there would be born a star,
Until at an intense throe of the dusk,

I started up, was pushed, I dare to say,
Out on the terrace, leaned and looked at last
Where the deliverer waited me : the same
Silent and solemn face, I first descried
At the spectacle, confronted mine once more.

So was that minute twice vouchsafed me, so
The manhood, wasted then, was still at watch
To save me yet a second time : no change
Here, though all else changed in the changing
        world !

I spoke on the instant, as my duty bade,
In some such sense as this, whatever the phrase.

" Friend, foolish words were borne from you to
        me ;
Your soul behind them is the pure strong wind,
Not dust and feathers which its breath may
        bear :
These to the witless seem the wind itself,
Since proving thus the first of it they feel.
If by mischance you blew offence my way,
The straws are dropt, the wind desists no whit,
And how such strays were caught up in the
        street
And took a motion from you, why inquire?
I speak to the strong soul, no weak disguise.
If it be truth, — why should I doubt it truth ? -
You serve God specially, as priests are bound,
And care about me, stranger as I am,
So far as wish my good, that — miracle
I take to imitate he wills you serve
By saving me, — what else can he direct ?
Here is the service. Since a long while now,
I am in course of being put to death :
While death concerned nothing but me, I bowed
The head and bade, in heart, my husband
        strike.
Now I imperil something more, it seems,
Something that 's trulier me than this myself,
Something I trust in God and you to save.
You go to Rome, they tell me : take me there,
Put me back with my people ! ”

                        He replied —
The first word I heard ever from his lips,
All himself in it, — an eternity
Of speech, to match the immeasurable depth
O' the soul that then broke silence — " I am
        yours.”

So did the star rise, soon to lead my step,
Lead on, nor pause before it should stand still
Above the House o' the Babe, — my babe to be,
That knew me first and thus made me know
        him,
That had his right of life and claim on mine,
And would not let me die till he was born,
But pricked me at the heart to save us both,
Saying, " Have you the will ? Leave God the
        way ! ”
And the way was Caponsacchi — " mine,” thank
        God !
He was mine, he is mine, he will be mine.

No pause i' the leading and the light ! I know,
Next night there was a cloud came, and not he :

But I prayed through the darkness till it broke
And let him shine. The second night, he came.

" The plan is rash ; the project desperate :
In such a flight needs must I risk your life,
Give food for falsehood, folly or mistake,
Ground for your husband's rancor and re-
      venge " —
So he began again, with the same face.
I felt that, the same loyalty — one star
Turning now red that was so white before —
One service apprehended newly : just
A word of mine and there the white was back !

" No, friend, for you will take me ! 'T is your-
      self
Risk all, not I, — who let you, for I trust
In the compensating great God : enough !
I know you : when is it that you will come ? "

" To-morrow at the day's dawn." Then I heard
What I should do : how to prepare for flight
And where to fly.

                    That night my husband bade
" — You, whom I loathe, beware you break my
      sleep
This whole night ! Couch beside me like the
      corpse
I would you were ! " The rest you know, I
      think —
How I found Caponsacchi and escaped.

And this man, men call sinner ? Jesus Christ !
Of whom men said, with mouths Thyself
      mad'st once,
" He hath a devil " — say he was Thy saint,
My Caponsacchi ! Shield and show — unshroud
In Thine own time the glory of the soul
If aught obscure, — if ink-spot, from vile pens
Scribbling a charge against him — (I was glad
Then, for the first time, that I could not
      write) —
Flirted his way, have flecked the blaze !

                              For me,
'T is otherwise : let men take, sift my thoughts
— Thoughts I throw like the flax for sun to
      bleach !
I did pray, do pray, in the prayer shall die,
" Oh, to have Caponsacchi for my guide ! "
Ever the face upturned to mine, the hand
Holding my hand across the world, — a sense
That reads, as only such can read, the mark
God sets on woman, signifying so
She should — shall peradventure — be divine ;
Yet 'ware, the while, how weakness mars the
      print
And makes confusion, leaves the thing men
      see,
— Not this man sees, — who from his soul, re-
      writes
The obliterated charter, — love and strength
Mending what 's marred. "So kneels a vo-
      tarist,
Weeds some poor waste traditionary plot
Where shrine once was, where temple yet may
      be,

Purging the place but worshipping the while,
By faith and not by sight, sight clearest so, —
Such way the saints work," — says Don Ce-
      lestine.
But I, not privileged to see a saint
Of old when such walked earth with crown and
      palm,
If I call " saint " what saints call something
      else —
The saints must bear with me, impute the fault
To a soul i' the bud, so starved by ignorance,
Stinted of warmth, it will not blow this year
Nor recognize the orb which Spring - flowers
      know.
But if meanwhile some insect with a heart
Worth floods of lazy music, spendthrift joy —
Some fire-fly renounced Spring for my dwarfed
      cup,
Crept close to me, brought lustre for the dark,
Comfort against the cold, — what though ex-
      cess
Of comfort should miscall the creature — sun ?
What did the sun to hinder while harsh hands
Petal by petal, crude and colorless,
Tore me ? This one heart gave me all the
      Spring !

Is all told ? There 's the journey : and where 's
      time
To tell you how that heart burst out in shine ?
Yet certain points do press on me too hard.
Each place must have a name, though I forget :
How strange it was — there where the plain
      begins
And the small river mitigates its flow —
When eve was fading fast, and my soul sank,
And I divined what surge of bitterness,
In overtaking me, would float me back
Whence I was carried by the striding day —
So, — " This gray place was famous once," said
      he —
And he began that legend of the place
As if in answer to the unspoken fear,
And told me all about a brave man dead,
Which lifted me and let my soul go on !
How did he know too — at that town's approach
By the rock-side — that in coming near the
      signs
Of life, the house-roofs and the church and
      tower,
I saw the old boundary and wall o' the world
Rise plain as ever round me, hard and cold,
As if the broken circlet joined again,
Tightened itself about me with no break, —
As if the town would turn Arezzo's self, —
The husband there, — the friends my enemies,
All ranged against me, not an avenue
To try, but would be blocked and drive me
      back
On him, — this other, . . . oh the heart in that !
Did not he find, bring, put into my arms
A new-born babe ? — and I saw faces beam
Of the young mother proud to teach me joy,
And gossips round expecting my surprise
At the sudden hole through earth that lets in
      heaven.
I could believe himself by his strong will
Had woven around me what I thought the world

We went along in, every circumstance,
Towns, flowers and faces, all things helped so
    well !
For, through the journey, was it natural
Such comfort should arise from first to last ?
As I look back, all is one milky way ;
Still bettered more, the more remembered, so
Do new stars bud while I but search for old,
And fill all gaps i' the glory, and grow him —
Him I now see make the shine everywhere.
Even at the last when the bewildered flesh,
The cloud of weariness about my soul
Clogging too heavily, sucked down all sense, —
Still its last voice was, "He will watch and
    care ;
Let the strength go, I am content : he stays !"
I doubt not he did stay and care for all —
From that sick minute when the head swam
    round,
And the eyes looked their last and died on
    him,
As in his arms he caught me, and, you say,
Carried me in, that tragical red eve,
And laid me where I next returned to life
In the other red of morning, two red plates
That crushed together, crushed the time be-
    tween,
And are since then a solid fire to me, —
When in, my dreadful husband and the world
Broke, — and I saw him, master, by hell's right,
And saw my angel helplessly held back
By guards that helped the malice — the lamb
    prone,
The serpent towering and triumphant — then
Came all the strength back in a sudden swell,
I did for once see right, do right, give tongue
The adequate protest : for a worm must turn
If it would have its wrong observed by God.
I did spring up, attempt to thrust aside
That ice-block 'twixt the sun and me, lay low
The neutralizer of all good and truth.
If I sinned so, — never obey voice more
O' the Just and Terrible, who bids us —
    "Bear !"
Not — "Stand by, bear to see my angels bear !"
I am clear it was on impulse to serve God
Not save myself, — no — nor my child unborn !
Had I else waited patiently till now ? —
Who saw my old kind parents, silly-sooth
And too much trustful, for their worst of faults,
Cheated, browbeaten, stripped and starved, cast
    out
Into the kennel: I remonstrated,
Then sank to silence, for, — their woes at end,
Themselves gone, — only I was left to plague.
If only I was threatened and belied,
What matter ? I could bear it and did bear ;
It was a comfort, still one lot for all :
They were not persecuted for my sake
And I, estranged, the single happy one.
But when at last, all by myself I stood
Obeying the clear voice which bade me rise,
Not for my own sake but my babe unborn,
And take the angel's hand was sent to help —
And found the old adversary athwart the path —
Not my hand simply struck from the angel's,
    but
The very angel's self made foul i' the face

By the fiend who struck there, — that I would
    not bear,
That only I resisted ! So, my first
And last resistance was invincible.
Prayers move God ; threats, and nothing else,
    move men !
I must have prayed a man as he were God
When I implored the Governor to right
My parents' wrongs : the answer was a smile.
The Archbishop, — did I clasp his feet enough,
Hide my face hotly on them, while I told
More than I dared make my own mother know ?
The profit was — compassion and a jest.
This time, the foolish prayers were done with,
    right
Used might. and solemnized the sport at once.
All was against the combat : vantage, mine ?
The runaway avowed, the accomplice-wife,
In company with the plan-contriving priest ?
Yet, shame thus rank and patent, I struck,
    bare,
At foe from head to foot in magic mail,
And off it withered, cobweb-armory
Against the lightning ! 'T was truth singed the
    lies
And saved me, not the vain sword nor weak
    speech !

You see, I will not have the service fail !
I say, the angel saved me : I am safe !
Others may want and wish, I wish nor want
One point o' the circle plainer, where I stand
Traced round about with white to front the
    world.
What of the calumny I came across,
What o' the way to the end ? — the end crowns
    all.
The judges judged aright i' the main, gave me
The uttermost of my heart's desire, a truce
From torture and Arezzo, balm for hurt,
With the quiet nuns, — God recompense the
    good !
Who said and sang away the ugly past.
And, when my final fortune was revealed,
What safety, while, amid my parents' arms,
My babe was given me ! Yes, he saved my
    babe :
It would not have peeped forth, the bird-like
    thing,
Through that Arezzo noise and trouble : back
Had it returned nor ever let me see !
But the sweet peace cured all, and let me live
And give my bird the life among the leaves
God meant him ! Weeks and months of quie-
    tude,
I could lie in such peace and learn so much —
Begin the task, I see how needful now,
Of understanding somewhat of my past, —
Know life a little, I should leave so soon.
Therefore, because this man restored my soul,
All has been right ; I have gained my gain, en-
    joyed
As well as suffered, — nay, got foretaste too
Of better life beginning where this ends —
All through the breathing-while allowed me
    thus,
Which let good premonitions reach my soul
Unthwarted, and benignant influence flow

And interpenetrate and change my heart,
Uncrossed by what was wicked, — nay, unkind.
For, as the weakness of my time drew nigh,
Nobody did me one disservice more,
Spoke coldly or looked strangely, broke the love
I lay in the arms of, till my boy was born,
Born all in love, with naught to spoil the bliss
A whole long fortnight: in a life like mine
A fortnight filled with bliss is long and much.
All women are not mothers of a boy,
Though they live twice the length of my whole
    life,
And, as they fancy, happily all the same.
There I lay, then, all my great fortnight long,
As if it would continue, broaden out
Happily more and more, and lead to heaven :
Christmas before me, — was not that a chance ?
I never realized God's birth before —
How he grew likest God in being born.
This time I felt like Mary, had my babe
Lying a little on my breast like hers.
So all went on till, just four days ago —
The night and the tap.

                    Oh, it shall be success
To the whole of our poor family ! My friends
. . . Nay, father and mother, — give me back
    my word !
They have been rudely stripped of life, disgraced
Like children who must needs go clothed too
    fine,
Carry the garb of Carnival in Lent.
If they too much affected frippery,
They have been punished and submit them-
    selves,
Say no word : all is over, they see God
Who will not be extreme to mark their fault
Or he had granted respite : they are safe.

For that most woeful man my husband once,
Who, needing respite, still draws vital breath,
I — pardon him ? So far as lies in me,
I give him for his good the life he takes,
Praying the world will therefore acquiesce.
Let him make God amends, — none, none to
    me
Who thank him rather that, whereas strange
    fate
Mockingly styled him husband and me wife,
Himself this way at least pronounced divorce,
Blotted the marriage-bond : this blood of mine
Flies forth exultingly at any door,
Washes the parchment white, and thanks the
    blow.
We shall not meet in this world nor the next,
But where will God be absent ? In his face
Is light, but in his shadow healing too :
Let Guido touch the shadow and be healed !
And as my presence was importunate, —
My earthly good, temptation and a snare, —
Nothing about me but drew somehow down
His hate upon me, — somewhat so excused
Therefore, since hate was thus the truth of
    him, —
May my evanishment forevermore
Help further to relieve the heart that cast
Such object of its natural loathing forth !
So he was made : he nowise made himself :

I could not love him, but his mother did.
His soul has never lain beside my soul ;
But for the unresisting body, — thanks !
He burned that garment spotted by the flesh.
Whatever he touched is rightly ruined : plague
It caught, and disinfection it had craved
Still but for Guido ; I am saved through him
So as by fire ; to him — thanks and farewell !

Even for my babe, my boy, there's safety
    thence —
From the sudden death of me, I mean : we poor
Weak souls, how we endeavor to be strong !
I was already using up my life, —
This portion, now, should do him such a good,
This other go to keep off such an ill !
The great life ; see, a breath and it is gone !
So is detached, so left all by itself
The little life, the fact which means so much.
Shall not God stoop the kindlier to his work,
His marvel of creation, foot would crush,
Now that the hand he trusted to receive
And hold it, lets the treasure fall perforce ?
The better ; he shall have in orphanage
His own way all the clearlier : if my babe
Outlived the hour — and he has lived two
    weeks —
It is through God who knows I am not by.
Who is it makes the soft gold hair turn black,
And sets the tongue, might lie so long at rest,
Trying to talk ? Let us leave God alone !
Why should I doubt he will explain in time
What I feel now, but fail to find the words ?
My babe nor was, nor is, nor yet shall be
Count Guido Franceschini's child at all —
Only his mother's, born of love not hate !
So shall I have my rights in after-time.
It seems absurd, impossible to-day ;
So seems so much else, not explained but
    known !

Ah ! Friends, I thank and bless you every one !
No more now : I withdraw from earth and
    man
To my own soul, compose myself for God.

Well, and there is more ! Yes, my end of
    breath
Shall bear away my soul in being true !
He is still here, not outside with the world,
Here, here, I have him in his rightful place !
'T is now, when I am most upon the move,
I feel for what I verily find — again
The face, again the eyes, again, through all,
The heart and its immeasurable love
Of my one friend, my only, all my own,
Who put his breast between the spears and
    me.
Ever with Caponsacchi ! Otherwise
Here alone would be failure, loss to me —
How much more loss to him, with life debarred
From giving life, love locked from love's dis-
    play,
The day-star stopped its task that makes night
    morn !
O lover of my life, O soldier-saint,
No work begun shall ever pause for death !
Love will be helpful to me more and more

I' the coming course, the new path I must
 tread —
My weak hand in thy strong hand, strong for
 that!
Tell him that if I seem without him now,
That 's the world's insight! Oh, he under-
 stands!
He is at Civita — do I once doubt
The world again is holding us apart?
He had been here, displayed in my behalf
The broad brow that reverberates the truth,
And flashed the word God gave him, back to
 man!
I know where the free soul is flown! My fate
Will have been hard for even him to bear:
Let it confirm him in the trust of God,
Showing how holily he dared the deed!
And, for the rest, — say, from the deed, no
 touch
Of harm came, but all good, all happiness,
Not one faint fleck of failure! Why explain?
What I see, oh, he sees and how much more!
Tell him, — I know not wherefore the true
 word
Should fade and fall unuttered at the last —
It was the name of him I sprang to meet
When came the knock, the summons and the
 end.
"My great heart, my strong hand are back
 again!"
I would have sprung to these, beckoning across
Murder and hell gigantic and distinct
O' the threshold, posted to exclude me heaven:
He is ordained to call and I to come!
Do not the dead wear flowers when dressed for
 God?
Say, — I am all in flowers from head to foot!
Say, — not one flower of all he said and did,
Might seem to flit unnoticed, fade unknown,
But dropped a seed, has grown a balsam-tree
Whereof the blossoming perfumes the place
At this supreme of moments! He is a priest;
He cannot marry therefore, which is right:
I think he would not marry if he could.
Marriage on earth seems such a counterfeit,
Mere imitation of the inimitable:
In heaven we have the real and true and sure.
'T is there they neither marry nor are given
In marriage but are as the angels: right,
Oh how right that is, how like Jesus Christ
To say that! Marriage-making for the earth,
With gold so much, — birth, power, repute so
 much,
Or beauty, youth so much, in lack of these!
Be as the angels rather, who, apart,
Know themselves into one, are found at length
Married, but marry never, no, nor give
In marriage; they are man and wife at once
When the true time is: here we have to wait
Not so long neither! Could we by a wish
Have what we will and get the future now,
Would we wish aught done undone in the past?
So, let him wait God's instant men call years;
Meantime hold hard by truth and his great
 soul,
Do out the duty! Through such souls alone
God stooping shows sufficient of his light
For us i' the dark to rise by. And I rise.

VIII

DOMINUS HYACINTHUS DE ARCH-
ANGELIS,

PAUPERUM PROCURATOR

Ah, my Giacinto, he 's no ruddy rogue,
Is not Cinone? What, to-day we 're eight?
Seven and one 's eight, I hope, old curly-pate!
— Branches me out his verb-tree on the slate,
Amo —as —avi —atum —are —ans,
Up to *—aturus,* person, tense, and mood,
Quies me cum subjunctivo (I could cry)
And chews Corderius with his morning crust!
Look eight years onward, and he 's perched,
 he 's perched
Dapper and deft on stool beside this chair,
Cinozzo, Cinoncello, who but he?
— Trying his milk-teeth on some crusty case
Like this, papa shall triturate full soon
To smooth Papinianian pulp!
 It trots
Already through my head, though noon be now,
Does supper-time and what belongs to eve.
Dispose, O Don, o' the day, first work then
 play!
— The proverb bids. And "then" means,
 won't we hold
Our little yearly lovesome frolic feast,
Cinuolo's birth-night, Cinicello's own,
That makes gruff January grin perforce!
For too contagious grows the mirth, the warmth
Escaping from so many hearts at once —
When the good wife, buxom and bonny yet,
Jokes the hale grandsire, — such are just the
 sort
To go off suddenly, — he who hides the key
O' the box beneath his pillow every night, —
Which box may hold a parchment (some one
 thinks)
Will show a scribbled something like a name
"Cinino, Ciniccino," near the end,
"To whom I give and I bequeath my lands,
Estates, tenements, hereditaments,
When I decease as honest grandsire ought."
Wherefore — yet this one time again perhaps —
Sha'n't my Orvieto fuddle his old nose!
Then, uncles, one or the other, well i' the
 world,
May — drop in, merely? — trudge through rain
 and wind,
Rather! The smell-feasts rouse them at the
 hint
There 's cookery in a certain dwelling-place!
Gossips, too, each with keepsake in his poke,
Will pick the way, thrid lane by lantern-light,
And so find door, put galligaskin off
At entry of a decent domicile
Cornered in snug Condotti, — all for love,
All to crush cup with Cinucciatolo!
 Well,
Let others climb the heights o' the court, the
 camp!
How vain are chambering and wantonness,
Revel and rout and pleasures that make mad!
Commend me to home-joy, the family board,
Altar and hearth! These, with a brisk career

A source of honest profit and good fame,
Just so much work as keeps the brain from rust,
Just so much play as lets the heart expand,
Honoring God and serving man, — I say,
These are reality, and all else, — fluff,
Nutshell and naught, — thank Flaccus for the phrase !
Suppose I had been Fisc, yet bachelor !

Why, work with a will, then ! Wherefore lazy now ?
Turn up the hour-glass, whence no sand-grain slips
But should have done its duty to the saint
O' the day, the son and heir that 's eight years old !
Let law come dimple Cinoncino's cheek,
And Latin dumple Cinarello's chin,
And while we spread him fine and toss him flat
This pulp that makes the pancake, trim our mass
Of matter into Argument the First,
Prime Pleading in defence of our accused,
Which, once a-waft on paper wing, shall soar,
Shall signalize before applausive Rome
What study, and mayhap some mother-wit,
Can do toward making Master fop and Fisc
Old bachelor Bottinius bite his thumb.
Now, how good God is ! How falls plumb to point
This murder, gives me Guido to defend
Now, of all days i' the year, just when the boy
Verges on Virgil, reaches the right age
For some such illustration from his sire,
Stimulus to himself ! One might wait years
And never find the chance which now finds me !
The fact is, there 's a blessing on the hearth,
A special providence for fatherhood !
Here 's a man, and what 's more, a noble, kills
— Not sneakingly but almost with parade —
Wife's father and wife's mother and wife's self
That 's mother's self of son and heir (like mine !)
— And here stand I, the favored advocate,
Who pluck this flower o' the field, no Solomon
Was ever clothed in glorious gold to match,
And set the same in Cinoncino's cap !
I defend Guido and his comrades — I !
Pray God, I keep me humble : not to me —
Non nobis, Domine, sed tibi laus !
How the fop chuckled when they made him Fisc !
We 'll beat you, my Bottinius, all for love,
All for our tribute to Cinotto's day !
Why, 'sbuddikins, old Innocent himself
May rub his eyes at the bustle, — ask " What 's this
Rolling from out the rostrum, as a gust
O' the Pro Milone had been prisoned there,
And rattled Rome awake ? " Awaken Rome,
How can the Pope doze on in decency ?
He needs must wake up also, speak his word,
Have his opinion like the rest of Rome,
About this huge, this hurly-burly case :
He wants who can excogitate the truth,

Give the result in speech, plain black and white,
To mumble in the mouth and make his own
— A little changed, good man, a little changed !
No matter, so his gratitude be moved,
By when my Giacintino gets of age,
Mindful of who thus helped him at a pinch,
Archangelus Procurator Pauperum —
And proved Hortensius Redivivus !
                                Whew !
To earn the Est-est, merit the minced herb
That mollifies the liver's leathery slice,
With here a goose-foot, there a cock's-comb stuck,
Cemented in an element of cheese !
I doubt if dainties do the grandsire good :
Last June he had a sort of strangling . . . bah !
He 's his own master, and his will is made.
So, liver fizz, law flit and Latin fly
As we rub hands o'er dish by way of grace !
May I lose cause if I vent one word more
Except — with fresh-cut quill we ink the white —
P-r-o-pro Guidone et Sociis.   There !

Count Guido married — or, in Latin due,
What ? Duxit in uxorem ? — commonplace !
Tædas jugales iniit, subiit, — ha !
He underwent the matrimonial torch ?
Connubio stabili sibi junxit, — hum !
In stable bond of marriage bound his own ?
That 's clear of any modern taint : and yet . .

Virgil is little help to who writes prose.
He shall attack me Terence with the dawn,
Shall Cinuccino ! Mum, mind business, Sir !
Thus circumstantially evolve we facts,
Ita se habet ideo series facti :
He wedded, — ah, with owls for augury !
Nupserat, heu sinistris avibus,
One of the blood Arezzo boasts her best,
Dominus Guido, nobili genere ortus,
Pompiliæ . . .

                        But the version afterward !
Curb we this ardor ! Notes alone, to-day,
The speech to-morrow, and the Latin last :
Such was the rule in Farinacci's time.
Indeed I hitched it into verse and good.
Unluckily, law quite absorbs a man,
Or else I think I too had poetized.
" Law is the pork substratum of the fry,
Goose-foot and cock's-comb are Latinity,"
And in this case, if circumstance assist,
We 'll garnish law with idiom, never fear !
Out-of-the-way events extend our scope :
For instance, when Bottini brings his charge,
" That letter which you say Pompilia wrote,
To criminate her parents and herself
And disengage her husband from the coil, —
That, Guido Franceschini wrote, say we :
Because Pompilia could not read nor write,
Therefore he pencilled her such letter first,
Then made her trace in ink the same again."
— Ha, my Bottini, have I thee on hip ?
How will he turn this and break Tully's pate ?
" Existimandum " (don't I hear the dog !)
" Quod Guido designaverit elementa

Dictæ epistolæ, quæ fuerint
(Superinducto ab ea calamo)
Notata atramento " — there 's a style ! —
" *Quia ipsa scribere nesciebat.*" Boh !
Now, my turn ! Either, *Insulse!* (I outburst)
Stupidly put ! Inane is the response,
Inanis est responsio, or the like —
To wit, that each of all those characters,
Quod singula elementa epistolæ,
Had first of all been traced for her by him,
Fuerant per eum prius designata,
And then, the ink applied a-top of that,
Et deinde, superinducto calamo,
The piece, she says, became her handiwork,
Per eam, efformata, ut ipsa asserit.
Inane were such response ! (a second time :)
Her husband outlined her the whole, forsooth ?
Vir ejus lineabat epistolam ?
What, she confesses that she wrote the thing,
Fatetur eam scripsisse, (scorn that scathes!)
That she might pay obedience to her lord ?
Ut viro obtemperaret, apices
(Here repeat charge with proper varied phrase)
Eo designante, ipsaque calamum
Super inducente ? By such argument,
Ita pariter, she seeks to show the same,
(Ay, by Saint Joseph and what saints you
please)
Epistolam ostendit, medius fidius,
No voluntary deed but fruit of force !
Non voluntarie sed coacte scriptam !
That 's the way to write Latin, friend my
Fisc !
Bottini is a beast, one barbarous :
Look out for him when he attempts to say
" Armed with a pistol, Guido followed her ! "
Will not I be beforehand with my Fisc,
Cut away phrase by phrase from underfoot !
Guido Pompiliam — Guido thus his wife
Following with igneous engine, shall I have ?
Armis munitus igneis persequens —
Arma sulphurea gestans, sulphury arms,
Or, might one style a pistol — popping-piece ?
Armatus breviori sclopulo ?
We 'll let him have been armed so, though it
make
Somewhat against us : I had thought to own —
Provided with a simple travelling-sword,
Ense solummodo viatorio
Instructus : but we 'll grant the pistol here :
Better we lost the cause than lacked the gird
At the Fisc's Latin, lost the Judge's laugh !
It 's Venturini that decides for style.
Tommati rather goes upon the law.
So, as to law, —

Ah, but with law ne'er hope
To level the fellow, — don't I know his trick !
How he draws up, ducks under, twists aside !
He 's a lean-gutted hectic rascal, fine
As pale-haired red-eyed ferret which pretends
'T is ermine, pure soft snow from tail to snout.
He eludes law by piteous looks aloft.
Lets Latin glance off as he makes appeal
To saint that 's somewhere in the ceiling-top :
Do you suppose I don't conceive the beast ?
Plague of the ermine-vermin ! For it takes,
It takes, and here 's the fellow Fisc, you see,

And Judge, you 'll not be long in seeing next !
Confound the fop — he 's now at work like me :
Enter his study, as I seem to do,
Hear him read out his writing to himself !
I know he writes as if he spoke : I hear
The hoarse shrill throat, see shut eyes, neck
shot-forth,
— I see him strain on tiptoe, soar and pour
Eloquence out, nor stay nor stint at all —
Perorate in the air, then quick to press
With the product ! What abuse of type and
sheet !
He 'll keep clear of my cast, my logic-throw,
Let argument slide, and then deliver swift
Some bowl from quite an unguessed point of
stand —
Having the luck o' the last word, the reply !
A plaguy cast, a mortifying stroke :
You face a fellow — cries, " So, there you
stand ?
But I discourteous jump clean o'er your head !
You take ship-carpentry for pilotage,
Stop rat-holes, while a sea sweeps through the
breach,—
Hammer and fortify at puny points ?
Do, clamp and tenon, make all tight and safe !
'T is here and here and here you ship a sea,
No good of your stopped leaks and littleness ! "

Yet what do I name " little and a leak " ?
The main defence o' the murder 's used to
death,
By this time, dry bare bones, no scrap we
pick :
Safer I worked the new, the unforeseen,
The nice by-stroke, the fine and improvised
Point that can titillate the brain o' the Bench
Torpid with over-teaching, long ago !
As if Tommati (that has heard, reheard
And heard again, first this side and then
that —
Guido and Pietro, Pietro and Guido, din
And deafen, full three years, at each long ear)
Don't want amusement for instruction now,
Won't rather feel a flea run o'er his ribs,
Than a daw settle heavily on his head !
Oh, I was young and had the trick of fence,
Knew subtle pass and push with careless
right —
My left arm ever quiet behind back,
With dagger ready . not both hands to blade !
Puff and blow, put the strength out, Blunder-
bore !
There 's my subordinate, young Spreti, now,
Pedant and prig, — he 'll pant away at proof,
That 's his way !

Now for mine — to rub some life
Into one's choppy fingers this cold day !
I trust Cinuzzo ties on tippet, guards
The precious throat on which so much depends
Guido must be all goose-flesh in his hole,
Despite the prison-straw : bad Carnival
For captives ! no sliced fry for him, poor
Count !

Carnival-time, — another providence !
The town a-swarm with strangers to amuse-

To edify, to give one's name and fame
In charge of, till they find, some future day,
Cintino come and claim it, his name too,
Pledge of the pleasantness they owe papa—
Who else was it cured Rome of her great
    qualms,
When she must needs have her own judgment?
    — ay,
When all her topping wits had set to work,
Pronounced already on the case : mere boys,
Twice Cineruggiolo's age with half his sense,
As good as tell me, when I cross the court,
" Master Arcangeli ! " (plucking at my gown)
" We can predict, we comprehend your play,
We 'll help you save your client." Tra-la-la !
I 've travelled ground, from childhood to this
    hour,
To have the town anticipate my track ?
The old fox takes the plain and velvet path,
The young hound's predilection, — prints the
    dew,
Don't he, to suit their pulpy pads of paw ?
No !   Burying nose deep down i' the briery
    bush,
Thus I defend Count Guido.
                        Where are we weak ?
First, which is foremost in advantage too,
Our murder, — we call, killing, — is a fact
Confessed, defended, made a boast of : good !
To think the Fisc claimed use of torture here,
And got thereby avowal plump and plain
That gives me just the chance I wanted, —
    scope
Not for brute-force but ingenuity,
Explaining matters, not denying them !
One may dispute, — as I am bound to do,
And shall, — validity of process here :
Inasmuch as a noble is exempt
From torture which plebeians undergo
In such a case : for law is lenient, lax,
Remits the torture to a nobleman
Unless suspicion be of twice the strength
Attaches to a man born vulgarly :
We don't card silk with comb that dresses
    wool.
Moreover, 't was severity undue
In this case, even had the lord been lout.
What utters, on this head, our oracle,
Our Farinacci, my Gamaliel erst,
In those immortal " Questions " ?   This I
    quote :
" Of all the tools at Law's disposal, sure
That named *Vigiliarum* is the best —
That is, the worst — to whoso needs must bear :
Lasting, as it may do, from some seven hours
To ten ; (beyond ten, we 've no precedent ;
Certain have touched their ten but, bah, they
    died !)
It does so efficaciously convince,
That — speaking by much observation here —
Out of each hundred cases, by my count,
Never I knew of patients beyond four
Withstand its taste, or less than ninety-six
End by succumbing : only martyrs four,
Of obstinate silence, guilty or no, — against
Ninety-six full confessors, innocent
Or otherwise, — so shrewd a tool have we ! "
No marvel either : in unwary hands,

Death on the spot is no rare consequence :
As indeed all but happened in this case
To one of ourselves, our young tough peasant
    friend
The accomplice called Baldeschi : they were
    rough,
Dosed him with torture as you drench a horse,
Not modify your treatment to a man :
So, two successive days he fainted dead,
And only on the third essay, gave up,
Confessed like flesh and blood.   We could re
    claim, —
Blockhead Bottini giving cause enough !
But no, — we 'll take it as spontaneously
Confessed : we 'll have the murder beyond
    doubt.
Ah, fortunate (the poet's word reversed)
Inasmuch as we know our happiness !
Had the antagonist left dubiety,
Here were we proving murder a mere myth,
And Guido innocent, ignorant, absent, — ay,
Absent !   He was — why, where should Chris-
    tian be ? —
Engaged in visiting his proper church,
The duty of us all at Christmas-time,
When Caponsacchi, the seducer, stung
To madness by his relegation, cast
About him and contrived a remedy
In murder : since opprobrium broke afresh,
By birth o' the babe, on him the imputed sire.
He it was quietly sought to smother up
His shame and theirs together, — killed the
    three,
And fled — (go seek him where you please to
    search) —
Just at the time when Guido, touched by
    grace,
Devotions ended, hastened to the spot,
Meaning to pardon his convicted wife,
" Neither do I condemn thee, go in peace ! " —
And thus arrived i' the nick of time to catch
The charge o' the killing, though great-
    heartedly
He came but to forgive and bring to life.
Doubt ye the force of Christmas on the soul ?
" Is thine eye evil because mine is good ? "

So, doubtless, had I needed argue here
But for the full confession round and sound !
Thus might you wrong some kingly alchem-
    ist, —
Whose concern should not be with showing brass
Transmuted into gold, but triumphing,
Rather, about his gold changed out of brass,
Not vulgarly to the mere sight and touch,
But in the idea, the spiritual display,
The apparition buoyed by wingèd words
Hovering above its birthplace in the brain, —
Thus would you wrong this excellent personage
Forced, by the gross need, to gird apron round,
Plant forge, light fire, ply bellows, — in a
    word,
Demonstrate : when a faulty pipkin's crack
May disconcert you his presumptive truth !
Here were I hanging to the testimony
Of one of these poor rustics — four, ye gods !
Whom the first taste of friend the Fiscal's cord
May drive into undoing my whole speech.

Undoing, on his birthday, — what is worse, —
My son and heir!

I wonder, all the same,
Not so much at those peasants' lack of heart ;
But — Guido Franceschini, nobleman,
Bear pain no better ! Everybody knows
It used once, when my father was a boy,
To form a proper, nay, important point
I' the education of our well-born youth,
That they took torture handsomely at need,
Without confessing in this clownish guise.
Each noble had his rack for private use,
And would, for the diversion of a guest,
Bid it be set up in the yard of arms,
And take thereon his hour of exercise, —
Command the varletry stretch, strain their
best,
While friends looked on, admired my lord could
smile
'Mid tugging which had caused an ox to roar.
Men are no longer men !

— And advocates
No longer Farinacci, let us add,
If I one more time fly from point proposed !
So, *Vindicatio,* — here begins the speech !
Honoris causa ; thus we make our stand :
Honor in us had injury, we prove.
Or if we fail to prove such injury
More than misprision of the fact, — what then ?
It is enough, authorities declare,
If the result, the deed in question now,
Be caused by confidence that injury
Is veritable and no figment : since,
What, though proved fancy afterward, seemed
fact
At the time, they argue shall excuse result.
That which we do, persuaded of good cause
For what we do, hold justifiable ! —
So casuists bid : man, bound to do his best,
They would not have him leave that best undone
And mean to do his worst, — though fuller light
Show best was worst and worst would have been
best.
Act by the present light ! — they ask of man.
Ultra quod hic non agitur, besides
It is not anyway our business here,
De probatione adulterii,
To prove what we thought crime was crime in-
deed,
Ad irrogandam pœnam, and require
Its punishment : such nowise do we seek :
Sed ad effectum, but 't is our concern,
Excusandi, here to simply find excuse,
Occisorem, for who did the killing-work,
Et ad illius defensionem, (mark
The difference) and defend the man, just that !
Quo casu levior probatio
Exuberaret, to which end far lighter proof
Suffices than the prior case would claim :
It should be always harder to convict,
In short, than to establish innocence.
Therefore we shall demonstrate first of all
That Honor is a gift of God to man
Precious beyond compare : which natural sense
Of human rectitude and purity, —
Which white, man's soul is born with, — brooks
no touch :

Therefore, the sensitivest spot of all,
Wounded by any wafture breathed from black,
Is — honor within honor, like the eye
Centred i' the ball — the honor of our wife.
Touch us o' the pupil of our honor, then,
Not actually, — since so you slay outright, -
But by a gesture simulating touch,
Presumable mere menace of such taint, —
This were our warrant for eruptive ire
" To whose dominion I impose no end."

(Virgil, now, should not be too difficult
To Cinoncino, — say, the early books.
Pen, truce to further gambols ! *Poscimur !*)

Nor can revenge of injury done here
To the honor proved the life and soul of us,
Be too excessive, too extravagant :
Such wrong seeks and must have complete re
venge.
Show we this, first, on the mere natural ground
Begin at the beginning, and proceed
Incontrovertibly. Theodoric,
In an apt sentence Cassiodorus cites,
Propounds for basis of all household law —
I hardly recollect it, but it ends,
" Bird mates with bird, beast genders with his
like,
And brooks no interference." Bird and beast?
The very insects . . . if they wive or no,
How dare I say when Aristotle doubts ?
But the presumption is they likewise wive,
At least the nobler sorts ; for take the bee
As instance, — copying King Solomon, —
Why that displeasure of the bee to aught
Which savors of incontinency, makes
The unchaste a very horror to the hive ?
Whence comes it bees obtain their epithet
Of *castæ apes,* notably "the chaste" ?
Because, ingeniously saith Scaliger,
(The young sage, — see his book of table-talk)
" Such is their hatred of immodest act,
They fall upon the offender, sting to death."
I mind a passage much confirmative
I' the Idyllist (though I read him Latinized) —
" Why," asks a shepherd, " is this bank unfit
For celebration of our vernal loves ? "
" Oh swain," returns the instructed shepherdess,
" Bees swarm here, and would quick resent our
warmth ! "
Only cold-blooded fish lack instinct here,
Nor gain nor guard connubiality :
But beasts, quadrupedal, mammiferous,
Do credit to their beasthood : witness him
That Ælian cites, the noble elephant,
(Or if not Ælian, somebody as sage)
Who seeing, much offence beneath his nose,
His master's friend exceed in courtesy
The due allowance to his master's wife,
Taught them good manners and killed both at
once,
Making his master and the world admire.
Indubitably, then, that master's self,
Favored by circumstance, had done the same
Or else stood clear rebuked by his own beast.
Adeo, ut qui honorem spernit, thus,
Who values his own honor not a straw, —
Et non recuperare curat, nor

Labors by might and main to salve its wound,
Se ulciscendo, by revenging him,
Nil differat a belluis, is a brute,
Quinimo irrationabilior
Ipsismet belluis, nay, contrariwise,
Much more irrational than brutes themselves,
Should be considered, *reputetur!* How?
If a poor animal feel honor smart,
Taught by blind instinct nature plants in him,
Shall man, — confessed creation's master-
    stroke,
Nay, intellectual glory, nay, a god,
Nay, of the nature of my Judges here, —
Shall man prove the insensible, the block,
The blot o' the earth he crawls on to disgrace?
(Come, that 's both solid and poetic!)   Man
Derogate, live for the low tastes alone,
Mean creeping cares about the animal life?
Absit such homage to vile flesh and blood!

(May Gigia have remembered, nothing stings
Fried liver out of its monotony
Of richness, like a root of fennel, chopped
Fine with the parsley: parsley-sprigs, I said —
Was there need I should say "and fennel too"?
But no, she cannot have been so obtuse!
To our argument!   The fennel will be chopped.)

From beast to man next mount we — ay, but,
    mind,
Still mere man, not yet Christian, — that, in·
    time!
Not too fast, mark you!   'T is on Heathen
    grounds
We next defend our act: then, fairly urge —
If this were done of old, in a green tree,
Allowed in the Spring rawness of our kind,
What may be licensed in the Autumn dry
And ripe, the latter harvest-tide of man?
If, with his poor and primitive half-lights,
The Pagan, whom our devils served for gods,
Could stigmatize the breach of marriage-vow
As that which blood, blood only might efface, —
Absolve the husband, outraged, whose revenge
Anticipated law, plied sword himself, —
How with the Christian in full blaze of noon?
Shall not he rather double penalty,
Multiply vengeance, than, degenerate,
Let privilege be minished, droop, decay?
Therefore set forth at large the ancient law!
Superabundant the examples be
To pick and choose from.   The Athenian Code,
Solon's, the name is serviceable, — then,
The Laws of the Twelve Tables, that fif-
    teenth, —
"Romulus" likewise rolls out round and large.
The Julian; the Cornelian: Gracchus' Law:
So old a chime, the bells ring of themselves!
Spreti can set that going if he please,
I point you, for my part, the belfry plain,
Intent to rise from dusk, *diluculum*,
Into the Christian day shall broaden next.

First, the fit compliment to His Holiness
Happily reigning: then sustain the point —
All that was long ago declared as law
By the natural revelation, stands confirmed
By Apostle and Evangelist and Saint, —

To wit — that Honor is man's supreme good.
Why should I balk Saint Jerome of his phrase?
Ubi honor non est, where no honor is,
Ibi contemptus est; and where contempt,
Ibi injuria frequens; and where that,
The frequent injury, *ibi et indignatio;*
And where the indignation, *ibi quies*
Nulla: and where there is no quietude,
Why, *ibi*, there, the mind is often cast
Down from the heights where it proposed to
    dwell,
Mens a proposito sæpe dejicitur.
And naturally the mind is so cast down,
Since harder 't is, *quum difficilius sit*,
Iram cohibere, to coerce one's wrath,
Quam miracula facere, than work miracles, - -
So Gregory smiles in his First Dialogue.
Whence we infer, the ingenuous soul, the mar
Who makes esteem of honor and repute,
Whenever honor and repute are touched,
Arrives at term of fury and despair,
Loses all guidance from the reason-check ·
As in delirium or a frenzy-fit,
Nor fury nor despair he satiates, — no,
Not even if he attain the impossible,
O'erturn the hinges of the universe
To annihilate — not whoso caused the smart
Solely, the author simply of his pain,
But the place, the memory, *vituperii*,
O' the shame and scorn: *quia*, — says Solomon,
(The Holy Spirit speaking by his mouth
In Proverbs, the sixth chapter near the end)
— Because, the zeal and fury of a man,
Zelus et furor viri, will not spare,
Non parcet, in the day of his revenge,
In die vindictæ, nor will acquiesce,
Nec acquiescet, through a person's prayers,
Cujusdam precibus, — *nec suscipiet*,
Nor yet take, *pro redemptione*, for
Redemption, *dona plurium*, gifts of friends,
Mere money-payment to compound for ache.
Who recognizes not my client's case?
Whereto, as strangely consentaneous here,
Adduce Saint Bernard in the Epistle writ
To Robertulus, his nephew: "Too much grief,
Dolor quippe nimius non deliberat,
Does not excogitate propriety,
Non verecundatur, nor knows shame at all,
Non consulit rationem, nor consults
Reason, *non dignitatis metuit*
Damnum, nor dreads the loss of dignity;
Modum et ordinem, order and the mode,
Ignorat, it ignores:" why, trait for trait,
Was ever portrait limned so like the life?
(By Cavalier Maratta, shall I say?
I hear he 's first in reputation now.)
Yes, that of Samson in the Sacred Text:
That 's not so much the portrait as the man!
Samson in Gaza was the antetype
Of Guido at Rome: observe the Nazarite!
Blinded he was, — an easy thing to bear:
Intrepidly he took imprisonment,
Gyves, stripes, and daily labor at the mill:
But when he found himself, i' the public place,
Destined to make the common people sport,
Disdain burned up with such an impetus
I' the breast of him, that, all the man one fire,
Moriatur, roared he, let my soul's self die,

Anima mea, with the Philistines!
So, pulled down pillar, roof, and death and all,
Multosque plures interfecit, ay,
And many more he killed thus, *moriens*,
Dying, *quam vivus*, than in his whole life,
Occiderat, he ever killed before.
Are these things writ for no example, Sirs?
One instance more, and let me see who doubts!
Our Lord himself, made all of mansuetude,
Sealing the sum of sufferance up, received
Opprobrium, contumely and buffeting
Without complaint: but when he found him-
  self
Touched in his honor never so little for once,
Then outbroke indignation pent before —
" *Honorem meum nemini dabo!* " " No,
My honor I to nobody will give!"
And certainly the example so hath wrought,
That whosoever, at the proper worth,
Apprises worldly honor and repute,
Esteems it nobler to die honored man
Beneath Mannaia, than live centuries
Disgraced in the eye o' the world. We find
  Saint Paul
No recreant to this faith delivered once:
" Far worthier were it that I died," cries he,
Expedit mihi magis mori, " than
That any one should make my glory void,"
Quam ut gloriam meam quis evacuei :
See, *ad Corinthienses:* whereupon
Saint Ambrose makes a comment with much
  fruit,
Doubtless my Judges long since laid to heart,
So I desist from bringing forward here.
(I can't quite recollect it.)

         Have I proved
Satis superque, both enough and to spare,
That Revelation old and new admits
The natural man may effervesce in ire,
O'erflood earth, o'erfroth heaven with foamy
  rage,
At the first puncture to his self-respect?
Then, Sirs, this Christian dogma, this law-bud
Full-blown now, soon to bask the absolute flower
Of Papal doctrine in our blaze of day, —
Bethink you, shall we miss one promise-streak,
One doubtful birth of dawn crepuscular,
One dew-drop comfort to humanity,
Now that the chalice teems with noonday wine?
Yea, argue Molinists who bar revenge —
Referring just to what makes out our case!
Under old dispensation, argue they,
The doom of the adulterous wife was death,
Stoning by Moses' law. " Nay, stone her not,
Put her away!" next legislates our Lord;
And last of all, " Nor yet divorce a wife!"
Ordains the Church, "she typifies ourself,
The Bride no fault shall cause to fall from
  Christ."
Then, as no jot nor tittle of the Law
Has passed away — which who presumes to
  doubt?
As not one word of Christ is rendered vain —
Which, could it be though heaven and earth
  should pass?
— Where do I find my proper punishment
For my adulterous wife, I humbly ask

Of my infallible Pope, — who now remits
Even the divorce allowed by Christ in lieu
Of lapidation Moses licensed me?
The Gospel checks the Law which throws the
  stone,
The Church tears the divorce-bill Gospel grants:
Shall wives sin and enjoy impunity?
What profits me the fulness of the days,
The final dispensation, I demand,
Unless Law, Gospel, and the Church subjoin,
" But who hath barred thee primitive revenge,
Which, like fire damped and dammed up, burns
  more fierce?
Use thou thy natural privilege of man,
Else wert thou found like those old ingrate
  Jews,
Despite the manna-banquet on the board,
A-longing after melons, cucumbers,
And such like trash of Egypt left behind!"

(There was one melon had improved our soup:
But did not Cinoncino need the rind
To make a boat with? So I seem to think.)

Law, Gospel, and the Church — from these we
  leap
To the very last revealment, easy rule
Befitting the well-born and thorough-bred
O' the happy day we live in, not the dark
O' the early rude and acorn-eating race.
" Behold," quoth James, " we bridle in a horse
And turn his body as we would thereby!"
Yea, but we change the bit to suit the growth,
And rasp our colt's jaw with a rugged spike
We hasten to remit our managed steed
Who wheels round at persuasion of a touch.
Civilization bows to decency;
The acknowledged use and wont: 't is manners.
  — mild
But yet imperative law — which make the man.
Thus do we pay the proper compliment
To rank, and that society of Rome
Hath so obliged us by its interest,
Taken our client's part instinctively,
As unaware defending its own cause.
What *dictum* doth Society lay down
I' the case of one who hath a faithless wife?
Wherewithal should the husband cleanse his
  way?
Be patient and forgive? Oh, language fails, —
Shrinks from depicturing his turpitude!
For if wronged husband raise not hue and cry,
Quod si maritus de adulterio non
Conquereretur, he 's presumed a — foh!
Presumitur leno: so, complain he must.
But how complain? At your tribunal, lords?
Far weightier challenge suits your sense, I wot!
You sit not to have gentlemen propose
Questions gentility can itself discuss.
Did not you prove that to our brother Paul?
The Abate, *quum judicialiter*
Prosequeretur, when he tried the law,
Guidonis causam, in Count Guido's case
Accidit ipsi, this befell himself,
Quod risum moverit et cachinnos, that
He moved to mirth and cachinnation, all
Or nearly all, *fere in omnibus*
Etiam sensatis et cordatis, men

Strong-sensed, sound-hearted, nay, the very
        Court,
Ipsismet in judicibus, I might add,
Non tamen dicam. In a cause like this,
So multiplied were reasons *pro* and *con,*
Delicate, intertwisted and obscure,
That Law refused loan of a finger-tip
To unravel, readjust the hopeless twine,
Since, half-a-dozen steps outside Law's seat,
There stood a foolish trifler with a tool
A-dangle to no purpose by his side,
Had clearly cut the embroilment in a trice.
Asserunt enim unanimiter
Doctores, for the Doctors all assert,
That husbands, *quod mariti,* must be held
Viles, cornuti reputantur, vile,
Fronts branching forth a florid infamy,
Si propriis manibus, if with their own hands,
Non sumunt, they fail straight to take revenge,
Vindictam, but expect the deed be done
By the Court — *expectant illam fieri*
Per judices, qui summopere rident, which
Gives an enormous guffaw for reply,
Et cachinnantur. For he ran away,
Deliquit enim, just that he might 'scape
The censure of both counsellors and crowd,
Ut vulgi et Doctorum evitaret
Censuram, and lest so he superadd
To loss of honor ignominy too,
Et sic ne istam quoque ignominiam
Amisso honori superadderet.
My lords, my lords, the inconsiderate step
Was — we referred ourselves to Law at all !
Twit me not with, " Law else had punished
        you ! "
Each punishment of the extra-legal step,
To which the high-born preferably revert,
Is ever for some oversight, some slip
I' the taking vengeance, not for vengeance' self.
A good thing, done unhandsomely, turns ill ;
And never yet lacked ill the law's rebuke.
For pregnant instance, let us contemplate
The luck of Leonardus, — see at large
Of Sicily's Decisions sixty-first.
This Leonard finds his wife is false : what
        then ?
He makes her own son snare her, and entice
Out of the town walls to a private walk,
Wherein he slays her with commodity.
They find her body half-devoured by dogs :
Leonard is tried, convicted, punished, sent
To labor in the galleys seven years long :
Why ? For the murder ? Nay, but for the
        mode !
Malus modus occidendi, ruled the Court,
An ugly mode of killing, nothing more !
Another fructuous sample, — see " *De Re*
Criminali," in Matthæus' divine piece.
Another husband, in no better plight,
Simulates absence, thereby tempts his wife ;
On whom he falls, out of sly ambuscade,
Backed by a brother of his, and both of them
Armed to the teeth with arms that law had
        blamed.
Nimis dolose, overwilily,
Fuisse operatum, did they work,
Pronounced the law : had all been fairly done
Law had not found him worthy, as she did,

Of four years' exile. Why cite more ? Enough
Is good as a feast — (unless a birthday-feast
For one's Cinuccio) so, we finish here.
My lords, we rather need defend ourselves
Inasmuch as, for a twinkling of an eye,
We hesitatingly appealed to law, —
Than need deny that, on mature advice,
We blushingly bethought us, bade revenge
Back to its simple proper private way
Of decent self-dealt gentlemanly death.
Judges, here is the law, and here beside,
The testimony ! Look to it !
                        Pause and breathe
So far is only too plain ; we must watch :
Bottini will scarce hazard an attack
Here : best anticipate the fellow's play,
And guard the weaker places — warily ask,
What if considerations of a sort,
Reasons of a kind, arise from out the strange
Peculiar unforeseen new circumstance
Of this our (candor owns) abnormal act,
To bar the right of us revenging so ?
" Impunity were otherwise your meed :
Go slay your wife and welcome," — may be
        urged, —
" But why the innocent old couple slay,
Pietro, Violante ? You may do enough,
Not too much, not exceed the golden mean :
Neither brute-beast nor Pagan, Gentile, Jew,
Nor Christian, no nor votarist of the mode,
Is justified to push revenge so far ! "

No, indeed ? Why, thou very sciolist !
The actual wrong, Pompilia seemed to do,
Was virtual wrong done by the parents here —
Imposing her upon us as their child —
Themselves allow : then, her fault was their
        fault,
Her punishment be theirs accordingly !
But wait a little, sneak not off so soon !
Was this cheat solely harm to Guido, pray ?
The precious couple you call innocent, —
Why, they were felons that Law failed to
        clutch,
Qui ut fraudarent, who that they might rob,
Legitime vocatos, folk law called,
Ad fidei commissum, true heirs to the Trust,
Partum supposuerunt, feigned this birth,
Immemores reos factos esse, blind
To the fact that, guilty, they incurred thereby.
Ultimi supplicii, hanging or what 's worse.
Do you blame us that we turn Law's instru-
        ments,
Not mere self-seekers, — mind the public weal,
Nor make the private good our sole concern ?
That having — shall I say — secured a thief,
Not simply we recover from his pouch
The stolen article our property,
But also pounce upon our neighbor's purse
We opportunely find reposing there,
And do him justice while we right ourselves ?
He owes us, for our part, a drubbing say,
But owes our neighbor just a dance i' the air
Under the gallows : so, we throttle him.
That neighbor's Law, that couple are the Thief,
We are the over-ready to help Law —-
Zeal of her house hath eaten us up : for which,
Can it be, Law intends to eat up us,

Crudum Priamum, devour poor Priam raw,
('T was Jupiter's own joke,) with babes to boot,
Priamique pisinnos, in Homeric phrase ?
Shame ! —— and so ends my period prettily.

But even, — prove the pair not culpable,
Free as unborn babe from connivance at,
Participation in, their daughter's fault :
Ours the mistake.   Is that a rare event ?
Non semel, it is anything but rare,
In contingentia facti, that by chance,
Impunes evaserunt, go scot-free,
Qui, such well-meaning people as ourselves,
Justo dolore moti, who aggrieved
With cause, *apposuerunt manus*, lay
Rough hands, *in innocentes*, on wrong heads.
Cite we an illustrative case in point :
Mulier Smirnea quœdam, good my lords,
A gentlewoman lived in Smyrna once,
Virum et filium ex eo conceptum, who,
Both husband and her son begot by him,
Killed, *interfecerat, ex quo*, because,
Vir filium suum perdiderat, her spouse
Had been beforehand with her, killed her son,
Matrimonii primi, of a previous bed.
Deinde accusata, then accused,
Apud Dolabellam, before him that sat
Proconsul, *nec duabus cœdibus*
Contaminatam liberare, nor
To liberate a woman doubly-dyed
With murder, *voluit*, made he up his mind,
Nec condemnare, nor to doom to death,
Justo dolore impulsam, one impelled
By just grief ; *sed remisit*, but sent her up
Ad Areopagum, to the Hill of Mars,
Sapientissimorum judicum
Cœtum, to that assembly of the sage
Paralleled only by my judges here ;
Ubi, cognito de causa, where, the cause
Well weighed, *responsum est*, they gave reply,
Ut ipsa et accusator, that both sides
O' the suit, *redirent*, should come back again,
Post centum annos, after a hundred years,
For judgment ; *et sic*, by which sage decree,
Duplici parricidio rea, one
Convicted of a double parricide,
Quamvis etiam innocentem, though in truth
Out of the pair, one innocent at least
She, *occidisset*, plainly had put to death,
Undequaque, yet she altogether 'scaped,
Evasit impunis.   See the case at length
In Valerius, fittingly styled *Maximus*,
That eighth book of his Memorable Facts.
Nor Cyriacus cites beside the mark :
Similiter uxor quœ mandaverat,
Just so, a lady who had taken care,
Homicidium viri, that her lord be killed,
Ex denegatione debiti,
For denegation of a certain debt,
Matrimonialis, he was loth to pay,
Fuit pecuniaria mulcta, was
Amerced in a pecuniary mulct,
Punita, et ad pœnam, and to pains,
Temporalem, for a certain space of time,
In monasterio, in a convent.

                    (Ay,
In monasterio !   He mismanages

In with the ablative, the accusative !
I had hoped to have hitched the villain into verse
For a gift, this very day, a complete list
O' the prepositions each with proper case,
Telling a story, long was in my head.
What prepositions take the accusative ?
Ad, to or at — *who saw the cat ?* — down to
Ob, for, because of, *keep her claws off !*   Tush !
Law in a man takes the whole liberty :
The muse is fettered : just as Ovid found !)

And now, sea widens and the coast is clear.
What of the dubious act you bade excuse ?
Surely things broaden, brighten, till at length
Remains — so far from act that needs de-
              fence —
Apology to make for act delayed
One minute, let alone eight mortal months
Of hesitation !   "Why procrastinate ? "
(Out with it, my Bottinius, ease thyself !)
"Right, promptly done, is twice right : right
              delayed
Turns wrong.   We grant you should have
              killed your wife,
But killed o' the moment, at the meeting her
In company with the priest: then did the
              tongue
O' the Brazen Head give license, 'Time is
              now ! '
Wait to make mind up ?   'Time is past' it
              peals.
Friend, you are competent to mastery
O' the passions that confessedly explain
An outbreak : you allow an interval,
And then break out as if time's clock still
              clanged.
You have forfeited your chance, and flat you
              fall
Into the commonplace category
Of men bound to go softly all their days,
Obeying law."

                    Now, which way make response ?
What was the answer Guido gave, himself ?
— That so to argue came of ignorance
How honor bears a wound : " For, wound,"
              said he,
" My body, and the smart soon mends and ends :
While, wound my soul where honor sits and
              rules,
Longer the sufferance, stronger grows the pain,
Being *ex incontinenti*, fresh as first."
But try another tack, urge common sense
By way of contrast : say — Too true, my lords !
We did demur, awhile did hesitate :
Since husband sure should let a scruple speak
Ere he slay wife, — for his own safety, lords !
Carpers abound in this misjudging world :
Moreover, there 's a nicety in law
That seems to justify them should they carp.
Suppose the source of injury a son, —
Father may slay such son yet run no risk :
Why graced with such a privilege ?   Because
A father so incensed with his own child,
Or must have reason, or believe he has :
Quia semper, seeing that in such event,
Presumitur, the law is bound suppose,
Quod capiat pater, that the sire must take,

Bonum consilium pro filio,
The best course as to what befits his boy,
Through instinct, *ex instinctu,* of mere love,
Amoris, and, *paterni,* fatherhood ;
Quam confidentiam, which confidence,
Non habet, law declines to entertain,
De viro, of the husband : where finds he
An instinct that compels him love his wife ?
Rather is he presumably her foe.
So, let him ponder long in this bad world
Ere do the simplest act of justice.

But
Again — and here we brush Bottini's breast —
Object you, " See the danger of delay,
Suppose a man murdered my friend last month :
Had I come up and killed him for his pains
In rage, I had done right, allows the law :
I meet him now and kill him in cold blood,
I do wrong, equally allows the law :
Wherein do actions differ, yours and mine ? "
In plenitudine intellectus es ?
Hast thy wits, Fisc ? To take such slayer's
    life,
Returns it life to thy slain friend at all ?
Had he stolen ring instead of stabbing friend, —
To-day, to-morrow, or next century,
Meeting the thief, thy ring upon his thumb,
Thou justifiably hadst wrung it thence :
So, couldst thou wrench thy friend's life back
    again,
Though prisoned in the bosom of his foe,
Why, law would look complacent on thy
    wrath.
Our case is, that the thing we lost, we found :
The honor, we were robbed of eight months
    since,
Being recoverable at any day
By death of the delinquent. Go thy ways !
Ere thou hast learned law, will be much to do,
As said the gaby while he shod the goose.

Nay, if you urge me, interval was none !
From the inn to the villa — blank or else a bar
Of adverse and contrarious incident
Solid between us and our just revenge !
What with the priest who flourishes his blade,
The wife who like a fury flings at us,
The crowd — and then the capture, the appeal
To Rome, the journey there, the jaunting
    thence
To shelter at the House of Convertites,
The visits to the Villa, and so forth,
Where was one minute left us all this while
To put in execution that revenge
We planned o' the instant ? — as it were,
    plumped down
O' the spot, some eight months since, which
    round sound egg,
Rome, more propitious than our nest, should
    hatch !
Object not, " You reached Rome on Christmas-
    eve,
And, despite liberty to act at once,
Waited a whole and indecorous week ! "
Hath so the Molinism, the canker, lords,
Eaten to our bone ? Is no religion left ?
No care for aught held holy by the Church ?

What, would you have us skip and miss those
    Feasts
O' the Natal Time, must we go prosecute
Secular business on a sacred day ?
Should not the merest charity expect,
Setting our poor concerns aside for once,
We hurried to the song matutinal
I' the Sistine, and pressed forward for the
    Mass
The Cardinal that 's Camerlengo chants,
Then rushed on to the blessing of the Hat
And Rapier, which the Pope sends to what
    prince
Has done most detriment to the Infidel —
And thereby whetted courage if 't were blunt ?
Meantime, allow we kept the house a week,
Suppose not we were idle in our mew !
Picture us raging here and raving there —
" ' Money ? ' I need none. ' Friends ? ' The
    word is null.
Restore the white was on that shield of mine
Borne at " . . . wherever might be shield to
    bear.
" I see my grandsire, he who fought so well
At " . . . here find out and put in time and
    place,
Or else invent the fight his grandsire fought :
" I see this ! I see that ! "

(See nothing else,
Or I shall scarce see lamb's fry in an hour !
What to the uncle, as I bid advance
The smoking dish ? " Fry suits a tender tooth !
Behooves we care a little for our kin —
You, Sir, — who care so much for cousinship
As come to your poor loving nephew's feast ! "
He has the reversion of a long lease yet —
Land to bequeath ! He loves lamb's fry, I
    know !)

Here fall to be considered those same six
Qualities ; what Bottini needs must call
So many aggravations of our crime,
Parasite-growth upon mere murder's back.
We summarily might dispose of such
By some off-hand and jaunty fling, some skit —
" So, since there 's proved no crime to aggra-
    vate,
A fico for your aggravations, Fisc ! "
No, — handle mischief rather, — play with
    spells
Were meant to raise a spirit, and laugh the
    while
We show that did he rise we stand his match !
Therefore, first aggravation : we made up —
Over and above our simple murderous selves —
A regular assemblage of armed men,
Coadunatio armatorum, — ay,
Unluckily it was the very judge
That sits in judgment on our cause to-day
Who passed the law as Governor of Rome :
" Four men armed " — though for lawful pur-
    pose, mark !
Much more for an acknowledged crime —
    " shall die."
We five were armed to the teeth, meant murder
    too ?
Why, that 's the very point that saves us Fisc

Let me instruct you. Crime nor done nor
    meant, —
You punish still who arm and congregate :
For wherefore use bad means to a good end ?
Crime being meant not done, — you punish still
The means to crime, whereon you haply pounce,
Though accident have balked them of effect.
But crime not only compassed but complete,
Meant and done too ? Why, since you have
    the end,
Be that your sole concern, nor mind those
    means
No longer to the purpose ! Murdered we ?
(— Which, that our luck was in the present
    case,
Quod contigisse in præsenti casu,
Is palpable, *manibus palpatum est —*)
Make murder out against us, nothing else !
Of many crimes committed with a view
To one main crime, Law overlooks the less,
Intent upon the large. Suppose a man
Having in view commission of a theft,
Climbs the town-wall : 't is for the theft he
    hangs,
In case he stands convicted of such theft :
Law remits whipping, due to who clomb wall
Through bravery or wantonness alone,
Just to dislodge a daw's nest, plant a flag.
So I interpret you the manly mind
Of him about to judge both you and me, —
Our Governor, who, being no Fisc, my Fisc,
Cannot have blundered on ineptitude !
Next aggravation, — that the arms themselves
Were specially of such forbidden sort
Through shape or length or breadth, as, prompt,
    Law plucks
From single hand of solitary man,
Making him pay the carriage with his life :
Delatio armorum, arms against the rule,
Contra formam constitutionis, of
Pope Alexander's blessed memory.
Such are the poniards with the double prong,
Horn-like, when tines make bold the antlered
    buck,
Each prong of brittle glass — wherewith to stab
And break off short and so let fragment stick
Fast in the flesh to baffle surgery :
Such being the Genoese blade with hooked edge
That did us service at the villa here.
Sed parcat mihi tam eximius vir,
But, — let so rare a personage forgive, —
Fisc, thy objection is a foppery !
Thy charge runs that we killed three inno-
    cents :
Killed, dost see ? Then, if killed, what matter
    how ? —
By stick or stone, by sword or dagger, tool
Long or tool short, round or triangular —
Poor slain folk find small comfort in the choice !
Means to an end, means to an end, my Fisc !
Nature cries out, " Take the first arms you
    find ! "
Furor ministrat arma : where 's a stone ?
Unde mî lapidem, where darts for me ?
Unde sagittas ? But subdue the bard
And rationalize a little. Eight months since,
Had we, or had we not, incurred your blame
For letting 'scape unpunished this bad pair ?

I think I proved that in last paragraph !
Why did we so ? Because our courage failed.
Wherefore ? Through lack of arms to fight the
    foe :
We had no arms or merely lawful ones,
An unimportant sword and blunderbuss,
Against a foe, pollent in potency,
The *amasius,* and our vixen of a wife.
Well then, how culpably do we gird loin
And once more undertake the high emprise,
Unless we load ourselves this second time
With handsome superfluity of arms,
Since better is " too much " than " not enough,"
And " *plus non vitiat,*" too much does no harm,
Except in mathematics, sages say.
Gather instruction from the parable !
At first we are advised — " A lad hath here
Seven barley loaves and two small fishes : what
Is that among so many ?" Aptly asked :
But put that question twice and, quite as apt,
The answer is, " Fragments, twelve baskets
    full ! "

And, while we speak of superabundance, fling
We word by the way to fools who cast their
    flout
On Guido — " Punishment were pardoned him,
But here the punishment exceeds offence :
He might be just, but he was cruel too ! "
Why, grant there seems a kind of cruelty
In downright stabbing people he could maim,
(If so you stigmatize the stern and strict)
Still, Guido meant no cruelty — may plead
Transgression of his mandate, over-zeal
O' the part of his companions : all he craved
Was, they should fray the faces of the folk,
Merely disfigure, nowise make them die.
Solummodo fassus est, he owns no more,
Dedisse mandatum, than that he desired,
Ad sfrisiandum, dicam, that they hack
And hew, i' the customary phrase, his wife,
Uxorem tantum, and no harm beside.
If his instructions then be misconceived,
Nay, disobeyed; impute you blame to him ?
Cite me no Panicollus to the point,
As adverse ! Oh, I quite expect his case —
How certain noble youths of Sicily
Having good reason to mistrust their wives,
Killed them and were absolved in consequence :
While others who had gone beyond the need
By mutilation of each paramour —
As Galba in the Horatian satire grieved
— These were condemned to the galleys, cast for
    guilt
Exceeding simple murder of a wife.
But why ? Because of ugliness, and not
Cruelty, in the said revenge, I trow !
Ex causa abscissionis partium ;
Qui nempe id facientes reputantur
Naturæ inimici, man revolts
Against them as the natural enemy.
Pray, grant to one who meant to slit the nose
And slash the cheek and slur the mouth, at
    most,
A somewhat more humane award than these
Obtained, these natural enemies of man !
Objectum funditus corruit, flat you fall,
My Fisc ! I waste no kick on you, but pass.

Third aggravation : that our act was done —
Not in the public street, where safety lies,
Not in the by-place, caution may avoid,
Wood, cavern, desert, spots contrived for
   crime, —
But in the very house, home, nook and nest,
O' the victims, murdered in their dwelling-place,
In domo ac habitatione propria,
Where all presumably is peace and joy.
The spider, crime, pronounce we twice a pest
When, creeping from congenial cottage, she
Taketh hold with her hands, to horrify
His household more, i' the palace of the king.
All three were housed and safe and confident.
Moreover, the permission that our wife
Should have at length *domum pro carcere,*
Her own abode in place of prison — why,
We ourselves granted, by our other self
And proxy Paolo : did we make such grant,
Meaning a lure ? — elude the vigilance
O' the jailer, lead her to commodious death,
While we ostensibly relented ?
                Ay,
Just so did we, nor otherwise, my Fisc !
Is vengeance lawful ?   We demand our right,
But find it will be questioned or refused
By jailer, turnkey, hangdog, — what know we ?
Pray, how is it we should conduct ourselves ?
To gain our private right — break public peace,
Do you bid us ? — trouble order with our broils ?
Endanger . . . shall I shrink to own . . . our-
   selves ? —
Who want no broken head nor bloody nose
(While busied slitting noses, breaking heads)
From the first tipstaff that may interfere !
Nam quicquid sit, for howsoever it be,
An de consensu nostro, if with leave
Or not, *a monasterio,* from the nuns,
Educta esset, she had been led forth,
Potuimus id dissimulare, we
May well have granted leave in pure pretence,
Ut aditum habere, that thereby
An entry we might compass, a free move
Potuissemus, to her easy death,
Ad eam occidendam.   Privacy
O' the hearth, and sanctitude of home, say you ?
Shall we give man's abode more privilege
Than God's ? — for in the churches where he
   dwells,
In quibus assistit Regum Rex, by means
Of his essence, *per essentiam,* all the same,
Et nihilominus, therein, *in eis,*
Ex justa via delinquens, whoso dares
To take a liberty on ground enough,
Is pardoned, *excusatur :* that 's our case —
Delinquent through befitting cause.   You hold,
To punish a false wife in her own house
Is graver than, what happens every day,
To hale a debtor from his hiding-place
In church protected by the Sacrament ?
To this conclusion have I brought my Fisc ?
Foxes have holes, and fowls o' the air their
   nests ;
Praise you the impiety that follows, Fisc ?
Shall false wife yet have where to lay her head ?
" *Contra Fiscum definitum est !* "   He 's done !
" *Surge et scribe,*" make a note of it !
— If I may dally with Aquinas' word.

Or in the death-throe does he mutter still,
Fourth aggravation, that we changed our garb,
And rusticized ourselves with uncouth hat,
Rough vest and goatskin wrappage ; murdered
   thus
Mutatione vestium, in disguise,
Whereby mere murder got complexed with wile,
Turned *homicidium ex insidiis ?*   Fisc,
How often must I round thee in the ears —
All means are lawful to a lawful end ?
Concede he had the right to kill his wife :
The Count indulged in a travesty ; why ?
De illa ut vindictam sumeret,
That on her he might lawful vengeance take,
Commodius, with more ease, *et tutius,*
And safelier : wants he warrant for the step ?
Read to thy profit how the Apostle once
For ease and safety, when Damascus raged,
Was let down in a basket by the wall,
To 'scape the malice of the governor
(Another sort of Governor boasts Rome !)
— Many are of opinion, — covered close,
Concealed with — what except that very cloak
He left behind at Troas afterward ?
I shall not add a syllable : Molinists may !
Well, have we more to manage ?   Ay, indeed !
Fifth aggravation, that our wife reposed
Sub potestate judicis, beneath
Protection of the judge, — her house was styled
A prison, and his power became its guard
In lieu of wall and gate and bolt and bar.
This is a tough point, shrewd, redoubtable :
Because we have to supplicate that judge
Shall overlook wrong done the judgment-seat.
Now, I might suffer my own nose be pulled,
As man : but then as father . . . if the Fisc
Touched one hair of my boy who held my hand
In confidence he could not come to harm
Crossing the Corso, at my own desire,
Going to see those bodies in the church —
What would you say to that, Don Hyacinth ?
This is the sole and single knotty point :
For, bid Tommati blink his interest,
You laud his magnanimity the while :
But balk Tommati's office, — he talks big !
" My predecessors in the place, — those sons
O' the prophets that may hope succeed me
   here, —
Shall I diminish their prerogative ?
Count Guido Franceschini's honor ! — well,
Has the Governor of Rome none ? "
                   You perceive.
The cards are all against us.   Make a push,
Kick over table, as shrewd gamesters do !
We, do you say, encroach upon the rights,
Deny the omnipotence o' the Judge forsooth ?
We, who have only been from first to last
Intending that his purpose should prevail,
Nay more, at times, anticipating it
At risk of his rebuke ?
               But wait awhile !
Cannot we lump this with the sixth and last
Of the aggravations — that the Majesty
O' the Sovereign here received a wound ? to
   wit,
Læsa Majestas, since our violence

Was out of envy to the course of law,
In odium litis? We cut short thereby
Three pending suits, promoted by ourselves
I' the main, — which worsens crime, *accedit ad
Exasperationem criminis!*

Yes, here the eruptive wrath with full effect !
How, did not indignation chain my tongue,
Could I repel this last, worst charge of all !
(There is a porcupine to barbecue ;
Gigia can jug a rabbit well enough,
With sour-sweet sauce and pine-pips ; but, good
    Lord,
Suppose the devil instigate the wench
To stew, not roast him ? Stew my porcupine ?
If she does, I know where his quills shall stick !
Come, I must go myself and see to things :
I cannot stay much longer stewing here.)
Our stomach . . . I mean, our soul is stirred
    within,
And we want words. We wounded Majesty ?
Fall under such a censure, we ? — who yearned
So much that Majesty dispel the cloud
And shine on us with healing on her wings,
That we prayed Pope *Majestas'* very self
To anticipate a little the tardy pack,
Bell us forth deep the authoritative bay
Should start the beagles into sudden yelp
Unisonous, — and, Gospel leading Law,
Grant there assemble in our own behoof
A Congregation, a particular Court,
A few picked friends of quality and place,
To hear the several matters in dispute,
Causes big, little, and indifferent,
Bred of our marriage like a mushroom-growth,
All at once (can one brush off such too soon ?)
And so with laudable dispatch decide
Whether we, in the main (to sink detail)
Were one the Pope should hold fast or let go.
" What, take the credit from the Law ? " you
    ask ?
Indeed, we did ! Law ducks to Gospel here :
Why should Law gain the glory and pronounce
A judgment shall immortalize the Pope ?
Yes : our self-abnegating policy
Was Joab's — we would rouse our David's
    sloth,
Bid him encamp against a city, sack
A place whereto ourselves had long laid seige,
Lest, taking it at last, it take our name
Nor be styled *Innocentinopolis.*
But no ! The modesty was in alarm,
The temperance refused to interfere,
Returned us our petition with the word
"*Ad judices suos,*" "Leave him to his
    Judge ! "
As who should say, " Why trouble my repose ?
Why consult Peter in a simple case,
Peter's wife's sister in her fever-fit
Might solve as readily as the Apostle's self ?
Are my Tribunals posed by aught so plain ?
Hath not my Court a conscience ? It is of age,
Ask it ! "

We do ask, — but, inspire reply
To the Court thou bidst me ask, as I have
    asked —
Th thou, who vigilantly dost attend

To even the few, the ineffectual words
Which rise from this our low and mundane
    sphere
Up to thy region out of smoke and noise,
Seeking corroboration from thy nod
Who art all justice — which means mercy too,
In a low noisy smoky world like ours
Where Adam's sin made peccable his seed !
We venerate the father of the flock,
Whose last faint sands of life, the fritterec
    gold,
Fall noiselessly, yet all too fast, o' the cone
And tapering heap of those collected years :
Never have these been hurried in their flow,
Though justice fain would jog reluctant arm,
In eagerness to take the forfeiture
Of guilty life : much less shall mercy sue
In vain that thou let innocence survive,
Precipitate no minim of the mass
O' the all-so precious moments of thy life,
By pushing Guido into death and doom !

(Our Cardinal engages to go read
The Pope my speech, and point its beauties
    out.
They say, the Pope has one half-hour, in
    twelve,
Of something like a moderate return
Of the intellectuals, — never much to lose ! —
If I adroitly plant this passage there,
The Fisc will find himself forestalled, I think,
Though he stand, beat till the old ear-drum
    break !
— Ah, boy of my own bowels, Hyacinth,
Wilt ever catch the knack, requite the pains
Of poor papa, become proficient too
I' the how and why and when, the time to
    laugh,
The time to weep, the time, again, to pray,
And all the times prescribed by Holy Writ ?
Well, well, we fathers can but care, but cast
Our bread upon the waters !)
                                In a word,
These secondary charges go to ground,
Since secondary, and superfluous, — motes
Quite from the main point : we did all and
    some,
Little and much, adjunct and principal,
Causa honoris. Is there such a cause
As the sake of honor ? By that sole test try
Our action, nor demand if more or less,
Because of the action's mode, we merit blame
Or maybe deserve praise ! The Court decides.
Is the end lawful ? It allows the means :
What we may do, we may with safety do,
And what means " safety " we ourselves mus;
    judge.
Put case a person wrongs me past dispute :
If my legitimate vengeance be a blow,
Mistrusting my bare arm can deal that blow,
I claim co-operation of a stick ;
Doubtful if stick be tough, I crave a sword ;
Diffident of ability in fence,
I fee a friend, a swordsman to assist :
Take one — he may be coward, fool or knave ?
Why not take fifty ? — and if these exceed
I' the due degree of drubbing, whom accuse
But the first author of the aforesaid wrong

Who put poor me to such a world of pains?
Surgery would have just excised a wart;
The patient made such pother, struggled so
That the sharp instrument sliced nose and all.
Taunt us not that our friends performed for
    pay!
Ourselves had toiled for simple honor's sake:
But country clowns want dirt they comprehend,
The piece of gold!   Our reasons, which suffice
Ourselves, be ours alone; our piece of gold
Be, to the rustic, reason he approves!
We must translate our motives like our speech,
Into the lower phrase that suits the sense
O' the limitedly apprehensive.   Let
Each level have its language! Heaven speaks
    first
To the angel, then the angel tames the word
Down to the ear of Tobit: he, in turn,
Diminishes the message to his dog,
And finally that dog finds how the flea
(Which else, importunate, might check his
    speed)
Shall learn its hunger must have holiday,
By application of his tongue or paw:
So many varied sorts of language here,
Each following each with pace to match the
    step,
Haud passibus æquis!

                Talking of which flea,
Reminds me I must put in special word
For the poor humble following, — the four
    friends,
Sicarii, our assassins caught and caged.
Ourselves are safe in your approval now:
Yet must we care for our companions, plead
The cause o' the poor, the friends (of old-world
    faith)
Who lie in tribulation for our sake.
Pauperum Procurator is my style:
I stand forth as the poor man's advocate:
And when we treat of what concerns the poor,
Et cum agatur de pauperibus,
In bondage, *carceratis,* for their sake,
In eorum causis, natural piety,
Pietas, ever ought to win the day,
Triumphare debet, quia ipsi sunt,
Because those very paupers constitute,
Thesaurus Christi, all the wealth of Christ.
Nevertheless I shall not hold you long
With multiplicity of proofs, nor burn
Candle at noontide, clarify the clear.
There beams a case refulgent from our
    books —
Castrensis, Butringarius, everywhere
I find it burn to dissipate the dark.
'T is this: a husband had a friend, which
    friend
Seemed to him over-friendly with his wife
In thought and purpose, — I pretend no more.
To justify suspicion or dispel,
He bids his wife make show of giving heed,
Semblance of sympathy — propose, in fine,
A secret meeting in a private place.
The friend, enticed thus, finds an ambuscade,
To wit, the husband posted with a pack
Of other friends, who fall upon the first
And beat his love and life out both at once.

These friends were brought to question for
    their help;
Law ruled, "The husband being in the right,
Who helped him in the right can scarce be
    wrong " —
Opinio, an opinion every way,
Multum tenenda cordi, heart should hold!
When the inferiors follow as befits
The lead o' the principal, they change their
    name,
And, *non dicuntur,* are no longer called
His mandatories, *mandatorii,*
But helpmates, *sed auxiliatores;* since
To that degree does honor's sake lend aid,
Adeo honoris causa est efficax,
That not alone, *non solum,* does it pour
Itself out, *se diffundat,* on mere friends
We bring to do our bidding of this sort,
In mandatorios simplices, but sucks
Along with it in wide and generous whirl,
Sed etiam assassinii qualitate
Qualificatos, people qualified
By the quality of assassination's self,
Dare I make use of such neologism,
Ut utar verbo.

                Haste we to conclude:
Of the other points that favor, leave some few
For Spreti; such as the delinquents' youth.
One of them falls short, by some months, of
    age
Fit to be managed by the gallows; two
May plead exemption from our law's award,
Being foreigners, subjects of the Granduke —
I spare that bone to Spreti, and reserve
Myself the juicier breast of argument —
Flinging the breast-blade i' the face o' the Fisc,
Who furnished me the tidbit: he must needs
Play off his privilege and rack the clowns, —
And they, at instance of the rack, confess
All four unanimously made resolve, —
The night o' the murder, in brief minute
    snatched
Behind the back of Guido as he fled, —
That, since he had not kept his promise, paid
The money for the murder on the spot,
So, reaching home again, might please ignore
The pact or pay them in improper coin, —
They one and all resolved, these hopeful
    friends,
'T were best inaugurate the morrow's light,
Nature recruited with her due repose,
By killing Guido as he lay asleep
Pillowed on wallet which contained their fee.

I thank the Fisc for knowledge of this fact:
What fact could hope to make more manifest
Their rectitude, Guido's integrity?
For who fails recognize the touching truth
That these poor rustics bore no envy, hate,
Malice nor yet uncharitableness
Against the people they had put to death?
In them, did such an act reward itself?
All done was to deserve the simple pay,
Obtain the bread clowns earn by sweat of
    brow,
And missing which, they missed of every
    thing —

Hence claimed pay, even at expense of life
To their own lord, so little warped (admire !)
By prepossession, such the absolute
Instinct of equity in rustic souls !
Whereas our Count, the cultivated mind,
He, wholly rapt in his serene regard
Of honor, he contemplating the sun,
Who hardly marks if taper blink below,
He, dreaming of no argument for death
Except a vengeance worthy noble hearts, —
Dared not so desecrate the deed, forsooth,
Vulgarize vengeance, as defray its cost
By money dug from out the dirty earth,
Irritant mere, in Ovid's phrase, to ill.
What though he lured base hinds by lucre's
     hope, —
The only motive they could masticate,
Milk for babes, not strong meat which men re-
     quire ?
The deed done, those coarse hands were soiled
     enough,
He spared them the pollution of the pay.
So much for the allegement, thine, my Fisc,
Quo nil absurdius, than which naught more
     mad,
Excogitari potest, may be squeezed
From out the cogitative brain of thee!

And now, thou excellent the Governor !
(Push to the peroration) *cœterum*
Enixe supplico, I strive in prayer,
Ut dominis meis, that unto the Court,
Benigna fronte, with a gracious brow,
Et oculis serenis, and mild eyes,
Perpendere placeat, it may please them weigh,
Quod dominus Guido, that our noble Count,
Occidit, did the killing in dispute,
Ut ejus honor tumulatus, that
The honor of him buried fathom-deep
In infamy, *in infamia,* might arise,
Resurgeret, as ghost breaks sepulchre !
Occidit, for he killed, *uxorem,* wife,
Quia illi fuit, since she was to him,
Opprobrio, a disgrace and nothing more !
Et genitores, killed her parents too,
Qui, who, *postposita verecundia,*
Having thrown off all sort of decency,
Filiam repudiarunt, had renounced
Their daughter, *atque declarare non*
Erubuerunt, nor felt blush tinge cheek,
Declaring, *meretricis genitam*
Esse, she was the offspring of a drab,
Ut ipse dehonestaretur, just
That so himself might lose his social rank !
Cujus mentem, and which daughter's heart and
     soul,
They, *perverterunt,* turned from the right
     course,
Et ad illicitos amores non
Dumtaxat pellexerunt, and to love
Not simply did alluringly incite,
Sed vi obedientiæ, but by force
O' the duty, *filialis,* daughters owe,
Coegerunt, forced and drove her to the deed:
Occidit, I repeat he killed the clan,
Ne scilicet amplius in dedecore,
Lest peradventure longer life might trail,
Viveret, link by link his turpitude,

Invisus consanguineis. hateful so
To kith and kindred, *a nobilibus*
Notatus, shunned by men of quality,
Relictus ab amicis, left i' the lurch
By friends, *ab omnibus derisus,* turned
A common hack-block to try edge of jokes.
Occidit, and he killed them here in Rome,
In Urbe, the Eternal City, Sirs,
Nempe quæ alias spectata est,
The appropriate theatre which witnessed once
Matronam nobilem, Lucretia's self,
Ablue e pudicitiæ maculas,
Wash off the spots of her pudicity,
Sanguine proprio, with her own pure blood ;
Quæ vidit, and which city also saw,
Patrem, Virginius, *undequaque,* quite,
Impunem, with no sort of punishment,
Nor, *et non illaudatum,* lacking praise,
Sed polluentem parricidio,
Imbrue his hands with butchery, *filiæ,*
Of chaste Virginia, to avoid a rape,
Ne raperetur ad stupra ; so to heart,
Tanti illi cordi fuit, did he take,
Suspicio, the mere fancy men might have,
Honoris amittendi, of fame's loss,
Ut potius voluerit filia
Orbari, he preferred to lose his child,
Quam illa incederet, rather than she walk
The ways an, *inhonesta,* child disgraced,
Licet non sponte, though against her will.
Occidit — killed them, I reiterate —
In propria domo, in their own abode,
Ut adultera et parentes, that each wretch,
Conscii agnoscerent, might both see and say,
Nullum locum, there 's no place, *nullumque esse*
Asylum, nor yet refuge of escape,
Impenetrabilem, shall serve as bar,
Honori læso, to the wounded one
In honor ; *neve ibi opprobria*
Continuarentur, killed them on the spot
Moreover, dreading lest within those walls
The opprobrium peradventure be prolonged,
Et domus quæ testis fuit turpium,
And that the domicile which witnessed crime
Esset et pœnæ, might watch punishment:
Occidit, killed, I round you in the ears,
Quia alio modo, since by other mode,
Non poterat ejus existimatio,
There was no possibility his fame,
Læsa, gashed griesly, *tam enormiter,*
Ducere cicatrices, might be healed :
Occidit ut exemplum præberet
Uxoribus, killed her, so to lesson wives
Jura conjugii, that the marriage-oath,
Esse servanda, must be kept henceforth :
Occidit denique, killed her, in a word,
Ut pro posse honestus viveret,
That he, please God, might creditably live.
Sin minus, but if fate willed otherwise,
Proprii honoris, of his outraged fame,
Offensi, by Mannaia, if you please,
Commiseranda victima caderet,
The pitiable victim he should fall !

Done ! I' the rough, i' the rough ! But done
     And, lo,
Landed and stranded lies my very speech,
My miracle, my monster of defence —

Leviathan into the nose whereof
I have put fish-hook, pierced his jaw with
thorn,
And given him to my maidens for a play!
I' the rough: to-morrow I review my piece
Tame here and there undue floridity.
It 's hard: you have to plead before these
priests
And poke at them with Scripture, or you pass
For heathen and, what 's worse, for ignorant
O' the quality o' the Court and what it likes
By way of illustration of the law.
To-morrow stick in this, and throw out that,
And, having first ecclesiasticized,
Regularize the whole, next emphasize,
Then latinize, and lastly Cicero-ize,
Giving my Fisc his finish. There 's my
speech!
And where 's my fry, and family and friends?
Where 's that huge Hyacinth I mean to hug
Till he cries out, "*Jam satis!* Let me
breathe!"
Now, what an evening have I earned to-day!
Hail, ye true pleasures, all the rest are false!
Oh, the old mother, oh, the fattish wife!
Rogue Hyacinth shall put on paper toque,
And wrap himself around with mamma's veil
Done up to imitate papa's black robe,
(I 'm in the secret of the comedy, —
Part of the program leaked out long ago!)
And call himself the Advocate o' the Poor,
Mimic Don father that defends the Count:
And for reward shall have a small full glass
Of manly red rosolio to himself,
— Always provided that he conjugate
Bibo, I drink, correctly — nor be found
Make the *perfectum, bipsi*, as last year!
How the ambitious do so harden heart
As lightly hold by these home-sanctitudes,
To me is matter of bewilderment —
Bewilderment! Because ambition's range
Is nowise tethered by domestic tie:
Am I refused an outlet from my home
To the world's stage? — whereon a man should
play
The man in public, vigilant for law,
Zealous for truth, a credit to his kind,
Nay, — since, employing talent so, I yield
The Lord his own again with usury, —
A satisfaction, yea, to God himself!
Well, I have modelled me by Agur's wish,
"Remove far from me vanity and lies,
Feed me with food convenient for me!" What
I' the world should a wise man require beyond?
Can I but coax the good fat little wife
To tell her fool of a father the mad prank
His scapegrace nephew played this time last
year
At Carnival! He could not choose, I think,
But modify that inconsiderate gift
O' the cup and cover (somewhere in the will
Under the pillow, some one seems to guess)
— Correct that clause in favor of a boy
The trifle ought to grace, with name engraved,
Would look so well, produced in future years
To pledge a memory, when poor papa
Latin and law are long since laid at rest —
Hyacintho dono dedit avus! Why,

The wife should get a necklace for her pains,
The very pearls that made Violante proud,
And Pietro pawned for half their value once,
Redeemable by somebody, *ne sit
Marita quæ rotundioribus
Onusta mammis . . . baccis ambulet:*
Her bosom shall display the big round balls,
No braver proudly borne by wedded wife!
With which Horatian promise I conclude.

Into the pigeon-hole with thee, my speech!
Off and away, first work, then play, play, play
Bottini, burn thy books, thou blazing ass!
Sing "Tra-la-la, for, lambkins, we must live!"

IX

JURIS DOCTOR JOHANNES – BAPTISTA
BOTTINIUS,

FISCI ET REV. CAM. APOSTOL. ADVOCATUS

Had I God's leave, how I would alter things!
If I might read instead of print my speech, —
Ay, and enliven speech with many a flower
Refuses obstinate to blow in print,
As wildings planted in a prim parterre, —
This scurvy room were turned an immense hall;
Opposite, fifty judges in a row;
This side and that of me, for audience — Rome:
And, where yon window is, the Pope should
hide —
Watch, curtained, but peep visibly enough.
A buzz of expectation! Through the crowd,
Jingling his chain and stumping with his staff,
Up comes an usher, louts him low, "The Court
Requires the allocution of the Fisc!"
I rise, I bend, I look about me, pause
O'er the hushed multitude: I count — One,
two —

Have ye seen, Judges, have ye, lights of law, —
When it may hap some painter, much in vogue
Throughout our city nutritive of arts,
Ye summon to a task shall test his worth,
To manufacture, as he knows and can,
A work may decorate a palace-wall,
Affords my lords their Holy Family,
Hath it escaped the acumen of the Court
How such a painter sets himself to paint?
Suppose that Joseph, Mary and her Babe
A-journeying to Egypt, prove the piece:
Why, first he sedulously practiseth,
This painter, — girding loin and lighting lamp, —
On what may nourish eye, make facile hand;
Getteth him studies (styled by draughtsmen so)
From some assistant corpse of Jew or Turk
Or, haply, Molinist, he cuts and carves, —
This Luca or this Carlo or the like.
To him the bones their inmost secret yield,
Each notch and nodule signify their use:
On him the muscles turn, in triple tier,
And pleasantly entreat the entrusted man
"Familiarize thee with our play that lifts
Thus, and thus lowers again, leg, arm and
foot!"

— Ensuring due correctness in the nude.
Which done, is all done? Not a whit, ye know!
He, — to art's surface rising from her depth,—
If some flax-polled soft-bearded sire be found,
May simulate a Joseph, (happy chance!) —
Limneth exact each wrinkle of the brow,
Loseth no involution, cheek or chap,
Till lo, in black and white, the senior lives!
Is it a young and comely peasant-nurse
That poseth? (be the phrase accorded me!)
Each feminine delight of florid lip,
Eyes brimming o'er and brow bowed down
        with love,
Marmoreal neck and bosom uberous, —
Glad on the paper in a trice they go
To help his notion of the Mother-maid:
Methinks I see it, chalk a little stumped!
Yea and her babe — that flexure of soft limbs,
That budding face imbued with dewy sleep,
Contribute each an excellence to Christ.
Nay, since he humbly lent companionship,
Even the poor ass, unpanniered and elate
Stands, perks an ear up, he a model too;
While clouted shoon, staff, scrip and water-
        gourd, —
Aught may betoken travel, heat and haste, —
No jot nor tittle of these but in its turn
Ministers to perfection of the piece:
Till now, such piece before him, part by
        part, —
Such prelude ended, — pause our painter may,
Submit his fifty studies one by one,
And in some sort boast "I have served my
        lords."

But what? And hath he painted once this
        while?
Or when ye cry, "Produce the thing required,
Show us our picture shall rejoice its niche,
Thy Journey through the Desert done in
        oils!" —
What, doth he fall to shuffling 'mid his sheets,
Fumbling for first this, then the other fact
Consigned to paper, — "studies," bear the
        term! —
And stretch a canvas, mix a pot of paste,
And fasten here a head and there a tail,
(The ass hath one, my Judges!) so dove-tail
Or, rather, ass-tail in, piece sorrily out —
By bits of reproduction of the life —
The picture, the expected Family?
I trow not! do I miss with my conceit
The mark, my lords? — not so my lords were
        served!
Rather your artist turns abrupt from these,
And preferably buries him and broods
(Quite away from aught vulgar and extern)
On the inner spectrum, filtered through the eye,
His brain-deposit, bred of many a drop,
E pluribus unum: and the wiser he!
For in that brain, — their fancy sees at work,
Could my lords peep indulged, — results alone,
Not processes which nourish such results,
Would they discover and appreciate, — life
Fed by digestion, not raw food itself,
No gobbets but smooth comfortable chyme
Secreted from each snapped-up crudity, —
Less distinct, part by part, but in the whole

Truer to the subject, — the main central truth
And soul o' the picture, would my Judges
        spy, —
Not those mere fragmentary studied facts
Which answer to the outward frame and
        flesh —
Not this nose, not that eyebrow, the other fact
Of man's staff, woman's stole or infant's clout,
But lo, a spirit-birth conceived of flesh,
Truth rare and real, not transcripts, fact and
        false.
The studies — for his pupils and himself!
The picture be for our eximious Rome
And — who knows? — satisfy its Governor,
Whose new wing to the villa he hath bought
(God give him joy of it) by Capena, soon
('T is bruited) shall be glowing with the brush
Of who hath long surpassed the Florentine,
The Urbinate and . . . what if I dared add,
Even his master, yea the Cortonese, —
I mean the accomplished Ciro Ferri, Sirs!
(— Did not he die? I 'll see before I print.)

End we exordium, Phœbus plucks my ear!
Thus then, just so and no whit otherwise,
Have I, — engaged as I were Ciro's self,
To paint a parallel, a Family,
The patriarch Pietro with his wise old wife
To boot (as if one introduced Saint Anne
By bold conjecture to complete the group)
And juvenile Pompilia with her babe,
Who, seeking safety in the wilderness,
Were all surprised by Herod, while out-
        stretched
In sleep beneath a palm-tree by a spring,
And killed — the very circumstance I paint,
Moving the pity and terror of my lords —
Exactly so have I, a month at least,
Your Fiscal, made me cognizant of facts,
Searched out, pried into, pressed the meaning
        forth
Of every piece of evidence in point,
How bloody Herod slew these innocents, —
Until the glad result is gained, the group
Demonstrably presented in detail,
Their slumber and his onslaught, — like as life.
Yea, and, availing me of help allowed
By law, discreet provision lest my lords
Be too much troubled by effrontery, —
The rack, law plies suspected crime withal —
(Law that hath listened while the lyrist sang
" Lene tormentum ingenio admoves,"
Gently thou joggest by a twinge the wit,
" Plerumque duro," else were slow to blab!)
Through this concession my full cup runs o'er:
The guilty owns his guilt without reserve.
Therefore by part and part I clutch my case
Which, in entirety now, — momentous task, —
My lords demand, so render them I must,
Since, one poor pleading more and I have done
But shall I ply my papers, play my proofs,
Parade my studies, fifty in a row,
As though the Court were yet in pupilage,
Claimed not the artist's ultimate appeal?
Much rather let me soar the height prescribed
And, bowing low, proffer my picture's self!
No more of proof, disproof, — such virtue was,
Such vice was never in Pompilia, now!

Far better say "Behold Pompilia!"—for
I leave the family as unmanageable,
And stick to just one portrait, but life-size.)
Hath calumny imputed to the fair
A blemish, mole on cheek or wart on chin,
Much more, blind hidden horrors best un-
     named?
Shall I descend to prove you, point by point,
Never was knock-knee known nor splay-foot
     found
In Phryne? (I must let the portrait go,
Content me with the model, I believe)—
—I prove this? An indignant sweep of hand,
Dash at and doing away with drapery,
And,—use your eyes, Athenians, smooth she
     smiles!
Or,—since my client can no longer smile,
And more appropriate instances abound,—
What is this Tale of Tarquin, how the slave
Was caught by him, preferred to Collatine?
Thou, even from thy corpse-clothes virginal,
Look'st the lie dead, Lucretia!
                    Thus at least
I, by the guidance of antiquity,
(Our one infallible guide,) now operate,
Sure that the innocence thus shown is safe;
Sure, too, that, while I plead, the echoes cry
(Lend my weak voice thy trump, sonorous
     Fame!)
"Monstrosity the Phrynean shape shall mar,
Lucretia's soul comport with Tarquin's lie,
When thistles grow on vines or thorns yield figs,
Or oblique sentence leave this judgment-seat!"

A great theme: may my strength be adequate!
For—paint Pompilia, dares my feebleness?
How did I unaware engage so much
—Find myself undertaking to produce
A faultless nature in a flawless form?
What's here? Oh, turn aside nor dare the
     blaze
Of such a crown, such constellation, say,
As jewels here thy front, Humanity!
First, infancy, pellucid as a pearl;
Then, childhood—stone which, dewdrop at the
     first,
(An old conjecture) sucks, by dint of gaze,
Blue from the sky and turns to sapphire so:
Yet both these gems eclipsed by, last and best,
Womanliness and wifehood opaline,
Its milk-white pallor,—chastity,—suffused
With here and there a tint and hint of flame,—
Desire,—the lapidary loves to find.
Such jewels bind conspicuously thy brow,
Pompilia, infant, child, maid, woman, wife—
Crown the ideal in our earth at last!
What should a faculty like mine do here?
Close eyes, or else, the rashlier hurry hand!

Which is to say,—lose no time but begin!
Sermocinando ne declamem, Sirs,
Ultra clepsydram, as our preachers smile,
Lest I exceed my hour-glass. Whereupon,
As Flaccus prompts, I dare the epic plunge—
Begin at once with marriage, up till when
Little or nothing would arrest your love,
In the easeful life o' the lady; lamb and lamb,
How do they differ? Know one, you know all

Manners of maidenhood: mere maiden she.
And since all lambs are like in more than fleece,
Prepare to find that, lamb-like, she too frisks—
O' the weaker sex, my lords, the weaker sex!
To whom, the Teian teaches us, for gift,
Not strength,—man's dower,—but beauty,
     nature gave,
"Beauty in lieu of spears, in lieu of shields!"
And what is beauty's sure concomitant,
Nay, intimate essential character,
But melting wiles, deliciousest deceits,
The whole redoubted armory of love?
Therefore of vernal pranks, dishevellings
O' the hair of youth that dances April in,
And easily-imagined Hebe-slips
O'er sward which May makes over-smooth for
     foot—
These shall we pry into?—or wiselier wink,
Though numerous and dear they may have
     been?

For lo, advancing Hymen and his pomp!
Discedunt nunc amores, loves, farewell!
Maneat amor, let love, the sole, remain!
Farewell to dewiness and prime of life!
Remains the rough determined day: dance
     done,
To work, with plough and harrow! What
     comes next?
'T is Guido henceforth guides Pompilia's step,
Cries, "No more friskings o'er the foodful glebe,
Else, 'ware the whip!" Accordingly,—first
     crack
O' the thong,—we hear that his young wife
     was barred,
Cohibita fuit, from the old free life,
Vitam liberiorem ducere.
Demur we? Nowise: heifer brave the hind?
We seek not there should lapse the natural law,
The proper piety to lord and king
And husband: let the heifer bear the yoke!
Only, I crave he cast not patience off,
This hind; for deem you she endures the whip,
Nor winces at the goad, nay, restive, kicks?
What if the adversary's charge be just,
And all untowardly she pursue her way
With groan and grunt, though hind strike ne'er
     so hard?
If petulant remonstrance made appeal,
Unseasonable, o'erprotracted,—if
Importunate challenge taxed the public ear
When silence more decorously had served
For protestation,—if Pompilian plaint
Wrought but to aggravate Guidonion ire,—
Why, such mishaps, ungainly though they be,
Ever companion change, are incident
To altered modes and novelty of life:
The philosophic mind expects no less,
Smilingly knows and names the crisis, sits
Waiting till old things go and new arrive.
Therefore, I hold a husband but inept
Who turns impatient at such transit-time,
As if this running from the rod would last!

Since, even while I speak, the end is reached:
Success awaits the soon-disheartened man.
The parents turn their backs and leave the
     house,

The wife may wail but none shall intervene :
He hath attained his object, groom and bride
Partake the nuptial bower no soul can see,
Old things are passed and all again is new,
Over and gone the obstacles to peace,
Novorum — tenderly the Mantuan turns
The expression, some such purpose in his eye —
Nascitur ordo ! Every storm is laid,
And forth from plain each pleasant herb may
          peep,
Each bloom of wifehood in abeyance late :
(Confer a passage in the Canticles.)

But what if, as 't is wont with plant and wife,
Flowers — after a suppression to good end,
Still, when they do spring forth — sprout here,
          spread there,
Anywhere likelier than beneath the foot
O' the lawful good-man gardener of the ground ?
He dug and dibbled, sowed and watered, — still
'T is a chance wayfarer shall pluck the increase.
Just so, respecting persons not too much,
The lady, foes allege, put forth each charm
And proper floweret of feminity
To whosoever had a nose to smell
Or breast to deck : what if the charge be true ?
The fault were graver had she looked with
          choice,
Fastidiously appointed who should grasp,
Who, in the whole town, go without the prize !
To nobody she destined donative,
But, first come was first served, the accuser
          saith.
Put case her sort of . . . in this kind . . .
          escapes
Were many and oft and indiscriminate —
Impute ye as the action were prepense,
The gift particular, arguing malice so ?
Which butterfly of the wide air shall brag
" I was preferred to Guido " — when 't is clear
The cup, he quaffs at, lay with olent breast
Open to gnat, midge, bee and moth as well ?
One chalice entertained the company ;
And if its peevish lord object the more,
Mistake, misname such bounty in a wife,
Haste we to advertise him — charm of cheek,
Lustre of eye, allowance of the lip,
All womanly components in a spouse,
These are no household-bread each stranger's
          bite
Leaves by so much diminished for the mouth
O' the master of the house at supper-time :
But rather like a lump of spice they lie,
Morsel of myrrh, which scents the neighborhood
Yet greets its lord no lighter by a grain.

Nay, even so, he shall be satisfied !
Concede we there was reason in his wrong,
Grant we his grievance and content the man !
For lo, Pompilia, she submits herself ;
Ere three revolving years have crowned their
          course,
Off and away she puts this same reproach
Of lavish bounty, inconsiderate gift
O' the sweets of wifehood stored to other ends :
No longer shall he blame " She none excludes,"
But substitute " She laudably sees all,
Searches the best out and selects the same."

For who is here, long sought and latest found,
Waiting his turn unmoved amid the whirl,
" *Constans in levitate*," — Ha, my lords ?
Calm in his levity, — indulge the quip ! —
Since 't is a levite bears the bell away,
Parades him henceforth as Pompilia's choice.
'T is no ignoble object, husband ! Doubt'st ?
When here comes tripping Flaccus with his
          phrase,
" Trust me, no miscreant singled from the mob,
*Crede non illum tibi de scelesta
Plebe delectum,*" but a man of mark,
A priest, dost hear ? Why then, submit thy-
          self !
Priest, ay, and very phœnix of such fowl,
Well-born, of culture, young and vigorous,
Comely too, since precise the precept points —
On the selected levite be there found
Nor mole nor scar nor blemish, lest the mind
Come all uncandid through the thwarting flesh !
Was not the son of Jesse ruddy, sleek,
Pleasant to look on, pleasant every way ?
Since well he smote the harp and sweetly sang,
And danced till Abigail came out to see,
And seeing smiled and smiling ministered
The raisin-cluster and the cake of figs,
With ready meal refreshed the gifted youth,
Till Nabal, who was absent shearing sheep,
Felt heart sink, took to bed (discreetly done —
They might have been beforehand with him else)
And died — would Guido have behaved as well ?
But ah, the faith of early days is gone,
Heu prisca fides ! Nothing died in him
Save courtesy, good sense and proper trust,
Which, when they ebb from souls they should
          o'erflow,
Discover stub, weed, sludge and ugliness.
(The Pope, we know, is Neapolitan
And relishes a sea-side simile.)
Deserted by each charitable wave,
Guido, left high and dry, shows jealous now !
Jealous avouched, paraded : tax the fool
With any peccadillo, he responds,
" Truly I beat my wife through jealousy,
Imprisoned her and punished otherwise,
Being jealous : now would threaten, sword in
          hand,
Now manage to mix poison in her sight,
And so forth : jealously I dealt, in fine."
Concede thus much, and what remains to prove ?
Have I to teach my masters what effect
Hath jealousy, and how, befooling men,
It makes false true, abuses eye and ear,
Turns mere mist adamantine, loads with sound
Silence, and into void and vacancy
Crowds a whole phalanx of conspiring foes ?
Therefore who owns " I watched with jealousy
My wife," adds " for no reason in the world ! "
What need that, thus proved madman, he re-
          mark
" The thing I thought a serpent proved an
          eel " ? —
Perchance the right Comacchian, six foot
          length,
And not an inch too long for that rare pie
(Master Arcangeli has heard of such)
Whose succulence makes fasting bearable ;
Meant to regale some moody splenetic

Who, pleasing to mistake the donor's gift,
Spying I know not what Lernæan snake
I' the luscious Lenten creature, stamps forsooth
The dainty in the dust.

Enough! Prepare,
Such lunes announced, for downright lunacy!
Insanit homo, threat succeeds to threat,
And blow redoubles blow, — his wife, the block.
But, if a block, shall not she jar the hand
That buffets her? The injurious idle stone
Rebounds and hits the head of him who flung.
Causeless rage breeds, i' the wife now, rageful cause,
Tyranny wakes rebellion from its sleep.
Rebellion, say I? — rather, self-defence,
Laudable wish to live and see good days,
Pricks our Pompilia now to fly the fool
By any means, at any price, — nay, more,
Nay, most of all, i' the very interest
O' the fool that, baffled of his blind desire
At any price, were truliest victor so.
Shall he effect his crime and lose his soul?
No, dictates duty to a loving wife!
Far better that the unconsummate blow,
Adroitly balked by her, should back again,
Correctively admonish his own pate!

Crime then, — the Court is with me? — she must crush;
How crush it? By all efficacious means;
And these, — why, what in woman should they be?
"With horns the bull, with teeth the lion fights;
To woman," quoth the lyrist quoted late,
"Nor teeth, nor horns, but beauty, Nature gave!"
Pretty i' the Pagan! Who dares blame the use
Of armory thus allowed for natural, —
Exclaim against a seeming-dubious play
O' the sole permitted weapon, spear and shield
Alike, resorted to i' the circumstance
By poor Pompilia? Grant she somewhat plied
Arts that allure, the magic nod and wink,
The witchery of gesture, spell of word,
Whereby the likelier to enlist this friend,
Yea stranger, as a champion on her side?
Such man, being but mere man, ('t was all she knew,)
Must be made sure by beauty's silken bond,
The weakness that subdues the strong, and bows
Wisdom alike and folly. Grant the tale
O' the husband, which is false, were proved and true
To the letter — or the letters, I should say,
Abominations he professed to find
And fix upon Pompilia and the priest, —
Allow them hers — for though she could not write,
In early days of Eve-like innocence
That plucked no apple from the knowledge-tree,
Yet, at the Serpent's word, Eve plucks and eats
And knows — especially how to read and write:

And so Pompilia, — as the move o' the maw,
Quoth Persius, makes a parrot bid "Good day!"
A crow salute the concave, and a pie
Endeavor at proficiency in speech, —
So she, through hunger after fellowship,
May well have learned, though late, to play the scribe:
As indeed, there 's one letter on the list
Explicitly declares did happen here.
"You thought my letters could be none of mine,"
She tells her parents — "mine, who wanted skill;
But now I have the skill, and write, you see!"
She needed write love-letters, so she learned,
"*Negatas artifex sequi voces*" — though
This letter nowise 'scapes the common lot,
But lies i' the condemnation of the rest,
Found by the husband's self who forged them all.
Yet, for the sacredness of argument,
For this once an exemption shall it plead —
Anything, anything to let the wheels
Of argument run glibly to their goal!
Concede she wrote (which were preposterous)
This and the other epistle, — what of it?
Where does the figment touch her candid fame?
Being in peril of her life — "my life,
Not an hour's purchase," as the letter runs, —
And having but one stay in this extreme,
Out of the wide world but a single friend —
What could she other than resort to him,
And how with any hope resort but thus?
Shall modesty dare bid a stranger brave
Danger, disgrace, nay death in her behalf —
Think to entice the sternness of the steel
Yet spare love's loadstone moving manly mind?
— Most of all, when such mind is hampered so
By growth of circumstance athwart the life
O' the natural man, that decency forbids
He stoop and take the common privilege,
Say frank "I love," as all the vulgar do.
A man is wedded to philosophy,
Married to statesmanship; a man is old;
A man is fettered by the foolishness
He took for wisdom and talked ten years since;
A man is, like our friend the Canon here,
A priest, and wicked if he break his vow:
Shall he dare love, who may be Pope one day?
Despite the coil of such encumbrance here,
Suppose this man could love, unhappily,
And would love, dared he only let love show!
In case the woman of his love speaks first,
From what embarrassment she sets him free!
"'T is I who break reserve, begin appeal,
Confess that, whether you love me or no,
I love you!" What an ease to dignity,
What help of pride from the hard high-backed chair
Down to the carpet where the kittens bask,
All under the pretence of gratitude!

From all which, I deduce — the lady here
Was bound to proffer nothing short of love

To the priest whose service was to save her.
    What?
Shall she propose him lucre, dust o' the mine,
Rubbish o' the rock, some diamond, muck-
    worms prize,
Some pearl secreted by a sickly fish?
Scarcely! She caters for a generous taste
'T is love shall beckon, beauty bid to breast.
Till all the Samson sink into the snare!
Because, permit the end — permit therewith
Means to the end!
                How say you, good my lords?
I hope you heard my adversary ring
The changes on this precept: now, let me
Reverse the peal! *Quia dato licito fine,*
Ad illum assequendum ordinata
Non sunt damnanda media, — licit end
Enough was found in mere escape from death,
To legalize our means illicit else
Of feigned love, false allurement, fancied fact.
Thus Venus losing Cupid on a day,
(See that *Idyllium Moschi*) seeking help,
In the anxiety of motherhood,
Allowably promised, "Who shall bring report
Where he is wandered to, my wingèd babe,
I give him for reward a nectared kiss;
But who brings safely back the truant's self,
His be a super-sweet makes kiss seem cold!"
Are not these things writ for example-sake?

To such permitted motive, then, refer
All those professions, else were hard explain,
Of hope, fear, jealousy, and the rest of love!
He is Myrtillus, Amaryllis she,
She burns, he freezes, — all a mere device
To catch and keep the man, may save her
    life,
Whom otherwise nor catches she nor keeps!
Worst, once, turns best now: in all faith, she
    feigns:
Feigning, — the liker innocence to guilt,
The truer to the life in what she feigns!
How if Ulysses, — when, for public good
He sunk particular qualms and played the spy,
Entered Troy's hostile gate in beggar's garb —
How if he first had boggled at this clout,
Grown dainty o'er that clack-dish? Grime is
    grace
To whoso gropes amid the dung for gold.

Hence, beyond promises, we praise each proof
That promise was not simply made to break,
Mere moonshine-structure meant to fade at
    dawn:
We praise, as consequent and requisite,
What, enemies allege, were more than words,
Deeds — meetings at the window, twilight-
    trysts,
Nocturnal entertainments in the dim
Old labyrinthine palace; lies, we know —
Inventions we, long since, turned inside out.
Must such external semblance of intrigue
Demonstrate that intrigue there lurks perdue?
Does every hazel-sheath disclose a nut?
He were a Molinist who dared maintain
That midnight meetings in a screened alcove
Must argue folly in a matron — since
So would he bring a slur on Judith's self,

Commended beyond women, that she lured
The lustful to destruction through his lust.
Pompilia took not Judith's liberty,
No falchion find you in her hand to smite,
No damsel to convey in dish the head
Of Holofernes, — style the Canon so —
Or is it the Count? If I entangle me
With my similitudes, — if wax wings melt,
And earthward down I drop, not mine the
    fault:
Blame your beneficence, O Court, O sun,
Whereof the beamy smile affects my flight!
What matter, so Pompilia's fame revive
I' the warmth that proves the bane of Icarus?

Yea, we have shown it lawful, necessary
Pompilia leave her husband, seek the house
O' the parents: and because 'twixt home and
    home
Lies a long road with many a danger rife,
Lions by the way and serpents in the path,
To rob and ravish, — much behooves she keep
Each shadow of suspicion from fair fame,
For her own sake much, but for his sake more,
The ingrate husband's. Evidence shall be,
Plain witness to the world how white she walks
I' the mire she wanders through ere Rome she
    reach.
And who so proper witness as a priest?
Gainsay ye? Let me hear who dares gainsay!
I hope we still can punish heretics!
"Give me the man," I say with him of Gath,
"That we may fight together!" None, I
    think:
The priest is granted me.

                Then, if a priest,
One juvenile and potent: else, mayhap,
That dragon, our Saint George would slay, slays
    him.
And should fair face accompany strong hand,
The more complete equipment: nothing mars
Work, else praiseworthy, like a bodily flaw
I' the worker: as 't is said Saint Paul himself
Deplored the check o' the puny presence, still
Cheating his fulmination of its flash,
Albeit the bolt therein went true to oak.
Therefore the agent, as prescribed, she takes, —
Both juvenile and potent, handsome too, —
In all obedience: "good," you grant again.
Do you? I would you were the husband, lords!
How prompt and facile might departure be!
How boldly would Pompilia and the priest
March out of door, spread flag at beat of drum,
But that inapprehensive Guido grants
Neither premiss nor yet conclusion here,
And, purblind, dreads a bear in every bush!
For his own quietude and comfort, then,
Means must be found for flight in masquerade
At hour when all things sleep — "Save
    jealousy!"
Right, Judges! Therefore shall the lady'
    wit
Supply the boon thwart nature balks him of,
And do him service with the potent drug
(Helen's nepenthe, as my lords opine)
Which respites blessedly each fretted nerve
O' the much-enduring man: accordingly,

There lies he, duly dosed and sound asleep,
Relieved of woes or real or raved about.
While soft she leaves his side, he shall not
    wake;
Nor stop who steals away to join her friend,
Nor do him mischief should he catch that friend
Intent on more than friendly office, — nay,
Nor get himself raw head and bones laid bare
In payment of his apparition!

                    Thus
Would I defend the step, — were the thing
    true
Which is a fable, — see my former speech, —
That Guido slept (who never slept a wink)
Through treachery, an opiate from his wife,
Who not so much as knew what opiates mean.

Now she may start: or hist, — a stoppage still!
A journey is an enterprise of cost!
As in campaigns, we fight but others pay,
Suis expensis, nemo militat.
'T is Guido's self we guard from accident,
Ensuring safety to Pompilia, versed
Nowise in misadventures by the way,
Hard riding and rough quarters, the rude fare,
The unready host. What magic mitigates
Each plague of travel to the unpractised wife?
Money, sweet Sirs! And were the fiction fact
She helped herself thereto with liberal hand
From out her husband's store, — what fitter
    use
Was ever husband's money destined to?
With bag and baggage thus did Dido once
Decamp, — for more authority, a queen!

So is she fairly on her route at last,
Prepared for either fortune: nay and if
The priest, now all aglow with enterprise,
Cool somewhat presently when fades the flush
O' the first adventure, clouded o'er belike
By doubts, misgivings how the day may die,
Though born with such auroral brilliance, — if
The brow seem over-pensive and the lip
'Gin lag and lose the prattle lightsome late, —
Vanquished by tedium of a prolonged jaunt
In a close carriage o'er a jolting road,
With only one young female substitute
For seventeen other Canons of ripe age
Were wont to keep him company in church, —
Shall not Pompilia haste to dissipate
The silent cloud that, gathering, bodes her
    bale? —
Prop the irresoluteness may portend
Suspension of the project, check the flight,
Bring ruin on them both? Use every means,
Since means to the end are lawful! What i'
    the way
Of wile should have allowance like a kiss
Sagely and sisterly administered,
Sororia saltem oscula? We find
Such was the remedy her wit applied
To each incipient scruple of the priest,
If we believe, — as, while my wit is mine
I cannot, — what the driver testifies,
Borsi, called Venerino, the mere tool
Of Guido and his friend the Governor, —
Avowal I proved wrung from out the wretch.

After long rotting in imprisonment,
As price of liberty and favor: long
They tempted, he at last succumbed, and lo
Counted them out full tale each kiss and more,
"The journey being one long embrace," quoth
    he.
Still, though we should believe the driver's lie,
Nor even admit as probable excuse,
Right reading of the riddle, — as I urged
In my first argument, with fruit perhaps —
That what the owl-like eyes (at back of head!)
O' the driver, drowsed by driving night and
    day,
Supposed a vulgar interchange of lips,
This was but innocent jog of head 'gainst head,
Cheek meeting jowl as apple may touch pear
From branch and branch contiguous in the
    wind,
When Autumn blusters and the orchard
    rocks: —
That rapid run and the rough road were cause
O' the casual ambiguity, no harm
I' the world to eyes awake and penetrative: —
Say, — not to grasp a truth I can release
And safely fight without, yet conquer still, —
Say, she kissed him, say, he kissed her again!
Such osculation was a potent means,
A very efficacious help, no doubt:
Such with a third part of her nectar did
Venus imbue: why should Pompilia fling
The poet's declaration in his teeth? —
Pause to employ what — since it had success,
And kept the priest her servant to the end —
We must presume of energy enough,
No whit superfluous, so permissible?

The goal is gained: day, night, and yet a day
Have run their round: a long and devious road
Is traversed, — many manners, various men
Passed in review, what cities did they see,
What hamlets mark, what profitable food
For after-meditation cull and store!
Till Rome, that Rome whereof — this voice
Would it might make our Molinists observe,
That she is built upon a rock nor shall
Their powers prevail against her! — Rome, I
    say,
Is all but reached; one stage more and they
    stop
Saved: pluck up heart, ye pair, and forward
    then!

Ah, Nature — baffled she recurs, alas!
Nature imperiously exacts her due,
Spirit is willing but the flesh is weak:
Pompilia needs must acquiesce and swoon,
Give hopes alike and fears a breathing-while.
The innocent sleep soundly: sound she sleeps,
So let her slumber, then, unguarded save
By her own chastity, a triple mail,
And his good hand whose stalwart arms have
    borne
The sweet and senseless burden like a babe
From coach to couch, — the serviceable
    strength!
Nay, what and if he gazed rewardedly
On the pale beauty prisoned in embrace,
Stooped over, stole a balmy breath perhaps

For more assurance sleep was not decease —
" *Ut vidi*," " how I saw ! " succeeded by
" *Ut perii*," " how I sudden lost my brains ! "
— What harm ensued to her unconscious quite ?
For, curiosity — how natural !
Importunateness — what a privilege
In the ardent sex !   And why curb ardor here ?
How can the priest but pity whom he saved ?
And pity is so near to love, and love
So neighborly to all unreasonableness !
As to love's object, whether love were sage
Or foolish, could Pompilia know or care,
Being still sound asleep, as I premised ?
Thus the philosopher absorbed by thought,
Even Archimedes, busy o'er a book
The while besiegers sacked his Syracuse,
Was ignorant of the imminence o' the point
O' the sword till it surprised him : let it stab,
And never knew himself was dead at all.
So sleep thou on secure whate'er betide !
For thou, too, hast thy problem hard to solve —
How so much beauty is compatible
With so much innocence !

            Fit place, methinks,
While in this task she rosily is lost,
To treat of and repel objection here
Which, — frivolous, I grant, — my mind mis-
    gives,
May somehow still have flitted, gadfly-like,
And teased the Court at times — as if, all said
And done, there seemed, the Court might nearly
    say,
In a certain acceptation, somewhat more
Of what may pass for insincerity,
Falsehood, throughout the course Pompilia
    took,
Than befits Christian.   Pagans held, we know,
Man always ought to aim at good and truth,
Not always put one thing in the same words :
Non idem semper dicere sed spectare
Debemus.   But the Pagan yoke was light ;
" Lie not at all," the exacter precept bids :
Each least lie breaks the law, — is sin, we
    hold.
I humble me, but venture to submit —
What prevents sin, itself is sinless, sure :
And sin, which hinders sin of deeper dye,
Softens itself away by contrast so.
Conceive me !   Little sin, by none at all,
Were properly condemned for great : but great,
By greater, dwindles into small again.
Now, what is greatest sin of womanhood ?
That which unwomans it, abolishes
The nature of the woman, — impudence.
Who contradicts me here ?   Concede me, then,
Whatever friendly fault may interpose
To save the sex from self-abolishment
Is three-parts on the way to virtue's rank !
And, what is taxed here as duplicity,
Feint, wile, and trick, — admitted for the
    nonce, —
What worse do one and all than interpose,
Hold, as it were, a deprecating hand,
Statuesquely, in the Medicean mode,
Before some shame which modesty would veil ?
Who blames the gesture prettily perverse ?
Thus, — lest ye miss a point illustrative, —

Admit the husband's calumny — allow
That the wife, having penned the epistle
    fraught
With horrors, charge on charge of crime she
    heaped
O' the head of Pietro and Violante — (still
Presumed her parents) — having dispatched the
    same
To their arch-enemy Paolo, through free choice
And no sort of compulsion in the world —
Put case she next discards simplicity
For craft, denies the voluntary act,
Declares herself a passive instrument
I' the husband's hands; that, duped by knavery,
She traced the characters she could not write,
And took on trust the unread sense which, read,
And recognized were to be spurned at once :
Allow this calumny, I reiterate !
Who is so dull as wonder at the pose
Of our Pompilia in the circumstance ?
Who sees not that the too-ingenuous soul,
Repugnant even at a duty done
Which brought beneath too scrutinizing glare
The misdemeanors, — buried in the dark, —
Of the authors of her being, was believed, —
Stung to the quick at her impulsive deed,
And willing to repair what harm it worked,
She — wise in this beyond what Nero proved,
Who, when folk urged the candid juvenile
To sign the warrant, doom the guilty dead,
" Would I had never learned to write ! " quoth
    he !
— Pompilia rose above the Roman, cried,
"To read or write I never learned at all ! "
O splendidly mendacious !

            But time fleets :
Let us not linger : hurry to the end,
Since flight does end, and that disastrously.
Beware ye blame desert for unsuccess,
Disparage each expedient else to praise,
Call failure folly !   Man's best effort fails.
After ten years' resistance Troy succumbed :
Could valor save a town, Troy still had stood.
Pompilia came off halting in no point
Of courage, conduct, her long journey through :
But nature sank exhausted at the close,
And, as I said, she swooned and slept all night.
Morn breaks and brings the husband : we assist
At the spectacle.   Discovery succeeds.
Ha, how is this ?   What moonstruck rage is
    here ?
Though we confess to partial frailty now,
To error in a woman and a wife,
Is 't by the rough way she shall be reclaimed ?
Who bursts upon her chambered privacy ?
What crowd profanes the chaste *cubiculum* ?
What outcries and lewd laughter, scurril gibe
And ribald jest to scare the ministrant
Good angels that commerce with souls in sleep ?
Why, had the worst crowned Guido to his
    wish,
Confirmed his most irrational surmise,
Yet there be bounds to man's emotion
    checks
To an immoderate astonishment.
'T is decent horror, regulated wrath,
Befit our dispensation : have we back

The old Pagan license? Shall a Vulcan clap
His net o' the sudden and expose the pair
To the unquenchable universal mirth?
A feat, antiquity saw scandal in
So clearly, that the nauseous tale thereof —
Demodocus his nugatory song —
Hath ever been concluded modern stuff
Impossible to the mouth of the grave Muse,
So, foisted into that Eighth Odyssey
By some impertinent pickthank. O thou fool,
Count Guido Franceschini, what didst gain
By publishing thy secret to the world?
Were all the precepts of the wise a waste —
Bred in thee not one touch of reverence?
Admit thy wife — admonish we the fool —
Were falseness' self, why chronicle thy shame?
Much rather should thy teeth bite out thy
tongue,
Dumb lip consort with desecrated brow,
Silence become historiographer,
And thou — thine own Cornelius Tacitus!
But virtue, barred, still leaps the barrier, lords!
— Still, moon-like, penetrates the encroaching
mist
And bursts, all broad and bare, on night, ye
know!
Surprised, then, in the garb of truth, perhaps,
Pompilia, thus opposed, breaks obstacle,
Springs to her feet, and stands Thalassian-pure,
Confronts the foe, — nay, catches at his sword
And tries to kill the intruder, he complains.
Why, so she gave her lord his lesson back,
Crowned him, this time, the virtuous woman's
way,
With an exact obedience; he brought sword,
She drew the same, since swords are meant to
draw.
Tell not me 't is sharp play with tools on edge!
It was the husband chose the weapon here
Why did not he inaugurate the game
With some gentility of apophthegm
Still pregnant on the philosophic page,
Some captivating cadence still a-lisp
O' the poet's lyre? Such spells subdue the
surge,
Make tame the tempest, much more mitigate
The passions of the mind, and probably
Had moved Pompilia to a smiling blush.
No, he must needs prefer the argument
O' the blow: and she obeyed, in duty bound,
Returned him buffet ratiocinative —
Ay, in the reasoner's own interest,
For wife must follow whither husband leads,
Vindicate honor as himself prescribes,
Save him the very way himself bids save!
No question but who jumps into a quag
Should stretch forth hand and pray us "Pull
me out
By the hand!" such were the customary cry:
But Guido pleased to bid "Leave hand alone!
Join both feet, rather, jump upon my head:
I extricate myself by the rebound!"
And dutifully as enjoined she jumped —
Drew his own sword and menaced his own life,
Anything to content a wilful spouse.

And so he was contented — one must do
Justice to the expedient which succeeds,

Strange as it seem: at flourish of the blade,
The crowd drew back, stood breathless and
abashed,
Then murmured, "This should be no wanton
wife,
No conscience-stricken sinner, caught i' the
act,
And patiently awaiting our first stone:
But a poor hard-pressed all-bewildered thing,
Has rushed so far, misguidedly perhaps,
Meaning no more harm than a frightened sheep.
She sought for aid; and if she made mistake
I' the man could aid most, why — so mortals
do:
Even the blessed Magdalen mistook
Far less forgivably: consult the place —
Supposing him to be the gardener,
'Sir,' said she, and so following." Why more
words?
Forthwith the wife is pronounced innocent:
What would the husband more than gain his
cause,
And find that honor flash in the world's eye,
His apprehension was lest soil had smirched?

So, happily the adventure comes to close
Whereon my fat opponent grounds his charge
Preposterous: at mid-day he groans "How
dark!"
Listen to me, thou Archangelic swine!
Where is the ambiguity to blame,
The flaw to find in our Pompilia? Safe
She stands, see! Does thy comment follow
quick,
"Safe, inasmuch as at the end proposed;
But thither she picked way by devious path —
Stands dirtied, no dubiety at all!
I recognize success, yet, all the same,
Importunately will suggestion prompt —
Better Pompilia gained the right to boast,
'No devious path, no doubtful patch was mine,
I saved my head nor sacrificed my foot!'
Why, being in a peril, show mistrust
Of the angels set to guard the innocent?
Why rather hold by obvious vulgar help
Of stratagem and subterfuge, excused
Somewhat, but still no less a foil, a fault,
Since low with high, and good with bad is
linked?
Methinks I view some ancient bas-relief.
There stands Hesione thrust out by Troy,
Her father's hand has chained her to a crag,
Her mother's from the virgin plucked the vest,
At a safe distance both distressful watch,
While near and nearer comes the snorting orc.
I look that, white and perfect to the end,
She wait till Jove dispatch some demigod;
Not that, — impatient of celestial club
Alcmena's son should brandish at the beast, —
She daub, disguise her dainty limbs with pitch
And so elude the purblind monster! Ay,
The trick succeeds, but 't is an ugly trick,
Where needs have been no trick!"

My answer? Faugh!
Nimis incongrue! Too absurdly put!
Sententiam ego teneo contrariam,
Trick, I maintain, had no alternative.

The heavens were bound with brass, — Jove far
    at feast
(No feast like that thou didst not ask me to,
Arcangeli, — I heard of thy regale !)
With the unblamed Æthiop, — Hercules spun
    wool
I' the lap of Omphale, while Virtue shrieked —
The brute came paddling all the faster. You
Of Troy, who stood at distance, where 's the aid
You offered in the extremity ? Most and least,
Gentle and simple, here the Governor,
There the Archbishop, everywhere the friends,
Shook heads and waited for a miracle,
Or went their way, left Virtue to her fate.
Just this one rough and ready man leapt forth !
— Was found, sole anti-Fabius (dare I say)
Who restored things, with no delay at all,
Qui haud cunctando rem restituit ! He,
He only, Caponsacchi 'mid a crowd,
Caught Virtue up, carried Pompilia off
Through gaping impotence of sympathy
In ranged Arezzo : what you take for pitch
Is nothing worse, belike, than black and blue,
Mere evanescent proof that hardy hands
Did yeoman's service, cared not where the gripe
Was more than duly energetic : bruised,
She smarts a little, but her bones are saved
A fracture, and her skin will soon show sleek.
How it disgusts when weakness, false-refined,
Censures the honest rude effective strength, —
When sickly dreamers of the impossible
Decry plain sturdiness which does the feat
With eyes wide open !

          Did occasion serve,
I could illustrate, if my lords allow ;
Quid vetat, what forbids I aptly ask
With Horace, that I give my anger vent,
While I let breathe, no less, and recreate,
The gravity of my Judges, by a tale ?
A case in point — what though an apologue
Graced by tradition ? — possibly a fact :
Tradition must precede all scripture, words
Serve as our warrant ere our books can be :
So, to tradition back we needs must go
For any fact's authority : and this
Hath lived so far (like jewel hid in muck)
On page of that old lying vanity
Called "Sepher Toldoth Yeschu:" God be
    praised,
I read no Hebrew, — take the thing on trust :
But I believe the writer meant no good
(Blind as he was to truth in some respects)
To our pestiferous and schismatic . . . well,
My lords' conjecture be the touchstone, show
The thing for what it is ! The author lacks
Discretion, and his zeal exceeds : but zeal, —
How rare in our degenerate day ! Enough !
Here is the story : fear not, I shall chop
And change a little, else my Jew would press
All too unmannerly before the Court.

It happened once, — begins this foolish Jew,
Pretending to write Christian history, —
That three, held greatest, best and worst of men,
Peter and John and Judas, spent a day
In toil and travel through the country-side
On some sufficient business — I suspect,

Suppression of some Molinism i' the bud.
Foot-sore and hungry, dropping with fatigue,
They reached by nightfall a poor lonely grange,
Hostel or inn : so, knocked and entered there.
"Your pleasure, great ones ? " — " Shelter,
    rest and food ! "
For shelter, there was one bare room above ;
For rest therein, three beds of bundled straw :
For food, one wretched starveling fowl, no
    more —
Meat for one mouth, but mockery for three.
"You have my utmost." How should supper
    serve ?
Peter broke silence : " To the spit with fowl !
And while 't is cooking, sleep ! — since beds
    there be,
And, so far, satisfaction of a want.
Sleep we an hour, awake at supper-time,
Then each of us narrate the dream he had,
And he whose dream shall prove the happiest
    point
The clearliest out the dreamer as ordained
Beyond his fellows to receive the fowl,
Him let our shares be cheerful tribute to,
His the entire meal, may it do him good ! "
Who could dispute so plain a consequence ?
So said, so done : each hurried to his straw,
Slept his hour's-sleep and dreamed his dream,
    and woke.
"I," commenced John, " dreamed that I gained
    the prize
We all aspire to : the proud place was mine,
Throughout the earth and to the end of time
I was the Loved Disciple : mine the meal ! "
" But I," proceeded Peter, " dreamed, a word
Gave me the headship of our company,
Made me the Vicar and Vice-gerent, gave
The keys of heaven and hell into my hand,
And o'er the earth, dominion : mine the meal ! "
" While I," submitted in soft under-tone
The Iscariot — sense of his unworthiness
Turning each eye up to the inmost white —
With long-drawn sigh, yet letting both lips
    smack,
" I have had just the pitifullest dream
That ever proved man meanest of his mates,
And born foot-washer and foot-wiper, nay
Foot-kisser to each comrade of you all !
I dreamed I dreamed ; and in that mimic dream
(Impalpable to dream as dream to fact)
Methought I meanly chose to sleep no wink
But wait until I heard my brethren snore ;
Then stole from couch, slipped noiseless o'er
    the planks,
Slid downstairs, furtively approached the
    hearth,
Found the fowl duly brown, both back and
    breast,
Hissing in harmony with the cricket's chirp,
Grilled to a point ; said no grace, but fell to,
Nor finished till the skeleton lay bare.
In penitence for which ignoble dream,
Lo, I renounce my portion cheerfully !
Fie on the flesh — be mine the ethereal gust,
And yours the sublunary sustenance !
See that whate'er be left ye give the poor ! "
Down the two scuttled, one on other's heel,
Stung by a fell surmise ; and found, alack.

A goodly savor, both the drumstick bones,
And that which henceforth took the appropri-
ate name
O' the Merry-thought, in memory of the fact
That to keep wide awake is man's best dream.

So, — as was said once of Thucydides
And his sole joke, "The lion, lo, hath
laughed !"—
Just so, the Governor and all that 's great
I' the city never meant that Innocence
Should quite starve while Authority sat at
meat ;
They meant to fling a bone at banquet's end :
Wished well to our Pompilia — in their dreams,
Nor bore the secular sword in vain — asleep.
Just so the Archbishop and all good like him
Went to bed meaning to pour oil and wine
I' the wounds of her, next day, — but long ere
day,
They had burned the one and drunk the other,
while
Just so, again, contrariwise, the priest
Sustained poor Nature in extremity
By stuffing barley-bread into her mouth,
Saving Pompilia (grant the parallel)
By the plain homely and straightforward way
Taught him by common sense. Let others
shriek
" Oh what refined expedients did we dream
Proved us the only fit to help the fair !"
He cried, "A carriage waits, jump in with
me !"

And now, this application pardoned, lords, —
This recreative pause and breathing-while, —
Back to beseemingness and gravity !
For Law steps in : Guido appeals to Law,
Demands she arbitrate, — does well for once.
O Law, of thee how neatly was it said
By that old Sophocles, thou hast thy seat
I' the very breast of Jove, no meanlier throned !
Here is a piece of work now, hitherto
Begun and carried on, concluded near,
Without an eye-glance cast thy sceptre's way ;
And, lo, the stumbling and discomfiture !
Well may you call them " lawless" means,
men take
To extricate themselves through mother-wit
When tangled haply in the toils of life !
Guido would try conclusions with his foe,
Whoe'er the foe was and whate'er the offence ;
He would recover certain dowry-dues :
Instead of asking Law to lend a hand,
What pother of sword drawn and pistol cocked,
What peddling with forged letters and paid
spies,
Politic circumvention ! — all to end
As it began — by loss of the fool's head,
First in a figure, presently in a fact.
It is a lesson to mankind at large.
How other were the end, would men be sage
And bear confidingly each quarrel straight,
O Law, to thy recipient mother-knees !
How would the children light come and prompt
go,
This, with a red-cheeked apple for reward,
The other, peradventure red-cheeked too

I' the rear, by taste of birch for punishment.
No foolish brawling murder any more !
Peace for the household, practice for the Fisc,
And plenty for the exchequer of my lords !
Too much to hope, in this world : in the next,
Who knows ? Since, why should sit the Twelve
enthroned
To judge the tribes, unless the tribes be judged ?
And 't is impossible but offences come :
So, all 's one lawsuit, all one long leet-day !

Forgive me this digression — that I stand
Entranced awhile at Law's first beam, outbreak
O' the business, when the Count's good ange
bade
" Put up thy sword, born enemy to the ear,
And let Law listen to thy difference !"
And Law does listen and compose the strife,
Settle the suit, how wisely and how well !
On our Pompilia, faultless to a fault,
Law bends a brow maternally severe,
Implies the worth of perfect chastity,
By fancying the flaw she cannot find.
Superfluous sifting snow, nor helps nor harms :
'T is safe to censure levity in youth,
Tax womanhood with indiscretion, sure !
Since toys, permissible to-day, become
Follies to-morrow : prattle shocks in church :
And that curt skirt which lets a maiden skip,
The matron changes for a trailing robe.
Mothers may aim a blow with half-shut eyes
Nodding above their spindles by the fire,
And chance to hit some hidden fault, else safe.
Just so, Law hazarded a punishment —
If applicable to the circumstance,
Why, well ! if not so apposite, well too.
" Quit the gay range o' the world," I hear her
cry,
" Enter, in lieu, the penitential pound :
Exchange the gauds of pomp for ashes, dust !
Leave each mollitious haunt of luxury !
The golden-garnished silken-couched alcove,
The many-columned terrace that so tempts
Feminine soul put foot forth, extend ear
To fluttering joy of lover's serenade, —
Leave these for cellular seclusion ! mask
And dance no more, but fast and pray !
avaunt —
Be burned, thy wicked townsman's sonnet-
book !
Welcome, mild hymnal by . . . some better
scribe !
For the warm arms were wont enfold thy flesh,
Let wire-shirt plough and whip-cord disci-
pline !"
If such an exhortation proved, perchance,
Inapplicable, words bestowed in waste,
What harm, since Law has store, can spend nor
miss ?

And so, our paragon submits herself,
Goes at command into the holy house,
And, also at command, comes out again :
For, could the effect of such obedience prove
Too certain, too immediate ? Being healed,
Go blaze abroad the matter, blessed one !
Art thou sound forthwith ? Speedily vacate
The step by pool-side, leave Bethesda free

To patients plentifully posted round,
Since the whole need not the physician! Brief,
She may betake her to her parents' place.
Welcome her, father, with wide arms once
    more;
Motion her, mother, to thy breast again!
For why? Since Law relinquishes the charge,
Grants to your dwelling-place a prison's style.
Rejoice you with Pompilia! golden days,
Redeunt Saturnia regna. Six weeks slip,
And she is domiciled in house and home
As though she thence had never budged at all.
And thither let the husband — joyous, ay,
But contrite also — quick betake himself,
Proud that his dove which lay among the pots
Hath mued those dingy feathers, — moulted
    now,
Shows silver bosom clothed with yellow gold!
So shall he tempt her to the perch she fled,
Bid to domestic bliss the truant back.

But let him not delay! Time fleets how fast,
And opportunity, the irrevocable,
Once flown will flout him! Is the furrow
    traced?
If field with corn ye fail preoccupy,
Darnel for wheat and thistle-beards for grain,
Infelix lolium, carduus horridus,
Will grow apace in combination prompt,
Defraud the husbandman of his desire.
Already — hist — what murmurs 'monish now
The laggard? — doubtful, nay, fantastic bruit
Of such an apparition, such return
Interdum, to anticipate the spouse,
Of Caponsacchi's very self! 'T is said,
When nights are lone and company is rare,
His visitations brighten winter up.
If so they did — which nowise I believe —
(How can I? — proof abounding that the priest,
Once fairly at his relegation-place,
Never once left it), still, admit he stole
A midnight march, would fain see friend again,
Find matter for instruction in the past,
Renew the old adventure in such chat
As cheers a fireside! He was lonely too,
He, too, must need his recreative hour.
Shall it amaze the philosophic mind
If he, long wont the empurpled cup to quaff,
Have feminine society at will,
Being debarred abruptly from all drink
Save at the spring which Adam used for wine,
Dreads harm to just the health he hoped to
    guard,
And, trying abstinence, gains malady?
Ask Tozzi, now physician to the Pope!
"Little by little break" — (I hear he bids
Master Arcangeli my antagonist,
Who loves good cheer, and may indulge too
    much:
So I explain the logic of the plea
Wherewith he opened our proceedings late) —
"Little by little break a habit, Don,
Become necessity to feeble flesh!"
And thus, nocturnal taste of intercourse
(Which never happened, — but, suppose it did)
May have been used to dishabituate
By sip and sip this drainer to the dregs
O' the draught of conversation, — heady stuff,

Brewage which, broached, it took two days and
    nights
To properly discuss i' the journey, Sirs!
Such power has second-nature, men call use,
That undelightful objects get to charm
Instead of chafe: the daily colocynth
Tickles the palate by repeated dose,
Old sores scratch kindly, the ass makes a push
Although the mill-yoke-wound be smarting yet,
For mill-door bolted on a holiday:
Nor must we marvel here if impulse urge
To talk the old story over now and then,
The hopes and fears, the stoppage and the
    haste, —
Subjects of colloquy to surfeit once.
"Here did you bid me twine a rosy wreath!"
"And there you paid my lips a compliment!"
"Here you admired the tower could be so
    tall!"
"And there you likened that of Lebanon
To the nose of the beloved!" Trifles! still,
"*Forsan et hæc olim,*" — such trifles serve
To make the minutes pass in winter-time.

Husband, return then, I re-counsel thee!
For, finally, of all glad circumstance
Should make a prompt return imperative,
What in the world awaits thee, dost suppose?
O' the sudden, as good gifts are wont befall,
What is the hap of our unconscious Count?
That which lights bonfire and sets cask a-tilt,
Dissolves the stubborn'st heart in jollity.
O admirable, there is born a babe,
A son, an heir, a Franceschini last
And best o' the stock! Pompilia, thine the
    palm!
Repaying incredulity with faith,
Ungenerous thrift of each marital debt
With bounty in profuse expenditure,
Pompilia scorns to have the old year end
Without a present shall ring in the new —
Bestows on her too-parsimonious lord
An infant for the apple of his eye,
Core of his heart, and crown completing life,
True *summum bonum* of the earthly lot!
"We," saith ingeniously the sage, "are born
Solely that others may be born of us."
So, father, take thy child, for thine that child,
Oh nothing doubt! In wedlock born, law
    holds
Baseness impossible: since "*filius est
Quem nuptiæ demonstrant,*" twits the text
Whoever dares to doubt.

                    Yet doubt he dares!
O faith, where art thou flown from out the
    world?
Already on what an age of doubt we fall!
Instead of each disputing for the prize,
The babe is bandied here from that to this.
Whose the babe? "*Cujum pecus?*" Guido's
    lamb?
"*An Melibœi?*" Nay, but of the priest!
"*Non sed Ægonis!*" Some one must be sire:
And who shall say, in such a puzzling strait,
If there were not vouchsafed some miracle
To the wife who had been harassed and abused
More than enough by Guido's family

For non-production of the promised fruit
Of marriage?　What if Nature, I demand,
Touched to the quick by taunts upon her sloth,
Had roused herself, put forth recondite power,
Bestowed this birth to vindicate her sway,
Like the strange favor Maro memorized
As granted Aristæus when his hive
Lay empty of the swarm? not one more bee —
Not one more babe to Franceschini's house!
And lo, a new birth filled the air with joy,
Sprung from the bowels of the generous steer,
A novel son and heir rejoiced the Count!
Spontaneous generation, need I prove
Were facile feat to Nature at a pinch?
Let whoso doubts, steep horsehair certain
　　weeks,
In water, there will be produced a snake ;
Spontaneous product of the horse, which horse
Happens to be the representative —
Now that I think on 't — of Arezzo's self,
The very city our conception blessed :
Is not a prancing horse the City-arms?
What sane eye fails to see coincidence?
Cur ego, boast thou, my Pompilia, then,
Desperem fieri sine conjuge
Mater — How well the Ovidian distich suits! —
Et parere intacto dummodo
Casta viro? such miracle was wrought!
Note, further, as to mark the prodigy,
The babe in question neither took the name
Of Guido, from the sire presumptive, nor
Giuseppe, from the sire potential, but
Gaetano — last saint of our hierarchy,
And newest namer for a thing so new!
What other motive could have prompted
　　choice?

Therefore be peace again : exult, ye hills!
Ye vales rejoicingly break forth in song!
Incipe, parve puer, begin, small boy,
Risu cognoscere patrem, with a laugh
To recognize thy parent!　Nor do thou
Boggle, O parent, to return the grace!
Nec anceps hære, pater, puero
Cognoscendo — one may well eke out the
　　prayer!
In vain!　The perverse Guido doubts his eyes,
Distrusts assurance, lets the devil drive.
Because his house is swept and garnished now,
He, having summoned seven like himself,
Must hurry thither, knock and enter in,
And make the last worse than the first, in-
　　deed!
Is he content?　We are.　No further blame
O' the man and murder!　They were stigma-
　　tized
Befittingly : the Court heard long ago
My mind o' the matter, which, outpouring full,
Has long since swept like surge, i' the simile
Of Homer, overborne both dyke and dam,
And whelmed alike client and advocate :
His fate is sealed, his life as good as gone,
On him I am not tempted to waste word.
Yet though my purpose holds, — which was and
　　is
And solely shall be to the very end,
To draw the true *effigies* of a saint,
Do justice to perfection in the sex, —

Yet let not some gross pamperer of the flesh
And niggard in the spirit's nourishment,
Whose feeding hath obfuscated his wit
Rather than law, — he never had, to lose —
Let not such advocate object to me
I leave my proper function of attack!
" What 's this to Bacchus? " — (in the classic
　　phrase,
Well used, for once) he hiccups probably.
O Advocate o' the Poor, thou born to make
Their blessing void — *beati pauperes!*
By painting saintship I depicture sin :
Beside my pearl, I prove how black thy jet,
And, through Pompilia's virtue, Guido's crime.

Back to her, then, — with but one beauty more,
End we our argument, — one crowning grace
Pre-eminent 'mid agony and death.
For to the last Pompilia played her part,
Used the right means to the permissible end,
And, wily as an eel that stirs the mud
Thick overhead, so baffling spearman's thrust,
She, while he stabbed her, simulated death,
Delayed, for his sake, the catastrophe,
Obtained herself a respite, four days' grace,
Whereby she told her story to the world,
Enabled me to make the present speech,
And, by a full confession, saved her soul.

Yet hold, even here would malice leer its last,
Gurgle its choked remonstrance : snake, hiss
　　free!
Oh, that 's the objection?　And to whom? —
　　not her
But me, forsooth — as, in the very act
Of both confession and (what followed close)
Subsequent talk, chatter and gossipry,
Babble to sympathizing he and she
Whoever chose besiege her dying-bed, —
As this were found at variance with my tale,
Falsified all I have adduced for truth,
Admitted not one peccadillo here,
Pretended to perfection, first and last,
O' the whole procedure — perfect in the end,
Perfect i' the means, perfect in everything,
Leaving a lawyer nothing to excuse,
Reason away and show his skill about!
— A flight, impossible to Adamic flesh,
Just to be fancied, scarcely to be wished,
And, anyhow, unpleadable in court!
" How reconcile," gasps Malice, " that with
　　this? "

Your " this," friend, is extraneous to the law,
Comes of men's outside meddling, the unskilled
Interposition of such fools as press
Out of their province.　Must I speak my
　　mind?
Far better had Pompilia died o' the spot
Than found a tongue to wag and shame the
　　law,
Shame most of all herself, — could friendship
　　fail,
And advocacy lie less on the alert :
But no, they shall protect her to the end!
Do I credit the alleged narration?　No!
Lied our Pompilia then, to laud herself?
Still, no!　Clear up what seems discrepancy?

The means abound : art 's long, though time is
  short ;
So, keeping me in compass, all I urge
Is — since, confession at the point of death,
Nam in articulo mortis, with the Church
Passes for statement honest and sincere,
Nemo presumitur reus esse, — then,
If sure that all affirmed would be believed,
'T was charity, in her so circumstanced,
To spend the last breath in one effort more
For universal good of friend and foe :
And, — by pretending utter innocence,
Nay, freedom from each foible we forgive, —
Re-integrate — not solely her own fame,
But do the like kind office for the priest
Whom telling the crude truth about might vex,
Haply expose to peril, abbreviate
Indeed the long career of usefulness
Presumably before him : while her lord,
Whose fleeting life is forfeit to the law, —
What mercy to the culprit if, by just
The gift of such a full certificate
Of his immitigable guiltiness,
She stifled in him the absurd conceit
Of murder as it were a mere revenge
— Stopped confirmation of that jealousy
Which, did she but acknowledge the first flaw,
The faintest foible, had emboldened him
To battle with the charge, balk penitence,
Bar preparation for impending fate !
Whereas, persuade him that he slew a saint
Who sinned not even where she may have sinned,
You urge him all the brisklier to repent
Of most and least and aught and everything !
Still, if this view of mine content you not,
Lords, nor excuse the genial falsehood here,
We come to our *Triarii*, last resource :
We fall back on the inexpugnable,
Submitting, — she confessed before she talked !
The sacrament obliterates the sin :
What is not, — was not, therefore, in a sense.
Let Molinists distinguish, " Souls washed white
But red once, still show pinkish to the eye ! "
We say, abolishment is nothingness,
And nothingness has neither head nor tail,
End nor beginning ! Better estimate
Exorbitantly, than disparage aught
Of the efficacity of the act, I hope !

Solvuntur tabulæ ? May we laugh and go ?
Well, — not before (in filial gratitude
To Law, who, mighty mother, waves adieu)
We take on us to vindicate Law's self !
For, — yea, Sirs, — curb the start, curtail the
  stare ! —
Remains that we apologize for haste
I' the Law, our lady who here bristles up,
" Blame my procedure ? Could the Court mis-
  take ?
(Which were indeed a misery to think) ;
Did not my sentence in the former stage
O' the business bear a title plain enough ?
Decretum " — I translate it word for word —
" ' Decreed : the priest, for his complicity
I' the flight and deviation of the dame,
As well as for unlawful intercourse,
Is banished three years : ' crime and penalty
Declared alike. If he be taxed with guilt,

How can you call Pompilia innocent ?
If both be innocent, have I been just ? ' "

Gently, O mother, judge men — whose mis-
  take
Is in the mere misapprehensiveness !
The *Titulus* a-top of your decree
Was but to ticket there the kind of charge
You in good time would arbitrate upon.
Title is one thing, — arbitration's self,
Probatio, quite another possibly.
Subsistit, there holds good the old response,
Responsio tradita, we must not stick,
Quod non sit attendendus Titulus,
To the Title, *sed Probatio*, but the Proof,
Resultans ex processu, the result
O' the Trial, and the style of punishment,
Et pœna per sententiam imposita.
All is tentative, till the sentence come :
An indication of what men expect,
But nowise an assurance they shall find.
Lords, what if we permissibly relax
The tense bow, as the law-god Phœbus bids,
Relieve our gravity at labor's close ?
I traverse Rome, feel thirsty, need a draught,
Look for a wine-shop, find it by the bough
Projecting as to say " Here wine is sold ! "
So much I know, — " sold : " but what sort of
  wine ?
Strong, weak, sweet, sour, home-made or foreign
  drink ?
That much must I discover by myself.
" Wine is sold," quoth the bough, " but good
  or bad,
Find, and inform us when you smack your lips ! "
Exactly so, Law hangs her title forth,
To show she entertains you with such case
About such crime. Come in ! she pours, you
  quaff.
You find the Priest good liquor in the main,
But heady and provocative of brawls :
Remand the residue to flask once more,
Lay it low where it may deposit lees,
I' the cellar : thence produce it presently,
Three years the brighter and the better !

                                    Thus,
Law's son, have I bestowed my filial help,
And thus I end, *tenax proposito ;*
Point to point as I purposed have I drawn
Pompilia, and implied as terribly
Guido : so, gazing, let the world crown Law —
Able once more, despite my impotence,
And helped by the acumen of the Court,
To eliminate, display, make triumph truth !
What other prize than truth were worth the
  pains ?

There 's my oration — much exceeds in length
That famed panegyric of Isocrates,
They say it took him fifteen years to pen.
But all those ancients could say anything !
He put in just what rushed into his head :
While I shall have to prune and pare and print.
This comes of being born in modern times
With priests for auditory. Still, it pays.

X

THE POPE

Like to Ahasuerus, that shrewd prince,
I will begin, — as is, these seven years now,
My daily wont, — and read a History
(Written by one whose deft right hand was dust
To the last digit, ages ere my birth)
Of all my predecessors, Popes of Rome :
For though mine ancient early dropped the pen,
Yet others picked it up and wrote it dry,
Since of the making books there is no end.
And so I have the Papacy complete
From Peter first to Alexander last ;
Can question each and take instruction so.
Have I to dare ! — I ask, how dared this Pope ?
To suffer ? Such-an-one, how suffered he ?
Being about to judge, as now, I seek
How judged once, well or ill, some other Pope ;
Study some signal judgment that subsists
To blaze on, or else blot, the page which seals
The sum up of what gain or loss to God
Came of his one more Vicar in the world.
So, do I find example, rule of life ;
So, square and set in order the next page,
Shall be stretched smooth o'er my own funeral
    cyst.

Eight hundred years exact before the year
I was made Pope, men made Formosus Pope,
Say Sigebert and other chroniclers.
Ere I confirm or quash the Trial here
Of Guido Franceschini and his friends,
Read, — How there was a ghastly Trial once
Of a dead man by a live man, and both, Popes :
Thus — in the antique penman's very phrase.

" Then Stephen, Pope and seventh of the name,
Cried out, in synod as he sat in state,
While choler quivered on his brow and beard,
' Come into court, Formosus, thou lost wretch,
That claimedst to be late Pope as even I ! '

" And at the word, the great door of the church
Flew wide, and in they brought Formosus' self,
The body of him, dead, even as embalmed
And buried duly in the Vatican
Eight months before, exhumed thus for the
    nonce.
They set it, that dead body of a Pope,
Clothed in pontific vesture now again,
Upright on Peter's chair as if alive.

" And Stephen, springing up, cried furiously,
' Bishop of Porto, wherefore didst presume
To leave that see and take this Roman see,
Exchange the lesser for the greater see,
— A thing against the canons of the Church ? '

" Then one — (a Deacon who, observing forms,
Was placed by Stephen to repel the charge,
Be advocate and mouthpiece of the corpse) —
Spoke as he dared, set stammeringly forth
With white lips and dry tongue, — as but a
    youth,
For frightful was the corpse-face to behold, —
How nowise lacked there precedent for this.

" But when, for his last precedent of all,
Emboldened by the Spirit, out he blurts,
' And, Holy Father, didst not thou thyself
Vacate the lesser for the greater see,
Half a year since change Arago for Rome ? '
'— Ye have the sin's defence now, synod mine !
Shrieks Stephen in a beastly froth of rage :
' Judge now betwixt him dead and me alive !
Hath he intruded, or do I pretend ?
Judge, judge ! ' — breaks wavelike one whole
    foam of wrath.

" Whereupon they, being friends and followers,
Said, ' Ay, thou art Christ's Vicar, and not he '
Away with what is frightful to behold !
This act was uncanonic and a fault.'

" Then, swallowed up in rage, Stephen ex-
    claimed,
' So, guilty ! So, remains I punish guilt !
He is unpoped, and all he did I damn :
The Bishop, that ordained him, I degrade :
Depose to laics those he raised to priests :
What they have wrought is mischief nor shall
    stand,
It is confusion, let it vex no more !
Since I revoke, annul and abrogate
All his decrees in all kinds : they are void !
In token whereof and warning to the world,
Strip me yon miscreant of those robes usurped,
And clothe him with vile serge befitting such !
Then hale the carrion to the market-place ;
Let the town-hangman chop from his right
    hand
Those same three fingers which he blessed
    withal ;
Next cut the head off, once was crowned for-
    sooth :
And last go fling them, fingers, head and trunk,
To Tiber that my Christian fish may sup ! '
— Either because of ΙΧΘΥΣ which means Fish
And very aptly symbolizes Christ,
Or else because the Pope is Fisherman,
And seals with Fisher's-signet.

                                " Anyway,
So said, so done : himself, to see it done,
Followed the corpse they trailed from street to
    street
Till into Tiber wave they threw the thing.
The people, crowded on the banks to see,
Were loud or mute, wept or laughed, cursed or
    jeered,
According as the deed addressed their sense ;
A scandal verily : and out spake a Jew,
' Wot ye your Christ had vexed our Herod
    thus ? '

" Now when, Formosus being dead a year,
His judge Pope Stephen tasted death in turn,
Made captive by the mob and strangled straight,
Romanus, his successor for a month,
Did make protest Formosus was with God,
Holy, just, true in thought and word and deed
Next Theodore, who reigned but twenty days,
Therein convoked a synod, whose decree
Did reinstate, repope the late unpoped,
And do away with Stephen as accursed.

So that when presently certain fisher-folk
(As if the queasy river could not hold
Its swallowed Jonas, but discharged the meal)
Produced the timely product of their nets,
The mutilated man, Formosus, — saved
From putrefaction by the embalmer's spice,
Or, as some said, by sanctity of flesh,
'Why, lay the body again,' bade Theodore,
'Among his predecessors, in the church
And burial-place of Peter!' which was done.
'And,' addeth Luitprand, 'many of repute,
Pious and still alive, avouch to me
That, as they bore the body up the aisle,
The saints in imaged row bowed each his head
For welcome to a brother-saint come back.'
As for Romanus and this Theodore,
These two Popes, through the brief reign
    granted each,
Could but initiate what John came to close
And give the final stamp to: he it was,
Ninth of the name, (I follow the best guides)
Who, — in full synod at Ravenna held
With Bishops seventy-four, and present too
Eude King of France with his Archbishopry, —
Did condemn Stephen, anathematize
The disinterment, and make all blots blank.
'For,' argueth here Auxilius in a place
De Ordinationibus, 'precedents
Had been, no lack, before Formosus long,
Of Bishops so transferred from see to see, —
Marinus, for example:' read the tract.

"But, after John, came Sergius, reaffirmed
The right of Stephen, cursed Formosus, nay
Cast out, some say, his corpse a second time,
And here, — because the matter went to
    ground,
Fretted by new griefs, other cares of the age, —
Here is the last pronouncing of the Church,
Her sentence that subsists unto this day.
Yet constantly opinion hath prevailed
I' the Church, Formosus was a holy man."

Which of the judgments was infallible?
Which of my predecessors spoke for God?
And what availed Formosus that this cursed,
That blessed, and then this other cursed again?
"Fear ye not those whose power can kill the
    body
And not the soul," saith Christ, "but rather
    those
Can cast both soul and body into hell!"

John judged thus in Eight Hundred Ninety
    Eight,
Exact eight hundred years ago to-day
When, sitting in his stead, Vicegerent here,
I must give judgment on my own behoof.
So worked the predecessor: now, my turn!

In God's name! Once more on this earth of
    God's,
While twilight lasts and time wherein to work,
I take his staff with my uncertain hand,
And stay my six and fourscore years, my due
Labor and sorrow, on his judgment-seat,
And forthwith think, speak, act, in place of
    him —

The Pope for Christ. Once more appeal is
    made
From man's assize to mine: I sit and see
Another poor weak trembling human wretch
Pushed by his fellows, who pretend the right,
Up to the gulf which, where I gaze, begins
From this world to the next, — gives way and
    way,
Just on the edge over the awful dark:
With nothing to arrest him but my feet.
He catches at me with convulsive face,
Cries "Leave to live the natural minute more!"
While hollowly the avengers echo "Leave?
None! So has he exceeded man's due share
In man's fit license, wrung by Adam's fall,
To sin and yet not surely die, — that we,
All of us sinful, all with need of grace,
All chary of our life, — the minute more
Or minute less of grace which saves a soul, —
Bound to make common cause with who craves
    time,
— We yet protest against the exorbitance
Of sin in this one sinner, and demand
That his poor sole remaining piece of time
Be plucked from out his clutch: put him to
    death!
Punish him now! As for the weal or woe
Hereafter, God grant mercy! Man be just,
Nor let the felon boast he went scot-free!"
And I am bound, the solitary judge,
To weigh the worth, decide upon the plea,
And either hold a hand out, or withdraw
A foot and let the wretch drift to the fall.
Ay, and while thus I dally, dare perchance
Put fancies for a comfort 'twixt this calm
And yonder passion that I have to bear, —
As if reprieve were possible for both
Prisoner and Pope, — how easy were reprieve!
A touch o' the hand-bell here, a hasty word
To those who wait, and wonder they wait long,
I' the passage there, and I should gain the
    life! —
Yea, though I flatter me with fancy thus,
I know it is but Nature's craven-trick.
The case is over, judgment at an end,
And all things done now and irrevocable:
A mere dead man is Franceschini here,
Even as Formosus centuries ago.
I have worn through this sombre wintry day,
With winter in my soul beyond the world's,
Over these dismalest of documents
Which drew night down on me ere eve befell, —
Pleadings and counter-pleadings, figure of fact
Beside fact's self, these summaries, to wit, —
How certain three were slain by certain five:
I read here why it was, and how it went,
And how the chief o' the five preferred ex-
    cuse,
And how law rather chose defence should lie, —
What argument he urged by wary word
When free to play off wile, start subterfuge,
And what the unguarded groan told, torture's
    feat
When law grew brutal, outbroke, overbore
And glutted hunger on the truth, at last, —
No matter for the flesh and blood between.
All's a clear rede and no more riddle now.
Truth, nowhere, lies yet everywhere in these —

Not absolutely in a portion, yet
Evolvable from the whole : evolved at last
Painfully, held tenaciously by me.
Therefore there is not any doubt to clear
When I shall write the brief word presently
And chink the hand-bell, which I pause to do.
Irresolute ? Not I, more than the mound
With the pine-trees on it yonder ! Some sur-
    mise,
Perchance, that since man's wit is fallible,
Mine may fail here ? Suppose it so, — what
    then ?
Say, — Guido, I count guilty, there 's no babe
So guiltless, for I misconceive the man !
What 's in the chance should move me from my
    mind ?
If, as I walk in a rough country-side,
Peasants of mine cry, " Thou art he can help,
Lord of the land and counted wise to boot :
Look at our brother, strangling in his foam,
He fell so where we find him, — prove thy
    worth ! "
I may presume, pronounce, " A frenzy-fit,
A falling-sickness or a fever-stroke !
Breathe a vein, copiously let blood at once ! "
So perishes the patient, and anon
I hear my peasants — " All was error, lore !
Our story, thy prescription : for there crawled
In due time from our hapless brother's breast
The serpent which had stung him : bleeding
    slew
Whom a prompt cordial had restored to health."
What other should I say than " God so willed :
Mankind is ignorant, a man am I :
Call ignorance my sorrow, not my sin ! "
So and not otherwise, in after-time,
If some acuter wit, fresh probing, sound
This multifarious mass of words and deeds
Deeper, and reach through guilt to innocence,
I shall face Guido's ghost nor blench a jot.
" God who set me to judge thee, meted out
So much of judging faculty, no more :
Ask him if I was slack in use thereof ! "
I hold a heavier fault imputable
Inasmuch as I changed a chaplain once,
For no cause, — no, if I must bare my heart, —
Save that he snuffled somewhat saying mass.
For I am 'ware it is the seed of act,
God holds appraising in his hollow palm,
Not act grown great thence on the world be-
    low,
Leafage and branchage, vulgar eyes admire.
Therefore I stand on my integrity,
Nor fear at all : and if I hesitate,
It is because I need to breathe awhile,
Rest, as the human right allows, review
Intent the little seeds of act, my tree, —
The thought, which, clothed in deed, I give the
    world
At chink of bell and push of arrased door.

O pale departure, dim disgrace of day !
Winter 's in wane, his vengeful worst art thou,
To dash the boldness of advancing March !
Thy chill persistent rain has purged our streets
Of gossipry ; pert tongue and idle ear
By this, consort 'neath archway, portico.
But wheresoe'er Rome gathers in the gray,

Two names now snap and flash from mouth to
    mouth —
(Sparks, flint and steel strike) — Guido and the
    Pope.
By this same hour to-morrow eve — aha,
How do they call him ? — the sagacious Swede
Who finds by figures how the chances prove,
Why one comes rather than another thing,
As, say, such dots turn up by throw of dice,
Or, if we dip in Virgil here and there
And prick for such a verse, when such shall
    point.
Take this Swede, tell him, hiding name and
    rank,
Two men are in our city this dull eve ;
One doomed to death, — but hundreds in such
    plight
Slip aside, clean escape by leave of law
Which leans to mercy in this latter time ;
Moreover in the plenitude of life
Is he, with strength of limb and brain adroit,
Presumably of service here : beside,
The man is noble, backed by nobler friends :
Nay, they so wish him well, the city's self
Makes common cause with who — house-magis-
    trate,
Patron of hearth and home, domestic lord —
But ruled his own, let aliens cavil.   Die ?
He 'll bribe a jailer or break prison first !
Nay, a sedition may be helpful, give
Hint to the mob to batter wall, burn gate,
And bid the favorite malefactor march.
Calculate now these chances of escape !
" It is not probable, but well may be."
Again, there is another man, weighed now
By twice eight years beyond the seven-times-
    ten,
Appointed overweight to break our branch.
And this man's loaded branch lifts, more than
    snow,
All the world's cark and care, though a bird's
    nest
Were a superfluous burden : notably
Hath he been pressed, as if his age were youth,
From to-day's dawn till now that day departs,
Trying one question with true sweat of soul,
" Shall the said doomed man fitlier die or live ? "
When a straw swallowed in his posset, stool
Stumbled on where his path lies, any puff
That 's incident to such a smoking flax,
Hurries the natural end and quenches him !
Now calculate, thou sage, the chances here,
Say, which shall die the sooner, this or that ?
" That, possibly, this in all likelihood."
I thought so : yet thou tripp'st, my foreign
    friend !
No, it will be quite otherwise, — to-day
Is Guido's last : my term is yet to run.

But say the Swede were right, and I forthwith
Acknowledge a prompt summons and lie dead :
Why, then I stand already in God's face
And hear, " Since by its fruit a tree is judged,
Show me thy fruit, the latest act of thine !
For in the last is summed the first and all, —
What thy life last put heart and soul into,
There shall I taste thy product." I must plead
This condemnation of a man to-day.

Not so! Expect nor question nor reply
At what we figure as God's judgment-bar!
None of this vile way by the barren words
Which, more than any deed, characterize
Man as made subject to a curse: no speech —
That still bursts o'er some lie which,lurks inside,
As the split skin across the coppery snake,
And most denotes man! since, in all beside,
In hate or lust or guile or unbelief,
Out of some core of truth the excrescence comes,
And, in the last resort, the man may urge
"So was I made, a weak thing that gave way
To truth, to impulse only strong since true,
And hated, lusted, used guile, forwent faith."
But when man walks the garden of this world
For his own solace, and, unchecked by law,
Speaks or keeps silence as himself sees fit,
Without the least incumbency to lie,
— Why, can he tell you what a rose is like,
Or how the birds fly, and not slip to false
Though truth serve better? Man must tell his
        mate
Of you, me and himself, knowing he lies,
Knowing his fellow knows the same, — will think
"He lies, it is the method of a man!"
And yet will speak for answer "It is truth"
To him who shall rejoin "Again a lie!"
Therefore these filthy rags of speech, this coil
Of statement, comment, query and response,
Tatters all too contaminate for use,
Have no renewing: He the Truth is, too,
The Word. We men, in our degree, may know
There, simply, instantaneously, as here
After long time and amid many lies,
Whatever we dare think we know indeed
— That I am I, as He is He, — what else?
But be man's method for man's life at least!
Wherefore, Antonio Pignatelli, thou
My ancient self, who wast no Pope so long
But studiedst God and man, the many years
I' the school, i' the cloister, in the diocese
Domestic, legate-rule in foreign lands, —
Thou other force in those old busy days
Than this gray ultimate decrepitude, —
Yet sensible of fires that more and more
Visit a soul, in passage to the sky,
Left nakeder than when flesh-robe was new —
Thou, not Pope but the mere old man o' the
        world,
Supposed inquisitive and dispassionate,
Wilt thou, the one whose speech I somewhat
        trust,
Question the after-me, this self now Pope,
Hear his procedure, criticise his work?
Wise in its generation is the world.

This is why Guido is found reprobate.
I see him furnished forth for his career,
On starting for the life-chance in our world,
With nearly all we count sufficient help:
Body and mind in balance, a sound frame,
A solid intellect: the wit to seek,
Wisdom to choose, and courage wherewithal
To deal in whatsoever circumstance
Should minister to man, make life succeed.
Oh, and much drawback! what were earth
        without?
Is this our ultimate stage, or starting-place

To try man's foot, if it will creep or climb,
'Mid obstacles in seeming, points that prove
Advantage for who vaults from low to high
And makes the stumbling-block a stepping-
        stone?
So, Guido, born with appetite, lacks food:
Is poor, who yet could deftly play-off wealth:
Straitened, whose limbs are restless till at large.
He, as he eyes each outlet of the cirque
And narrow penfold for probation, pines
After the good things just outside its grate,
With less monition, fainter conscience-twitch,
Rarer instinctive qualm at the first feel
Of greed unseemly, prompting grasp undue,
Than nature furnishes her main mankind, —
Making it harder to do wrong than right
The first time, careful lest the common ear
Break measure, miss the outstep of life's march.
Wherein I see a trial fair and fit
For one else too unfairly fenced about,
Set above sin, beyond his fellows here:
Guarded from the arch-tempter all must fight,
By a great birth, traditionary name,
Diligent culture, choice companionship,
Above all, conversancy with the faith
Which puts forth for its base of doctrine just,
"Man is born nowise to content himself,
But please God." He accepted such a rule,
Recognized man's obedience; and the Church,
Which simply is such rule's embodiment,
He clave to, he held on by, — nay, indeed,
Near pushed inside of, deep as layman durst,
Professed so much of priesthood as might sue
For priest's - exemption where the layman
        sinned, —
Go this arm frocked which, bare, the law would
        bruise,
Hence, at this moment, what's his last resource,
His extreme stay and utmost stretch of hope
But that, — convicted of such crime as law
Wipes not away save with a worldling's
        blood, —
Guido, the three-parts consecrate, may 'scape?
Nay, the portentous brothers of the man
Are veritably priests, protected each
May do his murder in the Church's pale,
Abate Paul, Canon Girolamo!
This is the man proves irreligiousest
Of all mankind, religion's parasite!
This may forsooth plead dinned ear, jaded
        sense,
The vice o' the watcher who bides near the bell,
Sleeps sound because the clock is vigilant,
And cares not whether it be shade or shine,
Doling out day and night to all men else!
Why was the choice o' the man to niche him-
        self
Perversely 'neath the tower where Time's own
        tongue
Thus undertakes to sermonize the world?
Why, but because the solemn is safe too,
The belfry proves a fortress of a sort,
Has other uses than to teach the hour:
Turns sunscreen, paravent and ombrifuge
To whoso seeks a shelter in its pale,
— Ay, and attractive to unwary folk
Who gaze at storied portal, statued spire,
And go home with full head but empty purse.

Nor dare suspect the sacristan the thief !
Shall Judas — hard upon the donor's heel,
To filch the fragments of the basket — plead .
He was too near the preacher's mouth, nor sat
Attent with fifties in a company ?
No, — closer to promulgated decree,
Clearer the censure of default.   Proceed !

I find him bound, then, to begin life well ;
Fortified by propitious circumstance,
Great birth, good breeding, with the Church for
    guide,
How lives he ?   Cased thus in a coat of proof,
Mailed like a man-at-arms, though all the while
A puny starveling, — does the breast pant big,
The limb swell to the limit, emptiness
Strive to become solidity indeed ?
Rather, he shrinks up like the ambiguous fish,
Detaches flesh from shell and outside show,
And steals by moonlight (I have seen the thing)
In and out, now to prey and now to skulk.
Armor he boasts when a wave breaks on beach,
Or bird stoops for the prize : with peril nigh, —
The man of rank, the much-befriended man,
The man almost affiliate to the Church,
Such is to deal with, let the world beware !
Does the world recognize, pass prudently ?
Do tides abate and sea-fowl hunt i' the deep ?
Already is the slug from out its mew,
Ignobly faring with all loose and free,
Sand-fly and slush-worm at their garbage-feast,
A naked blotch no better than they all :
Guido has dropped nobility, slipped the Church,
Plays trickster if not cut-purse, body and soul
Prostrate among the filthy feeders — faugh !
And when Law takes him by surprise at last,
Catches the foul thing on its carrion-prey,
Behold, he points to shell left high and dry,
Pleads " But the case out yonder is myself ! "
Nay, it is thou, Law prongs amid thy peers,
Congenial vermin ; that was none of thee,
Thine outside, — give it to the soldier-crab !

For I find this black mark impinge the man,
That he believes in just the vile of life.
Low instinct, base pretension, are these truth ?
Then, that aforesaid armor, probity,
He figures in, is falsehood scale on scale ;
Honor and faith, — a lie and a disguise,
Probably for all livers in this world,
Certainly for himself !   All say good words
To who will hear, all do thereby bad deeds
To who must undergo ; so thrive mankind !
See this habitual creed exemplified
Most in the last deliberate act ; as last,
So, very sum and substance of the soul
Of him that planned and leaves one perfect
    piece,
The sin brought under jurisdiction now,
Even the marriage of the man : this act
I sever from his life as sample, show
For Guido's self, intend to test him by,
As, from a cup filled fairly at the fount,
By the components we decide enough
Or to let flow as late, or stanch the source.

He purposes this marriage, I remark,
On no one motive that should prompt thereto —

Farthest, by consequence, from ends alleged
Appropriate to the action ; so they were :
The best, he knew and feigned, the worst he
    took.
Not one permissible impulse moves the man,
From the mere liking of the eye and ear,
To the true longing of the heart that loves,
No trace of these : but all to instigate,
Is what sinks man past level of the brute,
Whose appetite if brutish is a truth.
All is the lust for money : to get gold, —
Why, lie, rob, if it must be, murder !   Make
Body and soul wring gold out, lured within
The clutch of hate by love, the trap's pretence !
What good else get from bodies and from souls ?
This got, there were some life to lead thereby,
— What, where or how, appreciate those who
    tell
How the toad lives : it lives, — enough for me !
To get this good — but with a groan or so,
Then, silence of the victims — were the feat.
He foresaw, made a picture in his mind, —
Of father and mother stunned and echoless
To the blow, as they lie staring at fate's jaws
Their folly danced into, till the woe fell ;
Edged in a month by strenuous cruelty
From even the poor nook whence they watched
    the wolf
Feast on their heart, the lamb-like child his
    prey ;
Plundered to the last remnant of their wealth,
(What daily pittance pleased the plunderer
    dole,)
Hunted forth to go hide head, starve and die,
And leave the pale awe-stricken wife, past hope
Of help i' the world now, mute and motionless,
His slave, his chattel, to first use, then destroy.
All this, he bent mind how to bring about,
Put plain in act and life, as painted plain,
So have success, reach crown of earthly good,
In this particular enterprise of man,
By marriage — undertaken in God's face
With all these lies so opposite God's truth,
For end so other than man's end.

                                Thus scheme
Guido, and thus would carry out his scheme :
But when an obstacle first blocks the path,
When he finds none may boast monopoly
Of lies and trick i' the tricking lying world, —
That sorry timid natures, even this sort
O' the Comparini, want nor trick nor lie
Proper to the kind, — that as the gor-crow
    treats
The bramble-finch so treats the finch the moth,
And the great Guido is minutely matched
By this same couple, — whether true or false
The revelation of Pompilia's birth,
Which in a moment brings his scheme to
    naught, —
Then, he is piqued, advances yet a stage,
Leaves the low region to the finch and fly,
Soars to the zenith whence the fiercer fowl
May dare the inimitable swoop.   I see.
He draws now on the curious crime, the fine
Felicity and flower of wickedness ;
Determines, by the utmost exercise
Of violence, made safe and sure by craft.

To satiate malice, pluck one last arch-pang
From the parents, else would triumph out of
reach,
By punishing their child, within reach yet,
Who, by thought, word or deed, could nowise
wrong
I' the matter that now moves him. So plans he,
Always subordinating (note the point!)
Revenge, the manlier sin, to interest
The meaner, — would pluck pang forth, but
unclench
No gripe in the act, let fall no money-piece.
Hence a plan for so plaguing, body and soul,
His wife, so putting, day by day, hour by hour,
The untried torture to the untouched place,
As must precipitate an end foreseen,
Goad her into some plain revolt, most like
Plunge upon patent suicidal shame,
Death to herself, damnation by rebound
To those whose hearts he, holding hers, holds
still :
Such plan as, in its bad completeness, shall
Ruin the three together and alike,
Yet leave himself in luck and liberty,
No claim renounced, no right a forfeiture,
His person unendangered, his good fame
Without a flaw, his pristine worth intact, —
While they, with all their claims and rights that
cling,
Shall forthwith crumble off. him every side,
Scorched into dust, a plaything for the winds.
As when, in our Campagna, there is fired
The nest-like work that overruns a hut;
And, as the thatch burns here, there, every-
where,
Even to the ivy and wild vine, that bound
And blessed the home where men were happy
once,
There rises gradual, black amid the blaze,
Some grim and unscathed nucleus of the
nest, —
Some old malicious tower, some obscene tomb
They thought a temple in their ignorance,
And clung about and thought to lean upon —
There laughs it o'er their ravage, — where are
they ?
So did his cruelty burn life about,
And lay the ruin bare in dreadfulness,
Try the persistency of torment so
Upon the wife, that, at extremity,
Some crisis brought about by fire and flame,
The patient frenzy-stung must needs break
loose,
Fly anyhow, find refuge anywhere,
Even in the arms of who should front her first.
No monster but a man — while nature shrieked
" Or thus escape, or die !" The spasm arrived,
Not the escape by way of sin, — O God,
Who shall pluck sheep thou holdest, from thy
hand ?
Therefore she lay resigned to die, — so far
The simple cruelty was foiled. Why then,
Craft to the rescue, let craft supplement
Cruelty and show hell a masterpiece !
Hence this consummate lie, this love-intrigue,
Unmanly simulation of a sin,
With place and time and circumstance to
suit —

These letters false beyond all forgery —
Not just handwriting and mere authorship,
But false to body and soul they figure forth —
As though the man had cut out shape and
shape
From fancies of that other Aretine,
To paste below — incorporate the filth
With cherub faces on a missal-page !

Whereby the man so far attains his end
That strange temptation is permitted, — see,
Pompilia, wife, and Caponsacchi, priest,
Are brought together as nor priest nor wife
Should stand, and there is passion in the place,
Power in the air for evil as for good,
Promptings from heaven and hell, as if the
stars
Fought in their courses for a fate to be.
Thus stand the wife and priest, a spectacle,
I doubt not, to unseen assemblage there.
No lamp will mark that window for a shrine,
No tablet signalize the terrace, teach
New generations which succeed the old,
The pavement of the street is holy ground :
No bard describe in verse how Christ prevailed
And Satan fell like lightning ! Why repine ?
What does the world, told truth, but lie the
more ?

A second time the plot is foiled ; nor, now,
By corresponding sin for countercheck,
No wile and trick that baffle trick and wile, —
The play o' the parents ! Here the blot is
blanched
By God's gift of a purity of soul
That will not take pollution, ermine-like
Armed from dishonor by its own soft snow.
Such was this gift of God who showed for once
How he would have the world go white : it
seems
As a new attribute were born of each
Champion of truth, the priest and wife I
praise, —
As a new safeguard sprang up in defence
Of their new noble nature : so a thorn
Comes to the aid of and completes the rose —
Courage to wit, no woman's gift nor priest's,
I' the crisis ; might leaps vindicating right.
See how the strong aggressor, bad and bold,
With every vantage, preconcerts surprise,
Leaps of a sudden at his victim's throat
In a byway, — how fares he when face to face
With Caponsacchi ? Who fights, who fears
now ?
There quails Count Guido, armed to the chat-
tering teeth,
Cowers at the steadfast eye and quiet word
O' the Canon of the Pieve ! There skulks
crime
Behind law called in to back cowardice !
While out of the poor trampled worm the wife
Springs up a serpent !

But anon of these !
Him I judge now, — of him proceed to note,
Failing the first, a second chance befriends
Guido, gives pause ere punishment arrive.
The law he called, comes, hears, adjudicates

Nor does amiss i' the main, — secludes the wife
From the husband, respites the oppressed one,
    grants
Probation to the oppressor, could he know
The mercy of a minute's fiery purge !
The furnace-coals alike of public scorn,
Private remorse, heaped glowing on his head,
What if — the force and guile, the ore's alloy,
Eliminate, his baser soul refined —
The lost be saved even yet, so as by fire ?
Let him, rebuked, go softly all his days
And, when no graver musings claim their due,
Meditate on a man's immense mistake
Who, fashioned to use feet and walk, deigns
    crawl —
Takes the unmanly means — ay, though to
    ends
Man scarce should make for, would but reach
    through wrong, —
May sin, but nowise needs shame manhood so:
Since fowlers hawk, shoot, nay and snare the
    game,
And yet eschew vile practice, nor find sport
In torch-light treachery or the luring owl.

But how hunts Guido? Why, the fraudful
    trap —
Late spurned to ruin by the indignant feet
Of fellows in the chase who loved fair play —
Here he picks up its fragments to the least,
Lades him and hies to the old lurking-place
Where haply he may patch again, refit
The mischief, file its blunted teeth anew,
Make sure, next time, first snap shall break
    the bone.
Craft, greed and violence complot revenge :
Craft, for its quota, schemes to bring about
And seize occasion and be safe withal :
Greed craves its act may work both far and
    near,
Crush the tree, branch and trunk and root be-
    side,
Whichever twig or leaf arrests a streak
Of possible sunshine else would coin itself,
And drop down one more gold piece in the
    path :
Violence stipulates, " Advantage proved,
And safety sure, be pain the overplus !
Murder with jagged knife ! Cut but tear too !
Foiled oft, starved long, glut malice for
    amends ! "
And what, craft's scheme? scheme sorrowful
    and strange
As though the elements, whom mercy checked,
Had mustered hate for one eruption more,
One final deluge to surprise the Ark
Cradled and sleeping on its mountain-top :
Their outbreak-signal — what but the dove's
    coo,
Back with the olive in her bill for news
Sorrow was over ? 'T is an infant's birth,
Guido's first-born, his son and heir, that gives
The occasion : other men cut free their souls
From care in such a case, fly up in thanks
To God, reach, recognize his love for once :
Guido cries, " Soul, at last the mire is thine !
Lie there in likeness of a money-bag,
My babe's birth so pins down past moving now,

That I dare cut adrift the lives I late
Scrupled to touch lest thou escape with them !
These parents and their child my wife, — touch
    one,
Lose all ! Their rights determined on a head
I could but hate, not harm, since from each
    hair
Dangled a hope for me: now — chance and
    change !
No right was in their child but passes plain
To that child's child and through such child to
    me.
I am a father now, — come what come will,
I represent my child ; he comes between —
Cuts sudden off the sunshine of this life
From those three : why, the gold is in his curls !
Not with old Pietro's, Violante's head,
Not his gray horror, her more hideous black —
Go these, devoted to the knife ! "
                                    'T is done :
Wherefore should mind misgive, heart hesitate ?
He calls to counsel, fashions certain four
Colorless natures counted clean till now,
— Rustic simplicity, uncorrupted youth,
Ignorant virtue ! Here 's the gold o' the prime
When Saturn ruled, shall shock our leaden
    day —
The clown abash the courtier ! Mark it, bards !
The courtier tries his hand on clownship here,
Speaks a word, names a crime, appoints a
    price, —
Just breathes on what, suffused with all himself,
Is red-hot henceforth past distinction now
I' the common glow of hell. And thus they
    break
And blaze on us at Rome, Christ's birthnight-
    eve !
Oh angels that sang erst " On the earth, peace !
To man, good will ! " — such peace finds earth
    to-day !
After the seventeen hundred years, so man
Wills good to man, so Guido makes complete
His murder ! what is it I said ? — cuts loose
Three lives that hitherto he suffered cling,
Simply because each served to nail secure,
By a corner of the money-bag, his soul, —
Therefore, lives sacred till the babe's first
    breath
O'erweights them in the balance, — off they fly !

So is the murder managed, sin conceived
To the full : and why not crowned with triumph
    too ?
Why must the sin, conceived thus, bring forth
    death ?
I note how, within hair's-breadth of escape,
Impunity and the thing supposed success,
Guido is found when the check comes, the
    change,
The monitory touch o' the tether — felt
By few, not marked by many, named by none
At the moment, only recognized aright
I' the fulness of the days, for God's, lest sin
Exceed the service, leap the line: such check —
A secret which this life finds hard to keep,
And, often guessed, is never quite revealed —
Needs must trip Guido on a stumbling-block
Too vulgar, too absurdly plain i' the path !

Study this single oversight of care,
This hebetude that marred sagacity,
Forgetfulness of all the man best knew, —
How any stranger having need to fly,
Needs but to ask and have the means of flight.
Why, the first urchin tells you, to leave Rome,
Get horses, you must show the warrant, just
The banal scrap, clerk's scribble, a fair word
    buys,
Or foul one, if a ducat sweeten word, —
And straight authority will back demand,
Give you the pick o' the post-house ! — how
    should he,
Then, resident at Rome for thirty years,
Guido, instruct a stranger !   And himself
Forgets just this poor paper scrap, wherewith
Armed, every door he knocks at opens wide
To save him : horsed and manned, with such
    advance
O' the hunt behind, why, 't were the easy task
Of hours told on the fingers of one hand,
To reach the Tuscan frontier, laugh at home,
Light-hearted with his fellows of the place, —
Prepared by that strange shameful judgment,
    that
Satire upon a sentence just pronounced
By the Rota and confirmed by the Granduke, —
Ready in a circle to receive their peer,
Appreciate his good story how, when Rome,
The Pope-King and the populace of priests
Made common cause with their confederate
The other priestling who seduced his wife,
He, all unaided, wiped out the affront
With decent bloodshed and could face his
    friends,
Frolic it in the world's eye. Ay, such tale
Missed such applause, and by such oversight !
So, tired and footsore, those blood-flustered
    five
Went reeling on the road through dark and cold,
The few permissible miles, to sink at length,
Wallow and sleep in the first wayside straw,
As the other herd quenched, i' the wash o' the
    wave,
— Each swine, the devil inside him : so slept
    they,
And so were caught and caged — all through
    one trip,
One touch of fool in Guido the astute !
He curses the omission, I surmise,
More than the murder. Why, thou fool and
    blind,
It is the mercy-stroke that stops thy fate,
Hamstrings and holds thee to thy hurt, — but
    how ?
On the edge o' the precipice ! One minute more,
Thou hadst gone farther and fared worse, my
    son,
Fathoms down on the flint and fire beneath !
Thy comrades each and all were of one mind,
Thy murder done, to straightway murder thee
In turn, because of promised pay withheld.
So, to the last, greed found itself at odds
With craft in thee, and, proving conqueror,
Had sent thee, the same night that crowned thy
    hope,
Thither where, this same day, I see thee not,
Nor, through God's mercy, need, to-morrow, see.

Such I find Guido, midmost blotch of black
Discernible in this group of clustered crimes
Huddling together in the cave they call
Their palace, outraged day thus penetrates.
Around him ranged, now close and now remote,
Prominent or obscure to meet the needs
O' the mage and master, I detect each shape
Subsidiary i' the scene nor loathed the less,
All alike colored, all descried akin
By one and the same pitchy furnace stirred
At the centre : see, they lick the master's
    hand, —
This fox-faced horrible priest, this brother-brute
The Abate, — why, mere wolfishness looks well,
Guido stands honest in the red o' the flame,
Beside this yellow that would pass for white,
Twice Guido, all craft but no violence,
This copier of the mien and gait and garb
Of Peter and Paul, that he may go disguised,
Rob halt and lame, sick folk i' the temple-
    porch !
Armed with religion, fortified by law,
A man of peace, who trims the midnight lamp
And turns the classic page — and all for craft,
All to work harm with, yet incur no scratch !
While Guido brings the struggle to a close,
Paul steps back the due distance, clear o' the
    trap
He builds and baits. Guido I catch and judge ;
Paul is past reach in this world and my time :
That is a case reserved. Pass to the next,
The boy of the brood, the young Girolamo,
Priest, Canon, and what more ? nor wolf nor
    fox,
But hybrid, neither craft nor violence
Wholly, part violence part craft : such cross
Tempts speculation — will both blend one day,
And prove hell's better product ? Or subside
And let the simple quality emerge,
Go on with Satan's service the old way ?
Meanwhile, what promise, — what performance
    too !
For there 's a new distinctive touch, I see,
Lust — lacking in the two — hell's own blue tint
That gives a character and marks the man
More than a match for yellow and red. Once
    more,
A case reserved : why should I doubt ? Then
    comes
The gaunt gray nightmare in the furthest
    smoke,
The hag that gave these three abortions birth,
Unmotherly mother and unwomanly
Woman, that near turns motherhood to shame,
Womanliness to loathing : no one word,
No gesture to curb cruelty a whit
More than the she-pard thwarts her playsome
    whelps
Trying their milk-teeth on the soft o' the throat
O' the first fawn, flung, with those beseeching
    eyes,
Flat in the covert ! How should she but couch,
Lick the dry lips, unsheathe the blunted claw,
Catch 'twixt her placid eyewinks at what chance
Old bloody half-forgotten dream may flit,
Born when herself was novice to the taste,
The while she lets youth take its pleasure
    Last,

These God-abandoned wretched lumps of life,
These four companions, — country-folk this time,
Not tainted by the unwholesome civic breath,
Much less the curse o' the court ! Mere striplings too,
Fit to do human nature justice still !
Surely when impudence in Guido's shape
Shall propose crime and proffer money's-worth
To these stout tall rough bright-eyed black-haired boys,
The blood shall bound in answer to each cheek
Before the indignant outcry break from lip !
Are these i' the mood to murder, hardly loosed
From healthy autumn-finish of ploughed glebe,
Grapes in the barrel, work at happy end,
And winter near with rest and Christmas play ?
How greet they Guido with his final task —
(As if he but proposed " One vineyard more
To dig, ere frost come, then relax indeed ! ")
" Anywhere, anyhow and anywhy,
Murder me some three people, old and young,
Ye never heard the names of, — and be paid
So much ! " And the whole four accede at once.
Demur ? Do cattle bidden march or halt ?
Is it some lingering habit, old fond faith
I' the lord o' the land, instructs them, — birth-right badge
Of feudal tenure claims its slaves again ?
Not so at all, thou noble human heart !
All is done purely for the pay, — which, earned,
And not forthcoming at the instant, makes
Religion heresy, and the lord o' the land
Fit subject for a murder in his turn.
The patron with cut throat and rifled purse,
Deposited i' the roadside-ditch, his due,
Naught hinders each good fellow trudging home,
The heavier by a piece or two in poke,
And so with new zest to the common life,
Mattock and spade, plough-tail and wagon-shaft,
Till some such other piece of luck betide,
Who knows ? Since this is a mere start in life,
And none of them exceeds the twentieth year.
Nay, more i' the background yet ? Unnoticed forms
Claim to be classed, subordinately vile ?
Complacent lookers - on that laugh, — perchance
Shake head as their friend's horse - play grows too rough
With the mere child he manages amiss —
But would not interfere and make bad worse
For twice the fractious tears and prayers : thou know'st
Civility better, Marzi-Medici,
Governor for thy kinsman the Granduke !
Fit representative of law, man's lamp
I' the magistrate's grasp full-flare, no rushlight-end
Sputtering 'twixt thumb and finger of the priest !
Whose answer to the couple's cry for help
Is a threat, — whose remedy of Pompilia's wrong,
A shrug o' the shoulder, and facetious word

Or wink, traditional with Tuscan wits,
To Guido in the doorway. Laud to law !
The wife is pushed back to the husband, he
Who knows how these home-squabblings perse cute
People who have the public good to mind,
And work best with a silence in the court !

Ah, but I save my word at least for thee,
Archbishop, who art under, i' the Church,
As I am under God, — thou, chosen by both
To do the shepherd's office, feed the sheep —
How of this lamb that panted at thy foot
While the wolf pressed on her within crook reach ?
Wast thou the hireling that did turn and flee ?
With thee at least anon the little word !

Such denizens o' the cave now cluster round
And heat the furnace sevenfold : time indeed
A bolt from heaven should cleave roof and clear place,
Transfix and show the world, suspiring flame,
The main offender, scar and brand the rest
Hurrying, each miscreant to his hole : then flood
And purify the scene with outside day —
Which yet, in the absolutest drench of dark,
Ne'er wants a witness, some stray beauty-beam
To the despair of hell.

　　　　　　First of the first,
Such I pronounce Pompilia, then as now
Perfect in whiteness : stoop thou down, my child,
Give cne good moment to the poor old Pope
Heart-sick at having all his world to blame —
Let me look at thee in the flesh as erst,
Let me enjoy the old clean linen garb,
Not the new splendid vesture ! Armed and crowned,
Would Michael, yonder, be, nor crowned nor armed,
The less pre-eminent angel ? Everywhere
I see in the world the intellect of man,
That sword, the energy his subtle spear,
The knowledge which defends him like a shield —
Everywhere ; but they make not up, I think,
The marvel of a soul like thine, earth's flower
She holds up to the softened gaze of God !
It was not given Pompilia to know much,
Speak much, to write a book, to move man kind,
Be memorized by who records my time.
Yet if in purity and patience, if
In faith held fast despite the plucking fiend,
Safe like the signet stone with the new name
That saints are known by, — if in right returned
For wrong, most pardon for worst injury,
If there be any virtue, any praise, —
Then will this woman-child have proved — who knows ? —
Just the one prize vouchsafed unworthy me,
Seven years a gardener of the untoward ground
I till, — this earth, my sweat and blood manure
All the long day that barrenly grows dusk :
At least one blossom makes me proud at eve
Born 'mid the briers of my enclosure ! Still

(Oh, here as elsewhere, nothingness of man !)
Those be the plants, imbedded yonder South
To mellow in the morning, those made fat
By the master's eye, that yield such timid leaf,
Uncertain bud, as product of his pains !
While — see how this mere chance-sown, cleft-
      nursed seed,
That sprang up by the wayside 'neath the foot
Of the enemy, this breaks all into blaze,
Spreads itself, one wide glory of desire
To incorporate the whole great sun it loves
From the inch-height whence it looks and
      longs ! My flower,
My rose, I gather for the breast of God,
This I praise most in thee, where all I praise,
That having been obedient to the end
According to the light allotted, law
Prescribed thy life, still tried, still standing
      test, —
Dutiful to the foolish parents first,
Submissive next to the bad husband, — nay,
Tolerant of those meaner miserable
That did his hests, eked out the dole of pain, —
Thou, patient thus, couldst rise from law to
      law,
The old to the new, promoted at one cry
O' the trump of God to the new service, not
To longer bear, but henceforth fight, be found
Sublime in new impatience with the foe !
Endure man and obey God : plant firm foot
On neck of man, tread man into the hell
Meet for him, and obey God all the more !
Oh child that didst despise thy life so much
When it seemed only thine to keep or lose,
How the fine ear felt fall the first low word
"Value life, and preserve life for My sake ! "
Thou didst . . . how shall I say ? . . . receive
      so long
The standing ordinance of God on earth,
What wonder if the novel claim had clashed
With old requirement, seemed to supersede
Too much the customary law ? But, brave,
Thou at first prompting of what I call God,
And fools call Nature, didst hear, comprehend,
Accept the obligation laid on thee,
Mother elect, to save the unborn child,
As brute and bird do, reptile and the fly,
Ay and, I nothing doubt, even tree, shrub, plant
And flower o' the field, all in a common pact
To worthily defend the trust of trusts,
Life from the Ever Living : — didst resist —
Anticipate the office that is mine —
And with his own sword stay the upraised arm,
The endeavor of the wicked, and defend
Him who — again in my default — was there
For visible providence : one less true than thou
To touch, i' the past, less practised in the right,
Approved less far in all docility
To all instruction, — how had such an one
Made scruple " Is this motion a decree ? "
It was authentic to the experienced ear
O' the good and faithful servant. Go past me
And get thy praise, — and be not far to seek
Presently when I follow if I may !

And surely not so very much apart
Need I place thee, my warrior-priest, — in
      whom

What if I gain the other rose, the gold,
We grave to imitate God's miracle,
Greet monarchs with, good rose in its degree ?
Irregular noble scapegrace — son the same !
Faulty — and peradventure ours the fault
Who still misteach, mislead, throw hook and
      line,
Thinking to land leviathan forsooth,
Tame the scaled neck, play with him as a bird,
And bind him for our maidens ! Better bear
The King of Pride go wantoning awhile,
Unplagued by cord in nose and thorn in jaw,
Through deep to deep, followed by all that
      shine,
Churning the blackness hoary : He who made
The comely terror, He shall make the sword
To match that piece of netherstone his heart,
Ay, nor miss praise thereby ; who else shut fire
I' the stone, to leap from mouth at sword's first
      stroke,
In lamps of love and faith, the chivalry
That dares the right and disregards alike
The yea and nay o' the world ? Self-sacri-
      fice, —
What if an idol took it ? Ask the Church
Why she was wont to turn each Venus here, —
Poor Rome perversely lingered round, despite
Instruction, for the sake of purblind love, —
Into Madonna's shape, and waste no whit
Of aught so rare on earth as gratitude !
All this sweet savor was not ours but thine,
Nard of the rock, a natural wealth we name
Incense, and treasure up as food for saints,
When flung to us — whose function was to give
Not find the costly perfume. Do I smile ?
Nay, Caponsacchi, much I find amiss,
Blameworthy, punishable in this freak
Of thine, this youth prolonged, though age was
      ripe,
This masquerade in sober day, with change
Of motley too, — now hypocrite's disguise,
Now fool's-costume : which lie was least like
      truth,
Which the ungainlier, more discordant garb,
With that symmetric soul inside my son,
The churchman's or the worldling's, — let him
      judge,
Our adversary who enjoys the task !
I rather chronicle the healthy rage, —
When the first moan broke from the martyr-
      maid
At that uncaging of the beasts, —made bare
My athlete on the instant, gave such good
Great undisguised leap over post and pale
Right into the mid-cirque, free fighting-place.
There may have been rash stripping — every
      rag
Went to the winds, — infringement manifold
Of laws prescribed pudicity, I fear,
In this impulsive and prompt self-display !
Ever such tax comes of the foolish youth ;
Men mulct the wiser manhood, and suspect
No veritable star swims out of cloud.
Bear thou such imputation, undergo
The penalty I nowise dare relax, —
Conventional chastisement and rebuke.
But for the outcome, the brave starry birth
Conciliating earth with all that cloud.

Thank heaven as I do! Ay, such champion-
ship
Of God at first blush, such prompt cheery thud
Of glove on ground that answers ringingly
The challenge of the false knight, — watch we
long,
And wait we vainly for its gallant like
From those appointed to the service, sworn
His body-guard with pay and privilege —
White-cinct, because in white walks sanctity,
Red-socked, how else proclaim fine scorn of
flesh,
Unchariness of blood when blood faith begs !
Where are the men-at-arms with cross on coat ?
Aloof, bewraying their attire : whilst thou
In mask and motley, pledged to dance not
fight,
Sprang'st forth the hero ! In thought, word
and deed,
How throughout all thy warfare thou wast
pure,
I find it easy to believe : and if
At any fateful moment of the strange
Adventure, the strong passion of that strait,
Fear and surprise, may have revealed too
much, —
As when a thundrous midnight, with black air
That burns, raindrops that blister, breaks a
spell,
Draws out the excessive virtue of some
sheathed
Shut unsuspected flower that hoards and hides
Immensity of sweetness, — so, perchance,
Might the surprise and fear release too much
The perfect beauty of the body and soul
Thou savedst in thy passion for God's sake,
He who is Pity. Was the trial sore ?
Temptation sharp ? Thank God a second
time !
Why comes temptation but for man to meet
And master and make crouch beneath his foot,
And so be pedestalled in triumph ? Pray
" Lead us into no such temptations, Lord ! "
Yea, but, O Thou whose servants are the bold,
Lead such temptations by the head and hair,
Reluctant dragons, up to who dares fight,
That so he may do battle and have praise !
Do I not see the praise ? — that while thy mates
Bound to deserve i' the matter, prove at need
Unprofitable through the very pains
We gave to train them well and start them
fair, —
Are found too stiff, with standing ranked and
ranged,
For onset in good earnest, too obtuse
Of ear, through iteration of command,
For catching quick the sense of the real cry, —
Thou, whose sword-hand was used to strike the
lute,
Whose sentry-station graced some wanton's
gate,
Thou didst push forward and show mettle,
shame
The laggards, and retrieve the day. Well
done !
Be glad thou hast let light into the world,
Through that irregular breach o' the boundary,
— see

The same upon thy path and march assured,
Learning anew the use of soldiership,
Self-abnegation, freedom from all fear,
Loyalty to the life's end ! Ruminate,
Deserve the initiatory spasm, — once more
Work, be unhappy but bear life, my son !

And troop you, somewhere 'twixt the best and
worst,
Where crowd the indifferent product, all too
poor
Makeshift, starved samples of humanity !
Father and mother, huddle there and hide !
A gracious eye may find you ! Foul and fair,
Sadly mixed natures : self-indulgent, — yet
Self-sacrificing too : how the love soars,
How the craft, avarice, vanity and spite
Sink again ! So they keep the middle course,
Slide into silly crime at unaware,
Slip back upon the stupid virtue, stay
Nowhere enough for being classed, I hope
And fear. Accept the swift and rueful death
Taught, somewhat sternlier than is wont, what
waits
The ambiguous creature, — how the one black
tuft
Steadies the aim of the arrow just as well
As the wide faultless white on the bird's
breast !
Nay, you were punished in the very part
That looked most pure of speck, 't was honest
love
Betrayed you, — did love seem most worthy
pains,
Challenge such purging, since ordained survive
When all the rest of you was done with ? Go !
Never again elude the choice of tints !
White shall not neutralize the black, nor good
Compensate bad in man, absolve him so :
Life's business being just the terrible choice.

So do I see, pronounce on all and some
Grouped for my judgment now, — profess no
doubt
While I pronounce : dark, difficult enough
The human sphere, yet eyes grow sharp by use
I find the truth, dispart the shine from shade,
As a mere man may, with no special touch
O' the lynx-gift in each ordinary orb :
Nay, if the popular notion class me right,
One of wellnigh decayed intelligence, —
What of that ? Through hard labor and good
will,
And habitude that gives a blind man sight
At the practised finger-ends of him, I do
Discern, and dare decree in consequence,
Whatever prove the peril of mistake.
Whence, then, this quite new quick cold thrill,
— cloud-like,
This keen dread creeping from a quarter scarce
Suspected in the skies I nightly scan ?
What slacks the tense nerve, saps the wound-
up spring
Of the act that should and shall be, sends the
mount
And mass o' the whole man's-strength, — con-
globed so late —
Shudderingly into dust, a moment's work ?

While I stand firm, go fearless, in this world,
For this life recognize and arbitrate,
Touch and let stay, or else remove a thing,
Judge " This is right, this object out of place,"
Candle in hand that helps me and to spare, —
What if a voice deride me, " Perk and pry !
Brighten each nook with thine intelligence !
Play the good householder, ply man and maid
With tasks prolonged into the midnight, test
Their work and nowise stint of the due wage
Each worthy worker: but with gyves and whip
Pay thou misprision of a single point
Plain to thy happy self who lift'st the light,
Lament'st the darkling, — bold to all beneath !
What if thyself adventure, now the place
Is purged so well ?   Leave pavement and mount
        roof,
Look round thee for the light of the upper sky,
The fire which lit thy fire which finds default
In Guido Franceschini to his cost !
What if, above in the domain of light,
Thou miss the accustomed signs, remark
        eclipse ?
Shalt thou still gaze on ground nor lift a lid, —
Steady in thy superb prerogative,
Thy inch of inkling, — nor once face the doubt
I' the sphere above thee, darkness to be felt ? "

Yet my poor spark had for its source, the sun ;
Thither I sent the great looks which compel
Light from its fount : all that I do and am
Comes from the truth, or seen or else surmised,
Remembered or divined, as mere man may :
I know just so, nor otherwise.   As I know,
I speak, — what should I know, then, and how
        speak
Were there a wild mistake of eye or brain
As to recorded governance above ?
If my own breath, only, blew coal alight
I styled celestial and the morning-star ?
I, who in this world act resolvedly,
Dispose of men, their bodies and their souls,
As they acknowledge or gainsay the light
I show them, — shall I too lack courage ? —
        leave
I, too, the post of me, like those I blame ?
Refuse, with kindred inconsistency,
To grapple danger whereby souls grow strong ?
I am near the end ; but still not at the end ;
All to the very end is trial in life :
At this stage is the trial of my soul
Danger to face, or danger to refuse ?
Shall I dare try the doubt now, or not dare ?

O Thou, — as represented here to me
In such conception as my soul allows, —
Under Thy measureless, my atom width ! —
Man's mind, what is it but a convex glass
Wherein are gathered all the scattered points
Picked out of the immensity of sky,
To reunite there, be our heaven for earth,
Our known unknown, our God revealed to
        man ?
Existent somewhere, somehow, as a whole ;
Here, as a whole proportioned to our sense, —
There, (which is nowhere, speech must babble
        thus !)
In the absolute immensity, the whole

Appreciable solely by Thyself, —
Here, by the little mind of man, reduced
To littleness that suits his faculty,
In the degree appreciable too ;
Between Thee and ourselves — nay even,
        again,
Below us, to the extreme of the minute,
Appreciable by how many and what diverse
Modes of the life Thou madest be ! (why live
Except for love, — how love unless they know ?)
Each of them, only filling to the edge,
Insect or angel, his just length and breadth,
Due facet of reflection, — full, no less,
Angel or insect, as Thou framedst things.
I it is who have been appointed here
To represent Thee, in my turn, on earth,
Just as, if any philosophy know aught,
This one earth, out of all the multitude
Of peopled worlds, as stars are now supposed, —
Was chosen, and no sun-star of the swarm,
For stage and scene of Thy transcendent act
Beside which even the creation fades
Into a puny exercise of power.
Choice of the world, choice of the thing I am,
Both emanate alike from Thy dread play
Of operation outside this our sphere
Where things are classed and counted small or
        great, —
Incomprehensibly the choice is Thine !
I therefore bow my head and take Thy place.
There is, beside the works, a tale of Thee
In the world's mouth, which I find credible :
I love it with my heart : unsatisfied,
I try it with my reason, nor discept
From any point I probe and pronounce sound.
Mind is not matter nor from matter, but
Above, — leave matter then, proceed with
        mind !
Man's be the mind recognized at the height, —
Leave the inferior minds and look at man !
Is he the strong, intelligent and good
Up to his own conceivable height ?   Nowise.
Enough o' the low, — soar the conceivable
        height,
Find cause to match the effect in evidence,
The work i' the world, not man's but God's ;
        leave man !
Conjecture of the worker by the work :
Is there strength there ? — enough : intelli-
        gence ?
Ample : but goodness in a like degree ?
Not to the human eye in the present state,
An isoscele deficient in the base.
What lacks, then, of perfection fit for God
But just the instance which this tale supplies
Of love without a limit ?   So is strength,
So is intelligence ; let love be so,
Unlimited in its self-sacrifice,
Then is the tale true and God shows complete.
Beyond the tale, I reach into the dark,
Feel what I cannot see, and still faith stands :
I can believe this dread machinery
Of sin and sorrow, would confound me else,
Devised — all pain, at most expenditure
Of pain by Who devised pain — to evolve,
By new machinery in counterpart,
The moral qualities of man — how else ? —
To make him love in turn and be beloved,

Creative and self-sacrificing too,
And thus eventually God-like, (ay,
" I have said ye are Gods," — shall it be said
    for naught ?)
Enable man to wring, from out all pain,
All pleasure for a common heritage
To all eternity : this may be surmised,
The other is revealed, — whether a fact,
Absolute, abstract, independent truth,
Historic, not reduced to suit man's mind, —
Or only truth reverberate, changed, made pass
A spectrum into mind, the narrow eye, —
The same and not the same, else unconceived —
Though quite conceivable to the next grade
Above it in intelligence, — as truth
Easy to man were blindness to the beast
By parity of procedure, — the same truth
In a new form, but changed in either case :
What matter so intelligence be filled ?
To a child, the sea is angry, for it roars :
Frost bites, else why the tooth-like fret on
    face ?
Man makes acoustics deal with the sea's wrath,
Explains the choppy cheek by chymic law, —
To man and child remains the same effect
On drum of ear and root of nose, change cause
Never so thoroughly : so my heart be struck,
What care I, — by God's gloved hand or the
    bare ?
Nor do I much perplex me with aught hard,
Dubious in the transmitting of the tale, —
No, nor with certain riddles set to solve.
This life is training and a passage ; pass, —
Still, we march over some flat obstacle
We made give way before us ; solid truth
In front of it, what motion for the world ?
The moral sense grows but by exercise.
'T is even as man grew probatively
Initiated in Godship, set to make
A fairer moral world than this he finds,
Guess now what shall be known hereafter.
    Deal
Thus with the present problem : as we see,
A faultless creature is destroyed, and sin
Has had its way i' the world where God should
    rule.
Ay, but for this irrelevant circumstance
Of inquisition after blood, we see
Pompilia lost and Guido saved : how long ?
For his whole life : how much is that whole
    life ?
We are not babes, but know the minute's
    worth,
And feel that life is large and the world small,
So, wait till life have passed from out the
    world.
Neither does this astonish at the end,
That whereas I can so receive and trust,
Other men, made with hearts and souls the
    same,
Reject and disbelieve, — subordinate
The future to the present, — sin, nor fear.
This I refer still to the foremost fact,
Life is probation and the earth no goal
But starting-point of man : compel him strive,
Which means, in man, as good as reach the
    goal, —
Why institute that race, his life, at all ?

But this does overwhelm me with surprise,
Touch me to terror, — not that faith, the
    pearl,
Should be let lie by fishers wanting food, —
Nor, seen and handled by a certain few
Critical and contemptuous, straight consigned
To shore and shingle for the pebble it proves, —
But that, when haply found and known and
    named
By the residue made rich forevermore,
These, — that these favored ones, should in a
    trice
Turn, and with double zest go dredge for
    whelks,
Mud - worms that make the savory soup !
    Enough
O' the disbelievers, see the faithful few !
How do the Christians here deport them, keep
Their robes of white unspotted by the world ?
What is this Aretine Archbishop, this
Man under me as I am under God,
This champion of the faith, I armed and
    decked,
Pushed forward, put upon a pinnacle,
To show the enemy his victor, — see !
What 's the best fighting when the couple
    close ?
Pompilia cries, " Protect me from the wolf ! "
He — " No, thy Guido is rough, heady, strong,
Dangerous to disquiet : let him bide !
He needs some bone to mumble, help amuse
The darkness of his den with : so, the fawn
Which limps up bleeding to my foot and lies,
— Come to me, daughter ! — thus I throw him
    back ! "
Have we misjudged here, over - armed our
    knight,
Given gold and silk where plain hard steel
    serves best,
Enfeebled whom we sought to fortify,
Made an archbishop and undone a saint ?
Well, then, descend these heights, this pride of
    life,
Sit in the ashes with a barefoot monk
Who long ago stamped out the worldly sparks,
By fasting, watching, stone cell and wire
    scourge,
— No such indulgence as unknits the strength —
These breed the tight nerve and tough cuticle,
And the world's praise or blame runs rillet-
    wise
Off the broad back and brawny breast, we
    know !
He meets the first cold sprinkle of the world,
And shudders to the marrow. " Save this child ?
Oh, my superiors, oh, the Archbishop's self !
Who was it dared lay hand upon the ark
His betters saw fall nor put finger forth ?
Great ones could help yet help not : why should
    small ?
I break my promise : let her break her heart ! "
These are the Christians not the worldlings, not
The sceptics, who thus battle for the faith !
If foolish virgins disobey and sleep,
What wonder ? But, this time, the wise that
    watch,
Sell lamps and buy lutes, exchange oil for wine,
The mystic Spouse betrays the Bridegroom here

To our last resource, then! Since all flesh is
weak,
Bind weaknesses together, we get strength:
The individual weighed, found wanting, try
Some institution, honest artifice
Whereby the units grow compact and firm!
Each props the other, and so stand is made
By our embodied cowards that grow brave.
The Monastery called of Convertites,
Meant to help women because these helped
Christ, —
A thing existent only while it acts,
Does as designed, else a nonentity, —
For what is an idea unrealized? —
Pompilia is consigned to these for help.
They do help: they are prompt to testify
To her pure life and saintly dying days.
She dies, and lo, who seemed so poor, proves
rich!
What does the body that lives through helpful-
ness
To women for Christ's sake? The kiss turns
bite,
The dove's note changes to the crow's cry:
judge!
"Seeing that this our Convent claims of right
What goods belong to those we succor, be
The same proved women of dishonest life, —
And seeing that this Trial made appear
Pompilia was in such predicament, —
The Convent hereupon pretends to said
Succession of Pompilia, issues writ,
And takes possession by the Fisc's advice."
Such is their attestation to the cause
Of Christ, who had one saint at least, they
hoped:
But, is a title-deed to filch, a corpse
To slander, and an infant-heir to cheat?
Christ must give up his gains then! They unsay
All the fine speeches, — who was saint is whore.
Why, scripture yields no parallel for this!
The soldiers only threw dice for Christ's coat;
We want another legend of the Twelve
Disputing if it was Christ's coat at all,
Claiming as prize the woof of price — for why?
The Master was a thief, purloined the same,
Or paid for it out of the common bag!
Can it be this is end and outcome, all
I take with me to show as stewardship's fruit,
The best yield of the latest time, this year
The seventeen-hundredth since God died for
man?
Is such effect proportionate to cause?
And still the terror keeps on the increase
When I perceive . . . how can I blink the fact?
That the fault, the obduracy to good,
Lies not with the impracticable stuff
Whence man is made, his very nature's fault,
As if it were of ice the moon may gild
Not melt, or stone 't was meant the sun should
warm
Not make bear flowers, — nor ice nor stone to
blame:
But it can melt, that ice, can bloom, that stone,
Impassible to rule of day and night!
This terrifies me, thus compelled perceive,
Whatever love and faith we looked should spring
At advent of the authoritative star,

Which yet lie sluggish, curdled at the source, —
These have leapt forth profusely in old time,
These still respond with promptitude to-day,
At challenge of — what unacknowledged powers
O' the air, what uncommissioned meteors
warmth
By law, and light by rule should supersede?
For see this priest, this Caponsacchi, stung
At the first summons, — "Help for honor
sake,
Play the man, pity the oppressed!" — no pause,
How does he lay about him in the midst,
Strike any foe, right wrong at any risk,
All blindness, bravery and obedience! — blind?
Ay, as a man would be inside the sun,
Delirious with the plenitude of light
Should interfuse him to the finger-ends —
Let him rush straight, and how shall he go
wrong?
Where are the Christians in their panoply?
The loins we girt about with truth, the breasts
Righteousness plated round, the shield of faith,
The helmet of salvation, and that sword
O' the Spirit, even the word of God, — where
these?
Slunk into corners! Oh, I hear at once
Hubbub of protestation! "What, we monks,
We friars, of such an order, such a rule,
Have not we fought, bled, left our martyr-mark
At every point along the boundary-line
'Twixt true and false, religion and the world,
Where this or the other dogma of our Church
Called for defence?" And I, despite myself,
How can I but speak loud what truth speaks
low,
"Or better than the best, or nothing serves!
What boots deed, I can cap and cover straight
With such another doughtiness to match,
Done at an instinct of the natural man?"
Immolate body, sacrifice soul too, —
Do not these publicans the same? Outstrip!
Or else stop race you boast runs neck and neck,
You with the wings, they with the feet, — for
shame!
Oh, I remark your diligence and zeal!
Five years long, now, rounds faith into my ears,
"Help thou, or Christendom is done to death!"
Five years since, in the Province of To-kien,
Which is in China as some people know,
Maigrot, my Vicar Apostolic there,
Having a great qualm, issues a decree.
Alack, the converts use as God's name, not
Tien-chu but plain *Tien* or else mere *Shang-ti*,
As Jesuits please to fancy politic,
While, say Dominicans, it calls down fire, —
For *Tien* means heaven, and *Shang-ti*, supreme
prince,
While *Tien-chu* means the lord of heaven: all
cry,
"There is no business urgent for dispatch
As that thou send a legate, specially
Cardinal Tournon, straight to Pekin, there
To settle and compose the difference!"
So have I seen a potentate all fume
For some infringement of his realm's just right,
Some menace to a mud-built straw-thatched
farm
O' the frontier; while inside the mainland lie,

Quite undisputed-for in solitude,
Whole cities plague may waste or famine sap :
What if the sun crumble, the sands encroach,
While he looks on sublimely at his ease ?
How does their ruin touch the empire's bound ?

And is this little all that was to be ?
Where is the gloriously-decisive change,
Metamorphosis the immeasurable
Of human clay to divine gold, we looked
Should, in some poor sort, justify its price ?
Had an adept of the mere Rosy Cross
Spent his life to consummate the Great Work,
Would not we start to see the stuff it touched
Yield not a grain more than the vulgar got
By the old smelting-process years ago ?
If this were sad to see in just the sage
Who should profess so much, perform no more,
What is it when suspected in that Power
Who undertook to make and made the world,
Devised and did effect man, body and soul,
Ordained salvation for them both, and yet . . .
Well, is the thing we see, salvation ?
                                        I
Put no such dreadful question to myself,
Within whose circle of experience burns
The central truth, Power, Wisdom, Good-
        ness, — God :
I must outlive a thing ere know it dead :
When I outlive the faith there is a sun,
When I lie, ashes to the very soul, —
Some one, not I, must wail above the heap,
" He died in dark whence never morn arose."
While I see day succeed the deepest night —
How can I speak but as I know ? — my speech
Must be, throughout the darkness, " It will
        end :
The light that did burn, will burn ! "   Clouds
        obscure —
But for which obscuration all were bright ?
Too hastily concluded !   Sun-suffused,
A cloud may soothe the eye made blind by
        blaze, —
Better the very clarity of heaven :
The soft streaks are the beautiful and dear.
What but the weakness in a faith supplies
The incentive to humanity, no strength
Absolute, irresistible, comports ?
How can man love but what he yearns to help ?
And that which men think weakness within
        strength,
But angels know for strength and stronger
        yet —
What were it else but the first things made new,
But repetition of the miracle,
The divine instance of self-sacrifice
That never ends and aye begins for man ?
So, never I miss footing in the maze,
No, — I have light nor fear the dark at all.

But are mankind not real, who pace outside
My petty circle, world that 's measured me ?
And when they stumble even as I stand,
Have I a right to stop ear when they cry,
As they were phantoms who took clouds for
        crags,
Tripped and fell, where man's march might
        safely move ?

Beside, the cry is other than a ghost's,
When out of the old time there pleads some
        bard,
Philosopher, or both, and — whispers not,
But words it boldly.   " The inward work and
        worth
Of any mind, what other mind may judge
Save God who only knows the thing he made.
The veritable service he exacts ?
It is the outward product men appraise.
Behold, an engine hoists a tower aloft :
' I looked that it should move the mountain
        too ! '
Or else ' Had just a turret toppled down,
Success enough ! ' — may say the Machinist
Who knows what less or more result might be :
But we, who see that done we cannot do,
' A feat beyond man's force,' we men must say.
Regard me and that shake I gave the world !
I was born, not so long before Christ's birth
As Christ's birth haply did precede thy day, —
But many a watch before the star of dawn :
Therefore I lived, — it is thy creed affirms,
Pope Innocent, who art to answer me ! —
Under conditions, nowise to escape,
Whereby salvation was impossible.
Each impulse to achieve the good and fair,
Each aspiration to the pure and true,
Being without a warrant or an aim,
Was just as sterile a felicity
As if the insect, born to spend his life
Soaring his circles, stopped them to describe
(Painfully motionless in the mid-air)
Some word of weighty counsel for man's sake,
Some ' Know thyself ' or ' Take the golden
        mean ! '
— Forwent his happy dance and the glad ray,
Died half an hour the sooner and was dust.
I, born to perish like the brutes, or worse,
Why not live brutishly, obey brutes' law ?
But I, of body as of soul complete,
A gymnast at the games, philosopher
I' the schools, who painted, and made music,
        — all
Glories that met upon the tragic stage
When the Third Poet's tread surprised the
        Two, —
Whose lot fell in a land where life was great
And sense went free and beauty lay profuse,
I, untouched by one adverse circumstance,
Adopted virtue as my rule of life,
Waived all reward, loved but for loving's sake,
And, what my heart taught me, I taught the
        world,
And have been teaching now two thousand
        years.
Witness my work, — plays that should please,
        forsooth !
' They might please, they may displease, they
        shall teach,
For truth's sake,' so I said, and did, and do.
Five hundred years ere Paul spoke, Felix
        heard, —
How much of temperance and righteousness,
Judgment to come, did I find reason for,
Corroborate with my strong style that spared
No sin, nor swerved the more from branding
        brow

Because the sinner was called Zeus and God?
How nearly did I guess at that Paul knew?
How closely come, in what I represent
As duty, to his doctrine yet a blank?
And as that limner not untruly limns
Who draws an object round or square, which
  square
Or round seems to the unassisted eye,
Though Galileo's tube display the same
Oval or oblong, — so, who controverts
I rendered rightly what proves wrongly
  wrought
Beside Paul's picture? Mine was true for me.
I saw that there are, first and above all,
The hidden forces, blind necessities,
Named Nature, but the thing's self uncon-
  ceived:
Then follow — how dependent upon these,
We know not, how imposed above ourselves,
We well know — what I name the gods, a
  power
Various or one: for great and strong and good
Is there, and little, weak and bad there too,
Wisdom and folly: say, these make no God, —
What is it else that rules outside man's self?
A fact then, — always, to the naked eye, —
And so, the one revealment possible
Of what were unimagined else by man.
Therefore, what gods do, man may criticise,
Applaud, condemn, — how should he fear the
  truth? —
But likewise have in awe because of power,
Venerate for the main munificence,
And give the doubtful deed its due excuse
From the acknowledged creature of a day
To the Eternal and Divine. Thus, bold
Yet self-mistrusting, should man bear himself,
Most assured on what now concerns him most —
The law of his own life, the path he prints, —
Which law is virtue and not vice, I say, —
And least inquisitive where search least skills,
I' the nature we best give the clouds to keep.
What could I paint beyond a scheme like this
Out of the fragmentary truths where light
Lay fitful in a tenebrific time?
You have the sunrise now, joins truth to truth,
Shoots life and substance into death and void;
Themselves compose the whole we made before:
The forces and necessity grow God, —
The beings so contrarious that seemed gods,
Prove just his operation manifold
And multiform, translated, as must be,
Into intelligible shape so far
As suits our sense and sets us free to feel.
What if I let a child think, childhood-long,
That lightning, I would have him spare his eye,
Is a real arrow shot at naked orb?
The man knows more, but shuts his lids the
  same:
Lightning's cause comprehends nor man nor
  child.
Why then, my scheme, your better knowledge
  broke,
Presently readjusts itself, the small
Proportioned largelier, parts and whole named
  new:
So much, no more two thousand years have
  done!

Pope, dost thou dare pretend to punish me,
For not descrying sunshine at midnight,
Me who crept all-fours, found my way so far —
While thou rewardest teachers of the truth,
Who miss the plain way in the blaze of noon, —
Though just a word from that strong style of
  mine,
Grasped honestly in hand as guiding-staff,
Had pricked them a sure path across the bog,
That mire of cowardice and slush of lies
Wherein I find them wallow in wide day!"

How should I answer this Euripides?
Paul — 'tis a legend — answered Seneca,
But that was in the day-spring; noon is now,
We have got too familiar with the light.
Shall I wish back once more that thrill of
  dawn?
When the whole truth-touched man burned up,
  one fire?
— Assured the trial, fiery, fierce, but fleet,
Would, from his little heap of ashes, lend
Wings to that conflagration of the world
Which Christ awaits ere he makes all things
  new:
So should the frail become the perfect, rapt
From glory of pain to glory of joy; and so,
Even in the end, — the act renouncing earth,
Lands, houses, husbands, wives and children
  here, —
Begin that other act which finds all, lost,
Regained, in this time even, a hundredfold,
And, in the next time, feels the finite love
Blent and embalmed with the eternal life.
So does the sun ghastlily seem to sink
In those north parts, lean all but out of life,
Desist a dread mere breathing-stop, then slow
Re-assert day, begin the endless rise.
Was this too easy for our after-stage?
Was such a lighting-up of faith, in life,
Only allowed initiate, set man's step
In the true way by help of the great glow?
A way wherein it is ordained he walk,
Bearing to see the light from heaven still more
And more encroached on by the light of earth,
Tentatives earth puts forth to rival heaven,
Earthly incitements that mankind serve God
For man's sole sake, not God's and therefore
  man's.
Till at last, who distinguishes the sun
From a mere Druid fire on a far mount?
More praise to him who with his subtle prism
Shall decompose both beams and name the true
In such sense, who is last proves first indeed;
For how could saints and martyrs fail see
  truth
Streak the night's blackness? Who is faithful
  now,
Who untwists heaven's white from the yellow
  flare
O' the world's gross torch, without night's foil
  that helped
Produce the Christian act so possible
When in the way stood Nero's cross and
  stake, —
So hard now when the world smiles "Right and
  wise!
Faith points the politic, the thrifty way.

Will make who plods it in the end returns
Beyond mere fool's-sport and improvidence.
We fools dance through the cornfield of this
    life,
Pluck ears to left and right and swallow raw,
— Nay, tread, at pleasure, a sheaf underfoot,
To get the better at some poppy-flower, —
Well aware we shall have so much less wheat
In the eventual harvest : you meantime
Waste not a spike, — the richlier will you reap !
What then ? There will be always garnered
    meal
Sufficient for our comfortable loaf,
While you enjoy the undiminished sack ! "
Is it not this ignoble confidence,
Cowardly hardihood, that dulls and damps,
Makes the old heroism impossible ?

Unless . . . what whispers me of times to
    come ?
What if it be the mission of that age
My death will usher into life, to shake
This torpor of assurance from our creed,
Reintroduce the doubt discarded, bring
That formidable danger back, we drove
Long ago to the distance and the dark ?
No wild beast now prowls round the infant
    camp :
We have built wall and sleep in city safe :
But if some earthquake try the towers that
    laugh,
To think they once saw lions rule outside,
And man stand out again, pale, resolute,
Prepared to die, — which means, alive at last ?
As we broke up that old faith of the world,
Have we, next age, to break up this the new —
Faith, in the thing, grown faith in the report —
Whence need to bravely disbelieve report
Through increased faith i' the thing reports be-
    lie ?
Must we deny, — do they, these Molinists,
At peril of their body and their soul, —
Recognized truths, obedient to some truth
Unrecognized yet, but perceptible ? —
Correct the portrait by the living face,
Man's God, by God's God in the mind of man ?
Then, for the few that rise to the new height,
The many that must sink to the old depth,
The multitude found fall away ! A few,
E'en ere new law speak clear, may keep the
    old,
Preserve the Christian level, call good good
And evil evil, (even though razed and blank
The old titles,) helped by custom, habitude,
And all else they mistake for finer sense
O' the fact that reason warrants, — as before.
They hope perhaps, fear not impossibly,
At least some one Pompilia left the world
Will say " I know the right place by foot's feel,
I took it and tread firm there ; wherefore
    change ? "
But what a multitude will surely fall
Quite through the crumbling truth, late sub-
    jacent,
Sink to the next discoverable base,
Rest upon human nature, settle there
On what is firm, the lust and pride of life !
A mass of men, whose very souls even now

Seem to need re-creating, — so they slink
Worm-like into the mud, light now lays
    bare, —
Whose future we dispose of with shut eyes
And whisper — " They are grafted, barren
    twigs,
Into the living stock of Christ : may bear
One day, till when they lie death-like, not
    dead," —
Those who with all the aid of Christ succumb,
How, without Christ, shall they, unaided,
    sink ?
Whither but to this gulf before my eyes ?
Do not we end, the century and I ?
The impatient antimasque treads close on kibe
O' the very masque's self it will mock, — on
    me,
Last lingering personage, the impatient mime
Pushes already, — will I block the way ?
Will my slow trail of garments ne'er leave
    space
For pantaloon, sock, plume and castanet ?
Here comes the first experimentalist
In the new order of things, — he plays a priest ;
Does he take inspiration from the Church,
Directly make her rule his law of life ?
Not he : his own mere impulse guides the
    man —
Happily sometimes, since ourselves allow
He has danced, in gayety of heart, i' the main
The right step through the maze we bade him
    foot.
But if his heart had prompted him break loose
And mar the measure ? Why, we must sub-
    mit,
And thank the chance that brought him safe so
    far.
Will he repeat the prodigy ? Perhaps.
Can he teach others how to quit themselves,
Show why this step was right while that were
    wrong ?
How should he ? " Ask your hearts as I asked
    mine,
And get discreetly through the morrice too ;
If your hearts misdirect you, — quit the stage,
And make amends, — be there amends to
    make ! "
Such is, for the Augustin that was once,
This Canon Caponsacchi we see now.
" But my heart answers to another tune,"
Puts in the Abate, second in the suite ;
" I have my taste too, and tread no such step'
You choose the glorious life, and may, for me !
I like the lowest of life's appetites, —
So you judge, — but the very truth of joy
To my own apprehension which decides.
Call me knave and you get yourself called
    fool !
I live for greed, ambition, lust, revenge ;
Attain these ends by force, guile : hypocrite,
To-day perchance to-morrow recognized
The rational man, the type of common sense."
There 's Loyola adapted to our time !
Under such guidance Guido plays his part,
He also influencing in the due turn
These last clods where I track intelligence
By any glimmer, these four at his beck
Ready to murder any, and, at their own.

As ready to murder him, — such make the world!
And, first effect of the new cause of things,
There they lie also duly, — the old pair
Of the weak head and not so wicked heart,
With the one Christian mother, wife and girl,
— Which three gifts seem to make an angel up, —
The world's first foot o' the dance is on their heads!
Still, I stand here, not off the stage though close
On the exit: and my last act, as my first,
I owe the scene, and Him who armed me thus
With Paul's sword as with Peter's key. I smite
With my whole strength once more, ere end my part,
Ending, so far as man may, this offence.
And when I raise my arm, who plucks my sleeve?
Who stops me in the righteous function, — foe
Or friend? Oh, still as ever, friends are they
Who, in the interest of outraged truth
Deprecate such rough handling of a lie!
The facts being proved and incontestable,
What is the last word I must listen to?
Perchance — "Spare yet a term this barren stock,
We pray thee dig about and dung and dress
Till he repent and bring forth fruit even yet!"
Perchance — "So poor and swift a punishment
Shall throw him out of life with all that sin:
Let mercy rather pile up pain on pain
Till the flesh expiate what the soul pays else!"
Nowise! Remonstrants on each side commence
Instructing, there's a new tribunal now
Higher than God's — the educated man's!
Nice sense of honor in the human breast
Supersedes here the old coarse oracle —
Confirming none the less a point or so
Wherein blind predecessors worked aright
By rule of thumb: as when Christ said, — when, where?
Enough, I find it pleaded in a place, —
"All other wrongs done, patiently I take:
But touch my honor and the case is changed!
I feel the due resentment, — *nemini
Honorem trado* is my quick retort."
Right of Him, just as if pronounced to-day!
Still, should the old authority be mute
Or doubtful, or in speaking clash with new,
The younger takes permission to decide.
At last we have the instinct of the world
Ruling its household without tutelage:
And while the two laws, human and divine,
Have busied finger with this tangled case,
In pushes the brisk junior, cuts the knot,
Pronounces for acquittal. How it trips
Silverly o'er the tongue! "Remit the death!
Forgive, . . . well, in the old way, if thou please,
Decency and the relics of routine
Respected, — let the Count go free as air!
Since he may plead a priest's immunity, —
The minor orders help enough for that,
With Farinacci's license, — who decides
That the mere implication of such man,

So privileged, in any cause, before
Whatever Court except the Spiritual,
Straight quashes law-procedure, — quash it, then!
Remains a pretty loophole of escape
Moreover, that, beside the patent fact
O' the law's allowance, there's involved the weal
O' the Popedom: a son's privilege at stake,
Thou wilt pretend the Church's interest,
Ignore all finer reasons to forgive!
But herein lies the crowning cogency —
(Let thy friends teach thee while thou tellest beads)
That in this case the spirit of culture speaks,
Civilization is imperative.
To her shall we remand all delicate points
Henceforth, nor take irregular advice
O' the sly, as heretofore: she used to hint
Remonstrances, when law was out of sorts
Because a saucy tongue was put to rest,
An eye that roved was cured of arrogance:
But why be forced to mumble under breath
What soon shall be acknowledged as plain fact,
Outspoken, say, in thy successor's time?
Methinks we see the golden age return!
Civilization and the Emperor
Succeed to Christianity and Pope.
One Emperor then, as one Pope now: meanwhile,
Anticipate a little! We tell thee 'Take
Guido's life, sapped society shall crash,
Whereof the main prop was, is, and shall be
— Supremacy of husband over wife!'
Does the man rule i' the house, and may his mate
Because of any plea dispute the same?
Oh, pleas of all sorts shall abound, be sure,
One but allowed validity, — for, harsh
And savage, for, inept and silly-sooth,
For, this and that, will the ingenious sex
Demonstrate the best master e'er graced slave:
And there's but one short way to end the coil, —
Acknowledge right and reason steadily
I' the man and master: then the wife submits
To plain truth broadly stated. Does the time
Advise we shift — a pillar? nay, a stake
Out of its place i' the social tenement?
One touch may send a shudder through the heap
And bring it toppling on our children's heads!
Moreover, if ours breed a qualm in thee,
Give thine own better feeling play for once!
Thou, whose own life winks o'er the socket-edge,
Wouldst thou it went out in such ugly snuff
As dooming sons dead, e'en though justice prompt?
Why, on a certain feast, Barabbas' self
Was set free, not to cloud the general cheer:
Neither shalt thou pollute thy Sabbath close!
Mercy is safe and graceful. How one hears
The howl begin, scarce the three little taps
O' the silver mallet silent on thy brow, —
'His last act was to sacrifice a Count
And thereby screen a scandal of the Church!
Guido condemned, the Canon justified

Of course, — delinquents of his cloth go free ! '
And so the Luthers chuckle, Calvins scowl,
So thy hand helps Molinos to the chair
Whence he may hold forth till doom's day on
     just
These *petit-maître* priestlings, — in the choir,
Sanctus et Benedictus, with a brush
Of soft guitar-strings that obey the thumb,
Touched by the bedside, for accompaniment !
Does this give umbrage to a husband ?   Death
To the fool, and to the priest impunity !
But no impunity to any friend
So simply over-loyal as these four
Who made religion of their patron's cause,
Believed in him and did his bidding straight,
Asked not one question but laid down the lives
This Pope took, — all four lives together make
Just his own length of days, — so, dead they
     lie,
As these were times when loyalty 's a drug,
And zeal in a subordinate too cheap
And common to be saved when we spend life !
Come, 't is too much good breath we waste in
     words :
The pardon, Holy Father !   Spare grimace,
Shrugs and reluctance !   Are not we the world,
Art not thou Priam ? let soft culture plead
Hecuba-like, ' *non tali* ' (Virgil serves)
' *Auxilio*,' and the rest !   Enough, it works !
The Pope relaxes, and the Prince is loth,
The father's bowels yearn, the man's will
     bends,
Reply is apt.   Our tears on tremble, hearts
Big with a benediction, wait the word
Shall circulate through the city in a trice,
Set every window flaring, give each man
O' the mob his torch to wave for gratitude.
Pronounce then, for our breath and patience
     fail ! ''

I will, Sirs : but a voice other than yours
Quickens my spirit.   " *Quis pro Domino ?*
Who is upon the Lord's side ? '' asked the
     Count.
I, who write —
          " On receipt of this command,
Acquaint Count Guido and his fellows four
They die to-morrow : could it be to-night,
The better, but the work to do, takes time.
Set with all diligence a scaffold up,
Not in the customary place, by Bridge
Saint Angelo, where die the common sort ;
But since the man is noble, and his peers
By predilection haunt the People's Square,
There let him be beheaded in the midst,
And his companions hanged on either side :
So shall the quality see, fear, and learn.
All which work takes time : till to-morrow,
     then,
Let there be prayer incessant for the five ! ''

For the main criminal I have no hope
Except in such a suddenness of fate.
I stood at Naples once, a night so dark
I could have scarce conjectured there was earth
Anywhere, sky or sea or world at all :
But the night's black was burst through by a
     blaze —

Thunder struck blow on blow, earth groaned
     and bore,
Through her whole length of mountain visible :
There lay the city thick and plain with spires,
And, like a ghost disshrouded, white the sea.
So may the truth be flashed out by one blow,
And Guido see, one instant, and be saved.
Else I avert my face, nor follow him
Into that sad obscure sequestered state
Where God unmakes but to remake the soul
He else made first in vain ; which must not be
Enough, for I may die this very night :
And how should I dare die, this man let live ?

Carry this forthwith to the Governor !

XI

GUIDO

You are the Cardinal Acciaiuoli, and you,
Abate Panciatichi — two good Tuscan names :
Acciaiuoli — ah, your ancestor it was
Built the huge battlemented convent-block
Over the little forky flashing Greve
That takes the quick turn at the foot o' the
     hill
Just as one first sees Florence : oh those days !
'T is Ema, though, the other rivulet,
The one-arched brown brick bridge yawns over,
     — yes,
Gallop and go five minutes, and you gain
The Roman Gate from where the Ema's
     bridged :
Kingfishers fly there : how I see the bend
O'erturreted by Certosa which he built,
That Senescal (we styled him) of your House !
I do adjure you, help me, Sirs !   My blood
Comes from as far a source : ought it to end
This way, by leakage through their scaffold-
     planks
Into Rome's sink where her red refuse runs ?
Sirs, I beseech you by blood-sympathy,
If there be any vile experiment
In the air, — if this your visit simply prove,
When all 's done, just a well-intentioned trick,
That tries for truth truer than truth itself,
By startling up a man, ere break of day,
To tell him he must die at sunset, — pshaw !
That man 's a Franceschini ; feel his pulse,
Laugh at your folly, and let 's all go sleep !
You have my last word, — innocent am I
As Innocent my Pope and murderer,
Innocent as a babe, as Mary's own,
As Mary's self, — I said, say and repeat, —
And why, then, should I die twelve hours
     hence ?   I —
Whom, not twelve hours ago, the jailer bade
Turn to my straw-truss, settle and sleep sound
That I might wake the sooner, promptlier pay
His due of meat-and-drink-indulgence, cross
His palm with fee of the good-hand, beside,
As gallants use who go at large again !
For why ?   All honest Rome approved my part
Whoever owned wife, sister, daughter, — nay,
Mistress, — had any shadow of any right
That looks like right, and, all the more resolved

Held it with tooth and nail, — these manly men
Approved! I being for Rome, Rome was for
me.
Then, there's the point reserved, the subter-
fuge
My lawyers held by, kept for last resource,
Firm should all else — the impossible fancy! —
fail,
And sneaking burgess-spirit win the day.
The knaves! One plea at least would hold, —
they laughed, —
One grappling-iron scratch the bottom-rock
Even should the middle mud let anchor go!
I hooked my cause on to the Clergy's, — plea
Which, even if law tipped off my hat and plume,
Revealed my priestly tonsure, saved me so.
The Pope moreover, this old Innocent,
Being so meek and mild and merciful,
So fond o' the poor and so fatigued of earth,
So . . . fifty thousand devils in deepest hell!
Why must he cure us of our strange conceit
Of the angel in man's likeness, that we loved
And looked should help us at a pinch? He help?
He pardon? Here's his mind and message —
death!
Thank the good Pope! Now, is he good in
this,
Never mind, Christian, — no such stuff's ex-
tant, —
But will my death do credit to his reign,
Show he both lived and let live, so was good?
Cannot I live if he but like? "The Law!"
Why, just the law gives him the very chance,
The precise leave to let my life alone,
Which the archangelic soul of him (he says)
Yearns after! Here they drop it in his palm,
My lawyers, capital o' the cursed kind, —
Drop life to take and hold and keep: but no!
He sighs, shakes head, refuses to shut hand,
Motions away the gift they bid him grasp,
And of the coyness comes — that off I run
And down I go, he best knows whither! mind,
He knows, who sets me rolling all the same!
Disinterested Vicar of our Lord,
This way he abrogates and disallows,
Nullifies and ignores, — reverts in fine
To the good and right, in detriment of me!
Talk away! Will you have the naked truth?
He's sick of his life's supper, — swallowed lies:
So, hobbling bedward, needs must ease his maw
Just where I sit o' the doorsill. · Sir Abate,
Can you do nothing? Friends, we used to
frisk!
What of this sudden slash in a friend's face,
This cut across our good companionship
That showed its front so gay when both were
young?
Were not we put into a beaten path,
Bid pace the world, we nobles born and bred,
We body of friends with each his 'scutcheon
full
Of old achievement and impunity, —
Taking the laugh of morn and Sol's salute
As forth we fared, pricked on to breathe our
steeds
And take equestrian sport over the green
Under the blue, across the crop, — what care?
If we went prancing up hill and down dale,

In and out of the level and the straight,
By the bit of pleasant byway, where was harm?
Still Sol salutes me and the morning laughs:
I see my grandsire's hoofprints, — point the
spot
Where he drew rein, slipped saddle, and
stabbed knave
For daring throw gibe — much less, stone —
from pale:
Then back, and on, and up with the cavalcade.
Just so wend we, now canter, now converse,
Till, 'mid the jauncing pride and jaunty port,
Something of a sudden jerks at somebody —
A dagger is out, a flashing cut and thrust,
Because I play some prank my grandsire
played,
And here I sprawl: where is the company?
Gone!
A trot and a trample! Only I lie trapped,
Writhe in a certain novel springe just set
By the good old Pope: I'm first prize. Warn
me? Why?
Apprise me that the law o' the game is
changed?
Enough that I'm a warning, as I writhe,
To all and each my fellows of the file,
And make law plain henceforward past mis-
take,
"For such a prank, death is the penalty!"
Pope the Five Hundredth (what do I know or
care?)
Deputes your Eminency and Abateship
To announce that, twelve hours from this time,
he needs
I just essay upon my body and soul
The virtue of his brand-new engine, prove
Represser of the pranksome! I'm the first!
Thanks. Do you know what teeth you mean
to try
The sharpness of, on this soft neck and throat?
I know it, — I have seen and hate it, — ay,
As you shall, while I tell you! Let me talk,
Or leave me, at your pleasure! talk I must:
What is your visit but my lure to talk?
Nay, you have something to disclose? — a
smile,
At end of the forced sternness, means to mock
The heart-beats here? I call your two hearts
stone!
Is your charge to stay with me till I die?
Be tacit as your bench, then! Use your ears,
I use my tongue: how glibly yours will run
At pleasant supper-time . . . God's curse! . . .
to-night
When all the guests jump up, begin so brisk,
"Welcome, his Eminence who shrived the
wretch!
Now we shall have the Abate's story!"

Life!

How I could spill this overplus of mine
Among those hoar-haired, shrunk-shanked
odds and ends
Of body and soul old age is chewing dry!
Those windle-straws that stare while purblind
death
Mows here, mows there, makes hay of juicy me,
And misses just the bunch of withered weed

Would brighten hell and streak its smoke with
　　flame !
How the life I could shed yet never shrink,
Would drench their stalks with sap like grass
　　in May !
Is it not terrible, I entreat you, Sirs ?
With manifold and plenitudinous life,
Prompt at death's menace to give blow for
　　threat,
Answer his "Be thou not !" by "Thus I
　　am !" —
Terrible so to be alive yet die ?

How I live, how I see ! so, — how I speak !
Lucidity of soul unlocks the lips :
I never had the words at will before.
How I see all my folly at a glance !
" A man requires a woman and a wife : "
There was my folly ; I believed the saw.
I knew that just myself concerned myself,
Yet needs must look for what I seemed to lack,
In a woman, — why, the woman 's in the man !
Fools we are, how we learn things when too
　　late !
Overmuch life turns round my woman-side ;
The male and female in me, mixed before,
Settle of a sudden : I 'm my wife outright
In this unmanly appetite for truth,
This careless courage as to consequence,
This instantaneous sight through things and
　　through,
This voluble rhetoric, if you please, — 't is she !
Here you have that Pompilia whom I slew,
Also the folly for which I slew her !
　　　　　　　　　　Fool !
And, fool-like, what is it I wander from ?
What did I say of your sharp iron tooth ?
Ah, — that I know the hateful thing ! this way.
I chanced to stroll forth, many a good year
　　gone,
One warm Spring eve in Rome, and unaware
Looking, mayhap, to count what stars were out,
Came on your fine axe in a frame, that falls
And so cuts off a man's head underneath,
Mannaia, — thus we made acquaintance first :
Out of the way, in a by-part o' the town,
At the Mouth-of-Truth o' the river-side, you
　　know :
One goes by the Capitol : and wherefore coy,
Retiring out of crowded noisy Rome ?
Because a very little time ago
It had done service, chopped off head from
　　trunk,
Belonging to a fellow whose poor house
The thing must make a point to stand before.
Felice Whatsoever-was-the-name
Who stabled buffaloes and so gained bread,
(Our clowns unyoke them in the ground hard
　　by,)
And, after use of much improper speech,
Had struck at Duke Some-title-or-other's face,
Because he kidnapped, carried away and kept
Felice's sister who would sit and sing
I' the filthy doorway while she plaited fringe
To deck the brutes with, — on their gear it
　　goes, —
The good girl with the velvet in her voice.
So did the Duke, so did Felice, so

Did Justice, intervening with her axe.
There the man-mutilating engine stood
At ease, both gay and grim, like a Swiss guard
Off duty, — purified itself as well,
Getting dry, sweet and proper for next week, —
And doing incidental good, 't was hoped
To the rough lesson-lacking populace
Who now and then, forsooth, must right their
　　wrongs !
There stood the twelve-foot-square of scaffold,
　　railed
Considerately round to elbow-height,
For fear an officer should tumble thence
And sprain his ankle and be lame a month,
Through starting when the axe fell and head
　　too !
Railed likewise were the steps whereby 't was
　　reached.
All of it painted red : red, in the midst,
Ran up two narrow tall beams barred across,
Since from the summit, some twelve feet to
　　reach,
The iron plate with the sharp shearing edge
Had slammed, jerked, shot, slid, — I shall soon
　　find which !
And so lay quiet, fast in its fit place,
The wooden half-moon collar, now eclipsed
By the blade which blocked its curvature :
　　apart,
The other half, — the under half-moon board
Which, helped by this, completes a neck's em-
　　brace, —
Joined to a sort of desk that wheels aside
Out of the way when done with, — down you
　　kneel,
In you 're pushed, over you the other drops,
Tight you 're clipped, whiz, there 's the blade
　　cleaves its best,
Out trundles body, down flops head on floor,
And where 's your soul gone ? That, too, I
　　shall find !
This kneeling-place was red, red, never fear !
But only slimy-like with paint, not blood,
For why ? a decent pitcher stood at hand,
A broad dish to hold sawdust, and a broom
By some unnamed utensil, — scraper-rake, —
Each with a conscious air of duty done.
Underneath, loungers, — boys and some few
　　men, —
Discoursed this platter, named the other tool,
Just as, when grooms tie up and dress a steed,
Boys lounge and look on, and elucubrate
What the round brush is used for, what the
　　square, —
So was explained — to me the skill-less then —
The manner of the grooming for next world
Undergone by Felice What's-his-name.
There 's no such lovely month in Rome as
　　May —
May's crescent is no half-moon of red plank,
And came now tilting o'er the wave i' the west,
One greenish-golden sea, right 'twixt those bars
Of the engine — I began acquaintance with,
Understood, hated, hurried from before,
To have it out of sight and cleanse my soul !
Here it is all again, conserved for use :
Twelve hours hence, I may know more, not hate
　　worse.

That young May-moon-month! Devils of the
    deep!
Was not a Pope then Pope as much as now?
Used not he chirrup o'er the Merry Tales,
Chuckle, — his nephew so exact the wag
To play a jealous cullion such a trick
As wins the wife i' the pleasant story! Well?
Why do things change? Wherefore is Rome
    un-Romed?
I tell you, ere Felice's corpse was cold,
The Duke, that night, threw wide his palace-
    doors,
Received the compliments o' the quality
For justice done him, — bowed and smirked his
    best,
And in return passed round a pretty thing,
A portrait of Felice's sister's self,
Florid old rogue Albano's masterpiece,
As — better than virginity in rags —
Bouncing Europa on the back o' the bull:
They laughed and took their road the safelier
    home.
Ah, but times change, there's quite another
    Pope,
I do the Duke's deed, take Felice's place,
And, being no Felice, lout and clout,
Stomach but ill the phrase, "I lose my head!"
How euphemistic! Lose what? Lose your ring,
Your snuff-box, tablets, kerchief! — but, your
    head?
I learnt the process at an early age;
'Twas useful knowledge, in those same old
    days,
To know the way a head is set on neck.
My fencing-master urged, "Would you excel?
Rest not content with mere bold give-and-
    guard,
Nor pink the antagonist somehow-anyhow!
See me dissect a little, and know your game!
Only anatomy makes a thrust the thing."
Oh, Cardinal, those lithe live necks of ours!
Here go the vertebræ, here's *Atlas*, here
Axis, and here the symphyses stop short,
So wisely and well, — as, o'er a corpse, we
    cant, —
And here's the silver cord which . . . what's
    our word?
Depends from the gold bowl, which loosed (not
    " lost ")
Lets us from heaven to hell, — one chop, we're
    loose!
"And not much pain i' the process," quoth a
    sage:
Who told him? Not Felice's ghost, I think!
Such "losing" is scarce Mother Nature's mode.
She fain would have cord ease itself away,
Worn to a thread by threescore years and ten,
Snap while we slumber: that seems bearable.
I'm told one clot of blood extravasate
Ends one as certainly as Roland's sword, —
One drop of lymph suffused proves Oliver's
    mace, —
Intruding, either of the pleasant pair,
On the arachnoid tunic of my brain.
That's Nature's way of loosing cord! — but
    Art,
How of Art's process with the engine here,
When bowl and cord alike are crushed across,

Bored between, bruised through? Why, if
    Fagon's self,
The French Court's pride, that famed practi-
    tioner,
Would pass his cold pale lightning of a knife,
Pistoja-ware, adroit 'twixt joint and joint,
With just a "See how facile, gentlefolk!" —
The thing were not so bad to bear! Brute force
Cuts as he comes, breaks in, breaks on, breaks
    out
O' the hard and soft of you: is that the same?
A lithe snake thrids the hedge, makes throb no
    leaf:
A heavy ox sets chest to brier and branch,
Bursts somehow through, and leaves one hid-
    eous hole
Behind him!

          And why, why must this needs be?
Oh, if men were but good! They are not good,
Nowise like Peter: people called him rough,
But if, as I left Rome, I spoke the Saint,
— " *Petrus, quo vadis?* " — doubtless, I should
    hear,
" To free the prisoner and forgive his fault!
I plucked the absolute dead from God's own
    bar,
And raised up Dorcas, — why not rescue thee?"
What would cost one such nullifying word?
If Innocent succeeds to Peter's place,
Let him think Peter's thought, speak Peter's
    speech!
I say, he is bound to it: friends, how say you?
Concede I be all one bloodguiltiness
And mystery of murder in the flesh,
Why should that fact keep the Pope's mouth
    shut fast?
He execrates my crime, — good! — sees hell
    yawn
One inch from the red plank's end which I
    press, —
Nothing is better! What's the consequence?
How should a Pope proceed that knows his
    cue?
Why, leave me linger out my minute here,
Since close on death comes judgment and
    comes doom,
Not crib at dawn its pittance from a sheep
Destined ere dewfall to be butcher's-meat!
Think, Sirs, if I have done you any harm,
And you require the natural revenge,
Suppose, and so intend to poison me,
— Just as you take and slip into my draught
The paperful of powder that clears scores,
You notice on my brow a certain blue:
How you both overset the wine at once!
How you both smile, "Our enemy has the
    plague!"
Twelve hours hence he'll be scraping his bones
    bare
Of that intolerable flesh, and die,
Frenzied with pain: no need for poison here!
Step aside and enjoy the spectacle!"
Tender for souls are you, Pope Innocent!
Christ's maxim is — one soul outweighs the
    world!
Respite me, save a soul, then, curse the world!
"No," venerable sire, I hear you smirk,

"No: for Christ's gospel changes names, not
    things,
Renews the obsolete, does nothing more !
Our fire-new gospel is re-tinkered law,
Our mercy, justice, — Jove 's rechristened
    God, —
Nay, whereas, in the popular conceit,
'T is pity that old harsh Law somehow limps,
Lingers on earth, although Law's day be done,
Else would benignant Gospel interpose,
Not furtively as now, but bold and frank
O'erflutter us with healing in her wings,
Law being harshness, Gospel only love —
We tell the people, on the contrary,
Gospel takes up the rod which Law lets fall ;
Mercy is vigilant when justice sleeps !
Does Law permit a taste of Gospel-grace ?
The secular arm allow the spiritual power
To act for once ? — no compliment so fine
As that our Gospel handsomely turn harsh,
Thrust victim back on Law the nice and coy ! "
Yes, you do say so, — else you would forgive
Me, whom Law does not touch but tosses you !
Don't think to put on the professional face !
You know what I know, — casuists as you are,
Each nerve must creep, each hair start, sting
    and stand,
At such illogical inconsequence !
Dear my friends, do but see ! A murder 's
    tried,
There are two parties to the cause : I 'm one,
— Defend myself, as somebody must do :
I have the best o' the battle : that 's a fact,
Simple fact, — fancies find no place just now.
What though half Rome condemned me ? Half
    approved
And, none disputes, the luck is mine at last,
All Rome, i' the main, acquitting me : whereon,
What has the Pope to ask but " How finds
    Law ? "
" I find," replies Law, " I have erred this while :
Guilty or guiltless, Guido proves a priest,
No layman : he is therefore yours, not mine :
I bound him : loose him, you whose will is
    Christ's ! "   ·
And now what does this Vicar of our Lord,
Shepherd o' the flock, — one of whose charge
    bleats sore
For crook's help from the quag wherein it
    drowns ?
Law suffers him employ the crumpled end :
His pleasure is to turn staff, use the point,
And thrust the shuddering sheep, he calls a
    wolf,
Back and back, down and down to where hell
    gapes !
" Guiltless," cries Law — " Guilty," corrects
    the Pope !
" Guilty," for the whim's sake ! " Guilty," he
    somehow thinks,
And anyhow says : 't is truth ; he dares not lie !

Others should do the lying. That 's the cause
Brings you both here : I ought in decency
Confess to you that I deserve my fate,
Am guilty, as the Pope thinks, — ay, to the
    end,
Keep up the jest, lie on, lie ever, lie

I' the latest gasp of me ! What reason, Sirs ?
Because to-morrow will succeed to-day
For you, though not for me : and if I stick
Still to the truth, declare with my last breath,
I die an innocent and murdered man, —
Why, there 's the tongue of Rome will wag
    apace
This time to-morrow, — don't I hear the talk !
" So, to the last he proved impenitent ?
Pagans have said as much of martyred saints !
Law demurred, washed her hands of the whole
    case.
Prince Somebody said this, Duke Something,
    that.
Doubtless the man 's dead, dead enough, don't
    fear !
But, hang it, what if there have been a spice,
A touch of . . . eh ? You see, the Pope 's so
    old,
Some of us add, obtuse, — age never slips
The chance of shoving youth to face death
    first ! "
And so on. Therefore to suppress such talk
You two come here, entreat I tell you lies,
And end, the edifying way. I end,
Telling the truth ! Your self-styled shepherd
    thieves !
A thief — and how thieves hate the wolves we
    know :
Damage to theft, damage to thrift, all 's one !
The red hand is sworn foe of the black jaw.
That 's only natural, that 's right enough :
But why the wolf should compliment the thief
With shepherd's title, bark out life in thanks,
And, spiteless, lick the prong that spits him, —
    eh,
Cardinal ? My Abate, scarcely thus !
There, let my sheepskin-garb, a curse on 't, go —
Leave my teeth free if I must show my shag !
Repent ? What good shall follow ? If I pass
Twelve hours repenting, will that fact hold
    fast
The thirteenth at the horrid dozen's end ?
If I fall forthwith at your feet, gnash, tear,
Foam, rave, to give your story the due grace,
Will that assist the engine half-way back
Into its hiding-house ? — boards, shaking now,
Bone against bone, like some old skeleton bat
That wants, at winter's end, to wake and prey !
Will howling put the spectre back to sleep ?
Ah, but I misconceive your object, Sirs !
Since I want new life like the creature, — life,
Being done with here, begins i' the world away :
I shall next have " Come, mortals, and be
    judged ! "
There 's but a minute betwixt this and then :
So, quick, be sorry since it saves my soul !
Sirs, truth shall save it, since no lies assist !
Hear the truth, you, whatever you style your
    selves,
Civilization and society !
Come, one good grapple, I with all the world !
Dying in cold blood is the desperate thing ;
The angry heart explodes, bears off in blaze
The indignant soul, and I 'm combustion-ripe.
Why, you intend to do your worst with me !
That 's in your eyes ! You dare no more than
    death,

And mean no less. I must make up my mind!
So Pietro — when I chased him here and there,
Morsel by morsel cut away the life
I loathed — cried for just respite to confess
And save his soul : much respite did I grant!
Why grant me respite who deserve my doom?
Me — who engaged to play a prize, fight you,
Knowing your arms, and foil you, trick for
    trick,
At rapier-fence, your match and, maybe, more.
I knew that if I chose sin certain sins,
Solace my lusts out of the regular way
Prescribed me, I should find you in the path,
Have to try skill with a redoubted foe ;
You would lunge, I would parry, and make
    end.
At last, occasion of a murder comes :
We cross blades, I, for all my brag, break
    guard,
And in goes the cold iron at my breast,
Out at my back, and end is made of me.
You stand confessed the adroiter swordsman,
    — ay,
But on your triumph you increase, it seems,
Want more of me than lying flat on face:
I ought to raise my ruined head, allege
Not simply I pushed worse blade o' the pair,
But my antagonist dispensed with steel !
There was no passage of arms, you looked me
    low,
With brow and eye abolished cut and thrust,
Nor used the vulgar weapon ! This chance
    scratch,
This incidental hurt, this sort of hole
I' the heart of me ? I stumbled, got it so !
Fell on my own sword as a bungler may !
Yourself proscribe such heathen tools, and
    trust
To the naked virtue : it was virtue stood
Unarmed and awed me, — on my brow there
    burned
Crime out so plainly, intolerably red,
That I was fain to cry — " Down to the dust
With me, and bury there brow, brand and
    all ! "
Law had essayed the adventure, — but what 's
    Law ?
Morality exposed the Gorgon shield !
Morality and Religion conquer me.
If Law sufficed would you come here, entreat
I supplement law, and confess forsooth ?
Did not the Trial show things plain enough ?
" Ah, but a word of the man's very self
Would somehow put the keystone in its place
And crown the arch ! " Then take the word
    you want !

I say that, long ago, when things began,
All the world made agreement, such and such
Were pleasure-giving profit-bearing acts,
But henceforth extra-legal, nor to be :
You must not kill the man whose death would
    please
And profit you, unless his life stop yours
Plainly, and need so be put aside :
Get the thing by a public course, by law,
Only no private bloodshed as of old !
All of us, for the good of every one
Renounced such license and conformed to law :
Who breaks law, breaks pact therefore, helps
    himself
To pleasure and profit over and above the due,
And must pay forfeit, — pain beyond h¹
    share :
For, pleasure being the sole good in the world.
Any one's pleasure turns to some one's pain,
So, law must watch for every one, — say we,
Who call things wicked that give too much joy,
And nickname mere reprisal, envy makes,
Punishment: quite right ! thus the world goes
    round.
I, being well aware such pact there was,
I, in my time who found advantage come
Of law's observance and crime's penalty, —
Who, but for wholesome fear law bred in
    friends,
Had doubtless given example long ago,
Furnished forth some friend's pleasure with my
    pain,
And, by my death, pieced out his scanty life, —
I could not, for that foolish life of me,
Help risking law's infringement, — I broke
    bond,
And needs must pay price, — wherefore, here 's
    my head,
Flung with a flourish ! But, repentance too?
But pure and simple sorrow for law's breach
Rather than blunderer's-ineptitude ?
Cardinal, no ! Abate, scarcely thus !
'T is the fault, not that I dared try a fall
With Law and straightway am found under
    most,
But that I failed to see, above man's law,
God's precept you, the Christians, recognize ?
Colly my cow ! Don't fidget, Cardinal !
Abate, cross your breast and count your beads
And exorcise the devil, for here he stands
And stiffens in the bristly nape of neck,
Daring you drive him hence ! You, Christians
    both ?
I say, if ever was such faith at all
Born in the world, by your community
Suffered to live its little tick of time,
'T is dead of age, now, ludicrously dead ;
Honor its ashes, if you be discreet,
In epitaph only ! For, concede its death,
Allow extinction, you may boast unchecked
What feats the thing did in a crazy land
At a fabulous epoch, — treat your faith, that
    · way,
Just as you treat your relics : " Here 's a shred
Of saintly flesh, a scrap of blessed bone,
Raised King Cophetua, who was dead, to life
In Mesopotamy twelve centuries since,
Such was its virtue ! " — twangs the Sacristan,
Holding the shrine-box up, with hands lik₁
    feet
Because of gout in every finger-joint :
Does he bethink him to reduce one knob,
Allay one twinge by touching what he vaunts?
I think he half uncrooks fist to catch fee,
But, for the grace, the quality of cure, —
Cophetua was the man put that to proof !
Not otherwise, your faith is shrined and shown
And shamed at once : you banter while you
    bow !

Do you dispute this? Come, a monster-laugh,
A madman's laugh, allowed his Carnival
Later ten days than when all Rome, but he,
Laughed at the candle-contest : mine 's alight,
'T is just it sputter till the puff o' the Pope
End it to-morrow and the world turn Ash.
Come, thus I wave a wand and bring to pass
In a moment, in the twinkle of an eye,
What but that — feigning everywhere grows
    fact,
Professors turn possessors, realize
The faith they play with as a fancy now,
And bid it operate, have full effect
On every circumstance of life, to-day,
In Rome, — faith's flow set free at fountain-
    head !
Now, you 'll own, at this present, when I speak,
Before I work the wonder, there 's no man,
Woman or child in Rome, faith's fountain-head,
But might, if each were minded, realize
Conversely unbelief, faith's opposite —
Set it to work on life unflinchingly,
Yet give no symptom of an outward change :
Why should things change because men dis-
    believe ?
What 's incompatible, in the whited tomb,
With bones and rottenness one inch below ?
What saintly act is done in Rome to-day
But might be prompted by the devil, — "is "
I say not, — " has been, and again may be," —
I do say, full i' the face o' the crucifix
You try to stop my mouth with ! Off with it !
Look in your own heart, if your soul have eyes !
You shall see reason why, though faith were
    fled,
Unbelief still might work the wires and move
Man, the machine, to play a faithful part.
Preside your college, Cardinal, in your cape,
Or, — having got above his head, grown Pope, —
Abate, gird your loins and wash my feet !
Do you suppose I am at loss at all
Why you crook, why you cringe, why fast or
    feast ?
Praise, blame, sit, stand, lie or go ! — all of it,
In each of you, purest unbelief may prompt,
And wit explain to who has eyes to see.
But, lo, I wave wand, make the false the true !
Here 's Rome believes in Christianity !
What an explosion, how the fragments fly
Of what was surface, mask and make-believe !
Begin now, — look at this Pope's-halberdier
In wasp-like black and yellow foolery !
He, doing duty at the corridor,
Wakes from a muse and stands convinced of
    sin !
Down he flings halbert, leaps the passage-length,
Pushes into the presence, pantingly
Submits the extreme peril of the case
To the Pope's self, — whom in the world
    beside ? —
And the Pope breaks talk with ambassador,
Bids aside bishop, wills the whole world wait
Till he secure that prize, outweighs the world,
A soul, relieve the sentry of his qualm !
His Altitude the Referendary —
Robed right, and ready for the usher's word
To pay devoir — is, of all times, just then
'Ware of a master-stroke of argument.

Will cut the spinal cord . . . ugh, ugh ! . . . 1
    mean,
Paralyze Molinism forevermore !
Straight he leaves lobby, trundles, two and two,
Down steps to reach home, write, if but a word
Shall end the impudence : he leaves who likes
Go pacify the Pope : there 's Christ to serve !
How otherwise would men display their zeal ?
If the same sentry had the least surmise
A powder-barrel 'neath the pavement lay
In neighborhood with what might prove a
    match,
Meant to blow sky-high Pope and presence
    both —
Would he not break through courtiers, rank
    and file,
Bundle up, bear off, and save body so;
The Pope, no matter for his priceless soul ?
There 's no fool's-freak here, naught to soundly
    swinge,
Only a man in earnest, you 'll so praise
And pay and prate about, that earth shall ring !
Had thought possessed the Referendary
His jewel-case at home was left ajar,
What would be wrong in running, robes awry,
To be beforehand with the pilferer ?
What talk then of indecent haste ? Which
    means,
That both these, each in his degree, would do
Just that — for a comparative nothing's sake,
And thereby gain approval and reward —
Which, done for what Christ says is worth the
    world,
Procures the doer curses, cuffs and kicks.
I call such difference 'twixt act and act,
Sheer lunacy unless your truth on lip
Be recognized a lie in heart of you !
How do you all act, promptly or in doubt,
When there 's a guest poisoned at supper-time
And he sits chatting on with spot on cheek ?
" Pluck him by the skirt, and round him in the
    ears,
Have at him by the beard, warn anyhow ! "
Good ; and this other friend that 's cheat and
    thief
And dissolute, — go stop the devil's feast,
Withdraw him from the imminent hell-fire !
Why, for your life, you dare not tell your friend,
" You lie, and I admonish you for Christ ! "
Who yet dare seek that same man at the
    Mass
To warn him — on his knees, and tinkle near, —
He left a cask a-tilt, a tap unturned,
The Trebbian running : what a grateful jump
Out of the Church rewards your vigilance !
Perform that selfsame service just a thought
More maladroitly, — since a bishop sits
At function ! — and he budges not, bites lip, —
" You see my case : how can I quit my post ?
He has an eye to any such default.
See to it, neighbor, I beseech your love ! "
He and you know the relative worth of things,
What is permissible or inopportune.
Contort your brows ! You know I speak the
    truth :
Gold is called gold, and dross called dross, i' the
    Book :
Gold you let lie and dross pick up and prize !

— Despite your muster of some fifty monks
And nuns a-maundering here and mumping
  there,
Who could, and on occasion would, spurn dross,
Clutch gold, and prove their faith a fact so
  far, —
I grant you! Fifty times the number squeak
And gibber in the madhouse — firm of faith,
This fellow, that his nose supports the moon;
The other, that his straw hat crowns him Pope:
Does that prove all the world outside insane?
Do fifty miracle-mongers match the mob
That acts on the frank faithless principle,
Born-baptized-and-bred Christian-atheists, each
With just as much a right to judge as you, —
As many senses in his soul, and nerves
I' neck of him as I, — whom, soul and sense,
Neck and nerve, you abolish presently, —
I being the unit in creation now
Who pay the Maker, in this speech of mine,
A creature's duty, spend my last of breath
In bearing witness, even by my worst fault,
To the creature's obligation, absolute,
Perpetual: my worst fault protests, "The
  faith
Claims all of me: I would give all she claims,
But for a spice of doubt: the risk 's too rash:
Double or quits, I play, but, all or naught,
Exceeds my courage: therefore, I descend
To the next faith with no dubiety —
Faith in the present life, made last as long
And prove as full of pleasure as may hap,
Whatever pain it cause the world." I 'm
  wrong?
I 've had my life, whate'er I lose: I 'm right?
I 've got the single good there was to gain.
Entire faith, or else complete unbelief!
Aught between has my loathing and contempt,
Mine and God's also, doubtless: ask yourself,
Cardinal, where and how you like a man!
Why, either with your feet upon his head,
Confessed your caudatory, or, at large,
The stranger in the crowd who caps to you
But keeps his distance, — why should he pre-
  sume?
You want no hanger-on and dropper-off,
Now yours, and now not yours but quite his own,
According as the sky looks black or bright.
Just so I capped to and kept off from faith —
You promised trudge behind through fair and
  foul,
Yet leave i' the lurch at the first spit of rain.
Who holds to faith whenever rain begins?
What does the father when his son lies dead,
The merchant when his money-bags take wing,
The politican whom a rival ousts?
No case but has its conduct, faith prescribes:
Where 's the obedience that shall edify?
Why, they laugh frankly in the face of faith
And take the natural course, — this rends his
  hair
Because his child is taken to God's breast,
That gnashes teeth and raves at loss of trash
Which rust corrupts and thieves break through
  and steal,
And this, enabled to inherit earth
Through meekness, curses till your blood runs
  cold!

Down they all drop to my low level, rest
Heart upon dungy earth that 's warm and soft.
And let who please attempt the altitudes:
Each playing prodigal son of heavenly sire,
Turning his nose up at the fatted calf,
Fain to fill belly with the husks, we swine
Did eat by born depravity of taste!

Enough of the hypocrites. But you, Sirs,
  you —
Who never budged from litter where I lay,
And buried snout i' the draff-box while I fed,
Cried amen to my creed's one article —
"Get pleasure, 'scape pain, — give your prefer-
  ence
To the immediate good, for time is brief,
And death ends good and ill and everything!
What 's got is gained, what 's gained soon is
  gained twice,
And — inasmuch as faith gains most — feign
  faith!"
So did we brother-like pass word about:
— You, now, — like bloody drunkards but half-
  drunk,
Who fool men yet perceive men find them
  fools, —
Vexed that a titter gains the gravest mouth, —
O' the sudden you must needs reintroduce
Solemnity, straight sober undue mirth
By a blow dealt me your boon companion here,
Who, using the old license, dreamed of harm
No more than snow in harvest: yet it falls!
You check the merriment effectually
By pushing your abrupt machine i' the midst,
Making me Rome's example: blood for wine!
The general good needs that you chop and
  change!
I may dislike the hocus-pocus, — Rome,
The laughter-loving people, won't they stare
Chapfallen! — while serious natures sermonize,
"The magistrate, he beareth not the sword
In vain; who sins may taste its edge, we see!"
Why my sin, drunkards? Where have I abused
Liberty, scandalized you all so much?
Who called me, who crooked finger till I came,
Fool that I was, to join companionship?
I knew my own mind, meant to live my life,
Elude your envy, or else make a stand,
Take my own part and sell you my life dear.
But it was "Fie! No prejudice in the world
To the proper manly instinct! Cast your lot
Into our lap, one genius ruled our births,
We 'll compass joy by concert; take with us
The regular irregular way i' the wood;
You 'll miss no game through riding breast by
  breast,
In this preserve, the Church's park and pale,
Rather than outside where the world lies
  waste!"
Come, if you said not that, did you say this?
Give plain and terrible warning, "Live, enjoy!
Such life begins in death and ends in hell!
Dare you bid us assist your sins, us priests
Who hurry sin and sinners from the earth?
No such delight for us, why then for you?
Leave earth, seek heaven or find its opposite!'
Had you so warned me, not in lying words
But veritable deeds with tongues of flame,

That had been fair, that might have struck a man,
Silenced the squabble between soul and sense,
Compelled him to make mind up, take one course
Or the other, peradventure! — wrong or right,
Foolish or wise, you would have been at least
Sincere, no question, — forced me choose, indulge
Or else renounce my instincts, still play wolf
Or find my way submissive to your fold,
Be red-crossed on my fleece, one sheep the more.
But you as good as bade me wear sheep's-wool
Over wolf's-skin, suck blood and hide the noise
By mimicry of something like a bleat, —
Whence it comes that because, despite my care,
Because I smack my tongue too loud for once,
Drop baaing, here's the village up in arms!
Have at the wolf's throat, you who hate the breed!
Oh, were it only open yet to choose —
One little time more — whether I'd be free
Your foe, or subsidized your friend forsooth!
Should not you get a growl through the white fangs
In answer to your beckoning! Cardinal,
Abate, managers o' the multitude,
I'd turn your gloved hands to account, be sure!
You should manipulate the coarse rough mob:
'T is you I'd deal directly with, not them, —
Using your fears: why touch the thing myself
When I could see you hunt, and then cry "Shares!
Quarter the carcass or we quarrel; come,
Here's the world ready to see justice done!"
Oh, it had been a desperate game, but game
Wherein the winner's chance were worth the pains!
We'd try conclusions! — at the worst, what worse
Than this Mannaia-machine, each minute's talk
Helps push an inch the nearer me? Fool, fool!

You understand me and forgive, sweet Sirs?
I blame you, tear my hair and tell my woe —
All's but a flourish, figure of rhetoric!
One must try each expedient to save life.
One makes fools look foolisher fifty-fold
By putting in their place men wise like you,
To take the full force of an argument
Would buffet their stolidity in vain.
If you should feel aggrieved by the mere wind
O' the blow that means to miss you and maul them,
That's my success! Is it not folly, now,
To say with folk, "A plausible defence—
We see through notwithstanding, and reject"?
Reject the plausible they do, these fools,
Who never even make pretence to show
One point beyond its plausibility
In favor of the best belief they hold!
"Saint Somebody-or-other raised the dead:"
Did he? How do you come to know as much?
"Know it, what need? The story's plausible,
Avouched for by a martyrologist,
And why should good men sup on cheese and leeks
On such a saint's day, if there were no saint?"

I praise the wisdom of these fools, and straight
Tell them my story — "plausible, but false!"
False, to be sure! What else can story be
That runs — a young wife tired of an old spouse.
Found a priest whom she fled away with, — both
Took their full pleasure in the two-days' flight,
Which a gray-headed grayer-hearted pair
(Whose best boast was, their life had been a lie)
Helped for the love they bore all liars. Oh,
Here incredulity begins! Indeed?
Allow then, were no one point strictly true,
There's that i' the tale might seem like truth at least
To the unlucky husband, — jaundiced patch, —
Jealousy maddens people, why not him?
Say, he was maddened, so forgivable!
Humanity pleads that though the wife were true,
The priest true, and the pair of liars true,
They might seem false to one man in the world!
A thousand gnats make up a serpent's sting,
And many sly soft stimulants to wrath
Compose a formidable wrong at last,
That gets called easily by some one name
Not applicable to the single parts,
And so draws down a general revenge,
Excessive if you take crime, fault by fault.
Jealousy! I have known a score of plays,
Were listened to and laughed at in my time
As like the every-day life on all sides,
Wherein the husband, mad as a March hare,
Suspected all the world contrived his shame.
What did the wife? The wife kissed both eyes blind,
Explained away ambiguous circumstance,
And while she held him captive by the hand,
Crowned his head — you know what's the mockery —
By half her body behind the curtain. That's
Nature now! That's the subject of a piece
I saw in Vallombrosa Convent, made
Expressly to teach men what marriage was!
But say, "Just so did I misapprehend,
Imagine she deceived me to my face,"
And that's pretence too easily seen through!
All those eyes of all husbands in all plays,
At stare like one expanded peacock-tail,
Are laughed at for pretending to be keen
While horn-blind: but the moment I step forth —
Oh, I must needs o' the sudden prove a lynx
And look the heart, that stone-wall, through and through!
Such an eye, God's may be, — not yours nor mine.

Yes, presently . . . what hour is fleeting now?
When you cut earth away from under me,
I shall be left alone with, pushed beneath
Some such an apparitional dread orb
As the eye of God, since such an eye there glares:
I fancy it go filling up the void
Above my mote-self if it devours, or what
Proves wrath, immensity wreaks on nothingness
Just how I felt once, couching through the dark,
Hard by Vittiano; young I was, and gay,
And wanting to trap fieldfares: first a spark

Tipped a bent, as a mere dew-globule might
Any stiff grass-stalk on the meadow, — this
Grew fiercer, flamed out full, and proved the
    sun.
What do I want with proverbs, precepts here?
Away with man! What shall I say to God?
This, if I find the tongue and keep the mind —
" Do Thou wipe out the being of me, and smear
This soul from off Thy white of things, I blot!
I am one huge and sheer mistake, — whose
    fault?
Not mine at least, who did not make myself! "
Some one declares my wife excused me so!
Perhaps she knew what argument to use.
Grind your teeth, Cardinal, Abate, writhe!
What else am I to cry out in my rage,
Unable to repent one particle
O' the past? Oh, how I wish some cold wise
    man
Would dig beneath the surface which you
    scrape,
Deal with the depths, pronounce on my desert
Groundedly! I want simple sober sense,
That asks, before it finishes with a dog,
Who taught the dog that trick you hang him
    for?
You both persist to call that act a crime,
Which sense would call . . . yes, I maintain it,
    Sirs, . . .
A blunder! At the worst, I stood in doubt
On cross-road, took one path of many paths:
It leads to the red thing, we all see now,
But nobody saw at first: one primrose-patch
In bank, one singing-bird in bush, the less,
Had warned me from such wayfare: let me
    prove!
Put me back to the cross-road, start afresh!
Advise me when I take the first false step!
Give me my wife: how should I use my wife,
Love her or hate her? Prompt my action
    now!
There she is, there she stands alive and pale,
The thirteen-years'-old child, with milk for
    blood,
Pompilia Comparini, as at first,
Which first is only four brief years ago!
I stand too in the little ground-floor room
O' the father's house at Via Vittoria: see!
Her so-called mother — one arm round the
    waist
O' the child to keep her from the toys, let fall
At wonder I can live yet look so grim —
Ushers her in, with deprecating wave
Of the other, — and she fronts me loose at last,
Held only by the mother's finger-tip.
Struck dumb, for she was white enough before!
She eyes me with those frightened balls of
    black,
As heifer — the old simile comes pat —
Eyes tremblingly the altar and the priest.
The amazed look, all one insuppressive
    prayer, —
Might she but breathe, set free as heretofore,
Have this cup leave her lips unblistered, bear
Any cross anywhither anyhow,
So but alone, so but apart from me!
You are touched? So am I, quite otherwise,
If 't is with pity. I resent my wrong,

Being a man: I only show man's soul
Through man's flesh: she sees mine, it strikes
    her thus!
Is that attractive? To a youth perhaps —
Calf-creature, one-part boy to three-parts girl,
To whom it is a flattering novelty
That he, men use to motion from their path,
Can thus impose, thus terrify in turn
A chit whose terror shall be changed apace
To bliss unbearable when grace and glow,
Prowess and pride descend the throne and
    touch
Esther in all that pretty tremble, cured
By the dove o' the sceptre! But myself am
    old,
O' the wane at least, in all things: what do you
    say
To her who frankly thus confirms my doubt?
I am past the prime, I scare the woman-world,
Done-with that way: you like this piece of
    news?
A little saucy rose-bud minx can strike
Death-damp into the breast of doughty king
Though 't were French Louis, — soul I under-
    stand, —
Saying, by gesture of repugnance, just
" Sire, you are regal, puissant, and so forth,
But — young you have been, are not, nor will
    be! "
In vain the mother nods, winks, bustles up,
" Count, girls incline to mature worth like you!
As for Pompilia, what 's flesh, fish or fowl
To one who apprehends no difference,
And would accept you even were you old
As you are . . . youngish by her father's side?
Trim but your beard a little, thin your bush
Of eyebrow; and for presence, portliness,
And decent gravity, you beat a boy! "
Deceive yourself one minute, if you may,
In presence of the child that so loves age,
Whose neck writhes, cords itself against your
    kiss,
Whose hand you wring stark, rigid with de-
    spair!
Well, I resent this; I am young in soul,
Nor old in body, — thews and sinews here, —
Though the vile surface be not smooth as
    once, —
Far beyond that first wheelwork which went
    wrong
Through the untempered iron ere 't was proof:
I am the rock man worth ten times the
    crude, —
Would woman see what this declines to see,
Declines to say " I see," — the officious word
That makes the thing, pricks on the soul to
    shoot
New fire into the half-used cinder, flesh!
Therefore 't is she begins with wronging me,
Who cannot but begin with hating her.
Our marriage follows: there she stands again!
Why do I laugh? Why, in the very gripe
O' the jaws of death's gigantic skull, do I
Grin back his grin, make sport of my own
    pangs?
Why from each clashing of his molars, ground
To make the devil bread from out my grist,
Leaps out a spark of mirth, a hellish toy?

Take notice we are lovers in a church,
Waiting the sacrament to make us one
And happy! Just as bid, she bears herself,
Comes and kneels, rises, speaks, is silent, —
  goes:
So have I brought my horse, by word and blow,
To stand stock-still and front the fire he
  dreads.
How can I other than remember this,
Resent the very obedience? Gain thereby?
Yes, I do gain my end and have my will, —
Thanks to whom? When the mother speaks
  the word,
She obeys it — even to enduring me!
There had been compensation in revolt —
Revolt 's to quell : but martyrdom rehearsed,
But predetermined saintship for the sake
O' the mother? — " Go!" thought I, " we
  meet again ! "
Pass the next weeks of dumb contented death,
She lives, — wakes up, installed in house and
  home,
Is mine, mine all day-long, all night-long mine.
Good folk begin at me with open mouth :
" Now, at least, reconcile the child to life!
Study and make her love . . . that is, endure
The . . . hem ! the . . . all of you though
  somewhat old,
Till it amount to something, in her eye,
As good as love, better a thousand times, —
Since nature helps the woman in such strait,
Makes passiveness her pleasure : failing which,
What if you give up boy-and-girl-fools'-play
And go on to wise friendship all at once?
Those boys and girls kiss themselves cold, you
  know,
Toy themselves tired and slink aside full soon
To friendship, as they name satiety :
Thither go you and wait their coming!"
  Thanks,
Considerate advisers, — but, fair play!
Had you and I, friends, started fair at first,
We, keeping fair, might reach it, neck by
  neck,
This blessed goal, whenever fate so please :
But why am I to miss the daisied mile
The course begins with, why obtain the dust
Of the end precisely at the starting-point?
Why quaff life's cup blown free of all the
  beads,
The bright red froth wherein our beard should
  steep
Before our mouth essay the black o' the wine?
Foolish, the love-fit? Let me prove it such
Like you, before like you I puff things clear!
" The best 's to come, no rapture but content!
Not love's first glory but a sober glow,
Not a spontaneous outburst in pure boon,
So much as, gained by patience, care and toil,
Proper appreciation and esteem ! "
Go preach that to your nephews, not to me
Who, tired i' the midway of my life, would stop
And take my first refreshment, pluck a rose :
What 's this coarse woolly hip, worn smooth of
  leaf,
You counsel I go plant in garden-plot,
Water with tears, manure with sweat and
  blood,

In confidence the seed shall germinate
And, for its very best, some far-off day,
Grow big, and blow me out a dog-rose bell?
Why must your nephews begin breathing spice
O' the hundred-petalled Provence prodigy?
Nay, more and worse, — would such my root
  bear rose —
Prove really flower and favorite, not the kind
That 's queen, but those three leaves that make
  one cup
And hold the hedge-bird's breakfast, — then
  indeed
The prize though poor would pay the care and
  toil!
Respect we Nature that makes least as most,
Marvelous in the minim! But this bud,
Bit through and burned black by the tempter's
  tooth,
This bloom whose best grace was the slug out-
  side
And the wasp inside its bosom, — call you
  " rose " ?
Claim no immunity from a weed's fate
For the horrible present! What you call my
  wife
I call a nullity in female shape,
Vapid disgust, soon to be pungent plague,
When mixed with, made confusion and a curse
By two abominable nondescripts,
That father and that mother: think you see
The dreadful bronze our boast, we Aretines,
The Etruscan monster, the three-headed thing,
Bellerophon's foe! How name you the whole
  beast?
You choose to name the body from one head,
That of the simple kid which droops the eye,
Hangs the neck and dies tenderly enough :
I rather see the griesly lion belch
Flame out i' the midst, the serpent writhe her
  rings,
Grafted into the common stock for tail,
And name the brute, Chimæra, which I slew!
How was there ever more to be — (concede
My wife's insipid harmless nullity) —
Dissociation from that pair of plagues —
That mother with her cunning and her cant —
The eyes with first their twinkle of conceit,
Then, dropped to earth in mock-demureness, —
  now,
The smile self-satisfied from ear to ear,
Now, the prim pursed-up mouth's protruded
  lips,
With deferential duck, slow swing of head,
Tempting the sudden fist of man too much, —
That owl-like screw of lid and rock of ruff!
As for the father, — Cardinal, you know
The kind of idiot ! — such are rife in Rome,
But they wear velvet commonly ; good fools,
At the end of life, to furnish forth young folk
Who grin and bear with imbecility :
Since the stalled ass, the joker, sheds from jaw
Corn, in the joke, for those who laugh or
  starve.
But what say we to the same solemn beast
Wagging his ears and wishful of our pat,
When turned, with holes in hide and bones laid
  bare,
To forage for himself i' the waste o' the world,

Sir Dignity i' the dumps? Pat him? We drub
Self-knowledge, rather, into frowzy pate,
Teach Pietro to get trappings or go hang!
Fancy this quondam oracle in vogue
At Via Vittoria, this personified
Authority when time was, — Pantaloon
Flaunting his tom-fool tawdry just the same
As if Ash-Wednesday were mid-Carnival!
That 's the extreme and unforgivable
Of sins, as I account such. Have you stooped
For your own ends to bestialize yourself
By flattery of a fellow of this stamp?
The ends obtained or else shown out of reach,
He goes on, takes the flattery for pure truth, —
"You love, and honor me, of course: what next?"
What, but the trifle of the stabbing, friend? —
Which taught you how one worships when the shrine
Has lost the relic that we bent before.
Angry! And how could I be otherwise?
'T is plain: this pair of old pretentious fools
Meant to fool me: it happens, I fooled them.
Why could not these who sought to buy and sell
Me, — when they found themselves were bought and sold,
Make up their mind to the proved rule of right,
Be chattel and not chapman any more?
Miscalculation has its consequence;
But when the shepherd crooks a sheep-like thing
And meaning to get wool, dislodges fleece
And finds the veritable wolf beneath,
(How that stanch image serves at every turn!)
Does he, by way of being politic,
Pluck the first whisker grimly visible?
Or rather grow in a trice all gratitude,
Protest this sort-of-what-one-might-name sheep
Beats the old other curly-coated kind,
And shall share board and bed, if so it deign,
With its discoverer, like a royal ram?
Ay, thus, with chattering teeth and knocking knees,
Would wisdom treat the adventure! these, forsooth,
Tried whisker-plucking, and so found what trap
The whisker kept perdue, two rows of teeth —
Sharp, as too late the prying fingers felt.
What would you have? The fools transgress, the fools
Forthwith receive appropriate punishment:
They first insult me, I return the blow,
There follows noise enough: four hubbub months,
Now hue and cry, now whimpering and wail —
A perfect goose-yard cackle of complaint
Because I do not gild the geese their oats, —
I have enough of noise, ope wicket wide,
Sweep out the couple to go whine elsewhere.
Frightened a little, hurt in no respect,
And am just taking thought to breathe again,
Taste the sweet sudden silence all about,
When, there they raise it, the old noise I know,
At Rome i' the distance! "What, begun once more?

Whine on, wail ever, 't is the loser's right!"
But eh, what sort of voice grows on the wind?
Triumph it sounds and no complaint at all!
And triumph it is. My boast was premature:
The creatures, I turned forth, clapped wing and crew
Fighting-cock-fashion, — they had filched a pearl
From dung-heap, and might boast with cause enough!
I was defrauded of all bargained for:
You know, the Pope knows, not a soul but knows
My dowry was derision, my gain — muck,
My wife (the Church declared my flesh and blood)
The nameless bastard of a common whore:
My old name turned henceforth to . . . shall I say
"He that received the ordure in his face"?
And they who planned this wrong, performed this wrong,
And then revealed this wrong to the wide world,
Rounded myself in the ears with my own wrong, —
Why, these were (note hell's lucky malice, now!)
These were just they who, they alone, could act
And publish and proclaim their infamy,
Secure that men would in a breath believe,
Compassionate and pardon them, — for why?
They plainly were too stupid to invent,
Too simple to distinguish wrong from right, —
Inconscious agents they, the silly-sooth,
Of heaven's retributive justice on the strong
Proud cunning violent oppressor — me!
Follow them to their fate and help your best,
You Rome, Arezzo, foes called friends of me,
They gave the good long laugh to, at my cost!
Defray your share o' the cost, since you partook
The entertainment! Do! — assured the while,
That not one stab, I dealt to right and left,
But went the deeper for a fancy — this —
That each might do me twofold service, find
A friend's face at the bottom of each wound,
And scratch its smirk a little!
                                     Panciatichi!
There 's a report at Florence, — is it true? —
That when your relative the Cardinal
Built, only the other day, that barrack-bulk,
The palace in Via Larga, some one picked
From out the street a saucy quip enough
That fell there from its day's flight through the town,
About the flat front and the windows wide
And bulging heap of cornice, — hitched the joke
Into a sonnet, signed his name thereto,
And forthwith pinned on post the pleasantry:
For which he 's at the galleys, rowing now
Up to his waist in water, — just because
Panciatic and *lymphatic* rhymed so pat!
I hope, Sir, those who passed this joke on me
Were not unduly punished? What say you,
Prince of the Church, my patron? Nay, in deed,

I shall not dare insult your wits so much
As think this problem difficult to solve.
This Pietro and Violante then, I say,
These two ambiguous insects, changing name
And nature with the season's warmth or
    chill, —
Now, grovelled, grubbing toiling moiling ants,
A very synonym of thrift and peace, —
Anon, with lusty June to prick their heart,
Soared i' the air, winged flies for more offence,
Circled me, buzzed me deaf and stung me blind,
And stunk me dead with fetor in the face
Until I stopped the nuisance: there's my
    crime!
Pity I did not suffer them subside
Into some further shape and final form
Of execrable life? My masters, no!
I, by one blow, wisely cut short at once
Them and their transformations of disgust,
In the snug little Villa out of hand.
"Grant me confession, give bare time for
    that!" —
Shouted the sinner till his mouth was stopped.
His life confessed! — that was enough for me,
Who came to see that he did penance. 'S
    death!
Here's a coil raised, a pother and for what?
Because strength, being provoked by weakness,
    fought
And conquered, — the world never heard the
    like!
Pah, how I spend my breath on them, as if
'T was their fate troubled me, too hard to
    range
Among the right and fit and proper things!

Ay, but Pompilia, — I await your word, —
She unimpeached of crime, unimplicate
In folly, one of alien blood to these
I punish, why extend my claim, exact
Her portion of the penalty? Yes, friends,
I go too fast: the orator's at fault:
Yes, ere I lay her, with your leave, by them
As she was laid at San Lorenzo late,
I ought to step back, lead you by degrees,
Recounting at each step some fresh offence,
Up to the red bed, — never fear, I will!
Gaze at her, where I place her, to begin,
Confound me with her gentleness and worth!
The horrible pair have fled and left her now,
She has her husband for her sole concern:
His wife, the woman fashioned for his help,
Flesh of his flesh, bone of his bone, the bride
To groom as is the Church and Spouse to
    Christ:
There she stands in his presence: "Thy desire
Shall be to the husband, o'er thee shall he
    rule!"
— "Pompilia, who declare that you love God,
You know who said that: then, desire my love,
Yield me contentment and be ruled aright!"
She sits up, she lies down, she comes and goes,
Kneels at the couch-side, overleans the sill
O' the window, cold and pale and mute as
    stone,
Strong as stone also. "Well, are they not fled?
Am I not left, am I not one for all?
Speak a word, drop a tear, detach a glance,

Bless me or curse me of your own accord!
Is it the ceiling only wants your soul,
Is worth your eyes?" And then the eyes de
    scend,
And do look at me. Is it at the meal?
"Speak!" she obeys. "Be silent!" she
    obeys,
Counting the minutes till I cry "Depart,"
As brood-bird when you saunter past her eggs.
Departs she, just the same through door and
    wall
I see the same stone strength of white despair,
And all this will be never otherwise!
Before, the parents' presence lent her life:
She could play off her sex's armory,
Entreat, reproach, be female to my male,
Try all the shrieking doubles of the hare,
Go clamor to the Commissary, bid
The Archbishop hold my hands and stop my
    tongue,
And yield fair sport so: but the tactics change,
The hare stands stock-still to enrage the hound!
Since that day when she learned she was no
    child
Of those she thought her parents, — that their
    trick
Had tricked me whom she thought sole
    trickster late, —
Why, I suppose she said within herself,
"Then, no more struggle for my parents' sake!
And, for my own sake, why needs struggle
    be?"
But is there no third party to the pact?
What of her husband's relish or dislike
For this new game of giving up the game,
This worst offence of not offending more?
I'll not believe but instinct wrought in this,
Set her on to conceive and execute
The preferable plague: how sure they probe, —
These jades, the sensitivest soft of man!
The long black hair was wound now in a wisp,
Crowned sorrow better than the wild web late:
No more soiled dress, 't is trimness triumphs
    now,
For how should malice go with negligence?
The frayed silk looked the fresher for her
    spite!
There was an end to springing out of bed,
Praying me, with face buried on my feet,
Be hindered of my pastime, — so an end
To my rejoinder, "What, on the ground at
    last?
Vanquished in fight, a supplicant for life?
What if I raise you? 'Ware the casting down
When next you fight me!" Then, she lay
    there, mine:
Now, mine she is if I please wring her neck, —
A moment of disquiet, working eyes,
Protruding tongue, a long sigh, then no more, —
As if one killed the horse one could not ride!
Had I enjoined "Cut off the hair!" — why
    snap
The scissors, and at once a yard or so
Had fluttered in black serpents to the floor:
But till I did enjoin it, how she combs,
Uncurls and draws out to the complete length,
Plaits, places the insulting rope on head
To be an eyesore past dishevelment!

Is all done? Then sit still again and stare!
I advise — no one think to bear that look
Of steady wrong, endured as steadily
— Through what sustainment of deluding hope?
Who is the friend i' the background that notes
    all?
Who may come presently and close accounts?
This self-possession to the uttermost,
How does it differ in aught, save degree,
From the terrible patience of God?
                    "All which just means,
She did not love you!" Again the word is
    launched
And the fact fronts me! What, you try the
    wards
With the true key and the dead lock flies ope?
No, it sticks fast and leaves you fumbling still!
You have some fifty servants, Cardinal, —
Which of them loves you? Which subordinate
But makes parade of such officiousness
That — if there 's no love prompts it — love, the
    sham,
Does twice the service done by love, the true.
God bless us liars, where 's one touch of truth?
In what we tell the world, or world tells us,
Of how we love each other? All the same,
We calculate on word and deed, nor err, —
Bid such a man do such a loving act,
Sure of effect and negligent of cause,
Just as we bid a horse, with cluck of tongue,
Stretch his legs arch-wise, crouch his saddled
    back
To foot-reach of the stirrup — all for love,
And some for memory of the smart of switch
On the inside of the foreleg — what care we?
Yet where 's the bond obliges horse to man
Like that which binds fast wife to husband?
    God
Laid down the law: gave man the brawny arm
And ball of fist — woman the beardless cheek
And proper place to suffer in the side:
Since it is he can strike, let her obey!
Can she feel no love? Let her show the more,
Sham the worse, damn herself praiseworthily!
Who 's that soprano, Rome went mad about
Last week while I lay rotting in my straw?
The very jailer gossiped in his praise —
How, — dressed up like Armida, though a man;
And painted to look pretty, though a fright, —
He still made love so that the ladies swooned,
Being an eunuch. "Ah, Rinaldo mine!
But to breathe by thee while Jove slays us
    both!"
All the poor bloodless creature never felt,
Si, do, re, mi, fa, squeak and squall — for
    what?
Two gold zecchines the evening. Here 's my
    slave,
Whose body and soul depend upon my nod,
Can't falter out the first note in the scale
For her life! Why blame me if I take the life?
All women cannot give men love, forsooth!
No, nor all pullets lay the henwife eggs —
Whereat she bids them remedy the fault,
Brood on a chalk-ball: soon the nest is
    stocked —
Otherwise, to the plucking and the spit!
This wife of mine was of another mood —

Would not begin the lie that ends with truth,
Nor feign the love that brings real love about:
Wherefore I judged, sentenced, and punished
    her.
But why particularize, defend the deed?
Say that I hated her for no one cause
Beyond my pleasure so to do, — what then?
Just on as much incitement acts the world,
All of you! Look and like! You favor one,
Browbeat another, leave alone a third, —
Why should you master natural caprice?
Pure nature! Try: plant elm by ash in file;
Both unexceptionable trees enough,
They ought to overlean each other, pair
At top, and arch across the avenue
The whole path to the pleasaunce: do they so —
Or loathe, lie off abhorrent each from each?
Lay the fault elsewhere: since we must have
    faults,
Mine shall have been — seeing there 's ill in the
    end
Come of my course — that I fare somehow
    worse
For the way I took: my fault . . . as God 's
    my judge,
I see not where my fault lies, that 's the truth!
I ought . . . oh, ought in my own interest
Have let the whole adventure go untried,
This chance by marriage, — or else, trying it,
Ought to have turned it to account, some one
O' the hundred otherwises? Ay, my friend,
Easy to say, easy to do: step right
Now you 've stepped left and stumbled on the
    thing,
— The red thing! Doubt I any more than you
That practice makes man perfect? Give again
The chance, — same marriage and no other
    wife,
Be sure I 'll edify you! That 's because
I 'm practised, grown fit guide for Guido's self.
You proffered guidance, — I know, none so
    well, —
You laid down law and rolled decorum out,
From pulpit-corner on the gospel-side, —
Wanted to make your great experience mine,
Save me the personal search and pains so:
    thanks!
Take your word on life's use? When I take
    his —
The muzzled ox that treadeth out the corn,
Gone blind in padding round and round one
    path, —
As to the taste of green grass in the field!
What do you know o' the world that 's trodden
    flat
And salted sterile with your daily dung,
Leavened into a lump of loathsomeness?
Take your opinion of the modes of life,
The aims of life, life's triumph or defeat,
How to feel, how to scheme, and how to do
Or else leave undone? You preached long and
    loud
On high-days, "Take our doctrine upon trust!
Into the mill-house with you! Grind our corn,
Relish our chaff, and let the green grass grow!"
I tried chaff, found I famished on such fare,
So made this mad rush at the mill-house-door
Buried my head up to the ears in dew,

Browsed on the best : for which you brain me,
　　Sirs!
Be it so.　I conceived of life that way,
And still declare — life, without absolute use
Of the actual sweet therein, is death, not life.
Give me, — pay down, — not promise, which is
　　air, —
Something that 's out of life and better still,
Make sure reward, make certain punishment,
Entice me, scare me, — I 'll forego this life ;
Otherwise, no! — the less that words, mere wind,
Would cheat me of some minutes while they
　　plague,
Balk fulness of revenge here, — blame your-
　　selves
For this eruption of the pent-up soul
You prisoned first and played with afterward !
" Deny myself " meant simply pleasure you,
The sacred and superior, save the mark !
You, — whose stupidity and insolence
I must defer to, soothe at every turn, —
Whose swine-like snuffling greed and grunting
　　lust
I had to wink at or help gratify, —
While the same passions, — dared they perk in
　　me,
Me, the immeasurably marked, by God,
Master of the whole world of such as you, —
I, boast such passions ?　'T was, " Suppress
　　them straight !
Or stay, we 'll pick and choose before destroy.
Here 's wrath in you, a serviceable sword, —
Beat it into a ploughshare !　What 's this long
Lance-like ambition ?　Forge a pruning-hook,
May be of service when our vines grow tall !
But — sword used swordwise, spear thrust out
　　as spear ?
Anathema !　Suppression is the word ! "
My nature, when the outrage was too gross,
Widened itself an outlet over-wide
By way of answer, sought its own relief
With more of fire and brimstone than you
　　wished.
All your own doing : preachers, blame your-
　　selves !

'T is I preach while the hour-glass runs and
　　runs !
God keep me patient !　All I say just means —
My wife proved, whether by her fault or mine, —
That 's immaterial, — a true stumbling-block
I' the way of me her husband.　I but plied
The hatchet yourselves use to clear a path,
Was politic, played the game you warrant wins,
Plucked at law's robe a-rustle through the
　　courts,
Bowed down to kiss divinity's buckled shoe
Cushioned i' the church : efforts all wide the
　　aim !
Procedures to no purpose !　Then flashed truth.
The letter kills, the spirit keeps alive
In law and gospel : there be nods and winks
Instruct a wise man to assist himself
In certain matters, nor seek aid at all.
" Ask money of me," — quoth the clownish
　　saw, —
" And take my purse !　But, — speaking with
　　respect, —

Need you a solace for the troubled nose ?
Let everybody wipe his own himself ! "
Sirs, tell me free and fair !　Had things gone
　　well
At the wayside inn : had I surprised asleep
The runaways, as was so probable,
And pinned them each to other partridge-wise,
Through back and breast to breast and back,
　　then bade
Bystanders witness if the spit, my sword,
Were loaded with unlawful game for once —
Would you have interposed to damp the glow
Applauding me on every husband's cheek ?
Would you have checked the cry, " A judg-
　　ment, see !
A warning, note !　Be henceforth chaste, ye
　　wives,
Nor stray beyond your proper precinct,
　　priests ! "
If you had, then your house against itself
Divides, nor stands your kingdom any more.
Oh why, why was it not ordained just so ?
Why fell not things out so nor otherwise ?
Ask that particular devil whose task it is
To trip the all-but-at perfection, — slur
The line o' the painter just where paint leaves off
And life begins, — put ice into the ode
O' the poet while he cries " Next stanza — fire ! "
Inscribe all human effort with one word,
Artistry's haunting curse, the Incomplete !
Being incomplete, my act escaped success.
Easy to blame now !　Every fool can swear
To hole in net that held and slipped the fish.
But, treat my act with fair unjaundiced eye,
What was there wanting to a masterpiece
Except the luck that lies beyond a man ?
My way with the woman, now proved grossly
　　wrong,
Just missed of being gravely grandly right
And making mouths laugh on the other side.
Do, for the poor obstructed artist's sake,
Go with him over that spoiled work once more !
Take only its first flower, the ended act
Now in the dusty pod, dry and defunct !
I march to the Villa, and my men with me,
That evening, and we reach the door and stand.
I say . . . no, it shoots through me lightning-
　　like
While I pause, breathe, my hand upon the latch,
" Let me forebode !　Thus far, too much success :
I want the natural failure — find it where ?
Which thread will have to break and leave a
　　loop
I' the meshy combination, my brain's loom
Wove this long while, and now next minute
　　tests ?
Of three that are to catch, two should go free,
One must : all three surprised, — impossible !
Beside, I seek three and may chance on six, —
This neighbor, t' other gossip, — the babe's
　　birth
Brings such to fireside, and folks give them
　　wine, —
'T is late : but when I break in presently
One will be found outlingering the rest
For promise of a posset, — one whose shout
Would raise the dead down in the catacombs,
Much more the city-watch that goes its round.

When did I ever turn adroitly up
To sun some brick embedded in the soil,
And with one blow crush all three scorpions
there ?
Or Pietro or Violante shambles off —
It cannot be but I surprise my wife —
If only she is stopped and stamped on, good !
That shall suffice : more is improbable.
Now I may knock ! " And this once for my
sake
The impossible was effected : I called king,
Queen and knave in a sequence, and cards
came,
All three, three only ! So, I had my way,
Did my deed : so, unbrokenly lay bare
Each tænia that had sucked me dry of juice,
At last outside me, not an inch of ring
Left now to writhe about and root itself
I' the heart all powerless for revenge ! Hence-
forth
I might thrive : these were drawn and dead and
damned.
Oh, Cardinal, the deep long sigh you heave
When the load 's off you, ringing as it runs
All the way down the serpent-stair to hell !
No doubt the fine delirium flustered me,
Turned my brain with the influx of success
As if the sole need now were to wave wand
And find doors fly wide, — wish and have my
will, —
The rest o' the scheme would care for itself :
escape ?
Easy enough were that, and poor beside !
It all but proved so. — ought to quite have
proved,
Since, half the chances had sufficed, set free
Any one, with his senses at command,
From thrice the danger of my flight. But,
drunk,
Redundantly triumphant, — some reverse
Was sure to follow ! There 's no other way
Accounts for such prompt perfect failure then
And there on the instant. Any day o' the week,
A ducat slid discreetly into palm
O' the mute post-master, while you whisper
him —
How you the Count and certain four your
knaves,
Have just been mauling who was malapert,
Suspect the kindred may prove troublesome,
Therefore, want horses in a hurry, — that
And nothing more secures you any day
The pick o' the stable ! Yet I try the trick,
Double the bribe, call myself Duke for Count,
And say the dead man only was a Jew,
And for my pains find I am dealing just
With the one scrupulous fellow in all Rome —
Just this immaculate official stares,
Sees I want hat on head and sword in sheath,
Am splashed with other sort of wet than wine,
Shrugs shoulder, puts my hand by, gold and all,
Stands on the strictness of the rule o' the road !
" Where 's the Permission ? " Where 's the
wretched rag
With the due seal and sign of Rome's Police,
To be had for asking, half an hour ago ?
" Gone ? Get another, or no horses hence ! "
He dares not stop me, we five glare too grim,

But hinders, — hacks and hamstrings sure
enough,
Gives me some twenty miles of miry road
More to march in the middle of that night
Whereof the rough beginning taxed the strength
O' the youngsters, much more mine, both soul
and flesh,
Who had to think as well as act : dead-beat,
We gave in ere we reached the boundary
And safe spot out of this irrational Rome, —
Where, on dismounting from our steeds next
day,
We had snapped our fingers at you, safe and
sound,
Tuscans once more in blessed Tuscany,
Where laws make wise allowance, understand
Civilized life and do its champions right !
Witness the sentence of the Rota there,
Arezzo uttered, the Granduke confirmed,
One week before I acted on its hint, —
Giving friend Guillichini, for his love,
The galleys, and my wife your saint, Rome's
saint, —
Rome manufactures saints enough to know, —
Seclusion at the Stinche for her life.
All this, that all but was, might all have been,
Yet was not ! balked by just a scrupulous knave
Whose palm was horn through handling horses'
hoofs
And could not close upon my proffered gold !
What say you to the spite of fortune ? Well,
The worst 's in store : thus hindered, haled this
way
To Rome again by hangdogs, whom find I
Here, still to fight with, but my pale frail wife ?
— Riddled with wounds by one not like to
waste
The blows he dealt, — knowing anatomy, —
(I think I told you) bound to pick and choose
The vital parts ! 'T was learning all in vain !
She too must shimmer through the gloom o'
the grave,
Come and confront me — not at judgment-seat
Where I could twist her soul, as erst her flesh,
And turn her truth into a lie, — but there,
O' the death-bed, with God's hand between us
both,
Striking me dumb, and helping her to speak,
Tell her own story her own way, and turn
My plausibility to nothingness !
Four whole days did Pompilia keep alive,
With the best surgery of Rome agape
At the miracle, — this cut, the other slash,
And yet the life refusing to dislodge,
Four whole extravagant impossible days,
Till she had time to finish and persuade
Every man, every woman, every child
In Rome, of what she would : the selfsame she
Who, but a year ago, had wrung her hands,
Reddened her eyes and beat her breasts, re
hearsed
The whole game at Arezzo, nor availed
Thereby to move one heart or raise one hand
When destiny intends you cards like these,
What good of skill and preconcerted play ?
Had she been found dead, as I left her dead,
I should have told a tale brooked no reply :
You scarcely will suppose me found at fault

With that advantage ! "What brings me to Rome ?
Necessity to claim and take my wife :
Better, to claim and take my new-born babe, —
Strong in paternity a fortnight old,
When 't is at strongest : warily I work,
Knowing the machinations of my foe ;
I have companionship and use the night :
I seek my wife and child, — I find — no child
But wife, in the embraces of that priest
Who caused her to elope from me. These two,
Backed by the pander-pair who watch the while,
Spring on me like so many tiger-cats,
Glad of the chance to end the intruder. I —
What should I do but stand on my defence,
Strike right, strike left, strike thick and three-fold, slay,
Not all — because the coward priest escapes.
Last, I escape, in fear of evil tongues,
And having had my taste of Roman law."
What 's disputable, refutable here ? —
Save by just this one ghost-thing half on earth,
Half out of it. — as if she held God's hand
While she leant back and looked her last at me,
Forgiving me (here monks begin to weep)
Oh, from her very soul, commending mine
To heavenly mercies which are infinite, —
While fixing fast my head beneath your knife !
'T is fate, not fortune. All is of a piece !
When was it chance informed me of my youths ?
My rustic four o' the family, soft swains,
What sweet surprise had they in store for me,
Those of my very household. — what did Law
Twist with her rack-and-cord-contrivance late
From out their bones and marrow ? What but this —
Had no one of these several stumbling-blocks
Stopped me, they yet were cherishing a scheme,
All of their honest country homespun wit,
To quietly next day at crow of cock
Cut my own throat too, for their own behoof,
Seeing I had forgot to clear accounts
O' the instant, nowise slackened speed for that, —
And somehow never might find memory,
Once safe back in Arezzo. where things change,
And a court-lord needs mind no country lout.
Well, being the arch-offender, I die last, —
May, ere my head falls, have my eyesight free,
Nor miss them dangling high on either hand.
Like scarecrows in a hemp-field, for their pains !

And then my Trial, — 't is my Trial that bites
Like a corrosive, so the cards are packed,
Dice loaded. and my life-stake tricked away !
Look at my lawyers. lacked they grace of law,
Latin or logic? Were not they fools to the height,
Fools to the depth, fools to the level between,
O' the foolishness set to decide the case ?
They feign, they flatter ; nowise does it skill,
Everything goes against me : deal each judge
His dole of flattery and feigning, — why,
He turns and tries and snuffs and savors it,
As some old fly the sugar-grain, your gift ;

Then eyes your thumb and finger, brushes clean
The absurd old head of him, and whisks away,
Leaving your thumb and finger dirty. Faugh!

And finally, after this long-drawn range
Of affront and failure, failure and affront, —
This path, 'twixt crosses leading to a skull,
Paced by me barefoot, bloodied by my palms
From the entry to the end, — there 's light at length,
A cranny of escape : appeal may be
To the old man, to the father, to the Pope,
For a little life — from one whose life is spent,
A little pity — from pity's source and seat,
A little indulgence to rank, privilege,
From one who is the thing personified,
Rank, privilege, indulgence. grown beyond
Earth's bearing, even, ask Jansenius else !
Still the same answer, still no other tune
From the cicala perched at the tree-top
Than crickets noisy round the root, — 't is " Die ! "
Bids Law — " Be damned ! " adds Gospel, — nay,
No word so frank, — 't is rather, " Save yourself ! "
The Pope subjoins — " Confess and be absolved !
So shall my credit countervail your shame,
And the world see I have not lost the knack
Of trying all the spirits : yours, my son,
Wants but a fiery washing to emerge
In clarity ! Come, cleanse you, ease the ache
Of these old bones, refresh our bowels, boy ! "
Do I mistake your mission from the Pope ?
Then, bear his Holiness the mind of me !
I do get strength from being thrust to wall,
Successively wrenched from pillar and from post
By this tenacious hate of fortune, hate
Of all things in, under, and above earth.
Warfare, begun this mean unmanly mode,
Does best to end so, — gives earth spectacle
Of a brave fighter who succumbs to odds
That turn defeat to victory. Stab, I fold
My mantle round me ! Rome approves my act :
Applauds the blow which costs me life but keeps
My honor spotless : Rome would praise no more
Had I fallen, say, some fifteen years ago,
Helping Vienna when our Aretines
Flocked to Duke Charles and fought Turk Mustafa ;
Nor would you two be trembling o'er my corpse
With all this exquisite solicitude.
Why is it that I make such suit to live ?
The popular sympathy that 's round me now
Would break like bubble that o'er-domes a fly —
Solid enough while he lies quiet there,
But let him want the air and ply the wing,
Why, it breaks and bespatters him, what else ?
Cardinal, if the Pope had pardoned me,
And I walked out of prison through the crowd,
It would not be your arm I should dare press !
Then, if I got safe to my place again,
How sad and sapless were the years to come!

I go my old ways and find things grown gray ;
You priests leer at me, old friends look as-
    kance ;
The mob 's in love, I 'll wager, to a man,
With my poor young good beauteous murdered
    wife :
For hearts require instruction how to beat,
And eyes, on warrant of the story, wax
Wanton at portraiture in white and black
Of dead Pompilia gracing ballad-sheet,
Which eyes, lived she unmurdered and unsung,
Would never turn though she paced street as
    bare
As the mad penitent ladies do in France.
My brothers quietly would edge me out
Of use and management of things called mine ;
Do I command ? " You stretched command
    before ! "
Show anger ? " Anger little helped you once ! "
Advise ? " How managed you affairs of old ? "
My very mother, all the while they gird,
Turns eye up, gives confirmatory groan ;
For unsuccess, explain it how you will,
Disqualifies you, makes you doubt yourself,
—Much more, is found decisive by your friends.
Beside, am I not fifty years of age ?
What new leap would a life take, checked like
    mine
I' the spring at outset ? Where 's my second
    chance ?
Ay, but the babe . . . I had forgot my son,
My heir ! Now for a burst of gratitude !
There 's some appropriate service to intone,
Some gaudeamus and thanksgiving-psalm !
Old, I renew my youth in him, and poor
Possess a treasure, — is not that the phrase ?
Only I must wait patient twenty years —
Nourishing all the while, as father ought,
The excrescence with my daily blood of life.
Does it respond to hope, such sacrifice, —
Grows the wen plump while I myself grow
    lean ?
Why, here 's my son and heir in evidence,
Who stronger, wiser, handsomer than I
By fifty years, relieves me of each load, —
Tames my hot horse, carries my heavy gun,
Courts my coy mistress, — has his apt advice
On house-economy, expenditure,
And what not ? All which good gifts and great
    growth,
Because of my decline, he brings to bear
On Guido, but half apprehensive how
He cumbers earth, crosses the brisk young
    Count,
Who civilly would thrust him from the scene.
Contrariwise, does the blood-offering fail ?
There 's an ineptitude, one blank the more
Added to earth in semblance of my child ?
Then, this has been a costly piece of work,
My life exchanged for his ! — why he, not I,
Enjoy the world, if no more grace accrue ?
Dwarf me, what giant have you made of him ?
I do not dread the disobedient son —
I know how to suppress rebellion there,
Being not quite the fool my father was.
But grant the medium measure of a man,
The usual compromise 'twixt fool and sage,
—You know — the tolerably-obstinate,

The not-so-much-perverse but you may train,
The true son-servant that, when parent bids
" Go work, son, in my vineyard ! " makes reply
" I go, Sir ! " — Why, what profit in your son
Beyond the drudges you might subsidize,
Have the same work from, at a paul the head ?
Look at those four young precious olive-plants
Reared at Vittiano, — not on flesh and blood,
These twenty years, but black bread and sour
    wine !
I bade them put forth tender branch, hook, hold,
And hurt three enemies I had in Rome :
They did my hest as unreluctantly,
At promise of a dollar, as a son
Adjured by mumping memories of the past.
No, nothing repays youth expended so —
Youth, I say, who am young still : grant but
    leave
To live my life out, to the last I 'd live
And die conceding age no right of youth !
It is the will runs the renewing nerve
Through flaccid flesh that faints before the
    time.
Therefore no sort of use for son have I —
Sick, not of life's feast but of steps to climb
To the house where life prepares her feast, —
    of means
To the end : for make the end attainable
Without the means, — my relish were like
    yours.
A man may have an appetite enough
For a whole dish of robins ready cooked,
And yet lack courage to face sleet, pad snow,
And snare sufficiently for supper.

                                    Thus
The time 's arrived when, ancient Roman-like,
I am bound to fall on my own sword : why not
Say — Tuscan-like, more ancient, better still ?
Will you hear truth can do no harm nor good ?
I think I never was at any time
A Christian, as you nickname all the world,
Me among others : truce to nonsense now !
Name me, a primitive religionist —
As should the aboriginary be
I boast myself, Etruscan, Aretine,
One sprung — your frigid Virgil's fieriest word —
From fauns and nymphs, trunks and the heart
    of oak,
With — for a visible divinity —
The portent of a Jove Ægiochus
Descried 'mid clouds, lightning and thunder,
    couched
On topmost crag of your Capitoline :
'T is in the Seventh Æneid, — what, the
    Eighth ?
Right, — thanks, Abate, — though the Chris-
    tian 's dumb,
The Latinist 's vivacious in you yet !
I know my grandsire had our tapestry
Marked with the motto, 'neath a certain shield,
Whereto his grandson presently will give gules
To vary azure. First we fight for faiths,
But get to shake hands at the last of all :
Mine 's your faith too, — in Jove Ægiochus !
Nor do Greek gods, that serve as supplement,
Jar with the simpler scheme, if understood.
We want such intermediary race

To make communication possible ;
The real thing were too lofty, we too low,
Midway hang these : we feel their use so plain
In linking height to depth, that we doff hat
And put no question nor pry narrowly
Into the nature hid behind the names.
We grudge no rite the fancy may demand ;
But never, more than needs, invent, refine,
Improve upon requirement, idly wise
Beyond the letter, teaching gods their trade,
Which is to teach us : we 'll obey when taught.
Why should we do our duty past the need ?
When the sky darkens, Jove is wroth, — say
    prayer !
When the sun shines and Jove is glad, — sing
    psalm !
But wherefore pass prescription and devise
Blood-offering for sweat-service, lend the rod
A pungency through pickle of our own ?
Learned Abate, — no one teaches you
What Venus means and who 's Apollo here !
I spare you, Cardinal, — but, though you wince,
You know me, I know you, and both know
    that !
So, if Apollo bids us fast, we fast :
But where does Venus order we stop sense
When Master Pietro rhymes a pleasantry ?
Give alms prescribed on Friday, — but, hold
    hand
Because your foe lies prostrate, — where 's the
    word
Explicit in the book debars revenge ?
The rationale of your scheme is just
" Pay toll here, there pursue your pleasure
    free ! "
So do you turn to use the medium-powers,
Mars and Minerva, Bacchus and the rest,
And so are saved propitiating — whom ?
What all-good, all-wise, and all-potent Jove
Vexed by the very sins in man, himself
Made life's necessity when man he made ?
Irrational bunglers ! So, the living truth
Revealed to strike Pan dead, ducks low at last,
Prays leave to hold its own and live good days
Provided it go masque grotesquely, called
Christian not Pagan. Oh, you purged the sky
Of all gods save the One, the great and good,
Clapped hands and triumphed ! But the change
    came fast :
The inexorable need in man for life
(Life, you may mulct and minish to a grain
Out of the lump, so that the grain but live)
Laughed at your substituting death for life, —
And bade you do your worst : which worst was
    done
In just that age styled primitive and pure
When Saint this, Saint that, dutifully starved,
Froze, fought with beasts, was beaten and abused
And finally ridded of his flesh by fire :
He kept life-long unspotted from the world ! —
Next age, how goes the game, what mortal gives
His life and emulates Saint that, Saint this ?
Men mutter, make excuse, or mutiny,
In fine are minded all to leave the new,
Stick to the old, — enjoy old liberty,
No prejudice in enjoyment, if you please,
To the new profession : sin o' the sly, hence-
    forth !

The law stands though the letter kills : what
    then ?
The spirit saves as unmistakably.
Omniscience sees, Omnipotence could stop,
Omnibenevolence pardons : it must be,
Frown law its fiercest, there 's a wink some-
    where !

Such was the logic in this head of mine :
I, like the rest, wrote " poison " on my bread,
But broke and ate : — said " Those that use the
    sword
Shall perish by the same ; " then stabbed my
    foe.
I stand on solid earth, not empty air :
Dislodge me, let your Pope's crook hale me
    hence !
Not he, nor you ! And I so pity both,
I 'll make the true charge you want wit to
    make :
" Count Guido, who reveal our mystery,
And trace all issues to the love of life :
We having life to love and guard, like you,
Why did you put us upon self-defence ?
You well knew what prompt pass-word would
    appease
The sentry's ire when folk infringed his bounds,
And yet kept mouth shut : do you wonder then
If, in mere decency, he shot you dead ?
He can't have people play such pranks as yours
Beneath his nose at noonday : you disdained
To give him an excuse before the world
By crying ' I break rule to save our camp ! '
Under the old rule, such offence were death ;
And you had heard the Pontifex pronounce,
' Since you slay foe and violate the form,
Slaying turns murder, which were sacrifice
Had you, while, say, lawsuiting foe to death,
But raised an altar to the Unknown God,
Or else the Genius of the Vatican.'
Why then this pother ? — all because the Pope,
Doing his duty, cried ' A foreigner,
You scandalize the natives : here at Rome
Romano vivitur more : wise men, here,
Put the Church forward and efface themselves.
The fit defence had been, — you stamped on
    wheat,
Intending all the time to trample tares, —
Were fain extirpate, then, the heretic,
You now find, in your haste was slain a fool :
Nor Pietro, nor Violante, nor your wife
Meant to breed up your babe a Molinist !
Whence you are duly contrite. Not one word
Of all this wisdom did you urge : which slip
Death must atone for.' "
                        So, let death atone !
So ends mistake, so end mistakers ! — end
Perhaps to recommence, — how should I know ?
Only, be sure, no punishment, no pain
Childish, preposterous, impossible,
But some such fate as Ovid could foresee, —
Byblis in fluvium, let the weak soul end
In water, sed Lycaon in lupum, but
The strong become a wolf forevermore !
Change that Pompilia to a puny stream
Fit to reflect the daisies on its bank !
Let me turn wolf, be whole, and sate, for
    once, —

Wallow in what is now a wolfishness
Coerced too much by the humanity
That's half of me as well!   Grow out of man,
Glut the wolf-nature, — what remains but grow
Into the man again, be man indeed
And all man? Do I ring the changes right?
Deformed, transformed, reformed, informed,
      conformed!
The honest instinct, pent and crossed through
      life,
Let surge by death into a visible flow
Of rapture: as the strangled thread of flame
Painfully winds, annoying and annoyed,
Malignant and maligned, through stone and
      ore,
Till earth exclude the stranger: vented once,
It finds full play, is recognized atop
Some mountain as no such abnormal birth,
Fire for the mount, not streamlet for the vale!
Ay, of the water was that wife of mine —
Be it for good, be it for ill, no run
O' the red thread through that insignificance!
Again, how she is at me with those eyes!
Away with the empty stare! Be holy still,
And stupid ever! Occupy your patch
Of private snow that's somewhere in what
      world
May now be growing icy round your head,
And aguish at your footprint, — freeze not me,
Dare follow not another step I take,
Not with so much as those detested eyes,
No, though they follow but to pray me pause
On the incline, earth's edge that's next to hell!
None of your abnegation of revenge!
Fly at me frank, tug while I tear again!
There's God, go tell him, testify your worst!
Not she! There was no touch in her of hate!
And it would prove her hell, if I reached mine!
To know I suffered, would still sadden her,
Do what the angels might to make amends!
Therefore there's either no such place as hell,
Or thence shall I be thrust forth, for her sake,
And thereby undergo three hells, not one —
I who, with outlet for escape to heaven,
Would tarry if such flight allowed my foe
To raise his head, relieved of that firm foot
Had pinned him to the fiery pavement else!
So am I made, " who did not make myself: "
(How dared she rob my own lip of the word?)
Beware me in what other world may be! —
Pompilia, who have brought me to this pass!
All I know here, will I say there, and go
Beyond the saying with the deed. Some use
There cannot but be for a mood like mine,
Implacable, persistent in revenge.
She maundered, " All is over and at end:
I go my own road, go you where God will!
Forgive you? I forget you! " There's the
      saint
That takes your taste, you other kind of men!
How you had loved her! Guido wanted skill
To value such a woman at her worth!
Properly the instructed criticise,
" What's here, you simpleton have tossed to
      take
Its chance i' the gutter? This a daub, indeed?
Why, 't is a Rafael that you kicked to rags! "
Perhaps so: some prefer the pure design:

Give me my gorge of color, glut of gold
In a glory round the Virgin made for me!
Titian 's the man, not Monk Angelico
Who traces you some timid chalky ghost
That turns the church into a charnel: ay,
Just such a pencil might depict my wife!
She, — since she, also, would not change her
      self, —
Why could not she come in some heart-shaped
      cloud,
Rainbowed about with riches, royalty
Rimming her round, as round the tintless lawn
Guardingly runs the selvage cloth of gold?
I would have left the faint fine gauze un-
      touched,
Needle-worked over with its lily and rose,
Let her bleach unmolested in the midst,
Chill that selected solitary spot
Of quietude she pleased to think was life.
Purity, pallor grace the lawn no doubt
When there's the costly bordure to unthread
And make again an ingot: but what's grace
When you want meat and drink and clothes
      and fire?

A tale comes to my mind that's apposite —
Possibly true, probably false, a truth
Such as all truths we live by, Cardinal!
'T is said, a certain ancestor of mine
Followed — whoever was the potentate,
To Paynimrie, and in some battle, broke
Through more than due allowance of the foe,
And, risking much his own life, saved the
      lord's.
Battered and bruised, the Emperor scrambles
      up,
Rubs his eyes and looks round and sees my
      sire,
Picks a furze-sprig from out his hauberk-joint,
(Token how near the ground went majesty,)
And says, " Take this, and if thou get safe
      home,
Plant the same in thy garden-ground to grow:
Run thence an hour in a straight line, and stop:
Describe a circle round (for central point)
The furze aforesaid, reaching every way
The length of that hour's run: I give it
      thee, —
The central point, to build a castle there,
The space circumjacent, for fit demesne,
The whole to be thy children's heritage, —
Whom, for the sake, bid thou wear furze on
      cap! "
Those are my arms: we turned the furze a tree
To show more, and the greyhound tied thereto,
Straining to start, means swift and greedy
      both;
He stands upon a triple mount of gold —
By Jove, then, he's escaping from true gold
And trying to arrive at empty air!
Aha! the fancy never crossed my mind!
My father used to tell me, and subjoin,
" As for the castle, that took wings and flew:
The broad lands, — why, to traverse them to-
      day
Scarce tasks my gouty feet, and in my prime
I doubt not I could stand and spit so far:
But for the furze, boy, fear no lack of that,

So long as fortune leaves one field to grub !
Wherefore, hurrah for furze and loyalty ! "
What may I mean, where may the lesson lurk ?
" Do not bestow on man, by way of gift,
Furze without land for framework, — vaunt no
    grace
Of purity, no furze-sprig of a wife,
To me, i' the thick of battle for my bread,
Without some better dowry, — gold will do ! "
No better gift than sordid muck ? Yes, Sirs !
Many more gifts much better. Give them me !
O those Olimpias bold, those Biancas brave,
That brought a husband power worth Ormuz'
    wealth !
Cried, " Thou being mine, why, what but thine
    am I ?
Be thou to me law, right, wrong, heaven and
    hell !
Let us blend souls, blent, thou in me, to bid
Two bodies work one pleasure ! What are these
Called king, priest, father, mother, stranger,
    friend ?
They fret thee or they frustrate ? Give the
    word —
Be certain they shall frustrate nothing more !
And who is this young florid foolishness
That holds thy fortune in his pygmy clutch,
— Being a prince and potency, forsooth ! —
He hesitates to let the trifle go ?
Let me but seal up eye, sing ear to sleep
Sounder than Samson, — pounce thou on the
    prize
Shall slip from off my breast, and down couch-
    side,
And on to floor, and far as my lord's feet —
Where he stands in the shadow with the knife,
Waiting to see what Delilah dares do !
Is the youth fair ? What is a man to me
Who am thy call-bird ? Twist his neck — my
    dupe's, —
Then take the breast shall turn a breast
    indeed ! "
Such women are there ; and they marry
    whom ?   •
Why, when a man has gone and hanged himself
Because of what he calls a wicked wife, —
See, if the very turpitude bemoaned
Prove not mere excellence the fool ignores !
His monster is perfection, — Circe, sent
Straight from the sun, with wand the idiot
    blames
As not an honest distaff to spin wool !
O thou Lucrezia, is it long to wait
Yonder where all the gloom is in a glow
With thy suspected presence ? — virgin yet,
Virtuous again, in face of what 's to teach —
Sin unimagined, unimaginable, —
I come to claim my bride, — thy Borgia's self
Not half the burning bridegroom I shall be !
Cardinal, take away your crucifix !
Abate, leave my lips alone, — they bite !
Vainly you try to change what should not
    change,
And shall not. I have bared, you bathe my
    heart —
It grows the stonier for your saving dew !
You steep the substance, you would lubricate,
In waters that but touch to petrify !

You too are petrifactions of a kind :
Move not a muscle that shows mercy ; rave
Another twelve hours, every word were waste !
I thought you would not slay impenitence,
But teased, from men you slew, contrition
    first, —
I thought you had a conscience. Cardinal,
You know I am wronged ! — wronged, say, and
    wronged, maintain.
Was this strict inquisition made for blood
When first you showed us scarlet on your back,
Called to the College ? Your straightforward
    way
To your legitimate end, — I think it passed
Over a scantling of heads brained, hearts broke,
Lives trodden into dust ! — how otherwise ?
Such was the way o' the world, and so you
    walked.
Does memory haunt your pillow ? Not a whit.
God wills you never pace your garden-path,
One appetizing hour ere dinner-time,
But your intrusion there treads out of life
A universe of happy innocent things :
Feel you remorse about that damsel-fly
Which buzzed so near your mouth and flapped
    your face ?
You blotted it from being at a blow :
It was a fly, you were a man, and more,
Lord of created things, so took your course.
Manliness, mind, — these are things fit to save,
Fit to brush fly from : why, because I take
My course, must needs the Pope kill me ? —
    kill you !
You ! for this instrument, he throws away,
Is strong to serve a master, and were yours
To have and hold and get much good from out '
The Pope who dooms me needs must die next
    year ;
I 'll tell you how the chances are supposed
For his successor : first the Chamberlain,
Old San Cesario, — Colloredo, next, —
Then, one, two, three, four, I refuse to name ;
After these, comes Altieri ; then come you —
Seventh on the list you come, unless . . . ha, ha,
How can a dead hand give a friend a lift ?
Are you the person to despise the help
O' the head shall drop in pannier presently ?
So a child seesaws on or kicks away
The fulcrum-stone that 's all the sage requires
To fit his lever to and move the world.
Cardinal, I adjure you in God's name,
Save my life, fall at the Pope's feet, set forth
Things your own fashion, not in words like these
Made for a sense like yours who apprehend !
Translate into the Court-conventional
" Count Guido must not die, is innocent !
Fair, be assured ! But what an he were foul,
Blood-drenched and murder-crusted head to
    foot ?
Spare one whose death insults the Emperor,
Nay, outrages the Louis you so love !
He has friends who will avenge him ; enemies
Who will hate God now with impunity,
Missing the old coercive : would you send
A soul straight to perdition, dying frank
An atheist ? " Go and say this, for God's sake !
— Why, you don't think I hope you 'll say one
    word ?

Neither shall I persuade you from your stand
Nor you persuade me from my station: take
Your crucifix away, I tell you twice!

Come, I am tired of silence! Pause enough!
You have prayed: I have gone inside my soul
And shut its door behind me: 't is your torch
Makes the place dark: the darkness let alone
Grows tolerable twilight: one may grope
And get to guess at length and breadth and
  depth.
What is this fact I feel persuaded of —
This something like a foothold in the sea,
Although Saint Peter's bark scuds, billow-
  borne,
Leaves me to founder where it flung me first?
Spite of your splashing, I am high and dry!
God takes his own part in each thing he made;
Made for a reason, he conserves his work,
Gives each its proper instinct of defence.
My lamblike wife could neither bark nor bite,
She bleated, bleated, till for pity pure
The village roused up, ran with pole and prong
To the rescue, and behold the wolf's at bay!
Shall he try bleating? — or take turn or two,
Since the wolf owns some kinship with the fox,
And, failing to escape the foe by craft,
Give up attempt, die fighting quietly?
The last bad blow that strikes fire in at eye
And on to brain, and so out, life and all,
How can it but be cheated of a pang
If, fighting quietly, the jaws enjoy
One re-embrace in mid backbone they break,
After their weary work through the foe's flesh?
That's the wolf-nature. Don't mistake my
  trope!
A Cardinal so qualmish? Eminence,
My fight is figurative, blows i' the air,
Brain-war with powers and principalities,
Spirit-bravado, no real fisticuffs!
I shall not presently, when the knock comes,
Cling to this bench nor claw the hangman's face,
No, trust me! I conceive worse lots than mine.
Whether it be, the old contagious fit
And plague o' the prison have surprised me
  too,
The appropriate drunkenness of the death-hour
Crept on my sense, kind work o' the wine and
  myrrh, —
I know not, — I begin to taste my strength,
Careless, gay even. What's the worth of life?
The Pope 's dead now, my murderous old man,
For Tozzi told me so: and you, forsooth —
Why, you don't think, Abate, do your best,
You 'll live a year more with that hacking cough
And blotch of crimson where the cheek 's a pit?
Tozzi has got you also down in book!
Cardinal, only seventh of seventy near,
Is not one called Albano in the lot?
Go eat your heart, you 'll never be a Pope!
Inform me, is it true you left your love,
A Pucci, for promotion in the church?
She 's more than in the church — in the church-
  yard!
Plautilla Pucci, your affianced bride,
Has dust now in the eyes that held the love, —
And Martinez, suppose they make you Pope,
Stops that with veto, — so, enjoy yourself!

I see you all reel to the rock, you waves —
Some forthright, some describe a sinuous track,
Some, crested brilliantly, with heads above,
Some in a strangled swirl sunk who knows
  how,
But all bound whither the main-current sets
Rockward, an end in foam for all of you!
What if I be o'ertaken, pushed to the front
By all you crowding smoother souls behind,
And reach, a minute sooner than was meant,
The boundary whereon I break to mist?
Go to! the smoothest safest of you all,
Most perfect and compact wave in my train,
Spite of the blue tranquillity above,
Spite of the breadth before of lapsing peace,
Where broods the halcyon and the fish leaps
  free,
Will presently begin to feel the prick
At lazy heart, the push at torpid brain,
Will rock vertiginously in turn, and reel,
And, emulative, rush to death like me.
Later or sooner by a minute then,
So much for the untimeliness of death!
And, as regards the manner that offends,
The rude and rough, I count the same for gain.
Be the act harsh and quick! Undoubtedly
The soul 's condensed and, twice itself, expands
To burst through life, by alternation due,
Into the other state whate'er it prove.
You never know what life means till you die:
Even throughout life, 't is death that makes
  life live,
Gives it whatever the significance.
For see, on your own ground and argument,
Suppose life had no death to fear, how find
A possibility of nobleness
In man, prevented daring any more?
What's love, what's faith without a worst to
  dread?
Lack-lustre jewelry! but faith and love
With death behind them bidding do or die —
Put such a foil at back, the sparkle 's born!
From out myself how the strange colors come!
Is there a new rule in another world?
Be sure I shall resign myself: as here
I recognized no law I could not see,
There, what I see, I shall acknowledge too:
On earth I never took the Pope for God,
In heaven I shall scarce take God for the Pope.
Unmanned, remanned: I hold it probable —
With something changeless at the heart of me
To know me by, some nucleus that 's myself:
Accretions did it wrong? Away with them —
You soon shall see the use of fire!

                              Till when,
All that was, is; and must forever be.
Nor is it in me to unhate my hates, —
I use up my last strength to strike once more
Old Pietro in the wine-house-gossip-face,
To trample underfoot the whine and wile
Of beast Violante, — and I grow one gorge
To loathingly reject Pompilia's pale
Poison my hasty hunger took for food.
A strong tree wants no wreaths about its trunk,
No cloying cups, no sickly sweet of scent,
But sustenance at root, a bucketful.
How else lived that Athenian who died so-

Drinking hot bull's blood, fit for men like me?
I lived and died a man, and take man's chance,
Honest and bold : right will be done to such.

Who are these you have let descend my stair ?
Ha, their accursed psalm ! Lights at the sill !
Is it " Open " they dare bid you ? Treachery !
Sirs, have I spoken one word all this while
Out of the world of words I had to say ?
Not one word ! All was folly — I laughed and
    mocked !
Sirs, my first true word, all truth and no lie,
Is — save me notwithstanding ! Life is all !
I was just stark mad, — let the madman live
Pressed by as many chains as you please pile !
Don't open ! Hold me from them ! I am
    yours,
I am the Granduke's — no, I am the Pope's !
Abate,— Cardinal,— Christ,— Maria,—God, . . .
Pompilia, will you let them murder me ?

XII

THE BOOK AND THE RING

Here were the end, had anything an end :
Thus, lit and launched, up and up roared and
    soared
A rocket, till the key o' the vault was reached,
And wide heaven held, a breathless minute-
    space,
In brilliant usurpature : thus caught spark.
Rushed to the height, and hung at full of fame
Over men's upturned faces, ghastly thence,
Our glaring Guido : now decline must be.
In its explosion, you have seen his act,
By my power — maybe, judged it by your
    own, —
Or composite as good orbs prove, or crammed
With worse ingredients than the Wormwood
    Star.
The act, over and ended, falls and fades :
What was once seen, grows what is now de-
    scribed,
Then talked of, told about, a tinge the less
In every fresh transmission ; till it melts,
Trickles in silent orange or wan gray
Across our memory, dies and leaves all dark,
And presently we find the stars again.
Follow the main streaks, meditate the mode
Of brightness, how it hastes to blend with
    black !

After that February Twenty Two,
Since our salvation, Sixteen Ninety Eight,
Of all reports that were, or may have been,
Concerning those the day killed or let live,
Four I count only. Take the first that comes.
A letter from a stranger, man of rank,
Venetian visitor at Rome, — who knows,
On what pretence of busy idleness ?
Thus he begins on evening of that day.

" Here are we at our end of Carnival ;
Prodigious gayety and monstrous mirth,

And constant shift of entertaining show :
With influx, from each quarter of the globe,
Of strangers nowise wishful to be last
I' the struggle for a good place presently
When that befalls fate cannot long defer.
The old Pope totters on the verge o' the grave
You see, Malpichi understood far more
Than Tozzi how to treat the ailments : age,
No question, renders these inveterate.
Cardinal Spada, actual Minister,
Is possible Pope ; I wager on his head,
Since those four entertainments of his niece
Which set all Rome a-stare : Pope probably
Though Colloredo has his backers too,
And San Cesario makes one doubt at times :
Altieri will be Chamberlain at most.

" A week ago the sun was warm like May,
And the old man took daily exercise
Along the river-side ; he loves to see
That Custom-house he built upon the bank,
For, Naples-born, his tastes are maritime :
But yesterday he had to keep in-doors
Because of the outrageous rain that fell.
On such days the good soul has fainting-fits,
Or lies in stupor, scarcely makes believe
Of minding business, fumbles at his beads.
They say, the trust that keeps his heart alive
Is that, by lasting till December next,
He may hold Jubilee a second time,
And, twice in one reign, ope the Holy Doors.
By the way, somebody responsible
Assures me that the King of France has writ
Fresh orders : Fénelon will be condemned :
The Cardinal makes a wry face enough,
Having a love for the delinquent : still,
He 's the ambassador, must press the point.
Have you a wager too, dependent here ?

" Now, from such matters to divert awhile,
Hear of to-day's event which crowns the week,
Casts all the other wagers into shade.
Tell Dandolo I owe him fifty drops
Of heart's blood in the shape of gold zecchines !
The Pope has done his worst : I have to pay
For the execution of the Count, by Jove !
Two days since, I reported him as safe,
Re-echoing the conviction of all Rome :
Who could suspect its one deaf ear — the
    Pope's ?
But prejudices grow insuperable,
And that old enmity to Austria, that
Passion for France and France's pageant-king
(Of which, why pause to multiply the proofs
Now scandalously rife in Europe's mouth ?)
These fairly got the better in our man
Of justice, prudence, and *esprit de corps*,
And he persisted in the butchery.
Also, 't is said that in his latest walk
To that Dogana-by-the-Bank he built,
The crowd, — he suffers question, unrebuked,
Asked, ' Whether murder was a privilege
Only reserved for nobles like the Count ? '
And he was ever mindful of the mob.
Martinez, the Cæsarean Minister,
— Who used his best endeavors to spare blood,
And strongly pleaded for the life ' of one,'
Urged he. ' I may have dined at table with ! '

He will not soon forget the Pope's rebuff,
— Feels the slight sensibly, I promise you !
And but for the dissuasion of two eyes
That make with him foul weather or fine day,
He had abstained, nor graced the spectacle :
As it was, barely would he condescend
Look forth from the *palchetto* where he sat
Under the Pincian : we shall hear of this !
The substituting, too, the People's Square
For the out-o'-the-way old quarter by the
    Bridge,
Was meant as a conciliatory sop
To the mob ; it gave one holiday the more.
But the French Embassy might unfurl flag, —
Still the good luck of France to fling a foe !
Cardinal Bouillon triumphs properly !
Palchetti were erected in the Place,
And houses, at the edge of the Three Streets,
Let their front windows at six dollars each :
Anguisciola, that patron of the arts,
Hired one ; our Envoy Contarini too.

" Now for the thing ; no sooner the decree
Gone forth, — 't is four-and-twenty hours ago, —
Than Acciaiuoli and Panciatichi,
Old friends, indeed compatriots of the man,
Being pitched on as the couple properest
To intimate the sentence yesternight,
Were closeted ere cock-crow with the Count.
They both report their efforts to dispose
The unhappy nobleman for ending well,
Despite the natural sense of injury,
Were crowned at last with a complete success.
And when the Company of Death arrived
At twenty - hours, — the way they reckon
    here, —
We say, at sunset, after dinner-time, —
The Count was led down, hoisted up on car,
Last of the five, as heinousest, you know :
Yet they allowed one whole car to each man.
His intrepidity, nay, nonchalance,
As up he stood and down he sat himself,
Struck admiration into those who saw.
Then the procession started, took the way
From the New Prisons by the Pilgrim's Street.
The street of the Governo, Pasquin's Street,
(Where was stuck up, 'mid other epigrams,
A quatrain . . . but of all that, presently !)
The Place Navona, the Pantheon's Place,
Place of the Column, last the Corso's length,
And so debouched thence at Mannaia's foot
I' the Place o' the People. As is evident,
(Despite the malice, — plainly meant, I fear,
By this abrupt change of locality, —
The Square 's no such bad place to head and
    hang)
We had the titillation as we sat
Assembled, (quality in conclave, ha ?)
Of, minute after minute, some report
How the slow show was winding on its way.
Now did a car run over, kill a man,
Just opposite a pork-shop numbered Twelve :
And bitter were the outcries of the mob
Against the Pope : for, but that he forbids
The Lottery, why, Twelve were Tern Qua-
    tern !
Now did a beggar by Saint Agnes, lame
From his youth up, recover use of leg,

Through prayer of Guido as he glanced that
    way :
So that the crowd near crammed his hat with
    coin.
Thus was kept up excitement to the last,
— Not an abrupt out-bolting, as of yore,
From Castle, over Bridge and on to block,
And so all ended ere you well could wink !

" To mount the scaffold-steps, Guido was last
Here also, as atrociousest in crime.
We hardly noticed how the peasants died,
They dangled somehow soon to right and left,
And we remained all ears and eyes, could give
Ourselves to Guido undividedly,
As he harangued the multitude beneath.
He begged forgiveness on the part of God,
And fair construction of his act from men,
Whose suffrage he entreated for his soul,
Suggesting that we should forthwith repeat
A *Pater* and an *Ave*, with the hymn
Salve Regina Cœli, for his sake.
Which said, he turned to the confessor, crossed
And reconciled himself, with decency,
Oft glancing at Saint Mary's opposite,
Where they possess, and showed in shrine to-
    day,
The blessed *Umbilicus* of our Lord,
(A relic 't is believed no other church
In Rome can boast of) — then rose up, as brisk
Knelt down again, bent head, adapted neck,
And, with the name of Jesus on his lips,
Received the fatal blow.

        " The headsman showed
The head to the populace. Must I avouch
We strangers own to disappointment here ?
Report pronounced him fully six feet high,
Youngish, considering his fifty years,
And, if not handsome, dignified at least.
Indeed, it was no face to please a wife !
His friends say, this was caused by the cos-
    tume :
He wore the dress he did the murder in,
That is, a *just-a-corps* of russet serge,
Black camisole, coarse cloak of baracan
(So they style here the garb of goat's - hair
    cloth),
White hat and cotton cap beneath, poor Count,
Preservative against the evening dews
During the journey from Arezzo. Well,
So died the man, and so his end was peace ;
Whence many a moral were to meditate.
Spada — you may bet Dandolo — is Pope !
Now for the quatrain ! "

                No, friend, this will do !
You 've sputtered into sparks. What streak
    comes next ?
A letter : Don Giacinto Arcangeli,
Doctor and Proctor, him I made you mark
Buckle to business in his study late,
The virtuous sire, the valiant for the truth,
Acquaints his correspondent, — Florentine,
By name Cencini, advocate as well,
Socius and brother-in-the-devil to match, —
A friend of Franceschini, anyhow.

And knit up with the bowels of the case, —
Acquaints him (in this paper that I touch)
How their joint effort to obtain reprieve
For Guido had so nearly nicked the nine
And ninety and one over, — folk would say,
At Tarocs, — or succeeded, — in our phrase.
To this Cencini's care I owe the Book,
The yellow thing I take and toss once more, —
How will it be, my four-years'-intimate,
When thou and I part company anon ? —
'T was he, the " whole position of the case,"
Pleading and summary, were put before ;
Discreetly in my Book he bound them all,
Adding some three epistles to the point.
Here is the first of these, part fresh as penned,
The sand, that dried the ink, not rubbed away,
Though penned the day whereof it tells the
    deed :
Part — extant just as plainly, you know where,
Whence came t'·e other stuff, went, you know
    how,
To make the Ring that 's all but round and
    done.

" Late they arrived, too late, egregious Sir,
Those same justificative points you urge
Might benefit His Blessed Memory
Count Guido Franceschini now with God :
Since the Court, — to state things succinctly, —
    styled
The Congregation of the Governor,
Having resolved on Tuesday last our cause
I' the guilty sense, with death for punishment,
Spite of all pleas by me deducible
In favor of said Blessed Memory, —
I, with expenditure of pains enough,
Obtained a respite, leave to claim and prove
Exemption from the law's award, — alleged
The power and privilege o' the Clericate :
To which effect a courier was dispatched.
But ere an answer from Arezzo came,
The Holiness of our Lord the Pope (prepare !)
Judging it inexpedient to postpone
The execution of such sentence passed,
Saw fit, by his particular chirograph,
To derogate, dispense with privilege,
And wink at any hurt accruing thence
To Mother Church through damage of her son :
Also, to overpass and set aside
That other plea on score of tender age,
Put forth by me to do Pasquini good,
One of the four in trouble with our friend.
So that all five, to-day, have suffered death
With no distinction save in dying, — he,
Decollate by mere due of privilege,
The rest hanged decently and in order. Thus
Came the Count to his end of gallant man,
Defunct in faith and exemplarity :
Nor shall the shield of his great House lose
    shine
Thereby, nor its blue banner blush to red.
This, too, should yield sustainment to our
    hearts —
He had commiseration and respect
In his decease from universal Rome,
Quantum est hominum venustiorum,
The nice and cultivated everywhere :

Though, in respect of me his advocate,
Needs must I groan o'er my debility,
Attribute the untoward event o' the strife
To nothing but my own crass ignorance
Which failed to set the valid reasons forth,
Find fit excuse : such is the fate of war !
May God compensate us the direful blow
By future blessings on his family,
Whereof I lowly beg the next commands ;
— Whereto, as humbly, I confirm myself " . . .

And so forth, — follow name and place and
    date.
On next leaf —
            " *Hactenus senioribus !*
There, old fox, show the clients t' other side
And keep this corner sacred, I beseech !
You and your pleas and proofs were what folk
    call
Pisan assistance, aid that comes too late,
Saves a man dead as nail in post of door.
Had I but time and space for narrative !
What was the good of twenty Clericates
When Somebody's thick headpiece once was
    bent
On seeing Guido's drop into the bag ?
How these old men like giving youth a push !
So much the better : next push goes to him,
And a new Pope begins the century.
Much good I get by my superb defence !
But argument is solid and subsists,
While obstinacy and ineptitude
Accompany the owner to his tomb ;
What do I care how soon ? Beside, folks see !
Rome will have relished heartily the show,
Yet understood the motives, never fear,
Which caused the indecent change o' the Peo-
    ple's Place
To the People's Playground, — stigmatize the
    spite
Which in a trice precipitated things !
As oft the moribund will give a kick
To show they are not absolutely dead,
So feebleness i' the socket shoots its last,
A spirt of violence for energy !

" But thou, Cencini, brother of my breast,
O fox, whose home is 'mid the tender grape,
Whose couch in Tuscany by Themis' throne,
Subject to no such . . . best I shut my mouth
Or only open it again to say,
This pother and confusion fairly laid,
My hands are empty and my satchel lank.
Now then for both the Matrimonial Cause
And the case of Gomez ! Serve them hot and
    hot !

" *Reliqua differamus in crastinum !*
The impatient estafette cracks whip outside :
Still, though the earth should swallow him
    who swears
And me who make the mischief, in must slip –
My boy, your godson, fat-chaps Hyacinth,
Enjoyed the sight while Papa plodded here.
I promised him, the rogue, a month ago,
The day his birthday was, of all the days,
That if I failed to save Count Guido's head,
Cinuccio should at least go see it chopped

From trunk — 'So, latinize your thanks!'
    quoth I,
'That I prefer, *hoc malim*,' raps me out
The rogue: you notice the subjunctive? Ah!
Accordingly he sat there, bold in box,
Proud as the Pope behind the peacock-fans:
Whereon a certain lady-patroness
For whom I manage things (my boy in front,
Her Marquis sat the third in evidence;
Boys have no eyes nor ears save for the show)
'This time, Cintino,' was her sportive word,
When whiz and thump went axe and mowed
    lay man,
And folk could fall to the suspended chat,
'This time, you see, Bottini rules the roast,
Nor can Papa with all his eloquence
Be reckoned on to help as heretofore!'
Whereat Cinone pouts; then, sparkishly —
'Papa knew better than aggrieve his Pope,
And balk him of his grudge against our Count,
Else he'd have argued-off Bottini's' . . .
    what?
'His nose,' — the rogue! well parried of the
    boy!
He's long since out of Cæsar (eight years old)
And as for tripping in Eutropius . . . well,
Reason the more that we strain every nerve
To do him justice, mould a model-mouth,
A Bartolus-cum-Baldo for next age:
For that I purse the pieces, work the brain,
And want both Gomez and the marriage-case,
Success with which shall plaster aught of pate
That's broken in me by Bottini's flail,
And bruise his own, belike, that wags and
    brags.
Adverti supplico humiliter
Quod, don't the fungus see, the fop divine
That one hand drives two horses, left and
    right?
With this reign did I rescue from the ditch
The fortune of our Franceschini, keep
Unsplashed the credit of a noble House,
And set the fashionable cause at Rome
A-prancing till bystanders shouted ''ware!'
The other rein's judicious management
Suffered old Somebody to keep the pace,
Hobblingly play the roadster: who but he
Had his opinion, was not led by the nose
In leash of quibbles strung to look like law!
You'll soon see, — when I go to pay devoir
And compliment him on confuting me, —
If, by a back-swing of the pendulum,
Grace be not, thick and threefold, consequent.
'I must decide as I see proper, Don!
I'm Pope, I have my inward lights for guide.
Had learning been the matter in dispute,
Could eloquence avail to gainsay fact,
Yours were the victory, be comforted!'
Cinuzzo will be gainer by it all.
Quick then with Gomez, hot and hot next
    case!'"

Follows, a letter, takes the other side.
Tall blue-eyed Fisc whose head is capped with
    cloud,
Doctor Bottini, — to no matter who,
Writes on the Monday two days afterward.

Now shall the honest championship of right,
Crowned with success, enjoy at last, unblamed.
Moderate triumph! Now shall eloquence
Poured forth in fancied floods for virtue's sake,
(The print is sorrowfully dyked and dammed,
But shows where fain the unbridled force
    would flow,
Finding a channel) — now shall this refresh
The thirsty donor with a drop or two!
Here has been truth at issue with a lie:
Let who gained truth the day have handsome
    pride
In his own prowess! Eh? What ails the
    man?

———

" Well, it is over, ends as I foresaw:
Easily proved, Pompilia's innocence!
Catch them entrusting Guido's guilt to me
Who had, as usual, the plain truth to plead.
I always knew the clearness of the stream
Would show the fish so thoroughly, child might
    prong
The clumsy monster: with no mud to splash,
Small credit to lynx-eye and lightning-spear!
This Guido — (much sport he contrived to
    make,
Who at first twist, preamble of the cord,
Turned white, told all, like the poltroon he
    was!) —
Finished, as you expect, a penitent,
Fully confessed his crime, and made amends,
And, edifying Rome last Saturday,
Died like a saint, poor devil! That's the man
The gods still give to my antagonist:
Imagine how Arcangeli claps wing
And crows! 'Such formidable facts to face,
So naked to attack, my client here,
And yet I kept a month the Fisc at bay,
And in the end had foiled him of the prize
By this arch-stroke, this plea of privilege,
But that the Pope must gratify his whim,
Put in his word, poor old man, — let it pass!'
— Such is the cue to which all Rome responds
What with the plain truth given me to uphold,
And, should I let truth slip, the Pope at hand
To pick up, steady her on legs again,
My office turns a pleasantry indeed!
Not that the burly boaster did one jot
O' the little was to do — young Spreti's work!
But for him, — manikin and dandiprat,
Mere candle-end and inch of cleverness
Stuck on Arcangeli's save-all, — but for him
The spruce young Spreti, what is bad were
    worse!

" I looked that Rome should have the natural
    gird
At advocate with case that proves itself;
I knew Arcangeli would grin and brag:
But what say you to one impertinence
Might move a stone? That monk, you are to
    know,
That barefoot Augustinian whose report
O' the dying woman's words did detriment
To my best points it took the freshness from,
— That meddler preached to purpose yesterday
At San Lorenzo as a winding-up

O' the show which proved a treasure to the
    church.
Out comes his sermon smoking from the press :
Its text — ' Let God be true, and every man
A liar ' — and its application, this,
The longest-winded of the paragraphs,
I straight unstitch, tear out and treat you
    with :
'T is piping hot and posts through Rome to-
    day.
Remember it, as I engage to do !

" But if you rather be disposed to see
In the result of the long trial here, —
This dealing doom to guilt and doling praise
To innocency, — any proof that truth
May look for vindication from the world,
Much will you have misread the signs, I say.
God, who seems acquiescent in the main
With those who add ' So will he ever sleep ' —
Flutters their foolishness from time to time,
Puts forth his right-hand recognizably ;
Even as, to fools who deem he needs must right
Wrong on the instant, as if earth were heaven,
He wakes remonstrance — ' Passive, Lord,
    how long ? '
Because Pompilia's purity prevails,
Conclude you, all truth triumphs in the end ?
So might those old inhabitants of the ark,
Witnessing haply their dove's safe return,
Pronounce there was no danger, all the while
O' the deluge, to the creature's counterparts,
Aught that beat wing i' the world, was white
    or soft, —
And that the lark, the thrush, the culver too,
Might equally have traversed air, found earth,
And brought back olive-branch in unharmed
    bill.
Methinks I hear the Patriarch's warning
    voice —
' Though this one breast, by miracle, return,
No wave rolls by, in all the waste, but bears
Within it some dead dove-like thing as dear,
Beauty made blank and harmlessness de-
    stroyed ! '
How many chaste and noble sister-fames
Wanted the extricating hand, so lie
Strangled, for one Pompilia proud above
The welter, plucked from the world's calumny,
Stupidity, simplicity, — who cares ?

" Romans ! An elder race possessed your land
Long ago, and a false faith lingered still,
As shades do, though the morning-star be out.
Doubtless some pagan of the twilight-day
Has often pointed to a cavern-mouth,
Obnoxious to beholders, hard by Rome,
And said, — nor he a bad man, no, nor fool, —
Only a man born blind like all his mates, —
' Here skulk in safety, lurk, defying law,
The devotees to execrable creed,
Adoring — with what culture . . . Jove, avert
Thy vengeance from us worshippers of
    thee ! . . .
What rites obscene — their idol-god an Ass ! '
So went the word forth, so acceptance found,
So century re-echoed century,

Cursed the accursed, — and so, from sire to
    son,
You Romans cried, ' The offscourings of our
    race,
Corrupt within the depths there : fitly fiends
Perform a temple-service o'er the dead :
Child, gather garment round thee, pass nor
    pry ! '
Thus groaned your generations : till the time
Grew ripe, and lightning had revealed, belike,—
Through crevice peeped into by curious fear, —
Some object even fear could recognize
I' the place of spectres ; on the illumined wall,
To wit, some nook, tradition talks about,
Narrow and short, a corpse's length, no more :
And by it, in the due receptacle,
The little rude brown lamp of earthenware,
The cruse, was meant for flowers, but now held
    blood,
The rough-scratched palm-branch, and the
    legend left
Pro Christo. Then the mystery lay clear :
The abhorred one was a martyr all the time,
Heaven's saint whereof earth was not worthy.
    What ?
Do you continue in the old belief ?
Where blackness bides unbroke, must devils
    brood ?
Is it so certain not another cell
O' the myriad that make up the catacomb,
Contains some saint a second flash would show ?
Will you ascend into the light of day
And, having recognized a martyr's shrine,
Go join the votaries that gape around
Each vulgar god that awes the market-place ?
Are these the objects of your praising ? See !
In the outstretched right hand of Apollo, there,
Lies screened a scorpion : housed amid the
    folds
Of Juno's mantle lurks a centipede !
Each statue of a god were fitlier styled
Demon and devil. Glorify no brass
That shines like burnished gold in noonday
    glare,
For fools ! Be otherwise instructed, you !
And preferably ponder, ere ye judge,
Each incident of this strange human play
Privily acted on a theatre
That seemed secure from every gaze but
    God's, —
Till, of a sudden, earthquake laid wall low
And let the world perceive wild work inside,
And how, in petrifaction of surprise,
The actors stood, — raised arm and planted
    foot, —
Mouth as it made, eye as it evidenced,
Despairing shriek, triumphant hate, — trans-
    fixed,
Both he who takes and she who yields the life.

" As ye become spectators of this scene —
Watch obscuration of a pearl-pure fame
By vapory films, enwoven circumstance,
— A soul made weak by its pathetic want
Of just the first apprenticeship to sin,
Which thenceforth makes the sinning soul
    secure
From all foes save itself, soul's truliest foe, —

Since egg turned snake needs fear no ser-
    pentry, —
As ye behold this web of circumstance
Deepen the more for every thrill and throe,
Convulsive effort to disperse the films
And disenmesh the fame o' the martyr, — mark
How all those means, the unfriended one pur-
    sues,
To keep the treasure trusted to her breast,
Each struggle in the flight from death to life,
How all, by procuration of the powers
Of darkness, are transformed, — no single ray,
Shot forth to show and save the inmost star,
But, passed as through hell's prism, proceeding
    black
To the world that hates white : as ye watch, I
    say,
Till dusk and such defacement grow eclipse
By — marvellous perversity of man ! —
The inadequacy and inaptitude
Of that selfsame machine, that very law
Man vaunts, devised to dissipate the gloom,
Rescue the drowning orb from calumny,
— Hear law, appointed to defend the just,
Submit, for best defence, that wickedness
Was bred of flesh and innate with the bone
Borne by Pompilia's spirit for a space,
And no mere chance fault, passionate and
    brief :
Finally, when ye find, — after this touch
Of man's protection which intends to mar
The last pin-point of light and damn the disc, —
One wave of the hand of God amid the worlds
Bid vapor vanish, darkness flee away,
And let the vexed star culminate in peace
Approachable no more by earthly mist —
What I call God's hand, — you, perhaps, —
    mere chance
Of the true instinct of an old good man
Who happens to hate darkness and love light, —
In whom too was the eye that saw, not dim,
The natural force to do the thing he saw,
Nowise abated, — both by miracle, —
All this well pondered, — I demand assent
To the enunciation of my text
In face of one proof more that ' God is true
And every man a liar ' — that who trusts
To human testimony for a fact
Gets this sole fact — himself is proved a fool ;
Man's speech being false, if but by consequence
That only strength is true ! while man is weak,
And, since truth seem reserved for heaven not
    earth,
Plagued here by earth's prerogative of lies,
Should learn to love and long for what, one
    day,
Approved by life's probation, he may speak.

" For me, the weary and worn, who haply
    prompt
To mirth or pity, as I move the mood, —
A friar who glides unnoticed to the grave,
With these bare feet, coarse robe and rope-girt
    waist, —
I have long since renounced your world, ye
    know :
Yet what forbids I weigh the prize foregone,
The worldly worth ? I dare, as I were dead,

Disinterestedly judge this and that
Good ye account good : but God tries the heart.
Still, if you question me of my content
At having put each human pleasure by,
I answer, at the urgency of truth :
As this world seems, I dare not say I know
— Apart from Christ's assurance which de
    cides —
Whether I have not failed to taste much joy.
For many a doubt will fain perturb my choice —
Many a dream of life spent otherwise —
How human love, in varied shapes, might work
As glory, or as rapture, or as grace :
How conversancy with the books that teach,
The arts that help, — how, to grow good and
    great,
Rather than simply good, and bring thereby
Goodness to breathe and live, nor born, i' the
    brain,
Die there, — how these and many another gift
Of life are precious though abjured by me.
But, for one prize, best meed of mightiest man,
Arch-object of ambition, — earthly praise,
Repute o' the world, the flourish of loud trump,
The softer social fluting, — Oh, for these,
— No, my friends ! Fame, — that bubble which,
    world-wide
Each blows and bids his neighbor lend a breath,
That so he haply may behold thereon
One more enlarged distorted false fool's-face,
Until some glassy nothing grown as big
Send by a touch the imperishable to suds, —
No, in renouncing fame, my loss was light,
Choosing obscurity, my chance was well ! "

Didst ever touch such ampollosity
As the monk's own bubble, let alone its spite ?
What 's his speech for, but just the fame he
    flouts ?
How he dares reprehend both high and low,
Nor stoops to turn the sentence " God is true
And every man a liar — save the Pope
Happily reigning — my respects to him ! "
And so round off the period. Molinism
Simple and pure ! To what pitch get we next ?
I find that, for first pleasant consequence,
Gomez, who had intended to appeal
From the absurd decision of the Court,
Declines, though plain enough his privilege,
To call on help from lawyers any more —
Resolves earth's liars may possess the world,
Till God have had sufficiency of both :
So may I whistle for my job and fee !

But, for this virulent and rabid monk, —
If law be an inadequate machine,
And advocacy, froth and impotence,
We shall soon see, my blatant brother ! That 's
Exactly what I hope to show your sort !
For, by a veritable piece of luck,
The providence, you monks round period with,
All may be gloriously retrieved. Perpend !
That Monastery of the Convertites
Whereto the Court consigned Pompilia first,
— Observe, if convertite, why, sinner then,
Or what 's the pertinency of award ? —
And whither she was late returned to die.

— Still in their jurisdiction, mark again ! —
That thrifty Sisterhood, for perquisite,
Claims every piece whereof may die possessed
Each sinner in the circuit of its walls.
Now, this Pompilia seeing that, by death
O' the couple, all their wealth devolved on her,
Straight utilized the respite ere decease,
By regular conveyance of the goods
She thought her own, to will and to devise, —
Gave all to friends, Tighetti and the like,
In trust for him she held her son and heir,
Gaetano, — trust which ends with infancy :
So willing and devising, since assured
The justice of the court would presently
Confirm her in her rights and exculpate,
Re-integrate and rehabilitate —
Place her as, through my pleading, now she
    stands.
But here 's the capital mistake : the Court
Found Guido guilty, — but pronounced no word
About the innocency of his wife :
I grounded charge on broader base, I hope !
No matter whether wife be true or false,
The husband must not push aside the law,
And punish of a sudden : that 's the point :
Gather from out my speech the contrary !
It follows that Pompilia, unrelieved
By formal sentence from imputed fault,
Remains unfit to have and to dispose
Of property which law provides shall lapse :
Wherefore the Monastery claims its due.
And whose, pray, whose the office, but the Fisc's?
Who but I institute procedure next
Against the person of dishonest life,
Pompilia, whom last week I sainted so ?
I it is teach the monk what scripture means,
And that the tongue should prove a two-edged
    sword,
No axe sharp one side, blunt the other way,
Like what amused the town at Guido's cost !
Astræa redux ! I 've a second chance
Before the selfsame Court o' the Governor
Who soon shall see volte-face and chop, change
    sides.
Accordingly, I charge you on your life,
Send me with all dispatch the judgment late
O' the Florence Rota Court, confirmative
O' the prior judgment at Arezzo, clenched
Again by the Granducal signature,
Wherein Pompilia is convicted, doomed,
And only destined to escape through flight
The proper punishment. Send me the piece, —
I 'll work it ! And this foul-mouthed friar
    shall find
His Noah's-dove that brought the olive back
Turn into quite the other sooty scout,
The raven, Noah first put forth the ark,
Which never came back, but ate carcasses !
No adequate machinery in law ?
No power of life and death i' the learned
    tongue ?
Methinks I am already at my speech,
Startle the world with " Thou, Pompilia, thus ?
How is the fine gold of the Temple dim ! "
And so forth. But the courier bids me close,
And clip away one joke that runs through
    Rome,
Side by side with the sermon which I send.

How like the heartlessness of the old hunks
Arcangeli ! His Count is hardly cold,
The client whom his blunders sacrificed,
When somebody musts needs describe the
    scene —
How the procession ended at the church
That boasts the famous relic : quoth our brute,
" Why, that 's just Martial's phrase for ' make
    an end ' —
Ad umbilicum sic perventum est ! "
The callous dog, — let who will cut off head,
He cuts a joke, and cares no more than so !
I think my speech shall modify his mirth :
" How is the fine gold dim ! " — but send the
    piece !

Alack, Bottini, what is my next word
But death to all that hope ? The Instrument
Is plain before me, print that ends my Book
With the definitive verdict of the Court,
Dated September, six months afterward,
(Such trouble and so long the old Pope gave !)
" In restitution of the perfect fame
Of dead Pompilia, *quondam* Guido's wife,
And warrant to her representative
Domenico Tighetti, barred hereby,
While doing duty in his guardianship,
From all molesting, all disquietude,
Each perturbation and vexation brought
Or threatened to be brought against the heir
By the Most Venerable Convent called
Saint Mary Magdalen o' the Convertites
I' the Corso."
                    Justice done a second time !
Well judged, Marc Antony, *Locum-tenens*
O' the Governor, a Venturini too !
For which I save thy name, — last of the list !

Next year but one, completing his nine years
Of rule in Rome, died Innocent my Pope
— By some account, on his accession-day.
If he thought doubt would do the next age
    good,
'T is pity he died unapprised what birth
His reign may boast of, be remembered by —
Terrible Pope, too, of a kind, — Voltaire.

And so an end of all i' the story. Strain
Never so much my eyes, I miss the mark
If lived or died that Gaetano, child
Of Guido and Pompilia : only find,
Immediately upon his father's death,
A record, in the annals of the town —
That Porzia, sister of our Guido, moved
The Priors of Arezzo and their head
Its Gonfalonier to give loyally
A public attestation of the right
O' the Franceschini to all reverence —
Apparently because of the incident
O' the murder, — there 's no mention made o
    the crime,
But what else could have caused such urgency
To cure the mob, just then, of greediness
For scandal, love of lying vanity,
And appetite to swallow crude reports
That bring annoyance to their betters ? — bane
Which, here, was promptly met by antidote.
I like and shall translate the eloquence

Of nearly the worst Latin ever writ:
" Since antique time whereof the memory
Holds the beginning, to this present hour,
The Franceschini ever shone, and shine
Still i' the primary rank, supreme amid
The lustres of Arezzo, proud to own
In this great family, the flag-bearer,
Guide of her steps and guardian against foe, —
As in the first beginning, so to-day ! "
There, would you disbelieve the annalist,
Go rather by the babble of a bard ?
I thought, Arezzo, thou hadst fitter souls,
Petrarch, — nay, Buonarroti at a pinch,
To do thee credit as *vexillifer !*
Was it mere mirth the Patavinian meant,
Making thee out, in his veracious page,
Founded by Janus of the Double Face ?

Well, proving of such perfect parentage,
Our Gaetano, born of love and hate,
Did the babe live or die ?   I fain would find !
What were his fancies if he grew a man ?
Was he proud, — a true scion of the stock
Which bore the blazon, shall make bright my
        page —
Shield, Azure, on a Triple Mountain, Or,
A Palm-tree, Proper, whereunto is tied
A Greyhound, Rampant, striving in the slips ?
Or did he love his mother, the base-born,
And fight i' the ranks, unnoticed by the
        world ?

Such, then, the final state o' the story. So
Did the Star Wormwood in a blazing fall
Frighten awhile the waters and lie lost.
So did this old woe fade from memory :
Till after, in the fulness of the days,
I needs must find an ember yet unquenched,
And, breathing, blow the spark to flame. It
        lives,
If precious be the soul of man to man.

So, British Public, who may like me yet,
(Marry and amen !) learn one lesson hence
Of many which whatever lives should teach :
This lesson, that our human speech is naught,
Our human testimony false, our fame
And human estimation words and wind.
Why take the artistic way to prove so much ?
Because, it is the glory and good of Art,
That Art remains the one way possible
Of speaking truth, to mouths like mine at least.
How look a brother in the face and say,
" Thy right is wrong, eyes hast thou yet art
        blind ;
Thine ears are stuffed and stopped, despite their
        length :
And, oh, the foolishness thou countest faith ! "
Say this as silverly as tongue can troll —
The anger of the man may be endured,

The shrug, the disappointed eyes of him
Are not so bad to bear — but here 's the plague
That all this trouble comes of telling truth,
Which truth, by when it reaches him, looks
        false,
Seems to be just the thing it would supplant,
Nor recognizable by whom it left :
While falsehood would have done the work of
        truth.
But Art, — wherein man nowise speaks to men,
Only to mankind, — Art may tell a truth
Obliquely, do the thing shall breed the thought,
Nor wrong the thought, missing the mediate
        word.
So may you paint your picture, twice show
        truth,
Beyond mere imagery on the wall, —
So, note by note, bring music from your mind,
Deeper than ever e'en Beethoven dived, —
So write a book shall mean beyond the facts,
Suffice the eye and save the soul beside.

And save the soul ! If this intent save mine, —
If the rough ore be rounded to a ring,
Render all duty which good ring should do,
And, failing grace, succeed in guardianship, —
Might mine but lie outside thine, Lyric Love,
Thy rare gold ring of verse (the poet praised)
Linking our England to his Italy !

HELEN'S TOWER

Written at the request of the Earl of Dufferin
and Clandeboye, who had built a tower to the
memory of his mother, Helen, Countess of
Giffard, on a rock on his estate at Clandeboye,
Ireland, and printed in the *Pall Mall Gazette* of
December 28, 1883.

Who hears of Helen's Tower, may dream per-
        chance
    How the Greek Beauty from the Scæan Gate
    Gazed on old friends unanimous in hate,
Death-doom'd because of her fair countenance.

Hearts would leap otherwise, at thy advance,
    Lady, to whom this Tower is consecrate !
    Like hers, thy face once made all eyes elate,
Yet, unlike hers, was bless'd by every glance.

The Tower of Hate is outworn, far and strange :
    A transitory shame of long ago,
        It dies into the sand from which it sprang ;
But thine, Love's rock-built Tower, shall fear
        no change :
    God's self laid stable earth's foundation so,
        When all the morning-stars together sang.
April 26, 1870.

BALAUSTION'S ADVENTURE

INCLUDING

A TRANSCRIPT FROM EURIPIDES

"Our Euripides, the Human,
With his droppings of warm tears,
And his touches of things common
Till they rose to touch the spheres."

TO THE COUNTESS COWPER

IF I mention the simple truth, that this poem absolutely owes its existence to you, — who not only suggested, but imposed on me as a task, what has proved the most delight-ful of May-month amusements, — I shall seem honest, indeed, but hardly prudent ; for, how good and beautiful ought such a poem to be !

Euripides might fear little ; but I, also, have an interest in the performance ; and what wonder if I beg you to suffer that it make, in another and far easier sense, its nearest possible approach to those Greek qualities of goodness and beauty, by laying itself grate-fully at your feet ?   R. B.

LONDON, *July* 23, 1871.

AFTER the publication of the fourth volume of *The Ring and the Book* in February, 1869, Browning published nothing until March, 1871, when he printed *Hervé Riel* in the *Cornhill Magazine*, afterward including it in his first new volume of collected poems. In August of the same year appeared the first of his larger ventures in the field of Greek life. This poem was followed four years later by *Aristophanes' Apology*, and it is so intimately connected with *Balaustion's Adventure* that in this edition it is made to follow it, though the chronological sequence was broken, as will be seen, by the composition and publication of other considera-ble works. The motto at the head of the poem is from Mrs. Browning, and in the last lines of the poem Browning couples her with his friend Sir Frederick Leighton.

ABOUT that strangest, saddest, sweetest song
I, when a girl, heard in Kameiros once,
And, after, saved my life by ? Oh, so glad
To tell you the adventure !
                              Petalé,
Phullis, Charopé, Chrusion ! You must know,
This "after " fell in that unhappy time
When poor reluctant Nikias, pushed by fate,
Went falteringly against Syracuse ;
And there shamed Athens, lost her ships and men,
And gained a grave, or death without a grave.
I was at Rhodes — the isle, not Rhodes the town,
Mine was Kameiros — when the news arrived :
Our people rose in tumult, cried, " No more
Duty to Athens, let us join the League
And side with Sparta, share the spoil, — at worst,
Abjure a headship that will ruin Greece ! "
And so, they sent to Knidos for a fleet
To come and help revolters. Ere help came, —
Girl as I was, and never out of Rhodes
The whole of my first fourteen years of life,
But nourished with Ilissian mother's-milk, —
I passionately cried to who would hear

And those who loved me at Kameiros — " No !
Never throw Athens off for Sparta's sake —
Never disloyal to the life and light
Of the whole world worth calling world at all '
Rather go die at Athens, lie outstretched
For feet to trample on, before the gate
Of Diomedes or the Hippadai,
Before the temples and among the tombs,
Than tolerate the grim felicity
Of harsh Lakonia ! Ours the fasts and feasts,
Choës and Chutroi ; ours the sacred grove,
Agora, Dikasteria, Poikilé,
Pnux, Keramikos ; Salamis in sight,
Psuttalia, Marathon itself, not far !
Ours the great Dionusiac theatre,
And tragic triad of immortal fames,
Aischulos, Sophokles, Euripides !
To Athens, all of us that have a soul,
Follow me ! " And I wrought so with my prayer,
That certain of my kinsfolk crossed the strait
And found a ship at Kaunos ; well-disposed
Because the Captain — where did he draw breath
First but within Psuttalia ? Thither fled
A few like-minded as ourselves. We turned

The glad prow westward, soon were out at sea,
Pushing, brave ship with the vermilion cheek,
Proud for our heart's true harbor. But a wind
Lay ambushed by Point Malea of bad fame,
And leapt out, bent us from our course. Next day
Broke stormless, so broke next blue day and next.
" But whither bound in this white waste ? " we plagued
The pilot's old experience : " Cos or Crete ? "
Because he promised us the land ahead.
While we strained eyes to share in what he saw,
The Captain's shout startled us ; round we rushed !
What hung behind us but a pirate-ship
Panting for the good prize ! " Row ! harder row !
Row for dear life ! " the Captain cried : " 't is Crete,
Friendly Crete looming large there ! Beat th's craft
That 's but a keles, one-benched pirate-bark,
Lokrian, or that bad breed off Thessaly !
Only, so cruel are such water-thieves,
No man of you, no woman, child, or slave,
But falls their prey, once let them board our boat ! "
So, furiously our oarsmen rowed and rowed :
And when the oars flagged somewhat, dash and dip,
As we approached the coast and safety, so
That we could hear behind us plain the threats
And curses of the pirate panting up
In one more throe and passion of pursuit, —
Seeing our oars flag in the rise and fall,
I sprang upon the altar by the mast
And sang aloft — some genius prompting me —
That song of ours which saved at Salamis :
" O sons of Greeks, go, set your country free,
Free your wives, free your children, free the fanes
O' the Gods, your fathers founded, — sepulchres
They sleep in ! Or save all, or all be lost ! "
Then, in a frenzy, so the noble oars
Churned the black water white, that well away
We drew, soon saw land rise, saw hills grow up,
Saw spread itself a sea-wide town with towers,
Not fifty stadia distant ; and, betwixt
A large bay and a small, the islet-bar,
Even Ortugia's self — oh, luckless we !
For here was Sicily and Syracuse :
We ran upon the lion from the wolf.
Ere we drew breath, took counsel, out there came
A galley, hailed us. "Who asks entry here
In war-time ? Are you Sparta's friend or foe ? "
" Kaunians," — our Captain judged his best reply,
" The mainland-seaport that belongs to Rhodes ;
Rhodes that casts in her lot now with the League,
Forsaking Athens, — you have heard belike ! "
" Ay, but we heard all Athens in one ode
Just now ! we heard her in that Aischulos !

You bring a boatful of Athenians here,
Kaunians although you be : and prudence bids,
For Kaunos' sake, why, carry them unhurt
To Kaunos, if you will : for Athens' sake,
Back must you, though ten pirates blocked tne bay !
We want no colony from Athens here,
With memories of Salamis, forsooth,
To spirit up our captives, that pale crowd
I' the quarry, whom the daily pint of corn
Keeps in good order and submissiveness."
Then the gray Captain prayed them by the Gods,
And by their own knees, and their fathers' beards,
They should not wickedly thrust suppliants back,
But save the innocent on traffic bound —
Or, maybe, some Athenian family
Perishing of desire to die at home, —
From that vile foe still lying on its oars,
Waiting the issue in the distance. Vain !
Words to the wind ! And we were just about
To turn and face the foe, as some tired bird
Barbarians pelt at, drive with shouts away
From shelter in what rocks, however rude,
She makes for, to escape the kindled eye,
Split beak, crook'd claw o' the creature, cormorant
Or ossifrage, that, hardly baffled, hangs
Afloat i' the foam, to take her if she turn.
So were we at destruction's very edge,
When those o' the galley, as they had discussed
A point, a question raised by somebody,
A matter mooted in a moment, — " Wait ! "
Cried they (and wait we did, you may be sure).
" That song was veritable Aischulos,
Familiar to the mouth of man and boy,
Old glory : how about Euripides ?
The newer and not yet so famous bard,
He that was born upon the battle-day
While that song and the salpinx sounded him
Into the world, first sound, at Salamis —
Might you know any of his verses too ? "

Now, some one of the Gods inspired this speech :
Since ourselves knew what happened but last year —
How, when Gulippos gained his victory
Over poor Nikias, poor Demosthenes,
And Syracuse condemned the conquered force
To dig and starve i' the quarry, branded them —
Freeborn Athenians, brute-like in the front
With horse-head brands, — ah, " Region of the Steed " ! —
Of all these men immersed in misery,
It was found none had been advantaged so
By aught in the past life he used to prize
And pride himself concerning, — no rich man
By riches, no wise man by wisdom, no
Wiser man still (as who loved more the Muse)
By storing, at brain's edge and tip of tongue,
Old glory, great plays that had long ago
Made themselves wings to fly about the world, —
Not one such man was helped so at his need
As certain few that (wisest they of all)

Had, at first summons, oped heart, flung door
    wide
At the new knocking of Euripides,
Nor drawn the bolt with who cried " Deca-
    dence !
And, after Sophokles, be nature dumb ! "
Such, — and I see in it God Bacchos' boon
To souls that recognized his latest child,
He who himself, born latest of the Gods,
Was stoutly held impostor by mankind, —
Such were in safety : any who could speak
A chorus to the end, or prologize,
Roll out a rhesis, wield some golden length
Stiffened by wisdom out into a line,
Or thrust and parry in bright monostich,
Teaching Euripides to Syracuse —
Any such happy man had prompt reward :
If he lay bleeding on the battlefield
They stanched his wounds and gave him drink
    and food ;
If he were slave i' the house, for reverence
They rose up, bowed to who proved master
    now,
And bade him go free, thank Euripides !
Ay, and such did so : many such, he said,
Returning home to Athens, sought him out,
The old bard in the solitary house,
And thanked him ere they went to sacrifice.
I say, we knew that story of last year !

Therefore, at mention of Euripides,
The Captain crowed out, " Euoi, praise the
    God !
Oöp, boys, bring our owl-shield to the fore !
Out with our Sacred Anchor ! Here she
    stands,
Balaustion ! Strangers, greet the lyric girl !
Euripides ! Babai ! what a word there 'scaped
Your teeth's enclosure, quoth my grandsire's
    song !
Why, fast as snow in Thrace, the voyage
    through,
Has she been falling thick in flakes of him !
Frequent as figs at Kaunos, Kaunians said.
Balaustion, stand forth and confirm my speech !
Now it was some whole passion of a play ;
Now, peradventure, but a honey-drop
That slipt its comb i' the chorus. If there rose
A star, before I could determine steer
Southward or northward — if a cloud surprised
Heaven, ere I fairly hollaed ' Furl the sail ! '
She had at fingers' end both cloud and star ;
Some thought that perched there, tame and
    tunable,
Fitted with wings ; and still, as off it flew,
' So sang Euripides,' she said, ' so sang
The meteoric poet of air and sea,
Planets and the pale populace of heaven,
The mind of man, and all that 's made to soar ! '
And so, although she has some other name,
We only call her Wild-pomegranate-flower,
Balaustion ; since, where'er the red bloom burns
I' the dull dark verdure of the bounteous tree,
Dethroning, in the Rosy Isle, the rose,
You shall find food, drink, odor, all at once ;
Cool leaves to bind about an aching brow,
And, never much away, the nightingale.
Sing them a strophe, with the turn-again,

Down to the verse that ends all, proverb-like,
And save us, thou Baiaustion, bless the
    name ! "

But I cried, " Brother Greek ! better than so, —
Save us, and I have courage to recite
The main of a whole play from first to last ;
That strangest, saddest, sweetest song of his,
ALKESTIS ; which was taught, long years ago
At Athens, in Glaukinos' archonship,
But only this year reached our Isle o' the Rose
I saw it at Kameiros ; played the same,
They say, as for the right Lenean feast
In Athens ; and beside the perfect piece —
Its beauty and the way it makes you weep, —
There is much honor done your own loved God
Herakles, whom you house i' the city here
Nobly, the Temple wide Greece talks about !
I come a suppliant to your Herakles !
Take me and put me on his temple-steps,
To tell you his achievement as I may,
And, that told, he shall bid you set us free ! "

Then, because Greeks are Greeks, and hearts
    are hearts,
And poetry is power, — they all outbroke
In a great joyous laughter with much love :
" Thank Herakles for the good holiday !
Make for the harbor ! Row, and let voice
    ring,
' In we row, bringing more Euripides ! ' "
All the crowd, as they lined the harbor now,
" More of Euripides ! " — took up the cry.
We landed ; the whole city, soon astir,
Came rushing out of gates in common joy
To the suburb temple ; there they stationed me
O' the topmost step : and plain I told the play,
Just as I saw it ; what the actors said,
And what I saw, or thought I saw the while,
At our Kameiros theatre, clean-scooped
Out of a hillside, with the sky above
And sea before our seats in marble row :
Told it, and, two days more, repeated it,
Until they sent us on our way again
With good words and great wishes.
                      Oh, for me —
A wealthy Syracusan brought a whole
Talent and bade me take it for myself :
I left it on the tripod in the fane,
— For had not Herakles a second time
Wrestled with Death and saved devoted ones ? —
Thank-offering to the hero. And a band
Of captives, whom their lords grew kinder to
Because they called the poet countryman,
Sent me a crown of wild-pomegranate-flower :
So, I shall live and die Balaustion now.
But one — one man — one youth, — three days,
    each day, —
(If, ere I lifted up my voice to speak,
I gave a downward glance by accident,)
Was found at foot o' the temple. When we
    sailed,
There, in the ship too, was he found as well,
Having a hunger to see Athens too.
We reached Peiraieus ; when I landed — lo,
He was beside me. Anthesterion-month
Is just commencing : when its moon rounds full
We are to marry. O Euripides !

I saw the master: when we found ourselves
(Because the young man needs must follow me)
Firm on Peiraieus, I demanded first
Whither to go and find him. Would you think?
The story how he saved us made some smile:
They wondered strangers were exorbitant
In estimation of Euripides.
He was not Aischulos nor Sophokles:
— "Then, of our younger bards who boast the
         bay,
Had I sought Agathon, or Iophon,
Or, what now had it been Kephisophon?
A man that never kept good company,
The most unsociable of poet-kind,
All beard that was not freckle in his face!"

I soon was at the tragic house, and saw
The master, held the sacred hand of him
And laid it to my lips. Men love him not:
How should they? Nor do they much love his
         friend
Sokrates: but those two have fellowship:
Sokrates often comes to hear him read,
And never misses if he teach a piece.
Both, being old, will soon have company,
Sit with their peers above the talk. Meantime,
He lives as should a statue in its niche;
Cold walls enclose him, mostly darkness there,
Alone, unless some foreigner uncouth
Breaks in, sits, stares an hour, and so departs,
Brain-stuffed with something to sustain his life,
Dry to the marrow 'mid much merchandise.
How should such know and love the man?
                              Why, mark!
Even when I told the play and got the praise,
There spoke up a brisk little somebody,
Critic and whippersnapper, in a rage
To set things right: "The girl departs from
         truth!
Pretends she saw what was not to be seen,
Making the mask of the actor move, forsooth!
'Then a fear flitted o'er the wife's white face,' —
'Then frowned the father,'—'then the husband
         shook,' —
'Then from the festal forehead slipt each spray,
And the heroic mouth's gay grace was gone;' —
As she had seen each naked fleshly face,
And not the merely-painted mask it wore!"
Well, is the explanation difficult?
What's poetry except a power that makes?
And, speaking to one sense, inspires the rest,
Pressing them all into its service; so
That who sees painting, seems to hear as well
The speech that's proper for the painted mouth;
And who hears music, feels his solitude
Peopled at once — for how count heartbeats
         plain
Unless a company, with hearts which beat,
Come close to the musician, seen or no?
And who receives true verse at eye or ear,
Takes in (with verse) time, place, and person too,
So, links each sense on to its sister-sense,
Grace-like: and what if but one sense of three
Front you at once? The sidelong pair conceive
Through faintest touch of finest finger-tips, —
Hear, see and feel, in faith's simplicity,
Alike, what one was sole recipient of:
Who hears the poem, therefore, sees the play.

Enough and too much! Hear the play itself!
Under the grape-vines, by the streamlet-side,
Close to Baccheion; till the cool increase,
And other stars steal on the evening-star,
And so, we homeward flock i' the dusk, we
         five!
You will expect, no one of all the words
O' the play but is grown part now of my soul,
Since the adventure. 'T is the poet speaks:
But if I, too, should try and speak at times,
Leading your love to where my love, perchance,
Climbed earlier, found a nest before you knew —
Why, bear with the poor climber, for love's
         sake!
Look at Baccheion's beauty opposite,
The temple with the pillars at the porch!
See you not something beside masonry?
What if my words wind in and out the stone
As yonder ivy, the God's parasite?
Though they leap all the way the pillar leads,
Festoon about the marble, foot to frieze,
And serpentiningly enrich the roof,
Toy with some few bees and a bird or two, —
What then? The column holds the cornice
         up!

            ———

There slept a silent palace in the sun,
With plains adjacent and Thessalian peace —
Pherai, where King Admetos ruled the land.

Out from the portico there gleamed a God,
Apollon: for the bow was in his hand,
The quiver at his shoulder, all his shape
One dreadful beauty. And he hailed the house,
As if he knew it well and loved it much:
"O Admeteian domes, where I endured,
Even the God I am, to drudge awhile,
Do righteous penance for a reckless deed,
Accepting the slaves' table thankfully!"
Then told how Zeus had been the cause of all,
Raising the wrath in him which took revenge
And slew those forgers of the thunderbolt
Wherewith Zeus blazed the life from out the
         breast
Of Phoibos' son Asklepios (I surmise,
Because he brought the dead to life again),
And so, for punishment, must needs go slave,
God as he was, with a mere mortal lord: —
—Told how he came to King Admetos' land,
And played the ministrant, was herdsman there,
Warding all harm away from him and his
Till now; "For, holy as I am," said he,
"The lord I chanced upon was holy too:
Whence I deceived the Moirai, drew from death
My master, this same son of Pheres, — ay,
The Goddesses conceded him escape
From Hades, when the fated day should fall,
Could he exchange lives, find some friendly one
Ready, for his sake, to content the grave.
But trying all in turn, the friendly list,
Why, he found no one, none who loved so much,
Nor father, nor the aged mother's self
That bore him, no, not any save his wife,
Willing to die instead of him and watch
Never a sunrise nor a sunset more:
And she is even now within the house,
Upborne by pitying hands, the feeble frame

Gasping its last of life out ; since to-day
Destiny is accomplished, and she dies,
And I, lest here pollution light on me,
Leave, as ye witness, all my wonted joy
In this dear dwelling. Ay, — for here comes
    Death
Close on us of a sudden ! who, pale priest
Of the mute people, means to bear his prey
To the house of Hades. The symmetric step !
How he treads true to time and place and thing,
Dogging day, hour and minute, for death's-
    due !''

And we observed another Deity,
Half in, half out the portal, — watch and ward, —
Eying his fellow : formidably fixed,
Yet faltering too at who affronted him,
As somehow disadvantaged, should they strive.
Like some dread heapy blackness, ruffled wing,
Convulsed and cowering head that is all eye,
Which proves a ruined eagle who, too blind
Swooping in quest o' the quarry, fawn or kid,
Descried deep down the chasm 'twixt rock and
    rock,
Has wedged and mortised, into either wall
O' the mountain, the pent earthquake of his
    power;
So lies, half hurtless yet still terrible,
Just when — who stalks up, who stands front
    to front,
But the great lion-guarder of the gorge,
Lord of the ground, a stationed glory there !
Yet he too pauses ere he try the worst
O' the frightful unfamiliar nature, new
To the chasm, indeed, but elsewhere known
    enough,
Among the shadows and the silences
Above i' the sky : so, each antagonist
Silently faced his fellow and forbore.
Till Death shrilled, hard and quick, in spite
    and fear :

"Ha, ha, and what mayst thou do at the
    domes,
Why hauntest here, thou Phoibos ? Here
    again
At the old injustice, limiting our rights,
Balking of honor due us Gods o' the grave ?
Was 't not enough for thee to have delayed
Death from Admetos, — with thy crafty art
Cheating the very Fates, — but thou must arm
The bow-hand and take station, press 'twixt
    me
And Pelias' daughter, who then saved her
    spouse, —
Did just that, now thou comest to undo, —
Taking his place to die, Alkestis here ? ''

But the God sighed, "Have courage ! All my
    arms,
This time, are simple justice and fair words.''

Then each plied each with rapid interchange :

"What need of bow, were justice arms
    enough ? ''

"Ever it is my wont to bear the bow.''

"Ay, and with bow, not justice, help this
    house ! ''

"I help it, since a friend's woe·weighs me too.''

"And now, — wilt force from me this second
    corpse ? ''

"By force I took no corpse at first from thee.''

"How then is he above ground, not beneath ? ''

"He gave his wife instead of him, thy prey.''

"And prey, this time at least, I bear below ! ''

"Go take her ! — for I doubt persuading
    thee . . .''

"To kill the doomed one ?   What my function
    else ? ''

"No ! Rather, to dispatch the true mature.''

"Truly I take thy meaning, see thy drift ! ''

"Is there a way then she may reach old age ? ''

"No way ! I glad me in my honors too ! ''

"But, young or old, thou tak'st one life, no
    more ! ''

"Younger they die, greater my praise re-
    dounds ! ''

"If she die old, — the sumptuous funeral ! ''

"Thou layest down a law the rich would like.''

"How so ? Did wit lurk there and 'scape thy
    sense ? ''

"Who could buy substitutes would die old
    men.''

"It seems thou wilt not grant me, then, this
    grace ? ''

"This grace I will not grant : thou know'st
    my ways.''

"Ways harsh to men, hateful to Gods, at
    least ! ''

"All things thou canst not have : my rights
    for me ! ''

And then Apollon prophesied, — I think,
More to himself than to impatient Death,
Who did not hear or would not heed the
    while, —
For he went on to say, "Yet even so,
Cruel above the measure, thou shalt clutch
No life here ! Such a man do I perceive
Advancing to the house of Pheres now,
Sent by Eurustheus to bring out of Thrace,
The winter world, a chariot with its steeds !

He indeed, when Admetos proves the host,
And he the guest, at the house here, — he it is
Shall bring to bear such force, and from thy
    hands
Rescue this woman ! Grace no whit to me
Will that prove, since thou dost thy deed the
    same,
And earnest too my hate, and all for naught ! "

But how should Death or stay or understand ?
Doubtless, he only felt the hour was come,
And the sword free ; for he but flung some
    taunt —
" Having talked much, thou wilt not gain the
    more !
This woman, then, descends to Hades' hall
Now that I rush on her, begin the rites
O' the sword ; for sacred, to us Gods below,
That head whose hair this sword shall
    sanctify ! "

And, in the fire-flash of the appalling sword,
The uprush and the outburst, the onslaught
Of Death's portentous passage through the door,
Apollon stood a pitying moment-space :
I caught one last gold gaze upon the night
Nearing the world now : and the God was
    gone,
And mortals left to deal with misery,
As in came stealing slow, now this, now that
Old sojourner throughout the country-side,
Servants grown friends to those unhappy here :
And, cloudlike in their increase, all these
    griefs
Broke and began the over-brimming wail,
Out of a common impulse, word by word.

" What now may mean the silence at the door ?
Why is Admetos' mansion stricken dumb ?
Not one friend near, to say if we should mourn
Our mistress dead, or if Alkestis lives
And sees the light still, Pelias' child — to me,
To all, conspicuously the best of wives
That ever was toward husband in this world !
Hears any one or wail beneath the roof,
Or hands that strike each other, or the groan
Announcing all is done and naught to dread ?
Still not a servant stationed at the gates !
O Paian, that thou wouldst dispart the wave
O' the woe, be present ! Yet, had woe o'er-
    whelmed
The housemates, they were hardly silent thus :
It cannot be, the dead is forth and gone.
Whence comes thy gleam of hope ? I dare not
    hope :
What is the circumstance that heartens thee ?
How could Admetos have dismissed a wife
So worthy, unescorted to the grave ?
Before the gates I see no hallowed vase
Of fountain-water, such as suits death's door ;
Nor any clipt locks strew the vestibule,
Though surely these drop when we grieve the
    dead,
Nor hand sounds smitten against youthful
    hand,
The women's way. And yet — the appointed
    time —
How speak the word ? — this day is even the day

Ordained her for departing from its light.
O touch calamitous to heart and soul !
Needs must one, when the good are tortured so,
Sorrow, — one reckoned faithful from the
    first."

Then their souls rose together, and one sigh
Went up in cadence from the common mouth :
How " Vainly — anywhither in the world
Directing or land-labor or sea-search —
To Lukia or the sand-waste, Ammon's seat —
Might you set free their hapless lady's soul
From the abrupt Fate's footstep instant now.
Not a sheep-sacrificer at the hearths
Of Gods had they to go to : one there was
Who, if his eyes saw light still, — Phoibos'
    son, —
Had wrought so, she might leave the shadowy
    place
And Hades' portal : for he propped up Death's
Subdued ones, till the Zeus-flung thunder-
    flame
Struck him ; and now what hope of life were
    hailed
With open arms ? For, all the king could do
Is done already, — not one God whereof
The altar fails to reek with sacrifice :
And for assuagement of these evils — naught ! "

But here they broke off, for a matron moved
Forth from the house : and, as her tears flowed
    fast,
They gathered round. " What fortune shall we
    hear ?
For mourning thus, if aught affect thy lord,
We pardon thee : but lives the lady yet
Or has she perished ? — that we fain would
    know ! "

" Call her dead, call her living, each style
    serves,"
The matron said : " though grave-ward bowed,
    she breathed ;
Nor knew her husband what the misery meant
Before he felt it : hope of life was none :
The appointed day pressed hard ; the funeral
    pomp
He had prepared too."
                            When the friends broke out,
" Let her in dying know herself at least
Sole wife, of all the wives 'neath the sun wide,
For glory and for goodness ! " — " Ah, how else
Than best ? who controverts the claim ? " quoth
    she :
" What kind of creature should the woman
    prove
That has surpassed Alkestis ? — surelier shown
Preference for her husband to herself
Than by determining to die for him ?
But so much all our city knows indeed :
Hear what she did indoors and wonder then !
For, when she felt the crowning day was come,
She washed with river-waters her white skin,
And, taking from the cedar closets forth
Vesture and ornament, bedecked herself
Nobly, and stood before the hearth, and prayed
' Mistress, because I now depart the world,
Falling before thee the last time, I ask —

Be mother to my orphans! wed the one
To a kind wife, and make the other's mate
Some princely person : nor, as I who bore
My children perish, suffer that they too
Die all untimely, but live, happy pair,
Their full glad life out in the fatherland!'
And every altar through Admetos' house
She visited and crowned and prayed before,
Stripping the myrtle-foliage from the boughs,
Without a tear, without a groan, — no change
At all to that skin's nature, fair to see,
Caused by the imminent evil. But this done, —
Reaching her chamber, falling on her bed,
There, truly, burst she into tears and spoke :
'O bride-bed, where I loosened from my life
Virginity for that same husband's sake
Because of whom I die now — fare thee well!
Since nowise do I hate thee : me alone
Hast thou destroyed ; for, shrinking to betray
Thee and my spouse, I die : but thee, O bed,
Some other woman shall possess as wife —
Truer, no ! but of better fortune, say !'
— So falls on, kisses it till all the couch
Is moistened with the eyes' sad overflow.
But when of many tears she had her fill,
She flings from off the couch, goes headlong
    forth,
Yet — forth the chamber — still keeps turning
    back
And casts her on the couch again once more.
Her children, clinging to their mother's robe,
Wept meanwhile : but she took them in her
    arms,
And, as a dying woman might, embraced
Now one and now the other : 'neath the roof,
All of the household servants wept as well,
Moved to compassion for their mistress ; she
Extended her right hand to all and each,
And there was no one of such low degree
She spoke not to nor had an answer from.
Such are the evils in Admetos' house.
Dying, — why, he had died ; but, living, gains
Such grief as this he never will forget!"

And when they questioned of Admetos,
    "Well —
Holding his dear wife in his hands, he weeps ;
Entreats her not to give him up, and seeks
The impossible, in fine : for there she wastes
And withers by disease, abandoned now,
A mere dead weight upon her husband's arm.
Yet, none the less, although she breathe so
    faint,
Her will is to behold the beams o' the sun :
Since never more again, but this last once,
Shall she see sun, its circlet or its ray.
But I will go, announce your presence, —
    friends
Indeed ; since 't is not all so love their lords
As seek them in misfortune, kind the same :
But you are the old friends I recognize."

And at the word she turned again to go :
The while they waited, taking up the plaint
To Zeus again : "What passage from this
    strait ?
What loosing of the heavy fortune fast
About the palace ? Will such help appear,

Or must we clip the locks and cast around
Each form already the black peplos' fold ?
Clearly the black robe, clearly! All the same.
Pray to the Gods ! — like Gods' no power so
    great !
O thou king Paian, find some way to save !
Reveal it, yea, reveal it ! Since of old
Thou found'st a cure, why, now again become
Releaser from the bonds of Death, we beg,
And give the sanguinary Hades pause ! ''
So the song dwindled into a mere moan,
How dear the wife, and what her husband's
    woe ;
When suddenly —
            "Behold, behold !" breaks forth
" Here is she coming from the house indeed !
Her husband comes, too ! Cry aloud, lament,
Pheraian land, this best of women, bound —
So is she withered by disease away —
For realms below and their infernal king !
Never will we affirm there 's more of joy
Than grief in marriage ; making estimate
Both from old sorrows anciently observed,
And this misfortune of the king we see —
Admetos who, of bravest spouse bereaved,
Will live life's remnant out, no life at all ! ''

So wailed they, while a sad procession wound
Slow from the innermost o' the palace, stopped
At the extreme verge of the platform-front :
There opened, and disclosed Alkestis' self,
The consecrated lady, borne to look
Her last — and let the living look their last —
She at the sun, we at Alkestis.
                            We !
For would you note a memorable thing ?
We grew to see in that severe regard, —
Hear in that hard dry pressure to the point,
Word slow pursuing word in monotone, —
What Death meant when he called her conse-
    crate
Henceforth to Hades. I believe, the sword —
Its office was to cut the soul at once
From life, — from something in this world
    which hides
Truth, and hides falsehood, and so lets us live
Somehow. Suppose a rider furls a cloak
About a horse's head ; unfrightened, so,
Between the menace of a flame, between
Solicitation of the pasturage,
Untempted equally, he goes his gait
To journey's end : then pluck the pharos off!
Show what delusions steadied him i' the straight
O' the path, made grass seem fire and fire
    seem grass,
All through a little bandage o'er the eyes!
As certainly with eyes unbandaged now
Alkestis looked upon the action here,
Self-immolation for Admetos' sake ;
Saw, with a new sense, all her death would do,
And which of her survivors had the right,
And which the less right, to survive thereby.
For, you shall note, she uttered no one word
Of love more to her husband, though he wept
Plenteously, waxed importunate in prayer —
Folly's old fashion when its seed bears fruit.
I think she judged that she had bought the
    ware

O' the seller at its value, — nor praised him
Nor blamed herself, but, with indifferent eye,
Saw him purse money up, prepare to leave
The buyer with a solitary bale —
True purple — but in place of all that coin,
Had made a hundred others happy too,
If so willed fate or fortune!   What remained
To give away, should rather go to these
Than one with coin to clink and contemplate.
Admetos had his share and might depart,
The rest was for her children and herself.
(Charopé makes a face : but wait awhile !)
She saw things plain as Gods do : by one stroke
O' the sword that rends the life-long veil away.
(Also Euripedes saw plain enough :
But you and I, Charopé ! — you and I
Will trust his sight until our own grow clear.)

"Sun, and thou light of day, and heavenly
    dance
O' the fleet cloud - figure ! " (so her passion
    paused,
While the awe-stricken husband made his moan,
Muttered now this now that ineptitude :
"Sun that sees thee and me, a suffering pair,
Who did the Gods no wrong whence thou
    shouldst die ! ")
Then, as if caught up, carried in their course,
Fleeting and free as cloud and sunbeam are,
She missed no happiness that lay beneath :
"O thou wide earth, from these my palace
    roofs,
To distant nuptial chambers once my own
In that Iolkos of my ancestry ! " —
There the flight failed her.   " Raise thee,
    wretched one !
Give us not up !   Pray pity from the Gods ! "

Vainly Admetos : for " I see it — see
The two-oared boat !   The ferryer of the dead,
Charon, hand hard upon the boatman's-pole,
Calls me — even now calls — ' Why delayest
    thou ?
Quick !   Thou obstructest all made ready here
For prompt departure : quick, then ! ' "
                        " Woe is me !
A bitter voyage this to undergo,
Even i' the telling !   Adverse Powers above,
How do ye plague us ! "
                        Then a shiver ran :
" He has me — seest not ? — hales me, — who is
    it ? —
To the hall o' the Dead — ah, who but Hades'
    self,
He, with the wings there, glares at me, one gaze
All that blue brilliance, under the eyebrow !
What wilt thou do ?   Unhand me !   Such a
    way
I have to traverse, all unhappy one ! "

" Way — piteous to thy friends, but, most of all,
Me and thy children : ours assuredly
A common partnership in grief like this ! "

Whereat they closed about her ; but " Let be !
Leave, let me lie now !   Strength forsakes my
    feet.
Hades is here, and shadowy on my eyes

Comes the night creeping.   Children — chil-
    dren, now
Indeed, a mother is no more for you !
Farewell, O children, long enjoy the light ! "

" Ah me, the melancholy word I hear,
Oppressive beyond every kind of death !
No, by the Deities, take heart nor dare
To give me up — no, by our children too
Made orphans of !   But rise, be resolute,
Since, thou departed, I no more remain !
For in thee are we bound up, to exist
Or cease to be — so we adore thy love ! "

— Which brought out truth to judgment.   At
    this word
And protestation, all the truth in her
Claimed to assert itself : she waved away
The blue-eyed black-wing'd phantom, held in
    check
The advancing pageantry of Hades there,
And, with no change in her own countenance,
She fixed her eyes on the protesting man,
And let her lips unlock their sentence, — so !

" Admetos, — how things go with me thou
    seest, —
I wish to tell thee, ere I die, what things
I will should follow.   I — to honor thee,
Secure for thee, by my own soul's exchange,
Continued looking on the daylight here —
Die for thee — yet, if so I pleased, might live,
Nay, wed what man of Thessaly I would,
And dwell i' the dome with pomp and queenli-
    ness.
I would not, — would not live bereft of thee,
With children orphaned, neither shrank at all,
Though having gifts of youth wherein I joyed.
Yet, who begot thee and who gave thee birth,
Both of these gave thee up ; no less, a term
Of life was reached when death became them
    well,
Ay, well — to save their child and glorious die :
Since thou wast all they had, nor hope re-
    mained
Of having other children in thy place.
So, I and thou had lived out our full time,
Nor thou, left lonely of thy wife, wouldst groan
With children reared in orphanage : but thus
Some God disposed things, willed they so should
    be.
Be they so !   Now do thou remember this,
Do me in turn a favor — favor, since
Certainly I shall never claim my due,
For nothing is more precious than a life :
But a fit favor, as thyself wilt say,
Loving our children here no less than I,
If head and heart be sound in thee at least.
Uphold them, make them masters of my house,
Nor wed and give a step-dame to the pair,
Who, being a worse wife than I, through spite
Will raise her hand against both thine and
    mine.
Never do this at least, I pray to thee !
For hostile the new-comer, the step-dame,
To the old brood — a very viper she
For gentleness !   Here stand they, boy and
    girl ;

The boy has got a father, a defence
Tower-like, he speaks to and has answer from :
But thou, my girl, how will thy virginhood
Conclude itself in marriage fittingly ?
Upon what sort of sire-found yoke-fellow
Art thou to chance ? with all to apprehend —
Lest, casting on thee some unkind report,
She blast thy nuptials in the bloom of youth.
For neither shall thy mother watch thee wed,
Nor hearten thee in childbirth, standing by
Just when a mother's presence helps the most !
No, for I have to die : and this my ill
Comes to me, nor to-morrow, no, nor yet
The third day of the month, but now, even
    now,
I shall be reckoned among those no more.
Farewell, be happy ! And to thee, indeed,
Husband, the boast remains permissible
Thou hadst a wife was worthy ! and to you,
Children ; as good a mother gave you birth."

"Have courage !" interposed the friends.
  " For him
I have no scruple to declare — all this
Will he perform, except he fail of sense."

" All this shall be — shall be !" Admetos
    sobbed :
" Fear not ! And, since I had thee living,
    dead
Alone wilt thou be called my wife : no fear
That some Thessalian ever styles herself
Bride, hails this man for husband in thy place !
No woman, be she of such lofty line
Or such surpassing beauty otherwise !
Enough of children : gain from these I have,
Such only may the Gods grant ! since in thee
Absolute is our loss, where all was gain.
And I shall bear for thee no year-long grief,
But grief that lasts while my own days last,
    love !
Love ! For my hate is she who bore me, now :
And him I hate, my father : loving-ones
Truly, in word not deed ! But thou didst pay
All dearest to thee down, and buy my life,
Saving me so ! Is there not cause enough
That I who part with such companionship
In thee, should make my moan ? I moan, and
    more :
For I will end the feastings — social flow
O' the wine friends flock for, garlands and the
    Muse
That graced my dwelling. Never now for me
To touch the lyre, to lift my soul in song
At summons of the Lydian flute ; since thou
From out my life hast emptied all the joy !
And this thy body, in thy likeness wrought
By some wise hand of the artificers,
Shall lie disposed within my marriage-bed :
This I will fall on, this enfold about,
Call by thy name, — my dear wife in my arms
Even though I have not, I shall seem to have —
A cold delight, indeed, but all the same
So should I lighten of its weight my soul !
And, wandering my way in dreams perchance,
Thyself wilt bless me : for, come when they
    will,
Even by night our loves are sweet to see.

But were the tongue and tune of Orpheus
    mine,
So that to Koré crying, or her lord,
In hymns, from Hades I might rescue thee —
Down would I go, and neither Plouton's dog
Nor Charon, he whose oar sends souls across,
Should stay me till again I made thee stand
Living, within the light ! But, failing this,
There, where thou art, await me when I die,
Make ready our abode, my housemate still !
For in the selfsame cedar, me with thee
Will I provide that these our friends shall
    place,
My side lay close by thy side ! Never, corpse
Although I be, would I division bear
From thee, my faithful one of all the world ! "

So he stood sobbing : nowise insincere,
But somehow child-like, like his children, like
Childishness the world over. What was new
In this announcement that his wife must die ?
What particle of pain beyond the pact
He made, with eyes wide open, long ago —
Made and was, if not glad, content to make ?
Now that the sorrow, he had called for, came,
He sorrowed to the height : none heard him say,
However, what would seem so pertinent,
" To keep this pact, I find surpass my power :
Rescind it, Moirai ! Give me back her life,
And take the life I kept by base exchange !
Or, failing that, here stands your laughing-
    stock
Fooled by you, worthy just the fate o' the fool
Who makes a pother to escape the best
And gain the worst you wiser Powers allot ! "
No, not one word of this : nor did his wife
Despite the sobbing, and the silence soon
To follow, judge so much was in his thought —
Fancy that, should the Moirai acquiesce,
He would relinquish life nor let her die.
The man was like some merchant who, in
    storm,
Throws the freight over to redeem the ship :
No question, saving both were better still.
As it was, — why, he sorrowed, which sufficed.
So, all she seemed to notice in his speech
Was what concerned her children. Children,
    too,
Bear the grief and accept the sacrifice.
Rightly rules nature : does the blossomed
    bough
O' the grape-vine, or the dry grape's self, bleed
    wine ?

So, bending to her children all her love,
She fastened on their father's only word
To purpose now, and followed it with this :
" O children, now yourselves have heard these
    things —
Your father saying he will never wed
Another woman to be over you,
Nor yet dishonor me ! "

                     " And now at least
I say it, and I will accomplish too ! "

" Then, for such promise of accomplishment,
Take from my hand these children ! "

"Thus I take—
Dear gift from the dear hand!"

"Do thou become
Mother, now, to these children in my place!"

"Great the necessity, I should be so,
At least, to these bereaved of thee!"

"Child—child!
Just when I needed most to live, below
Am I departing from you both!"

"Ah me!
And what shall I do, then, left lonely thus?"

"Time will appease thee: who is dead is
naught."

"Take me with thee—take, by the Gods
below!"

"We are sufficient, we who die for thee."

"O Powers, ye widow me of what a wife!"

"And truly the dimmed eye draws earthward
now!"

"Wife, if thou leav'st me, I am lost indeed!"

"She once was—now is nothing, thou mayst
say."

"Raise thy face, nor forsake thy children
thus!"

"Ah, willingly indeed I leave them not!
But—fare ye well, my children!"

"Look on them—
Look!"

"I am nothingness."

"What dost thou? Leav'st . . ."

"Farewell!"
And in the breath she passed away.
"Undone—me miserable!" moaned the king,
While friends released the long-suspended sigh.
"Gone is she: no wife for Admetos more!"

Such was the signal: how the woe broke forth,
Why tell?—or how the children's tears ran
fast
Bidding their father note the eyelids' stare,
Hands' droop, each dreadful circumstance of
death.

Ay, she hears not, she sees not: I and you,
T is plain, are stricken hard and have to
bear!"
Was all Admetos answered; for, I judge,
He only now began to taste the truth:
The thing done lay revealed, which undone
thing,
Rehearsed for fact by fancy, at the best,

Never can equal. He had used himself
This long while (as he muttered presently)
To practise with the terms, the blow involved
By the bargain, sharp to bear, but bearable
Because of plain advantage at the end.
Now that, in fact not fancy, the blow fell—
Needs must he busy him with the surprise.
"Alkestis—not to see her nor be seen,
Hear nor be heard of by her, any more
To-day, to-morrow, to the end of time—
Did I mean this should buy my life?" thought
he.

So, friends came round him, took him by the
hand,
Bade him remember our mortality,
Its due, its doom: how neither was he first,
Nor would be last, to thus deplore the loved.

"I understand," slow the words came at last.
"Nor of a sudden did the evil here
Fly on me: I have known it long ago,
Ay, and essayed myself in misery;
Nothing is new. You have to stay, you friends,
Because the next need is to carry forth
The corpse here: you must stay and do your
part,
Chant proper pæan to the God below;
Drink-sacrifice he likes not. I decree
That all Thessalians over whom I rule
Hold grief in common with me; let them shear
Their locks, and be the peplos black they show!
And you who to the chariot yoke your steeds,
Or manage steeds one-frontleted,—I charge,
Clip from each neck with steel the mane away!
And through my city, nor of flute nor lyre
Be there a sound till twelve full moons succeed.
For I shall never bury any corpse
Dearer than this to me, nor better friend:
One worthy of all honor from me, since
Me she has died for, she and she alone."

With that, he sought the inmost of the house,
He and his dead, to get grave's garniture,
While the friends sang the pæan that should
peal.
"Daughter of Pelias, with farewell from me,
I' the house of Hades have thy unsunned home!
Let Hades know, the dark-haired deity,—
And he who sits to row and steer alike,
Old corpse-conductor, let him know he bears
Over the Acherontian lake, this time,
I' the two-oared boat, the best—oh, best by far
Of womankind! For thee, Alkestis Queen!
Many a time those haunters of the Muse
Shall sing thee to the seven-stringed mountain
shell,
And glorify in hymns that need no harp,
At Sparta when the cycle comes about,
And that Karneian month wherein the moon
Rises and never sets the whole night through:
So too at splendid and magnificent
Athenai. Such the spread of thy renown,
And such the lay that, dying, thou hast left
Singer and sayer. Oh that I availed
Of my own might to send thee once again
From Hades' hall, Kokutos' stream, by help
O' the oar that dips the river, back to-day!"

So, the song sank to prattle in her praise:
" Light, from above thee, lady, fall the earth,
Thou only one of womankind to die,
Wife for her husband! If Admetos take
Anything to him like a second spouse —
Hate from his offspring and from us shall be
His portion, let the king assure himself!
No mind his mother had to hide in earth
Her body for her son's sake, nor his sire
Had heart to save whom he begot, — not they,
The white-haired wretches! only thou it was,
I' the bloom of youth, didst save him and so
    die!
Might it be mine to chance on such a mate
And partner! For there 's penury in life
Of such allowance: were she mine at least,
So wonderful a wife, assuredly
She would companion me throughout my days
And never once bring sorrow! "
                    A great voice —
" My hosts here! "
        Oh, the thrill that ran through us!
Never was aught so good and opportune
As that great interrupting voice! For see!
Here maundered this dispirited old age
Before the palace; whence a something crept
Which told us well enough without a word
What was a-doing inside, — every touch
O' the garland on those temples, tenderest
Disposure of each arm along its side,
Came putting out what warmth i' the world
    was left.
Then, as it happens at a sacrifice
When, drop by drop, some lustral bath is
    brimmed:
Into the thin and clear and cold, at once
They slaughter a whole wine-skin; Bacchos'
    blood
Sets the white water all aflame even so,
Sudden into the midst of sorrow, leapt
Along with the gay cheer of that great voice,
Hope, joy, salvation: Herakles was here!
Himself, o' the threshold, sent his voice on first
To herald all that human and divine
I' the weary happy face of him, — half God,
Half man, which made the god-part God the
    more.

" Hosts mine," he broke upon the sorrow with,
" Inhabitants of this Pheraian soil,
Chance I upon Admetos inside here? "

The irresistible sound wholesome heart
O' the hero, — more than all the mightiness
At labor in the limbs that, for man's sake,
Labored and meant to labor their life-long, —
This drove back, dried up sorrow at its source.
How could it brave the happy weary laugh
Of who had bantered sorrow, " Sorrow here?
What have you done to keep your friend from
    harm?
Could no one give the life I see he keeps?
Or, say there 's sorrow here past friendly help,
Why waste a word or let a tear escape
While other sorrows wait you in the world,
And want the life of you, though helpless
    here? "
Clearly there was no telling such an one

How, when their monarch tried who loved him
    more
Than he loved them, and found they loved, as
    he,
Each man, himself, and held, no otherwise,
That, of all evils in the world, the worst
Was — being forced to die, whate'er death
    gain:
How all this selfishness in him and them
Caused certain sorrow which they sang about, —
I think that Herakles, who held his life
Out on his hand, for any man to take —
I think his laugh had marred their threnody.

" He is in the house," they answered. After
    all,
They might have told the story, talked their
    best
About the inevitable sorrow here,
Nor changed nor checked the kindly nature, —
    no!
So long as men were merely weak, not bad,
He loved men: were they Gods he used to help?
" Yea, 'heres' son is in-doors, Herakles.
But say, what sends thee to Thessalian soil,
Brought by what business to this Pherai
    town? "

" A certain labor that I have to do
Eurustheus the Tirunthian," laughed the God.

" And whither wendest — on what wandering
Bound now? " (They had an instinct, guessed
    what meant
Wanderings, labors, in the God's light mouth.)

" After the Thrakian Diomedes' car
With the four horses."

            " Ah, but canst thou that?
Art inexperienced in thy host to be? "

" All-inexperienced: I have never gone
As yet to the land o' the Bistones."

            " Then, look
By no means to be master of the steeds
Without a battle! "
            " Battle there may be:
I must refuse no labor, all the same."

" Certainly, either having slain a foe
Wilt thou return to us, or, slain thyself,
Stay there! "
        " And, even if the game be so,
The risk in it were not the first I run."

" But, say thou overpower the lord o' the place,
What more advantage dost expect thereby? "

" I shall drive off his horses to the king."

" No easy handling them to bit the jaw! "

" Easy enough; except, at least, they breathe
Fire from their nostrils! "
            " But they mince up men
With those quick jaws! "

"You talk of provender
For mountain-beasts, and not mere horses'
    food!"

"Thou mayst behold their mangers caked
    with gore!"

"And of what sire does he who bred them boast
Himself the son?"
                    "Of Ares, king o' the targe —
Thrakian, of gold throughout."
                              Another laugh.
"Why, just the labor, just the lot for me
Dost thou describe in what I recognize!
Since hard and harder, high and higher yet,
Truly this lot of mine is like to go
If I must needs join battle with the brood
Of Ares: ay, I fought Lukaon first,
And again, Kuknos: now engage in strife
This third time, with such horses and such lord.
But there is nobody shall ever see
Alkmené's son shrink foemen's hand before!"

— "Or ever hear him say" (the Chorus
    thought)
"That death is terrible; and help us so
To chime in — ' terrible beyond a doubt,
And, if to thee, why, to ourselves much more :
Know what has happened, then, and sympa-
    thize'!"
Therefore they gladly stopped the dialogue,
Shifted the burden to new shoulder straight,
As, "Look where comes the lord o' the land,
    himself,
Admetos, from the palace!" they outbroke
In some surprise, as well as much relief.
What had induced the king to waive his right
And luxury of woe in loneliness?

Out he came quietly; the hair was clipt,
And the garb sable; else no outward sign
Of sorrow as he came and faced his friend.
Was truth fast terrifying tears away?
"Hail, child of Zeus, and sprung from Perseus
    too!"
The salutation ran without a fault.

"And thou, Admetos, King of Thessaly!"

"Would, as thou wishest me, the grace might
    fall!
But my good-wisher, that thou art, I know."

"What's here? these shorn locks, this sad
    show of thee?"

"I must inter a certain corpse to-day."

"Now, from thy children God avert mis-
    chance!"

"They live, my children; all are in the house!"

"Thy father — if 't is he departs indeed,
His age was ripe at least."

                    "My father lives,
And she who bore me lives too, Herakles."

"It cannot be thy wife Alkestis gone?"

"Twofold the tale is, I can tell of her."

"Dead dost thou speak of her, or living yet?"

"She is — and is not: hence the pain to me!"

"I learn no whit the more, so dark thy speech!"

"Know'st thou not on what fate she needs
    must fall?"

"I know she is resigned to die for thee."

"How lives she still, then, if submitting so?"

"Eh, weep her not beforehand! wait till then!"

"Who is to die is dead; doing is done."

"To be and not to be are thought diverse."

"Thou judgest this — I, that way, Herakles!"

"Well, but declare what causes thy complaint!
Who is the man has died from out thy friends?"

"No man: I had a woman in my mind."

"Alien, or some one born akin to thee?"

"Alien: but still related to my house."

"How did it happen then that here she died?"

"Her father dying left his orphan here."

"Alas, Admetos — would we found thee gay,
Not grieving!"

                    "What as if about to do
Subjoinest thou that comment?"
                              "I shall seek
Another hearth, proceed to other hosts."

"Never, O king, shall that be!   No such ill
Betide me!"
              "Nay, to mourners should there come
A guest, he proves importunate!"
                              "The dead —
Dead are they: but go thou within my house!"

"'T is base carousing beside friends who
    mourn."

"The guest-rooms, whither we shall lead thee,
    lie
Apart from ours."
                    "Nay, let me go my way!
Ten-thousandfold the favor I shall thank!"

"It may not be thou goest to the hearth
Of any man but me!" so made an end
Admetos, softly and decisively,
Of the altercation.   Herakles forbore:
And the king bade a servant lead the way,
Open the guest-rooms ranged remote from view

O' the main hall, tell the functionaries, next,
They had to furnish forth a plenteous feast:
And then shut close the doors o' the hall, mid-
    way,
" Because it is not proper friends who feast
Should hear a groaning or be grieved," quoth
    he.

Whereat the hero, who was truth itself,
Let out the smile again, repressed awhile
Like fountain-brilliance one forbids to play.
He did too many grandnesses, to note
Much in the meaner things about his path:
And stepping there, with face towards the sun,
Stopped seldom to pluck weeds or ask their
    names.
Therefore he took Admetos at the word:
This trouble must not hinder any more
A true heart from good will and pleasant ways.
And so, the great arm, which had slain the
    snake,
Strained his friend's head a moment in embrace
On that broad breast beneath the lion's hide,
Till the king's cheek winced at the thick rough
    gold ;
And then strode off, with who had care of
    him,
To the remote guest-chamber: glad to give
Poor flesh and blood their respite and relief
In the interval 'twixt fight and fight again —
All for the world's sake. Our eyes followed
    him,
Be sure, till those mid-doors shut us outside.
The king, too, watched great Herakles go off
All faith, love, and obedience to a friend.

And when they questioned him, the simple
    ones,
"What dost thou? Such calamity to face,
Lies full before thee — and thou art so bold
As play the host, Admetos? Hast thy wits? "
He replied calmly to each chiding tongue:
" But if from house and home I forced away
A coming guest, wouldst thou have praised me
    more?
No, truly! since calamity were mine,
Nowise diminished : while I showed myself
Unhappy and inhospitable too:
So adding to my ills this other ill,
That mine were styled a stranger-hating house.
Myself have ever found this man the best
Of entertainers when I went his way
To parched and thirsty Argos."
                     " If so be —
Why didst thou hide what destiny was here,
When one came that was kindly, as thou
    say'st? "

" He never would have willed to cross my door
Had he known aught of my calamities.
And probably to some of you I seem
Unwise enough in doing what I do ;
Such will scarce praise me : but these halls of
    mine
Know not to drive off and dishonor guests."

And so, the duty done, he turned once more
To go and busy him about his dead.

As for the sympathizers left to muse,
There was a change, a new light thrown on
    things,
Contagion from the magnanimity
O' the man whose life lay on his hand so light,
As up he stepped, pursuing duty still
" Higher and harder," as he laughed and said.
Somehow they found no folly now in the act
They blamed erewhile : Admetos' private grief
Shrank to a somewhat pettier obstacle
I' the way o' the world: they saw good days
    had been,
And good days, peradventure, still might be,
Now that they overlooked the present cloud
Heavy upon the palace opposite.
And soon the thought took words and music
    thus : —

" Harbor of many a stranger, free to friend,
Ever and always, O thou house o' the man
We mourn for ! Thee, Apollon's very self,
The lyric Puthian, deigned inhabit once,
Become a shepherd here in thy domains,
And pipe, adown the winding hillside paths,
Pastoral marriage-poems to thy flocks
At feed: while with them fed in fellowship,
Through joy i' the music, spot-skin lynxes ; ay,
And lions too, the bloody company,
Came, leaving Othrus' dell; and round thy
    lyre,
Phoibos, there danced the speckle-coated fawn,
Pacing on lightsome fetlock past the pines
Tress-topped, the creature's natural boundary
Into the open everywhere ; such heart
Had she within her, beating joyous beats,
At the sweet reassurance of thy song !
Therefore the lot o' the master is, to live
In a home multitudinous with herds,
Along by the fair-flowing Boibian lake,
Limited, that ploughed land and pasture-plain,
Only where stand the sun's steeds, stabled west
I' the cloud, by that mid-air which makes the
    clime
Of those Molossoi: and he rules as well
O'er the Aigaian, up to Pelion's shore, —
Sea-stretch without a port ! Such lord have
    we:
And here he opens house now, as of old,
Takes to the heart of it a guest again:
Though moist the eyelid of the master, still
Mourning his dear wife's body, dead but
    now ! "

And they admired : nobility of soul
Was self-impelled to reverence, they saw :
The best men ever prove the wisest too:
Something instinctive guides them still aright.
And on each soul this boldness settled now,
That one who reverenced the Gods so much
Would prosper yet : (or — I could wish it
    ran —
Who venerates the Gods i' the main will still
Practise things honest though obscure to
    judge).

They ended, for Admetos entered now ;
Having disposed all duteously indoors,
He came into the outside world again,

Quiet as ever: but a quietude
Bent on pursuing its descent to truth,
As who must grope until he gain the ground
O' the dungeon doomed to be his dwelling now.
Already high o'er head was piled the dusk,
When something pushed to stay his downward
    step,
Pluck back despair just reaching its repose.
He would have bidden the kind presence there
Observe that, — since the corpse was coming
    out,
Cared for in all things that befit the case,
Carried aloft, in decency and state,
To the last burial-place and burning pile, —
'T were proper friends addressed, as custom
    prompts,
Alkestis bound on her last journeying.

" Ay, for we see thy father," they subjoined,
" Advancing as the aged foot best may ;
His servants, too: each bringing in his hand
Adornments for thy wife, all pomp that 's due
To the downward-dwelling people." And in
    truth,
By slow procession till they filled the stage,
Came Pheres, and his following, and their gifts.
You see, the worst of the interruption was,
It plucked back, with an over-hasty hand,
Admetos from descending to the truth,
(I told you) — put him on the brink again,
Full i' the noise and glare where late he stood:
With no fate fallen and irrevocable,
But all things subject still to chance and
    change :
And that chance — life, and that change —
    happiness.
And with the low strife came the little mind :
He was once more the man might gain so
    much,
Life too and wife too, would his friends but
    help !
All he felt now was that there faced him one
Supposed the likeliest, in emergency,
To help: and help, by mere self-sacrifice
So natural, it seemed as if the sire
Must needs lie open still to argument,
Withdraw the rash decision, not to die
But rather live, though death would save his
    son : —
Argument like the ignominious grasp
O' the drowner whom his fellow grasps as
    fierce,
Each marvelling that the other needs must
    hold
Head out of water, though friend choke there-
    by.

And first the father's salutation fell.
Burdened he came, in common with his child,
Who lost, none would gainsay, a good chaste
    spouse :
Yet such things must be borne, though hard to
    bear.
"So, take this tribute of adornment, deep
In the earth let it descend along with her !
Behooves we treat the body with respect
— Of one who died, at least, to save thy life,
Kept me from being childless, nor allowed

That I, bereft of thee, should peak and pine
In melancholy age ! she, for the sex,
All of her sisters, put in evidence,
By daring such a feat, that female life
Might prove more excellent than men suppose.
O thou Alkestis ! " out he burst in fine,
" Who, while thou savedst this my son, didst
    raise
Also myself from sinking, —hail to thee !
Well be it with thee even in the house
Of Hades ! I maintain, if mortals must
Marry, this sort of marriage is the sole
Permitted those among them who are wise ! "

So his oration ended. Like hates like :
Accordingly Admetos, —full i' the face
Of Pheres, his true father, outward shape
And inward fashion, body matching soul, —
Saw just himself when years should do their
    work
And reinforce the selfishness inside
Until it pushed the last disguise away :
As when the liquid metal cools i' the mould,
Stands forth a statue : bloodless, hard, cold
    bronze.
So, in old Pheres, young Admetos showed,
Pushed to completion : and a shudder ran,
And his repugnance soon had vent in speech :
Glad to escape outside, nor, pent within,
Find itself there fit food for exercise.

" Neither to this interment called by me
Comest thou, nor thy presence I account
Among the covetable proofs of love.
As for thy tribute of adornment, — no !
Ne'er shall she don it, ne'er in debt to thee
Be buried ! What is thine, that keep thou
    still !
Then it behooved thee to commiserate
When I was perishing : but thou — who stood'st
Foot-free o' the snare, wast acquiescent then
That I, the young, should die, not thou, the
    old —
Wilt thou lament this corpse thyself hast slain ?
Thou wast not, then, true father to this flesh ;
Nor she, who makes profession of my birth
And styles herself my mother, neither she
Bore me : but, come of slave's blood, I was cast
Stealthily 'neath the bosom of thy wife !
Thou showedst, put to touch, the thing thou
    art,
Nor I esteem myself born child of thee !
Otherwise, thine is the preëminence
O'er all the world in cowardice of soul :
Who, being the old man thou art, arrived
Where life should end, didst neither will nor
    dare
Die for thy son, but left the task to her,
The alien woman, whom I well might think
Own, only mother both and father too !
And yet a fair strife had been thine to strive,
— Dying for thy own child ; and brief for thee
In any case, the rest of time to live ;
While I had lived, and she, our rest of time,
Nor I been left to groan in solitude.
Yet certainly all things which happy man
Ought to experience, thy experience grasped.
Thou wast a ruler through the bloom of youth

And I was son to thee, recipient due
Of sceptre and demesne, — no need to fear
That dying thou shouldst leave an orphan
house
For strangers to despoil. Nor yet wilt thou
Allege that as dishonoring, forsooth,
Thy length of days, I gave thee up to die, —
I, who have held thee in such reverence !
And in exchange for it, such gratitude
Thou, father, —thou award'st me, mother
mine !
Go, lose no time, then, in begetting sons
Shall cherish thee in age, and, when thou diest,
Deck up and lay thee out as corpses claim !
For never I, at least, with this my hand
Will bury thee : it is myself am dead
So far as lies in thee. But if I light
Upon another savior, and still see
The sunbeam, — his, the child I call myself,
His, the old age that claims my cherishing.
How vainly do these aged pray for death,
Abuse the slow drag of senility !
But should death step up, nobody inclines
To die, nor age is now the weight it was ! "

You see what all this poor pretentious talk
Tried at, — how weakness strove to hide itself
In bluster against weakness, — the loud word
To hide the little whisper, not so low
Already in that heart beneath those lips !
Ha, could it be, who hated cowardice
Stood confessed craven, and who lauded so
Self-immolating love, himself had pushed
The loved one to the altar in his place ?
Friends interposed, would fain stop further play
O' the sharp-edged tongue : they felt love's
champion here
Had left an undefended point or two,
The antagonist might profit by ; bade " Pause !
Enough the present sorrow ! Nor, O son,
Whet thus against thyself thy father's soul ! "

Ay, but old Pheres was the stouter stuff !
Admetos, at the flintiest of the heart,
Had so much soft in him as held a fire :
The other was all iron, clashed from flint
Its fire, but shed no spark and showed no
bruise.
Did Pheres crave instruction as to facts ?
He came, content, the ignoble word, for him,
Should lurk still in the blackness of each
breast,
As sleeps the water-serpent half surmised :
Not brought up to the surface at a bound,
By one touch of the idly-probing spear,
Reed-like against unconquerable scale.
He came pacific, rather, as strength should,
Bringing the decent praise, the due regret,
And each banality prescribed of old.
Did he commence " Why let her die for you ? "
And rouse the coiled and quiet ugliness,
" What is so good to man as man's own life ? "
No : but the other did : and, for his pains,
Out, full in face of him, the venom leapt.

" And whom dost thou make bold, son — Lud-
ian slave,
Or Phrygian whether, money made thy ware,

To drive at with revilings ? Know'st thou
not
I, a Thessalian, from Thessalian sire
Spring and am born legitimately free ?
Too arrogant art thou ; and, youngster words
Casting against me, having had thy fling,
Thou goest not off as all were ended so !
I gave thee birth indeed and mastership
I' the mansion, brought thee up to boot : there
ends
My owing, nor extends to die for thee !
Never did I receive it as a law
Hereditary, no, nor Greek at all,
That sires in place of sons were bound to die.
For, to thy sole and single self wast thou
Born, with whatever fortune, good or bad ;
Such things as bear bestowment, those thou
hast ;
Already ruling widely, broad lands, too,
Doubt not but I shall leave thee in due time :
For why ? My father left me them before.
Well then, where wrong I thee ? — of what de-
fraud ?
Neither do thou die for this man, myself,
Nor let him die for thee ! — is all I beg.
Thou joyest seeing daylight : dost suppose
Thy father joys not too ? Undoubtedly,
Long I account the time to pass below,
And brief my span of days ; yet sweet the
same :
Is it otherwise to thee who, impudent,
Didst fight off this same death, and livest now
Through having sneaked past fate apportioned
thee,
And slain thy wife so ? Cryest cowardice
On me, I wonder, thou — whom, poor poltroon,
A very woman worsted, daring death
Just for the sake of thee, her handsome spark ?
Shrewdly hast thou contrived how not to die
Forevermore now : 't is but still persuade
The wife, for the time being, to take thy
place !
What, and thy friends who would not do the
like,
These dost thou carp at, craven thus thyself ?
Crouch and be silent, craven ! Comprehend
That, if thou lovest so that life of thine,
Why, everybody loves his own life too :
So, good words, henceforth ! If thou speak us
ill,
Many and true an ill thing shalt thou hear ! "

There you saw leap the hydra at full length !
Only, the old kept glorying the more,
The more the portent thus uncoiled itself,
Whereas the young man shuddered head to foot,
And shrank from kinship with the creature.
Why
Such horror, unless what he hated most,
Vaunting itself outside, might fairly claim
Acquaintance with the counterpart at home ?
I would the Chorus here had plucked up heart,
Spoken out boldly and explained the man,
If not to men, to Gods. That way, I think,
Sophokles would have led their dance and song.
Here, they said simply, " Too much evil spoke
On both sides ! " As the young before, so now
They bade the old man leave abusing thus.

" Let him speak, — I have spoken ! " said the
    youth :
And so died out the wrangle by degrees,
In wretched bickering. " If thou wince at fact,
Behooved thee not prove faulty to myself ! "

" Had I died for thee I had faulted more ! "

" All 's one, then, for youth's bloom and age to
    die ? "

" Our duty is to live one life, not two ! "

" Go then, and outlive Zeus, for aught I
    care ! "

" What, curse thy parents with no sort of
    cause ? "

" Curse, truly ! All thou lovest is long life ! "

" And dost not thou, too, all for love of life,
Carry out now, in place of thine, this corpse ? "

" Monument, rather, of thy cowardice,
Thou worst one ! "

            " Not for me she died, I hope !
That, thou wilt hardly say ! "
                    " No ; simply this :
Would, some day, thou mayst come to need
    myself ! "

" Meanwhile, woo many wives — the more will
    die ! "

" And so shame thee who never dared the like ! "

" Dear is this light o' the sun-god — dear, I
    say ! "

" Proper conclusion for a beast to draw ! "

" One thing is certain : there 's no laughing
    now,
As out thou bearest the poor dead old man ! "

" Die when thou wilt, thou wilt die infamous ! "

" And once dead, whether famed or infamous,
I shall not care ! "
            " Alas and yet again !
How full is age of impudency ! "
                    " True !
Thou couldst not call thy young wife impu-
    dent :
She was found foolish merely."

                " Get thee gone !
And let me bury this my dead ! "
                    " I go.
Thou buriest her whom thou didst murder
    first ;
Whereof there 's some account to render yet
Those kinsfolk by the marriage-side ! I think,
Brother Akastos may be classed with me,
Among the beasts, not men, if he omit
Avenging upon thee his sister's blood ! "

" Go to perdition, with thy housemate too !
Grow old all childlessly, with child alive,
Just as ye merit ! for to me, at least,
Beneath the same roof ne'er do ye return.
And did I need by heralds' help renounce
The ancestral hearth, I had renounced the
    same !
But we — since this woe, lying at our feet
I' the path, is to be borne — let us proceed
And lay the body on the pyre."
                    I think,
What, through this wretched wrangle, kept
    the man
From seeing clear — beside the cause I gave —
Was, that the woe, himself described as full
I' the path before him, there did really lie —
Not roll into the abyss of dead and gone.
How, with Alkestis present, calmly crowned,
Was she so irrecoverable yet —
The bird, escaped, that 's just on bough above,
The flower, let flutter half-way down the
    brink ?
Not so detached seemed lifelessness from life
But — one dear stretch beyond all straining
    yet —
And he might have her at his heart once more,
When, in the critical minute, up there comes
The father and the fact, to trifle time !

" To the pyre ! " an instinct prompted : pallid
    face,
And passive arm and pointed foot, when these
No longer shall absorb the sight, O friends,
Admetos will begin to see indeed
Who the true foe was, where the blows should
    fall !

So, the old selfish Pheres went his way,
Case-hardened as he came ; and left the youth,
(Only half selfish now, since sensitive)
To go on learning by a light the more,
As friends moved off, renewing dirge the while :

" Unhappy in thy daring ! Noble dame,
Best of the good, farewell ! With favoring
    face
May Hermes the infernal, Hades too,
Receive thee ! And if there, — ay, there, —
    some touch
Of further dignity await the good,
Sharing with them, mayst thou sit throned by
    her
The Bride of Hades, in companionship ! "

Wherewith, the sad procession wound away,
Made slowly for the suburb sepulchre.
And lo, — while still one's heart, in time and
    tune,
Paced after that symmetric step of Death
Mute-marching, to the mind's eye, at the head
O' the mourners — one hand pointing out their
    path
With the long pale terrific sword we saw,
The other leading, with grim tender grace,
Alkestis quieted and consecrate, —
Lo, life again knocked laughing at the door !
The world goes on, goes ever, in and through,
And out again o' the cloud. We faced about.

Fronted the palace where the mid-hall gate
Opened — not half, nor half of half, perhaps —
Yet wide enough to let out light and life,
And warmth, and bounty, and hope, and joy, at
    once.
Festivity burst wide, fruit rare and ripe
Crushed in the mouth of Bacchos, pulpy-prime,
All juice and flavor, save one single seed
Duly ejected from the God's nice lip,
Which lay o' the red edge, blackly visible —
To wit, a certain ancient servitor:
On whom the festal jaws o' the palace shut,
So, there he stood, a much-bewildered man.
Stupid ?   Nay, but sagacious in a sort:
Learned, life-long, i' the first outside of things,
Though bat for blindness to what lies beneath
And needs a nail-scratch ere 't is laid you bare.
This functionary was the trusted one
We saw deputed by Admetos late
To lead in Herakles and help him, soul
And body, to such snatched repose, snapped-
    up
Sustainment, as might do away the dust
O' the last encounter, knit each nerve anew
For that next onset sure to come at cry
O' the creature next assailed, — nay, should it
    prove
Only the creature that came forward now
To play the critic upon Herakles !

" Many the guests," — so he soliloquized
In musings burdensome to breast before,
When it seemed not too prudent tongue should
    wag, —
" Many, and from all quarters of this world,
The guests I now have known frequent our
    house,
For whom I spread the banquet ; but than this,
Never a worse one did I yet receive
At the hearth here !   One who seeing, first of
    all,
The master's sorrow, entered gate the same,
And had the hardihood to house himself.
Did things stop there !   But, modest by no
    means,
He took what entertainment lay to hand,
Knowing of our misfortune, — did we fail
In aught of the fit service, urged us serve
Just as a guest expects !   And in his hands
Taking the ivied goblet, drinks and drinks
The unmixed product of black mother-earth,
Until the blaze o' the wine went round about
And warmed him : then he crowns with myrtle
    sprigs
His head, and howls discordance — twofold lay
Was thereupon for us to listen to —
This fellow singing, namely, nor restrained
A jot by sympathy with sorrows here —
While we o' the household mourned our mis-
    tress — mourned,
That is to say, in silence — never showed
The eyes, which we kept wetting, to the
    guest —
For there Admetos was imperative.
And so, here am I helping make at home
A guest, some fellow ripe for wickedness,
Robber or pirate, while she goes her way
Out of our house : and neither was it mine

To follow in procession, nor stretch forth
Hand, wave my lady dear a last farewell,
Lamenting who to me and all of us
Domestics was a mother : myriad harms
She used to ward away from every one,
And mollify her husband's ireful mood.
I ask then, do I justly hate or no
This guest, this interloper on our grief ? "

" Hate him and justly ! "   Here 's the proper
    judge
Of what is due to the house from Herakles !
This man of much experience saw the first
O' the feeble duckings-down at destiny,
When King Admetos went his rounds, poor
    soul,
A-begging somebody to be so brave
As die for one afraid to die himself —
" Thou, friend ?   Thou, love ?   Father or
    mother, then !
None of you ?   What, Alkestis must Death
    catch ?
O best of wives, one woman in the world !
But nowise droop : our prayers may still assist :
Let us try sacrifice ; if those avail
Nothing and Gods avert their countenance,
Why, deep and durable our grief will be ! "
Whereat the house, this worthy at its head,
Re-echoed " deep and durable our grief ! "
This sage, who justly hated Herakles,
Did he suggest once " Rather I than she ! "
Admonish the Turannos — " Be a man !
Bear thine own burden, never think to thrust
Thy fate upon another and thy wife !
It were a dubious gain could death be doomed
That other, and no passionatest plea
Of thine, to die instead, have force with fate ;
Seeing thou lov'st Alkestis : what were life
Unlighted by the loved one ?   But to live —
Not merely live unsolaced by some thought,
Some word so poor — yet solace all the same —
As ' Thou i' the sepulchre, Alkestis, say !
Would I, or would not I, to save thy life,
Die, and die on, and die forevermore ? '
No ! but to read red-written up and down
The world ' This is the sunshine, this the shade,
This is some pleasure of earth, sky or sea,
Due to that other, dead that thou mayst live ! '
Such were a covetable gain to thee ?
Go die, fool, and be happy while 't is time ! "
One word of counsel in this kind, methinks,
Had fallen to better purpose than Ai, ai,
Pheu, pheu, e, papai, and a pother of praise
O' the best, best, best one !   Nothing was to
    hate
In King Admetos, Pheres, and the rest
O' the household down to his heroic self !
This was the one thing hateful : Herakles
Had flung into the presence, frank and free,
Out from the labor into the repose,
Ere out again and over head and ears
I' the heart of labor, all for love of men :
Making the most o' the minute, that the soul
And body, strained to height a minute since,
Might lie relaxed in joy, this breathing-space,
For man's sake more than ever ; till the bow,
Restrung o' the sudden, at first cry for help,
Should send some unimaginable shaft

True to the aim and shatteringly through
The plate-mail of a monster, save man so.
He slew the pest o' the marish yesterday:
To-morrow he would bit the flame-breathed
    stud
That fed on man's-flesh: and this day between —
Because he held it natural to die,
And fruitless to lament a thing past cure,
So, took his fill of food, wine, song and flowers,
Till the new labor claimed him soon enough, —
" Hate him and justly ! "
                True, Charopé mine !
The man surmised not Herakles lay hid
I' the guest ; or, knowing it, was ignorant
That still his lady lived — for Herakles ;
Or else judged lightness needs must indicate
This or the other caitiff quality:
And therefore — had been right if not so wrong !
For who expects the sort of him will scratch
A nail's depth, scrape the surface just to see
What peradventure underlies the same ?

So, he stood petting up his puny hate,
Parent-wise, proud of the ill-favored babe.
Not long ! A great hand, careful lest it crush,
Startled him on the shoulder : up he stared,
And over him, who stood but Herakles !
There smiled the mighty presenceè, all one smile
And no touch more of the world-weary God,
Through the brief respite. Just a garland's
    grace
About the brow, a song to satisfy
Head, heart and breast, and trumpet-lips at
    once,
A solemn draught of true religious wine,
And — how should I know ? — half a mountain-
    goat
Torn up and swallowed down, — the feast was
    fierce
But brief: all cares and pains took wing and
    flew,
Leaving the hero ready to begin
And help mankind, whatever woe came next,
Even though what came next should be naught
    more
Than the mean querulous mouth o' the man, re-
    marked
Pursing its grievance up till patience failed
And the sage needs must rush out, as we saw,
To sulk outside and pet his hate in peace.
By no means would the Helper have it so :
He who was just about to handle brutes
In Thrace, and bit the jaws which breathed the
    flame, —
Well, if a good laugh and a jovial word
Could bridle age which blew bad humors forth,
That were a kind of help, too !
             " Thou, there ! " hailed
This grand benevolence the ungracious one —
" Why look'st so solemn and so thought-ab-
    sorbed ?
To guests a servant should not sour-faced be,
But do the honors with a mind urbane.
While thou, contrariwise, beholding here
Arrive thy master's comrade, hast for him
A churlish visage, all one beetle-brow —
Having regard to grief that 's out-of-door !
Come hither, and so get to grow more wise !

Things mortal — know'st the nature that they
    have ?
No, I imagine ! whence could knowledge spring ?
Give ear to me, then ! For all flesh to die,
Is Nature's due ; nor is there any one
Of mortals with assurance he shall last
The coming morrow : for, what 's born of chance
Invisibly proceeds the way it will,
Not to be learned, no fortune-teller's prize.
This, therefore, having heard and known
    through me,
Gladden thyself ! Drink ! Count the day-by-
    day
Existence thine, and all the other — chance !
Ay, and pay homage also to by far
The sweetest of divinities for man,
Kupris ! Benignant Goddess will she prove !
But as for aught else, leave and let things be !
And trust my counsel, if I seem to speak
To purpose — as I do, apparently.
Wilt not thou, then, — discarding overmuch
Mournfulness, do away with this shut door,
Come drink along with me, be-garlanded
This fashion ? Do so, and — I well know
    what —
From this stern mood, this shrunk-up state of
    mind,
The pit-pat fall o' the flagon-juice down throat,
Soon will dislodge thee from bad harborage !
Men being mortal should think mortal-like :
Since to your solemn, brow-contracting sort,
All of them, — so I lay down law at least, —
Life is not truly life but misery."

Whereto the man with softened surliness:
" We know as much : but deal with matters,
    now,
Hardly befitting mirth and revelry."

" No intimate, this woman that is dead :
Mourn not too much ! For, those o' the house
    itself,
Thy masters live, remember ! "

                " Live indeed ?
Ah, thou know'st naught o' the woe within
    these walls ! "

" I do — unless thy master spoke me false
Somehow ! "
           " Ay, ay, too much he loves a guest,
Too much, that master mine ! " so muttered he.

" Was it improper he should treat me well,
Because an alien corpse was in the way ? "

" No alien, but most intimate indeed ! "

" Can it be, some woe was, he told me not ? "

" Farewell and go thy way ! Thy cares for
    thee —
To us, our master's sorrow is a care."

" This word begins no tale of alien woe ! "

" Had it been other woe than intimate,
I could have seen thee feast, nor felt amiss."

" What! have I suffered strangely from my
    host ? "

" Thou cam'st not at a fit reception-time:
With sorrow here beforehand: and thou seest
Shorn hair, black robes."
                    " But who is it that 's dead ?
Some child gone ? or the aged sire perhaps ? "

" Admetos' wife, then ! she has perished,
    guest ! "

" How sayest ?   And did ye house me, all the
    same ? "

" Ay : for he had thee in that reverence
He dared not turn thee from his door away ! "

" O hapless, and bereft of what a mate ! "

" All of us now are dead, not she alone ! "

" But I divined it ! seeing, as I did,
His eye that ran with tears, his close-clipt hair,
His countenance !   Though he persuaded me,
Saying it was a stranger's funeral
He went with to the grave: against my wish,
He forced on me that I should enter doors,
Drink in the hall o' the hospitable man
Circumstanced so !   And do I revel yet
With wreath on head ?   But — thou to hold thy
    peace,
Nor tell me what a woe oppressed my friend !
Where is he gone to bury her ?   Where am I
To go and find her ? "
                    " By the road that leads
Straight to Larissa, thou wilt see the tomb,
Out of the suburb, a carved sepulchre."

So said he, and therewith dismissed himself
Inside to his lamenting: somewhat soothed,
However, that he had adroitly spoilt
The mirth of the great creature: oh, he marked
The movement of the mouth, how lip pressed
    lip,
And either eye forgot to shine, as, fast,
He plucked the chaplet from his forehead,
    dashed
The myrtle-sprays down, trod them under-
    foot !
And all the joy and wonder of the wine
Withered away, like fire from off a brand
The wind blows over — beacon though it be,
Whose merry ardor only meant to make
Somebody all the better for its blaze,
And save lost people in the dark: quenched
    now !

Not long quenched !   As the flame, just hurried
    off
The brand's edge, suddenly renews its bite,
Tasting some richness caked i' the core o' the
    tree, —
Pine, with a blood that 's oil, — and triumphs
    up
Pillar-wise to the sky and saves the world:
So, in a spasm and splendor of resolve,
All at once did the God surmount the man.

" O much-enduring heart and hand of mine !
Now show what sort of son she bore to Zeus,
That daughter of Elektruon, Tiruns' child,
Alkmené ! for that son must needs save now
The just-dead lady : ay, establish here
I' the house again Alkestis, bring about
Comfort and succor to Admetos so !
I will go lie in wait for Death, black-stoled
King of the corpses !   I shall find him, sure,
Drinking, beside the tomb, o' the sacrifice:
And if I lie in ambuscade, and leap
Out of my lair, and seize — encircle him
Till one hand join the other round about —
There lives not who shall pull him out from me
Rib-mauled, before he let the woman go !
But even say I miss the booty, — say,
Death comes not to the boltered blood, — why
    then,
Down go I, to the unsunned dwelling-place
Of Koré and the king there, — make demand,
Confident I shall bring Alkestis back,
So as to put her in the hands of him
My host, that housed me, never drove me off:
Though stricken with sore sorrow, hid the
    stroke,
Being a noble heart and honoring me !
Who of Thessalians, more than this man, loves
The stranger ? Who, that now inhabits Greece ?
Wherefore he shall not say the man was vile
Whom he befriended, — native noble heart ! "

So, one look upward, as if Zeus might laugh
Approval of his human progeny, —
One summons of the whole magnific frame,
Each sinew to its service, — up he caught,
And over shoulder cast, the lion-shag,
Let the club go, — for had he not those hands ?
And so went striding off, on that straight way
Leads to Larissa and the suburb tomb.
Gladness be with thee, Helper of our world !
I think this is the authentic sign and seal
Of Godship, that it ever waxes glad,
And more glad, until gladness blossoms, bursts
Into a rage to suffer for mankind,
And recommence at sorrow : drops like seed
After the blossom, ultimate of all.
Say, does the seed scorn earth and seek the
    sun ?
Surely it has no other end and aim
Than to drop, once more die into the ground,
Taste cold and darkness and oblivion there:
And thence rise, tree-like grow through pain to
    joy,
More joy and most joy, — do man good again.

So, to the struggle off strode Herakles.
When silence closed behind the lion-garb,
Back came our dull fact settling in its place,
Though heartiness and passion half-dispersed
The inevitable fate.   And presently
In came the mourners from the funeral,
One after one, until we hoped the last
Would be Alkestis and so end our dream.
Could they have really left Alkestis lone
I' the wayside sepulchre !   Home, all save she !
And when Admetos felt that it was so,
By the stand-still: when he lifted head and
    face

From the two hiding hands and peplos' fold,
And looked forth, knew the palace, knew the
    hills,
Knew the plains, knew the friendly frequence
    there,
And no Alkestis any more again,
Why, the whole woe billow-like broke on him.

" O hateful entry, hateful countenance
O' the widowed halls ! " — he moaned. " What
    was to be ?
Go there ? Stay here ? Speak, not speak ? All
    was now
Mad and impossible alike ; one way
And only one was sane and safe — to die :
Now he was made aware how dear is death,
How lovable the dead are, how the heart
Yearns in us to go hide where they repose,
When we find sunbeams do no good to see,
Nor earth rests rightly where our footsteps
    fall.
His wife had been to him the very pledge,
Sun should be sun, earth — earth ; the pledge
    was robbed,
Pact broken, and the world was left no world."
He stared at the impossible, mad life :
Stood, while they urged " Advance — advance !
    Go deep
Into the utter dark, thy palace-core ! "
They tried what they called comfort, " touched
    the quick
Of the ulceration in his soul," he said,
With memories, — " once thy joy was thus and
    thus ! "
True comfort were to let him fling himself
Into the hollow grave o' the tomb, and so
Let him lie dead along with all he loved.

One bade him note that his own family
Boasted a certain father whose sole son,
Worthy bewailment, died : and yet the sire
Bore stoutly up against the blow and lived ;
For all that he was childless now, and prone
Already to gray hairs, far on in life.
Could such a good example miss effect ?
Why fix foot, stand so, staring at the house,
Why not go in, as that wise kinsman would ?

" Oh that arrangement of the house I know !
How can I enter, how inhabit thee
Now that one cast of fortune changes all ?
Oh me, for much divides the then from now !
Then — with those pine-tree torches, Pelian
    pomp
And marriage-hymns, I entered, holding high
The hand of my dear wife ; while many-voiced
The revelry that followed me and her
That's dead now, — friends felicitating both,
As who were lofty-lineaged, each of us
Born of the best, two wedded and made one ;
Now — wail is wedding-chant's antagonist,
And, for white peplos, stoles in sable state
Herald my way to the deserted couch ! "

The one word more they ventured was, " This
    grief
Befell thee witless of what sorrow means,
Close after prosperous fortune : but, reflect !

Thou hast saved soul and body. Dead, thy
    wife —
Living, the love she left. What 's novel here ?
Many the man, from whom Death long ago
Loosed the life-partner ! "
                    Then Admetos spoke :
Turned on the comfort, with no tears, this
    time.
He was beginning to be like his wife.
I told you of that pressure to the point,
Word slow pursuing word in monotone,
Alkestis spoke with ; so Admetos, now,
Solemnly bore the burden of the truth.
And as the voice of him grew, gathered
    strength,
And groaned on, and persisted to the end,
We felt how deep had been descent in grief,
And with what change he came up now to light,
And left behind such littleness as tears.

" Friends, I account the fortune of my wife
Happier than mine, though it seem otherwise :
For, her indeed no grief will ever touch,
And she from many a labor pauses now,
Renowned one ! Whereas I, who ought not live,
But do live, by evading destiny,
Sad life am I to lead, I learn at last !
For how shall I bear going in-doors here ?
Accosting whom ? By whom saluted back,
Shall I have joyous entry ? Whither turn ?
Inside, the solitude will drive me forth,
When I behold the empty bed — my wife's —
The seat she used to sit upon, the floor
Unsprinkled as when dwellers loved the cool,
The children that will clasp my knees about,
Cry for their mother back : these servants too
Moaning for what a guardian they have lost !
Inside my house such circumstance awaits,
Outside, — Thessalian people's marriage-feasts
And gatherings for talk will harass me,
With overflow of women everywhere ;
It is impossible I look on them —
Familiars of my wife and just her age !
And then, whoever is a foe of mine,
And lights on me — why, this will be his word —
' See there ! alive ignobly, there he skulks
That played the dastard when it came to die,
And, giving her he wedded, in exchange,
Kept himself out of Hades safe and sound,
The coward ! Do you call that creature — man ?
He hates his parents for declining death,
Just as if he himself would gladly die ! '
This sort of reputation shall I have,
Beside the other ills enough in store.
Ill-famed, ill-faring, — what advantage, friends,
Do you perceive I gain by life for death ? "

That was the truth. Vexed waters sank to
    smooth :
'T was only when the last of bubbles broke,
The latest circlet widened all away
And left a placid level, that up swam
To the surface the drowned truth, in dreadful
    change.
So, through the quiet and submission, — ay,
Spite of some strong words — (for you miss the
    tone)
The grief was getting to be infinite —

Grief, friends fell back before.　Their office
　　shrank
To that old solace of humanity ! —
" Being born mortal, bear grief ! Why born
　　else ? "
And they could only meditate anew.

" They, too, upborne by airy help of song,
And haply science, which can find the stars,
Had searched the heights : had sounded depths
　　as well
By catching much at books where logic lurked,
Yet nowhere found they aught could overcome
Necessity: not any medicine served,
Which Thrakian tablets treasure, Orphic voice
Wrote itself down upon : nor remedy
Which Phoibos gave to the Asklepiadai ;
Cutting the roots of many a virtuous herb
To solace overburdened mortals.　None !
Of this sole goddess, never may we go
To altar nor to image : sacrifice
She hears not.　All to pray for is — ' Approach !
But, oh, no harder on me, awful one,
Than heretofore !　Let life endure thee still !
For, whatsoe'er Zeus' nod decree, that same
In concert with thee hath accomplishment.
Iron, the very stuff o' the Chaluboi,
Thou, by sheer strength, dost conquer and
　　subdue ;
Nor, of that harsh abrupt resolve of thine,
Any relenting is there ! '
　　　　　　　" O my king !
Thee also, in the shackles of those hands,
Not to be shunned, the Goddess grasped !　Yet,
　　bear !
Since never wilt thou lead from underground
The dead ones, wail thy worst !　If mortals
　　die, —
The very children of immortals, too,
Dropped 'mid our darkness, these decay as
　　sure !
Dear indeed was she while among us : dear,
Now she is dead, must she forever be :
Thy portion was to clasp, within thy couch,
The noblest of all women as a wife.
Nor be the tomb of her supposed some heap
That hides mortality : but like the Gods
Honored, a veneration to a world
Of wanderers !　Oft the wanderer, struck there-
　　by,
Who else had sailed past in his merchant-ship,
Ay, he shall leave ship, land, long wind his way
Up to the mountain-summit, till there break
Speech forth, ' So, this was she, then, died of
　　old
To save her husband !　now, a deity
She bends above us.　Hail, benignant one !
Give good ! '　Such voices so will supplicate.
But — can it be ?　Alkmené's offspring comes,
Admetos ! — to thy house advances here ! "

I doubt not, they supposed him decently
Dead somewhere in that winter world of
　　Thrace —
Vanquished by one o' the Bistones, or else
Victim to some mad steed's voracity —
For did not friends prognosticate as much ?
It were a new example to the point,

That " children of immortals, dropped by
　　stealth
Into our darkness, die as sure as we ! "
A case to quote and comfort people with :
But, as for lamentation, ai and pheu,
Right-minded subjects kept them for their
　　lord.

Ay, he it was advancing !　In he strode,
And took his stand before Admetos, — turned
Now by despair to such a quietude,
He neither raised his face nor spoke, this time,
The while his friend surveyed him steadily.
That friend looked rough with fighting : had he
　　strained
Worst brute to breast was ever strangled yet ?
Somehow, a victory — for there stood the
　　strength,
Happy, as always ; something grave, perhaps
The great vein-cordage on the fret-worked
　　front,
Black-swollen, beaded yet with battle-dew
The yellow hair o' the hero ! — his big frame
A-quiver with each muscle sinking back
Into the sleepy smooth it leaped from late.
Under the great guard of one arm, there leant
A shrouded something, live and woman-like,
Propped by the heartbeats 'neath the lion-coat.
When he had finished his survey, it seemed,
The heavings of the heart began subside,
The helpful breath returned, and last the smile
Shone out, all Herakles was back again,
As the words followed the saluting hand.

" To friendly man, behooves we freely speak,
Admetos ! — nor keep buried, deep in breast,
Blame we leave silent.　I assuredly
Judged myself proper, if I should approach
By accident calamities of thine,
To be demonstrably thy friend : but thou
Told'st me not of the corpse then claiming
　　care,
That was thy wife's, but didst instal me guest
I' the house here, as though busied with a
　　grief
Indeed, but then, mere grief beyond thy gate :
And so, I crowned my head, and to the Gods
Poured my libations in thy dwelling-place,
With such misfortune round me.　And I
　　blame —
Certainly blame thee, having suffered thus !
But still I would not pain thee, pained enough :
So let it pass !　Wherefore I seek thee now,
Having turned back again though onward
　　bound,
That I will tell thee.　Take and keep for me
This woman, till I come thy way again,
Driving before me, having killed the king
O' the Bistones, that drove of Thrakian steeds'
In such case, give the woman back to me !
But should I fare, — as fare I fain would not,
Seeing I hope to prosper and return, —
Then, I bequeath her as thy household slave.
She came into my hands with good hard toil !
For, what find I, when started on my course,
But certain people, a whole country-side,
Holding a wrestling-bout ? as good to me
As a new labor : whence I took. and here

Come keeping with me, this, the victor's prize.
For, such as conquered in the easy work,
Gained horses which they drove away: and
    such
As conquered in the harder, — those who
    boxed
And wrestled, — cattle; and, to crown the
    prize,
A woman followed. Chancing as I did,
Base were it to forego this fame and gain !
Well, as I said, I trust her to thy care :
No woman I have kidnapped, understand !
But good hard toil has done it : here I come !
Some day, who knows? even thou wilt praise
    the feat ! "

Admetos raised his face and eyed the pair :
Then, hollowly and with submission, spoke,
And spoke again, and spoke time after time,
When he perceived the silence of his friend
Would not be broken by consenting word.
As a tired slave goes adding stone to stone
Until he stop some current that molests,
So poor Admetos piled up argument
Vainly against the purpose all too plain
In that great brow acquainted with command.

" Nowise dishonoring, nor amid my foes
Ranking thee, did I hide my wife's ill fate ;
But it were grief superimposed on grief,
Shouldst thou have hastened to another home.
My own woe was enough for me to weep !
But, for this woman, — if it so may be, —
Bid   some   Thessalian, — I   entreat   thee,
    king ! —
Keep her, — who has not suffered like myself !
Many of the Pheraioi welcome thee.
Be no reminder to me of my ills !
I could not, if I saw her come to live,
Restrain the tear ! Inflict on me, diseased,
No new disease : woe bends me down enough !
Then, where could she be sheltered in my house,
Female and young too ? For that she is young,
The vesture and adornment prove. Reflect !
Should such an one inhabit the same roof
With men ? And how, mixed up, a girl, with
    youths,
Shall she keep pure, in 'that case ? No light
    task
To curb the May-day youngster, Herakles !
I only speak because of care for thee.
Or must I, in avoidance of such harm,
Make her to enter, lead her life within
The chamber of the dead one, all apart ?
How shall I introduce this other, couch
This where Alkestis lay ? A double blame
I apprehend : first, from the citizens —
Lest some tongue of them taunt that I betray
My benefactress, fall into the snare
Of a new fresh face : then, the dead one's self, —
Will she not blame me likewise ? Worthy, sure,
Of worship from me ! circumspect my ways,
And jealous of a fault, are bound to be.
But thou, — O woman, whosoe'er thou art, —
Know, thou hast all the form, art like as like
Alkestis, in the bodily shape ! Ah me !
Take — by the Gods — this woman from my
    sight,

Lest thou undo me, the undone before !
Since I seem — seeing her — as if I saw
My own wife ! And confusions cloud my
    heart,
And from my eyes the springs break forth !
    Ah me
Unhappy — how I taste for the first time
My misery in all its bitterness ! "

Whereat the friends conferred : " The chance,
    in truth,
Was an untoward one — none said otherwise.
Still, what a God comes giving, good or bad,
That, one should take and bear with. Take
    her, then ! "

Herakles, — not unfastening his hold
On that same misery, beyond mistake
Hoarse in the words, convulsive in the face, —
" I would that I had such a power," said he,
' As to lead up into the light again
Thy very wife, and grant thee such a grace ! "

" Well do I know thou wouldst : but where the
    hope ?
There is no bringing back the dead to light."

" Be not extravagant in grief, no less !
Bear it, by augury of better things ! "

" 'T is easier to advise ' bear up,' than bear ! "

" But how carve way i' the life that lies be-
    fore,
If bent on groaning ever for the past ? "

" I myself know that : but a certain love
Allures me to the choice I shall not change."

" Ay, but, still loving dead ones, still makes
    weep."

" And let it be so ! She has ruined me,
And still more than I say : that answers all."

" Oh, thou hast lost a brave wife : who dis-
    putes ? "

" So brave a one — that he whom thou be-
    hold'st
Will never more enjoy his life again ! "

" Time will assuage ! The evil yet is young ! "

" Time, thou mayst say, will ; if time mean —
    to die."

" A wife — the longing for new marriage-joys
Will stop thy sorrow ! "
                    " Hush, friend, — hold thy peace !
What hast thou said ! I could not credit ear ! "

" How then ? Thou wilt not marry, then, but
    keep
A widowed couch ? "
                    " There is not any one
Of womankind shall couch with whom thou
    seest ! "

" Dost think to profit thus in any way
The dead one ? "
      " Her, wherever she abide,
My duty is to honor."
          " And I praise —
Indeed I praise thee ! Still, thou hast to pay
The price of it, in being held a fool ! "

" Fool call me — only one name call me not !
Bridegroom ! "
      " No : it was praise, I portioned thee,
Of being good true husband to thy wife ! "

" When I betray her, though she is no more,
May I die ! "
      And the thing he said was true :
For out of Herakles a great glow broke.
There stood a victor worthy of a prize :
The violet-crown that withers on the brow
Of the half-hearted claimant. Oh, he knew
The signs of battle hard fought and well won,
This queller of the monsters ! — knew his friend
Planted firm foot, now, on the loathly thing
That was Admetos late ! "would die," he
    knew,
Ere let the reptile raise its crest again.
If that was truth, why try the true friend
    more ?

" Then, since thou canst be faithful to the
    death,
Take, deep into thy house, my dame ! " smiled
    he.

" Not so ! — I pray, by thy Progenitor ! "

" Thou wilt mistake in disobeying me ! "

" Obeying thee, I have to break my heart ! "

" Obey me ! Who knows but the favor done
May fall into its place as duty too ? "

So, he was humble, would decline no more
Bearing a burden : he just sighed, " Alas !
Would thou hadst never brought this prize
    from game ! "

" Yet, when I conquered there, thou con-
    queredst ! "

" All excellently urged ! Yet — spite of all,
Bear with me ! let the woman go away ! "

" She shall go, if needs must : but ere she go,
See if there *is* need ! "
      " Need there is ! At least,
Except I make thee angry with me, so ! "

" But I persist, because I have my spice
Of intuition likewise : take the dame ! "

" Be thou the victor, then ! But certainly
Thou dost thy friend no pleasure in the act ! "

" Oh, time will come when thou shalt praise
    me ! Now —
Only obey ! "

" Then, servants, since my house
Must needs receive this woman, take her
    there ! "

" I shall not trust this woman to the care
Of servants."
      " Why, conduct her in, thyself,
If that seem preferable ! "
          " I prefer,
With thy good leave, to place her in thy
    hands ! "

" I would not touch her ! Entry to the
    house —
That, I concede thee."
      " To thy sole right hand
I mean to trust her ! "
      " King ! Thou wrenchest this
Out of me by main force, if I submit ! "

" Courage, friend ! Come, stretch hand forth !
    Good ! Now touch
The stranger-woman ! "
      " There ! A hand I stretch —
As though it meant to cut off Gorgon's head ! "

" Hast hold of her ? "
      " Fast hold."
      " Why, then, hold fast
And have her ! and, one day, asseverate
Thou wilt, I think, thy friend, the son of Zeus,
He was the gentle guest to entertain !
Look at her ! See if she, in any way,
Present thee with resemblance of thy wife ! "

Ah, but the tears come, find the words at fault !
There is no telling how the hero twitched
The veil off : and there stood, with such fixed
    eyes
And such slow smile, Alkestis' silent self !
It was the crowning grace of that great heart,
To keep back joy : procrastinate the truth
Until the wife, who had made proof and found
The husband wanting, might essay once more,
Hear, see, and feel him renovated now —
Able to do, now, all herself had done,
Risen to the height of her : so, hand in hand,
The two might go together, live and die.

Beside, when he found speech, you guess the
    speech.
He could not think he saw his wife again :
It was some mocking God that used the bliss
To make him mad ! Till Herakles must help :
Assure him that no spectre mocked at all ;
He was embracing whom he buried once.
Still, — did he touch, might he address the
    true, —
True eye, true body of the true live wife ?

And Herakles said, smiling, " All was truth.
Spectre ? Admetos had not made his guest
One who played ghost-invoker, or such cheat :
Oh, he might speak and have response, in time
All heart could wish was gained now — life for
    death :
Only, the rapture must not grow immense :
Take care, nor wake the envy of the Gods ! "

"O thou, of greatest Zeus true son,"—so
spoke
Admetos when the closing word must come,
"Go ever in a glory of success,
And save, that sire, his offspring to the end!
For thou hast—only thou—raised me and
mine
Up again to this light and life!" Then asked
Tremblingly, how was trod the perilous path
Out of the dark into the light and life:
How it had happened with Alkestis there.

And Herakles said little, but enough—
How he engaged in combat with that king
O' the dæmons: how the field of contest lay
By the tomb's self: how he sprang from am-
buscade,
Captured Death, caught him in that pair of
hands.

But all the time, Alkestis moved not once
Out of the set gaze and the silent smile;
And a cold fear ran through Admetos' frame:
"Why does she stand and front me, silent
thus?"

Herakles solemnly replied, "Not yet
Is it allowable thou hear the things
She has to tell thee; let evanish quite
That consecration to the lower Gods,
And on our upper world the third day rise!
Lead her in, meanwhile; good and true thou
art,
Good, true, remain thou! Practise piety
To stranger-guests the old way! So, farewell!
Since forth I fare, fulfil my urgent task
Set by the king, the son of Sthenelos."

Fain would Admetos keep that splendid smile
Ever to light him. "Stay with us, thou heart!
Remain our house-friend!"

"At some other day!
Now, of necessity, I haste!" smiled he.

"But mayst thou prosper, go forth on a foot
Sure to return! Through all the tetrarchy,
Command my subjects that they institute
Thanksgiving-dances for the glad event,
And bid each altar smoke with sacrifice!
For we are minded to begin a fresh
Existence, better than the life before;
Seeing I own myself supremely blest."

Whereupon all the friendly moralists
Drew this conclusion: chirped, each beard to
each:
"Manifold are thy shapings, Providence!
Many a hopeless matter Gods arrange.
What we expected never came to pass:
What we did not expect Gods brought to bear;
So have things gone, this whole experience
through!"

Ah, but if you had seen the play itself!
They say, my poet failed to get the prize:

Sophokles got the prize,—great name! They
say,
Sophokles also means to make a piece,
Model a new Admetos, a new wife:
Success to him! One thing has many sides.
The great name! But no good supplants a good.
Nor beauty undoes beauty. Sophokles
Will carve and carry a fresh cup, brimful
Of beauty and good, firm to the altar-foot,
And glorify the Dionusiac shrine:
Not clash against this crater in the place
Where the God put it when his mouth had
drained,
To the last dregs, libation lifeblood-like,
And praised Euripides forevermore—
The Human with his droppings of warm tears.

Still, since one thing may have so many sides,
I think I see how,—far from Sophokles,—
You, I, or any one might mould a new
Admetos, new Alkestis. Ah, that brave
Bounty of poets, the one royal race
That ever was, or will be, in this world!
They give no gift that bounds itself and ends
I' the giving and the taking: theirs so breeds
I' the heart and soul o' the taker, so trans-
mutes
The man who only was a man before,
That he grows godlike in his turn, can give—
He also: share the poets' privilege,
Bring forth new good, new beauty, from the
old.
As though the cup that gave the wine, gave,
too,
The God's prolific giver of the grape,
That vine, was wont to find out, fawn around
His footstep, springing still to bless the dearth,
At bidding of a Mainad. So with me:
For I have drunk this poem, quenched my
thirst,
Satisfied heart and soul—yet more remains!
Could we too make a poem? Try at least,
Inside the head, what shape the rose-mists take!

When God Apollon took, for punishment,
A mortal form and sold himself a slave
To King Admetos till a term should end,—
Not only did he make, in servitude,
Such music, while he fed the flocks and herds,
As saved the pasturage from wrong or fright,
Curing rough creatures of ungentleness:
Much more did that melodious wisdom work
Within the heart o' the master: there, ran wild
Many a lust and greed that grow to strength
By preying on the native pity and care,
Would else, all undisturbed, possess the land.

And these the God so tamed, with golden
tongue,
That, in the plenitude of youth and power,
Admetos vowed himself to rule thenceforth
In Pherai solely for his people's sake,
Subduing to such end each lust and greed
That dominates the natural charity.

And so the struggle ended. Right ruled might:
And soft yet brave, and good yet wise, the man
Stood up to be a monarch; having learned

The worth of life, life's worth would he bestow
On all whose lot was cast, to live or die,
As he determined for the multitude.
So stands a statue : pedestalled sublime,
Only that it may wave the thunder off,
And ward, from winds that vex, a world below.

And then, — as if a whisper found its way
E'en to the sense o' the marble, — "Vain thy
      vow !
The royalty of its resolve, that head
Shall hide within the dust ere day be done :
That arm, its outstretch of beneficence,
Shall have a speedy ending on the earth :
Lie patient, prone, while light some cricket
      leaps
And takes possession of the masterpiece,
To sit, sing louder as more near the sun.
For why ? A flaw was in the pedestal ;
Who knows ? A worm's work ! Sapped, the
      certain fate
O' the statue is to fall, and thine to die ! "

Whereat the monarch, calm, addressed himself
To die, but bitterly the soul outbroke —
"O prodigality of life, blind waste
I' the world, of power profuse without the will
To make life do its work, deserve its day !
My ancestors pursued their pleasure, poured
The blood o' the people out in idle war,
Or took occasion of some weary peace
To bid men dig down deep or build up high,
Spend bone and marrow that the king might
      feast
Entrenched and buttressed from the vulgar
      gaze.
Yet they all lived, nay, lingered to old age :
As though Zeus loved that they should laugh
      to scorn
The vanity of seeking other ends
In rule, than just the ruler's pastime. They
Lived ; I must die."
                   And, as some long last moan
Of a minor suddenly is propped beneath
By note which, new-struck, turns the wail that
      was
Into a wonder and a triumph, so
Began Alkestis : "Nay, thou art to live !
The glory that, in the disguise of flesh,
Was helpful to our house, — he prophesied
The coming fate : whereon, I pleaded sore
That he, — I guessed a God, who to his couch
Amid the clouds must go and come again,
While we were darkling, — since he loved us
      both,
He should permit thee, at whatever price,
To live and carry out to heart's content
Soul's purpose, turn each thought to very deed,
Nor let Zeus lose the monarch meant in thee.

"To which Apollon, with a sunset smile,
Sadly — 'And so should mortals arbitrate !
It were unseemly if they aped us Gods,
And, mindful of our chain of consequence,
Lost care of the immediate earthly link :
Forwent the comfort of life's little hour,
In prospect of some cold abysmal blank
Alien eternity, — unlike the time

They know, and understand to practise with, —
No, — our eternity — no heart's blood, bright
And warm outpoured in its behoof, would
      tinge
Never so palely, warm a whit the more :
Whereas retained and treasured — left to beat
Joyously on, a life's length, in the breast
O' the loved and loving — it would throb itself
Through, and suffuse the earthly tenement,
Transform it, even as your mansion here
Is love-transformed into a temple-home
Where I, a God, forget the Olympian glow,
I' the feel of human richness like the rose :
Your hopes and fears, so blind and yet so sweet
With death about them. Therefore, well in
      thee
To look, not on eternity, but time :
To apprehend that, should Admetos die,
All, we Gods purposed in him, dies as sure :
That, life's link snapping, all our chain is lost.
And yet a mortal glance might pierce, me-
      thinks,
Deeper into the seeming dark of things,
And learn, no fruit, man's life can bear, will
      fade :
Learn, if Admetos die now, so much more
Will pity for the frailness found in flesh,
Will terror at the earthly chance and change
Frustrating wisest scheme of noblest soul,
Will these go wake the seeds of good asleep
Throughout the world : as oft a rough wind
      sheds
The unripe promise of some field-flower, —
      true !
But loosens too the level, and lets breathe
A thousand captives for the year to come.
Nevertheless, obtain thy prayer, stay fate !
Admetos lives — if thou wilt die for him ! '

"So was the pact concluded that I die,
And thou live on, live for thyself, for me,
For all the world. Embrace and bid me hail,
Husband, because I have the victory —
Am, heart, soul, head to foot, one happiness ! "

Whereto Admetos, in a passionate cry :
"Never, by that true word Apollon spoke !
All the unwise wish is unwished, O wife !
Let purposes of Zeus fulfil themselves,
If not through me, then through some other
      man !
Still, in myself he had a purpose too,
Inalienably mine, to end with me :
This purpose — that, throughout my earthly
      life,
Mine should be mingled and made up with
      thine, —
And we two prove one force and play one part
And do one thing. Since death divides the
      pair,
'T is well that I depart and thou remain
Who wast to me as spirit is to flesh :
Let the flesh perish, be perceived no more,
So thou, the spirit that informed the flesh,
Bend yet awhile, a very flame above
The rift I drop into the darkness by, —
And bid remember, flesh and spirit once
Worked in the world, one body, for man's sake.

Never be that abominable show
Of passive death without a quickening life —
Admetos only, no Alkestis now!"

Then she: "O thou Admetos, must the pile
Of truth on truth, which needs but one truth
  more
To tower up in completeness, trophy-like,
Emprise of man, and triumph of the world,
Must it go ever to the ground again
Because of some faint heart or faltering hand,
Which we, that breathless world about the
  base,
Trusted should carry safe to altitude,
Superimpose o' the summit, our supreme
Achievement, our victorious coping-stone?
Shall thine, Beloved, prove the hand and heart
That fail again, flinch backward at the truth
Would cap and crown the structure this last
  time, —
Precipitate our monumental hope
And strew the earth ignobly yet once more?
See how, truth piled on truth, the structure
  wants,
Waits justs the crowning truth I claim of thee!
Wouldst thou, for any joy to be enjoyed,
For any sorrow that thou mightst escape,
Unwill thy will to reign a righteous king?
Nowise! And were there two lots, death and
  life, —
Life, wherein good resolve should go to air,
Death, whereby finest fancy grew plain fact
I' the reign of thy survivor, — life or death?
Certainly death, thou choosest. Here stand I
The wedded, the beloved one: hadst thou
  loved
Her who less worthily could estimate
Both life and death than thou? Not so should
  say
Admetos, whom Apollon made come court
Alkestis in a car, submissive brutes
Of blood were yoked to, symbolizing soul
Must dominate unruly sense in man.
Then, shall Admetos and Alkestis see
Good alike, and alike choose, each for each,
Good, — and yet, each for other, at the last,
Choose evil? What? thou soundest in my soul
To depths below the deepest, reachest good
In evil, that makes evil good again,
And so allottest to me that I live
And not die — letting die, not thee alone,
But all true life that lived in both of us?
Look at me once ere thou decree the lot!"

Therewith her whole soul entered into his,
He looked the look back, and Alkestis died.

And even while it lay, i' the look of him,
Dead, the dimmed body, bright Alkestis' soul
Had penetrated through the populace
Of ghosts, was got to Koré, — throned and
  crowned
The pensive queen o' the twilight, where she
  dwells
Forever in a muse, but half away
From flowery earth she lost and hankers for, —
And there demanded to become a ghost
Before the time.

Whereat the softened eyes
Of the lost maidenhood that lingered still
Straying among the flowers in Sicily,
Sudden was startled back to Hades' throne
By that demand: broke through humanity
Into the orbed omniscience of a God,
Searched at a glance Alkestis to the soul,
And said — while a long slow sigh lost itself
I' the hard and hollow passage of a laugh:

"Hence, thou deceiver! This is not to die,
If, by the very death which mocks me now,
The life, that 's left behind and past my power,
Is formidably doubled. Say, there fight
Two athletes, side by side, each athlete armed
With only half the weapons, and no more,
Adequate to a contest with their foe:
If one of these should fling helm, sword and
  shield
To fellow — shieldless, swordless, helmless
  late —
And so leap naked o'er the barrier, leave
A combatant equipped from head to heel,
Yet cry to the other side, 'Receive a friend
Who fights no longer!' 'Back, friend, to the
  fray!'
Would be the prompt rebuff; I echo it.
Two souls in one were formidable odds:
Admetos must not be himself and thou!"

And so, before the embrace relaxed a whit,
The lost eyes opened, still beneath the look;
And lo, Alkestis was alive again,
And of Admetos' rapture who shall speak?

So, the two lived together long and well.
But never could I learn, by word of scribe
Or voice of poet, rumor wafts our way,
That — of the scheme of rule in righteousness,
The bringing back again the Golden Age,
Which, rather than renounce, our pair would
  die —
That ever one faint particle came true,
With both alive to bring it to effect:
Such is the envy Gods still bear mankind!

So might our version of the story prove,
And no Euripidean pathos plague
Too much my critic-friend of Syracuse.

"Besides your poem failed to get the prize:
(That is, the first prize: second prize is none.)
Sophokles got it!" Honor the great name!
All cannot love two great names; yet some do:
I know the poetess who graved in gold,
Among her glories that shall never fade,
This style and title for Euripides,
The Human with his droppings of warm tears.

I know, too, a great Kaunian painter, strong
As Herakles, though rosy with a robe
Of grace that softens down the sinewy strength:
And he has made a picture of it all.
There lies Alkestis dead, beneath the sun,
She longed to look her last upon, beside
The sea, which somehow tempts the life in us
To come trip over its white waste of waves,
And try escape from earth, and fleet as free.

Behind the body, I suppose there bends
Old Pheres in his hoary impotence ;
And women-wailers in a corner crouch
— Four, beautiful as you four — yes, indeed ! —
Close, each to other, agonizing all,
As fastened, in fear's rhythmic sympathy,
To two contending opposite. There strains
The might o' the hero 'gainst his more than
    match,
— Death, dreadful not in thew and bone, but
    like
The envenomed substance that exudes some dew
Whereby the merely honest flesh and blood
Will fester up and run to ruin straight,
Ere they can close with, clasp and overcome

The poisonous impalpability
That simulates a form beneath the flow
Of those gray garments ; I pronounce that
    piece
Worthy to set up in our Poikilé !

And all came, — glory of the golden verse,
And passion of the picture, and that fine
Frank outgush of the human gratitude
Which saved our ship and me, in Syracuse, —
Ay, and the tear or two which slipt perhaps
Away from you, friends, while I told my tale,
— It all came of this play that gained no prize :
Why crown whom Zeus has crowned in sou'
    before ?

ARISTOPHANES' APOLOGY

INCLUDING A TRANSCRIPT FROM EURIPIDES, BEING

THE LAST ADVENTURE OF BALAUSTION

οὐκ ἔσθω κενέβρει' · ὁπόταν δὲ θύῃς τι, κάλει με.

"I eat no carrion; when you sacrifice
Some cleanly creature — call me for a slice !"

WIND, wave, and bark, bear Euthukles and me,
Balaustion, from — not sorrow but despair,
Not memory but the present and its pang !
Athenai, live thou hearted in my heart :
Never, while I live, may I see thee more,
Never again may these repugnant orbs
Ache themselves blind before the hideous
    pomp,
The ghastly mirth which mocked thine over-
    throw
— Death's entry, Haides' outrage !
                 Doomed to die, —
Fire should have flung a passion of embrace
About thee till, resplendently inarmed,
(Temple by temple folded to his breast,
All thy white wonder fainting out in ash,)
Lightly some vaporous sigh of soul escaped
And so the Immortals bade Athenai back !
Or earth might sunder and absorb thee, save,
Buried below Olumpos and its gods,
Akropolis to dominate her realm
For Koré, and console the ghosts ; or, sea,
What if thy watery plural vastitude,
Rolling unanimous advance, had rushed,
Might upon might, a moment, — stood, one
    stare,
Sea-face to city-face, thy glaucous wave
Glassing that marbled last magnificence, —
Till fate's pale tremulous foam-flower tipped
    the gray,
And when wave broke and overswarmed, and,
    sucked

To bounds back, multitudinously ceased,
Let land again breathe unconfused with sea,
Attiké was, Athenai was not now !

Such end I could have borne, for I had shared.
But this which, glanced at, aches within my
    orbs
To blinding, — bear me thence, bark, wind and
    wave !
Me, Euthukles, and, hearted in each heart,
Athenai, undisgraced as Pallas' self,
Bear to my birthplace, Helios' island-bride,
Zeus' darling : thither speed us, homeward-
    bound,
Wafted already twelve hours' sail away
From horror, nearer by one sunset Rhodes !

Why should despair be ? Since, distinct above
Man's wickedness and folly, flies the wind
And floats the cloud, free transport for our
    soul
Out of its fleshly durance dim and low, —
Since disembodied soul anticipates
(Thought-borne as now in rapturous unrestraint)
Above all crowding, crystal silentness,
Above all noise, a silver solitude : —
Surely, where thought so bears soul, soul in
    time
May permanently bide, " assert the wise,"
There live in peace, there work in hope once
    more —
Oh, nothing doubt, Philemon ! Greed and strife,

Hatred and cark and care, what place have
    they
In yon blue liberality of heaven?
How the sea helps! How rose-smit earth will
    rise
Breast-high thence, some bright morning, and
    be Rhodes!
Heaven, earth and sea, my warrant — in their
    name,
Believe — o'er falsehood, truth is surely
    sphered,
O'er ugliness beams beauty, o'er this world
Extends that realm where "as the wise assert,"
Philemon, thou shalt see Euripides
Clearer than mortal sense perceived the man!

A sunset nearer Rhodes, by twelve hours'
    sweep
Of surge secured from horror? Rather say,
Quieted out of weakness into strength.
I dare invite, survey the scene my sense
Staggered to apprehend: for, disenvolved
From the mere outside anguish and contempt,
Slowly a justice centred in a doom
Reveals itself. Ay, pride succumbed to pride,
Oppression met the oppressor and was matched.
Athenai's vaunt braved Sparté's violence
Till, in the shock, prone fell Peiraios, low
Rampart and bulwark lay, as — timing stroke
Of hammer, axe, and beam hoist, poised and
    swung —
The very flute-girls blew their laughing best,
In dance about the conqueror while he bade
Music and merriment help enginery
Batter down, break to pieces all the trust
Of citizens once, slaves now. See what walls
Play substitute for the long double range
Themistoklean, heralding a guest
From harbor on to citadel! Each side
Their senseless walls demolished stone by stone,
See, — outer wall as stonelike, heads and
    hearts, —
Athenai's terror-stricken populace!
Prattlers, tongue-tied in crouching abjectness, —
Braggarts, who wring hands 'wont to flourish
    swords —
Sophist and rhetorician, demagogue,
(Argument dumb, authority a jest,)
Dikast and heliast, pleader, litigant,
Quack-priest, sham-prophecy-retailer, scout
O' the customs, sycophant, whate'er the style,
Altar-scrap-snatcher, pimp and parasite, —
Rivalities at truce now each with each,
Stupefied mud-banks, — such an use they serve!
While the one order which performs exact
To promise, functions faithful last as first,
What is it but the city's lyric troop,
Chantress and psaltress, flute-girl, dancing-girl?
Athenai's harlotry takes laughing care
Their patron miss no pipings, late she loved,
But deathward tread at least the kordax-step.

Die then, who pulled such glory on your heads!
There let it grind to powder! Perikles!
The living are the dead now: death be life!
Why should the sunset yonder waste its wealth?
Prove thee Olumpian! If my heart supply
Inviolate the structure, — true to type,

Build me some spirit-place no flesh shall find,
As Pheidias may inspire thee; slab on slab,
Renew Athenai, quarry out the cloud,
Convert to gold yon west extravagance!
'Neath Propulaia, from Akropolis
By vapory grade and grade, gold all the way,
Step to thy snow-Pnux, mount thy Bema-cloud,
Thunder and lighten thence a Hellas through
That shall be better and more beautiful
And too august for Sparté's foot to spurn!
Chasmed in the crag, again our Theatre
Predominates, one purple: Staghunt-month,
Brings it not Dionusia? Hail, the Three!
Aischulos, Sophokles, Euripides
Compete, gain prize or lose prize, godlike still.
Nay, lest they lack the old god-exercise —
Their noble want the unworthy, — as of old,
(How otherwise should patience crown their
    might?)
What if each find his ape promoted man,
His censor raised for antic service still?
Some new Hermippos to pelt Perikles,
Kratinos to swear Pheidias robbed a shrine,
Eruxis — I suspect, Euripides,
No brow will ache because with mop and mow
He gibes my poet! There 's a dog-faced dwarf
That gets to godship somehow, yet retains
His apehood in the Egyptian hierarchy,
More decent, indecorous just enough:
Why should not dog-ape, graced in due degree,
Grow Momos as thou Zeus? Or didst thou sigh
Rightly with thy Makaria? "After life,
Better no sentiency than turbulence;
Death cures the low contention." Be it so!
Yet progress means contention, to my mind.

Euthukles, who, except for love that speaks,
Art silent by my side while words of mine
Provoke that foe from which escape is vain
Henceforward, wake Athenai's fate and fall, —
Memories asleep as, at the altar-foot,
Those Furies in the Oresteian song, —
Do I amiss, who wanting strength use craft,
Advance upon the foe I cannot fly,
Nor feign a snake is dormant though it gnaw?
That fate and fall, once bedded in our brain,
Roots itself past upwrenching; but coaxed
    forth,
Encouraged out to practise fork and fang, —
Perhaps, when satiate with prompt sustenance,
It may pine, likelier die than if left swell
In peace by our pretension to ignore,
Or pricked to threefold fury, should our
    stamp
Bruise and not brain the pest.

                A middle course!
What hinders that we treat this tragic theme
As the Three taught when either woke some
    woe,
— How Klutaimnestra hated, what the pride
Of Iokasté, why Medeia clove
Nature asunder. Small rebuked by large,
We felt our puny hates refine to air,
Our poor prides sink, prevent the humbling
    hand,
Our petty passions purify their tide.
So, Euthukles, permit the tragedy

To re-enact itself, this voyage through,
Till sunsets end and sunrise brighten Rhodes!
Majestic on the stage of memory,
Peplosed and kothorned, let Athenai fall
Once more, nay, oft again till life conclude,
Lent for the lesson : Choros, I and thou !
What else in life seems piteous any more
After such pity, or proves terrible
Beside such terror ?

           Still — since Phrunichos
Offended, by too premature a touch
Of that Milesian smart-place freshly frayed —
(Ah, my poor people, whose prompt remedy
Was — fine the poet, not reform thyself!)
Beware precipitate approach ! Rehearse
Rather the prologue, well a year away,
Than the main misery, a sunset old.
What else but fitting prologue to the piece
Style an adventure, stranger than my first
By so much as the issue it enwombed
Lurked big beyond Balaustion's littleness ?
Second supreme adventure !   O that Spring,
That eve I told the earlier to my friends !
Where are the four now, with each red-ripe
    mouth
Crumpled so close, no quickest breath it fetched
Could disengage the lip-flower furled to bud
For fear Admetos — shivering head and foot,
As with sick soul and blind averted face
He trusted hand forth to obey his friend —
Should find no wife in her cold hand's response,
Nor see the disenshrouded statue start
Alkestis, live the life and love the love !
I wonder, does the streamlet ripple still,
Out-smoothing galingale and watermint
Its mat-floor ? while at brim, 'twixt sedge and
    sedge,
What bubblings past Baccheion, broadened
    much,
Pricked by the reed and fretted by the fly,
Oared by the boatman-spider's pair of arms !
Lenaia was a gladsome month ago —
Euripides had taught "Andromedé : "
Next month, would teach " Kresphontes " —
    which same month
Some one from Phokis, who companioned me
Since all that happened on those temple-steps,
Would marry me and turn Athenian too.
Now ! if next year the masters let the slaves
Do Bacchic service and restore mankind
That trilogy whereof, 't is noised, one play
Presents the Bacchai, — no Euripides
Will teach the choros, nor shall we be tinged
By any such grand sunset of his soul,
Exiles from dead Athenai, — not the live
That 's in the cloud there with the new-born
    star !

Speak to the infinite intelligence,
Sing to the everlasting sympathy !
Winds belly sail, and drench of dancing brine
Buffet our boat-side, so the prore bound free !
Condense our voyage into one great day
Made up of sunset-closes : eve by eve,
Resume that memorable night-discourse
When — like some meteor-brilliance, fire and
    filth,

Or say, his own Amphitheos, deity
And dung, who, bound on the gods' embassage,
Got men's acknowledgement in kick and cuff —
We made acquaintance with a visitor
Ominous, apparitional, who went
Strange as he came, but shall not pass away.
Let us attempt that memorable talk,
Clothe the adventure's every incident
With due expression : may not looks be told,
Gesture made speak, and speech so amplified
That words find blood-warmth which, cold
    writ, they lose ?

Recall the night we heard the news from
    Thrace,
One year ago, Athenai still herself.

We two were sitting silent in the house,
Yet cheerless hardly. Euthukles, forgive !
I somehow speak to unseen auditors.
Not *you*, but — Euthukles had entered, grave,
Grand, may I say, as who brings laurel-branch
And message from the tripod : such it proved.

He first removed the garland from his brow,
Then took my hand and looked into my face.

" Speak good words ! " much misgiving fal-
    tered I.

" Good words, the best, Balaustion ! He is
    crowned,
Gone with his Attic ivy home to feast,
Since Aischulos required companionship.
Pour a libation for Euripides ! "

When we had sat the heavier silence out —
" Dead and triumphant still ! " began reply
To my eye's question. " As he willed, he
    worked :
And, as he worked, he wanted not, be sure,
Triumph his whole life through, submitting
    work
To work's right judges, never to the wrong,
To competency, not ineptitude.
When he had run life's proper race and worked
Quite to the stade's end, there remained to try
The stade's turn, should strength dare the
    double course.
Half the diaulos reached, the hundred plays
Accomplished, force in its rebound sufficed
To lift along the athlete and ensure
A second wreath, proposed by fools for first,
The statist's olive as the poet's bay.
Wiselier, he suffered not a twofold aim
Retard his pace, confuse his sight ; at once
Poet and statist ; though the multitude
Girded him ever ' All thine aim thine art ?
The idle poet only ? No regard
For civic duty, public service, here ?
We drop our ballot-bean for Sophokles !
Not only could he write " Antigoné,"
But — since (we argued) whoso penned that
    piece
Might just as well conduct a squadron, —
    straight
Good-naturedly he took on him command,
Got laughed at, and went back to making plays,

Having allowed us our experiment
Respecting the fit use of faculty.'
No whit the more did athlete slacken pace.
Soon the jeers grew: ' Cold hater of his kind,
A sea-cave suits him, not the vulgar hearth !
What need of tongue-talk, with a bookish store
Would stock ten cities ? ' Shadow of an ass !
No whit the worse did athlete touch the mark
And, at the turning-point, consign his scorn
O' the scorners to that final trilogy
' Hupsipule,' ' Phoinissai,' and the Match
Of Life Contemplative with Active Life,
Zethos against Amphion. Ended so?
Nowise ! — began again ; for heroes rest
Dropping shield's oval o'er the entire man,
And he who thus took Contemplation's prize
Turned stade-point but to face Activity.
Out of all shadowy hands extending help
For life's decline pledged to youth's labor
    still,
Whatever renovation flatter age, —
Society with pastime, solitude
With peace, — he chose the hand that gave the
    heart,
Bade Macedonian Archelaos take
The leavings of Athenai, ash once flame.
For fifty politicians' frosty work,
One poet's ash proved ample and to spare :
He propped the state and filled the treasury,
Counselled the king as might a meaner soul,
Furnished the friend with what shall stand in
    stead
Of crown and sceptre, star his name about
When these are dust ; for him, Euripides
Last the old hand on the old phorminx flung,
Clashed thence ' Alkaion,' maddened ' Pen-
    theus ' up ;
Then music sighed itself away, one moan
Iphigeneia made by Aulis' strand ;
With her and music died Euripides.

" The poet-friend who followed him to Thrace,
Agathon, writes thus much : the merchant-
    ship
Moreover brings a message from the king
To young Euripides, who went on board
This morning at Mounuchia : all is true."

I said " Thank Zeus for the great news and
    good ! "

" Nay, the report is running in brief fire
Through the town's stubbly furrow," he re-
    sumed :
— " Entertains brightly what their favorite
    styles
' The City of Gapers ' for a week perhaps,
Supplants three luminous tales, but yesterday
Pronounced sufficient lamps to last the month :
How Glauketes, outbidding Morsimos,
Paid market-price for one Kopaic eel
A thousand drachmai, and then cooked his
    prize
Not proper conger-fashion but in oil
And nettles, as man fries the foam-fish-kind ;
How all the captains of the triremes, late
Victors at Arginousai, on return
Will, for return, be straightway put to death ;

How Mikon wagered a Thessalian mime
Trained him by Lais, looked on as complete,
Against Leogoras' blood-mare koppa-marked,
Valued six talents, — swore, accomplished so,
The girl could swallow at a draught, nor
    breathe,
A choinix of unmixed Mendesian wine ;
And having lost the match will — dine on
    herbs !
Three stories late aflame, at once extinct,
Outblazed by just ' Euripides is dead ' !

" I met the concourse from the Theatre,
The audience flocking homeward : victory
Again awarded Aristophanes
Precisely for his old play chopped and
    changed,
' The Female Celebrators of the Feast ' —
That Thesmophoria, tried a second time.
' Never such full success ! ' — assured the folk,
Who yet stopped praising to have word of mouth
With ' Euthukles, the bard's own intimate,
Balaustion's husband, the right man to ask.'

" ' Dead, yes, but how dead, may acquaintance
    know ?
You were the couple constant at his cave :
Tell us now, is it true that women, moved
By reason of his liking Krateros ' . . .

" I answered ' He was loved by Sokrates.'

" ' Nay,' said another, ' envy did the work !
For, emulating poets of the place,
One Arridaios, one Krateues, both
Established in the royal favor, these ' . . .

" ' Protagoras instructed him,' said I.

" ' Phu,' whistled Comic Platon, ' hear the
    fact !
'T was well said of your friend by Sophokles,
" He hate our women ? In his verse, belike.
But when it comes to prose-work, — ha, ha,
    ha ! "
New climes don't change old manners : so, it
    chanced,
Pursuing an intrigue one moonless night
With Arethousian Nikodikos' wife,
(Come now, his years were simply seventy-
    five,)
Crossing the palace-court, what haps he on
But Archelaos' pack of hungry hounds ?
Who tore him piecemeal ere his cry brought
    help.'

" I asked : Did not you write ' The Festivals ' ?
You best know what dog tore him when alive.
You others, who now make a ring to hear,
Have not you just enjoyed a second treat,
Proclaimed that ne'er was play more worthy
    prize
Than this, myself assisted at, last year,
And gave its worth to, — spitting on the same ?
Appraise no poetry, — price cuttlefish,
Or that seaweed-alphestes, scorpion-sort,
Much famed for mixing mud with fantasy
On midnights ! I interpret no foul dreams."

If so said Euthukles, so could not I,
Balaustion, say.   After " Lusistraté "
No more for me of " people's privilege,"
No witnessing " the Grand old Comedy
Coeval with our freedom, which, curtailed,
Were freedom's deathblow : relic of the past,
When Virtue laughingly told truth to Vice,
Uncensured, since the stern mouth, stuffed with
     flowers,
Through poetry breathed satire, perfumed blast
Which sense snuffed up while searched unto
     the bone ! "
I was a stranger : " For first joy," urged
     friends,
" Go hear our Comedy, some patriot piece
That plies the selfish advocates of war
With argument so unevadable
That crash fall Kleons whom the finer play
Of reason, tickling, deeper wounds no whit
Than would a spear-thrust from a savory-stalk !
No : you hear knave and fool told crime and
     fault,
And see each scourged his quantity of stripes.
Rough dealing, awkward language,' whine
     our fops :
The world 's too squeamish now to bear plain
     words
Concerning deeds it acts with gust enough :
But, thanks to wine-lees and democracy,
We 've still our stage where truth calls spade a
     spade !
Ashamed ?   Phuromachos' decree provides
The sex may sit discreetly, witness all,
Sorted, the good with good, the gay with gay,
Themselves unseen, no need to force a blush.
A Rhodian wife and ignorant so long ?
Go hear next play ! "

               I heard " Lusistraté."
Waves, said to wash pollution from the world,
Take that plague-memory, cure that pustule
     caught
As, past escape, I sat and saw the piece
By one appalled at Phaidra's fate, — the chaste,
Whom, because chaste, the wicked goddess
     chained
To that same serpent of unchastity
She loathed most, and who, coiled so, died dis-
     traught
Rather than make submission, loose one limb
Love-wards, at lambency of honeyed tongue,
Or torture of the scales which scraped her snow
— I say, the piece by him who charged this piece
(Because Euripides shrank not to teach,
If gods be strong and wicked, man, though
     weak,
May prove their match by willing to be good)
With infamies the Scythian's whip should cure —
" Such outrage done the public — Phaidra
     named !
Such purpose to corrupt ingenuous youth,
Such insult cast on female character ! " —
Why, when I saw that bestiality —
So beyond all brute-beast imagining,
That when, to point the moral at the close,
Poor Salabaccho, just to show how fair
Was " Reconciliation," stripped her charms,
That exhibition simply bade us breathe,

Seemed something healthy and commendable
After obscenity grotesqued so much
It slunk away revolted at itself.
Henceforth I had my answer when our sage
Pattern-proposing seniors pleaded grave,
" You fail to fathom here the deep design !
All 's acted in the interest of truth,
Religion, and those manners old and dear
Which made our city great when citizens
Like Aristeides and like Miltiades
Wore each a golden tettix in his hair."
What do they wear now under — Kleophon ?

Well, for such reasons; — I am out of breath,
But loathsomeness we needs must hurry past, -
I did not go to see, nor then nor now,
The " Thesmophoriazousai." But, since males
Choose to brave first, blame afterward, nor
     brand
Without fair taste of what they stigmatize,
Euthukles had not missed the first display,
Original portrait of Euripides
By " Virtue laughingly reproving Vice : "
" Virtue," — the author, Aristophanes,
Who mixed an image out of his own depths,
Ticketed as I tell you. Oh, this time
No more pretension to recondite worth !
No joke in aid of Peace, no demagogue
Pun-pelleted from Pnux, no kordax-dance
Overt helped covertly the Ancient Faith !
All now was muck, home-produce, honestman
The author's soul secreted to a play
Which gained the prize that day we heard the
     death.

I thought " How thoroughly death alters things !
Where is the wrong now, done our dead and
     great ?
How natural seems grandeur in relief,
Cliff-base with frothy spites against its calm ! "

Euthukles interposed — he read my thought —

" O'er them, too, in a moment came the change.
The crowd 's enthusiastic, to a man :
Since, rake as such may please the ordure-heap
Because of certain sparkles presumed ore,
At first flash of true lightning overhead,
They look up, nor resume their search too soon.
The insect-scattering sign is evident,
And nowhere winks a firefly rival now,
Nor bustles any beetle of the brood
With trundled dung-ball meant to menace
     heaven.
Contrariwise, the cry is ' Honor him ! '
' A statue in the theatre ! ' wants one ;
Another ' Bring the poet's body back,
Bury him in Peiraios : o'er his tomb
Let Alkamenes carve the music-witch,
The songstress-siren, meed of melody :
Thoukudides invent his epitaph ! '
To-night the whole town pays its tribute thus."

Our tribute should not be the same, my friend !
Statue ? Within our heart he stood, he stands !
As for the vest outgrown now by the form,
Low flesh that clothed high soul, — a vesture's
     fate —

Why, let it fade, mix with the elements
There where it, falling, freed Euripides!
But for the soul that 's tutelary now
Till time end, o'er the world to teach and bless —
How better hail its freedom than by first
Singing, we two, its own song back again,
Up to that face from which flowed beauty — face
Now abler to see triumph and take love
Than when it glorified Athenai once?

The sweet and strange Alkestis, which saved
    me,
Secured me — you, ends nowise, to my mind,
In pardon of Admetos. Hearts are fain
To follow cheerful weary Herakles
Striding away from the huge gratitude,
Club shouldered, lion-fleece round loin and flank,
Bound on the next new labor "height o'er height
Ever surmounting, — destiny's decree!"
Thither He helps us: that 's the story's end;
He smiling said so, when I told him mine —
My great adventure, how Alkestis helped.
Afterward, when the time for parting fell,
He gave me, with two other precious gifts,
This third and best, consummating the grace,
"Herakles," writ by his own hand, each line.

"If it have worth, reward is still to seek.
Somebody, I forget who, gained the prize
And proved arch-poet: time must show!" he
    smiled /
"Take this, and, when the noise tires out, judge
    me —
Some day, not slow to dawn, when somebody —
Who? I forget — proves nobody at all!"

Is not that day come? What if you and I
Re-sing the song, inaugurate the fame?
We have not waited to acquaint ourselves
With song and subject; we can prologize
How, at Eurustheus' bidding, — hate strained
    hard, —
Herakles had departed, one time more,
On his last labor, worst of all the twelve;
Descended into Haides, thence to drag
The triple-headed hound, which sun should see
Spite of the god whose darkness whelped the
    Fear.
Down went the hero, "back — how should he
    come?"
So laughed King Lukos, an old enemy,
Who judged that absence testified defeat
Of the land's loved one, — since he saved the
    land
And for that service wedded Megara
Daughter of Thebai, realm her child should rule.
Ambition, greed and malice seized their prey,
The Heraclean House, defenceless left,
Father and wife and child, to trample out
Trace of its hearth-fire : since extreme old age
Wakes pity, woman's wrong wins championship,
And child may grow up man and take revenge.
Hence see we that, from out their palace-home
Hunted, for last resource they cluster now
Couched on the cold ground, hapless supplicants
About their court-yard altar, — Household Zeus
It is, the Three in funeral garb beseech,
Delaying death so, till deliverance come —

When did it ever? — from the deep and dark.
And thus breaks silence old Amphitruon's
    voice. . . .
Say I not true thus far, my Euthukles?

Suddenly, torch-light! knocking at the door,
Loud, quick, "Admittance for the revels'
    lord!"
Some unintelligible Komos-cry —
Raw-flesh red, no cap upon his head,
Dionusos, Bacchos, Phales, Iacchos,
In let him reel with the kid-skin at his heel,
Where it buries in the spread of the bushy myrtle-
    bed!
(Our Rhodian Jackdaw-song was sense to that!)
Then laughter, outbursts ruder and more rude,
Through which, with silver point, a fluting
    pierced,
And ever "Open, open, Bacchos bids!"

But at last — one authoritative word,
One name of an immense significance :
For Euthukles rose up, threw wide the door.

There trooped the Choros of the Comedy
Crowned and triumphant; first, those flushed
    Fifteen,
Men that wore women's garb, grotesque disguise.
Then marched the Three, — who played Mnesi-
    lochos,
Who, Toxotes, and who, robed right, masked
    rare,
Monkeyed our Great and Dead to heart's content
That morning in Athenai. Masks were down
And robes doffed now; the sole disguise was
    drink.

Mixing with these — I know not what gay crowd,
Girl-dancers, flute-boys, and pre-eminent
Among them, — doubtless draped with such re-
    serve
As stopped fear of the fifty-drachma fine
(Beside one's name on public fig-tree nailed)
Which women pay who in the streets walk
    bare, —
Behold Elaphion of the Persic dance!
Who lately had frisked fawn-foot, and the rest,
— All for the Patriot Cause, the Antique Faith,
The Conservation of True Poesy —
Could I but penetrate the deep design!
Elaphion, more Peiraios-known as "Phaps,"
Tripped at the head of the whole banquet-band
Who came in front now, as the first fell back ;
And foremost — the authoritative voice,
The revels-leader, he who gained the prize,
And got the glory of the Archon's feast —
There stood in person Aristophanes.

And no ignoble presence! On the bulge
Of the clear baldness, — all his head one brow, —
True, the veins swelled, blue network, and
    there surged
A red from cheek to temple, — then retired
As if the dark-leaved chaplet damped a
    flame, —
Was never nursed by temperance or health.
But huge the eyeballs rolled back native fire,
Imperiously triumphant : nostrils wide

Waited their incense; while the pursed mouth's
  pout
Aggressive, while the beak supreme above,
While the head, face, nay, pillared throat
  thrown back,
Beard whitening under like a vinous foam,
These made a glory, of such insolence —
I thought, — such domineering deity
Hephaistos might have carved to cut the brine
For his gay brother's prow, imbrue that path
Which, purpling, recognized the conqueror.
Impudent and majestic: drunk, perhaps,
But that's religion; sense too plainly snuffed:
Still, sensuality was grown a rite.

What I had disbelieved most proved most true.
There was a mind here, mind a-wantoning
At ease of undisputed mastery
Over the body's brood, those appetites.
Oh, but he grasped them grandly, as the god
His either struggling handful, — hurtless snakes
Held deep down, strained hard off from side
  and side!
Mastery his, theirs simply servitude,
So well could firm fist help intrepid eye.
Fawning and fulsome, had they licked and
  hissed?
At mandate of one muscle, order reigned.
They had been wreathing much familiar now
About him on his entry; but a squeeze
Choked down the pests to place: their lord
  stood free.

Forward he stepped: I rose and fronted him.

"Hail, house, the friendly to Euripides!"
(So he began) "Hail, each inhabitant!
You, lady? What, the Rhodian? Form and
  face,
Victory's self upsoaring to receive
The poet? Right they named you . . . some
  rich name,
Vowel-buds thorned about with consonants,
Fragrant, felicitous, rose-glow enriched
By the Isle's unguent: some diminished end
In *ion*, Kallistion? delicater still,
Kubelion or Melittion, — or, suppose
(Less vulgar love than bee or violet)
Phibalion, for the mouth split red-fig-wise,
Korakinidion for the coal-black hair,
Nettarion, Phabion for the darlingness?
But no, it was some fruit-flower, Rhoidion
  . . . ha,
We near the balsam-bloom — Balaustion!
  Thanks,
Rhodes! Folk have called me Rhodian, do
  you know?
Not fools so far! Because, if Helios wived,
As Pindaros sings somewhere prettily,
Here blooms his offspring, earth-flesh with sun-
  fire,
Rhodes' blood and Helios' gold. My phorminx,
  boy!
Why does the boy hang back and balk an ode
Tiptoe at spread of wing? But like enough,
Sunshine frays torchlight. Witness whom you
  scare,
Superb Balaustion! Look outside the house!

Pho, you have quenched my Komos by first
  frown,
Struck dead all joyance: not a fluting puffs
From idle cheekband! Ah, my Choros too?
You've eaten cuckoo-apple? Dumb, you
  dogs?
So much good Thasian wasted on your throats
And out of them not one *Threttanelo?*
Neblaretai! Because this earth-and-sun
Product looks wormwood and all bitter herbs?
Well, do I blench, though me she hates the most
Of mortals? By the cabbage, off they slink!
You, too, my Chrusomelolonthion-Phaps,
Girl-goldling-beetle-beauty? You, abashed,
Who late, supremely unabashable,
Propped up my play at that important point
When Artamouxia tricks the Toxotes?
Ha, ha, — thank Hermes for the lucky
  throw, —
We came last comedy of the whole seven,
So went all fresh to judgment well-disposed
For who should fatly feast them, eye and ear,
We two between us! What, you fail your
  friend?
Away then, free me of your cowardice!
Go, get you the goat's breakfast! Fare afield,
Ye circumcised of Egypt, pigs to sow,
Back to the Priest's or forward to the crows,
So you but rid me of such company!
Once left alone, I can protect myself
From statuesque Balaustion pedestalled
On much disapprobation and mistake!
She dares not beat the sacred brow, beside!
Bacchos' equipment, ivy safeguards well
As Phoibos' bay.

                "They take me at my word!
One comfort is, I shall not want them long,
The Archon's cry creaks, creaks, 'Curtail ex-
  pense!'
The war wants money, year the twenty-sixth!
Cut down our Choros number, clip costume,
Save birds' wings, beetles' armor, spend the
  cash
In three-crest skull-caps, three days' salt-fish-
  slice,
Three-banked-ships for these sham-ambassa-
  dors,
And what not: any cost but Comedy's!
'No Choros'—soon will follow; what care I?
Archinos and Agurrhios, scrape your flint,
Flay your dead dog, and curry favor so!
Choros in rags, with loss of leather next,
We lose the boys' vote, lose the song and dance,
Lose my Elaphion! Still, the actor stays.
Save but my acting, and the baldhead bard
Kudathenaian and Pandionid,
Son of Philippos, Aristophanes
Surmounts his rivals now as heretofore,
Though stinted to mere sober prosy verse —
'Manners and men,' so squeamish gets the
  world!
No more 'Step forward, strip for anapæsts!'
No calling naughty people by their names,
No tickling audience into gratitude
With chickpease, barleygroats and nuts and
  plums,
No setting Salabaccho" . . .

As I turned —

"True, lady, I am tolerably drunk:
The proper inspiration! Otherwise, —
Phrunichos, Choirilos! — had Aischulos
So foiled you at the goat-song? Drink's a
god.
How else did that old doating driveller
Kratinos foil me, match my masterpiece
The 'Clouds'? I swallowed cloud-distilment
— dew
Undimmed by any grape-blush, knit my brow
And gnawed my style and laughed my learned-
est;
While he worked at his 'Willow-wicker-flask,'
Swigging at that same flask by which he swore,
Till, sing and empty, sing and fill again,
Somehow result was — what it should not be
Next time, I promised him and kept my word!
Hence, brimful now of Thasian . . . I'll be
bound,
Mendesian, merely: triumph-night, you know,
The High Priest entertains the conqueror,
And, since war worsens all things, stingily
The rascal starves whom he is bound to stuff,
Choros and actors and their lord and king
The poet: supper, still he needs must spread —
And this time all was conscientious fare:
He knew his man, his match, his master —
made
Amends, spared neither fish, flesh, fowl nor
wine:
So merriment increased, I promise you,
Till — something happened."

Here he strangely paused,

"After that, — Well, it either was the cup
To the Good Genius, our concluding pledge,
That wrought me mischief, decently un-
mixed, —
Or, what if, when *that* happened, need arose
Of new libation? Did you only know
What happened! Little wonder I am drunk."

Euthukles, o'er the boat-side, quick, what
change,
Watch, in the water! But a second since,
It laughed a ripply spread of sun and sea,
Ray fused with wave, to never disunite.
Now, sudden all the surface, hard and black,
Lies a quenched light, dead motion: What the
cause?
Look up and lo, the menace of a cloud
Has solemnized the sparkling, spoil the sport!
Just so, some overshadow, some new care
Stopped all the mirth and mocking on his face
And left there only such a dark surmise
— No wonder if the revel disappeared,
So did his face shed silence every side!
I recognized a new man fronting me.

"So!" he smiled, piercing to my thought at
once,
"You see myself? Balaustion's fixed regard
Can strip the proper Aristophanes
Of what our sophists, in their jargon, style
His accidents? My soul sped forth but now

To meet your hostile survey, — soul unseen,
Yet veritably cinct for soul-defence
With satyr sportive quips, cranks, boss and
spike,
Just as my visible body paced the street,
Environed by a boon companionship
Your apparition also puts to flight.
Well, what care I, if, unaccoutred twice,
I front my foe — no comicality
Round soul, and body-guard in banishment?
Thank your eyes' searching, undisguised I
stand:
The merest female child may question me.
Spare not, speak bold, Balaustion!'"

I did speak:

"Bold speech be — welcome to this honored
hearth,
Good Genius! Glory of the poet, glow
O' the humorist who castigates his kind,
Suave summer-lightning lambency which plays
On stag-horned tree, misshapen crag askew,
Then vanishes with unvindictive smile
After a moment's laying black earth bare.
Splendor of wit that springs a thunderball —
Satire — to burn and purify the world,
True aim, fair purpose: just wit justly strikes
Injustice, — right, as rightly quells the wrong,
Finds out in knaves', fools', cowards' armory
The tricky tinselled place fire flashes through,
No damage else, sagacious of true ore;
Wit, learned in the laurel, leaves each wreath
O'er lyric shell or tragic barbiton, —
Though alien gauds be singed, — undesecrate,
The genuine solace of the sacred brow.
Ay, and how pulses flame a patriot-star
Steadfast athwart our country's night of things,
To beacon, would she trust no meteor-blaze,
Athenai from the rock she steers for straight!
O light, light, light, I hail light everywhere,
No matter for the murk that was, — perchance,
That will be, — certes, never should have been
Such orb's associate!

"Aristophanes!
'The merest female child may question you?'
Once, in my Rhodes, a portent of the wave
Appalled our coast: for many a darkened day,
Intolerable mystery and fear.
Who snatched a furtive glance through crannied
peak,
Could but report of snake-scale, lizard-limb, —
So swam what, making whirlpools as it went,
Madded the brine with wrath or monstrous
sport.
''T is Tuphon, loose, unmanacled from mount.'
Declared the priests, 'no way appeasable
Unless perchance by virgin-sacrifice!'
Thus grew the terror and o'erhung the doom —
Until one eve a certain female-child
Strayed in safe ignorance to seacoast edge,
And there sat down and sang to please herself.
When all at once, large-looming from his wave,
Out leaned, chin hand-propped, pensive on the
ledge,
A sea-worn face, sad as mortality,
Divine with yearning after fellowship.

He rose but breast-high. So much god she saw ;
So much she sees now, and does reverence ! "

Ah, but there followed tail-splash, frisk of fin !
Let cloud pass, the sea's ready laugh outbreaks.
No very godlike trace retained the mouth
Which mocked with —

          "So, He taught you tragedy !
I always asked 'Why may not women act ? '
Nay, wear the comic visor just as well ;
Or, better, quite cast off the face-disguise
And voice-distortion, simply look and speak,
Real women playing women as men — men !
I shall not wonder if things come to that,
Some day when I am distant far enough.
Do you conceive the quite new Comedy
When laws allow ? laws only let girls dance,
Pipe, posture, — above all, Elaphinize,
Provided they keep decent — that is, dumb.
Ay, and, conceiving, I would execute,
Had I but two lives : one were overworked !
How penetrate encrusted prejudice,
Pierce ignorance three generations thick
Since first Sousarion crossed our boundary ?
He battered with a big Megaric stone ;
Chionides felled oak and rough-hewed thence
This club I wield now, having spent my life
In planing knobs and sticking studs to shine ;
Somebody else must try mere polished steel ! "

Emboldened by the sober mood's return,
"Meanwhile," said I, "since planed and
    studded club
Once more has pashed competitors to dust,
And poet proves triumphant with that play
Euthukles found last year unfortunate, —
Does triumph spring from smoothness still more
    smoothed,
Fresh studs sown thick and threefold ? In
    plain words,
Have you exchanged brute - blows, — which
    teach the brute
Man may surpass him in brutality, —
For human fighting, or true god-like force
Which breathes persuasion nor needs fight at
    all ?
Have you essayed attacking ignorance,
Convicting folly, by their opposites,
Knowledge and wisdom ? not by yours for ours,
Fresh ignorance and folly, new for old,
Greater for less, your crime for our mistake !
If so success at last have crowned desert,
Bringing surprise (dashed haply by concern
At your discovery such wild waste of strength
— And what strength ! — went so long to keep
    in vogue
Such warfare — and what warfare ! — shamed
    so fast,
So soon made obsolete, as fell their foe
By the first arrow native to the orb,
First onslaught worthy Aristophanes) —
Was this conviction's entry that same strange
'Something that happened ' to confound your
    feast ? "

" Ah, did he witness then my play that failed,
First ' Thesmophoriazousai '? Well and good !

But did he also see — your Euthukles —
My ' Grasshoppers,' which followed and failed
    too,
Three months since, at the ' Little-in-the-
    Fields ' ? "

"To say that he did see that First — should
    say
He never cared to see its following."

" There happens to be reason why I wrote
First play and second also. Ask the cause !
I warrant you receive, ere talk be done,
Fit answer, authorizing either act.
But here 's the point : as Euthukles made vow
Never again to taste my quality,
So I was minded next experiment
Should tickle palate — yea, of Euthukles !
Not by such utter change, such absolute
A topsyturvy of stage-habitude
As you and he want, — Comedy built fresh,
By novel brick and mortar, base to roof, —
No, for I stand too near and look too close !
Pleasure and pastime yours, spectators brave,
Should I turn art's fixed fabric upside down !
Little you guess how such tough work tasks
    soul !
Not overtasks, though : give fit strength fair
    play,
And strength 's a demiourgos ! Art renewed ?
Ay, in some closet where strength shuts out —
    first
The friendly faces, sympathetic cheer :
' More of the old provision, none supplies
So bounteously as thou, — our love, our pride,
Our author of the many a perfect piece !
Stick to that standard, change were deca-
    dence ! '
Next, the unfriendly : ' This time, strain will
    tire,
He 's fresh, Ameipsias thy antagonist ! '
— Or better, in some Salaminian cave
Where sky and sea and solitude make earth
And man and noise one insignificance,
Let strength propose itself, — behind the
    world, —
Sole prize worth winning, work that satisfies
Strength it has dared and done strength's utter-
    most !
After which, — clap-to closet and quit cave, —
Strength may conclude in Archelaos' court,
And yet esteem the silken company
So much sky-scud, sea-froth, earth-thistledown,
For aught their praise or blame should joy or
    grieve.
Strength amid crowds as late in solitude
May lead the still life, ply the wordless task :
Then only, when seems need to move or speak,
Moving — for due respect, when statesmen pass,
(Strength, in the closet, watched how spiders
    spin !)
Speaking — when fashion shows intelligence,
(Strength, in the cave, oft whistled to the
    gulls !)
In short, has learnt first, practised afterwards !
Despise the world and reverence yourself, —
Why, you may unmake things and remake
    things,

And throw behind you, unconcerned enough,
What 's made or marred : ' you teach men, are
not taught ! '
So marches off the stage Euripides !

" No such thin fare feeds flesh and blood like
mine,
No such faint fume of fancy sates my soul,
No such seclusion, closet, cave or court,
Suits either : give me Iostephanos
Worth making happy what coarse way she
will —
O happy-maker, when her cries increase
About the favorite ! 'Aristophanes !
More grist to mill, here 's Kleophon to grind !
He 's for refusing peace, though Sparté cede
Even Dekeleia ! Here 's Kleonumos
Declaring — though he threw away his shield,
He 'll thrash you till you lay your lyre aside !
Orestes bids mind where you walk of nights —
He wants your cloak as you his cudgelling.
Here 's, finally, Melanthios fat with fish,
The gormandizer-spendthrift-dramatist !
So, bustle ! Pounce on opportunity !
Let fun a-screaming in Parabasis,
Find food for folk agape at either end,
Mad for amusement ! Times grow better
too,
And should they worsen, why, who laughs, for-
gets.
In no case, venture boy-experiments !
Old wine 's the wine : new poetry drinks raw :
Two plays a season is your pledge, beside ;
So, give us " Wasps " again, grown hornets
now ! ' "

Then he changed.

" Do you so detect in me —
Brow-bald, chin-bearded, me, curved cheek,
carved lip,
Or where soul sits and reigns in either eye —
What suits the — stigma, I say, — style say you,
Of ' Wine-lees-poet ' ? Bravest of buffoons,
Less blunt than Telekleides, less obscene
Than Murtilos, Hermippos : quite a match
In elegance for Eupolis himself, .
Yet pungent as Kratinos at his best ?
Graced with traditional immunity
Ever since, much about my grandsire's time,
Some funny village-man in Megara,
Lout-lord and clown-king, used a privilege,
As due religious drinking-bouts came round,
To daub his phiz, — no, that was afterward, —
He merely mounted cart with mates of choice
And traversed country, taking house by house,
At night, — because of danger in the freak, —
Then hollaed ' Skin-flint starves his laborers ! '
Clench-fist stows figs away, cheats government !
Such an one likes to kiss his neighbor's wife,
And beat his own ; while such another . . .
Boh ! '
Soon came the broad day, circumstantial tale,
Dancing and verse, and there 's our Comedy,
There 's Mullos, there 's Euetes, there 's the
stock
I shall be proud to graft my powers upon !
Protected ? Punished quite as certainly

When Archons pleased to lay down each his
law, —
Your Morucheides-Surakosios sort, —
Each season, ' No more naming citizens,
Only abuse the vice, the vicious spare !
Observe, henceforth no Areopagite
Demean his rank by writing Comedy ! '
(They one and all could write the ' Clouds ' of
course.)
' Needs must we nick expenditure, allow
Comedy half a choros, supper — none,
Times being hard, while applicants increase
For, what costs cash, the Tragic Trilogy.'
Lofty Tragedians ! How they lounge aloof
Each with his Triad, three plays to my one,
Not counting the contemptuous fourth, the frank
Concession to mere mortal levity,
Satyric pittance tossed our beggar-world !
Your proud Euripides from first to last
Doled out some five such, never deigned us
more !
And these — what curds and whey for marrowy
wine !
That same Alkestis you so rave about
Passed muster with him for a Satyr-play,
The prig ! — why trifle time with toys and skits
When he could stuff four ragbags sausage-wise
With sophistry, with bookish odds and ends,
Sokrates, meteors, moonshine, ' Life 's not
Life,'
' The tongue swore, but unsworn the mind re-
mains,'
And fifty such concoctions, crabtree-fruit
Digested while, head low and heels in heaven,
He lay, let Comics laugh — for privilege !
Looked puzzled on, or pityingly off,
But never dreamed of paying gibe by jeer,
Buffet by blow : plenty of proverb-pokes
At vice and folly, wicked kings, mad mobs !
No sign of wincing at my Comic lash,
No protest against infamous abuse,
Malignant censure, — naught to prove I scourged
With tougher thong than leek-and-onion-plait !
If ever he glanced gloom, aggrieved at all,
The aggriever must be — Aischulos perhaps :
Or Sophokles he 'd take exception to.
— Do you detect in me — in me, I ask,
The man like to accept this measurement
Of faculty, contentedly sit classed
Mere Comic Poet — since I wrote ' The
Birds ' ? "

I thought there might lurk truth in jest's dis-
guise.

" Thanks ! " he resumed, so quick to construe
smile !
" I answered — in my mind — these gapers
thus :
Since old wine 's ripe and new verse raw, you
judge —
What if I vary vintage-mode and mix
Blossom with must, give nosegay to the brew,
Fining, refining, gently, surely, till
The educated taste turns unawares
From customary dregs to draught divine ?
Then answered — with my lips : More ' Wasps
you want ?

Come next year and I give you 'Grasshoppers'!
And 'Grasshoppers' I gave them, — last
     month's play.
They formed the Choros.   Alkibiades,
No longer Triphales but Trilophos,
(Whom I called Darling-of-the-Summertime,
Born to be nothing else but beautiful
And brave, to eat, drink, love his life away)
Persuades the Tettix (our Autochthon-brood,
That sip the dew and sing on olive-branch
Above the ant-and-emmet populace)
To summon all who meadow, hill and dale
Inhabit — bee, wasp, woodlouse, dragonfly —
To band themselves against red nipper-nose
Stagbeetle, huge Taügetan (you guess —
Sparté) Athenai needs must battle with,
Because her sons are grown effeminate
To that degree — so morbifies their flesh
The poison-drama of Euripides,
Morals and music — there's no antidote
Occurs save warfare which inspirits blood,
And brings us back perchance the blessed time
When (Choros takes up tale) our commonalty
Firm in primeval virtue, antique faith,
Ere earwig-sophist plagued or pismire-sage,
Cockered no noddle up with A, b, g,
Book-learning, logic-chopping, and the moon,
But just employed their brains on '*Ruppapai*,
Row, boys, munch barley-bread, and take your
     ease —
Mindful, however, of the tier beneath ! '
Ah, golden epoch ! while the nobler sort
(Such needs must study, no contesting that !)
Wore no long curls but used to crop their hair,
Gathered the tunic well about the ham,
Remembering 't was soft sand they used for
     seat
At school-time, while — mark this — the lesson
     long,
No learner ever dared to cross his legs !
Then, if you bade him take the myrtle-bough
And sing for supper — 't was some grave ro-
     maunt
How man of Mitulené, wondrous wise,
Jumped into hedge, by mortals quickset called,
And there, anticipating Oidipous,
Scratched out his eyes and scratched them in
     again.
None of your Phaidras, Augés, Kanakés,
To mincing music, turn, trill, tweedle-trash,
Whence comes that Marathon is obsolete !
Next, my Antistrophé was — praise of Peace:
Ah, could our people know what Peace implies !
Home to the farm and furrow !   Grub one's
     vine,
Romp with one's Thratta, pretty serving-girl,
When wifie 's busy bathing !   Eat and drink,
And drink and eat, what else is good in life ?
Slice hare, toss pancake, gayly gurgle down
The Thasian grape in celebration due
Of Bacchos !   Welcome, dear domestic rite,
When wife and sons and daughters, Thratta
     too,
Pour pea-soup as we chant delectably
In Bacchos reels, his tunic at his heels !
Enough, you comprehend, — I do at least !
Then, — be but patient, — the Parabasis !
Pray !   For in that I also pushed reform.

None of the self-laudation, vulgar brag,
Vainglorious rivals cultivate so much !
No !   If some merest word in Art's defence
Justice demanded of me, — never fear !
Claim was preferred, but dignifiedly.
A cricket asked a locust (winged, you know)
What he had seen most rare in foreign parts ?
'I have flown far,' chirped he, 'North, East,
     South, West,
And nowhere heard of poet worth a fig
If matched with Bald-head here, Aigina's
     boast,
Who in this play bids rivalry despair
Past, present, and to come, so marvellous
His Tragic, Comic, Lyric excellence !
Whereof the fit reward were (not to speak
Of dinner every day at public cost
I' the Prutaneion) supper with yourselves,
My Public, best dish offered bravest bard ! '
No more !   no sort of sin against good taste !
Then, satire, — Oh, a plain necessity !
But I won't tell you: for — could I dispense
With one more gird at old Ariphrades ?
How scorpion-like he feeds on human flesh —
Ever finds out some novel infamy
Unutterable, inconceivable,
Which all the greater need was to describe
Minutely, each tail-twist at ink-shed time . . .
Now, what 's your gesture caused by ?   What
     you loathe,
Don't I loathe doubly, else why take such pains
To tell it you ?   But keep your prejudice !
My audience justified you !   Housebreakers !
This pattern-purity was played and failed
Last Rural Dionusia — failed !   for why ?
Ameipsias followed with the genuine stuff.
He had been mindful to engage the Four —
Karkinos and his dwarf-crab-family —
Father and sons, they whirled like spinning-
     tops,
Choros gigantically poked his fun,
The boys' frank laugh relaxed the seniors'
     brow,
The skies re-echoed victory's acclaim,
Ameipsias gained his due, I got my dose
Of wisdom for the future.   Purity ?
No more of that next month, Athenai mine !
Contrive new cut of robe who will, — I patch
The old exomis, add no purple sleeve !
The Thesmophoriazousai, smartened up
With certain plaits, shall please, I promise you !

" Yes, I took up the play that failed last year,
And re-arranged things ; threw adroitly in —
No Parachoregema — men to match
My women there already ; and when these
(I had a hit at Aristullos here,
His plan how womankind should rule the roast)
Drove men to plough — ' A-field, ye cribbed of
     cape ! '
Men showed themselves exempt from service
     straight
Stupendously, till all the boys cried ' Brave ! '
Then for the elders, I bethought me too,
Improved upon Mnesilochos' release
From the old bowman, board and binding-strap
I made his son-in-law Euripides
Engage to put both shrewish wives away —

'Gravity,' one, the other 'Sophist-lore' —
And mate with the Bald Bard's hetairai
twain —
Goodhumor' and 'Indulgence:' on they
tripped,
Murrhiné, Akalanthis, — 'beautiful
Their whole belongings' — crowd joined choros
there!
And while the Toxotes wound up his part
By shower of nuts and sweetmeats on the mob,
The woman-choros celebrated New
Kalligeneia, the frank last-day rite.
Brief, I was chairéd and caressed and crowned
And the whole theatre broke out a-roar,
Echoed my admonition — choros-cap —
Rivals of mine, your hands to your faces!
Summon no more the Muses, the Graces,
Since here by my side they have chosen their
places!
And so we all flocked merrily to feast, —
I, my choragos, choros, actors, mutes
And flutes aforesaid, friends in crowd, no fear,
At the Priest's supper; and hilarity
Grew none the less that, early in the piece,
Ran a report, from row to row close-packed,
Of messenger's arrival at the Port
With weighty tidings, 'Of Lusandros' flight,'
Opined one; 'That Euboia penitent
Sends the Confederation fifty ships,'
Preferred another; while 'The Great King's
Eye
Has brought a present for Elaphion here,
That rarest peacock Kompolakuthes!'
Such was the supposition of a third.
'No matter what the news,' friend Strattis
laughed,
'It won't be worse for waiting: while each
click
Of the klepsudra sets a shaking grave
Resentment in our shark's-head, boiled and
spoiled
By this time: dished in Sphettian vinegar,
Silphion and honey, served with cocks'-brain-
sauce!
So, swift to supper, Poet! No mistake,
This play; nor, like the unflavored "Grass-
hoppers,"
Salt without thyme!' Right merrily we
supped,
Till — something happened.

"Out it shall, at last!

"Mirth drew to ending, for the cup was
crowned
To the Triumphant! 'Kleonclapper erst,
Now, Plier of a scourge Euripides
Fairly turns tail from, flying Attiké
For Makedonia's rocks and frosts and bears,
Where, furry grown, he growls to match the
squeak
Of girl-voiced, crocus-vested Agathon!
Ha ha, he he!' When suddenly a knock —
Sharp, solitary, cold, authoritative.

"'Babaiax! Sokrates a-passing by,
A-peering in, for Aristullos' sake,
To put a question touching Comic Law?'

"No! Enters an old pale-swathed majesty,
Makes slow mute passage through two ranks as
mute,
(Strattis stood up with all the rest, the sneak!)
Gray brow still bent on ground, upraised at
length
When, our Priest reached, full front the vision
paused.

"'Priest!' — the deep tone succeeded the
fixed gaze —
'Thou carest that thy god have spectacle
Decent and seemly; wherefore, I announce
That, since Euripides is dead to-day,
My Choros, at the Greater Feast, next month,
Shall, clothed in black, appear ungarlanded!'

"Then the gray brow sank low, and Sophokles
Re-swathed him, sweeping doorward: mutely
passed
'Twixt rows as mute, to mingle possibly
With certain gods who convoy age to port;
And night resumed him.

"When our stupor broke,
Chirpings took courage, and grew audible.

"'Dead — so one speaks now of Euripides!'
'Ungarlanded dance Choros, did he say?
I guess the reason: in extreme old age
No doubt such have the gods for visitants.
Why did he dedicate to Herakles
An altar else, but that the god, turned Judge,
Told him in dream who took the crown of
gold?
He who restored Akropolis the theft,
Himself may feel perhaps a timely twinge
At thought of certain other crowns he filched
From — who now visits Herakles the Judge.
Instance "Medeia"! that play yielded palm
To Sophokles; and he again — to whom?
Euphorion! Why? Ask Herakles the
Judge!'
'Ungarlanded, just means — economy!
Suppress robes, chaplets, everything suppress
Except the poet's present! An old tale
Put capitally by Trugaios — eh?
News from the world of transformation
strange!
How Sophokles is grown Simonides,
And — aged, rotten — all the same, for greed
Would venture on a hurdle out to sea!
So jokes Philonides. Kallistratos
Retorts, Mistake! Instead of stinginess —
The fact is, in extreme decrepitude,
He has discarded poet and turned priest,
Priest of Half-Hero Alkon: visited
In his own house too by Asklepios' self,
So he avers. Meanwhile, his own estate
Lies fallow; Iophon 's the manager, —
Nay, touches up a play, brings out the same,
Asserts true sonship. See to what you sink
After your dozen-dozen prodigies!
Looking so old — Euripides seems young,
Born ten years later.'

"'Just his tricky style!
Since, stealing first away, he wins first word

Out of good-natured rival Sophokles,
Procures himself no bad panegyric.
Had fate willed otherwise, himself were taxed
To pay survivor's-tribute, — harder squeezed
From anybody beaten first to last,
Than one who, steadily a conqueror,
Finds that his magnanimity is tasked
To merely make pretence and — beat itself ! '

" So chirped the feasters though suppressedly.

" But I — what else do you suppose ? — had
    pierced
Quite through friends' outside-straining, foes'
    mock-praise,
And reached conviction hearted under all.
Death's rapid line had closed a life's account,
And cut off, left unalterably clear
The summed-up value of Euripides.

" Well, it might be the Thasian ! Certainly
There sang suggestive music in my ears ;
And, through — what sophists style — the wall
    of sense
My eyes pierced : death seemed life and life
    seemed death,
Envisaged that way, now, which I, before,
Conceived was just a moon-struck mood.
    Quite plain
There re-insisted, — ay, each prim stiff phrase
Of each old play, my still-new laughing-stock,
Had meaning, well worth poet's pains to state,
Should life prove half true life's term, — death,
    the rest.
As for the other question, late so large,
Now all at once so little, — he or I, —
Which better comprehended playwright
    craft, —
There, too, old admonition took fresh point.
As clear recurred our last word-interchange
Two years since, when I tried with ' Ploutos.'
    ' Vain ! '
Saluted me the cold grave-bearded bard —
' Vain, this late trial, Aristophanes !
None balks the genius with impunity !
You know what kind,'s the nobler, what makes
    grave
Or what makes grin : there 's yet a nobler still,
Possibly, — what makes wise, not grave, — and
    glad,
Not grinning : whereby laughter joins with
    tears,
Tragic and Comic Poet prove one power,
And Aristophanes becomes our Fourth —
Nay, greatest ! Never needs the Art stand still,
But those Art leans on lag, and none like you,
Her strongest of supports, whose step aside
Undoes the march : defection checks advance
Too late adventured ! See the " Ploutos "
    here !
This step decides your foot from old to new —
Proves you relinquish song and dance and jest,
Discard the beast, and, rising from all-fours,
Fain would paint, manlike, actual human life,
Make veritable men think, say and do.
Here 's the conception : which to execute,
Where,'s force ? Spent ! Ere the race began,
    was breath

O' the runner squandered on each friendly
    fool —
Wit-fireworks fizzed off while day craved no
    flame :
How should the night receive her due of fire
Flared out in Wasps and Horses, Clouds and
    Birds,
Prodigiously a-crackle ? Rest content !
The new adventure for the novel man
Born to that next success myself foresee
In right of where I reach before I rest.
At end of a long course, straight all the way,
Well may there tremble somewhat into ken
The untrod path, clouds veiled from earlier
    gaze !
None may live two lives : I have lived mine
    through,
Die where I first stand still. You retrograde.
I leave my life's work. I compete with you,
My last with your last, my " Antiope " —
" Phoinissai " — with this " Ploutos " ? No, I
    think !
Ever shall great and awful Victory
Accompany my life — in Maketis
If not Athenai. Take my farewell, friend !
Friend, — for from no consummate excellence
Like yours, whatever fault may countervail,
Do I profess estrangement : murk the marsh,
Yet where a solitary marble block
Blanches the gloom, there let the eagle perch !
You show — what splinters of Pentelikos,
Islanded by what ordure ! Eagles fly,
Rest on the right place, thence depart as free ;
But 'ware man's footstep, would it traverse
    mire
Untainted ! Mire is safe for worms that
    crawl.'

" Balaustion ! Here are very many words,
All to portray one moment's rush of thought, —
And much they do it ! Still, you understand.
The Archon, the Feast-master, read their sum
And substance, judged the banquet-glow ex-
    tinct,
So rose, discreetly if abruptly, crowned
The parting cup, — ' To the Good Genius,
    then ! '

" Up starts young Strattis for a final flash :
' Ay, the Good Genius ! To the Comic Muse,
She who evolves superiority,
Triumph and joy from sorrow, unsuccess
And all that 's incomplete in human life ;
Who proves such actual failure transient wrong,
Since out of body uncouth, halt and maimed —
Since out of soul grotesque, corrupt or blank —
Fancy, uplifted by the Muse, can flit
To soul and body, reinstate them Man :
Beside which perfect man, how clear we see
Divergency from type was earth's effect !
Escaping whence by laughter, — Fancy's
    feat, —
We right man's wrong, establish true for
    false, —
Above misshapen body, uncouth soul,
Reach the fine form, the clear intelligence —
Above unseemliness, reach decent law, —
By laughter : attestation of the Muse

That low-and-ugsome is not signed and sealed
Incontrovertibly man's portion here,
Or, if here, — why, still high-and-fair exists
In that ethereal realm where laughs our soul
Lift by the Muse. Hail thou her ministrant !
Hail who accepted no deformity
In man as normal and remediless,
But rather pushed it to such gross extreme
That, outraged, we protest by eye's recoil
The opposite proves somewhere rule and law !
Hail who implied, by limning Lamachos,
Plenty and pastime wait on peace, not war !
Philokleon — better bear a wrong than plead,
Play the litigious fool to stuff the mouth
Of dikast with the due three-obol fee !
The Paphlagonian — stick to the old sway
Of few and wise, not rabble-government !
Trugaios, Pisthetairos, Strepsiades, —
Why multiply examples ? Hail, in fine,
The hero of each painted monster — so
Suggesting the unpictured perfect shape !
Pour out ! A laugh to Aristophanes !'

"'Stay, my fine Strattis' — and I stopped ap-
     plause —
'To the Good Genius — but the Tragic Muse !
She who instructs her poet, bids man's soul
Play man's part merely nor attempt the gods'
Ill-guessed of ! Task humanity to height,
Put passion to prime use, urge will, unshamed
When will's last effort breaks in impotence !
No power forego, elude : no weakness, — plied
Fairly by power and will, — renounce, deny !
Acknowledge, in such miscalled weakness,
     strength
Latent : and substitute thus things for words !
Make man run life's race fairly, — legs and
     feet,
Craving no false wings to o'erfly its length !
Trust on, trust ever, trust to end — in truth !
By truth of extreme passion, utmost will,
Shame back all false display of either force —
Barrier about such strenuous heat and glow,
That cowardice shall shirk contending, — cant,
Pretension, shrivel at truth's first approach !
Pour to the Tragic Muse's ministrant
Who, as he pictured pure Hippolutos,
Abolished our earth's blot Ariphrades ;
Who, as he drew Bellerophon the bold,
Proclaimed Kleonumos incredible ;
Who, as his Theseus towered up man once more,
Made Alkibiades shrink boy again !
A tear — no woman's tribute, weak exchange
For action, water spent and heart's-blood
     saved —
No man's regret for greatness gone, ungraced
Perchance by even that poor meed, man's
     praise —
But some god's superabundance of desire,
Yearning of will to 'scape necessity, —
Love's overbrimming for self-sacrifice,
Whence good might be, which never else may be,
By power displayed, forbidden this strait
     sphere, —
Effort expressible one only way —
Such tear from me fall to Euripides !'

"The Thasian ! — All, the Thasian. I account !

"Whereupon outburst the whole company
Into applause and — laughter, would you think ?

"'The unrivalled one ! How, never at a loss,
He turns the Tragic on its Comic side
Else imperceptible ! Here's death itself —
Death of a rival, of an enemy, —
Scarce seen as Comic till the master-touch
Made it acknowledge Aristophanes !
Lo, that Euripidean laurel-tree
Struck to the heart by lightning ! Sokrates
Would question us, with buzz of "how" and
     "why,"
Wherefore the berry's virtue, the bloom's vice,
Till we all wished him quiet with his friend ;
Agathon would compose an elegy,
Lyric bewailment fit to move a stone,
And, stones responsive, we might wince, 't is
     like ;
Nay, with most cause of all to weep the least,
Sophokles ordains mourning for his sake
While we confess to a remorseful twinge : —
Suddenly, who but Aristophanes,
Prompt to the rescue, puts forth solemn hand,
Singles us out the tragic tree's best branch,
Persuades it groundward and, at tip, appends,
For votive-visor, Faun's goat-grinning face !
Back it flies, evermore with jest a-top,
And we recover the true mood, and laugh !'

"I felt as when some Nikias, — ninny-like
Troubled by sunspot-portent, moon-eclipse, —
At fault a little, sees no choice but sound
Retreat from foeman ; and his troops mistake
The signal, and hail onset in the blast,
And at their joyous answer, *alalé*, —
Back the old courage brings the scattered wits :
He wonders what his doubt meant, quick con-
     firms
The happy error, blows the charge amain.
So I repaired things.

          "'Both be praised,' thanked I.
'You who have laughed with Aristophanes,
You who wept rather with the Lord of Tears !
Priest, do thou, president alike o'er each,
Tragic and Comic function of the god,
Help with libation to the blended twain !
Either of which who serving, only serves —
Proclaims himself disqualified to pour
To that Good Genius — complex Poetry,
Uniting each god-grace, including both :
Which, operant for body as for soul,
Masters alike the laughter and the tears,
Supreme in lowliest earth, sublimest sky.
Who dares disjoin these, — whether he ignores
Body or soul, whichever half destroys, —
Maims the else perfect manhood, perpetrates
Again the inexpiable crime we curse —
Hacks at the Hermai, halves each guardian
     shape
Combining, nowise vainly, prominence
Of august head and enthroned intellect,
With homelier symbol of asserted sense, —
Nature's prime impulse, earthly appetite.
For, when our folly ventures on the freak,
Would fain abolish joy and fruitfulness,
Mutilate nature — what avails the Head

Left solitarily predominant, —
Unbodied soul, — not Hermes, both in one?
I, no more than our City, acquiesce
In such a desecration, but defend
Man's double nature — ay, wert thou its foe!
Could I once more, thou cold Euripides,
Encounter thee, in naught would I abate
My warfare, nor subdue my worst attack
On thee whose life-work preached "Raise soul,
    sink sense!
Evirate Hermes!" — would avenge the god,
And justify myself. Once face to face,
Thou, the argute and tricksy, shouldst not wrap,
As thine old fashion was, in silent scorn
The breast that quickened at the sting of truth,
Nor turn from me, as, if the tale be true,
From Lais when she met thee in thy walks,
And questioned why she had no rights as thou.
Not so shouldst thou betake thee, be assured,
To book and pencil, deign me no reply!
I would extract an answer from those lips
So closed and cold, were mine the garden-chance!
Gone from the world! Does none remain to
    take
Thy part and ply me with thy sophist-skill?
No sun makes proof of his whole potency
For gold and purple in that orb we view:
The apparent orb does little but leave blind
The audacious, and confused the worshipping;
But, close on orb's departure, must succeed
The serviceable cloud, — must intervene,
Induce expenditure of rose and blue,
Reveal what lay in him was lost to us.
So, friends, what hinders, as we homeward go,
If, privileged by triumph gained to-day,
We clasp that cloud our sun left saturate,
The Rhodian rosy with Euripides?
Not of my audience on my triumph-day,
She nor her husband! After the night's news
Neither will sleep but watch; I know the mood.
Accompany! my crown declares my right!'

"And here you stand with those warm golden
    eyes!

"In honest language, I am scarce too sure
Whether I really felt, indeed expressed
Then, in that presence, things I now repeat:
Nor half, nor any one word, — will that do?
Maybe, such eyes must strike conviction, turn
One's nature bottom upwards, show the base —
The live rock latent under wave and foam:
Superimposure these! Yet solid stuff
Will ever and anon, obeying star,
(And what star reaches rock-nerve like an eye?)
Swim up to surface, spout or mud or flame,
And find no more to do than sink as fast.

"Anyhow, I have followed happily
The impulse, pledged my Genius with effect,
Since, come to see you, I am shown — myself!"

I answered:

        "One of us declared for both
'Welcome the glory of Aristophanes.'
The other adds: and, — if that glory last,
Nor marsh-born vapor creep to veil the same, —

Once entered, share in our solemnity!
Commemorate, as we, Euripides!'"

"What?" he looked round, "I darken the
    bright house?
Profane the temple of your deity?
That's true! Else wherefore does he stand
    portrayed?
What Rhodian paint and pencil saved so much,
Beard, freckled face, brow — all but breath, I
    hope!
Come, that's unfair: myself am somebody,
Yet my pictorial fame's just potter's work, —
I merely figure on men's drinking-mugs!
I and the Flat-nose, Sophroniskos' son,
Oft make a pair. But what's this lies be-
    low?
His table-book and graver, playwright's tool!
And lo, the sweet psalterion, strung and screwed,
Whereon he tried those le-é-é-é-és
And ke-é-é-é-és and turns and trills,
Lovely lark's tirra-lirra, lad's delight!
Aischulos' bronze-throat eagle-bark at blood
Has somehow spoiled my taste for twitterings!
With . . . what, and did he leave you 'Her-
    akles'?
The 'Frenzied Hero,' one unfractured sheet,
No pine-wood tablets smeared with treacherous
    wax —
Papuros perfect as e'er tempted pen!
This sacred twist of bay-leaves dead and sere
Must be that crown the fine work failed to
    catch, —
No wonder! This might crown 'Antiope.'
'Herakles' triumph? In your heart perhaps!
But elsewhere? Come now, I'll explain the
    case,
Show you the main mistake. Give me the
    sheet!"

I interrupted:

        "Aristophanes!
The stranger-woman sues in her abode —
'Be honored as our guest!' But, call it —
    shrine,
Then 'No dishonor to the Daimon!' bids
The priestess 'or expect dishonor's due!'
You enter fresh from your worst infamy,
Last instance of long outrage; yet I pause,
Withhold the word a-tremble on my lip,
Incline me, rather, yearn to reverence, —
So you but suffer that I see the blaze
And not the bolt, — the splendid fancy-fling,
Not the cold iron malice, the launched lie
Whence heavenly fire has withered; impotent,
Yet execrable, leave it 'neath the look
Of yon impassive presence! What he scorned,
His life long, need I touch, offend my foot,
To prove that malice missed its mark, that lie
Cumbers the ground, returns to whence it came?
I marvel, I deplore, — the rest be mute!
But, throw off hate's celestiality, —
Show me, apart from song-flash and wit-flame,
A mere man's hand ignobly clenched against
Yon supreme calmness, — and I interpose,
Such as you see me! Silk breaks lightning't
    blow!"

He seemed to scarce so much as notice me,
Aught I had spoken, save the final phrase :
Arrested there.

          " Euripides grown calm !
Calmness supreme means dead and therefore
    safe,"
He muttered ; then more audibly began —

" Dead ! Such must die ! Could people com-
    prehend !
There 's the unfairness of it ! So obtuse
Are all : from Solon downward with his saw,
' Let none revile the dead, — no, though the
    son,
Nay, far descendant, should revile thyself ! ' —
To him who made Elektra, in the act
Of wreaking vengeance on her worst of foes,
Scruple to blame, since speech that blames
    insults
Too much the very villain life-released.
Now, *I* say, only after death, begins
That formidable claim, — immunity
Of faultiness from fault's due punishment !
The living, who defame me, — why, they live :
Fools, — I best prove them foolish by their life,
Will they but work on, lay their work by mine,
And wait a little, one Olympiad, say !
Then, where 's the vital force, mine froze
    beside ?
The sturdy fibre, shamed my brittle stuff ?
The school-correctness, sure of wise award
When my vagaries cease to tickle taste ?
Where 's censure that must sink me, judgment
    big
Awaiting just the word posterity
Pants to pronounce ?   Time's wave breaks,
    buries — *whom*,
Fools, when myself confronts you four years
    hence ?
But die, ere next Lenaia, — safely so
You 'scape me, slink with all your ignorance,
Stupidity and malice, to that hole
O'er which survivors croak ' Respect the
    dead ! '
Ay, for I needs must !   But allow me clutch
Only a carrion-handful, lend it sense,
(Mine, not its own, or could it answer me ?)
And question, ' You, I pluck from hiding-place,
Whose cant was, certain years ago, my " Clouds "
Might last until the swallows came with Spring—
Whose chatter, " Birds " are unintelligible,
Mere psychologic puzzling : poetry ?
List, the true lay to rock a cradle with !
O man of Mitulené, wondrous wise ! '
— Would not I rub each face in its own filth
To tune of ' Now that years have come and
    gone,
How does the fact stand ? What 's demon-
    strable
By time, that tries things ? — your own test,
    not mine
Who think men are, were, ever will be fools,
Though somehow fools confute fools, — as these,
    you !
Don't mumble to the sheepish twos and threes
You cornered and called " audience ! " face this
    me

Who know, and can, and — helped by fifty
    years —
Do pulverize you pygmies, then as now ! '

" Ay, now as then, I pulverize the brood,
Balaustion ! Mindful, from the first, where foe
Would hide head safe when hand had flung its
    stone,
I did not turn cheek and take pleasantry,
But flogged while skin could purple and flesh
    start,
To teach fools whom they tried conclusions
    with.
First face a-splutter at me got such splotch
Of prompt slab mud as, filling mouth to maw,
Made its concern thenceforward not so much
To criticise me as go cleanse itself.
The only drawback to which huge delight, —
(He saw it, how he saw it, that calm cold
Sagacity you call Euripides !)
— Why, 't is that, make a muckheap of a man,
There, pillared by your prowess, he remains,
Immortally immerded.   Not so he !
Men pelted him but got no pellet back.
He reasoned, I 'll engage, — ' Acquaint the
    world
Certain minuteness butted at my knee ?
Dogface Eruxis, the small satirist, —
What better would the manikin desire
Than to strut forth on tiptoe, notable
As who so far up fouled me in the flank ? '
So dealt he with the dwarfs : we giants, too,
Why must we emulate their pin-point play ?
Render imperishable — impotence,
For mud throw mountains ?   Zeus, by mud un-
    reached, —
Well, 't was no dwarf he heaved Olumpos at ! "

My heart burned up within me to my tongue.

" And why must men remember, ages hence,
Who it was rolled down rocks, but refuse too —
Strattis might steal from ! mixture-monument,
Recording what ?   ' I, Aristophanes,
Who boast me much inventive in my art,
Against Euripides thus volleyed muck
Because, in art, he too extended bounds.
I — patriot, loving peace and hating war, —
Choosing the rule of few, but wise and good,
Rather than mob-dictature, fools and knaves
However multiplied their mastery, —
Despising most of all the demagogue,
(Noisome air-bubble, buoyed up, borne along
By kindred breath of knave and fool below,
Whose hearts swell proudly as each puffing face
Grows big, reflected in that glassy ball,
Vacuity, just bellied out to break
And righteously bespatter friends the first,)
I loathing, — beyond less puissant speech
Than my own god-grand language to declare, —
The fawning, cozenage and calumny
Wherewith such favorite feeds the populace
That fan and set him flying for reward : —
I who, detecting what vice underlies
Thought's superstructure, — fancy's sludge
    and slime
'Twixt fact's sound floor and thought's mere
    surface-growth

Of hopes and fears which root no deeplier down
Than where all such mere fungi breed and
  bloat —
Namely, man's misconception of the God : —
I, loving, hating, wishful from my soul
That truth should triumph, falsehood have
  defeat,
— Why, all my soul's supremacy of power
Did I pour out in volley just on him
Who, his whole life long, championed every
  cause
I called my heart's cause, loving as I loved,
Hating my hates, spurned falsehood, championed
  truth, —
Championed truth not by flagellating foe
With simple rose and lily, gibe and jeer,
Sly wink of boon-companion o'er the bowze
Who, while he blames the liquor, smacks the
  lip,
Blames, doubtless, but leers condonation too, —
No, the balled fist broke brow like thunder-
  bolt,
Battered till brain flew ! Seeing which descent,
None questioned that was first acquaintance-
  ship,
The avenger's with the vice he crashed through
  bone.
Still, he displeased me ; and I turned from foe
To fellow-fighter, flung much stone, more
  mud, —
But missed him, since he lives aloof, I see.'
Pah ! stop more shame, deep-cutting glory
  through,
Nor add, this poet, learned, — found no taunt
Tell like ' That other poet studies books ! '
Wise, — cried ' At each attempt to move our
  hearts,
He uses the mere phrase of daily life ! '
Witty, — ' His mother was a herb-woman ! '
Veracious, honest, loyal, fair and good, —
' It was Kephisophon who helped him write ! '

" Whence, — oh the tragic end of Comedy ! —
Balaustion pities Aristophanes.
For, who believed him ? Those who laughed
  so loud ?
They heard him call the sun Sicilian cheese !
Had he called true cheese — curd, would muscle
  move ?
What made them laugh but the enormous lie ?
' Kephisophon wrote " Herakles " ? ha, ha,
What can have stirred the wine-dregs, soured
  the soul,
And set a-lying Aristophanes ?
Some accident at which he took offence !
The Tragic Master in a moody muse
Passed him unhailing, and it hurts — it hurts !
Beside, there 's license for the Wine-lees-
  song ! ' "

Blood burnt the cheekbone, each black eye
  flashed fierce.

" But this exceeds our license ! Stay awhile —
That 's the solution ! both are foreigners,
The fresh-come Rhodian lady, and her spouse
The man of Phokis : newly resident,
Nowise instructed — that explains it all !

No born and bred Athenian but would smile,
Unless frown seemed more fit for ignorance.
These strangers have a privilege !

                     " You blame "
(Presently he resumed with milder mien)
" Both theory and practice — Comedy :
Blame her from altitudes the Tragic friend
Rose to, and upraised friends along with him,
No matter how. Once there, all 's cold and
  fine,
Passionless, rational ; our world beneath
Shows (should you condescend to grace so much
As glance at poor Athenai) grimly gross —
A population which, mere flesh and blood,
Eats, drinks, and kisses, falls to fisticuffs,
Then hugs as hugely : speaks too as it acts,
Prodigiously talks nonsense, — townsmen needs
Must parley in their town's vernacular.
Such world has, of two courses, one to choose :
Unworld itself, — or else go blackening off
To its crow-kindred, leave philosophy
Her heights serene, fit perch for owls like you.
Now, since the world demurs to either course,
Permit me, — in default of boy or girl,
So they be reared Athenian, good and true, —
To praise what you most blame ! Hear Art's
  defence !
I 'll prove our institution, Comedy,
Coeval with the birth of freedom, matched
So nice with our Republic, that its growth
Measures each greatness, just as its decline
Would signalize the downfall of the pair.
Our Art began when Bacchos . . . never
  mind !
You and your master don't acknowledge gods :
' They are not, no, they are not ! ' well, — began
When the rude instinct of our race outspoke,
Found, — on recurrence of festivity
Occasioned by black mother-earth's good will
To children, as they took her vintage-gifts, —
Found — not the least of many benefits —
That wine unlocked the stiffest lip, and loosed
The tongue late dry and reticent of joke,
Through custom's gripe which gladness thrusts
  aside.
So, emulating liberalities,
Heaven joined with earth for that god's day at
  least,
Renewed man's privilege, grown obsolete,
Of telling truth nor dreading punishment,
Whereon the joyous band disguised their forms
With skins, beast-fashion, daubed each phiz
  with dregs,
Then hollaed ' Neighbor, you are fool, you —
  knave,
You — hard to serve, you — stingy to reward ! '
The guiltless crowed, the guilty sunk their
  crest,
And good folk gained thereby, 't was evident.
Whence, by degrees, a birth of happier thought,
The notion came — not simply this to say,
But this to do — prove, put in evidence,
And act the fool, the knave, the harsh, the
  hunks,
Who *did* prate, cheat, shake fist, draw purse-
  string tight,
As crowd might see, which only heard before,

"So played the Poet, with his man of parts ;
And all the others, found unqualified
To mount cart and be persons, made the mob,
Joined choros, fortified their fellows' fun,
Anticipated the community,
Gave judgment which the public ratified.
Suiting rough weapon doubtless to plain truth,
They flung, for word-artillery, why — filth ;
Still, folks who wiped the unsavory salute
From visage, would prefer the mess, to wit —
Steel, poked through midriff with a civil
    speech,
As now the way is : then, the kindlier mode
Was — drub not stab, rib-roast not scarify !
So did Sousarion introduce, and so
Did I, acceding, find the Comic Art :
Club, — if I call it, — notice what 's implied !
An engine proper for rough chastisement,
No downright slaying : with impunity —
Provided crabtree, steeped in oily joke,
Deal only such a bruise as laughter cures.
I kept the gained advantage : stickled still
For club - law — stout fun and allowanced
    thumps —
Knocked in each knob a crevice to hold joke
As fig-leaf holds the fat-fry.

            " Next, whom thrash ?
Only the coarse fool and the clownish knave ?
Higher, more artificial, composite
Offence should prove my prowess, eye and arm !
Not who robs henroost, tells of untaxed figs,
Spends all his substance on stewed ellops-fish,
Or gives a pheasant to his neighbor's wife :
No ! strike malpractice that affects the State,
The common weal — intriguer or poltroon,
Venality, corruption, what care I
If shrewd or witless merely ? — so the thing
Lay sap to aught that made Athenai bright
And happy, change her customs, lead astray
Youth or age, play the demagogue at Pnux,
The sophist in Palaistra, or — what 's worst,
As widest mischief, — from the Theatre
Preach innovation, bring contempt on oaths,
Adorn licentiousness, despise the Cult.
Are such to be my game ? Why, then there
    wants
Quite other cunning than a cudgel-sweep !
Grasp the old stout stock, but new tip with
    steel
Each boss, if I would bray — no callous hide
Simply, but Lamachos in coat of proof,
Or Kleon cased about with impudence !
Shaft pushed no worse while point pierced
    sparkling so
That none smiled ' Sportive, what seems sav-
    agest,
— Innocuous anger, spiteless rustic mirth ! '
Yet spiteless in a sort, considered well,
Since I pursued my warfare till each wound
Went through the mere man, reached the prin-
    ciple
Worth purging from Athenai. Lamachos ?
No, I attacked war's representative ;
Kleon ? No, flattery of the populace ;
Sokrates ? No, but that pernicious seed
Of sophists whereby hopeful youth is taught
To jabber argument, chop logic, pore

On sun and moon, and worship Whirligig.
Oh, your tragedian, with the lofty grace,
Aims at no other and effects as much ?
Candidly : what 's a polished period worth,
Filed curt sententiousness of loaded line,
When he who deals out doctrine, primly steps
From just that selfsame moon he maunders of,
And, blood-thinned by his pallid nutriment,
Proposes to rich earth-blood — purity ?
In me, 't was equal-balanced flesh rebuked
Excess alike in stuff-guts Glauketes
Or starveling Chairephon ; I challenged both, —
Strong understander of our common life,
I urged sustainment of humanity.
Whereas when your tragedian cries up Peace —
He 's silent as to cheese-cakes Peace may chew ;
Seeing through rabble-rule, he shuts his eye
To what were better done than crowding
    Pnux —
That 's dance ' *Threttanelo*, the Kuklops
    drunk ! '

" My power has hardly need to vaunt itself !
Opposers peep and mutter, or speak plain :
' No naming names in Comedy ! ' votes one,
' Nor vilifying live folk ! ' legislates
Another, ' urge amendment on the dead ! '
' Don't throw away hard cash,' supplies a third,
' But crib from actor's dresses, choros-treats ! '
Then Kleon did his best to bully me :
Called me before the Law Court : ' Such a play
Satirized citizens with strangers there,
Such other,' — why, its fault was in myself !
I was, this time, the stranger, privileged
To act no play at all, — Egyptian, I —
Rhodian or Kameirensian, Aiginete,
Lindian, or any foreigner he liked —
Because I can't write Attic, probably !
Go ask my rivals, — how they roughed my
    fleece,
And how, shorn pink themselves, the huddled
    sheep
Shiver at distance from the snapping shears !
Why must they needs provoke me ?

            " All the same,
No matter for my triumph, I foretell
Subsidence of the day-star : quench his beams ?
No Aias e'er was equal to the feat
By throw of shield, tough-hided seven times
    seven,
'Twixt sky and earth ! 't is dullards soft and
    sure
Who breathe against his brightest, here a sigh
And there a ' So let be, we pardon you ! '
Till the minute mist hangs a block, has tamed
Noonblaze to ' twilight mild and equable,'
Vote the old women spinning out of doors.
Give me the earth-spasm, when the lion ramped
And the bull gendered in the brave gold flare !
Oh, you shall have amusement, — better still,
Instruction ! no more horse-play, naming names,
Taxing the fancy when plain sense will serve !
Thearion, now, my friend who bakes you bread,
What 's worthier limning than his household
    life ?
His whims and ways, his quarrels with the
    spouse,

And how the son, instead of learning knead
Kilikian loaves, brings heartbreak on his sire
By buying horseflesh branded *San*, each flank,
From shrewd Menippos who imports the ware :
While pretty daughter Kepphé too much haunts
The shop of Sporgilos the barber ! brave !
Out with Thearion's meal-tub politics
In lieu of Pisthetairos, Strepsiades !
That 's your exchange ? O Muse of Megara !
Advise the fools ' *Feed babe on weasel-lap*
For wild-boar's marrow, Cheiron's hero-pap,
And rear, for man — Ariphrades, mayhap !'
Yes, my Balaustion, yes, my Euthukles,
That 's *your* exchange, — who, foreigners in fact
And fancy, would impose your squeamishness
On sturdy health, and substitute such brat
For the right offspring of us Rocky Ones,
Because babe kicks the cradle, — crows, not
    mewls !

" Which brings me to the prime fault, poison-
    speck
Whence all the plague springs — that first feud
    of all
'Twixt me and you and your Euripides.
' Unworld the world,' frowns he, my opposite.
I cry, ' Life ! ' ' Death,' he groans, ' our better
    Life ! '
Despise what is — the good and graspable,
Prefer the out of sight and in at mind,
To village-joy, the well-side violet-patch,
The jolly club-feast when our field 's in soak,
Roast thrushes, hare-soup, pea-soup, deep
    washed down
With Peparethian ; the prompt paying off
That black-eyed brown-skinned country-fla-
    vored wench
We caught among our brushwood foraging :
On these look fig-juice, curdle up life's cream,
And fall to magnifying misery !
Or, if you condescend to happiness,
Why, talk, talk, talk about the empty name
While thing's self lies neglected 'neath your
    nose !
I need particular discourtesy
And private insult from Euripides
To render contest with him credible ?
Say, all of me is outraged ! one stretched sense,
I represent the whole Republic, — gods,
Heroes, priests, legislators, poets, — prone,
And pummelled into insignificance,
If will in him were matched with power of
    stroke.
For see what he has changed or hoped to
    change !
How few years since, when he began the fight,
Did there beat life indeed Athenai through !
Plenty and peace, then ! Hellas thundersmote
The Persian. He himself had birth, you say,
That morn salvation broke at Salamis,
And heroes still walked earth. Themistokles —
Surely his mere back-stretch of hand could still
Find, not so lost in dark, Odusseus ? — he
Holding as surely on to Herakles, —
Who touched Zeus, link by link, the unrup-
    tured chain !
Were poets absent ? Aischulos might hail —
With Pindaros, Theognis, — whom for sire ?

Homeros' self, departed yesterday !
While Hellas, saved and sung to, then and
    thus, —
Ah, people, — ah, lost antique liberty !
We lived, ourselves, undoubted lords of earth :
Wherever olives flourish, corn yields crop
To constitute our title — ours such land !
Outside of oil and breadstuff, — barbarism !
What need of conquest ? Let barbarians starve !
Devote our whole strength to our sole defence,
Content with peerless native products, home,
Beauty profuse in earth's mere sights and
    sounds,
Such men, such women, and such gods their
    guard !
The gods ? he worshipped best who feared
    them most,
And left their nature uninquired into,
— Nature ? their very names ! pay reverence,
Do sacrifice for our part, theirs would be
To prove benignantest of playfellows.
With kindly humanism they countenanced
Our emulation of divine escapes
Through sense and soul : soul, sense are made
    to use ;
Use each, acknowledging its god the while !
Crush grape, dance, drink, indulge, for Bac-
    chos' sake !
'T is Aphrodité's feast-day — frisk and fling,
Provided we observe our oaths, and house
Duly the stranger : Zeus takes umbrage else !
Ah, the great time — had I been there to taste !
Perikles, right Olumpian, — occupied
As yet with getting an Olumpos reared
Marble and gold above Akropolis, —
Wisely so spends what thrifty fools amassed
For cut-throat projects. Who carves Proma-
    chos ?
Who writes the Oresteia ?

                              " Ah, the time !
For, all at once, a cloud has blanched the blue,
A cold wind creeps through the close vineyard-
    rank,
The olive-leaves curl, violets crisp and close
Like a nymph's wrinkling at the bath's first
    splash
On breast. (Your pardon !) There 's a restless
    change,
Deterioration. Larks and nightingales
Are silenced, here and there a gor-crow grim
Flaps past, as scenting opportunity.
Where Kimon passaged to the Boulé once,
A starveling crew, unkempt, unshorn, un-
    washed,
Occupy altar-base and temple-step,
Are minded to indoctrinate our youth !
How call these carrion kill-joys that intrude ?
' Wise men,' their nomenclature ! Prodikos —
Who scarce could, unassisted, pick his steps
From way Theseia to the Tripods' way, —
This empty noddle comprehends the sun, —
How he 's Aigina's bigness, wheels no whit
His way from east to west, nor wants a steed !
And here 's Protagoras sets wrongheads right,
Explains what virtue, vice, truth, falsehood
    mean,
Makes all we seemed to know prove ignorance

Yet knowledge also, since, on either side
Of any question, something is to say,
Nothing to 'stablish, all things to disturb!
And shall youth go and play at kottabos,
Leaving unsettled whether moon-spots breed?
Or dare keep Choes ere the problem 's solved —
Why should I like my wife who dislikes me?
' But sure the gods permit this, censure that? '
So tell them! straight the answer 's in your
    teeth:
' You relegate these points, then, to the gods?
What and where are they? ' What my sire
    supposed,
And where yon cloud conceals them! ' Till
    they 'scape,
And scramble down to Leda, as a swan,
Europa, as a bull! why not as — ass
To somebody? Your sire was Zeus perhaps!
Either — away with such ineptitude!
Or, wanting energy to break your bonds,
Stick to the good old stories, think the rain
Is — Zeus distilling pickle through a sieve!
Think thunder 's thrown to break Theoros'
    head
For breaking oaths first! Meanwhile let our-
    selves
Instruct your progeny you prate like fools
Of father Zeus, who 's but the atmosphere,
Brother Poseidon, otherwise called — sea,
And son Hephaistos — fire and nothing else!
Over which nothings there 's a something still,
"Necessity," that rules the universe
And cares as much about your Choes-feast
Performed or intermitted, as you care
Whether gnats sound their trump from head or
    tail! '
When, stupefied at such philosophy,
We cry, ' Arrest the madmen, governor!
Pound hemlock and pour bull's-blood, Peri-
    kles! '
Would you believe? The Olumpian bends his
    brow,
Scarce pauses from his building! 'Say they
    thus?
Then, they say wisely. Anaxagoras,
I had not known how simple proves eclipse
But for thy teaching! Go, fools, learn like me! '

" Well, Zeus nods: man must reconcile him-
    self,
So, let the Charon's-company harangue,
And Anaxagoras be — as we wish!
A comfort is in nature: while grass grows
And water runs, and sesame pricks tongue,
And honey from Brilesian hollow melts
On mouth, and Bacchis' flavorous lip beats
    both,
You will not be untaught life's use, young man?
Pho! My young man just proves that pan-
    niered ass
Said to have borne Youth strapped on his stout
    back,
With whom a serpent bargained, bade him swap
The priceless boon for — water to quench
    thirst!
What 's youth to my young man? In love
    with age,
He Spartanizes, argues, fasts and frowns,

Denies the plainest rules of life, long since
Proved sound; sets all authority aside,
Must simply recommence things, learn ere act,
And think out thoroughly how youth should
    pass —
Just as if youth stops passing, all the same!

" One last resource is left us — poetry!
' Vindicate nature, prove Plataian help,
Turn out, a thousand strong, all right and
    tight,
To save Sense, poet! Bang the sophist-brood
Would cheat man out of wholesome sustenance
By swearing wine is water, honey — gall,
Saperdion — the Empousa! Panic-smit,
Our juveniles abstain from Sense and starve:
Be yours to disenchant them! Change things
    back!
Or better, strain a point the other way
And handsomely exaggerate wronged truth!
Lend wine a glory never gained from grape,
Help honey with a snatch of him we style
The Muses' Bee, baybloom-fed Sophokles,
And give Saperdion a Kimberic robe! '

" ' I, his successor,' gruff the answer grunts,
' Incline to poetize philosophy,
Extend it rather than restrain; as thus —
Are heroes men? No more, and scarce as
    much,
Shall mine be represented. Are men poor?
Behold them ragged, sick, lame, halt and
    blind!
Do they use speech? Ay, street-terms, market-
    phrase!
Having thus drawn sky earthwards, what
    comes next
But dare the opposite, lift earth to sky?
Mere puppets once, I now make womankind,
For thinking, saying, doing, match the male.
Lift earth? I drop to, dally with, earth's
    dung!
— Recognize in the very slave — man's mate,
Declare him brave and honest, kind and true,
And reasonable as his lord, in brief.
I paint men as they are — so runs my boast —
Not as they should be: paint — what 's part of
    man,
— Women and slaves, — not as, to please your
    pride,
They should be, but your equals, as they are.
Oh, and the Gods! Instead of abject mien,
Submissive whisper, while my Choros cants,
" Zeus, — with thy cubit's length of attributes, —
May I, the ephemeral, ne'er scrutinize
Who made the heaven and earth and all things
    there! "
Myself shall say . . . Ay, ' Herakles ' may
    help!
Give me, — I want the very words, — attend! "

He read. Then — " Murder 's out, — ' There
    are no Gods,'
Man has no master, owns, by consequence,
No right, no wrong, except to please or plague!
His nature: what man likes be man's sole law
Still, since he likes Saperdion, honey, figs,
Man may reach freedom by your roundabout!

' Never believe yourselves the freer thence !
There are no gods, but there 's " Necessity," —
Duty enjoined you, fact in figment's place,
Throned on no mountain, native to the mind !
Therefore deny yourselves Saperdion, figs
And honey, for the sake of — what I dream,
A-sitting with my legs up ! '

            " Infamy !
The poet casts in calm his lot with these
Assailants of Apollon ! Sworn to serve
Each Grace, the Furies call him minister —
He, who was born for just that roseate world
Renounced so madly, where what 's false is
    fact,
Where he makes beauty out of ugliness,
Where he lives, life itself disguised for him
As immortality — so works the spell,
The enthusiastic mood which marks a man
Muse-mad, dream-drunken, wrapt around by
    verse,
Encircled with poetic atmosphere,
As lark emballed by its own crystal song,
Or rose enmisted by that scent it makes !
No, this were unreality ! the real
He wants, not falsehood, — truth alone he
    seeks,
Truth, for all beauty ! Beauty, in all truth —
That 's certain somehow ! Must the eagle lilt
Lark-like, needs fir-tree blossom rose-like ?
    No !
Strength and utility charm more than grace,
And what 's most ugly proves most beautiful.
So much assistance from Euripides !

" Whereupon I betake me, since needs must,
To a concluding — ' Go and feed the crows !
Do ! Spoil your art as you renounce your life,
Poetize your so precious system, do,
Degrade the hero, nullify the god,
Exhibit women, slaves and men as peers, —
Your castigation follows prompt enough !
When all 's concocted upstairs, heels o'erhead,
Down must submissive drop the masterpiece
For public praise or blame : so, praise away,
Friend Sokrates, wife's-friend Kephisophon !
Boast innovations, cramp phrase, uncouth
    song,
Hard matter and harsh manner, gods, men,
    slaves
And women jumbled to a laughing-stock
Which Hellas shall hold sides at lest she split !
Hellas, on these, shall have her word to say ! '

" She has it and she says it — there 's the
    curse ! —
She finds he makes the shag-rag hero-race,
The noble slaves, wise women, move as much
Pity and terror as true tragic types :
Applauds inventiveness — the plot so new,
The turn and trick subsidiary so strange !
She relishes that homely phrase of life,
That common town-talk, more than trumpet-
    blasts ;
Accords him right to chop and change a myth :
What better right had he, who told the tale
In the first instance, to embellish fact ?
This last may disembellish yet improve !

Both find a block : this man carves back to
    bull
What first his predecessor cut to sphinx :
Such genuine actual roarer, nature's brute,
Intelligible to our time, was sure
The old-world artist's purpose, had he worked
To mind ; this both means and makes the
    thing !
If, past dispute, the verse slips oily-bathed
In unctuous music — say, effeminate —
We also say, like Kuthereia's self,
A lulling effluence which enswathes some isle
Where hides a nymph, not seen but felt the
    more.
That 's Hellas' verdict !

            " Does Euripides
Even so far absolved, remain content ?
Nowise ! His task is to refine, refine,
Divide, distinguish, subtilize away
Whatever seemed a solid planting-place
For footfall, — not in that phantasmal sphere
Proper to poet, but on vulgar earth
Where people used to tread with confidence.
There 's left no longer one plain positive
Enunciation incontestable
Of what is good, right, decent here on earth.
Nobody now can say, ' This plot is mine,
Though but a plethron square, — my duty ! ' —
    ' Yours ?
Mine, or at least not yours,' snaps somebody !
And, whether the dispute be parent-right
Or children's service, husband's privilege
Or wife's submission, there 's a snarling straight,
Smart passage of opposing ' yea ' and ' nay,'
' Should,' ' should not,' till, howe'er the contest
    end,
Spectators go off sighing ' Clever thrust !
Why was I so much hurried to pay debt,
Attend my mother, sacrifice an ox,
And set my name down " for a trireme, good " ?
Something I might have urged on t' other side !
No doubt, Chresphontes or Bellerophon
We don't meet every day ; but Stab-and-stitch
The tailor — ere I turn the drachmas o'er
I owe him for a chiton, as he thinks,
I 'll pose the blockhead with an argument ! '

" So has he triumphed, your Euripides !
Oh, I concede, he rarely gained a prize :
That 's quite another matter ! cause for that !
Still, when 't was got by Ions, Iophons,
Off he would pace confoundedly superb,
Supreme, no smile at movement in his mouth
Till Sokrates winked, whispered : out it broke !
And Aristullos jotted down the jest,
While Iophons or Ions, bay on brow,
Looked queerly, and the foreigners — like
    you —
Asked o'er the border with a puzzled smile,
— ' And so, you value Ions, Iophons,
Euphorions ! How about Euripides ? '
(Eh, brave bard's-champion ? Does the anger
    boil ?
Keep within bounds a moment, — eye and lip
Shall loose their doom on me, their fiery worst !)
What strangers ? Archelaos heads the file !
He sympathizes, he concerns himself,

He pens epistle, each successless play :
' Athenai sinks effete ; there 's younger blood
In Makedonia.   Visit where I rule !
Do honor to me and take gratitude !
Live the guest's life, or work the poet's way,
Which also means the statesman's : he who
       wrote
" Erechtheus " may seem rawly politic
At home where Kleophon is ripe ; but here
My council-board permits him choice of seats.'

" Now, this was operating, — what should prove
A poison-tree, had flowered far on to fruit
For many a year, — when I was moved, first
       man,
To dare the adventure, down with root and
       branch.
So, from its sheath I drew my Comic steel,
And dared what I am now to justify.
A serious question first, though !

                       " Once again !
Do you believe, when I aspired in youth,
I made no estimate of power at all,
Nor paused long, nor considered much, what
       class
Of fighters I might claim to join, beside
That class wherewith I cast in company ?
Say, you — profuse of praise no less than
       blame —
Could not I have competed — franker phrase
Might trulier correspond to meaning — still,
Competed with your Tragic paragon ?
Suppose me minded simply to make verse,
To fabricate, parade resplendent arms,
Flourish and sparkle out a Trilogy, —
Where was the hindrance ?   But my soul bade
       ' Fight !
Leave flourishing for mock-foe, pleasure-time ;
Prove arms efficient on real heads and hearts ! '
How ? With degeneracy sapping fast
The Marathonian muscle, nerved of old
To maul the Mede, now strung at best to help
— How did I fable ? — War and Hubbub mash
To mincemeat Fatherland and Brotherhood,
Pound in their mortar Hellas, State by State,
That greed might gorge, the while frivolity
Rubbed hands and smacked lips o'er the
       dainty dish !
Authority, experience — pushed aside
By any upstart who pleads throng and press,
O' the people ! ' Think, say, do thus ! ' Where-
fore, pray ?
' We are the people : who impugns our right
Of choosing Kleon that tans hide so well,
Huperbolos that turns out lamps so trim,
Hemp-seller Eukrates or Lusikles
Sheep-dealer, Kephalos the potter's son,
Diitriphes who weaves the willow-work
To go round bottles, and Nausikudes
The meal-man ? Such we choose and more,
       their mates,
To think and say and do in our behalf ! '
While sophistry wagged tongue, emboldened
       still,
Found matter to propose, contest, defend,
'Stablish, turn topsyturvy, — all the same,
No matter what, provided the result

Were something new in place of something
       old, —
Set wagging by pure insolence of soul
Which needs must pry into, have warrant for
Each right, each privilege good policy
Protects from curious eye and prating mouth !
Everywhere lust to shape the world anew,
Spurn this Athenai as we find her, build
A new impossible Cloudcuckooburg
For feather-headed birds, once solid men,
Where rules, discarding jolly habitude,
Nourished on myrtle-berries and stray ants,
King Tereus who, turned Hoopoe Triple-Crest,
Shall terrify and bring the gods to terms !

" Where was I ?   Oh ! Things ailing thus — I
       ask,
What cure ? Cut, thrust, hack, hew at heap-on-
       heaped
Abomination with the exquisite
Palaistra-tool of polished Tragedy ?
Erechtheus shall harangue Amphiktuon,
And incidentally drop word of weight
On justice, righteousness, so turn aside
The audience from attacking Sicily ! —
The more that Choros, after he recounts
How Phrixos rode the ram, the far-famed
       Fleece,
Shall add — at last fall of grave dancing-foot —
' Aggression never yet was helped by Zeus ! '
That helps or hinders Alkibiades ?
As well expect, should Pheidias carve Zeus' self
And set him up, some half a mile away,
His frown would frighten sparrows from your
       field !
Eagles may recognize their lord, belike,
But as for vulgar sparrows, — change the god,
And plant some big Priapos with a pole !
I wield the Comic weapon rather — hate !
Hate ! honest, earnest, and directest hate —
Warfare wherein I close with enemy,
Call him one name and fifty epithets,
Remind you his great-grandfather sold bran,
Describe the new exomion, sleeveless coat
He knocked me down last night and robbed
       me of,
Protest he voted for a tax on air !
And all this hate — if I write Comedy —
Finds tolerance, most like — applause, perhaps
True veneration ; for I praise the god
Present in person of his minister,
And pay — the wilder my extravagance —
The more appropriate worship to the Power
Adulterous, night-roaming, and the rest :
Otherwise, — that originative force
Of nature, impulse stirring death to life,
Which, underlying law, seems lawlessness,
Yet is the outbreak which, ere order be,
Must thrill creation through, warm stocks and
       stones,
Phales Iacchos.

               " Comedy for me !
Why not for you, my Tragic masters ? Sneaks
Whose art is mere desertion of a trust !
Such weapons lay to hand, the ready club,
The clay - ball, on the ground a stone to
       snatch, —

Arms fit to bruise the boar's neck, break the
    chine
O' the wolf, — and you must impiously — de-
    spise?
No, I 'll say, furtively let fall that trust
Consigned you !   'T was not ' take or leave
    alone,'
But ' take and, wielding, recognize your god
In his prime attributes !'   And though full soon
You sneaked, subsided into poetry,
Nor met your due reward, still, — heroize
And speechify and sing-song and forego
Far as you may your function, — still its pact
Endures, one piece of early homage still
Exacted of you ; after your three bouts
At hoitytoity, great men with long words,
And so forth, — at the end, must tack itself
The genuine sample, the Satyric Play,
Concession, with its wood-boys' fun and freak,
To the true taste of the mere multitude.
Yet, there again ! What does your Still-at-itch,
Always-the-innovator ?   Shrugs and shirks !
Out of his fifty Trilogies, some five
Are somehow suited : Satyrs dance and sing,
Try merriment, a grimly prank or two,
Sour joke squeezed through pursed lips and
    teeth on edge,
Then quick on top of toe to pastoral sport,
Goat-tending and sheep-herding, cheese and
    cream,
Soft grass and silver rillets, country-fare —
When throats were promised Thasian ! Five
    such feats, —
Then frankly off he threw the yoke : next
    Droll,
Next festive drama, covenanted fun,
Decent reversion to indecency,
Proved — your ' Alkestis ' ! There 's quite fun
    enough.
Herakles drunk ! From out fate's blackening
    wave
Calamitous, just zigzags some shot star,
Poor promise of faint joy, and turns the laugh
On dupes whose fears and tears were all in
    waste !

" For which sufficient reasons, in truth's name,
I closed with whom you count the Meaner
    Muse,
Classed me with Comic Poets who should weld
Dark with bright metal, show their blade may
    keep
Its adamantine birthright though ablaze
With poetry, the gold, and wit, the gem,
And strike mere gold, unstiffened out by steel,
Or gem, no iron joints its strength around,
From hand of — posturer, not combatant !

" Such was my purpose : it succeeds, I say !
Have not we beaten Kallikratidas,
Not humbled Sparté ?   Peace awaits our word,
Spite of Theramenes, and fools his like.
Since my previsions — warranted too well
By the long war now waged and worn to end —
Had spared such heritage of misery,
My after-counsels scarce need fear repulse.
Athenai, taught prosperity has wings,
Cages the glad recapture. Demos, see,

From folly's premature decrepitude
Boiled young again, emerges from the stew
Of twenty-five years' trouble, sits and sways,
One brilliance and one balsam, — sways and
    sits
Monarch of Hellas ! ay, and, sage again,
No longer jeopardizes chieftainship,
No longer loves the brutish demagogue
Appointed by a bestial multitude,
But seeks out sound advisers.   Who are they ?
Ourselves, of parentage proved wise and good !
To such may hap strains thwarting quality,
(As where shall want its flaw mere human
    stuff ?)
Still, the right grain is proper to right race ;
What 's contrary, call curious accident !
Hold by the usual !   Orchard-grafted tree,
Not wilding, racehorse-sired, not rouncey-born,
Aristocrat, no sausage-selling snob !
Nay, why not Alkibiades, come back
Filled by the Genius, freed of petulance,
Frailty, — mere youthfulness that 's all at
    fault, —
Advanced to Perikles and something more ?
— Being at least our duly born and bred, —
Curse on what chaunoprockt first gained his
    ear
And got his . . . well, once true man in right
    place,
Our commonalty soon content themselves
With doing just what they are born to do,
Eat, drink, make merry, mind their own affairs
And leave state-business to the larger brain !
I do not stickle for their punishment ;
But certain culprits have a cloak to twitch,
A purse to pay the piper : flog, say I,
Your fine fantastics, paragons of parts,
Who choose to play the important !   Far from
    side
With us, their natural supports, allies, —
And, best by brain, help who are best by birth
To fortify each weak point in the wall
Built broad and wide and deep for permanence
Between what 's high and low, what 's rare
    and vile, —
They cast their lot perversely in with low
And vile. lay flat the barrier, lift the mob
To dizzy heights where Privilege stood firm.
And then, simplicity become conceit, —
Woman, slave, common soldier, artisan,
Crazy with new - found worth, new - fangled
    claims, —
These must be taught next how to use their
    heads
And hands in driving man's right to mob's
    rule !
What fellows thus inflame the multitude ?
Your Sokrates, still crying ' Understand !'
Your Aristullos, — ' Argue !'   Last and worst,
Should, by good fortune, mob still hesitate,
Remember there 's degree in heaven and earth,
Cry ' Aischulos enjoined us fear the gods,
And Sophokles advised respect the kings !'
Why, your Euripides informs them — Gods ?
They are not ! Kings ? They are, but . . .
    do not I,
In ' Suppliants,' make my Theseus, — yours
    no more. —

Fire up at insult of who styles him King?
Play off that Herald, I despise the most,
As patronizing kings' prerogative
Against a Theseus proud to dare no step
Till he consult the people?

       "Such as these —
Ah, you expect I am for strangling straight?
Nowise, Balaustion! All my roundabout
Ends at beginning, with my own defence!
I dose each culprit just with — Comedy.
Let each be doctored in exact the mode
Himself prescribes: by words, the word-monger —
My words to his words, — my lies, if you like,
To his lies. Sokrates I nickname thief,
Quack, necromancer; Aristullos, — say,
Male Kirké who bewitches and bewrays
And changes folk to swine; Euripides, —
Well, I acknowledge! Every word is false,
Looked close at; but stand distant and stare through,
All's absolute indubitable truth
Behind lies, truth which only lies declare!
For come, concede me truth's in thing not word,
Meaning not manner! Love smiles 'rogue' and 'wretch'
When 'sweet' and 'dear' seem vapid; Hate adopts
Love's 'sweet' and 'dear,' when 'rogue' and 'wretch' fall flat;
Love, Hate — are truths, then, each, in sense not sound.
Further: if Love, remaining Love, fell back
On 'sweet' and 'dear,' — if Hate, though Hate the same,
Dropped down to 'rogue' and 'wretch,' — each phrase were false.
Good! and now grant I hate no matter whom
With reason: I must therefore fight my foe,
Finish the mischief which made enmity.
How? By employing means to most hurt him
Who much harmed me. What way did he do harm?
Through word or deed? Through word? with word, wage war!
Word with myself directly? As direct
Reply shall follow: word to you, the wise,
Whence indirectly came the harm to me?
What wisdom I can muster waits on such!
Word to the populace which, misconceived
By ignorance and incapacity,
Ends in no such effect as follows cause
When I, or you the wise, are reasoned with,
So damages what I and you hold dear?
In that event, I ply the populace
With just such word as leavens their whole lump
To the right ferment for my purpose. *They*
Arbitrate properly between us both?
They weigh my answer with his argument,
Match quip with quibble, wit with eloquence?
All they attain to understand is — blank!
Two adversaries differ; which is right
And which is wrong, none takes on him to say,
Since both are unintelligible. Pooh!
Swear my foe's mother vended herbs she stole,

They fall a-laughing! Add, — his household drudge
Of all-work justifies that office well,
Kisses the wife, composing him the play, —
They grin at whom they gaped in wonderment,
And go off — 'Was he such a sorry scrub?
This other seems to know! we praised too fast!'
When then, my lies have done the work of truth,
Since 'scrub,' improper designation, means
Exactly what the proper argument
— Had such been comprehensible — proposed
To proper audience — were I graced with such —
Would properly result in; so your friend
Gets an impartial verdict on his verse,
'The tongue swears, but the soul remains unsworn!'

"There, my Balaustion! All is summed and said.
No other cause of quarrel with yourself!
Euripides and Aristophanes
Differ: he needs must round our difference
Into the mob's ear; with the mob I plead.
You angrily start forward 'This to me?'
No speck of this on you the thrice refined!
Could parley be restricted to us two,
My first of duties were to clear up doubt
As to our true divergence each from each.
Does my opinion so diverge from yours?
Probably less than little — not at all!
To know a matter, for my very self
And intimates — that's one thing: to imply
By 'knowledge' — loosing whatsoe'er I know
Among the vulgar who, by mere mistake,
May brain themselves and me in consequence, —
That's quite another. 'O the daring flight!
This only bard maintains the exalted brow,
Nor grovels in the slime nor fears the gods!'
Did *I* fear — *I* play superstitious fool,
Who, with the due proviso, introduced,
Active and passive, their whole company
As creatures too absurd for scorn itself?
Zeus? I have styled him — 'slave, mere thrashing-block!'
I'll tell you: in my very next of plays,
At Bacchos' feast, in Bacchos' honor, full
In front of Bacchos' representative.
I mean to make main-actor — Bacchos' self!
Forth shall he strut, apparent, first to last,
A blockhead, coward, braggart, liar, thief,
Demonstrated all these by his own mere
Xanthias the man-slave: such man shows such god
Shamed to brute-beastship by comparison!
And when ears have their fill of his abuse,
And eyes are sated with his pummelling, —
My Choros taking care, by, all the while
Singing his glory, that men recognize
A god in the abused and pummelled beast, —
Then, should one ear be stopped of auditor,
Should one spectator shut revolted eye, —
Why, the Priest's self will first raise outraged voice:
'Back, thou barbarian, thou ineptitude!

Does not most license hallow best our day,
And least decorum prove its strictest rite?
Since Bacchos bids his followers play the fool,
And there's no fooling like a majesty
Mocked at, — who mocks the god, obeys the
  law —
Law which, impute but indiscretion to,
And . . . why, the spirit of Euripides
Is evidently active in the world!'
Do I stop here? No! feat of flightier force!
See Hermes! what commotion raged, — re-
  flect! —
When imaged god alone got injury
By drunkards' frolic! How Athenai stared
Aghast, then fell to frenzy, fit on fit, —
Ever the last, the longest! At this hour,
The craze abates a little: so, my Play
Shall have up Hermes: and a Karion, slave,
(Since there's no getting lower) calls our friend
The profitable god, we honor so,
Whatever contumely fouls the mouth —
Bids him go earn more honest livelihood
By washing tripe in well-trough — wash he
  does,
Duly obedient! Have I dared my best?
Asklepios, answer! — deity in vogue,
Who visits Sophokles familiarly,
If you believe the old man, — at his age,
Living is dreaming, and strange guests haunt
  door
Of house, belike, peep through and tap at
  times
When a friend yawns there, waiting to be
  fetched, —
At any rate, to memorize the fact,
He has spent money, set an altar up
In the god's temple, now in much repute.
That temple-service trust me to describe —
Cheaters and choused, the god, his brace of
  girls,
Their snake, and how they manage to snap
  gifts
'And consecrate the same into a bag,'
For whimsies done away with in the dark!
As if, a stone's throw from that theatre
Whereon I thus unmask their dupery,
The thing were not religious and august!

"Of Sophokles himself — nor word nor sign
Beyond a harmless parody or so!
He founds no anti-school, upsets no faith,
But, living, lets live, the good easy soul
Who, — if he saves his cash, unpoetlike,
Loves wine and — never mind what other
  sport,
Boasts for his father just a swordblade-smith,
Proves but queer captain when the people
  claim,
For one who conquered with 'Antigone,'
The right to undertake a squadron's charge, —
And needs the son's help now to finish plays,
Seeing his dotage calls for governance
And Iophon to share his property, —
Why, of all this, reported true, I breathe
Not one word — true or false, I like the man!
Sophokles lives and lets live: long live he!
Otherwise, — sharp the scourge and hard the
  blow!

"And what's my teaching but — accept the
  old,
Contest the strange! acknowledge work that's
  done,
Misdoubt men who have still their work to do!
Religions, laws and customs, poetries,
Are old? So much achieved victorious truth!
Each work was product of a lifetime, wrung
From each man by an adverse world: for why?
He worked, destroying other older work
Which the world loved and so was loth to lose.
Whom the world beat in battle — dust and ash!
Who beat the world, left work in evidence,
And wears its crown till new men live new
  lives,
And fight new fights, and triumph in their
  turn.
I mean to show you on the stage! you'll see
My Just Judge only venture to decide
Between two suitors, which is god, which man,
By thrashing both of them as flesh can bear.
You shall agree, — whichever bellows first,
He's human; who holds longest out, divine:
That is the only equitable test!
Cruelty? Pray, who pricked them on to court
My thong's award? Must they needs domi-
  nate?
Then I — rebel! Their instinct grasps the
  new?
Mine bids retain the old: a fight must be,
And which is stronger the event will show.
Oh, but the pain! Your proved divinity
Still smarts all reddened? And the rightlier
  served!
Was not some man's-flesh in him, after all?
Do let us lack no frank acknowledgment
There's nature common to both gods and men!
All of them — spirit? What so winced was
  clay!
Away pretence to some exclusive sphere
Cloud-nourishing a sole selected few
Fume-fed with self-superiority!
I stand up for the common coarse-as-clay
Existence, — stamp and ramp with heel and
  hoof
On solid vulgar life, you fools disown!
Make haste from your unreal eminence,
And measure lengths with me upon that ground
Whence this mud-pellet sings and summons
  you!
I know the soul, too, how the spark ascends
And how it drops apace and dies away.
I am your poet-peer, man thrice your match!
I too can lead an airy life when dead,
Fly like Kinesias when I'm cloud-ward bound;
But here, no death shall mix with life it mars!

"So, my old enemy who caused the fight,
Own I have beaten you, Euripides!
Or, — if your advocate would contravene, —
Help him, Balaustion! Use the rosy strength!
I have not done my utmost, — treated you
As I might Aristullos, mint-perfumed, —
Still, let the whole rage burst in brave attack!
Don't pay the poor ambiguous compliment
Of fearing any pearl-white knuckled fist
Will damage this broad buttress of a brow!
Fancy yourself my Aristonumos,

Ameipsias or Sannurion : punch and pound !
Three cuckoos who cry 'cuckoo'! much I
   care !
They boil a stone ! *Neblaretai ! Rattei !* "

Cannot your task have end here, Euthukles ?
Day by day glides our galley on its path :
Still sunrise and still sunset, Rhodes half-
   reached,
And still, my patient scribe ! no sunset's peace
Descends more punctual than that brow's in-
   cline
O'er tablets which your serviceable hand
Prepares to trace. Why treasure up, forsooth,
These relics of a night that make me rich,
But, half-remembered merely, leave so poor
Each stranger to Athenai and her past ?
For — how remembered ! As some greedy hind
Persuades a honeycomb, beyond the due,
To yield its hoarding, — heedless what alloy
Of the poor bee's own substance taints the gold
Which, unforced, yields few drops, but pur-
   ity, —
So would you fain relieve of load this brain,
Though the hived thoughts must bring away,
   with strength,
What words and weakness, strength's recepta-
   cle —
Wax from the store ! Yet, — aching soothed
   away, —
Accept the compound ! No suspected scent
But proves some rose was rifled, though its
   ghost
Scarce lingers with what promised musk and
   myrrh.
No need of farther squeezing ! What remains
Can only be Balaustion, just her speech !

Ah, but — because speech serves a purpose
   still ! —

He ended with that flourish. I replied :

" Fancy myself your Aristonumos ?
Advise me, rather, to remain myself,
Balaustion, — mindful what mere mouse con-
   fronts
The forest-monarch Aristophanes !
I who, a woman, claim no quality
Beside the love of all things lovable
Created by a power pre-eminent
In knowledge, as in love I stand perchance,
— You, the consummately-creative ! How
Should I, then, dare deny submissive trust
To any process aiming at result
Such as you say your songs are pregnant with ?
Result, all judge : means, let none scrutinize
Save those aware how glory best is gained
By daring means to end, ashamed of shame,
Constant in faith that only good works good,
While evil yields no fruit but impotence !
Graced with such plain good, I accept the
   means !
Nay, if result itself in turn become
Means, — who shall say ? — to ends still loftier
   yet, —

Though still the good prove hard to under-
   stand,
The bad still seemingly predominate, —
Never may I forget which order bears
The burden, toils to win the great reward,
And finds, in failure, the grave punishment,
So, meantime, claims of me a faith I yield !
Moreover, a mere woman, I recoil
From what may prove man's-work permissi-
   ble,
Imperative. Rough strokes surprise : what
   then ?
Some lusty armsweep needs must cause the
   crash
Of thorn and bramble, ere those shrubs, those
   flowers,
We fain would have earth yield exclusively,
Are sown, matured and garlanded for boys
And girls, who know not how the growth was
   gained.
Finally, am I not a foreigner ?
No born and bred Athenian, — isled about,
I scarce can drink, like you, at every breath,
Just some particular doctrine which may best
Explain the strange thing I revolt against —
How — by involvement, who may extricate ? —
Religion perks up through impiety,
Law leers with license, folly wise-like frowns,
The seemly lurks inside the abominable.
But opposites, — each neutralizes each
Haply by mixture : what should promise death,
May haply give the good ingredient force,
Disperse in fume the antagonistic ill.
This institution, therefore, — Comedy, —
By origin, a rite ; by exercise,
Proved an achievement tasking poet's power
To utmost, eking legislation out
Beyond the legislator's faculty,
Playing the censor where the moralist
Declines his function, far too dignified
For dealing with minute absurdities ;
By efficacy, — virtue's guard, the scourge
Of vice, each folly's fly-flap, arm in aid
Of all that 's righteous, customary, sound
And wholesome ; sanctioned therefore, — better
   say,
Prescribed for fit acceptance of this age
By, not alone the long recorded roll
Of earlier triumphs, but, success to-day —
(The multitude as prompt recipient still
Of good gay teaching from that monitor
They crowned this morning — Aristophanes —
As when Sousarion's car first traversed street) —
This product of Athenai — *I* dispute,
Impugn ? There 's just one only circumstance
Explains that ! I, poor critic, see, hear, feel ;
But eyes, ears, senses prove me — foreigner !
Who shall gainsay that the raw new-come guest
Blames oft, too sensitive ? On every side
Of — larger than your stage — life's spectacle,
Convention here permits and there forbids
Impulse and action, nor alleges more
Than some mysterious 'So do all, and so
Does no one : ' which the hasty stranger blames
Because, who bends the head unquestioning,
Transgresses, turns to wrong what else were
   right,
By failure of a reference to law

Beyond convention ; blames unjustly, too —
As if, through that defect, all gained were lost
And slave-brand set on brow indelibly ; —
Blames unobservant or experienceless
That men, like trees, if stout and sound and
    sane,
Show stem no more affected at the root
By bough's exceptional submissive dip
Of leaf and bell, light danced at end of spray
To windy fitfulness in wayward sport, —
No more lie prostrate, — than low files of flower
Which, when the blast goes by, unruffled raise
Each head again o'er ruder meadow-wreck
Of thorn and thistle that refractory
Demurred to cower at passing wind's caprice.
Why shall not guest extend like charity,
Conceive how, — even when astounded most
That natives seem to acquiesce in muck
Changed by prescription, they affirm, to gold, —
Such may still bring to test, still bear away
Safely and surely much of good and true
Though latent ore, themselves unspecked, un-
    spoiled ?
Fresh bathed i' the icebrook, any hand may pass
A placid moment through the lamp's fierce
    flame :
And who has read your ' Lemnians,' seen ' The
    Hours,'
Heard ' Female-Playhouse-seat-Preoccupants,'
May feel no worse effect than, once a year,
Those who leave decent vesture, dress in rags
And play the mendicant, conform thereby
To country's rite, and then, no beggar-taint
Retained, don vesture due next morrow-day.
What if I share the stranger's weakness then ?
Well, could I also show his strength, his sense
Untutored, ay ! — but then untampered with !

" I fancy, though the world seems old enough,
Though Hellas be the sole unbarbarous land,
Years may conduct to such extreme of age,
And outside Hellas so isles new may lurk,
That haply, — when and where remain a
    dream ! —
In fresh days when no Hellas fills the world,
In novel lands as strange where, all the same,
Their men and women yet behold, as we,
Blue heaven, black earth, and love, hate, hope
    and fear,
Over again, unhelped by Attiké —
Haply some philanthropic god steers bark,
Gift-laden, to the lonely ignorance
Islanded, say, where mist and snow mass hard
To metal — ay, those Kassiterides !
Then asks : ' Ye apprehend the human form.
What of this statue, made to Pheidias' mind,
This picture, as it pleased our Zeuxis paint ?
Ye too feel truth, love beauty : judge of these ! '
Such strangers may judge feebly, stranger-like :
' Each hair too indistinct — for, see our own !
Hands, not skin-colored as these hands we have,
And lo, the want of due decorum here !
A citizen, arrayed in civic garb,
Just as he walked your streets apparently,
Yet wears no sword by side, adventures thus,
In thronged Athenai ! foolish painter's-freak !
While here 's his brother-sculptor found at fault
Still more egregiously, who shames the world,

Shows wrestler, wrestling at the public games,
Atrociously exposed from head to foot ! '
Sure, the Immortal would impart at once
Our slow-stored knowledge, how small truths
    suppressed
Conduce to the far greater truth's display, —
Would replace simple by instructed sense,
And teach them how Athenai first so tamed
The natural fierceness that her progeny
Discarded arms nor feared the beast in man :
Wherefore at games, where earth's wise grati-
    tude,
Proved by responsive culture, claimed the prize
For man's mind, body, each in excellence, —
When mind had bared itself, came body's turn,
And only irreligion grudged the gods
One naked glory of their master-work
Where all is glorious rightly understood, —
The human frame ; enough that man mistakes :
Let him not think the gods mistaken too !

" But, peradventure, if the stranger's eye
Detected . . . Ah, too high my fancy-flight !
Pheidias, forgive, and Zeuxis bear with me —
How on your faultless should I fasten fault
Of my own framing, even ? Only say, —
Suppose the impossible were realized,
And some as patent incongruity,
Unseemliness, — of no more warrant, there
And then, than now and here, whate'er the time
And place, — I say, the Immortal, — who can
    doubt ? —
Would never shrink, but own, ' The blot escaped
Our artist : thus he shows humanity ! '

" May stranger tax one peccant part in thee,
Poet, three-parts divine ! May I proceed ?

" ' Comedy is prescription and a rite.'
Since when ? No growth of the blind antique
    time,
' It rose in Attiké with liberty ;
When freedom falls, it too will fall.' Scarce so !
Your games, — the Olumpian, Zeus gave birth
    to these ;
Your Puthian, — these were Phoibos' institute.
Isthmian, Nemeian, — Theseus, Herakles
Appointed each, the boys and barbers say !
Earth's day is growing late : where 's Comedy ?
' Oh, that commenced an age since, — two, be-
    like, —
In Megara, whence here they brought the thing ! '
Or I misunderstand, or here 's the fact —
Your grandsire could recall that rustic song,
How such-an-one was thief, and miser such,
And how, — immunity from chastisement
Once promised to bold singers of the same
By daylight on the drunkard's holiday, —
The clever fellow of the joyous troop
Tried acting what before he sang about,
Acted and stole, or hoarded, acting too :
While his companions ranged a-row, closed up
For Choros, — bade the general rabblement
Sit, see, hear, laugh, — not join the dance them-
    selves.
Soon, the same clever fellow found a mate,
And these two did the whole stage-mimicking,
Still closer in approach to Tragedy, —

So led the way to Aristophanes,
Whose grandsire saw Sousarion, and whose
    sire —
Chionides ; yourself wrote ' Banqueters '
When Aischulos had made ' Prometheus,' nay,
All of the marvels ; Sophokles, — I 'll cite,
' Oidipous ' — and Euripides — I bend
The head — ' Medeia ' henceforth awed the
    world !
' Banqueters,' ' Babylonians ' — next come you !
Surely the great days that left Hellas free
Happened before such advent of huge help,
Eighty-years-late assistance ? Marathon,
Plataia, Salamis were fought, I think,
Before new educators stood reproved,
Or foreign legates blushed, excepted to !
Where did the helpful rite pretend its rise ?
Did it break forth, as gifts divine are wont,
Plainly authentic, incontestably
Adequate to the helpful ordinance ?
Founts, dowered with virtue, pulse out pure
    from source ;
'T is there we taste the god's benign intent :
Not when, — fatigued away by journey, foul
With brutish trampling, — crystal sinks to slime,
And lymph forgets the first salubriousness.
Sprang Comedy to light thus crystal-pure ?
' Nowise ! ' yourself protest with vehemence ;
' Gross, bestial, did the clowns' diversion break ;
Every successor paddled in the slush ;
Nay, my contemporaries one and all
Gay played the mudlark till I joined their game ;
Then was I first to change buffoonery
For wit, and stupid filth for cleanly sense,
Transforming pointless joke to purpose fine,
Transfusing rude enforcement of home-law —
" Drop knave's-tricks, deal more neighbor-like,
    ye boors ! " —
With such new glory of poetic breath
As, lifting application far past use
O' the present, launched it o'er men's lowly
    heads
To future time, when high and low alike
Are dead and done with, while my airy power
Flies disengaged, as vapor from what stuff
It — say not, dwelt in — fitlier, dallied with
To forward work, which done, — deliverance
    brave, —
It soars away, and mud subsides to dust.
Say then, myself invented Comedy ! '

" So mouths full many a famed Parabasis !
Agreed ! No more, then, of prescriptive use,
Authorization by antiquity,
For what offends our judgment ! 'T is your
    work,
Performed your way : not work delivered you
Intact, intact producible in turn.
Everywhere have you altered old to new —
Your will, your warrant : therefore, work must
    stand
Or stumble by intrinsic worth. What worth ?
Its aim and object ! Peace you advocate,
And war would fain abolish from the land :
Support religion, lash irreverence,
Yet laughingly administer rebuke
To superstitious folly, — equal fault !
While innovating rashness, lust of change,

New laws, new habits, manners, men and
    things,
Make your main quarry, — ' oldest ' meaning
    ' best.'
You check the fretful litigation-itch,
Withstand mob-rule, expose mob-flattery,
Punish mob-favorites ; most of all press hard
On sophists who assist the demagogue,
And poets their accomplices in crime.
Such your main quarry, — by the way, you
    strike
Ignobler game, mere miscreants, snob or scamp,
Cowardly, gluttonous, effeminate :
Still with a bolt to spare when dramatist
Proves haply unproficient in his art,
Such aims — alone, no matter for the means —
Declare the unexampled excellence
Of their first author — Aristophanes !

" Whereat — Euripides, oh, not thyself —
Augustlier than the need ! — thy century
Of subjects dreamed and dared and done, be-
    fore
' Banqueters ' gave dark earth enlightenment,
Or ' Babylonians ' played Prometheus here, —
These let me summon to defend thy cause !
Lo, as indignantly took life and shape
Labor by labor, all of Herakles, —
Palpably fronting some o'erbold pretence
' Eurustheus slew the monsters, purged the
    world ! '
So shall each poem pass you and imprint
Shame on the strange assurance. You praised
    Peace ?
Sing him full-face, Kresphontes ! ' Peace ' the
    theme ?
' Peace, in whom depths of wealth lie, — of the
    blest
Immortals beauteousest, —
Come ! for the heart within me dies away,
So long dost thou delay !
Oh, I have feared lest old age, much annoy,
Conquer me, quite outstrip the tardy joy,
Thy gracious triumph-season I would see,
The song, the dance, the sport, profuse of
    crowns to be.
But come ! for my sake, goddess great and dear,
Come to the city here !
Hateful Sedition drive thou from our homes,
With Her who madly roams
Rejoicing in the steel against the life
That 's whetted — banish Strife ! '

" Shall I proceed ? No need of next and next!
That were too easy, play so presses play,
Trooping tumultuous, each with instance apt,
Each eager to confute the idle boast !
What virtue but stands forth panegyrized,
What vice, unburned by stigma, in the books
Which bettered Hellas, — beyond graven gold
Or gem-indenture, sung by Phoibos' self
And saved in Kunthia's mountain treasure-
    house —
Ere you, man, moralist, were youth or boy ?
— Not praise which, in the proffer, mocks the
    praised
By sly admixture of the blameworthy
And enforced coupling of base fellowship, —

Not blame which gloats the while it frowning
    laughs,
' Allow one glance on horrors — laughable ! ' —
This man's entire of heart and soul, discharged
Its love or hate, each unalloyed by each,
On objects worthy either ; earnestness,
Attribute him, and power ! but novelty ?
Nor his nor yours a doctrine — all the world's !
What man of full-grown sense and sanity
Holds other than the truth, — wide Hellas
    through, —
Though truth he acts discredit truth he holds ?
What imbecile has dared to formulate
' Love war, hate peace, become a litigant ! ' —
And so preach on, reverse each rule of right
Because he quarrels, combats, goes to law ?
No, for his comment runs, with smile or sigh
According to heart's temper, ' Peace were best,
Except occasions when we put aside
Peace, and bid all the blessings in her gift
Quick join the crows, for sake of Marathon ! '

" ' Nay,' you reply ; for one, whose mind with-
    stands
His heart, and, loving peace, for conscience'
    sake
Wants war, — you find a crowd of hypocrites
Whose conscience means ambition, grudge and
    greed.
On such, reproof, sonorous doctrine, melts
Distilled like universal but thin dew
Which all too sparsely covers country : dear,
No doubt, to universal crop and clown,
Still, each bedewed keeps his own head-gear
    dry
With upthrust *skiadeion*, shakes adroit
The droppings to his neighbor. No ! collect
All of the moisture, leave unhurt the heads
Which nowise need a washing, save and store
And dash the whole condensed to one fierce
    spout
On some one evil-doer, sheltered close, —
The fool supposed, — till you beat guard away,
And showed your audience, not that war was
    wrong,
But Lamachos absurd, — case, crests and all, —
Not that democracy was blind of choice,
But Kleon and Huperbolos were shams :
Not superstition vile, but Nikias crazed, —
The concrete for the abstract ; that 's the way !
What matters Choros crying ' Hence, impure ! '
You cried ' Ariphrades does thus and thus ! '
Now, earnestness seems never earnest more
Than when it dons for garb — indifference ;
So, there 's much laughing : but, compensative,
When frowning follows laughter, then indeed
Scout innuendo, sarcasm, irony ! —
Wit's polished warfare glancing at first graze
From off hard headpiece, coarsely-coated brain
O' the commonalty — whom, unless you prick
To purpose, what avails that finer pates
Succumb to simple scratching ? Those — not
    these —
'T is Multitude, which, moved, fines Lamachos,
Banishes Kleon and burns Sokrates,
House over head, or, better, poisons him.
Therefore in dealing with King Multitude,
Club-drub the callous numskulls ! In and in

Beat this essential consequential fact
That here they have a hater of the three,
Who hates in word, phrase, nickname, epithet
And illustration, beyond doubt at all !
And similarly, would you win assent
To — Peace, suppose ? You tickle the tough
    hide
With good plain pleasure her concomitant —
And, past mistake again, exhibit Peace —
Peace, vintager and festive, cheesecake-time,
Hare-slice-and-peasoup-season, household-joy ;
Theoria's beautiful belongings match
Opora's lavish condescendings : brief,
Since here the people are to judge, you press
Such argument as people understand :
If with exaggeration — what care you ?

" Have I misunderstood you in the main ?
No ! then must answer be, such argument,
Such policy, no matter what good love
Or hate it help, in practice proves absurd,
Useless and null : henceforward intercepts
Sober effective blow at what you blame,
And renders nugatory rightful praise
Of thing or person. The coarse brush has
    daubed —
What room for the finer limner's pencil-mark ?
Blame ? You curse, rather, till who blames
    must blush —
Lean to apology or praise, more like !
Does garment, simpered o'er as white, prove
    gray ?
' Black, blacker than Acharnian charcoal, black
Beyond Kimmerian, Stugian blackness black,'
You bawl, till men sigh ' nearer snowiness ! '
What follows ? What one faint-rewarding fall
Of foe belabored ne'er so lustily ?
Laugh Lamachos from out the people's heart ?
He died, commanding, ' hero,' say yourself !
Gibe Nikias into privacy ? — nay, shake
Kleon a little from his arrogance
By cutting him to shoe-sole-shreds ? I think,
He ruled his life long, and, when time was ripe,
Died fighting for amusement, — good tough
    hide !
Sokrates still goes up and down the streets,
And Aristullos puts his speech in book,
When both should be abolished long ago.
Nay, wretchedest of rags, Ariphrades —
You have been fouling that redoubtable
Harp-player, twenty years, with what effect ?
Still he strums on, strums ever cheerily,
And earns his wage, — ' Who minds a joke ? '
    men say.
No, friend ! The statues stand — mud-stained
    at most —
Titan or pygmy : what achieves their fall
Will be, long after mud is flung and spent,
Some clear thin spirit-thrust of lightning —
    truth !

" Your praise, then — honey-smearing helps
    your friend,
More than blame's ordure-smirch hurts foe,
    perhaps ?
Peace, now, misunderstood, ne'er prized
    enough,
You have interpreted to ignorance

Till ignorance opes eye, bat-blind before,
And for the first time knows Peace means the
    power
On maw of pancake, cheese-cake. barley-cake,
No stop nor stint to stuffing. While, in camp,
Who fights chews rancid tunny, onions raw,
Peace sits at cosy feast with lamp and fire,
Complaisant smooth-sleeked flute-girls giggling
    gay.
How thick and fast the snow falls, freezing War
Who shrugs, campaigns it, and may break a
    shin
Or twist an ankle! come, who hesitates
To give Peace, over War, the preference?
Ah, friend — had this indubitable fact
Haply occurred to poor Leonidas,
How had he turned tail on Thermopulai!
It cannot be that even his few wits
Were addled to the point that, so advised,
Preposterous he had answered — 'Cakes are
    prime,
Hearth-sides are snug, sleek dancing-girls have
    worth,
And yet — for country's sake, to save our gods
Their temples, save our ancestors their tombs,
Save wife and child and home and liberty, —
I would chew sliced salt-fish, bear snow — nay,
    starve,
If need were, — and by much prefer the
    choice!'
Why, friend, your genuine hero, all the while,
Has been — who served precisely for your butt —
Kleonumos that, wise, cast shield away
On battle-ground; cried 'Cake my buckler be,
Embossed with cream-clot! peace, not war, I
    choose,
Holding with Dikaiopolis!' Comedy
Shall triumph, Dikaiopolis win assent,
When Miltiades shall next shirk Marathon,
Themistokles swap Salamis for — cake,
And Kimon grunt 'Peace, grant me dancing-
    girls!'
But sooner, hardly! twenty-five years since,
The war began, — such pleas for Peace have
    reached
A reasonable age. The end shows all!
And so with all the rest you advocate!
'Wise folk leave litigation! 'ware the wasps!
Whoso loves law and lawyers, heliast-like,
Wants hemlock!' None shows that so funnily.
But, once cure madness, how comports himself
Your sane exemplar, what's our gain thereby?
Philokleon turns Bdelukleon! just this change,—
New sanity gets straightway drunk as sow,
Cheats baker-wives, brawls, kicks, cuffs, curses
    folk,
Parades a shameless flute-girl, bandies filth
With his own son who cured his father's cold
By making him catch fever — funnily!
But as for curing love of lawsuits — faugh!

"And how does new improve upon the old
— Your boast — in even abusing? Rough, may
    be —
Still, honest was the old mode. 'Call thief —
    thief!'
But never call thief even — murderer!
Much less call fop and fribble, worse one whit

Than fribble and fop! Spare neither! beat
    your brains
For adequate invective, — cut the life
Clean out each quality, — but load your lash
With no least lie, or we pluck scourge from
    hand!
Does poet want a whipping, write bad verse,
Inculcate foul deeds? There's the fault to
    flog!
You vow, 'The rascal cannot read nor write,
Spends more in buying fish than Morsimos,
Somebody helps his Muse and courts his wife,
His uncle deals in crockery. and last —
Himself's a stranger!' That's the cap and
    crown
Of stinging-nettle, that's the master-stroke!
What poet-rival, — after 'housebreaker,'
'Fish-gorging,' 'midnight footpad,' and so
    forth, —
Proves not, beside, 'a stranger'? Chased from
    charge
To charge, and, lie by lie, laughed out of
    court, —
Lo, wit's sure refuge, satire's grand resource —
All, from Kratinos downward — 'strangers'
    they!
Pity the trick's too facile! None so raw
Among your playmates but have caught the
    ball
And sent it back as briskly to — yourself!
You too, my Attic, are styled 'stranger' —
    Rhodes,
Aigina, Lindos or Kameiros, — nay,
'T was Egypt reared (if Eupolis be right)
Who wrote the comedy (Kratinos vows)
Kratinos helped a little! Kleon's self
Was nigh promoted Comic, when he haled
My poet into court, and o'er the coals
Hauled and re-hauled 'the stranger, — insolent,
Who brought out plays, usurped our privilege!'
Why must you Comics one and all take stand
On lower ground than truth from first to last?
Why all agree to let folk disbelieve,
So laughter but reward a funny lie?
Repel such onslaughts — answer, sad and grave,
Your fancy-fleerings — who would stoop so low?
Your own adherents whisper, — when disgust
Too menacingly thrills Logeion through
At — Perikles invents this present war
Because men robbed his mistress of three
    maids —
Or — Sokrates wants burning, house o'er
    head, —
'What, so obtuse, not read between the lines?
Our poet means no mischief! All should
    know —
Ribaldry here implies a compliment!
He deals with things, not men, — his men are
    things —
Each represents a class, plays figure-head
And names the ship: no meaner than the first
Would serve; he styles a trireme "Sokrates"—
Fears "Sokrates" may prove unseaworthy,
(That's merely — "Sophists are the bane of
    boys")
Rat-riddled ("they are capable of theft")
Rotten or whatsoe'er shows ship-disease,
("They war with gods and worship whirligig.")

You never took the joke for earnest? scarce
Supposed mere figure-head meant entire ship,
And Sokrates — the whole fraternity? '

" This then is Comedy, our sacred song,
Censor of vice, and virtue's guard as sure :
Manners-instructing, morals' stop-estray,
Which, born a twin with public liberty,
Thrives with its welfare, dwindles with its
      wane !
Liberty? what so exquisitely framed
And fitted to suck dry its life of life
To last faint fibre? — since that life is truth.
You who profess your indignation swells
At sophistry, when specious words confuse
Deeds right and wrong, distinct before, you
      say —
(Though all that's done is — dare veracity,
Show that the true conception of each deed
Affirmed, in vulgar parlance, ' wrong ' or ' right,'
Proves to be neither, as the hasty hold,
But, change your side, shoots light, where dark
      alone
Was apprehended by the vulgar sense) —
You who put sophistry to shame, and shout
' There's but a single side to man and thing ;
A side so much more big than thing or man
Possibly can be, that — believe 't is true ?
Such were too marvellous simplicity ! ' —
Confess, those sophists whom yourself depict,
(— Abide by your own painting !) what they
      teach,
They wish at least their pupil to believe,
And, what believe, to practise ! Did *you* wish
Hellas should haste, as taught, with torch in
      hand,
And fire the horrid Speculation-shop ?
Straight the shop's master rose and showed the
      mob
What man was your so monstrous Sokrates ;
Himself received amusement, why not they ?
Just as did Kleon first play magistrate
And bid you put your birth in evidence —
Since no unbadged buffoon is licensed here
To shame us all when foreign guests may mock —
Then, — birth established, fooling licensed you, —
He, duty done, resumed mere auditor.
Laughed with the loudest at his Lamia-shape,
Kukloboros-roaring, and the camel-rest.
Nay, Aristullos, — once your volley spent
On the male-Kirké and her swinish crew, —
PLATON, — so others call the youth we love, —
Sends your performance to the curious king —
' Do you desire to know Athenai's knack
At turning seriousness to pleasantry ?
Read this ! One Aristullos means myself.
The author is indeed a merry grig ! '
Nay, it would seem as if yourself were bent
On laying down the law, ' Tell lies I must —
Aforethought and of purpose, no mistake ! '
When forth yourself step, tell us from the stage,
' Here you behold the King of Comedy —
Me, who, the first, have purged my every piece
From each and all my predecessors' filth,
Abjured those satyr-adjuncts sewn to bid
The boys laugh, satyr-jokes whereof not one
Least sample but would make my hair turn
      gray

Beyond a twelvemonth's ravage ! I renounce
Mountebank-claptrap, such as firework-fizz
And torchflare, or else nuts and barleycorns
Scattered among the crowd, to scramble for
And stop their mouths with ; no such stuff
      shames me !
Who — what's more serious — know both when
      to strike
And when to stay my hand : once dead, my foe,
Why, done, my fighting ! *I* attack a corpse ?
I spare the corpse-like even ! punish age ?
I pity from my soul that sad effete
Toothless old mumbler called Kratinos ! once
My rival, — now, alack, the dotard slinks
Ragged and hungry to what hole's his home ;
Ay, slinks through byways where no passenger
Flings him a bone to pick. You formerly
Adored the Muses' darling : dotard now,
Why, he may starve ! O mob most mutable ! '
So you harangued in person ; while, — to point
Precisely out, these were but lies you
      launched, —
Prompt, a play followed primed with satyr-
      frisks,
No spice spared of the stomach-turning stew,
Full-fraught with torch-display, and barley-
      throw,
And Kleon, dead enough, bedaubed afresh ;
While daft Kratinos — home to hole trudged he,
Wrung dry his wit to the last vinous dregs,
Decanted them to ' Bottle,' — beat, next
      year, —
' Bottle ' and dregs — your best of ' Clouds '
      and dew !
Where, Comic King, may keenest eye detect
Improvement on your predecessors' work
Except in lying more audaciously ?

" Why — genius ! That's the grandeur, that's
      the gold —
That's *you* — superlatively true to touch —
Gold, leaf or lump — gold, anyhow the mass
Takes manufacture and proves Pallas' casque
Or, at your choice, simply a cask to keep
Corruption from decay. Your rivals' hoard
May ooze forth, lacking such preservative :
Yours cannot — gold plays guardian far too
      well !
Genius, I call *you* : dross, your rivals share ;
Ay, share and share alike, too ! says the world,
However you pretend supremacy
In aught beside that gold, your very own.
Satire ? ' Kratinos for our satirist ! '
The world cries. Elegance ? ' Who elegant
As Eupolis ? ' resounds as noisily.
Artistic fancy ? Choros-creatures quaint ?
Magnes invented ' Birds ' and ' Frogs ' enough ,
Archippos punned, Hegemon parodied,
To heart's content, before you stepped on stage.
Moral invective ? Eupolis exposed
' That prating beggar, he who stole the cup,'
Before your ' Clouds ' rained grime on Sokrates ;
Nay, what beat ' Clouds ' but ' Konnos,' muck
      for mud ?
Courage ? How long before, well-masked, you
      poured
Abuse on Eukrates and Lusikles,
Did Telekleides and Hermippos pelt

Their Perikles and Kumon ? standing forth,
Bareheaded, not safe crouched behind a
name, —
Philonides or else Kallistratos,
Put forth, when danger threatened, — mask for
face,
To bear the brunt, — if blame fell, take the
blame, —
If praise . . . why, frank laughed Aristoph-
anes
' They write such rare stuff ? No, I promise
you ! '
Rather, I see all true improvements, made
Or making, go against you — tooth and nail
Contended with ; 't is still Moruchides,
'T is Euthumenes, Surakosios, nay,
Argurrhios and Kinesias, — common sense
And public shame, these only cleanse your sty !
Coerced, prohibited, — you grin and bear,
And, soon as may be, hug to heart again
The banished nastiness too dear to drop !
Krates could teach and practise festive song
Yet scorn scurrility ; as gay and good,
Pherekrates could follow. *Who* loosed hold,
Must let fall rose-wreath, stoop to muck once
more ?
Did your particular self advance in aught,
Task the sad genius — steady slave the while —
To further — say, the patriotic aim ?
No, there 's deterioration manifest
Year by year, play by play ! survey them all,
From that boy's-triumph when ' Acharnes '
dawned,
To ' Thesmophoriazousai,' — this man's-shame !
There, truly, patriot zeal so prominent
Allowed friends' plea perhaps : the baser stuff
Was but the nobler spirit's vehicle.
Who would imprison, unvolatilize
A violet's perfume, blends with fatty oils
Essence too fugitive in flower alone ;
So, calling unguent — violet, call the play —
Obscenity impregnated with ' Peace ' !
But here 's the boy grown bald, and here 's the
play
With twenty years' experience : where 's one
spice
Of odor in the hogs'-lard ? what pretends
To aught except a grease-pot's quality ?
Friend, sophist-hating ! know, — worst sophistry
Is when man's own soul plays its own self false,
Reasons a vice into a virtue, pleads
' I detail sin to shame its author ' — not
' I shame Ariphrades for sin's display ! '
' I show Opora to commend Sweet Home ' —
Not ' I show Bacchis for the striplings' sake ! '

" Yet all the same — O genius and O gold —
Had genius ne'er diverted gold from use
Worthy the temple, to do copper's work
And coat a swine's trough — which abundantly
Might furnish Phoibos' tripod, Pallas' throne !
Had you, I dream, discarding all the base,
The brutish, spurned alone convention's watch
And ward against invading decency
Disguised as license, law in lawlessness,
And so, re-ordinating outworn rule,
Made Comedy and Tragedy combine,
Prove some new Both-yet-neither, all one bard,

Euripides with Aristophanes
Co-operant ! this, reproducing Now
As that gave Then existence : Life to-day,
This, as that other — Life dead long ago !
The mob decrees such feat no crown, perchance,
But — why call crowning the reward of quest ?
Tell him, my other poet, ·· where thou walk'st
Some rarer world than e'er Ilissos washed !

" But dream goes idly in the air. To earth !
Earth's question just amounts to — which suc-
ceeds,
Which fails of two life-long antagonists ?
Suppose my charges all mistake ! assume
Your end, despite ambiguous means, the best --
The only ! you and he, a patriot-pair,
Have striven alike for one result — say, Peace !
You spoke your best straight to the arbiters —
Our people : have you made them end this war
By dint of laughter and abuse and lies
And postures of Opora ? Sadly — No !
This war, despite your twenty-five years' work,
May yet endure until Athenai falls,
And freedom falls with her. So much for you !
Now, the antagonist Euripides —
Has he succeeded better ? Who shall say ?
He spoke quite o'er the heads of Kleon's crowd
To a dim future, and if there he fail,
Why, you are fellows in adversity.
But that 's unlike the fate of wise words
launched
By music on their voyage. Hail, Depart,
Arrive, Glad Welcome ! Not my single wish —
Yours also wafts the white sail on its way,
Your nature too is kingly. All beside
I call pretension, — no true potentate,
Whatever intermediary be crowned,
Zeus or Poseidon, where the vulgar sky
Lacks not Triballos to complete the group.
I recognize — behind such phantom-crew —
Necessity, Creation, Poet's Power,
Else never had I dared approach, appeal
To poetry, power, Aristophanes !
But I trust truth's inherent kingliness,
Trust who, by reason of much truth, shall
reign
More or less royally — may prayer but push
His sway past limit, purge the false from true !
Nor, even so, had boldness nerved my tongue
But that the other king stands suddenly,
In all the grand investiture of death,
Bowing your knee beside my lowly head —
Equals one moment !

" Now, arise and go !
Both have done homage to Euripides ! "

Silence pursued the words : till he broke out —

" Scarce so ! This constitutes, I may believe,
Sufficient homage done by who defames
Your poet's foe, since you account me such ;
But homage-proper, — pay it by defence
Of him, direct defence and not oblique,
Not by mere mild admonishment of me ! "

" Defence ? The best, the only ! " I replied.
" A story goes — When Sophokles, last year,

Cited before tribunal by his son
(A poet — to complete the parallel),
Was certified unsound of intellect,
And claimed as only fit for tutelage,
Since old and doting and incompetent
To carry on this world's work, — the defence
Consisted just in his reciting (calm
As the verse bore, which sets our heart a-swell
And voice a-heaving too tempestuously)
That choros-chant ' The station of the steed,
Stranger ! thou comest to, — Kolonos white ! '
Then he looked round and all revolt was dead.
You know the one adventure of my life —
What made Euripides Balaustion's friend.
When I last saw him, as he bade farewell,
' I sang another " Herakles," ' smiled he ;
' It gained no prize : your love be prize I gain !
Take it — the tablets also where I traced
The story first with stulos pendent still —
Nay, the psalterion may complete the gift,
So, should you croon the ode bewaiing Age,
Yourself shall modulate — same notes, same
    strings —
With the old friend who loved Balaustion once.'
There they lie ! When you broke our solitude,
We were about to honor him once more
By reading the consummate Tragedy.
Night is advanced ; I have small mind to sleep ;
May I go on, and read, — so make defence,
So test true godship ? You affirm, not I,
— Beating the god, affords such test : I hold
That when rash hands but touch divinity,
The chains drop off, the prison-walls dispart,
And — fire — he fronts mad Pentheus ! Dare we
    try ? "

Accordingly I read the perfect piece.

HERAKLES

Amphitruon. Zeus' Couchmate, — who of
    mortals knows not me,
Argive Amphitruon whom Alkaios sired
Of old, as Perseus him, I — Herakles ?
My home, this Thebai where the earth-born
    spike
Of Sown-ones burgeoned: Ares saved from
    these
A handful of their seed that stocks to-day
With children's children Thebai, Kadmos
    built.
Of these had Kreon birth, Menoikeus' child,
King of the country, — Kreon that became
The father of this woman, Megara,
Whom, when time was, Kadmeians one and all
Pealed praise to, marriage-songs with fluted
    help,
While to my dwelling that grand Herakles
Bore her, his bride. But, leaving Thebes —
    where I
Abode perforce — this Megara and those
Her kinsmen, the desire possessed my son
Rather to dwell in Argos, that walled work,
Kuklopian city, which I fly, myself,
Because I slew Elektruon. Seeking so
To ease away my hardships and once more
Inhabit his own land, for my return

Heavy the price he pays Eurustheus there —
The letting in of light on this choked world !
Either he promised, vanquished by the goad
Of Heré, or because fate willed it thus.
The other labors — why, he toiled them
    through ;
But for this last one — down by Tainaros,
Its mouth, to Haides' realm descended he
To drag into the light the three-shaped hound
Of Hell: whence Herakles returns no more.
Now, there 's an old-world tale, Kadmeians
    have,
How Dirké's husband was a Lukos once,
Holding the seven-towered city here in sway
Before they ruled the land, white - steeded
    pair,
The twins Amphion, Zethos, born to Zeus.
This Lukos' son, — named like his father too,
No born Kadmeian but Euboia's gift, —
Comes and kills Kreon, lords it o'er the land,
Falling upon our town sedition-sick.
To us, akin to Kreon, just that bond
Becomes the worst of evils, seemingly ;
For, since my son in the earth's abysms,
This man of valor, Lukos, lord and king,
Seeks now to slay these sons of Herakles,
And slay his wife as well, — by murder thus
Thinking to stamp out murder, — slay too me,
(If me 't is fit you count among men still, —
Useless old age,) and all for fear lest these,
Grown men one day, exact due punishment
Of blo 'dshed and their mother's father's fate.
I theref re, since he leaves me in these domes,
The children's household guardian, — left, when
    earth's
Dark dread he underwent, that son of mine, —
I, with their mother, lest his boys should die,
Sit at this altar of the savior Zeus
Which, glory of triumphant spear, he raised
Conquering — my nobly-born ! — the Minuai.
Here do we guard our station, destitute
Of all things, drink, food, raiment, on bare
    ground
Couched side by side : sealed out of house and
    home
Sit we in a resourcelessness of help.
Our friends — why, some are no true friends, I
    see !
The rest, that are true, want the means to aid.
So operates in man adversity :
Whereof may never anybody — no,
Though half of him should really wish me
    well, —
Happen to taste ! a friend-test faultless, that !
    Megara. Old man, who erst did raze the Ta-
    phian town,
Illustriously, the army-leader, thou,
Of speared Kadmeians — how gods play men
    false !
I, now, missed nowise fortune in my sire,
Who, for his wealth, was boasted mighty once,
Having supreme rule, — for the love of which
Leap the long lances forth at favored breasts, —
And having children too : and me he gave
Thy son, his house with that of Herakles
Uniting by the far-famed marriage-bed.
And now these things are dead and flown away
While thou and I await our death, old man,

These Herakleian boys too, whom — my chicks —
I save beneath my wings like brooding bird.
But one or other falls to questioning.
"O mother," cries he, "where in all the world
Is father gone to? What's he doing? when
Will he come back?" At fault through tender years,
They seek their sire. For me, I put them off,
Telling them stories; at each creak of doors,
All wonder "Does he come?" — and all a-foot
Make for the fall before the parent knee.
Now then, what hope, what method of escape
Facilitatest thou? — for, thee, old man,
I look to, — since we may not leave by stealth
The limits of the land, and guards, more strong
Than we, are at the outlets: nor in friends
Remain to us the hopes of safety more.
Therefore, whatever thy decision be,
Impart it for the common good of all!
Lest now should prove the proper time to die,
Though, being weak, we spin it out and live.

Amph. Daughter, it scarce is easy, do one's best,
To blurt out counsel, things at such a pass.
Meg. You want some sorrow more, or so love life?
Amph. I both enjoy life, and love hopes beside.
Meg. And I; but hope against hope — no, old man!
Amph. In these delayings of an ill lurks cure.
Meg. But bitter is the meantime, and it bites.
Amph. Oh, there may be a run before the wind
From out these present ills, for me and thee,
Daughter, and yet may come my son, thy spouse!
But hush! and from the children take away
Their founts aflow with tears, and talk them calm,
Steal them by stories — sad theft, all the same!
For, human troubles — they grow weary too;
Neither the wind-blasts always have their strength,
Nor happy men keep happy to the end:
Since all things change — their natures part in twain;
And that man's bravest therefore, who hopes on,
Hopes ever: to despair is coward-like.
Choros. These domes that overroof,
This long-used couch, I come to, having made
A staff my prop, that song may put to proof
The swan-like power, age-whitened, — poet's aid
Of sobbed-forth dirges — words that stand aloof
From action now: such am I — just a shade
With night for all its face, a mere night-dream —
And words that tremble too: howe'er they seem,
Devoted words, I deem.

O of a father ye unfathered ones,
O thou old man, and thou whose groaning stuns —
Unhappy mother — only us above,
Nor reaches him below in Haides' realm, thy love!
— (Faint not too soon, urge forward foot and limb
Way-weary, nor lose courage — as some horse
Yoked to the car whose weight recoils on him
Just at the rock-ridge that concludes his course!
Take by the hand, the peplos, any one
Whose foothold fails him, printless and fordone!
Aged, assist along me aged too,
Who, — mate with thee in toils when life was new,
And shields and spears first made acquaintanceship, —
Stood by thyself and proved no bastard-slip
Of fatherland when loftiest glory grew.) —
See now, how like the sire's
Each eyeball fiercely fires!
What though ill-fortune have not left his race?
Neither is gone the grand paternal grace!
Hellas! O what — what combatants, destroyed
In these, wilt thou one day seek — seek, and find all void!

Pause! for I see the ruler of this land,
Lukos, now passing through the palace-gate.
Lukos. The Herakleian couple — father, wife —
If needs I must, I question: "must" forsooth?
Being your master — all I please, I ask.
To what time do you seek to spin out life?
What hope, what help see, so as not to die?
Is it you trust the sire of these, that's sunk
In Haides, will return? How past the pitch,
Suppose you have to die, you pile the woe —
Thou, casting, Hellas through, thy empty vaunts
As though Zeus helped thee to a god for son;
And thou, that thou wast styled our best man's wife!
Where was the awful in his work wound up,
If he did quell and quench the marshy snake
Or the Nemeian monster whom he snared
And — says, by throttlings of his arm, he slew?
With these do you outwrestle me? Such feats
Shall save from death the sons of Herakles
Who got praise, being naught, for bravery
In wild-beast-battle, otherwise a blank?
No man to throw on left arm buckler's weight,
Not he, nor get in spear's reach! bow he bore —
True coward's-weapon: shoot first and then fly!
No bow-and-arrow proves a man is brave,
But who keeps rank, — stands, one unwinking stare
As, ploughing up, the darts come, — brave is he.
My action has no impudence, old man!
Providence, rather: for I own I slew
Kreon, this woman's sire, and have his seat.
Nowise I wish, then, to leave, these grown up,

.Avengers on me, payment for my deeds.

   Amph. As to the part of Zeus in his own
      child,
Let Zeus defend that! As to mine, 't is me
The care concerns to show by argument
The folly of this fellow, — Herakles,
Whom I stand up for! since to hear thee
    styled —
Cowardly — that is unendurable.
First then, the infamous (for I account
Amongst the words denied to human speech,
Timidity ascribed thee, Herakles!)
This I must put from thee, with gods in proof.
Zeus' thunder I appeal to, those four steeds
Whereof he also was the charioteer
When, having shut down the earth's Giant-
    growth —
(Never shaft flew but found and fitted flank) —
Triumph he sang in common with the gods.
The Kentaur-race, four-footed insolence —
Go ask at Pholoé, vilest thou of kings,
Whom they would pick out and pronounce best
    man,
If not my son, "the seeming-brave," say'st
    thou!
But Dirphus, thy Abantid mother-town,
Question her, and she would not praise, I
    think!
For there's no spot, where having done some
    good,
Thy country thou might'st call to witness
    worth.
Now, that allwise invention, archer's-gear,
Thou blamest: hear my teaching and grow
    sage!
A man in armor is his armor's slave,
And, mixed with rank and file that want to
    run,
He dies because his neighbors have lost heart.
Then, should he break his spear, no way
    remains
Of warding death off, — gone that body-guard,
His one and only; while, whatever folk
Have the true bow-hand, — here's the one main
    good, —
Though he have sent ten thousand shafts
    abroad,
Others remain wherewith the archer saves
His limbs and life, too, — stands afar and
    wards
Away from flesh the foe that vainly stares
Hurt by the viewless arrow, while himself
Offers no full front to those opposite,
But keeps in thorough cover: there's the
    point
That's capital in combat — damage foe,
Yet keep a safe skin — foe not out of reach
As you are! Thus my words contrast with
    thine,
And such, in judging facts, our difference.
These children, now, why dost thou seek to
    slay?
What have they done thee? In a single point
I count thee wise — if, being base thyself,
Thou dread'st the progeny of nobleness,
Yet this bears hard upon us, all the same,
If we must die — because of fear in thee —
A death 't were fit thou suffer at our hands,

Thy betters, did Zeus rightly judge us all.
If therefore thou art bent on sceptre-sway,
Thyself, here — suffer us to leave the land,
Fugitives! nothing do by violence,
Or violence thyself shalt undergo
When the gods' gale may chance to change for
    thee!
Alas, O land of Kadmos, — for 't is thee
I mean to close with, dealing out the due
Revilement, — in such sort dost thou defend
Herakles and his children? Herakles
Who, coming, one to all the world, against
The Minuai, fought them and left Thebes an
    eye
Unblinded henceforth to front freedom with!
Neither do I praise Hellas, nor shall brook
Ever to keep in silence that I count
Towards my son, craven of cravens — her
Whom it behooved go bring the young ones
    here
Fire, spears, arms — in exchange for seas made
    safe,
And cleansings of the land, his labor's price.
But fire, spears, arms, — O children, neither
    Thebes
Nor Hellas has them for you! 'T is myself,
A feeble friend, ye look to: nothing now
But a tongue's murmur, for the strength is
    gone
We had once, and with age are limbs a-shake
And force a-flicker! Were I only young,
Still with the mastery o'er bone and thew,
Grasping first spear that came, the yellow locks
Of this insulter would I bloody so —
Should send him skipping o'er the Atlantic
    bounds
Out of my arm's reach through poltroonery!

   Cho. Have not the really good folk starting-
    points
For speech to purpose, — though rare talkers
    they?

   Luk. Say thou against us words thou towerest
    with!
I, for thy words, will deal thee blows, their
    due.
Go, some to Helikon, to Parnasos
Some, and the clefts there! Bid the woodmen
    fell
Oak-trunks, and, when the same are brought
    inside
The city, pile the altar round with logs,
Then fire it, burn the bodies of them all,
That they may learn thereby, no dead man
    rules
The land here, but 't is I, by acts like these!
As for you, old sirs, who are set against
My judgments, you shall groan for — not alone
The Herakleian children, but the fate
Of your own house beside, when faring ill
By any chance: and you shall recollect
Slaves are you of a tyranny that 's mine!

   Cho. O progeny of earth, — whom Ares
    sowed
When he laid waste the dragon's greedy jaw —
Will ye not lift the staves, right-hand supports,
And bloody this man's irreligious head?
Who, being no Kadmeian, rules, — the
    wretch. —

Our easy youth : an interloper too !
But not of me, at least, shalt thou enjoy
Thy lordship ever ; nor my labor's fruit —
Hand worked so hard for — have ! A curse
  with thee,
Whence thou didst come, there go and tyran-
  nize !
For never while I live shalt thou destroy
The Herakleian children : not so deep
Hides he below ground, leaving thee their
  lord !
But we bear both of you in mind, — that thou,
The land's destroyer, dost possess the land,
While he who saved it, loses every right.
I play the busybody — for I serve
My dead friends when they need friends' ser-
  vice most ?
O right-hand, how thou yearnest to snatch
  spear
And serve indeed ! in weakness dies the wish,
Or I had stayed thee calling me a slave,
And nobly drawn my breath at home in Thebes
Where thou exultest ! — city that 's insane,
Sick through sedition and bad government,
Else never had she gained for master — thee !
  Meg. Old friends, I praise you : since a
    righteous wrath
For friend's sake well becomes a friend. But no!
On our account in anger with your lord,
Suffer no injury ! Hear my advice,
Amphitruon, if I seem to speak aright.
Oh, yes, I love my children ! how not love
What I brought forth, what toiled for ? and to
  die —
Sad I esteem too ; still, the fated way
Who stiffens him against, that man I count
Poor creature ; us, who are of other mood,
Since we must die, behooves us meet our death
Not burnt to cinders, giving foes the laugh —
To me, worse ill than dying, that ! we owe
Our houses many a brave deed, now to pay.
Thee, indeed, gloriously men estimate
For spear-work, so that unendurable
Were it that thou shouldst die a death of
  shame.
And for my glorious husband, where wants he
A witness that he would not save his boys
If touched in their good fame thereby ? since
  birth
Bears ill with baseness done for children's
  sake,
My husband needs must be my pattern here.
See now thy hope — how much I count thereon !
Thou thinkest that thy son will come to light :
And, of the dead, who came from Haides
  back ?
But we with talk this man might mollify :
Never ! Of all foes, fly the foolish one !
Wise, well-bred people, make concession to !
Sooner you meet respect by speaking soft.
Already it was in my mind — perchance
We might beg off these children's banishment ;
But even that is sad, involving them
In safety, ay — and piteous poverty !
Since the host's visage for the flying friend
Has, only one day, the sweet look, 't is said.
Dare with us death, which waits thee, dared or
  no !

We call on thine ancestral worth, old man !
For who out-labors what the gods appoint
Shows energy, but energy gone mad.
Since what must — none e'er makes what must
  not be !
  Cho. Had any one, while yet my arms were
    strong,
Been scorning thee, he easily had ceased.
But we are naught, now ; thine henceforth to
  see —
Amphitruon, how to push aside these fates !
  Amph. Nor cowardice nor a desire of life
Stops me from dying : but I seek to save
My son his children. Vain ! I set my heart,
It seems, upon impossibility.
See, it is ready for the sword, this throat
To pierce, divide, dash down from precipice !
But one grace grant us, king, we supplicate !
Slay me and this unhappy one before
The children, lest we see them — impious
  sight ! —
Gasping the soul forth, calling all the while
On mother and on father's father ! Else,
Do as thy heart inclines thee ! No resource
Have we from death, and we resign ourselves.
  Meg. And I too supplicate : add grace to
    grace,
And, though but one man, doubly serve us
  both !
Let me bestow adornment of the dead
Upon these children ! Throw the palace wide !
For now we are shut out. Thence these shall
  share
At least so much of wealth was once their
  sire's !
  Luk. These things shall be. Withdraw the
    bolts, I bid
My servants ! Enter and adorn yourselves !
I grudge no peploi ; but when these ye wind
About your bodies, — that adornment done, —
Then I shall come and give you to the grave.
  Meg. O children, follow this unhappy foot,
Your mother's, into your ancestral home,
Where others have the power, are lords in
  truth,
Although the empty name is left us yet !
  Amph. O Zeus, in vain I had thee marriage-
    mate,
In vain I called thee father of my child !
Thou wast less friendly far than thou didst
  seem.
I, the mere man, o'ermatch in virtue thee
The mighty god : for I have not betrayed
The Herakleian children, — whereas thou
Hadst wit enough to come clandestinely
Into the chamber, take what no man gave,
Another's place ; and when it comes to help
Thy loved ones, there thou lackest wit indeed !
Thou art some stupid god or born unjust.
  Cho. Even a dirge, can Phoibos suit
In song to music jubilant
For all its sorrow : making shoot
His golden plectron o'er the lute,
Melodious ministrant.   .
And I, too, am of mind to raise,
Despite the imminence of doom,
A song of joy, outpour my praise
To him — what is it rumor says ? —

Whether — now buried in the ghostly gloom
Below ground — he was child of Zeus indeed,
Or mere Amphitruon's mortal seed —
To him I weave the wreath of song, his labor's
    meed.
For, is my hero perished in the feat ? .
The virtues of brave toils, in death complete,
These save the dead in song, — their glory-
    garland meet !

First, then, he made the wood
Of Zeus a solitude,
Slaying its lion-tenant ; and he spread
The tawniness behind — his yellow head
Enmuffled by the brute's, backed by that grin
    of dread.
The mountain-roving savage Kentaur-race
He strewed with deadly bow about their place,
Slaying with wingèd shafts : Peneios knew,
Beauteously-eddying, and the long tracts too
Of pasture trampled fruitless, and as well
Those desolated haunts Mount Pelion under,
And, grassy up to Homolé, each dell
Whence, having filled their hands with pine-
    tree plunder,
Horse-like was wont to prance from, and sub-
    due
The land of Thessaly, that bestial crew.
The golden-headed spot-back'd stag he slew,
That robber of the rustics : glorified
Therewith the goddess who in hunter's pride
Slaughters the game along Oinoé's side.
And, yoked abreast, he brought the chariot-
    breed
To pace submissive to the bit, each steed
That in the bloody cribs of Diomede
Champed and, unbridled, hurried down that
    gore
For grain, exultant the dread feast before —
Of man's flesh: hideous feeders they of yore !
All as he crossed the Hebros' silver-flow
Accomplished he such labor, toiling so
For Mukenaian tyrant ; ay, and more —
He crossed the Melian shore
And, by the sources of Amauros, shot
To death that strangers'-pest
Kuknos, who dwelt in Amphanaia : not
Of fame for good to guest !

And next, to the melodious maids he came,
Inside the Hesperian court-yard : hand must
    aim
At plucking gold fruit from the appled leaves,
Now he had killed the dragon, backed like
    flame,
Who guards the unapproachable he weaves
Himself all round, one spire about the same.
And into those sea-troughs of ocean dived
The hero, and for mortals calm contrived,
Whatever oars should follow in his wake.
And under heaven's mid-seat his hands thrust
    he,
At home with Atlas: and, for valor's sake,
Held the gods up their star-faced mansionry.
Also, the rider-host of Amazons
About Maiotis many-streamed, he went
To conquer through the billowy Euxin once,
Having collected what an armament

Of friends from Hellas, all on conquest bent
Of that gold-garnished cloak, dread girdle-
    chase !
So Hellas gained the girl's barbarian grace
And at Mukenai saves the trophy still —
Go wonder there, who will !

And the ten-thousand-headed hound
Of many a murder, the Lernaian snake
He burned out, head by head, and cast around
His darts a poison thence, — darts soon to
    slake
Their rage in that three-bodied herdsman's gore
Of Erutheia. Many a running more
He made for triumph and felicity,
And, last of toils, to Haides, never dry
Of tears, he sailed : and there he, luckless, ends
His life completely, nor returns again.
The house and home are desolate of friends,
And where the children's life-path leads them,
    plain
I see, — no step retraceable, no god
Availing, and no law to help the lost !
The oar of Charon marks their period,
Waits to end all. Thy hands, these roofs ac-
    cost ! —
To thee, though absent, look their uttermost !

But if in youth and strength I flourished still,
Still shook the spear in fight, did power match
    will
In these Kadmeian co-mates of my age,
They would, — and I, — when warfare was to
    wage,
Stand by these children ; but I am bereft
Of youth now, lone of that good genius left !

But hist, desist ! for here come these, —
Draped as the dead go, under and over, —
Children long since — now hard to discover —
Of the once so potent Herakles !
And the loved wife dragging, in one tether
About her feet, the boys together ;
And the hero's aged sire comes last !
Unhappy that I am ! Of tears which rise, —
How am I all unable to hold fast,
Longer, the aged fountains of these eyes !
  Meg. Be it so ! Who is priest, who butcher
    here
Of these ill-fated ones, or stops the breath
Of me, the miserable ? Ready, see,
The sacrifice — to lead where Haides lives !
O children, we are led — no lovely team
Of corpses — age, youth, motherhood, all mixed !
O sad fate of myself and these my sons
Whom with these eyes I look at, this last time !
I, indeed, bore you: but for enemies
I brought you up to be a laughing-stock,
Matter for merriment, destruction-stuff !
Woe 's me !
Strangely indeed my hopes have struck me down
From what I used to hope about you once —
The expectation from your father's talk !
For thee, now, thy dead sire dealt Argos to:
Thou wast to have Eurustheus' house one day,
And rule Pelasgia where the fine fruits grow ;
And, for a stole of state, he wrapped about
Thy head with that the lion-monster bore,

That which himself went wearing armor-wise.
And thou wast King of Thebes — such chariots
  there !
Those plains I had for portion — all for thee,
As thou hadst coaxed them out of who gave
  birth
To thee, his boy : and into thy right hand
He thrust the guardian-club of Daidalos, —
Poor guardian proves the gift that plays thee
  false !
And upon thee he promised to bestow
Oichalia — what, with those far-shooting shafts,
He ravaged once ; and so, since three you were,
With threefold kingdoms did he build you up
To very towers, your father, — proud enough,
Prognosticating, from your manliness
In boyhood, what the manhood's self would be.
For my part, I was picking out for you
Brides, suiting each with his alliance — this
From Athens, this from Sparté, this from
  Thebes —
Whence, suited — as stern-cables steady ship —
You might have hold on life gods bless. All
  gone !
Fortune turns round and gives us — you, the
  Fates
Instead of brides — me, tears for nuptial baths,
Unhappy in my hoping ! And the sire
Of your sire — he prepares the marriage-feast
Befitting Haides who plays father now —
Bitter relationship ! Oh me ! which first —
Which last of you shall I to bosom fold ?
To whom shall I fit close, his mouth to mine ?
Of whom shall I lay hold and ne'er let go ?
How would I gather, like the brown-winged bee,
The groans from all, and, gathered into one,
Give them you back again, a crowded tear !
Dearest, if any voice be heard of men
Dungeoned in Haides, thee — to thee I speak !
Here is thy father dying, and thy boys !
And I too perish, famed as fortunate
By mortals once, through thee ! Assist them !
  Come !
But come ! though just a shade, appear to me !
For, coming, thy ghost-grandeur would suffice,
Such cowards are they in thy presence, these
Who kill thy children now thy back is turned !
  Amph. Ay, daughter, bid the powers below
  assist !
But I will rather, raising hand to heaven,
Call thee to help, O Zeus, if thy intent
Be, to these children, helpful anyway,
Since soon thou wilt be valueless enough !
And yet thou hast been called and called ; in
  vain
I labor : for we needs must die, it seems.
Well, aged brothers — life 's a little thing !
Such as it is, then, pass life pleasantly
From day to night, nor once grieve all the while !
Since Time concerns him not about our hopes,—
To save them, — but his own work done, flies off.
Witness myself, looked up to among men,
Doing noteworthy deeds : when here comes fate
Lifts me away, like feather skyward borne,
In one day ! Riches then and glory, — whom
These are found constant to, I know not.
  Friends,
Farewell ! the man who loved you all so much,

Now, this last time, my mates, ye look upon !
  Meg. Ha !
O father, do I see my dearest ? Speak !
  Amph. No more than thou canst, daughter —
  dumb like thee !
  Meg. Is this he whom we heard was under
  ground ?
  Amph. Unless at least some dream in day we
  see !
  Meg. What do I say ? what dreams insanely
  view ?
This is no other than thy son, old sire !
Here, children ! hang to these paternal robes,
Quick, haste, hold hard on him, since here 's
  your true
Zeus that can save — and every whit as well !
  Herakles. Oh, hail, my palace, my hearth's
  propula, —
How glad I see thee as I come to light !
Ha, what means this ? My children I behold
Before the house in garments of the grave,
Chapleted, and, amid a crowd of men,
My very wife — my father weeping too,
Whatever the misfortune ! Come, best take
My station nearer these and learn it all !
Wife, what new sorrow has approached our
  home ?
  Meg. O dearest ! light flashed on thy father
  now !
Art thou come ? art thou saved and dost thou
  fall
On friends in their supreme extremity ?
  Her. How say'st thou ? Father ! what 's the
  trouble here ?
  Meg. Undone are we ! — but thou, old man,
  forgive
If first I snatch what thou shouldst say to him !
For somehow womanhood wakes pity more.
Here are my children killed and I undone !
  Her. Apollon, with what preludes speech be-
  gins !
  Meg. Dead are my brothers and old father too,
  Her. How say'st thou ? — doing what ? — by
  spear-stroke whence ?
  Meg. Lukos destroyed them — the land's noble
  king !
  Her. Met them in arms ? or through the
  land's disease ?
  Meg. Sedition : and he sways seven-gated
  Thebes.
  Her. Why then came fear on the old man
  and thee ?
  Meg. He meant to kill thy father, me, our
  boys.
  Her. How say'st thou ? Fearing what from
  orphanage ?
  Meg. Lest they should some day pay back
  Kreon's death.
  Her. And why trick out the boys corpse-
  fashion thus ?
  Meg. These wraps of death we have already
  donned.
  Her. And you had died through violence ?
  Woe 's me !
  Meg. Left bare of friends : and thou wast
  dead, we heard.
  Her. And whence came on you this faint
  heartedness ?

Meg. The heralds of Eurustheus brought the news.

Her. And why was it you left my house and hearth?

Meg. Forced thence: thy father — from his very couch!

Her. And no shame at insulting the old man?

Meg. Shame, truly! no near neighbors *he* and Shame!

Her. And so much, in my absence, lacked I friends?

Meg. Friends, — are there any to a luckless man?

Her. The Minuai-war I waged, — they spat forth these?

Meg. Friendless — again I tell thee — is ill-luck.

Her. Will not you cast these hell-wraps from your hair
And look on light again, and with your eyes
Taste the sweet change from nether dark to day?
While I — for now there needs my handi-work —
First I shall go, demolish the abodes
Of these new lordships; next hew off the head
Accurst and toss it for the dogs to trail.
Then, such of the Kadmeians as I find
Were craven though they owed me grati-tude, —
Some I intend to handle with this club
Renowned for conquest; and with wingèd shafts
Scatter the others, fill Ismenos full
With bloody corpses, — Dirké's flow so white
Shall be incarnadined. For, whom, I pray,
Behooves me rather help than wife and child
And aged father? Farewell, "Labors" mine!
Vainly I wrought them: my true work lay here!
My business is to die defending these, —
If for their father's sake they meant to die.
Or how shall we call brave the battling it
With snake and lion, as Eurustheus bade,
If yet I must not labor death away
From my own children? "Conquering Her-akles"
Folk will not call me as they used, I think!
The right thing is for parents to assist
Children, old age, the partner of the couch.

Amph. True, son! thy duty is — be friend to friends
And foe to foes: yet — no more haste than needs!

Her. Why, father, what is over-hasty here?

Amph. Many a pauper — seeming to be rich,
As the word goes — the king calls partisan.
Such made a riot, ruined Thebes to rob
Their neighbor: for, what good they had at home
Was spent and gone, — flew off through idle-ness.
You came to trouble Thebes, they saw: since seen,
Beware lest, raising foes, a multitude,
You stumble where you apprehend no harm.

Her. If all Thebes saw me, not a whit care I.

But seeing as I did a certain bird
Not in the lucky seats, I knew some woe
Was fallen upon the house: so, purposely,
By stealth I made my way into the land.

Amph. And now, advancing, hail the hearth with praise
And give the ancestral home thine eye to see!
For he himself will come, thy wife and sons
The drag-forth — slaughter — slay me too, — this king!
But, here remaining, all succeeds with thee —
Gain lost by no false step. So, this thy town
Disturb not, son, ere thou right matters here!

Her. Thus will I do, for thou say'st well; my home
Let me first enter! Since at the due time
Returning from the unsunned depths where dwells
Haides' wife Koré, let me not affront
Those gods beneath my roof, I first should hail!

Amph. For didst thou really visit Haides, son?

Her. Ay — dragged to light, too, his three-headed beast.

Amph. By fight didst conquer — or through Koré's gift?

Her. Fight: well for me, I saw the Orgies first!

Amph. And is he in Eurustheus' house, the brute?

Her. Chthonia's grove, Hermion's city, holds him now.

Amph. Does not Eurustheus know thee back on earth?

Her. No: I would come first and see mat-ters here.

Amph. But how wast thou below ground such a time?

Her. I stopped, from Haides, bringing The-seus up.

Amph. And where is he? — bound o'er the plain for home?

Her. Gone glad to Athens — Haides' fugi-tive!
But, up, boys! follow father into house!
There's a far better going-in for you
Truly, than going-out was! Nay, take heart,
And let the eyes no longer run and run!
And thou, O wife, my own, collect thy soul
Nor tremble now! Leave grasping, all of you,
My garments! I'm not winged, nor fly from friends!
Ah, —
No letting go for these, who all the more
Hang to my garments! Did you foot indeed
The razor's edge? Why, then I'll carry them —
Take with my hands these small craft up, and tow
Just as a ship would. There! don't fear I shirk
My children's service! this way, men are men,
No difference! best and worst, they love their boys
After one fashion: wealth they differ in —
Some have it, others not; but each and all
Combine to form the children-loving race.

Cho. Youth is a pleasant burden to me ;
But age on my head, more heavily
Than the crags of Aitna, weighs and weighs,
And darkening cloaks the lids and intercepts
the rays.
Never be mine the preference
Of an Asian empire's wealth, nor yet
Of a house all gold, to youth, to youth
That 's beauty, whatever the gods dispense !
Whether in wealth we joy, or fret
Paupers, — of all God's gifts most beautiful, in
truth !

But miserable murderous age I hate !
Let it go to wreck, the waves adown,
Nor ever by rights plague tower or town
Where mortals bide, but still elate
With wings, on ether, precipitate,
Wander them round — nor wait !

But if the gods, to man's degree,
Had wit and wisdom, they would bring
Mankind a twofold youth, to be
Their virtue's sign-mark, all should see,
In those with whom life's winter thus grew
spring.
For when they died, into the sun once more
Would they have traversed twice life's race-
course o'er ;
While ignobility had simply run
Existence through, nor second life begun,
And so might we discern both bad and good
As surely as the starry multitude
Is numbered by the sailors, one and one.
But now the gods by no apparent line
Limit the worthy and the base define ;
Only, a certain period rounds, and so
Brings man more wealth, — but youthful vigor,
no !

Well ! I am not to pause
Mingling together — wine and wine in cup —
The Graces with the Muses up —
Most dulcet marriage : loosed from music's laws,
No life for me !
But where the wreaths abound, there ever may
I be !
And still, an aged bard, I shout Mnemosuné —
Still chant of Herakles the triumph-chant,
Companioned by the seven-stringed tortoise-
shell
And Libuan flute, and Bromios' self as well,
God of the grape, with man participant !
Not yet will we arrest their glad advance —
The Muses who so long have led me forth to
dance !
A paian — hymn the Delian girls indeed,
Weaving a beauteous measure in and out
His temple-gates, Latona's goodly seed ;
And paians — I too, these thy domes about,
From these gray cheeks, my king, will swan-
like shout —
Old songster ! Ay, in song it starts off brave —
" Zeus' son is he ! " and yet, such grace of birth
Surpassing far, to man his labors gave
Existence, one calm flow without a wave,
Having destroyed the beasts, the terrors of the
earth.

Luk. From out the house Amphitruon comes
— in time !
For 't is a long while now since ye bedecked
Your bodies with the dead-folks' finery.
But quick ! the boys and wife of Herakles —
Bid them appear outside this house, keep pact
To die, and need no bidding but your own !
Amph. King ! you press hard on me sore-
pressed enough,
And give me scorn — beside my dead ones here.
Meet in such matters were it, though you reign,
To temper zeal with moderation. Since
You do impose on us the need to die —
Needs must we love our lot, obey your will.
Luk. Where 's Megara, then ? Alkmené's
grandsons, where ?
Amph. She, I think, — as one figures from
outside, —
Luk. Well, this same thinking, — what af-
fords its ground ?
Amph. — Sits suppliant on the holy altar-
steps, —
Luk. Idly indeed a suppliant to save life !
Amph. — And calls on her dead husband,
vainly too !
Luk. For he 's not come, nor ever will arrive.
Amph. Never — at least, if no god raise him
up.
Luk. Go to her, and conduct her from the
house !
Amph. I should partake the murder, doing
that.
Luk. We, — since thou hast a scruple in the
case, —
Outside of fears, we shall march forth these
lads,
Mother and all. Here, follow me, my folk —
And gladly so remove what stops our toils !
Amph. Thou — go then ! March where needs
must ! What remains —
Perhaps concerns another. Doing ill,
Expect some ill be done thee !
                              Ha, old friends !
On he strides beautifully ! in the toils
O' the net, where swords spring forth, will he
be fast —
Minded to kill his neighbors — the arch-knave !
I go, too — I must see the falling corpse !
For he has sweets to give — a dying man,
Your foe, that pays the price of deeds he did.
Cho. Troubles are over ! He the great king
once,
Turns the point, tends for Haides, goal of life !
O justice, and the gods' back-flowing fate !
Amph. Thou art come, late indeed, where
death pays crime —
These insults heaped on better than thyself !
Cho. Joy gives this outburst to my tears :
Again
Come round those deeds, his doing, which of
old
He never dreamed himself was to endure —
King of the country ! But enough, old man !
Indoors, now, let us see how matters stand —
If somebody be faring as I wish !
Luk. Ah me — me !
Cho. This strikes the keynote — music to
my mind.

Merry i' the household! Death takes up the
    tune!
The king gives voice, groans murder's prelude
    well!
   Luk. O all the land of Kadmos! slain by
    guile!
   Clo. Ay, for who slew first? Paying back thy
    due,
Resign thee! make, for deeds done, mere
    amends!
Who was it grazed the gods through lawless-
    ness —
Mortal himself, threw up his fools'-conceit
Against the blessed heavenly ones — as though
Gods had no power? Old friends, the impious
    man
Exists not any more! The house is mute.
Turn we to song and dance! For, those I love,
Those I wish well to, well fare they, to wish!

Dances, dances and banqueting
To Thebes, the sacred city through,
Are a care! for, change and change
Of tears to laughter, old to new,
Our lays, glad birth, they bring, they bring!
He is gone and past, the mighty king!
And the old one reigns, returned — Oh, strange!
From the Acherontian harbor too!
Advent of hope, beyond thought's widest
    range!
To the gods, the gods, are crimes a care,
And they watch our virtue, well aware
That gold and that prosperity drive man
Out of his mind — those charioteers who hale
Might-without-right behind them: face who
    can
Fortune's reverse which time prepares, nor
    quail?
— He who evades law and in lawlessness
Delights him, — he has broken down his
    trust —
The chariot, riches haled — now blackening in
    the dust!

Ismenos, go thou garlanded!
Break into dance, ye ways, the polished bed
O' the seven-gated city! Dirké, thou
Fair-flowing, with the Asopiad sisters all,
Leave your sire's stream, attend the festival
Of Herakles, one choir of nymphs, sing triumph
    now!
O woody rock of Puthios and each home
O the Helikonian Muses, ye shall come
With joyous shouting to my walls, my town
Where saw the light that Spartan race, those
    "Sown,"
Brazen-shield-bearing chiefs, whereof the band
With children's children renovates our land,
To Thebes a sacred light!
O combination of the marriage rite —
Bed of the mortal-born and Zeus, who couched
Beside the nymph of Perseus' progeny!
For credible, past hope, becomes to me
That nuptial story long ago avouched,
O Zeus! and time has turned the dark to bright,
And made one blaze of truth the Herakleidan
    might —
His, who emerged from earth's pavilion, left

Plouton's abode, the nether palace-cleft.
Thou wast the lord that nature gave me — not
That baseness born and bred — my king, by lot!
— Baseness made plain to all, who now regard
The match of sword with sword in fight, —
If to the gods the Just and Right
Still pleasing be, still claim the palm's award.

Horror!
Are we come to the selfsame passion of fear,
Old friends? — such a phantasm fronts me here
Visible over the palace-roof!
In flight, the laggard limb
Bestir! and haste aloof
From that on the roof there — grand and grim!
O Paian, king!
Be thou my safeguard from the woeful thing!
   Iris. Courage, old men! beholding here —
    Night's birth —
Madness, and me the handmaid of the gods,
Iris: since to your town we come, no plague —
Wage war against the house of but one man
From Zeus and from Alkmené sprung, they say.
Now, till he made an end of bitter toils,
Fate kept him safe, nor did his father Zeus
Let us once hurt him, Heré nor myself.
But, since he has toiled through Eurustheus'
    task,
Heré desires to fix fresh blood on him —
Slaying his children: I desire it too.

Up then, collecting the unsoftened heart,
Unwedded virgin of black Night! Drive, drag
Frenzy upon the man here — whirls of brain
Big with child-murder, while his feet leap gay!
Let go the bloody cable its whole length!
So that, — when o'er the Acherousian ford
He has sent floating, by self-homicide,
His beautiful boy-garland, — he may know
First, Heré's anger, what it is to him,
And then learn mine. The gods are vile indeed
And mortal matters vast, if he 'scape free!
   Madness. Certes, from well-born sire and
    mother too
Had I my birth, whose blood is Night's and
    Heaven's;
But here 's my glory, — not to grudge the good!
Nor love I raids against the friends of man.
I wish, then, to persuade, — before I see
You stumbling, you and Heré! trust my
    words!
This man, the house of whom ye hound me to,
Is not unfamed on earth nor gods among;
Since, having quelled waste land and savage
    sea,
He alone raised again the falling rights
Of gods — gone ruinous through impious men.
Desire no mighty mischief, I advise!
   Iris. Give thou no thought to Heré's faulty
    schemes!
   Mad. Changing her step from faulty to
    fault-free!
   Iris. Not to be wise, did Zeus' wife send thee
    here!
   Mad. Sun, thee I cite to witness — doing
    what I loathe to do!
But since indeed to Heré and thyself I must
    subserve.

And follow you quick, with a whiz, as the
    hounds a-hunt with the huntsman,
— Go I will ! and neither the sea, as it groans
Nor earthquake, no, nor the bolt of thunder
    gasping out heaven's labor-throe,
Shall cover the ground as I, at a bound, rush
    with its waves so furiously,
    into the bosom of Herakles !
And home I scatter, and house I batter,
Having first of all made the children fall, —
And he who felled them is never to know
He gave birth to each child that received the
    blow,
Till the Madness, I am, have let him go !

Ha, behold, already he rocks his head — he is
    off from the starting-place !
Not a word, as he rolls his frightful orbs, from
    their sockets wrenched in the ghastly
    race !
And the breathings of him he tempers and
    times no more than a bull in act to toss,
And hideously he bellows invoking the Keres,
    daughters of Tartaros.
Ay, and I soon will dance thee madder, and
    pipe thee quite out of thy mind with fear !
So, up with the famous foot, thou Iris, march to
    Olumpos, leave me here !
Me and mine, who now combine, in the dread-
    ful shape no mortal sees,
And now are about to pass, from without, inside
    of the home of Herakles !
Cho. Ototototoi, — groan ! Away is mown
Thy flower, Zeus' offspring, City !
Unhappy Hellas, who dost cast (the pity !)
Who worked thee all the good,
Away from thee, — destroyest in a mood
Of madness him, to death whom pipings dance !
There goes she, in her chariot — groans, her
    brood —
And gives her team the goad, as though adrift
For doom, Night's Gorgon, Madness, she whose
    glance
Turns man to marble ! with what hissings lift
Their hundred heads the snakes, her head's in-
    heritance !
Quick has the god changed fortune : through
    their sire
Quick will the children, that he saved, ex-
    pire !
O miserable me ! O Zeus ! thy child —
Childless himself — soon vengeance, hunger-
    wild,
Craving for punishment, will lay how low —
Loaded with many a woe !

O palace-roofs ! your courts about,
A measure begins all unrejoiced
By the tympanies and the thyrsos hoist
Of the Bromian revel-rout !
O ye domes ! and the measure proceeds
For blood, not such as the cluster bleeds
Of the Dionusian pouring-out !

Break forth, fly, children ! fatal this —
Fatal the lay that is piped, I wis !
Ay, for he hunts a children-chase —
Never shall Madness lead her revel

And leave no trace in the dwelling-place !
Ai ai, because of the evil !
Ai ai, the old man — how I groan
For the father, and not the father alone !
She who was nurse of his children, — small
Her gain that they ever were born at all !

See ! See !
A whirlwind shakes hither and thither
The house — the roof falls in together !
Ha, ha ! what dost thou, son of Zeus ?
A trouble of Tartaros broke loose,
Such as once Pallas on the Titan thundered,
Thou sendest on thy domes, roof-shattered and
    wall-sundered !
    Messenger. O bodies white with age ! —
    Cho.   What cry, to me —
What, dost thou call with ?
    Mes.   There's a curse indoors !
    Cho. I shall not bring a prophet: you suffice !
    Mes. Dead are the children !
    Cho.   Ai ai !
    Mes.   Groan ! for, groans
Suit well the subject ! Dire the children's
    death,
Dire too the parent's hands that dealt the fate.
No one could tell worse woe than we have
    borne !
    Cho. How dost thou that same curse —
    curse, cause for groan
The father's on the children, make appear ?
Tell in what matter they were hurled from
    heaven
Against the house — these evils ; and recount
The children's hapless fate, O Messenger !
    Mes. The victims were before the hearth of
    Zeus
A household-expiation: since the king
O' the country, Herakles had killed and cast
From out the dwelling ; and a beauteous choir
Of boys stood by his sire, too, and his wife.
And now the basket had been carried round
The altar in a circle, and we used
The consecrated speech. Alkmené's son —
Just as he was about, in his right hand,
To bear the torch, that he might dip into
The cleansing-water — came to a stand-still ;
And, as their father yet delayed, his boys
Had their eyes on him. But he was himself
No longer : lost in rollings of the eyes ;
Out-thrusting eyes — their very roots — like
    blood !
Froth he dropped down his bushy-bearded
    cheek,
And said — together with a madman's laugh —
" Father ! why sacrifice, before I slay
Eurustheus ? why have twice the lustral fire,
And double pains, when 't is permitted me
To end, with one good hand-sweep, matters
    here ?
Then, — when I hither bring Eurustheus'
    head, —
Then for these just slain, wash hands once for
    all !
Now, — cast drink-offerings forth, throw bas-
    kets down !
Who gives me bow and arrows, who my club ?
I go to that Mukenai ! One must match

Crowbars and mattocks, so that — those sunk
    stones
The Kuklops squared with picks and plumb-line
    red —
I, with my bent steel, may o'ertumble town ! "
Which said, he goes and — with no car to
    have —
Affirms he has one ! mounts the chariot-board,
And strikes, as having really goad in hand !
And two ways laughed the servants — laugh
    with awe ;
And one said, as each met the other's stare,
" Playing us boys' tricks ? or is master mad ? "
But, up he climbs, and down along the roof,
And, dropping into the men's place, maintains
He 's come to Nisos city, when he 's come
Only inside his own house ! then reclines
On floor, for couch, and, as arrived indeed,
Makes himself supper ; goes through some
    brief stay,
Then says he 's traversing the forest-flats
Of Isthmos ; thereupon lays body bare
Of bucklings, and begins a contest with
— No one ! and is proclaimed the conqueror —
He by himself — having called out to hear
— Nobody ! Then, if you will take his word,
Blaring against Eurustheus horribly,
He 's at Mukenai. But his father laid
Hold of the strong hand and addressed him
    thus :
" O son, what ails thee ? Of what sort is this
Extravagance ? Has not some murder-craze,
Bred of those corpses thou didst just dispatch,
Danced thee drunk ? " But he, — taking him
    to crouch,
Eurustheus' sire, that apprehensive touched
His hand, a suppliant, — pushes him aside,
Gets ready quiver, and bends low against
His children — thinking them Eurustheus' boys
He means to slay. They, horrified with fear,
Rushed here and there, — this child, into the
    robes
O' the wretched mother, — this, beneath the
    shade
O' the column, — and this other, like a bird,
Cowered at the altar-foot. The mother shrieks,
" Parent — what dost thou ? — kill thy chil-
    dren ? " So
Shriek the old sire and crowd of servitors.
But he, outwinding him, as round about
The column ran the boy, a horrid whirl
O' the lathe his foot described ! — stands op-
    posite,
Strikes through the liver ! and supine the boy
Bedews the stone shafts, breathing out his life.
But " Victory " he shouted ! boasted thus :
" Well, this one nestling of Eurustheus —
    dead —
Falls by me, pays back the paternal hate ! "
Then bends bow on another who was crouched
At base of altar — overlooked, he thought —
And now prevents him, falls at father's knee,
Throwing up hand to beard and cheek above.
" O dearest ! " cries he, " father, kill me not !
Yours, I am — your boy : not Eurustheus' boy
You kill now ! " But he, rolling the wild eye
Of Gorgon, — as the boy stood all too close
For deadly bowshot, — mimicry of smith

Who batters red-hot iron, — hand o'er head
Heaving his club, on the boy's yellow hair
Hurls it and breaks the bone. This second
    caught, —
He goes, would slay the third, one sacrifice
He and the couple ; but, beforehand here,
The miserable mother catches up,
Carries him inside house and bars the gate.
Then he, as he were at those Kuklops' work,
Digs at, heaves doors up, wrenches doorposts
    out,
Lays wife and child low with the selfsame
    shaft.
And this done, at the old man's death he
    drives ;
But there came, as it seemed to us who saw,
A statue — Pallas with the crested head,
Swinging her spear — and threw a stone which
    smote
Herakles' breast and stayed his slaughter-rage,
And sent him safe to sleep. He falls to
    ground —
Striking against the column with his back —
Column which, with the falling of the roof,
Broken in two, lay by the altar-base.
And we, foot-free now from our several flights,
Along with the old man, we fastened bonds
Of rope-noose to the column, so that he,
Ceasing from sleep, might not go adding deeds
To deeds done. And he sleeps a sleep, poor
    wretch,
No gift of any god ! since he has slain
Children and wife. For me, I do not know
What mortal has more misery to bear.
    Cho. A murder there was which Argolis
Holds in remembrance, Hellas through,
As, at that time, best and famousest :
Of those, the daughters of Danaos slew.
A murder indeed was that ! but this
Outstrips it, straight to the goal has pressed.
I am able to speak of a murder done
To the hapless Zeus-born offspring, too —
Proknè's son, who had but one —
Or a sacrifice to the Muses, say
Rather, who Itus sing alway,
Her single child ! But thou, the sire
Of children three — O thou consuming fire ! —
In one outrageous fate hast made them all
    expire !
And this outrageous fate —
What groan, or wail, or deadmen's dirge,
Or choric dance of Haides shall I urge
The Muse to celebrate ?

Woe ! woe ! behold !
The portalled palace lies unrolled,
This way and that way, each prodigious fold !
Alas for me ! these children, see,
Stretched, hapless group, before their father —
    he
The all-unhappy, who lies sleeping out
The murder of his sons, a dreadful sleep !
And bonds, see, all about, —
Rope-tangle, ties and tether, — these
Tightenings around the body of Herakles
To the stone columns of the house made fast !

But — like a bird that grieves

For callow nestlings some rude hand bereaves —
See, here, a bitter journey overpast,
The old man — all too late — is here at last !
Amph. Silently, silently, aged Kadmeians !
Will ye not suffer my son, diffused
Yonder, to slide from his sorrows in sleep ?
Cho. And thee, old man, do I, groaning, weep,
And the children too, and the head there —
   used
Of old to the wreaths and paians !
Amph. Farther away ! Nor beat the breast,
Nor wail aloud, nor rouse from rest
The slumberer — asleep, so best !
Cho. Ah me — what a slaughter !
Amph.   Refrain — refrain !
Ye will prove my perdition !
Cho.   Unlike water,
Bloodshed rises from earth again !
Amph. Do I bid you bate your breath, in
   vain —
Ye elders ? Lament in a softer strain !
Lest he rouse himself, burst every chain,
And bury the city in ravage — bray
Father and house to dust away !
Cho. I cannot forbear — I cannot forbear !
Amph. Hush ! I will learn his breathings :
   there !
I will lay my ears close.
Cho.   What, he sleeps ?
Amph. Ay, — sleeps ! A horror of slumber
   keeps
The man who has piled
On wife and child
Death and death, as he shot them down
With clang o' the bow.
Cho.   Wail —
Amph.   Even so !
Cho. — The fate of the children —
Amph.   Triple woe !
Cho. — Old man, the fate of thy son !
Amph. Hush, hush ! Have done !
He is turning about !
He is breaking out !
Away ! I steal
And my body conceal,
Before he arouse,
In the depths of the house !
Cho. Courage ! The Night
Maintains her right
On the lids of thy son there, sealed from sight !
Amph. See, see ! To leave the light
And, wretch that I am, bear one last ill,
I do not avoid ; but if he kill
Me, his own father, and devise
Beyond the present miseries
A misery more ghastly still —
And to haunt him, over and above
Those here who, as they used to love,
Now hate him, what if he have with these
My murder, the worst of Erinues ?
Cho. Then was the time to die, for thee,
When ready to wreak in the full degree
Vengeance on those
Thy consort's foes
Who murdered her brothers ! glad, life's close,
With the Taphioi down,
And sacked their town
Clustered about with a wash of sea !

Amph. To flight — to flight !
Away from the house, troop off, old men !
Save yourselves out of the maniac's sight !
He is rousing himself right up : and then,
Murder on murder heaping anew,
He will revel in blood your city through !
Cho. O Zeus, why hast, with such unmeas-
   ured hate,
Hated thy son, whelmed in this sea of woes ?
Her. Ha, —
In breath indeed I am — see things I ought —
Æther, and earth, and these the sunbeam-
   shafts !
But then — some billow and strange whirl of
   sense
I have fallen into ! and breathings hot I
   breathe —
Smoked upwards, not the steady work from
   lungs.
See now ! Why, bound — at moorings like a
   ship, —
About my young breast and young arm, to this
Stone piece of carved work broke in half, do I
Sit, have my rest in corpses' neighborhood ?
Strewn on the ground are wingèd darts, and bow
Which played my brother-shieldman, held in
   hand, —
Guarded my side, and got my guardianship !
I cannot have gone back to Haides — twice
Begun Eurustheus' race I ended thence ?
But I nor see the Sisupheian stone,
Nor Plouton, nor Demeter's sceptred maid !
I am struck witless sure ! Where can I be ?
Ho there ! what friend of mine is near or far —
Some one to cure me of bewilderment ?
For naught familiar do I recognize.
Amph. Old friends, shall I go close to these
   my woes ?
Cho. Ay, and let me too, — nor desert your
   ills !
Her. Father, why weepest thou, and buriest
   up
Thine eyes, aloof so from thy much-loved son ?
Amph. O child ! — for, faring badly, mine
   thou art !
Her. Do I fare somehow ill, that tears should
   flow ?
Amph. Ill, — would cause any god who bore
   to groan !
Her. That's boasting, truly ! still, you state
   no hap.
Amph. For, thyself seest — if in thy wits
   again.
Her. Heyday ! How riddlingly that hint re-
   turns !
Amph. Well, I am trying — art thou sane and
   sound !
Her. Say if thou lay'st aught strange to my
   life's charge !
Amph. If thou no more art Haides-drunk, —
   I tell !
Her. I bring to mind no drunkenness of soul.
Amph. Shall I unbind my son, old men, or
   what ?
Her. And who was binder, tell ! — not *that*,
   my deed !
Amph. Mind that much of misfortune — past
   the rest !

Her. Enough! from silence, I nor learn nor
   wish.
Amph. O Zeus, dost witness here throned
   Heré's work?
Her. But have I had to bear aught hostile
   thence?
Amph. Let be the goddess — bury thine own
   guilt!
Her. Undone! What is the sorrow thou wilt
   say?
Amph. Look! See the ruins of thy children
   here!
Her. Ah me! What sight do wretched I be-
   hold?
Amph. Unfair fight, son, this fight thou fas-
   tenedst
On thine own children!
Her.   What fight? Who slew these?
Amph. Thou and thy bow, and who of gods
   was cause.
Her. How say'st? What did I? Ill-announ-
   cing sire!
Amph. — Go mad! Thou askest a sad clear-
   ing up!
Her. And am I also murderer of my wife?
Amph. All the work here was just one hand's
   work — thine!
Her. Ai ai — for groans encompass me — a
   cloud!
Amph. For these deeds' sake do I begroan
   thy fate!
Her. Did I break up my house or dance it
   down?
Amph. I know just one thing — all 's a woe
   with thee!
Her. But where did the craze catch me,
   where destroy?
Amph. When thou didst cleanse hands at the
   altar-flame.
Her. Ah me! why is it then I save my life —
Proved murderer of my dearest ones, my boys?
Shall not I rush to the rock-level's leap,
Or, darting sword through breast and all, be-
   come
My children's blood-avenger? or, this flesh
Burning away with fire, so thrust away
The infamy, which waits me there, from
   life?
Ah, but, — a hindrance to my purposed death,
Theseus arrives, my friend and kinsman, here!
Eyes will be on me! my child-murder-plague
In evidence before friends loved so much!
O me, what shall I do? Where, taking wing
Or gliding underground, shall I seek out
A solitariness from misery?
I will pull night upon my muffled head!
Let this wretch here content him with his
   curse
Of blood: I would pollute no innocents!
   Theseus. I come, — with others who await be-
   side
Asopos' stream, the armed Athenian youth, —
Bring thy son, old man, spear's fight-fellow-
   ship!
For a bruit reached the Erechtheidai's town
That, having seized the sceptre of this realm,
Lukos prepares you battle-violence.
So, paying good back, — Herakles began,

Saving me down there, — I have come, old man,
If aught, of my hand or my friends', you want.
What 's here? Why all these corpses on the
   ground?
Am I perhaps behindhand — come too late
For newer ill? Who killed these children
   now?
Whose wife was she, this woman I behold?
Boys, at least, take no stand in reach of spear!
Some other woe than war, I chance upon!
   Amph. O thou, who sway'st the olive-bear-
   ing height! —
   Thes. Why hail'st thou me with woeful pre-
   lude thus?
   Amph. Dire sufferings have we suffered from
   the gods.
   Thes. These boys, — who are they, thou art
   weeping o'er?
   Amph. He gave them birth, indeed, my hap-
   less son!
Begot, but killed them — dared their bloody
   death.
   Thes. Speak no such horror!
   Amph.   Would I might obey!
   Thes. O teller of dread tidings!
   Amph.   Lost are we —
Lost — flown away from life!
   Thes.   What sayest thou?
What did he?
   Amph.   Erring through a frenzy-fit,
He did all, with the arrows dipt in dye
Of hundred-headed Hudra.
   Thes.   Heré's strife!
But who is this among the dead, old man?
   Amph. Mine, mine, this progeny — the labor-
   plagued,
Who went with gods once to Phlegruia's plain,
And in the giant-slaying war bore shield!
   Thes. Woe — woe! What man was born mis-
   chanceful thus!
   Amph. Thou couldst not know another mortal
   man
Toil-weary, more outworn by wanderings.
   Thes. And why i' the peploi hides he his sad
   head?
   Amph. Not daring meet thine eye, thy friend-
   liness
And kinship, — nor that children's - blood
   about!
   Thes. But *I* come to who shared my woe with
   me!
Uncover him!
   Amph.   O child, put from thine eyes
The peplos, throw it off, show face to sun!
Woe's weight well matched contends with tears
   in thee.
I supplicate thee, falling at thy cheek
And knee and hand, and shedding this old
   tear!
O son, remit the savage lion's mood,
Since to a bloody, an unholy race
Art thou led forth, if thou be resolute
To go on adding ill to ill, my child!
   Thes. Let me speak! Thee, who sittest —
   seated woe —
I call upon to show thy friends thine eye!
For there 's no darkness has a cloud so black
May hide thy misery thus absolute.

Why, waving hand, dost sign me — murder's
    done?
Lest a pollution strike me, from thy speech?
Naught care I to — with thee, at least — fare ill:
For I had joy once! *Then*, — soul rises to, —
When thou didst save me from the dead to
    light!
Friends' gratitude that tastes old age, I loathe,
And him who likes to share when things look
    fine,
But, sail along with friends in trouble — no!
Arise, uncover thine unhappy head!
Look on us! Every man of the right race
Bears what, at least, the gods inflict, nor
    shrinks.
  Her. Theseus, hast seen this match — my
    boys with me?
  Thes. I heard of, now I see the ills thou
    sign'st.
  Her. Why then hast thou displayed my head
    to sun?
  Thes. Why? mortals bring no plague on aught
    divine!
  Her. Fly, O unhappy, this my impious
    plague!
  Thes. No plague of vengeance flits to friends
    from friends.
  Her. I praise thee! But I helped thee, —
    that is truth.
  Thes. And I, advantaged then, now pity
    thee.
  Her. — The pitiable, — my children's mur-
    derer!
  Thes. I mourn for thy sake, in this altered
    lot.
  Her. Hast thou found others in still greater
    woe?
  Thes. Thou, from earth, touchest heaven, one
    huge distress!
  Her. Accordingly, I am prepared to die.
  Thes. Think'st thou thy threats at all import
    the gods?
  Her. Gods please themselves: to gods I give
    their like.
  Thes. Shut thy mouth, lest big words bring
    bigger woe!
  Her. I am full fraught with ills — no stowing
    more!
  Thes. Thou wilt do — what, then? Whither
    moody borne?
  Her. Dying, I go below earth whence I came.
  Thes. Thou hast used words of — what man
    turns up first!
  Her. While thou, being outside sorrow,
    schoolest me.
  Thes. The much-enduring Herakles talks
    thus? —
  Her. Not the so much-enduring: measure's
    past!
  Thes. — Mainstay to mortals, and their
    mighty friend?
  Her. They nowise profit me: but Heré rules.
  Thes. Hellas forbids thou shouldst ineptly
    die.
  Her. But hear, then, how I strive by argu-
    ments
Against thy teachings! I will ope thee out
My life — past, present — as unlivable.

First, I was born of this man, who had slain
His mother's aged sire, and, sullied so,
Married Alkmené, she who gave me birth.
Now, when the basis of a family
Is not laid right, what follows needs must fall;
And Zeus, whoever Zeus is, formed me foe
To Heré (take not thou offence, old man!
Since father, in Zeus' stead, account I thee)
And, while I was at suck yet, frightful snakes
She introduced among my swaddling-clothes, —
That bedfellow of Zeus! — to end me so.
But when I gained the youthful garb of flesh,
The labors I endured — what need to tell?
What lions ever, or three-bodied brutes,
Tuphons or giants, or the four-legg'd swarms
Of Kentaur-battle, did not I end out?
And that hound, headed all about with heads
Which cropped up twice, the Hudra, having
    slain —
I both went through a myriad other toils
In full drove, and arrived among the dead
To convoy, as Eurustheus bade, to light
Haides' three-headed dog and doorkeeper.
But then I, — wretch, — dared this last labor
    — see!
Slew my sons, keystone-coped my house with
    ills.
To such a strait I come! nor my dear Thebes
Dare I inhabit, — and, suppose I stay?
Into what fane or festival of friends
Am I to go? My curse scarce courts accost!
Shall I seek Argos? How, if fled from home?
But say, — I hurry to some other town!
And there they eye me, as notorious now, —
Kept by sharp tongue-taunts under lock and
    key —
"Is not this he, Zeus' son, who murdered once
Children and wife? Let him go rot else-
    where!"
To any man renowned as happy once,
Reverses are a grave thing; but to whom
Evil is old acquaintance, there's no hurt
To speak of, he and misery are twins.
To this degree of woe I think to come:
For earth will utter voice forbidding me
To touch the ground, and sea — to pierce the
    wave,
The river-springs — to drink, and I shall play
Ixion's part quite out, the chained and wheeled!
And best of all will be, if so I 'scape
Sight from one man of those Hellenes, — once
I lived among, felicitous and rich!
Why ought I then to live? What gain accrues
From good-for-nothing, wicked life I lead?
In fine, let Zeus' brave consort dance and sing,
Stamp foot, the Olumpian Zeus' own sandal-
    trick!
What she has willed, that brings her will to
    pass —
The foremost man of Hellas pedestalled,
Up, over, and down whirling! Who would
    pray
To such a goddess? — that, begrudging Zeus
Because he loved a woman, ruins me —
Lover of Hellas, faultless of the wrong!
  Thes. This strife is from no other of the gods
Than Zeus' wife; rightly apprehend, as well,
Why, to no death — thou meditatest now —

I would persuade thee, but to bear thy woes!
None, none of mortals boasts a fate unmixed,
Nor gods — if poets' teaching be not false.
Have not they joined in wedlock against law
With one another ? not, for sake of rule,
Branded their sires in bondage ? Yet they
  house,
All the same, in Olumpos, carry heads
High there, notorious sinners though they be !
What wilt thou say, then, if thou, mortal-born,
Bearest outrageously fate gods endure ?
Leave Thebes, now, pay obedience to the law,
And follow me to Pallas' citadel !
There, when thy hands are purified from stain,
House will I give thee, and goods shared alike.
What gifts I hold too from the citizens
For saving twice seven children, when I slew
The Knosian bull, these also give I thee.
And everywhere about the land are plots
Apportioned me : these, named by thine own
  name,
Shall be henceforward styled by all men
  thine,
Thy life-long ; but at death, when Haides-
  bound,
All Athens shall uphold the honored one
With sacrifices, and huge marble heaps:
For that 's a fair crown our Hellenes grant
Their people — glory, should they help the
  brave !
And I repay thee back this grace for thine
That saved me, now that thou art lorn of
  friends —
Since, when the gods give honor, friends may
  flit:
For, a god's help suffices, if he please.
  Her. Ah me, these words are foreign to my
  woes!
I neither fancy gods love lawless beds,
Nor, that with chains they bind each other's
  hands,
Have I judged worthy faith, at any time ;
Nor shall I be persuaded — one is born
His fellows' master ! since God stands in
  need —
If he is really God — of naught at all.
These are the poets' pitiful conceits !
But this it was I pondered, though woe-
  whelmed —
" Take heed lest thou be taxed with cowardice
Somehow in leaving thus the light of day ! "
For whoso cannot make a stand against
These same misfortunes, neither could with-
  stand
A mere man's dart, oppose death, strength to
  strength.
Therefore unto thy city I will go
And have the grace of thy ten thousand gifts.
There ! I have tasted of ten thousand toils
As truly — never waived a single one,
Nor let these runnings drop from out my eyes!
Nor ever thought it would have come to this —
That I from out my eyes do drop tears! Well !
At present, as it seems, one bows to fate.
So be it ! Old man, thou seest my exile —
Seest, too, me — my children's murderer !
These give thou to the tomb, and deck the dead,
Doing them honor with thy tears — since me

Law does not sanction ! Propping on her
  breast,
And giving them into their mother's arms,
  — Reinstitute the sad community
Which I, unhappy, brought to nothingness —
Not by my will ! And, when earth hides the
  dead,
Live in this city ! — sad, but, all the same,
Force thy soul to bear woe along with me !
O children, who begat and gave you birth —
Your father — has destroyed you ! naught you
  gain
By those fair deeds of mine I laid you up,
As by main-force I labored glory out
To give you, — that fine gift of fatherhood !
And thee, too, O my poor one, I destroyed.
Not rendering like for like, as when thou
  kept'st
My marriage-bed inviolate, — those long
Household-seclusions draining to the dregs
Inside my house ! O me, my wife, my boys —
And — O myself, how, miserably moved.
Am I disyoked now from both boys and wife !
Oh, bitter those delights of kisses now —
And bitter these my weapons' fellowship !
For I am doubtful whether shall I keep
Or cast away these arrows which will clang
Ever such words out, as they knock my side —
" Us — thou didst murder wife and children
  with !
Us — child-destroyers — still thou keepest
  thine ! "
Ha, shall I bear them in my arms, then ? What
Say for excuse ? Yet, naked of my darts
Wherewith I did my bravest, Hellas through,
Throwing myself beneath foot to my foes,
Shall I die basely ? No ! relinquishment
Of these must never be, — companions once,
We sorrowfully must observe the pact !
In just one thing, co-operate with me
Thy sad friend, Theseus ! Go along with him
To Argos, and in concert get arranged
The price my due for bringing there the Hound !
O land of Kadmos, Theban people all,
Shear off your locks, lament one wide lament,
Go to my children's grave and, in one strain,
Lament the whole of us — my dead and me —
Since all together are foredone and lost,
Smitten by Heré's single stroke of fate !
  Thes. Rise up now from thy dead ones !
  Tears enough,
Poor friend !
  Her.   I cannot : for my limbs are fixed.
  Thes. Ay : even these strong men fate over-
  throws !
  Her. Woe !
Here might I grow a stone, nor mind woes
  more !
  Thes. Cease ! Give thy hand to friendly
  helpmate now !
  Her. Nay, but I wipe off blood upon thy
  robes !
  Thes. Squeeze out and spare no drop ! I take
  it all !
  Her. Of sons bereaved, I have thee like my
  son !
  Thes. Give to my neck thy hand ! 't is I will
  lead.

Her. Yoke - fellows friendly — one heart-
broken, though !
Ꝺ father ! such a man we need for friend !
Amph. Certes, the land that bred him boasts
good sons !
Her. Turn me round, Theseus — to behold my
boys !
Thes. What ? will the having such a love-
charm soothe ?
Her. I want it ; and to press my father's
breast.
Amph. See here, O son ! for, what I love
thou seek'st !
Thes. Strange ! Of thy labors no more
memory ?
Her. All those were less than these, those
ills I bore !
Thes. Who sees thee grow a woman, — will
not praise !
Her. I live low to thee ? Not so once, I
think !
Thes. Too low by far ! "Famed Herakles"
— where 's he ?
Her. Down amid evils, of what kind wast
thou ?
Thes. As far as courage — least of all man-
kind !
Her. How say'st, then, *I* in evils shrink to
naught ?
Thes. Forward !
Her.   Farewell, old father !
Amph.   Thou too, son !
Her. Bury the boys as I enjoined !
Amph.   And *me* —
Who will be found to bury now, my child ?
Her. Myself !
Amph.   When, coming ?
Her.   When thy task is done.
Amph. How ?
Her. I will have thee carried forth from
Thebes
To Athens. But bear in the children, earth
Is burdened by ! Myself, — who with these
shames
Have cast away my house, — a ruined hulk,
I follow — trailed by Theseus — on my way ;
And whoso rather would have wealth and
strength
Than good friends, reasons foolishly therein !
Cho. And we depart, with sorrow at heart,
Sobs that increase with tears that start ;
The greatest of all our friends of yore
We have lost forevermore !

When the long silence ended, — " Our best
friend —
Lost, our best friend ! " he muttered musingly.
Then, " Lachares the sculptor " (half aloud)
"Sinned he or sinned he not ? 'Outrageous
sin ! '
Shuddered our elders, ' Pallas should be
clothed :
He carved her naked.' ' But more beautiful ! '
Answers this generation : ' Wisdom formed
For love not fear ! ' And there the statue
stands,
Entraps the eye severer art repels.

Moreover, Pallas wields the thunderbolt,
Yet has not struck the artist all this while.
Pheidias and Aischulos ? Euripides
And Lachares ? But youth will have its way !
The ripe man ought to be as old as young —
As young as old. I too have youth at need.
Much may be said for stripping wisdom bare !

" And who 's ' our best friend ' ? You play
kottabos ;
Here 's the last mode of playing. Take a
sphere
With orifices at due interval,
Through topmost one of which, a throw adroit
Sends wine from cup, clean passage, from out
side
To where, in hollow midst, a manikin
Suspended ever bobs with head erect
Right underneath whatever hole 's a-top
When you set orb a-rolling : plumb, he gets
Ever this benediction of the splash.
An other-fashioned orb presents him fixed :
Of all the outlets, he fronts only one,
And only when that one — and rare the
chance —
Comes uppermost, does he turn upward too :
He can't turn all sides with the turning orb.
Inside this sphere of life — all objects, sense
And soul perceive — Euripides hangs fixed,
Gets knowledge through the single aperture
Of High and Right : with visage fronting these
He waits the wine thence ere he operate,
Work in the world and write a tragedy.
When that hole happens to revolve to point,
In drops the knowledge, waiting meets reward.
But, duly in rotation, Low and Wrong —
When these enjoy the moment's altitude,
His heels are found just where his head should
be !
No knowledge that way ! *I* am movable, —
To slightest shift of orb make prompt response,
Face Low and Wrong and Weak and all the rest,
And still drink knowledge, wine-drenched every
turn, —
Equally favored by their opposites.
Little and Bad exist, are natural :
Then let me know them, and be twice as great
As he who only knows one phase of life !
So doubly shall I prove ' best friend of man,'
If I report the whole truth — Viee, perceived
While he shut eyes to all but Virtue there.
Man 's made of both : and both must be of use
To somebody : if not to him, to me.
While, as to your imaginary Third,
Who, — stationed (by mechanics past my guess)
So as to take in every side at once,
And not successively, — may reconcile
The High and Low in tragicomic verse, —
He shall be hailed superior to us both
When born — in the Tin-islands ! Meantime,
here
In bright Athenai, I contest the claim,
Call myself Iostephanos' ' best friend,'
Who took my own course, worked as I descried
Ordainment, stuck to my first faculty !

" For, listen ! There 's no failure breaks the
heart.

Whate'er be man's endeavor in this world,
Like the rash poet's when he — nowise fails
By poetizing badly, — Zeus or makes
Or mars a man, so — at it, merrily !
But when, — made man, — much like myself,
 — equipt
For such and such achievement, — rash he turns
Out of the straight path, bent on snatch of
 feat
From — who's the appointed fellow born
 thereto, —
Crows take him ! — in your Kassiterides ?
Half-doing his work, leaving mine untouched,
That were the failure ! Here I stand, heart-
 whole,
No Thamuris !

   " Well thought of, Thamuris !
Has zeal, pray, for ' best friend ' Euripides
Allowed you to observe the honor done
His elder rival, in our Poikilé ?
You don't know ? Once and only once, trod
 stage,
Sang and touched lyre in person, in his youth,
Our Sophokles, — youth, beauty, dedicate
To Thamuris who named the tragedy.
The voice of him was weak ; face, limbs and
 lyre,
These were worth saving: Thamuris stands
 yet
Perfect as painting helps in such a case.
At least you know the story, for ' best friend '
Enriched his ' Rhesos ' from the Blind Bard's
 store ;
So haste and see the work, and lay to heart
What it was struck me when I eyed the piece !
Here stands a poet punished for rash strife
With Powers above his power, who see with
 sight
Beyond his vision, sing accordingly
A song, which he must needs dare emulate !
Poet, remain the man nor ape the Muse !

" But — lend me the psalterion ! Nay, for
 once —
Once let my hand fall where the other's lay !
I see it, just as I were Sophokles,
That sunrise and combustion of the east ! "

And then he sang — are these unlike the words ?

Thamuris marching, — lyre and song of
 Thrace —
(Perpend the first, the worst of woes that were,
Allotted lyre and song, ye poet-race !)

Thamuris from Oichalia, feasted there
By kingly Eurutos of late, now bound
For Dorion at the uprise broad and bare

Of Mount Pangaios (ore with earth enwound
Glittered beneath his footstep) — marching gay
And glad, Thessalia through, came, robed and
 crowned,

From triumph on to triumph, 'mid a ray
Of early morn, — came, saw and knew the spot
Assigned him for his worst of woes, that day.

Balura — happier while its name was not —
Met him, but nowise menaced ; slipt aside,
Obsequious river, to pursue its lot

Of solacing the valley — say, some wide
Thick busy human cluster, house and home,
Embanked for peace, or thrift that thanks the
 tide.

Thamuris, marching, laughed " Each flake of
 foam "
(As sparklingly the ripple raced him by)
" Mocks slower clouds adrift in the blue
 dome ! "

For Autumn was the season : red the sky
Held morn's conclusive signet of the sun
To break the mists up, bid them blaze and die.

Morn had the mastery as, one by one,
All pomps produced themselves along the tract
From earth's far ending to near heaven begun.

Was there a ravaged tree ? it laughed compact
With gold, a leaf-ball crisp, high-brandished
 now,
Tempting to onset frost which late attacked.

Was there a wizened shrub, a starveling bough,
A fleecy thistle filched from by the wind,
A weed, Pan's trampling hoof would disallow ?

Each, with a glory and a rapture twined
About it, joined the rush of air and light
And force: the world was of one joyous mind.

Say not the birds flew ! they forebore their
 right —
Swam, revelling onward in the roll of things.
Say not the beasts' mirth bounded ! that was
 flight —

How could the creatures leap, no lift of wings ?
Such earth's community of purpose, such
The ease of earth's fulfilled imaginings, —

So did the near and far appear to touch
I' the moment's transport, — that an inter-
 change
Of function, far with near, seemed scarce too
 much ;

And had the rooted plant aspired to range
With the snake's license, while the insect
 yearned
To glow fixed as the flower it were not
 strange —

No more than if the fluttery tree-top turned
To actual music, sang itself aloft ;
Or if the wind, impassioned chantress, earned

The right to soar embodied in some soft
Fine form all fit for cloud-companionship,
And, blissful, once touch beauty chased so oft.

Thamuris, marching, let no fancy slip
Born of the fiery transport ; lyre and song

Were his, to smite with hand and launch from
   lip —

Peerless recorded, since the list grew long
Of poets (saith Homeros) free to stand
Pedestalled 'mid the Muses' temple-throng,

A statued service, laurelled, lyre in hand,
(Ay, for we see them) — Thamuris of Thrace
Predominating foremost of the band.

Therefore the morn-ray that enriched his face,
If it gave lambent chill, took flame again
From flush of pride ; he saw, he knew the
   place.

What wind arrived with all the rhythms from
   plain,
Hill, dale, and that rough wildwood inter-
   spersed ?
Compounding these to one consummate strain,

It reached him, music ; but his own outburst
Of victory concluded the account,
And that grew song which was mere music erst.

"Be my Parnassos, thou Pangaian mount !
And turn thee, river, nameless hitherto !
Famed shalt thou vie with famed Pieria's
   fount !

Here I await the end of this ado :
Which wins — Earth's poet or the Heavenly
   Muse." . . .

But song broke up in laughter. "Tell the
   rest,
Who may ! *I* have not spurned the common
   life,
Nor vaunted mine a lyre to match the Muse
Who sings for gods, not men ! Accordingly,
I shall not decorate her vestibule —
Mute marble, blind the eyes and quenched the
   brain,
Loose in the hand a bright, a broken lyre !
— Not Thamuris but Aristophanes !

"There ! I have sung content back to myself,
And started subject for a play beside.
My next performance shall content you both.
Did 'Prelude-Battle' maul 'best friend' too
   much ?
Then 'Main-Fight' be my next song, fairness'
   self !
Its subject — Contest for the Tragic Crown.
Ay, you shall hear none else but Aischulos
Lay down the law of Tragedy, and prove
'Best friend' a stray-away, — no praise denied
His manifold deservings, never fear —
Nor word more of the old fun ! Death de-
   fends !
Sound admonition has its due effect.
Oh, you have uttered weighty words, believe !
Such as shall bear abundant fruit, next year,
In judgment, regular, legitimate.
Let Bacchos' self preside in person ! Ay —
For there 's a buzz about those 'Bacchanals'
Rumor attributes to your great and dead

For final effort : just the prodigy
Great dead men leave, to lay survivors low !
— Until we make acquaintance with our fate
And find, fate's worst done, we, the same, sur-
   vive
Perchance to honor more the patron-god,
Fitlier inaugurate a festal year.
Now that the cloud has broken, sky laughs
   blue,
Earth blossoms youthfully ! Athenai breathes !
After a twenty-six years' wintry blank
Struck from her life, — war-madness, one long
   swoon,
She wakes up : Arginousai bids good cheer !
We have disposed of Kallikratidas ;
Once more will Sparté sue for terms, — who
   knows ?
Cede Dekeleia, as the rumor runs :
Terms which Athenai, of right mind again,
Accepts — she can no other ! Peace declared,
Have my long labors borne their fruit or no ?
Grinned coarse buffoonery so oft in vain ?
Enough — it simply saved you. Saved ones,
   praise
Theoria's beauty and Opora's breadth !
Nor, when Peace realizes promised bliss,
Forget the Bald Bard, Envy ! but go burst
As the cup goes round, and the cates abound,
Collops of hare, with roast spinks rare !
Confess my pipings, dancings, posings served
A purpose : guttlings, guzzlings, had their use !
Say whether light Muse, Rosy-finger-tips,
Or, 'best friend's' Heavy-hand, Melpomené,
Touched lyre to purpose, played Amphion's
   part,
And built Athenai to the skies once more !
Farewell, brave couple ! Next year, welcome
   me !"

No doubt, in what he said that night, sincere !
One story he referred to, false or fact,
Was not without adaptability.
They do say — Laïs the Corinthian once
Chancing to see Euripides (who paced
Composing in a garden, tablet-book
In left hand, with appended stulos prompt) —
"Answer me," she began, "O Poet, — this !
What didst intend by writing in thy play,
Go hang, thou filthy doer ?" Struck on heap,
Euripides, at the audacious speech —
"Well now," quoth he, "thyself art just the
   one
I should imagine fit for deeds of filth !"
She laughingly retorted his own line
"What 's filth, — unless who does it, thinks it
   so ?"

So might he doubtless think. "Farewell,"
   said we.

And he was gone, lost in the morning-gray,
Rose-streaked and gold to eastward. Did we
   dream ?
Could the poor twelve-hours hold this argu-
   ment
We render durable from fugitive.
As duly at each sunset's droop of sail.

Delay of oar, submission to sea-might,
I still remember, you as duly dint
Remembrance, with the punctual rapid style,
Into — what calm cold page !

      Thus soul escapes
From eloquence made captive : thus mere
  words
— Ah, would the lifeless body stay ! But no :
Change upon change till, — who may recognize
What did soul service, in the dusty heap ?
What energy of Aristophanes
Inflames the wreck Balaustion saves to show ?
Ashes be evidence how fire — with smoke —
All night went lamping on ! But morn must
  rise.
The poet — I shall say — burned up and, blank,
Smouldered this ash, now white and cold
  enough.

Nay, Euthukles ! for best, though mine it be,
Comes yet ! Write on, write ever, wrong no
  word !

Add, first, — he gone, if jollity went too,
Some of the graver mood, which mixed and
  marred,
Departed likewise. Sight of narrow scope
Has this meek consolation : neither ills
We dread, nor joys we dare anticipate,
Perform to promise. Each soul sows a seed —
Euripides and Aristophanes ;
Seed bears crop, scarce within our little lives ;
But germinates — perhaps enough to judge —
Next year ?

   Whereas, next year brought harvest-time !
For, next year came, and went not, but is now,
Still now, while you and I are bound for Rhodes
That 's all but reached ! — and harvest has it
  brought,
Dire as the homicidal dragon-crop !
Sophokles had dismissal ere it dawned,
Happy as ever ; though men mournfully
Plausive, — when only soul could triumph now,
And Iophon produced his father's play, —
Crowned the consummate song where Oidipous
Dared the descent 'mid earthquake-thundering,
And hardly Theseus' hands availed to guard
Eyes from the horror, as their grove disgorged
Its dread ones, while each daughter sank to
  ground.

Then Aristophanes, on heel of that,
Triumphant also, followed with his " Frogs : "
Produced at next Lenaia, — three months
  since, —
The promised Main-Fight, loyal, license-free ! ·
As if the poet, primed with Thasian juice,
(Himself swore — wine that conquers every kind
For long abiding in the head) could fix
Thenceforward any object in its truth,
Through eyeballs bathed by mere Castalian dew,
Nor miss the borrowed medium, — vinous drop
That colors all to the right crimson pitch
When mirth grows mockery, censure takes the
  tinge
Of malice !

     All was Aristophanes :
There blazed the glory, there shot black the
  shame !
Ay, Bacchos did stand forth, the Tragic God
In person ! and when duly dragged through
  mire, —
Having lied, filched, played fool, proved coward,
  flung
The boys their dose of fit indecency,
And finally got trounced to heart's content,
At his own feast, in his own theatre
(— Oh, never fear ! 'T was consecrated sport,
Exact tradition, warranted no whit
Offensive to instructed taste, — indeed,
Essential to Athenai's liberty,
Could the poor stranger understand !) why,
  then —
He was pronounced the rarely-qualified
To rate the work, adjust the claims to worth,
Of Aischulos (of whom, in other mood,
This same appreciative poet pleased
To say, " He 's all one stiff and gluey piece
Of back of swine's-neck ! ") — and of Chatter-
  box
Who, " twisting words like wool," usurped his
  seat
In Plouton's realm : " the arch-rogue, liar,
  scamp
That lives by snatching-up of altar-orts,"
— Who failed to recognize Euripides ?

Then came a contest for supremacy —
Crammed full of genius, wit and fun and freak.
No spice of undue spite to spoil the dish
Of all sorts, — for the Mystics matched the Frogs
In poetry, no Seiren sang so sweet ! —
Till, pressed into the service (how dispense
With Phaps-Elaphion and free foot-display ?)
The Muse of dead Euripides danced frank,
Rattled her bits of tile, made all too plain
How baby-work like " Herakles " had birth !
Last, Bacchos — candidly disclaiming brains
Able to follow finer argument —
Confessed himself much moved by three main
  facts :
First, — if you stick a " Lost his flask of oil "
At pause of period, you perplex the sense, —
Were it the Elegy for Marathon !
Next, if you weigh two verses, " car " — the
  word,
Will outweigh " club " — the word, in each
  packed line !
And — last, worst fact of all ! in rivalry
The younger poet dared to improvise
Laudation less distinct of — Triphales ?
(Nay, that served when ourself abused the
  youth !)
Pheidippides — (nor that 's appropriate now !)
Then, — Alkibiades, our city's hope,
Since times change and we Comics should change
  too !
These three main facts, well weighed, drew
  judgment down,
Conclusively assigned the wretch his fate —
" Fate due," admonished the sage Mystic choir,
" To sitting, prate-apace, with Sokrates,
Neglecting music and each tragic aid ! "
— All wound-up by a wish " We soon may cease

From certain griefs, and warfare, worst of
    them!"
—Since, deaf to Comedy's persistent voice,
War still raged, still was like to rage. In vain
Had Sparté cried once more, " But grant us
    Peace,
We give you Dekeleia back!" Too shrewd
Was Kleophon to let escape, forsooth,
The enemy — at final gasp, besides!

So, Aristophanes obtained the prize,
And so Athenai felt she had a friend
Far better than her "best friend," lost last
    year ;
And so, such fame had "Frogs" that, when
    came round
This present year, those Frogs croaked gay again
At the great Feast, Elaphebolion-month.
Only — there happened Aigispotamoi !

And, in the midst of the frog-merriment,
Plump o' the sudden, pounces stern King Stork
On the light-hearted people of the marsh !
Spartan Lusandros swooped precipitate,
Ended Athenai, rowed her sacred bay
With oars which brought a hundred triremes
    back
Captive !

      And first word of the conqueror
Was " Down with those Long Walls, Peiraios'
    pride !
Destroy, yourselves, your bulwarks ! Peace
    needs none !"
And " We obey " they shuddered in their dream.

But, at next quick imposure of decree —
" No longer democratic government !
Henceforth such oligarchy as ourselves
Please to appoint you !" — then the horror-
    stung
Dreamers awake ; they started up a-stare
At the half-helot captain and his crew
—Spartans, "men used to let their hair grow
    long,
To fast, be dirty, and just — Sokratize " —
Whose word was " Trample on Themistokles !"

So, as the way is with much misery,
The heads swam, hands refused their office,
    hearts
Sunk as they stood in stupor. " Wreck the
    Walls ?
Ruin Peiraios ? — with our Pallas armed
For interference ? — Herakles apprised,
And Theseus hasting ? Lay the Long Walls
    low ? "

Three days they stood, stared, — stonier than
    their walls.

Whereupon, sleep who might, Lusandros woke :
Saw the prostration of his enemy,
Utter and absolute beyond belief,
Past hope of hatred even. I surmise
He also probably saw fade in fume
Certain fears, bred of Bakis-prophecy,
Nor apprehended any more that gods

And heroes, — fire, must glow forth, guard the
    ground
Where prone, by sober day-dawn, corpse-like lay
Powerless Athenai, late predominant
Lady of Hellas, — Sparté's slave-prize now !
Where should a menace lurk in those slack
    limbs ?
What was to move his circumspection ? Why
Demolish just Peiraios ?

           "Stay ! " bade he :
" Already promise-breakers ? True to type,
Athenians ! past, and present, and to come, —
The fickle and the false ! No stone dislodged,
No implement applied, yet three days' grace
Expire ! Forbearance is no longer-lived.
By breaking promise, terms of peace you
    break —
Too gently framed for falsehood, fickleness !
All must be reconsidered — yours the fault ! "

Wherewith, he called a council of allies.
Pent-up resentment used its privilege, —
Outburst at ending : this the summed result.

" Because we would avenge no transient wrong
But an eternity of insolence,
Aggression, — folly, no disasters mend,
Pride, no reverses teach humility, —
Because too plainly were all punishment,
Such as comports with less obdurate crime,
Evadable by falsehood, fickleness —
Experience proves the true Athenian type, —
Therefore, 't is need we dig deep down into
The root of evil ; lop nor bole nor branch.
Look up, look round and see, on every side,
What nurtured the rank tree to noisome fruit !
We who live hutted (so they laugh) not housed,
Build barns for temples, prize mud-monuments,
Nor show the sneering stranger aught but —
    men, —
Spartans take insult of Athenians just
Because they boast Akropolis to mount,
And Propulaia to make entry by,
Through a mad maze of marble arrogance
Such as you see — such as let none see more !
Abolish the detested luxury !
Leave not one stone upon another, raze
Athenai to the rock ! Let hill and plain
Become a waste, a grassy pasture-ground
Where sheep may wander, grazing goats depend
From shapeless crags once columns ! so at last
Shall peace inhabit there, and peace enough."

Whereon, a shout approved " Such peace be-
    stow ! "

Then did a Man of Phokis rise — O heart !
Rise — when no bolt of Zeus disparted sky,
No omen-bird from Pallas scared the crew,
Rise — when mere human argument could
    stem
No foam-fringe of the passion surging fierce,
Baffle no wrath-wave that o'er barrier broke —
Who was the Man of Phokis rose and flung
A flower i' the way of that fierce foot's advance,
Which — stop for ? — nay, had stamped down
    sword's assault !

Could it be *He* stayed Sparté with the snatch —
" Daughter of Agamemnon, late my liege,
Elektra, palaced, once a visitant
To thy poor rustic dwelling, now I come ? "

Ay, facing fury of revenge, and lust
Of hate, and malice moaning to appease
Hunger on prey presumptuous, prostrate now —
Full in the hideous faces — last resource,
You flung that choric flower, my Euthukles !

And see, as through some pinhole, should the
    wind
Wedgingly pierce but once, in with a rush
Hurries the whole wild weather, rends to rags
The weak sail stretched against the outside
    storm —
So did the power of that triumphant play
Pour in, and oversweep the assembled foe !
Triumphant play, wherein our poet first
Dared bring the grandeur of the Tragic Two
Down to the level of our common life,
Close to the beating of our common heart.
Elektra ?   'T was Athenai, Sparté's ice
Thawed to, while that sad portraiture ap-
    pealed —
Agamemnonian lady, lost by fault
Of her own kindred, cast from house and home,
Despoiled of all the brave inheritance,
Dowered humbly as befits a herdsman's mate,
Partaker of his cottage, clothed in rags,
Patient performer of the poorest chares,
Yet mindful, all the while, of glory past
When she walked darling of Mukenai, dear
Beyond Orestes to the King of Men !

So, because Greeks are Greeks, though Sparté's
    brood,
And hearts are hearts, though in Lusandros'
    breast,
And poetry is power, and Euthukles
Had faith therein to, full-face, fling the same —
Sudden, the ice-thaw !   The assembled foe,
Heaving and swaying with strange friendliness,
Cried, " Reverence Elektra ! " — cried, " Ab-
    stain
Like that chaste Herdsman, nor dare violate
The sanctity of such reverse !   Let stand
Athenai ! "

Mindful of that story's close,
Perchance, and how, — when he, the Herds-
    man chaste,
Needs apprehend no break of tranquil sleep, —
All in due time, a stranger, dark, disguised,
Knocks at the door : with searching glance,
    notes keen,
Knows quick, through mean attire and disre-
    spect,
The ravaged princess !   Ay, right on, the clutch
Of guiding retribution has in charge
The author of the outrage !   While one hand,
Elektra's, pulls the door behind, made fast
On fate, — the other strains, prepared to push
The victim-queen, should she make frightened
    pause
Before that serpentining blood which steals
Out of the darkness where, a pace beyond,

Above the slain Aigisthos, bides his blow
Dreadful Orestes !

Klutaimnestra, wise
This time, forebore ; Elektra held her own ;
Saved was Athenai through Euripides,
Through Euthukles, through — more than evei
    — me,
Balaustion, me, who, Wild-pomegranate-flower,
Felt my fruit triumph, and fade proudly so !

But next day, as ungracious minds are wont,
The Spartan, late surprised into a grace,
Grew sudden sober at the enormity,
And grudged, by daybreak, midnight's easy
    gift ;
Splenetically must repay its cost
By due increase of rigor, doglike snatch
At aught still left dog to concede like man.
Rough sea, at flow of tide, may lip, perchance,
Smoothly the land-line reached as for repose —
Lie indolent in all unquestioned sway ;
But ebbing, when needs must, all thwart and
    loth,
Sea claws at sand relinquished strugglingly.
So, harsh Lusandros — pinioned to inflict
The lesser penalty alone — spoke harsh,
As minded to embitter scathe by scorn.

" Athenai's self be saved then, thank the Lyre !
If Tragedy withdraws her presence — quick,
If Comedy replace her, — whaɩ more just ?
Let Comedy do service, frisk away,
Dance off stage these indomitable stones,
Long Walls, Peiraian bulwarks !   Hew and
    heave,
Pick at, pound into dust each dear defence !
Not to the Kommos — *elelelelu*
With breast bethumped, as Tragic lyre prefers,
But Comedy shall sound the flute, and crow
At kordax-end — the hearty slapping-dance !
Collect those flute-girls — trash who flattered
    ear
With whistlings, and fed eye with caper-cuts,
While we Lakonians supped black broth or
    crunched
Sea-urchin, conchs and all, unpricked — coarse
    brutes !
Command they lead off step, time steady
    stroke
To spade and pickaxe, till demolished lie
Athenai's pride in powder ! "

Done that day —
That sixteenth famed day of Munuchion-month !
The day when Hellas ᶜought at Salamis,
The very day Euripides was born,
Those flute-girls — Phaps-Elaphion at their
    head —
Did blow their best, did dance their worst, the
    while
Sparté pulled down the walls, wrecked wide
    the works,
Laid low each merest molehill of defence,
And so the Power, Athenai, passed away !

We would not see its passing !   Ere I knew
The issue of their counsels, — crouching low

And shrouded by my peplos, — I conceived,
Despite the shut eyes, the stopped ears, — by
          count
Only of heart-beats, telling the slow time, —
Athenai's doom was signed and signified
In that assembly, — ay, but knew there
          watched
One who would dare and do, nor bate at all
The stranger's licensed duty, — speak the
          word
Allowed the Man from Phokis! Naught re-
          mained
But urge departure, flee the sights and sounds,
Hideous exultings, wailings worth contempt,
And pressed to other earth, new heaven, by sea
That somehow ever prompts to 'scape despair.

Help rose to heart's wish ; at the harbor-side,
The old gray mariner did reverence
To who had saved his ship, still weather-tight
As when with prow gay-garlanded she praised
The hospitable port and pushed to sea.
" Convoy Balaustion back to Rhodes, for sake
Of her and her Euripides ! " laughed he.

Rhodes, — shall it not be there, my Euthukles,
Till this brief trouble of a lifetime end,
That solitude — two make so populous ! —
For food finds memories of the past suffice,
Maybe, anticipations, — hope so swells, —
Of some great future we, familiar once
With who so taught, should hail and entertain ?
He lies now in the little valley, laughed
And moaned about by those mysterious
          streams,
Boiling and freezing, like the love and hate
Which helped or harmed him through his
          earthly course.

They mix in Arethousa by his grave.
The warm spring, traveller, dip thine arms
          into,
Brighten thy brow with ! Life detests black
          cold !

I sent the tablets, the psalterion, so
Rewarded Sicily ; the tyrant there
Bestowed them worthily in Phoibos' shrine.
A gold-graved writing tells — " I also loved
The poet, Free Athenai cheaply prized —
King Dionusios, — Archelaos-like ! "

And see if young Philemon, — sure one day
To do good service and be loved himself, —
If he too have not made a votive verse !
" Grant, in good sooth, our great dead, all the
          same,
Retain their sense, as certain wise men say,
I 'd hang myself — to see Euripides ! "
Hands off, Philemon ! nowise hang thyself,
But pen the prime plays, labor the right life,
And die at good old age as grand men use, —
Keeping thee, with that great thought, warm
          the while, —
That he does live, Philemon ! Ay, most sure !
" He lives ! " hark, — waves say, winds sing
          out the same,
And yonder dares the citied ridge of Rhodes
Its headlong plunge from sky to sea, disparts
North bay from south, — each guarded calm,
          that guest
May enter gladly, blow what wind there will, —
Boiled round with breakers, to no other cry !
All in one choros, — what the master-word
They take up ? — hark ! " There are no gods,
          no gods !
Glory to God — who saves Euripides ! "

PRINCE HOHENSTIEL–SCHWANGAU

SAVIOUR OF SOCIETY

Ὕδραν φονεύσας, μυρίων τ' ἄλλων πόνων
διῆλθον ἀγέλας . . .
τὸ λοίσθιον δὲ τόνδ' ἔτλην τάλας πόνον,
. . . δῶμα θριγκῶσαι κακοῖς.

I slew the Hydra, and from labor pass'd
To labor — tribes of labors! Till, at last,
Attempting one more labor, in a trice,
Alack, with ills I *crowned the edifice.*

THIS poem, written in Scotland in 1871,
shortly after the downfall of Napoleon III.,
was published in December of the same year.
The suggestion of the emperor is transparent,
and Browning writing in January, 1872, to Miss
Isa Blagden, says of it : " I am glad you have
got my little book, and seen for yourself
whether I make the best or the worst of the
case. I think, in the main, he meant to do
what I say, and, but for weakness — grown
more apparent in his last years than formerly
— would have done what I say he did not. I

thought badly of him at the beginning of his career, *et pour cause:* better afterward, on the strength of the promises he made, and gave indications of intending to redeem. I think him very weak in the last miserable year. At his worst I prefer him to Thiers's best. I am told my little thing is succeeding — sold 1400 in the first five days, and before any notice appeared." And again, to the same correspondent: "I am glad you like what the editor of the *Edinburgh* calls my eulogium on the second empire — which it is not, any more than

what another wiseacre affirms it to be, 'a scandalous attack on the old constant friend of England' — it is just what I imagine the man might, if he pleased, say for himself." Mrs. Browning's well-known enthusiasm for Napoleon III. as instanced in her poems unquestionably gave distinctness to Browning's own reflections. The motto is from the *Hercules Furens* of Euripides, vv. 1276-1280, and the translation is presumably by Browning. There is a palace Hohen-Schwangau, built by the Bavarian mad king Ludwig.

You have seen better days, dear? So have
    I —
And worse too, for they brought no such bud-
    mouth
As yours to lisp "You wish you knew me!"
    Well,
Wise men, 't is said, have sometimes wished
    the same,
And wished and had their trouble for their
    pains.
Suppose my Œdipus should lurk at last
Under a pork-pie hat and crinoline,
And, latish, pounce on Sphinx in Leicester
    Square?
Or likelier, what if Sphinx in wise old age,
Grown sick of snapping foolish people's heads,
And jealous for her riddle's proper rede, —
Jealous that the good trick which served the
    turn
Have justice rendered it, nor class one day
With friend Home's stilts and tongs and
    medium-ware, —
What if the once redoubted Sphinx, I say,
(Because night draws on, and the sands in-
    crease,
And desert-whispers grow a prophecy,)
Tell all to Corinth of her own accord,
Bright Corinth, not dull Thebes, for Laïs'
    sake,
Who finds me hardly gray, and likes my nose,
And thinks a man of sixty at the prime?
Good! It shall be! Revealment of myself!
But listen, for we must co-operate;
I don't drink tea: permit me the cigar!

First, how to make the matter plain, of
    course —
What was the law by which I lived. Let's
    see:
Ay, we must take one instant of my life
Spent sitting by your side in this neat room:
Watch well the way I use it, and don't laugh!
Here's paper on the table, pen and ink:
Give me the soiled bit — not the pretty rose!
See! having sat an hour, I 'm rested now,
Therefore want work: and spy no better work
For eye and hand and mind that guides them
    both,
During this instant, than to draw my pen
From blot One — thus — up, up to blot Two —
    thus —
Which I at last reach, thus, and here 's my line

Five inches long and tolerably straight:
Better to draw than leave undrawn, I think,
Fitter to do than let alone, I hold,
Though better, fitter, by but one degree.
Therefore it was that, rather than sit still
Simply, my right-hand drew it while my left
Pulled smooth and pinched the moustache to a
    point.

Now I permit your plump lips to unpurse:
"So far, one possibly may understand
Without recourse to witchcraft!" True, my
    dear.
Thus folks begin with Euclid, — finish, how?
Trying to square the circle! — at any rate,
Solving abstruser problems than this first,
"How find the nearest way 'twixt point and
    point."
Deal but with moral mathematics so —
Master one merest moment's work of mine,
Even this practising with pen and ink, —
Demonstrate why I rather plied the quill
Than left the space a blank, — you gain a fact,
And God knows what a fact 's worth! So pro-
    ceed
By inference from just this moral fact
— I don't say, to that plaguy quadrature,
"What the whole man meant, whom you wish
    you knew,"
But, what meant certain things he did of old,
Which puzzled Europe, — why, you 'll find
    them plain,
This way, not otherwise: I guarantee,
Understand one, you comprehend the rest.
Rays from all round converge to any point:
Study the point then ere you track the rays!
The size o' the circle 's nothing; subdivide
Earth, and earth's smallest grain of mustard-
    seed,
You count as many parts, small matching large,
If you can use the mind's eye: otherwise,
Material optics, being gross at best,
Prefer the large and leave our mind the small—
And pray how many folk have minds can see?
Certainly you — and somebody in Thrace
Whose name escapes me at the moment. You —
Lend me your mind then! Analyze with me
This instance of the line 'twixt blot and blot
I rather chose to draw than leave a blank,
Things else being equal. You are taught
    thereby
That 't is my nature, when I am at ease.

Rather than idle out my life too long,
To want to do a thing — to put a thought,
Whether a great thought or a little one,
Into an act, as nearly as may be.
Make what is absolutely new — I can't,
Mar what is made already well enough —
I won't : but turn to best account the thing
That 's half-made — that I can. Two blots, you
    saw
I knew how to extend into a line
Symmetric on the sheet they blurred before —
Such little act sufficed, this time, such thought.

Now, we 'll extend rays, widen out the verge,
Describe a larger circle ; leave this first
Clod of an instance we began with, rise
To the complete world many clods effect.
Only continue patient while I throw,
Delver-like, spadeful after spadeful up,
Just as truths come, the subsoil of me, mould
Whence spring my moods : your object, — just
    to find,
Alike from handlift and from barrow-load,
What salts and silts may constitute the earth —
If it be proper stuff to blow man glass,
Or bake him pottery, bear him oaks or wheat—
What 's born of me, in brief ; which found,
    all 's known.
If it were genius did the digging-job,
Logic would speedily sift its product smooth
And leave the crude truths bare for poetry ;
But I 'm no poet, and am stiff i' the back.
What one spread fails to bring, another may.
In goes the shovel and out comes scoop — as
    here !

I live to please myself. I recognize
Power passing mine, immeasurable, God —
Above me, whom he made, as heaven beyond
Earth — to use figures which assist our sense.
I know that he is there as I am here,
By the same proof, which seems no proof at all,
It so exceeds familiar forms of proof.
Why " there," not " here " ? Because, when
    I say " there "
I treat the feeling with distincter shape
That space exists between us : I, — not he, —
Live, think, do human work here — no machine.
His will moves, but a being by myself,
His, and not he who made me for a work,
Watches my working, judges its effect,
But does not interpose. He did so once,
And probably will again some time — not now,
Life being the minute of mankind, not God's,
In a certain sense, like time before and time
After man's earthly life, so far as man
Needs apprehend the matter. Am I clear ?
Suppose I bid a courier take to-night —
(. . Once for all, let me talk as if I smoked
Yet in the Residenz, a personage :
I must still represent the thing I was,
Galvanically make dead muscle play,
Or how shall I illustrate muscle's use ?)
I could then, last July, bid courier take
Message for me, post-haste, a thousand miles.
I bid him, since I have the right to bid,
And, my part done so far, his part begins ;
He starts with due equipment, will and power,

Means he may use, misuse, not use at all,
At his discretion, at his peril too.
I leave him to himself : but, journey done,
I count the minutes, call for the result
In quickness and the courier quality,
Weigh its worth, and then punish or reward
According to proved service ; not before.
Meantime, he sleeps through noontide, rides till
    dawn,
Sticks to the straight road, tries the crooked
    path,
Measures and manages resource, trusts, doubts
Advisers by the wayside, does his best
At his discretion, lags or launches forth,
(He knows and I know) at his peril too.
You see ? Exactly thus men stand to God :
I with my courier, God with me. Just so
I have his bidding to perform ; but mind
And body, all of me, though made and meant
For that sole service, must consult, concert
With my own self and nobody beside,
How to effect the same : God helps not else.
'T is I who, with my stock of craft and strength,
Choose the directer cut across the hedge,
Or keep the foot-track that respects a crop.
Lie down and rest, rise up and run, — live spare,
Feed free, — all that 's my business : but, ar-
    rive,
Deliver message, bring the answer back,
And make my bow, I must : then God will
    speak,
Praise me or haply blame as service proves.
To other men, to each and every one,
Another law ! what likelier ? God, perchance,
Grants each new man, by some as new a mode,
Intercommunication with himself,
Wreaking on finiteness infinitude ;
By such a series of effects, gives each
Last his own imprint : old yet ever new
The process : 't is the way of Deity.
How it succeeds, he knows : I only know
That varied modes of creatureship abound,
Implying just as varied intercourse
For each with the creator of them all.
Each has his own mind and no other's mode.
What mode may yours be ? I shall sympathize !
No doubt, you, good young lady that you are,
Despite a natural naughtiness or two,
Turn eyes up like a Pradier Magdalen
And see an outspread providential hand
Above the owl's-wing aigrette — guard and
    guide —
Visibly o'er your path, about your bed,
Through all your practisings with London-town.
It points, you go ; it stays fixed, and you stop ;
You quicken its procedure by a word
Spoken, a thought in silence, prayer and praise
Well, I believe that such a hand may stoop,
And such appeals to it may stave off harm,
Pacify the grim guardian of this Square,
And stand you in good stead on quarter-day :
Quite possible in your case ; not in mine.
" Ah, but I choose to make the difference,
Find the emancipation ? " No, I hope !
If I deceive myself, take noon for night,
Please to become determinedly blind
To the true ordinance of human life,
Through mere presumption — that is my affair,

And truly a grave one ; but as grave I think
Your affair, yours, the specially observed, —
Each favored person that perceives his path
Pointed him, inch by inch, and looks above
For guidance, through the mazes of this world,
In what we call its meanest life-career
— Not how to manage Europe properly,
But how keep open shop, and yet pay rent,
Rear household, and make both ends meet, the
    same.
I say, such man is no less tasked than I
To duly take the path appointed him
By whatsoever sign he recognize.
Our insincerity on both our heads !
No matter what the object of a life,
Small work or large, — the making thrive a
    shop,
Or seeing that an empire take no harm, —
There are known fruits to judge obedience by.
You 've read a ton's weight, now, of news-
    paper —
Lives of me, gabble about the kind of prince —
You know my work i' the rough ; I ask you,
    then,
Do I appear subordinated less
To hand-impulsion, one prime push for all,
Than little lives of men, the multitude
That cried out, every quarter of an hour,
For fresh instructions, did or did not work,
And praised in the odd minutes ?

                    Eh, my dear ?
Such is the reason why I acquiesced
In doing what seemed best for me to do,
So as to please myself on the great scale,
Having regard to immortality
No less than life — did that which head and
    heart
Prescribed my hand, in measure with its means
Of doing — used my special stock of power —
Not from the aforesaid head and heart alone,
But every sort of helpful circumstance,
Some problematic and some nondescript :
All regulated by the single care
I' the last resort — that I made thoroughly serve
The when and how, toiled where was need, re-
    posed
As resolutely at the proper point,
Braved sorrow, courted joy, to just one end :
Namely, that just the creature I was bound
To be, I should become, nor thwart at all
God's purpose in creation. I conceive
No other duty possible to man, —
Highest mind, lowest mind, — no other law
By which to judge life failure or success :
What folk call being saved or cast away.

Such was my rule of life ; I worked my best,
Subject to ultimate judgment, God's not man's.
Well then, this settled, — take your tea, I beg,
And meditate the fact, 'twixt sip and sip, —
This settled — why I pleased myself, you saw
By turning blot and blot into a line,
O' the little scale, — we 'll try now (as your
    tongue
Tries the concluding sugar-drop) what 's meant
To please me most o' the great scale. Why,
    just now,

With nothing else to do within my reach,
Did I prefer making two blots one line
To making yet another separate
Third blot, and leaving those I found unlinked ?
It meant, I like to use the thing I find,
Rather than strive at unfound novelty :
I make the best of the old, nor try for new.
Such will to act, such choice of action's way,
Constitute — when at work on the great scale,
Driven to their farthest natural consequence
By all the help from all the means — my own
Particular faculty of serving God,
Instinct for putting power to exercise
Upon some wish and want o' the time, I prove
Possible to mankind as best I may.
This constitutes my mission, — grant the
    phrase, —
Namely, to rule men — men within my reach,
To order, influence and dispose them so
As render solid and stability
Mankind in particles, the light and loose,
For their good and my pleasure in the act.
Such good accomplished proves twice good to
    me —
Good for its own sake, as the just and right,
And, in the effecting also, good again
To me its agent, tasked as suits my taste.

Is this much easy to be understood
At first glance ? Now begin the steady gaze !

My rank — (if I must tell you simple truth —
Telling were else not worth the whiff o' the
    weed
I lose for the tale's sake) — dear, my rank i'
    the world
Is hard to know and name precisely : err
I may, but scarcely overestimate
My style and title. Do I class with men
Most useful to their fellows ? Possibly, —
Therefore, in some sort, best ; but, greatest
    mind
And rarest nature ? Evidently no.
A conservator, call me, if you please,
Not a creator nor destroyer : one
Who keeps the world safe. I profess to trace
The broken-circle of society,
Dim actual order, I can redescribe
Not only where some segment silver-true
Stays clear, but where the breaks of black
    commence
Baffling you all who want the eye to probe —
As I make out yon problematic thin
White paring of your thumb-nail outside there,
Above the plaster-monarch on his steed —
See an inch, name an ell, and prophesy
O' the rest that ought to follow, the round
    moon
Now hiding in the night of things : that round,
I labor to demonstrate moon enough
For the month's purpose, — that society,
Render efficient for the age's need :
Preserving you in either case the old,
Nor aiming at a new and greater thing,
A sun for moon, a future to be made
By first abolishing the present law :
No such proud task for me by any means !
History shows you men whose master-touch

Not so much modifies as makes anew:
Minds that transmute nor need restore at all.
A breath of God made manifest in flesh
Subjects the world to change, from time to
    time,
Alters the whole conditions of our race
Abruptly, not by unperceived degrees
Nor play of elements already there,
But quite new leaven, leavening the lump,
And liker, so, the natural process. See!
Where winter reigned for ages — by a turn
I' the time, some star-change, (ask geologists,)
The ice-tracts split, clash, splinter and disperse,
And there 's an end of immobility,
Silence, and all that tinted pageant, base
To pinnacle, one flush from fairy-land
Dead-asleep and deserted somewhere, — see! —
As a fresh sun, wave, spring and joy outburst.
Or else the earth it is, time starts from trance,
Her mountains tremble into fire, her plains
Heave blinded by confusion: what result?
New teeming growth, surprises of strange life
Impossible before, a world broke up
And re-made, order gained by law destroyed.
Not otherwise, in our society
Follow like portents, all as absolute
Regenerations: they have birth at rare
Uncertain unexpected intervals
O' the world, by ministry impossible
Before and after fulness of the days:
Some dervish desert-spectre, swordsman, saint,
Lawgiver, lyrist, — oh, we know the names!
Quite other these than I. Our time requires
No such strange potentate, — who else would
    dawn, —
No fresh force till the old have spent itself.
Such seems the natural economy.
To shoot a beam into the dark, assists:
To make that beam do fuller service, spread
And utilize such bounty to the height,
That assists also, — and that work is mine.
I recognize, contemplate, and approve
The general compact of society,
Not simply as I see effected good,
But good i' the germ, each chance that 's possi-
    ble
I' the plan traced so far: all results, in short,
For better or worse of the operation due
To those exceptional natures, unlike mine,
Who, helping, thwarting, conscious, unaware,
Did somehow manage to so far describe
This diagram left ready to my hand,
Waiting my turn of trial. I see success,
See failure, see what makes or mars through-
    out.
How shall I else but help complete this plan
Of which I know the purpose and approve,
By letting stay therein what seems to stand,
And adding good thereto of easier reach
To-day than yesterday?

        So much, no more!
Whereon, "No more than that?" — inquire
    aggrieved
Half of my critics: "nothing new at all?
The old plan saved, instead of a sponged slate
And fresh-drawn figure?" — while, "So much
    as that?"

Object their fellows of the other faith:
" Leave uneffaced the crazy labyrinth
Of alteration and amendment, lines
Which every dabster felt in duty bound
To signalize his power of pen and ink
By adding to a plan once plain enough?
Why keep each fool's bequeathment, scratch
    and blur
Which overscrawl and underscore the piece —
Nay, strengthen them by touches of your
    own?"

Well, that 's my mission, so I serve the world,
Figure as man o' the moment, — in default
Of somebody inspired to strike such change
Into society — from round to square,
The ellipsis to the rhomboid, how you please,
As suits the size and shape o' the world he
    finds.
But this I can, — and nobody my peer, —
Do the best with the least change possible:
Carry the incompleteness on, a stage,
Make what was crooked straight, and rough-
    ness smooth,
And weakness strong: wherein if I succeed,
It will not prove the worst achievement, sure,
In the eyes at least of one man, one I look
Nowise to catch in critic company:
To wit, the man inspired, the genius' self
Destined to come and change things thoroughly.
He, at least, finds his business simplified,
Distinguishes the done from undone, reads
Plainly what meant and did not mean this
    time
We live in, and I work on, and transmit
To such successor: he will operate
On good hard substance, not mere shade and
    shine.
Let all my critics, born to idleness
And impotency, get their good, and have
Their hooting at the giver: I am deaf —
Who find great good in this society,
Great gain, the purchase of great labor. Touch
The work I may and must, but — reverent
In every fall o' the finger-tip, no doubt.
Perhaps I find all good there 's warrant for
I' the world as yet: nay, to the end of time, —
Since evil never means part company
With mankind, only shift side and change
    shape.
I find advance i' the main, and notably
The Present an improvement on the Past,
And promise for the Future — which shall
    prove
Only the Present with its rough made smooth,
Its indistinctness emphasized; I hope
No better, nothing newer for mankind,
But something equably smoothed everywhere,
Good, reconciled with hardly-quite-as-good,
Instead of good and bad each jostling each.
"And that 's all?" Ay, and quite enough for
    me!
We have toiled so long to gain what gain I find
I' the Present, — let us keep it! We shall toil
So long before we gain — if gain God grant —
A Future with one touch of difference
I' the heart of things, and not their outside
    face, —

Let us not risk the whiff of my cigar
For Fourier, Comte, and all that ends in smoke !

This I see clearest probably of men
With power to act and influence, now alive :
Juster than they to the true state of things ;
In consequence, more tolerant that, side
By side, shall co-exist and thrive alike
In the age, the various sorts of happiness
Moral, mark ! — not material — moods o' the
     mind
Suited to man and man his opposite :
Say, minor modes of movement — hence to
     there,
Or thence to here, or simply round about —
So long as each toe spares its neighbor's kibe,
Nor spoils the major march and main advance.
The love of peace, care for the family,
Contentment with what 's bad but might be
     worse —
Good movements these ! and good, too, dis-
     content,
So long as that spurs good, which might be
     best,
Into becoming better, anyhow :
Good — pride of country, putting hearth and
     home
I' the background, out of undue prominence :
Good — yearning after change, strife, victory,
And triumph. Each shall have its orbit
     marked,
But no more, — none impede the other's path
In this wide world, — though each and all
     alike,
Save for me, fain would spread itself through
     space
And leave its fellow not an inch of way.
I rule and regulate the course, excite,
Restrain : because the whole machine should
     march
Impelled by those diversely-moving parts,
Each blind to aught beside its little bent.
Out of the turnings round and round inside,
Comes that straightforward world-advance, I
     want,
And none of them supposes God wants too
And gets through just their hindrance and my
     help.
I think that to have held the balance straight
For twenty years, say, weighing claim and
     claim
And giving each its due, no less no more,
This was good service to humanity,
Right usage of my power in head and heart,
And reasonable piety beside.
Keep those three points in mind while judging
     me !
You stand, perhaps, for some one man, not
     men, —
Represent this or the other interest,
Nor mind the general welfare, — so, impugn
My practice and dispute my value : why ?
You man of faith, I did not tread the world
Into a paste, and thereof make a smooth
Uniform mound whereon to plant your flag,
The lily-white, above the blood and brains !
Nor yet did I, you man of faithlessness,
So roll things to the level which you love,

That you could stand at ease there and survey
The universal Nothing undisgraced
By pert obtrusion of some old church-spire
I' the distance ! Neither friend would I con-
     tent,
Nor, as the world were simply meant for him,
Thrust out his fellow and mend God's mistake.
Why, you two fools, — my dear friends all the
     same, —
Is it some change o' the world and nothing else
Contents you ? Should whatever was, not be ?
How thanklessly you view things ! There 's
     the root
Of the evil, source of the entire mistake :
You see no worth i' the world, nature and life,
Unless we change what is to what may be,
Which means, — may be, i' the brain of one of
     you !
" Reject what is ? " — all capabilities —
Nay, you may style them chances if you
     choose —
All chances, then, of happiness that lie
Open to anybody that is born,
Tumbles into this life and out again, —
All that may happen, good and evil too,
I' the space between, to each adventurer
Upon this 'sixty, Anno Domini :
A life to live — and such a life ! a world
To learn, one's lifetime in, — and such a
     world !
How did the foolish ever pass for wise
By calling life a burden, man a fly
Or worm or what 's most insignificant ?
" O littleness of man ! " deplores the bard ;
And then, for fear the Powers should punish
     him,
" O grandeur of the visible universe
Our human littleness contrasts withal !
O sun, O moon, ye mountains and thou sea,
Thou emblem of immensity, thou this,
That and the other, — what impertinence
In man to eat and drink and walk about
And have his little notions of his own,
The while some wave sheds foam upon the
     shore ! "
First of all, 't is a lie some three-times thick :
The bard, — this sort of speech being poetry, —
The bard puts mankind well outside himself
And then begins instructing them : " This way
I and my friend the sea conceive of you !
What would you give to think such thoughts
     as ours
Of you and the sea together ? " Down they go
On the humbled knees of them : at once they
     draw
Distinction, recognize no mate of theirs
In one, despite his mock humility,
So plain a match for what he plays with. Next,
The turn of the great ocean-playfellow,
When the bard, leaving Bond Street very far
From ear-shot, cares not to ventriloquize,
But tells the sea its home-truths : " You, my
     match ?
You, all this terror and immensity
And what not ? Shall I tell you what you are ?
Just fit to hitch into a stanza, so
Wake up and set in motion who 's asleep
O' the other side of you in England, else

Unaware, as folk pace their Bond Street now,
Somebody here despises them so much!
Between us, — they are the ultimate! to them
And their perception go these lordly thoughts:
Since what were ocean — mane and tail, to
    boot —
Mused I not here, how make thoughts think-
    able?
Start forth my stanza and astound the world!
Back, billows, to your insignificance!
Deep, you are done with!"

        Learn, my gifted friend,
There are two things i' the world, still wiser
    folk
Accept — intelligence and sympathy.
You pant about unutterable power
I' the ocean, all you feel but cannot speak?
Why, that's the plainest speech about it all.
You did not feel what was not to be felt.
Well, then, all else but what man feels is
    naught —
The wash o' the liquor that o'erbrims the cup
Called man, and runs to waste adown his side,
Perhaps to feed a cataract, — who cares?
I'll tell you: all the more I know mankind,
The more I thank God, like my grandmother,
For making me a little lower than
The angels, honor-clothed and glory-crowned:
This is the honor, — that no thing I know,
Feel or conceive, but I can make my own
Somehow, by use of hand or head or heart:
This is the glory, — that in all conceived,
Or felt or known, I recognize a mind
Not mine but like mine, — for the double joy, —
Making all things for me and me for Him.
There's folly for you at this time of day!
So think it! and enjoy your ignorance
Of what — no matter for the worthy's name —
Wisdom set working in a noble heart.
When he, who was earth's best geometer
Up to that time of day, consigned his life
With its results into one matchless book,
The triumph of the human mind so far,
All in geometry man yet could do:
And then wrote on the dedication-page
In place of name the universe applauds,
"But, God, what a geometer art Thou!"
I suppose Heaven is, through Eternity,
The equalizing, ever and anon,
In momentary rapture, great with small,
Omniscience with intelligency, God
With man, — the thunder-glow from pole to
    pole
Abolishing, a blissful moment-space,
Great cloud alike and small cloud, in one fire —
As sure to ebb as sure again to flow
When the new receptivity deserves
The new completion. There's the Heaven for
    me.
And I say, therefore, to live out one's life
I' the world here, with the chance, — whether
    by pain
Or pleasure be the process, long or short
The time, august or mean the circumstance
To human eye, — of learning how set foot
Decidedly on some one path to Heaven,
Touch segment in the circle whence all lines

Lead to the centre equally, red lines
Or black lines, so they but produce them-
    selves —
This, I do say, — and here my sermon ends, —
This makes it worth our while to tenderly
Handle a state of things which mend we might,
Mar we may, but which meanwhile helps so far.
Therefore my end is — save society!

"And that's all?" twangs the never-failing
    taunt
O' the foe — "No novelty, creativeness,
Mark of the master that renews the age?"
"Nay, all that?" rather will demur my judge
I look to hear some day, nor friend nor foe —
"Did you attain, then, to perceive that God
Knew what he undertook when he made
    things?"
Ay: that my task was to co-operate
Rather than play the rival, chop and change
The order whence comes all the good we know,
With this, — good's last expression to our
    sense, —
That there's a further good conceivable
Beyond the utmost earth can realize:
And, therefore, that to change the agency,
The evil whereby good is brought about —
Try to make good do good as evil does —
Were just as if a chemist, wanting white,
And knowing black ingredients bred the dye,
Insisted these too should be white forsooth!
Correct the evil, mitigate your best,
Blend mild with harsh, and soften black to
    gray
If gray may follow with no detriment
To the eventual perfect purity!
But as for hazarding the main result
By hoping to anticipate one half
In the intermediate process, — no, my friends!
This bad world, I experience and approve;
Your good world, — with no pity, courage,
    hope,
Fear, sorrow, joy, — devotedness, in short,
Which I account the ultimate of man,
Of which there's not one day nor hour but
    brings,
In flower or fruit, some sample of success,
Out of this same society I save —
None of it for me! That I might have none,
I rapped your tampering knuckles twenty years.
Such was the task imposed me, such my end.

Now for the means thereto. Ah, confidence —
Keep we together or part company?
This is the critical minute! "Such my end?"
Certainly; how could it be otherwise?
Can there be question which was the right
    task —
To save or to destroy society?
Why, even prove that, by some miracle,
Destruction were the proper work to choose,
And that a torch best remedies what's wrong
I' the temple, whence the long procession
    wound
Of powers and beauties, earth's achievements
    all,
The human strength that strove and over-
    threw, —

The human love that, weak itself, crowned
    strength, —
The instinct crying, "God is whence I
    came ! " —
The reason laying down the law, " And such
His will i' the world must be ! " — the leap and
    shout
Of genius, " For I hold his very thoughts,
The meaning of the mind of him ! " — nay,
    more
The ingenuities, each active force
That turning in a circle on itself
Looks neither up nor down but keeps the spot,
Mere creature-like and, for religion, works,
Works only and works ever, makes and shapes
And changes, still wrings more of good from
    less,
Still stamps some bad out, where was worst
    before,
So leaves the handiwork, the act and deed,
Were it but house and land and wealth, to show
Here was a creature perfect in the kind —
Whether as bee, beaver, or behemoth,
What 's the importance ? he has done his work
For work 's sake, worked well, earned a crea-
    ture's praise ; —
I say, concede that same fane, whence deploys
Age after age, all this humanity,
Diverse but ever dear, out of the dark
Behind the altar into the broad day
By the portal — enter, and, concede there
    mocks
Each lover of free motion and much space
A perplexed length of apse and aisle and
    nave,
Pillared roof and carved screen, and what care
    I ? —
Which irk the movement and impede the
    march, —
Nay, possibly, bring flat upon his nose
At some odd breakneck angle, by some freak
Of old-world artistry, that personage
Who, could he but have kept his skirts from
    grief
And catching at the hooks and crooks about,
Had stepped out on the daylight of our time
Plainly the man of the age, — still, still, I bar
Excessive conflagration in the case.
" Shake the flame freely ! " shout the multi-
    tude:
The architect approves I stuck my torch
Inside a good stout lantern, hung its light
Above the hooks and crooks, and ended so.
To save society was well : the means
Whereby to save it, — there begins the doubt
Permitted you, imperative on me ;
Were mine the best means? Did I work
    aright
With powers appointed me? — since powers de-
    nied
Concern me nothing.

                Well, my work reviewed
Fairly, leaves more hope than discouragement.
First, there 's the deed done : what I found, I
    leave, —
What tottered, I kept stable : if it stand
One month, without sustainment, still thank me

The twenty years' sustainer ! Now, observe,
Sustaining is no brilliant self-display
Like knocking down or even setting up :
Much bustle these necessitate ; and still
To vulgar eye, the mightier of the myth
Is Hercules, who substitutes his own
For Atlas' shoulder and supports the globe
A whole day, — not the passive and obscure
Atlas who bore, ere Hercules was born,
And is to go on bearing that same load
When Hercules turns ash on Œta's top.
'T is the transition-stage, the tug and strain,
That strike men : standing still is stupid-like.
My pressure was too constant on the whole
For any part's eruption into space
'Mid sparkles, crackling, and much praise of
    me.
I saw that, in the ordinary life,
Many of the little make a mass of men
Important beyond greatness here and there ;
As certainly as, in life exceptional,
When old things terminate and new commence,
A solitary great man 's worth the world.
God takes the business into his own hands
At such time : who creates the novel flower
Contrives to guard and give it breathing-room :
I merely tend the cornfield, care for crop,
And weed no acre thin to let emerge
What prodigy may stifle there perchance,
— No, though my eye have noted where he
    lurks.
Oh those mute myriads that spoke loud to me —
The eyes that craved to see the light, the
    mouths
That sought the daily bread and nothing more,
The hands that supplicated exercise,
Men that had wives, and women that had babes,
And all these making suit to only live !
Was I to turn aside from husbandry,
Leave hope of harvest for the corn, my care,
To play at horticulture, rear some rose
Or poppy into perfect leaf and bloom
When, 'mid the furrows, up was pleased to
    sprout
Some man, cause, system, special interest
I ought to study, stop the world meanwhile?
" But I am Liberty, Philanthropy,
Enlightenment, or Patriotism, the power
Whereby you are to stand or fall ! " cries each:
" Mine and mine only be the flag you flaunt ! "
And, when I venture to object, " Meantime,
What of yon myriads with no flag at all —
My crop which, who flaunts flag must tread
    across ? "
" Now, this it is to have a puny mind ! "
Admire my mental prodigies : " down —
    down —
Ever at home o' the level and the low,
There bides he brooding ! Could he look
    above,
With less of the owl and more of the eagle eye,
He 'd see there 's no way helps the little cause
Like the attainment of the great. Dare first
The chief emprise ; dispel yon cloud between
The sun and us ; nor fear that, though our
    heads
Find earlier warmth and comfort from his ray,
What lies about our feet, the multitude,

Will fail of benefaction presently.
Come now, let each of us awhile cry truce
To special interests, make common cause
Against the adversary — or perchance
Mere dullard to his own plain interest!
Which of us will you choose? — since needs
must be
Some one o' the warring causes you incline
To hold, i' the main, has right and should pre-
vail:
Why not adopt and give it prevalence?
Choose strict Faith or lax Incredulity, —
King, Caste, and Cultus — or the Rights of
Man,
Sovereignty of each Proudhon o'er himself,
And all that follows in just consequence!
Go free the stranger from a foreign yoke;
Or stay, concentrate energy at home;
Succeed! — when he deserves, the stranger will.
Comply with the Great Nation's impulse, print
By force of arms, — since reason pleads in vain,
And, 'mid the sweet compulsion, pity weeps, —
Hohenstiel-Schwangau on the universe!
Snub the Great Nation, cure the impulsive itch
With smartest fillip on a restless nose
Was ever launched by thumb and finger! Bid
Hohenstiel-Schwangau first repeal the tax
On pig-tails and pomatum, and then mind
Abstruser matters for next century!
Is your choice made? Why then, act up to
choice!
Leave the illogical touch now here now there
I' the way of work, the tantalizing help
First to this, then the other opposite:
The blowing hot and cold, sham policy,
Sure ague of the mind and nothing more,
Disease of the perception or the will,
That fain would hide in a fine name! Your
choice,
Speak it out and condemn yourself thereby!"

Well, Leicester Square is not the Residenz:
Instead of shrugging shoulder, turning friend
The deaf ear, with a wink to the police —
I 'll answer — by a question, wisdom's mode.
How many years, o' the average, do men
Live in this world? Some score, say computists.
Quintuple me that term and give mankind
The likely hundred, and with all my heart
I 'll take your task upon me, work your way,
Concentrate energy on some one cause:
Since, counseller, I also have my cause,
My flag, my faith in its effect, my hope
In its eventual triumph for the good
O' the world. And once upon a time, when I
Was like all you, mere voice and nothing more,
Myself took wings, soared sunward, and thence
sang,
"Look where I live i' the loft, come up to me,
Groundlings, nor grovel longer! gain this
height,
And prove you breathe here better than below!
Why, what emancipation far and wide
Will follow in a trice! They too can soar,
Each tenant of the earth's circumference
Claiming to elevate humanity,
They also must attain such altitude,
Live in the luminous circle that surrounds

The planet, not the leaden orb itself.
Press out, each point, from surface to yon verge
Which one has gained and guaranteed your
realm!"
Ay, still my fragments wander, music-fraught,
Sighs of the soul, mine once, mine now, and
mine
Forever! Crumbled arch, crushed aqueduct.
Alive with tremors in the shaggy growth
Of wild-wood, crevice-sown, that triumphs there
Imparting exultation to the hills!
Sweep of the swathe when only the winds walk
And waft my words above the grassy sea
Under the blinding blue that basks o'er
Rome, —
Hear ye not still — "Be Italy again"?
And ye, what strikes the panic to your heart?
Decrepit council-chambers, — where some lamp
Drives the unbroken black three paces off
From where the graybeards huddle in debate,
Dim cowls and capes, and midmost glimmers
one
Like tarnished gold, and what they say is
doubt,
And what they think is fear, and what suspends
The breath in them is not the plaster-patch
Time disengages from the painted wall
Where Rafael moulderingly bids adieu,
Nor tick of the insect turning tapestry
Which a queen's finger traced of old, to dust;
But some word, resonant, redoubtable,
Of who once felt upon his head a hand
Whereof the head now apprehends his foot.
"Light in Rome, Law in Rome, and Liberty
O' the soul in Rome — the free Church, the
free State!
Stamp out the nature that 's best typified
By its embodiment in Peter's Dome,
The scorpion-body with the greedy pair
Of outstretched nippers, either colonnade
Agape for the advance of heads and hearts!"
There 's one cause for you! one and only one,
For I am vocal through the universe,
I' the workshop, manufactory, exchange
And market-place, seaport and custom-house
O' the frontier: listen if the echoes die —
"Unfettered commerce! Power to speak and
hear,
And print and read! The universal vote!
Its rights for labor!" This, with much beside,
I spoke when I was voice and nothing more,
But altogether such an one as you
My censors. "Voice, and nothing more, in-
deed!"
Re-echoes round me: "that 's the censure,
there 's
Involved the ruin of you soon or late!
Voice, — when its promise beat the empty air:
And nothing more, — when solid earth 's your
stage,
And we desiderate performance, deed
For word, the realizing all you dreamed
In the old days: now, for deed, we find at door
O' the council-chamber posted, mute as mouse,
Hohenstiel-Schwangau, sentry and safeguard
O' the graybeards all a-chuckle, cowl to cape,
Who challenge Judas, — that 's endearment's
style, —

To stop their mouths or let escape grimace,
While they keep cursing Italy and him.
The power to speak, hear, print and read is
    ours?
Ay, we learn where and how, when clapped
    inside
A convict-transport bound for cool Cayenne!
The universal vote we have: its urn,
We also have where votes drop, fingered-o'er
By the universal Prefect. Say, Trade 's free
And Toil turned master out o' the slave it was:
What then? These feed man's stomach, but
    his soul
Craves finer fare, nor lives by bread alone,
As somebody says somewhere. Hence you
    stand
Proved and recorded either false or weak,
Faulty in promise or performance: which?"
Neither, I hope. Once pedestalled on earth,
To act not speak, I found earth was not air.
I saw that multitude of mine, and not
The nakedness and nullity of air
Fit only for a voice to float in free.
Such eyes I saw that craved the light alone,
Such mouths that wanted bread and nothing
    else,
Such hands that supplicated handiwork,
Men with the wives, and women with the babes,
Yet all these pleading just to live, not die!
Did I believe one whit less in belief,
Take truth for falsehood, wish the voice re-
    voked
That told the truth to heaven for earth to hear?
No, this should be, and shall; but when and
    how?
At what expense to these who average
Your twenty years of life, my computists?
" Not bread alone," but bread before all else
For these: the bodily want serve first, said I;
If earth-space and the lifetime help not here,
Where is the good of body having been?
But, helping body, if we somewhat balk
The soul of finer fare, such food 's to find
Elsewhere and afterward — all indicates,
Even this selfsame fact that soul can starve
Yet body still exist its twenty years:
While, stint the body, there 's an end at once
O' the revel in the fancy that Rome 's free,
And superstition 's fettered, and one prints
Whate'er one pleases, and who pleases reads
The same, and speaks out and is spoken to,
And divers hundred thousand fools may vote
A vote untampered with by one wise man,
And so elect Barabbas deputy
In lieu of his concurrent. I who trace
The purpose written on the face of things,
For my behoof and guidance — (whoso needs
No such sustainment, sees beneath my signs,
Proves, what I take for writing, penmanship,
Scribble and flourish with no sense for me
O' the sort I solemnly go spelling out, —
Let him! there 's certain work of mine to show
Alongside his work: which gives warranty
Of shrewder vision in the workman — judge!)
I who trace Providence without a break
I' the plan of things, drop plumb on this plain
    print
Of an intention with a view to good,

That man is made in sympathy with man
At outset of existence, so to speak;
But in dissociation, more and more,
Man from his fellow, as their lives advance
In culture; still humanity, that 's born
A mass, keeps flying off, fining away
Ever into a multitude of points,
And ends in isolation, each from each:
Peerless above i' the sky, the pinnacle, —
Absolute contact, fusion, all below
At the base of being. How comes this about?
This stamp of God characterizing man
And nothing else but man in the universe —
That, while he feels with man (to use man
    speech)
I' the little things of life, its fleshly wants
Of food and rest and health and happiness,
Its simplest spirit-motions, loves and hates,
Hopes, fears, soul-cravings on the ignoblest scale,
O' the fellow - creature, — owns the bond at
    base, —
He tends to freedom and divergency
In the upward progress, plays the pinnacle
When life 's at greatest (grant again the
    phrase!
Because there 's neither great nor small in life).
" Consult thou for thy kind that have the eyes
To see, the mouths to eat, the hands to work,
Men with the wives, and women with the
    babes!"
Prompts Nature. " Care thou for thyself alone
I' the conduct of the mind God made thee with!
Think, as if man had never thought before!
Act, as if all creation hung attent
On the acting of such faculty as thine,
To take prime pattern from thy masterpiece!"
Nature prompts also: neither law obeyed
To the uttermost by any heart and soul
We know or have in record: both of them
Acknowledged blindly by whatever man
We ever knew or heard of in this world.
" Will you have why and wherefore, and the
    fact
Made plain as pikestaff?" modern Science asks.
" That mass man sprung from was a jelly-lump
Once on a time; he kept an after-course
Through fish and insect, reptile, bird and beast,
Till he attained to be an ape or last but one.
Or last but one. And if this doctrine shock
In aught the natural pride" . . . Friend, ban-
    ish fear,
The natural humility replies.
Do you suppose, even I, poor potentate,
Hohenstiel - Schwangau, who once ruled the
    roast, —
I was born able at all points to ply
My tools? or did I have to learn my trade,
Practise as exile ere perform as prince?
The world knows something of my ups and
    downs:
But grant me time, give me the management
And manufacture of a model me,
Me fifty-fold, a prince without a flaw, —
Why, there 's no social grade, the sordidest,
My embryo potentate should blink and 'scape,
King, all the better he was cobbler once,
He should know, sitting on the throne, how
    tastes

Life to who sweeps the doorway. But life 's
  hard,
Occasion rare ; you cut probation short,
And, being half-instructed, on the stage
You shuffle through your part as best you can,
And bless your stars, as I do. God takes time.
I like the thought he should have lodged me
  once
I' the hole, the cave, the hut, the tenement,
The mansion and the palace ; made me learn
The feel o' the first, before I found myself
Loftier i' the last, not more emancipate ;
From first to last of lodging, I was I,
And not at all the place that harbored me.
Do I refuse to follow farther yet
I' the backwardness, repine if tree and flower,
Mountain or streamlet were my dwelling-place
Before I gained enlargement, grew mollusc ?
As well account that way for many a thrill
Of kinship, I confess to, with the powers
Called Nature: animate, inanimate,
In parts or in the whole, there 's something there
Man-like that somehow meets the man in me.
My pulse goes altogether with the heart
O' the Persian, that old Xerxes, when he stayed
His march to conquest of the world, a day
I' the desert, for the sake of one superb
Plane-tree which queened it there in solitude :
Giving her neck its necklace, and each arm
Its armlet, suiting soft waist, snowy side,
With cincture and apparel. Yes, I lodged
In those successive tenements ; perchance
Taste yet the straitness of them while I stretch
Limb and enjoy new liberty the more.
And some abodes are lost or ruinous ;
Some, patched-up and pieced-out, and so trans-
  formed
They still accommodate the traveller
His day of lifetime. Oh, you count the links,
Descry no bar of the unbroken man ?
Yes, — and who welds a lump of ore, suppose
He likes to make a chain and not a bar,
And reach by link on link, link small, link large,
Out to the due length — why, there 's fore-
  thought still
Outside o' the series, forging at one end,
While at the other there 's — no matter what
The kind of critical intelligence
Believing that last link had last but one
For parent, and no link was, first of all,
Fitted to anvil, hammered into shape.
Else, I accept the doctrine, and deduce
This duty, that I recognize mankind,
In all its height and depth and length and
  breadth.
Mankind i' the main have little wants, not large :
I, being of will and power to help, i' the main,
Mankind, must help the least wants first. My
  friend,
That is, my foe, without such power and will,
May plausibly concentrate all he wields,
And do his best at helping some large want,
Exceptionally noble cause, that 's seen
Subordinate enough from where I stand.
As he helps, I helped once, when like himself,
Unable to help better, work more wide ;
And so would work with heart and hand to-day,
Did only computists confess a fault,

And multiply the single score by five,
Five only, give man's life its hundred years.
Change life, in me shall follow change to match !
Time were then, to work here, there, every-
  where,
By turns and try experiment at ease !
Full time to mend as well as mar : why wait
The slow and sober uprise all around
O' the building ? Let us run up, right to roof,
Some sudden marvel, piece of perfectness,
And testify what we intend the whole !
Is the world losing patience ? "Wait !" say we:
"There 's time : no generation needs to die
Unsolaced ; you 've a century in store !"
But, no : I sadly let the voices wing
Their way i' the upper vacancy, nor test
Truth on this solid as I promised once.
Well, and what is there to be sad about ?
The world 's the world, life 's life, and nothing
  else.
'T is part of life, a property to prize,
That those o' the higher sort engaged i' the
  world,
Should fancy they can change its ill to good,
Wrong to right, ugliness to beauty : find
Enough success in fancy turning fact,
To keep the sanguine kind in countenance
And justify the hope that busies them :
Failure enough, — to who can follow change
Beyond their vision, see new good prove ill
I' the consequence, see blacks and whites of life
Shift square indeed, but leave the checkered face
Unchanged i' the main, — failure enough for
  such,
To bid ambition keep the whole from change,
As their best service. I hope naught beside.
No, my brave thinkers, whom I recognize,
Gladly, myself the first, as, in a sense,
All that our world 's worth, flower and fruit of
  man !
Such minds myself award supremacy
Over the common insignificance,
When only Mind 's in question, — Body bows
To quite another government, you know.
Be Kant crowned king o' the castle in the air !
Hans Slouch — his own, and children's mouths
  to feed
I' the hovel on the ground — wants meat, nor
  chews
"The Critique of Pure Reason" in exchange.
But, now, — suppose I could allow your claims
And quite change life to please you, — would it
  please ?
Would life comport with change and still be life ?
Ask, now, a doctor for a remedy :
There 's his prescription. Bid him point you out
Which of the five or six ingredients saves
The sick man. "Such the efficacy ?
Then why not dare and do things in one dose
Simple and pure, all virtue, no alloy
Of the idle drop and powder ?" What 's his
  word ?
The efficacy, neat, were neutralized :
It wants dispersing and retarding, — nay,
Is put upon its mettle, plays its part
Precisely through such hindrance everywhere,
Finds some mysterious give and take i' the case
Some gain by opposition, he foregoes

Should he unfetter the medicament.
So with this thought of yours that fain would
    work
Free in the world : it wants just what it finds —
The ignorance, stupidity, the hate,
Envy and malice and uncharitableness
That bar your passage, break the flow of you
Down from those happy heights where many a
    cloud
Combined to give you birth and bid you be
The royalest of rivers : on you glide
Silverly till you reach the summit-edge,
Then over, on to all that ignorance,
Stupidity, hate, envy, bluffs and blocks,
Posted to fret you into foam and noise.
What of it ?   Up you mount in minute mist,
And bridge the chasm that crushed your qui-
    etude,
A spirit-rainbow, earthborn jewelry
Outsparkling the insipid firmament
Blue above Terni and its orange-trees.
Do not mistake me ! You, too, have your rights !
Hans must not burn Kant's house above his head
Because he cannot understand Kant's book :
And still less must Hans' pastor burn Kant's self
Because Kant understands some books too well.
But, justice seen to on this little point,
Answer me, is it manly, is it sage
To stop and struggle with arrangements here
It took so many lives, so much of toil,
To tinker up into efficiency ?
Can't you contrive to operate at once, —
Since time is short and art is long, — to show
Your quality i' the world, whate'er you boast,
Without this fractious call on folks to crush
The world together just to set you free,
Admire the capers you will cut perchance,
Nor mind the mischief to your neighbors ?

                                    " Age !
Age and experience bring discouragement,"
You taunt me : I maintain the opposite.
Am I discouraged who — perceiving health,
Strength, beauty, as they tempt the eye of soul,
Are uncombinable with flesh and blood —
Resolve to let my body live its best,
And leave my soul what better yet may be
Or not be, in this life or afterward ?
— In either fortune, wiser than who waits
Till magic art procure a miracle.
In virtue of my very confidence
Mankind ought to outgrow its babyhood ;
I prescribe rocking, deprecate rough hands,
While thus the cradle holds it past mistake.
Indeed, my task 's the harder — equable
Sustainment everywhere, all strain, no push —
Whereby friends credit me with indolence,
Apathy, hesitation. "Stand stock-still
If able to move briskly ? ' All a-strain ' —
So must we compliment your passiveness ?
Sound asleep, rather ! "

                        Just the judgment passed
Upon a statue, luckless like myself,
I saw at Rome once ! 'T was some artist's
    whim
To cover all the accessories close
I' the group, and leave you only Laocoön

With neither sons nor serpents to denote
The purpose of his gesture.   Then a crowd
Was called to try the question, criticise
Wherefore such energy of legs and arms,
Nay, eyeballs, starting from the socket. One —
I give him leave to write my history —
Only one said, " I think the gesture strives
Against some obstacle we cannot see."
All the rest made their minds up. " 'T is a
    yawn
Of sheer fatigue subsiding to repose :
The statue 's ' Somnolency ' clear enough ! "

There, my arch stranger-friend, my audience
    both
And arbitress, you have one half your wish,
At least : you know the thing I tried to do !
All, so far, to my praise and glory — all
Told as befits the self-apologist, —
Who ever promises a candid sweep
And clearance of those errors miscalled crimes
None knows more, none laments so much as he,
And ever rises from confession, proved
A god whose fault was — trying to be man.
Just so, fair judge, — if I read smile aright —
I condescend to figure in your eyes
As biggest heart and best of Europe's friends,
And hence my failure.   God will estimate
Success one day ; and, in the mean time — you !

I daresay there 's some fancy of the sort
Frolicking round this final puff I send
To die up yonder in the ceiling-rose, —
Some consolation-stakes, we losers win !
A plague of the return to " I — I — I
Did this, meant that, hoped, feared the other
    thing ! "
Autobiography, adieu !   The rest
Shall make amends, be pure blame, history
And falsehood : not the ineffective truth,
But Thiers-and-Victor-Hugo exercise.
Hear what I never was, but might have been
I' the better world where goes tobacco-smoke !
Here lie the dozen volumes of my life :
(Did I say "lie" ? the pregnant word will
    serve.)
Cut on to the concluding chapter, though !
Because the little hours begin to strike.
Hurry Thiers-Hugo to the labor's end !

Something like this the unwritten chapter
    reads.

Exemplify the situation thus !
Hohenstiel-Schwangau, being, no dispute,
Absolute mistress, chose the Assembly, first,
To serve her : chose this man, its President
Afterward, to serve also, — specially
To see that folk did service one and all.
And now the proper term of years was out,
When the Head-servant must vacate his place ;
And nothing lay so patent to the world
As that his fellow-servants one and all
Were — mildly to make mention — knaves or
    fools,
Each of them with his promise flourished full
I' the face of you by word and impudence,
Or filtered slyly out by nod and wink

And nudge upon your sympathetic rib —
That not one minute more did knave or fool
Mean to keep faith and serve as he had sworn
Hohenstiel-Schwangau, once her Head away.
Why should such swear except to get the
    chance,
When time should ripen and confusion bloom,
Of putting Hohenstielers-Schwangauese
To the true use of human property —
Restoring souls and bodies, this to Pope,
And that to King, that other to his planned
Perfection of a Share-and-share-alike,
That other still, to Empire absolute
In shape of the Head-servant's very self
Transformed to Master whole and sole? each
    scheme
Discussible, concede one circumstance —
That each scheme's parent were, beside him-
    self,
Hohenstiel-Schwangau, not her serving-man
Sworn to do service in the way she chose
Rather than his way : way superlative,
Only, — by some infatuation, — his
And his and his and every one's but hers
Who stuck to just the Assembly and the Head.
I make no doubt the Head, too, had his dream
Of doing sudden duty swift and sure
On all that heap of untrustworthiness —
Catching each vaunter of the villany
He meant to perpetrate when time was ripe,
Once the Head-servant fairly out of doors, —
And, caging here a knave and there a fool,
Cry, " Mistress of your servants, these and me,
Hohenstiel-Schwangau ! I, their trusty Head,
Pounce on a pretty scheme concocting here
That 's stopped, extinguished by my vigilance.
Your property is safe again : but mark !
Safe in these hands, not yours, who lavish
    trust
Too lightly.   Leave my hands their charge
    awhile !
I know your business better than yourself :
Let me alone about it ! Some fine day,
Once we are rid of the embarrassment,
You shall look up and see your longings
    crowned ! "
Such fancy might have tempted him be false,
But this man chose truth and was wiser so.
He recognized that for great minds i' the world
There is no trial like the appropriate one
Of leaving little minds their liberty
Of littleness to blunder on through life,
Now aiming at right ends by foolish means,
Now, at absurd achievement through the aid
Of good and wise endeavor — to acquiesce
In folly's life-long privilege, though with power
To do the little minds the good they need,
Despite themselves, by just abolishing
Their right to play the part and fill the place
I' the scheme of things He schemed who made
    alike
Great minds and little minds, saw use for each.
Could the orb sweep those puny particles
It just half-lights at distance, hardly leads
I' the leash — sweep out each speck of them
    from space
They anticise in with their days and nights
And whirlings round and dancings off, forsooth,

And all that fruitless individual life
One cannot lend a beam to but they spoil —
Sweep them into itself and so, one star,
Preponderate henceforth i' the heritage
Of heaven !   No ! in less senatorial phrase,
The man endured to help, not save outright
The multitude by substituting him
For them, his knowledge, will and way, for
    God's :
Nor change the world, such as it is, and was
And will be, for some other, suiting all
Except the purpose of the maker. No !
He saw that weakness, wickedness will be,
And therefore should be : that the perfect man,
As we account perfection — at most pure
O' the special gold, whate'er the form it take,
Head-work or heart-work, fined and thrice
    refined
I' the crucible of life, whereto the powers
Of the refiner, one and all, are flung
To feed the flame, he saw that e'en the block,
Such perfect man holds out triumphant, breaks
Into some poisonous ore, gold's opposite,
At the very purest, so compensating
Man's Adversary — what if we believe ?
For earlier stern exclusion of his stuff.
See the sage, with the hunger for the truth,
And see his system that 's all true, except
The one weak place that 's stanchioned by a
    lie !
The moralist, who walks with head erect
I' the crystal clarity of air so long,
Until a stumble, and the man 's one mire !
Philanthropy undoes the social knot
With axe-edge, makes love room 'twixt head
    and trunk :
Religion — but, enough, the thing 's too clear !
Well, if these sparks break out i' the greenest
    tree,
Our topmost of performance, yours and mine,
What will be done i' the dry ineptitude
Of ordinary mankind, bark and bole,
All seems ashamed of but their mother-earth ?
Therefore throughout Head's term of servitude
He did the appointed service, and forebore
Extraneous action that were duty else,
Done by some other servant, idle now
Or mischievous : no matter, each his own —
Own task, and, in the end, own praise or blame !
He suffered them strut, prate, and brag their
    best,
Squabble at odds on every point save one,
And there shake hands, — agree to trifle time,
Obstruct advance with, each, his cricket-cry,
" Wait till the Head be off the shoulders here !
Then comes my King, my Pope, my Autocrat,
My Socialist Republic to her own —
To-wit, that property of only me,
Hohenstiel-Schwangau who conceits herself
Free, forsooth, and expects I keep her so ! "
— Nay, suffered when, perceiving with dismay
Head's silence paid no tribute to their noise,
They turned on him. " Dumb menace in that
    mouth,
Malice in that unstridulosity !
He cannot but intend some stroke of state
Shall signalize his passage into peace
Out of the creaking, — hinder transference

O' the Hohenstielers-Schwangauese to king,
Pope, autocrat, or socialist republic! That 's
Exact the cause his lips unlocked would cry!
Therefore be stirring: brave, beard, bully him!
Dock, by the million, of its friendly joints,
The electoral body short at once! who did,
May do again, and undo us beside;
Wrest from his hands the sword for self-de-
    fence,
The right to parry any thrust in play
We peradventure please to meditate!"
And so forth; creak, creak, creak: and ne'er
    a line
His locked mouth oped the wider, till at last
O' the long degraded and insulting day,
Sudden the clock told it was judgment-time.
Then he addressed himself to speak indeed
To the fools, not knaves: they saw him walk
    straight down
Each step of the eminence, as he first engaged,
And stand at last o' the level, — all he swore.
"People, and not the people's varletry,
This is the task you set myself and these!
Thus I performed my part of it, and thus
They thwarted me throughout, here, here and
    here:
Study each instance! yours the loss, not mine.
What they intend now is demonstrable
As plainly: here 's such man, and here 's such
    mode
Of making you some other than the thing
You, wisely or unwisely, choose to be,
And only set him up to keep you so.
Do you approve this? Yours the loss, not
    mine.
Do you condemn it? There 's a remedy.
Take me — who know your mind, and mean
    your good,
With clearer brain and stouter arm than they,
Or you, or haply anybody else —
And make me master for the moment! Choose
What time, what power you trust me with: I
    too
Will choose as frankly ere I trust myself
With time and power: they must be adequate
To the end and aim, since mine the loss, with
    yours,
If means be wanting; once their worth ap-
    proved,
Grant them, and I shall forthwith operate —
Ponder it well! — to the extremest stretch
O' the power you trust me: if with unsuccess,
God wills it, and there 's nobody to blame."

Whereon the people answered with a shout,
"The trusty one! no tricksters any more!"
How could they other? He was in his place.

What followed? Just what he foresaw, what
    proved
The soundness of both judgments, — his, o' the
    knaves
And fools, each trickster with his dupe, — and
    theirs,
The people's, in what head and arm could help.
There was uprising, masks dropped, flags un-
    furled,
Weapons outflourished in the wind, my faith!

Heavily did he let his fist fall plumb
On each perturber of the public peace,
No matter whose the wagging head it broke —
From bald-pate craft and greed and impudence
Of night-hawk at first chance to prowl and prey
For glory and a little gain beside,
Passing for eagle in the dusk of the age, —
To florid head-top, foamy patriotism
And tribunitial daring, breast laid bare
Through confidence in rectitude, with hand
On private pistol in the pocket: these
And all the dupes of these, who lent themselves
As dust and feather do, to help offence
O' the wind that whirls them at you, then sub-
    sides
In safety somewhere, leaving filth afloat,
Annoyance you may brush from eyes and
    beard, —
These he stopped: bade the wind's spite howl
    or whine
Its worst outside the building, wind conceives
Meant to be pulled together and become
Its natural playground so. What foolishness
Of dust or feather proved importunate
And fell 'twixt thumb and finger, found them
    gripe
To detriment of bulk and buoyancy.
Then followed silence and submission. Next,
The inevitable comment came on work
And work's cost: he was censured as profuse
Of human life and liberty: too swift
And thorough his procedure, who had lagged
At the outset, lost the opportunity
Through timid scruples as to right and wrong.
"There 's no such certain mark of a small
    mind "
(So did Sagacity explain the fault)
"As when it needs must square away and sink
To its own small dimensions, private scale
Of right and wrong, — humanity i' the large,
The right and wrong of the universe, forsooth!
This man addressed himself to guard and
    guide
Hohenstiel-Schwangau. When the case de-
    mands
He frustrate villany in the egg, unhatched,
With easy stamp and minimum of pang
E'en to the punished reptile, ' There 's my oath
Restrains my foot,' objects our guide and
    guard,
' I must leave guardianship and guidance now:
Rather than stretch one handbreadth of the
    law,
I am bound to see it break from end to end.
First show me death i' the body politic:
Then prescribe pill and potion, what may
    please
Hohenstiel-Schwangau! all is for her sake:
'T was she ordained my service should be so.
What if the event demonstrate her unwise,
If she unwill the thing she willed before?
I hold to the letter and obey the bond
And leave her to perdition loyally.'
Whence followed thrice the expenditure we
    blame
Of human life and liberty: for want
O' the by-blow, came deliberate butcher's
    work!"

'Elsewhere go carry your complaint!" bade
  he.
'Least, largest, there's one law for all the
  minds,
Here or above: be true at any price!
'T is just o' the great scale, that such happy
  stroke
Of falsehood would be found a failure. Truth
Still stands unshaken at her base by me,
Reigns paramount i' the world, for the large
  good
O' the long late generations, — I and you
Forgotten like this buried foolishness!
Not so the good I rooted in its grave."

This is why he refused to break his oath,
Rather appealed to the people, gained the
  power
To act as he thought best, then used it, once
For all, no matter what the consequence
To knaves and fools. As thus began his sway,
So, through its twenty years, one rule of right
Sufficed him: govern for the many first,
The poor mean multitude, all mouths and eyes:
Bid the few, better favored in the brain,
Be patient, nor presume on privilege,
Help him or else be quiet, — never crave
That he help them, — increase, forsooth, the
  gulf
Yawning so terribly 'twixt mind and mind
I' the world here, which his purpose was to
  block
At bottom, were it by an inch, and bridge,
If by a filament, no more, at top.
Equalize things a little! And the way
He took to work that purpose out, was plain
Enough to intellect and honesty
And — superstition, style it if you please,
So long as you allow there was no lack
O' the quality imperative in man —
Reverence. You see deeper? thus saw he,
And by the light he saw, must walk: how else
Was he to do his part? a man's, with might
And main, and not a faintest touch of fear,
Sure he was in the hand of God who comes
Before and after, with a work to do
Which no man helps nor hinders. Thus the
  man, —
So timid when the business was to touch
The uncertain order of humanity,
Imperil, for a problematic cure
Of grievance on the surface, any good
I' the deep of things, dim yet discernible, —
This same man, so irresolute before,
Show him a true excrescence to cut sheer,
A devil's graft on God's foundation-stock,
Then — no complaint of indecision more!
He wrenched out the whole canker, root and
  branch,
Deaf to who cried that earth would tumble in
At its four corners if he touched a twig.
Witness that lie of lies, arch-infamy,
When the Republic, with her life involved
In just this law — "Each people rules itself
Its own way, not as any stranger please " —
Turned, and for first proof she was living, bade
Hohenstiel-Schwangau fasten on the throat
Of the first neighbor that claimed benefit

O' the law herself established: "Hohenstiel
For Hohenstielers! Rome, by parity
Of reasoning, for Romans? That's a jest
Wants proper treatment, — lancet - puncture
  suits
The proud flesh: Rome ape Hohenstiel for-
  sooth!"
And so the siege and slaughter and success
Whereof we nothing doubt that Hohenstiel
Will have to pay the price, in God's good time
Which does not always fall on Saturday
When the world looks for wages. Anyhow,
He found this infamy triumphant. Well:
Sagacity suggested, make this speech!
"The work was none of mine: suppose wrong
  wait,
Stand over for redressing? Mine for me,
My predecessors' work on their own head!
Meantime, there's plain advantage, should we
  leave
Things as we find them. Keep Rome mana-
  cled
Hand and foot: no fear of unruliness!
Her foes consent to even seem our friends
So long, no longer. Then, there's glory got
By boldness and bravado to the world:
The disconcerted world must grin and bear
The old saucy writing, — 'Grunt thereat who
  may,
So shall things be, for such my pleasure is —
Hohenstiel-Schwangau's.' How that reads in
  Rome,
I' the capitol where Brennus broke his pate,
And lends a flourish to our journalists!"
Only, it was nor read nor flourished of,
Since, not a moment did such glory stay
Excision of the canker! Out it came,
Root and branch, with much roaring, and some
  blood,
And plentiful abuse of him from friend
And foe. Who cared? Not Nature, who as-
  suaged
The pain and set the patient on his legs
Promptly: the better! had it been the worse,
'T is Nature you must try conclusions with,
Not he, since nursing canker kills the sick
For certain, while to cut may cure, at least.
"Ah," groaned a second time Sagacity,
"Again the little mind, precipitate,
Rash, rude, when even in the right, as here!
The great mind knows the power of gentleness,
Only tries force because persuasion fails.
Had this man, by prelusive trumpet-blast,
Signified, 'Truth and Justice mean to come,
Nay, fast approach your threshold! Ere they
  knock,
See that the house be set in order, swept
And garnished, windows shut, and doors
  thrown wide!
The free State comes to visit the free Church:
Receive her! or . . . or . . . never mind what
  else!'
Thus moral suasion heralding brute force,
How had he seen the old abuses die,
And new life kindle here, there, everywhere,
Roused simply by that mild yet potent spell —
Beyond or beat of drum or stroke of sword —
Public opinion!"

" How, indeed ? " he asked,
" When all to see, after some twenty years,
Were your own fool-face waiting for the sight,
Faced by as wide a grin from ear to ear
O' the knaves who, while the fools were wait-
    ing, worked —
Broke yet another generation's heart —
Twenty years' respite helping! Teach your
    nurse
' Compliance with, before you suck, the teat ! '
Find what that means, and meanwhile hold
    your tongue ! "

Whereof the war came which he knew must
    be.

Now, this had proved the dry-rot of the race
He ruled o'er, that, i' the old day, when was
    need
They fought for their own liberty and life,
Well did they fight, none better : whence, such
    love
Of fighting somehow still for fighting's sake
Against no matter whose the liberty
And life, so long as self-conceit should crow
And clap the wing, while justice sheathed her
    claw, —
That what had been the glory of the world
When thereby came the world's good, grew its
    plague
Now that the champion-armor, donned to dare
The dragon once, was clattered up and down
Highway and by-path of the world at peace,
Merely to mask marauding, or for sake
O' the shine and rattle that apprised the fields
Hohenstiel-Schwangau was a fighter yet,
And would be, till the weary world suppressed
Her peccant humors out of fashion now.
Accordingly the world spoke plain at last,
Promised to punish who next played with fire.

So, at his advent, such discomfiture
Taking its true shape of beneficence,
Hohenstiel-Schwangau, half-sad and part-wise,
Sat : if with wistful eye reverting oft
To each pet weapon, rusty on its peg,
Yet, with a sigh of satisfaction too
That, peacefulness become the law, herself
Got the due share of godsends in its train,
Cried shame and took advantage quietly.
Still, so the dry-rot had been nursed into
Blood, bones and marrow, that, from worst to
    best,
All, — clearest brains and soundest hearts save
    here, —
All had this lie acceptable for law
Plain as the sun at noonday — " War is best,
Peace is worst ; peace we only tolerate
As needful preparation for new war :
War may be for whatever end we will —
Peace only as the proper help thereto.
Such is the law of right and wrong for us
Hohenstiel-Schwangau : for the other world,
As naturally, quite another law.
Are we content ? The world is satisfied.
Discontent? Then the world must give us
    leave
To strike right, left, and exercise our arm

Torpid of late through overmuch repose,
And show its strength is still superlative
At somebody's expense in life or limb :
Which done, — let peace succeed and last a
    year ! "
Such devil's-doctrine so was judged God's law,
We say, when this man stepped upon the stage,
That it had seemed a venial fault at most
Had he once more obeyed Sagacity.
" You come i' the happy interval of peace,
The favorable weariness from war :
Prolong it ! artfully, as if intent
On ending peace as soon as possible.
Quietly so increase the sweets of ease
And safety, so employ the multitude,
Put hod and trowel so in idle hands,
So stuff and stop up wagging jaws with bread,
That selfishness shall surreptitiously
Do wisdom's office, whisper in the ear
Of Hohenstiel-Schwangau, there 's a pleasant
    feel
In being gently forced down, pinioned fast
To the easy arm-chair by the pleading arms
O' the world beseeching her to there abide
Content with all the harm done hitherto,
And let herself be petted in return,
Free to re-wage, in speech and prose and verse,
The old unjust wars, nay — in verse and prose
And speech, — to vaunt new victories, shall
    prove
A plague o' the future, — so that words suffice
For present comfort, and no deeds denote
That — tired of illimitable line on line
Of boulevard-building, tired o' the theatre
With the tuneful thousand in their thrones
    above,
For glory of the male intelligence,
And Nakedness in her due niche below,
For illustration of the female use —
That she, 'twixt yawn and sigh, prepares to
    slip
Out of the arm-chair, wants fresh blood again
From over the boundary, to color-up
The sheeny sameness, keep the world aware
Hohenstiel-Schwangau's arm needs exercise
Despite the petting of the universe !
Come, you 're a city-builder : what 's the way
Wisdom takes when time needs that she entice
Some fierce tribe, castled on the mountain-peak,
Into the quiet and amenity
O' the meadow-land below ? By crying ' Done
With fight now, down with fortress ' ? Rather
    — ' Dare
On, dare ever, not a stone displaced ! '
Cries Wisdom : ' Cradle of our ancestors,
Be bulwark, give our children safety still !
Who of our children please may stoop and taste
O' the valley-fatness, unafraid, — for why ?
At first alarm they have thy mother-ribs
To run upon for refuge ; foes forget
Scarcely that Terror on her vantage-coign,
Couchant supreme among the powers of air,
Watches — prepared to pounce — the country
    wide !
Meanwhile the encouraged valley holds its own,
From the first hut's adventure in descent,
Half home, half hiding-place, — to dome and
    spire

Befitting the assured metropolis :
Nor means offence to the fort which caps the
	crag,
All undismantled of a turret-stone,
And bears the banner-pole that creaks at times
Embarrassed by the old emblazonment,
When festal days are to commemorate :
Otherwise left untenanted, no doubt,
Since, never fear, our myriads from below
Would rush, if needs were, man the walls again,
Renew the exploits of the earlier time
At moment's notice !   But till notice sound,
Inhabit we in ease and opulence ! '
And so, till one day thus a notice sounds,
Not trumpeted, but in a whisper-gust
Fitfully playing through mute city streets
At midnight weary of day's feast and game —
'Friends, your famed fort 's a ruin past repair !
Its use is — to proclaim it had a use
Obsolete long since.   Climb and study there
How to paint barbican and battlement
I' the scenes of our new theatre !   We fight
Now — by forbidding neighbors to sell steel
Or buy wine, not by blowing out their brains !
Moreover, while we let time sap the strength
O' the walls omnipotent in menace once,
Neighbors would seem to have prepared sur-
	prise —
Run up defences in a mushroom-growth,
For all the world like what we boasted : brief —
Hohenstiel-Schwangau's policy is peace ! ' "

Ay, so Sagacity advised him filch
Folly from fools ; handsomely substitute
The dagger o' lath, while gay they sang and
	danced,
For that long dangerous sword they liked to
	feel,
Even at feast-time, clink and make friends
	start.
No ! he said : " Hear the truth, and bear the
	truth,
And bring the truth to bear on all you are
And do, assured that only good comes thence
Whate'er the shape good take !   While I have
	rule,
Understand ! — war for war's sake, war for sake
O' the good war gets you as war's sole excuse,
Is damnable and damned shall be.   You want
Glory ?   Why so do I, and so does God.
Where is it found, — in this paraded shame, —
One particle of glory ?   Once you warred
For liberty against the world, and won :
There was the glory.   Now, you fain would war
Because the neighbor prospers overmuch, —
Because there has been silence half-an-hour,
Like Heaven on earth, without a cannon-shot
Announcing Hohenstielers-Schwangauese
Are minded to disturb the jubilee, —
Because the loud tradition echoes faint,
And who knows but posterity may doubt
If the great deeds were ever done at all,
Much less believe, were such to do again,
So the event would follow : therefore, prove
The old power, at the expense of somebody !
Oh, Glory, — gilded bubble, bard and sage
So nickname rightly, — would thy dance endure
One moment, would thy vaunting make believe

Only one eye thy ball was solid gold,
Hadst thou less breath to buoy thy vacancy
Than a whole multitude expends in praise,
Less range for roaming than from head to head
Of a whole people ?   Flit, fall, fly again,
Only, fix never where the resolute hand
May prick thee, prove the glassy lie thou art !
Give me real intellect to reason with,
No multitude, no entity that apes
One wise man, being but a million fools !
How and whence wishest glory, thou wise one ?
Wouldst get it, — didst thyself guide Provi-
	dence, —
By stinting of his due each neighbor round
In strength and knowledge and dexterity
So as to have thy littleness grow large
By all those somethings once, turned nothings
	now,
As children make a molehill mountainous
By scooping out a trench around their pile,
And saving so the mudwork from approach ?
Quite otherwise the cheery game of life,
True yet mimetic warfare, whereby man
Does his best with his utmost, and so ends
The victor most of all in fair defeat.
Who thinks, — would he have no one think be-
	side ?
Who knows, who does, — save his must learning
	die
And action cease ?   Why, so our giant proves
No better than a dwarf, once rivalry
Prostrate around him.   Let the whole race stand
For him to try conclusions fairly with !
Show me the great man would engage his peer
Rather by grinning ' Cheat, thy gold is brass ! '
Than granting ' Perfect piece of purest ore !
Still, is it less good mintage, this of mine ? '
Well, and these right and sound results of soul
I' the strong and healthy one wise man, — shall
	such
Be vainly sought for, scornfully renounced
I' the multitude that make the entity —
The people ? — to what purpose, if no less,
In power and purity of soul, below
The reach of the unit than, by multiplied
Might of the body, vulgarized the more,
Above, in thick and threefold brutishness ?
See !   you accept such one wise man, myself :
Wiser or less wise, still I operate
From my own stock of wisdom, nor exact
Of other sort of natures you admire,
That whoso rhymes a sonnet pays a tax,
Who paints a landscape dips brush at his cost,
Who scores a septett true for strings and wind
Mulcted must be — else how should I impose
Properly, attitudinize aright,
Did such conflicting claims as these divert
Hohenstiel-Schwangau from observing me ?
Therefore, what I find facile, you be sure,
With effort or without it, you shall dare —
You, I aspire to make my better self
And truly the Great Nation.   No more war
For war's sake, then !   and, — seeing, wickedness
Springs out of folly, — no more foolish dread
O' the neighbor waxing too inordinate
A rival, through his gain of wealth and ease !
What ? — keep me patient, Powers ! — the peo-
	ple here.

Earth presses to her heart, nor owns a pride
Above her pride i' the race all flame and air
And aspiration to the boundless Great,
The incommensurably Beautiful —
Whose very falterings groundward come of
    flight
Urged by a pinion all too passionate
For heaven and what it holds of gloom and
    glow:
Bravest of thinkers, bravest of the brave
Doers, exalt in Science, rapturous
In Art, the — more than all — magnetic race
To fascinate their fellows, mould mankind
Hohenstiel-Schwangau-fashion, — these, what?
    — these
Will have to abdicate their primacy
Should such a nation sell them steel untaxed,
And such another take itself, on hire
For the natural sennight, somebody for lord
Unpatronized by me whose back was turned?
Or such another yet would fain build bridge,
Lay rail, drive tunnel, busy its poor self
With its appropriate fancy: so there's —
    flash —
Hohenstiel-Schwangau up in arms at once!
Genius has somewhat of the infantine:
But of the childish, not a touch nor taint
Except through self-will, which, being foolish-
    ness,
Is certain, soon or late, of punishment.
Which Providence avert! — and that it may
Avert what both of us would so deserve,
No foolish dread o' the neighbor, I enjoin!
By consequence, no wicked war with him,
While I rule!

            "Does that mean — no war at all
When just the wickedness I here proscribe
Comes, haply, from the neighbor? Does my
    speech
Precede the praying that you beat the sword
To ploughshare, and the spear to pruning-hook,
And sit down henceforth under your own vine
And fig-tree through the sleepy summer month,
Letting what hurly-burly please explode
On the other side the mountain-frontier? No,
Beloved! I foresee and I announce
Necessity of warfare in one case,
For one cause: one way, I bid broach the blood
O' the world. For truth and right, and only
    right
And truth, — right, truth, on the absolute scale
    of God,
No pettiness of man's admeasurement, —
In such case only, and for such one cause,
Fight your hearts out, whatever fate betide
Hands energetic to the uttermost!
Lie not! Endure no lie which needs your heart
And hand to push it out of mankind's path —
No lie that lets the natural forces work
Too long ere lay it plain and pulverized —
Seeing man's life lasts only twenty years!
And such a lie, before both man and God,
Proving, at this time present, Austria's rule
O'er Italy, — for Austria's sake the first,
Italy's next, and our sake last of all,
Come with me and deliver Italy!
Smite hip and thigh until the oppressor leave

Free from the Adriatic to the Alps
The oppressed one! We were they who laid
    her low
In the old bad day when Villany braved Truth
And Right, and laughed 'Henceforward, God
    deposed,
Satan we set to rule forevermore
I' the world!' — whereof to stop the conse-
    quence,
And for atonement of false glory there
Gaped at and gabbled over by the world,
I purpose to get God enthroned again
For what the world will gird at as sheer shame
I' the cost of blood and treasure. 'All for
    naught —
Not even, say, some patch of province, splice
O' the frontier? — some snug honorarium-fee
Shut into glove and pocketed apace?'
(Questions Sagacity) 'in deference
To the natural susceptibility
Of folks at home, unwitting of that pitch
You soar to, and misdoubting if Truth, Right
And the other such augustnesses repay
Expenditure in coin o' the realm, — but prompt
To recognize the cession of Savoy
And Nice as marketable value!' No,
Sagacity, go preach to Metternich,
And, sermon ended, stay where he resides!
Hohenstiel-Schwangau, you and I must march
The other road! war for the hate of war,
Not love, this once!" So Italy was free.

What else noteworthy and commendable
I' the man's career? — that he was resolute —
No trepidation, much less treachery
On his part, should imperil from its poise
The ball o' the world, heaved up at such expense
Of pains so far, and ready to rebound,
Let but a finger maladroitly fall,
Under pretence of making fast and sure
The inch gained by late volubility,
And run itself back to the ancient rest
At foot o' the mountain. Thus he ruled, gave
    proof
The world had gained a point, progressive so,
By choice, this time, as will and power con-
    curred,
O' the fittest man to rule; not chance of birth,
Or such-like dice-throw. Oft Sagacity
Was at his ear: "Confirm this clear advance,
Support this wise procedure! You, elect
O' the people, mean to justify their choice
And out-king all the kingly imbeciles;
But that's just half the enterprise: remains
You find them a successor like yourself,
In head and heart and eye and hand and aim,
Or all done's undone; and whom hope to
    mould
So like you as the pupil Nature sends,
The son and heir's completeness which you
    lack?
Lack it no longer! Wed the pick o' the world,
Where'er you think you find it. Should she be
A queen, — tell Hohenstielers-Schwangauese,
'So do the old enthroned decrepitudes
Acknowledge, in the rotten hearts of them,
Their knell is knolled, they hasten to make
    peace

With the new order, recognize in me
Your right to constitute what king you will,
Cringe therefore crown in hand and bride on
   arm,
To both of us: we triumph, I suppose! '
Is it the other sort of rank ? — bright eye,
Soft smile, and so forth, all her queenly boast ?
Undaunted the exordium — ' I, the man
O' the people, with the people mate myself :
So stand, so fall.   Kings, keep your crowns and
   brides !
Our progeny (if Providence agree)
Shall live to tread the baubles underfoot
And bid the scarecrows consort with their kin.
For son, as for his sire, be the free wife
In the free state ! ' "

               That is, Sagacity
Would prop up one more lie, the most of all
Pernicious fancy that the son and heir
Receives the genius from the sire, himself
Transmits as surely, — ask experience else !
Which answers, — never was so plain a truth
As that God drops his seed of heavenly flame
Just where he wills on earth : sometimes
   where man
Seems to tempt — such the accumulated store
Of faculties — one spark to fire the heap ;
Sometimes where, fireball-like, it falls upon
The naked unpreparèdness of rock,
Burns, beaconing the nations through their
   night.
Faculties, fuel for the flame ?   All helps
Come, ought to come, or come not, crossed by
   chance,
From culture and transmission.   What 's your
   want
I' the son and heir ?   Sympathy, aptitude,
Teachableness, the fuel for the flame ?
You 'll have them for your pains: but the
   flame's self,
The novel thought of God shall light the world ?
No, poet, though your offspring rhyme and
   chime
I' the cradle, — painter, no, for all your pet
Draws his first eye, beats Salvatore's boy, —
And thrice no, statesman, should your progeny
Tie bib and tucker with no tape but red,
And make a foolscap-kite of protocols !
Critic and copyist and bureaucrat
To heart's content !   The seed o' the apple-
   tree
Brings forth another tree which bears a crab !
'T is the great gardener grafts the excellence
On wildings where he will.

                  " How plain I view,
Across those misty years 'twixt me and
   Rome " —
(Such the man's answer to Sagacity)
" The little wayside temple, halfway down
To a mild river that makes oxen white
Miraculously, un-mouse-colors skin,
Or so the Roman country people dream !
I view that sweet small shrub-embedded shrine
On the declivity, was sacred once
To a transmuting Genius of the land,
Could touch and turn its dunnest natures bright,

— Since Italy means the Land of the Ox, we
   know.
Well, how was it the due succession fell
From priest to priest who ministered i' the cool
Calm fane o' the Clitumnian god ?   The sire
Brought forth a son and sacerdotal sprout,
Endowed instinctively with good and grace
To suit the gliding gentleness below —
Did he ?   Tradition tells another tale.
Each priest obtained his predecessor's staff,
Robe, fillet and insignia, blamelessly,
By springing out of ambush, soon or late,
And slaying him : the initiative rite
Simply was murder, save that murder took,
I' the case, another and religious name.
So it was once, is now, shall ever be
With genius and its priesthood in this world :
The new power slays the old — but handsomely.
There he lies, not diminished by an inch
Of stature that he graced the altar with,
Though somebody of other bulk and build
Cries, ' What a goodly personage lies here
Reddening the water where the bulrush roots !
May I conduct the service in his place,
Decently and in order, as did he,
And, as he did not, keep a wary watch
When meditating 'neath yon willow shade ! '
Find out your best man, sure the son of him
Will prove best man again, and, better still
Somehow than best, the grandson-prodigy !
You think the world would last another day
Did we so make us masters of the trick
Whereby the works go, we could pre-arrange
Their play and reach perfection when we please?
Depend on it, the change and the surprise
Are part o' the plan : 't is we wish steadiness ;
Nature prefers a motion by unrest,
Advancement through this force which jostles
   that.
And so, since much remains i' the world to
   see,
Here 's the world still, affording God the
   sight."
Thus did the man refute Sagacity,
Ever at this old whisper in his ear :
" Here are you picked out, by a miracle,
And placed conspicuously enough, folks say
And you believe, by Providence outright
Taking a new way — nor without success —
To put the world upon its mettle : good !
But Fortune alternates with Providence;
Resource is soon exhausted.   Never count
On such a happy hit occurring twice !
Try the old method next time ! "

                  " Old enough,"
(At whisper in his ear, the laugh outbroke,)
" And mode the most discredited of all,
By just the men and women who make boast
They are kings and queens thereby !   Mere
   self-defence
Should teach them, on one chapter of the law
Must be no sort of trifling — chastity :
They stand or fall, as their progenitors
Were chaste or unchaste.   Now, run eye
   around
My crowned acquaintance, give each life its
   look

And no more, — why, you 'd think each life
          was led
Purposely for example of what pains
Who leads it took to cure the prejudice,
And prove there 's nothing so unprovable
As who is who, what son of what a sire,
And — inferentially — how faint the chance
That the next generation needs to fear
Another fool o' the selfsame type as he
Happily regnant now by right divine
And luck o' the pillow !   No : select your lord
By the direct employment of your brains
As best you may, — bad as the blunder prove,
A far worse evil stank beneath the sun
When some legitimate blockhead managed so
Matters that high time was to interfere,
Though interference came from hell itself
And not the blind mad miserable mob
Happily ruled so long by pillow-luck
And divine right, — by lies in short, not truth.
And meanwhile use the allotted minute . . ."

———

                                        One, —
Two, three, four, five — yes, five the pendulum
          warns !
Eh ?   Why, this wild work wanders past all
          bound
And bearing !   Exile, Leicester Square, the life
I' the old gay miserable time, rehearsed,
Tried on again like cast clothes, still to serve
At a pinch, perhaps ?   " Who 's who ? " was
          aptly asked,
Since certainly I am not I !   since when ?
Where is the bud-mouthed arbitress ?   A nod
Out-Homering Homer !   Stay — there flits the
          clue
I fain would find the end of !   Yes, — " Mean-
          while,
Use the allotted minute ! "   Well, you see,
(Veracious and imaginary Thiers,
Who map out thus the life I might have led,
But did not, — all the worse for earth and
          me, —
Doff spectacles, wipe pen, shut book, decamp !)
You see 't is easy in heroics !   Plain
Pedestrian speech shall help me perorate.
Ah, if one had no need to use the tongue !
How obvious and how easy 't is to talk
Inside the soul, a ghostly dialogue —
Instincts with guesses, — instinct, guess, again
With dubious knowledge, half - experience :
          each
And all the interlocutors alike
Subordinating, — as decorum bids,
Oh, never fear ! but still decisively, —
Claims from without that take too high a tone,
— (" God wills this, man wants that, the dig-
          nity
Prescribed a prince would wish the other
          thing ") —
Putting them back to insignificance
Beside one intimatest fact — myself
Am first to be considered, since I live
Twenty years longer and then end, perhaps !
But, where one ceases to soliloquize,
Somehow the motives, that did well enough

I' the darkness, when you bring them into
          light
Are found, like those famed cave-fish, to lack
          eye
And organ for the upper magnitudes.
The other common creatures, of less fine
Existence, that acknowledge earth and heaven,
Have it their own way in the argument.
Yes, forced to speak, one stoops to say — one's
          aim
Was — what it peradventure should have
          been :
To renovate a people, mend or end
That bane come of a blessing meant the
          world —
Inordinate culture of the sense made quick
By soul, — the lust o' the flesh, lust of the eye,
And pride of life, — and, consequent on these,
The worship of that prince o' the power o' the
          air
Who paints the cloud and fills the emptiness
And bids his votaries, famishing for truth,
Feed on a lie.

          Alack, one lies one's self
Even in the stating that one's end was truth,
Truth only, if one states as much in words !
Give me the inner chamber of the soul
For obvious easy argument !   't is there
One pits the silent truth against a lie —
Truth which breaks shell a careless simple bird,
Nor wants a gorget nor a beak filed fine,
Steel spurs and the whole armory o' the tongue,
To equalize the odds.   But, do your best,
Words have to come : and somehow words
          deflect
As the best cannon ever rifled will.

" Deflect " indeed !   nor merely words from
          thoughts
But names from facts : " Clitumnus " did I
          say ?
As if it had been his ox-whitening wave
Whereby folk practised that grim cult of old —
The murder of their temple's priest by who
Would qualify for his succession.   Sure —
Nemi was the true lake's style.   Dream had
          need
Of the ox-whitening peace of prettiness
And so confused names, well known once
          awake.

So, i' the Residenz yet, not Leicester Square,
Alone, — no such congenial intercourse ! —
My reverie concludes, as dreaming should,
With daybreak : nothing done and over yet,
Except cigars !   The adventure thus may be,
Or never needs to be at all : who knows ?
My Cousin-Duke, perhaps, at whose hard head
— Is it, now — is this letter to be launched,
The sight of whose gray oblong, whose grim
          seal,
Set all these fancies floating for an hour ?

Twenty years are good gain, come what come
          will !
Double or quits !   The letter goes !   Or stays ?

FIFINE AT THE FAIR

DONE ELVIRE

Vous plaît-il, don Juan, nous éclaircir ces beaux mystères?

DON JUAN

Madame, à vous dire la vérité . . .

DONE ELVIRE

Ah! que vous savez mal vous défendre pour un homme de cour,
et qui doit être accoutumé à ces sortes de choses! J'ai pitié de vous
voir la confusion que vous avez. Que ne vous armez-vous le front
d'une noble effronterie? Que ne me jurez-vous que vous êtes
toujours dans les mêmes sentimens pour moi, que vous m'aimez
toujours avec une ardeur sans égale, et que rien n'est capable de
vous détacher de moi que la mort? — (MOLIERE, *Don Juan*, Acte i
Sc 3.)

DONNA ELVIRA

Don Juan, might you please to help one give a guess,
Hold up a candle, clear this fine mysteriousness?

DON JUAN

Madam, if needs I must declare the truth, — in short . .

DONNA ELVIRA

Fie, for a man of mode, accustomed at the court
To such a style of thing, how awkwardly my lord
Attempts defence! You move compassion, that's the word—
Dumb-foundered and chapfallen! Why don't you arm your brow
With noble impudence? Why don't you swear and vow
No sort of change is come to any sentiment
You ever had for me? Affection holds the bent,
You love me now as erst, with passion that makes pale
All ardor else: nor aught in nature can avail
To separate us two, save what, in stopping breath,
May peradventure stop devotion likewise — death!

PROLOGUE

AMPHIBIAN

THE fancy I had to-day,
   Fancy which turned a fear!
I swam far out in the bay,
   Since waves laughed warm and clear.

I lay and looked at the sun,
   The noon-sun looked at me:
Between us two, no one
   Live creature, that I could see.

Yes! There came floating by
   Me, who lay floating too,
Such a strange butterfly!
   Creature as dear as new:

Because the membraned wings
   So wonderful, so wide,
So sun-suffused, were things
   Like soul and naught beside.

A handbreadth overhead!
   All of the sea my own,
It owned the sky instead;
   Both of us were alone.

I never shall join its flight,
   For, naught buoys flesh in air.
If it touch the sea — good night!
   Death sure and swift waits there.

Can the insect feel the better
   For watching the uncouth play
Of limbs that slip the fetter,
   Pretend as they were not clay?

Undoubtedly I rejoice
   That the air comports so well
With a creature which had the choice
   Of the land once. Who can tell?

What if a certain soul
   Which early slipped its sheath,
And has for its home the whole
   Of heaven, thus look beneath.

Thus watch one who, in the world,
  Both lives and likes life's way,
Nor wishes the wings unfurled
  That sleep in the worm, they say?

But sometimes when the weather
  Is blue, and warm waves tempt
To free one's self of tether,
  And try a life exempt

From worldly noise and dust,
  In the sphere which overbrims
With passion and thought, — why, just
  Unable to fly, one swims!

By passion and thought upborne,
  One smiles to one's self — "They fare
Scarce better, they need not scorn
  Our sea, who live in the air!"

Emancipate through passion
  And thought, with sea for sky,
We substitute, in a fashion,
  For heaven — poetry:

Which sea, to all intent,
  Gives flesh such noon-disport
As a finer element
  Affords the spirit-sort.

Whatever they are, we seem:
  Imagine the thing they know;
All deeds they do, we dream;
  Can heaven be else but so?

And meantime, yonder streak
  Meets the horizon's verge;
That is the land, to seek
  If we tire or dread the surge:

Land the solid and safe —
  To welcome again (confess!)
When, high and dry, we chafe
  The body, and don the dress.

Does she look, pity, wonder
  At one who mimics flight,
Swims — heaven above, sea under,
  Yet always earth in sight?

FIFINE AT THE FAIR

I

O TRIP and skip, Elvire! Link arm in arm
  with me!
Like husband and like wife, together let us see
The tumbling-troop arrayed, the strollers on
  their stage,
Drawn up and under arms, and ready to engage.

II

Now, who supposed the night would play us
  such a prank?
— That what was raw and brown, rough pole
  and shaven plank,
Mere bit of hoarding, half by trestle propped,
  half tub,

Would flaunt it forth as brisk as butterfly from
  grub?
This comes of sun and air, of Autumn afternoon,
And Pornic and Saint Gille, whose feast affords
  the boon —
This scaffold turned parterre, this flower-bed in
  full blow,
Bateleurs, baladines! We shall not miss the
  show!
They pace and promenade; they presently will
  dance:
What good were else i' the drum and fife? O
  pleasant land of France!

III

Who saw them make their entry? At wink
  of eve, be sure!
They love to steal a march, nor lightly risk the
  lure.
They keep their treasure hid, nor stale (impro-
  vident)
Before the time is ripe, each wonder of their
  tent —
Yon six-legged sheep, to wit, and he who beats
  a gong,
Lifts cap and waves salute, exhilarates the
  throng —
Their ape of many years and much adventure,
  grim
And gray with pitying fools who find a joke in
  him.
Or, best, the human beauty, Mimi, Toinette,
  Fifine,
Tricot fines down if fat, padding plumps up if
  lean,
Ere, shedding petticoat, modesty, and such toys,
They bounce forth, squalid girls transformed
  to gamesome boys.

IV

No, no, thrice, Pornic, no! Perpend the
  authentic tale!
'Twas not for every Gawain to gaze upon the
  Grail!
But whoso went his rounds, when flew bat,
  flitted midge,
Might hear across the dusk, — where both
  roads join the bridge,
Hard by the little port, — creak a slow caravan,
A chimneyed house on wheels; so shyly-
  sheathed, began
To broaden out the bud which, bursting un-
  aware,
Now takes away our breath, queen-tulip of the
  Fair!

V

Yet morning promised much: for, pitched
  and slung and reared
On terrace 'neath the tower, 'twixt tree and
  tree appeared
An airy structure; how the pennon from its
  dome,
Frenetic to be free, makes one red stretch for
  home!
The home far and away, the distance where
  lives joy,

The cure, at once and ever, of world and
    world's annoy ;
Since, what lolls full in front, a furlong from
    the booth,
But ocean-idleness, sky-blue and millpond-
    smooth ?

VI

Frenetic to be free ! And, do you know,
    there beats
Something within my breast, as sensitive ? —
    repeats
The fever of the flag ? My heart makes just
    the same
Passionate stretch, fires up for lawlessness, lays
    claim
To share the life they lead : losels, who have
    and use
The hour what way they will, — applaud them
    or abuse
Society, whereof myself am at the beck,
Whose call obey, and stoop to burden stiffest
    neck !

VII

Why is it that whene'er a faithful few com-
    bine
To cast allegiance off, play truant, nor repine,
Agree to bear the worst, forego the best in
    store
For us who, left behind, do duty as of yore, —
Why is it that, disgraced, they seem to relish
    life the more ?
— Seem as they said, " We know a secret
    passing praise
Or blame of such as you ! Remain ! we go our
    ways
With something you o'erlooked, forgot or
    chose to sweep
Clean out of door : our pearl picked from your
    rubbish-heap.
You care not for your loss, we calculate our
    gain.
All 's right. Are you content ? Why, so let
    things remain !
To the wood then, to the wild : free life, full
    liberty ! "
And when they rendezvous beneath the in-
    clement sky,
House by the hedge, reduced to brute-com-
    panionship,
— Misguided ones who gave society the slip,
And find too late how boon a parent they de-
    spised,
What ministration spurned, how sweet and
    civilized —
Then, left alone at last with self-sought wretch-
    edness,
No interloper else ! — why is it, can we guess ? —
At somebody's expense, goes up so frank a
    laugh ?
As though they held the corn, and left us only
    chaff
From garners crammed and closed. And we
    indeed are clever
If we get grain as good, by threshing straw for-
    ever !

VIII

Still, truants as they are and purpose yet to
    be,
That nowise needs forbid they venture — as
    you see —
To cross confine, approach the once familiar
    roof
O' the kindly race their flight estranged : stand
    half aloof,
Sidle half up, press near, and proffer wares for
    sale
— In their phrase, — make in ours, white levy
    of black mail.
They, of the wild, require some touch of us the
    tame,
Since clothing, meat and drink, mean money
    all the same.

IX

If hunger, proverbs say, allures the wolf
    from wood,
Much more the bird must dare a dash at some-
    thing good :
Must snatch up, bear away in beak, the trifle-
    treasure
To wood and wild, and then — oh, how enjoy at
    leisure !
Was never tree-built nest, you climbed and
    took, of bird,
(Rare city-visitant, talked of, scarce seen or
    heard,)
But, when you would dissect the structure,
    piece by piece,
You found, enwreathed amid the country-
    product — fleece
And feather, thistle-fluffs and bearded windle-
    straws —
Some shred of foreign silk, unravelling of
    gauze,
Bit, maybe, of brocade, mid fur and blow-bell-
    down :
Filched plainly from mankind, dear tribute
    paid by town,
Which proved how oft the bird had plucked up
    heart of grace,
Swooped down at waif and stray, made fur-
    tively our place
Pay tax and toll, then borne the booty to en-
    rich
Her paradise i' the waste ; the how and why of
    which,
That is the secret, there the mystery that
    stings !

X

For, what they traffic in, consists of just the
    things
We, — proud ones who so scorn dwellers with-
    out the pale,
Bateleurs, baladines, white leviers of black
    mail, —
I say, they sell what we most pique us that we
    keep !
How comes it, all we hold so dear they count
    so cheap ?

XI

What price should you impose, for instance, on
    repute,
Good fame, your own good fame and family's
    to boot?
Stay start of quick moustache, arrest the angry
    rise
Of eyebrow! All I asked is answered by sur-
    prise.
Now tell me: are you worth the cost of a cigar?
Go boldly, enter booth, disburse the coin at bar
Of doorway where presides the master of the
    troop,
And forthwith you survey his Graces in a
    group,
Live Picture, picturesque no doubt and close
    to life:
His sisters, right and left; the Grace in front,
    his wife.
Next, who is this performs the feat of the Tra-
    peze?
Lo, she is launched, look — fie, the fairy! —
    how she flees
O'er all those heads thrust back, — mouths,
    eyes, one gape and stare, —
No scrap of skirt impedes free passage through
    the air,
Till, plumb on the other side, she lights and
    laughs again,
That fairy-form, whereof each muscle, nay,
    each vein
The curious may inspect, — his daughter that
    he sells
Each rustic for five sous. Desiderate aught
    else
O' the vendor? As you leave his show, why,
    joke the man!
"You cheat: your six-legged sheep, I recollect,
    began
Both life and trade, last year, trimmed prop-
    erly and clipt,
As the Twin-headed Babe, and Human Nonde-
    script!"
What does he care? You paid his price, may
    pass your jest.
So values he repute, good fame, and all the
    rest!

XII

But try another tack; say: "I indulge ca-
    price,
Who am Don and Duke, and Knight, beside, o'
    the Golden Fleece.
And, never mind how rich. Abandon this
    career!
Have hearth and home, nor let your woman-
    kind appear
Without as multiplied a coating as protects
An onion from the eye! Become, in all respects,
God-fearing householder, subsistent by brain-
    skill,
Hand-labor; win your bread whatever way
    you will,
So it be honestly, — and, while I have a purse,
Means shall not lack!" — his thanks will be
    the roundest curse
That ever rolled from lip.

XIII

Now, what is it? — returns
The question — heartens so this losel that he
    spurns
All we so prize? I want, put down in black
    and white,
What compensating joy, unknown and infin-
    ite,
Turns lawlessness to law, makes destitution —
    wealth,
Vice — virtue, and disease of soul and body —
    health?

XIV

Ah, the slow shake of head, the melancholy
    smile,
The sigh almost a sob! What's wrong, was
    right erewhile?
Why are we two at once such ocean-width
    apart?
Pale fingers press my arm, and sad eyes probe
    my heart.
Why is the wife in trouble?

XV

This way, this way, Fifine!
Here's she, shall make my thoughts be surer
    what they mean!
First let me read the signs, portray you past
    mistake
The gypsy's foreign self, no swarth our sun
    could bake.
Yet where's a woolly trace degrades the wiry
    hair?
And note the Greek-nymph nose, and — oh, my
    Hebrew pair
Of eye and eye — o'erarched by velvet of the
    mole —
That swim as in a sea, that dip and rise and
    roll,
Spilling the light around! While either ear is
    cut
Thin as a dusk-leaved rose carved from a
    cocoanut.
And then, her neck! now, grant you had the
    power to deck,
Just as your fancy pleased, the bistre-length of
    neck,
Could lay, to shine against its shade, a moon-
    like row
Of pearls, each round and white as bubble
    Cupids blow
Big out of mother's milk, — what pearl-moon
    would surpass
That string of mock-turquoise, those alman-
    dines of glass,
Where girlhood terminates? for with breasts'-
    birth commence
The boy, and page-costume, till pink and im-
    pudence
End admirably all: complete the creature
    trips
Our way now, brings sunshine upon her span-
    gled hips,
As here she fronts us full, with pose half-
    frank, half-fierce!

XVI

Words urged in vain, Elvire! You waste
　　your quart and tierce,
Lunge at a phantom here, try fence in fairy-
　　land.
For me, I own defeat, ask but to understand
The acknowledged victory of whom I call my
　　queen,
Sexless and bloodless sprite: though mischiev-
　　ous and mean,
Yet free and flower-like too, with loveliness
　　for law,
And self-sustainment made morality.

XVII
A flaw
Do you account i' the lily, of lands which
　　travellers know,
That, just as golden gloom supersedes Northern
　　snow
I' the chalice, so, about each pistil, spice is
　　packed, —
Deliriously - drugged scent, in lieu of odor
　　lacked,
With us, by bee and moth, their banquet to en-
　　hance
At morn and eve, when dew, the chilly suste-
　　nance,
Needs mixture of some chaste and temperate
　　perfume ?
I ask, is she in fault who guards such golden
　　gloom,
Such dear and damning scent, by who cares
　　what devices,
And takes the idle life of insects she entices
When, drowned to heart's desire, they satiate
　　the inside
O' the lily, mark her wealth and manifest her
　　pride ?

XVIII

But, wiser, we keep off, nor tempt the acrid
　　juice ;
Discreet we peer and praise, put rich things to
　　right use.
No flavorous venomed bell, — the rose it is, I
　　wot,
Only the rose, we pluck and place, unwronged
　　a jot,
No worse for homage done by every devotee,
I' the proper loyal throne, on breast where rose
　　should be.
Or if the simpler sweets we have to choose
　　among,
Would taste between our teeth, and give its toy
　　the tongue, —
O gorgeous poison-plague, on thee no hearts are
　　set !
We gather daisy meek, or maiden violet :
I think it is Elvire we love, and not Fifine.

XIX

" How does she make my thoughts be sure of
　　what they mean ? "
Judge and be just ! Suppose, an age and time
　　long past
Renew for our behoof one pageant more, the last

O' the kind, sick Louis liked to see defile be-
　　tween
Him and the yawning grave, its passage served
　　to screen.
With eye as gray as lead, with cheek as brown
　　as bronze,
Here where we stand, shall sit and suffer Louis
　　Onze :
The while from yonder tent parade fortn, not
　　— oh, no —
Bateleurs, baladines ! but range themselves
　　a-row
Those well-sung women-worthies whereof loud
　　fame still finds
Some echo linger faint, less in our hearts than
　　minds.

XX

See, Helen ! pushed in front o' the world's
　　worst night and storm.
By Lady Venus' hand on shoulder : the sweet
　　form
Shrinkingly prominent, though mighty, like a
　　moon
Outbreaking from a cloud, to put harsh things
　　in tune,
And magically bring mankind to acquiesce
In its own ravage, — call no curse upon, but
　　bless
(Beldame, a moment since) the outbreaking
　　beauty, now,
That casts o'er all the blood a candor from her
　　brow.
See, Cleopatra ! bared, the entire and sinuous
　　wealth
O' the shining shape ; each orb of indolent ripe
　　health,
Captured, just where it finds a fellow-orb as fine
I' the body : traced about by jewels which out-
　　line,
Fire-frame, and keep distinct, perfections — lest
　　they melt
To soft smooth unity ere half their hold be
　　felt :
Yet, o'er that white and wonder, a soul's pre-
　　dominance
I' the head so high and haught — except one
　　thievish glance,
From back of oblong eye, intent to count the
　　slain.
Hush, — oh, I know, Elvire ! Be patient, more
　　remain !
What say you to Saint ? . . . Pish ! Whatever
　　Saint you please,
Cold-pinnacled aloft o' the spire, prays calm the
　　seas
From Pornic Church, and oft at midnight
　　(peasants say)
Goes walking out to save from shipwreck:
　　well she may !
For think how many a year has she been con-
　　versant
With naught but winds and rains, sharp cour-
　　tesy and scant
O' the wintry snow that coats the pent-house of
　　her shrine,
Covers each knee, climbs near, but spares the
　　smile benign

Which seems to say, " I looked for scarce so
    much from earth ! ' '
She follows, one long thin pure finger in the
    girth
O' the girdle — whence the folds of garment,
    eye and eye,
Besprent with fleurs-de-lys, flow down and
    multiply
Around her feet, — and one, pressed hushingly
    to lip :
As if, while thus we made her march, some
    foundering ship
Might miss her from her post, nearer to God
    halfway
In heaven, and she inquired, " Who that treads
    earth can pray ?
I doubt if even she, the unashamed ! though,
    sure,
She must have stripped herself only to clothe
    the poor.''

XXI

    This time, enough 's a feast, not one more
    form, Elvire !
Provided you allow that, bringing up the rear
O' the bevy I am loth to — by one bird — cur-
    tail,
First note may lead to last, an octave crown the
    scale,
And this feminity be followed — do not
    flout ! —
By — who concludes the masque with curtsey,
    smile and pout,
Submissive-mutinous ? No other than Fifine
Points toe, imposes haunch, and pleads with
    tambourine !

XXII

" Well, what 's the meaning here, what does
    the masque intend,
Which, unabridged, we saw file past us, with
    no end
Of fair ones, till Fifine came, closed the cata-
    logue ? "

XXIII

    Task fancy yet again ! Suppose you cast this
    clog
Of flesh away (that weeps, upbraids, with-
    stands my arm)
And pass to join your peers, paragon charm with
    charm,
As I shall show you may, — prove best of
    beauty there !
Yourself confront yourself ! This, help me to
    declare
That yonder-you, who stand beside these, brav-
    ing each
And blinking none, beat her who lured to Troy-
    town beach
The purple prows of Greece, — nay, beat Fi-
    fine ; whose face,
Mark how I will inflame, when seigneur-like I
    place
I' the tambourine, to spot the strained and
    piteous blank
Of pleading parchment, see, no less than a
    whole franc !

XXIV

Ah, do you mark the brown o' the cloud,
    made bright with fire
Through and through ? as, old wiles succeed-
    ing to desire,
Quality (you and I) once more compassion-
    ate
A hapless infant, doomed (fie on such partial
    fate !)
To sink the inborn shame, waive privilege of
    sex,
And posture as you see, support the nods and
    becks
Of clowns that have their stare, nor always pay
    its price ;
An infant born perchance as sensitive and nice
As any soul of you, proud dames, whom des-
    tiny
Keeps uncontaminate from stigma of the sty
She wallows in ! You draw back skirts from
    filth like her
Who, possibly, braves scorn, if, scorned, she
    minister
To age, want, and disease of parents one or
    both ;
Nay, peradventure, stoops to degradation, loth
That some just-budding sister, the dew yet on
    the rose,
Should have to share in turn the ignoble trade,
    — who knows ?

XXV

    Ay, who indeed ! Myself know nothing, but
    dare guess
That off she trips in haste to hand the
    booty . . . yes,
'Twixt fold and fold of tent, there looms he,
    dim-discerned,
The ogre, lord of all those lavish limbs have
    earned !
— Brute-beast-face, — ravage, scar, scowl and
    malignancy, —
O' the Strong Man, whom (no doubt, her hus-
    band) by and by
You shall behold do feats : lift up nor quail be-
    neath
A quintal in each hand, a cart-wheel 'twixt his
    teeth.
Oh, she prefers sheer strength to ineffective
    grace,
Breeding and culture ! seeks the essential in
    the case !
To him has flown my franc ; and welcome, if
    that squint
O' the diabolic eye so soften through absinthe,
That for once, tambourine, tunic and tricot
    'scape
Their customary curse " Not half the gain o'
    the ape ! "
Ay, they go in together !

XXVI

                Yet still her phantom stays
Opposite, where you stand : as steady 'neath
    our gaze, —
The live Elvire's and mine, — though fancy
    stuff and mere

Illusion ; to be judged — dream-figures — with-
out fear
Or favor, those the false, by you and me the
true.

XXVII

" What puts it in my head to make yourself
judge you ? "
Well, it may be, the name of Helen brought to
mind
A certain myth I mused in years long left be-
hind :
How she that fled from Greece with Paris whom
she loved,
And came to Troy, and there found shelter, and
so proved
Such cause of the world's woe, — how she, old
stories call
This creature, Helen's self, never saw Troy at
all.
Jove had his fancy-fit, must needs take empty
air,
Fashion her likeness forth, and set the phan-
tom there
I' the midst for sport, to try conclusions with
the blind
And blundering race, the game create for Gods,
mankind :
Experiment on these, — establish who would
yearn
To give up life for her, who, other-minded,
spurn
The best her eyes could smile, — make half the
world sublime,
And half absurd, for just a phantom all the
time !
Meanwhile true Helen's self sat, safe and far
away,
By a great river-side, beneath a purer day,
With solitude around, tranquillity within ;
Was able to lean forth, look, listen, through
the din
And stir ; could estimate the worthlessness or
worth
Of Helen who inspired such passion to the
earth,
A phantom all the time ! That put it in my
head
To make yourself judge you — the phantom-
wife instead
O' the tearful true Elvire !

XXVIII

I thank the smile at last
Which thins away the tear ! Our sky was
overcast,
And something fell ; but day clears up : if
there chanced rain,
The landscape glistens more. I have not vexed
in vain
Elvire : because she knows, now she has stood
the test,
How, this and this being good, herself may still
be best
O' the beauty in review ; because the flesh that
claimed
Unduly my regard, she thought, the taste, she
blamed

In me, for things externe, was all mistake, she
finds, —
Or will find, when I prove that bodies show me
minds,
That, through the outward sign, the inward
grace allures,
And sparks from heaven transpierce earth's
coarsest covertures,
All by demonstrating the value of Fifine !

XXIX

Partake my confidence ! No creature 's made
so mean
But that, some way, it boasts, could we investi-
gate,
Its supreme worth : fulfils, by ordinance of
fate,
Its momentary task, gets glory all its own,
Tastes triumph in the world, pre-eminent, alone.
Where is the single grain of sand, 'mid millions
heaped
Confusedly on the beach, but, did we know, has
leaped
Or will leap, would we wait, i' the century,
some once,
To the very throne of things ? — earth's
brightest for the nonce,
When sunshine shall impinge on just that
grain's facette
Which fronts him fullest, first, returns his ray
with jet
Of promptest praise, thanks God best in crea-
tion's name !
As firm is my belief, quick sense perceives the
same
Self-vindicating flash illustrate every man
And woman of our mass, and prove, throughout
the plan,
No detail but, in place allotted it, was prime
And perfect.

XXX

Witness her, kept waiting all this time !
What happy angle makes Fifine reverberate
Sunshine, least sand-grain, she, of shadiest so-
cial state ?
No adamantine shield, polished like Helen
there,
Fit to absorb the sun, regorge him till the glare,
Dazing the universe, draw Troy-ward those
blind beaks
Of equal-sided ships rowed by the well-greaved
Greeks !
No Asian mirror, like yon Ptolemaic witch
Able to fix sun fast and tame sun down, en-
rich,
Not burn the world with beams thus flatter-
ingly rolled
About her, head to foot, turned slavish snakes
of gold !
And oh, no tinted pane of oriel sanctity,
Does our Fifine afford, such as permits supply
Of lustrous heaven, revealed, far more than
mundane sight
Could master, to thy cell, pure Saint ! where,
else too bright,
So suits thy sense the orb, that, what outside
was noon,

Pales, through thy lozenged blue, to meek
    benefic moon!
What then? does that prevent each dunghill,
    we may pass
Daily, from boasting too its bit of looking-glass,
Its sherd which, sun-smit, shines, shoots arrowy
    fire beyond
That satin-muffled mope, your sulky diamond?

XXXI

And now, the mingled ray she shoots, I de-
    compose.
Her antecedents, take for execrable! Gloze
No whit on your premiss: let be, there was no
    worst
Of degradation spared Fifine: ordained from
    first
To last, in body and soul, for one life-long
    debauch,
The Pariah of the North, the European Nautch!
This, far from seek to hide, she puts in evidence
Calmly, displays the brand, bids pry without
    offence
Your finger on the place. You comment,
    " Fancy us
So operated on, maltreated, mangled thus!
Such torture in our case, had we survived an
    hour?
Some other sort of flesh and blood must be,
    with power
Appropriate to the vile, unsensitive, tough-
    thonged,
In lieu of our fine nerve! Be sure, she was
    not wronged
Too much: you must not think she winced at
    prick as we!"
Come, come, that's what you say, or would,
    were thoughts but free.

XXXII

Well then, thus much confessed, what won-
    der if there steal
Unchallenged to my heart the force of one
    appeal
She makes, and justice stamp the sole claim
    she asserts?
So absolutely good is truth, truth never hurts
The teller, whose worst crime gets somehow
    grace, avowed.
To me, that silent pose and prayer proclaimed
    aloud:
" Know all of me outside, the rest be emptiness
For such as you! I call attention to my dress,
Coiffure, outlandish features, lithe memorable
    limbs,
Piquant entreaty, all that eye-glance overskims.
Does this give pleasure? Then, repay the
    pleasure, put
Its price i' the tambourine! Do you seek
    further? Tut!
I'm just my instrument, — sound hollow:
    mere smooth skin
Stretched o'er gilt framework, I; rub-dub,
    naught else within —
Always, for such as you! — if I have use else-
    where, —
If certain bells, now mute, can jingle, need you
    care?

Be it enough, there's truth i' the pleading,
    which comports
With no word spoken out in cottages or courts,
Since all I plead is, ' Pay for just the sight you
    see,
And give no credit to another charm in me!'
Do I say, like your Love? ' To praise my face
    is well,
But, who would know my worth, must search
    my heart to tell!'
Do I say, like your Wife? ' Had I passed in
    review
The produce of the globe, my man of men were
    — you!'
Do I say, like your Helen? ' Yield yourself
    up, obey
Implicitly, nor pause to question, to survey
Even the worshipful! prostrate you at my
    shrine!
Shall you dare controvert what the world
    counts divine?
Array your private taste, own liking of the
    sense,
Own longing of the soul, against the impudence
Of history, the blare and bullying of verse?
As if man ever yet saw reason to disburse
The amount of what sense liked, soul longed
    for, — given, devised
As love, forsooth, — until the price was recog-
    nized
As moderate enough by divers fellow-men!
Then, with his warrant safe that these would
    love too, then,
Sure that particular gain implies a public loss,
And that no smile he buys but proves a slash
    across
The face, a stab into the side of somebody —
Sure that, along with love's main-purchase, he
    will buy
Up the whole stock of earth's uncharitableness,
Envy and hatred, — then, decides he to profess
His estimate of one, by love discerned, though
    dim
To all the world beside: since what's the
    world to him?'
Do I say, like your Queen of Egypt? ' Who
    foregoes
My cup of witchcraft — fault be on the fool!
    He knows
Nothing of how I pack my wine-press, turn its
    winch
Three-times-three, all the time to song and
    dance, nor flinch
From charming on and on, till at the last I
    squeeze
Out the exhaustive drop that leaves behind
    mere lees
And dregs, vapidity, thought essence hereto-
    fore!
Sup of my sorcery, old pleasures please no more!
Be great, be good, love, learn, have potency of
    hand
Or heart or head, — what boots? You die, nor
    understand
What bliss might be in life: you ate the grapes,
    but knew
Never the taste of wine, such vintage as I
    brew!'

Do I say, like your Saint? 'An exquisitest
    touch
Bides in the birth of things: no after-time can
    much
Enhance that fine, that faint, fugitive first of
    all!
What color paints the cup o' the May-rose, like
    the small
Suspicion of a blush which doubtfully begins?
What sound outwarbles brook, while, at the
    source, it wins
That moss and stone dispart, allow its bub-
    blings breathe?
What taste excels the fruit, just where sharp
    flavors sheathe
Their sting, and let encroach the honey that
    allays?
And so with soul and sense; when sanctity
    betrays
First fear lest earth below seem real as heaven
    above,
And holy worship, late, change soon to sinful
    love —
Where is the plenitude of passion which en-
    dures
Comparison with that, I ask of amateurs?'
Do I say, like Elvire" . . .

          XXXIII

    (Your husband holds you fast,
Will have you listen, learn your character at
    last!)
"Do I say? — like her mixed unrest and dis-
    content,
Reproachfulness and scorn, with that submis-
    sion blent
So strangely, in the face, by sad smiles and gay
    tears, —
Quiescence which attacks, rebellion which en-
    dears, —
Say? 'As you loved me once, could you but
    love me now!
Years probably have graved their passage on
    my brow,
Lips turn more rarely red, eyes sparkle less
    than erst;
Such tribute body pays to time; but, un-
    amerced,
The soul retains, nay, boasts old treasure
    multiplied.
Though dew-prime flee, — mature at noonday,
    love defied
Chance, the wind, change, the rain: love stren-
    uous all the more
For storm, struck deeper root and choicer fruit-
    age bore,
Despite the rocking world; yet truth struck
    root in vain:
While tenderness bears fruit, you praise, not
    taste again.
Why? They are yours, which once were hardly
    yours, might go
To grace another's ground: and then — the
    hopes we know,
The fears we keep in mind! — when, ours to ar-
    bitrate,
Your part was to bow neck, bid fall decree of
    fate.

Then, O the knotty point — white-night's work
    to revolve —
What meant that smile, that sigh? Not Solon's
    self could solve!
Then, O the deep surmise what one word might
    express,
And if what seemed her "No" may not have
    meant her "Yes!"
Then, such annoy, for cause — calm welcome,
    such acquist
Of rapture if, refused her arm, hand touched
    her wrist!
Now, what's a smile to you? Poor candle
    that lights up
The decent household gloom which sends you
    out to sup.
A tear? worse! warns that health requires you
    keep aloof
From nuptial chamber, since rain penetrates
    the roof!
Soul, body got and gained, inalienably safe
Your own, become despised; more worth has
    any waif
Or stray from neighbor's pale: pouch that, —
    't is pleasure, pride,
Novelty, property, and larceny beside!
Preposterous thought! to find no value fixed in
    things,
To covet all you see, hear, dream of, till fate
    brings
About that, what you want, you gain; then
    follows change.
Give you the sun to keep, forthwith must fancy
    range:
A goodly lamp, no doubt, — yet might you
    catch her hair
And capture, as she frisks, the fen-fire dancing
    there!
What do I say? at least a meteor's half in
    heaven;
Provided filth but shine, my husband hankers
    even
After putridity that's phosphorescent, cribs
The rustic's tallow-rush, makes spoil of urchins'
    squibs,
In short, prefers to me — chaste, temperate,
    serene —
What sputters green and blue, this fizgig called
    Fifine!'"

          XXXIV

So all your sex mistake! Strange that so
    plain a fact
Should raise such dire debate! Few families
    were racked
By torture self-supplied, did Nature grant but
    this —
That women comprehend mental analysis!

          XXXV

Elvire, do you recall when, years ago, our
    home
The intimation reached, a certain pride of
    Rome,
Authenticated piece, in the third, last and best
Manner — whatever, fools and connoisseurs con-
    test, —
No particle disturbed by rude restorer's touch,

The palaced picture-pearl, so long eluding
 clutch
Of creditor, at last, the Rafael might — could
 we
But come to terms — change lord, pass from
 the Prince to me?
I think you recollect my fever of a year:
How the Prince would, and how he would not;
 now, — too dear
That promise was, he made his grandsire so
 long since,
Rather to boast " I own a Rafael " than " am
 Prince ! "
And now, the fancy soothed — if really sell he
 must
His birthright for a mess of pottage — such a
 thrust
I' the vitals of the Prince were mollified by
 balm,
Could he prevail upon his stomach to bear
 qualm,
And bequeath Liberty (because a purchaser
Was ready with the sum — a trifle !) yes, trans-
 fer
His heart at all events to that land where, at
 least,
Free institutions reign ! And so, its price in-
 creased
Fivefold (Americans are such importunates !),
Soon must his Rafael start for the United
 States.
Oh, alternating bursts of hope now, then despair!
At last, the bargain 's struck, I 'm all but beg-
 gared, there
The Rafael faces me, in fine, no dream at all,
My housemate, evermore to glorify my wall.
A week must pass, before heart-palpitations
 sink,
In gloating o'er my gain, so late I edged the
 brink
Of doom; a fortnight more, I spend in Para-
 dise :
" Was outline e'er so true, could coloring entice
So calm, did harmony and quiet so avail ?
How right, how resolute, the action tells the
 tale ! "
A month, I bid my friends congratulate their
 best :
" You happy Don ! " (to me): " The block-
 head ! " (to the rest) :
" No doubt he thinks his daub original, poor
 dupe ! "
Then I resume my life : one chamber must not
 coop
Man's life in, though it boast a marvel like my
 prize.
Next year, I saunter past with unaverted
 eyes,
Nay, loll and turn my back : perchance to over-
 look
With relish, leaf by leaf, Doré's last picture-
 book.

XXXVI

Imagine that a voice reproached me from its
 frame :
" Here do I hang, and may ! Your Rafael, just
 the same,

'T is only you that change; no ecstasies of
 yore !
No purposed suicide distracts you any more ! "
Prompt would my answer meet such frivolous
 attack :
" You misappropriate sensations. What men
 lack,
And labor to obtain, is hoped and feared about
After a fashion ; what they once obtain, makes
 doubt,
Expectancy's old fret and fume, henceforward
 void.
But do they think to hold such havings un-
 alloyed
By novel hopes and fears, of fashion just as
 new,
To correspond i' the scale ? Nowise, I promise
 you !
Mine you are, therefore mine will be, as fit to
 cheer
My soul and glad my sense to-day as this-day-
 year.
So, any sketch or scrap, pochade, caricature,
Made in a moment, meant a moment to endure,
I snap at, seize, enjoy, then tire of, throw aside,
Find you in your old place. But if a servant
 cried
' Fire in the gallery ! ' — methinks, were I en-
 gaged
In Doré, elbow-deep, picture-books million-
 paged
To the four winds would pack, sped by the
 heartiest curse
Was ever launched from lip, to strew the uni-
 verse.
Would not I brave the best o' the burning,
 bear away
Either my perfect piece in safety, or else stay
And share its fate, be made its martyr, nor re-
 pine ?
Inextricably wed, such ashes mixed with
 mine ! "

XXXVII

For which I get the eye, the hand, the heart,
 the whole
O' the wondrous wife again !

XXXVIII

     But no, play out your rôle
I' the pageant ! 'T is not fit your phantom
 leave the stage :
I want you, there, to make you, here, confess
 you wage
Successful warfare, pique those proud ones, and
 advance
Claim to . . . equality ? nay, but predomi-
 nance
In physique o'er them all, where Helen heads
 the scene
Closed by its tiniest of tail-tips, pert Fifine.
How ravishingly pure you stand in pale con-
 straint !
My new-created shape, without or touch or
 taint,
Inviolate of life and worldliness and sin —
Fettered, I hold my flower, her own cup's
 weight would win

From off the tall slight stalk a-top of which
   she turns
And trembles, makes appeal to one who
   roughly earns
Her thanks instead of blame, (did lily only
   know,)
By thus constraining length of lily, letting snow
Of cup-crown, that's her face, look from its
   guardian stake,
Superb on all that crawls beneath, and mutely
   make
Defiance, with the mouth's white movement of
   disdain,
To all that stoops, retires, and hovers round
   again !
How windingly the limbs delay to lead up,
   reach
Where, crowned, the head waits calm : as if
   reluctant, each,
That eye should traverse quick such lengths
   of loveliness,
From feet, which just are found embedded in
   the dress
Deep swathed about with folds and flowings
   virginal,
Up to the pleated breasts, rebellious 'neath
   their pall,
As if the vesture's snow were moulding sleep
   not death,
Must melt and so release ; whereat, from the
   fine sheath,
The flower-cup-crown starts free, the face is
   unconcealed,
And what shall now divert me, once the sweet
   face revealed,
From all I loved so long, so lingeringly left ?

XXXIX

Because indeed your face fits into just the
   cleft
O' the heart of me, Elvire, makes right and
   whole once more
All that was half itself without you ! As be-
   fore,
My truant finds its place ! Doubtlessly sea-
   shells yearn,
If plundered by sad chance : would pray their
   pearls return,
Let negligently slip away into the wave !
Never may eyes desist, those eyes so gray and
   grave,
From their slow sure supply of the effluent soul
   within !
And, would you humor me ? I dare to ask,
   unpin
The web of that brown hair ! O'erwash o' the
   sudden, but
As promptly, too, disclose, on either side, the jut
Of alabaster brow ! So part rich rillets dyed
Deep by the woodland leaf, when down they
   pour, each side
O' the rock-top, pushed by Spring !

XL

               " And where i' the world is all
This wonder, you detail so trippingly, espied ?
My mirror would reflect a tall, thin, pale, deep-
   eyed

Personage, pretty once, it may be, doubtless
   still
Loving, — a certain grace yet lingers, if you
   will, —
But all this wonder, where ? "

XLI

              Why, where but in the sense
And soul of me, Art's judge ? Art is my
   evidence
That something was, is, might be ; but no more
   thing itself,
Than flame is fuel. Once the verse-book laid
   on shelf,
The picture turned to wall, the music fled
   from ear, —
Each beauty, born of each, grows clearer and
   more clear,
Mine henceforth, ever mine !

XLII

              But if I would retrace
Effect, in Art, to cause, — corroborate, erase
What 's right or wrong i' the lines, test fancy in
   my brain
By fact which gave it birth ? I re-peruse in
   vain
The verse, I fail to find that vision of delight
I' the Bazzi's lost-profile, eye-edge so exqui-
   site.
And, music : what ? that burst of pillared
   cloud by day
And pillared fire by night, was product, must
   we say,
Of modulating just, by enharmonic change, —
The augmented sixth resolved, — from out the
   straighter range
Of D sharp minor — leap of disimprisoned
   thrall —
Into thy light and life, D major natural ?

XLIII

Elvire, will you partake in what I shall impart ?
I seem to understand the way heart chooses
   heart
By help of the outside form, — a reason for our
   wild
Diversity in choice, — why each grows recon-
   ciled
To what is absent, what superfluous in the mask
Of flesh that 's meant to yield, — did nature ply
   her task
As artist should, — precise the features of the
   soul,
Which, if in any case they found expression,
   whole
I' the traits, would give a type, undoubtedly
   display
A novel, true, distinct perfection in its way.
Never shall I believe any two souls were made
Similar ; granting, then, each soul of every
   grade
Was meant to be itself, prove in itself com-
   plete,
And, in completion, good, — nay, best o' the
   kind, — as meet
Needs must it be that show on the outside cor-
   respond

With inward substance, — flesh, the dress which
  soul has donned,
Exactly reproduce, — were only justice done
Inside and outside too, — types perfect every
  one.
How happens it that here we meet a mystery
Insoluble to man, a plaguy puzzle ?   Why
Each soul is either made imperfect, and de-
  serves
As rude a face to match ; or else a bungler
  swerves,
And nature, on a soul worth rendering aright,
Works ill, or proves perverse, or, in her own
  despite,
— Here too much, there too little, — bids each
  face, more or less,
Retire from beauty, make approach to ugliness ?
And yet succeeds the same : since, what is want-
  ing to success,
If somehow every face, no matter how deform,
Evidence, to some one of hearts on earth, that,
  warm
Beneath the veriest ash, there hides a spark of
  soul
Which, quickened by love's breath, may yet
  pervade the whole
O' the gray, and, free again, be fire ? — of
  worth the same,
Howe'er produced, for, great or little, flame is
  flame.
A mystery, whereof solution is to seek.

XLIV

I find it in the fact that each soul, just as weak
Its own way as its fellow, — departure from de-
  sign
As flagrant in the flesh, — goes striving to com-
  bine
With what shall right the wrong, the under or
  above
The standard : supplement unloveliness by love.
— Ask Plato else !   And this corroborates the
  sage,
That Art, — which I may style the love of lov-
  ing, rage
Of knowing, seeing, feeling the absolute truth
  of things
For truth's sake, whole and sole, not any good,
  truth brings
The knower, seer, feeler, beside, — instinctive
  Art
Must fumble for the whole, once fixing on a part
However poor, surpass the fragment, and aspire
To reconstruct thereby the ultimate entire.
Art, working with a will, discards the super-
  flux,
Contributes to defect, toils on till, — *fiat lux*, —
There 's the restored, the prime, the individual
  type !

XLV

Look, for example now !   This piece of broken
  pipe
(Some shipman's solace erst) shall act as crayon ;
  and
What tablet better serves my purpose than the
  sand ?

—Smooth slab whereon I draw, no matter with
  what skill,
A face, and yet another, and yet another still.
There lie my three prime types of beauty !

XLVI

                              Laugh your best !
" Exaggeration and absurdity ? "   Confessed !
Yet, what may that face mean, no matter for
  its nose,
A yard long, or its chin, a foot short ?

XLVII

                              " You suppose,
Horror ? "   Exactly !   What 's the odds if,
  more or less
By yard or foot, the features do manage to ex-
  press
Such meaning in the main ?   Were I of Gé-
  rôme's force,
Nor feeble as you see, quick should my crayon
  course
O'er outline, curb, excite, till, — so completion
  speeds
With Gérôme well at work, — observe how
  brow recedes,
Head shudders back on spine, as if one haled
  the hair,
Would have the full-face front what pin-point
  eye's sharp stare
Announces ; mouth agape to drink the flowing
  fate,
While chin protrudes to meet the burst o' the
  wave : elate
Almost, spurred on to brave necessity, expend
All life left, in one flash, as fire does at its end.
Retrenchment and addition effect a masterpiece,
Not change i' the motive : here diminish, there
  increase —
And who wants Horror, has it.

XLVIII

                              Who wants some other show
Of soul, may seek elsewhere — this second of
  the row ?
What does it give for germ, monadic mere in-
  tent
Of mind in face, faint first of meanings ever
  meant ?
Why, possibly, a grin, that, strengthened, grows
  a laugh ;
That, softened, leaves a smile ; that, tempered,
  bids you quaff
At such a magic cup as English Reynolds once
Compounded : for the witch pulls out of you
  response
Like Garrick's to Thalia, however due may be
Your homage claimed by that stiff-stoled Mel-
  pomene !

XLIX

And just this one face more !   Pardon the
  bold pretence !
May there not lurk some hint, struggle toward
  evidence
In that compressed mouth, those strained nos-
  trils, steadfast eyes

Of utter passion, absolute self-sacrifice,
Which — could I but subdue the wild grotesque,
    refine
That bulge of brow, make blunt that nose's
    aquiline,
And let, although compressed, a point of pulp
    appear
I' the mouth — would give at last the portrait
    of Elvire ?

L

Well, and if so succeed hand-practice on awry
Preposterous art-mistake, shall soul-proficiency
Despair, — when exercised on nature, which at
    worst
Always implies success, — however crossed and
    curst
By failure, — such as art would emulate in vain ?
Shall any soul despair of setting free again
Trait after trait, until the type as wholly start
Forth, visible to sense, as that minutest part,
(Whate'er the chance,) which first arresting eye,
    warned soul
That, under wrong enough and ravage, lay the
    whole
O' the loveliness it " loved " — I take the ac-
    cepted phrase ?

LI

So I account for tastes : each chooses, none
    gainsays
The fancy of his fellow, a paradise for him,
A hell for all beside. You can but crown the
    brim
O' the cup ; if it be full, what matters less or
    more ?
Let each, i' the world, amend his love, as I, o'
    the shore,
My sketch, and the result as undisputed be !
Their handiwork to them, and my Elvire to me :
— Result more beautiful than beauty's self,
    when lo,
What was my Rafael turns my Michelagnolo !

LII

For, we two boast, beside our pearl, a dia-
    mond.
I' the palace-gallery, the corridor beyond,
Upheaves itself a marble, a magnitude man-
    shaped
As snow might be. One hand — the Master's —
    smoothed and scraped
That mass, he hammered on and hewed at, till
    he hurled
Life out of death, and left a challenge : for the
    world,
Death still, — since who shall dare, close to the
    image, say
If this be purposed Art, or mere mimetic play
Of Nature ? — wont to deal with crag or cloud,
    as stuff
To fashion novel forms, like forms we know,
    enough
For recognition, but enough unlike the same,
To leave no hope ourselves may profit by her
    game ;
Death therefore to the world. Step back a pace
    or two !

And then, who dares dispute the gradual birth
    its due
Of breathing life, or breathless immortality,
Where out she stands, and yet stops short, half
    bold, half shy,
Hesitates on the threshold of things, since
    partly blent
With stuff she needs must quit, her native ele-
    ment
I' the mind o' the Master, — what 's the crea-
    ture, dear-divine
Yet earthly-awful too, so manly-feminine,
Pretends this white advance ? What startling
    brain-escape
Of Michelagnolo takes elemental shape ?
I think he meant the daughter of the old man
    o' the sea,
Emerging from her wave, goddess Eidotheé —
She who, in elvish sport, spite with benevolence
Mixed Mab-wise up, must needs instruct the
    Hero whence
Salvation dawns o'er that mad misery of his
    isle.
Yes, she imparts to him, by what a pranksome
    wile
He may surprise her sire, asleep beneath a rock,
When he has told their tale, amid his webfoot
    flock
Of sea-beasts, " fine fat seals with bitter
    breath ! " laughs she
At whom she likes to save, no less : Eidotheé,
Whom you shall never face evolved, in earth, in
    air,
In wave ; but, manifest i' the soul's domain,
    why, there
She ravishingly moves to meet you, all through
    aid
O' the soul ! Bid shine what should, dismiss
    into the shade
What should not be, — and there triumphs the
    paramount
Emprise o' the Master ! But, attempt to make
    account
Of what the sense, without soul's help perceives ?
    I bought
That work — (despite plain proof, whose hand
    it was had wrought
I' the rough : I think we trace the tool of triple
    tooth,
Here, there, and everywhere) — bought dearly
    that uncouth
Unwieldy bulk, for just ten dollars — " Bulk,
    would fetch —
Converted into lime — some five pauls ! "
    grinned a wretch,
Who, bound on business, paused to hear the
    bargaining,
And would have pitied me " but for the fun o'
    the thing ! "

LIII

Shall such a wretch be — you ? Must —
    while I show Elvire
Shaming all other forms, seen as I see her here
I' the soul, — this other-you perversely look out-
    side,
And ask me, " Where i' the world is charm to
    be descried

I' the tall thin personage, with paled eye, pen-
  sive face,
Any amount of love, and some remains of
  grace ? ''
See yourself in my soul !

LIV

And what a world for each
Must somehow be i' the soul, — accept that
  mode of speech, —
Whether an aura gird the soul, wherein it
  seems
To float and move, a belt of all the glints and
  gleams
It struck from out that world, its weaklier fel-
  lows found
So dead and cold ; or whether these not so
  much surround,
As pass into the soul itself, add worth to worth,
As wine enriches blood, and straightway send it
  forth,
Conquering and to conquer, through all eter-
  nity,
That 's battle without end.

LV

I search but cannot see
What purpose serves the soul that strives, or
  world it tries
Conclusions with, unless the fruit of victories
Stay, one and all, stored up and guaranteed its
  own
Forever, by some mode whereby shall be made
  known
The gain of every life. Death reads the title
  clear —
What each soul for itself conquered from out
  things here :
Since, in the seeing soul, all worth lies, I
  assert, —
And naught i' the world, which, save for soul
  that sees, inert
Was, is, and would be ever, — stuff for trans-
  muting, — null
And void until man's breath evoke the beau-
  tiful —
But, touched aright, prompt yields each particle
  its tongue
Of elemental flame, — no matter whence flame
  sprung
From gums and spice, or else from straw and
  rottenness,
So long as soul has power to make them burn,
  express
What lights and warms henceforth, leaves only
  ash behind,
Howe'er the chance: if soul be privileged to
  find
Food so soon that, by first snatch of eye, suck
  of breath,
It can absorb pure life: or, rather, meeting
  death
I' the shape of ugliness, by fortunate recoil
So put on its resource, it find therein a foil
For a new birth of life, the challenged soul's
  response
To ugliness and death, — creation for the
  nonce.

LVI

I gather heart through just such conquests
  of the soul,
Through evocation out of that which, on the
  whole,
Was rough, ungainly, partial accomplishment,
  at best,
And — what, at worst, save failure to spit at
  and detest ? —
— Through transference of all, achieved in vis-
  ible things,
To where, secured from wrong, rest soul's
  imaginings —
Through ardor to bring help just where com-
  pletion halts,
Do justice to the purpose, ignore the slips and
  faults —
And, last, through waging with deformity a
  fight
Which wrings thence, at the end, precise its
  opposite.
I praise the loyalty o' the scholar, — stung by
  taunt
Of fools, '' Does this evince thy Master men so
  vaunt ?
Did he then perpetrate the plain abortion
  here ? '' —
Who cries, '' His work am I ! full fraught by
  him, I clear
His fame from each result of accident and
  time,
Myself restore his work to its fresh morning-
  prime,
Not daring touch the mass of marble, fools
  deride,
But putting my idea in plaster by its side,
His, since mine ; I, he made, vindicate who
  made me ! ''

LVII

For you must know, I too achieved Eidotheé,
In silence and by night — dared justify the
  lines
Plain to my soul, although, to sense, that triple-
  tine's
Achievement halt halfway, break down, or
  leave a blank.
If she stood forth at last, the Master was to
  thank !
Yet may there not have smiled approval in his
  eyes —
That one at least was left who, born to recog-
  nize
Perfection in the piece imperfect, worked, that
  night,
In silence, such his faith, until the apposite
Design was out of him, truth palpable once
  more ?
And then — for at one blow, its fragments
  strewed the floor —
Recalled the same to live within his soul as
  heretofore.

LVIII

And, even as I hold and have Eidotheé,
I say, I cannot think that gain, — which would
  not be

Except a special soul had gained it, — that
        such gain
Can ever be estranged, do aught but appertain
Immortally, by right firm, indefeasible,
To who performed the feat, through God's
        grace and man's will !
Gain, never shared by those who practised with
        earth's stuff,
And spoiled whate'er they touched, leaving its
        roughness rough,
Its blankness bare, and, when the ugliness
        opposed,
Either struck work or laughed "He doted or
        he dozed ! "

LIX

While, oh, how all the more will love become
        intense
Hereafter, when "to love" means yearning to
        dispense,
Each soul, its own amount of gain through its
        own mode
Of practising with life, upon some soul which
        owed
Its treasure, all diverse and yet in worth the
        same,
To new work and changed way ! Things fur-
        nish you rose-flame,
Which burn up red, green, blue, nay, yellow
        more than needs,
For me, I nowise doubt ; why doubt a time
        succeeds
When each one may impart, and each receive,
        both share
The chemic secret, learn, — where I lit force,
        why there
You drew forth lambent pity, — where I found
        only food
For self-indulgence, you still blew a spark at
        brood
I' the grayest ember, stopped not till self-
        sacrifice imbued
Heaven's face with flame ? What joy, when
        each may supplement
The other, changing each, as changed, till,
        wholly blent,
Our old things shall be new, and, what we both
        ignite,
Fuse, lose the varicolor in achromatic white !
Exemplifying law, apparent even now
In the eternal progress, — love's law, which I
        avow
And thus would formulate : each soul lives,
        longs and works
For itself, by itself, because a lodestar lurks,
An other than itself, — in whatsoe'er the niche
Of mistiest heaven it hide, whoe'er the Glum-
        dalclich
May grasp the Gulliver : or it, or he, or she —
Theosutos e broteios eper kekramene, —
(For fun's sake, where the phrase has fastened,
        leave it fixed !
So soft it says, — "God, man, or both together
        mixed ! ")
This, guessed at through the flesh, by parts
        which prove the whole,
This constitutes the soul discernible by soul
— Elvire, by me !

LX

" And then " — (pray you, permit remain
This hand upon my arm ! — your cheek dried,
        if you deign,
Choosing my shoulder) — "then ! " — (Stand
        up for, boldly state
The objection in its length and breadth !)
" You abdicate,
With boast yet on your lip, soul's empire, and
        accept
The rule of sense ; the Man, from monarch's
        throne has stept —
Leapt, rather, at one bound, to base, and there
        lies, Brute.
You talk of soul, — how soul, in search of soul
        to suit,
Must needs review the sex, the army, rank and
        file
Of womankind, report no face nor form so
        vile
But that a certain worth, by certain signs, may
        thence
Evolve itself and stand confessed — to soul —
        by sense.
Sense ? Oh, the loyal bee endeavors for the
        hive !
Disinterested hunts the flower-field through,
        alive
Not one mean moment, no, — suppose on flower
        he light, —
To his peculiar drop, petal-dew perquisite,
Matter-of-course snatched snack : unless he
        taste, how try ?
This, light on tongue-tip laid, allows him pack
        his thigh,
Transport all he counts prize, provision for the
        comb,
Food for the future day, — a banquet, but at
        home !
Soul ? Ere you reach Fifine's, some flesh may
        be to pass !
That bombéd brow, that eye, a kindling chrys-
        opras,
Beneath its stiff black lash, inquisitive how
        speeds
Each functionary limb, how play of foot suc-
        ceeds,
And how you let escape or duly sympathize
With gastro-knemian grace, — true, your soul
        tastes and tries,
And trifles time with these, but, fear not, will
        arrive
At essence in the core, bring honey home to
        hive,
Brain-stock and heart-stuff both — to strike
        objectors dumb —
Since only soul affords the soul fit pabulum !
Be frank for charity ! Who is it you de-
        ceive —
Yourself or me or God, with all this make
        believe ? "

LXI

And frank I will respond as you interrogate.
Ah, Music, wouldst thou help ! Words strug-
        gle with the weight
So feebly of the False, thick element between

Our soul, the True, and Truth! which, but
    that intervene
False shows of things, were reached as easily
    by thought
Reducible to word, as now by yearnings
    wrought
Up with thy fine free force, O Music, that
    canst thrid,
Electrically win a passage through the lid
Of earthly sepulchre, our words may push
    against,
Hardly transpierce as thou! Not dissipate,
    thou deign'st,
So much as tricksily elude what words attempt
To heave away, i' the mass, and let the soul,
    exempt
From all that vapory obstruction, view, instead
Of glimmer underneath, a glory overhead.
Not feebly, like our phrase, against the barrier
    go
In suspirative swell the authentic notes I know,
By help whereof, I would our souls were found
    without
The pale, above the dense and dim which breeds
    the doubt!
But Music, dumb for you, withdraws her help
    from me;
And, since to weary words recourse again must
    be,
At least permit they rest their burden here and
    there,
Music-like: cover space! My answer, — need
    you care
If it exceed the bounds, reply to questioning
You never meant should plague? Once fairly
    on the wing,
Let me flap far and wide!

LXII

               For this is just the time,
The place, the mood in you and me, when all
    things chime.
Clash forth life's common chord, whence, list
    how there ascend
Harmonics far and faint, till our perception
    end, —
Reverberated notes whence we construct the
    scale
Embracing what we know and feel and are!
    How fail
To find or, better, lose your question, in this
    quick
Reply which nature yields, ample and catholic?
For, arm in arm, we too have reached, nay,
    passed, you see,
The village-precinct; sun sets mild on Sainte-
    Marie —
We only catch the spire, and yet I seem to
    know
What's hid i' the turn o' the hill: how all the
    graves must glow
Soberly, as each warms its little iron cross,
Flourished about with gold, and graced (if
    private loss
Be fresh) with stiff rope-wreath of yellow crisp
    bead-blooms
Which tempt down birds to pay their supper,
    'mid the tombs,

With prattle good as song, amuse the dead
    awhile,
If couched they hear beneath the matted camo-
    mile!

LXIII

Bid them good-by before last friend has
    sung and supped!
Because we pick our path and need our eyes, —
    abrupt
Descent enough, — but here's the beach, and
    there's the bay,
And, opposite, the streak of Île Noirmoutier.
Thither the waters tend; they freshen as they
    haste,
At feel o' the night-wind, though, by cliff and
    cliff embraced,
This breadth of blue retains its self-possession
    still;
As you and I intend to do, who take our fill
Of sights and sounds — soft sound, the countless
    hum and skip
Of insects we disturb, and that good fellow-
    ship
Of rabbits our footfall sends huddling, each to
    hide
He best knows how and where; and what
    whirred past, wings wide?
That was an owl, their young may justlier
    apprehend!
Though you refuse to speak, your beating heart,
    my friend,
I feel against my arm, — though your bent head
    forbids
A look into your eyes, yet, on my cheek, their
    lids
That ope and shut, soft send a silken thrill the
    same.
Well, out of all and each these nothings, comes
    — what came
Often enough before, the something that would
    aim
Once more at the old mark: the impulse to at
    last
Succeed where hitherto was failure in the past,
And yet again essay the adventure. Clearlier
    sings
No bird to its couched corpse, "Into the truth
    of things —
Out of their falseness rise, and reach thou, and
    remain!"

LXIV

"That rise into the true out of the false —
    explain?"
May an example serve? In yonder bay I bathed,
This sunny morning: swam my best, then hung,
    half swathed
With chill, and half with warmth, i' the chan-
    nel's midmost deep:
You know how one — not treads, but stands in
    water? Keep
Body and limbs below, hold head back, uplift
    chin,
And, for the rest, leave care! If brow, eyes,
    mouth, should win
Their freedom, — excellent! If they must
    brook the surge,

No matter though they sink, let but the nose
    emerge.
So, all of me in brine lay soaking: did I care
One jot? I kept alive by man's due breath of
    air
I' the nostrils, high and dry. At times, o'er
    these would run
The ripple, even wash the wavelet, — morning's
    sun
Tempted advance, no doubt: and always flash
    of froth,
Fish-outbreak, bubbling by, would find me no-
    thing loth
To rise and look around ; then all was overswept
With dark and death at once. But trust the
    old adept !
Back went again the head, a merest motion
    made,
Fin-fashion, either hand, and nostril soon con-
    veyed
Assurance light and life were still in reach as
    erst :
Always the last and — wait and watch — some-
    times the first.
Try to ascend breast-high ? wave arms wide
    free of tether ?
Be in the air and leave the water altogether ?
Under went all again, till I resigned myself
To only breathe the air, that 's footed by an
    elf,
And only swim the water, that 's native to a fish.
But there is no denying that, ere I curbed my
    wish,
And schooled my restive arms, salt entered
    mouth and eyes
Often enough — sun, sky, and air so tantalize !
Still, the adept swims, this accorded, that de-
    nied ;
Can always breathe, sometimes see and be sat-
    isfied !

LXV

I liken to this play o' the body — fruitless
    strife
To slip the sea and hold the heaven — my
    spirit's life
'Twixt false, whence it would break, and true,
    where it would bide.
I move in, yet resist, am upborne every side
By what I beat against, an element too gross
To live in, did not soul duly obtain her dose
Of life-breath, and inhale from truth's pure
    plenitude
Above her, snatch and gain enough to just illude
With hope that some brave bound may baffle
    evermore
The obstructing medium, make who swam
    henceforward soar :
— Gain scarcely snatched when, foiled by the
    very effort, souse,
Underneath ducks the soul, her truthward
    yearnings dowse
Deeper in falsehood ! ay, but fitted less and less
To bear in nose and mouth old briny bitterness
Proved alien more and more : since each experi-
    ence proves
Air — the essential good, not sea, wherein who
    moves

Must thence, in the act, escape, apart from will
    or wish.
Move a mere hand to take water-weed, jelly-fish,
Upward you tend ! And yet our business with
    the sea
Is not with air, but just o' the water, watery:
We must endure the false, no particle of which
Do we acquaint us with, but up we mount a pitch
Above it, find our head reach truth, while hands
    explore
The false below : so much while here we bathe,
    — no more !

LXVI

Now, there is one prime point (hear and be
    edified !)
One truth more true for me than any truth
    beside —
To-wit, that I am I, who have the power to
    swim,
The skill to understand the law whereby each
    limb
May bear to keep immersed, since, in return,
    made sure
That its mere movement lifts head clean
    through coverture.
By practice with the false, I reach the true ?
    Why, thence
It follows, that the more I gain self-confidence,
Get proof I know the trick, can float, sink, rise,
    at will,
The better I submit to what I have the skill
To conquer in my turn, even now, and by and by
Leave wholly for the land, and there laugh,
    shake me dry
To last drop, saturate with noonday — no need
    more
Of wet and fret, plagued once : on Pornic's
    placid shore,
Abundant air to breathe, sufficient sun to feel !
Meantime I buoy myself : no whit my senses reel
When over me there breaks a billow ; nor, elate
Too much by some brief taste, I quaff intem-
    perate
The air, o'ertop breast-high the wave-environ-
    ment.
Full well I know the thing I grasp, as if intent
To hold, — my wandering wave, — will not be
    grasped at all :
The solid-seeming grasped, the handful great
    or small
Must go to nothing, glide through fingers fast
    enough ;
But none the less, to treat liquidity as stuff —
Though failure — certainly succeeds beyond its
    aim,
Sends head above, past thing that hands miss,
    or the same.

LXVII

So with this wash o' the world, wherein life-
    long we drift ;
We push and paddle through the foam by mak-
    ing shift
To breathe above at whiles when, after deepest
    duck
Down underneath the show, we put forth hand
    and pluck

At what seems somehow like reality — a soul.
I catch at this and that, to capture and control,
Presume I hold a prize, discover that my pains
Are run to naught : my hands are balked, my head regains
The surface where I breathe and look about, a space.
The soul that helped me mount ? Swallowed up in the race
O' the tide, come who knows whence, gone gayly who knows where !
I thought the prize was mine ; I flattered myself there.
It did its duty, though : I felt it, it felt me ;
Or, where I look about and breathe, I should not be.
The main point is — the false fluidity was bound
Acknowledge that it frothed o'er substance, nowise found
Fluid, but firm and true. Man, outcast, "howls," — at rods ? —
If "sent in playful spray a-shivering to his gods ! "
Childishest childe, man makes thereby no bad exchange.
Stay with the flat-fish, thou ! We like the upper range
Where the "gods " live, perchance the dæmons also dwell :
Where operates a Power, which every throb and swell
Of human heart invites that human soul approach,
"Sent " near and nearer still, however "spray " encroach
On "shivering " flesh below, to altitudes, which gained,
Evil proves good, wrong right, obscurity explained,
And "howling " childishness. Whose howl have we to thank.
If all the dogs 'gan bark and puppies whine, till sank
Each yelper's tail 'twixt legs ? for Huntsman Common-sense
Came to the rescue, bade prompt thwack of thong dispense
Quiet i' the kennel ; taught that ocean might be blue,
And rolling and much more, and yet the soul have, too,
Its touch of God's own flame, which he may so expand,
"Who measurèd the waters i' the hollow of his hand,"
That ocean's self shall dry, turn dewdrop in respect
Of all-triumphant fire, matter with intellect
Once fairly matched ; bade him who egged on hounds to bay,
Go curse, i' the poultry yard, his kind : " there let him lay "
The swan's one addled egg : which yet shall put to use,
Rub breast-bone warm against, so many a sterile goose !

LXVIII

No, I want sky not sea, prefer the larks to shrimps,
And never dive so deep but that I get a glimpse
O' the blue above, a breath of the air around. Elvire,
I seize — by catching at the melted beryl here,
The tawny hair that just has trickled off, — Fifine !
Did not we two trip forth to just enjoy the scene,
The tumbling-troop arrayed, the strollers on their stage,
Drawn up and under arms, and ready to engage —
Dabble, and there an end, with foam and froth o'er face,
Till suddenly Fifine suggested change of place ?
Now we taste æther, scorn the wave, and interchange apace
No ordinary thoughts, but such as evidence
The cultivated mind in both. On what pretence
Are you and I to sneer at who lent help to hand,
And gave the lucky lift ?

LXIX

Still sour ? I understand !
One ugly circumstance discredits my fair plan —
That Woman does the work : I waive the help of Man.
"Why should experiment be tried with only waves,
When solid spars float round ? Still some Thalassia saves
Too pertinaciously, as though no Triton, bluff
As e'er blew brine from conch, were free to help enough !
Surely, to recognize a man, his mates serve best !
Why is there not the same or greater interest
In the strong spouse as in the pretty partner, pray,
Were recognition just your object, as you say,
Amid this element o' the false ? "

LXX

We come to terms.
I need to be proved true ; and nothing so confirms
One's faith in the prime point that one 's alive, not dead,
In all Descents to Hell whereof I ever read,
As when a phantom there, male enemy or friend,
Or merely stranger-shade, is struck, is forced suspend
His passage : " You that breathe, along with us the ghosts ? "
Here, why must it be still a woman that accosts ?

Because, one woman 's worth, in that respect, such hairy hosts
Of the other sex and sort ! Men ? Say you have the power
To make them yours, rule men, throughout life's little hour,

According to the phrase ; what follows ? Men,
you make,
By ruling them, your own : each man for his
own sake
Accepts you as his guide, avails him of what
worth
He apprehends in you to sublimate his earth
With fire : content, if so you convoy him
through night,
That you shall play the sun, and he, the satel-
lite,
Pilfer your light and heat and virtue, starry
pelf,
While, caught up by your course, he turns upon
himself.
Women rush into you, and there remain ab-
sorbed.
Beside, 't is only men completely formed, full-
orbed,
Are fit to follow track, keep pace, illustrate so
The leader : any sort of woman may bestow
Her atom on the star, or clod she counts for
such, —
Each little making less bigger by just that
much.
Women grow you, while men depend on you at
best.
And what dependence ! Bring and put him to
the test,
Your specimen disciple, a handbreadth sepa-
rate
From you, he almost seemed to touch before !
Abate
Complacency you will, I judge, at what 's di-
vulged !
Some flabbiness you fixed, some vacancy out-
bulged,
Some — much — nay, all, perhaps, the outward
man 's your work :
But, inside man ? — find him, wherever he may
lurk,
And where 's a touch of you in his true self ?

LXXII

I wish
Some wind would waft this way a glassy bub-
ble-fish
O' the kind the sea inflates, and show you, once
detached
From wave . . . or no, the event is better told
than watched :
Still may the thing float free, globose and opal-
ine
All over, save where just the amethysts com-
bine
To blue their best, rim-round the sea-flower
with a tinge
Earth's violet never knew ! Well, 'neath that
gem-tipped fringe,
A head lurks — of a kind — that acts as stom-
ach too ;
Then comes the emptiness which out the water
blew
So big and belly-like, but, dry of water drained,
Withers away nine-tenths. Ah, but a tenth
remained !
That was the creature's self : no more akin to
sea,

Poor rudimental head and stomach, you agree,
Than sea 's akin to sun who yonder dips his
edge.

LXXIII

But take the rill which ends a race o'er yon-
der ledge
O' the fissured cliff, to find its fate in smoke
below !
Disengage that, and ask — what news of life,
you know
It led, that long lone way, through pasture,
plain and waste ?
All 's gone to give the sea ! no touch of earth,
no taste
Of air, reserved to tell how rushes used to
bring
The butterfly and bee, and fisher-bird that 's
king
O' the purple kind, about the snow-soft silver-
sweet
Infant of mist and dew ; only these atoms fleet,
Embittered evermore, to make the sea one
drop
More big thereby — if thought keep count
where sense must stop.

LXXIV

The full-blown ingrate, mere recipient of the
brine,
That takes all and gives naught, is Man ; the
feminine
Rillet that, taking all and giving naught in
turn,
Goes headlong to her death i' the sea, without
concern
For the old inland life, snow-soft and silver-
clear,
That 's woman — typified from Fifine to Elvire.

LXXV

Then, how diverse the modes prescribed to
who would deal
With either kind of creature ! 'T is Man, you
seek to seal
Your very own ? Resolve, for first step, to
discard
Nine-tenths of what you are ! To make, you
must be marred, —
To raise your race, must stoop, — to teach them
aught, must learn
Ignorance, meet halfway what most you hope
to spurn
I' the sequel. Change yourself, dissimulate the
thought
And vulgarize the word, and see the deed be
brought
To look like nothing done with any such intent
As teach men — though perchance it teach, by
accident !
So may you master men : assured that if you
show
One point of mastery, departure from the low
And level, — head or heart-revolt at long dis-
guise,
Immurement, stifling soul in mediocrities, —
If inadvertently a gesture, much more, word
Reveal the hunter no companion for the herd,

His chance of capture 's gone. Success means,
    they may snuff,
Examine, and report, — a brother, sure enough,
Disports him in brute-guise; for skin is truly
    skin,
Horns, hoofs, are hoofs and horns, and all, out-
    side and in,
Is veritable beast, whom fellow-beasts resigned
May follow, made a prize in honest pride, be-
    hind
One of themselves and not creation's upstart
    lord!
Well, there 's your prize i' the pound — much
    joy may it afford
My Indian! Make survey and tell me, — was it
    worth
You acted part so well, went all-fours upon
    earth
The live-long day, brayed, belled, and all to
    bring to pass
That stags should deign eat hay when winter
    stints them grass?

LXXVI

So much for men, and how disguise may make
    them mind
Their master. But you have to deal with
    womankind?
Abandon stratagem for strategy! Cast quite
The vile disguise away, try truth clean-opposite
Such creep-and-crawl, stand forth all man and,
    might it chance,
Somewhat of angel too! — whate'er inheritance,
Actual on earth, in heaven prospective, be your
    boast,
Lay claim to! Your best self revealed at utter-
    most, —
That 's the wise way o' the strong! And e'en
    should falsehood tempt
The weaker sort to swerve, — at least the lie 's
    exempt
From slur, that 's loathlier still, of aiming to
    debase
Rather than elevate its object. Mimic grace,
Not make deformity your mask! Be sick by
    stealth,
Nor   traffic   with   disease — malingering   in
    health!
No more of: "Countrymen, I boast me one
    like you —
My lot, the common strength, the common
    weakness too!
I think the thoughts you think; and if I have
    the knack
Of fitting thoughts to words, you peradventure
    lack,
Envy me not the chance, yourselves more for-
    tunate!
Many the loaded ship self-sunk through treas-
    ure freight,
Many the pregnant brain brought never child
    to birth,
Many the great heart broke beneath its girdle-
    girth!
Be mine the privilege to supplement defect,
Give dumbness voice, and let the laboring in-
    tellect
Find utterance in word, or possibly in deed!

What though I seem to go before? 't is you that
    lead!
I follow what I see so plain — the general mind
Projected pillar-wise, flame kindled by the
    kind,
Which dwarfs the unit — me — to insignifi-
    cance!
Halt you, I stop forthwith, — proceed, I too ad-
    vance!"

LXXVII

Ay, that 's the way to take with men you
    wish to lead,
Instruct and benefit. Small prospect you suc-
    ceed
With women so! Be all that 's great and good
    and wise,
August, sublime — swell out your frog the
    right ox-size —
He 's buoyed like a balloon, to soar, not burst,
    you 'll see!
The more you prove yourself, less fear the
    prize will flee
The captor. Here you start after no pompous
    stag
Who condescends be snared, with toss of horn,
    and brag
Of bray, and ramp of hoof; you have not to
    subdue
The foe through letting him imagine he snares
    you!
'T is rather with . . .

LXXVIII

Ah, thanks! quick — where the dipping disk
Shows red against the rise and fall o' the fin!
    there frisk
In shoal the — porpoises? Dolphins, they shall
    and must
Cut through the freshening clear — dolphins,
    my instance just!
'T is fable, therefore truth: who has to do with
    these,
Needs never practice trick of going hands and
    knees
As beasts require. Art fain the fish to capti-
    vate?
Gather thy greatness round, Arion! Stand in
    state,
As when the banqueting thrilled conscious —
    like a rose
Throughout its hundred leaves at that approach
    it knows
Of music in the bird — while Corinth grew one
    breast
A-throb for song and thee; nay, Periander
    pressed
The Methymnæan hand, and felt a king indeed,
    and guessed
How Phœbus' self might give that great mouth
    of the gods
Such a magnificence of song! The pillar nods,
Rocks roof, and trembles door, gigantic, post
    and jamb,
As harp and voice rend air — the shattering
    dithyramb!
So stand thou, and assume the robe that tingles
    yet

With triumph; strike the harp, whose every
golden fret
Still smoulders with the flame, was late at
fingers' end —
So, standing on the bench o' the ship, let voice
expend
Thy soul, sing, unalloyed by meaner mode,
thine own,
The Orthian lay; then leap from music's lofty
throne
Into the lowest surge, make fearlessly thy
launch !
Whatever storm may threat, some dolphin will
be stanch !
Whatever roughness rage, some exquisite sea-
thing
Will surely rise to save, will bear — palpita-
ting —
One proud humility of love beneath its load —
Stem tide, part wave, till both roll on, thy
jewell'd road
Of triumph, and the grim o' the gulf grow
wonder-white
I' the phosphorescent wake ; and still the ex-
quisite
Sea-thing stems on, saves still, palpitatingly
thus,
Lands safe at length its load of love at Tænarus,
True woman-creature !

LXXIX

Man? Ah, would you prove what power
Marks man, — what fruit his tree may yield,
beyond the sour
And stinted crab, he calls love-apple, which
remains
After you toil and moil your utmost, — all, love
gains
By lavishing manure ? — try quite the other
plan !
And, to obtain the strong true product of a
man,
Set him to hate a little !   Leave cherishing his
root,
And rather prune his branch, nip off the petti-
est shoot
Superfluous on his bough !   I promise, you
shall learn
By what grace came the goat, of all beasts else,
to earn
Such favor with the god o' the grape : 't was
only he
Who, browsing on its tops, first stung fertility
Into the stock's heart, stayed much growth of
tendril-twine,
Some faintish flower, perhaps, but gained the
indignant wine,
Wrath of the red press !   Catch the puniest of
the kind —
Man-animalcule, starved body, stunted mind,
And, as you nip the blotch 'twixt thumb and
finger-nail,
Admire how heaven above and earth below
avail
No jot to soothe the mite, sore at God's prime
offence
In making mites at all, — coax from its impo-
tence

One virile drop of thought, or word, or deed, by
strain
To propagate for once — which nature rendered
vain,
Who lets first failure stay, yet cares not to re-
cord
Mistake that seems to cast opprobrium on the
Lord !
Such were the gain from love's best pains !
But let the elf
Be touched with hate, because some real man
bears himself
Manlike in body and soul, and, since he lives,
must thwart
And furify and set a-fizz this counterpart
O' the pismire that's surprised to efferves-
cence, if,
By chance, black bottle come in contact with
chalk cliff,
Acid with alkali !   Then thrice the bulk, out
blows
Our insect, does its kind, and cuckoo-spits some
rose !

LXXX

No — 't is ungainly work, the ruling men, at
best !
The graceful instinct's right : 't is women
stand confessed
Auxiliary, the gain that never goes away,
Takes nothing and gives all : Elvire, Fifine,
't is they
Convince, — if little, much, no matter ! — one
degree
The more, at least, convince unreasonable me
That I am, anyhow, a truth, though all else seem
And be not : if I dream, at least I know I
dream.
The falsity, beside, is fleeting : I can stand
Still, and let truth come back, — your steady-
ing touch of hand
Assists me to remain self-centred, fixed amid
All on the move. Believe in me, at once you
bid
Myself believe that, since one soul has disen-
gaged
Mine from the shows of things, so much is fact :
I waged
No foolish warfare, then, with shades, myself a
shade,
Here in the world — may hope my pains will be
repaid !
How false things are, I judge : how change-
able, I learn :
When, where, and how it is I shall see truth
return,
That I expect to know, because Fifine knows
me ! —
How much more, if Elvire !

LXXXI

"And why not, only she ?
Since there can be for each, one Best, no more,
such Best,
For body and mind of him, abolishes the rest
O' the simply Good and Better. You please
select Elvire
To give you this belief in truth, dispel the fear

Yourself are, after all, as false as what sur-
    rounds ;
And why not be content? When we two
    watched the rounds
The boatman made, 'twixt shoal and sandbank,
    yesterday,
As, at dead slack of tide, he chose to push his
    way,
With oar and pole, across the creek, and reach
    the isle
After a world of pains — my word provoked
    your smile,
Yet none the less deserved reply : ''T were
    wiser wait
The turn o' the tide, and find conveyance for
    his freight —
How easily — within the ship to purpose
    moored,
Managed by sails, not oars ! But no, — the
    man 's allured
By liking for the new and hard in his exploit !
First come shall serve ! He makes — coura-
    geous and adroit —
The merest willow-leaf of boat do duty, bear
His merchandise across : once over, needs he
    care
If folk arrive by ship, six hours hence, fresh
    and gay ? '
No : he scorns commonplace, affects the un-
    usual way ;
And good Elvire is moored, with not a breath
    to flap
The yards of her, no lift of ripple to o'erlap
Keel, much less, prow. What care ? since
    here 's a cockle-shell,
Fifine, that 's taut and crank, and carries just
    as well
Such seamanship as yours ! "

LXXXII

Alack, our life is lent,
From first to last, the whole, for this experi-
    ment
Of proving what I say — that we ourselves are
    true !
I would there were one voyage, and then no
    more to do
But tread the firm-land, tempt the uncertain
    sea no more
I would we might dispense with change of
    shore for shore
To evidence our skill, demonstrate — in no
    dream
It was, we tided o'er the trouble of the stream.
I would the steady voyage, and not the fitful
    trip, —
Elvire, and not Fifine, — might test our sea-
    manship.
But why expend one's breath to tell you,
    change of boat
Means change of tactics too ? Come see the
    same afloat
To-morrow, all the change, new stowage fore
    and aft
O' the cargo ; then, to cross requires new
    sailor-craft !
To-day, one step from stern to bow keeps boat
    in trim :

To-morrow, some big stone — or woe to boat
    and him ! --
Must ballast both. That man stands for Mind,
    paramount
Throughout the adventure : ay, howe'er you
    make account,
'T is mind that navigates, — skips over, twists
    between
The bales i' the boat, — now gives importance
    to the mean,
And now abates the pride of life, accepts all
    fact,
Discards all fiction, — steers Fifine, and cries, i'
    the act,
" Thou art so bad, and yet so delicate a brown !
Wouldst tell no end of lies : I talk to smile or
    frown !
Wouldst rob me : do men blame a squirrel,
    lithe and sly,
For pilfering the nut she adds to hoard ? Nor
    I."
Elvire is true, as truth, honesty's self, alack !
The worse ! too safe the ship, the transport
    there and back
Too certain ! one may loll and lounge and
    leave the helm,
Let wind and tide do work : no fear that
    waves o'erwhelm
The steady-going bark, as sure to feel her
    way
Blindfold across, reach land, next year as yes-
    terday !
How can I but suspect, the true feat were to
    slip
Down side, transfer myself to cockle-shell from
    ship,
And try if, trusting to sea-tracklessness, I
    class
With those around whose breast grew oak and
    triple brass :
Who dreaded no degree of death, but, with dry
    eyes,
Surveyed the turgid main and its monstrosi-
    ties —
And rendered futile so, the prudent Power's
    decree
Of separate earth and disassociating sea ;
Since, how is it observed, if impious vessels
    leap
Across, and tempt a thing they should not
    touch — the deep?
(See Horace to the boat, wherein, for Athens
    bound,
When Virgil must embark — Jove keep him
    safe and sound ! —
The poet bade his friend start on the watery
    road,
Much reassured by this so comfortable ode.)

LXXXIII

Then, never grudge my poor Fifine her com-
    pliment !
The rakish craft could slip her moorings in the
    tent,
And, hoisting every stitch of spangled canvas,
    steer
Through divers rocks and shoals, — in fine, de-
    posit here

Your Virgil of a spouse, in Attica: yea, thrid
The mob of men, select the special virtue hid
In him, forsooth, and say — or rather, smile so
  sweet,
" Of all the multitude, you — I prefer to cheat !
Are you for Athens bound ? I can perform the
  trip,
Shove little pinnace off, while yon superior
  ship,
The Elvire, refits in port ! " So, off we push
  from beach
Of Pornic town, and lo, ere eye can wink, we
  reach
The Long Walls, and I prove that Athens is no
  dream,
For there the temples rise ! they are, they
  nowise seem !
Earth is not all one lie, this truth attests me
  true !
Thanks therefore to Fifine ! Elvire, I 'm back
  with you !
Share in the memories ! Embark I trust we
  shall
Together some fine day, and so, for good and
  all,
Bid Pornic Town adieu, — then, just the strait
  to cross,
And we reach harbor, safe, in Iostephanos !

LXXXIV

How quickly night comes ! Lo, already 't is
  the land
Turns sea-like ; overcrept by gray, the plains
  expand,
Assume significance ; while ocean dwindles,
  shrinks
Into a pettier bound : its plash and plaint,
  methinks,
Six steps away, how both retire, as if their
  part
Were played, another force were free to prove
  her art,
Protagonist in turn ! Are you unterrified ?
All false, all fleeting too ! And nowhere things
  abide,
And everywhere we strain that things should
  stay, — the one
Truth, that ourselves are true !

LXXXV

A word, and I have done.
Is it not just our hate of falsehood, fleeting-
  ness,
And the mere part, things play, that constitutes
  express
The inmost charm of this Fifine and all her
  tribe ?
Actors ! We also act, but only they inscribe
Their style and title so, and preface, only they,
Performance with " A lie is all we do or say."
Wherein but there can be the attraction.
  Falsehood's bribe,
That wins so surely o'er to Fifine and her
  tribe
The liking, nay the love of who hate Falsehood
  most,
Except that these alone of mankind make their
  boast

" Frankly, we simulate ! " To feign, means —
  to have grace
And so get gratitude ! This ruler of the race,
Crowned, sceptred, stoled to suit, — 't is not
  that you detect
The cobbler in the king, but that he makes
  effect
By seeming the reverse of what you know to
  be
The man, the mind, whole form, fashion, and
  quality.
Mistake his false for true, one minute, — there 's
  an end
Of the admiration ! Truth, we grieve at or
  rejoice :
'T is only falsehood, plain in gesture, look and
  voice,
That brings the praise desired, since profit
  comes thereby.
The histrionic truth is in the natural lie.
Because the man who wept the tears was, all
  the time,
Happy enough ; because the other man, a-grime
With guilt was, at the least, as white as I and
  you ;
Because the timid type of bashful maidhood,
  who
Starts at her own pure shade, already numbers
  seven
Born babes and, in a month, will turn their
  odd to even ;
Because the saucy prince would prove, could
  you unfurl
Some yards of wrap, a meek and meritorious
  girl —
Precisely as you see success attained by each
O' the mimes, do you approve, not foolishly
  impeach
The falsehood !

LXXXVI

That 's the first o' the truths found : all
  things, slow
Or quick i' the passage, come at last to that,
  you know !
Each has a false outside, whereby a truth is
  forced
To issue from within : truth, falsehood, are
  divorced
By the excepted eye, at the rare season, for
The happy moment. Life means — learning to
  abhor
The false, and love the true, truth treasured
  snatch by snatch,
Waifs counted at their worth. And when with
  strays they match
I' the particolored world, — when, under foul,
  shines fair,
And truth, displayed i' the point, flashes forth
  everywhere
I' the circle, manifest to soul, though hid from
  sense,
And no obstruction more affects this confi-
  dence,
When faith is ripe for sight, — why, reason-
  ably, then
Comes the great clearing-up. Wait threescore
  years and ten !

LXXXVII

Therefore I prize stage - play, the honest
     cheating ; thence
The impulse pricked, when fife and drum bade
     Fair commence,
To bid you trip and skip, link arm in arm with
     me,
Like husband and like wife, and so together
     see
The tumbling-troop arrayed, the strollers on
     their stage
Drawn up and under arms, and ready to en-
     gage.
And if I started thence upon abstruser
     themes . . .
Well, 't was a dream, pricked too !

LXXXVIII

                    A poet never dreams :
We prose-folk always do : we miss the proper
     duct
For thoughts on things unseen, which stagnate
     and obstruct
The system, therefore ; mind, sound in a body
     sane,
Keeps thoughts apart from facts, and to one
     flowing vein
Confines its sense of that which is not, but
     might be,
And leaves the rest alone. What ghosts do
     poets see ?
What demons fear ? what man or thing misap-
     prehend ?
Unchecked, the channel 's flush, the fancy 's
     free to spend
Its special self aright in manner, time and
     place.
Never believe that who create the busy race
O' the brain, bring poetry to birth, such act
     performed,
Feel trouble them, the same, such residue as
     warmed
My prosy blood, this morn, — intrusive fancies,
     meant
For outbreak and escape by quite another
     vent !
Whence follows that, asleep, my dreamings oft
     exceed
The bound.   But you shall hear.

LXXXIX

         I smoked.   The webs o' the weed,
With many a break i' the mesh, were floating
     to re-form
Cupola-wise above : chased thither by soft
     warm
Inflow of air without ; since I — of mind to
     muse, to clench
The gain of soul and body, got by their noon-
     day drench
In sun and sea — had flung both frames o' the
     window wide,
To soak my body still and let soul soar beside.
In came the country sounds and sights and
     smells — that fine
Sharp needle in the nose from our fermenting
     wine !

In came a dragon-fly with whir and stir, then
     out,
Off and away : in came, — kept coming, rather,
     — pout
Succeeding smile, and take-away still close on
     give, —
One loose long creeper-branch, tremblingly sen-
     sitive
To risks, which blooms and leaves, — each leaf
     tongue-broad, each bloom
Midfinger-deep, — must run by prying in the
     room
Of one who loves and grasps and spoils and
     speculates.
All so far plain enough to sight and sense :
     but, weights,
Measures and numbers, — ah, could one apply
     such test
To other visitants that came at no request
Of who kept open house, — to fancies manifold
From this four-cornered world, the memories
     new and old,
The antenatal prime experience — what know
     I ? —
The initiatory love preparing us to die —
Such were a crowd to count, a sight to see, a
     prize
To turn to profit, were but fleshly ears and
     eyes
Able to cope with those o' the spirit !

XC

                    Therefore, — since
Thought hankers after speech, while no speech
     may evince
Feeling like music, — mine, o'erburdened with
     each gift
From every visitant, at last resolved to shift
Its burden to the back of some musician dead
And gone, who feeling once what I feel now,
     instead
Of words, sought sounds, and saved forever, in
     the same,
Truth that escapes prose, — nay, puts poetry to
     shame.
I read the note, I strike the key, I bid *record*
The instrument, — thanks greet the veritable
     word !
And not in vain I urge : " O dead and gone
     away,
Assist who struggles yet, thy strength become
     my stay,
Thy record serve as well to register — I felt
And knew thus much of truth ! With me,
     must knowledge melt
Into surmise and doubt and disbelief, unless
Thy music reassure — I gave no idle guess,
But gained a certitude, I yet may hardly keep !
What care ? since round is piled a monumental
     heap
Of music that conserves the assurance, thou as
     well
Wast certain of the same ! thou, master of the
     spell,
Mad'st moonbeams marble, didst *record* what
     other men
Feel only to forget ! " Who was it helped me,
     then ?

What master's work first came responsive to
    my call,
Found my eye, fixed my choice?

XCI

Why, Schumann's " Carnival " !
My choice chimed in, you see, exactly with the
    sounds
And sights of yestereve, when, going on my
    rounds,
Where both roads join the bridge, I heard
    across the dusk
Creak a slow caravan, and saw arrive the husk
O' the spice-nut, which peeled off this morning,
    and displayed,
'Twixt tree and tree, a tent whence the red
    pennon made
Its vivid reach for home and ocean-idleness —
And where, my heart surmised, at that same
    moment, — yes, —
Tugging her tricot on — yet tenderly, lest stitch
Announce the crack of doom, reveal disaster
    which
Our Pornic's modest stock of merceries in vain
Were ransacked to retrieve, — there, cautiously
    a-strain,
(My heart surmised) must crouch in that tent's
    corner, curved
Like Spring-month's russet moon, some girl by
    fate reserved
To give me once again the electric snap and
    spark
Which prove, when finger finds out finger in
    the dark
O' the world, there's fire and life and truth
    there, link but hands
And pass the secret on. Lo, link by link, ex-
    pands
The circle, lengthens out the chain, till one
    embrace
Of high with low is found uniting the whole
    race,
Not simply you and me and our Fifine, but all
The world: the Fair expands into the Carni-
    val,
And Carnival again to . . . ah, but that 's my
    dream !

XCII

I somehow played the piece : remarked on
    each old theme
I' the new dress ; saw how food o' the soul, the
    stuff that 's made
To furnish man with thought and feeling, is
    purveyed
Substantially the same from age to age, with
    change
Of the outside only for successive feasters,
    Range
The banquet-room o' the world, from the dim
    farthest head
O' the table, to its foot, for you and me be-
    spread,
This merry morn, we find sufficient fare, I trow.
But, novel ? Scrape away the sauce ; and taste,
    below,
The verity o' the viand, — you shall perceive
    there went

To board-head just the dish which other condi-
    ment
Makes palatable now : guests came, sat down,
    fell-to,
Rose up, wiped mouth, went way, — lived,
    died, — and never knew
That generations yet should, seeking sustenance,
Still find the selfsame fare, with somewhat to
    enhance
Its flavor, in the kind of cooking. As with hates
And loves and fears and hopes, so with what
    emulates
The same, expresses hates, loves, fears, and
    hopes in Art :
The forms, the themes — no one without its
    counterpart
Ages ago ; no one but, mumbled the due time
I' the mouth of the eater, needs be cooked
    again in rhyme,
Dished up anew in paint, sauce-smothered fresh
    in sound,
To suit the wisdom-tooth, just cut, of the age,
    that 's found
With gums obtuse to gust and smack which
    relished so
The meat o' the meal folk made some fifty
    years ago.
But don't suppose the new was able to efface
The old without a struggle, a pang ! The
    commonplace
Still clung about his heart, long after all the rest
O' the natural man, at eye and ear, was caught,
    confessed
The charm of change, although wry lip and
    wrinkled nose
Owned ancient virtue more conducive to repose
Than modern nothings roused to somethings by
    some shred
Of pungency, perchance garlic in amber's stead.
And so on, till one day, another age, by due
Rotation, pries, sniffs, smacks, discovers old is
    new,
And sauce, our sires pronounced insipid, proves
    again
Sole piquant, may resume its titillating reign —
With music, most of all the arts, since change is
    there
The law, and not the lapse : the precious means
    the rare,
And not the absolute in all good save surprise.
So I remarked upon our Schumann's victories
Over the commonplace, how faded phrase grew
    fine,
And palled perfection — piqued, up-startled by
    that brine,
His pickle — bit the mouth and burnt the
    tongue aright,
Beyond the merely good no longer exquisite :
Then took things as I found, and thanked with-
    out demur
The pretty piece — played through that move-
    ment, you prefer
Where dance and shuffle past, — he scolding
    while she pouts,
She canting while he calms, — in those eternal
    bouts
Of age, the dog — with youth, the cat — by
    rose-festoon

Tied teasingly enough — Columbine, Pantaloon :
She, toe-tips and *staccato*, — *legato*, shakes his
    poll
And shambles in pursuit, the senior. *Fi la
    folle !*
Lie to him ! get his gold and pay its price !
    begin
Your trade betimes, nor wait till you 've wed
    Harlequin
And need, at the week's end, to play the du-
    teous wife,
And swear you still love slaps and leapings
    more than life !
Pretty ! I say.

XCIII

        And so, I somehow-nohow played
The whole o' the pretty piece ; and then . . .
    whatever weighed
My eyes down, furled the films about my wits ?
    suppose,
The morning-bath, — the sweet monotony of
    those
Three keys, flat, flat and flat, never a sharp at
    all, —
Or else the brain's fatigue, forced even here to
    fall
Into the same old track, and recognize the
    shift
From old to new, and back to old again, and, —
    swift
Or slow, no matter, — still the certainty of
    change,
Conviction we shall find the false, where'er we
    range,
In art no less than nature : or what if wrist were
    numb,
And over-tense the muscle, abductor of the
    thumb,
Taxed by those tenths' and twelfths' uncon-
    scionable stretch ?
Howe'er it came to pass, I soon was far to
    fetch —
Gone off in company with Music !

XCIV

        Whither bound
Except for Venice ? She it was, by instinct
    found
Carnival-country proper, who far below the
    perch
Where I was pinnacled, showed, opposite,
    Mark's Church,
And, underneath, Mark's Square, with those
    two lines of street,
Procuratié-sides, each leading to my feet —
Since from above I gazed, however I got there.

XCV

And what I gazed upon was a prodigious Fair,
Concourse immense of men and women, crowned
    or casqued,
Turbaned or tiar'd, wreathed, plumed, hatted
    or wigged, but masked —
Always masked, — only, how ? No face-shape,
    beast or bird,
Nay, fish and reptile even, but some one had
    preferred,

From out its frontispiece, feathered or scaled
    or curled,
To make the vizard whence himself should
    view the world,
And where the world believed himself was
    manifest.
Yet when you came to look, mixed up among
    the rest
More funnily by far, were masks to imitate
Humanity's mishap : the wrinkled brow, bald
    pate,
And rheumy eyes of Age, peak'd chin and
    parchment chap,
Were signs of day-work done, and wage-time
    near, — mishap
Merely ; but, Age reduced to simple greed and
    guile,
Worn apathetic else as some smooth slab, ere-
    while
A clear-cut man-at-arms i' the pavement, till
    foot's tread
Effaced the sculpture, left the stone you saw
    instead, —
Was not that terrible beyond the mere un-
    couth ?
Well, and perhaps the next revolting you was
    Youth,
Stark ignorance and crude conceit, half smirk,
    half stare
On that frank fool-face, gay beneath its head
    of hair
Which covers nothing.

XCVI

        These, you are to understand,
Were the mere hard and sharp distinctions.
    On each hand,
I soon became aware, flocked the infinitude
Of passions, loves and hates, man pampers till
    his mood
Becomes himself, the whole sole face we name
    him by,
Nor want denotement else, if age or youth
    supply
The rest of him : old, young, — classed crea-
    ture : in the main
A love, a hate, a hope, a fear, each soul
    astrain
Some one way through the flesh — the face, an
    evidence
O' the soul at work inside ; and, all the more
    intense,
So much the more grotesque.

XCVII

        " Why should each soul be tasked
Some one way, by one love or else one hate ? "
    I asked.
When it occurred to me, from all these sights
    beneath
There rose not any sound : a crowd, yet dumb
    as death !

XCVIII

Soon I knew why. (Propose a riddle, and
    't is solved
Forthwith — in dream !) They spoke ; but,
    since on me devolved

To see, and understand by sight, — the vulgar
   speech
Might be dispensed with. " He who cannot
   see, must reach
As best he may the truth of men by help of
   words
They please to speak, must fare at will of who
   affords
The banquet," — so I thought. " Who sees
   not, hears and so
Gets to believe ; myself it is that, seeing,
   know,
And, knowing, can dispense with voice and
   vanity
Of speech. What hinders then, that, drawing
   closer, I
Put privilege to use, see and know better still
These *simulacra*, taste the profit of my skill,
Down in the midst ? "

XCIX

      And plumb I pitched into the square —
A groundling like the rest. What think you
   happened there ?
Precise the contrary of what one would expect !
For, — whereas, so much more monstrosities
   deflect
From nature and the type, as you the more
   approach
Their precinct, — here, I found brutality en-
   croach
Less on the human, lie the lightlier as I looked
The nearlier on these faces that seemed but
   now so crook'd
And clawed away from God's prime purpose.
   They diverged
A little from the type, but somehow rather urged
To pity than disgust : the prominent, before,
Now dwindled into mere distinctness, nothing
   more.
Still, at first sight, stood forth undoubtedly the
   fact
Some deviation was : in no one case there
   lacked
The certain sign and mark, say hint, say, trick
   of lip
Or twist of nose, that proved a fault in work-
   manship,
Change in the prime design, some hesitancy
   here
And there, which checked the man and let
   the beast appear ;
But that was all.

C

      All ; yet enough to bid each tongue
Lie in abeyance still. They talked, themselves
   among,
Of themselves, to themselves : I saw the
   mouths at play,
The gesture that enforced, the eye that strove
   to say
The same thing as the voice, and seldom gained
   its point
— That this was so, I saw ; but all seemed out
   of joint
I' the vocal medium 'twixt the world and me.
   I gained

Knowledge by notice, not by giving ear, —
   attained
To truth by what men seemed, not said : to me
   one glance
Was worth whole histories of noisy utterance,
— At least, to me in dream.

CI

      And presently I found
That, just as ugliness had withered, so unwound
Itself, and perished off, repugnance to what
   wrong
Might linger yet i' the make of man. My will
   was strong
I' the matter ; I could pick and choose, project
   my weight :
(Remember how we saw the boatman trim his
   freight !)
Determine to observe, or manage to escape,
Or make divergency assume another shape
By shift of point of sight in me the observer:
   thus
Corrected, added to, subtracted from, — dis-
   cuss
Each variant quality, and brute-beast touch
   was turned
Into mankind's safeguard ! Force, guile, were
   arms which earned
My praise, not blame at all : for we must learn
   to live,
Case-hardened at all points, not bare and
   sensitive,
But plated for defence, nay, furnished for
   attack,
With spikes at the due place, that neither front
   nor back
May suffer in that squeeze with nature, we find
   — life.
Are we not here to learn the good of peace
   through strife,
Of love through hate, and reach knowledge by
   ignorance ?
Why, those are helps thereto, which late we
   eyed askance,
And nicknamed unaware ! Just so, a sword
   we call
Superfluous, and cry out against, at festival :
Wear it in time of war, its clink and clatter
   grate
O' the ear to purpose then !

CII

      I found, one must abate
One's scorn of the soul's casing, distinct from
   the soul's self —
Which is the centre-drop : whereas the pride in
   pelf,
The lust to seem the thing it cannot be, the
   greed
For praise, and all the rest seen outside, —
   these indeed
Are the hard polished cold crystal environment
Of those strange orbs unearthed i' the Druid
   temple, meant
For divination (so the learned please to think)
Wherein you may admire one dewdrop roll and
   wink,
All unaffected by — quite alien to — what sealed

And saved it long ago : though how it got con-
gealed
I shall not give a guess, nor how, by power
occult,
The solid surface-shield was outcome and result
Of simple dew at work to save itself amid
The unwatery force around ; protected thus,
dew slid
Safe through all opposites, impatient to absorb
Its spot of life, and last forever in the orb
We, now, from hand to hand pass with impunity.

CIII

And the delight wherewith I watch this
crowd must be
Akin to that which crowns the chemist when he
winds
Thread up and up, till clue be fairly clutched,
— unbinds
The composite, ties fast the simple to its mate,
And, tracing each effect back to its cause, elate,
Constructs in fancy, from the fewest primitives,
The complex and complete, all diverse life, that
lives
Not only in beast, bird, fish, reptile, insect, but
The very plants and earths and ores. Just so
I glut
My hunger both to be and know the thing I am,
By contrast with the thing I am not ; so,
through sham
And outside, I arrive at inmost real, probe
And prove how the nude form obtained the
checkered robe.

CIV

— Experience, I am glad to master soon or
late,
Here, there, and everywhere i' the world, with-
out debate !
Only, in Venice why ? What reason for Mark's
Square
Rather than Timbuctoo ?

CV

And I became aware,
Scarcely the word escaped my lips, that swift
ensued
In silence and by stealth, and yet with certitude,
A formidable change of the amphitheatre
Which held the Carnival ; although the human
stir
Continued just the same amid that shift of
scene.

CVI

For as on edifice of cloud i' the gray and
green
Of evening, — built about some glory of the
west,
To barricade the sun's departure, — manifest,
He plays, pre-eminently gold, gilds vapor, crag
and crest
Which bend in rapt suspense above the act and
deed
They cluster round and keep their very own,
nor heed
The world at watch ; while we, breathlessly at
the base

O' the castellated bulk, note momently the
mace
Of night fall here, fall there, bring change with
every blow,
Alike to sharpened shaft and broadened portico
I' the structure : heights and depths, beneath
the leaden stress,
Crumble and melt and mix together, coalesce,
Re-form, but sadder still, subdued yet more and
more
By every fresh defeat, till wearied eyes need
pore
No longer on the dull impoverished decadence
Of all that pomp of pile in towering evidence
So lately : —

CVII

Even thus nor otherwise, meseemed
That if I fixed my gaze awhile on what I
dreamed
Was Venice' Square, Mark's Church, the
scheme was straight unschemed,
A subtle something had its way within the
heart
Of each and every house I watched, with coun-
terpart
Of tremor through the front and outward face,
until
Mutation was at end ; impassive and stock-still
Stood now the ancient house, grown — new, is
scarce the phrase,
Since older, in a sense, — altered to . . . what
i' the ways,
Ourselves are wont to see, coerced by city, town,
Or village, anywhere i' the world, pace up or
down
Europe ! In all the maze, no single tenement
I saw, but I could claim acquaintance with.

CVIII

There went
Conviction to my soul, that what I took of late
For Venice was the world ; its Carnival — the
state
Of mankind, masquerade in life-long perma-
nence
For all time, and no one particular feast-day.
Whence
'T was easy to infer what meant my late dis-
gust
At the brute-pageant, each grotesque of greed
and lust
And idle hate, and love as impotent for good —
When from my pride of place I passed the in-
terlude
In critical review ; and what, the wonder that
ensued
When, from such pinnacled pre-eminence, I
found
Somehow the proper goal for wisdom was the
ground
And not the sky, — so, slid sagaciously betimes
Down heaven's baluster-rope, to reach the mob
of mimes
And mummers ; whereby came discovery there
was just
Enough and not too much of hate, love, greed
and lust,

Could one discerningly but hold the balance,
 shift
The weight from scale to scale, do justice to the
 drift
Of nature, and explain the glories by the
 shames
Mixed up in man, one stuff miscalled by differ-
 ent names
According to what stage i' the process turned
 his rough,
Even as I gazed, to smooth — only get close
 enough!
— What was all this except the lesson of a life?

CIX

And — consequent upon the learning how from
 strife
Grew peace — from evil, good — came know-
 ledge that, to get
Acquaintance with the way o' the world, we
 must nor fret
Nor fume, on altitudes of self-sufficiency,
But bid a frank farewell to what — we think —
 should be,
And, with as good a grace, welcome what is —
 we find.

CX

Is — for the hour, observe! Since something
 to my mind
Suggested soon the fancy, nay, certitude that
 change,
Never suspending touch, continued to derange
What architecture, we, walled up within the
 cirque
O' the world, consider fixed as fate, not fairy-
 work.
For those were temples, sure, which tremblingly
 grew blank
From bright, then broke afresh in triumph, —
 ah, but sank
As soon, for liquid change through artery and
 vein
O' the very marble wound its way! And first a
 stain
Would startle and offend amid the glory; next,
Spot swift succeeded spot, but found me less
 perplexed
By portents; then, as 't were, a sleepiness soft
 stole
Over the stately fane, and shadow sucked the
 whole
Façade into itself, made uniformly earth
What was a piece of heaven; till, lo, a second
 birth,
And the veil broke away because of something
 new
Inside, that pushed to gain an outlet, paused in
 view
At last, and proved a growth of stone or brick
 or wood
Which, alien to the aim o' the Builder, some-
 how stood
The test, could satisfy, if not the early race
For whom he built, at least our present popu-
 lace,
Who must not bear the blame for what, blamed,
 proves mishap

Of the Artist: his work gone, another fills the
 gap,
Serves the prime purpose so. Undoubtedly
 there spreads
Building around, above, which makes men lift
 their heads
To look at, or look through, or look — for aught
 I care —
Over: if only up, it is, not down, they stare.
" Commercing with the skies," and not the
 pavement in the Square.

CXI

But are they only temples that subdivide, col-
 lapse,
And tower again, transformed? Academies,
 perhaps!
Domes where dwells Learning, seats of Science,
 bower and hall
Which house Philosophy — do these, too, rise
 and fall,
Based though foundations be on steadfast
 mother-earth,
With no chimeric claim to supermundane birth,
No boast that, dropped from cloud, they did
 not grow from ground?
Why, these fare worst of all! these vanish and
 are found
Nowhere, by who tasks eye some twice within
 his term
Of threescore years and ten, for tidings what
 each germ
Has burgeoned out into, whereof the promise
 stunned
His ear with such acclaim, — praise-payment to
 refund
The praisers, never doubt, some twice before
 they die
Whose days are long i' the land.

CXII

                        Alack, Philosophy!
Despite the chop and change, diminished or in-
 creased,
Patched-up and plastered-o'er, Religion stands
 at least
I' the temple-type. But thou? Here gape I,
 all agog
These thirty years, to learn how tadpole turns
 to frog;
And thrice at least have gazed with mild aston-
 ishment,
As, skyward up and up, some fire-new fabric
 sent
Its challenge to mankind, that, clustered under-
 neath
To hear the word, they straight believe, ay, in
 the teeth
O' the Past, clap hands, and hail triumphant
 Truth's outbreak —
Tadpole-frog-theory propounded past mistake!
In vain! A something ails the edifice, it bends,
It bows, it buries . . . Haste! cry " Heads
 below " to friends —
But have no fear they find, when smother shall
 subside,
Some substitution perk with unabated pride
I' the predecessor's place!

CXIII

No, — the one voice which failed
Never, the preachment's coign of vantage
nothing ailed, —
That had the luck to lodge i' the house not
made with hands !
And all it preached was this : " Truth builds
upon the sands,
Though stationed on a rock : and so her work
decays,
And so she builds afresh, with like result.
Naught stays
But just the fact that Truth not only is, but
fain
Would have men know she needs must be, by
each so plain
Attempt to visibly inhabit where they dwell."
Her works are work, while she is she ; that
work does well
Which lasts mankind their lifetime through,
and lets believe
One generation more, that, though sand run
through sieve,
Yet earth now reached is rock, and what we
moderns find
Erected here is Truth, who, 'stablished to her
mind
I' the fulness of the days, will never change in
show
More than in substance erst : men thought
they knew ; we know !

CXIV

Do you, my generation ? Well, let the blocks
prove mist
I' the main enclosure, — church and college, if
they list,
Be something for a time, and everything anon,
And anything awhile, as fit is off or on,
Till they grow nothing, soon to reappear no
less
As something, — shape reshaped, till out of
shapelessness
Come shape again as sure ! no doubt, or round
or square
Or polygon its front, some building will be
there,
Do duty in that nook o' the wall o' the world
where once
The Architect saw fit precisely to ensconce
College or church, and bid such bulwark guard
the line
O' the barrier round about, humanity's confine.

CXV

Leave watching change at work i' the greater
scale, on these
The main supports, and turn to their interstices
Filled up by fabrics too, less costly and less
rare,
Yet of importance, yet essential to the Fair
They help to circumscribe, instruct, and regu-
late !
See, where each booth-front boasts, in letters
small or great,
Its speciality, proclaims its privilege to stop
A breach, beside the best !

CXVI

Here History keeps shop,
Tells how past deeds were done, so and not
otherwise :
" Man ! hold truth evermore ! forget the early
lies ! "
There sits Morality, demure behind her stall,
Dealing out life and death : " This is the thing
to call
Right, and this other, wrong ; thus think, thus
do, thus say,
Thus joy, thus suffer ! — not to-day as yester-
day —
Yesterday's doctrine dead, this only shall en-
dure !
Obey its voice and live ! " — enjoins the dame
demure.
While Art gives flag to breeze, bids drum beat,
trumpet blow,
Inviting eye and ear to yonder raree-show.
Up goes the canvas, hauled to height of pole.
I think,
We know the way — long lost, late learned —
to paint ! A wink
Of eye, and lo, the pose ! the statue on its
plinth !
How could we moderns miss the heart o' the
labyrinth
Perversely all these years, permit the Greek
seclude
His secret till to-day ? And here 's another
feud
Now happily composed : inspect this quartet-
score !
Got long past melody, no word has Music more
To say to mortal man ! But is the bard to be
Behindhand ? Here 's his book, and now per-
haps you see
At length what poetry can do !

CXVII

Why, that 's stability
Itself, that change on change we sorrowfully
saw
Creep o'er the prouder piles ! We acquiesced
in law
When the fine gold grew dim i' the temple,
when the brass
Which pillared that so brave abode where
Knowledge was,
Bowed and resigned the trust ; but, bear all
this caprice,
Harlequinade where swift to birth succeeds
decease
Of hue at every turn o' the tinsel-flag which
flames
While Art holds booth in Fair ? Such glories
chased by shames
Like these, distract beyond the solemn and
august
Procedure to decay, evanishment in dust,
Of those marmoreal domes, — above vicissi-
tude,
We used to hope !

CXVIII

" So, all is change, in fine," pursued

The preachment to a pause. When — " All is
  permanence ! "
Returned a voice. Within? without? No
  matter whence
The explanation came : for, understand, I
  ought
To simply say — " I saw," each thing I say " I
  thought."
Since ever, as, unrolled, the strange scene-
  picture grew
Before me, sight flashed first, though mental
  comment too
Would follow in a trice, come hobblingly to
  halt.

CXIX

So, what did I see next but, — much as when
  the vault
I' the west, — wherein we watch the vapory,
  manifold
Transfiguration, — tired turns blaze to black,
  — behold,
Peak reconciled to base, dark ending feud
  with bright,
The multiform subsides, becomes the definite.
Contrasting life and strife, where battle they i'
  the blank
Severity of peace in death, for which we thank
One wind that comes to quell the concourse,
  drive at last
Things to a shape which suits the close of things,
  and cast
Palpably o'er vexed earth heaven's mantle of
  repose ?

CXX

Just so, in Venice' Square, that things were at
  the close
Was signalled to my sense ; for I perceived
  arrest
O' the change all round about. As if some im-
  pulse pressed
Each gently into each, what was distinctness,
  late,
Grew vague, and, line from line no longer
  separate,
No matter what its style, edifice . . . shall I
  say,
Died into edifice ? I find no simpler way
Of saying how, without or dash or shock or
  trace
Of violence, I found unity in the place
Of temple, tower, — nay, hall and house and
  hut, — one blank
Severity of peace in death ; to which they
  sank
Resigned enough, till . . . ah, conjecture, I
  beseech,
What special blank did they agree to, all and
  each ?
What common shape was that wherein they
  mutely merged
Likes and dislikes of form, so plain before ?

CXXI

    I urged
Your step this way, prolonged our path of en-
  terprise

To where we stand at last, in order that your
  eyes
Might see the very thing, and save my tongue
  describe
The Druid monument which fronts you. Could
  I bribe
Nature to come in aid, illustrate what I mean,
What wants there she should lend to solemnize
  the scene ?

CXXII

How does it strike you, this construction
  gaunt and gray —
Sole object, these piled stones, that gleam un-
  ground-away
By twilight's hungry jaw, which champs fine
  all beside
I' the solitary waste we grope through ? Oh,
  no guide
Need we to grope our way and reach the mon-
  strous door
Of granite ! Take my word, the deeper you ex-
  plore
That caverned passage, filled with fancies to
  the brim,
The less will you approve the adventure ! such
  a grim
Bar-sinister soon blocks abrupt your path, and
  ends
All with a cold dread shape, — shape whereon
  Learning spends
Labor, and leaves the text obscurer for the
  gloss,
While Ignorance reads right — recoiling from
  that Cross !
Whence came the mass and mass, strange
  quality of stone
Unquarried anywhere i' the region round ?
  Unknown !
Just as unknown, how such enormity could be
Conveyed by land, or else transported over sea,
And laid in order, so, precisely each on each,
As you and I would build a grotto where the
  beach
Sheds shell — to last an hour : this building
  lasts from age
To age the same. But why ?

CXXIII

    Ask Learning ! I engage
You get a prosy wherefore, shall help you to
  advance
In knowledge just as much as helps you Igno-
  rance
Surmising, in the mouth of peasant-lad or lass,
" I heard my father say he understood it was
A building, people built as soon as earth was
  made
Almost, because they might forget (they were
  afraid)
Earth did not make itself, but came of Some-
  body.
They labored that their work might last, and
  show thereby
He stays, while we and earth, and all things
  come and go.
Come whence? Go whither.? That, when
  come and gone, we know

Perhaps, but not while earth and all things
   need our best
Attention : we must wait and die to know the
   rest.
Ask, if that 's true, what use in setting up the
   pile ?
To make one fear and hope : remind us, all the
   while
We come and go, outside there 's Somebody
   that stays ;
A circumstance which ought to make us mind
   our ways,
Because, — whatever end we answer by this
   life, —
Next time, best chance must be for who, with
   toil and strife,
Manages now to live most like what he was
   meant
Become : since who succeeds so far, 't is evi-
   dent,
Stands foremost on the file ; who fails, has less
   to hope
From new promotion. That 's the rule — with
   even a rope
Of mushrooms, like this rope I dangle ! those
   that grew
Greatest and roundest, all in life they had to
   do,
Gain a reward, a grace they never dreamed, I
   think ;
Since, outside white as milk and inside black as
   ink,
They go to the Great House to make a dainty
   dish
For Don and Donna ; while this basket-load, I
   wish
Well off my arm, it breaks, — no starveling of
   the heap
But had his share of dew, his proper length of
   sleep
I' the sunshine : yet, of all, the outcome is —
   this queer
Cribbed quantity of dwarfs which burden bas-
   ket here
Till I reach home ; 't is there that, having run
   their rigs,
They end their earthly race, are flung as food
   for pigs.
Any more use I see ? Well, you must know,
   there lies
Something, the Curé says, that points to myste-
   ries
Above our grasp : a huge stone pillar, once up-
   right,
Now laid at length, half-lost — discreetly shun-
   ning sight
I' the bush and brier, because of stories in the
   air —
Hints what it signified, and why was stationed
   there,
Once on a time. In vain the Curé tasked his
   lungs —
Showed, in a preachment, how, at bottom of the
   rungs
O' the ladder, Jacob saw, where heavenly an-
   gels stept
Up and down, lay a stone which served him,
   while he slept,

For pillow ; when he woke, he set the same up-
   right
As pillar, and a-top poured oil : things requisite
To instruct posterity, there mounts from floor
   to roof,
A staircase, earth to heaven ; and also put in
   proof,
When we have scaled the sky, we well may let
   alone
What raised us from the ground, and — paying
   to the stone
Proper respect, of course — take staff and go
   our way,
Leaving the Pagan night for Christian break of
   day.
' For,' preached he, ' what they dreamed, these
   Pagans, wide-awake
We Christians may behold. How strange, then,
   were mistake
Did anybody style the stone, — because of drop
Remaining there from oil which Jacob poured
   a-top, —
Itself the Gate of Heaven, itself the end, and not
The means thereto !' Thus preached the Curé,
   and no jot
The more persuaded people but that, what once
   a thing
Meant and had right to mean, it still must
   mean. So cling
Folk somehow to the prime authoritative
   speech,
And so distrust report, it seems as they could
   reach
Far better the arch-word, whereon their fate
   depends.
Through rude charactery, than all the grace it
   lends,
That lettering of your scribes ! who flourish
   pen apace
And ornament the text, they say — we say,
   efface.
Hence, when the earth began its life afresh in
   May,
And fruit-trees bloomed, and waves would wan-
   ton, and the bay
Ruffle its wealth of weed, and stranger-birds
   arrive,
And beasts take each a mate, — folk, too,
   found sensitive,
Surmised the old gray stone upright there,
   through such tracts
Of solitariness and silence, kept the facts
Entrusted it, could deal out doctrine, did it
   please :
No fresh and frothy draught, but liquor on the
   lees,
Strong, savage, and sincere : first bleedings from
   a vine
Whereof the product now do Curés so refine
To insipidity, that, when heart sinks, we strive
And strike from the old stone the old restora-
   tive.
' Which is ? ' — why, go and ask our grandames
   how they used
To dance around it, till the Curé disabused
Their ignorance, and bade the parish in a band
Lay flat the obtrusive thing that cumbered so
   the land !

And there, accordingly, in bush and brier it —
　' bides
Its time to rise again!' (so somebody derides,
That 's pert from Paris,) ' since, yon spire, you
　keep erect
Yonder, and pray beneath, is nothing, I suspect,
But just the symbol's self, expressed in slate
　for rock,
Art's smooth for Nature's rough, new chip
　from the old block!'
There, sir, my say is said! Thanks, and Saint
　Gille increase
The wealth bestowed so well!"—wherewith
　he pockets piece,
Doffs cap, and takes the road. I leave in
　Learning's clutch
More money for his book, but scarcely gain as
　much.

CXXIV

To this it was, this same primeval monument,
That, in my dream, I saw building with build-
　ing blent
Fall: each on each they fast and founderingly
　went
Confusion-ward; but thence again subsided fast,
Became the mound you see. Magnificently
　massed
Indeed, those mammoth-stones, piled by the
　Protoplast
Temple-wise in my dream! beyond compare
　with fanes
Which, solid-looking late, had left no least re-
　mains
I' the bald and blank, now sole usurper of the
　plains
Of heaven, diversified and beautiful before.
And yet simplicity appeared to speak no more
Nor less to me than spoke the compound. At
　the core,
One and no other word, as in the crust of late,
Whispered, which, audible through the transi-
　tion-state,
Was no loud utterance in even the ultimate
Disposure. For as some imperial chord sub-
　sists,
Steadily underlies the accidental mists
Of music springing thence, that run their mazy
　race
Around, and sink, absorbed, back to the triad
　base, —
So, out of that one word, each variant rose and
　fell
And left the same " All 's change, but perma-
　nence as well."
— Grave note whence — list aloft! — harmonics
　sound, that mean:
" Truth inside, and outside, truth also; and
　between
Each, falsehood that is change, as truth is
　permanence.
The individual soul works through the shows
　of sense
(Which, ever proving false, still promise to be
　true)
Up to an outer soul as individual too;
And, through the fleeting, lives to die into the
　fixed,

And reach at length ' God, man, or both to-
　gether mixed,'
Transparent through the flesh, by parts which
　prove a whole,
By hints which make the soul discernible by
　soul —
Let only soul look up, not down, not hate but
　love,
As truth successively takes shape, one grade
　above
Its last presentment, tempts as it were truth
　indeed
Revealed this time; so tempts, till we attain to
　read
The signs aright, and learn, by failure, truth is
　forced
To manifest itself through falsehood; whence
　divorced
By the excepted eye, at the rare season, for
The happy moment, truth instructs us to abhor
The false, and prize the true, obtainable
　thereby.
Then do we understand the value of a lie;
Its purpose served, its truth once safe deposited,
Each lie, superfluous now, leaves, in the singer's
　stead,
The indubitable song; the historic personage
Put by, leaves prominent the impulse of his age;
Truth sets aside speech, act, time, place, in-
　deed, but brings
Nakedly forward now the principle of things
Highest and least."

CXXV

Wherewith change ends. What change to
　dread
When, disengaged at last from every veil, in-
　stead
Of type remains the truth? once — falsehood:
　but anon
Theosuton e broteion eper kekramenon,
Something as true as soul is true, though veils
　between
Prove false and fleet away. As I mean, did he
　mean,
The poet whose bird-phrase sits, singing in my
　ear
A mystery not unlike? What through the
　dark and drear
Brought comfort to the Titan? Emerging
　from the lymph,
" God, man, or mixture " proved only to be a
　nymph:
" From whom the clink on clink of metal "
　(money, judged
Abundant in my purse) " struck " (bumped at,
　till it budged)
" The modesty, her soul's habitual resident "
(Where late the sisterhood were lively in their
　tent)
" As out of wingèd ear " (that caravan on
　wheels)
" Impulsively she rushed, no slippers to her
　heels,"
And " Fear not, friends we flock! " soft smiled
　the sea-Fifine —
Primitive of the veils (if he meant what I
　mean)

The poet's Titan learned to lift, ere "Three-
    formed Fate,
Moirai Trimorphoi," stood unmasked the Ulti-
    mate.

CXXVI

Enough o' the dream! You see how poetry
    turns prose.
Announcing wonder-work, I dwindle at the
    close
Down to mere commonplace old facts which
    everybody knows.
So dreaming disappoints! The fresh and
    strange at first,
Soon wears to trite and tame, nor warrants the
    outburst
Of heart with which we hail those heights, at
    very brink
Of heaven, whereto one least of lifts would lead,
    we think,
But wherefrom quick decline conducts our
    step, we find,
To homely earth, old facts familiar left behind.
Did not this monument, for instance, long
    ago
Say all it had to say, show all it had to show,
Nor promise to do duty more in dream?

CXXVII

                            Awaking so,
What if we, homeward-bound, all peace and
    some fatigue,
Trudge, soberly complete our tramp of near a
    league,
Last little mile which makes the circuit just,
    Elvire?
We end where we began: that consequence is
    clear.
All peace and some fatigue, wherever we were
    nursed
To life, we bosom us on death, find last is first
And thenceforth final too.

CXXVIII

                "Why final? Why the more
Worth credence now than when such truth
    proved false before?"
Because a novel point impresses now: each lie
Redounded to the praise of man, was victory
Man's nature had both right to get, and might
    to gain,
And by no means implied submission to the
    reign
Of other quite as real a nature, that saw fit
To have its way with man, not man his way
    with it.
This time, acknowledgment and acquiescence
    quell
Their contrary in man; promotion proves as
    well
Defeat: and Truth, unlike the False with
    Truth's outside,
Neither plumes up his will nor puffs him out
    with pride.
I fancy, there must lurk some cogency i' the
    claim,
Man, such abatement made, submits to, all the
    same.

Soul finds no triumph, here, to register like
    Sense
With whom 't is ask and have, — the want,
    the evidence
That the thing wanted, soon or late, will be
    supplied.
This indeed plumes up will; this, sure, puffs
    out with pride,
When, reading records right, man's instincts
    still attest
Promotion comes to Sense because Sense likes
    it best;
For bodies sprouted legs, through a desire to run:
While hands, when fain to filch, got fingers one
    by one,
And nature, that's ourself, accommodative
    brings
To bear that, tired of legs which walk, we now
    bud wings
Since of a mind to fly. Such savor in the nose
Of Sense would stimulate Soul sweetly, I sup-
    pose,
Soul with its proper itch of instinct, prompting
    clear
To recognize soul's self soul's only master here
Alike from first to last. But if time's pressure,
    light's
Or rather dark's approach, wrest thoroughly
    the rights
Of rule away, and bid the soul submissive bear
Another soul than it play master everywhere
In great and small, — this time, I fancy, none
    disputes
There's something in the fact that such con-
    clusion suits
Nowise the pride of man, nor yet chimes in with
    attributes
Conspicuous in the lord of nature. He receives
And not demands — not first likes faith and
    then believes.

CXXIX

And as with the last essence, so with its first
    faint type.
Inconstancy means raw, 't is faith alone means
    ripe
I' the soul which runs its round: no matter how
    it range
From Helen to Fifine, Elvire bids back the
    change
To permanence. Here, too, love ends where
    love began.
Such ending looks like law, because the natural
    man
Inclines the other way, feels lordlier free than
    bound.
Poor pabulum for pride when the first love is
    found
Last also! and, so far from realizing gain,
Each step aside just proves divergency in vain.
The wanderer brings home no profit from his
    quest
Beyond the sad surmise that keeping house
    were best
Could life begin anew. His problem posed
    aright
Was — "From the given point evolve the in-
    finite!"

Not—"Spend thyself in space, endeavoring to joint
Together, and so make infinite, point and point:
Fix into one Elvire a Fair-ful of Fifines!"
Fifine, the foam-flake, she: Elvire, the sea's self, means
Capacity at need to shower how many such!
And yet we left her calm profundity, to clutch
Foam-flutter, bell on bell, that, bursting at a touch,
Blistered us for our pains. But wise, we want no more
O' the fickle element. Enough of foam and roar!
Land-locked, we live and die henceforth: for here's the villa door.

CXXX

How pallidly you pause o' the threshold! Hardly night,
Which drapes you, ought to make real flesh and blood so white!
Touch me, and so appear alive to all intents!
Will the saint vanish from the sinner that repents?
Suppose you are a ghost! A memory, a hope,
A fear, a conscience! Quick! Give back the hand I grope
I' the dusk for!

CXXXI

That is well. Our double horoscope
I cast, while you concur. Discard that simile
O' the fickle element! Elvire is land not sea—
The solid land, the safe. All these word-bubbles came
O' the sea, and bite like salt. The unlucky bath's to blame.
This hand of yours on heart of mine, no more the bay
I beat, nor bask beneath the blue! In Pornic, say,
The Mayor shall catalogue me duly domiciled,
Contributable, good-companion of the guild
And mystery of marriage. I stickle for the town,
And not this tower apart; because, though, halfway down,
Its mullions wink o'erwebbed with bloomy greenness, yet
Who mounts to staircase top may tempt the parapet,
And sudden there's the sea! No memories to arouse,
No fancies to delude! Our honest civic house
Of the earth be earthy too!—or graced perchance with shell
Made prize of long ago, picked haply where the swell
Menaced a little once—or seaweed-branch that yet
Dampens and softens, notes a freak of wind, a fret
Of wave: though, why on earth should sea-change mend or mar
The calm contemplative householders that we are?

So shall the seasons fleet, while our two selves abide:
E'en past astonishment how sunrise and spring-tide
Could tempt one forth to swim; the more if time appoints
That swimming grow a task for one's rheumatic joints.
Such honest civic house, behold, I constitute
Our villa! Be but flesh and blood, and smile to boot!
Enter for good and all! then fate bolt fast the door,
Shut you and me inside, never to wander more!

CXXXII

Only,—you do not use to apprehend attack!
No doubt, the way I march, one idle arm, thrown slack
Behind me, leaves the open hand defenceless at the back,
Should an impertinent on tiptoe steal, and stuff
—Whatever can it be? A letter sure enough,
Pushed betwixt palm and glove! That largess of a franc?
Perhaps inconsciously,—to better help the blank
O' the nest, her tambourine, and, laying egg, persuade
A family to follow, the nest-egg that I laid
May have contained—but just to foil suspicious folk—
Between two silver whites a yellow double yolk!
Oh, threaten no farewell! five minutes shall suffice
To clear the matter up. I go, and in a trice
Return; five minutes past, expect me! If in vain—
Why, slip from flesh and blood, and play the ghost again!

EPILOGUE

THE HOUSEHOLDER

Savage I was sitting in my house, late, lone:
Dreary, weary with the long day's work:
Head of me, heart of me, stupid as a stone:
Tongue-tied now, now blaspheming like a Turk;
When, in a moment, just a knock, call, cry,
Half a pang and all a rapture, there again were we!—
"What, and is it really you again?" quoth I:
"I again, what else did you expect?" quoth She.

"Never mind, hie away from this old house—
Every crumbling brick embrowned with sin and shame!
Quick, in its corners ere certain shapes arouse!
Let them—every devil of the night—lay claim,
Make and mend, or rap and rend, for me!
Good-by!

God be their guard from disturbance at their
glee,
Till, crash, comes down the carcass in a heap ! "
quoth I :
" Nay, but there 's a decency required ! "
quoth She.

" Ah, but if you knew how time has dragged,
days, nights !
All the neighbor-talk with man and maid —
such men !
All the fuss and trouble of street-sounds,
window-sights :
All the worry of flapping door and echoing
roof ; and then,
All the fancies . . . Who were they had leave,
dared try
Darker arts that almost struck despair in
me ?

If you knew but how I dwelt down here ! "
quoth I :
" And was I so better off up there ? " quoth
She.

" Help and get it over ! *Reunited to his wife*
(How draw up the paper lets the parish-
people know ?)
Lies M. or N., departed from this life,
Day the this or that, month and year the so and
so.
What i' the way of final flourish ? Prose,
verse ? Try !
Affliction sore long time he bore, or, what is it
to be ?
Till God did please to grant him ease. Do end ! "
quoth I :
" I end with — Love is all, and Death is
naught ! " quoth She.

RED COTTON NIGHT-CAP COUNTRY

OR

TURF AND TOWERS

TO MISS THACKERAY

THIS poem, dated January 23, 1873, was pub-
lished in the early summer of the same year.
Browning had been staying with his sister at
St. Aubin, in Normandy, and there met Miss
Thackeray, who was to tell a tale of the White
Cotton Night-cap Country, but a tragedy then
just coming to a culmination in the courts sup-
plied Browning with the more suggestive title
which he adopted. Mr. Cooke records : —
" In the poem as written the names of the
actors and places were correctly given, but
when the poem was being revised in proof-
sheets they were changed from prudential
reasons, because the last act in the tragedy
occurred only a brief period prior to the writing
of the poem.

" Browning submitted the proof-sheets of the
poem to his friend Lord Coleridge, then the
English Attorney-General, afterwards Chief
Justice, who thought that a case of libel might
lie for what was said, however improbable such
action might be. He accordingly changed the
names to fictitious ones. It was the year follow-
ing this, and the publication of the poem, that
the appeal against the judgment in favor of the
will of Mellerio was dismissed, and the case
finally set at rest in harmony with the conclu-
sion reached by the poet."
In the second edition of her *Hand-Book* Mrs.
Orr gives the correct names, as furnished to her
by Browning himself. These names will be
found in the notes at the end of this volume.

I

AND so, here happily we meet, fair friend !
Again once more, as if the years rolled back
And this our meeting-place were just that
Rome
Out in the champaign, say, o'er-rioted
By verdure, ravage, and gay winds that war
Against strong sunshine settled to his sleep ;
Or on the Paris Boulevard, might it prove,
You and I came together saunteringly,

Bound for some shop-front in the Place Ven-
dôme —
Goldsmithy and Golconda mine, that makes
" The Firm - Miranda " blazed about the
world —
Or, what if it were London, where my toe
Trespassed upon your flounce ? " Small
blame," you smile,
Seeing the Staircase Party in the Square
Was Small and Early, and you broke no
rib.

Even as we met where we have met so oft,
Now meet we on this unpretending beach
Below the little village: little, ay!
But pleasant, may my gratitude subjoin?
Meek, hitherto un-Murrayed bathing-place,
Best loved of seacoast-nookful Normandy!
That, just behind you, is mine own hired
house:
With right of pathway through the field in
front,
No prejudice to all its growth unsheaved
Of emerald luzern bursting into blue.
Be sure I keep the path that hugs the wall,
Of mornings, as I pad from door to gate!
Yon yellow — what if not wild-mustard
flower? —
Of that, my naked sole makes lawful prize,
Bruising the acrid aromatics out,
Till, what they preface, good salt savors sting
From, first, the sifted sands, then sands in slab,
Smooth save for pipy wreath-work of the
worm:
(Granite and mussel-shell are ground alike
To glittering paste, — the live worm troubles
yet.)
Then, dry and moist, the varech limit-line,
Burnt cinder-black, with brown uncrumpled
swathe
Of berried softness, sea-swoln thrice its size;
And, lo, the wave protrudes a lip at last,
And flecks my foot with froth, nor tempts in
vain.

Such is Saint-Rambert, wilder very much
Than Joyeux, that famed Joyous-Gard of
yours,
Some five miles farther down; much homelier
too —
Right for me, — right for you the fine and fair!
Only, I could endure a transfer — wrought
By angels famed still, through our country-
side,
For weights they fetched and carried in old
time
When nothing like the need was — transfer,
just
Of Joyeux church, exchanged for yonder prig,
Our brand-new stone cream-colored master-
piece.

Well — and you know, and not since this one
year,
The quiet seaside country? So do I:
Who like it, in a manner, just because
Nothing is prominently likable
To vulgar eye without a soul behind,
Which, breaking surface, brings before the ball
Of sight, a beauty buried everywhere.
If we have souls, know how to see and use,
One place performs, like any other place,
The proper service every place on earth
Was framed to furnish man with: serves alike
To give him note that, through the place he
sees,
A place is signified he never saw,
But, if he lack not soul, may learn to know.
Earth's ugliest walled and ceiled imprisonment
May suffer, through its single rent in roof,

Admittance of a cataract of light
Beyond attainment through earth's palace-
panes
Pinholed athwart their windowed filigree
By twinklings sobered from the sun outside.
Doubtless the High Street of our village here
Imposes hardly as Rome's Corso could:
And our projected race for sailing-boats
Next Sunday, when we celebrate our Saint,
Falls very short of that attractiveness,
That artistry in festive spectacle,
Paris ensures you when she welcomes back
(When shall it be?) the Assembly from Ver
sailles;
While the best fashion and intelligence
Collected at the counter of our Mayor
(Dry-goods he deals in, grocery beside)
What time the post-bag brings the news from
Vire, —
I fear me much, it scarce would hold its
own,
That circle, that assorted sense and wit,
With Five-o'clock Tea in a house we know.

Still, 't is the check that gives the leap its lift.
The nullity of cultivated souls,
Even advantaged by their news from Vire,
Only conduces to enforce the truth
That, thirty paces off, this natural blue
Broods o'er a bag of secrets, all unbroached,
Beneath the bosom of the placid deep,
Since first the Post Director sealed them safe;
And formidable I perceive this fact —
Little Saint-Rambert touches the great sea.
From London, Paris, Rome, where men are
men,
Not mice, and mice not Mayors presumably,
Thought scarce may leap so fast, alight so far.
But this is a pretence, you understand,
Disparagement in play, to parry thrust
Of possible objector: nullity
And ugliness, the taunt be his, not mine
Nor yours, — I think we know the world too
well!
Did you walk hither, jog it by the plain,
Or jaunt it by the highway, braving bruise
From springless and uncushioned vehicle?
Much, was there not, in place and people both,
To lend an eye to? and what eye like yours —
The learned eye is still the loving one!
Our land; its quietude, productiveness,
Is length and breadth of grain-crop, meadow-
ground,
Its orchards in the pasture, farms a-field,
And hamlets on the road-edge, naught you
missed
Of one and all the sweet rusticities!
From stalwart strider by the wagon-side,
Brightening the acre with his purple blouse,
To those dark-featured comely women-folk,
Healthy and tall, at work, and work indeed,
On every cottage doorstep, plying brisk
Bobbins that bob you ladies out such lace!
Oh, you observed! and how that nimble play
Of finger formed the sole exception, bobbed
The one disturbance to the peace of things,
Where nobody esteems it worth his while,
If time upon the clock-face goes asleep,

To give the rusted hands a helpful push.
Nobody lifts an energetic thumb
And index to remove some dead and gone
Notice which, posted on the barn, repeats
For truth what two years' passage made a lie.
Still is for sale, next June, that same châ-
   teau
With all its immobilities, — were sold
Duly next June behind the last but last ;
And, woe 's me, still placards the Emperor
His confidence in war he means to wage,
God aiding and the rural populace.
No : rain and wind must rub the rags away
And let the lazy land untroubled snore.

Ah, in good truth ? and did the drowsihead
So suit, so soothe the learned loving eye,
That you were minded to confer a crown,
(Does not the poppy boast such ?) — call the
   land
By one slow hither-thither stretching, fast
Subsiding-into-slumber sort of name,
Symbolic of the place and people too,
" *White Cotton Night-cap Country ?* "   Excel-
   lent !
For they do, all, dear women young and old,
Upon the heads of them bear notably
This badge of soul and body in repose ;
Nor its fine thimble fits the acorn-top,
Keeps woolly ward above that oval brown,
Its placid feature, more than muffler makes
A safeguard, circumvents intelligence
In. — what   shall   evermore   be   named   and
   famed,
If happy nomenclature aught avail,
" *White Cotton Night-cap Country.* "

                        Do I hear —
Oh, better, very best of all the news —
You mean to catch and cage the wingèd word,
And make it breed and multiply at home
Till Norman idlesse stock our England too ?
Normandy shown minute yet magnified
In one of those small books, the truly great,
We never know enough, yet know so well ?
How I foresee the cursive diamond-dints, —
Composite pen that plays the pencil too, —
As, touch the page and up the glamour goes,
And filmily o'er grain-crop, meadow-ground,
O'er orchard in the pasture, farm a-field,
And hamlet on the road-edge, floats and forms
And falls, at lazy last of all, the Cap
That crowns the country ! we, awake outside,
Farther than ever from the imminence
Of what cool comfort, what close coverture
Your magic, deftly weaving, shall surround
The unconscious captive with.   Be theirs to
   drowse
Trammelled, and ours to watch the trammel-
   trick !
Ours be it, as we con the book of books,
To wonder how is winking possible !

All hail, " White Cotton Night-cap Country,"
   then !
And yet, as on the beach you promise book, —
On beach, mere razor-edge 'twixt earth and
   sea,

I stand at such a distance from the world
That 't is the whole world which obtains regard,
Rather than any part, though part presumed
A perfect little province in itself,
When wayfare made acquaintance first there-
   with.
So standing, therefore, on this edge of things,
What if the backward glance I gave, return
Loaded with other spoils of vagrancy
Than I dispatched it for, till I propose
The question — puzzled by the sudden store
Officious fancy plumps beneath my nose —
" Which sort of Night-cap have you glorified ? "

You would be gracious to my ignorance :
What other Night-cap than the normal one ? —
Old honest guardian of man's head and hair
In its elastic yet continuous, soft,
No less persisting, circumambient gripe, —
Night's notice, life is respited from day !
Its form and fashion vary, suiting so
Each seasonable want of youth and age.
In infancy, the rosy naked ball
Of brain, and that faint golden fluff it bears,
Are smothered from disaster, — nurses know
By what foam-fabric ; but when youth suc-
   ceeds,
The sterling value of the article
Discards adornment, cap is cap henceforth
Unfeathered by the futile row on row.
Manhood strains hard a sturdy stocking-stuff
O'er well-deserving head and ears : the cone
Is tassel-tipt, commendably takes pride,
Announcing workday done and wages pouched,
And liberty obtained to sleep, nay, snore.
Unwise, he peradventure shall essay
The sweets of independency for once —
Waive its advantage on his wedding-night :
Fool, only to resume it, night the next,
And never part companionship again.
Since, with advancing years, night's solace
   soon
Intrudes upon the daybreak dubious life
Persuades it to appear the thing it is
Half - sleep ; and so, encroaching more and
   more,
It lingers long past the abstemious meal
Of morning, and, as prompt to serve, precedes
The supper-summons, gruel grown a feast.
Finally, when the last sleep finds the eye
So tired it cannot even shut itself,
Does not a kind domestic hand unite
Friend to friend, lid from lid to part no more,
Consigned alike to that receptacle
So bleak without, so warm and white within ?

" Night-caps, night's comfort of the human
   race :
Their usage may be growing obsolete,
Still, in the main, the institution stays.
And though yourself may possibly have lived,
And probably will die, undignified —
The Never-night-capped — more experienced
   folk
Laugh you back answer — What should Night-
   cap be
Save Night-cap pure and simple ?   Sorts of
   such ?

Take cotton for the medium, cast an eye
This side to comfort, lambswool, or the like,
That side to frilly cambric costliness,
And all between proves Night-cap proper.''
    Add
" Fiddle ! " and I confess the argument.

Only, your ignoramus here again
Proceeds as tardily to recognize
Distinctions : ask him what a fiddle means,
And " Just a fiddle " seems the apt reply.
Yet, is not there, while we two pace the beach,
This blessed moment, at your Kensington,
A special Fiddle-Show and rare array
Of all the sorts were ever set to cheek,
'Stablished on clavicle, sawn bow-hand-wise,
Or touched lute-fashion and forefinger-plucked ?
I doubt not there be duly catalogued
Achievements all and some of Italy,
Guarnerius, Straduarius, — old and new,
Augustly rude, refined to finicking,
This mammoth with his belly full of blare,
That mouse of music — inch-long silvery wheeze,
And here a specimen has effloresced
Into the scroll-head, there subsides supreme,
And with the tailpiece satisfies mankind.
Why should I speak of woods, grains, stains
    and streaks,
The topaz varnish or the ruby gum ?
We preferably pause where tickets teach,
" Over this sample would Corelli croon,
Grieving, by minors, like the cushat-dove,
Most dulcet Giga, dreamiest Saraband."
" From this did Paganini comb the fierce
Electric sparks, or to tenuity
Pull forth the inmost wailing of the wire —
No cat-gut could swoon out so much of soul ! ''

Three hundred violin-varieties
Exposed to public view ! And dare I doubt
Some future enterprise shall give the world
Quite as remarkable a Night-cap-show ?
Methinks, we, arm-in-arm, that festal day,
Pace the long range of relics shrined aright,
Framed, glazed, each cushioned curiosity,
And so begin to smile and to inspect :
" Pope's sickly head-sustainment, damped with
    dews
Wrung from the all-unfair fight : such a frame —
Though doctor and the devil helped their
    best —
Fought such a world that, waiving doctor's
    help,
Had the mean devil at its service too !
Voltaire's imperial velvet ! Hogarth eyed
The thumb-nail record of some alley-phiz,
Then chucklingly clapped yonder cosiness
On pate, and painted with true flesh and blood !
Poor hectic Cowper's soothing sarsnet-stripe ! ''
And so we profit by the catalogue,
Somehow our smile subsiding more and more,
Till we decline into . . . but no ! shut eyes
And hurry past the shame uncoffined here,
The hangman's toilet ! If we needs must trench,
For science' sake which craves completeness
    still,
On the sad confine, not the district's self,
The object that shall close review may be . . .

Well, it is French, and here are we in France :
It is historic, and we live to learn,
And try to learn by reading story-books.
It is an incident of 'Ninety-two,
And, twelve months since, the Commune had
    the sway.
Therefore resolve that, after all the Whites
Presented you, a solitary Red
Shall pain us both, a minute and no more !
Do not you see poor Louis pushed to front
Of palace-window, in persuasion's name,
A spectacle above the howling mob
Who tasted, as it were, with tiger-smack,
The outstart, the first spurt of blood on brow,
The Phrygian symbol, the new crown of thorns,
The Cap of Freedom ? See the feeble mirth
At odds with that half-purpose to be strong
And merely patient under misery !
And note the ejaculation, ground so hard
Between his teeth, that only God could hear,
As the lean pale proud insignificance
With the sharp-featured liver-worried stare
Out of the two gray points that did him stead,
And passed their eagle-owner to the front
Better than his mob-elbowed undersize, —
The Corsican lieutenant commented,
" Had I but one good regiment of my own,
How soon should volleys to the due amount
Lay stiff upon the street-flags this canaille !
As for the droll there, he that plays the king,
And screws out smile with a Red night-cap on,
He 's done for ! somebody must take his place."
White Cotton Night-cap Country : excellent !
Why not Red Cotton Night-cap Country too ?

" Why not say swans are black and blackbirds
    white,
Because the instances exist ? " you ask.
" Enough that white, not red, predominates.
Is normal, typical, in cleric phrase
Quod semel, semper, et ubique." Here,
Applying such a name to such a land,
Especially you find inopportune,
Impertinent, my scruple whether white
Or red describes the local color best.
" Let be," (you say,) " the universe at large
Supplied us with exceptions to the rule,
So manifold, they bore no passing-by, —
Little Saint-Rambert has conserved at least
The pure tradition : white from head to heel,
Where is a hint of the ungracious hue ?
See, we have traversed with hop, step, and
    jump,
From heel to head, the main-street in a trice,
Measured the garment (help my metaphor !)
Not merely criticised the cap, forsooth ;
And were you pricked by that collecting-itch,
That pruriency for writing o'er your reds,
' Rare, rarer, rarest, not rare but unique,' —
The shelf, Saint-Rambert, of your cabinet,
Unlabelled, — virginal, no Rahab-thread
For blushing token of the spy's success, —
Would taunt with vacancy, I undertake !
What, yonder is your best apology,
Pretence at most approach to naughtiness,
Impingement of the ruddy on the blank ?
This is the criminal Saint-Rambertese
Who smuggled in tobacco, half-a-pound !

The Octroi found it out and fined the wretch.
This other is the culprit who dispatched
A hare, he thought a hedgehog, (clods obstruct,)
Unfurnished with Permission for the Chase !
As to the womankind — renounce from those
The hope of getting a companion-tinge,
First faint touch promising romantic fault ! ''

Enough : there stands Red Cotton Night-cap
    shelf —
A cavern's ostentatious vacancy —
My contribution to the show ; while yours —
Whites heap your row of pegs from every hedge
Outside, and house inside Saint-Rambert here —
We soon have come to end of. See, the church
With its white steeple gives your challenge
    point,
Perks as it were the night-cap of the town,
Starchedly warrants all beneath is matched
By all above, one snowy innocence !

You put me on my mettle. British maid
And British man, suppose we have it out
Here in the fields, decide the question so ?
Then, British fashion, shake hands hard again,
Go home together, friends the more confirmed
That one of us — assuredly myself —
Looks puffy about eye, and pink at nose ?
Which '' pink '' reminds me that the arduous-
    ness
We both acknowledge in the enterprise,
Claims, counts upon a large and liberal
Acceptance of as good as victory
In whatsoever just escapes defeat.
You must be generous, strain point, and call
Victory, any the least flush of pink
Made prize of, labelled scarlet for the nonce —
Faintest pretension to be wrong and red
And picturesque, that varies by a splotch
The righteous flat of insipidity.

Quick to the quest, then — forward, the firm
    foot !
Onward, the quarry-overtaking eye !
For, what is this, by way of march-tune, makes
The musicalest buzzing at my ear
By reassurance of that promise old,
Though sins as scarlet they shall be as wool ?
Whence — what fantastic hope do I deduce ?
I am no Liebig : when the dyer dyes
A texture, can the red dye prime the white ?
And if we washed well, wrung the texture hard,
Would we arrive, here, there and everywhere,
At a fierce ground beneath the surface meek ?

I take the first chance, rub to threads what rag
Shall flutter snowily in sight. For see !
Already these few yards upon the rise,
Our back to brave Saint-Rambert, how we
    reach
The open, at a dozen steps or strides !
Turn round and look about, a breathing-while !
There lie, outspread at equidistance, thorpes
And villages and towns along the coast,
Distinguishable, each and all alike,
By white persistent Night-cap, spire on spire.
Take the left : yonder town is — what say you
If I say '' Londres ''? Ay, the mother-mouse

(Reversing fable, as truth can and will)
Which gave our mountain of a London birth !
This is the Conqueror's country, bear in mind,
And Londres-district blooms with London-pride.
Turn round ; La Roche, to right, where oysters
    thrive :
Monlieu — the lighthouse is a telegraph ;
This, full in front, Saint-Rambert ; then suc-
    ceeds
Villeneuve, and Pons the Young with Pons the
    Old,
And — ere faith points to Joyeux, out of sight,
A little nearer — oh, La Ravissante !

There now is something like a Night-cap spire,
Donned by no ordinary Notre-Dame !
For, one of the three safety-guards of France,
You front now, lady ! Nothing intercepts
The privilege, by crow-flight, two miles far.
She and her sisters Lourdes and La Salette
Are at this moment hailed the cynosure
Of poor dear France, such waves have buffeted
Since she eschewed infallibility
And chose to steer by the vague compass-box.
This same midsummer month, a week ago,
Was not the memorable day observed
For reinstatement of the misused Three
In old supremacy forevermore ?
Did not the faithful flock in pilgrimage
By railway, diligence, and steamer — nay,
On foot with staff and scrip, to see the sights
Assured them ? And I say best sight was
    here :
And nothing justified the rival Two
In their pretension to equality ;
Our folk laid out their ticket-money best,
And wiseliest, if they walked, wore shoe away ;
Not who went farther only to fare worse.
For, what was seen at Lourdes and La Salette
Except a couple of the common cures
Such as all three can boast of, any day ?
While here it was, here and by no means there,
That the Pope's self sent two great real gold
    crowns
As thick with jewelry as thick could stick,
His present to the Virgin and her Babe —
Provided for — who knows not ? — by that
    fund,
Count Alessandro Sforza's legacy,
Which goes to crown some Virgin every year.
But this year, poor Pope was in prison-house,
And money had to go for something else ;
And therefore, though their present seemed
    the Pope's,
The faithful of our province raised the sum
Preached and prayed out of — nowise purse
    alone.
Gentle and simple paid in kind, not cash,
The most part : the great lady gave her brooch,
The peasant-girl, her hairpin ; 't was the rough
Bluff farmer mainly who, — admonished well
By wife to care lest his new colewort-crop
Stray sorrowfully sparse like last year's seed, —
Lugged from reluctant pouch the fifty-franc,
And had the Curé's hope that rain would cease.
And so, the sum in evidence at length,
Next step was to obtain the donative
By the spontaneous bounty of the Pope —

No easy matter, since his Holiness
Had turned a deaf ear, long and long ago,
To much entreaty on our Bishop's part,
Commendably we boast. "But no," quoth he,
"Image and image needs must take their turn:
Here stand a dozen as importunate."
Well, we were patient; but the cup ran o'er
When — who was it pressed in and took the
     prize
But our own offset, set far off indeed
To grow by help of our especial name,
She of the Ravissante — in Martinique!
"What!" cried our patience at the boiling-
     point,
"The daughter crowned, the mother's head
     goes bare?
Bishop of Raimbaux!" — that's our diocese —
"Thou hast a summons to repair to Rome,
Be efficacious at the Council there:
Now is the time or never! Right our wrong!
Hie thee away, thou valued Morillon,
And have the promise, thou who hast the
     vote!"
So said, so done, so followed in due course
(To cut the story short) this festival,
This famous Twenty-second, seven days since.

Oh, but you heard at Joyeux! Pilgrimage,
Concourse, procession with, to head the host,
Cardinal Mirecourt, quenching lesser lights:
The leafy street-length through, decked end to
     end
With August-strippage, and adorned with flags,
That would have waved right well but that it
     rained
Just this picked day, by some perversity.
And so were placed, on Mother and on Babe,
The pair of crowns: the Mother's, you must
     see!
Miranda, the great Paris goldsmith, made
The marvel, — he's a neighbor: that's his
     park
Before you, tree-topped wall we walk toward.
His shop it was turned out the masterpiece,
Probably at his own expenditure;
Anyhow, his was the munificence
Contributed the central and supreme
Splendor that crowns the crown itself, The
     Stone.
Not even Paris, ransacked, could supply
That gem: he had to forage in New York,
This jeweller, and country-gentleman,
And most undoubted devotee beside!
Worthily wived, too: since his wife it was
Bestowed "with friendly hand" — befitting
     phrase
The lace which trims the coronation-robe —
Stiff wear — a mint of wealth on the brocade.
Do go and see what I saw yesterday!
And, for that matter, see in fancy still,
Since . . .

          There now! Even for unthankful me,
Who stuck to my devotions at high-tide
That festal morning, never had a mind
To trudge the little league and join the crowd —
Even for me is miracle vouchsafed!
How pointless proves the sneer at miracles!

As if, contrariwise to all we want
And reasonably look to find, they graced
Merely those graced-before, grace helps no
     whit,
Unless, made whole, they need physician still.
I — sceptical in every inch of me —
Did I deserve that, from the liquid name
"Miranda," — faceted as lovelily
As his own gift, the gem, — a shaft should
     shine,
Bear me along, another Abaris,
Nor let me light till, lo, the Red is reached,
And yonder lies in luminosity!

Look, lady! where I bade you glance but now!
Next habitation, though two miles away, —
No tenement for man or beast between, —
That, park and domicile, is country-seat
Of this same good Miranda! I accept
The augury. Or there, or nowhere else,
Will I establish that a Night-cap gleams
Of visionary Red, not White for once!
"Heaven," saith the sage, "is with us, here
     inside
Each man:" "Hell also," simpleness sub-
     joins,
By White and Red describing human flesh.

And yet as we continue, quicken pace,
Approach the object which determines me
Victorious or defeated, more forlorn
My chance seems, — that is certainty at least.
Halt midway, reconnoitre! Either side
The path we traverse (turn and see) stretch
     fields
Without a hedge: one level, scallop-striped
With bands of beet and turnip and luzern,
Limited only by each color's end,
Shelves down — we stand upon an eminence —
To where the earth-shell scallops out the sea,
A sweep of semicircle; and at edge —
Just as the milk-white incrustations stud
At intervals some shell-extremity,
So do the little growths attract us here,
Towns with each name I told you: say, they
     touch
The sea, and the sea them, and all is said,
So sleeps and sets to slumber that broad blue!
The people are as peaceful as the place.
This, that I call "the path" is road, highway;
But has there passed us by a market-cart,
Man, woman, child, or dog to wag a tail?
True, I saw weeders stooping in a field;
But — formidably white the Cap's extent!

Round again! Come, appearance promises!
The boundary, the park-wall, ancient brick,
Upholds a second wall of tree-heads high
Which overlean its top, a solid green.
That surely ought to shut in mysteries!
A jeweller — no unsuggestive craft!
Trade that admits of much romance, indeed.
For, whom but goldsmiths used old monarchs
     pledge
Regalia to, or seek a ransom from,
Or pray to furnish dowry, at a pinch,
According to authentic story-books?
Why, such have revolutionized this land

With diamond-necklace-dealing ! not to speak
Of families turned upside-down, because
The gay wives went and pawned clandestinely
Jewels, and figured, till found out, with paste,
Or else redeemed them — how, is horrible !
Then there are those enormous criminals
That love their ware and cannot lose their love,
And murder you to get your purchase back.
Others go courting after such a stone,
Make it their mistress, marry for their wife,
And find out, some day, it was false the while,
As ever wife or mistress, man too fond
Has named his Pilgrim, Hermit, Ace of Hearts.

Beside — what style of edifice begins
To grow in sight at last and top the scene ?
That gray roof, with the range of lucarnes,
   four
I count, and that erection in the midst —
Clock-house, or chapel-spire, or what, above ?
Conventual, that, beyond manorial, sure !
And reason good ; for Clairvaux, such its name,
Was built of old to be a Priory,
Dependence on that Abbey-for-the-Males
Our Conqueror founded in world-famous Caen,
And where his body sought the sepulture,
It was not to retain : you know the tale.
Such Priory was Clairvaux, prosperous
Hundreds of years ; but nothing lasts below,
And when the Red Cap pushed the Crown aside,
The Priory became, like all its peers,
A National Domain : which, bought and sold
And resold, needs must change, with ownership.
Both outside show and inside use ; at length
The messuage, three-and-twenty years ago,
Became the purchase of rewarded worth
Impersonate in Father — I must stoop
To French phrase for precision's sake, I fear —
Father Miranda, goldsmith of renown :
By birth a Madrilene, by domicile
And sojourning accepted French at last.
His energy it was which, trade transferred
To Paris, throve as with a golden thumb,
Established in the Place Vendôme. He bought
Not building only, but belongings far
And wide, at Gonthier there, Monlieu, Ville-
   neuve,
A plentiful estate : which, twelve years since,
Passed, at the good man's natural demise,
To Son and Heir Miranda — Clairvaux here,
The Paris shop, the mansion — not to say
Palatial residence on Quai Rousseau,
With money, movables, a mine of wealth —
And young Léonce Miranda got it all.

Ah, but — whose might the transformation be ?
Were you prepared for this, now ? As we
   talked,
We walked, we entered the half-privacy,
The partly-guarded precinct : passed beside
The little paled-off islet, trees and turf,
Then found us in the main ash-avenue
Under the blessing of its branchage-roof :
Till, on emergence, what affronts our gaze ?
Priory — Conqueror — Abbey-for-the-Males —
Hey, presto, pass, who conjured all away ?
Look through the railwork of the gate : a park
— Yes, but à l'Anglaise, as they compliment !

Grass like green velvet, gravel-walks like gold,
Bosses of shrubs, embosomings of flowers,
Lead you — through sprinkled trees of tiny
   breed
Disporting, within reach of coverture.
By some habitual acquiescent oak
Or elm, that thinks, and lets the youngsters
   laugh —
Lead, lift at last your soul that walks the air,
Up to the house-front, or its back perhaps —
Whether façade or no, one coquetry
Of colored brick and carved stone ! Stucco ?
   Well,
The daintiness is cheery, that I know,
And all the sportive floral framework fits
The lightsome purpose of the architect.
Those lucarnes which I called conventual, late,
Those are the outlets in the mansard-roof ;
And, underneath, what long light elegance
Of windows here suggests how brave inside
Lurk eyeballed gems they play the eyelids to !
Festive arrangements look through such, be
   sure !
And now the tower a-top, I took for clock's
Or bell's abode, turns out a quaint device,
Pillared and temple-treated Belvedere —
Pavilion safe within its railed-about
Sublimity of area — whence what stretch,
Of sea and land, throughout the seasons'
   change,
Must greet the solitary ! Or suppose,
— If what the husband likes, the wife likes
   too, —
The happy pair of students cloistered high,
Alone in April kiss when Spring arrives !
Or no, he mounts there by himself to meet
Winds, welcome wafts of sea-smell, first white
   bird
That flaps thus far to taste the land again,
And all the promise of the youthful year ;
Then he descends, unbosoms straight his store
Of blessings in the bud, and both embrace,
Husband and wife, since earth is Paradise,
And man at peace with God. You see it all ?

Let us complete our survey, go right round
The place : for here, it may be, we surprise
The Priory, — these solid walls, big barns,
Gray orchard-grounds, huge four-square stores
   for stock,
Betoken where the Church was busy once.
Soon must we come upon the Chapel's self.
No doubt next turn will treat us to . . . Aha,
Again our expectation proves at fault !
Still the bright graceful modern — not to say
Modish adornment, meets us : Parc Anglais,
Tree-sprinkle, shrub-embossment as before.
See, the sun splits on yonder bauble world
Of silvered glass concentring, every side,
All the adjacent wonder, made minute
And touched grotesque by ball-convexity !
Just so, a sense that something is amiss,
Something is out of sorts in the display,
Affects us, past denial, everywhere.
The right erection for the Fields, the Wood,
(Fields — but Elysées, wood — but de Boulogne)
Is peradventure wrong for wood and fields
When Vire, not Paris, plays the Capital.

So may a good man have deficient taste ;
Since Son and Heir Miranda, he it was
Who, six years now elapsed, achieved the work
And truly made a wilderness to smile.
Here did their domesticity reside,
A happy husband and as happy wife,
Till . . . how can I in conscience longer keep
My little secret that the man is dead
I, for artistic purpose, talk about
As if he lived still ?   No, these two years now
Has he been dead.   You ought to sympathize,
Not mock the sturdy effort to redeem
My pledge, and wring you out some tragedy
From even such a perfect commonplace !
Suppose I boast the death of such desert
My tragic bit of Red ?   Who contravenes
Assertion that a tragedy exists
In any stoppage of benevolence,
Utility, devotion above all ?
Benevolent ?   There never was his like :
For poverty, he had an open hand
. . . Or stop — I use the wrong expression
       here —
An open purse, then, ever at appeal ;
So that the unreflecting rather taxed
Profusion than penuriousness in alms.
One, in his day and generation, deemed
Of use to the community ?   I trust,
Clairvaux thus renovated, regalized,
Paris expounded thus to Normandy,
Answers that question.   Was the man devout ?
After a life — one mere munificence
To Church and all things churchly, men or
       mice, —
Dying, his last bequeathment gave land, goods,
Cash, every stick and stiver, to the Church,
And notably to that church yonder, that
Beloved of his soul, La Ravissante —
Wherefrom, the latest of his gifts, the Stone
Gratefully bore me as on arrow-flash
To Clairvaux, as I told you.

                              " Ay, to find
Your Red desiderated article,
Where every scratch and scrape provokes my
       White
To all the more superb a prominence !
Why, 't is the story served up fresh again —
How it befell the restive prophet old
Who came and tried to curse but blessed the
       land.
Come, your last chance ! he disinherited
Children : he made his widow mourn too much
By this endowment of the other Bride —
Nor understood that gold and jewelry
Adorn her in a figure, not a fact.
You make that White I want, so very white,
'T is I say now — some trace of Red should be
Somewhere in this Miranda-sanctitude ! "

Not here, at all events, sweet mocking friend !
For he was childless: and what heirs he had
Were an uncertain sort of Cousinry
Scarce claiming kindred so as to withhold
The donor's purpose though fantastical :
Heirs, for that matter, wanting no increase
Of wealth, since rich already as himself ;
Heirs that had taken trouble off his hands,

Bought that productive goldsmith-business he,
With abnegation wise as rare, renounced
Precisely at a time of life when youth,
Nigh on departure, bids mid-age discard
Life's other loves and likings in a pack,
To keep, in lucre, comfort worth them all.
This Cousinry are they who boast the shop
Of " Firm-Miranda, London and New York."
Cousins are an unconscionable kind ;
But these — pretension surely on their part
To share inheritance were too absurd !

" Remains then, he dealt wrongly by his wife,
Despoiled her somehow by such testament ? "
Farther than ever from the mark, fair friend !
The man's love for his wife exceeded bounds
Rather than failed the limit.   'T was to live
Hers and hers only, to abolish earth
Outside — since Paris holds the pick of earth —
He turned his back, shut eyes, stopped ears, to
       all
Delicious Paris tempts her children with,
And fled away to this far solitude —
She peopling solitude sufficiently !
She, partner in each heavenward flight sublime,
Was, with each condescension to the ground,
Duly associate also : hand in hand,
. . . Or side by side, I say by preference —
On every good work sidlingly they went.
Hers was the instigation — none but she
Willed that, if death should summon first her
       lord,
Though she, sad relict, must drag residue
Of days encumbered by this load of wealth —
(Submitted to with something of a grace
So long as her surviving vigilance
Might worthily administer, convert
Wealth to God's glory and the good of man,
Give, as in life, so now in death, effect
To cherished purpose) — yet she begged and
       prayed
That, when no longer she could supervise
The House, it should become a Hospital :
For the support whereof, lands, goods, and
       cash
Alike will go, in happy guardianship,
To yonder church, La Ravissante : who debt
To God and man undoubtedly will pay.

" Not of the world, your heroine ! "

                              Do you know
I saw her yesterday — set eyes upon
The veritable personage, no dream ?
I in the morning strolled this way, as oft,
And stood at entry of the avenue.
When, out from that first garden-gate, we gazed
Upon and through, a small procession swept —
Madame Miranda with attendants five.
First, of herself : she wore a soft and white
Engaging dress, with velvet stripes and squares
Severely black, yet scarce discouraging :
Fresh Paris-manufacture !   (Vire's would do ?
I doubt it, but confess my ignorance.)
Her figure ? somewhat small and darling-like.
Her face ? well, singularly colorless,
For first thing : which scarce suits a blonde
       you know.

Pretty you would not call her : though perhaps
Attaining to the ends of prettiness,
And somewhat more, suppose enough of soul.
Then she is forty full : you cannot judge
What beauty was her portion at eighteen,
The age she married at. So, colorless
I stick to, and if featureless I add,
Your notion grows completer : for, although
I noticed that her nose was aquiline,
The whole effect amounts with me to — blank !
I never saw what I could describe.
The eyes, for instance, unforgettable
Which ought to be, are out of mind as sight.

Yet is there not conceivably a face,
A set of wax-like features, blank at first,
Which, as you bendingly grow warm above,
Begins to take impressment from your breath ?
Which, as your will itself were plastic here
Nor needed exercise of handicraft,
From formless moulds itself to correspond
With all you think and feel and are — in fine
Grows a new revelation of yourself,
Who know now for the first time what you
     want ?
Here has been something that could wait awhile,
Learn your requirement, nor take shape before,
But, by adopting it, make palpable
Your right to an importance of your own,
Companions somehow were so slow to see !
— Far delicater solace to conceit
Than should some absolute and final face,
Fit representative of soul inside,
Summon you to surrender — in no way
Your breath's impressment, nor, in stranger's
     guise,
Yourself — or why of force to challenge you ?
Why should your soul's reflection rule your
     soul ?
(" You " means not you, nor me, nor any one
Framed, for a reason I shall keep suppressed,
To rather want a master than a slave :
The slavish still aspires to dominate !)
So, all I say is, that the face, to me
One blur of blank, might flash significance
To who had seen his soul reflected there
By that symmetric silvery phantom-like
Figure, with other five processional.
The first, a black-dressed matron — maybe,
     maid —
Mature, and dragonish of aspect, — marched ;
Then four came tripping in a joyous flock,
Two giant goats and two prodigious sheep
Pure as the arctic fox that suits the snow,
Tripped, trotted, turned the march to merri-
     ment,
But ambled at their mistress' heel — for why ?
A rod of guidance marked the Châtelaine,
And ever and anon would sceptre wave,
And silky subject leave meandering.
Nay, one great naked sheep-face stopped to ask
Who was the stranger, snuffed inquisitive
My hand that made acquaintance with its nose,
Examined why the hand — of man at least —
Patted so lightly, warmly, so like life !
Are they such silly natures after all ?
And thus accompanied, the paled-off space,
Isleted shrubs and verdure, gained the group ;

Till, as I gave a furtive glance, and saw
Her back-hair was a block of solid gold,
The gate shut out my harmless question —
     Hair
So young and yellow, crowning sanctity,
And claiming solitude . . . can hair be false ?

" Shut in the hair and with it your last hope,
Yellow might on inspection pass for Red ! —
Red, Red, where is the tinge of promised Red
In this old tale of town and country life,
This rise and progress of a family ?
First comes the bustling man of enterprise,
The fortune-founding father, rightly rough,
As who must grub and grab, play pioneer.
Then, with a light and airy step, succeeds
The son, surveys the fabric of his sire,
And enters home, unsmirched from top to toe.
Polish and education qualify
Their fortunate possessor to confine
His occupancy to the first-floor suite
Rather than keep exploring needlessly
Where dwelt his sire content with cellarage :
Industry bustles underneath, no doubt,
And supervisors should not sit too close.
Next, rooms built, there 's the furniture to buy,
And what adornment like a worthy wife ?
In comes she like some foreign cabinet,
Purchased indeed, but purifying quick
What space receives it from all traffic-taint.
She tells of other habits, palace-life ;
Royalty may have pried into those depths
Of sandal-wooded drawer, and set a-creak
That pygmy portal pranked with lazuli.
More fit by far the ignoble we replace
By objects suited to such visitant,
Than that we desecrate her dignity
By neighborhood of vulgar table, chair,
Which haply helped old age to smoke and doze.
The end is, an exchange of city stir
And too intrusive burgess-fellowship,
For rural isolated elegance,
Careless simplicity, how preferable !
There one may fairly throw behind one's back
The used-up worn-out Past, we want away,
And make a fresh beginning of stale life.
' In just the place ' — does any one object ? —
' Where aboriginal gentility
Will scout the upstart, twit him with each
     trick
Of townish trade-mark that stamps word and
     deed,
And most of all resent that here town-dross
He daubs with money-color to deceive ! '
Rashly objected ! Is there not the Church
To intercede and bring benefic truce
At outset ? She it is shall equalize
The laborers i' the vineyard, last as first.
Pay court to her, she stops impertinence.
' Duke, once your sires crusaded it, we know :
Our friend the newcomer observes, no less,
Your chapel, rich with their emblazonry,
Wants roofing — might he but supply the
     means !
Marquise, you gave the honor of your name,
Titular patronage, abundant will
To what should be an Orphan Institute :
Gave everything but funds, in brief ; and these

Our friend, the lady newly resident,
Proposes to contribute, by your leave !'
Brothers and sisters lie they in thy lap,
Thou none-excluding, all-collecting Church !
Sure, one has half a foot i' the hierarchy
Of birth, when 'Nay, my dear,' laughs out the
    Duke,
'I'm the crown's cushion-carrier, but the
    crown—
Who gave its central glory, I or you ?'
When Marquise jokes, 'My quest, forsooth ?
    Each doit
I scrape together goes for Peter-pence
To purvey bread and water in his bonds
For Peter's self imprisoned — Lord, how long ?
Yours, yours alone the bounty, dear my dame,
You plumped the purse, which, poured into the
    plate,
Made the Archbishop open brows so broad !
And if you really mean to give that length
Of lovely lace to edge the robe !' . . . Ah,
    friends,
Gem better serves so than by calling crowd,
Round shop-front to admire the million's-
    worth !
Lace gets more homage than from lorgnette-
    stare,
And comment coarse to match, (should one
    display
One's robe a trifle o'er the baignoire-edge,)
'Well may she line her slippers with the like,
If minded so ! their shop it was produced
That wonderful *parure*, the other day,
Whereof the Baron said, it beggared him.'
And so the paired Mirandas built their house,
Enjoyed their fortune, sighed for family,
Found friends would serve their purpose quite
    as well,
And come, at need, from Paris — anyhow,
With evident alacrity, from Vire —
Endeavor at the chase, at least succeed
In smoking, eating, drinking, laughing, and
Preferring country, oh so much to town !
Thus lived the husband ; though his wife
    would sigh
In confidence, when Countesses were kind,
'Cut off from Paris and society !'
White, White, I once more round you in the
    ears !
Though you have marked it, in a corner, yours
Henceforth, — Red-lettered 'Failure,' very
    plain,
I shall acknowledge, on the snowy hem
Of ordinary Night-cap ! Come, enough !
We have gone round its cotton vastitude,
Or half-round, for the end's consistent still,
A *cul-de-sac* with stoppage at the sea.
Here we return upon our steps. One look
May bid good-morning — properly good-night —
To civic bliss, Miranda and his mate !
Are we to rise and go ?"

        No, sit and stay !
Now comes my moment, with the thrilling
    throw
Of curtain from each side a shrouded case.
Don't the rings shriek an ominous "Ha ! ha !
So you take Human Nature upon trust " ?

List but with like trust to an incident
Which speedily shall make quite Red enough
Burn out of yonder spotless napery !
Sit on the little mound here, whence you seize
The whole of the gay front sun-satisfied,
One laugh of color and embellishment !
Because it was there, — past those laurustines,
On that smooth gravel-sweep 'twixt flowers
    and sward, —
There tragic death befell ; and not one grace
Outspread before you but is registered
In that sinistrous coil these last two years
Were occupied in winding smooth again.

"True ?" Well, at least it was concluded so,
Sworn to be truth, allowed by Law as such,
(With my concurrence, if it matter here,)
A month ago : at Vire they tried the case.

II

Monsieur Léonce Miranda, then, . . . but
    stay !
Permit me a preliminary word,
And, after, all shall go so straight to end !

Have you, the travelled lady, found yourself
Inside a ruin, fane or bath or cirque,
Renowned in story, dear through youthful
    dream ?
If not, — imagination serves as well.
Try fancy-land, go back a thousand years,
Or forward, half the number, and confront
Some work of art gnawn hollow by Time's
    tooth, —
Hellenic temple. Roman theatre,
Gothic cathedral, Gallic Tuileries,
But ruined, one and whichsoe'er you like.
Obstructions choke what still remains intact,
Yet proffer change that's picturesque in turn ;
Since little life begins where great life ends,
And vegetation soon amalgamates,
Smooths novel shape from out the shapeless old,
Till broken column, battered cornice-block,
The centre with a bulk half weeds and flowers,
Half relics you devoutly recognize.
Devoutly recognizing, — hark, a voice
Not to be disregarded ! " Man worked here
Once on a time ; here needs again to work ;
Ruins obstruct, which man must remedy."
Would you demur " Let Time fulfil his task,
And, till the scythe-sweep find no obstacle,
Let man be patient " ?

        The reply were prompt :
" Glisteningly beneath the May-night moon,
Herbage and floral coverture bedeck
Yon splintered mass amidst the solitude :
Wolves occupy the background, or some snake
Glides by at distance : picturesque enough !
Therefore, preserve it ? Nay, pour daylight
    in, —
The mound proves swarming with humanity.
There never was a thorough solitude,
Now you look nearer : mortal busy life
First of all brought the crumblings down on
    pate,

Which trip man's foot still, plague his passage
      much,
And prove — what seems to you so picturesque
To him is . . . but experiment yourself
On how conducive to a happy home
Will be the circumstance, your bed for base
Boasts tessellated pavement, — equally
Affected by the scorpion for his nest, —
While what o'er-roofs bed is an architrave,
Marble, and not unlikely to crush man
To mummy, should its venerable prop,
Some figtree-stump, play traitor underneath.
Be wise! Decide! For conservation's sake,
Clear the arena forthwith! lest the tread
Of too-much-tried impatience trample out
Solid and unsubstantial to one blank
Mud-mixture, picturesque to nobody, —
And, task done, quarrel with the parts intact
Whence came the filtered fine dust, whence
      the crash
Bides but its time to follow. Quick conclude
Removal, time effects so tardily,
Of what is plain obstruction; rubbish cleared,
Let partial-ruin stand while ruin may,
And serve world's use, since use is manifold.
Repair wreck, stanchion wall to heart's content,
But never think of renovation pure
And simple, which involves creation too:
Transform and welcome! Yon tall tower may
      help
(Though built to be a belfry and naught else)
Some Father Secchi, to tick Venus off
In transit: never bring there bell again,
To damage him aloft, brain us below,
When new vibrations bury both in brick!"

Monsieur Léonce Miranda, furnishing
The application at his cost, poor soul!
Was instanced how, — because the world lay
      strewn
With ravage of opinions in his path,
And neither he, nor any friendly wit,
Knew and could teach him which was firm,
      which frail,
In his adventure to walk straight through life
The partial-ruin, — in such enterprise,
He straggled into rubbish, struggled on,
And stumbled out again observably.
"Yon buttress still can back me up," he
      judged:
And at a touch down came both he and it.
"A certain statue, I was warned against,
Now, by good fortune, lies well underfoot,
And cannot tempt to folly any more:"
So, lifting eye, aloft since safety lay,
What did he light on? the Idalian shape,
The undeposed, erectly Victrix still!
"These steps ascend the labyrinthine stair
Whence, darkling and on all-fours, out I stand
Exalt and safe, and bid low earth adieu —
For so instructs 'Advice to who would
      climb:'"
And all at once the climbing landed him
— Where, is my story.

                        Take its moral first.
Do you advise a climber? Have respect
To the poor head, with more or less of brains

To spill, should breakage follow your advice!
Head-break to him will be heart-break to you
For having preached "Disturb no ruins here!
Are not they crumbling of their own accord?
Meantime, let poets, painters keep a prize!
Beside, a sage pedestrian picks his way."
A sage pedestrian — such as you and I!
What if there trip, in merry carelessness,
And come to grief, a weak and foolish child?
Be cautious how you counsel climbing, then!

Are you adventurous and climb yourself?
Plant the foot warily, accept a staff,
Stamp only where you probe the standing-point,
Move forward, well assured that move you may:
Where you mistrust advance, stop short, there
      stick!
This makes advancing slow and difficult?
Hear what comes of the endeavor of brisk youth
To foot it fast and easy! Keep this same
Notion of outside mound and inside mash,
Towers yet intact round turfy rottenness,
Symbolic partial-ravage, — keep in mind!
Here fortune placed his feet who first of all
Found no incumbrance, till head found . . .
      But hear!

This son and heir then of the jeweller,
Monsieur Léonce Miranda, at his birth,
Mixed the Castilian passionate blind blood
With answerable gush, his mother's gift,
Of spirit, French and critical and cold.
Such mixture makes a battle in the brain,
Ending as faith or doubt gets uppermost;
Then will has way a moment, but no more:
So nicely balanced are the adverse strengths,
That victory entails reverse next time.
The tactics of the two are different
And equalize the odds: for blood comes first,
Surrounding life with undisputed faith.
But presently a new antagonist,
By scarce-suspected passage in the dark,
Steals spirit, fingers at each crevice found
Athwart faith's stronghold, fronts the aston-
      ished man:
"Such pains to keep me far, yet here stand I,
Your doubt inside the faith-defence of you!"

With faith it was friends bulwarked him about
From infancy to boyhood; so, by youth,
He stood impenetrably circuited,
Heaven-high and low as hell: what lacked he
      thus,
Guarded against aggression, storm or sap?
What foe would dare approach? Historic
      Doubt?
Ay, were there some half-knowledge to attack!
Batter doubt's best, sheer ignorance will beat.
Acumen metaphysic? — drills its way
Through what, I wonder! A thick feather-
      bed
Of thoughtlessness, no operating tool —
Framed to transpierce the flint-stone — fumbles
      at,
With chance of finding an impediment!
This Ravissante, now: when he saw the church
For the first time, and to his dying-day,
His firm belief was that the name fell fit

From the Delivering Virgin, niched and known;
As if there wanted records to attest
The appellation was a pleasantry,
A pious rendering of Rare Vissante,
The proper name which erst our province bore.
He would have told you that Saint Aldabert
Founded the church, (Heaven early favored France,)
About the second century from Christ;
Though the true man was Bishop of Raimbaux,
Eleventh in succession, Eldobert,
Who flourished after some six hundred years.
He it was brought the image "from afar,"
(Made out of stone the place produces still,)
"Infantine Art divinely artless," (Art
In the decrepitude of Decadence,)
And set it up a-working miracles
Until the Northmen's fury laid it low,
Not long, however: an egregious sheep,
Zealous with scratching hoof and routing horn,
Unearthed the image in good Mailleville's time,
Count of the country. "If the tale be false,
Why stands it carved above the portal plain?"
Monsieur Léonce Miranda used to ask.
To Londres went the prize in solemn pomp,
But, liking old abode and loathing new,
Was borne — this time, by angels — back again.
And, reinaugurated, miracle
Succeeded miracle, a lengthy list,
Until indeed the culmination came —
Archbishop Chaumont prayed a prayer and vowed
A vow — gained prayer and paid vow properly —
For the conversion of Prince Vertgalant.
These facts, sucked in along with mother's-milk,
Monsieur Léonce Miranda would dispute
As soon as that his hands were flesh and bone,
Milk-nourished two-and-twenty years before.
So fortified by blind Castilian blood,
What say you to the chances of French cold
Critical spirit, should Voltaire besiege
"Alp, Apennine, and fortified redoubt"?
Ay, would such spirit please to play faith's game
Faith's way, attack where faith ·defends so well!
But then it shifts, tries other strategy.
Coldness grows warmth, the critical becomes
Unquestioning acceptance. "Share and share
Alike in facts, to truth add other truth!
Why with old truth needs new truth disagree?"

Thus doubt was found invading faith, this time,
By help of not the spirit but the flesh:
Fat Rabelais chuckled, where faith lay in wait
For lean Voltaire's grimace — French, either foe.
Accordingly, while round about our friend
Ran faith without a break which learned eye
Could find at two-and-twenty years of age,
The twenty-two-years-old frank footstep soon
Assured itself there spread a standing-space
Flowery and comfortable, nowise rock
Nor pebble-pavement roughed for champion's tread

Who scorns discomfort, pacing at his post.
Tall, long-limbed, shoulder right and shoulder left,
And 'twixt *acromia* such a latitude,
Black heaps of hair on head, and blacker bush
O'er-rioting chin, cheek and throat and chest, —
His brown meridional temperament
Told him — or rather pricked into his sense
Plainer than language — "Pleasant station here!
Youth, strength, and lustihood can sleep on turf
Yet pace the stony platform afterward:
First signal of a foe and up they start!
Saint Eldobert, at all such vanity,
Nay — sinfulness, had shaken head austere.
Had he? But did Prince Vertgalant? And yet,
After how long a slumber, of what sort,
Was it, he stretched octogenary joints,
And, nigh on Day-of-Judgment trumpet-blast,
Jumped up and manned wall, brisk as any bee?"

Nor Rabelais nor Voltaire, but Sganarelle,
You comprehend, was pushing through the chink!
That stager in the saint's correct costume,
Who ever has his speech in readiness
For thick-head juvenility at fault:
"Go pace yon platform and play sentinel!
You won't? The worse! but still a worse might hap.
Stay then, provided that you keep in sight
The battlement, one bold leap lands you by!
Resolve not desperately 'Wall or turf,
Choose this, choose that, but no alternative!'
No! Earth left once were left for good and all:
'With Heaven you may accommodate yourself.'"

Saint Eldobert — I much approve his mode;
With sinner Vertgalant I sympathize;
But histrionic Sganarelle, who prompts
While pulling back, refuses yet concedes, —
Whether he preach in chair, or print in book,
Or whisper due sustainment to weak flesh,
Counting his sham beads threaded on a lie —
Surely, one should bid pack that mountebank!
Surely, he must have momentary fits
Of self-sufficient stage-forgetfulness,
Escapings of the actor-lassitude
When he allows the grace to show the grin,
Which ought to let even thickheads recognize
(Through all the busy and benefic part, —
Bridge-building, or rock-riving, or good clean
Transport of church and congregation both
From this to that place with no harm at all,)
The Devil, that old stager, at his trick
Of general utility, who leads
Downward, perhaps, but fiddles all the way!

Therefore, no sooner does our candidate
For saintship spotlessly emerge soul-cleansed
From First Communion to mount guard at post,
Paris-proof, top to toe, than up there start
The Spirit of the Boulevard — you know Who —
With jocund "So. a structure fixed as fate,

Faith's tower joins on to tower, no ring more
    round,
Full fifty years at distance, too, from youth!
Once reach that precinct and there fight your
    best,
As looking back you wonder what has come
Of daisy-dappled turf you danced across!
Few flowers that played with youth shall
    pester age,
However age esteem the courtesy ;
And Eldobert was something past his prime,
Stocked Caen with churches ere he tried hand
    here.
Saint - Sauveur, Notre - Dame, Saint - Pierre,
    Saint-Jean
Attest his handiwork commenced betimes.
He probably would preach that turf is mud.
Suppose it mud, through mud one picks a way,
And when, clay-clogged, the struggler steps to
    stone,
He uncakes shoe, arrives in manlier guise
Than carried pick-a-back by Eldobert
Big-baby-fashion, lest his leathers leak !
All that parade about Prince Vertgalant
Amounts to — your Castilian helps enough —
Inveni ovem quæ perierat.
But ask the pretty votive statue-thing
What the lost sheep's meantime amusements
    were
Till the Archbishop found him ! That stays
    blank :
They washed the fleece well and forgot the
    rest.
Make haste, since time flies, to determine,
    though ! "

Thus opportunely took up parable, —
Admonishing Miranda just emerged
Pure from The Ravissante and Paris-proof, —
Saint Sganarelle : then slipped aside, changed
    mask,
And made re-entry as a gentleman
Born of the Boulevard, with another speech,
I spare you.

          So, the year or two revolved,
And ever the young man was dutiful
To altar and to hearth : had confidence
In the whole Ravissantish history.
Voltaire ? Who ought to know so much of
    him, —
Old sciolist, whom only boys think sage, —
As one whose father's house upon the Quai
Neighbored the very house where that Voltaire
Died mad and raving, not without a burst
Of squibs and crackers too significant ?
Father and mother hailed their best of sons,
Type of obedience, domesticity,
Never such an example inside doors !
Outside, as well not keep too close a watch ;
Youth must be left to some discretion there.
And what discretion proved, I find deposed
At Vire, confirmed by his own words : to wit,
How, with the spriteliness of twenty-five,
Five — and not twenty, for he gave their names
With laudable precision — were the few
Appointed by him unto mistress-ship ;
While, meritoriously the whole long week

A votary of commerce only, week
Ended, " at shut of shop on Saturday,
Do I, as is my wont, get drunk," he writes
In airy record to a confidant.
" Bragging and lies ! " replies the apologist :
" And do I lose by that ? " laughed Somebody,
At the Court-edge a-tiptoe, 'mid the crowd,
In his own clothes, a-listening to men's Law.

Thus while, prospectively a combatant,
The volunteer bent brows, clenched jaws, and
    fierce
Whistled the march-tune " Warrior to the
    wall ! "
Something like flowery laughters round his feet
Tangled him of a sudden with " Sleep first ! "
And fairly flat upon the turf sprawled he,
And let strange creatures make his mouth their
    home.

Anyhow, 't is the nature of the soul
To seek a show of durability,
Nor, changing, plainly be the slave of change.
Outside the turf, the towers : but, round the
    turf,
A tent may rise, a temporary shroud,
Mock-faith to suit a mimic dwelling-place :
Tent which, while screening jollity inside
From the external circuit — evermore
A menace to who lags when he should march —
Yet stands a-tremble, ready to collapse
At touch of foot : turf is acknowledged grass,
And grass, though pillowy, held contemptible
Compared with solid rock, the rampired ridge.
To truth a pretty homage thus we pay
By testifying — what we dally with,
Falsehood, (which, never fear we take for
    truth !)
We may enjoy, but then — how we despise !

Accordingly, on weighty business bound,
Monsieur Léonce Miranda stooped to play,
But, with experience, soon reduced the game
To principles, and thenceforth played by rule :
Rule, dignifying sport as sport, proclaimed
No less that sport was sport, and nothing more.
He understood the worth of womankind, —
To furnish man — provisionally — sport :
Sport transitive — such earth's amusements
    are :
But, seeing that amusements pall by use,
Variety therein is requisite.
And since the serious work of life were wronged
Should we bestow importance on our play,
It follows, in such womankind-pursuit,
Cheating is lawful chase. We have to spend
An hour — they want a lifetime thrown away :
We seek to tickle sense — they ask for soul,
As if soul had no higher ends to serve !
A stag-hunt gives the royal creature law :
Bat-fowling is all fair with birds at roost,
The lantern and the clap-net suit the hedge.
Which must explain why, bent on Boulevard
    game,
Monsieur Léonce Miranda decently
Was prudent in his pleasure — passed himself
Off on the fragile fair about his path
As the gay devil rich in mere good looks,

Youth, hope -- what matter though the purse
    be void ?
" If I were only young Miranda, now,
Instead of a poor clerkly drudge at desk
All day, poor artist vainly bruising brush
On palette, poor musician scraping gut
With horsehair teased that no harmonics come !
Then would I love with liberality,
Then would I pay ! — who now shall be repaid,
Repaid alike for present pain and past,
If Mademoiselle permit the contre-danse,
Sing ' Gay in garret youth at twenty lives,'
And afterward accept a lemonade ! "

Such sweet facilities of intercourse
Afford the Winter-Garden and Mabille !
" Oh, I unite " — runs on the confidence,
Poor fellow, that was read in open Court,
— " Amusement with discretion : never fear
My escapades cost more than market-price !
No durably-attached Miranda-dupe,
Sucked dry of substance by two clinging lips,
Promising marriage, and performing it !
Trust me, I know the world, and know myself,
And know where duty takes me — in good
    time ! "

Thus fortified and realistic, then,
At all points thus against illusion armed,
He wisely did New Year inaugurate
By playing truant to the favored five :
And sat installed at " The Varieties," —
Playhouse appropriately named, — to note
(Prying amid the turf that 's flowery there)
What primrose, firstling of the year, might push
The snows aside to deck his buttonhole —
Unnoticed by that outline sad, severe,
(Though fifty good long years removed from
    youth,)
That tower and tower, — our image bear in
    mind !

No sooner was he seated than, behold,
Out burst a polyanthus ! He was 'ware
Of a young woman niched in neighborhood ;
And ere one moment flitted, fast was he
Found captive to the beauty evermore,
For life, for death, for heaven, for hell, her own.
Philosophy, bewail thy fate ! Adieu,
Youth realistic and illusion-proof !
Monsieur Léonce Miranda, — hero late
Who " understood the worth of womankind,"
" Who found therein — provisionally — sport," —
Felt, in the flitting of a moment, fool
Was he, and folly all that seemed was wise,
And the best proof of wisdom's birth would be
That he made all endeavor, body, soul,
By any means, at any sacrifice
Of labor, wealth, repute, and (— well, the time
For choosing between heaven on earth, and
    heaven
In heaven, was not at hand immediately —)
Made all endeavor, without loss incurred
Of one least minute, to obtain her love.
" Sport transitive ? " " Variety required ? "
" In loving were a lifetime thrown away ? "
How singularly may young men mistake !
The fault must be repaired with energy.

Monsieur Léonce Miranda ate her up
With eye-devouring ; when the unconscious fair
Passed from the close-packed hall, he pressed
    behind ;
She mounted vehicle, he did the same,
Coach stopped, and cab fast followed, at one
    door —
Good house in unexceptionable street.
Out stepped the lady, — never think, alone !
A mother was not wanting to the maid,
Or, maybe, wife, or widow, might one say ?
Out stepped and properly down flung himself
Monsieur Léonce Miranda at her feet —
And never left them after, so to speak,
For twenty years, till his last hour of life,
When he released them, as precipitate.
Love proffered and accepted then and there !
Such potency in word and look has truth.

Truth I say, truth I mean : this love was true,
And the rest happened by due consequence.
By which we are to learn that there exists
A falsish false, for truth 's inside the same,
And truth that 's only half true, falsish truth.
The better for both parties ! folks may taunt
That half your rock-built wall is rubble-heap :
Answer them, half their flowery turf is stones !
Our friend had hitherto been decking coat
If not with stones, with weeds that stones befit,
With dandelions — " primrose-buds," smirked
    he ;
This proved a polyanthus on his breast,
Prize-lawful or prize-lawless, flower the same.
So with his other instance of mistake :
Was Christianity the Ravissante ?

And what a flower of flowers he chanced on
    now !
To primrose, polyanthus I prefer
As illustration, from the fancy-fact
That out of simple came the composite
By culture : that the florist bedded thick
His primrose-root in ruddle, bullock's blood,
Ochre and devils'-dung, for aught I know,
Until the pale and pure grew fiery-fine,
Ruby and topaz, rightly named anew.
This lady was no product of the plain ;
Social manure had raised a rarity.
Clara de Millefleurs (note the happy name)
Blazed in the full-blown glory of her Spring.
Peerlessly perfect, form and face : for both —
" Imagine what, at seventeen, may have proved
Miss Pages, the actress : Pages herself, my
    dear ! "

Noble she was, the name denotes : and rich ?
" The apartment in this Coliseum Street,
Furnished, my dear, with such an elegance,
Testifies wealth, my dear, sufficiently !
What quality, what style and title, eh ?
Well now, waive nonsense, you and I are boys
No longer : somewhere must a screw be slack !
Don't fancy, Duchesses descend at door
From carriage - step to stranger prostrate
    stretched,
And bid him take heart, and deliver mind,
March in and make himself at ease forthwith, —
However broad his chest and black his beard,
And comely his belongings, — all through love

Protested in a world of ways save one —
Hinting at marriage ! ” — marriage which yet
    means
Only the obvious method, easiest help
To satisfaction of love's first demand,
That love endure eternally : “ my dear,
Somewhere or other must a screw be slack ! ”

Truth is the proper policy : from truth —
Whate'er the force wherewith you fling your
    speech, —
Be sure that speech will lift you, by rebound,
Somewhere above the lowness of a lie !
Monsieur Léonce Miranda heard too true
A tale — perhaps I may subjoin, too trite !
As the meek martyr takes her statued stand
Above our pity, claims our worship just
Because of what she puts in evidence,
Signal of suffering, badge of torture borne
In days gone by, shame then, but glory now,
Barb, in the breast, turned aureole for the front !
So, half timidity, composure half,
Clara de Millefleurs told her martyrdom.

Of poor though noble parentage, deprived
Too early of a father's guardianship,
What wonder if the prodigality
Of nature in the girl, whose mental gifts
Matched her external dowry, form and face —
If these suggested a too prompt resource
To the resourceless mother ? “ Try the Stage,
And so escape starvation !   Prejudice
Defames Mimetic Art : be yours to prove
That gold and dross may meet and never mix,
Purity plunge in pitch yet soil no plume ! ”

All was prepared in London — (you conceive
The natural shrinking from publicity
In Paris, where the name excites remark) —
London was ready for the grand début ;
When some perverse ill-fortune, incident
To art mimetic, some malicious thrust
Of Jealousy who sidles 'twixt the scenes,
Or pops up sudden from the prompter's hole, —
Somehow the brilliant bubble burst in suds.
Want followed : in a foreign land, the pair !
Oh, hurry over the catastrophe —
Mother too sorely tempted, daughter tried
Scarcely so much as circumvented, say !
Caged unsuspecting artless innocence !

Monsieur Léonce Miranda tell the rest ! —
The rather that he told it in a style
To puzzle Court Guide students, much more
    me.
“ Brief, she became the favorite of Lord N.,
An aged but illustrious Duke, thereby
Breaking the heart of his competitor,
The Prince of O.   Behold her palaced straight
In splendor, clothed in diamonds,” (phrase how
    fit !)
“ Giving tone to the City by the Thames !
Lord N., the aged but illustrious Duke,
Was even on the point of wedding her —
Giving his name to her ” (why not to us ?)
“ But that her better angel interposed.
She fled from such a fate to Paris back.
A fortnight since : conceive Lord N.'s despair !

Duke as he is, there 's no invading France.
He must restrict pursuit to postal plague
Of writing letters daily, duly read
As darlingly she hands them to myself,
The privileged supplanter, who therewith
Light a cigar and see abundant blue ” —
(Either of heaven or else Havana-smoke,)
“ Think ! she, who helped herself to diamonds
    late,
In passion of disinterestedness
Now — will accept no tribute of my love
Beyond a paltry ring, three Louis'-worth !
Little she knows I have the rummaging
Of old Papa's shop in the Place Vendôme ! ”
So wrote entrancedly to confidant,
Monsieur Léonce Miranda.   Surely now,
If Heaven, that see all, understands no less,
It finds temptation pardonable here,
It mitigates the promised punishment,
It recognizes that to tarry just
An April hour amid such dainty turf
Means no rebellion against task imposed
Of journey to the distant wall one day ?
Monsieur Léonce Miranda puts the case !
Love, he is purposed to renounce, abjure ;
But meanwhile, is the case a common one ?
Is it the vulgar sin, none hates as he ?
Which question, put directly to “ his dear ”
(His brother — I will tell you in a trice),
Was doubtless meant, by due meandering,
To reach, to fall not unobserved before
The auditory cavern 'neath the cope
Of Her, the placable, the Ravissante.
But here 's the drawback, that the image
    smiles,
Smiles on, smiles ever, says to supplicant
“ Ay, ay, ay ” — like some kindly weathercock
Which, stuck fast at Set Fair, Favonian
    Breeze,
Still warrants you from rain, though Auster's
    lead
Bring down the sky above your cloakless
    mirth.
Had he proposed this question to, nor “ dear ”
Nor Ravissante, but prompt to the Police,
The Commissary of his Quarter, now —
There had been shaggy eyebrows elevate
With twinkling apprehension in each orb
Beneath, and when the sudden shut of mouth
Relaxed, — lip pressing lip, lest out should
    plump
The pride of knowledge in too frank a flow, —
Then, fact on fact forthcoming, dose were
    dealt
Of truth remedial, in sufficiency
To save a chicken threatened with the pip,
Head-staggers and a tumble from its perch.

Alack, it was the lady's self that made
The revelation, after certain days
— Nor so unwisely !   As the haschisch-man
Prepares a novice to receive his drug,
Adroitly hides the soil with sudden spread
Of carpet ere he seats his customer :
Then shows him how to smoke himself about
With Paradise ; and only when, at puff
Of pipe, the Houri dances round the brain
Of dreamer, does he judge no need is now

For circumspection and punctiliousness;
He may resume the serviceable scrap
That made the votary unaware of muck.
Just thus the lady, when her brewage — love —
Was well a-fume about the novice-brain,
Saw she might boldly pluck from underneath
Her lover the preliminary lie.

Clara de Millefleurs, of the noble race,
Was Lucie Steiner, child to Dominique
And Magdalen Commercy ; born at Sierck,
About the bottom of the Social Couch.
The father having come and gone again,
The mother and the daughter found their way
To Paris, and professed mode-merchandise,
Were milliners, we English roughlier say ;
And soon a fellow-lodger in the house,
Monsieur Ulysse Muhlhausen, young and smart,
Tailor by trade, perceived his house-mate's
    youth,
Smartness, and beauty over and above.
Courtship was brief, and marriage followed
    quick,
And quicklier — impecuniosity.
The young pair quitted Paris to reside
At London : which repaid the compliment
But scurvily, since not a whit the more
Trade prospered by the Thames than by the
    Seine.
Failing all other, as a last resource,
" He would have trafficked in his wife," — she
    said.
If for that cause they quarrelled, 't was, I fear,
Rather from reclamation of her rights
To wifely independence, than as wronged
Otherwise by the course of life proposed :
Since, on escape to Paris back again,
From horror and the husband, — ill-exchanged
For safe maternal home recovered thus, —
I find her domiciled and dominant
In that apartment, Coliseum Street,
Where all the splendid magic met and mazed
Monsieur Léonce Miranda's venturous eye.
Only, the same was furnished at the cost
Of some one notable in days long since,
Carlino Centofanti : he it was,
Found entertaining unawares — if not
An angel, yet a youth in search of one.

Why this revealment after reticence ?
Wherefore, beginning " Millefleurs," end at all
Steiner, Muhlhausen, and the ugly rest ?
Because the unsocial purse-controlling wight,
Carlino Centofanti, made aware
By misadventure that his bounty, crumbs
From table, comforted a visitant,
Took churlish leave, and left, too, debts to
    pay.
Loaded with debts, the lady needs must bring
Her soul to bear assistance from a friend
Beside that paltry ring, three Louis'-worth ;
And therefore might the little circumstance
That Monsieur Léonce had the rummaging
Of old Papa's shop in the Place Vendôme,
Pass, perhaps, not so unobservably.

Frail shadow of a woman in the flesh,
These very eyes of mine saw yesterday,

Would I re-tell this story of your woes,
Would I have heart to do you detriment
By pinning all this shame and sorrow plain
To that poor chignon, — staying with me still,
Though form and face have well-nigh faded
    now, —
But that men read it, rough in brutal print,
As two years since some functionary's voice
Rattled all this — and more by very much —
Into the ear of vulgar Court and crowd ?
Whence, by reverberation, rumblings grew
To what had proved a week-long roar in France
Had not the dreadful cannonry drowned all.
Was, now, the answer of your advocate
More than just this ? " The shame fell long
    ago,
The sorrow keeps increasing : God forbid
We judge man by the faults of youth in age ! "
Permit me the expression of a hope
Your youth proceeded like your avenue,
Stepping by bush, and tree, and taller tree,
Until, columnar, at the house they end.
So might your creeping youth columnar rise
And reach, by year and year, symmetrical,
To where all shade stops short, shade's service
    done.
Bushes on either side, and boughs above,
Darken, deform the path else sun would
    streak ;
And, cornered halfway somewhere, I suspect
Stagnation and a horse-pond : hurry past !
For here 's the house, the happy half-and-half
Existence — such as stands for happiness
True and entire, howe'er the squeamish talk !
Twenty years long, you may have loved this
    man ;
He must have loved you ; that 's a pleasant life,
Whatever was your right to lead the same.
The white domestic pigeon pairs secure,
Nay, does mere duty by bestowing egg
In authorized compartment, warm and safe,
Boarding about, and gilded spire above,
Hoisted on pole, to dogs' and cats' despair !
But I have spied a veriest trap of twigs
On tree-top, every straw a thievery,
Where the wild dove — despite the fowler's
    snare,
The sportsman's shot, the urchin's stone —
    crooned gay,
And solely gave her heart to what she hatched,
Nor minded a malignant world below.
I throw first stone forsooth ? 'T is mere assault
Of playful sugarplum against your cheek,
Which, if it makes cheek tingle, wipes off
    rouge !
You, my worst woman ? Ah, that touches
    pride,
Puts on his mettle the exhibitor
Of Night-caps, if you taunt him " This, no
    doubt, —
Now we have got to Female-garniture, —
Crowns your collection, Reddest of the row ! "
O unimaginative ignorance
Of what dye's depth keeps best apart from
    worst
In womankind ! — how heaven's own pure may
    seem
To blush aurorally beside such blanched

Divineness as the women-wreaths named White :
While hell, eruptive and fuliginous,
Sickens to very pallor as I point
Her place to a Red clout called woman too !
Hail, heads that ever had such glory once
Touch you a moment, like God's cloven tongues
Of fire ! your lambent aureoles lost may leave
You marked yet, dear beyond true diadems !
And hold, each foot, nor spurn, to man's dis-
        grace,
What other twist of fetid rag may fall !
Let slink into the sewer the cupping-cloth !

Lucie, much solaced, I re-finger you,
The medium article ; if ruddy-marked
With iron-mould, your cambric, — clean at
        least
From poison-speck of rot and purulence !
Lucie Muhlhausen said — "Such thing am I :
Love me, or love me not ! "   Miranda said,
" I do love, more than ever, most for this."
The revelation of the very truth
Proved the concluding necessary shake
Which bids the tardy mixture crystallize
Or else stay ever liquid : shoot up shaft,
Durably diamond, or evaporate —
Sluggish solution through a minute's slip.
Monsieur Léonce Miranda took his soul
In both his hands, as if it were a vase,
To see what came of the convulsion there,
And found, amid subsidence, love new-born
So sparklingly resplendent, old was new.
" Whatever be my lady's present, past,
Or future, this is certain of my soul,
I love her ! in despite of all I know,
Defiance of the much I have to fear,
I venture happiness on what I hope,
And love her from this day forevermore !
No prejudice to old profound respect
For certain Powers !   I trust they bear in mind
A most peculiar case, and straighten out
What 's crooked there, before we close accounts.
Renounce the world for them — some day I
        will :
Meantime, to me let her become the world ! "

Thus, mutely might our friend soliloquize
Over the tradesmen's bills, his Clara's gift —
In the apartment, Coliseum Street,
Carlino Centofanti's legacy,
Provided rent and taxes were discharged —
In face of Steiner now, De Millefleurs once,
The tailor's wife and runaway confessed.

On such a lady if election light,
(According to a social prejudice,)
If henceforth " all the world " she constitute
For any lover, — needs must he renounce
Our world in ordinary, walked about
By couples loving as its laws prescribe, —
Renunciation sometimes difficult.
But, in this instance, time and place and thing
Combined to simplify experiment,
And make Miranda, in the current phrase,
Master the situation passably.

For first facility, his brother died —
Who was, I should have told you, confidant,

Adviser, referee, and substitute,
All from a distance : but I knew how soon
This younger brother, lost in Portugal,
Had to depart and leave our friend at large.
Cut off abruptly from companionship
With brother-soul of bulk about as big,
(Obvious recipient — by intelligence
And sympathy, poor little pair of souls —
Of much affection and some foolishness,)
Monsieur Léonce Miranda, meant to lean
By nature, needs must shift the leaning-place
To his love's bosom from his brother's neck,
Or fall flat unrelieved of freight sublime.

Next died the lord of the Aladdin's cave,
Master o' the mint, and keeper of the keys
Of chests chokefull with gold and silver changed
By Art to forms where wealth forgot itself,
And caskets where reposed each pullet-egg
Of diamond, slipping flame from fifty slants.
In short, the father of the family
Took his departure also from our scene,
Leaving a fat succession to his heir
Monsieur Léonce Miranda, — " fortunate,
If ever man was, in a father's death,"
(So commented the world, — not he, too kind,
Could that be, rather than scarce kind enough)
Indisputably fortunate so far,
That little of incumbrance in his path,
Which money kicks aside, would lie there long.

And finally, a rough but wholesome shock,
An accident which comes to kill or cure,
A jerk which mends a dislocated joint !
Such happy chance, at cost of twinge, no doubt,
Into the socket back again put truth,
And stopped the limb from longer dragging
        lie.
For love suggested, " Better shamble on,
And bear your lameness with what grace you
        may ! "
And but for this rude wholesome accident,
Continuance of disguise and subterfuge,
Retention of first falsehood as to name
And nature in the lady, might have proved
Too necessary for abandonment.
Monsieur Léonce Miranda probably
Had else been loath to cast the mask aside,
So politic, so self-preservative,
Therefore so pardonable — though so wrong !
For see the bugbear in the background !
        Breathe
But ugly name, and wind is sure to waft
The husband news of the wife's whereabout:
From where he lies perdue in London town,
Forth steps the needy tailor on the stage,
Deity-like from dusk machine of fog,
And claims his consort, or his consort's worth
In rubies which her price is far above.
Hard to propitiate, harder to oppose, —
Who but the man's self came to banish fear,
A pleasant apparition, such as shocks
A moment, tells a tale, then goes for good !

Monsieur Ulysse Muhlhausen proved no less
Nor more than " Gustave," lodging opposite
Monsieur Léonce Miranda's diamond-cave
And ruby-mine, and lacking little thence

Save that its gnome would keep the captive safe,
Never return his Clara to his arms.
For why? He was become the man in vogue,
The indispensable to who went clothed
Nor cared encounter Paris fashion's blame, —
Such miracle could London absence work.
Rolling in riches — so translate " the vogue " —
Rather his object was to keep off claw
Should griffin scent the gold, should wife lay
    claim
To lawful portion at a future day,
Than tempt his partner from her private spoils.
Best forage each for each, nor coupled hunt!

Pursuantly, one morning, — knock at door
With knuckle, dry authoritative cough,
And easy stamp of foot, broke startlingly
On household slumber, Coliseum Street:
"Admittance in the name of Law!" In
    marched
The Commissary and subordinate.
One glance sufficed them. " A marital pair:
We certify, and bid good morning, sir!
Madame, a thousand pardons!" Whereupon
Monsieur Ulysse Muhlhausen, otherwise
Called "Gustave" for conveniency of trade,
Deposing in due form complaint of wrong,
Made his demand of remedy — divorce
From bed, board, share of name, and part in
    goods.
Monsieur Léonce Miranda owned his fault,
Protested his pure ignorance, from first
To last, of rights infringed in " Gustave's "
    case :
Submitted him to judgment. Law decreed
" Body and goods be henceforth separate!"
And thereupon each party took its way,
This right, this left, rejoicing, to abide
Estranged yet amicable, opposites
In life as in respective dwelling-place.
Still does one read on his establishment
Huge-lettered " Gustave," — gold out-glittering
" Miranda, goldsmith," just across the street —
" A first-rate hand at riding-habits " — say
The instructed — " special cut of chamber-
    robes."

Thus by a rude in seeming — rightlier judged
Beneficent surprise, publicity
Stopped further fear and trembling, and what
    tale
Cowardice thinks a covert : one bold splash
Into the mid-shame, and the shiver ends,
Though cramp and drowning may begin per-
    haps.

To cite just one more point which crowned
    success :
Madame, Miranda's mother, most of all
An obstacle to his projected life
In license, as a daughter of the Church,
Duteous, exemplary, severe by right —
Moreover one most thoroughly beloved
Without a rival till the other sort
Possessed her son, — first storm of anger spent,
She seemed, though grumblingly and grudg-
    ingly,
To let be what needs must be, acquiesce.

" With heaven — accommodation possible!"
Saint Sganarelle had preached with such effect,
She saw now mitigating circumstance.
" The erring one was most unfortunate,
No question : but worse Magdalens repent.
Were Clara free, did only Law allow,
What fitter choice in marriage could have
    made
Léonce or anybody?" 'T is alleged
And evidenced, I find, by advocate,
" Never did she consider such a tie
As baleful, springe to snap whate'er the cost."
And when the couple were in safety once
At Clairvaux, motherly, considerate,
She shrank not from advice. " Since safe you
    be,
Safely abide! for winter, I know well,
Is troublesome in a cold country-house.
I recommend the south room that we styled,
Your sire and I, the winter-chamber."

                                        Chance
Or purpose, — who can read the mystery? —
Combined, I say, to bid " Intrench yourself,
Monsieur Léonce Miranda, on this turf,
About this flower, so firmly that, as tent
Rises on every side around you both,
The question shall become, — Which arrogates
Stability, this tent or those far towers?
May not the temporary structure suit
The stable circuit, co-exist in peace? —
Always until the proper time, no fear!
' Lay flat your tent!' is easier said than done."

So, with the best of auspices, betook
Themselves Léonce Miranda and his bride —
Provisionary — to their Clairvaux house,
Never to leave it — till the proper time.

I told you what was Clairvaux-Priory
Ere the improper time : an old demesne
With memories, — relic half, and ruin
    whole, —
The very place, then, to repair the wits
Worn out with Paris-traffic, when its lord,
Miranda's father, took his month of ease
Purchased by industry. What contrast here!
Repose, and solitude, and healthy ways!
That ticking at the back of head, he took
For motion of an inmate, stopped at once,
Proved nothing but the pavement's rattle left
Behind at Paris : here was holiday!
Welcome the quaint succeeding to the spruce,
The large and lumbersome and — might be
    breathe
In whisper to his own ear — dignified
And gentry-fashioned old-style haunts of sleep!
Palatial gloomy chambers for parade,
And passage-lengths of lost significance,
Never constructed as receptacle,
At his odd hours, for him their actual lord
By dint of diamond-dealing, goldsmithry.
Therefore Miranda's father chopped and
    changed
Nor roof-tile nor yet floor-brick, undismayed
By rains a-top or rats at bottom there.
Such contrast is so piquant for a month!
But now arrived quite other occupants

Whose cry was " Permanency, — life and death
Here, here, not elsewhere, change is all we
  dread ! "
Their dwelling-place must be adapted, then,
To inmates, no mere truants from the town,
No temporary sojourners, forsooth,
At Clairvaux : change it into Paradise !

Fair friend, — who listen and let talk, alas ! —
You would, in even such a state of things,
Pronounce, — or am I wrong ? — for bidding
  stay
The old-world inconvenience, fresh as found.
All folk of individuality
Prefer to be reminded, now and then,
Though at the cost of vulgar cosiness,
That the shell-outside only harbors man
The vital and progressive, meant to build,
When build he may, with quite a difference,
Some time, in that far land we dream about,
Where every man is his own architect.
But then the couple here in question, each
At one in project for a happy life,
Were by no acceptation of the word
So individual that they must aspire
To architecture all-appropriate,
And, therefore, in this world impossible :
They needed house to suit the circumstance,
Proprietors, not tenants for a term.
Despite a certain marking, here and there,
Of fleecy black or white distinguishment,
These vulgar sheep wore the flock's uniform.
They love the country, *they* renounce the town ?
They gave a kick, as our Italians say,
To Paris ere it turned and kicked themselves !
Acquaintances might prove too hard to seek,
Or the reverse of hard to find, perchance,
Since Monsieur Gustave's apparition there.
And let me call remark upon the list
Of notabilities invoked, in Court
At Vire, to witness, by their phrases culled
From correspondence, what was the esteem
Of those we pay respect to, for " the pair
Whereof they knew the inner life," 't is said.
Three, and three only, answered the appeal.
First Monsieur Vaillant, music-publisher,
" Begs Madame will accept civilities."
Next Alexandre Dumas, — sire, not son, —
" Sends compliments to Madame and to you."
And last — but now prepare for England's
  voice !
I will not mar nor make — here 's word for
  word —
" A rich proprietor of Paris, he
To whom belonged that beauteous *Bagatelle*
Close to the wood of Boulogne, Hertford hight,
Assures of homages and compliments
Affectionate " — not now Miranda but
" Madame Muhlhausen." (Was this friend, the
  Duke
Redoubtable in rivalry before ?)
Such was the evidence when evidence
Was wanted, then if ever, to the worth
Whereat acquaintances in Paris prized
Monsieur Léonce Miranda's household charm.
No wonder, then, his impulse was to live,
In Norman solitude, the Paris life :
Surround himself with Art transported thence,

And nature like those famed Elysian Fields :
Then, warm up the right color out of both,
By Boulevard friendships tempted to come
  taste
How Paris lived again in little there.

Monsieur Léonce Miranda practised Art.
Do let a man for once live as man likes !
Politics ?   Spend your life, to spare the
  world's :
Improve each unit by some particle
Of joy the more, deteriorate the orb
Entire, your own : poor profit, dismal loss !
Write books, paint pictures, or make music —
  since
Your nature leans to such life-exercise !
Ay, but such exercise begins too soon,
Concludes too late, demands life whole and
  sole,
Artistry being battle with the age
It lives in !   Half life, — silence, while you
  learn
What has been done ; the other half, — attempt
At speech, amid world's wail of wonderment —
" Here's something done was never done be-
  fore ! "
To be the very breath that moves the age
Means not to have breath drive you bubble-
  like
Before it — but yourself to blow : that 's
  strain ;
Strain's worry through the lifetime, till there 's
  peace ;
We know where peace expects the artist-soul.

Monsieur Léonce Miranda knew as much.
Therefore in Art he nowise cared to be
Creative ; but creation, that had birth
In storminess long years before was born
Monsieur Léonce Miranda, — Art, enjoyed
Like fleshly objects of the chase that tempt
In cookery, not in capture — these might feast
The dilettante, furnish tavern-fare
Open to all with purses open too.
To sit free and take tribute seigneur-like —
Now, not too lavish of acknowledgment,
Now, self-indulgently profuse of pay.
Always Art's seigneur, not Art's serving-man,
Whate'er the style and title and degree, —
That is the quiet life and easy death
Monsieur Léonce Miranda would approve
Wholly — provided (back I go again
To the first simile) that while glasses clink,
And viands steam, and banqueting laughs high,
All that 's outside the temporary tent,
The dim grim outline of the circuit-wall,
Forgets to menace " Soon or late will drop
Pavilion, soon or late you needs must march,
And laggards will be sorry they were slack !
Always — unless excuse sound plausible ! "

Monsieur Léonce Miranda knew as much :
Whence his determination just to paint
So creditably as might help the eye
To comprehend how painter's eye grew dim
Ere it produced L'Ingegno's piece of work —
So to become musician that his ear
Should judge, by its own tickling and turmoil.

Who made the Solemn Mass might well die
  deaf —
So cultivate a literary knack
That, by experience how it wiles the time,
He might imagine how a poet, rapt
In rhyming wholly, grew so poor at last
By carelessness about his banker's-book,
That the Sieur Boileau (to provoke our smile)
Began abruptly, — when he paid devoir
To Louis Quatorze as he dined in state, —
" Sire, send a drop of broth to Pierre Corneille
Now dying and in want of sustenance ! "
— I say, these half-hour playings at life's toil,
Diversified by billiards, riding, sport —
With now and then a visitor — Dumas,
Hertford — to check no aspiration's flight —
While Clara, like a diamond in the dark,
Should extract shining from what else were
  shade,
And multiply chance rays a million-fold, —
How could he doubt that all offence outside, —
Wrong to the towers, which, pillowed on the
  turf,
He thus shut eyes to, — were as good as gone ?

So, down went Clairvaux-Priory to dust,
And up there rose, in lieu, yon structure gay
Above the Norman ghosts: and where the
  stretch
Of barren country girdled house about,
Behold the Park, the English preference !
Thus made undoubtedly a desert smile
Monsieur Léonce Miranda.

                              Ay, but she ?
One should not so merge soul in soul, you
  think ?
And I think : only, let us wait, nor want
Two things at once — her turn will come in
  time.
A cork-float danced upon the tide, we saw,
This morning, blinding-bright with briny dews :
There was no disengaging soaked from sound,
Earth-product from the sister-element.
But when we turn, the tide will turn, I think,
And bare on beach will lie exposed the buoy :
A very proper time to try, with foot
And even finger, which was buoying wave,
Which merely buoyant substance, — power to
  lift,
And power to be sent skyward passively.
Meanwhile, no separation of the pair !

III

And so slipt pleasantly away five years
Of Paradisiac dream ; till, as there flit
Premonitory symptoms, pricks of pain,
Because the dreamer has to start awake
And find disease dwelt active all the while
In head or stomach through his night-long
  sleep, —
So happened here disturbance to content.

Monsieur Léonce Miranda's last of cares,
Ere he composed himself, had been to make
Provision that, while sleeping safe he lay,

Somebody else should, dragon-like, let fall
Never a lid, coiled round the apple-stem,
But watch the precious fruitage. Somebody
Kept shop, in short, played Paris substitute.
Himself, shrewd, well-trained, early-exercised,
Could take in, at an eye-glance, luck or loss —
Know commerce throve, though lazily uplift
On elbow merely : leave his bed forsooth ?
Such active service was the substitute's.

But one October morning, at first drop
Of appled gold, first summons to be grave
Because rough Autumn's play turns earnest
  now,
Monsieur Léonce Miranda was required
In Paris to take counsel, face to face,
With Madame-mother : and be rated, too,
Roundly at certain items of expense
Whereat the government provisional,
The Paris substitute and shopkeeper,
Shook head, and talked of funds inadequate:
Oh, in the long run, — not if remedy
Occurred betimes ! Else, — tap the generous bole
Too near the quick, — it withers to the root —
Leafy, prolific, golden apple-tree,
" Miranda," sturdy in the Place Vendôme !

" What is this reckless life you lead ? " began
Her greeting she whom most he feared and
  loved,
Madame Miranda. " Luxury, extravagance
Sardanapalus' self might emulate, —
Did your good father's money go for this ?
Where are the fruits of education, where
The morals which at first distinguished you,
The faith which promised to adorn your age ?
And why such wastefulness outbreaking now,
When heretofore you loved economy ?
Explain this pulling-down and building-up
Poor Clairvaux, which your father bought be-
  cause
Clairvaux he found it, and so left to you,
Not a gilt-gingerbread big baby-house !
True, we could somehow shake head and shut
  eye
To what was past prevention on our part —
This reprehensible illicit bond :
We, in a manner, winking, watched consort
Our modest well-conducted pious son
With Delilah : we thought the smoking flax
Would smoulder soon away and end in snuff !
Is spark to strengthen, prove consuming fire ?
No lawful family calls Clairvaux 'home' —
Why play that fool of Scripture whom the voice
Admonished 'Whose to-night shall be those
  things
Provided for thy morning jollity ? '
To take one specimen of pure caprice
Out of the heap conspicuous in the plan, —
Puzzle of change, I call it, — titled big
' Clairvaux Restored : ' what means this Bel-
  vedere ?
This Tower, stuck like a fool's-cap on the
  roof —
Do you intend to soar to heaven from thence ?
Tower, truly ! Better had you planted turf —
More fitly would you dig yourself a hole
Beneath it for the final journey's help !

O we poor parents — could we prophesy ! "
Léonce was found affectionate enough
To man, to woman, child, bird, beast, alike ;
But all affection, all one fire of heart
Flaming toward Madame-mother. Had she
    posed
The question plainly at the outset " Choose !
Cut clean in half your all-the-world of love,
The mother and the mistress : then resolve,
Take me or take her, throw away the one ! " —
He might have made the choice and marred
    my tale.
But, much I apprehend, the problem put
Was, " Keep both halves, yet do no detriment
To either ! Prize each opposite in turn ! " "
Hence, while he prized at worth the Clairvaux-
    life
With all its tolerated naughtiness,
He, visiting in fancy Quai Rousseau,
Saw, cornered in the cosiest nook of all,
That range of rooms through number Thirty-
    three,
The lady-mother bent o'er her Bézique
While Monsieur Curé This, and Sister That, —
Superior of no matter what good House —
Did duty for Duke Hertford and Dumas,
Nay — at his mother's age — for Clara's self.
At Quai Rousseau, things comfortable thus,
Why should poor Clairvaux prove so trouble-
    some ?
She played at cards, he built a Belvedere.
But here 's the difference : she had reached the
    Towers
And there took pastime : he was still on Turf —
Though fully minded that, when once he
    marched,
No sportive fancy should distract him more.

In brief, the man was angry with himself,
With her, with all the world and much beside :
And so the unseemly words were interchanged
Which crystallize what else evaporates,
And make mere misty petulance grow hard
And sharp inside each softness, heart and soul.
Monsieur Léonce Miranda flung at last
Out of doors, fever-flushed : and there the
    Seine
Rolled at his feet, obsequious remedy
For fever, in a cold autumnal flow.
" Go and be rid of memory in a bath ! "
Craftily whispered Who besets the ear
On such occasions.

                    Done as soon as dreamed.
Back shivers poor Léonce to bed — where else ?
And there he lies a month 'twixt life and death,
Raving. " Remorse of conscience ! " friends
    opine.
" Sirs, it may partly prove so," represents
Beaumont — (the family physician, he
Whom last year's Commune murdered, do you
    mind ?)
Beaumont reports, " There is some active cause,
More than mere pungency of quarrel past, —
Cause that keeps adding other food to fire.
I hear the words and know the signs, I say !
Dear Madame, you have read the Book of
    Saints,

How Antony was tempted ? As for me,
Poor heathen, 't is by pictures I am taught.
I say then, I see standing here, — between
Me and my patient, and that crucifix
You very properly would interpose —
A certain woman-shape, one white appeal,
' Will you leave me, then, me, me, me for her ? '
Since cold Seine could not quench this flame,
    since flare
Of fever does not redden it away, —
Be rational, indulgent, mute — should chance
Come to the rescue — Providence, I mean —
The while I blister and phlebotomize ! ' "

Well, somehow rescued by whatever power,
At month's end, back again conveyed himself
Monsieur Léonce Miranda, worn to rags,
Nay, tinder : stuff irreparably spoiled,
Though kindly hand should stitch and patch its
    best.
Clairvaux in Autumn is restorative.
A friend stitched on, patched ever. All the
    same,
Clairvaux looked grayer than a month ago.
Unglossed was shrubbery, unglorified
Each copse, so wealthy once ; the garden-plots,
The orchard-walks, showed dearth and dreari-
    ness.
The sea lay out at distance crammed by cloud
Into a leaden wedge ; and sorrowful
Sulked field and pasture with persistent rain.
Nobody came so far from Paris now :
Friends did their duty by an invalid
Whose convalescence claimed entire repose.
Only a single ministrant was stanch
At quiet reparation of the stuff —
Monsieur Léonce Miranda, worn to rags :
But she was Clara and the world beside.

Another month, the year packed up his plagues
And sullenly departed, peddler-like,
As apprehensive old-world ware might show
To disadvantage when the newcomer,
Merchant of novelties, young 'Sixty-eight,
With brand-new bargains, whistled o'er the lea.
Things brightened somewhat o'er the Christmas
    hearth,
As Clara plied assiduously her task.

" Words are but words and wind. Why let the
    wind
Sing in your ear, bite, sounding, to your brain ?
Old folk and young folk, still at odds, of course !
Age quarrels because Spring puts forth a leaf
While Winter has a mind that boughs stay bare ;
Or rather — worse than quarrel — age descries
Propriety in preaching life to death.
' Enjoy nor youth, nor Clairvaux, nor poor me ? '
Dear Madame, you enjoy your age, 't is thought !
Your number Thirty-three on Quai Rousseau
Cost fifty times the price of Clairvaux, tipped
Even with our prodigious Belvedere :
You entertain the Curé, — we, Dumas :
We play charades, while you prefer Bézique :
Do lead your own life and let ours alone !
Cross Old Year shall have done his worst, my
    friend !
Here comes gay New Year with a gift, no doubt !

Look up and let in light that longs to shine —
One flash of light, and where will darkness
    hide ?
Your cold makes me too cold, love ! Keep me
    warm ! "

Whereat Léonce Miranda raised his head
From his two white thin hands, and forced a
    smile,
And spoke : " I do look up, and see your light
Above me ! Let New Year contribute warmth —
I shall refuse no fuel that may blaze."
Nor did he. Three days after, just a spark
From Paris, answered by a snap at Caen
Or whither reached the telegraphic wire :
" Quickly to Paris ! On arrival, learn
Why you are wanted ! " Curt and critical !

Off starts Léonce, one fear from head to foot ;
Caen, Rouen, Paris, as the railway helps ;
Then come the Quai and Number Thirty-three.
" What is the matter, concierge ? " — a gri-
    mace !
He mounts the staircase, makes for the main
    seat
Of dreadful mystery which draws him there —
Bursts in upon a bedroom known too well —
There lies all left now of the mother once.
Tapers define the stretch of rigid white,
Nor want there ghastly velvets of the grave.
A blackness sits on either side at watch,
Sisters, good souls but frightful all the same,
Silent : a priest is spokesman for his corpse.
" Dead, through Léonce Miranda ! stricken
    down
Without a minute's warning, yesterday !
What did she say to you, and you to her,
Two months ago ? This is the consequence !
The doctors have their name for the disease ;
I, you, and God say — heart-break, nothing
    more ! "
Monsieur Léonce Miranda, like a stone
Fell at the bedfoot and found respite so,
While the priest went to tell the company.
What follows you are free to disbelieve.
It may be true or false that this good priest
Had taken his instructions, — who shall
    blame ? —
From quite another quarter than, perchance,
Monsieur Léonce Miranda might suppose
Would offer solace in such pressing need.
All he remembered of his kith and kin
Was, they were worthily his substitutes
In commerce, did their work and drew their
    pay.
But *they* remembered, in addition, this —
They fairly might expect inheritance,
As nearest kin, called Family by law
And gospel both. Now, since Miranda's life
Showed nothing like abatement of distaste
For conjugality, but preference
Continued and confirmed of that smooth chain
Which slips and leaves no knot behind, no
    heir —
Presumption was, the man, become mature,
Would at a calculable day discard
His old and outworn . . . what we blush to
    name,

And make society the just amends ;
Scarce by a new attachment — Heaven for-
    bid !
Still less by lawful marriage : that 's reserved
For those who make a proper choice at first —
Not try both courses and would grasp in age
The very treasure, youth preferred to spurn !
No ! putting decently such thought aside,
The penitent must rather give his powers
To such a reparation of the past
As, edifying kindred, makes them rich.
Now, how would it enrich prospectively
The Cousins, if he lavished such expense
On Clairvaux ? — pretty as a toy, but then
As toy, so much productive and no more !
If all the outcome of the goldsmith's shop
Went to gild Clairvaux, where remain the
    funds
For Cousinry to spread out lap and take ?
This must be thought of and provided for.
I give it you a mere conjecture, mind !
To help explain the wholesome unannounced
Intelligence, the shock that startled guilt,
The scenic show, much yellow, black and
    white
By taper-shine, the nuns — portentous pair,
And, more than all, the priest's admonish-
    ment —
" No flattery of self ! You murdered her !
The gray lips, silent now, reprove by mine.
You wasted all your living, rioted
In harlotry — she warned and I repeat !
No warning had she, for she needed none :
If this should be the last yourself receive ? "
Done for the best, no doubt, though clumsily, —
Such, and so startling, the reception here.
You hardly wonder if down fell at once
The tawdry tent, pictorial, musical,
Poetical, besprent with hearts and darts ;
Its cobweb-work, betinselled stitchery,
Lay dust about our sleeper on the turf,
And showed the outer towers distinct and
    dread.

Senseless he fell, and long he lay, and much
Seemed salutary in his punishment
To planners and performers of the piece.
When pain ends, pardon prompt may operate.
There was a good attendance close at hand,
Waiting the issue in the great saloon,
Cousins with consolation and advice.

All things thus happily performed to point,
No wonder at success commensurate.
Once swooning stopped, once anguish subse-
    quent
Raved out, — a sudden resolution chilled
His blood and changed his swimming eyes to
    stone,
As the poor fellow raised himself upright,
Collected strength, looked, once for all, his
    look,
Then, turning, put officious help aside
And passed from out the chamber. " For af-
    fairs ! "
So he announced himself to the saloon :
" We owe a duty to the living too ! " —
Monsieur Léonce Miranda tried to smile.

How did the hearts of Cousinry rejoice
At their stray sheep returning thus to fold,
As, with a dignity, precision, sense,
All unsuspected in the man before,
Monsieur Léonce Miranda made minute
Detail of his intended scheme of life
Thenceforward and forever.   " Vanity
Was ended : its redemption must begin —
And, certain, would continue ; but since life
Was awfully uncertain — witness here ! —
Behooved him lose no moment but discharge
Immediate burden of the world's affairs
On backs that kindly volunteered to crouch.
Cousins, with easier conscience, blamelessly
Might carry on the goldsmith's trade, in brief,
Uninterfered with by its lord who late
Was used to supervise and take due tithe.
A stipend now sufficed his natural need :
Themselves should fix what sum allows man
     live.
But half a dozen words concisely plain
Might, first of all, make sure that, on demise,
Monsieur Léonce Miranda's property
Passed by bequeathment, every particle,
To the right heirs, the cousins of his heart.
As for that woman — they would understand !
This was a step must take her by surprise !
It were too cruel did he snatch away
Decent subsistence. She was young, and fair,
And . . . and attractive ! Means must be sup-
     plied
To save her from herself, and from the world,
And . . . from anxieties might haunt him else
When he were fain have other thoughts in
     mind."

It was a sight to melt a stone, that thaw
Of rigid disapproval into dew
Of sympathy, as each extended palm
Of cousin hasted to enclose those five
Cold fingers, tendered so mistrustfully,
Despairingly of condonation now !
You would have thought, — at every fervent
     shake,
In reassurance of those timid tips, —
The penitent had squeezed, considerate,
By way of fee into physician's hand
For physicking his soul, some diamond knob.

And now let pass a week. Once more behold
The same assemblage in the same saloon,
Waiting the entry of protagonist
Monsieur Léonce Miranda.   " Just a week
Since the death-day, — was ever man trans-
     formed
Like this man ? " questioned cousin of his
     mate.

Last seal to the repentance had been set
Three days before, at Sceaux in neighborhood
Of Paris where they laid with funeral pomp
Mother by father. Let me spare the rest :
How the poor fellow, in his misery,
Buried hot face and bosom, where heaped snow
Offered assistance, at the grave's black edge,
And there lay, till uprooted by main force
From where he prayed to grow and ne'er again
Walk earth unworthily as heretofore.

It is not with impunity priests teach
The doctrine he was dosed with from his
     youth —
" Pain to the body — profit to the soul ;
Corporeal pleasure — so much woe to pay
When disembodied spirit gives account."

However, woe had done its worst, this time.
Three days allow subsidence of much grief.
Already, regular and equable,
Forward went purpose to effect. At once
The testament was written, signed and sealed.
Disposer of the commerce — that took time,
And would not suffer by a week's delay ;
But the immediate, the imperious need,
The call demanding of the Cousinry
Co-operation, what convened them thus,
Was — how and when should deputation march
To Coliseum Street, the old abode
Of wickedness, and there acquaint — oh,
     shame !
Her, its old inmate, who had followed up
And lay in wait in the old haunt for prey —
That they had rescued, they possessed Léonce,
Whose loathing at recapture equalled theirs —
Upbraid that sinner with her sinfulness,
Impart the fellow-sinner's firm resolve
Never to set eyes on her face again :
Then, after stipulations strict but just,
Hand her the first instalment — moderate
Enough, no question — of her salary :
Admonish for the future, and so end. —
All which good purposes, decided on
Sufficiently, were waiting full effect
When presently the culprit should appear.

Somehow appearance was delayed too long ;
Chatting and chirping sunk inconsciously
To silence, nay, uneasiness, at length
Alarm, till — anything for certitude ! —
A peeper was commissioned to explore,
At keyhole, what the laggard's task might
     be —
What caused so palpable a disrespect !

Back came the tiptoe cousin from his quest.
" Monsieur Léonce was busy," he believed,
" Contemplating — those love-letters, perhaps,
He always carried, as if precious stones,
About with him. He read, one after one,
Some sort of letters. But his back was turned.
The empty coffer open at his side,
He leant on elbow by the mantelpiece
Before the hearth-fire ; big and blazing too."

" Better he shovelled them all in at once,
And burned the rubbish ! " was a cousin's
     quip,
Warming his own hands at the fire the while,
I told you, snow had fallen outside, I think.

When suddenly a cry, a host of cries,
Screams, hubbub and confusion thrilled the
     room.
All by a common impulse rushed thence,
     reached
The late death-chamber, tricked with trappings
     still,

Skulls, crossbones, and such moral broidery.
Madame Muhlhausen might have played the
   witch,
Dropped down the chimney and appalled Lé-
   once
By some proposal, "Parting touch of hand!"
If she but touched his foolish hand, you know!

Something had happened quite contrariwise.
Monsieur Léonce Miranda, one by one,
Had read the letters and the love they held,
And, that task finished, had required his soul
To answer frankly what the prospect seemed
Of his own love's departure — pledged to part!
Then, answer being unmistakable,
He had replaced the letters quietly,
Shut coffer, and so, grasping either side
By its convenient handle, plunged the whole —
Letters and coffer and both hands to boot —
Into the burning grate and held them there.
" Burn, burn, and purify my past! " said he,
Calmly, as if he felt no pain at all.

In vain they pulled him from the torture-place:
The strong man, with the soul of tenfold
   strength,
Broke from their clutch: and there again
   smiled he,
The miserable hands re-bathed in fire —
Constant to that ejaculation, " Burn,
Burn, purify! " And when, combining force,
They fairly dragged the victim out of reach
Of further harm, he had no hands to hurt —
Two horrible remains of right and left,
" Whereof the bones, phalanges formerly,
Carbonized, were still crackling with the
   flame,"
Said Beaumont. And he fought them all the
   while:
" Why am I hindered when I would be pure?
Why leave the sacrifice still incomplete?
She holds me, I must have more hands to
   burn! "
They were the stronger, though, and bound
   him fast.

Beaumont was in attendance presently.
" What did I tell you? Preachment to the
   deaf!
I wish he had been deafer when they preached.
Those priests! But wait till next Republic
   comes! "

As for Léonce, a single sentiment
Possessed his soul and occupied his tongue —
Absolute satisfaction at the deed.
Never he varied, 't is observable,
Nor in the stage of agonies (which proved
Absent without leave, — science seemed to
   think),
Nor yet in those three months' febricity
Which followed, — never did he vary tale —
Remaining happy beyond utterance.
" Ineffable beatitude " — I quote
The words, I cannot give the smile — " such
   bliss
Abolished pain! Pain might or might not be :
He felt in heaven, where flesh desists to fret.

Purified now and henceforth, all the past
Reduced to ashes with the flesh defiled !
Why all those anxious faces round his bed ?
What was to pity in their patient, pray,
When doctor came and went, and Cousins
   watched?
— Kindness, but in pure waste!" he said and
   smiled.
And if a trouble would at times disturb
The ambrosial mood, it came from other source
Than the corporeal transitory pang.
" If sacrifice be incomplete!" cried he —
" If ashes have not sunk reduced to dust,
To nullity ! If atoms coalesce
Till something grow, grow, get to be a shape
I hate, I hoped to burn away from me !
She is my body, she and I are one,
Yet, all the same, there, there at bedfoot stands
The woman wound about my flesh and blood,
There, the arms open, the more wonderful,
The whiter for the burning . . . Vanish thou!
Avaunt, fiend's self found in the form I wore!"

" Whereat," said Beaumont, " since his hands
   were gone,
The patient in a frenzy kicked and kicked
To keep off some imagined visitant.
So will it prove as long as priests may preach
Spiritual terrors!" groaned the evidence
Of Beaumont that his patient was stark mad —
Produced in time and place : of which anon.
" Mad, or why thus insensible to pain?
Body and soul are one thing, with two names
For more or less elaborated stuff."

Such is the new *Religio Medici*.
Though antiquated faith held otherwise,
Explained that body is not soul, but just
Soul's servant : that, if soul be satisfied,
Possess already joy or pain enough,
It uses to ignore, as master may,
What increase, joy or pain, its servant brings —
Superfluous contribution : soul, once served,
Has naught to do with body's service more.
Each, speculated on exclusively,
As if its office were the only one,
Body or soul, either shows service paid
In joy and pain, that 's blind and objectless —
A servant's toiling for no master's good —
Or else shows good received and put to use,
As if within soul's self grew joy and pain,
Nor needed body for a ministrant.
I note these old unscientific ways:
Poor Beaumont cannot : for the Commune
   ruled
Next year, and ere they shot his priests, shot
   him.

Monsieur Léonce Miranda raved himself
To rest ; lay three long months in bliss or bale,
Inactive, anyhow: more need that heirs,
His natural protectors, should assume
The management, bestir their cousinship,
And carry out that purpose of reform
Such tragic work now made imperative.
A deputation, with austerity,
Nay, sternness, bore her sentence to the fiend
Aforesaid, — she at watch for turn of wheel

And fortune's favor, Street — you know the
    name.
A certain roughness seemed appropriate :
    " You —
Steiner, Muhlhausen, whatsoe'er your name,
Cause whole and sole of this catastrophe ! " —
And so forth, introduced the embassage.

" Monsieur Léonce Miranda was divorced
Once and forever from his — ugly word.
Himself had gone for good to Portugal ;
They came empowered to act and stipulate.
Hold ! no discussion ! Terms were settled now :
So much of present and prospective pay,
But also — good engagement in plain terms
She never seek renewal of the past ! "

This little harmless tale produced effect.
Madame Muhlhausen owned her sentence just,
Its execution gentle. " Stern their phrase,
These kinsfolk with a right she recognized —
But kind its import probably, which now
Her agitation, her bewilderment,
Rendered too hard to understand, perhaps.
Let them accord the natural delay,
And she would ponder and decide. Meantime,
So far was she from wish to follow friend
Who fled her, that she would not budge from
    place —
Now that her friend was fled to Portugal, —
Never ! She leave this Coliseum Street ?
No, not a footstep ! " she assured them.

                                        So —
They saw they might have left that tale untold
When, after some weeks more were gone to
    waste,
Recovery seemed incontestable,
And the poor mutilated figure, once
The gay and glancing fortunate young spark,
Miranda, humble and obedient took
The doctor's counsel, issued sad and slow
From precincts of the sick-room, tottered down,
And out, and into carriage for fresh air,
And so drove straight to Coliseum Street,
And tottered upstairs, knocked, and in a trice
Was clasped in the embrace of whom you
    know —
With much asseveration, I omit,
Of constancy henceforth till life should end.
When all this happened, — " What reward,"
    cried she,
" For judging her Miranda by herself !
For never having entertained a thought
Of breaking promise, leaving home forsooth,
To follow who was fled to Portugal !
As if she thought they spoke a word of truth !
She knew what love was, knew that he loved
    her ;
The Cousinry knew nothing of the kind."

I will not scandalize you and recount
How matters made the morning pass away.
Not one reproach, not one acknowledgment,
One explanation : all was understood !
Matters at end, the home-uneasiness
Cousins were feeling at this jaunt prolonged
Was ended also by the entry of —

Not simply him whose exit had been made
By mild command of doctor " Out with you !
I warrant we receive another man ! "
But — would that I could say, the married pair !
And, quite another man assuredly,
Monsieur Léonce Miranda took on him
Forthwith to bid the trio, priest and nuns,
Constant in their attendance all this while,
Take his thanks and their own departure too ;
Politely but emphatically. Next,
The Cousins were dismissed : " No protest,
    pray !
Whatever I engaged to do is done,
Or shall be — I but follow your advice :
Love I abjure : the lady, you behold,
Is changed as I myself ; her sex is changed :
This is my Brother — He will tend me now,
Be all my world henceforth as brother should.
Gentlemen, of a kinship I revere,
Your interest in trade is laudable ;
I purpose to indulge it : manage mine,
My goldsmith-business in the Place Vendôme,
Wholly — through purchase at the price ad-
    judged
By experts I shall have assistance from.
If, in conformity with sage advice,
I leave a busy world of interests
I own myself unfit for — yours the care
That any world of other aims, wherein
I hope to dwell, be easy of access
Through ministration of the moneys due,
As we determine, with all proper speed,
Since I leave Paris to repair my health.
Say farewell to our Cousins, Brother mine ! "

And, all submissiveness, as brother might,
The lady curtsied gracefully, and dropt
More than mere curtsey, a concluding phrase
So silver-soft, yet penetrative too,
That none of it escaped the favored ears :
" Had I but credited one syllable,
I should to-day be lying stretched on straw,
The produce of your miserable rente !
Whereas, I hold him — do you comprehend ? "
Cousin regarded cousin, turned up eye,
And took departure, as our Tuscans laugh,
Each with his added palm-breadth of long
    nose, —
Curtailed but imperceptibly, next week,
When transfer was accomplished, and the trade
In Paris did indeed become their own,
But bought by them and sold by him on terms
'Twixt man and man, — might serve 'twixt
    wolf and wolf,
Substitute " bit and clawed " for " signed and
    sealed " —
Our ordinary business-terms, in short.
Another week, and Clairvaux broke in bloom
At end of April, to receive again
Monsieur Léonce Miranda, gentleman,
Ex-jeweller and goldsmith : never more —
According to the purpose he professed —
To quit this paradise, his property,
This Clara, his companion : so it proved.

The Cousins, each with elongated nose,
Discussed their bargain, reconciled them soon
To hard necessity, disbursed the cash,

And hastened to subjoin, wherever type
Proclaimed " Miranda " to the public, " Called
Now Firm-Miranda." There, a colony,
They flourish underneath the name that still
Maintains the old repute, I understand.
They built their Clairvaux, dream-Château, in
    Spain,
Perhaps — but Place Vendôme is waking
    worth :
Oh, they lost little ! — only, man and man
Hardly conclude transactions of the kind
As cousin should with cousin, — cousins think.
For the rest, all was honorably done,
So, ere buds break to blossom, let us breathe !
Never suppose there was one particle
Of recrudescence — wound, half-healed before,
Set freshly running — sin, repressed as such,
New loosened as necessity of life !
In all this revocation and resolve,
Far be sin's self-indulgence from your thought !
The man had simply made discovery,
By process I respect if not admire,
That what was, was : — that turf, his feet had
    touched,
Felt solid just as much as yonder towers
He saw with eyes, but did not stand upon,
And could not, if he would, reach in a leap.
People had told him flowery turf was false
To footstep, tired the traveller soon, beside :
That was untrue. They told him " One fair
    stride
Plants on safe platform, and secures man rest."
That was untrue. Some varied the advice :
" Neither was solid, towers no more than
    turf : "
Double assertion, therefore twice as false.
" I like these amateurs " — our friend had
    laughed,
Could he turn what he felt to what he thought,
And, that again, to what he put in words :
" I like their pretty trial, proof of paste
Or precious stone, by delicate approach
Of eye askance, fine feel of finger-tip,
Or touch of tongue inquisitive for cold.
I tried my jewels in a crucible :
Fierce fire has felt them, licked them, left
    them sound.
Don't tell me that my earthly love is sham,
My heavenly fear a clever counterfeit !
Each may oppose each, yet be true alike ! "

To build up, independent of the towers,
A durable pavilion o'er the turf,
Had issued in disaster. " What remained
Except, by tunnel, or else gallery,
To keep communication 'twixt the two,
Unite the opposites, both near and far,
And never try complete abandonment
Of one or other ? " so he thought, not said.
And to such engineering feat, I say,
Monsieur Léonce Miranda saw the means
Precisely in this revocation prompt
Of just those benefits of worldly wealth
Conferred upon his Cousinry — all but !

This Clairvaux — you would know, were you
    at top
Of yonder crowning grace, its Belvedere —

Is situate in one angle-niche of three,
At equidistance from Saint-Rambert — there
Behind you, and The Ravissante, beside —
There : steeple, steeple, and this Clairvaux-top
(A sort of steeple) constitute a trine,
With not a tenement to break each side,
Two miles or so in length, if eye can judge.

Now this is native land of miracle.
Oh, why, why, why, from all recorded time,
Was miracle not wrought once, only once,
To help whoever wanted help indeed ?
If on the day when Spring's green girlishness
Grew nubile, and she trembled into May,
And our Miranda climbed to clasp the Spring
A-tiptoe o'er the sea, those wafts of warmth,
Those cloudlets scudding under the bare blue,
And all that new sun, that fresh hope about
His airy place of observation, — friend,
Feel with me that if just then, just for once,
Some angel, — such as the authentic pen
Yonder records a daily visitant
Of ploughman Claude, rheumatic in the joints,
And spinster Jeanne, with megrim troubled
    sore, —
If such an angel, with naught else to do,
Had taken station on the pinnacle
And simply said, " Léonce, look straight be-
    fore !
Neither to right hand nor to left : for why ?
Being a stupid soul, you want a guide
To turn the goodness in you to account
And make stupidity submit itself.
Go to Saint-Rambert ! Straightway get such
    guide !
There stands a man of men. You, jeweller,
Must needs have heard how once the biggest
    block
Of diamond now in Europe lay exposed
'Mid specimens of stone and earth and ore,
On huckster's stall, — Navona names the
    Square,
And Rome the city for the incident, —
Labelled ' quartz-crystal, price one halfpenny.'
Haste and secure that ha'p'worth, on your
    life !
That man will read you rightly head to foot,
Mark the brown face of you, the bushy beard,
The breadth 'twixt shoulderblades, and through
    each black
Castilian orbit, see into your soul.
Talk to him for five minutes — nonsense, sense,
No matter what — describe your horse, your
    hound, —
Give your opinion of the policy
Of Monsieur Rouher, — will he succor Rome ?
Your estimate of what may outcome be
From Œcumenical Assemblage there !
After which samples of intelligence,
Rapidly run through those events you call
Your past life, tell what once you tried to do,
What you intend on doing this next May !
There he stands, reads an English newspaper,
Stock-still, and now, again upon the move,
Paces the beach to taste the Spring, like you,
Since both are human beings in God's eye.
He will have understood you, I engage.
Endeavor, for your part, to understand

He knows more, and loves better, than the
    world
That never heard his name, and never may.
He will have recognized, ere breath be spent
And speech at end, how much that 's good in
    man,
And generous, and self-devoting, makes
Monsieur Léonce Miranda worth his help ;
While sounding to the bottom ignorance
Historical and philosophical
And moral and religious, all one couch
Of crassitude, a portent of its kind.
Then, just as he would pityingly teach
Your body to repair maltreatment, give
Advice that you should make those stumps to
    stir
With artificial hands of caoutchouc,
So would he soon supply your crippled soul
With crutches, from his own intelligence,
Able to help you onward in the path
Of rectitude whereto your face is set,
And counsel justice — to yourself, the first,
To your associate, very like a wife
Or something better, — to the world at large,
Friends, strangers, horses, hounds, and Cous-
    inry —
All which amount of justice will include
Justice to God. Go and consult his voice ! ''
Since angel would not say this simple truth,
What hinders that my heart relieve itself,
Milsand, who makest warm my wintry world,
And wise my heaven, if there we consort too ?
Monsieur Léonce Miranda turned, alas,
Or was turned, by no angel, t' other way,
And got him guidance of The Ravissante.

Now, into the originals of faith,
Yours, mine, Miranda's, no inquiry here !
Of faith, as apprehended by mankind,
The causes, were they caught and catalogued,
Would too distract, too desperately foil
Inquirer. How may analyst reduce
Quantities to exact their opposites,
Value to zero, then bring zero back
To value of supreme preponderance ?
How substitute thing meant for thing ex-
    pressed ?
Detect the wire-thread through that fluffy silk
Men call their rope, their real compulsive
    power ?
Suppose effected such anatomy,
And demonstration made of what belief
Has moved believer — were the consequence
Reward at all ? would each man straight de-
    duce,
From proved reality of cause, effect
Conformable — believe and unbelieve
According to your True thus disengaged
From all his heap of False called reason first ?

No : hand once used to hold a soft thick twist,
Cannot now grope its way by wire alone :
Childhood may catch the knack, scarce Youth,
    not Age !
That 's the reply rewards you. Just as well
Remonstrate to yon peasant in the blouse
That, had he justified the true intent
Of Nature who composed him thus and thus,

Weakly or strongly, here he would not stand
Struggling with uncongenial earth and sky,
But elsewhere tread the surface of the globe,
Since one meridian suits the faulty lungs,
Another bids the sluggish liver work.
" Here I was born, for better or for worse :
I did not choose a climate for myself ;
Admit, my life were healthy, led elsewhere,"
(He answers,) " how am I to migrate, pray ? ''

Therefore the course to take is — spare your
    pains,
And trouble uselessly with discontent
Nor soul nor body, by parading proof
That neither haply had known ailment, placed
Precisely where the circumstance forbade
Their lot should fall to either of the pair.
But try and, what you find wrong, remedy,
Accepting the conditions : never ask
" How came you to be born here with those
    lungs,
That liver ? '' But bid asthma smoke a pipe,
Stramonium, just as if no Tropics were,
And ply with calomel the sluggish duct,
Nor taunt " The born Norwegian breeds no
    bile ! ''
And as with body, so proceed with soul :
Nor less discerningly, where faith you found,
However foolish and fantastic, grudge
To play the doctor and amend mistake,
Because a wisdom were conceivable
Whence faith had sprung robust above disease,
Far beyond human help, that source of things !
Since, in the first stage, so to speak, — first
    stare
Of apprehension at the invisible, —
Begins divergency of mind from mind,
Superior from inferior : leave this first !
Little you change there ! What comes after-
    ward —
From apprehended thing, each inference
With practicality concerning life,
This you may test and try, confirm the right
Or contravene the wrong which reasons there.
The offspring of the sickly faith must prove
Sickly act also : stop a monster-birth !
When water 's in the cup, and not the cloud,
Then is the proper time for chemic test :
Belief permits your skill to operate
When, drop by drop condensed from misty
    heaven,
'T is wrung out, lies a bowl-full in the fleece.
How dew by spoonfuls came, let Gideon say :
What purpose water serves, your word or two
May teach him, should he fancy it lights fire.

Concerning, then, our vaporous Ravissante —
How fable first precipitated faith. —
Silence you get upon such point from me.
But when I see come posting to the pair
At Clairvaux, for the cure of soul-disease,
This Father of the Mission, Parish-priest,
This Mother of the Convent, Nun I know —
They practise in that second stage of things ;
They boast no fresh distillery of faith ;
'T is dogma in the bottle, bright and old,
They bring ; and I pretend to pharmacy.
They undertake the cure with all my heart !

He trusts them, and they surely trust them-
    selves.
I ask no better.   Never mind the cause,
Fons et origo of the malady :
Apply the drug with courage !   Here 's our
    case.
Monsieur Léonce Miranda asks of God,
— May a man, living in illicit tie,
Continue, by connivance of the Church,
No matter what amends he please to make
Short of forthwith relinquishing the sin ?
Physicians, what do you propose for cure ?

Father and Mother of The Ravissante,
Read your own records, and you find prescribed
As follows, when a couple out of sorts
Rather than gravely suffering, sought your
    skill
And thereby got their health again.   Perpend !
Two and a half good centuries ago,
Luc de la Maison Rouge, a nobleman
Of Claise, (the river gives this country name,)
And, just as noblewoman, Maude his wife,
Having been married many happy years
Spent in God's honor and man's service too,
Conceived, while yet in flower of youth and
    hope,
The project of departing each from each
Forever, and dissolving marriage-bonds
That both might enter a religious life.
Needing, before they came to such resolve,
Divine illumination, — course was clear, —
They visited your church in pilgrimage,
On Christmas morn : communicating straight,
They heard three Masses proper for the day,
" It is incredible with what effect " —
Quoth the Cistercian monk I copy from —
And, next day, came, again communicants,
Again heard Masses manifold, but now
With added thanks to Christ for special grace
And consolation granted : in the night,
Had been divorce from marriage, manifest
By signs and tokens.   So, they made great
    gifts,
Left money for more Masses, and returned
Homeward rejoicing — he, to take the rules,
As Brother Dionysius, Capucin !
She, to become first postulant, then nun
According to the rules of Benedict,
Sister Scolastica : so ended they,
And so do I — not end nor yet commence
One note or comment.   What was done was
    done.
Now, Father of the Mission, here 's your case !
And, Mother of the Convent, here 's its cure !
If separation was permissible,
And that decree of Christ " What God hath
    joined
Let no man put asunder " nullified
Because a couple, blameless in the world,
Had the conceit that, still more blamelessly,
Out of the world, by breach of marriage-vow,
Their life was like to pass, — you oracles
Of God, — since holy Paul says such you are, —
Hesitate, not one moment, to pronounce
When questioned by the pair now needing help,
" Each from the other go, you guilty ones,
Preliminary to your least approach

Nearer the Power that thus could strain a
    point
In favor of a pair of innocents
Who thought their wedded hands not clean
    enough
To touch and leave unsullied their souls' snow
Are not your hands found filthy by the world,
Mere human law and custom ?   Not a step
Nearer till hands be washed and purified ! "

What they did say is immaterial, since
Certainly it was nothing of the kind.
There was no washing hands of him (alack,
You take me ? — in the figurative sense !)
But, somehow, gloves were drawn o'er dirt and
    all,
And practice with the Church procured there-
    by.
Seeing that, — all remonstrance proved in vain
Persuasives tried and terrors put to use,
I nowise question, — still the guilty pair
Only embraced the closelier, obstinate, —
Father and Mother went from Clairvaux back
Their weary way, with heaviness of heart,
I grant you, but each palm well crossed with
    coin,
And nothing like a smutch perceptible.
Monsieur Léonce Miranda might compound
For sin ? — no, surely ! but by gifts — prepare
His soul the better for contrition, say !

Gift followed upon gift, at all events.
Good counsel was rejected, on one part :
Hard money, on the other — may we hope
Was unreflectingly consigned to purse ?

Two years did this experiment engage
Monsieur Léonce Miranda : how, by gifts
To God and to God's poor, a man might stay
In sin and yet stave off sin's punishment.
No salve could be conceived more nicely mixed
For this man's nature : generosity, —
Susceptibility to human ills,
Corporeal, mental, — self-devotedness
Made up Miranda — whether strong or weak
Elsewhere, may be inquired another time.
In mercy he was strong, at all events.
Enough ! he could not see a beast in pain,
Much less a man, without the will to aid ;
And where the will was, oft the means were
    too,
Since that good bargain with the Cousinry.

The news flew fast about the countryside
That, with the kind man, it was ask and have ;
And ask and have they did.   To instance
    you : —
A mob of beggars at The Ravissante
Clung to his skirts one day, and cried " We
    thirst ! "
Forthwith he bade a cask of wine be broached
To satisfy all comers, till, dead-drunk
So satisfied, they strewed the holy place.
For this was grown religious and a rite :
Such slips of judgment, gifts irregular,
Showed but as spillings of the golden grist
On either side the hopper, through blind zeal ;
Steadily the main stream went pouring on

From mill to mouth of sack — held wide and
          close
By Father of the Mission, Parish-priest,
And Mother of the Convent, Nun I know,
With such effect that, in the sequel, proof
Was tendered to the Court at Vire, last month,
That in these same two years, expenditure
At quiet Clairvaux rose to the amount
Of Forty Thousand English Pounds: whereof
A trifle went, no inappropriate close
Of bounty, to supply the Virgin's crown
With that stupendous jewel from New York,
Now blazing as befits the Star of Sea.

Such signs of grace, outward and visible,
I rather give you, for your sake and mine,
Than put in evidence the inward strife,
Spiritual effort to compound for fault
By payment of devotion — thank the phrase !
That payment was as punctual, do not doubt,
As its far easier fellow.   Yesterday
I trudged the distance from The Ravissante
To Clairvaux, with my two feet : but our friend,
The more to edify the country-folk,
Was wont to make that journey on both knees.
" Maliciously perverted incident ! "
Snarled the retort, when this was told at Vire :
" The man paid mere devotion as he passed,
Knelt decently at just each wayside shrine ! "
Alas, my lawyer, I trudged yesterday —
On my two feet, and with both eyes wide ope, —
The distance, and could find no shrine at all !
According to his lights, I praise the man.
Enough ! incessant was devotion, say —
With her, you know of, praying at his side.
Still, there be relaxations of the tense :
Or life indemnifies itself for strain,
Or finds its very strain grow feebleness.
Monsieur Léonce Miranda's days were passed
Much as of old, in simple work and play.
His first endeavor, on recovery
From that sad ineffectual sacrifice,
Had been to set about repairing loss :
Never admitting, loss was to repair.
No word at any time escaped his lips
— Betrayed a lurking presence, in his heart,
Of sorrow ; no regret for mischief done —
Punishment suffered, he would rather say.
Good-tempered schoolboy-fashion, he preferred
To laugh away his flogging, fair price paid
For pleasure out of bounds : if needs must be,
Get pleasure and get flogged a second time !
A sullen subject would have nursed the scars
And made excuse, for throwing grammar by,
That bench was grown uneasy to the seat.
No : this poor fellow cheerfully got hands
Fit for his stumps, and what hands failed to do,
The other members did in their degree —
Unwonted service. With his mouth alone
He wrote, nay, painted pictures — think of that !
He played on a piano pedal-keyed,
Kicked out — if it was Bach's — good music
          thence.
He rode, that 's readily conceivable,
But then he shot and never missed his bird,
With other feats as dexterous : I infer
He was not ignorant what hands are worth,
When he resolved on ruining his own.

So the two years passed somehow — who shall
          say
Foolishly, — as one estimates mankind,
The work they do, the play they leave un-
          done ? —
Two whole years spent in that experiment
I told you of, at Clairvaux all the time,
From April on to April : why that month
More than another, notable in life ?
Does the awakening of the year arouse
Man to new projects, nerve him for fresh feats
Of what proves, for the most part of mankind
Playing or working, novel folly too ?
At any rate, I see no slightest sign
Of folly (let me tell you in advance),
Nothing but wisdom meets me manifest
In the procedure of the Twentieth Day
Of April, 'Seventy, — folly's year in France.

It was delightful Spring, and out of doors
Temptation to adventure. Walk or ride ?
There was a wild young horse to exercise,
And teach the way to go, and pace to keep :
Monsieur Léonce Miranda chose to ride.
So, while they clapped soft saddle straight on
          back,
And bitted jaw to satisfaction, — since
The partner of his days must stay at home,
Teased by some trifling legacy of March
To throat or shoulder, — visit duly paid
And " farewell " given and received again, —
As chamber-door considerately closed
Behind him, still five minutes were to spend.
How better, than by clearing, two and two,
The staircase-steps and coming out aloft
Upon the platform yonder (raise your eyes !)
And tasting, just as those two years before,
Spring's bright advance upon the tower a-top,
The feature of the front, the Belvedere ?

Look at it for a moment while I breathe.

IV

Ready to hear the rest ?   How good you are !

Now for this Twentieth splendid day of Spring,
All in a tale, — sun, wind, sky, earth and sea, —
To bid man, " Up, be doing ! " Mount the stair,
Monsieur Léonce Miranda mounts so brisk,
And look — ere his elastic foot arrive —
Your longest, far and wide, o'er fronting space.
Yon white streak — Havre lighthouse ! Name
          and name,
How the mind runs from each to each relay,
Town after town, till Paris' self be touched,
Superlatively big with life and death
To all the world, that very day perhaps !
He who stepped out upon the platform here,
Pinnacled over the expanse, gave thought
Neither to Rouher nor Ollivier, Roon
Nor Bismarck, Emperor nor King, but just
To steeple, church, and shrine, The Ravissante !

He saw Her, whom myself saw, but when Spring
Was passing into Fall : not robed and crowned
As, thanks to him, and her you know about.

She stands at present ; but She smiled the same.
Thither he turned — to never turn away.

He thought . . .

     (Suppose I should prefer " He said " ?
Along with every act — and speech is act —
There go, a multitude impalpable
To ordinary human faculty,
The thoughts which give the act significance.
Who is a poet needs must apprehend
Alike both speech and thoughts which prompt
    to speak.
Part these, and thought withdraws to poetry :
Speech is reported in the newspaper.)

He said, then, probably no word at all,
But thought as follows — in a minute's space —
One particle of ore beats out such leaf !

" This Spring-morn I am forty-three years old :
In prime of life, perfection of estate
Bodily, mental, nay, material too, —
My whole of worldly fortunes reach their height.
Body and soul alike on eminence :
It is not probable I ever raise
Soul above standard by increase of worth,
Nor reasonably may expect to lift
Body beyond the present altitude.

" Behold me, Lady called The Ravissante !
Such as I am, I — gave myself to you
So long since, that I cannot say ' I give.'
All my belongings, what is summed in life,
I have submitted wholly — as man might,
At least, as I might, who am weak, not strong,—
Wholly, then, to your rule and governance,
So far as I had strength.   My weakness was —
I felt a fascination, at each point
And pore of me, a Power as absolute
Claiming that soul should recognize her sway.
Oh, you were no whit clearlier Queen, I see,
Throughout the life that rolls out ribbon-like
Its shot-silk length behind me, than the strange
Mystery — how shall I denominate
The unrobed One ? Robed you go and crowned
    as well,
Named by the nations : she is hard to name,
Though you have spelt out certain characters
Obscure upon what fillet binds her brow,
Lust of the flesh, lust of the eye, life's pride.
' So call her, and contemn the enchantress ! ' —
    ' Crush
The despot, and recover liberty ! '
Cried despot and enchantress at each ear.
You were conspicuous and pre-eminent,
Authoritative and imperial, — you
Spoke first, claimed homage : did I hesitate ?
Born for no mastery, but servitude.
Men cannot serve two masters, says the Book ;
Master should measure strength with master,
    then,
Before on servant is imposed a task.
You spoke first, promised best, and threatened
    most ;
The other never threatened, promised, spoke
A single word, but, when your part was done,
Lifted a finger, and I, prostrate, knew

Films were about me, though you stood aloof
Smiling or frowning ' Where is power like mine
To punish or reward thee ?   Rise, thou fool !
Will to be free, and, lo, I lift thee loose ! '
Did I not will, and could I rise a whit ?
Lay I, at any time, content to lie ?
' To lie, at all events, brings pleasure : make
Amends by undemanded pain ! ' I said.
Did not you prompt me ?   ' Purchase now by
    pain
Pleasure hereafter in the world to come ! '
I could not pluck my heart out, as you bade :
Unbidden, I burned off my hands at least.
My soul retained its treasure ; but my purse
Lightened itself with much alacrity.
Well, where is the reward ? what promised
    fruit
Of sacrifice in peace, content ? what sense
Of added strength to bear or to forbear ?
What influx of new light assists me now
Even to guess you recognize a gain
In what was loss enough to mortal me ?
But she, the less authoritative voice,
Oh, how distinct enunciating, how
Plain dealing !   Gain she gave was gain indeed !
That, you deny : that, you contemptuous call
Acorns, swine's food not man's meat !   ' Spurn
    the draff ! '
Ay, but those life-tree apples I prefer,
Am I to die of hunger till they drop ?
Husks keep flesh from starvation, anyhow.
Give those life-apples ! — one, worth woods of
    oak,
Worth acorns by the wagon-load, — one shoot
Through heart and brain, assurance bright and
    brief
That you, my Lady, my own Ravissante,
Feel, through my famine, served and satisfied,
Own me, your starveling, soldier of a sort !
Your soldier ! do I read my title clear
Even to call myself your friend, not foe ?
What is the pact between us but a truce ?
At best I shall have staved off enmity,
Obtained a respite, ransomed me from wrath.
I pay, instalment by instalment, life,
Earth's tribute-money, pleasures great and
    small,
Whereof should at the last one penny piece
Fall short, the whole heap becomes forfeiture.
You find in me deficient soldiership :
Want the whole life or none. I grudge that
    whole,
Because I am not sure of recompense :
Because I want faith. Whose the fault ? I
    ask.
If insufficient faith have done thus much,
Contributed thus much of sacrifice,
More would move mountains, you are warrant.
    Well,
Grant, you, the grace, I give the gratitude !
And what were easier ?   ' Ask and have ' folk
    call
Miranda's method : ' Have, nor need to ask ! '
So do they formulate your quality
Superlative beyond my human grace.
The Ravissante, you ravish men away
From puny aches and petty pains, assuaged
By man's own art with small expenditure

Of pill or potion, unless, put to shame,
Nature is roused and sets things right herself.
Your miracles are grown our commonplace ;
No day but pilgrim hobbles his last mile,
Kneels down and rises up, flings crutch away,
Or else appends it to the reverend heap
Beneath you, votive cripple-carpentry.
Some few meet failure — oh, they wanted faith,
And may betake themselves to La Salette,
Or seek Lourdes, so that hence the scandal
    limp !
The many get their grace and go their way
Rejoicing, with a tale to tell, — most like,
A staff to borrow, since the crutch is gone,
Should the first telling happen at my house,
And teller wet his whistle with my wine.
I tell this to a doctor and he laughs :
' Give me permission to cry — Out of bed,
You loth rheumatic sluggard ! Cheat yon chair
Of laziness, its gouty occupant ! —
You should see miracles performed ! But now,
I give advice, and take as fee ten francs,
And do as much as does your Ravissante.
Send her that case of cancer to be cured
I have refused to treat for any fee,
Bring back my would-be patient sound and
    whole,
And see me laugh on t'other side my mouth ! '
Can he be right, and are you hampered thus !
Such pettiness restricts a miracle
Wrought by the Great Physician, who hears
    prayer,
Visibly seated in your mother-lap !
He, out of nothing, made sky, earth, and sea,
And all that in them is, man, beast, bird, fish,
Down to this insect on my parapet.
Look how the marvel of a minim crawls !
Were I to kneel among the halt and maimed,
And pray ' Who mad'st the insect with ten
    legs,
Make me one finger grow where ten were
    once ! '
The very priests would thrust me out of church.
' What folly does the madman dare expect ?
No faith obtains — in this late age, at least —
Such cure as that ! We ease rheumatics,
    though ! '

" Ay, bring the early ages back again,
What prodigy were unattainable ?
I read your annals. Here came Louis Onze,
Gave thrice the sum he ever gave before
At one time, some three hundred crowns, to
    wit —
On pilgrimage to pray for — health, he found ?
Did he ? I do not read it in Commines.
Here sent poor joyous Marie-Antoinette
To thank you that a Dauphin dignified
Her motherhood — called Duke of Normandy
And Martyr of the Temple, much the same
As if no robe of hers had dressed you rich ;
No silver lamps, she gave, illume your shrine !
Here, following example, fifty years
Ago, in gratitude for birth again
Of yet another destined King of France,
Did not the Duchess fashion with her hands,
And frame in gold and crystal, and present
A bouquet made of artificial flowers ?

And was he King of France, and is not he
Still Count of Chambord ?

                    " Such the days of faith,
And such their produce to encourage mine !
What now, if I too count without my host ?
I too have given money, ornament,
And ' artificial flowers ' — which, when I
    plucked,
Seemed rooting at my heart and real enough :
What if I gain thereby nor health of mind,
Nor youth renewed which perished in its prime,
Burnt to a cinder 'twixt the red-hot bars,
Nor gain to see my second baby-hope
Of managing to live on terms with both
Opposing potentates, the Power and you,
Crowned with success ? I dawdle out my days
In exile here at Clairvaux, with mock love,
That gives, while whispering ' Would I dared
    refuse ! ' —
What the loud voice declares my heart's free
    gift !
Mock worship, mock superiority
O'er those I style the world's benighted ones,
That irreligious sort I pity so,
Dumas and even Hertford, who is Duke.

" Impiety ? Not if I know myself !
Not if you know the heart and soul I bare,
I bid you cut, hack, slash, anatomize,
Till peccant part be found and flung away !
Demonstrate where I need more faith !
    Describe
What act shall evidence sufficiency
Of faith, your warrant for such exercise
Of power, in my behalf, as all the world,
Except poor praying me, declares profuse ?
Poor me ? It is that world, not me alone,
That world which prates of fixed laws and the
    like,
I fain would save, poor world so ignorant !
And your part were — what easy miracle ?
Oh, Lady, could I make your want like mine ! "

Then his face grew one luminosity.

" Simple, sufficient ! Happiness at height !
I solve the riddle, I persuade mankind.
I have been just the simpleton who stands —
Summoned to claim his patrimonial rights —
At shilly-shally, may he knock or no
At his own door in his own house and home
Whereof he holds the very title-deeds !
Here is my title to this property,
This power you hold for profit of myself
And all the world at need — which need is
    now !

" My title — let me hear who controverts !
Count Mailleville built yon church. Why did he
    so ?
Because he found your image. How came
    that ?
His shepherd told him that a certain sheep
Was wont to scratch with hoof and scrape with
    horn
At ground where once the Danes had razed a
    church.

Thither he went, and there he dug, and thence
He disinterred the image he conveyed
In pomp to Londres yonder, his domain.
You liked the old place better than the new.
The Count might surely have divined as much:
He did not; some one might have spoke a
    word —
No one did. A mere dream had warned enough,
That back again in pomp you best were borne:
No dream warned, and no need of convoy was;
An angel caught you up and clapped you
    down, —
No mighty task; you stand one metre high,
And people carry you about at times.
Why, then, did you despise the simple course?
Because you are the Queen of Angels: when
You front us in a picture, there flock they,
Angels around you, here and everywhere.

"Therefore, to prove indubitable faith,
Those angels that acknowledge you their queen,
I summon them to bear me to your feet
From Clairvaux through the air, an easy trip!
Faith without flaw! I trust your potency,
Benevolence, your will to save the world —
By such a simplest of procedures, too!
Not even by affording angel-help,
Unless it please you: there 's a simpler mode:
Only suspend the law of gravity,
And, while at back, permitted to propel,
The air helps onward, let the air in front
Cease to oppose my passage through the midst!

"Thus I bestride the railing, leg o'er leg,
Thus, lo, I stand, a single inch away,
At dizzy edge of death, — no touch of fear,
As safe on tower above as turf below!
Your smile enswathes me in beatitude,
You lift along the votary — who vaults,
Who, in the twinkling of an eye, revives,
Dropt safely in the space before the church —
How crowded, since this morn is market-day!
I shall not need to speak. The news will run
Like wild-fire. 'Thousands saw Miranda's
    flight!'
'T is telegraphed to Paris in a trice.
The Boulevard is one buzz — 'Do you believe?
Well, this time, thousands saw Miranda's
    flight:
You know him, goldsmith in the Place Ven-
    dôme.'
In goes the Empress to the Emperor:
'Now — will you hesitate to make disgorge
Your wicked King of Italy his gains,
Give the Legations to the Pope once more?'
Which done, — why, grace goes back to oper-
    ate,
They themselves set a good example first,
Resign the empire twenty years usurped,
And Henry, the Desired One, reigns o'er
    France!
Regenerated France makes all things new!
My house no longer stands on Quai Rousseau,
But Quai rechristened Alacoque: a quai
Where Renan burns his book, and Veuillot
    burns
Renan beside, since Veuillot rules the roast,
Re-edits now indeed 'The Universe.'

O blessing, O superlatively big
With blessedness beyond all blessing dreamed
By man! for just that promise has effect,
' Old things shall pass away and all be new!'
Then, for a culminating mercy-feat,
Wherefore should I dare dream impossible
That I too have my portion in the change?
My past with all its sorrow, sin and shame,
Becomes a blank, a nothing! There she stands,
Clara de Millefleurs, all deodorized,
Twenty years' stain wiped off her innocence!
There never was Muhlhausen, nor at all
Duke Hertford: naught that was, remains, ex-
    cept
The beauty, — yes, the beauty is unchanged!
Well, and the soul too, that must keep the
    same!
And so the trembling little virgin hand
Melts into mine, that 's back again, of course!
— Think not I care about my poor old self!
I only want my hand for that one use,
To take her hand, and say ' I marry you —
Men, women, angels, you behold my wife!
There is no secret, nothing wicked here,
Nothing she does not wish the world to know!'
None of your married women have the right
To mutter ' Yes, indeed, she beats us all
In beauty, — but our lives are pure at least!'
Bear witness, for our marriage is no thing
Done in a corner! 'T is The Ravissante
Repairs the wrong of Paris. See, She smiles,
She beckons, She bids ' Hither, both of you!'
And may we kneel? And will you bless us
    both?
And may I worship you, and yet love her?
Then!"—
        A sublime spring from the balustrade
About the tower so often talked about,
A flash in middle air, and stone-dead lay
Monsieur Léonce Miranda on the turf.

A gardener who watched, at work the while
Dibbling a flower-bed for geranium-shoots,
Saw the catastrophe, and, straightening back,
Stood up and shook his brows. "Poor soul,
    poor soul,
Just what I prophesied the end would be!
Ugh — the Red Night-cap!" (as he raised the
    head)
"This must be what he meant by those strange
    words
While I was weeding larkspurs, yesterday,
' Angels would take him!' Mad!"

                    No! sane, I say,
Such being the conditions of his life,
Such end of life was not irrational.
Hold a belief, you only half-believe,
With all-momentous issues either way, —
And I advise you imitate this leap,
Put faith to proof, be cured or killed at once!
Call you men, killed through cutting cancer
    out,
The worse for such an act of bravery?
That 's more than I know. In my estimate,
Better lie prostrate on his turf at peace,
Than, wistful, eye, from out the tent, the
    tower,

Racked with a doubt, " Will going on bare
    knees
All the way to The Ravissante and back,
Saying my Ave Mary all the time,
Somewhat excuse if I postpone my march ?
— Make due amends for that one kiss I gave
In gratitude to her who held me out
Superior Fricquot's sermon, hot from press,
A-spread with hands so sinful yet so smooth ? "

And now, sincerely do I pray she stand,
Clara, with interposing sweep of robe,
Between us and this horror ! Any screen
Turns white by contrast with the tragic pall ;
And her dubiety distracts at least,
As well as snow, from such decided black.
With womanhood, at least, we have to do :
Ending with Clara — is the word too kind ?

Let pass the shock ! There's poignancy enough
When what one parted with, a minute since,
Alive and happy, is returned a wreck —
All that was, all that seemed about to be,
Razed out and ruined now forevermore,
Because a straw descended on this scale
Rather than that, made death o'erbalance life.
But think of cage-mates in captivity,
Inured to day-long, night-long vigilance
Each of the other's tread and angry turn
If behind prison bars the jailer knocked :
These whom society shut out, and thus
Penned in, to settle down and regulate
By the strange law, the solitary life —
When death divorces such a fellowship,
Theirs may pair off with that prodigious woe
Imagined of a ghastly brotherhood —
One watcher left in lighthouse out at sea,
With leagues of surf between the land and
    him,
Alive with his dead partner on the rock ;
One galley-slave, whom curse and blow com-
    pel
To labor on, ply oar — beside his chain,
Encumbered with a corpse-companion now.
Such these : although, no prisoners, self-en-
    trenched,
They kept the world off from their barricade.

Memory, gratitude, was poignant, sure,
Though pride brought consolation of a kind.
Twenty years long had Clara been — of whom
The rival, nay, the victor, past dispute ?
What if in turn The Ravissante at length
Proved victor — which was doubtful — any-
    how,
Here lay the inconstant with, conspicuous too,
The fruit of his good fortune !

                  " Has he gained
By leaving me ? " she might soliloquize :
" All love could do, I did for him. I learned
By heart his nature, what he loved and loathed.
Leaned to with liking, turned from with dis-
    taste.
No matter what his least velleity,
I was determined he should want no wish,
And in conformity administered
To his requirement ; most of joy I mixed

With least of sorrow in life's daily draught,
Twenty years long, life's proper average.
And when he got to quarrel with my cup,
Would needs out-sweeten honey, and discard
That gall-drop we require lest nectar cloy, —
I did not call him fool, and vex my friend,
But quietly allowed experiment,
Encouraged him to spice his drink, and now
Grate *lignum vitæ*, now bruise so-called grains
Of Paradise, and pour now, for perfume,
Distilment rare, the rose of Jericho,
Holy-thorn, passion-flower, and what know I ?
Till beverage obtained the fancied smack.
'T was wild-flower-wine that neither helped nor
    harmed
Who sipped and held it for restorative —
What harm ? But here has he been through
    the hedge
Straying in search of simples, while my back
Was turned a minute, and he finds a prize,
Monkshood and belladonna ! O my child,
My truant little boy, despite the beard,
The body two feet broad and six feet long,
And what the calendar counts middle age —
You wanted, did you, to enjoy a flight ?
Why not have taken into confidence
Me, that was mother to you ? — never mind
What mock disguise of mistress held you mine !
Had you come laughing, crying, with request,
' Make me fly, mother ! ' I had run upstairs
And held you tight the while I danced you
    high
In air from tower-top, singing ' Off we go
(On pilgrimage to Lourdes some day next
    month),
And swift we soar (to Rome with Peter-pence),
And low we light (at Paris where we pick
Another jewel from our store of stones
And send it for a present to the Pope) ! '
So, dropt indeed you were, but on my knees,
Rolling and crowing, not a whit the worse
For journey to your Ravissante and back.
Now, no more Clairvaux — which I made you
    build,
And think an inspiration of your own —
No more fine house, trim garden, pretty park,
Nothing I used to busy you about,
And make believe you worked for my sur-
    prise !
What weariness to me will work become
Now that I need not seem surprised again !
This boudoir, for example, with the doves
(My stupid maid has damaged, dusting one)
Embossed in stucco o'er the looking-glass
Beside the toilet-table ! dear — dear me ! "

Here she looked up from her absorbing grief,
And round her, crow-like grouped, the Cous-
    inry,
(She grew aware) sat witnesses at watch.
For, two days had elapsed since fate befell
The courser in the meadow, stretched so stark.
They did not cluster on the tree-tops, close
Their sooty ranks, caw and confabulate
For nothing : but, like calm determined crows,
They came to take possession of their corpse.
And who shall blame them ? Had not they the
    right ?

One spoke. " They would be gentle, not aus-
tere.
They understood, and were compassionate.
Madame Muhlhausen lay too abject now
For aught but the sincerest pity ; still,
Since plain speech salves the wound it seems to
make,
They must speak plainly — circumstances
spoke !
Sin had conceived and brought forth death in-
deed.
As the commencement, so the close of things :
Just what might be expected all along !
Monsieur Léonce Miranda launched his youth
Into a cesspool of debauchery,
And, if he thence emerged all dripping slime,
— Where was the change except from thin to
thick,
One warm rich mud-bath, Madame ? — you, in
place
Of Paris-drainage and distilment, you
He never needed budge from, boiled to rags !
True, some good instinct left the natural man,
Some touch of that deep dye wherewith imbued
By education, in his happier day,
The hopeful offspring of high parentage
Was fleece-marked moral and religious sheep, —
Some ruddle, faint reminder (we admit),
Stuck to Miranda, rubbed he ne'er so rude
Against the goatly coarseness : to the last,
Moral he styled himself, religious too !
Which means — what ineradicable good
You found, you never left till good's self proved
Perversion and distortion, nursed to growth
So monstrous, that the tree-stock, dead and
dry,
Were seemlier far than such a heap grotesque
Of fungous flourishing excrescence. Here,
Sap-like affection, meant for family,
Stole off to feed one sucker fat — yourself ;
While branchage, trained religiously aloft
To rear its head in reverence to the sun,
Was pulled down earthward, pegged and pick-
eted,
By topiary contrivance, till the tree
Became an arbor where, at vulgar ease,
Sat superstition grinning through the loops.
Still, nature is too strong or else too weak
For cockney treatment : either, tree springs
back
To pristine shape, or else degraded droops,
And turns to touchwood at the heart. So
here —
Body and mind, at last the man gave way.
His body — there it lies, what part was left
Unmutilated ! for, the strife commenced
Two years ago, when, both hands burnt to ash,
— A branch broke loose, by loss of what choice
twigs !
As for his mind — behold our register
Of all its moods, from the incipient mad,
Nay, mere erratic, to the stark insane,
Absolute idiocy or what is worse !
All have we catalogued — extravagance
In worldly matters, luxury absurd,
And zeal as crazed in its expenditure
Of nonsense called devotion. Don't we know
— We Cousins, bound in duty to our kin, —

What mummeries were practised by you two
At Clairvaux ? Not a servant got discharge
But came and told his grievance, testified
To acts which turn religion to a farce.
And as the private mock, so patent — see —
The public scandal ! Ask the neighborhood —
Or rather, since we asked them long ago,
Read what they answer, depositions down,
Signed, sealed and sworn to ! Brief, the man
was mad.
We are his heirs and claim our heritage.
Madame Muhlhausen, — whom good taste for-
bids
We qualify as do these documents, —
Fear not lest justice stifle mercy's prayer !
True, had you lent a willing ear at first,
Had you obeyed our call two years ago,
Restrained a certain insolence of eye,
A volubility of tongue, that time,
Your prospects had been none the worse, per-
haps.
Still, fear not but a decent competence
Shall smooth the way for your declining age !
What we propose, then " . . .

                    Clara dried her eyes,
Sat up, surveyed the consistory, spoke
After due pause, with something of a smile.

" Gentlemen, kinsfolk of my friend defunct,
In thus addressing me — of all the world ! —
You much misapprehend what part I play.
I claim no property you speak about.
You might as well address the park-keeper,
Harangue him on some plan advisable
For covering the park with cottage-plots.
He is the servant, no proprietor,
His business is to see the sward kept trim,
Untrespassed over by the indiscreet :
Beyond that, he refers you to myself —
Another servant of another kind —
Who again — quite as limited in act —
Refer you, with your projects, — can I else ?
To who in mastery is ultimate,
The Church. The Church is sole administrant,
Since sole possessor of what worldly wealth
Monsieur Léonce Miranda late possessed.
Often enough has he attempted, nay,
Forced me, wellnigh, to occupy the post
You seemingly suppose I fill, — receive
As gift the wealth intrusted me as grace.
This — for quite other reasons than appear
So cogent to your perspicacity —
This I refused ; and, firm as you could wish,
Still was my answer, ' We two understand
Each one the other. I am intimate
— As how can be mere fools and knaves — or,
say,
Even your Cousins ? — with your love to me,
Devotion to the Church. Would Providence
Appoint, and make me certain of the same,
That I survive you (which is little like,
Seeing you hardly overpass my age
And more than match me in abundant health)
In such case, certainly I would accept
Your bounty : better I than alien hearts
Should execute your planned benevolence
To man, your proposed largess to the Church,

But though I be survivor, — weakly frame,
With only woman's wit to make amends, —
When I shall die, or while I am alive,
Cannot you figure me an easy mark
For hypocritical rapacity,
Kith, kin and generation, crouching low,
Ever on the alert to pounce on prey ?
Far be it I should say they profited
By that first frenzy-fit themselves induced,—
Cold-blooded scenical buffoons at sport
With horror and damnation o'er a grave :
That were too shocking — I absolve them
   there !
Nor did they seize the moment of your swoon
To rifle pocket, wring a paper thence,
Their Cousinly dictation, and enrich
Thereby each mother's son as heart could wish,
Had nobody supplied a codicil.
But when the pain, poor friend ! had prostrated
Your body, though your soul was right once
   more,
I fear they turned your weakness to account !
Why else to me, who agonizing watched,
Sneak, cap in hand, now bribe me to forsake
My maimed Léonce, now bully, cap on head,
The impudent pretension to assuage
Such sorrows as demanded Cousins' care ? —
*For you rejected, hated, fled me, far
In foreign lands you laughed at me !* — they
   judged.
And, think you, will the unkind one hesitate
To try conclusions with my helplessness, —
To pounce on and misuse your derelict,
Helped by advantage that bereavement lends
Folk, who, while yet you lived, played tricks
   like these ?
You only have to die, and they detect,
In all you said and did, insanity !
Your faith was fetish-worship, your regard
For Christ's prime precept which endows the
   poor
And strips the rich, a craze from first to last !
They so would limn your likeness, paint your
   life,
That if it ended by some accident, —
For instance, if, attempting to arrange
The plants below that dangerous Belvedere
I cannot warn you from sufficiently,
You lost your balance and fell headlong — fine
Occasion, such, for crying *Suicide !*
Non compos mentis, naturally next,
Hands over Clairvaux to a Cousin-tribe
Who nor like me nor love The Ravissante :
Therefore be ruled by both ! Life-interest
In Clairvaux, — conservation, guardianship
Of earthly good for heavenly purpose, — give
Such and no other proof of confidence !
Let Clara represent The Ravissante ! '
— To whom accordingly, he then and there
Bequeathed each stick and stone, by testament
In holograph, mouth managing the quill :
Go, see the same in Londres, if you doubt ! "

Then smile grew laugh, as sudden up she stood
And out she spoke : intemperate the speech !

" And now, sirs, for your special courtesy,
Your candle held up to the character

Of Lucie Steiner, whom you qualify
As coming short of perfect womanhood.
Yes, kindly critics, truth for once you tell !
True is it that through childhood, poverty,
Sloth, pressure of temptation, I succumbed,
And, ere I found what honor meant, lost mine.
So was the sheep lost, which the Shepherd
   found
And never lost again. My friend found me ;
Or better say, the Shepherd found us both —
Since he, my friend, was much in the same mire
When first we made acquaintance. Each
   helped each, —
A twofold extrication from the slough ;
And, saving me, he saved himself. Since then,
Unsmirched we kept our cleanliness of coat.
It is his perfect constancy, you call
My friend's main fault — he never left his
   love !
While as for me, I dare your worst, impute
One breach of loving bond, these twenty years,
To me whom only cobwebs bound, you count !
' He was religiously disposed in youth ! '
That may be, though we did not meet at
   church.
Under my teaching did he, like you scamps,
Become Voltairian — fools who mock his
   faith ?
' Infirm of body ! ' I am silent there :
Even yourselves acknowledge service done,
Whatever motive your own souls supply
As inspiration. Love made labor light."

Then laugh grew frown, and frown grew terri-
   ble.
Do recollect what sort of person shrieked —
" Such was I, saint or sinner, what you please :
And who is it casts stone at me but you ?
By your own showing, sirs, you bought and
   sold,
Took what advantage bargain promised bag,
Abundantly did business, and with whom ?
The man whom you pronounce imbecile, push
Indignantly aside if he presume
To settle his affairs like other folk !
How is it you have stepped into his shoes,
And stand there, bold as brass, ' Miranda, late ;
Now, Firm-Miranda ' ? Sane, he signed away
That little birthright, did he ? Hence to
   trade !
I know and he knew who 't was dipped and
   ducked,
Truckled and played the parasite in vain,
As now one, now the other, here you cringed,
Were feasted, took our presents, you — those
   drops,
Just for your wife's adornment ! you — that
   spray
Exactly suiting, as most diamonds would,
Your daughter on her marriage ! No word
   then
Of somebody the wanton ! Hence, I say,
Subscribers to the ' Siècle,' every snob —
For here the post brings me the ' Univers ' !
Home and make money in the Place Vendôme,
Sully yourselves no longer by my sight,
And, when next Schneider wants a new *parure*
Be careful lest you stick there by mischance

That stone beyond compare intrusted you
To kindle faith with, when, Miranda's gift,
Crowning the very crown, The Ravissante
Shall claim it! As to Clairvaux — talk to
    Her!
She answers by the Chapter of Raimbaux!"
Vituperative, truly! All this wrath
Because the man's relations thought him mad!
Whereat, I hope you see the Cousinry
Turn each to other, blankly dolorous,
Consult a moment, more by shrug and shrug
Than mere man's language, — finally conclude
To leave the reprobate untroubled now
In her unholy triumph, till the Law
Shall right the injured ones ; for gentlemen
Allow the female sex, this sort at least,
Its privilege. So, simply "Cockatrice!" —
"Jezebel!" — "Queen of the Camellias!" —
    cried
Cousin to cousin, as yon hinge a-creak
Shut out the party, and the gate returned
To custody of Clairvaux. "Pretty place!
What say you, when it proves our property,
To trying a concurrence with La Roche,
And laying down a rival oyster-bed?
Where the park ends, the sea begins, you
    know."
So took they comfort till they came to Vire.

But I would linger, fain to snatch a look
At Clara as she stands in pride of place,
Somewhat more satisfying than my glance
So furtive, so near futile, yesterday,
Because one must be courteous. Of the masks
That figure in this little history,
She only has a claim to my respect,
And one-eyed, in her French phrase, rules the
    blind.
Miranda hardly did his best with life :
He might have opened eye, exerted brain,
Attained conception as to right and law
In certain points respecting intercourse
Of man with woman — love, one likes to say ;
Which knowledge had dealt rudely with the
    claim
Of Clara to play representative
And from perdition rescue soul, forsooth!
Also, the sense of him should have sufficed
For building up some better theory
Of how God operates in heaven and earth,
Than would establish Him participant
In doings yonder at The Ravissante.
The heart was wise according to its lights
And limits ; but the head refused more sun,
And shrank into its mew, and craved less
    space.
Clara, I hold the happier specimen, —
It may be, through that artist-preference
For work complete, inferiorly proposed,
To incompletion, though it aim aright.
Morally, no! Aspire, break bounds! I say,
Endeavor to be good, and better still,
And best! Success is naught, endeavor 's all.
But intellect adjusts the means to ends,
Tries the low thing, and leaves it done, at
    least ;
No prejudice to high thing, intellect
Would do and will do, only give the means.

Miranda, in my picture-gallery,
Presents a Blake ; be Clara — Meissonnier!
Merely considered so by artist, mind!
For, break through Art and rise to poetry,
Bring Art to tremble nearer, touch enough
The verge of vastness to inform our soul
What orb makes transit through the dark
    above,
And there 's the triumph! — there the incom-
    plete,
More than completion, matches the immense, —
Then, Michelagnolo against the world!
With this proviso, let me study her
Approvingly, the finished little piece!
Born, bred, with just one instinct, — that of
    growth, —
Her quality was, caterpillar-like,
To all-unerringly select a leaf
And without intermission feed her fill,
Become the Painted Peacock, or belike
The Brimstone-wing, when time of year should
    suit ;
And 't is a sign (say entomologists)
Of sickness, when the creature stops its meal
One minute, either to look up at heaven,
Or turn aside for change of aliment.
No doubt there was a certain ugliness
In the beginning, as the grub grew worm :
She could not find the proper plant at once,
But crawled and fumbled through a whole
    parterre.
Husband Muhlhausen served for stuff not long:
Then came confusion of the slimy track
From London, "where she gave the tone
    awhile,"
To Paris : let the stalks start up again,
Now she is off them, all the greener they!
But, settled on Miranda, how she sucked,
Assimilated juices, took the tint,
Mimicked the form and texture of her food!
Was he for pastime? Who so frolic-fond
As Clara? Had he a devotion-fit?
Clara grew serious with like qualm, be sure!
In health and strength he, — healthy too and
    strong,
She danced, rode, drove, took pistol-practice,
    fished,
Nay, "managed sea-skiff with consummate
    skill."
In pain and weakness, he, — she patient watched
And whiled the slow drip-dropping hours away.
She bound again the broken self-respect,
She picked out the true meaning from mistake,
Praised effort in each stumble, laughed "Well-
    climbed!"
When others groaned "None ever grovelled
    so!"
"Rise, you have gained experience!" was her
    word :
"Lie satisfied, the ground is just your place!"
They thought appropriate counsel. "Live, not
    die,
And take my full life to eke out your own :
That shall repay me and with interest!
Write! — is your mouth not clever as my
    hand?
Paint! — the last Exposition warrants me,
Plenty of people must ply brush with toes.

And as for music — look, what folk nickname
A lyre, those ancients played to ravishment, —
Over the pendule, see, Apollo grasps
A three-stringed gimcrack which no Liszt could
    coax
Such music from as jew's-harp makes to-day !
Do your endeavor like a man, and leave
The rest to ' fortune who assists the bold ' —
Learn, you, the Latin which you taught me
    first,
You clever creature — clever, yes, I say ! "

If he smiled " Let us love, love's wrong comes
    right,
Shows reason last of all ! Necessity
Must meanwhile serve for plea — so, mind not
    much
Old Fricquot's menace ! " — back she smiled
    " Who minds ? "
If he sighed " Ah, but She is strict, they say,
For all Her mercy at The Ravissante,
She scarce will be put off so ! " — straight a sigh
Returned " My lace must go to trim Her gown ! "
I nowise doubt she inwardly believed
Smiling and sighing had the same effect
Upon the venerated image. What
She did believe in, I as little doubt,
Was — Clara's self's own birthright to sustain
Existence, grow from grub to butterfly,
Upon unlimited Miranda-leaf ;
In which prime article of faith confirmed,
According to capacity, she fed
On and on till the leaf was eaten up,
That April morning. Even then, I praise
Her forethought which prevented leafless stalk
Bestowing any hoarded succulence
On earwig and black-beetle squat beneath ; —
Clairvaux, that stalk whereto her hermitage
She tacked by golden throw of silk, so fine,
So anything but feeble, that her sleep
Inside it, through last winter, two years long,
Recked little of the storm and strife without.
" But — loved him ? " Friend, I do not praise
    her love !
True love works never for the loved one so,
Nor spares skin - surface, smoothening truth
    away.
Love bids touch truth, endure truth, and em-
    brace
Truth, though, embracing truth, love crush
    itself.
" Worship not me, but God ! " the angels urge :
That is love's grandeur : still, in pettier love
The nice eye can distinguish grade and grade.
Shall mine degrade the velvet green and puce
Of caterpillar, palmer-worm — or what —
Ball in and out of ball, each ball with brush
Of Venus' eye-fringe round the turquoise egg
That nestles soft, — compare such paragon
With any scarabæus of the brood
Which, born to fly, keeps wing in wing-case,
    walks
Persistently a-trundling dung on earth ?

Egypt may venerate such hierophants,
Not I — the couple yonder, Father Priest
And Mother Nun, who came and went and
    came,

Beset this Clairvaux, trundled money-muck
To midden and the main heap oft enough,
But never bade unshut from sheath the gauze,
Nor showed that, who would fly, must let fall
    filth,
And warn " Your jewel, brother, is a blotch :
Sister, your lace trails ordure ! Leave your
    sins,
And so best gift with Crown and grace with
    Robe ! "

The superstition is extinct, you hope ?
It were, with my good will ! Suppose it so,
Bethink you likewise of the latest use
Whereto a Night-cap is convertible,
And draw your very thickest, thread and
    thrum,
O'er such a decomposing face of things,
Once so alive, it seemed immortal too !

This happened two years since. The Cousinry
Returned to Paris, called in help from Law,
And in due form proceeded to dispute
Monsieur Léonce Miranda's competence,
Being insane, to make a valid Will.

Much testimony volunteered itself ;
The issue hardly could be doubtful — but
For that sad 'Seventy which must intervene,
Provide poor France with other work to mind
Than settling lawsuits, even for the sake
Of such a party as The Ravissante.
It only was this Summer that the case
Could come and be disposed of, two weeks
    since,
At Vire — Tribunal Civil — Chamber First.

Here, issued with all regularity,
I hold the judgment — just, inevitable,
Nowise to be contested by what few
Can judge the judges ; sum and substance,
    thus : —

" Inasmuch as we find, the Cousinry,
During that very period when they take
Monsieur Léonce Miranda for stark mad,
Considered him to be quite sane enough
For doing much important business with —
Nor showed suspicion of his competence
Until, by turning of the tables, loss
Instead of gain accrued to them thereby, —
Plea of incompetence we set aside.

— " The rather, that the dispositions, sought
To be impugned, are natural and right,
Nor jar with any reasonable claim
Of kindred, friendship, or acquaintance here.
Nobody is despoiled, none overlooked ;
Since the testator leaves his property
To just that person whom, of all the world,
He counted he was most indebted to.
In mere discharge, then, of conspicuous debt,
Madame Muhlhausen has priority.
Enjoys the usufruct of Clairvaux.

" Next,
Such debt discharged, such life determining,
Such earthly interest provided for,

Monsieur Léonce Miranda may bequeath,
In absence of more fit recipient, fund
And usufruct together to the Church
Whereof he was a special devotee.

" — Which disposition, being consonant
With a long series of such acts and deeds
Notorious in his lifetime, needs must stand,
Unprejudiced by eccentricity
Nowise amounting to distemper : since,
In every instance signalized as such,
We recognize no overleaping bounds,
No straying out of the permissible :
Duty to the Religion of the Land, —
Neither excessive nor inordinate.

" The minor accusations are dismissed ;
They prove mere freak and fancy, boyish mood
In age mature of simple kindly man.
Exuberant in generosities
To all the world : no fact confirms the fear
He meditated mischief to himself
That morning when he met the accident
Which ended fatally.   The case is closed."

How otherwise ?   So, when I grazed the skirts,
And had the glimpse of who made, yesterday, —
Woman and retinue of goats and sheep, —
The sombre path one whiteness, vision-like,
As out of gate, and in at gate again,
They wavered, — she was lady there for life :
And, after life — I hope, a white success
Of some sort, wheresoever life resume
School interrupted by vacation — death ;
Seeing that home she goes with prize in hand,
Confirmed the Châtelaine of Clairvaux.

True,
Such prize fades soon to insignificance.
Though she have eaten her Miranda up,
And spun a cradle-cone through which she
    pricks
Her passage, and proves peacock-butterfly,
This Autumn — wait a little week of cold !
Peacock and death's-head-moth end much the
    same.
And could she still continue spinning, — sure,
Cradle would soon crave shroud for substitute,
And o'er this life of hers distaste would drop
Red-cotton-Nightcap-wise.

How say you, friend ?
Have I redeemed my promise ? Smile assent
Through the dark Winter-gloom between us
    both !
Already, months ago and miles away,
I just as good as told you, in a flash,
The while we paced the sands before my house,
All this poor story — truth and nothing else.
Accept that moment's flashing, amplified,
Impalpability reduced to speech,
Conception proved by birth, — no other change !
Can what Saint-Rambert flashed me in a
    thought,
Good gloomy London make a poem of ?
Such ought to be whatever dares precede,
Play ruddy herald-star to your white blaze
About to bring us day. How fail imbibe
Some foretaste of effulgence ? Sun shall wax,
And star shall wane : what matter, so star tell
The drowsy world to start awake, rub eyes,
And stand all ready for morn's joy a-blush ?

THE INN ALBUM

THE story told in this poem was suggested to
Browning, but not followed in all its details, by
an adventure of Lord De Ros, a friend of Wel-
lington's and mentioned frequently by Greville

in his *Memoirs*. The circumstances of De Ros's
villainy were much talked of in London at the
time of their occurrence, just before the middle
of this century.

I

" THAT oblong book's the Album ; hand it
    here !
Exactly ! page on page of gratitude
For breakfast, dinner, supper, and the view !
I praise these poets, they leave margin-space ;
Each stanza seems to gather skirts around,
And primly, trimly, keep the foot's confine,
Modest and maidlike ; lubber prose o'ersprawls
And straddling stops the path from left to right.
Since I want space to do my cipher-work,
Which poem spares a corner ? What comes
    first ?
' Hail, calm acclivity, salubrious spot ! '
(Open the window, we burn daylight, boy !)
Or see — succincter beauty, brief and bold —
' If a fellow can dine On rump-steaks and port
    wine,

He needs not despair Of dining well here ' —
' Here ! '   I myself could find a better rhyme !
That bard 's a Browning ; he neglects the form :
But ah, the sense, ye gods, the weighty sense !
Still, I prefer this classic. Ay, throw wide !
I 'll quench the bits of candle yet unburnt.
A minute's fresh air, then to cipher-work !
Three little columns hold the whole account :
Ecarté, after which Blind Hookey, then
Cutting-the-Pack, five hundred pounds the cut.
'T is easy reckoning : I have lost, I think."

Two personages occupy this room
Shabby-genteel, that 's parlor to the inn
Perched on a view-commanding eminence ;
— Inn which may be a veritable house
Where somebody once lived and pleased good
    taste
Till tourists found his coigne of vantage out,

And fingered blunt the individual mark,
And vulgarized things comfortably smooth.
On a sprig-pattern-papered wall there brays
Complaint to sky Sir Edwin's dripping stag;
His couchant coast-guard creature corresponds;
They face the Huguenot and Light o' the
     World.
Grim o'er the mirror on the mantelpiece,
Varnished and coffined, *Salmo ferox* glares,
— Possibly at the List of Wines which, framed
And glazed, hangs somewhat prominent on peg.

So much describes the stuffy little room —
Vulgar flat smooth respectability :
Not so the burst of landscape surging in,
Sunrise and all, as he who of the pair
Is, plain enough, the younger personage
Draws sharp the shrieking curtain, sends aloft
The sash, spreads wide and fastens back to wall
Shutter and shutter, shows you England's best.
He leans into a living glory-bath
Of air and light where seems to float and move
The wooded watered country, hill and dale
And steel-bright thread of stream, a-smoke
     with mist,
A-sparkle with May morning, diamond drift
O' the sun-touched dew.   Except the red-roofed
     patch
Of half a dozen dwellings that, crept close
For hillside shelter, make the village-clump,
This inn is perched above to dominate —
Except such sign of human neighborhood,
" And this surmised rather than sensible "
There's nothing to disturb absolute peace,
The reign of English nature — which means art
And civilized existence.   Wildness' self
Is just the cultured triumph.   Presently
Deep solitude, be sure, reveals a Place
That knows the right way to defend itself :
Silence hems round a burning spot of life.
Now, where a Place burns, must a village brood,
And where a village broods, an inn should
     boast—
Close and convenient : here you have them both.
This inn, the Something-arms — the family's —
(Don't trouble Guillim : heralds leave out half !)
Is dear to lovers of the picturesque,
And epics have been planned here ; but who plan
Take holy orders and find work to do.
Painters are more productive, stop a week,
Declare the prospect quite a Corot, — ay,
For tender sentiment,— themselves incline
Rather to handsweep large and liberal ;
Then go, but not without success achieved
— Haply some pencil-drawing, oak or beech,
Ferns at the base and ivies up the bole,
On this a slug, on that a butterfly.
Nay, he who hooked the *salmo* pendent here,
Also exhibited, this same May-month,
" *Foxgloves : a study* " — so inspires the scene,
The air, which now the younger personage
Inflates him with till lungs o'erfraught are fain
Sigh forth a satisfaction might bestir
Even those tufts of tree-tops to the South
I' the distance where the green dies off to gray,
Which, easy of conjecture, front the Place ;
He eyes them, elbows wide, each hand to
     cheek.

His fellow, the much older — either say
A youngish-old man or man oldish-young —
Sits at the table : wicks are noisome-deep
In wax, to detriment of plated ware ;
Above — piled, strewn — is store of playing
     cards,
Counters and all that's proper for a game.
He sets down, rubs out figures in the book,
Adds and subtracts, puts back here, carries
     there,
Until the summed-up satisfaction stands
Apparent, and he pauses o'er the work :
Soothes what of brain was busy under brow,
By passage of the hard palm, curing so
Wrinkle and crowfoot for a second's space ;
Then lays down book and laughs out.   No mis-
     take,
Such the sum-total — ask Colenso else !

Roused by which laugh, the other turns, laughs
     too —
The youth, the good strong fellow, rough per-
     haps.

" Well, what's the damage — three, or four, or
     five ?
How many figures in a row ? Hand here !
Come now, there's one expense all yours not
     mine —
Scribbling the people's Album over, leaf
The first and foremost too !   You think, per-
     haps,
They'll only charge you for a brand-new book
Nor estimate the literary loss ?
Wait till the small account comes !   ' *To one
     night's*
Lodging,' for — ',beds' they can't say, — '*pound
     or so ;*
Dinner, Apollinaris, — *what they please,*
Attendance not included ;' last looms large
' *Defacement of our Album, late enriched
With* ' — let's see what !   Here, at the window,
     though !
Ay, breathe the morning and forgive your
     luck !
Fine enough country for a fool like me
To own, as next month I suppose I shall !
Eh ?   True fool's-fortune ! so console yourself.
Let's see, however — hand the book, I say !
Well, you've improved the classic by romance.
Queer reading !   Verse with parenthetic prose —
' *Hail, calm acclivity, salubrious spot !* '
(Three-two fives) ' *life how profitably spent* '
(Five-naught, five-nine fives) ' *yonder humble cot ;*'
(More and more naughts and fives) ' *in mild
     content ;*
*And did my feelings find the natural vent
In friendship and in love, how blest my lot !* '
Then follow the dread figures — five !   ' *Con
     tent ?* '
That's appetite !   Are you content as he —
Simpkin the sonneteer ?   *Ten thousand pounds*
Give point to his effusion — by so much
Leave me the richer and the poorer you
After our night's play ; who's content the
     most,
If, you, or Simpkin ? "
               So the polished snob.

The elder man, refinement every inch
From brow to boot-end, quietly replies:

"Simpkin's no name I know. I had my whim."

"Ay, had you! And such things make friend-
ship thick.
Intimates, I may boast we were; henceforth,
Friends — shall it not be? — who discard re-
serve,
Use plain words, put each dot upon each i,
Till death us twain do part? The bargain's
struck!
Old fellow, if you fancy — (to begin —)
I failed to penetrate your scheme last week,
You wrong your poor disciple. Oh, no airs!
Because you happen to be twice my age
And twenty times my master, must perforce
No blink of daylight struggle through the web
There's no unwinding? You entoil my legs,
And welcome, for I like it: blind me, — no!
A very pretty piece of shuttle-work
Was that — your mere chance question at the
club —
' Do you go anywhere this Whitsuntide?
I'm off for Paris, there's the Opera — there's
The Salon, there's a china-sale, — beside
Chantilly; and, for good companionship,
There's Such-and-such and So-and-so. Suppose
We start together?' 'No such holiday!'
I told you: *'Paris and the rest be hanged!*
Why plague me who am pledged to home-de-
lights?
I'm the engaged now; through whose fault but
yours?
On duty. As you well know. Don't I drowse
The week away down with the Aunt and Niece?
No help: it's leisure, loneliness, and love.
'Wish I could take you; but fame travels fast, —
A man of much newspaper-paragraph,
You scare domestic circles; and beside
Would not you like your lot, that second taste
Of nature and approval of the grounds!
You might walk early or lie late, so shirk
Week-day devotions: but stay Sunday o'er,
And morning church is obligatory:
No mundane garb permissible, or dread
The butler's privileged monition! No!
Pack off to Paris, nor wipe tear away!'
Whereon how artlessly the happy flash
Followed, by inspiration! *''Tell you what —*
Let's turn their flank, try things on t' other side!
Inns for my money! Liberty's the life!
We'll lie in hiding: there's the crow-nest nook,
The tourist's joy, the Inn they rave about,
Inn that's out — out of sight and out of mind
And out of mischief to all four of us —
Aunt and niece, you and me. At night arrive;
At morn, find time for just a Pisgah-view
Of my friend's Land of Promise; then depart.
And while I'm whizzing onward by first train,
Bound for our own place (since my Brother sulks
And says I shun him like the plague) yourself —
Why, you have stepped thence, start from plat-
form, gay
Despite the sleepless journey, — love lends
wings, —
Hug aunt and niece who, none the wiser, wait

The faithful advent! Eh?' 'With all my
heart,'
Said I to you; said I to mine own self:
' Does he believe I fail to comprehend
He wants just one more final friendly snack
At friend's exchequer ere friend runs to earth,
Marries, renounces yielding friends such sport?'
And did I spoil sport, pull face grim, — nay,
grave?
Your pupil does you better credit! No!
I parleyed with my pass-book, — rubbed my
pair
At the big balance in my banker's hands, —
Folded a check cigar-case-shape, — just wants
Filling and signing, — and took train, resolved
To execute myself with decency
And let you win — if not Ten thousand quite,
Something by way of wind-up-farewell burst
Of firework-nosegay! Where's your fortune
fled?
Or is not fortune constant after all?
You lose ten thousand pounds: had I lost half
Or half that, I should bite my lips, I think.
You man of marble! Strut and stretch my best
On tiptoe, I shall never reach your height.
How does the loss feel! Just one lesson more!"

The more refined man smiles a frown away.

"The lesson shall be — only boys like you
Put such a question at the present stage.
I had a ball lodge in my shoulder once,
And, full five minutes, never guessed the fact;
Next day, I felt decidedly: and still,
At twelve years' distance, when I lift my arm
A twinge reminds me of the surgeon's probe.
Ask me, this day month, how I feel my luck!
And meantime please to stop impertinence,
For — don't I know its object? All this chaff
Covers the corn, this preface leads to speech,
This boy stands forth a hero. *'There, my lord!*
Our play was true play, fun not earnest! I
Empty your purse, inside out, while my poke
Bulges to bursting! You can badly spare
A doit, confess now, Duke though brother be!
While I'm gold-daubed so thickly, spangles
drop
And show my father's warehouse-apron: pshaw!
Enough! We've had a palpitating night!
Good morning! Breakfast and forget our
dreams!
My mouth's shut, mind! I tell nor man nor
mouse.'
There, see! He don't deny it! Thanks, my boy!
Hero and welcome — only, not on me
Make trial of your 'prentice-hand! Enough!
We've played, I've lost and owe ten thousand
pounds,
Whereof I muster, at the moment, — well,
What's for the bill here and the back to town.
Still, I've my little character to keep;
You may expect your money at month's end."

The young man at the window turns round
quick —
A clumsy giant handsome creature; grasps
In his large red the little lean white hand
Of the other, looks him in the sallow face.

" I say now — is it right to so mistake
A fellow, force him in mere self-defence
To spout like Mister *Mild Acclivity*
In album-language ? You know well enough
Whether I like you — *like* 's no album-word,
Anyhow : point me to one soul beside
In the wide world I care one straw about !
I first set eyes on you a year ago ;
Since when you 've done me good — I 'll stick to
  it —
More than I got in the whole twenty-five
That make my life up, Oxford years and all —
Throw in the three I fooled away abroad,
Seeing myself and nobody more sage
Until I met you, and you made me man
Such as the sort is and the fates allow.
I do think, since we two kept company,
I 've learnt to know a little — all through you !
It 's nature if I like you. Taunt away !
As if I need you teaching me my place —
The snob I am, the Duke your brother is,
When just the good you did was — teaching me
My own trade, how a snob and millionaire
May lead his life and let the Duke's alone,
Clap wings, free jackdaw, on his steeple-perch,
Burnish his black to gold in sun and air,
Nor pick up stray plumes, strive to match in
  strut
Regular peacocks who can't fly an inch
Over the courtyard-paling. Head and heart
(That 's album-style) are older than you know,
For all your knowledge : boy, perhaps — ay, boy
Had his adventure, just as he were man —
His ball-experience in the shoulder-blade,
His bit of life-long ache to recognize,
Although he bears it cheerily about,
Because you came and clapped him on the back,
Advised him ' *Walk and wear the aching off ! '*
Why, I was minded to sit down for life
Just in Dalmatia, build a seaside tower
High on a rock, and so expend my days
Pursuing chemistry or botany
Or, very like, astronomy because
I noticed stars shone when I passed the place :
Letting my cash accumulate the while
In England — to lay out in lump at last
As Ruskin should direct me ! All or some
Of which should I have done or tried to do,
And preciously repented, one fine day,
Had you discovered Timon, climbed his rock
And scaled his tower, some ten years thence,
  suppose,
And coaxed his story from him ! Don't I see
The pair conversing ! It 's a novel writ
Already, I 'll be bound, — our dialogue !
' *What ? '* cried the elder and yet youthful man —
So did the eye flash 'neath the lordly front,
And the imposing presence swell with scorn,
As the haught high-bred bearing and dispose
Contrasted with his interlocutor
The flabby low-born who, of bulk before,
Had steadily increased, one stone per week,
Since his abstention from horse-exercise : —
' *What ? you, as rich as Rothschild, left, you say*
London the very year you came of age,
Because your father manufactured goods —
Commission-agent hight of Manchester —
Partly, and partly through a baby case

Of disappointment I 've pumped out at last —
And here you spend life's prime in gaining flesh
And giving science one more asteroid ? '
Brief, my dear fellow, you instructed me,
At Alfred's and not Istria ! proved a snob
May turn a million to account although
His brother be no Duke, and see good days
Without the girl he lost and some one gained.
The end is, after one year's tutelage,
Having, by your help, touched society,
Polo, Tent-pegging, Hurlingham, the Rink —
I leave all these delights, by your advice,
And marry my young pretty cousin here
Whose place, whose oaks ancestral you behold.
(Her father was in partnership with mine —
Does not his purchase look a pedigree ?)
My million will be tails and tassels smart
To this plump-bodied kite, this house and land
Which, set a-soaring, pulls me, soft as sleep,
Along life's pleasant meadow, — arm left free
To lock a friend's in, — whose, but yours, old
  boy ?
Arm in arm glide we over rough and smooth,
While hand, to pocket held, saves cash from
  cards.
Now, if you don't esteem ten thousand pounds
(— Which I shall probably discover snug
Hid somewhere in the column-corner capped
With ' *Credit,*' based on ' *Balance,*' — which, I
  swear,
By this time next month I shall quite forget
Whether I lost or won — ten thousand pounds,
Which at this instant I would give . . . let 's
  see,
For Galopin — nay, for that Gainsborough
Sir Richard won't sell, and, if bought by me,
Would get my glance and praise some twice a
  year, —)
Well, if you don't esteem that price dirt-cheap
For teaching me Dalmatia was mistake —
Why then, my last illusion-bubble breaks,
My one discovered phœnix proves a goose,
My cleverest of all companions — oh,
Was worth nor ten pence nor ten thousand
  pounds !
Come ! Be yourself again ! So endeth here
The morning's lesson ! Never while life lasts
Do I touch card again. To breakfast now !
To bed — I can't say, since you needs must
  start
For station early — oh, the down-train still,
First plan and best plan — townward trip be
  hanged !
You 're due at your big brother's — pay that
  debt,
Then owe me not a farthing ! Order eggs —
And who knows but there 's trout obtainable ? "

The fine man looks wellnigh malignant : then —

" Sir, please subdue your manner ! Debts are
  debts :
I pay mine — debts of this sort — certainly.
What do I care how you regard your gains,
Want them or want them not ? The thing I
  want
Is — not to have a story circulate
From club to club — how, bent on clearing out,

Young So-and-so, young So-and-so cleaned me,
Then set the empty kennel flush again,
Ignored advantage and forgave his friend —
For why ? There was no wringing blood from
    stone !
Oh, don't be savage ! You would hold your
    tongue,
Bite it in two, as man may ; but those small
Hours in the smoking-room, when instance apt
Rises to tongue's root, tingles on to tip,
And the thinned company consists of six
Capital well-known fellows one may trust !
Next week, it 's in the ' World.' No, thank you
    much.
I owe ten thousand pounds : I 'll pay them ! "

                  " Now, —
This becomes funny. You 've made friends
    with me :
I can't help knowing of the ways and means !
Or stay ! they say your brother closets up
Correggio's long lost Leda : if he means
To give you that, and if you give it me " . . .

" *I* polished snob off to aristocrat ?
You compliment me ! father's apron still
Sticks out from son's court-vesture ; still silk
    purse
Roughs finger with some bristle sow-ear-born !
Well, neither I nor you mean harm at heart !
I owe you and shall pay you : which premised,
Why should what follows sound like flattery ?
The fact is — you do compliment too much
Your humble master, as I own I am ;
You owe me no such thanks as you protest.
The polisher needs precious stone no less
Than precious stone needs polisher : believe
I struck no tint from out you but I found
Snug lying first 'neath surface hairbreadth-deep !
Beside, I liked the exercise : with skill
Goes love to show skill for skill's sake. You
    see,
I 'm old and understand things : too absurd
It were you pitched and tossed away your life,
As diamond were Scotch-pebble ! all the more,
That I myself misused a stone of price.
Born and bred clever — people used to say
Clever as most men, if not something more —
Yet here I stand a failure, cut awry
Or left opaque, — no brilliant named and known.
Whate'er my inner stuff, my outside 's blank ;
I 'm nobody — or rather, look that same —
I 'm — who I am — and know it ; but I hold
What in my hand out for the world to see ?
What ministry, what mission, or what book
— I 'll say, book even ? Not a sign of these !
I began — laughing — '*All these when I like !* '
I end with — well, you 've hit it ! — ' *This boy's
    check
For just as many thousands as he 'll spare !* '
The first — I could, and would not ; your spare
    cash
I would, and could not : have no scruple, pray,
But, as I hoped to pocket yours, pouch mine
— When you are able ! ' "

            " Which is — when to be ?
I 've heard, great characters require a fall

Of fortune to show greatness by uprise :
They touch the ground to jollily rebound,
Add to the Album ! Let a fellow share
Your secret of superiority !
I know, my banker makes the money breed
Money ; I eat and sleep, he simply takes
The dividends and cuts the coupons off,
Sells out, buys in, keeps doubling, tripling cash.
While I do nothing but receive and spend.
But you, spontaneous generator, hatch
A wind-egg ; cluck, and forth struts Capital
As Interest to me from egg of gold.
I am grown curious : pay me by all means !
How will you make the money ? "

            " Mind your own -
Not my affair. Enough : or money, or
Money's worth, as the case may be, expect
Ere month's end, — keep but patient for a
    month !
Who 's for a stroll to station ? Ten 's the time ;
Your man, with my things, follow in the trap ;
At stoppage of the down-train, play the arrived
On platform, and you 'll show the due fatigue
Of the night-journey, — not much sleep, — per-
    haps,
Your thoughts were on before you — yes, in-
    deed,
You join them, being happily awake
With thought's sole object as she smiling sits
At breakfast-table. I shall dodge meantime
In and out station-precinct, wile away
The hour till up my engine pants and smokes.
No doubt, she goes to fetch you. Never fear !
She gets no glance at me, who shame such
    saints ! "

              II

So, they ring bell, give orders, pay, depart
Amid profuse acknowledgment from host
Who well knows what may bring the younger
    back.
They light cigar, descend in twenty steps
The " *calm acclivity*," inhale — beyond
Tobacco's balm — the better smoke of turf
And wood fire, — cottages at cookery
I' the morning, — reach the main road straight-
    ening on
'Twixt wood and wood, two black walls full of
    night
Slow to disperse, though mists thin fast before
The advancing foot, and leave the flint-dust
    fine
Each speck with its fire-sparkle. Presently
The road's end with the sky's beginning mix
In one magnificence of glare, due East,
So high the sun rides, — May 's the merry
    month.

They slacken pace : the younger stops abrupt,
Discards cigar, looks his friend full in face.

" All right ; the station comes in view at end ;
Five minutes from the beech-clump, there you
    are !
I say : let 's halt, let 's borrow yonder gate
Of its two magpies, sit and have a talk ! "

Do let a fellow speak a moment ! More
I think about and less I like the thing —
No, you must let me ! Now, be good for once !
Ten thousand pounds be done for, dead and
    damned !
We played for love, not hate : yes, hate ! I hate
Thinking you beg or borrow or reduce
To strychnine some poor devil of a lord
Licked at Unlimited Loo. I had the cash
To lose — you knew that !— lose and none the
    less
Whistle to-morrow : it 's not every chap
Affords to take his punishment so well !
Now, don't be angry with a friend whose fault
Is that he thinks — upon my soul, I do —
Your head the best head going. Oh, one sees
Names in the newspaper — great This, great
    That,
Gladstone, Carlyle, the Laureate : — much I
    care !
Others have their opinion, I keep mine :
Which means — by right you ought to have the
    things
I want a head for. Here 's a pretty place,
My cousin's place, and presently my place,
Not yours ! I 'll tell you how it strikes a man.
My cousin 's fond of music and of course
Plays the piano (it won't be for long !)
A brand-new bore she calls a ' *semi-grand* '
Rosewood and pearl, that blocks the drawing-
    room,
And cost no end of money. Twice a week
Down comes Herr Somebody and seats him-
    self,
Sets to work teaching — with his teeth on
    edge —
I 've watched the rascal. ' *Does he play first-
    rate ?* '
I ask : ' *I rather think so,*' answers she —
' *He 's What 's-his-Name !* ' — ' *Why give you
    lessons then ?* ' —
' *I pay three guineas and the train beside.*' —
' *This instrument, has he one such at home ?* ' —
' *He ? Has to practise on a table-top,
When he can't hire the proper thing.*' — ' *I see !
You* 've the piano, he the skill, and God
The distribution of such gifts.*' So here :
After your teaching, I shall sit and strum
Polkas on this piano of a Place
You 'd make resound with ' *Rule Britannia* ' ! ''

         '' Thanks !
I don't say but this pretty cousin's place,
Appendaged with your million, tempts my
    hand
As key-board I might touch with some effect.''

'' Then, why not have obtained the like ?
    House, land,
Money, are things obtainable, you see,
By clever head-work : ask my father else !
You, who teach me, why not have learned,
    yourself ?
Played like Herr Somebody with power to
    thump
And flourish and the rest, not bend demure
Pointing out blunders — ' *Sharp, not natural !
Permit me — on the black key use the thumb !* '

There 's some fatality, I 'm sure ! You say
' *Marry the cousin, that 's your proper move !* '
And I do use the thumb and hit the sharp :
You should have listened to your own head's
    hint,
As I to you ! The puzzle 's past my power,
How you have managed — with such stuff, such
    means —
Not to be rich nor great nor happy man :
Of which three good things where 's a sign at
    all ?
Just look at Dizzy ! Come, — what tripped
    your heels ?
Instruct a goose that boasts wings and can't
    fly !
I wager I have guessed it ! — never found
The old solution of the riddle fail !
' *Who was the woman ?*' I don't ask, but —
    ' *Where
I' the path of life stood she who tripped you ?* ' ''

                '' Goose
You truly are ! I own to fifty years.
Why don't I interpose and cut out — you ?
Compete with five - and - twenty ? Age, my
    boy ! ''

'' Old man, no nonsense ! — even to a boy
That 's ripe at least for rationality
Rapped into him, as maybe mine was, once !
I 've had my small adventure lesson me
Over the knuckles ! — likely, I forget
The sort of figure youth cuts now and then,
Competing with old shoulders but young head
Despite the fifty grizzling years ! ''

                '' Aha ?
Then that means — just the bullet in the blade
Which brought Dalmatia on the brain, — that,
    too,
Came of a fatal creature ? Can't pretend
Now for the first time to surmise as much !
Make a clean breast ! Recount ! a secret 's
    safe
'Twixt you, me, and the gate-post ! ''

             '' — Can't pretend,
Neither, to never have surmised your wish !
It 's no use, — case of unextracted ball —
Winces at finger-touching. Let things be ! ''

'' Ah, if you love your love still ! I hate
    mine.''

'' I can't hate.''

         '' I won't teach you ; and won't tell
You, therefore, what you please to ask of me :
As if I, also, may not have my ache ! ''

'' My sort of ache ? No, no ! and yet — per-
    haps !
All comes of thinking you superior still.
But live and learn ! I say ! Time 's up !
    Good jump !
You old, indeed ! I fancy there 's a cut
Across the wood, a grass-path : shall we try ?
It 's venturesome, however ! ''

"Stop, my boy!
Don't think I 'm stingy of experience! Life
— It 's like this wood we leave. Should you
and I
Go wandering about there, though the gaps
We went in and came out by were opposed
As the two poles still, somehow, all the same
By nightfall we should probably have chanced
On much the same main points of interest —
Both of us measured girth of mossy trunk,
Stript ivy from its strangled prey, clapped
hands
At squirrel, sent a fir-cone after crow,
And so forth, — never mind what time betwixt.
So in our lives; allow I entered mine
Another way than you: 't is possible
I ended just by knocking head against
That plaguy low-hung branch yourself began
By getting bump from; as at last you too
May stumble o'er that stump which first of all
Bade me walk circumspectly. Head and feet
Are vulnerable both, and I, foot-sure,
Forgot that ducking down saves brow from
bruise.
I, early old, played young man four years since
And failed confoundedly: so, hate alike
Failure and who caused failure, — curse her
cant!"

"Oh, I see! You, though somewhat past the
prime,
Were taken with a rosebud beauty! Ah —
But how should chits distinguish? She admired
Your marvel of a mind, I 'll undertake!
But as to body . . . nay, I mean . . . that is,
When years have told on face and figure" . . .

"Thanks,
Mister *Sufficiently-Instructed!* Such
No doubt was bound to be the consequence
To suit your self-complacency: she liked
My head enough, but loved some heart beneath
Some head with plenty of brown hair a-top
After my young friend's fashion! What be-
comes
Of that fine speech you made a minute since
About the man of middle age you found
A formidable peer at twenty-one?
So much for your mock-modesty! and yet
I back your first against this second sprout
Of observation, insight, what you please.
My middle age, Sir, had too much success!
It 's odd : my case occurred four years ago —
I finished just while you commenced that turn
I' the wood of life that takes us to the wealth
Of honeysuckle, heaped for who can reach.
Now, I don't boast: it's bad style, and beside,
The feat proves easier than it looks: I plucked
Full many a flower unnamed in that bouquet
(Mostly of peonies and poppies, though!)
Good-nature sticks into my buttonhole.
Therefore it was with nose in want of snuff
Rather than Ess or Psidium, that I chanced
On what — so far from 'rosebud beauty' . . .
Well —
She 's dead: at least you never heard her name;
She was no courtly creature, had nor birth
Nor breeding — mere fine-lady-breeding: but

Oh, such a wonder of a woman! Grand
As a Greek statue! Stick fine clothes on that,
Style that a Duchess or a Queen, — you know,
Artists would make an outcry: all the more,
That she had just a statue's sleepy grace
Which broods o'er its own beauty. Nay, her
fault
(Don't laugh!) was just perfection: for suppose
Only the little flaw, and I had peeped
Inside it, learned what soul inside was like.
At Rome some tourist raised the grit beneath
A Venus' forehead with his whittling-knife —
I wish — now — I had played that brute,
brought blood
To surface from the depths I fancied chalk!
As it was, her mere face surprised so much
That I stopped short there, struck on heap, as
stares
The cockney stranger at a certain bust
With drooped eyes, — she 's the thing I have in
mind, —
Down at my Brother's. All sufficient prize —
Such outside! Now, — confound me for a
prig! —
Who cares? I 'll make a clean breast once for
all!
Beside, you 've heard the gossip. My life long
I 've been a woman-liker, — liking means
Loving and so on. There 's a lengthy list
By this time I shall have to answer for —
So say the good folk: and they don't guess
half —
For the worst is, let once collecting-itch
Possess you, and, with perspicacity,
Keeps growing such a greediness that theft
Follows at no long distance, — there 's the fact!
I knew that on my Leporello-list
Might figure this, that, and the other name
Of feminine desirability,
But if I happened to desire inscribe,
Along with these, the only Beautiful —
Here was the unique specimen to snatch
Or now or never. 'Beautiful' I said —
'Beautiful' say in cold blood, — boiling then
To tune of ' *Haste, secure whate'er the cost
This rarity, die in the act, be damned,
So you complete collection, crown your list!* '
It seemed as though the whole world, once
aroused
By the first notice of such wonder's birth,
Would break bounds to contest my prize with
me
The first discoverer, should she but emerge
From that safe den of darkness where she dozed
Till I stole in, that country-parsonage
Where, country-parson's daughter, motherless,
Brotherless, sisterless, for eighteen years
She had been vegetating lily-like.
Her father was my brother's tutor, got
The living that way: him I chanced to see —
Her I saw — her the world would grow one eye
To see, I felt no sort of doubt at all!
' *Secure her!* ' cried the devil: ' *afterward
Arrange for the disposal of the prize!* '
The devil's doing! yet I seem to think —
Now, when all 's done, — think with ' *a head
reposed* '
In French phrase — hope I think I meant to do

All requisite for such a rarity
When I should be at leisure, have due time
To learn requirement. But in evil day —
Bless me, at week's end, long as any year,
The father must begin, ' *Young Somebody,*
Much recommended — for I break a rule —
Comes here to read, next Long Vacation.' —
' *Young !* '
That did it. Had the epithet been ' *rich,*'
' *Noble,*' ' *a genius,*' even ' *handsome,*' — but
— ' *Young* ' *!* "

" I say — just a word ! I want to know —
You are not married ? "

"I ? "

" Nor ever were ? "

" Never ! Why ? "

" Oh, then — never mind ! Go on !
I had a reason for the question."

" Come, —
You could not be the young man ? "

" No, indeed !
Certainly — if you never married her ! "

" That I did not : and there 's the curse, you 'll
see !
Nay, all of it 's one curse, my life's mistake
Which nourished with manure that 's war-
ranted
To make the plant bear wisdom, blew out full
In folly beyond fieldflower-foolishness !
The lies I used to tell my womankind !
Knowing they disbelieved me all the time
Though they required my lies, their decent
due,
This woman — not so much believed, I 'll say,
As just anticipated from my mouth :
Since being true, devoted, constant — she
Found constancy, devotion, truth, the plain
And easy commonplace of character.
No mock-heroics but seemed natural
To her who underneath the face, I knew
Was fairness' self, possessed a heart, I judged
Must correspond in folly just as far
Beyond the common, — and a mind to match, —
Not made to puzzle conjurers like me
Who, therein, proved the fool who fronts you,
Sir,
And begs leave to cut short the ugly rest !
' *Trust me !* ' I said : she trusted. ' *Marry me !* '
Or rather, ' *We are married: when, the rite ?* '
That brought on the collector's next-day qualm
At counting acquisition's cost. There lay
My marvel, there my purse more light by much
Because of its late lie-expenditure :
Ill-judged such moment to make fresh de-
mand —
To cage as well as catch my rarity !
So, I began explaining. At first word
Outbroke the horror. ' *Then, my truths were*
lies ! '
I tell you, such an outbreak, such new strange

All-unsuspected revelation — soul
As supernaturally grand as face
Was fair beyond example — that at once
Either I lost — or, if it please you, found
My senses, — stammered somehow — ' *Jest ! and*
now,
Earnest ! *Forget all else but — heart has loved,*
Does love, shall love you ever ! *take the hand !*'
Not she ! no marriage for superb disdain,
Contempt incarnate ! "

" Yes, it 's different, —
It 's only like in being four years since.
I see now ! "

" Well, what did disdain do next,
Think you ? "

" That 's past me : did not marry you ! —
That 's the main thing I care for, I suppose.
Turned nun, or what ? "

" Why, married in a month
Some parson, some smug crop-haired smooth-
chinned sort
Of curate-creature, I suspect, — dived down,
Down, deeper still, and came up somewhere
else —
I don't know where — I 've not tried much to
know,
In short, she 's happy : what the clodpoles call
' Countrified ' with a vengeance ! leads the life
Respectable and all that drives you mad :
Still — where, I don't know, and that 's best
for both."

" Well, that she did not like you, I conceive.
But why should you hate her, I want to
know ? "

" My good young friend, — because or her or
else
Malicious Providence I have to hate.
For, what I tell you proved the turning-point
Of my whole life and fortune toward success
Or failure. If I drown, I lay the fault
Much on myself who caught at reed not rope,
But more on reed which, with a packthread's
pith,
Had buoyed me till the minute's cramp could
thaw
And I strike out afresh and so be saved.
It 's easy saying — I had sunk before,
Disqualified myself by idle days
And busy nights, long since, from holding hard
On cable, even, had fate cast me such !
You boys don't know how many times men fail
Perforce o' the little to succeed i' the large,
Husband their strength, let slip the petty prey,
Collect the whole power for the final pounce !
My fault was the mistaking man's main prize
For intermediate boy's diversion ; clap
Of boyish hands here frightened game away
Which, once gone, goes forever. Oh, at first
I took the anger easily, nor much
Minded the anguish — having learned that
storms
Subside and teapot-tempests are akin.

Time would arrange things, mend whate'er
    might be
Somewhat amiss; precipitation, eh?
Reason and rhyme prompt — reparation! Tiffs
End properly in marriage and a dance!
I said 'We'll marry, make the past a blank' —
And never was such damnable mistake!
That interview, that laying bare my soul,
As it was first, so was it last chance — one
And only. Did I write? Back letter came
Unopened as it went. Inexorable
She fled, I don't know where, consoled herself
With the smug curate-creature: chop and
    change!
Sure am I, when she told her shaveling all
His Magdalen's adventure, tears were shed,
Forgiveness evangelically shown,
'Loose hair and lifted eye,' — as some one says.
And now, he's worshipped for his pains, the
    sneak!"

"Well, but your turning-point of life, — what's
    here
To hinder you contesting Finsbury
With Orton, next election? I don't see" . . .

"Not you! But *I* see. Slowly, surely, creeps
Day by day o'er me the conviction — here
Was life's prize grasped at, gained, and then
    let go!
— That with her — maybe, for her — I had felt
Ice in me melt, grow steam, drive to effect
Any or all the fancies sluggish here
I' the head that needs the hand she would not
    take
And I shall never lift now. Lo, your wood —
Its turnings which I likened life to! Well, —
There she stands, ending every avenue,
Her visionary presence on each goal
I might have gained had we kept side by side!
Still string nerve and strike foot? Her frown
    forbids:
The steam congeals once more: I'm old
    again!
Therefore I hate myself — but how much
    worse
Do not I hate who would not understand,
Let me repair things — no, but sent a-slide
My folly falteringly, stumblingly
Down, down, and deeper down until I drop
Upon — the need of your ten thousand pounds
And consequently loss of mine! I lose
Character, cash, nay, common-sense itself
Recounting such a lengthy cock-and-bull
Adventure, lose my temper in the act" . . .

"And lose beside, — if I may supplement
The list of losses, — train and ten-o'clock!
Hark, pant and puff, there travels the swart
    sign!
So much the better! You're my captive now!
I'm glad you trust a fellow: friends grow
    thick
This way — that's twice said; we were thick-
    ish, though,
Even last night, and, ere night comes again,
I prophesy good luck to both of us!
For see now! — back to 'balmy eminence'

Or '*calm acclivity*' or what's the word!
Bestow you there an hour, concoct at ease
A sonnet for the Album, while I put
Bold face on, best foot forward, make for
    house,
March in to aunt and niece, and tell the
    truth —
(Even white-lying goes against my taste
After your little story.) Oh, the niece
Is rationality itself! The aunt —
If she's amenable to reason too —
Why, you stopped short to pay her due respect,
And let the Duke wait (I'll work well the
    Duke).
If she grows gracious, I return for you;
If thunder's in the air, why — bear your doom,
Dine on rump-steaks and port, and shake the
    dust
Of aunty from your shoes as off you go
By evening-train, nor give the thing a thought
How you shall pay me — that's as sure as fate,
Old fellow! Off with you, face left about!
Yonder's the path I have to pad. You see,
I'm in good spirits, God knows why! Perhaps
Because the woman did not marry you
— Who look so hard at me, — and have the
    right,
One must be fair and own."

                              The two stand still
Under an oak.

              "Look here!" resumes the youth.
"I never quite knew how I came to like
You — so much — whom I ought not court at
    all:
Nor how you had a leaning just to me
Who am assuredly not worth your pains,
For there must needs be plenty such as you
Somewhere about, — although I can't say
    where, —
Able and willing to teach all you know;
While — how can you have missed a score like
    me
With money and no wit, precisely each
A pupil for your purpose, were it — ease
Fool's poke of tutor's *honorarium*-fee?
And yet, howe'er it came about, I felt
At once my master : you as prompt descried
Your man, I warrant, so was bargain struck.
Now, these same lines of liking, loving, run
Sometimes so close together they converge —
Life's great adventures — you know what I
    mean —
In people. Do you know, as you advanced,
It got to be uncommonly like fact
We two had fallen in with — liked and loved
Just the same woman in our different ways?
I began life — poor groundling as I prove —
Winged and ambitious to fly high: why not?
There's something in 'Don Quixote' to the
    point,
My shrewd old father used to quote and
    praise —
'*Am I born man?*' asks Sancho; '*being man,
By possibility I may be Pope!*'
So, Pope I meant to make myself, by step
And step, whereof the first should be to find

A perfect woman; and I tell you this —
If what I fixed on, in the order due
Of undertakings, as next step, had first
Of all disposed itself to suit my tread,
And I had been, the day I came of age,
Returned at head of poll for Westminster
— Nay, and moreover summoned by the Queen
At week's end, when my maiden-speech bore
        fruit,
To form and head a Tory ministry —
It would not have seemed stranger, no, nor
        been
More strange to me, as now I estimate,
Than what did happen — sober truth, no dream.
I saw my wonder of a woman, — laugh,
I 'm past that ! — in Commemoration-week.
A plenty have I seen since, fair and foul, —
With eyes, too, helped by your sagacious wink ;
But one to match that marvel — no least trace,
Least touch of kinship and community !
The end was — I did somehow state the fact,
Did, with no matter what imperfect words,
One way or other give to understand
That woman, soul and body were her slave
Would she but take, but try them — any test
Of will, and some poor test of power beside :
So did the strings within my brain grow tense
And capable of . . . hang similitudes !
She answered kindly but beyond appeal.
' No sort of hope for me, who came too late.
She was another's. Love went — mine to her,
Hers just as loyally to some one else.'
Of course ! I might expect it ! Nature's law —
Given the peerless woman, certainly
Somewhere shall be the peerless man to match !
I acquiesced at once, submitted me
In something of a stupor, went my way.
I fancy there had been some talk before
Of somebody — her father or the like —
To coach me in the holidays, — that 's how
I came to get the sight and speech of her, —
But I had sense enough to break off sharp,
Save both of us the pain."

                    " Quite right there ! "

                                " Eh ?
Quite wrong, it happens ! Now comes worst of
        all !
Yes, I did sulk aloof and let alone
The lovers — I disturb the angel-mates ? "

" Seraph paired off with cherub ! "

                        " Thank you ! While
I never plucked up courage to inquire
Who he was, even, — certain-sure of this,
That nobody I knew of had blue wings
And wore a star-crown as he needs must do, —
Some little lady, — plainish, pock-marked girl, —
Finds out my secret in my woeful face,
Comes up to me at the Apollo Ball,
And pityingly pours her wine and oil
This way into the wound : ' Dear f-f-friend,
Why waste affection thus on — must I say,
A somewhat worthless object ? Who 's her choice —
Irrevocable as deliberate —
Out of the wide world ? I shall name no names —

But there 's a person in society,
Who, blessed with rank and talent, has grown
        gray
In idleness and sin of every sort
Except hypocrisy : he 's thrice her age,
A byword for ' successes with the sex '
As the French say — and, as we ought to say,
Consummately a liar and a rogue,
Since — show me where 's the woman won without
The help of this one lie which she believes —
That — never mind how things have come to pass,
And let who loves have loved a thousand times —
All the same he now loves her only, loves
Her ever ! if by ' won ' you just mean ' sold,'
That 's quite another compact. Well, this scamp,
Continuing descent from bad to worse,
Must leave his fine and fashionable prey
(Who — fathered, brothered, husbanded, — are
        hedged
About with thorny danger) and apply
His arts to this poor country ignorance
Who sees forthwith in the first rag of man
Her model hero ! Why continue waste
On such a woman treasures of a heart
Would yet find solace, — yes, my f-f-friend —
In some congenial — fiddle-diddle-dee ? ' "

" Pray, is the pleasant gentleman described
Exact the portrait which my ' f-f-friends '
Recognize as so like ? 'T is evident
You half surmised the sweet original
Could be no other than myself, just now !
Your stop and start were flattering ! "

                            " Of course
Caricature 's allowed for in a sketch !
The longish nose becomes a foot in length,
The swarthy cheek gets copper-colored, — still,
Prominent beak and dark-hued skin are facts :
And ' parson's daughter ' — ' young man coach-
        able ' —
' Elderly party ' — ' four years since ' — were facts
To fasten on, a moment ! Marriage, though —
That made the difference, I hope."

                            " All right !
I never married ; wish I had — and then
Unwish it : people kill their wives, sometimes !
I hate my mistress, but I 'm murder-free.
In your case, where 's the grievance ? You
        came last,
The earlier bird picked up the worm. Suppose
You, in the glory of your twenty-one,
Had happened to precede myself ! 't is odds
But this gigantic juvenility,
This offering of a big arm's bony hand —
I 'd rather shake than feel shake me, I know —
Had moved my dainty mistress to admire
An altogether new Ideal — deem
Idolatry less due to life's decline
Productive of experience, powers mature
By dint of usage, the made man — no boy
That 's all to make ! I was the earlier bird —
And what I found, I let fall ; what you missed,
Who is the fool that blames you for ? "

                            " Myself —
For nothing, everything ! For finding out

She, whom I worshipped, was a worshipper
In turn of . . . but why stir up settled mud?
She married him — the fifty-years-old rake —
How you have teased the talk from me! At
    last
My secret 's told you. I inquired no more,
Nay, stopped ears when informants unshut
    mouth;
Enough that she and he live, deuce take where,
Married and happy, or else miserable —
It 's 'Cut-the-pack;' she turned up ace or
    knave,
And I left Oxford, England, dug my hole
Out in Dalmatia, till you drew me thence
Badger-like, — ' Back to London ' was the
    word —
' Do things, a many, there, you fancy hard,
I 'll undertake are easy ! ' — the advice.
I took it, had my twelvemonth's fling with
    you —
(Little hand holding large hand pretty tight
For all its delicacy — eh, my lord ?)
Until when, t' other day, I got a turn
Somehow and gave up tired : and ' Rest ! ' bade
    you,
' Marry your cousin, double your estate,
And take your ease by all means ! ' So, I loll
On this the springy sofa, mine next month —
Or should loll, but that you must needs beat
    rough
The very down you spread me out so smooth.
I wish this confidence were still to make !
Ten thousand pounds ? You owe me twice the
    sum
For stirring up the black depths ! There 's
    repose
Or, at least, silence when misfortune seems
All that one has to bear ; but folly — yes,
Folly, it all was ! Fool to be so meek,
So humble, — such a coward rather say !
Fool, to adore the adorer of a fool !
Not to have faced him, tried (a useful hint)
My big and bony, here, against the bunch
Of lily-colored five with signet-ring,
Most like, for little-finger's sole defence —
Much as you flaunt the blazon there ! I grind
My teeth, that bite my very heart, to think —
To know I might have made that woman mine
But for the folly of the coward — know —
Or what 's the good of my apprenticeship
This twelvemonth to a master in the art ?
Mine — had she been mine — just one moment
    mine
For honor, for dishonor — anyhow,
So that my life, instead of stagnant . . . Well,
You 've poked and proved stagnation is not
    sleep —
Hang you ! "

            " Hang you for an ungrateful goose !
All this means — I who since I knew you first
Have helped you to conceit yourself this cock
O' the dunghill with all hens to pick and
    choose —
Ought to have helped you when shell first was
    chipped
By chick that wanted prompting ' Use the spur ! '
While I was elsewhere putting mine to use.

As well might I blame you who kept aloof,
Seeing you could not guess I was alive,
Never advised me ' Do as I have done —
Reverence such a jewel as your luck
Has scratched up to enrich unworthiness ! '
As your behavior was, should mine have been,
— Faults which we both, too late, are sorry for:
Opposite ages, each with its mistake :
' If youth but would — if age but could,' you know.
Don't let us quarrel ! Come, we 're — young
    and old —
Neither so badly off. Go you your way,
Cut to the Cousin ! I 'll to Inn, await
The issue of diplomacy with Aunt,
And wait my hour on ' calm acclivity '
In rumination manifold — perhaps
About ten thousand pounds I have to pay ! "

III

Now, as the elder lights the fresh cigar
Conducive to resource, and saunteringly
Betakes him to the left-hand backward path, —
While, much sedate, the younger strides away
To right and makes for — islanded in lawn
And edged with shrubbery — the brilliant bit
Of Barry's building that 's the Place, — a pair
Of women, at this nick of time, one young,
One very young, are ushered with due pomp
Into the same Inn-parlor — " disengaged
Entirely now ! " the obsequious landlord smiles,
" Since the late occupants — whereof but one
Was quite a stranger " — (smile enforced by
    bow)
" Left, a full two hours since, to catch the train,
Probably for the stranger's sake ! "   (Bow, smile,
And backing out from door soft-closed behind.)

Woman and girl, the two, alone inside,
Begin their talk : the girl, with sparkling eyes —
" Oh, I forewent him purposely ! but you,
Who joined at — journeyed from the Junction
    here —
I wonder how he failed your notice. Few
Stop at our station : fellow-passengers
Assuredly you were — I saw indeed
His servant, therefore he arrived all right.
I wanted, you know why, to have you safe
Inside here first of all, so dodged about
The dark end of the platform ; that 's his
    way —
To swing from station straight to avenue
And stride the half a mile for exercise.
I fancied you might notice the huge boy.
He soon gets o'er the distance ; at the house
He 'll hear I went to meet him and have
    missed ;
He 'll wait. No minute of the hour''s too much
Meantime for our preliminary talk :
First word of which must be — oh, good beyond
Expression of all goodness — you to come ! ' "

The elder, the superb one, answers slow.

" There was no helping that. You called for
    me,
Cried, rather : and my old heart answered you

Still, thank me! since the effort breaks a
    vow —
At least, a promise to myself."

                    " I know!
How selfish get you happy folk to be!
If I should love my husband, must I needs
Sacrifice straightway all the world to him,
As you do? Must I never dare leave house
On this dread Arctic expedition, out
And in again, six mortal hours, though you,
You even, my own friend forevermore,
Adjure me — fast your friend till rude love
    pushed
Poor friendship from her vantage — just to
    grant
The quarter of a whole day's company
And counsel? This makes counsel so much
    more
Need and necessity. For here 's my block
Of stumbling : in the face of happiness
So absolute, fear chills me. If such change
In heart be but love's easy consequence,
Do I love? If to marry mean — let go
All I now live for, should my marriage be? "

The other never once has ceased to gaze
On the great elm-tree in the open, posed
Placidly full in front, smooth bole, broad branch,
And leafage, one green plenitude of May.
The gathered thought runs into speech at last.

" O you exceeding beauty, bosomful
Of lights and shades, murmurs and silences,
Sun-warmth, dew-coolness, — squirrel, bee and
    bird,
High, higher, highest, till the blue proclaims
' *Leave earth, there 's nothing better till next step*
Heavenward ! ' — so, off flies what has wings to
    help ! "

And henceforth they alternate. Says the
    girl —

" That 's saved then : marriage spares the early
    taste."

" Four years now, since my eye took note of
    tree ! "

" If I had seen no other tree but this
My life long, while yourself came straight, you
    said,
From tree which overstretched you and was
    just
One fairy tent with pitcher-leaves that held
Wine, and a flowery wealth of suns and moons,
And magic fruits whereon the angels feed —
I looking out of window on a tree
Like yonder — otherwise well-known, much-
    liked,
Yet just an English ordinary elm —
What marvel if you cured me of conceit
My elm's bird-bee-and-squirrel tenantry
Was quite the proud possession I supposed ?
And there is evidence you tell me true.
The fairy marriage-tree reports itself
Good guardian of the perfect face and form,

Fruits of four years' protection ! Married
    friend,
You are more beautiful than ever ! "

                       " Yes :
I think that likely. I could well dispense
With all thought fair in feature, mine or no,
Leave but enough of face to know me by —
With all found fresh in youth except such
    strength
As lets a life-long labor earn repose
Death sells at just that price, they say ; and
    so,
Possibly, what I care not for, I keep."

" How you must know he loves you ! Chill,
    before,
Fear sinks to freezing. Could I sacrifice —
Assured my lover simply loves my soul —
One nose-breadth of fair feature ? No, indeed !
Your own love " . . .

                " The preliminary hour —
Don't waste it ! "

                " But I can't begin at once !
The angel's self that comes to hear me speak
Drives away all the care about the speech.
What an angelic mystery you are —
Now — that is certain ! when I knew you first,
No break of halo and no bud of wing !
I thought I knew you, saw you, round and
    through,
Like a glass ball ; suddenly, four years since,
You vanished, how and whither ? Mystery !
Wherefore ? No mystery at all : you loved,
Were loved again, and left the world of course :
Who would not ? Lapped four years in fairy-
    land,
Out comes, by no less wonderful a chance,
The changeling, touched athwart her trellised
    bliss
Of blush-rose bower by just the old friend's
    voice
That 's now struck dumb at her own potency.
I talk of my small fortunes ? Tell me yours
Rather ! The fool I ever was — I am,
You see that : the true friend you ever had,
You have, you also recognize. Perhaps,
Giving you all the love of all my heart,
Nature, that 's niggard in me, has denied
The after-birth of love there 's some one claims,
— This huge boy, swinging up the avenue ;
And I want counsel : is defect in me,
Or him who has no right to raise the love ?
My cousin asks my hand : he 's young enough,
Handsome, — my maid thinks, — manly 's more
    the word :
He asked my leave to ' *drop* ' the elm-tree there,
Some morning before breakfast. Gentleness
Goes with the strength, of course. He 's hon-
    est too,
Limpidly truthful. For ability —
All 's in the rough yet. His first taste of life
Seems to have somehow gone against the
    tongue :
He travelled, tried things — came back, tried
    still more —

He says he 's sick of all. He 's fond of me
After a certain careless-earnest way
I like : the iron 's crude, — no polished steel
Somebody forged before me. I am rich —
That 's not the reason, he 's far richer : no,
Nor is it that he thinks me pretty, — frank
Undoubtedly on that point ! He saw once
The pink of face-perfection — oh, not you —
Content yourself, my beauty ! — for she proved
So thoroughly a cheat, his charmer . . . nay,
He runs into extremes, I 'll say at once,
Lest you say ! Well, I understand he wants
Some one to serve, something to do : and both
Requisites so abound in me and mine
That here 's the obstacle which stops consent —
The smoothness is too smooth, and I mistrust
The unseen cat beneath the counterpane.
Therefore I thought — ' *Would she but judge for
   me,*
Who, judging for herself, succeeded so ! '
Do I love him, does he love me, do both
Mistake for knowledge — easy ignorance ?
Appeal to its proficient in each art !
I got rough-smooth through a piano-piece,
Rattled away last week till tutor came,
Heard me to end, then grunted '*Ach, mein Gott !
Sagen Sie " easy " ? Every note is wrong !
All thumped mit wrist — we 'll trouble fingers now.
The Fräulein will please roll up Raff again
And exercise at Czerny for one month !* '
Am I to roll up cousin, exercise
At Trollope's novels for one month ? Pro-
   nounce ! "

" Now, place each in the right position first,
Adviser and advised one ! I perhaps
Am three — nay, four years older ; am, beside,
A wife : advantages — to balance which,
You have a full fresh joyous sense of life
That finds you out life's fit food everywhere,
Detects enjoyment where I, slow and dull,
Fumble at fault. Already, these four years,
Your merest glimpses at the world without
Have shown you more than ever met my gaze ;
And now, by joyance you inspire joy, — learn
While you profess to teach, and teach, although
Avowedly a learner. I am dazed
Like any owl by sunshine which just sets
The sparrow preening plumage ! Here 's to spy
— Your cousin ! You have scanned him all
   your life,
Little or much ; I never saw his face.
You have determined on a marriage — used
Deliberation therefore — I 'll believe
No otherwise, with opportunity
For judgment so abounding ! Here stand I —
Summoned to give my sentence, for a whim,
(Well, at first cloud-fleck thrown athwart your
   blue,)
Judge what is strangeness' self to me, — say
   ' *Wed !* '
Or ' *Wed not !* ' whom you promise I shall
   judge
Presently, at propitious lunch-time, just
While he carves chicken ! Sends he leg for
   wing ?
That revelation into character
And conduct must suffice me ! Quite as well

Consult with yonder solitary crow
That eyes us from your elm-top ! "

                                " Still the same
Do you remember, at the library
We saw together somewhere, those two books
Somebody said were notice-worthy ? One
Lay wide on table, sprawled its painted leaves
For all the world's inspection ; shut on shelf
Reclined the other volume, closed, clasped
   locked —
Clear to be let alone. Which page had we
Preferred the turning over of ? You were,
Are, ever will be the locked lady, hold
Inside you secrets written, — soul absorbed,
My ink upon your blotting-paper. I —
What trace of you have I to show in turn ?
Delicate secrets ! No one juvenile
Ever essayed at croquet and performed
Superiorly but I confided you
The sort of hat he wore and hair it held.
While you ? One day a calm note comes by
   post —
' *I am just married, you may like to hear.* '
Most men would hate you, or they ought ; we
   love
What we fear, — *I* do ! ' *Cold* ' I shall expect
My cousin calls you. I — dislike not him,
But (if I comprehend what loving means)
Love you immeasurably more — more — more
Than even he who, loving you his wife,
Would turn up nose at who impertinent,
Frivolous, forward — *loves* that excellence
Of all the earth he bows in worship to !
And who 's this paragon of privilege ?
Simply a country parson : his the charm
That worked the miracle ! Oh, too absurd —
But that you stand before me as you stand !
Such beauty does prove something, everything !
Beauty 's the prize-flower which dispenses eye
From peering into what has nourished root —
Dew or manure : the plant best knows its
   place.
Enough, from teaching youth and tending age
And hearing sermons, — haply writing tracts, —
From such strange love-besprinkled compost,
   lo,
Out blows this triumph ! Therefore love 's the
   soil
Plants find or fail of. You, with wit to find,
Exercise wit on the old friend's behalf,
Keep me from failure ! Scan and scrutinize
This cousin ! Surely he 's as worth your pains
To study as my elm-tree, crow and all,
You still keep staring at. I read your
   thoughts."

" At last ? "

                " At first ! ' *Would, tree, a-top of thee
I wingèd were, like crow perched moveless there,
And so could straightway soar, escape this bore,
Back to my nest where broods whom I love best —
The parson o'er his parish — garish — rarish,* ' —
Oh, I could bring the rhyme in if I tried :
The Album here inspires me ! Quite apart
From lyrical expression, have I read
The stare aright, and sings not soul just so ? "

" Or rather *so ?* ' *Cool comfortable elm*
That men make coffins out of, — none for me
At the expense, so thou permit I glide
Under y ferny feet, and there sleep, sleep,
Nor dr d awaking though in heaven itself ! ' "

The younger looks with face struck sudden
     white.
The elder answers its inquiry.

                                   " Dear,
You are a guesser, not a ' *clairvoyante.*'
I 'll so far open you the locked and shelved
Volume, my soul, that you desire to see,
As let you profit by the title-page " —

" *Paradise Lost ?* "

                      " *Inferno !* — All which comes
Of tempting me to break my vow. Stop here !
Friend, whom I love the best in the whole
     world,
Come at your call, be sure that I will do
All your requirement — see and say my mind.
It may be that by sad apprenticeship
I have a keener sense : I 'll task the same.
Only indulge me, — here let sight and speech
Happen, — this Inn is neutral ground, you
     know !
I cannot visit the old house and home,
Encounter the old sociality
Abjured forever. Peril quite enough
In even this first — last, I pray it prove —
Renunciation of my solitude !
Back, you, to house and cousin ! Leave me
     here,
Who want no entertainment, carry still
My occupation with me. While I watch
The shadow inching round those ferny feet,
Tell him '*A school-friend wants a word with
     me*
Up at the inn: time, tide, and train won't wait:
I must go see her — on and off again —
You 'll keep me company? ' Ten minutes'
     talk,
With you in presence, ten more afterward
With who, alone, convoys me station-bound,
And I see clearly — and say honestly
To-morrow: pen shall play tongue's part, you
     know.
Go — quick ! for I have made our hand-in-
     hand
Return impossible. So scared you look, —
If cousin does not greet you with ' *What ghost
Has crossed your path ?* ' I set him down ob-
     tuse."

And after one more look, with face still white,
The younger does go, while the elder stands
Occupied by the elm at window there.

                    IV

Occupied by the elm ; and, as its shade
Has crept clock-hand-wise till it ticks at fern
Five inches further to the South, — the door
Opens abruptly, some one enters sharp,

The elder man returned to wait the youth :
Never observes the room's new occupant,
Throws hat on table, stoops quick, elbow-
     propped
Over the Album wide there, bends down brow
A cogitative minute, whistles shrill,
Then, — with a cheery-hopeless laugh-and-lose
Air of defiance to fate visibly
Casting the toils about him — mouths once
     more
' *Hail, calm acclivity, salubrious spot !* '
Then clasps-to cover, sends book spinning off
T' other side table, looks up, starts erect
Full-face with her who — roused from that ab-
     struse
Question ' *Will next tick tip the fern or no ?* ' —
Fronts him as fully.

                              All her languor breaks,
Away withers at once the weariness
From the black-blooded brow, anger and hate
Convulse.   Speech follows slowlier, but at
     last —

" You here !   I felt, I knew it would befall !
Knew, by some subtle undivinable
Trick of the trickster, I should, silly-sooth,
Late or soon, somehow be allured to leave
Safe hiding and come take of him arrears,
My torment due on four years' respite ! Time
To pluck the bird's healed breast of down o'er
     wound !
Have your success ! Be satisfied this sole
Seeing you has undone all heaven could do
These four years, puts me back to you and
     hell !
What will next trick be, next success ? No
     doubt
When I shall think to glide into the grave,
There will you wait disguised as beckoning
     Death,
And catch and capture me forevermore !
But, God, though I am nothing, be thou all !
Contest him for me ! Strive, for he is strong ! "

Already his surprise dies palely out
In laugh of acquiescing impotence.
He neither gasps nor hisses: calm and plain —

" I also felt and knew — but otherwise !
You out of hand and sight and care of me
These four years, whom I felt, knew, all the
     while . . .
Oh, it 's no superstition ! It 's a gift
O' the gamester that he snuffs the unseen
     powers
Which help or harm him. Well I knew what
     lurked,
Lay perdue paralyzing me, — drugged, drowsed
And damnified my soul and body both !
Down and down, see where you have dragged
     me to,
You and your malice ! I was, four years
     since,
— Well, a poor creature ! I became a knave.
I squandered my own pence : I plump my purse
With other people's pounds. I practised play
Because I liked it : play turns labor now

Because there's profit also in the sport.
I gamed with men of equal age and craft:
I steal here with a boy as green as grass
Whom I have tightened hold on slow and sure
This long while, just to bring about to-day
When the boy beats me hollow, buries me
In ruin who was sure to beggar him.
Oh, time indeed I should look up and laugh
' Surely she closes on me !' Here you stand ! "

And stand she does: while volubility,
With him, keeps on the increase, for his tongue
After long locking-up is loosed for once.

" Certain the taunt is happy ! " he resumes:
" So, I it was allured you — only I
— I, and none other — to this spectacle —
Your triumph, my despair — you woman-fiend
That front me ! Well, I have my wish, then !
    See
The low wide brow oppressed by sweeps of hair
Darker and darker as they coil and swathe
The crowned corpse-wanness whence the eyes
    burn black,
Not asleep now ! not pin-points dwarfed be-
    neath
Either great bridging eyebrow — poor blank
    beads —
Babies, I've pleased to pity in my time:
How they protrude and glow immense with hate!
The long triumphant nose attains — retains
Just the perfection ; and there's scarlet-skein
My ancient enemy, her lip and lip,
Sense-free, sense-frighting lips clenched cold
    and bold
Because of chin, that based resolve beneath !
Then the columnar neck completes the whole
Greek-sculpture-baffling body ! Do I see?
Can I observe ? You wait next word to come ?
Well, wait and want ! since no one blight I bid
Consume one least perfection. Each and all,
As they are rightly shocking now to me,
So may they still continue ! Value them?
Ay, as the vendor knows the money-worth
Of his Greek statue, fools aspire to buy,
And he to see the back of ! Let us laugh !
You have absolved me from my sin at least !
You stand stout, strong, in the rude health of
    hate,
No touch of the tame timid nullity
My cowardice, forsooth, has practised on !
Ay, while you seemed to hint some fine fifth act
Of tragedy should freeze blood, end the farce,
I never doubted all was joke. I kept,
Maybe, an eye alert on paragraphs,
Newspaper-notice, — let no inquest slip,
Accident, disappearance : sound and safe
Were you, my victim, not of mind to die !
So, my worst fancy that could spoil the smooth
Of pillow, and arrest descent of sleep,
Was ' Into what dim hole can she have dived,
She and her wrongs, her woe that's wearing flesh
And blood away?' Whereas, see, sorrow swells !
Or, fattened, fulsome, have you fed on me,
Sucked out my substance ? How much gloss, I
    pray,
O'erbloomed those hair-swathes when there
    crept from you

To me that craze, else unaccountable,
Which urged me to contest our county-seat
With whom but my own brother's nominee ?
Did that mouth's pulp glow ruby from carmine
While I misused my moment, pushed, — one
    word, —
One hair's-breadth more of gesture, — idiot-like
Past passion, floundered on to the grotesque,
And lost the heiress in a grin ? At least,
You made no such mistake ! You tickled fish,
Landed your prize the true artistic way !
How did the smug young curate rise to tune
Of ' Friend, a fatal fact divides us. Love
Suits me no longer. I have suffered shame,
Betrayal : past is past ; the future — yours —
Shall never be contaminate by mine !
I might have spared me this confession, not
— Oh, never by some hideousest of lies,
Easy, impenetrable ! No ! but say,
By just the quiet answer — " I am cold."
Falsehood avaunt, each shadow of thee, hence !
Had happier fortune willed . . . but dreams are
    vain.
Now, leave me — yes, for pity's sake ! ' Aha,
Who fails to see the curate as his face
Reddened and whitened, wanted handkerchief
At wrinkling brow and twinkling eye, until
Out burst the proper ' Angel, whom the fiend
Has thought to smirch, — thy whiteness, at one
    wipe
Of holy cambric, shall disgrace the swan !
Mine be the task ' . . . and so forth ! Fool? not
    he !
Cunning in flavors, rather ! What but sour
Suspected makes the sweetness doubly sweet,
And what stings love from faint to flamboyant
But the fear-sprinkle ? Even horror helps —
' Love's flame in me by such recited wrong
Drenched, quenched, indeed ? It burns the fierce-
    lier thence !'
Why, I have known men never love their wives
Till somebody — myself, suppose — had
    ' drenched
And quenched love,' so the blockheads whined :
    as if
The fluid fire that lifts the torpid limb
Were a wrong done to palsy. But I thrilled
No palsied person : half my age, or less,
The curate was, I'll wager : o'er young blood
Your beauty triumphed ! Eh, but — was it he ?
Then, it was he, I heard of ! None beside !
How frank you were about the audacious boy
Who fell upon you like a thunderbolt —
Passion and protestation ! He it was
Reserved in petto ! Ay, and ' rich ' beside —
' Rich ' — how supremely did disdain curl nose !
All that I heard was — ' wedded to a priest ;'
Informants sunk youth, riches and the rest.
And so my lawless love disparted loves,
That loves might come together with a rush !
Surely this last achievement sucked me dry :
Indeed, that way my wits went. Mistress-queen,
Be merciful and let your subject slink
Into dark safety ! He's a beggar, see —
Do not turn back his ship, Australia-bound,
And bid her land him right amid some crowd
Of creditors, assembled by your curse !
Don't cause the very rope to crack (you can !)

Whereon he spends his last (friend's) sixpenee,
   just
The moment when he hoped to hang himself !
Be satisfied you beat him ! ''

                              She replies —

" Beat him ! I do. To all that you confess
Of abject failure, I extend belief.
Your very face confirms it : God is just !
Let my face — fix your eyes ! — in turn confirm
What I shall say. All-abject 's but half truth ;
Add to all-abject knave as perfect fool !
So is it you probed human nature, *so*
Prognosticated of me ? Lay these words
To heart then, or where God meant heart should
   lurk !
That moment when you first revealed yourself,
My simple impulse prompted — end forthwith
The ruin of a life uprooted thus
To surely perish ! How should such spoiled tree
Henceforward balk the wind of its worst sport,
Fail to go falling deeper, falling down
From sin to sin until some depth were reached
Doomed to the weakest by the wickedest
Of weak and wicked human-kind ? But when,
That self-display made absolute, — behold
A new revealment ! — round you pleased to veer,
Propose me what should prompt annul the past,
Make me ' *amends by marriage* ' — in your
   phrase,
Incorporate me henceforth, body and soul,
With soul and body which mere brushing past
Brought leprosy upon me — ' *marry* ' these !
Why, then despair broke, reassurance dawned,
Clear-sighted was I that who hurled contempt
As I — thank God ! — at the contemptible,
Was scarce an utter weakling. Rent away
By treason from my rightful pride of place,
I was not destined to the shame below.
A cleft had caught me : I might perish there,
But thence to be dislodged and whirled at last
Where the black torrent sweeps the sewage —
   no !
' *Bare breast be on hard rock*,' laughed out my
   soul
In gratitude, ' *howe'er rock's grip may grind !*
The plain, rough, wretched holdfast shall suffice
This wreck of me ! ' The wind, — I broke in
   bloom
At passage of, — which stripped me bole and
   branch,
Twisted me up and tossed me here, — turns
   back,
And, playful ever, would replant the spoil ?
Be satisfied, not one least leaf that 's mine
Shall henceforth help wind's sport to exercise !
Rather I give such remnant to the rock
Which never dreamed a straw would settle
   there.
Rock may not thank me, may not feel my
   breast,
Even : enough that *I* feel, hard and cold,
Its safety my salvation. Safe and saved,
I lived, live. When the tempter shall persuade
His prey to slip down, slide off, trust the
   wind, —
Now that I know if God or Satan be

Prince of the Power of the Air, — then, then,
   indeed,
Let my life end and degradation too ! ''

" Good ! '' he smiles, " true Lord Byron ! ''
   ' *Tree and rock :*
Rock,' — there 's advancement ! He 's at first
   a youth,
Rich, worthless therefore ; next he grows a
   priest :
Youth, riches prove a notable resource,
When to leave me for their possessor gluts
Malice abundantly ; and now, last change,
The young rich parson represents a rock
— Bloodstone, no doubt. He 's Evangelical ?
Your Ritualists prefer the Church for spouse ! ''

She speaks.

                " I have a story to relate.
There was a parish-priest, my father knew,
Elderly, poor : I used to pity him
Before I learned what woes are pity-worth.
Elderly was grown old now, scanty means
Were straitening fast to poverty, beside
The ailments which await in such a case.
Limited every way, a perfect man
Within the bounds built up and up since birth
Breast-high about him till the outside world
Was blank save o'erhead one blue bit of sky —
Faith : he had faith in dogma, small or great,
As in the fact that if he clave his skull
He 'd find a brain there : who proves such a fact
No falsehood by experiment at price
Of soul and body ? The one rule of life
Delivered him in childhood was ' *Obey !*
Labor ! ' He had obeyed and labored — tame,
True to the mill-track blinked on from above.
Some scholarship he may have gained in youth :
Gone — dropt or flung behind. Some blossom-
   flake,
Spring's boon, descends on every vernal head,
I used to think ; but January joins
December, as his year had known no May ;
Trouble its snow-deposit, — cold and old !
I heard it was his will to take a wife,
A helpmate. Duty bade him tend and teach —
How ? with experience null, nor sympathy
Abundant, — while himself worked dogma
   dead,
Who would play ministrant to sickness, age,
Womankind, childhood ? These demand a
   wife.
Supply the want, then ! theirs the wife ; for
   him —
No coarsest sample of the proper sex
But would have served his purpose equally
With God's own angel, — let but knowledge
   match
Her coarseness : zeal does only half the work.
I saw this — knew the purblind honest drudge
Was wearing out his simple blameless life,
And wanted help beneath a burden — borne
To treasure-house or dust-heap, what cared I ?
Partner he needed : I proposed myself,
Nor much surprised him — duty was so clear !
Gratitude ? What for ? Gain of Paradise —
Escape, perhaps, from the dire penalty

Of who hides talent in a napkin? No:
His scruple was — should I be strong enough
— In body? since of weakness in the mind,
Weariness in the heart — no fear of these?
He took me as these Arctic voyagers
Take an aspirant to their toil and pain:
Can he endure them? — that's the point, and
   not
— Will he? Who would not, rather! Where-
   upon,
I pleaded far more earnestly for leave
To give myself away, than you to gain
What you called priceless till you gained the
   heart
And soul and body! which, as beggars serve
Extorted alms, you straightway spat upon.
Not so my husband, — for I gained my suit,
And had my value put at once to proof.
Ask him! These four years I have died away
In village-life. The village? Ugliness
At best and filthiness at worst, inside.
Outside, sterility — earth sown with salt
Or what keeps even grass from growing fresh.
The life? I teach the poor and learn, myself,
That commonplace to such stupidity
Is all-recondite. Being brutalized
Their true need is brute-language, cheery
   grunts
And kindly cluckings, no articulate
Nonsense that's elsewhere knowledge. Tend
   the sick,
Sickened myself at pig-perversity,
Cat-craft, dog-snarling — maybe, snapping" . . .

               " Brief:
You eat that root of bitterness called Man
— Raw: I prefer it cooked, with social sauce!
So, he was not the rich youth after all!
Well, I mistook. But somewhere needs must
   be
The compensation. If not young nor rich" . . .

" You interrupt!"

        " Because you've daubed enough
Bistre for background. Play the artist now,
Produce your figure well-relieved in front!
The contrast — do not I anticipate?
Though neither rich nor young — what then?
   'T is all
Forgotten, all this ignobility,
In the dear home, the darling word, the smile,
The something sweeter" . . .

           " Yes, you interrupt.
I have my purpose and proceed. Who lives
With beasts assumes beast-nature, look and
   voice,
And, much more, thought, for beasts think.
   Selfishness
In us met selfishness in them, deserved
Such answer as it gained. My husband, bent
On saving his own soul by saving theirs, —
They, bent on being saved if saving soul
Included body's getting bread and cheese
Somehow in life and somehow after death, —
Both parties were alike in the same boat,
One danger, therefore one equality.

Safety induces culture: culture seeks
To institute, extend and multiply
The difference between safe man and man,
Able to live alone now; progress means
What but abandonment of fellowship?
We were in common danger, still stuck close.
No new books, — were the old ones mastered
   yet?
No pictures and no music: these divert
— What from? the staving danger off! You
   paint
The waterspout above, you set to words
The roaring of the tempest round you?
   Thanks!
Amusement? Talk at end of the tired day
Of the more tiresome morrow! I transcribed
The page on page of sermon-scrawlings —
   stopped
Intellect's eye and ear to sense and sound —
Vainly: the sound and sense would penetrate
To brain and plague there in despite of me
Maddened to know more moral good were done
Had we two simply sallied forth and preached
I' the 'Green' they call their grimy, — I with
   twang
Of long-disused guitar, — with cut and slash
Of much-misvalued horsewhip he, — to bid
The peaceable come dance, the peace-breaker
Pay in his person! Whereas — Heaven and
   Hell,
Excite with that, restrain with this! — so dealt
His drugs my husband; as he dosed himself,
He drenched his cattle: and, for all my part
Was just to dub the mortar, never fear
But drugs, hand pestled at, have poisoned
   nose!
Heaven he let pass, left wisely undescribed:
As applicable therefore to the sleep
I want, that knows no waking — as to what's
Conceived of as the proper prize to tempt
Souls less world-weary: there, no fault to find!
But Hell he made explicit. After death,
Life: man created new, ingeniously
Perfect for a vindictive purpose now,
That man, first fashioned in beneficence,
Was proved a failure; intellect at length
Replacing old obtuseness, memory
Made mindful of delinquent's bygone deeds
Now that remorse was vain, which life-long lay
Dormant when lesson might be laid to heart;
New gift of observation up and down
And round man's self, new power to apprehend
Each necessary consequence of act
In man for well or ill — things obsolete —
Just granted to supplant the idiocy
Man's only guide while act was yet to choose,
With ill or well momentously its fruit;
A faculty of immense suffering
Conferred on mind and body, — mind, erewhile
Unvisited by one compunctious dream
During sin's drunken slumber, startled up,
Stung through and through by sin's significanc
Now that the holy was abolished — just
As body which, alive, broke down beneath
Knowledge, lay helpless in the path to good,
Failed to accomplish aught legitimate,
Achieve aught worthy, — which grew old in
   youth,

And at its longest fell a cut-down flower, —
Dying, this too revived by miracle
To bear no end of burden now that back
Supported torture to no use at all,
And live imperishably potent — since
Life's potency was impotent to ward
One plague off which made earth a hell before.
This doctrine, which one healthy view of
things,
One sane sight of the general ordinance —
Nature — and its particular object — man, —
Which one mere eye-cast at the character
Of Who made these and gave man sense to
boot,
Had dissipated once and evermore, —
This doctrine I have dosed our flock withal.
Why? Because none believed it. *They* desire
Such Heaven and dread such Hell, whom every
day
The alehouse tempts from one, a dog-fight bids
Defy the other? All the harm is done
Ourselves — done my good husband who in
youth
Perhaps read Dickens, done myself who still
Could play both Bach and Brahms. Such life
I lead —
Thanks to you, knave! You learn its qual-
ity —
Thanks to me, fool!"

                              He eyes her earnestly,
But she continues.

          " — Life which, thanks once more
To you, arch-knave as exquisitest fool,
I acquiescingly — I gratefully
Take back again to heart! and hence this
speech
Which yesterday had spared you. Four years
long
Life — I began to find intolerable,
Only this moment. Ere your entry just,
The leap of heart which answered, spite of me,
A friend's first summons, first provocative,
Authoritative, nay, compulsive call
To quit, though for a single day, my house
Of bondage — made return seem horrible.
I heard again a human lucid laugh
All trust, no fear ; again saw earth pursue
Its narrow busy way amid small cares,
Smaller contentments, much weeds, some few
flowers, —
Never suspicious of a thunderbolt
Avenging presently each daisy's death.
I recognized the beech-tree, knew the thrush
Repeated his old music-phrase, — all right,
How wrong was I, then! But your entry
broke
Illusion, bade me back to bounds at once.
I honestly submit my soul : which sprang
At love, and losing love lies signed and sealed
'*Failure.*' No love more? then, no beauty
more
Which tends to breed love! Purify my
powers,
Effortless till some other world procures
Some other chance of prize! or, if none be, —
Nor second world nor chance, — undesecrate

Die then this aftergrowth of heart, surmised
Where May's precipitation left June blank!
Better have failed in the high aim, as I,
Than vulgarly in the low aim succeed
As, God be thanked, I do not! Ugliness
Had I called beauty, falsehood — truth, and
you —
My lover! No — this earth's unchanged for
me,
By his enchantment whom God made the
Prince
O' the Power o' the Air, into a Heaven : there
is
Heaven, since there is Heaven's simulation —
earth.
I sit possessed in patience ; prison-roof
Shall break one day and Heaven beam over-
head."

His smile is done with ; he speaks bitterly.

" Take my congratulations, and permit
I wish myself had proved as teachable!
— Or, no! until you taught me, could I learn,
A lesson from experience ne'er till now
Conceded? Please you listen while I show
How thoroughly you estimate my worth
And yours — the immeasurably superior! I
Believed at least in one thing, first to last, —
Your love to me : I was the vile and you
The precious ; I abused you, I betrayed,
But doubted — never! Why else go my way
Judas-like plodding to this Potters' Field
Where fate now finds me? What has dinned
my ear
And dogged my step? The spectre with the
shriek
' *Such she was, such were you, whose punishment
Is just!* ' And such she was not, all the while!
She never owned a love to outrage, faith
To pay with falsehood! For, my heart knows
this —
Love once and you love always. Why, it 's
down
Here in the Album : every lover knows
Love may use hate but — turn to hate, itself —
Turn even to indifference — no, indeed!
Well, I have been spellbound, deluded like
The witless negro by the Obeah-man
Who bids him wither : so, his eye grows dim,
His arm slack, arrow misses aim and spear
Goes wandering wide, — and all the woe be-
cause
He proved untrue to Fetish, who, he finds,
Was just a feather-phantom! I wronged love,
Am ruined, — and there was no love to
wrong!"

" No love? Ah, dead love! I invoke thy
ghost
To show the murderer where thy heart poured
life
At summons of the stroke he doubts was dealt
On pasteboard and pretence! Not love, my
love?
I changed for you the very laws of life :
Made you the standard of all right, all fair.
No genius but you could have been, no sage,

No sufferer — which is grandest — for the
  truth !
My hero — where the heroic only hid
To burst from hiding, brighten earth one day !
Age and decline were man's maturity ;
Face, form were nature's type : more grace,
  more strength,
What had they been but just superfluous
  gauds,
Lawless divergence ? I have danced through
  day
On tiptoe at the music of a word,
Have wondered where was darkness gone as
  night
Burst out in stars at brilliance of a smile !
Lonely, I placed the chair to help me seat
Your fancied presence ; in companionship,
I kept my finger constant to your glove
Glued to my breast ; then — where was all the
  world ?
I schemed — not dreamed — how I might die
  some death
Should save your finger aching ! Who creates
Destroys, he only : I had laughed to scorn
Whatever angel tried to shake my faith
And make you seem unworthy : you yourself
Only could do that ! With a touch 't was done.
'Give me all, trust me wholly !' At the word,
I did give, I did trust — and thereupon
The touch did follow. Ah, the quiet smile,
The masterfully-folded arm in arm,
As trick obtained its triumph one time more !
In turn, my soul too triumphs in defeat :
Treason like faith moves mountains : love is
  gone !"

He paces to and fro, stops, stands quite close
And calls her by her name. Then —

                "God forgives :
Forgive you, delegate of God, brought near
As never priests could bring him to this soul
That prays you both — forgive me ! I abase —
Know myself mad and monstrous utterly
In all I did that moment ; but as God
Gives me this knowledge — heart to feel and
  tongue
To testify — so be you gracious too !
Judge no man by the solitary work
Of — well, they do say and I can believe —
The devil in him : his, the moment, — mine
The life — your life !"

           He names her name again.

"You were just — merciful as just, you were
In giving me no respite : punishment
Followed offending. Sane and sound once
  more,
The patient thanks decision, promptitude,
Which flung him prone and fastened him from
  hurt,
Haply to others, surely to himself.
I wake and would not you had spared one
  pang.
All 's well that ends well !"

           Yet again her name.

"Had you no fault ? Why must you change,
  forsooth,
Parts, why reverse positions, spoil the play ?
Why did your nobleness look up to me,
Not down on the ignoble thing confessed ?
Was it your part to stoop, or lift the low ?
Wherefore did God exalt you ? Who would
  teach
The brute man's tameness and intelligence
Must never drop the dominating eye :
Wink — and what wonder if the mad fit break,
Followed by stripes and fasting ? Sound and
  sane,
My life, chastised now, couches at your foot.
Accept, redeem me ! Do your eyes ask 'How ?'
I stand here penniless, a beggar ; talk
What idle trash I may, this final blow
Of fortune fells me. I disburse, indeed,
This boy his winnings ? when each bubble-
  scheme
That danced athwart my brain, a minute since,
The worse the better, — of repairing straight
My misadventure by fresh enterprise,
Capture of other boys in foolishness
His fellows, — when these fancies fade away
At first sight of the lost so long, the found
So late, the lady of my life, before
Whose presence I, the lost, am also found
Incapable of one least touch of mean
Expedient, I who teemed with plot and wile —
That family of snakes your eye bids flee !
Listen ! Our troublesomest dreams die off
In daylight : I awake, and dream is — where ?
I rouse up from the past : one touch dispels
England and all here. I secured long since
A certain refuge, solitary home
To hide in, should the head strike work one
  day,
The hand forget its cunning, or perhaps
Society grow savage, — there to end
My life's remainder, which, say what fools will,
Is or should be the best of life, — its fruit,
All tends to, root and stem and leaf and flower.
Come with me, love, loved once, loved only,
  come,
Blend loves there ! Let this parenthetic doubt
Of love, in me, have been the trial test
Appointed to all flesh at some one stage
Of soul's achievement, — when the strong man
  doubts
His strength, the good man whether goodness
  be,
The artist in the dark seeks, fails to find
Vocation, and the saint forswears his shrine.
What if the lover may elude, no more
Than these, probative dark, must search the
  sky
Vainly for love, his soul's star ? But the orb
Breaks from eclipse : I breathe again : I love !
Tempted, I fell ; but fallen — fallen lie
Here at your feet, see ! Leave this poor pre-
  tence
Of union with a nature and its needs
Repugnant to your needs and nature ! Nay,
False, beyond falsity you reprehend
In me, is such mock marriage with such mere
Man-mask as — whom you witless wrong, beside,
By that expenditure of heart and brain

He recks no more of than would yonder tree
If watered with your life-blood : rains and dews
Answer its ends sufficiently, while me
One drop saves — sends to flower and fruit at
    last
The laggard virtue in the soul which else
Cumbers the ground ! Quicken me ! Call me
    yours —
Yours and the world's — yours and the world's
    and God's !
Yes, for you can, you only ! Think ! Confirm
Your instinct ! Say, a minute since, I seemed
The castaway you count me, — all the more
Apparent shall the angelic potency
Lift me from out perdition's deep of deeps
To light and life and love ! — that 's love for
    you —
Love that already dares match might with
    yours.
You loved one worthy, — in your estimate, —
When time was ; you descried the unworthy
    taint,
And where was love then ? No such test could
    e'er
Try my love : but you hate me and revile ;
Hatred, revilement — had you these to bear,
Would you, as I do, nor revile, nor hate,
But simply love on, love the more, perchance ?
Abide by your own proof ! ' *Your love was
    love :*
Its ghost knows no forgetting ! ' Heart of mine,
Would that I dared remember ! Too unwise
Were he who lost a treasure, did himself
Enlarge upon the sparkling catalogue
Of gems to her his queen who trusted late
The keeper of her caskets ! Can it be
That I, custodian of such relic still
As your contempt permits me to retain,
All I dare hug to breast is — ' *How your glove
Burst and displayed the long thin lily streak !* '
What may have followed — that is forfeit now !
I hope the proud man has grown humble !
    True —
One grace of humbleness absents itself —
Silence ! yet love lies deeper than all words,
And not the spoken but the speechless love
Waits answer ere I rise and go my way."

Whereupon, yet one other time the name.

To end she looks the large deliberate look,
Even prolongs it somewhat ; then the soul
Bursts forth in a clear laugh that lengthens on,
On, till — thinned, softened, silvered, one
    might say
The bitter runnel hides itself in sand,
Moistens the hard gray grimly comic speech.

" Ay — give the baffled angler even yet
His supreme triumph as he hales to shore
A second time the fish once 'scaped from
    hook —
So artfully has new bait hidden old
Blood-imbrued iron ! Ay, no barb 's beneath
The gilded minnow here ! You bid break trust,
This time, with who trusts me, — not simply
    bid
Me trust you, me who ruined but myself,

In trusting but myself ! Since, thanks to you,
I know the feel of sin and shame, — be sure,
I shall obey you and impose them both
On one who happens to be ignorant
Although my husband — for the lure is love,
Your love ! Try other tackle, fisher-friend !
Repentance, expiation, hopes and fears, ·
What you had been, may yet be, would I but
Prove helpmate to my hero — one and all
These silks and worsteds round the hook seduce
Hardly the late torn throat and mangled
    tongue.
Pack up, I pray, the whole assortment prompt !
Who wonders at variety of wile
In the Arch-cheat ? You are the Adversary !
Your fate is of your choosing : have your
    choice !
Wander the world, — God has some end to
    serve,
Ere he suppress you ! He waits : I endure,
But interpose no finger-tip, forsooth,
To stop your passage to the pit. Enough
That I am stable, uninvolved by you
In the rush downwards : free I gaze and fixed ;
Your smiles, your tears, prayers, curses move
    alike
My crowned contempt. You kneel ? Prostrate
    yourself !
To earth, and would the whole world saw you
    there ! "

Whereupon — " All right ! " carelessly begins
Somebody from outside, who mounts the stair,
And sends his voice for herald of approach :
Half in half out the doorway as the door
Gives way to push.

          " Old fellow, all 's no good !
The train 's your portion ! Lay the blame on
    me !
I 'm no diplomatist, and Bismarck's self
Had hardly braved the awful Aunt at broach
Of proposition — so has world-repute
Preceded the illustrious stranger ! Ah ! " —

Quick the voice changes to astonishment,
Then horror, as the youth stops, sees, and knows.

The man who knelt starts up from kneeling,
    stands
Moving no muscle, and confronts the stare.

One great red outbreak buries — throat and
    brow —
The lady's proud pale queenliness of scorn :
Then her great eyes that turned so quick, be-
    come
Intenser : — quail at gaze, not they indeed !

              V

It is the young man shatters silence first.

" Well, my lord — for indeed my lord you are,
I little guessed how rightly — this last proof
Of lordship-paramount confounds too much
My simple headpiece ! Let 's see how we stand

Each to the other ! how we stood i' the game
Of life an hour ago, — the magpies, stile,
And oak-tree witnessed. Truth exchanged for
    truth —
My lord confessed his four-years-old affair —
How he seduced and then forsook the girl
Who married somebody and left him sad.
My pitiful experience was — I loved
A girl whose gown's hem had I dared to touch
My finger would have failed me, palsy-fixed.
She left me, sad enough, to marry — whom ?
A better man, — then possibly not you !
How does the game stand ? Who is who and
    what
Is what, o' the board now, since an hour went
    by ?
My lord's ' *seduced, forsaken, sacrificed,*'
Starts up, my lord's familiar instrument,
Associate and accomplice, mistress-slave —
Shares his adventure, follows on the sly !
— Ay, and since ' bag and baggage ' is a
    phrase —
Baggage lay hid in carpet-bag belike,
Was but unpadlocked when occasion came
For holding council, since my back was turned,
On how invent ten thousand pounds which,
    paid,
Would lure the winner to lose twenty more,
Beside refunding these ! Why else allow
The fool to gain them ? So displays herself
The lady whom my heart believed — oh, laugh !
Noble and pure : whom my heart loved at once,
And who at once did speak truth when she said
' *I am not mine now but another's* ' — thus
Being that other's ! Devil's-marriage, eh ?
' *My lie weds thine till lucre us do part ?* '
But pity me the snobbish simpleton,
You two aristocratic tiptop swells
At swindling ! Quits, I cry ! Decamp content
With skin I 'm peeled of : do not strip bones
    bare —
As that you could, I have no doubt at all !
O you two rare ones ! Male and female, Sir !
The male there smirked, this morning, ' *Come,
    my boy* —
*Out with it ! You 've been crossed in love, I
    think :
I recognize the lover's hangdog look ;
Make a clean breast and match my confidence,
For, I 'll be frank, I too have had my fling,
Am punished for my fault, and smart enough !
Where now the victim hides her head, God
    knows !* '
Here loomed her head, life-large, the devil
    knew !
Look out, Salvini ! Here 's your man, your
    match !
He and I sat applauding, stall by stall,
Last Monday — ' *Here 's Othello* ' was our word,
' *But where 's Iago ?* ' Where ? Why, there !
    And now
The fellow-artist, female specimen —
Oh, lady, you must needs describe yourself !
He 's great in art, but you — how greater still
— (If I can rightly, out of all I learned,
Apply one bit of Latin that assures
' *Art means just art's concealment* ') — tower your-
    self !

For he stands plainly visible henceforth —
Liar and scamp : while you, in artistry
Prove so consummate — or I prove perhaps
So absolute an ass — that — either way —
You still do seem to me who worshipped you
And see you take the homage of this man,
Your master, who played slave and knelt, no
    doubt,
Before a mistress in his very craft . . .
Well, take the fact, I nor believe my eyes,
Nor trust my understanding ! Still you seem
Noble and pure as when we had the talk
Under the tower, beneath the trees, that day.
And there 's the key explains the secret : **down**
He knelt to ask your leave to rise a grade
I' the mystery of humbug : well he may !
For how you beat him ! Half an hour ago,
I held your master for my best of friends ;
And now I hate him ! Four years since, you
    seemed
My heart's one love : well, and you so remain !
What 's he to you in craft ? "

                    She looks him through.

" My friend, 't is just that friendship have its
    turn —
Interrogate thus me whom one, of foes
The worst, has questioned and is answered by.
Take you as frank an answer ! answers both
Begin alike so far, divergent soon
World-wide — I own superiority
Over you, over him. As him I searched,
So do you stand seen through and through by me
Who, this time, proud, report your crystal
    shrines
A dewdrop, plain as amber prisons round
A spider in the hollow heart his house !
Nowise are you that thing my fancy feared
When out you stepped on me, a minute since,
— This man's confederate ! no, you step not
    thus
Obsequiously at beck and call to help
At need some second scheme, and supplement
Guile by force, use my shame to pinion me
From struggle and escape ! I fancied that !
Forgive me ! Only by strange chance, — most
    strange
In even this strange world, — you enter now,
Obtain your knowledge. Me you have not
    wronged
Who never wronged you — least of all, my
    friend,
That day beneath the College tower and trees,
When I refused to say, — ' *not friend, but love !* '
Had I been found as free as air when first
We met, I scarcely could have loved you. No —
For where was that in you which claimed return
Of love ? My eyes were all too weak to probe
This other's seeming, but that seeming loved
The soul in me, and lied — I know too late !
While your truth was truth : and I knew at once
My power was just my beauty — bear the word —
As I must bear, of all my qualities,
To name the poorest one that serves my soul
And simulates myself ! So much in me
You loved, I know : the something that 's be-
    neath

Heard not your call, — uncalled, no answer
    comes !
For, since in every love, or soon or late,
Soul must awake and seek out soul for soul,
Yours, overlooking mine then, would, some day,
Take flight to find some other ; so it proved —
Missing me, you were ready for this man.
I apprehend the whole relation: his —
The soul wherein you saw your type of worth
At once, true object of your tribute. Well
Might I refuse such half-heart's homage ! Love
Divining, had assured you I no more
Stand his participant in infamy
Than you — I need no love to recognize
As simply dupe and nowise fellow-cheat !
Therefore accept one last friend's-word, — your
    friend's,
All men's friend, save a felon's. Ravel out
The bad embroilment howsoe'er you may,
Distribute as it please you praise or blame
To me — so you but fling this mockery far —
Renounce this rag-and-feather hero-sham,
This poodle clipt to pattern, lion-like !
Throw him his thousands back, and lay to heart
The lesson I was sent, — if man discerned
Ever God's message, — just to teach. I judge —
To far another issue than could dream
Your cousin, — younger, fairer, as befits —
Who summoned me to judgment's exercise.
I find you, save in folly, innocent.
And in my verdict lies your fate ; at choice
Of mine your cousin takes or leaves you.
    ' Take ! '
I bid her — for you tremble back to truth !
She turns the scale, — one touch of the pure
    hand
Shall so press down, emprison past relapse
Farther vibration 'twixt veracity —
That 's honest solid earth — and falsehood, theft
And air, that 's one illusive emptiness !
That reptile capture you ? I conquered him :
You saw him cower before me ! Have no fear
He shall offend you farther. Spare to spurn —
Safe let him slink hence till some subtler Eve
Than I, anticipate the snake — bruise head
Ere he bruise heel — or, warier than the first,
Some Adam purge earth's garden of its pest
Before the slaver spoil the Tree of Life !

"You ! Leave this youth, as he leaves you, as I
Leave each ! There 's caution surely extant yet
Though conscience in you were too vain a claim.
Hence quickly ! Keep the cash but leave un-
    soiled
The heart I rescue and would lay to heal
Beside another's ! Never let her know
How near came taint of your companionship ! "

"Ah " — draws a long breath with a new
    strange look
The man she interpellates — soul astir
Under its covert, as, beneath the dust,
A coppery sparkle all at once denotes
The hid snake has conceived a purpose.

              " Ah "
Innocence should be crowned with ignorance ?
Desirable indeed, but difficult !

As if yourself, now, had not glorified
Your helpmate by imparting him a hint
Of how a monster made the victim bleed
Ere crook and courage saved her — hint, I say,—
Not the whole horror, — that were needless
    risk, —
But just such inkling, fancy of the fact,
As should suffice to qualify henceforth
The shepherd, when another lamb would stray,
For warning ' ' Ware the wolf ! ' No doubt at all,
Silence is generosity, — keeps wolf
Unhunted by flock's warder ! Excellent,
Did — generous to me, mean — just to him !
But, screening the deceiver, lamb were found
Outraging the deceitless ! So, — he knows !
And yet, unharmed I breathe — perchance,
    repent —
Thanks to the mercifully-politic ! "

" Ignorance is not innocence but sin —
Witness yourself ignore what after-pangs
Pursue the plague-infected. Merciful
Am I ? Perhaps ! the more contempt, the less
Hatred ; and who so worthy of contempt
As you that rest assured I cooled the spot
I could not cure, by poisoning, forsooth,
Whose hand I pressed there ? Understand for
    once
That, sick, of all the pains corroding me
This burnt the last and nowise least — the need
Of simulating soundness. I resolved —
No matter how the struggle tasked weak flesh —
To hide the truth away as in a grave
From — most of all — my husband: he nor
    knows
Nor ever shall be made to know your part,
My part, the devil's part, — I trust, God's part
In the foul matter. Saved, I yearn to save
And not destroy : and what destruction like
The abolishing of faith in him, that 's faith
In me as pure and true ? Acquaint some child
Who takes yon tree into his confidence,
That, where he sleeps now, was a murder done,
And that the grass which grows so thick, he
    thinks,
Only to pillow him is product just
Of what lies festering beneath ! 'T is God
Must bear such secrets and disclose them. Man ?
The miserable thing I have become
By dread acquaintance with my secret — you —
That thing had he become by learning me —-
The miserable, whom his ignorance
Would wrongly call the wicked : ignorance
Being, I hold, sin ever, small or great.
No, he knows nothing ! "

             " He and I alike
Are bound to you for such discreetness, then.
What if our talk should terminate awhile ?
Here is a gentleman to satisfy,
Settle accounts with, pay ten thousand pounds
Before we part — as, by his face, I fear,
Results from your appearance on the scene.
Grant me a minute's parley with my friend !
Which scarce admits of a third personage !
The room from which you made your entry first
So opportunely — still untenanted —
What if you please return there ? Just a word

To my young friend first — then, a word to you,
And you depart to fan away each fly
From who, grass-pillowed, sleeps so sound at
    home ! ”

“ So the old truth comes back !   A wholesome
    change, —
At last the altered eye, the rightful tone !
But even to the truth that drops disguise
And stands forth grinning malice which but now
Whined so contritely — I refuse assent
Just as to malice.   I, once gone, come back ?
No, my lord !   I enjoy the privilege
Of being absolutely loosed from you
Too much — the knowledge that your power is
    null
Which was omnipotence.   A word of mouth,
A wink of eye would have detained me once,
Body and soul your slave ; and now, thank
    God,
Your fawningest of prayers, your frightfulest
Of curses — neither would avail to turn
My footstep for a moment ! ”

                    “ Prayer, then, tries
No such adventure.   Let us cast about
For something novel in expedient : take
Command, — what say you ?   I profess myself
One fertile in resource.   Commanding, then,
I bid — not only wait there, but return
Here, where I want you !   Disobey and — good !
On your own head the peril ! ”

                    “ Come ! ” breaks in
The boy with his good glowing face.   “ Shut up !
None of this sort of thing while I stand here
— Not to stand that !   No bullying, I beg !
I also am to leave you presently
And never more set eyes upon your face —
You won’t mind that much ; but — I tell you
    frank —
I do mind having to remember this
For your last word and deed — my friend who
    were !
Bully a woman you have ruined, eh ?
Do you know, — I give credit all at once
To all those stories everybody told
And nobody but I would disbelieve :
They all seem likely now, — nay, certain, sure !
I daresay you did cheat at cards that night
The row was at the Club : ‘ sauter la coupe ’ —
That was your ‘ cut,’ for which your friends
    ‘ cut ’ you ;
While I, the booby, ‘ cut ’ — acquaintanceship
With who so much as laughed when I said
    ‘ luck ! ’
I daresay you had bets against the horse
They doctored at the Derby ; little doubt,
That fellow with the sister found you shirk
His challenge and did kick you like a ball,
Just as the story went about !   Enough :
It only serves to show how well advised,
Madam, you were in bidding such a fool
As I, go hang.   You see how the mere sight
And sound of you suffice to tumble down
Conviction topsy-turvy : no, — that ’s false, —
There ’s no unknowing what one knows ; and
    yet

Such is my folly that, in gratitude
For . . . well, I ’m stupid ; but you seemed to
    wish
I should know gently what I know, should slip
Softly from old to new, not break my neck
Between beliefs of what you were and are.
Well then, for just the sake of such a wish
To cut no worse a figure than needs must
In even eyes like mine, I ’d sacrifice
Body and soul !   But don’t think danger -
    pray ! —
Menaces either !   He do harm to us ?
Let me say ‘ us ’ this one time !   You ’d allow
I lent perhaps my hand to rid your ear
Of some cur’s yelping — hand that ’s fortified,
Into the bargain, with a horsewhip ?   Oh,
One crack and you shall see how curs decamp ! —
My lord, you know your losses and my gains.
Pay me my money at the proper time !
If cash be not forthcoming — well, yourself
Have taught me, and tried often, I ’ll engage,
The proper course : I post you at the Club,
Pillory the defaulter.   Crack, to-day,
Shall, slash, to-morrow, slice through flesh and
    bone !
There, Madam, you need mind no cur, I
    think ! ”

“ Ah, what a gain to have an apt no less
Than grateful scholar !   Nay, he brings to mind
My knowledge till he puts me to the blush,
So long has it lain rusty !   Post my name !
That were indeed a wheal from whipcord !
    Whew !
I wonder now if I could rummage out
— Just to match weapons — some old scorpion-
    scourge !
Madam, you hear my pupil, may applaud
His triumph o’er the master.   I — no more
Bully, since I ’m forbidden : but entreat —
Wait and return — for my sake, no ! but just
To save your own defender, should he chance
Get thwacked through awkward flourish of
    his thong.
And what if — since all waiting ’s weary work —
I help the time pass ’twixt your exit now
And entry then ? for — pastime proper — here ’s
The very thing, the Album, verse and prose
To make the laughing minutes launch away !
Each of us must contribute.   I ’ll begin —
‘ Hail, calm acclivity, salubrious spot ! ’
I ’m confident I beat the bard, — for why ?
My young friend owns me an Iago — him
Confessed, among the other qualities,
A ready rhymer.   Oh, he rhymed !   Here goes !
— Something to end with ‘ horsewhip ! ’   No,
    that rhyme
Beats me ; there ’s ‘ cowslip,’ ‘ boltsprit,’
    nothing else !
So, Tennyson take my benison, — verse for
    bard,
Prose suits the gambler’s book best !   Dared
    and done ! ”

Wherewith he dips pen, writes a line or two,
Closes and clasps the cover, gives the book,
Bowing the while, to her who hesitates,
Turns half away, turns round again, at last

Takes it as you touch carrion, then retires.
The door shuts fast the couple.

VI

                                        With a change
Of his whole manner, opens out at once
The Adversary.

                    " Now, my friend, for you !
You who, protected late, aggressive grown,
Brandish, it seems, a weapon I must 'ware !
Plain speech in me becomes respectable
Henceforth because courageous ; plainly, then —
(Have lash well loose, hold handle tight and
    light !)
Throughout my life's experience, you indulged
Yourself and friend by passing in review
So courteously but now, I vainly search
To find one record of a specimen
So perfect of the pure and simple fool
As this you furnish me. Ingratitude
I lump with folly, — all 's one lot, — so — fool !
Did I seek you or you seek me ? Seek ? sneak
For service to, and service you would style —
And did style — godlike, scarce an hour ago !
Fool, there again, yet not precisely there
First-rate in folly : since the hand you kissed
Did pick you from the kennel, did plant firm
Your footstep on the pathway, did persuade
Your awkward shamble to true gait and pace,
Fit for the world you walk in. Once a-strut
On that firm pavement which your cowardice
Was for renouncing as a pitfall, next
Came need to clear your brains of their conceit
They cleverly could distinguish who was who,
Whatever folk might tramp the thoroughfare.
Men, now — familiarly you read them off,
Each phiz at first sight ! Oh, you had an eye !
Who couched it ? made you disappoint each
    fox
Eager to strip my gosling of his fluff
So golden as he cackled ' Goose trusts lamb ' ?
' Ay, but I saved you — wolf defeated fox —
Wanting to pick your bones myself ? ' then, wolf
Has got the worst of it with goose for once.
I, penniless, pay you ten thousand pounds
(— No gesture, pray ! I pay ere I depart !)
And how you turn advantage to account
Here 's the example ! Have I proved so wrong
In my peremptory ' debt must be discharged ' ?
Oh, you laughed lovelily, were loth to leave
The old friend out at elbows, pooh, a thing
Not to be thought of ! I must keep my cash,
And you forget your generosity !
Ha ha ! I took your measure when I laughed
My laugh to that ! First quarrel — nay, first
    faint
Pretence at taking umbrage — ' Down with debt,
Both interest and principal ! — The Club,
Exposure and expulsion ! — stamp me out ! '
That 's the magnanimous magnificent
Renunciation of advantage ! Well,
But whence and why did you take umbrage,
    Sir ?
Because your master, having made you know
Somewhat of men, was minded to advance,

Expound you women, still a mystery !
My pupil pottered with a cloud on brow,
A clod in breast : had loved, and vainly loved :
Whence blight and blackness, just for all the
    world
As Byron used to teach us boys.   Thought I —
' Quick rid him of that rubbish !   Clear the cloud,
And set the heart a-pulsing ! ' — heart, this time :
'T was nothing but the head I doctored late
For ignorance of Man ; now heart 's to dose,
Palsied by over-palpitation due
To Woman-worship — so, to work at once
On first avowal of the patient's ache !
This morning you described your malady, —
How you dared love a piece of virtue — lost
To reason, as the upshot showed : for scorn
Fitly repaid your stupid arrogance ;
And, parting, you went two ways, she resumed
Her path — perfection, while forlorn you paced
The world that 's made for beasts like you and
    me.
My remedy was — tell the fool the truth !
Your paragon of purity had plumped
Into these arms at their first outspread —
    ' fallen
My victim,' she prefers to turn the phrase —
And, in exchange for that frank confidence,
Asked for my whole life present and to come —
Marriage : a thing uncovenanted for !
Never so much as put in question ! Life —
Implied by marriage — throw that trifle in
And round the bargain off, no otherwise
Than if, when we played cards, because you
    won
My money you should also want my head !
That, I demurred to : we but played ' for
    love ' —
She won my love ; had she proposed for stakes,
' Marriage,' — why, that 's for whist, a wiser
    game.
Whereat she raved at me, as losers will,
And went her way. So far the story 's known,
The remedy 's applied, no farther — which
Here 's the sick man's first honorarium for —
Posting his medicine-monger at the Club !
That being, Sir, the whole you mean my fee —
In gratitude for such munificence
I 'm bound in common honesty to spare
No droplet of the draught : so, — pinch your
    nose,
Pull no wry faces ! — drain it to the dregs !
I say ' She went off ' — ' went off,' you subjoin,
' Since not to wedded bliss, as I supposed,
Sure to some convent : solitude and peace
Help her to hide the shame from mortal view,
With prayer and fasting.' No, my sapient Sir !
Far wiselier, straightway she betook herself
To a prize-portent from the donkey-show
Of leathern long-ears that compete for palm
In clerical absurdity : since he,
Good ass, nor practises the shaving-trick,
The candle-crotchet, nonsense which repays
When you 've young ladies congregant, — but
    schools
The poor, — toils, moils, and grinds the mill,
    nor means
To stop and munch one thistle in this life
Till next life smother him with roses : just

The parson for her purpose ! Him she stroked
Over the muzzle ; into mouth with bit,
And on to back with saddle, — there he stood,
The serviceable beast who heard, believed
And meekly bowed him to the burden, —
  borne
Off in a canter to seclusion — ay,
The lady's lost ! But had a friend of mine
— While friend he was — imparted his sad case
To sympathizing counsellor, full soon
One cloud at least had vanished from his brow.
' Don't fear ! ' had followed reassuringly —
' The lost will in due time turn up again,
Probably just when, weary of the world,
You think of nothing less than settling-down
To country life and golden days, beside
A dearest best and brightest virtuousest
Wife : who needs no more hope to hold her own
Against the naughty-and-repentant — no,
Than water-gruel against Roman punch ! '
And as I prophesied, it proves ! My youth, —
Just at the happy moment when, subdued
To spooniness, he finds that youth fleets fast,
That town-life tires, that men should drop
  boys'-play,
That property, position have, no doubt,
Their exigency with their privilege,
And if the wealthy wed with wealth, how dire
The double duty ! — in, behold, there beams
Our long-lost lady, form and face complete !
And where 's my moralizing pupil now,
Had not his master missed a train by chance ?
But, by your side instead of whirled away,
How have I spoiled scene, stopped catastrophe,
Struck flat the stage-effect I know by heart !
Sudden and strange the meeting — improvised ?
Bless you, the last event she hoped or dreamed !
But rude sharp stroke will crush out fire from
  flint —
Assuredly from flesh. ' 'T is you ? ' ' Myself ! '
' Changed ? ' ' Changeless ! ' ' Then, what's
  earth to me ? ' ' To me
What's heaven ? ' ' So, — thine ! ' ' And thine ! '
  ' And likewise mine ! '
Had laughed ' Amen ' the devil, but for me
Whose intermeddling hinders this hot haste,
And bids you, ere concluding contract, pause —
Ponder one lesson more, then sign and seal
At leisure and at pleasure, — lesson's price
Being, if you have skill to estimate,
— How say you ? — I'm discharged my debt in
  full !
Since paid you stand, to farthing uttermost,
Unless I fare like that black majesty
A friend of mine had visit from last Spring.
Coasting along the Cape-side, he 's becalmed
Off an uncharted bay, a novel town
Untouched at by the trader : here 's a chance !
Out paddles straight the king in his canoe,
Comes over bulwark, says he means to buy
Ship's cargo — being rich and having brought
A treasure ample for the purpose. See !
Four dragons, stalwart blackies, guard the
  same
Wrapped round and round : its hulls, a multi-
  tude, —
Palm-leaf and cocoa-mat and goat's-hair cloth
All duly braced about with bark and board, —

Suggest how brave, 'neath coat, must kernel
  be !
At length the peeling is accomplished, plain
The casket opens out its core, and lo
— A brand-new British silver sixpence — bid
That 's ample for the Bank, — thinks majesty !
You are the Captain ; call my sixpence cracked
Or copper ; ' what I've said is calumny ;
The lady's spotless ! ' Then, — I'll prove my
  words,
Or make you prove them true as truth — your-
  self,
Here, on the instant ! I'll not mince my
  speech,
Things at this issue. When she enters, then,
Make love to her ! No talk of marriage now —
The point - blank bare proposal ! Pick no
  phrase —
Prevent all misconception ! Soon you'll see
How different the tactics when she deals
With an instructed man, no longer boy
Who blushes like a booby. Woman's wit !
Man, since you have instruction, blush no more !
Such your five minutes' profit by my pains,
'T is simply now, — demand and be possessed !
Which means — you may possess — may strip
  the tree
Of fruit desirable to make one wise !
More I nor wish nor want : your act 's your act.
My teaching is but — there 's the fruit to pluck
Or let alone at pleasure. Next advance
In knowledge were beyond you ! Don't expect
I bid a novice — pluck, suck, send sky-high
Such fruit, once taught that neither crab nor
  sloe
Falls readier prey to who but robs a hedge,
Than this gold apple to my Hercules.
Were you no novice but proficient — then,
Then, truly, I might prompt you — Touch and
  taste,
Try flavor and be tired as soon as I !
Toss on the prize to greedy mouths agape,
Betake yours, sobered as the satiate grow,
To wise man's solid meal of house and land,
Consols and cousin ! but, my boy, my boy,
Such lore 's above you !

                    Here 's the lady back !
So, Madam, you have conned the Album-page
And come to thank its last contributor ?
How kind and condescending ! I retire
A moment, lest I spoil the interview,
And mar my own endeavor to make friends —
You with him, him with you, and both with
  me !
If I succeed — permit me to inquire
Five minutes hence ! Friends bid good-by,
  you know." —
And out he goes.

VII

                    She, face, form, bearing, one
Superb composure —

                    " He has told you all ?
Yes, he has told you all, your silence says —

What gives him, as he thinks, the mastery
Over my body and my soul ! — has told
That instance, even, of their servitude
He now exacts of me ?   A silent blush !
That's well, though better would white igno-
rance
Beseem your brow, undesecrate before —
Ay, when I left you !   I too learn at last
— Hideously learned as I seemed so late —
What sin may swell to.   Yes, — I needed
learn
That, when my prophet's rod became the snake
I fled from, it would, one day, swallow up
— Incorporate whatever serpentine
Falsehood and treason and unmanliness
Beslime earth's pavement : such the power of
Hell,
And so beginning, ends no otherwise
The Adversary !   I was ignorant,
Blameworthy — if you will ; but blame I take
Nowise upon me as I ask myself
— *You* — how can you, whose soul I seemed to
read
The limpid eyes through, have declined so
deep,
Even with him for consort ?   I revolve
Much memory, pry into the looks and words
Of that day's walk beneath the College wall,
And nowhere can distinguish, in what gleams
Only pure marble through my dusky past,
A dubious cranny where such poison-seed
Might harbor, nourish what should yield to-day
This dread ingredient for the cup I drink.
Do not I recognize and honor truth
In seeming ? — take your truth, and for return,
Give you my truth, a no less precious gift ?
You loved me :   I believed you.   I replied
— How could I other ? — ' *I was not my own,*'
No longer had the eyes to see, the ears
To hear, the mind to judge, since heart and soul
Now were another's.   My own right in me,
For well or ill, consigned away — my face
Fronted the honest path, deflection whence
Had shamed me in the furtive backward look
At the late bargain — fit such chapman's
phrase !
As though — less hasty and more provident —
Waiting had brought advantage.   Not for me
The chapman's chance !   Yet while thus much
was true,
I spared you — as I knew you then — one more
Concluding word which, truth no less, seemed
best
Buried away forever.   Take it now,
Its power to pain is past !   Four years — that
day —
Those limes that make the College avenue !
I would that — friend and foe — by miracle,
I had, that moment, seen into the heart
Of either, as I now am taught to see !
I do believe I should have straight assumed
My proper function, and sustained a soul,
— Nor aimed at being just sustained myself
By some man's soul — the weaker woman's-
want !
So had I missed the momentary thrill
Of finding me in presence of a god,
But gained the god's own feeling when he gives

Such thrill to what turns life from death be
fore.
' *Gods many and Lords many,*' says the Book :
You would have yielded up your soul to me
— Not to the false god who has burned its clay
In his own image.   I had shed my love
Like Spring dew on the clod all flowery thence,
Not sent up a wild vapor to the sun
That drinks and then disperses.   Both of us
Blameworthy, — I first meet my punishment —
And not so hard to bear.   I breathe again !
Forth from those arms' enwinding leprosy
At last I struggle — uncontaminate :
Why must I leave *you* pressing to the breast
That's all one plague-spot ?   Did you love me
once ?
Then take love's last and best return !   I
think,
Womanliness means only motherhood ;
All love begins and ends there, — roams
enough,
But, having run the circle, rests at home.
Why is your expiation yet to make ?
Pull shame with your own hands from your
own head
Now, — never wait the slow envelopment
Submitted to by unelastic age !
One fierce throe frees the sapling : flake on
flake
Lull till they leave the oak snow-stupefied.
Your heart retains its vital warmth — or why
That blushing reassurance ?   Blush, young
blood !
Break from beneath this icy premature
Captivity of wickedness — I warn
Back, in God's name !   No fresh encroachment
here !
This May breaks all to bud — no winter now !
Friend, we are both forgiven !   Sin no more !
I am past sin now, so shall you become !
Meanwhile I testify that, lying once,
My foe lied ever, most lied last of all.
He, waking, whispered to your sense asleep
The wicked counsel, — and assent might seem ;
But, roused, your healthy indignation breaks
The idle dream-pact.   You would die — not
dare
Confirm your dream-resolve, — nay, find the
word
That fits the deed to bear the light of day !
Say I have justly judged you !   then farewell
To blushing — nay, it ends in smiles, not tears !
Why tears now ?   I have justly judged, thank
God !"

He does blush boy-like, but the man speaks
out,
— Makes the due effort to surmount himself.

"I don't know what he wrote — how should I ?
Nor
How he could read my purpose, which, it
seems,
He chose to somehow write — mistakenly
Or else for mischief's sake.   I scarce believe
My purpose put before you fair and plain
Would need annoy so much ; but there's my
luck —

From first to last I blunder. Still, one more
Turn at the target, try to speak my thought!
Since he could guess my purpose, won't you read
Right what he set down wrong ? He said —
    let 's think !
Ay, so ! — he did begin by telling heaps
Of tales about you. Now, you see — suppose
Any one told me — my own mother died
Before I knew her — told me — to his cost ! —
Such tales about my own dead mother : why,
You would not wonder surely if I knew,
By nothing but my own heart's help, he lied,
Would you ? No reason 's wanted in the case.
So with you ! In they burnt on me, his tales,
Much as when madhouse-inmates crowd around,
Make captive any visitor and scream
All sorts of stories of their keeper — he 's
Both dwarf and giant, vulture, wolf, dog, cat,
Serpent and scorpion, yet man all the same ;
Sane people soon see through the gibberish !
I just made out, you somehow lived somewhere
A life of shame — I can't distinguish more —
Married or single — how, don't matter much :
Shame which himself had caused — that point
    was clear,
That fact confessed — that thing to hold and
    keep.
Oh, and he added some absurdity
— That you were here to make me — ha, ha,
    ha ! —
Still love you, still of mind to die for you,
Ha, ha — as if that needed mighty pains !
Now, foolish as . . . but never mind myself ;
— What I am, what I am not, in the eye
Of the world, is what I never cared for much.
Fool then or no fool, not one single word
In the whole string of lies did I believe,
But this — this only — if I choke, who
    cares ? —
I believe somehow in your purity
Perfect as ever ! Else what use is God ?
He is God, and work miracles he can !
Then, what shall I do ? Quite as clear, my
    course !
They 've got a thing they call their Labyrinth
I' the garden yonder : and my cousin played
A pretty trick once, led and lost me deep
Inside the briery maze of hedge round hedge ;
And there might I be staying now, stock-still,
But that I laughing bade eyes follow nose
And so straight pushed my path through let
    and stop
And soon was out in the open, face all
    scratched,
But well behind my back the prison-bars
In sorry plight enough, I promise you !
So here : I won my way to truth through
    lies —
Said, as I saw light, — if her shame be shame
I 'll rescue and redeem her, — shame 's no
    shame ?
Then, I 'll avenge, protect — redeem myself
The stupidest of sinners ! Here I stand !
Dear, — let me once dare call you so, — you
    said,
Thus ought you to have done, four years ago,
Such things and such ! Ay, dear, and what
    ought I ?

You were revealed to me : where 's gratitude,
Where 's memory even, where the gain of you
Discernible in my low after-life
Of fancied consolation ? why, no horse
Once fed on corn, will, missing corn, go munch
Mere thistles like a donkey ! I missed you,
And in your place found — him, made him my
    love,
Ay, did I, — by this token, that he taught
So much beast-nature that I meant . . . God
    knows
Whether I bow me to the dust enough ! . .
To marry — yes, my cousin here ! I hope
That was a master-stroke ! Take heart of
    hers,
And give her hand of mine with no more heart
Than now you see upon this brow I strike !
What atom of a heart do I retain
Not all yours ? Dear, you know it ! Easily
May she accord me pardon when I place
My brow beneath her foot, if foot so deign,
Since uttermost indignity is spared —
Mere marriage and no love ! And all this time
Not one word to the purpose ! Are you free ?
Only wait ! only let me serve — deserve
Where you appoint and how you see the good !
I have the will — perhaps the power — at least
Means that have power against the world. For
    time —
Take my whole life for your experiment !
If you are bound — in marriage, say — why,
    still,
Still, sure, there 's something for a friend to do,
Outside ? A mere well-wisher, understand !
I 'll sit, my life long, at your gate, you know,
Swing it wide open to let you and him
Pass freely, — and you need not look, much less
Fling me a ' *Thank you — are you there, old
    friend ?* '
Don't say that even : I should drop like shot !
So I feel now at least : some day, who knows ?
After no end of weeks and months and years
You might smile ' *I believe you did your best !* '
And that shall make my heart leap — leap such
    leap
As lands the feet in Heaven to wait you there !
Ah, there 's just one thing more ! How pale
    you look !
Why ? Are you angry ? If there 's, after all,
Worst come to worst — if still there somehow
    be
The shame — I said was no shame, — none, I
    swear ! —
In that case, if my hand and what it holds, —
My name, — might be your safeguard now —
    at once —
Why, here 's the hand — you have the heart !
    Of course —
No cheat, no binding you, because I 'm bound,
To let me off probation by one day,
Week, month, year, lifetime ! Prove as you
    propose !
Here 's the hand with the name to take or leave !
That 's all — and no great piece of news, I
    hope ! "

" Give me the hand, then ! " she cries hastily.
" Quick, now ! I hear his footstep ! "

Hand in hand
The couple face him as he enters, stops
Short, stands surprised a moment, laughs away
Surprise, resumes the much-experienced man.

" So, you accept him ? "

              " Till us death do part ! "

" No longer ? Come, that 's right and rational !
I fancied there was power in common sense,
But did not know it worked thus promptly.
      Well —
At last each understands the other, then ?
Each drops disguise, then ? So, at supper-time
These masquerading people doff their gear,
Grand Turk his pompous turban, Quakeress
Her stiff-starched bib and tucker, — make-be-
      lieve
That only bothers when, ball-business done,
Nature demands champagne and *mayonnaise*.
Just so has each of us sage three abjured
His and her moral pet particular
Pretension to superiority,
And, cheek by jowl, we henceforth munch and
      joke !
Go, happy pair, paternally dismissed
To live and die together — for a month,
Discretion can award no more ! Depart
From whatsoe'er the calm sweet solitude
Selected — Paris not improbably —
At month's end, when the honeycomb 's left
      wax,
— You, daughter, with a pocketful of gold
Enough to find your village boys and girls
In duffel cloaks and hobnailed shoes from May
To — what 's the phrase ? — Christmas-come-
      never-mas !
You, son and heir of mine, shall reappear
Ere Spring-time, that 's the ring-time, lose one
      leaf,
And — not without regretful smack of lip
The while you wipe it free of honey-smear —
Marry the cousin, play the magistrate,
Stand for the county, prove perfection's pink —
Master of hounds, gay-coated dine — nor die
Sooner than needs of gout, obesity,
And sons at Christ Church ! As for me, — ah
      me,
I abdicate — retire on my success,
Four years well occupied in teaching youth
— My son and daughter the exemplary !
Time for me to retire now, having placed
Proud on their pedestal the pair : in turn,
Let them do homage to their master ! You, —
Well, your flushed cheek and flashing eye pro-
      claim
Sufficiently your gratitude: you paid
The *honorarium*, the ten thousand pounds
To purpose, did you not ? I told you so !
And you, — but, bless me, why so pale — so
      faint
At influx of good fortune ? Certainly,
No matter how or why or whose the fault,
I save your life — save it, nor less nor more !
You blindly were resolved to welcome death
In that black boor-and-bumpkin-haunted hole
Of his, the prig with all the preachments ! *You*

Installed as nurse and matron to the crones
And wenches, while there lay a world outside
Like Paris (which again I recommend),
In company and guidance of — first, this,
Then — all in good time — some new friend as
      fit —
What if I were to say, some fresh myself.
As I once figured ? Each dog has his day,
And mine 's at sunset : what should old dog do
But eye young litters' frisky puppyhood ?
Oh, I shall watch this beauty and this youth
Frisk it in brilliance ! But don't fear ! Dis-
      creet,
I shall pretend to no more recognize
My quondam pupils than the doctor nods
When certain old acquaintances may cross
His path in Park, or sit down prim beside
His plate at dinner-table : tip nor wink
Scares patients he has put, for reason good,
Under restriction, — maybe, talked sometimes
Of douche or horsewhip to, — for why ? be-
      cause
The gentleman would crazily declare
His best friend was — Iago ! Ay, and worse —
The lady, all at once grown lunatic,
In suicidal monomania vowed,
To save her soul, she needs must starve herself !
They 're cured now, both, and I tell nobody.
Why don't you speak ? Nay, speechless, each
      of you
Can spare — without unclasping plighted
      troth —
At least one hand to shake ! Left-hands will
      do —
Yours first, my daughter ! Ah, it guards — it
      gripes
The precious Album fast — and prudently !
As well obliterate the record there
On page the last : allow me tear the leaf !
Pray, now !   And afterward, to make amends,
What if all three of us contribute each
A line to that prelusive fragment, — help
The embarrassed bard who broke out to break
      down
Dumfoundered at such unforeseen success ?
' *Hail, calm acclivity, salubrious spot* '
You begin — *place aux dames !* I 'll prompt
      you then !
' *Here do I take the good the gods allot !* '
Next you, Sir ! What, still sulky ? Sing, O
      Muse !
' *Here does my lord in full discharge his shot !* '
Now for the crowning flourish ! mine shall
      be " . . .

" Nothing to match your first effusion, mar
What was, is, shall remain your masterpiece !
Authorship has the alteration-itch !
No, I protest against erasure. Read,
My friend ! " (she gasps out). " Read and
      quickly read
' *Before us death do part,*' what made you mine
And made me yours — the marriage-license
      here !
Decide if he is like to mend the same ! "

And so the lady, white to ghastliness,
Manages somehow to display the page

With left-hand only, while the right retains
The other hand, the young man's, — dreaming-
     drunk
He, with this drench of stupefying stuff,
Eyes wide, mouth open, — half the idiot's stare
And half the prophet's insight, — holding tight,
All the same, by his one fact in the world —
The lady's right-hand : he but seems to read —
Does not, for certain ; yet, how understand
Unless he reads ?

                    So, understand he does,
For certain. Slowly, word by word, *she reads*
Aloud that license — or that warrant, say.

" *One against two — and two that urge their odds*
To uttermost — I needs must try resource !
Madam, I laid me prostrate, bade you spurn
Body and soul : you spurned and safely spurned
So you had spared me the superfluous taunt
' *Prostration means no power to stand erect,*
Stand, trampling on who trampled — prostrate
     now ! '
So, with my other fool-foe : I was fain
Let the boy touch me with the buttoned foil,
And him the infection gains, he too must needs
Catch up the butcher's cleaver. Be it so !
Since play turns earnest, here 's my serious fence.
He loves you ; he demands your love : both know
What love means in my language. Love him
     then ?
Pursuant to a pact, love pays my debt :
Therefore, deliver me from him, thereby
Likewise delivering from me yourself !
For, hesitate — much more, refuse consent —
I tell the whole truth to your husband. Flat
Cards lie on table, in our gamester-phrase !
Consent — you stop my mouth, the only way."

" I did well, trusting instinct : knew your
     hand
Had never joined with his in fellowship
Over this pact of infamy. You known —
As he was known through every nerve of me.
Therefore I ' *stopped his mouth the only way* '
But *my* way ! none was left for you, my
     friend —
The loyal — near, the loved one ! No — no — no !
Threaten ? Chastise ? The coward would but
     quail.
Conquer who can, the cunning of the snake !
Stamp out his slimy strength from tail to head,
And still you leave vibration of the tongue.
His malice had redoubled — not on me
Who, myself, choose my own refining fire —
But on poor unsuspicious innocence ;
And, — victim, — to turn executioner
Also — that feat effected, forky tongue
Had done indeed its office ! Once snake's
     ' *mouth* '
Thus ' *open* ' — how could mortal ' *stop it* ' ? "

                         " So ! "

A tiger-flash — yell, spring, and scream : hal-
     loo !
Death 's out and on him, has and holds him —
     ugh !

But *ne trucidet coram populo*
Juvenis senem ! Right the Horatian rule !

There, see how soon a quiet comes to pass !

                    VIII

The youth is somehow by the lady's side.
His right-hand grasps her right-hand once
     again.
Both gaze on the dead body. Hers the word.

" And that was good but useless. Had I lived,
The danger was to dread : but, dying now —
Himself would hardly become talkative,
Since talk no more means torture. Fools —
     what fools
These wicked men are ! Had I borne four
     years,
Four years of weeks and months and days and
     nights,
Inured me to the consciousness of life
Coiled round by his life, with the tongue to
     ply, —
But that I bore about me, for prompt use
At urgent need, the thing that ' *stops the mouth* '
And stays the venom ? Since such need was
     now
Or never, — how should use not follow need ?
Bear witness for me, I withdraw from life
By virtue of the license — warrant, say,
That blackens yet this Album — white again,
Thanks still to my one friend who tears the
     page !
Now, let me write the line of supplement,
As counselled by my foe there : ' *each a line !* ' "

And she does falteringly write to end.

" *I die now through the villain who lies dead,*
Righteously slain. He would have outraged me,
So, my defender slew him. God protect
The right ! Where wrong lay, I bear witness
     now.
Let man believe me, whose last breath is spent
In blessing my defender from my soul ! "

And so ends the Inn Album.

                         As she dies,
Begins outside a voice that sounds like song,
And is indeed half song though meant for
     speech
Muttered in time to motion — stir of heart
That unsubduably must bubble forth
To match the fawn-step as it mounts the stair.

" All 's ended and all 's over ! Verdict found
' *Not guilty* ' — prisoner forthwith set free,
'Mid cheers the Court pretends to disregard !
Now Portia, now for Daniel, late severe.
At last appeased, benignant ! ' *This young*
     man —
Hem — has the young man's foibles but no fault.
He 's virgin soil — a friend must cultivate.
I think no plant called " love " grows wild — a
     friend

May introduce, and name the bloom, the fruit!'
Here somebody dares wave a handkerchief —
She 'll want to hide her face with presently !
Good-by then !   ' *Cigno fedel, cigno fedel,*
Addio !' Now, was ever such mistake —
Ever such foolish ugly omen ?   Pshaw !
Wagner, beside ! '*Amo te solo, te*
Solo amai !' That 's worth fifty such !
But, mum, the grave face at the opened door ! "

And so the good gay girl, with eyes and
          cheeks

Diamond and damask, — cheeks so white ere
          while
Because of a vague fancy, idle fear
Chased on reflection ! — pausing, taps discreet ;
And then, to give herself a countenance,
Before she comes upon the pair inside,
Loud — the oft-quoted,   long - laughed - over
          line —
" ' *Hail, calm acclivity, salubrious spot !'*
Open the door ! "

                    No : let the curtain fall !

PACCHIAROTTO

AND

HOW HE WORKED IN DISTEMPER

WITH OTHER POEMS

PROLOGUE

OH, the old wall here !   How I could pass
    Life in a long midsummer day,
My feet confined to a plot of grass,
    My eyes from a wall not once away !

And lush and lithe do the creepers clothe
    Yon wall I watch, with a wealth of green :
Its bald red bricks draped, nothing loth,
    In lappets of tangle they laugh between.

Now, what is it makes pulsate the robe ?
    Why tremble the sprays ?   What life o'er-
      brims
The body, — the house, no eye can probe, —
    Divined as, beneath a robe, the limbs ?

And there again !   But my heart may guess
    Who tripped behind ; and she sang perhaps :
So, the old wall throbbed, and its life's excess
    Died out and away in the leafy wraps !

Wall upon wall are between us : life
    And song should away from heart to heart !
I — prison-bird, with a ruddy strife
    At breast, and a lip whence storm-notes
      start —

Hold on, hope hard in the subtle thing
    That 's spirit : though cloistered fast, soar
      free ;
Account as wood, brick, stone, this ring
    Of the rueful neighbors, and — forth to thee !

OF PACCHIAROTTO, AND HOW HE
WORKED IN DISTEMPER

I

QUERY : was ever a quainter
Crotchet than this of the painter

Giacomo Pacchiarotto
Who took " Reform " for his motto ?

II

He, pupil of old Fungaio,
Is always confounded (heigho !)
With Pacchia, contemporaneous
No question, but how extraneous
In the grace of soul, the power
Of hand, — undoubted dower
Of Pacchia who decked (as *we* know,
My Kirkup !) San Bernardino,
Turning the small dark Oratory
To Siena's Art-laboratory,
As he made its straitness roomy
And glorified its gloomy,
With Bazzi and Beccafumi.
(Another heigho for Bazzi :
How people miscall him Razzi !)

III

This Painter was of opinion
Our earth should be his dominion
Whose Art could correct to pattern
What Nature had slurred — the slattern !
And since, beneath the heavens,
Things lay now at sixes and sevens,
Or, as he said, *sopra-sotto* —
Thought the painter Pacchiarotto
Things wanted reforming, therefore.
" Wanted it " — ay, but wherefore ?
When earth held one so ready
As he to step forth, stand steady
In the middle of God's creation
And prove to demonstration
What the dark is, what the light is,
What the wrong is, what the right is,
What the ugly, what the beautiful,
What the restive, what the dutiful,
In Mankind profuse around him ?
Man, devil as now he found him,
Would presently soar up angel

At the summons of such evangel,
And owe — what would Man *not* owe
To the painter Pacchiarotto?
Ay, look to thy laurels, Giotto!

IV

But Man, he perceived, was stubborn,
Grew regular brute, once cub born;
And it struck him as expedient —
Ere he tried to make obedient
The wolf, fox, bear, and monkey
By piping advice in one key, —
That his pipe should play a prelude
To something heaven-tinged not hell-hued,
Something not harsh but docile,
Man-liquid, not Man-fossil —
Not fact, in short, but fancy —
By a laudable necromancy
He would conjure up ghosts — a circle
Deprived of the means to work ill
Should his music prove distasteful
And pearls to the swine go wasteful.
To be rent of swine — that *was* hard!
With fancy he ran no hazard:
Fact might knock him o'er the mazard.

V

So, the painter Pacchiarotto
Constructed himself a grotto
In the quarter of Stalloreggi —
As authors of note allege ye.
And on each of the whitewashed sides of it
He painted — (none far and wide so fit
As he to perform in fresco) —
He painted nor cried *quiesco*
Till he peopled its every square foot
With Man — from the Beggar barefoot
To the Noble in cap and feather;
All sorts and conditions together.
The Soldier in breastplate and helmet
Stood frowningly — hail fellow well met —
By the Priest armed with bell, book, and can-
  dle.
Nor did he omit to handle
The Fair Sex, our brave distemperer:
Not merely King, Clown, Pope, Emperor —
He diversified too his Hades
Of all forms, pinched Labor and paid Ease,
With as mixed an assemblage of Ladies.

VI

Which work done, dry, — he rested him,
Cleaned palette, washed brush, divested him
Of the apron that suits *frescanti*,
And, bonnet on ear stuck jaunty,
This hand upon hip well planted,
That, free to wave as it wanted,
He addressed in a choice oration
His folk of each name and nation,
Taught its duty to every station.
The Pope was declared an arrant
Impostor at once, I warrant.
The Emperor — truth might tax him
With ignorance of the maxim
" Shear sheep but nowise flay them!"
And the Vulgar that obey them,
The Ruled, well-matched with the Ruling,

They failed not of wholesome schooling
On their knavery and their fooling.
As for Art — where's decorum? Pooh-poohed
  it is
By Poets that plague us with lewd ditties,
And Painters that pester with nudities!

VII

Now, your rater and debater
Is balked by a mere spectator
Who simply stares and listens
Tongue-tied, while eye nor glistens
Nor brow grows hot and twitchy,
Nor mouth, for a combat itchy,
Quivers with some convincing
Reply — that sets him wincing?
Nay, rather — reply that furnishes
Your debater with just what burnishes
The crest of him, all one triumph,
As you see him rise, hear him cry " Humph!
Convinced am I? This confutes me?
Receive the rejoinder that suits me!
Confutation of vassal for prince meet —
Wherein all the powers that convince meet,
And mash my opponent to mincemeat!"

VIII

So, off from his head flies the bonnet,
His hip loses hand planted on it,
While t' other hand, frequent in gesture,
Slinks modestly back beneath vesture,
As — hop, skip and jump, — he's along with
Those weak ones he late proved so strong
  with!
Pope, Emperor, lo, he's beside them,
Friendly now, who late could not abide them,
King, Clown, Soldier, Priest, Noble, Burgess;
And his voice, that out-roared Boanerges,
How minikin-mildly it urges
In accents how gentled and gingered
Its word in defence of the injured!
" Oh, call him not culprit, this Pontiff!
Be hard on this Kaiser ye won't if
Ye take into con-si-der-ation
What dangers attend elevation!
The Priest — who expects him to descant
On duty with more zeal and less cant?
He preaches but rubbish he's reared in.
The Soldier, grown deaf (by the mere din
Of battle) to mercy, learned tippling
And what not of vice while a stripling.
The Lawyer — his lies are conventional.
And as for the Poor Sort — why mention all
Obstructions that leave barred and bolted
Access to the brains of each dolt-head?"

IX

He ended, you wager? Not half! A bet?
Precedence to males in the alphabet!
Still, disposed of Man's A B C, there's X
Y Z want assistance, — the Fair Sex!
How much may be said in excuse of
Those vanities — males see no use of —
From silk shoe on heel to laced poll's-hood;
What's their frailty beside our own falsehood?
The boldest, most brazen of . . . trumpets,
How kind can they be to their dumb pets!

Of their charms — how are most frank, how few
    venal !
While as for those charges of Juvenal —
Quæ nemo dixisset in toto
Nisi (œdepol) ore illoto —
He dismissed every charge with an " *Apage !* "

X

Then, cocking (in Scotch phrase) his cap
    a-gee,
Right hand disengaged from the doublet
— Like landlord, in house he had sublet
Resuming of guardianship gestion,
To call tenants' conduct in question —
Hop, skip, jump, to inside from outside
Of chamber, he lords, ladies, louts eyed
With such transformation of visage
As fitted the censor of this age.
No longer an advocate tepid
Of frailty, but champion intrepid
Of strength, — not of falsehood but verity, —
He, one after one, with asperity
Stripped bare all the cant-clothed abuses,
Disposed of sophistic excuses,
Forced folly each shift to abandon,
And left vice with no leg to stand on.
So crushing the force he exerted,
That Man at his foot lay converted !

XI

True — Man bred of paint-pot and mortar !
But why suppose folks of this sort are
More likely to hear and be tractable
Than folks all alive and, in fact, able
To testify promptly by action
Their ardor, and make satisfaction
For misdeeds *non verbis sed factis* ?
" With folks all alive be my practice
Henceforward !   O mortar, paint-pot O,
Farewell to ye ! " cried Pacchiarotto,
" Let only occasion intérpose ! "

XII

It did so : for, pat to the purpose
Through causes I need not examine,
There fell upon Siena a famine.
In vain did the magistrates busily
Seek succor, fetch grain out of Sicily,
Nay, throw mill and bakehouse wide open —
Such misery followed as no pen
Of mine shall depict ye.   Faint, fainter
Waxed hope of relief : so, our painter,
Emboldened by triumph of recency,
How could he do other with decency
Than rush in this strait to the rescue,
Play schoolmaster, point as with fescue
To each and all slips in Man's spelling
The law of the land ? — slips now telling
With monstrous effect on the city,
Whose magistrates moved him to pity
As, bound to read law to the letter,
They minded their hornbook no better.

XIII

I ought to have told you, at starting,
How certain, who itched to be carting

Abuses away clean and thorough
From Siena, both province and borough,
Had formed themselves into a company
Whose swallow could bolt in a lump any
Obstruction of scruple, provoking
The nicer throat's coughing and choking :
Fit Club, by as fit a name dignified
Of " Freed Ones " — " *Bardotti* " — which sig
    nified
" Spare-Horses " that walk by the wagon
The team has to drudge for and drag on.
This notable Club Pacchiarotto
Had joined long since, paid scot and lot to,
As free and accepted " Bardotto."
The Bailiwick watched with no quiet eye
The outrage thus done to society,
And noted the advent especially
Of Pacchiarotto their fresh ally.

XIV

These Spare-Horses forthwith assembled :
Neighed words whereat citizens trembled
As oft as the chiefs, in the Square by
The Duomo, proposed a way whereby
The city were cured of disaster.
" Just substitute servant for master,
Make Poverty Wealth and Wealth Poverty,
Unloose Man from overt and covert tie,
And straight out of social confusion
True Order would spring ! "   Brave illusion —
Aims heavenly attained by means earthy !

XV

Off to these at full speed rushed our wor
    thy, —
Brain practised and tongue no less tutored,
In argument's armor accoutred, —
Sprang forth, mounted rostrum, and essayed
Proposals like those to which " Yes " said
So glibly each personage painted
O' the wall-side wherewith you 're acquainted.
He harangued on the faults of the Bailiwick :
" Red soon were our State-candle's paly wick,
If wealth would become but interfluous,
Fill voids up with just the superfluous ;
If ignorance gave way to knowledge
— Not pedantry picked up at college
From Doctors, Professors *et cætera* —
(*They* say : ' *kai ta loipa* '— like better a
Long Greek string of *kappas, taus, lambdas*,
Tacked on to the tail of each damned ass) —
No knowledge we want of this quality,
But knowledge indeed — practicality
Through insight's fine universality !
If you shout ' *Bailiffs, out on ye all !   Fie,*
Thou Chief of our forces, Amalfi,
Who shieldest the rogue and the clotpoll ! '
If you pounce on and poke out, with what
    pole
I leave ye to fancy, our Siena's
Beast-litter of sloths and hyenas — "
(Whoever to scan this is ill able
Forgets the town's name 's a dissyllable) —
" If, this done, ye did — as ye might — place
For once the right man in the right place,
If you listened to me " . . .

XVI

At which last "If "
There flew at his throat like a mastiff
One Spare-Horse — another and another !
Such outbreak of tumult and pother,
Horse-faces a-laughing and fleering,
Horse-voices a-mocking and jeering,
Horse-hands raised to collar the caitiff
Whose impudence ventured the late "If " —
That, had not fear sent Pacchiarotto
Off tramping, as fast as could trot toe,
Away from the scene of discomfiture —
Had he stood there stock-still in a dumb fit —
    sure
Am I he had paid in his person
Till his mother might fail to know her son,
Though she gazed on him never so wistful,
In the figure so tattered and tristful.
Each mouth full of curses, each fist full
Of cuffings — behold, Pacchiarotto,
The pass which thy project has got to,
Of trusting, nigh ashes still hot — tow !
(The paraphrase — which I much need — is
From Horace " *per ignes incedis.*")

XVII

Right and left did he dash helter-skelter
In agonized search of a shelter.
No purlieu so blocked and no alley
So blind as allowed him to rally
His spirits and see — nothing hampered
His steps if he trudged and not scampered
Up here and down there in a city
That 's all ups and downs, more the pity
For folks who would outrun the constable.
At last he stopped short at the one stable
And sure place of refuge that 's offered
Humanity.   Lately was coffered
A corpse in its sepulchre, situate
By St. John's Observance.   "Habituate
Thyself to the strangest of bedfellows,
And, kicked by the live, kiss the dead fellows ! "
So Misery counselled the craven.
At once he crept safely to haven
Through a hole left unbricked in the structure.
Ay, Misery, in have you tucked your
Poor client and left him conterminous
With — pah ! — the thing fetid and verminous !
(I gladly would spare you the detail,
But History writes what I retail.)

XVIII

Two days did he groan in his domicile :
"Good Saints, set me free and I promise I 'll
Abjure all ambition of preaching
Change, whether to minds touched by teaching
— The smooth folk of fancy, mere figments
Created by plaster and pigments, —
Or to minds that receive with such rudeness
Dissuasion from pride, greed and lewdness,
— The rough folk of fact, life's true specimens
Of mind — ' *haud in posse sed esse mens* '
As it was, is, and shall be forever
Despite of my utmost endeavor.
O live foes I thought to illumine,
Henceforth lie untroubled your gloom in !

I need my own light, every spark, as
I couch with this sole friend — a carcase ! "

XIX

Two days thus he maundered and rambled ;
Then, starved back to sanity, scrambled
From out his receptacle loathsome.
"A spectre ! " — declared upon oath some
Who saw him emerge and (appalling
To mention) his garments a-crawling
With plagues far beyond the Egyptian.
He gained, in a state past description,
A convent of months, the Observancy.

XX

Thus far is a fact : I reserve fancy
For Fancy's more proper employment :
And now she waves wing with enjoyment,
To tell ye how preached the Superior,
When somewhat our painter's exterior
Was sweetened.   He needed (no mincing
The matter) much soaking and rinsing,
Nay, rubbing with drugs odoriferous,
Till, rid of his garments pestiferous,
And, robed by the help of the Brotherhood
In odds and ends, — this gown and t' other
    hood, —
His empty inside first well-garnished, —
He delivered a tale round, unvarnished.

XXI

"Ah, Youth ! " ran the Abbot's admonish-
    ment,
"Thine error scarce moves my astonishment.
For — why shall I shrink from asserting ? —
Myself have had hopes of converting
The foolish to wisdom, till, sober,
My life found its May grow October.
I talked and I wrote, but, one morning,
Life's Autumn bore fruit in this warning :
' *Let tongue rest, and quiet thy quill be !*
Earth is earth and not heaven, and ne'er will be.'
Man's work is to labor and leaven —
As best he may — earth here with heaven ;
'T is work for work's sake that he 's needing :
Let him work on and on as if speeding
Work's end, but not dream of succeeding !
Because if success were intended,
Why, heaven would begin ere earth ended.
A Spare-Horse ?   Be rather a thill-horse,
Or — what 's the plain truth — just a mill-
    horse !
Earth's a mill where we grind and wear
    mufflers :
A whip awaits shirkers and shufflers
Who slacken their pace, sick of lugging
At what don't advance for their tugging.
Though round goes the mill, we must still post
On and on as if moving the mill-post.
So, grind away, mouth-wise and pen-wise,
Do all that we can to make men wise !
And if men prefer to be foolish,
Ourselves have proved horse-like not mulish :
Sent grist, a good sackful, to hopper,
And worked as the Master thought proper.
Tongue I wag, pen I ply, who am Abbot ;

Stick, thou, Son, to daub-brush and dab-pot!
But, soft! I scratch hard on the scab hot?
Though cured of thy plague, there may linger
A pimple I fray with rough finger?
So soon could my homily transmute
Thy brass into gold? Why, the man's mute!"

XXII

"Ay, Father, I'm mute with admiring
How Nature's indulgence untiring
Still bids us turn deaf ear to Reason's
Best rhetoric — clutch at all seasons
And hold fast to what's proved untenable!
Thy maxim is — Man's not amenable
To argument: whereof by consequence —
Thine arguments reach me: a non-sequence!
Yet blush not discouraged, O Father!
I stand unconverted, the rather
That nowise I need a conversion.
No live man (I cap thy assertion)
By argument ever could take hold
Of me. 'T was the dead thing, the clay-cold,
Which grinned '*Art thou so in a hurry*
That out of warm light thou must scurry
And join me down here in the dungeon
Because, above, one's Jack and one — John,
One's swift in the race, one — a hobbler,
One's a crowned king and one — a capped cobbler,
Rich and poor, sage and fool, virtuous, vicious?
Why complain? Art thou so unsuspicious
That all's for an hour of essaying
Who's fit and who's unfit for playing
His part in the after-construction
— Heaven's Piece whereof Earth's the Induction?
Things rarely go smooth at Rehearsal.
Wait patient the change universal,
And act, and let act, in existence!
For, as thou art clapped hence or hissed hence,
Thou hast thy promotion or otherwise.
And why must wise thou have thy brother wise
Because in rehearsal thy cue be
To shine by the side of a booby?
No polishing garnet to ruby!
All's well that ends well — through Art's magic.
Some end, whether comic or tragic,
The Artist has purposed, be certain!
Explained at the fall of the curtain —
In showing thy wisdom at odds with
That folly: he tries men and gods with
No problem for weak wits to solve meant,
But one worth such Author's evolvement.
So, back nor disturb play's production
By giving thy brother instruction
To throw up his fool's-part allotted!
Lest haply thyself prove besotted
When stript, for thy pains, of that costume
Of sage, which has bred the imposthume
I prick to relieve thee of, — Vanity!'

XXIII

"So, Father, behold me in sanity!
I'm back to the palette and mahlstick:
And as for Man — let each and all stick
To what was prescribed them at starting!
Once planted as fools — no departing
From folly one inch, *sæculorum*

In sæcula! Pass me the jorum,
And push me the platter — my stomach
Retains, through its fasting, still some ache —
And then, with your kind *Benedicite*,
Good-by!'"

XXIV

I have told with simplicity
My tale, dropped those harsh analytics,
And tried to content you, my critics,
Who greeted my early uprising!
I knew you through all the disguising,
Droll dogs, as I jumped up, cried "Heyday!
This Monday is — what else but May-day?
And these in the drabs, blues, and yellows,
Are surely the privileged fellows.
So, saltbox and bones, tongs and bellows!"
(I threw up the window) "Your pleasure?"

XXV

Then he who directed the measure —
An old friend — put leg forward nimbly,
"We critics as sweeps out your chimbly!
Much soot to remove from your flue, sir!
Who spares coal in kitchen an't you, sir!
And neighbors complain it's no joke, sir,
— You ought to consume your own smoke, sir!"

XXVI

Ah, rogues, but my housemaid suspects
you —
Is confident oft she detects you
In bringing more filth into my house
Than ever you found there! I'm pious,
However: 't was God made you dingy
And me — with no need to be stingy
Of soap, when 't is sixpence the packet.
So, dance away, boys, dust my jacket,
Bang drum and blow fife — ay, and rattle
Your brushes, for that's half the battle!
Don't trample the grass, — hocus-pocus
With grime my Spring snowdrop and crocus, —
And, what with your rattling and tinkling,
Who knows but you give me an inkling
How music sounds, thanks to the jangle
Of regular drum and triangle?
Whereby, tap-tap, chink-chink, 't is proven
I break rule as bad as Beethoven.
"That chord now — a groan or a grunt is 't?
Schumann's self was no worse contrapuntist.
No ear! or if ear, so tough-gristled —
He thought that he sung while he whistled!"

XXVII

So, this time I whistle, not sing at all,
My story, the largest I fling at all
And every the rough there whose *aubade*
Did its best to amuse me, — nor *so* bad!
Take my thanks, pick up largess, and scamper
Off free, ere your mirth gets a damper!
You've Monday, your one day, your fun-day,
While mine is a year that's all Sunday.
I've seen you, times — who knows how
many? —
Dance in here, strike up, play the zany,
Make mouths at the Tenant, hoot warning

You 'll find him decamped next May-morning ;
Then scuttle away, glad to 'scape hence
With — kicks ? no, but laughter and ha'pence !
Mine 's freehold, by grace of the grand Lord
Who lets out the ground here, — my landlord :
To him I pay quit-rent — devotion ;
Nor hence shall I budge, I 've a notion,
Nay, here shall my whistling and singing
Set all his street's echoes a-ringing
Long after the last of your number
Has ceased my front-court to encumber
While, treading down rose and ranunculus,
You *Tommy-make-room-for-your-Uncle* us !
Troop, all of you — man or homunculus,
Quick march ! for Xanthippe, my housemaid,
If once on your pates she a souse made
With what, pan or pot, bowl or *skoramis*,
First comes to her hand — things were more
    amiss !
I would not for worlds be your place in —
Recipient of slops from the basin !
You, Jack-in-the-Green, leaf-and-twiggishness
Won't save a dry thread on your priggishness !
While as for Quilp-Hop-o'-my-thumb there,
Banjo-Byron that twangs the strum-strum
    there —
He 'll think as the pickle he curses,
I 've discharged on his pate his own verses !
" Dwarfs are saucy," says Dickens : so, sauced
    in
Your own sauce,[1] . . .

XXVIII

But, back to my Knight of the Pencil,
Dismissed to his fresco and stencil !
Whose story — begun with a chuckle,
And   throughout   timed   by   raps   of   the
    knuckle, —
To small enough purpose were studied
If it ends with crown cracked or nose bloodied.
Come, critics, — not shake hands, excuse me !
But — say have you grudged to amuse me
This once in the forty-and-over
Long years since you trampled my clover
And scared from my house-eaves each sparrow
I never once harmed by that arrow
Of song, *karterotaton belos,*
(Which Pindar declares the true *melos,*)
I was forging and filing and finishing,
And no whit my labors diminishing
Because, though high up in a chamber
Where none of your kidney may clamber
Your hullabaloo would approach me ?
Was   it   "grammar"   wherein   you   would
    " coach " me —
You, — pacing in even that paddock
Of language allotted you *ad hoc,*
With a clog at your fetlocks, — you — scorners
Of me free of all its four corners ?
Was   it   "clearness   of   words   which   convey
    thought " ?
Ay, if words never needed enswathe aught
But ignorance, impudence, envy
And malice — what word-swathe would then vie

[1] No, please ! For
    " Who would be satirical
        On a thing so very small ? " — *Printer's Devil.*

With yours for a clearness crystalline ?
But had you to put in one small line
Some thought big and bouncing — as noddle
Of goose, born to cackle and waddle
And bite at man's heel as goose-wont is,
Never felt plague its puny *os frontis* —
You 'd know, as you hissed, spat and sput-
    tered,
Clear cackle is easily uttered !

XXIX

Lo, I 've laughed out my laugh on this mirth-
    day !
Beside, at week's end, dawns my birthday,
That *hebdome, hieron emar* —
(More things in a day than you deem are !)
— *Tei gar Apollona chrusaora*
Egeinato Leto. So, gray or ray
Betide me, six days hence, I 'm vexed here
By no sweep, that 's certain, till next year !
" Vexed ? " — roused from what else were in
    sipid ease !
Leave snoring abed to Pheidippides !
We 'll up and work ! won't we, Euripides ?

AT THE " MERMAID "

The figure that thou here seest . . . Tut !
Was it for gentle Shakespeare put ?
            B. JONSON. (*Adapted.*)

I — " NEXT Poet ? " No, my hearties,
    I nor am nor fain would be !
Choose your chiefs and pick your parties,
    Not one soul revolt to me !
I, forsooth, sow song-sedition ?
    I, a schism in verse provoke ?
I, blown up by bard's ambition,
    Burst — your bubble-king ? You joke.

Come, be grave ! The sherris mantling
    Still about each mouth, mayhap,
Breeds you insight — just a scantling —
    Brings me truth out — just a scrap.
Look and tell me ! Written, spoken,
    Here 's my life-long work : and where
— Where 's your warrant or my token
    I 'm the dead king's son and heir ?

Here 's my work : does work discover —
    What was rest from work — my life ?
Did I live man's hater, lover ?
    Leave the world at peace, at strife ?
Call earth ugliness or beauty ?
    See things there in large or small ?
Use to pay its Lord my duty ?
    Use to own a lord at all ?

Blank of such a record, truly,
    Here 's the work I hand, this scroll,
Yours to take or leave ; as duly,
    Mine remains the unproffered soul.
So much, no whit more, my debtors —
    How should one like me lay claim
To that largess elders, betters
    Sell you cheap their souls for — fame ?

Which of you did I enable
  Once to slip inside my breast,
There to catalogue and label
  What I like least, what love best,
Hope and fear, believe and doubt of,
  Seek and shun, respect — deride ?
Who has right to make a rout of
  Rarities he found inside ?

Rarities or, as he 'd rather,
  Rubbish such as stocks his own :
Need and greed (oh, strange) the Father
  Fashioned not for him alone !
Whence — the comfort set a-strutting,
  Whence — the outcry " Haste, behold !
Bard's breast open wide, past shutting,
  Shows what brass we took for gold ! "

Friends, I doubt not he 'd display you
  Brass — myself call orichalc, —
Furnish much amusement ; pray you
  Therefore, be content I balk
Him and you, and bar my portal !
  Here 's my work outside : opine
What 's inside me mean and mortal !
  Take your pleasure, leave me mine !

Which is — not to buy your laurel
  As last king did, nothing loth.
Tale adorned and pointed moral
  Gained him praise and pity both.
Out rushed sighs and groans by dozens,
  Forth by scores oaths, curses flew :
Proving you were cater-cousins,
  Kith and kindred, king and you !

Whereas do I ne'er so little
  (Thanks to sherris), leave ajar
Bosom's gate — no jot nor tittle
  Grow we nearer than we are.
Sinning, sorrowing, despairing,
  Body-ruined, spirit-wrecked, —
Should I give my woes an airing, —
  Where 's one plague that claims respect ?

Have you found your life distasteful ?
  My life did and does smack sweet.
Was your youth of pleasure wasteful ?
  Mine I saved and hold complete.
Do your joys with age diminish ?
  When mine fail me, I 'll complain.
Must in death your daylight finish ?
  My sun sets to rise again.

What, like you, he proved — your Pilgrim —
  This our world a wilderness,
Earth still gray and heaven still grim,
  Not a hand there his might press,
Not a heart his own might throb to,
  Men all rogues and women — say,
Dolls which boys' heads duck and bob to,
  Grown folk drop or throw away ?

My experience being other,
  How should I contribute verse
Worthy of your king and brother ?
  Balaam-like I bless, not curse.

I find earth not gray but rosy,
  Heaven not grim but fair of hue.
Do I stoop ? I pluck a posy.
  Do I stand and stare ? All 's blue.

Doubtless I am pushed and shoved by
  Rogues and fools enough : the more
Good luck mine, I love, am loved by
  Some few honest to the core.
Scan the near high, scout the far low !
  " But the low come close : " what then ?
Simpletons ? My match is Marlowe ;
  Sciolists ? My mate is Ben.

Womankind — " the cat-like nature,
  False and fickle, vain and weak " —
What of this sad nomenclature
  Suits my tongue, if I must speak ?
Does the sex invite, repulse so,
  Tempt, betray, by fits and starts ?
So becalm but to convulse so,
  Decking heads and breaking hearts ?

Well may you blaspheme at fortune !
  I " threw Venus " (Ben, expound !)
Never did I need importune
  Her, of all the Olympian round.
Blessings on my benefactress !
  Cursings suit — for aught I know —
Those who twitched her by the back tress,
  Tugged and thought to turn her — so !

Therefore, since no leg to stand on
  Thus I 'm left with, — joy or grief
Be the issue, — I abandon
  Hope or care you name me Chief !
Chief and king and Lord's anointed,
  I ? — who never once have wished
Death before the day appointed :
  Lived and liked, not poohed and pished !

" Ah, but so I shall not enter,
  Scroll in hand, the common heart —
Stopped at surface : since at centre
  Song should reach Welt-schmerz, world
    smart ! "
" Enter in the heart ? " Its shelly
  Cuirass guard mine, fore and aft !
Such song " enters in the belly
  And is cast out in the draught."

Back then to our sherris-brewage !
  " Kingship " quotha ? I shall wait —
Waive the present time : some new age . . .
  But let fools anticipate !
Meanwhile greet me — " friend, good fellow,
  Gentle Will," my merry men !
As for making Envy yellow
  With " Next Poet " — (Manners, Ben !)

HOUSE

Shall I sonnet-sing you about myself ?
  Do I live in a house you would like to see ?
Is it scant of gear, has it store of pelf ?
  " Unlock my heart with a sonnet-key ? "

Invite the world, as my betters have done?
  "Take notice: this building remains on view,
Its suites of reception every one,
  Its private apartment and bedroom too;

"For a ticket, apply to the Publisher."
  No: thanking the public, I must decline.
A peep through my window, if folk prefer;
  But, please you, no foot over threshold of
    mine!

I have mixed with a crowd and heard free talk
  In a foreign land where an earthquake chanced
And a house stood gaping, naught to balk
  Man's eye wherever he gazed or glanced.

The whole of the frontage shaven sheer,
  The inside gaped: exposed to day,
Right and wrong and common and queer,
  Bare, as the palm of your hand, it lay.

The owner? Oh, he had been crushed, no
    doubt!
  "Odd tables and chairs for a man of wealth!
What a parcel of musty old books about!
  He smoked, — no wonder he lost his health!

"I doubt if he bathed before he dressed.
  A brasier? — the pagan, he burned perfumes!
You see it is proved, what the neighbors guessed:
  His wife and himself had separate rooms."

Friends, the goodman of the house at least
  Kept house to himself till an earthquake came:
'T is the fall of its frontage permits you feast
  On the inside arrangement you praise or blame.

Outside should suffice for evidence:
  And whoso desires to penetrate
Deeper, must dive by the spirit-sense —
  No optics like yours, at any rate!

'Hoity-toity! A street to explore,
  Your house the exception! 'With this same key
Shakespeare unlocked his heart,' once more!"
  Did Shakespeare? If so, the less Shakespeare
    he!

SHOP

So, friend, your shop was all your house!
  Its front, astonishing the street,
Invited view from man and mouse
  To what diversity of treat
Behind its glass — the single sheet!

What gimcracks, genuine Japanese:
  Gape-jaw and goggle-eye, the frog;
Dragons, owls, monkeys, beetles, geese;
  Some crush-nosed human-hearted dog:
Queer names, too, such a catalogue!

I thought "And he who owns the wealth
  Which blocks the window's vastitude,
— Ah, could I peep at him by stealth
  Behind his ware, pass shop, intrude
On house itself, what scenes were viewed!

"If wide and showy thus the shop,
  What must the habitation prove?
The true house with no name a-top —
  The mansion, distant one remove,
Once get him off his traffic-groove!

"Pictures he likes, or books perhaps;
  And as for buying most and best,
Commend me to these city chaps!
  Or else he 's social, takes his rest
On Sundays, with a Lord for guest.

"Some suburb-palace, parked about
  And gated grandly, built last year:
The four-mile walk to keep off gout;
  Or big seat sold by bankrupt peer:
But then he takes the rail, that 's clear.

"Or, stop! I wager, taste selects
  Some out-o'-the-way, some all-unknown
Retreat: the neighborhood suspects
  Little that he who rambles lone
Makes Rothschild tremble on his throne!"

Nowise! Nor Mayfair residence
  Fit to receive and entertain, —
Nor Hampstead villa's kind defence
  From noise and crowd, from dust and drain, —
Nor country-box was soul's domain!

Nowise! At back of all that spread
  Of merchandise, woe 's me, I find
A hole i' the wall where, heels by head,
  The owner couched, his ware behind,
— In cupboard suited to his mind.

For why? He saw no use of life
  But, while he drove a roaring trade,
To chuckle "Customers are rife!"
  To chafe "So much hard cash outlaid,
Yet zero in my profits made!

"This novelty costs pains, but — takes?
  Cumbers my counter! Stock no more!
This article, no such great shakes,
  Fizzes like wildfire? Underscore
The cheap thing — thousands to the fore!"

'T was lodging best to live most nigh
  (Cramp, coffinlike as crib might be)
Receipt of Custom; ear and eye
  Wanted no outworld: "Hear and see
The bustle in the shop!" quoth he.

My fancy of a merchant-prince
  Was different. Through his wares we groped
Our darkling way to — not to mince
  The matter — no black den where moped
The master if we interloped!

Shop was shop only: household-stuff?
  What did he want with comforts there?
"Walls, ceiling, floor, stay blank and rough,
  So goods on sale show rich and rare!
'Sell and scud home,' be shop's affair!"

What might he deal in? Gems, suppose!
  Since somehow business must be done

At cost of trouble, — see, he throws
   You choice of jewels, every one,
Good, better, best, star, moon, and sun !

Which lies within your power of purse ?
   This ruby that would tip aright
Solomon's sceptre ? Oh, your nurse
   Wants simply coral, the delight
Of teething baby, — stuff to bite !

How e'er your choice fell, straight you took
   Your purchase, prompt your money rang
On counter, — scarce the man forsook
   His study of the "Times," just swang
Till-ward his hand that stopped the clang, —

Then off made buyer with a prize,
   Then seller to his "Times" returned ;
And so did day wear, wear, till eyes
   Brightened apace, for rest was earned :
He locked door long ere candle burned.

And whither went he ? Ask himself,
   Not me ! To change of scene, I think.
Once sold the ware and pursed the pelf,
   Chaffer was scarce his meat and drink,
Nor all his music — money-chink.

Because a man has shop to mind
   In time and place, since flesh must live,
Needs spirit lack all life behind,
   All stray thoughts, fancies fugitive,
All loves except what trade can give ?

I want to know a butcher paints,
   A baker rhymes for his pursuit,
Candlestick-maker much acquaints
   His soul with song, or, haply mute,
Blows out his brains upon the flute !

But — shop each day and all day long !
   Friend, your good angel slept, your star
Suffered eclipse, fate did you wrong !
   From where these sorts of treasures are,
There should our hearts be — Christ, how far !

PISGAH–SIGHTS

When sanctioning a volume of *Selections* from
his poems, Browning made a third of *Pisgah-
Sights* to consist of the *Proem* to *La Saisiaz.*

I

Over the ball of it,
   Peering and prying,
How I see all of it,
   Life there, outlying !
Roughness and smoothness,
   Shine and defilement,
Grace and uncouthness :
   One reconcilement.

Orbed as appointed,
   Sister with brother
Joins, ne'er disjointed
   One from the other.

All 's lend-and-borrow ;
   Good, see, wants evil,
Joy demands sorrow,
   Angel weds devil !

" Which things must — *why* be ? '
   Vain our endeavor !
So shall things aye be
   As they were ever.
" Such things should *so* be ! "
   Sage our desistence !
Rough-smooth let globe be,
   Mixed — man's existence !

Man — wise and foolish,
   Lover and scorner,
Docile and mulish —
   Keep each his corner !
Honey yet gall of it !
   There 's the life lying,
And I see all of it,
   Only, I 'm dying !

II

Could I but live again
   Twice my life over,
Would I once strive again ?
   Would not I cover
Quietly all of it —
   Greed and ambition —
So, from the pall of it,
   Pass to fruition ?

" Soft ! " I 'd say, " Soul mine !
   Three-score and ten years,
Let the blind mole mine
   Digging out deniers !
Let the dazed hawk soar,
   Claim the sun's rights too !
Turf 't is thy walk 's o'er,
   Foliage thy flight 's to."

Only a learner,
   Quick one or slow one,
Just a discerner,
   I would teach no one.
I am earth's native :
   No rearranging it !
I be creative,
   Chopping and changing it ?

March, men, my fellows !
   Those who, above me,
(Distance so mellows)
   Fancy you love me :
Those who, below me,
   (Distance makes great so)
Free to forego me,
   Fancy you hate so !

Praising, reviling,
   Worst head and best head,
Past me defiling,
   Never arrested,
Wanters, abounders,
   March, in gay mixture,
Men, my surrounders !
   I am the fixture.

So shall I fear thee,
  Mightiness yonder !
Mock-sun — more near thee,
  What is to wonder ?
So shall I love thee,
  Down in the dark, — lest
Glowworm I prove thee,
  Star that now sparklest !

FEARS AND SCRUPLES

In answer to a letter of inquiry, addressed to him by Mr. W. G. Kingsland, Browning wrote the following in regard to the meaning of this poem : " I think that the point I wanted to illustrate was this : Where there is a genuine love of the ' letters ' and ' actions ' of the invisible ' friend,' — however these may be disadvantaged by an inability to meet the objections to their authenticity or historical value urged by ' experts ' who assume the privilege of learning over ignorance, — it would indeed be a wrong to the wisdom and goodness of the ' friend ' if he were supposed capable of overlooking the actual ' love ' and only considering the ' ignorance ' which, failing to in any degree affect ' love,' is really the highest evidence that ' love ' exists. So I *meant*, whether the result be clear or no."

HERE 's my case. Of old I used to love him,
  This same unseen friend, before I knew :
Dream there was none like him, none above him, —
  Wake to hope and trust my dream was true.

Loved I not his letters full of beauty ?
  Not his actions famous far and wide ?
Absent, he would know I vowed him duty ;
  Present, he would find me at his side.

Pleasant fancy ! for I had but letters,
  Only knew of actions by hearsay :
He himself was busied with my betters ;
  What of that ? My turn must come some day.

" Some day " proving — no day ! Here 's the puzzle.
  Passed and passed my turn is. Why complain ?
He 's so busied ! If I could but muzzle
  People's foolish mouths that give me pain !

" Letters ? " (hear them !) " You a judge of writing ?
  Ask the experts ! How they shake the head
O'er these characters, your friend's inditing —
  Call them forgery from A to Z !

" Actions ? Where 's your certain proof " (they bother)
  " He, of all you find so great and good,
He, he only, claims this, that, the other
  Action — claimed by men, a multitude ? "

I can simply wish I might refute you,
  Wish my friend would, — by a word, a wink, —
Bid me stop that foolish mouth, — you brute you !
  He keeps absent, — why, I cannot think.

Never mind ! Though foolishness may flout me,
  One thing 's sure enough : 't is neither frost,
No, nor fire, shall freeze or burn from out me
  Thanks for truth — though falsehood, gained — though lost.

All my days, I 'll go the softlier, sadlier,
  For that dream's sake ! How forget the thrill
Through and through me as I thought " The gladlier
  Lives my friend because I love him still ! "

Ah, but there 's a menace some one utters !
  " What and if your friend at home play tricks ?
Peep at hide-and-seek behind the shutters ?
  Mean your eyes should pierce through solid bricks ?

" What and if he, frowning, wake you, dreamy ?
  Lay on you the blame that bricks — conceal ?
Say ' *At least I saw who did not see me,*
  Does see now, and presently shall feel ' ? "

" Why, that makes your friend a monster ! " say you :
  " Had his house no window ? At first nod,
Would you not have hailed him ? " Hush, I pray you !
  What if this friend happened to be — God ?

NATURAL MAGIC

ALL I can say is — I saw it !
The room was as bare as your hand.
I locked in the swarth little lady, — I swear,
From the head to the foot of her — well, quite as bare !
" No Nautch shall cheat me," said I, " taking my stand
At this bolt which I draw ! " And this bolt — I withdraw it,
And there laughs the lady, not bare, but embowered
With — who knows what verdure, o'erfruited, o'erflowered ?
Impossible ! Only — I saw it !

All I can sing is — I feel it !
This life was as blank as that room ;
I let you pass in here. Precaution, indeed ?
Walls, ceiling and floor, — not a chance for a weed !
Wide opens the entrance : where 's cold now, where 's gloom ?
No May to sow seed here, no June to reveal it,

Behold you enshrined in these blooms of your
    bringing,
These fruits of your bearing — nay, birds of
    your winging !
A fairy-tale ! Only — I feel it !

MAGICAL NATURE

Flower — I never fancied, jewel — I profess
    you !
    Bright I see and soft I feel the outside of a
        flower.
Save but glow inside and — jewel, I should
    guess you,
    Dim to sight and rough to touch : the glory is
        the dower.

You, forsooth, a flower ? Nay, my love, a
    jewel —
    Jewel at no mercy of a moment in your
        prime !
Time may fray the flower-face : kind be time
    or cruel,
    Jewel, from each facet, flash your laugh at
        time !

BIFURCATION

We were two lovers ; let me lie by her,
My tomb beside her tomb. On hers inscribe —
" I loved him ; but my reason bade prefer
Duty to love, reject the tempter's bribe
Of rose and lily when each path diverged,
And either I must pace to life's far end
As love should lead me, or, as duty urged,
Plod the worn causeway arm-in-arm with
    friend.
So, truth turned falsehood : ' How I loathe a
    flower,
How prize the pavement !' still caressed his
    ear —
The deafish friend's — through life's day, hour
    by hour,
As he laughed (coughing) ' Ay, it would ap-
    pear !'
But deep within my heart of hearts there hid
Ever the confidence, amends for all,
That heaven repairs what wrong earth's jour-
    ney did,
When love from life-long exile comes at call.
Duty and love, one broad way, were the best —
Who doubts ? But one or other was to choose,
I chose the darkling half, and wait the rest
In that new world where light and darkness
    fuse."

Inscribe on mine — " I loved her : love's track
    lay
O'er sand and pebble, as all travellers know.
Duty led through a smiling country, gay
With greensward where the rose and lily blow.
' Our roads are diverse : farewell, love !' said
    she :
''T is duty I abide by : homely sward
And not the rock-rough picturesque for me !
Above, where both roads join, I wait reward.

Be you as constant to the path whereon
I leave you planted !' But man needs must
    move,
Keep moving — whither, when the star is gone
Whereby he steps secure nor strays from love ?
No stone but I was tripped by, stumbling-block
But brought me to confusion. Where I fell,
There I lay flat, if moss disguised the rock,
Thence, if flint pierced, I rose and cried ' All 's
    well !
Duty be mine to tread in that high sphere
Where love from duty ne'er disparts, I trust,
And two halves make that whole, whereof — since
    here
One must suffice a man — why, this one must ! ' "

Inscribe each tomb thus : then, some sage
    acquaint
The simple — which holds sinner, which holds
    saint !

NUMPHOLEPTOS

The Browning Society became so puzzled
over the interpretation of this poem that
through Dr. Furnivall it applied to the poet for
an explanation and he replied : " Is not the key
to the meaning of the poem in its title νυμφόληπ-
τος [caught or rapt by a nymph] not γυναικε-
ραστής [a woman lover] ? An allegory, that is,
of an impossible ideal object of love, accepted
conventionally as such by a man who, all the
while, cannot quite blind himself to the demon-
strable fact that the possessor of knowledge
and purity obtained without the natural conse-
quences of obtaining them by achievement —
not inheritance, — such a being is imaginary,
not real, a nymph and no woman ; and only
such an one would be ignorant of and surprised
at the results of a lover's endeavor to emulate
the qualities which the beloved is entitled to
consider as pre-existent to earthly experience,
and independent of its inevitable results. I
had no particular woman in my mind ; certainly
never intended to personify wisdom, philosophy,
or any other abstraction ; and the orb, raying
color out of whiteness, was altogether a fancy
of my own. The 'seven spirits' are in the
Apocalypse, also in Coleridge and Byron, — a
common image."

Still you stand, still you listen, still you
    smile !
Still melts your moonbeam through me, white
    awhile,
Softening, sweetening, till sweet and soft
Increase so round this heart of mine, that oft
I could believe your moonbeam-smile has past
The pallid limit, lies, transformed at last
To sunlight and salvation — warms the soul
It sweetens, softens ! Would you pass that
    goal,

Gain love's birth at the limit's happier verge,
And, where an iridescence lurks, but urge
The hesitating pallor on to prime
Of dawn! — true blood-streaked, sun-warmth, action-time,
By heart-pulse ripened to a ruddy glow
Of gold above my clay — I scarce should know
From gold's self, thus suffused! For gold means love.
What means the sad slow silver smile above
My clay but pity, pardon? — at the best,
But acquiescence that I take my rest,
Contented to be clay, while in your heaven
The sun reserves love for the Spirit-Seven
Companioning God's throne they lamp before,
— Leaves earth a mute waste only wandered o'er
By that pale soft sweet disempassioned moon
Which smiles me slow forgiveness! Such, the boon
I beg? Nay, dear, submit to this — just this
Supreme endeavor! As my lips now kiss
Your feet, my arms convulse your shrouding robe,
My eyes, acquainted with the dust, dare probe
Your eyes above for — what, if born, would blind
Mine with redundant bliss, as flash may find
The inert nerve, sting awake the palsied limb,
Bid with life's ecstasy sense overbrim
And suck back death in the resurging joy —
Love, the love whole and sole without alloy!

Vainly! The promise withers! I employ
Lips, arms, eyes, pray the prayer which finds the word,
Make the appeal which must be felt, not heard,
And none the more is changed your calm regard:
Rather, its sweet and soft grow harsh and hard —
Forbearance, then repulsion, then disdain.
Avert the rest! I rise, see! — make, again
Once more, the old departure for some track
Untried, yet through a world which brings me back
Ever thus fruitlessly to find your feet,
To fix your eyes, to pray the soft and sweet
Which smile there — take from his new pilgrimage
Your outcast, once your inmate, and assuage
With love — not placid pardon now — his thirst
For a mere drop from out the ocean erst
He drank at! Well, the quest shall be renewed.
Fear nothing! Though I linger, unembued
With any drop, my lips thus close. I go!
So did I leave you, I have found you so,
And doubtlessly, if fated to return,
So shall my pleading persevere and earn
Pardon — not love — in that same smile, I learn,
And lose the meaning of, to learn once more,
Vainly!

       What fairy track do I explore?
What magic hall return to, like the gem
Centuply-angled o'er a diadem?

You dwell there, hearted; from your midmost home
Rays forth — through that fantastic world I roam
Ever — from centre to circumference,
Shaft upon colored shaft: this crimsons thence,
That purples out its precinct through the waste.
Surely I had your sanction when I faced,
Fared forth upon that untried yellow ray
Whence I retrack my steps? They end to-day
Where they began, before your feet, beneath
Your eyes, your smile: the blade is shut in sheath,
Fire quenched in flint; irradiation, late
Triumphant through the distance, finds its fate,
Merged in your blank pure soul, alike the source
And tomb of that prismatic glow: divorce
Absolute, all-conclusive! Forth I fared,
Treading the lambent flamelet: little cared
If now its flickering took the topaz tint,
If now my dull-caked path gave sulphury hint
Of subterranean rage — no stay nor stint
To yellow, since you sanctioned that I bathe,
Burnish me, soul and body, swim and swathe
In yellow license. Here I reek suffused
With crocus, saffron, orange, as I used
With scarlet, purple, every dye o' the bow
Born of the storm-cloud. As before, you show
Scarce recognition, no approval, some
Mistrust, more wonder at a man become
Monstrous in garb, nay — flesh disguised as well,
Through his adventure. Whatsoe'er befell,
I followed, wheresoe'er it wound, that vein
You authorized should leave your whiteness stain
Earth's sombre stretch beyond your midmost place
Of vantage, — trode that tinct whereof the trace
On garb and flesh repel you! Yes, I plead
Your own permission — your command, indeed,
That who would worthily retain the love
Must share the knowledge shrined those eyes above,
Go boldly on adventure, break through bounds
O' the quintessential whiteness that surrounds
Your feet, obtain experience of each tinge
That bickers forth to broaden out, impinge
Plainer his foot its pathway all distinct
From every other. Ah, the wonder, linked
With fear, as exploration manifests
What agency it was first tipped the crests
Of unnamed wildflower, soon protruding grew
Portentous 'mid the sands, as when his hue
Betrays him and the burrowing snake gleams through;
Till, last . . . but why parade more shame and pain?
Are not the proofs upon me? Here again
I pass into your presence, I receive
Your smile of pity, pardon, and I leave . . .
No, not this last of times I leave you, mute,
Submitted to my penance, so my foot
May yet again adventure, tread, from source
To issue, one more ray of rays which course
Each other, at your bidding, from the sphere
Silver and sweet, their birthplace, down that drear

Dark of the world, — you promise shall return
Your pilgrim jewelled as with drops o' the urn
The rainbow paints from, and no smatch at
    all
Of ghastliness at edge of some cloud-pall
Heaven cowers before, as earth awaits the fall
O' the bolt and flash of doom. Who trusts your
    word
Tries the adventure : and returns — absurd
As frightful — in that sulphur-steeped disguise
Mocking the priestly cloth-of-gold, sole prize
The arch-heretic was wont to bear away
Until he reached the burning. No, I say :
No fresh adventure ! No more seeking love
At end of toil, and finding, calm above
My passion, the old statuesque regard,
The sad petrific smile !

            O you — less hard
And hateful than mistaken and obtuse
Unreason of a she-intelligence !
You very woman with the pert pretence
To match the male achievement ! Like enough !
Ay, you were easy victors, did the rough
Straightway efface itself to smooth, the gruff
Grind down and grow a whisper, — did man's
    truth
Subdue, for sake of chivalry and ruth,
Its rapier-edge to suit the bulrush-spear
Womanly falsehood fights with ! O that ear
All fact pricks rudely, that thrice-superfine
Feminity of sense, with right divine
To waive all process, take result stain-free
From out the very muck wherein . . .

                Ah me !
The true slave's querulous outbreak ! All the
    rest
Be resignation ! Forth at your behest
I fare. Who knows but this — the crimson-
    quest —
May deepen to a sunrise, not decay
To that cold sad sweet smile ? — which I obey.

APPEARANCES

And so you found that poor room dull,
    Dark, hardly to your taste, my dear ?
Its features seemed unbeautiful :
    But this I know — 't was there, not here,
You plighted troth to me, the word
Which — ask that poor room how it heard.

And this rich room obtains your praise
    Unqualified, — so bright, so fair,
So all whereat perfection stays ?
    Ay, but remember — here, not there,
The other word was spoken ! — Ask
This rich room how you dropped the mask !

ST. MARTIN'S SUMMER

No protesting, dearest !
    Hardly kisses even !
        Don't we both know how it ends ?
How the greenest leaf turns serest,

Bluest outbreak — blankest heaven,
    Lovers — friends ?

You would build a mansion,
    I would weave a bower
        — Want the heart for enterprise.
Walls admit of no expansion :
    Trellis-work may haply flower
        Twice the size.

What makes glad Life's Winter ?
    New buds, old blooms after.
        Sad the sighing " How suspect
Beams would ere mid-Autumn splinter.
    Rooftree scarce support a rafter,
        Walls lie wrecked ? "

You are young, my princess !
    I am hardly older :
        Yet — I steal a glance behind !
Dare I tell you what convinces
    Timid me that you, if bolder,
        Bold — are blind ?

Where we plan our dwelling
    Glooms a graveyard surely !
        Headstone, footstone moss may drape,
Name, date, violets hide from spelling, —
    But, though corpses rot obscurely,
        Ghosts escape.

Ghosts ! O breathing Beauty,
    Give my frank word pardon !
        What if I — somehow, somewhere —
Pledged my soul to endless duty
    Many a time and oft ? Be hard on
        Love — laid there ?

Nay, blame grief that 's fickle,
    Time that proves a traitor,
        Chance, change, all that purpose warps, —
Death who spares to thrust the sickle
    Laid Love low, through flowers which later
        Shroud the corpse !

And you, my winsome lady,
    Whisper with like frankness !
        Lies nothing buried long ago ?
Are yon — which shimmer 'mid the shady
    Where moss and violet run to rankness —
        Tombs or no ?

Who taxes you with murder ?
    My hands are clean — or nearly !
        Love being mortal needs must pass.
Repentance ? Nothing were absurder.
    Enough : we felt Love's loss severely ;
        Though now — alas !

Love's corpse lies quiet therefore,
    Only Love's ghost plays truant,
        And warns us have in wholesome awe
Durable mansionry ; that 's wherefore
    I weave but trellis-work, pursuant
        — Life, to law.

The solid, not the fragile,
    Tempts rain and hail and thunder.

If bower stand firm at Autumn's close,
Beyond my hope, — why, boughs were agile ;
If bower fall flat, we scarce need wonder
    Wreathing — rose !

So, truce to the protesting,
    So, muffled be the kisses !
    For, would we but avow the truth,
Sober is genuine joy.   No jesting !
    Ask else Penelope, Ulysses —
    Old in youth !

For why should ghosts feel angered ?
    Let all their interference
    Be faint march-music in the air !
'Up !   Join the rear of us the vanguard !
Up, lovers, dead to all appearance,
    Laggard pair ! ''

The while you clasp me closer,
    The while I press you deeper,
    As safe we chuckle, — under breath, —
Yet all the slyer, the jocoser, —
    " So, life can boast its day, like leap-year,
    Stolen from death ! ''

Ah me — the sudden terror !
    Hence quick — avaunt, avoid me,
    You cheat, the ghostly flesh-disguised !
Nay, all the ghosts in one !   Strange error !
    So, 't was Death's self that clipped and
        coyed me,
    Loved — and lied !'

Ay, dead loves are the potent !
    Like any cloud they used you,
    Mere semblance you, but substance they !
Build we no mansion, weave we no tent !
    Mere flesh — their spirit interfused you !
    Hence, I say !

All theirs, none yours the glamour !
    Theirs each low word that won me,
    Soft look that found me Love's, and left
What else but you — the tears and clamor
    That 's all your very own !   Undone me —
    Ghost-bereft !

HERVÉ RIEL

This ballad was printed first in the *Cornhill
Magazine* for March, 1871.   In a letter to Mr.
George Smith, one of the publishers of the
magazine, Browning stated that he intended to
devote the proceeds of the poem to the aid of
the people of Paris suffering from the Franco-
German war.   The publisher generously sec-
onded his resolve and paid one hundred pounds
for the poem.

I

On the sea and at the Hogue, sixteen hundred
        ninety-two,
    Did the English fight the French, — woe to
        France !

And, the thirty-first of May, helter-skelter
        through the blue,
    Like a crowd of frightened porpoises a shoal of
        sharks pursue,
    Came crowding ship on ship to Saint Malo
        on the Rance,
With the English fleet in view.

II

'T was the squadron that escaped, with the vic
        tor in full chase ;
    First and foremost of the drove, in his great
        ship, Damfreville ;
    Close on him fled, great and small,
        Twenty-two good ships in all ;
And they signalled to the place
    " Help the winners of a race !
    Get us guidance, give us harbor, take us
        quick — or, quicker still,
    Here 's the English can and will ! ''

III

Then the pilots of the place put out brisk and
        leapt on board ;
    " Why, what hope or chance have ships like
        these to pass ? '' laughed they :
    " Rocks to starboard, rocks to port, all the
        passage scarred and scored,
    Shall the ' Formidable ' here with her twelve
        and eighty guns
        Think to make the river-mouth by the single
            narrow way,
    Trust to enter where 't is tricklish for a craft of
            twenty tons,
        And with flow at full beside ?
    Now, 't is slackest ebb of tide.
    Reach the mooring ?   Rather say,
While rock stands or water runs,
    Not a ship will leave the bay ! ''

IV

Then was called a council straight.
Brief and bitter the debate :
    " Here 's the English at our heels ; would you
            have them take in tow
All that 's left us of the fleet, linked together
        stern and bow,
For a prize to Plymouth Sound ?
Better run the ships aground ! ''
    (Ended Damfreville his speech).
    " Not a minute more to wait !
    Let the Captains all and each
    Shove ashore, then blow up, burn the vessel
        on the beach !
France must undergo her fate.

V

" Give the word ! ''   But no such word
Was ever spoke or heard ;
    For up stood, for out stepped, for in struck
        amid all these
    — A Captain ?   A Lieutenant ?   A Mate — first,
        second, third ?
    No such man of mark, and meet
    With his betters to compete !

But a simple Breton sailor pressed by
    Tourville for the fleet,
A poor coasting-pilot he, Hervé Riel the Croi-
    sickese.

VI

And "What mockery or malice have we
    here?" cries Hervé Riel:
"Are you mad, you Malouins? Are you
    cowards, fools, or rogues?
Talk to me of rocks and shoals, me who took
    the soundings, tell
On my fingers every bank, every shallow, every
    swell
    'Twixt the offing here and Grève where the
    river disembogues?
Are you bought by English gold? Is it love
    the lying 's for?
    Morn and eve, night and day,
    Have I piloted your bay,
Entered free and anchored fast at the foot of
    Solidor.
    Burn the fleet and ruin France? That were
    worse than fifty Hogues!
    Sirs, they know I speak the truth! Sirs,
    believe me there 's a way!
Only let me lead the line,
    Have the biggest ship to steer,
    Get this 'Formidable' clear,
Make the others follow mine,
And I lead them, most and least, by a passage
    I know well,
    Right to Solidor past Grève,
    And there lay them safe and sound;
    And if one ship misbehave,
    — Keel so much as grate the ground,
Why, I 've nothing but my life, — here 's my
    head!" cries Hervé Riel.

VII

Not a minute more to wait.
"Steer us in, then, small and great!
    Take the helm, lead the line, save the squa-
    dron!" cried its chief.
Captains, give the sailor place!
He is Admiral, in brief.
Still the north-wind, by God's grace!
See the noble fellow's face
As the big ship, with a bound,
Clears the entry like a hound,
Keeps the passage as its inch of way were the
    wide sea's profound!
    See, safe through shoal and rock,
    How they follow in a flock,
Not a ship that misbehaves, not a keel that
    grates the ground,
    Not a spar that comes to grief!
The peril, see, is past,
All are harbored to the last,
And just as Hervé Riel hollas "Anchor!" —
    sure as fate,
Up the English come — too late!

VIII

So, the storm subsides to calm:
    They see the green trees wave
    On the heights o'erlooking Grève.

Hearts that bled are stanched with balm.
"Just our rapture to enhance,
    Let the English rake the bay,
    Gnash their teeth and glare askance
    As they cannonade away!
'Neath rampired Solidor pleasant riding on the
    Rance!"
How hope succeeds despair on each Captain's
    countenance!
Out burst all with one accord,
    "This is Paradise for Hell!
    Let France, let France's King
    Thank the man that did the thing!"
What a shout, and all one word,
    "Hervé Riel!"
As he stepped in front once more,
    Not a symptom of surprise
    In the frank blue Breton eyes,
Just the same man as before.

IX

Then said Damfreville, "My friend,
I must speak out at the end,
    Though I find the speaking hard.
Praise is deeper than the lips:
You have saved the King his ships,
    You must name your own reward.
'Faith, our sun was near eclipse!
Demand whate'er you will,
France remains your debtor still.
Ask to heart's content and have! or my name 's
    not Damfreville."

X

Then a beam of fun outbroke
On the bearded mouth that spoke,
As the honest heart laughed through
Those frank eyes of Breton blue:
"Since I needs must say my say,
    Since on board the duty 's done,
    And from Malo Roads to Croisic Point, what
    is it but a run? —
Since 't is ask and have, I may —
    Since the others go ashore —
Come! A good whole holiday!
    Leave to go and see my wife, whom I call the
    Belle Aurore!"
    That he asked and that he got, — nothing
    more.

XI

Name and deed alike are lost:
Not a pillar nor a post
    In his Croisic keeps alive the feat as it befell;
Not a head in white and black
On a single fishing-smack,
In memory of the man but for whom had gone
    to wrack
    All that France saved from the fight whence
    England bore the bell.
Go to Paris: rank on rank
    Search the heroes flung pell-mell
On the Louvre, face and flank!
    You shall look long enough ere you come to
    Hervé Riel.
So, for better and for worse,

Hervé Riel, accept my verse!
In my verse, Hervé Riel, do thou once more
Save the squadron, honor France, love thy wife
    the Belle Aurore!

A FORGIVENESS

I AM indeed the personage you know.
As for my wife, — what happened long ago —
You have a right to question me, as I
Am bound to answer.

                      ("Son, a fit reply!"
The monk half spoke, half ground through his
    clenched teeth,
At the confession-grate I knelt beneath.)

Thus then all happened, Father! Power and
    place
I had as still I have. I ran life's race,
With the whole world to see, as only strains
His strength some athlete whose prodigious
    gains
Of good appall him: happy to excess, —
Work freely done should balance happiness
Fully enjoyed; and, since beneath my roof
Housed she who made home heaven, in heaven's
    behoof
I went forth every day, and all day long
Worked for the world. Look, how the laborer's
    song
Cheers him! Thus sang my soul, at each sharp
    throe
Of laboring flesh and blood — "She loves me
    so!"

One day, perhaps such song so knit the nerve
That work grew play and vanished. "I deserve
Haply my heaven an hour before the time!"
I laughed, as silverly the clockhouse-chime
Surprised me passing through the postern-gate
— Not the main entry where the menials wait
And wonder why the world's affairs allow
The master sudden leisure. That was how
I took the private garden-way for once.

Forth from the alcove, I saw start, ensconce
Himself behind the porphyry vase, a man.

My fancies in the natural order ran:
"A spy, — perhaps a foe in ambuscade, —
A thief, — more like, a sweetheart of some maid
Who pitched on the alcove for tryst perhaps."

"Stand there!" I bid.

                Whereat my man but wraps
His face the closelier with uplifted arm
Whereon the cloak lies, strikes in blind alarm
This and that pedestal as, — stretch and stoop, —
Now in, now out of sight, he thrids the group
Of statues, marble god and goddess ranged
Each side the pathway, till the gate's exchanged
For safety: one step thence, the street, you
    know!

Thus far I followed with my gaze. Then, slow,
Near on admiringly, I breathed again,

And — back to that last fancy of the train —
" A danger risked for hope of just a word
With — which of all my nest may be the bird
This poacher covets for her plumage, pray?
Carmen? Juana? Carmen seems too gay
For such adventure, while Juana's grave
— Would scorn the folly. I applaud the knave!
He had the eye, could single from my brood
His proper fledgeling!"

                As I turned, there stood
In face of me, my wife stone-still stone-white.
Whether one bound had brought her, — at first
    sight
Of what she judged the encounter, sure to be
Next moment, of the venturous man and me, —
Brought her to clutch and keep me from my
    prey:
Whether impelled because her death no day
Could come so absolutely opportune
As now at joy's height, like a year in June
Stayed at the fall of its first ripened rose;
Or whether hungry for my hate — who
    knows? —
Eager to end an irksome lie, and taste
Our tingling true relation, hate embraced
By hate one naked moment: — anyhow
There stone-still stone-white stood my wife, but
    now
The woman who made heaven within my house.
Ay, she who faced me was my very spouse
As well as love — you are to recollect!

"Stay!" she said. "Keep at least one soul
    unspecked
With crime, that's spotless hitherto — your
    own!
Kill me who court the blessing, who alone
Was, am, and shall be guilty, first to last!
The man lay helpless in the toils I cast
About him, helpless as the statue there
Against that strangling bell-flower's bondage:
    tear
Away and tread to dust the parasite,
But do the passive marble no despite!
I love him as I hate you. Kill me! Strike
At one blow both infinitudes alike
Out of existence — hate and love! Whence love?
That's safe inside my heart, nor will remove
For any searching of your steel, I think.
Whence hate? The secret lay on lip, at brink
Of speech, in one fierce tremble to escape,
At every form wherein your love took shape,
At each new provocation of your kiss.
Kill me!"

            We went in.

                    Next day after this.
I felt as if the speech might come. I spoke —
Easily, after all.

            "The lifted cloak
Was screen sufficient: I concern myself
Hardly with laying hands on who for pelf —
Whate'er the ignoble kind — may prowl and
    brave
Cuffing and kicking proper to a knave

Detected by my household's vigilance.
Enough of such! As for my love-romance —
I, like our good Hidalgo, rub my eyes
And wake and wonder how the film could rise
Which changed for me a barbers' basin straight
Into — Mambrino's helm? I hesitate
Nowise to say — God's sacramental cup!
Why should I blame the brass which, burnished
     up,
Will blaze, to all but me, as good as gold?
To me — a warning I was overbold
In judging metals. The Hidalgo waked
Only to die, if I remember, — staked
His life upon the basin's worth, and lost:
While I confess torpidity at most
In here and there a limb; but, lame and halt,
Still should I work on, still repair my fault
Ere I took rest in death, — no fear at all!
Now, work — no word before the curtain
     fall!"

The "curtain"? That of death on life, I
     meant:
My "word," permissible in death's event,
Would be — truth, soul to soul; for, otherwise,
Day by day, three years long, there had to rise
And, night by night, to fall upon our stage —
Ours, doomed to public play by heritage —
Another curtain, when the world, perforce
Our critical assembly, in due course
Came and went, witnessing, gave praise or
     blame
To art-mimetic. It had spoiled the game
If, suffered to set foot behind our scene,
The world had witnessed how stage-king and
     queen,
Gallant and lady, but a minute since
Enarming each the other, would evince
No sign of recognition as they took
His way and her way to whatever nook
Waited them in the darkness either side
Of that bright stage where lately groom and
     bride
Had fired the audience to a frenzy-fit
Of sympathetic rapture — every whit
Earned as the curtain fell on her and me,
— Actors. Three whole years, nothing was to
     see
But calm and concord: where a speech was
     due
There came the speech; when the smiles were
     wanted too,
Smiles were as ready. In a place like mine,
Where foreign and domestic cares combine,
There's audience every day and all day long;
But finally the last of the whole throng
Who linger lets one see his back. For her —
Why, liberty and liking: I aver,
Liking and liberty! For me — I breathed,
Let my face rest from every wrinkle wreathed
Smile-like about the mouth, unlearned my task
Of personation till next day bade mask,
And quietly betook me from that world
To the real world, not pageant: there unfurled
In work, its wings, my soul, the fretted power.
Three years I worked, each minute of each
     hour
Not claimed by acting: — work I may dispense

With talk about, since work in evidence,
Perhaps in history; who knows or cares?

After three years, this way, all unawares,
Our acting ended. She and I, at close
Of a loud night-feast, led, between two rows
Of bending male and female loyalty,
Our lord the king down staircase, while, held
     high
At arm's length did the twisted tapers' flare
Herald his passage from our palace, where
Such visiting left glory evermore.
Again the ascent in public, till at door
As we two stood by the saloon — now blank
And disencumbered of its guests — there sank
A whisper in my ear, so low and yet
So unmistakable!

                    "I half forget
The chamber you repair to, and I want
Occasion for one short word — if you grant
That grace — within a certain room you called
Our 'Study,' for you wrote there while I
     scrawled
Some paper full of faces for my sport.
That room I can remember. Just one short
Word with you there, for the remembrance'
     sake!"

"Follow me thither!" I replied.

                              We break
The gloom a little, as with guiding lamp
I lead the way, leave warmth and cheer, by
     damp
Blind disused serpentining ways afar
From where the habitable chambers are, —
Ascend, descend stairs tunnelled through the
     stone, —
Always in silence, — till I reach the lone
Chamber sepulchred for my very own
Out of the palace-quarry. When a boy,
Here was my fortress, stronghold from annoy.
Proof-positive of ownership; in youth
I garnered up my gleanings here — uncouth
But precious relics of vain hopes, vain fears;
Finally, this became in after-years
My closet of entrenchment to withstand
Invasion of the foe on every hand —
The multifarious herd in bower and hall,
State-room, — rooms whatsoe'er the style,
     which call
On masters to be mindful that, before
Men, they must look like men and something
     more.
Here, — when our lord the king's bestowment
     ceased
To deck me on the day that, golden-fleeced,
I touched ambition's height, — 't was here,
     released
From glory (always symbolled by a chain!)
No sooner was I privileged to gain
My secret domicile than glad I flung
That last toy on the table — gazed where hung
On hook my father's gift, the arquebus —
And asked myself, "Shall I envisage thus
The new prize and the old prize, when I reach
Another year's experience? — own that each

Equalled advantage — sportsman's — states-
man's tool?
That brought me down an eagle, this — a fool!"

Into which room on entry, I set down
The lamp, and turning saw whose rustled gown
Had told me my wife followed, pace for pace.
Each of us looked the other in the face.
She spoke. "Since I could die now" . . .

(To explain
Why that first struck me, know — not once
again
Since the adventure at the porphyry's edge
Three years before, which sundered like a
wedge
Her soul from mine, — though daily, smile to
smile,
We stood before the public, — all the while
Not once had I distinguished, in that face
I paid observance to, the faintest trace
Of feature more than requisite for eyes
To do their duty by and recognize:
So did I force mine to obey my will
And pry no further. There exists such skill, —
Those know who need it. What physician
shrinks
From needful contact with a corpse? He
drinks
No plague so long as thirst for knowledge — not
An idler impulse — prompts inquiry. What,
And will you disbelieve in power to bid
Our spirit back to bounds, as though we chid
A child from scrutiny that 's just and right
In manhood? Sense, not soul, accomplished
sight,
Reported daily she it was — not how
Nor why a change had come to cheek and
brow.)

"Since I could die now of the truth concealed,
Yet dare not, must not die, — so seems revealed
The Virgin's mind to me, — for death means
peace
Wherein no lawful part have I, whose lease
Of life and punishment the truth avowed
May haply lengthen, — let me push the shroud
Away, that steals to muffle ere is just
My penance-fire in snow! I dare —. I must
Live, by avowal of the truth — this truth —
I loved you! Thanks for the fresh serpent's
tooth
That, by a prompt new pang more exquisite
Than all preceding torture, proves me right!
I loved you yet I lost you! May I go
Burn to the ashes, now my shame you know?"

I think there never was such — how express? —
Horror coquetting with voluptuousness,
As in those arms of Eastern workmanship —
Yataghan, kandjar, things that rend and rip,
Gash rough, slash smooth, help hate so many
ways,
Yet ever keep a beauty that betrays
Love still at work with the artificer
Throughout his quaint devising. Why prefer,
Except for love's sake, that a blade should
writhe

And bicker like a flame? — now play the
scythe
As if some broad neck tempted, — now con-
tract
And needle off into a fineness lacked
For just that puncture which the heart de-
mands?
Then, such adornment! Wherefore need our
hands
Enclose not ivory alone, nor gold
Roughened for use, but jewels? Nay, behold!
Fancy my favorite — which I seem to grasp
While I describe the luxury. No asp
Is diapered more delicate round throat
Than this below the handle! These denote
— These mazy lines meandering, to end
Only in flesh they open — what intend
They else but water-purlings — pale contrast
With the life-crimson where they blend at
last?
And mark the handle's dim pellucid green,
Carved, the hard jadestone, as you pinch a
bean,
Into a sort of parrot-bird! He pecks
A grape-bunch; his two eyes are ruby-specks
Pure from the mine: seen this way, — glassy
blank,
But turn them, — lo, the inmost fire, that
shrank
From sparkling, sends a red dart right to aim!
Why did I choose such toys? Perhaps the
game
Of peaceful men is warlike, just as men
War-wearied get amusement from that pen
And paper we grow sick of — statesfolk tired
Of merely (when such measures are required)
Dealing out doom to people by three words,
A signature and seal: we play with swords
Suggestive of quick process. That is how
I came to like the toys described you now,
Store of which glittered on the walls and
strewed
The table, even, while my wife pursued
Her purpose to its ending. "Now you know
This shame, my three years' torture, let me go,
Burn to the very ashes! You — I lost,
Yet you — I loved!"

The thing I pity most
In men is — action prompted by surprise
Of anger: men? nay, bulls — whose onset lies
At instance of the firework and the goad!
Once the foe prostrate, — trampling once be-
stowed, —
Prompt follows placability, regret,
Atonement. Trust me, blood-warmth never
yet
Betokened strong will! As no leap of pulse
Pricked me, that first time, so did none con-
vulse
My veins at this occasion for resolve.
Had that devolved which did not then devolve
Upon me, I had done — what now to do
Was quietly apparent.

"Tell me who
The man was, crouching by the porphyry
vase!"

"No, never! All was folly in his case,
All guilt in mine. I tempted, he complied."

"And yet you loved me?"

         "Loved you. Double-dyed
In folly and in guilt, I thought you gave
Your heart and soul away from me to slave
At statecraft. Since my right in you seemed
    lost,
I stung myself to teach you, to your cost,
What you rejected could be prized beyond
Life, heaven, by the first fool I threw a fond
Look on, a fatal word to."

         "And you still
Love me? Do I conjecture well or ill?."

"Conjecture — well or ill! I had three years
To spend in learning you."

       "We both are peers
In knowledge, therefore: since three years are
    spent
Ere thus much of yourself *I* learn — who went
Back to the house, that day, and brought my
    mind
To bear upon your action, uncombined
Motive from motive, till the dross, deprived
Of every purer particle, survived
At last in native simple hideousness,
Utter contemptibility, nor less
Nor more. Contemptibility — exempt
How could I, from its proper due — contempt?
I have too much despised you to divert
My life from its set course by help or hurt
Of your all-despicable life — perturb
The calm I work in, by — men's mouths to curb,
Which at such news were clamorous enough —
Men's eyes to shut before my broidered stuff
With the huge hole there, my emblazoned wall
Blank where a scutcheon hung, — by, worse
    than all,
Each day's procession, my paraded life
Robbed and impoverished through the wanting
    wife
— Now that my life (which means — my work)
    was grown
Riches indeed! Once, just this worth alone
Seemed work to have, that profit gained thereby
Of good and praise would — how rewardingly! —
Fall at your feet, — a crown I hoped to cast
Before your love, my love should crown at last.
No love remaining to cast crown before,
My love stopped work now: but contempt the
    more
Impelled me task as ever head and hand,
Because the very fiends weave ropes of sand
Rather than taste pure hell in idleness,
Therefore I kept my memory down by stress
Of daily work I had no mind to stay
For the world's wonder at the wife away.
Oh, it was easy all of it, believe,
For I despised you! But your words retrieve
Importantly the past. No hate assumed
The mask of love at any time! There gloomed
A moment when love took hate's semblance,
    urged

By causes you declare; but love's self purged
Away a fancied wrong I did both loves
— Yours and my own: by no hate's help, it
    proves,
Purgation was attempted. Then, you rise
High by how many a grade! I did despise —
I do but hate you. Let hate's punishment
Replace contempt's! First step to which as-
    cent —
Write down your own words I re-utter you!
'*I loved my husband and I hated — who
He was, I took up as my first chance, mere
Mud-ball to fling and make love foul with!*' Here
Lies paper!"

    "Would my blood for ink suffice!"

"It may: this minion from a land of spice,
Silk, feather — every bird of jewelled breast —
This poniard's beauty, ne'er so lightly prest
Above your heart there" . . .

        "Thus?"

        "It flows, I see.
Dip there the point and write!"

        "Dictate to me!
Nay, I remember."

        And she wrote the words
I read them. Then — "Since love, in you
    affords
License for hate, in me, to quench (I say)
Contempt — why, hate itself has passed away
In vengeance — foreign to contempt. Depart
Peacefully to that death which Eastern art
Imbued this weapon with, if tales be true!
Love will succeed to hate. I pardon you —
Dead in our chamber!"

        True as truth the tale.
She died ere morning; then, I saw how pale
Her cheek was ere it wore day's paint-disguise,
And what a hollow darkened 'neath her eyes,
Now that I used my own. She sleeps, as erst
Beloved, in this your church: ay, yours!

        Immersed
In thought so deeply, Father? Sad, perhaps?
For whose sake, hers or mine or his who wraps
— Still plain I seem to see! — about his head
The idle cloak, — about his heart (instead
Of cuirass) some fond hope he may elude
My vengeance in the cloister's solitude?
Hardly, I think! As little helped his brow
The cloak then, Father — as your grate helps
    now!

CENCIAJA

Ogni cencio vuol entrare in bucato. — Italian Proverb.

Mr. Buxton Forman, the editor of Shelley,
upon asking Browning the precise value at-
tached to the terminal *aja* in the title of his
poem, received the following answer: —

"19 Warwick Crescent, W., *July* 27, '76.

"Dear Mr. Buxton Forman: There can be no objection to such a simple statement as you have inserted, if it seems worth inserting. 'Fact,' it is. Next: 'aia' is generally an accumulative yet depreciative termination: 'Cenciaja' — a bundle of rags — a trifle. The proverb means 'every poor creature will be pressing into the company of his betters,' and I used it to deprecate the notion that I intended anything of the kind. Is it any contribution to 'all connected with Shelley,' if I mention that my 'Book' (*The Ring and the Book*) [rather the 'old square yellow book' from which the details were taken] has a reference to the reason given by Farinacci, the advocate of the Cenci, of his failure in the defence of Beatrice? 'Fuisse punitam Beatricem (he declares) poenâ ultimi supplicii, non quia ex intervallo occidi mandavit insidiantem suo honori, sed quia ejus exceptionem non probavi tibi. *Prout, et idem firmiter sperabatur de sorore Beatrice si propositam excusationem probasset, prout non probavit.*' That is, she expected to avow the main outrage, and did not: in conformity with her words, 'That which I ought to confess, that will I confess; that to which I ought to assent, to that I assent; and that which I ought to deny, that will I deny.' Here is another Cenciaja!

"Yours very sincerely, Robert Browning."

May I print, Shelley, how it came to pass
That when your Beatrice seemed — by lapse
Of many a long month since her sentence fell —
Assured of pardon for the parricide —
By intercession of stanch friends, or, say,
By certain pricks of conscience in the Pope
Conniver at Francesco Cenci's guilt, —
Suddenly all things changed and Clement grew
"Stern," as you state, "nor to be moved nor bent,
But said these three words coldly 'She *must* die;'
Subjoining '*Pardon? Paolo Santa Croce
Murdered his mother also yestereve,
And he is fled: she shall not flee at least!*'"
— So, to the letter, sentence was fulfilled?
Shelley, may I condense verbosity
That lies before me, into some few words
Of English, and illustrate your superb
Achievement by a rescued anecdote,
No great things, only new and true beside?
As if some mere familiar of a house
Should venture to accost the group at gaze
Before its Titian, famed the wide world through,
And supplement such pictured masterpiece
By whisper, "Searching in the archives here,
I found the reason of the Lady's fate,
And how by accident it came to pass
she wears the halo and displays the palm:
Who, haply, else had never suffered — no,
Nor graced our gallery, by consequence."
Who loved the work would like the little news:

Who lauds your poem lends an ear to me
Relating how the penalty was paid
By one Marchese dell' Oriolo, called
Onofrio Santa Croce otherwise,
For his complicity in matricide
With Paolo his own brother, — he whose crime
And flight induced "those three words — She must die."
Thus I unroll you then the manuscript.

"God's justice" — (of the multiplicity
Of such communications extant still,
Recording, each, injustice done by God
In person of his Vicar-upon-earth,
Scarce one but leads off to the selfsame tune)—
"God's justice, tardy though it prove perchance
Rests never on the track until it reach
Delinquency. In proof I cite the case
Of Paolo Santa Croce."

Many times
The youngster, — having been importunate
That Marchesine Costanza, who remained
His widowed mother, should supplant the heir
Her elder son, and substitute himself
In sole possession of her faculty, —
And meeting just as often with rebuff, —
Blinded by so exorbitant a lust
Of gold, the youngster straightway tasked his wits,
Casting about to kill the lady — thus.

He first, to cover his iniquity,
Writes to Onofrio Santa Croce, then
Authoritative lord, acquainting him
Their mother was contamination — wrought
Like hell-fire in the beauty of their House
By dissoluteness and abandonment
Of soul and body to impure delight.

Moreover, since she suffered from disease,
Those symptoms which her death made manifest
Hydroptic, he affirmed were fruits of sin
About to bring confusion and disgrace
Upon the ancient lineage and high fame
O' the family, when published. Duty bound,
He asked his brother — what a son should do?

Which when Marchese dell' Oriolo heard
By letter, being absent at his land
Oriolo, he made answer, this, no more:
"It must behoove a son, — things haply so, —
To act as honor prompts a cavalier
And son, perform his duty to all three,
Mother and brothers" — here advice broke off.

By which advice informed and fortified
As he professed himself — since bound by birth
To hear God's voice in primogeniture —
Paolo, who kept his mother company
In her domain Subiaco, straightway dared
His whole enormity of enterprise,
And, falling on her, stabbed the lady dead;
Whose death demonstrated her innocence,
And happened, — by the way, — since Jesu Christ
Died to save man, just sixteen hundred years.

Costanza was of aspect beautiful
Exceedingly, and seemed, although in age
Sixty about, to far surpass her peers
The coëtaneous dames, in youth and grace.

Done the misdeed, its author takes to flight,
Foiling thereby the justice of the world:
Not God's however, — God, be sure, knows
    well
The way to clutch a culprit. Witness here!
The present sinner, when he least expects,
Snug-cornered somewhere i' the Basilicate,
Stumbles upon his death by violence.
A man of blood assaults a man of blood
And slays him somehow. This was afterward:
Enough, he promptly met with his deserts,
And, ending thus, permits we end with him,
And push forthwith to this important point —
His matricide fell out, of all the days,
Precisely when the law-procedure closed
Respecting Count Francesco Cenci's death
Chargeable on his daughter, sons and wife.
" Thus patricide was matched with matricide,"
A poet not inelegantly rhymed:
Nay, fratricide — those Princes Massimi! —
Which so disturbed the spirit of the Pope
That all the likelihood Rome entertained
Of Beatrice's pardon vanished straight,
And she endured the piteous death.

                  Now see
The sequel — what effect commandment had
For strict inquiry into this last case,
When Cardinal Aldobrandini (great
His efficacy — nephew to the Pope!)
Was bidden crush — ay, though his very hand
Got soil i' the act — crime spawning everywhere!
Because, when all endeavor had been used
To catch the aforesaid Paolo, all in vain —
" Make perquisition," quoth our Eminence,
" Throughout his now deserted domicile!
Ransack the palace, roof and floor, to find
If haply any scrap of writing, hid
In nook or corner, may convict — who knows? —
Brother Onofrio of intelligence
With brother Paolo, as in brotherhood
Is but too likely: crime spawns everywhere."

And, every cranny searched accordingly,
There comes to light — O lynx-eyed Cardinal! —
Onofrio's unconsidered writing-scrap,
The letter in reply to Paolo's prayer,
The word of counsel that — things proving so,
Paolo should act the proper knightly part,
And do as was incumbent on a son,
A brother — and a man of birth, be sure!

Whereat immediately the officers
Proceeded to arrest Onofrio — found
At football, child's play, unaware of harm,
Safe with his friends, the Orsini, at their seat
Monte Giordano; as he left the house
He came upon the watch in wait for him
Set by the Barigel, — was caught and caged.

News of which capture being, that same hour,
Conveyed to Rome, forthwith our Eminence
Commands Taverna, Governor and Judge,

To have the process in especial care,
Be, first to last, not only president
In person, but inquisitor as well,
Nor trust the by-work to a substitute:
Bids him not, squeamish, keep the bench, but
    scrub
The floor of Justice, so to speak, — go try
His best in prison with the criminal:
Promising, as reward for by-work done
Fairly on all-fours, that, success obtained
And crime avowed, or such connivency
With crime as should procure a decent death —
Himself will humbly beg — which means, pro-
    cure —
The Hat and Purple from his relative
The Pope, and so repay a diligence
Which, meritorious in the Cenci-case,
Mounts plainly here to Purple and the Hat.

Whereupon did my lord the Governor
So masterfully exercise the task
Enjoined him, that he, day by day, and week
By week, and month by month, from first to
    last
Toiled for the prize: now, punctual at his place,
Played Judge, and now, assiduous at his post,
Inquisitor — pressed cushion and scoured plank,
Early and late. Noon's fervor and night's
    chill,
Naught moved whom morn would, purpling,
    make amends!
So that observers laughed as, many a day,
He left home, in July when day is flame,
Posted to Tordinona-prison, plunged
Into a vault where daylong night is ice,
There passed his eight hours on a stretch, con-
    tent,
Examining Onofrio: all the stress
Of all examination steadily
Converging into one pin-point, — he pushed
Tentative now of head and now of heart.
As when the nut-hatch taps and tries the nut
This side and that side till the kernel sound, —
So did he press the sole and single point
— What was the very meaning of the phrase
" *Do as beseems an honored cavalier*"?

Which one persistent question-torture, —
    plied
Day by day, week by week, and month by
    month,
Morn, noon and night, — fatigued away a mind
Grown imbecile by darkness, solitude,
And one vivacious memory gnawing there
As when a corpse is coffined with a snake:
— Fatigued Onofrio into what might seem
Admission that perchance his judgment groped
So blindly, feeling for an issue — aught
With semblance of an issue from the toils
Cast of a sudden round feet late so free,
He possibly might have envisaged, scarce
Recoiled from — even were the issue death
— Even her death whose life was death and
    worse!
Always provided that the charge of crime,
Each jot and tittle of the charge were true.
In such a sense, belike, he might advise
His brother to expurgate crime with . . . well.

With blood, if blood must follow on "*the course*
Taken as might beseem a cavalier."

Whereupon process ended, and report
Was made without a minute of delay
To Clement, who, because of those two crimes
O' the Massimi and Cenci flagrant late,
Must needs impatiently desire result.

Result obtained, he bade the Governor
Summon the Congregation and despatch.
Summons made, sentence passed accordingly
— Death by beheading. When his death-decree
Was intimated to Onofrio, all
Man could do — that did he to save himself.
'T was much, the having gained for his defence
The Advocate o' the Poor, with natural help
Of many noble friendly persons fain
To disengage a man of family,
So young too, from his grim entanglement:
But Cardinal Aldobrandini ruled
There must be no diversion of the law.
Justice is justice, and the magistrate
Bears not the sword in vain. Who sins must
       die.

So, the Marchese had his head cut off,
With Rome to see, a concourse infinite,
In Place Saint Angelo beside the Bridge :
Where, demonstrating magnanimity
Adequate to his birth and breed, — poor boy ! —
He made the people the accustomed speech,
Exhorted them to true faith, honest works,
And special good behavior as regards
A parent of no matter what the sex,
Bidding each son take warning from himself.
Truly, it was considered in the boy
Stark staring lunacy, no less, to snap
So plain a bait, be hooked and hauled ashore
By such an angler as the Cardinal !
Why make confession of his privity
To Paolo's enterprise ? Mere sealing lips —
Or, better, saying " When I counselled him
' *To do as might beseem a cavalier,*'
What could I mean but ' *Hide our parent's*
       shame
As Christian ought, by aid of Holy Church !
Bury it in a convent — ay, beneath
Enough dotation to prevent its ghost
From troubling earth ! ' " Mere saying thus, —
       't is plain,
Not only were his life the recompense.
But he had manifestly proved himself
True Christian, and in lieu of punishment
Got praise of all men ! — so the populace.

Anyhow, when the Pope made promise good
(That of Aldobrandini, near and dear)
And gave Taverna, who had toiled so much,
A Cardinal's equipment, some such word
As this from mouth to ear went saucily :
" Taverna's cap is dyed in what he drew
From Santa Croce's veins ! " So joked the
world.

I add : Onofrio left one child behind,
A daughter named Valeria, dowered with
       grace

Abundantly of soul and body, doomed
To life the shorter for her father's fate.
By death of her, the Marquisate returned
To that Orsini House from whence it came :
Oriolo having passed as donative
To Santa Croce from their ancestors.

And no word more ? By all means ! Would
       you know
The authoritative answer, when folk urged
"What made Aldobrandini, hound-like stanch
Hunt out of life a harmless simpleton ? "
The answer was — " Hatred implacable,
By reason they were rivals in their love."
The Cardinal's desire was to a dame
Whose favor was Onofrio's.   Pricked with
       pride,
The simpleton must ostentatiously
Display a ring, the Cardinal's love-gift,
Given to Onofrio as the lady's gage ;
Which ring on finger, as he put forth hand
To draw a tapestry, the Cardinal
Saw and knew, gift and owner, old and young ;
Whereon a fury entered him — the fire
He quenched with what could quench fire only
       — blood.
Nay, more : "there want not who affirm to
       boot,
The unwise boy, a certain festal eve,
Feigned ignorance of who the wight might be
That pressed too closely on him with a crowd.
He struck the Cardinal a blow : and then,
To put a face upon the incident,
Dared next day, smug as ever, go pay court
I' the Cardinal's antechamber. Mark and
       mend,
Ye youth, by this example how may greed
Vainglorious operate in worldly souls ! ' "

So ends the chronicler, beginning with
" God's justice, tardy though it prove per-
       chance,
Rests never till it reach delinquency."
Ay, or how otherwise had come to pass
That Victor rules, this present year, in Rome ?

FILIPPO BALDINUCCI ON THE PRIVI-
LEGE OF BURIAL

A REMINISCENCE OF A. D. 1676

" No, boy, we must not " — so began
My Uncle (he 's with God long since),
A-petting me, the good old man !
" We must not " — and he seemed to wince,
And lost that laugh whereto had grown
       His chuckle at my piece of news,
How cleverly I aimed my stone —
" I fear we must not pelt the Jews !

" When I was young indeed, — ah, faith
       Was young and strong in Florence too !
We Christians never dreamed of scathe
       Because we cursed or kicked the crew.
But now — well, well ! The olive-crops
       Weighed double then, and Arno's pranks
Would always spare religious shops
       Whenever he o'erflowed his banks !

"I'll tell you" — and his eye regained
  Its twinkle — "tell you something choice!
Something may help you keep unstained
  Your honest zeal to stop the voice
Of unbelief with stone-throw — spite
  Of laws, which modern fools enact,
That we must suffer Jews in sight
  Go wholly unmolested! Fact!

"There was, then, in my youth, and yet
  Is, by our San Frediano, just
Below the Blessed Olivet,
  A wayside ground wherein they thrust
Their dead, — these Jews, — the more our
    shame!
Except that, so they will but die,
Christians perchance incur no blame
  In giving hogs a hoist to sty.

"There, anyhow, Jews stow away
  Their dead; and — such their insolence —
Slink at odd times to sing and pray
  As Christians do — all make-pretence! —
Which wickedness they perpetrate
  Because they think no Christians see.
They reckoned here, at any rate,
  Without their host: ha, ha! he, he!

"For, what should join their plot of ground
  But a good Farmer's Christian field?
The Jews had hedged their corner round
  With bramble-bush to keep concealed
Their doings: for the public road
  Ran betwixt this their ground and that
The Farmer's, where he ploughed and sowed,
  Grew corn for barn and grapes for vat.

"So, properly to guard his store
  And gall the unbelievers too,
He builds a shrine and, what is more,
  Procures a painter whom I knew,
One Buti (he's with God), to paint
  A holy picture there — no less
Than Virgin Mary free from taint
  Borne to the sky by angels: yes!

"Which shrine he fixed, — who says him nay? —
  A-facing with its picture-side
Not, as you'd think, the public way,
  But just where sought these hounds to hide
Their carrion from that very truth
  Of Mary's triumph: not a hound
Could act his mummeries uncouth
  But Mary shamed the pack all round!

"Now, if it was amusing, judge!
  — To see the company arrive,
Each Jew intent to end his trudge
  And take his pleasure (though alive)
With all his Jewish kith and kin
  Below ground, have his venom out,
Sharpen his wits for next day's sin,
  Curse Christians, and so home, no doubt!

"Whereas, each phiz upturned beholds
  Mary, I warrant, soaring brave!
And in a trice, beneath the folds
  Of filthy garb which gowns each knave,

Down drops it — there to hide grimace,
  Contortion of the mouth and nose
At finding Mary in the place
  They'd keep for Pilate, I suppose!

"At last, they will not brook — not they!
  Longer such outrage on their tribe:
So, in some hole and corner, lay
  Their heads together — how to bribe
The meritorious Farmer's self
  To straight undo his work, restore
Their chance to meet and muse on pelf —
  Pretending sorrow, as before!

"Forthwith, a posse, if you please,
  Of Rabbi This and Rabbi That
Almost go down upon their knees
  To get him lay the picture flat.
The spokesman, eighty years of age,
  Gray as a badger, with a goat's
Not only beard but bleat, 'gins wage
  War with our Mary. Thus he dotes: —

"'Friends, grant a grace! How Hebrews
    toil
Through life in Florence — why relate
To those who lay the burden, spoil
  Our paths of peace? We bear our fate.
But when with life the long toil ends,
  Why must you — the expression craves
Pardon, but truth compels me, friends! —
  Why must you plague us in our graves?

"'Thoughtlessly plague, I would believe!
  For how can you — the lords of ease
By nurture, birthright — e'en conceive
  Our luxury to lie with trees
And turf, — the cricket and the bird
  Left for our last companionship:
No harsh deed, no unkindly word,
  No frowning brow nor scornful lip!

"'Death's luxury, we now rehearse
  While, living, through your streets we fare
And take your hatred: nothing worse
  Have we, once dead and safe, to bear!
So we refresh our souls, fulfil
  Our works, our daily tasks; and thus
Gather you grain — earth's harvest — still
  The wheat for you, the straw for us.

"'What flouting in a face, what harm.
  In just a lady borne from bier
By boys' heads, wings for leg and arm?'
  You question. Friends, the harm is here —
That just when our last sigh is heaved,
  And we would fain thank God and you
For labor done and peace achieved,
  Back comes the Past in full review!

"'At sight of just that simple flag,
  Starts the foe-feeling serpent-like
From slumber. Leave it lulled, nor drag —
  Though fangless — forth what needs must strike
When stricken sore, though stroke be vain
  Against the mailed oppressor! Give
Play to our fancy that we gain
  Life's rights when once we cease to live!

" ' Thus much to courtesy, to kind,
  To conscience! Now to Florence folk!
There 's core beneath this apple-rind,
  Beneath this white-of-egg there 's yolk!
Beneath this prayer to courtesy,
  Kind, conscience — there 's a sum to pouch!
How many ducats down will buy
  Our shame's removal, sirs? Avouch!

" ' Removal, not destruction, sirs!
  Just turn your picture! Let it front
The public path! Or memory errs,
  Or that same public path is wont
To witness many a chance befall
  Of lust, theft, bloodshed — sins enough,
Wherein our Hebrew part is small.
  Convert yourselves!' — he cut up rough.

'Look you, how soon a service paid
  Religion yields the servant fruit!
A prompt reply our Farmer made
  So following: ' Sirs, to grant your suit
Involves much danger! How? Transpose
  Our Lady? Stop the chastisement,
All for your good, herself bestows?
  What wonder if I grudge consent?

" ' — Yet grant it: since, what cash I take
  Is so much saved from wicked use.
We know you! And, for Mary's sake,
  A hundred ducats shall induce
Concession to your prayer. One day
  Suffices: Master Buti's brush
Turns Mary round the other way,
  And deluges your side with slush.

" ' Down with the ducats therefore!' Dump,
  Dump, dump it falls, each counted piece,
Hard gold. Then out of door they stump,
  These dogs, each brisk as with new lease
Of life, I warrant, — glad he 'll die
  Henceforward just as he may choose,
Be buried and in clover lie!
  Well said Esaias — ' stiff-necked Jews! '

" Off posts without a minute's loss
  Our Farmer, once the cash in poke,
And summons Buti — ere its gloss
  Have time to fade from off the joke —
To chop and change his work, undo
  The done side, make the side, now blank,
Recipient of our Lady — who,
  Displaced thus, had these dogs to thank!

" Now, boy, you 're hardly to instruct
  In technicalities of Art!
My nephew's childhood sure has sucked
  Along with mother's-milk some part
Of painter's-practice — learned, at least,
  How expeditiously is plied
A work in fresco — never ceased
  When once begun — a day, each side.

" So, Buti — (he 's with God) — begins:
  First covers up the shrine all round
With hoarding; then, as like as twins,
  Paints, t' other side the burial-ground,

New Mary, every point the same;
  Next, sluices over, as agreed,
The old; and last — but, spoil the game
  By telling you? Not I, indeed!

" Well, ere the week was half at end,
  Out came the object of this zeal,
This fine alacrity to spend
  Hard money for mere dead men's weal!
How think you? That old spokesman Jew
  Was High Priest, and he had a wife
As old, and she was dying too,
  And wished to end in peace her life!

" And he must humor dying whims,
  And soothe her with the idle hope
They 'd say their prayers and sing their hymns
  As if her husband were the Pope!
And she did die — believing just
  This privilege was purchased! Dead
In comfort through her foolish trust!
  ' Stiff-necked ones,' well Esaias said!

" So, Sabbath morning, out of gate
  And on to way, what sees our arch
Good Farmer? Why, they hoist their freight -
  The corpse — on shoulder, and so, march!
' Now for it, Buti!' In the nick
  Of time 't is pully-hauly, hence
With hoarding! O'er the wayside quick
  There 's Mary plain in evidence!

" And here 's the convoy halting: right!
  Oh, they are bent on howling psalms
And growling prayers, when opposite!
  And yet they glance, for all their qualms,
Approve that promptitude of his,
  The Farmer's — duly at his post
To take due thanks from every phiz,
  Sour smirk — nay, surly smile almost!

" Then earthward drops each brow again;
  The solemn task 's resumed; they reach
Their holy field — the unholy train:
  Enter its precinct, all and each,
Wrapt somehow in their godless rites;
  Till, rites at end, up-waking, lo,
They lift their faces! What delights
  The mourners as they turn to go?

" Ha, ha! he, he! On just the side
  They drew their purse-strings to make quit
Of Mary, — Christ the Crucified
  Fronted them now — these biters bit!
Never was such a hiss and snort,
  Such screwing nose and shooting lip!
Their purchase — honey in report —
  Proved gall and verjuice at first sip!

" Out they break, on they bustle, where,
  A-top of wall, the Farmer waits
With Buti: never fun so rare!
  The Farmer has the best: he rates
The rascal, as the old High Priest
  Takes on himself to sermonize —
Nay, sneer, ' We Jews supposed, at least,
  Theft was a crime in Christian eyes!'

"'Theft?' cries the Farmer. 'Eat your
        words!
Show me what constitutes a breach
Of faith in aught was said or heard!
I promised you in plainest speech
I'd take the thing you count disgrace
And put it here — and here't is put!
Did you suppose I'd leave the place
Blank therefore, just your rage to glut?

"'I guess you dared not stipulate
For such a damned impertinence!
So, quick, my graybeard, out of gate
And in at Ghetto! Haste you hence!
As long as I have house and land,
To spite you irreligious chaps,
Here shall the Crucifixion stand —
Unless you down with cash, perhaps!'

"So snickered he and Buti both.
The Jews said nothing, interchanged
A glance or two, renewed their oath
To keep ears stopped and hearts estranged
From grace, for all our Church can do;
Then off they scuttle: sullen jog
Homewards, against our Church to brew
Fresh mischief in their synagogue.

"But next day — see what happened, boy!
See why I bid you have a care
How you pelt Jews! The knaves employ
Such methods of revenge, forbear
No outrage on our faith, when free
To wreak their malice! Here they took
So base a method — plague o' me
If I record it in my Book!

"For, next day, while the Farmer sat
Laughing with Buti, in his shop,
At their successful joke, — rat-tat, —
Door opens, and they're like to drop
Down to the floor as in there stalks
A six-feet-high herculean-built
Young he-Jew with a beard that balks
Description. 'Help ere blood be spilt!'

— "Screamed Buti: for he recognized
Whom but the son, no less no more,
Of that High Priest his work surprised
So pleasantly the day before!
Son of the mother, then, whereof
The bier he lent a shoulder to,
And made the moans about, dared scoff
At sober Christian grief — the Jew!

"'Sirs, I salute you! Never rise!
No apprehension!' (Buti, white
And trembling like a tub of size,
Had tried to smuggle out of sight
The picture's self — the thing in oils,
You know, from which a fresco's dashed
Which courage speeds while caution spoils)
'Stay and be praised, sir, unabashed!

"'Praised, — ay, and paid too: for I come
To buy that very work of yours.
My poor abode, which boasts — well, some
Few specimens of Art, secures,

Haply, a masterpiece indeed
If I should find my humble means
Suffice the outlay. So, proceed!
Propose — ere prudence intervenes!'

"On Buti, cowering like a child,
These words descended from aloft,
In tone so ominously mild,
With smile terrifically soft
To that degree — could Buti dare
(Poor fellow) use his brains, think twice?
He asked, thus taken unaware,
No more than just the proper price!

"'Done!' cries the monster. 'I disburse
Forthwith your moderate demand.
Count on my custom — if no worse
Your future work be, understand,
Than this I carry off! No aid!
My arm, sir, lacks nor bone nor thews:
The burden's easy, and we're made,
Easy or hard, to bear — we Jews!'

"Crossing himself at such escape,
Buti by turns the money eyes
And, timidly, the stalwart shape
Now moving doorwards; but, more wise,
The Farmer — who, though dumb, this while
Had watched advantage — straight conceived
A reason for that tone and smile
So mild and soft! The Jew — believed!

"Mary in triumph borne to deck
A Hebrew household! Pictured where
No one was used to bend the neck
In praise or bow the knee in prayer!
Borne to that domicile by whom?
The son of the High Priest! Through
        what?
An insult done his mother's tomb!
Saul changed to Paul — the case came pat!

"'Stay, dog-Jew . . . gentle sir, that is!
Resolve me! Can it be, she crowned, —
Mary, by miracle, — oh bliss! —
My present to your burial-ground?
Certain, a ray of light has burst
Your vale of darkness! Had you else,
Only for Mary's sake, unpursed
So much hard money? Tell — oh, tell's!'

"Round — like a serpent that we took
For worm and trod on — turns his bulk
About the Jew. First dreadful look
Sends Buti in a trice to skulk
Out of sight somewhere, safe — alack!
But our good Farmer faith made bold:
And firm (with Florence at his back)
He stood, while gruff the gutturals rolled —

"'Ay, sir, a miracle was worked,
By quite another power, I trow,
Than ever yet in canvas lurked,
Or you would scarcely face me now!
A certain impulse did suggest
A certain grasp with this right-hand,
Which probably had put to rest
Our quarrel, — thus your throat once spanned.

" ' But I remembered me, subdued
  That impulse, and you face me still !
And soon a philosophic mood
  Succeeding (hear it, if you will !)
Has altogether changed my views
  Concerning Art. Blind prejudice !
Well may you Christians tax us Jews
  With scrupulosity too nice !

" ' For, don't I see, — let 's issue join ! —
  Whenever I 'm allowed pollute
(I — and my little bag of coin)
  Some Christian palace of repute, —
Don't I see stuck up everywhere
  Abundant proof that cultured taste
Has Beauty for its only care,
  And upon Truth no thought to waste ?

" ' 'Jew, since it must be, take in pledge
  Of payment ' — so a Cardinal
Has sighed to me as if a wedge
  Entered his heart — ' this best of all
My treasures ! ' Leda, Ganymede
  Or Antiope : swan, eagle, ape,
(Or what 's the beast of what 's the breed,)
  And Jupiter in every shape !

" ' Whereat if I presume to ask
  ' But, Eminence, though Titian's whisk
Of brush have well performed its task,
  How comes it these false godships frisk
In presence of — what yonder frame
  Pretends to image ? Surely, odd
It seems, you let confront The Name
  Each beast the heathen called his god ! '

" ' Benignant smiles me pity straight
  The Cardinal. ' 'T is Truth, we prize !
Art 's the sole question in debate !
  These subjects are so many lies.
We treat them with a proper scorn
  When we turn lies — called gods forsooth —
To lies' fit use, now Christ is born.
  Drawing and coloring are Truth.

" ' 'Think you I honor lies so much
  As scruple to parade the charms
Of Leda — Titian, every touch —
  Because the thing within her arms
Means Jupiter who had the praise
  And prayer of a benighted world ?
He would have mine too, if, in days
  Of light, I kept the canvas furled ! '

" ' So ending, with some easy gibe.
  What power has logic ! I, at once,
Acknowledged error in our tribe
  So squeamish that, when friends ensconce
A pretty picture in its niche
  To do us honor, deck our graves,
We fret and fume and have an itch
  To strangle folk — ungrateful knaves !

" ' No, sir ! Be sure that — what 's its style,
  Your picture ? — shall possess ungrudged
A place among my rank and file
  Of Ledas and what not — be judged

Just as a picture ! and (because
  I fear me much I scarce have bought
A Titian) Master Buti's flaws
  Found there, will have the laugh.flaws ought !

" So, with a scowl, it darkens door —
  This bulk — no longer ! Buti makes
Prompt glad re-entry ; there 's a score
  Of oaths, as the good Farmer wakes
From what must needs have been a trance,
  Or he had struck (he swears) to ground
The bold bad mouth that dared advance
  Such doctrine the reverse of sound !

" Was magic here ? Most like ! For, since,
  Somehow our city's faith grows still
More and more lukewarm, and our Prince
  Or loses heart or wants the will
To check increase of cold. 'T is ' Live
  And let live ! Languidly repress
The Dissident ! In short, — contrive
  Christians must bear with Jews : no less ! '

" The end seems, any Israelite
  Wants any picture, — pishes, poohs,
Purchases, hangs it full in sight
  In any chamber he may choose !
In Christ's crown, one more thorn we rue !
  In Mary's bosom, one more sword !
No, boy, you must not pelt a Jew !
  O Lord, how long ? How long, O Lord ? "

EPILOGUE

μεστοὶ . . .
οἱ δ' ἀμφορῆς οἴνου μέλανος ἀνθοσμίου.

" THE poets pour us wine — "
  Said the dearest poet I ever knew,
Dearest and greatest and best to me.
You clamor athirst for poetry —
We pour. " But when shall a vintage be " —
  You cry — " strong grape, squeezed gold from
    screw.
Yet sweet juice, flavored flowery-fine ?
  That were indeed the wine ! "

One pours your cup — stark strength,
  Meat for a man ; and you eye the pulp
Strained, turbid still, from the viscous blood
Of the snaky bough : and you grumble " Good !
For it swells resolve, breeds hardihood ;
  Dispatch it, then, in a single gulp ! "
So, down, with a wry face, goes at length
  The liquor : stuff for strength.

One pours your cup — sheer sweet,
  The fragrant fumes of a year condensed :
Suspicion of all that 's ripe or rathe,
From the bud on branch to the grass in swathe
" We suck mere milk of the seasons," saith
  A curl of each nostril — " dew, dispensed
Nowise for nerving man to feat :
  Boys sip such honeyed sweet ! "

And thus who wants wine strong,
  Waves each sweet smell of the year away :

Who likes to swoon as the sweets suffuse
His brain with a mixture of beams and dews
Turned syrupy drink — rough strength eschews:
 " What though in our veins your wine-stock
        stay ?
The lack of the bloom does our palate wrong.
     Give us wine sweet, not strong ! "

Yet wine is — some affirm —
     Prime wine is found in the world somewhere,
Of portable strength with sweet to match.
You double your heart its dose, yet catch —
As the draught descends — a violet-smatch,
     Softness — however it came there,
Through drops expressed by the fire and worm :
     Strong sweet wine — some affirm.

Body and bouquet both ?
     'T is easy to ticket a bottle so ;
But what was the case in the cask, my friends ?
Cask ?   Nay,   the vat — where the maker
        mends
His strong with his sweet (you suppose) and
        blends
His rough with his smooth, till none can know
How it comes you may tipple, nothing loth,
     Body and bouquet both.

" You " being just — the world.
     No poets — who turn, themselves, the winch
Of the press ; no critics — I 'll even say,
(Being flustered and easy of faith, to-day,)
Who for love of the work have learned the way
     Till themselves produce home-made, at a
        pinch :
No !   You are the world, and wine ne'er purled
     Except to please the world !

" For, oh the common heart !
     And, ah the irremissible sin
Of poets who please themselves, not us !
Strong wine yet sweet wine pouring thus,
How please still — Pindar and Æschylus ! —
     Drink — dipt into by the bearded chin
Alike and the bloomy lip — no part
     Denied the common heart !

" And might we get such grace,
     And did you moderns but stock our vault
With the true half-brandy half-attar-gul,
How would seniors indulge at a hearty pull
While juniors tossed off their thimbleful !
     Our Shakespeare and Milton escaped your
        fault,
So, they reign supreme o'er the weaker race
     That wants the ancient grace ! "

If I paid myself with words
     (As the French say well) I were dupe in-
        deed !
I were found in belief that you quaffed and
        bowsed
At your Shakespeare the whole day long,
        caroused
In your Milton pottle-deep nor drowsed
     A moment of night — toped on, took heed
Of nothing like modern cream-and-curds.
     Pay me with deeds, not words !

For — see your cellarage !
     There are forty barrels with Shakespeare's
        brand.
Some five or six are abroach : the rest
Stand spigoted, fauceted.   Try and test
What yourselves call best of the very best !
     How comes it that still untouched they
        stand ?
Why don't you try tap, advance a stage
     With the rest in cellerage ?

For — see your cellarage !
     There are four big butts of Milton's brew.
How comes it you make old drips and drops
Do duty, and there devotion stops ?
Leave such an abyss of malt and hops
     Embellied in butts which bungs still glue ?
You hate your bard !   A fig for your rage !
     Free him from cellarage !

'T is said I brew stiff drink,
     But the deuce a flavor of grape is there.
Hardly a May-go-down, 't is just
A sort of a gruff Go-down-it-must —
No Merry-go-down, no gracious gust
     Commingles the racy with Springtide's rare !
" What wonder," say you, " that we cough,
     and blink
     At Autumn's heady drink ? " "

Is it a fancy, friends ?
     Mighty and mellow are never mixed,
Though mighty and mellow be born at once.
Sweet for the future, — strong for the nonce !
Stuff you should stow away, ensconce
     In the deep and dark, to be found fast-fixed
At the century's close : such time strength
        spends
     A-sweetening for my friends !

And then — why, what you quaff
     With a smack of lip and a cluck of tongue,
Is leakage and leavings — just what haps
From the tun some learned taster taps
With a promise " Prepare your watery chaps !
     Here 's properest wine for old and young !
Dispute its perfection — you make us laugh !
     Have faith, give thanks, but — quaff ! "

Leakage, I say, or — worse —
     Leavings suffice pot-valiant souls.
Somebody, brimful, long ago,
Frothed flagon he drained to the dregs ; and, lo,
Down whisker and beard what an overflow !
     Lick spilth that has trickled from classic
        jowls,
Sup the single scene, sip the only verse —
     Old wine, not new and worse !

I grant you : worse by much !
     Renounce that new where you never gained
One glow at heart, one gleam at head,
And stick to the warrant of age instead !
No dwarf's-lap !   Fatten, by giants fed !
     You fatten, with oceans of drink undrained ?
You feed — who would choke did a cobweb
        smutch
     The Age you love so much ?

A mine 's beneath a moor :
  Acres of moor roof fathoms of mine
Which diamonds dot where you please to
    dig ;
Yet who plies spade for the bright and big ?
Your product is — truffles, you hunt with a
    pig !
  Since bright-and-big, when a man would
    dine,
Suits badly : and therefore the Koh-i-noor
  May sleep in mine 'neath moor !

Wine, pulse in might from me !
  It may never emerge in must from vat,
Never fill cask nor furnish can,
Never end sweet, which strong began —
God's gift to gladden the heart of man ;
  But spirit 's at proof, I promise that !
No sparing of juice spoils what should be
  Fit brewage — mine for me.

Man's thoughts and loves and hates !
  Earth is my vineyard, these grew there :
From grape of the ground, I made or marred
My vintage ; easy the task or hard,
Who set it — his praise be my reward !
  Earth's yield ! Who yearn for the Dark
    Blue Sea's,
Let them " lay, pray, bray " — the addle-pates !
  Mine be Man's thoughts, loves, hates !

But some one says, " Good Sir ! "
  ('T is a worthy versed in what concerns
The making such labor turn out well,)
" You don't suppose that the nosegay-smell
Needs always come from the grape ? Each
    bell
  At your foot, each bud that your culture
    spurns,
The very cowslip would act like myrrh
  On the stiffest brew — good Sir !

" Cowslips, abundant birth
  O'er meadow and hillside, vineyard too,
— Like a schoolboy's scrawlings in and out
Distasteful lesson-book — all about
Greece and Rome, victory and rout —
  Love-verses instead of such vain ado !
So, fancies frolic it o'er the earth
  Where thoughts have rightlier birth.

" Nay, thoughtlings they themselves :
  Loves, hates — in little and less and least !
Thoughts ? ' What is a man beside a mount ! '

Loves ? ' Absent — poor lovers the minutes
    count ! '
Hates ? ' Fie — Pope's letters to Martha
    Blount ! '
  These furnish a wine for a children's-feast :
Insipid to man, they suit the elves
  Like thoughts, loves, hates themselves."

And, friends, beyond dispute
  I too have the cowslips dewy and dear.
Punctual as Springtide forth peep they :
I leave them to make my meadow gay.
But I ought to pluck and impound them, eh ?
  Not let them alone, but deftly shear
And shred and reduce to — what may suit
  Children, beyond dispute ?

And, here 's May-month, all bloom,
  All bounty : what if I sacrifice ?
If I out with shears and shear, nor stop
Shearing till prostrate, lo, the crop ?
And will you prefer it to ginger-pop
  When I 've made you wine of the memories
Which leave as bare as a churchyard tomb
  My meadow, late all bloom ?

Nay, what ingratitude
  Should I hesitate to amuse the wits
That have pulled so long at my flask, nor
    grudged
The headache that paid their pains, nor budged
From bunghole before they sighed and judged
  " Too rough for our taste, to-day, befits
The racy and right when the years conclude ! "
    Out on ingratitude !

Grateful or ingrate — none,
  No cowslip of all my fairy crew
Shall help to concoct what makes you wink,
And goes to your head till you think you think !
I like them alive : the printer's ink
  Would sensibly tell on the perfume too.
I may use up my nettles, ere I 've done ;
  But of cowslips — friends get none !

Don't nettles make a broth
  Wholesome for blood grown lazy and thick ?
Maws out of sorts make mouths out of taste.
My Thirty-four Port — no need to waste
On a tongue that 's fur and a palate — paste !
  A magnum for friends who are sound ! the
    sick —
I 'll posset and cosset them, nothing loth,
  Henceforward with nettle-broth !

THE AGAMEMNON OF ÆSCHYLUS

MAY I be permitted to chat a little, by way of recreation, at the end of a somewhat toilsome and perhaps fruitless adventure ?

If, because of the immense fame of the following Tragedy, I wished to acquaint myself with it, and could only do so by the help of a translator, I should require him to be literal at every cost save that of absolute violence to our language. The use of certain allowable constructions which, happening to be out of daily favor, are all the more appropriate to archaic workmanship, is no violence : but I would be tolerant for once — in the case of so immensely famous an original — of even a clumsy attempt to furnish me with the very turn of each phrase in as Greek a fashion as English will bear : while, with respect to amplifications and embellishments, — anything rather than, with the good farmer, experience that most signal of mortifications, " to gape for Æschylus and get Theognis." I should especially decline — what may appear to brighten up a passage — the employment of a new word for some old one, — πόνος, or μέγας, or τέλος, with its congeners, recurring four times in three lines : for though such substitution may be in itself perfectly justifiable, yet this exercise of ingenuity ought to be within the competence of the unaided English reader if he likes to show himself ingenious. Learning Greek teaches Greek, and nothing else : certainly not common sense, if that have failed to precede the teaching. Further, — if I obtained a mere strict bald version of thing by thing, or at least word pregnant with thing, I should hardly look for an impossible transmission of the reputed magniloquence and sonority of the Greek ; and this with the less regret, inasmuch as there is abundant musicality elsewhere, but nowhere else than in his poem the ideas of the poet. And lastly, when presented with these ideas, I should expect the result to prove very hard reading indeed if it were meant to resemble Æschylus, ξυμβαλεῖν οὐ ῥᾴδιος, " not easy to understand," in the opinion of his stoutest advocate among the ancients ; while, I suppose, even modern scholarship sympathizes with that early declaration of the redoubtable Salmasius, when, looking about for an example of the truly obscure for the benefit of those who found obscurity in the sacred books, he protested that this particular play leaves them all behind in this respect, with their " Hebraisms, Syriasms, Hellenisms, and the whole of such bag and baggage." [1] For, over and above the proposed ambiguity of the Chorus, the text is sadly corrupt, probably interpolated, and certainly mutilated ; and no unlearned person enjoys the scholar's privilege of trying his fancy upon each obstacle whenever he comes to a stoppage, and effectually clearing the way by suppressing what seems to lie in it.

All I can say for the present performance is, that I have done as I would be done by, if need were. Should anybody, without need, honor my translation by a comparison with the original, I beg him to observe that " following no editor exclusively, I keep to the earlier readings so long as sense can be made out of them, but disregard, I hope, little of importance in recent criticism so far as I have fallen in with it. Fortunately, the poorest translation, provided only it be faithful, — though it reproduce all the artistic confusion of tenses, moods, and persons, with which the original teems, — will not only suffice to display what an eloquent friend maintains to be the all-in-all of poetry — " the action of the piece " — but may help to illustrate his assurance that " the Greeks are the highest models of expression, the unapproached masters of the grand style : their expression is so excellent because it is so admirably kept in its right degree of prominence, because it is so simple and so well subordinated, because it draws its force directly from the pregnancy of the matter which it conveys . . . not a word wasted, not a sentiment capriciously thrown in, stroke on stroke ! " [2] So may all happen !

Just a word more on the subject of my spelling — in a transcript from the Greek and there exclusively — Greek names and places precisely as does the Greek author. I began this practice, with great innocency of intention, some six-and-thirty years ago. Leigh Hunt, I remember, was accustomed to speak of his gratitude, when ignorant of Greek, to those writers (like Goldsmith) who had obliged him by using English characters, so that he might relish, for instance, the smooth quality of such

---

[1] " Quis Æschylum possit affirmare Græce nunc scienti magis patere explicabilem quam Evangelia aut Epistolas Apostolicas ? Unus ejus Agamemnon obscuritate superat quantum est librorum sacrorum cum suis Hebraismis et Syriasmis et tota Hellenisticæ supellectili vel farragine." — SALMASIUS de Hellenistica, Epist. Dedic.

[2] *Poems* by MATTHEW ARNOLD, Preface.

a phrase as "hapalunetai galené;" he said also that Shelley was indignant at "Firenze" having displaced the Dantesque "Fiorenza," and would contemptuously English the intruder "Firence." I supposed I was doing a simple thing enough: but there has been till lately much astonishment at os and us, ai and oi, representing the same letters in Greek. Of a sudden, however, whether in translation or out of it, everybody seems committing the offence, although the adoption of u for v still presents such difficulty that it is a wonder how we have hitherto escaped "Eyripides." But there existed a sturdy Briton who, Ben Jonson informs us, wrote "The Life of the Emperor Anthony Pie"—whom we now acquiesce in as Antoninus Pius: for "with time and patience the mulberry leaf becomes satin." Yet there is on all sides much profession of respect for what Keats called "vowelled Greek"—"consonanted," one would expect; and, in a criticism upon a late admirable translation of something of my own, it was deplored that, in a certain verse corresponding in measure to the fourteenth of the sixth Pythian Ode, "neither Professor Jebb in his Greek, nor Mr. Browning in his English, could emulate that matchlessly musical γόνον ἰδὼν κάλλιστον ἀνδρῶν." Now, undoubtedly, "Seeing her son the fairest of men" has more sense than sound to boast of: but then, would not an Italian roll us out "Rimirando il figliuolo bellissimo degli uomini?" whereat Pindar, no less than Professor Jebb and Mr. Browning, τριακτῆρος οἴχεται τυχών.

It is recorded in the Annals of Art[1] that there was once upon a time, practising so far north as Stockholm, a painter and picture-cleaner—sire of a less unhappy son—Old Muytens: and the annalist, Baron de Tessé, has not concealed his profound dissatisfaction at Old Muytens' conceit "to have himself had something to do with the work of whatever master of eminence might pass through his hands." Whence it was—the Baron goes on to deplore—that much detriment was done to that excellent piece "The Recognition of Achilles," by Rubens, through the perversity of Old Muytens, "who must needs take on him to beautify every nymph of the twenty by the bestowment of a widened eye and an enlarged mouth." I, at least, have left eyes and mouths everywhere as I found them, and this conservatism is all that claims praise for—what is, after all ἀκέλευστος ἄμισθος ἀοιδά. No, neither "uncommanded" nor "unrewarded:" since it was commanded of me by my venerated friend Thomas Carlyle, and rewarded will it indeed become, if I am permitted to dignify it by the prefatory insertion of his dear and noble name.   R. B.

LONDON, October 1, 1877.

[1] Lettres à un jeune Prince, traduites du Suédois.

AGAMEMNON

PERSONS OF THE DRAMA

WARDER.
CHOROS OF OLD MEN.
KLUTAIMNESTRA.
TALTHUBIOS, Herald.
AGAMEMNON.
AIGISTHOS.
KASSANDRA.

Warder. The gods I ask deliverance from these labors,
Watch of a year's length whereby, slumbering through it
On the Atreidai's roofs on elbow,—dog-like—
I know of nightly star-groups the assemblage,
And those that bring to men winter and summer,
Bright dynasts, as they pride them in the æther
—Stars, when they wither, and the uprisings of them.
And now on ward I wait the torch's token,
The glow of fire, shall bring from Troia message
And word of capture: so prevails audacious
The man's-way-planning hoping heart of woman.
But when I, driven from night-rest, dew-drenched, hold to
This couch of mine—not looked upon by visions,
Since fear instead of sleep still stands beside me,

So as that fast I fix in sleep no eyelids—
And when to sing or chirp a tune I fancy,
For slumber such song-remedy infusing,
I wail then, for this House's fortune groaning,
Not, as of old, after the best ways governed.
Now, lucky be deliverance from these labors,
At good news—the appearing dusky fire!
O hail, thou lamp of night, a day-long lightness
Revealing, and of dances the ordainment!
Halloo, halloo!
To Agamemnon's wife I show, by shouting,
That, from bed starting up at once, i' the household
Joyous acclaim, good-omened to this torch-blaze,
She send aloft if haply Ilion's city
Be taken, as the beacon boasts announcing.
Ay, and, for me, myself will dance a prelude,
For, that my masters' dice drop right, I'll reckon:
Since thrice-six has it thrown to me, this signal.
Well, may it hap that, as he comes, the loved hand
O' the household's lord I may sustain with this hand!
As for the rest, I'm mute: on tongue a big ox

Has trodden. Yet this House, if voice it take
   should,
Most plain would speak. So, willing I myself
   speak
To those who know : to who know not — I 'm
   blankness.
   Choros. The tenth year this, since Priamos'
   great match,
King Menelaos, Agamemnon King,
— The strenuous yoke-pair of the Atreidai's
   honor
Two-throned, two-sceptred, whereof Zeus was
   donor —
Did from this land the aid, the armament dis-
   patch,
The thousand-sailored force of Argives clamor-
   ing
" Ares " from out the indignant breast, as fling
Passion forth vultures which, because of grief
Away, — as are their young ones, — with the
   thief,
Lofty above their brood-nests wheel in ring,
Row round and round with oar of either wing,
Lament the bedded chicks, lost labor that was
   love :
Which hearing, one above
— Whether Apollon, Pan or Zeus — that wail,
Sharp-piercing bird-shriek of the guests who
   fare
Housemates with gods in air —
Such-an-one sends, against who these assail,
What, late-sent, shall not fail
Of punishing — Erinus. Here as there,
The Guardian of the Guest, Zeus, the excelling
   one,
Sends against Alexandros either son
Of Atreus : for that wife, the many-husbanded,
Appointing many a tug that tries the limb,
While the knee plays the prop in dust, while,
   shred
To morsels, lies the spear-shaft ; in those
   grim
Marriage-prolusions when their Fury wed
Danaoi and Troes, both alike. All 's said :
Things are where things are, and, as fate has
   willed,
So shall they be fulfilled.
Not gently-grieving, not just doling out
The drops of expiation — no, nor tears dis-
   tilled —
Shall he we know of bring the hard about
To soft — that intense ire
At those mock rites unsanctified by fire.
But we pay naught here : through our flesh, age-
   weighed,
Left out from who gave aid
In that day, — we remain,
Staying on staves a strength
The equal of a child's at length.
For when young marrow in the breast doth
   reign,
That 's the old man's match, — Ares out of
   place
In either : but in oldest age's case,
Foliage a-fading, why, he wends his way
On three feet, and, no stronger than a child,
Wanders about gone wild,
A dream in day.

But thou, Tundareus' daughter, Klutaimnestra
   queen,
What need ? What new ? What having heard
   or seen,
By what announcement's tidings, everywhere.
Settest thou, round about, the sacrifice aflare ?
For, of all gods the city-swaying,
Those supernal, those infernal,
Those of the fields', those of the mart's
   obeying, —
The altars blaze with gifts ;
And here and there, heaven-high the torch up-
   lifts
Flame — medicated with persuasions mild,
With foul admixture unbeguiled —
Of holy unguent, from the clotted chrism
Brought from the palace, safe in its abysm.
Of these things, speaking what may be in-
   deed
Both possible and lawful to concede,
Healer do thou become ! — of this solicitude
Which, now, stands plainly forth of evil mood,
And, then . . . but from oblations, hope, to-
   day
Gracious appearing, wards away
From soul the insatiate care,
The sorrow at my breast, devouring there !

Empowered am I to sing
The omens, what their force which, journey-
   ing,
Rejoiced the potentates :
(For still, from God, inflates
My breast, song-suasion : age,
Born to the business, still such war can wage)
— How the fierce bird against the Teukris land
Dispatched, with spear and executing hand,
The Achaian's two-throned empery — o'er
   Hellas' youth
Two rulers with one mind :
The birds' king to these kings of ships, on high,
— The black sort, and the sort that 's white
   behind, —
Appearing by the palace, on the spear-throw
   side,
In right sky-regions, visible far and wide, —
Devouring a hare-creature, great with young,
Balked of more racings they, as she from whom
   they sprung !
Ah, Linos, say — ah, Linos, song of wail !
But may the good prevail !

The prudent army-prophet seeing two
The Atreidai, two their tempers, knew
Those feasting on the hare
The armament-conductors were ;
And thus he spoke, explaining signs in view.
" In time, this outset takes the town of
   Priamos :
But all before its towers, — the people's wealth
   that was,
Of flocks and herds, — as sure, shall booty-
   sharing thence
Drain to the dregs away, by battle violence.
Only, have care lest grudge of any god disturb
With cloud the unsullied shine of that great
   force, the curb
Of Troia. struck with damp

Beforehand in the camp !
For envyingly is
The virgin Artemis
Toward — her father's flying hounds — this
House —
The sacrificers of the piteous
And cowering beast,
Brood and all, ere the birth : she hates the
eagles' feast.
Ah, Linos, say — ah, Linos, song of wail !
But may the good prevail !

" Thus ready is the beauteous one with help
To those small dewdrop things fierce lions
whelp,
And udder-loving litter of each brute
That roams the mead ; and therefore makes
she suit,
The fair one, for fulfilment to the end
Of things these signs portend —
Which partly smile, indeed, but partly scowl —
The phantasms of the fowl.
I call Ieïos Paian to avert
She work the Danaoi hurt
By any thwarting waftures, long and fast
Holdings from sail of ships :
And sacrifice, another than the last,
She for herself precipitate —
Something unlawful, feast for no man's lips,
Builder of quarrels, with the House cognate —
Having in awe no husband : for remains
A frightful, backward-darting in the path,
Wily house-keeping chronicler of wrath,
That has to punish that old children's fate ! "
Such things did Kalchas, — with abundant
gains
As well, — vociferate,
Predictions from the birds, in journeying,
Above the abode of either king.
With these, symphonious, sing —
Ah, Linos, say — ah, Linos, song of wail !
But may the good prevail !

Zeus, whosoe'er he be, — if that express
Aught dear to him on whom I call —
So do I him address.
I cannot liken out, by all
Admeasurement of powers,
Any but Zeus for refuge at such hours,
If veritably needs I must
From off my soul its vague care-burden thrust.

Not — whosoever was the great of yore,
Bursting to bloom with bravery all round —
Is in our mouths : he was, but is no more.
And who it was that after came to be,
Met the thrice-throwing wrestler, — he
Is also gone to ground.
But " Zeus " — if any, heart and soul, that
name —
Shouting the triumph-praise — proclaim,
Complete in judgment shall that man be found.
Zeus, who leads onward mortals to be wise,
Appoints that suffering masterfully teach.
In sleep, before the heart of each,
A woe-remembering travail sheds in dew
Discretion, — ay, and melts the unwilling too
By what, perchance, may be a graciousness

Of gods, enforced no less, —
As they, commanders of the crew,
Assume the awful seat.

And then the old leader of the Achaian fleet,
Disparaging no seer —
With bated breath to suit misfortune's inrush
here
— (What time it labored, that Achaian host,
By stay from sailing, — every pulse at length
Emptied of vital strength, —
Hard over Kalchis shore-bound, current-crost
In Aulis station, — while the winds which post
From Strumon, ill-delayers, famine-fraught,
Tempters of man to sail where harborage is
naught,
Spendthrifts of ships and cables, turning time
To twice the length, — these carded, by delay,
To less and less away
The Argeians' flowery prime :
And when a remedy more grave and grand
Than aught before — yea, for the storm and
dearth —
The prophet to the foremost in command
Shrieked forth, as cause of this
Adducing Artemis,
So that the Atreidai striking staves on earth
Could not withhold the tear) —
Then did the king, the elder, speak this clear.

" Heavy the fate, indeed — to disobey !
Yet heavy if my child I slay,
The adornment of my household : with the
tide
Of virgin-slaughter, at the altar-side,
A father's hands defiling : which the way
Without its evils, say ?
How shall I turn fleet-fugitive,
Failing of duty to allies ?
Since for a wind-abating sacrifice
And virgin blood, — 't is right they strive,
Nay, madden with desire.
Well may it work them — this that they re-
quire ! "

But when he underwent necessity's
Yoke-trace, — from soul blowing unhallowed
change
Unclean, abominable, — thence — another
man —
The audacious mind of him began
Its wildest range.
For this it is gives mortals hardihood —
Some vice-devising miserable mood
Of madness, and first woe of all the brood.
The sacrificer of his daughter — strange ! —
He dared become, to expedite
Woman-avenging warfare, — anchors weighed
With such prelusive rite !

Prayings and callings " Father " — naught
they made
Of these, and of the virgin-age, —
Captains heart-set on war to wage !
His ministrants, vows done, the father bade —
Kid-like, above the altar, swathed in pall,
Take her — lift high, and have no fear at all,
Head-downward, and the fair mouth's guard

And frontage hold, — press hard
From utterance a curse against the House
By dint of bit — violence bridling speech.
And as to ground her saffron-vest she shed,
She smote the sacrificers all and each
With arrow sweet and piteous,
From the eye only sped, —
Significant of will to use a word,
Just as in pictures : since, full many a time,
In her sire's guest-hall, by the well-heaped
    board
Had she made music, — lovingly with chime
Of her chaste voice, that unpolluted thing,
Honored the third libation, — paian that should
    bring
Good fortune to the sire she loved so well.

What followed — those things I nor saw nor
    tell.
But Kalchas' arts — whate'er they indicate —
Miss of fulfilment never : it is fate.
True, justice makes, in sufferers, a desire
To know the future woe preponderate.
But — hear before is need !
To that, farewell and welcome ! 't is the same,
    indeed,
As grief beforehand : clearly, part for part,
Conformably to Kalchas' art,
Shall come the event.
But be they as they may, things subsequent, —
What is to do, prosperity betide
E'en as we wish it ! — we, the next allied,
Sole guarding barrier of the Apian land.

I am come, reverencing power in thee,
O Klutaimnestra ! For 't is just we bow
To the ruler's wife, — the male-seat man-be-
    reaved.
But if thou, having heard good news, — or
    none, —
For good news' hope dost sacrifice thus wide,
I would hear gladly : art thou mute, — no
    grudge !
  Klutaimnestra. Good-news-announcer, may —
    as is the by-word —
Morn become, truly, — news from Night his
    mother !
But thou shalt learn joy past all hope of hear-
    ing.
Priamos' city have the Argeioi taken.
  Cho. How sayest ? The word, from want of
    faith, escaped me.
  Klu. Troia the Achaioi hold : do I speak
    plainly ?
  Cho. Joy overcreeps me, calling forth the
    tear-drop.
  Klu. Right ! for, that glad thou art, thine
    eye convicts thee.
  Cho. For — what to thee, of all this, trusty
    token ?
  Klu. What 's here ! how else ? unless the
    god have cheated.
  Cho. Haply thou flattering shows of dreams
    respectest ?
  Klu. No fancy would I take of soul sleep-
    burdened.
  Cho. But has there puffed thee up some un-
    winged omen ?

  Klu. As a young maid's my mind thou
    mockest grossly.
  Cho. Well, at what time was — even sacked,
    the city ?
  Klu. Of this same mother Night — the dawn,
    I tell thee.
  Cho. And who of messengers could reach this
    swiftness ?
  Klu. Hephaistos — sending a bright blaze
    from Idé !
Beacon did beacon send, from fire the poster,
Hitherward : Idé to the rock Hermaian
Of Lemnos : and a third great torch o' the
    island
Zeus' seat received in turn, the Athoan sum-
    mit.
And, — so upsoaring as to stride sea over,
The strong lamp-voyager, and all for joyance —
Did the gold-glorious splendor, any sun like,
Pass on — the pine-tree — to Makistos' watch-
    place ;
Who did not, — tardy, — caught, no wits about
    him,
By sleep, — decline his portion of the missive.
And far the beacon's light, on stream Euri-
    pos
Arriving, made aware Messapios' warders.
And up they lit in turn, played herald on-
    wards,
Kindling with flame a heap of gray old
    heather.
And, strengthening still, the lamp, decaying
    nowise,
Springing o'er Plain Asopos, — fullmoon-
    fashion
Effulgent, — toward the crag of Mount Kitha-
    iron,
Roused a new rendering-up of fire the escort —
And light, far escort, lacked no recognition
O' the guard — as burning more than burnings
    told you.
And over Lake Gorgopis light went leaping,
And, at Mount Aigiplanktos safe arriving,
Enforced the law — " to never stint the fire-
    stuff."
And they send, lighting up with ungrudged
    vigor,
Of flame a huge beard, ay, the very foreland
So as to strike above, in burning onward,
The look-out which commands the Strait
    Saronic,
Then did it dart until it reached the outpost
Mount Arachnaios here, the city's neighbor ;
And then darts to this roof of the Atreidai
This light of Idé's fire not unforefathered !
Such are the rules prescribed the flambeau-
    bearers :
He beats that 's first and also last in running.
Such is the proof and token I declare thee,
My husband having sent me news from Troia.
  Cho. The gods, indeed, anon will I pray,
    woman !
But now, these words to hear, and sate my
    wonder
Thoroughly, I am fain — if twice thou tell
    them.
  Klu. Troia do the Achaioi hold, this same
    day.

I think a noise — no mixture — reigns i' the
    city.
Sour wine and unguent pour thou in one
    vessel —
Standers-apart, not lovers, would'st thou style
    them :
And so, of captives and of conquerors, partwise
The voices are to hear, of fortune diverse.
For those, indeed, upon the bodies prostrate
Of husbands, brothers, children upon parents
— The old men, from a throat that 's free no
    longer,
Shriekingly wail the death-doom of their dear-
    est :
While these — the after-battle hungry labor,
Which prompts night-faring, marshals them to
    breakfast
On the town's store, according to no billet
Of sharing, but as each drew lot of fortune.
In the spear-captured Troic habitations
House they already : from the frosts upæthral
And dews delivered, will they, luckless crea-
    tures,
Without a watch to keep, slumber all night
    through.
And if they fear the gods, the city-guarders,
And if the gods' structures of the conquered
    country,
They may not — capturers — soon in turn be
    captive.
But see no prior lust befall the army
To sack things sacred — by gain-cravings van-
    quished !
For there needs homeward the return's sal-
    vation,
To round the new limb back o' the double race-
    course.
And guilty to the gods if came the army,
Awakened up the sorrow of those slaughtered
Might be — should no outbursting evils happen.
But may good beat — no turn to see i' the
    balance !
For, many benefits I want the gain of.
    Cho. Woman, like prudent man thou kindly
    speakest.
And I, thus having heard thy trusty tokens,
The gods to rightly hail forthwith prepare
    me ;
For, grace that must be paid has crowned our
    labors.

O Zeus the king, and friendly Night
Of these brave boons bestower —
Thou who didst fling on Troia's every tower
The o'er-roofing snare, that neither great thing
    might,
Nor any of the young ones, overpass
Captivity's great sweep-net — one and all
Of Até held in thrall !
Ay, Zeus I fear — the guest's friend great —
    who was
The doer of this, and long since bent
The bow on Alexandros with intent
That neither wide o' the white
Nor o'er the stars the foolish dart should light.
The stroke of Zeus — they have it, as men say !
This, at least, from the source track forth we
    may !

As he ordained, so has he done.
" No " — said some one —
" The gods think fit to care
Nowise for mortals, such
As those by whom the good and fair
Of things denied their touch
Is trampled ! " but he was profane.
That they do care, has been made plain
To offspring of the over-bold,
Outbreathing " Ares " greater than is just —
Houses that spill with more than they can hold,
More than is best for man. Be man's what
    must
Keep harm off, so that in himself he find
Sufficiency — the well-endowed of mind !
For there 's no bulwark in man's wealth to him
Who, through a surfeit, kicks — into the dim
And disappearing — Right's great altar.

                         Yes —
It urges him, the sad persuasiveness,
Até's insufferable child that schemes
Treason beforehand : and all cure is vain.
It is not hidden : out it glares again,
A light dread-lamping-mischief, just as gleams
The badness of the bronze ;
Through rubbing, puttings to the touch,
Black-clotted is he, judged at once.
He seeks — the boy — a flying bird to clutch,
The insufferable brand
Setting upon the city of his land
Whereof not any god hears prayer ;
While him who brought about such evils there,
That unjust man, the god in grapple throws.
Such an one, Paris goes
Within the Atreidai's house —
Shamed the guest's beard by robbery of the
    spouse.

And, leaving to her townsmen throngs a-spread
With shields, and spear-thrusts of sea-arma-
    ment,
And bringing Ilion, in a dowry's stead,
Destruction — swiftly through the gates she
    went,
Daring the undareable. But many a groan out-
    broke
From prophets of the House as thus they
    spoke.
" Woe, woe the House, the House and Rulers,
    — woe
The marriage-bed and dints
A husband's love imprints !
There she stands silent ! meets no honor —
    no
Shame — sweetest still to see of things gone long
    ago !
And, through desire of one across the main,
A ghost will seem within the house to reign :
And hateful to the husband is the grace
Of well-shaped statues : from — in place of
    eyes,
Those blanks — all Aphrodité dies.

" But dream-appearing mournful fantasies —
There they stand, bringing grace that 's vain.
For vain 't is, when brave things one seems to
    view :

The fantasy has floated off, hands through ;
Gone, that appearance, — nowise left to creep, —
On wings, the servants in the paths of sleep ! ''
Woes, then, in household and on hearth, are
    such
As these — and woes surpassing these by much.
But not these only : everywhere —
For those who from the land
Of Hellas issued in a band,
Sorrow, the heart must bear,
Sits in the home of each, conspicuous there.
Many a circumstance, at least,
Touches the very breast.
For those
Whom any sent away, — he knows :
And in the live man's stead,
Armor and ashes reach
The house of each.

For Ares, gold-exchanger for the dead,
And balance-holder in the fight o' the spear,
Due-weight from Ilion sends —
What moves the tear on tear —
A charred scrap to the friends :
Filling with well-packed ashes every urn,
For man — that was — the sole return.
And they groan — praising much, the while,
Now this man as experienced in the strife,
Now that, fallen nobly on a slaughtered pile,
Because of — not his own — another's wife.
But things there be, one barks,
When no man harks :
A surreptitious grief that 's grudge
Against the Atreidai who first sought the judge.
But some there, round the rampart, have
In Ilian earth, each one his grave :
All fair-formed as at birth,
It hid them — what they have and hold — the
    hostile earth.

And big with anger goes the city's word,
And pays a debt by public curse incurred.
And ever with me — as about to hear
A something night-involved — remains my
    fear :
Since of the many-slayers — not
Unwatching are the gods.
The black Erinues, at due periods —
Whoever gains the lot
Of fortune with no right —
Him, by life's strain and stress
Back-again-beaten from success,
They strike blind : and among the out-of-sight
For who has got to be, avails no might.
The being praised outrageously
Is grave, for at the eyes of such an one
Is launched, from Zeus, the thunder-stone.
Therefore do I decide
For so much and no more prosperity
Than of his envy passes unespied.
Neither a city-sacker would I be,
Nor life, myself by others captive, see.

A swift report has gone our city through,
From fire, the good-news messenger : if true,
Who knows ? Or is it not a god-sent lie ?
Who is so childish and deprived of sense
That, having, at announcements of the flame

Thus novel, felt his own heart fired thereby,
He then shall, at a change of evidence,
Be worsted just the same ?
It is conspicuous in a woman's nature,
Before its view to take a grace for granted :
Too trustful, — on her boundary, usurpature
Is swiftly made ;
But swiftly, too, decayed,
The glory perishes by woman vaunted.
   Klu. Soon shall we know — of these light-
    bearing torches,
And beacons and exchanges, fire with fire —
If they are true, indeed, or if, dream-fashion,
This gladsome light came and deceived our
    judgment.
Yon herald from the shore I see, o'ershadowed
With boughs of olive : dust, mud's thirsty
    brother,
Close neighbors on his garb, thus testify me
That neither voiceless, nor yet kindling for thee
Mountain-wood-flame, shall he explain by fire-
    smoke :
But either tell out more the joyance, speak-
    ing . . .
Word contrary to which, I ought but love it !
For may good be — to good that 's known —
    appendage !
   Cho. Whoever prays for aught else to this
    city
— May he himself reap fruit of his mind's
    error !
   Herald. Ha, my forefathers' soil of earth Ar-
    geian !
Thee, in this year's tenth light, am I returned
    to —
Of many broken hopes, on one hope chancing ;
For never prayed I, in this earth Argeian
Dying, to share my part in tomb the dearest.
Now, hail thou earth, and hail thou also, sun-
    light,
And Zeus, the country's lord, and king the Pu-
    thian
From bow no longer urging at us arrows !
Enough, beside Skamandros, cam'st thou ad-
    verse :
Now, contrary, be saviour thou and healer,
O king Apollon ! And gods conquest-granting,
All — I invoke too. and my tutelary
Hermes, dear herald, heralds' veneration, —
And Heroes our forthsenders, — friendly, once
    more
The army to receive, the war-spear's leavings !
Ha, mansions of my monarchs, roofs beloved,
And awful seats, and deities sun-fronting —
Receive with pomp your monarch, long time
    absent !
For he comes bringing light in night-time to you,
In common with all these — king Agamemnon.
But kindly greet him — for clear shows your
    duty —
Who has dug under Troia with the mattock
Of Zeus the Avenger, whereby plains are out-
    ploughed,
Altars unrecognizable, and god's shrines,
And the whole land's seed thoroughly has per-
    ished.
And such a yoke-strap having cast round Troia,
The elder king Atreides, happy man — he

Comes to be honored, worthiest of what mortals
Now are. Nor Paris nor the accomplice-city
Outvaunts their deed as more than they are
    done-by :
For, in a suit for rape and theft found guilty,
He missed of plunder and, in one destruction,
Fatherland, house and home has mowed to
    atoms :
Debts the Priamidai have paid twice over.
  Cho. Hail, herald from the army of Achai-
    ans !
  Her. I hail : — to die, will gainsay gods no
    longer !
  Cho. Love of this fatherland did exercise
    thee ?
  Her. So that I weep, at least, with joy, my
    eyes full.
  Cho. What, of this gracious sickness were ye
    gainers ?
  Her. How now ? instructed, I this speech
    shall master.
  Cho. For those who loved you back, with
    longing stricken.
  Her. This land yearned for the yearning
    army, say'st thou ?
  Cho. So as to set me oft, from dark mind,
    groaning.
  Her. Whence came this ill mind — hatred to
    the army ?
  Cho. Of old, I use, for mischief's physic, si-
    lence.
  Her. And how, the chiefs away, did you fear
    any ?
  Cho. So that now — late thy word — much
    joy were — dying !
  Her. For well have things been worked out :
    these, — in much time,
Some of them, one might say, had luck in fall-
    ing,
While some were faulty : since who, gods ex-
    cepted,
Goes, through the whole time of his life, un-
    grieving ?
For labors should I tell of, and bad lodgments,
Narrow deckways ill-strewn, too, — what the
    day's woe
We did not groan at getting for our portion ?
As for land-things, again, on went more hatred !
Since beds were ours hard by the foemen's ram-
    parts,
And, out of heaven and from the earth, the
    meadow
Dews kept a-sprinkle, an abiding damage
Of vestures, making hair a wild-beast matting.
Winter, too, if one told of·it — bird-slaying —
Such as, unbearable, Idaian snow brought —
Or heat, when waveless, on its noontide couches
Without a wind, the sea would slumber falling
— Why must one mourn these ? O'er and gone
    is labor :
O'er and gone is it, even to those dead ones,
So that no more again they mind uprising.
Why must we tell in numbers those deprived
    ones,
And the live man be vexed with fate's fresh
    outbreak ?
Rather, I bid full farewell to misfortunes !
For us, the left from out the Argeian army,

The gain beats, nor does sorrow counterbalance.
So that 't is fitly boasted of, this sunlight,
By us, o'er sea and land the aery flyers,
" Troia at last taking, the band of Argives
Hang up such trophies to the gods of Hellas
Within their domes — new glory to grow an-
    cient ! "
Such things men having heard must praise the
    city
And army - leaders : and the grace which
    wrought them —
Of Zeus, shall honored be. Thou hast my whole
    word.
  Cho. O'ercome by words, their sense I do not
    gainsay.
For, aye this breeds youth in the old — " to
    learn well."
But these things most the house and Klutaim-
    nestra
Concern, 't is likely : while they make me rich,
    too.
  Klu. I shouted long ago, indeed, for joyance,
When came that first night-messenger of fire
Proclaiming Ilion's capture and dispersion.
And some one, girding me, said, " Through
    fire-bearers
Persuaded — Troia to be sacked now, thinkest ?
Truly, the woman's way, — high to lift heart
    up ! "
By such words I was made seem wit-bewildered :
Yet still I sacrificed ; and, — female-song
    with, —
A shout one man and other, through the city,
Set up, congratulating in the gods' seats,
Soothing the incense-eating flame right fra-
    grant.
And now, what 's more, indeed, why need'st thou
    tell me ?
I of the king himself shall learn the whole
    word :
And, — as may best be, — I my revered hus-
    band
Shall hasten, as he comes back, to receive : for —
What 's to a wife sweeter to see than this light
(Her husband, by the god saved, back from
    warfare)
So as to open gates ? This tell my husband —
To come at soonest to his loving city.
A faithful wife at home may he find, coming !
Such an one as he left — the dog o' the house-
    hold —
Trusty to him, adverse to the ill-minded,
And, in all else, the same : no signet-impress
Having done harm to, in that time's duration.
I know nor pleasure, nor blameworthy con-
    verse
With any other man more than — bronze-dip-
    pings !
  Her. Such boast as this — brimful of the
    veracious —
Is for a high-born dame not bad to send forth !
  Cho. Ay, she spoke thus to thee — that hast
    a knowledge
From clear interpreters — a speech most seemly !
But speak, thou, herald ! Menelaos I ask of :
If he, returning, back in safety also
Will come with you — this land's beloved chief-
    tain ?

Her. There's no way I might say things
false and pleasant
For friends to reap the fruits of through a long
time.
Cho. How then, if, speaking good, things true
thou chance on ?
Her. For not well-hidden things become they,
sundered.
The man has vanished from the Achaic army,
He and his ship too. I announce no falsehood.
Cho. Whether forth - putting openly from
Ilion,
Or did storm — wide woe — snatch him from
the army ?
Her. Like topping bowman, thou hast touched
the target,
And a long sorrow hast succinctly spoken.
Cho. Whether, then, of him, as a live or dead
man
Was the report by other sailors bruited ?
Her. Nobody knows so as to tell out clearly
Excepting Helios who sustains earth's nature.
Cho. How say'st thou then, did storm the
naval army
Attack and end, by the celestials' anger ?
Her. It suits not to defile a day auspicious
With ill-announcing speech : distinct each god's
due :
And when a messenger with gloomy visage
To a city bears a fall'n host's woes — God ward
off ! —
One popular wound that happens to the city,
And many sacrificed from many households —
Men, scourged by that two-thonged whip Ares
loves so,
Double spear-headed curse, bloody yoke-cou-
ple, —
Of woes like these, doubtless, whoe'er comes
weighted,
Him does it suit to sing the Erinues' paian.
But who, of matters saved a glad-news-bringer,
Comes to a city in good estate rejoicing. . . .
How shall I mix good things with evil, telling
Of storm against the Achaioi, urged by gods'
wrath ?
For they swore league, being arch-foes before
that,
Fire and the sea : and plighted troth approved
they,
Destroying the unhappy Argeian army.
At night began the bad-wave-outbreak evils ;
For, ships against each other Threkian breezes
Shattered : and these, butted at in a fury
By storm and typhoon, with surge rain-resound-
ing, —
Off they went, vanished, through a bad herd's
whirling.
And, when returned the brilliant light of
Helios,
We view the Aigaian sea on flower with corpses
Of men Achaian and with naval ravage.
But us indeed, and ship, unhurt i' the hull too,
Either some one outstole us or outprayed us —
Some god — no man it was the tiller touching.
And Fortune, savior, willing on our ship sat.
So as it neither had in harbor wave-surge
Nor ran aground against a shore all rocky.
And then, the water-Haides having fled from

In the white day, not trusting to our fortune,
We chewed the cud in thoughts — this novel
sorrow
O' the army laboring and badly pounded.
And now — if any one of them is breathing —
They talk of us as having perished : why not ?
And we — that they the same fate have, ima-
gine.
May it be for the best ! Meneleos, then,
Foremost and specially to come, expect thou !
If (that is) any ray o' the sun reports him
Living and seeing too — by Zeus' contrivings,
Not yet disposed to quite destroy the lineage —
Some hope is he shall come again to household.
Having heard such things, know, thou truth art
hearing !
Cho. Who may he have been that named
thus wholly with exactitude —
(Was he some one whom we see not, by forecast-
ings of the future
Guiding tongue in happy mood ?)
— Her with battle for a bridegroom, on all
sides contention-wooed,
Helena ? Since — mark the suture ! —
Ship's-Hell, Man's-Hell, City's-Hell,
From the delicately - pompous curtains that
pavilion well,
Forth, by favor of the gale
Of earth-born Zephuros did she sail.
Many shield-bearers, leaders of the pack,
Sailed too upon their track,
Theirs who had directed oar,
Then visible no more,
To Simois' leaf-luxuriant shore —
For sake of strife all gore !

To Ilion Wrath, fulfilling her intent,
This marriage-care — the rightly named so —
sent :
In after-time, for the tables' abuse
And that of the hearth-partaker Zeus,
Bringing to punishment
Those who honored with noisy throat
The honor of the bride, the hymenæal note
Which did the kinsfolk then to singing urge.
But, learning a new hymn for that which was,
The ancient city of Priamos
Groans probably a great and general dirge,
Denominating Paris
" The man that miserably marries : " —
She who, all the while before,
A life, that was a general dirge
For citizens' unhappy slaughter, bore.

And thus a man, by no milk's help,
Within his household reared a lion's whelp
That loved the teat
In life's first festal stage :
Gentle as yet,
A true child-lover, and, to men of age,
A thing whereat pride warms ;
And oft he had it in his arms
Like any new-born babe, bright-faced, to hand
Wagging its tail, at belly's strict command.

But in due time upgrown,
The custom of progenitors was shown :
For — thanks for sustenance repaying

With ravage of sheep slaughtered —
It made unbidden feast ;
With blood the house was watered,
To household came a woe there was no staying :
Great mischief many-slaying !
From God it was — some priest
Of Até, in the house, by nurture thus increased.

At first, then, to the city of Ilion went
A soul, as I might say, of windless calm —
Wealth's quiet ornament,
An eyes'-dart bearing balm,
Love's spirit-biting flower.
But — from the true course bending —
She brought about, of marriage, bitter ending :
Ill-resident, ill-mate, in power
Passing to the Priamidai — by sending
Of Hospitable Zeus —
Erinus for a bride, — to make brides mourn,
her dower.

Spoken long ago
Was the ancient saying
Still among mortals staying :
" Man's great prosperity at height of rise
Engenders offspring nor unchilded dies ;
And, from good fortune, to such families,
Buds forth insatiate woe."
Whereas, distinct from any,
Of my own mind I am :
For 't is the unholy deed begets the many,
Resembling each its dam.
Of households that correctly estimate,
Ever a beauteous child is born of Fate.
But ancient Arrogance delights to generate
Arrogance, young and strong 'mid mortals'
sorrow,
Or now, or then, when comes the appointed
morrow.
And she bears young Satiety ;
And, fiend with whom nor fight nor war can
be,
Unholy Daring — twin black Curses
Within the household, children like their
nurses.

But Justice shines in smoke-grimed habita-
tions,
And honors the well-omened life ;
While, — gold-besprinkled stations
Where the hands' filth is rife,
With backward-turning eyes
Leaving, — to holy seats she hies,
Not worshipping the power of wealth
Stamped with applause by stealth :
And to its end directs each thing begun.

Approach then, my monarch, of Troia the
sacker, of Atreus the son !
How ought I address thee, how ought I revere
thee, — nor yet overhitting
Nor yet underbending the grace that is fitting ?
Many of mortals hasten to honor the seeming-
to-be —
Passing by justice : and, with the ill-faring, to
groan as he groans all are free.
But no bite of the sorrow their liver has reached
to :

They say with the joyful, — one outside on
each, too,
As they force to a smile smileless faces.
But whoever is good at distinguishing races
In sheep of his flock — it is not for the eyes
Of a man to escape such a shepherd's surprise,
As they seem, from a well-wishing mind,
In watery friendship to fawn and be kind.
Thou to me, then, indeed, sending an army for
Helena's sake,
(I will not conceal it,) wast — oh, by no help of
the Muses ! — depicted
Not well of thy midriff the rudder directing, —
convicted
Of bringing a boldness they did not desire to
the men with existence at stake.
But now — from no outside of mind, nor un-
lovingly — gracious thou art
To those who have ended the labor, fulfilling
their part ;
And in time shalt thou know, by inquiry in-
structed,
Who of citizens justly, and who not to purpose,
the city conducted.
    Agamemnon. First, indeed, Argos, and the
gods, the local,
'T is right addressing — those with me the
partners
In this return and right things done the city
Of Priamos : gods who, from no tongue hear-
ing
The rights o' the cause, for Ilion's fate man-
slaught'rous
Into the bloody vase, not oscillating,
Put the vote-pebbles, while, o' the rival vessel,
Hope rose up to the lip-edge : filled it was not.
By smoke the captured city is still conspicuous :
Até's burnt-offerings live : and, dying with
them,
The ash sends forth the fulsome blasts of
riches.
Of these things, to the gods grace many-mind-
ful
'T is right I render, since both nets outrageous
We built them round with, and, for sake of
woman,
It did the city to dust — the Argeian monster,
The horse's nestling, the shield-bearing people
That made a leap, at setting of the Pleiads,
And, vaulting o'er the tower, the raw-flesh-
feeding
Lion licked up his fill of blood tyrannic.
I to the gods indeed prolonged this preface ;
But — as for *thy* thought, I remember hear-
ing —
I say the same, and thou co-pleader hast me.
Since few of men this faculty is born with
To honor, without grudge, their friend success-
ful.
For moody, on the heart, a poison seated
Its burden doubles to who gained the sickness :
By his own griefs he is himself made heavy,
And out-of-door prosperity seeing groans at.
Knowing, I 'd call (for well have I experi-
enced)
" Fellowship's mirror," " phantom of a
shadow,"
Those seeming to be mighty gracious to me :

While just Odusseus — he who sailed not will-
    ing —
When joined on, was to me the ready trace-
    horse.
This of him, whether dead or whether living,
I say. For other city - and - gods' concern-
    ment —
Appointing common courts, in full assemblage
We will consult. And as for what holds
    seemly
How it may lasting stay well, must be coun-
    selled :
While what has need of medicines Paionian
We, either burning or else cutting kindly,
Will make endeavor to turn pain from sickness.
And now into the domes and homes by altar
Going, I to the gods first raise the right-hand —
They who, far sending, back again have
    brought me.
And Victory, since she followed, fixed remain
    she !
    Klu. Men, citizens, Argeians here, my wor-
    ships !
I shall not shame me, consort-loving manners
To tell before you: for in time there dies off
The diffidence from people. Not from others
Learning, I of myself will tell the hard life
I bore so long as this man was 'neath Ilion.
First: for a woman, from the male divided,
To sit at home alone, is monstrous evil —
Hearing the many rumors back-revenging :
And for now This to come, now That bring
    after
Woe, and still worse woe, bawling in the house-
    hold !
And truly, if so many wounds had chanced on
My husband here, as homeward used to dribble
Report, he 's pierced more than a net to speak
    of !
While, were he dying (as the words abounded)
A triple-bodied Geruon the Second,
Plenty above — for loads below I count not —
Of earth a three-share cloak he 'd boast of
    taking,
Once only dying in each several figure !
Because of such-like rumors back-revenging,
Many the halters from my neck, above head,
Others than *I* loosed — loosed from neck by
    main force !
From this cause, sure, the boy stands not
    beside me —
Possessor of our troth-plights, thine and mine
    too —
As ought Orestes : be not thou astonished !
For, him brings up our well-disposed guest-
    captive
Strophios the Phokian — ills that told on both
    sides
To me predicting — both of thee 'neath Ilion
The danger, and if anarchy's mob-uproar
Should overthrow thy council ; since 't is born
    with
Mortals, — whoe'er has fallen, the more to kick
    him.
Such an excuse, I think, no cunning carries !
As for myself — why, of my wails the rushing
Fountains are dried up : not in them a drop
    more !

And in my late-to-bed eyes I have damage
Bewailing what concerned thee, those torch-
    holdings
Forever unattended to. In dreams — why,
Beneath the light wing-beats o' the gnat, I
    woke up
As he went buzzing — sorrows that concerned
    thee
Seeing, that filled more than their fellow-sleep-
    time.
Now, all this having suffered, from soul grief-
    free
I would style this man here the dog o' the
    stables,
The savior forestay of the ship, the high roof's
Ground-prop, son sole-begotten to his father,
— Ay, land appearing to the sailors past hope,
Loveliest day to see after a tempest,
To the wayfaring-one athirst a well-spring,
— The joy, in short, of 'scaping all that 's —
    fatal !
I judge him worth addresses such as these are
— Envy stand off ! — for many those old evils
We underwent. And now, to me — dear head-
    ship ! —
Dismount thou from this car, not earthward
    setting
The foot of thine, O king, that 's Ilion's spoiler !
Slave-maids, why tarry ? — whose the task
    allotted
To strew the soil o' the road with carpet-spread-
    ings.
Immediately be purple-strewn the pathway,
So that to home unhoped may lead him —
    Justice !
As for the rest, care shall — by no sleep con-
    quered —
Dispose things — justly (gods to aid !) appointed.
    Aga. Offspring of Leda, of my household
    warder,
Suitably to my absence hast thou spoken,
For long the speech thou didst outstretch ! But
    aptly
To praise — from others ought to go this favor.
And for the rest, — not me, in woman's fashion,
Mollify, nor — as mode of barbarous man is —
To me gape forth a groundward-falling clamor !
Nor, strewing it with garments, make my pas-
    sage
Envied ! Gods, sure, with these behooves we
    honor :
But, for a mortal on these varied beauties
To walk — to me, indeed, is nowise fear-free.
I say — as man, not god, to me do homage !
Apart from foot-mats both and varied vestures,
Renown is loud, and — not to lose one's senses,
God's greatest gift. Behooves we him call
    happy
Who has brought life to end in loved wellbeing.
If all things I might manage thus — brave
    man, I !
    Klu. Come now, this say, nor feign a feeling
    to me !
    Aga. With feeling, know indeed, I do not
    tamper !
    Klu. Vowed'st thou to the gods, in fear, to
    act thus ?
    Aga. If any, *I* well knew resolve I outspoke.

Klu. What think'st thou Priamos had done,
 thus victor?
Aga. On varied vests — I do think — he had
 passaged.
Klu. Then, do not, struck with awe at human
 censure. . . .
Aga. Well, popular mob-outcry much avails
 too !
Klu. Ay, but the unenvied is not the much
 valued.
Aga. Sure, 't is no woman's part to long for
 battle !
Klu. Why, to the prosperous, even suits a
 beating !
Aga. What ? thou this beating us in war dost
 prize too ?
Klu. Persuade thee ! power, for once, grant
 me — and willing !
Aga. But if this seem so to thee — shoes, let
 some one
Loose under, quick — foot's serviceable car-
riage !
And me, on these sea-products walking, may no
Grudge from a distance, from the god's eye,
 strike at !
For great shame were my strewment-spoiling —
 riches !
Spoiling with feet, and silver-purchased tex-
tures !
Of these things, thus then. But this female-
stranger
Tenderly take inside ! Who conquers mildly
God, from afar, benignantly regardeth.
For, willing, no one wears a yoke that's ser-
vile :
And she, of many valuables, outpicked
The flower, the army's gift, myself has fol-
lowed.
So — since to hear thee, I am brought about
 thus, —
I go into the palace — purples treading.
 Klu. There is the sea — and what man shall
 exhaust it ? —
Feeding much purple's worth-its-weight-in-
silver
Dye, ever fresh and fresh, our garments' tinc-
ture ;
At home, such wealth, king, we begin — by
 gods' help —
With having, and to lack, the household knows
 not.
Of many garments had I vowed a treading
(In oracles if fore-enjoined the household)
Of this dear soul the safe-return-price scheming !
For, root existing, foliage goes up houses,
O'erspreading shadow against Seirios dog-star ;
And, thou returning to the hearth domestic,
Warmth, yea, in winter dost thou show return-
ing.
And when, too, Zeus works, from the green-
 grape acrid,
Wine — then, already, cool in houses cometh —
The perfect man his home perambulating !
Zeus, Zeus Perfecter, these my prayers perfect
 thou !
Thy care be — yea — of things thou mayst make
 perfect !
 Cho. Wherefore to me, this fear —

Groundedly stationed here
Fronting my heart, the portent-watcher — flits
 she ?
Wherefore should prophet-play
The uncalled and unpaid lay,
Nor — having spat forth fear, like bad dreams
 — sits she
On the mind's throne beloved — well-suasive
 Boldness ?
For time, since, by a throw of all the hands,
The boat's stern-cables touched the sands,
Has passed from youth to oldness, —
When under Ilion rushed the ship-borne bands.

And from my eyes I learn —
Being myself my witness — their return.
Yet, all the same, without a lyre, my soul,
Itself its teacher too, chants from within
Erinus' dirge, not having now the whole
Of Hope's dear boldness : nor my inwards sin —
The heart that 's rolled in whirls against the
 mind
Justly presageful of a fate behind.
But I pray — things false, from my hope, may
 fall
Into the fate that 's not-fulfilled-at-all !

Especially a⁺ least, of health that 's great
The term 's insatiable : for, its weight
— A neighbor, with a common wall between —
Ever will sickness lean ;
And destiny, her course pursuing straight,
Has struck man's ship against a reef unseen.
Now, when a portion, rather than the treasure,
Fear casts from sling, with peril in right measure,
It has not sunk — the universal freight,
(With misery freighted over-full,)
Nor has fear whelmed the hull.
Then too the gift of Zeus,
Two-handedly profuse,
Even from the furrows' yield for yearly use
Has done away with famine, the disease ;
But blood of man to earth once falling, — deadly,
 black, —
In times ere these, —
Who may, by singing spells, call back ?
Zeus had not else stopped one who rightly knew
The way to bring the dead again.
But, did not an appointed Fate constrain
The Fate from gods, to bear no more than due,
My heart, outstripping what tongue utters,
Would have all out : which now, in darkness,
 mutters
Moodily grieved, nor ever hopes to find
How she a word in season may unwind
From out the enkindling mind.
 Klu. Take thyself in, thou too — I say, Kas
 sandra !
Since Zeus — not angrily — in household placed
 thee
Partaker of hand-sprinklings, with the many
Slaves stationed, his the Owner's altar close to.
Descend from out this car, nor be high-minded !
And truly they do say Alkmene's child once
Bore being sold, slaves' barley-bread his living.
If, then, necessity of this lot o'erbalance,
Much is the favor of old-wealthy masters :
For those who, never hoping, made fine harvest

Are harsh to slaves in all things, beyond meas-
ure.
Thou hast — with us — such usage as law war-
rants.
  Cho. To thee it was, she paused plain speech
from speaking.
Being inside the fatal nets — obeying,
Thou mayst obey : but thou mayst disobey too !
  Klu. Why, if she is not, in the swallow's
fashion,
Possessed of voice that 's unknown and barbaric,
I, with speech — speaking in mind's scope —
persuade her.
  Cho. Follow ! The best — as things now stand
— she speaks of.
Obey thou, leaving this thy car-enthronement !
  Klu. Well, with this thing at door, for me no
leisure
To waste time : as concerns the hearth mid-
navelled,
Already stand the sheep for fireside slaying
By those who never hoped to have such favor.
If thou, then, aught of this wilt do, delay not !
But if thou, being witless, tak'st no word in,
Speak thou, instead of voice, with hand as Kars
do !
  Cho. She seems a plain interpreter in need of,
The stranger ! and her way — a beast's new-
captured !
  Klu. Why, she is mad, sure, — hears her own
bad senses, —
Who, while she comes, leaving a town new-
captured,
Yet knows not how to bear the bit o' the bridle
Before she has out-frothed her bloody fierceness.
Not I — throwing away more words — will
shamed be !
  Cho. But I, — for I compassionate, — will
chafe not.
Come, O unhappy one, this car vacating,
Yielding to this necessity, prove yoke's use !
  Kassandra. Otototoi, Gods, Earth —
Apollon, Apollon !
  Cho. Why didst thou " ototoi " concerning
Loxias ?
Since he is none such as to suit a mourner.
  Kas. Otototoi, Gods, Earth, —
Apollon, Apollon !
  Cho. Ill-boding here again the god invokes she
— Nowise empowered in woes to stand by help-
ful.
  Kas. Apollon, Apollon,
Guard of the ways, my destroyer !
For thou hast quite, this second time, destroyed
me.
  Cho. To prophesy she seems of her own evils :
Remains the god-gift to the slave-soul present.
  Kas. Apollon, Apollon,
Guard of the ways, my destroyer !
Ha, whither hast thou led me ? to what roof
now ?
  Cho. To the Atreidai's roof : if this thou
know'st not,
I tell it thee, nor this wilt thou call falsehood.
  Kas. How ! how !
God-hated, then ! Of many a crime it knew —
Self-slaying evils, halters too :
Man's-shambles, blood-besprinkler of the ground !

  Cho. She seems to be good-nosed, the stranger :
dog-like,
She snuffs indeed the victims she will find there.
  Kas. How ! how !
By the witnesses here I am certain now !
These children bewailing their slaughters —
flesh dressed in the fire
And devoured by their sire !
  Cho. Ay, we have heard of thy soothsaying
glory,
Doubtless : but prophets none are we in scent
of !
  Kas. Ah, gods, what ever does she meditate ?
What this new anguish great ?
Great in the house here she meditates ill
Such as friends cannot bear, cannot cure it :
and still
Off stands all Resistance
Afar in the distance !
  Cho. Of these I witless am — these prophe-
syings.
But those I knew : for the whole city bruits
them.
  Kas. Ah, unhappy one, this thou consum-
matest ?
Thy husband, thy bed's common guest,
In the bath having brightened. . . . How shall
I declare
Consummation ? It soon will be there :
For hand after hand she outstretches,
At life as she reaches !
  Cho. Nor yet I 've gone with thee ! for —
after riddles —
Now, in blind oracles, I feel resourceless.
  Kas. Eh, eh, papai, papai,
What this, I espy ?
Some net of Haides undoubtedly !
Nay, rather, the snare
Is she who has share
In his bed, who takes part in the murder there
But may a revolt —
Unceasing assault —
On the Race, raise a shout
Sacrificial, about
A victim — by stoning —
For murder atoning !
  Cho. What this Erinus which i' the house
thou callest
To raise her cry ? Not me thy word enlightens !
To my heart has run
A drop of the crocus-dye :
Which makes for those
On earth by the spear that lie,
A common close
With life's descending sun.
Swift is the curse begun !
  Kas. How ! how !
See — see quick !
Keep the bull from the cow !
In the vesture she catching him, strikes him
now
With the black-horned trick,
And he falls into the watery vase !
Of the craft-killing caldron I tell thee the case ?
  Cho. I would not boast to be a topping critic
Of oracles : but to some sort of evil
I liken these. From oracles, what good speech
To mortals, beside, is sent ?

It comes of their evils : these arts word-abound-
ing that sing the event
Bring the fear 't is their office to teach.
   Kas. Ah me, ah me —
Of me unhappy, evil-destined fortunes !
For I bewail my proper woe
As, mine with his, all into one I throw.
Why hast thou hither me unhappy brought ?
— Unless that I should die with him — for
   naught ?
What else was sought ?
   Cho. Thou art some mind-mazed creature,
   god-possessed :
And all about thyself dost wail
A lay — no lay !
Like some brown nightingale
Insatiable of noise, who — well away ! —
From her unhappy breast
Keeps moaning Itus, Itus, and his life
With evils, flourishing on each side, rife.
   Kas. Ah me, ah me,
The fate o' the nightingale, the clear resounder !
For a body wing-borne have the gods cast
   round her,
And sweet existence, from misfortunes free :
But for myself remains a sundering
With spear, the two-edged thing !
   Cho. Whence hast thou this on-rushing god-
   involving pain
And spasms in vain ?
For, things that terrify,
With changing unintelligible cry
Thou strikest up in tune, yet all the while
After that Orthian style !
Whence hast thou limits to the oracular road,
That evils bode ?
   Kas. Ah me, the nuptials, the nuptials of
   Paris, the deadly to friends !
Ah me, of Skamandros the draught
Paternal ! There once, to these ends,
On thy banks was I brought,
The unhappy ! And now, by Kokutos and
   Acheron's shore
I shall soon be, it seems, these my oracles
   singing once more !
   Cho. Why this word, plain too much,
Hast thou uttered ? A babe might learn of
   such !
I am struck with a bloody bite — here under —
At the fate woe-wreaking
Of thee shrill-shrieking :
To me who hear — a wonder !
   Kas. Ah me, the toils — the toils of the
   city
The wholly destroyed : ah, pity,
Of the sacrificings my father made
In the ramparts' aid —
Much slaughter of grass-fed flocks — that
   afforded no cure
That the city should not, as it does now, the
   burthen endure !
But I, with the soul on fire,
Soon to the earth shall cast me and expire !
   Cho. To things, on the former consequent,
Again hast thou given vent :
And 't is some evil-meaning fiend doth move
   thee,
Heavily falling from above thee,

To melodize thy sorrows — else, in singing,
Calamitous, death-bringing !
And of all this the end
I am without resource to apprehend.
   Kas. Well then, the oracle from veils no
   longer
Shall be outlooking, like a bride new-married :
But bright it seems, against the sun's uprisings
Breathing, to penetrate thee : so as, wave-like,
To wash against the rays a woe much greater
Than this. I will no longer teach by riddles.
And witness, running with me, that of evils
Done long ago, I nosing track the footstep !
For, this same roof here — never quits a Choros
One-voiced, not well-tuned since no " well " it
   utters :
And truly having drunk, to get more courage,
Man's blood — the Komos keeps within the
   household
— Hard to be sent outside — of sister Furies :
They hymn their hymn — within the house
   close sitting —
The first beginning curse : in turn spit forth at
The Brother's bed, to him who spurned it
   hostile.
Have I missed aught, or hit I like a bowman ?
False prophet am I, — knock at doors, a bab-
   bler ?
Henceforward witness, swearing now, I know
   not
By other's word the old sins of this household !
   Cho. And how should oath, bond honorably
   binding,
Become thy cure ? No less I wonder at thee
— That thou, beyond sea reared, a strange-
   tongued city
Shouldst hit in speaking, just as if thou stood'st
   by !
   Kas. Prophet Apollon put me in this office.
   Cho. What, even though a god, with longing
   smitten ?
   Kas. At first, indeed, shame was to me to
   say this.
   Cho. For, more relaxed grows every one who
   fares well.
   Kas. But he was athlete to me — huge grace
   breathing !
   Cho. Well, to the work of children, went ye
   law's way ?
   Kas. Having consented, I played false to
   Loxias.
   Cho. Already when the wits inspired pos-
   sessed of ?
   Kas. Already townsmen all their woes I fore-
   told.
   Cho. How wast thou then unhurt by Loxias'
   anger ?
   Kas. I no one aught persuaded, when I
   sinned thus.
   Cho. To us, at least, now sooth to say thou
   seemest.
   Kas. Halloo, halloo, ah, evils !
Again, straightforward foresight's fearful labor
Whirls me, distracting with prelusive last-lays !
Behold ye those there, in the household
   seated, —
Young ones, — of dreams approaching to the
   figures ?

Children, as if they died by their beloveds —
Hands they have filled with flesh, the meal domestic —
Entrails and vitals both, most piteous burthen,
Plain they are holding! — which their father tasted!
For this, I say, plans punishment a certain
Lion ignoble, on the bed that wallows,
House-guard (ah, me!) to the returning master
— Mine, since to bear the slavish yoke behooves me!
The ships' commander, Ilion's desolator,
Knows not what things the tongue of the lewd she-dog
Speaking, outspreading, shiny-souled, in fashion
Of Até hid, will reach to, by ill fortune!
Such things she dares — the female, the male's slayer!
She is . . . how calling her the hateful bite-beast
May I hit the mark? Some amphisbaina — Skulla
Housing in rocks, of mariners the mischief,
Revelling Haides' mother, — curse, no truce with,
Breathing at friends! How piously she shouted,
The all-courageous, as at turn of battle!
She seems to joy at the back-bringing safety!
Of this, too, if I naught persuade, all 's one!
Why?
What is to be will come! And soon thou, present,
"True prophet all too much" wilt pitying style me!
Cho. Thuestes' feast, indeed, on flesh of children,
I went with, and I shuddered. Fear too holds me
Listing what 's true as life, nowise out-imaged!
Kas. I say, thou Agamemnon's fate shalt look on!
Cho. Speak good words, O unhappy! Set mouth sleeping!
Kas. But Paian stands in no stead to the speech here.
Cho. Nay, if the thing be near: but never be it!
Kas. Thou, indeed, prayest: they to kill are busy!
Cho. Of what man is it ministered, this sorrow?
Kas. There again, wide thou look'st of my foretellings.
Cho. For, the fulfiller's scheme I have not gone with.
Kas. And yet too well I know the speech Hellenic.
Cho. For Puthian oracles, thy speech, and hard too!
Kas. Papai: what fire this! and it comes upon me!
Ototoi, Lukeion Apollon, ah me — me!
She, the two-footed lioness that sleeps with
The wolf, in absence of the generous lion,
Kills me the unhappy one: and as a poison
Brewing, to put my price too in the anger,

She vows, against her mate this weapon whetting
To pay him back the bringing me, with slaughter.
Why keep I then these things to make me laughed at,
Both wands and, round my neck, oracular fillets?
Thee, at least, ere my own fate will I ruin:
Go, to perdition falling! Boons exchange we —
Some other Até in my stead make wealthy!
See there — himself, Apollon stripping from me
The oracular garment! having looked upon me
— Even in these adornments, laughed by friends at,
As good as foes, i' the balance weighed: and vainly —
For, called crazed stroller, — as I had been gypsy,
Beggar, unhappy, starved to death, — I bore it.
And now the Prophet — prophet me undoing,
Has led away to these so deadly fortunes!
Instead of my sire's altar, waits the hack-block
She struck with first warm bloody sacrificing!
Yet nowise unavenged of gods will death be:
For there shall come another, our avenger,
The mother-slaying scion, father's doomsman:
Fugitive, wanderer, from this land an exile,
Back shall he come, — for friends, copestone these curses!
For there is sworn a great oath from the gods that
Him shall bring hither his fallen sire's prostration.
Why make I then, like an indweller, moaning?
Since at the first I foresaw Ilion's city
Suffering as it has suffered: and who took it,
Thus by the judgment of the gods are faring.
I go, will suffer, will submit to dying!
But, Haides' gates — these same I call, I speak to,
And pray that on an opportune blow chancing,
Without a struggle, — blood the calm death bringing
In easy outflow, — I this eye may close up!
Cho. O much unhappy, but, again, much learned
Woman, long hast thou outstretched! But if truly
Thou knowest thine own fate, how comes that, like to
A god-led steer, to altar bold thou treadest?
Kas. There 's no avoidance, — strangers, no! Some time more!
Cho. He last is, anyhow, by time advantaged.
Kas. It comes, the day: I shall by flight gain little.
Cho. But know thou patient art from thy brave spirit!
Kas. Such things hears no one of the happy-fortuned.
Cho. But gloriously to die — for man is grace, sure!
Kas. Ah, sire, for thee and for thy noble children!
Cho. But what thing is it? What fear turns thee backwards?

Kas. Alas, alas!

Cho. Why this " alas " ? if 't is no spirit's loathing . . .

Kas. Slaughter blood-dripping does the household smell of !

Cho. How else ? This scent is of hearth-sacrifices.

Kas. Such kind of steam as from a tomb is proper !

Cho. No Surian honor to the House thou speak'st of !

Kas. But I will go, — even in the household wailing

My fate and Agamemnon's. Life suffice me !

Ah, strangers !

I cry not " ah " — as bird at bush — through terror

Idly ! to me, the dead thus much bear witness:

When, for me — woman, there shall die a woman,

And, for a man ill-wived, a man shall perish !

This hospitality I ask as dying.

Cho. O sufferer, thee — thy foretold fate I pity.

Kas. Yet once for all, to speak a speech, I fain am :

No dirge, mine for myself ! The sun I pray to,

Fronting his last light ! — to my own avengers —

That from my hateful slayers they exact too

Pay for the dead slave — easy-managed hand's work !

Cho. Alas for mortal matters ! Happy-fortuned, —

Why, any shade would turn them : if unhappy,

By throws the wetting sponge has spoiled the picture !

And more by much in mortals this I pity.

The being well-to-do —

Insatiate a desire of this

Born with all mortals is,

Nor any is there who

Well-being forces off, aroints

From roofs whereat a finger points,

" No more come in ! " exclaiming. This man, too,

To take the city of Priamos did the celestials give,

And, honored by the god, he homeward comes ;

But now if, of the former, he shall pay

The blood back, and, for those who ceased to live,

Dying, for deaths in turn new punishment he dooms —

Who, being mortal, would not pray

With an unmischievous

Daimon to have been born — who would not, hearing thus ?

Aga. Ah me ! I am struck — a right-aimed stroke within me !

Cho. Silence ! Who is it shouts " stroke " — " right-aimedly," a wounded one ?

Aga. Ah me ! indeed again, — a second, struck by !

Cho. This work seems to me completed by this " Ah me " of the king's ;

But we somehow may together share in solid counsellings.

Cho. 1. I, in the first place, my opinion tell you:

— To cite the townsmen, by help-cry, to house here.

Cho. 2. To me, it seems we ought to fall upon them

At quickest — prove the fact by sword fresh-flowing !

Cho. 3. And I, of such opinion the partaker,

Vote — to do something : not to wait — the main point !

Cho. 4. 'T is plain to see: for they prelude as though of

A tyranny the signs they gave the city.

Cho. 5. For we waste time ; while they, — this waiting's glory

Treading to ground, — allow the hand no slumber.

Cho. 6. I know not — chancing on some plan — to tell it :

'T is for the doer to plan of the deed also.

Cho. 7. And I am such another : since I 'm schemeless

How to raise up again by words — a dead man !

Cho. 8. What, and, protracting life, shall we give way thus

To the disgracers of our home, these rulers ?

Cho. 9. Why, 't is unbearable : but to die is better :

For death than tyranny is the riper finish !

Cho. 10. What, by the testifying " Ah me " of him,

Shall we prognosticate the man as perished ?

Cho. 11. We must quite know ere speak these things concerning :

For to conjecture and " quite know " are two things.

Cho. 12. This same to praise I from all sides abound in —

Clearly to know, Atreides, what he 's doing !

Klu. Much having been before to purpose spoken,

The opposite to say I shall not shamed be :

For how should one, to enemies, — in semblance,

Friends, — enmity proposing, — sorrow's net-frame

Enclose, a height superior to outleaping ?

To me, indeed, this struggle of old — not mindless

Of an old victory — came : with time, I grant you !

I stand where I have struck, things once accomplished :

And so have done, — and this deny I shall not, —

As that his fate was nor to fly nor ward off.

A wrap-round with no outlet, as for fishes,

I fence about him — the rich woe of the garment :

I strike him twice, and in a double " Ah me ! "

He let his limbs go — *there !* And to him, fallen,

The third blow add I, giving — of Below-ground

Zeus, guardian of the dead — the votive favor.

Thus in the mind of him he rages, falling,

And blowing forth a brisk blood-spatter, strikes
me
With the dark drop of slaughterous dew, — re-
joicing
No less than, at the god-given dewy-comfort,
The sown-stuff in its birth-throes from the
calyx.
Since so these things are, — Argives, my re-
vered here, —
Ye may rejoice — if ye rejoice : but I — boast !
If it were fit on corpse to pour libation,
That would be right — right over and above,
too !
The cup of evils in the house he, having
Filled with such curses, himself coming drinks
of.

Cho. We wonder at thy tongue : since bold-
mouthed truly
Is she who in such speech boasts o'er her hus-
band !

Klu. Ye test me as I were a witless woman :
But I — with heart intrepid — to you knowers
Say (and thou — if thou wilt or praise or blame
me,
Comes to the same) — this man is Agamem-
non,
My husband, dead, the work of the right hand
here,
Ay, of a just artificer : so things are.

Cho. What evil, O woman, food or drink,
earth-bred
Or sent from the flowing sea,
Of such having fee
Didst thou set on thee
This sacrifice
And popular cries
Of a curse on thy head ?
Off thou hast thrown him, off hast cut
The man from the city : but
Off from the city thyself shalt be
Cut — to the citizens
A hate immense !

Klu. Now, indeed, thou adjudgest exile to
me,
And citizens' hate, and to have popular curses :
Nothing of this against the man here bringing,
Who, no more awe-checked than as 't were a
beast's fate, —
With sheep abundant in the well-fleeced graze-
flocks, —
Sacrificed *his* child, — dearest fruit of travail
To me, — as song-spell against Threkian blow-
ings.
Not *him* did it behoove thee hence to banish
— Pollution's penalty ? But hearing *my* deeds
Justicer rough thou art ! Now, this I tell thee :
To threaten thus — me, one prepared to have
thee
(On like conditions, thy hand conquering) o'er
me
Rule : but if God the opposite ordain us,
Thou shalt learn — late taught, certes — to be
modest.

Cho. Greatly-intending thou art :
Much-mindful, too, hast thou cried
(Since thy mind, with its slaughter-outpouring
part,
Is frantic) that over the eyes, a patch

Of blood — with blood to match
Is plain for a pride !
Yet still, bereft of friends, thy fate
Is — blow with blow to expiate !

Klu. And this thou hearest — of my oaths,
just warrant !
By who fulfilled things for my daughter, Jus-
tice,
Até, Erinus, — by whose help I slew him, —
Not mine the fancy — Fear will tread my
palace
So long as on my hearth there burns a fire,
Aigisthos as before well-caring for me ;
Since he to me is shield, no small, of boldness.
Here does he lie — outrager of this female,
Dainty of all the Chruseids under Ilion ;
And she — the captive, the soothsayer also
And couchmate of this man, oracle-speaker,
Faithful bedfellow, — ay, the sailors' benches
They wore in common, nor unpunished did so,
Since he is — thus ! While, as for her, — swan-
fashion,
Her latest having chanted, — dying wailing
She lies, — to him, a sweetheart : me she
brought to
My bed's by-nicety, the whet of dalliance.

Cho. Alas, that some
Fate would come
Upon us in quickness —
Neither much sickness
Neither bed-keeping —
And bear unended sleeping,
Now that subdued
Is our keeper, the kindest of mood !
Having borne, for a woman's sake, much
strife —
By a woman he withered from life !
Ah me !
Law-breaking Helena who, one,
Hast many, so many souls undone
'Neath Troia ! and now the consummated
Much-memorable curse
Hast thou made flower-forth, red
With the blood no rains disperse,
That which was then in the House —
Strife all-subduing, the woe of a spouse.

Klu. Nowise, of death the fate —
Burdened by these things — supplicate !
Nor on Helena turn thy wrath
As the man-destroyer, as "she who hath,
Being but one,
Many and many a soul undone
Of the men, the Danaoi " —
And wrought immense annoy !

Cho. Daimon, who fallest
Upon this household and the double-raced
Tantalidai, a rule, minded like theirs displaced,
Thou rulest me with, now,
Whose heart thou gallest !
And on the body, like a hateful crow,
Stationed, all out of tune, his chant to chant
Doth Something vaunt !

Klu. Now, of a truth, hast thou set upright
Thy mouth's opinion, —
Naming the Sprite,
The triply-gross,
O'er the race that has dominion :
For through him it is that Eroy

The carnage-licker
In the belly is bred : ere ended quite
Is the elder throe — new ichor !
    Cho. Certainly, great of might
And heavy of wrath, the Sprite
Thou tellest of, in the palace
(Woe, woe !)
— An evil tale of a fate
By Até's malice
Rendered insatiate !
Oh, oh, —
King, king, how shall I beweep thee ?
From friendly soul what ever say ?
Thou liest where webs of the spider o'ersweep
    thee
In impious death, life breathing away.
O me — me !
This couch, not free !
By a slavish death subdued thou art,
From the hand, by the two-edged dart.
    Klu. Thou boastest this deed to be mine:
But leave off styling me
" The Agamemnonian wife ! "
For, showing himself in sign
Of the spouse of the corpse thou dost see,
Did the ancient bitter avenging-ghost
Of Atreus, savage host,
Pay the man here as price —
A full-grown for the young one's sacrifice.
    Cho. That no cause, indeed, of this killing
      art thou,
Who shall be witness-bearer ?
How shall he bear it — how?
But the sire's avenging-ghost might be in the
    deed a sharer.
He is forced on and on
By the kin-born flowing of blood,
— Black Ares : to where, having gone,
He shall leave off, flowing done,
At the frozen-child's-flesh food.
King, king, how shall I beweep thee !
From friendly soul what ever say ?
Thou liest where webs of the spider o'ersweep
    thee,
In impious death, life breathing away.
Oh, me — me !
This couch not free !
By a slavish death subdued thou art,
From the hand, by the two-edged dart.
    Klu. No death " unfit for the free "
Do I think this man's to be,:
For did not himself a slavish curse
To his household decree ?
But the scion of him, myself did nurse —
That much-bewailed Iphigeneia, he
Having done well by, — and as well, nor worse,
Been done to, — let him not in Haides loudly
Bear himself proudly !
Being by sword-destroying death amerced
For that sword's punishment himself inflicted
    first.
    Cho. I at a loss am left —
Of a feasible scheme of mind bereft —
Where I may turn: for the house is falling:
I fear the bloody crash of the rain
That ruins the roof as it bursts amain :
The warning-drop
Has come to a stop.

Destiny doth Justice whet
For other deed of hurt, on other whetstones yet.
Woe, earth, earth — would thou hadst taken *me*
Ere I saw the man I see,
On the pallet-bed
Of the silver-sided bath-vase, dead !
Who is it shall bury him, who
Sing his dirge ? Can it be true
That *thou* wilt dare this same to do —
Having slain thy husband, thine own,
To make his funeral moan :
And for the soul of him, in place
Of his mighty deeds, a graceless grace
To wickedly institute ? By whom
Shall the tale of praise o'er the tomb
At the god-like man be sent —
From the truth of his mind as he toils intent ?
    Klu. It belongs not to thee to declare
This object of care !
By us did he fall — down there !
Did he die — down there ! and down, no less,
We will bury him there, and not beneath
The wails of the household over his death :
But Iphigeneia, — with kindliness, —
His daughter, — as the case requires, —
Facing him full, at the rapid-flowing
Passage of Groans shall — both hands throwing
Around him — kiss that kindest of sires !
    Cho. This blame comes in the place of blame :
Hard battle it is to judge each claim.
" He is borne away who bears away:
And the killer has all to pay."
And this remains while Zeus is remaining,
" The doer shall suffer in time " — for, such his
    ordaining.
Who may cast out of the House its cursed
    brood ?
The race is to Até glued !
    Klu. Thou hast gone into this oracle
With a true result. For me, then, — I will
— To the Daimon of the Pleisthenidai
Making an oath — with all these things comply
Hard as they are to bear. For the rest —
Going from out this House, a guest,
May he wear some other family
To naught, with the deaths of kin by kin !
And — keeping a little part of my goods —
Wholly am I contented in
Having expelled from the royal House
These frenzied moods
The mutually-murderous.
    Aigisthos. O light propitious of day justice-
    bringing !
I may say truly, now, that men's avengers,
The gods from high, of earth behold the sor
    rows —
Seeing, as I have, i' the spun robes of the Eri-
    nues,
This man here lying, — sight to me how
    pleasant ! —
His father's hands' contrivances repaying.
For Atreus, this land's lord, of this man father,
Thuestes, my own father — to speak clearly —
His brother too, — being i' the rule contested, —
Drove forth to exile from both town and house-
    hold :
And, coming back, to the hearth turned, a sup-
    pliant,

Wretched Thuestes found the fate assured him
— Not to die, bloodying his paternal threshold
Just there: but host-wise this man's impious
  father
Atreus, soul-keenly more than kindly, — seem-
  ing
To joyous hold a flesh-day, — to my father
Served up a meal, the flesh of his own chil-
  dren.
The feet indeed and the hands' top divisions
He hid, high up and isolated sitting :
But, their unshowing parts in ignorance taking,
He forthwith eats food — as thou seest — per-
  dition
To the race: and then, 'ware of the deed ill-
  omened,
He shrieked O ! — falls back, vomiting, from
  the carnage,
And fate on the Pelopidai past bearing
He prays down — putting in his curse together
The kicking down o' the feast — that so might
  perish
The race of Pleisthenes entire : and thence is
That it is given thee to see this man prostrate.
And I was rightly of this slaughter stitch-
  man :
Since me, — being third from ten, — with my
  poor father
He drives out — being then a babe in swathe-
  bands :
But, grown up, back again has justice brought
  me :
And of this man I got hold — being without-
  doors —
Fitting together the whole scheme of ill-will.
So, sweet, in fine, even to die were to me,
Seeing as I have, this man i' the toils of
  justice !
Cho. Aigisthos, arrogance in ills I love not.
Dost thou say — willing, thou didst kill the
  man here,
And, alone, plot this lamentable slaughter ?
I say — thy head in justice will escape not
The people's throwing — know that ! — stones
  and curses !
Aig. Thou such things soundest — seated at
  the lower
Oarage to those who rule at the ship's mid-
  bench ?
Thou shalt know, being old, how heavy is
  teaching
To one of the like age — bidden be modest !
But chains and old age and the pangs of fasting
Stand out before all else in teaching, — pro-
  phets
At souls'-cure ! Dost not, seeing aught, see
  this too ?
Against goads kick not, lest tript-up thou suf-
  fer !
Cho. Woman, thou, — of him coming new
  from battle
Houseguard — thy husband's bed the while
  disgracing, —
For the Army-leader didst thou plan this fate
  too ?
Aig. These words too are of groans the
  prime-begetters !
Truly a tongue opposed to Orpheus hast thou :

For he led all things by his voice's grace-charm,
But thou, upstirring them by these wild yelp-
  ings,
Wilt lead them ! Forced, thou wilt appear the
  tamer !
Cho. So — thou shalt be my king then of
  the Argeians —
Who, not when for this man his fate thou
  plannedst,
Daredst to do this deed — thyself the slayer !
Aig. For, to deceive him was the wife's part,
  certes !
I was looked after — foe, ay, old-begotten !
But out of this man's wealth will I endeavor
To rule the citizens : and the no-man-minder
— Him will I heavily yoke — by no means
  trace-horse,
A corned-up colt ! but that bad friend in dark-
  ness,
Famine its housemate, shall behold him gentle.
Cho. Why then, this man here, from a
  coward spirit,
Didst not thou slay thyself ? But, — helped,
  — a woman,
The country's pest, and that of gods o' the
  country,
Killed him ! Orestes, where may he see light
  now ?
That coming hither back, with gracious for-
  tune,
Of both these he may be the all-conquering
  slayer ?
Aig. But since this to do thou thinkest —
  and not talk — thou soon shalt know !
Up then, comrades dear ! the proper thing to
  do — not distant this !
Cho. Up then ! hilt in hold, his sword let
  every one aright dispose !
Aig. Ay, but I myself too, hilt in hold, do
  not refuse to die !
Cho. Thou wilt die, thou say'st, to who
  accept it. We the chance demand !
Klu. Nowise, O belovedest of men, may we
  do other ills !
To have reaped away these, even, is a harvest
  much to me !
Go, both thou and these the old men, to the
  homes appointed each,
Ere ye suffer ! It behooved one do these things
  just as we did :
And if of these troubles, there should be
  enough — we may assent
— By the Daimon's heavy heel unfortunately
  stricken ones !
So a woman's counsel hath it — if one judge it
  learning-worth.
Aig. But to think that these at me the idle
  tongue should thus o'erbloom,
And throw out such words — the Daimon's
  power experimenting on —
And, of modest knowledge missing, — me, the
  ruler, . . .
Cho. Ne'er may this befall Argeians —
  wicked man to fawn before !
Aig. Anyhow, in after-days, will I, yes, I,
  be at thee yet !
Cho. Not if hither should the Daimon make
  Orestes straightway come !

Aig. Oh, I know, myself, that fugitives on
    hopes are pasture-fed !
Cho. Do thy deed, get fat, defiling justice,
    since the power is thine !
Aig. Know that thou shalt give me satisfac-
    tion for this folly's sake !

Cho. Boast on, bearing thee audacious, like a
    cock his females by !
Klu. Have not thou respect for these same
    idle yelpings ! I and thou
Will arrange it, o'er this household ruling
    excellently well.

LA SAISIAZ

DEDICATED TO MRS. SUTHERLAND ORR

MISS A. EGERTON-SMITH was, at the time
of her death, one of Browning's oldest women
friends. "He first met her," says Mrs. Suther-
land Orr, "as a young woman in Florence when
she was visiting there; and the love for and
proficiency in music soon asserted itself as a
bond of sympathy between them. They did
not, however, see much of each other till he
had finally left Italy, and she also had made
her home in London. . . . Mr. Browning was
one of the very few persons whose society she
cared to cultivate : and for many years the com-
mon musical interest took the practical, and for
both of them convenient, form, of their going
to concerts together." Browning was at La
Saisiaz, under the Salève, when Miss Egerton-
Smith, who was also domiciled there, died sud-
denly in the autumn of 1877, and it was after
the shock of her loss that he composed the
poem to which he gave the title of their sum-
mer resort. The poem is dated November 9,
1877.

GOOD, to forgive ;
    Best, to forget !
    Living, we fret ;
Dying, we live.
Fretless and free,
    Soul, clap thy pinion !
    Earth have dominion,
Body, o'er thee !

Wander at will,
    Day after day, —
    Wander away,
Wandering still —
Soul that canst soar !
    Body may slumber:
    Body shall cumber
Soul-flight no more.

Waft of soul's wing !
    What lies above ?
    Sunshine and Love,
Skyblue and Spring !
Body hides — where ?
    Ferns of all feather,
    Mosses and heather,
Yours be the care !

LA SAISIAZ

A. E. S. SEPTEMBER 14, 1877.

DARED and done: at last I stand upon the
    summit, Dear and True !
Singly dared and done ; the climbing both of us
    were bound to do.
Petty feat and yet prodigious : every side my
    glance was bent
O'er the grandeur and the beauty lavished
    through the whole ascent.
Ledge by ledge, out broke new marvels, now
    minute and now immense :
Earth's most exquisite disclosure, heaven's own
    God in evidence !
And no berry in its hiding, no blue space in its
    outspread,
Pleaded to escape my footstep, challenged my
    emerging head,
(As I climbed or paused from climbing, now
    o'erbranched by shrub and tree,
Now built round by rock and boulder, now at
    just a turn set free,
Stationed face to face with — Nature ? rather
    with Infinitude,)
— No revealment of them all, as singly I my
    path pursued,
But a bitter touched its sweetness, for the
    thought stung " Even so
Both of us had loved and wondered just the
    same, five days ago ! "
Five short days, sufficient hardly to entice,
    from out its den
Splintered in the slab, this pink perfection of
    the cyclamen ;
Scarce enough to heal and coat with amber gum
    the sloe-tree's gash,
Bronze the clustered wilding apple, redden ripe
    the mountain-ash :
Yet of might to place between us — Oh the bar-
    rier ! Yon Profound
Shrinks beside it, proves a pin-point: barrier
    this, without a bound !
Boundless though it be, I reach you : somehow
    seem to have you here
— Who are there. Yes, there you dwell now,
    plain the four low walls appear ;
Those are vineyards, they enclose from ; and
    the little spire which points

—That's Collonge, henceforth your dwelling.
  All the same, howe'er disjoints
Past from present, no less certain you are here,
  not there : have dared,
Done the feat of mountain-climbing, — five
  days since, we both prepared
Daring, doing, arm in arm, if other help should
  haply fail.
For you asked, as forth we sallied to see sunset
  from the vale,
"Why not try for once the mountain, — take a
  foretaste, snatch by stealth
Sight and sound, some unconsidered fragment
  of the hoarded wealth ?
Six weeks at its base, yet never once have we
  together won
Sight or sound by honest climbing : let us two
  have dared and done
Just so much of twilight journey as may prove
  to-morrow's jaunt
Not the only mode of wayfare — wheeled to
  reach the eagle's haunt ! "
So, we turned from the low grass-path you were
  pleased to call "your own,"
Set our faces to the rose-bloom o'er the sum-
  mit's front of stone
Where Salève obtains, from Jura and the sunken
  sun she hides,
Due return of blushing "Good Night," rosy as
  a borne-off bride's,
For his masculine "Good Morrow" when, with
  sunrise still in hold,
Gay he hails her, and, magnific, thrilled her
  black length burns to gold.
Up and up we went, how careless — nay, how
  joyous ! All was new,
All was strange. "Call progress toilsome ?
  that were just insulting you !
How the trees must temper noontide ! Ah, the
  thicket's sudden break !
What will be the morning glory, when at dusk
  thus gleams the lake ?
Light by light puts forth Geneva : what a land
  — and, of the land,
Can there be a lovelier station than this spot
  where now we stand ?
Is it late, and wrong to linger ? True, to-mor-
  row makes amends.
Toilsome progress ? child's play, call it —
  specially when one descends !
There, the dread descent is over — hardly our
  adventure, though !
Take the vale where late we left it, pace the
  grass-path, 'mine,' you know !
Proud completion of achievement ! " And we
  paced it, praising still
That soft tread on velvet verdure as it wound
  through hill and hill ;
And at very end there met us, coming from
  Collonge, the pair
— All our people of the Chalet — two, enough
  and none to spare.
So, we made for home together, and we reached
  it as the stars
One by one came lamping — chiefly that pre-
  potency of Mars —
And your last word was " I owe you this enjoy-
  ment ! " — met with " Nay :

With yourself it rests to have a month of mor-
  rows like to-day ! "
Then the meal, with talk and laughter, and the
  news of that rare nook
Yet untroubled by the tourist, touched on by
  no travel-book,
All the same — though latent — patent, hybrid
  birth of land and sea,
And (our travelled friend assured you) — if
  such miracle might be —
Comparable for completeness of both blessings
  — all around
Nature, and, inside her circle, safety from
  world's sight and sound —
Comparable to our Saisiaz. "Hold it fast and
  guard it well !
Go and see and vouch for certain, then come
  back and never tell
Living soul but us ; and haply, prove our sky
  from cloud as clear,
There may we four meet, praise fortune just as
  now, another year ! "

Thus you charged him on departure : not with-
  out the final charge,
" Mind to-morrow's early meeting ! We must
  leave our journey marge
Ample for the wayside wonders : there's the
  stoppage at the inn
Three-parts up the mountain, where the hard-
  ships of the track begin ;
There's the convent worth a visit ; but, the
  triumph crowning all —
There's Salève's own platform facing glory
  which strikes greatness small,
— Blanc, supreme above his earth-brood, nee-
  dles red and white and green,
Horns of silver, fangs of crystal set on edge in
  his demesne.
So, some three weeks since, we saw them : so,
  to-morrow we intend
You shall see them likewise ; therefore Good
  Night till to-morrow, friend ! "
Last, the nothings that extinguish embers of a
  vivid day :
" What might be the Marshal's next move,
  what Gambetta's counter-play ? "
Till the landing on the staircase saw escape
  the latest spark :
" Sleep you well ! " " Sleep but as well, you ! "
  — lazy love quenched, all was dark.

Nothing dark next day at sundawn ! Up I
  rose and forth I fared :
Took my plunge within the bath-pool, pacified
  the watch-dog scared,
Saw proceed the transmutation — Jura's black
  to one gold glow,
Trod your level path that let me drink the
  morning deep and slow,
Reached the little quarry — ravage recom-
  pensed by shrub and fern —
Till the overflowing ardors told me time was
  for return.
So, return I did, and gayly. But, for once,
  from no far mound
Waved salute a tall white figure. " Has her
  sleep been so profound ?

Foresight, rather, prudent saving strength for
day's expenditure!
Ay, the chamber-window's open: out and on
the terrace, sure!"

No, the terrace showed no figure, tall, white,
leaning through the wreaths,
Tangle-twine of leaf and bloom that intercept
the air one breathes,
Interpose between one's love and Nature's
loving, hill and dale
Down to where the blue lake's wrinkle marks
the river's inrush pale
— Mazy Arve: whereon no vessel but goes
sliding white and plain,
Not a steamboat pants from harbor but one
hears pulsate amain,
Past the city's congregated peace of homes
and pomp of spires
— Man's mild protest that there's something
more than Nature, man requires,
And that, useful as is Nature to attract the
tourist's foot,
Quiet slow sure money-making proves the
matter's very root, —
Need for body, — while the spirit also needs a
comfort reached
By no help of lake or mountain, but the texts
whence Calvin preached.
" Here's the veil withdrawn from landscape:
up to Jura and beyond,
All awaits us ranged and ready; yet she vio-
lates the bond,
Neither leans nor looks nor listens: why is
this?" A turn of eye
Took the whole sole answer, gave the undis-
puted reason " why "!

This dread way you had your summons! No
premonitory touch,
As you talked and laughed ('t is told me) scarce
a minute ere the clutch
Captured you in cold forever. Cold? nay,
warm you were as life
When I raised you, while the others used, in
passionate poor strife,
All the means that seemed to promise any aid,
and all in vain.
Gone you were, and I shall never see that
earnest face again
Grow transparent, grow transfigured with the
sudden light that leapt
At the first word's provocation, from the
heart-deeps where it slept.

Therefore, paying piteous duty, what seemed
You have we consigned
Peacefully to — what I think were, of all earth-
beds, to your mind
Most the choice for quiet, yonder: low walls
stop the vines' approach,
Lovingly Salève protects you; village-sports
will ne'er encroach
On the stranger lady's silence, whom friends
bore so kind and well
Thither "just for love's sake," — such their
own word was: and who can tell?

You supposed that few or none had known and
loved you in the world:
Maybe! flower that's full-blown tempts the
butterfly, not flower that's furled.
But more learned sense unlocked you, loosed
the sheath and let expand
Bud to bell and outspread flower-shape at the
least warm touch of hand
— Maybe, throb of heart, beneath which —
quickening farther than it knew —
Treasure oft was disembosomed, scent all
strange and unguessed hue.
Disembosomed, re-embosomed, — must one
memory suffice,
Prove I knew an Alpine-rose which all beside
named Edelweiss?

Rare thing, red or white, you rest now: two
days slumbered through; and since
One day more will see me rid of this same scene
whereat I wince,
Tetchy at all sights and sounds and pettish at
each idle charm
Proffered me who pace now singly where we
two went arm in arm, —
I have turned upon my weakness: asked, " And
what, forsooth, prevents
That, this latest day allowed me, I fulfil of
her intents
One she had the most at heart — that we should
thus again survey
From Salève Mont Blanc together?" There-
fore, — dared and done to-day
Climbing, — here I stand: but you — where?

If a spirit of the place
Broke the silence, bade me question, promised
answer, — what disgrace
Did I stipulate " Provided answer suit my
hopes, not fears!"
Would I shrink to learn my lifetime's limit —
days, weeks, months or years?
Would I shirk assurance on each point whereat
I can but guess —
" Does the soul survive the body? Is there
God's self, no or yes?"
If I know my mood, 't were constant — come
in whatsoe'er uncouth
Shape it should, nay, formidable — so the
answer were but truth.

Well, and wherefore shall it daunt me, when
't is I myself am tasked,
When, by weakness weakness questioned,
weakly answers — weakly asked?
Weakness never needs be falseness: truth is
truth in each degree
— Thunder-pealed by God to Nature, whis-
pered by my soul to me.
Nay, the weakness turns to strength and tri-
umphs in a truth beyond:
" Mine is but man's truest answer — how were
it did God respond?"
I shall no more dare to mimic such response in
futile speech,
Pass off human lisp as echo of the sphere-song
out of reach,

Than, — because it well may happen yonder,
  where the far snows blanch
Mute Mont Blanc, that who stands near them
  sees and hears an avalanche, —
I shall pick a clod and throw, — cry, "Such
  the sight and such the sound !
What though I nor see nor hear them ?   Others
  do, the proofs abound ! "
Can I make my eye an eagle's, sharpen ear to
  recognize
Sound o'er league and league of silence ?   Can
  I know, who but surmise ?
If I dared no self-deception when, a week
  since, I and you
Walked and talked along the grass-path, pass-
  ing lightly in review
What seemed hits and what seemed misses in a
  certain fence-play, — strife
Sundry minds of mark engaged in "On the
  Soul and Future Life," —
If I ventured estimating what was come of par-
  ried thrust,
Subtle stroke, and, rightly, wrongly, estimat-
  ing could be just
—Just, though life so seemed abundant in the
  form which moved by mine,
I might well have played at feigning, fooling,
  —laughed "What need opine
Pleasure must succeed to pleasure, else past
  pleasure turns to pain,
And this first life claims a second, else I count
  its good no gain ? " —
Much less have I heart to palter when the
  matter to decide
Now becomes "Was ending ending once and
  always, when you died ? "
Did the face, the form I lifted as it lay, reveal
  the loss
Not alone of life but soul ?   A tribute to yon
  flowers and moss,
What of you remains beside ?   A memory !
  Easy to attest
"Certainly from out the world that one be-
  lieves who knew her best
Such was good in her, such fair, which fair
  and good were great perchance
Had but fortune favored, bidden each shy
  faculty advance ;
After all — who knows another ?   Only as I
  know, I speak."
So much of you lives within me while I live
  my year or week.
Then my fellow takes the tale up, not unwilling
  to aver
Duly in his turn, "I knew him best of all, as he
  knew her :
Such he was, and such he was not, and such
  other might have been
But that somehow every actor, somewhere in
  this earthly scene,
Fails." And so both memories dwindle, yours
  and mine together linked,
Till there is but left for comfort, when the
  last spark proves extinct,
This — that somewhere new existence led by
  men and women new
Possibly attains perfection coveted by me and
  you.

While ourselves, the only witness to what work
  our life evolved,
Only to ourselves proposing problems proper to
  be solved
By ourselves alone, — who working ne'er shall
  know if work bear fruit
Others reap and garner, heedless how produced
  by stalk and root, —
We who, darkling, timed the day's birth, —
  struggling, testified to peace, —
Earned, by dint of failure, triumph, — we, cre-
  ative thought, must cease
In created word, thought's echo, due to impulse
  long since sped !
Why repine ?   There's ever some one lives
  although ourselves be dead !

Well, what signifies repugnance ?   Truth is
  truth howe'er it strike.
Fair or foul the lot apportioned life on earth, we
  bear alike.
Stalwart body idly yoked to stunted spirit,
  powers, that fain
Else would soar, condemned to grovel, ground-
  lings through the fleshly chain, —
Help that hinders, hindrance proved but help
  disguised when all too late, —
Hindrance is the fact acknowledged, howsoe'er
  explained as Fate,
Fortune, Providence : we bear, own life a bur-
  den more or less.
Life thus owned unhappy, is there supplemental
  happiness
Possible and probable in life to come ? or must
  we count
Life a curse and not a blessing, summed-up in
  its whole amount,
Help and hindrance, joy and sorrow ?
           Why should I want courage here ?
I will ask and have an answer, — with no favor,
  with no fear,
From myself. How much, how little, do I in-
  wardly believe
True that controverted doctrine ?   Is it fact to
  which I cleave,
Is it fancy I but cherish, when I take upon my
  lips
Phrase the solemn Tuscan fashioned, and de-
  clare the soul's eclipse
Not the soul's extinction ? take his "I believe
  and I declare —
Certain am I — from this life I pass into a bet-
  ter, there
Where that lady lives of whom enamored was
  my soul " — where this
Other lady, my companion dear and true, she
  also is ?

I have questioned and am answered. Ques-
  tion, answer presuppose
Two points : that the thing itself which ques-
  tions, answers, — is, it knows ;
As it also knows the thing perceived outside it-
  self, — a force
Actual ere its own beginning, operative
  through its course,
Unaffected by its end, — that this thing like-
  wise needs must be;

Call this — God, then, call that — soul, and
  both — the only facts for me.
Prove them facts? that they o'erpass my power
  of proving, proves them such:
Fact it is I know I know not something which
  is fact as much.
What before caused all the causes, what effect
  of all effects
Haply follows, — these are fancy. Ask the
  rush if it suspects
Whence and how the stream which floats it had
  a rise, and where and how
Falls or flows on still! What answer makes the
  rush except that now
Certainly it floats and is, and, no less certain
  than itself,
Is the everyway external stream that now
  through shoal and shelf
Floats it onward, leaves it — maybe — wrecked
  at last, or lands on shore
There to root again and grow and flourish sta-
  ble evermore.
— Maybe! mere surmise not knowledge: much
  conjecture styled belief,
What the rush conceives the stream means
  through the voyage blind and brief.
Why, because I doubtless am, shall I as doubt-
  less be? "Because
God seems good and wise." Yet under this our
  life's apparent laws
Reigns a wrong which, righted once, would give
  quite other laws to life.
"He seems potent." Potent here, then: why
  are right and wrong at strife?
Has in life the wrong the better? Happily life
  ends so soon!
Right predominates in life? Then why two
  lives and double boon?
"Anyhow, we want it: wherefore want?"
  Because, without the want,
Life, now human, would be brutish: just that
  hope, however scant,
Makes the actual life worth leading; take the
  hope therein away,
All we have to do is surely not endure another
  day.
This life has its hopes for this life, hopes that
  promise joy: life done —
Out of all the hopes, how many had complete
  fulfilment? None.
"But the soul is not the body:" and the breath
  is not the flute;
Both together make the music: either marred
  and all is mute.
Truce to such old sad contention whence, ac-
  cording as we shape
Most of hope or most of fear, we issue in a half-
  escape:
"We believe" is sighed. I take the cup of
  comfort proffered thus,
Taste and try each soft ingredient, sweet infu-
  sion, and discuss
What their blending may accomplish for the
  cure of doubt, till — slow,
Sorrowful, but how decided! needs must I o'er-
  turn it — so!
Cause before, effect behind me — blanks! The
  midway point I am,

Caused, itself — itself efficient: in that narrow
  space must cram
All experience — out of which there crowds con-
  jecture manifold,
But, as knowledge, this comes only — things
  may be as I behold,
Or may not be, but, without me and above me,
  things there are;
I myself am what I know not — ignorance which
  proves no bar
To the knowledge that I am, and, since I am,
  can recognize
What to me is pain and pleasure: this is sure,
  the rest — surmise.
If my fellows are or are not, what may please
  them and what pain, —
Mere surmise: my own experience — that is
  knowledge, once again!

I have lived, then, done and suffered, loved and
  hated, learnt and taught
This — there is no reconciling wisdom with a
  world distraught,
Goodness with triumphant evil, power with fail-
  ure in the aim,
If — (to my own sense, remember! though none
  other feel the same!)
If you bar me from assuming earth to be a pu-
  pil's place,
And life, time — with all their chances, changes
  — just probation-space,
Mine, for me. But those apparent other mor-
  tals — theirs, for them?
Knowledge stands on my experience: all outside
  its narrow hem,
Free surmise may sport and welcome! Pleas-
  ures, pains affect mankind
Just as they affect myself? Why, here's my
  neighbor color-blind,
Eyes like mine to all appearance: "green as
  grass" do I affirm?
"Red as grass" he contradicts me; — which
  employs the proper term?
Were we two the earth's sole tenants, with no
  third for referee,
How should I distinguish? Just so, God must
  judge 'twixt man and me.
To each mortal peradventure earth becomes a
  new machine,
Pain and pleasure no more tally in our sense
  than red and green;
Still, without what seems such mortal's plea-
  sure, pain, my life were lost
— Life, my whole sole chance to prove — al-
  though at man's apparent cost —
What is beauteous and what ugly, right to strive
  for, right to shun,
Fit to help and fit to hinder, — prove my forces
  every one,
Good and evil, — learn life's lesson, hate of evil,
  love of good,
As 't is set me, understand so much as may be
  understood —
Solve the problem: "From thine apprehended
  scheme of things, deduce
Praise or blame of its contriver, shown a niggard
  or profuse

In each good or evil issue! nor miscalculate alike
Counting one the other in the final balance, which to strike,
Soul was born and life allotted : ay, the show of things unfurled
For thy summing-up and judgment, — thine, no other mortal's world ! "

What though fancy scarce may grapple with the complex and immense
— " His own world for every mortal ? " Postulate omnipotence !
Limit power, and simple grows the complex : shrunk to atom size,
That which loomed immense to fancy low before my reason lies, —
I survey it and pronounce it work like other work : success
Here and there, the workman's glory, — here and there, his shame no less,
Failure as conspicuous. Taunt not " Human work ape work divine ? "
As the power, expect performance! God's be God's as mine is mine !
God whose power made man and made man's wants, and made, to meet those wants,
Heaven and earth which, through the body, prove the spirit's ministrants,
Excellently all, — did he lack power or was the will in fault
When he let blue heaven be shrouded o'er by vapors of the vault,
Gay earth drop her garlands shrivelled at the first infecting breath
Of the serpent pains which herald, swarming in, the dragon death ?
What, no way but this that man may learn and lay to heart how rife
Life were with delights would only death allow their taste to life ?
Must the rose sigh " Pluck — I perish ! " must the eve weep " Gaze — I fade ! "
— Every sweet warn " 'Ware my bitter ! " every shine bid " Wait my shade " ?
Can we love but on condition, that the thing we love must die ?
Needs there groan a world in anguish just to teach us sympathy —
Multitudinously wretched that we, wretched too, may guess
What a preferable state were universal happiness ?
Hardly do I so conceive the outcome of that power which went
To the making of the worm there in yon clod its tenement,
Any more than I distinguish aught of that which, wise and good,
Framed the leaf, its plain of pasture, dropped the dew, its fineless food.
Nay, were fancy fact, were earth and all it holds illusion mere,
Only a machine for teaching love and hate and hope and fear
To myself, the sole existence, single truth 'mid falsehood, — well !

If the harsh throes of the prelude die not off into the swell
Of that perfect piece they sting me to become a-strain for, — if
Roughness of the long rock-clamber lead not to the last of cliff,
First of level country where is sward my pilgrim-foot can prize, —
Plainlier ! if this life's conception new life fail to realize, —
Though earth burst and proved a bubble glassing hues of hell, one huge
Reflex of the devil's doings — God's work by no subterfuge —
(So death's kindly touch informed me as it broke the glamour, gave
Soul and body both release from life's long nightmare in the grave)—
Still, — with no more Nature, no more Man as riddle to be read,
Only my own joys and sorrows now to reckon real instead, —
I must say — or choke in silence — " Howsoever came my fate,
Sorrow did and joy did nowise — life well weighed — preponderate."
By necessity ordained thus ? I shall bear as best I can ;
By a cause all-good, all-wise, all-potent ? No, as I am man !
Such were God : and was it goodness that the good within my range
Or had evil in admixture or grew evil's self by change ?
Wisdom — that becoming wise meant making slow and sure advance
From a knowledge proved in error to acknowledged ignorance ?
Power ! 't is just the main assumption reason most revolts at ! power
Unavailing for bestowment on its creature of an hour,
Man, of so much proper action rightly aimed and reaching aim,
So much passion, — no defect there, no excess, but still the same, —
As what constitutes existence, pure perfection bright as brief
For yon worm, man's fellow-creature, on yon happier world — its leaf !
No, as I am man, I mourn the poverty I must impute :
Goodness, wisdom, power, all bounded, each a human attribute !

But, O world outspread beneath me! only for myself I speak,
Nowise dare to play the spokesman for my brothers strong and weak,
Full and empty, wise and foolish, good and bad, in every age,
Every clime, I turn my eyes from, as in one or other stage
Of a torture writhe they, Job-like couched on dung and crazed with blains
—Wherefore ? whereto ? ask the whirlwind what the dread voice thence explains !

I shall "vindicate no way of God's to man,"
        nor stand apart,
"Laugh, be candid," while I watch it traversing
        the human heart!
Traversed heart must tell its story uncommented
        on: no less
Mine results in, "Only grant a second life; I
        acquiesce
In this present life as failure, count misfortune's
        worst assaults
Triumph, not defeat, assured that loss so much
        the more exalts
Gain about to be. For at what moment did I
        so advance
Near to knowledge as when frustrate of escape
        from ignorance?
Did not beauty prove most precious when its
        opposite obtained
Rule, and truth seem more than ever potent
        because falsehood reigned?
While for love — Oh how but, losing love, does
        whoso loves succeed
By the death-pang to the birth-throe — learning
        what is love indeed?
Only grant my soul may carry high through
        death her cup unspilled,
Brimming though it be with knowledge, life's
        loss drop by drop distilled,
I shall boast it mine — the balsam, bless each
        kindly wrench that wrung
From life's tree its inmost virtue, tapped the
        root whence pleasure sprung,
Barked the bole, and broke the bough, and
        bruised the berry, left all grace
Ashes in death's stern alembic, loosed elixir in
        its place!"

Witness, Dear and True, how little I was 'ware
        of — not your worth
— That I knew, my heart assures me — but of
        what a shade on earth
Would the passage from my presence of the
        tall white figure throw
O'er the ways we walked together! Somewhat
        narrow, somewhat slow,
Used to seem the ways, the walking: narrow
        ways are well to tread
When there's moss beneath the footstep,
        honeysuckle overhead:
Walking slow to beating bosom surest solace
        soonest gives,
Liberates the brain o'erloaded — best of all
        restoratives.
Nay, do I forget the open vast where soon or
        late converged
Ways though winding? — world-wide heaven-
        high sea where music slept or surged
As the angel had ascendant, and Beethoven's
        Titan mace
Smote the immense to storm, Mozart would by
        a finger's lifting chase?
Yes, I knew — but not with knowledge such as
        thrills me while I view
Yonder precinct which henceforward holds and
        hides the Dear and True.
Grant me (once again) assurance we shall each
        meet each some day,

Walk — but with how bold a footstep! on a
        way — but what a way!
— Worst were best, defeat were triumph, utter
        loss were utmost gain.
Can it be, and must, and will it?

                        Silence! Out of fact's domain
Just surmise prepared to mutter hope, and als
        fear — dispute
Fact's inexorable ruling, "Outside fact, surmise
        be mute!"
Well!
        Ay, well and best, if fact's self I may force
        the answer from!
'T is surmise I stop the mouth of! Not above
        in yonder dome
All a rapture with its rose-glow, — not around,
        where pile and peak
Strainingly await the sun's fall, — not beneath,
        where crickets creak,
Birds assemble for their bedtime, soft the tree-
        top swell subsides, —
No, nor yet within my deepest sentient self the
        knowledge hides.
Aspiration, reminiscence, plausibilities of trust
— Now the ready "Man were wronged else,"
        now the rash "and God unjust" —
None of these I need. Take thou, my soul, thy
        solitary stand,
Umpire to the champions Fancy, Reason, as on
        either hand
Amicable war they wage and play the foe in thy
        behoof!
Fancy thrust and Reason parry! Thine the
        prize who stand aloof!

FANCY

I concede the thing refused: henceforth no
        certainty more plain
Than this mere surmise that after body dies
        soul lives again.
Two, the only facts acknowledged late, are now
        increased to three —
God is, and the soul is, and, as certain, after
        death shall be.
Put this third to use in life, the time for using
        fact!

REASON

                                        I do:
Find it promises advantage, coupled with the
        other two.
Life to come will be improvement on the life
        that's now; destroy
Body's thwartings, there's no longer screen
        betwixt soul and soul's joy.
Why should we expect new hindrance, novel
        tether? In this first
Life, I see the good of evil, why our world
        began at worst:
Since time means amelioration, tardily enough
        displayed,
Yet a mainly onward moving, never wholly
        retrograde.
We know more though we know little, we grow
        stronger though still weak,

Partly see though all too purblind, stammer though we cannot speak.
There is no such grudge in God as scared the ancient Greek, no fresh
Substitute of trap for drag-net, once a breakage in the mesh.
Dragons were, and serpents are, and blindworms will be : ne'er emerged
Any new-created python for man's plague since earth was purged.
Failing proof, then, of invented trouble to replace the old,
O'er this life the next presents advantage much and manifold :
Which advantage — in the absence of a fourth and farther fact
Now conceivably surmised, of harm to follow from the act —
I pronounce for man's obtaining at this moment. Why delay?
Is he happy? happiness will change : anticipate the day!
Is he sad? there 's ready refuge : of all sadness death 's prompt cure!
Is he both, in mingled measure? cease a burden to endure!
Pains with sorry compensations, pleasures stinted in the dole,
Power that sinks and pettiness that soars, all halved and nothing whole,
Idle hopes that lure man onward, forced back by as idle fears —
What a load he stumbles under through his glad sad seventy years,
When a touch sets right the turmoil, lifts his spirit where, flesh-freed,
Knowledge shall be rightly named so, all that seems to be truth indeed!
Grant his forces no accession, nay, no faculty's increase,
Only let what now exists continue, let him prove in peace
Power whereof the interrupted unperfected play enticed
Man through darkness, which to lighten any spark of hope sufficed, —
What shall then deter his dying out of darkness into light?
Death itself perchance, brief pain that 's pang, condensed and infinite?
But at worst, he needs must brave it one day, while, at best, he laughs —
Drops a drop within his chalice, sleep not death his science quaffs!
Any moment claims more courage, when, by crossing cold and gloom,
Manfully man quits discomfort, makes for the provided room
Where the old friends want their fellow, where the new acquaintance wait,
Probably for talk assembled, possibly to sup in state!
I affirm and reaffirm it therefore : only make as plain
As that man now lives, that, after dying, man will live again, —
Make as plain the absence, also, of a law to contravene

Voluntary passage from this life to that by change of scene, —
And I bid him — at suspicion of first cloud athwart his sky,
Flower's departure, frost's arrival — never hesitate, but die !

FANCY

Then I double my concession : grant, along with new life sure
This same law found lacking now : ordain that, whether rich or poor
Present life is judged in aught man counts advantage — be it hope,
Be it fear that brightens, blackens most or least his horoscope, —
He, by absolute compulsion such as made him live at all,
Go on living to the fated end of life whate'er befall.
What though, as on earth he darkling grovels, man descry the sphere,
Next life's — call it, heaven of freedom, close above and crystal-clear?
He shall find — say, hell to punish who in aught curtails the term,
Fain would act the butterfly before he has played out the worm !
God, soul, earth, heaven, hell, — five facts now : what is to desiderate ?

REASON

Nothing ! Henceforth man's existence bows to the monition "Wait !
Take the joys and bear the sorrows — neither with extreme concern !
Living here means nescience simply : 't is next life that helps to learn.
Shut those eyes, next life will open, — stop those ears, next life will teach
Hearing's office, — close those lips, next life will give the power of speech !
Or, if action more amuse thee than the passive attitude,
Bravely bustle through thy being, busy thee for ill or good,
Reap this life's success or failure ! Soon shall things be unperplexed
And the right and wrong, now tangled, lie unravelled in the next."

FANCY

Not so fast ! Still more concession ! not alone do I declare
Life must needs be borne, — I also will that man become aware
Life has worth incalculable, every moment that he spends
So much gain or loss for that next life which on this life depends.
Good, done here, be there rewarded, — evil, worked here, there amerced !
Six facts now, and all established, plain to man the last as first.

REASON

There was good and evil, then, defined to man by this decree ?

Was — for at its promulgation both alike have
  ceased to be.
Prior to this last announcement, " Certainly as
  God exists,
As He made man's soul, as soul is quenchless
  by the deathly mists,
Yet is, all the same, forbidden premature
  escape from time
To eternity's provided purer air and brighter
  clime, —
Just so certainly depends it on the use to which
  man turns
Earth, the good or evil done there, whether
  after death he earns
Life eternal, — heaven, the phrase be, or eter-
  nal death, — say, hell.
As his deeds, so proves his portion, doing ill or
  doing well ! "
— Prior to this last announcement, earth was
  man's probation-place :
Liberty of doing evil gave his doing good a
  grace ;
Once lay down the law, with Nature's simple
  "Such effects succeed
Causes such, and heaven or hell depends upon
  man's earthly deed
Just as surely as depends the straight or else
  the crooked line
On his making point meet point or with or else
  without incline," —
Thenceforth neither good nor evil does man,
  doing what he must.
Lay but down that law as stringent " Wouldst
  thou live again, be just ! "
As this other " Wouldst thou live now, regu-
  larly draw thy breath !
For, suspend the operation, straight law's
  breach results in death " —
And (provided always, man, addressed this
  mode, be sound and sane)
Prompt and absolute obedience, never doubt,
  will law obtain !
Tell not me " Look round us ! nothing each
  side but acknowledged law,
Now styled God's — now, Nature's edict ! "
  Where 's obedience without flaw
Paid to either?   What 's the adage rife in
  man's mouth ?   Why, " The best
I both see and praise, the worst I follow " —
  which, despite professed
Seeing, praising, all the same he follows, since
  he disbelieves
In the heart of him that edict which for truth
  his head receives.
There 's evading and persuading and much mak-
  ing law amends
Somehow, there 's the nice distinction 'twixt
  fast foes and faulty friends,
— Any consequence except inevitable death
  when, " Die,
Whoso breaks our law ! " they publish, God
  and Nature equally.
Law that 's kept or broken — subject to man's
  will and pleasure !   Whence ?
How comes law to bear eluding ?   Not be-
  cause of impotence :
Certain laws exist already which to hear means
  to obey ;

Therefore not without a purpose these man
  must, while those man may
Keep and, for the keeping, haply gain approval
  and reward.
Break through this last superstructure, all is
  empty air — no sward
Firm like my first fact to stand on, " God there
  is, and soul there is,"
And soul's earthly life-allotment : wherein, by
  hypothesis,
Soul is bound to pass probation, prove its
  powers, and exercise
Sense and thought on fact, and then, from fact
  educing fit surmise,
Ask itself, and of itself have solely answer,
  " Does the scope
Earth affords of fact to judge by warrant fu-
  ture fear or hope ? "

Thus have we come back full circle : fancy's
  footsteps one by one
Go their round conducting reason to the point
  where they begun,
Left where we were left so lately, Dear and
  True !   When, half a week
Since, we walked and talked and thus I told
  you, how suffused a cheek
You had turned me had I sudden brought the
  blush into the smile
By some word like "Idly argued ! you know
  better all the while ! "
Now, from me — Oh not a blush, but, how much
  more, a joyous glow,
Laugh triumphant, would it strike did your
  "Yes, better I do know "
Break, my warrant for assurance ! which assur-
  ance may not be
If, supplanting hope, assurance needs must
  change this life to me.
So, I hope — no more than hope, but hope — no
  less than hope, because
I can fathom, by no plumb-line sunk in life's
  apparent laws,
How I may in any instance fix where change
  should meetly fall
Nor involve, by one revisal, abrogation of them
  all :
— Which again involves as utter change in life
  thus law-released,
Whence the good of goodness vanished when
  the ill of evil ceased,
Whereas, life and laws apparent reinstated, —
  all we know,
All we know not, — o'er our heaven again cloud
  closes, until, lo, —
Hope the arrowy, just as constant, comes to
  pierce its gloom, compelled
By a power and by a purpose which, if no one
  else beheld,
I behold in life, so — hope !

Sad summing-up of all to say !
Athanasius contra mundum, why should he hope
  more than they ?
So are men made notwithstanding, such mag-
  netic virtue darts
From each head their fancy haloes to their un-
  resisting hearts !

Here I stand, methinks a stone's throw from
　　yon village I this morn
Traversed for the sake of looking one last look
　　at its forlorn
Tenement's ignoble fortune: through a crev-
　　ice, plain its floor
Piled with provender for cattle, while a dung-
　　heap blocked the door.
In that squalid Bossex, under that obscene red
　　roof, arose,
Like a fiery flying serpent from its egg, a soul
　　— Rousseau's.
Turn thence! Is it Diodati joins the glimmer
　　of the lake?
There I plucked a leaf, one week since, — ivy,
　　plucked for Byron's sake.
Famed unfortunates! And yet, because of that
　　phosphoric fame
Swathing blackness' self with brightness till
　　putridity looked flame,
All the world was witched: and wherefore?
　　what could lie beneath, allure
Heart of man to let corruption serve man's head
　　as cynosure?
Was the magic in the dictum "All that's good
　　is gone and past;
Bad and worse still grows the present, and the
　　worst of all comes last:
Which believe — for I believe it"? So
　　preached one his gospel-news;
While melodious moaned the other, "dying
　　day with dolphin-hues!
Storm, for loveliness and darkness like a wo-
　　man's eye! Ye mounts
Where I climb to 'scape my fellow, and thou sea
　　wherein he counts
Not one inch of vile dominion! What were
　　your especial worth
Failed ye to enforce the maxim 'Of all objects
　　found on earth
Man is meanest, much too honored when com-
　　pared with — what by odds
Beats him — any dog: so, let him go a-howling
　　to his gods!'
Which believe — for I believe it!" Such the
　　comfort man received
Sadly since perforce he must: for why? the
　　famous bard believed!

Fame! Then, give me fame, a moment! As
　　I gather at a glance
Human glory after glory vivifying yon ex-
　　panse,
Let me grasp them altogether, hold on high and
　　brandish well
Beacon-like above the rapt world ready, whether
　　heaven or hell
Send the dazzling summons earthward, to sub-
　　mit itself the same,
Take on trust the hope or else despair flashed
　　full on face by — Fame!
Thanks, thou pine-tree of Makistos, wide thy
　　giant torch I wave!
Know ye whence I plucked the pillar, late with
　　sky for architrave?
This the trunk, the central solid Knowledge,
　　kindled core, began

Tugging earth-deeps, trying heaven-heights,
　　rooted yonder at Lausanne.
This which flits and spits, the aspic, — sparkles
　　in and out the boughs
Now, and now condensed, the python, coiling
　　round and round allows
Scarce the bole its due effulgence, dulled by
　　flake on flake of Wit —
Laughter so bejewels Learning, — what but
　　Ferney nourished it?
Nay, nor fear — since every resin feeds the
　　flame — that I dispense
With yon Bossex terebinth-tree's all-explosive
　　Eloquence:
No, be sure! nor, any more than thy resplen-
　　dency, Jean-Jacques,
Dare I want thine, Diodati! What though
　　monkeys and macaques
Gibber "Byron"? Byron's ivy rears a branch
　　beyond the crew,
Green forever, no deciduous trash macaques
　　and monkeys chew!
As Rousseau, then, eloquent, as Byron prime
　　in poet's power, —
Detonations, fulgurations, smiles — the rain-
　　bow, tears — the shower, —
Lo, I lift the coruscating marvel — Fame! and,
　　famed, declare
— Learned for the nonce as Gibbon, witty as
　　wit's self Voltaire . . .
Oh, the sorriest of conclusions to whatever man
　　of sense
'Mid the millions stands the unit, takes no flare
　　for evidence!
Yet the millions have their portion, live their
　　calm or troublous day,
Find significance in fireworks: so, by help of
　　mine, they may
Confidently lay to heart and lock in head their
　　life long — this:
"He there with the brand flamboyant, broad
　　o'er night's forlorn abyss,
Crowned by prose and verse; and wielding,
　　with Wit's bauble, Learning's rod" . . .
Well? Why, he at least believed in Soul, was
　　very sure of God!

———

So the poor smile played, that evening: pallid
　　smile long since extinct
Here in London's mid-November! Not so
　　loosely thoughts were linked,
Six weeks since as I, descending in the sunset
　　from Salève,
Found the chain, I seemed to forge there, flaw-
　　less till it reached your grave, —
Not so filmy was the texture, but I bore it in
　　my breast
Safe thus far. And since I found a something
　　in me would not rest
Till I, link by link, unravelled any tangle of
　　the chain,
— Here it lies, for much or little! I have lived
　　all o'er again
That last pregnant hour: I saved it, just as I
　　could save a root
Disinterred for reinterment when the time best
　　helps to shoot.

Life is stocked with germs of torpid life; but
 may I never wake
Those of mine whose resurrection could not be
 without earthquake!

Rest all such, unraised forever! Be this, sad
 yet sweet, the sole
Memory evoked from slumber! Least part
 this: then what the whole?

THE TWO POETS OF CROISIC

Written immediately after *La Saisiaz*, being dated January 15, 1878.

Such a starved bank of moss
 Till, that May-morn,
Blue ran the flash across:
 Violets were born!

Sky — what a scowl of cloud
 Till, near and far,
Ray on ray split the shroud:
 Splendid, a star!

World — how it walled about
 Life with disgrace
Till God's own smile came out:
 That was thy face!

I

"Fame!" Yes, I said it and you read it.
 First,
 Praise the good log-fire! Winter howls with-
  out.
Crowd closer, let us! Ha, the secret nursed
 Inside yon hollow, crusted roundabout
With copper where the clamp was, — how the
  burst
 Vindicates flame the stealthy feeder! Spout
Thy splendidest — a minute and no more?
So soon again all sobered as before?

II

Nay, for I need to see your face! One stroke
 Adroitly dealt, and lo, the pomp revealed!
Fire in his pandemonium, heart of oak
 Palatial, where he wrought the works con-
  cealed
Beneath the solid-seeming roof I broke,
 As redly up and out and off they reeled
Like disconcerted imps, those thousand sparks
From fire's slow tunnelling of vaults and arcs!

III

Up, out, and off, see! Were you never used, —
 You now, in childish days or rather nights, —
As I was, to watch sparks fly? not amused
 By that old nurse-taught game which gave
  the sprites
Each one his title and career, — confused
 Belief 't was all long over with the flights
From earth to heaven of hero, sage, and bard,
And bade them once more strive for Fame's
 award?

IV

New long bright life! and happy chance be-
 fell —
 That I know — when some prematurely lost

Child of disaster bore away the bell
 From some too-pampered son of fortune,
  crossed
Never before my chimney broke the spell!
 Octogenarian Keats gave up the ghost,
While — never mind Who was it cumbered
  earth —
Sank stifled, span-long brightness, in the birth.

V

Well, try a variation of the game!
 Our log is old ship-timber, broken bulk.
There's sea-brine spirits up the brimstone
  flame,
 That crimson-curly spiral proves the hulk
Was saturate with — ask the chloride's name
 From somebody who knows! I shall not sulk
If yonder greenish tonguelet licked from brass
Its life, I thought was fed on copperas.

VI

Anyhow, there they flutter! What may be
 The style and prowess of that purple one?
Who is the hero other eyes shall see
 Than yours and mine? That yellow, deep to
  dun —
Conjecture how the sage glows, whom not we
 But those unborn are to get warmth by!
  Son
O' the coal, — as Job and Hebrew name a
 spark, —
What bard, in thy red soaring, scares the dark?

VII

Oh and the lesser lights, the dearer still
 That they elude a vulgar eye, give ours
The glimpse repaying astronomic skill
 Which searched sky deeper, passed those
  patent powers
Constellate proudly, — swords, scrolls, harps,
  that fill
 The vulgar eye to surfeit, — found best
  flowers
Hid deepest in the dark, — named unplucked
 grace
Of soul, ungathered beauty, form or face!

VIII

Up with thee, mouldering ash men never knew,
 But I know! flash thou forth, and figure
  bold,
Calm and columnar as yon flame I view!
 Oh and I bid thee, — to whom fortune doled
Scantly all other gifts out — bicker blue,
 Beauty for all to see, zinc's uncontrolled

Flake-brilliance! Not my fault if these were
    shown,
Grandeur and beauty both, to me alone.

IX

No! as the first was boy's play, this proves
    mere
    Stripling's amusement : manhood's sport be
        grave !
Choose rather sparkles quenched in mid career,
    Their boldness and their brightness could not
        save
(In some old night of time on some lone drear
    Sea-coast, monopolized by crag or cave)
— Save from ignoble exit into smoke,
Silence, oblivion, all death-damps that choke !

X

Launched by our ship-wood, float we, once
    adrift
    In fancy to that land-strip waters wash,
We both know well ! Where uncouth tribes
    made shift
Long since to just keep life in, billows dash
Nigh over folk who shudder at each lift
    Of the old tyrant tempest's whirlwind-lash
Though they have built the serviceable town
Tempests but tease now, billows drench, not
    drown.

XI

Croisic, the spit of sandy rock which juts
    Spitefully northward, bears nor tree nor
        shrub
To tempt the ocean, show what Guérande shuts
    Behind her, past wild Batz whose Saxons grub
The ground for crystals grown where ocean
        gluts
    Their promontory's breadth with salt: all
        stub
Of rock and stretch of sand, the land's last
        strife
To rescue a poor remnant for dear life.

XII

And what life ! Here was, from the world to
    choose,
    The Druids' chosen chief of homes : they
        reared
— Only their women, — 'mid the slush and
    ooze
Of yon low islet, — to their sun, revered
In strange stone guise, — a temple. May-dawn
    dews
    Saw the old structure levelled ; when there
        peered
May's earliest eve-star, high and wide once
    more
Up towered the new pile perfect as before:

XIII

Seeing that priestesses — and all were such —
    Unbuilt and then rebuilt it every May,
Each alike helping — well, if not too much !
    For, 'mid their eagerness to outstrip day
And get work done, if any loosed her clutch
    And let a single stone drop, straight a prey

Herself fell, torn to pieces, limb from limb,
By sisters in full chorus glad and grim.

XIV

And still so much remains of that gray cult,
    That even now, of nights, do women steal
To the sole Menhir standing, and insult
    The antagonistic church-spire by appeal
To power discrowned in vain, since each adult
    Believes the gruesome thing she clasps may
        heal
Whatever plague no priestly help can cure :
Kiss but the cold stone, the event is sure !

XV

Nay more : on May-morns, that primeval rite
    Of temple-building, with its punishment
For rash precipitation, lingers, spite
    Of all remonstrance ; vainly are they shent,
Those girls who form a ring and, dressed in
    white,
    Dance round it, till some sister's strength be
        spent :
Touch but the Menhir, straight the rest turn
        roughs
From gentles, fall on her with fisticuffs.

XVI

Oh and, for their part, boys from door to door
    Sing unintelligible words to tunes
As obsolete : " scraps of Druidic lore,"
    Sigh scholars, as each pale man importunes
Vainly the mumbling to speak plain once more.
    Enough of this old worship, rounds and
        runes !
They serve my purpose, which is but to show
Croisic to-day and Croisic long ago.

XVII

What have we sailed to see, then, wafted there
    By fancy from the log that ends its days
Of much adventure 'neath skies foul or fair,
    On waters rough or smooth, in this good
        blaze
We two crouch round so closely, bidding care
    Keep outside with the snow-storm ? Some-
        thing says
" Fit time for story-telling ! " I begin —
Why not at Croisic, port we first put in ?

XVIII

Anywhere serves : for point me out the place
    Wherever man has made himself a home,
And there I find the story of our race
    In little, just at Croisic as at Rome.
What matters the degree ? the kind I trace.
    Druids their temple, Christians have their
        dome :
So with mankind ; and Croisic, I 'll engage,
With Rome yields sort for sort, in age for age.

XIX

No doubt, men vastly differ : and we need
    Some strange exceptional benevolence
Of nature's sunshine to develop seed
    So well, in the less-favored clime, that thence

We may discern how shrub means tree indeed
  Though dwarfed till scarcely shrub in evi-
    dence .
Man in the ice-house or the hot-house ranks
With beasts or gods : stove-forced, give warmth
    the thanks !

XX

While, is there any ice-checked ? Such shall
    learn
I am thankworthy, who propose to slake
His thirst for tasting how it feels to turn
  Cedar from hyssop-on-the-wall. I wake
No memories of what is harsh and stern
In ancient Croisic-nature, much less rake
The ashes of her last warmth till out leaps
Live Hervé Riel, the single spark she keeps.

XXI

Take these two, see, each outbreak, — spirt
    and spirt
Of fire from our brave billet's either edge
Which — call maternal Croisic ocean-girt !
  These two shall thoroughly redeem my
    pledge.
One flames fierce gules, its feebler rival —
    vert,
  Heralds would tell you : heroes, I allege,
They both were : soldiers, sailors, statesmen,
    priests,
Lawyers, physicians — guess what gods or
    beasts !

XXII

None of them all, but — poets, if you please ?
  " What, even there, endowed with knack of
    rhyme,
Did two among the aborigines
  Of that rough region pass the ungracious
    time
Suiting, to rumble-tumble of the sea's,
  The songs forbidden a serener clime ?
Or had they universal audience — that 's
To say, the folk of Croisic, ay, and Batz ? "

XXIII

Open your ears ! Each poet in his day
  Had such a mighty moment of success
As pinnacled him straight, in full display,
  For the whole world to worship — nothing
    less !
Was not the whole polite world Paris, pray ?
  And did not Paris, for one moment — yes,
Worship these poet-flames, our red and green,
One at a time, a century between ?

XXIV

And yet you never heard their names ! Assist,
  Clio, Historic Muse, while I record
Great deeds ! Let fact, not fancy, break the
    mist
  And bid each sun emerge, in turn play lord
Of day, one moment ! Hear the annalist
  'Tell a strange story, true to the least word !
At Croisic, sixteen hundred years and ten
Since Christ, forth flamed yon liquid ruby,
    then.

XXV

Know him henceforth as René Gentilhomme
  — Appropriate appellation ! noble birth
And knightly blazon, the device wherefrom
  Was " Better do than say " ! In Croisic's
    dearth
Why prison his career while Christendom
  Lay open to reward acknowledged worth ?
He therefore left it at the proper age
And got to be the Prince of Condé's page.

XXVI

Which Prince of Condé, whom men called
    " The Duke,"
  — Failing the king, his cousin, of an heir,
(As one might hold hap, would, without rebuke,
  Since Anne of Austria, all the world was
    ware,
Twenty-three years long sterile, scarce could
    look
  For issue) — failing Louis of so rare
A godsend, it was natural the Prince
Should hear men call him " Next King " too,
    nor wince.

XXVII

Now, as this reasonable hope, by growth
  Of years, nay, tens of years, looked plump
    almost
To bursting, — would the brothers, childless
    both,
  Louis and Gaston, give but up the ghost —
Condé, called " Duke " and " Next King,"
    nothing loth
  Awaited his appointment to the post,
And wiled away the time, as best he might,
Till Providence should settle things aright.

XXVIII

So, at a certain pleasure-house, withdrawn
  From cities where a whisper breeds offence,
He sat him down to watch the streak of dawn
  Testify to first stir of Providence ;
And, since dull country life makes courtiers
    yawn,
  There wanted not a poet to dispense
Song's remedy for spleen-fits all and some,
Which poet was Page René Gentilhomme.

XXIX

A poet born and bred, his very sire
  A poet also, author of a piece
Printed and published, " Ladies — their attire : "
  Therefore the son, just born at his decease,
Was bound to keep alive the sacred fire,
  And kept it, yielding moderate increase
Of songs and sonnets, madrigals, and much
Rhyming thought poetry and praised as such.

XXX

Rubbish unutterable (bear in mind !)
  Rubbish not wholly without value, though,
Being to compliment the Duke designed
  And bring the complimenter credit so, —
Pleasure with profit happily combined.
  Thus René Gentilhomme rhymed, rhymed
    till — lo,

This happened, as he sat in an alcove
Elaborating rhyme for "love" — *not* "dove."

XXXI

He was alone : silence and solitude
  Befit the votary of the Muse. Around,
Nature — not our new picturesque and rude,
  But trim tree-cinctured stately garden-
    ground —
Breathed polish and politeness. All-imbued
  With these, he sat absorbed in one profound
Excogitation, " Were it best to hint
Or boldly boast ' She loves me — Araminte ' ? "

XXXII

When suddenly flashed lightning, searing sight
  Almost, so close to eyes ; then, quick on flash,
Followed the thunder, splitting earth down-
    right
Where René sat a-rhyming : with huge crash
Of marble into atoms infinite —
  Marble which, stately, dared the world to
    dash
The stone-thing proud, high-pillared, from its
    place :
One flash, and dust was all that lay at base.

XXXIII

So, when the horrible confusion loosed
  Its wrappage round his senses, and, with
    breath,
Seeing and hearing by degrees induced
  Conviction what he felt was life, not death —
His fluttered faculties came back to roost
  One after one, as fowls do : ay, beneath,
About his very feet there, lay in dust
Earthly presumption paid by heaven's disgust.

XXXIV

For, what might be the thunder-smitten thing
  But, pillared high and proud, in marble guise,
A ducal crown — which meant " Now Duke :
    Next, King " ?
Since such the Prince was, not in his own
    eyes
Alone, but all the world's. Pebble from sling
  Prostrates a giant ; so can pulverize
Marble pretension — how much more, make
    moult
A peacock-prince his plume — God's thunder-
    bolt !

XXXV

That was enough for René, that first fact
  Thus flashed into him. Up he looked : all
    blue
And bright the sky above ; earth firm, compact
  Beneath his footing, lay apparent too ;
Opposite stood the pillar : nothing lacked
  There, but the Duke's crown : see, its frag-
    ments strew
The earth, — about his feet lie atoms fine
Where he sat nursing late his fourteenth line !

XXXVI

So, for the moment, all the universe
  Being abolished, all 'twixt God and him, —

Earth's praise or blame, its blessing or its curse,
  Of one and the same value, — to the brim
Flooded with truth for better or for worse, —
  He pounces on the writing-paper, prim
Keeping its place on table : not a dint
Nor speck had damaged " Ode to Araminte."

XXXVII

And over the neat crowquill calligraph
  His pen goes blotting, blurring, as an ox
Tramples a flower-bed in a garden, — laugh
  You may ! — so does not he, whose quick
    heart knocks
Audibly at his breast : an epitaph
  On earth's break-up, amid the falling rocks,
He might be penning in a wild dismay,
Caught with his work half-done on Judgment
    Day.

XXXVIII

And what is it so terribly he pens,
  Ruining " Cupid, Venus, wile and smile,
Hearts, darts," and all his day's *divinior mens*
  Judged necessary to a perfect style ?
Little recks René, with a breast to cleanse,
  Of Rhadamanthine law that reigned erewhile :
Brimful of truth, truth's outburst will con-
    vince
(Style or no style) who bears truth's brunt — the
    Prince.

XXXIX

" Condé, called ' Duke,' be called just ' Duke,'
    not more,
  To life's end ! ' Next King ' thou forsooth
    wilt be ?
Ay, when this bauble, as it decked before
  Thy pillar, shall again, for France to see,
Take its proud station there ! Let France adore
  No longer an illusive mock-sun — thee —
But keep her homage for Sol's self, about
To rise and put pretenders to the rout !

XL

" What ? France so God-abandoned that her
    root
  Regal, though many a Spring it gave no sign,
Lacks power to make the bole, now branchless,
    shoot
  Greenly as ever ? Nature, though benign,
Thwarts ever the ambitious and astute.
  In store for such is punishment condign :
Sure as thy Duke's crown to the earth was
    hurled,
So sure, next year, a Dauphin glads the world ! "

XLI

Which penned — some forty lines to this effect —
  Our René folds his paper, marches brave
Back to the mansion, luminous, erect,
  Triumphant, an emancipated slave.
There stands the Prince. " How now ? My
    Duke's-crown wrecked ?
  What may this mean ? " The answer René
    gave
Was — handing him the verses, with the due
Incline of body : " Sir, God's word to you ! "

XLII

The Prince read, paled, was silent; all around,
　The courtier-company, to whom he passed
The paper, read, in equal silence bound.
　René grew also by degrees aghast
At his own fit of courage — palely found
　Way of retreat from that pale presence:
　　classed
Once more among the cony-kind. "Oh, son,
It is a feeble folk!" saith Solomon.

XLIII

Vainly he apprehended evil: since,
　When, at the year's end, even as foretold,
Forth came the Dauphin who discrowned the
　　Prince
Of that long-craved mere visionary gold,
'T was no fit time for envy to evince
　Malice, be sure! The timidest grew bold:
Of all that courtier-company not one
But left the semblance for the actual sun.

XLIV

And all sorts and conditions that stood by
　At René's burning moment, bright escape
Of soul, bore witness to the prophecy.
　Which witness took the customary shape
Of verse; a score of poets in full cry
　Hailed the inspired one. Nantes and Tours
　　agape,
Soon Paris caught the infection; gaining strength,
How could it fail to reach the Court at length?

XLV

"O poet!" smiled King Louis, "and besides,
　O prophet! Sure, by miracle announced,
My babe will prove a prodigy. Who chides
　Henceforth the unchilded monarch shall be
　　trounced
For irreligion: since the fool derides
　Plain miracle by which this prophet pounced
Exactly on the moment I should lift
Like Simeon, in my arms, a babe, 'God's gift!'

XLVI

"So call the boy! and call this bard and seer
　By a new title! him I raise to rank
Of 'Royal Poet:' poet without peer!
　Whose fellows only have themselves to thank
If humbly they must follow in the rear
　My René. He's the master: they must clank
Their chains of song, confessed his slaves; for
　why?
They poetize, while he can prophesy!"

XLVII

So said, so done; our René rose august,
　"The Royal Poet;" straightway put in type
His poem-prophecy, and (fair and just
　Procedure) added, — now that time was ripe
For proving friends did well his word to trust, —
　Those attestations, tuned to lyre or pipe,
Which friends broke out with when he dared
　foretell
The Dauphin's birth: friends trusted, and did
　well.

XLVIII

Moreover he got painted by Du Pré,
　Engraved by Daret also; and prefixed
The portrait to his book: a crown of bay
　Circled his brows, with rose and myrtle mixed.
And Latin verses, lovely in their way,
　Described him as "the biforked hill betwixt:
Since he hath scaled Parnassus at one jump,
Joining the Delphic quill and Getic trump."

XLIX

Whereof came . . . What, it lasts, our spirt
　　thus long
　— The red fire? That's the reason must
　　excuse
My letting flicker René's prophet-song
　No longer; for its pertinacious hues
Must fade before its fellow joins the throng
　Of sparks departed up the chimney, dues
To dark oblivion. At the word, it winks,
Rallies, relapses, dwindles, deathward sinks.

L

So does our poet. All this burst of fame,
　Fury of favor, Royal Poetship,
Prophetship, book, verse, picture — thereof
　　came
　— Nothing! That's why I would not let
　　outstrip
Red his green rival flamelet: just the same
　Ending in smoke waits both! In vain we rip
The past, no further faintest trace remains
Of René to reward our pious pains.

LI

Somebody saw a portrait framed and glazed
　At Croisic. "Who may be this glorified
Mortal unheard-of hitherto?" amazed
　That person asked the owner by his side,
Who proved as ignorant. The question raised
　Provoked inquiry; key by key was tried
On Croisic's portrait-puzzle, till back flew
The wards at one key's touch, which key was
　— Who?

LII

The other famous poet! Wait thy turn,
　Thou green, our red's competitor! Enough
Just now to note 't was he that itched to learn
　(A hundred years ago) how fate could puff
Heaven-high (a hundred years before), then
　　spurn
To suds so big a bubble in some huff:
Since green too found red's portrait, — having
　heard
Hitherto of red's rare self not one word.

LIII

And he with zeal addressed him to the task
　Of hunting out, by all and any means,
　— Who might the brilliant bard be, born to
　　bask
Butterfly-like in shine which kings and
　　queens
And baby-dauphins shed? Much need to ask!
　Is fame so fickle that what perks and preens

The eyed wing, one imperial minute, dips
  Next sudden moment into blind eclipse?

LIV

After a vast expenditure of pains,
  Our second poet found the prize he sought:
Urged in his search by something that re-
    strains
    From undue triumph famed ones who have
      fought,
Or simply, poetizing, taxed their brains:
    Something that tells such — dear is triumph
      bought
If it means only basking in the midst
Of fame's brief sunshine, as thou, René, didst.

LV

For, what did searching find at last but this?
  Quoth somebody, "I somehow somewhere
    seem
To think I heard one old De Chevaye is
  Or was possessed of René's works!" which
    gleam
Of light from out the dark proved not amiss
  To track, by correspondence on the theme;
And soon the twilight broadened into day,
For thus to question answered De Chevaye.

LVI

" True it is, I did once possess the works
  You want account of — works — to call them
    so, —
Comprised in one small book : the volume lurks
  (Some fifty leaves *in duodecimo*)
'Neath certain ashes which my soul it irks
  Still to remember, because long ago
That and my other rare shelf-occupants
Perished by burning of my house at Nantes.

LVII

" Yet of that book one strange particular
  Still stays in mind with me " — and there-
    upon
Followed the story. " Few the poems are;
  The book was two-thirds filled up with this
    one,
And sundry witnesses from near and far
  That here at least was prophesying done
By prophet, so as to preclude all doubt,
Before the thing he prophesied about."

LVIII

That 's all he knew, and all the poet learned,
  And all that you and I are like to hear
Of René; since not only book is burned
  But memory extinguished, — nay, I fear,
Portrait is gone too : nowhere I discerned
  A trace of it at Croisic. "Must a tear
Needs fall for that?" you smile. " How
    fortune fares
With such a mediocrity, who cares ? "

LIX

Well, I care — intimately care to have
  Experience how a human creature felt
In after-life, who bore the burden grave
  Of certainly believing God had dealt

For once directly with him : did not rave
  — A maniac, did not find his reason melt
— An idiot, but went on, in peace or strife,
The world's way, lived an ordinary life.

LX

How many problems that one fact would solve!
  An ordinary soul, no more, no less,
About whose life earth's common sights re
    volve,
  On whom is brought to bear, by thunder
    stress,
This fact — God tasks him, and will not ab
    solve
  Task's negligent performer ! Can you guess
How such a soul — the task performed to
    point —
Goes back to life nor finds things out of joint ?

LXI

Does he stand stock-like henceforth ? or pro-
    ceed
  Dizzily, yet with course straightforward still,
Down-trampling vulgar hindrance ? — as the
    reed
  Is crushed beneath its tramp when that blind
    will
Hatched in some old-world beast's brain bids
    it speed
  Where the sun wants brute-presence to fulfil
Life's purpose in a new far zone, ere ice
Enwomb the pasture-tract its fortalice.

LXII

I think no such direct plain truth consists
  With actual sense and thought and what
    they take
To be the solid walls of life : mere mists —
  How such would, at that truth's first pier-
    cing, break
Into the nullity they are ! — slight lists
  Wherein the puppet-champions wage, for
    sake
Of some mock-mistress, mimic war : laid low
At trumpet-blast, there 's shown the world, one
    foe !

LXIII

No, we must play the pageant out, observe
  The tourney-regulations, and regard
Success — to meet the blunted spear nor
    swerve,
  Failure — to break no bones yet fall on
    sward ;
Must prove we have — not courage ? well then
    — nerve !
  And, at the day's end, boast the crown's
    award —
Be warranted as promising to wield
Weapons, no sham, in a true battlefield.

LXIV

Meantime, our simulated thunderclaps
  Which tell us counterfeited truths — these
    same
Are — sound, when music storms the soul, per
    haps ?
  —Sight, beauty, every dart of every aim

That touches just, then seems, by strange re-
        lapse,
    To fall effectless from the soul it came
As if to fix its own, but simply smote
And startled to vague beauty more remote ?

LXV

So do we gain enough — yet not too much —
    Acquaintance with that outer element
Wherein there 's operation (call it such !)
    Quite of another kind than we the pent
On earth are proper to receive. Our hutch
    Lights up at the least chink : let roof be
        rent —
How inmates huddle, blinded at first spasm,
Cognizant of the sun's self through the chasm !

LXVI

Therefore, who knows if this our René's quick
    Subsidence from as sudden noise and glare
Into oblivion was impolitic ?
    No doubt his soul became at once aware
That, after prophecy, the rhyming-trick
    Is poor employment : human praises scare
Rather than soothe ears all a-tingle yet
With tones few hear and live, but none forget.

LXVII

There 's our first famous poet !   Step thou
        forth
    Second consummate songster ! See, the tongue
Of fire that typifies thee, owns thy worth
    In yellow, purple mixed its green among,
No pure and simple resin from the North,
    But composite with virtues that belong
To Southern culture ! Love not more than
        hate
Helped to a blaze . . . But I anticipate.

LXVIII

Prepare to witness a combustion rich
    And riotously splendid, far beyond
Poor René's lambent little streamer which
    Only played candle to a Court grown fond
By baby-birth : this soared to such a pitch,
    Alternately such colors doffed and donned,
That when I say it dazzled Paris — please
Know that it brought Voltaire upon his knees !

LXIX

Who did it, was a dapper gentleman,
    Paul Desforges Maillard, Croisickese by
        birth,
Whose birth that century ended which began
    By similar bestowment on our earth
Of the aforesaid René. Cease to scan
    The ways of Providence ! See Croisic's
        dearth —
Not Paris in its plenitude — suffice
To furnish France with her best poet twice !

LXX

Till he was thirty years of age, the vein
    Poetic yielded rhyme by drops and spirts :
In verses of society had lain
    His talent chiefly ; but the Muse asserts
Privilege most by treating with disdain
    Epics the bard mouths out, or odes he blurts

Spasmodically forth. Have people time
And patience nowadays for thought in rhyme ?

LXXI

So, his achievements were the quatrain's inch
    Of homage, or at most the sonnet's ell
Of admiration : welded lines with clinch
    Of ending word and word, to every belle
In Croisic's bounds ; these, brisk as any finch,
    He twittered till his fame had reached as
        well
Guérande as Batz ; but there fame stopped, for
        — curse
On fortune — outside lay the universe !

LXXII

That 's Paris. Well, — why not break bounds
        and send
    Song onward till it echo at the gates
Of Paris whither all ambitions tend,
    And end too, seeing that success there sates
The soul which hungers most for fame ? Why
        spend
    A minute in deciding, while, by Fate's
Decree, there happens to be just the prize
Proposed there, suiting souls that poetize ?

LXXIII

A prize indeed, the Academy's own self
    Proposes to what bard shall best indite
A piece describing how, through shoal and shelf,
    The Art of Navigation, steered aright,
Has, in our last king's reign, — the lucky elf, —
    Reached, one may say, Perfection's haven
        quite,
And there cast anchor. At a glance one sees
The subject's crowd of capabilities !

LXXIV

Neptune and Amphitrité ! Thetis, who
    Is either Tethys or as good — both tag !
Triton can shove along a vessel too :
    It 's Virgil ! Then the winds that blow or
        lag, —
De Maille, Vendôme, Vermandois ! Toulouse
        blew
    Longest, we reckon : he must puff the flag
To fullest outflare ; while our lacking nymph
Be Anne of Austria, Regent o'er the lymph !

LXXV

Promised, performed ! Since *irritabilis gens*
    Holds of the feverish impotence that strives
To stay an itch by prompt resource to pen's
    Scratching itself on paper ; placid lives,
Leisurely works mark the *divinior mens :*
    Bees brood above the honey in their hives ;
Gnats are the busy bustlers. Splash and
        scrawl, —
Completed lay thy piece, swift penman Paul !

LXXVI

To Paris with the product ! This dispatched,
    One had to wait the Forty's slow and sure
Verdict, as best one might. Our penman
        scratched
    Away perforce the itch that knows no cure
But daily paper-friction : more than matched

His first feat by a second — tribute pure
And heartfelt to the Forty when their voice
Should peal with one accord "Be Paul our
    choice!"

LXXVII

Scratch, scratch went much laudation of that
    sane
And sound Tribunal, delegates august
Of Phœbus and the Muses' sacred train —
Whom every poetaster tries to thrust
From where, high-throned, they dominate the
    Seine:
Fruitless endeavor, — fail it shall and must!
Whereof in witness have not one and all
The Forty voices pealed " Our choice be Paul "?

LXXVIII

Thus Paul discounted his applause. Alack
For human expectation! Scarcely ink
Was dry when, lo, the perfect piece came
    back
Rejected, shamed! Some other poet's clink
" Thetis and Tethys " had seduced the pack
Of pedants to declare perfection's pink
A singularly poor production. "Whew!
The Forty are stark fools, I always knew! "

LXXIX

First fury over (for Paul's race — to wit,
Brain-vibrios — wriggle clear of protoplasm
Into minute life that 's one fury-fit),
" These fools shall find a bard's enthusiasm
Comports with what should counterbalance it —
Some knowledge of the world! No doubt,
    orgasm
Effects the birth of verse which, born, demands
Prosaic ministration, swaddling-bands!

LXXX

" Verse must be cared for at this early stage,
    Handled, nay dandled even. I should play
Their game indeed if, till it grew of age,
    I meekly let these dotards frown away
My bantling from the rightful heritage
    Of smiles and kisses! Let the public say
If it be worthy praises or rebukes,
My poem, from these Forty old perukes! "

LXXXI

So, by a friend, who boasts himself in grace
    With no less than the Chevalier La Roque, —
Eminent in those days for pride of place,
    Seeing he had it in his power to block
The way or smooth the road to all the race
    Of literators trudging up to knock
At Fame's exalted temple-door — for why?
He edited the Paris " Mercury: " —

LXXXII

By this friend's help the Chevalier receives
    Paul's poem, prefaced by the due appeal
To Cæsar from the Jews. As duly heaves
    A sigh the Chevalier, about to deal
With case so customary — turns the leaves,
    Finds nothing there to borrow, beg, or steal —
Then brightens up the critic's brow deep-lined.
" The thing may be so cleverly declined! "

LXXXIII

Down to desk, out with paper, up with quill,
    Dip and indite! " Sir, gratitude immense
For this true draught from the Pierian rill!
    Our Academic clodpoles must be dense
Indeed to stand unirrigated still.
    No less, we critics dare not give offence
To grandees like the Forty: while we mock,
We grin and bear. So, here 's your piece! La
    Roque."

LXXXIV

" There now! " cries Paul: " the fellow can't
    avoid
Confessing that my piece deserves the palm;
And yet he dares not grant me space enjoyed
    By every scribbler he permits embalm
His crambo in the Journal's corner! Cloyed
    With stuff like theirs, no wonder if a qualm
Be caused by verse like mine: though that 's
    no cause
For his defrauding me of just applause.

LXXXV

" Aha, he fears the Forty, this poltroon?
    First let him fear me! Change smooth speech
    to rough!
I 'll speak my mind out, show the fellow soon
    Who is the foe to dread: insist enough
On my own merits till, as clear as noon,
    He sees I am no man to take rebuff
As patiently as scribblers may and must!
Quick to the onslaught, out sword, cut and
    thrust! "

LXXXVI

And thereupon a fierce epistle flings
    Its challenge in the critic's face. Alack!
Our bard mistakes his man! The gauntlet rings
    On brazen visor proof against attack.
Prompt from his editorial throne up springs
    The insulted magnate, and his mace falls,
    thwack,
On Paul's devoted brainpan, — quite away
From common courtesies of fencing-play!

LXXXVII

" Sir, will you have the truth? This piece of
    yours
    Is simply execrable past belief.
I shrank from saying so; but, since naught
    cures
    Conceit but truth, truth 's at your service!
    Brief,
Just so long as ' The Mercury ' endures,
    So long are you excluded by its Chief
From corner, nay, from cranny! Play the cock
O' the roost, henceforth, at Croisic! " wrote
    La Roque.

LXXXVIII

Paul yellowed, whitened, as his wrath from red
    Waxed incandescent. Now, this man of
    rhyme
Was merely foolish, faulty in the head
    Not heart of him: conceit 's a venial crime.
" Oh by no means malicious! " cousins said:
    Fussily feeble, — harmless all the time,

Piddling at so-called satire — well-advised,
He held in most awe whom he satirized.

LXXXIX

Accordingly his kith and kin — removed
  From emulation of the poet's gift
By power and will — these rather liked, nay,
    loved
  The man who gave his family a lift
Out of the Croisic level ; disapproved
  Satire so trenchant." Thus our poet sniffed
Home-incense, though too churlish to unlock
"The Mercury's" box of ointment was La
  Roque.

XC

But when Paul's visage grew from red to
    white,
  And from his lips a sort of mumbling fell
Of who was to be kicked, — " And serve him
    right ! "
  A gay voice interposed, " Did kicking well
Answer the purpose ! Only — if I might
  Suggest as much — a far more potent spell
Lies in another kind of treatment. Oh,
Women are ready at resource, you know !

XCI

" Talent should minister to genius ! good :
  The proper and superior smile returns.
Hear me with patience ! Have you understood
  The only method whereby genius earns
Fit guerdon nowadays ? In knightly mood
  You entered lists with visor up ; one learns
Too late that, had you mounted Roland's crest,
' Room ! ' they had roared — La Roque with all
  the rest !

XCII

" Why did you first of all transmit your piece
  To those same priggish Forty unprepared
Whether to rank you with the swans or geese
  By friendly intervention ? If they dared
Count you a cackler, — wonders never cease !
  I think it still more wondrous that you bared
Your brow (my earlier image) as if praise
Were gained by simple fighting nowadays !

XCIII

" Your next step showed a touch of the true
    means
  Whereby desert is crowned : not force but
    wile
Came to the rescue. ' Get behind the scenes ! '
  Your friend advised : he writes, sets forth
    your style
And title, to such purpose intervenes
  That you get velvet-compliment three-pile ;
And, though ' The Mercury ' said ' nay,' nor
    stock
Nor stone did his refusal prove La Roque.

XCIV

" Why must you needs revert to the high hand,
  Imperative procedure — what you call
'Taking on merit your exclusive stand ' ?
  Stand, with a vengeance ! Soon you went to
    wall.

You and your merit ! Only fools command
  When folks are free to disobey them, Paul !
You 've learnt your lesson, found out what 's
    o'clock,
By this uncivil answer of La Roque.

XCV

" Now let me counsel ! Lay this piece on shelf
  — Masterpiece though it be ! From out your
    desk
Hand me some lighter sample, verse the elf
  Cupid inspired you with, no god grotesque
Presiding o'er the Navy ! I myself
  Hand-write what 's legible yet picturesque ;
I 'll copy fair and femininely frock
Your poem masculine that courts La Roque !

XCVI

" Deidamia he — Achilles thou !
  Ha, ha, these ancient stories come so apt !
My sex, my youth, my rank I next avow
  In a neat prayer for kind perusal. Sapped
I see the walls which stand so stoutly now !
  I see the toils about the game entrapped
By honest cunning ! Chains of lady's-smock,
Not thorn and thistle, tether fast La Roque ! "

XCVII

Now, who might be the speaker sweet and arch
  That laughed above Paul's shoulder as it
    heaved
With the indignant heart ? — bade steal a
    march
  And not continue charging ? Who conceived
This plan which set our Paul, like pea you
    parch
  On fire-shovel, skipping, of a load relieved,
From arm-chair moodiness to escritoire
Sacred to Phœbus and the tuneful choir ?

XCVIII

Who but Paul's sister ! named of course like
    him
  " Desforges ; " but, mark you, in those days
    a queer
Custom obtained, — who knows whence grew
    the whim ? —
  That people could not read their title clear
To reverence till their own true names, made
    dim
  By daily mouthing, pleased to disappear,
Replaced by brand-new bright ones : Arouet,
For instance, grew Voltaire ; Desforges — Mal-
  crais.

XCIX

" Demoiselle Malcrais de la Vigne " — because
  The family possessed at Brederac
A vineyard, — few grapes, many hips-and-
    haws, —
  Still a nice Breton name. As breast and
    back
Of this vivacious beauty gleamed through
    gauze,
  So did her sprightly nature nowise lack
Lustre when draped, the fashionable way,
In " Malcrais de la Vigne," — more short,
  " Malcrais."

C

Out from Paul's escritoire behold escape
  The hoarded treasure! verse falls thick and
    fast,
Sonnets and songs of every size and shape.
  The lady ponders on her prize; at last
Selects one which — O angel and yet ape! —
  Her malice thinks is probably surpassed
In badness by no fellow of the flock,
Copies it fair, and "Now for my La Roque!"

CI

So, to him goes, with the neat manuscript,
  The soft petitionary letter. "Grant
A fledgeling novice that with wing unclipt
  She soar her little circuit, habitant
Of an old manor; buried in which crypt,
  How can the youthful châtelaine but pant
For disemprisonment by one *ad hoc*
Appointed 'Mercury's' Editor, La Roque?"

CII

'T was an epistle that might move the Turk!
  More certainly it moved our middle-aged
Pen-driver drudging at his weary work,
  Raked the old ashes up and disengaged
The sparks of gallantry which always lurk
  Somehow in literary breasts, assuaged
In no degree by compliments on style;
Are Forty wagging beards worth one girl's
    smile?

CIII

In trips the lady's poem, takes its place
  Of honor in the gratified Gazette,
With due acknowledgment of power and
    grace;
Prognostication, too, that higher yet
The Breton Muse will soar: fresh youth, high
    race.
Beauty and wealth have amicably met
That Demoiselle Malcrais may fill the chair
Left vacant by the loss of Deshoulières.

CIV

"There!" cried the lively lady. "Who was
    right —
You in the dumps, or I the merry maid
Who know a trick or two can baffle spite
  Tenfold the force of this old fool's? Afraid
Of Editor La Roque? But come! next flight
  Shall outsoar — Deshoulières alone? My
    blade,
Sappho herself shall you confess outstript!
Quick, Paul, another dose of manuscript!"

CV

And so, once well a-foot, advanced the game:
  More and more verses, corresponding gush
On gush of praise, till everywhere acclaim
  Rose to the pitch of uproar. "Sappho?
    Tush!
Sure 'Malcrais on her Parrot' puts to shame
  Deshoulières' pastorals, clay not worth a rush
Beside this find of treasure, gold in crock,
Unearthed in Brittany, — nay, ask La Roque!"

CVI

Such was the Paris tribute. "Yes," you sneer,
  "Ninnies stock Noodledom, but folk more
    sage
Resist contagious folly, never fear!"
  Do they? Permit me to detach one page
From the huge Album which from far and
    near
  Poetic praises blackened in a rage
Of rapture! and that page shall be — who
    stares
Confounded now, I ask you º — just Voltaire's!

CVII

Ay, sharpest shrewdest steel that ever stabbed
  To death Imposture through the armor-
    joints!
How did it happen that gross Humbug grabbed
  Thy weapons, gouged thine eyes out? Fate
    appoints
That pride shall have a fall, or I had blabbed
  Hardly that Humbug, whom thy soul aroints,
Could thus cross-buttock thee caught unawares,
And dismalest of tumbles proved — Voltaire's!

CVIII

See his epistle extant yet, wherewith
  "Henri" in verse and "Charles" in prose he
    sent
To do her suit and service! Here's the pith
  Of half a dozen stanzas — stones which went
To build that simulated monolith —
  Sham love in due degree with homage blent
As sham — which in the vast of volumes scares
The traveller still: "That stucco-heap — Vol-
    taire's?"

CIX

"O thou, whose clarion-voice has overflown
  The wilds to startle Paris that's one ear!
Thou who such strange capacity hast shown
  For joining all that's grand with all that's
    dear,
Knowledge with power to please — Deshou-
    lières grown
  Learned as Dacier in thy person! mere
Weak fruit of idle hours, these crabs of mine
I dare lay at thy feet, O Muse divine!

CX

"Charles was my task-work only; Henri trod
  My hero erst, and now, my heroine — she
Shall be thyself! True — is it true, great God!
  Certainly love henceforward must not be!
Yet all the crowd of Fine Arts fail — how
    odd! —
  Tried turn by turn, to fill a void in me!
There's no replacing love with these, alas!
Yet all I can I do to prove no ass.

CXI

"I labor to amuse my freedom; but
  Should any sweet young creature slavery
    preach,
And — borrowing thy vivacious charm, the
    slut! —
  Make me, in thy engaging words, a speech,
Soon should I see myself in prison shut

THE TWO POETS OF CROISIC

With all imaginable pleasure." Reach
The washhand-basin for admirers! There's
A stomach-moving tribute — and Voltaire's!

CXII

Suppose it a fantastic billet-doux,
  Adulatory flourish, not worth frown!
What say you to the Fathers of Trévoux?
  These in their Dictionary have her down
Under the heading " Author: " " Malcrais, too,
  Is 'Author' of much verse that claims re-
    nown."
While Jean-Baptiste Rousseau . . . but why
    proceed?
Enough of this — something too much, indeed!

CXIII

At last La Roque, unwilling to be left
  Behindhand in the rivalry, broke bounds
Of figurative passion hilt and heft,
  Plunged his huge downright love through
    what surrounds
The literary female bosom; reft
  Away its veil of coy reserve with " Zounds!
I love thee, Breton Beauty! All's no use!
Body and soul I love, — the big word's loose!"

CXIV

He's greatest now and to de-struc-ti-on
  Nearest. Attend the solemn word I quote,
O Paul! There's no pause at per-fec-ti-on.
  Thus knolls thy knell the Doctor's bronzèd
    throat!
Greatness a period hath, no sta-ti-on!
  Better and truer verse none ever wrote
(Despite the antique outstretched a-i-on)
Than thou, revered and magisterial Donne!

CXV

Flat on his face, La Roque, and — pressed to
    heart
  His dexter hand — Voltaire with bended
    knee!
Paul sat and sucked-in triumph; just apart
  Leaned over him his sister. "Well?"
    smirks he,
And "Well?" she answers, smiling — woman's
    art
  To let a man's own mouth, not hers, decree
What shall be next move which decides the
    game:
Success? She said so. Failure? His the
    blame.

CXVI

"Well!" this time forth affirmatively comes
  With smack of lip, and long-drawn sigh
    through teeth
Close clenched o'er satisfaction, as the gums
  Were tickled by a sweetmeat teased beneath
Palate by lubricating tongue: " Well! crumbs
  Of comfort these, undoubtedly! no death
Likely from famine at Fame's feast! 'tis clear
I may put claim in for my pittance, Dear!

CXVII

"La Roque, Voltaire, my lovers? Then dis-
    guise

Has served its turn, grows idle; let it drop!
I shall to Paris, flaunt there in men's eyes
  My proper manly garb and mount a-top
The pedestal that waits me, take the prize
  Awarded Hercules. He threw a sop
To Cerberus who let him pass, you know,
Then, following, licked his heels: exactly so!

CXVIII

" I like the prospect — their astonishment,
  Confusion: wounded vanity, no doubt,
Mixed motives; how I see the brows quick
    bent!
  'What, sir, yourself, none other, brought
    about
This change of estimation? Phœbus sent
  His shafts as from Diana?' Critic pout
Turns courtier smile: 'Lo, him we took for
    her!
Pleasant mistake! You bear no malice, sir?'

CXIX

" Eh, my Diana?" But Diana kept
  Smilingly silent with fixed needle-sharp
Much-meaning eyes that seemed to intercept
  Paul's very thoughts ere they had time to
    warp
From earnest into sport the words they leapt
  To life with — changed as when maltreated
    harp
Renders in tinkle what some player-prig
Means for a grave tune though it proves a jig.

CXX

" What, Paul, and are my pains thus thrown
    away,
  My lessons end in loss?" at length fall slow
The pitying syllables, her lips allay
  The satire of by keeping in full flow,
Above their coral reef, bright smiles at play:
  " Can it be, Paul thus fails to rightly know
And altogether estimate applause
As just so many asinine hee-haws?

CXXI

" I thought to show you" . . . "Show me,"
    Paul inbroke,
  " My poetry is rubbish, and the world
That rings with my renown a sorry joke!
  What fairer test of worth than that, form
    furled,
I entered the arena? Yet you croak
  Just as if Phœbé and not Phœbus hurled
The dart and struck the Python! What, he
    crawls
Humbly in dust before your feet, not Paul's?

CXXII

" Nay, 't is no laughing matter though absurd
  If there's an end of honesty on earth!
La Roque sends letters, lying every word!
  Voltaire makes verse, and of himself makes
    mirth
To the remotest age! Rousseau's the third
  Who, driven to despair amid such dearth
Of people that want praising, finds no one
More fit to praise than Paul the simpleton!

CXXIII

"Somebody says — if a man writes at all
    It is to show the writer's kith and kin
He was unjustly thought a natural ;
    And truly, sister, I have yet to win
Your favorable word, it seems, for Paul
    Whose poetry you count not worth a pin
Though well enough esteemed by these Vol-
        taires,
Rousseaus and such-like : let them quack, who
        cares ? "

CXXIV

" — To Paris with you, Paul ! Not one word's
        waste
    Further : my scrupulosity was vain !
Go triumph ! Be my foolish fears effaced
    From memory's record ! Go, to come again
With glory crowned, — by sister re-embraced,
    Cured of that strange delusion of her brain
Which led her to suspect that Paris gloats
On male limbs mostly when in petticoats ! "

CXXV

So laughed her last word, with the little touch
    Of malice proper to the outraged pride
Of any artist in a work too much
    Shorn of its merits. " By all means, be tried
The opposite procedure ! Cast your crutch
    Away, no longer crippled, nor divide
The credit of your march to the World's Fair
With sister Cherry-cheeks who helped you
        there ! "

CXXVI

Crippled, forsooth ! What courser sprightlier
        pranced
    Paris-ward than did Paul ? Nay, dreams
        lent wings :
He flew, or seemed to fly, by dreams en-
        tranced.
    Dreams ? wide-awake realities : no things
Dreamed merely were the missives that ad-
        vanced
    The claim of Malcrais to consort with kings
Crowned by Apollo — not to say with queens
Cinctured by Venus for Idalian scenes.

CXXVII

Soon he arrives, forthwith is found before
    The outer gate of glory. Bold tic-toc
Announces there's a giant at the door.
    "Ay, sir, here dwells the Chevalier La
        Roque."
"Lackey ! Malcrais — mind, no word less nor
        more ! —
    Desires his presence. I 've unearthed the
        brock :
Now, to transfix him ! " There stands Paul
        erect,
Inched out his uttermost, for more effect.

CXXVIII

A bustling entrance : " Idol of my flame !
    Can it be that my heart attains at last
Its longing ? that you stand, the very same
        As in my visions ? . . . Ha ! hey, how ? "
            aghast

Stops short the rapture. "Oh, my boy's to
        blame !
    You merely are the messenger ! Too fast
My fancy rushed to a conclusion. Pooh !
Well, sir, the lady's substitute is — who ? "

CXXIX

Then Paul's smirk grows inordinate. "Shake
        hands !
    Friendship not love awaits you, master mine,
Though nor Malcrais nor any mistress stands
    To meet your ardor ! So, you don't divine
Who wrote the verses wherewith ring the
        land's
    Whole length and breadth ? Just he where-
        of no line
Had ever leave to blot your Journal — eh ?
Paul Desforges Maillard — otherwise Malcrais ! "

CXXX

And there the two stood, stare confronting
        smirk,
    A while uncertain which should yield the
        pas.
In vain the Chevalier beat brain for quirk
    To help in this conjuncture ; at length,
        " Bah !
Boh ! Since I 've made myself a fool, why
        shirk
    The punishment of folly ? Ha, ha, ha,
Let me return your handshake ! " Comic sock
For tragic buskin prompt thus changed La
Roque.

CXXXI

" I 'm nobody — a wren-like journalist ;
    You 've flown at higher game and winged
        your bird,
The golden eagle ! That 's the grand acquist !
    Voltaire's sly Muse, the tiger-cat, has purred
Prettily round your feet ; but if she missed
    Priority of stroking, soon were stirred
The dormant spitfire. To Voltaire ! away,
Paul Desforges Maillard, otherwise Malcrais ! "

CXXXII

Whereupon, arm in arm, and head in air,
    The two begin their journey. Need I say,
La Roque had felt the talon of Voltaire,
    Had a long-standing little debt to pay,
And pounced, you may depend, on such a rare
    Occasion for its due discharge ? So, gay
And grenadier-like, marching to assault,
They reach the enemy's abode, there halt.

CXXXIII

" I 'll be announcer ! " quoth La Roque : " I
        know,
    Better than you, perhaps, my Breton bard,
How to procure an audience ! He 's not slow
    To smell a rat, this scamp Voltaire ! Dis-
        card
The petticoats too soon, — you 'll never show
    Your haut-de-chausses and all they 've made
        or marred
In your true person. Here 's his servant.
        Pray,
Will the great man see Demoiselle Malcrais ? "

CXXXIV

Now, the great man was also, no whit less,
  The man of self-respect, — more great man
  he !
And bowed to social usage, dressed the dress,
  And decorated to the fit degree
His person ; 't was enough to bear the stress
  Of battle in the field, without, when free
From outside foes, inviting friends' attack
By — sword in hand ? No, — ill-made coat on
  back.

CXXXV

And, since the announcement of his visitor
  Surprised him at his toilet, — never glass
Had such solicitation ! " Black, now — or
  Brown be the killing wig to wear ? Alas,
Where 's the rouge gone, this cheek were better
  for
A tender touch of ? Melted to a mass,
All my pomatum ! There 's at all events
A devil — for he 's got among my scents ! "

CXXXVI

So, " barbered ten times o'er," as Antony
  Paced to his Cleopatra, did at last
Voltaire proceed to the fair presence : high
  In color, proud in port, as if a blast
Of trumpet bade the world " Take note ! draws
  nigh
To Beauty, Power ! Behold the Iconoclast,
The Poet, the Philosopher, the Rod
Of iron for imposture ! Ah my God ! "

CXXXVII

For there stands smirking Paul, and — what
  lights fierce
The situation as with sulphur flash —
There grinning stands La Roque ! No carte-
  and-tierce
Observes the grinning fencer, but, full dash
From breast to shoulder-blade, the thrusts
  transpierce
That armor against which so idly clash
The swords of priests and pedants ! Victors
  there,
Two smirk and grin who have befooled — Vol-
  taire !

CXXXVIII

A moment's horror ; then quick turn-about
  On high-heeled shoe, — flurry of ruffles,
  flounce
Of wig-ties and of coat-tails, — and so out
  Of door banged wrathfully behind, goes —
  bounce —
Voltaire in tragic exit ! vows, no doubt,
  Vengeance upon the couple. Did he trounce
Either, in point of fact ? His anger's flash
Subsided if a culprit craved his cash.

CXXXIX

As for La Roque, he having laughed his laugh
  To heart's content, — the joke defunct at
  once,
Dead in the birth, you see, — its epitaph
  Was sober earnest. " Well, sir, for the
  nonce,

You 've gained the laurel ; never hope to graff
  A second sprig of triumph there ! Ensconce
Yourself again at Croisic : let it be
Enough you mastered both Voltaire and — me !

CXL

" Don't linger here in Paris to parade
  Your victory, and have the very boys
Point at you ! ' There 's the little mouse
  which made
Believe those two big lions that its noise,
  Nibbling away behind the hedge, conveyed
  Intelligence that — portent which destroys
All courage in the lion's heart, with horn
That 's fable — there lay couched the unicorn ! '

CXLI

" Beware us, now we 've found who fooled us !
  Quick
To cover ! ' In proportion to men's fright,
  Expect their fright's revenge ! ' quoth politic
  Old Macchiavelli. As for me, — all 's right :
I 'm but a journalist. But no pin's prick
  The tooth leaves when Voltaire is roused to
  bite !
So, keep your counsel, I advise ! Adieu !
Good journey ! Ha, ha, ha, Malcrais was —
  you ! "

CXLII

" — Yes, I 'm Malcrais, and somebody beside,
  You snickering monkey ! " thus winds up
  the tale
Our hero, safe at home, to that black-eyed
  Cherry-cheeked sister, as she soothes the
  pale
Mortified poet. " Let their worst be tried,
  I'm their match henceforth — very man and
  male !
Don't talk to me of knocking-under ! man
And male must end what petticoats began !

CXLIII

" How woman-like it is to apprehend
  The world will eat its words ! why, words
  transfixed
To stone, they stare at you in print, — at end,
  Each writer's style and title ! Choose be-
  twixt
Fool and knave for his name, who should intend
  To perpetrate a baseness so unmixed
With prospect of advantage ! What is writ
Is writ : they 've praised me, there 's an end of
  it !

CXLIV

" No, Dear, allow me ! I shall print these
  same
Pieces, with no omitted line, as Paul's.
Malcrais no longer, let me see folk blame
  What they — praised simply ? — placed on
  pedestals,
Each piece a statue in the House of Fame !
  Fast will they stand there, though their
  presence galls
The envious crew : such show their teeth,
  perhaps,
And snarl, but never bite ! I know the chaps ! '

CXLV

O Paul, oh, piteously deluded! Pace
  Thy sad sterility of Croisic flats,
Watch, from their southern edge, the foamy
    race
Of high-tide as it heaves the drowning mats
Of yellow-berried web-growth from their place,
  The rock-ridge, when, rolling as far as Batz,
One broadside crashes on it, and the crags,
That needle under, stream with weedy rags!

CXLVI

Or, if thou wilt, at inland Bergerac,
  Rude heritage but recognized domain,
Do as two here are doing: make hearth crack
  With logs until thy chimney roar again
Jolly with fire-glow! Let its angle lack
  No grace of Cherry-cheeks thy sister, fain
To do a sister's office and laugh smooth
Thy corrugated brow — that scowls forsooth!

CXLVII

Wherefore? Who does not know how these
    La Roques,
  Voltaires, can say and unsay, praise and
    blame,
.rove black white, white black, play at para-
    dox
  And, when they seem to lose it, win the
    game?
Care not thou what this badger, and that fox,
  His fellow in rascality, call "fame!"
Fiddlepin's end! Thou hadst it, — quack,
    quack, quack!
Have quietude from geese at Bergerac!

CXLVIII

Quietude! For, be very sure of this!
  A twelvemonth hence, and men shall know
    or care
As much for what to-day they clap or hiss
  As for the fashion of the wigs they wear,
Then wonder at. There 's fame which, bale or
    bliss, —
  Got by no gracious word of great Voltaire
Or not-so-great La Roque, — is taken back
By neither, any more than Bergerac!

CXLIX

Too true! or rather, true as ought to be!
  No more of Paul the man, Malcrais the maid,
Thenceforth forever! One or two, I see,
  Stuck by their poet: who the longest stayed
Was Jean-Baptiste Rousseau, and even he
  Seemingly saddened as perforce he paid
A rhyming tribute: "After death, survive —
He hoped he should: and died while yet
    alive!"

CL

No, he hoped nothing of the kind, or held
  His peace and died in silent good old age.
Him it was, curiosity impelled
  To seek if there were extant still some page
Of his great predecessor, rat who belled
  The cat once, and would never deign engage
In after-combat with mere mice, — saved from
More sonneteering, — René Gentilhomme.

CLI

Paul's story furnished forth that famous play
  Of Piron's "Métromanie:" there you 'll
    find
He 's Francaleu, while Demoiselle Malcrais
  Is Demoiselle No-end-of-names-behind!
As for Voltaire, he 's Damis. Good and gay
  The plot and dialogue, and all 's designed
To spite Voltaire: at "Something" such the
    laugh
Of simply "Nothing!" (see his epitaph).

CLII

But truth, truth, that 's the gold! and all the
    good
  I find in fancy is, it serves to set
Gold's inmost glint free, gold which comes up
    rude
  And rayless from the mine. All fume and
    fret
Of artistry beyond this point pursued
  Brings out another sort of burnish: yet
Always the ingot has its very own
Value, a sparkle struck from truth alone.

CLIII

Now, take this sparkle and the other spirt
  Of fitful flame, — twin births of our gray
    brand
That 's sinking fast to ashes! I assert,
  As sparkles want but fuel to expand
Into a conflagration no mere squirt
  Will quench too quickly, so might Croisic
    strand,
Had Fortune pleased posterity to chowse,
Boast of her brace or beacons luminous.

CLIV

Did earlier Agamemnons lack their bard?
  But later bards lacked Agamemnon too!
How often frustrate they of fame's award
  Just because Fortune, as she listed, blew
Some slight bark's sails to bellying, mauled
    and marred
  And forced to put about the First-rate!
    True,
Such tacks but for a time: still — small-craft
    ride
At anchor, rot while Beddoes breasts the tide!

CLV

Dear, shall I tell you? There 's a simple test
  Would serve, when people take on them to
    weigh
The worth of poets. "Who was better, best,
  This, that, the other bard?" (Bards none
    gainsay
As good, observe! no matter for the rest.)
  "What quality preponderating may
Turn the scale as it trembles?" End the
    strife
By asking "Which one led a happy life?"

CLVI

If one did, over his antagonist
  That yelled or shrieked or sobbed or wept or
    wailed
Or simply had the dumps, — dispute who list. —

I count him victor. Where his fellow failed,
Mastered by his own means of might, — acquist
Of necessary sorrows, — he prevailed,
A strong since joyful man who stood distinct
Above slave-sorrows to his chariot linked.

CLVII

Was not his lot to feel more? What meant
    "feel"
Unless to suffer! Not, to see more?
    Sight —
What helped it but to watch the drunken reel
Of vice and folly round him, left and right,
One dance of rogues and idiots! Not, to deal
    More with things lovely? What provoked
        the spite
Of filth incarnate, like the poet's need
Of other nutriment than strife and greed!

CLVIII

Who knows most, doubts most; entertaining
    hope,
    Means recognizing fear; the keener sense
Of all comprised within our actual scope
    Recoils from aught beyond earth's dim and
        dense.
Who, grown familiar with the sky, will grope
    Henceforward among groundlings? That's
        offence
Just as indubitably: stars abound
O'erhead, but then — what flowers make glad
    the ground!

CLIX

So, force is sorrow, and each sorrow, force:
    What then? since Swiftness gives the char-
        ioteer
The palm, his hope be in the vivid horse
    Whose neck God clothed with thunder, not
        the steer
Sluggish and safe! Yoke Hatred, Crime, Re-
    morse,
    Despair: but ever 'mid the whirling fear,
Let, through the tumult, break the poet's face
Radiant, assured his wild slaves win the race!

CLX

Therefore I say . . . no, shall not say, but
    think,
    And save my breath for better purpose.
        White
From gray our log has burned to: just one
    blink
That quivers, loth to leave it, as a sprite
The outworn body. Ere your eyelids' wink
    Punish who sealed so deep into the night
Your mouth up, for two poets dead so long, —
Here pleads a live pretender: right your
    wrong!

What a pretty tale you told me
    Once upon a time
— Said you found it somewhere (scold me!)
Was it prose or was it rhyme,
Greek or Latin? Greek, you said,
While your shoulder propped my head.

Anyhow there's no forgetting
    This much if no more,
That a poet (pray, no petting!)
Yes, a bard, sir, famed of yore,
Went where suchlike used to go,
Singing for a prize, you know.

Well, he had to sing, nor merely
    Sing but play the lyre;
Playing was important clearly
Quite as singing: I desire,
Sir, you keep the fact in mind
For a purpose that's behind.

There stood he, while deep attention
    Held the judges round,
— Judges able, I should mention,
To detect the slightest sound
Sung or played amiss: such ears
Had old judges, it appears!

None the less he sang out boldly.
    Played in time and tune,
Till the judges, weighing coldly
Each note's worth, seemed, late or soon,
Sure to smile "In vain one tries
Picking faults out: take the prize!"

When, a mischief! Were they seven
    Strings the lyre possessed?
Oh, and afterwards eleven,
    Thank you! Well, sir, — who had guessed
Such ill luck in store? — it happed
One of those same seven strings snapped.

All was lost, then! No! a cricket
    (What "cicada"? Pooh!)
— Some mad thing that left its thicket
    For mere love of music — flew
With its little heart on fire,
Lighted on the crippled lyre.

So that when (Ah, joy!) our singer
    For his truant string
Feels with disconcerted finger,
    What does cricket else but fling
Fiery heart forth, sound the note
Wanted by the throbbing throat?

Ay and, ever to the ending,
    Cricket chirps at need,
Executes the hand's intending,
    Promptly, perfectly, — indeed
Saves the singer from defeat
With her chirrup low and sweet.

Till, at ending, all the judges
    Cry with one assent
"Take the prize — a prize who grudges
    Such a voice and instrument?
Why, we took your lyre for harp,
So it shrilled us forth F sharp!"

Did the conqueror spurn the creature,
    Once its service done?
That's no such uncommon feature
    In the case when Music's son

Finds his Lotte's power too spent
For aiding soul-development.

No! This other, on returning
    Homeward, prize in hand,
Satisfied his bosom's yearning:
    (Sir, I hope you understand!)
— Said " Some record there must be
Of this cricket's help to me!"

So, he made himself a statue:
    Marble stood, life-size ;
On the lyre, he pointed at you,
    Perched his partner in the prize ;
Never more apart you found
Her, he throned, from him, she crowned.

That's the tale : its application?
    Somebody I know
Hopes one day for reputation
    Through his poetry that's — Oh,
All so learned and so wise
And deserving of a prize!

If he gains one, will some ticket,
    When his statue 's built,
Tell the gazer " 'T was a cricket
    Helped my crippled lyre, whose lilt
Sweet and low, when strength usurped
Softness' place i' the scale, she chirped?

" For as victory was nighest,
    While I sang and played, —
With my lyre at lowest, highest,
    Right alike, — one string that made
' Love ' sound soft was snapt in twain,
Never to be heard again, —

" Had not a kind cricket fluttered,
    Perched upon the place
Vacant left, and duly uttered
    ' Love, Love, Love,' whene'er the bass
Asked the treble to atone
For its somewhat sombre drone."

But you don't know music! Wherefore
    Keep on casting pearls

To a — poet? All I care for
    Is — to tell him that a girl's
" Love " comes aptly in when gruff
    Grows his singing. (There, enough!)

OH LOVE! LOVE

Translation of a lyric in the *Hyppolytus* of
Euripides, and printed by J. P. Mahaffy in his
Euripides, 1879. Mr. Mahaffy writes: " Mr.
Browning has honored me with the following
translation of these stanzas, so that the general
reader may not miss the meaning or the spirit
of the ode. The English metre, though not a
strict reproduction, gives an excellent idea of
the original."

I

OH Love ! Love, thou that from the eyes dif-
        fusest
Yearning, and on the soul sweet grace indu-
        cest —
Souls against whom thy hostile march is made —
Never to me be manifest in ire,
Nor, out of time and tune, my peace invade !
Since neither from the fire —
No, nor from the stars — is launched a bolt
        more mighty
Than that of Aphrodité
Hurled from the hands of Love, the boy with
        Zeus for sire.

II

Idly, how idly, by the Alpheian river
And in the Pythian shrines of Phœbus, quiver
Blood-offerings from the bull, which Hellas
        heaps :
While Love we worship not — the Lord of men !
Worship not him, the very key who keeps
Of Aphrodité, when
She closes up her dearest chamber-portals :
— Love, when he comes to mortals,
Wide-wasting, through those deeps of woes be-
        yond the deep !

DRAMATIC IDYLS

FIRST SERIES

THE *Dramatic Idyls*, a group of poems which indicated a return to Browning's earlier manner, furnished the title for two successive volumes, the first series published in 1879, the second the year following. The poems in the first series were composed while Browning and his sister were sojourning in a mountain hotel near the summit of the Splügen Pass in the summer of 1878. So stimulated was Browning by the mountain air that he composed with extraordinary rapidity, even for him, bringing down upon himself his sister's determined caution.

MARTIN RELPH

My grandfather says he remembers he saw, when
    a youngster long ago,
On a bright May day, a strange old man, with a
    beard as white as snow,
Stand on the hill outside our town like a monu-
    ment of woe,
And, striking his bare bald head the while, sob out
    the reason — so !

If I last as long as Methuselah I shall never for-
    give myself :
But — God forgive me, that I pray, unhappy
    Martin Relph,
As coward, coward I call him — him, yes, him !
    Away from me !
Get you behind the man I am now, you man
    that I used to be !

What can have sewed my mouth up, set me
    a-stare, all eyes, no tongue ?
People have urged, " You visit a scare too hard
    on a lad so young !
You were taken aback, poor boy," they urge,
    " no time to regain your wits :
Besides it had maybe cost your life." Ay, there
    is the cap which fits !

So, cap me, the coward, — thus ! No fear ! A
    cuff on the brow does good :
The feel of it hinders a worm inside which bores
    at the brain for food.
See now, there certainly seems excuse : for a
    moment, I trust, dear friends,
The fault was but folly, no fault of mine, or if
    mine, I have made amends !

For, every day that is first of May, on the hill-
    top, here stand I,
Martin Relph, and I strike my brow, and pub-
    lish the reason why,
When there gathers a crowd to mock the fool.
    No fool, friends, since the bite
Of a worm inside is worse to bear : pray God I
    have balked him quite !

I 'll tell you. Certainly much excuse ! It came
    of the way they cooped
Us peasantry up in a ring just here, close hud-
    dling because tight-hooped
By the red-coats round us villagers all : they
    meant we should see the sight

And take the example, — see, not speak, for
    speech was the Captain's right.

" You clowns on the slope, beware ! " cried he :
    " This woman about to die
Gives by her fate fair warning to such acquaint-
    ance as play the spy.
Henceforth who meddle with matters of state
    above them perhaps will learn
That peasants should stick to their plough-
    tail, leave to the King the King's con-
    cern.

" Here 's a quarrel that sets the land on fire, be-
    tween King George and his foes :
What call has a man of your kind — much less,
    a woman — to interpose ?
Yet you needs must be meddling, folk like you,
    not foes — so much the worse !
The many and loyal should keep themselves
    unmixed with the few perverse.

" Is the counsel hard to follow ? I gave it you
    plainly a month ago,
And where was the good ? The rebels have
    learned just all that they need to know.
Not a month since in we quietly marched : a
    week, and they had the news,
From a list complete of our rank and file to a
    note of our caps and shoes.

" All about all we did and all we were doing
    and like to do !
Only, I catch a letter by luck, and capture who
    wrote it, too.
Some of you men look black enough, but the
    milk-white face demure
Betokens the finger foul with ink : 't is a woman
    who writes, be sure !

" Is it ' Dearie, how much I miss your mouth ! '
    — good natural stuff, she pens ?
Some sprinkle of that, for a blind, of course :
    with talk about cocks and hens,
How ' robin has built on the apple-tree, and our
    creeper which came to grief
Through the frost, we feared, is twining afresh
    round casement in famous leaf.'

" But all for a blind ! She soon glides frank
    into ' Horrid the place is grown
With Officers here and Privates there, no nook
    we may call our own :

And Farmer Giles has a tribe to house, and
    lodging will be to seek
For the second Company sure to come ('t is
    whispered) on Monday week.'

" And so to the end of the chapter ! There !
    The murder, you see, was out :
Easy to guess how the change of mind in the
    rebels was brought about !
Safe in the trap would they now lie snug, had
    treachery made no sign :
But treachery meets a just reward, no matter
    if fools malign !

" That traitors had played us false, was proved
    — sent news which fell so pat :
And the murder was out — this letter of love,
    the sender of this sent that !
'T is an ugly job, though, all the same — a
    hateful, to have to deal
With a case of the kind, when a woman 's
    in fault : we soldiers need nerves of
    steel !

" So, I gave her a chance, despatched post-haste
    a message to Vincent Parkes
Whom she wrote to ; easy to find he was, since
    one of the King's own clerks,
Ay, kept by the King's own gold in the town
    close by where the rebels camp :
A sort of a lawyer, just the man to betray our
    sort — the scamp !

" ' If her writing is simple and honest and only
    the lover-like stuff it looks,
And if you yourself are a loyalist, nor down in
    the rebels' books,
Come quick,' said I, ' and in person prove you
    are each of you clear of crime,
Or martial law must take its course : this day
    next week 's the time ! '

" Next week is now : does he come ? Not he !
    Clean gone, our clerk, in a trice !
He has left his sweetheart here in the lurch :
    no need of a warning twice !
His own neck free, but his partner's fast in the
    noose still, here she stands
To pay for her fault. 'T is an ugly job : but
    soldiers obey commands.

" And hearken wherefore I make a speech !
    Should any acquaintance share
The folly that led to the fault that is now to be
    punished, let fools beware !
Look black, if you please, but keep hands
    white : and, above all else, keep wives —
Or sweethearts or what they may be — from
    ink ! Not a word now, on your lives ! "

Black ? but the Pit's own pitch was white to
    the Captain's face — the brute
With the bloated cheeks and the bulgy nose
    and the bloodshot eyes to suit !
He was muddled with wine, they say : more
    like, he was out of his wits with fear ;

He had but a handful of men, that 's true, — a
    riot might cost him dear.

And all that time stood Rosamund Page, with
    pinioned arms and face
Bandaged about, on the turf marked out for
    the party's firing-place.
I hope she was wholly with God : I hope 't was
    his angel stretched a hand
To steady her so, like the shape of stone you
    see in our church-aisle stand.

I hope there was no vain fancy pierced the
    bandage to vex her eyes,
No face within which she missed without, no
    questions and no replies —
" Why did you leave me to die ? " — " Be-
    cause " . . . Oh, fiends, too soon you
    grin
At merely a moment of hell, like that — such
    heaven as hell ended in !

Let mine end too ! He gave the word, up went
    the guns in a line.
Those heaped on the hill were blind as dumb,
    — for, of all eyes, only mine
Looked over the heads of the foremost rank.
    Some fell on their knees in prayer,
Some sank to the earth, but all shut eyes, with
    a sole exception there.

That was myself, who had stolen up last, had
    sidled behind the group :
I am highest of all on the hill-top, there stand
    fixed while the others stoop !
From head to foot in a serpent's twine am I
    tightened : I touch ground ?
No more than a gibbet's rigid corpse which the
    fetters rust around !

Can I speak, can I breathe, can I burst — aught
    else but see, see, only see ?
And see I do — for there comes in sight — a
    man, it sure must be ! —
Who staggeringly, stumblingly rises, falls, rises,
    at random flings his weight
On and on, anyhow onward — a man that 's
    mad he arrives too late !

Else why does he wave a something white high-
    flourished above his head ?
Why does not he call, cry, — curse the fool ! —
    why throw up his arms instead ?
O take this fist in your own face, fool ! Why
    does not yourself shout " Stay !
Here 's a man comes rushing, might and main,
    with something he 's mad to say " ?

And a minute, only a moment, to have hell-fire
    boil up in your brain,
And ere you can judge things right, choose
    heaven, — time 's over, repentance vain !
They level : a volley, a smoke and the clearing
    of smoke : I see no more
Of the man smoke hid, nor his frantic arms, nor
    the something white he bore.

But stretched on the field, some half-mile off,
 is an object. Surely dumb,
Deaf, blind were we struck, that nobody heard,
 not one of us saw him come !
Has he fainted through fright ? One may well
 believe ! What is it he holds so fast ?
Turn him over, examine the face ! Heyday !
 What, Vincent Parkes at last ?

Dead ! dead as she, by the selfsame shot : one
 bullet has ended both,
Her in the body and him in the soul. They
 laugh at our plighted troth.
"Till death us do part ? " Till death us do
 join past parting — that sounds like
Betrothal indeed ! O Vincent Parkes, what
 need has my fist to strike ?

I helped you : thus were you dead and wed :
 one bound, and your soul reached hers !
There is clenched in your hand the thing, signed,
 sealed, the paper which plain avers
She is innocent, innocent, plain as print, with
 the King's Arms broad engraved :
No one can hear, but if any one high on the hill
 can see, she 's saved !

And torn his garb and bloody his lips with
 heart-break — plain it grew
How the week's delay had been brought about :
 each guess at the end proved true.
It was hard to get at the folk in power : such
 waste of time ! and then
Such pleading and praying, with, all the while,
 his lamb in the lions' den !

And at length when he wrung their pardon out,
 no end to the stupid forms —
The license and leave : I make no doubt —
 what wonder if passion warms
The pulse in a man if you play with his heart ?
 — he was something hasty in speech ;
Anyhow, none would quicken the work : he
 had to beseech, beseech !

And the thing once signed, sealed, safe in his
 grasp, — what followed but fresh delays ?
For the floods were out, he was forced to take
 such a roundabout of ways !
And 't was " Halt there ! " at every turn of
 the road, since he had to cross the thick
Of the red-coats : what did they care for him
 and his " Quick, for God's sake, quick ! "

Horse ? but he had one : had it how long ? till
 the first knave smirked " You brag
Yourself a friend of the King's ? then lend to a
 King's friend here your nag ! "
Money to buy another ? Why, piece by piece
 they plundered him still,
With their " Wait you must, — no help : if
 aught can help you, a guinea will ! "

And a borough there was — I forget the name
 — whose Mayor must have the bench
Of Justices ranged to clear a doubt : for
 " Vincent," thinks he, sounds French !

It well may have driven him daft, God knows !
 all man can certainly know
Is — rushing and falling and rising, at last he
 arrived in a horror — so !

When a word, cry, gasp, would have rescued
 both ! Ay, bite me ! The worm begins
At his work once more. Had cowardice proved
 — that only — my sin of sins !
Friends, look you here ! Suppose . . . suppose
 . . . But mad I am, needs must be !
Judas the Damned would never have dared
 such a sin as I dream ! For, see !

Suppose I had sneakingly loved her myself, my
 wretched self, and dreamed
In the heart of me " She were better dead than
 happy and his ! " — while gleamed
A light from hell as I spied the pair in a per-
 fectest embrace,
He the savior and she the saved, — bliss born
 of the very murder-place !

No ! Say I was scared, friends ! Call me fool
 and coward, but nothing worse !
Jeer at the fool and gibe at the coward ! 'T was
 ever the coward's curse
That fear breeds fancies in such : such take
 their shadow for substance still,
— A fiend at their back. I liked poor Parkes,
 — loved Vincent, if you will !

And her — why, I said " Good morrow " to her,
 " Good even," and nothing more :
The neighborly way ! She was just to me as
 fifty had been before.
So, coward it is and coward shall be ! There 's
 a friend, now ! Thanks ! A drink
Of water I wanted : and now I can walk, get
 home by myself, I think.

PHEIDIPPIDES

Χαίρετε, νικῶμεν.

First I salute this soil of the blessed, river and
 rock !
Gods of my birthplace, dæmons and heroes,
 honor to all !
Then I name thee, claim thee for our patron,
 co-equal in praise
— Ay, with Zeus the Defender, with Her of
 the ægis and spear !
Also, ye of the bow and the buskin, praised be
 your peer,
Now, henceforth and forever, — O latest to
 whom I upraise
Hand and heart and voice ! For Athens, leave
 pasture and flock !
Present to help, potent to save, Pan — patron
 I call !

Archons of Athens, topped by the tettix, see, I
 return !
See, 't is myself here standing alive, no spectre
 that speaks !

Crowned with the myrtle, did you command
  me, Athens and you,
⁵⁶ Run, Pheidippides, run and race, reach Sparta
  for aid !
Persia has come, we are here, where is She ? "
  Your command I obeyed,
Ran and raced : like stubble, some field which
  a fire runs through,
Was the space between city and city : two
  days, two nights did I burn
Over the hills, under the dales, down pits and
  up peaks.

Into their midst I broke : breath served but for
  " Persia has come !
Persia bids Athens proffer slaves'-tribute, water
  and earth ;
Razed to the ground is Eretria — but Athens,
  shall Athens sink,
Drop into dust and die — the flower of Hellas
  utterly die,
Die, with the wide world spitting at Sparta,
  the stupid, the stander-by ?
Answer me quick, what help, what hand do
  you stretch o'er destruction's brink ?
How, — when ? No care for my limbs ! —
  there 's lightning in all and some —
Fresh and fit your message to bear, once lips
  give it birth ! "

O my Athens — Sparta love thee ? Did Sparta
  respond ?
Every face of her leered in a furrow of envy,
  mistrust,
Malice, — each eye of her gave me its glitter
  of gratified hate !
Gravely they turned to take counsel, to cast for
  excuses. I stood
Quivering, — the limbs of me fretting as fire
  frets, an inch from dry wood :
" Persia has come, Athens asks aid, and still
  they debate ?
Thunder, thou Zeus ! Athene, are Spartans a
  quarry beyond
Swing of thy spear ? Phoibos and Artemis,
  clang them ' Ye must ' ! "

No bolt launched from Olumpos ! Lo, their
  answer at last !
" Has Persia come, — does Athens ask aid, —
  may Sparta befriend ?
Nowise precipitate judgment — too weighty
  the issue at stake !
Count we no time lost time which lags through
  respect to the gods !
Ponder that precept of old, ' No warfare, what-
  ever the odds
In your favor, so long as the moon, half-orbed,
  is unable to take
Full-circle her state in the sky ! ' Already she
  rounds to it fast :
Athens must wait, patient as we — who judg-
  ment suspend."

Athens, — except for that sparkle, — thy name,
  I had mouldered to ash !
That sent a blaze through my blood; off, off
  and away was I back,

— Not one word to waste, one look to lose on
  the false and the vile !
Yet " O gods of my land ! " I cried, as each
  hillock and plain,
Wood and stream, I knew, I named, rushing
  past them again,
" Have ye kept faith, proved mindful of honors
  we paid you erewhile ?
Vain was the filleted victim, the fulsome liba-
  tion ! Too rash
Love in its choice, paid you so largely service
  so slack !

" Oak and olive and bay, — I bid you cease to
  enwreathe
Brows made bold by your leaf ! Fade at the
  Persian's foot,
You that, our patrons were pledged, should
  never adorn a slave !
Rather I hail thee, Parnes, — trust to thy wild
  waste tract !
Treeless, herbless, lifeless mountain ! What
  matter if slacked
My speed may hardly be, for homage to crag
  and to cave
No deity deigns to drape with verdure ? at
  least I can breathe,
Fear in thee no fraud from the blind, no lie
  from the mute ! "

Such my cry as, rapid, I ran over Parnes'
  ridge ;
Gully and gap I clambered and cleared till,
  sudden, a bar
Jutted, a stoppage of stone against me, block-
  ing the way.
Right ! for I minded the hollow to traverse,
  the fissure across :
" Where I could enter. there I depart by !
  Night in the fosse ?
Athens to aid ? Though the dive were through
  Erebos, thus I obey —
Out of the day dive, into the day as bravely
  arise ! No bridge
Better ! " — when — ha ! what was it I came on,
  of wonders that are ?

There, in the cool of a cleft, sat he — majestical
  Pan !
Ivy drooped wanton, kissed his head, moss
  cushioned his hoof :
All the great god was good in the eyes grave-
  kindly — the curl
Carved on the bearded cheek, amused at a
  mortal's awe,
As, under the human trunk, the goat-thighs
  grand I saw.
" Halt, Pheidippides ! " — halt I did, my brain
  of a whirl :
" Hither to me ! Why pale in my presence ? "
  he gracious began :
" How is it, — Athens, only in Hellas, holds me
  aloof ?

" Athens, she only, rears me no fane, makes
  me no feast !
Wherefore ? Than I what godship to Athens
  more helpful of old ?

Go, bid Athens take heart, laugh Persia to
    scorn, have faith
In the temples and tombs! Go, say to Athens,
    'The Goat-God saith:
When Persia — so much as strews not the soil
    — is cast in the sea,
Then praise Pan who fought in the ranks with
    your most and least,
Goat-thigh to greaved-thigh, made one cause
    with the free and the bold!'

"Say Pan saith: 'Let this, foreshowing the
    place, be the pledge!'"
(Gay, the liberal hand held out this herbage I
    bear
— Fennel — I grasped it a-tremble with dew —
    whatever it bode)
"While, as for thee" . . . But enough! He
    was gone. If I ran hitherto —
Be sure that, the rest of my journey, I ran no
    longer, but flew.
Parnes to Athens — earth no more, the air was
    my road:
Here am I back. Praise Pan, we stand no
    more on the razor's edge!
Pan for Athens, Pan for me! I too have a
    guerdon rare!

Then spoke Miltiades. "And thee, best run-
    ner of Greece,
Whose limbs did duty indeed, — what gift is
    promised thyself?
Tell it us straightway, — Athens the mother
    demands of her son!"
Rosily blushed the youth: he paused: but,
    lifting at length
His eyes from the ground, it seemed as he
    gathered the rest of his strength
Into the utterance — " Pan spoke thus: 'For
    what thou hast done
Count on a worthy reward! Henceforth be
    allowed thee release
From the racer's toil, no vulgar reward in
    praise or in pelf!'

"I am bold to believe, Pan means reward the
    most to my mind!
Fight I shall, with our foremost, wherever this
    fennel may grow, —
Pound — Pan helping us — Persia to dust, and,
    under the deep,
Whelm her away forever; and then, — no
    Athens to save, —
Marry a certain maid, I know keeps faith to
    the brave, —
Hie to my house and home: and, when my
    children shall creep
Close to my knees, — recount how the God was
    awful yet kind,
Promised their sire reward to the full — re-
    warding him — so!"

Unforeseeing one! Yes, he fought on the Mara-
    thon day:
So, when Persia was dust, all cried "To Akro-
    polis!

Run, Pheidippides, one race more! the meed is
    thy due!
'Athens is saved, thank Pan,' go shout!" He
    flung down his shield,
Ran like fire once more: and the space 'twixt
    the Fennel-field
And Athens was stubble again, a field which a
    fire runs through,
Till in he broke: "Rejoice, we conquer!"
    Like wine through clay,
Joy in his blood bursting his heart, he died —
    the bliss!

So, to this day, when friend meets friend, the
    word of salute
Is still "Rejoice!" — his word which brought
    rejoicing indeed.
So is Pheidippides happy forever, — the noble
    strong man
Who could race like a god, bear the face of a
    god, whom a god loved so well;
He saw the land saved he had helped to save,
    and was suffered to tell
Such tidings, yet never decline, but, gloriously
    as he began,
So to end gloriously — once to shout, thereafter
    be mute:
"Athens is saved!" — Pheidippides dies in the
    shout for his meed.

HALBERT AND HOB

HERE is a thing that happened. Like wild
    beasts whelped, for den,
In a wild part of North England, there lived
    once two wild men
Inhabiting one homestead, neither a hovel nor
    hut,
Time out of mind their birthright: father and
    son, these — but —
Such a son, such a father! Most wildness by
    degrees
Softens away: yet, last of their line, the wild-
    est and worst were these.

Criminals, then? Why, no: they did not mur-
    der and rob;
But, give them a word, they returned a blow —
    old Halbert as young Hob:
Harsh and fierce of word, rough and savage of
    deed,
Hated or feared the more — who knows? — the
    genuine wild-beast breed.

Thus were they found by the few sparse folk of
    the countryside;
But how fared each with other? E'en beasts
    couch, hide by hide,
In a growling, grudged agreement: so, father
    and son aye curled
The closelier up in their den because the last of
    their kind in the world.

Still, beast irks beast on occasion. One Christ-
    mas night of snow,
Came father and son to words — such words!
    more cruel because the blow

To crown each word was wanting, while taunt
    matched gibe, and curse
Competed with oath in wager, like pastime in
    hell, — nay, worse :
For pastime turned to earnest, as up there
    sprang at last
The son at the throat of the father, seized him
    and held him fast.

"Out of this house you go !" (there followed a
    hideous oath) —
"This oven where now we bake, too hot to
    hold us both !
If there 's snow outside, there 's coolness : out
    with you, bide a spell
In the drift and save the sexton the charge of a
    parish shell ! "

Now, the old trunk was tough, was solid as
    stump of oak
Untouched at the core by a thousand years :
    much less had its seventy broke
One whipcord nerve in the muscly mass from
    neck to shoulder-blade
Of the mountainous man, whereon his child's
    rash hand like a feather weighed.

Nevertheless at once did the mammoth shut his
    eyes,
Drop chin to breast, drop hands to sides, stand
    stiffened — arms and thighs
All of a piece — struck mute, much as a sentry
    stands,
Patient to take the enemy's fire : his captain so
    commands.

Whereat the son's wrath flew to fury at such
    sheer scorn
Of his puny strength by the giant eld thus act-
    ing the babe new-born :
And "Neither will this turn serve ! " yelled he.
    "Out with you ! Trundle, log !
If you cannot tramp and trudge like a man, try
    all-fours like a dog ! "

Still the old man stood mute. So, logwise, —
    down to floor
Pulled from his fireside place, dragged on from
    hearth to door, —
Was he pushed, a very log, staircase along,
    until
A certain turn in the steps was reached, a yard
    from the house-door-sill.

Then the father opened eyes — each spark of
    their rage extinct, —
Temples, late black, dead-blanched, — right-
    hand with left-hand linked, —
He faced his son submissive ; when slow the
    accents came,
They were strangely mild though his son's rash
    hand on his neck lay all the same.

"Hob, on just such a night of a Christmas long
    ago,
For such a cause, with such a gesture, did I
    drag — so —

My father down thus far : but, softening here
    I heard
A voice in my heart, and stopped : you wait for
    an outer word,

"For your own sake, not mine, soften you too !
    Untrod
Leave this last step we reach, nor brave the
    finger of God !
I dared not pass its lifting : I did well. I nor
    blame
Nor praise you. I stopped here : and, Hob, do
    you the same ! "

Straightway the son relaxed his hold of the
    father's throat.
They mounted, side by side, to the room again :
    no note
Took either of each, no sign made each to
    either : last
As first, in absolute silence, their Christmas-
    night they passed.

At dawn, the father sate on, dead, in the self-
    same place,
With an outburst blackening still the old bad
    fighting-face :
But the son crouched all a-tremble like any
    lamb new-yeaned.

When he went to the burial, some one's staff he
    borrowed, — tottered and leaned.
But his lips were loose, not locked, — kept mut-
    tering, mumbling. "There !
At his cursing and swearing ! " the youngsters
    cried : but the elders thought "In
    prayer."
A boy threw stones : he picked them up and
    stored them in his vest.

So tottered, muttered, mumbled he, till he
    died, perhaps found rest.
"Is there a reason in nature for these hard
    hearts ? " O Lear,
That a reason out of nature must turn them
    soft, seems clear !

IVÀN IVÀNOVITCH

"THEY tell me, your carpenters," quoth I to
    my friend the Russ,
"Make a simple hatchet serve as a tool-box
    serves with us.
Arm but each man with his axe, 't is a hammer
    and saw and plane
And chisel, and — what know I else ?   We
    should imitate in vain
The mastery wherewithal, by a flourish of just
    the adze,
He cleaves, clamps, dovetails in, — no need of
    our nails and brads, —
The manageable pine : 't is said he could shave
    himself
With the axe, — so all adroit, now a giant and
    now an elf,
Does he work and play at once ! "

Quoth my friend the Russ to me,
Ay, that and more beside on occasion ! It
    scarce may be
You never heard tell a tale told children, time
    out of mind,
By father and mother and nurse, for a moral
    that 's behind,
Which children quickly seize. If the incident
    happened at all,
We place it in Peter's time when hearts were
    great not small,
Germanized, Frenchified. I wager 't is old to
    you
As the story of Adam and Eve, and possibly
    quite as true."

In the deep of our land, 't is said, a village
    from out the woods
Emerged on the great main-road 'twixt two
    great solitudes.
Through forestry right and left, black verst
    and verst of pine,
From village to village runs the road's long
    wide bare line.
Clearance and clearance break the else-uncon-
    quered growth
Of pine and all that breeds and broods there,
    leaving loth
Man's inch of masterdom, — spot of life, spirt
    of fire, —
To star the dark and dread, lest right and rule
    expire
Throughout the monstrous wild, a-hungered to
    resume
Its ancient sway, suck back the world into its
    womb:
Defrauded by man's craft which clove from
    North to South
This highway broad and straight e'en from the
    Neva's mouth
To Moscow's gates of gold. So, spot of life
    and spirt
Of fire aforesaid, burn, each village death-
    begirt
By wall and wall of pine — unprobed un-
    dreamed abyss.

Early one winter morn, in such a village as
    this,
Snow-whitened everywhere except the middle
    road
Ice-roughed by track of sledge, there worked
    by his abode
Ivàn Ivànovitch, the carpenter, employed
On a huge shipmast trunk; his axe now
    trimmed and toyed
With branch and twig, and now some chop
    athwart the bole
Changed bole to billets, bared at once the sap
    and soul.
About him, watched the work his neighbors
    sheepskin-clad ;
Each bearded mouth puffed steam, each gray
    eye twinkled glad
To see the sturdy arm which, never stopping
    play,

Proved strong man's blood still boils, freeze
    winter as he may.
Sudden, a burst of bells. Out of the road, on
    edge
Of the hamlet — horse's hoofs galloping.
    " How, a sledge ?
What 's here ? " cried all as — in, up to the
    open space,
Workyard and market-ground, folk's common
    meeting-place, —
Stumbled on, till he fell, in one last bound for
    life,
A horse : and, at his heels, a sledge held —
    " Dmìtri's wife !
Back without Dmìtri too ! and children —
    where are they ?
Only a frozen corpse ! "

          They drew it forth : then — " Nay,
Not dead, though like to die ! Gone hence a
    month ago :
Home again, this rough jaunt — alone through
    night and snow —
What can the cause be ? Hark — Droug, old
    horse, how he groans :
His day 's done ! Chafe away, keep chafing,
    for she moans :
She 's coming to ! Give here : see, motherkin,
    your friends !
Cheer up, all safe at home ! Warm inside
    makes amends
For outside cold, — sup quick ! Don't look as
    we were bears !
What is it startles you ? What strange ad-
    venture stares
Up at us in your face ? You know friends —
    which is which ?
I 'm Vàssili, he 's Sergeì, Ivàn Ivànovitch " —

At the word, the woman's eyes, slow-wander-
    ing till they neared
The blue eyes o'er the bush of honey-colored
    beard,
Took in full light and sense and — torn to rags,
    some dream
Which hid the naked truth — O loud and long
    the scream
She gave, as if all power of voice within her
    throat
Poured itself wild away to waste in one dread
    note !
Then followed gasps and sobs, and then the
    steady flow
Of kindly tears : the brain was saved, a man
    might know.
Down fell her face upon the good friend's
    propping knee ;
His broad hands smoothed her head, as fain to
    brush it free
From fancies, swarms that stung like bees
    unhived. He soothed —
"Loukèria, Loùscha ! " — still he, fondling,
    smoothed and smoothed.
At last her lips formed speech.

          " Ivan, dear — you indeed,
You, just the same dear you ! While I . . . Oh,
    intercede,

Sweet Mother, with thy Son Almighty — let his
    might
Bring yesterday once more, undo all done last
    night !
But this time yesterday, Ivàn, I sat like you,
A child on either knee, and, dearer than the
    two,
A babe inside my arms, close to my heart —
    that 's lost
In morsels o'er the snow !   Father, Son, Holy
    Ghost,
Cannot you bring again my blessed yesterday ? "

When no more tears would flow, she told her
    tale : this way.

" Maybe, a month ago, — was it not ? — news
    came here,
They wanted, deeper down, good workmen fit
    to rear
A church and roof it in.   ' We 'll go,' my
    husband said :
' None understands like me to melt and mould
    their lead.'
So, friends here helped us off — Ivàn, dear,
    you the first !
How gay we jingled forth, all five — (my heart
    will burst) —
While Dmìtri shook the reins, urged Droug
    upon his track !

" Well, soon the month ran out, we just were
    coming back,
When yesterday — behold, the village was on
    fire !
Fire ran from house to house.   What help, as,
    nigh and nigher,
The flames came furious ?   ' Haste,' cried
    Dmìtri, ' men must do
The little good man may : to sledge and in with
    you,
You and our three !   We check the fire by
    laying flat
Each building in its path, — I needs must stay
    for that, —
But you . . . no time for talk !   Wrap round
    you every rug,
Cover the couple close, — you 'll have the babe
    to hug.
No care to guide old Droug, he knows his way,
    by guess,
Once start him on the road : but chirrup, none
    the less !
The snow lies glib as glass and hard as steel,
    and soon
You 'll have rise, fine and full, a marvel of a
    moon.
Hold straight up, all the same, this lighted
    twist of pitch !
Once home and with our friend Ivàn Ivànovitch,
All 's safe : I have my pay in pouch, all 's right
    with me,
So I but find as safe you and our precious
    three !
Off, Droug ! ' — because the flames had reached
    us, and the men
Shouted ' But lend a hand, Dmìtri — as good
    as ten !'

" So, in we bundled — I, and those God gave
    me once ;
Old Droug, that 's stiff at first, seemed youth-
    ful for the nonce :
He understood the case, galloping straight
    ahead.
Out came the moon : my twist soon dwindled,
    feebly red
In that unnatural day — yes, daylight, bred
    between
Moonlight and snow-light, lamped those grotto-
    depths which screen
Such devils from God's eye.   Ah, pines, how
    straight you grow,
Nor bend one pitying branch, true breed of
    brutal snow !
Some undergrowth had served to keep the
    devils blind
While we escaped outside their border !

                " Was that — wind ?
Anyhow, Droug starts, stops, back go his ears,
    he snuffs,
Snorts, — never such a snort !   then plunges,
    knows the sough 's
Only the wind : yet, no — our breath goes up
    too straight !
Still the low sound, — less low, loud, louder, at
    a rate
There 's no mistaking more !   Shall I lean out
    — look — learn
The truth whatever it be ?   Pad, pad !   At
    last, I turn —

" 'T is the regular pad of the wolves in pursuit
    of the life in the sledge !
An army they are : close-packed they press like
    the thrust of a wedge :
They increase as they hunt : for I see, through
    the pine-trunks ranged each side,
Slip forth new fiend and fiend, make wider and
    still more wide
The four-footed steady advance.   The fore-
    most — none may pass :
They are elders and lead the line, eye and eye
    — green-glowing brass !
But a long way distant still.   Droug, save us !
    He does his best :
Yet they gain on us, gain, till they reach, —
    one reaches . . . How utter the rest ?
O that Satan-faced first of the band !   How he
    lolls out the length of his tongue,
How he laughs and lets gleam his white teeth !
    He is on me, his paws pry among
The wraps and the rugs !   O my pair, my twin-
    pigeons, lie still and seem dead !
Stepàn, he shall never have you for a meal, —
    here 's your mother instead !
No, he will not be counselled — must cry, poor
    Stiòpka, so foolish ! though first
Of my boy-brood, he was not the best : nay,
    neighbors have called him the worst :
He was puny, an undersized slip, — a darling to
    me, all the same !
But little there was to be praised in the boy,
    and a plenty to blame.
I loved him with heart and soul, yes — but
    deal him a blow for a fault,

He would sulk for whole days.   'Foolish boy!
   lie still or the villain will vault,
Will snatch you from over my head!' No use!
   he cries, screams, — who can hold
Fast a boy in a frenzy of fear! It follows — as
   I foretold!
The Satan-face snatched and snapped: I
   tugged, I tore — and then
His brother too needs must shriek! If one
   must go, 't is men
The Tsar needs, so we hear, not ailing boys!
   Perhaps
My hands relaxed their grasp, got tangled in
   the wraps!
God, he was gone! I looked: there tumbled
   the cursed crew,
Each fighting for a share: too busy to pursue!
That's so far gain at least: Droug, gallop an-
   other verst
Or two, or three — God sends we beat them,
   arrive the first!
A mother who boasts two boys was ever ac-
   counted rich:
Some have not a boy: some have, but lose him,
   — God knows which
Is worse: how pitiful to see your weakling
   pine
And pale and pass away! Strong brats, this
   pair of mine!

"O misery! for while I settle to what near
   seems
Content, I am 'ware again of the tramp, and
   again there gleams —
Point and point — the line, eyes, levelled
   green brassy fire!
So soon is resumed your chase? Will nothing
   appease, naught tire
The furies? And yet I think — I am certain
   the race is slack,
And the numbers are nothing like. Not a quar-
   ter of the pack!
Feasters and those full-fed are staying behind
   . . . Ah, why?
We'll sorrow for that too soon! Now, — gallop,
   reach home, and die,
Nor ever again leave house, to trust our life in
   the trap
For life — we call a sledge! Teriòscha, in my
   lap!
Yes, I'll lie down upon you, tight-tie you with
   the strings
Here — of my heart! No fear, this time, your
   mother flings . . .
Flings? I flung? Never! But think! — a
   woman, after all,
Contending with a wolf! Save you I must and
   shall,
Terentii!
   "How now? What, you still head the race,
Your eyes and tongue and teeth crave fresh
   food, Satan-face?
There and there! Plain I struck green fire
   out! Flash again?
All a poor fist can do to damage eyes proves
   vain!
My fist — why not crunch that? He is wanton
   for . . . O God,

Why give this wolf his taste? Common wolves
   scrape and prod
The earth till out they scratch some corpse —
   mere putrid flesh!
Why must this glutton leave the faded, choose
   the fresh?
Terentii — God, feel! — his neck keeps fast
   thy bag
Of holy things, saints' bones, this Satan-face
   will drag
Forth, and devour along with him, our Pope
   declared
The relics were to save from danger!

       "Spurned, not spared!
'T was through my arms, crossed arms, he —
   nuzzling now with snout,
Now ripping, tooth and claw — plucked, pulled
   Terentii out,
A prize indeed! I saw — how could I else but
   see? —
My precious one — I bit to hold back — pulled
   from me!
Up came the others, fell to dancing — did the
   imps! —
Skipped as they scampered round. There's
   one is gray, and limps:
Who knows but old bad Màrpha — she always
   owed me spite
And envied me my births — skulks out of
   doors at night
And turns into a wolf, and joins the sisterhood,
And laps the youthful life, then slinks from
   out the wood,
Squats down at door by dawn, spins there de-
   mure as erst
— No strength, old crone, — not she! — to
   crawl forth half a verst!

"Well, I escaped with one: 'twixt one and
   none there lies
The space 'twixt heaven and hell. And see, a
   rose-light dyes
The endmost snow: 't is dawn, 't is day, 't is
   safe at home!
We have outwitted you! Ay, monsters, snarl
   and foam,
Fight each the other fiend, disputing for a
   share, —
Forgetful, in your greed, our finest off we bear,
Tough Droug and I, — my babe, my boy that
   shall be man,
My man that shall be more, do all a hunter can
To trace and follow and find and catch and
   crucify
Wolves, wolfkins, all your crew! A thousand
   deaths shall die
The whimperingest cub that ever squeezed the
   teat!
'Take that!' we'll stab you with, — 'the ten-
   derness we met
When, wretches, you danced round, — not this,
   thank God — not this!
Hellhounds, we balk you!'

      "But — Ah, God above! — Bliss, bliss, —
Not the band, no! And yet — yes, for Droug
   knows him! One —

This only of them all has said 'She saves a
son!'
His fellows disbelieve such luck: but he be-
lieves,
He lets them pick the bones, laugh at him in
their sleeves:
He's off and after us, — one speck, one spot,
one ball
Grows bigger, bound on bound, — one wolf as
good as all!
Oh, but I know the trick! Have at the snaky
tongue!
That's the right way with wolves! Go, tell
your mates I wrung
The panting morsel out, left you to howl your
worst!
Now for it — now! Ah me! I know him —
thrice-accurst
Satan-face, — him to the end my foe!

                    "All fight's in vain:
This time the green brass points pierce to my
very brain.
I fall — fall as I ought — quite on the babe I
guard:
I overspread with flesh the whole of him. Too
hard
To die this way, torn piecemeal? Move hence?
Not I — one inch!
Gnaw through me, through and through: flat
thus I lie nor flinch!
O God, the feel of the fang furrowing my
shoulder! — see!
It grinds — it grates the bone. O Kìrill under
me,
Could I do more? Besides he knew wolf's way
to win:
I clung, closed round like wax: yet in he
wedged and in,
Past my neck, past my breasts, my heart, until
. . . how feels
The onion-bulb your knife parts, pushing
through its peels,
Till out you scoop its clove wherein lie stalk
and leaf
And bloom and seed unborn?

                    "That slew me: yes, in brief,
I died then, dead I lay doubtlessly till Droug
stopped
Here, I suppose. I come to life, I find me
propped
Thus, — how or when or why — I know not.
Tell me, friends,
All was a dream: laugh quick and say the
nightmare ends!
Soon I shall find my house: 't is over there: in
proof,
Save for that chimney heaped with snow,
you 'd see the roof
Which holds my three — my two — my one —
not one?

                    "Life's mixed
With misery, yet we live — must live. The
Satan fixed
His face on mine so fast, I took its print as
pitch

Takes what it cools beneath. Ivàn Ivànovitch,
'T is you unharden me, you thaw, disperse the
thing!
Only keep looking kind, the horror will not
cling.
Your face smooths fast away each print of
Satan. Tears
— What good they do! Life's sweet, and all
its after-years,
Ivàn Ivànovitch, I owe you! Yours am I!
May God reward you, dear!"

                    Down she sank. Solemnly
Ivàn rose, raised his axe, — for fitly, as she
knelt,
Her head lay: well-apart, each side, her arms
hung, — dealt
Lightning-swift thunder-strong one blow — no
need of more!
Headless she knelt on still: that pine was
sound at core
(Neighbors were used to say) — cast-iron-ker-
nelled — which
Taxed for a second stroke Ivàn Ivànovitch.

The man was scant of words as strokes. "It
had to be:
I could no other: God it was, bade 'Act for
me!'"
Then stooping, peering round — what is it now
he lacks?
A proper strip of bark wherewith to wipe his
axe.
Which done, he turns, goes in, closes the door
behind.
The others mute remain, watching the blood-
snake wind
Into a hiding-place among the splinter-heaps.

At length, still mute, all move: one lifts —
from where it steeps
Redder each ruddy rag of pine — the head:
two more
Take up the dripping body: then, mute still
as before,
Move in a sort of march, march on till march-
ing ends
Opposite to the church; where halting, — who
suspends,
By its long hair, the thing, deposits in its place
The piteous head: once more the body shows
no trace
Of harm done: there lies whole the Loùscha,
maid and wife
And mother, loved until this latest of her life.
Then all sit on the bank of snow which bounds
a space
Kept free before the porch of judgment: just
the place!

Presently all the souls, man, woman, child,
which make
The village up, are found assembling for the
sake
Of what is to be done. The very Jews are
there:
A Gypsy-troop, though bound with horses for
the Fair,

Squats with the rest. Each heart with its con-
ception seethes
And simmers, but no tongue speaks: one may
say, — none breathes.

Anon from out the church totters the Pope —
the priest —
Hardly alive, so old, a hundred years at least.
With him, the Commune's head, a hoary senior
too,
Stàrosta, that 's his style, — like Equity Judge
with you, —
Natural Jurisconsult: then, fenced about with
furs,
Pomeschìk, — Lord of the Land, who wields —
and none demurs —
A power of life and death. They stoop, survey
the corpse.

Then, straightened on his staff, the Stàrosta —
the thorpe's
Sagaciousest old man — hears what you just
have heard,
From Droug's first inrush, all, up to Ivàn's
last word —
" God bade me act for him: I dared not dis-
obey ! "

Silence — the Pomeschìk broke with " A wild
wrong way
Of righting wrong — if wrong there were, such
wrath to rouse !
Why was not law observed ? What article
allows
Whoso may please to play the judge, and, judg-
ment dealt,
Play executioner, as promptly as we pelt
To death, without appeal, the vermin whose
sole fault
Has been — it dared to leave the darkness of its
vault,
Intrude upon our day ! Too sudden and too
rash !
What was this woman's crime ? Suppose the
church should crash
Down where I stand, your lord : bound are my
serfs to dare
Their utmost that I 'scape: yet, if the crashing
scare
My children — as you are, — if sons fly, one and
all,
Leave father to his fate, — poor cowards though
I call
The runaways, I pause before I claim their life
Because they prized it more than mine. I would
each wife
Died for her husband's sake, each son to save
his sire :
'T is glory, I applaud — scarce duty, I require.
Ivàn Ivànovitch has done a deed that 's named
Murder by law and me: who doubts, may
speak unblamed ! "

All turned to the old Pope. " Ay, children, I
am old —
How old, myself have got to know no longer.
Rolled
Quite round, my orb of life, from infancy to age,

Seems passing back again to youth. A certain
stage
At least I reach, or dream I reach, where I dis-
cern
Truer truths, laws behold more lawlike than we
learn
When first we set our foot to tread the course I
trod
With man to guide my steps: who leads me
now is God.
' Your young men shall see visions : ' and in my
youth I saw
And paid obedience to man's visionary law :
' Your old men shall dream dreams: ' and, in
my age, a hand
Conducts me through the cloud round law to
where I stand
Firm on its base, — know cause, who, before,
knew effect.

" The world lies under me : and nowhere I detect
So great a gift as this — God's own — of human
life.
' Shall the dead praise thee ? ' No ! ' The
whole live world is rife,
God, with thy glory,' rather ! Life then, God's
best of gifts,
For what shall man exchange ? For life — when
so he shifts
The weight and turns the scale, lets life for life
restore
God's balance, sacrifice the less to gain the
more,
Substitute — for low life, another's or his own —
Life large and liker God's who gave it : thus
alone
May life extinguish life that life may trulier be !
How low this law descends on earth, is not for
me
To trace : complexed becomes the simple, intri-
cate
The plain, when I pursue law's winding. 'T is
the straight
Outflow of law I know and name: to law, the
fount
Fresh from God's footstool, friends, follow while
I remount.

" A mother bears a child: perfection is com-
plete
So far in such a birth. Enabled to repeat
The miracle of life, — herself was born so just
A type of womankind, that God sees fit to trust
Her with the holy task of giving life in turn.
Crowned by this crowning pride, how say you,
should she spurn
Regality — discrowned, unchilded, by her choice
Of barrenness exchanged for fruit which made
rejoice
Creation, though life's self were lost in giving
birth
To life more fresh and fit to glorify God's earth ?
How say you, should the hand God trusted with
life's torch
Kindled to light the world — aware of sparks
that scorch,
Let fall the same ? Forsooth, her flesh a fire-
flake stings :

The mother drops the child! Among what
   monstrous things
Shall she be classed? Because of motherhood,
   each male
Yields to his partner place, sinks proudly in the
   scale:
His strength owned weakness, wit — folly, and
   courage — fear,
Beside the female proved male's mistress —
   only here.
The fox-dam, hunger-pined, will slay the felon
   sire
Who dares assault her whelp: the beaver,
   stretched on fire,
Will die without a groan: no pang avails to
   wrest
Her young from where they hide — her sanctu-
   ary breast.
What's here then? Answer me, thou dead one,
   as, I trow,
Standing at God's own bar, he bids thee answer
   now!
Thrice crowned wast thou — each crown of
   pride, a child — thy charge!
Where are they? Lost? Enough: no need
   that thou enlarge
On how or why the loss: life left to utter 'lost'
Condemns itself beyond appeal. The soldier's
   post
Guards from the foe's attack the camp he senti-
   nels:
That he no traitor proved, this and this only
   tells —
Over the corpse of him trod foe to foe's success.
Yet — one by one thy crowns torn from thee —
   thou no less
To scare the world, shame God, — livedst! I
   hold he saw
The unexampled sin, ordained the novel law,
Whereof first instrument was first intelligence
Found loyal here. I hold that, failing human
   sense,
The very earth had oped, sky fallen, to efface
Humanity's new wrong, motherhood's first dis-
   grace.
Earth oped not, neither fell the sky, for prompt
   was found
A man and man enough, head-sober and heart-
   sound,
Ready to hear God's voice, resolute to obey.
Ivàn Ivànovitch, I hold, has done, this day,
No otherwise than did, in ages long ago,
Moses when he made known the purport of that
   flow
Of fire athwart the law's twain-tables! I pro-
   claim
Ivàn Ivànovitch God's servant!"

              At which name
Uprose that creepy whisper from out the crowd,
   is wont,
To swell and surge and sink when fellow-men
   confront
A punishment that falls on fellow flesh and
   blood,
Appallingly beheld — shudderingly understood,
No less, to be the right, the just, the merciful.
"God's servant!" hissed the crowd.

When the Amen grew dull
And died away and left acquittal plain ad-
   judged,
"Amen!" last sighed the lord. "There's
   none shall say I grudged
Escape from punishment in such a novel case.
Deferring to old age and holy life, — be grace
Granted! say I. No less, scruples might shake
   a sense
Firmer than I boast mine. Law's law, and
   evidence
Of breach therein lies plain, — blood-red-bright,
   — all may see!
Yet all absolve the deed: absolved the deed
   must be!

"And next — as mercy rules the hour — me-
   thinks 't were well
You signify forthwith its sentence, and dispel
The doubts and fears, I judge, which busy now
   the head
Law puts a halter round — a halo — you, in-
   stead!
Ivàn Ivànovitch — what think you he expects
Will follow from his feat? Go, tell him — law
   protects
Murder, for once: no need he longer keep be-
   hind
The Sacred Pictures — where skulks Innocence
   enshrined,
Or I missay! Go, some! You others, haste
   and hide
The dismal object there: get done, whate'er
   betide!"

So, while the youngers raised the corpse, the
   elders trooped
Silently to the house: where halting, some one
   stooped,
Listened beside the door; all there was silent
   too.
Then they held counsel; then pushed door
   and, passing through,
Stood in the murderer's presence.
                        Ivàn Ivànovitch
Knelt, building on the floor that Kremlin rare
   and rich
He deftly cut and carved on lazy winter nights.
Some five young faces watched, breathlessly, as,
   to rights,
Piece upon piece, he reared the fabric nigh
   complete.
Stèscha, Ivàn's old mother, sat spinning by the
   heat
Of the oven where his wife Kàtia stood baking
   bread.
Ivàn's self, as he turned his honey-colored head,
Was just in act to drop, 'twixt fir-cones, — each
   a dome, —
The scooped-out yellow gourd presumably the
   home
Of Kolokol the Big: the bell, therein to hitch,
— An acorn-cup — was ready: Ivàn Ivànovitch
Turned with it in his mouth.

                  They told him he was free
As air to walk abroad. "How otherwise?"
   asked he.

TRAY

This poem describes an actual incident witnessed in Paris by a friend of Browning's, and with accuracy of detail. The poem was written as a protest against vivisection, which the poet called "an infamous practice." He was early associated with Miss Frances Power Cobbe in her efforts to prevent vivisection; and he was a vice-president of the "Victoria Street Society for the Protection of Animals." Dr. Berdoe says, "He always expressed the utmost abhorrence of the practices which it opposes." To Miss Cobbe he wrote in 1874: "You have heard, 'I take an equal interest with yourself in the effort to suppress vivisection.' I dare not so honor my mere wishes and prayers as to put them for a moment beside your noble acts; but this I know, I would rather submit to the worst of deaths, so far as pain goes, than have a single dog or cat tortured on the pretence of sparing me a twinge or two." He goes even so far as to say that the person not willing to sign the petition against vivisection certainly could not be numbered among his friends. To Miss Stackpoole he wrote in April, 1883: "I despise and abhor the pleas on behalf of that infamous practice, vivisection." G. W. COOKE.

SING me a hero! Quench my thirst
Of soul, ye bards!

    Quoth Bard the first:
"Sir Olaf, the good knight, did don
His helm and eke his habergeon " . . .
Sir Olaf and his bard ———!

"That sin-scathed brow " (quoth Bard the second),
"That eye wide ope as though Fate beckoned
My hero to some steep, beneath
Which precipice smiled tempting death " . . .
You too without your host have reckoned!

"A beggar-child " (let 's hear this third!)
"Sat on a quay's edge: like a bird
Sang to herself at careless play,
And fell into the stream. 'Dismay!
Help, you the standers-by!' None stirred.

'Bystanders reason, think of wives
And children ere they risk their lives.
Over the balustrade has bounced
A mere instinctive dog, and pounced
Plumb on the prize. 'How well he dives!

" 'Up he comes with the child, see, tight
In mouth, alive too, clutched from quite
A depth of ten feet — twelve, I bet!
Good dog! What, off again? There 's yet
Another child to save? All right!

" How strange we saw no other fall!
It 's instinct in the animal.
Good dog! But he 's a long while under:
If he got drowned I should not wonder —
Strong current, that against the wall!

" ' Here he comes, holds in mouth this time
— What may the thing be? Well, that 's prime!
Now, did you ever? Reason reigns
In man alone, since all Tray's pains
Have fished — the child's doll from the slime!'

" And so, amid the laughter gay,
Trotted my hero off, — old Tray, —
Till somebody, prerogatived
With reason, reasoned: 'Why he dived,
His brain would show us, I should say.

" 'John, go and catch — or, if needs be,
Purchase — that animal for me!
By vivisection, at expense
Of half-an-hour and eighteenpence,
How brain secretes dog's soul, we 'll see!' "

NED BRATTS

Written from memory of Bunyan's story of old Tod in *The Life and Death of Mr. Badman.*

'T WAS Bedford Special Assize, one daft Midsummer's Day:
A broiling blasting June, — was never its like, men say.
Corn stood sheaf-ripe already, and trees looked yellow as that;
Ponds drained dust-dry, the cattle lay foaming around each flat.
Inside town, dogs went mad, and folk kept bibbing beer,
While the parsons prayed for rain. 'T was horrible, yes — but queer:
Queer — for the sun laughed gay, yet nobody moved a hand
To work one stroke at his trade: as given to understand
That all was come to a stop, work and such worldly ways,
And the world's old self about to end in a merry blaze,
Midsummer's day moreover was the first of Bedford Fair;
With Bedford Town's tag-rag and bobtail a-bowsing there.

But the Court House, Quality crammed: through doors ope, windows wide,
High on the Bench you saw sit Lordships side by side.
There frowned Chief Justice Jukes, fumed learned Brother Small,
And fretted their fellow Judge: like threshers, one and all,
Of a reek with laying down the law in a furnace. Why?
Because their lungs breathed flame — the regular crowd forbye —

From gentry pouring in — quite a nosegay, to be
    sure !
How else could they pass the time, six mortal
    hours endure
Till night should extinguish day, when matters
    might haply mend ?
Meanwhile no bad resource was — watching be-
    gin and end
Some trial for life and death, in a brisk five
    minutes' space,
And betting which knave would 'scape, which
    hang, from his sort of face.

So, their Lordships toiled and moiled, and a
    deal of work was done
(I warrant) to justify the mirth of the crazy sun,
As this and t' other lout, struck dumb at the
    sudden show
Of red robes and white wigs, boggled nor
    answered " Boh ! "
When asked why he, Tom Styles, should not —
    because Jack Nokes
Had stolen the horse — be hanged : for Judges
    must have their jokes,
And louts must make allowance — let 's say,
    for some blue fly
Which punctured a dewy scalp where the
    frizzles stuck awry —
Else Tom had fleered scot-free, so nearly over
    and done
Was the main of the job. Full-measure, the
    gentles enjoyed their fun,
As a twenty-five were tried, rank puritans
    caught at prayer
In a cow-house and laid by the heels, — have at
    'em, devil may care ! —
And ten were prescribed the whip, and ten a
    brand on the cheek,
And five a slit of the nose — just leaving enough
    to tweak.

Well, things at jolly high-tide, amusement
    steeped in fire,
While noon smote fierce the roof's red tiles to
    heart's desire,
The Court a-simmer with smoke, one ferment
    of oozy flesh,
One spirituous humming musk mount-mounting
    until its mesh
Entoiled all heads in a fluster, and Serjeant
    Postlethwayte
— Dashing the wig oblique as he mopped his
    oily pate —
Cried " Silence, or I grow grease ! No loophole
    lets in air ?
Jurymen, — Guilty, Death ! Gainsay me if
    you dare ! "
— Things at this pitch, I say, — what hubbub
    without the doors ?
What laughs, shrieks, hoots and yells, what
    rudest of uproars ?

Bounce through the barrier throng a bulk comes
    rolling vast !
Thumps, kicks, — no manner of use ! — spite of
    them rolls at last
Into the midst a ball, which, bursting, brings
    to view

Publican Black Ned Bratts and Tabby his big
    wife too :
Both in a muck-sweat, both . . . were never
    such eyes uplift
At the sight of yawning hell, such nostrils —
    snouts that sniffed
Sulphur, such mouths agape ready to swallow
    flame !
Horrified, hideous, frank fiend-faces ! yet, all
    the same,
Mixed with a certain . . . eh ? how shall I dare
    style — mirth
The desperate grin of the guess that, could they
    break from earth,
Heaven was above, and hell might rage in
    impotence
Below the saved, the saved !

           " Confound you ! (no offence !)
Out of our way, — push, wife ! Yonder their
    Worships be ! "
Ned Bratts has reached the bar, and " Hey,
    my Lords," roars he,
" A Jury of life and death, Judges the prime
    of the land,
Constables, javelineers, — all met, if I under-
    stand,
To decide so knotty a point as whether 't was
    Jack or Joan
Robbed the henroost, pinched the pig, hit the
    King's Arms with a stone,
Dropped the baby down the well, left the
    tithesman in the lurch,
Or, three whole Sundays running, not once
    attended church !
What a pother — do these deserve the parish-
    stocks or whip,
More or less brow to brand, much or little nose
    to snip, —
When, in our Public, plain stand we — that 's
    we stand here
I and my Tab, brass-bold, brick-built of beef
    and beer,
— Do not we, slut ? Step forth and show your
    beauty, jade !
Wife of my bosom — that 's the word now !
    What a trade
We drove ! None said us nay : nobody loved
    his life
So little as wag a tongue against us, — did they,
    wife ?
Yet they knew us all the while, in their hearts,
    for what we are
— Worst couple, rogue and quean, unhanged —
    search near and far !
Eh, Tab ? The peddler, now — o'er his noggin
    — who warned a mate
To cut and run, nor risk his pack where its loss
    of weight
Was the least to dread, — aha, how we two
    laughed a-good
As, stealing round the midden, he came on
    where I stood
With billet poised and raised,   you, ready with
    the rope, —
Ah, but that 's past, that 's sin repented of, we
    hope !

Men knew us for that same, yet safe and sound
    stood we !
The lily-livered knaves knew too (I 've balked
    a d———)
Our keeping the ' Pied Bull ' was just a mere
    pretence :
Too slow the pounds make food, drink, lodging,
    from out the pence !
There 's not a stoppage to travel has chanced,
    this ten long year,
No break into hall or grange, no lifting of nag
    or steer,
Not a single roguery, from the clipping of a
    purse
To the cutting of a throat, but paid us toll.
    Od's curse !
When Gypsy Smouch made bold to cheat us of
    our due,
—Eh, Tab? the Squire's strong-box we helped
    the rascal to
I think he pulled a face, next Sessions' swinging-
    time !
He danced the jig that needs no floor, — and,
    here 's the prime,
'T was Scroggs that houghed the mare ! Ay,
    those were busy days !

" Well, there we flourished brave, like scrip-
    ture-trees called bays,
Faring high, drinking hard, in money up to head
— Not to say, boots and shoes, when . . .
    Zounds, I nearly said —
Lord, to unlearn one 's language ! How shall
    we labor, wife ?
Have you, fast hold, the Book ? Grasp, grip it,
    for your life !
See, sirs, here 's life, salvation ! Here 's —
    hold but out my breath —
When did I speak so long without once swear-
    ing ? 'Sdeath,
No, nor unhelped by ale since man and boy !
    And yet
All yesterday I had to keep my whistle wet
While reading Tab this Book : book ? don't
    say ' book ' — they 're plays,
Songs, ballads, and the like : here 's no such
    strawy blaze,
But sky wide ope, sun, moon,,and seven stars
    out full-flare !
Tab, help and tell ! I 'm hoarse. A mug ! or
    — no, a prayer !
Dip for one out of the Book ! Who wrote it in
    the Jail
—He plied his pen unhelped by beer, sirs, I 'll
    be bail !

" I 've got my second wind. In trundles she —
    that 's Tab.
' Why, Gammer, what 's come now, that —
    bobbing like a crab
On Yule-tide bowl — your head 's a-work and
    both your eyes
Break loose ? Afeard, you fool ? As if the
    dead can rise !
Say — Bagman Dick was found last May with
    fuddling-cap
Stuffed in his mouth : to choke 's a natural
    mishap ! '

' Gaffer, be — blessed,' cries she, ' and Bagman
    Dick as well !
I, you, and he are damned : this Public is our
    hell :
We live in fire : live coals don't feel ! — once
    quenched, they learn —
Cinders do, to what dust they moulder while
    they burn ! '

" ' If you don't speak straight out,' says I —
    belike I swore —
' A knobstick, well you know the taste of, shall,
    once more,
Teach you to talk, my maid !' She ups with
    such a face,
Heart sunk inside me. ' Well, pad on, my
    prate-apace ! '

" ' I 've been about those laces we need for . . .
    never mind !
If henceforth they tie hands, 't is mine they 'll
    have to bind.
You know who makes them best — the Tinker
    in our cage,
Pulled-up for gospelling, twelve years ago : no
    age
To try another trade, — yet, so he scorned to
    take
Money he did not earn, he taught himself the
    make
Of laces, tagged and tough — Dick Bagman
    found them so !
Good customers were we ! Well, last week,
    you must know,
His girl, — the blind young chit, who hawks
    about his wares, —
She takes it in her head to come no more —
    such airs
These hussies have ! Yet, since we need a
    stoutish lace, —
" I 'll to the jail-bird father, abuse her to his
    face ! "
So, first I filled a jug to give me heart, and then,
Primed to the proper pitch, I posted to their
    den —
Patmore, they style their prison ! I tip the
    turnkey, catch
My heart up, fix my face, and fearless lift the
    latch —
Both arms akimbo, in bounce with a good
    round oath
Ready for rapping out : no " Lawks " nor " By
    my troth ! "

" ' There sat my man, the father. He looked
    up : what one feels
When heart that leapt to mouth drops down
    again to heels !
He raised his hand . . . Hast seen, when
    drinking out the night,
And in, the day, earth grow another something
    quite
Under the sun's first stare? I stood a very stone.

" ' " Woman ! " (a fiery tear he put in every
    tone),
" How should my child frequent your house
    where lust is sport.

Violence — trade? Too true! I trust no vague
   report.
Her angel's hand, which stops the sight of sin,
   leaves clear
The other gate of sense, lets outrage through
   the ear.
What has she heard! — which, heard shall
   never be again.
Better lack food than feast, a Dives in the —
   wain
Or reign or train — of Charles! " (His language
   was not ours:
'T is my belief, God spoke: no tinker has such
   powers.)
" Bread, only bread they bring — my laces: if
   we broke
Your lump of leavened sin, the loaf's first
   crumb would choke! "

" 'Down on my marrow-bones! Then all at
   once rose he:
His brown hair burst a-spread, his eyes were
   suns to see:
Up went his hands: " Through flesh, I reach,
   I read thy soul!
So may some stricken tree look blasted, bough
   and bole,
Champed by the fire-tooth, charred without,
   and yet, thrice-bound
With dreriment about, within may life be found,
A prisoned power to branch and blossom as be-
   fore,
Could but the gardener cleave the cloister,
   reach the core,
Loosen the vital sap: yet where shall help be
   found?
Who says ' How save it? ' — nor ' Why cumbers
   it the ground? '
Woman, that tree art thou! All sloughed
   about with scurf,
Thy stag-horns fright the sky, thy snake-roots
   sting the turf!
Drunkenness, wantonness, theft, murder gnash
   and gnarl
Thine outward, case thy soul with coating like
   the marle
Satan stamps flat upon each head beneath his
   hoof!
And how deliver such? The strong men keep
   aloof,
Lover and friend stand far, the mocking ones
   pass by,
Tophet gapes wide for prey: lost soul, despair
   and die!
What then? ' Look unto me and be ye saved! '
   saith God:
' I strike the rock, outstreats the life-stream at
   my rod! [1]
Be your sins scarlet, wool shall they seem like,
   — although
As crimson red, yet turn white as the driven
   snow! ' "

"' There, there, there! All I seem to some-
   how understand

[1] They did not eat
His flesh, nor suck those oils which thence outstreat.
     Donne's *Progress of the Soul*, line 344.

Is — that, if I reached home, 't was through the
   guiding hand
Of his blind girl which led and led me through
   the streets
And out of town and up to door again. What
   greets
First thing my eye, as limbs recover from their
   swoon?
A book — this Book she gave at parting.
   " Father's boon —
The Book he wrote: it reads as if he spoke
   himself:
He cannot preach in bonds, so, — take it down
   from shelf
When you want counsel, — think you hear his
   very voice!

" ' Wicked dear Husband, first despair and
   then rejoice!
Dear wicked Husband, waste no tick of moment
   more,
Be saved like me, bald trunk! There 's green-
   ness yet at core,
Sap under slough! Read, read! '

       " Let me take breath, my lords!
I 'd like to know, are these — hers, mine, or
   Bunyan's words?
I 'm 'wildered — scarce with drink, — nowise
   with drink alone!
You 'll say, with heat: but heat 's no stuff to
   split a stone
Like this black boulder — this flint heart of
   mine: the Book —
That dealt the crashing blow! Sirs, here 's
   the fist that shook
His beard till Wrestler Jem howled like a just-
   lugged bear!
You had brained me with a feather: at once I
   grew aware
Christmas was meant for me. A burden at
   your back,
Good Master Christmas? Nay, — yours was
   that Joseph's sack,
— Or whose it was, — which held the cup, —
   compared with mine!
Robbery loads my loins, perjury cracks my chine,
Adultery . . . nay, Tab, you pitched me as I
   flung!
One word, I 'll up with fist . . . No, sweet
   spouse, hold your tongue!

" I 'm hasting to the end. The Book, sirs —
   take and read!
You have my history in a nutshell, — ay, indeed!
It must off, my burden! See, — slack straps
   and into pit,
Roll, reach the bottom, rest, rot there — a
   plague on it!
For a mountain 's sure to fall and bury Bedford
   Town,
' Destruction ' — that 's the name, and fire shall
   burn it down!
Oh, 'scape the wrath in time! Time 's now, if
   not too late.
How can I pilgrimage up to the wicket-gate?
Next comes Despond the slough: not that I
   fear to pull

Through mud, and dry my clothes at brave
  House Beautiful —
But it's late in the day, I reckon: had I left
  years ago
Town, wife, and children dear . . . Well,
  Christmas did, you know! —
Soon I had met in the valley and tried my cud-
  gel's strength
On the enemy horned and winged, a-straddle
  across its length!
Have at his horns, thwick — thwack: they
  snap, see! Hoof and hoof —
Bang, break the fetlock-bones! For love's
  sake, keep aloof
Angels! I'm man and match, — this cudgel
  for my flail, —
To thresh him, hoofs and horns, bat's wing and
  serpent's tail!
A chance gone by! But then, what else does
  Hopeful ding
Into the deafest ear except — hope, hope 's the
  thing?
Too late i' the day for me to thrid the wind-
  ings: but
There's still a way to win the race by death's
  short cut!
Did Master Faithful need climb the Delightful
  Mounts?
No, straight to Vanity Fair, — a fair, by all ac-
  counts,
Such as is held outside, — lords, ladies, grand
  and gay, —
Says he in the face of them, just what you hear
  me say.
And the Judges brought him in guilty, and
  brought him out
To die in the market-place — St. Peter's Green's
  about
The same thing: there they flogged, flayed,
  buffeted, lanced with knives,
Pricked him with swords, — I'll swear, he'd
  full a cat's nine lives, —
So to his end at last came Faithful, — ha, ha, he!
Who holds the highest card? for there stands
  hid, you see,
Behind the rabble-rout, a chariot, pair and all:
He's in, he's off, he's up, through clouds, at
  trumpet-call,
Carried the nearest way to Heaven-gate! Odds
  my life —
Has nobody a sword to spare? not even a knife?
Then hang me, draw and quarter! Tab — do
  the same by her!
O Master Worldly-Wiseman . . . that's Master
  Interpreter,
Take the will, not the deed! Our gibbet's
  handy, close:
Forestall Last Judgment-Day! Be kindly, not
  morose!
There wants no earthly judge-and-jurying: here
  we stand —
Sentence our guilty selves: so, hang us out of
  hand!
Make haste for pity's sake! A single moment's
  loss
Means — Satan's lord once more: his whisper
  shoots across
All singing in my heart, all praying in my brain,

'It comes of heat and beer!' — hark how he
  guffaws plain!
'To-morrow you'll wake bright, and, in a safe
  skin, hug
Your sound selves, Tab and you, over a foam-
  ing jug!
You've had such qualms before, time out of
  mind!' He's right!
Did not we kick and cuff and curse away, that
  night
When home we blindly reeled, and left poor
  humpback Joe
I' the lurch to pay for what . . . somebody
  did, you know!
Both of us maundered then, 'Lame humpback,
  — never more
Will he come limping. drain his tankard at our
  door!
He'll swing, while — somebody' . . . Says Tab,
  'No, for I'll peach!'
'I'm for you, Tab,' cries I, 'there's rope
  enough for each!'
So blubbered we, and bussed, and went to bed
  upon
The grace of Tab's good thought: by morning,
  all was gone!
We laughed — 'What's life to him, a cripple
  of no account?'
Oh, waves increase around — I feel them mount
  and mount!
Hang us! To-morrow brings Tom Bearward
  with his bears:
One new black-muzzled brute beats Sackerson,
  he swears:
(Sackerson, for my money!) And, baiting o'er,
  the Brawl
They lead on Turner's Patch, — lads, lasses, up
  tails all, —
I'm i' the thick o' the throng! That means
  the Iron Cage,
— Means the Lost Man inside! Where's hope
  for such as wage
War against light? Light's left, light's here,
  I hold light still,
So does Tab — make but haste to hang us both!
  You will?"

I promise, when he stopped you might have
  heard a mouse
Squeak, such a death-like hush sealed up the
  old Mote House.
But when the mass of man sank meek upon his
  knees,
While Tab, alongside, wheezed a hoarse "Do
  hang us, please!"
Why, then the waters rose, no eye but ran with
  tears,
Hearts heaved, heads thumped, until, paying
  all past arrears
Of pity and sorrow, at last a regular scream
  outbroke
Of triumph, joy, and praise.

          My Lord Chief Justice spoke,
First mopping brow and cheek, where still, for
  one that budged,
Another bead broke fresh: "What Judge, that
  ever judged

Since first the world began, judged such a case
    as this?
Why, Master Bratts, long since, folks smelt
    you out, I wis!
I had my doubts, i' faith, each time you played
    the fox
Convicting geese of crime in yonder witness-
    box —
Yea, much did I misdoubt, the thief that stole
    her eggs
Was hardly goosey's self at Reynard's game, i'
    feggs!
Yet thus much was to praise — you spoke to
    point, direct —
Swore you heard, saw the theft: no jury could
    suspect —
Dared to suspect, — I 'll say, — a spot in white
    so clear:
Goosey was throttled, true: but thereof godly
    fear
Came of example set, much as our laws in-
    tend;
And, though a fox confessed, you proved the
    Judge's friend.
What if I had my doubts? Suppose I gave
    them breath,
Brought you to bar: what work to do, ere
    'Guilty, Death'
Had paid our pains! What heaps of witnesses
    to drag
From holes and corners, paid from out the
    County's bag!
Trial three dog-days long! *Amicus Curiæ* —
    that 's
Your title, no dispute — truth-telling Master
    Bratts!
Thank you, too, Mistress Tab! Why doubt
    one word you say?
Hanging you both deserve, hanged both shall
    be this day!
The tinker needs must be a proper man. I 've
    heard

He lies in Jail long since: if Quality's good
    word
Warrants me letting loose, — some householder,
    I mean —
Freeholder, better still, — I don't say but —
    between
Now and next Sessions . . . Well! Consider
    of his case,
I promise to, at least: we owe him so much
    grace.
Not that — no, God forbid! — I lean to think,
    as you,
The grace that such repent is any jail-bird's due:
I rather see the fruit of twelve years' pious
    reign —
Astræa Redux, Charles restored his rights
    again!
— Of which, another time! I somehow feel a
    peace
Stealing across the world. May deeds like
    this increase!
So, Master Sheriff, stay that sentence I pro-
    nounced
On those two dozen odd: deserving to be
    trounced
Soundly, and yet . . . well, well, at all events
    dispatch
This pair of — shall I say, sinner-saints? — ere
    we catch
Their jail-distemper too. Stop tears, or I 'll in'
    dite
All weeping Bedfordshire for turning Bunyan-
    ite!"

So, forms were galloped through. If Justice,
    on the spur,
Proved somewhat expeditious, would Quality
    demur?
And happily hanged were they, — why lengthen
    out my tale? —
Where Bunyan's Statue stands facing where
    stood his Jail.

SECOND SERIES

" You are sick, that 's sure," — they say:
" Sick of what? " — they disagree.
" 'T is the brain," — thinks Doctor A;
" 'T is the heart," — holds Doctor B;
"The liver — my life I 'd lay!"
" The lungs!" "The lights!"
                                                    Ah me!

So ignorant of man's whole
Of bodily organs plain to see —
So sage and certain, frank and free,
About what 's under lock and key —
Man's soul!

ECHETLOS

HERE is a story, shall stir you! Stand up,
    Greeks dead and gone,
Who breasted, beat Barbarians, stemmed Per-
    sia rolling on,
Did the deed and saved the world, for the day
    was Marathon!

No man but did his manliest, kept rank and
    fought away
In his tribe and file: up, back, out, down —
    was the spear-arm play:
Like a wind-whipt branchy wood, all spear
    arms a-swing that day!

But one man kept no rank, and his sole arm
    plied no spear,
As a flashing came and went, and a form i' the
    van, the rear,
Brightened the battle up, for he blazed now
    there, now here.

Nor helmed nor shielded, he! but, a goat-skin
    all his wear,
Like a tiller of the soil, with a clown's limbs
    broad and bare,
Went he ploughing on and on: he pushed with
    a ploughman's share.

Did the weak mid-line give way, as tunnies on
    whom the shark
Precipitates his bulk? Did the right-wing
    halt when, stark
On his heap of slain lay stretched Kallimachos
    Polemarch?

Did the steady phalanx falter? To the rescue,
    at the need,
The clown was ploughing Persia, clearing
    Greek earth of weed,
As he routed through the Sakian and rooted up
    the Mede.

But the deed done, battle won, — nowhere to
    be descried
On the meadow, by the stream, at the marsh,
    — look far and wide
From the foot of the mountain, no, to the last
    blood-plashed sea-side, —

Not anywhere on view blazed the large limbs
    thonged and brown,
Shearing and clearing still with the share
    before which — down
To the dust went Persia's pomp, as he ploughed
    for Greece, that clown!

How spake the Oracle? "Care for no name
    at all!
Say but just this: 'We praise one helpful
    whom we call
The Holder of the Ploughshare.' The great
    deed ne'er grows small."

Not the great name! Sing — woe for the
    great name Mîltiadés
And its end at Paros isle! Woe for Themis-
    tokles
—Satrap in Sardis court! Name not the
    clown like these!

CLIVE

Browning had this story from Mrs. Jameson
as early as 1846, she in turn having just heard
Macaulay tell it. Clive's telling the story a
week before his death is Browning's invention.

I AND Clive were friends — and why not?
    Friends! I think you laugh, my lad.

Clive it was gave England India, while your
    father gives — egad,
England nothing but the graceless boy who
    lures him on to speak —
"Well, Sir, you and Clive were comrades —"
    with a tongue thrust in your cheek!
Very true: in my eyes, your eyes, all the
    world's eyes, Clive was man,
I was, am, and ever shall be — mouse, nay,
    mouse of all its clan
Sorriest sample, if you take the kitchen's esti-
    mate for fame;
While the man Clive — he fought Plassy,
    spoiled the clever foreign game,
Conquered and annexed and Englished!

            Never mind! As o'er my punch
(You away) I sit of evenings, — silence, save for
    biscuit crunch,
Black, unbroken, — thought grows busy, thrids
    each pathway of old years,
Notes this forthright, that meander, till the
    long-past life appears
Like an outspread map of country plodded
    through, each mile and rood,
Once, and well remembered still, — I'm star-
    tled in my solitude
Ever and anon by — what's the sudden mock-
    ing light that breaks
On me as I slap the table till no rummer-glass
    but shakes
While I ask — aloud, I do believe, God help
    me! — "Was it thus?
Can it be that so I faltered, stopped when just
    one step for us —"
(Us, — you were not born, I grant, but surely
    some day born would be)
"—One bold step had gained a province"
    (figurative talk, you see)
"Got no end of wealth and honor, — yet I
    stood stock-still no less?"
— "For I was not Clive," you comment: but it
    needs no Clive to guess
Wealth were handy, honor ticklish, did no
    writing on the wall
Warn me "Trespasser, 'ware man-traps!"
    Him who braves that notice — call
Hero! none of such heroics suit myself who
    read plain words,
Doff my hat, and leap no barrier. Scripture
    says, the land's the Lord's:
Louts then — what avail the thousand, noisy
    in a smock-frocked ring,
All-agog to have me trespass, clear the fence,
    be Clive their king?
Higher warrant must you show me ere I set one
    foot before
T' other in that dark direction, though I stand
    forevermore
Poor as Job and meek as Moses. Evermore?
    No! By and by
Job grows rich and Moses valiant, Clive turns
    out less wise than I.
Don't object "Why call him friend, then?"
    Power is power, my boy, and still
Marks a man, — God's gift magnific, exercised
    for good or ill.

You 've your boot now on my hearth-rug,
  tread what was a tiger's skin :
Rarely such a royal monster as I lodged the
  bullet in !
True, he murdered half a village, so his own
  death came to pass ;
Still, for size and beauty, cunning, courage —
  ah, the brute he was !
Why, that Clive, — that youth, that greenhorn,
  that quill-driving clerk, in fine, —
He sustained a siege in Arcot . . . But the
  world knows ! Pass the wine.

Where did I break off at ? How bring Clive
  in ? Oh, you mentioned "fear" !
Just so : and, said I, that minds me of a story
  you shall hear.

We were friends then, Clive and I : so, when
  the clouds, about the orb
Late supreme, encroaching slowly, surely,
  threatened to absorb
Ray by ray its noontide brilliance, — friendship
  might, with steadier eye
Drawing near, bear what had burned else, now
  no blaze — all majesty.
Too much bee's-wing floats my figure ? Well,
  suppose a castle 's new :
None presume to climb its ramparts, none find
  foothold sure for shoe
'Twixt those squares and squares of granite
  plating the impervious pile
As his scale-mail's warty iron cuirasses a croco-
  dile.
Reels that castle thunder-smitten, storm-dis-
  mantled ? From without
Scrambling up by crack and crevice, every
  cockney prates about
Towers — the heap he kicks now ! turrets —
  just the measure of his cane !
Will that do ? Observe moreover — (same si-
  militude again) —
Such a castle seldom crumbles by sheer stress
  of cannonade :
'T is when foes are foiled and fighting 's fin-
  ished that vile rains invade,
Grass o'ergrows, o'ergrows till night-birds con-
  gregating find no holes
Fit to build in like the topmost sockets made
  for banner-poles.
So Clive crumbled slow in London, crashed at
  last.

                          A week before,
Dining with him, — after trying churchyard
  chat of days of yore, —
Both of us stopped, tired as tombstones, head-
  piece, foot-piece, when they lean
Each to other, drowsed in fog-smoke, o'er a
  coffined Past between.
As I saw his head sink heavy, guessed the soul's
  extinguishment
By the glazing eyeball, noticed how the furtive
  fingers went
Where a drug-box skulked behind the honest
  liquor, — "One more throw
Try for Clive !" thought I : "Let 's venture
  some good rattling question !" So —

"Come Clive, tell us" — out I blurted —
  "what to tell in turn, years hence,
When my boy — suppose I have one — asks me
  on what evidence
I maintain my friend of Plassy proved a war-
  rior every whit
Worth your Alexanders, Cæsars, Marlboroughs
  and — what said Pitt ? —
Frederick the Fierce himself ! Clive told me
  once" — I want to say —
"Which feat out of all those famous doings bore
  the bell away
— In his own calm estimation, mark you, not
  the mob's rough guess —
Which stood foremost as evincing what Clive
  called courageousness !
Come ! what moment of the minute, what
  speck-centre in the wide
Circle of the action saw your mortal fairly dei-
  fied ?
(Let alone that filthy sleep-stuff, swallow bold
  this wholesome Port !)
If a friend has leave to question, — when were
  you most brave, in short ? "

Up he arched his brows o' the instant — for-
  midably Clive again.
"When was I most brave ? I 'd answer, were
  the instance half as plain
As another instance that 's a brain-lodged crys-
  tal — curse it ! — here
Freezing when my memory touches — ugh ! —
  the time I felt most fear.
Ugh ! I cannot say for certain if I showed fear
  — anyhow,
Fear I felt, and, very likely, shuddered, since
  I shiver now."

"Fear !" smiled I. "Well, that 's the rarer :
  that 's a specimen to seek,
Ticket up in one's museum, *Mind-Freaks, Lord
  Clive's Fear, Unique !* "

Down his brows dropped. On the table pain-
  fully he pored as though
Tracing, in the stains and streaks there,
  thoughts encrusted long ago.
When he spoke 't was like a lawyer reading
  word by word some will,
Some blind jungle of a statement, — beating on
  and on until
Out there leaps fierce life to fight with.

                    "This fell in my factor-days.
Desk-drudge, slaving at Saint David's, one
  must game, or drink, or craze.
I chose gaming : and, — because your high-
  flown gamesters hardly take
Umbrage at a factor's elbow if the factor pays
  his stake, —
I was winked at in a circle where the company
  was choice,
Captain This and Major That, men high of
  color, loud of voice,
Yet indulgent, condescending to the modest
  juvenile
Who not merely risked but lost his hard-earned
  guineas with a smile.

"Down I sat to cards, one evening, — had for
my antagonist
Somebody whose name's a secret — you'll know
why — so, if you list,
Call him Cock o' the Walk, my scarlet son of
Mars from head to heel!
Play commenced: and, whether Cocky fancied
that a clerk must feel
Quite sufficient honor came of bending over one
green baize,
I the scribe with him the warrior, guessed no
penman dared to raise
Shadow of objection should the honor stay but
playing end
More or less abruptly, — whether disinclined he
grew to spend
Practice strictly scientific on a booby born to
stare
At — not ask of — lace-and-ruffles if the hand
they hide plays fair, —
Anyhow, I marked a movement when he bade
me 'Cut!'

"I rose.
'Such the new manœuvre, Captain? I'm a
novice: knowledge grows.
What, you force a card, you cheat, Sir?'

"Never did a thunder-clap
Cause emotion, startle Thyrsis locked with
Chloe in his lap,
As my word and gesture (down I flung my
cards to join the pack)
Fired the man of arms, whose visage, simply
red before, turned black.

When he found his voice, he stammered 'That
expression once again!'

"'Well, you forced a card and cheated!'

"'Possibly a factor's brain,
Busied with his all-important balance of ac-
counts, may deem
Weighing words superfluous trouble: *cheat* to
clerkly ears may seem
Just the joke for friends to venture: but we
are not friends, you see!
When a gentleman is joked with, — if he's
good at repartee,
He rejoins, as do I — Sirrah, on your knees,
withdraw in full!
Beg my pardon, or be sure a kindly bullet
through your skull
Lets in light and teaches manner to what brain
it finds! Choose quick —
Have your life snuffed out or, kneeling, pray
me trim yon candle-wick!'

"'Well, you cheated!'
"Then outbroke a howl from all the friends
around.
To his feet sprang each in fury, fists were
clenched and teeth were ground.
'End it! no time like the present! Captain,
yours were our disgrace!
No delay, begin and finish! Stand back, leave
the pair a space!

Let civilians be instructed: henceforth simply
ply the pen,
Fly the sword! This clerk's no swordsman?
Suit him with a pistol, then!
Even odds! A dozen paces 'twixt the most
and least expert
Make a dwarf a giant's equal: nay, the dwarf,
if he's alert,
Likelier hits the broader target!'

"Up we stood accordingly.
As they handed me the weapon, such was my
soul's thirst to try
Then and there conclusions with this bully,
tread on and stamp out
Every spark of his existence, that, — crept
close to, curled about
By that toying tempting teasing fool-forefinger's
middle joint, —
Don't you guess? — the trigger yielded. Gone
my chance! and at the point
Of such prime success moreover: scarce an
inch above his head
Went my ball to hit the wainscot. He was
living, I was dead.

"Up he marched in flaming triumph — 't was
his right, mind! — up, within
Just an arm's length. 'Now, my clerkling,'
chuckled Cocky with a grin
As the levelled piece quite touched me, 'Now,
Sir Counting-House, repeat
That expression which I told you proved bad
manners! Did I cheat?'

"'Cheat you did, you knew you cheated, and,
this moment, know as well.
As for me, my homely breeding bids you —
fire and go to Hell!'

"Twice the muzzle touched my forehead.
Heavy barrel, flurried wrist,
Either spoils a steady lifting. Thrice: then,
'Laugh at Hell who list,
I can't! God's no fable either. Did this
boy's eye wink once? No!
There's no standing him and Hell and God all
three against me, — so,
I did cheat!'

"And down he threw the pistol, out rushed
— by the door
Possibly, but, as for knowledge if by chimney,
roof or floor,
He effected disappearance — I'll engage no
glance was sent
That way by a single starer, such a blank aston-
ishment
Swallowed up their senses: as for speaking —
mute they stood as mice.

"Mute not long, though! Such reaction, such
a hubbub in a trice!
'Rogue and rascal! Who'd have thought it?
What's to be expected next,
When His Majesty's Commission serves a
sharper as pretext

For . . . But where's the need of wasting
time now? Naught requires delay:
Punishment the Service cries for: let disgrace
be wiped away
Publicly, in good broad daylight! Resigna-
tion? No, indeed!
Drum and fife must play the Rogue's-March,
rank and file be free to speed
Tardy marching on the rogue's part by appli-
ance in the rear
— Kicks administered shall right this wronged
civilian, — never fear,
Mister Clive, for — though a clerk — you bore
yourself — suppose we say —
Just as would beseem a soldier?

    " 'Gentlemen, attention — pray!
First, one word!'

" I passed each speaker severally in review.
When I had precise their number, names and
styles, and fully knew
Over whom my supervision thenceforth must
extend, — why, then —

" 'Some five minutes since, my life lay — as you
all saw, gentlemen —
At the mercy of your friend there. Not a
single voice was raised
In arrest of judgment, not one tongue — before
my powder blazed —
Ventured " Can it be the youngster blundered,
really seemed to mark
Some irregular proceeding? We conjecture in
the dark,
Guess at random, — still, for sake of fair play
— what if for a freak,
In a fit of absence, — such things have been! —
if our friend proved weak
— What's the phrase? — corrected fortune!
Look into the case, at least!'"
Who dared interpose between the altar's victim
and the priest?
Yet he spared me! You eleven! Whosoever,
all or each,
To the disadvantage of the man who spared
me, utters speech
— To his face, behind his back, — that speaker
has to do with me:
Me who promise, if positions change and mine
the chance should be,
Not to imitate your friend and waive ad-
vantage!'

    " Twenty-five
Years ago this matter happened: and 't is
certain," added Clive,
" Never, to my knowledge, did Sir Cocky have
a single breath
Breathed against him: lips were closed through-
out his life, or since his death,
For if he be dead or living I can tell no more
than you.
All I know is — Cocky had one chance more;
how he used it, — grew
Out of such unlucky habits, or relapsed, and
back again

Brought the late-ejected devil with a score
more in his train, —
That's for you to judge. Reprieval I procured,
at any rate.
Ugh — the memory of that minute's fear makes
gooseflesh rise! Why prate
Longer? You've my story, there's your
instance: fear I did, you see!"

" Well " — I hardly kept from laughing — "if
I see it thanks must be
Wholly to your Lordship's candor. Not that
— in a common case —
When a bully caught at cheating thrusts a
pistol in one's face,
I should under-rate, believe me, such a trial to
the nerve!
'T is no joke, at one-and-twenty, for a youth to
stand nor swerve.
Fear I naturally look for — unless, of all men
alive,
I am forced to make exception when I come to
Robert Clive.
Since at Arcot, Plassy, elsewhere, he and death
— the whole world knows —
Came to somewhat closer quarters."

    Quarters? Had we come to blows,
Clive and I, you had not wondered — up he
sprang so, out he rapped
Such a round of oaths — no matter! I'll en-
deavor to adapt
To our modern usage words he — well, 't was
friendly license — flung
At me like so many fire-balls, fast as he could
wag his tongue.

" You — a soldier? You — at Plassy? Yours
the faculty to nick
Instantaneously occasion when your foe, if
lightning-quick,
— At his mercy, at his malice, — has you,
through some stupid inch
Undefended in your bulwark? Thus laid open,
— not to flinch
— That needs courage, you'll concede me.
Then, look here! Suppose the man,
Checking his advance, his weapon still ex-
tended, not a span
Distant from my temple, — curse him! — quiet-
ly had bade me, ' There!
Keep your life, calumniator! — worthless life I
freely spare:
Mine you freely would have taken — murdered
me and my good fame
Both at once — and all the better! Go, and
thank your own bad aim
Which permits me to forgive you!' What if,
with such words as these,
He had cast away his weapon? How should
I have borne me, please?
Nay, I'll spare you pains and tell you. This,
and only this, remained —
Pick his weapon up and use it on myself. If
so had gained
Sleep the earlier, leaving England probably to
pay on still

Rent and taxes for half India, tenant at the
  Frenchman's will."

"Such the turn," said I, " the matter takes
  with you? Then I abate
— No, by not one jot nor tittle, — of your act
  my estimate.
Fear — I wish I could detect there: courage
  fronts me, plain enough —
Call it desperation, madness — never mind !
  for here 's in rough
Why, had mine been such a trial, fear had
  overcome disgrace.
True, disgrace were hard to bear: but such a
  rush against God's face
— None of that for me, Lord Plassy, since I go
  to church at times,
Say the creed my mother taught me ! Many
  years in foreign climes
Rub some marks away — not all, though ! We
  poor sinners reach life's brink,
Overlook what rolls beneath it, recklessly
  enough, but think
There 's advantage in what 's left us — ground
  to stand on, time to call
' Lord, have mercy ! ' ere we topple over — do
  not leap, that 's all ! ' "

Oh, he made no answer, re-absorbed into his
  cloud. I caught
Something like " Yes — courage : only fools
  will call it fear."
          If aught
Comfort you, my great unhappy hero Clive, in
  that I heard,
Next week, how your own hand dealt you
  doom, and uttered just the word
" Fearfully courageous ! " — this, be sure, and
  nothing else I groaned.
I 'm no Clive, nor parson either : Clive's
  worst deed — we 'll hope condoned.

MULÉYKEH

If a stranger passed the tent of Hóseyn, he
  cried " A churl's ! "
Or haply " God help the man who has neither
  salt nor bread ! "
— " Nay," would a friend exclaim, " he needs
  nor pity nor scorn
More than who spends small thought on the
  shore-sand, picking pearls,
— Holds but in light esteem the seed-sort,
  bears instead
On his breast a moon-like prize, some orb
  which of night makes morn.

" What if no flocks and herds enrich the son of
  Sinán?
They went when his tribe was mulct, ten thou-
  sand camels the due,
Blood-value paid perforce for a murder done of
  old.
' God gave them, let them go ! But never since
  time began,

Muléykeh, peerless mare, owned master the
  match of you,
And you are my prize, my Pearl: I laugh at
  men's land and gold ! '

" So in the pride of his soul laughs Hóseyn —
  and right, I say.
Do the ten steeds run a race of glory? Out-
  stripping all,
Ever Muléykeh stands first steed at the victor's
  staff.
Who started, the owner's hope, gets shamed
  and named, that day.
' Silence,' or, last but one, is ' The Cuffed,' as
  we use to call
Whom the paddock's lord thrusts forth.
  Right, Hóseyn, I say, to laugh ! "

" Boasts he Muléykeh the Pearl ? " the
  stranger replies : " Be sure
On him I waste nor scorn nor pity, but lavish
  both
On Duhl the son of Sheybán, who withers
  away in heart
For envy of Hóseyn's luck. Such sickness
  admits no cure.
A certain poet has sung, and sealed the same
  with an oath,
' For the vulgar — flocks and herds ! The
  Pearl is a prize apart.' "

Lo, Duhl the son of Sheybán comes riding to
  Hóseyn's tent,
And he casts his saddle down, and enters and
  " Peace ! " bids he.
" You are poor, I know the cause: my plenty
  shall mend the wrong.
'T is said of your Pearl — the price of a hun-
  dred camels spent
In her purchase were scarce ill paid : such pru-
  dence is far from me
Who proffer a thousand. Speak ! Long
  parley may last too long."

Said Hóseyn, " You feed young beasts a many,
  of famous breed,
Slit-eared, unblemished, fat, true offspring of
  Múzennem :
There stumbles no weak-eyed she in the line
  as it climbs the hill.
But I love Muléykeh's face : her forefront
  whitens indeed
Like a yellowish wave's cream-crest. Your
  camels — go gaze on them !
Her fetlock is foam-splashed too. Myself am
  the richer still."

A year goes by : lo, back to the tent again
  rides Duhl.
" You are open-hearted, ay — moist-handed, a
  very prince.
Why should I speak of sale ? Be the mare
  your simple gift !
My son is pined to death for her beauty : my
  wife prompts ' Fool,
Beg for his sake the Pearl ! Be God the
  rewarder, since

God pays debts seven for one : who squanders
  on Him shows thrift.' "

Said Hóseyn, " God gives each man one life,
  like a lamp, then gives
That lamp due measure of oil : lamp lighted —
  hold high, wave wide
Its comfort for others to share ! once quench
  it, what help is left ?
The oil of your lamp is your son : I shine while
  Muléykeh lives.
Would I beg your son to cheer my dark if
  Muléykeh died ?
It is life against life : what good avails to the
  life-bereft ? "

Another year, and — hist ! What craft is it
  Duhl designs ?
He alights not at the door of the tent as he did
  last time,
But, creeping behind, he gropes his stealthy
  way by the trench
Half-round till he finds the flap in the folding,
  for night combines
With the robber — and such is he : Duhl,
  covetous up to crime,
Must wring from Hóseyn's grasp the Pearl, by
  whatever the wrench.

" He was hunger-bitten, I heard : I tempted
  with half my store,
And a gibe was all my thanks. Is he generous
  like Spring dew ?
Account the fault to me who chaffered with
  such an one !
He has killed, to feast chance comers, the
  creature he rode : nay, more —
For a couple of singing-girls his robe has he
  torn in two :
I will beg ! Yet I nowise gained by the tale of
  my wife and son.

" I swear by the Holy House, my head will
  I never wash
Till I filch his Pearl away. Fair dealing I
  tried, then guile,
And now I resort to force. He said we must
  live or die :
Let him die, then, — let me live ! Be bold —
  but not too rash !
I have found me a peeping-place : breast, bury
  your breathing while
I explore for myself ! Now, breathe ! He
  deceived me not, the spy !

" As he said — there lies in peace Hóseyn —
  how happy ! Beside
Stands tethered the Pearl : thrice winds her
  headstall about his wrist :
'T is therefore he sleeps so sound — the moon
  through the roof reveals.
And, loose on his left, stands too that other,
  known far and wide,
Buhéyseh, her sister born : fleet is she yet ever
  missed
The winning tail's fire-flash a-stream past the
  thunderous heels.

" No less she stands saddled and bridled, this
  second, in case some thief
Should enter and seize and fly with the first, as
  I mean to do.
What then ? The Pearl is the Pearl : once
  mount her we both escape."
Through the skirt-fold in glides Duhl, — so a
  serpent disturbs no leaf
In a bush as he parts the twigs entwining a nest :
  clean through,
He is noiselessly at his work : as he planned, he
  performs the rape.

He has set the tent-door wide, has buckled the
  girth, has clipped
The headstall away from the wrist he leaves
  thrice bound as before,
He springs on the Pearl, is launched on the
  desert like bolt from bow.
Up starts our plundered man : from his breast
  though the heart be ripped,
Yet his mind has the mastery : behold, in a
  minute more,
He is out and off and away on Buhéyseh, whose
  worth we know !

And Hóseyn — his blood turns flame, he has
  learned long since to ride,
And Buhéyseh does her part, — they gain —
  they are gaining fast
On the fugitive pair, and Duhl has Ed-Dárraj
  to cross and quit,
And to reach the ridge El-Sabán, — no safety
  till that be spied !
And Buhéyseh is, bound by bound, but a horse-
  length off at last,
For the Pearl has missed the tap of the heel,
  the touch of the bit.

She shortens her stride, she chafes at her rider
  the strange and queer :
Buhéyseh is mad with hope — beat sister she
  shall and must,
Though Duhl, of the hand and heel so clumsy,
  she has to thank.
She is near now, nose by tail — they are neck
  by croup — joy ! fear !
What folly makes Hóseyn shout " Dog Duhl,
  Damned son of the Dust,
Touch the right ear and press with your foot
  my Pearl's left flank ! "

And Duhl was wise at the word, and Muléykeh
  as prompt perceived
Who was urging redoubled pace, and to hear
  him was to obey,
And a leap indeed gave she, and evanished
  forevermore.
And Hóseyn looked one long last look as who,
  all bereaved,
Looks, fain to follow the dead so far as the liv-
  ing may :
Then he turned Buhéyseh's neck slow home-
  ward, weeping sore.

And, lo, in the sunrise, still sat Hóseyn upon
  the ground

Weeping: and neighbors came, the tribesmen
      of Bénu-Asád
In the vale of green Er-Rass, and they ques-
      tioned him of his grief ;
And he told from first to last how, serpent-like,
      Duhl had wound
His way to the nest, and how Duhl rode like an
      ape, so bad !
And how Buhéyseh did wonders, yet Pearl re-
      mained with the thief.

And they jeered him, one and all : " Poor
      Hóseyn is crazed past hope !
How else had he wrought himself his ruin, in
      fortune's spite ?
To have simply held the tongue were a task for
      boy or girl,
And here were Muléykeh again, the eyed like
      an antelope,
The child of his heart by day, the wife of his
      breast by night ! " —
" And the beaten in speed ! " wept Hóseyn.
" You never have loved my Pearl."

PIETRO OF ABANO

Petrus Aponensis — there was a magician !
When that strange adventure happened, which
      I mean to tell my hearers,
Nearly had he tried all trades — beside physi-
      cian,
Architect, astronomer, astrologer, — or worse :
How else, as the old books warrant, was he able,
All at once, through all the world, to prove the
      promptest of appearers
Where was prince to cure, tower to build as
      high as Babel,
Star to name or sky-sign read, — yet pouch, for
      pains, a curse ?

— Curse : for when a vagrant, — foot-sore,
      travel-tattered,
Now a young man, now an old man, Turk or
      Arab, Jew or Gypsy, —
Proffered folk in passing — Oh, for pay, what
      mattered ? —
" I 'll be doctor, I 'll play builder, star I 'll
      name — sign read ! "
Soon as prince was cured, tower built, and fate
      predicted,
" Who may you be ? " came the question ;
      when he answered " *Petrus ipse*,"
" Just as we divined ! " cried folk — " A
      wretch convicted
Long ago of dealing with the devil — you in-
      deed ! "

So, they cursed him roundly, all his labor's pay-
      ment,
Motioned him — the convalescent prince would
      — to vacate the presence :
Babylonians plucked his beard and tore his rai-
      ment,
Drove him from that tower he built : while,
      had he peered at stars,
Town howled " Stone the quack who styles our
      Dog-star — Sirius ! "

Country yelled " Aroint the churl who prophe-
      sies we take no pleasance
Under vine and fig-tree, since the year 's deliri-
      ous,
Bears no crop of any kind, — all through the
      planet Mars ! "

Straightway would the whilom youngster grow
      a grisard,
Or, as case might hap, the hoary eld drop off
      and show a stripling.
Town and country groaned — indebted to a
      wizard !
" Curse — nay, kick and cuff him — fit requital
      of his pains !
Gratitude in word or deed were wasted truly !
Rather make the Church amends by crying out
      on, cramping, crippling
One who, on pretence of serving man, serves
      duly
Man's arch foe : not ours, be sure, but Satan's
      — his the gains ! "

Peter grinned and bore it, such disgraceful
      usage :
Somehow, cuffs and kicks and curses seem or-
      dained his like to suffer :
Prophet's pay with Christians, now as in the
      Jews' age,
Still is — stoning : so, he meekly took his wage
      and went,
— Safe again was found ensconced in those old
      quarters,
Padua's blackest blindest by-street, — none the
      worse, nay, somewhat tougher :
" Calculating," quoth he, " soon I join the mar-
      tyrs,
Since, who magnify my lore on burning me are
      bent." [1]

Therefore, on a certain evening, to his alley
Peter slunk, all bruised and broken, sore in
      body, sick in spirit,
Just escaped from Cairo where he launched a
      galley
Needing neither sails nor oars nor help of wind
      or tide,
— Needing, but the fume of fire to set a-flying
Wheels like mad which whirled you quick —
      North, South, where'er you pleased re-
      quire it, —
That is — would have done so had not priests
      come prying,
Broke his engine up and bastinadoed him be-
      side.

As he reached his lodging, stopped there unmo-
      lested,
(Neighbors feared him, urchins fled him, few
      were bold enough to follow)
While his fumbling fingers tried the lock and
      tested
Once again the queer key's virtue, oped the sul-
      len door, —
Some one plucked his sleeve, cried, " Master,
      pray your pardon !

[1] See note at end of volume.

Grant a word to me who patient wait you in
your archway's hollow!
Hard on you men's hearts are: be not your
heart hard on
Me who kiss your garment's hem, O Lord of
magic lore!

"Mage — say I, who no less, scorning tittle-tat-
tle,
To the vulgar give no credence when they
prate of Peter's magic,
Deem his art brews tempest, hurts the crops
and cattle,
Hinders fowls from laying eggs and worms from
spinning silk,
Rides upon a he-goat, mounts at need a broom-
stick:
While the price he pays for this (so turns to
comic what was tragic)
Is — he may not drink — dreads like the Day
of Doom's tick —
One poor drop of sustenance ordained mere men
— that 's milk!

"Tell such tales to Padua! Think me no such
dullard!
Not from these benighted parts did I derive my
breath and being!
I am from a land whose cloudless skies are
colored
Livelier, suns orb largelier, airs seem incense,
— while, on earth —
What, instead of grass, our fingers and our
thumbs cull,
Proves true moly! sounds and sights there
help the body's hearing, seeing,
Till the soul grows godlike: brief, — you front
no numskull
Shaming by ineptitude the Greece that gave
him birth!

"Mark within my eye its iris mystic-let-
tered —
That 's my name! and note my ear — its swan-
shaped cavity, my emblem!
Mine 's the swan-like nature born to fly unfet-
tered
Over land and sea in search of knowledge —
food for song.
Art denied the vulgar! Geese grow fat on
barley,
Swans require ethereal provend, undesirous to
resemble 'em —
Soar to seek Apollo — favored with a parley
Such as, Master, you grant me — who will not
hold you long.

"Leave to learn to sing — for that your swan
petitions:
Master, who possess the secret, say not nay to
such a suitor!
All I ask is — bless mine, purest of ambitions!
Grant me leave to make my kind wise, free,
and happy! How?
Just by making me — as you are mine — their
model!
Geese have goose-thoughts: make a swan their
teacher first, then coadjutor, —

Let him introduce swan-notions to each nod-
dle, —
Geese will soon grow swans, and men become
what I am now!

"That 's the only magic — had but fools dis-
cernment,
Could they probe and pass into the solid through
the soft and seeming!
Teach me such true magic — now, and no ad-
journment!
Teach your art of making fools subserve the
man of mind!
Magic is the power we men of mind should
practice,
Draw fools to become our drudges — docile
henceforth, never dreaming —
While they do our hests for fancied gain — the
fact is
What they toil and moil to get proves false-
hood: truth 's behind!

"See now! you conceive some fabric — say, a
mansion
Meet for monarch's pride and pleasure: this is
truth — a thought has fired you,
Made you fain to give some cramped concept
expansion,
Put your faculty to proof, fulfil your nature's
task.
First you fascinate the monarch's self: he fan-
cies
He it was devised the scheme you execute as he
inspired you:
He in turn sets slaving insignificances
Toiling, moiling till your structure stands there
— all you ask!

"Soon the monarch 's known for what he was
— a ninny:
Soon the rabble-rout leave labor, take their
work-day wage and vanish:
Soon the late puffed bladder, pricked, shows
lank and skinny —
'Who was its inflator?' ask we, 'whose the
giant lungs'
Petri en pulmones! What though men prove
ingrates?
Let them — so they stop at crucifixion — buffet,
ban and banish!
Peter's power 's apparent: human praise — its
din grates
Harsh as blame on ear unused to aught save
angels' tongues.

"Ay, there have been always, since our world
existed,
Mages who possessed the secret — needed but to
stand still, fix eye
On the foolish mortal: straight was he enlisted
Soldier, scholar, servant, slave — no matter for
the style!
Only through illusion; ever what seemed
profit —
Love or lucre — justified obedience to the Ipse
dixi:
Work done — palace reared from pavement up
to soffit —

Was it strange if builders smelt out cheating
  all the while ?

" Let them pelt and pound, bruise, bray you in
  a mortar !
What 's the odds to you who seek reward of
  quite another nature ?
You 've enrolled your name where sages of
  your sort are,
— Michael of Constantinople, Hans of Halber-
  stadt !
Nay and were you nameless, still you 've your
  conviction
You it was and only you — what signifies the
  nomenclature ? —
Ruled the world in fact, though how you ruled
  be fiction
Fit for fools : true wisdom's magic you — if
  e'er man — had 't !

" But perhaps you ask me, ' Since each igno-
  ramus
While he profits by such magic persecutes the
  benefactor,
What should I expect but — once I render
  famous
You as Michael, Hans, and Peter — just one
  ingrate more ?
If the vulgar prove thus, whatsoe'er the pelf
  be,
Pouched through my beneficence — and doom
  me dungeoned, chained, or racked, or
Fairly burned outright — how grateful will
  yourself be
When, his secret gained, you match your —
  master just before ? '

" That 's where I await you ! Please, revert a
  little !
What do folk report about you if not this —
  which, though chimeric,
Still, as figurative, suits you to a tittle —
That, — although the elements obey your nod
  and wink,
Fades or flowers the herb you chance to smile
  or sigh at,
While your frown bids earth quake palled by
  obscuration atmospheric, —
Brief, although through nature naught resists
  your *fiat*,
There 's yet one poor substance mocks you —
  milk you may not drink !

" Figurative language ! . Take my explanation !
Fame with fear, and hate with homage, these
  your art procures in plenty.
All 's but daily dry bread : what makes moist
  the ration ?
Love, the milk that sweetens man his meal —
  alas, you lack :
I am he who, since he fears you not, can love
  you.
Love is born of heart not mind, *de corde natus
  haud de mente ;*
Touch my heart and love 's yours, sure as shines
  above you
Sun by day and star by night though earth
  should go to wrack !

" Stage by stage you lift me — kiss by kiss I
  hallow
Whose but your dear hand my helper, punctual
  as at each new impulse
I approach my aim ? Shell chipped, the eaglet
  callow
Needs a parent's pinion-push to quit the eyrie's
  edge :
But once fairly launched forth, denizen of ether.
While each effort sunward bids the blood more
  freely through each limb pulse,
Sure the parent feels, as gay they soar together,
Fully are all pains repaid when love redeems
  its pledge ! "

Then did Peter's tristful visage lighten some-
  what,
Vent a watery smile as though inveterate mis-
  trust were thawing.
" Well, who knows ? " he slow broke silence.
  " Mortals — come what
Come there may — are still the dupes of hope
  there 's luck in store.
Many scholars seek me, promise mounts and
  marvels :
Here stand I to witness how they step 'twixt
  me and clapper-clawing !
Dry bread, — that I 've gained me : truly I
  should starve else :
But of milk, no drop was mine ! Well, shuffle
  cards once more ! "

At the word of promise thus implied, our
  stranger —
What can he but cast his arms, in rapture of
  embrace, round Peter ?
" Hold ! I choke ! " the mage grunts. " Shall
  I in the manger
Any longer play the dog ? Approach, my calf,
  and feed !
Bene . . . won't you wait for grace ? " But
  sudden incense
Wool-white, serpent-solid, curled up — perfume
  growing sweet and sweeter
Till it reached the young man's nose and seemed
  to win sense
Soul and all from out his brain through nostril :
  yes, indeed !

Presently the young man rubbed his eyes.
  " Where am I ?
Too much bother over books ! Some reverie
  has proved amusing.
What did Peter prate of ? 'Faith, my brow is
  clammy !
How my head throbs, how my heart thumps !
  Can it be I swooned ?
Oh, I spoke my speech out — cribbed from
  Plato's tractate,
Dosed him with ' the Fair and Good,' swore —
  Dog of Egypt — I was choosing
Plato's way to serve men ! What 's the hour ?
  Exact eight !
Home now, and to-morrow never mind how
  Plato mooned !

" Peter has the secret ! Fair and Good are
  products

(So he said) of Foul and Evil: one must bring
     to pass the other.
Just as poisons grow drugs, steal through
     sundry odd ducts
Doctors name, and ultimately issue safe and
     changed.
You 'd abolish poisons, treat disease with
     dainties
Such as suit the sound and sane? With all
     such kickshaws vain you pother!
Arsenic 's the stuff puts force into the faint
     eyes,
Opium sets the brain to rights — by cark and
     care deranged.

"What, he 's safe within door? — would escape
     — no question —
Thanks, since thanks and more I owe, and
     mean to pay in time befitting.
What most presses now is — after night's
     digestion,
Peter, of thy precepts! — promptest practice of
     the same.
Let me see! The wise man, first of all, scorns
     riches:
But to scorn them must obtain them: none
     believes in his permitting
Gold to lie ungathered: who picks up, then
     pitches
Gold away — philosophizes: none disputes his
     claim.

"So with worldly honors: 't is by abdicating,
Incontestably he proves he could have kept the
     crown discarded.
Sulla cuts a figure, leaving off dictating:
Simpletons laud private life? 'The grapes are
     sour,' laugh we.
So, again — but why continue? All 's tumultu-
     ous
Here: my head 's a-whirl with knowledge.
     Speedily shall be rewarded
He who taught me! Greeks prove ingrates?
     So insult you us?
When your teaching bears its first-fruits, Peter
     — wait and see! "

As the word, the deed proved; ere a brief
     year's passage,
Fop — that fool he made the jokes on — now he
     made the jokes for, gratis:
Hunks — that hoarder, long left lonely in his
     crass age —
Found now one appreciative deferential friend:
Powder-paint-and-patch, Hag Jezebel — recov-
     ered,
Strange to say, the power to please, got court-
     ship till she cried Jam satis!
Fop be-flattered, Hunks be-friended, Hag be-
     lovered —
Nobody o'erlooked, save God — he soon attained
     his end.

As he lounged at ease one morning in his villa,
(Hag's the dowry) estimated (Hunks' bequest)
     his coin in coffer,
Mused on how a fool's good word (Fop's word)
     could fill a

Social circle with his praise, promote him man
     of mark, —
All at once — "An old friend fain would see
     your Highness! "
There stood Peter, skeleton and scarecrow,
     plain writ Phi-lo-so-pher
In the woe-worn face — for yellowness and dry-
     ness,
Parchment — with a pair of eyes — one hope
     their feeble spark.

" Did I counsel rightly? Have you, in ac-
     cordance,
Prospered greatly, dear my pupil? Sure, at
     just the stage I find you,
When your hand may draw me forth from the
     mad war-dance
Savages are leading round your master — down,
     not dead.
Padua wants to burn me: balk them, let me
     linger
Life out — rueful though its remnant — hid in
     some safe hold behind you!
Prostrate here I lie: quick, help with but a
     finger
Lest I house in safety's self — a tombstone o'er
     my head!

" Lodging, bite and sup, with — now and then —
     a copper
— Alms for any poorer still, if such there be, —
     is all my asking.
Take me for your bedesman, — nay, if you think
     proper,
Menial merely, — such my perfect passion for
     repose!
Yes, from out your plenty Peter craves a pit-
     tance
— Leave to thaw his frozen hands before the
     fire whereat you 're basking!
Double though your debt were, grant this boon
     — remittance
He proclaims of obligation: 't is himself that
     owes! "

" Venerated Master — can it be, such treatment
Learning meets with, magic fails to guard you
     from, by all appearance?
Strange! for, as you entered, — what the
     famous feat meant,
I was full of, — why you reared that fabric,
     Padua's boast.
Nowise for man's pride, man's pleasure, did
     you slyly
Raise it, but man's seat of rule whereby the
     world should soon have clearance
(Happy world) from such a rout as now so vilely
Handles you — and hampers me, for which I
     grieve the most.

"Since if it got wind you now were my familiar,
How could I protect you — nay, defend myself
     against the rabble?
Wait until the mob, now masters, willy-nilly
     are
Servants as they should be: then has gratitude
     full play!
Surely this experience shows how unbefitting

'T is that minds like mine should rot in ease
and plenty. Geese may gabble,
Gorge, and keep the ground: but swans are
soon for quitting
Earthly fare — as fain would I, your swan, if
taught the way.

"Teach me, then, to rule men, have them at
my pleasure !
Solely for their good, of course, — impart a
secret worth rewarding,
Since the proper life's - prize ! Tantalus's
treasure
Aught beside proves, vanishes, and leaves no
trace at all.
Wait awhile, nor press for payment prema-
turely !
)ver-haste defrauds you. Thanks ! since, —
even while I speak, — discarding
Sloth and vain delights, I learn how — swiftly,
surely —
Magic sways the sceptre, wears the crown and
wields the ball !

"Gone again — what, is he? 'Faith, he's soon
disposed of !
Peter's precepts work already, put within my
lump their leaven !
Ay, we needs must don glove would we pluck
the rose — doff
Silken garment would we climb the tree and
take its fruit.
Why sharp thorn, rough rind? To keep un-
violated
Either prize ! We garland us, we mount from
earth to feast in heaven,
Just because exist what once we estimated
Hindrances which, better taught, as helps we
now compute.

"Foolishly I turned disgusted from my fel-
lows !
Pits of ignorance — to fill, and heaps of preju-
dice — to level —
Multitudes in motley, whites and blacks and
yellows —
What a hopeless task it seemed to discipline
the host !
Now I see my error. Vices act like virtues
— Not alone because they guard — sharp thorns
— the rose we first dishevel,
Not because they scrape, scratch — rough rind
— through the dirt-shoes
Bare feet cling to bole with, while the half-
mooned boot we boast.

"No, my aim is nobler, more disinterested !
Man shall keep what seemed to thwart him,
since it proves his true assistance,
Leads to ascertaining which head is the best
head,
Would he crown his body, rule its members —
lawless else.
Ignorant the horse stares, by deficient vision
Takes a man to be a monster, lets him mount,
then, twice the distance
Horse could trot unridden, gallops — dream
Elysian ! —

Dreaming that his dwarfish guide's a giant, —
jockeys tell 's."

Brief, so worked the spell, he promptly had a
riddance:
Heart and brain no longer felt the pricks which
passed for conscience-scruples:
Free henceforth his feet, — *Per Bacco*, how
they did dance
Merrily through lets and checks that stopped
the way before !
Politics the prize now, — such adroit adviser,
Opportune suggester, with the tact that triples
and quadruples
Merit in each measure, — never did the Kaiser
Boast as subject such a statesman, friend, and
something more !

As he, up and down, one noonday, paced his closet
— Council o'er, each spark (his hint) blown
flame, by colleagues' breath applauded,
Strokes of statecraft hailed with "*Salomo si
nôsset !*"
(His the nostrum) — every throw for luck come
double-six, —
As he, pacing, hugged himself in satisfaction,
Thump — the door went. "What, the Kaiser ?
By none else were I defrauded
Thus of well-earned solace. Since 't is fate's
exaction, —
Enter, Liege my Lord ! Ha, Peter, you here ?
Teneor vix !"

"Ah, Sir, none the less, contain you, nor wax
irate !
You so lofty, I so lowly, — vast the space which
yawns between us !
Still, methinks, you — more than ever — at a
high rate
Needs must prize poor Peter's secret since it
lifts you thus.
Grant me now the boon whereat before you
boggled !
Ten long years your march has moved — one
triumph — (though *e* 's short) — *hactēnus*,
While I down and down disastrously have
joggled
Till I pitch against Death's door, the true *Nec
Ultra Plus.*

"Years ago — some ten 't is — since I sought
for shelter,
Craved in your whole house a closet, out of all
your means a comfort.
Now you soar above these: as is gold to spelter
So is power — you urged with reason — para-
mount to wealth.
Power you boast in plenty: let it grant me
refuge !
House-room now is out of question: find for
me some stronghold — some fort —
Privacy wherein, immured, shall this blind
deaf huge
Monster of a mob let stay the soul I'd save by
stealth !

"Ay, for all too much with magic have I tam
pered !

— Lost the world, and gained, I fear, a certain
　　place I 'm to describe loth !
Still, if prayer and fasting tame the pride long
　　pampered,
Mercy may be mine : amendment never comes
　　too late.
How can I amend beset by cursers, kickers ?
Pluck this brand from out the burning ! Once
　　away, I take my Bible-oath,
Never more — so long as life's weak lamp-flame
　　flickers —
No, not once I 'll tease you, but in silence bear
　　my fate ! "

" Gently, good my Genius, Oracle unerring !
Strange now ! can you guess on what — as in
　　you peeped — it was I pondered ?
You and I are both of one mind in preferring
Power to wealth, but — here 's the point —
　　what sort of power, I ask ?
Ruling men is vulgar, easy, and ignoble :
Rid yourself of conscience, quick you have at
　　beck and call the fond herd.
But who wields the crozier, down may fling the
　　crow-bill :
That 's the power I covet now ; soul's sway o'er
　　souls — my task !

" ' Well but,' you object, ' you have it, who by
　　glamour
Dress up lies to look like truths, mask folly in
　　the garb of reason :
Your soul acts on theirs, sure, when the people
　　clamor,
Hold their peace, now fight now fondle, — ear-
　　wigged through the brains.'
Possibly ! but still the operation 's mundane,
Grosser than a taste demands which — craving
　　manna — kecks at peason —
Power o'er men by wants material : why should
　　one deign
Rule by sordid hopes and fears — a grunt for
　　all one's pains ?

" No, if men must praise me, let them praise to
　　purpose !
Would we move the world, not earth but
　　heaven must be our fulcrum — *pou sto !*
Thus I seek to move it : Master, why intérpose —
Balk my climbing close on what 's the ladder's
　　topmost round ?
Statecraft 't is I step from : when by priest-
　　craft hoisted
Up to where my foot may touch the highest
　　rung which fate allows toe,
Then indeed ask favor. On you shall be
　　foisted
No excuse : I 'll pay my debt, each penny of
　　the pound !

" Ho, my knaves without there ! Lead this
　　worthy downstairs !
No farewell, good Paul — nay, Peter — what 's
　　your name remembered rightly ?
Come, he 's humble : out another would have
　　flounced — airs
Suitors often give themselves when our sort
　　bow them forth.

Did I touch his rags ? He surely kept his dis-
　　tance :
Yet, there somehow passed to me from him —
　　where'er the virtue might lie —
Something that inspires my soul — Oh, by as-
　　sistance
Doubtlessly of Peter ! — still, he 's worth just
　　what he 's worth !

" 'T is my own soul soars now : soaring — how ?
　　By crawling !
I 'll to Rome, before Rome's feet the tempora!
　　supreme lay prostrate !
' Hands ' (I 'll say) ' proficient once in pulling,
　　hauling
This and that way men as I was minded — feet
　　now clasp ! '
Ay, the Kaiser's self has wrung them in his
　　fervor !
Now — they only sue to slave for Rome, nor at
　　one doit the cost rate.
Rome's adopted child — no bone, no muscle,
　　nerve or
Sinew of me but I 'll strain, though out my life
　　I gasp ! "

As he stood one evening proudly — (he had
　　traversed
Rome on horseback — peerless pageant ! —
　　claimed the Lateran as new Pope) —
Thinking " All 's attained now ! Pontiff ! Who
　　could have erst
Dreamed of my advance so far when, some ten
　　years ago,
I embraced devotion, grew from priest to
　　bishop,
Gained the Purple, bribed the Conclave, got
　　the Two-thirds, saw my coop ope,
Came out — what Rome hails me ! O were
　　there a wish-shop,
Not one wish more would I purchase — lord of
　　all below !

" Ha — who dares intrude now — puts aside the
　　arras ?
What, old Peter, here again, at such a time, in
　　such a presence ?
Satan sends this plague back merely to em-
　　barrass
Me who enter on my office — little needing
　　you !
'Faith, I 'm touched myself by age, but you
　　look Tithon !
Were it vain to seek of you the sole prize left —
　　rejuvenescence ?
Well, since flesh is grass which time must lay
　　his scythe on,
Say your say and so depart and make no more
　　ado ! "

Peter faltered — coughing first by way of pro-
　　logue —
" Holiness, your help comes late : a death at
　　ninety little matters.
Padua, build poor Peter's pyre now, on log roll
　　log,
Burn away — I 've lived my day ! Yet here 's
　　the sting in death —

I 've an author's pride: I want my Book's survival:
See, I 've hid it in my breast to warm me 'mid the rags and tatters!
Save it — tell next age your Master had no rival!
Scholar's debt discharged in full, be ' Thanks ' my latest breath! ''

" Faugh, the frowsy bundle — scribblings harum-scarum
Scattered o'er a dozen sheepskins! What 's the name of this farrago ?
Ha — ' *Conciliator Differentiarum* ' —
Man and book may burn together, cause the world no loss!
Stop — what else ? A tractate — eh, ' *De Speciebus*
Ceremonialis Ma-gi-æ ? ' I dream sure! Hence, away, go,
Wizard, — quick avoid me! Vain you clasp my knee, buss
Hand that bears the Fisher's ring or foot that boasts the Cross!

" Help! The old magician clings like an octopus!
Ah, you rise now — fuming, fretting, frowning, if I read your features!
Frown, who cares? We 're Pope — once Pope, you can't unpope us!
Good — you muster up a smile : that 's better! Still so brisk ?
All at once grown youthful? But the case is plain! Ass —
Here I dally with the fiend, yet know the Word — compels all creatures
Earthly, heavenly, hellish. *Apage, Sathanas Dicam verbum Salomonis* — '' " *dicite!* '' When — whisk! —

What was changed? The stranger gave his eyes a rubbing:
There smiled Peter's face turned back a moment at him o'er the shoulder,
As the black-door shut, bang! " So he 'scapes a drubbing! ''
(Quoth a boy who, unespied, had stopped to hear the talk.)
" That 's the way to thank these wizards when they bid men
Benedicite! What ails you? You, a man, and yet no bolder ?
Foreign Sir, you look but foolish! " " *Idmen, idmen!* ''
Groaned the Greek. " O Peter, cheese at last I know from chalk! ''

Peter lived his life out, menaced yet no martyr,
Knew himself the mighty man he was — such knowledge all his guerdon,
Left the world a big book — people but in part err
When they style a true *Scientiæ Com-pen-di-um :*
" *Admirationem incutit* '' they sourly
Smile, as fast they shut the folio which myself was somehow spurred on
Once to ope : but love — life's milk which daily, hourly,

Blockheads lap — O Peter, still thy taste of love 's to come!

Greek, was your ambition likewise doomed to failure ?
True, I find no record you wore purple, walked with axe and fasces,
Played some antipope's part: still, friend, don't turn tail, you 're
Certain, with but these two gifts, to gain earth's prize in time!
Cleverness uncurbed by conscience — if you ransacked
Peter's book you 'd find no potent spell like these to rule the masses ;
Nor should want example, had I not to transact
Other business. Go your ways, you 'll thrive! So ends my rhyme.

When these parts Tiberius — not yet Cæsar — travelled,
Passing Padua, he consulted Padua's Oracle of Geryon
(God three-headed, thrice wise) just to get unravelled
Certain tangles of his future. " Fling at Abano
Golden dice," it answered : " dropt within the fount there,
Note what sum the pips present! " And still we see each die, the very one,
Turn up, through the crystal, — read the whole account there
Where 't is told by Suetonius, — each its highest throw.

Scarce the sportive fancy-dice I fling show " Venus : ''
Still — for love of that dear land which I so oft in dreams revisit —
I have — oh, not sung! but lilted (as — between us —
Grows my lazy custom) this its legend. What the lilt ?

DOCTOR ——

A RABBI told me: On the day allowed
Satan for carping at God's rule, he came,
Fresh from our earth, to brave the angel-
    crowd.

"What is the fault now?" "This I find to
    blame:
Many and various are the tongues below,
Yet all agree in one speech, all proclaim

"'Hell has no might to match what earth can
    show:
Death is the strongest-born of Hell, and yet
Stronger than Death is a Bad Wife, we know.'

"Is it a wonder if I fume and fret—
Robbed of my rights, since Death am I, and
    mine
The style of Strongest? Men pay Nature's
    debt

"Because they must at my demand; decline
To pay it henceforth surely men will please,
Provided husbands with bad wives combine

"To baffle Death. Judge between me and
    these!"
"Thyself shalt judge. Descend to earth in
    shape
Of mortal, marry, drain from froth to lees

"The bitter draught, then see if thou escape
Concluding, with men sorrowful and sage,
A Bad Wife's strength Death's self in vain
    would ape!"

How Satan entered on his pilgrimage,
Conformed himself to earthly ordinance,
Wived and played husband well from youth to
    age

Intrepidly—I leave untold, advance
Through many a married year until I reach
A day when—of his father's countenance

The very image, like him too in speech
As well as thought and deed,—the union's
    fruit
Attained maturity. "I needs must teach

"My son a trade: but trade, such son to suit,
Needs seeking after. He a man of war?
Too cowardly! A lawyer wins repute—

"Having to toil and moil, though—both which
    are
Beyond this sluggard. There's Divinity:
No, that's my own bread-winner—that be
    far

"From my poor offspring! Physic? Ha, we'll
    try
If this be practicable. Where's my wit?
Asleep?—since, now I come to think . . . Ay,
    ay!

"Hither, my son! Exactly have I hit
On a profession for thee. *Medicus*—
Behold, thou art appointed! Yea, I spit

"Upon thine eyes, bestow a virtue thus
That henceforth not this human form I wear
Shalt thou perceive alone, but—one of us

"By privilege—thy fleshly sight shall bear
Me in my spirit-person as I walk
The world and take my prey appointed there.

"Doctor once dubbed—what ignorance shall
    balk
Thy march triumphant? Diagnose the gout
As colic, and prescribe it cheese for chalk—

"No matter! All's one: cure shall come
    about
And win thee wealth—fees paid with such a
    roar
Of thanks and praise alike from lord and lout

"As never stunned man's ears on earth before.
'How may this be?' Why, that's my skeptic!
    Soon
Truth will corrupt thee, soon thou doubt'st no
    more!

"Why is it I bestow on thee the boon
Of recognizing me the while I go
Invisibly among men, morning, noon,

"And night, from house to house, and—quick
    or slow—
Take my appointed prey? They summon thee
For help, suppose: obey the summons! so!

"Enter, look round! Where's Death? Know
    —I am he,
Satan who work all evil: I who bring
Pain to the patient in whate'er degree.

"I, then, am there: first glance thine eye shall
    fling
Will find me—whether distant or at hand,
As I am free to do my spiriting.

"At such mere first glance thou shalt under-
    stand
Wherefore I reach no higher up the room
Than door or window, when my form is
    scanned.

"Howe'er friends' faces please to gather gloom,
Bent o'er the sick,—howe'er himself de-
    sponds,—
In such case Death is not the sufferer's doom.

"Contrariwise, do friends rejoice my bonds
Are broken, does the captive in his turn
Crow 'Life shall conquer'? Nip these foolish
    fronds

"Of hope a-sprout, if haply thou discern
Me at the head—my victim's head, be sure!
Forth now! This taught thee, little else to
    learn!"

And forth he went. Folk heard him ask de-
    mure,
" How do you style this ailment? (There he
    peeps,
My father through the arras!) Sirs, the cure

" Is plain as A B C! Experience steeps
Blossoms of pennyroyal half an hour
In sherris.   *Sumat!* — Lo, hcw sound he
    sleeps —

" The subject you presumed was past the power
Of Galen to relieve!" Or else, " How 's this?
Why call for help so tardily? Clouds lour

" Portentously   indeed,   Sirs!   (Naught 's
    amiss:
He 's at the bed-foot merely.) Still, the storm
May pass averted — not by quacks, I wis,

" Like you, my masters! You, forsooth, per-
    form
A miracle? Stand, sciolists, aside!
Blood, ne'er so cold, at ignorance grows
    warm!"

Which boasting by result was justified,
Big as might words be: whether drugged or
    left
Drugless, the patient always lived, not died.

Great the heir's gratitude, so nigh bereft
Of all he prized in this world: sweet the smile
Of disconcerted rivals: " Cure? — say, theft

" From Nature in despite of Art — so style
This off-hand kill-or-cure work! You did
    much,
I had done more: folk cannot wait awhile!"

But did the case change? was it — " Scarcely
    such
The symptoms as to warrant our recourse
To your skill, Doctor! Yet since just a touch

" Of pulse, a taste of breath, has all the force
With you of long investigation claimed
By others, — tracks an ailment to its source

" Intuitively, — may we ask unblamed
What from this pimple you prognosticate?"
" Death!" was the answer, as he saw and
    named

The coucher by the sick man's head. " Too
    late
You send for my assistance. I am bold
Only by Nature's leave, and bow to Fate!

" Besides, you have my rivals: lavish gold!
How comfortably quick shall life depart
Cosseted by attentions manifold!

" One day, one hour ago, perchance my art
Had done some service. Since you have your-
    selves
Chosen — before the horse — to put the cart,

" Why, Sirs, the sooner that the sexton delves
Your patient's grave the better! How you
    stare
— Shallow, for all the deep books on your
    shelves!

" Fare you well, fumblers!" Do I need de-
    clare
What name and fame, what riches recompensed
The Doctor's practice? Never anywhere

Such an adept as daily evidenced
Each new vaticination! Oh, not he
Like dolts who dallied with their scruples
    fenced

With subterfuge, nor gave out frank and free
Something decisive! If he said " I save
The patient," saved he was: if " Death will be

" His portion," you might count him dead.
    Thus brave,
Behold our worthy, sans competitor
Throughout the country, on the architrave

Of Glory's temple golden-lettered for
Machaon *redivivus!* So, it fell
That, of a sudden, when the Emperor

Was smit by sore disease, I need not tell
If any other Doctor's aid was sought
To come and forthwith make the sick Prince
    well.

" He will reward thee as a monarch ought.
Not much imports the malady; but then,
He clings to life and cries like one distraught

" For thee — who, from a simple citizen,
Mayst look to rise in rank, — nay, haply wear
A medal with his portrait, — always when

" Recovery is quite accomplished. There!
Pass to the presence!" Hardly has he crossed
The chamber's threshold when he halts, aware

Of who stands sentry by the head. All 's lost.
" Sire, naught avails my art: you near the goal,
And end the race by giving up the ghost."

" How?" cried the monarch: " Names upon
    your roll
Of half my subjects rescued by your skill —
Old and young, rich and poor — crowd cheek by
    jowl

" And yet no room for mine? Be saved I will!
Why else am I earth's foremost potentate?
Add me to these and take as fee your fill

" Of gold — that point admits of no debate
Between us: save me, as you can and must, —
Gold, till your gown's pouch cracks beneath the
    weight!"

This touched the Doctor. " Truly a home-
    thrust,

Parent, you will not parry ! Have I dared
Entreat that you forego the meal of dust

" — Man that is snake's meat — when I saw
    prepared
Your daily portion ? Never ! Just this once,
Go from his head, then, — let his life be
    spared ! "

Whisper met whisper in the gruff response ;
" Fool, I must have my prey : no inch I budge
From where thou see'st me thus myself en-
    sconce."

" Ah," moaned the sufferer, " by thy look I
    judge
Wealth fails to tempt thee : what if honors
    prove
More efficacious ? Naught to him I grudge

" Who saves me. Only keep my head above
The cloud that 's creeping round it — I 'll
    divide
My empire with thee ! No ? What 's left but
    — love ?

" Does love allure thee ? Well then, take as
    bride
My only daughter, fair beyond belief !
Save me — to-morrow shall the knot be tied ! "

" Father, you hear him ! Respite ne'er so
    brief
Is all I beg : go now and come again
Next day, for aught I care : respect the grief

" Mine will be if thy first-born sues in vain ! "
" Fool, I must have my prey ! " was all he
    got
In answer. But a fancy crossed his brain.

" I have it ! Sire, methinks a meteor shot
Just now across the heavens and neutralized
Jove's salutary influence : 'neath the blot

" Plumb are you placed now : well that I sur-
    mised
The cause of failure ! Knaves, reverse the
    bed ! "
" Stay ! " groaned the monarch, " I shall be
    capsized —

" Jolt — jolt — my heels uplift where late my
    head
Was lying — sure I 'm turned right round at
    last !
What do you say now, Doctor ? " Naught he
    said,

For why ? With one brisk leap the Antic
    passed
From couch-foot back to pillow, — as before,
Lord of the situation. Long aghast

The Doctor gazed, then " Yet one trial more
Is left me " inwardly he uttered. " Shame
Upon thy flinty heart ! Do I implore

" This trifling favor in the idle name
Of mercy to the moribund ? I plead
The cause of all thou dost affect : my aim

" Befits my author ! Why would I succeed ?
Simply that by success I may promote
The growth of thy pet virtues — pride and
    greed.

" But keep thy favors ! — curse thee ! I devote
Henceforth my service to the other side.
No time to lose : the rattle 's in his throat.

" So, — not to leave one last resource untried, —
Run to my house with all haste, somebody !
Bring me that knobstick thence, so often plied

" With profit by the astrologer — shall I
Disdain its help, the mystic Jacob's-Staff ?
Sire, do but have the courage not to die

" Till this arrive ! Let none of you dare laugh !
Though rugged its exterior, I have seen
That implement work wonders, send the chaff

" Quick and thick flying from the wheat — I
    mean,
By metaphor, a human sheaf it threshed
Flail-like. Go fetch it ! Or — a word between

Just you and me, friend ! — go bid, unabashed,
My mother, whom you 'll find there, bring the
    stick
Herself — herself, mind ! " Out the lackey
    dashed

Zealous upon the errand. Craft and trick
Are meat and drink to Satan : and he grinned
— How else ? — at an excuse so politic

For failure : scarce would Jacob's-Staff rescind
Fate's firm decree ! And ever as he neared
The agonizing one, his breath like wind

Froze to the marrow, while his eye-flash seared
Sense in the brain up : closelier and more close
Pressing his prey, when at the door appeared

— Who but his Wife the Bad ? Whereof one
    dose,
One grain, one mite of the medicament,
Sufficed him. Up he sprang. One word, too
    gross

To soil my lips with, — and through ceiling went
Somehow the Husband. " That a storm 's
    dispersed
We know for certain by the sulphury scent !

" Hail to the Doctor ! Who but one so versed
In all Dame Nature's secrets had prescribed
The staff thus opportunely ? Style him first

" And foremost of physicians ! " " I 've imbibed
Elixir surely," smiled the prince, — " have
    gained
New lease of life. Dear Doctor, how you
    bribed

"Death to forego me, boots not: you've ob-
    tained
My daughter and her dowry. Death, I've heard,
Was still on earth the strongest power that
    reigned,

"Except a Bad Wife!" Whereunto demurred
Nowise the Doctor, so refused the fee
— No dowry, no bad wife!

                "You think absurd
This tale?"— the Rabbi added: " True, our
    Talmud
Boasts sundry such: yet — have our elders
    erred
In thinking there's some water there, not all
    mud?"
I tell it, as the Rabbi told it me.

PAN AND LUNA

Si credere dignum est. — Georgic, III. 390.

OH, worthy of belief I hold it was,
Virgil, your legend in those strange three lines!
No question, that adventure came to pass
One black night in Arcadia: yes, the pines,
Mountains and valleys mingling made one mass
Of black with void black heaven: the earth's
    confines,
The sky's embrace, — below, above, around,
All hardened into black without a bound.

Fill up a swart stone chalice to the brim
With fresh-squeezed yet fast-thickening poppy-
    juice:
See how the sluggish jelly, late a-swim,
Turns marble to the touch of who would loose
The solid smooth, grown jet from rim to rim,
By turning round the bowl! So night can fuse
Earth with her all-comprising sky. No less,
Light, the least spark, shows air and emptiness.

And thus it proved when — diving into space,
Stript of all vapor, from each web of mist
Utterly film-free — entered on her race
The naked Moon, full-orbed antagonist
Of night and dark, night's dowry: peak to base,
Upstarted mountains, and each valley, kissed
To sudden life, lay silver-bright: in air
Flew she revealed, Maid-Moon with limbs all
    bare.

Still as she fled, each depth — where refuge
    seemed —
Opening a lone pale chamber, left distinct
Those limbs: 'mid still-retreating blue, she
    teemed
Herself with whiteness, — virginal, uncinct
By any halo save what finely gleamed
To outline not disguise her: heaven was linked
In one accord with earth to quaff the joy,
Drain beauty to the dregs without alloy.

Whereof she grew aware. What help? When,
    lo,
A succorable cloud with sleep lay dense:

Some pinetree-top had caught it sailing slow,
And tethered for a prize: in evidence
Captive lay fleece on fleece of piled-up snow
Drowsily patient: flake-heaped how or whence,
The structure of that succorable cloud,
What matter? Shamed she plunged into its
    shroud.

Orbed — so the woman-figure poets call
Because of rounds on rounds — that apple-
    shaped
Head which its hair binds close into a ball
Each side the curving ears — that pure undraped
Pout of the sister paps — that . . . Once for
    all,
Say — her consummate circle thus escaped
With its innumerous circlets, sank absorbed,
Safe in the cloud — O naked Moon full-orbed!

But what means this? The downy swathes
    combine,
Conglobe, the smothery coy-caressing stuff
Curdles about her! Vain each twist and twine
Those lithe limbs try, encroached on by a fluff
Fitting as close as fits the dented spine
Its flexible ivory outside-flesh: enough!
The plumy drifts contract, condense, constringe,
Till she is swallowed by the feathery springe.

As when a pearl slips lost in the thin foam
Churned on a sea-shore, and, o'er-frothed, con-
    ceits
Herself safe-housed in Amphitrite's dome, —
If, through the bladdery wave-worked yeast,
    she meets
What most she loathes and leaps from, — elf
    from gnome
No gladlier, — finds that safest of retreats
Bubble about a treacherous hand wide ope
To grasp her — (divers who pick pearls so
    grope) —

So lay this Maid-Moon clasped around and
    caught
By rough red Pan, the god of all that tract:
He it was schemed the snare thus subtly wrought
With simulated earth-breath, — wool-tufts
    packed
Into a billowy wrappage. Sheep far-sought
For spotless shearings yield such: take the fact
As learned Virgil gives it, — how the breed
Whitens itself forever: yes, indeed!

If one forefather ram, though pure as chalk
From tinge on fleece, should still display a
    tongue
Black 'neath the beast's moist palate, prompt
    men balk
The propagating plague: he gets no young:
They rather slay him, — sell his hide to calk
Ships with, first steeped in pitch, — nor hands
    are wrung
In sorrow for his fate: protected thus,
The purity we love is gained for us.

So did Girl-Moon, by just her attribute
Of unmatched modesty betrayed, lie trapped,
Bruised to the breast of Pan, half god half brute,

Raked by his bristly boar-sward while he lapped
— Never say, kissed her ! that were to pollute
Love's language — which moreover proves un-
    apt
To tell how she recoiled — as who finds thorns
Where she sought flowers — when, feeling, she
    touched — horns !

Then — does the legend say ? — first moon-
    eclipse
Happened, first swooning-fit which puzzled sore
The early sages ? Is that why she dips
Into the dark, a minute and no more,
Only so long as serves her while she rips
The cloud's womb through and, faultless as
    before,
Pursues her way ? No lesson for a maid
Left she, a maid herself thus trapped, betrayed ?

Ha, Virgil ? Tell the rest, you ! " To the deep
Of his domain the wildwood, Pan forthwith
Called her, and so she followed " — in her sleep,
Surely ? — " by no means spurning him." The
    myth
Explain who may ! Let all else go, I keep
— As of a ruin just a monolith —
Thus much, one verse of five words, each a boon :
Arcadia, night, a cloud, Pan, and the moon.

The first ten lines that follow were printed as
epilogue to the second series of *Dramatic Idyls;*
the second ten were added to them by Brown-
ing in the album of a young American girl in
Venice, October, 1880. See *The Century* for
November, 1882.

" Touch him ne'er so lightly, into song he broke :
Soil so quick-receptive, — not one feather-seed,
Not one flower-dust fell but straight its fall awoke
Vitalizing virtue : song would song succeed
Sudden as spontaneous — prove a poet-soul ! "
                                          Indeed ?
Rock 's the song-soil rather, surface hard and bare :
Sun and dew their mildness, storm and frost their rage
Vainly both expend, — few flowers awaken there :
Quiet in its cleft broods — what the after-age
Knows and names a pine, a nation's heritage.

Thus I wrote in London, musing on my betters,
Poets dead and gone ; and lo, the critics cried,
" Out on such a boast ! " as if I dreamed that fetters
Binding Dante bind up — me ! as if true pride
Were not also humble !
                    So I smiled and sighed
As I oped your book in Venice this bright morning,
Sweet new friend of mine ! and felt the clay or sand,
Whatsoe'er my soil be, break — for praise or scorning —
Out in grateful fancies — weeds ; but weeds expand
Almost into flowers, held by such a kindly hand.

THE BLIND MAN TO THE MAIDEN

Browning translated the following from a
German poem in Wilhelmine von Hillern's
novel *The Hour Will Come* at the request of
Mrs. Clara Bell, the translator of the novel.
It there appeared as the work of an anonymous
friend, but was reprinted as Browning's in *The
Whitehall Review* for March 1, 1883.

THE blind man to the maiden said,
  " O thou of hearts the truest,
Thy countenance is hid from me ;
Let not my question anger thee !
  Speak, though in words the fewest.

" Tell me, what kind of eyes are thine ?
  Dark eyes, or light ones rather ? "
" My eyes are a decided brown —
So much, at least, by looking down,
  From the brook's glass I gather."

" And is it red — thy little mouth ?
  That too the blind must care for."
" Ah ! I would tell it soon to thee,
Only — none yet has told it me.
  I cannot answer, therefore.

" But dost thou ask what heart I have —
  There hesitate I never.
In thine own breast 't is borne, and so
'T is thine in weal, and thine in woe,
  For life, for death — thine ever ! "

GOLDONI

The following sonnet was written by Brown-
ing for the album of the Committee of the
Goldoni monument, erected in Venice in 1883.

GOLDONI — good, gay, sunniest of souls, —
  Glassing half Venice in that verse of thine, —
  What though it just reflect the shade and shine
Of common life, nor render, as it rolls,
Grandeur and gloom ? Sufficient for thy shoals
  Was Carnival ; Parini's depths enshrine
  Secrets unsuited to that opaline
Surface of things which laughs along thy scrolls
There throng the people : how they come and go
  Lisp the soft language, flaunt the bright
      garb, — see, —
On Piazza, Calle, under Portico
  And over Bridge ! Dear king of Comedy,
Be honored ! thou that didst love Venice so,
  Venice, and we who love her, all love thee !
VENICE, *November* 27, 1883.

JOCOSERIA

THIS collection of poems was published in 1883. The title of the volume is mentioned in a foot-note to the *Note* at the end of *Paracelsus*, where the poet speaks of "such rubbish as Melander's *Jocoseria*." In a letter, accompanying a copy of the volume, sent to a friend, Browning wrote : " The title is taken from the work of Melander (Schwartzmann), reviewed, by a curious coincidence, in the *Blackwood* of this month [February, 1883]. I referred to it in a note to *Paracelsus*. The two Hebrew quotations [in the note to Jochanan Hakkadosh] (put in to give a grave look to what is mere fun and invention) being translated amount to (1) ' A Collection of Lies ' ; and (2), an old saying, ' From Moses to Moses arose none like Moses.' "

WANTING IS — WHAT?

This is in the nature of a prelude to the entire group of poems.

WANTING is — what?
Summer redundant,
Blueness abundant,
— Where is the blot?
Beamy the world, yet a blank all the same,
— Framework which waits for a picture to
    frame :
What of the leafage, what of the flower?
Roses embowering with naught they embower !
Come then, complete incompletion, O comer,
Pant through the blueness, perfect the sum-
    mer !
    Breathe but one breath
    Rose-beauty above,
    And all that was death
    Grows life, grows love,
    Grows love !

DONALD

This story which Browning had from the lips of the hero has also been told in prose by Sir Walter Scott.

" WILL you hear my story also,
    — Huge Sport, brave adventure in plenty? "
The boys were a band from Oxford,
    The oldest of whom was twenty.

The bothy we held carouse in
    Was bright with fire and candle ;
Tale followed tale like a merry-go-round
    Whereof Sport turned the handle.

In our eyes and noses — turf-smoke :
    In our ears a tune from the trivet,
Whence " Boiling, boiling," the kettle sang,
    " And ready for fresh Glenlivet."

So, feat capped feat, with a vengeance :
    Truths, though, — the lads were loyal :
" Grouse, five-score brace to the bag !
    Deer, ten hours' stalk of the Royal ! "

Of boasting, not one bit, boys !
    Only there seemed to settle
Somehow above your curly heads,
    — Plain through the singing kettle,

Palpable through the cloud,
    As each new-puffed Havana
Rewarded the teller's well-told tale, —
    This vaunt " To Sport — Hosanna !

" Hunt, fish, shoot,
    Would a man fulfil life's duty !
Not to the bodily frame alone
    Does Sport give strength and beauty,

" But character gains in — courage ?
    Ay, Sir, and much beside it !
You don't sport, more 's the pity ;
    You soon would find, if you tried it,

" Good sportsman means good fellow,
    Sound-hearted he, to the centre ;
Your mealy-mouthed mild milksops
    — There 's where the rot can enter !

" There 's where the dirt will breed,
    The shabbiness Sport would banish !
Oh no, Sir, no ! In your honored case
    All such objections vanish.

" 'T is known how hard you studied :
    A Double-First — what, the jigger !
Give me but half your Latin and Greek,
    I 'll never again touch trigger !

" Still, tastes are tastes, allow me !
    Allow, too, where there 's keenness
For Sport, there 's little likelihood
    Of a man's displaying meanness ! "

So, put on my mettle, I interposed.
    " Will you hear my story ? " quoth I.
" Never mind how long since it happed,
    I sat, as we sit, in a bothy ;

" With as merry a band of mates, too,
    Undergrads all on a level :
(One 's a Bishop, one 's gone to the Bench,
    And one 's gone — well, to the Devil.)

" When, lo, a scratching and tapping !
　In hobbled a ghastly visitor.
Listen to just what he told us himself
　— No need of our playing inquisitor ! "

———————

Do you happen to know in Ross-shire
　Mount Ben . . . but the name scarce mat-
　　ters :
Of the naked fact I am sure enough,
Though I clothe it in rags and tatters.

You may recognize Ben by description ;
　Behind him — a moor's immenseness :
Up goes the middle mount of a range,
Fringed with its firs in denseness.

Rimming the edge, its fir-fringe, mind !
　For an edge there is, though narrow ;
From end to end of the range, a strip
Of path runs straight as an arrow.

And the mountaineer who takes that path
　Saves himself miles of journey
He has to plod if he crosses the moor
Through heather, peat, and burnie.

But a mountaineer he needs must be,
　For, look you, right in the middle
Projects bluff Ben — with an end in *ich* —
Why planted there, is a riddle :

Since all Ben's brothers little and big
　Keep rank, set shoulder to shoulder,
And only this burliest out must bulge
Till it seems — to the beholder

From down in the gully, — as if Ben's breast,
　To a sudden spike diminished,
Would signify to the boldest foot
" All further passage finished ! "

Yet the mountaineer who sidles on
　And on to the very bending,
Discovers, if heart and brain be proof,
No necessary ending.

Foot up, foot down, to the turn abrupt
　Having trod, he, there arriving,
Finds — what he took for a point was breadth,
A mercy of Nature's contriving.

So, he rounds what, when 't is reached, proves
　　straight,
　From one side gains the other :
The wee path widens — resume the march,
And he foils you, Ben my brother !

But Donald — (that name, I hope, will do) —
　I wrong him if I call " foiling "
The tramp of the callant, whistling the while
As blithe as our kettle 's boiling.

He had dared the danger from boyhood up,
　And now, — when perchance was waiting
A lass at the brig below, — 'twixt mount
And moor would he stand debating ?

Moreover this Donald was twenty-five,
　A glory of bone and muscle :
Did a fiend dispute the right of way,
Donald would try a tussle.

Lightsomely marched he out of the broad
　On to the narrow and narrow ;
A step more, rounding the angular rock,
Reached the front straight as an arrow.

He stepped it, safe on the ledge he stood,
　When — whom found he full-facing ?
What fellow in courage and wariness too,
Had scouted ignoble pacing,

And left low safety to timid mates,
　And made for the dread dear danger,
And gained the height where — who **could**
　　guess
He would meet with a rival ranger ?

'T was a gold-red stag that stood and stared,
　Gigantic and magnific,
By the wonder — ay, and the peril — struck
Intelligent and pacific :

For a red deer is no fallow deer
　Grown cowardly through park-feeding ;
He batters you like a thunderbolt
If you brave his haunts unheeding.

I doubt he could hardly perform *volte-face*
　Had valor advised discretion :
You may walk on a rope, but to turn on a rope
No Blondin makes profession.

Yet Donald must turn, would pride permit,
　Though pride ill brooks retiring :
Each eyed each — mute man, motionless beast —
Less fearing than admiring.

These are the moments when quite new sense,
　To meet some need as novel,
Springs up in the brain : it inspired resource :
　— " Nor advance nor retreat but — grovel ! "

And slowly, surely, never a whit
　Relaxing the steady tension
Of eye-stare which binds man to beast, —
By an inch and inch declension,

Sank Donald sidewise down and down :
　Till flat, breast upwards, lying
At his six-foot length, no corpse more still,
　— " If he cross me ! The trick 's worth try-
　　ing."

Minutes were an eternity ;
　But a new sense was created
In the stag's brain too ; he resolves ! Slow,
　　sure,
With eye-stare unabated,

Feelingly he extends a foot
　Which tastes the way ere it touches
Earth's solid and just escapes man's soft,
Nor hold of the same unclutches

Till its fellow foot, light as a feather whisk,
  Lands itself no less finely :
So a mother removes a fly from the face
  Of her babe asleep supinely.

And now 't is the haunch and hind-foot's turn
  — That 's hard: can the beast quite raise
    it ?
Yes, traversing half the prostrate length,
  His hoof-tip does not graze it.

Just one more lift ! But Donald, you see,
  Was sportsman first, man after :
A fancy lightened his caution through,
  — He wellnigh broke into laughter :

" It were nothing short of a miracle !
  Unrivalled, unexampled —
All sporting feats with this feat matched
  Were down and dead and trampled ! "

The last of the legs as tenderly
  Follows the rest : or never
Or now is the time ! His knife in reach,
  And his right-hand loose — how clever !

For this can stab up the stomach's soft,
  While the left-hand grasps the pastern.
A rise on the elbow, and — now 's the time
  Or never : this turn 's the last turn !

I shall dare to place myself by God
  Who scanned — for he does — each feature
Of the face thrown up in appeal to him
  By the agonizing creature.

Nay, I hear plain words: " Thy gift brings
    this ! "
Up he sprang, back he staggered,
Over he fell, and with him our friend
  — At following game no laggard.

Yet he was not dead when they picked next
    day
From the gully's depth the wreck of him ;
His fall had been stayed by the stag beneath
  Who cushioned and saved the neck of him.

But the rest of his body — why, doctors said,
  Whatever could break was broken ;
Legs, arms, ribs, all of him looked like a toast
  In a tumbler of port-wine soaken.

" That your life is left you, thank the stag ! "
  Said they when — the slow cure ended —
They opened the hospital-door, and thence
  — Strapped, spliced, main fractures mended,

And minor damage left wisely alone, —
  Like an old shoe clouted and cobbled,
Out — what went in a Goliath wellnigh, —
  Some half of a David hobbled.

" You must ask an alms from house to house :
  Sell the stag's head for a bracket,
With its grand twelve tines — I 'd buy it my-
    self —
And use the skin for a jacket ! "

He was wiser, made both head and hide
  His win-penny : hands and knees on,
Would manage to crawl — poor crab — by the
    roads
In the misty stalking-season.

And if he discovered a bothy like this,
  Why, harvest was sure : folk listened.
He told his tale to the lovers of Sport :
  Lips twitched, cheeks glowed, eyes glistened.

And when he had come to the close, and spread
  His spoils for the gazers' wonder,
With " Gentlemen, here 's the skull of the stag
  I was over, thank God, not under ! " —

The company broke out in applause ;
  " By Jingo, a lucky cripple !
Have a munch of grouse and a hunk of bread,
  And a tug, besides, at our tipple ! "

And " There 's my pay for your pluck ! " cried
    This,
  " And mine for your jolly story ! "
Cried That, while T' other — but he was
    drunk —
Hiccupped " A trump, a Tory ! "

I hope I gave twice as much as the rest ;
  For, as Homer would say, " within grate
Though teeth kept tongue," my whole soul
    growled,
  " Rightly rewarded, — Ingrate ! "

SOLOMON AND BALKIS

SOLOMON King of the Jews and the Queen of
    Sheba, Balkis,
Talk on the ivory throne, and we well may con-
    jecture their talk is
Solely of things sublime : why else has she
    sought Mount Zion,
Climbed the six golden steps, and sat betwixt
    lion and lion ?

She proves him with hard questions : before
    she has reached the middle
He smiling supplies the end, straight solves
    them riddle by riddle ;
Until, dead-beaten at last, there is left no spirit
    in her,
And thus would she close the game whereof she
    was first beginner :

" O wisest thou of the wise, world's marvel and
    wellnigh monster,
One crabbed question more to construe or *vulgo
    conster*,
Who are those, of all mankind, a monarch of
    perfect wisdom
Should open to, when they knock at *spheteron do*
    — that 's, his dome ? "

The King makes tart reply : " Whom else but
    the wise his equals
Should he welcome with heart and voice ? —
    since, king though he be, such weak walls

Of circumstance — power and pomp — divide
    souls each from other
That whoso proves kingly in craft I needs must
    acknowledge my brother.

"Come poet, come painter, come sculptor,
    come builder — whate'er his condition,
Is he prime in his art? We are peers! My
    insight has pierced the partition
And hails — for the poem, the picture, the
    statue, the building — my fellow!
Gold 's gold though dim in the dust: court-
    polish soon turns it yellow,

'But tell me in turn, O thou to thy weakling
    sex superior,
That for knowledge hast travelled so far yet
    seemest nowhit the wearier, —
Who are those, of all mankind, a queen like
    thyself, consummate
In wisdom, should call to her side with an
    affable ' Up hither, come, mate ' ? "

"The Good are my mates — how else? Why
    doubt it ? " the Queen upbridled:
"Sure even above the Wise, — or in travel my
    eyes have idled, —
I see the Good stand plain : be they rich, poor,
    shrewd, or simple,
If Good they only are. . . . Permit me to drop
    my wimple!"

And, in that bashful jerk of her body, she —
    peace, thou scoffer ! —
Jostled the King's right-hand stretched court-
    ously help to proffer,
And so disclosed a portent: all unaware the
    Prince eyed
The Ring which bore the Name — turned out-
    side now from inside !

The truth-compelling Name ! — and at once,
    " I greet the Wise — oh,
Certainly welcome such to my court — with
    this proviso :
The building must be my temple, my person
    stand forth the statue,
The picture my portrait prove, and the poem
    my praise — you cat, you ! "

But Solomon nonplussed ? Nay ! " Be truth-
    ful in turn ! " so bade he :
"See the Name, obey its hest ! " And at once
    subjoins the lady,
— " Provided the Good are the young, men
    strong and tall and proper,
Such servants I straightway enlist, — which
    means " . . . But the blushes stop her.

"Ah, Soul," the Monarch sighed, "that
    wouldst soar yet ever crawlest,
How comes it thou canst discern the greatest
    yet choose the smallest,
Unless because heaven is far, where wings find
    fit expansion,
While creeping on all-fours suits, suffices the
    earthly mansion ?

"Aspire to the Best ! But which ? There are
    Bests and Bests so many,
With a *habitat* each for each, earth's Best as
    much Best as any !
On Lebanon roots the cedar — soil lofty, yet
    stony and sandy —
While hyssop, of worth in its way, on the wall
    grows low but handy.

"Above may the Soul spread wing, spurn body
    and sense beneath her ;
Below she must condescend to plodding un-
    buoyed by ether.
In heaven I yearn for knowledge, account all
    else inanity ;
On earth I confess an itch for the praise of fools
    — that 's Vanity.

"It is naught, it will go, it can never presume
    above to trouble me ;
But here, — why, it toys and tickles and teases,
    howe'er I redouble me
In a doggedest of endeavors to play the indif-
    ferent. Therefore,
Suppose we resume discourse ? Thou hast
    travelled thus far: but wherefore ?

"Solely for Solomon's sake, to see whom earth
    styles Sagest ? "
Through her blushes laughed the Queen.
    " For the sake of a Sage ? The gay
    jest !
On high, be communion with Mind — there,
    Body concerns not Balkis :
Down here, — do I make too bold ? Sage
    Solomon, — one fool's small kiss ! "

CRISTINA AND MONALDESCHI

AH, but how each loved each, Marquis !
    Here 's the gallery they trod
    Both together, he her god,
    She his idol, — lend your rod,
Chamberlain ! — ay, there they are — " *Quis
    Separabit ?* " — plain those two
    Touching words come into view,
    Apposite for me and you:

Since they witness to incessant
    Love like ours : King Francis, he —
    Diane the adored one, she —
    Prototypes of you and me.
Everywhere is carved her Crescent
    With his Salamander-sign —
    Flame-fed creature : flame benign
    To itself or, if malign,

Only to the meddling curious,
    — So, be warned, Sir ! Where 's my head
    How it wanders ! What I said
    Merely meant — the creature, fed
Thus on flame, was scarce injurious
    Save to fools who woke its ire,
    Thinking fit to play with fire.
    'T is the Crescent you admire ?

Then, be Diane ! I 'll be Francis.
  Crescents change, — true ! — wax and wane,
  Woman-like : male hearts retain
  Heat nor, once warm, cool again.
So, we figure — such our chance is —
  I as man and you as . . . What ?
  Take offence ? My Love forgot
  He plays woman, I do not ?

I — the woman ? See my habit,
  Ask my people ! Anyhow,
  Be we what we may, one vow
  Binds us, male or female. Now, —
Stand, Sir ! Read ! " *Quis separabit ?* "
  Half a mile of pictured way
  Past these palace-walls to-day
  Traversed, this I came to say.

You must needs begin to love me ;
  First I hated, then, at best,
  — Have it so ! — I acquiesced ;
  Pure compassion did the rest.
From below thus raised above me,
  Would you, step by step, descend,
  Pity me, become my friend,
  Like me, like less, loathe at end ?

That 's the ladder's round you rose by !
  That — my own foot kicked away,
  Having raised you : let it stay,
  Serve you for retreating ? Nay.
Close to me you climbed : as close by,
  Keep your station, though the peak
  Reached proves somewhat bare and bleak !
  Woman 's strong if man is weak.

Keep here, loving me forever !
  Love's look, gesture, speech, I claim :
  Act love, lie love, all the same —
  Play as earnest were our game !
Lonely I stood long : 't was clever
  When you climbed, before men's eyes,
  Spurned the earth and scaled the skies,
  Gained my peak and grasped your prize.

Here you stood, then, to men's wonder ;
  Here you tire of standing ? Kneel !
  Cure what giddiness you feel,
  This way ! Do your senses reel ?
Not unlikely ! What rolls under ?
  Yawning death in yon abyss
  Where the waters whirl and hiss
  Round more frightful peaks than this.

Should my buffet dash you thither . . .
  But be sage ! No watery grave
  Needs await you : seeming brave
  Kneel on safe, dear timid slave !
You surmised, when you climbed hither,
  Just as easy were retreat
  Should you tire, conceive unmeet
  Longer patience at my feet ?

Me as standing, you as stooping, —
  Who arranged for each the pose ?
  Lest men think us friends turned foes,
  Keep the attitude you chose !

Men are used to this same grouping —
  I and you like statues seen.
  You and I, no third between,
  Kneel and stand ! That makes the scene.

Mar it — and one buffet . . . Pardon !
  Needless warmth — wise words in waste !
  'T was prostration that replaced
  Kneeling, then ? A proof of taste.
Crouch, not kneel, while I mount guard on
  Prostrate love — become no waif,
  No estray to waves that chafe
  Disappointed — love 's so safe !

Waves that chafe ? The idlest fancy !
  Peaks that scare ? I think we know
  Walls enclose our sculpture : so
  Grouped, we pose in Fontainebleau.
Up now ! Wherefore hesitancy ?
  Arm in arm and cheek by cheek,
  Laugh with me at waves and peak !
  Silent still ? Why, pictures speak.

See, where Juno strikes Ixion,
  Primatice speaks plainly ! Pooh —
  Rather, Florentine Le Roux !
  I 've lost head for who is who —
So it swims and wanders ! Fie on
  What still proves me female ! Here,
  By the staircase ! — for we near
  That dark " Gallery of the Deer."

Look me in the eyes once ! Steady !
  Are you faithful now as erst
  On that eve when we two first
  Vowed at Avon, blessed and cursed
Faith and falsehood ? Pale already ?
  Forward ! Must my hand compel
  Entrance — this way ? Exit — well.
  Somehow, somewhere. Who can tell ?

What if to the selfsame place in
  Rustic Avon, at the door
  Of the village church once more,
  Where a tombstone paves the floor
By that holy-water basin
  You appealed to — " As, below.
  This stone hides its corpse, e'en so
  I your secrets hide " ? What ho !

Friends, my four ! You, Priest, confess him.
  I have judged the culprit there :
  Execute my sentence ! Care
  For no mail such cowards wear !
Done, Priest ? Then, absolve and bless him !
  Now — you three, stab thick and fast,
  Deep and deeper ! Dead at last ?
  Thanks, friends — Father, thanks ! Aghast?

What one word of his confession
  Would you tell me, though I lured
  With that royal crown abjured
  Just because its bars immured
Love too much ? Love burst compression,
  Fled free, finally confessed
  All its secrets to that breast
  Whence . . . let Avon tell the rest !

MARY WOLLSTONECRAFT AND FUSELI

OH, but is it not hard, Dear?
  Mine are the nerves to quake at a mouse:
If a spider drops I shrink with fear:
  I should die outright in a haunted house;
While for you — did the danger dared bring
    help —
From a lion's den I could steal his whelp,
With a serpent round me, stand stock-still,
Go sleep in a churchyard, — so would will
Give me the power to dare and do
Valiantly — just for you!

Much amiss in the head, Dear,
  I toil at a language, tax my brain
Attempting to draw — the scratches here!
  I play, play, practise, and all in vain:
But for you — if my triumph brought you pride,
I would grapple with Greek Plays till I died,
Paint a portrait of you — who can tell?
Work my fingers off for your "Pretty well:"
Language and painting and music too,
Easily done — for you!

Strong and fierce in the heart, Dear,
  With — more than a will — what seems a
    power
To pounce on my prey, love outbroke here
  In flame devouring and to devour.
Such love has labored its best and worst
To win me a lover; yet, last as first,
I have not quickened his pulse one beat,
Fixed a moment's fancy, bitter or sweet:
Yet the strong fierce heart's love's labor's due,
Utterly lost, was — you!

ADAM, LILITH, AND EVE

ONE day, it thundered and lightened.
Two women, fairly frightened,
Sank to their knees, transformed, transfixed,
At the feet of the man who sat betwixt;
And "Mercy!" cried each — "if I tell the truth
Of a passage in my youth!"

Said This: "Do you mind the morning
I met your love with scorning?
As the worst of the venom left my lips,
I thought, 'If, despite this lie, he strips
The mask from my soul with a kiss — I crawl
His slave, — soul, body, and all!'"

Said That: "We stood to be married;
The priest, or some one, tarried;
'If Paradise-door prove locked?' smiled you.
I thought, as I nodded, smiling too,
'Did one, that's away, arrive — nor late
Nor soon should unlock Hell's gate!'"

It ceased to lighten and thunder.
Up started both in wonder,
Looked round and saw that the sky was clear,
Then laughed "Confess you believed us, Dear!"
"I saw through the joke!" the man replied
They re-seated themselves beside.

IXION

HIGH in the dome, suspended, of Hell, sad tri-
    umph, behold us!
  Here the revenge of a God, there the amends
    of a Man.
Whirling forever in torment, flesh once mortal,
    immortal
  Made — for a purpose of hate — able to die
    and revive,
Pays to the uttermost pang, then, newly for
    payment replenished,
  Doles out — old yet young — agonies ever
    afresh;
Whence the result above me: torment is bridged
    by a rainbow, —
  Tears, sweat, blood, — each spasm, ghastly
    once, glorified now.
Wrung, by the rush of the wheel ordained my
    place of reposing,
  Off in a sparklike spray, — flesh become vapor
    through pain, —
Flies the bestowment of Zeus, soul's vaunted
    bodily vesture,
  Made that his feats observed gain the approval
    of Man, —
Flesh that he fashioned with sense of the earth
    and the sky and the ocean,
  Framed should pierce to the star, fitted to
    pore on the plant, —
All, for a purpose of hate, re-framed, re-fash-
    ioned, re-fitted,
  Till, consummate at length, — lo, the employ-
    ment of sense!
Pain's mere minister now to the soul, once
    pledged to her pleasure —
  Soul, if untrammelled by flesh, unapprehen-
    sive of pain!
Body, professed soul's slave, which serving be-
    guiled and betrayed her,
  Made things false seem true, cheated through
    eye and through ear,
Lured thus heart and brain to believe in the
    lying reported, —
  Spurn but the trait'rous slave, uttermost
    atom, away,
What should obstruct soul's rush on the real,
    the only apparent?
  Say I have erred, — how else? Was I Ixion
    or Zeus?
Foiled by my senses I dreamed; I doubtless
    awaken in wonder:
  This proves shine, that — shade? Good was
    the evil that seemed?
Shall I, with sight thus gained, by torture be
    taught I was blind once?
  Sisuphos, teaches thy stone — Tantalos,
    teaches thy thirst
Aught which unaided sense, purged pure, less
    plainly demonstrates?
  No, for the past was dream: now that the
    dreamers awake,
Sisuphos scouts low fraud, and to Tantalos
    treason is folly.
  Ask of myself, whose form melts on the
    murderous wheel,

What is the sin which throe and throe prove
    sin to the sinner !
Say the false charge was true, — thus do I
    expiate, say,
Arrogant thought, word, deed, — mere man
    who conceited me godlike,
Sat beside Zeus, my friend — knelt before
    Heré, my love !
What were the need but of pitying power to
    touch and disperse it,
Film-work — eye's and ear's — all the dis-
    traction of sense ?
How should the soul not see, not hear, — per-
    ceive and as plainly
Render, in thought, word, deed, back again
    truth — not a lie ?
" Ay, but the pain is to punish thee ! " Zeus,
    once more for a pastime,
Play the familiar, the frank ! Speak and
    have speech in return !
I was of Thessaly king, there ruled and a peo-
    ple obeyed me :
Mine to establish the law, theirs to obey it or
    die :
Wherefore ? Because of the good to the peo-
    ple, because of the honor
Thence accruing to me, king, the king's law
    was supreme.
What of the weakling, the ignorant criminal ?
    Not who, excuseless,
Breaking my law braved death, knowing his
    deed and its due —
Nay, but the feeble and foolish, the poor trans-
    gressor, of purpose
No whit more than a tree, born to erectness of
    bole,
Palm or plane or pine, we laud if lofty, colum-
    nar —
Loathe if athwart, askew, — leave to the axe
    and the flame !
Where is the vision may penetrate earth and
    beholding acknowledge
Just one pebble at root ruined the straight-
    ness of stem ?
Whose fine vigilance follows the sapling, ac-
    counts for the failure,
— Here blew wind, so it bent : there the snow
    lodged, so it broke ?
Also the tooth of the beast, bird's bill, mere bite
    of the insect
Gnawed, gnarled, warped their worst : passive
    it lay to offence.
King — I was man, no more : what I recognized
    faulty I punished,
Laying it prone : be sure, more than a man
    had I proved,
Watch and ward o'er the sapling at birthtime
    had saved it, nor simply
Owned the distortion's excuse, — hindered it
    wholly : nay, more —
Even a man, as I sat in my place to do judg-
    ment, and pallid
Criminals passing to doom shuddered away at
    my foot,
Could I have probed through the face to the
    heart, read plain a repentance,
Crime confessed fools' play, virtue ascribed to
    the wise,

Had I not stayed the consignment to doom, not
    dealt the renewed ones
Life to retraverse the past, light to retrieve
    the misdeed ?
Thus had I done, and thus to have done much
    more it behooves thee,
Zeus who madest man — flawless or faulty,
    thy work !
What if the charge were true, as thou mouthest,
    — Ixion the cherished
Minion of Zeus grew vain, vied with the god-
    ships and fell,
Forfeit through arrogance ? Stranger ! I
    clothed, with the grace of our hu-
    man,
Inhumanity — gods, natures I likened to ours.
Man among men I had borne me till gods for-
    sooth must regard me
— Nay, must approve, applaud, claim as a
    comrade at last.
Summoned to enter their circle, I sat — their
    equal, how other ?
Love should be absolute love, faith is in ful-
    ness or naught.
" I am thy friend, be mine ! " smiled Zeus : " If
    Heré attract thee,"
Blushed the imperial cheek, " then — as thy
    heart may suggest ! "
Faith in me sprang to the faith, my love hailed
    love as its fellow,
" Zeus, we are friends — how fast ! Heré, my
    heart for thy heart ! "
Then broke smile into fury of frown, and the
    thunder of " Hence, fool ! "
Then through the kiss laughed scorn " Limbs
    or a cloud was to clasp ? "
Then from Olumpos to Erebos, then from the
    rapture to torment,
Then from the fellow of gods — misery's
    mate, to the man !
— Man henceforth and forever, who lent from
    the glow of his nature
Warmth to the cold, with light colored the
    black and the blank.
So did a man conceive of your passion, you pas-
    sion-protesters !
So did he trust, so love — being the truth of
    your lie !
You to aspire to be Man ! Man made you who
    vainly would ape him :
You are the hollowness, he — filling you, fal-
    sifies void.
Even as — witness the emblem, Hell's sad tri-
    umph suspended,
Born of my tears, sweat, blood — bursting to
    vapor above —
Arching my torment, an iris ghostlike startles
    the darkness,
Cold white — jewelry quenched — justifies,
    glorifies pain.
Strive, mankind, though strife endure through
    endless obstruction,
Stage after stage, each rise marred by as cer-
    tain a fall !
Baffled forever — yet never so baffled but, e'en
    in the baffling,
When Man's strength proves weak, checked
    in the body or soul,

Whatsoever the medium, flesh or essence, —
    Ixion's
Made for a purpose of hate, — clothing the
    entity Thou,
— Medium whence that entity strives for the
    Not-Thou beyond it,
Fire elemental, free, frame unencumbered,
    the All, —
Never so baffled but — when, on the verge of
    an alien existence,
Heartened to press, by pangs burst to the in-
    finite Pure,
Nothing is reached but the ancient weakness
    still that arrests strength,
Circumambient still, still the poor human ar-
    ray,
Pride and revenge and hate and cruelty — all it
    has burst through,
Thought to escape, — fresh formed, found in
    the fashion it fled,
Never so baffled but — when Man pays the price
    of endeavor,
Thunderstruck, downthrust, Tartaros-doomed
    to the wheel, —
Then, ay, then, from the tears and sweat and
    blood of his torment,
E'en from the triumph of Hell, up let him
    look and rejoice !
What is the influence, high o'er Hell, that
    turns to a rapture
Pain — and despair's murk mist blends in a
    rainbow of hope ?
What is beyond the obstruction, stage by stage
    though it baffle ?
Back must I fall, confess " Ever the weakness
    I fled " ?
No, for beyond, far, far is a Purity all-unob-
    structed !
Zeus was Zeus — not Man: wrecked by his
    weakness, I whirl.
Out of the wreck I rise — past Zeus to the Po-
    tency o'er him !
I — to have hailed him my friend ! I — to
    have clasped her — my love !
Pallid birth of my pain, — where light, where
    light is, aspiring
Thither I rise, whilst thou — Zeus, keep the
    godship and sink !

JOCHANAN HAKKADOSH

" This now, this other story makes amends
And justifies our Mishna," quoth the Jew
Aforesaid. " Tell it, learnedest of friends ! "

A certain morn broke beautiful and blue
O'er Schiphaz city, bringing joy and mirth,
— So had ye deemed ; while the reverse was true,

Since one small house there gave a sorrow birth
In such black sort that, to each faithful eye,
Midnight, not morning settled on the earth.

How else, when it grew certain thou wouldst die,
Our much-enlightened master, Israel's prop,
Eximious Jochanan Ben Sabbathai ?

Old, yea, but, undiminished of a drop,
The vital essence pulsed through heart and
    brain ;
Time left unsickled yet the plenteous crop

On poll and chin and cheek, whereof a skein
Handmaids might weave — hairs silk-soft, sil-
    ver-white,
Such as the wool-plant's ; none the less in vain

Had Physic striven her best against the spite
Of fell disease : the Rabbi must succumb ;
And, round the couch whereon in piteous plight

He lay a-dying, scholars, — awe-struck, dumb
Throughout the night-watch, — roused them-
    selves and spoke
One to the other : " Ere death's touch benumb

" His active sense, — while yet 'neath Reason's
    yoke
Obedient toils his tongue, — befits we claim
The fruit of long experience, bid this oak

" Shed us an acorn which may, all the same,
Grow to a temple-pillar, — dear that day ! —
When Israel's scattered seed finds place and
    name

" Among the envious nations. Lamp us, pray,
Thou the Enlightener ! Partest hence in peace ?
Hailest without regret — much less, dismay —

" The hour of thine approximate release
From fleshly bondage soul hath found obstruct ?
Calmly envisagest the sure increase

" Of knowledge ? Eden's tree must hold un-
    plucked
Some apple, sure, has never tried thy tooth,
Juicy with sapience thou hast sought, not
    sucked ?

" Say, does age acquiesce in vanished youth ?
Still towers thy purity above — as erst —
Our pleasant follies ? Be thy last word —
    truth ! "

The Rabbi groaned ; then, grimly, " Last as first
The truth speak I — in boyhood who began
Striving to live an angel, and, amerced

" For such presumption, die now hardly man.
What have I proved of life ? To live, indeed,
That much I learned : but here lies Jochanan

" More luckless than stood David when, to speed
His fighting with the Philistine, they brought
Saul's harness forth : whereat, ' Alack, I need

" ' Armor to arm me, but have never fought
With sword and spear, nor tried to manage
    shield,
Proving arms' use, as well-trained warrior ought

" ' Only a sling and pebbles can I wield ! '
So he : while I, contrariwise, ' No trick
Of weapon helpful on the battlefield

"'Comes unfamiliar to my theoric:
But, bid me put in practice what I know,
Give me a sword — it stings like Moses' stick,

"'A serpent I let drop apace.' E'en so,
I, — able to comport me at each stage
Of human life as never here below

"Man played his part, — since mine the heri-
tage
Of wisdom carried to that perfect pitch,
Ye rightly praise, — I, therefore, who, thus
sage,

"Could sure act man triumphantly, enrich
Life's annals, with example how I played
Lover, Bard, Soldier, Statist, — (all of which

"Parts in presentment failing, cries invade
The world's ear — 'Ah, the Past, the pearl-
gift thrown
To hogs, time's opportunity we made

"'So light of, only recognized when flown!
Had we been wise!') — in fine, I — wise
enough, —
What profit brings me wisdom never shown

"Just when its showing would from each re-
buff
Shelter weak virtue, threaten back to bounds
Encroaching vice, tread smooth each track too
rough

"For youth's unsteady footstep, climb the
rounds
Of life's long ladder, one by slippery one,
Yet make no stumble? Me hard fate con-
founds

"With that same crowd of wailers I outrun
By promising to teach another cry
Of more hilarious mood than theirs, the sun

"I look my last at is insulted by.
What cry, — ye ask? Give ear on every side!
Witness yon Lover! 'How entrapped am I!

"'Methought, because a virgin's rose-lip vied
With ripe Khubbezleh's, needs must beauty
mate
With meekness and discretion in a bride:

"'Bride she became to me who wail — too
late —
Unwise I loved!' That's one cry. 'Mind's
my gift:
I might have loaded me with lore, full weight

"'Pressed down and running over at each rift
O' the brain-bag where the famished clung and
fed.
I filled it with what rubbish! — would not sift

"'The wheat from chaff, sound grain from
musty — shed
Poison abroad as oft as nutriment —
And sighing say but as my fellows said,

"'Unwise I learned!' That's two. 'In
dwarf's-play spent
Was giant's prowess: warrior all unversed
In war's right waging, I struck brand, was
lent

"'For steel's fit service, on mere stone — and
cursed
Alike the shocked limb and the shivered steel,
Seeing too late the blade's true use which erst

"How was I blind to! My cry swells the
peal —
Unwise I fought!' That's three. But where-
fore waste
Breath on the wailings longer? Why reveal

"A root of bitterness whereof the taste
Is noisome to Humanity at large?
First we get Power, but Power absurdly placed

"In Folly's keeping, who resigns her charge
To Wisdom when all Power grows nothing
worth:
Bones marrowless are mocked with helm and
targe

"When, like your Master's, soon below the
earth
With worms shall warfare only be. Fare-
well,
Children! I die a failure since my birth!"

"Not so!" arose a protest, as, pell-mell,
They pattered from his chamber to the street,
Bent on a last resource. Our Targums tell

That such resource there is. Put case, there
meet
The Nine Points of Perfection — rarest
chance —
Within some saintly teacher whom the fleet

Years, in their blind implacable advance,
O'ertake before fit teaching born of these
Have magnified his scholars' countenance, —

If haply folk compassionating please
To render up — according to his store,
Each one — a portion of the life he sees

Hardly worth saving when 't is set before
Earth's benefit should the Saint, Hakkadosh,
Favored thereby, attain to full fourscore —

If such contribute (Scoffer, spare thy "Bosh!")
A year, a month, a day, an hour — to eke
Life out, — in him away the gift shall wash

That much of ill-spent time recorded, streak
The twilight of the so-assisted sage
With a new sunrise: truth, though strange to
speak!

Quick to the doorway, then, where youth and
age,
All Israel, thronging, waited for the last
News of the loved one. "'T is the final stage:

"Art's utmost done, the Rabbi's feet tread fast
The way of all flesh!" So announced that apt
Olive-branch Tsaddik: "Yet, O Brethren, cast

"No eye to earthward! Look where heaven
    has clapped
Morning's extinguisher — yon ray-shot robe
Of sun-threads — on the constellation mapped

"And mentioned by our Elders, — yea, from
    Job
Down to Satam, — as figuring forth — what?
Perpend a mystery! Ye call it *Dob*,

"'The Bear': I trow, a wiser name than
    that
Were *Aish* — 'The Bier': a corpse those four
    stars hold,
Which — are not those Three Daughters weep-
    ing at

"*Banoth?* I judge so: list while I unfold
The reason. As in twice twelve hours this
    Bier
Goes and returns, about the east-cone rolled,

"So may a setting luminary here
Be rescued from extinction, rolled anew
Upon its track of labor, strong and clear,

"About the Pole — that Salem, every Jew
Helps to build up when thus he saves some
    Saint
Ordained its architect. Ye grasp the clue

"To all ye seek? The Rabbi's lamp-flame faint
Sinks: would ye raise it? Lend then life from
    yours,
Spare each his oil-drop! Do I need acquaint

"The Chosen how self-sacrifice ensures
Tenfold requital? — urge ye emulate
The fame of those Old Just Ones death procures

"Such praise for, that 't is now men's sole de-
    bate
Which of the Ten, who volunteered at Rome
To die for glory to our Race, was great

"Beyond his fellows? Was it thou — the comb
Of iron carded, flesh from bone, away,
While thy lips sputtered through their bloody
    foam

"Without a stoppage (O brave Akiba!)
'Hear, Israel, our Lord God is One'? Or thou,
Jischab? — who smiledst, burning, since there
    lay,

"Burning along with thee, our Law! I trow,
Such martyrdom might tax flesh to afford:
While that for which I make petition now,

"To what amounts it? Youngster, wilt thou
    hoard
Each minute of long years thou look'st to spend
In dalliance with thy spouse? Hast thou so
    soared,

"Singer of songs, all out of sight of friend
And teacher, warbling like a woodland bird,
There's left no Selah, 'twixt two psalms, to
    lend

"Our late-so-tuneful quirist? Thou, averred
The fighter born to plant our lion-flag
Once more on Zion's mount, — doth all-un-
    heard,

"My pleading fail to move thee? Toss some
    rag
Shall stanch our wound, some minute never
    missed
From swordsman's lustihood like thine! Wilt
    lag

"In liberal bestowment, show close fist
When open palm we look for, — thou, wide-
    known
For statecraft? whom, 't is said, and if thou
    list,

"The Shah himself would seat beside his
    throne,
So valued were advice from thee" . . . But
    here
He stopped short: such a hubbub! Not alone

From those addressed, but far as well as near
The crowd brought into clamor: "Mine, mine,
    mine —
Lop from my life the excrescence, never fear!

"At me thou lookedst, markedst me! As-
    sign
To me that privilege of granting life —
Mine, mine!" Then he: "Be patient! I
    combine

"The needful portions only, wage no strife
With Nature's law nor seek to lengthen out
The Rabbi's day unduly. 'T is the knife

"I stop, — would cut its thread too short.
    About
As much as helps life last the proper term,
The appointed Fourscore, — that I crave, and
    scout

"A too-prolonged existence. Let the worm
Change at fit season to the butterfly!
And here a story strikes me, to confirm

"This judgment. Of our worthies, none ranks
    high
As Perida who kept the famous school:
None rivalled him in patience: none! For
    why?

"In lecturing it was his constant rule,
Whatever he expounded, to repeat
— Ay, and keep on repeating, lest some fool

"Should fail to understand him fully — (feat
Unparalleled, Uzzean!) — do ye mark? —
Five hundred times! So might he entrance
    beat

"For knowledge into howsoever dark
And dense the brain-pan. Yet it happed, at
    close
Of one especial lecture, not one spark

"Of light was found to have illumed the rows
Of pupils round their pedagogue. 'What, still
Impenetrable to me? Then—here goes!'

"And for a second time he sets the rill
Of knowledge running, and five hundred times
More re-repeats the matter—and gains *nil*.

"Out broke a voice from heaven: 'Thy patience
    climbs
Even thus high. Choose! Wilt thou, rather,
    quick
Ascend to bliss—or, since thy zeal sublimes

"'Such drudgery, will thy back still bear its
    crick,
Bent o'er thy class,—thy voice drone spite of
    drouth,—
Five hundred years more at thy desk wilt
    stick?'

"'To heaven with me!' was in the good man's
    mouth,
When all his scholars—cruel-kind were they!—
Stopped utterance, from East, West, North and
    South,

"Rending the welkin with their shout of
    'Nay—
No heaven as yet for our instructor! Grant
Five hundred years on earth for Perida!'

"And so long did he keep instructing! Want
Our Master no such misery! I but take
Three months of life marital. Ministrant

"Be thou of so much, Poet! Bold I make,
Swordsman, with thy frank offer!—and con-
    clude,
Statist, with thine! One year,—ye will not
    shake

"My purpose to accept no more. So rude?
The very boys and girls, forsooth, must press
And proffer their addition? Thanks! The
    mood

"Is laudable, but I reject, no less,
One month, week, day of life more. Leave my
    gown,
Ye overbold ones! Your life's gift, you guess,

"Were good as any? Rudesby, get thee down!
Set my feet free, or fear my staff! Farewell,
Seniors and saviors, sharers of renown

"With Jochanan henceforward!" Straight-
    way fell
Sleep on the sufferer; who awoke in health,
Hale everyway, so potent was the spell.

O the rare Spring-time! Who is he by stealth
Approaches Jochanan?—embowered that sits
Under his vine and figtree 'mid the wealth

Of garden-sights and sounds, since intermits
Never the turtle's coo, nor stays nor stints
The rose her smell. In homage that befits

The musing Master, Tsaddik, see, imprints
A kiss on the extended foot, low bends
Forehead to earth, then, all-obsequious, hints

"What if it should be time? A period ends -
That of the Lover's gift—his quarter-year
Of lustihood: 't is just thou make amends,

"Return that loan with usury: so, here
Come I, of thy Disciples delegate,
Claiming our lesson from thee. Make appear

"Thy profit from experience! Plainly state
How men should Love!" Thus he: and to
    him thus
The Rabbi: "Love, ye call it?—rather, Hate!

"What wouldst thou? Is it needful I discuss
Wherefore new sweet wine, poured in bottles
    caked
With old strong wine's deposit, offers us

"Spoilt liquor we recoil from, thirst-unslaked?
Like earth-smoke from a crevice, out there
    wound—
Languors and yearnings: not a sense but ached

"Weighed on by fancied form and feature,
    sound
Of silver word and sight of sunny smile:
No beckoning of a flower-branch, no profound

"Purple of noon-oppression, no light wile
O' the West wind, but transformed itself till—
    brief—
Before me stood the phantasy ye style

"Youth's love, the joy that shall not come to
    grief,
Born to endure, eternal, unimpaired
By custom the accloyer, time the thief.

"Had Age's hard cold knowledge only spared
That ignorance of Youth! But now the dream,
Fresh as from Paradise, alighting fared

"As fares the pigeon, finding what may seem
Her nest's safe hollow holds a snake inside
Coiled to enclasp her. See, Eve stands supreme

"In youth and beauty! Take her for thy
    bride!
What Youth deemed crystal, Age finds out was
    dew
Morn set a-sparkle, but which noon quick dried

"While Youth bent gazing at its red and blue
Supposed perennial,—never dreamed the sun
Which kindled the display would quench it too.

"Graces of shape and color — every one
With its appointed period of decay
When ripe to purpose! 'Still, these dead and
    done,

"'Survives the woman-nature — the soft sway
Of undefinable omnipotence ·
O'er our strong male-stuff, we of Adam's
    clay.'

"Ay, if my physics taught not why and whence
The attraction! Am I like the simple steer
Who, from his pasture lured inside the fence,

"Where yoke and goad await him, holds that
    mere
Kindliness prompts extension of the hand
Hollowed for barley, which drew near and
    near

"His nose — in proof that, of the hornèd band,
The farmer best affected him? Beside,
Steer, since his calfhood, got to understand

"Farmers a many in the world so wide
Were ready with a handful just as choice
Or choicer — maize and cummin, treats untried.

"Shall I wed wife, and all my days rejoice
I gained the peacock? 'Las me, round I look,
And lo — 'With me thou wouldst have blamed
    no voice

"'Like hers that daily deafens like a rook:
I am the phœnix!' — 'I, the lark, the dove,
— The owl,' for aught knows he who blindly
    took

"Peacock for partner, while the vale, the
    grove,
The plain held bird-mates in abundance.
    There!
Youth, try fresh capture! Age has found out
    Love

"Long ago. War seems better worth man's
    care.
But leave me! Disappointment finds a balm
Haply in slumber." "This first step o' the
    stair

"To knowledge fails me, but the victor's palm
Lies on the next to tempt him overleap
A stumbling-block. Experienced, gather calm,

"Thou excellence of Judah, cured by sleep
Which ushers in the Warrior, to replace
The Lover! At due season I shall reap

"Fruit of my planting!" So, with length-
    ened face,
Departed Tsaddik: and three moons more
    waxed
And waned, and not until the summer-space

Waned likewise, any second visit taxed
The Rabbi's patience. But at three months' end
Behold, supine beneath a rock, relaxed

The sage lay musing till the noon should spend
Its ardor. Up comes Tsaddik, who but he,
With "Master, may I warn thee, nor offend,

"That time comes round again? We look to
    see
Sprout from the old branch — not the young-
    ling twig —
But fruit of sycamine : deliver me,

"To share among my fellows, some plump fig
Juicy as seedy! That same man of war,
Who, with a scantling of his store, made big

"Thy starveling nature, caused thee, safe from
    scar,
To share his gains by long acquaintanceship
With bump and bruise and all the knocks that
    are

"Of battle dowry, — he bids loose thy lip,
Explain the good of battle! Since thou know'st,
Let us know likewise! Fast the moments slip,

"More need that we improve them!" — "Ay,
    we boast,
We warriors in our youth, that with the sword
Man goes the swiftliest to the uttermost —

"Takes the straight way through lands yet un-
    explored
To absolute Right and Good, — may so obtain
God's glory and man's weal too long ignored,

"Too late attained by preachments all in
    vain —
The passive process. Knots get tangled worse
By toying with : does cut cord close again?

"Moreover there is blessing in the curse
Peace-praisers call war. What so sure evolves
All the capacities of soul, proves nurse

"Of that self-sacrifice in men which solves
The riddle — *Wherein differs Man from beast?*
Foxes boast cleverness and courage wolves :

"Nowhere but in mankind is found the least
Touch of an impulse 'To our fellows — good
I' the highest! — not diminished but increased

"'By the condition plainly understood
— Such good shall be attained at price of hurt
I' the highest to ourselves!' Fine sparks,
    that brood

"Confusedly in Man, 't is war bids spurt
Forth into flame : as fares the meteor-mass,
Whereof no particle but holds inert

"Some seed of light and heat, however crass
The enclosure, yet avails not to discharge
Its radiant birth before there come to pass

"Some push external, — strong to set at large
Those dormant fire-seeds, whirl them in a trice
Through heaven, and light up earth from
    marge to marge :

"Since force by motion makes — what erst was
    ice —
Crash into fervency and so expire,
Because some Djinn has hit on a device

"For proving the full prettiness of fire !
Ay, thus we prattle — young: but old — why,
    first,
Where 's that same Right and Good — (the wise
    inquire) —

"So absolute, it warrants the outburst
Of blood, tears, all war's woeful consequence,
That comes of the fine flaring ? Which plague
    cursed

"The more your benefited Man — offence,
Or what suppressed the offender ? Say it did —
Show us the evil cured by violence,

"Submission cures not also ! Lift the lid
From the maturing crucible, we find
Its slow sure coaxing-out of virtue, hid

"In that same meteor-mass, hath uncombined
Those particles and, yielding for result
Gold, not mere flame, by so much leaves be-
    hind

"The heroic product.   E'en the simple cult
Of Edom's children wisely bids them turn
Cheek to the smiter with ' Sic Jesus vult.'

"Say there 's a tyrant by whose death we earn
Freedom, and justify a war to wage :
Good ! — were we only able to discern

"Exactly how to reach and catch and cage
Him only and no innocent beside !
Whereas the folk whereon war wreaks its rage

" — How shared they his ill-doing ? Far and
    wide
The victims of our warfare strew the plain,
Ten thousand dead, whereof not one but died

"In faith that vassals owed their suzerain
Life : therefore each paid tribute — honest
    soul —
To that same Right and Good ourselves are
    fain

"To call exclusively our end.   From bole
(Since ye accept in me a sycamine)
Pluck, eat, digest a fable — yea, the sole

"Fig I afford you ! ' Dost thou dwarf my
    vine ? '
(So did a certain husbandman address
The tree which faced his field.) ' Receive con-
    dign

"' Punishment, prompt removal by the stress
Of axe I forthwith lay unto thy root ! '
Long did he hack and hew, the root no less

"As long defied him, for its tough strings
    shoot

As deep down as the boughs above aspire :
All that he did was — shake to the tree's foot

"Leafage and fruitage, things we most require
For shadow and refreshment : which good deed
Thoroughly done, behold the axe-haft tires

"His hand, and he desisting leaves unfreed
The vine he hacked and hewed for. Comes a
    frost,
One natural night's work, and there 's little
    need

"Of hacking, hewing : lo, the tree 's a ghost !
Perished it starves, black death from topmost
    bough
To farthest-reaching fibre ! Shall I boast

"My rough work — warfare — helped more ?
    Loving, now —
That, by comparison, seems wiser, since
The loving fool was able to avow

"He could effect his purpose, just evince
Love's willingness, — once 'ware of what she
    lacked,
His loved one, — to go work for that, nor wince

"At self-expenditure : he neither hacked
Nor hewed, but when the lady of his field
Required defence because the sun attacked.

"He, failing to obtain a fitter shield,
Would interpose his body, and so blaze,
Blest in the burning. Ah, were mine to wield

"The intellectual weapon — poet-lays, —
How preferably had I sung one song
Which . . . but my sadness sinks me : go your
    ways !

"I sleep out disappointment." "Come along,
Never lose heart ! There 's still as much again
Of our bestowment left to right the wrong

"Done by its earlier moiety — explain
Wherefore, who may ! The Poet's mood comes
    next.
Was he not wishful the poetic vein

"Should pulse within him ? Jochanan, thou
    reck'st
Little of what a generous flood shall soon
Float thy clogged spirit free and unperplexed

"Above dry dubitation ! Song 's the boon
Shall make amends for my untoward mistake
That Joshua-like thou couldst bid sun and
    moon —

"Fighter and Lover, — which for most men
    make
All they descry in heaven, — stand both stock-
    still
And lend assistance. Poet shalt thou wake ! ' "

Autumn brings Tsaddik. "Ay, there speeds
    the rill

Loaded with leaves: a scowling sky, beside:
The wind makes olive-trees up yonder hill

"Whiten and shudder — symptoms far and wide
Of gleaning-time's approach; and glean good
　　store
May I presume to trust we shall, thou tried

"And ripe experimenter! Three months more
Have ministered to growth of Song: that graft
Into thy sterile stock has found at core

"Moisture, I warrant, hitherto unquaffed
By boughs, however florid, wanting sap
Of prose-experience which provides the draught

"Which song-sprouts, wanting, wither: vain
　　we tap
A youngling stem all green and immature;
Experience must secrete the stuff, our hap

"Will be to quench Man's thirst with, glad and
　　sure
That fancy wells up through corrective fact:
Missing which test of truth, though flowers
　　allure

"The goodman's eye with promise, soon the
　　pact
Is broken, and 't is flowers — mere words — he
　　finds
When things — that 's fruit — he looked for.
　　Well, once cracked

"The nut, how glad my tooth the kernel grinds!
Song may henceforth boast substance! There-
　　fore, hail
Proser and poet, perfect in both kinds!

"Thou from whose eye hath dropped the en-
　　vious scale
Which hides the truth of things and substitutes
Deceptive show, unaided optics fail

"To transpierce, — hast entrusted to the lute's
Soft but sure guardianship some unrevealed
Secret shall lift mankind above the brutes

"As only knowledge can?" "A fount un-
　　sealed"
(Sighed Jochanan) "should seek the heaven in
　　leaps
To die in dew-gems — not find death, congealed

"By contact with the cavern's nether deeps,
Earth's secretest foundation where, enswathed
In dark and fear, primeval mystery sleeps —

"Petrific fount wherein my fancies bathed
And straight turned ice. My dreams of good
　　and fair
In soaring upwards had dissolved, unscathed

"By any influence of the kindly air,
Singing, as each took flight, 'The Future —
　　that 's
Our destination, mists turn rainbows there,

"'Which sink to fog, confounded in the flats
O' the Present! Day 's the song-time for the
　　lark,
Night for her music boasts but owls and bats.

"'And what 's the Past but night — the deep
　　and dark
Ice-spring I speak of, corpse-thicked with its
　　drowned
Dead fancies which no sooner touched the
　　mark

"'They aimed at — fact — than all at once
　　they found
Their film-wings freeze, henceforth unfit to
　　reach
And roll in ether, revel — robed and crowned

"'As truths confirmed by falsehood all and
　　each —
Sovereign and absolute and ultimate!
Up with them, skyward, Youth, ere Age im-
　　peach

"'Thy least of promises to reinstate
Adam in Eden!' Sing on, ever sing,
Chirp till thou burst! — the fool cicada's fate.

"Who holds that after Summer next comes
　　Spring,
Than Summer's self sun-warmed, spice-scented
　　more.
Fighting was better! There, no fancy-fling

"Pitches you past the point was reached of
　　yore
By Samsons, Abners, Joabs, Judases,
The mighty men of valor who, before

"Our little day, did wonders none profess
To doubt were fable and not fact, so trust
By fancy-flights to emulate much less.

"Were I a Statesman, now! Why, that were
　　just
To pinnacle my soul, mankind above,
A-top the universe: no vulgar lust

"To gratify — fame, greed, at this remove
Looked down upon so far — or overlooked
So largely, rather — that mine eye should rove

"World-wide and rummage earth, the many-
　　nooked,
Yet find no unit of the human flock
Caught straying but straight comes back
　　hooked and crooked

"By the strong shepherd who, from out his
　　stock
Of aids proceeds to treat each ailing fleece,
Here stimulate to growth, curtail and dock

"There, baldness or excrescence, — that, with
　　grease,
This, with up-grubbing of the bristly patch
Born of the tick-bite. How supreme a peace

"Steals o'er the Statist, — while, in wit, a
    match
For shrewd Ahithophel, in wisdom . . . well,
His name escapes me — somebody, at watch

"And ward, the fellow of Ahithophel
In guidance of the Chosen!" — at which word
Eyes closed and fast asleep the Rabbi fell.

"Cold weather!" shivered Tsaddik. "Yet
    the hoard
Of the sagacious ant shows garnered grain,
Ever abundant most when fields afford

"Least pasture, and alike disgrace the plain
Tall tree and lowly shrub. 'T is so with us
Mortals: our age stores wealth ye seek in vain

"While busy youth culls just what we discuss
At leisure in the last days: and the last
Truly are these for Jochanan, whom thus

"I make one more appeal to! Thine amassed
Experience, now or never, let escape
Some portion of! For I perceive aghast

"The end approaches, while they jeer and
    jape,
These sons of Shimei: 'Justify your boast!
What have ye gained from Death by twelve
    months' rape?

"Statesman, what cure hast thou for — least
    and most —
Popular grievances? What nostrum, say,
Will make the Rich and Poor, expertly dosed,

"Forget disparity, bid each go gay,
That, with his bauble, — with his burden, this?
Propose an alkahest shall melt away

"Men's lacquer, show by prompt analysis
Which is the metal, which the make-believe,
So that no longer brass shall find, gold miss

"Coinage and currency? Make haste, retrieve
The precious moments, Master!" Whereunto
There snarls an "Ever laughing in thy sleeve,

"Pert Tsaddik? Youth indeed sees plain a
    clue
To guide man where life's wood is intricate:
How shall he fail to thrid its thickest through

"When every oak-trunk takes the eye? Elate
He goes from hole to brushwood, plunging
    finds —
Smothered in briers — that the small 's the
    great!

"All men are men: I would all minds were
    minds!
Whereas 't is just the many's mindless mass
That most needs helping: laborers and hinds

"We legislate for — not the cultured class
Which law-makes for itself nor needs the whip
And bridle, — proper help for mule and ass,

"Did the brutes know! In vain our states-
    manship
Strives at contenting the rough multitude:
Still the ox cries ' 'T is me thou shouldst equip

"'With equine trappings!' or, in humbler
    mood,
'Cribful of corn for me! and, as for work —
Adequate rumination o'er my food!'

"Better remain a Poet! Needs it irk
Such an one if light, kindled in his sphere,
Fail to transfuse the Mizraim cold and murk

"Round about Goshen? Though light disap-
    pear,
Shut inside, — temporary ignorance
Got outside of, lo, light emerging clear

"Shows each astonished starer the expanse
Of heaven made bright with knowledge!
    That 's the way,
The only way — I see it at a glance —

"To legislate for earth! As poet . . . Stay!
What is . . . I would that . . . were it . . . I
    had been . . .
O sudden change, as if my arid clay

"Burst into bloom!" . . . "A change indeed.
    I ween,
And change the last!" sighed Tsaddik as he
    kissed
The closing eyelids. "Just as those serene

"Princes of Night apprised me! Our acquist
Of life is spent, since corners only four
Hath Aisch, and each in turn was made desist

"In passage round the Pole (O Mishna's lore —
Little it profits here!) by strenuous tug
Of friends who eked out thus to full fourscore

"The Rabbi's years. I see each shoulder shrug!
What have we gained? Away the Bier may
    roll!
To-morrow, when the Master's grave is dug,

"In with his body I may pitch the scroll
I hoped to glorify with, text and gloss,
My Science of Man's Life: one blank 's the
    whole!

"Love, war, song, statesmanship — no gain, all
    loss,
The stars' bestowment! We on our return
To-morrow merely find — not gold but dross,

"The body not the soul. Come, friends, we
    learn
At least thus much by our experiment —
That — that . . . well, find what, whom it may
    concern!'"

But next day through the city rumors went
Of a new persecution; so, they fled
All Israel, each man, — this time, — from his
    tent,

Tsaddik among the foremost. When, the dread
Subsiding, Israel ventured back again
Some three months after, to the cave they sped

Where lay the Sage, — a reverential train !
Tsaddik first enters. "What is this I view ?
The Rabbi still alive ?   No stars remain

"Of Aisch to stop within their courses. True,
I mind me, certain gamesome boys must urge
Their offerings on me : can it be — one threw

"Life at him and it stuck ? There needs the
        scourge
To teach that urchin manners ! Prithee, grant
Forgiveness if we pretermit thy dirge

"Just to explain no friend was ministrant,
This time, of life to thee ! Some jackanapes,
I gather, has presumed to foist his scant

"Scurvy unripe existence — wilding grapes
Grass-green and sorrel-sour — on that grand
        wine,
Mighty as mellow, which, so fancy shapes

"May fitly image forth this life of thine
Fed on the last low fattening lees — condensed
Elixir, no milk-mildness of the vine !

"Rightly with Tsaddik wert thou now incensed
Had he been witting of the mischief wrought
When, for elixir, verjuice he dispensed ! "

And slowly woke, —like Shushan's flower be-
        sought
By over-curious handling to unloose
The curtained secrecy wherein she thought

Her captive bee, 'mid store of sweets to choose,
Would loll, in gold pavilioned lie unteased,
Sucking on, sated never, — whose, O whose

Might seem that countenance, uplift, all eased
Of old distraction and bewilderment,
Absurdly happy ?   " How ye have appeased

"The strife within me, bred this whole con-
        tent,
This utter acquiescence in my past,
Present and future life, — by whom was lent

"The power to work this miracle at last, —
Exceeds my guess. Though — *ignorance con-
firmed
By knowledge* sounds like paradox, I cast

"Vainly about to tell you — fitlier termed —
Of calm struck by encountering opposites,
Each nullifying either ! Henceforth wormed

"From out my heart is every snake that bites
The dove that else would brood there : doubt,
        which kills
With hiss of ' What if sorrows end delights ? '

" Fear which stings ease with ' Work the Master
        wills ! '

Experience which coils round and strangles
        quick
Each hope with ' Ask the Past if hoping skills

" ' To work accomplishment, or proves a trick
Wiling thee to endeavor ! Strive, fool, stop
Nowise, so live, so die — that 's law ! why kick

" 'Against the pricks ? '   All out-wormed !
        Slumber, drop
Thy films once more and veil the bliss within !
Experience strangle hope ? Hope waves a-top

"Her wings triumphant ! Come what will, I
        win,
Whoever loses ! Every dream's assured
Of soberest fulfilment. Where 's a sin

"Except in doubting that the light, which
        lured
The unwary into darkness, meant no wrong
Had I but marched on bold, nor paused immured

"By mists I should have pressed through,
        passed along
My way henceforth rejoicing ? Not the boy's
Passionate impulse he conceits so strong,

"Which, at first touch, truth, bubble-like, de-
        stroys, —
Not the man's slow conviction ' Vanity
Of vanities — alike my griefs and joys ! '

" Ice ! — thawed (look up) each bird, each insect
        by —
(Look round) by all the plants that break in
        bloom,
(Look down) by every dead friend's memory

"That smiles ' Am I the dust within my
        tomb ? '
Not either, but both these — amalgam rare —
Mix in a product, not from Nature's womb,

"But stuff which He the Operant — who shall
        dare
Describe His operation ? — strikes alive
And thaumaturgic. I nor know nor care

"How from this tohu-bohu — hopes which dive,
And fears which soar — faith, ruined through
        and through
By doubt, and doubt, faith treads to dust —
        revive

"In some surprising sort, — as see, they do ! —
Not merely foes no longer but fast friends.
What does it mean unless — O strange and
        new

"Discovery ! — this life proves a wine-press —
        blends
Evil and good, both fruits of Paradise,
Into a novel drink which — who intends

"To quaff, must bear a brain for ecstasies
Attempered, not this all-inadequate
Organ which, quivering within me, dies

" — Nay, lives! — what, how, — too soon, or
  else too late —
I was — I am " . . . (" He babbleth!" Tsad-
  dik mused)

" O Thou Almighty, who canst reinstate

" Truths in their primal clarity, confused
By man's perception, which is man's and made
To suit his service, — how, once disabused

" Of reason which sees light half shine half
  shade,
Because of flesh, the medium that adjusts
Purity to his visuals, both an aid

" And hindrance, — how to eyes earth's air en-
  crusts,
When purged and perfect to receive truth's
  beam
Pouring itself on the new sense it trusts

" With all its plenitude of power, — how seem
The intricacies now, of shade and shine,
Oppugnant natures — Right and Wrong, we
  deem

" Irreconcilable ? O eyes of mine,
Freed now of imperfection, ye avail
To see the whole sight, nor may uncombine

" Henceforth what, erst divided, caused you
  quail —
So huge the chasm between the false and true,
The dream and the reality ! All hail,

" Day of my soul's deliverance — day the new,
The never-ending ! What though every shape
Whereon I wreaked my yearning to pursue

" Even to success each semblance of escape
From my own bounded self to some all-fair
All-wise external fancy, proved a rape

" Like that old giant's, feigned of fools — on air,
Not solid flesh ? How otherwise ? To love —
That lesson was to learn not here — but there —

" On earth, not here ! 'T is there we learn, —
  there prove
Our parts upon the stuff we needs must spoil,
Striving at mastery, there bend above

" The spoiled clay potsherds, many a year of toil
Attests the potter tried his hand upon,
Till sudden he arose, wiped free from soil

" His hand, cried ' So much for attempt — anon
Performance ! Taught to mould the living vase,
What matter the cracked pitchers dead and
  gone ? '

" Could I impart and could thy mind embrace
The secret, Tsaddik !" "Secret none to me !"
Quoth Tsaddik, as the glory on the face

Of Jochanan was quenched. " The truth I see
Of what that excellence of Judah wrote,
Doughty Halaphta. This a case must be

" Wherein, though the last breath have passed
  the throat,
So that ' The man is dead ' we may pronounce,
Yet is the Ruach — (thus do we denote

" The imparted Spirit) — in no haste to bounce
From its entrusted Body, — some three days
Lingers ere it relinquish to the pounce

" Of hawk-clawed Death his victim. Further
  says
Halaphta, ' Instances have been, and yet
Again may be, when saints, whose earthly ways

" ' Tend to perfection, very nearly get
To heaven while still on earth : and, as a fine
Interval shows where waters pure have met

" ' Waves brackish, in a mixture, sweet with
  brine,
That 's neither sea nor river but a taste
Of both — so meet the earthly and divine

" ' And each is either.' Thus I hold him
  graced —
Dying on earth, half inside and half out,
Wholly in heaven, who knows ? My mind em-
  braced

" Thy secret, Jochanan, how dare I doubt ?
Follow thy Ruach, let earth, all it can,
Keep of the leavings !" Thus was brought about

The sepulture of Rabbi Jochanan :
Thou hast him, — sinner-saint, live-dead, boy-
  man, —
Schiphaz, on Bendimir, in Farzistan !

NOTE. — This story can have no better authority than
that of the treatise, existing dispersedly in fragments
of Rabbinical writing, מֶשֶׁךְ שֶׁל רַבִּים בָּדִים,
from which I might have helped myself more liberally.
Thus, instead of the simple reference to "Moses' stick,"
— but what if I make amends by attempting three illus-
trations, when some thirty might be composed on the
same subject, equally justifying that pithy proverb

מִמְּשֶׁה עַד מֹשֶׁה לֹא קָם כְּמֹשֶׁה.

I

MOSES the Meek was thirty cubits high,
  The staff he strode with — thirty cubits long ;
  And when he leapt, so muscular and strong
Was Moses that his leaping neared the sky
By thirty cubits more : we learn thereby
  He reached full ninety cubits — am I wrong ? —
  When, in a fight slurred o'er by sacred song,
With staff outstretched he took a leap to try
The just dimensions of the giant Og.
  And yet he barely touched — this marvel lacked
Posterity to crown earth's catalogue
  Of marvels — barely touched — to be exact —
The giant's ankle-bone, remained a frog
  That fain would match an ox in stature : fact !

II

And this same fact has met with unbelief !
  How saith a certain traveller ? " Young, I chanced
  To come upon an object — if thou canst,

Guess me its name and nature! 'T was, in brief,
 White, hard, round, hollow, of such length, in chief,
   — And this is what especially enhanced
 My wonder — that it seemed, as I advanced,
 Never to end.   Bind up within thy sheaf
 Of marvels, this — Posterity!   I walked
   From end to end, — four hours walked I, who go
 A goodly pace, — and found — I have not balked
   Thine expectation, Stranger?   Ay or No? —
 'T was but Og's thighbone, all the while, I stalked
   Alongside of: respect to Moses, though!

III

Og's thighbone — if ye deem its measure strange,
   Myself can witness to much length of shank
 Even in birds.   Upon a water's bank
 Once halting, I was minded to exchange
 Noon heat for cool.   Quoth I, " On many a grange
   I have seen storks perch — legs both long and lank:
   Yon stork's must touch the bottom of this tank,
 Since on its top doth wet no plume derange
 Of the smooth breast.   I 'll bathe there!"   "Do not
   so!"
   Warned me a voice from heaven.   " A man let drop
 His axe into that shallow rivulet —
   As thou accountest — seventy years ago:
 It fell and fell and still without a stop
 Keeps falling, nor has reached the bottom yet."

NEVER THE TIME AND THE PLACE

NEVER the time and the place
   And the loved one all together!
 This path — how soft to pace!
   This May — what magic weather!
 Where is the loved one's face?
 In a dream that loved one's face meets mine,
   But the house is narrow, the place is bleak
 Where, outside, rain and wind combine
   With a furtive ear, if I strive to speak,
   With a hostile eye at my flushing cheek,
 With a malice that marks each word, each sign!
 O enemy sly and serpentine,
   Uncoil thee from the waking man!
     Do I hold the Past
     Thus firm and fast
 Yet doubt if the Future hold I can?
 This path so soft to pace shall lead
 Through the magic of May to herself indeed!
 Or narrow if needs the house must be,
 Outside are the storms and strangers: we —
 Oh, close, safe, warm sleep I and she,
   — I and she!

PAMBO

SUPPOSE that we part (work done, comes play)
   With a grave tale told in crambo
 — As our hearty sires were wont to say —
   Whereof the hero is Pambo?

Do you happen to know who Pambo was?
   Nor I — but this much have heard of him:

He entered one day a college-class,
   And asked — was it so absurd of him? —

" May Pambo learn wisdom ere practise it?
   In wisdom I fain would ground me:
 Since wisdom is centred in Holy Writ,
   Some psalm to the purpose expound me!"

" That psalm," the Professor smiled, " shall be
   Untroubled by doubt which dirtieth
 Pellucid streams when an ass like thee
   Would drink there — the Nine-and-thirtieth.

" Verse First: *I said I will look to my ways
   That I with my tongue offend not.*
 How now?   Why stare?   Art struck in amaze?
   Stop, stay!   The smooth line hath an end knot!

" He 's gone! — disgusted my text should prove
   Too easy to need explaining?
 Had he waited, the blockhead might find I move
   To matter that pays remaining!"

Long years went by, when — " Ha, who 's this?
   Do I come on the restive scholar
 I had driven to Wisdom's goal, I wis,
   But that he slipped the collar?

" What?   Arms crossed, brow bent, thought-
       immersed?
   A student indeed!   Why scruple
 To own that the lesson proposed him first
   Scarce suited so apt a pupil?

" Come back!   From the beggarly elements
   To a more recondite issue
 We pass till we reach, at all events,
   Some point that may puzzle . . . Why 'pish'
       you?"

From the ground looked piteous up the head:
   " Daily and nightly, Master,
 Your pupil plods through that text you read,
   Yet gets on never the faster.

" At the selfsame stand, — now old, then young,
   I will look to my ways — were doing
 As easy as saying! — *that I with my tongue
   Offend not* — and 'scape pooh-poohing

" From sage and simple, doctor and dunce?
   Ah, nowise!   Still doubts so muddy
 The stream I would drink at once, — but once
   That — thus I resume my study!"

Brother, brother, I share the blame,
   Arcades sumus ambo!
 Darkling, I keep my sunrise-aim,
   Lack not the critic's flambeau,
 And *look to my ways*, yet, much the same,
   Offend with my tongue — like Pambo!

FERISHTAH'S FANCIES

His genius was jocular, but, when disposed, he could be very serious. — Article "Shakespear," JEREMY COLLIER'S *Historical etc. Dictionary*, 2d edition, 1701.

You, Sir, I entertain you for one of my Hundred; only, I do not like the fashion of your garments: you will say they are Persian: but let them be changed. — *King Lear*, Act III. Sc. 6.

THERE is a loose connection between this group of poems and certain forms of Oriental literature, notably *The Fables of Bidpai* or Pilpay, Firdausi's *Shâh-Nâmeh*, and the *Book of Job*; specific instances may easily be noted; but Browning himself said in a letter to a friend, written soon after the publication of *Ferishtah's Fancies:* " I hope and believe that one or two careful readings of the Poem will make its sense clear enough. Above all, pray allow for the Poet's inventiveness in any case, and do not suppose there is more than a thin disguise of a few Persian names and allusions. There was no such person as Ferishtah — the stories are all inventions. . . . The Hebrew quotations are put in for a purpose, as a direct acknowledgment that certain doctrines may be found in the Old Book, which the Concoctors of Novel Schemes of Morality put forth as discoveries of their own."

PROLOGUE

PRAY, Reader, have you eaten ortolans
    Ever in Italy?
Recall how cooks there cook them: for my plan 's
    To — Lyre with Spit ally.
They pluck the birds, — some dozen luscious lumps,
    Or more or fewer, —
Then roast them, heads by heads and rumps by rumps,
    Stuck on a skewer.
But first, — and here 's the point I fain would press, —
    Don't think I 'm tattling! —
They interpose, to curb its lusciousness,
    — What, 'twixt each fatling?
First comes plain bread, crisp, brown, a toasted square:
    Then, a strong sage-leaf:
(So we find books with flowers dried here and there
    Lest leaf engage leaf.)
First, food — then, piquancy — and last of all
    Follows the thirdling:
Through wholesome hard, sharp soft, your tooth must bite
    Ere reach the birdling.
Now, were there only crust to crunch, you 'd wince:
    Unpalatable!
Sage-leaf is bitter-pungent — so 's a quince:
    Eat each who 's able!
But through all three bite boldly — lo, the gust!
    Flavor — no fixture —
Flies permeating flesh and leaf and crust
    In fine admixture.
So with your meal, my poem: masticate
    Sense, sight, and song there!

Digest these, and I praise your peptics' state,
    Nothing found wrong there.
Whence springs my illustration who can tell?
    — The more surprising
That here eggs, milk, cheese, fruit suffice so well
    For gormandizing.
A fancy-freak by contrast born of thee,
    Delightful Gressoney!
Who laughest " Take what is, trust what may be!"
    That 's Life's true lesson, — eh?

MAISON DELAPIERRE,
    Gressoney St. Jean, Val d'Aosta,
        September 12, '83.

I. THE EAGLE

This poem is drawn quite closely from *The Fables of Bidpai.*

DERVISH — (though yet un-dervished, call him so
No less beforehand: while he drudged our way,
Other his worldly name was: when he wrote
Those versicles we Persians praise him for,
— True fairy-work — Ferishtah grew his style) —
Dervish Ferishtah walked the woods one eve,
And noted on a bough a raven's nest
Whereof each youngling gaped with callow beak
Widened by want; for why? beneath the tree
Dead lay the mother-bird. " A piteous chance!
How shall they 'scape destruction?" sighed the sage
— Or sage about to be, though simple still.
Responsive to which doubt, sudden there swooped
An eagle downward, and behold he bore
(Great-hearted) in his talons flesh wherewith

He stayed their craving, then resought the sky.
"Ah, foolish, faithless me !" the observer
   smiled,
" Who toil and moil to eke out life, when, lo,
Providence cares for every hungry mouth ! "
To profit by which lesson, home went he,
And certain days sat musing, — neither meat
Nor drink would purchase by his handiwork.
Then — for his head swam and his limbs grew
   faint —
Sleep overtook the unwise one, whom in dream
God thus admonished : "Hast thou marked
   my deed ?
Which part assigned by providence dost judge
Was meant for man's example ? Should he
   play
The helpless weakling, or the helpful strength
That captures prey and saves the perishing ?
Sluggard, arise : work, eat, then feed who
   lack ! "

Waking, " I have arisen, work I will,
Eat, and so following. Which lacks food the
   more,
Body or soul in me ? I starve in soul :
So may mankind : and since men congregate
In towns, not woods, — to Ispahan forthwith ! "

Round us the wild creatures, overhead the trees,
Underfoot the moss-tracks, — life and love with these !
I to wear a fawn-skin, thou to dress in flowers :
All the long lone summer-day, that greenwood life of
   ours !

Rich-pavilioned, rather, — still the world without, —
Inside — gold-roofed silk-walled silence round about !
Queen it thou on purple, — I, at watch, and ward
Couched beneath the columns, gaze, thy slave, love's
   guard !

So, for us no world ? Let throngs press thee to me !
Up and down amid men, heart by heart fare we !
Welcome squalid vesture, harsh voice, hateful face !
God is soul, souls I and thou : with souls should souls
   have place.

II. THE MELON-SELLER

GOING his rounds one day in Ispahan, —
Halfway on Dervishhood, not wholly there, —
Ferishtah, as he crossed a certain bridge,
Came startled on a well-remembered face.
"Can it be ? What, turned melon-seller —
   thou ?
Clad in such sordid garb, thy seat yon step
Where dogs brush by thee and express con-
   tempt ?
Methinks, thy head-gear is some scooped-out
   gourd !
Nay, sunk to slicing up, for readier sale,
One fruit whereof the whole scarce feeds a
   swine ?
Wast thou the Shah's Prime Minister, men saw
Ride on his right-hand while a trumpet blew
And Persia hailed the Favorite ? Yea, twelve
   years
Are past, I judge, since that transcendency,
And thou didst peculate and art abased ;

No less, twelve years since, thou didst hold in
   hand
Persia, couldst halve and quarter, mince its
   pulp
As pleased thee, and distribute — melon-like —
Portions to whoso played the parasite,
Or suck — thyself — each juicy morsel. How
Enormous thy abjection, — hell from heaven,
Made tenfold hell by contrast ! Whisper me !
Dost thou curse God for granting twelve years'
   bliss
Only to prove this day 's the direr lot ? "

Whereon the beggar raised a brow, once more
Luminous and imperial, from the rags.
" Fool, does thy folly think my foolishness
Dwells rather on the fact that God appoints
A day of woe to the unworthy one,
Than that the unworthy one, by God's award,
Tasted joy twelve years long ? Or buy a slice,
Or go to school ! "
          To school Ferishtah went ;
And, schooling ended, passed from Ispahan
To Nishapur, that Elburz looks above
— Where they dig turquoise : there kept school
   himself,
The melon-seller's speech, his stock in trade.
Some say a certain Jew adduced the word
Out of their book, it sounds so much the same.
את־הטוב נקבל מאת האלהים
ואת־הרע לא נקבל : In Persian phrase,
" Shall we receive good at the hand of God
And evil not receive ? " But great wits jump.

Wish no word unspoken, want no look away !
What if words were but mistake, and looks — too sud-
   den, say !
Be unjust for once, Love ! Bear it — well I may !

Do me justice always ? Bid my heart — their shrine —
Render back its store of gifts, old looks and words of
   thine
— Oh, so all unjust — the less deserved, the more di-
   vine?

III. SHAH ABBAS

ANYHOW, once full Dervish, youngsters came
To gather up his own words, 'neath a rock
Or else a palm, by pleasant Nishapur.

Said some one, as Ferishtah paused abrupt,
Reading a certain passage from the roll
Wherein is treated of Lord Ali's life :
" Master, explain this incongruity !
When I dared question ' It is beautiful,
But is it true ? ' — thy answer was ' In truth
Lives beauty.' I persisting — ' Beauty — yes,
In thy mind and in my mind, every mind
That apprehends : but outside — so to speak —
Did beauty live in deed as well as word,
Was this life lived, was this death died — not
   dreamed ? '
' Many attested it for fact,' saidst thou.
' Many ! ' but mark, Sir ! Half as long ago
As such things were, — supposing that they
   were, —

Reigned great Shah Abbas: he too lived and
　died
— How say they? Why, so strong of arm, of foot
So swift, he stayed a lion in his leap
On a stag's haunch, — with one hand grasped
　the stag,
With one struck down the lion: yet, no less,
Himself, that same day, feasting after sport.
Perceived a spider drop into his wine,
Let fall the flagon, died of simple fear.
So all say, — so dost thou say?"

　　　　　　　　" Wherefore not?"
Ferishtah smiled: " though strange, the story
　stands
Clear-chronicled: none tells it otherwise:
The fact's eye-witness bore the cup, beside."

" And dost thou credit one cup-bearer's tale,
False, very like, and futile certainly,
Yet hesitate to trust what many tongues
Combine to testify was beautiful
In deed as well as word? No fool's report,
Of lion, stag and spider, but immense
With meaning for mankind, thy race, thyself?"

Whereto the Dervish: " First amend, my son,
Thy faulty nomenclature, call belief
Belief indeed, nor grace with such a name
The easy acquiescence of mankind
In matters nowise worth dispute, since life
Lasts merely the allotted moment. Lo —
That lion-stag-and-spider tale leaves fixed
The fact for us that somewhen Abbas reigned,
Died, somehow slain, — a useful registry, —
Which therefore we — ' believe ' ? Stand for-
　ward, thou,
My Yakub, son of Yusuf, son of Zal!
I advertise thee that our liege, the Shah
Happily regnant, hath become assured,
By opportune discovery, that thy sires,
Son by the father upwards, track their line
To — whom but that same bearer of the cup
Whose inadvertency was chargeable
With what therefrom ensued, disgust and
　death
To Abbas Shah, the over-nice of soul?
Whence he appoints thee, — such his clem-
　ency, —
Not death, thy due, but just a double tax
To pay, on thy particular bed of reeds
Which flower into the brush that makes a broom
Fit to sweep ceilings clear of vermin. Sure,
Thou dost believe the story nor dispute
That punishment should signalize its truth?
Down therefore with some twelve dinars!
　Why start,
— The stag's way with the lion hard on
　haunch?
' Believe the story? ' — how thy words throng
　fast! —
' Who saw this, heard this, said this, wrote
　down this,
That and the other circumstance to prove
So great a prodigy surprised the world?
Needs must thou prove me fable can be fact
Or ere thou coax one piece from out my
　pouch!' "

" There we agree, Sir : neither of us knows,
Neither accepts that tale on evidence
Worthy to warrant the large word— belief.
Now I get near thee! Why didst pause ab
　rupt,
Disabled by emotion at a tale
Might match — be frank! — for credibility
The figment of the spider and the cup?
— To wit, thy roll's concerning Ali's life,
Unevidenced — thine own word! Little boots
Our sympathy with fiction! When I read
The annals and consider of Tahmasp
And that sweet sun-surpassing star his love,
I weep like a cut vine-twig, though aware
Zurah's sad fate is fiction, since the snake
He saw devour her, — how could such exist,
Having nine heads? No snake boasts more
　than three!
I weep, then laugh — both actions right alike.
But thou, Ferishtah, sapiency confessed,
When at the Day of Judgment God shall ask
' Didst thou believe? ' — what wilt thou plead?
　Thy tears?
(Nay, they fell fast and stain the parchment
　still.)
What if thy tears meant love? Love lacking
　ground
— Belief, — avails thee as it would avail
My own pretence to favor since, forsooth,
I loved the lady — I who needs must laugh
To hear a snake boasts nine heads: they have
　three!' "

" Thanks for the well-timed help that 's born,
　behold,
Out of thy words, my son, — belief and love!
Hast heard of Ishak son of Absal? Ay,
The very same we heard of, ten years since,
Slain in the wars: he comes back safe and
　sound, —
Though twenty soldiers saw him die at
　Yezdt, —
Just as a single mule-and-baggage boy
Declared 't was like he some day would, — for
　why?
The twenty soldiers lied, he saw him stout,
Cured of all wounds at once by smear of salve,
A Mubid's manufacture: such the tale.
Now, when his pair of sons were thus apprised
Effect was twofold on them. ' Hail! ' crowed
　This:
' Dearer the news than dayspring after night!
The cure-reporting youngster warrants me
Our father shall make glad our eyes once more,
For whom, had outpoured life of mine sufficed
To bring him back, free broached were every
　vein!'
' Avaunt, delusive tale-concocter, news
Cruel as meteor simulating dawn!'
Whimpered the other: ' Who believes this boy,
Must disbelieve his twenty seniors: no,
Return our father shall not! Might my death
Purchase his life, how promptly would the dole
Be paid as due!' Well, ten years pass, —
　aha,
Ishak is marching homeward, — doubts, not he,
Are dead and done with! So, our townsfolk
　straight

Must take on them to counsel.   ' Go thou gay,
Welcome thy father, thou of ready faith !
Hide thee, contrariwise, thou faithless one,
Expect paternal frowning, blame and blows ! '
So do our townsfolk counsel : dost demur ? "

" Ferishtah like those simpletons — at loss
In what is plain as pikestaff ?   Pish ! Suppose
The trustful son had sighed 'So much the
    worse !
Returning means — retaking heritage
Enjoyed these ten years, who should say me
    nay ? '
How would such trust reward him ?   Trustless-
    ness
— O' the other hand — were what procured
    most praise
To him who judged return impossible,
Yet hated heritage procured thereby.
A fool were Ishak if he failed to prize
Mere head's work less than heart's work : no
    fool he ! "

" Is God less wise ?   Resume the roll ! "   They
    did.

You groped your way across my room i' the drear dark
    dead of night ;
At each fresh step a stumble was : but, once your lamp
    alight,
Easy and plain you walked again : so soon all wrong
    grew right !

What lay on floor to trip your foot ?   Each object, late
    awry,
Looked fitly placed, nor proved offence to footing free
    — for why ?
The lamp showed all, discordant late, grown simple
    symmetry.

Be love your light and trust your guide, with these
    explore my heart !
No obstacle to trip you then, strike hands and souls
    apart !
Since rooms and hearts are furnished so, — light shows
    you, — needs love start ?

IV. THE FAMILY

A CERTAIN neighbor lying sick to death,
Ferishtah grieved beneath a palm-tree, whence
He rose at peace : whereat objected one
" Gudarz our friend gasps in extremity.
Sure, thou art ignorant how close at hand
Death presses, or the cloud, which fouled so
    late
Thy face, had deepened down not lightened
    off."

" I judge there will be respite, for I prayed."

" Sir, let me understand, of charity !
Yestereve, what was thine admonishment ?
' All-wise, all-good, all-mighty — God is such ! '
How then should man, the all-unworthy, dare
Propose to set aside a thing ordained ?
To pray means — substitute man's will for
    God's :
Two best wills cannot be : by consequence,

What is man bound to but — assent, say I ?
Rather to rapture of thanksgiving ; since
That which seems worst to man to God is best,
So, because God ordains it, best to man.
Yet man — the foolish, weak, and wicked —
    prays !
Urges ' My best were better, didst Thou
    know ' ! "

" List to a tale.   A worthy householder
Of Shiraz had three sons, beside a spouse
Whom, cutting gourds, a serpent bit, whereon
The offended limb swelled black from foot to
    fork.
The husband called in aid a leech renowned
World-wide, confessed the lord of surgery,
And bade him dictate — who forthwith de-
    clared
' Sole remedy is amputation.'   Straight
The husband sighed ' Thou knowest : be it so ! '
His three sons heard their mother sentenced :
    ' Pause ! '
Outbroke the elder : ' Be precipitate
Nowise, I pray thee !   Take some gentler way,
Thou sage of much resource !   I will not doubt
But science still may save foot, leg, and thigh ! '
The next in age snapped petulant : ' Too rash !
No reason for this maiming !   What, Sir
    Leech,
Our parent limps henceforward while we leap ?
Shame on thee !   Save the limb thou must and
    shalt ! '
' Shame on yourselves, ye bold ones ! ' followed
    up
The brisk third brother, youngest, pertest too :
' The leech knows all things, we are ignorant ;
What he proposes, gratefully accept !
For me, had I some unguent bound to heal
Hurts in a twinkling, hardly would I dare
Essay its virtue and so cross the sage
By cure his skill pronounces folly.   Quick !
No waiting longer !   There the patient lies :
Out then with implements and operate ! ' "

" Ah, the young devil ! "

                    " Why, his reason chimed
Right with the Hakim's."

                    " Hakim's, ay — but chit's ?
How ? what the skilled eye saw and judged of
    weight
To overbear a heavy consequence,
That — shall a sciolist affect to see ?
All he saw — that is, all such oaf should see,
Was just the mother's suffering."

                    " In my tale,
Be God the Hakim : in the husband's case,
Call ready acquiescence — aptitude
Angelic, understanding swift and sure :
Call the first son — a wise humanity,
Slow to conceive but duteous to adopt :
See in the second son — humanity,
Wrong-headed yet right-hearted, rash but kind,
Last comes the cackler of the brood, our chit
Who, aping wisdom all beyond his years,
Thinks to discard humanity itself :

Fares like the beast which should affect to fly
Because a bird with wings may spurn the
    ground,
So, missing heaven and losing earth — drops
    how
But hell-ward ?   No, be man and nothing
    more —
Man who, as man conceiving, hopes and fears,
And craves and deprecates, and loves, and
    loathes,
And bids God help him, till death touch his
    eyes
And show God granted most, denying all."

Man I am and man would be, Love — merest man and
    nothing more.
Bid me seem no other !   Eagles boast of pinions — let
    them soar !
I may put forth angel's plumage, once unmanned, but
    not before.

Now on earth, to stand suffices, — nay, if kneeling
    serves, to kneel :
Here I front me, here I find the all of heaven that
    earth can feel :
Sense looks straight, — not over, under, — perfect sees
    beyond appeal.

Good you are and wise, full circle : what to me were
    more outside ?
Wiser wisdom, better goodness ?   Ah, such want the
    angel's wide
Sense to take and hold and keep them !   Mine at least
    has never tried.

V. THE SUN

" AND what might that bold man's announce-
    ment be " —
Ferishtah questioned — " which so moved thine
    ire
That thou didst curse, nay, cuff and kick — in
    short,
Confute the announcer ?   Wipe those drops
    away
Which start afresh upon thy face at mere
Mention of such enormity : now, speak ! "

" He scrupled not to say — (thou warrantest,
O patient Sir, that I unblamed repeat
Abominable words which blister tongue ?)
God once assumed on earth a human shape :
(Lo, I have spitten !)   Dared I ask the grace,
Fain would I hear, of thy subtility,
From out what hole in man's corrupted heart
Creeps such a maggot : fancies verminous
Breed in the clots there, but a monster born
Of pride and folly like this pest — thyself
Only canst trace to egg-shell it hath chipped."

The sun rode high.   " During our ignorance " —
Began Ferishtah — " folk esteemed as God
Yon orb : for argument, suppose him so, —
Be it the symbol, not the symbolized,
I and thou safelier take upon our lips.
Accordingly, yon orb that we adore
— What is he ?   Author of all light and life :
Such one must needs be somewhere : this is he.
Like what ?   If I may trust my human eyes,

A ball composed of spirit-fire, whence springs
— What, from this ball, my arms could circle
    round ?
All I enjoy on earth.   By consequence,
Inspiring me with — what ?   Why, love and
    praise.
I eat a palatable fig — there 's love
In little : who first planted what I pluck,
Obtains my little praise, too : more of both
Keeps due proportion with more cause for each.
So, more and ever more, till most of all
Completes experience, and the orb, descried
Ultimate giver of all good, perforce
Gathers unto himself all love, all praise,
Is worshipped — which means loved and praised
    at height.
Back to the first good : 't was the gardener gave
Occasion to my palate's pleasure : grace,
Plain on his part, demanded thanks on mine.
Go up above this giver, — step by step,
Gain a conception of what — (how and why,
Matters not now) — occasioned him to give,
Appointed him the gardener of the ground, —
I mount by just progression slow and sure
To some prime giver — here assumed yon orb —
Who takes my worship.   Whom have I in
    mind,
Thus worshipping, unless a man, my like
Howe'er above me ?   Man, I say — how else,
I being man who worship ?   Here 's my hand
Lifts first a mustard-seed, then weight on
    weight
Greater and ever greater, till at last
It lifts a melon, I suppose, then stops —
Hand-strength expended wholly : so, my love
First lauds the gardener for the fig his gift,
Then, looking higher, loves and lauds still more,
Who hires the ground, who owns the ground,
    Sheikh, Shah,
On and away, away and ever on,
Till, at the last, it loves and lauds the orb
Ultimate cause of all to laud and love.
Where is the break, the change of quality
In hand's power, soul's impulsion ?   Gift was
    grace,
The greatest as the smallest.   Had I stopped
Anywhere in the scale, stayed love and praise
As so far only fit to follow gift,
Saying, ' I thanked the gardener for his fig,
But now that, lo, the Shah has filled my purse
With tomans which avail to purchase me
A fig-tree forest, shall I pay the same
With love and praise, the gardener's proper
    fee ? '
Justly would whoso bears a brain object,
' Giving is giving, gift claims gift's return,
Do thou thine own part, therefore : let the Shah
Ask more from one has more to pay.'   Per-
    chance
He gave me from his treasure less by much
Than the soil's servant : let that be !   My part
Is plain — to meet and match the gift and gift
With love and love, with praise and praise, till
    both
Cry ' All of us is thine, we can no more ! '
So shall I do man's utmost — man to man .
For as our liege the Shah's sublime estate
Merely enhaloes, leaves him man the same,

So must I count that orb I call a fire
(Keep to the language of our ignorance)
Something that 's fire and more beside : mere
　　fire
— Is it a force which, giving, knows it gives,
And wherefore, so may look for love and praise
From me, fire's like so far, however less
In all beside ?　Prime cause this fire shall be,
Uncaused, all-causing : hence begin the gifts,
Thither must go my love and praise — to what ?
Fire ?　Symbol fitly serves the symbolized
Herein, — that this same object of my thanks,
While to my mind nowise conceivable
Except as mind no less than fire, refutes
Next moment mind's conception : fire is fire —
While what I needs must thank, must needs in-
　　clude
Purpose with power, — humanity like mine,
Imagined, for the dear necessity,
One moment in an object which the next
Confesses unimaginable.　Power !
— What need of will, then ?　Naught opposes
　　power :
Why, purpose ? any change must be for worse :
And what occasion for beneficence
When all that is, so is and so must be ?
Best being best now, change were for the
　　worse.
Accordingly discard these qualities
Proper to imperfection, take for type
Mere fire, eject the man, retain the orb, —
The perfect and, so, inconceivable, —
And what remains to love and praise ?　A
　　stone
Fair-colored proves a solace to my eye,
Rolled by my tongue brings moisture curing
　　drouth,
And struck by steel emits a useful spark :
Shall I return it thanks, the insentient thing ?
No, — man once, man forever — man in soul
As man in body : just as this can use
Its proper senses only, see and hear,
Taste, like or loathe according to its law
And not another creature's, — even so
Man's soul is moved by what, if it in turn
Must move, is kindred soul : receiving good
— Man's way — must make man's due acknow-
　　ledgment,
No other, even while he reasons out
Plainly enough that, were the man unmanned,
Made angel of, angelic every way,
The love and praise that rightly seek and find
Their man-like object now, — instructed more,
Would go forth idly, air to emptiness.
Our human flower, sun-ripened, proffers scent
Though reason prove the sun lacks nose to feed
On what himself made grateful : flower and
　　man,
Let each assume that scent and love alike
Being once born, must needs have use !　Man's
　　part
Is plain — to send love forth, — astray, perhaps :
No matter, he has done his part."

　　　　　　　　　　　　　" Wherefrom
What is to follow — if I take thy sense —
But that the sun — the inconceivable
Confessed by man — comprises, all the same,

Man's every-day conception of himself —
No less remaining unconceived ! "

　　　　　　　　　　　　　" Agreed ! "

" Yet thou, insisting on the right of man
To feel as man, not otherwise, — man, bound
By man's conditions neither less nor more,
Obliged to estimate as fair or foul,
Right, wrong, good, evil, what man's faculty
Adjudges such, — how canst thou, — plainly
　　bound
To take man's truth for truth and only truth, —
Dare to accept, in just one case, as truth
Falsehood confessed ?　Flesh simulating fire —
Our fellow-man whom we his fellows know
For dust — instinct with fire unknowable !
Where 's thy man-needed truth — its proof, nay
　　print
Of faintest passage on the tablets traced
By man, termed knowledge ?　'T is conceded
　　thee,
We lack such fancied union — fire with flesh :
But even so, to lack is not to gain
Our lack's suppliance : where 's the trace of
　　such
Recorded ? "

　　　　　　　　" What if such a tracing were ?
If some strange story stood, — whate'er its
　　worth, —
That the immensely yearned-for, once befell,
— The sun was flesh once ? — (keep the fig-
　　ure !) "

　　　　　　　　　　　　　" How ?
An union inconceivable was fact ? "

" Son, if the stranger have convinced himself
Fancy is fact — the sun, besides a fire,
Holds earthly substance somehow fire pervades
And yet consumes not, — earth, he understands,
With essence he remains a stranger to, —
Fitlier thou saidst ' I stand appalled before
Conception unattainable by me
Who need it most ' — than this — ' What ?
　　boast he holds
Conviction where I see conviction's need,
Alas, — and nothing else ?　then what remains
But that I straightway curse, cuff, kick the
　　fool ! ' "

　　　　　　　　———————

Fire is in the flint : true, once a spark escapes,
Fire forgets the kinship, soars till fancy shapes
Some befitting cradle where the babe had birth —
Wholly heaven 's the product, unallied to earth.
Splendors recognized as perfect in the star ! —
In our flint their home was, housed as now they are.

VI. MIHRAB SHAH

Quoth an inquirer, " Praise the Merciful !
My thumb which yesterday a scorpion nipped
(It swelled and blackened) — lo, is sound again !
By application of a virtuous root
The burning has abated : that is well.
But now methinks I have a mind to ask, —

Since this discomfort came of culling herbs
Nor meaning harm, — why needs a scorpion be?
Yea, there began, from when my thumb last
    throbbed,
Advance in question-framing, till I asked
Wherefore should any evil hap to man —
From ache of flesh to agony of soul —
Since God's All-mercy mates All-potency?
Nay, why permits he evil to himself —
Man's sin, accounted such? Suppose a world
Purged of all pain, with fit inhabitant —
Man pure of evil in thought, word, and deed —
Were it not well? Then, wherefore otherwise?
Too good result? But he is wholly good!
Hard to effect? Ay, were he impotent!
Teach me, Ferishtah!"

              Said the Dervish: "Friend,
My chance, escaped to-day, was worse than
    thine:
I, as I woke this morning, raised my head,
Which never tumbled but stuck fast on neck.
Was not I glad and thankful!"

              "How could head
Tumble from neck, unchopped — inform me
    first!
Unless we take Firdausi's tale for truth,
Who ever heard the like?"

              "The like might hap
By natural law: I let my staff fall thus —
It goes to ground, I know not why. Suppose,
Whene'er my hold was loosed, it skyward
    sprang
As certainly, and all experience proved
That, just as staves when unsupported sink,
So, unconfined, they soar?"

              "Let such be law —
Why, a new chapter of sad accidents
Were added to humanity's mischance,
No doubt at all, and as a man's false step
Now lays him prone on earth, contrariwise,
Removal from his shoulder of a weight
Might start him upwards to perdition. Ay!
But, since such law exists in just thy brain,
I shall not hesitate to doff my cap
For fear my head take flight."

              "Nor feel relief
Finding it firm on shoulder. Tell me, now!
What were the bond 'twixt man and man,
    dost judge,
Pain once abolished? Come, be true! Our
    Shah —
How stands he in thy favor? Why that
    shrug?
Is not he lord and ruler?"

              "Easily!
His mother bore him, first of those four wives
Provided by his father, such his luck:
Since when his business simply was to breathe
And take each day's new bounty. There he
    stands —
Where else had I stood, were his birth-star
    mine?

No, to respect men's power, I needs must see
Men's bare hands seek, find, grasp and wield
    the sword
Nobody else can brandish! Bless his heart,
'T is said, he scarcely counts his fingers right!"

"Well, then — his princely doles! from every
    feast
Off go the feasted with the dish they ate
And cup they drank from, — nay, a change
    besides
Of garments" . . .

              "Sir, put case, for service done, —
Or best, for love's sake, — such and such a slave
Sold his allowance of sour lentil-soup
To herewith purchase me a pipe-stick, — nay,
If he, by but one hour, cut short his sleep
To clout my shoe, — that were a sacrifice!"

"All praise his gracious bearing."

              "All praise mine —
Or would praise did they never make approach
Except on all-fours, crawling till I bade,
'Now that with eyelids thou hast touched the
    earth,
Come close and have no fear, poor nothingness!'
What wonder that the lady-rose I woo
And palisade about from every wind,
Holds herself handsomely? The wilding, now,
Ruffled outside at pleasure of the blast,
That still lifts up with something of a smile
Its poor attempt at bloom" . . .

              "A blameless life,
Where wrong might revel with impunity —
Remember that!"

              "The falcon on his fist —
Reclaimed and trained and belled and beautified
Till she believes herself the Simorgh's match —
She only deigns destroy the antelope,
Stoops at no carrion-crow: thou marvellest?

"So be it, then! He wakes no love in thee
For any one of divers attributes
Commonly deemed love-worthy. All the same,
I would he were not wasting, slow but sure,
With that internal ulcer" . . .

              "Say'st thou so?
How should I guess? Alack, poor soul! But
    stay —
Sure in the reach of art some remedy
Must lie to hand: or if it lurk, — that leech
Of fame in Tebriz, why not seek his aid?
Couldst not thou, Dervish, counsel in the
    case?"

"My counsel might be — what imports a pang
The more or less, which puts an end to one
Odious in spite of every attribute
Commonly deemed love-worthy?"

              "Attributes?
Faugh! — nay, Ferishtah, — 't is an ulcer,
    think!

Attributes, quotha? Here's poor flesh and
    blood,
Like thine and mine and every man's, a prey
To hell-fire! Hast thou lost thy wits for
    once?"

" Friend, here they are to find and profit by!
Put pain from out the world, what room were
    left
For thanks to God, for love to Man? Why
    thanks, —
Except for some escape, whate'er the style,
From pain that might be, name it as thou
    mayst?
Why love, — when all thy kind, save me, sup-
    pose,
Thy father, and thy son, and . . . well, thy
    dog,   .
To eke the decent number out — we few
Who happen — like a handful of chance stars
From the unnumbered host — to shine o'erhead
And lend thee light, — our twinkle all thy
    store, —
We only take thy love! Mankind, forsooth?
Who sympathizes with their general joy
Foolish as undeserved? But pain — see God's
Wisdom at work! — man's heart is made to
    judge
Pain deserved nowhere by the common flesh
Our birthright, — bad and good deserve alike
No pain, to human apprehension! Lust,
Greed, cruelty, injustice crave (we hold)
Due punishment from somebody, no doubt:
But ulcer in the midriff! that brings flesh
Triumphant from the bar whereto arraigned
Soul quakes with reason. In the eye of God
Pain may have purpose and be justified:
Man's sense avails to only see, in pain,
A hateful chance no man but would avert
Or, failing, needs must pity. Thanks to God
And love to man, — from man take these away,
And what is man worth? Therefore, Mihrab
    Shah,
Tax me my bread and salt twice over, claim
Laila my daughter for thy sport, — go on!
Slay my son's self, maintain thy poetry
Beats mine, — thou meritest a dozen deaths!
But — ulcer in the stomach, — ah, poor soul,
Try a fig-plaster: may it ease thy pangs!"

So, the head aches and the limbs are faint!
    Flesh is a burden — even to you!
Can I force a smile with a fancy quaint?
    Why are my ailments none or few?

In the soul of me sits sluggishness:
    Body so strong and will so weak:
The slave stands fit for the labor — yes,
    But the master's mandate is still to seek.

You, now — what if the outside clay
    Helped, not hindered the inside flame?
My dim to-morrow — your plain to-day,
    Yours the achievement, mine the aim?

So were it rightly, so shall it be!
    Only, while earth we pace together
For the purpose apportioned you and me,
    Closer we tread for a common tether.

You shall sigh, " Wait for his sluggish soul!
    Shame he should lag, not lamed as I!"
May not I smile, " Ungained her goal:
    Body may reach her — by and by"?

VII. A CAMEL-DRIVER

" How of his fate, the Pilgrims' soldier-guide
Condemned " (Ferishtah questioned), " for he
    slew
The merchant whom he convoyed with his
    bales
— A special treachery?"

                    "Sir, the proofs were plain:
Justice was satisfied: between two boards
The rogue was sawn asunder, rightly served."

" With all wise men's approval — mine at
    least."

" Himself, indeed, confessed as much. 'I die
Justly' (groaned he) ' through over-greediness
Which tempted me to rob: but grieve the most
That he who quickened sin at slumber, — ay,
Prompted and pestered me till thought grew
    deed, —
The same is fled to Syria and is safe,
Laughing at me thus left to pay for both.
My comfort is that God reserves for him
Hell's hottest '" . . .

                    " Idle words."

                        " Enlighten me!
Wherefore so idle? Punishment by man
Has thy assent, — the word is on thy lips.
By parity of reason, punishment
By God should likelier win thy thanks and
    praise."

" Man acts as man must: God, as God beseems.
A camel-driver, when his beast will bite,
Thumps her athwart the muzzle; why?"

                        " How else
Instruct the creature — mouths should munch
    not bite?"

" True, he is man, knows but man's trick to
    teach.
Suppose some plain word, told her first of all,
Had hindered any biting?"

                        " Find him such.
And fit the beast with understanding first!
No understanding animals like Rakhsh
Nowadays, Master! Till they breed on earth,
For teaching — blows must serve."

                        " Who deals the blow —
What if by some rare method, — magic, say, —
He saw into the biter's very soul,
And knew the fault was so repented of
It could not happen twice?"

                        " That's something: still
I hear, methinks, the driver say, ' No less

Take thy fault's due! Those long-necked
    sisters, see,
Lean all a-stretch to know if biting meets
Punishment or enjoys impunity.
For their sakes — thwack!'"

        "The journey home at end,
The solitary beast safe-stabled now,
In comes the driver to avenge a wrong
Suffered from six months since, — apparently
With patience, nay, approval: when the jaws
Met i' the small o' the arm. 'Ha, Ladykin,
Still at thy frolics, girl of gold?' laughed he:
'Eat flesh? Rye-grass content thee rather with,
Whereof accept a bundle!' Now, — what
    change!
Laughter by no means! Now 't is, 'Fiend, thy
    frisk
Was fit to find thee provender, didst judge?
Behold this red-hot twy-prong, thus I stick
To hiss i' the soft of thee!'"

        "Behold? behold
A crazy noddle, rather! Sure the brute
Might wellnigh have plain speech coaxed out of
    tongue,
And grow as voluble as Rakhsh himself
At such mad outrage. 'Could I take thy mind,
Guess thy desire? If biting was offence,
Wherefore the rye-grass bundle, why each
    day's
Patting and petting, but to intimate
My playsomeness had pleased thee? Thou en-
    dowed
With reason, truly!'"

        "Reason aims to raise
Some makeshift scaffold-vantage midway,
    whence
Man dares, for life's brief moment, peer below:
But ape omniscience? Nay! The ladder lent
To climb by, step and step, until we reach
The little foothold-rise allowed mankind
To mount on and thence guess the sun's sur-
    vey —
Shall this avail to show us world-wide truth
Stretched for the sun's descrying? Reason
    bids,
'Teach, Man, thy beast his duty first of all
Or last of all, with blows if blows must be, —
How else accomplish teaching?' Reason adds,
'Before man's First, and after man's poor Last,
God operated and will operate.'
— Process of which man merely knows this
    much, —
That nowise it resembles man's at all,
Teaching or punishing."

        "It follows, then,
That any malefactor I would smite
With God's allowance, God himself will spare
Presumably. No scapegrace? Then, rejoice
Thou snatch-grace safe in Syria!"

        "Friend, such view
Is but man's wonderful and wide mistake.
Man lumps his kind i' the mass: God singles
    thence

Unit by unit. Thou and God exist —
So think! — for certain: think the mass —
    mankind —
Disparts, disperses, leaves thyself alone!
Ask thy lone soul what laws are plain to thee, —
Thee and no other, — stand or fall by them!
That is the part for thee: regard all else
For what it may be — Time's illusion. This
Be sure of — ignorance that sins, is safe.
No punishment like knowledge! Instance,
    now!
My father's choicest treasure was a book
Wherein he, day by day and year by year,
Recorded gains of wisdom for my sake
When I should grow to manhood. While a
    child,
Coming upon the casket where it lay
Unguarded, — what did I but toss the thing
Into a fire to make more flame therewith,
Meaning no harm? So acts man three-years
    old!
I grieve now at my loss by witlessness,
But guilt was none to punish. Man mature —
Each word of his I lightly held, each look
I turned from — wish that wished in vain —
    nay, will
That willed and yet went all to waste — 't is these
Rankle like fire. Forgiveness? rather grant
Forgetfulness! The past is past and lost.
However near I stand in his regard,
So much the nearer had I stood by steps
Offered the feet which rashly spurned their
    help
That I call Hell; why further punishment?"

        When I vexed you and you chid me,
          And I owned my fault and turned
        My cheek the way you bid me,
          And confessed the blow well earned, —

        My comfort all the while was
          — Fault was faulty — near, not quite!
        Do you wonder why the smile was?
        O'erpunished wrong grew right.

        But faults, you ne'er suspected,
        Nay, praised, no faults at all, —
        Those would you had detected —
        Crushed eggs whence snakes could crawl!

VIII. TWO CAMELS

QUOTH one: "Sir, solve a scruple! No true
    sage
I hear of, but instructs his scholar thus:
'Wouldst thou be wise? Then mortify thy-
    self!
Balk of its craving every bestial sense!
Say, "If I relish melons — so do swine!
Horse, ass, and mule consume their provender
Nor leave a pea-pod: fasting feeds the soul."'
Thus they admonish: while thyself, I note,
Eatest thy ration with an appetite,
Nor fallest foul of whoso lieks his lips
And sighs — 'Well-saffroned was that barley
    soup!'
Can wisdom coexist with — gorge-and-swill,
I say not, — simply sensual preference

For this or that fantastic meat and drink?
Moreover, wind blows sharper than its wont
This morning, and thou hast already donned
Thy sheepskin over-garment: sure the sage
Is busied with conceits that soar above
A petty change of season and its chance
Of causing ordinary flesh to sneeze?
I always thought, Sir " . . .

             "Son," Ferishtah said,
" Truth ought to seem as never thought before.
How if I give it birth in parable?
A neighbor owns two camels, beasts of price
And promise, destined each to go, next week,
Swiftly and surely with his merchandise
From Nishapur to Sebzevar, no truce
To tramp, but travel, spite of sands and drouth,
In days so many, lest they miss the Fair.
Each falls to meditation o'er his crib
Piled high with provender before the start.
Quoth this: 'My soul is set on winning praise
From goodman lord and master, — hump to hoof,
I dedicate me to his service. How?
Grass, purslane, lupines, and I know not what,
Crammed in my manger? Ha, I see — I see!
No, master, spare thy money! I shall trudge
The distance and yet cost thee not a doit
Beyond my supper on this mouldy bran.'
'Be magnified, O master, for the meal
So opportunely liberal!' quoth that.
'What use of strength in me but to surmount
Sands and simooms, and bend beneath thy bales
No knee until I reach the glad bazaar?
Thus I do justice to thy fare: no sprig
Of toothsome chervil must I leave unchewed!
Too bitterly should I reproach myself
Did I sink down in sight of Sebzevar,
Remembering how the merest mouthful more
Had heartened me to manage yet a mile!'
And so it proved: the too-abstemious brute
Midway broke down, his pack rejoiced the
    thieves,
His carcass fed the vultures: not so he
The wisely thankful, who, good market-drudge,
Let down his lading in the market-place,
No damage to a single pack. Which beast,
Think ye, had praise and patting and a brand
Of good-and-faithful-servant fixed on flank?
So, with thy squeamish scruple. What imports
Fasting or feasting? Do thy day's work, dare
Refuse no help thereto, since help refused
Is hindrance sought and found. Win but the
    race —
Who shall object 'He tossed three wine-cups off,
And, just at starting, Lilith kissed his lips'?

"More soberly, — consider this, my Son!
Put case I never have myself enjoyed,
Known by experience what enjoyment means,
How shall I — share enjoyment? — no, in-
    deed! —
Supply it to my fellows, — ignorant,
As so I should be of the thing they crave,
How it affects them, works for good or ill.
Style my enjoyment self-indulgence — sin —
Why should I labor to infect my kind
With sin's occasion, bid them too enjoy,
Who else might neither catch nor give again

Joy's plague, but live in righteous misery?
Just as I cannot, till myself convinced,
Impart conviction, so, to deal forth joy
Adroitly, needs must I know joy myself.
Renounce joy for my fellows' sake? That's joy
Beyond joy; but renounced for mine, not theirs?
Why, the physician called to help the sick,
Cries 'Let me, first of all, discard my health!'
No, Son: the richness hearted in such joy
Is in the knowing what are gifts we give,
Not in a vain endeavor not to know!
Therefore, desire joy and thank God for it!
The Adversary said, — a Jew reports, —
הֶחִנָּם רֵא אִיּוֹב אֱלֹהִים:
In Persian phrase, 'Does Job fear God for
    naught?'
Job's creatureship is not abjured, thou fool!
He nowise isolates himself and plays
The independent equal, owns no more
Than himself gave himself, so why thank God?
A proper speech were this מֵאֱלֹהִים
'Equals we are, Job, labor for thyself,
Nor bid me help thee: bear, as best flesh may,
Pains I inflict not nor avail to cure:
Beg of me nothing thou thyself mayst win
By work, or waive with magnanimity,
Since we are peers acknowledged, — scarcely
    peers,
Had I implanted any want of thine
Only my power could meet and gratify.'
No: rather hear, at man's indifference —
'Wherefore did I contrive for thee that ear
Hungry for music, and direct thine eye
To where I hold a seven-stringed instrument,
Unless I meant thee to beseech me play?'"

Once I saw a chemist take a pinch of powder
— Simple dust it seemed — and half-unstop a phial:
— Out dropped harmless dew. "Mixed nothings make"
    (quoth he)
"Something!" So they did: a thunderclap, but
    louder —
Lightning-flash, but fiercer — put spectators' nerves to
    trial:
Sure enough, we learned what was, imagined what
    might be.

Had I no experience how a lip's mere tremble,
Look's half hesitation, cheek's just change of color,
These effect a heartquake, — how should I conceive
What a heaven there may be? Let it but resemble
Earth myself have known! No bliss that's finer, fuller,
Only — bliss that lasts, they say, and fain would I be-
    lieve.

IX. CHERRIES

"What, I disturb thee at thy morning-meal:
Cherries so ripe already? Eat apace!
I recollect thy lesson yesterday.
Yet — thanks, Sir, for thy leave to inter-
    rupt" . . .

"Friend, I have finished my repast, thank
    God!"

"There now, thy thanks for breaking fast on
    fruit! —

Thanks being praise, or tantamount thereto.
Prithee consider, have not things degree,
Lofty and low ? Are things not great and small,
Thence claiming praise and wonder more or less ?
Shall we confuse them, with thy warrant too,
Whose doctrine otherwise begins and ends
With just this precept, ' Never faith enough
In man as weakness, God as potency ' ?
When I would pay soul's tribute to that same,
Why not look up in wonder, bid the stars
Attest my praise of the All-mighty One ?
What are man's puny members and as mean
Requirements weighed with Star-King Mush-
      tari ?
There is the marvel ! ''

                  " Not to man — that 's me.
List to what happened late, in fact or dream.
A certain stranger, bound from far away,
Still the Shah's subject, found himself before
Ispahan palace-gate. As duty bade,
He enters in the courts, will, if he may,
See so much glory as befits a slave
Who only comes, of mind to testify
How great and good is shown our lord the Shah.
In he walks, round he casts his eye about,
Looks up and down, admires to heart's content,
Ascends the gallery, tries door and door,
None says his reverence nay: peeps in at each,
Wonders at all the unimagined use,
Gold here and jewels there, — so vast, that hall —
So perfect yon pavilion ! — lamps above
Bidding look up from luxuries below, —
Evermore wonder topping wonder, — last —
Sudden he comes upon a cosy nook,
A nest-like little chamber, with his name,
His own, yea, his and no mistake at all,
Plain o'er the entry, — what, and he descries
Just those arrangements inside, — oh, the
      care ! —
Suited to soul and body both, — so snug
The cushion — nay, the pipe-stand furnished so !
Whereat he cries aloud, — what think'st thou,
      Friend ?
' That these my slippers should be just my
      choice,
Even to the color that I most affect,.
Is nothing : ah, that lamp, the central sun,
What must it light within its minaret
I scarce dare guess the good of ! Who lives
      there ?
That let me wonder at, — no slipper toys
Meant for the foot, forsooth, which kicks them
      — thus ! '

" Never enough faith in omnipotence, —
Never too much, by parity, of faith
In impuissance, man's — which turns to strength
When once acknowledged weakness every way.
How ? Hear the teaching of another tale.

" Two men once owed the Shah a mighty sum,
Beggars they both were: this one crossed his
      arms
And bowed his head, — ' whereof,' sighed he,
      ' each hair
Proved it a jewel, how the host's amount
Were idly strewn for payment at thy feet ! '

' Lord, here they lie, my havings poor and
      scant !
All of the berries on my currant-bush,
What roots of garlic have escaped the mice,
And some five pippins from the seedling tree, —
Would they were half-a-dozen ! Anyhow,
Accept my all, poor beggar that I am ! '
' Received in full of all demands ! ' smiled back
The apportioner of every lot of ground
From inch to acre. Littleness of love
Befits the littleness of loving thing.
What if he boasted ' Seeing I am great,
Great must my corresponding tribute be ' ?
Mushtari, — well, suppose him seven times seven
The sun's superior, proved so by some sage :
Am I that sage ? To me his twinkle blue
Is all I know of him and thank him for,
And therefore I have put the same in verse —
' Like yon blue twinkle, twinks thine eye, my
      Love ! '

Neither shalt thou be troubled overmuch
Because thy offering — littleness itself —
Is lessened by admixture sad and strange
Of mere man's motives, — praise with fear, and
      love
With looking after that same love's reward.
Alas, Friend, what was free from this alloy, —
Some smatch thereof, — in best and purest love
Proffered thy earthly father ? Dust thou art,
Dust shalt be to the end. Thy father took
The dust, and kindly called the handful — gold
Nor cared to count what sparkled here and
      there
Sagely unanalytic. Thank, praise, love
(Sum up thus) for the lowest favors first,
The commonest of comforts ! aught beside
Very omnipotence had overlooked
Such needs, arranging for thy little life.
Nor waste thy power of love in wonderment
At what thou wiselier lettest shine unsoiled
By breath of word. That this last cherry soothes
A roughness of my palate, that I know:
His Maker knows why Mushtari was made.''

Verse-making was least of my virtues : I viewed with
      despair
Wealth that never yet was but might be — all that verse-
      making were
If the life would but lengthen to wish, let the mind be
      laid bare.
So I said " To do little is bad, to do nothing is worse '' —
      And made verse.

Love-making, — how simple a matter ! No depths to
      explore,
No heights in a life to ascend ! No disheartening Before,
No affrighting Hereafter, — love now will be love ever
      more.
So I felt " To keep silence were folly : '' — all language
      above,
      I made love.

X. PLOT-CULTURE

" Ay, but, Ferishtah,'' — a disciple smirked, —
" That verse of thine ' How twinks thine eye,
      my Love,
Blue as yon star-beam ! ' much arrides myself

Who haply may obtain a kiss therewith
This eve from Laila where the palms abound —
My youth, my warrant — so the palms be close !
Suppose when thou art earnest in discourse
Concerning high and holy things, — abrupt
I out with — ' Laila's lip, how honey-sweet ! ' —
What say'st thou, were it scandalous or no ?
I feel thy shoe sent flying at my mouth
For daring — prodigy of impudence —
Publish what, secret, were permissible.
Well, — one slide further in the imagined
    slough, —
Knee-deep therein, (respect thy reverence !) —
Suppose me well aware thy very self
Stooped prying through the palm-screen, while
    I dared
Solace me with caressings all the same ?
Unutterable, nay — unthinkable,
Undreamable a deed of shame ! Alack,
How will it fare shouldst thou impress on me
That certainly an Eye is over all
And each, to mark the minute's deed, word,
    thought,
As worthy of reward or punishment ?
Shall I permit my sense an Eye-viewed shame,
Broad daylight perpetration, — so to speak, —
I had not dared to breathe within the Ear,
With black night's help about me ? Yet I stand
A man, no monster, made of flesh not cloud :
Why made so, if my making prove offence
To Maker's eye and ear ? "

           " Thou wouldst not stand
Distinctly Man," — Ferishtah made reply,
" Not the mere creature, — did no limit-line
Round thee about, apportion thee thy place
Clean-cut from out and off the illimitable, —
Minuteness severed from immensity.
All of thee for the Maker, — for thyself,
Workings inside the circle that evolve
Thine all, — the product of thy cultured plot.
So much of grain the ground's lord bids thee
    yield :
Bring sacks to granary in Autumn ! spare
Daily intelligence of this manure,
That compost, how they tend to feed the soil :
There thou art master sole and absolute
— Only, remember doomsday ! Twit'st thou me
Because I turn away my outraged nose
Shouldst thou obtrude thereon a shovelful
Of fertilizing kisses ? Since thy sire
Wills and obtains thy marriage with the maid,
Enough ! Be reticent, I counsel thee,
Nor venture to acquaint him, point by point,
What he procures thee. Is he so obtuse ?
Keep thy instruction to thyself ! My ass —
Only from him expect acknowledgment,
The while he champs my gift, a thistle-bunch,
How much he loves the largess : of his love
I only tolerate so much as tells
By wrinkling nose and inarticulate grunt,
The meal, that heartens him to do my work,
Tickles his palate as I meant it should."

———

Not with my Soul, Love ! — bid no soul like mine
  Lap thee around nor leave the poor Sense room !

Soul, — travel-worn, toil-weary, — would confine
  Along with Soul, Soul's gains from glow and gloom.
Captures from soarings high and divings deep.
Spoil-laden Soul, how should such memories sleep ?
  Take Sense, too — let me love entire and whole —
    Not with my Soul !

Eyes shall meet eyes and find no eyes between,
  Lips feed on lips, no other lips to fear !
No past, no future — so thine arms but screen
  The present from surprise ! not there, 't is here —
Not then, 't is now : — back, memories that intrude !
Make, Love, the universe our solitude,
  And, over all the rest, oblivion roll —
    Sense quenching Soul !

XI. A PILLAR AT SEBZEVAR

" KNOWLEDGE deposed, then ! " — groaned
    whom that most grieved
As foolishest of all the company.
" What, knowledge, man's distinctive attribute,
He doffs that crown to emulate an ass
Because the unknowing long-ears loves at least
Husked lupines, and belike the feeder's self
— Whose purpose in the dole what ass divines ? "

" Friend," quoth Ferishtah, " all I seem to know
Is — I know nothing save that love I can
Boundlessly, endlessly. My curls were crowned
In youth with knowledge, — off, alas, crown
    slipped
Next moment, pushed by better knowledge still
Which nowise proved more constant : gain, to-
    day,
Was toppling loss to-morrow, lay at last
— Knowledge, the golden ? — lacquered igno-
    rance !
As gain — mistrust it ! Not as means to gain :
Lacquer we learn by : cast in fining-pot,
We learn, when what seemed ore assayed proves
    dross, —
Surelier true gold's worth, guess how purity
I' the lode were precious could one light on ore
Clarified up to test of crucible.
The prize is in the process : knowledge means
Ever-renewed assurance by defeat
That victory is somehow still to reach,
But love is victory, the prize itself :
Love — trust to ! Be rewarded for the trust
In trust's mere act. In love success is sure,
Attainment — no delusion, whatsoe'er
The prize be : apprehended as a prize,
A prize it is. Thy child as surely grasps
An orange as he fails to grasp the sun
Assumed his capture. What if soon he finds
The foolish fruit unworthy grasping ? Joy
In shape and color, — that was joy as true —
Worthy in its degree of love — as grasp
Of sun were, which had singed his hand beside
What if he said the orange held no juice
Since it was not that sun he hoped to suck ?
This constitutes the curse that spoils our life
And sets man maundering of his misery,
That there 's no meanest atom he obtains
Of what he counts for knowledge but he cries
' Hold here, — I have the whole thing, — know.
    this time,
Nor need search farther ! ' Whereas, strew his
    path

With pleasures, and he scorns them while he
    stoops :
' This fitly call'st thou pleasure, pick up this
And praise it, truly ? I reserve my thanks
For something more substantial.' Fool not thus
In practising with life and its delights !
Enjoy the present gift, nor wait to know
The unknowable. Enough to say ' I feel
Love's sure effect, and, being loved, must love
The love its cause behind, — I can and do ! '
Nor turn to try thy brain-power on the fact,
(Apart from as it strikes thee, here and now —
Its how and why, i' the future and elsewhere)
Except to — yet once more, and ever again,
Confirm thee in thy utter ignorance :
Assured that, whatsoe'er the quality
Of love's cause, save that love was caused
    thereby,
This — nigh upon revealment as it seemed
A minute since — defies thy longing looks,
Withdrawn into the unknowable once more.
Wholly distrust thy knowledge, then, and trust
As wholly love allied to ignorance !
There lies thy truth and safety. Love is praise,
And praise is love ! Refine the same, contrive
An intellectual tribute — ignorance
Appreciating ere approbative
Of knowledge that is infinite ? With us,
The small, who use the knowledge of our
    kind
Greater than we, more wisely ignorance
Restricts its apprehension, sees and knows
No more than brain accepts in faith of sight,
Takes first what comes first, only sure so far.
By Sebzevar a certain pillar stands
So aptly that its gnomon tells the hour ;
What if the townsmen said ' Before we thank
Who placed it, for his serviceable craft,
And go to dinner since its shade tells noon,
Needs must we have the craftsman's purpose
    clear
On half a hundred more recondite points
Than a mere summons to a vulgar meal ! '
Better they say ' How opportune the help !
Be loved and praised, thou kindly-hearted sage
Whom Hudhud taught, — the gracious spirit-
    bird, —
How to construct the pillar, teach the time ! '
So let us say — not ' Since we know, we love,'
But rather ' Since we love, we know enough.'
Perhaps the pillar by a spell controlled
Mushtari in his courses ? Added grace
Surely I count it that the sage devised,
Beside celestial service, ministry
To all the land, by one sharp shade at noon
Falling as folk foresee. Once more, then,
    Friend —
(What ever in those careless ears of thine
Withal I needs must round thee) — knowledge
    doubt
Even wherein it seems demonstrable !
Love, — in the claim for love, that 's gratitude
For apprehended pleasure, nowise doubt !
Pay its due tribute, — sure that pleasure is,
While knowledge may be, at the most. See,
    now !
Eating my breakfast, I thanked God. — ' For
    love

Shown in the cherries' flavor ? Consecrate
So petty an example ? ' There 's the fault !
We circumscribe omnipotence. Search sand
To unearth water : if first handful scooped
Yields thee a draught, what need of digging
    down
Full fifty fathoms deep to find a spring
Whereof the pulse might deluge half the land ?
Drain the sufficient drop, and praise what
    checks
The drouth that glues thy tongue, — what more
    would help
A brimful cistern ? Ask the cistern's boon
When thou wouldst solace camels : in thy case,
Relish the drop and love the lovable ! "

" And what may be unlovable ? "

               " Why, hate !
If out of sand comes sand and naught but sand,
Affect not to be quaffing at mirage,
Nor nickname pain as pleasure. That, belike,
Constitutes just the trial of thy wit
And worthiness to gain promotion, — hence,
Proves the true purpose of thine actual life.
Thy soul's environment of things perceived,
Things visible and things invisible,
Fact, fancy — all was purposed to evolve
This and this only — was thy wit of worth
To recognize the drop's use, love the same,
And loyally declare against mirage
Though all the world asseverated dust
Was good to drink ? Say, ' what made moist
    my lip,
That I acknowledged moisture : ' thou art
    saved !

For why ? The creature and creator stand
Rightly related so. Consider well !
Were knowledge all thy faculty, then God
Must be ignored : love gains him by first leap.
Frankly accept the creatureship : ask good
To love for : press bold to the tether's end
Allotted to this life's intelligence !
' So we offend ? ' Will it offend thyself
If — impuissance praying potency —
Thy child beseech that thou command the sun
Rise bright to-morrow — thou, he thinks su-
    preme
In power and goodness, why shouldst thou
    refuse ?
Afterward, when the child matures, perchance
The fault were greater if, with wit full-grown,
The stripling dared to ask for a dinar,
Than that the boy cried ' Pluck Sitara down
And give her me to play with ! ' 'T is for him
To have no bounds to his belief in thee :
For thee it also is to let her shine
Lustrous and lonely, so best serving him ! "

Ask not one least word of praise !
  Words declare your eyes are bright ?
What then meant that summer day's
Silence spent in one long gaze ?
  Was my silence wrong or right ?

Words of praise were all to seek !
  Face of you and form of you,

Did they find the praise so weak
When my lips just touched your cheek —
Touch which let my soul come through?

XII. A BEAN-STRIPE: ALSO APPLE-
EATING

" LOOK, I strew beans " . . .

(Ferishtah, we premise,
Strove this way with a scholar's cavilment
Who put the peevish question: " Sir, be frank!
A good thing or a bad thing — Life is which?
Shine and shade, happiness and misery
Battle it out there: which force beats, I
ask?
If I pick beans from out a bushelful —
This one, this other, — then demand of thee
What color names each justly in the main, —
' Black ' I expect, and ' White ' ensues reply:
No hesitation for what speck, spot, splash
Of either color's opposite, intrudes
To modify thy judgment. Well, for beans
Substitute days, — show, ranged in order, Life—
Then, tell me its true color! Time is short,
Life's days compose a span, — as brief be
speech!
Black I pronounce for, like the Indian Sage, —
Black — present, past, and future, interspersed
With blanks, no doubt, which simple folk style
Good
Because not Evil: no, indeed? Forsooth,
Black's shade on White is White too! What's
the worst
Of Evil but that, past, it overshades
The else-exempted present? — memory,
We call the plague! ' Nay, but our memory
fades
And leaves the past unsullied! ' Does it so?
Why, straight the purpose of such breathing-
space,
Such respite from past ills, grows plain enough!
What follows on remembrance of the past?
Fear of the future! Life, from birth to death,
Means — either looking back on harm escaped,
Or looking forward to that harm's return
With tenfold power of harming. Black, not
White,
Never the whole consummate quietude
Life should be, troubled by no fear! — nor
hope —
I 'll say, since lamplight dies in noontide, hope
Loses itself in certainty. Such lot
Man's might have been: I leave the conse-
quence
To bolder critics or the Primal Cause;
Such am not I: but, man — as man I speak:
Black is the bean-throw: evil is the Life! '")

" Look, I strew beans," — resumed Ferishtah,
— " beans
Blackish and whitish; what they figure forth
Shall be man's sum of moments, bad and
good,
That make up Life, — each moment when he
feels
Pleasure or pain, his poorest fact of sense,
Consciousness anyhow: there 's stand the first;

Whence next advance shall be from points to
line,
Singulars to a series, parts to whole,
And moments to the Life.. How look they now.
Viewed in the large, those little joys and griefs
Ranged duly all a-row at last, like beans
— These which I strew? This bean was white,
this — black,
Set by itself, — but see if good and bad
Each following either in companionship,
Black have not grown less black and white less
white,
Till blackish seems but dun, and whitish —
gray,
And the whole line turns — well, or black to
thee
Or white belike to me — no matter which:
The main result is — both are modified
According to our eye's scope, power of range
Before and after. Black dost call this bean?
What, with a whiteness in its wake, which —
see —
Suffuses half its neighbor? — and, in turn,
Lowers its pearliness late absolute,
Frowned upon by the jet which follows hard —
Else wholly white my bean were. Choose a
joy!
Bettered it was by sorrow gone before,
And sobered somewhat by the shadowy sense
Of sorrow which came after or might come.
Joy, sorrow, — by precedence, subsequence —
Either on each, make fusion, mix in Life
That 's both and neither wholly: gray or dun?
Dun thou decidest? gray prevails, say I:
Wherefore? Because my view is wide enough,
Reaches from first to last nor winks at all:
Motion achieves it: stop short — fast we
stick, —
Probably at the bean that 's blackest.

"Since —
Son, trust me, — this I know and only this —
I am in motion, and all things beside
That circle round my passage through their
midst, —
Motionless, these are, as regarding me:
— Which means, myself I solely recognize.
They too may recognize themselves, not me,
For aught I know or care: but plain they serve
This, if no other purpose — stuff to try
And test my power upon of raying light
And lending hue to all things as I go
Moonlike through vapor. Mark the flying orb!
Think'st thou the halo, painted still afresh
At each new cloud-fleece pierced and passaged
through,
This was and is and will be evermore
Colored in permanence? The glory swims
Girdling the glory-giver, swallowed straight
By night's abysmal gloom, unglorified
Behind as erst before the advancer: gloom?
Faced by the onward-faring, see, succeeds
From the abandoned heaven a next surprise,
And where 's the gloom now? — silver-smitten
straight,
One glow and variegation! So with me,
Who move and make — myself — the black, the
white,

The good, the bad, of life's environment.
Stand still ! black stays black : start again !
    there 's white
Asserts supremacy : the motion 's all
That colors me my moment : seen as joy ? —
I have escaped from sorrow, or that was
Or might have been : as sorrow ? — thence shall
    be
Escape as certain : white preceded black,
Black shall give way to white as duly, — so,
Deepest in black means white most imminent,
Stand still, — have no before, no after ! — life
Proves death, existence grows impossible
To man like me. 'What else is blessed sleep
But death, then ? ' Why, a rapture of release
From toil, — that 's sleep's approach : as cer-
    tainly,
The end of sleep means, toil is triumphed o'er :
These round the blank inconsciousness between
Brightness and brightness, either pushed to
    blaze
Just through that blank's interposition. Hence
The use of things external : man — that 's I —
Practise thereon my power of casting light,
And calling substance, — when the light I cast
Breaks into color, — by its proper name
— A truth and yet a falsity : black, white,
Names each bean taken from what lay so close
And threw such tint : pain might mean pain
    indeed
Seen in the passage past it, — pleasure prove
No mere delusion while I pause to look, —
Though what an idle fancy was that fear
Which overhung and hindered pleasure's hue !
While now, again, pain's shade enhanced the
    shine
Of pleasure, else no pleasure ! Such effects
Came of such causes. Passage at an end, —
Past, present, future pains and pleasures fused
So that one glance may gather blacks and
    whites
Into a lifetime, — like my bean-streak there,
Why, white they whirl into, not black — for
    me ! ''

" Ay, but for me ? The indubitable blacks,
Immeasurable miseries, here, there
And everywhere i' the world — world outside
    thine
Paled off so opportunely, — body's plague,
Torment of soul, — where 's found thy fellow-
    ship
With wide humanity all round about
Reeling beneath its burden ? What 's despair ?
Behold that man, that woman, child — nay,
    brute !
Will any speck of white unblacken life
Splashed, splotched, dyed hell-deep now from
    end to end
For him or her or it — who knows ? Not I ! ''

" Nor I, Son ! 'It' shall stand for bird, beast,
    fish,
Reptile, and insect even : take the last !
There 's the palm-aphis, minute miracle
As wondrous every whit as thou or I :
Well, and his world 's the palm-frond, there
    he 's born,

Lives, breeds, and dies in that circumference,
An inch of green for cradle, pasture-ground,
Purlieu and grave : the palm's use, ask of him !
'To furnish these,' replies his wit : ask thine —
Who see the heaven above, the earth below,
Creation everywhere, — these, each and all
Claim certain recognition from the tree
For special service rendered branch and bole,
Top-tuft and tap-root : — for thyself, thus seen,
Palms furnish dates to eat, and leaves to shade,
— Maybe, thatch huts with, — have another use
Than strikes the aphis. So with me, my Son !
I know my own appointed patch i' the world,
What pleasures me or pains there : all out-
    side —
How he, she, it, and even thou, Son, live,
Are pleased or pained, is past conjecture, once
I pry beneath the semblance, — all that 's fit,
To practise with, — reach where the fact may
    lie
Fathom-deep lower. There 's the first and last
Of my philosophy. Blacks blur thy white ?
Not mine ! The aphis feeds, nor finds his leaf
Untenable, because a lance-thrust, nay,
Lightning strikes sere a moss-patch close be-
    side,
Where certain other aphids live and love.
Restriction to his single inch of white,
That 's law for him, the aphis : but for me,
The man, the larger-souled, beside my stretch
Of blacks and whites, I see a world of woe
All round about me : one such burst of black
Intolerable o'er the life I count
White in the main, and, yea — white's faintest
    trace
Were clean abolished once and evermore.
Thus fare my fellows, swallowed up in gloom
So far as I discern : how far is that ?
God's care be God's ! 'T is mine — to boast no
    joy
Unsobered by such sorrows of my kind
As sully with their shade my life that shines."

" Reflected possibilities of pain,
Forsooth, just chasten pleasure ! Pain itself, —
Fact and not fancy, does not this affect
The general color ? ''

                " Here and there a touch
Taught me, betimes, the artifice of things —
That all about, external to myself,
Was meant to be suspected, — not revealed
Demonstrably a cheat, — but half seen through,
Lest white should rule unchecked along the
    line
Therefore white may not triumph. All the
    same,
Of absolute and irretrievable
And all-subduing black, — black's soul of black
Beyond white's power to disintensify, —
Of that I saw no sample : such may wreck
My life and ruin my philosophy
To - morrow, doubtless : hence the constant
    shade
Cast on life's shine, — the tremor that intrudes
When firmest seems my faith in white. Dost
    ask
'Who is Ferishtah, hitherto exempt

From black experience? Why, if God be just,
Were sundry fellow-mortals singled out
To undergo experience for his sake,
Just that the gift of pain, bestowed on them,
In him might temper to the due degree
Joy's else-excessive largess?' Why, indeed!
Back are we brought thus to the starting-
point—
Man's impotency, God's omnipotence,
These stop my answer. Aphis that I am,
How leave my inch-allotment, pass at will
Into my fellow's liberty of range,
Enter into his sense of black and white,
As either, seen by me from outside, seems
Predominatingly the color? Life,
Lived by my fellow, shall I pass into
And myself live there? No—no more than
pass
From Persia, where in sun since birth I bask
Daily, to some ungracious land afar,
Told of by travellers, where the night of snow
Smothers up day, and fluids lose themselves
Frozen to marble. How I bear the sun,
Beat though he may unduly, that I know:
How blood once curdled ever creeps again,
Baffles conjecture: yet since people live
Somehow, resist a clime would conquer me,
Somehow provided for their sake must dawn
Compensative resource. 'No sun, no grapes,—
Then, no subsistence!'—were it wisely said?
Or this well-reasoned—'Do I dare feel warmth
And please my palate here with Persia's vine,
Though, over-mounts,—to trust the travel-
ler,—
Snow, feather-thick, is falling while I feast?
What if the cruel winter force his way
Here also?' Son, the wise reply were this:
When cold from over-mounts spikes through
and through
Blood, bone and marrow of Ferishtah,—then,
Time to look out for shelter—time, at least,
To wring the hands and cry 'No shelter serves!'
Shelter, of some sort, no experienced chill
Warrants that I despair to find."

" No less,
Doctors have differed here; thou say'st thy
say ;
Another man's experience masters thine,
Flat controverted by the sourly-Sage,
The Indian witness who, with faculty
Fine as Ferishtah's, found no white at all
Chequer the world's predominating black,
No good oust evil from supremacy,
So that Life's best was that it led to death.
How of his testimony?"

" Son, suppose
My camel told me: 'Threescore days and ten
I traversed hill and dale, yet never found
Food to stop hunger, drink to stay my drouth ;
Yet, here I stand alive, which take in proof
That to survive was found impossible!'
'Nay, rather take thou, non-surviving beast,'
(Reply were prompt,) 'on flank this thwack of
staff
Nowise affecting flesh that 's dead and dry !
Thou wincest? Take correction twice, amend

Next time thy nomenclature! Call white
white!'
The sourly-Sage, for whom life's best was death,
Lived out his seventy years, looked hale,
laughed loud,
Liked—above all—his dinner,—lied, in
short."

" Lied is a rough phrase: say he fell from
truth
In climbing towards it!—sure less faulty so
Than had he sat him down and stayed content
With thy safe orthodoxy, 'White, all white,
White everywhere for certain I should see
Did I but understand how white is black,
As clearer sense than mine would.' Clearer
sense, —
Whose may that be? Mere human eyes I
boast,
And such distinguish colors in the main,
However any tongue, that 's human too,
Please to report the matter. Dost thou blame
A soul that strives but to see plain, speak true,
Truth at all hazards? Oh, this false for real,
This emptiness which feigns solidity,—
Ever some gray that 's white and dun that 's
black, —
When shall we rest upon the thing itself
Not on its semblance?—Soul—too weak, for-
sooth,
To cope with fact—wants fiction everywhere !
Mine tires of falsehood: truth at any cost !''

" Take one and try conclusions—this, sup-
pose !
God is all-good, all-wise, all-powerful: truth ?
Take it and rest there. What is man? Not
God:
None of these absolutes therefore,—yet him-
self,
A creature with a creature's qualities.
Make them agree, these two conceptions !
Each
Abolishes the other. Is man weak,
Foolish and bad? He must be Ahriman,
Co-equal with an Ormuzd, Bad with Good,
Or else a thing made at the Prime Sole Will,
Doing a maker's pleasure—with results
Which—call, the wide world over, 'what must
be '—
But, from man's point of view, and only point
Possible to his powers, call—evidence
Of goodness, wisdom, strength? we mock our-
selves
In all that 's best of us,—man 's blind but
sure
Craving for these in very deed not word,
Reality and not illusions. Well, —
Since these nowhere exist—nor there where
cause
Must have effect, nor here where craving means
Craving unfollowed by fit consequence
And full supply, aye sought for, never found—
These—what are they but man's own rule of
right ?
A scheme of goodness recognized by man,
Although by man unrealizable,—
Not God's with whom to will were to perform :

Nowise performed here, therefore never willed.
What follows but that God, who could the
     best,
Has willed the worst, — while man, with power
     to match
Will with performance, were deservedly
Hailed the supreme — provided . . . here 's the
     touch
That breaks the bubble . . . this concept of
     man's
Were man's own work, his birth of heart and
     brain,
His native grace, no alien gift at all.
The bubble breaks here.   Will of man create ?
No more than this my hand which strewed the
     beans
Produced them also from its finger-tips.
Back goes creation to its source, source prime
And ultimate, the single and the sole."

" How reconcile discordancy, — unite
Notion and notion — God that only can
Yet does not, — man that would indeed
But just as surely cannot, — both in one ?
What help occurs to thy intelligence ? "

" Ah, the beans, — or, — example better yet, —
A carpet-web I saw once leave the loom
And lie at gorgeous length in Ispahan !
The weaver plied his work with lengths of silk
Dyed each to match some jewel as it might,
And wove them, this by that. ' How comes it,
     friend,' —
(Quoth I) — ' that while, apart, this fiery hue,
That watery dimness, either shocks the eye,
So blinding bright, or else offends again,
By dulness, — yet the two, set each by each,
Somehow produce a color born of both,
A medium profitable to the sight ? '
' Such medium is the end whereat I aim,' —
Answered my craftsman: ' there 's no single
     tinct
Would satisfy the eye's desire to taste
The secret of the diamond : join extremes
Results a serviceable medium-ghost,
The diamond's simulation. Even so
I needs must blend the quality of man
With quality of God, and so assist
Mere human sight to understand my Life,
What is, what should be, — understand thereby
Wherefore I hate the first and love the last, —
Understand why things so present themselves
To me, placed here to prove I understand.
Thus, from beginning runs the chain to end,
And binds me plain enough.   By consequence,
I bade thee tolerate, — not kick and cuff
The man who held that natures did in fact
Blend so, since so thyself must have them blend
In fancy, if it take a flight so far."

" A power, confessed past knowledge, nay,
     past thought,
— Thus thought thus known ! "

               " To know of, think about —
Is all man's sum of faculty effects
When exercised on earth's least atom, Son !
What was, what is, what may such atom be ?

No answer !   Still, what seems it to man's
     sense ?
An atom with some certain properties
Known about, thought of as occasion needs,
— Man's — but occasions of the universe ?
Unthinkable, unknowable to man.
Yet, since to think and know fire through and
     through
Exceeds man, is the warmth of fire unknown,
Its uses — are they so unthinkable ?
Pass from such obvious power to powers un-
     seen,
Undreamed of save in their sure consequence :
Take that, we spoke of late, which draws to
     ground
The staff my hand lets fall : it draws, at least —
Thus much man thinks and knows, if nothing
     more."

" Ay, but man puts no mind into such power !
He neither thanks it, when an apple drops,
Nor prays it spare his pate while underneath.
Does he thank Summer though it plumped the
     rind ?
Why thank the other force — whate'er its
     name —
Which gave him teeth to bite and tongue to
     taste
And throat to let the pulp pass ?   Force and
     force,
No end of forces !   Have they mind like man ? "

" Suppose thou visit our lord Shalim-Shah,
Bringing thy tribute as appointed. ' Here
Come I to pay my due ! '   Whereat one slave
Obsequious spreads a carpet for thy foot,
His fellow offers sweetmeats, while a third
Prepares a pipe : what thanks or praise have
     they ?
Such as befit prompt service.   Gratitude
Goes past them to the Shah whose gracious nod
Set all the sweet civility at work ;
But for his ordinance, I much suspect,
My scholar had been left to cool his heels
Uncarpeted, or warm them — likelier still —
With bastinado for intrusion.   Slaves
Needs must obey their master : ' force and
     force,
No end of forces,' act as bids some force
Supreme o'er all and each : where find that
     one ?
How recognize him ?   Simply as thou didst
The Shah — by reasoning ' Since I feel a debt.
Behooves me pay the same to one aware
I have my duty, he his privilege.'
Didst thou expect the slave who charged thy
     pipe
Would serve as well to take thy tribute-bag
And save thee further trouble ? "

                         " Be it so !
The sense within me that I owe a debt
Assures me — somewhere must be somebody
Ready to take his due.   All comes to this —
Where due is, there acceptance follows : find
Him who accepts the due ! and why look far ?
Behold thy kindred compass thee about !
Ere thou wast born and after thou shalt die,

Heroic man stands forth as Shahan-Shah.
Rustem and Gew, Gudarz and all the rest,
How come they short of lordship that's to
    seek?
Dead worthies! but men live undoubtedly
Gifted as Sindokht, sage Sulayman's match,
Valiant like Kawah: ay, and while earth lasts
Such heroes shall abound there — all for thee
Who profitest by all the present, past,
And future operation of thy race.
Why, then, o'erburdened with a debt of thanks,
Look wistful for some hand from out the clouds
To take it, when, all round, a multitude
Would ease thee in a trice?''

                    "Such tendered thanks
Would tumble back to who craved riddance,
    Son!
— Who but my sorry self? See! stars are
    out—
Stars which, unconscious of thy gaze beneath,
Go glorifying, and glorify thee too
—- Those Seven Thrones, Zurah's beauty, weird
    Parwin!
Whether shall love and praise to stars be paid
Or — say — some Mubid who, for good to thee
Blind at thy birth, by magic all his own
Opened thine eyes, and gave the sightless sight,
Let the stars' glory enter? Say his charm
Worked while thyself lay sleeping: as he went
Thou wakedst: 'What a novel sense have I!
Whom shall I love and praise?' 'The stars,
    each orb
Thou standest rapt beneath,' proposes one:
'Do not they live their life, and please them-
    selves,
And so please thee? What more is requisite?'
Make thou this answer: 'If indeed no mage
Opened my eyes and worked a miracle,
Then let the stars thank me who apprehend
That such an one is white, such other blue!
But for my apprehension both were blank.
Cannot I close my eyes and bid my brain
Make whites and blues, conceive without stars'
    help,
New qualities of color? were my sight
Lost or misleading, would yon red — I judge
A ruby's benefaction — stand for aught
But green from vulgar glass? Myself appraise
Lustre and lustre: should I overlook
Fomalhaut and declare some fen-fire king,
Who shall correct me, lend me eyes he trusts
No more than I trust mine? My mage for me!
I never saw him: if he never was,
I am the arbitrator!' No, my Son!
Let us sink down to thy similitude:
I eat my apple, relish what is ripe —
The sunny side, admire its rarity
Since half the tribe is wrinkled, and the rest
Hide commonly a maggot in the core, —
And down Zerdusht goes with due smack of
    lips:
But — thank an apple? He who made my
    mouth
To masticate, my palate to approve,
My maw to further the concoction — Him
I thank, — but for whose work, the orchard's
    wealth

Might prove so many gall-nuts — stocks or
    stones
For aught that I should think, or know, or
    care.''

———————

"Why from the world," Ferishtah smiled, "should
    thanks
    Go to this work of mine? If worthy praise,
Praised let it be and welcome: as verse ranks,
    So rate my verse: if good therein outweighs
    Aught faulty judged, judge justly! Justice says?
Be just to fact, or blaming or approving:
But — generous? No, nor loving!

"Loving! what claim to love has work of mine?
    Concede my life were emptied of its gains
To furnish forth and fill work's strict confine,
    Who works so for the world's sake — he complains
    With cause when hate, not love, rewards his pains.
I looked beyond the world for truth and beauty:
Sought, found, and did my duty.''

EPILOGUE

OH, Love — no, Love! All the noise below,
    Love,
    Groanings all and moanings — none of Life I
        lose!
All of Life's a cry just of weariness and woe,
    Love —
    "Hear at least, thou happy one!" How can
        I, Love, but choose?

Only, when I do hear, sudden circle round
    me
    — Much as when the moon's might frees a
        space from cloud —
Iridescent splendors: gloom — would else con-
    found me —
    Barriered off and banished far — bright-
        edged the blackest shroud!

Thronging through the cloud-rift, whose are
    they, the faces
    Faint revealed yet sure divined, the famous
        ones of old?
"What" — they smile — "our names, our
    deeds so soon erases
    Time upon his tablet where Life's glory lies
        enrolled?

"Was it for mere fool's-play, make-believe
    and mumming,
    So we battled it like men, not boylike sulked
        or whined?
Each of us heard clang God's 'Come!' and
    each was coming:
    Soldiers all, to forward-face, not sneaks to
        lag behind!

"How of the field's fortune? That concerned
    our Leader!
    Led, we struck our stroke nor cared for do-
        ings left and right:
Each as on his sole head, failer or succeeder,
    Lay the blame or lit the praise: no care for
        cowards: fight!"

Then the cloud-rift broadens, spanning earth
 that 's under,
 Wide our world displays its worth, man's
  strife and strife's success ;
All the good and beauty, wonder crowning
  wonder,
 Till my heart and soul applaud perfection,
  nothing less.

Only, at heart's utmost joy and triumph, terror
 Sudden turns the blood to ice : a chill wind
  disencharms
All the late enchantment ! What if all be
  error —
 If the halo irised round my head were, Love,
  thine arms ?

Palazzo Giustinian-Recanati, VENICE :
 December 1, 1883.

RAWDON BROWN

" Tutti ga i so gusti, e mi go i mii."
   (*Venetian saying.*)

Mr. Rawdon Brown was an Englishman who
went to Venice on some temporary errand, and
lived there for forty years, dying in that city in
the summer of 1883. He had an enthusiastic
love for Venice, and is mentioned in books of
travel as one who knew the city thoroughly.
The Venetian saying means that " everybody
follows his taste as I follow mine." Toni was
the gondolier and attendant of Brown. The in-
scription on Brown's tomb is given in the third
and fourth lines. G. W. COOKE.

SIGHED Rawdon Brown : " Yes, I 'm departing,
 Toni !
I needs must, just this once before I die,
 Revisit England : *Anglus* Brown am I,
Although my heart 's Venetian. Yes, old
 crony —
Venice and London — London 's ' Death the
 bony '
 Compared with Life — that 's Venice ! What
  a sky,
A sea, this morning ! One last look ! Good-by,
Cà Pesaro ! No, lion — I 'm a coney
To weep ! I 'm dazzled ; 't is that sun I view
 Rippling the . . . the . . . *Cospetto*, Toni !
  Down
 With carpet-bag, and off with valise-straps !
Bella Venezia, non ti lascio più ! "
 Nor did Brown ever leave her : well, per-
  haps
 Browning, next week, may find himself quite
  Brown !
November 28, 1883.

THE FOUNDER OF THE FEAST

Inscribed in an Album presented to Mr.
Arthur Chappell, of the Saint James Hall
Saturday and Monday popular concerts.

" ENTER my palace," if a prince should say —
 " Feast with the Painters ! See, in bounteous
  row,
 They range from Titian up to Angelo ! "
Could we be silent at the rich survey ?
A host so kindly, in as great a way
 Invites to banquet, substitutes for show
 Sound that 's diviner still, and bids us know
Bach like Beethoven ; are we thankless, pray ?

Thanks, then, to Arthur Chappell, — thanks
 to him
 Whose every guest henceforth not idly vaunts
 " Sense has received the utmost Nature
  grants,
My cup was filled with rapture to the brim,
 When, night by night, — ah, memory, how it
  haunts ! —
 Music was poured by perfect ministrants,
By Halle, Schumann, Piatti, Joachim.
 April 5, 1884.

THE NAMES

At Dr. F. J. Furnivall's suggestion, Brown-
ing was asked to contribute a sonnet to the
Shakesperean Show-Book of the "Shakesperean
Show" held in Albert Hall, London, on May
29-31, 1884, to pay off the debt on the Hospital
for Women, in Fulham Road. The poet sent
to the committee a sonnet on the names of Je-
hovah and Shakespeare.

SHAKESPEARE ! — to such name's sounding,
 what succeeds
 Fitly as silence ? Falter forth the spell, —
 Act follows word, the speaker knows full
  well,
Nor tampers with its magic more than needs.
Two names there are : That which the Hebrew
 reads
 With his soul only : if from lips it fell,
 Echo, back thundered by earth, heaven and
  hell,
Would own " Thou didst create us ! " Naught
 impedes
We voice the other name, man's most of might,
 Awesomely, lovingly : let awe and love
Mutely await their working, leave to sight
 All of the issue as — below — above —
Shakespeare's creation rises : one remove,
Though dread — this finite from that infinite.
 March 12, 1884.

EPITAPH

ON LEVI LINCOLN THAXTER

Born in Watertown, Massachusetts, February 1, 1824.
Died May 31, 1884.

Mr. Thaxter was early a student of Browning's
genius and in his later years gave readings from
his poems, which were singularly interpretative.
The boulder over his grave bears these lines.

THOU, whom these eyes saw never ! Say friends
    true
Who say my soul, helped onward by my song,
Though all unwittingly, has helped thee too ?
I gave of but the little that I knew :
How were the gift requited, while along
Life's path I pace, couldst thou make weak-
    ness strong !
Help me with knowledge — for Life's Old —
    Death's New !
R. B. to L. L. T., *April*, 1885.

WHY I AM A LIBERAL

Contributed to a volume edited by Andrew
Reid, in which a number of leaders of English
thought answered the question, "Why I am a
Liberal ? "

"WHY ? " Because all I haply can and do,
All that I am now, all I hope to be, —
Whence comes it save from fortune setting
    free
Body and soul the purpose to pursue,
God traced for both ? If fetters, not a few,
Of prejudice, convention, fall from me,
These shall I bid men — each in his de
    gree
Also God-guided — bear, and gayly, too ?

But little do or can the best of us :
    That little is achieved through Liberty.
Who, then, dares hold, emancipated thus,
    His fellow shall continue bound ? Not I,
Who live, love, labor freely, nor discuss
    A brother's right to freedom. That i
    " Why."

PARLEYINGS WITH CERTAIN PEOPLE OF IMPORTANCE IN THEIR DAY

IN MEMORIAM J. MILSAND, OBIIT IV. SEPTEMBER, MDCCCLXXXVI.
Absens Absentem Auditque Videtque.

APOLLO AND THE FATES

A PROLOGUE

(Hymn in Mercurium, v. 559. Eumenides, vv. 693-4,
697-8. Alcestis, vv. 12, 33.)

Apollo. (*From above.*) Flame at my footfall,
    Parnassus ! Apollo,
Breaking ablaze on thy topmost peak,
Burns thence, down to the depths — dread
    hollow —
Haunt of the Dire Ones. Haste ! They
    wreak
Wrath on Admetus whose respite I seek.

The Fates. (*Below. Darkness.*) Dragonwise
    couched in the womb of our Mother,
Coiled at thy nourishing heart's core,
    Night !
Dominant Dreads, we, one by the other,
    Deal to each mortal his dole of light
On earth — the upper, the glad, the bright.

Clotho. Even so : thus from my loaded spin-
    dle
Plucking a pinch of the fleece, lo, "Birth"
Brays from my bronze lip : life I kindle :
Look, 't is a man ! go, measure on earth
The minute thy portion, whatever its worth !

Lachesis. Woe-purfled, weal-prankt, — if it
    speed, if it linger, —
Life's substance and show are determined by
    me,
Who, meting out, mixing with sure thumb and
    finger,

Lead life the due length : is all smoothness
    and glee,
All tangle and grief ? Take the lot, my decree !

Atropos. — Which I make an end of : the
    smooth as the tangled
My shears cut asunder : each snap shrieks
    " One more
Mortal makes sport for us Moirai who dangled
    The puppet grotesquely till earth's solid floor
Proved film he fell through, lost in Naught as
    before."

Clo. I spin thee a thread. Live, Admetus !
    Produce him !
Lac. Go, — brave, wise, good, happy ! Now
    chequer the thread !
He is slaved for, yet loved by a god. I unloose
    him
A goddess-sent plague. He has conquered,
    is wed,
Men crown him, he stands at the height, —
Atr.   He is . . .
Apollo. (*Entering : Light.*)   " Dead ? '

Nay, swart spinsters ! So I surprise you
    Making and marring the fortunes of Man ?
Huddling — no marvel, your enemy eyes you —
    Head by head bat-like, blots under the ban
Of daylight earth's blessing since time began !

The Fates. Back to thy blest earth, prying
    Apollo !
Shaft upon shaft transpierce with thy beams
Earth to the centre, — spare but this hollow
Hewn out of Night's heart, where our
    mystery seems

Mewed from day's malice : wake earth from
    her dreams !

Apol. Crones, 't is your dusk selves I startle
    from slumber :
Day's god deposes you — queens Night-
    crowned !
— Plying your trade in a world ye encumber,
Fashioning Man's web of life — spun, wound,
Left the length ye allot till a clip strews the
    ground !

Behold I bid truce to your doleful amuse-
    ment —
Annulled by a sunbeam !
The Fates.   Boy, are not we peers ?
Apol. You with the spindle grant birth:
    whose inducement
But yours — with the niggardly digits — en-
    dears
To mankind chance and change, good and evil ?
    Your shears . . .

Atr. Ay, mine end the conflict : so much is
    no fable.
We spin, draw to length, cut asunder : what
    then ?
So it was, and so is, and so shall be : art able
To alter life's law for ephemeral men ?
Apol. Nor able nor willing. To threescore
    and ten

Extend but the years of Admetus ! Disaster
    O'ertook me, and, banished by Zeus, I be-
    came
A servant to one who forbore me though mas-
    ter :
True lovers were we. Discontinue your
    game,
Let him live whom I loved, then hate on, all
    the same !

The Fates. And what if we granted — law-
    flouter, use-trampler —
His life at the suit of an upstart ? Judge,
    thou —
Of joy were it fuller, of span because ampler ?
For love's sake, not hate's, end Admetus —
    ay, now —
Not a gray hair on head, nor a wrinkle on
    brow !

For, boy, 't is illusion: from thee comes a glim-
    mer
Transforming to beauty life blank at the
    best.
Withdraw — and how looks life at worst, when
    to shimmer
Succeeds the sure shade, and Man's lot
    frowns — confessed
Mere blackness chance-brightened ? Whereof
    shall attest

The truth this same mortal, the darling thou
    stylest,
Whom love would advantage, — eke out,
    day by day,
A life which 't is solely thyself reconcilest

Thy friend to endure, — life with hope : take
    away
Hope's gleam from Admetus, he spurns it.
    For, say —

What 's infancy ? Ignorance, idleness, mis-
    chief :
Youth ripens to arrogance, foolishness, greed:
Age — impotence, churlishness, rancor : call *this*
    chief
Of boons for thy loved one ? Much rather
    bid speed
Our function, let live whom thou hatest indeed !

Persuade thee, bright boy-thing ! Our eld be
    instructive !
Apol. And certes youth owns the experience
    of age.
Ye hold then, grave seniors, my beams are
    productive
— They solely — of good that 's mere sem-
    blance, engage
Man's eye — gilding evil, Man's true heritage ?

The Fates. So, even so ! From without, — at
    due distance
If viewed, — set a-sparkle, reflecting thy
    rays, —
Life mimics the sun: but withdraw such
    assistance,
The counterfeit goes, the reality stays —
An ice-ball disguised as a fire-orb.
Apol.   What craze

Possesses the fool then whose fancy conceits
    him
As happy ?
The Fates. Man happy ?
Apol.   If otherwise —solve
This doubt which besets me ! What friend
    ever greets him
Except with " Live long as the seasons re-
    volve,"
Not " Death to thee straightway " ? Your
    doctrines absolve

Such hailing from hatred : yet Man should
    know best.
He talks it, and glibly, as life were a load
Man fain would be rid of : when put to the test,
He whines " Let it lie, leave me trudging the
    road
That is rugged so far, but methinks " . . .
The Fates.   Ay, 't is owed

To that glamour of thine, he bethinks him
    " Once past
The stony, some patch, nay, a smoothness of
    swarth
Awaits my tired foot : life turns easy at last " —
Thy largess so lures him, he looks for reward
Of the labor and sorrow.
Apol.   It seems, then — debarred

Of illusion — (I needs must acknowledge the
    plea)
Man desponds and despairs. Yet, — still
    further to draw

Due profit from counsel, — suppose there should
    be
Some power in himself, some compensative
    law
By virtue of which, independently . . .

The Fates.   Faugh!
Strength hid in the weakling!
           What bowl-shape hast there,
Thus laughingly proffered? A gift to our
    shrine?
Thanks — worsted in argument! Not so? De-
    clare
Its purpose!
Apol.   I proffer earth's product, not mine.
Taste, try, and approve Man's invention of —
    WINE!

The Fates. We feeding suck honeycombs.
Apol.   Sustenance meagre!
Such fare breeds the fumes that show all
    things amiss.
Quaff wine, — how the spirits rise nimble and
    eager,
Unscale the dim eyes! To Man's cup grant
    one kiss
Of your lip, then allow — no enchantment like
    this!

Clo. Unhook wings, unhood brows! Dost
    hearken?
Lach.   I listen:
I see — smell the food these fond mortals
    prefer
To our feast, the bee's bounty!
Atr.   The thing leaps! But — glisten
Its best, I withstand it — unless all concur
In adventure so novel.
Apol.   Ye drink?
The Fates.   . We demur.

Apol. Sweet Trine, be indulgent nor scout
    the contrivance
Of Man — Bacchus-prompted! The juice, I
    uphold,
Illuminates gloom without sunny connivance,
Turns fear into hope and makes cowardice
    bold, —
Touching all that is leadlike in life turns it
    gold!

The Fates. Faith foolish as false!
Apol.   But essay it, soft sisters!
Then mock as ye may. Lift the chalice to lip!
Good: thou next — and thou! Seems the web,
    to you twisters
Of life's yarn, so worthless?
Clo.   Who guessed that one sip
Would impart such a lightness of limb?
Lach.   I could skip

In a trice from the pied to the plain in my
    woof!
What parts each from either? A hair's
    breadth, no inch.
Once learn the right method of stepping aloof,
    Though on black next foot falls, firm I fix it,
    nor flinch,

— Such my trust white succeeds!
Atr.   One could live — at a pinch!

Apol. What, beldames? Earth's yield, by
    Man's skill, can effect
Such a cure of sick sense that ye spy the re-
    lation
Of evil to good? But drink deeper, correct
Blear sight more convincingly still! Take
    your station
Beside me, drain dregs! Now for edification!

Whose gift have ye gulped? Thank not me
    but my brother,
Blithe Bacchus, our youngest of godships.
    'T was he
Found all boons to all men, by one god or other
Already conceded, so judged there must be
New guerdon to grace the new advent, you
    see!

Else how would a claim to Man's homage arise?
The plan lay arranged of his mixed woe and
    weal,
So disposed — such Zeus' will — with design to
    make wise
The witless — that false things were mingled
    with real,
Good with bad: such the lot whereto law set
    the seal.

Now, human of instinct — since Semele's son,
    Yet minded divinely — since fathered by Zeus,
With naught Bacchus tampered, undid not
    things done,
Owned wisdom anterior, would spare wont
    and use,
Yet change — without shock to old rule — in-
    troduce.

Regard how your cavern from crag-tip to base
Frowns sheer, height and depth adamantine,
    one death!
I rouse with a beam the whole rampart, displace
No splinter — yet see how my flambeau, be-
    neath
And above, bids this gem wink, that crystal
    unsheathe!

Withdraw beam — disclosure once more Night
    forbids you
Of spangle and sparkle — Day's chance-gift,
    surmised
Rock's permanent birthright: my potency rids
    you
No longer of darkness, yet light — recog-
    nized —
Proves darkness a mask: day lives on though
    disguised.

If Bacchus by wine's aid avail so to fluster
Your sense, that life's fact grows from adverse
    and thwart
To helpful and kindly by means of a cluster —
Mere hand-squeeze, earth's nature sublimed
    by Man's art —
Shall Bacchus claim thanks wherein Zeus has
    no part?

Zeus — wisdom anterior? No, maids, be admonished!
  If morn's touch at base worked such wonders, much more
Had noontide in absolute glory astonished
  Your den, filled a-top to o'erflowing. I pour
No such mad confusion. 'T is Man's to explore

Up and down, inch by inch, with the taper his reason:
  No torch, it suffices — held deftly and straight.
Eyes, purblind at first, feel their way in due season,
  Accept good with bad, till unseemly debate
Turns concord — despair, acquiescence in fate.

Who works this but Zeus? Are not instinct and impulse,
  Not concept and incept his work through Man's soul
On Man's sense? Just as wine ere it reach brain must brim pulse,
  Zeus' flash stings the mind that speeds body to goal,
Bids pause at no part but press on, reach the whole.

For petty and poor is the part ye envisage
  When — (quaff away, cummers!) — ye view, last and first,
As evil Man's earthly existence. Come! Is age,
  Is infancy — manhood — so uninterspersed
With good — some faint sprinkle?
  Clo.   I 'd speak if I durst.

Apol. Draughts dregward loose tongue-tie.
Lach.   I 'd see, did no web
Set eyes somehow winking.
Apol.   Drains-deep lies their purge
— True collyrium!
Atr. Words, surging at high-tide, soon ebb
From starved ears.
Apol. Drink but down to the source, they resurge.
Join hands! Yours and yours too! A dance or a dirge?

Cho. Quashed be our quarrel! Sourly and smilingly,
  Bare and gowned, bleached limbs and browned,
Drive we a dance, three and one, reconcilingly,
  Thanks to the cup where dissension is drowned,
Defeat proves triumphant and slavery crowned.

Infancy? What if the rose-streak of morning
  Pale and depart in a passion of tears?
Once to have hoped is no matter for scorning!
  Love once — e'en love's disappointment endears!
A minute's success pays the failure of years.

Manhood — the actual? Nay, praise the potential!
  (Bound upon bound, foot it around!)
What *is*? No, what *may* be — sing! that 's Man's essential!
  (Ramp, tramp, stamp and compound
Fancy with fact — the lost secret is found!)

Age? Why, fear ends there: the contest concluded,
Man *did* live his life, *did* escape from the fray:
Not scratchless but unscathed, he somehow eluded
  Each blow fortune dealt him, and conquers to-day:
To-morrow — new chance and fresh strength, — might we say?

Laud then Man's life — no defeat but a triumph!
          [*Explosion from the earth's centre.*
Clo. Ha, loose hands!
Lach.   I reel in a swound.
Atro. Horror yawns under me, while from on high — humph!
Lightnings astound, thunders resound,
Vault-roof reverberates, groans the ground!
                              [*Silence.*
Apol. I acknowledge.
The Fates. Hence, trickster! Straight sobered are we!
The portent assures 't was our tongue spoke the truth,
Not thine. While the vapor encompassed us three
We conceived and bore knowledge — a bantling uncouth,
Old brains shudder back from: so — take it, rash youth!

Lick the lump into shape till a cry comes!
Apol.   I hear.
The Fates. Dumb music, dead eloquence! Say it, or sing!
What was quickened in us and thee also?
Apol.   I fear.
The Fates. Half female, half male — go, ambiguous thing!
While we speak — perchance sputter — pick up what we fling!

Known yet ignored, nor divined nor unguessed,
  Such is Man's law of life. Do we strive to declare
What is ill, what is good in our spinning? Worst, best,
  Change hues of a sudden: now here and now there
Flits the sign which decides: all about yet nowhere.

'T is willed so, — that Man's life be lived, first to last,
  Up and down, through and through — not in portions, forsooth,
To pick and to choose from. Our shuttles fly fast,
  Weave living, not life sole and whole: as age — youth,
So death completes living, shows life in its truth.

Man learningly lives: till death helps him — no lore!
  It is doom and must be. Dost submit?
Apol.   I assent —
Concede but Admetus! So much if no more

Of my prayer grant as peace-pledge ! Be gra-
cious, though, blent,
Good and ill, love and hate streak your life-gift !
The Fates.   Content !

Such boon we accord in due measure. Life's
term
We lengthen should any be moved for love's
sake
To forego life's fulfilment, renounce in the
germ
Fruit mature — bliss or woe — either infinite.
Take
Or leave thy friend's lot: on his head be the
stake !

Apol. On mine, griesly gammers ! Admetus,
I know thee !
Thou prizest the right these unwittingly give
Thy subjects to rush, pay obedience they owe
thee !
Importunate one with another they strive
For the glory to die that their king may survive.

Friends rush : and who first in all Pheræ ap-
pears
But thy father to serve as thy substitute ?
Clo.   Bah !
Apol. Ye wince ?   Then his mother, well
stricken in years,
Advances her claim — or his wife —
Lach.   Tra-la-la !
Apol. But he spurns the exchange, rather
dies !
Atro.   Ha, ha, ha !
                    [*Apollo ascends. Darkness.*

WITH BERNARD DE MANDEVILLE

I

Ay, this same midnight, by this chair of mine,
Come and review thy counsels : art thou still
Stanch to their teaching ? — not as fools opine
Its purport might be, but as subtler skill
Could, through turbidity, the loaded line
Of logic casting, sound deep, deeper, till
It touched a quietude and reached a shrine
And recognized harmoniously combine
Evil with good, and hailed truth's triumph —
thine,
Sage dead long since, Bernard de Mandeville !

II

Only, 't is no fresh knowledge that I crave,
Fuller truth yet, new gainings from the grave ;
Here we alive must needs deal fairly, turn
To what account Man may Man's portion, learn
Man's proper play with truth in part, before
Entrusted with the whole. I ask no more
Than smiling witness that I do my best
With doubtful doctrine : afterwards the rest !
So, silent face me while I think and speak !
A full disclosure ? Such would outrage law.
Law deals the same with soul and body : seek
Full truth my soul may, when some babe, I saw
A new-born weakling, starts up strong — not
weak —

Man every whit, absolved from earning awe,
Pride, rapture, if the soul attains to wreak
Its will on flesh, at last can thrust, lift, draw,
As mind bids muscle — mind which long has
striven,
Painfully urging body's impotence
To effort whereby — once law's barrier riven,
Life's rule abolished — body might dispense
With infancy's probation, straight be given
— Not by foiled darings, fond attempts back-
driven,
Fine faults of growth, brave sins which saint
when shriven —
To stand full-statured in magnificence.

III

No : as with body so deals law with soul
That 's stung to strength through weakness,
strives for good
Through evil, — earth its race-ground, heaven
its goal,
Presumably : so far I understood
Thy teaching long ago. But what means this
— Objected by a mouth which yesterday
Was magisterial in antithesis
To half the truths we hold, or trust we may,
Though tremblingly the while ? "No sign "
— groaned he —
" No stirring of God's finger to denote
He wills that right should have supremacy
On earth, not wrong ! How helpful could we
quote
But one poor instance when he interposed
Promptly and surely and beyond mistake
Between oppression and its victim, closed
Accounts with sin for once, and bade us wake
From our long dream that justice bears no
sword,
Or else forgets whereto its sharpness serves !
So might we safely mock at what unnerves
Faith now, be spared the sapping fear's increase
That haply evil's strife with good shall cease
Never on earth. Nay, after earth, comes peace
Born out of life-long battle ? Man's lip curves
With scorn : there, also, what if justice swerves
From dealing doom, sets free by no swift stroke
Right fettered here by wrong, but leaves life's
yoke —
Death should loose man from — fresh laid, past
release ? "

IV

Bernard de Mandeville, confute for me
This parlous friend who captured or set free
Thunderbolts at his pleasure, yet would draw
Back, panic-stricken by some puny straw
Thy gold-rimmed amber-headed cane had
whisked
Out of his pathway if the object risked
Encounter, 'scaped thy kick from buckled shoe !
As when folk heard thee in old days pooh-pooh
Addison's tye-wig preachment, grant this
friend —
(Whose groan I hear, with guffaw at the end
Disposing of mock-melancholy) — grant
His bilious mood one potion, ministrant
Of homely wisdom, healthy wit ! For, hear !
" With power and will, let preference appear

By intervention ever and aye, help good
When evil's mastery is understood
In some plain outrage, and triumphant wrong
Tramples weak right to nothingness : nay, long
Ere such sad consummation brings despair
To right's adherents, ah, what help it were
If wrong lay strangled in the birth — each head
Of the hatched monster promptly crushed,
    instead
Of spared to gather venom ! We require
No great experience that the inch-long worm,
Free of our heel, would grow to vomit fire,
And one day plague the world in dragon form.
So should wrong merely peep abroad to meet
Wrong's due quietus, leave our world's way
    safe
For honest walking."

v

              Sage, once more repeat
Instruction ! 'T is a sore to soothe not chafe.
Ah, Fabulist, what luck, could I contrive
To coax from thee another " Grumbling
    Hive " !
My friend himself wrote fables short and sweet :
Ask him — " Suppose the Gardener of Man's
    ground
Plants for a purpose, side by side with good,
Evil — (and that he does so — look around !
What does the field show ?) — were it under-
    stood
That purposely the noxious plant was found
Vexing the virtuous, poison close to food,
If, at first stealing-forth of life in stalk
And leaflet-promise, quick his spud should
    balk
Evil from budding foliage, bearing fruit ?
Such timely treatment of the offending root
Might strike the simple as wise husbandry,
But swift sure extirpation would scarce suit
Shrewder observers. Seed once sown thrives :
    why
Frustrate its product, miss the quality
Which sower binds himself to count upon ?
Had seed fulfilled the destined purpose, gone
Unhindered up to harvest — what know I
But proof were gained that every growth of
    good
Sprang consequent on evil's neighborhood ? "
So said your shrewdness : true — so did not
    say
That other sort of theorists who held
Mere unintelligence prepared the way
For either seed's upsprouting : you repelled
Their notion that both kinds could sow them-
    selves.
True ! but admit 't is understanding delves
And drops each germ, what else but folly
    thwarts
The doer's settled purpose ? Let the sage
Concede a use to evil, though there starts
Full many a burgeon thence, to disengage
With thumb and finger lest it spoil the yield
Too much of good's main tribute ! But our
    main
Tough - tendoned mandrake - monster — purge
    the field
Of him for once and all ? It follows plain

Who set him there to grow beholds repealed
His primal law : his ordinance proves vain :
And what beseems a king who cannot reign,
But to drop sceptre valid arm should wield ?

VI

" Still there 's a parable " — retorts my friend ·
"Shows agriculture with a difference !
What of the crop and weeds which solely blend
Because, once planted, none may pluck them
    thence ?
The Gardener contrived thus ? Vain pretence !
An enemy it was who unawares
Ruined the wheat by interspersing tares.
Where 's our desiderated forethought ?
    Where 's
Knowledge, where power and will in evidence ?
'T is Man's-play merely ! Craft foils rectitude,
Malignity defeats beneficence.
And grant, at very last of all, the feud
'Twixt good and evil ends, strange thoughts in-
    trude
Though good be garnered safely, and good's foe
Bundled for burning. Thoughts steal : ' Even
    so —
Why grant tares leave to thus o'ertop, o'ertower
Their field-mate, boast the stalk and flaunt
    the flower,
Triumph one sunny minute ? Knowledge,
    power,
And will thus worked ? ' Man's fancy makes
    the fault !
Man, with the narrow mind, must cram inside
His finite God's infinitude, — earth's vault
He bids comprise the heavenly far and wide,
Since Man may claim a right to understand
What passes understanding. So, succinct
And trimly set in order, to be scanned
And scrutinized, lo — the divine lies linked
Fast to the human, free to move as moves
Its proper match : awhile they keep the grooves,
Discreetly side by side together pace,
Till sudden comes a stumble incident
Likely enough to Man's weak-footed race,
And he discovers — wings in rudiment,
Such as he boasts, which full-grown, free-
    distent
Would lift him skyward, fail of flight while
    pent
Within humanity's restricted space.
Abjure each fond attempt to represent
The formless, the illimitable ! Trace
No outline, try no hint of human face
Or form or hand ! "

VII

            Friend, here 's a tracing meant
To help a guess at truth you never knew.
Bend but those eyes now, using mind's eye too,
And note — sufficient for all purposes —
The ground-plan — map you long have yearned
    for — yes,
Make out in markings -- more what artist
    can ? —
Goethe's Estate in Weimar, — just a plan !
A is the House, and B the Garden-gate,
And C the Grass-plot — you 've the whole
    estate

Letter by letter, down to Y the Pond,
And Z the Pigsty. Do you look beyond
The algebraic signs, and captious say
" Is A the House ? But where 's the Roof to
  A,
Where 's Door, where 's Window ? Needs
  must House have such ! "
Ay, that were folly. Why so very much
More foolish than our mortal purblind way
Of seeking in the symbol no mere point
To guide our gaze through what were else inane,
But things — their solid selves ? " Is, joint
  by joint,
Orion man-like, — as these dots explain
His constellation ? Flesh composed of suns —
How can such be ? " exclaim the simple ones.
Look through the sign to the thing signified —
Shown nowise, point by point at best descried,
Each an orb's topmost sparkle : all beside
Its shine is shadow : turn the orb one jot —
Up flies the new flash to reveal 't was not
The whole sphere late flamboyant in your ken !

VIII

" What need of symbolizing ? Fitlier men
Would take on tongue mere facts — few, faint
  and far,
Still facts not fancies : quite enough they are,
That Power, that Knowledge, and that Will,
  — add then
Immensity, Eternity : these jar
Nowise with our permitted thought and
  speech.
Why human attributes ? "

                    A myth may teach :
Only, who better would expound it thus
Must be Euripides, not Æschylus.

IX

Boundingly up through Night's wall dense and
  dark,
Embattled crags and clouds, outbroke the Sun
Above the conscious earth, and one by one
Her heights and depths absorbed to the last
  spark
His fluid glory, from the far fine ridge
Of mountain-granite which, transformed to
  gold,
Laughed first the thanks back, to the vale's
  dusk fold
On fold of vapor-swathing, like a bridge
Shattered beneath some giant's stamp. Night
  wist
Her work done and betook herself in mist
To marsh and hollow, there to bide her time
Blindly in acquiescence. Everywhere
Did earth acknowledge Sun's embrace sublime,
Thrilling her to the heart of things : since
  there
No ore ran liquid, no spar branched anew,
No arrowy crystal gleamed, but straightway
  grew
Glad through the inrush — glad nor more nor
  less
Than, 'neath his gaze, forest and wilderness,
Hill, dale, land, sea, the whole vast stretch and
  spread,

The universal world of creatures bred
By Sun's munificence, alike gave praise —
All creatures but one only : gaze for gaze,
Joyless and thankless, who — all scowling
  can —
Protests against the innumerous praises ?
  Man,
Sullen and silent.

                    Stand thou forth then, state
Thy wrong, thou sole aggrieved — disconso-
  late —
While every beast, bird, reptile, insect, gay
And glad acknowledges the bounteous day !

X

Man speaks now : " What avails Sun's earth-
  felt thrill
To me ? Sun penetrates the ore, the plant —
They feel and grow : perchance with subtler
  skill
He interfuses fly, worm, brute, until
Each favored object pays life's ministrant
By pressing, in obedience to his will,
Up to completion of the task prescribed,
So stands and stays a type. Myself imbibed
Such influence also, stood and stand complete —
The perfect Man, — head, body, hands and
  feet,
True to the pattern : but does that suffice ?
How of my superadded mind which needs
— Not to be, simply, but to do, and pleads
For — more than knowledge that by some
  device
Sun quickens matter : mind is nobly fain
To realize the marvel, make — for sense
As mind — the unseen visible, condense
— Myself — Sun's all-pervading influence
So as to serve the needs of mind, explain
What now perplexes. Let the oak increase
His corrugated strength on strength, the palm
Lift joint by joint her fan-fruit, ball and balm, —
Let the coiled serpent bask in bloated peace, —
The eagle, like some skyey derelict,
Drift in the blue, suspended, glorying, —
The lion lord it by the desert-spring, —
What know or care they of the power which
  pricked
Nothingness to perfection ? I, instead,
When all-developed still am found a thing
All-incomplete : for what though flesh had
  force
Transcending theirs — hands able to unring
The tightened snake's coil, eyes that could out
  course
The eagle's soaring, voice whereat the king
Of carnage couched discrowned ? Mind seeks
  to see,
Touch, understand, by mind inside of me,
The outside mind — whose quickening I attain
To recognize — I only. All in vain
Would mind address itself to render plain
The nature of the essence. Drag what lurks
Behind the operation — that which works
Latently everywhere by outward proof —
Drag that mind forth to face mine ? No ! aloof
I solely crave that one of all the beams
Which do Sun's work in darkness, at my will

Should operate — myself for once have skill
To realize the energy which streams
Flooding the universe. Above, around,
Beneath — why mocks that mind my own thus
    found
Simply of service, when the world grows dark,
To half-surmise — were Sun's use understood,
I might demonstrate him supplying food,
Warmth, life, no less the while ? To grant
    one spark
Myself may deal with — make it thaw my
    blood
And prompt my steps, were truer to the mark
Of mind's requirement than a half-surmise
That somehow secretly is operant,
A power all matter feels, mind only tries
To comprehend ! Once more — no idle vaunt
'Man comprehends the Sun's self !' Myste-
    ries
At source why probe into ? Enough : display,
Make demonstrable, how, by night as day,
Earth's centre and sky's outspan, all 's informed
Equally by Sun's efflux ! — source from whence
If just one spark I drew, full evidence
Were mine of fire ineffably enthroned —
Sun's self made palpable to Man ! "

XI

                                    Thus moaned
Man till Prometheus helped him, — as we
    learn, —
Offered an artifice whereby he drew
Sun's rays into a focus, — plain and true,
The very Sun in little : made fire burn
And henceforth do Man service — glass - con-
    globed
Though to a pin-point circle — all the same
Comprising the Sun's self, but Sun disrobed
Of that else-unconceived essential flame
Borne by no naked sight. Shall mind's eye
    strive
Achingly to companion as it may
The supersubtle effluence, and contrive
To follow beam and beam upon their way
Hand-breadth by hand-breadth, till sense faint —
    confessed
Frustrate, eluded by unknown unguessed
Infinitude of action ? Idle quest !
Rather ask aid from optics. Sense, descry
The spectrum — mind, infer immensity !
Little ? In little, light, warmth, life are
    blessed —
Which, in the large, who sees to bless ? Not I
More than yourself : so, good my friend, keep
    still
Trustful with — me ? with thee, sage Mande-
    ville !

WITH DANIEL BARTOLI

I

Don, the divinest women that have walked
Our world were scarce those saints of whom we
    talked.
My saint, for instance — worship if you will !
'T is pity poets need historians' skill :
What legendary 's worth a chronicle ?

II

Come, now ! A great lord once upon a time
Visited — oh a king, of kings the prime,
To sign a treaty such as never was :
For the king's minister had brought to pass
That this same duke — so style him — must
    engage
Two of his dukedoms as an heritage
After his death to this exorbitant
Craver of kingship. " Let who lacks go scant,
Who owns much, give the more to ! " Why
    rebuke ?
So bids the devil, so obeys the duke.

III

Now, as it happened, at his sister's house
— Duchess herself — indeed the very spouse
Of the king's uncle, — while the deed of gift
Whereby our duke should cut his rights adrift
Was drawing, getting ripe to sign and seal —
What does the frozen heart but uncongeal
And, shaming his transcendent kin and kith,
Whom do the duke's eyes make acquaintance
    with ?
A girl. " What, sister, may this wonder be ? "
" Nobody ! Good as beautiful is she,
With gifts that match her goodness, no faint
    flaw
I' the white : she were the pearl you think you
    saw,
But that she is — what corresponds to white ?
Some other stone, the true pearl's opposite,
As cheap as pearls are costly. She 's — now,
    guess
Her parentage ! Once — twice — thrice ? Foiled,
    confess !
Drugs, duke, her father deals in — faugh, the
    scents ! —
Manna and senna — such medicaments
For payment he compounds you. Stay — stay
    — stay !
I 'll have no rude speech wrong her ! Whither
    away,
The hot-head ? Ah, the scapegrace ! She de-
    serves
Respect — compassion, rather ! right it serves
My folly, trusting secrets to a fool !
Already at it, is he ? She keeps cool —
Helped by her fan's spread. Well, our state
    atones
For thus much license, and words break no
    bones ! "
(Hearts, though, sometimes.)

IV

                        Next morn 't was " Reason, rate,
Rave, sister, on till doomsday ! Sure as fate,
I wed that woman — what a woman is
Now that I know, who never knew till this ! "
So swore the duke. " I wed her : once again —
Rave, rate, and reason — spend your breath in
    vain ! "

V

At once was made a contract firm and fast,
Published the banns were, only marriage, last,
Required completion when the Church's rite

Should bless and bid depart, make happy quite
The coupled man and wife forevermore:
Which rite was soon to follow. Just before —
All things at all but end — the folk o' the bride
Flocked to a summons. Pomp the duke defied:
" Of ceremony — so much as empowers,
Naught that exceeds, suits best a tie like
    ours " —
He smiled — " all else were mere futility.
We vow, God hears us : God and you and I —
Let the world keep at distance ! This is why
We choose the simplest forms that serve to
    bind
Lover and lover of the human kind,
No care of what degree — of kings or clowns —
Come blood and breeding. Courtly smiles and
    frowns
Miss of their mark, would idly soothe or strike
My style and yours — in one style merged
    alike —
God's man and woman merely. Long ago
'T was rounded in my ears ' Duke, wherefore
    slow
To use a privilege ? Needs must one who
    reigns
Pay reigning's due : since statecraft so or-
    dains —
Wed for the commonweal's sake ! law pre-
    scribes
One wife : but to submission license bribes
Unruly nature : mistresses accept
— Well, at discretion ! ' Prove I so inept
A scholar, thus instructed ? Dearest, be
Wife and all mistresses in one to me,
Now, henceforth, and forever ! " So smiled he.

VI

Good : but the minister, the crafty one,
Got ear of what was doing — all but done —
Not sooner, though, than the king's very self,
Warned by the sister on how sheer a shelf
Royalty's ship was like to split. " I bar
The abomination ! Mix with muck my star ?
Shall earth behold prodigiously enorbed
An upstart marsh-born meteor sun-absorbed ?
Nuptial me no such nuptials ! " " Past dis-
    pute,
Majesty speaks with wisdom absolute,"
Admired the minister : " yet, all the same,
I would we may not — while we play his game,
The ducal meteor's — also lose our own,
The solar monarch's : we relieve your throne
Of an ungracious presence, like enough :
Balked of his project he departs in huff,
And so cuts short — dare I remind the king ? —
Our not so unsuccessful bargaining.
The contract for eventual heritage
Happens to *pari passu* reach the stage
Attained by just this other contract, — each
Unfixed by signature though fast in speech.
Off goes the duke in dudgeon — off withal
Go with him his two dukedoms past recall.
You save a fool from tasting folly's fruit,
Obtain small thanks thereby, and lose to boot
Sagacity's reward. The jest is grim :
The man will mulct you — for amercing him ?
Nay, for . . . permit a poor similitude !
A witless wight in some fantastic mood

Would drown himself : you plunge into the
    wave,
Pluck forth the undeserving : he, you save,
Pulls you clean under also for your pains.
Sire, little need that I should tax my brains
To help your inspiration ! " " Let him sink !
Always contriving " — hints the royal wink —
" To keep ourselves dry while we claim his
    clothes."

VII

Next day, the appointed day for plighting
    troths
At eve, — so little time to lose, you see,
Before the Church should weld indissolubly
Bond into bond, wed these who, side by side,
Sit each by other, bold groom, blushing bride,—
At the preliminary banquet, graced
By all the lady's kinsfolk come in haste
To share her triumph, — lo, a thunderclap !
" Who importunes now ? " " Such is my mis-
    hap —
In the king's name ! No need that any stir
Except this lady ! " bids the minister :
" With her I claim a word apart, no more :
For who gainsays — a guard is at the door.
Hold, duke ! Submit you, lady, as I bow
To him whose mouthpiece speaks his pleasure
    now !
It well may happen I no whit arrest
Your marriage : be it so, — we hope the best !
By your leave, gentles ! Lady, pray you,
    hence !
Duke, with my soul and body's deference ! "

VIII

Doors shut, mouth opens and persuasion flows
Copiously forth. " What flesh shall dare op-
    pose
The king's command ? The matter in debate
— How plain it is ! Yourself shall arbitrate,
Determine. Since the duke affects to rate
His prize in you beyond all goods of earth,
Accounts as naught old gains of rank and birth,
Ancestral obligation, recent fame,
(We know his feats) — nay, ventures to dis-
    claim
Our will and pleasure almost — by report —
Waives in your favor dukeliness, in short, —
We — ('t is the king speaks) — who might forth-
    with stay
Such suicidal purpose, brush away
A bad example shame would else record, —
Lean to indulgence rather. At his word
We take the duke : allow him to complete
The cession of his dukedoms, leave our feet
Their footstool when his own head, safe in
    vault,
Sleeps sound. Nay, would the duke repair his
    fault
Handsomely, and our forfeited esteem
Recover, — what if wisely he redeem
The past, — in earnest of good faith, at once
Give us such jurisdiction for the nonce
As may suffice — prevent occasion slip —
And constitute our actual ownership ?
Concede this — straightway be the marriage
    blessed

By warrant of this paper ! Things at rest,
This paper duly signed, down drops the bar,
To-morrow you become — from what you are,
The druggist's daughter — not the duke's mere
    spouse,
But the king's own adopted : heart and house
Open to you — the idol of a court
' Which heaven might copy ' — sing our poet-
    sort.
In this emergency, on you depends
The issue : plead what bliss the king intends !
Should the duke frown, should arguments and
    prayers,
Nay, tears if need be, prove in vain, — who
    cares ?
We leave the duke to his obduracy,
Companionless, — you, madam, follow me
Without, where divers of the body-guard
Wait signal to enforce the king's award
Of strict seclusion : over you at least
Vibratingly the sceptre threats increased
Precipitation ! How avert its crash ? "

IX

" Re-enter, sir ! A hand that 's calm, not rash,
Averts it ! " quietly the lady said.
" Yourself shall witness."
                At the table's head
Where, mid the hushed guests, still the duke
    sat glued
In blank bewilderment, his spouse pursued
Her speech to end — syllabled quietude.

X

" Duke, I, your duchess of a day, could take
The hand you proffered me for love's sole sake,
Conscious my love matched yours ; as you, my-
    self
Would waive, when need were, all but love —
    from pelf
To potency. What fortune brings about
Haply in some far future, finds me out,
Faces me on a sudden here and now.
The better ! Read — if beating heart allow —
Read this, and bid me rend to rags the shame !
I and your conscience — hear and grant our
    claim !
Never dare alienate God's gift you hold
Simply in trust for him ! Choose muck for
    gold ?
Could you so stumble in your choice, cajoled
By what I count my least of worthiness
— The youth, the beauty, — you renounce
    them — yes,
With all that 's most too : love as well you lose.
Slain by what slays in you the honor ! Choose !
Dear — yet my husband — dare I love you
    yet ? "

XI

How the duke's wrath o'erboiled, — words,
    words, and yet
More words, — I spare you such fool's fever-
    fret.
They were not of one sort at all, one size,
As souls go — he and she. 'T is said, the eyes
Of all the lookers-on let tears fall fast.
The minister was mollified at last :

" Take a day, — two days even, ere through
    pride
You perish, — two days' counsel — then de-
    cide ! "

XII

" If I shall save his honor and my soul ?
Husband, — this one last time, — you tear the
    scroll ?
Farewell, duke ! Sir, I follow in your train ! "

XIII

So she went forth : they never met again,
The duke and she. The world paid compli-
    ment
(Is it worth noting ?) when, next day, she sent
Certain gifts back — " jewelry fit to deck
Whom you call wife." I know not round what
    neck
They took to sparkling, in good time — weeks
    thence.

XIV

Of all which was the pleasant consequence,
So much and no more — that a fervid youth,
Big - hearted boy, — but ten years old, in
    truth —
Laid this to heart and loved, as boyhood can,
The unduchessed lady : boy and lad grew man :
He loved as man perchance may : did mean-
    while
Good soldier-service, managed to beguile
The years, no few, until he found a chance :
Then, as at trumpet-summons to advance,
Outbroke the love that stood at arms so long,
Brooked no withstanding longer. They were
    wed.
Whereon from camp and court alike he fled,
Renounced the sun-king, dropped off into night,
Evermore lost, a ruined satellite :
And, oh, the exquisite deliciousness
That lapped him in obscurity ! You guess
Such joy is fugitive : she died full soon.
He did his best to die — as sun, so moon
Left him, turned dusk to darkness absolute.
Failing of death — why, saintship seemed to
    suit :
Yes, your sort, Don ! He trembled on the
    verge
Of monkhood : trick of cowl and taste of
    scourge
He tried : then, kicked not at the pricks per-
    verse,
But took again, for better or for worse,
The old way in the world, and, much the same
Man o' the outside, fairly played life's game.

XV

" Now, Saint Scholastica, what time she fared
In Paynimrie, behold, a lion glared
Right in her path ! Her waist she promptly
    strips
Of girdle, binds his teeth within his lips,
And, leashed all lamblike, to the Soldan's
    court
Leads him." Ay, many a legend of the sort
Do you praiseworthily authenticate :
Spare me the rest. This much of no debate

Admits: my lady flourished in grand days
When to be duchess was to dance the hays
Up, down, across the heaven amid its host:
While to be hailed the sun's own self almost —
So close the kinship — was — was —

       Saint, for this.
Be yours the feet I stoop to — kneel and
  kiss !
So human ?   Then the mouth too, if you will !
Thanks to no legend but a chronicle.

XVI

One leans to like the duke, too : up we 'll patch
Some sort of saintship for him — not to match
Hers — but man's best and woman's worst
  amount
So nearly to the same thing, that we count
In man a miracle of faithfulness
If, while unfaithful somewhat, he lay stress
On the main fact that love, when love indeed,
Is wholly solely love from first to last —
Truth — all the rest a lie.   Too likely, fast
Enough that necklace went to grace the throat
— Let 's say, of such a dancer as makes doat
The senses when the soul is satisfied —
Trogalia, say the Greeks — a sweetmeat tried
Approvingly by sated tongue and teeth,
Once body's proper meal consigned beneath
Such unconsidered munching.

XVII

       Fancy's flight
Makes me a listener when, some sleepless night,
The duke reviewed his memories, and aghast
Found that the Present intercepts the Past
With such effect as when a cloud enwraps
The moon and, moon-suffused, plays moon per-
  haps
To who walks under, till comes, late or soon,
A stumble : up he looks, and lo, the moon
Calm, clear, convincingly herself once more !
How could he 'scape the cloud that thrust be-
  tween
Him and effulgence ?   Speak, fool — duke, I
  mean !

XVIII

"Who bade you come, brisk-marching bold
  she-shape,
  A terror with those black-balled worlds of
  eyes,
That black hair bristling solid-built from nape
  To crown its coils about ?   O dread surmise !
Take, tread on, trample under past escape
  Your capture, spoil and trophy !   Do — de-
  vise
Insults for one who, fallen once, ne'er shall
  rise !

"Mock on, triumphant o'er the prostrate
  shame !
  Laugh ' Here lies he among the false to
  Love —
Love's loyal liegeman once : the very same
  Who, scorning his weak fellows, towered
  above
Inconstancy : yet why his faith defame ?

Our eagle's victor was at least no dove,
No dwarfish knight picked up our giant's
  glove —

"'When, putting prowess to the proof, faith
  urged
  Her champion to the challenge : had it
  chanced
That merely virtue, wisdom, beauty — merged
  All in one woman — merely these advanced
Their claim to conquest, — hardly had he purged
  His mind of memories, dearnesses enhanced
Rather than harmed by death, nor, disen-
  tranced,

"' Promptly had he abjured the old pretence
  To prove his kind's superior — first to last
Display erect on his heart's eminence
  An altar to the never-dying Past.
For such feat faith might boast fit play of
  fence
  And easily disarm the iconoclast
Called virtue, wisdom, beauty : impudence

"' Fought in their stead, and how could faith
  but fall ?
  There came a bold she-shape brisk-marching,
  bent
No inch of her imperious stature, tall
  As some war-engine from whose top was sent
One shattering volley out of eye's black ball,
  And prone lay faith's defender ! '   Mockery
  spent ?
Malice discharged in full ?   In that event,

" My queenly impudence, I cover close,
  I wrap me round with love of your black hair,
Black eyes, black every wicked inch of those
  Limbs' war-tower tallness : so much truth
  lives there
'Neath the dead heap of lies.   And yet — who
  knows ?
  What if such things are ?   No less, such
  things were,
Then was the man your match whom now you
  dare

" Treat as existent still.   A second truth !
  They held — this heap of lies you rightly
  scorn —
A man who had approved himself in youth
  More than a match for — you ? for sea-foam
  born
Venus herself : you conquer him forsooth ?
  'T is me his ghost : he died since left and lorn,
As needs must Samson when his hair is shorn.

" Some day, and soon, be sure himself will rise,
  Called into life by her who long ago
Left his soul whiling time in flesh-disguise.
  Ghosts tired of waiting can play tricks, you
  know !
Tread, trample me — such sport we ghosts de-
  vise,
  Waiting the morn - star's reappearance —
  though
You think we vanish scared by the cock's
  crow."

WITH CHRISTOPHER SMART

I

It seems as if . . . or did the actual chance
Startle me and perplex ? Let truth be said !
How might this happen? Dreaming, blindfold
  led
By visionary hand, did soul's advance
Precede my body's, gain inheritance
Of fact by fancy — so that when I read
At length with waking eyes your Song, instead
Of mere bewilderment, with me first glance
Was but full recognition that in trance
Or merely thought's adventure some old day
Of dim and done-with boyishness, or — well,
Why might it not have been, the miracle
Broke on me as I took my sober way
Through veritable regions of our earth
And made discovery, many a wondrous one ?

II

Anyhow, fact or fancy, such its birth :
I was exploring some huge house, had gone
Through room and room complacently, no
  dearth
Anywhere of the signs of decent taste,
Adequate culture : wealth had run to waste
Nowise, nor penury was proved by stint :
All showed the Golden Mean without a hint
Of brave extravagance that breaks the rule.
The master of the mansion was no fool
Assuredly, no genius just as sure !
Safe mediocrity had scorned the lure
Of now too much and now too little cost,
And satisfied me sight was never lost
Of moderate design's accomplishment
In calm completeness. On and on I went
With no more hope than fear of what came
  next,
Till lo, I push a door, sudden uplift
A hanging, enter, chance upon a shift
Indeed of scene ! So — thus it is thou deck'st
High heaven, our low earth's brick-and-mortar
  work ?

III

It was the Chapel. That a star, from murk
Which hid, should flashingly emerge at last,
Were small surprise : but from broad day I
  passed
Into a presence that turned shine to shade.
There fronted me the Rafael Mother-Maid,
Never to whom knelt votarist in shrine
By Nature's bounty helped, by Art's divine
More varied — beauty with magnificence —
Than this : from floor to roof one evidence
Of how far earth may rival heaven. No niche
Where glory was not prisoned to enrich
Man's gaze with gold and gems, no space but
  glowed
With color, gleamed with carving — hues which
  owed
Their outburst to a brush the painter fed
With rainbow-substance — rare shapes never
  wed
To actual flesh and blood, which, brain-born
  once,

Became the sculptor's dowry, Art's response
To earth's despair. And all seemed old yet
  new :
Youth, — in the marble's curve, the canvas'
  hue,
Apparent, — wanted not the crowning thrill
Of age the consecrator. Hands long still
Had worked here — could it be, what lent them
  skill
Retained a power to supervise, protect,
Enforce new lessons with the old, connect
Our life with theirs ? No merely modern touch
Told me that here the artist, doing much,
Elsewhere did more, perchance does better,
  lives —
So needs must learn.

IV

                    Well, these provocatives
Having fulfilled their office, forth I went
Big with anticipation — well-nigh fear —
Of what next room and next for startled eyes
Might have in store, surprise beyond surprise.
Next room and next and next — what followed
  here ?
Why, nothing ! not one object to arrest
My passage — everywhere too manifest
The previous decent null and void of best
And worst, mere ordinary right and fit,
Calm commonplace which neither missed, nor
  hit
Inch-high, inch-low, the placid mark proposed.

V

Armed with this instance, have I diagnosed
Your case, my Christopher ? The man was
  sound
And sane at starting : all at once the ground
Gave way beneath his step, a certain smoke
Curled up and caught him, or perhaps down
  broke
A fireball wrapping flesh and spirit both
In conflagration. Then — as heaven were loth
To linger — let earth understand too well
How heaven at need can operate — off fell
The flame-robe, and the untransfigured man
Resumed sobriety, — as he began,
So did he end nor alter pace, not he !

VI

Now, what I fain would know is — could it be
That he — whoe'er he was that furnished forth
The Chapel, making thus, from South to
  North,
Rafael touch Leighton, Michelagnolo
Join Watts, was found but once combining so
The elder and the younger, taking stand
On Art's supreme, — or that yourself who sang
A Song where flute-breath silvers trumpet-
  clang,
And stations you for once on either hand
With Milton and with Keats, empowered to
  claim
Affinity on just one point — (or blame
Or praise my judgment, thus it fronts you
  full) —
How came it you resume the void and null,
Subside to insignificance, — live, die

— Proved plainly two mere mortals who drew
    nigh
One moment — that, to Art's best hierarchy,
This, to the superhuman poet-pair?
What if, in one point only, then and there
The otherwise all-unapproachable
Allowed impingement? Does the sphere pre-
    tend
To span the cube's breadth, cover end to end
The plane with its embrace? No, surely!
    Still,
Contact is contact, sphere's touch no whit less
Than cube's superimposure. Such success
Befell Smart only out of throngs between
Milton and Keats that donned the singing-
    dress —
Smart, solely of such songmen, pierced the
    screen
'Twixt thing and word, lit language straight
    from soul, —
Left no fine film-flake on the naked coal
Live from the censer — shapely or uncouth,
Fire-suffused through and through, one blaze
    of truth
Undeadened by a lie, — (you have my mind) —
For, think! this blaze outleapt with black be-
    hind
And blank before, when Hayley and the
    rest . . .
But let the dead successors worst and best
Bury their dead: with life be my concern —
Yours with the fire-flame: what I fain would
    learn
Is just — (suppose me haply ignorant
Down to the common knowledge, doctors
    vaunt)
Just this — why only once the fire-flame was:
No matter if the marvel came to pass
The way folk judged — if power too long sup-
    pressed
Broke loose and maddened, as the vulgar
    guessed
Or simply brain-disorder (doctors said),
A turmoil of the particles disturbed,
Brain's workaday performance in your head,
Spurred spirit to wild action health had curbed,
And so verse issued in a cataract
Whence prose, before and after, unperturbed
Was wont to wend its way. Concede the fact
That here a poet was who always could —
Never before did — never after would —
Achieve the feat: how were such fact ex-
    plained?

VII

Was it that when, by rarest chance, there
    fell
Disguise from Nature, so that Truth remained
Naked, and whoso saw for once could tell
Us others of her majesty and might
In large, her lovelinesses infinite
In little, — straight you used the power where-
    with
Sense, penetrating as through rind to pith
Each object, thoroughly revealed might view
And comprehend the old things thus made new,
So that while eye saw, soul to tongue could
    trust

Thing which struck word out, and once more
    adjust
Real vision to right language, till heaven's
    vault
Pompous with sunset, storm-stirred sea's as-
    sault
On the swilled rock-ridge, earth's embosomed
    brood
Of tree and flower and weed, with all the life
That flies or swims or crawls, in peace or strife,
Above, below, — each had its note and name
For Man to know by, — Man who, now — the
    same
As erst in Eden, needs that all he sees
Be named him ere he note by what degrees
Of strength and beauty to its end Design
Ever thus operates — (your thought and mine,
No matter for the many dissident) —
So did you sing your Song, so truth found vent
In words for once with you?

VIII

    Then — back was furled
The robe thus thrown aside, and straight the
    world
Darkened into the old oft-catalogued
Repository of things that sky, wave, land,
Or show or hide, clear late, accretion-clogged
Now, just as long ago, by tellings and
Re-tellings to satiety, which strike
Muffled upon the ear's drum. Very like
None was so startled as yourself when friends
Came, hailed your fast-returning wits:
    "Health mends
Importantly, for — to be plain with you —
This scribble on the wall was done — in lieu
Of pen and paper — with — ha, ha! — your key
Denting it on the wainscot! Do you see
How wise our caution was? Thus much we
    stopped
Of babble that had else grown print: and
    lopped
From your trim bay-tree this unsightly bough —
Smart's who translated Horace! Write us
    now" . . .
Why, what Smart did write — never afterward
One line to show that he, who paced the sward,
Had reached the zenith from his madhouse cell.

IX

Was it because you judged (I know full well
You never had the fancy) — judged — as some —
That who makes poetry must reproduce
Thus ever and thus only, as they come,
Each strength, each beauty, everywhere diffuse
Throughout creation, so that eye and ear,
Seeing and hearing, straight shall recognize,
At touch of just a trait, the strength appear, —
Suggested by a line's lapse see arise
All evident the beauty, — fresh surprise
Startling at fresh achievement? "So, indeed,
Wallows the whale's bulk in the waste of brine,
Nor otherwise its feather-tufts make fine
Wild Virgin's Bower when stars faint off to
    seed!"
(My prose — your poetry I dare not give,
Purpling too much my mere gray argument.)
— Was it because you judged — when fugitive

Was glory found, and wholly gone and spent
Such power of startling up deaf ear, blind eye,
At truth's appearance, — that you humbly bent
The head and, bidding vivid work good-by,
Doffed lyric dress and trod the world once more
A drab-clothed decent proseman as before?
Strengths, beauties, by one word's flash thus
　　laid bare
— That was effectual service: made aware
Of strengths and beauties, Man but hears the
　　text,
Awaits your teaching. Nature? What comes
　　next?
Why all the strength and beauty? — to be
　　shown
Thus in one word's flash, thenceforth let alone
By Man who needs must deal with aught that's
　　known
Never so lately and so little? Friend,
First give us knowledge, then appoint its use!
Strength, beauty are the means: ignore their
　　end?
As well you stopped at proving how profuse
Stones, sticks, nay stubble lie to left and right
Ready to help the builder, — careless quite
If he should take, or leave the same to strew
Earth idly, — as by word's flash bring in view
Strength, beauty, then bid who beholds the
　　same
Go on beholding. Why gains unemployed?
Nature was made to be by Man enjoyed
First; followed duly by enjoyment's fruit,
Instruction — haply leaving joy behind:
And you, the instructor, would you slack pursuit
Of the main prize, as poet help mankind
Just to enjoy, there leave them? Play the fool,
Abjuring a superior privilege?
Please simply when your function is to rule —
By thought incite to deed? From edge to edge
Of earth's round, strength and beauty every-
　　where
Pullulate — and must you particularize
All, each and every apparition? Spare
Yourself and us the trouble! Ears and eyes
Want so much strength and beauty, and no less
Nor more, to learn life's lesson by. Oh, yes —
The other method's favored in our day!
The end ere the beginning: as you may
Master the heavens before you study earth,
Make you familiar with the meteor's birth
Ere you descend to scrutinize the rose!
I say, o'erstep no least one of the rows
That lead man from the bottom where he plants
Foot first of all, to life's last ladder-top:
Arrived there, vain enough will seem the vaunts
Of those who say — "We scale the skies, then
　　drop
To earth — to find, how all things there are loth
To answer heavenly law: we understand
The meteor's course, and lo, the rose's growth —
How other than should be by law's command!"
Would not you tell such — "Friends, beware
　　lest fume
Offuscate sense: learn earth first ere presume
To teach heaven legislation. Law must be
Active in earth or nowhere: earth you see, —
Or there or not at all, Will, Power and Love
Admit discovery, — as below, above

Seek next law's confirmation! But reverse
The order, where's the wonder things grow
　　worse
Than, by the law your fancy formulates,
They should be? Cease from anger at the fates
Which thwart themselves so madly. Live and
　　learn,
Not first learn and then live, is our concern.

WITH GEORGE BUBB DODINGTON

I

Ah, George Bubb Dodington Lord Melcombe,
　　— no,
Yours was the wrong way! — always under-
　　stand,
Supposing that permissibly you planned
How statesmanship — your trade — in outward
　　show
Might figure as inspired by simple zeal
For serving country, king and commonweal,
(Though service tire to death the body, tease
The soul from out an o'ertasked patriot-drudge)
And yet should prove zeal's outward show agrees
In all respects — right reason being judge —
With inward care that, while the statesman
　　spends
Body and soul thus freely for the sake
Of public good, his private welfare take
No harm by such devotedness. Intends
Scripture aught else — let captious folk in-
　　quire —
Which teaches "Laborers deserve their hire,
And who neglects his household bears the bell
Away of sinning from an infidel"?
Wiselier would fools that carp bestow a thought
How birds build nests; at outside, roughly
　　wrought,
Twig knots with twig, loam plasters up each
　　chink,
Leaving the inmate rudely lodged — you think?
Peep but inside! That specious rude-and-
　　rough
Covers a domicile where downy fluff
Embeds the ease-deserving architect,
Who toiled and moiled not merely to effect
'Twixt sprig and spray a stop-gap in the teeth
Of wind and weather, guard what swung be-
　　neath
From upset only, but contrived himself
A snug interior, warm and soft and sleek.
Of what material? Oh, for that, you seek
How nature prompts each volatile! Thus — pelf
Smoothens the human mudlark's lodging, power
Demands some hardier wrappage to embrace
Robuster heart-beats: rock, not tree nor tower,
Contents the building eagle: rook shoves close
To brother rook on branch, while crow morose
Apart keeps balance perched on topmost bough.
No sort of bird but suits his taste somehow:
Nay, Darwin tells of such as love the bower —
His bower-birds opportunely yield us yet
The lacking instance when at loss to get
A feathered parallel to what we find
The secret motor of some mighty mind
That worked such wonders — all for vanity!
Worked them to haply figure in the eye

Of intimates as first of — doers' kind?
Actors', that work in earnest sportively,
Paid by a sourish smile.   How says the Sage?
Birds born to strut prepare a platform-stage
With sparkling stones and speckled shells, all
     sorts
Of slimy rubbish, odds and ends and orts,
Whereon to pose and posture and engage
The priceless female simper.

II

                    I have gone
Thus into detail, George Bubb Dodington,
Lest, when I take you presently to task
For the wrong way of working, you should ask
" What fool conjectures that profession means
Performance? that who goes behind the scenes
Finds, — acting over, — still the soot-stuff
     screens
Othello's visage, still the self-same cloak's
Bugle-bright-blackness half reveals half chokes
Hamlet's emotion, as ten minutes since? "
No, each resumes his garb, stands — Moor or
     prince —
Decently draped : just so with statesmanship !
All outside show, in short, is sham — why
     wince ?
Concede me — while our parley lasts ! You trip
Afterwards — lay but this to heart ! (there
     lurks
Somewhere in all of us a lump which irks
Somewhat the spriteliest-scheming brain that's
     bent
On brave adventure, would but heart consent !)
— Here trip you, that — your aim allowed as
     right —
Your means thereto were wrong. Come, we,
     this night,
Profess one purpose, hold one principle,
Are at odds only as to — not the will
But way of winning solace for ourselves
— No matter if the ore for which zeal delves
Be gold or coprolite, while zeal's pretence
Is — we do good to men at — whose expense
But ours? who tire the body, tease the soul,
Simply that, running, we may reach fame's goal
And wreathe at last our brows with bay — the
     State's
Disinterested slaves, nay — please the Fates —
Saviors and nothing less : such lot has been !
Statesmanship triumphs pedestalled, serene, —
O happy consummation ! — brought about
By managing with skill the rabble-rout
For which we labor (never mind the name —
People or populace, for praise or blame)
Making them understand — their heaven, their
     hell,
Their every hope and fear is ours as well.
Man's cause — what other can we have at heart ?
Whence follows that the necessary part
High o'er Man's head we play, — and freelier
     breathe
Just that the multitude which gasps beneath
May reach the level where unstifled stand
Ourselves at vantage to put forth a hand,
Assist the prostrate public.   'T is by right
Merely of such pretence, we reach the height

Where storms abound, to brave — nay, court
     their stress,
Though all too well aware — of pomp the less,
Of peace the more !   But who are we, to spurn
For peace' sake, duty's pointing ? Up, then —
     earn
Albeit no prize we may but martyrdom !
Now, such fit height to launch salvation from,
How get and gain ?   Since help must needs be
     craved
By would-be saviours of the else-unsaved,
How coax them to co-operate, lend a lift,
Kneel down and let us mount ?

III

                    You say, " Make shift
By sham — the harsh word : preach and teach,
     persuade
Somehow the Public — not despising aid
Of salutary artifice — we seek
Solely their good : our strength would raise the
     weak,
Our cultivated knowledge supplement
Their rudeness, rawness : why to us were lent
Ability except to come in use ?
Who loves his kind must by all means induce
That kind to let his love play freely, press
In Man's behalf to full performance ! "

IV

                              Yes —
Yes, George, we know ! — whereat they hear,
     believe,
And bend the knee, and on the neck receive
Who fawned and cringed to purpose ? Not so,
     George !
Try simple falsehood on shrewd folk who forge
Lies of superior fashion day by day
And hour by hour ?   With craftsmen versed as
     they
What chance of competition when the tools
Only a novice wields ?   Are knaves such fools ?
Disinterested patriots, spare your tongue
The tones thrice-silvery, cheek save smiles it
     flung
Pearl-like profuse to swine — a herd, whereof
No unit needs be taught, his neighbor's trough
Scarce holds for who but grunts and whines the
     husks
Due to a wrinkled snout that shows sharp tusks.
No animal — much less our lordly Man —
Obeys its like : with strength all rule began,
The stoutest awes the pasture.   Soon succeeds
Discrimination, — nicer power Man needs
To rule him than is bred of bone and thew :
Intelligence must move strength's self.   This
     too
Lasts but its time : the multitude at length
Looks inside for intelligence and strength
And finds them here and there to pick and
     choose :
" All at your service, mine, see ! "   Ay, but
     who 's
My George, at this late day, to make his boast
" In strength, intelligence, I rule the roast,
Beat, all and some, the ungraced who crowd
     your ranks ? "

" Oh, but I love, would lead you, gain your
thanks
By unexampled yearning for Man's sake —
Passion that solely waits your help to take
Effect in action ! " George, which one of us
But holds with his own heart communion thus :
" I am, if not of men the first and best,
Still — to receive enjoyment — properest :
Which since by force I cannot, nor by wit
Most likely — craft must serve in place of it.
Flatter, cajole ! If so I bring within
My net the gains which wit and force should
win,
What hinders ? " 'T is a trick we know of old :
Try, George, some other of tricks manifold !
The multitude means mass and mixture — right !
Are mixtures simple, pray, or composite ?
Dive into Man, your medley : see the waste !
Sloth-stifled genius, energy disgraced
By ignorance, high aims with sorry skill,
Will without means and means in want of will
— Sure we might fish, from out the mothers' sons
That welter thus, a dozen Dodingtons !
Why call up Dodington, and none beside,
To take his seat upon our backs and ride
As statesman conquering and to conquer ? Well,
The last expedient, which must needs excel
Those old ones — this it is, — at any rate
To-day's conception thus I formulate :
As simple force has been replaced, just so
Must simple wit be : men have got to know
Such wit as what you boast is nowise held
The wonder once it was, but, paralleled
Too plentifully, counts not, — puts to shame
Modest possessors like yourself who claim,
By virtue of it merely, power and place
— Which means the sweets of office. Since our
race
Teems with the like of you, some special gift,
Your very own, must coax our hands to lift,
And backs to bear you : is it just and right
To privilege your nature ?

v

" State things quite
Other than so " — make answer ! " I pretend
No such community with men. Perpend
My key to domination : Who would use
Man for his pleasure needs must introduce
The element that awes Man. Once for all,
His nature owns a Supernatural
In fact as well as phrase — which found must be
— Where, in this doubting age ? Old mystery
Has served its turn — seen through and sent
adrift
To nothingness : new wizard-craft makes shift
Nowadays shorn of help by robe and book, —
Otherwise, elsewhere, for success must look
Than chalked-ring, incantation-gibberish.
Somebody comes to conjure : that 's he ? Pish !
He 's like the roomful of rapt gazers, — there 's
No sort of difference in the garb he wears
From ordinary dressing, — gesture, speech,
Deportment, just like those of all and each
That eye their master of the minute. Stay !
What of the something — call it how you may —
Uncanny in the — quack ? That 's easy said !
Notice how the Professor turns no head

And yet takes cognizance of who accepts,
Denies, is puzzled as to the adept's
Supremacy, yields up or lies in wait
To trap the trickster ! Doubtless, out of date
Are dealings with the devil : yet, the stir
Of mouth, its smile half smug half sinister,
Mock-modest boldness masked in diffidence, —
What if the man have — who knows how or
whence ? —
Confederate potency unguessed by us —
Prove no such cheat as he pretends ? "

vi

Ay, thus
Had but my George played statesmanship's
new card
That carries all ! " Since we " — avers the
Bard —
" All of us have one human heart " — as good
As say — by all of us is understood
Right and wrong, true and false — in rough, at
least,
We own a common conscience. God, man,
beast —
How should we qualify the statesman-shape
I fancy standing with our world agape ?
Disguise, flee, fight against with tooth and nail
The outrageous designation ! " Quack " men
quail
Before ? You see, a little year ago
They heard him thunder at the thing which, lo,
To-day he vaunts for unscathed, while what erst
Heaven-high he lauded, lies hell-low, accursed !
And yet where 's change ? Who, awe-struck,
cares to point
Critical finger at a dubious joint
In armor, true *œs triplex*, breast and back
Binding about, defiant of attack,
An imperturbability that 's — well,
Or innocence or impudence — how tell
One from the other ? Could ourselves broach
lies,
Yet brave mankind with those unaltered eyes,
Those lips that keep the quietude of truth ?
Dare we attempt the like ? What quick uncouth
Disturbance of thy smug economy,
O coward visage ! Straight would all descry
Back on the man's brow the boy's blush once
more !
No : he goes deeper — could our sense explore —
Finds conscience beneath conscience such as
ours.
Genius is not so rare, — prodigious powers —
Well, others boast such, — but a power like this
Mendacious intrepidity — *quid vis ?*
Besides, imposture plays another game,
Admits of no diversion from its aim
Of captivating hearts, sets zeal aflare
In every shape at every turn, — nowhere
Allows subsidence into ash. By stress
Of what does guile succeed but earnestness,
Earnest word, look and gesture ? Touched
with aught
But earnestness, the levity were fraught
With ruin to guile's film - work. Grave is
guile ;
Here no act wants its qualifying smile,
Its covert pleasantry to neutralize

The outward ardor. Can our chief despise
Even while most he seems to adulate?
As who should say "What though it be my
        fate
To deal with fools? Among the crowd must
        lurk
Some few with faculty to judge my work
Spite of its way which suits, they understand,
The crass majority : — the Sacred Band,
No duping them forsooth!" So tells a touch
Of subintelligential nod and wink —
Turning foes friends. Coarse flattery moves
        the gorge :
Mine were the mode to awe the many, George!
They guess you half despise them while most
        bent
On demonstrating that your sole intent
Strives for their service. Sneer at them?
        Yourself
'T is you disparage, — tricksy as an elf,
Scorning what most you strain to bring to pass,
Laughingly careless, — triply cased in brass, —
While pushing strenuous to the end in view.
What follows? Why, you formulate within
The vulgar headpiece this conception : "Win
A master-mind to serve us needs we must,
One who, from motives we but take on trust,
Acts strangelier — haply wiselier than we
        know
Stronglier, for certain. Did he say 'I throw
Aside my good for yours, in all I do
Care nothing for myself and all for you' —
We should both understand and disbelieve :
Said he, 'Your good I laugh at in my sleeve,
My own it is I solely labor at,
Pretending yours the while' — that, even that,
We, understanding well, give credence to,
And so will none of it. But here 't is through
Our recognition of his service, wage
Well earned by work, he mounts to such a stage
Above competitors as all save Bubb
Would agonize to keep. Yet — here's the
        rub —
So slightly does he hold by our esteem
Which solely fixed him fast there, that we seem
Mocked every minute to our face, by gibe
And jest — scorn insuppressive : what ascribe
The rashness to? Our pay and praise to
        boot —
Do these avail him to tread under foot
Something inside us all and each, that stands
Somehow instead of somewhat which com-
        mands
'Lie not'? Folk fear to jeopardize their soul,
Stumble at times, walk straight upon the
        whole, —
That 's nature's simple instinct : what may be
The portent here, the influence such as we
Are strangers to?"—

                    VII
                    Exact the thing I call
Man's despot, just the Supernatural
Which, George, was wholly out of — far be-
        yond
Your theory and practice. You had conned
But to reject the precept "To succeed
In gratifying selfishness and greed,

Asseverate such qualities exist
Nowise within yourself! then make acquist
By all means, with no sort of fear!" Alack,
That well-worn lie is obsolete! Fall back
On still a working pretext — "Hearth and
        Home,
The Altar, love of England, hate of Rome" —
That 's serviceable lying — that perchance
Had screened you decently : but 'ware ad-
        vance
By one step more in perspicacity
Of these our dupes! At length they get to see
As through the earlier, this the latter plea —
And find the greed and selfishness at source!
Ventum est ad triarios : last resource
Should be to what but — exquisite disguise
Disguise-abjuring, truth that looks like lies,
Frankness so sure to meet with unbelief?
Say — you hold in contempt —not them in
        chief —
But first and foremost your own self! No use
In men but to make sport for you, induce
The puppets now to dance, now stand stock-
        still,
Now knock their heads together, at your will
For will's sake only — while each plays his
        part
Submissive : why? through terror at the
        heart :
"Can it be — this bold man, whose hand we saw
Openly pull the wires, obeys some law
Quite above Man's — nay, God's?" On face
        fall they.
This was the secret missed, again I say,
Out of your power to grasp conception of,
Much less employ to purpose. Hence the scoff
That greets your very name : folk see but one
Fool more, as well as knave, in Dodington.

                WITH FRANCIS FURINI

                        I

NAY, that, Furini, never I at least
Mean to believe! What man you were I
        know,
While you walked Tuscan earth, a painter-
        priest,
Something about two hundred years ago.
Priest — you did duty punctual as the sun
That rose and set above Saint Sano's church,
Blessing Mugello : of your flock not one
But showed a whiter fleece because of smirch,
Your kind hands wiped it clear from : were
        they poor?
Bounty broke bread apace, — did marriage lag
For just the want of moneys that ensure
Fit hearth-and-home provision? — straight your
        bag
Unplumped itself, — reached hearts by way of
        palms
Goodwill's shake had but tickled. All about
Mugello valley, felt some parish qualms
At worship offered in bare walls without
The comfort of a picture? — prompt such need
Our painter would supply, and throngs to see
Witnessed that goodness — no unholy greed
Of gain — had coaxed from Don Furini — he

Whom princes might in vain implore to toil
For worldly profit — such a masterpiece.
Brief — priest, you poured profuse God's wine
    and oil
Praiseworthily, I know : shall praising cease
When, priestly vesture put aside, mere man,
You stand for judgment ? Rather — what ac-
    claim
— " Good son, good brother, friend in whom we
    scan
No fault nor flaw " — salutes Furini's name,
The loving as the liberal ! Enough :
Only to ope a lily, though for sake
Of setting free its scent, disturbs the rough
Loose gold about its anther. I shall take
No blame in one more blazon, last of all —
Good painter were you : if in very deed
I styled you great — what modern art dares
    call
My word in question ? Let who will take heed
Of what he seeks and misses in your brain
To balance that precision of the brush
Your hand could ply so deftly : all in vain
Strives poet's power for outlet when the push
Is lost upon a barred and bolted gate
Of painter's impotency. Agnolo —
Thine were alike the head and hand, by fate
Doubly endowed ! Who boasts head only — woe
To hand's presumption should brush emulate
Fancy's free passage by the pen, and show
Thought wrecked and ruined where the inex-
    pert
Foolhardy fingers half grasped, half let go
Film-wings the poet's pen arrests unhurt !
No — painter such as that miraculous
Michael, who deems you ? But the ample gift
Of gracing walls else blank of this our house
Of life with imagery, one bright drift
Poured forth by pencil, — man and woman
    mere,
Glorified till half owned for gods, — the dear
Fleshly perfection of the human shape, —
This was apportioned you whereby to praise
Heaven and bless earth. Who clumsily essays,
By slighting painter's craft, to prove the ape
Of poet's pen-creation, just betrays
Twofold ineptitude.

         II

        By such sure ways
Do I return, Furini, to my first
And central confidence — that he I proved
Good priest, good man, good painter, and re-
    hearsed
Praise upon praise to show — not simply loved
For virtue, but for wisdom honored too
Needs must Furini be, — it follows — who
Shall undertake to breed in me belief
That, on his death-bed, weakness played the
    thief
With wisdom, folly ousted reason quite ?
List to the chronicler ! With main and might —
So fame runs — did the poor soul beg his
    friends
To buy and burn his hand-work, make amends
For having reproduced therein — (Ah me !
Sighs fame — that 's friend Filippo) — nudity !
Yes, I assure you : he would paint — not men

Merely — a pardonable fault — but when
He had to deal with — oh, not mother Eve
Alone, permissibly in Paradise
Naked and unashamed, — but dared achieve
Dreadful distinction, at soul-safety's price,
By also painting women — (why the need ?)
Just as God made them : there, you have the
    truth !
Yes, rosed from top to toe in flush of youth,
One foot upon the moss-fringe, would some
    Nymph
Try, with its venturous fellow, if the lymph
Were chillier than the slab-stepped fountain-
    edge ;
The while a-heap her garments on its ledge
Of boulder lay within hand's easy reach,
— No one least kid-skin cast around her !
    Speech
Shrinks from enumerating case and case
Of — were it but Diana at the chase,
With tunic tucked discreetly hunting-high !
No, some Queen Venus set our necks awry,
Turned faces from the painter's all-too-frank
Triumph of flesh ! For — whom had he to
    thank
— This self-appointed nature-student ? Whence
Picked he up practice ? By what evidence
Did he unhandsomely become adept
In simulating bodies ? How except
By actual sight of such ? Himself confessed
The enormity : quoth Philip, " When I pressed
The painter to acknowledge his abuse
Of artistry else potent — what excuse
Made the infatuated man ? I give
His very words : ' Did you but know, as I,
— O scruple-splitting sickly-sensitive
Mild-moral-monger, what the agony
Of Art is ere Art satisfy herself
In imitating Nature — (Man, poor elf,
Striving to match the finger-mark of Him
The immeasurably matchless) — gay or grim,
Pray, would your smile be ? Leave mere fools
    to tax
Art's high-strung brain's intentness as so lax
That, in its mid-throe, idle fancy sees
The moment for admittance ! ' Pleadings
    these —
Specious, I grant." So adds, and seems to wince
Somewhat, our censor — but shall truth con-
    vince
Blockheads like Baldinucci ?

         III

           I resume
My incredulity : your other kind
Of soul, Furini, never was so blind,
Even through death-mist, as to grope in gloom
For cheer beside a bonfire piled to turn
Ashes and dust all that your noble life
Did homage to life's Lord by, — bid them burn
— These Baldinucci blockheads — pictures rife
With record, in each rendered loveliness,
That one appreciative creature's debt
Of thanks to the Creator, more or less,
Was paid according as heart's-will had met
Hand's-power in Art's endeavor to express
Heaven's most consummate of achievements
    bless

Earth by a semblance of the seal God set
On woman his supremest work. I trust
Rather, Furini, dying breath had vent
In some fine fervor of thanksgiving just
For this — that soul and body's power you
    spent —
Agonized to adumbrate, trace in dust
That marvel which we dream the firmament
Copies in star-device when fancies stray
Outlining, orb by orb, Andromeda —
God's best of beauteous and magnificent
Revealed to earth — the naked female form.
Nay, I mistake not: wrath that 's but luke-
    warm
Would boil indeed were such a critic styled
Himself an artist: artist ! Ossa piled
Topping Olympus — the absurd which crowns
The extravagant — whereat one laughs, not
    frowns.
Paints he ?   One bids the poor pretender take
His sorry self, a trouble and disgrace,
From out the sacred presence, void the place
Artists claim only.   What — not merely wake
Our pity that suppressed concupiscence —
A satyr masked as matron — makes pretence
To the coarse blue-fly's instinct — can perceive
No better reason why she should exist —
— God's lily - limbed and blushrose - bosomed
    Eve —
Than as a hot-bed for the sensualist
To fly-blow with his fancies, make pure stuff
Breed him back filth — this were not crime
    enough ?
But further — fly to style itself — nay, more —
To steal among the sacred ones, crouch down
Though but to where their garments sweep the
    floor —
— Still catching some faint sparkle from the
    crown
Crowning transcendent Michael, Leonard,
Rafael, — to sit beside the feet of such,
Unspurned because unnoticed, then reward
Their toleration — mercy overmuch —
By stealing from the throne-step to the fools
Curious outside the gateway, all-agape
To learn by what procedure, in the schools
Of Art, a merest man in outward shape
May learn to be Correggio ! Old and young,
These learners got their lesson : Art was just
A safety - screen — (Art, which Correggio's
    tongue
Calls " Virtue ") — for a skulking vice : mere
    lust
Inspired the artist when his Night and Morn
Slept and awoke in marble on that edge
Of heaven above our awe-struck earth : lust-
    born
His Eve low bending took the privilege
Of life from what our eyes saw — God's own
    palm
That put the flame forth — to the love and
    thanks
Of all creation save this recreant !

IV

Calm
Our phrase, Furini ! Not the artist-ranks
Claim riddance of an interloper : no —

This Baldinucci did but grunt and sniff
Outside Art's pale — ay, grubbed, where pine
    trees grow,
For pignuts only.

V

You the Sacred ! If
Indeed on you has been bestowed the dower
Of Art in fulness, graced with head and hand,
Head — to look up not downwards, hand — of
    power
To make head's gain the portion of a world
Where else the uninstructed ones too sure
Would take all outside beauty — film that 's
    furled
About a star — for the star's self, endure
No guidance to the central glory, — nay,
(Sadder) might apprehend the film was fog,
Or (worst) wish all but vapor well away,
And sky's pure product thickened from earth's
    bog —
Since so, nor seldom, have your worthiest
    failed
To trust their own soul's insight — why ? except
For warning that the head of the adept
May too much prize the hand, work unassailed
By scruple of the better sense that finds
An orb within each halo, bids gross flesh
Free the fine spirit-pattern, nor enmesh
More than is meet a marvel, custom blinds
Only the vulgar eye to. Now, less fear
That you, the foremost of Art's fellowship,
Will oft — will ever so offend ! But — hip
And thigh — smite the Philistine ! *You* —
    slunk here —
Connived at, by too easy tolerance,
Not to scrape palette simply or squeeze brush,
But dub your very self an Artist ? Tush —
You, of the daubings, is it, dare advance
This doctrine that the Artist-mind must needs
Own to affinity with yours — confess
Provocative acquaintance, more or less,
With each impurely-peevish worm that breeds
Inside your brain's receptacle ?

VI

Enough.
Who owns " I dare not look on diadems
Without an itch to pick out, purloin gems
Others contentedly leave sparkling " — gruff
Answers the guard of the regalia : " Why —
Consciously kleptomaniac — thrust yourself
Where your illicit craving after pelf
Is tempted most — in the King's treasury ?
Go elsewhere ! Sort with thieves, if thus you
    feel —
When folk clean-handed simply recognize
Treasure whereof the mere sight satisfies —
But straight your fingers are on itch to steal !
Hence with you ! "
              Pray, Furini !

VII

              " Bounteous God,
Deviser and dispenser of all gifts
To soul through sense, — in Art the soul uplifts
Man's best of thanks ! What but thy measur-
    ing-rod

Meted forth heaven and earth? more intimate,
Thy very hands were busied with the task
Of making, in this human shape, a mask —
A match for that divine. Shall love abate
Man's wonder? Nowise! True — true — all
    too true —
No gift but, in the very plenitude
Of its perfection, goes maimed, misconstrued
By wickedness or weakness: still, some few
Have grace to see thy purpose, strength to mar
Thy work by no admixture of their own,
— Limn truth not falsehood, bid us love alone
The type untampered with, the naked star!"

VIII

And, prayer done, painter — what if you should
    preach?
Not as of old when playing pulpiteer
To simple-witted country folk, but here
In actual London try your powers of speech
On us the cultured, therefore skeptical —
What would you? For, suppose he has his
    word
In faith's behalf, no matter how absurd,
This painter-theologian? One and all
We lend an ear — nay, Science takes thereto —
Encourages the meanest who has racked
Nature until he gains from her some fact,
To state what truth is from his point of view,
Mere pin-point though it be: since many such
Conduce to make a whole, she bids our friend
Come forward unabashed and haply lend
His little life-experience to our much
Of modern knowledge. Since she so insists,
Up stands Furini.

IX

"Evolutionists!
At truth I glimpse from depths, you glance from
    heights,
Our stations for discovery opposites, —
How should ensue agreement? I explain:
'T is the tip-top of things to which you strain
Your vision, until atoms, protoplasm,
And what and whence and how may be the
    spasm
Which sets all going, stop you: down perforce
Needs must your observation take its course,
Since there 's no moving upwards: link by link
You drop to where the atoms somehow think,
Feel, know themselves to be: the world's
    begun,
Such as we recognize it. Have you done
Descending? Here 's ourself, — Man, known
    to-day,
Duly evolved at last, — so far, you say,
The sum and seal of being's progress. Good!
Thus much at least is clearly understood —
Of power does Man possess no particle:
Of knowledge — just so much as shows that
    still
It ends in ignorance on every side:
But righteousness — ah, Man is deified
Thereby, for compensation! Make survey
Of Man's surroundings, try creation — nay,
Try emulation of the minimized
Minuteness fancy may conceive! Surprised
Reason becomes by two defeats for one —

Not only power at each phenomenon
Baffled, but knowledge also in default —
Asking what *is* minuteness — yonder vault
Speckled with suns, or this the millionth —
    thing,
How shall I call? — that on some insect's wing
Helps to make out in dyes the mimic star?
Weak, ignorant, accordingly we are:
What then? The worse for Nature! Where
    began
Righteousness, moral sense except in Man?
True, he makes nothing, understands no whit:
Had the initiator-spasm seen fit
Thus doubly to endow him, none the worse
And much the better were the universe.
What does Man see or feel or apprehend
Here, there, and everywhere, but faults to
    mend,
Omissions to supply, — one wide disease
Of things that are, which Man at once would
    ease
Had will but power and knowledge? failing
    both —
Things must take will for deed — Man, nowise
    loth,
Accepts pre-eminency: mere blind force —
Mere knowledge undirected in its course
By any care for what is made or marred
In either's operation — *these* award
The crown to? Rather let it deck thy brows,
Man, whom alone a righteousness endows
Would cure the wide world's ailing! Who
    disputes
Thy claim thereto? Had Spasm more attributes
Than power and knowledge in its gift, before
Man came to pass? The higher that we soar,
The less of moral sense like Man's we find:
No sign of such before, — what comes behind,
Who guesses! But until there crown our sight
The quite new — not the old mere infinite
Of changings, — some fresh kind of sun and
    moon, —
Then, not before, shall I expect a boon
Of intuition just as strange, which turns
Evil to good, and wrong to right, unlearns
All Man's experience learned since Man was he.
Accept in Man, advanced to this degree,
The Prime Mind, therefore! neither wise nor
    strong —
Whose fault? but were he both, then right, not
    wrong
As now, throughout the world were paramount
According to his will, — which I account
The qualifying faculty. He stands
Confessed supreme — the monarch whose com-
    mands
Could he enforce, how bettered were the world!
He 's at the height this moment — to be hurled
Next moment to the bottom by rebound
Of his own peal of laughter. All around
Ignorance wraps him, — whence and how and
    why
Things are, — yet cloud breaks and lets blink
    the sky
Just overhead, not elsewhere! What assures
His optics that the very blue which lures
Comes not of black outside it, doubly dense?
Ignorance overwraps his moral sense.

Winds him about, relaxing, as it wraps,
So much and no more than lets through perhaps
The murmured knowledge — ' Ignorance exists.'

x

" I at the bottom, Evolutionists,
Advise beginning, rather. I profess
To know just one fact — my self-conscious-
        ness, —
'Twixt ignorance and ignorance enisled, —
Knowledge : before me was my Cause — that 's
        styled
God : after, in due course succeeds the rest, —
All that my knowledge comprehends — at
        best —
At worst, conceives about in mild despair.
Light needs must touch on either darkness :
        where ?
Knowledge so far impinges on the Cause
Before me, that I know — by certain laws
Wholly unknown, whate'er I apprehend
Within, without me, had its rise : thus blend
I, and all things perceived, in one Effect.
How far can knowledge any ray project
On what comes after me — the universe ?
Well, my attempt to make the cloud disperse
Begins — not from above but underneath :
I climb, you soar, — who soars soon loses breath
And sinks, who climbs keeps one foot firm on
        fact
Ere hazarding the next step : soul's first act
(Call consciousness the soul — some name we
        need)
Getting itself aware, through stuff decreed
Thereto (so call the body) — who has stept
So far, there let him stand, become adept
In body ere he shift his station thence
One single hair's breadth. Do I make pretence
To teach, myself unskilled in learning ? Lo,
My life's work ! Let my pictures prove I know
Somewhat of what this fleshly frame of ours
Or is or should be, how the soul empowers
The body to reveal its every mood
Of love and hate, pour forth its plenitude
Of passion. If my hand attained to give
Thus permanence to truth else fugitive,
Did not I also fix each fleeting grace
Of form and feature — save the beauteous
        face —
Arrest decay in transitory might
Of bone and muscle — cause the world to bless
Forever each transcendent nakedness
Of man and woman ?   Were such feats
        achieved
By sloth, or strenuous labor unrelieved,
— Yet lavished vainly ?   Ask that underground
(So may I speak) of all on surface found
Of flesh-perfection ! Depths on depths to probe
Of all-inventive artifice, disrobe
Marvel at hiding under marvel, pluck
Veil after veil from Nature — were the luck
Ours to surprise the secret men so name,
That still eludes the searcher — all the same,
Repays his search with still fresh proof — ' Ex-
        terne,
Not inmost, is the Cause, fool ! Look and
        learn ! '
Thus teach my hundred pictures : firm and fast

There did I plant my first foot. And the
        next ?
Nowhere !   'T was put forth and withdrawn
        perplexed
At touch of what seemed stable and proved
        stuff
Such as the colored clouds are : plain enough
There lay the outside universe : try Man —
My most immediate ! and the dip began
From safe and solid into that profound
Of ignorance I tell you surges round
My rock-spit of self-knowledge.   Well and ill,
Evil and good irreconcilable
Above, beneath, about my every side, —
How did this wild confusion far and wide
Tally with my experience when my stamp —
So far from stirring — struck out, each a lamp,
Spark after spark of truth from where I
        stood —
Pedestalled triumph ?   Evil there was good,
Want was the promise of supply, defect
Ensured completion, — where and when and
        how ?
Leave that to the First Cause ! Enough that
        now,
Here where I stand, this moment's me and
        mine,
Shows me what is, permits me to divine
What shall be. Wherefore ? Nay, how other-
        wise ?
Look at my pictures ! What so glorifies
The body that the permeating soul
Finds there no particle elude control
Direct, or fail of duty, — most obscure
When most subservient ? Did that Cause en-
        sure
The soul such raptures as its fancy stings
Body to furnish when, uplift by wings
Of passion, here and now, it leaves the earth,
Loses itself above, where bliss has birth —
(Heaven, be the phrase) — did that same Cause
        contrive
Such solace for the body, soul must dive
At drop of fancy's pinion, condescend
To bury both alike on earth, our friend
And fellow, where minutely exquisite
Low lie the pleasures, now and here — no herb
But hides its marvel, peace no doubts perturb
In each small mystery of insect life —
— Shall the soul's Cause thus gift the soul, yet
        strife
Continue still of fears with hopes, — for why ?
What if the Cause, whereof we now descry
So far the wonder-working, lack at last
Will, power, benevolence — a protoplast,
No consummator, sealing up the sum
Of all things, — past and present and to
        come —
Perfection ? No, I have no doubt at all !
There 's my amount of knowledge — great or
        small,
Sufficient for my needs : for see ! advance
Its light now on that depth of ignorance
I shrank before from — yonder where the
        world
Lies wreck-strewn, — evil towering, prone good
        — hurled
From pride of place, on every side. For me

Patience, beseech you!) knowledge can but be
Of good by knowledge of good's opposite —
Evil, — since, to distinguish wrong from right,
Both must be known in each extreme, beside —
(Or what means knowledge — to aspire or bide
Content with half-attaining? Hardly so!)
Made to know on, know ever, I must know
All to be known at any halting-stage
Of my soul's progress, such as earth, where
    wage
War, just for soul's instruction, pain with joy,
Folly with wisdom, all that works annoy
With all that quiets and contents, — in brief,
Good strives with evil.

                   " Now then for relief,
Friends, of your patience kindly curbed so long-
' What? ' snarl you, ' is the fool's conceit thus
    strong —
Must the whole outside world in soul and sense
Suffer, that he grow sage at its expense? '
By no means ! 'T is by merest touch of toe
I try — not trench on — ignorance, just know —
And so keep steady footing : how you fare,
Caught in the whirlpool — that's the Cause's
    care,
Strong, wise, good, — this I know at any rate
In my own self, — but how may operate
With you — strength, wisdom, goodness — no
    least blink
Of knowledge breaks the darkness round me.
    Think !
Could I see plain, be somehow certified
All was illusion, — evil far and wide
Was good disguised, — why, out with one huge
    wipe
Goes knowledge from me. Type needs anti-
    type:
As night needs day, as shine needs shade, so
    good
Needs evil: how were pity understood
Unless by pain? Make evident that pain
Permissibly masks pleasure — you abstain
From outstretch of the finger-tip that saves
A drowning fly. Who proffers help of hand
To weak Andromeda exposed on strand
At mercy of the monster? Were all true,
Help were not wanting: ' But 't is false,' cry
    you,
' Mere fancy-work of paint and brush ! ' No
    less,
Were mine the skill, the magic, to impress
Beholders with a confidence they saw
Life, — veritable flesh and blood in awe
Of just as true a sea-beast, — would they stare
Simply as now, or cry out, curse and swear,
Or call the gods to help, or catch up stick
And stone, according as their hearts were
    quick
Or sluggish ? Well, some old artificer
Could do as much, — at least, so books aver, —
Able to make believe, while I, poor wight,
Make fancy, nothing more. Though wrong
    were right,
Could we but know — still wrong must needs
    seem wrong
To do right's service, prove men weak or
    strong.

Choosers of evil or of good. ' No such
Illusion possible ! ' Ah, friends, you touch
Just here my solid standing-place amid
The wash and welter, whence all doubts are
    bid
Back to the ledge they break against in foam,
Futility : my soul, and my soul's home
This body, — how each operates on each,
And how things outside, fact or feigning, teach
What good is and what evil, — just the same,
Be feigning or be fact the teacher, — blame
Diffidence nowise if, from this I judge
My point of vantage, not an inch I budge.
All — for myself — seems ordered wise and
    well
Inside it, — what reigns outside, who can tell ?
Contrariwise, who needs be told ' The space
Which yields thee knowledge, — do its bounds
    embrace
Well-willing and wise-working, each at height ?
Enough : beyond thee lies the infinite —
Back to thy circumscription ! '

                        " Back indeed !
Ending where I began — thus : retrocede,
Who will, — what comes first, take first, I ad-
    vise !
Acquaint you with the body ere your eyes
Look upward: this Andromeda of mine —
Gaze on the beauty, Art hangs out for sign
There 's finer entertainment underneath.
Learn how they ministrate to life and death —
Those incommensurably marvellous
Contrivances which furnish forth the house
Where soul has sway ! Though Master keep
    aloof,
Signs of his presence multiply from roof
To basement of the building. Look around,
Learn thoroughly, — no fear that you confound
Master with messuage ! He 's away, no doubt,
But what if, all at once, you come upon
A startling proof — not that the Master gone
Was present lately — but that something —
    whence
Light comes — has pushed him into residence ?
Was such the symbol's meaning, — old, un-
    couth —
That circle of the serpent, tail in mouth ?
Only by looking low, ere looking high,
Comes penetration of the mystery."

                        XI

Thanks ! After sermonizing, psalmody !
Now praise with pencil, Painter ! Fools attaint
Your fame, forsooth, because its power inclines
To livelier colors, more attractive lines
Than suit some orthodox sad sickly saint
— Gray male emaciation, haply streaked
Carmine by scourgings — or they want, far
    worse —
Some self-scathed woman, framed to bless not
    curse
Nature that loved the form whereon hate
    wreaked
The wrongs you see. No, rather paint some full
Benignancy, the first and foremost boon
Of youth, health, strength, — show beauty's
    May, ere June

Undo the bud's blush, leave a rose to cull
— No poppy, neither! yet less perfect-pure,
Divinely-precious with life's dew besprent.
Show saintliness that's simply innocent
Of guessing sinnership exists to cure
All in good time! In time let age advance
And teach that knowledge helps — not igno-
    rance —
The healing of the nations. Let my spark
Quicken your tinder! Burn with — Joan of
    Arc!
Not at the end, nor midway when there grew
The brave delusions, when rare fancies flew
Before the eyes, and in the ears of her
Strange voices woke imperiously astir:
No, — paint the peasant girl all peasant-like,
Spirit and flesh — the hour about to strike
When this should be transfigured, that in-
    flamed,
By heart's admonishing "Thy country shamed,
Thy king shut out of all his realm except
One sorry corner!" and to life forth leapt
The indubitable lightning "Can there be
Country and king's salvation — all through
    me?"
Memorize that burst's moment, Francis!
    Tush—
None of the nonsense-writing! Fitlier brush
Shall clear off fancy's film-work and let show
Not what the foolish feign but the wise know —
Ask Sainte-Beuve else! — or better, Quicherat,
The downright-digger into truth that's — Bah,
Bettered by fiction? Well, of fact thus much
Concerns you, that "of prudishness no touch
From first to last defaced the maid; anon,
Camp-use compelling" — what says D'Alen-
    çon
Her fast friend? — "though I saw while she
    undressed
How fair she was — especially her breast —
Never had I a wild thought!" — as indeed
I nowise doubt. Much less would she take
    heed —
When eve came, and the lake, the hills around
Were all one solitude and silence, — found
Barriered impenetrably safe about, —
Take heed of interloping eyes shut out,
But quietly permit the air imbibe
Her naked beauty till . . . but hear the
    scribe!
Now as she fain would bathe, one even-tide,
God's maid, this Joan, from the pool's edge she
    spied
The fair blue bird clowns call the Fisher-king:
And " 'Las, sighed she, my Liege is such a thing
As thou, lord but of one poor lonely place
Out of his whole wide France: were mine the
    grace
To set my Dauphin free as thou, blue bird!"
Properly Martin-fisher — that's the word,
Not yours nor mine: folk said the rustic
    oath
In common use with her was — "By my
    troth"?
No, — "By my Martin"! Paint this! Only,
    turn
Her face away — that face about to burn
Into an angel's when the time is ripe!

That task's beyond you. Finished, Francis?
    Wipe
Pencil, scrape palette, and retire content!
"*Omnia non omnibus*" — no harm is meant!

WITH GERARD DE LAIRESSE

The Art of Painting by Gerard le Lairesse,
translated by J. F. Fritsch, was the "tome" to
which Browning refers as having interested him
when he was a boy and so given rise to this
poem. The song at the end of the poem was
first printed in a small volume called *The New
Amphion*, published for the Edinburgh Uni-
versity Union Fancy Fair in 1886.

I

AH, but — because you were struck blind,
    could bless
Your sense no longer with the actual view
Of man and woman, those fair forms you drew
In happier days so duteously and true, —
Must I account my Gerard de Lairesse
All sorrow-smitten? He was hindered too
— Was this no hardship? — from producing,
    plain
To us who still have eyes, the pageantry
Which passed and passed before his busy brain
And, captured on his canvas, showed our sky
Traversed by flying shapes, earth stocked with
    brood
Of monsters, — centaurs bestial, satyrs lewd, —
Not without much Olympian glory, shapes
Of god and goddess in their gay escapes
From the severe serene: or haply paced
The antique ways, god-counselled, nymph-em-
    braced,
Some early human kingly personage.
Such wonders of the teeming poet's-age
Were still to be: nay, these indeed began —
Are not the pictures extant? — till the ban
Of blindness struck both palette from his
    thumb
And pencil from his finger.

II

                    Blind — not dumb,
Else, Gerard, were my inmost bowels stirred
With pity beyond pity: no, the word
Was left upon your unmolested lips:
Your mouth unsealed, despite of eyes' eclipse,
Talked all brain's yearning into birth. I lack
Somehow the heart to wish your practice back
Which boasted hand's achievement in a score
Of veritable pictures, less or more,
Still to be seen: myself have seen them, —
    moved
To pay due homage to the man I loved
Because of that prodigious book he wrote
On Artistry's Ideal, by taking note,
Making acquaintance with his artist-work.
So my youth's piety obtained success'
Of all too dubious sort: for, though it irk
To tell the issue, few or none would guess
From extant lines and colors, De Lairesse.

Your faculty, although each deftly-grouped
And aptly-ordered figure-piece was judged
Worthy a prince's purchase in its day.
Bearded experience bears not to be duped
Like boyish fancy : 't was a boy that budged
No foot's breath from your visioned steps away
The while that memorable " Walk " he trudged
In your companionship, — the Book must say
Where, when and whither, — " Walk," come
    what come may,
No measurer of steps on this our globe
Shall ever match for marvels. Faustus' robe,
And Fortunatus' cap were gifts of price :
But — oh, your piece of sober sound advice
That artists should descry abundant worth
In trivial commonplace, nor groan at dearth
If fortune bade the painter's craft be plied
In vulgar town and country ! Why despond
Because hemmed round by Dutch canals?
    Beyond
The ugly actual, lo, on every side
Imagination's limitless domain
Displayed a wealth of wondrous sounds and
    sights
Ripe to be realized by poet's brain
Acting on painter's brush ! " Ye doubt?
    Poor wights,
What if I set example, go before,
While you come after, and we both explore
Holland turned Dreamland, taking care to note
Objects whereto my pupils may devote
Attention with advantage ? "

III
                    So commenced
That " Walk " amid true wonders — none to
    you,
But huge to us ignobly common-sensed,
Purblind, while plain could proper optics view
In that old sepulchre by lightning split,
Whereof the lid bore carven, — any dolt
Imagines why, — Jove's very thunderbolt :
You who could straight perceive, by glance at
    it,
This tomb must needs be Phaeton's ! In a
    trice,
Confirming that conjecture, close on hand,
Behold, half out, half in the ploughed-up sand,
A chariot-wheel explained its bolt-device :
What other than the Chariot of the Sun
Ever let drop the like ? Consult the tome —
I bid inglorious tarriers-at-home —
For greater still surprise the while that " Walk "
Went on and on, to end as it begun,
Chokefull of chances, changes, every one
No whit less wondrous. What was there to balk
Us, who had eyes, from seeing ? You with none
Missed not a marvel : wherefore ? Let us talk.

IV
Say am I right ? Your sealed sense moved
    your mind,
Free from obstruction, to compassionate
Art's power left powerless, and supply the blind
With fancies worth all facts denied by fate.
Mind could invent things, add to — take away,
At pleasure, leave out trifles mean and base
Which vex the sight that cannot say them nay

But, where mind plays the master, have no place,
And bent on banishing was mind, be sure,
All except beauty from its mustered tribe
Of objects apparitional which lure
Painter to show and poet to describe —
That imagery of the antique song
Truer than truth's self. Fancy's rainbow-birth
Conceived 'mid clouds in Greece, could glance
    along
Your passage o'er Dutch veritable earth,
As with ourselves, who see, familiar throng
About our pacings men and women worth
Nowise a glance — so poets apprehend —
Since naught avails portraying them in verse :
While painters turn upon the heel, intend
To spare their work the critic's ready curse
Due to the daily and undignified.

V
I who myself contentedly abide
Awake, nor want the wings of dream, — who
    tramp
Earth's common surface, rough, smooth, dry or
    damp,
— I understand alternatives, no less
Conceive your soul's leap, Gerard de Lairesse !
How were it could I mingle false with true,
Boast, with the sights I see, your vision too?
Advantage would it prove or detriment
If I saw double ? Could I gaze intent
On Dryope plucking the blossoms red,
As you, whereat her lote-tree writhed and bled,
Yet lose no gain, no hard fast wide-awake
Having and holding nature for the sake
Of nature only — nymph and lote-tree thus
Gained by the loss of fruit not fabulous,
Apple of English homesteads, where I see
Nor seek more than crisp buds a struggling bee
Uncrumples, caught by sweet he clambers
    through ?
Truly, a moot point : make it plain to me,
Who, bee-like, sate sense with the simply true,
Nor seek to heighten that sufficiency
By help of feignings proper to the page —
Earth's surface-blank whereon the elder age
Put color, poetizing — poured rich life
On what were else a dead ground — nothing-
    ness —
Until the solitary world grew rife
With Joves and Junos, nymphs and satyrs. Yes,
The reason was, fancy composed the strife
'Twixt sense and soul : for sense, my De Lai-
    resse,
Cannot content itself with outward things,
Mere beauty: soul must needs know whence
    there springs —
How, when and why — what sense but loves
    nor lists
To know at all.

VI
                Not one of man's acquists
Ought he resignedly to lose, methinks :
So, point me out which was it of the links
Snapt first, from out the chain which used to
    bind
Our earth to heaven, and yet for you, since blind,
Subsisted still efficient and intact?

Oh, we can fancy too! but somehow fact
Has got to — say, not so much push aside
Fancy, as to declare its place supplied
By fact unseen but no less fact the same,
Which mind bids sense accept. Is mind to
    blame,
Or sense, — does that usurp, this abdicate?
First of all, as you "walked" — were it too late
For us to walk, if so we willed? Confess
We have the sober feet still, De Lairesse!
Why not the freakish brain too, that must needs
Supplement nature — not see flowers and weeds
Simply as such, but link with each and all
The ultimate perfection — what we call
Rightly enough the human shape divine?
The rose? No rose unless it disentwine
From Venus' wreath the while she bends to kiss
Her deathly love?

VII

Plain retrogression, this!
No, no: we poets go not back at all:
What you did we could do — from great to small
Sinking assuredly: if this world last
One moment longer when Man finds its Past
Exceed its Present — blame the Protoplast!
If we no longer see as you of old,
'T is we see deeper. Progress for the bold!
You saw the body, 't is the soul we see.
Try now! Bear witness while you walk with me,
I see as you: if we loose arms, stop pace,
'T is that you stand still, I conclude the race
Without your company. Come, walk once more
The "Walk:" if I to-day as you of yore
See just like you the blind — then sight shall cry
— The whole long day quite gone through —
    victory!

VIII

Thunders on thunders, doubling and redoubling
Doom o'er the mountain, while a sharp white
    fire
Now shone, now sheared its rusty herbage,
    troubling
Hardly the fir-boles, now discharged its ire
Full where some pine-tree's solitary spire
Crashed down, defiant to the last: till — lo,
The motive of the malice! — all aglow,
Circled with flame there yawned a sudden rift
I' the rock-face, and I saw a form erect
Front and defy the outrage, while — as checked,
Chidden, beside him dauntless in the drift —
Cowered a heaped creature, wing and wing out-
    spread
In deprecation o'er the crouching head
Still hungry for the feast foregone awhile.
O thou, of scorn's unconquerable smile,
Was it when this — Jove's feathered fury —
    slipped
Gore-glutted from the heart's core whence he
    ripped —
This eagle-hound — neither reproach nor
    prayer —
Baffled, in one more fierce attempt to tear
Fate's secret from thy safeguard, — was it then
That all these thunders rent earth, ruined air
To reach thee, pay thy patronage of men?
He thundered, — to withdraw, as beast to lair,

Before the triumph on thy pallid brow.
Gather the night again about thee now,
Hate on, love ever! Morn is breaking there —
The granite ridge pricks through the mist,
    turns gold
As wrong turns right. O laughters manifold
Of ocean's ripple at dull earth's despair!

IX

But morning's laugh sets all the crags alight
Above the baffled tempest: tree and tree
Stir themselves from the stupor of the night,
And every strangled branch resumes its right
To breathe, shakes loose dark's clinging dregs,
    waves free
In dripping glory. Prone the runnels plunge,
While earth, distent with moisture like a sponge,
Smokes up, and leaves each plant its gem to see,
Each grass-blade's glory-glitter. Had I known
The torrent now turned river? — masterful
Making its rush o'er tumbled ravage — stone
And stub which barred the froths and foams:
    no bull
Ever broke bounds in formidable sport
More overwhelmingly, till lo, the spasm
Sets him to dare that last mad leap: report
Who may — his fortunes in the deathly chasm
That swallows him in silence! Rather turn
Whither, upon the upland, pedestalled
Into the broad day-splendor, whom discern
These eyes but thee, supreme one, rightly called
Moon-maid in heaven above and, here below,
Earth's huntress-queen? I note the garb suc-
    cinct
Saving from smirch that purity of snow
From breast to knee — snow's self with just the
    tinct
Of the apple-blossom's heart-blush. Ah, the
    bow
Slack-strung her fingers grasp, where, ivory-
    linked
Horn curving blends with horn, a moonlike pair
Which mimic the brow's crescent sparkling so —
As if a star's live restless fragment winked
Proud yet repugnant, captive in such hair!
What hope along the hillside, what far bliss
Lets the crisp hair-plaits fall so low they kiss
Those lucid shoulders? Must a morn so blithe
Needs have its sorrow when the twang and hiss
Tell that from out thy sheaf one shaft makes
    writhe
Its victim, thou unerring Artemis?
Why did the chamois stand so fair a mark
Arrested by the novel shape he dreamed
Was bred of liquid marble in the dark
Depths of the mountain's womb which ever
    teemed
With novel births of wonder? Not one spark
Of pity in that steel-gray glance which gleamed
At the poor hoof's protesting as it stamped
Idly the granite? Let me glide unseen
From thy proud presence: well mayst thou be
    queen
Of all those strange and sudden deaths which
    damped
So oft Love's torch and Hymen's taper lit
For happy marriage till the maidens paled
And perished on the temple-step, assailed

By — what except to envy must man's wit
Impute that sure implacable release
Of life from warmth and joy? But death
    means peace.

X

Noon is the conqueror, — not a spray, nor leaf,
Nor herb, nor blossom but has rendered up
Its morning dew : the valley seemed one cup
Of cloud-smoke, but the vapor's reign was brief;
Sun-smitten, see, it hangs — the filmy haze —
Gray-garmenting the herbless mountain-side,
To soothe the day's sharp glare: while far and
    wide
Above unclouded burns the sky, one blaze
With fierce immitigable blue, no bird
Ventures to spot by passage. E'en of peaks
Which still presume there, plain each pale point
    speaks
In wan transparency of waste incurred
By over-daring : far from me be such !
Deep in the hollow, rather, where combine
Tree, shrub and brier to roof with shade and
    cool
The remnant of some lily-strangled pool,
Edged round with mossy fringing soft and fine.
Smooth lie the bottom slabs, and overhead
Watch elder, bramble, rose, and service-tree
And one beneficent rich barberry
Jewelled all over with fruit-pendants red.
What have I seen ! O Satyr, well I know
How sad thy case, and what a world of woe
Was hid by the brown visage furry-framed
Only for mirth: who otherwise could think —
Marking thy mouth gape still on laughter's
    brink,
Thine eyes a-swim with merriment unnamed
But haply guessed at by their furtive wink?
And all the while a heart was panting sick
Behind that shaggy bulwark of thy breast —
Passion it was that made those breath-bursts
    thick
I took for mirth subsiding into rest.
So, it was Lyda — she of all the train
Of forest-thridding nymphs, — 't was only she
Turned from thy rustic homage in disdain,
Saw but that poor uncouth outside of thee,
And, from her circling sisters, mocked a pain
Echo had pitied — whom Pan loved in vain —
For she was wishful to partake thy glee,
Mimic thy mirth — who loved her not again,
Savage for Lyda's sake. She crouches there —
Thy cruel beauty, slumberously laid
Supine on heaped-up beast-skins, unaware
Thy steps have traced her to the briery glade,
Thy greedy hands disclose the cradling lair,
Thy hot eyes reach and revel on the maid !

XI

Now, what should this be for? The sun's de-
    cline
Seems as he lingered lest he lose some act
Dread and decisive, some prodigious fact
Like thunder from the safe sky's sapphirine
About to alter earth's conditions, packed
With fate for nature's self that waits, aware
What mischief unsuspected in the air
Menaces momently a cataract.

Therefore it is that yonder space extends
Untrenched upon by any vagrant tree,
Shrub, weed well-nigh ; they keep their bounds,
    leave free
The platform for what actors ? Foes or friends,
Here come they trooping silent : heaven sus-
    pends
Purpose the while they range themselves. I see !
Bent on a battle, two vast powers agree
This present and no after-contest ends
One or the other's grasp at rule in reach
Over the race of man — host fronting host,
As statue statue fronts — wrath-molten each,
Solidified by hate, — earth halved almost,
To close once more in chaos. Yet two shapes
Show prominent, each from the universe
Of minions round about him, that disperse
Like cloud-obstruction when a bolt escapes.
Who flames first ? Macedonian, is it thou ?
Ay, and who fronts thee, King Darius, drapes
His form with purple, fillet-folds his brow.

XII

What, then the long day dies at last ? Abrupt
The sun that seemed, in stooping, sure to melt
Our mountain-ridge, is mastered : black the
    belt
Of westward crags, his gold could not corrupt,
Barriers again the valley, lets the flow
Of lavish glory waste itself away
— Whither ? For new climes, fresh eyes breaks
    the day ?
Night was not to be baffled. If the glow
Were all that 's gone from us ! Did clouds,
    afloat
So filmily but now, discard no rose,
Sombre throughout the fleeciness that grows
A sullen uniformity. I note
Rather displeasure, — in the overspread
Change from the swim of gold to one pale lead
Oppressive to malevolence, — than late
Those amorous yearnings when the aggregate
Of cloudlets pressed that each and all might sate
Its passion and partake in relics red
Of day's bequeathment: now, a frown instead
Estranges, and affrights who needs must fare
On and on till his journey ends: but where ?
Caucasus ? Lost now in the night. Away
And far enough lies that Arcadia.
The human heroes tread the world's dark way
No longer. Yet I dimly see almost —
Yes, for my last adventure ! 'T is a ghost.
So drops away the beauty ! There he stands
Voiceless, scarce strives with deprecating
    hands . . .

XIII

Enough ! Stop further fooling, De Lairesse !
My fault, not yours ! Some fitter way express
Heart's satisfaction that the Past indeed
Is past, gives way before Life's best and last,
The all-including Future ! What were life
Did soul stand still therein, forego her strife
Through the ambiguous Present to the goal
Of some all-reconciling Future ? Soul,
Nothing has been which shall not bettered be
Hereafter, — leave the root, by law's decree
Whence springs the ultimate and perfect tree !

Busy thee with unearthing root ? Nay, climb —
Quit trunk, branch, leaf and flower — reach,
    rest sublime
Where fruitage ripens in the blaze of day !
O'erlook, despise, forget, throw flower away,
Intent on progress ?   No whit more than stop
Ascent therewith to dally, screen the top
Sufficiency of yield by interposed
Twistwork bold foot gets free from. Wherefore
    glozed
The poets — " Dream afresh old godlike shapes,
Recapture ancient fable that escapes,
Push back reality, repeople earth
With vanished falseness, recognize no worth
In fact new-born unless 't is rendered back
Pallid by fancy, as the western rack
Of fading cloud bequeaths the lake some gleam
Of its gone glory ! "

XIV

Let things be — not seem,
I counsel rather, — do, and nowise dream !
Earth's young significance is all to learn :
The dead Greek lore lies buried in the urn
Where who seeks fire finds ashes.   Ghost, for-
    sooth !
What was the best Greece babbled of as truth ?
" A shade, a wretched nothing, — sad, thin,
    drear,
Cold, dark, it holds on to the lost loves here,
If have have haply sprinkled o'er the dead
Three charitable dust-heaps, made mouth red
One moment by the sip of sacrifice :
Just so much comfort thaws the stubborn ice
Slow-thickening upward till it choke at length
The last faint flutter craving — not for strength,
Not beauty, not the riches and the rule
O'er men that made life life indeed." Sad
    school
Was Hades ! Gladly, — might the dead but
    slink
To life back, — to the dregs once more would
    drink
Each interloper, drain the humblest cup
Fate mixes for humanity.

XV

Cheer up, —
Be death with me, as with Achilles erst,
Of Man's calamities the last and worst :
Take it so ! By proved potency that still
Makes perfect, be assured, come what come will,
What once lives never dies — what here attains
To a beginning, has no end, still gains
And never loses aught : when, where, and how —
Lies in Law's lap. What 's death then ? Even
    now
With so much knowledge is it hard to bear
Brief interposing ignorance ? Is care
For a creation found at fault just there —
There where the heart breaks bond and out-
    runs time,
To reach not follow what shall be ?

XVI

Here 's rhyme
Such as one makes now, — say, when Spring
    repeat

That miracle the Greek Bard sadly greets :
" Spring for the tree and herb — no Spring for
    us ! "
Let Spring come : why, a man salutes her
    thus :

Dance, yellows and whites and reds, —
Lead your gay orgy, leaves, stalks, heads
Astir with the wind in the tulip-beds !

There 's sunshine ; scarcely a wind at all
Disturbs starved grass and daisies small
On a certain mound by a churchyard wall.

Daisies and grass be my heart's bedfellows
On the mound wind spares and sunshine mel-
    lows :
Dance you, reds and whites and yellows !

WITH CHARLES AVISON

The manuscript of the *Grand March* written
by Avison was in the possession of Browning's
father, and a copy is given at the end of the
poem. The *Relfe* who is two or three times
mentioned was Browning's teacher of music,
who was a learned contrapuntist.

I

How strange ! — but, first of all, the little face
Which led my fancy forth. This bitter morn
Showed me no object in the stretch forlorn
Of garden-ground beneath my window, backed
By yon worn wall wherefrom the creeper,
    tacked
To clothe its brickwork, hangs now, rent and
    racked
By five months' cruel winter, — showed no torn
And tattered ravage worse for eyes to see
Than just one ugly space of clearance, left
Bare even of the bones which used to be
Warm wrappage, safe embracement : this one
    cleft —
— Oh, what a life and beauty filled it up
Startlingly, when methought the rude clay cup
Ran over with poured bright wine ! 'T was a
    bird
Breast-deep there, tugging at his prize, de-
    terred
No whit by the fast-falling snow-flake : gain
Such prize my blackcap must by might and
    main —
The cloth-shred, still a-flutter from its nail
That fixed a spray once. Now, what told the
    tale
To thee, — no townsman but born orchard-
    thief, —
That here — surpassing moss-tuft, beard from
    sheaf
Of sun-scorched barley, horsehairs long and
    stout,
All proper country-pillage — here, no doubt,
Was just the scrap to steal should line thy nest
Superbly ? Off he flew, his bill possessed
The booty sure to set his wife's each wing
Greenly a-quiver. How they climb and cling,

Hang parrot-wise to bough, these blackcaps! Strange
Seemed to a city-dweller that the finch
Should stray so far to forage : at a pinch,
Was not the fine wool's self within his range
—Filchings on every fence? But no: the need
Was of this rag of manufacture, spoiled
By art, and yet by nature near unsoiled,
New-suited to what scheming finch would breed
In comfort, this uncomfortable March.

II

Yet — by the first pink blossom on the larch! —
This was scarce stranger than that memory, —
In want of what should cheer the stay-at-home,
My soul, —must straight clap pinion, well-nigh roam
A century back, nor once close plume, descry
The appropriate rag to plunder, till she pounced —
Pray, on what relic of a brain long still?
What old-world work proved forage for the bill
Of memory the far-flyer? "March" announced,
I verily believe, the dead and gone
Name of a music-maker: one of such
In England as did little or did much,
But, doing, had their day once. Avison!
Singly and solely for an air of thine,
Bold-stepping "March," foot stept to ere my hand
Could stretch an octave, I o'erlooked the band
Of majesties familiar, to decline
On thee — not too conspicuous on the list
Of worthies who by help of pipe or wire
Expressed in sound rough rage or soft desire —
Thou, whilom of Newcastle organist!

III

So much could one — well, thinnish air effect!
Am I ungrateful? for, your March, styled "Grand,"
Did veritably seem to grow, expand,
And greaten up to title as, unchecked,
Dream-marchers marched, kept marching, slow and sure,
In time, to tune, unchangeably the same,
From nowhere into nowhere, — out they came,
Onward they passed, and in they went. No lure
Of novel modulation pricked the flat
Forthright persisting melody, — no hint
That discord, sound asleep beneath the flint,
Struck — might spring spark-like, claim due tit-for-tat,
Quenched in a concord. No! Yet, such the might
Of quietude's immutability,
That somehow coldness gathered warmth, well-nigh
Quickened — which could not be! — grew burning-bright
With fife-shriek, cymbal-clash and trumpet-blare,

To drum-accentuation: pacing turned
Striding, and striding grew gigantic, spurned
At last the narrow space 'twixt earth and air,
So shook me back into my sober self.

IV

And where woke I? The March had set me down
There whence I plucked the measure, as his brown
Frayed flannel-bit my blackcap. Great John Relfe,
Master of mine, learned, redoubtable,
It little needed thy consummate skill
To fitly figure such a bass! The key
Was — should not memory play me false — well, C.
Ay, with the Greater Third, in Triple Time,
Three crochets to a bar: no change, I grant,
Except from Tonic down to Dominant.
And yet — and yet — if I could put in rhyme
The manner of that marching! — which had stopped
— I wonder, where? — but that my weak self dropped
From out the ranks, to rub eyes disentranced
And feel that, after all the way advanced,
Back must I foot it, I and my compeers,
Only to reach, across a hundred years,
The bandsman Avison whose little book
And large tune thus had led me the long way
(As late a rag my blackcap) from to-day
And to-day's music-manufacture, — Brahms,
Wagner, Dvorak, Liszt, — to where — trumpets, shawms,
Show yourselves joyful! — Handel reigns — supreme?
By no means! Buononcini's work is theme
For fit laudation of the impartial few:
(We stand in England, mind you!) Fashion too
Favors Geminiani — of those choice
Concertos: nor there wants a certain voice
Raised in thy favor likewise, famed Pepusch
Dear to our great-grandfathers! In a bush
Of Doctor's wig, they prized thee timing beats
While Greenway trilled "Alexis." Such were feats
Of music in thy day — dispute who list —
Avison, of Newcastle organist!

V

And here 's your music all alive once more —
As once it was alive, at least: just so
The figured worthies of a waxwork-show
Attest — such people, years and years ago,
Looked thus when outside death had life be low,
—Could say "We are now" not "We were of yore,"
— "Feel how our pulses leap!" and not "Explore —
Explain why quietude has settled o'er
Surface once all awork!" Ay, such a "Suite"
Roused heart to rapture, such a "Fugue" would catch
Soul heavenwards up, when time was: why attach
Blame to exhausted faultlessness, no match

For fresh achievement? Feat once — ever
   feat!
How can completion grow still more complete?
Hear Avison! He tenders evidence
That music in his day as much absorbed
Heart and soul then as Wagner's music now,
Perfect from centre to circumference —
Orbed to the full can be but fully orbed:
And yet — and yet — whence comes it that
   "O Thou" —
Sighed by the soul at eve to Hesperus —
Will not again take wing and fly away
(Since fatal Wagner fixed it fast for us)
In some unmodulated minor? Nay.
Even by Handel's help!

VI

                    I state it thus:
There is no truer truth obtainable
By Man than comes of music. "Soul" —
   (accept
A word which vaguely names what no adept
In word-use fits and fixes so that still
Thing shall not slip word's fetter and remain
Innominate as first, yet, free again,
Is no less recognized the absolute
Fact underlying that same other fact
Concerning which no cavil can dispute
Our nomenclature when we call it " Mind " —
Something not Matter) — "Soul," who seeks
   shall find
Distinct beneath that something. You exact
An illustrative image? This may suit.

VII

We see a work : the worker works behind,
Invisible himself. Suppose his act
Be to o'erarch a gulf : he digs, transports,
Shapes and, through enginery — all sizes,
   sorts,
Lays stone by stone until a floor compact
Proves our bridged causeway. So works Mind
   — by stress
Of faculty, with loose facts, more or less,
Builds up our solid knowledge : all the same,
Underneath rolls what Mind may hide not
   tame,
An element which works beyond our guess,
Soul, the unsounded sea — whose lift of surge,
Spite of all superstructure, lets emerge,
In flower and foam, Feeling from out the deeps
Mind arrogates no mastery upon —
Distinct indisputably. Has there gone
To dig up, drag forth, render smooth from
   rough
Mind's flooring, — operosity enough?
Still the successive labor of each inch,
Who lists may learn : from the last turn of
   winch
That let the polished slab-stone find its place,
To the first prod of pickaxe at the base
Of the unquarried mountain, — what was all
Mind's varied process except natural,
Nay, easy even, to descry, describe,
After our fashion? "So worked Mind: its
   tribe
Of senses ministrant above, below,
Far, near, or now or haply long ago

Brought to pass knowledge." But Soul's sea
   — drawn whence,
Fed how, forced whither, — by what evidence
Of ebb and flow, that 's felt beneath the tread,
Soul has its course 'neath Mind's work over-
   head, —
Who tells of, tracks to source the founts of
   Soul ?
Yet wherefore heaving sway and restless roll
This side and that, except to emulate
Stability above? To match and mate
Feeling with knowledge, — make as manifest
Soul's work as Mind's work, turbulence as rest,
Hates, loves, joys, woes, hopes, fears, that rise
   and sink
Ceaselessly, passion's transient flit and wink,
A ripple's tinting or a spume-sheet's spread
Whitening the wave, — to strike all this life
   dead,
Run mercury into a mould like lead,
And henceforth have the plain result to show —
How we Feel, hard and fast as what we Know —
This were the prize and is the puzzle ! — which
Music essays to solve: and here 's the hitch
That balks her of full triumph else to boast.

VIII

All Arts endeavor this, and she the most
Attains thereto, yet fails of touching: why?
Does Mind get Knowledge from Art's min-
   istry?
What 's known once is known ever: Arts
   arrange,
Dissociate, re-distribute, interchange
Part with part, lengthen, broaden, high or
   deep
Construct their bravest, — still such pains
   produce
Change, not creation: simply what lay loose
At first lies firmly after, what design
Was faintly traced in hesitating line
Once on a time, grows firmly resolute
Henceforth and evermore. Now, could we
   shoot
Liquidity into a mould, — some way
Arrest Soul's evanescent moods, and keep
Unalterably still the forms that leap
To life for once by help of Art ! — which yearns
To save its capture: Poetry discerns,
Painting is 'ware of passion's rise and fall,
Bursting, subsidence, intermixture — all
A-seethe within the gulf. Each Art a-strain
Would stay the apparition, — nor in vain:
The Poet's word-mesh, Painter's sure and
   swift
Color-and-line-throw — proud the prize they
   lift !
Thus felt Man and thus looked Man, — passions
   caught
I' the midway swim of sea, — not much, if
   aught,
Of nether-brooding loves, hates, hopes and
   fears,
Enwombed past Art's disclosure. Fleet the
   years,
And still the Poet's page holds Helena
At gaze from topmost Troy — "But where are
   they,

My brothers, in the armament I name
Hero by hero ? Can it be that shame
For their lost sister holds them from the war ? "
— Knowing not they already slept afar
Each of them in his own dear native land.
Still on the Painter's fresco, from the hand
Of God takes Eve the life-spark whereunto
She trembles up from nothingness. Outdo
Both of them, Music ! Dredging deeper yet,
Drag into day, — by sound, thy master-net, —
The abysmal bottom-growth, ambiguous thing
Unbroken of a branch, palpitating
With limbs' play and life's semblance ! There
    it lies,
Marvel and mystery, of mysteries
And marvels, most to love and laud thee for !
Save it from chance and change we most ab-
    hor !
Give momentary feeling permanence,
So that thy capture hold, a century hence,
Truth's very heart of truth as, safe to-day,
The Painter's Eve, the Poet's Helena
Still rapturously bend, afar still throw
The wistful gaze ! Thanks, Homer, Angelo !
Could Music rescue thus from Soul's profound,
Give feeling immortality by sound,
Then were she queenliest of Arts ! Alas —
As well expect the rainbow not to pass !
" Praise ' Radamisto ' — love attains therein
To perfect utterance ! Pity — what shall win
Thy secret like ' Rinaldo ' ? " — so men said:
Once all was perfume — now, the flower is
    dead —
They spied tints, sparks have left the spar !
    Love, hate,
Joy, fear, survive, — alike importunate
As ever to go walk the world again,
Nor ghost-like pant for outlet all in vain
Till Music loose them, fit each filmily
With form enough to know and name it by
For any recognizer sure of ken
And sharp of ear, no grosser denizen
Of earth than needs be. Nor to such appeal
Is Music long obdurate : off they steal —
How gently, dawn-doomed phantoms ! back
    come they
Full-blooded with new crimson of broad day —
Passion made palpable once more. Ye look
Your last on Handel ? Gaze your first on
    Gluck !
Why wistful search, O waning ones, the chart
Of stars for you while Haydn, while Mozart
Occupies heaven ? These also, fanned to fire,
Flamboyant wholly, — so perfections tire, —
Whiten to wanness, till . . . let others note
The ever-new invasion !

IX

                            I devote
Rather my modicum of parts to use
What power may yet avail to re-infuse
(In fancy, please you !) sleep that looks like
    death
With momentary liveliness, lend breath
To make the torpor half inhale. O Relfe,
An all-unworthy pupil, from the shelf
Of thy laboratory, dares unstop
Bottle, ope box, extract thence pinch and drop

Of dusts and dews a many thou didst shrine
Each in its right receptacle, assign
To each its proper office, letter large
Label and label, then with solemn charge,
Reviewing learnedly the list complete
Of chemical reactives, from thy feet
Push down the same to me, attent below,
Power in abundance : armed wherewith I go
To play the enlivener. Bring good antique
    stuff !
Was it alight once ? Still lives spark enough
For breath to quicken, run the smouldering
    ash
Red right-through. What, " stone-dead " were
    fools so rash
As style my Avison, because he lacked
Modern appliance, spread out phrase unracked
By modulations fit to make each hair
Stiffen upon his wig ? See there — and there !
I sprinkle my reactives, pitch broadcast
Discords and resolutions, turn aghast
Melody's easy-going, jostle law
With license, modulate (no Bach in awe)
Change enharmonically (Hudl to thank)
And lo, upstart the flamelets, — what was
    blank
Turns scarlet, purple, crimson ! Straightway
    scanned
By eyes that like new lustre — Love once more
Yearns through the Largo, Hatred as before
Rages in the Rubato : e'en thy March,
My Avison, which, sooth to say — (ne'er arch
Eyebrows in anger !) — timed, in Georgian
    years
The step precise of British Grenadiers
To such a nicety, — if score I crowd,
If rhythm I break, if beats I vary, — tap
At bar's off-starting turns true thunder-clap,
Ever the pace augmented till — what 's here ?
Titanic striding toward Olympus !

X

                            Fear
No such irreverent innovation ! Still
Glide on, go rolling, water-like, at will —
Nay, were thy melody in monotone,
The due three-parts dispensed with !

XI

                            This alone
Comes of my tiresome talking : Music's throne
Seats somebody whom somebody unseats,
And whom in turn — by who knows what new
    feats
Of strength — shall somebody as sure push
    down,
Consign him dispossessed of sceptre, crown,
And orb imperial — whereto ? Never dream
That what once lived shall ever die ! They
    seem
Dead — do they ? lapsed things lost in limbo ?
    Bring
Our life to kindle theirs, and straight each
    king
Starts, you shall see, stands up, from head to
    foot
No inch that is not Purcell ! Wherefore ? (Suit
Measure to subject, first — no marching on

Yet in thy bold C major, Avison,
As suited step a minute since : no : wait —
Into the minor key first modulate —
Gently with A, now — in the Lesser Third !)

XII

Of all the lamentable debts incurred
By Man through buying knowledge, this were
    worst :
That he should find his last gain prove his
    first
Was futile — merely nescience absolute,
Not knowledge in the bud which holds a fruit
Haply undreamed of in the soul's Spring-tide,
Pursed in the petals Summer opens wide,
And Autumn, withering, rounds to perfect
    ripe, —
Not this, — but ignorance, a blur to wipe
From human records, late it graced so much.
" Truth — this attainment ? Ah, but such and
    such
Beliefs of yore seemed inexpugnable
When we attained them ! E'en as they, so
    will
This their successor have the due morn, noon,
Evening and night — just as an old - world
    tune
Wears out and drops away, until who hears
Smilingly questions — ' This it was brought
    tears
Once to all eyes, — this roused heart's rapture
    once ? '
So will it be with truth that, for the nonce,
Styles itself truth perennial : 'ware its wile !
Knowledge turns nescience, — foremost on the
    file,
Simply proves first of our delusions."

XIII

              Now —
Blare it forth, bold C major ! Lift thy brow,
Man, the immortal, that wast never fooled
With gifts no gifts at all, nor ridiculed —
Man knowing — he who nothing knew ! As
    Hope,
Fear, Joy, and Grief, — though ampler stretch
    and scope
They seek and find in novel rhythm, fresh
    phrase, —
Were equally existent in far days
Of Music's dim beginning — even so,
Truth was at full within thee long ago,
Alive as now it takes what latest shape
May startle thee by strangeness. Truths es-
    cape
Time's insufficient garniture : they fade,
They fall — those sheathings now grown sere,
    whose aid
Was infinite to truth they wrapped, saved fine
And free through March frost : May dews
    crystalline
Nourish truth merely, — does June boast the
    fruit
As — not new vesture merely but, to boot,
Novel creation ? Soon shall fade and fall
Myth after myth — the husk-like lies I call
New truth's corolla-safeguard : Autumn comes,
So much the better !

XIV

          Therefore — bang the drums
Blow the trumpets, Avison ! March-motive ?
    that's
Truth which endures resetting. Sharps and flats,
Lavish at need, shall dance athwart thy score
When ophicleide and bombardon's uproar
Mate the approaching trample, even now
Big in the distance — or my ears deceive —
Of federated England, fitly weave
March-music for the Future !

XV

               Or suppose
Back, and not forward, transformation goes ?
Once more some sable-stoled procession — say
From Little-ease to Tyburn — wends its way,
Out of the dungeon to the gallows-tree
Where heading, hacking, hanging is to be
Of half-a-dozen recusants — this day
Three hundred years ago ! How duly drones
Elizabethan plain-song — dim antique
Grown clarion-clear the while I humbly wreak
A classic vengeance on thy March ! It
    moans —
Larges and Longs and Breves displacing quite
Crotchet-and-quaver pertness — brushing bars
Aside and filling vacant sky with stars
Hidden till now that day return to night.

XVI

Nor night nor day : one purpose move us both,
Be thy mood mine ! As thou wast minded,
    Man 's
The cause our music champions : I were loth
To think we cheered our troop to Preston Pans
Ignobly : back to times of England's best !
Parliament stands for privilege — life and limb
Guards Hollis, Haselrig, Strode, Hampden,
    Pym,
The famous Five. There 's rumor of arrest
Bring up the Train Bands, Southwark ! They
    protest :
Shall we not all join chorus ? Hark the hymn,
— Rough, rude, robustious — homely heart a-
    throb,
Harsh voice a-hallo, as beseems the mob !
How good is noise ! what 's silence but de-
    spair
Of making sound match gladness never there ?
Give me some great glad " subject," glorious
    Bach,
Where cannon-roar not organ-peal we lack !
Join in, give voice robustious rude and rough, —
Avison helps — so heart lend noise enough !

Fife, trump, drum, sound ! and singers then
Marching say " Pym, the man of men ! "
Up, heads, your proudest, — out throats, your
    loudest —
" Somerset's Pym ! "

Strafford from the block, Eliot from the den,
Foes, friends, shout " Pym, our citizen ! "
Wail, the foes he quelled, — hail, the friends
    he held,
" Tavistock's Pym ! "

Hearts prompt heads, hands that ply the pen
Teach babes unborn the where and when.
— Tyrants, he braved them, — patriots, he
    saved them —
" Westminster's Pym ! "

Lustily.

FUST AND HIS FRIENDS

AN EPILOGUE

(*Inside the House of Fust, Mayence, 1457.*)

First Friend. Up, up, up — next step of the
    staircase
Lands us, lo, at the chamber of dread !
Second Friend. Locked and barred ?
Third Friend.   Door open — the rare case!
Fourth Friend.   Ay, there he leans — lost
    wretch !
Fifth Friend.   His head
Sunk on his desk 'twixt his arms outspread !

Sixth Friend. Hallo, — wake, man, ere God
    thunderstrike Mayence
— Mulct for thy sake who art Satan's, John
    Fust !
Satan installed here, God's rule in abeyance,
Mayence some morning may crumble to dust.
Answer our questions thou shalt and thou must !

Seventh Friend. Softly and fairly ! Wherefore
    a-gloom ?
Greet us, thy gossipry, cousin and sib !
Raise the forlorn brow, Fust ! Make room —
Let daylight through arms which, enfolding
    thee, crib
From those clenched lids the comfort of sun-
    shine !
First Friend.   So glib

Thy tongue slides to " comfort " already ?
    Not mine !
Behoove us deal roundly : the wretch is dis-
    traught
— Too well I guess wherefore ! Behooves a
    Divine
— Such as I, by grace, boast me — to threaten
    one caught
In the enemy's toils, — setting " comfort " at
    naught.

Second Friend. Nay, Brother, so hasty? I
    heard — nor long since —
Of a certain Black Art'sman who, — help-
    lessly bound
By rash pact with Satan, — through paying —
    why mince
The matter? — fit price to the Church, —
    safe and sound
Full a year after death in his grave-clothes was
    found.

Whereas 't is notorious the Fiend claims his
    due
During lifetime, — comes clawing, with talons
    aflame,
The soul from the flesh-rags left smoking and
    blue:
So it happed with John Faust; lest John
    Fust fare the same, —
Look up, I adjure thee by God's holy name!

For neighbors and friends — no foul hell-brood
    flock we!
Saith Solomon "Words of the wise are as
    goads:"
Ours prick but to startle from torpor, set free
Soul and sense from death's drowse!
First Friend.   And soul, wakened, unloads
Much sin by confession: no mere palinodes!

— "I was youthful and wanton, am old yet no
    sage:
When angry I cursed, struck and slew: did I
    want?
Right and left did I rob: though no war I
    dared wage
With the Church (God forbid!) — harm her
    least ministrant —
Still I outraged all else. Now that strength is
    grown scant,

"I am probity's self" — no such bleatings as
    these!
But avowal of guilt so enormous, it balks
Tongue's telling. Yet penitence prompt may
    appease
God's wrath at thy bond with the Devil who
    stalks
— Strides hither to strangle thee!
Fust.   Childhood so talks. —

Not rare wit nor ripe age — ye boast them, my
    neighbors! —
Should lay such a charge on your townsman,
    this Fust
Who, known for a life spent in pleasures and
    labors
If freakish yet venial, could scarce be induced
To traffic with fiends.
First Friend.   So, my words have unloosed

A plie from those pale lips corrugate but now?
Fust. Lost count me, yet not as ye lean to
    surmise.
First Friend. To surmise? to establish!
    Unbury that brow!
Look up, that thy judge may read clear in
    thine eyes!

Second Friend. By your leave, Brother
    Barnabite! Mine to advise!

— Who arraign thee, John Fust! What was
    bruited erewhile
Now bellows through Mayence. All cry —
    thou hast trucked
Salvation away for lust's solace! Thy smile
Takes its hue from hell's smoulder!
Fust.   Too certain! I sucked
— Got drunk at the nipple of sense.
Second Friend.   Thou hast ducked —

Art drowned there, say rather! Faugh —
    fleshly disport!
How else but by help of Sir Belial didst win
That Venus-like lady, no drudge of thy sort
Could lure to become his accomplice in sin?
Folk nicknamed her Helen of Troy!
First Friend.   Best begin

At the very beginning. Thy father, — all knew,
A mere goldsmith . . .
Fust. Who knew him, perchance may know
    this —
He dying left much gold and jewels no few:
Whom these help to court with, but seldom
    shall miss
The love of a leman: true witchcraft, I wis!

First Friend. Dost flout me? 'T is said, in
    debauchery's guild
Admitted prime guttler and guzzler — O
    swine! —
To honor thy headship, those tosspots so swilled
That out of their table there sprouted a vine
Whence each claimed a cluster, awaiting thy
    sign

To out knife, off mouthful: when — who could
    suppose
Such malice in magic? — each sot woke and
    found
Cold steel but an inch from the neighbor's red
    nose
He took for a grape-bunch!
Fust.   Does that so astound
Sagacity such as ye boast, — who surround

Your mate with eyes staring, hairs standing
    erect
At his magical feats? Are good burghers
    unversed
In the humors of toping? Full oft, I suspect,
Ye, counting your fingers, call thumbkin their
    first,
And reckon a groat every guilder disbursed.

What marvel if wags, while the skinker fast
    brimmed
Their glass with rare tipple's enticement,
    should gloat
— Befooled and beflustered — through optics
    drink-dimmed —
On this draught and that, till each found in
    his throat
Our Rhenish smack rightly as Raphal? For,
    note —

They fancied — their fuddling deceived them so
　　grossly —
That liquor sprang out of the table itself
Through　gimlet-holes　drilled　there, — nor
　　noticed how closely
The skinker kept plying my guests, from the
　　shelf
O'er their heads, with the potable madness.
　　No elf

Had need to persuade them a vine rose umbra-
　　geous,
Fruit-bearing, thirst-quenching! Enough!
　　I confess
To many such fool-pranks, but none so out-
　　rageous
That Satan was called in to help me: ex-
　　cess
I own to, I grieve at — no more and no less.

Second Friend. Strange honors were heaped
　　on thee — medal for breast,
Chain for neck, sword for thigh: not a lord
　　of the land
But acknowledged thee peer! What ambition
　　possessed
A goldsmith by trade, with craft's grime on
　　his hand,
To seek such associates?
Fust.　　　　Spare taunts! Understand —

I submit me! Of vanities under the sun,
　　Pride seized me at last as concupiscence
　　first,
Crapulosity ever: true Fiends, every one,
　　Haled this way and that my poor soul: thus
　　amerced —
Forgive and forget me!
　　First Friend.　　Had flesh sinned the worst,

Yet help were in counsel: the Church could
　　absolve:
But say not men truly thou barredst escape
By signing and sealing . . .
　　Second Friend.　　　On me must devolve
The task of extracting . . .
　　First Friend.　　　Shall Barnabites ape
Us Dominican experts?
　　Seventh Friend.　　Nay, Masters, — agape

When Hell yawns for a soul, 't is myself claim
　　the task
Of extracting, by just one plain question,
　　God's truth!
Where 's Peter Genesheim thy partner? I
　　ask
Why, cloistered up still in thy room, the pale
　　youth
Slaves tongue-tied — thy trade brooks no tat-
　　tling forsooth!

No less he, thy *famulus,* suffers entrapping,
　　Succumbs to good fellowship: barrel a-broach
Runs freely nor needs any subsequent tapping:
　　Quoth Peter, "That room, none but I dare
　　approach,
Holds secrets will help me to ride in my coach."

He prattles, we profit: in brief, he assures
　　Thou hast taught him to speak so that all
　　men may hear
— Each alike, wide world over, Jews, Pagans,
　　Turks, Moors,
The same as we Christians — speech heard
　　far and near
At one and the same magic moment!
Fust.　　　　　　That 's clear!

Said he — how?
　　Seventh Friend. Is it like he was licensed to
　　learn?
Who doubts but thou dost this by aid of the
　　Fiend?
Is it so? So it is, for thou smilest! Go, burn
To ashes, since such proves thy portion, un-
　　screened
By bell, book and candle! Yet lately I
　　weened

Balm yet was in Gilead, — some healing in
　　store
For the friend of my bosom. Men said thou
　　wast sunk
In a sudden despondency: not, as before,
　　Fust gallant and gay with his pottle and punk,
But sober, sad, sick as one yesterday drunk!

Fust. Spare Fust, then, thus contrite! — who,
　　youthful and healthy,
Equipped for life's struggle with culture of
　　mind,
Sound flesh and sane soul in coherence, born
　　wealthy,
Nay, wise — how he wasted endowment de-
　　signed
For the glory of God and the good of mankind!

That much were misused such occasions of
　　grace
Ye well may upbraid him, who bows to the
　　rod.
But this should bid anger to pity give place —
　　He has turned from the wrong, in the right
　　path to plod,
Makes amends to mankind and craves pardon
　　of God.

"Yea, friends, even now from my lips the
　　Heureka —
Soul saved!" was nigh bursting — unduly
　　elate!
Have I brought Man advantage, or hatched —
　　so to speak — a
Strange serpent, no cygnet? 'T is this I de-
　　bate
Within me. Forbear, and leave Fust to his
　　fate!

First Friend. So abject, late lofty? Me-
　　thinks I spy respite.
Make clean breast, discover what mysteries
　　hide
In thy room there!
　　Second Friend. Ay, out with them! Do
　　Satan despite!

Remember what caused his undoing was pride !
First Friend. Dumb devil ! Remains one resource to be tried !

Second Friend. Exorcise !
Seventh Friend. Nay, first — is there any remembers
In substance that potent " *Ne pulvis* " — a psalm
Whereof some live spark haply lurks 'mid the embers
Which choke in my brain. Talk of " Gilead and balm " ?
I mind me, sung half through, this gave such a qualm

To Asmodeus inside of a Hussite, that, queasy,
He broke forth in brimstone with curses. I 'm strong
In — at least the commencement : the rest should go easy,
Friends helping. " *Ne pulvis et ignis* " . . .
Sixth Friend.   All wrong !
Fifth Friend. I 've conned till I captured the whole.
Seventh Friend.   Get along !

" *Ne pulvis et cinis superbe te geras,*
Nam fulmina " . . .
Sixth Friend. Fiddlestick ! Peace, dolts and dorrs !
Thus runs it " *Ne Numinis fulmina feras* " —
Then " *Hominis perfidi justa sunt sors*
Fulmen et grando et horrida mors."

Seventh Friend. You blunder . . . " *Irati ne.*"
Sixth Friend.   Mind your own business !
Fifth Friend. I do not so badly, who gained the monk's leave
To study an hour his choice parchment. A dizziness
May well have surprised me. No Christian dares thieve,
Or I scarce had returned him his treasure. These cleave :

" *Nos pulvis et cinis, trementes, gementes,*
Venimus " — some such word — " *ad te, Domine !*
Da lumen, juvamen, ut sancta sequentes
Cor . . . corda " . . . Plague take it !
Seventh Friend.   — " *erecta sint spe :* "
Right text, ringing rhyme, and ripe Latin for me !

Sixth Friend. A Canon's self wrote it me fair : I was tempted
To part with the sheepskin.
Seventh Friend. Didst grasp and let go
Such a godsend, thou Judas ? My purse had been emptied
Ere part with the prize !
Fust.   Do I dream ? Say ye so ?
Clouds break, then ! Move, world ! I have gained my " *Pou sto* " !

I am saved : Archimedes, salute me !
Omnes.   Assistance !

Help, Angels ! He summons . . . Aroint thee ! — by name,
His familiar !
Fust. Approach !
Omnes.   Devil, keep thy due distance !
Fust. Be tranquillized, townsmen ! The knowledge ye claim
Behold, I prepare to impart. Praise or blame, —

Your blessing or banning, whatever betide me,
At last I accept. The slow travail of years,
The long-teeming brain's birth — applaud me, deride me, —
At last claims revealment. Wait !
Seventh Friend.   Wait till appears
Uncaged Archimedes cooped-up there ?
Second Friend.   Who fears ?

Here 's have at thee !
Seventh Friend. Correctly now ! " *Pulvis et cinis* " . . .
Fust. The verse ye so value, it happens I hold
In my memory safe from *initium* to *finis.*
Word for word, I produce you the whole, plain enrolled,
Black letters, white paper — no scribe's red and gold !

Omnes. Aroint thee !
Fust.   I go and return.
                (*He enters the inner room.*)
First Friend.   Ay, 't is " *ibis* "
No doubt : but as boldly " *redibis* " — who 'll say ?
I rather conjecture " *in Orco peribis !* "
Seventh Friend. Come, neighbors !
Sixth Friend.   I 'm with you ! Show courage and stay
Hell's outbreak ? Sirs, cowardice here wins the day !

Fifth Friend. What luck had that student of Bamberg who ventured
To peep in the cell where a wizard of note
Was busy in getting some black deed debentured
By Satan ? In dog's guise there sprang at his throat
A flame-breathing fury. Fust favors, I note,

An ugly huge lurcher !
Seventh Friend.   If I placed reliance
As thou, on the beads thou art telling so fast,
I 'd risk just a peep through the keyhole.
Sixth Friend.   Appliance
Of ear might be safer. Five minutes are past.
Omnes. Saints, save us ! The door is thrown open at last !

Fust (*re-enters, the door closing behind him*).
As I promised, behold I perform ! Apprehend you
The object I offer is poison or pest ?
Receive without harm from the hand I extend you

A gift that shall set every scruple at rest !
Shrink back from mere paper-strips ? Try
 them and test !

Still hesitate ? Myk, was it thou who lament-
 edst
 Thy five wits clean failed thee to render
 aright
A poem read once and no more ? — who re-
 pentedst
 Vile pelf had induced thee to banish from
 sight
The characters none but our clerics indite ?

Take and keep !
 First Friend. Blessed Mary and all Saints
 about her !
 Second Friend. What imps deal so deftly, —
 five minutes suffice
To play thus the penman ?
 Third Friend. By Thomas the Doubter,
 Five minutes, no more !
 Fourth Friend. Out on arts that entice
Such scribes to do homage !
 Fifth Friend. Stay ! Once — and now
 twice —

Yea, a third time, my sharp eye completes the
 inspection
 Of line after line, the whole series, and
 finds
Each letter join each — not a fault for detec-
 tion !
 Such upstrokes, such downstrokes, such
 strokes of all kinds
In the criss-cross, all perfect !
 Sixth Friend. There 's nobody minds

His quill-craft with more of a conscience, o'er-
 scratches
 A sheepskin more nimbly and surely with
 ink,
Than Paul the Sub-Prior: here 's paper that
 matches
 His parchment with letter on letter, no link
Overleapt — underlost !
 Seventh Friend. No erasure, I think —

No blot, I am certain !
 Fust. Accept the new treasure !
 Sixth Friend. I remembered full half !
 Seventh Friend. But who other than I
(Bear witness, bystanders !) when he broke the
 measure
Repaired fault with "*fulmen*" ?
 Fust. Put bickerings by !
Here 's for thee — thee — and thee, too: at
 need a supply

 (*Distributing Proofs.*)

For Mayence, though seventy times seven
 should muster !
 How now ? All so feeble of faith that no
 face
Which fronts me but whitens — or yellows,
 were juster ?
Speak out lest I summon my Spirits !
 Omnes. Grace — grace !

Call none of thy — helpmates ! We 'll answer
 apace !

My paper — and mine — and mine also — they
 vary
 In nowise — agree in each tittle and jot !
Fust, how — why was this ?
 Fust. Shall such "*Cur*" miss a "*quare*" ?
Within, there ! Throw doors wide ! Be-
 hold who complot
To abolish the scribe's work — blur, blunder
 and blot !

 (*The doors open, and the Press is discovered in oper-
 ation.*)

Brave full-bodied birth of this brain that con-
 ceived thee
 In splendor and music, — sustained the slow
 drag
Of the days stretched to years dim with doubt,
 — yet believed thee,
 Had faith in thy first leap of life ! Pulse
 might flag —
— Mine fluttered how faintly ! — Arch-moment
 might lag

Its longest — I bided, made light of endurance,
 Held hard by the hope of an advent which —
 dreamed,
Is done now : night yields to the dawn's reas-
 surance :
 I have thee — I hold thee — my fancy that
 seemed,
My fact that proves palpable ! Ay, Sirs, I
 schemed

Completion that 's fact : see this Engine — be
 witness
 Yourselves of its working ! Nay, handle my
 Types !
Each block bears a Letter : in order and fitness
 I range them. Turn, Peter, the winch !
 See, it gripes
What 's under ! Let loose — draw ! In regu-
 lar stripes

Lies plain, at one pressure, your poem —
 touched, tinted,
 Turned out to perfection ! The sheet, late a
 blank,
Filled — ready for reading, — not written but
 PRINTED !
 Omniscient omnipotent God, thee I thank,
Thee ever, thee only ! — thy creature that
 shrank

From no task thou, Creator, imposedst !
 Creation
 Revealed me no object, from insect to Man,
But bore thy hand's impress : earth glowed
 with salvation :
 "Hast sinned ? Be thou saved, Fust ! Con-
 tinue my plan,
Who spake and earth was : with my word
 things began.

"As sound so went forth, to the sight be ex-
 tended

Word's mission henceforward !   The task I
  assign,
Embrace — thy allegiance to evil is ended !
Have cheer, soul impregnate with purpose !
  Combine
Soul and body, give birth to my concept —
  called thine !

"Far and wide, North and South, East and
    West, have dominion
  O'er thought, wingèd wonder, O Word !
    Traverse world
In sun-flash and sphere-song !   Each beat of
    thy pinion
Bursts night, beckons day : once Truth's ban-
    ner unfurled,
Where's Falsehood ?   Sun-smitten, to nothing-
    ness hurled ! "

More humbly — so, friends, did my fault find
    redemption.
  I sinned, soul-entoiled by the tether of sense :
My captor reigned master :   I plead no exemp-
    tion,
From Satan's award to his servant : defence
From the fiery and final assault would be —
    whence ?

By making — as man might — to truth restitu-
    tion !
  Truth is God : trample lies and lies' father,
    God's foe !
Fix fact fast :   truths change by an hour's
    revolution :
What deed's very doer, unaided, can show
How 't was done a year — month — week —
    day — minute ago ?

At best, he relates it — another reports it —
  A third — nay, a thousandth records it : and
    still
Narration, tradition, no step but distorts it,
  As down from truth's height it goes sliding
    until
At the low level lie-mark it stops — whence no
    skill

Of the scribe, intervening too tardily, rescues
  — Once fallen — lost fact from lie's fate
    there.   What scribe
— Eyes horny with poring, hands crippled with
    desk-use,
Brains fretted by fancies — the volatile tribe
That tease weary watchers — can boast that no
    bribe

Shuts eye and frees hand and remits brain
    from toiling ?
  Truth gained — can we stay, at whatever the
    stage,
Truth a-slide, — save her snow from its ulti-
    mate soiling
In mire, — by some process, stamp promptly
    on page
Fact spoiled by pen's plodding, make truth
    heritage

Not merely of clerics, but poured out, full
    measure,
  On clowns — every mortal endowed with a
    mind ?
Read, gentle and simple !   Let labor win leis-
    ure
At last to bid truth do all duty assigned,
Not pause at the noble but pass to the hind !

How bring to effect such swift sure simultane-
    ous
  Unlimited multiplication ?   How spread
By an arm-sweep a hand-throw — no helping
    extraneous —
Truth broadcast o'er Europe ?   " The gold-
    smith," I said,
" Graves limning on gold : why not letters on
    lead ? "

So, Tuscan artificer, grudge not thy pardon
  To me who played false, made a furtive
    descent,
Found the sly secret workshop, — thy genius
    kept guard on
Too slackly for once, — and surprised thee
    low-bent
O'er thy labor — some chalice thy tool would
    indent

With a certain free scroll-work framed round
    by a border
  Of foliage and fruitage : no scratching so fine,
No shading so shy but, in ordered disorder,
  Each flourish came clear, — unbewildered by
    shine,
On the gold, irretrievably right, lay each line.

How judge if thy hand worked thy will ?   By
    reviewing,
  Revising again and again, piece by piece,
Tool's performance, — this way, as I watched.
    'T was through glueing
A paper-like film-stuff — thin, smooth, void
    of crease,
On each cut of the graver : press hard ! at re-
    lease,

No mark on the plate but the paper showed
    double :
  His work might proceed : as he judged —
    space or speck
Up he filled, forth he flung — was relieved thus
    from trouble
Lest wrong — once — were right never more :
    what could check
Advancement, completion ?   Thus lay at my
    beck —

At my call — triumph likewise !   " For," cried
    I, " what hinders
  That graving turns Printing ?   Stamp one
    word — not one
But fifty such, phœnix-like, spring from death's
    cinders, —
Since death is word's doom, clerics hide from
    the sun

As some churl closets up this rare chalice."
  Go, run

Thy race now, Fust's child! High, O Printing,
    and holy
  Thy mission! These types, see, I chop and
    I change
Till the words, every letter, a pageful, not slowly
  Yet surely lies fixed: last of all, I arrange
A paper beneath, stamp it, loosen it!
  First Friend.   Strange!

Second Friend. How simple exceedingly!
Fust.   Bustle, my Schœffer!
Set type, — quick, Genesheim! Turn screw
    now!
  Third Friend.   Just that!
Fourth Friend. And no such vast miracle!
Fust.   " Plough with my heifer,
Ye find out my riddle," quoth Samson, and pat
He speaks to the purpose. Grapes squeezed in
    the vat

Yield to sight and to taste what is simple — a
    liquid
  Mere urchins may sip: but give time, let fer-
    ment —
You 've wine, manhood's master! Well, "*rec-
    tius si quid
Novistis im-per-ti-te !* " Wait the event,
Then weigh the result! But, whate'er Thy
    intent,

O Thou, the one force in the whole variation
  Of visible nature, — at work — do I doubt? —
From Thy first to our last, in perpetual crea-
    tion —
  A film hides us from Thee — 'twixt inside
    and out,
A film, on this earth where Thou bringest about

New marvels, new forms of the glorious, the
    gracious,
  We bow to, we bless for: no star bursts
    heaven's dome
But Thy finger impels it, no weed peeps auda-
    cious
  Earth's clay-floor from out, but Thy finger
    makes room
For one world's-want the more in Thy Cosmos :
    presume

Shall Man, Microcosmos, to claim the concep-
    tion
  Of grandeur, of beauty, in thought, word or
    deed?
I toiled, but Thy light on my dubiousest step
    shone :
  If I reach the glad goal, is it I who succeed
Who stumbled at starting tripped up by a reed,

Or Thou? Knowledge only and absolute, glory
  As utter be Thine who concedest a spark
Of Thy spheric perfection to earth's transitory
  Existences! Nothing that lives, but Thy
    mark
Gives law to — life's light: what is doomed to
    the dark?

Where 's ignorance? Answer, creation! What
    height,
  What depth has escaped Thy commandment
    — to Know?
What birth in the ore-bed but answers aright
  Thy sting at its heart which impels — bids
    " E'en so,
Not otherwise move or be motionless, — grow,

" Decline, disappear!" Is the plant in default
  How to bud, when to branch forth? The
    bird and the beast
— Do they doubt if their safety be found in
    assault
  Or escape? Worm or fly, of what atoms the
    least
But follows light's guidance, — will famish, not
    feast?

In such various degree, fly and worm, ore and
    plant,
  All know, none is witless: around each, a
    wall
Encloses the portion, or ample or scant,
  Of Knowledge: beyond which one hair's
    breadth, for all
Lies blank — not so much as a blackness — a pall

Some sense unimagined must penetrate : plain
  Is only old license to stand, walk or sit,
Move so far and so wide in the narrow domain
  Allotted each nature for life's use : past it
How immensity spreads does he guess? Not a
    whit.

Does he care? Just as little. Without? No,
    within
  Concerns him? he Knows. Man Ignores —
    thanks to Thee
Who madest him know, but — in knowing —
    begin
  To know still new vastness of knowledge
    must be
Outside him — to enter, to traverse, in fee

Have and hold! " Oh, Man's ignorance!" hear
    the fool whine!
  How were it, for better or worse, didst thou
    grunt
Contented with sapience — the lot of the swine
  Who knows he was born for just truffles to
    hunt? —
Monks' Paradise — " *Semper sint res uti sunt!* "

No, Man's the prerogative — knowledge once
    gained —
  To ignore, — find new knowledge to press for,
    to swerve
In pursuit of, no, not for a moment : attained —
  Why, onward through ignorance! Dare and
    deserve!
As still to its asymptote speedeth the curve,

So approximates Man — Thee, who, reachable
    not,
  Hast formed him to yearningly follow Thy
    whole
Sole and single omniscience!

               Such, friends, is my lot :
I am back with the world : one more step to
   the goal
Thanks for reaching I render — Fust's help to
   Man's soul !

Mere mechanical help ? So the hand gives a toss
   To the falcon, — aloft once, spread pinions
   and fly,
Beat air far and wide, up and down and across !
   My Press strains a-tremble : whose masterful
   eye
Will be first, in new regions, new truth to
   descry ?

Give chase, soul ! Be sure each new capture
   consigned
To my Types will go forth to the world, like
   God's bread
— Miraculous food not for body but mind,
   Truth's manna ! How say you ? Put case
   that, instead
Of old leasing and lies, we superiorly fed

These Heretics, Hussites . . .
   First Friend.   First answer my query !
If saved, art thou happy ?
   Fust.   I was and I am.
   First Friend. Thy visage confirms it : how
   comes, then, that — weary
And woe-begone late — was it show, was it
   sham ? —
We found thee sunk thiswise ?
   Second Friend.   — In need of the dram

From the flask which a provident neighbor
   might carry !
Fust. Ah, friends, the fresh triumph soon
   flickers, fast fades !
I hailed Word's dispersion : could heartleaps
   but tarry !
Through me does Print furnish Truth wings ?
   The same aids
Cause Falsehood to range just as widely. What
   raids

On a region undreamed of does Printing en‹
   able
Truth's foe to effect ! Printed leasing and lies
May speed to the world's farthest corner —
   gross fable
No less than pure fact — to impede, neutralize,
Abolish God's gift and Man's gain !
   First Friend.   Dost surmise

What struck me at first blush ? Our Beghards,
   Waldenses,
Jeronimites, Hussites — does one show his
   head,
Spout heresy now ? Not a priest in his senses
Deigns answer mere speech, but piles fagots
   instead,
Refines as by fire, and, him silenced, all 's said.

Whereas if in future I pen an opuscule
Defying retort, as of old when rash tongues
Were easy to tame, — straight some knave of
   the Huss-School
Prints answer forsooth ! Stop invisible lungs ?
The barrel of blasphemy broached once, who
   bungs ?

   Second Friend. Does my sermon, next Easter,
   meet fitting acceptance ?
Each captious disputative boy has his quirk
" *An cuique credendum sit ?* " Well, the Church
   kept " *ans* "
In order till Fust set his engine at work !
What trash will come flying from Jew, Moor,
   and Turk

When, goosequill, thy reign o'er the world is
   abolished !
   Goose — ominous name ! With a goose woe
   began :
Quoth Huss — which means " goose " in his
   idiom unpolished —
" Ye burn now a Goose : there succeeds me a
   Swan
Ye shall find quench your fire ! "
   Fust.   I foresee such a man.

ASOLANDO

TO MRS. ARTHUR BRONSON

To whom but you, dear Friend, should I dedicate verses — some few written, all of them supervised, in the comfort of your presence, and with yet another experience of the gracious hospitality now bestowed on me since so many a year, — adding a charm even to my residences at Venice, and leaving me little regret for the surprise and delight at my visits to Asolo in bygone days ?

I unite, you will see, the disconnected poems by a title-name popularly ascribed to the inventiveness of the ancient secretary of Queen Cornaro whose palace-tower still overlooks us : *Asolare* — " to disport in the open air, amuse one's self at random." The objection that such a word nowhere occurs in the works of the Cardinal is hardly important — Bembo was too thorough a purist to conserve in print a term which in talk he might possibly toy with : but the word is more likely derived from a Spanish source. I use it for

love of the place, and in requital of your pleasant assurance that an early poem of mine
first attracted you thither — where and elsewhere, at La Mura as Cà Alvisi, may all happi-
ness attend you !   Gratefully and affectionately yours,

ASOLO: *October* 15, 1889.   R. B.

THE greater part of *Asolando* was written in
1888–89, though in one instance at least an early
poem was included in the collection. The title
of the volume is explained in the dedication.
The book, by a strange coincidence, was pub-
lished on the day of Browning's death.

PROLOGUE

" THE Poet's age is sad : for why ?
   In youth, the natural world could show
No common object but his eye
   At once involved with alien glow —
His own soul's iris-bow.

" And now a flower is just a flower :
   Man, bird, beast are but beast, bird, man —
Simply themselves, uncinct by dower
   Of dyes which, when life's day began,
Round each in glory ran."

Friend, did you need an optic glass,
   Which were your choice ? A lens to drape
In ruby, emerald, chrysopras,
   Each object — or reveal its shape
Clear outlined, past escape,

The naked very thing ? — so clear
   That, when you had the chance to gaze,
You found its inmost self appear
   Through outer seeming — truth ablaze,
Not falsehood's fancy-haze ?

How many a year, my Asolo,
   Since — one step just from sea to land —
I found you, loved yet feared you so —
   For natural objects seemed to stand
Palpably fire-clothed ! No —

No mastery of mine o'er these !
   Terror with beauty, like the Bush
Burning but unconsumed. Bend knees,
   Drop eyes to earthward ! Language ? Tush !
Silence 't is awe decrees.

And now ? The lambent flame is — where ?
   Lost from the naked world : earth, sky,
Hill, vale, tree, flower, — Italia's rare
   O'er-running beauty crowds the eye —
But flame ? The Bush is bare.

Hill, vale, tree, flower — they stand distinct,
   Nature to know and name. What then ?
A Voice spoke thence which straight unlinked
   Fancy from fact : see, all 's in ken :
Has once my eyelid winked ?

No, for the purged ear apprehends
   Earth's import, not the eye late dazed .
The Voice said, " Call my works thy friends !
   At Nature dost thou shrink amazed ?
God is it who transcends."

ASOLO: *September* 6, 1889.

ROSNY

WOE, he went galloping into the war,
   Clara, Clara !
Let us two dream : shall he 'scape with a
   sear ?
Scarcely disfigurement, rather a grace
Making for manhood which nowise we mar :
   See, while I kiss it, the flush on his face —
   Rosny, Rosny !

Light does he laugh : " With your love in my
   soul " —
   (Clara, Clara !)
" How could I other than — sound, safe, and
   whole —
Cleave who opposed me asunder, yet stand
Scatheless beside you, as, touching love's goal,
   Who won the race kneels, craves reward at
   your hand —
   Rosny, Rosny ? "

Ay, but if certain who envied should see !
   Clara, Clara,
Certain who simper : " The hero for me
   Hardly of life were so chary as miss
Death — death and fame — that 's love's guer-
   don when She
Boasts, proud bereaved one, her choice fell on
   this
   Rosny, Rosny ! "

So, — go on dreaming, — he lies mid a heap
   (Clara, Clara,)
Of the slain by his hand : what is death but a
   sleep ?
Dead, with my portrait displayed on his
   breast :
Love wrought his undoing : " No prudence
   could keep
The love-maddened wretch from his fate."
   That is best.
   Rosny, Rosny !

DUBIETY

I WILL be happy if but for once :
   Only help me, Autumn weather,
Me and my cares to screen, ensconce
   In luxury's sofa-lap of leather !

Sleep ? Nay, comfort — with just a cloud
   Suffusing day too clear and bright :
Eve's essence, the single drop allowed
   To sully, like milk, Noon's water-white.

Let gauziness shade, not shroud, — adjust,
　Dim and not deaden, — somehow sheathe
Aught sharp in the rough world's busy thrust,
　If it reach me through dreaming's vapor-
　　wreath.

Be life so, all things ever the same !
　For, what has disarmed the world? Out-
　　side,
Quiet and peace : inside, nor blame
　Nor want, nor wish whate'er betide.

What is it like that has happened before ?
　A dream ?　No dream, more real by much.
A vision ?　But fanciful days of yore
　Brought many : mere musing seems not
　　such.

Perhaps but a memory, after all !
　— Of what came once when a woman leant
To feel for my brow where her kiss might
　　fall.
Truth ever, truth only the excellent !

NOW

Out of your whole life give but a moment !
All of your life that has gone before,
All to come after it, — so you ignore,
So you make perfect the present, — condense,
In a rapture of rage, for perfection's endow-
　ment,
Thought and feeling and soul and sense —
Merged in a moment which gives me at
　last
You around me for once, you beneath me,
　above me —
Me — sure that despite of time future, time
　past, —
This tick of our life-time's one moment you
　love me !
How long such suspension may linger ? Ah,
　Sweet —
The moment eternal — just that and no more —
When ecstasy's utmost we clutch at the core
While cheeks burn, arms open, eyes shut and
　lips meet !

HUMILITY

What girl but, having gathered flowers,
Stript the beds and spoilt the bowers,
From the lapful light she carries
Drops a careless bud ? — nor tarries
To regain the waif and stray :
"Store enough for home " — she 'll say.

So say I too : give your lover
Heaps of loving — under, over,
Whelm him — make the one the wealthy !
Am I all so poor who — stealthy
Work it was ! — picked up what fell :
Not the worst bud — who can tell ?

POETICS

"So say the foolish ! "　Say the foolish so,
　Love ?
"Flower she is, my rose " — or else, " My
　very swan is she " —
Or perhaps, " Yon maid-moon, blessing earth
　below, Love,
That art thou ! " — to them, belike : no such
　vain words from me.

" Hush, rose, blush ! no balm like breath," I
　chide it :
" Bend thy neck its best, swan, — hers the
　whiter curve ! "
Be the moon the moon : my Love I place be-
　side it :
What is she ?　Her human self, — no lower
　word will serve.

SUMMUM BONUM

All the breath and the bloom of the year in
　the bag of one bee :
All the wonder and wealth of the mine in the
　heart of one gem :
In the core of one pearl all the shade and the
　shine of the sea :
Breath and bloom, shade and shine, — won-
　der, wealth, and — how far above them —
　　Truth, that 's brighter than gem,
　　Trust, that 's purer than pearl, —
Brightest truth, purest trust in the universe —
　all were for me
In the kiss of one girl.

A PEARL, A GIRL

A simple ring with a single stone,
　To the vulgar eye no stone of price :
Whisper the right word, that alone —
　Forth starts a sprite, like fire from ice,
And lo, you are lord (says an Eastern scroll)
　Of heaven and earth, lord whole and sole
　　Through the power in a pearl.

A woman ('t is I this time that say)
　With little the world counts worthy praise
Utter the true word — out and away
　Escapes her soul : I am wrapt in blaze,
Creation's lord, of heaven and earth
Lord whole and sole — by a minute's birth —
　Through the love in a girl !

SPECULATIVE

Others may need new life in Heaven —
　Man, Nature, Art — made new, assume !
Man with new mind old sense to leaven,
　Nature, — new light to clear old gloom,
Art that breaks bounds, gets soaring-room.

I shall pray : " Fugitive as precious —
　Minutes which passed, — return, remain !

Let earth's old life once more enmesh us,
  You with old pleasure, me — old pain,
So we but meet nor part again ! "

WHITE WITCHCRAFT

When a boy Browning had a humble friend
in the person of a toad. "He visited it daily
where it burrowed under a white rosetree, an-
nouncing himself by a pinch of gravel dropped
into its hole ; and the creature would crawl
forth, allow its head to be gently tickled, and
reward the act with a loving glance of its soft
full eyes."   MRS. ORR.

IF you and I could change to beasts, what
      beast should either be ?
Shall you and I play Jove for once ?   Turn fox
  then, I decree !
Shy wild sweet stealer of the grapes !   Now do
  your worst on me !

And thus you think to spite your friend —
    turned loathsome ?   What, a toad ?
So, all men shrink and shun me !   Dear men,
    pursue your road !
Leave but my crevice in the stone, a reptile's fit
    abode !

Now say your worst, Canidia !   "He 's loath-
    some, I allow :
There may or may not lurk a pearl beneath his
    puckered brow :
But see his eyes that follow mine — love lasts
    there, anyhow."

BAD DREAMS

I

LAST night I saw you in my sleep :
  And how your charm of face was changed !
I asked, "Some love, some faith you keep ?"
  You answered, "Faith gone, love estranged."

Whereat I woke — a twofold bliss :
  Waking was one, but next there came
This other : "Though I felt, for this,
  My heart break, I loved on the same."

BAD DREAMS

II

You in the flesh and here —
  Your very self !   Now, wait !
One word !   May I hope or fear ?
  Must I speak in love or hate ?
Stay while I ruminate !

The fact and each circumstance
  Dare you disown ?   Not you !
That vast dome, that huge dance,
  And the gloom which overgrew
A — possibly festive crew !

For why should men dance at all —
  Why women — a crowd of both —
Unless they are gay ?   Strange ball -
  Hands and feet plighting troth,
Yet partners enforced and loth !

Of who danced there, no shape
  Did I recognize : thwart, perverse,
Each grasped each, past escape
  In a whirl or weary or worse :
Man's sneer met woman's curse,

While he and she toiled as if
  Their guardian set galley-slaves
To supple chained limbs grown stiff :
  Unmanacled trulls and knaves —
The lash for who misbehaves !

And a gloom was, all the while,
  Deeper and deeper yet
O'ergrowing the rank and file
  Of that army of haters — set
To mimic love's fever-fret.

By the wall-side close I crept,
  Avoiding the livid maze,
And, safely so far, outstepped
  On a chamber — a chapel, says
My memory or betrays —

Closet-like, kept aloof
  From unseemly witnessing
What sport made floor and roof
  Of the Devil's palace ring
While his Damned amused their king.

Ay, for a low lamp burned,
  And a silence lay about
What I, in the midst, discerned
  Though dimly till, past doubt,
'T was a sort of throne stood out —

High seat with steps, at least :
  And the topmost step was filled
By — whom ?   What vestured priest ?
  A stranger to me, — his guild,
His cult, unreconciled

To my knowledge how guild and cult
  Are clothed in this world of ours :
I pondered, but no result
  Came to — unless that Giaours
So worship the Lower Powers.

When suddenly who entered ?
  Who knelt — did you guess I saw ?
Who — raising that face were centred
  Allegiance to love and law
So lately — off-casting awe,

Down-treading reserve, away
  Thrusting respect . . . but mine
Stands firm — firm still shall stay !
  Ask Satan ! for I decline
To tell — what I saw, in fine !

Yet here in the flesh you come —
  Your same self, form and face, —

In the eyes, mirth still at home !
  On the lips, that commonplace
Perfection of honest grace !

Yet your errand is — needs must be —
  To palliate — well, explain,
Expurgate in some degree
  Your soul of its ugly stain.
Oh, you — the good in grain —

How was it your white took tinge ?
  " A mere dream " — never object !
Sleep leaves a door on hinge
  Whence soul, ere our flesh suspect,
Is off and away: detect

Her vagaries when loose, who can !
  Be she pranksome, be she prude,
Disguise with the day began :
  With the night — ah, what ensued
From draughts of a drink hell-brewed ?

Then She : " What a queer wild dream !
  And perhaps the best fun is —
Myself had its fellow — I seem
  Scarce awake from yet. 'T was this —
Shall I tell you ? First, a kiss !

" For the fault was just your own, —
  'T is myself expect apology :
You warned me to let alone
  (Since our studies were mere philology)
That ticklish (you said) Anthology.

" So I dreamed that I passed *exam*
  Till a question posed me sore :
' Who translated this epigram
  By — an author we best ignore ? '
And I answered, ' Hannah More ' ¡ "

BAD DREAMS

III

THIS was my dream : I saw a Forest
  Old as the earth, no track nor trace
Of unmade man. Thou, Soul, explorest —
  Though in a trembling rapture — space
Immeasurable ! Shrubs, turned trees,
Trees that touch heaven, support its freize
Studded with sun and moon and star :
While — oh, the enormous growths that bar
Mine eye from penetrating past
  Their tangled twine where lurks — nay, lives
Royally lone, some brute-type cast
  I' the rough, time cancels, man forgives.

On, Soul ! I saw a lucid City
  Of architectural device
Every way perfect. Pause for pity,
  Lightning ! nor leave a cicatrice
On those bright marbles, dome and spire,
Structures palatial, — streets which mire
Dares not defile, paved all too fine
For human footstep's smirch, not thine —
Proud solitary traverser,
  My Soul, of silent lengths of way —
With what ecstatic dread, aver,
  Lest life start sanctioned by thy stay !

Ah, but the last sight was the hideous !
  A City, yes, — a Forest, true, —
But each devouring each. Perfidious
  Snake-plants had strangled what I knew
Was a pavilion once : each oak
Held on his horns some spoil he broke
By surreptitiously beneath
Upthrusting : pavements, as with teeth,
Griped huge weed widening crack and split
  In squares and circles stone-work erst.
Oh, Nature — good ! Oh, Art — no whit
Less worthy ! Both in one — accurst !

BAD DREAMS

IV

IT happened thus : my slab, though new,
  Was getting weather-stained, — beside,
Herbage, balm, peppermint o'ergrew
Letter and letter : till you tried
Somewhat, the Name was scarce descried.

That strong stern man my lover came :
  — Was he my lover ? Call him, pray,
My life's cold critic bent on blame
  Of all poor I could do or say
To make me worth his love one day —

One far day when, by diligent
  And dutiful amending faults,
Foibles, all weaknesses which went
  To challenge and excuse assaults
Of culture wronged by taste that halts —

Discrepancies should mar no plan
  Symmetric of the qualities
Claiming respect from — say — a man
  That's strong and stern. " Once more he pries
Into me with those critic eyes ! "

No question ! so — " Conclude, condemn
  Each failure my poor self avows !
Leave to its fate all you contemn !
  There 's Solomon's selected spouse :
Earth needs must hold such maids — choose
  them ! "

Why, he was weeping ! Surely gone
  Sternness and strength : with eyes to ground.
And voice a broken monotone —
  " Only be as you were ! Abound
In foibles, faults, — laugh, robed and crowned.

" As Folly's veriest queen, — care I
  One feather-fluff ? Look pity, Love,
On prostrate me — your foot shall try
  This forehead's use — mount thence above,
And reach what Heaven you dignify ! "

Now, what could bring such change about ?
  The thought perplexed : till, following
His gaze upon the ground, — why, out
  Came all the secret ! So, a thing
Thus simple has deposed my king !

For, spite of weeds that strove to spoil
  Plain reading on the lettered slab,

My name was clear enough — no soil
  Effaced the date when one chance stab
Of scorn . . . if only ghosts might blab!

INAPPREHENSIVENESS

WE two stood simply friend-like side by side,
Viewing a twilight country far and wide,
Till she at length broke silence. "How it towers
Yonder, the ruin o'er this vale of ours!
The West's faint flare behind it so relieves
Its rugged outline — sight perhaps deceives,
Or I could almost fancy that I see
A branch wave plain — belike some wind-sown
  tree
Chance-rooted where a missing turret was.
What would I give for the perspective glass
At home, to make out if 't is really so!
Has Ruskin noticed here at Asolo
That certain weed-growths on the ravaged wall
Seem" . . . something that I could not say at all,
My thought being rather — as absorbed she
  sent
Look onward after look from eyes distent
With longing to reach Heaven's gate left ajar —
"Oh, fancies that might be, oh, facts that are!
What of a wilding? By you stands, and may
So stand unnoticed till the Judgment Day,
One who, if once aware that your regard
Claimed what his heart holds, — woke, as from
  its sward
The flower, the dormant passion, so to speak —
Then what a rush of life would startling wreak
Revenge on your inapprehensive stare
While, from the ruin and the West's faint flare,
You let your eyes meet mine, touch what you
  term
Quietude — that 's an universe in germ —
The dormant passion needing but a look
To burst into immense life!"
                              "No, the book
Which noticed how the wall-growths wave,"
  said she,
"Was not by Ruskin."
                      I said, "Vernon Lee."

WHICH?

So, the three Court-ladies began
  Their trial of who judged best
In esteeming the love of a man:
Who preferred with most reason was thereby
  confessed
Boy-Cupid's exemplary catcher and cager;
An Abbé crossed legs to decide on the wager.

First the Duchesse: "Mine for me —
  Who were it but God's for Him,
And the King's for — who but he?
Both faithful and loyal, one grace more shall
  brim
His cup with perfection: a lady's true lover,
He holds — save his God and his king — none
  above her."

"I require" — outspoke the Marquise —
  "Pure thoughts, ay, but also fine deeds:

Play the paladin must he, to please
My whim, and — to prove my knight's service
  exceeds
Your saint's and your loyalist's praying and
  kneeling —
Show wounds, each wide mouth to my mercy
  appealing."

  Then the Comtesse: "My choice be a
    wretch,
    Mere losel in body and soul,
  Thrice accurst! What care I, so he stretch
Arms to me his sole savior, love's ultimate
  goal,
Out of earth and men's noise — names of 'in-
  fidel,' 'traitor,'
Cast up at him? Crown me, crown's adjudi-
  cator!"

  And the Abbé uncrossed his legs,
    Took snuff, a reflective pinch,
  Broke silence: "The question begs
Much pondering ere I pronounce. Shall I
  flinch?
The love which to one and one only has refer-
  ence
Seems terribly like what perhaps gains God's
  preference."

THE CARDINAL AND THE DOG

This poem was written in May, 1842, at the
same time as the *Pied Piper*, both having been
written at the request of Macready's little son,
who was confined to the house by illness and
wanted Browning to write him some poems for
which he could make pictures.

CRESCENZIO, the Pope's Legate at the High
    Council, Trent,
— Year Fifteen hundred twenty-two, March
    Twenty-five — intent
On writing letters to the Pope till late into the
    night,
Rose, weary, to refresh himself, and saw a
    monstrous sight:
(I give mine Author's very words: he penned,
    I reindite.)

A black Dog of vast bigness, eyes flaming, ears
    that hung
Down to the very ground almost, into the
    chamber sprung
And made directly for him, and laid himself
    right under
The table where Crescenzio wrote — who called
    in fear and wonder
His servants in the ante-room, commanded
    every one
To look for and find out the beast: but, look-
    ing, they found none.

The Cardinal fell melancholy, then sick, soon
    after died:
And at Verona, as he lay on his death-bed, he
    cried

Aloud to drive away the Dog that leapt on his
  bedside.
Heaven keep us Protestants from harm : the
  rest . . . no ill betide !

THE POPE AND THE NET

WHAT, he on whom our voices unanimously ran,
Made Pope at our last Conclave ?   Full low his
  life began :
His father earned the daily bread as just a
  fisherman.

So much the more his boy minds book, gives
  proof of mother-wit,
Becomes first Deacon, and then Priest, then
  Bishop : see him sit
No less than Cardinal erelong, while no one
  cries " Unfit ! "

But some one smirks, some other smiles, jogs
  elbow and nods head :
Each winks at each : " I'-faith, a rise ! Saint
  Peter's net, instead
Of sword and keys, is come in vogue ! " You
  think he blushes red ?

Not he, of humble holy heart !   " Unworthy
  me ! " he sighs :
" From fisher's drudge to Church's prince — it
  is indeed a rise : .
So, here 's my way to keep the fact forever in
  my eyes ! "

And straightway in his palace-hall, where
  commonly is set
Some coat-of-arms, some portraiture ancestral,
  lo, we met
His mean estate's reminder in his fisher-father's
  net !

Which step conciliates all and some, stops cavil
  in a trice :
" The humble holy heart that holds of new-
  born pride no spice !
He 's just the saint to choose for Pope ! "
  Each adds, " 'T is my advice."

So, Pope he was : and when we flocked — its
  sacred slipper on —
To kiss his foot, we lifted eyes, alack, the thing
  was gone —
That guarantee of lowlihead, — eclipsed that
  star which shone !

Each eyed his fellow, one and all kept silence.
  I cried, " Pish !
I 'll make me spokesman for the rest, express
  the common wish.
Why, Father, is the net removed ? " " Son, it
  hath caught the fish."

THE BEAN-FEAST

HE was the man — Pope Sixtus, that Fifth,
  that swineherd's son :

He knew the right thing, did it, and thanked
  God when 't was done :
But of all he had to thank for, my fancy some-
  how leans
To thinking, what most moved him was a cer-
  tain meal on beans.

For one day, as his wont was, in just enough
  disguise
As he went exploring wickedness, — to see with
  his own eyes
If law had due observance in the city's entrail
  dark
As well as where, i' the open, crime stood an
  obvious mark, —

He chanced, in a blind alley, on a tumble-down
  once house
Now hovel, vilest structure in Rome the ruinous :
And, as his tact impelled him, Sixtus adven-
  tured bold,
To learn how lowliest subjects bore hunger,
  toil, and cold.

There sat they at high-supper — man and wife,
  lad and lass,
Poor as you please, but cleanly all and care-
  free : pain that was
— Forgotten, pain as sure to be let bide aloof
  its time, —
Mightily munched the brave ones — what
  mattered gloom or grime ?

Said Sixtus, " Feast, my children ! who works
  hard needs eat well.
I 'm just a supervisor, would hear what you
  can tell.
Do any wrongs want righting ? The Father
  tries his best,
But, since he 's only mortal, sends such as I to
  test
The truth of all that 's told him — how folk
  like you may fare :
Come ! — only don't stop eating — when mouth
  has words to spare —

" You " — smiled he — " play the spokesman,
  bell-wether of the flock !
Are times good, masters gentle ? Your griev-
  ances unlock !
How of your work and wages ? — pleasures, if
  such may be —
Pains, as such are for certain." Thus smiling
  questioned he.

But somehow, spite of smiling, awe stole upon
  the group —
An inexpressible surmise : why should a priest
  thus stoop —
Pry into what concerned folk ? Each visage
  fell. Aware,
Cries Sixtus interposing : " Nay, children, have
  no care !

" Fear nothing ! Who employs me requires
  the plain truth. Pelf
Beguiles who should inform me : so, I inform
  myself.

See!" And he drew his hood back, let the
    close vesture ope,
Showed face, and where on tippet the cross
    lay: 't was the Pope.

Imagine the joyful wonder! "How shall the
    like of us —
Poor souls — requite such blessing of our rude
    bean-feast?" "Thus —
Thus amply!" laughed Pope Sixtus. "I early
    rise, sleep late:
Who works may eat: they tempt me, your
    beans there: spare a plate!"

Down sat he on the door-step: 't was they this
    time said grace:
He ate up the last mouthful, wiped lips, and
    then, with face
Turned heavenward, broke forth thankful:
    "Not now, that earth obeys
Thy word in mine, that through me the peoples
    know Thy ways —

"But that Thy care extendeth to Nature's
    homely wants,
And, while man's mind is strengthened, Thy
    goodness nowise scants
Man's body of its comfort, — that I whom kings
    and queens
Crouch to, pick crumbs from off my table,
    relish beans!
The thunders I but seem to launch, there plain
    Thy hand all see:
That I have appetite, digest, and thrive — that
    boon 's for me."

MUCKLE-MOUTH MEG

FROWNED the Laird on the Lord: "So, red-
    handed I catch thee?
Death-doomed by our Law of the Border!
We 've a gallows outside and a chiel to dispatch
    thee:
Who trespasses — hangs: all 's in order."

He met frown with smile, did the young English
    gallant:
    Then the Laird's dame: "Nay, Husband, I
    beg!
He 's comely: be merciful! Grace for the
    callant
    — If he marries our Muckle-mouth Meg!

"No mile-wide-mouthed monster of yours do I
    marry:
    Grant rather the gallows!" laughed he.
"Foul fare kith and kin of you — why do you
    tarry?"
    "To tame your fierce temper!" quoth she.

"Shove him quick in the Hole, shut him fast
    for a week:
    Cold, darkness, and hunger work wonders:
Who lion-like roars now, mouse-fashion will
    squeak,
And 'it rains' soon succeed to 'it thun-
    ders.'"

A week did he bide in the cold and the dark
    — Not hunger: for duly at morning
In flitted a lass, and a voice like a lark
    Chirped, "Muckle-mouth Meg still ye 're
    scorning?

"Go hang, but here 's parritch to hearten ye
    first!"
    "Did Meg's muckle-mouth boast within some
Such music as yours, mine should match it or
    burst:
    No frog-jaws! So tell folk, my Winsome!"

Soon week came to end, and, from Hole's door
    set wide,
    Out he marched, and there waited the lassie:
"Yon gallows, or Muckle-mouth Meg for a
    bride!
    Consider! Sky 's blue and turf 's grassy:

"Life 's sweet: shall I say ye wed Muckle-
    mouth Meg?"
    "Not I," quoth the stout heart: "too eerie
The mouth that can swallow a bubblyjock's
    egg;
    Shall I let it munch mine? Never, Dearie!

"Not Muckle-mouth Meg? Wow, the obstinate
    man!
    Perhaps he would rather wed me!"
"Ay, would he — with just for a dowry your
    can!"
    "I 'm Muckle-mouth Meg," chirruped she.

"Then so — so — so — so — " as he kissed her
    apace —
    "Will I widen thee out till thou turnest
From Margaret Minnikin - mou', by God's
    grace,
    To Muckle-mouth Meg in good earnest!"

ARCADES AMBO

A. You blame me that I ran away?
    Why, Sir, the enemy advanced:
    Balls flew about, and — who can say
    But one, if I stood firm, had glanced
    In my direction? Cowardice?
    I only know we don't live twice,
    Therefore — shun death, is my advice.

B. Shun death at all risks? Well, at some?
    True, I myself, Sir, though I scold
    The cowardly, by no means come
    Under reproof as overbold
    — I, who would have no end of brutes
    Cut up alive to guess what suits
    My case and saves my toe from shoots.

THE LADY AND THE PAINTER

She. YET womanhood you reverence,
        So you profess!
He.   With heart and soul
She. Of which fact this is evidence!
        To help Art-study, — for some dole

Of certain wretched shillings, — you
Induce a woman — virgin too —
To strip and stand stark-naked ?

He.   True.
She. Nor feel you so degrade her ?
He.   What
   — (Excuse the interruption) — clings
Half-savage-like around your hat ?
She.   Ah, do they please you ? Wild-bird-
      wings !
Next season, — Paris-prints assert, —
We must go feathered to the skirt :
My modiste keeps on the alert.

Owls, hawks, jays — swallows most ap-
     prove.
He.   Dare I speak plainly ?
She.   Oh, I trust !
He. Then, Lady Blanche, it less would move
   In heart and soul of me disgust
Did you strip off those spoils you wear,
And stand — for thanks, not shillings —
     bare
To help Art like my Model there.
She well knew what absolved her —
     praise
In me for God's surpassing good,
Who granted to my reverent gaze
A type of purest womanhood.
You — clothed with murder of his best
Of harmless beings — stand the test !
What is it *you* know ?
She.   That you jest !

PONTE DELL' ANGELO, VENICE

STOP rowing ! This one of our bye-canals
O'er a certain bridge you have to cross
That 's named, " Of the Angel : " listen why !
The name " Of the Devil " too much appalls
Venetian acquaintance, so — his the loss,
While the gain goes . . . look on high !

An angel visibly guards yon house :
Above each scutcheon — a pair — stands he,
Enfolds them with droop of either wing :
The family's fortune were perilous
Did he thence depart — you will soon agree,
If I hitch into verse the thing.

For, once on a time, this house belonged
To a lawyer of note, with law and to spare,
But also with overmuch lust of gain :
In the matter of law you were nowise wronged,
But alas for the lucre ! He picked you bare
To the bone. Did folk complain ?

" I exact," growled he, " work's rightful due :
'T is folk seek me, not I seek them.
Advice at its price ! They succeed or fail,
Get law in each case — and a lesson too :
Keep clear of the Courts — is advice *ad rem :*
They 'll remember, I 'll be bail ! "

So, he pocketed fee without a qualm.
What reason for squeamishness ? Labor done,
To play he betook him with lightened heart,

Ate, drank, and made merry with song or
    psalm,
Since the yoke of the Church is an easy one —
Fits neck nor causes smart.

Brief : never was such an extortionate
Rascal — the word has escaped my teeth !
And yet — (all 's down in a book no ass
Indited, believe me !) — this reprobate
Was punctual at prayer-time : gold lurked be-
    neath
Alloy of the rankest brass.

For, play the extortioner as he might,
Fleece folk each day and all day long,
There was this redeeming circumstance :
He never lay down to sleep at night
But he put up a prayer first, brief yet strong,
" Our Lady avert mischance ! "

Now it happened at close of a fructuous week
" I must ask," quoth he, " some Saint to dine .
I want that widow well out of my ears
With her ailing and wailing. Who bade her
    seek
Redress at my hands ? ' She was wronged !'
    Folk whine
If to Law wrong right appears.

" Matteo da Bascio — he 's my man !
No less than Chief of the Capucins :
His presence will surely suffumigate
My house — fools think lies under a ban
If somebody loses what somebody wins.
Hark, there he knocks at the grate !

" Come in, thou blessed of Mother Church !
I go and prepare — to bid, that is,
My trusty and diligent servitor
Get all things in readiness. Vain the search
Through Venice for one to compare with this
My model of ministrants : for —

" For — once again, nay, three times over,
My helpmate 's an ape ! so intelligent,
I train him to drudge at household work :
He toils and he moils, I live in clover :
Oh, you shall see ! There 's a goodly scent —
From his cooking, or I 'm a Turk !

" Scarce need to descend and supervise :
I 'll do it, however : wait here awhile ! "
So, down to the kitchen gayly scuttles
Our host, nor notes the alarmed surmise
Of the holy man. " O depth of guile !
He blindly guzzles and guttles,

" While — who is it dresses the food and pours
The liquor ? Some fiend — I make no doubt —
In likeness of — which of the loathly brutes ?
An ape ! Where hides he ? No bull that gores,
No bear that hugs — 't is the mock and flout
Of an ape, fiend's face that suits.

" So — out with thee, creature, wherever thou
    hidest !
I charge thee, by virtue of . . . right do I
    judge !

There skulks he perdue, crouching under the
    bed.
Well done! What, forsooth, in beast's shape
    thou confidest?
I know and would name thee but that I be-
    grudge
Breath spent on such carrion. Instead —

"I adjure thee by ——" "Stay!" laughed
    the portent that rose
From floor up to ceiling: "No need to adjure!
See Satan in person, late ape by command
Of Him thou adjurest in vain. A saint's nose
Scents brimstone though incense be burned for
    a lure.
Yet, hence! for I'm safe, understand!

"'T is my charge to convey to fit punishment's
    place
This lawyer, my liegeman, for cruelty wrought
On his clients, the widow and orphan, poor souls
He has plagued by exactions which proved
    law's disgrace,
Made equity void and to nothingness brought
God's pity. Fiends, on with fresh coals!"

"Stay!" nowise confounded, withstands Hell
    its match:
"How comes it, were truth in this story of
    thine,
God's punishment suffered a minute's delay?
Weeks, months have elapsed since thou squat-
    tedst at watch
For a spring on thy victim: what caused thee
    decline
Advantage till challenged to-day?"

"That challenge I meet with contempt," quoth
    the fiend.
"Thus much I acknowledge: the man's
    armed in mail:
I wait till a joint's loose, then quick ply my
    claws.
Thy friend's one good custom — he knows not
    — has screened
His flesh hitherto from what else would assail:
At 'Save me, Madonna!' I pause.

"That prayer did the losel but once pretermit,
My pounce were upon him. I keep me attent:
He's in safety but till he's caught napping.
    Enough!"
"Ay, enough!" smiles the Saint — "for the
    biter is bit,
The spy caught in somnolence. Vanish! I'm
    sent
To smooth up what fiends do in rough."

"I vanish? Through wall or through roof?"
    the ripost
Grinned gayly. "My orders were — 'Leave
    not unharmed
The abode of this lawyer! Do damage to prove
'T was for something thou quittedst the land
    of the lost —
To add to their number this unit!' Though
    charmed
From descent there, on earth that 's above

"I may haply amerce him." "So do, and be-
    gone,
I command thee! For, look! Though there 's
    doorway behind
And window before thee, go straight through
    the wall,
Leave a breach in the brickwork, a gap in the
    stone
For who passes to stare at!" "Spare speech!
    I'm resigned:
Here goes!" roared the goblin, as all —

Wide bat-wings, spread arms and legs, tail out
    a-stream,
Crash obstacles went, right and left, as he
    soared
Or else sank, was clean gone through the hole
    anyhow.
The Saint returned thanks: then a satisfied
    gleam
On the bald polished pate showed that triumph
    was scored.
"To dinner with appetite now!"

Down he trips. "In good time!" smirks the
    host. "Didst thou scent
Rich savor of roast meat? Where hides he,
    my ape?
Look alive, be alert! He's away to wash
    plates.
Sit down, Saint! What 's here? Dost exam-
    ine a rent
In the napkin thou twistest and twirlest?
    Agape . . .
Ha, blood is it drips nor abates

"From thy wringing a cloth, late was laven-
    dered fair?
What means such a marvel?" "Just this does
    it mean:
I convince and convict thee of sin!" answers
    straight
The Saint, wringing on, wringing ever — oh,
    rare! —
Blood — blood from a napery snow not more
    clean.
"A miracle shows thee thy state!

"See'— blood thy extortions have wrung from
    the flesh
Of thy clients who, sheep-like, arrived to be
    shorn,
And left thee — or fleeced to the quick or so
    flayed
That, behold, their blood gurgles and grumbles
    afresh
To accuse thee! Ay, down on thy knees, get
    up sworn
To restore! Restitution once made,

"Sin no more! Dost thou promise? Absolved,
    then, arise!
Upstairs follow me! Art amazed at yon
    breach?
Who battered and shattered and scattered, es-
    cape
From thy purlieus obtaining? That Father of
    Lies

Thou wast wont to extol for his feats, all and
each
The Devil 's disguised as thine ape ! ''

Be sure that our lawyer was torn by remorse,
Shed tears in a flood, vowed and swore so to
alter
His ways that how else could our Saint but de-
clare
He was cleansed of past sin ?   '' For sin future
— fare worse
Thou undoubtedly wilt,'' warned the Saint,
'' shouldst thou falter
One whit ! ''   '' Oh, for that have no care !

'' I am firm in my purposed amendment. But,
prithee,
Must ever affront and affright me yon gap ?
Who made it for exit may find it of use
For entrance as easy. If, down in his smithy
He forges me fetters — when heated, mayhap,
He 'll up with an armful ! Broke loose —

'' How bar him out henceforth ? ''   '' Judi-
ciously urged ! ''
Was the good man's reply. '' How to balk
him is plain.
There 's nothing the Devil objects to so much,
So speedily flies from, as one of those purged
Of his presence, the angels who erst formed his
train —
His, their emperor.   Choose one of such !

'' Get fashioned his likeness and set him on
high
At back of the breach thus adroitly filled up :
Display him as guard of two scutcheons, thy
arms :
I warrant no devil attempts to get by
And disturb thee so guarded. Eat, drink, dine,
and sup,
In thy rectitude, safe from alarms ! ''

So said and so done. See, the angel has place
Where the Devil has passage ! All 's down in
a book.
Gainsay me ? Consult it !   Still faithless ?
Trust *me* ?
Trust Father Boverio who gave me the case
In his Annals — gets of it, by hook or by crook,
Two confirmative witnesses : three

Are surely enough to establish an act :
And thereby we learn — would we ascertain
truth —
To trust wise tradition which took, at the time,
Note that served till slow history ventured on
fact,
Though folk have their fling at tradition for-
sooth !
Row, boys, fore and aft, rhyme and chime !

BEATRICE SIGNORINI

THIS strange thing happened to a painter once :
Viterbo boasts the man among her sons
Of note, I seem to think : his ready tool

Picked up its precepts in Cortona's school —
That 's Pietro Berretini, whom they call
Cortona, these Italians : greatish-small,
Our painter was his pupil, by repute
His match if not his master absolute,
Though whether he spoiled fresco more or less,
And what 's its fortune, scarce repays your
guess.
Still, for one circumstance, I save his name
— Francesco Romanelli : do the same !
He went to Rome and painted : there he knew
A wonder of a woman painting too —
For she, at least, was no Cortona's drudge :
Witness that ardent fancy-shape — I judge
A semblance of her soul — she called, '' Desire ''
With starry front for guide, where sits the fire
She left to brighten Buonarroti's house.
If you see Florence, pay that piece your vows,
Though blockhead Baldinucci's mind, imbued
With monkish morals, bade folk '' Drape the
nude
And stop the scandal ! '' quoth the record prim
I borrow this of : hang his book and him !
At Rome, then, where these fated ones met
first,
The blossom of his life had hardly burst
While hers was blooming at full beauty's
stand :
No less Francesco — when half-ripe he scanned
Consummate Artemisia — grew one want
To have her his and make her ministrant
With every gift of body and of soul
To him. In vain. Her sphery self was whole —
Might only touch his orb at Art's sole point.
Suppose he could persuade her to enjoint
Her life — past, present, future — all in his
At Art's sole point by some explosive kiss
Of love through lips, would love's success de-
feat
Artistry's haunting curse — the Incomplete ?
Artists no doubt they both were, — what beside
Was she ? who long had felt heart, soul spread
wide
Her life out, knowing much and loving well,
On either side Art's narrow space where fell
Reflection from his own speck : but the germ
Of individual genius — what we term
The very self, the God-gift whence had grown
Heart's life and soul's life — how make that
his own ?
Vainly his Art, reflected, smiled in small
On Art's one facet of her ampler ball ;
The rest, touch-free, took in, gave back
heaven, earth,
All where he was not. Hope, well-nigh ere
birth
Came to Desire, died off all-unfulfilled.
'' What though in Art I stand the abler-
skilled,''
(So he conceited : mediocrity
Turns on itself the self-transforming eye)
'' If only Art were suing, mine would plead
To purpose : man — by nature I exceed
Woman the bounded : but how much beside
She boasts, would sue in turn and be denied !
Love her ? My own wife loves me in a sort
That suits us both : she takes the world's report
Of what my work is worth, and, for the rest,

Concedes that, while his consort keeps her
    nest,
The eagle soars a licensed vagrant, lives
A wide free life which she at least forgives —
Good Beatricé Signorini ! Well
And wisely did I choose her. But the spell
To subjugate this Artemisia — where ?
She passionless ? — she resolute to care
Nowise beyond the plain sufficiency
Of fact that she is she and I am I
— Acknowledged arbitrator for us both
In her life as in mine which she were loth
Even to learn the laws of ? No, and no,
Twenty times over ! Ay, it must be so :
I for myself, alas ! ''
                    Whereon, instead
Of the checked lover's-utterance — why, he said
— Leaning over her easel : '' Flesh is red ''
(Or some such just remark) — '' by no means
    white
As Guido's practice teaches : you are right.''
Then came the better impulse : '' What if
    pride
Were wisely trampled on, whate'er betide ?
If I grow hers, not mine — join lives, confuse
Bodies and spirits, gain her not but lose
Myself to Artemisia ? That were love !
Of two souls — one must bend, one rule above :
If I crouch under proudly, lord turned slave,
Were it not worthier both than if she gave
Herself — in treason to herself — to me ? ''

And, all the while, he felt it could not be.
Such love was true love : love that way who
    can !
Some one that's born half woman, not whole
    man :
For man, prescribed man better or man worse,
Why, whether microcosm or universe,
What law prevails alike through great and
    small,
The world and man — world's miniature we
    call ?
Male is the master. '' That way'' smiled and
    sighed
Our true male estimator — '' puts her pride
My wife in making me the outlet whence
She learns all Heaven allows : 't is my pretence
To paint : her lord should do what else but
    paint ?
Do I break brushes, cloister me turned saint ?
Then, best of all suits sanctity her spouse
Who acts for Heaven, allows and disallows
At pleasure, past appeal, the right, the wrong
In all things. That's my wife's way. But this
    strong
Confident Artemisia — an adept
In Art does she conceit herself ? ' Except
In just this instance,' tell her, ' no one draws
More rigidly observant of the laws
Of right design : yet here, — permit me hint, —
If the acromion had a deeper dint,
That shoulder were perfection.' What surprise
— Nay scorn, shoots black fire from those
    startled eyes !
She to be lessoned in design forsooth !
I'm doomed and done for, since I spoke the
    truth.

Make my own work the subject of dispute —
Fails it of just perfection absolute
Somewhere ? Those motors, flexors, — don't I
    know
Ser Santi, styled ' Tirititototo
The pencil-prig,' might blame them ? Yet my
    wife —
Were he and his nicknamer brought to life,
Tito and Titian, to pronounce again —
Ask her who knows more — I or the great
    Twain,
Our colorist and draughtsman !
                        '' I help her,
Not she helps me ; and neither shall demur
Because my portion is '' — he chose to think —
'' Quite other than a woman's : I may drink
At many waters, must repose by none —
Rather arise and fare forth, having done
Duty to one new excellence the more,
Abler thereby, though impotent before
So much was gained of knowledge. Best de-
    part,
From this last lady I have learned by heart ! ''

Thus he concluded of himself — resigned
To play the man and master : '' Man boasts
    mind :
Woman, man's sport calls mistress, to the same
Does body's suit and service. Would she claim
— My placid Beatricé-wife — pretence
Even to blame her lord if, going hence,
He wistfully regards one whom — did fate
Concede — he might accept queen, abdicate
Kingship because of ? — one of no meek sort
But masterful as he : man's match in short ?
Oh, there 's no secret I were best conceal !
Bicé shall know ; and should a stray tear steal
From out the blue eye, stain the rose cheek —
    bah !
A smile, a word's gay reassurance — ah,
With kissing interspersed, — shall make amends,
Turn pain to pleasure.''
                    '' What, in truth so ends
Abruptly, do you say, our intercourse ? ''
Next day, asked Artemisia : '' I 'll divorce
Husband and wife no longer. Go your ways,
Leave Rome ! Viterbo owns no equal, says
The by-word, for fair women : you, no doubt,
May boast a paragon all specks without,
Using the painter's privilege to choose
Among what 's rarest. Will your wife refuse
Acceptance from — no rival — of a gift ?
You paint the human figure I make shift
Humbly to reproduce : but, in my hours
Of idlesse, what I fain would paint is — flowers.
Look now ! ''
            She twitched aside a veiling cloth.
'' Here is my keepsake — frame and picture
    both :
For see, the frame is all of flowers festooned
About an empty space, — left thus, to wound
No natural susceptibility :
How can I guess ? 'T is you must fill, not I,
The central space with — her whom you like
    best !
That is your business, mine has been the rest.
But judge ! ''
            How judge them ? Each of us, in flowers,

Chooses his love, allies it with past hours,
Old meetings, vanished forms and faces : no —
Here let each favorite unmolested blow
For one heart's homage, no tongue's banal praise,
Whether the rose appealingly bade "Gaze
Your fill on me, sultana who dethrone
The gaudy tulip ! " or 't was "Me alone
Rather do homage to, who lily am,
No unabashed rose ! " "Do I vainly cram
My cup with sweets, your jonquil ? " "Why
  forget
Vernal endearments with the violet ? "
So they contested yet concerted, all
As one, to circle round about, enthral
Yet, self-forgetting, push to prominence
The midmost wonder, gained no matter whence.

There 's a tale extant, in a book I conned
Long years ago, which treats of things beyond
The common, antique times and countries queer
And customs strange to match. "'T is said,
  last year,"
(Recounts my author) "that the King had mind
To view his kingdom — guessed at from behind
A palace-window hitherto. Announced
No sooner was such purpose than 't was pounced
Upon by all the ladies of the land —
Loyal but light of life : they formed a band
Of loveliest ones but lithest also, since
Proudly they all combined to bear their prince.
Backs joined to breasts, — arms, legs, — nay,
  ankles, wrists,
Hands, feet, I know not by what turns and
  twists,
So interwoven lay that you believed
'T was one sole beast of burden which received
The monarch on its back, of breadth not scant,
Since fifty girls make one white elephant."
So with the fifty flowers which shapes and hues
Blent, as I tell, and made one fast yet loose
Mixture of beauties, composite, distinct
No less in each combining flower that linked
With flower to form a fit environment
For — whom might be the painter's heart's in-
  tent
Thus, in the midst enhaloed, to enshrine ?

"This glory-guarded middle space — is mine ?
For me to fill ? "
  "For you, my Friend ! We part,
Never perchance to meet again. Your Art —
What if I mean it — so to speak — shall wed
My own, be witness of the life we led
When sometimes it has seemed our souls near
  found
Each one the other as its mate — unbound
Had yours been haply from the better choice
— Beautiful Bicé : 't is the common voice,
The crowning verdict. Make whom you like best
Queen of the central space, and manifest
Your predilection for what flower beyond
All flowers finds favor with you. I am fond
Of — say — yon rose's rich predominance,
While you — what wonder ? — more affect the
  glance
The gentler violet from its leafy screen
Ventures : so — choose your flower and paint
  your queen ! "

Oh, but the man was ready, head as hand,
Instructed and adroit. "Just as you stand,
Stay and be made — would Nature but relent --
By Art immortal ! "
  Every implement
In tempting reach — a palette primed, each
  squeeze
Of oil-paint in its proper patch — with these,
Brushes, a veritable sheaf to grasp !
He worked as he had never dared.
  "Unclasp
My Art from yours who can ! " — he cried at
  length,
As down he threw the pencil — "Grace from
  Strength
Dissociate, from your flowery fringe detach
My face of whom it frames, — the feat will
  match
With that of Time should Time from me extract
Your memory, Artemisia ! " And in fact, —
What with the pricking impulse, sudden glow
Of soul — head, hand coöperated so
That face was worthy of its frame, 't is said —
Perfect, suppose !
  They parted. Soon instead
Of Rome was home, — of Artemisia — well,
The placid-perfect wife. And it befell
That after the first incontestably
Blessedest of all blisses (— wherefore try
Your patience with embracings and the rest
Due from Calypso's all-unwilling guest
To his Penelope ?) — there somehow came
The coolness which as duly follows flame.
So, one day, "What if we inspect the gifts
My Art has gained us ? "
  Now the wife uplifts
A casket-lid, now tries a medal's chain
Round her own lithe neck, fits a ring in vain
— Too loose on the fine finger, — vows and
  swears
The jewel with two pendent pearls like pears
Betters a lady's bosom — witness else !
And so forth, while Ulysses smiles.
  "Such spells
Subdue such natures — sex must worship toys
— Trinkets and trash : yet, ah, quite other joys
Must stir from sleep the passionate abyss
Of — such an one as her I know — not this
My gentle consort with the milk for blood !
Why, did it chance that in a careless mood
(In those old days, gone — never to return —
When we talked — she to teach and I to learn)
I dropped a word, a hint which might imply
Consorts exist — how quick flashed fire from
  eye,
Brow blackened, lip was pinched by furious lip !
I needed no reminder of my slip :
One warning taught me wisdom. Whereas
  here . . .
Aha, a sportive fancy ! Eh, what fear
Of harm to follow ? Just a whim indulged !

"My Beatricé, there 's an undivulged
Surprise in store for you : the moment 's fit
For letting loose a secret : out with it !
Tributes to worth, you rightly estimate
These gifts of Prince and Bishop, Church and
  State :

Yet, may I tell you? Tastes so disagree!
There 's one gift, preciousest of all to me,
I doubt if you would value as well worth
The obvious sparkling gauds that men unearth
For toy-cult mainly of you womankind;
Such make you marvel, I concede : while blind
The sex proves to the greater marvel here
I veil to balk its envy. Be sincere!
Say, should you search creation far and wide,
Was ever face like this?"

                        He drew aside
The veil, displayed the flower-framed portrait
                        kept
For private delectation.
                        No adept
In florist's lore more accurately named
And praised or, as appropriately, blamed
Specimen after specimen of skill,
Than Bicé. "Rightly placed the daffodil —
Scarcely so right the blue germander. Gray
Good mouse-ear! Hardly your auricula
Is powdered white enough. It seems to me
Scarlet not crimson, that anemone:
But there 's amends in the pink saxifrage.
O darling dear ones, let me disengage
You innocents from what your harmlessness
Clasps lovingly! Out thou from their caress,
Serpent!"
              Whereat forth-flashing from her coils
On coils of hair, the *spilla* in its toils
Of yellow wealth, the dagger-plaything kept
To pin its plaits together, life-like leapt
And — woe to all inside the coronal!
Stab followed stab, — cut, slash, she ruined all
The masterpiece. Alack for eyes and mouth
And dimples and endearment — North and
              South,
East, West, the tatters in a fury flew:
There yawned the circlet. What remained to
              do?
She flung the weapon, and, with folded arms
And mien defiant of such low alarms
As death and doom beyond death, Bicé stood
Passively statuesque, in quietude
Awaiting judgment.
                        And out judgment burst
With frank unloading of love's laughter, first
Freed from its unsuspected source. Some
              throe
Must needs unlock love's prison-bars, let flow
The joyance.
              "Then you ever were, still are,
And henceforth shall be — no occulted star
But my resplendent Bicé, sun-revealed,
Full-rondure! Woman-glory unconcealed,
So front me, find and claim and take your
              own —
My soul and body yours and yours alone,
As you are mine, mine wholly! Heart's love,
              take —
Use your possession — stab or stay at will
Here — hating, saving — woman with the skill
To make man beast or god!"
                        And so it proved:
For, as beseemed new godship, thus he loved,
Past power to change, until his dying-day, —
Good fellow! And I fain would hope — some say

Indeed for certain — that our painter's toils
At fresco-splashing, finer stroke in oils,
Were not so mediocre after all ;
Perhaps the work appears unduly small
From having loomed too large in old esteem,
Patronized by late Papacy. I seem
Myself to have cast eyes on certain work
In sundry galleries, no judge needs shirk
From moderately praising. He designed
Correctly, nor in color lagged behind
His age: but both in Florence and in Rome
The elder race so make themselves at home
That scarce we give a glance to ceilingfuls
Of such like as Francesco. Still, one culls
From out the heaped laudations of the time
The pretty incident I put in rhyme.

FLUTE-MUSIC, WITH AN ACCOMPANI
                        MENT

He. AH, the bird-like fluting
       Through the ash-tops yonder —
    Bullfinch-bubblings, soft sounds suiting
       What sweet thoughts, I wonder?
    Fine-pearled notes that surely
       Gather, dewdrop-fashion,
    Deep-down in some heart which purely
       Secretes globuled passion —
    Passion insuppressive —
       Such is piped, for certain ;
    Love, no doubt, nay, love excessive
       'T is, your ash-tops curtain.

    Would your ash-tops open
       We might spy the player —
    Seek and find some sense which no pen
       Yet from singer, sayer,
    Ever has extracted:
       Never, to my knowledge,
    Yet has pedantry enacted
       That, in Cupid's College,
    Just this variation
       Of the old, old yearning
    Should by plain speech have salvation,
       Yield new men new learning.

    "Love!" but what love, nicely
       New from old disparted,
    Would the player teach precisely?
       First of all, he started
    In my brain Assurance —
       Trust — entire Contentment —
    Passion proved by much endurance ;
       Then came — not resentment,
    No, but simply Sorrow :
       What was seen had vanished :
    Yesterday so blue! To-morrow
       Blank, all sunshine banished.

    Hark! 'T is Hope resurges,
       Struggling through obstruction —
    Forces a poor smile which verges
       On Joy's introduction.
    Now, perhaps, mere Musing :
       "Holds earth such a wonder?
    Fairy-mortal, soul-sense-fusing
       Past thought's power to sunder!"

What ? calm Acquiescence ?
  "Daisied turf gives room to
Trefoil, plucked once in her presence —
  Growing by her tomb too ! "

She. All 's your fancy-spinning !
  Here 's the fact : a neighbor
Never-ending, still beginning,
  Recreates his labor :
Deep o'er desk he drudges,
  Adds, divides, subtracts and
Multiplies, until he judges
  Noonday-hour's exact sand ·
Shows the hour-glass emptied :
  Then comes lawful leisure,
Minutes rare from toil exempted,
  Fit to spend in pleasure.

Out then with — what treatise ?
  Youth's Complete Instructor
How to play the Flute. Quid petis ?
  Follow Youth's conductor
On and on, through *Easy,*
  Up to *Harder, Hardest*
Flute-piece, till thou, flautist wheezy,
  Possibly discardest
Tootlings hoarse and husky,
  Mayst expend with courage
Breath — on tunes once bright, now dusky —
  Meant to cool thy porridge.

That 's an air of Tulou's
  He maltreats persistent,
Till as lief I 'd hear some Zulu's
  Bone-piped bag, breath-distent,
Madden native dances.
  I 'm the man's familiar :
Unexpectedness enhances
  What your ear's auxiliar
— Fancy — finds suggestive.
  Listen ! That 's *legato*
Rightly played, his fingers restive
  Touch as if *staccato.*

He. Ah, you trick-betrayer !
  Telling tales, unwise one ?
So the secret of the player
  Was — he could surprise one
Well-nigh into trusting
  Here was a musician
Skilled consummately, yet lusting
  Through no vile ambition
After making captive
  All the world, — rewarded
Amply by one stranger's rapture,
  Common praise discarded.

So, without assistance
  Such as music rightly
Needs and claims, — defying distance,
  Overleaping lightly
Obstacles which hinder,
  He, for my approval,
All the same and all the kinder
  Made mine what might move all
Earth to kneel adoring :
  Took — while he piped Gounod's

Bit of passionate imploring —
  Me for Juliet : who knows ?

No ! as you explain things,
  All 's mere repetition,
Practise-pother : of all vain things
  Why waste pooh or pish on
Toilsome effort — never
  Ending, still beginning
After what should pay endeavor
  — Right-performance ? winning
Weariness from you who,
  Ready to admire some
Owl's fresh hooting — Tu-whit, tu-who —
  Find stale thrush-songs tiresome.

She. Songs, Spring thought perfection,
  Summer criticises :
What in May escaped detection,
  August, past surprises,
Notes, and names each blunder.
  You, the just-initiate,
Praise to heart's content (what wonder ?)
  Tootings I hear vitiate
Romeo's serenading —
  I who, times full twenty,
Turned to ice — no ash-tops aiding —
  At his *caldamente.*

So, 't was distance altered
  Sharps to flats ? The missing
Bar when syncopation faltered
  (You thought — paused for kissing !)
Ash-tops too felonious
  Intercepted ? Rather
Say — they well-nigh made euphonious
  Discord, helped to gather
Phrase, by phrase, turn patches
  Into simulated
Unity which botching matches, —
  Scraps redintegrated.

He. Sweet, are you suggestive
  Of an old suspicion
Which has always found me restive
  To its admonition
When it ventured whisper
  " Fool, the strifes and struggles
Of your trembler — blusher — lisper
  Were so many juggles,
Tricks tried — oh, so often ! —
  Which once more do duty,
Find again a heart to soften,
  Soul to snare with beauty."

Birth-blush of the briar-rose,
  Mist-bloom of the hedge-sloe,
Some one gains the prize : admire rose
  Would he, when noon's wedge — slow
Sure, has pushed, expanded
  Rathe pink to raw redness ?
Would he covet sloe when sanded
  By road-dust to deadness ?
So — restore their value !
  Ply a water-sprinkle !
Then guess sloe is fingered, shall you ?
  Find in rose a wrinkle ?

Here what played Aquarius?
  Distance — ash-tops aiding,
Reconciled scraps else contrarious,
  Brightened stuff fast fading.
Distance — call your shyness:
  Was the fair one peevish?
Coyness softened out of slyness.
  Was she cunning, thievish,
All-but-proved impostor?
  Bear but one day's exile,
Ugly traits were wholly lost or
  Screened by fancies flexile —

Ash-tops these, you take me?
  Fancies' interference
Changed . . .
        But since I sleep, don't wake me!
  What if all 's appearance?
Is not outside seeming
  Real as substance inside?
Both are facts, so leave me dreaming:
  If who loses wins I 'd
Ever lose, — conjecture,
  From one phrase trilled deftly,
All the piece. So, end your lecture,
  Let who lied be left lie!

"IMPERANTE AUGUSTO NATUS EST —"

WHAT it was struck the terror into me?
This, Publius: closer! while we wait our turn
I 'll tell you. Water's warm (they ring inside)
At the eighth hour, till when no use to bathe.

Here in the vestibule where now we sit,
One scarce stood yesterday, the throng was such
Of loyal gapers, folk all eye and ear
While Lucius Varius Rufus in their midst
Read out that long-planned late-completed piece,
His Panegyric on the Emperor.
"Nobody like him," little Flaccus laughed,
"At leading forth an Epos with due pomp!
Only, when godlike Cæsar swells the theme,
How should mere mortals hope to praise aright?
Tell me, thou offshoot of Etruscan kings!"
Whereat Mæcenas smiling sighed assent.

I paid my quadrans, left the Thermæ's roar
Of rapture as the poet asked, "What place
Among the godships Jove, for Cæsar's sake,
Would bid its actual occupant vacate
In favor of the new divinity?"
And got the expected answer, "Yield thine own!" —
Jove thus dethroned, I somehow wanted air,
And found myself a-pacing street and street,
Letting the sunset, rosy over Rome,
Clear my head dizzy with the hubbub — say,
As if thought's dance therein had kicked up dust
By trampling on all else: the world lay prone,
As — poet-propped, in brave hexameters —
Their subject triumphed up from man to God.
Caius Octavius Cæsar the August —
Where was escape from his prepotency?

I judge I may have passed — how many piles
Of structure dropt like doles from his free hand
To Rome on every side? Why, right and left,
For temples you 've the Thundering Jupiter,
Avenging Mars, Apollo Palatine:
How count Piazza, Forum — there 's a third
All but completed. You 've the Theatre
Named of Marcellus — all his work, such work! —
One thought still ending, dominating all —
With warrant Varius sang, "Be Cæsar God!"
By what a hold arrests he Fortune's wheel,
Obtaining and retaining heaven and earth
Through Fortune, if you like, but favor — no!
For the great deeds flashed by me, fast and thick
As stars which storm the sky on autumn nights —
Those conquests! but peace crowned them, — so, of peace
Count up his titles only — these, in few —
Ten years Triumvir, Consul thirteen times,
Emperor, nay — the glory topping all —
Hailed Father of his Country, last and best
Of titles, by himself accepted so:
And why not? See but feats achieved in Rome —
Not to say, Italy — he planted there
Some thirty colonies — but Rome itself
All new-built, "marble now, brick once," he boasts:
This Portico, that Circus. Would you sail?
He has drained Tiber for you: would you walk?
He straightened out the long Flaminian Way.
Poor? Profit by his score of donatives!
Rich — that is, mirthful? Half-a-hundred games
Challenge your choice! There 's Rome — for you and me
Only? The centre of the world besides!
For, look the wide world over, where ends Rome?
To sunrise? There 's Euphrates — all between!
To sunset? Ocean and immensity:
North, stare till Danube stops you: South, see Nile,
The Desert and the earth-upholding Mount.
Well may the poet-people each with each
Vie in his praise, our company of swans,
Virgil and Horace, singers — in their way —
Nearly as good as Varius, though less famed:
Well may they cry, "No mortal, plainly God!"

Thus to myself myself said, while I walked:
Or would have said, could thought attain to speech,
Clean baffled by enormity of bliss
The while I strove to scale its heights and sound
Its depths — this masterdom o'er all the world
Of one who was but born — like you, like me,
Like all the world he owns — of flesh and blood.
But he — how grasp, how gauge his own conceit
Of bliss to me near inconceivable?
Or, since such flight too much makes reel the brain,
Let's sink — and so take refuge, as it were,
From life's excessive altitude — to life's

Breathable wayside shelter at its base !
If looms thus large this Cæsar to myself
— Of senatorial rank and somebody —
How must he strike the vulgar nameless crowd,
Innumerous swarm that 's nobody at all ?
Why, — for an instance, — much as yon gold
    shape
Crowned, sceptred, on the temple opposite —
Fulgurant Jupiter — must daze the sense
Of — say, yon outcast begging from its step !
" What, Anti-Cæsar, monarch in the mud,
As he is pinnacled above thy pate ?
Ay, beg away ! thy lot contrasts full well
With his whose bounty yields thee this sup-
    port —
Our Holy and Inviolable One,
Cæsar, whose bounty built the fane above !
Dost read my thought ? Thy garb, alack, dis-
    plays
Sore usage truly in each rent and stain —
Faugh ! Wash though in Suburra ! 'Ware
    the dogs
Who may not so disdain a meal on thee !
What, stretchest forth a palm to catch my
    alms ?
Aha, why yes : I must appear — who knows ? —
I, in my toga, to thy rags and thee —
Quæstor — nay, Ædile, Censor — Pol ! perhaps
The very City-Prætor's noble self !
As to me Cæsar, so to thee am I ?
Good : nor in vain shall prove thy quest, poor
    rogue !
Hither — hold palm out — take this quarter-
    as ! "

And who did take it ? As he raised his head,
(My gesture was a trifle — well — abrupt,)
Back fell the broad flap of the peasant's-hat.
The homespun cloak that muffled half his
    cheek
Dropped somewhat, and I had a glimpse —
    just one !
One was enough. Whose — whose might be
    the face ?
That unkempt careless hair — brown, yellow-
    ish —
Those sparkling eyes beneath their eyebrows'
    ridge
(Each meets each, and the hawk-nose rules
    between)
— That was enough, no glimpse was needed
    more !
And terrifyingly into my mind
Came that quick-hushed report was whispered
    us,
" They do say, once a year in sordid garb
He plays the mendicant, sits all day long,
Asking and taking alms of who may pass,
And so averting, if submission help,
Fate's envy, the dread chance and change of
    things
When Fortune — for a word, a look, a
    naught —
Turns spiteful and — the petted lioness —
Strikes with her sudden paw, and prone falls
    each
Who patted late her neck superiorly,

Or trifled with those claw - tips velvet-
    sheathed."
"He 's God ! " shouts Lucius Varius Rufus :
    " Man
And worms'-meat any moment ! " mutters low
Some Power, admonishing the mortal-born.

Ay, do you mind ? There 's meaning in the
    fact
That whoso conquers, triumphs, enters Rome,
Climbing the Capitolian, soaring thus
To glory's summit, — Publius, do you mark —
Ever the same attendant who, behind,
Above the Conqueror's head supports the crown
All-too-demonstrative for human wear,
— One hand's employment — all the while re-
    serves
Its fellow, backward flung, to point how, close
Appended from the car, beneath the foot
Of the up-borne exulting Conqueror,
Frown — half-descried — the instruments of
    shame,
The malefactor's due. Crown, now — Cross,
    when ?

Who stands secure ? Are even Gods so safe ?
Jupiter that just now is dominant —
Are not there ancient dismal tales how once
A predecessor reigned ere Saturn came,
And who can say if Jupiter be last ?
Was it for nothing the gray Sibyl wrote
" Cæsar Augustus regnant, shall be born
In blind Judæa " — one to master him,
Him and the universe ? An old-wife's tale ?

Bath-drudge ! Here, slave ! No cheating !
    Our turn next.
No loitering, or be sure you taste the lash !
Two strigils, two oil-drippers, each a sponge !

DEVELOPMENT

My Father was a scholar and knew Greek.
When I was five years old, I asked him once
" What do you read about ? "
           " The siege of Troy."
" What is a siege, and what is Troy ? "
                    Whereat
He piled up chairs and tables for a town,
Set me a-top for Priam, called our cat
— Helen, enticed away from home (he said)
By wicked Paris, who couched somewhere
    close
Under the footstool, being cowardly,
But whom — since she was worth the pains,
    poor puss —
Towzer and Tray, — our dogs, the Atreidai, —
    sought
By taking Troy to get possession of
— Always when great Achilles ceased to sulk,
(My pony in the stable) — forth would prance
And put to flight Hector — our page-boy's self.
This taught me who was who and what was
    what :
So far I rightly understood the case
At five years old ; a huge delight it proved

And still proves — thanks to that instructor
    sage
My Father, who knew better than turn straight
Learning's full flare on weak-eyed ignorance,
Or, worse yet, leave weak eyes to grow sand-
    blind,
Content with darkness and vacuity.

It happened, two or three years afterward,
That — I and playmates playing at Troy's
    Siege —
My Father came upon our make-believe.
" How would you like to read yourself the tale
Properly told, of which I gave you first
Merely such notion as a boy could bear ?
Pope, now, would give you the precise account
Of what, some day, by dint of scholarship,
You 'll hear — who knows ? — from Homer's
    very mouth.
Learn Greek by all means, read the ' Blind Old
    Man,
Sweetest of Singers' — *tuphlos* which means
    "blind,'
Hedistos which means ' sweetest.'   Time
    enough !
Try, anyhow, to master him some day ;
Until when, take what serves for substitute,
Read Pope, by all means ! ''
                    So I ran through Pope,
Enjoyed the tale — what history so true ?
Also attacked my Primer, duly drudged,
Grew fitter thus for what was promised next —
The very thing itself, the actual words,
When I could turn — say, Buttmann to account.

Time passed, I ripened somewhat : one fine
    day,
" Quite ready for the Iliad, nothing less ?
There 's Heine, where the big books block the
    shelf :
Don't skip a word, thumb well the Lexicon ! ''

I thumbed well and skipped nowise till I
    learned
Who was who, what was what, from Homer's
    tongue,
And there an end of learning.   Had you asked
The all-accomplished scholar, twelve years old,
" Who was it wrote the Iliad ? '' — what a
    laugh !
" Why, Homer, all the world knows : of his
    life
Doubtless some facts exist : it 's everywhere :
We have not settled, though, his place of birth :
He begged, for certain, and was blind beside :
Seven cities claimed him — Scio, with best
    right,
Thinks Byron.   What he wrote ?   Those
    Hymns we have.
Then there 's the ' Battle of the Frogs and
    Mice,'
That 's all — unless they dig ' Margites ' up
(I 'd like that) nothing more remains to know.''

Thus did youth spend a comfortable time ;
Until — '' What 's this the Germans say in fact
That Wolf found out first ? It 's unpleasant
    work

Their chop and change, unsettling one's be-
    lief :
All the same, where we live, we learn, that 's
    sure.''
So, I bent brow o'er *Prolegomena*.
And after Wolf, a dozen of his like
Proved there was never any Troy at all,
Neither   Besiegers   nor   Besieged, — nay,
    worse, —
No actual Homer, no authentic text,
No warrant for the fiction I, as fact,
Had treasured in my heart and soul so long —
Ay, mark you ! and as fact held still, still
    hold,
Spite of new knowledge, in my heart of hearts
And soul of souls, fact's essence freed and
    fixed
From accidental fancy's guardian sheath.
Assuredly thenceforward — thank my stars ! —
However it got there, deprive who could —
Wring from the shrine my precious tenantry,
Helen, Ulysses, Hector and his Spouse,
Achilles and his Friend ? — though Wolf — ah,
    Wolf !
Why must he needs come doubting. spoil a
    dream ?

But then, " No dream 's worth waking " —
    Browning says :
And here 's the reason why I tell thus much.
I, now mature man, you anticipate,
May blame my Father justifiably
For letting me dream out my nonage thus,
And only by such slow and sure degrees
Permitting me to sift the grain from chaff,
Get truth and falsehood known and named as
    such.
Why did he ever let me dream at all,
Not bid me taste the story in its strength ?
Suppose my childhood was scarce qualified
To rightly understand mythology,
Silence at least was in his power to keep :
I might have — somehow — correspondingly —
Well, who knows by what method, gained my
    gains,
Been taught, by forthrights not meanderings,
My aim should be to loathe, like Peleus' son,
A lie as Hell's Gate, love my wedded wife,
Like Hector, and so on with all the rest.
Could not I have excogitated this
Without believing such man really were ?
That is — he might have put into my hand
The " Ethics " ?   In translation, if you please,
Exact, no pretty lying that improves,
To suit the modern taste : no more, no less —
The " Ethics : " 't is a treatise I find hard
To read aright now that my hair is gray,
And I can manage the original.
At five years old — how ill had fared its leaves ?
Now, growing double o'er the Stagirite,
At least I soil no page with bread and milk,
Nor crumple, dogs-ear and deface — boys' way.

REPHAN

Suggested by a very early recollection of a
prose story by the noble woman and imagina-

tive writer, Jane Taylor, of Norwich, [more correctly, of Ongar]. R. B.

How I lived, ere my human life began
In this world of yours, — like you, made man, —
When my home was the Star of my God Re-
phan ?

Come then around me, close about,
World-weary earth-born ones ! Darkest doubt
Or deepest despondency keeps you out ?

Nowise ! Before a word I speak,
Let my circle embrace your worn, your weak,
Brow-furrowed old age, youth's hollow cheek —

Diseased in the body, sick in soul,
Pinched poverty, satiate wealth, — your whole
Array of despairs ! Have I read the roll ?

All here ? Attend, perpend ! O Star
Of my God Rephan, what wonders are
In thy brilliance fugitive, faint and far !

Far from me, native to thy realm,
Who shared its perfections which o'erwhelm
Mind to conceive. Let drift the helm,

Let drive the sail, dare unconfined
Embark for the vastitude, O Mind,
Of an absolute bliss ! Leave earth behind !

Here, by extremes, at a mean you guess :
There, all 's at most — not more, not less:
Nowhere deficiency nor excess.

No want — whatever should be, is now :
No growth — that 's change, and change comes
— how
To royalty born with crown on brow ?

Nothing begins — so needs to end :
Where fell it short at first ? Extend
Only the same, no change can mend !

I use your language : mine — no word
Of its wealth would help who spoke, who heard,
To a gleam of intelligence. None preferred,

None felt distaste when better and worse
Were uncontrastable : bless or curse
What — in that uniform universe ?

Can your world's phrase, your sense of things
Forth-figure the Star of my God ? No springs,
No winters throughout its space. Time brings

No hope, no fear : as to-day, shall be
To-morrow : advance or retreat need we
At our stand-still through eternity ?

All happy : needs must we so have been,
Since who could be otherwise ? All serene :
What dark was to banish, what light to screen ?

Earth's rose is a bud that 's checked or grows
As beams may encourage or blasts oppose :
Our lives leapt forth, each a full-orbed rose —

Each rose sole rose in a sphere that spread
Above and below and around — rose-red :
No fellowship, each for itself instead.

One better than I — would prove I lacked
Somewhat : one worse were a jarring fact
Disturbing my faultlessly exact.

How did it come to pass there lurked
Somehow a seed of change that worked
Obscure in my heart till perfection irked ? —

Till out of its peace at length grew strife —
Hopes, fears, loves, hates, — obscurely rife, —
My life grown a-tremble to turn your life ?

Was it Thou, above all lights that are,
Prime Potency, did Thy hand unbar
The prison-gate of Rephan my Star ?

In me did such potency wake a pulse
Could trouble tranquillity that lulls
Not lashes inertion till throes convulse

Soul's quietude into discontent ?
As when the completed rose bursts. rent
By ardors till forth from its orb are sent

New petals that mar — unmake the disk —
Spoil rondure : what in it ran brave risk,
Changed apathy's calm to strife, bright, brisk,

Pushed simple to compound, sprang and spread
Till, fresh-formed, faceted, floreted,
The flower that slept woke a star instead ?

No mimic of Star Rephan ! How long
I stagnated there where weak and strong,
The wise and the foolish, right and wrong,

Are merged alike in a neutral Best,
Can I tell ? No more than at whose behest
The passion arose in my passive breast,

And I yearned for no sameness but difference
In thing and thing, that should shock my sense
With a want of worth in them all, and thence

Startle me up, by an Infinite
Discovered above and below me — height
And depth alike to attract my flight,

Repel my descent : by hate taught love.
Oh, gain were indeed to see above
Supremacy ever — to move, remove,

Not reach — aspire yet never attain
To the object aimed at ! Scarce in vain, —
As each stage I left nor touched again.

To suffer, did pangs bring the loved one bliss,
Wring knowledge from ignorance, — just for
this —
To add one drop to a love-abyss !

Enough : for you doubt, you hope, O men,
You fear, you agonize, die : what then ?
Is an end to your life's work out of ken ?

Have you no assurance that, earth at end,
Wrong will prove right? Who made shall mend
In the higher sphere to which yearnings tend?

Why should I speak? You divine the test.
When the trouble grew in my pregnant breast
A voice said, "So wouldst thou strive, not rest?

"Burn and not smoulder, win by worth,
Not rest content with a wealth that's dearth?
Thou art past Rephan, thy place be Earth!"

REVERIE

I KNOW there shall dawn a day
— Is it here on homely earth?
Is it yonder, worlds away,
Where the strange and new have birth,
That Power comes full in play?

Is it here, with grass about,
Under befriending trees,
When shy buds venture out,
And the air by mild degrees
Puts winter's death past doubt?

Is it up amid whirl and roar
Of the elemental flame
Which star-flecks heaven's dark floor,
That, new yet still the same,
Full in play comes Power once more?

Somewhere, below, above,
Shall a day dawn — this I know —
When Power, which vainly strove
My weakness to o'erthrow,
Shall triumph. I breathe, I move,

I truly am, at last!
For a veil is rent between
Me and the truth which passed
Fitful, half-guessed, half-seen,
Grasped at — not gained, held fast.

I for my race and me
Shall apprehend life's law:
In the legend of man shall see
Writ large what small I saw
In my life's: tale both agree.

As the record from youth to age
Of my own, the single soul —
So the world's wide book: one page
Deciphered explains the whole
Of our common heritage.

How but from near to far
Should knowledge proceed, increase?
Try the clod ere test the star!
Bring our inside strife to peace
Ere we wage, on the outside, war!

So, my annals thus begin:
With body, to life awoke
Soul, the immortal twin
Of body which bore soul's yoke
Since mortal and not akin.

By means of the flesh, grown fit,
Mind, in surview of things,
Now soared, anon alit
To treasure its gatherings
From the ranged expanse — to-wit,

Nature, — earth's, heaven's wide show.
Which taught all hope, all fear:
Acquainted with joy and woe,
I could say, "Thus much is clear,
Doubt annulled thus much: I know.

"All is effect of cause:
As it would, has willed and done
Power: and my mind's applause
Goes, passing laws each one,
To Omnipotence, lord of laws."

Head praises, but heart refrains
From loving's acknowledgment.
Whole losses outweigh half-gains:
Earth's good is with evil blent:
Good struggles but evil reigns.

Yet since Earth's good proved good —
Incontrovertibly
Worth loving — I understood
How evil — did mind descry
Power's object to end pursued —

Were haply as cloud across
Good's orb, no orb itself:
Mere mind — were it found at loss
Did it play the tricksy elf
And from life's gold purge the dross?

Power is known infinite:
Good struggles to be — at best
Seems — scanned by the human sight,
Tried by the senses' test —
Good palpably: but with right

Therefore to mind's award
Of loving, as power claims praise?
Power — which finds naught too hard,
Fulfilling itself all ways
Unchecked, unchanged: while barred,

Baffled, what good began
Ends evil on every side.
To Power submissive man
Breathes, "E'en as Thou art, abide!"
While to good "Late-found, long-sought

"Would Power to a plenitude
But liberate, but enlarge
Good's strait confine, — renewed
Were ever the heart's discharge
Of loving!" Else doubts intrude.

For you dominate, stars all!
For a sense informs you — brute,
Bird, worm, fly, great and small,
Each with your attribute
Or low or majestical!

Thou earth that embosomest
Offspring of land and sea —

How thy hills first sank to rest,
  How thy vales bred herb and tree
Which dizen thy mother-breast —

Do I ask ? "Be ignorant
  Ever !" the answer clangs:
Whereas if I plead world's want,
  Soul's sorrows and body's pangs,
Play the human applicant, —

Is a remedy far to seek ?
  I question and find response :
I — all men, strong or weak,
  Conceive and declare at once
For each want its cure. "Power, speak !

"Stop change, avert decay
  Fix life fast, banish death,
Eclipse from the star bid stay,
  Abridge of no moment's breath
One creature ! Hence, Night, hail, Day !"

What need to confess again
  No problem this to solve
By impotence ? Power, once plain
  Proved Power — let on Power devolve
Good's right to co-equal reign !

Past mind's conception — Power !
  Do I seek how star, earth, beast,
Bird, worm, fly, gain their dower
  For life's use, most and least ?
Back from the search I cower.

Do I seek what heals all harm,
  Nay, hinders the harm at first,
Saves earth ? Speak, Power, the charm !
  Keep the life there unamerced
By chance, change, death's alarm !

As promptly as mind conceives,
  Let Power in its turn declare
Some law which wrong retrieves,
  Abolishes everywhere
What thwarts, what irks, what grieves !

Never to be ! and yet
  How easy it seems — to sense
Like man's — if somehow met
  Power with its match — immense
Love, limitless, unbeset

By hindrance on every side !
  Conjectured, nowise known,
Such may be : could man confide
  Such would match — were Love but shown
Script of the veils that hide —

Power's self now manifest !
  So reads my record: thine,
O world, how runs it ? Guessed
  Were the purport of that prime line,
Prophetic of all the rest !

"In a beginning God
  Made heaven and earth." Forth flashed
Knowledge : from star to clod

Man knew things : doubt abashed
Closed its long period.

Knowledge obtained Power praise.
  Had Good been manifest,
Broke out in cloudless blaze,
  Unchequered as unrepressed,
In all things Good at best —

Then praise — all praise, no blame —
  Had hailed the perfection. No !
As Power's display, the same
  Be Good's — praise forth shall flow
Unisonous in acclaim !

Even as the world its life,
  So have I lived my own —
Power seen with Love at strife,
  That sure, this dimly shown,
— Good rare and evil rife.

Whereof the effect be — faith
  That, some far day, were found
Ripeness in things now rathe,
  Wrong righted, each chain unbound,
Renewal born out of scathe.

Why faith — but to lift the load,
  To leaven the lump, where lies
Mind prostrate through knowledge owed
  To the loveless Power it tries
To withstand, how vain ! In flowed

Ever resistless fact :
  No more than the passive clay
Disputes the potter's act,
  Could the whelmed mind disobey
Knowledge the cataract.

But, perfect in every part,
  Has the potter's moulded shape,
Leap of man's quickened heart,
  Throe of his thought's escape,
Stings of his soul which dart

Through the barrier of flesh, till keen
  She climbs from the calm and clear,
Through turbidity all between,
  From the known to the unknown here,
Heaven's "Shall be," from Earth's "Has
    been" ?

Then life is — to wake not sleep,
  Rise and not rest, but press
From earth's level where blindly creep
  Things perfected, more or less,
To the heaven's height, far and steep,

Where, amid what strifes and storms
  May wait the adventurous quest,
Power is Love — transports, transforms
  Who aspired from worst to best,
Sought the soul's world, spurned the worms'

I have faith such end shall be :
  From the first, Power was — I knew.
Life has made clear to me

That, strive but for closer view,
Love were as plain to see.

When see?   When there dawns a day,
   If not on the homely earth,
Then yonder, worlds away,
   Where the strange and new have birth,
And Power comes full in play.

EPILOGUE

In regard to the third verse of this poem the *Pall Mall Gazette* of February 1, 1890, related this incident: "One evening, just before his death-illness, the poet was reading this from a proof to his daughter-in-law and sister. He said: 'It almost looks like bragging to say this, and as if I ought to cancel it; but it 's the simple truth; and as it 's true, it shall stand.'"

At the midnight in the silence of the sleep-time,
   When you set your fancies free,
Will they pass to where — by death, fools think,
   imprisoned —

Low he lies who once so loved you, whom you
   loved so,
      — Pity me?

Oh to love so, be so loved, yet so mistaken!
   What had I on earth to do
With the slothful, with the mawkish, the un-
   manly?
Like the aimless, helpless, hopeless, did I drivel
      — Being — who?

One who never turned his back but marched
   breast forward,
   Never doubted clouds would break,
Never dreamed, though right were worsted,
   wrong would triumph,
Held we fall to rise, are baffled to fight better,
   Sleep to wake.

No, at noonday in the bustle of man's work-time
   Greet the unseen with a cheer!
Bid him forward, breast and back as either
   should be,
"Strive and thrive!" cry "Speed, — fight on,
   fare ever
      There as here!"

APPENDIX

I. AN ESSAY ON SHELLEY

SHELLEY's influence on Browning is so frequently referred to, that it seems best, inasmuch as this *Essay* is the only distinct piece of prose in Browning's writings, to print it here in the Appendix to his *Complete Poetic and Dramatic Writings*. The paper was written in 1852 at the request of Mr. Moxon, the publisher, under the circumstances named in the first paragraph of the *Essay*. Before the book was actually published, it was discovered to be a fabrication and was immediately suppressed. A very few copies only escaped the publisher's hands; apparently, those only which went to the depositories of copyright matter. The present copy is taken from the one issued in 1888 by the Shelley Society, London, under the editorship of W. Tyas Harden.

AN opportunity having presented itself for the acquisition of a series of unedited letters by Shelley, all more or less directly supplementary to and illustrative of the collection already published by Mr. Moxon, that gentleman has decided on securing them. They will prove an acceptable addition to a body of correspondence, the value of which, towards a right understanding of its author's purpose and work, may be said to exceed that of any similar contribution exhibiting the worldly relations of a poet whose genius has operated by a different law.

Doubtless we accept gladly the biography of an objective poet, as the phrase now goes ; one whose endeavor has been to reproduce things external (whether the phenomena of the scenic universe, or the manifested action of the human heart and brain), with an immediate reference, in every case, to the common eye and apprehension of his fellow-men, assumed capable of receiving and profiting by this reproduction. It has been obtained through the poet's double faculty of seeing external objects more clearly, widely, and deeply than is possible to the average mind, at the same time that he is so acquainted and in sympathy with its narrower comprehension as to be careful to supply it with no other materials than it can combine into an intelligible whole. The auditory of such a poet will include, not only the intelligences which, save for such assistance, would have missed the deeper meaning and enjoyment of the original objects, but also the spirits of a like endowment with his own, who, by means of his abstract, can forthwith pass to the reality it was made from, and either corroborate their impressions of things known already, or supply themselves with new from whatever shows in the inexhaustible variety of existence may have hitherto escaped their knowledge. Such a poet is properly the ποιητής, the fashioner ; and the thing fashioned, his poetry, will of necessity be substantive, projected from himself and distinct. We are ignorant what the inventor of *Othello* conceived of that fact as he beheld it in completeness, how he accounted for it, under what known law he registered its nature, or to what unknown law he traced its coincidence. We learn only what he intended we should learn by that particular exercise of his power, — the fact itself, — which, with its infinite significances, each of us receives for the first time as a creation, and is hereafter left to deal with, as, in proportion to his own intelligence, he best may. We are ignorant, and would fain be otherwise.

Doubtless, with respect to such a poet, we covet his biography. We desire to look back upon the process of gathering together in a lifetime the materials of the work we behold entire ; of elaborating, perhaps under difficulty and with hindrance, all that is familiar to our admiration in the apparent facility of success. And the inner impulse of this effort and operation, what induced it ? Did a soul's delight in its own extended sphere of vision set it, for the gratification of an insuppressible power, on labor, as other men are set on rest ? Or did a sense of duty or of love lead it to communicate its own sensations to mankind ? Did an irresistible sympathy with men compel it to bring down and suit its own provision of knowledge and beauty to their narrow scope ? Did the personality of such an one stand like an open watch-tower in the midst of the territory it is erected to gaze on, and were the storms and calms, the stars and meteors, its watchman was wont to report of, the habitual variegation of his every-day life, as they glanced across its open door or lay reflected on its four-square parapet ? Or did some sunken and darkened chamber of imagery witness, in the artificial illumination of every storied compartment we are permitted to contemplate, how rare and precious were the outlooks through here and there an embrasure upon a world beyond, and how blankly would have pressed on the artificer the boundary of his daily life, except for the amorous diligence with which he had rendered permanent by art whatever came to diversify the gloom ? Still, fraught with instruction and interest as such details undoubtedly are, we can, if needs be, dispense with them. The man passes, the work remains. The work speaks for itself, as we say; and the biography of the worker is no more necessary to an understanding or enjoyment of it than is a model or anatomy of some tropical tree to the right tasting of the fruit we are familiar with on the market-stall, — or a geologist's map and stratification to the prompt recognition of the hill-top, our landmark of every day.

We turn with stronger needs to the genius of an opposite tendency, — the subjective poet of modern classification. He, gifted like the objective poet with the fuller perception of nature and man, is impelled to embody the thing he perceives, not so much with reference to the many below as to the one above him, the supreme Intelligence which apprehends all things in their absolute truth, — an ultimate view ever aspired to, if but partially attained, by the poet's own soul. Not what man sees, but what God sees, — the *Ideas* of Plato, seeds of creation lying burningly on the Divine Hand, — it is toward these that he struggles. Not with the combination of humanity in action, but with the primal elements of humanity, he has to do; and he digs where he stands, — preferring to seek them in his own soul as the nearest reflex of that absolute Mind, according to the intuitions of which he desires to perceive and speak. Such a poet does not deal habitually with the picturesque groupings and tempestuous tossings of the forest trees, but with their roots and fibres naked to the chalk and stone. He does not paint pictures and hang them on the walls, but rather carries them on the retina of his own eyes: we must look deep into his human eyes to see those pictures on them. He is rather a seer, accordingly, than a fashioner, and what he produces will be less a work than an effluence. That effluence cannot be easily considered in abstraction from his personality, — being indeed the very radiance and aroma of his personality, projected from it but not separated. Therefore, in our approach to the poetry, we necessarily approach the personality of the poet; in apprehending it we apprehend him, and certainly we cannot love it without loving him. Both for love's and for understanding's sake we desire to know him, and, as readers of his poetry, must be readers of his biography also.

I shall observe, in passing, that it seems not so much from any essential distinction in the faculty of the two poets, or in the nature of the objects contemplated by either, as in the more immediate adaptability of these objects to the distinct purpose of each, that the objective poet, in his appeal to the aggregate human mind, chooses to deal with the doings of men (the result of which dealing, in its pure form, when even description, as suggesting a describer, is dispensed with, is what we call dramatic poetry); while the subjective poet, whose study has been himself, appealing through himself to the absolute Divine mind, prefers to dwell upon those external scenic appearances which strike out most abundantly and uninterruptedly his inner light and power, selects that silence of the earth and sea in which he can best hear the beating of his individual heart, and leaves the noisy, complex, yet imperfect exhibitions of nature in the manifold experience of man around him, which serve only to distract and suppress the working of his brain. These opposite tendencies of genius will be more readily descried in their artistic effect than in their moral spring and cause. Pushed to an extreme and manifested as a deformity, they will be seen plainest of all in the fault of either artist when, subsidiarily to the human interest of his work, his occasional illustrations from scenic nature are introduced as in the earlier works of the originative painters, — men and women filling the foreground with consummate mastery, while mountain, grove, and rivulet show like an anticipatory revenge on that succeeding race of landscape-painters, whose "figures" disturb the perfection of their earth and sky. It would be idle to inquire, of these two kinds of poetic faculty in operation, which is the higher or even rarer endowment. If the subjective might seem to be the ultimate requirement of every age, the objective, in the strictest state, must still retain its original value. For it is with this world, as starting point and basis alike, that we shall always have to concern ourselves: the world is not to be learned and thrown aside, but reverted to and relearned. The spiritual comprehension may be infinitely subtilized, but the raw material it operates upon must remain. There may be no end of the poets who communicate to us what they see in an object with reference to their own individuality: what it was before they saw it, in reference to the aggregate human mind, will be as desirable to know as ever. Nor is there any reason why these two modes of poetic faculty may not issue hereafter from the same poet in successive perfect works, examples of which, according to what are now considered the exigencies of art, we have hitherto possessed in distinct individuals only. A mere running in of the one faculty upon the other is, of course, the ordinary circumstance. Far more rarely it happens that either is found so decidedly prominent and superior as to be pronounced comparatively pure; while of the perfect shield, with the gold and the silver side set up for all comers to challenge, there has yet been no instance. Either faculty in its eminent state is doubtless conceded by Providence as a best gift to men, according to their especial want. There is a time when the general eye has, so to speak, absorbed its fill of the phenomena around it, whether spiritual or material, and desires rather to learn the exacter significance of what it possesses than to receive any augmentation of what is possessed. Then is the opportunity for the poet of loftier vision to lift his fellows, with their half-apprehensions, up to his own sphere, by intensifying the import of details and rounding the universal meaning. The influence of such an achievement will not soon die out. A tribe of successors

(Homerides), working more or less in the same spirit, dwell on his discoveries and reinforce his doctrine; till, at unawares, the world is found to be subsisting wholly on the shadow of a reality, on sentiments diluted from passions, on the tradition of a fact, the convention of a moral, the straw of last year's harvest. Then is the imperative call for the appearance of another sort of poet, who shall at once replace this intellectual rumination of food swallowed long ago, by a supply of the fresh and living swathe; getting at new substance by breaking up the assumed wholes into parts of independent and unclassed value, careless of the unknown laws for recombining them (it will be the business of yet another poet to suggest those hereafter), prodigal of objects for men's outer and not inner sight; shaping for their uses a new and different creation from the last, which it displaces by the right of life over death, — to endure until, in the inevitable process, its very sufficiency to itself shall require at length an exposition of its affinity to something higher, when the positive yet conflicting facts shall again precipitate themselves under a harmonizing law, and one more degree will be apparent for a poet to climb in that mighty ladder, of which, however cloud-involved and undefined may glimmer the topmost step, the world dares no longer doubt that its gradations ascend.

Such being the two kinds of artists, it is naturally, as I have shown, with the biography of the subjective poet that we have the deeper concern. Apart from his recorded life altogether, we might fail to determine with satisfactory precision to what class his productions belong, and what amount of praise is assignable to the producer. Certainly, in the fact of any conspicuous achievement of genius, philosophy no less than sympathetic instinct warrants our belief in a great moral purpose having mainly inspired even where it does not visibly look out of the same. Greatness in a work suggests an adequate instrumentality; and none of the lower incitements, however they may avail to initiate or even effect many considerable displays of power, simulating the nobler inspiration to which they are mistakenly referred, have been found able, under the ordinary conditions of humanity, to task themselves to the end of so exacting a performance as a poet's complete work. As soon will the galvanism, that provokes to violent action the muscles of a corpse, induce it to cross the chamber steadily: sooner. The love of displaying power for the display's sake; the love of riches, of distinction, of notoriety; the desire of a triumph over rivals, and the vanity in the applause of friends, — each and all of such whetted appetites grow intenser by exercise, and increasingly sagacious as to the best and readiest means of self-appeasement: while for any of their ends, whether the money or the pointed finger of the crowd, or the flattery and hate to heart's content, there are cheaper prices to pay, they will all find soon enough, than the bestowment of a life upon a labor hard, slow, and not sure. Also, assuming the proper moral aim to have produced a work, there are many and various states of an aim: it may be more intense than clear-sighted, or too easily satisfied with a lower field of activity than a steadier aspiration would reach. All the bad poetry in the world (accounted poetry, that is, by its affinities) will be found to result from some one of the infinite degrees of discrepancy between the attributes of the poet's soul, occasioning a want of correspondency between his work and the verities of nature, — issuing in poetry, false under whatever form, which shows a thing, not as it is to mankind generally, nor as it is to the particular describer, but as it is supposed to be for some unreal neutral mood, midway between both and of value to neither, and living its brief minute simply through the indolence of whoever accepts it or his incapacity to denounce a cheat. Although of such depths of failure there can be no question here, we must in every case betake ourselves to the review of a poet's life ere we determine some of the nicer questions concerning his poetry, — more especially if the performance we seek to estimate aright has been obstructed and cut short of completion by circumstances, — a disastrous youth or a premature death. We may learn from the biography whether his spirit invariably saw and spoke from the last height to which it had attained. An absolute vision is not for this world, but we are permitted a continual approximation to it, every degree of which in the individual, provided it exceed the attainment of the masses, must procure him a clear advantage. Did the poet ever attain to a higher platform than where he rested and exhibited a result? Did he know more than he spoke of?

I concede, however, in respect to this subject of our study as well as some few other illustrious examples, that the unmistakable quality of the verse would be evidence enough, under usual circumstances, not only of the kind and degree of the intellectual but of the moral constitution of Shelley; the whole personality of the poet shining forward from the poems, without much need of going further to seek it. The "Remains" — produced within a period of ten years, and at a season of life when other men of at all comparable genius have hardly done more than prepare the eye for future sight and the tongue for speech — present us with the complete enginery of a poet, as signal in the excellence of its several aptitudes as transcendent in the combination of effects, — examples, in fact, of the whole poet's function of beholding with an understanding keenness the universe, nature and man, in their actual state of perfection in imperfection; of the whole poet's virtue of being untempted, by the manifold partial developments of beauty and good on every side, into leaving them the ultimates he found them, — induced by the facility of the gratification of his own sense of those qualities, or by the pleasure of acquiescence in the shortcomings of his predecessors in art, and the pain of disturbing their conventionalisms, — the whole poet's virtue, I repeat, of looking higher than any manifestation yet made of both beauty and good, in order to suggest from the utmost realization of the one a corresponding capability in the other, and out of the calm, purity, and energy of nature to reconstitute and store up, for the forthcoming stage of man's being, a gift in repayment of that former gift in which man's own thought and passion had been lavished by the poet on the else-incompleted magnificence of the sunrise, the else-uninterpreted mystery of the lake, — so drawing out, lifting up, and assimilating this ideal of a future man, thus descried as possible, to the present reality of the poet's soul already arrived at the higher state of development, and still aspirant to elevate and extend itself in conformity with its still-improving perceptions of, no longer the eventual Human, but the actual Divine. In conjunction with which noble and rare powers came the subordinate power of delivering these attained results to the world in an embodiment of verse more closely answering to and indicative of the process of the informing spirit, (failing, as it occasionally does, in art, only to succeed in highest art), — with a diction more adequate to the task in its natural and acquired richness, its material color and spiritual transparency, — the whole being moved by and suffused with a music at once of the soul and the sense, expressive both of an external might of sincere passion and an internal fitness and consonancy, — than can be attributed to any other writer whose record is among us. Such was the spheric poetical faculty of Shelley, as its own self-sacrificing central light, radiating equally through immaturity and accomplishment, through many fragments and occasional completion, reveals it to a competent judgment.

But the acceptance of this truth by the public has been retarded by certain objections which cast us back on the evidence of biography, even with Shelley's poetry in our hands. Except for the particular character of these objections, indeed, the non-appreciation of his contemporaries would simply class, now that it is over, with a series of experiences which have necessarily happened, and needlessly been wondered at, ever since the world began, and concerning which any present anger may well be moderated, no less in justice to our forerunners than in policy to ourselves. For the misapprehensiveness of his age is exactly what a poet is sent to remedy; and the interval between his operation and the generally perceptible effect of it is no greater, less indeed, than in many other departments of great human effort. The "E pur si muove" of the astronomer was as bitter a word as any uttered before or since by a poet over his rejected living work, in that depth of conviction which is so like despair.

But in this respect was the experience of Shelley peculiarly unfortunate, — that the disbelief in him as a man even preceded the disbelief in him as a writer; the misconstruction of his moral nature preparing the way for the misappreciation of his intellectual labors. There existed from the beginning — simultaneous with, indeed anterior to, his earliest noticeable works, and not brought forward to counteract any impression they had succeeded in making — certain charges against his private character and life, which, if substantiated to their whole breadth, would materially disturb, I do not attempt to deny, our reception and enjoyment of his works, however wonderful the artistic qualities of these. For we are not sufficiently supplied with instances of genius of his order to be able to pronounce certainly how many of its constituent parts have been tasked and strained to the production of a given lie, and how high and pure a mood of the creative mind may be dramatically simulated as the poet's habitual and exclusive one. The doubts, therefore, arising from such a question, required to be set at rest, as they were effectually, by those early authentic notices of Shelley's career and the corroborative accompaniment of his letters, in which not only the main tenor and principal result of his life, but the purity and beauty of many of the processes which had conduced to them, were made apparent enough for the general reader's purpose, — whoever lightly condemned Shelley first, on the evidence of reviews and gossip, as lightly acquitting him now, on that of memoirs and correspondence. Still, it is advisable to lose no opportunity of strengthening and completing the chain of biographical testimony; much more, of course, for the sake of the poet's original lovers, whose volunteered sacrifice of particular principle in favor of absorbing sympathy we might desire to dispense with, than for the sake of his foolish haters, who have long since diverted upon other objects their obtuseness or malignancy. A full life of Shelley should be written at once, while the materials for it continue in reach; not to minister to the curiosity of the public, but to obliterate the last stain of that false life which was forced on the public's attention before it had any curiosity on the matter, — a biography composed in harmony with the present general disposition to have faith in him, yet not shrinking from a candid statement of all ambiguous passages, through a reasonable confidence that the most doubtful of them will be found consistent with a belief in the eventual perfection of his character, according to the poor limits of our humanity. Nor will men persist in confounding, any more than God confounds, with genuine infidelity and atheism of the heart those passionate, impatient struggles of a boy towards distant truth and love, made in the dark, and ended by one sweep of the natural seas before the full moral sunrise could shine out on him. Crude convictions of boyhood, conveyed in imperfect and inapt forms of speech, — for such things all boys have been pardoned. There are growing-pains, accompanied by temporary distortion, of the soul also. And it would be hard indeed upon this young Titan of genius, murmuring in divine music his human ignorances through his very thirst for knowledge, and his rebellion in mere aspiration to law, if the melody itself substantiated the error, and the tragic cutting short of life perpetuated into sins such faults as, under happier circumstances, would have been left behind by the consent of the most arrogant moralist, forgotten on the lowest steps of youth.

The responsibility of presenting to the public a biography of Shelley does not, however, lie with me: I have only to make it a little easier by arranging these few supplementary letters, with a recognition of the value of the whole collection. This value I take to consist in a most truthful conformity of the Correspondence, in its limited degree, with the moral and intellectual character of the writer as displayed in the highest manifestations of his genius. Letters and poems are obviously an act of the same mind, produced by the same law, only differing in the application to the individual or collective understanding. Letters and poems may be used indifferently as the basement of our opinion upon the writer's character; the finished expression of a sentiment in the poems giving light and significance to the rudiments of the same in the letters, and these again, in their incipiency and unripeness, authenticating the exalted mood and reattaching it to the personality of the writer. The musician speaks on the note he sings with; there is no change in the scale as he diminishes the volume into familiar intercourse. There is nothing of that jarring between the man and the author, which has been found so amusing or so melancholy; no dropping of the tragic mask as the crowd melts away; no mean discovery of the real motives of a life's achievement, often in other lives laid bare as pitifully as when, at the close of a holiday, we catch sight of the internal lead-pipes and wood-valves to which, and not to the ostensible conch and dominant Triton of the fountain, we have owed our admired waterwork. No breaking out, in household privacy, of hatred, anger, and scorn, incongruous with the higher mood, and suppressed artistically in the book; no brutal return to self-delighting, when the audience of philanthropic schemes is out of hearing; no indecent stripping off the grander feeling and rule of life as too costly and cumbrous for every-day wear. Whatever Shelley was, he was with an admirable sincerity. It was not always truth that he thought and spoke; but in the purity of truth he spoke and thought always. Everywhere is apparent his belief in the existence of Good, to which Evil is an accident; his faithful holding by what he assumed to be the former going everywhere in company with the tenderest pity for those acting or suffering on the opposite hypothesis. For he was tender, though tenderness is not always the characteristic of very sincere natures; he was eminently both tender and sincere. And not only do the same affection and yearning after the well-being of his kind appear in the letters as in the poems, but they express themselves by the same theories and plans, however crude and unsound. There is no reservation of a subtler, less costly, more serviceable remedy for his own ill than he has proposed for the general one; nor does he ever contemplate an object on his own account from a less elevation than he uses in exhibiting it to the world. How shall we help believing Shelley to have been, in his ultimate attainment, the splendid spirit of his own best poetry, when we find even his carnal speech to agree faithfully, at faintest as at strongest, with the tone and rhythm of his most oracular utterances?

For the rest, these new letters are not offered as presenting any new feature of the poet's character. Regarded in themselves, and as the substantive productions of a man, their importance would be slight. But they possess interest beyond their limits, in confirming the evidence just dwelt on, of the poetical mood of Shelley being only the intensification of his habitual mood; the same tongue only speaking, for want of the special excitement to sing. The very first letter, as one instance for all, strikes the key-note of the predominating sentiment of Shelley throughout his whole life — his sympathy with the oppressed. And when we see him at so early an age, casting out, under the influence of such a sympathy, letters and pamphlets on every side, we accept it as the simple exemplification of the sincerity, with which, at the close of his life, he spoke of himself, as —

> "One whose heart a stranger's tear might wear
> As water-drops the sandy fountain stone;
> Who loved and pitied all things, and could moan
> For woes which others hear not, and could see
> The absent with the glass of phantasy,
> And near the poor and trampled sit and weep,
> Following the captive to his dungeon deep —
> One who was as a nerve o'er which do creep
> The else-unfelt oppressions of this earth."

Such sympathy with his kind was evidently developed in him to an extraordinary and even morbid degree, at a period when the general intellectual powers it was impatient to put in motion were immature or deficient.

I conjecture, from a review of the various publications of Shelley's youth, that one of the causes of his failure at the outset was the peculiar *practicalness* of his mind, which was not without a determinate effect on his progress in theorizing. An ordinary youth, who turns his attention to similar subjects, discovers falsities, incongruities, and various points for amendment, and, in the natural advance of the purely critical spirit unchecked by considerations of remedy, keeps up before his young eyes so many instances of the same error and wrong, that he finds himself unawares arrived at the startling conclusion, that all must be changed — or nothing: in the face of which plainly impossible achievement, he is apt (looking perhaps a little more serious by the time he touches at the decisive issue) to feel, either carelessly or considerately, that his own attempting a single piece of service would be worse than useless even, and to refer the whole task to another age and person — safe in proportion to his incapacity. Wanting words to speak, he has never made a fool of himself by speaking. But, in Shelley's case, the early fervor and power to *see* was accompanied by as precocious a fertility to *contrive:* he endeavored to realize as he went on idealizing; every wrong had simultaneously its remedy, and, out of the strength of his hatred for the former, he took the strength of his confidence in the latter—till suddenly he stood pledged to the defence of a set of miserable little expedients, just as if they represented great principles, and to an attack upon various great principles, really so, without leaving himself time to examine whether because they were antagonistical to the remedy he had suggested, they must therefore be identical or even essentially connected with the wrong he sought to cure, —playing with blind passion into the hands of his enemies, and dashing at whatever red cloak was held forth to him, as the cause of the fireball he had last been stung with—mistaking Churchdom for Christianity, and for marriage, "the sale of love" and the law of sexual oppression.

Gradually, however, he was leaving behind him this low practical dexterity, unable to keep up with his widening intellectual perception; and, in exact proportion as he did so, his true power strengthened and proved itself. Gradually he was raised above the contemplation of spots and the attempt at effacing them, to the great Abstract Light, and through the discrepancy of the creation, to the sufficiency of the First Cause. Gradually he was learning that the best way of removing abuses is to stand fast by truth. Truth is one, as they are manifold; and innumerable negative effects are produced by the upholding of one positive principle. I shall say what I think, — had Shelley lived he would have finally ranged himself with the Christians; his very instinct for helping the weaker side (if numbers make strength), his very "hate of hate," which at first mistranslated itself into delirious Queen Mab notes and the like, would have got clear-sighted by exercise. The preliminary step to following Christ, is the leaving the dead to bury their dead — not clamoring on his doctrine for an especial solution of difficulties which are referable to the general problem of the universe. Already he had attained to a profession of "a worship to the Spirit of good within, which requires (before it sends that inspiration forth, which impresses its likeness upon all it creates) devoted and disinterested homage," *as Coleridge says*, — and Paul likewise. And we find in one of his last exquisite fragments, avowedly a record of one of his own mornings and its experience, as it dawned on him at his soul and body's best in his boat on the Serchio — that as surely as

"The stars burnt out in the pale blue air,
  And the thin white moon lay withering there —
  Day had kindled the dewy woods,
  And the rocks above, and the stream below,
  And the vapors in their multitudes,
  And the Apennine's shroud of summer snow —
  Day had awakened all things that be ; "

just so surely, he tells us (stepping forward from this delicious dance-music, choragus-like, into the grander measure befitting the final enunciation), —

"All rose to do the task He set to each,
  Who shaped us to His ends and not our own ;
  The million rose to learn, and One to teach
  What none yet ever knew or can be known."

No more difference than this, from David's pregnant conclusion so long ago !

Meantime, as I call Shelley a moral man, because he was true, simple-hearted, and brave, and because what he acted corresponded to what he knew, so I call him a man of religious mind, because every audacious negative cast up by him against the Divine was interpenetrated with a mood of reverence and adoration, — and because I find him everywhere taking for granted some of the capital dogmas of Christianity, while most vehemently denying their historical basement. There is such a thing as an efficacious knowledge of and belief in the politics of Junius, or the poetry of Rowley, though a man should at the same time dispute the title of Chatterton to the one, and consider the author of the other, as Byron wittily did, "really, truly, nobody at all."[1]

There is even such a thing, we come to learn wonderingly in these very letters, as a profound sensibility and adaptitude for art, while the science of the percipient is so little advanced as to admit of his stronger admiration for Guido (and Carlo Dolce !) than for Michael Angelo. A Divine Being has Himself said, that "a word against the Son of man shall be forgiven to a man," while "a word against the Spirit of God" (implying a general deliberate preference of perceived evil to perceived good) "shall not be forgiven to a man." Also, in religion, one earnest and unextorted assertion of belief should outweigh, as a matter of testimony, many assertions of unbelief. The fact that there is a gold-region is established by finding one lump, though you miss the vein never so often.

He died before his youth ended. In taking the measure of him as a man, he must be considered on the whole and at his ultimate spiritual stature, and not to be judged of at the immaturity and by the mistakes of ten years before : that, indeed, would be to judge of the author of "Julian and Maddalo" by "Zastrozzi." Let the whole truth be told of his worst mistake. I believe, for my own part, that if anything could now shame or grieve Shelley, it would be an attempt to vindicate him at the expense of another.

In forming a judgment, I would, however,

[1] Or, to take our illustrations from the writings of Shelley himself, there is such a thing as admirably appreciating a work by Andrea Verochio, — and fancifully characterizing the Pisan Torre Guelfa by the Ponte a Mare, black against the sunsets, — and consummately painting the islet of San Clemente with its penitentiary for rebellious priests, to the west between Venice and the Lido — while you believe the first to be a fragment of an antique sarcophagus, — the second, Ugolino's Tower of Famine (the vestiges of which should be sought for in the Piazza de' Cavalieri) — and the third (as I convinced myself last summer at Venice), San Servolo with its mad-house — which, far from being "windowless," is as full of windows as a barrack.

press on the reader the simple justice of considering tenderly his constitution of body as well as mind, and how unfavorable it was to the steady symmetries of conventional life ; the body, in the torture of incurable disease, refusing to give repose to the bewildered soul, tossing in its hot fever of the fancy, — and the laudanum - bottle making but a perilous and pitiful truce between these two. He was constantly subject to " that state of mind " (I quote his own note to *Hellas*) "in which ideas may be supposed to assume the force of sensation, through the confusion of thought, with the objects of thought, and excess of passion animating the creations of the imagination : " in other words, he was liable to remarkable delusions and hallucinations. The nocturnal attack in Wales, for instance, was assuredly a delusion ; and I venture to express my own conviction, derived from a little attention to the circumstances of either story, that the idea of the enamored lady following him to Naples, and of the " man in the cloak " who struck him at the Pisan post-office, were equally illusory, — the mere projection, in fact, from himself, of the image of his own love and hate.

> " To thirst and find no fill — to wail and wander
> With short unsteady step — to pause and ponder —
> To feel the blood run through the veins and tingle
> When busy thought and blind sensation mingle, —
> To nurse the image of *unfelt caresses*
> Till dim imagination just possesses
> The half-created shadow " —

of unfelt caresses, — and of unfelt blows as well : to such conditions was his genius subject. It was not at Rome only (where he heard a mystic voice exclaiming, " Cenci, Cenci," in reference to the tragic theme which occupied him at the time), — it was not at Rome only that he mistook the cry of " old rags." The habit of somnambulism is said to have extended to the very last days of his life.

Let me conclude with a thought of Shelley as a poet. In the hierarchy of creative minds, it is the presence of the highest faculty that gives first rank, in virtue of its kind, not degree ; no pretension of a lower nature, whatever the completeness of development of, variety of effect, impeding the precedency of the rarer endowment though only in the germ. The contrary is sometimes maintained ; it is attempted to make the lower gifts (which are potentially included in the higher faculty) of independent value, and equal to some exercise of the special function. For instance, should not a poet possess common sense ? Then the possession of abundant common sense implies a step towards becoming a poet. Yes ; such a step as the lapidary's, when, strong in the fact of carbon entering largely into the composition of the diamond, he heaps up a sack of charcoal in order to compete with the Koh-i-noor. I pass at once, therefore, from Shelley's minor excellences to his noblest and predominating characteristic. This I call his simultaneous perception of Power and Love in the absolute, and of Beauty and Good in the concrete, while he throws, from his poet's station between both, swifter,

subtler, and more numerous films for the connection of each with each, than have been thrown by any modern artificer of whom I have knowledge ; proving how, as he says,

> " The spirit of the worm within the sod
> In love and worship blends itself with God."

I would rather consider Shelley's poetry as a sublime fragmentary essay towards a presentment of the correspondency of the universe to Deity, of the natural to the spiritual, and of the actual to the ideal, than I would isolate and separately appraise the worth of many detachable portions which might be acknowledged as utterly perfect in a lower moral point of view, under the mere conditions of art. It would be easy to take my stand on successful instances of objectivity in Shelley : there is the unrivalled *Cenci ;* there is the *Julian and Maddalo* too ; there is the magnificent *Ode to Naples :* why not regard, it may be said, the less organized matter as the radiant elemental foam and solution, out of which would have been evolved, eventually, creations as perfect even as those ? But I prefer to look for the highest attainment, not simply the high, — and, seeing it, I hold by it. There is surely enough of the work " Shelley " to be known enduringly among men, and, I believe, to be accepted of God, as human work may ; and around the imperfect proportions of such, the most elaborated productions of ordinary art must arrange themselves as inferior illustrations.

It is because I have long held these opinions in assurance and gratitude, that I catch at the opportunity offered to me of expressing them here ; knowing that the alacrity to fulfil an humble office conveys more love than the acceptance of the honor of a higher one, and that better, therefore, than the signal service it was the dream of my boyhood to render to his fame and memory, may be the saying of a few inadequate words upon these scarcely more important supplementary letters of Shelley.

II. NOTES AND ILLUSTRATIONS

Page 2. PAULINE. A translation of the passage from Cornelius Agrippa may be found in Cooke, p. 285.

V. A. XX. *i. e.*, Vixi annos viginti. I was twenty years old.

Page 3.

> *Had not the glow I felt at his award*

> *Sun-treader, life and light be thine forever.*

The whole passage refers to Shelley. Many annotations to the poem are given in *Poet-Lore*, January and February, 1889.

Page 9. *O God, where does this tend — these struggling aims ?*

Browning appends the following note, a translation of which may be found in Cooke, p. 332.

" Je crains bien que mon pauvre ami ne soit pas toujours parfaitement compris dans ce qui reste à lire de cet étrange fragment, mais il est moins propre que tout autre à éclaircir ce qui de sa nature ne peut jamais être que songe et confusion.

D'ailleurs je ne sais trop si en cherchant à mieux co-ordonner certaines parties l'on ne courrait pas le risque de nuire au seul mérite auquel une production si singulière peut prétendre, celui de donner une idée assez précise du genre qu'elle n'a fait qu' ébaucher. Ce début sans prétention, ce remuement des passions qui va d'abord en accroissant et puis s'appaise par degrés, ces élans de l'âme, ce retour soudain sur soimême, et par-dessus tout, la tournure d'esprit tout particulière de mon ami, rendent les changemens presque impossibles. Les raisons qu'il fait valoir ailleurs, et d'autres encore plus puissantes, ont fait trouver grâce à mes yeux pour cet écrit qu'autrement je lui eusse conseillé de jeter au feu. Je n'en crois pas moins au grand principe de toute composition — à ce principe de Shakespeare, de Rafaelle, de Beethoven, d'où il suit que la concentration des idées est dûe bien plus à leur conception qu'à leur mise en exécution: j'ai tout lieu de craindre que la première de ces qualités ne soit encore étrangere à mon ami, et je doute fort qu'un redoublement de travail lui fasse acquerir la seconde. Le mieux serait de brûler ceci; mais que faire?

"Je crois que dans ce qui suit il fait allusion à un certain examen qu'il fit autrefois de l'âme ou plutôt de son âme, pour decouvrir la suite des objets auxquels il lui serait possible d'attendre, et dont chacun une fois obtenu devait former une espèce de plateau d'où l'on pouvait apercevoir d'autres buts, d'autres projets, d'autres jouissances qui, à leur tour, devaient être surmontes. Il en resultait que l'oubli et le sommeil devaient tout terminer. Cette idée, que je ne saisis pas parfaitement, lui est peutêtre aussi inintelligible qu'à moi."   PAULINE.

Page 12. PARACELSUS. The following historical note and comment was provided by Browning to accompany the poem. The notes indicated by the superior numbers in the text will be found at the end of the article.

The liberties I have taken with my subject are very trifling; and the reader may skip the foregoing scenes between the leaves of any memoir of Paracelsus he pleases, by way of commentary. To prove this, I subjoin a popular account, translated from the *Biographie Universelle*, Paris, 1822, which I select, not as the best, certainly, but as being at hand, and sufficiently concise for my purpose. I also append a few notes, in order to correct those parts which do not bear out my own view of the character of Paracelsus; and have incorporated with them a notice or two, illustrative of the poem itself.

"PARACELSUS (Philippus Aureolus Theophrastus Bombastus ab Hohenheim) was born in 1493 at Einsiedeln,[1] a little town in the canton of Schwyz, some leagues distant from Zurich. His father, who exercised the profession of medicine at Villach in Carinthia, was nearly related to George Bombast de Hohenheim, who became afterward Grand Prior of the Order of Malta: consequently Paracelsus could not spring from the dregs of the people, as Thomas Erastus, his sworn enemy, pretends.[*] It appears that his elementary education was much neglected, and that he spent part of his youth in pursuing the life common to the travelling *literati* of the age; that is to say, in wandering from country to country, predicting the future by astrology and cheiromancy, evoking apparitions, and practising the different operations of magic and alchemy, in which he had been initiated whether by his father or by various ecclesiastics, among the number of whom he particularizes the Abbot Tritheim,[2] and many German bishops.

"As Paracelsus displays everywhere an ignorance of the rudiments of the most ordinary knowledge, it is not probable that he ever studied seriously in the schools: he contented himself with visiting the universities of Germany, France, and Italy; and in spite of his boasting himself to have been the ornament of those institutions, there is no proof of his having legally acquired the title of Doctor, which he assumes. It is only known that he applied himself long, under the direction of the wealthy Sigismond Fugger of Schwatz, to the discovery of the Magnum Opus.

"Paracelsus travelled among the mountains of Bohemia, in the east, and in Sweden, in order to inspect the labors of the miners, to be initiated in the mysteries of the oriental adepts, and to observe the secrets of nature and the famous mountain of loadstone.[3] He professes also to have visited Spain, Portugal, Prussia, Poland, and Transylvania; everywhere communicating freely, not merely with the physicians, but the old women, charlatans, and conjurers of these several lands. It is even believed that he extended his journeyings as far as Egypt and Tartary, and that he accompanied the son of the Khan of the Tartars to Constantinople, for the purpose of obtaining the secret of the tincture of Trismegistus from a Greek who inhabited that capital.

"The period of his return to Germany is unknown: it is only certain that, at about the age of thirty-three, many astonishing cures which he wrought on eminent personages procured him such a celebrity, that he was called in 1526, on the recommendation of Œcolampadius,[4] to fill a chair of physic and surgery at the University of Basle. There Paracelsus began by burning publicly in the amphitheatre the works of Avicenna and Galen, assuring his auditors that the latchets of his shoes were more instructed than those two physicians; that all universities, all writers put together, were less gifted than the hairs of his beard and of the crown of his head; and that, in a word, he was to be re-

---

[*] I shall disguise M. Renauldin's next sentence a little.

[b] Hic (Erastus sc.) Paracelsum trimum a milite quodam, alii a nse exectum ferunt: constat imberbem illum, mulierumque osorem fuisse." A standing High-Dutch joke in those days at the expense of a number of learned men, as may be seen by referring to such rubbish as Melander's *Jocoseria*, etc. In the prints from his por-

trait by Tintoretto, painted a year before his death, Paracelsus is *barbatulus*, at all events. But Erastus was never without a good reason for his faith — *e. g.*, "Helvetium fuisse (Paracelsum) vix credo, vix enim ea regio tale monstrum ediderit." (*De Medicine Nova*.)

garded as the legitimate monarch of medicine,
'You shall follow me,' cried he, 'you, Avicenna,
Galen, Rhasis, Montagnana, Mesues, you, gen-
tlemen of Paris, Montpellier, Germany, Cologne,
Vienna,* and whomsoever the Rhine and Dan-
ube nourish; you who inhabit the isles of the
sea; you, likewise, Dalmatians, Athenians:
thou, Arab; thou, Greek; thou, Jew: all shall
follow me, and the monarchy shall be mine.' †
"But at Basle it was speedily perceived
that the new Professor was no better than an
egregious quack. Scarcely a year elapsed be-
fore his lectures had fairly driven away an audi-
ence incapable of comprehending their emphatic
jargon. That which above all contributed to
sully his reputation was the debauched life he
led. According to the testimony of Oporinus,
who lived two years in his intimacy, Paracelsus
scarcely ever ascended the lecture-desk unless
half drunk, and only dictated to his secretaries
when in a state of intoxication: if summoned
to attend the sick, he rarely proceeded thither
without previously drenching himself with wine.
He was accustomed to retire to bed without
changing his clothes; sometimes he spent the
night in pot-houses with peasants, and in the
morning knew no longer what he was about;
and, nevertheless, up to the age of twenty-five
his only drink had been water.[5]
"At length, fearful of being punished for a
serious outrage on a magistrate,[6] he fled from
Basle towards the end of the year 1527, and took
refuge in Alsatia, whither he caused Oporinus
to follow with his chemical apparatus.
"He then entered once more upon the career
of ambulatory theosophist.‡ Accordingly we
find him at Colmar in 1528; at Nuremberg in
1529; at St. Gall in 1531; at Pfeffers in 1535;
and at Augsburg in 1536: he next made some
stay in Moravia, where he still further com-
promised his reputation by the loss of many dis-
tinguished patients, which compelled him to be-
take himself to Vienna; from thence he passed
into Hungary; and in 1538 was at Villach,
where he dedicated his *Chronicle* to the States
of Carinthia, in gratitude for the many kind-
nesses with which they had honored his father.
Finally, from Mindelheim, which he visited in
1540, Paracelsus proceeded to Salzburg, where
he died in the hospital of St. Stephen (*Sebastian*
is meant), Sept. 24, 1541." — (Here follows a
criticism on his writings, which I omit.)

[1] *Paracelsus* would seem to be a fantastic ver-
sion of *Von Hohenheim;* Einsiedeln is the Lat-

inized Eremus, whence Paracelsus is sometimes
called, as in the correspondence of Erasmus,
Eremita. Bombast, his proper name, probably
acquired, from the characteristic phraseology
of his lectures, that unlucky signification which
it has ever since retained.

[2] Then Bishop of Spanheim, and residing at
Würzburg in Franconia; a town situated in a
grassy fertile country, whence its name, Herbi-
polis. He was much visited there by learned
men, as may be seen by his *Epistolæ Familiares,*
Hag. 1536: among others, by his stanch friend
Cornelius Agrippa, to whom he dates thence,
in 1510, a letter in answer to the dedicatory epis-
tle prefixed to the treatise *De Occult. Philosoph.*
which last contains the following ominous allu-
sion to Agrippa's sojourn: "Quum nuper te-
cum, R. P. in cœnobia tuo apud Herbipolim ali-
quamdiu conversatus, multa de chymicis, multa
de magicis, multa de cabalisticis, cæterisque
quæ adhuc in occulto delitescunt, arcanis scien-
tiis atque artibus una contulissemus," etc.

[3] "Inexplebilis illa aviditas naturæ perscru-
tandi secreta et reconditarum supellectile scien-
tiarum animum locupletandi, uno eodemque
loco diu persistere non patiebatur, sed Mercurii
instar, omnes terras, nationes et urbes perlus-
trandi igniculos supponebat, ut cum viris naturæ
scrutatoribus, chymicis præsertim, ore tenus
conferret, et quæ diurturnis laboribus nocturnis-
que vigiliis invenerant una vel altera communica-
tione obtineret." (BITISKIUS in *Præfat.*) "Pa-
tris auxilio primum, deinde propria industria
doctissimos viros in Germania, Italia, Gallia,
Hispania, aliisque Europæ regionibus, nactus
est præceptores; quorum liberali doctrina, et
potissimum propria inquisitione ut qui esset in-
genio acutissimo ac fere divino, tantum profecit,
ut multi testati sint, in universa philosophia,
tam ardua, tam arcana et abdita eruisse mor-
talium neminem." (MELCH. ADAM, in *Vit.
Germ. Medic.*) "Paracelsus qui in intima na-
turæ viscera sic penitus introierit, metallorum
stirpiumque vires et facultates tam incredibili
ingenii acumine exploraverit ac perviderit, ad
morbos omnes vel desperatos et opinione homi-
num insanabiles percurandum; ut cum Theo-
phrasto nata primum medicina perfectaque
videtur." (PETRI RAMI, *Orat. de Basilea.*) His
passion for wandering is best described in his
own words: "Ecce amatorem adolescentem
difficillimi itineris haud piget, ut venustam sal-
tem puellam vel fœminam aspiciat: quanto

---

* Erastus, who relates this, here oddly remarks,
"mirum quod non et Garamantos, Indos et *Anglos* ad-
junxit." Not so wonderful neither, if we believe what
another adversary "had heard somewhere," — that all
Paracelsus' system came of his pillaging "Anglum
quendam, Rogerium Bacchonem."
† See his works, *passim.* I must give one specimen:
— Somebody had been styling him "Luther alter."
"And why not?" (he asks, as he well might.) "Lu-
ther is abundantly learned, therefore you hate him and
me; but we are at least a match for you. — Nam et
contra vos et vestros universos principes Avicennam,
Galenum, Aristotelem, etc. me satis superque munitum
esse novi. Et vertex iste meus calvus ac depilis multo

plura et sublimiora novit quam vester vel Avicenna vel
universæ academiæ. Prodite, et signum date, qui viri
sitis, quid roboris habeatis? quid autem sitis? Doc-
tores et magistri, pediculos pectentes et fricantes podi-
cem." (*Frag. Med.*)
‡ "So migratory a life could afford Paracelsus but
little leisure for application to books, and accordingly
he informs us that for the space of ten years he never
opened a single volume, and that his whole medical
library was not composed of six sheets: in effect, the in-
ventory drawn up after his death states that the only
books which he left were the Bible, the New Testament,
the Commentaries of St. Jerome on the Gospels, a
printed volume on Medicine, and seven manuscripts."

minus nobilissimarum artium amore laboris ac cujuslibet tædii pigebit ? " etc. (*Defensiones Septem adversus æmulos suos.* 1573. Def. 4ta " De peregrinationibus et exilio.")

4 The reader may remember that it was in conjunction with Œcolampadius, then Divinity Professor at Basle, that Zuinglius published in 1528 an answer to Luther's Confession of Faith ; and that both proceeded in company to the subsequent conference with Luther and Melancthon at Marburg. Their letters fill a large volume. — *D. D. Johannis Œcolampadii et Huldrichi Zuinglii Epistolarum lib. quatuor.* Bas. 1536. It must be also observed that Zuinglius began to preach in 1516, and at Zurich in 1519, and that in 1525 the Mass was abolished in the cantons. The tenets of Œcolampadius were supposed to be more evangelical than those up to that period maintained by the glorious German, and our brave Bishop Fisher attacked them as the fouler heresy : — " About this time arose out of Luther's school one Œcolampadius, like a mighty and fierce giant ; who, as his master had gone beyond the Church, went beyond his master (or else it had been impossible he could have been reputed the better scholar), who denied the real presence ; him, this worthy champion (the Bishop) sets upon, and with five books (like so many smooth stones taken out of the river that doth always run with living water) slays the Philistine ; which five books were written in the year of our Lord 1526, at which time he had governed the See of Rochester twenty years." (*Life of Bishop Fisher,* 1655.) Now, there is no doubt of the Protestantism of Paracelsus, Erasmus, Agrippa, etc., but the nonconformity of Paracelsus was always scandalous. L. Crasso (*Elogj. d'Huomini Letterati.* Ven. 1666) informs us that his books were excommunicated by the Church. Quenstedt (*de Patr. Doct.*) affirms " nec tantum novæ medicinæ, verum etiam novæ theologiæ autor est." Delrio, in his *Disquisit Magicar.,* classes him among those " partim atheos, partim hæreticos " (lib. I. cap. 3). " Omnino tamen multa theologica in ejusdem scriptis plane atheismum olent, ac duriuscule sonant in auribus vere Christiani." (D. GABRIELIS CLAUDERI SCHEDIASMA, *de Tinct. Univ. Norimb.* 1736.) I shall only add one more authority : — " Oporinus dicit se (Paracelsum) aliquando Lutherum et Papam, non minus quam nunc Galenum et Hippocratem redacturum in ordinem minabatur, neque enim eorum qui hactenus in scripturam sacram scripsissent, sive veteres, sive recentiores, quenquam scripturæ nucleum recte eruisse, sed circa corticem et quasi membranam tantum hærere." (TH. ERASTUS, *Disputant. de Med. Nova.*) These and similar notions had their due effect on Oporinus, who, says Zuingerus, in his *Theatrum,* " longum vale dixit ei (Paracelso), ne ob præ-

ceptoris, alioqui amicissimi, horrendas blasphemias, ipse quoque aliquando pœnas Deo Opt. Max. lueret."

5 His defenders allow the drunkenness. Take a sample of their excuses : " Gentis hoc, non viri vitiolum est, a Taciti seculo ad nostrum usque non interrupto filo devolutum, sinceritati forte Germanæ eoævum, et nescio an aliquo consanguinitatas vinculo junctum." (BITISKIUS.) The other charges were chiefly trumped up by Oporinus : " Domi, quod Oporinus amanuensis ejus sæpe narravit, nunquam nisi potus ad explicanda sua accessit, atque in medio conclavi ad columnam τετυψωμένος adsistens, apprehenso manibus capulo ensis, cujus κοίλωμα hospitium præbuit, ut aiunt, spiritui familiari, imaginationes aut concepta sua protulit : — alii illud quod in capulo habuit, ab ipso Azoth appellatum, medicinam fuisse præstantissimam aut lapidem Philosophicum putant." (MELCH. ADAM.) This famous sword was no laughing-matter in those days, and it is now a material feature in the popular idea of Paracelsus. I recollect a couple of allusions to it in our own literature, at the moment.

> Ne had been known the Danish Gonswart,
> Or Paracelsus with his long sword.
> *Volpone,* Act ii. Sc. 2.

> Bumbastus kept a devil's bird
> Shut in the pummel of his sword,
> That taught him all the cunning pranks
> Of past and future mountebanks.
> *Hudibras,* Part ii. Cant. 3.

This Azoth was simply " *laudanum suum.*" But in his time he was commonly believed to possess the double tincture — the power of curing diseases and transmuting metals. Oporinus often witnessed, as he declares, both these effects, as did also Franciscus, the servant of Paracelsus, who describes, in a letter to Neander, a successful projection at which he was present, and the results of which, good golden ingots, were confided to his keeping. For the other quality, let the following notice vouch among many others : — " Degebat Theophrastus Norimbergæ procitus a medentibus illius urbis, et vaniloquus deceptorque proclamatus, qui, ut laboranti famæ subveniat, viros quosdam authoritatis summæ in Republica illa adit, et infamiæ amoliendæ, artique suæ asserendæ, specimen ejus pollicetur editurum, nullo stipendio vel accepto pretio, horum faciles præbentium aures jussu elephantiacos aliquot, a communione hominum cæterorum segregatos, et in valetudinarium detrusos, alieno arbitrio eliguntur, quos virtute singulari remediorum suorum Theophrastus a fœda Græcorum lepra mundat, pristinæque sanitati restituit ; conservat illustre harum curationum urbs in archivis suis testimonium." (BITISKIUS.)* It is to be remarked that Oporinus afterwards repented of his treach-

---

* The premature death of Paracelsus casts no manner of doubt on the fact of his having possessed the Elixir Vitæ : the alchemists have abundant reasons to adduce, from which I select the following, as explanatory of a property of the Tincture not calculated on by its votaries : — " Objectionem illam, quod Paracelsus

non fuerit longævus, non nulli quoque solvunt per rationes physicas : vitæ nimiarum abbreviationem fortasse talibus accidere posse, ab Tincturam frequentiore ac largiore dosi sumtam, dum a summe efficaci et penetrabili hujus virtute calor innatus quasi suffocatur." (GABRIELIS CLAUDERI SCHEDIASMA.)

ery : " Sed resipuit tandem, et quem vivum convitiis insectatus fuerat defunctum veneratione prosequutus, infames famæ præceptoris morsus in remorsus conscientiæ conversi pœnitentia, heu nimis tarda, vulnera clausere exanimi quæ spiranti inflixerant." For these " bites " of Oporinus, see Disputat. Erasti, and Andreæ Jocisci *Oratio de Vit. ob Opor[i]; for the " remorse," Mic. Toxita in pref. Testamenti*, and Conringius (otherwise an enemy of Paracelsus), who says it was contained in a letter from Oporinus to Doctor Vegerus.*

Whatever the moderns may think of these marvellous attributes, the title of Paracelsus to be considered the father of modern chemistry is indispu⁺able. Gerardus Vossius, *De Philos[a] et Philos[um] sectis*, thus prefaces the ninth section of cap. 9, *De Chymia* — " Nobilem hanc medicinæ partem, diu sepultam avorum ætate, quasi ab orco revocavit Th. Paracelsus." I suppose many hints lie scattered in his neglected books, which clever appropriators have since developed with applause. Thus, it appears from his treatise *De Phlebotomia*, and elsewhere, that he had discovered the circulation of the blood and the sanguinification of the heart ; as did after him Realdo Colombo, and still more perfectly Andrea Cesalpino of Arezzo, as Bayle and Bartoli observe. Even Lavater quotes a passage from his work *De Natura Rerum*, on practical Physiognomy, in which the definitions and axioms are precise enough : he adds, " though an astrological enthusiast, a man of prodigious genius." See Holcroft's Translation, vol. iii. p. 179 — " The Eyes." While on the subject of the writings of Paracelsus, I may explain a passage in the third part of the Poem. He was, as I have said, unwilling to publish his works, but in effect did publish a vast number. Valentius (*in Præfat in Paramyr.*) declares " quod ad librorum Paracelsi copiam attinet, audio, a Germanis prope trecentos recenseri." " O fœcunditas ingenii ! " adds he, appositely. Many of these were, however, spurious ; and Fred. Bitiskius gives his good edition (3 vols. fol. Gen. 1658) " rejectis suppositis solo ipsius nomine superbientibus quorum ingens circumfertur numerus." The rest were " charissimum et pretiosissimum authoris pignus, extorsum potius ab illo quam obtentum." " Jam minime eo volente atque jubente hæc ipsius scripta in lucem prodisse videntur ; quippe quæ muro inclusa ipso absente, servi cujusdam indicio, furto surrepta atque sublata sunt," says Valentius. These have been the study of a host of commentators, amongst whose labors are most notable, Petri Severini, *Idea Medicinæ Philosophiæ*, Bas. 1571; Mic. Toxetis, *Onomastica*, Arg. 1574 ; Dornei, *Dict. Parac.* Franc. 1584; and *P[i] Phil-os[æ] Compendium cum scholiis auctore Leone Suavio.* Paris. (This last, a good book.)

6 A disgraceful affair. One Liechtenfels, a canon, having been rescued *in extremis* by the "*laudanum*" of Paracelsus, refused the stip-

* For a good defence of Paracelsus I refer the reader to Olaus Borrichius' treatise — *Hermetis etc. Sapientia vindicata*, 1674. Or, if he is no more learned than my-

ulated fee, and was supported in his meanness by the authorities, whose interference Paracelsus would not brook. His own liberality was allowed by his bitterest foes, who found a ready solution of his indifference to profit in the aforesaid sword-handle and its guest. His freedom from the besetting sin of a profession he abhorred—(as he curiously says somewhere, " Quis quæso deinceps honorem deferat professione tali, quæ a tam facinorosis nebulonibus obitur et administratur ? ") — is recorded in his epitaph, which affirms — " Bona sua in pauperes distribuenda collocandaque erogavit," *honoravit*, or *ordinavit* — for accounts differ.

Page 52. Act I. sc. 2. LADY CARLISLE and WENTWORTH.

Lady Carlisle, whose part was taken by Helen Faucit, afterward Lady Martin, was in history daughter to the ninth Earl of Northumberland. In 1639 she had been for three years a widow.

Page 71.

> . . . *Consign*
> *To the low ground once more the ignoble Term,*
> *And raise the Genius on his orb again.*

The *term* was a statue representing the Roman term, the god who presides over boundaries. The *genius* was the image that represented the guardian spirit. Mr. Browning commenting on this passage has said : " Suppose the enemies of a man to have thrown down the image and replaced it by a mere *Term*, and you have what I put into Strafford's head." " Putting the Genius on the pedestal usurped by the Term means — or tries to mean — substituting eventually the true notion of Strafford's endeavor and performance in the world for what he conceives to be the ignoble and distorted conception of these by his contemporary judge."

Page 90. BOCAFOLI and PLARA.

" Purely supposititious poets. Browning chooses to invent them as types of two opposite poetic defects ; Bocafoli as the writer of stark-naked or totally jejune and inartistic psalms : Plara as the writer of petted and over-finikin sonnets." [W. M. ROSSETTI.]

Page 101. *Patron-friend*. Walter Savage Landor.

Page 101. *Eyebright*.

"Stands for 'Euphrasia,' its Greek equivalent, and refers to one of Mr. Browning's oldest friends," Miss Euphrasia Fanny Haworth. [MRS. ORR.]

Page 129. *Asolo*.

It is interesting to note the choice of scene for *Pippa Passes* in view of the dedicatory letter of Browning's latest volume *Asolando*. In a letter written on his first journey to Italy he speaks of " delicious Asolo."

Page 137.

> *Kate ? The Cornaro doubtless, who renounced*
> *The crown of Cyprus to be lady here*
> *At Asolo.*

Caterina Cornaro, the daughter of a wealthy and noble citizen of Venice, was born in 1454. self in such matters, I mention simply that Paracelsus introduced the use of Mercury and Laudanum.

In 1471 she married the king of Cyprus. He died the next year and for seven years Caterina was nominal queen, but Venice compelled her at the end of that time to resign, and gave her for residence Castle Asolo.

Page 138. BLUPHOCKS.

The curious Biblical scholia on this character is Browning's own. It is said that the name was simply another way of spelling Blue Fox, a slang-phrase for the Edinburgh Review.

Page 168. THE LABORATORY.

Which is the poison to poison her, prithee?

D. G. Rossetti's first water-color was an illustration of this poem, and bore beneath it this line.

Page 169. CRISTINA.

The Cristina of this poem is fashioned after Cristina Maria, daughter of Francis I., King of the Two Sicilies. She was born in 1806 ; was married in 1829 to Ferdinand VII. King of Spain ; became Regent in 1833, on the death of the king ; and in 1843 her daughter ascended the throne as Isabel II. Her life was given to intrigue, and to the use of tyrannical power. She was hated by those she ruled, and despised by them because of her personal character.

Page 175. A TOCCATA OF GALUPPI'S.

Baldassere Galuppi was born near Venice in 1706, and died in Venice in 1785. He was in London for three or four years, and was a most prolific composer.

Page 176. *You 're wroth— can you slay your snake like Apollo?*

In a volume of selections from his poem, revised by Browning himself, occurs the following note on this line, by the poet.

"A word on the line about Apollo the snake-slayer, which my friend Professor Colvin condemns, believing that the god of the Belvedere grasps no bow, but the ægis, as described in the 15th Iliad. Surely the text represents that portentous object (θοῦριν, δεινήν, ἀμφιδάσειαν, ἀριπρεπέ' — μαρμαρέην) as 'shaken violently' or 'held immovably' by both hands, not a single one, and that the left hand : —

ἀλλὰ σύ γ' ἐν χείρεσσι λάβ' αἰγίδα θυσανόεσσαν τὴν μάλ' ἐπισσείων φοβέειν ἥρωας Ἀχαιούς.

and so on, τὴν ἄρ' ὃ γ' ἐν χείρεσσιν ἔχων — χερσὶν ἔχ' ἀτρέμα, κ.τ.λ. Moreover, while he shook it he 'shouted enormously,' σεῖσ', ἐπὶ δ' αὐτὸς αὖσε μαλά μέγα, which the statue does not. Presently when Teukros, on the other side, plies the bow, it is τόξον ἔχων ἐν χειρὶ παλίντονον. Besides, by the act of discharging an arrow, the right arm and hand are thrown back as we see, — a quite gratuitous and theatrical display in the case supposed. The conjecture of Flaxman that the statue was suggested by the bronze Apollo Alexikakos of Kalamis, mentioned by Pausanias, remains probable ; though the 'hardness' which Cicero considers to distinguish the artist's workmanship from that of Muron is not by any means apparent in our marble copy, if it be one. — Feb. 16, 1880."

Page 181.

The last four lines of the ninth section of *Saul* which ended the first part in *Bells and Pomegranates*, were as follows, 1845 : —

"On one head the joy and the pride, even rage like the throe
That opes the rock, helps its glad labor, and lets the gold go —
And ambition that sees a man lead it — oh, all of these — all
Combine to unite in one creature — Saul ! "

Page 191. RESPECTABILITY.

"These two unconventional Bohemian lovers," says Professor Corson, " strolling together at night, at their own sweet will, see down the court along which they are strolling, three lampions flare, which indicate some big place or other where the respectables do congregate ; and the woman says to the companion, with a humorous sarcasm, Put forward your best foot ! that is, we must be very correct passing along here in this brilliant light. By the lovers are evidently meant George Sand (the speaker) and Jules Sandeau, with whom she lived in Paris, after she left her husband, M. Dudevant. They took just such unconventional night-strolls together, in the streets of Paris."

Page 194. THE GUARDIAN ANGEL.

The picture which Browning describes, called *L' Angelo Custode*, is in the church of St. Augustine at Fano ; and it "represents an angel standing with outstretched wings by a little child. The child is half-kneeling on a kind of pedestal, while the angel joins its hands in prayer ; its gaze is directed upwards towards the sky, from which cherubs are looking down." It is not regarded as one of his chief pictures, but it interested Browning because of the subject, and its simple pathos.

Page 194. *Alfred, dear friend.*

Alfred Domett, the hero of *Waring*, an early friend of Browning, and at the time living in New Zealand. Mrs. Orr writes : " When he read the apostrophe to ' Alfred, dear friend,' he had reached the last line before it occurred to him that the person invoked could be he."

Page 254. INSTANS TYRANNUS.

The title of this poem was suggested by Horace's ode, III. iii. 1. beginning

Justum et tenacem propositi virum,
Non civium ardor prava jubentium
Non vultus instantis tyranni.

Page 264. WARING.

Alfred Domett, son of Nathaniel Domett, was born at Camberwell Grove, Surrey, May 20, 1811. His father was a seaman under Nelson, and a gallant sailor. Alfred entered St. John's College, Cambridge, in 1829 ; but after a residence of three years he left without graduation. His attention was early turned to literature, and in 1832 he published a volume of poems. He also contributed to *Blackwood's Magazine* various lyrics which attracted attention to him as a rising poet. One of these was *A Christmas Hymn*, which is the best known of all his poems, and has been highly praised. It may be found in several poetical collections, and among them *Festival Poems*. In 1839, in the same magazine, he published a poem on *Venice*. Domett was called to the bar in 1841, and lived in the Middle Temple with Joseph Arnold, who became Chief Justice of Bombay.

He was handsome and attractive, well received in society, and a favorite with his literary friends. Before this, however, he had spent two years in travelling in America, including a winter in the backwoods of Canada ; and then two years more in Switzerland, Italy, and other Continental countries. In 1842 he was persuaded to go to New Zealand by his cousin, William Young, whose father was a large land owner there, in connection with the New Zealand Company. In May, 1842, he went out to that colony among the earliest settlers. It was immediately after his departure that Browning wrote his *Waring*, which describes his friend very accurately, and the circumstances of his sudden absence from London. On arriving in New Zealand, Domett found that his cousin had just been drowned. He settled in the county of Wairoa, on the North Island. In *The Guardian Angel* Browning addressed him : —

> " Where are you, dear old friend ?
> How rolls the Wairoa at your world's far end ? "

Soon after his arrival Domett was made a magistrate with a salary of £700 a year. Before leaving England Domett was permanently lamed by an accident to one of his legs, which saved his life soon after he reached the colony, for it prevented his accepting the invitation of some treacherous native chiefs to a banquet at which all the English guests were killed. In his *Narrative of the Wairou Massacre*, 1843, he described this event.

In 1848 he was made the Colonial Secretary for the southern part of the North Island ; and in 1851 he was also appointed the Civil Secretary for the whole of New Zealand, holding both offices until the introduction of the new constitution, in 1853. Having resigned these offices, he accepted one of more work and less remuneration, as Commissioner of Crown Lands, and Resident Magistrate at Hawke's Bay ; and of this district he had virtually the sole official management. In 1859 he represented the town of Nelson in the House of Representatives, and he was reëlected the following year.

In 1862, at a critical moment in the affairs of New Zealand, Domett was called upon to form a new government, which he successfully accomplished, becoming the Prime Minister.

In 1871, Domett returned to London, and took up his residence at Phillimore Terrace, Kensington; and afterwards at St. Charles's Square, North Kensington. He had married a handsome English lady while yet a resident in New Zealand. He saw much of Browning ; he became an interested member of the Browning Society, and one of its vice-presidents. " His grand white head," says Mr. F. J. Furnivall, " was to be seen at all the Society's performances and at several of its meetings. He naturally preferred Mr. Browning's early works to the later ones. He could not be persuaded to write any account of his early London days. Mr. Domett produced with pride his sea-stained copy of Browning's *Bells and Pomegranates*. A sterling, manly, independent nature was Alfred Domett's. He impressed every one with whom he came in contact, and is deeply regretted by his remaining friends."

In 1872 Domett published in London his *Ranolf and Amohia, a South-Sea Day Dream*, a poem descriptive of New Zealand, its scenery, and the legends and habits of the Maori inhabitants. This poem was afterwards revised, enlarged, and published in two volumes. In 1877 appeared a volume of his short poems, including those published before he went to New Zealand, under the title of *Flotsam and Jetsam, Rhymes Old and New*. [G. W. COOKE.]

Page 280.

> *He settled Hoti's business — let it be !*
> *Properly based Oun —*
> *Gave us the doctrine of the enclitic De.*

— *Hoti* is the Greek particle ὅτι, that, etc. — *Oun* is the Greek particle οὖν, then, now then, etc. — *The enclitic De* is the Greek δε, which Browning refers to in a letter to the London *Daily News* of Nov. 21, 1874 : " To the Editor: Sir, — In a clever article this morning you speak of ' the doctrine of enclitic De ' — ' which, with all deference to Mr. Browning, in point of fact does not exist.' No, not to Mr. Browning : but pray defer to Herr Buttmann, whose fifth list of ' enclitics ' ends with ' the inseparable *De* ' — or to Curtius, whose fifth list ends also with ' *De* (meaning " *towards* " and as a demonstrative appendage).' That this is not to be confounded with the accentuated ' De, meaning *but* ' was the ' doctrine ' which the Grammarian bequeathed to those capable of receiving it. — I am, sir, yours obediently, R. B."

Page 287. CHILDE ROLAND TO THE DARK TOWER CAME.

In an article describing a visit to the poet, Rev. John W. Chadwick speaks of this tapestry and Mr. Browning's comments on the poem : — " Upon the lengthwise wall of the room, above the Italian furniture, sombre and richly carved, was a long, wide band of tapestry, on which I thought I recognized the miserable horse of Childe Roland's pilgrimage : —

> " ' One stiff blind horse, his every bone a-stare,
> Stood stupefied, however he came there :
> Thrust out past service from the devil's stud ! '

I asked Mr. Browning if the beast of the tapestry was the beast of the poem ; and he said yes, and descanted somewhat on his lean monstrosity. But only a Browning could have evolved the stanzas of the poem from the woven image. I further asked him if he had said that he only wrote *Childe Roland* for its realistic imagery, without any moral purpose, — a notion to which Mrs. Sutherland Orr has given currency ; and he protested that he never had. When I asked him if constancy to an ideal — ' He that endureth to the end shall be saved ' — was not a sufficient understanding of the central purpose of the poem, he said, ' Yes, just about that.' "

Page 337. ARTEMIS PROLOGIZES.

Mrs. Orr prints in her *Handbook* a note from Browning with reference to the attacks upon him for the form he adopted in the printing of Greek names. It is in reply to an article in the

Nineteenth Century, for January, 1886, written by Mr. Frederick Harrison. "I have just noticed," wrote Browning, "in this month's *Nineteenth Century* that it is inquired by a humorous objector to the practice of spelling (under exceptional conditions) Greek proper names as they are spelled in Greek literature, why the same principle should not be adopted by Ægyptologists, Hebraists, Sanscrittists, Accadians, Moabites, Hittites, and Cuneiformists? Adopt it by all means whenever the particular language enjoyed by any fortunate possessor of these shall, like Greek, have been for about three hundred years insisted upon in England, as an acquisition of paramount importance at school and college, for every aspirant to distinction in learning, even at the cost of six or seven years' study — a sacrifice considered well worth making for even an imperfect acquaintance with the most perfect language in the world. Further, it will be adopted whenever the letters substituted for those in ordinary English use shall do no more than represent to the unscholarly what the scholar accepts without scruple, when, for the hundredth time, he reads the word which, for once, he has occasion to write in English, and which he concludes must be as euphonic as the rest of a language renowned for euphony. And finally, the practice will be adopted whenever the substituted letters effect no sort of organic change, so as to jostle the word from its pride of place in English verse or prose. 'Themistokles' fits in quietly everywhere, with or without the 'k;' but in a certain poetical translation I remember by a young friend, of the *Anabasis*, beginning thus felicitously, '*Cyrus the Great and Artaxerxes (Whose temper bloodier than a Turk's is) Were children both of the mild, pious, And happy monarch King Darius;* who fails to see that, although a correct 'Kuraush' may pass, yet 'Darayavash' disturbs the metre as well as the rhyme? It seems, however, that 'Themistokles' may be winked at; not so the 'harsh and subversive "Kirke."' But let the objector ask somebody with no knowledge to subvert, how he supposes 'Circe' is spelled in Greek, and the answer will be, 'With a soft *c*.' Inform him that no such letter exists, and he guesses, 'Then with *s*, if there be anything like it.' Tell him that to eye and ear equally, his own *k* answers the purpose, and you have at all events taught him that much, if little enough — and why does he live unless to learn a little!" This note is signed "R. B." Its date is January 4, 1886.

Page 341. JOHANNES AGRICOLA IN MEDITATION.

"'Antinomians, so denominated for rejecting the Law as a thing of no use under the Gospel dispensation: they say, that good works do not further, nor evil works hinder salvation; that the child of God cannot sin, that God never chastiseth him, that murder, drunkenness, etc., are sins in the wicked but not in him, that the child of grace being once assured of salvation, afterwards never doubteth, . . . that God doth not love any man for his holiness, that sanctification is no evidence of justification, etc.

Pontanus, in his *Catalogue of Heresies*, says John Agricola was the author of this sect, A. D. 1535.' *Dictionary of all Religions*, 1704."

"Browning," says Mr. Cooke, "does not correctly represent the teachings of Agricola, though his poem is correct so far as many Antinomians are concerned. Agricola held that the Law and the Gospel are incompatible, that the Law is only for the Jew, and that the spirit of Christ abolishes it for the Christian. The moral obligations, however, he held were for the Christian as much as for any other person. In the New Testament he found all the principles and motives necessary to give true impulse and guidance to the Christian. It was the use made of his teachings by fanatics which cast an odium on the name of Antinomians; and it is this fanatical and sentimental religion which Browning has interpreted correctly in his poem. Many of the Antinomians taught what is attributed to them in the *Dictionary of all Religions*, from which Browning quoted when his poem was first published."

Page 348. THE BISHOP ORDERS HIS TOMB. "I know no other piece of modern English, prose or poetry, in which there is so much told, as in these lines, of the Renaissance spirit, — its worldliness, inconsistency, pride, hypocrisy, ignorance of itself, love of art, of luxury, and of good Latin. It is nearly all that I said of the central Renaissance in thirty pages of the *Stones of Venice*, put into as many lines, Browning's being also the antecedent work. The worst of it is that this kind of concentrated writing needs so much solution before the reader can fairly get the good of it, that people's patience fails them, and they give the thing up as insoluble; though, truly, it ought to be to the current of common thought like Saladin's talisman, dipped in clear water, not soluble altogether, but making the element medicinal." [JOHN RUSKIN.]

Page 387. *Is not his love at issue still with sin.*

In the first edition there followed this line: *Closed with and cast and conquered, crucified.*

Page 602. BALAUSTION'S ADVENTURE.

Mr. Richard G. Moulton, in the *Transactions of the Browning Society*, 1890-1891, offers a detailed criticism of Browning's poem as a reproduction of the thought of Euripides, especially in regard to the character of Admetus. The chief points will be found in Berdoe's *The Browning Cyclopaedia*.

Page 699. PRINCE HOHENSTIEL-SCHWANGAU.

Of the description of the succession of Roman high priests, Mrs. Orr says: "Mr. Browning desires me to say that he has been wrong in associating this custom with the little temple by the river Clitumnus, which he describes from personal knowledge. That to which the tradition refers stood by the lake of Nemi."

Page 736. RED COTTON NIGHT-CAP COUNTRY.

The equivalents in point of fact of names are as follows.

The Firm Miranda = Mellerio Brothers.

St. Rambert=St. Aubin. Joyeux, Joyous-Gard = Lion, Lionesse.
Vire = Caen.
St. Rambertese =St. Aubinese.
Londres = Douvres.
London = Dover. La Roche = Courcelle.
Monlieu =Bernières. Villeneuve = Langrune.
Pons = Luc. La Ravissante = La Délivrande.
Raimbaux = Bayeux. Morillon = Hugonin.
Mirecourt = Bonnechose.
New York = Madrid.
Clairvaux ='Tailleville. Gonthier = Bény.
Rousseau = Voltaire. Léonce = Antoine.
Of "Firm Miranda, London and New York" = "Mellerio Brothers;" Meller, people say.
Rare Vissante = Dell Yvrande. Aldabert = Regnobert. Eldobert = Ragnobert. Mailleville = Beaudoin. Chaumont = Quelen. Vertgalant = Talleyrand.
Ravissantish = Délivrandish.
Clara de Millefleurs = Anna de Beaupré.
Coliseum Street = Miromesnil Street.
Steiner = Mayer. Commercy = Larocy. Sierck = Metz.
Muhlhausen = Debacker. Carlino Centofanti = Miranda di Mongino.
Portugal = Italy.
Vaillant = Mériel.
Thirty-three = Twenty-five.
Beaumont = Pasquier.
Sceaux = Garges.
The "guide" recommended to Miranda was M. Joseph Milsand, who was always at St. Aubin during the bathing season, and who was an old friend of Browning's.
Luc de la Maison Rouge = Jean de la Becquetière. Claise = Vire. Maude = Anne.
Dionysius = Eliezer. Scholastica = Elizabeth.
Twentieth = Thirteenth.
Fricquot = Picot.
Page 802. *My Kirkup.*
Baron Kirkup, a connoisseur in literature and art, who was numbered among Browning's Florentine friends. He was ennobled by the King of Italy, because of his literary and patriotic services to his country. He discovered a portrait of Dante in the Bargello at Florence.
Page 827. EPILOGUE.
The poet referred to is Mrs. Browning in *Wine of Cyprus.*
Page 880. IVÀN IVÀNOVITCH.
Mr. Nathan Haskell Dole, the author of a *History of Russia*, and the translator of Tolstoi and other Russian authors, furnishes for Mr. Cooke's *Browning Guide Book* the following notes : —
"A *verst* is about .66 of a mile (3500 feet). — I take it the *highway broad and straight from the Neva's mouth to Moscow's gates of gold* must refer to the legend that when the first railroad was built from one city to the other, the Emperor Nicholas ordered that it should run absolutely straight, himself marking it with a ruler on the map. I do not think the old highway ran straight. — *Ivàn Ivànovitch* is equivalent to John Johnson, or more correctly Jack Jackson, *Ivàn* being the familiar of *Ioànn*, John. The

ending *vitch*, however, is not exactly an equivalent to son ; it really means father. — *Droug*, more correctly spelt *druk* (pronounced drook), means friend. — Browning's *motherkin* corresponds to the Russian *màtushka*, and is an endearing diminutive of *mc:*, mother ; it is always applied to any old peasant woman; it is a familiar form of address, often applied to any woman or even girl. — *Vàssili* (accented by Browning incorrectly on the first syllable) should be spelt *Vasìli :* it is our Basil. — *Lukeria* is a colloquial form of *Glikeria, Glycera ;* the proper diminutive is *Lusha* and also *Lushka*. — Browning makes one odd mistake in the poem ; it would be impossible for the breath to go up straight when the people were riding fast in a Russian sledge.— He speaks of *twin pigeons;* the most familiar term of endearment in Russian is *golùbchik*, which is the diminutive of the word for pigeon. — *Stiòpka* is the proper diminutive of *Stepàn*, Stephen ; the *io* merely represents the sound of the *e* (as in yelk) with which it is written in Russian.— *Pope* should not be with a capital ; it simply means priest. — *Marpha* should be spelt *Marfa ;* it is our Martha, but the Russians cannot pronounce *th ;* they represent it by *f*. — *Pomeschìk* should be *pomyeschìk ;* it means merely a landed proprietor. — *Stàrosta* is correctly accented ; it is the bailiff of a village, also overseer, inspector ; it merely means old man (from *stàrost*, old age, *star*, old.)— *Kremlin* is better *kreml ;* it is any fortress, but especially the fortress of Moscow. — *Kàtia* is the diminutive of *Yekaterìna*, Katherine. — *Kòlokol* is pronounced as though it were two syllables, accent on the first. — I am not certain about the correctness of *Teriòscha*. It should have no *c :* nor should *Stèscha*."
Page 899. PIETRO OF ABANO.

> "Studiando le mie cifre col compasso,
> Rilevo che sarò presto sotterra,
> Perchè del mio saper si fa gran chiasso,
> E gl' ignoranti m' hanno mosso guerra."

Said to have been found in a well at Abano in the last century. They were extemporaneously Englished thus : not as Father Prout chose to prefer them : —

> Studying my ciphers with the compass,
> I reckon — I soon shall be below-ground ;
> Because, of my lore folk make great rumpus,
> And war on myself makes each dull rogue round.
>   R. B.

Page 914. CRISTINA AND MONALDESCHI.
The subjects of this poem are Queen Christina of Sweden, daughter of Gustavus Adolphus, and her master of horse.
Page 955. WITH DANIEL BARTOLI.
A learned and ingenious writer. "Fu Gesuita e Storico della Compagnia ; onde scrisse lunghissime storie, le quali sarebbero lette se non fossero ripiene traboccanti di tutte le superstizioni. . . . Egli vi ha ficcati dentro tanti miracoloni, che diviene una noia insopportabile a chiunque voglia leggere quelle storie : e anche a me, non mi bastò l'ammio di proseguire molto avanti." — ANGELO CERUTTI.

III. A LIST OF MR. BROWNING'S POEMS AND DRAMAS

ARRANGED IN THE ORDER OF FIRST PUBLICA-
TION IN BOOK FORM

THE following list is drawn from the careful Bibliography, prepared by Mr. Thomas J. Wise, and published in *The Athenaeum* for August 11, 25, September 29, October 27, 1894.

1833. Pauline : A Fragment of a Confession.
1835. Paracelsus.
1837. Strafford : An Historical Tragedy.
1840. Sordello.
1841. Bells and Pomegranates. No. I. Pippa Passes.
1842. Bells and Pomegranates. No. II. King Victor and King Charles.
1843. Bells and Pomegranates. No. III. Dramatic Lyrics.

Contents

Cavalier Tunes :
  (1) Marching Along.
  (2) Give a Rouse.
  (3) My Wife Gertrude.
Italy and France.
Camp and Cloister.
In a Gondola.
Artemis Prologizes.
Waring.
Queen-Worship.
  (1) Rudel and the Lady of Tripoli.
  (2) Cristina.
Madhouse Cells.
Through the Metidja to Abd-el-Kadr. 1842.
The Pied Piper of Hamelin.

1843. Bells and Pomegranates. No. IV. The Return of the Druses. A Tragedy in five Acts.
1843. Bells and Pomegranates. No. V. A Blot in the 'Scutcheon. A Tragedy in three Acts.
1844. Bells and Pomegranates. No. VI. Colombe's Birthday. A Play in five Acts.
1845. Bells and Pomegranates. No. VII. Dramatic Romances and Lyrics.

Contents

"How they brought the Good News from Ghent to Aix."
Pictor Ignotus.
Italy in England.
England in Italy.
The Lost Leader.
The Lost Mistress.
Home Thoughts from Abroad.
The Tomb at St. Praxed's.
Garden Fancies :
  (1) The Flower's Name.
  (2) Sibrandus Schafnaburgensis.
France and Spain :
  (1) The Laboratory.
  (2) The Confessional.
The Flight of the Duchess.
Earth's Immortalities.

Song : "Nay but you, who do not love her."
The Boy and the Angel.
Night and Morning.
Claret and Tokay.
Saul.
Time's Revenges.
The Glove.

1846. Bells and Pomegranates. No. VIII. and last. Luria; and A Soul's Tragedy.
1850. Christmas-Eve and Easter-Day.
1855. Cleon.
1855. The Statue and the Bust.
1855. Men and Women. In two volumes.

Contents. I.

Love among the Ruins.
A Lovers' Quarrel.
Evelyn Hope.
Up at a Villa — down in the City. (As Distinguished by an Italian Person of Quality.)
A Woman's Last Word.
Fra Lippo Lippi.
A Toccata of Galuppi's.
By the Fireside.
Any Wife to Any Husband.
An Epistle containing the Strange Medical Experience of Karshish, the Arab Physician.
Mesmerism.
A Serenade at the Villa.
My Star.
Instans Tyrannus.
A Pretty Woman.
"Childe Roland to the Dark Tower came."
Respectability.
A Light Woman.
The Statue and the Bust.
Love in a Life.
Life in a Love.
How it strikes a Contemporary.
The Last Ride Together.
The Patriot — An Old Story.
Master Hugues of Saxe-Gotha.
Bishop Blougram's Apology.
Memorabilia.

Contents. II.

Andrea del Sarto. (Called "The Faultless Painter.")
Before.
After.
In Three Days.
In a Year.
Old Pictures in Florence.
In a Balcony. — First Part.
In a Balcony. — Second Part.
In a Balcony. — Third Part.
Saul.
"De Gustibus — "
Women and Roses.
Protus.
Holy-Cross Day. (On which the Jews were forced to attend an Annual Christian Sermon in Rome.)

Fates; concluded by another between John Fust and his Friends.

1890. Asolando: Fancies and Facts.

Contents

Prologue.
Rosny.
Dubiety.
Now.
Humility.
Poetics.
Summum Bonum.
A Pearl, A Girl.
Speculative.
White Witchcraft.
Bad Dreams: I.
"   "   II.
"   "   III.
Bad Dreams: IV.
Inapprehensiveness.
Which ?
The Cardinal and the Dog.
The Pope and the Net.
The Bean-Feast.
Muckle-mouth Meg.
Arcades Ambo.
The Lady and the Painter.
Ponte dell' Angelo, Venice.
Beatrice Signorini.
Flute-Music, with an Accompaniment.
" Imperante Augusto natus est — "
Development.
Rephan.
Reverie.
Epilogue.

INDEX OF FIRST LINES OF POEMS

GENERAL INDEX OF TITLES

[The titles of major works and general divisions are set in SMALL CAPITALS.*]*